The Environmental Resource Handbook

2013/14

Seventh Edition

The Environmental Resource Handbook

Associations
Research Centers
Environmental Health
Publications
Educational Programs
Environmental Law
Trade Shows
Environmental Statistics
Green City Rankings
Grants
Government Agencies
Consultants
Green Product Catalogs
Web Sites

A Universal Reference Book

Grey House Publishing

PUBLISHER: Leslie Mackenzie
EDITORIAL DIRECTOR: Laura Mars
STATISTICS EDITOR: David Garoogian

PRODUCTION MANAGER: Kristen Thatcher
PRODUCTION ASSISTANTS: Jael Bridgemahon, Brittany O'Brien

MARKETING DIRECTOR: Jessica Moody

A Universal Reference Book
Grey House Publishing, Inc.
4919 Route 22
Amenia, NY 12501
518.789.8700
FAX 518.789.0545
www.greyhouse.com
E-MAIL: books@greyhouse.com

First edition published 2001
Seventh edition published 2013
Printed in Canada

The environmental resource handbook. – 7th Ed. (2013/14)
1014 p. 27.5 cm.
Annual
Spine title: ERH
1. Environmental protection – United States – Directories. 2. Environmental agencies – United States – Directories. 3. Conservation of natural resources – Societies, etc. – Directories. 4. Nature conservation – Societies, etc. – Directories. 5. Environmental protection – United States – Bibliography. 6. Conservation of natural resources – Bibliography. 7. Nature conservation – Bibliography. I. Grey House Publishing, Inc. II. Title: ERH.
GE20.E586
1. 363'7 – dc21.

RC108 .C645 616' .0025'73 96-640803
ISBN: 978-1-61925-115-1

Table of Contents

SECTION ONE: RESOURCES

SECTION TWO: STATISTICS & RANKINGS

Introduction

This seventh edition of *The Environmental Resource Handbook* offers immediate access to a unique combination of more than 6,200 resources and nearly 350 statistical and ranking charts, tables and maps, all revised with the most current information available.

Hailed as a "must-have resource" for environmentalists, educators, researchers and students of environmental studies, this new edition is comprehensive and thoughtfully arranged for easy and efficient use. In addition to the new listings, you'll find 4,111 emails, 5,639 web sites, and 7,847 key contacts – thousands of ways to reach exactly who you need.

Section One: Resources

Includes 15 major chapters from **Associations** to **Green Product Catalogs,** and 68 subchapters that further organize the wealth of information in this directory by specific environmental issues from **Air & Climate** to **Water Resources**.

1. **Associations & Organizations** disseminate information, host seminars, provide educational literature and promote studies. These 1,445 listings are defined by both national categories and state listings.

2. **Awards & Honors** list 87 organizations that recognize education and business professionals for excellence in environmental sciences.

3. **Conferences & Trade Shows** include large conventions, as well as small, specialized conferences. The 84 listings in this section include who, what, when, where and why.

4. **Consultants** offer information on environmental consulting services – 378 in all –including hazardous material screening, construction requirements, and habitat conservation.

5. **Environmental Health** addresses health issues caused by the environment. These 161 listings are divided into two sections of Associations – both general and those that focus on environmental issues affecting **Pediatric Health** – plus a third section on pediatric health publications.

6. **Environmental Law** offers 57 resources that offer legal solutions and advocacy that are needed when environmental issues turn into legal ones.

7. **Financial Resources** include 215 grants, foundations and scholarships that offer financing for educational programs, research and environmental clean-up programs.

8. **Government Agencies & Programs** list 1,144 Federal and State agencies. This section ends with a separate by-state list of National Forests, Parks, and Refuges.

9. **Publications** include books and periodicals that focus on the environment as a business, course of study, subject of activism, and scientific research. In addition to individual publications, this section includes **Environmental Library Collections** and **Publishers** – for a total of 832 listings.

10. **Research Centers** helps those looking to research environmental issues. The 1,017 centers listed here are divided into two categories – those that operate within universities, and those that are run by commercial corporations.

11. **Educational Resources & Programs** are divided into two sections – public and private educational institutions, and workshops and camps. These 258 listings offer environmental educational experiences in a wide variety of specific topics for beginning students, professionals new to the work force, and seasoned environmentalists.

12. **Industry Websites, Online Databases**, and **Videos** offer a total of 533 ways to connect electronically to environmental resources.

13. **Green Product Catalogs** lists 27 of the best catalogs for environmentally friendly products for home, office and everything in between, from tree-free paper to cruelty-free aromatherapy products.

Section Two: Statistics & Rankings

The hundreds of tables, charts and maps in this section comprise 17 main topics from **Agriculture** to **UV Index,** plus valuable **Green Metro Area Rankings.** These been updated with the most current data available and include a variety of maps, graphs, and pie charts to make the information as accessible as possible.

> *"...Some charts document consumption and production back to the 1940s and will prove valuable to researchers seeking to identify broader trends."*
>
> **Library Journal**

You will find a great number of state statistics and rankings, making it easy to compile environmental snapshots by state, as well as to compare individual states, counties, and regions of the country. This section is designed to show which communities are taking an active role in protecting our environment and preserving our natural resources. Using the most current data available from more than 40 sources, this section helps complete the picture for those doing research, conducting business, or providing education and consulting services.

Section Three: Appendices

- **Abbreviations & Acronyms**, provided by the Environmental Protection Agency, contains over 1,000 listings that identify and define the political and educational language of the industry.
- **Glossary of Terms**, also from the EPA, defines nearly 2,000 commonly used environmental terms in non-technical language.

Section Four: Indexes

- **Entry**: Lists all entries alphabetically, identified by record number.
- **Geographic**: Lists entries alphabetically by state.
- **Subject**: Facilitates a fine-tuned search of resources and statistical tables by more than 250 specific environmental categories.

In addition to this print directory, *The Environmental Resource Handbook* is available for subscription on G.O.L.D. Grey House OnLine Databases. This gives you immediate access to the most valuable US environmental contacts, plus offers easy-to-use keyword searches, organization type and subject searches, hotlinks to web sites and emails, and so much more. Call 800-562-2139 for a free trial of the new G.O.L.D. OnLine Database, or visit http://gold.greyhouse.com for more information.

User Guide

Descriptive listings in *The Environmental Resource Handbook (ERH)* are organized into 15 chapters and 68 subchapters. You will find the following types of listings throughout the book:

- Associations & Organizations
- Conferences & Trade Shows
- Print & Electronic Media
- Foundations
- Government Agencies
- Research Centers
- Educational Programs
- Catalogs

Below is a sample listing illustrating the kind of information that is or might be included in an Association entry. Each numbered item of information is described in the paragraphs on the following page.

12345 **Water Environment Association of South Central US**
1762 South Major Drive
Suite 200
New Orleans, LA 98087

800-000-0000
058-884-0709
058-884-0568

info@wenvi.com
www.wenvi.com

Barbara Pierce, Executive Director
Diane Watkins, Marketing Director
Robert Goldfarb, Administrative Assistant
Ann Klein, Wastewater Consultant

The mission of the Association is to develop and disseminate information concerning waste quality management and the nature, collection, treatment, and disposal of wastewater. The Association publishes information, including a monthly magazine, manages a web site, and offers workshops and consultation on health and legal issues. A variety of educational programs are offered throughout the year on the history, ecology and culture of local rivers and streams, both on site, and in community schools.

Founded 1964

18 pages

Monthly

User Key

Record Number: Entries are listed alphabetically within each category and numbered ,sequentially. Entry numbers, rather than page number, are used in the indexes to refer to listings.

Title: Formal name of company or association. Where association names are completely capitalized, the listing will appear at the beginning of the alphabetized section.

Address: Location or permanent address of the association.

Toll-Free Number: This is listed when provided by the association.

Phone Number: The listed phone number is usually for the main office of the association, but may also be for the sales, marketing, or public relations office as provided.

Fax Number: This is listed when provided by the association.

E-Mail: This is listed when provided, and is generally the main office e-mail.

Web Site: This is listed when provided, and is also referred to as an URL address. These web sites are accessed through the Internet by typing http://before the URL address.

Key Personnel: Names and titles of department heads of the association.

Association Description: This paragraph contains a brief description of the association and their services.

Year Founded: The year in which the association was established or founded. If there has been a name change, the founding date is usually for the earliest name under which it was known.

Number of Pages: Number of pages if the listing is a publication.

Frequency: How often it is published if it is a publication.

Associations & Organizations

National: Air & Climate

1 **Action Environment**
38 Tobin Crescent 709-722-1925
A1A-2J3
To take an active role in protecting, restoring and enhancing the environment; committed to taking an advocacy and activist role in our community.
Majorie Evans, Contact

2 **Action on Smoking & Health (ASH)**
1000 10080 Jasper Avenue 780-426-7867
Edmonton, AB T5J 1-1V9 Fax: 780-426-7872
E-mail: website@ash.ca
http://www.ash.ca
To reduce and prevent tobacco use.

3 **Air and Waste Management Association**
One Gateway Center, 3rd Floor 412-232-3444
420 Fort Duquesne Boulevard 800-270-3444
Pittsburgh, PA 15222-1435 Fax: 412-232-3450
E-mail: info@awma.org
http://www.awma.org
A nonprofit, nonpartisan professional organization that enhances knowledge and expertise by providing a neutral forum for information exchange, professional development, networking opportunities, public education, and outreach to more than 8000 environmental professionals in 65 countries.
Founded: 1907
Sara Head, President
Micheal Miller, President Elect

4 **American Clean Skies Foundation**
750 1st Street NE 202-682-6294
Suite 1100 Fax: 202-682-3050
Washington, DC 20002 http://www.cleanskies.org
Promotes a cleaner, low-carbon environment through expanded use of natural gas, renewables and efficiency.
Founded: 2007
Gregory Staple, CEO

5 **American Meteorological Society**
45 Beacon Street 617-227-2425
Boston, MA 2108-3693 Fax: 617-742-8718
E-mail: amsinfo@ametsoc.org
http://www.ametsoc.org
Promotes the development and dissemination of information and education on the atmospheric and related oceanic and hydrologic sciences and the advancement of their professional applications.
Founded: 1919 14,000 Members
J. Marshall Shepherd, President
William B. Gail, President Elect

6 **Center for Clean Air Policy**
750 First Street NE 202-408-9260
Suite 940 Fax: 202-408-8896
Washington, DC 20002 http://www.ccap.org
significantly advances cost-effective and pragmatic air quality and climate policy through analysis, dialogue and education to reach a broad range of policy-makers and stakeholders worldwide.
Founded: 1985
Ned Helme, President
Leila Yim Surratt, Director

7 **Clean Air Council**
135 S 19th Street 215-567-4004
Suite 300 Fax: 215-567-5791
Philadelphia, PA 19103 E-mail: joe_minott@cleanair.org
http://www.cleanair.org
A member-supported, non-profit environmental organization dedicated to protecting everyone's right to breathe clean air. Works through public education, community advocacy, and government oversight to ensure enforcement of environmental laws.
Founded: 1967
Russ Allen, President
Patrick J Feeley, Vice President

8 **Climate Institute**
900 17th Street NW 202-552-4723
Suite 700 Fax: 202-737-6410
Washington, DC 20006 E-mail: info@climate.org
http://www.climate.org
Catalyze innovative and practical policy solutions to protect the balance between climate and life on Earth.
Founded: 1986
Sir Crispin Tickell, Chairman
John C. Topping Jr., President & CEO

9 **Conservation International**
2011 Crystal Drive 703-341-2400
Suite 500 800-429-5660
Arlington, VA 22202 http://www.conservation.org
Building a strong foundation of science, partnership and field demonstration, CI empowers societies to responsibly and sustainably care for nature, our global biodiversity, for the well-being of humanity.
Peter A. Seligmann, Chairman/CEO
Niels Crone, Chief Operating Officer

10 **Institute for Global Environmental Strategies**
1600 Wilson Boulevard 703-312-0823
Suite 600 Fax: 703-312-8657
Arlington, VA 22209 E-mail: info@strategies.org
http://www.strategies.org
A leader in Earth and space science education, communication and outreach, and in fostering national and international cooperation in global Earth observations.
Wayne T. Chen, Chairman
Nancy Colleton, President

11 **Institute of Clean Air Companies**
2025 M Street, NW 202-367-1114
Suite 800 Fax: 202-367-2114
Washington, DC 20036 E-mail: icacinfo@icac.com
http://www.icac.com
The national association of companies that supply air pollution monitoring and control systems, equipment, and services for stationery sources. Members are leading manufacturers of equipment to monitor and control emissions of particulate, VOC, SO2, NOx, air toxics and greenhouse gases.
Founded: 1960
Betsy Natz, Director
Doug Austin, Director of Govt. Affairs

12 **Institute of Global Environment and Society**
4041 Powder Mill Road 301-595-7000
Suite 302 Fax: 301-595-9793
Calverton, MD 20705-3106 E-mail: www@cola.iges.org
http://www.iges.org
Established to improve understanding and prediction of the variations of the Earth's climate through scientific research and the tools necessary to carry out this research with society as a whole.
Jagadish Shukla, President
Anastasia Shukla, Business Manager

13 **International Center for Arid and Semiarid Land Studies: Texas Tech University**
Texas Tech University
601 Indiana Avenue 806-742-3667
PO Box 45004 Fax: 806-742-1286
Lubbock, TX 79409-5004 http://www.iaff.ttu.edu/home/icasals
The purpose is to stimulate, coordinate and implement teaching, research, and public service activities concerning all aspects of the world's arid and semiarid regions, their people and their problems.
Founded: 1966
Bob Crosier, Director
Dawn Cepica, Int'l Faculty Counsel

14 **International Research Institute for Climate and Society**
Monell Building, 61 Route 9W 845-680-4468
PO Box 1000 E-mail: info@iri.columbia.edu
Palisades, NY 10964-1000 http://iri.columbia.edu
Enhances the society's capability to understand, anticipate and manage the impacts of seasonal climate fluctuations in order to improve human welfare and the environment, especially in developing countries.
Prof. Ed Sarachik, Chairman
Dr. Mark Cane, Director

15 **National Association of Clean Air Agencies**
444 North Capitol Street NW 202-624-7864
Suite 307 Fax: 202-624-7863
Washington, DC 20001 E-mail: 4cleanair@4cleanair.org
http://www.4cleanair.org
State and local air pollution control officials formed NACAA (formerly STAPPA/ALAPCO) to improve their effectiveness as managers of air quality programs. It encourages the exchange of information among officials, enhances communication and cooperation among federal, state and local regulatory agencies, and promotes good management of air resources.
Dave J. Shaw, Co-President
Barry R. Walterstein, Co-President

National: Business & Education

16 **20/20 Vision**
1463 E. Republican St. #182 206-686-2777
Seattle, WA 98112 Fax: 301-587-1848
E-mail: vision@2020vision.org
http://www.2020vision.org
A national grassroots nonprofit organization that works to increase citizen participation in public policy related to peace and the environment. Each month 20/20 Vision produces an action-alert postcard so members can quickly andeasily contact policymakers and weigh in on timely issues. Works with government and corporations and collaborates with dozens of groups and experts.
Founded: 1994
Charles Hamilton, Co-Owner
Martin Potter, Co-Owner

17 **American Association of Zoo Keepers**
3601 SW 29th Street 785-273-9149
Suite 133 Fax: 785-273-1980
Topeka, KS 66614-2054 E-mail: ed.hansen@aazk.org
http://www.aazk.org
AAZK is a nonprofit 501(c)(3) volunteer organization made up of professional zoo keepers and other interested persons dedicated to professional anmical care and conservation.
Bob Cisneros, President
Penny Jolly, Vice President

18 **American Chemical Society**
1155 16th Street Northwest 202-872-4600
Washington, DC 20036 800-227-5558
Fax: 202-872-4615
E-mail: help@acs.org
http://www.chemistry.org
Promotes the public perception and understanding of chemistry and the chemical sciences through public outreach programs and public awareness campaigns.
Marinda Li Wu, President
Tom Barton, President Elect

19 **American Chemistry Council**
700 Second St., NE 202-249-7000
Washington, DC 20002 Fax: 202-249-6100
http://www.americanchemistry.com
Represents the companies that make the products that make a modern life possible, while working to protect the environment, public health, and the security of our nation.
Founded: 1872
Calvin M Dooley, President/CEO
Roger D. Bernstein, Vice President

20 **American Federation of Teachers**
555 New Jersey Avenue NW 202-879-4400
Washington, DC 20001 Fax: 202-879-4597
http://www.aft.org
Founded to represent the economic, social and professional interests of classroom teachers.
Founded: 1916 1.4 Million Members
Randi Weingarten, President
Loretta Johnson, Executive VP

21 **American Forest & Paper Association**
1111 Nineteenth St NW 202-463-2700
Suite 800 800-878-8878
Washington, DC 20036 E-mail: info@afandpa.org
http://www.afandpa.org
The national trade association of the forest, paper, and wood products industry and advances public policies that promote a strong and sustainable US forest products industry in the global marketplace.
Founded: 1993
Donna Harman, President/CEO
Elizabeth VanDersal, Senior Advisor

22 **American National Standards Institute**
1899 L Street NW 202-293-8020
11th Floor Fax: 202-293-9287
Washington, DC 20036 http://www.ansi.org
The Institute's mission is to enhance both the global competitiveness of US business and the US quality of life by promoting and facilitating voluntary consensus standards and conformity assessment systems, and safeguarding theirintegrity.
Founded: 1918
Joe Bhatia, President/CEO
James T. Pauley, Chairman

23 **American Public Works Association**
2345 Grand Boulevard 816-472-6100
Suite 700 800-848-2792
Kansas City, MO 64108-2625 Fax: 816-472-1610
http://www.apwa.net
An international educational and professional association of public agencies, private sector companies, and individuals dedicated to providing high quality public works goods and services.
Founded: 1937
Elizabeth Treadway, President

24 **American Society for Testing and Materials International**
100 Barr Harbor Drive 610-832-9585
PO Box C700 877-909-2786
West Conshohocken, PA 19428-2959 http://www.astm.org
One of the largest voluntary standards development organization in the world-a trusted source for technical standards for materials, products, systems, and services.
Founded: 1898
James Thomas, President
Kenneth Pearson, Senior Vice President

25 **Association for Educational Communications**
320 W 8th Street 812-335-7675
Suite 101 877-677-AECT
Bloomington, IN 47404-3745 E-mail: aect@aect.org
http://www.aect.org
The mission of the Association for Educational Communications and Technology is to provide leadership in educational communications and technology by linking professionals holding a common interest in the use of educational technologyand its application to the learning process.
Mark Childress, President
Stephen Harmon, President Elect

26 **Association of American Geographers**
1710 16th Street NW 202-234-1450
Washington, DC 20009-3198 Fax: 202-234-2744
E-mail: gaia@aag.org
http://www.aag.org

The Association of American Geographers (AAG) is a scientific and educational society whose 6,500 members share interests in the theory, methods, and practice of geography. These interests are cultivated through Annual Meetings, twoscholarly journals (the Annals of the Association of American Geographers and The Professional Geographer), a monthly AAG Newsletter, and the activities of its two affinity groups, nine regional divisions and 53 specialty groups.
Founded: 1904
Kenneth E. Foote, President
Audrey L. Koboyashi, Vice President

27 **Association of Environmental and Resource Economists (AERE)**
1616 P Street NW 202-328-5125
Suite 600 Fax: 202-939-3460
Washington, DC 20036 E-mail: voigt@rff.org
http://www.aere.org

Offers a way to exchange ideas, stimulate research, and promote graduate training in resource and environmental economics. Members come from academic institutions, the public sector, and private industry.
Founded: 1979
Alan J. Krupnick, President
Prof. Don Fullerton, Vice President

28 **Association of State Wetland Managers**
32 Tandberg Trail 208-892-3399
Suite 2A Fax: 207-892-3089
Windham, ME 4062 E-mail: aswm@aswm.org
http://www.aswm.org

Nonprofit organization dedicated to the protection and restoration of the nations wetlands. Our goal is to help public and private wetland decision-makers utilize the best possible scientific information and techniques in wetland delineation, assessment, mapping, planning, regulation, acquisition, restoration, and other management.
Founded: 1983
Dave Davis, Chairman
Jeanne Christie, Executive Director

29 **Association of Zoos and Aquariums**
8403 Colesville Road 301-562-0777
Suite 710 Fax: 301-562-0888
Silver Springs, MD 20910-3314 E-mail: generalinquiry@aza.org
http://www.aza.org

Non profit organization dedicated to the advancement of accredited zoos and aquariums in the areas of animal care, wildlife conservation, education and science.
Founded: 1924
Tom Schmid, President/CEO
Jackie Ogden, Chairman Elect

30 **Bank Information Center**
1100 H Street NW 202-737-7752
Suite 650 Fax: 202-737-1155
Washington, DC 20005 E-mail: info@bicusa.org
http://www.bicusa.org

The Bank Information Center partners with civil society to help countries influence the World Bank and other international financial institutions to promote social and economic justice and ecological sustainability.
Katie Redford, Chairman
Charly Moore, Treasurer

31 **Biotechnology Industry Organization**
1201 Maryland Avenue NW 202-962-9200
Suite 900 Fax: 202-488-6301
Washington, DC 20024 E-mail: info@bio.org
http://www.bio.org

The mission of BIO is to be the champion of biotechnology and the advocate for its member organizations-both large and small.
Founded: 1993
James C Greenwood, President/CEO
Kenneth Lisaius, Vice President

32 **Bureau of Land Management**
Environmental Education Program
1849 C Street NW 202-208-3801
Rm. 5665 Fax: 202-208-5242
Washington, DC 20240 E-mail: director@blm.gov
http://www.blm.gov

Provides public education about public lands resources and management issues. Identifies educational needs and resource gaps and collaborates with partner groups, volunteers, schools, and other agencies. This group also makes products and programs available to BLM field offices, communities and schools.
Bob Abbey, Director
Mike Pool, Deputy Director

33 **Business for Social Responsibility**
5 Union Square W 212-370-7707
6th Floor Fax: 646-758-8150
New York, NY 10003 E-mail: connect@bsr.org
http://www.bsr.org

Works with its global network of more than 250 member companies to develop sustainable business strategies and solutions through consulting, research and cross-sector collaboration.
Founded: 1992
Aron Cramer, President/CEO
Pamela Passman, Vice President

34 **CERES (Coalition for Environmentally Responsible Economies)**
99 Chauncy Street 617-247-0700
6th Floor Fax: 617-267-5400
Boston, MA 2111 E-mail: info@ceres.org
http://www.ceres.org

A national network of investors, environmental organizations and other public interest groups working with companies and investors to address sustainability challenges such as global climate change.
Founded: 1989
Anne Stausboll, Co-Chair
Norman L. Dean, Co-Chair

35 **CO2 Science**
PO Box 25697 480-966-3719
Tempe, AZ 85285-5697 E-mail: contactus@co2science.org
http://www.co2science.org

Reviews articles, books, and other educational materials, attempting to separate reality from rhetoric in the debate that surrounding the subject of carbon dioxide and global change. The Center maintains on-line intructions on how toconduct CO2 enrichment and depletion experiments in its Global Change Laboratory.
Craig D. Idso, Founder
Sherwood D. Idso, President

36 **Center for Policy Alternatives**
1875 Connecticut Avenue NW 202-387-6030
Suite 710 Fax: 202-387-8529
Washington, DC 20009 E-mail: info@cfpa.org
http://www.stateaction.org

The nation's leading nonpartisan progressive public policy and leadership development center serving state legislators, state policy organizations, and state grassroots leaders. CPA is a 501 (c)(3) nonprofit corporation with thesethree unique programs: Leadership Development; Policy Tools; and Network Building.
Founded: 1976
Nan Grogan-Orrock, Co-Chair
Tim McFeeley, Executive Director

37 **Chelonian Research Institute**
402 South Central Avenue 407-365-6347
Oviedo, FL 32765 Fax: 407-977-5142
E-mail: chelonianri@aol.com
http://http://www.chelonian.org

Dedicated to the study and conservation of turtles and tortoises worldwide
Founded: 1992
Peter C.H. Pritchard, President
Russell A. Mittermeier, President

38 **Chemical Producers and Distributors Association**
1730 Rhode Island Ave NW 202-386-7407
Suite 812 Fax: 202-386-7409
Washington, DC 20036 E-mail: cpda@cpda.com
http://www.claraweb.us
The preeminent US based trade association representing the interests of generic pesticide registrants, with a membership that includes manufacturers, formulators, and distributors of pesticide products. Membership also includesmanufacturers and suppliers of inert ingredients used to enhance the delivery and efficacy of pesticide products.
Dr Susan Ferenc, President
Diane Schute, Communications/Programs Dir

39 **Chlorine Institute**
1300 Wilson Boulevard 703-894-4140
Suite 525 Fax: 703-894-4130
Arlington, VA 22209 E-mail: info@cl2.com
http://www.chlorineinstitute.org
Exists to support the chlor-alkali industry and serve the public by fostering continuous improvements to safety and the protection of human health and the environment connected with the production, distribution and use of chlorine,sodium and potassium hydoroxides, and sodium hypochlorite; and the distribution and use of hydrogen chloride.
Founded: 1924 220 Members
Arthur E Dungan, President

40 **Consumer Specialty Products Association**
1667 K Street NW 202-872-8110
Suite 300 Fax: 202-872-8114
Washington, DC 20006 E-mail: info@cspa.org
http://www.cspa.org
To foster high standards for the industry; concern for the health, safety and environmental impacts of its products; address legislative and regulatory challenges at the federal, state and local level; meet the needs of industry fortechnical and legal guidance; provide a forum to share ideas for scientific and marketing excellence.
Founded: 1914
Christopher Cathcart, President/CEO
Keith Fulk, Senior Vice President

41 **Corps Network**
1100 G Street NW 202-737-6272
Suite 1000 Fax: 202-737-6277
Washington, DC 20005 E-mail: sprouty@corpsnetwork.org
http://www.nascc.org
A proud advocate and representative of the nation's Service and Conservation Corps. The number one goal is to sustain and grow the Corps movement. The Corps Network's member Service and Conservation Corps operate in 42 state and the District of Columbia. Over 26,000 Corps members, ages 16-25, contribute and generate more than 16 million hours of service annually.
Founded: 1985
Joel D. Holdrop, Chairman
David B. Smith, Vice Chairman

42 **Council of State Governments**
33250 North Island Avenue 847-548-2289
Wildwood, IL 60030 Fax: 859-244-8001
E-mail: membership@csg.org
http://www.csg.org
A region-based forum that fosters the exchange of insights and ideas to help state officials shape public policy. CSG serves the executive, judicial and legislative branches of state government through leadership education, research and information services.
Founded: 1933
Carol Juet, Director
David Akins, Executive Director

43 **Earth First!**
PO Box 964 561-320-3840
Lake Worth, FL 33460 E-mail: collective@earthfirstjournal.org
http://www.earthfirstjournal.org
Earth First! was founded in response to a compromising and increasingly corporate environmental community.
Founded: 1979

44 **Earth Share**
7735 Old Georgetown Road 240-333-0300
Suite 900 800-875-3863
Bethesda, MD 20814 Fax: 240-333-0301
E-mail: info@earthshare.org
http://www.earthshare.org
Mission is to engage individuals and organization in creating a healthy and sustainable environment.
Founded: 1988
Kalman Stein, President/CEO
Steven J. Kravitz, CFO

45 **Ecological Society of America**
1990 M Street NW 202-833-8773
Suite 700 Fax: 202-833-8775
Washington, DC 20036 E-mail: esahq@esa.org
http://www.esa.org
To promote ecological science by improving communication among ecologists; raise the public's level of awareness of the importance of ecological science; increase the resources available for the conduct of ecological science; andensure the appropriate use of ecological science in environmental decision making by enhancing communication between the ecological community and policy-makers.
Founded: 1915
Katherine S. McCarter, Executive Director
Elizabeth Biggs, CFO

46 **Environmental Council of the States**
50 F Street NW 202-266-4920
Suite 350 Fax: 202-266-4937
Washington, DC 20001 E-mail: ecos@sso.org
http://www.ecos.org
National non profit and non partisan association of state and territorial environmental agency leaders. Its purpose is to improve the capability of state environmental agencies and their leaders to protect and improve human health and the environment of the United States of America.
Founded: 1993
R Steven Brown, Executive Director
Carolyn Hanson, Deputy Executive Director

47 **Environmental Industry Associations**
4301 Connecticut Avenue NW 202-244-4700
Suite 300 800-424-2869
Washington, DC 20008 Fax: 202-966-4824
http://www.envasns.org
The Environmental Industry Associations (EIA) is the parent organization for the National Solid Waste Management Association and the Waste Equipment Technology Association. Through these two associations, EIA represents companies and individuals who manage solid and medical wastes; manufacture and distribute waste equipment; and to provide environmental management, consulting and pollution-prevention-related services.

48 **Environmental Media Association**
8909 W Olympic Blvd 323-556-2790
Suite 200 Fax: 323-556-2791
Beverly Hills, CA 90211 E-mail: ema@ema-online.org
http://www.ema-online.org
Dedicated to the broadcast of balanced news about the environment.
Founded: 1989
Debbie Levin, President
Greg Baldwin, Executive Director

49 **Federal Wildlife Association**
FWOA Secretary

PO Box 144
Washington, KS 66968
E-mail: fwoasecretary@aol.com
http://www.fwoa.org
Dedicated to the protection of wildlife, the enforcement of federal wildlife law, the fostering of cooperation and communication among federal wildlife officers, and the perpetuation, enhancement and defense of the wildlife enforcementprofession.
Dave Hubbard, President
John Brooks, Vice President

50 **Federation of Environmental Technologists**
W175 N11081 Stonewood Drive
Suite 203
Germantown, WI 53022
262-437-1700
Fax: 262-437-1702
E-mail: info@fetinc.org
http://www.fetinc.org
A nonprofit organization formed to assist industry in interpretation of and compliance with environmental regulations.
Founded: 1982 600-700 Members
Barbara Hurula, Executive Director
Julie Jansett, Executive Assistant

51 **Florida Center for Environmental Studies**
5353 Parkside Drive
Building SR
Jupiter, FL 33458
561-799-8554
Fax: 56 - 7 - 85
E-mail: jjolley@ces.fau.edu
http://www.ces.fau.edu/
Represents the ten state universities and the major private universities in regard to environmental studies and research.
Founded: 1995
Jeffrey Nettesheim, President
Dan Brady, Chairman

52 **Forestry Conservation Communications Association**
National Office
122 Baltimore Street
Gettysburg, PA 17325
717-338-1505
Fax: 717-334-5656
E-mail: ed@fcca-usa.org
http://www.fcca-usa.org
A national organization; some of whose functions, such as that of frequency coordination, are conducted on a regional level. A certified frequency coordinator for all public safety frequencies, in cluding those in the 700 MHz and 800MHz bands
Lloyd M. Mitchell, President
Roy Mott, Vice President

53 **Get America Working!**
1700 N Moore Street
Arlington, VA 22209
E-mail: info@getamericaworking.org
http://www.getamericaworking.org
A non-profit national organization whose mission is to create 70 million jobs through structural changes in the US economy.
Marca Bristo, President
Sandra Nathan, Vice President

54 **Global Environmental Management Initiative**
1155 15th Street NW
Suite 500
Washington, DC 20005
202-296-7449
Fax: 202-296-7442
E-mail: info@gemi.org
http://www.gemi.org
Business helping business improve EHS performance, shareholder value and corporate citizenship.
Founded: 1990
Neville Dias, Chairman
Lori Williams, Vice Chairman

55 **Green America**
1612 K Street NW
Suite 600
Washington, DC 20006
800-584-7336
E-mail: ccafaq.htm
http://www.greenamerica.org
Formerly known as Co-op America, whose mission is to harness economic power-the strength of consumers, investors, businesses, and the marketplace-to create a socially just and environmentally sustainable society.
Founded: 1982
Alisa Gravitz, President
Larry Giammo, Executive Director

56 **Green Media Toolshed**
1915 I Street NW
Suite 700
Washington, DC 20006
202-659-7710
Fax: 86 - 8 - 52
E-mail: info@greenmediatoolshed.org
http://www.netcentriccampaigns.org
Green Media Toolshed is a nonprofit organization that provides the environmental community with access to a host of high quality communications tools for an affordable cost.
Founded: 2000
Martin Kearns, Executive Director
Bobbi Russell, Associate Director

57 **Green Seal**
1001 Connecticut Avenue NW
Suite 827
Washington, DC 20036-5525
202-872-6400
Fax: 202-872-4324
E-mail: greenseal@greenseal.org
http://www.greenseal.org
An independent non-profit organization dedicated to safeguarding the environment and transforming the marketplace by promoting the manufacture, purchase, and use of environmentally responsible products and services.
Founded: 1989
Garry Petersen, Chairman
Paul Walitsky, Treasurer

58 **Greenpeace USA**
702 H Street NW
Suite 300
Washington, DC 20001
202-462-1177
http://www.greenpeace.org
Greenpeace is the leading independent campaigning organization that uses non-violent direct action and creative communication to expose global environmental problems and to promote solutions that are essential to a green and peacefulfuture.
Founded: 1971
Phil Radford, Executive Director

59 **H John Heinz III Center for Science**
900 17th Street NW
Suite 700
Washington, DC 20006
202-737-6307
Fax: 202-737-6410
E-mail: info@heinzctr.org
http://www.heinzctr.org
The Center is a nonpartisan, nonprofit institute dedicated to improving the scientific and economic foundation for environmental policy through nmultisectoral collaboration. The Heinz Center fosters collaboration among industry, environmental organizations, academia, and all levels of government in each of its program areas.
Founded: 1995
Conn Nugent, President
Tom Nichols, Vice President

60 **Halogenated Solvents Industry Alliance**
1530 Wilson Boulevard
Suite 690
Arlington, VA 22209
703-875-0683
Fax: 703-875-0675
E-mail: info@hsia.org
http://www.hsia.org
The mission is to present the interests of users and producers of chlorinated solvents. To promote the continued safe use of these products and to promote the use of sound science in assessing their potential health effects.
Founded: 1980

61 **Honor the Earth**
PO Box 63
Callaway, MN 56521
218-375-3200
E-mail: info@honorearth.org
http://www.honorearth.org
Honor the Earth is a Native-led organization, established by Winona LaDuke and Indigo Girls Amy Ray and Emily Saliers, in 1993 to address the two primary needs of the Native environmental movement: the need to break the geographic andpolitical isolation of Native communities and the need to increase financial resources for organizing and change.
Founded: 1993
Winona LaDuke, Founder/Author/Activist
Amy Ray, Founder

62 **Institute for Earth Education**
Cedar Cove
Greenville, WV 24945
304-832-6404
Fax: 304-832-6077
E-mail: info@ieetree.org
http://www.eartheducation.org

The Institute for Earth Education is the world's alternative agency-and industry-sponsored supplemental environmental education. IEE develops and disseminates instructional programs aimed at helping people live more lightly, harmoniously, and joyously with the natural world.
Fran McKeever, Branch Coordinator

63 **Institute of Clean Air Companies**
2025 M Street NW
Suite 800
Washington, DC 20036
202-367-1114
Fax: 202-367-2114
E-mail: icacinfo@icac.com
http://www.icac.com

The nonprofit national association of companies working in the stationary source air pollution control and monitoring sector. Members include leading system and component suppliers of monitoring and control technologies for PM, NOx, SO2, Hg, VOCs and other HAPs.
Vince Albanese, President
Michael Durham, Vice President

64 **Institute of Environmental Sciences and Technology**
2340 S Arlington Heights Rd
Suite 100
Arlington Heights, IL 60005
84 - 9 - 01
Fax: 84 - 9 - 41
E-mail: information@iest.org
http://www.iest.org

An international professional society that serves the environmental sciences in the areas of contamination control in electronics manufacturing and pharmaceutical processes, design, test and evaluation of commercial and militaryequipment and product reliability issues.
Greg Winn, President
John Weaver, Fiscal Vice President

65 **Institute of Hazardous Materials Management**
11900 Parklawn Drive
Suite 450
Rockville, MD 20852-2624
301-984-8969
Fax: 301-984-1516
E-mail: info@ihmm.org
http://www.ihmm.org

A nonprofit organization that protects the environment and the public's health and safety through the administration of credentials recognizing professionals who have demonstrated a high level of knowledge, expertise, and excellence inthe management of hazardous materials.
Founded: 1984
W. Ashton Haus, Chairman
Allison A. King, Director

66 **International Center for the Solution of Environmental Problems**
5120 Woodway Drive
Suite 8009
Houston, TX 77056
713-527-8711
Fax: 713-961-5157
E-mail: icsep@airmail.net
http://http://icsep.com

To anticipate and detect environmental problems and either solve the problems or design and demonstrate their solutions using scientific methods in concert with nature. To provide environmental information.
Founded: 1975
Leonel Castillo, Immigration Expert

67 **Interstate Mining Compact Commission**
445A Carlisle Drive
Herndon, VA 20170
703-709-8654
Fax: 703-709-8655
E-mail: bbotsis@imcc.isa.us.
http://www.imcc.isa.us

A multi-state governmental agency/organization that represents the natural resource interests of its member states.
Founded: 1970
Gregory E Conrad, Executive Director
Beth A Botsis, Diretor of Programs

68 **Jane Goodall Institute for Wildlife Research, Education and Conservation**
1595 Spring Hill Road
Suite 550
Vienna, VA 22182
703-682-9220
Fax: 703-682-9312
E-mail: webmaster@janegoodall.org
http://www.janegoodall.org

A tax-exempt, nonprofit corporation, founded to concentrate on research, education and conservation of wildlife, pursuant to the life work of Jane Goodall.
William Johnston, President/CEO
Rich Hays, Executive Vice President

69 **Land Improvement Contractors of America**
3080 Ogden Avenue
Suite 300
Lisle, IL 60532
630-548-1984
Fax: 630-548-9189
E-mail: nlica@aol.com
http://www.licanational.com

Organization composed primarily of small contractors whose activities related to the conservation, use and improvement of land and water resources ranging from grading, excavating, paving, landscaping, wetland development, drainage,and site preparation. Strives to improve the climate within which members conduct their businesses by working for better legislation and regulations.
Founded: 1951
Merlin Welch, Chairman
Steve Miller, President

70 **National Association for Environmental Management**
1612 K Street NW
Suite 1102
Washington, DC 20006
202-986-6616
800-391-6236
Fax: 202-530-4408
E-mail: programs@naem.org
http://www.naem.org

Provides peer-to-peer networking for EHS managers; develop EHS professionals as leaders; advance the integration of EHS into business as a value driver; and promote the growth and implementation of EHS management systems worldwide; so,as to offer tangible benefits to the regulated entity and other stakeholders.
Founded: 1990
Carol Singer Neuvelt, Executive Director
Virginia Hoekenga, Deputy Director

71 **National Association of Biology Teachers**
1313 Dolley Madison Blvd
Suite 402
McLean, VA 22101
703-264-9696
800-406-0775
Fax: 703-790-7672
E-mail: office@nabt.org
http://www.nabt.org

Includes more than 9,000 educators who share experience and expertise with colleagues from around the globe; keep up with trends and developments; and grow professionally. The NABT empowers educators to provide the best biology andlife science education for all students.
Mark Little, President
Stacey Kiser, President Elect

72 **National Association of Environmental Professionals**
PO Box 460
Collingswood, NJ 8108
856-283-7816
Fax: 856-210-1619
E-mail: naep@bowermanagementservices.com
http://www.naep.org

NAEP is a multidisciplinary association dedicated to the advancement of environmental professionals in the US and abroad, and a forum for state-of-the-art information on environmental planning, research and management. A network ofprofessional contacts and a resource for structured career development, this organization is a strong proponent of ethics and the highest standards of practice in the environmental professions.
Harold Draper, President
Brock Hoegh, Vice President

73 **National Conference of State Legislatures**
7700 E First Place
Denver, CO 80230
303-364-7700
Fax: 303-364-7800
http://www.ncsl.org

The National Conference of State Legislatures serves the legislators and staffs of the nation's 50 states and its commonwealths and territories. NCSL is a bipartisan organization with three objectives: to improve the quality andeffectiveness of state legislatures; to foster interstate communications and cooperation; and to ensure states a strong cohesive voice in the federal system.
Founded: 1975
William T Pound, Executive Director

74 **National Council for Science and the Environment**
1101 17th Street NW 202-530-5810
Suite 250 Fax: 202-628-4311
Washington, DC 20036 E-mail: info@ncseonline.org
http://www.ncseonline.org
National nonprofit organization working to improve the scientific basis for making decisions on environmental issues. The Council promotes a new crosscutting approach to environmental science that integrates interdisciplinary research, scientific assessment, environmental education and communication of science-based information to decision makers and the public.
A. Karim Ahmed, President
Micheal Carvalho, Managing Partner

75 **National Energy Foundation**
4516 Sout 700 East 800-616-8326
Suite 100 800-616-8326
Salt Lake City, UT 84107 Fax: 801-908-5400
E-mail: info@nef1.org
http://www.nef1.org
A nonprofit educational organization dedicated to the development, dissemination and implementation of supplemental educational materials and programs primarily related to the environment, conservation, science, energy, water, and natural resources.
Founded: 1976
Robert Poulson, President
Gary Swan, Vice President

76 **National Environmental Education Foundation**
4301 Connecticut Avenue NW 202-833-2933
Suite 160 Fax: 202-261-6464
Washington, DC 20008 http://www.neefusa.org
Provides objective environmental information and education to help Americans live better. Environmental education programs include those tailored to the adult public, for health professionals, and in the schools.
S. Decker Anstrom, Chairman
JL Armstrong, Vice Chair

77 **National Environmental Trust**
Washington, DC 20004 202-552-2000
Fax: 202-552-2299
E-mail: info@pewtrusts.org
http://www.net.org
Informs citizens about environmental problems and how they affect human health and quality of life. The Trust uses public education campaigns and modern communication techniques to localize the impacts of national problems.
Founded: 1994
Rebecca W. Rimel, President
Rebecca A. Cornejo, Senior Officer

78 **National FFA Organization**
PO Box 68960 317-802-6060
6060 FFA Drive Fax: 317-802-6051
Indianapolis, IN 46268-0960 http://www.ffa.org
The organization (formerly Future Farmers of America) is dedicated to making a positive difference in the lives of young people by developing their potential for premier leadership, personal growth and career success throughagricultural education.
Founded: 1928
Steve A. Brown, Advisor
Sherene R. Donaldson, Executive Secretary

79 **National Geographic Society**
1145 17th Street NW 202-857-7000
Washington, DC 20036 800-647-5463
Fax: 202-775-6141
http://www.nationalgeographic.com
Its mission, in a nutshell, is to inspire people to care about the planet. Programs support scientific fieldwork and expeditions; encourage geography education for students; and promote natural and cultural conservation.
Founded: 1888
John Fahey, President/CEO
Terrence B Adamson, Executive VP

80 **National Governors Association**
Hall of States 202-624-5300
444 N Capitol St, Suite 267 Fax: 202-624-5313
Washington, DC 20001 E-mail: webmaster@nga.org
http://www.nga.org
The Association works closely with the administration and Congress on state and federal policy issues, serves as a vehicle for sharing knowledge of innovative programs among states, and provides technical assistance and consultant services to governors on a wide range of management and policy issues. Part of the organization is the Center for Best Practices which undertakes demonstration projects and provides anticipatory research on important policy issues.
Founded: 1908
Dan Crippin, Executive Director
Barry Anderson, Deputy Director

81 **National Institute for Global Environmental Change**
University of California, Davis
2850 Spafford Street 530-757-3350
Suite A Fax: 530-756-6499
Davis, CA 95618 E-mail: nigec@ucdavis.edu
http://nigec.ucdavis.edu
Sponsored by the Office of Science at the US Department of Energy, the institute is operated by the University of California under a cooperative agreement. Its overall mission is to assist the nation in its response to human-induced climate and environmental change.
Dr Lawrence B Coleman, Interim National Director
Thanos Toulopoulos, Program & Info Systems

82 **National Network of Forest Practitioners**
8 North Court Street 740-593-8733
Suite 411 Fax: 401-273-6508
Athens, OH 45701 E-mail: info@nnfp.org
http://www.nnfp.org
Promotes the mutual well-being of workers, rural communities and forests by supporting individuals and groups that build sustainable relationships between forests and people.
Colin Donohue, Executive Director
Chris Demel, Financial Manager

83 **National Parent Teachers Association**
1250 N. Pitt Street 703-518-1200
Alexandria, VA 22314 800-300-4782
Fax: 703-836-0942
E-mail: info@pta.org
http://www.pta.org
Part of the mission of the National PTA is to support and speak on behalf of children and youth in the school, in the community and before governmental bodies and other organizations. School Construction and Environmental Health is one of the program focuses where the National PTA aims to ensure that facilities are free from health and environmental hazards.
Charles J. Saylors, President
Betsy Landers, President Elect

84 **National Religious Partnership for the Environment**
116 East 27th Street 212-532-7436
10th Floor Fax: 413-253-1414
New York, NY 10016-8942 E-mail: nrpe@nrpe.org
http://www.nrpe.org
The mission of the National Religious Partnership for the Environment is to permanently integrate issues of environmental

sustainability and justice across all aspects of organized religious life.
Dr. Joan Brown Campbell, Chairman
Rabbi Steve Gutow, Vice Chairman

85 National Solid Waste Management Association
Environmental Industry Associations
4301 Connecticut Avenue NW 202-244-4700
Suite 300 800-424-2869
Washington, DC 20008 Fax: 202-966-4824
E-mail: membership@envasns.org
http://www.nswma.org; www.envasns.org
The trade association that represents the private scetor companies in North America that provide solid, hazardous and medical waste collection, recycling and disposal services, and companies that provide professionals and consulting services to the waste services industry.
Founded: 1962
Bruce J Parker, President/CEO
Chaz Miller, Director

86 Nature's Classroom
19 Harrington Rd 508-248-2741
Charlton, MA 01507 800-433-8375
E-mail: info@naturesclassroom.org
http://www.naturesclassroom.org
Nature's Classroom is a residential environmental education program, at fifteen wonderful sites in New York and New England. We give students, and teachers, the chance to experience education from another perspective, outside the walls of the classroom. After spending time in Nature's Classroom, living and learning together, students develop a sense of community, a confidence in themselves and an appreciation for others that carries over to the school community.
Dr. John Santos, Director

87 Noise Free America
PO Box 14 877-664-7366
Asheville, NC 28802 E-mail: noisefree@hotmail.com
http://www.noisefree.org
A national non-profit organization aimed at reducing noise pollution in the community. Their main focus is on noises from boom cars, leaf blowers, motorcycles and car alarms.
Founded: 2001

88 North American Association for Environmental Education
2000 P Street NW 202-419-0412
Suite 540 Fax: 202-419-0415
Washington, DC 20036 E-mail: brian@naaee.org
http://www.naaee.org
A professional association for environmental education that promotes excellence in environmental education and serves environmental educators for the purpose of achieving environmental literacy in order for present and futuregenerations to benefit from a safe and health environment and a better quality of life.
Founded: 1971
Jose Pepe Marcos-Iga, President
Michael A. Marzolla, President Elect

89 Office of Environmental Affairs
Environmental Education
100 Cambidge Street 617-626-1000
Suite 900 Fax: 617-626-1181
Boston, MA 2114 E-mail: env.internet@state.ma.us
http://www.state.ma.us/envir
A resource for environmental literacy, whose goal is to reconnect people to the natural world, and to inspire a sense of public responsibility. Learn how to link to our collective health, making a difference through our decisions andchoices.
Martha Coakley, Attorney General

90 Orion Society
187 Main Street 413-528-4422
Great Barrington, MA 1230 888-909-6568
E-mail: orion@orionsociety.org
http://www.orionsociety.org
A nonprofit organization supported by donations from individuals, families and foundations, and corporate and government grants. Mission is to inform, inspire, and engage individuals and grassroots organizations in becoming a significant cultural force for healing nature and community.
Founded: 1982
Alison Hawthorn Deming, Chairman
H Emerson Blake, Executive Director

91 Public Citizen
1600 20th Street NW 202-588-1000
Washington, DC 20009 http://www.citizen.org
A consumer advocacy organization founded to represent consumer interests in Congress, the executive branch, and the courts.
Founded: 1971
Robert Weissman, President
Margrete Strand Rangnes, Executive Vice President

92 Public Employees for Environmental Responsibility (PEER)
2000 P Street NW 202-265-7337
Suite 240 Fax: 202-265-4192
Washington, DC 20036 E-mail: info@peer.org
http://www.peer.org
A national non-profit alliance of local, state and federal scientists, law enforcement officers, land managers and other professionals dedicated to upholding environmental laws and values.
Frank Buono, Chairman
Louis Clark, Executive Director

93 Renew America
1200 18th Street NW 202-721-1545
Suite 1100 Fax: 202-467-5780
Washington, DC 20036 http://www.solstice.crest.org
Renew America is a nonprofit organization founded in 1989. They coordinate a network of community and environment groups, businesses, government leaders and civic activists to exchange ideas and expertise for improving the enviroment. By finding and promoting programs that work, Renew America helps inspire communities and businesses to meet today's environmental challenges.
Founded: 1989
Kenneth Brown, Executive Director
L Hunter Lovins, President

94 Renewable Fuels Association
425 Third Street, SW 202-289-3835
Suite 1150 Fax: 202-289-7519
Washington, DC 20024 E-mail: info@ethanolrfa.org
http://www.ethanolrfa.org
The national trade association for the US ethanol industry, promotes policies, regulations and research and development initiative that will lead to the increased production and use of fuel ethanol.
Founded: 1981
Bob Dinneen, President/CEO
Alex Obuchowski, CFO

95 Roger Tory Peterson Institute of Natural History
311 Curtis Street 716-665-2473
Jamestown, NY 14701 800-758-6841
Fax: 716-665-3794
E-mail: mail@rtpi.org
http://www.rtpi.org
Nature education organization that works on the national level, with an audience of primarily adults who are interested in gaining skills for educating young people about the natural world. RTPI also houses the life's work of Roger Tory Peterson.
Founded: 1984
Twan Leenders, President
Mark Baldwin, Director of Education

96 Silicones Environmental, Health and Safety Council of North America
700 2nd Street NE 202-249-7000
Washington, DC 20002 Fax: 202-249-6100
E-mail: sehsc@americanchemistry.com
http://www.sehsc.com

An organization of North America silicone chemical producers and importers. It promotes the safe use of silicones through product stewardship and environmental, health and safety research. It focuses on coordinating research and submitting it for peer review through independent advisory boards and publication of peer-reviewed literature.
Karluss Thomas, Executive Director

97 **Smithsonian Institution**
Smithsonian Information
PO Box 37012 — 202-633-1000
SI Building Room 153 — E-mail: info@si.edu
Washington, DC 20013 — http://www.si.edu
Independent trust instrumental of the United States holding more than 140 million artifacts and specimens in its trust for the public interest and knowledge. Also a center for research dedicated to public education, national service, scholarship in the arts, sciences, and history.
Founded: 1846
Cristian Samper, Secretary

98 **Society of American Foresters**
5400 Grosvenor Lane — 301-897-8720
Bethesda, MD 20814-2198 — 866-897-8720
E-mail: membership@safnet.org
http://www.safnet.org
To advance the science, education, technology, and practice of forestry; to enhance the competency of its members; to establish professional excellence; and to use the knowledge, skills, and conservation ethic of the profession to ensure the continued health and use of forest ecosystems present and future of availability of forest resources to benefit society.
Founded: 1900
Joan Meyer Cox, President
Michael T. Goergen Jr., Executive Vice President

99 **Student Pugwash USA**
1015 18th Street NW — 202-429-8900
Suite 704 — 800-969-2784
Washington, DC 20036 — Fax: 202-429-8905
E-mail: spusa@spusa.org
http://www.spusa.org
Promotes social responsibility in science and technology. Prepare science, technology and policy students to make social responsibility a guiding focus of their academic and professional endeavors.
Sharlissa Moore, President
Kyle Gracey, Vice President

100 **Synthetic Organic Chemical Manufacturers Association**
1850 M Street NW — 202-721-4100
Suite 700 — Fax: 202-296-8120
Washington, DC 20036-5810 — E-mail: info@socma.com
http://www.socma.com
The leading international trade association serving the small and mid-sized batch chemical manufacturers. Advocates flexible policies grounded in sound science and works to ensure that Congress and the regulatory agencies do not adopt a one-size fits-all approach to the industry.
Founded: 1921
Lawrence D. Sloan, President/CEO
Dave Herder, Vice President

101 **U.S. Global Change Research Information Office**
1717 Pennsylvania Avenue NW — 202-223-6262
Suite 250 — Fax: 202-223-3065
Washington, DC 20006 — E-mail: information@gcrio.org
http://www.gcrio.org
The U.S. Global Change Research Information Office (GCRIO) provides access to data and information on climate change research, adaptation/mitigation strategies and technologies and global change-related educational resources on behalf of the various US federal agencies that are involved in the US Global Change Research Program.
Founded: 1993

102 **United Nations Environment Programme New York Office**
2 UN Plaza — 212-963-8210
Room DC2-803 — Fax: 212-963-7341
New York, NY 10017 — E-mail: unepnyo@un.org
http://www.unep.org/newyork
Provides leadership and to encourage partnership in caring for the environment by inspiring, informing, and enabling nationals and peoples to improve their quality of life without compromising that of future generations.
Founded: 1972
Achim Steiner, Executive Director
Christophe Bouvier, Chief

103 **University of North Texas**
Center for Environmental Philosophy
1704 W Mulberry — 940-565-2727
Suite 370 — Fax: 940-565-4439
Denton, TX 76201 — E-mail: cep@unt.edu.
http://www.cep.unt.edu
Conducts environmental research and offers environmental education as is relates to decisions we make when dealing with environmental issues.
Jan Dickson, Executive Director

104 **Welder Wildlife Foundation**
PO Box 1400 — 361-364-2643
Sinton, TX 78387 — Fax: 361-364-2650
E-mail: welderfoundation@welderwildlife.org
http://www.welderwildlife.org
A private non profit organization that has gained international recognition through its research program. The mission of the Foundation is to conduct research and education in the fields of wildlife management and conservation and other closely related fields.
Founded: 1954
Terry Blankenship, Director
Selma Glasscock, Assistant Director

National: Design & Architecture

105 **ABS Group**
American Bureau of Shipping
16855 Northchase Drive — 281-673-2800
Houston, TX 77060 — 1 8-0 7-9 11
Fax: 281-673-2950
http://www.abs-group.com
A subsidiary of American Bureau of Shipping offering risk management, safety, quality and environmental consulting and certification services to a wide range of industries and companies throughout the world.
Founded: 1990
Tony Nassif, President/CEO
Gary Graham, Vice President

106 **American Society of Landscape Architects**
636 Eye Street NW — 202-898-2444
Washington, DC 20001-3736 — 888-999-2752
Fax: 202-898-1185
E-mail: info@asla.org
http://www.asla.org
To lead, to educate and to participate in the careful stewardship, wise planning and artful design of our cultural and natural environments.
Founded: 1899
Thomas R. Travella, President
Mark A. Focht, President Elect

107 **Environmental Action Foundation Associated General Contractors of America**
2300 Wilson Boulevard — 703-548-3118
Suite 400 — 800-242-1767
Arlington, VA 22201 — Fax: 703-548-3119
E-mail: info@agc.org
http://www.agc.org

The mission is demonstrating the construction industry's commitment to improving the environment and quality of the life through: improving environmental education, supporting sensible application of environmental laws, promoting environmental awareness campaigns and assisting in environmental litigation.
Founded: 1999
Paul W. Diederich, President
Alan L. Landes, Senior Vice President

108 **Environmental Design Research Association**
1760 Old Meadow Road 703-506-2895
Suite 500 Fax: 703-506-3266
McLean, VA 22102 E-mail: edra@edra.org
http://www.edra.org

Advances and disseminates behavior and design research toward improving understanding of the relationships between people and their environments.
Founded: 1968
Mallika Bose, Chairman
Rula Awwad-Raferty, Chairman Elect

109 **Land Improvement Contractors of America**
3080 Ogden Avenue 630-548-1984
Suite 300 Fax: 630-548-9189
Lisle, IL 60532 E-mail: nlica@aol.com
http://www.licanational.com

Organization composed primarily of small contractors whose activities related to the conservation, use and improvement of land and water resources ranging from grading, excavating, paving, landscaping, wetland development, drainage, and site preparation. Strives to improve the climate within which members conduct their businesses by working for better legislation and regulations.
Founded: 1951
Merlin Welch, Chairman
Steve Miller, President

110 **Rocky Mountain Institute**
2317 Snowmass Creek Road 970-927-3851
Snowmass, CO 81654-9118 http://www.rmi.org

An independent, entrepreneurial, nonprofit think and do tank. Envisage a world thriving, verdant, and secure, for all.
Michael Potts, President
Kathy Wight, Executive Assistant

National: Disaster Preparedness & Response

111 **Global Response**
215 Prospect Street 617-441-5400
Cambridge, MA 2139 Fax: 617-441-5417
E-mail: culturalsurvival@cs.org
http://www.globalresponse.org

Provides a worldwide connection for a better global environment through effective letter-writing campaigns. Empowers people of all ages, cultures, and nationalities to protect the environment by creating partnerships for effective citizen action.
Sarah Fuller, President
Richard A. Grounds, Vice Chairman

112 **International Association of Wildland Fire**
1418 Washburn Street 406-531-8264
Missoula, MT 59801 888-440-4293
E-mail: iawf@iawfonline.org
http://www.iawfonline.org

A professional association representing members of the global wild land fire community. It facilitates communication and provides leadership for the wild land fire community.
Dan Bailey, President
Kris Johnson, Vice President

113 **National Association of Flood and Stormwater Management Agencies**
PO Box 56764 202-289-8625
Washington, DC 20040 Fax: 202-530-3389
E-mail: info@nafsma.org
http://www.nafsma.org

They are an organization of public agencies whose function is the protection of lives, property and economic activity from the adverse impacts of storm and flood waters. The mission of the association is to advocate public policy, encourage technologies and conduct education programs which facilitate and enhance the achievement of the public service functions of its members.
Founded: 1978
James Fiedler, President
Dusty Williams, Vice President

114 **National Council on Radiation Protection and Measurements**
7910 Woodmont Avenue 301-657-2652
Suite 400 Fax: 301-907-8768
Bethesda, MD 20814-3095 E-mail: ncrp@ncrponline.org
http://www.ncrponline.org

The National Council on Radiation Protection and Measurements (NCRP) seeks to formulate and widely disseminate information, guidance and recommendations on radiation protection and measurements which represent the consensus of leading scientific thinking.
Founded: 1964
J.R. Cassata, Executive Director

115 **National Fire Protection Association**
1 Batterymarch Park 617-770-3000
Quincy, MA 2169-7471 800-344-3555
Fax: 617-770-0700
E-mail: custserv@nfpa.org
http://www.nfpa.org

Reduces the worldwide burden of fire and other hazards on the quality of life by providing and advocating consensus codes and standards, research, training and education.
Founded: 1896 81,000 members
James M. Shannon, President/CEO
Philip C. Stittleburg, Chairman

116 **Natural Hazards Center**
University of Colorado
1440 15th Street 303-492-6818
Boulder, CO 80302 Fax: 303-492-2151
E-mail: hazctr@colorado.edu
http://www.colorado.edu/hazards

Advances and communicates knowledge on hazards mitigation and disaster preparedness, response, and recovery. Using an all-hazards and interdisciplinary framework, the Center fosters information sharing and integration of activities among researchers, practitioners, and policy makers from around the world; supports and conducts research; and provides educational opportunities for the next generation of hazards scholars and professionals.
Founded: 1976
Kathleen Tierney, Director
Dennis S. Mileti, Senior Research Scientist

117 **Office of Response and Restoration-NOAA**
National Oceanic and Atmospheric Administration
National Ocean Service 301-713-4248
1305 East West Highway Fax: 301-713-4389
Silver Spring, MD 20910 E-mail: orr.webmaster@noaa.gov
http://response.restoration.noaa.gov/

Protects coastal and marine resources, mitigates threats, reduces harm, and restores ecological function. Provides comprehensive solutions to environmental hazards caused by oil, chemicals, and marine debris.

118 **Safety Equipment Institute**
1307 Dolley Madison Boulevard 703-442-5732
Suite 3A Fax: 703-442-5756
McLean, VA 22101 E-mail: info@seinet.org
http://www.seinet.org

A private, nonprofit organization established to administer the first non-governmental, third-party certification program to test and certify a broad range of safety equipment products.
Founded: 1981
Patricia A. Gleason, President
Stephen Sanders, Technical Director

National: Energy & Transportation

119 **Alliance to Save Energy**
1850 M Street NW 202-857-0666
Suite 600 Fax: 202-331-9588
Washington, DC 20036 E-mail: info@ase.org
http://www.ase.org

A non-profit coalition of business, government, environmental and consumer leaders. Promotes energy efficient worldwide to achieve a healthier economy, a cleaner environment and greater energy security.
Founded: 1977
Kateri Callahan, President
Brian Castelli, Executive Vice President

120 **Alternative Energy Resources Organization**
432 N Last Chance Gulch 406-443-7272
Helena, MT 59601 Fax: 406-442-9120
E-mail: aero@aeromt.org
http://www.aeromt.org

A grassroots nonprofit organization dedicated to solutions that promote resource conservation and local economic vitality. Nurtures individuals and community self reliance through programs that support sustainable agriculture, renewable energy and environmental quality.
Founded: 1974
Bryan Von Lossberg, Executive Director
Kevin Moore, Program Manager

121 **American Coal Ash Association**
15200 East Girard Avenue 720-870-7897
Suite 3050 Fax: 720-870-7889
Aurora, CO 80014 E-mail: info@acaa-usa.org
http://www.acca-usa.org

ACAA's mission is to advance the management and use of coal combustion products in ways that are environmentally responsible, technically sound, commercially competitive and more supportive of a sustainable global community.
Thomas H Adams, Executive Director

122 **American Council for an Energy-Efficient Economy**
529 14th Street NW 202-507-4000
Suite 600 Fax: 202 429 2248
Washington, DC 20045-1000 E-mail: info@aceee.org
http://www.aceee.org

A nonprofit organization dedicated to advancing energy efficiency as a means of promoting both economic prosperity and environmental protection. Fulfills its mission by: conducting technical and policy assessments; advising governments and utilities; publishing books, conference proceedings and research reports and informing consumers.
Founded: 1980
Scott Bernstein, President
Carl Blumstein, Chairman

123 **American Gas Association**
400 North Capitol Street NW 202-824-7000
Washington, DC 20001 Fax: 202-824-7115
http://www.aga.org

The Association represents 202 local energy companies that deliver natural gas throughout the United States.
Founded: 1918
Ronald W. Jibson, President/Chairman/CEO
Dave McCurdy, President/CEO

124 **American Petroleum Institute**
1220 L Street NW 202-682-8000
Washington, DC 20005-4070 http://www.api.org

API is the major national trade association representing all aspects of the nation's oil and natural gas industry. There 400 corporate members that include producers, refiners, pipeline operators, and service companies. The association's broad range of programs include: advocacy, research and statistics, certification, standards, and education.
Founded: 1911
Jack N. Gerard, President

125 **American Public Power Association**
1875 Connecticut Ave NW 202-467-2900
Suite 1200 800-515-2772
Washington, DC 20009-5715 Fax: 202-467-2910
E-mail: mrufe@appanet.org
http://www.publicpower.org

The American Public Power Association (APPA) is the service organization for the nation's more than 2,000 community-owned electric utilities that serve more than 43 million Americans. It was created as a non-profit, non-partisan organization. Its purpose is to advance the public policy interests of its members and their consumers, and provide member services to ensure adequate, reliable electricity at a reasonable price with the proper protection of the environment.
Founded: 1940
Phyllis Currie, Chairman
J. Gary Stauffer, Chairman Elect

126 **American Solar Energy Society**
4760 Walnut Street 303-443-3130
Suite 106 Fax: 303-443-3212
Boulder, CO 80301 E-mail: ases@ases.org
http://www.ases.org

Nonprofit association of solar professionals and grassroots advocates. The mission is to speed the transition to a sustainable energy economy.
David G. Hill, Chairman
Bill Poulin, Treasurer

127 **Association of Energy Engineers**
4025 Pleasantdale Road 770-447-5083
Suite 420 Fax: 770-446-3969
Atlanta, GA 30340 E-mail: info@aeecenter.org
http://www.aeecenter.org

A nonprofit professional society that promotes the scientific and educational interests of those engaged in the energy industry and fosters action for sustainable development.
Founded: 1977
Albert Thumann, Executive Director
Ruth Whitlock, Executive Administrator

128 **Civil Engineering Forum for Innovation (CEFI)**
American Society of Civil Engineers
1801 Alexander Bell Drive 703-295-6314
Reston, VA 20191 Fax: 202-833-6315
E-mail: sskemp@asce.org
http://www.content.asce.org/cefi

Established by the ASCE to strengthen the profession and industry through public policy and technical innovation. It is focused on advancing the engineering profession.
Susan Skemp, Executive VP
Laurie Hanson, Executive Assistant

129 **Clean Fuels Development Coalition**
4641 Montgomery Avenue 301-718-0077
Suite 350 Fax: 301-718-0606
Bethesda, MD 20814 E-mail: cfdcinc@aol.com
http://www.cleanfuelsdc.org

Actively supports the increased production and use of fuels that can reduce air pollution and oil imports.
Doug Durante, Executive Director

130 **Compressed Gas Association**
14501 George Carter Way 703-788-2700
Suite 103 Fax: 703-961-1831
Chantilly, VA 20151 E-mail: cga@cganet.com
http://www.cganet.com

The mission of the CGA is to promote the safe manufacture, transportation, storage, trans filling, and disposal of industrial and medical gases and their containers.
Founded: 1913

131 Consumer Energy Council of America
2737 Devonshire Place NW 202-468-8440
Suite 102 Fax: 703-690-5920
Washington, DC 20008 E-mail: info@cecarf.org
http://www.cecarf.org

A senior public interest organization in the US focusing on energy, telecommunications and other network industries that provide essential services to consumers.
Founded: 1973
Ellen Berman, CEO
Richard Aiken, President

132 Environmental Coalition on Nuclear Power
433 Orlando Avenue 814-237-3900
State College, PA 16803-3477 Fax: 814-237-3900
E-mail: johnstrud@uplink.net

Groups and individuals concerned with the nuclear power and energy policies. Maintains speakers' bureau and conducts research and educational programs.
Dr Judith Johnsrud, Director

133 Institute for Energy and Environmental Research (IEER)
6935 Laurel Ave, Suite 201 301-270-5500
Suite 201 Fax: 301-270-3029
Takoma Park, MD 20912 E-mail: info@ieer.org
http://www.ieer.org

IEER's aim is to provide people with literature which has a quality equal to that in scientific journals, but which doesn't require you to go back to college to get a degree in science to understand it. Our focus has been mainly on two areas: ozone layer depletion and energy-related climate issues; and environmental and security aspects of nuclear weapons production and nuclear technology.
Founded: 1987
Arjun Makhijani, President

134 International Association for Energy Economics
28790 Chagrin Boulevard 216-464-5365
Suite 350 E-mail: iaee@iaee.org
Cleveland, OH 44122 http://www.iaee.org

A non-profit, professional organization that provides an interdisciplinary forum for the exchange of ideas, experiences and issues among professionals interested in the field of energy economics.
Founded: 1977
David Newbery, President
Omowumi Lledare, President Elect

135 Interstate Oil and Gas Compact Commission
900 NE 23rd Street 405-525-3556
Oklahoma City, OK 73105 Fax: 405-525-3592
E-mail: iogcc@iogcc.state.ok.us
http://www.iogcc.state.ok.us

A multi-state government agency that is passionate about advancing the quality of life for all Americans. Works to ensure our nation's oil and natural gas resources are conserved and maximized while protecting health, safety and the environment.
Dr. Robert Bentley, Chairman
Mike Smith, Executive Director

136 NW Energy Coalition
811 1st Avenue 206-621-0094
Suite 305 Fax: 206-621-0097
Seattle, WA 98104 E-mail: nwec@nwenergy.org
http://www.nwenergy.org

The Coalition is an alliance of over 100 environmental, civic and human service organizations, progressive utilities and businesses in Oregon, Washington, Idaho, Montana, Alaska and British Columbia. They promote renewable energy and energy conservation, consumer protection, low-income energy assistance, and fish and wildlife restoration on the Columbia and Snake Rivers.
1981 pages
Sara Patton, Executive Director
Nancy Hirsh, Policy Director

137 National Energy Foundation
4516 Sout 700 East 801-908-5800
Suite 100 800-616-8326
Salt Lake City, UT 84107 Fax: 801-908-5400
E-mail: info@nef1.org
http://www.nef1.org

A nonprofit educational organization dedicated to the development, dissemination and implementation of supplemental educational materials and programs primarily related to the environment, conservation, science, energy, water, and natural resources.
Founded: 1976
Robert Poulson, President
Gary Swan, Vice President

138 Northwest Energy Efficiency Alliance (NEEA)
421 SW Sixth Avenue 503-688-5400
Suite 600 800-411-0834
Portland, OR 97204 Fax: 503-688-5447
http://www.neea.org

A non-profit organization working to maximize energy efficiency in the Pacific Northwest through the acceleration and adoption of energy-efficient products, services and practices.
Sushanah Boston, Project Manager

139 Northwest Power and Conservation Council
851 SW 6th Avenue 503-222-5161
Suite 1100 800-452-5161
Portland, OR 97204 Fax: 503-820-2370
E-mail: info@nwcouncil.org
http://www.nwcouncil.org

Develops and maintains a regional power plan and a fish and wildlife program to balance the Northwest's environment and energy needs.
Bruce A. Measure, Chair
Dick Wallace, Vice Chair

140 Renewable Fuels Association
425 Third Street, SW 202-289-3835
Suite 1150 Fax: 202-289-7519
Washington, DC 20024 E-mail: info@ethanolrfa.org
http://www.ethanolrfa.org

The national trade association for the US ethanol industry, promotes policies, regulations and research and development initiatives that will lead to the increased production and use of fuel ethanol.
Founded: 1981
Bob Dinneen, President/CEO
Mary Giglio, Director

141 Rocky Mountain Institute
2317 Snowmass Creek Road 970-927-3851
Snowmass, CO 81654-9118 http://www.rmi.org
An independent, entrepreneurial, nonprofit think-and-do tank that envisages a world thriving, verdant, and secure, for all.
Founded: 1982
Michael Potts, President
Kathy Wight, Executive Assistant

National: Environmental Engineering

142 American Academy of Environmental Engineers
130 Holiday Court 410-266-3311
Suite 100 Fax: 410-266-7653
Annapolis, MD 21401 E-mail: info@aaee.net
http://www.aaee.net

Dedicated to excellence in the practice of environmental engineering to ensure the public health, safety, and welfare to enable humankind to co-exist in harmony with nature.
Founded: 1955
Joseph S Cavaretta, Executive Director
J. Sammi Olmo, Manager

143 American Institute of Chemical Engineers
3 Park Avenue 203-702-7660
New York, NY 10016-5991 800-242-4363
Fax: 203-775-5177
http://www.aiche.org
Organization for chemical engineering professionals. AIChE has the breadth of resources and expertise you need whether you are in core process industries or emerging areas, such as nanobiotechnology.
Founded: 1908 40,000 Members
Phillip R. Westmoreland, President
Otis Shelton, President Elect

144 American Institute of Chemists
315 Chestnut Street 215-873-8224
Philadelphia, PA 19106-2702 Fax: 215-629-5224
E-mail: info@theaic.org
http://www.theaic.org
To advance the chemical sciences by establishing high professional standards of practice and to emphasize the professional, ethical, economic, and social status of its members for the benefit of society as a whole.
Founded: 1923
Dr. David Manuto, President
Dr. Jerry Jasinski, Chairman

145 American Society of Agricultural and Biological Engineers
2950 Niles Road 269-429-0300
St Joseph, MI 49085 800-371-2723
Fax: 269-429-3852
E-mail: hq@asabe.org
http://www.asabe.org
An educational and scientific organization dedicated to the advancement of engineering applicable to agricultural, food, and biological systems.
Founded: 1907 9,000 Members
Ronald L. McAllister, President
Sonia M. Maassel Jacobsen, President Elect

146 American Society of Civil Engineers
1801 Alexander Bell Road 703-295-6000
Reston, VA 20191 800-548-2723
Fax: 703-295-6333
http://www.asce.org
Represents members of the civil engineering profession worldwide, and is the oldest national engineering society.
Founded: 1852 133,000 Members
Gregory E. DiLoreto, President
Randall S. Over, President Elect

147 American Society of Safety Engineers
1800 E Oakton Street 847-699-2929
Des Plaines, IL 60018 Fax: 847-768-3434
E-mail: customerservice@asse.org
http://www.asse.org
The oldest and largest professional safety organization whose members manage, supervise and consult on safety, health, and environmental issues in industry, insurance, government and education.
Founded: 1911 32,000 Members
Richard A. Pollock, President
Kathy A. Seabrook, President Elect

148 American Society of Sanitary Engineering
18927 Hickory Creek Drive 708-995-3019
Suite 220 Fax: 708-479-6139
Mokena, IL 60448 E-mail: info@asse-plumbing.org
http://www.asse-plumbing.org
A nonprofit organization that is comprised of individuals and sustaining members who represent all disciplines of the Plumbing Industry.
Founded: 1906
Steve Silber, President
Douglas A. Marian, First Vice President

149 Association for Environmental Health and Sciences
150 Fearing Street 413-549-5170
Amherst, MA 1002 Fax: 413-549-0579
E-mail: paul@aehs.com
http://www.aehsfoundation.org
The AEHS was created to facilitate communication and foster cooperation among professionals concerned with the challenge of soil protection and cleanup. Members represent the many disciplines involved in making decisions and solving problems affecting soils.
Founded: 2009
Paul Kostecki, Executive Director
Ed Calabrese, Editor in Chief

150 Association of Energy Engineers
4025 Pleasantdale Road 770-447-5083
Suite 420 Fax: 770-446-3969
Atlanta, GA 30340 E-mail: info@aeecenter.org
http://www.aeecenter.org
A non profit professional society that promotes the scientific and educational interests of those engaged in the energy industry and fosters action for sustainable development.
Founded: 1977 9,500 Members
Eric A. Woodroof, President
Gary Hogsett, President Elect

151 Association of Environmental Engineering and Science Professors
Business Office 813-973-6969
27236 Edenfield Drive Fax: 217-355-9232
Wesley Chapel, FL 33544 E-mail: joanne@aeesp.org
http://www.aeesp.org
The association is made up of professors of worldwide academic programs who provide education in the sciences and technologies of environmental protection. It has more than 700 members.
Founded: 1963
Mark R. Wiesner, President
Jennifer G. Becker, President Elect

152 Association of Ground Water Scientists and Engineers
601 Dempsey Road 614-898-7791
Westerville, OH 43081 800-551-7379
Fax: 614-898-7786
E-mail: ngwa@ngwa.org
http://www.ngwa.org/agwse
The Scientists and Engineers membership division of the National Ground Water Association (NGWA).
Founded: 1948
Art Becker, President
John Pitz, President Elect

153 Environmental and Engineering Geophysical Society
1720 South Bellaire Street 303-531-7517
Suite 110 Fax: 303-820-3844
Denver, CO 80222 E-mail: staff@eegs.org
http://www.eegs.org
An applied scientific organization with 700 members. Among its goals are the promotion of the science of geophysics especially as it is applied to environmental and engineering problems; and to foster common scientific interests of geophysicists and their colleagues in other related sciences and engineering.
Founded: 1992 650 Members
Catherine Skokan, President
Moe Moyamez, President Elect

154 Institute for Alternative Futures
100 North Pitt Street 703-684-5880
Suite 235 Fax: 703-684-0640
Alexandria, VA 22314 E-mail: futurist@altfutures.com
http://www.altfutures.com

A nonprofit research and educational organization that specializes in aiding organization and individuals to more wisely choose and create their preferred futures.
Founded: 1977
Jonathan Peck, President
Clement Bezold, Chairman

155 **Institute of Noise Control Engineering**
100 E Washington Street 217-528-9945
Springfield, IL 62701 Fax: 283-654-6545
E-mail: ibo@inceusa.org
http://www.inceusa.org
A non-profit professional organization incorporated with the primary purpose to promote engineering solutions to environmental, product, machinery, industrial and other noise problems.
Eric Wood, President
Gordon Ebitt, President Elect

156 **Inter-American Association of Sanitary and Environmental Engineering**
USAIDIS 703-247-8730
PO Box 7737 Fax: 703-243-9004
McLean, VA 22106 E-mail: turnerje@cdm.com
http://www.aidis-usa.org
To further the goals of AIDIS Inter-Americana through programs and services that promote sound environmental practices, policies, management, and education to improve the quality of life throughout the Americas.
Quincalee Brown, President
Jacqueline Rose, Senior Vice President

157 **National Registry of Environmental Professionals (NREP)**
PO Box 2099 847-724-6631
Glenview, IL 60025 Fax: 847-724-4223
E-mail: nrep@nrep.org
http://www.nrep.org
The NREP are dedicated to professionally and legally enhancing the recognition of those individuals who possess the education, training, and experience as qualified environmental engineers, technologists, managers, technicians, and scientists. We aim to consolidate such recognition into a single, viable source so that the public at large, the government, insurers, and employers can easily see, understand, and justify the importance of these individuals.
Scott Spear, Chairperson
Richard Young, Executive Director

158 **NatureServe**
4600 N. Fairfax Dr. 703-908-1800
7th Floor Fax: 703-229-1670
Arlington, VA 22203 http://www.natureserve.org
Provides the scientific basis for conservation action. Collects and manages local information on plants, animals and ecosystems and develops related information products, data management tools and conservation services.
Mary Klein, President & CEO

National: Environmental Health

159 **Bonneville Environmental Foundation**
240 SW 1st Avenue 503-248-1905
Portland, OR 97204 Fax: 503-248-1908
E-mail: info@b-e-f.org
http://www.b-e-f.org
Strives to protect against two major threats to the globe; climate change and the degradation of world freshwater resources.
Founded: 1998
Angus Duncan, Founder & President
Todd Reeve, CEO

160 **Greenguard Environmental Institute**
2211 Newmarket Parkway, Suite 110 770-984-9903
Marietta, GA 30067 800-427-9681
Fax: 770-980-0072
E-mail: environment@ul.com
http://www.greenguard.org
The Greenguard Environmental Institute aims to protect human health and improve quality of life by enhancing indoor air quality and reducing people's exposure to chemicals and other pollutants.
Founded: 2001
Henning Bloech, Executive Director
Dr. Marilyn Black, Founder

161 **Inform, Inc.**
PO Box 320403 E-mail: ramsey@informinc.org
Brooklyn, NY 11232 http://www.informinc.org
Publishes reports covering chemical hazard prevention, solid waste prevention, extended producer responsibility and sustainable transportation. Educates the public about the environmental effects of various consumer products through media.
Founded: 1973
Virginia Ramsey, President

National: Gaming & Hunting

162 **Action Volunteers for Animals (AVA)**
PO Box 64578 416-439-8770
Unionville, ON L3R-0M9 http://www.actionvolunteersforanimals.com
An organization of people who are active on behalf of non-human animals, and who give their time and energy without monetary reward.
Founded: 1972

163 **American Bass Association**
402 N Prospect Avenue 310-376-1026
Redondo Beach, CA 90277 Fax: 310-376-5072
E-mail: feedback@americanbass.com
http://www.americanbass.com
American Bass develops and institutes programs that will protect, enhance and improve the environment and natural resources while providing high value to sponsors and advertisers through quality run events and promotions. They are involved in such programs as: stocking bass in public lakes, planting trees, and protection of natural spawning and juvenile fish.
David Plotnik, President

164 **American Birding Association**
1618 W Colorado Ave 719-578-9703
Colorado Springs, CO 80904 800-850-2473
Fax: 719-578-1480
E-mail: member@aba.org
http://www.aba.org
The Association represents the interests of birdwatchers in various arenas, and helps birders increase their knowledge, skills, and enjoyment of birding. ABA also contributes to bird conservation by linking the skills of its members to on-the-ground projects. ABA promotes field-birding skills through meetings, workshops, equipment, and guided involvement in birding, promoting national and international birders networks and publications.
Founded: 1969
Jeffrey A. Gordon, President/CEO
Bill Stewart, Director

165 **American Eagle Foundation**
PO Box 333 865-429-0157
Pigeon Forge, TN 37868 800-232-4537
Fax: 865-429-4743
E-mail: eaglemail@eagles.org
http://www.eagles.org
Not-for-profit organization of concerned citizens and professionals to develop and conduct bald eagle and environmental recov-

ery programs in the United States and to assist private, state and federal projects that do the same.
Founded: 1985
Al Louis Cecere, President/CEO
Christine Blackpool, Wildlife Program Coordinator

166 American Fisheries Society
5410 Grosvenor Lane 301-897-8616
Bethesda, MD 20814 Fax: 301-897-8096
E-mail: main@fisheries.org
http://www.fisheries.org

The American Fisheries Society (AFS) is an international professional and scientific organization of nearly 9,000 fisheries managers and aquatic scientists. Founded in 1870, AFS is the worlds oldest and largest organization dedicated to strengthening the fisheries profession, advancing fisheries science and conserving fisheries resource. AFS chapters exist worldwide and throughout North America.
Ghassan N. Rassam, Executive Director
Myja Merritt, Office Administration Mgr

167 American Humane Association
1400 16th Street NW 303-792-9900
Suite 360 800-227-4645
Washington, DC 20036 Fax: 303-792-5333
E-mail: info@americanhumane.org
http://www.americanhumane.org

The Associations mission, as a network of individuals and organizations, is to prevent cruelty, abuse, neglect and exploitation of children and animals and to assure that their interests and well-being are fully, effectively, and humanely guaranteed by an aware and caring society.
Founded: 1877
Robin R. Ganzert, President/CEO
Dale Austin, Chief Operating Officer

168 American Livestock Breeds Conservancy
PO Box 477 919-542-5704
Pittsboro, NC 27312 Fax: 919-545-0022
E-mail: albc@albc-usa.org
http://www.albc-usa.org

Protects genetic diversity in livestock and poultry species through the conservation and promotion of endangered breeds. These rare breeds are a part of our national heritage and represent a unique piece of the earth's bio-diversity.
Founded: 1977
Charles Taft, Chairman
Karen Thornton, Vice Chair

169 American Medical Fly Fishing Association
PO Box 768 570-769-7375
Lock Haven, PA 17745 E-mail: amffa@cub.kcnet.org
http://www.amffa.org

The Association began with the idea of combining professional medical interests with that of then interest in fly fishing and to promote conservation of the natural resources as pertains to the sport and support those causes and efforts oriented towards these latter goals. The organization has grown steadily over the years and presently is a strong and viable organization.
Founded: 1969
Veryl F. Frye MD, Secretary/Treasurer

170 American Pheasant and Waterfowl Society
6220 Bullbeggar Road E-mail: alpat@apexotics.com
Withams, VA 23488 http://www.apws.org

To promote the rights and interest of the members to keep pheasants, waterfowl, and other upland aquatic and ornamental birds. To collect and distribute pertinent and scientific data and information relating to these rights. The society advocates and encourages public appreciation and understanding of wildlife conservation and publishes a monthly magazine.
$25/Year
Al Novosad, President
Terry Smith, Secretary

171 American Society of Ichthyologists and Herpetologists
PO Box 1897 305-348-1235
Lawrence, KA 66044-8897 800-627-0326
Fax: 305-348-4172
E-mail: asih@allenpress.com
http://www.asih.org

The Society is dedicated to the scientific study of fishes, amphibians and reptiles. Its mission is to increase knowledge about these organisms, to disseminate that knowledge through publications, conferences, symposia, and other means, and to encourage and support young scientists who will make future advances in these fields.
Founded: 1913
Michael E. Douglas, President
Steven J. Beaupre, Vice President

172 American Society of Mammalogists
PO Box 7060 800-627-0629
Lawrence, KS 66044 Fax: 785-843-1274
E-mail: dodell@cfl.rr.com
http://www.mammalsociety.org

Established for the purpose of promoting interest in the study of mammals. There are over 4,500 members and they provide information for public policy, resources management, conservation and education.
Founded: 1919
Robert M Timm, President
Nancy Solomon, VP

173 Animal Protection Institute
1122 S Street 916-447-3085
Sacramento, CA 95811 Fax: 916-447-3070
E-mail: info@api4animals.org
http://www.bornfreeusa.org

A national animal advocacy nonprofit organization established to advocate for the protection of animals from cruelty and exploitation. Its primary campaign areas include: farmed animals, companion animals, compassionate consumerism, wildlife protection, and animals used in entertainment.
Founded: 1968
Prashant K. Khetan, Chairman
Errol Antzis, Treasurer

174 Birds of Prey Foundation
2290 S 104th Street 303-460-0674
Broomfield, CO 80020 E-mail: raptor@birds-of-prey.org
http://www.birds-of-prey.org

Treats injured and orphaned wildlife, primarily raptors, such as eagles, hawks, falcons and owls and return healthy members of the breeding population to the natural habitat; fosters compassion for wildlife in distress and teach new generations through mentorships, internships, lectures, and volunteer programs; seeks protection for raptors in the wild through education, invention and interventions.
Sigrid Ueblacker, President/Executive Director
Brenda Leap, Secretary

175 Cetacean Society International
PO Box 953 203-770-8615
Georgetown, CT 6829 Fax: 860-561-0187
E-mail: rossiter@csiwhalesalive.org
http://www.csiwhalesalive.org

All volunteer, nonprofit conservation, educational and research organization to benefit whales, dolphins, porpoises and the marine environment. Promotes education and conservation programs, including whale and dolphin watching, and non-invasive, benign research. Advocates for laws and treaties to prevent commercial whaling, habitat destruction and other harmful or destructive human interactions. CSI's world goal is to minimize cetacean killing and captures and to enhance public awareness.
William Rossiter, President

176 Federal Wildlife Officers Association
PO Box 206 http://www.fwoa.org
Amesbury, MA 1913

An organization dedicated to the protection of wildlife, the enforcement of federal wildlife law, the fostering of cooperation and communication among federal wildlife officers, and the per-

petuation, enhancement and defense of the wildlife enforcement profession.
Dave Hubbard, President
John Brooks, Vice President

177 Foundation for North American Wild Sheep
720 Allen Avenue 307-527-6261
Cody, WY 82414 Fax: 307-527-7117
E-mail: fnaws@fnaws.org
http://www.wildsheepfoundation.org
The Foundation's mission is to promote and enhance populations of indigenous wild sheep on the North American continent, and to fund programs for the professional management of these populations, while keeping administrative costs to a minimum.
Founded: 1974
Mark Hansen, Chairman
Louis Rupp, Vice Chairman

178 Friends of the Australian Koala Foundation
214 W 29th Street 212-967-8200
Suite 1002 Fax: 212-967-7292
New York, NY 10001 E-mail: akf@savethekoala.com
http://www.savethekoala.com
Founded: 1986
Deborah Tabart, CEO
Lorraine O'Keefe, Administration & Finance

179 Friends of the Earth
1100 15th Street NW 202-783-7400
11th Floor 877-843-8687
Washington, DC 20005 Fax: 202-783-0444
E-mail: foe@foe.org
http://www.foe.org
National nonprofit advocacy organization dedicated to protecting the planet from environmental degradation; preserving biological, cultural and ethnic diversity, and empowering citizens to have an influential voice in decisions affecting the quality of their environment and their lives.
Founded: 1969
Erich Pica, President
Nick Berning, Director of Communications

180 Fund for Animals
200 West 57th Street 212-246-2096
New York, NY 10019 866-720-2676
Fax: 212-246-2633
E-mail: info@fundforanimals.org
http://www.fundforanimals.org/about/
The Fund for Animals was founded in 1967 by author/humanitarian Cleveland Amory to speak for those who can't. In 2005, The Fund for Animals merged with The Humane Society of the United States, to avoid duplication of program and increase strength and coordination in the areas of legislation, litigation, humane education and disaster relief.
Founded: 1967
Marian Probst, Chair

181 Game Conservancy USA
49 Locust Ave 203-661-7900
Suite 104 Fax: 203-661-7997
New Canaan, CT 06840 E-mail: gbignell@gcusa.org
http://www.gcusa.org
Seeks to increase support for research of conservation of game and wildlife habitats in the US and UK through an expanding membership base.
Bruce D. Sargent, President
John M.B. O'Connor, Treasurer

182 Hawk Migration Association of North America
P.O. Box 721 E-mail: info@hmana.org
Plymouth, NH 3264 http://www.hmana.org
The mission is to conserve raptor populations through the scientific study, enjoyment and appreciation of raptor migration.
Founded: 1974
Will Weber, Chair
Laurie Goodrich, Vice Chair

183 Hawkwatch International
2240 South 900 East 801-484-6808
Salt Lake City, UT 84106 800-726-4295
Fax: 801-484-6810
E-mail: hwi@hawkwatch.org
http://www.hawkwatch.org
Their mission is to monitor and protect hawks, eagles, other birds of prey and their environment through research, education and conservation.
Founded: 1986
Nancy Matro, Chair
Rachel Hayes, Treasurer

184 Humane Society of the United States
2100 L Street NW 202-452-1100
Washington, DC 20037 Fax: 202-778-6132
E-mail: corprelations@hsus.org
http://www.humanesociety.org
HSUS is the nation's largest animal-protection organization with more than 5 million constituents. The HSUS was founded to promote the humane treatment of animals, to foster respect, understanding, and compassion for all creatures. Today our message of care and protection embraces not only the animal kingdom but also the Earth and its environment. To achieve our goals we work through legal, educational, legislative and investigative means.
Founded: 1954
Wayne Pacelle, President/CEO
Michael Markarian, VP/COO

185 International Association for Bear Research and Management
1300 College Road 907-459-7238
Fairbanks, AK 99071 Fax: 907-451-9723
http://www.bearbiology.com
A Volunteer organization open to professional biologists, wildlife managers and others dedicated to the conservation of all species of bears. Consists of several hundred members from over 20 countries. Supports the scientific management of bears through research and distribution of information.
Frank Van Manen, President
Harry Reynolds, Vice President

186 International Society for Endangered Cats
709 A.N.Shoreline Blvd 630-240-4797
Mountain View, CA 94043 Fax: 614-487-8769
http://www.isec.org/isec-left-index.htm
A not-for-profit organization dedicated to the conservation of wild cats throughout the world. Most species of wild cats are threatened or endangered in all or parts of their native ranges and, unless action is taken in the near future, many will be lost to extinction. The society's goals are to raise public understanding and knowledge of wild cats and support and facilitate research on ecology, captive breeding and reintroduction of cats to their native habitats.
Ted Semon, President/Director
Dr. Peter Swan, President/Vice President

187 International Wild Waterfowl Association
500 Sylvian Heights Park Way 425-334-8223
PO Drawer 368 Fax: 425-397-8136
Scotland Neck, NC 27874 E-mail: dye@greatnorthern.net
http://www.wildwaterfowl.org
IWWA is committed to protecting and enhancing wild waterflow habitats. Supports the captive breeding and restoration of endangered species, and supports the establishment and maintenance of genetically diverse and disease-free captive populations of endangered waterfowl.
Walter Sturgeon, President

188 International Wildlife Coalition
Whale Adoption Program
70 East Falmouth Highway 508-548-8328
PO Box 388 Fax: 508-548-8542
East Falmouth, MA 2536 http://www.iwc.org
Adoption fees are used to help purchase rescue and research vessels, hire crews, and rescue whales and other marine mammals

from fishing nets, conduct crucial research, and help enforce wildlife protection laws and treaties.
Daniel J Morast, President

189 International Wildlife Conservation Society
PO Box 34 310-476-9305
Pacific Palisades, CA 90272 Fax: 212-220-7114
E-mail: peterb@internationalwildlife.org
http://www.internationalwildlife.org
John G Robinson, Director

190 International Wolf Center
1396 Highway 169 Ely 763-560-7374
Minneapolis, MN 55731 Fax: 763-560-7368
E-mail: mortiz@wolf.org
http://www.wolf.org
The International Wolf Center advances the survival of the wolf populations by teaching about wolves, their relationship to wildlands and the human role in their future.
Founded: 1985
Nancy Jo Tubbs, Chair
L. David Mech, Vice Chair

191 Last Chance Forever
PO Box 460993 210-499-4080
San Antonio, TX 78246-0993 Fax: 210-499-4305
E-mail: raptor@ddc.net
http://www.lastchanceforever.org
Dedicated to the rehabilitation of sick, injured and orphaned birds of prey, scientific investigation, and also just as importantly, the education of the public.
Founded: 1978
John A Karger, Executive Director

192 Muskies
PO Box 120870 701-239-9540
New Brighton, MN 58112 E-mail: info@muskiesinc.org
http://www.muskiesinc.org
Supports growth and interest in the sport of Muskie fishing. We are reaching out to protect our existing fisheries and to develop new fisheries.
Founded: 1966
Greg Wells, President

193 National Bison Association
8690 Wolff Ct. #200 303-292-2833
Westminster, CO 80031 Fax: 303-845-081
E-mail: info@bisoncentral.com
http://www.bisoncentral.com
Created from a merger of the American Bison Association and the National Buffalo Association, the NBA has over 2400 members in all 50 states and 16 foreign countries. It is a nonprofit association which promotes the preservation, production and marketing of bison. NBA activities and services serve to better inform and educate our members and the general public about bison.
Founded: 1995
Peter Cook, President
Bruce Anderson, Vice President

194 National Endangered Species Act Reform Coalition
1050 Thomas Jefferson Street NW 202-333-7481
6th Floor Fax: 202-338-2461
Washington, DC 20007 E-mail: nesarc@vnf.com
http://www.nesarc.org
A broad based coalition of roughly 150 member organizations, representing millions of individuals across the United States, that is dedicated to bringing balance back to Endangered Species Act. Our membership includes rural irrigators, municipalities, farmers, electric utilities and many other individuals and organizations that are directly affected by the ESA.
Nancy Macan McNally, Executive Director
Jordan Smith, Associate Director

195 National Hunters Association
PO Box 820 919-365-7157
Knightdale, NC 27545 Fax: 919-366-2142
E-mail: nhadvs@worldnet.att.net
http://www.nationalhunters.com
Our organization is dedicated to preserving the rights of hunters, promoting hunter safety among the youth and all hunters by demanding game controls and hunting laws, maintaining the rights to use and own firearms and protecting the environment and maintaining a healthy habitat.
D Smith, President
Faye Smith, Secretary/Treasurer

196 National Marine Fisheries Service Office of Protective Resources
1315 East-West Highway 301-713-2322
Silver Spring, MD 20910 Fax: 301-713-0376
E-mail: jim.lecky@noaa.gov
http://www.nmfs.noaa.gov
James H Lecky, Director

197 National Rifle Association of America
11250 Waples Mill Road 703-267-1000
Fairfax, VA 22030 800-672-3888
Fax: 703-267-3909
http://www.nra.org
Founded: 1871
Chris Cox, Executive Director

198 National Shooting Sports Foundation
11 Mile Hill Road 203-426-1320
Newtown, CT 6470-2359 Fax: 203-426-1087
E-mail: info@nssf.org
http://www.nssf.org
Leading trade association of the firearms and recreational shooting sports industry. A nonprofit communications and marketing organization, the NSSF manages a variety of programs designed to promote a better understanding of and a more active participation in the shooting sports.
Founded: 1961
Robert L. Scott, Chairman
Stephen Hornady, Co-Vice Chairman

199 National Trappers Association
524 5th Street 812-277-9670
Bedford, IN 47421 Fax: 812-277-9672
E-mail: ntaheadquarters@nationaltrappers.com
http://www.nationaltrapper.com
To promote conservation, legislation and administrative procedures; to save and faithfully defend from waste the natural resources of the United States; to promote environmental education programs; and to promote a continued annual fur harvest using the best tools presently available for that purpose.
Steve Fitzwater, President

200 National Walking Horse Association
4059 Iron Works Parkway 859-252-6942
Suite 4 Fax: 859-252-0640
Lexington, KY 40511 http://www.nwha.com
An alliance of people committed to preserving and fostering the natural abilities and welfare of the Walking Horse. Improves the lives of horses and people by encouraging responsibility and sportsmanship. Promotes educational and recreational activities, while preserving the unique qualities of the Walking Horse.
Lori Snyder-Lowe, President
Margaret Hershberger, Vice President

201 National Wildlife Federation
11100 Wildlife Center Drive 202-797-6800
Reston, VA 20190 800-822-9919
Fax: 202-797-6646
http://www.nwf.org
The National Wildlife Federation is the largest member-supported conservation group, uniting individuals, organizations, businesses and government to protect wildlife, wild places and the environment.
Larry J Schweiger, President/CEO
Jaime Matyas, Executive Vice President/COO

202 National Wildlife Federation: Office of Federal and International Affairs
1400 16th Street NW 202-797-6800
Washington, DC 20036 Fax: 202-797-6646

A field office of the NWF staffed by people experienced on policy issues, grassroots outreach, law, government affairs, and media. The Office educates, mobilizes and advocates to preserve and strengthen protection for wildlife and wildplaces.

203 Native American Fish and Wildlife Society
From The Eagle's Nest
8333 Greenwood BLVD 303-466-1725
Suite 260 866-890-7258
Denver, CO 80221 Fax: 303-466-5414
http://www.nafws.org

National tribal organization to develop a national communications network for the exchange of information and management techniques related to self-determined tribal fish and wildlife management.
Founded: 1983
D. Fred Matt, Executive Director
Ronald R. Rodgers, Deputy Director

204 North American Bear Society
4061 E Hartford Avenue 602-971-2338
PO Box 555774 Fax: 602-971-2100
Phoenix, AZ 85078 E-mail: bearsociety@nonline.com
http://www.nonprofitnet.com/nabs

To support the conservation and management of bear populations throughout North America for the benefit of the general public and future generations. Dedicated to the conservation and management of the indigenous bears of North America.
William T Smaltz, Founder

205 North American Native Fishes Association
123 W Mount Airy Avenue E-mail: nanfa@att.net
Philadelphia, PA 19119 http://www.nanfa.org

NANFA is dedicated to the enjoyment, study and conservation of the continent's native fishes. The objectives are: to increase and disseminate knowledge about fishes and their habitats among aquarium hobbyists, biologists, fish and wildlife officials, anglers, educators, students and others, through publications, electronic media, regional and national meetings, and other means; to promote the conservation and the protection/restoration of natural habitats; to advance the captive husbandry.

206 Organization of Wildlife Planners
500 Lafayette Road http://www.owpweb.org
PO Box 25
Saint Paul, MN 55155

A professional organization of creative, committed people concerned with the management and future of government agencies that manage fish and wildlife populations and habitat. The purpose of OWP is to improve fish and wildlife resource management capabilities through informed decision-making.
Founded: 1978
Verdie J. Abel, President
Michele Beucler, President Elect

207 POWS Wildlife Rehabilitation Center
15305 44th Avenue West 425-743-1884
PO Box 1037 Fax: 425-742-5711
Lynnwood, WA 98046 E-mail: kparker@paws.org
http://www.paws.org/wildlife

Each wildlife patient requires individualized, specialized care. But for every animal the goal is identical: rehabilitation and release into the wild.
Kip Parker, Director

208 Pacific Whale Foundation
300 Maalaea Road 808-249-8811
Suite 211 800-942-5311
Wailuku, HI 96793 Fax: 808-243-9021
E-mail: info@pacificwhale.org
http://www.pacificwhale.org

Mission is to promote appreciation, understanding and protection of whales, dolphins, coral reefs, and our planet's oceans. We accomplish this by educating the public from a scientific perspective about the marine environment.
Founded: 1980
Gregory Kaufman, President

209 People for the Ethical Treatment of Animals
501 Front Street 757-622-7382
Norfolk, VA 23510 Fax: 757-622-0457
E-mail: info@peta.org
http://www.peta.org

With more than 850,000 members, PETA is the largest animal rights organization in the world. Also dedicated to establishing and protecting the rights of all animals. Operates under the simple principal that animals are not ours to eat, wear, experiment on, or use for entertainment.
Founded: 1980
Ingrid Newkirk, President

210 Pheasants Forever
1783 Buerkle Circle 651-773-2000
St. Paul, MN 55110 877-773-2070
Fax: 651-773-5500
E-mail: contact@pheasantsforever.org
http://www.pheasantsforever.org

A non profit organization dedicated to the protection and enhancement of pheasant and other wildlife populations in North America. This mission is carried out through habitat improvement, land management, public awareness, and education.
Founded: 1983
Howard K Vincent, President/CEO
Robert P. Larson, Chairman

211 Pope and Young Club
273 Mill Creek Road 507-867-4144
PO Box 548 Fax: 507-867-4144
Chatfield, MN 55923 E-mail: admin@pope-young.com
http://www.pope-young.org

The Pope and Young Club is one of North America's leading bow hunting and conservation organizations. Founded in 1961 as a nonprofit scientific organization, the Club is patterned after the prestigious Boone and Crockett Club. The Club advocates and encourages responsible bow hunting by promoting quality, fair chase hunting, and sound conservation practices. Today it fosters and nourishes bow hunting excellence and acts in the best interest of our bow hunting heritage everywhere.
Founded: 1961
Donald Ace Morgan, President

212 Purple Martin Conservation Association
301 Peninsula Drive 814-833-7656
Suite 6 Fax: 814-833-2451
Erie, PA 16505 E-mail: generalinfo@purplemartin.org
http://www.purplemartin.org

The only organization devoted exclusively to the scientific study of purple martins, their biology, and habitat requirements.
Founded: 1986
James R. Hill, Founder
John Tautin, Executive Director

213 Safari Club International
4800 W Gates Pass Road 520-620-1220
Tucson, AZ 85745-9490 888-486-8724
Fax: 520-622-1205
http://www.safariclub.org/

A leader in wildlife conservation, hunter education, and protecting the freedom to hunt.
John Whipple, President
Mike J. Borel, Vice President

214 Scientists Center for Animal Welfare
2660 NE Highway 20 301-345-3500
Suite 610-115 Fax: 301-345-3503
Bend, OR 97701 E-mail: INFO@SCAW.COM
http://WWW.SCAW.COM

A nonprofit educational association of individuals whose mission is to promote humane care, use, and management of animals involved in research, testing or education in laboratory, agricultural, wildlife or other settings.
Founded: 1978
Randall J. Nelson, President
Paul G. Braunschweiger, Vice President

215 Sea Shepherd Conservation Society
PO Box 2616 — 360-370-5650
Friday Harbor, WA 98250 — Fax: 360-370-5651
E-mail: info@seasheperd.org
http://www.seashepherd.org
The mandate of this organization was mammal protection and conservation with an immediate goal of shutting down illegal whaling and sealing operations. We are committed to the eradication of private whaling, poaching, shark finning, unlawful habitat destruction, and violations of established laws in the world's oceans.
Founded: 1977
Marnie Gaede, President
Robert Wintner, Vice President

216 Sea Turtle Restoration Project
PO Box 370 — 415-488-0370
Forest Knolls, CA 94933 — Fax: 415-488-0372
E-mail: info@seaturtles.org
http://www.seaturtles.org
Fights to protect endangered sea turtle populations in ways that meet the ecological needs of the sea turtles and the oceans and the needs of the local communities who share the beaches and waters with these gentle, beautiful creatures.
Founded: 1989
Erica Heimberg, Managing Director
Todd Steiner, Executive Director

217 Society for Animal Protective Legislation
900 Pennsylvania Ave SE — 202-337-2334
Washington, DC 20003 — Fax: 202-338-9478
E-mail: awi@awionline.org
http://www.awionline.org
Prepares information for use by Members of Congress and their staffs to protect animals. Also sends action alerts to individuals and organizations interested in animal protective legislation, informing them of ways in which they may help.
Founded: 1955
Christine Stevens, President
Charles M. Jabbour, Treasurer

218 Society of Tympanuchus Cupido Pinnatus
College of Natural Resources — 715-346-3859
University of Wisconsin-Stevens Point — Fax: 715 346 3624
Stevens Point, WI 54481 — E-mail: eanderso@uwsp.edu
http://www.uwsp.edu/wildlife/programs
Russell Schallert, President

219 Sportsman's Network
111 S Main Street — 859-824-6526
PO Box 257 — 800-680-8058
Dry Ridge, KY 41035 — Fax: 606-824-0556
E-mail: sportsman@sportsmansnetwork.org
http://www.sportsmansnetwork.org
To raise awareness of animal wildlife conservation issues through various forms of public media and to address the subject in all appropriate ways including hunting, fishing, trapping, and related activities.
William Krebs, Treasurer

220 Trout Unlimited
1300 North 17th Street — 703-522-0200
Suite 500 — 800-834-2419
Arlington, VA 22209-2404 — Fax: 703-284-9400
E-mail: trout@tu.org
http://www.tu.org
Mission: To conserve. protect and restore North America's trout and salmon fisheries and their watersheds. We accomplish this mission on local, state and national levels with an extensive and dedicated volunteer network.
Founded: 1959
Hillary Coley, CFO/CAO
Elizabeth Maclin, Vice President

221 Trumpeter Swan Society
12615 County Road 9 — 763-694-7851
Plymouth, MN 55441-1248 — Fax: 763-476-1514
E-mail: ttss@trumpeterswansociety.org
http://www.trumpeterswansociety.org
Private, nonprofit organization dedicated to assuring the vitality and welfare of wild Trumpeter Swan populations, and to restoring the species to as much of its former range as possible.
Founded: 1968
John Cornley, Executive Director
Becky Abel, Associate Director

222 US Sportsmen's Alliance
801 Kingsmill Parkway — 614-888-4868
Columbus, OH 43229 — Fax: 614-888-0326
E-mail: info@USSPORTSMEN.org
http://www.ussportsmen.org
The US Sportsmen's Alliance is a national non-profit association that protects hunting, fishing and trapping and scientific wildlife management programs.
Founded: 1978
Walter Bud Pidgeon Jr, President/CEO
Douglas Jeanneret, Vice President

223 Waterfowl USA
Waterfowl Building — 803-637-5767
Box 50 — Fax: 803-637-6983
Edgefield, SC 29824 — E-mail: president@waterfowlusa.org
http://www.waterfowlusa.org
National non profit, conservation organization, dedicated to using funds in the areas in which they were raised for local and state waterfowl projects. Founded by biologists for the purpose of preserving and improving wintering and breeding habitat within the United States.
Founded: 1983
Roger L White, President/CEO

224 Whitetails Unlimited
2100 Michigan Street — 920-743-6777
PO Box 720 — 800-274-5471
Sturgeon Bay, WI 54235 — Fax: 920-743-4658
http://www.whitetailsunlimited.com
A national conservation organization that has remained true to its mission and has made great strides in the field of conservation. They have gained the reputation of being the nation's premier organization dedicating resources to the betterment of the white-tail deer and its environment.
Founded: 1982
Jeffrey Schinkten, President
Peter J. Gerl, Executive Director

225 Wilderness Society
1615 M Street NW — 800-843-9453
Washington, DC 20036 — E-mail: member@tws.org
http://www.wilderness.org
Protects the wilderness and inspires Americans to care for the wild places.
Founded: 1935
Jamie Williams, President
Thomas Tepper, Vice President

226 Wildlife Trust
460 West 34th Street — 212-380-4460
17th Floor — Fax: 212-380-4465
New York, NY 10001-2320 — http://www.ecohealthalliance.org
Works in the United States and worldwide to save threatened species from extinction, protect habitat, and link nature protection with health through collaborative projects with local scientists. They also communicate our results to educators, health professionals, policy experts and civic leaders.
Founded: 1971
Ellen Shedlarz, Chairman
Oliver Engert, Vice Chairman

227 **Xerces Society**
628 NE Broadway
Suite 200
Portland, OR 97232
503-232-6639
Fax: 503-233-6794
E-mail: info@xerces.org
http://www.xerces.org

An international non profit organization dedicated to protecting biological diversity through inverterate conservation. The Society advocates for invertebrates and their habitats by working with scientists, land managers, educators, and citizens on conservation and education projects. Core programs focus on endangered species, native pollinators, and watershed health.
Founded: 1971
Scott Hoffman Black, Executive Director
Mace Vaughan, Conservation Director

National: Habitat Preservation & Land Use

228 **Abundant Life Seeds**
PO Box 158
Cottage Grove, OR 97424
541-942-9547
800-626-0866
Fax: 888-657-3131
E-mail: info@territorialseed.com
http://www.territorialseed.com

Focuses on the genetic diversity of rare and endangered food crops. Offers varieties grown using only certified organic or biodynamic farming methods.
Founded: 1975

229 **Agricultural Resources Center-Pesticide Education Project**
CB #3456 Manning Hill
Chapel Hill, NC 27599-3456
919-833-5333
877-667-7729
E-mail: info@PESTed.org
http://www.ibiblio.org

Fawn Pattison, Executive Director
Billie Karel, Program Coordinator

230 **Aldo Leopold Foundation**
E13701 Levee Road
PO Box 77
Baraboo, WI 53913-0077
608-355-0279
Fax: 608-356-7309
E-mail: mail@aldoleopold.org
http://www.aldoleopold.org

The Aldo Leopold Foundation is a 501 (c)3 nonprofit organization that works to promote the philosophy of Aldo Leopold and the land ethic he so eloquently defined in his writing. The foundation actively integrates programs on land stewardship, environmental education and scientific research to promote care of natural resources and have an ethical relationship between people and land.
Founded: 1982
Wellington B Huffaker IV, President/Executive Director
Jennifer Anstett, Membership Associate

231 **America the Beautiful Fund**
725 15th Street NW
Suite 605
Washington, DC 20005
202-638-1649
Fax: 202-638-2175
E-mail: info@america-the-beautiful.org
http://www.america-the-beautiful.org

America the Beautiful Fund encourages volunteer citizen efforts to protect the natural and historic beauty of America. Programs include Operation Green Plant: Free Seeds!, which provides free seeds and bulbs for environmental education and preservation, community gardens and hunger relief.
Founded: 1965
Nanine Bilski, President/CEO
Kay Lautman, VP

232 **American Cave Conservation Association**
119 E Main Street
PO Box 409
Horse Cave, KY 42749
270-786-1466
Fax: 270-786-1467
E-mail: acca@caven.org
http://www.cavern.org/acca

A national nonprofit association dedicated to the protection of caves, karst lands and groundwater. The ACCA operates the American Cave Museum and Karst Center, an educational center that includes the American Cave Museum and Hidden River Cave.
Founded: 1978
David G Foster, Executive Director
Peggy A Nims, Community Outreach

233 **American Conservation Association**
1350 New York Ave NW
Suite 300
Washington, DC 20005
202-624-9365
Fax: 202-289-1396

Operative private organization dedicated to promote the knowledge and understanding of conservation, to preserve the live beauty of the landscape and the natural resources and organisms in areas of the United States and others, and to educate to the public in the adapted use of these areas.
Charles Clusen, Executive Director
R Greathead, Secretary

234 **American Council on the Environment**
1301 20th Street NW
Suite 113
Washington, DC 20036
202-659-1900
John H Gullett, Executive Officer

235 **American Geological Institute**
4220 King Street
Alexandria, VA 22302-1502
703-379-2480
Fax: 703-379-7563
E-mail: asm@agiweb.org
http://www.agiweb.org

Comprised of more than 50 scientific and professional associations that represent more than 120,000 geologists, geophysicists, and other earth scientists. Provides information services to geoscientists, serves as a voice of shared interests in the profession, plays a major role in strengthening geoscience education, and strives to increase public awareness of the vital role the geosciences play in society's use of resources and interaction with the environment.
Founded: 1948
P. Patrick Leahy, Executive Director
Patrick Burks, Controller

236 **American Institute of Fishery Research Biologists**
1315 E West Highway
Silver Spring, MD 20910
http://www.aifrb.org
Steve Cadrin, President
Allen Shimada, Treasurer

237 **American Land Conservancy**
1388 Sutter Street
Suite 810
San Francisco, CA 94109
415-912-3660
Fax: 415-749-3011
E-mail: mail@alcnet.org
http://www.alcnet.org

ALC is dedicated to the preservation of land and water as enduring public resources, to protect and enhance our nation's natural, ecological historical, recreational, and scenic heritage.
Kerry O'Toole, President

238 **American Lands**
230 N. Highland Street
Arlington, VA 22201
703-216-8624
E-mail: info@americanlands.org
http://www.americanlands.org

America's wildlife and wildlands continue to be threatened by logging, road building, grazing, off road vehicles and mining. A broad coalition of activists and organizations is dedicated to protecting our forest heritage and restoring ecological integrity to the landscape.
Jim Jontz, Executive Director
Randi Spivak, President

239 **American Littoral Society**
18 Hartshorne Drive
Suite 1
Highlands, NJ 07732
732-291-0055
Fax: 732-291-3551
E-mail: alssj@earthlink.net
http://www.littoralsociety.org

The American Littoral Society is an environmental organization concerned about issues that affect the littoral zone: that area on the beach between low and high tide. The American Littoral Soci-

ety is a national, nonprofit, public-interest organization comprised of over 6,000 professional and amateur naturalists.
Richard G. Lathrop, President
Peter Hetzler, Vice President

240 American Public Gardens Association
351 Longwood Road — 610-708-3010
Kenneth Square, PA 19348 — Fax: 610-444-3594
E-mail: mquigley@publicgardens.org
http://www.publicgardens.org
Formerly the American Association of Botanical Gardens and Arboreta. APGA is committed to increasing the knowledge of public garden professionals through information sharing, professional development, education, research and plant conservation.
Founded: 1940
Casey Sclar, Executive Director
Vivian Lovingood, Office Manager

241 American Shore and Beach Preservation Association
5460 Beaujolais Lane — 239-489-2616
Fort Myers, FL 33919 — Fax: 239-489-9917
E-mail: exdir@asbpa.org
http://www.asbpa.org
Dedicated to preserving, protecting and enhancing the beaches, shores and other coastal resources of America, recognizing their important quality-of-life assets.
Founded: 1926
Harry Simmons, President
Kate & Ken Gooderham, Executive Directors

242 Antarctica Project
1630 Connecticut Avenue NW — 202-234-2480
3rd Floor — Fax: 202-387-4823
Washington, DC 20009 — E-mail: secretariat@asoc.org
http://www.asoc.org
The only conservation organization in the world that works exclusively for Antarctica. Leads domestic and international campaigns to protect Antarctica's pristine wilderness and environment, as the international secretariat for the Antarctic and Southern Ocean Coalition (ASOC). ASOC is a global coalition with 214 member organizations working in 41 countries on six continents.
Beth Clark, Director
Josh Stevens, Campaign Associate

243 Arctic Network
PO Box 102252 — 907-272-2452
Anchorage, AK 99510 — Fax: 907-272-2453
Works to the conserve Arctic ecosystem. Focus includes indigenous cultures.

244 Association for Conservation Information
1000 Assembly Street — 843-762-5032
PO Box 167 — Fax: 843-734-3951
Columbia, SC 29202
ACI, the Association for Conservation Information, is a nonprofit association of information and education professionals representing state, federal and Canadian agencies and private conservation organizations.
Bob Campbell, President

245 Association for Environmental Health and Sciences
150 Fearing Street — 413-549-5170
Amherst, MA 01002 — Fax: 413-549-0579
E-mail: paul@aehs.com
http://www.aehs.com
The AEHS was created to facilitate communication and foster cooperation among professionals concerned with the challenge of soil protection and cleanup. Members represent the many disciplines involved in making decisions and solving problems affecting soils. AEHS recognizes that widely acceptable solutions to the problem can be found only through the integration of scientific and technological discovery, social and political judgment and hands on practice.
Paul Kostecki PhD, Executive Director
Cindy Langlois, Managing Director

246 Association for Natural Resources Enforcement Training
Missouri Department of Conservation — 573-751-4115
Box 180 — E-mail: yamnil@mail.conservation.state.mo.us
Jefferson City, MO 65102 — http://www.dirdid.com\anret
Dave Windsor, VP

247 Association of Consulting Foresters of America, Inc
312 Montgomery Street — 703-548-0990
Suite 208 — 888-540-8733
Alexandria, VA 22314 — Fax: 703-548-6395
E-mail: director@acf-foresters.org
http://www.acf-foresters.org
To protect the public welfare and property in the practice of forestry. To raise the professional standards and work of ACF Consultants and all other consulting foresters. To develop and expand the services of ACF Consultants.
Lynn C Wilson, Executive Director

248 Association of Field Ornithologists
University of Maine at Machias
9 O'Brian Avenue — http://www.afonet.org
Machias, ME 04654
Society of professional and amateur ornithologists dedicated to the scientific study and dissemination of information about birds in their natural habitats. Especially active in bird-banding and development of field techniques. Encourages participation of amateurs in research, and emphasizes conservation biology of birds.
Founded: 1922
Charles Duncan, President

249 Association of Great Lakes Outdoor Writers
123 2nd Ave, Suite 100 — 425-775-7282
PO Box 1749 — 877-472-4569
Edmonds, WA 98020 1749 — Fax: 425-778-9615
E-mail: aglow@aglow.org
http://www.aglow.info
Dedicated to communicating the outdoor experience in word and image.
Jane Hansen Hoyt, President/CEO
Rick Allen, Director

250 Association of Partners for Public Lands
2401 Blueridge Ave — 301-946-9475
Suite 303 — Fax: 301-946-9478
Wheaton, MD 20902 — E-mail: appl@appl.org
http://www.appl.org
To provide the highest levels of program and service to public agencies entrusted with the care of America's natural and cultural heritage.
Dan Puskar, Executive Director

251 Association of State Wetland Managers
32 Tandberg Trail — 207-892-3399
Suite 2A — Fax: 207-892-3089
Windham, ME 04062 — E-mail: aswm@aswm.org
http://www.aswm.org
Nonprofit organization dedicated to the protection and restoration of the nations wetlands. Our goal is to help public and private wetland decision-makers utilize the best possible scientific information and techniques in wetland delineation, assessment, mapping, planning, regulation, acquisition, restoration, and other management.
Founded: 1983
Jeanne Christie, Executive Director
Jon Kusler, Associate Director

252 Bat Conservation International
PO Box 162603 — 512-327-9721
Austin, TX 78716 — 800-538-2287
Fax: 512-327-9724
E-mail: batinfo@batcon.org
http://www.batcon.org
Dedicated to preserving and restoring bat populations and habitats around the world. Uses a non-confrontational approach to educate the public about the ecological and economic value of bats, advance scientific knowledge about bats and the ecosystems that

rely on them and preserve critical bat habitats through win-win solutions that benefit both humans and bats.
Founded: 1982 $35/Yr
Andrew Walker, Executive Director
Linda Moore, Director Administration

253 Big Thicket Association
PO Box 198 936-274-1181
Saratoga, TX 77585 E-mail: director@bigthicket.org
http://www.btatx.org
Formed to save remnants of the once extensive historic Big Thicket forests with its remarkable diversity.
Founded: 1964
Dr Bruce Drury, President
Elaine Allums, Secretary

254 Birds of Prey Foundation
2290 S 104th Street 303-460-0674
Broomfield, CO 80020 E-mail: raptor@birds-of-prey.org
http://www.birds-of-prey.org
The foundation seeks protection for raptors in the wild through education, invention and intervention; treats injured and orphaned wildlife; and works continuously to improve the quality of care and housing of captive raptors everywhere.
Sigrid Ueblacker, Executive Officer
Brenda Leap, Secretary

255 Boone and Crockett Club
250 Station Drive 406-542-1888
Missoula, MT 59801 Fax: 406-542-0784
E-mail: bcclub@boone-crockett.org
http://www.boone-crockett.org
Organization founded by Theodore Roosevelt with the vision of establishing a coalition of dedicated conservationists and sportsmen to provide leadership in the issues affecting hunting, wildlife and wildlife habitat.
Founded: 1887
William A. Demmer, President
Marshall J. Collins Jr., Treasurer

256 Brotherhood of the Jungle Cock
PO Box 576 E-mail: bosleywright@hotmail.com
Glen Burnie, MD 21061 http://www.flyfishersofvirginia.org/bojc.htm
Founded: 1940
Steve Lewis, President

257 Camp Fire Conservation Fund
230 Campfire Road 914-769-5508
Chappaqua, NY 10514-2419 Fax: 914-923-0977
E-mail: lvallen491@aol.com
The fund is a wildlife and habitat conservation organization that has been around for over 100 years.
Gordon Whiting, President

258 Canyonlands Field Institute
1320 South Highway 191 435-259-7750
PO Box 68 800-860-5262
Moab, UT 84532 Fax: 435-259-2335
E-mail: info@cfimoab.org
http://www.cfimoab.org
To increase understanding of, connection to and care for the Colorado Plateau, expand perception of and appreciation for the beauty and integrity of the natural world, improve the quality of field oriented, experiential teaching and learning for students and adults and to encourage individuals to be involved in the care of their own home places.
Founded: 1984
Karla VanderZanden, Executive Director
Dave Montgomery, Operations Manager

259 Caribbean Conservation Corporation & Sea Turtle Survival League
4424 NW 13th Street 352-373-6441
Suite B-11 800-678-7853
Gainesville, FL 32609 Fax: 352-375-2449
E-mail: stc@conserveturtles.org
http://www.conserveturtles.org
Strives to ensure the survival of sea turtles within the Wider Caribbean basin and Atlantic through research, education, training, advocacy and protection of habitats. CCC was the first marine turtle conservation organization in the world, and has more than 40 years of experience in national and international sea turtle conservation, research and educational endeavors.
Founded: 1959
David Godfrey, Executive Director
Gary Appelson, Policy Coordinator

260 Carrying Capacity Network
1629 K Street NW 202-296-4548
Suite 300 Fax: 202-296-4609
Washington, DC 20006 E-mail: info@carryingcapacity.org
http://www.carryingcapacity.org
An information exchange network. Interests include resource conservation, population stabilization and environmental protection.

261 Center for Clean Air Policy
750 1st Street Northeast 202-408-9260
Suite 940 Fax: 202-408-8896
Washington, DC 20002 E-mail: communications@ccap.org
http://www.ccap.org
A leader in climate and air quality policy, it advances cost-effective and pragmatic policies. International and domestic programs focus on these four major areas: GHG Emission and Mitigation Economics; Emerging Technologies and Technology Investment; Transportation and Land Use; and Adaptation.
Founded: 1985
Ned Helme, President
Micheal Comstock, Manager

262 Center for Humans and Nature
20 N. Wacker Drive 312-629-5060
Suite 2807 Fax: 312-629-5061
Chicago, IL 60606 http://www.humansandnature.com
Works to explore and promote human responsibilities in relation to nature.
Founded: 2003
Brooke Hecht, President

263 Center for Plant Conservation
4344 Shaw Blvd 314-577-9450
St. Louis, MO 63110 Fax: 314-577-9465
http://www.mobot.org/CPC/
The CPC is a consortium of 28 American botanical gardens and arboreta whose mission is to conserve and restore the rare native plants of the US To meet this end, they are involved in plant conservation, research and education. This site includes information about the National Collection of Endangered Plants, which is maintained by the group.

264 Center for Wildlife Information
PO Box 8289 406-721-8985
Missoula, MT 59807 E-mail: bearinfo@cfwi.org
http://www.centerforwildlifeinformation.org
Chuck Bartlebaugh, Contact

265 Center for the Study of Tropical Birds
218 Conway 210-828-5306
San Antonio, TX 78209 Fax: 210-828-9732
E-mail: office@cstBbnc.org
http://www.cstbinc.org
Devoted to the conservation of neotropical birdlife through collaborative programs of research and education.
Jack Eitniear, President/Chairman
Thomas Rueckle, Treasurer

266 Clean Sites
1199 N Fairfax Street 703-519-2135
Suite 400 Fax: 703-548-8733
Alexandria, VA 22314 E-mail: cses@cleansites.com
http://www.cleansites.com
We apply sound project management principles, real-world experience, and cost control measures to find creative solutions to environmental remediation and land reuse problems.
Douglas Ammon, Contact

267 Committee for Conservation and Care of Chimpanzees
3819 48th Street NW — 202-362-1993
Washington, DC 20016 — Fax: 202-686-3402
Dr. Geza Teleki, Chairman

268 Committee for the Preservation of the Tule Elk
PO Box 3696
San Diego, CA 92103
Jolene W Steigerwalt, Secretary

269 Community Greens Shared Parks in Urban Blocks
1700 N Moore Street, 20th Floor — 703-527-8300
Suite 2000 — Fax: 703-527-8383
Arlington, VA 22209 — E-mail: info@ashoka.org
http://www.communitygreens.org
Community Greens aims to transform the interiors of urban blocks across the US into resplendent shared parks and gardens that are owned and managed by the residents who live around them. These community greens would provide a green oasis for hassled city dwellers, offer a safe place for children to interact, increase home values and improve a sense of community. They would also help the environment by providing microhabitats for birds and small wildlife, clean the air and reduce urban sprawl.
Kate Herrod, Director

270 Conservation Education Association
3914 Foxdale Road — 573-751-4115
New Bloomfield, MO 65063
Dedicated to the education of individuals from all walks of life who are interested in making a difference to the environment. The association offers workshops, advocacy, literature and hands-on events.

271 Conservation Education Center
2473 160th Road — 641-747-0000
Guthrie Center, IA 50115 — Fax: 641-747-3951
E-mail: ajay.winter@dnr.state.ia.us
We are an educational facility serving 20,000 participants each year. We focus on hands-on natural resource topics.
A.J. Winter, Specialist

272 Conservation International
2011 Crystal Drive — 703-341-2400
Suite 500 — 800-429-5660
Arlington, VA 22202 — Fax: 202-887-5188
http://www.conservation.org
Our mission is to conserve the Earth's living natural heritage, our global biodiversity, and to demonstrate that human societies are able to live harmoniously with nature.
Peter A Seligmann, Chairman of the Board
Harrison Ford, Vice Chair

273 Conservation Management Institute
School of Natural Resources
1900 Kraft Drive — 540-231-7348
Suite 250 — Fax: 540-231-8825
Blackburg, VA 24061 — E-mail: CMInfo@vt.edu
http://www.cmi.vt.edu
To better address multi-disciplinary research questions that affect conservation management effectiveness in Virginia, North America and the world. Faculty from research institutions work collaboratively on projects ranging from endangered species propagation to natural resource-based satellite imagery interpretation.
Founded: 2000
Scott Kloper, Executive Director

274 Conservation Treaty Support Fund
3705 Cardiff Road — 301-654-3150
Chevy Chase, MD 20815 — 800-654-3150
Fax: 301-652-6390
E-mail: ctsf@conservationtreaty.org
http://www.conservationtreaty.org
CTSF's mission is to support the major inter-governmental treaties which conserve wild natural resources and habitat for their own sake and the benefit of people. These include the Endangered Species Convention and the International Wetlands Convention. CTSF raises support for treaty projects from individuals, corporations, foundations and government agencies. It also develops educational and informational materials including videos and the CITES Endangered Species Book.
Founded: 1986
George A Furness Jr, President

275 Counterpart International
2345 Crystal Drive — 571-447-5700
Suite 301 — Fax: 703-412-5035
Arlington, VA 22202 — E-mail: communications@counterpart.org
http://www.counterpart.org
Promotes socioeconomics, health care, biodiversity, and natural resource management in over 60 countries.
Joan C. Parker, President/CEO
Sibel Berzeg, Vice President

276 Defenders of Wildlife
1130 17th Street NW — 202-682-9400
Washington, DC 20036 — 800-385-9712
Fax: 202-682-1331
E-mail: defenders@mail.defenders.org
http://www.defenders.org
Dedicated to the protection of all native wild animals and plants in their natural communities. Focus is placed on what scientists consider two of the most serious environmental threats to the planet: the accelerating rate of extinction of species and the associated loss of biological diversity, and habitat alteration and destruction. Long known for leadership on endangered species issues.
Jamie Rappaport Clark, President/CEO
Donald Barry, Ex-Vice President

277 Delta Wildlife
PO Box 276 — 601-686-3370
Stoneville, MS 38776 — Fax: 601-686-1700
E-mail: teycoo@yahoo.com
http://www.nawf.org/dwf/
Recognizing the need for an aggressive, but reasonable effort to develop wildlife, in 1990, one-hundred agri-business leaders, representing every country in Mississippi Delta, had the vision and dedication to form Delta Wildlife so they and others could do more for conservation.
Bill Kennedy, Chairman

278 Department of Fisheries, Wildlife and Conservation Biology
University of Minnesota
200 Hodson Hall — 612-624-3600
1980 Folwell Avenue — Fax: 612-625-5299
St Paul, MN 55108 — E-mail: cuthb001@umn.edu
http://fwcb.cfans.umn.edu
Fosters a high quality natural environment by contributing to the management, protection, and sustainable use of fisheries and wildlife resources through teaching, research and outreach.
Founded: 1972
Francesca Cuthbert, Interim Department Head
Betsy Chastain, Program Coordinator

279 Desert Fishes Council
PO Box 337 — 760-872-8751
Bishop, CA 93515 — Fax: 760-872-8751
E-mail: phil@desertfishes.org
http://www.desertfishes.org
The mission of the Desert Fishes Council is to preserve the biological integrity of desert aquatic ecosystems and their associated life forms, to hold symposia to report related research and management endeavors, and to effect rapid dissemination of information concerning activities of the Council and its members.
Heidi B. Blasius, President
Phil Pister, Executive Secretary

280 Desert Protective Council
PO Box 3635 — 619-342-5524
San Diego, CA 92163-1635 — E-mail: terryweiner@dpcinc.org
http://www.dpcinc.org
To safeguard for wise and reverent use by this and succeeding generations those desert areas of unique scenic, scientific, histor-

ical, spiritual or recreational value and to educate children and adults to a better understanding of the deserts.
Founded: 1954
Janet Anderson, President
Larry Klaasen, Treasurer

281 Desert Tortoise Council
PO Box 1568 909-884-9700
Ridgecrest, CA 93556 E-mail: mojotort@yahoo.com
http://www.deserttortoise.org
The Council is a private, nonprofit organization made up of hundreds of professionals, and lay-persons from all walks of life, from across the United States, and several continents. We share a common fascination with wild desert tortoises and environment they depend upon.
Founded: 1976
Bruce Palmer, Chair
Joe Probst, Chair Elect

282 Dragonfly Society of the Americas
Bulletin of American Odonatology
2091 Partridge Lane 607-722-4939
Binghamton, NY 13903 E-mail: tdonnel@binghamton.edu
http://www.afn.org/~iori/dsaintro.html
The Dragonfly Society of the Americas was organized in 1988. It is a nonprofit society whose purpose is to encourage scientific research, habitat preservation and aesthetic enjoyment of Odonata (dragon flies).
TW Donnelly, Editor

283 Ducks Unlimited
One Waterfowl Way 901-758-3825
Memphis, TN 38120 800-453-8257
Fax: 847-438-9236
http://www.ducks.org
The mission is to fulfill the annual life cycle needs of North American waterfowl by protecting, enhancing, restoring and managing important wetlands and associated uplands.
George Dunkling Jr., President
Dale Hall, CEO

284 Eagle Nature Foundation
300 E Hickory Street 815-594-2306
Apple River, IL 61001 Fax: 815-594-2305
E-mail: eaglenature.tni@juno.com
http://www.eaglenature.com
A nonprofit organization dedicated to the preservation of the bald eagle, our national symbol, and other endangered species from extinction and to increase public awareness of unique endangered plants and animals. They monitor bald eagle and other endangered species populations, strive to preserve habitat essential to their survival, and develops materials for schools to inform students about the needs of the bald eagle and how we can help preserve and protect their natural environment.
Founded: 1995
Terrence N Ingram, Founder/President
Eugene Small, Vice President

285 Earth Ecology Foundation
612 N 2nd Street 559-442-3034
Fresno, CA 93702
Erik Wunstell, Director

286 Earth Island Institute
2150 Allston Way 510-859-9100
Suite 460 Fax: 510-859-9091
San Francisco, CA 94704-1375E-mail: johnknox@earthisland.org
http://www.earthisland.org
A non-profit, public interest, membership organization that supports people who are creating solutions to protect our shared planet.
Founded: 1982
John Knox, Executive Director
Dave Phillips, Executive Director

287 Elephant Interest Group
106 E Hickory Grove 313-540-3947
Bloomfield Hills, MI 48304 http://www.webdirectory.com
Hezy Shoshani, Contact

288 Elsa Wild Animal Appeal USA
PO Box 675 630-833-8896
Elmhurst, IL 60126 http://www.2ca.com/fullefx/2king4.htm
Donald A Rolla, President

289 Endangered Species Coalition
PO Box 65195 240-353-2765
Washington, DC 20035 E-mail: esc@stopextinction.org
http://www.stopextinction.org
The Coalition is one of the most unique organizations in the United States. An organization of organizations that supports endangered species issues for over 430 environmental, religious, scientific, humane, and business groups around the country. The vast majority of our member groups are small, local grassroots organizations, who struggle to protect species and habitats in their region.
Brock Evans, President
Julie Fox Gorte, Treasurer

290 Ford Foundation
320 E 43rd Street 212-573-5000
New York, NY 10017 Fax: 212-599-4584
http://www.fordfoundation.org
Concerned with natural resource preservation. Provides funding for environmental projects throughout the world.
Luis A. Ubinas, President
Ricardo A. Castro, Vice President

291 Forest Guild
PO Box 519 505-983-8992
Santa Fe, NM 87504 Fax: 505-986-0798
E-mail: info@forestguild.org
http://www.forestguild.org
The Forest Trust merged with Forest Stewards Guild to form Forest Guild. The practice of conservation forestry and the promotion of stewardship are central to the guild's mission.
Founded: 1984
Mike DeBonis, Executive Director

292 Forest History Society
701 Vickers Avenue 919-682-9319
Durham, NC 27701-3162 Fax: 919-682-2349
E-mail: stevena@duke.edu
http://www.foresthistory.org
Brings lessons of forest and conservation history to bear on current issues in natural resource management. Identifies, collects, preserves, interprets and disseminates information on forest and conservation history with the goals of improving the public's understanding of the forest industry and forest products; providing original resource material to researchers writing forest history, to assure accuracy on facts and interpretation; and facilitating development of natural resource policy.
Steven Anderson, President

293 Friends of Acadia
43 Cottage Street 207-288-3340
PO Box 45 800-625-0321
Bar Harbor, ME 04609 Fax: 207-288-8938
E-mail: info@friendsofacadia.org
http://www.friendsofacadia.org
The mission of Friends of Acadia is to preserve and protect the outstanding natural beauty, ecological vitality and cultural distinctiveness of Acadia National Park and the surrounding communities. Their methods are: raises and donates private funds to park and communities; advocates before legislatures and agencies; counters threats to park; and represents users in betterment of its operations.
Founded: 1986
David MacDonald, President/CEO
Mike Staggs, Manager

294 Friends of the Sea Lion Marine Mammal Center
20612 Laguna Canyon Road 949-494-3050
Laguna Beach, CA 92651 Fax: 949-494-2802
E-mail: info@fslmmc.org
http://www.fslmmc.org
Friends of the Sea Lion Marine Mammal Center is a nonprofit organization staffed by dedicated volunteers and funded by donations. Its mission is to rescue, medically treat and rehabilitate seals and sea lions that are stranded along Orange County, California beaches due to injury and illness; release healthy animals back to their natural habitat; and increase public awareness of the marine environment through education and research.
WH Ford, Executive Officer

295 Friends of the Sea Otter
PO Box 223260 831-373-2747
Carmel, CA 93922 Fax: 831-373-2749
E-mail: info@seaotters.org
http://www.seaotters.org
Friends of the Sea Otter is a nonprofit organization founded in 1968 dedicated to the protection of a threatened species, the Southern Sea Otter, as well as Sea Otters throughout their north pacific range, and all sea otter habitat.
Frank Reynolds, Program Manager
Jim Curland, Program Director

296 Garden Club of America
14 E 60th Street 212-753-8287
New York, NY 10022 Fax: 212-753-0134
E-mail: gca@gcamerica.org
http://www.gcamerica.org
To stimulate the knowledge and love of gardening, to share the advantages of association by means of educational meetings, conferences, correspondence and publications, and to restore, improve, and protect the quality of the environment through educational programs and action in the fields of conservation and civic improvement.
Frederik Hansen, President

297 George Wright Society
PO Box 65 906-487-9722
Hancock, MI 49930 Fax: 906-487-9405
http://www.georgewright.org
Concerned with the preservation of natural and cultural parks in the United States.
Gary E. Davis, Treasurer

298 Global Coral Reef Alliance
324 Bedford Road 914-238-8788
Chappaqua, NY 10514 Fax: 914-238-8768
E-mail: goreau@bestweb.net
http://www.people.fas.harvard.edu/~goreau
A nonprofit organization for the protection and sustainable management of coral reef.
Dr. Thomas J Goreau, President

299 Gopher Tortoise Council
Florida Museum of Natural History
PO Box 117800 904-362-1721
University of Florida http://www.gohertortoisecouncil.org
Gainesville, FL 32611
Formed by a group of biologists and others concerned about the range-wide decline of the gopher tortoise.
Founded: 1978
Jennifer Howze, Co-Chair
Rachael Sulker, Co-Chair

300 Grand Canyon Trust
2601 N Fort Valley 928-774-7488
Flagstaff, AZ 86001 888-428-5550
E-mail: info@grandcanyontrust.org
http://www.grandcanyontrust.org
The mission of The Grand Canyon Trust is to protect and restore the canyon country of the Colorado Plateau. Our vision for this unique region 100 years from now is of a landscape still characterized by vast open spaces and dominated by wildness and of healthy and restored natural ecosystems.
Founded: 1985
Bill Hedden, Executive Director
Darcy Allen, Director of Administration

301 Grassland Heritage Foundation
PO Box 394 785-748-0955
Shawnee Mission, KS 66201 http://www.grasslandheritage.org
Grassland Heritage Foundation is a nonprofit membership organization to prairie preservation and education.
Founded: 1976
Angie Babbit, President
Joyce Wolf, Vice President

302 Great Bear Foundation
802 E Front St 406-829-9378
PO Box 9383 Fax: 406-829-9379
Missoula, MT 59807-9383 E-mail: gbf@greatbear.org
http://www.greatbear.org
The Foundation was established to promote conservation of wild bears and their natural habitat worldwide.
Liz Sedler, President
Brian Horejsi, Vice President

303 Hawkwatch International
2240 South 900 East 801-484-6808
Salt Lake City, UT 84106 800-726-4295
Fax: 801-484-6810
E-mail: hwi@hawkwatch.org
http://www.hawkwatch.org
Thier mission is to monitor and protect hawks, eagles, other birds of prey and their environment through research, education and conservation.
Founded: 1986
Nancy Matro, Chairman
Caroline Goldman, Executive Director

304 Henry A Wallace Institute for Alternative Agriculture
9200 Edmonston Road 301-441-8777
Suite 117 Fax: 301-220-0164
Greenbelt, MD 20770 E-mail: hawiaa@access.digex.net
http://www.hawiaa.org
The Institute is a nonprofit, tax-exempt, research and education organization established in 1983 to encourage and facilitate the adoption of low-cost, resource-conserving, and environmentally sound farming systems. Provides leadership, policy research and analysis to influence national agricultural educational and research institutions, producer groups, farmers, scientists, advocates, and other organizations that provide agricultural research, education, and information services.
Founded: 1983
I Garth Youngberg, Executive Director

305 Holy Land Conservation Fund
969 Park Avenue 718-965-1057
New York, NY 10028
Bertel Bruun, President

306 Humane Society of the United States
2100 L Street NW 202-452-1100
Washington, DC 20037 Fax: 202-778-6132
E-mail: corprelations@hsus.org
http://www.humanesociety.org
HSUS is the nation's largest animal-protection organization with more than 5 million constituents. The HSUS was founded in 1954 to promote the humane treatment of animals, to foster respect, understanding, and compassion for all creatures. Today our message of care and protection embraces not only the animal kingdom but also the Earth and its environment. To achieve our goals we work through legal, educational, legislative and investigative means.
Founded: 1954
Wayne Pacelle, President/CEO
Michael Markarian, Executive VP/COO

307 Hummingbird Society
6560 Highway 179 928-284-2251
Suite 124 800-529-3699
Sedona, AZ 86351 Fax: 928-284-2251
E-mail: info@hummingbirdsociety.org
http://www.hummingbirdsociety.org

Nonprofit corporation organized for the purpose of encouraging international understanding and conservation of hummingbirds by publishing and disseminating information, promoting and supporting scientific study and protecting habitat.
Founded: 1996
Dr Robert L Gell, President
Dr H Ross Hawkins, Executive Director/Secretary

308 Inland Bird Banding Association
1409 Childs Road East 419-447-0005
Bellevue, NE 68005 E-mail: jingold@pilot.lsus.edu
http://www.aves.net/inlandbba/

Inland Bird Banding Association was organized in 1922, and now supports the largest membership of any bird banding association in America. Inland Bird Banding Association is an organization for all individuals interested in the serious study of birds, their life-history, ecology, and conservation.
Founded: 1922
James Ingold, President
Vernon Kleen, Vice President

309 Institute for Conservation Leadership
6930 Carroll Ave 301-270-2900
Suite 1050 Fax: 301-270-0610
Takoma Park, MD 20912 http://www.icl.org

The mission of this Institute is to train and empower volunteer leaders and to build volunteer institutions that protect and conserve the Earth's environment. We lend a helping hand to our dedicated friends in pursuit of a better world for everyone.
Dianne Russell, President
Margaret Bond, Director

310 Institute for the Human Environment
PO Box 552 707-935-9335
Vineburg, CA 95487

Community planning and land use.
Norman Gilroy, President
Shelley Arrowsmith, Vice President

311 International Association for Bear Research and Management
2841 Forest Avenue 510-549-3116
Berkley, CA 94705 E-mail: ucumari@aol.com
http://www.bearbiology.com

The International Association for Bear Research and Management (IBA)is a nonprofit tax-exempt volunteer organization open to professional biologists, wildlife managers and others dedicated to the conservation of all species of bears. The organization consists of several hundred members from over 20 countries. It supports the scientific management of the bears through research and distribution of information.
Bernie Peyton, Secretary

312 International Association of Theoretical and Applied Limnology
University of Alabama
Department of Biology 205-348-1793
Tuscaloosa, AL 35487 http://www.limnology.org

To further the study and understanding of all aspects of limnology. Promotes and communicates new and emerging knowledge among limnologists to advance the understanding of inland aquatic ecosystems and their management.
Prof. Dr. Brian Moss, President
Dr. Morten Sondergaard, Treasurer/Secretary

313 International Bird Rescue Research Center
PO Box 2171 707-207-0380
Long Beach, CA 90801 818-222-9453
Fax: 707-207-0395
E-mail: jlewis@ibrrc.org
http://www.bird-rescue.org

Dedicated to mitigating the human impact on aquatic birds and other wildlife, worldwide. This is achieved through emergency response, education, research and planning.
Founded: 1972
Jay Holcomb, Director
Andrew Harman, Communications Manager

314 International Council for Bird Preservation, US Section
World Wildlife Fund
1250 24th Street NW 202-467-8348
Washington, DC 20037 Fax: 202-293-9342
E-mail: abc@mnsinc.com
http://www.worldwildlife.org

Founded: 1994
Carter Roberts, President/CEO
Marcia Marsh, COO

315 International Crane Foundation
E-11376 Shady Lane Road 608-356-9462
PO Box 447 Fax: 608-356-9465
Baraboo, WI 53913 E-mail: cranes@savingcranes.org
http://www.savingcranes.org

Works worldwide to conserve cranes and the wetland and grasslands communities on which they depend. Dedicated to providing experience, knowledge, and inspiration to involve people in resolving threats to these ecosystems.
Founded: 1973
Richard Beilfuss, President/CEO
Robert Dohmen, Secretary

316 International Ecology Society
R Kramer
909 Sepulveda Blvd 651-774-4971
11th Floor 800-835-8857
El Segundo, CA 90245 http://www.businessfinance.com
Richard Kramer, President
Corey Pierce, Founder/COO

317 International Erosion Control Association
3001 S Lincoln Ave 970-879-3010
Suite A Fax: 970-879-8563
Steamboat Springs, CO 80487 E-mail: ecinfo@ieca.org
http://www.ieca.org

An organization dedicated to minimizing accelerated soil erosion. IECA offers an annual conference, chapter events, training courses as well as a variety of topic specific publications and a quarterly news letter.
Founded: 1972
Philip Handley, President
Beth Chesson, Secretary

318 International Fund for Animal Welfare
290 Summer Street 508-744-2000
Yarmouth Port, MA 02675 800-932-4329
Fax: 508-744-2009
E-mail: info@ifaw.org
http://www.ifaw.org

IFAW's mission is to improve the welfare of the wild and domestic animals throughout the world by reducing commercial exploitation of animals, protecting wildlife habitats, and assisting animals in distress. We seek to motivate the public to prevent cruelty to animals and to promote animal welfare and conservation policies that advance the well-being of both animals and people.
Azzedine Downes, President/CEO
Thom Maul, CFO

319 International Osprey Foundation
PO Box 250 941-472-1862
Sanibel Island, FL 33957 http://www.sancap.com

Nonprofit corporation dedicated to the continuing recovery and preservation of the osprey, others in the raptor family, wildlife and the environment as a whole. Conducts monitoring activities and accumulates data specific to the breeding activities of the osprey population. Publishes newsletter, issues grants for researchers whose studies involve environmental concerns. Directs and

participates in all areas of wildlife and habitat maintenance and restoration.
Tim Gardner, President
Anne Mitchell, VP

320 International Snow Leopard Trust
4649 Sunnyside Avenue N 206-632-2421
Suite 325 Fax: 206-632-3967
Seattle, WA 98103 E-mail: info@snowleopard.org
http://www.snowleopard.org
The trust is dedicated to the conservation of the endangered Snow Leopard and its mountain ecosystem. Since its founding by Helen Freeman, ISLT has worked on more than 100 projects with local people throughout Central Asia. Focus is on small, creative and sustainable programs to make conservation happen now and in the future. Has hosted snow leopard symposia and developed the Snow Leopard Information Management System. This allows for range-wide comparison and sharing of information.
Founded: 1981
Brad Rutherford, Executive Director
Katie Yankula, Office Manager

321 International Society for the Preservation of the Tropical Rainforest
3302 N Burton Avenue 626-572-0233
Rosemead, CA 91770 800-932-4329
Fax: 818-990-3333
E-mail: pard_expeditions@yahoo.com
http://www.isptr-pard.org/orderlist.html
ISPTR is mandated to publish, inform policy makers and the pub lic, as well as conduct programs toward the conservation of tropical forests, fauna and flora and tribal peoples globally.
Founded: 1994
Roxanne Kremer, Executive Director

322 International Society for the Protection of Mustangs and Burros
PO Box 55 605-964-6866
Lantry, SD 57636-0055 Fax: 605-430-2088
E-mail: ispmb@lakotanetwork.com
http://www.ispmb.com
Dedicated to preserving wild horses/burros and their habitats. We also run a rescue program and purchase slaughter bound wild horses and burros, placing them in permanent loving homes, or transporting entire herds of horses.
Karen Sussman, President

323 International Union for Conservation of Nature and Natural Resources
World Conservation Union
1630 Connecticut Avenue NW 202-387-4826
Washington, DC 20009 Fax: 202-387-4823
E-mail: postmaster@iucnus.org
http://www.iucn.org
Founded: 1948
Russell Mittermeier, Chairman
Gary Allport, Senior Conservation Policy A

324 International Union for the Conservation of Nature's Primate Specialist Group
2011 Crystal Drive 703-341-2400
Suite 500 800-429-5660
Arlington, VA 22202 Fax: 202-887-5188
http://www.conservation.org
The mission is to conserve the Earth's living natural heritage, our global biodiversity, and to demonstrate that human societies are able to live harmoniously with nature.
Peter A. Seligmann, Chairman
Harrison Ford, Vice Chair

325 International Wildlife Rehabilitation Council
PO Box 3197 408-271-2685
Eugene, OR 97403 Fax: 408-271-9285
E-mail: office@theiwrc.org
http://www.theiwrc.org
A nonprofit international membership organization. Founded in 1972, the IWRC works to enhance the integrity of native wildlife systems and conserve biological diversity worldwide, through rehabilitation of wildlife, support of rehabilitators, public education and advocacy.
Founded: 1974
Lynn Miller, President
Rebekah Weiss, Vice President

326 Island Conservation Effort
2161 Delaware Ave 831-359-4787
Suite A Fax: 305-663-9941
Santa Cruz, CA 95060 http://www.islandconservation.org
David Hartwell, Chairman
John Dawson, Vice Chair

327 Izaak Walton League of America
707 Conservation Lane 301-548-0150
Gaithersburg, MD 20878 800-453-5463
Fax: 301-548-0146
E-mail: info@iwla.org
http://www.iwla.org
The mission is to conserve, maintain, protect and restore the soil, forest water and other natural resources of the United States and other lands; to promote means and opportunities for the education of the public with respect to such resources and their enjoyment and wholesome utilization.
Founded: 1922
Robert Chapman, President
Shawn Gallagher, Vice President

328 Jackson Hole Preserve
30 Rockefeller Plaza 212-649-5819
Room 5600 Fax: 212-649-5729
New York, NY 10112 http://www.undueinfluence.com
Founded: 1940
Laurance Rockefeller, Chairman of the Board
Clayton Frye, President

329 Life of the Land
76 N King Street 808-533-3454
Suite 203 Fax: 808-533-0993
Honolulu, HI 96817 E-mail: henry@lifeoftheland.net
http://www.lifeofthelandhawaii.org
Hawaii's own environmental and community action group protecting our fragile natural and cultural resources through research, education, advocacy and litigation.
Founded: 1970
Kapua Sproat, President
Henry Curtis, Executive Director

330 Lighthawk
304 Main Street, Suite 14 307-332-3242
PO Box 653 Fax: 888-297-0156
Lander, WY 82850 E-mail: sfo@lighthawk.org
http://www.lighthawk.org
Nonprofit organization founded in 1979, addresses critical environmental issues by providing an aerial perspective on areas of concern in the US, Canada and Central America. Using small aircraft, we fly partner organizations, elected officials, industry and media representatives, activists, and indigenous groups over protected and threatened regions. Our program flights give passengers both intellectual and visceral understanding of what is at stake.
Founded: 1979
C. Rudy Engholm, Executive Director
Laura Armstrong, Director

331 Marin Conservation League
175 N Redwood Drive 415-472-6170
Suite 135 Fax: 415-472-1404
San Rafael, CA 94903 E-mail: mcl@conservationleague.org
http://www.conservationleague.org
The Marin Conservation League is an a nonprofit organization founded in 1934 to preserve, protect and enhance the natural assets of Marin County for all people. MCL is Marin's oldest, locally based environmental organization, championing a sound balance between the needs of Marin's citizens and its beautiful and fragile environment.
David Schnap, President
Jana Haehl, First Vice President

332 Mineral Policy Center
1612 K Street NW 202-887-1872
Suite 808 Fax: 202-887-1875
Washington, DC 20006 E-mail: info@earthworksaction.org
http://www.mineralpolicy.org

Mining causes serious environmental problems for local communities across the United States and throughout the world. From the perpetual water pollution caused by mine drainage to cyanide spills and heavy metals contamination; from the desecration of sacred sites to the creation of toxic waste rock- mining creates devastating environmental consequences. Mineral Policy Center carries out research and publishes comprehensive reports on the environmental impacts of mining.

Stephen D'Esposito, President/CEO
Cathy Carlson, Policy Advisor

333 Monitor Consortium of Conservation Groups
1506 19th Street NW 202-234-6576
Washington, DC 20036
Craig VanNote, Executive VP

334 Mountain Institute
3000 Connecticut Avenue NW 202-234-4050
Suite 101 Fax: 202-234-4051
Washington, DC 20008 E-mail: summit@mountain.org
http://www.mountain.org

The Mountain Institute's objectives are to: conserve high priority mountain eco-systems; increase environmentally and culturally sustainable livelihoods for mountain communities; and promote support for mountain cultures and issues through advocacy, education and outreach.

Founded: 1972
Andrew Taber, Executive Director
Chris Czarnecki, Program Officer

335 National Association of Conservation Districts
509 Capitol Court NE 202-547-6223
Washington, DC 20002-4937 Fax: 202-547-6450
E-mail: krysta-harden@nacdnet.org
http://www.nacdnet.org

A nongovernmental, nonprofit organization representing 3000 local soil and water conservation districts as well as the 17,000 that serve on their governing boards. Among its goals are: provide useful information to the districts and their state associations; represent them as a national unified voice; analyze programs and policy issues that have an impact on local districts; and offer needed and cost-effective services.

Founded: 1946
John Larson, CEO
Bethany Shively, Director Communications

336 National Audubon Society
225 Varick Street 212-979-3000
New York, NY 10014 800-274-4201
Fax: 212-979-3188
E-mail: audubon@emailcustomerservice.com
http://www.audubon.org

The National Audubon Society is one of the oldest, largest, and most powerful nature appreciation and conservation organizations in the country. NAS works on a broad range of concerns related to the protection of the world's ecosystems; preserving wetlands, population planning, eliminating acid rain and reducing air pollution, promoting environmental justice, and protecting water quality.

Founded: 1905
David Yarnold, President/CEO
John Beavers, Vice President

337 National Audubon Society: Project Puffin
311 Main Street 207-596-5566
Rockland, ME 04841 Fax: 607-257-6231
E-mail: puffin@audubon.org
http://www.projectpuffin.org

Established in 1973 in an effort to learn how to restore puffins to historic nesting islands in the Gulf of Maine. Although puffins are abundant in Newfoundland, Iceland and Britain, they are rare in Maine. Project Puffin has a year round staff of six which increases to include more than 50 biologists and researchers during the seabird breeding season in spring and summer. The project is based in Ithaca, New York and the Todd Wildlife Sanctuary in mid-coast Maine.

Founded: 1973
Stephen W. Kress, Director
Rosalie Borzik, Associate Director

338 National Conservation Foundation
509 Capitol Court NE 202-547-6223
Washington, DC 20002 Fax: 202-547-6450
E-mail: libbysimon@conservationfoundation.com
http://www.nacdnet.org

Founded: 1982
Donald Spickler, Chairman
Clear Spring, Managing Director

339 National Council for Environmental Balance
4169 Westport Road 502-896-8731
PO Box 7732 Fax: 502-339-1745
Louisville, KY 40257 http://www.exxonsecrets.org
Irwin Tucker, President

340 National Fish and Wildlife Foundation
1133 15th Street, NW 202-857-0166
Suite 1100 Fax: 202-857-0162
Washington, DC 20005 E-mail: decarolis@nfwf.org
http://www.nfwf.org

The National Fish and Wildlife Foundation is a nonprofit organization dedicated to the conservation of fish, wildlife, and plants and the habitats on which they depend. Among its goals are species habitat protection, environmental education, public policy development, natural resource management, habitat and ecosystem rehabilitation and restoration, and leadership training for conservation professionals.

Founded: 1984
Don J. McGrath, Chairman
Jeff Trandahl, CEO/Executive Director

341 National Forest Foundation
Fort Missoula Road 202-298-6740
Building 27, Suite 3 Fax: 406-542-2810
Missoula, MT 59804 E-mail: bpossiel@nationalforests.org
http://www.natlforests.org

The official nonprofit partner of the USDA Forest Service. To accept and administer private contributions, undertaking activities that further the purposes for which the National Forest System was established and conducting educational, technical, and other activities that support the multiple use, research, and forestry programs administered by the Forest Service.

Bill Possiel, President
Mary Mitsos, Executive Vice President

342 National Garden Clubs
4401 Magnolia Avenue 314-776-7574
St Louis, MO 63110 800-550-6007
Fax: 314-776-5108
E-mail: headquarters@gardenclub.org
http://www.gardenclub.org

National Garden Clubs is a nonprofit educational organization with its headquarters in St. Louis, Missouri, US. It is composed of 50 State Garden Clubs and the National Capital Area, 8,858 member garden clubs and 235,316 members. In addition, NGC proudly recognizes 200 International Affiliates from Canada to Mexico and South America.

Founded: 1891
Linda Nelson, President
Sandra Robinson, First Vice President

343 National Grange
1616 H Street NW 202-628-3507
Washington, DC 20006 888-447-2643
Fax: 202-347-1091
E-mail: rfrederick@nationalgrange.org
http://www.nationalgrange.org

The Grange is a family based community organization with a special interest in agriculture and rural America, as well as in legislative efforts regarding these issues.
Founded: 1867
Ed Luttrell, President
Jessie Cope, Executive Assistant

344 National Institute for Urban Wildlife
10921 Trotting Ridge Way 301-596-3311
Columbia, MD 21044
Promotes the preservation of wildlife in urban settings, providing support to individuals and organizations involved in maintaining a place for wildlife in expanding American cities and suburbs. The Institute conducts research exploring the relationship between humans and wildlife in these habitats, publicizes urban wildlife management methods, and raises public awareness of the value of wildlife in city settings. The Institute also provides consulting services.
Founded: 1973

345 National Military Fish and Wildlife Association
12428 Pinecrest Lane 540-663-4186
Newburg, MD 20664 Fax: 540-663-4016
E-mail: nmfwa@nmfwa.org
http://www.nmfwa.org
David McNaughton, President
Todd Wills, President Elect

346 National Park Foundation
1201 Eye Street NW 202-354-6460
Suite 550B Fax: 202-371-2066
Washington, DC 20005 E-mail: ask-npf@nationalparks.org
http://www.nationalparks.org
Mission is to strengthen the connection between the American people and their National Parks by raising private funds, making strategic grants, creating innovative partnerships and increasing public awareness.
John L. Lau III, Vice Chair

347 National Park Trust
401 E Jefferson Street 301-279-7275
Suite 203 866-281-5971
Rockville, MD 20850 Fax: 301-279-7211
E-mail: npt@parktrust.org
http://www.parktrust.org
Founded: 1983
Grace K Lee, Executive Director
Shana Newman Fajardo, Development Director

348 National Parks Conservation Association
777 6th Street NW 800-628-7275
Suite 700 Fax: 202-659-0650
Washington, DC 20001-3723 E-mail: npca@npca.org
http://www.npca.org
Since 1919, the National Parks Conservation Association has been the voice of the American people in the fight to safeguard the scenic beauty, wildlife, and historical and cultural treasures of the largest and most diverse park system in the world.
Founded: 1916
Theresa Pierno, Acting President
Ron Tipton, Senior Vice President

349 National Prairie Grouse Technical Council
Wildlife Research Center
317 W Prospect Road 414-559-4278
Fort Collins, CO 80526 Fax: 970-490-2621
Russell C. Schallert, President
Greg Septon, Executive Director

350 National Recreation and Park Association
Parks and Recreation Magazine
22377 Belmont Ridge Road 703-858-0784
Ashburn, VA 20148 Fax: 703-858-0794
E-mail: customerservice@nrpa.org
http://www.nrpa.org
The NRPA, headquartered in Ashburn Virginia, is a national nonprofit organization devoted to advancing park, recreation and conservation efforts that enhance the quality of life for all Americans. The Association works to extend social, health, cultural and economic benefits of parks and recreation, through its network of 23,000 recreation and park professionals and civic leaders. NRPA encourages recreation initiatives for youth in high-risk environments.
Founded: 1965
John A Thorner, Executive Director
M Lauren Yost, Human Resources Manager

351 National Speleological Society
2813 Cave Avenue 256-852-1300
Huntsville, AL 35810-4431 Fax: 256-851-9241
E-mail: nss@caves.org
http://www.caves.org
Founded for the purpose of advancing the study, conservation, exploration, and knowledge of caves. More than 12,000 members in 200 grottos conduct regular meetings to bring cavers together within their general area to coordinate activities which may include mapping, cleaning and investigating sensitive caves.
William Tozer, President
Stephanie Searles, Operations Manager

352 National Tree Society
910 East Aliso Street 805-646-4756
Ojai, CA 93023 Fax: 775-248-6035
E-mail: tncinfo@natural-connection.com
http://www.natural-connection.com
Organization to preserve the earth's biosphere by planting and caring for trees. Seeks to raise public understanding of the need for trees and the role they play in maintaining a healthy environment; works to acquire forest and other lands to ensure the continued growth of trees on such lands; establishes nurseries to supply the trees.
Gregory W Davis, Contact

353 National Trust for Historic Preservation
1785 Massachusetts Avenue NW 202-588-6000
Washington, DC 20036 800-944-6847
Fax: 202-588-6038
E-mail: feedback@nthp.org
http://www.nthp.org
Provides leadership, education, resources and advocacy to save America's diverse historic places and revitalize our communities.
Founded: 1949
Richard Moe, President
David J Brown, Executive Vice President

354 National Wildflower Research Center
Lady Bird Johnson Wildflower Center
4801 Lacross Avenue 512-471-1525
Austin, TX 78739 Fax: 512-471-1551
E-mail: facilityrentals@wildflower.org
http://www.wildflower.org
Combines native plants with local culture, reflecting the specifics and peculiarities of Central Texas Hill Country ecosystems. Walking through the center, you'll find native plants in gardens and natural areas, an unparalleled rainwater collection and storage system, recycled building materials, American folk art, environmentally conscious construction and engaging educational facilities— all designed to learn to live more gently on the land.
Founded: 1897
Robert A. Wooster, President
Larry McNeill, Vice President

355 National Wildlife Federation
PO Box 1583 800-822-9919
Merrifield, VA 22116-1583 http://www.nwf.org
Gives voice to the wildlife conservation values that are part of our country's heritage.
Founded: 1936
Larry Schweiger, President/CEO
Jaime Matyas, Executive Vice President

356 **National Wildlife Refuge Association**
5335 Wisconsin Avenue NW 202-333-9075
Suite 521 877-396-NWRA
Washington, DC 20015 Fax: 202-333-9077
E-mail: nwra@refugeassociation.org
http://www.refugeassociation.org
Aims to protect, enhance and expand the National Wildlife Refuge System lands, set aside by the American public to protect our country's diverse wildlife heritage.
Founded: 1975
Stuart Watson, Chair
Kathy Woodward, Vice Chair

357 **National Wildlife Rehabilitators Association**
2625 Clearwater Rd 320-230-9920
Suite 110 Fax: 320-230-3077
St. Cloud, MN 56301 E-mail: nwra@nwrawildlife.org
http://www.nwrawildlife.org
The National Wildlife Rehabilitators Association is a nonprofit international membership organization committed to promoting and improving the integrity and professionalism of wildlife rehabilitation and contributing to the preservation of natural ecosystems.
Founded: 1982
Sandy Woltman, President
January O. Bill, Vice President

358 **National Woodland Owners Association**
374 Maple Avenue E 703-255-2700
Suite 310 Fax: 703-281-9200
Vienna, VA 22180 E-mail: info@woodlandowners.org
http://www.woodlandowners.org/
NWOA is independent of the forest products industry and forestry agencies. They independently work with all organizations to promote non-industrial forestry and the best interests of woodland owners.
Founded: 1983
Keith A Argow, President
Trish Hugg, Member Services Coordinator

359 **Natural Area Council**
725 15th street NW 202-638-1649
Suite 605 Fax: 202-638-2175
Washington, DC 20005 http://www.america-the-beautiful.org
Founded: 1965
Nanine Bilski, President

360 **Natural Areas Association**
PO Box 1504 541-317-0199
Bend, OR 97709 E-mail: info@naturalarea.org
http://www.naturalarea.org/
To advance the preservation of natural diversity. To inform, unite and support persons engaged in identifying, protecting, managing, and studying natural areas and biological diversity across landscapes and ecosystems.
Founded: 1980
Lisa Smith, Executive Director
Deb Kraus, Director Of Operations

361 **Natural Resources Defense Council**
40 West 20th Street 212-727-2700
New York, NY 10011 Fax: 212-727-1773
E-mail: nrdcinfo@nrdc.org
http://www.nrdc.org
Mission: To safeguard the Earth: its people, its plants and animals, and natural systems on which all life depends.
Founded: 1990
Daniel R. Tishman, President/CEO
Frederick A.O. Schwarz Jr., Chief

362 **Neighborhood Parks Council**
PO Box 170160 415-621-3260
San Francisco, CA 94117-0160 Fax: 415-703-0889
E-mail: feedback@sfparksalliance.org
http://www.sfparksalliance.org
Neighborhood Parks Council (NPC) advocates for a superior, equitable and sustainable park and recreation system. NPC provides leadership and support to park users through community-driven stewardship, education, planning and research.
Founded: 1996
Matthew O'Grady, Executive Director
Rosemary Cameron, President

363 **Nicodemus Wilderness Project**
PO Box 40712 E-mail: mail@wildernessproject.org
Albuquerque, NM 87196-0712 http://www.wildernessproject.org
The Nicodemus Wilderness Project was founded because of the need for environmental restoration, stewardship, and projection of neglected public lands.
Robert K. Dudley, President/Executive Director
Yih Ming Hsu, Vice President/Volunteer Pro

364 **North American Bluebird Society (NABS)**
PO Box 7844 330-359-5511
Bloomington, IN 47407 Fax: 330-359-5455
E-mail: info@nabluebirdsociety.org
http://www.nabluebirdsociety.org
Nonprofit conservation, education and research organization, promotes the recovery of the bluebirds and other native cavity-nesting bird species. NABS supports conservation through such continent wide programs as the Transcontinental Bluebird Trail and the NABS Nestbox Approval Process. NABS also produces award-winning educational materials.
Founded: 1977
Sherry Linn, President
Gwen Tietz, Treasurer

365 **North American Crane Working Group**
PO Box 566 http://www.nacwg.org
Gambier, OH 43022
NACWG is an organization of professional biologists, aviculturists, land managers and other interested individuals dedicated to the conservation of cranes and their habitats in North America. They sponsor a North American Crane Workshop every 3-4 years, promulgates technical information including a published Proceedings of a North American Workshop and a semi-annual newsletter, address conservation issues affecting cranes and their habitat, promote appropriate research on crane conservation.
Tom Hoffman, Contact

366 **North American Falconers Association**
3509 Whippoorwill Cove E-mail: nafaprez@yahoo.com
White Hall, AR 71602 http://www.n-a-f-a.org
Provides communication among and disseminates relevant information to interested members; scientific study of raptorial species, their care, welfare and training; promotes conservation of the birds of prey and an appreciation of their value in nature and in wildlife conservation programs; urges recognition of falconry as a legal field sport; and establishes traditions which will aid, perpetuate and further the welfare of falconry and raptors it employs.
Founded: 1961
Darryl A Perkins, President
Rusty Scarborough, Secretary

367 **North American Loon Fund**
PO Box 329 603-528-4711
Holderness, NH 03245 800-462-5666
http://www.facstaff.uww.edu
The North American Loon Fund's mission is to promote the preservation of loons and their lake habitats through research, public education, and the involvement of people who share their lakes with loons.
Linda O'Bara, Director

368 **North American Wildlife Park Foundation Wolf Park**
4008 East 800 North 765-567-2265
Battle Ground, IN 47920 Fax: 765-567-4299
E-mail: admin@wolfpark.org
http://www.wolfpark.org/
Founded: 1972
Elizabeth Rose, Managing Director
Pat Goodmann, Senior

369 North American Wolf Society
PO Box 3242
Boulder, CO 80307

370 Open Space Institute
1350 Broadway 212-290-8200
Suite 201 Fax: 212-290-3441
New York, NY 10018 E-mail: info@osiny.org
http://www.osiny.org

Protects land for public benefit and supports the efforts of citizen activists working to improve environmental regulations in their communities.
Kim Elliman, President/CEO
Robert Anderberg, Vice President

371 Openlands Project
25 E Washington Street 312-427-4256
Suite 1650 Fax: 312-427-6251
Chicago, IL 60602-1708 E-mail: info@openlands.org
http://www.openlands.org

Nonprofit project, founded in 1963, is an independent, nonprofit organization dedicated to preserving and enhancing public open space in northeastern Illinois. Openlands bridges political boundaries and build consensus on open spacegoals and regional growth strategies.
Founded: 1963
Gerald W. Adelmann, President/CEO
Robert Megquier, COO

372 Organization for Bat Conservation
39221 Woodward Ave 248-645-3232
P.O. Box 801 Fax: 517-339-5618
Bloomfield Hills, MI 48303 E-mail: info@batconservation.org
http://www.batconservation.org

A nonprofit organization, our mission is to preserve bats and their habitats through education, collaboration, and research. We also work with local health departments and government agencies to aid in public health issues associated with bats, and we have trained field biologists to research endangered bats.
Rob Mies, Executive Director

373 Ozark Society
PO Box 2914 479-587-8757
Little Rock, AR 72203 E-mail: racross@uark.edu
http://www.ozarksociety.net

The Ozark Society has remained a strong regional organization because is has not allowed itself to be diverted from its principal purpose: the preservation of wild and scenic rivers, wilderness and unique natural areas. Its primary focus is the Ozark-Ouachita region and its associated bottom land habitat.
Founded: 1962
Bob Cross, President

374 Ozarks Resource Center
PO Box 3 417-679-4773
Brixey, MO 65618 Fax: 417-679-4773
E-mail: jlorrain@goin.missouri.org
http://www.ic.org/resources

The purpose of the organization is to provide research, education, technical assistance and dissemination of information on: renewable resource-based appropriate technology, environmentally responsible practices, sustainable agriculture, community economic development and self-reliance for the family, farm community, the Ozarks and their bioregions.
Janice Lorrain, Executive Director

375 Partners in Parks
Department of Parks and Recreation
Citrus Ranch Park 202-364-7244
2910 Portola Parkway Fax: 202-255-2364
Tustin Ranch, CA 92782 E-mail: partpark@cqi.com
http://www.partnersinparks.org

Organize and direct volunteers for work in city parks and trails. Outdoor work can be as simple as litter pick-up to trail cleaning, tree planting, etc.
Founded: 1988
David Kekil, Secretary/Treasurer

376 Peregrine Fund
5668 W Flying Hawk Lane 208-362-3716
Boise, ID 83709 Fax: 208-362-2376
E-mail: tpf@peregrinefund.org
http://www.peregrinefund.org

The Peregrine Fund was founded to restore the Peregrine Falcon, which was removed from the U.S. Endangered Species List in 1999. That success has encouraged the organization to expand its focus and apply its experience and understanding to raptor conservation efforts on behalf of 87 species in 61 countries worldwide, including the California Condor and Aplomado Falcon in the United States. The organization is non-political, solution-oriented, and hands-on.
Founded: 1970
J Peter Penny, President
Richard T. Watson, Vice President

377 Public Lands Foundation
PO Box 7226 703-790-1988
Arlington, VA 22207 Fax: 703-893-1500
E-mail: leaplf@erols.com
http://www.publicland.org

Founded in 1987, the Public Lands Foundation is a private nonprofit organization dedicated to the proper use and protection of the public lands administrated by the Bureau of Land Management, implementation of the Federal Land Policy and Management Act, and professional land management by professional employees.
Ed Shepard, President
Ed Spang, Vice President

378 Quail Unlimited
308 3rd Ave 229-883-3209
Albany, GA 31701 Fax: 229-883-3979
http://www.qu.org

Quail Unlimited was established in 1981 to battle the problem of dwindling quail and wildlife habitat. Quail Unlimited is the only national conservation organization dedicated to the wise management of America's wild quail as a valuable and renewable resource.
Bill Bowles, President
Debbie Powell, Administrative Assistant

379 RARE Conservation
1310 North Courthouse Road 703-522-5070
Suite 110 Fax: 703-522-5027
Arlington, VA 22201 E-mail: info@rareconservation.org
http://www.rareconservation.org

They work globally to equip people in the most threatened natural areas with tools and the motivation needed to care for their natural resources.
Founded: 1973
Edward Soule, Chairman
Nancy Mackinnon, Vice Chair

380 Rainforest Alliance
233 Broadway 212-677-1900
28th Floor Fax: 212-677-2187
New York, NY 10279 E-mail: info@ra.org
http://www.rainforest-alliance.org

Dedicated to tropical forest conservation for the benefit of the global community.
Founded: 1987
Daniel R. Katz, Chairman
Roger Deromedi, Vice Chair

381 Raptor Education Foundation
PO Box 200 400 303-680-8500
Denver, CO 80220 Fax: 303-680-8502
E-mail: raptor2@usaref.org
http://www.usaref.org

One of the most important challenges facing the world today is the preservation, protection and appropriate use of natural resources. The environmental decisions made today will have a monumental impact on wildlife on a global scale and affect the overall quality of life for mankind. We must strive to restore and maintain a level of dynamic balance in nature and minimize the

rate at which species of animals, plants and other natural resources are declining.
Founded: 1980
Peter Reshetniak, Chairman
Ann Price, Secretary

382 Ruffed Grouse Society
451 McCormick Road 412-262-4044
Coraopolis, PA 15108 888-564-6747
Fax: 412-262-9207
E-mail: RGS@ruffedgrousesociety.org
http://www.ruffedgrousesociety.org

The Ruffed Grouse Society's role in conservation of wildlife habitat is to enhance the environment for the Ruffed Grouse, American Woodcock, and other forest wildlife that require or utilize thick, young forests. Since forests are dynamic and constantly changing and man has virtually eliminated the fires that shaped much of the forested land we know today, forests must be managed.
Founded: 1961
Gaylen J. Byker, Chair
James Oliver, Treasurer

383 Save the Dunes Council
444 Barker Road 219-879-3937
Michigan City, IN 46360 Fax: 219-872-4875
E-mail: tom@savedunes.org
http://www.savedunes.org

The Save the Dunes Council of northwest Indiana was founded in 1952, one of the oldest grassroots conservation organizations in the country. Its objectives are to maintain and restore the integrity and quality of the natural environment of the Indiana Dunes region. The hard work of their members led to the establishment of the Indiana Dunes National Lakeshore in 1966; the group continues to work on a wide variety of issues concerning the Dunes and the environmental quality of the area.
Founded: 1952
Ryan Strode, President
Erin Argyilan, Vice President

384 Save the Manatee Club
500 N Maitland Avenue 407-539-0990
Maitland, FL 32751 800-432-5646
Fax: 407-539-0871
E-mail: membership@savethemanatee.org
http://www.savethemanatee.org

Save the Manatee Club (SMC) is a nonprofit organization, established in 1981 by US Senator Bob Graham and singer/songwriter Jimmy Buffett so the general public could participate in conservation efforts to save endangered manatees from extinction. The purpose of SMC is to promote public awareness and education; fund manatee research, rescue, and rehabilitation efforts; lobby for the protection of manatees and their habitat, and take appropriate legal action.
Founded: 1981
Patrick M. Rose, Executive Director
Carlene Nall, Administrative Assistant

385 Save the Whales
Animal Welfare Institute
900 Pennsylvania Ave SE 202-337-2332
Washington, DC 20003 Fax: 202-446-2131
E-mail: awi@awionline.org
http://www.awionline.org

Save the Whales' purpose is to educate children and adults about marine mammals, their environment and their preservation. Founded in 1977, Save the Whale is a 801(c)(3) Educational Nonprofit Corporation.
Founded: 1951
Cathy Liss, President
Charles M. Jabbour, Treasurer

386 Scenic America
1785 Massachusetts Avenue NW 202-638-1839
Washington, DC 20036 Fax: 202-638-3171
E-mail: tracy@scenic.org
http://www.scenic.org

A national nonprofit organization dedicated solely to protecting natural beauty and distinctive community character. They provide technical assistance across the nation and through our state affiliates on scenic byways, billboard and sign control, context sensitive highway design, wireless telecommunications tower location, transportation enhancements, and other scenic conservation. We advance our number one goal, to build a citizen movement for scenic conservation through education.
Mary Tracy, President
Max Ashburn, Communications Director

387 Sierra Club
85 Second Street 415-977-5500
2nd Floor Fax: 415-977-5799
San Francisco, CA 94105 E-mail: information@sierraclub.org
http://www.sierraclub.org

To advance the preservation and protection of the natural environment by empowering the citizenry, especially democratically-based grassroots organizations, with charitable resources to further the cause of environmental protection. The vehicle through which The Sierra Club Foundation generally fulfills its charitable mission.
Founded: 1892
Allison Chin, President
Carl Pope, Executive Director

388 Smithsonian Institution
SI Building, Room 153, MRC 010 202-357-2700
PO Box 37012 Fax: 202-357-2426
Washington, DC 20013-7012 E-mail: info@si.edu
http://www.si.edu
G. Wayne Clough, Secretary

389 Society for Marine Mammalogy
7600 San Point Way NE PO Box 206-526-4016
Seattle, WA 98115 Fax: 206-526-6615
http://www.marinemammalscience.org

To evaluate and promote the educational, scientific and managerial advancement of marine mammal science. Gather and disseminate to members of the Society, the public and private institutions, scientific, technical and management information through publications and meetings. Provide scientific information, as required, on matters related to the conservation and management of marine mammal resources.
Founded: 1981
Helene Marsh, President
Nick Gales, President Elect

390 Sonoran Institute
44 E Broadway Blvd 520-290-0828
Suite 350 Fax: 520-290-0969
Tucson, AZ 85701 E-mail: afast@sonoraninstitute.org
http://www.sonoraninstitute.org

Nonprofit organization that works collaboratively with local people and interests to conserve and restore important natural landscapes in western North America, engaging partners such as landowners, public land managers, local leaders, commmunity residents and nongovernmental organizations. Community Stewardship is an innovative approach to conservation.
Founded: 1990
Maria Baier, CEO
Sharea Escalante, Controller

391 Tall Timbers Research Station
Tall Timbers
13093 Henry Beadel Drive 850-893-4153
Tallahassee, FL 32312 Fax: 850-668-7781
E-mail: rose@ttrs.org
http://www.talltimbers.org

Dedicated to protecting wildlands and preserving natural habitats. Promotes public education on the importance of natural disturbances to the environment and the subsequent need for wildlife and land management. Conducts fire ecology research and other biological research programs through the Tall Timbers Research Station. Operates museum.
Founded: 1958
William E. Palmer, President/CEO
Melissa Proctor, Controller

392 Theodore Roosevelt Conservation Alliance
27 Fort Missola Road 406-549-0101
Suite 4K 877-770-8722
Missoula, MT 59804 Fax: 406-549-7402
E-mail: info@trca.org
http://www.trca.org
To inform and engage Americans to foster our conservation legacy while working to nurture, enhance and protect our fish, wildlife and habitat resources in our National Forest System.
Founded: 1991
Kristen Munson, Executive Assistant
Robert Munson, Executive Director

393 Tread Lightly!
353 E 400 S 801-627-0077
Suite 100 800-966-9900
Salt Lake City, UT 84111 Fax: 801-621-8633
E-mail: treadlightly@treadlightly.org
http://www.treadlightly.org
National nonprofit organization dedicated to proactively protecting recreation access and opportunities through education and stewardship.
Founded: 1990
Lori McCullough, Executive Director
Jill Scott, Assistant Director

394 TreePeople
12601 Mulholland Drive 818-753-4600
Beverly Hills, CA 90210 Fax: 818-753-4635
E-mail: info@treepeople.org
http://www.treepeople.org
To inspire the people of Los Angeles to take personal responsibility for their environment, training and supporting them as they plant and care for trees and improve the neighborhoods in which they live, work and play. Through education, planting projects, policy development and research, the organization is helping lead the promotion of integrated urban watershed management.
Founded: 1973
Andy Lipkis, President/Founder
Tom Hansen, Executive Director

395 Trees for Life
3006 W St Louis 316-945-6929
Wichita, KS 67203-5129 Fax: 316-945-0909
E-mail: info@treesforlife.org
http://www.treesforlife.org
Empowers people by demonstrating that in helping each other, they can unleash extraordinary power that impacts lives. By planting fruit trees in developing countries, we protect the environment and provide a low-cost, self-renewing source of food for a large number of people. Activities include three elements: education, health and environment.
Founded: 1984
Balbir S. Mathur, President
David Kimble, Executive Director

396 Trust for Public Land
101 Montgomery Street 415-495-4014
Suite 900 800-714-5263
San Francisco, CA 94104 Fax: 415-495-4103
E-mail: info@tpl.org
http://www.tpl.org
A national nonprofit land conservation organization working to protect land for human enjoyment and well-being. Initiatives include: Parks for People; Working Lands; Natural Lands; Heritage Lands; and Land & Water.
Founded: 1972
William B. Rogers, President/CEO
Page Knudsen Cowles, Chair

397 UNEP: United Nations Environment Programme/Regional Office for North America
900 17h St, NW 202-785-0465
Suite 506 Fax: 202-785-2096
Washington, DC 20006 http://www.unep.org
It's mission is to provide leadership and encourage partnership in caring for the environment by inspiring, informing, and enabling nations and peoples to improve their quality of life without compromising that of future generations.
Achim Steiner, Executive Director
Angela Cropper, Deputy Executive Director

398 Unexpected Wildlife Refuge: New Beaver Defenders
PO Box 765 856-697-3541
Newfield, NJ 08344-0765 Fax: 856-697-5081
E-mail: info@unexpectedwildliferefuge.org
http://www.unexpectedwildliferefuge.org
The refuge includes 540 acres of swamps, bogs, forests and lakes and is home to seven active beaver lodges.
Sarah Summerville, Director
Helga Tacreiter, President

399 Way of Nature Fellowship
PO Box 3388 877-818-1881
Tucson, AZ 85722-3388 E-mail: info@sacredpassage.com
http://www.sacredpassage.com
John P Milton, President

400 Western Hemisphere Shorebird Reserve Network
125 Manomet Point Road 508-224-6521
PO Box 1770 Fax: 508-224-9220
Manomet, MA 02345 E-mail: info@whsrn.org
http://www.whsrn.org
WHSRN is a voluntary, community-based coalition of over 185 organizations across the US and other countries in the Western Hemisphere that have joined together to protect, restore and manage critical wetland habitats for migratory birds.
Charles D. Duncan, Director
Meredith Gutowski Morehouse, Conservation Specialist

401 Western Society of Naturalists
California State University
18111 Nordhoff Street 818-677-3256
Northridge, CA 91330 Fax: 818-677-2034
E-mail: presofc@csun.edu
http://www.csun.edu
Members include researchers, educators, academics and others with an interest in the area's biology, particularly its marine life. Membership is $15.00 per year for individuals and $7.00 for students.
Dianne F. Harrison, President

402 Whooping Crane Conservation Association
8803 Pine Run 337-234-6339
Spanish Fort, AL 36527 E-mail: webadmin@whoopingcrane.com
http://www.whoopingcrane.com
The mission is to advance conservation, protection and propagation of the Whooping Crane population, to prevent its extinction, to establish and maintain a captive management program for the perpetuation of the species. We collect and disseminate knowledge of this species; and advocate and encourage public appreciation and understanding of the Whooping Crane's educational, scientific and economic values.

403 Wild Canid Survival and Research Center
PO Box 1544 636-938-5900
La Porte, CO 80535-1544 Fax: 636-938-6490
E-mail: wildcanidcenter@onemain.com
http://www.wolfsanctuary.org
A private nonprofit conservation organization dedicated to the preservation of the wolf and other endangered canids through education, research and captive breeding.
Founded: 1971
Shelley Coldiron, Executive Director
Michelle Hecker, Administrative Assistant

404 Wild Horse Organized Assistance
PO Box 555 702-851-4817
Reno, NV 89504 http://www.wildhorseorganizedassistance.org
The mission is to save diminishing herds of wild horses in the Western United States.
Founded: 1971
Dawn Y Lappin, Executive Director

405 Wild Horses of America Registry
6212 E Sweetwater 602-991-0273
Scottsdale, AZ 85254 Fax: 602-991-2920
E-mail: 103053.1112@campuserve.com
http://www.ispmb.com
Recognizes wild horses and burros of America that have been removed from public lands.
Karen Sussman, Registrar

406 Wilderness Society
1615 M Street NW 800-846-9453
Washington, DC 20036 E-mail: member@tws.org
http://www.wilderness.org
Protects the wilderness and inspires Americans to care for the wild places.
Founded: 1935
Jamie Williams, President
Thomas Tepper, Vice President

407 Wilderness Watch
PO Box 9175 406-542-2048
Missoula, MT 59807 Fax: 406-542-7714
E-mail: wild@wildernesswatch.org
http://www.wildernesswatch.org
Keep It Wild! we are America's leading citizens' voice for protecting our nation's designated wilderness and wild rivers.
Founded: 1989
George Nickas, Executive Director
Jeff Smith, Development Director

408 Wildlife Action
PO Box 866 843-464-8473
Mullins, SC 29574 800-753-2264
Fax: 843-464-8859
E-mail: info@wildlifeaction.com
http://www.wildlifeaction.com
Raises public awareness about wildlife habitat, security, protection and management; protects the rivers and wetlands from unnecessary destruction and development and works to reduce poaching, trespassing and other illegal outdoor activities.
Founded: 1977
Gault Beeson Jr., President
Ian Beeson, Secretary

409 Wildlife Conservation Society
2300 Southern Boulevard 718-220-5100
Bronx, NY 10460 Fax: 718-220-2685
E-mail: feedback@wcs.org
http://www.wcs.org
WCS is at work in 53 nations across Africa, Latin America and North America, protecting wild landscapes that are home to a variety of species from butterflies to tigers. We uniquely combine the resources of wildlife parks in New York with field projects around the globe to inspire care for nature, provide leadership in environmental education, and help sustain our planet's biological diversity.
Founded: 1895
Steven Sanderson, President
Richard Lattios, Vice President

410 Wildlife Disease Association
PO Box 7065 785-843-1235
Lawrence, KS 66044-7065 800-627-0629
Fax: 785-843-1274
E-mail: wda@allenpress.com
http://www.wildlifedisease.org
Our mission is to acquire, disseminate and apply knowledge of the health and diseases of wild animals in relation to their biology, conservation and interactions with human and domestic animals.
Founded: 1952
Dolores Gavier Widen, President
Thierry Work, VP

411 Wildlife Forever
2700 Freeway Boulevard 763-253-0222
Suite 1000 Fax: 763-560-9961
Minneapolis, MN 55430-1779 E-mail: info@wildlifeforever.com
http://www.wildlifeforever.com
Wildlife Forever conserves America's wildlife heritage through preservation of habitat, conservation education and management of fish and wildlife.
Founded: 1987
Douglas Grann, President/CEO

412 Wildlife Habitat Enhancement Council
8737 Colesville Road 301-588-8994
Suite 800 Fax: 301-588-4629
Silver Spring, MD 20910 E-mail: Whc@wildlifehc.org
http://www.wildlifehc.org
The Wildlife Habitat Council is a nonprofit groups of corporations, conservations, and individuals dedicated to protecting and enhancing wildlife habitat.
Founded: 1998
Margaret O'Gorman, President
Laurie Coran, Vice President

413 Wildlife Management Institute
1440 Upper Bermudian Road 717-677-4480
Gardners, PA 17324 E-mail: info@wildlifemgt.org
http://www.wildlifemgt.org
WMI is a private, nonprofit, scientific and educational organization. It is committed to the conservation, enhancement and professional management of North America's wildlife and other natural resources.
Founded: 1946
Steven A Williams, President

414 Wildlife Society
5410 Grosvenor Lane 301-897-9700
Suite 200 Fax: 301-530-2471
Bethesda, MD 20814 E-mail: tws@wildlife.org
http://www.wildlife.org
A nonprofit scientific and educational organization that serves professionals such as government agencies, academia, industry, and non-government organizations in all areas related to the conservation of wildlife and natural resources management.
Founded: 1937
Ken Williams, Executive Director
Jane Jorgenson, Manager

415 Wilson Ornithological Society
OSNA 254-399-9636
5400 Bosque Boulevard, Ste 680 E-mail: business@osnabirds.org
Waco, TX 76710 http://www.wilsonsociety.org
World-wide organization of approximately 2,500 people who share a curiosity about birds.
Founded: 1888
Dr Dale Kennedy, President
John A Smallwood, Secretary

416 Windstar Foundation
2317 Snowmass Creek Road 303-927-4777
Snowmass, CO 81654 Fax: 970-927-4779
E-mail: webhelp@wstar.org
http://www.wstar.org
Windstar is a nonprofit environmental education organization which promotes a holistic approach to addressing environmental concerns. Founded in 1976 for singer/songwriter and environmentalist John Denver along with Aikido Master TomCrum.
Founded: 1976
Ron Deutschendorf, President
Pam Peterson, Secretary

417 Wolf Education and Research Center
PO Box 12604 208-924-6960
Portland, OR 97212 888-422-1110
E-mail: info@wolfcenter.org
http://www.wolfcenter.org
Dedicated to providing public education concerning the gray wolf anf its habitat in the Northern Rocky Mountains. Provides

the public with the rare opportunity to observe and learn about wolves in their natural habitat.
Chris Anderson, President
Sharon Lander, Treasurer

418 Wolf Fund
PO Box 471 — 307-733-0740
Moose, WY 83012 — Fax: 307-733-0962
Renee Askins, Executive Officer

419 Wolf Haven International
3111 Offut Lake Road SE — 360-264-4695
Tenino, WA 98589 — 800-448-9653
Fax: 360-264-4639
E-mail: info@wolfhaven.org
http://www.wolfhaven.org
Wolf Haven International's objectives include protection of the remaining wild wolves and their habitat, promotion of wolf re-establishment in historic ranges, provision of a sanctuary for captive wolves, and public education on the value of all wildlife.
Founded: 1982
Diane Gallegos, Executive Director
Patt Poinsett, Director of Marketing & Deve

420 World Bird Sanctuary
125 Bald Eagle Ridge Road — 636-938-6193
Valley Park, MO 63088 — Fax: 636-938-9464
E-mail: info@worldbirdsanctuary.org
http://www.worldbirdsantuary.org
The World Bird Sanctuary's mission is to preserve the earth's biological diversity and to secure the future of threatened bird species in their natural environment. We work to fulfill that mission through education, propagation, field studies and rehabilitation.
Walter Crawford Jr., Executive Director
Jeff Meshach, Director

421 World Forestry Center
4033 SW Canyon Road — 503-228-1367
Portland, OR 97221 — Fax: 503-228-4608
E-mail: mail@worlforestry.org
http://www.worldforestry.org
They educate and inform people about the world's forests and trees and their importance to all life, in order to promote a balanced and sustainable future. The WFC also operates a museum in Portland, OR, with local, national, and international programs and three demonstration forests.
Founded: 1964
Gary Hartshorn PhD, President/CEO
Mark Reed, Operations Director

422 World Nature Association
PO Box 673 — 301-593-2522
Silver Spring, MD 20901 — Fax: 301-593-2522
Donald H Messersmith, President

423 World Wildlife Fund
1250 24th Street NW — 202-293-4800
PO Box 97180 — 800-225-5993
Washington, DC 20090 — Fax: 202-293-9211
http://www.worldwildlife.org
Dedicated to protecting endangered species and their habitats through field work, advocacy, policy engagement, pioneering work, and education. The largest multinational conservation organization in the world. WWF works in 100 countries and is supported by 1.2 million members in the US and almost 5 million members globally.
Founded: 1960
Carter Roberts, President/CEO
Marcia Marsh, COO

National: Recycling & Pollution Prevention

424 Abandoned Mined Lands Reclamation Council
One Natural Resources Way — 217-782-0588
Springfield, IL 62701-1271 — Fax: 217-524-4819
http://dnr.state.il.us
Currently reclaiming abandoned mine lands in Illinois
Founded: 1974
Joe Angleton, Executive Director

425 Acoustical Society of America
Suite 1NO1 — 516-576-2360
2 Huntington Quadrangle — Fax: 516-576-2377
Melville, NY 11747 — E-mail: asa@aip.org
http://asa.aip.org/
For years the society has been involved in studies of noise as far as measurements, effects, and ways of reducing noise to improve the human environment.
Founded: 1929
Gilles A Daigle, President
Charles E Schmid, Executive Director

426 Air and Waste Management Association
One Gateway Center, 3rd Floor — 412-232-3444
420 Fort Duquesne Boulevard — 800-270-3444
Pittsburgh, PA 15222-1435 — Fax: 412-232-3450
E-mail: info@awma.org
http://www.awma.org
The Air and Waste Management Association (A&WMA) is a non-profit, nonpartisan professional organization that provides information, networking opportunities, public educational and professional development to more than 9,000environmental professionals in 65 countries.
Founded: 1907
Jim Powell, Executive Director
Mary Korzen, Receptionist

427 Association of Battery Recyclers
PO Box 290286 — 813-626-6151
Tampa, FL 33687 — Fax: 813-622-8388
E-mail: info@batteryrecyclers.com
http://www.batteryrecyclers.com
To keep members abreast of environmental, health, and safety requirements that affect our industry. The association meets two times a year and membership consists of recyclers of lead-acid batteries and their components, manufacturers and environmental consulting services.
Founded: 1984
Joyce Morales, Sectary Treasurer
Earl Cornette, Chairman

428 Association of Energy Engineers
4025 Pleasantdale Road — 770-447-5083
Suite 420 — Fax: 770-446-3969
Atlanta, GA 30340 — E-mail: info@aeecenter.org
http://www.aeecenter.org
A non profit professional society that promotes the scientific and educational interests of those engaged in the energy industry and fosters action for sustainable development.
Albert Thumann, Executive Director
Ruth Whitlock, Executive Administrator

429 Association of State and Territorial Solid Waste Management Officials
444 N Capitol Street NW — 202-624-5828
Suite 315 — Fax: 202-624-7875
Washington, DC 20001 — E-mail: swmtrina@sso.org
http://www.astswmo.org
To enhance and promote effective state and territorial waste management programs, and affect national waste management policies.
Founded: 1974
Dania Rodriguez, Executive Director
Allison Goldberg, Program & IS Associate

430 **Container Recycling Institute**
4361 Keystone Ave 310-559-7451
Culver City, CA 90232 E-mail: info@container-recycling.org
http://www.container-recycling.org

A nonprofit organization that studies and promotes policies and programs that increase recovery and recycling of beverage containers, and shift the social and environmental costs associated with manufacturing, recycling and disposal of container and packaging waste from government and taxpayers to producers and consumers.
Founded: 1991
Susan V. Collins, President
Sue Herrschaft, Programs Manager

431 **Earth Regeneration Society**
1442A Walnut Street 510-849-4155
Number 57 Fax: 510-849-0183
Berkeley, CA 94709 E-mail: csiri@igc.apc.org
http://www.imaja.com

The Earth Regeneration Society does research and education on climate change, ozone, and pollution, and calls for full employment and full social support based on survival programs and national and international networking.
Alden Bryant, President

432 **Environmental Industry Associations**
4301 Connecticut Avenue NW 202-244-4700
Suite 300 800-424-2869
Washington, DC 20008 Fax: 202-966-4818
E-mail: membership@envasns.org
http://www.envasns.org

The Environmental Industry Associations (EIA) is the parent organization for the National Solid Waste Management Association and the Waste Equipment Technology Association. It supports these through research and administrative, legal, federal affairs and public relations resources.
Bruce Parker, President

433 **Get Oil Out**
914 Anacapa Street 805-965-1519
Santa Barbara, CA 93102 E-mail: getoilout.goo@verizon.net
http://www.getoilout.org

A Santa Barbara public group dedicated to the protection of the Santa Barbara Channel and coastline from the environmental, economic and esthetic impact of oil development. The organization was formed in response to a 1969 accident that blackened the beaches, poisoned the ocean's water and killed many creatures that depend on clean water for survival.
John Abraham Powell, President

434 **GrassRoots Recycling Network**
672 Robinson Road 707-321-7883
Sebastopol, CA 95472 E-mail: linda@grrn.org
http://www.grrn.org

A national network of waste reduction activists and recycling professionals. The voice calling for Zero Waste in the United States by promoting the message that individuals must go beyond recycling and go upstream to the headwaters of the waste stream which is the industrial designer's desk.
Rick Anthony, Board President
Portia Sinott, Program Director

435 **Hazardous Waste Resource Center**
Environmental Technology Council
1112 16th Street NW 202-783-0870
Suite 420 Fax: 202-737-2038
Washington, DC 20036 E-mail: mail@etc.org
http://www.etc.org

The Environmental Technology Council (ETC) is a trade association of commercial environmental firms the recycle, treat and dispose of industrial and hazardous wastes; and firms involved in cleanup of contaminated sites.
Founded: 1982
David R Case, Executive Director
Scott Slesunger, VP Goverment Affairs

436 **Institute of Clean Air Companies**
2025 M Street NW 202-367-1114
Suite 800 Fax: 202-367-2114
Washington, DC 20036 E-mail: icacinfo@icac.com
http://www.icac.com

To promote the air pollution control industry and encourage improvement of engineering and technical systems. Members are leading manufacturers of equipment to monitor and control emissions of particulate, VOC, SO2, NOX, and air toxics.
Betsy Natz, Executive Director
Laura Somerville, Administrative Manager

437 **Institute of Scrap Recycling Industries**
1615 L Street NW 202-662-8500
Suite 600 Fax: 202-626-0900
Washington, DC 20036-5610 E-mail: robinweiner@isri.org
http://www.isri.org

Trade association that represents more than 1,200 companies of the scrap processing and recycling industry.
Robin K. Weiner, President
David Krohne, Director Communications

438 **Kids Against Pollution**
311 Main Street 315-266-0185
3rd Floor Fax: 315-266-0186
Utica, NY 13501 E-mail: christine@kidsagainstpollution.org
http://www.kidsagainstpollution.org

Nonprofit organization of active youth dedicated to solving and preventing pollution problems through educational projects and events in order to protect children's health and the planet.
Founded: 1987
Christine Shahin, Director

439 **Manufacturers of Emission Controls Association**
2020 North 14th Street 202-296-4797
Suite 220 Fax: 202-331-1388
Arlington, VA 22201 E-mail: asantos@meca.org
http://www.meca.org

Offers current and relevant technical information on emission control technology thereby facilitating strong state, federal and local air quality programs that promote public health, environmental quality and industrial progress.
Founded: 1976
Bruce I Bertelsen, Executive Director

440 **Municipal Waste Management Association**
1620 Eye Street NW 202-293-7330
Suite 300 Fax: 202-293-2352
Washington, DC 20006 E-mail: info@usmayors.org
http://www.usmayors.org/USCM/mwma

MWMA promotes operational efficiencies, facilitates information, fosters innovation and promotes legislation advocacy around Superfund, brown fields redevelopment, clean air and water, and waste energy regulations.
Founded: 1982
Susan Jarvis, Senior Program Manager
Ted Fischer, Director Membership Services

441 **NORA An Association of Responsible Recyclers**
7250 Heritage Village Plaza 703-753-4277
Suite 201 Fax: 703-753-2445
Gainesville, VA 20155 E-mail: sparker@noranews.org
http://www.noranews.org

A trade association that represents almost 200 leading companies in the liquid recycling industry. It defends and promotes the liquid recycling industry and business.
Scott D Parker, Executive Director
Casey Parker, Associate Director

442 **National Association for PET Container Resources**
PO Box 1327 707-996-4207
Sonoma, CA 95476 Fax: 707-935-1998
E-mail: information@napcor.com
http://www.napcor.com

A trade association formed in 1987, that helps communities establish recycling programs and conducts promotional and educational activities to promote PET plastic container recycling. The

members of NAPCOR are manufacturers of polyester resins and bottles.
Founded: 1987
Dennis Sabourin, Executive Director
Kate Eagles, Communications

443 National Association of Chemical Recyclers
1900 Main Street NW — 202-296-1725
Suite 750 — Fax: 202-296-2530
Washington, DC 20036 — E-mail: info@nacr-r2.org

The National Association of Chemical Recyclers is comprised of companies that recycle solvents and other chemicals for reuse by industry. Its members include both large conglomerates and smaller companies. The association's responsible recycling program ensures that all recyclers adhere to the same standards and regulations members in the association pledge to meet the ten principles of responsible recycling.
Brenda Pulley, Executive Director
Christopher Goebel, Director

444 National Association of Clean Air Agencies
444 North Capitol Street NW — 202-624-7864
Suite 307 — Fax: 202-624-7863
Washington, DC 20001 — E-mail: 4cleanair@4cleanair.org
http://www.4cleanair.org

State and local air pollution control officials formed NACAA (formerly STAPPA/ALAPCO) to improve their effectiveness as managers of air quality programs. It encourages the exchange of information among officials, enhances communication and cooperation among federal, state and local regulatory agencies, and promotes good management of air resources.
Dave J. Shaw, Co-President
Barry R. Wallerstein, Co-President

445 National Council for Air and Stream Improvements
4815 Emperor Boulevard — 919-941-6400
Canterbury Hall, Ste 110 — Fax: 919-941-6401
Durham, NC 27703 — E-mail: ryeske@ncasi.org
http://www.ncasi.org

The Council is a technical organization devoted to finding solutions to environmental protection problems in the manufacture of pulp, paper, and wood products in industrial forestry. It now has about 75 member companies.
Founded: 1943
Ronald Yeske, President

446 National Recycling Coalition
1220 L Street NW — 202-789-1430
Suite 100-155 — Fax: 202-789-1431
Washington, DC 20005 — E-mail: info@NRCrecycle.org
http://www.nrc-recycle.org

Nonprofit advocacy group with members from all aspects of the waste reduction, reuse and recycling industries. It is dedicated to the advancement and improvement of recycling, waste prevention, composting and reuse.
Founded: 1978
Mark Lichtenstein, President
Jeff Cooper, Chairperson of Board

447 Noise Pollution Clearinghouse
PO Box 1137 — 888-200-8332
Montpelier, VT 05601-1137 — E-mail: freenpc@nonoise.org
http://www.nonoise.org

A national non-profit organization with extensive online noise related resources. Creates more civil cities and more natural rural and wilderness areas by reducing noise pollution at the source.

448 Public Citizen
1600 20th Street NW — 202-588-1000
Washington, DC 20009 — Fax: 202-588-7796
E-mail: pcmail@citizen.org
http://www.citizen.org

Founded as a consumer advocacy organization to represent consumer interests in Congress, the executive branch, and the courts. Among other things it fights for clean, safe and sustainable energy sources and strong health, safety and environmental protections.
Founded: 1971
Joan Claybrook, President

449 Secondary Materials and Recycled Textiles Association
2105 Laurel Bush Road — 443-640-1050
Suite 200 — Fax: 443-640-1086
Bel Air, MD 21015 — E-mail: smartasn@erols.com
http://www.smartasn.org

Since 1932, SMART has represented the interests of companies dealing with pre-consumer and post-consumer recyclable textile materials. This material includes fibers, remnants, recycled clothing and shoes, and other related materials. SMART members also manufacture and distribute industrial and commercial wipers.
Founded: 1932
Jackie King, Executive Director
Casey Joseph, Association Coordinator

450 Solid Waste Association of North America
1100 Wayne Ave — 301-585-2898
Suite 700 — 800-467-9262
Silver Spring, MD 20910 — Fax: 301-589-7068
E-mail: info@swana.org
http://www.swana.org

SWANA is dedicated to education and training of its members by advancing the practice of environmentally and economically sound management of solid waste in North America.
Founded: 1965
John Skinner, CEO/Executive Director
Shelby Truxon, Program Manager

451 Steel Recycling Institute
680 Andersen Drive — [illegible]
Pittsburgh, PA 15220 — 800-937-1226
Fax: 412-922-3213
E-mail: jimw@recycle-steel.org
http://www.recycle-steel.org

The Steel Recycling Institute, a unit of the American Iron and Steel Institute, is an industry association that promotes and sustains the recycling of all steel products. The SRI educates the solid waste industry, government, business and ultimately the consumer about the benefit of steel's infinite recycling cycle.
Founded: 1988
Bill Heenan, President
Gregory L Crawford, VP Operations

National: Sustainable Development

452 Alliance for Sustainability
1521 University Avenue SE — 612-250-0389
Minneapolis, MN 55414 — Fax: 612-379-9004
E-mail: iasa@mtn.org
http://www.afs.nonprofitoffice.com

The Mission of the Alliance is to bring about personal, organizational and planetary sustainability through support of projects that are ecologically sound, economically viable, socially just and humane. The Alliance for Sustanability is a Minnesota-based, tax-deductible nonprofit supporting model sustainability projects on the local, national and international levels.
Founded: 1983
Sean Gosiewski, Program Director

453 American Crop Protection Association
1156 15th Street NW — 202-296-1585
Suite 400 — Fax: 202-463-0474
Washington, DC 20005 — http://www.croplifeamerica.org

ACPA promotes the environmentally sound use of crop protection products for the economical production of safe, high quality, abundant food, fiber and other crops.
Founded: 1933
Jay Vroom, President/CEO
Bill Kuckuck, Vice President/COO

454 American Forest Foundation
1111 19th Street NW 202-463-2462
Suite 780 888-889-4466
Washington, DC 20036 Fax: 202-463-2461
E-mail: info@forestfoundation.org
http://www.forestfoundation.org

A nonprofit 501 (C)(3) conservation and education organization that strives to ensure the sustainability of America's family forests for present and future generations. The vision is to create a future where North American forests are sustained by the public which understands and values the social, economic, and environmental benefits they provide to our communities, our nation, and our world.
Founded: 1982
Tom Martin, President/CEO
Melissa Moeller, Manager

455 American Forests
734 15th Street NW 202-737-1944
Suite 800 800-368-5748
Washington, DC 20005 Fax: 202-737-2457
E-mail: info@amfor.org
http://www.americanforests.org

Works to protect, restore and enhance the natural capital of trees and forests. Healthy forests filter water, remove air pollution, catch carbon, and provide homes for wildlife.
Founded: 1875
Scott Steen, CEO
Rebecca Walker, Vice President/CFO

456 American Planning Association
122 S Michigan Avenue 312-431-9100
Suite 1600 Fax: 312-431-9985
Chicago, IL 60603 http://www.planning.org

The American Planning Association is a nonprofit public interest and research organization representing 30,000 practicing officials, and citizens involved with urban and rural planning issues. Sixty-five percent of APA's members are employed by state and local government agencies. These members are involved, on a day-to-day basis, in formulating planning policies and preparing land use regulations.
Frank So, Executive Director

457 American Society of Agronomy
5585 Guilford Road 608-273-8080
Madison, WI 53711-5801 Fax: 608-273-2021
E-mail: headquarters@agronomy.org
http://www.agronomy.org

ASA is dedicated to development of agricultural interests in harmony with environmental and human values. The Society supports scientific, educational and professional activities that enhance communication and technology transfer among agronomists and those in related disciplines on topics of local, regional, national and international significance.
Ellen Bergfeld, CEO
Wes Meixelsperger, CFO

458 Ancient Forest International
PO Box 1850 707-923-4475
Redway, CA 95560 Fax: 707-923-4475
E-mail: afi@ancientforests.org
http://www.ancientforests.org

Ancient Forest International has been instrumental in the protection of primary forests around the world. With the help of its international ancient forest network, AFL develops opportunities for wildlands philanthropists and communities to work together to acquire and protect strategic and invaluable forestlands. AFL has helped coordinate the purchase of nearly a million acres of ecologically critical forested land, primarily along the Pacific coast of North and South America.
Founded: 1989

459 Association of Fish and Wildlife Agencies
444 N Capitol Street NW 202-624-7890
Suite 725 Fax: 202-624-7891
Washington, DC 20001 E-mail: info@fishwildlife.org
http://www.fishwildlife.org

Mission is to promote the sustainable use of natural resources; encourage cooperation and coordination of fish and wildlife management at all levels of government; develop coalitions among conservation organizations or promote fish and wildlife interests; encourage the professional management of fish and wildlife; foster public understanding of the need for conservation.
Founded: 1902
Jeff Vonk, President
Ron Regan, Executive Director

460 Atlantic Center for the Environment Quebec-Labrador Foundation
QLF-Atlantic Center for the Environment
55 S Main Street 978-356-0038
Ipswich, MA 01938 Fax: 978-356-7322
E-mail: webmaster@qlf.org
http://www.qlf.org

A not-for-profit corporation in the United States and a registered Charity in Canada. QLF exists to support the rural communities and environment of eastern Canada and New England and to create models for stewardship of natural resources and cultural heritage that can be applied worldwide.
Founded: 1963
Lawrence B Morris, President
Elizabeth Alling, Executive Vice President

461 CONCERN
PO Box 5892 202-328-8160
Washington, DC 20016 Fax: 202-387-3378
E-mail: concern@concern.org
http://www.sustainable.org

CONCERN is a national nonprofit environmental education organization with a focus on sustainable communities. CONCERN disseminates examples of successful initiatives, offers numerous resources and guidelines for action, serves as a clearinghouse for information and collaborates with others to carry out its programs. Through its Sustainable Communities Network CONCERN seeks to increase public understanding of and participation in initiatives that are environmentally and socially sound.
Founded: 1970
Susan Boyd, Director

462 Center for Ecoliteracy
2150 Allston Way 510-845-4595
Suite 2700 E-mail: info@ecoliteracy.org
Berkeley, CA 94702-1377 http://www.ecoliteracy.org

The Center for Ecoliteracy is dedicated to fostering a profound understanding of the natural world, grounded in direct experience that leads to sustainable patterns of living.
Zenobia Barlow, Executive Director
Jeanne Henry, Administrative Manager

463 Conservation Fund
1655 N Fort Myer Drive 703-525-6300
Suite 1300 Fax: 703-525-4610
Arlington, VA 22209-3199 http://www.conservationfund.org

Forges partnerships to protect America's legacy of land and water resources. Through land acquisition, community initiatives and leadership training, the Fund and its partners demonstrate sustainable conservation solutions emphasizing the integration of economic and environmental goals.
Founded: 1985
Lawrence A. Selzer, President/CEO
David K. Phillips, Vice President/CFO

464 Earth Island Institute
2150 Allston Way 510-859-9100
Suite 460 Fax: 510-859-9091
Berkeley, CA 94704-1375 E-mail: johnknox@earthisland.org
http://www.earthisland.org

A non-profit, public interest, membership organization that supports people who are creating solutions to protect our shared planet.
Founded: 1982
John Knox, Executive Director
Kevin Connelly, Associate Director

465 **Environmental Policy Center Global Cities Project**
2962 Fillmore Street 415-775-0791
San Francisco, CA 94123 Fax: 415-775-4159
E-mail: epc@globalcities.org
http://www.globalcities.org

Provides assistance and information on sustainable development and environmental conservation to communities within North America.

466 **Environmental and Energy Study Institute**
1112 16th Street NW 202-628-1400
Suite 300 888-788-3378
Washington, DC 20036-4819 Fax: 202-628-1825
E-mail: eesi@eesi.org
http://www.eesi.org

They are a nonprofit organization dedicated to promoting environmentally sustainable societies. EESI believes meeting this goal requires transitions to social and economic patterns that sustain people, the environment and the natural resources upon which present and future generations depend.
Founded: 1984
Carol Werner, Executive Director

467 **Forest History Society**
Forest History Society
701 Vickers Avenue 919-682-9319
Durham, NC 27701 Fax: 919-682-2349
E-mail: recluce2@duke.edu
http://www.foresthistory.org

A non-profit educational institution that links the past to the future by identifying, collecting, preserving, interpreting, and disseminating information on the history of people, forests, and their related resources.
Founded: 1946
Steven Anderson, President
Cheryl Oakes, Librarian

468 **Friends of the Earth**
1100 15th Street NW 202-783-7400
11th Floor 877-843-8687
Washington, DC 20005 Fax: 202 783 0444
E-mail: foe@foe.org
http://www.foe.org

National nonprofit advocacy organization dedicated to protecting the planet from environmental degradation; preserving biological, cultural and ethnic diversity, and empowering citizens to have an influential voice in decisions affecting the quality of their environment and their lives.
Founded: 1969
Erich Pica, President
Anna Prow, Managing Director

469 **Global Action Network**
50 California Street 415-477-2303
Suite 3325 Fax: 415-477-2334
San Francisco, CA 94111 http://www.globalactionnetwork.org

A new model of relationship development and community building for the reproductive health field that employs an Internet-based model of networking proven successful in other sectors. Our goal is to provide resources and opportunities for Network members to share knowledge, collaborate with other individuals working in the field, engage in mentoring relationships, and utilize online contacts and information to build networks with communities around the world.
Founded: 1998
Andrea Johnston, Co-Director
Jessica Klein, Program Associate

470 **Global Committee of Parliamentarians on Population and Development**
345 E 45th Street 212-953-7947
12th Floor Fax: 212-557-2061
New York, NY 10017

471 **Global Tomorrow Coalition**
1325 G Street NW 202-628-4016
Suite 1010 Fax: 202-628-4018
Washington, DC 20005

Global Tomorrow Coalition - a national leadership alliance on sustainable development, with membership in business and industry, conservation and environment, education and community planning, and social issues and development.
Donald R Lesh, President

472 **Institute for Agriculture and Trade Policy**
2105 First Avenue South 612-870-0453
Minneapolis, MN 55404 Fax: 612-870-4846
http://www.iatp.org

IATP works locally and globally at the intersection of policy and practice to ensure fair and sustainable food, farm and trade systems.
Founded: 1980
Jim Harkness, President
Emily Barker, Program Associate

473 **Institute for Sustainable Communities**
535 Stone Cutters Way 802-229-2900
Montpelier, VT 05602 Fax: 802-229-2919
E-mail: isc@iscvt.org
http://www.iscvt.org

Promotes sustainable environmental practices in the US and around the world. It leads transformative community-driven projects for environmental problem solving and other challenges.
Founded: 1991
George Hamilton, President
Steve Adams, Senior Program Director, US

474 **Institute for the Human Environment**
PO Box 552 707-935-9335
Vineburg, CA 95487

Community planning and land use.
Norman Gilroy, President
Shelley Arrowsmith, Vice President

475 **International Mountain Society**
810 East 10th Street 613-523-8891
Lawrence, KS 66044 E-mail: mrd-journal@peertrack.net
http://www.mrd-journal.org

An association registered in Berne, Switzerland, for the purpose of advancing knowledge and disseminating information about mountain research and development throughout the world. Aims to promote sustainable mountain development through improved communication among institutions and individuals, with a particular focus on mountain eco-regions in the developing world. Collaborates with like-minded institutions, and is a joint publisher of the journal Mountain Research and Development.
Dr Jack Ives, President

476 **International Society of Arboriculture**
PO Box 3129 217-355-9411
Champaign, IL 61826 888-472-8733
Fax: 217-355-9516
E-mail: isa@isa-arbor.com
http://www.isa-arbor.com

Through research, technology, and education promote the professional practice of arboriculture and foster a greater public awareness of the benefits of trees.
Founded: 1924
Jim Skiera, Executive Director
Jerri Moorman, Executive Assistant

477 **International Society of Tropical Foresters**
5400 Grosvenor Lane 301-897-8720
Bethesda, MD 20814-2198 866-897-8720
Fax: 301-897-3690
E-mail: membership@safnet.org
http://www.safnet.org

The International Society of Tropical Foresters, Inc. (ISTF) is a nonprofit organization committed to the protection, wise management and rational use of the world's tropical forests. Established in 1950, ISTF has about 1500 members in more than 100 countries. Financial support comes from membership dues, donations and grants. ISTF sponsors meetings, promotes chapters in

other countries, maintains a web site and has chapters at universities.
Founded: 1900 24 pages
Michael Goergen, Chief Executive
Larry Burner, CFO

478 Interstate Mining Compact Commission
445A Carlisle Drive 703-709-8654
Herndon, VA 20170 Fax: 703-709-8655
E-mail: bbotsis@imcc.isa.us
http://www.imcc.isa.us

A multi-state governmental organization which represents its 24 member states on issues of mining and environmental regulations. It works closely with several federal agencies such as Office of Surface Mining Reclamation and Enforcement, US EPA, and US Bureau of Land Management.
Founded: 1970
Gregory E Conrad, Executive Director
Beth A Botsis, Diretor of Programs

479 Island Resources Foundation
1718 P Street NW 202-265-9712
Suite T-4 Fax: 202-232-0748
Washington, DC 20036 E-mail: bpotter-@-irf.org
http://www.irf.org

Island Resources Foundation is a private, nonprofit research and education organization based at Red Hook in St. Thomas, US Virgin Islands, dedicated to solving the environmental problems of developing in small tropical island.
Founded: 1972
Bruce Potter, President
Charles Consolvo, Secretary

480 Kids for Saving Earth Worldwide
37955 Bridge Road 763-559-1234
North Branch, MN 55442 Fax: 651-674-5005
E-mail: kse@kidsforsavingearth.org
http://www.kidsforsavingearth.org/

To help protect the Earth through kids and adults. To educate and inspire them to participate in Earth-saving actions.
Tessa Hill, President

481 Kids for Saving the Earth Worldwide
37955 Bridge Road 763-559-1234
North Branch, MN 55442 Fax: 651-674-5005
E-mail: kse@kidsforsavingearth.org
http://www.kidsforsavingearth.org/

To help protect the Earth through kids and adults. To educate and inspire them to participate in Earth-saving actions.
Tessa Hill, President/Director

482 Land Institute
2440 E Water Well Road 785-823-5376
Salina, KS 67401 Fax: 785-823-8728
E-mail: info@landinstitute.org
http://www.landinstitute.org

This nonprofit research and education organization is engaged in a 25-year research program that marries ecology and agronomy to produce a Natural Systems Agriculture. The Land Institute is developing perennial grain plants to be grown in fields of mixed species patterned after native prairies. These domestic prairies will be plowed rarely, need few manufactured inputs because they will provide their own fertility and manage pests and diseases. Year-round roots will hold soils from erosion.
Founded: 2000
Wes Jackson, President
Scott Seirer, Managing Director

483 Land Trust Alliance
1660 L Street NW 202-638-4725
Suite 1100 Fax: 202-638-4730
Washington, DC 20036 E-mail: lta@lta.org
http://www.landtrustalliance.org

National leader of the private land conservation movement, promoting voluntary land conservation across the country and providing resources, leadership and training to the nation's 1200 plus nonprofit, grassroots land trusts, helping them to protect important open spaces. Provides an array of programs, including direct grants to land trusts, training programs, answers to more than 3,000 inquiries for technical assistance each year, and one-on-one mentoring.
Founded: 1983
Rand Wentworth, President
Mary Pope Hutson, Executive Vice President

484 Manomet Center for Conservation Sciences
125 Manomet Point Road 508-224-6521
Plymouth, MA 02360 Fax: 508-224-9220
E-mail: info@manomet.org
http://www.manomet.org

Manomet mission is to conserve natural resources for the benefit of wildlife and human populations. Through research and collaboration. Builds science-based, cooperative solutions to environmental problems.
Founded: 1970
John Hagan, President
Beth Brazil, Foundations Manager

485 Manufacturers of Emission Controls Association
2020 North 14th Street 202-296-4797
Suite 220 Fax: 202-331-1388
Arlington, VA 22201 E-mail: asantos@meca.org
http://www.meca.org

Offers current and relevant technical information on emissions control technology thus helping to strengthen state, federal and local air quality programs in promoting public health, environmental quality, and industrial progress.
Founded: 1976
Joe Kubsh, Executive Director

486 National Association of State Departments of Agriculture
4350 North Fairfax Drive 202-296-9680
Suite 910 Fax: 202-296-9686
Arlington, VA 22203 E-mail: nasda@nasda.org
http://www.nasda.org

This organization's mission is to support and promote the American agriculture industry, while protecting consumers and the environment, through the development, implementation, and communication of sound public policy and programs. There are twenty national organizations affiliated with NASDA. They are made up of persons of similar responsibilities with the state departments of agriculture and other agencies of state government.
Founded: 1915
Stephen Haterius, CEO
Megan McDonald, Assistant Director

487 National Association of State Land Reclamationists
Southern Illinois University 618-536-5521
Coal Research Center Fax: 618-453-7346
Carbondale, IL 62901 E-mail: President@notes.siu.edu
http://www.siu.edu

As a nationally recognized authority on the reclamation of mined lands, the National Association of State Land Reclamationists (NASLR) advocates the use of research, innovative technology and professional discourse to foster the restoration of lands and waters affected by mining related activities.
Founded: 1869
Anna Caswell, Secretary/Treasurer

488 National Audubon Society: Everglades Campaign
444 Brickell Avenue 305-371-6399
Suite 850 Fax: 305-371-6398
Miami, FL 33131 E-mail: danderson@audubon.org
http://www.audubonofflorida.org

The mission of the NAS Everglades Conservation Office is to ensure the restoration and conservation of the Greater Everglades Ecosystem in order to achieve an ecologically and economically sustainable South Florida. Our Miami-based office has a five-part program including science, education, advocacy, outreach and grassroots action.
Founded: 1886
David Anderson, Executive Director
John Flicker, President

489 **National Environmental Development Association**
1440 New York Avenue NW 202-638-1230
Suite 300 Fax: 202-639-8685
Washington, DC 20005
Companies and others concerned with balancing environmental and economic interests to obtain both a clean environment and a strong economy.
Andrew McElwaine, Director

490 **National FFA Organization**
6060 FFA Drive 317-802-6060
PO Box 68960 Fax: 317-802-6061
Indianapolis, IN 46268-960 http://www.ffa.org
The organization (formerly Future Farmers of America) is dedicated to making a positive difference in the lives of young people by developing their potential for premier leadership, personal growth and career success through agricultural education.
Founded: 1928
Larry Case, CEO/National Advisor
C Coleman Harris, Executive Secretary

491 **National Forestry Association**
374 Maple Avenue East 703-255-2700
Suite 310 800-476-8733
Vienna, VA 22180 Fax: 703-281-9200
E-mail: info@woodlandowners.org
http://www.nationalforestry.net
Nation's largest referral program to link up private forest owners with professional foresters. To be supplemented with a new innovative Forest Practices Certification program for landowners. Landowners who complete the review process and follow designated practices will be certified by the National Forestry Association.
Founded: 1981
Keith A. Argow, President/CEO
Dale Ting, Treasurer

492 **National Gardening Association**
237 Commerce Street 802-863-5251
Suite 101 Fax: 802-864-6889
Williston, VT 05945 E-mail: alisonw@garden.org
http://www.garden.org
The mission of the National Gardening Association is to sustain and renew the fundamental links between people, plants and the earth. NGA achieves its mission through youth and community gardening programs, industry research, free gardening information and memberships.
Founded: 1973
Mike Metallo, President
Tony Vargo, VP

493 **National Mining Association**
101 Constitution Avenue NW 202-463-2600
Suite 500E Fax: 202-463-2666
Washington, DC 20001 E-mail: craulston@nma.org
http://www.nma.org
The mission of the National Mining Association is to create and maintain a broad base of political support in Congress, the administration and the media for the mining industry of the US. In doing so, a secondary goal is to help our nation and the world realize the full promise and potential of the natural resources derived from America's mining industry.
Founded: 1917
Hal Quinn, President/CEO
Carol Raulston, Communications

494 **Native Forest Council**
PO Box 2190 541-688-2600
Eugene, OR 97402 Fax: 541-461-2156
E-mail: info@forestcouncil.org
http://www.forestcouncil.org
To provide visionary leadership and to ensure the integrity of public land ecosystems without compromising people or forests.
Founded: 1987
Timothy Hermach, President/Founder
Ed Dorsch, Vice President

495 **Native Seeds/SEARCH**
3061 N Campbell Ave 520-622-5561
Tucson, AZ 85719 866-622-5561
Fax: 520-622-5591
E-mail: web@nativeseeds.org
http://www.nativeseeds.org
Promote the use of ancient crops and their wild relatives by gathering, safeguarding, and distributing their seeds, while sharing benefits with traditional communities. Work to preserve knowledge about their uses. Through research, training, and community education, works to protect biodiversity and to celebrate cultural diversity.
Founded: 1983
Suzanne Nelson, Conservation
Julie Evans, Marketing/Operations

496 **Natural Land Institute**
320 South 3rd Street 815-964-6666
Rockford, IL 61104 Fax: 815-964-6661
E-mail: info@naturalland.org
http://www.naturalland.org
Dedicated to preserving land and natural diversity for future generations. Since 1958, NLI has protected, managed, and restored thousands of acres throughout Illinois and southern Wisconsin. These include prairies, forests, wetlands, and river corridors.
Founded: 1958
Kerry Leigh, Executive Director
Jill Kennay, Assisstant Director

497 **Natural Resources Council of America**
11100 Wiodlise Centre Drive 703-438-6000
Reston, VA 20190 Fax: 703-438-3570
E-mail: nrca@naturalresourcescouncil.org
http://www.naturalresourcescouncil.org
The Council dedicated to strengthening the conservation movement as a whole. For more than 50 years the Council has been the Crossroads of Conservation, keeping conservationists connected, informed and prepared to face the challenges of the future. The Council provides their membership- more than 85 conservation groups and nearly 100 individual supporters- with unique networking opportunities, valuable leadership training and cost-saving services.
Founded: 1946
Andrea Yank, Executive Director
Carlton Gleed, Program Coordinator

498 **Negative Population Growth**
2861 Duke St 703-370-9510
Suite 36 Fax: 703-370-9514
Alexandria, VA 22314 E-mail: npg@npg.org
http://www.npg.org
Leader in the movement for a sound population policy and advocates a smaller and truly sustainable population through voluntary incentives for smaller families and reduced immigration levels.
Founded: 1972
Donald Mann, President
Craig Lewis, Executive Vice President

499 **New England Coalition for Sustainable Population**
PO Box 1163 603-283-6686
Montpelier, VT 05601 E-mail: plumb.george@gmail.com
http://www.necsp.org
Provides progressive leadership and programs to educate the public about population stabilization and its beneficial relationship to environmental conservation, human rights and sustainable economic development.
Joseph Bish, Executive Director

500 **Pacific Institute for Studies in Development, Environment and Security**
654 13th Street 510-251-1600
Oakland, CA 94612 Fax: 510-251-2203
E-mail: info@pacinst.org
http://www.pacinst.org

Nonprofit policy research group, bringing knowledge to power on issues of environmental, economical development, and international peace and security.
Founded: 1987
Dr. Peter H. Gleick, President
Pete Stanga, COO

501 Panos Institute
1322 18th Street, NW 202-429-0730
Suite 26 Fax: 202-223-7947
Washington, DC 20036 E-mail: panoswashington@aol.com
http://www.panosinst.org
Founded in 1986, the Panos Institute is an international, nonprofit, nongovernmental organization with offices in Budapest, London, Paris, and Washington DC, working to raise public understanding of sustainable development issues.
Founded: 1986
Melanie Oliviero, Executive Director

502 Pinchot Institute for Conservation
1616 P Street NW 202-797-6580
Suite 100 Fax: 202-797-6583
Washington, DC 20036 E-mail: pinchot@pinchot.org
http://www.pinchot.org
Strives to advance conservation and sustainable natural resource management by developing innovative, practical, and broadly-supported solutions to conservation challenges and opportunities. This is accomplished through nonpartisan research, education and technical assistance.
Founded: 1963
V Alaric Sample, President
Jennifer Yeager, CFO

503 Population Communications International
777 United Nations Plaza 212-687-3366
5th Floor Fax: 212-661-4188
New York, NY 10017 E-mail: info@mediaimpact.org
http://www.mediaimpact.org
PCI's mission is to work creatively with the media and other organizations to motivate individuals and communities to make choices that influence population trends encouraging sustainable development and environmental protection.
Founded: 1985
Sean Southey, Executive Director
Brenda Campos, Program Director

504 Population Connection
2120 L Street NW 202-332-2200
Suite 500 800-767-1956
Washington, DC 20037 Fax: 202-332-2302
E-mail: info@populationconnection.org
http://www.populationconnection.org/
A national nonprofit organization working to slow population growth and achieve a sustainable balance between the Earth's people and its resources. They seek to protect the environment and ensure a high quality of life for present and future generations.
Founded: 1965
John Seager, President/CEO
Jessie Duarte, Membership Manager

505 Population Crisis Committee
1120 19th Street NW 202-659-1833
Washington, DC 20036 Fax: 202-293-1795
J Joseph Speidel, President

506 Population Institute
107 2nd Street NE 202-544-3300
Washington, DC 20002 888-787-0038
Fax: 202-544-0068
E-mail: info@populationinstitute.org
http://www.populationinstitute.org
The Population Institute is the World's largest independent nonprofit, educational organization dedicated exclusively to achieving a more equitable balance between the worlds population, environment, and resources. Established in 1969, the Institute, with members in 172 countries, is headquartered on Capitol Hill in Washington DC. The Institute uses a variety of resources and programs to bring its concerns about the consequences of rapid population growth to the forefront of the national agenda.
Founded: 1969
Robert Walker, President
William Ryerson, CEO

507 Population Reference Bureau
1875 Connecticut Avenue NW 202-483-1100
Suite 520 800-877-9881
Washington, DC 20009-5728 Fax: 202-328-3937
E-mail: popref@prb.org
http://www.prb.org
PRB informs policymakers, educators, the media, and concerned citizens working in the public interest around the world through a broad range of activities, including publications, information services, seminars and workshops, and technical support. They work with both public-sector and private-sector partners.
Founded: 1929
Wendy Baldwin, President/CEO
James Scott, CFO/COO

508 Population Resource Center
15 Roszel Road 609-452-2822
Princeton, NJ 08540 Fax: 609-452-0010
E-mail: prc@prcnj.org
http://www.prcdc.org
The mission of the Population Resource Center is to promote the use of accurate population data and sound, objective analysis of these data in the making of public policy.
Founded: 1985
Jane S De Lung, President
Linda Rosen, Director of Policy Analysis

509 Population: Environment Balance
1629 K Street NW 202-955-5700
Suite 300 800-866-8269
Washington, DC 20006 Fax: 202-955-6161
E-mail: info@balance.org
http://www.balance.org
Population Environment Balance is a national, nonprofit membership organization dedicated to maintaining the quality of the United States population stabilization.
Founded: 1973
Aaron Beckwith, Vice President

510 Population: Environmental Council
1629 K Street NW 202-955-5700
Suite 300 Fax: 202-955-6161
Washington, DC 20006 E-mail: info@balance.org
http://www.balance.org
Population-Environment Balance is dedicated to public education regarding the adverse effects of population growth on the environment. Founded in 1973, Population-Environment Balance has 8,800 members. It advocates measures that would encourage population stabilization.
Founded: 1973
Aaron Beckwith, Vice President

511 Rainforest Relief
PO Box 298 718-398-3760
New York, NY 10008-298 Fax: 718-398-3760
E-mail: info@rainforestrelief.org
http://www.rainforestrelief.org
Rainforest relief works to end the loss of the world's tropical and temperate rainforests by reducing the demand for materials for which rainforests are destroyed. These include rainforest woods such as mahogany, lauan and cedar, agricultural products such as bananas, chocolate, coffee and cut flowers, and mining products such as petroleum, gold, aluminum and copper. Rainforest relief works through research, education and non-violent direct action campaigns.
Founded: 1989
Tim Keating, Executive Director
Jeff Lockwood, West Coast Chapter Director

512 **Rural Advancement Foundation International USA**
274 Pittsboro Elementary School Roa 919-542-1396
Pittsboro, NC 27312 Fax: 919-542-0069
E-mail: regina@raiusa.org
http://www.rafiusa.org
RAFI USA is a nonprofit organization promoting community, equity and sustainability for family farmers and rural communities. Our headquarters serves as a model for green building. In addition to day lighting, solar and energy conservation features, the building showcases the use of salvaged materials from the deconstruction of an 1830s farmhouse.
Founded: 1990
Scott Marlow, Executive Director
Benny Bunting, Program Manager

513 **Save America's Forests**
4 Library Court SE 202-544-9219
Washington, DC 20003 Fax: 202-544-7462
E-mail: info@saveamericasforests.org
http://www.saveamericasforests.org
A nationwide campaign to end clear cutting and protect and restore our America's wild and natural forests. A coalition of groups throughout America working together to protect each other's local forests and to protect our nation's forests and forests throughout the world. A network of individual citizens from the country, the cities, and the suburbs who love forests and want to save them.
Founded: 1994
Carl Ross, Executive Director

514 **Society for Ecological Restoration**
1017 O Street NW 202-299-9518
Washington, AZ 85701 Fax: 520-622-5491
E-mail: info@ser.org
http://www.ser.org
To serve the growing field of Ecological Restoration through facilitating dialogue among restorationists; encouraging research, promoting awareness and public support for restoration and restorative management; contributing to public policy discussions; recognizing those who have made outstanding contributions to the field of restoration; and promoting ecological restoration around the globe.
Founded: 1987
Steve Bosak, Executive Director
Levi Wickwire, Program Manager

515 **Southface Energy Institute**
241 Pine Street NE 404-872-3549
Atlanta, GA 30308 Fax: 404-872-5009
E-mail: info@southface.org
http://www.southface.org
An environmental nonprofit working to promote sustainable homes, workplaces and communities through education, research, advocacy and technical assistance.
Founded: 1978
Michael Halicki, COO
Dennis Creech, Executive Director

516 **Synthetic Organic Chemical Manufacturers Association**
1850 M Street NW 202-721-4100
Suite 700 Fax: 202-296-8120
Washington, DC 20036-5810 E-mail: info@socma.com
http://www.socma.com
A trade association that serves the specialty, batch and custom chemical industry. SOCMA member companies make the products and refine the raw materials that make our standard of living possible; from pharmaceuticals to cosmetics, soaps to plastics, and all manner of industrial and construction products. SOCMA promotes innovative, safe and environmentally responsible operations, which are internationally competitive and contribute to a healthy, productive economy.
Founded: 1921
Larry Sloan, President/CEO
Diane McMahon, Director Business Operations

517 **World Environment Center**
734 15th Street NW 202-312-1370
Suite 720 Fax: 202-637-2411
Washington, DC 20005 E-mail: info@wec.org
http://www.wec.org
The World Environment Center is an independent, global non-profit, non-advocacy organization that advances sustainable development worldwide through the business practices of member companies and in partnership with governments, multi-lateral organizations, private sector organizations, universities and other stake holders.
Founded: 1974
Gwen Davidow, Director

518 **Worldwatch Institute**
1776 Massachusetts Avenue NW 202-452-1999
Suite 800 Fax: 202-296-7365
Washington, DC 20036 http://www.worldwatch.org
The Worldwatch Institute is an independent, nonprofit environmental research organization in Washington DC. Its mission is to foster a sustainable society in which human needs are met in ways that do not threaten the health of the natural environment or future generations. To this end, this Institute conducts interdisciplinary research on emerging global issues, the results of which are published and disseminated to decision-makers and the media.
Founded: 1974
Christopher Flavin, President
Leanne Mitchell, Director Communications

National: Travel & Tourism

519 **American Association for Physical Activity and Recreation**
1900 Association Drive 703-476-3400
Reston, VA 20191-1598 800-213-7193
Fax: 703-476-9527
E-mail: aapar@aahperd.org
http://www.aahperd.org
The AALR and the AAALF (American Association for Active Lifestyles and Fitness) have merged are in the process of reorganizing. The American Association for Leisure and Recreation (AALR) serves recreation professionals, practitioners, educators, and students who advance the profession and enhance the quality of life of all Americans through creative and meaningful leisure and recreation experiences.
Founded: 2005
Gale Wiedow, President
Dolly D. Lambdin, President Elect

520 **American Hiking Society**
1422 Fenwick Lane 301-565-6704
Silver Spring, MD 20910 800-972-8608
Fax: 301-565-6714
E-mail: info@americanhiking.org
http://www.americanhiking.org
American Hiking Society is a recreation based conservation organization working to cultivate a nation of hikers dedicated to establishing, protecting, and maintaining foot trails in America. The more than 10,000 individual members and hiking club members contribute to this national effort.
Founded: 1976
Gregory A Miller, President
Celina Montorfano, VP Programs

521 **American Recreation Coalition**
1200 G Street NW 202-682-9530
Suite 650 Fax: 202-682-9529
Washington, DC 20005-3832 E-mail: arc@funoutdoors.com
http://www.funoutdoors.com
Washington based nonprofit that partners to enhance and protect outdoor recreational opportunities and resources. ARC also monitors legislative and regulatory proposals that influence recreation.
Founded: 1979
Derrick Crandall, President
Catherine Ahern, Vice President

522 **American Whitewater**
PO Box 1540 828-586-1930
Cullowhee, NC 28723 866-262-8429
Fax: 828-586-2840
E-mail: membership@amwhitewater.org
http://www.americanwhitewater.org/
Restores rivers adversely affected by hydropower dams, eliminates water degradation, improves public land management and protects public access to rivers for responsible recreational use.
Founded: 1954
Norwood Scott, President
Chris Bell, Vice President

523 **Association of Zoos and Aquariums**
8403 Colesville Road 301-562-0777
Suite 710 Fax: 301-562-0888
Silver Spring, MD 20910-3314 E-mail: membership@aza.org
http://www.aza.org
As the leading accrediting organization for zoos and aquariums, it is dedicated to the advancement of accredited zoos and aquariums in the area of animal care, wildlife conservation, education and science.
Founded: 1924
Jim Maddy, President/CEO
Kris Vehrs, Executive Director

524 **Federation of Western Outdoor Clubs**
PO Box 129 E-mail: jack.jan.indiancreek@mailbug.com
Selma, OR 97538 http://www.federationofwesternoutdoorclubs.org
The Federation is composed of organizations that engage in hiking, camping, birding and other similar activities that rely on an outdoor environment where natural conditions predominate. Organizations in the West that have such programs, and that have an active interest in protecting the natural environment, are invited to affiliate.
Founded: 1932
Raelene Gold, President
Jack Walker, Treasurer

525 **Green Hotels Association**
PO Box 420212 713-789-8889
Houston, TX 77242 Fax: 713-789-9786
E-mail: green@greenhotels.com
http://www.greenhotels.com
Helping hotels save water, energy, solid and money world wide; to become environmentally-friendly properties.
Founded: 1993
Patricia Griffin, President

526 **Lighthawk**
304 Main Street, Suite 14 307-332-3242
PO Box 653 Fax: 307-332-1641
Lander, WY 82520 E-mail: info@lighthawk.org
http://www.lighthawk.org
Nonprofit organization founded in 1979, addresses critical environmental issues by providing an aerial perspective on areas of concern in the US, Canada and Central America. Using small aircraft, they fly partner organizations, electedofficials, industry and media representatives, activists, and indigenous groups over protected and threatened regions. Program flights give passengers both intellectual and visceral understanding of what is at stake.
Founded: 1979
C. Rudy Engholm, Executive Director
Bev Gabe, Communications Manager

527 **National Association of Recreation Resource Planners**
PO Box 221 814-927-8212
Marienville, PA 16239 Fax: 814-927-6659
E-mail: brenda@recpro.org
http://www.recpro.org
NARRP, is an organization comprised of outdoor recreation professionals and others interested in recreation resource planning. It is a nationwide organization with members in nearly every state representing federal and state agencies, land managers, consultants, and academic institutions. The mission of NARRP is to Advance the Art, the Science and the Profession of Recreation Resource Planning: and enhance the provision of recreation opportunities for all Americans.
Sergio Capozzi, President
Mary Donze, Vice President

528 **National Association of State Outdoor Recreation Liaison Officers**
105H ABNR University of Missouri 573-353-2702
Columbia, MO 65211-7230 Fax: 573-882-9521
E-mail: nasorlo@embavqmail.com
http://www.nasorlo.org
An association of gubernatorial appointed state and territorial officials that work across the nation to provide places for outdoor recreation through the use of the Land and Water Conservation Fund.
Doug Eiken, Executive Director
Tim Hagsett, President

529 **National Council of State Tourism Directors**
TIA
1100 New York Avenue NW 202-408-8422
Suite 450 Fax: 202-408-1255
Washington, DC 20005 E-mail: feedback@tia.org
http://www.tia.org/councils/NCSTD/
The first council of the TIA it brings together tourism directors from all 50 states, DC, and territories to serve as a: unified voice, catalyst for developing programs for the benefit of all, and harmonizer in the diversity of needs, priorities and values.
Founded: 1969
Todd Davidson, Chairman

530 **National Wildlife Federation: Expeditions**
11100 Wildlife Center Drive 202-797-6800
Reston, VA 20190 800-606-9563
Fax: 202-797-6646
E-mail: expeditions@nwf.org
http://www.nwf.org
Travel with the NWF with expert guides, in an environmentally-sensitive way, and into natural ecosystems. The National Wildlife Federation is the largest member-supported conservation group, uniting individuals, organizations, businesses and government to protect wildlife, wild places and the environment.
Larry J Schweiger, President/CEO
Jamie Matyas, Executive Vice President/COO

531 **Rails-to-Trails Conservancy**
The Duke Ellington Building
2121 Ward Ct NW 202-331-9696
5th Floor Fax: 202-331-9680
Washington, DC 20037 E-mail: railtrails@railtrails.org
http://www.railtrails.org
A nonprofit organization working with communities to preserve unused rail corridors by transforming them into trails, enhancing the health of American's environment, economy, neighborhoods and people.
Founded: 1986
Keith Laughlin, President
Jeff Ciabotti, VP Trail Development

532 **Safari Club International**
4800 W Gates Pass Road 520-620-1220
Tucson, AZ 85745-9490 888-486-8724
Fax: 520-622-1205
http://www.safariclub.org/
A leader in wildlife conservation, hunter education, and protecting the freedom to hunt.
John Whipple, President
John W Nelson, Vice President

533 **Wilderness Education Association**
2150 N 107th Street 812-855-4095
Suite 205 Fax: 812-855-8697
Seattle, WA 98133 http://www.weainfo.org/

WEA provides professional instruction, leadership training and wilderness travel. Promoting safe, ethical and professional wilderness leaders.
Founded: 1977
Mike McGowan, President
Ricky Haro, Vice President

National: Water Resources

534 **Adopt-A-Stream Foundation**
Northwest Stream Center 425-316-8592
600-128th Street SE Fax: 425-338-1423
Everett, WA 98208 E-mail: aasf@streamkeeper.org
http://www.streamkeeper.org
The mission of the AASF is to teach people how to become stewards of their watershed. That mission is carried out by conducting classes, producing environmental education materials, and providing local communitites stram and wetlandrestoration technical assistance.
Founded: 1985
Tom Murdoch, Executive Director

535 **American Canal Society**
117 Main Street 610-691-0956
Freemansburg, PA 18017 http://www.americancanals.org
Dedicated to Historic Canal Research, Preservation, Restoration, and Parks. Promotes the wise use of America's many historic canal resources through research, preservation, restoriation, recreation, and parks. Acts as a nationalclearing house of canal information and co-operates with local, state, and international canal societies, groups, and individuals to identify historic canal resources, to publicize canal history, activities, and problems, and to take action onthreatened canals and sites
Founded: 1972
David G Barber, President
Charles W Derr, Secretary/Treasurer

536 **American Ground Water Trust**
50 Pleasant Street Ste 2 603-228-5444
Concord, NH 03301 Fax: 603-228-6557
E-mail: trustinfo@agwt.org
http://www.agwt.org
A not-for-profit education organization. Promotes opportunity, cooperation and action among individuals, groups and organizations in order to educate the public, and further its mission: to protect ground water, promote publicawareness of the environment and economic importance of groundwater and provide accurate information to assist public participation in water resources decisions and management.
Founded: 1986
Kevin McGinnis, Chairman
Andrew Stone, Executive Director

537 **American Rivers**
1101 14th Street NW 202-347-7550
Suite 1400 877-347-7550
Washington, DC 20005 Fax: 202-347-9240
E-mail: outreach@americanrivers.org
http://www.americanrivers.org
The only national organization that is dedicated to protecting and restoring rivers nationwide. Founded over 30 years ago it now has over 65,000 members and supports nationwide and two regional and six field offices.
Founded: 1973
William Robert Irwin, President
Cathy Duley, Membership Director

538 **American Rivers: Northeast Region**
1101 14th Street NW 202-347-7550
Suite 1400 877-347-7550
Washington, DC 20005 Fax: 202-347-9240
E-mail: feedback@americanrivers.org
http://www.americanrivers.org
American Rivers is the only national organization standing up for healthy rivers so our communities can thrive.
William Robert Irwin, President
Cathy Duley, Membership Director

539 **American Shore and Beach Preservation Association**
5460 Beaujolais Lane 239-489-2616
Fort Myers, FL 33919 Fax: 239-489-9917
E-mail: exdir@asbpa.org
http://www.asbpa.org
This Association is formed in recognition of the fact that shores of our oceans, lakes and rivers constitute important assets for promoting the health and physical well-being of the people of this nation, and that their contiguity togo out great centers of population affords an opportunity for wholesome and necessary rest and recreation not equally available in any other form. The purpose of the Association is to bring together for cooperation and mutural helpfulness.
Founded: 1926
Harry Simmons, President
Kate & Ken Gooderham, Executive Directors

540 **American Water Resources Association**
PO Box 1626 540-687-8390
Middleburg, VA 20118 Fax: 540-687-8395
E-mail: info@awra.org
http://www.awra.org
Founded in 1964, the American Water Resources Association is a non-profit professional association dedicated to the advancement of men and women in water resources management, research, and education. AWRA's membership ismultidisciplinary; its diversity is its hallmark. It is the professional home of a wide variety of water resources experts including engineers, educators, foresters, biologists, ecologists, geographers, managers, regulators, hydrologists andattorneys.
Carol R. Collier, President
Kenneth D. Reid, Executive Vice President

541 **American Water Works Association**
6666 W Quincy Avenue 303-794-7711
Denver, CO 80235 800-926-7337
Fax: 303-347-0804
http://www.awwa.org
Dedicated to the promotion of public health and welfare in the provision of drinking water of unquestionable quality and sufficient quantity. AWWA must be proactive and effective in advancing the technology, science, management andgovernment policies relative to the stewardship of water.
Founded: 1881
Darcy Burke, Executive Director
JoAnn Taniguchi, Secretary

542 **Association of Ground Water Scientists and Engineers**
601 Dempsey Road 614-898-7791
Westerville, OH 43081 800-551-7379
Fax: 614-898-7786
E-mail: smasters@ngwa.org
http://www.ngwa.org/agwse
The Scientists and Engineers membership division of the NGWA. The mission of the National Ground Water Association is to enhance the skills and credibility of all ground water professionals, develop and exchange industry knowledge, andpromote the ground water industry and understanding of ground water resources.
Sandy Masters, Liaison

543 **Association of Metropolitan Sewerage Agencies**
1816 Jefferson Place NW 202-833-2672
Washington, DC 20036 Fax: 202-833-4657
E-mail: info@nacwa.org
http://www.amsa-cleanwater.org
Represents the interests of the country's wastewater treatment agencies, true environmental practitioners that serve the majority of the sewered population in the US, and collectively treat and reclaim more than 17 billion gallons of wastewater each day. Maintains a key role in the development of environmental legislation,

and works closely with federal regulatory agencies in the implementation of environmental programs.
Ken Kirk, Executive Director

544 Association of Metropolitan Water Agencies
1620 I Street NW 202-331-2820
Suite 500 Fax: 202-785-1845
Washington, DC 20006 E-mail: info@amwa.net
http://www.amwa.net
An organization of the largest publicly owned drinking water systems in the nation.
Founded: 1981
Diane VanDe Hei, Executive Director
Michael Arceneaux, Deputy Executive Director

545 Association of State Floodplain Managers
575 D'Onofrio Drive 608-828-3000
Suite 200 Fax: 608-828-6319
Madison, WI 53719 E-mail: asfpm@floods.org
http://www.floods.org
The Association is an organization of professionals involved in floodplain management, flood hazard mitigation, the National Flood Insurance Program, and flood preparedness, warning and recovery.
Founded: 1977
Larry Larson, Director Emeritus
Diane Brown, Outreach and Events Manager

546 Association of State Wetland Managers
32 Tandberg Trail 207-892-3399
Suite 2A Fax: 207-892-3089
Windham, ME 04062 E-mail: aswm@aswm.org
http://www.aswm.org
Nonprofit organization dedicated to the protection and restoration of the nations wetlands. Our goal is to help public and private wetland decision-makers utilize the best possible scientific information and techniques in wetland delineation, assessment, mapping, planning, regulation, acquisition, restoration, and other management.
Founded: 1983
Jeanne Christie, Executive Director
Jon Kusler, Associate Director

547 Association of State and Interstate Water Pollution Control Administrators
750 1st Street NE 202-898-0905
Suite 1010 Fax: 202-898-0929
Washington, DC 20002 E-mail: admin1@aswipca.org
http://www.asiwpca.org
Maintain and enhance the quality of the nation's water resources and protect the public health through improving the State's capability to develop and implement effective Federal and State water management programs.
Roberta Savage, Executive Director
Linda Eichmiller, Deputy Director

548 Blue Ocean Institute
Stony Brook University 631-632-3763
Stony Brook, NY 11794-5000 http://www.blueocean.org
Inspires a closer relationship with the sea through science, art and literature. Shares information that enlightens personal choice. Instills hope and helps restore living abundance in the sea.
Founded: 2003
Carl Safina, President

549 CEDAM International
1 Fox Road 914-271-5365
Croton on Hudson, NY 10520 Fax: 914-271-4723
E-mail: cedamint@aol.com
http://www.cedam.org
Conservation, Education, Diving, Awareness and Marine research International is a nonprofit organization dedicated to the understanding, protection and preservation of the world's marine resources. Through our expeditions, CEDAMInternational volunteer divers actively participate in scientific research and conservation-oriented education projects. The results of our findings and efforts are disseminated to both the scientific and lay communities. The CEDA also publishes anannual newsletter.
Susan Sammon, Director

550 Center for Coastal Studies
115 Bradford Street 508-487-3623
Provincetown, MA 02657 Fax: 508-487-4695
E-mail: ccs@coastalstudies.org
http://www.coastalstudies.org
Private nonprofit organization for research, conservation and education in the coastal and marine environments.
Richard Delaney, President

551 Center for Great Lakes Environmental Education
PO Box 56 E-mail: info@greatlakesed.org
Buffalo, NY 14205 http://www.greatlakesed.org
Mission leads to awareness of and access to information about Great Lakes environmental subjects by promoting learning links for teachers, students and other stakeholders in the international Great Lakes-St Lawrence basin ecosystem.

552 Center for Marine Conservation
2029 K Street, NW 202-429-5609
Washington, DC 20006 800-519-1541
Fax: 202-872-0619
E-mail: info@oceanconservancy.org
http://www.cmc-ocean.org
The mission of the CMC is to protect ocean ecosystems and conserve the global abundance and diversity of marine wildlife. Through sciencebased advocacy, research and public education, CMC informs, inspires and empowers people to speakand act for the oceans.
Roger Rufe Jr, President
Thomas J Tepper, Senior VP Operations

553 Center for Watershed Protection
8390 Main Street 410-461-8323
Second Floor Fax: 410-461-8324
Ellicott City, MD 21043 E-mail: center@cwp.org
http://www.cwp.org
The center is a nonprofit 501(c)3 organization dedicated to finding new ways to protect and restore our nation's streams, lakes, rivers and estuaries. The center publishes numerous technical publications on all aspects of watershedprotection, including stormwater management, watershed planning and better site design. Publications are available online.
Founded: 1992
Hye Yeong Kwon, Executive Director
Karen Cappiella, Program Manager Research

554 Center for the Great Lakes
435 N Michigan Avenue 312-263-0785
Suite 1408 Fax: 312-201-0683
Chicago, IL 60611
Daniel K Ray, Director

555 Clean Harbors Cooperative
4601 Tremley Point Road 908-862-7500
Linden, NJ 07036 Fax: 908-862-7560
E-mail: chcllc@aol.com
http://www.apicom.org/members.html
Edward M Wirkowski, Manager
Dennis J McCarthy, Director

556 Clean Water Action
1010 Vermont Avenue NW 410-235-8808
Suite 400 Fax: 410-235-8816
Washington, DC 20005 E-mail: cwa@cleanwater.org
http://www.cleanwateraction.org
National citizens' organization working for clean, safe and affordable water, prevention of health-threatening pollution, creation of environmentally-safe jobs and businesses, and empowerment of people to make democracy work.Organizes strong grassroots groups, coalitions and campaigns to protect our

environment, health, economic well-being and community quality of life.
Founded: 1972
Robert Wendelgass, President
Peter Lockwood, Treasurer

557 **Clean Water Fund**
1010 Vermont Avenue, NW 202-895-0432
Suite 400 Fax: 202-895-0438
Washington, DC 20005 E-mail: cwf@cleanwater.org
http://www.cleanwaterfund.org
Brings diverse communities together to work for changes that improve our lives, promoting sensible solutions for people and the environment.
Founded: 1972
Peter Lockwood, President
Robert Wendelgass, Executive VP

558 **Clean Water Network**
1200 New York Avenue NW 202-298-2421
Suite 400 Fax: 202-289-1060
Washington, DC 20005 E-mail: info@cwn.org
http://www.cleanwaternetwork.org
A nonprofit network of over 1,000 organizations that deal with clean water issues covered by the Clean Water Act. Our member organizations consist of a variety of organizations representing environmentalists, family farmers, recreationanglers, commercial fishermen, surfers, boaters, faith communities, labor unions and civic associations. We publish a monthly newsletter and various reports.
Natalie Roy, Executive Director

559 **Coastal Conservation Association**
6919 Portwest 713-626-4234
Suite 100 800-201-3474
Houston, TX 77024 Fax: 713-951-3801
E-mail: ccantl@joincca.org
http://www.joincca.org/
A national nonprofit organization of 17 coastal state chapters dedicated to the conservation and preservation of marine resources.
Founded: 1977
Pat Murray, VP/Director Conservation
Ted Venker, Director Communications

560 **Coastal Society**
PO Box 3590 757-565-0999
Williamsburg, VA 23187-3590 Fax: 757-565-0299
E-mail: coastalsoc@aol.com
http://www.thecoastalsociety.org
Organization of private sector, academic, government professionals and students dedicated to actively addressing emerging coastal issues by fostering dialogue, forging partnerships and promoting communication and education.
Founded: 1975
Kate Killerlain Morrison, President
Gerhard Kuska, President Elect

561 **Cook Inletkeeper**
PO Box 3269 907-235-4068
3734 Ben Walters Lane Fax: 907-235-4069
Homer, AK 99603 E-mail: keeper@inletkeeper.org
http://www.inletkeeper.org
Dedicated to protecting the vast Cook Inlet watershed and the life it sustains; it is a community-based nonprofit organization that combines education, advocacy and science to reach this goal.
Founded: 1995
Bob Shavelson, Executive Director

562 **Coral Reef Alliance**
351 Caliornia Street 415-834-0900
Suite 650 Fax: 415-834-0999
San Francisco, CA 94104 E-mail: info@coral.org
http://www.coral.org
Unites and empowers communities to save coral reefs. Provides tools, education, and inspiration to residents of coral reef destinations to support local projects that benefit both reefs and people. Originally founded in 1994 togalvanize te dive community for conservation, CORAL has grown from a small grassroots organization into the only international nonprofit organization that works exclusively to protect our planet's coral reefs.
Founded: 1994
Michael Webster, Executive Director
Lisa Owens Viani, Communications Manager

563 **Earth Island Institute**
2150 Allston Way 415-788-3666
Suite 4600 Fax: 415-788-7324
Berkeley, CA 94704-1375 E-mail: johnknox@earthisland.org
http://www.earthisland.org
A non-profit, public interest, membership organization that supports people who are creating solutions to protect our shared planet.
Founded: 1982
John Knox, Executive Director
Kevin Connelly, Associate Director

564 **Ecological Society of America**
1990 M St, NW 202-833-8773
Suite 700 Fax: 202-833-8775
Washington, DC 20036 E-mail: esahq@esa.org
http://www.esa.org
To promote ecological science by improving communication among ecologists; raise the public's level of awareness of the importance of ecological science; increase the resources available for the conduct of ecological science; and ensure the appropriate use of ecological science in environmental decision making by enhancing communication between the ecological community and policy-makers.
Founded: 1915
Elizabeth Biggs, CFO
Katherine S McCarter, Executive Director

565 **Emergency Committee to Save America's Marine Resources**
1552 Osprey Court 732-223-5729
Manasquan Park, NJ 08736 Fax: 732-528-1056
E-mail: cristori@aol.com
Founded: 1955
Allan J Ristori, Chairman

566 **Foresta Institute for Ocean and Mountain Studies**
2400 E Speedway 520-881-6174
Suite 118-293 Fax: 520-323-2751
Tucson, AZ 85716
Works to educate teachers and youth about environmental conservation.

567 **Freshwater Society**
2500 Shadywood Road 952-471-9773
Excelsior, MN 55331 888-471-9773
Fax: 952-471-7685
E-mail: freshwater@freshwater.org
http://www.freshwater.org
Founded: 1968
Tom Skramstad, Chairman
Stuart E. Grubb, Vice Chair

568 **Future Fisherman Foundation**
1001 North Fairfax Street 703-519-9691
Suite 501 Fax: 703-519-1872
Alexandria, VA 22314 E-mail: info@asafishing.org
http://www.asafishing.org
The Future Fisherman Foundation supports groups that offers training in fishing and aquatic resource stewardship by developing curriculum materials for environmental and angler education. Working through state fish and wildlifeagencies, the foundation strives to increase aquatic resource education by using available federal funds.
Mike Nussman, Preisdent/CEO
Gordon Robertson, Vice President

569 Gaia Institute
400 City Island Avenue 718-885-1906
Bronx, NY 10464 Fax: 718-885-0882
E-mail: Gaia@gaia-inst.org
http://www.gaia-inst.org

The purpose of the Gaia Institute is to test through demostration the means by which ecological components of backyards, communities, towns and cities, as well as watersheds and estuaries, can be enhanced through integratedwastes-into-resources technologies.
Founded: 1972
Paul S Mankiewicz, Director
Julie A Mankiewicz, PhD, Director

570 Global Water Policy Project
107 Larkspur Drive 413-256-4808
Amherst, MA 01002 E-mail: info@globalwaterpolicy.org
http://www.globalwaterpolicy.org

Global Water Policy Projects aims to promote the preservation and sustainable use of Earth's fresh water through research, writing, outreach, and public speaking.
Founded: 1994
Sandra Postel, Founder/Director

571 Great Lakes United
4525 Rue DeRouen 514-396-3333
Montreal Quebec, QC H1V 1 Fax: 514-396-0297
E-mail: glu@glu.org
http://www.glu.org

Great Lakes United is an international coalition dedicated to preserving and restoring the Great Lakes-St. Lawrence River ecosystem. Great Lakes United is made up of member organizations representing environmentalists, conservationists, hunters and anglers, labor unions, community groups, and programs, and promotes citizen action and grassroots leadership to assure.
Founded: 1982
Derek Stack, Executive Director
Patty O'Donnell, President

572 International Association for Environmental Hydrology
2607 Hopeton Drive 210-344-5418
San Antonio, TX 78230 Fax: 210-344-9941
E-mail: hydroweb@mail.org
http://www.hydroweb.com

573 International Desalination Association
94 Central Street, Suite 200 978-887-0410
PO Box 387 Fax: 978-887-0411
Topsfield, MA 01983 E-mail: info@idadesal.org
http://www.idadesal.org

IDA is committed to the development and promotion of the appropriate use of desalination and desalination technology worldwide. We endeavor to carry out these goals by encouraging research and development, exchanging, promoting communication and disseminating information.
Founded: 1972
Corrado Sommariva, President
Fady Juez, First Vice President

574 International Oceanographic Foundation
4600 Rickenbacker Causeway 305-361-4000
Miami, FL 33149-1098 Fax: 305-361-4711
http://www.rsmas.miami.edu

International Oceanographic Foundation (IOF) is a nonprofit supporting organization to the University of Miami's Rosenstiel School of Marine and Atmospheric Science. IOF was chartered in 1953 to encourage scientific investigation of the sea, to provide the public with current, accurate and unbiased information pertaining to marine environments and to promote awareness of the importance of Earth's oceans to humankind. IOF is a 501(c)(3) nonprofit organization, contributions are tax deductable.
Founded: 1953
Otis B Brown, Dean

575 International Rivers
2150 Allston Way 510-848-1155
Suite 300 Fax: 510-848-1008
Berkeley, CA 94704-1378 E-mail: info@internationalrivers.org
http://www.internationalrivers.org

Mission is to protect rivers and defend the rights of communities that depend on them. We oppose destructive dams and the development model they advance, and encourage better was of meeting people's needs for water, energy and protection from damaging floods. To achieve this mission, we collaborate with a network of local communities, social movements, non-governmental organizations and other partners.
Founded: 1985
Jason Rainey, Executive Director
Elisabeth Sabel, Foundations Director

576 International Water Resources Association
Southern Illinois University Carbondale
4535 Faner Hall 618-453-5138
Carbondale, IL 62901-6899 Fax: 618-453-6465
E-mail: iwra@siu.edu
http://www.iwra.siu.edu

IWRA strives to improve water management worldwide through dialogue, education, and research. It seeks to improve water resources outcomes by improving our collective understanding of the physical, biological, chemical, institutional, and socioeconomic aspects of water.
Founded: 1972 160 pages
ISSN: 0250-8060
Benedykt Dziegielewski, Executive Director
John W Nicklow, Treasurer

577 Interstate Council on Water Policy
505 North Ivy Street 202-466-7287
Arlington, VA 22220-1707 Fax: 202-646-6210
http://www.icwp.org

The Interstate Council on Water Policy is the national organization of state and regional water resource management agencies. It provides a means to exchange information, ideas, and experience and to work with federal agencies, which share water management responsibilities. In particular, ICWP focuses on water quality and water quantity issues, and on the dynamic interface state and federal roles.
Founded: 1959
Joe Hoffman, Executive Director

578 Marine Technology Society
1100 H Street NW 202-717-8705
Suite LL100 Fax: 202-347-4302
Washington, DC 20005 E-mail: membership@mtsociety.org
http://www.mtsociety.org

Addresses coastal zone management, marine mineral and energy resources, marine environmental protection, and ocean engineering issues.
Founded: 1963
Richard Lawson, Executive Director

579 National Association for State and Local River Conservation Programs
8630 Fenton Street 301-589-9455
Suite 910 Fax: 301-589-6121
Silver Spring, MD 20910
Barry Beasley, President

580 National Association of Clean Water Agencies
1816 Jefferson Place NW 202-833-2672
Washington, DC 20039 Fax: 202-833-4657
E-mail: info@nacwa.org
http://www.nacwa.org

The NACWA is a recognized leader in environmental policy and a technical resource on water quality and ecosystem protection issues. It represents the interests of the country's wastewater treatment agencies and true environmentalpractioners.
Ken Kirk, Executive Director
Paula Dannenfeldt, Deputy Executive Director

581 **National Association of Flood and Stormwater Management Agencies**
PO Box 56764 202-218-4122
Washington, DC 20040 Fax: 202-478-1734
E-mail: info@nasma.org
http://www.nafsma.org
The National Association of Flood and Stormwater Management Agencies is an organization of public agencies whose function is the protection of lives, property and economic activity from the adverse impacts of storm and flood waters.The mission of the association is to advocate public policy, encourage technologies and conduct education programs which facilitate and enhance the adchievement of the public service functions of its members.
Founded: 1978
Susan Gilson, Executive Director
Kerry Wilson, Membership Services

582 **National Audubon Society: Living Oceans Program**
550 S Bay Avenue 516-859-3032
Islip, NY 11751 Fax: 516-581-5268
E-mail: mlee@audubon.org
http://www.audubon.org/campaign/10
Living Oceans is the marine conservation program of National Audubon Society. Audubon's Living Oceans uses science-based policy analysis, education and grassroots advocacy to put science to work on behalf of marine fish and ocean ecosystems.
Carl Safina, Director
Mercedes Lee, Assistant Director

583 **National Boating Federation**
PO Box 4111 Fax: 360-297-3505
Annapolis, MD 21403-4111 E-mail: rpdavid@capecod.net
http://www.n-b-f.org
Nonprofit, all volunteer organization that represents over 2 million of America's boaters. It is an alliance of yacht and boating clubs, recreational boating organizations and includes associate and individual members.
Founded: 1966
Marlene Barrington, President
Margot J Brown, Executive Director

584 **National Coalition for Marine Conservation**
4 Royal Street SE 703-777-0037
Leesburg, VA 20175 Fax: 703-777-1107
E-mail: christine@savethefish.org
http://www.wildoceans.org
National Coalition for Marine Conservation is dedicated exclusively to conserving ocean fish, preventing overfishing, reducing bycatch, and protecting marine habitat.
Founded: 1973
Ken Hinman, President
Pam Lyons Gromen, Executive Director

585 **National Council for Air and Stream Improvements**
4815 Emperor Boulevard 919-941-6400
Canterbury Hall, Ste 110 Fax: 919-941-6401
Durham, NC 27703 E-mail: ryeske@ncasi.org
http://www.ncasi.org
The Council is a technical organization devoted to finding solutions to environmental protection problems in the manufacture of pulp, paper, and wood products in industrial forestry. It now has about 75 member companies.
Founded: 1943
Ronald Yeske, President

586 **National Ground Water Association**
601 Dempsey Road 614-898-7791
Westerville, OH 43081 800-551-7379
Fax: 614-898-7786
E-mail: ngwa@ngwa.org
http://www.ngwa.org
The mission of the National Ground Water Association is to provide professional and technical leadership for the advancement of the ground water industry and for the protection, promotion, and responsible development and use of groundwater resources.
Founded: 1948
Daniel T. Meyer, President
Griffin Crosby, President Elect

587 **National Institutes for Water Resources**
University of Massachusetts Water Resources Center
47 Harkness Road 413-253-5686
Pelham, MA 01002 Fax: 413-253-1309
E-mail: godfrey@tei.umass.edu
http://www.snr.unl.edu/niwr
The National Institutes for Water Resources is a network of Research Institutes in every state. They conduct basic and applied research to solve water problems unique to their area. The programmatic responsibilities stipulated by theWater resources Research Act provide a unified focus for the federal and non-federal components of the Institute Program.
Founded: 1970
Reagan Waskom, President
Brian Haggard, President Elect

588 **National Water Center**
5473 Highway 23N E-mail: peace@ipa.net
Eureka Springs, AR 72631 http://www.nationalwatercenter.org
Strives to look at water with the broadest ideas of ecological balance and harmony. Support appropriate technology, bioregionalism, composting toilets, dowsing, ecology, flow forms, stream monitoring, vibrational water, watershed planning.
Barbara Helen Harmony, President

589 **National Water Resources Association**
3800 North Fairfax Drive 703-524-1544
Suite 4 Fax: 703-524-1548
Arlington, VA 22203 E-mail: nwra@nwra.org
http://www.nwra.org
The National Water Resources Association consists of individuals or groups, such as irrigation districts, canal companies and conservancy districts, municipalities and the public in general, who are interested in water resource development projects. It was started in 1932 and now has about 5,000 members.
Founded: 1932
Tom Myrum, President
Dave Koland, First Vice President

590 **National Watershed Coalition**
1023 Manvel, Suite D 405-627-0670
PO Box 556 E-mail: nwchdqtrs@sbcglobal.net
Chandler, OK 74834 http://www.watershedcoalition.org
A nonprofit Coalition made up of national, regional, state, and local organizations, associations, and individuals, that advocate dealing with natural resource problems and issues using watersheds as the planning and implementation unit.
Founded: 1989
Dr Dan Sebert PhD, CEO/Executive Director

591 **National Waterways Conference**
1100 North Glebe Road 703-243-4090
Suite 1010 Fax: 866-371-1390
Arlington, VA 22201 E-mail: info@waterways.org
http://www.waterways.org
Coalition of trade and regional associations that have an interest in national waterways policy issues.
Amy W. Larson, President
Carole Wright, Director

592 **National Xeriscape Council**
PO Box 163172 512-392-6225
Austin, TX 78716 http://www.xeriscape.org
Systematic concept for saving water in landscaped areas.

593 **North American Benthological Society**
PO Box 7065 E-mail: webmaster@benthos.org
Lawrence, KS 66044 http://www.freshwater-science.org
An international scientific organization that promotes better understanding of biotic communities of lake and stream bottoms and their role in aquatic ecosystems.
Founded: 1953
Dave Penrose, President
Randy Fuller, President Elect

594 North American Lake Management Society
PO Box 5443 608-233-2836
Madison, WI 53705-443 Fax: 608-233-3186
E-mail: info@nalms.org
http://www.nalms.org
Their focus is on lake management for a wide variety of uses, but they also get involved with other issues on a watershed level: land, streams, wetlands, and estuaries. The society forges partnerships among citizens, scientists andprofessionals to foster the management and protection of lakes and reservoirs.
Founded: 1980
Philip Forsberg, Program Manager
Greg Arenz, Membership Coordinator

595 Ocean Champions
202 San Jose Avenue 831-462-2550
Capitola, CA 95010 Fax: 831-462-2542
http://www.oceanchampions.org
Environmental organization connected to a political action committee focused solely on oceans and ocean wildlife.
Founded: 2003
Mike Dunmyer, Executive Director

596 Ocean Conservancy
1300 19th Street NW 202-429-5609
8th Floor 800-519-1541
Washington, DC 20036 Fax: 202-872-0619
E-mail: webmaster@oceanconservancy.org
http://www.oceanconservancy.org
To conserve and protect the oceans. Advocate for the oceans, with an emphasis on conserving and protecting significant parts of our oceans.
Founded: 1972
Andreas Merkl, President/CEO
Larry Amon, CFO

597 Oceana
1350 Connecticut Ave NW 202-833-3900
5th Floor 877-762-3262
Washington, DC 20036 Fax: 202-833-2070
E-mail: info@oceana.org
http://www.oceana.org
Oceana is a nonprofit international advocacy organization dedicated to protecting and restoring the world's oceans through policy advocacy, science, law and public education. Oceana's constituency includes members and activists frommore than 190 countries and territories who are committed to saving the world's marine environment. In 2002, American Oceans Campaign became part of Oceana's international effort to protect ocean eco-systems and sustain the circle of life.
Founded: 2001
Andrew Sharpless, CEO
Valarie Van Cleave, Treasurer

598 Oceanic Society
30 Sir Francis Drake Blvd 415-441-1106
PO Box 437 800-326-7491
Ross, CA 94957 Fax: 415-474-3395
E-mail: office@oceanic-society.org
http://www.oceanic-society.org
Founded for the protection of the marine environment, environmental education and conservation-based field research.
Founded: 1969
Birgit Winning, President
Roderic Mast, Executive Vice President

599 River Network
520 SW 6th Avenue 503-241-3506
Suite 1130 800-423-6747
Portland, OR 97204 Fax: 503-241-9256
E-mail: info@rivernetwork.org
http://www.rivernetowrk.org
River Network is a national nonprofit organization for citizen groups working for river and watershed protection. Thier mission is to help people understand, protect and restore rivers and their watersheds. They provide conservationpartners with with information training, consultation, grants, referrals to other service organizations and networking opportunities.
Founded: 1988
Don Elder, President/CEO
Susan Schwartz, CAO

600 Scientific Committee on Oceanic Research: Department of Earth and Planetary Science
242 Garland Hall 410-516-4070
3400 N Charles Street Fax: 410-516-4019
Baltimore, MD 21218 E-mail: scor@jhu.edu
http://www.jhu.edu
The Scientific Committee on Oceanic Research (SCOR), is an international nonprofit organization whose purpose is to encourage international cooperation in a branch of ocean research.
Founded: 1957
Ronald J. Daniels, President
Phil Spector, Vice President

601 Seacoast Anti-Pollution League
163 Court Street 603-431-5089
PO Box 1136 E-mail: info@sapl.org
Portsmouth, NH 03802 http://www.sapl.org
A nonprofit environmental group that makes it our business to monitor threats to public health and safety, wildlife, and ecosystems in our-and your-community.
Founded: 1969
David Hills, President

602 Soil and Water Conservation Society
945 SW Ankeny Road 515-289-2331
Ankeny, IA 50023-9723 800-843-7645
Fax: 515-289-1227
E-mail: memberservices@swcs.org
http://www.swcs.org
Their mission is to foster the science and art of natural resource conservation. Their work targets the conservation of soil, water, and related natural resources.
Founded: 1943
Craig A Cox, Executive Director
Lindey Krug, Member Services

603 Steamboaters
1665 Evergreen Drive 541-688-4980
Eugene, OR 97404 Fax: 541-607-3763
E-mail: steamboaters@jeffnet.org
http://www.steamboaters.org
Nonprofit organization dedicated to work to restore the North Umpqua river system's wild fish stocks, particularly steelhead, to a sustainable level that is consistent with optimum natural population levels. Protect, preserve andrestore fish habitat, including adequate and consistent flows of high quality water in the North Umpqua and its tributaries.
Founded: 1975
Joe Ferguson, President

604 Surfrider Foundation
942 Calle Negocio 949-492-8170
Suite 350 Fax: 949-492-8142
San Clemente, CA 92673 E-mail: info@surfrider.org
http://www.surfrider.org
A nonprofit organization that works to protect the world's oceans, waves and beaches. The organization largely focuses on issues such as; water quality, beach access, beach and surf spot preservation and sustaining marine and coastalecosystems.
Founded: 1984
Jim Moriarty, CEO

605 The Groundwater Foundation
5561 S 48th Street 402-434-2740
Suite 215 800-858-4844
Lincoln, NE 68516 Fax: 402-434-2742
E-mail: info@groundwater.org
http://www.groundwater.org
The Groundwater Foundation is a nonprofit organization that is dedicated to informing the public about one of our greatest hidden resources, groundwater. Since 1985, our programs and publications present the benefits everyone receivesfrom groundwater

and the risks that threaten groundwater quality. We make learning about groundwater fun and understandable for kids and adults alike.
Founded: 1985
Jane Griffin, President
Cindy Kreifels, Executive VP

606 United Citizens Coastal Protection League
PO Box 46 760-753-7477
Cardiff By The Sea, CA 92007
Founded: 1982
Robert Bonde, Executive Director

607 Water Environment Federation
601 Wythe Street 703-684-2400
Alexandria, VA 22314-1994 800-666-0206
Fax: 703-684-2492
E-mail: inquiry@wef.org
http://www.wef.org

A not-for-profit technical and educational organization with members from varied disciplines who work toward the WEF vision of preservation and enhancement of the global water environment.
Founded: 1928
William Bertera, Executive Director
Lori Harrison, Media Relations

608 Water Quality Association
4151 Naperville Road 630-505-0160
Lisle, IL 60532-3696 Fax: 630-505-9637
E-mail: info@mail.wqa.org
http://www.wqa.org

Nonprofit international trade association representing the water treatment industry.
Founded: 1974
Dave Haataja, CEO/Executive Director
Thomas Palkon, Vice President/COO

609 Water Resources Congress
2300 Claredon Boulevard 703-525-4881
Suite 404 Fax: 703-527-1693
Arlington, VA 22201
Kathleen A Phelps, Executive Director

610 Western Hemisphere Shorebird Reserve Network
125 Manomet Point Road 508-224-6521
PO Box 1770 Fax: 508-224-9220
Manomet, MA 02345 E-mail: info@whsrn.org
http://www.whsrn.org

WHSRN is a voluntary, community-based coalition of over 185 organizations across the US and other countries in the Western Hemisphere that have joined together to protect, restore and manage critical wetland habitats for migratory birds.
Charles Duncan, Executive Director
Meredith Gutowski Morehouse, Conservation Specialist

611 Wildlands Conservancy
3701 Orchid Place 610-965-4397
Emmaus, PA 18049 Fax: 610-965-7223
E-mail: info@wildlandspa.org
http://www.wildlandspa.org

Wildlands Conservancy is a nonprofit organization dedicated to preserving precious land, river restoration, keeping our waterways healthy, teaching the community about nature and caring for orphaned or injured wildlife.
Founded: 1973
Christopher Kocher, President
Sara Phillips, Executive Administrator

612 World Aquaculture Society
143 JM Parker Coliseum 225-578-3137
Louisiana State University Fax: 225-578-3493
Baton Rouge, LA 70803 E-mail: carolm@was.org
http://www.was.org

The World Aquaculture Society is an international nonprofit society, whose commitment to excellence in science, technology, education and information exchange, will contribute to progressive and sustainable development of aquaculture throughout the world.
Founded: 1970
Carol Mendoza, Home Office Director

Alabama

613 Alabama Association of Soil & Water Conservation Districts
PO Box 304800 334-242-2620
Montgomery, AL 36130-4800 Fax: 334-242-0551
E-mail: phyllis.mcguire@swcc.alabama.gov
http://www.swcc.state.al.us

The function of the NRCS at the local level is to provide technical leadership, delivery of special programs, and overall leadership of each office.
Founded: 1937
Stephen Cauthen, Executive Director
Pat Conner, Administrative Manager

614 Alabama Environmental Council
City Council Office 205-322-3126
2717 7th Avenue S 800-982-4364
Birmingham, AL 35203 Fax: 205-254-2603
E-mail: stateoffice@aeconline.ws
http://www.aeconline.ws

Statewide grassroots. The oldest environmental advocacy and education organization dedicated to the preservation and protection of Alabama's natural heritage.
Founded: 1967
Ouida Fritschi, President
Larry Crenshaw, Secretary

615 Alabama National Safety Council: Birmingham
2125 Data Office Drive 205-328-7233
Suite 102 800-457-7233
Birmingham, AL 35244 Fax: 205-328-1467
E-mail: info@nsc.org
http://www.alabama.nsc.org

The National Safety Council's network of chapters conducts safety, health and environmental efforts at the community level, providing training, conferences, workshops, consultation, newsletters, updates and safety support materials, as well as valuable networking avenues. Our network extends the Council's visibility and provides a local voice for advocating issues that can educate, inform, protect, and save lives.
Donny Ward, Executive Director

616 Alabama Solar Association
PO Box 143 256-650-5120
Huntsville, AL 35804-143 Fax: 256-650-5119
E-mail: isimon1027@aol.com
http://www.al-solar.org

A non-profit organization leading the US to a sustainable energy economy.
Erwin H Simon, Contact

617 Alabama Waterfowl Association
1346 Country Road #11 205-259-2509
Scottsboro, AL 35768 E-mail: awa@alabamawaterfowl.org
http://www.alabamawaterfowl.org

A state voice for over 12,000 Alabama waterfowl hunters, concerning the waterfowl hunting season and the federal migratory bird regulations in Alabama. AWA networks with other state waterfowl associations in the North American waterfowl federation for wetlands conservation.
Jerry Davis, CEO
Gary Benefield, Executive Director

618 Alabama Wildlife Federation
3050 Lanark Road 334-285-4550
Millbrook, AL 36054 800-822-9453
Fax: 334-285-4959
E-mail: awf@alabamawildlife.org
http://www.alabamawildlife.org

Mission is to promote the conservation of Alabama's wildlife and related natural resources, as a basis for the social and economic prosperity of present and future generations, through wise use and responsible stewardship of our wildlife, forests, fish, soils, water and air.
Founded: 1935
Tim L. Gothard, Executive Director
Carol Turner, Office Manager

619 **American Society of Landscape Architects: Alabama Chapter**
http://www.alabamasla.org
The national professional association representing landscape architects.
Stephen Schrader, President
Ben Wieseman, President-Elect

620 **BASS Anglers Sportsman Society**
3500 Blue Lake Drive 334-272-9530
Suite 330 Fax: 334-270-7148
Birmingham, AL 35243 E-mail: bassmaster@customerservice.com
http://www.bassmaster.com
Goal is to create a credible and honorable tournament trail, to improve our environment by uniting and amplifying the voices of anglers and to secure a future for our youth.
Founded: 1967
Gary Jones, Federation Director

621 **National Safety Council: Tennessee Valley Office)**
2042 Beltline Road SW 256-308-1133
Building A, Suite 110 Fax: 256-308-1161
Decatur, AL 35601 E-mail: alabama@nsc.org
Network of chapters conducts safety, health and environmental efforts at the community level, providing training, conferences, workshops, consultation, newsletters, updates and safety support materials, as well as valuable networking avenues.
Donny Ward, Executive Director

622 **Nature Conservancy: Colorado Field Office**
2424 Spruce Street 303-444-2950
Boulder, CO 80302 Fax: 303-444-2986
E-mail: colorado@tnc.org
http://www.nature.org/wherewework/
The mission of the Nature Conservancy is to preserve plants, animals and natural communities that represent the diversity of life on earth by protecting the lands and waters they need to survive. To date, the conservation and its more than one million members have been responsible for the protection of more than 12 million acres in 50 states.
Founded: 1951

623 **Sierra Club**
1330 21st Way S 251-599-8699
Suite 110 E-mail: maggie@campmcdowell.com
Birmingham, AL 35205 http://alabama.sierraclub.org
To advance the preservation and protection of the natural environment by empowering the citizenry, especially democratically-based grassroots organizations, with charitable resources to further the cause of environmental protection. The vehicle through which The Sierra Club Foundation generally fulfills its charitable mission.
Founded: 1908
Margaret Wade Johnston, Chair
David Underhill, Secretary

Alaska

624 **Alaska Conservation Alliance**
PO Box 100660 907-258-6171
Anchorage, AK 99510 Fax: 907-258-6177
E-mail: info@akvoice.org
http://www.akvoice.org
Statewide non-profit organization whose primary mission is to protect Alaska's natural environment through voter education and engagement, and advocacy.
Founded: 1997
Andy Moderow, Executive Director
Betty Jo Pritchett, Office Manager

625 **Alaska Natural Resource & Outdoor Education**
200 W. 34th Street 907-292-1772
Suite 1007 Fax: 907-207-1795
Anchorage, AK 99503 E-mail: info@anroe.org
http://www.anroe.wordpress.com
Mission is to promote and implement excellence in natural resource, outdoor, and environmental education for all Alaskans
Founded: 1986
Courtney Sullivan, President
Kristen Romanoff, Secretary

626 **Alaska Wildlife Alliance**
PO Box 202022 907-277-0897
Anchorage, AK 99520 Fax: 907-277-7423
E-mail: info@akwildlife.org
http://www.akwildlife.org
Mission is the protection of Alaska's natural wildlife for its intrinsic value as well as for the benefit of present and future generations.
Founded: 1978
Tina M Brown, President
Art Greenwalt, Vice President

627 **American Lung Association of Alaska**
500 Airport Maintenance Rd 907-276-5864
Anchorage, AK 99518 Fax: 503-924-4120
E-mail: info@lungmtpacific.org
http://www.aklung.org
Promoting lung health and preventing lung disease in Alaska.
Founded: 1934
Marge Larson, COO

628 **American Society of Landscape Architects: Alaska Chapter**
Municipality of Anchorage 907-343-8368
PO Box 196650 888-999-2752
Anchorage, AK 99519 Fax: 907-343-8088
E-mail: info@asla.org
http://www.akasla.org
National professional association representing landscape architects.
Founded: 1899
Peter Briggs, President
Nancy Casey, President-Elect

629 **Audubon Alaska**
Nation Audubon Society
441 West Fifth Ave 907-276-7034
Suite 300 Fax: 907-276-5069
Anchorage, AK 99501 http://www.ak.audubon.org
Founded in 1977, this office has played a crucial role in protecting the Great Land and its extraordinary ecosystems through a combination of science and stewardship, public policy, and education. The mission is to conserve Alaska's natural ecosystems, for the benefit and enjoyment of current and future generations.
Founded: 1977
Nils Warnock, Executive Director
Robyn Langlie, Office Manager

630 **Bureau of Land Management**
222 W 7th Avenue 907-271-5960
#13 Fax: 907-271-3684
Anchorage, AK 99513 E-mail: ak_akso_public_room@blm.gov
http://www.blm.gov
A nonprofit scientific and educational organization that serves professionals such as government agencies, academia, industry, and non-government organizations in all areas related to the conservation of wildlife and natural resources management.
Bud C. Cribley, State Director
Ted Murphy, Associate State Director

631 National Wildlife Federation Alaska Regional Center
750 W. 2nd Avenue 206-285-8707
Anchorage, AK 99501 800-937-2026
Fax: 206-285-8698
http://www.nwf.org/pacific-region/alaska.aspx

It is committed to protecting Alaska's wildlife and wild places by working in partnership with concerned citizens, grassroots groups, and communities. They also offer the Alaska Youth for Environmental Action program which is designed to help youth become stronger and more effective environmental leaders.
Founded: 1988
Beth Pratt, Director
Jennifer Murck, Manager

632 Northern Alaska Environmental Center
830 College Road 907-452-5021
Fairbanks, AK 99701-1535 Fax: 907-452-3100
E-mail: info@northern.org
http://www.northern.org

Promotes conservation of the environment in Interior and Arctic Alaska through advocacy, education, and sustainable resource stewardship.
Founded: 1971
David Arnold, Executive Director
Kristen Sullivan, Office Manager

633 Sierra Club
750 W 2nd Ave 907-258-6807
Suite 100 Fax: 907-258-6807
Anchorage, AK 99501 E-mail: dan.ritzman@sierraclub.org
http://www.alaska.sierraclub.org

The Alaska Chapter of the Sierra Club works to protect the last frontier from the damage of logging, drilling and the like. It strives for renewable energy, sustainable use of resources, preservation of wild places, and the smart growth of urban areas.
Founded: 1892
Dan Ritzman, Executive Director
Lindsey Hajduk, Associate Manager

634 Trustees for Alaska
1026 W 4th Avenue 907-276-4244
Suite 201 Fax: 907-276-7110
Anchorage, AK 99501 E-mail: ecolaw@trustees.org
http://www.trustees.org

A public interest law firm whose mission is to provide legal counsel to sustain and protect Alaska's natural environment. We represent local and national environmental groups, Alaska Native villages, nonprofit organizations, community groups, hunters, fishers and others where the outcome of our advocacy could benefit Alaska's environment.
Founded: 1974
Trish Rolfe, Executive Director
Brittany Hales, Office Manager

635 Wildlife Society: Alaska Chapter
1271 Lowbush Lane 907-456-8682
Fairbanks, AK 99709 Fax: 907-257-2774
E-mail: www.membership@wildlife.org
http://www.wildlife.org/chapters/ak

A nonprofit scientific and educational organization that serves professionals such as government agencies, academia, industry, and non-government organizations in all areas related to the conservation of wildlife and natural resources management.
Founded: 1971
Kris Hundertmark, President
Michelle Davis, Branch Manager

Arizona

636 American Lung Association: Arizona
The American Lung Association
2819 East Broadway 520-323-1812
Tucson, AZ 85716-5309 800-586-4872
Fax: 520-323-1816
http://www.lungusa.org/south/

The mission of the American Lung Association is to prevent lung disease and promote lung health.
Founded: 1912
Dominic San Angelo, Executive Director
Mary Dillon, Program Manager

637 Arizona ASLA: American Society of Landscape Architects
PO Box 28393 602-258-8668
Tempe, AZ 85285 Fax: 602-273-6814
http://www.azasla.org

The Arizona state affiliate of the American Society of Landscape Architects.
Irene Ugata, President
Aaron Allan, President Elect

638 Arizona Automotive Recyclers Association
1030 E. Baseline Rd. 480-609-3999
#105-1025 E-mail: admin@aara.com
Tempe, AZ 85283 http://www.aara.com

A group of automotive recyclers that know quality, value and service go hand in hand.
Founded: 1910
Mike Pierson Jr, President
Layla Ressler, VP

639 Arizona BASS Chapter Federation
PO Box 1505 623-434-3520
Tempe, AZ 85280-1505 Fax: 480-773-7019
http://www.azbassfederation.com

Bass fishing tournament organization.
Founded: 1972
Greg Krueger, President
Tim Price, Vice President

640 Arizona Chapter, National Safety Council
1606 W Indian School Road 602-264-2394
Phoenix, AZ 85015-5232 Fax: 602-277-5485
E-mail: main@acnsc.org
http://www.acnsc.org

Purpose is to educate and motivate people to live safer and healthier lives whether at home, work, school, play or on the highway.
Founded: 1949
John Keeler, President
Margaret Cather, Executive Director

641 Arizona Solar Energy Industries Association
Solar Energy Industries Association
3008N Civic Center Plaza 602-253-8180
Scottsdale, AZ 85251 Fax: 602-258-3422
E-mail: mneary@arizonasolarindustry.org
http://www.arizonasolarindustry.org

A non-profit trade association representing local, national and international solar companies in the Arizona market.
Michael L. Neary, Executive Director

642 Arizona Water Well Association
1030 E Baseline Road 480-609-3999
#105-1025 Fax: 480-609-3939
Tempe, AZ 85283 E-mail: admin@azwwa.org
http://www.azwwa.org

Promotes protection and wise development of underground water resources.
Founded: 1957
Larry Cofelt, President
Nathan Little, President Elect

643 Arizona-Sonora Desert Museum
2021 N Kinney Road 520-883-2702
Tucson, AZ 85743 Fax: 520-883-2500
E-mail: info@desertmuseum.org
http://www.desertmuseum.org

A museum, zoo and botanical garden center. The Sonora Desert of New Mexico and North America is the primary focus.
Founded: 1952
Patricia Engels, Chair
Francis Boyle, Secretary

644 **Center for Biological Diversity**
PO Box 710 520-623-5252
Tucson, AZ 85702-0710 866-357-3349
Fax: 520-623-9797
E-mail: center@biologicaldiversity.org
http://www.biologicaldiversity.org
Works through science, law and creative media to secure a future for all species, great or small, hovering on the brink of extinction.
Kieran Suckling, Executive Director
Linda Wells, Finance Director

645 **Sierra Club**
202 E McDowell Road 602-253-8633
Suite 277 E-mail: sierraclubinfo@gmail.com
Phoenix, AZ 85004 http://www.arizona.sierraclub.org
The Grand Canyon Chapter is made up of six groups that utilize conservation, political and legislative activism, administrative work, and outings to protect the state.
Jim Vaaler, Chair
Sandy Bahr, Outreach Director

Arkansas

646 **American Society of Landscape Architects: Arkansas Chapter**
Dept of Landscape Architecture 202-898-2444
230 Memorial Hall 800-999-2752
Fayetteville, AR 72701 Fax: 202-898-1185
E-mail: contact@arasla.org
http://www.arasla.org
Founded in 1899, the American Society of Landscape Architects is the national professional association representing landscape architects.
Founded: 1899
Fran Beatty, President
Travis G Brooks, President-Elect

647 **Arkansas Association of Conservation Districts**
101 E Capitol 501-682-2915
Suite 350 Fax: 501-682-3991
Little Rock, AR 72201 E-mail: Randy.Young@mail.state.ar.us
http://www.aracd.org
Affiliated with the National Association of Conservation Districts. Membership is $25.00 per year for individuals and $1,200.00 per year for organizations and companies.
Founded: 1937
Charles Glover, President
Rocky Harrell, First Vice President

648 **Arkansas Environmental Federation**
1400 W Markham Street 501-374-0263
Suite 302 Fax: 501-374-8752
Little Rock, AR 72201 http://www.environmentark.org
Formerly the Arkansas Federation of Water and Air Users. Membership is $25.00 per year for individuals and $200.00 to $2,070.02 per year for organizations.
Founded: 1967
Randy Thurman, Executive Director
Elyse Cullen, Communication Director

649 **Arkansas Respiratory Health Association**
211 Natural Resources Drive 501-224-5864
Little Rock, AR 72205 Fax: 501-224-5645
E-mail: lcollers@lungark.org
http://www.arkresp.org
Mission of the Arkansas Respiratory Health Association is to prevent lung disease and promote lung health through education, advocacy and research.

650 **Sierra Club**
1400 West Markham Street 501-301-8280
Suite 302 E-mail: sierraclubinfo@gmail.com
Little Rock, AR 72201 http://arkansas.sierraclub.org
To practice and promote responsible use of the earth's ecosystems and resources; educate and enlist humanity to protect and restore the quality of the natural environment.
Randy Thurman, Executive Director
Marge Brookins, Office Manager

California

651 **American Fisheries Society: Fish Health Section**
California State University
California State University 510-885-3000
25800 Carlos Bee Blvd Fax: 510-885-4747
Hayward, CA 94542 E-mail: eric.cheatham@csueastbay.com
http: //www20.csueastbay.edu
Goals and missions are to maintain an association of persons involved in safe-guarding the health of fish and other aquatic animals.
Leroy M. Morishito, President

652 **American Lung Association of California**
American Lung Association
424 Pendleton Way 510-638-5864
Oakland, CA 94621 Fax: 510-638-8984
E-mail: rmcginnis@alac.org
http: //www.californialung.org
Fights lung disease through education, community service, advocacy and research.
Founded: 1904
Janet Warner, Chief Executive Officer
Ben Abate, President

653 **American Lung Association of California: Redwood Empire Branch**
115 Talbot Avenue 707-527-5864
Santa Rosa, CA 95404 Fax: 707-542-6111
E-mail: tjohnson@ala.org
http: //www.californialung.org
Fighting lung disease through education, community service, advocacy and research.
Founded: 1953
Karen Fulton, Vice President
Terrie Johnson, Manager

654 **American Lung Association of California: East Bay Branch**
American Lung Association
1900 Powell Street 510-893-5474
Suite 800 Fax: 510-893-9008
Emeryville, CA 94608 E-mail: eastbaylung@alaebay.org
http: //www.alaebay.org
The American Lung Association of the East Bay, serves the Greater Bay Area. Serves the people that live and work in the 7 Bay Area counties.
Founded: 1904
Karen Fulton, President
Anita Lee, Vice President

655 **American Lung Association of California: Superior Branch**
10 Landing Circle 530-345-5864
Suite 1 800-586-4872
Chico, CA 95973 Fax: 530-345-6035
E-mail: sbrantley@alac.org
http: //www.lungusa2.org
The American Lung Association of California and its offices statewide work to prevent lung disease and promote lung health.
Founded: 1904
Stephen R O'Kane, Chairman
Don Brunson, Vice Chairman

656 **American Lung Association of Central California**
American Lung Association

4948 North Arthur 559-222-4800
Fresno, CA 93705 800-586-4872
Fax: 559-221-2081
E-mail: myang@alac.org
http: //www.lungusa.org/associations/states/california/

The American Lung Association of California and its offices statewide work to prevent lung disease and to promote lung health.

Founded: 1904

Michael Peterson MD, Chairman of the Board

Josette Merce Bello, CEO

657 American Lung Association of Sacramento: Emigrant Trails

921 11th Street 916-442-4446
Suite 700 800-586-4872
Sacramento, CA 95814 Fax: 916-442-8585
E-mail: pknepprath@alac.org
http: //www.californialung.org

The American Lung Association of California and its offices statewide work to prevent lung disease and promote lung health.

Founded: 1917

Earl Wisthycombe, President

Jane Hagerdorn, CFO

658 American Lung Association of San Diego & Imperial Counties

American Lung Association
2750 Fourth Avenue 619-297-3901
San Diego, CA 92103 800-586-4872
Fax: 619-297-8402
E-mail: info@lungsandiego.org
http: //www.lungsandiego.org

The mission of the American Lung Association is to prevent lung disease and promote lung health.

Founded: 1904

Janie Davis, Chief Executive Officer

Yolanda Orres, Manager

659 American Lung Association of Santa Barbara and Ventura Counties

American Lung Association
1510 San Andres Street 805-963-1426
Santa Barbara, CA 93101 800-586-4872
Fax: 805-456-0892
E-mail: jayne@lungsbvc.org
http://www.californialung.org

The American Lung Association of California and its offices statewide work to prevent lung disease and to promote lung health.

Founded: 1904

John Kirkwood, President

Charles A Heinrich, Chairman

660 American Lung Association of the Central Coast

550 Camino El Estero 831-373-7306
Suite 100 800-586-4872
Monterey, CA 93940 Fax: 831-373-5530
E-mail: admin@alaccoast.org
http://www.californialung.org

The American Lung Association of California and its offices statewide work to prevent lung disease and promote lung health.

Founded: 1953

Karen Fulton, Chief Executive Officer

John Morrison, Vice President

661 American Rivers: California Region: Fairfax

2150 Allston Way 510-809-8010
Suite 320 E-mail: outreach@americanrivers.org
Berkeley, CA 94704 http://www.americanrivers.org

American Rivers is the only national organization standing up for healthy rivers so our communities can thrive.

Founded: 1973

Rebecca Wodder, President

Fay Augustyn, Conservation Associate

662 American Rivers: California Region:Nevada City

PO Box 559 530-478-5672
Nevada City, CA 95959 Fax: 530-478-5849
E-mail: outreach@americanrivers.org
http://www.americanrivers.org

The conservation organization standing up for healthy rivers so communities can thrive. American Rivers protects and restores America's rivers for the benefit of people, wildlife and nature.

Founded: 1973 65,000 Members

Rebecca Wodder, President

Fay Augustyn, Conservation Associate

663 American Society of Landscape Architects: Sierra Chapter

1400 S Street 916-447-7400
Suite 100 Fax: 916-447-8270
Sacramento, CA 95811 E-mail: asla-sierra@sbcglobal.net
http://www.asla-sierra.org

Founded in 1899, the American Society of Landscape Architects is the national professional association representing landscape architects.

Meredith Branstad, President

Michael Scheele, President-Elect

664 American Society of Landscape Architects: Northern California Chapter

5 Third Street 415-974-5430
Suite 724 Fax: 415-543-2112
San Francisco, CA 94103 E-mail: staff@asla-ncc.admn.org
http://host.asla.org/chapters/norcal

Founded in 1899, the American Society of Landscape Architects is the national professional association representing landscape architects.

Founded: 1899

Jeffrey George, President

Joe Owen, Executive Director

665 American Society of Landscape Architects: San Diego Chapter

1050 Rosecrans Street 619-225-8155
Suite B Fax: 619-225-8151
San Diego, CA 92106 E-mail: aslasd@sbcglobal.net
http://www.asla-sandiego.org

Founded in 1899, the American Society of Landscape Architects is the national professional association representing landscape architects.

Tim Jachlewski Jr., President

Patricia Trauth, President Elect

666 American Society of Landscape Architects: Southern California Chapter

1100 Irvine Boulevard 714-838-3615
Suite 371 Fax: 714-730-6296
Tustin, CA 92780 E-mail: sccasla@aol.com
http://host.asla.org/chapters/southca

Founded in 1899, the American Society of Landscape Architects is the national professional association representing landscape architects.

Andrew Bowden, President-Elect

Vicki Phillipy, Executive Director

667 Asian Pacific Environmental Network

310 8th Street 510-834-8920
Suite 309 Fax: 510-834-8926
Oakland, CA 94607 E-mail: info@apen4ej.org
http://www.apen4ej.org

The Asian Pacific Environmental Network (APEN) empowers low-income Asian Pacific Islander (API) communities to take action on environmental and social justice issues. APEN builds organizations in disempowered API communities to develop lasting capacity of the community to achieve solutions to problems affecting people's lives.

Founded: 1991

Roger Kim, Executive Director

Miya Yoshitani, Associate Director

668 **Bio Integral Resource Center**
PO Box 7414 510-524-2567
Berkeley, CA 94707 Fax: 510-524-1758
E-mail: birc@igc.org
http://www.birc.org
The goal of the Bio Integral Resources Center is to reduce pesticide use by educating the public about effective, less toxic alternatives for pest problems.
Founded: 1979
Dr. William Quarles, Executive Director

669 **Breathe California Golden Gate Public Health Partnership**
2171 Junipero Serra Boulevard 650-994-5864
Suite 720 Fax: 650-994-4601
Daly City, CA 94014 E-mail: info@ggbreathe.org
http://www.ggbreathe.org
Through grassroots education, advocacy and services, Breathe California fights lung disease, advocates for clean air, and advances public health.
Founded: 1908
Linda Civitello, President/CEO
Elias Trevino, Vice President Operations

670 **Breathe California Of Los Angeles County**
5858 Wilshire Boulevard 323-935-8050
Suite 300 Fax: 323-935-1873
Los Angeles, CA 90036 http://www.breathela.org
Formerly the American Lung Association of Los Angeles County, is dedicated to providing communities in Los Angeles County with the resources needed to promote clean air initiatives through its continued commitment to researcheducation, and advocacy.
Founded: 1903
Jud Schoendorf, Chair
Lawrence M. Lebowsky, Chair Elect

671 **Breathe California of the Bay Area: Alameda, Santa Clara & San Benito Counties**
1469 Park Avenue 408-998-5865
San Jose, CA 95126 Fax: 408-998-0578
E-mail: info@lungsrus.org
http://www.lungsrus.org
Fights lung disease in all its forms and works with its communities to promote lung health.
Founded: 1904
Margo Leathers Sidener, Executive Director
Steve French, Development Director

672 **California Academy of Sciences Library**
55 Music Concourse Drive 415-321-8000
Golden Gate Park Fax: 415-321-8633
San Francisco, CA 94118 E-mail: info@calacademy.org
http://www.calacademy.org
Founded in 1853 to survey and study the vast resources of California and beyond, the California Academy of Sciences is the oldest scientific institution in the West. The Academy has grown to become the 4th largest natural historymuseum in the country. The academy's mission is to explore, explain, and protect the natural world.
Founded: 1853
Gregory C. Farrington, Executive Director
Allison Brown, CFO

673 **California Air Resources Board**
State of California
PO Box 2815 916-322-2990
Sacremento, CA 95812 800-242-4450
Fax: 916-445-5025
E-mail: helpline@arb.ca.gov
http://www.arb.ca.gov
The California ARB is the state agency charged with coordinating efforts to attain and maintain ambient air quality standards, conduct research into the causes of and solutions to air pollution and its adverse health impacts, andattack systematically the serious problem caused by motor vehicles, which are the major source of air pollution in many areas of the state. The California ARB's mission is to promote and protect public health, welfare and ecological resources.
Founded: 1967
Mary Nichols, Chairman
James Goldstene, Executive Officer

674 **California Association of Environmental Health**
3700 Chaney Court 530-676-0715
Carmichael, CA 95608 Fax: 530-676-0515
E-mail: justin@ccdeh.com
http://www.ccdeh.com
Environmental Health Departments provide the delivery of Local Environmental Health Programs.
Justin Malan, Executive Director
Sheryl Baldwin, CCDEH Manager

675 **California Association of Resource Conservation Districts**
801 K Street 916-457-7904
18th Floor Fax: 916-457-7934
Sacramento, CA 95814 E-mail: info@carcd.org
http://www.carcd.org
CARCD is a voluntary association whose primary purpose is to provide a unified means for California Resource Conservation Districts (RCDs) to meet major conservation goals.
Karen Buhr, Executive Director
Emily Sutherland, Office Manager

676 **California BASS Chapter Federation**
13350 Racquet Court 858-748-9459
Poway, CA 92064 E-mail: info@californiabass.org
http://www.californiabass.org
The Bass Federation Conservation Dept is dedicated to the preservation, restoration, enhancement and public access to their resources.
Founded: 1969
Scott Sweet, President
Larry Wilson, VP

677 **California Birth Defects Monitoring Program**
1947 Center Street 510-981-5300
Berkeley, CA 94704 Fax: 510-981-5395
E-mail: info@cbdmp.org
http://www.repcoupons.org
The California Birth Defects Monitoring Program is a public health program devoted to finding the causes of birth defects so they can be prevented. The program is funded through the California Department of Health Services and isjointly operated with the March of Dimes Birth Defects Foundation.
Founded: 1982
Janet Berreman, Health Officer
Kate Clayton, Health Promotion, Chief

678 **California Certified Organic Farmers**
2155 Delaware Avenue 831-423-2263
Suite 150 Fax: 831-423-4528
Santa Cruz, CA 95060 E-mail: ccof@ccof.org
http://www.ccof.org
Premier organic certification since 1973, for growers, processors, handlers, packers, retailers. Public education of organic, and advocacy for public policy to support organic. Newsletter subscriptions available through a supportingmembership program.
Founded: 1973
Jake Lewin, Chief Certification Officer
Peggy Miars, Executive Director

679 **California Council for Environmental and Economic Balance**
100 Spear Street 415-512-7890
Suite 805 Fax: 415-512-7897
San Francisco, CA 94105 E-mail: cceeb@cceeb.org
http://www.cceeb.org
A coalition of California business, labor and public leaders which strive to advance collaborative strategies for a sound California.
Founded: 1976
Victor Weisser, President
Bill Quinn, Executive Director

680 California Renewable Fuels Council
1516 Ninth Street 916-654-4058
MS-29 800-555-7794
Sacramento, CA 95814-5512 E-mail: renewable@energy.state.ca.us
http://www.energy.ca.gov/renewables
Lobbying organization
Founded: 2002
Robert Weisenmiller, Chairman
James Boyd, Vice Chair

681 California Solar Energy Industries Association
1107 9th Street 916-747-6987
Suite 820 Fax: 707-374-4767
Sacramento, CA 95814 E-mail: info@calseia.org
http://www.calseia.org
Promotes the growth of California's solar energy industry. Membership is $325-650 per year.
Founded: 1977
Les Nelson, President
Pat Redgate, Vice President

682 California Trappers Association (CTA)
907 Holmes Flat Road 707-222-4259
Attn: Rita Clark, Membership Secretary 888-457-2873
Redcrest, CA 95569 E-mail: chris.adamski@fwmedia.com
http://www.trapperpredatorcaller.com
CTA's primary concern is California's fur bearing mammals, and the category of small predatory mammals. Approximately 20 of the association's 2,400 members do lengthy studies and assist State and Federal Agencies in the field with their biologists. Educational forums and talks are hosted at local universities. Farming agencies and timber companies commonly use their services. Members commonly work for numerous environmental public projects, both public and governmental.
Founded: 1863
John Clark, President
James C Schmerker Jr, Vice President

683 California Waterfowl Association
1346 Blue Oaks Blvd 916-648-1406
Roseville, CA 95678 Fax: 916-648-1665
E-mail: cwa_hq@calwaterfowl.org
http://www.calwaterfowl.org
A statewide nonprofit organization whose principal objectives are the preservation, protection, and enhancement of California's waterfowl resources, wetlands, and associated hunting heritage.
Founded: 1945
John Carlson Jr., President
Colby Heaton, CFO

684 California Wildlife Foundation
428 13th Street 510-208-4436
10th Floor, Suite A Fax: 510-268-9948
Oakland, CA 94612 E-mail: info@californiawildlifefoundation.org
http://www.californiawildlifefoundation.org
A nonprofit organization dedicated to the conservation, enhancement, scientific management and wise use of all our natural resources. It seeks to accomplish these objectives through education, scientific research, charitable donationsand support projects and other organizations having compatible purposes.
Ellen Maldonaldo, Secretary
James Lightbody, Treasurer

685 Californians for Population Stabilization (CAPS)
1129 State Street 805-564-6626
Suite 3-D Fax: 805-564-6636
Santa Barbara, CA 93101 E-mail: info@capsweb.org
http://www.capsweb.org
A nonprofit, public interest organization that works to protect California's environment and quality of life by turning the tide of population growth.
Founded: 1986
Diana Hull PhD, President
Ben Zuckerman, Vice President

686 Colorado River Board of California
770 Fairmont Avenue 818-500-1625
Suite 100 Fax: 818-543-4685
Glendale, CA 91203-1068 E-mail: crb@crb.ca.gov
http://www.crb.ca.gov
Established to protect California's rights and interests in the resources provided by the Colorado River and to represent California in discussions and negotiations regarding the Colorado River and its management.
Founded: 1937
Christopher Harris, Executive Director

687 Communities for a Better Environment
6325 Pacific Blvd 510-302-0430
Suite 300 Fax: 510-302-0437
Huntington Park, CA 90255 E-mail: cbeca@mail.com
http://www.cbecal.org
Nonprofit statewide, multiracial, urban environmental health and justice organization that works with urban communities and grassroots organizations, using science based research, legal tactics and organizing strategies to prevent airand water pollution, eliminate toxic hazards and improve public health. Long-term goals are to develop an environmentally sustainable manufacturing base, minimize the use of toxins, expand pollution prevention strategies and involve people most atrisk.
Bill Gallegos, Executive Director
Bahram Fazeli, Policy Director

688 Concerned Citizens of South Central Los Angeles
4111 S Central Avenue 213-846-2505
Suite 101 Fax: 213-846-2508
Los Angelos, CA 90011 E-mail: info@ccscla.org
http://www.ccscla.org/
The mission of the Concerned Citizens of South Central Los Angeles is to fight for social, economic and environmental justice and to encourage resident participation in the process.
Founded: 1985
Robin Cannon, President
Noreen McClendon, Executive Director & VP

689 Desert Tortoise Preserve Committee
Tortoise T-R-A-C-K-S
4067 Mission Inn Avenue 951-683-3872
Riverside, CA 92501 Fax: 951-683-6949
E-mail: dtpc@pacbell.net
http://www.tortoise-tracks.org
A non-profit organization formed to promote the welfare of the desert tortoise in its native wild state.
Mary Kotschwar, Preserve Manager

690 Earth Island Institute
2150 Allston Way 510-859-9100
Suite 460 Fax: 510-859-9091
Berkeley, CA 94704-1375 http://www.earthisland.org
A non-profit, public interest, membership organization that supports people who are creating solutions to protect our shared planet.
John Knox, Executive Director
Kevin Connelly, Associate Director

691 Environmental Defense Center
906 Garden Street 805-708-0127
Santa Barbara, CA 93101 Fax: 805-962-3152
E-mail: help@rain.org
http://www.rain.org
The Environmental Defense Center is a nonprofit, public interest organization that provides legal, educational and advocacy support to advance environmental quality. EDC primarily serves community groups on California's South CentralCoast. EDC selects cases and projects that preserve the environment for future generations, protect human health, promote appropriate management and use of natural resources, and enhance the character of the community.
Linda Krop, Executive Director

692 Environmental Health Coalition
2727 Hoover Avenue 619-474-0220
Suite 202 Fax: 619-474-1210
National City, CA 91950 E-mail: ehc@environmentalhealth.org
http://www.environmentalhealth.org
One of the oldest and most effective grassroots organizations in the US, using social change strategies to achieve environmental and social justice. We believe that justice is accomplished by empowered communities acting together tomake social change. We organize and advocate to protect public health and the environment threatened by toxic pollution. EHC supports broad efforts that create a just society which foster a healthy and sustainable quality of life.
Founded: 1985
Diane Takvorian, Executive Director
Tony Pettina, CFO

693 Environmental Health Network
PO Box 1155 415-541-5075
Larkspur, CA 94977-1155 E-mail: fdadockets@oc.fda.gov
http://www.ehnca.org
Nonprofit, volunteer organization, whose main goal is to promote public awareness of environmental sensitivities and causative factors. EHN's focus is on issues of access and developments relating to the health and welfare of theenvironmentally sensitive.
Barb Wilkie, President

694 Friends of the River
1418 20th Street 916-442-3155
Suite 100 888-464-2477
Sacramento, CA 95811 Fax: 916-442-3396
E-mail: info@friendsoftheriver.org
http://www.friendsoftheriver.org
Friends of the River is dedicated to preserving and restoring California's rivers, streams, and their watersheds as well as advocating for sustainable water management.
Founded: 1973
Bob Cushman, President
Mark DuBois, Director Emeritus

695 Heal the Bay
1444 9th Street 310-451-1500
Santa Monica, CA 90401 Fax: 310-496-1902
http://www.healthebay.com
A nonprofit organization based in Santa Monica, California dedicated to protecting Santa Monica Bay, as well as, all Southern California coastal waters and watersheds.
Founded: 1985
Alix Hobbs, Acting Executive Director
Sylvie Makara, Executive Assistant

696 Institute of International Education
Institute of International Education, New York
530 Bush Street, Suite 1000 415-362-6520
San Francisco, CA 94108 Fax: 415-392-4667
E-mail: iiesf@iie.org
http://www.iie.org
An independent non-profit organization that is a world leader in the exchange of people and ideas.
Founded: 1919
Allen Goodman, President
Tricia Tierney, Director

697 Laotian Organizing Project
310 8th Street 510-236-4616
Suite 309 Fax: 510-236-4572
Oakland, CA 94607 E-mail: apen@apen4ej.org
http://www.apen4ej.org/organize_lop.htm
The Laotian Organization Project (LOP), a project of the Asian Pacific Environmental Network, is a membership-based organization of Laotian residents in Richmond and San Pablo, California. LOP works to bring people from the Laotiancommunity together to identify problems, develop solutions, and take action for a more healthy, safe, and just community.
Amber Chan, PAO Lead Organizer
Roger Kim, Executive Director

698 League to Save Lake Tahoe
2608 Lake Tahoe Blvd 530-541-5388
South Lake Tahoe, CA 96150 Fax: 530-541-5454
E-mail: info@keeptahoeblue.org
http://www.keeptahoeblue.org
Our mission is the preservation and restoration of the magnificent natural attributes of the Tahoe Basin's waters, forests, wildlife and landscape for the enjoyment of present and future generations.
Founded: 1957
Darcie Goodman Collins, Executive Director
Jesse Patterson, Deputy Director

699 Marine Mammal Center
2000 Bunker Road 415-289-7325
Fort Cronkite Fax: 415-289-7333
Sausalito, CA 94965-2619 http://www.marinemammalcenter.org
A nonprofit veterinary research hospital and educational cetner dedicated to the rescue and rehabilitation of ill and injured marine mammals, primarily elephant seals, harbor seals, and California sea lions.
Founded: 1975
Dr Jeff Boehm, Executive Director
Marci Davis, CFO/COO

700 Mountain Lion Foundation
PO Box 1896 916-442-2666
Sacramento, CA 95812 800-319-7621
Fax: 916-442-2871
E-mail: mlf@mountainlion.org
http://www.mountainlion.org
A national nonprofit conservation and education organization dedicated to protecting the mountain lion, its wild habitat, and the wildlife that shares that habitat-for present and future generations. The Foundation is dedicated to theproposition that much can be done to preserve the cougar as a viable species of this effort can assure the survival of other species.
Founded: 1986
Tim Dunbar, Executive Director
Lynn Cullens, Communications Director

701 National Institute for Global Environmental Change: Western Regional Center
University of Califonia-Davis
1 Shields Avenue 530-752-7300
Davis, CA 95616 Fax: 530-752-7302
E-mail: westgec@ucdavis.edu
http://www.ucdavis.edu/
This overview provides insight into the major environmental programs and permitting requirements governing industrial processes and activities.
Founded: 1990
Dr. Susin Ustin, Director

702 National Safety Council: California Chapter
1121 Spring Lake Drive 630-285-1121
Itasca, IL 60143-7615 800-621-7615
Fax: 630-285-1315
E-mail: customerservice@nsc.org
http://www.nsc.org
Mission is to educate and influence people to prevent accidental injury and death. Vision is to make our world safer.
Janet Froetscher, President
Patrick Phelan, CFO

703 Nature Conservancy: Western Division Office
4245 North Fairfax Drive 415-777-0487
Suite 100 800-628-6860
Arlington, VA 22203-1606 Fax: 415-777-0244
E-mail: comment@tnc.org
http://www.nature.org
A leading conservation organization working around the world to protect ecologically important lands and waters for nature and people.
Mark Burgett, President
Mick Sweeney, CFO

704 **NorCal Solar/Northern California Solar Energy Society**
PO Box 3008 510-705-8813
Berkeley, CA 94703 Fax: 510-548-8896
E-mail: info@norcalsolar.org
http://www.norcalsolar.org

A non-profit educational organization whose mission is to accelerate the use of solar energy technology through the exchange of information.
Founded: 1975
Emily Barry, Operations Manager
Jamie Cutlip, Secretary

705 **Northcoast Environmental Center**
1385 8th Street 707-822-6918
Suite 226 Fax: 707-822-0827
Arcata, CA 95521 E-mail: nec@yournec.org
http://www.yournec.org

A nonprofit educational organization devoted to illuminating people concerning the Biosphere. It has a library, information and referral, radio show, nationally circulated newsletter and national membership. It is focused on theredwood region and northwest California and the Bioregion along the California-Oregon border.
Founded: 1971
Dan Ehresman, Executive Director

706 **Outdoor Programs**
University of California San Francisco
Milborry Union 125 West 415-476-2078
500 Parnassus Ave Fax: 502-620-7415
San Francisco, CA 94143-232 E-mail: outdoors@cls.ucsf.edu
http://www.campuslifeservices.ucsf.edu

Creates outdoor experiences for students, staff and families in UCSF and the local community.
Founded: 1970
Kirk McLaughlin, Parnassus Prog. Supervisor
Colleen Massey, Mission Bay Prog. Supervisor

707 **Pesticide Action Network North America**
161 Telegraph Ave 510-788-9020
Suite 1200 E-mail: panna@panna.org
San Francisco, CA 94612 http://www.panna.org

Pesticide Action Network North American advocates the adoption of ecologically sound practices in place of hazardous pesticide use. PANNA works with more than 100 affiliated organizations in Canada, Mexico and US, as well as withPesticide Action Network partners around the world to demand that development agencies and governments redirect support from pesticides to safe alternatives.
Founded: 1984
Judy Hatcher, Executive Director
Leticia Tirrez, Office Manager

708 **Pesticide Education Center**
PO Box 225279 415-665-4722
San Francisco, CA 94122-5279 Fax: 415-665-2693
E-mail: pec@igc.org
http://www.pesticides.org

The mission of the Pesticide Education Center is to educate the public about the adverse health effects of exposure to pesticides in the home, community and at work.
Founded: 1988
Marion Moses, President

709 **Rainforest Action Network**
425 Bush Street 415-398-4404
Suite 300 Fax: 415-398-2732
San Francisco, CA 94108 E-mail: answers@ran.org
http://www.ran.org

Rainforest Action Network works to protect the Earth's rainforest and support the rights of their inhabitants through education, grassroots organizing, and non-violent direct action.
Founded: 1985
Amanda Starbuck, Energy & Finance Prog. Dir.
Scott Parkin, Global Finance Campaigner

710 **Redwood Empire Solar Living Association**
c/o Solar Living Institute
13771 S Highway 101 707-472-2450
Hopland, CA 95449 E-mail: sli@solarliving.org
http://www.solarliving.org

The Solar Living Institute joined the ASES (American Solar Energy Society) as the Redwood Empire Solar Living Association (RESLA). RESLA includes these seven counties in northwest CA: Del Norte, Humboldt, Lake, Mendocino, Siskiyou, Sonoma, Trinity. The Institute promotes sustainable living through environmental education.
Karen Kallen, Managing Director
Hannah Bird, Programs Manager

711 **San Diego Renewable Energy Society (SDRES)**
PO Box 927203 E-mail: info@sdres.org
San Diego, CA 92192 http://sdres.org

A regional chapter of the American Solar Energy Society and membership nonprofit organization dedicated to increasing intelligent use of renewable and sustainable energy technologies in San Diego County. Members are encouraged todevelop and create new technology and applications for alternate energy.
Stephen T. Johnston, Chairman
Jake Lincoln, Treasurer

712 **Save San Francisco Bay Association**
1330 Broadway 510-452-9261
Suite 1800 Fax: 510-452-9266
Oakland, CA 94612-2519 E-mail: info@savesfbay.org
http://www.savesfbay.org

Save the Bay has worked for over 40 years to protect the San Francisco Bay-Delta from pollution, fill, shoreline destruction and fresh water diversion. We have launched a century of renewal to restore bay fish and wildlife, reclaimtidal wetlands and make the bay safe and accessible to all.
Founded: 1961
David Lewis, Executive Director
Robin Erickson, Director Finance/Admin.

713 **Scenic California**
2215 5th Street 510-883-0390
Berkeley, CA 94710 Fax: 510-883-0391
E-mail: sceniccalifornia@lsa-assoc.com
http://www.sceniccalifornia.org

Scenic America is the only national nonprofit organization dedicated to protecting natural beauty and distinctive community character. We provide technical assistance across the nation and through affiliates on scenic byways, billboardand sign control, context sensitive highway design, wireless telecommunications tower location, transportation enhancements, and other scenic conservation issues.
Sheila Brady, Manager

714 **Sierra Club: Angeles Chapter**
3435 Wilshire Blvd 213-387-4287
Suite 660 Fax: 213-387-5383
Los Angeles, CA 90010-1904 http://www.angeles.sierraclub.org

The Angeles Chapter has 58,000 members located in Los Angeles and Orange counties.
Founded: 1920
Ron Silverman, Executive Director
Jennifer Robinson, Program Manager

715 **Sierra Club: Kern Kaweah Chapter**
PO Box 3357 661-323-5569
Bakersfield, CA 93385-3357 http://www.kernkaweah.sierraclub.org

To advance the preservation and protection of the natural environment by empowering the citizenry, especially democratically-based grassroots organizations, with charitable resources to further the cause of environmental protection.
Stephen Montgomery, Chair
Gordon Nipp, Vice Chair

716 **Sierra Club: Loma Prieta Chapter**
3921 East Bayshore Road 650-390-8411
Suite 204 Fax: 650-390-8497
Palo Alto, CA 94303 E-mail: melissa.hippard@sierraclub.org
http://www.lomaprieta.sierraclub.org

One of the largest chapters of the Sierra Club.
Founded: 1933
Megan Fluke, Development Manager
Kenneth Rosales, Conservation Coordinator

717 Sierra Club: Los Padres Chapter
PO Box 31241 805-965-9719
Santa Barbara, CA 93130-1241 E-mail: motodata@adelphia.net
http://www.lospadres.sierraclub.org
The Chapter represents the members in Ventura and Santa Barbara counties in Southern California.
Gerry Ching, Chair
David Gold, Vice Chair

718 Sierra Club: Mother Lode Chapter
909 12th Street 916-557-1100
Suite 202 Fax: 916-557-9669
Sacramento, CA 95814 E-mail: info@mlc.sierraclub.org
http://motherlode.sierraclub.org
The 20,000 members of this chapter come from a large region stretching from Stanislaus County to the Oregon border to the north, the California/Nevada border in the east and to the west of the Central Valley.
Andy Sawyer, Chair
Barbara Williams, Vice Chair

719 Sierra Club: Redwood Chapter
55A Ridgeway Avenue 707-544-7651
PO Box 466 Fax: 707-544-9861
Santa Rosa, CA 95402 E-mail: penningt@sonic.net
http://www.redwood.sierraclub.org
The Club's purpose is to protect and restore wild places, public health and wildlife for future generations.
Victoria Brandon, Chair
Steve Birdlebough, Vice Chair

720 Sierra Club: San Diego Chapter
8304 Clairemont Mesa Blvd 619-299-1743
Suite 101 Fax: 619-299-1742
San Diego, CA 92111 E-mail: san-diego.chapter@sierraclub.org
http://www.sandiego.sierraclub.org
A nonprofit organization dedicated to preserving, protecting and enjoying the earth.
Cheryl Reiff, Chapter Coordinator
Martha Bertles, Office

721 Sierra Club: San Francisco Bay Chapter
2530 San Pablo Avenue 510-848-0800
Suite I Fax: 510-848-3383
Berkeley, CA 94702 E-mail: info@sfbaysc.org
http://www.sanfranciscobay.sierraclub.org
Represents over 30,000 members from Alameda, Contra Costa, Marin and SF. Nonprofit, member-supported, public interest organization that promotes enjoyment and preservation of the national and local forests, waters, wildlife andwilderness. In addition to a wide variety of environmental and conservation interests and activities, it is active in the areas of pollution prevention and climate change.
Founded: 1924
Arthur Feinstein, Chair
Glenn Kirby, Vice Chair

722 Sierra Club: San Gorgonio Chapter
4079 Mission Inn Avenue 951-684-6203
Riverside, CA 92501-3204 Fax: 951-684-6172
E-mail: ralphsalisbury@charter.net
http://www.sangorgonio.sierraclub.org
To explore, enjoy and protect the wild places of the earth, to practice and promote the responsible use of the earth's ecosystems and resources; to educate and enlist humanity to protect and restore the quality of the natural and humanenvironment; and to use all lawful means to carry out these objectives.
Ralph Salisbury, Chair
Bill Cunningham, Vice Chair

723 Sierra Club: Tehipite Chapter
PO Box 5396 559-229-4031
Fresno, CA 93755-5396 E-mail: tehipite.chapter@sierraclub.org
http://www.tehipite.sierraclub.org
The Sierra Club is dedicated to protecting the quality of life in Fresno County from unwise land development.
Bill Fjellbo, Chair
Gary Lasky, Vice Chair

724 Sierra Club: Ventana Chapter
PO Box 5667 831-624-8032
Carmel, CA 93921 Fax: 831-624-3371
E-mail: chapter@ventana.sierraclub.org
http://www.ventana.sierraclub.org
To protect, preserve, and restore the wilderness qualities and biodiversity of the public lands within California's northern Santa Lucia Mountains and Big Sur coast.
Rita Dalessio, Chair
Mary Gale, Secretary

725 Society for the Conservation of Bighorn Sheep
PO Box 94182 310-679-2102
Pasadena, CA 91109 E-mail: info@scbs-desertbighorn.com
http://www.desertbighorn.cjb.net/
Mission and ultimate goal is the full restoration of the California Desert Bighorn to its historic habitat and the establishment of self-sustaining populations throughout those ranges.
Founded: 1964
John Nelson, President

726 Southern California Chapter: American Solar Energy Society
4760 Walnut Street 303-443-3130
Suite 106 Fax: 303-443-3212
Boulder, CA 80301 E-mail: ases@ases.org
http://www.ases.org
The American Solar Energy Society (ASES) is the United States section of the International Solar Energy Society (ASES) a non profit organization dedicated to the development and adoption of renewable energy in all its forms.
Seth Masia, Executive Director
Gina Johnson, Editor

727 Southwestern Herpetologists Society
PO Box 7469 818-503-2052
Van Nuys, CA 91409 E-mail: webmaster@swhs.org
http://www.swhs.org
To further serve members in central California. Open to anyone interested in the study and conservation of reptiles and amphibians.
Founded: 1954
Bud James, President
Sabine Bradley Phillips, Vice President

728 Urban Habitat Program
Presido Station
1212 Broadway 510-839-9510
Suite 500 Fax: 510-839-9610
Oakland, CA 94612 E-mail: contact@urbanhabitatprogram.org
http://www.urbanhabitat.org
Dedicated to building a multicultural majority that provides urban environmental leadership in order to create socially just, ecologically sustainable communities in the Bay Area.
Founded: 1989
Allen Fernandez Smith, President/CEO
Josy McEldowney, Office Manager

729 Western Occupational and Environmental Medical Association
575 Market Street 415-764-4918
Suite 2125 Fax: 415-764-4915
San Francisco, CA 94105 E-mail: woema@hp-assoc.com
http://www.woema.org
The mission is to represent and be a resource to members in the profession and practice of occupational and environmental medi-

cine and to enhance their efforts to promote and improve health in the workplace.
Founded: 1941
Shannon Jamieson, Executive Director

730 Yellowstone Grizzly Foundation
2515 Wilshire Blvd 307-734-8643
Santa Monica, CA 90403 http://www.grizzlypeople.com
A non-profit organization dedicated to the conservation of the threatened grizzly bear in the greater Yellowstone Ecosystem. YGF pursues the conservation of the Yellowstone Grizzly by conducting independent research and a wide range of education programs.

Colorado

731 American Lung Association of Colorado
American Lung Association
5600 Greenwood Plaza Boulevard 303-388-4327
Suite 100 Fax: 303-377-1102
Greenwood Village, CO 80111 E-mail: info@lungcolorado.org
http://www.lung.org/associations/states/colorado
The mission of the American Lung Association is to prevent lung disease and to promote lung health.
Founded: 1904
Curt Huber, Executive Director
Durban Swartz, Program Manager

732 American Society of Landscape Architects: Colorado Chapter
PO Box 200822 303-748-0321
Denver, CO 80220 Fax: 303-220-5833
E-mail: info@aslacolorado.org
http://www.aslacolorado.org
Serves as the state professional society representing landscape architects in Colorado and Wyoming. Promotes the landscape architecture profession and advances the practice through advocacy, education, communication and networking
Founded: 1973
Abraham Medina, President
Robb Kerg, President-Elect

733 Aspen Global Change Institute
104 Midland Ave 970-925-7376
Suite 205 Fax: 970-925-7097
Basalt, CO 81621 E-mail: agcimail@agci.org
http://www.agci.org
A Colorado nonprofit dedicated to furthering the understanding of Earth systems through interdisciplinary science meetings, publications, and educational programs about global environmental change.
John Katzenberger, President
Michael Stranahan, Secretary/Treasurer

734 Association of Midwest Fish and Game Law Enforcement Officers
Division of Wildlife
6060 Broadway 303-291-7223
Denver, CO 80216 http://www.midwestgamewarden.org
Lead group among wildlife enforcement organizations in the development and maintenance of training for field officers that protects the resource and benefits the citizens of our countries, provinces and states.
Founded: 1944
Bob Thompson, Executive Secretary

735 Colorado Association of Conservation Districts
PO Box 4138 719-686-0020
Woodland Park, CO 80866 E-mail: cacd.contact.us@gmail.com
http://www.cascd.com
Promotes soil and water conservation. Membership is $15.00 per year for individuals and $250.00 per year for organizations.
12 pages Quarterly
Jerry Schwien, Author
Gary Moyer, President
Brian Nuefeld, Vice President

736 Colorado BASS Chapter Federation
4485 Enchanted Circle North 719-597-2304
Colorado Springs, CO 80917 E-mail: noznut36@comcast.net
http://www.coloradobassfederation.org
Main purpose is to stimulate public awareness of bass fishing as a major sport and to offer the Colorado Department of Wildlife and other organizations moral and political support and encouragement.
Audrey McKenney, President
Dave Gerhardt, Vice President

737 Colorado Forestry Association
1413 Ash 970-221-1336
Ft. Collins, CO 80521 E-mail: billgheerardi@comcast.net
http://www.coloradoforestry.org/
The original mission was to support conservation, management and renewal of forests through forestry legislation, public education and creation of forest reserves.
Founded: 1884
Bill Gherardi, President
Bill Carpenter, Vice President

738 Colorado Renewable Energy Society
3245 Eliot Street 303-806-5317
Denver, CO 80211 E-mail: info@cres-energy.org
http://www.cres-energy.org
Nonprofit membership organization that works for the sensible adoption of cost-effective energy efficient and renewable energy technologies by Colorado businesses and consumers.
Lorrie McAllister, Executive Director
Pat Grossman, Membership Director

739 Colorado Safety Association
4730 Oakland Street 303-373-1937
Suite 500 800-727-0519
Denver, CO 80239 Fax: 303-373-1955
E-mail: melodye@coloradosafety.org
http://www.coloradosafety.org
Not-for-profit, non-governmental educational organization specializing in occupational safety and health issues.
Liz Couture, Executive Director
Chris Baker, Program Manager

740 Colorado Solar Energy Industries Association
1536 Wynkoop Street 303-333-7342
Suite 300 Fax: 303-604-6988
Denver, CO 80202 E-mail: info@coseia.org
http://www.coseia.org
Represents and serves energy professionals and renewable energy users. We promote the use of solar energy and conservation to improve the environment and create a sustainable future.
Founded: 1989

741 Colorado Trappers Association
PO Box 397 970-268-5554
Empire, CO 80438 E-mail: steve@coloradotrapper.com
http://www.coloradotrapper.com/
An organization dedicated to promoting wildlife education and management, and upholding the ideals of our unique trapping heritage.
Otis Latham, President
Dan Gates, Vice President

742 Colorado Water Congress
1580 Logan Street 303-837-0812
Suite 700 Fax: 303-837-1607
Denver, CO 80203 E-mail: info@cowatercongress.org
http://www.cowatercongress.org

Protects and conserves Colorado's water resources by means of advocacy and education.
Founded: 1958
Doug Kemper, Executive Director
Emily Brumit, Communications Coordinator

743 **Colorado Wildlife Federation**
1410 Grant Street 303-987-0400
Suite C-313 Fax: 303-987-0200
Denver, CO 80203 E-mail: cwfed@coloradowildlife.org
http://www.coloradowildlife.org
Mission is to promote the conservation, sound management, and sustainable use of Colorado's wildlife and wildlife habitat through education and advocacy.
Founded: 1953
Suzanne O'Neill, Executive Director

744 **Keystone Center and Keystone Science School**
Keystone Center & Science School
1628 Sts. John Road 970-513-5800
Keystone, CO 80435 Fax: 970-262-0152
E-mail: info@keystone.org
http://www.keystone.org
Nonprofit public policy and educational organization founded in 1975. Strives to develop creative problem-solving processes that assist diverse parties address issues of importance and to provide qualified science education throughhands-on inquiry of the natural world. Keystone Center pursues this end through its two divisions, the Science and Public Policy Program and the Keystone Science School.
Founded: 1975
Robert W Craig, President
Dirk Forrister, Managing Director

745 **National Wildlife Federation Rocky Mountain Natural Resource Center**
11100 Wildlife Center Drive 303-786-8001
Reston, VA 20190 800-822-9919
Fax: 303-786-8911
http://www.nwf.org
Protects and restores wildlife habitat on tribal lands and is involved with other issues that impact wildlife and wild places of the West and Great Plains regions.
Larry Schweiger, President/CEO
Jaime Matyas, Executive Vice President/COO

746 **Sierra Club-Rocky Mountain Chapter**
1536 Wynkoop Street 303-861-8819
4th Floor Fax: 303-449-6520
Denver, CO 80202 E-mail: dan.disner@rmc.sierraclub.org
http://www.rmc.sierraclub.org
To advance the preservation and protection of the natural environment by empowering the citizenry, especially democratically based grassroots organizations with charitable resources to further the cause of environmental protection, thevehicle through which the Sierra Club Foundation generally fulfills its charitable mission.
Susan Lefever, Director
Dan Disner, Chapter Coordinator

Connecticut

747 **American Association in Support of Ecological Initiatives**
45 Wyllys Ave 860-685-2000
Middletown, CT 06459 Fax: 860-347-8459
E-mail: wwasch@wesleyan.edu
http://www.wesleyan.edu
AASEI is a US 501 nonprofit organization which supports international environmental initiatives in Russian Nature Reserves. In cooperation with Russia and foreign scientists, students, and universities, AASEI organizes scientific research projects, academic internships, work camps, environmental exchanges, and eco-tourism. Our aim is to provide practical support to Russian Reserves, expand opportunities for international scientific research, and promote international understanding.
Founded: 1994
Michael S. Roth, President
Brendan Sweeney, President

748 **American Lung Association of Connecticut**
American Lung Association
45 Ash Street 860-289-5401
East Hartford, CT 06108 800-586-4872
Fax: 860-289-5405
E-mail: bcase@alact.org
http://www.alact.org
The American Lung Association of Connecticut offers a wide variety of lung health services to the people of Connecticut.
Founded: 1904
John Zinn, Chief Executive Officer
Margaret LaCroix, Vice President

749 **American Society of Landscape Architects: Connecticut Chapter**
370 James Street 203-966-7071
4th Floor 800-878-1474
New Haven, CT 06513 Fax: 203-972-0770
E-mail: brobinsonla@gmail.com
http://www.ctasla.org
As a chapter of the ASLA, it aims to lead, educate and participate in the careful stewardship, wise planning, and artful design of cultural and natural environments.
Brian A Robinson, President-Elect
Jeff Mills, Executive Director

750 **Connecticut Audubon Society**
2325 Burr Street 203-259-6305
Fairfield, CT 06824 Fax: 203-254-7673
E-mail: communicationsdir@ctaudubon.org
http://www.ctaudubon.org
A statewide, nonprofit, membership organization dedicated to protecting the Connecticut environment by providing citizens of all ages with top-quality education and outdoor experiences. Each year, through school programs, teachertraining workshops, youth activities, adult and family trips, community events and legislative initiatives, the Society reaches more than 175,000 people.
Robert Martinez, President
Barbara Strickland, Chairman

751 **Connecticut Botanical Society**
PO Box 9004 860-439-2144
New Haven, CT 06532-4 E-mail: lemmon@snet.net
http://www.ct-botanical-society.org
A group of amateur and professional botanists who share an interest in the plants and habitats of Connecticut and the surrounding region. The goals are to increase knowledge of the state's flora, to accumulate a permanent botanicalrecord, and to promote conservation and public awareness of the state's rich natural heritage.
Founded: 1903
Glenn Dreyer, President

752 **Connecticut Forest and Park Association**
16 Meriden Road 860-346-2372
Rockfall, CT 06481 Fax: 860-347-7463
E-mail: info@ctwoodlands.org
http://www.ctwoodlands.org
An organization for forest and wildlife conservation. Develops outdoor recreation and natural resources. Provides forest management, construction of hiking trails and consultation in the areas of forestry and environment.
Founded: 1895
Eric Hammerling, Executive Director
Teresa Peters, Office Manager

753 **Connecticut Fund for the Environment**
Fact Sheet
142 Temple Street 203-787-0646
Suite 305 Fax: 203-787-0246
New Haven, CT 06510 E-mail: protect@cfenv.org
http://www.ctenvironment.org

States non-profit legal champion for the environment. CFE utilizes law, science and education to better air and water quality, control toxic contamination, minimize the adverse impacts of highways and traffic congestion, protect publicwater supplies, and preserve the open space and wetlands so crucial to both the state's citizens and its wildlife.
Founded: 1978
Donald S. Strait, Executive Director
Lois Greene, Development Associate

754 **Friends of Animals**
777 Post Road 203-656-1522
Suite 205 Fax: 203-656-0267
Darien, CT 06820 E-mail: info@friendsofanimals.org
http://www.friendsofanimals.org
A non-profit, international animal advocacy organization that works to cultivate a respectful view of non-human animals, free-living and domestic.
Founded: 1957
Priscilla Feral, President
Sally Malanga, Secretary/Treasurer

755 **Litchfield Environmental Council: Berkshire**
Oriion Grassroots Network
The Roraback Bldg 860-435-2004
115 Main Street, PO Box 668 E-mail: wml61@comcast.net
North Canaan, CT 06018 http://www.berklitchfieldenviro.org
To promote an understanding of both the environmental and economic needs, and of the preservation and conservation issues, within the bioregion.
Ellery Sinclair, Executive Secretary
B Blake Levitt, Communications Director

756 **Save the Sound**
142 Temple Street 203-422-2563
Suite 301 800-729-3547
New Haven, CT 06510 Fax: 203-967-2677
E-mail: savethesound@snet.net
http://www.savethesound.org
Save the Sound Inc is a nonprofit membership organization dedicated to the restoration, protection and appreciation of Long Island Sound and its watershed through education, research and advocacy.
Founded: 1972
John Atkin, President

757 **Sierra Club**
645 Farmington Avenue 860-236-4405
Hartford, CT 06105-2946 http://connecticut.sierraclub.org
To advance the preservation and protection of the natural environment by empowering the citizenry, especially democratically based grassroots organizations with charitable resources to further the cause of environmental protection, thevehicle through which the Sierra Club Foundation generally fulfills its charitable mission.
John Blake, Chair
John Calandrelli, Chapter Coordinator

District of Columbia

758 **African American Environmentalists Association**
1629 K Street NW 443-569-5102
Suite 300 http://www.aaenvironment.com
Washington, DC 20036
A national, nonprofit environmental organization dedicated to protecting the environment, enhancing human, animal and plant ecologies, promoting the efficient use of natural resources and increasing Afrian American participation in theenvironmental movement.
Founded: 1985
Norris McDonald

759 **Alliance for Climate Protection**
901 E Street NW 202-628-1999
Washington, DC 20004-2037 http://www.climateproject.org
Seeks to uncover the complete truth about the climate crisis in a way that ignites the moral courage in each of us.
Maggie L Fox, President/CEO

760 **Alliance to Save Energy**
1850 M Street NW 202-857-0666
Suite 600 http://www.ase.org
Washington, DC 20036
A nonprofit organization that promotes efficiency worldwide through research, education and advocacy. Strives to be the world's premier organization promoting energy efficiency to achieve a healthier economy, a cleaner environment andgreater energy security.
Kateri Callahan, President
Brian Castelli, Executive Vice President

761 **American Lung Association**
1301 Pennsylvania Ave NW 202-785-3355
Suite 800 Fax: 202-452-1805
Washington, DC 20004 http://www.midlandlung.org
Serves the Counties of: Arenac, Bay, Genessee, Gladwin, Huron, Lapeer, Livingston, Midland, Saginaw, Sanliac, Shiawassee and Tuscola.
Founded: 1906
Tracy Ross, CEO

762 **American Lung Association of the District of Columbia**
1301 Pennsylvania Ave NW 202-785-3355
Suite 800 Fax: 202-682-5874
Washington, DC 20004 E-mail: info@lung.org
http://www.lung.org
The core of the American Lung Association's mission is to help promote lung health and prevent lung disease
Katrina Jones, Project Coordinator

763 **American Rivers: Mid-Atlantic Region**
1101 14th Street NW 202-347-7550
Suite 1400 877-347-7550
Washington, DC 20005 Fax: 202-347-9240
E-mail: akober@americanrivers.org
http://www.americanrivers.org
William Robert Irvin, President
Chris Alford, Associate Director

764 **American Society of Landscape Architects: Potomac Chapter**
PO Box 18184 703-838-5095
Washington, DC 20036 E-mail: potomachapterasla@gmail.com
http://www.potomacasla.org
Serves the metro DC area. It advocates responsible design and use of land and advances the professional success of its members.
Ron Kagawa, President

765 **Casey Trees**
3030 12th Street NE 202-833-4010
Washington, DC 20017 Fax: 202-833-4092
http://www.caseytree.org
Works to restore, enhance and protect the tree canopy of the nation's capital.
Founded: 2001
Mark Buscaino, Executive Director

766 **Environmental Working Group**
1436 U Street NW 202-667-6982
Suite 100 Fax: 202-232-2592
Washington, DC 20009 http://www.ewg.org
The Environmental Working Group is a small, computer powered research organization dedicated to improving environmental protection through the analysis of federal and state regulatory policies and performance and through technicalassistance and education.
Founded: 1993
Ken Cook, President
Richard Wiles, Senior Vice President

767 **Human Environment Center**
1930 18th Street NW
Suite 24
Washington, DC 20009
202-588-8036
Fax: 202-588-9422
Hector Eriksen-Mendoza, Executive Director

768 **Institute of Scrap Recycling Industries**
1615 L Street NW
Suite 600
Washington, DC 20036
202-662-8500
Fax: 202-626-0900
E-mail: maryanngreene@isri.org
http://www.isri.org
Founded: 1987
Robin K Weiner, President
Maryann Greene, Executive Assistant

769 **Resources for the Future**
1616 P Street NW
Washington, DC 20036
202-328-5000
Fax: 202-939-3460
http://www.rff.org
A nonprofit and nonpartisan organization that conducts independent research, rooted primarily in economics and other social sciences on environmental, energy, natural resource and environmental health issues.
Founded: 1952
Philip Sharp, President
Mike Viola, Development Assistant

770 **Sierra Club**
50 F Street NW
Washington, DC 20001
202-548-4581
Fax: 202-244-4438
E-mail: amanda.brinton@sierraclub.org
http://dc.sierraclub.org
The more than 3,200 members of the DC Chapter are actively involved in local conservation and political efforts in conjunction with the national Sierra Club mission.
Karen Cordry, Treasurer
Debby Cooney, Secretary

771 **Society for Occupational and Environmental Health**
1010 Vermont Avenue NW
#513
Washington, DC 20005
202-347-4976
888-347-2632
Fax: 202-347-4950
E-mail: kkirkland@aoec.org
http://www.soeh.org
Provides a neutral forum where occupational safety and health and environmental issues can be discussed and resolved. Actively seeks to improve the quality of both working and living places.
Ronald D Dobbin, President
Katherine H Kirkland, Executive Director

772 **Washington, DC: Chesapeake Region Safety Council**
Rutherford Business Center
17 Governor's Court
Baltimore, MD 21244
410-298-4770
800-875-4770
Fax: 410-281-1350
E-mail: safety@chesapeakesc.org
http://www.chesapeakesc.org
A private, non-profit, non-governmental public service organization whose mission is to provide the safety training and education that will reduce disabling injuries and save lives.
Dave Minford, CEO
Connie Schultheis, Vice President

Delaware

773 **American Lung Association of Delaware**
630 Churchmans Road
Suite 202
Newark, DE 19702
302-737-6414
Fax: 302-737-126
E-mail: llyons@lungingo.org
http://www.lunginfo.org
Since the turn of the century, we have been fighting lung disease through education, community services, advocacy and research. Lung disease, including asthma, emphysema, and lung cancer, is the third leading cause of death in America.
Founded: 1904
Harold P. Wimmer, President/CEO
Susan DeNardo, Director Development

774 **Atlantic Waterfowl Council**
Division of Fish and Wildlife
89 Kings Highway
Dover, DE 19901
302-739-5295
Fax: 302-739-6157
http://www.flyways.us/flyways/atlantic
Committed to the preservation and advancement of waterfowl.
Founded: 1948
William C Wagner II, Chairman

775 **Delaware Association of Conservation Districts**
509 Capitol Court NE
Washington, DC 20002-4937
202-547-6223
Fax: 202-547-6450
E-mail: terry.pepper@state.de.us
http://www.nacdnet.org/delaware
Mandated to preserve and protect our state's soil, water and coastal resources.
John Larson, CEO

776 **Delaware BASS Chapter Federation**
2453 S State Street
Camden, DE 19901
302-698-9257
800-463-6062
Fax: 720-302-1230
E-mail: pr@deltbf.org
http://www.deltbf.com
An organization striving to represent the interests of local Bass chapters on a state wide basis. We offer the Delaware Department of Natural Resources & Environmental Control our organized and political support and encouragement. TheDFB promotes full adherence to all conservation codes of existing regulatory standards.
Founded: 1975
Ron Horton, President
Gary Brandt, Vice President

777 **Delaware Greenways**
1910 Rockland Road
Wilmington, DE 19803
302-655-7275
Fax: 302-655-7274
E-mail: greenways@dca.net
http://www.delawaregreenways.org/
Committed to the preservation and advancement of Delaware's natural, scenic, historic, cultural, and recreational resources. Works to accomplish this in preserving and connecting open space greenways, increasing opportunities forwalking and biking and creating more livable communities.
Founded: 1990
David Hunt, Managing Director
Donna Deery, Administrative Coordinator

778 **Delaware Nature Society**
Delaware Nature Society
3511 Barley Mill Road
PO Box 700
Hockessin, DE 19707
302-239-2334
Fax: 302-239-2473
E-mail: dnsinfo@delawarenaturesociety.org
http://www.delawarenaturesociety.org
DNS members benefit from discounts and free admissions, previews and special programs, priority registration, guest passes, and more. Memberships begin at $30 for the college student, through $1000 as a member of the Director's Circle.to many species of amphibians, birds, mammals, fish, reptiles, and native plants.
Michael Riska, Executive Director

779 **Delaware: Chesapeake Region Safety Council**
Rutherford Business Center
17 Governor's Court
Baltimore, MD 21244
410-298-4770
800-875-4770
Fax: 410-281-1350
E-mail: safety@chesapeakesc.org
http://www.chesapeakesc.org
A private, non-profit non-governmental public service organization whose mission is to provide the safety training and education that will reduce disabling injuries and save lives.

780 **Save Wetlands and Bays**
41 Beaver Circle 302-945-8578
Lewes, DE 19958
Henry Glowiak, President

781 **Sierra Club**
100 West 10th Street 302-468-4550
Suite 106 E-mail: delaware.chapter@sierraclub.org
Wilmington, DE 19801 http://delaware.sierraclub.org
John Irwin, Chair
Matt Urban, Vice Chair

Florida

782 **American Fisheries Society: Agriculture Economics Section**
University of California
PO Box 240 352-392-4991
Gainsville, FL 32611 Fax: 352-392-3646
E-mail: adams@fred.ifas.ufl.edu
Committed to the preservation and advancement of Florida's natural resources.
Charles Adams, President

783 **American Lung Association of Florida**
American Lung Association
6852 Belfort Oaks Place 904-743-2933
Jacksonville, FL 32216 800-940-2933
Fax: 904-743-2916
E-mail: alaf@lungfla.org
http://www.lung.org/associations/states/florida
The mission of the American Lung Association is to prevent lung disease and promote lung health.
Founded: 1904
Pablo Mila, Director

784 **American Lung Association: Central Area Office**
American Lung Association
851 Outer Road 407-425-5864
Orlando, FL 32814-6652 800-586-4872
Fax: 407-425-2876
E-mail: alafcentral@lungfla.org
http://www.lung.org/associations/states/florida/about-us/local-offi
The mission of the American Lung Association is to prevent lung disease and promote lung health.
Founded: 1904
Martha Bogdan, Chief Executive

785 **American Lung Association: Gulfcoast Area**
American Lung Association
8950 Dr. Martin Luther King St N 727-347-6133
Suite 205 Fax: 727-345-0287
Saint Petersburg, FL 33702 E-mail: alagf@lungfla.org
http://www.lung.org/associations/states/florida/about-us/local-offi
The mission of the American Lung Association is to prevent lung disease and to promote lung health.
Founded: 1904
Shirley Westrate, Area Executive Director

786 **American Lung Association: Gulfcoast Area: Southwest Office**
American Lung Association
662 Astarias Circle 239-908-2680
Fort Meyers, FL 33919 Fax: 239-908-2608
E-mail: alafgcfm@lungfla.org
http://www.lung.org/associations/states/florida/about-us/local-offi
The mission of the American Lung Association is to prevent lung disease and to promote lung health
Founded: 1904
Darius Joseph, President
Shirley M Westrate, Chief Operating Officer

787 **American Lung Association: Gulfcoast Area: South Bay Office**
3333 Clark Road 941-377-5864
Suite 100 Fax: 941-342-6099
Sarasota, FL 34231
The mission of the American Lung Association is to prevent lung disease and to promote lung health.

788 **American Lung Association: North Area: Northwest Office**
American Lung Association
4300 Bayou Boulevard 850-478-5864
Suite 2 800-586-4872
Pensacola, FL 32503 Fax: 850-474-6354
E-mail: alafnw@networktel.net
http://www.lungfla.org
The mission of the American Lung Association is to prevent lung disease and to promote lung health.
Founded: 1904
John L Kirkwood, President

789 **American Lung Association: North Area: Big Bend Office**
539 Silver Slipper Lane 850-386-2065
Suite A Fax: 850-422-1894
Tallahassee, FL 32303 E-mail: alafbb@lungfla.org
http://www.lung.org/associations/states/florida/about-us/local-offi
The mission of the American Lung Association is to prevent lung disease and to promote lung health.
Brenda Olsen, Director of Governmental Aff
Kelsey Ryan, President

790 **American Lung Association: North Area: Daytona Office**
American Lung Association
412 S. Palmetto Avenue 386-255-6447
Daytona Beach, FL 32114 800-LUN- USA
Fax: 386-253-2410
E-mail: alafspaceport@cfl.rr.com
http://www.lungusa.org/
The mission of the American Lung Association is to prevent lung disease and to promote lung health
Founded: 1904
Charles A Heinrich, Chairman
Robert A Green, Vice Chairman

791 **American Lung Association: South Area Office**
2020 South Andrews Avenue 954-524-4657
Fort Lauderdale, FL 33316-3430 800-524-8010
Fax: 954-524-3162
E-mail: alafsouth@lungfla.org
http://www.lung.org/associations/states/florida/about-us/local-offi
The mission of the American Lung Association is to prevent lung disease and to promote lung health.
Founded: 1904
Denise Grimsley, President

792 **American Lung Association: Southeast Area Office**
American Lung Association: Florida
2701 North Australian Avenue 561-659-7644
Suite 100 800-LUN-GUSA
West Palm Beach, FL 33407-4526 Fax: 561-835-8967
E-mail: alafse@lungfla.org
http://www.lung.org/associations/states/florida/about-us/local-offi
The mission of the American Lung Association is to save lives by improving lung health and preventing lung disease.
Founded: 1937
Carol A Ruggeri, Executive Director

793 **American Lung Association: Southeast Area: Belle Glade Office**
American Lung Association of Florida
136 South Main Street 561-993-3632
Belle Glade, FL 33430 800-586-4872
Fax: 561-993-3433
E-mail: amlungself@enhaleexhale.org
http://www.lungusa.org

The mission of the American Lung Association is to prevent lung disease and to promote lung health.
Founded: 1904
Paul Polisena, President
James Sugarman, Executive Director

794 **American Lung Association: Gulfcoast Area: Nature Coast Office**
American Lung Association
PO Box 1445
Inverness, FL 34451
352-860-0616
800-586-4872
Fax: 352-860-0336
http://www.lungusa.org
The mission of the American Lung Association is to prevent lung disease and to promote lung health
Founded: 1904

795 **American Lung Association: Gulfcoast Area: East Bay Office**
110 Carolon Parkway
St. Petersburg, FL 33716
813-962-4448
Fax: 727-345-0287
The mission of the American Lung Association is to prevent lung disease and to promote lung health.

796 **Association of Battery Recyclers**
PO Box 290286
Tampa, FL 33687
813-626-6151
Fax: 813-622-8388
E-mail: info@batteryrecyclers.com
http://www.americasbatteryrecyclers.com
To keep members abreast of environmental, health, and safety requirements that affect our industry.
Founded: 1984
Earl Cornette, President
Joyce Morales Caramella, Secretary

797 **Audubon of Florida**
Travenier Science Center
444 Brickell Ave
Suite 850
Miami, FL 33131-2403
305-371-6399
Fax: 305-371-6398
E-mail: wmones@audubon.org
http://www.fl.audubon.org
The science center is the research arm of the Everglades Campaign. The mission of Audubon of Florida is to ensure the restoration and conservation of the Greater Everglades Ecosystem in order to achieve an ecologically and economicallysustainable South Florida. Our Everglades Conservation office has a five-part program including science, education, advocacy, outreach and grassroots action.
Founded: 1938
Eric Draper, Executive Director
Victoria Johnston, Development Associate

798 **Citizens for a Scenic Florida**
4401 Emerson Street
Suite 10
Jacksonville, FL 32207
904-396-0037
Fax: 904-398-4647
E-mail: scenicfl@scenicflorida.org
http://www.scenicflorida.org
Promotes and carries out programs that protect natural beauty in the environment, protect historical and cultural resources; promotes education of the public about such issues; and coordinates local, regional and state efforts to preserve and enhance visual resources.
William C Jonson, President
Trudy Barker, Executive Vice President

799 **Florida Chapter: American Society of Landscape Architects**
722 Vassar Street
Orlando, FL 32804
407-443-0071
E-mail: tom.bohn@flasla.org
http://www.flasla.org
A non-profit association, operating under the national professional society, that represents the landscape architecture profession throughout the state of Florida.
Thomas Bohn, Executive Director
Diane Story, Administrative Assistant

800 **Florida Defenders of the Environment**
4424 NW 13th Street
Suite C-8
Gainesville, FL 32607
352-378-8465
Fax: 352-377-0869
E-mail: fde@fladefenders.org
http://www.fladefenders.org
One of the oldest and most accomplished conservation organizations in Florida with a network of scientists, economists and other professionals dedicated to preserving and protecting the state's natural resources. FDE's top priority iscurrently the restoration of a 16-mile stretch of the Ocklawaha River and its 9,000-acre floodplain forest by removal of Rodman Dam- the last vestige of the Cross-Florida Barge Canal.
Founded: 1969
Erin Condon, Executive Director

801 **Florida Environmental Health Association**
PO Box 160848
Altamonte Springs, FL 32716-848
407-790-0347
E-mail: fehaweb@feha.org
http://www.feha.org
Promotes public health by means of advanced environmental control.
Founded: 1967
Sonia Cruz, Executive Director

802 **Florida Forestry Association**
PO Box 1696
Tallahassee, FL 32302
850-222-5646
Fax: 850-222-6179
E-mail: info@forestfla.org
http://www.floridaforest.org
Mission is to promote the responsible use of Florida's forests. This is accomplished through a variety of programsand services designed to keep the state of Florida green while it grows.
Founded: 1923
Alan Shelby, Executive Vice President
Debbie Bryant, Director of Member Services

803 **Florida Keys Wild Bird Rehabilitation Center**
93997 Overseas Highway
Tavernier, FL 33070
305-852-4486
Fax: 305-852-3186
E-mail: info@fkwbc.org
http://www.fkwbc.org
The mission is to reduce the suffering of sick and injured wild birds, to reduce the incidents of their injury and environmental hazards that place these birds at the risk through education.
Horn Bruce, President
Laura Quinn, Executive Director

804 **Florida Ornithological Society**
143 Beacon Lane
Jupiter, FL 33469
850-942-2489
E-mail: necox@nettally.com
http://www.fosbirds.org
The purpose of the organization is to promote field ornithology and to facilitate contact between those persons interested in birds.
Founded: 1972
Dave Goodwin, President
Ann Paul, Vice President

805 **Florida Public Interest Research Group**
310 N Monroe Street
Tallahassee, FL 32301
850-224-3321
Fax: 850-224-1310
E-mail: info@floridapirg.org
http://www.floridapirg.org
State wide, nonprofit, public interest advocacy organization that focuses primarily on environmental and consumer protection.
Michael Russo, Federal Program Director
Ed Mierzwinski, Consumer Program Director

806 **Florida Renewable Energy Association**
PO Box 560272
Orlando, FL 32856-272
407-710-8705
E-mail: FREAInformation@gmail.com
http://www.cleanenergyflorida.org
Dedicated to expanding the use of clean, renewable energy technologies through public awareness, political advocacy, and individual initiative.
Robert Stonerock Jr., President
Craig Williams, Executive Director

807 Florida Solar Energy Industries Association
2555 Porter Lake Drive 407-339-2010
Suite 106 800-426-5899
Sarasota, FL 34240 Fax: 407-260-1582
E-mail: wendy@FlaSEIA.org
http://www.flaseia.org

A nonprofit professional association of companies involved in the solar energy industry.
Founded: 1977
Wendy Parker Barsell, Executive Director

808 Florida Trail Association
5415 SW 13th Street 352-378-8823
Gainesville, FL 32608 Fax: 352-378-4550
E-mail: fta@floridatrail.org
http://www.florida-trail.org

Builds, maintains and preserves the Florida Trail, a 1300 mile trail from Big Cypress Preserve to Gulf Islands National Seashore for hikers and backpackers. Sponsors hikes and canoe trips.
Founded: 1964
Janet Akerson, Administrative Director
Eric Mason, Trail Program Director

809 International Association for Hydrogen Energy
5794 SW 40 Street 305-284-4666
303 Fax: 305-284-4792
Miami, FL 33155 E-mail: info@iahe.org
http://www.iahe.org

Advances the day when hydrogen energy will become the principal means by which the world will achieve its long-sought goal of abundant clean energy. Toward this end, the Association endeavors to inform scientists and the public of theimportant role of hydrogen energy in the planning of an inexhaustible and clean energy system through its publications (International Journal of Hydrogen Energy) and conferences.
Founded: 1974
T Nejat Veziroglu, President
Matthew M. Mench, Executive Director

810 International Game Fish Association
300 Gulf Stream Way 954-927-2628
Dania Beach, FL 33004 Fax: 954-924-4299
E-mail: hq@igfa.org
http://www.igfa.org

Founded as record-keeper and to maintain fishing rules. Today, emphasis is on conservation and education. Encourages youngsters to enter the sport and maintains a huge library on the subject of fishing. Has a network of well over 300representatives around the world, many of whom are conservation leaders in their communities.
Founded: 1939
Rob Kramer, President
Michael J. Myatt, COO

811 Keep Florida Beautiful
193 Rainbow Street 321-543-4582
Meritt Island, FL 32952 Fax: 850-385-4020
http://www.gogreenfl.org

Non-profit organization dedicated to litter prevention, beautification and community improvement, and minimization of the impacts of waste on communities.
Jeff Koons, Chairman

812 Legal Environmental Assistance Foundation (LEAF)
1114 Thomasville Road 850-681-2591
Suite E Fax: 850-224-1275
Tallahassee, FL 32303 E-mail: cvalencic@leaflaw.org
http://www.leaflaw.org

To protect human health and life-sustaining natural resources from pollution in Florida, Georgia and Alabama.
Founded: 1979
David Lupder, President
Cynthia Valencic, Vice President

813 National Wildlife Federation: Everglades Project
PO Box 1583 239-643-4111
Merrifield, VA 22116-1583 800-822-9919
Fax: 239-643-5130
E-mail: adamsk@nwf.org
http://www.nwf.org

To advocate and support restoration of the greater Everglades ecosystem and protection of the western Everglades through planning, education and management activities. We seek to re-create a more natural hydrologic flow through thegreater Everglades that ensures the long-term viability of native habitats, threatened and endangered species and associated wildlife.
Founded: 1934
Larry Schweiger, President
Jaime Matyas, Executive Vice President/COO

814 Pelican Man's Bird Sanctuary
1708 Ken Thompson Parkway 941-388-4444
Sarasota, FL 34236 Fax: 941-388-3258
E-mail: mail@pelicanman.org
http://www.pelicanman.org

Southwest Florida's largest rescue and rehabilitation center for wildlife, emphasizing, but not limited to, birds.
Mona Schonbrunn PhD, President
Tonya Clauss, Director of Vet. Medicine

815 Reef Relief
PO Box 430 305-294-3100
Key West, FL 33041 Fax: 305-293-9515
E-mail: info@relier.org
http://www.reefrelief.org

Reef Relief is a global nonprofit membership organization dedicated to preserve and protect living coral reef ecosystems.
Founded: 1986
Peter Anderson, President
Bob Cardenas, Vice President

816 Sanibel-Captiva Conservation Foundation
3333 Sanibel-Captiva Road 239-472-2329
PO Box 839 Fax: 239-472-6421
Sanibel, FL 33957 E-mail: sccf@sccf.org
http://www.sccf.org

Land acquisition, native plant nursery, environmental education, habitat management, marine laboratory. Dedicated to the preservation of natural resources and wildlife habitat on and around the barrier islands.
Founded: 1967
Erick Lindblad, Executive Director
Wendy Cerdan, Business Manager

817 Sierra Club
1990 Central Avenue 727-824-8813
St Petersburg, FL 33712 Fax: 727-824-0936
E-mail: frank.jackalone@sierraclub.org
http://florida.sierraclub.org

To advance the preservation and protection of the natural environment by empowering the citizenry, especially democratically-based grassroots organizations, with charitable resources to further the cause of environmental protection.
Debbie Matthews, Chair
John Glenn, Conservation Chair

818 Society of Environmental Toxicology and Chemistry
SETAC N America Office
229 South Baylan Street 850-469-1500
2nd Floor Fax: 850-469-9778
Pensacola, FL 32502 E-mail: setac@setac.org
http://www.setac.org

Provides a forum for individuals and institutions engaged in study of environmental issues, management and conservation of natural resources, environmental education and environmental research and development.
Founded: 1979
Mimi Meredith, Sr Manager

819 South Florida Chapter, National Safety Council
4171 West Hillsboro Boulevard
Suite 5
Coconut Creek, FL 33073
954-422-5757
800-392-5101
Fax: 954-418-9290
E-mail: occupational@safetycouncil.com
http://www.safetycouncil.com

Not-for-profit, non-governmental, public service organization dedicated to the safety and health of the Broward, Dade, Palm Beach and surrounding communities.
Michael Walters, VP Operations

820 Suncoast Seabird Sanctuary
18328 Gulf Blvd
Indian Shores, FL 33785
727-391-6211
800-406-3400
Fax: 727-399-2923
E-mail: seabird@seabirdsanctuary.com
http://www.seabirdsanctuary.com

The sanctuary is the largest wild bird hospital in the United States dedicated to the rescue, repair, rehabilitation and hopeful release of sick and injured native birds. Over 600 birds permanently reside at our beachfront sanctuary. We are open free of charge to the public 365 days a year. Tours and educational programs are available.
Founded: 1971
Ralph Heath Jr, Founder/Director
Michelle Simoneau, Marketing/PR Manager

821 Tallahassee Museum of History and Natural Science
3945 Museaum Drive
Tallassee, FL 32310
850-575-8684
Fax: 850-574-8243
E-mail: rdaws@tallasseemuseum.org
http://www.tallahasseemuseum.org

One of the few museums in the nation combining a natural habitat zoo of indigenous wildlife, a collection of historical buildings and artifacts and an environmental science center on a beautiful 52 acre lake side setting.
Founded: 1957
Russell S. Daws, Executive Director/CEO
Steve Carbol, Director Education

822 Wildlife Foundation of Florida
PO Box 11010
Tallahassee, FL 32302
850-922-1066
800-988-4889
Fax: 850-921-5786
E-mail: info@wildlifeflorida.org
http://www.wildlifefoundationflorida.org

Goal is to ensure that Florida's wildlife survives and thrives for future generations of Florida residents and visitors.
Founded: 1994
Will Bradford, CFO
Brett Boston, Executive Director

Georgia

823 Agency for Toxic Substances and Disease Registry
Centre for Disease Control
4770 Buford Highway NE
Atlanta, GA 30341
404-639-3311
800-232-4636
Fax: 770-488-4178
E-mail: atsdric@cdc.gov
http://www.atsdr.cdc.gov

To prevent exposure and adverse human health effects and diminished quality of life associated with exposure to hazardous substances from waste sites, unplanned releases, and other sources of pollution present in the environment. ATSDRis an operating division of the US Department of Health and Human Services. It divides its activities between those related to a particular site and those related to a specific hazardous substance.
Founded: 1987
Julie Gerberding, Director
Henry Falk, Associate Director

824 American Academy of Sanitarians
1568 Le Grande Circle
Lawrenceville, GA 30043
678-407-1051
Fax: 678-407-1051
http://www.sanitarians.org

A nonprofit corporation governed to carry out the programs and to meet the objectives stated in its constitution by laws.
Gary P. Noonan, Executive Secretary/Treas.

825 American Lung Association of Georgia
American Lung Association
2452 Spring Road
Smyrna, GA 30080
770-434-5864
800-586-4872
Fax: 770-319-0349
E-mail: alaga@lungga.org
http://www.lung.org/associations/states/georgia

The mission of the American Lung Association is to prevent lung disease and promote lung health.
Founded: 1904
Charles A Heinrich, Chairman
Robert A Green, Vice-Chairman

826 American Society of Landscape Architects: Georgia Chapter
PO Box 18622
Savannah, GA 31126
202-898-2444
E-mail: info@gaasla.org
http://www.gaasla.org

A local source of professional support to practicing professionals.
450 Members
Mark Bullard, Treasurer

827 Center for a Sustainable Coast
221 Mallory Street
Suite B
St. Simons Island, GA 31522
912-638-3612
Fax: 912-638-3615
E-mail: susdev@gate.net
http://www.sustainablecoast.org

The purpose of the non-profit membership organization is to improve the responsible use, protection, and conservation of coastal Georgia's resources- natural historic, and economic.
Founded: 1997
David Kyler, Executive Director
Helen Alexander, Administrative Assistant

828 Centers for Disease Control and Prevention
United States of health and human services
1600 Clifton Road NE
Atlanta, GA 30333
404-639-3311
800-232-4636
Fax: 404-639-7111
http://www.cdc.gov

Protects the public health of the nation by providing leadership and direction in the prevention and control of diseases and other preventable conditions and responding to public health emergencies.
Founded: 1946
Julie Louise Gerberding, Director
William Gimson, Chief Operating Officer

829 Coastal Conservation Association of Georgia
Coastal Conservation Association
2807-A Roger Lacey Ave
Savannah, GA 30458
912-927-0280
Fax: 912-927-7764
E-mail: info@ccaga.org
http://www.ccaga.org

A non-profit organization dedicated to promoting the preservation, conservation, restoration and protection of the marine fisheries and habitats of the Georgia coast both in shore and offshore, for the benefit and responsibleutilization by the general public.
Founded: 1986
Michael D. Denmark, Executive Director
Bill Schwickrath, Secretary

830 Coosa River Basin Initiative
408 Broad Street
Rome, GA 30161
706-232-2724
Fax: 706-235-9066
E-mail: jcook@coosa.org
http://www.coosa.org

We are a nonprofit environmental advocacy organization dedicated to creating a cleaner, healthier, more economically viable Coosa River Basin.
Joe Cook, Executive Director
Amos Tuck, Program Coordinator

831 Council of State and Territorial Epidemiologists (CSTE)
2872 Woodcock Boulevard 770-458-3811
Suite 250 Fax: 770-458-8516
Atlanta, GA 30341 E-mail: fellowship@cste.org
http://www.cste.org

The Council of State and Territorial Epidemiologists is an organization of epidemiologists working together to establish effective relationships amoung state and other epidemiologists, to consult and advise with appropriate disciplinesin other health agencies, and to provide technical assistance to the Association of State and Territorial Health Officials.
Founded: 1951
Tim Jones, President
Lauene Mascola, Vice President

832 Earth Share of Georgia
1447 Peachtree Street 404-873-3173
Suite 214 Fax: 404-873-3135
Atlanta, GA 30309 E-mail: info@earthsharega.org
http://www.earthsharega.org

Nonprofit federation of local, national and global environmental groups addressing the critical environmental issues. ESGA raises funds for these groups through workplace giving campaigns, special events and individual contributions.
Founded: 1992
Madeline L. Reamy, Executive Director
Jackie Furlong, Admin. & Comm. Director

833 Environmental Justice Resource Center
223 James Brawley Drive SW 404-880-6911
Atlanta, GA 30314 Fax: 404-880-6909
E-mail: ejrc@cau.edu
http://www.ejrc.cau.edu

Since 1994, a research, policy and information clearinghouse on issues related to environmental justice, race and the environment, civil rights, facility siting, land use planning, brownfields, transportation equity, suburban sprawland Smart Growth. The overall goal of the center is to assist, support, train and educate people of color, students, professionals and grassroots community leaders with the goal of facilitating their inclusion into the mainstream of environmentaldecision-making.
Robert Bullard, Director
Michelle Dawkins, Program Manager

834 Georgia Association of Conservation District Supervisors
PO Box 111 706-542-3065
Athens, GA 30603 E-mail: info@gacds.org
http://www.gacds.org

Dedicated to the protection and conservation of the state's natual resources
Founded: 1943 370 Members
Christa Carrell, Executive Director

835 Georgia Chapter, National Safety Council
5161 Brook Hollow Parkway 770-729-0077
Suite 220 Fax: 770-729-0044
Norcross, GA 30071 E-mail: georgia@nsc.org
http://georgia.nsc.org

Mission is to educate and influence people to prevent accidental injury and death. Raising awareness about safety issues that affect all of us regardless of industry, helps make our world a safer place.
Bob Wilson, Executive Director

836 Georgia Conservancy
817 West Peachtree Street 404-876-2900
Suite 200 Fax: 404-872-9229
Atlanta, GA 30308 E-mail: mail@gaconservancy.org
http://www.georgiaconservancy.org

A catalyst for the stewardship of our natural environment through education, principled advocacy, and inclusive decision-making in order to make Georgia a premier environmental state.
Founded: 1967
Pierre Howard, President
Allie Kelly, Senior VP

837 Georgia Environmental Health Association
397 Eastman Highway 706-595-5478
Hawkinsville, GA 31036 E-mail: clerk@gehaorg.net
http://www.geha-online.org

A non-profit, professional organization, dedicated to promoting, supporting, training, and registering individuals working in environmental health fields throughout government, academia, industry and business.
Allison Strickland, President
Kathy Worthington, VP

838 Georgia Environmental Organization
108 E Ponce De Leon Ave 404-892-3573
Suite 210 E-mail: geoco@geoco.org
Decatur, GA 30030 http://www.environmentgeorgia.org

Devoted to the preservation of the natural diversity of the plant and animal species, and their habitats, through the prevention of environmental degradation and destruction.
Olin Ivey, Executive Director

839 Georgia Federation of Forest Owners
900 Circle 75 Parkway 404-325-2954
Suite 205 800-325-2954
Atlanta, GA 30339 Fax: 404-325-2955
E-mail: info@forestlandowners.com
http://www.forestlandowners.com

The most active, independent landowners group in the country.
Joe Hopkins, President
Scott Rowland, President Elect

840 Georgia Solar Energy Association
1199 Euclid Ave 404-522-4775
Atlanta, GA 30307 E-mail: admin@gasolar.org
http://www.gasolar.org

The Georgia Chapter of the American Solar Energy Society. A nonprofit organization working to promote renewable energy in the state of Georgia through education, research and advocacy.
Julie Hairston, Communications Director
Norene Quinn, Operations Manager

841 Georgia Trappers Association
PO Box 613 912-782-5417
Metter, GA 30439 E-mail: info@gatrappersassoc.com
http://www.gatrappersassoc.com

Non profit organization interested in promoting the education and growth of hunting, fishing, and trapping while maintaining the highest standards of sportsmanship.
Russ Carter, President
Randy Zerwig, Treasurer

842 Georgia Water and Pollution Control Association
1655 Enterprise Way 770-618-8690
Marietta, GA 30067 Fax: 770-618-8695
E-mail: info@gwpca.org
http://www.gwpca.org

The GW+PCA is dedicated to education, dissemination of technical and scientific information, increased public understanding and promotion of sound public laws and programs in the water resources and related environmental fields.Founded in 1932.
Jack C Dozier, Executive Director
Bill Cannon, President

843 Georgia Wildlife Federation
11600 Hazelbrand Road 770-787-7887
Covington, GA 30094 Fax: 770-787-9229
E-mail: gwf@gwf.org
http://www.gwf.org

A member supported, not-for-profit conservation organization and the state affiliate of the NationaL Wildlife Federation.
Founded: 1936
Todd Holbrook, President/CEO
Deanne Harris, Conservation Resources Mngr

844 Human Ecology Action League (HEAL)
PO Box 509 770-389-4519
Stockbridge, GA 30281 Fax: 770-389-4520
E-mail: healnatnl@aol.com
http://www.healnatl.org

The Human Ecology Action League Inc (HEAL) is a nonprofit organization founded in 1977 to serve those whose health has been adversely affected by environment exposures; to provide information to those who are concerned about the healtheffects of chemicals; and to alert the general public about the potential dangers of chemicals. Referrals to local HEAL chapters and other support groups are available from the League.
Founded: 1977
Katherine P Collier, Manager

845 **Mountain Conservation Trust of Georgia**
104 N Main Street 706-253-4077
Suite B3 Fax: 706-253-4078
Jasper, GA 30143 E-mail: info@mctga.org
http://www.mctga.org
Dedicated to the permanent conservation of the scenic beauty and natural resources of the mountains and foothills of North Georgia through land protection, education and collaborative partnerships.
Founded: 1994
Dan Pool, Vice President
Clay Johnston, President

846 **National Wildlife Federation Southeastern Natural Resource Center**
730 Peachtree Street NE 404-876-8733
Suite 1000 Fax: 404-892-1744
Atlanta, GA 30308 E-mail: online.nwf.org/southeastern
http://www.nwf.org
Works to protect the ecosystems of the Southeastern US including the coastal plain estuaries, the everglades, the Appalachian highlands, and public lands.
Larry Schweiger, President/CEO
Jaime Matyas, Executive VP/COO

847 **Nature Conservancy: Georgia Chapter**
100 Peachtree NW 404-873-6946
Suite 2250 Fax: 404-873-6984
Atlanta, GA 30303 E-mail: comment@tnc.org
http://www.nature.org
A leading conservation organization working around the world to protect ecologically important lands and waters for nature and people.
Founded: 1951
Tavia McCuean, VP
Allen Harrison, Director of Operations

848 **Sierra Club: Georgia Chapter**
743 E College Ave 404-607-1262
Suite B Fax: 404-876-5260
Decatur, GA 30030 E-mail: georgia.chapter@sierraclub.org
http://georgia.sierraclub.org
A grassroots organization dedicated to the preservation, protection and enjoyment of our environment. We work towards those goals through public education, political advocacy, an active outings program and litigation when necessary.
Sybil Cypress, Assistant Director

849 **The Clean Air Campaign**
55 Park Place 877-253-2624
Suite 250 http://www.cleanaircampaign.org
Atlanta, GA 30303
A not-for-profit organization that motivates Georgians to take action to improve air quality and reduce traffic congestion.
Founded: 1996
Tedra Cheatham, Executive Director

850 **Trees Atlanta**
225 Chester Ave 404-522-4097
Atlanta, GA 30316 Fax: 404-522-6855
E-mail: info@treesatlanta.org
http://www.treesatlanta.org
A non-profit citizen's group dedicated to protecting and improving our urban environment by planting and conserving trees.
Founded: 1985
Connie Veates, Co-Executive Director/COO
Greg Levine, Co-Executive Director/CPO

851 **Upper Chattahoochee Riverkeeper**
3 Puritan Mill 404-352-9828
916 Joseph Lowery Boulevard Fax: 404-352-8676
Atlanta, GA 30318 E-mail: sbethea@ucriverkeeper.org
http://www.ucriverkeeper.org
Mission is to advocate and secure the protection and stewardship of the chattahoochee River, its tributaries and watershed, in order to restore and preserve their ecological health for the people, fish and wildlife that depend on theRiver system.
Founded: 1994
Sally Bethea, Executive Director
David Lee Simmons, Communications Director

Hawaii

852 **American Lung Association in Hawaii**
650 Iwilei Road 808-537-5966
Suite 208 Fax: 808-537-5971
Honolulu, HI 96817 E-mail: lleslie@ala-hawaii.org
http://www.ala-hawaii.org
Mission is to prevent lung disease and promote lung health. We strive to reach this goal by delivering customer driven quality programs to fight lung disease, developing the financial base to support these activities, and engaging thecommitment of our board staff, volunteers and customers.
Founded: 1929
Lorraine Leslei, Executive Director
Debbie Apolo, Tobacco Control Manager

853 **American Lung Association of Hawaii: East Hawaii Office**
39 Ululani Street 808-935-1206
Hilo, HI 96720 Fax: 808-935-7474
E-mail: cfernandes@ala-hawaii.org
http://www.ala-hawaii.org
The mission of the American Lung Association is to prevent lung disease and to promote lung health.
Founded: 1929
Mary Miller, CEO
Malcolm Koga, President

854 **American Lung Association of Hawaii: Kauai Office**
29992 Umi Street 808-245-4142
Lihue, HI 96766 Fax: 808-245-8488
E-mail: alahkaui@pixi.com
http://www.ala-hawaii.org/
The mission of the American Lung Association is to prevent lung disease and to promote lung health.
Malcolm Koga, President
Sterling Yee, Vice President

855 **American Lung Association of Hawaii: Maui Office**
American Lung Association of Hawaii
95 Mahalani Street 808-244-5110
Cameron Center, Suite 1A Fax: 808-242-9041
Wailuku, HI 96793 E-mail: lbrady@ala-hawaii.org
http://www.ala-hawaii.org
The mission of the American Lung association is to prevent lung disease and to promote lung health.
Founded: 1929
Mary Miller, President
Didier Decler, VP Finance

856 **American Lung Association of Hawaii: West Hawaii Office**
American Lung Association
74-5588 Pawai Place 808-326-4755
Building P 800-LUN- USA
Kailua-Kona, HI 96740 Fax: 808-326-9149
E-mail: alahkona@pixi.com
http://www.lungusa.org/site/
The mission of the American Lung Association is to prevent lung disease and to promote lung health.
Founded: 1904
James M Anderson, Secretary

857 American Society of Landscape Architects: Hawaii Chapter
1164 Bishop Street, Suite 124 808-521-5631
Box 246 E-mail: info@hawaiiasla.org
Honululu, HI 96813 http://www.hawaiiasla.org
The purpose of the society is the advancement of knowledge, education, and skill in the art and science of landscape architecture as an instrument of service for the public welfare.
Founded: 1969
Kyle Sasaki, President
Wayne Baldwin, Treasurer

858 Big Island Rain Forest Action Group
223 South King Street 808-966-7622
Suite 400 E-mail: mpoffice@earhtjustice.org
Honolulu, HI 96813 http://www.earthjustice.org
Founded: 1989
Jim Albertini, Coordinator

859 EarthTrust
Windward Environmental Center
1118 Maunawili Road 808-261-5339
Kailua, HI 96734 Fax: 206-202-3893
E-mail: sue@flipperfund.com
http://www.earthtrust.org
EarthTrust is the impossible missions team for wildlife and the environment. Its low-overhead high-tech campaigns are always positive and effective. Dedicated to saving marine mammals, reforming unsustainable fisheries and ending the trade in endangered species around the world. EarthTrust is a relatively small organization which may have directly saved more marine wildlife biomass than any other organization in history.
Founded: 1976
Don White, President

860 Flipper Foundation
Windward Environmental Center
1118 Maunawili Road 808-261-5339
Kailua, HI 96734 Fax: 815-333-1158
E-mail: sue@flipperfund.com
http://www.earthtrust.org
The Flipper Foundation exists to save dolphins and to revolutionize consumer control over environmental destruction by world fisheries. Its mission is to establish and maintain the highest world standard of dolphin safety and fisheriessustainability; to educate consumers worldwide while directly granting funds to save marine mammals and their habitats. Its primary way of accomplishing this is to engage fishery firms in voluntary partnerships to phase out destructive fishingtechnologies.
Founded: 1992
Don White, President

861 Greenpeace Foundation
Windward Environmental Center
1118 Maunawili Road 808-263-4388
Kailua, HI 96734 Fax: 630-604-6129
E-mail: email@gpfdn.com
http://www.greenpeacefoundation.com
The oldest and original Greenpeace organization in the US Greenpeace Foundation is dedicated to peaceful no-nonsense environmental advocacy. Greenpeace Foundation seeks to preserve biodiversity on a green and peaceful planet. Proudlyunaffiliated with Greenpeace International we make no apologies for standing up for the earth; a human voice for the majority of earth's life which has none so that citizens may have a voice in what sort of planet we will leave to our children andtheirs.
Founded: 1976
Sharon Sue White, President

862 Hawaii Association of Conservation Districts
PO Box 430 808-323-3209
Kealakekua, HI 96750 Fax: 808-248-7725
E-mail: grirobins@aol.com
http://www.nacdnet.org/hawaii
HACD coordinates and facilitates partners and governmental agenciesin identifying and implimenting projects and practiceswith cultural sensitivity to assure the protection of Hawaii's environment.
David Nobriga, President
Mike Tulang, Executive Director

863 Hawaii Nature Center
875 Iao Valley Road 808-955-0100
Wailuku, HI 96793 Fax: 808-955-0116
E-mail: hawaiinaturecenter@hawaii.rr.com
http://www.hawaiinaturecenter.org
The Hawaii Nature Center is a private nonprofit organization specializing in environmental education field program for children, adults and families. Its mission is to foster awareness appreciation and understanding of Hawaii andencourage wise stewardship of the Islands. The Nature Center provides full day field trips for 20,000 students on two islands each year and features an interactive nature museum at its field site on Maui.
Founded: 1981
Dyanna Okazaki, Executive Director
Serena O'Grady, Administrative Assistant

864 Hawaiian Botanical Society
University of Hawaii
3190 Maile Way 808-956-8072
Room 101 Fax: 808-956-3923
Honolulu, HI 96822 E-mail: botany@hawaii.edu
http://www.botany.hawaii.edu
Dedicated to the understanding and preservation of hawaii's fauna and wildlife.
Founded: 1924
Eileen Helmstetter, President
Vickie Caraway, Vice President

865 Nature Conservancy: Hawaii Chapter
Nature Conservancy
923 Nuuanu Avenue 808-537-4508
Honolulu, HI 96817 E-mail: hawaii@tnc.org
http://www.nature.org
The mission is to preserve the plants, animals, and natural communities that represent the diversity of life on earth by protecting the lands and waters they need to survive.
Founded: 1903
Suzanne Case, Executive Director
Steven McCormick, President/CEO

866 Sierra Club
PO Box 2577 808-538-6616
Honolulu, HI 96803 Fax: 808-537-9019
E-mail: hawaii.chapter@sierraclub.org
http://www.hi.sierraclub.org
To explore, enjoy and protect wild places and the environment, the club uses a multi-pronged approach to protecting and restoring Hawaii's environmental quality. Through the volunteer efforts of group leaders they conduct interpretiveand educational outings; lead fun and challenging hikes; conduct service projects involving fencing, cleaning streams, trail building and noxious plant control; and advocate and lobby for environmental protection.
Robert D. Harris, Director
Helen Chong, Treasurer

Idaho

867 American Lung Association of Idaho/Nevada: Boise Office
1412 W Idaho 208-345-5864
Suite 100 Fax: 775-829-5850
Boise, ID 83702 E-mail: jflynn@lungmtpacific.org
http://www.lungs.org/associations/states/idaho/local-offices
The mission of the American Heart Association is to prevent lung disease and to promote lung health.
Founded: 1904

868 **American Society of Landscape Architects: Idaho/Montana Chapter**
c/o Hatchmueller PC
611 Sherman Avenue
Coeur d'Alene, ID 83814
E-mail: keithd@architectswest.com
http://www.imasla.org
Works to increase public's awareness of and appreciation for the profession of landscape architecture.
Keith Dixon, President
Jolene Rieck, President-Elect

869 **Energy Products of Idaho**
3586 W Industrial Loop
Coeur d' Alene, ID 83815-6016
208-765-1611
Fax: 208-765-0503
E-mail: cda.sales@outotec.com
http://www.outotec.com/us
EPI is a world leader in the development and implementation of proprietary and patented technologies used to convert biomass and other waste fuels into usable forms of energy. Since 1973, EPI has pioneered and perfected fluidized bedand related technologies forutility, industrial and commercial uses. Although our primary focus remains our world renowned fluidized bed technologies, our vast experience has lead to a stable of superior auxiliary and related proprietarytechnologies.
Founded: 1973
Pertti Korhonen, President/CEO
Robin Lindahl, Executive VP

870 **Idaho Association of Soil Conservation Districts**
9173 W Barnes Drive
Suite C
Boise, ID 83709
208-665-6989
Fax: 208-376-6858
http://www.iascd.org
Provides action at the local level for promoting wise and beneficial conservation of natural resources with emphasis on soil and water.
Founded: 1944
Nancy Weatherstone, Executive Assistant

871 **Idaho Conservation League**
PO Box 844
710 North Sixth Street
Boise, ID 83701
208-345-6933
877-345-6933
Fax: 208-344-0344
E-mail: icl@wildidaho.org
http://www.idahoconservation.org
The mission of the League is to preserve Idaho's clean water, wilderness and quality of life through citizen action, public education, and professional advocacy.
Founded: 1973
Rick Johnson, Executive Director
Justin Hayes, Program Director

872 **Idaho Forest Owners Association**
233 E. Palouse River Drive
PO Box 9748
Moscow, ID 83843
208-883-4488
Fax: 208-883-1098
E-mail: NWManage@consulting-foresters.com
http://www.consulting-foresters.com
A full service forestry consulting firm. Provides the best forest planning and management practices for forest landowners throughout the Inland Northwest area.
Founded: 1983
Vincent P. Corrao, Manager
Gary Ellingson, Manager

873 **Sierra Club-Northern Rockies Chapter**
503 W Franklin Street
Boise, ID 83702
208-384-1023
E-mail: jessica.ruehrwein@sierraclub.org
http://idaho.sierraclub.org
The Northern Rockies Chapter represents over 4,000 members in Idaho and eastern Washington.
Katie Swanson, Manager
Brian Himes, Manager

Illinois

874 **American College of Occupational and Environmental Medicine**
25 Northwest Point Blvd
Suite 700
Elk Grove Village, IL 60007-1030
847-818-1800
Fax: 847-818-9266
http://www.acoem.org
Made up of physicians in industry, government, academia, private practice and the military, who promote the health of workers through preventive medicine, clinical care, research and education.
Founded: 1916
Ronald R. Loeppke, President
Kathryn L. Mueller, President Elect

875 **American Lung Association of Illinois/Iowa**
American Lung Association
2530 73rd Street
Des Moines, IA 50322
515-309-9507
800-586-4872
Fax: 217-787-5916
E-mail: info@lungia.org
http://www.lungusa.org/site
Founded: 1904
Harold Wimmer, CEO
Lori Younker, Manager

876 **American Lung Association: Chicagoland Collar Counties**
American Lung Association
55 W Wacker
Suite 800
Chicago, IL 62711
217-787-5864
Fax: 630-260-1111
E-mail: info@lungil.org
http://www.lungil.org
Founded: 1904
Herald Wimmer, Chief Executive Officer
Ted Schlake, Senior Manager

877 **American Lung Association: Northern Illinois**
1330 East State Street
Rockford, IL 61104
815-962-6412
Fax: 815-962-6413
E-mail: info@lungil.org
http://www.lungusa.org
Founded: 1904
James M Anderson, Secretary

878 **American Lung Association: Southwestern Illinois**
American Lung Association
1600 Golfview Drive
Suite 260
Colinsville, IL 62234
618-344-8891
800-586-4872
Fax: 618-344-8933
E-mail: info@lungil.org
http://www.lungfla.org
Founded: 1917
Tina Barnard, President
Harold Wimmer, Executive Director

879 **American Medical Association**
515 N State Street
Chicago, IL 60654
800-621-8335
http://www.ama-assn.org
Medical doctors concerned with environmentally related health issues.
Founded: 1847
John C Nelson, President

880 **American Society of Landscape Architects: Illinois Chapter**
PO Box 4566
Oak Brook, IL 60522-4566
630-833-4516
Fax: 630-833-4030
E-mail: info@il-asla.org
http://www.il-asla.org
The Illinois Chapter is one of the larger ASLA chapters with over 500 members.
Founded: 1899
Christopher Gent, President
J. Christopher Lannert, President Elect

881 **Audubon Council of Illinois**
Illinois Audubon Society
PO Box 2547
Springfield, IL
217-544-2473
Fax: 217-544-7433
http://www.illinoisaudubon.org

David Yarnold, President/CEO
Mary Beth Henson, CFO

882 **Chicago Chapter: National Safety Council**
1121 Spring Lake Drive
Suite 100
Itasca, IL 60143
630-775-2213
800-621-2855
Fax: 630-775-2136
E-mail: chicago@nsc.org
http://www.chicago.nsc.org

Alan McMillian, President

883 **Chicago Zoological Society**
Brookfield Zoo
3300 Golf Road
Brookfield, IL 60513
708-688-8000
800-201-0784
E-mail: bzadmin@brookfieldzoo.org
http://www.brookfieldzoo.org

To inspire conservation leadership by connecting people with wildlife and nature.
Founded: 1934
Stuart D. Strahl, President/CEO

884 **Eagle Nature Foundation**
Eagle Nature Foundation, LTD
300 E. Hickory St.
Apple River, IL 61001
815-594-2306
Fax: 815-594-2305
E-mail: eaglenature.tni@juno.com
http://www.eaglenature.com

A nonprofit organization dedicated to the preservation of the bald eagle, our national symbol, and other endangered species from extinction and to increase public awareness of unique endangered plants and animals. We monitor bald eagle and other endangered species populations and strive to preserve habitat essential to their survival. We develop materials for schools to inform students about the needs of the bald eagle and how we can help preserve and protect their naturalenvironment.
Founded: 1995
Terrence N Ingram, Chief Executive Officer
Eugene Small, Vice President

885 **Environmental Education Association of Illinois**
1505 N Broadway
Urbana, IL 61801
815-479-5779
Fax: 815-479-5766
E-mail: EEAssociationIllinois@gmail.com
http://www.eeai.net

Patricia Brown, President
Kirsten Hope Walker, Treasurer

886 **Great Lakes Sport Fishing Council**
PO Box 297
Elmhurst, IL 60126
630-941-1351
Fax: 630-941-1196
E-mail: hdqtrs@great-lakes.org
http://www.great-lakes.org

Our mission is to inform and educate the outdoor recreational community (sport fishing, boating and general public) through educational outreach programs about natural resource conservation and enhancement, wise conservation and boating policies, and the spread of unintentional introductions on nonindigenous aquatic nuisance species (exotics).
Founded: 1971
Dan Thomas, President
Robert Mitchell, Vice President

887 **Illinois Association of Conservation Districts**
9313 Bull Valley Road
Woodstock, IL 60098
815-338-7664
Fax: 815-338-2773
E-mail: conserveone@aol.com

Founded: 1972
John Todt, President
Ken Fiske, Assistant Secretary

888 **Illinois Association of Environmental Professionals**
PO Box 81551
Chicago, IL 60681
773-325-2771
E-mail: kkopija@cbbel.com
http://www.iaepnetwork.org

Enhnacing environmental awareness for the businesses, communities and citizens of Illinois.
Nathan Quaglia, President
Gregory Merritt, VP

889 **Illinois Audubon Society**
PO Box 2547
Springfield, IL 62708
217-544-2473
Fax: 217-544-7433
E-mail: director@pdnt.com
http://www.illinoisaudubon.org

A membership organization dedicated to the preservation of Illinois Wildlife and the habitats which support them. Has sanctuaries, conservation education and land acquisition programs and publishes quarterly magazines and newsletters.
Founded: 1897
Tom Clay, Executive Director
Jo Fessett, Assistant

890 **Illinois Environmental Council**
230 Broadway
Suite 150
Springfield, IL 62701
217-544-5954
Fax: 217-544-5958
E-mail: iec@ilenviro.org
http://www.ilenviro.org

Coalition of over 70 environmental, conservation and health groups.
Founded: 1975
Jennifer Walling, Executive Director
Mary Pemberton, Administrative Director

891 **Illinois Prairie Path**
P.O. Box 1086
Wheaton, IL 60187
630-752-0120
http://www.ipp.org
Founded: 1905
Ray Bartels, President

892 **Illinois Recycling Association**
PO Box 3717
Oak Park, IL 60303
708-358-0050
Fax: 708-358-0051
E-mail: info@illinoisrecycles.org
http://www.illinoisrecycles.org

The association's mission is to encourage the responsible use of resources and protecting the environment by promoting effective programs and practices regarding waste reduction, re-use of materials, and recycling.
Founded: 1980
Marta Keane, President
Debra Hopgood, VP

893 **Illinois Solar Energy Association**
1281 E Brummel Ave
Elk Grove Village, IL 60007
312-376-8245
Fax: 630-420-1517
E-mail: contactisea@illinoissolar.org
http://www.illinoissolar.org

Its mission is to provide energy education to the Illinois public and promote the widespread application of solar, renewable and sustainable energy methods and technologies.
Founded: 1975
Shannon Fulton, President
Leslie McCain, Executive Director

894 **Lake Michigan Federation**
17 North State Street
Suite 1390
Chicago, IL 60602
312-939-0838
Fax: 313-939-2708
E-mail: chicago@greatlakes.org
http://www.mygreatlakes.org

Works to restore fish and wildlife habitat, conserve land and water and eliminate pollution in the watershed of America's largest lake. We achieve these through education, research, law, science, economics and strategic partnerships.
Founded: 1971

895 **Nature Conservancy: Illinois Chapter**
8 S Michigan Avenue
Suite 900
Chicago, IL 60603
312-580-2100
Fax: 312-346-5606
E-mail: illinois@tnc.org
http://www.nature.org
Founded: 1915
Steven J McCormick, Chief Executive Officer

896 **Outside Chicagoland: Iowa/Illinois Safety Council**
6200 Aurora Ave
Suite 604 W
Urbandale, IA 50322
515-276-4724
800-568-2495
Fax: 515-276-8038
E-mail: iiscadmin@iisc.org
http://www.iisc.org
Our mission is to educate society to adopt safety, health, and environmental practices and to provide high quality, value added training and services.
Laura Johnson, Executive Director
Dawn Gunderson, Communications Director

897 **Prairie Rivers Network**
Prairie Rivers Network
1902 Fox Drive
Suite G
Champaign, IL 61820
217-344-2371
Fax: 217-344-2381
E-mail: info@prairierivers.org
http://www.prairierivers.org
The only statewide river conservation organization in Illinois. They strive to protect rivers and streams of Illinois and to promote the lasting health and beauty of watershed communities by providing information, sound science andhands-on assistance. They also help individuals and community groups become effective river conservation leaders.
Founded: 1967
Brad Walker, Program Coordinator

898 **Respiratory Health Association of Metropolitan Chicago**
1440 West Washington Boulevard
Chicago, IL 60607
312-243-2000
888-880-5864
Fax: 312-243-3954
E-mail: burbaszewski@lungchicago.org
http://www.lungchicago.org
Founded: 1906
Joel Africk, President/CEO
Chris Byrne, Development Director

899 **Safer Pest Control Project**
Safer Pest Control Project
4611 N Ravenswood Ave.
Suite 107
Chicago, IL 60640
773-878-7378
Fax: 773-878-8250
E-mail: general@pesticideaction.org
http://www.spcpweb.org
Dedicated to reducing the health risks and environmental impacts of pesticides and promoting safer alternatives in Illinois.
Founded: 1994
Ruth Kerzee, Executive Director
Kristin Weiss, Development Director

900 **Sierra Club: Illinois Chapter**
70 East Lake Street
Suite 1500
Chicago, IL 60601
312-251-1680
Fax: 312-251-1780
E-mail: illinois.chapter@sierraclub.org
http://illinois.sierraclub.org
The Illinois Chapter is a statewide organization representing more than 26,000 individuals committed to protecting the Illinois environment.
Jack Darin, Director
Jennifer Hensley, Program Manager

Indiana

901 **Acres Land Trust**
1802 Chapman Road
Huntertown, IN 46748
260-637-2273
Fax: 260-637-2273
E-mail: acres@acreslandtrust.org
http://www.acreslandtrust.org
Exists to collect and protect the lasdst of the natural habitats in northeast Indiana and to teach Hoosiers the value of keeping natural tracts intact.
Founded: 1960
Steven Hammer, President
Jason Kissel, Executive Director

902 **American Lung Association of Indiana: Northern Office**
American Lung Association
115 West Washington Street
Suite 1180 South
Indianapolis, IN 46204
317-819-1181
Fax: 317-819-1187
E-mail: info@lungin.org
http://www.lungin.org
Audrey Ferguson, Master Trainer

903 **American Lung Association of Indiana: State Office & Support Office**
American Lung Association
9445 Delegates Row
Indianapolis, IN 46240
317-573-3900
800-586-4872
Fax: 317-573-3909
E-mail: info@lungin.org
http://www.lungin.org
Founded: 1904
Audrey Ferguson, Master Trainer

904 **American Society of Landscape Architects: Indiana Chapter**
PO Box 441195
Indianapolis, IN 46244-1195
E-mail: office@inasla.org
http://www.inasla.org
Members include private sector landscape architects, public practitioners, scholars, government officials and other professionals representing landscape architecture, planning, preservation and ecology.
200 Members
Katie Clark, President
Stacy Haviland, President Elect

905 **Bison World**
National Bison Association
20100 State Road 37
Noblesville, IN 46060
317-214-1060
Fax: 317-214-3988
E-mail: info@bisonworld.org
http://www.bisonworld.org
An organization of bison producers dedicated to awareness of the healthy properties of bison meat and bison production.
Founded: 1978
Dave Carter, Executive Director
Merle Maas, Chairman of Board

906 **Conservation Technology Information Center**
3495 Kent Ave
Suite J100
West Lafayette, IN 47906
765-494-9555
Fax: 765-494-5969
E-mail: ctic@ctic.org
http://www.ctic.purdue.edu
A nonprofit organization dedicated to environmentally responsible and economically viable agricultural decision-making.
Founded: 1982
Karen Scanlon, Executive Director
Tammy Taylor, Operations Manager

907 **Dj Case And Associates Wildlife Society**
Dj Case And Associates
317 East Jefferson Blvd.
Mishawaka, IN 46545
574-258-0100
Fax: 574-258-0189
E-mail: info@djcase.com
http://www.djcase.com
a nonprofit scientific and educational organization that serves professionals such as government agencies, academia, industry, and non-government organizations. In all areas related to the conservation of wildlife and natural resources management.
Dave Case, President
Phil Seng, Vice President

908 **Indiana Audubon Society**
Indiana Audubon Society Inc.

3497 S Bird Sanctuary Road 765-827-0908
Connersville, IN 47331 Fax: 765-825-9788
E-mail: indianaaudubon@yahoo.com
http://www.indianaudubon.org

Founded: 1898
Brad Bumgardner, President
Robert Ripma, VP

909 **Indiana Forestry and Woodland Owners Association**
Purdue University
West Lafayette, IN 47907 765-494-4600
E-mail: steward1@inwoodlands.org
http://www.inwoodlands.org

Founded: 1977
Dan Shaver, President
Lynn Andrews, Treasurer

910 **Indiana State Trappers Association**
6420 Street Road 47 N 812-939-3215
Crawfordsville, IN 47933 http://www.indianatrappers.org
Ken Brosman, President

911 **Indiana Water Environment Association Purdue University**
200 S Meridian Street 317-686-2664
Suite 410 Fax: 317-686-2672
Indianapolis, IN 46225 E-mail: hcheslek@greeley-hansen.com
http://www.indianawea.org

Scott Grimes, Executive Director
Julia Whitson, Associate Manager

912 **Sierra Club**
1100 W 42nd Street 317-822-3750
Suite 140 E-mail: sierra@netdirect.net
Indianapolis, IN 46208 http://www.hoosier.sierraclub.org
Indiana/Hoosier Chapter of the Sierra Club
Founded: 1975
Steve Francis, Chair
Dick Miller, Vice Chair

913 **Wildlife Society**
1010 Yeardley Lane 219-258-0100
Mishawaka, IN 46544 Fax: 219-258-0189
E-mail: phil@djcase.com

A nonprofit scientific and educational organization that serves professionals such as government agencies, academia, industry, and non-government organizations in all areas related to the conservation of wildlife and natural resources management.
Phil Seng, President

Iowa

914 **American Lung Association of Iowa**
2530 73rd Street 515-309-9507
Des Moines, IA 50322 Fax: 515-334-9564
E-mail: info@lungia.org
http://www.lungia.org

Founded: 1904

915 **American Society of Landscape Architects: Iowa Chapter**
200 W 2nd Ave 515-442-2451
Indianola, IA 50125 Fax: 866-442-6751
E-mail: ia-asla@assocserv.com
http://www.iaasla.org

The chapter organizes educational and social activities for its more than 155 members.
Founded: 1899
Laura Peters, President
Jim Harbaugh, President Elect

916 **Asla Iowa Chapter**
200 W 2nd Ave 515-442-2451
Indianola, IA 50125 Fax: 866-442-6751
E-mail: ia-asla@assocserv.com
http://www.iaasla.org

Laura Peters, President
Jim Harbaugh, President Elect

917 **Indian Creek Nature Center**
6665 Otis Road SE 319-362-0664
Cedar Rapids, IA 52403 Fax: 319-362-2876
E-mail: naturecenter@indiancreeknaturecenter.org
http://www.indiancreeknaturecenter.org

A private nonprofit organization open to the public. The Nature Center provides about 300 acres of natural land and provides an array of educational programs.
Founded: 1973
John Myers, Exec. Director Of Operations
Dana Wood, Office Manager

918 **Iowa Academy of Science**
Iowa Academy of Science
UNI - 175 Baker Hall 319-273-2581
2607 Campus Street Fax: 319-273-2807
Cedar Falls, IA 50614-0508 E-mail: iascience@uni.edu
http://www.iacad.org

Iowa Academy of Science is a professional scientific organization.
Founded: 1875
Craig Johnson, Executive Director
Marcy Seavey, Program Director

919 **Iowa Association of Soil and Water Conservation District Commissioners**
945 SW Ankeny Road 515-289-8300
Suite A E-mail: clarc.lindahl@cdiowa.org
Ankeny, IA 50023 http://www.cdiowa.org
Bernie Bolton, Secretary

920 **Iowa BASS Chapter Federation**
3282 Midway 319-393-1481
Marion, IA 52302 E-mail: mail@iabass.com
http://www.iabass.com

Tom Bowler, President

921 **Iowa Native Plant Society**
Iowa State University
Botany Department, 341A Bessey Hall 515-294-9499
Iowa State University Fax: 515-294-1337
Ames, IA 50011 E-mail: mottll@grinnell.edu
http://www.public.iastate.edu

An organization of amateur and professional botanists and native plant enthusiasts who are interested in the scientific, educational and cultural aspects, as well as the preservation and conservation of the native plants of Iowa. The Society was organized in 1995 to create a forum where plant enthusiasts, gardeners and professional botanists could exchange ideas and coordinate activities such as field trips, work shops, and restoration of natural areas.
Larissa Mottl, President
Connie Mutel, Vice President

922 **Iowa Renewable Fuels Association**
5505 NW 88th Street 515-252-6249
100 Fax: 515-225-0781
Johnston, IA 50131-2948 E-mail: info@iowarfa.org
http://www.iowarfa.org

Brings together ethanol and biodiesel producers to promote the development and growth of the state's renewable fuels industry through education and infrastructure development.
Walter Wendland, President
Monte Shaw, Executive Director

923 **Iowa Trappers Association**
Gene Purdy
122 2nd Street
Fontanelle, IA 50846
641-682-3937
Fax: 641-682-9092
E-mail: cegrillo@fbcom.net
http://www.iowatrappers.com
Spencer Hill, President
Chris Grillot, Secretary

924 **Iowa Wildlife Rehabilitators Association**
328 Main Street
Suite 208
Ames, IA 50010
515-233-1379
http://www.iowawildlifecenter.org
Marlene Ehresman, Executive Director

925 **Iowa-Illinois Safety Council**
6200 Aurora Ave
Suite 604 W
Urbandale, IA 50322
515-276-4724
800-568-2495
Fax: 515-276-8038
E-mail: iiscadmin@iisc.org
http://www.iisc.org

Our mission is to educate society to adopt safety, health and environmental practices and to provide high quality, value added training and services.
1200 Members
Laura Johnson, Executive Director
Dawn Gunderson, Communications Director

926 **Macbride Raptor Project**
6301 Kirkwood Boulevard SW
Cedar Rapids, IA 52406
319-335-9293
Fax: 319-398-4493
E-mail: rec-services@uiowa.org
http://www.macbrideraptorproject.org
A nonprofit organization jointly sponsored by the University of Iowa and Kirkwood Community College. The project has two main facilities, the educational display facility and rehabilitation flight cage at the Macbride Nature Recreational Area and the medical clinic on the Kirkwood Campus.
Founded: 1985
Jodeane Cancilla, Project Coordinator
Luke Hart, Project Assistant

927 **Nature Conservancy: Iowa Chapter**
505 5th Ave
Suite 930
Des Moines, IA 50309
515-244-5044
800-628-6860
Fax: 515-244-8890
E-mail: iowa@tnc.org
http://http://nature.org

Founded: 1951
Jan Glendening, State Director

928 **Practical Farmers of Iowa**
600 Fifth Street
Suite 100
Ames, IA 50010
515-232-5661
Fax: 515-232-5649
http://www.practicalfarmers.org
Teresa Opheim, Executive Director
Patrick Burke, Office Manager

929 **Sierra Club**
3839 Merle Hay Road
Suite 280
Des Moines, IA 50310
515-277-8868
E-mail: iowa.chapter@sierraclub.org
http://iowa.sierraclub.org
With approximately 6,000 members, the Iowa Chapter has been working together to protect the community and the planet.
Founded: 1972
Jane Clark, Chair
Debbie Neustadt, Vice Chair

930 **Soil and Water Conservation Society**
945 SW Ankeny Road
Ankeny, IA 50023-9723
515-289-2331
Fax: 515-289-1227
E-mail: swcs@swcs.org
http://www.swcs.org

Fosters the science and the art of soil, water and related natural resource management to achieve sustainability. Promote and practice an ethic recognizing the interdependence of people and the environment.
Founded: 1943
Jim Gulliford, Executive Director
Chrissy Rhodes, Program Coordinator

931 **State of Iowa Woodlands Associations**
204 Park Rd
Iowa City, IA 52246
515-233-1161
Fax: 515-233-1131
http://www.iowawoodlandsowners.org
Al Wagner, President
Chuck Semler, VP

Kansas

932 **American Lung Association of Kansas**
6701 W 64th Street Suite 110
Cloverleaf Office Park Bldg #5
Overland Park, KS 66202
913-912-7190
Fax: 913-912-7206
E-mail: inquiries@breathehealthy.org
http://www.lung.org/associations/charters/plains-gulf
William Voigt, Chair

933 **Arkansas River Compact Administration**
109 SW 9th Street
2nd Floor
Topeka, KS 66612-1283
785-296-3710
Fax: 785-296-1176
http://www.ksda.gov/interstate_water_issues/
Protecting Kansas' interests in interstate rivers.
David Barfield, Chief Engineer & Director

934 **Audubon of Kansas**
210 Southwind Place
Manhattan, KS 66503
785-537-4385
Fax: 785-537-4395
E-mail: aok@audubonofkansas.org
http://www.audubonofkansas.org

Founded: 1999
Ryan Klataske, Special Projects Coordinator
Ron Klataske, Executive Director

935 **Heartland Renewable Energy Society**
8214 W 75th Street
Overland Park, KS 66204
816-224-5550
E-mail: info@heartlandrenewable.org
http://www.heartlandrenewable.org
The Missouri/Kansas Chapter of the American Solar Energy Society.
Craig Wolfe, President
Shauna Zahner, Secretary

936 **Kansas Academy of Science**
1700 SW College Avenue
Topeka, KS 66621
785-231-1010
E-mail: webmaster@washburn.edu
http://www.kansasacademyscience.org

Founded: 1868
Brian Maricle, President
Eric Trump, President Elect

937 **Kansas Association for Conservation and Environmental Education**
2610 Claflin Road
Manhatten, KS 66502-2743
785-532-3322
Fax: 785-532-3305
E-mail: ldowney@kacee.edu
http://www.kacee.org

Statewide no-profit dedicated to promoting quality sound, non-biased environmental education in Kansas through professional development and technical assistance.
Laura Downey, Executive Director
Jolene Amtower, Office Manager

938 **Kansas BASS Chapter Federation**
9712 Juniper Lane
Overland Park, KS 66207
913-385-2277
http://www.kbcf.com
The purpose is to stimulate public awareness of bass fishing as a major sport.
Eric Strong, President

939 **Kansas Natural Resources Council**
PO Box 2635 316-265-0767
Topeka, KS 66601 E-mail: lerick@ksu.edu
http://www.knrc.ws
Protect the quality and supplies of Kansas' water. Support sustainable family farming practices that respect and restore the land and the community. Ensure a competitive energy market where renewable resources and conservation can flourish. Reduce the exposure to hazardous and nuclear wastes. Encourage environmentally sound industrial practices.
Founded: 1980
Larry Erickson, President

940 **Kansas Rural Center**
PO Box 133 785-873-3431
Whiting, KS 66552 E-mail: ksrc@rainbowtel.net
http://www.kansasruralcenter.org
A non-profit promoting the long-term health of the land and its people through research, education and advocacy. KRC is committed to economically viable, environmentally sound, and socially sustainable rural culture.
Founded: 1979
Julie Mettenburg, Executive Director
Mary Fund, Communications Director

941 **Kansas Wildflower Society**
2045 Constant Avenue 785-864-3453
Lawrence, KS 66047 Fax: 785-864-5093
http://www.naturalkansas.org
Dwight Platt, President
Cynthia Ford, Secretary

942 **Kansas Wildscape Foundation**
2500 W 6th 785-843-9453
Suite G 866-655-4377
Lawrence, KS 66049 Fax: 785-843-6379
E-mail: wildscape@sunflower.com
http://www.kansaswildscape.org
Founded: 1991
Charlie Black, Executive Director
Lynn Gontino, Development Director

943 **North Dakota Natural Science Society**
Department of Biological Sciences
600 Park Street 785-628-4214
Hays, KS 67601 Fax: 785-628-4156
E-mail: efinck@fhsu.edu
http://www.fhsu.edu/biology/pn/prarienat.htm
Regional organization with interests in the natural history of grasslands and the Great Plains.
Founded: 1967
Chris Deperno, President

944 **Safety & Health Council of Western Missouri & Kansas**
5829 Troost Avenue 816-842-5223
Kansas City, MO 64110 Fax: 816-842-6226
E-mail: shc@safetycouncilmoks.com
http://www.safetycouncilmoks.com
Is a private not-for-profit community service organization which has been helping to make our community a safer place to live, work and play. We are dedicated to preventing unintentional injuries where ever they occur.
Kathy Zents, Executive Director

945 **Sierra Club**
9844 Georgia 913-707-3296
Kansas City, KS 66109 E-mail: info@kansas.sierraclub.org
http://kansas.sierraclub.org
Protection of the Kansas environment through education, and the practice and promotion of responsible ecosystem and resource use.
Yvonne Cather, Chair
Craig Lubow, Vice Chair

946 **Wildlife Society**
Kansas State University
205 Ackert 758-532-0978
Manhattan, KS 66506 E-mail: wildlife@ksu.edu
A nonprofit scientific and educational organization that serves professionals such as government agencies, academia, industry, and non-government organizations in all areas related to the conservation of wildlife and natural resources management.
Jason Tarwater, President

Kentucky

947 **American Lung Association of Kentucky**
American Lung Association
4100 Churchman Ave 502-363-2652
Louisville, KY 40215 800-586-4872
E-mail: bgottschalk@midlandlung.org
http://www.kylung.org
Founded: 1905
Jim Sugarman, Executive Director

948 **American Society of Landscape Architects: Kentucky Chapter**
163 West Short Drive 859-246-2753
Suite 351 Fax: 859-246-2754
Lexington, KY 40507 E-mail: ky.labd@ky.gov
http://www.kyasla.com
Jane A. Gardner, Executive Director

949 **Kentucky Association for Environmental Education**
KAEE
PO Box 1208 425-814-5095
Frankfort, KY 40602 http://www.kaee.org
John Rudolph, President
Bob Oliver, Secretary

950 **Kentucky Audubon Council**
Kentucky Audubon Council
306 Hoover Hill Road 270-298-4237
Hartford, KY 42347 E-mail: kac@kentuckyaudubon.org
http://www.kentuckyaudubon.org
Serves as an effective support and coordinating organization to the Commonwealth's Audubon Society Chapters and members of the National Audubon Society.
Brenda Little, President
Pat Tuttle, VP

951 **Kentucky Resources Council**
PO Box 1070 502-875-2428
Frankfort, KY 40602 800-372-7181
Fax: 502-875-2845
E-mail: fitzKRC@aol.com
http://www.kyrc.org
Tom Fitzgerald, Director

952 **Land Between the Lakes Association**
345 Maintenance Road 800-455-5897
Golden Pond, KY 42211 E-mail: information@friendsoflbl.org
http://www.friendsoflbl.org
Assists with the education, improvement, promotion, conservation, and wise use of the USDA Forest Service's Land Between The Lakes National Recreation Area.
John Rufli, Executive Director

953 **Nature Conservancy: Kentucky Chapter**
114 Woodland Ave 859-259-9655
Lexington, KY 40502 Fax: 859-259-9678
E-mail: kentucky@tnc.org
http://www.nature.org
Founded: 1951
Jim Aldrich, State Director
Lisa Morris, Office Manager

954 **Scenic Kentucky**
Scenic Kentucky

PO Box 23317
Louisville, KY 40223
502-489-9497
Fax: 502-489-5278
E-mail: info@scenickentucky.org
http://www.scenickentucky.org

Scenic America is the only national nonprofit organization dedicated to protecting natural beauty and distinctive community character. We provide technical assistance across the nation and through affiliates on scenic byways, billboard and sign control, context sensitive highway design, wireless telecommunications tower location, transportation enhancements, and other scenic conservation issues.

Paul Bergmann, Executive Director
Marlene Grissom, President

955 Sierra Club
PO Box 1368
Lexington, KY 40588-1368
859-296-4335
E-mail: alicehowell@insightbb.com
http://kentucky.sierraclub.org

Advances the preservation and protection of the natural environment by empowering the citizenry, especially democratically-based grassroots organizations, with charitable resources to further the cause of environmental protection. The vehicle through which The Sierra Club Foundation generally fulfills its charitable mission.

Founded: 1968
Alice Howell, Chair
Sherry Otto, Chapter Coordinator

956 Southeastern Association of Fish and Wildlife Agencies
1 Sportsman's Lane
Frankfort, KY 40601
800-858-1549
E-mail: info.center@ky.gov
http://http://fw.ky.gov/

Dr. Johathan W. Gassett, Commissioner

Louisiana

957 American Lung Association of Louisiana
2325 Severn Avenue
Suite 8
Metairie, LA 70001-6918
504-828-5864
800-586- 872
Fax: 504-828-5867
E-mail: inquiries@breathehealthy.org
http://www.louisianalung.org

A resource for information and data on lung diseases with a focus on education and prevention.

Founded: 1904
Thomas P Lotz, Executive Director
Steven M Lee, Program Director

958 American Society of Landscape Architects: Louisiana Chapter
Brown+Danos Landdesign Inc
3347 Nicholson Drive
Unit a214
Baton Rouge, LA 70802
225-571-9534
E-mail: ce_list@lcasla.org
http://www.lcasla.org

Haley Blakeman, President
Greg Grandy, President-Elect

959 Calcasieu Parish Animal Control and Protection Department
Department of Animal Services
1015 Pithon Street
PO Box 1583
Lake Charles, LA 70602
337-721-3500
Fax: 337-437-3399
E-mail: administration@cppj.net
http://cpac.cppj.net

David Marcantel, Operations Supervisor

960 Louisiana Association of Conservation Districts
663 Holmes Road
Keatchie, LA 71046
318-933-5375
Fax: 318-872-3178
http://www.laconservationdistricts.org

Bruce Frazier, President
John Compton, Secretary/Treasurer

961 Louisiana BASS Chapter Federation
603 Terri Drive
Luling, LA 70070
504-785-9069
E-mail: webmaster@nybassfed.com
http://www.nybassfed.com

Kevin Gaubert, President
Elvis Jeanminette, Vice President

962 Louisiana Wildlife Federation
PO Box 65239
Audubon Station
Baton Rouge, LA 70896-5239
225-344-6707
Fax: 225-344-6707
E-mail: lwf@lawildlifefed.org
http://www.lawildlifefed.org

Founded: 1940
Warren Singer, President
Clinton Mouser, Treasurer

963 National Safety Council: Ark-La-Tex Chapter
8101 Kingston Road
#107
Shreveport, LA 71108
318-687-7550
800-595-7550
Fax: 318-687-7298
E-mail: info@nscaltchapter.org
http://www.nscaltchapter.org

Specialists in professional safety training.

Larry Holbert, Executive Director
Dana Gunn, Assistant Director

964 Nature Conservancy: Louisiana Chapter
PO Box 4125
Baton Rouge, LA 70821
225-338-1040
Fax: 225-338-0103
E-mail: lafo@tnc.org
http://http://www.nature.org

Founded: 1957

Steve McCormack, President

965 Sierra Club: Delta Chapter
PO Box 52503
Lafayette, LA 70505
504-891-9642
E-mail: chair@louisiana.sierraclub.org
http://la.sierraclub.org

Advances the cause of protecting Louisiana's environment in a variety of ways including lobbying the state legislature in Baton Rouge, raising public awareness about climate change, working to keep the Atchafalaya Basin river swamp alive and wild, and sponsoring a Mercury Public Education Campaign.

Martin Haywood, Chair

966 Tulane Environment Law Clinic
Tulane University
6823 St. Charles Avenue
New Orleans, LA 70118
504-865-5794
800-873-9283
E-mail: pr@tulane.edu
http://www.tulane.edu

Since 1989, the Tulane Law School, through its Environmental Law Clinic, has provided free legal assistance on wide variety of environmental issues. In addition, the Clinic assists community groups with scientific and organizational issues.

Founded: 1989
Scott S. Cowen, President

967 Wildlife Society
200 Quail Drive
Baton Rouge, LA 70808
225-765-2800
http://www.wlf.state.la.us

A nonprofit scientific and educational organization that serves professionals such as government agencies, academia, industry and non-government organizations in all areas related to the conservation of wildlife and natural resources management.

Kathleen Babineaux Blanco, Governor

Maine

968 American Lung Association of Maine
122 State Street
Augusta, ME 04330
207-622-6394
800-499-5864
Fax: 639-426-2919
E-mail: info@lungne.org
http://www.lungne.org

Leads the lung health promotion and lung disease prevention for Maine.
Founded: 1911
Edward Miller, Senior VP
Norman Anderson, Regional Director EHR

969 Atlantic Salmon Federation
PO Box 807 506-529-4581
Calais, ME 04619-807 506-529-1033
800-565-5666
Fax: 506-529-1070
Fax: 506-529-4438
E-mail: savesalmon@asf.ca
http://www.asf.ca

An international non-profit organization that promotes the conservation and wise management of wild Atlantic salmon and their environment.
Bill Taylor, President/CEO
Elizabeth Ames, Executive Assistant

970 Maine Association of Conservation Commissions
168 Cushman Hill Road 207-665-2577
Woodstock, ME 04219 Fax: 207-443-6913
E-mail: meacc@meacc.net
http://www.meacc.net
Founded: 1973
Robert C Cummings, Executive Director

971 Maine Association of Conservation Districts
1197 Washington Ave 207-878-0857
PO Box 541 E-mail: info@maineswcds.org
Portland, ME 04112 http://www.maineswcds.org
The statewide voice of Maine's 16 local conservation districts. By working with landowners, organizations and government, districts have helped to protect our soil, water, forestry, wildlife and other natural resources for over 60years.

972 Maine Audubon
20 Gilsland Farm Road 207-781-2330
Falmouth, ME 04105 Fax: 207-781-0974
E-mail: info@maineaudubon.org
http://www.maineaudubon.org

Maine Audubon works to conserve Maine's wildlife and wildlife habitat by engaging people of all ages in education, conservation and action.
Founded: 1843
Elyse Tipton, Communications Director
Kevin Karley, Executive Director

973 Maine Coast Heritage Trust
1 Bowdoin Mill Island 207-729-7366
Suite 201 Fax: 207-729-6863
Topsham, ME 04086 E-mail: info@mcht.org
http://www.mcht.org
Conserves and stewards Maine's coastal lands and islands for their renowned scenic beauty, outdoor recreational opportunities, ecological diversity and working landscapes.
Founded: 1970
Tim Glidden, President
Karin Marchetti Ponte, General Counsel

974 Sierra Club
44 Oak Street 207-761-5616
Suite 301 Fax: 207-773-6690
Portland, ME 04101-3936 E-mail: maine.chapter@sierraclub.org
http://maine.sierraclub.org
Becky Bartovic, Co-Chair
Joan Saxe, Co-Chair

975 Small Woodland Owners Association of Maine
153 Hospital Street 207-626-0005
PO Box 836 877-467-9626
Augusta, ME 04332-836 E-mail: info@swoam.org
http://www.swoam.org
Promoting sound forest management and strengthening long-term woodland stewardship.
Founded: 1975
Thomas C. Doak, Executive Director
Debra L. Ladd, Administrative Assistant

Massachusetts

976 Alternatives for Community and Environment
2181 Washington St 617-442-3343
Suite 301 Fax: 617-442-2425
Roxbury, MA 02119 E-mail: info@ace-ej.org
http://www.ace-ej.org
Builds the power of communities of color and lower income communities in New England to eradicate environmental racism and classism and achieve environmental justice. We believe that everyone has the right to a healthy environment andto be decision-makers in issues affecting our communities.
Founded: 1994
Kalila Barnett, Executive Director
Eugene B Benson, Prog. Director/Legal Counsel

977 Association for Environmental Health and Sciences
150 Fearing Street 413-549-5170
Amherst, MA 01002 Fax: 413-549-0579
E-mail: info@AEHS.com
http://www.aehs.com

The AEHS was created to facilitate communication and foster cooperation among professionals concerned with the challenge of soil protection and cleanup. Members represent the many disciplines involved in making decisions and solving problems affecting soils. AEHS recognizes that widely acceptable solutions to the problem can be found only through the integration of scientific and technological discovery, social and political judgement and hands on practice.
Paul Kostecki PhD, Executive Director
Cindy Langlois, Managing Director

978 Boston Society of Landscape Architects
19 Harrison Street 508-620-5018
Framingham, MA 01702 Fax: 508-879-4892
E-mail: ChapterOffice@BSLAweb.org
http://www.bslaweb.org

The Boston Chapter of the American Society of Landscape Architects (ASLA). It consists of landscape architects in the states of Massachusetts, New Hampshire and Maine.
Kathleen Ogden, President
Tim Nickerson, President Elect

979 Earthwatch Institute
114 Western Ave 978-461-0081
Boston, MA 02134 800-776-0188
Fax: 978-461-2332
E-mail: info@earthwatch.org
http://www.earthwatch.org
Earthwatch is a diverse community of scientists, educators, students, businesspeople, and resolute explorers who work together to get the fullest benefit from scientific expeditions. In addition to 150 dedicated staff in the United States, England, Australia, and Japan, Earthwatch supports more than 130 scientists each year and builds networks of hundreds of students and teachers.
Founded: 1971
Whitney L Johnson, Chairman
Ruth C Scheer, Vice Chairman

980 Environmental League of Massachusetts
14 Beacon Street 617-742-2553
Suite 714 Fax: 617-742-9656
Boston, MA 02108 E-mail: info@environmentalleague.org
http://www.environmentalleague.org
Dedicated to protecting the air, water, and land for the people of the commonwealth. We do this by voicing citizens' concerns, ed-

ucating the public, advocating for strong environmental laws, and ensuring that our laws are implemented and enforced.
Founded: 1898
George Bachrach, President
Eileen Mullen, Office Manager

981 Ethnobotany Specialist Group
Oxford Street
Cambridge, MA 02138
617-495-2326
Fax: 617-495-5667

982 Genesis Fund/National Birth Defects Center
1347 Main Street
2nd Floor
Waltham, MA 02451
781-890-4282
800-322-5014
Fax: 781-487-2361
E-mail: nbdc@thegenesisfund.org
http://www.thegenesisfund.org
The National Birth Defects Center provides diagnosis and treatment to children born with birth defects, genetic diseases and mental retardation. The Center consists of physicians and consultants in pediatrics, genetics, orthopedics, cardiology, neurology, ophthalmology, endocrinology, cranial facial surgery, plastic surgery, and other specialties.
Founded: 1984
Erica D'Agostino, Executive Director
Caroline Hobbs, VP, Administration

983 MASSPIRG
44 Winter Street, 4th Floor
Boston, MA 02108
617-292-4800
Fax: 617-292-8057
E-mail: www.masspirg/about-us/contact-us
http://www.masspirg.org
MASSPIRG is an advocate for the public interest. When consumers are cheated or the voices of ordinary citizens are drowned out by special interest lobbyists, MASSPIRG speaks up and takes action. We uncover threats to public health and well-being and fight to end them, using time-tested tool of investigative research, media exposes, grassroots organizing, advocacy and litigations. Their mission is to deliver persistent, result-oriented public interest activism.

984 Massachusetts Association of Conservation Districts
319 Littleton Road
Suite 205
Westford, MA 01886
978-692-9395
Fax: 978-392-1305
http://www.middlesexconservation.org
Founded: 1947
Frances Gillespie, Plant Sale Coordinator
Elizabeth McGuire, Administrator

985 Massachusetts Association of Conservation Commissions
10 Juniper Road
Belmont, MA 02478
617-489-3930
Fax: 617-489-3935
E-mail: staff@maccweb.org
http://www.maccweb.org
We educate and advocate on behalf of all 351 Conservation Commissions in Massachusetts. We also host the MACC Annual Environment Conference, the largest such event in New England, with over 40 workshops and nearly 50 exhibitors on the first Saturday of March at the College of the Holy Cross in Worcester.
Founded: 1961
Eugene Benson, Executive Director
Michele Girard, Associate Director

986 Massachusetts Audubon Society
208 S Great Road
Lincoln, MA 01773
781-259-9500
800-AUD-UBON
E-mail: webmaster@massaudubon.org
http://www.massaudubon.org
Works to protect the nature of Massachusetts for people and wildlife. Together with more than 100,000 members, we care for 32,000 acres of conservation land, provide educational programs for 200,000 children and adults annually, andadvocate for sound environmental policies at local, state, and federal levels.
Founded: 1896
Laura A Johnson, President

987 Massachusetts Environmental Education Society
290 Turnpike Road
PO Box 105
Westboro, MA 01581
508-792-7270
Fax: 508-792-7275
E-mail: admin@mees.org
http://www.mees.org
Dedicated to the promotion, preservation and improvement of environmental education in the State of Massachusetts. A non-profit organization whose members include classroom teachers, environmental educators, outdoor leaders,naturalists and administrators committed to encouraging education and awareness of the inter-relationship of the natural world, and re-establishing the balance between nature and people.
Founded: 1977
Amy Nelson, President

988 Massachusetts Forest Landowners Association
249 Lakeside Ave
Marlborough, MA 01752-4503
617-455-9918
E-mail: massforests@verizon.net
http://www.massforests.org
MFLA's mission is to be exemplary stewards of our forest resources, and help others understand, respect, care for, and use this renewable resource. The only statewide, non-profit organization with an exclusive focus on the forests and trees of Massachusetts. Focuses on positive, constructive ways of improving and ensuring the health, care, and use of the trees, forests and associated resources of the state for generations to come.
Founded: 1970
Jeffrey D. Hutchins, Executive Director
Gregory Cox, Program Director

989 Massachusetts Trapper's Association
277 Main Street
Spencer, MA 01562
508-868-8896
E-mail: flat.tail@verizon.net
http://www.masstrappers.org
An organization founded for the purpose of preserving the tradition of fur harvesting, while promoting education and perseverance into the future. Today, the Association's focus is to maintain our trapping priviledges, regain those that have been lost, and to encourage and promote education of trappers, seasoned and inexperienced, as well as those unfamiliar with our sport.
Malcolm Spencer, President

990 Massachusetts Water Pollution Control Association
PO Box 60
Rochdale, MA 01542
774-276-9722
Fax: 774-670-9956
E-mail: mwpca2011@yahoo.com
http://www.mwpca.org
John Connor, Secretary/Treasurer

991 Mount Grace Land Conservation Trust
1461 Old Keene Road
Athol, MA 01331
978-248-2043
Fax: 978-248-2053
E-mail: landtrust@mountgrace.org
http://www.mountgrace.org
Protects significant natural, agricultural, and scenic areas and encourages land stewardship in N Central Massachusetts for the benefit of the environment, the economy, and future generations. Mount Grace has protected over 11,000acres of land. We currently own 1,270 acres of land and we hold conservation restrictions on 2,164 acres.
Founded: 1986
Leigh Youngblood, Executive Director
David Graham Wolf, Deputy Director

992 National Association of School Nurses
1100 Wayne Ave
Suite 925
Silver Spring, MA 20910
240-821-1130
866-627-6767
Fax: 301-585-1791
E-mail: nasn@nasn.org
http://www.nasn.org
The mission of The National Association of School Nurses is to advance the practice of school nursing and provide leadership in the delivery of quality health programs to school communities.
Founded: 1979
Linda Davis Alldritt, President
Carolyn Duff, President Elect

993 **New England Water Environment Association**
10 Tower Office Park — 781-939-0908
Suite 601 — Fax: 781-939-0907
Woburn, MA 01801-2155 — E-mail: mail@newea.org
http://www.newea.org

A not-for-profit organization whose objective is the advancement of fundamental knowledge and technology of design, construction, operation and management of waste treatment works and other water pollution contral activities anddedication to the preservation of water quality and water resources.
Founded: 1929
Elizabeth Cutone, Executive Director
Linda Austin, Office Manager

994 **Northeast Sustainable Energy Association**
50 Miles Street — 413-774-6051
Greenfield, MA 01301 — Fax: 413-774-6053
E-mail: nesea@nesea.org
http://www.nesea.org

NESEA is a leading regional membership organization focused on promoting the understanding, development, and adoption of energy conservation and non-polluting renewable energy technologies. It works to bring clean electricity, green transportation, and healthy, efficient buildings into everyday use.
Founded: 1974
Jennifer Marrapese, Executive Director
Mary Biddle, Deputy Executive Director

995 **Save the Harbor/Save the Bay**
Boston Fish Pier — 617-451-2860
212 Northern Ave, Suite 304 W — Fax: 617-451-0496
Boston, MA 02210 — http://www.savetheharbor.org

Mission is to restore and protect the harbor and the bay, and to reconnect them with Bostonians from every neighborhood, regional residents and visitors alike, so that we can all enjoy the benefits of the enormous public and private investment in our revitalized harbo and waterfront.
Founded: 1986
Patricia Foley, President
Matt Wolfe, VIce President

996 **Sierra Club**
10 Milk Street — 617-423-5775
Suite 632 — Fax: 617-423-5858
Boston, MA 02108-4621 — E-mail: office@sierraclubmass.org
http://www.sierraclubmass.org

James Bryan McCaffrey, Director
Alexander Oster, Administrator

997 **Walden Pond Advisory Committee**
Page Road — 781-259-9544
Lincoln, MA 01773 — http://www.concordnet.org
Founded: 1975

998 **Walden Woods Project**
44 Baker Farm Rd — 781-259-4700
Lincoln, MA 01773-3004 — 800-554-3569
Fax: 781-259-4710
E-mail: wwproject@walden.org
http://www.walden.org
Founded: 1990

Maryland

999 **Alliance for the Chesapeake Bay: Baltimore Office**
6600 York Road — 410-377-6270
Suite 100 — Fax: 410-377-7144
Baltimore, MD 21212 — E-mail: mail@acb-online.org
http://www.acb-online.org

A regional nonprofit organization that builds and fosters partnerships to protect and to restore the Bay and its rivers. The Alliance develops methods and tools for restoration activities and trains citizens to use them. Also mobilizes decision-makers, stakeholders, and other citizens to learn about Bay issues and participate in resolving them. Provides analysis, information and evaluation of Bay policies, proposals, and institutions.
Founded: 1971
David Bancroft, President
Darlin Hicks, Finance Director

1000 **American Fisheries Society: Equal Opportunities**
5410 Grosvenor Lane — 301-897-8616
Bethesda, MD 20814 — Fax: 301-897-8096
E-mail: feuker@fisheries.org
http://www.fisheries.org

The section of the American Fisheries Society promotes the representation and involvement of diverse ethnic, racial and cultural groups and women in the fisheries profession. The group fosters mentoring of under-represented groups, administers awards for travel and academic achievement and provides information on social and professional diversity in fisheries.
Gus Rassam, Executive Director
Shawn Johnston, Administrative Coordinator

1001 **American Lung Association of Maryland**
211 East Lombard Street — 443-451-4950
Suite 260 — 800-642-1184
Baltimore, MD 21202 — Fax: 410-560-0829
E-mail: lungmd@lungusa.org
http://www.lungmaryland.org

Founded as the Maryland Tuberculosis Association, and although the focus of the Association has changed since a cure for TB was found, we remain constant in working toward the mission - to prevent lung disease and promote lung health.
Founded: 1919
Stephen Peregoy, President/CEO

1002 **American Society of Landscape Architects: Maryland Chapter**
PO Box 4825 — http://www.mdasla.org
Baltimore, MD 21211

The professoinal assocation ofr landscape architects in Maryland. Promotes the landscape architecture profession and advances the practice through advocacy, education, communication, and fellowship.
Founded: 1972 — 370 Members
Colleen Bathon, President
Naomi Reetz, Executive Director

1003 **Audubon Naturalist Society of the Central Atlantic States**
8940 Jones Mill Road — 301-652-9188
Chevy Chase, MD 20815 — Fax: 301-951-7179
E-mail: contact@audubonnaturalist.org
http://www.audubonnaturalist.org

Fosters stewardship of the region's environment by educating citizens about the natural world, promoting conservation of biodiversity, and protecting wildlife habitat. The independent nonprofit society focuses its efforts in the mid-Atlantic region.
Founded: 1897
Neal Fitzpatrick, Executive Director
Lisa Alexander, Deputy Director

1004 **Center for Chesapeake Communities**
192 Duke Of Gloucester Street — 410-267-8595
Annapolis, MD 21401 — Fax: 410-267-8597
http://www.chesapeakecommunities.org

Technical assistance on environmental, land use, energy and water quality issues for local government in Chesapeake Bay Watershed.
Gary Allen, Executive Director

1005 **Chesapeake Bay Foundation**
Save The Bay Maryland Office
Philip Merrill Environmental Center — 410-268-8816
6 Herndon Avenue — 888-728-3229
Annapolis, MD 21403 — Fax: 410-268-6687
E-mail: chesapeake@cbf.org
http://www.cbf.org

Fights for strong and effective laws and regulations. CBF also works cooperatively with government, business, and citizens in partnerships to protect and restore the Bay. Their mission is: Save

the Bay, defined as achieving a HealthIndex for the Bay of 70 by the year 2050.
Founded: 1966
William C Baker, President
Fay R. Nance, CFO

1006 **Chesapeake Wildlife Heritage**
Chesapeake Wildlife Heritage 410-822-5100
PO Box 1745 Fax: 410-822-4016
Easton, MD 21601 E-mail: info@cheswildlife.org
http://www.cheswildlife.org
Dedicated to creating, restoring and protecting wildlife habitat and establishing a more sustainable agriculture through direct action, education and research in partnership with private landowners.
Founded: 1980
Ned Gerber, Executive Director
Chris Pupke, Development Director

1007 **Eastern Shore Land Conservancy**
PO Box 169 410-827-9756
Queenstown, MD 21658 Fax: 410-827-5765
E-mail: info@eslc.org
http://www.eslc.org
Mission is to sustain the Eastern Shore's rich landscapes through strategic land conservation and cound land use planning.
Founded: 1990
Robert J Etgen, Executive Director

1008 **Environmental Health Education Center**
University of Maryland, School of Nursing
655 W Lombard Street 410-706-1849
Room 665 Fax: 410-706-0295
Baltimore, MD 21201 E-mail: cehn@cehn.org
http://www.cehn.org/environmental_health_education_center
The overall mission of the Center is to engage in research and provide training and education programs on topics related to occupational and environmental health and safety. Our focus is broad and the workplace, community and home areall included in our defination of environment. The audiences for our training and education programs include professionals, labor, and industry and community members. Through our efforts we hope to prevent occupation and/or environment related injuriesand illnesses.
Nsedu Obot Witherspoon, Executive Director
Joanne Perodin, Program Manager

1009 **Institute of Hazardous Materials Management**
11900 Parklawn Drive 301-984-8969
Suite 450 Fax: 301-984-1516
Rockville, MD 20852 E-mail: info@ihmm.org
http://www.ihmm.org
Mission is to provide recognition for professionals engaged in the management and engineering control of hazardous materials who have attained the required level of education, experience and competence; foster continued professionaldevelopment of Certified Hazardous Materials Managers (CHMM).
Founded: 1984
Jeffrey H. Greenwald, Executive Director
S. Chrissy Warner, Communications Director

1010 **Izaak Walton League of America**
707 Conservation Lane 301-548-0150
Gaithersburg, MD 20878 E-mail: info@iwla.org
http://www.iwla.org
One of the nation's oldest and most respected conservation organizations. With a powerful grassroots network of nearly 300 local chapters nationwide, the League takes a common-sense approach toward protecting our country's nautralheritage and improving outdoor recreation opportunities for all Americans.
Founded: 1922
Scott Kovarovics, Executive Director
Marybeth Garrett, Administrative Assistant

1011 **Maryland Association of Soil Conservation Districts**
53 Slama Road 410-956-5771
Edgewater, MD 21037-1423 Fax: 410-956-0161
E-mail: lynnehoot@aol.com
http://www.mascd.net
Founded: 1956
R Calvert Steuart, President
Marguerite Guare, Office Secretary

1012 **Maryland BASS Chapter Federation**
PO Box 3620 301-842-3200
Baltimore, MD 21214 E-mail: web@mdbass.com
http://www.mdbass.com
Roger Trageser, President
Dick Brown, 1st Vice President

1013 **Maryland Native Plant Society**
PO Box 4877 E-mail: info@mdflora.org
Silver Spring, MD 20914 http://www.mdflora.org
Promote awareness, appreciation, and conservation of Maryland's native plants and their habitats.
Founded: 1992
Kirsten Johnson, President
Carolyn Fulton, Secretary

1014 **Maryland Recyclers Coalition**
c/o Mariner Management 888-496-3196
PO Box 1046 Fax: 301-238-4579
Laurel, MD 20725 E-mail: info@marylandrecyclers.org
http://www.marylandrecyclers.org
Mission is to promote sustainable reduction, reuse and recycling of materials otherwise destined for disposal and promote and increase buying products made with recycled material content. Seeks to accomplish this mission through a combination of education programs, advocacy activities to affect public policy, technical assistance efforts, and the development of markets to purchase recycled materials and manufacture products with recycled content.
Virginia Lipscomb, Vice President
Brian Ryerson, President

1015 **Multiple Chemical Sensitivity Referral and Resources**
508 Westgate Road 410-362-6400
Baltimore, MD 21229 Fax: 410-448-3317
E-mail: adonnay@mcsrr.org
http://www.mcsrr.org
A non-profit organization engaged in professional outreach, patient support and public advocacy devoted to the diagnosis, treatment, accommodation and prevention of Multiple Chemical Sensitivity disorders.
Founded: 1994
Albert Donnay MHS, Co-Founder/Executive Directo

1016 **Nature Conservancy: Maryland/DC Chapter**
5410 Grosvenor Lane 301-897-8570
Suite 100 800-628-6860
Bethesda, MD 20814 Fax: 301-897-0858
E-mail: egray@tnc.org
http://www.tnc.org
To preserve the plants, animals and natural communities that represent the diversity of life on Earth by protecting the lands and waters they need to survive.
Founded: 1950
Elizabeth Gray, Executive Director
Lindsay Renick Mayer, Media Relations Contact

1017 **Potomac Region Solar Energy Association**
PO Box 27 301-880-7045
Harwood, MD 20776 866-477-5369
E-mail: contact@mases.us
http://www.prsea.org
A non-profit organization whose purposes are to further the development, use of, and support for solar energy and related arts, sciences, and technologies with concern for the economic, environmental, and social fabric of the region.
John Essig, Chair
Matthew Stewart, Vice Chair

1018 **Rachel Carson Council**
PO Box 10779
Silver Spring, MD 20914
301-593-7507
E-mail: rccouncil@aol.com
http://www.rachelcarsoncouncil.com
An association for the integrity of the environment, seeks to inform and advise the public about the effects of pesticides that threaten the health, welfare, and survival of living organisms and biological systems.
Founded: 1965
Diana Post, Executive Director

1019 **Sierra Club**
7338 Baltimore Avenue
Suite 101A
College Park, MD 20740
301-277-7111
Fax: 301-277-6699
E-mail: josh.tulkin@sierraclub.org
http://maryland.sierraclub.org
A grassroots environmental organization which promotes appreciation of nature with hikes and outtings. We work to protect the environment in Maryland through legislative and grassroots organizing efforts.
Founded: 1865
Michael Martin, Chair
Ron Henry, Vice Chair

1020 **White Lung Association**
PO Box 1483
Baltimore, MD 21203
410-243-5864
Fax: 410-254-4602
E-mail: jfite@whitelung.org
http://www.whitelung.org
National nonprofit organization dedicated to the education of the public to the hazards of asbestos exposure. Has developed programs of public education and consults with victims of asbestos exposure, school boards, building owners,government agencies and others interested in identifying asbestos hazards and developing control programs.
James Fite, Executive Director

1021 **Wildfowl Trust of North America**
600 Discovery Lane
PO Box 519
Grasonville, MD 21638
410-827-6694
E-mail: info@bayrestoration.org
http://www.bayrestoration.org
Mission is to be responsible and protactive environmentally. We strive to improve the health of the Chesapeake Bay. Specifically, we promote environmental stewardship at the 510-acre site, the Chesapeake Bay Environmental Center, through education, restoration and conservation.
Founded: 1979
Judy Wink, Executive Director
Vicki Paulas, Assistant Director

1022 **Wildlife Society**
5410 Grosvenor Lane
Suite 200
Bethesda, MD 20814
301-897-9770
Fax: 301-530-2471
E-mail: tws@wildlife.org
http://www.wildlife.org
An international, non-profit scientific and educational organization serving and representing wildlife professionals in all areas of wildlife conservation and resource management. Our goal is to promote excellence in wildlifestewardship through science and education.
Founded: 1937
Ken Williams, Executive Director
Yanin Walker, Operations Director

Michigan

1023 **American Lung Association of Michigan**
American Lung Association
1475 E 12 Mile Road
Madison Heights, MI 48071
248-784-2000
800-543-5864
Fax: 248-784-2008
E-mail: midland@midland.org
http://www.alam.org
Founded: 1904
Ray Maloni, Interim CEO

1024 **American Lung Association of Michigan: Capital Region Office**
American Lung Association
403 Seymour Avenue
Lansing, MI 48933
517-484-4541
800-678-5864
Fax: 517-484-2118
E-mail: alam@alam.org
http://www.alam.org
Serves the Counties of: Clare, Clinton, Eaton, Gratiot, Hillsdale, Ingham, Ionia, Isabella, Jackson, Lenawee, Mecosta, Montcalm and Osceola.
Founded: 1904
Kevin M Chan, Managing Director
Stephen D Moore, President

1025 **American Lung Association of Michigan: Grand Valley Region**
c/o Wege Center for Health and Learning
300 Lafayette Street SE
Suite 3400
Grand Rapids, MI 49503
616-752-5051
Fax: 616-752-6972
Serves the Counties of: Allegan, Barry, Berrien, Branch, Calhoun, Cass, Kalamazoo, Kent, Muskegon, Newago, Oceana, Ottowa, St. Joseph and Van Buren.

1026 **American Society of Landscape Architects: Michigan Chapter**
1000 W St Joseph Highway
Suite 200
Lansing, MI 48915
517-485-4116
Fax: 517-485-9408
E-mail: manager@michiganasla.org
http://www.michiganasla.org
Founded: 1899
Mark Robinson, President
Sulin Kotowicz, President Elect

1027 **Association of Midwest Fish and Wildlife Agencies**
PO Box 30028
Lansing, MI 48909
517-373-1263
Fax: 517-373-6705
http://www.mafwa.org
Founded: 1934
Jon Gassett, President
Becky Humphries, Director-at-Large

1028 **Ecology Center of Ann Arbor**
339 E Liberty
Suite 300
Ann Arbor, MI 48104
734-761-3186
Fax: 734-663-2414
E-mail: info@ecocenter.org
http://www.ecocenter.org
A member-based, nonprofit environmental organization that is now a regional leader that works for a safe and healthly environment where people live, work, and play.
Founded: 1970
Mike Garfield, Director
Terry Gallagher, Communications Director

1029 **Great Lakes Commission**
Eisenhower Corporate Park
2805 S Industrial Highway
Suite 100
Ann Arbor, MI 48104-6791
734-971-9135
Fax: 734-971-9150
E-mail: landrews@glc.org
http://www.glc.org
A bi-national public agency dedicated to the use, management and protection of the water, land and other natural resources of the Great Lakes-St Lawrence system.
Founded: 1955
Tim A Eder, Executive Director

1030 **Great Lakes Renewable Energy Association**
PO Box 714
East Lansing, MI 48826
517-646-6269
Fax: 517-646-8584
E-mail: info@glrea.org
http://www.glrea.org
A non-profit organization that educates, advocates, promotes, and publicly demonstrates renewable energy technologies.
John Saver, Executive Director
Mary McGraw, Treasurer

1031 Home Chemical Awareness Coalition
Michigab State University
Natural Resource Building
E Lansing, MI 48824
517-355-9578
Fax: 517-353-8994
Cynthia Frigden, Chairperson

1032 Michigan Association of Conservation Districts
3001 Coolidge Road
Suite 250
East Lansing, MI 48823
517-324-4421
Fax: 517-324-4435
E-mail: lori.phalen@macd.org
http://www.macd.org

A non-governmental, non-profit organization, established to represent and provide services to Michigan's 80 Conservation Districts.
Lori Phalen, Executive Director

1033 Michigan BASS Chapter Federation
1010 S W Avenue
Jackson, MI 49203
517-789-1008
Fax: 517-789-5603
E-mail: psacks@michiganbass.net
http://www.michiganbass.org

Paul Sacks, President

1034 Michigan Forest Association
6120 S Clinton Trail
Eaton Rapids, MI 48827
517-663-3423
E-mail: miforest@acd.net
http://www.michiganforests.com

To promote good management on all forest land, to educate our members about good forest practices and stewardship of the land, and to inform the general public about forestry issues and the benefits of good forest management.

1035 Michigan Natural Areas Council
c/o Matthaei Botanical Gardens
1800 N Dixboro Road
Ann Arbor, MI 48109
E-mail: mnac@cyberspace.org
http://www.cyberspace.org/~mnac
Founded: 1946
Phyllis Higman, Chair

1036 Michigan United Conservation Clubs
2101 Wood Street
PO Box 30235
Lansing, MI 48912
517-371-1041
Fax: 517-371-1505
http://www.mucc.org

The largest statewide conservation organization with nearly 100,000 members and more than 500 affiliated clubs. MUCC works to conserve Michigan's wildlife, fisheries, waters, forests, air, and soils by providing information, educationand advocacy.
Founded: 1937
Dennis Muchmore, Executive Director

1037 National Wildlife Federation Great Lakes Natural Resource Center
213 W Liberty
Suite 200
Ann Arbor, MI 48104
734-769-3351
Fax: 734-769-1449
E-mail: greatlakes@nwf.org
http://www.nwf.org/greatlakes

Responsible for the National Wildlife Federation's eight state Great Lakes region. The Great Lakes are of global importance but have been used as a garbage dump. The federation has scientists, lawyers, organizers and educators allcontributing their skills to make a change on the health of these freshwater seas.
Larry Schweiger, President/CEO
Jaime Matyas, Executive VP/COO

1038 Nature Conservancy: Michigan Chapter
101 E Grand River
Lansing, MI 48906
517-316-0300
Fax: 517-316-9886
E-mail: michigan@tnc.org
http://www.nature.org/michigan

The mission of The Nature Conservancy is to preserve the plants, animals and natural communities that represent the diversity of life on Earth by protecting the lands and waters they need to survive.
Founded: 1952
Helen Taylor, State Director

1039 Scenic Michigan
445 E Mitchell Street
Petoskey, MI 49770
231-347-1171
Fax: 231-347-1185
E-mail: info@scenicmichigan.org
http://www.scenicmichigan.org

An affiliate of the national non-profit organization Scenic America. Work to enhance the scenic beauty of Michigan's communities and roadsides. The principal activity is informing the public of the economic, social and culturalbenefits of highway beautification. Promotes and sponsors programs to encourage natural beauty in the environment, enhance landscapes, protect historical and cultural resources, and improve community appeareance.
Founded: 1996
Abby Dart, Executive Director
Jim Lagowski, President

1040 Sierra Club: Mackinac Chapter
109 E Grand River Avenue
Lansing, MI 48906-4348
517-484-2372
Fax: 517-484-3108
E-mail: mackinac.chapter@sierraclub.org
http://michigan.sierraclub.org

To advance the preservation and protection of the natural environment by empowering the citizenry, especially democratically-based grassroots organizations, with charitable resources to further the cause of environmental protection.
Founded: 1967
Anne Woiwode, State Director
Gail Philbin, Assistant Director

1041 Wildflower Association of Michigan
3853 Farrell Road
Hastings, MI 49058
269-948-2496
700-333-6459
Fax: 269-948-2957
E-mail: wam@iserv.net
http://www.wildflowersmich.org

A nonprofit organization whose mission is to promote, coordinate, and participate in education, enjoyment, science, and stewardship of native wildflowers and their habitats - including promoting public education of proper principles,ethics, and methods of landscaping with native wildflowers and associated habitats.
Founded: 1986
Chad Hughson, President
Trish Hacker-Hennig, 1st Vice President

1042 Wildlife Society: Michigan Chapter
Michigan State University
Department of Natural Resources
Room 13
East Lansing, MI 48824
517-353-2042
Fax: 517-432-1699
E-mail: campa@msu.edu
http://www.wildlife.org/chapters/mi/index.cfm?tname=officers

A nonprofit scientific and educational organization that serves professionals such as government agencies, academia, industry, and non-government organizations in all areas related to the conservation of wildlife and natural resources management.
Founded: 1982
Brent Rudolph, President-Elect
Scott Winterstein, President

Minnesota

1043 American Lung Association in Minnesota
490 Concordia Avenue
Saint Paul, MN 55103
651-227-8014
800-586-4872
Fax: 651-227-5459
E-mail: info@lungmn.org
http://www.lungmn.org

To save lives, improve lung health, and prevent lung disease.
Founded: 1903
Penny Fena, Executive Director
Harold Wimmer, CEO

1044 American Lung Association of Minnesota: Greater Minnesota Branch Office
424 West Superior Street
Suite 203
Duluth, MN 55802
218-726-4721
800-548-8252
Fax: 218-726-4722
E-mail: info@alamn.org
http://www.alamn.org/

To prevent lung disease and promote lung health.
Founded: 1903
Jerry Orr, Chief Executive Officer

1045 American Society of Landscape Architects: Minnesota Chapter
International Market Square
275 Market Street, Suite 54
Minneapolis, MN 55405-1627
612-339-0797
Fax: 612-338-7981
E-mail: info@asla-mn.org
http://www.asla-mn.org

Ellen Stewart, President
Tom Moua, Association Manager

1046 Institute for Agriculture and Trade Policy
2105 First Avenue S
Minneapolis, MN 55404
612-870-0453
Fax: 612-870-4846
E-mail: iatp@iatp.org
http://www.iatp.org

Promotes resilient family farms, rural communitites and ecosystems around the world through research and education, science and technology, and advocacy.
Founded: 1987
Jim Harkness, President
Emily Barker, Program Associate

1047 Minnesota Association of Soil and Water Conservation Districts
Soil and Water Conservation Districts
255 Kellogg Blvd E
Suite 101
St. Paul, MN 55101
651-690-9028
Fax: 651-690-9065
http://www.maswcd.org

MASWCD is a nonprofit organization which exists to provide leadership and a common voice for Minnesota's soil and water conservation districts and to maintain a positive, results-oriented relationship with rule making agencies,partners and legislators; expanding education opportunities for the districts so they may carry out effective conservation programs.
Founded: 1952
Ken Pederson, President
Steve Sunderland, Vice President

1048 Minnesota BASS Chapter Federation
PO Box 225
Howard Lake, MN 55349
612-339-5609
E-mail: jbarnett@mnbfn.org
http://www.mnbfn.org

Mission is to stimulate public awareness of bass fishing as a major sport; to offer our State Conservation Department, our organized and moral and political supports and encouragement, to promote full adherence to, and enforcement ofexisting conservation regulations; to promote and encourage youth fishing and teach youth the importance of Catch and Release; to improve our skills as bass anglers through a friendly exchange of ideas and techniques used in tournament fishing.
Peter Perovich, President
Mark Gomez, VP

1049 Minnesota Conservation Federation
542 Snelling Avenue S
#104
Saint Paul, MN 55116
651-690-3077
800-531-3077
Fax: 651-690-2208
E-mail: info@mncf.org
http://www.mncf.org

A common sense conservation organization made up of hunters, anglers and others who are dedicated to the enjoyment, education and ethical use of our natural resources.
Founded: 1936
Steve Maurice, President

1050 Minnesota Ground Water Association
4779 126th Street North
White Bear Lake, MN 55110
952-832-2740
Fax: 612-385-3292
E-mail: office@mgwa.org
http://www.mgwa.org

A non-profit, volunteer organization which promotes public policy and scientific education about ground water.
Founded: 2000
Robert Tipping, President
Eric Mohring, President Elect

1051 Minnesota Renewable Energy Society
2928 Fifth Avenue S
Minneapolis, MN 55408
612-308-4757
E-mail: info@mnrenewables.org
http://www.mnrenewables.org

A member-run, non-profit organzation founded to promote the use of, and to engage in advocacy for, renewable energies in Minnesota through education and through the demonstration of practical applications.
Founded: 1978
Laura Burrington, Managing Director

1052 Minnesota Wings Society
Bobwhite Quail Society of Minnesota
PO Box 11323
Minneapolis, MN 55411
612-588-2966
E-mail: wtcn.nature@att.net
http://www.nmu.edu/sbp/us_off.html

Founded: 1975
Thurman Tucker, President
Martin Hanson, Secretary

1053 Nature Conservancy: Minnesota Chapter
1101 W River Park Way
Suite 200
Minneapolis, MN 55415-1291
612-331-0750
Fax: 612-331-0770
E-mail: minnesota@tnc.org
http://www.nature.org

Aims to preserve plants, animals, and natural communities that represent the diversity of life on Earth by protecting the lands and waters they need to survive.
Founded: 1951
Steven McCormick, President/CEO

1054 Parks and Trails Council of Minnesota
275 E 4th Street
Suite 250
Saint Paul, MN 55101-1651
651-726-2457
800-944-0707
Fax: 651-726-2458
E-mail: info@parksandtrails.org
http://www.parksandtrails.org

Mission: To acquire, protect and enhance critical lands for the public's enjoyment now and in the future.
Founded: 1954
Brett Feldman, Executive Director
Jess Mann, Administrative Assistant

1055 Raptor Center
The College of Veterinary Sciences
University of Minnesota
1920 Fitch Avenue
St.Paul, MN 55108
612-624-4745
Fax: 612-624-8740
E-mail: raptor@umn.edu
http://www.raptor.cvm.umn.edu

Specializes in the medical care, rehabilitation, and conservation of eagles, hawks, owls and falcons. In addition to treating approxminately 800 birds a year, the internationally known program reaches more than 240,000 people each year through public education programs and events, provides training in avian medicine and surgery for veterinarians from around the world, and identifies emerging issues related to raptor health and populations.
Founded: 1974
Dr Julia Ponder, Executive Director

1056 Sierra Club-North Star Chapter
2327 E Franklin Avenue
Suite 1
Minneapolis, MN 55406-1024
612-659-9124
Fax: 612-659-9129
http://www.northstar.sierraclub.org

To advance the preservation and protection of the natural environment by empowering the citizenry, especially democratically based grassroots organizations, with charitable resources to fur-

ther the cause of environmental protection,the vehicle through which The Sierra Club Foundation generally fulfills its charitable mission.
Margaret Levin, State Director
Alexis Boyer, Conservation Director

Mississippi

1057 **American Lung Association of Mississippi**
PO Box 2178
Ridgeland, MS 39158
601-206-5810
800-586-4872
Fax: 601-206-5813
E-mail: inquiries@breathehealthy.org
http://www.lung.org/associations/charters/plains-gulf
To prevent lung disease and promote lung health through direct assistance, education programs, advocacy and research.
Founded: 1914
Sandra Holman, President
Robin Robinson, Vice President

1058 **American Society of Landscape Architects: Mississippi Chapter**
PO Box 55726
Jackson, MS 39296
601-898-0775
Fax: 601-898-9112
http://www.msasla.org
George Ewing III, President
Robert Mercier, President-Elect

1059 **Crosby Arboretum**
Mississippi State University
370 Ridge Road
Picayune, MS 39466
601-799-2311
Fax: 601-799-2372
E-mail: crosbyar@datastar.net
http://www.crosbyarboretum.msstate.edu
Dedicated to educating the public about their environment. This mission is carried out by preserving, protecting, and displaying plants native to the Pearl River Drainage Basin ecosystem, providing environmental and botanical research opportunities, and offering cultural, scientific, and recreational programs.
Patricia Drackett, Director
Richelle Stafne, Senior Curator/Assistant Dir

1060 **Mississippi Solar Energy Society**
211 Popes Road
Carthage, MS 39051
601-656-6161
Sammy C Germany, Contact

1061 **Mississippi Wildlife Federation**
517 Cobblestone Court
Suite 2
Madison, MS 39110-7570
601-605-1790
Fax: 601-605-1794
E-mail: cshropshire@mswf.org
http://www.mswildlife.org
Established to advance the protectin of wildlife in Mississippi
Founded: 1946
Brad Young, Executive Director
Melanie Starns, Office Manager

1062 **National Flyway Council: Mississippi Office Section of Wildlife Natural Resources**
North American Flyways
PO Box 30444
Lansing, MI 48909
517-373-1263
Fax: 517-373-6705
E-mail: humphrir@state.mi.us
http://www.npwrc.usgs.gov/info/flyway/flychair.htm
Roger Holmes, Chairman
Joshua L Sandt, Deputy Director

1063 **Sierra Club**
921 North Congress Street
Jackson, MS 39202
601-352-1026
Fax: 601-355-1506
E-mail: louie.miller@sierraclub.org
http://mississippi.sierraclub.org
The Chapter is currently involved with the air pollution concern that local residents were exposed to after Hurricane Katrina. The general mission is to advance the preservation and protection of the natural environment by empowering the citizenry, especially democratically-based grassroots organizations, with charitable resources to further the cause of environmental protection.
Michael Berk, Chairman
Rose Johnson, Vice Chair

Missouri

1064 **American Fisheries Society: North Central Division**
420 New Haven Road
Columbia, MO 65201
573-875-5399
Fax: 573-876-1896
E-mail: pamela_haverland@usgs.gov
Pamela Haverland, President

1065 **American Lung Association of Missouri**
1118 Hampton Avenue
Saint Louis, MO 63139-3196
314-645-5505
800-586-4872
Fax: 314-645-7128
E-mail: inquiries@breathehealthy.org
http://www.lung.org/associations/charters/plains-gulf
Founded: 1904

1066 **American Lung Association of Missouri: Southeast Missouri Office**
PO Box 482
Cape Girardeau, MO 63702
573-204-7552
Fax: 866-929-5682
http://www.lungusa2.org/missouri/
Founded: 1907

1067 **American Lung Association of Missouri: Kansas City Office**
6701 W 64th Street Suite 110
Cloverleaf Office Park Bldg #5
Overland Park, MO 63139
816-842-5242
Fax: 816-842-5470
E-mail: inquiries@breathehealthy.org
http://www.lungusa.org
Founded: 1904

1068 **American Lung Association of Missouri: Southwest Missouri Office**
2053-D South Waverly
Springfield, MO 65804
417-883-7177
Fax: 417-883-7026
http://www.lungusa2.org/missouri
Founded: 1907

1069 **American Society of Landscape Architects: Prairie Gateway Chapter**
104 W 9th Street
Suite 101
Kansas City, MO 64105
816-421-1054
http://www.pgasla.org
Represents membership from the states of Kansas and Missouri. The purpose is to promote the profession of landscape architecture and advancement of the practice through advocacy, education, communication, and fellowship.
Cale Doornbos, President
David Contag, President-Elect

1070 **American Society of Landscape Architects: St Louis Chapter**
PO Box 11594
Clayton, MO 63105
314-206-4313
E-mail: exdir@stlouisasla.org
http://www.stlouisasla.org
Represents the eastern half of Missouri and is responsible for the promotion and legislation of the landscape architect profession in the St Louis region.
Elizabeth Graff, Executive Director

1071 **Missouri Audubon Council**
301 Riverlands Way
West Alton, MO 63386
636-899-0090
Fax: 636-899-2655
E-mail: missouri@audubon.org
http://http://mo.audubon.org

To conserve and restore natural ecosystems, focusing on birds and other wildlife, and their habitats for the benfit of humanity and the earth's biological diversity.
Founded: 1990
Patricia Hagen, Executive Director/VP
Debra McStay, Operations Director

1072 Missouri Forest Products Association
611 E Capitol Ave 573-634-3252
Jefferson City, MO 65101 Fax: 573-636-2591
E-mail: moforest@moforest.org
http://www.moforest.org
Brings together timberland owners, forest products companies, state agencies, and professional foresters to promote good forest stewardship throughout the state. A membership organization that works together to educate and assistprimary and secondary wood processors, and timberland owners through programs, educational opportunities, publications, and membership benefits.
Brian Brookshire, Executive Director
Tammy Homefeldt, Communications Manager

1073 Missouri Prairie Foundation
PO Box 200 579-356-7828
Columbia, MO 65205 888-843-6739
Fax: 573-442-0260
E-mail: missouriprairie@yahoo.com
http://www.moprairie.org
Works with public and private partners to protect and restore our prairie and native grassland communities through land acquisition, management, education and research.
Founded: 1966
John Wingo, President
Dorris Sherrick, VP

1074 Missouri Public Interest Research Group
10 S Euclid Ave 314-454-1713
Suite H Fax: 314-454-0787
Saint Louis, MO 63108 E-mail: info@mopirg.org
http://www.mopirg.org
To deliver persistent, result-oriented public interest activism that protects our environment, encourages a fair, sustainable economy, and fosters responsive, democratic government.
Founded: 1972
Steve Blackledge, Deputy Director
Ed Mierzwinski, Consumer Program Director

1075 Missouri Stream Team: Missouri Department of Conservation
728 W Main 800-781-1989
Jefferson City, MO 65101 E-mail: streamteam@mdc.mo.gov
http://www.mostreamteams.org
A working partnership of citizens who are concerned about Missouri Stream. The Stream Team Program Provides an opportunity for all interested to get involved in river conservation.
Sherry Fischer, Supervisor, Stream Services

1076 Rocky Mountain Elk Foundation
5705 Grant Creek 406-523-4500
Missoula, MT 59808 800-225-5355
http://www.rmef.org
Committed to conserving, restoring and enhancing natural habitats; promoting the sound management of wild, free-ranging elk, which may be hunted orotherwise enjoyed; fostering cooperation among federal, state, tribal and privateorganization and individuals in wildlife management and habitat conservation; and educating members and the public about habitat conservation, the value of hunting, hunting ethics and wildlife management.
Founded: 1984 155,000 Members
M David Allen, President/CEO
Rod Triepke, COO

1077 Safety Council of the Ozarks
1111 South Glenstone 417-869-2121
Springfield, MO 65804 800-334-1349
Fax: 417-869-2133
E-mail: dbiggs@nscoazarks.org
http://www.nscozarks.org
Dedicated to interpreting current safety & health issues and developing practical, cost effective, methodologies based on best practices for protecting human life, property and the environment.
Debora S Biggs, Executive Director
Jane Whillock, Office Manager

1078 Scenic Missouri
3963 Wyoming Street 314-265-5328
St Louis, MO 63116 E-mail: info@scenicmissouri.org
http://www.scenicmissouri.org
To preserve and enhance the scenic beauty of Missouri
John Regenbogen, Executive Director

1079 Sierra Club
7164 Manchester Avenue 314-644-1011
Maplewood, MO 63143 800-628-5333
E-mail: missouri.chapter@sierraclub.org
http://missouri.sierraclub.org
Jim Turner, Chair
Henry Robertson, Vice Chair

1080 Society for Environmental Geochemistry and Health
1870 Miner Circle 573-341-4831
Rolla, MO 65409 Fax: 303-556-4822
http://www.segh.net
Established to provide a forum for scientists from various disciplines to work together in understanding the interaction between the geochemical environment and the health of plants, animals, and humans.
Founded: 1971
Xiangdong Li, President

Montana

1081 American Lung Association of the Northern Rockies
825 Helena Avenue 406-442-6556
Helena, MT 59601-3459 Fax: 406-442-2346
E-mail: ala-nr@ala-nr.org
http://www.ala-nr.org

1082 Chemical Injury Information Network
PO Box 301 406-547-2255
White Sulphur Springs, MT 59645 Fax: 406-547-2455
http://www.ciin.org
A support and advocacy organization dealing with Multiple Chemical Sensitivities. It is run by the chemically injured for the benefit of the chemically injured, crediable research into MCS, and the empowerment of the chemicallyinjured.
Founded: 1990
Cinthia Wilson, Executive Director
John Wilson, President

1083 Craighead Environmental Research Institute
201 S Wallace Avenue 405-585-8705
Suite B2D Fax: 406-587-5951
Bozeman, MT 59715 E-mail: info@craigheadresearch.org
http://craigheadresearch.org
A network of biologists dedicated to providing reliable information, through innovative research and state-of-the-art conservation planning, to foster ecologically sound management of wildlife and their habitats. CERI focuses its efforts in the Yellowstone-to-Yukon and Coastal Rainforest regions of North America
Lance Craighead, Executive Director
Jonquil Nelson, Development Director

1084 Craighead Wildlife: Wetlands Institute
5200 Upper Miller Creek Road 406-251-3867
Missoula, MT 59803 Fax: 406-251-5069
http://www.grizzlybear.org
John A Mitchell PhD, Director

1085 **Foundation for Research on Economics and the Environment (FREE)**
662 Ferguson Avenue
Suite 2
Bozeman, MT 59718
406-585-1776
Fax: 406-585-3000
http://www.free-eco.org
FREE mission is to advance conservation and environmental values consistent with individuals freedom and responsibility. The Foundation's intellectual entrepreneurs develop environmental policies featuring private property rights, market incentives, and voluntary organizations. FREE achieves its mission by working with leaders in universities, businesses, environmental groups, government, the media, and think tanks.
John A. Baden, Chairman

1086 **Greater Yellowstone Coalition**
215 S Wallace
Bozeman, MT 59715
406-586-1593
800-775-1834
Fax: 406-556-2839
E-mail: gyc@greateryellowstone.org
http://www.greateryellowstone.org
People protecting the lands, waters, and wildlife of the Greater Yellowstone Ecosystem, now and for future generations.
Founded: 1983
Caroline Byrd, Executive Director
Jeff Welsch, Communications Director

1087 **Montana Association of Conservation Districts**
1101 11th Ave
Helena, MT 59601
406-443-5711
Fax: 406-443-0174
E-mail: mail@macdnet.org
http://www.macdnet.org
Montana's 58 Conservation Districts utilize locally-led and largely non-regulatory approaches to successfully address general natural resource issues. CD's have a decades-long history of conserving our state's resources by helping local people match their needs with technical and financial resources, thereby getting good conservation practices on the ground to benefit all of Montanans.
Sarah Carlson, Executive Director

1088 **Montana Audubon**
PO Box 595
Helena, MT 59624
406-443-3949
Fax: 406-443-7144
E-mail: mtaudubon@mtaudubon.org
http://www.mtaudubon.org
Promotes appreciation, knowledge and conservation of native birds, other wildlife, and their habitats.
Founded: 1976
Steve Hoffman, Executive Director
Norane Freistandt, Development Director

1089 **Montana Environmental Information Center**
107 W Lawrence St
#N-6
Helena, MT 59601
406-443-2520
Fax: 406-443-2507
E-mail: meic@meic.org
http://www.meic.org
MEIC's purpose is to protect and restore Montana's natural environment. It works to do this by: monitoring and influencing the decisions and activities of the state, local and federal governments; educating individuals and by assisting individuals and other nonprofit organizations.
Jim Jensen, Executive Director
Anne Hedges, Program Director

1090 **Montana Land Reliance**
324 Fuller Avenue
PO Box 355
Helena, MT 59624-355
406-443-7027
Fax: 406-443-7061
E-mail: info@mtlandreliance.org
http://www.mtlandreliance.org
Montana's only private, statewide land trust, an apolitical, nonprofit corporation. Our mission is to provide permanent protection for private lands that are ecologically significant for agricultural production, fish and wildlifehabitat and scenic open space.
Lois Delger-DeMars, Operations Manager
Doug Mitchell, Managing Director

1091 **Montana Water Environment Association**
516 N Park Street
Suite A
Helena, MT 59601
406-449-7913
Fax: 406-449-6350

1092 **Montana Wildlife Federation**
5530 North Montana Ave
Helena, MT 59601
404-458-0227
800-517-7256
Fax: 403-458-0373
E-mail: mwf@mtwf.org
http://www.montanawildlife.com
An organization of conservation minded people who share a mission to protect and enhance Montana's piblic wildlife, lands, waters and fair chase hunting and fishing heritage.
Skip Kowalski, President
Joe Perry, Treasurer

1093 **Rocky Mountain Elk Foundation**
5705 Grant Creek
Missoula, MT 59808
406-523-4500
800-225-5355
http://www.rmef.org
Committed to conserving, restoring and enhancing natural habitats; promoting the sound management of wild, free-ranging elk, which may be hunted or otherwise enjoyed; fostering cooperation among federal, state, tribal and private organizations and individuals in wildlife management and habitat conservation; and educating members and the public about habitat conservation, the value of hunting, hunting ethics and wildlife management.
155,000 Members
M David Allen, President/CEO
Rod Triepke, COO

1094 **Sierra Club**
PO Box 1290
Bozeman, MT 59771
406-582-8365
Fax: 408-582-9417
http://montana.sierraclub.org
To advance the preservation and protection of the natural environment by empowering the citizenry, especially democratically-based grassroots organizations, with charitable resources to further the cause of environmental protection. The vehicle through which The Sierra Club Foundation generally fulfills its charitable mission.
Jeff van den Noort, Chair
Ron Mueller, Vice Chair

1095 **Wildlife Society**
3630 Columbus
Butte, MT 59701
406-533-3445
Fax: 406-533-3600
E-mail: montanatws@montanatws.org
http://www.montanatws.org
A nonprofit scientific and educational organization that serves professionals such as government agencies, academia, industry, and non-government organizations in all areas related to the conservation of wildlife and natural resources management.
Founded: 1937
Brian Logan, President
Tom Carlsen, President Elect

Nebraska

1096 **American Lung Association of Nebraska**
8990 West Dodge
Suite 226
Omaha, NE 68114
402-572-3030
Fax: 402-572-3028
E-mail: inquiries@breathehealthy.org
http://www.lung.org/associations/charters/plains-gulf
Founded: 1904
Sara Dreiling, CEO

1097 **American Society of Landscape Architects: Great Plains Chapter**
c/o HDR Engineering
8404 Indian Hills Drive
Omaha, NE 68114
402-399-1399
Fax: 402-392-6713
E-mail: jay.gordon@HDRINC
http://www.asla.org/chapters/greatplains
Chad Kucker, President
Mark Jobman, President-Elect

1098 **Iowa Prairie Network**
6736 Laurel
Omaha, NE 68104
402-571-6230
Fax: 402-571-6230
E-mail: pollockg@top.net
http://www.iowaprairienetwork.org

Glenn Pollock, President
David Hansen, Director

1099 **Nature Conservancy: Nebraska Chapter**
1007 Leavenworth Street
Omaha, NE 68102
402-342-0282
Fax: 402-342-0474
E-mail: nebraska@tnc.org
http://www.nature.org

The mission of the Nature Conservancy is to preserve the plants, animals and natural communities that represent the diversity of life on Earth by protecting the lands and waters they need to survive.
Founded: 1915
Mace Hack, State Director
Ralph Jones, Conservation Data Manager

1100 **Nebraska Association of Resource Districts**
601 S 12th Street
Suite 201
Lincoln, NE 68508
402-471-7670
Fax: 402-471-7677
E-mail: nard@nrdnet.org
http://www.nrdnet.org

The mission is to assist NRDs in a coordinated effort to accomplish collectively what mat not be accomplished individually to conserve, sustain, and improve our natural resources and environment.
Dean E Edson, Executive Director
Jeanne Dryburgh, Office Manager

1101 **Nebraska BASS Chapter Federation**
National B.A.S. S. Chapter Federation
1310 Kozy Drive
Columbus, NE 68601
402-563-2297
E-mail: admin@nebraskabass.com
http://www.nebraskabass.com

Joe Citta Jr., President
Duve Knuth, Vice President

1102 **Nebraska Wildlife Federation**
PO Box 81437
Lincoln, NE 68501
402-477-1008
Fax: 402-994-2021
E-mail: nebraskawildlife@windstream.net
http://www.nebraskawildlife.org

A state-wide, non-profit membership organization dedicated to fish and wildlife conservation through environmental education, fish and wildlife conservation, and common sense public policy.
Founded: 1970
Duane Hovorka, Executive Director
John Atkieson, Energy Policy Director

1103 **Sierra Club**
PO Box 4664
Omaha, NE 68104
http://sierra.nebraska.org

The Nebraska Chapter is divided into four groups and is active in statewide programs in conservation; legislative involvement; outings and programs.
Dick Boyd, Chair
JoEllen Polzien, Vice Chair

1104 **Wildlife Society**
The Wildlife Society
45090 Elm Island Road
Gibbon, NE 68840
308-865-5308
Fax: 308-865-5309
E-mail: mhumpert@lycosmail.com
http://www.wildlifeconsult.com/netws/

A nonprofit scientific and educational organization that serves professionals such as government agencies, academia, industry, and non-government organizations in all areas related to the conservation of wildlife and natural resources management.
Founded: 1937
Chris Helzer, President
Renae Held, Secretary

Nevada

1105 **American Lung Association of Nevada**
10615 Double R Bldv
Reno, NV 89521-8920
775-829-5864
Fax: 775-829-5850
E-mail: dszabo@lungnevada.org

Founded: 1904
Dorothy Szabo, Office Manager

1106 **American Society of Landscape Architects: Nevada Chapter**
c/o Stone Peak Services
PO Box 97986
Las Vegas, NV 89193
702-274-2013
Fax: 702-454-3097
E-mail: info@NVASLA.com
http://www.nvasla.org

Caryl Davies, President
Brad Theurer, President Elect

1107 **Nevada Wildlife Federation**
PO Box 71238
Reno, NV 89570
775-885-0405
Fax: 775-885-0405
E-mail: nvwf@nvwf.org
http://www.nvwf.org

The federation represents the views of hunters, fisherman and anyone who deeply cares about our wildlife and wild lands.
Robert Gaudet, President
Anita Wagner, Treasurer

1108 **Sierra Club: Toiyabe Chapter**
PO Box 8096
Reno, NV 89507
702-323-3162
http://nevada.sierraclub.org

The Toiyabe Chapter (Eastern Sierra) serves Nevada and Eastern California. Advances the preservation and protection of the natural environment by empowering the citizenry, especially democratically-based grassroots organizations, with charitable resources to further the cause of environmental protection.
David Von Seggern, Chair
David Hornbeck, Chapter Vice Chair

1109 **Solar NV**
817 S Main St
Las Vegas, NV 89101
702-507-0093
Fax: 702-507-0093
E-mail: info@solarnv.org
http://www.solarnv.org

The Southern Nevada Chapter of the American Solar Energy Society. Educates Southern Nevadans about the benefits of renewable energy and to encourage and promote the use of sustainable energy technology.

1110 **Sunrise Sustainable Resources Group**
PO Box 19074
Reno, NV 89511
775-348-7192
E-mail: president@sunrisenevada.org
http://www.sunrisenevada.org

Empowers Nevadans to use resources responsibly through education, advocacy and community.
Founded: 1996
Philip Moore, President
Brian Bass, VP

1111 **Tahoe Regional Planning Agency**
PO Box 5310
Stateline, NV 89449
702-588-4547
Fax: 702-588-4527
E-mail: trpa@trpa.org
http://www.trpa.org

To cooperatively lead the effort to preserve, restore and enhance the unique natural and human environment of the Lake Tahoe region now and in the future.
John Singlaub, Executive Director

New Hampshire

1112 **American Bass Association of New Hampshire**
235 Ridgeview Road
Weare, NH 03281
603-529-2642
John Cowan, President

1113 **Audubon Society of New Hampshire**
84 Silk Farm Road
Concord, NH 03301
603-224-9909
Fax: 603-226-0902
E-mail: nha@audubon.org
http://www.nhaudubon.org

A nonprofit state wide membership organization that is dedicated to the conservation of wildlife and habitat throughout the state. The mission is to protect New Hampshire's natural environment for wildlife and for people.
Founded: 1914
Michael J Bartlett, President/CEO
Carol Foss, Director, Conservation

1114 **Breathe New Hampshire**
145 Hollis Street
Unit C
Manchester, NH 03101
603-669-2411
800-835-8647
Fax: 603-645-6220
E-mail: info@breathenh.org
http://www.breathnh.org

Formerly the American Lung Association of New Hampshire, is committed to eliminating lung disease and improving the quality of life for those with lung disease in New Hampshire.
Founded: 1916
Dan Fortin, President/CEO
Susan Berry, Program Manager

1115 **Nature Conservancy: New Hampshire Chapter**
22 Bridge Street
4th Floor
Concord, NH 03301
603-224-5853
Fax: 603-228-2459
E-mail: naturenewhampshire@tnc.org
http://www.nature.org

The mission of the Nature Conservancy is to preserve the plants, animals, and nature communities that represent the diversity of life on earth by protecting the lands and waters they need to survive.
Founded: 1987
Sydney Allen, State Director
Jim O'Brien, Media Relations Contact

1116 **New Hampshire Association of Conservation Commissions**
54 Portsmouth Street
Concord, NH 03301
603-224-7867
Fax: 603-228-0423
E-mail: info@nhacc.org
http://www.nhacc.org

The New Hampshire Association of Conservation Commissions is a private, non-profit association of municipal conservation commissions. Its purpose is to foster conservation and appropriate use of New Hampshire's natural resources by providing assistance to conservation commissions, facilitating communication and cooperation among commissions, and helping to create a climate in which commissions can be successful.
Founded: 1970
Gene Harrington, President
Paul Dionne, Vice President

1117 **New Hampshire Association of Conservation Districts**
PO Box 533
Conway, NH 03818
603-796-2615
Fax: 603-796-2600
E-mail: director@nhacd.org
http://www.nhacd.org

Provides statewide coordination, representation, and leadership for Conservation Districts to conserve, protect, and promote responsible use of New Hampshire's natural resources.
Founded: 1946
Michele L Tremblay, Executive Director

1118 **New Hampshire Lakes Association (NH Lakes)**
14 Horseshoe Pond Lane
Concord, NH 03301
603-226-0299
Fax: 603-224-9442
E-mail: info@nhlakes.org
http://www.nhlakes.org

A nonprofit, tax-exempt volunteer organization established by the merger of two citizens' groups, each with a history of accomplishments in the protection of lakes. Works on issues concerning shoreland and watershed protection; water quality improvement; boating safety; lake environment education; and fisheries and wildlife preservation.
Founded: 1992
Tom O'Brien, President
Andrea LaMoreaux, Vice President

1119 **New Hampshire Wildlife Federation**
54 Portsmouth Street
Concord, NH 03301
603-224-5953
Fax: 603-228-0423
E-mail: info@nhwf.org
http://www.nhwf.org

A non-profit member organization promoting conservation, environmental education, sportsmanship, and outdoor activities such as hunting, fishing, trapping, camping and photography. The mission is to be the leading advocate for the promotion and protection of hunting, fishing and trapping as well as the conservation of fish and wildlife habitat.
Founded: 1933
Janice Boynton, President

1120 **Northeast Resource Recovery Association**
2101 Dover Road
Epsom, NH 03234
603-736-4401
Fax: 603-736-4402
E-mail: info@nrra.net
http://www.recyclewithus.org

The Northeast Resource Recovery Association is a pro-active nonprofit working with its membership to make their recycling programs strong, efficient, and financially successful by providing cooperative marketing, cooperative purchasing, education and networking opportunities; developing innovative recycling programs; creating sustainable alternatives to reduce the volume and toxicity of the waste, and educating and informing local officials about recycling and solid waste issues.
Founded: 1981
Rick Cooper, President
Paula Dow, Executive Director

New Jersey

1121 **American Bass Association of Eastern Pennsylvania/New Jersey**
7 Logan Drive
Somerville, NJ 08876
908-526-7721
Fax: 908-685-0970
E-mail: ehargraves@sdamechanical.com
http://www.aba-of-eastern-pa-nj.com

Organized with three primary purposes for: to ensure the future of fishing through the protection and enhancement of the fishery resource; to promote bass fishing across America as a major sport; and to introduce youngsters to the joy of fishing, sportsmanship and instill in them an appreciation of the life-giving waters of America.
Founded: 1974
Fred Eurick, President
Mark Dilatush, Vice President

1122 **American Society of Landscape Architects: New Jersey Chapter**
414 River View Plaza
Trenton, NJ 08611-3420
609-393-7500
Fax: 609-393-9891
E-mail: info@njasla.org
http://www.njasla.net

Founded: 1901
Tmothy N. Delorm, President
Ilonka Angalet, President Elect

1123 **Association of New Jersey Environmental Commissions**
PO Box 157
Mendham, NJ 07945
973-539-7547
Fax: 973-539-7713
E-mail: info@anjec.org
http://www.anjec.org

To promote the public interest in natural resource protection, sustainable development and reclamation and to support environ-

mental commissions and open space committees working with citizens and other non-profit organizations.
Sandy Batty, Executive Director
Kerry Miller, Assistant Director

1124 Clean Ocean Action
18 Hartshorne Drive, Suite 2 732-872-0111
Sandy Hook, NJ 07732 Fax: 732-872-8041
E-mail: info@CleanOceanAction.org
http://www.cleanoceanaction.org
A broad-based coalition of over 150 groups and individuals that work to clean up and protect the waters of the New York and New Jersey coasts.
Founded: 1984
Cindy Zipf, Executive Director
Mary-Beth Thompson, Operations Director

1125 Edison Facilities
2890 Woodbridge Avenue 732-321-6754
Ms 100 Fax: 732-321-4381
Edison, NJ 08837

1126 Environmental and Occupational Health Science Institute
Rutgers University
170 Frelinghuysen Road 848-445-0200
PO Box 1179 Fax: 732-445-0131
Piscataway, NJ 08854 http://eohsi.rutgers.edu
Sponsors research, education and service programs in a setting that fosters interaction among experts in environmental health, toxicology, occupational health, exposure assessment, public policy and health education. The Institute also serves as an unbiased source of expertise about environmental problems for communities, employers and government in all areas of occupational and environmental health, toxicology and risk assessment.
Kenneth Reuhl, Interim Director
Howard Kipen, Associate Director

1127 New Jersey BASS Chapter Federation
77 Kenvil Avenue 201-584-9387
Succasunna, NJ 07876 E-mail: amgoing@verizon.net
http://www.njbassfed.org
An organization of chapters dedicated to the sport of bass fishing.
Founded: 1917
Tony Going, President
Forest R Honeywell, Executive Director

1128 New Jersey Department of Health and Senior Services
PO Box 360 609-292-7837
Trenton, NJ 08625-360 800-367-6543
http://www.state.nj.us/health
The mission of the Child and Adolescent Health Program is to promote optimum health and development of the children of New Jersey through the promotion of preventive services, linkages with primary medical care and healthy physical and psychosocial environments.
Heather Howard, Commission erector
Jon S Corzine, Governor

1129 New Jersey Environmental Lobby
204 W State Street 609-396-3774
Trenton, NJ 08608 Fax: 609-396-4521
http://www.njenvironment.org
Nonprofit organization devoted to lobbying for legislation and/or regulations that will preserve and protect New Jersey's natural resources and environment — both natural and built — and protect the public health.
Founded: 1969
Anne Poole, President

1130 New Jersey Public Interest Research Group
143 E State Street 609-394-8155
Suite 6 http://www.njpirg.org
Trenton, NJ 08608
Delivers persistent, result-oriented public interest activism that protects consumers, encourages a fair, sustainable economy, and fosters responsive, democratic government.
Jennifer Kim, State Director
Peter Skopec, Program Associate

1131 New York/New Jersey Trail Conference
156 Ramapo Valley Road 201-512-9348
Route 202 Fax: 201-512-9012
Mahwah, NJ 07430-1199 E-mail: office@nynjtc.org
http://www.nynjtc.org
A federation of 104 hiking clubs and environmental organizations and 10,000 individuals dedicated to building and maintaining marked hiking trails and protecting related open spaces in the bi-state region.

1132 Passaic River Coalition
330 Speedwell Ave 973-532-9830
Morristown, NJ 07059 Fax: 973-889-9172
E-mail: prc@passaicriver.org
http://www.passaicriver.org
Interested in preserving, maintaining and/or enhancing the water quality and quantity in the Passaic River Basin. Advocates on related issues, carries out projects that further its goals, and participates in land acquisition activities in order to provide open space.
Founded: 1969
Ella Filippone, Executive Director
Kate Kelleher, Administrative Assistant

1133 Sierra Club: NJ Chapter
145 West Hanover Street 609-656-7612
Trenton, NJ 08618 Fax: 609-656-7618
E-mail: njsierra1@verizon.net
http://newjersey.sierraclub.org
Mission is to explore, enjoy, and protect the wild places of the earth; to practice and promote the responsible use of the earth's ecosystems and resources; to educate and enlist humanity to protect and restore the quality of the natural and human environments.
Jeff Tittel, Chapter Director
Kate Millsaps, Program Assistant

New Mexico

1134 American Society of Landscape Architects: New Mexico
School of Architecture & Planhttp://gt.asla.org/chapters/newmexico/
2414 Central Ave SE
Albuquerque, NM 87131
Statewide professional organization that is open to landscape architects and their associates.
C Patricia Westbrook, President
Laurie Firor, President-Elect

1135 Holistic Management International
5941 Jefferson Street NE 505-842-5252
Suite B Fax: 505-843-7900
Albuquerque, NM 87109 E-mail: hmi@holisticmanagement.org
http://www.holisticmanagement.org
Enhance the efficiency, natural health, productivity and profitability of their land; increase natural annual profits; provide a framework for family, owners, managers, foreman, communal agriculturalists and other ranch/farm stakeholders to work together toward a common future; and enable development agencies working with marginalized farmers or pastoral people to break the cycle of food and water insecurity.
Founded: 1984
Peter Holter, CEO
Tracy Favre, Sr Director Contract Sales

1136 National Parks Conservation Association
777 6th Street NW 800-628-7275
Suite 700 Fax: 202-659-0650
Washington, DC 20001-3723 E-mail: npca@npca.org
http://www.npca.org

To protect and enhance America's National Parks for presents and future generations.
Founded: 1919
Theresa Pierno, Acting President
Ron Tipton, Senior VP

1137 Nature Conservancy: New Mexico Chapter
Nature Conservancy
212 E Marcy Street
Suite 200
Santa Fe, NM 87501
505-988-3867
800-628-6860
Fax: 505-988-4095
E-mail: nm@tnc.org
http://www.nature.org
Founded: 1951
Tracey Stone, Media Contact

1138 New Mexico Association of Conservation Districts
163 Trail Canyon Road
Carlsbad, NM 88220
505-981-2400
Fax: 505-981-2400
http://www.nmacd.org
To facilitate conservation of natural resources in New Mexico by providing opportunities & quality support to local conservation districts through representative & leadership.
Founded: 1946
Kenny Salazar, President
Jim Berlier, VP

1139 New Mexico Association of Soil and Water Conservation
163 Trail Canyon Road
Carlsbad, NM 88220
505-981-2400
Fax: 505-981-2422
Kenny Salazar, President
Jim Berlier, VP

1140 New Mexico Center for Wildlife Law
University of New Mexico School of Law
Albuquerque, NM 87131
E-mail: cbyers@unm.edu
http://ipl.unm.edu
Provides expertise in wildlife and biodiversity law and policy, including training, youth education, facilitation, legislation, research, teaching and publication.
Founded: 1990
Carolyn Byers, Director

1141 New Mexico Rural Water Association
8336 Washington Place NE
Albuquerque, NM 87113
505-884-1031
800-819-9893
Fax: 505-884-1032
E-mail: nmrwa@nmrwa.org
http://www.nmrwa.org
A non-profit membership organization that provides free training and technical assistance to water and wastewater systems.
David Kenneke, President
Clarence Aragon, Secretary/Treasurer

1142 New Mexico Solar Energy Association
1009 Bradbury SE
#35
Albuquerque, NM 87106
505-246-0400
Fax: 505-246-2251
E-mail: info@nmsea.org
http://www.nmsea.org
An educational nonprofit organization dedicated to the promotion of solar energy and related sustainable practices. Membership includes building contractors, architects, planners, educators and others who support renewable energy.
Founded: 1972
Mary McArthur, Executive Director

1143 Sierra Club: Rio Grande Chapter
142 Truman NE
Albuquerque, NM 87108
505-243-7767
Fax: 505-243-7771
E-mail: daniel.lorimier@sierraclub.org
http://nmsierraclub.org
Founded: 1892
John Buchser, Chair
Norma McCallan, Vice Chair

1144 Wildlife Society
PO Box 35936
Albuquerque, NM 87176
505-992-8651
800-299-0196
E-mail: triley@trcp.org
http://www.leopold.nmsu.edu
A nonprofit scientific and educational organization that serves professionals such as government agencies, academia, industry, and non-government organizations in all areas related to the conservation of wildlife and natural resources management.
Founded: 1937
Terry Z Riley, President
Valerie A Williams, Secretary

New York

1145 Adirondack Council
103 Hand Avenue
PO Box D-2, #3
Elizabethtown, NY 12932
518-873-2240
877-873-2240
Fax: 518-873-6675
E-mail: info@adirondackcouncil.org
http://www.adirondackcouncil.org
A not-for-profit environmental group that has been working since 1975 to protect the open-space resources of New York State's six million acre Adirondack Park and to help sustain the natural and human communities of the region. Based in the Adirondacks with a second office in Albany, the Adirondack Council has a staff of 15 and a strong and vocal membership in all 50 states.
Founded: 1975
William C. Janeway, Executive Director
Elaine Burke, Operations Director

1146 Adirondack Land Trust
PO Box 65
Keene Valley, NY 12943
518-576-2082
E-mail: adirondacks@tnc.org
http://www.nature.org
Dedicated to protecting open space, working landscapes such as farmlands and managed forests, as well as other lands contributing to the quality of life of Adirondack residents.
Founded: 1984

1147 Adirondack Mountain Club
310 Hamilton Street
Albany, NY 12210-1738
518-668-4447
Fax: 518-449-3875
E-mail: info@adk.org
http://www.adk.org
Dedicated to the protection and responsible recreational use of the New York State Forest Preserve, and other parks, wild lands, and waters vital to the members and chapters.
Founded: 1922
Neil Woodworth, Executive Director
James Bird, President

1148 American Council on Science and Health
1995 Broadway
Suite 202
New York, NY 10023-5882
212-362-7044
866-905-2694
Fax: 212-362-4919
E-mail: acsh@acsh.org
http://www.acsh.org
A consumer education organization based in New York City that promotes scientifically balanced evaluations of food, chemicals and the environment, and their relationship to human health.
Founded: 1978
Elizabeth M Whelan, President
Gilbert Ross MD, Medical/Executive Director

1149 American Lung Association of New York State: Albany Office
155 Washington Avenue
Suite 210
Albany, NY 12210
518-465-2013
Fax: 518-465-2926
http://www.lungusa2.org

1150 American Lung Association of New York State: Long Island Office
700 Veterans Memorial Highway
Hauppauge, NY 11788
631-265-3848
Fax: 631-265-6123

1151 American Lung Association of the City of New York
116 John Street
30th Floor
New York, NY 10038
212-889-3370
Fax: 212-889-3375
E-mail: infonyc@alany.org
http://www.alany.org
Mission is to prevent lung disease and promote lung health - is realized through a broad variety of community education programs, research projects and advocacy initiatives.
Deborah Carlto, CEO

1152 American Rivers: Mid-Atlantic Region
1 Danker Avenue
Albany, NY 12206
518-482-2631
Fax: 518-482-2632
http://www.americanrivers.org
Stephanie Lindloff, Director

1153 American Society of Landscape Architects: New York Upstate Chapter
PO Box 227
East Rochester, NY 14445
585-586-6906
Fax: 585-385-6053
E-mail: asla@riversorg.com
http://www.nyuasla.org
Landscape Architecture is a comprehensive discipline of land analysis, planning, design, management, preservation, and rehabilitation. The New York Upstate Chapter of ASLA promotes the landscape architecture profession and advances the practice through advocacy, education, communication, and fellowship amongst Landscape Architects and allied professionals.
Andy Hart, President
Joy Kuebler, President Elect

1154 American Society of Landscape Architects: New York Chapter
148 West 37th Street
13th Floor
New York, NY 10018-6909
212-269-2987
E-mail: director@aslany.org
http://www.aslany.org
Susannah Drake, President
Kathy Shea, Executive Director

1155 Catskill Forest Association
PO Box 336
Arkville, NY 12406
845-586-3054
Fax: 845-586-4071
E-mail: cfa@catskill.net
http://www.catskillforest.org
A non-profit organization dedicated to enhancing all aspects of the forest in New York's Catskill region.
Founded: 1982
Jim Waters, Executive Director
Robert L. Bishop II, VP

1156 Cornell Lab of Ornithology
159 Sapsucker Woods Road
Ithaca, NY 14850
607-254-2437
800-843-2473
E-mail: cornellbirds@cornell.edu
http://www.birds.cornell.edu
The Lab uses the best science and technology, and inspires the widest range of people and organizations-to solve critical problems facing wildlife. The mission is to interpret and conserve the earth's biological diversity through research, education, and citizen science focused on birds.
Founded: 1950
John W. Fitzpatrick, Director

1157 Environmental Action Coalition
625 Broadway
9th Floor
New York, NY 10012
212-677-1601
Fax: 212-505-8613
E-mail: eac@eacnyc.org
http://www.eacnyc.org
A network of concerned citizens who devote time and money to spreading information on ecological and environmental clean-up efforts. Offers environmental education and sponsors programs for professionals in the field, citizen activists, volunteers, teachers, students and labor leaders.
Paul C Berizzi, Executive Director

1158 Federation of New York State Bird Clubs
New York Birders
PO Box 440
Loch Sheldrake, NY 12759
E-mail: mkoeneke@a-znet.com
http://www.fnysbc.com
The objectives are to document the ornithology of New York State; to foster interest in and appreciation of birds; and to protect birds and their habitats.
Sue Adadair, Treasurer

1159 Great Lakes United
State University College at Buffalo
Cassety Hall
1300 Elmwood Avenue
Buffalo, NY 14222
716-886-0142
Fax: 716-204-9521
E-mail: glu@glu.org
http://www.glu.org
Founded: 1982
Derek Stack, Executive Director

1160 Hudsonia Limited
30 Campus Road
PO Box 5000
Annandale, NY 12504
845-758-7053
Fax: 845-758-7033
http://www.hudsonia.org
A not-for-profit institute for research, education, and technical assistance in the environmental sciences.
Founded: 1981
Erik Kiviat Phd, Executive Director
Robert E Schmidt Phd, Associate Director

1161 INFORMBuilding Environmental Literacy
PO Box 320403
Brooklyn, NY 11232
212-361-2400
E-mail: ramsey@informinc.org
http://www.informinc.org
INFORM prides itself on more than three decades of identifying innovative technologies, practices and products that provide practical solutions to complex environmental and health-related problems.
Founded: 1974
Virginia Ramsey, President
Lauren Menson, Senior Manager

1162 In Our Backyards
540 President St.
3rd Floor
Brooklyn, NY 11215
917-464-4515
E-mail: info@ioby.org
http://www.ioby.org
Strives to deepen civic engagement in cities by connecting individuals directly to community-led, neighbor funded environmental projects in their neighborhoods.
Founded: 2008
Erin Barnes, Co-Founder & Exec. Director
Brandon Whitney, Co-Founder & COO

1163 Montefiore Medical Center Lead Poisoning Prevention Program
3415 Bainbridge Avenue
Bronx, NY 10467-2940
718-920-4943
E-mail: montekids@montefiore.org
http://www.montekids.org
The Montefiore Lead Poisoning Prevention Program addresses all aspects of childhood lead poisoning from diagnosis and treatment to education and research. Their mission is to treat lead-poisoned children and their families and to educate families at risk, other medical providers and local, state and national legislators and policy makers.
Steven M Safyer, President/CEO

1164 Nature Conservancy: New York Long Island Chapter
The Nature Conservancy
250 Lawerence Hill Road
Cold Spring Harbor, NY 11724
631-367-3225
800-628-6860
Fax: 516-367-4715
E-mail: comment@tnc.org
http://www.nature.org
Founded: 1951
Henry M Paulson Jr, Chairman
Steven J McCormick, President/CEO

1165 New York Association of Conservation Districts
245 Hartley Road
Amsterdam, NY 12010
518-857-0060
E-mail: nyacd@nycap.rr.com
http://www.nyacd.org

Provides leadership in the wise use of soil, water, and related natural resources.
Founded: 1958
Tom Nichols, President
Judy Littrell, Executive Director

1166 New York Forest Owners Association
PO Box 541
Lima, NY 14485
585-624-3385
800-836-3566
E-mail: lgooding@nyfoa.org
http://www.nyfoa.org

Promotes sustainable forestry practices and improved stewardship on privately owned woodlands in New York State. A not-for-profit group of people who care about NYS trees and forests and are interested in the thoughtful management of private forests for the benefit of current and future generations.
Founded: 1905
Jim Minor, President

1167 New York Healthy Schools Network
773 Madison Ave
Albany, NY 12208
518-462-0632
Fax: 518-462-0433
E-mail: info@healthyschools.org
http://www.healthyschools.org

A national environmental health organization that does research, information, education, coalition-building, and advocacy to ensure that every child has a healthy learning environment that is clean and in good repair.
Founded: 1995
Claire L Barnett, Executive Director

1168 New York State Council of Landscape Architects
52 South Pearl Street
3rd Floor
Albany, NY 12207
518-465-5176
E-mail: kmatthews@mnlandscape.com
http://www.nyscla.org
Charles P May, President
Erin Reynolds, Secretary

1169 New York State Department of Environmental Conservation
625 Broadway
Albany, NY 12233
518-402-8540
Fax: 518-402-9016
http://www.dec.ny.gov

DEC protects, improves and conserves the state's land, water, air, fish, wildlife and other resources to enhance the health, safety and welfare of the people and their overall economic and social well-being.
Andrew M Cuomo, Governor
Geo Martins, Commissioner

1170 New York State Ornithology Society
PO Box 296
Somers, NY 10589
E-mail: president1@nybirds.org
http://www.nybirds.org

The objectives of the Federation are to document the ornithology of New York State; to foster interest in and appreciation of birds; and to protect birds and their habitats.
Founded: 1947
Gail Kirch, President
Kathy Schneider, Vice President

1171 New York Turtle and Tortoise Society
1214 W Boston Post Road
PO Box 267
Mamaroneck, NY 10543
212-459-4803
800-847-7332
E-mail: qanda@nytts.org
http://www.nytts.org

A nonprofit organization dedicated to the conservation, preservation of habitat, and the promotion of proper husbandry and captive propagation of turtles and tortoises. The Society emphasizes the education of its members and the public in all areas relevant to the appreciation of these unique animals.

1172 New York Water Environment Association
525 Plum Street
Suite 102
Syracuse, NY 13204
315-422-7811
877-556-9932
Fax: 315-422-3851
E-mail: pcr@nywea.org
http://www.nywea.org

The New York Water Environment Association is a nonprofit educational association dedicated to the development and dissemination of information concerning water quality management and the nature, collection, treatment, and disposal of wastewater. Founded in 1929, the Association has over 2,100 members. The NYWEA is a member association of the Water Environment Federation.
Founded: 1929
Patricia Cerro-Reehil, Executive Director

1173 Parks and Trails New York
29 Elk Street
Albany, NY 12207
518-434-1583
Fax: 518-427-0067
E-mail: ptny@ptny.org
http://www.ptny.org

The only organization working statewide to protect New York's parks and help communities create new parks. A non-profit organization whose mission is to expand, protect and promote a network of parks, trails, and open spaces throughout our state for use and enjoyment by all.
Founded: 1985
Judith C Mower, Chairman
David Bronston, Vice Chairman

1174 Rene Dubos Center for Human Environments
279 Bronxville Road
Bronxville, NY 10708
914-337-1636
Fax: 914-771-5206
E-mail: info@dubos.org
http://www.dubos.org

The Rene Dubos Center for Human Environments is a non-profit education and research organization focused on the social and humanistic aspects of environmental problems.
Noel Brown, President

1175 Riverkeeper
20 Secor Road
Ossining, NY 10562
800-21 -IVER
Fax: 914-478-4527
E-mail: info@riverkeeper.org
http://www.riverkeeper.org

A member supported watchdog organization dedicated to defending Hudson River and its tributaries and protecting the drinking water supply of nine million New York City and Hudson Valley residents.
Founded: 1966
Dr Howard A Rubin, Chairman
Peggy Cullen, Secretary

1176 Sagamore Institute
PO Box 40
Sagamore Road
Raquette Lake, NY 13436
315-354-5311
Fax: 315-354-5851
E-mail: info@greatcampsagamore.org
http://www.greatcampsagamore.org

A non-profit corporation dedicated to the stewardship of Great Camp Sagamore, in Raquette Lake, NY, and to its use for educational and interpretive purposes.
Founded: 1973
Beverly Bridger, Executive Director
Dr Michael Wilson, Associate Director

1177 Scenic Hudson
One Civic Center Plaza
Suite 200
Poughkeepsie, NY 12601
845-473-4440
Fax: 845-473-2648
E-mail: info@scenichudson.org
http://www.scenichudson.org

Scenic Hudson works to protect and restore the Hudson River and its majestic landscape as an irreplaceable national treasure and a vital resource for residents and visitors.
Founded: 1963
James C Goodfellow, Chairman
Lisina M Hoch, Vice Chairman

1178 Selikoff Clinical Center for Occupational & Environmental Medicine
Mount Sinai School of Medicine
Department of Community Medicine
1 Gustave Levy Place, Box 1043
New York, NY 10029-6574
212-241-6500
Fax: 212-241-6696
http://www.mssm.edu/cpm

Internationally respected diagnostic referral center and an important interface between the research programs of the Division of Environmental Health Science and populations exposed to environmental hazards.

1179 **Sierra Club: Atlantic Chapter**
353 Hamilton Street
Albany, NY 12210
518-426-9144
Fax: 518-427-0381
E-mail: chaptercoord@newyork.sierraclub.org
http://newyork.sierraclub.org

The Atlantic Chapter applies the principles of the national Sierra Club to the environmental issues facing New York State.
Jeff Bohner, Chairman
Carl Arnold, Vice Chairman

1180 **Sierra Club: New York City Office**
85 Second Street
2nd Floor
San Francisco, CA 94105
415-977-5500
Fax: 415-977-5797
E-mail: ne.field@sierraclub.org
http://www.sierraclub.org

Part of the national Sierra Club with over 700,000 members, headquarters in San Francisco, offices in Washington DC, and staff in state capitals around the nation. Our mission is to enjoy and protect the earth's ecosystems and resources, and to enlist others to do the same. The Atlantic Chapter consists of 32,000 members in 11 local groups throughout New York State. We use the media, grassroots education and personal contact to bring our issues to our communities and our public officials.
Founded: 1892 Quarterly
Michael Brune, Executive Director

1181 **Sierra Club: Northeast Office**
85 Washington Street
Saratoga Springs, NY 12866
518-587-9166
Fax: 518-583-9062
E-mail: ne.field@sierraclub.org
http://newyork.sierraclub.org

To advance the preservation and protection of the natural environment by empowering the citizenry, especially democratically based grassroots organizations with charitable resources to further the cause of environmental protection, the vehicle through which The Sierra Club Foundation generally fulfills its charitable mission.
Founded: 1892

1182 **Tug Hill Tomorrow Land Trust**
PO Box 6063
Watertown, NY 13601
315-779-8240
Fax: 315-782-6192
E-mail: thtomorr@northnet.org
http://www.tughilltomorrowlandtrust.org

A regional, private, nonprofit founded by a group of Tug Hill residents to serve the region of 2,100 square miles serving portions of Jefferson, Lewis, Oneida & Oswego Counties. The mission is two-fold: increase awareness and appreciation of the Tug Hill Region through education; and to help retain the forest, farm, recreation, and wild land of the region through voluntary, private land protection efforts.
Founded: 1990
Linda Garrett, Executive Director
Kalie Gerenser Brady, Community Programs Manager

1183 **Waterkeeper Alliance**
17 Battery Place
Suite 1329
New York, NY 10004
212-747-0622
Fax: 212-747-0611
E-mail: info1@waterkeeper.org
http://www.waterkeeper.org

Provides a way for communities to stand up for their right to clean water and for the wise and equitable use of water resources, both locally and globally. The vision of the Waterkeeper movement is for fishable, swimmable and drinkable waterways worldwide.
Marc A Yaggi, Executive Director
Sharon Khan, International Director

1184 **West Harlem Environmental Action**
1854 Amsterdam Avenue(at 152nd Stre
2nd Floor
New York, NY 10031
212-961-1000
Fax: 212-961-1015
E-mail: peggy@weact.org
http://www.weact.org

A non-profit, community-based, environmental justice organization dedicated to building community power to fight environmental racism and improve environmental health, protection and policy in communities of color.
Peggy M Shepard, Executive Director
Ceci. D Corbin-Mark, Deputy Director

1185 **Women's Environment and Development Organization**
355 Lexington Avenue
3rd Floor
New York, NY 10017
212-973-0325
Fax: 212-973-0335
E-mail: wedo@wedo.org
http://www.wedo.org

An international organization that advocates for women's equality in global policy. It seeks to empower women as decision makers to achieve economic, social and gender justice, a healthy, peaceful planet and human rights for all.
Founded: 1990
Cate Owren, Executive Director
Dona Weeks, Finance Manager

North Carolina

1186 **Acid Rain Foundation**
1410 Varsity Drive
Raleigh, NC 27606
919-828-9443
Fax: 919-515-3593
Dr. Harriett S Stubbs, Executive Director

1187 **American Lung Association of North Carolina**
514 Daniels
St. # 109
Raleigh, NC 27605
919-424-6069
800-892-5650
Fax: 919-856-8530
E-mail: lungnc@lungusa.org
http://www.lungnc.org

The voluntary health organization dedicated to eliminating lung disease and fostering healthy breathing for all people through prevention, outreach, education, research and advocacy.
Founded: 1904
Dennis C. Alexander, Regional Executive Director
Marc Ittelson, Regional Development Dir.

1188 **American Society of Landscape Architects: North Carolina Chapter**
1829 East Franklin Street
Suite 600
Chapel Hill, NC 27514
919-215-3117
888-999-2752
Fax: 919-278-2647
E-mail: manager@ncasla.org
http://www.ncasla.org

Founded: 1899
Ed Johnson, President
Matt Langston, Trustee

1189 **Carolina Bird Club**
1809 Lakepark Drive
Raleigh, NC 27612
910-791-9034
Fax: 910-791-7228
E-mail: hq@carolinabirdclub.org
http://www.carolinabirdclub.org

A nonprofit educational and scientific association, open to anyone interested in the study and conservation of wildlife, particularly birds. Meets each winter, spring and fall. Meeting sites are selected to give participants an opportunity to see many different kinds of birds. Guided field trips, informative programs and business sessions are combined for an exciting weekend of meeting with people who share an enthusiasm and concern for birds.
Founded: 1937
Katherine Higgi Wilmington, President

1190 **Center for the Evaluation of Risks to Human Reproduction**
NIEHS EC-32
PO Box 12233
Research Triangle Park, NC 27709
919-541-3455
Fax: 919-316-4511
E-mail: shelby@niehs.nih.gov
http://cerhr.niehs.nih.gov

Established to serve as an environmental health resource to the public and to regulatory and health agencies. The Center provides scientifically-based, uniform assessments of the potential for ad-

verse effects on reproduction and development caused by agents to which humans may be exposed.
Founded: 1998
Dr Michael D Shelby, Director

1191 Environmental Educators of North Carolina
PO Box 4904
Chapel Hill, NC 27515
919-250-1050
Fax: 919-250-1058
E-mail: eenc@rtpnet.org
http://www.eenc.org
To promote excellence in professional development and facilitate networking opportunities, inspiring educators to create an environmentally literate citizenry.
Renee Strnad, President

1192 Forest History Society
701 Williams Vickers Avenue
Durham, NC 27701
919-682-9319
Fax: 919-682-2349
E-mail: coakes@duke.edu
http://www.foresthistory.org
The Forest History is a non-profit educational institution that links the past to the future by indentifying, collecting, preserving, interpreting, and disseminating information on the history of people, forests, and their related resources.
Founded: 1946
Steven Anderson, President
Andrea H. Anderson, Administrative Assistant

1193 North Carolina Association of Soil & Water Conservation Districts
PO Box 27943
Raleigh, NC 27611
919-715-6104
Fax: 919-602-5777
E-mail: ncaswcd@gmail.com
http://www.ncaswcd.org
An independent nonpartisan conservation organization created to represent the interests of 96 local soil and water conservation districts and the 492 district supervisors who direct their local district's conservation programs.
Founded: 1944
Tommy Houser, President
John Langdon, First Vice President

1194 North Carolina Chapter of the Wildlife Society
PO Box 37742
Raleigh, NC 27627
704-732-1391
E-mail: admin@nctws.org
http://www.nctws.org
Seeks to provide a forum for wildlife professionals and others to interact to improve wildlife conservation and management while fostering high professional standards and ethics for its members
Founded: 1983
Kendrick Weeks, President
Kelly Douglass, Secretary

1195 North Carolina Coastal Federation
3609 N.C. 24 Ocean
Newport, NC 28570
252-393-8185
800-232-6210
Fax: 252-393-7508
http://www.nccoast.org
Works with citizens to safeguard the state's coastal rivers, creeks, sounds and beaches. The state's only non-profit organization focused exclusively on protecting and restoring the coast of North Carolina through education, advocacy, and habitat preservation and restoration.
Founded: 1982
Todd Miller, Executive Director
Dick Bierly, President

1196 North Carolina Museum of Natural Sciences
11 W Jones Street
Raleigh, NC 27601
919-707-9800
Fax: 919-733-1573
E-mail: museum@naturalsciences.org
http://www.naturalsciences.org
Founded: 1985
Angela B Baker-James, Executive Director
Katey Ahmann, Deputy Director of Education

1197 North Carolina Native Plant Society
c/o North Carolina Botanical Garden
PO Box 10815
Greensboro, NC 27404
E-mail: terry@ncwildflower.org
http://www.ncwildflower.org
The purpose of the Society is to promote enjoyment and conservation of native plants and their habitats through education, protection, and propagation.
Tom Harville, President
Ullana Stuart, Secretary

1198 North Carolina Sustainable Energy Association
PO Box 6465
Raleigh, NC 27628
919-832-7601
E-mail: info@energync.org
http://www.ncsustainableenergy.org
A non-profit membership organization of individuals and businesses interested in sustainable energy. Works to ensure a sustainable future by promoting renewable energy and energy efficiency in North Carolina through education, public policy and economic development.
Founded: 1978
Ivan Urlaub, Executive Director
Van Crandall, Development Director

1199 Sierra Club: North Carolina Chapter
19 W. Hargett St.
Suite 210
Raleigh, NC 27601
919-833-8467
E-mail: nc.sierraclub.org
http://info@nc.sierraclub.org
The North Carolina Chapter currently has 19,000 members and 13 local statewide groups.
Founded: 1970
Molly Diggins, State Director
Robert Scull, Chairman

1200 Southeastern Association of Fish and Wildlife Agencies
PO Box 2040
Maggie Valley, NC 28751
850-545-6001
E-mail: seafwa@aol.com
http://www.seafwa.org
An organization whose members are the state agencies with primary responsibility for management and protection of the fish and wildlife resources in 16 states.
John Frampton, Director
Robert Cook, Executive Director

North Dakota

1201 American Lung Association in North Dakota
212 North 2nd Street
Bismarck, ND 58501-3819
701-223-5613
800-586-4872
Fax: 701-223-5727
E-mail: info@lungnd.org
http://www.lungnd.org
Offers a wide array of lung health services to the people of North Dakota. The mission is to save lives, improve lung health and prevent lung disease. ALAND advocates for clean in-/outdoor air quality; provides asthma management resources; provides prevention and cessation programs and services; monitors lung health; and are
Judy Mourhess, Associate, Program Services
Lewis Bartfield, President/CEO

1202 International Association for Impact Assessment
1330 23rd Street S
Suite C
Fargo, ND 58103
701-297-7908
Fax: 701-297-7917
E-mail: info@iaia.org
http://www.iaia.org
The International Association for Impact Assessment is an interdisciplinary society dedicated to developing international capacity to anticipate, plan and manage the consequences of development. The Association has over 2,500 members in over 100 nations. IAIA seeks to ensure that political, environmental, social and technological dimensions of decisions are understood by those making them.
Founded: 1980
Rita Hamm, CEO
Loreley Fortuny, Special Project Associate

1203 **North Dakota Association of Soil Conservation Districts**
3310 University Drive 701-223-8518
Bismarck, ND 58504 E-mail: kathy@lincolnoakes.com
http://ndascd.org

The purpose is to further the widespread application of sound and practical soil and water conservation practices in North Dakota. The goal is to provide quality membership services and nursery products to carry out the soil conservation program of the soil conservation districts of North Dakota.
Brian Johnston, CEO
Jim Cart, President

Ohio

1204 **American Lung Association of Ohio**
1950 Arlingate Lane 614-279-1700
Columbus, OH 43228 800-586-4872
Fax: 614-279-4940
E-mail: alao@ohiolung.org
http://www.ohiolung.org

Helps Ohioans breathe easier. We lead the fight to prevent lung disease through our mission to promote lung health through research, education, community service, and advocacy.
Founded: 1901
Barry Gottschalk, President/CEO
Robert Singletary, Vice President

1205 **American Lung Association of Ohio: Northeast Region**
6100 Rockside Wood 216-524-5864
Suite 260 800-586-4872
Independence, OH 44131 Fax: 216 524-7647
E-mail: alao@ohiolung.org
http://www.ohiolung.org

Founded: 1901

1206 **American Lung Association of Ohio: Northwest Region**
226 State Route 61 419-663-5864
Norwalk, OH 44857 Fax: 419 668 2575
E-mail: northwest@ohiolung.org
http://www.ohiolung.org

1207 **American Lung Association of Ohio: Southwest Region**
4050 Executive Park Drive 513-985-3990
#402 Fax: 513-985-3995
Cincinnati, OH 45241 E-mail: alao@ohiolung.org
http://www.ohiolung.org

1208 **American Society of Landscape Architects: Ohio Chapter**
579 High Street 614-436-4431
Worthington, OH 43085 Fax: 614-436-4451
E-mail: ocasla@ocasla.org
http://www.ocasla.org

Richard Espe, President
Beth Adamson, Association Manager

1209 **Central Ohio Anglers and Hunters Club**
2045 Morse Road 614-265-6565
Columbus, OH 43229 http://www.dnr.state.oh.us
Doug Eakens, President

1210 **Cincinnati Nature Center**
4949 Tealtown Road 513-831-1711
Milford, OH 45150 Fax: 513-831-8052
E-mail: cnc@cincynature.org
http://www.cincynature.org

To inspire passion for nature and promote environmentally responsible choices through experience and education.
Founded: 1965
Bill Hopple, Executive Director
Diana Ritterholz, Exec. Administrative Asst.

1211 **Great Lakes Tomorrow**
9315 Glenwood Trail 440-838-4176
Brecksville, OH 44141 Fax: 440-838-4176
E-mail: jcowdeni@ibm.net
James W Cowden, Director

1212 **Green Energy Ohio**
7870 Olentangy River Road 614-985-6131
Suite 304 Fax: 614-888-9716
Columbus, OH 43235 E-mail: geo@greenenergyohio.org
http://www.greenenergyohio.org

Green Energy Ohio promotes renewable energy statewide by acting as a clearinghouse for information for Ohioans on sustainable energy.
Jim Gravelle, President
William Spratley, Executive Director

1213 **Holden Arboretum**
9500 Sperry Road 440-946-4400
Kirtland, OH 44094 E-mail: holden@holdenarb.org
http://www.holdenarb.org

Connects people with nature for inspiration and enjoyment, fosters learning and promotes conservation.
Founded: 1931
Clem Hamilton, President/ CEO
Deborah Ryan, Executive Assistant

1214 **League of Ohio Sportsmen**
642 West Broad Street 614-224-8970
Columbus, OH 43215 Fax: 614-224-8971
E-mail: president@leagueofohiosportsmen.org
http://www.leagueofohiosportsmen.org

Dedicated to supporting conservation, restoration, and education that promotes the wise use and enjoyment of our natural resources including wildlife management.
Founded: 1908
Larry Mitchell Sr, President
John Hobbs, Vice President

1215 **Native Plant Society of Northeastern Ohio**
10761 Pekin Road 440-286-9504
Newbury, OH 44065 E-mail: npsohio@hotmail.com
Mission is to promote conservation of all native plants and native plant communities through habitat protection and other means; to encourage public education and appreciation of native plants; to support proper ethics and methods of natural landscaping; to encourage surveys and research on native plants and publication of the information; to promote cooperation with other programs and organizations concerned with the conservation of natural resources.
Judy Barnhart, President
Peggy Duvette, Executive Director

1216 **Nature Conservancy: Ohio Chapter**
6375 Riverside Drive 614-717-2770
Suite 100 Fax: 614-717-2777
Dublin, OH 43017 E-mail: ohio@tnc.org
http://www.nature.org

A global conservation organization dedicated to preserving plants, animals and natural communities that represent the diversity of life on Earth by protecting the lands and water they need to survive. Since its inception in 1951, TheNature Conservancy has protected more than 12 million acres in the US and helped through partnerships preserve more tan 80 million acres in Latin America, the Caribbean, Canada, Asia and the Pacific.
Founded: 1915
Frank E. Loy, Secretary
Mark R. Tercek, President and CEO

1217 **Ohio Alliance for the Environment**
14 Beck St 614-833-4223
Canal Winchester, OH 43110 Fax: 614-833-4223
E-mail: probasco@ohioalliance.org
http://www.ohioalliance.org

Founded: 1978
Peggy Smith, Executive Director
Mike Parkes, President

1218 **Ohio BASS Chapter Federation**
43 Portsmouth Rd
Gallipolis, OH 45631
740-446-9810
Fax: 740-446-9819
E-mail: jdoss@zoomnet.net
http://www.ohiobass.org

Jim Doss, President

1219 **Ohio Energy Project**
200 E. Wilson Bridge Road
Suite 320
Worthington, OH 43085
614-785-1717
Fax: 614-785-1731
E-mail: rsmith@ohioenergy.org
http://www.ohioenergy.org

An organization providing energy and energy efficiency education using current complete and unbrased information, as well as hands-on, engaging and innovative techniques. OEP's kids teching kids approach also helps develop leadershipteam work and presentation skills. An affiliate of NEED, OEP has been named a National Energy Champion and one of the Top 12 Environmental Education Programs in Ohio.
Debby Yerkes, Executive Director
Sue Tenney, Education Coordinator

1220 **Ohio Environmental Council**
1207 Grandview Avenue
Suite 201
Columbus, OH 43212
614-487-7506
Fax: 614-487-7510
E-mail: oec@theOEC.org
http://www.theoec.org

The state's premier advocate for our air, land and water.
Kieth Dimoff, Executive Director
Lisa Estrella, Executive Assistant

1221 **Ohio Federation of Soil and Water Conservation Districts**
2045 Morse Road
Columbus, OH 43229
614-784-1900
Fax: 614-784-9181
E-mail: laurahollingsworth@ofswcd.org
http://www.ofswcd.org

To provide leadership and support to the board supervisors, soil and water conservation districts, and their partners through grassroots programs that promote natural resource stewardship.
Founded: 1943
Joe Glassmeyer, President
Kris Swartz, Vice President

1222 **Ohio Parks and Recreation Association**
1069-A W Main Street
Westerville, OH 43081
614-895-2222
800-238-1108
Fax: 614-895-3050
E-mail: opra@opraonline.org
http://www.opraonline.org

A non-profit, public interest organization representing over 1200 professionals and citizen board members involved in providing leisure facilities and opportunities to all Ohioans as well as the tourists who visit the state each year.Dedicated to the promotion of parks and recreation services for all Ohioans and the sound stewardship of Ohio's natural resources.
Founded: 1938
Woody Woodward, Executive Director
Mindy McInturf, Business Manager

1223 **Sierra Club**
131 N High Street
Suite 605
Columbus, OH 43215
614-461-0734
Fax: 614-461-0710
E-mail: Enid.Nagel@thomson.com
http://ohio.sierraclub.org

To advance the preservation and protection of the natural environment by empowering the citizenry, especially democratically-based grassroots organizations, with charitable resources to further the cause of environmental protection.The vehicle through which The Sierra Club Foundation generally fulfills its charitable mission.
Robert Shields, Chairman
Linda Reeder, Tresurer

1224 **Wildlife Society**
952 Lima Avenue
Box A
Findlay, OH 45840
419-424-5000
Fax: 419-422-4875

A nonprofit scientific and educational organization that serves professionals such as government agencies, academia, industry, and non-government organizations in all areas related to the conservation of wildlife and natural resources management.
J Butterworth, President

Oklahoma

1225 **American Fisheries Society: Fisheries Management Section**
OK Fish RS Laboratory
5410 Grosvenor Lane
Bethesda, MD 20184
301-897-8616
Fax: 301-897-8096
E-mail: main@fisheries.org
http://www.fisheries.org

Founded: 1870
Shawn Johnston, Administrative Coordinator
Guss Rassam, Executive Director

1226 **American Lung Association of Oklahoma**
1010 E 8th Street
Tulsa, OK 74120
918-747-3441
Fax: 918-747-4629
E-mail: mcrump@oklung.org
http://www.oklung.org

Margaret Crump, Contact

1227 **American Lung Association: Oklahoma City Office**
11212 N May Ave #405
Oklahoma City, OK 73120
405-748-4674
Fax: 405-748-6274
E-mail: jwilliams@breathehealthy.org
http://www.breathehealthy.oth

Founded: 1904
Heather Griswold, Contact

1228 **Nature Conservancy: Oklahoma Chapter**
2727 E 21st Street
Suite 102
Tulsa, OK 74114
918-585-1117
Fax: 918-585-2383
E-mail: mfuhr@tnc.org
http://www.tnc-oklahoma.org

Mike Fuhr, State Director
Eileen Jobin, Director of Operations

1229 **Oklahoma Association of Conservation Districts**
PO Box 107
Chelsea, OK 74016
405-340-8884
Fax: 405-842-8744
E-mail: claypope@pldi.net
http://www.oacd.us

Provides leadership, resources, and partnership opportunities for conservation districts and those who manage the land to enhance out natural resources for a better Oklahoma.
Clay Pope, Exeucitve Director
Kim Farber, President

1230 **Oklahoma BASS Chapter Federation**
17316 E 110 Street N
Owasso, OK 74055
E-mail: okgwg1@cox.net
http://www.okbass.org
Founded: 1972
Gary Gunter, President

1231 **Oklahoma Ornithological Society**
PO Box 2931
Claremore, OK 74018
918-343-7701
Fax: 918-343-7563
E-mail: info@okbirds.org
http://www.okbirds.org

Founded: 1982
Doug Wood, President
Claudia Glass, Secretary

1232 **Sierra Club**
PO Box 60644
Oklahoma City, OK 73146
405-286-2277
E-mail: c.wesner@bcglobal.net
http://oklahoma.sierraclub.org

To explore, enjoy and protect the planet; to practice the responsible use of the earth's ecosystem and resources; to educate and enlist humanity; to protect and restore the quality of the natural and

human environmenta; and to use alllawfule means to carry out those objectives.
Jody Harlan, Chair
David Brown, Treasurer

Oregon

1233 **American Lung Association of Oregon**
7420 Southwest Bridgeport Road 503-924-4094
Suite 200 E-mail: info@lungoregon.org
Tigard, OR 97224 http://www.lungoregon.org
The oldest, nationwide, non-profit, voluntary public health organization in Oregon. Governed by a voluntary Board of Directors, we are the only community health agency dedicated solely to fighting lung disease and promoting lung healthin Oregon.
Founded: 1972
Dana Kaye, Executive Director

1234 **American Rivers: Northwest Region:Portland**
320 SW Stark Street 503-827-8648
Suite 412 Fax: 503-827-8654
Portland, OR 97204 http://www.americanrivers.org
American Rivers is the only national organization standing up for healthy rivers so our communities can thrive. Through national advocacy, innovative solutions and our growing network of strategic partners, we protect and promote ourrivers as valuable assests that are vital to our health, safety and quality of life.
Founded: 1992
J David Moryc, Associate Director Programs

1235 **American Society of Landscape Architects: Oregon Chapter**
147 SE 102nd Avenue Portland 503-227-6156
Oregon, OR 97216 Fax: 503-253-9172
E-mail: info@aslaoregon.org
http://www.aslaoregon.org

Kurt Lango, President
Amy Cooney, VP Chapter Services

1236 **Columbia Basin Fish and Wildlife Authority**
851 SW Sixth Avenue, Suite 260 503-229-0191
Pacific Centre Fax: 503-229-0443
Portland, OR 97204 http://www.cbfwa.org
A non-profit corporation to provide an opportunity for the Agencies and Tribes of the Pacific Northwest to become directly involved in the fiscal, administrative and managerial aspects of jointly funded activities.
Founded: 1993
Jann Eckman, President
Dave Statler, Vice President

1237 **Ecotrust**
721 NW Ninth Avenue 503-227-6225
Suite 200 Fax: 503-222-1517
Portland, OR 97209 E-mail: contact@ecotrust.org
http://www.ecotrust.org
To inspire fresh thinking that creates economic opportunity, social equity and environmental well-being.
Astrid Scholz, President
Adam Lane, CFO/COO

1238 **Natural Resources Information Council**
StreamNet Library
Dean Walton 541-346-2871
520 University of Oregon Fax: 541-346-3485
Eugene, OR 97403 E-mail: dpwalton@uoregon.edu
http://www.nric.info
The main purpose of NRIC is to facilitate the exchange of information among librarians specializing in natural resource libraries and collections in both public (government, academic), and private (NGO, consulting) organizations.
Founded: 1993
Dean Walton, President

1239 **Northwest Coalition for Alternatives to Pesticides**
PO Box 1393 541-344-5044
Eugene, OR 97440 Fax: 541-344-6923
E-mail: info@pesticide.org
http://www.pesticide.org
Protects the health of people and the environment by advancing alternatives to pesticides.
Founded: 1977
Kim Leval, Executive Director
Shelly Connor, Development Director

1240 **Northwest Power and Conservation Council**
851 SW Sixth Avenue 503-222-5161
Suite 1100 800-452-5161
Portland, OR 97204 Fax: 503-820-2370
E-mail: info@nwcouncil.org
http://www.nwcouncil.org/contact/or.asp
The council develops and maintains a regional power plan and a fish and wildlife program to balance the Northwest's environment and energy needs.
Brill Bradbury, Council Chair

1241 **Oregon Refuse and Recycling Association**
PO Box 2186 503-588-1837
Salem, OR 97308 800-527-7624
Fax: 503-399-7784
E-mail: orrainfo@orra.net
http://www.orra.net
A 200 member voluntary association of solid waste management companies and businesses which specialize in offering equipment and services important to the industry. ORRA provides legislative advocacy, education, group insurance,meeting facilities and advice on regulatory matters to its memebers.
Founded: 1965
Kristen Mitchell, Executive Director
Kimera Coady, Executive Assistant

1242 **Oregon State Public Interest Research Group**
1536 SE 11th Avenue 503-231-4181
Suite A E-mail: info@ospirg.org
Portland, OR 97214 http://www.ospirg.org
OSPIRG's mission is to deliver persistent, result-oriented public interest activism that protects consumers, encourages a fair, sustainable economy, and fosters responsive democratic government.
Founded: 1983
David Rosenfeld, Executive Director
Julie Titus, Development Director

1243 **Oregon Trout**
65 SW Yamhill Street 503-222-9091
Suite 200 Fax: 503-222-9187
Portland, OR 97204 E-mail: info@thefreshwatertrust.org
http://www.ortrout.org
A statewide non-profit organization headquartered in Portland, Oregon with satellite offices in Bandon, Bend, Corvallis and Medford. Oregon Trout works to restore freshwater health through innovation and education.
Founded: 1983
Joe S. Whitworth, President
Alan Hortan, Managing Director

1244 **Oregon Water Resources Congress**
437 Union Street NE 503-363-0121
Salem, OR 97301 Fax: 503-371-4926
E-mail: owrc_info@yahoo.com
http://www.owrc.org
To promote the protection and use of water rights and the wise stewardship of water resources.
Founded: 1912
April Snell, Executive Director
Ken Crick, Office Manager

1245 **Oregon Wild**
5825 N Greeley 503-283-6343
Portland, OR 97217 Fax: 503-283-0756
E-mail: rm@oregonwild.org
http://www.oregonwild.org

Formerly Oregon Natural Resources Council, Oregon Wild works to protect and restore Oregon's wildlands, wildlife and waters as an enduring leagacy for all Oregonians.
Founded: 1974
Sean Stevens, Executive Director
Jonathan Jelen, Development Coordinator

1246 **Pacific Rivers Council**
PO Box 10798
Eugene, OR 97440
541-345-0119
Fax: 541-345-0710
E-mail: info@pacrivers.org
http://www.pacrivers.org
One of the most influential river conservation organizations in the United States. The mission is to protect and restore rivers, their watersheds, and native aquatic species.
Founded: 1987
Holly Spencer, Acting Executive Director

1247 **Rising Tide North America**
268 Bush St
Box # 3717
San Francisco, CA 94101
E-mail: contact@risingtidenorthamerica.org
http://www.risingtidenorthamerica.org
An international, all-volunteer, grassroots network of groups and individuals who organize locally, promote community-based solutions to the climate crisis and take direct action to confront the root causes of climate change.

1248 **Sierra Club-Oregon Chapter**
1821 SE Ankeny St
Portland, OR 97214
503-238-0442
Fax: 503-238-6281
E-mail: oregon.chapter@sierraclub.org
http://oregon.sierraclub.org
Non profit member supported organization that promotes conservation of the state's natural environment for the public interest by influencing public policy decisions.
Chris Smith, State Forest Program Coordin
Brian Pasko, Chapter Director

1249 **Solar Oregon**
205 SE Grand Ave
Suite 205
Portland, OR 97214
844-272-3477
E-mail: info@solaror.org
http://www.solaror.org
A non-profit membership organization providing public education and community outreach to encourage Oregonians to choose solar energy
Christopher Luttkus, President
Michael VanDerwater, Executive Director

1250 **University of Oregon Environmental Studies Program**
5223 University of Oregon
Eugene, OR 97403
541-346-5070
Fax: 541-346-5954
E-mail: ecopeers@uoregon.edu
http://envs.uoregon.edu
Environmental Studies crosses the boundaries of traditional disciplines, challenging faculty and students to look at the relationship between humans and their environment from a new perspective. They are dedicated to gaining greaterunderstanding of the natural world from an ecological perspective; devising policy and behavior that address contemporary environmental problems; and promoting a rethinking of basic cultural premises, ways of structuring knowledge and the rootmetaphors of society.
Founded: 1983
Alan Dickman, Program Director
RaDonna Aymong, Office Manager

1251 **Wildlife Society**
PO Box 2378
Corvallis, OR 97339
541-937-2131
Fax: 541-937-3401
To promote wise conservation and management of wildlife resources in Oregon by serving and representing wildlife professionals.
Mark Penninger, President

Pennsylvania

1252 **Air and Waste Management Association**
One Gateway Center, 3rd Floor
420 Fort Duquesne Boulevard
Pittsburgh, PA 15222
412-232-3444
800-270-3444
Fax: 412-232-3450
E-mail: info@awma.org
http://www.awma.org
A nonprofit, nonpartisan professional organization that enhances knowledge and expertise by providing a neutral forum for information exchange, professional development, networking opportunities, public education, and outreach to morethan 9000 environmental professionals in 65 countries. A&WMA also promotes global enviromnetal responsibility and increases the effectivenessof organization to make critical decisions that benefit society.
Founded: 1907
Jim Powell, Executive Director
Bill Braun, Director

1253 **Alliance for the Chesapeake Bay**
3310 Market Street
Suite A
Camp Hill, PA 17011
717-737-8622
Fax: 717-737-8650
E-mail: acbpa@acb-online.org
http://www.acb-online.org
Founded: 1971
David Bancroft, President

1254 **American Lung Association of the Mid-Atlantic**
3001 Old Gettysburg Road
Camp Hill, PA 17011
717-541-5864
Fax: 717-541-8828
E-mail: dbrown@lunginfo.org
http://www.lunginfo.org
The mission of the American Lung Association is to save lives through the prevention of lung disease and the promotion of lung health. Covers PA, WV, & NJ areas.
Founded: 1904
Kenneth G Hysdock, Board Chair

1255 **American Society of Landscape Architects: Pennsylvania/Delaware Chapter**
908 North Second Street
Harrisburg, PA 19102
717-441-6041
E-mail: info@padeasla.org
http://www.padeasla.org
Founded: 1899
Adam Supplee, President
John D Wanner, Executive Director

1256 **Appalachian States Low-Level Radioactive Waste Commission**
Pennsylvania DEP/BRP
400 Market Street, 13th Floor
Harrisburg, PA 17101
410-537-3345
Fax: 410-537-4133
E-mail: kmcginty@state.pa.us
http://www.dep.state.pa.us
The commission was ratified by Maryland, Delaware, Pennsylvania and West Virginia to assure intertstate cooperation for the proper packaging and transportation of low-level radioactive waste. Pennsylvania is the host state and handlesthe administrative duties of the commission at this time.
Founded: 1986
Kathleen A McGinty, Chair/Executive Director
Richard R Janati, Administrator

1257 **Audubon Society of Western Pennsylvania at the Beechwood Farms Nature Reserve**
614 Dorseyville Road
Pittsburgh, PA 15238
412-963-6100
Fax: 412-963-6761
E-mail: aswp@aswp.org
http://www.aswp.org/
To inspire and educate the people of southwestern Pennsylvania to be respectful and responsible stewards of the natural world.
Founded: 1916
Sally Tarhi, President
Danforth Fales, Vice President

1258 Brandywine Conservancy
PO Box 141
Chadds Ford, PA 19317
610-388-2700
Fax: 610-388-1197
E-mail: emc@brandywine.org
http://www.brandywineconservancy.org

The Conservancy is a nonprofit land and water conservation organization protecting natural resources in southeastern PA and northern DE. It provides conservation services to landowners, farmers and municipalities through acomprehensive approach to cutting-edge environmental planning and management. Through conservation easements, historic preservation, and water protection efforts, the Conservancy has been instrumental in permanently protecting more than 43,000 acresof land.
Founded: 1967
George A Weymouth, Chairman
Jeffrey M Nielsen, Vice President

1259 Global Education Motivators
9601 Germantown Avenue
Philadelphia, PA 19118
215-248-1150
877-451-7925
Fax: 215-248-7056
E-mail: gem@chc.edu
http://www.gem-ngo.org

A non-profit organization to help schools meet the complex challenges of living in a global society.
Founded: 1981
Wayne Jacoby, President
Sabrina Cusimano, Director of Programs

1260 Hawk Mountain Sanctuary Association
1700 Hawk Mountain Road
Kempton, PA 19529
610-756-6961
Fax: 601-756-4468
http://www.hawkmountain.org

To conserve birds of prey worldwide by providing leadership in raptor conservation science and education, and by maintaining Hawk Mountain Sanctuary as a model observation, research and education facility.
Wendy Mclean, Chairman
Peter Bennett, Vice Chairman

1261 Nature Conservancy: Pennsylvania Chapter
Nature Conservancy
2101 North Front Street
Building # 1 Suite 200
Harrisburg, PA 17110
717-232-6001
866-298-1267
Fax: 717-232-6061
E-mail: pa_chapter@tnc.org
http://http://nature.org/wherewework/northamerica/states/pennsylvan

Founded: 1951
Bill Kunze, State Director
Nels Johnson, Deputy State Director

1262 Penn State Institutes of Energy and the Environment
Land and Water Research Building
University Park, PA 16802
814-863-0291
Fax: 814-865-3378
E-mail: plc103@psu.edu
http://www.environment.psu.edu

The mission is to expand Penn State's capacity to pursue the newest frontiers in energy and environmental research by encouraging cooperation across disciplines and the participation of local, state, federal and internationalstakeholders.
Tom Richard, Director

1263 Pennsylvania Association of Accredited Environmental Laboratories
316 Roosevelt Street
Sayre, PA 18840
570-888-4768
Fax: 570-882-8538
E-mail: judygraves@paael.org
http://www.paael.org

A non-profit association of PA DEP accredited laboratories and related industry representatives which takes a leadership role in promoting the advancement of environmental laboratories by: providing educational opportunities,professional development, and a forum for information exchange; providing an arena for memebers to effectively interact with state and national regulatory agencies; and encouraging ethical conduct of environmental laboratories.
Founded: 1987
Judy Graves, Executive Director

1264 Pennsylvania Association of Conservation Districts
25 N Front Street
Harrisburg, PA 17101
717-238-7223
Fax: 717-238-7201
E-mail: pacd@pacd.org
http://www.pacd.org

A nonprofit organization that supports, enhances and promotes Pennsylvania's Conservation Districts and their programs. PACd provides districts with education and information to help them in their work in land and water conservation.
Founded: 1950
Robert Maiden, Executive Director

1265 Pennsylvania BASS Chapter Federation
769 N Cottage Road
Mercer, PA 16137
http://www.pabass.com

A non-profit service organization comprised of seven geographically divided districts across the state.
Mark Heckaman, President

1266 Pennsylvania Environmental Council
130 Locust Street
Suite 200
Harrisburg, PA 17101
717-230-8044
Fax: 717-230-8045
E-mail: bhill@pecpa.org
http://www.pecpa.org

Protects and restores the natural and built environments through innovation, collaboration, education and advocacy.
Brian Hill, President/CEO
Michael Hudson, VP/COO

1267 Pennsylvania Forestry Association
PO Box 1278
Mechanicsburg, PA 17055
717-766-5371
800-835-8065
E-mail: info@paforestry.org
http://pfa.cas.psu.edu

A broad-based citizens organization, provides leadership in sound forest management advice and education and promotes wise stewardship to private land owners, resulting in benefits for the resident of the Commonwealth.
Founded: 1886
David J Alerich, President
Robert Piper, Vice President

1268 Pennsylvania Resources Council
3606 Providence Road
Newtown Square, PA 19073
610-353-1555
Fax: 610-353-6257
E-mail: vanclief@prc.org
http://www.prc.org

To promote conservation of our natural resources and protection of scenic beauty through public education and outreach in a collaborative effort with government agencies, business, charitable foundations and other nonprofitorganizations.
Founded: 1939
Larry Myers, Executive Director
Barley Van Clief, Regional Director

1269 Pocono Environmental Education Center
538 Emery Road
Dingsman Ferry, PA 18328
570-828-2319
Fax: 570-828-9695
E-mail: peec@peec.org
http://www.peec.org

PEEC enhances environmental awareness, knowledge, and appreciation through hands-on experience in a natural outdoor classroom. Located in the Delaware Water Gap Nat'l Rec Area, PEEC is open year-round and welcomes school groupsfamilies, retreats, and volunteers.
Founded: 1972

1270 Rodale Institute
611 Siegfriedale Road
Kutztown, PA 19530
610-683-1400
Fax: 610-683-8548
E-mail: info@rodaleinst.org
http://www.rodaleinstitute.org

Works with people worldwide to achieve a regenerative food system thaty renews environmental and human health working with the philosophy that healthy soil = healthy food = healthy people.
Tim LaSalle, President

1271 Sierra Club: Pennsylvania Chapter
PO Box 606
Harrisburg, PA 17108
717-232-0101
Fax: 717-238-6330
E-mail: pennsylvania.chapter@sierraclub.org
http://pennsylvania.sierraclub.org
Includes 10 local Sierra Club groups. Emphasis is on state environmental policy advocacy, outings, education and local environmental protection efforts.
Jeff Schmidt, Senior Chapter Director
Carli Timpson, Administrative Assistant

1272 Western Pennsylvania Conservancy
800 Waterfront Drive
Pittsburgh, PA 15222
412-288-2777
866-564-6972
Fax: 412-231-1414
E-mail: info@paconserve.org
http://www.paconserve.org
Protects, conserves and restores land and water for the diversity of the region's plants, animals and their ecosystems. Through science-based strategies, collaboration, leadership and recognition of the relationship between humankindand nature, WPC achieves tangible conservation outcomes for present and future generations.
Susan Fitzsimmons, Chairman
Stephen G Robinson, Vice Chairman

Rhode Island

1273 American Lung Association of Rhode Island
260 West Exchange Street
Suite 102 B
Providence, RI 02903
401-421-6487
Fax: 401-331-5266
E-mail: info@lungne.org
http://www.lungusa.org/rhodeisland
Offers a wide variety of lung health services to the people of Rhode Island

1274 American Society of Landscape Architects:Rhode Island Chapter
http://www.riasla.org
The purpose shall be the advancement of knowledge, education, and skill in the art and science of landscape architecture as an instrument of service in the public welfare.
Jennifer Judge, President
Kurt Van Dexter, President-Elect

1275 Audubon Society of Rhode Island
12 Sanderson Road
Smithfield, RI 02917
401-949-5454
Fax: 401-949-5788
E-mail: audubon@asri.org
http://www.asri.org
An independent, nonprofit, state organization dedicated to the conservation of wildlife habitat, the education of young and old about natural ecosystems and the need to preserve them, and advocacy in order to promote continued effortsat preserving our natural heritage.
Founded: 1897
Lawrence Taft, Executive Director

1276 Nature Conservancy: Rhode Island Chapter
159 Waterman Street
Providence, RI 02906
401-331-7110
Fax: 401-273-4902
E-mail: ri@tnc.org
http://www.nature.org
An international nonprofit organization dedicated to preserving the plants, animals and natural communities that represent the diversity of life on Earth by protecting the lands and waters they need to survive.
John Cook, Regional Managing Director

1277 Sierra Club: Rhode Island Chapter
42 Rice Street
Providence, RI 02907
401-521-4734
E-mail: abels.collins@sierraclub.org
http://rhodeisland.sierraclub.org
Represents one of 64 chapters across the U.S. and Canada.
2500 Members
Ben Jones, Chapter Chairman
Abel Collins, Program Manager

South Carolina

1278 American Lung Association of South Carolina
44-A Markfield Drive
Charleston, SC 29407
843-556-8451
Fax: 843-766-3294
E-mail: alasc1@lungs.org
http://www.lungsc.org
Marcia Williams Ehd, Chairwoman
William R Cook MD, Chair-Elect

1279 American Lung Association of South Carolina: Coastal Region
1941 Savage Road
Suite 200-A
Charleston, SC 29407
843-556-8451
Fax: 843-556-3332
E-mail: scatlin@lungsc.org
Sally Catlin, Regional Director

1280 American Lung Association of South Carolina: Upstate Region
11 Brendan Way
B-2
Greenville, SC 29615
864-233-0517
Fax: 864-233-2124
E-mail: altompkins@lungsc.org
Al Tompkins, Regional Director

1281 American Rivers: Southeast Region
1001 Washington Street
Suite 301
Columbia, SC 29201
803-771-7114
Fax: 803-771-7580
http://www.americanrivers.org

1282 American Society of Landscape Architects: South Carolina Chapter
7 Lafayette Place
Hilton Head Island, SC 29926
843-681-6618
Fax: 843-681-7086
http://www.scasla.org
Robert Hewitt, President
Jamie Hairfield, President Elect

1283 Carolina Recycling Association
Greenville
PO Box 1296
Greenville, SC 29602
877-972-0007
Fax: 919-545-9060
E-mail: staff@cra-recycle.org
http://www.cra-recycle.org
Conserves resources by advancing waste reducation and recycling throughout the Carolinas
Founded: 1989
Kerry Krumsiek, Executive Director
Anna Shirley, Office Manager

1284 Friends of the Reedy River
PO Box 9351
Greensville, SC 29604
864-255-8946
http://www.friendsofthereedyriver.org
The Reedy River is an economic and social resource for the community that impacts our quality of life. Maintaining and protecting its health, above and below the surface, is pivotal in maintaining the natural, social and economicalhealth of the Upstate of South Carolina.
Kathryn Moore, President
Rita Barker, Vice President

1285 Nature Conservancy: South Carolina Chapter
PO Box 5475
Columbia, SC 29250
803-254-9049
Fax: 803-252-7134
E-mail: southcarolina@tnc.org
http://www.nature.org
Nonprofit conservation organization dedicated to preserving the plants, animals and natural communities that represent the diver-

sity of life on Earth by protecting the lands and waters they need to survive. Buys significant tracts ofland in its project areas and later re-sells the tracts to a public agency partner such as US Fish and Wildlife Service, US Forest Service and the SC Department of Natural Resources. Also supports and encourages conservation easements.
Mark Robertson, Executive Director

1286 **Sierra Club: South Carolina Chapter**
1314 Lincoln Street
Suite 211
Columbia, SC 29202
803-256-8487
Fax: 803-256-8448
http://southcarolina.sierraclub.org
Kurt Henning, Chapter Coordinator

1287 **South Atlantic Fishery Management Council**
4055 Faber Place Drive
Suite 201
North Charleston, SC 29405
843-571-4366
866-SAF-C 10
Fax: 843-769-4520
E-mail: safmc@safmc.net
http://www.safmc.net
Responsible for the conservation and management of fish stocks within the federal 200-mile limit of the Atlantic off the coasts of North Carolina, South Carolina, Georgia and east Florida to Key West.
Robert Mahood, Executive Director
Gregg Waugh, Deputy Executive Director

1288 **South Carolina BASS Chapter Federation**
1469 Schurlknight Road
St. Stephen, SC 29479
803-567-4680
Tony Bennett, President

1289 **South Carolina Native Plant Society**
PO Box 1324
Greenville, SC 29602
E-mail: jeffbeacham@gmail.com
http://www.scnps.org
A non-profit ogranization committed to the preservation and protection of native plant communities in South Carolina.
Jeff Beacham, President

1290 **South Carolina Solar Council**
PO Box 402
Columbia, SC 29201
803-691-4576
E-mail: info@scsolarcouncil.org
Todd Delello, Chairman

1291 **Southern Appalachian Botanical Society**
Newberry College
2100 College Street
Newberry, SC 29108
803-321-5257
Fax: 803-321-5636
E-mail: charles.horn.@newberry.edu
http://www.sabs.appstate.edu
This is a professional organization for those interested in botanical research, especially in the areas of ecology, floristics and systematics. To this end, we publish a journal, CASTANEA, and a newsletter, CHINQUAPIN.
Founded: 1936
Dr Wendy Zomlefer, President
Charles Horn, Treasurer

South Dakota

1292 **American Lung Association of South Dakota**
108 E. 38th Street
Sioux Falls, SD 57105
202-785-3355
800-586-4872
Fax: 202-452-1805
E-mail: lung@americanlungsd.org
http://www.lungusa.org
Founded: 1904
John F Emanuel JD, Secretary/Treasurer
Ross P Lanzafame, Chairman

1293 **Great Plains Native Plant Society**
PO Box 461
Hot Springs, SD 57747
605-745-3397
Fax: 605-745-3397
E-mail: info@gpnps.org
http://www.gpnps.org
Mission is to engage in scientific research regarding plants of the Great Plains of North America; to disseminate this knowledge through the creation of one or more educational botanic gardens of plants of the Great Plains, featuringbut not limited to Barr's discoveries; and to engage in any educational activities which may further public familiarity with plants of the Great Plains, their uses and enjoyment.
Founded: 1984

1294 **Sierra Club: South Dakota Chapter**
PO Box 1624
Rapid City, SD 57709
605-348-1345
Fax: 605-348-1344
http://southdakota.sierraclub.org
Jim Heisinger, Chair
Todd Jensen, Secretary

1295 **South Dakota Association of Conservation Districts**
PO Box 275
Pierre, SD 57501
605-895-4099
Fax: 605-895-9424
http://www.sdconservation.org
Mission is to lead, represent and assist South Dakota's conservation districts in promoting a healthy environment. Specific areas of concern include wind and water erosion, water quality and quantity including preservation of theMissouri main stem dams, air quality, forestry, rangeland, wildlife and recreation.
Founded: 1942
Angela Ehlers, Executive Director

1296 **South Dakota Ornithologists Union**
3108 South Holly Avenue
Sioux Falls, SD 57105
605-677-6175
Fax: 605-677-6557
E-mail: sfbirdclub@sio.midco.net
http://www.sdou.org
To encourage the study of birds in South Dakota and to promote the study of orinthology by more closely uniting the students of this branch of natural science.
Founded: 1949
Nancy Drilling, President
Ricky Olson, Vice President

1297 **South Dakota Wildlife Federation**
PO Box 7075
Pierre, SD 57501
605-224-7524
Fax: 605-224-7524
E-mail: sdwf@mncomm.com
http://www.sdwf.org
Represents the interests of all South Dakotans in wildelife, out door recreation, natural resources, and a quality environment.
Founded: 1945
Rose Jensen, Director District

1298 **Wildlife Society**
Box 218
DeSmet, SD 57231
605-854-9105
E-mail: paul.coughlin@state.sd.us
A nonprofit scientific and educational organization that serves professionals such as government agencies, academia, industry, and non-government organizations in all areas related to the conservation of wildlife and natural resources management.
Founded: 1937
Will Morlock, South Dakota State President

Tennessee

1299 **American Lung Association of Tennessee: Southeast Office**
1466 Riverside Drive
Suite D
Chattanooga, TN 37406
423-629-1098
800-432-5864
Fax: 423-629-0054
E-mail: scudabac@midlandlung.org
http://www.lungtn.org
Founded: 1910

1300 **American Lung Association of Tennessee:Middle Region**
State Office
One Vantage Way, Suite D220
Nashville, TN 37228
615-329-1151
800-432-5864
Fax: 615-329-1723
E-mail: gbost@midlandlung.org
http://www.alatn.org

Founded: 1910

1301 **American Society of Landscape Architects: Tennessee Chapter**
E-mail: hollie@tnasla.org
http://www.tnasla.org

Larry Mizell, President
Henry Minor, President-Elect

1302 **Kids for a Clean Environment**
PO Box 158254
Nashville, TN 37215
615-331-7381
Fax: 615-333-9879
E-mail: kidsface@mindspring.com
http://www.kidsface.org

Established to help children who wanted to learn more about the world in which they live, provide a way for children to be involved in the protection of nature and connect children with other children who share their concerns aboutglobal environmental issues.
Founded: 1989
Melissa Poe, Founder

1303 **Nature Conservancy: Tennessee Chapter**
2021 21st Avenue South
Suite C-400
Nashville, TN 37212
615-383-9909
800-628-6860
Fax: 615-383-9717
E-mail: tennessee@tnc.org
http://www.nature.org

The Tennessee Chapter has protected more than 220,000 acres in the state.
Founded: 1951
Gina Hancock, State Director
Paul Kingsbury, Communications Manager

1304 **Scenic Tennessee**
45 Burris Court
Mount Juliet, TN 37122
615-758-8647
E-mail: margedavis@comcast.net
http://www.scenictennessee.org

The only organization in the state devoted exclusively to issues of scenic beauty.
Marge Davis Ph D, President
Jay Nevans, Vice President

1305 **Sierra Club: Tennessee Chapter**
3340 Perimeter Hill Drive
Nashville, TN 37211
615-837-3773
http://tennessee.sierraclub.org

Keven Routon, Chair
Angela Garrone, Vice Chair

1306 **Tennessee Association of Conservation Districts**
PO Box 107
Hickory Valley, TN 38042
731-764-2909
Fax: 731-658-6726
E-mail: barry.lake@tnacd.org
http://tnacd.org

Founded: 1982
Ray Weaver, President
John Leeman, Vice President

1307 **Tennessee Citizens for Wilderness Planning**
130 Tabor Road
Oak Ridge, TN 37830
865-481-0286
E-mail: groton87@comcast.net
http://www.tcwp.org

Dedicated to achieving and perpetuating protection of natural lands and waters by means of public ownership, legislation, or cooperation of the private sector.
Founded: 1966
Jimmy Groton, President
Sandra Goss, Executive Director

1308 **Tennessee Environmental Council**
One Vantage Way
Suite E-250
Nashville, TN 37228
615-248-6500
Fax: 615-248-6500
E-mail: tec@tectn.org
http://www.tectn.org

The mission of the Tennessee Environmental Council is to educate and advocate for the conservation and improvement of Tennessee's environment, communities, and public health.
Founded: 1970
Don Safer, Chairman
Mary Mastin, Board Secretary

1309 **Tennessee Woodland Owners Association**
PO Box 1400
Crossville, TN 38557
615-484-5535
Fax: 915-484-1924
E-mail: reharrison@multipro.com

Robert Harrison, Secretary/Treasurer

1310 **Toxicology Information Response Center**
1060 Commerce Park
MS 6480
Oak Ridge, TN 37830
865-576-1746
Fax: 865-574-9888
E-mail: slusherkg@ornl.gov
http://www.ornl.gov/TechResources/tirc/hmepg.html

TIRC provides customer search services to both scientific and public communities as a convenient and efficient way to obtain comprehensive scientific information on any subject of interest.
Founded: 1971
Kim Slusher, Administrator

1311 **Wildlife Society**
Ellington Agricultural Center
PO Box 40747
Nashville, TN 37204
423-253-8416
E-mail: mdodson@fs.fed.us
http://www.utm.edu/TN-TWS

A nonprofit scientific and educational organization that serves professionals such as government agencies, academia, industry, and non-government organizations in all areas related to the conservation of wildlife and natural resources management.
Founded: 1968 $10/Year
Ed Warr, President
Tim White, President-Elect

Texas

1312 **American Environmental Health Foundation**
8345 Walnut Hill Lane
Suite 225
Dallas, TX 75231
214-361-9515
800-428-2343
Fax: 214-361-2534
E-mail: aehf@aehf.com
http://www.aehf.com

The Environmental Health Foundation's mission is two-fold: to fund scientific and/or medical research into the causes of environmentally linked disease; and to educate the public about environmentally linked illness and how to preventexposure through lifestyle changes.
Founded: 1975
William Rea, Founder
David Hicks, Director

1313 **American Lung Association of Texas: Central Region**
5926 Balcones Drive
Suite 100
Austin, TX 78731
512-467-6753
Fax: 512-467-7621
E-mail: inquiries@breathehealthy.org
http://www.texaslung.org

Laura Chapman, Senior Program Director

1314 **American Lung Association of Texas:Alamo and Southern Region**
7475 Callaghan Road
Suite 140
San Antonio, TX 78230
210-308-8978
Fax: 210-308-8992
E-mail: alasoutx@texaslung.org
http://www.texaslung.org

Jerilyn Miller, Senior Program Director
Linda Nichols, Regional VP/Advocacy

1315 American Lung Association of Texas:Dallas/Ft Worth Region
8150 Brookriver Drive
S-102
Dallas, TX 75247
214-631-5864
800-586-4872
Fax:214-630-8092
E-mail:inquiries@breathehealthy.org
http://www.texaslung.org

Sara Dreiling, CEO
Yolanda Sims, Program Director

1316 American Lung Association of Texas:Houston and Southeast Region
2030 North Loop West
Suite 250
Houston, TX 77018
713-629-5864
800-586-4872
Fax:713-629-5825
E-mail:batkins@texaslung.org
http://www.texaslung.org

Bob Atkins, Regional VP Development
Chantel L Henderson, Program Coordinator

1317 American Lung Association of Texas:Western Region
4141 Pinnacle Street
Suite 212
El Paso, TX 79902
915-532-6776
800-252-5864
Fax:915-532-7231
E-mail:terrazas@texaslung.org
http://www.texaslung.org

Miguel Escobedo, Program Coordinator

1318 American Socicty of Landscape Architects:Texas Chapter
1709 Buttercup Creek Blvd.
Cedar Park, TX 78613
512-627-4570
Fax:512-249-9885
E-mail:bclifford@team-psc.cpm
http://www.texasasla.org

Brent Clifford, President
Jennifer Fontana,CAE, Executive Director

1319 Association of Texas Soil and Water Conservation Districts
4311 South 31st Street
Suite 125
Temple, TX 76502
254-773-2250
800-792-3485
Fax:254-773-3311
E-mail:bwhite@tsswcb.state.tx.us
http://www.tsswcb.state.tx.us/swcds/atswcd

The nonprofit organization attempts to make owners and operators of agricultural land aware of the need to conserve and protect the soil and water resources in Texas. It promotes SWCDs (soil and water conservation districts) througheducational, scientific, charitable, and religious activities.
Scott Buckles, President

1320 Big Bend Natural History Association
PO Box 196
Big Bend National Park, TX 79834
432-477-2236
Fax:432-477-2234
E-mail:info@bigbendbookstore.org
http://www.bigbendbookstore.org

The association's goal is to educate the public and increase their appreciation of the Big Bend Area. It conducts seminars, publishes and supplies books, maps and other materials.
Founded:1956
Mike Boren, Executive Director

1321 Center for Environmental Philosophy
University of North Texas
1155 Union Circle # 310980
Denton, TX 76203
940-565-2727
Fax:940-565-4439
E-mail:cep@unt.edu.
http://www.cep.unt.edu

Publishes the journal Environmental Ethics, maintains a reprint book series in environmental philosophy, promotes education in the field of environmental philosophy, sponsors conference, workshops.
Founded:1979
Eugene C Hargrove, President
Alexandria K. Poole, Associate Director

1322 National Wildlife Federation Gulf States Natural Resource Center
44 East Avenue
Suite 200
Austin, TX 78701
512-476-9805
Fax:512-476-9810
E-mail:kaderka@nwf.org
http://online.nwf.org/gulfstates

The focus of the four state region (TX, LA, OK, MO) is to restore clean rivers and estuaries, conserve wetlands and natural river systems, protect wildlife populations, promote sustainable land and water use, and educate the public onthese issues.
Susan Kaderka, Regional Executive Director
Lacey McCormick, Communications Manager

1323 North Plains Groundwater Conservation District
603 E 1st Street
PO Box 795
Dumas, TX 79029
806-935-6401
Fax:806-935-6633
E-mail:kwelch@northplainsgcd.org.
http://www.npwd.org

Founded:1949
Steven Walthour, General Manager
Casey Tice, Compliance Coordinator

1324 Scenic Texas
3015 Richmond Ave
Suite 220
Houston, TX 77098
713-533-9149
Fax:713-629-0485
E-mail:scenic@scenictexas.org
http://www.scenictexas.org

Scenic Texas is a nonprofit organization dedicated to the preservation and enhancement of the tstate's visual environemnt. It seeks and supports public policies which promote scenic conservation and beautification and limits harmfulactions to the visual environment.
Founded:1967
Amanda McClanahan, Program Director
Anne Culver, Executive Vice President

1325 Sierra Club:Lone Star Chapter
PO Box 1931
Austin, TX 78767-1931
512-477-1729
Fax:512-477-8526
E-mail:lonestar.chapter@sierraclub.org
http://texas.sierraclub.org

The Lone Star Chapter consists of over 25,000 members and serves as the grassroots communications center. The chapter also represents memebers as they fight at the state level to protect and conserve Texas' diverse natural heritage.
Founded:1965
Scheleen Walker, Chapter Director
Neil Carman, Clean Air Director

1326 Texas Conservation Alliance
PO Box 822554
Dallas, TX 75382
512-327-4119
E-mail:TCA@TCAtexas.org
http://tconr.org

Formerly the Texas Committee on Natural Resources. A statewide conservation organization protecting native wildlife habitat and urging the wise and efficient use of natural resources.
Founded:1970
Janice Bezanson, Executive Director

1327 Texas Environmental Health Association
PO Box 889
Wolfforth, TX 79382
806-855-4277
E-mail:steve.berry@myteha.org
http://www.myteha.org

A professional nonprofit educational organization that was originally founded as the Texas Association of Sanitarians and then merged with the National Environmental Health Association and changed its name in 1971. For professionals inall program areas of the environmental health field.
Founded:1956
Janet Tucker, President
Jodie Heilman-Halter, Executive Director

1328 Texas Solar Energy Society
PO Box 1447
Austin, TX 78767
512-326-3391
800-465-5049
Fax:512-444-0333
E-mail:info@txses.org
http://www.txses.org

Their mission is to increase the awareness of the potential of solar and other renewable energy applications and promote the wise use of these sustainable and non-polluting resources.
Lucy Stolzenburg, Executive Director
Chris Boyer, Chairman

1329 **Texas State Soil and Water Conservation Board (TSSWCB)**
4311 South 31st Street 254-773-2250
Suite 125 800-792-3485
Temple, TX 76502 Fax:254-773-3311
http://www.tsswcb.state.tx.us
The state agency that administers Texas' soil and water conservation laws and coordinates conservation and nonpoint source pollution abatement programs through the State. The Board is composed of 7 members, 2 Governor appointed and 5landowners, from across Texas, and is the lead state agency for planning, management, and abatement of agricultural and silvicultural (forestry) nonpoint source pollution, and administers the Texas Brush Control Program. There are regional officesthroughout Texas.
Founded: 1939
Vicky Davis, Administrative Coordinator
Rex Isom, Executive Director

1330 **Texas Water Conservation Association**
221 E 9th Street
Suite 206 512-472-7216
Austin, TX 78701 Fax: 512-472-0537
E-mail: drobbins@twca.org
http://www.twca.org
Devoted to conserving, developing, protecting, and using water resources in the state of Texas for all beneficial purposes.
Founded: 1944
Luana T. Buckner, President
Leroy Goodson, General Manager

Utah

1331 **American Fisheries Society: Water Quality Section**
324 25th Street 801-625-5358
Ogden, UT 84401 Fax: 801-625-5756
E-mail: glampman@fs.fed.us
Section objectives are to: maintain an association of persons involved in the protection of watersheds, water quality, and aquatic habitat, and the abatement of water pollution and aquatic habitat and water deterioration.
Gina Lampman, President

1332 **American Lung Association in Utah**
1930 South 1100 East 801-484-4456
Salt Lake City, UT 84106 Fax: 801-484-5461
E-mail: info@lungutah.org
http://www.lungutah.org
The American Lung Association is committed to preventing lung disease and promoting lung health, through education, research, and advocacy.
Founded: 1904
W. Glenn Lanham, Executive Director
Sara Kecor, Office Coordinator

1333 **American Society of Landscape Architects: Utah Chapter**
636 Eye Street NW 202-898-2444
Washington, DC 20001 888-999-2752
Fax: 202-898-1185
E-mail: info@asla.org
http://host.asla.org/chapters/utahasla

1334 **Grand Canyon Trust: Utah Office**
HC 64
PO Box 1801 435-259-5284
Maob, UT 84532 Fax: 435-259-5348
http://www.grandcanyontrust.org
A regional, non-profit conservation organization that advocates collaborative, common sense solutions to the significant problems affecting the region's natural resources. Our work is focused in the greater Grand Canyon region ofnorthern Arizona, and in the forests and red rock country of central and southern Utah.
Bill Hedden, Executive Director

1335 **Jack H Berryman Institute**
Utah State University 435-797-2436
5230 Old Main Hill NR 206 Fax: 435-797-1871
Logan, UT 84322-5271 http://www.berrymaninstitute.org
The Berryman Institute is a national organization based in the Department of Wildland Resources at Utah State University and the Department of Wildlife & Fisheries at Mississippi State University. The Berryman Institute is dedicatedto improving human-wildlife relationships and resolving human-wildlife conflicts through teaching, research, and extension.
Dr. Terry A. Messmer, Director
Dr. Mike Conover, Editor in Chief

1336 **Nature Conservancy: Utah Chapter**
559 E South Temple 801-531-0999
Salt Lake City, UT 84102 Fax: 801-531-1003
E-mail: utah@tnc.org
http://www.tnc.org/utah
Founded: 1951
Dave Livermore, State Director

1337 **Sierra Club**
423 W 800 S STE A103 801-467-9294
Salt Lake City, UT 84101 E-mail: utah.chapter@sierraclub.org
http://utah.sierraclub.org
To advance the preservation and protection of the natural environment by empowering the citizenry, especially democratically-based grassroots organizations, with charitable resources to further the cause of environmental protection.The vehicle through which The Sierra Club Foundation generally fulfills its charitable mission.
Founded: 1892
Marion Klaus, Chair
Leslie Hugo, Secretary

1338 **Southern Utah Wilderness Alliance**
425 East 100 South 801-486-3161
Salt Lake City, UT 84111 E-mail: info@suwa.org
http://www.suwa.org
The mission is the preservation of the outstanding wilderness at the heartof the Colorado Plateau, and the mangement of these lands in their natural state for the benefit of all Americans.
Founded: 1983
Scott Groene, Executive Director

1339 **Utah Association of Conservation Districts**
1860 N 100 E 435-753-6029
Logan, UT 84341 Fax: 435-755-2117
http://www.uacd.org
A nonprofit corporation representing Utah's 38 soil conservation districts. Provides technicians and planners to design conservation projects for private landowners, staff to coordinate watershed and conservation district projects andconservation education outreach.
Gordon L Younker, Executive VP
Susan Jackson, Executive Assistant

1340 **Utah Association of Soil Conservation Districts**
1860 N 100 E 435-753-6029
Logan, UT 84341 Fax: 435-753-4037
William Rigby, Executive Board Member

1341 **Utah Division of Wildlife Resources**
1594 West North Temple 801-538-4700
Suite 2110 Box 146301 E-mail: dwrcomment@utah.gov
Salt Lake City, UT 84114-6301 http://wildlife.utah.gov
Serve people of Utah as trustee and guardian of the state's wildlife.

1342 **Utah Solar Energy Association**
7414 S State 801-566-5620
Midvale, UT 84047 Fax: 801-566-0708
E-mail: info@UTSOLAR.org
http://utsolar.org

Organized to promote the usage of renewable energy, with a focus on solar energy, through education, public outreach, participation in policy development and other activities to accomplish the goals of the organization.

Vermont

1343 **American Lung Association of Vermont**
30 Farrell St. 802-863-6817
South Burlington, VT 05403 Fax: 802-863-6818
E-mail: info@vtlung.org
http://www.lungusa2.org/vermont/
Offers a wide variety of lung health services to the people of Vermont.
Robert C. Uerz, Executive Director

1344 **American Society of Landscape Architects: Vermont Chapter**
497 Ethan Allen Road E-mail: patrick.mclean@stantec.com
Chester http://host.asla.org/chapters/vermont/index.cfm
Vermont, VT 05143
The chapter holds monthly meetings to encourage dialogue among practioners and members, collaborate with those in related fields, and embrace professional guidelines.
Kevin O Connor, CEO
Scott Leonard, CTO

1345 **Bluebirds Across Vermont Project**
The Birdhouse Network
255 Sherman Hollow Road 802-434-3068
Green Mountain Abdubon Society Fax: 802-434-4686
Huntington, VT 05462 E-mail: bluebirdhousing@ellijay.com
http://www.cornell.edu
Jim Shallow, Executive Director

1346 **Conservation and Research Foundation**
PO Box 909 913-268-0076
Shelburne, VT 05482 Fax: 913-268-0076
http://www.conservationresearch.wordpress.com
Founded: 1953
Mary Wetzel, President

1347 **National Wildlife Federation Northeastern Natural Resource Center**
58 State Street 802-229-0650
Montpelier, VT 05602 800-822-9919
Fax: 802-229-4532
http://www.nwf.org
The Northeastern Field Office works with state-based affiliates and like-minded organizations to protect valuable woods, water and wildlife resources across New England through education, advocacy and research.
Larry J Schweiger, President/CEO

1348 **Noise Pollution Clearinghouse**
PO Box 1137 888-200-8332
Montpelier, VT 05601 http://www.nonoise.org
A national non-profit organization with extensive online noise related resources. The mission of the Clearinghouse is to create more civil cities and more natural rural and wilderness areas by reducing noise pollutions at the source.

1349 **Northeast Recycling Council**
139 Main Street 802-254-3636
Suite 401 Fax: 802-254-5870
Brattleboro, VT 05301 E-mail: info@nerc.org
http://www.nerc.org
To advance an environmentally sustainable economy by promoting source and toxicity reduction, recycling, and the purchasing of environmentally preferable products and services.
Lynn Rubinstein, Executive Director
Mary Ann Remolador, Assistant Director

1350 **Sierra Club: Vermont Chapter**
149 State Street 802-229-6399
Montpelier, VT 05601 E-mail: sierraclub.vt@gmail.com
http://vermont.sierraclub.org

1351 **Vermont Association of Conservation Districts**
PO Box 566 802-496-5162
Waitsfield, VT 05673 Fax: 802-329-2057
E-mail: jill.arace@vacd.org
http://www.vacd.org
A non-profit organization of Vermont's 14 Conservation Districts whose mission is to help the Districts carry out natural resource oriented programs at the local level.
Jonathan Chamberlin, President
D. Jill Arace, Executive Director

1352 **Vermont BASS Chapter Federation**
Bassin' USA
19 Pinewood Road 802-223-7793
Montpelier, VT 05602 E-mail: nsk@together.net
http://www.bassinusa.com
Founded: 1968
Brendan Cucinello, President

1353 **Vermont Haulers and Recyclers Association**
PO Box 976 802-864-3615
Williston, VT 05495 Fax: 802-660-8553
http://www.zella.com

1354 **Vermont Land Trust**
8 Bailey Avenue 802-223-5234
Montpelier, VT 05602 800-639-1709
Fax: 802-223-4223
E-mail: info@vlt.org
http://www.vlt.org
One of the most effective land trusts in the country. Its primary focus is on permanently conserving productive, recreational, and scenic lands vital to Vermont's and rural economy and environment.
Founded: 1977
Gil Livingston, President
Rick Provost, Director of Finance

1355 **Vermont Public Interest Research Group**
141 Main Street 802-223-5221
Suite 6 Fax: 802 223 6855
Montpelier, VT 05602 E-mail: vpirg@vpirg.org
http://www.vpirg.org
The largest nonprofit consumer and environmental advocacy organization in the state, with approximately 20,000 members and supporters. VPIRG's mission is to promote and protect the health of Vermont's people, environment andlocally-based economy by informing and mobilizing citizens statewide.
Founded: 1972
Paul Burns, Executive Director
Colleen Thomas, Associate Director

1356 **Vermont State-Wide Environmental Education Programs**
713 Elm St. 802-985-8686
Montpelier, VT 05602 http://vermontsweep.org
Susan Clark, Chair

Virginia

1357 **American Bird Conservancy**
4249 Loudoun Ave 540-253-5780
PO Box 249 888-247-3624
The Plains, VA 20198-2237 Fax: 540-253-5782
http://www.abcbirds.org
A not-for-profit organization whose mission is to conserve native birds and their habitats throughout the Americas.
George H Fenwick, President
Warren F Cooke, Chairman

1358 American Lung Association of Virginia
9702 Gayton Road
#110
Richmond, VA 23238
804-955-4910
800-586-4872
E-mail: lungva@lungusa.org
http://www.lungvirginia.org

To promote lung health and prevent lung disease.
Founded: 1909
Dennis C Alexander, Regional Executive Director
Billie Murray, Program Manager

1359 American Society of Landscape Architects: Virginia Chapter
2415-B Westwood Avenue
Richmond, VA 23230
804-523-2901
Fax: 804-288-3551
E-mail: mary.kidd@vaasla.org
http://www.vaasla.org

Founded: 1899
Barry Frankenfield, President
Jimmy Shepherd, President-Elect

1360 Arlington Outdoor Education Association
Phoebe Hall Knipling Outdoor Laboratory
PO Box 5646
Arlington, VA 22205
703-228-7650
Fax: 540-349-3336
http://www.outdoorlab.org

Founded to own and operate the Phoebe Hall Knipling Outdoor Laboratory. Its primary purpose is to provide a facility and support a school program designed to give urban school children who live in Arlington, Virginia, an opportunity tolearn science, outdoor skills, arts and humanities in a natural setting.
Founded: 1967
Mike Nardolilli, President
Lisa Fues, Vice President

1361 Ashoka
1700 N Moore Street
Suite 2000, 20th Floor
Arlington, VA 22209
703-527-8300
Fax: 703-527-8383
E-mail: info@ashoka.org
http://www.ashoka.org

Strives to shape a global, entrepreneurial, competitive citizen sector: one that allows social entrepreneurs to thrive and enables the world's citizens to think and act as changemakers.
Bill Drayton, CEO/Chair
Diana Wells, President

1362 Association for Facilities Engineering
12801 Worldgate Drive
Suite 500
Herndon, VA 20170
571-203-7171
Fax: 571-766-2142
E-mail: info@AFE.org
http://www.afe.org

The premier organization for facility engineers and maintenance personnel. Unites a large community of likeminded professionals for networking opportunities, knowledge-sharing, and support, as well as offers members a world variety ofeducational opportunities, training, and certification for career advancement.
Larry Ross, CPE, President & Chairman
Wayne P. Saya, Sr., CPE, Executive Director

1363 Audubon Society of Northern Virginia
11100 Wildlife Center Drive
Suite 100
Reston, VA 20190
703-438-6008
E-mail: info@audubonva.org
http://www.audubonva.org

To conserve and restore natural ecosystems. ASNV carries out conservation, education and advocacy programs throughout the region from Alexandria to Manassas in Fairfax, Prince William, Loudoun and Arlington counties, and beyond.
Founded: 1980
Terrence Liercke, President
Bill Brown, Treasurer

1364 Center for Health, Environment and Justice
PO Box 6806
Falls Church, VA 22040
703-237-2249
E-mail: chej@chej.org
http://www.chej.org

Works to build healthy communities, with social justice, economic well-being, and democratic governance. Through training, coalition-building and one-on-one technical and organizing assistance, the Center works to level the playingfield so that people can have a say in the environmental policies and decisions that affect their health and well-being.
Founded: 1981
Louis Marie Gibbs, Executive Director
Sharon Franklin, Finance/Administration Direc

1365 Center for a New American Dream
455 Second Street SE
Suite 101
Charlottesville, VA 22902
301-891-3683
E-mail: newdream@newdream.org
http://www.newdream.org

Seeks to cultivate a new American dream - one that emphasizes community, ecological sustainability, and a celebration of non-material values, while upholding the spirit of the traditional American dream of life, liberty, and thepursuit of happiness.
Founded: 1997
Wendy Philleo, Executive Director

1366 Chesapeake Bay Foundation
Capitol Place
1108 E Main Street
Suite 1600
Richmond, VA 23219
804-780-1392
Fax: 804-648-4011
E-mail: chesapeake@cbf.org
http://www.cbf.org

Founded: 1964
Ann Jennings, Executive Director
John Fowler, Senior Scientist

1367 Citizens Clearinghouse for Hazardous Waste
PO Box 6806
Falls Church, VA 22040-6806
703-237-2249
E-mail: info@chej.org
http://www.chej.org

Nonprofit organization serves citizens' groups, individuals and small municipalities working to solve hazardous and solid waste problems. Supplies information needed to understand, prevent, reduce or eliminate exposure to toxicchemicals through customized assistance, both in-house and on referral, a research library and service, publications and newsletters.
Founded: 1981
Louis Marie Gibbs, Executive Director
Stephen Lester, Science Director

1368 Nature Conservancy
490 Westfield Road
Charlottesville, VA 22901
434-295-6106
800-628-6860
E-mail: mlipford@tnc.org
http://www.nature.org

To preserve the plants, animals and natural communities that represent the diversity of life on Earth by protecting the lands and waters they need to survive.
Michael L Lipford, Executive Director

1369 Potomac Appalachian Trail Club
118 Park Street SE
Vienna, VA 22180
703-242-0315
Fax: 703-242-0968
E-mail: info@patc.net
http://www.patc.net

A volunteer-based organization, founded by the men and women who planned and built the Appalachian Trail. The Club now manages over 1000 miles of hiking trails in the Mid-Atlantic region, along with cabins, shelters, and hundreds ofacres of conserved land.
Founded: 1927
John Hedrick, President
Tom Avey, Secretary

1370 Scenic Virginia
4 East Main Street
Suite 2A
Richmond, VA 23219
804-643-8439
Fax: 804-643-8438
E-mail: email@scenicvirginia.org
http://www.scenicva.org

The sole statewide organization in the Commonwealth dedicated to the preservation, protection and enhancement of Virginia's scenic beauty and community character. Promotes and sponsors programs that enhance landscapes, promote tourismand eco-

nomic development, encourage natural beauty in the environment, preserve historical and cultural resources, and improve community appearance.
Founded: 1998
Cecelia S Howell, President
Barry W Starke, Vice President

1371 **Sierra Club: Virginia Chapter**
422 East Franklin Street
Suite 302
Richmond, VA 23219
804-225-9113
Fax: 804-225-9114
E-mail: glen.besa@sierraclub.org
http://virginia.sierraclub.org
To advance the preservation and protection of the natural environment by empowering the citizenry, especially democratically-based grassroots organizations, with charitable resources to further the cause of environmental protection.The vehicle through which The Sierra Club Foundation generally fulfills its charitable mission.
Glen Besa, Director

1372 **Spill Control Association of America**
103 Oronoco Street
Suite 200
Alexandria, VA 22314
571-451-0433
E-mail: info@scaa-spill.org
http://www.scaa-spill.org
Organized to actively promote the interests of all groups within the spill response community. The organization represents spill response contractors, manufacturers, distributors, consultants, instructors, government & traininginstitutions and corporation working in the industry.
Founded: 1973
John Parker, President
Jackie King, Executive Director

1373 **Student Conservation Association**
4245 North Fairfax Drive
Arlington, VA 22203
603-543-1700
Fax: 603-543-1828
E-mail: dcinfo@thesca.org
http://www.thesca.org
To build the next generation of conservation leaders and inspire lifelong stewardship of our environment and communities by engaging young people in hands-on service to the land.
Founded: 1957
Martha H Talbot, Co-Founder
Dale Penny, President/CEO

1374 **Teratology Society**
1821 Michael Faraday Drive
Suite 300
Reston, VA 20190
703-438-3104
Fax: 703-438-3113
E-mail: tshq@teratology.org
http://teratology.org/
A multidisciplinary scientific society founded in 1960, the members of which study the causes and biological processes leading to abnormal development and birth defects at the fundamental and clinical level, and appropriate measuresfor prevention.

1375 **Trout Unlimited**
1300 North 17th Street
Suite 500
Arlington, VA 22209
703-522-0200
800-834-2419
Fax: 703-284-9400
E-mail: trout@tu.org
http://www.tu.org
Mission: To conserve, protect and restore North America's trout and salmon fisheries and their watersheds. We accomplish this mission on local, state and national levels with an extensive and dedicated volunteer network.
Founded: 1959
Chris Wood, President/CEO
Steve Moyer, Vice President

1376 **Virginia Association of Soil and Water Conservation Districts**
7308 Hanover Green Drive
Suite 100
Mechanicsville, VA 23111
804-559-0324
Fax: 804-559-0325
E-mail: info@vaswcd.org
http://www.vaswcd.org
The Virginia Association of Soil and Water Conservation Districts (VASWCD) is a private nonprofit association of 47 soil and water conservation districts in Virginia. It is a voluntary, nongovernmental association of Virginia'sdistricts that provides and promotes leadership in the conservation of natural resources through stewardship and education programs.
Founded: 1930
Wilkie W Chaffin PhD, President

1377 **Virginia Conservation Network**
422 E Franklin Street
Suite 303
Richmond, VA 23219
804-644-0283
Fax: 804-644-0286
E-mail: vcn@vcna.org
http://www.vcnva.org
Devoted to advancing a common, environmentally sound vision for Virginia. The network's membership is comprised of more than 115 member organizations committed to protecting Virginia's natural resources.
Founded: 1990
Nathan Lott, Executive Director
Dana Roberts, Outreach and Events Manager

1378 **Virginia Forestry Association**
3808 Augusta Avenue
Richmond, VA 23230
804-278-8733
Fax: 804-278-8774
E-mail: vfa@vaforestry.org
http://www.vaforestry.org
Promotes stewardship and wise use of the Commonwealth's forest resources for the economic and environmental benefits of all Virginians.
Founded: 1943
Paul Howe, Executive Director

1379 **Virginia Native Plant Society**
400 Blandy Farm Lane
Unit 2
Boyce, VA 22620
540-837-1600
Fax: 540-837-1523
E-mail: vnpsofa@shentel.net
http://www.vnps.org
A statewide organization with approximately 2000 members supported primarily by dues and contributions. The Society's programs emphasize public education, protection of endangered species, habitat preservation, and encouragement ofappropriate landscape use of natice plants.
Founded: 1982
Sally Anderson, President

1380 **Virginia Waste Industries Association**
508 Somerset Avenue
Richmond, VA 23226
757-686-5960
Fax: 757-686-0010
E-mail: mdobson@envasns.org
http://www.vwia.com
To promote the management of waste in a manner that is environmentally responsible, efficient, profitable, and ethical while benefiting the public and protecting the employees.
Mike Dobson, Manager

1381 **Water Environment Federation**
601 Wythe Street
Alexandria, VA 22314
703-684-2400
800-666-0206
Fax: 703-684-2492
E-mail: inquiry@wef.org
http://www.wef.org
A not-for-profit technical and educational organization with 32,000 individual members and 80 affiliated Member Associations representing and additional 50,000 water quality professionals throughout the world. WEF and its memberassociations proudly work to achieve our mission of preserving and enhancing the global water environment.
Founded: 1928
Jeff Eger, Executive Director

Washington

1382 **American Lung Association of Washington: Spokane Branch**
American Lung Association

1817 East Springfield
Suite E
Spokane, WA 99202
509-325-6516
800-732-9339
Fax: 509-323-5380
E-mail: alaw@alaw.org
http://www.alaw.org

The mission of the American Lung Association is to prevent lung disease and to promote lung health.
Founded: 1904
Marina Cofer-Wildsmith, Chief Executive Officer
Leanne Noren, Chief Operations Officer

1383 American Lung Association of Washington: Eastern Region
110 South 9th Avenue
Yakima, WA 98902
509-248-4384
Fax: 509-248-4943
E-mail: alaw@alaw.org
http://www.alaw.org

The mission of the American Lung Association is to eliminate lung disease and to promote lung health.
Founded: 1906
Marina Cofer-Wildsmith, Chief Execuive Officer

1384 American Lung Association of Washington:Western Region
American Lung Association
223 Tacoma Avenue South
Tacoma, WA 98402
253-272-8777
Fax: 253-593-8827
E-mail: lnoren@alaw.org
http://www.ala.org

The mission of the American Lung Association is to prevent lung disease and to promote lung health.
Founded: 1905
marina Cofer-Wildsmith, Chief Executive Director
leanne Noren, Operations Officer

1385 American Lung Association- Mountain Pacific
2625 Third Avenue
Seattle, WA 98121
206-441-5100
800-586-4872
Fax: 206-441-3277
E-mail: alaw@alaw.org
http://www.alaw.org

Mission is to save lives by improving lung health and preventing lung disease.
Founded: 1906
Renee Klein, President/CEO

1386 American Rivers: Northwest Region Seattle
4005 20th Ave West
Suite 221
Seattle, WA 98199
206-213-0330
Fax: 206-213-0334
E-mail: arnw@amrivers.org
http://www.americanrivers.org

American Rivers is the only national organization standing up for healthy rivers so our community can thrive. Through national advocacy, innovative solutions and our growing network of strategic partners, we protect and promote ourrivers as valuable assests that are vital to our health, safety and quality of life.
Founded: 1992
Ross Freeman, Associate Director
Amy Souers Kober, Communications Director

1387 American Society of Landscape Architects: Washington Chapter
603 Stewart Street
Suite 610
Seattle, WA 98101
206-443-9484
Fax: 425-450-9077
E-mail: office@wasla.org
http://www.wasla.org

Mission is to lead, to educate and to participate in the careful stewardship, wise planning and artful design of our cultural and natural environments.
Founded: 1899
Curtis LaPierre, President
Christopher Overdorf, President-Elect

1388 Conservation Northwest
1208 Bay Street
#201
Bellingham, WA 98225
360-671-9950
Fax: 360-671-8429
E-mail: wild@conservationnw.org
http://www.conservationnw.org

A non-profit organization with 4 offices and 23 staff around the state that are supported by 5,000 families and hundreds of volunteers who together provide 70 percent of our funding.
Founded: 1988
Heidi Wills, President
Michel Girard, Vice President

1389 Environmental Education Association of Washington
Environmental Education Association of Washington
EEAW
P.O. Box 6277
Olympia, WA 98507
360-943-6643
Fax: 360-497-7132
E-mail: eeaw@eeaw.org
http://www.eeaw.org

Dedicated to increasing the awareness of and support for environmental education in the state of Washington.
Founded: 1991
Deb Abrahamson, President
Wendy Church, Executive Director

1390 Friends of Discovery Park
PO Box 99662
Seattle, WA 98199
206-285-6862
888-291-6104
Fax: 253-872-6668
E-mail: info@discoveryparkfriends.org
http://www.discoveryparkfriends.org

An all-volunteer group formed to defend the integrity of Discovery Park and to create and protect there an open space of quiet and tranquility, a sanctuary where the words of man are minimized.
Founded: 1970
Valerie Cholvin, President

1391 Friends of the San Juans
PO Box 1344
Friday Harbor, WA 98250
360-378-2319
877-757-3629
Fax: 360-378-2324
E-mail: friends@sanjuans.org
http://www.sanjuans.org

Mission is to protect the land, water, sea and livability of the San Juan islands through science, education, law and citizen action.
Founded: 1979
San Olson, President
Janet Alderton, Vice President

1392 Great Peninsula Conservancy
3721, Kitsap Way
Suite 5
Bremerton, WA 98312
360-373-3500
866-373-3504
Fax: 360-377-0239
E-mail: info@greatpeninsula.org
http://www.greatpeninsula.org

The Great Peninsula Conservancy is a private nonprofit land trust dedicated to forever protecting the rural landscapes, natural habitat and open spaces of our region.
Founded: 2000
Sandr S Bortner, Executive Director
Kate Kuhlman, Operations Director

1393 International Bicycle Fund
4887 Columbia Drive South
Seattle, WA 98108
206-767-0848
Fax: 206-767-0848
E-mail: ibike@ibike.org
http://www.ibike.org

A non-governmental, nonprofit, advocacy organization, promoting sustainable transport and international understanding. Major areas of activity are non-motorized urban planning, economic development, bike safety education, responsibletravel and bicycle tourism, and cross-cultural, educational programs.
Founded: 1983
David Mozer, President
John Dowlin, Executive Director

1394 Issaquah Alps Trails Club
PO Box 351
Issaquah, WA 98027
425-392-3571
E-mail: Webmaster@issaquahalps.org
http://www.issaquahalps.org

Mission is to act as custodian of the trails and the lush, open tree-covered mountaintops known as the Issaquah Alps. Offers

free guided hikes and a voice for protection of our open spaces, trails, and quality of life.
Founded: 1979
David Kapler, President

1395 Mountaineers Conservation Division
The Mountaineers
7700 Sand Point Way
North East
Seattle, WA 98115
206-521-6000
800-573-8484
Fax: 206-523-6763
E-mail: clubmail@mountaineers.org
http://www.mountaineers.org

Mission is to be the premier outdoor recreation club, dedicated to the responsible employment and protection of natural areas.
Founded: 1906
Gavin Woody, President
Dan Lauren, President-Elect

1396 Nature Conservancy: Washington Chapter
217 Pine Street
Suite 1100
Seattle, WA 98101
206-343-4344
800-628-6860
Fax: 206-343-5608
E-mail: washington@tnc.org
http://www.tnc-washington.org

A leading conservation organization working around the world to protect ecologically important lands and waters for nature and people.
Founded: 1951
John Rose, Chairman

1397 North Cascades Conservation Council
PO Box 95980
Seattle, WA 98145
360-296-5159
E-mail: ncccinfo@northcascades.org
http://www.northcascades.org

Mission is to protect and preserve the North Cascade's scenic, scientific, recreational, educational, and wilderness values.
Founded: 1957
Karl Forsgaard, President

1398 Olympic Park Associates
1905 Bothell-Everett Highway
#270
MillCreek, WA 98012
206-364-3933
Fax: 206-364-6379
E-mail: info@olympicparkassociates.org
http://www.drizzle.com/~rdpayne/opa.html/

An organization working to preseve Olympic Park's wilderness, beauty and spelndor.
Founded: 1948
Donna Osseward, President
John Bridge, Secretary

1399 Olympic Region Clean Air Agency
2940-B Limited Lane, NW
Olympia, WA 98502
360-539-7610
800-422-5623
Fax: 360-491-6308
E-mail: info@orcaa.org
http://www.orcaa.org

A local government agency charged with regulatory and enforcement authority for air quality issues. It is one of the seven such regional air pollution control agencies in Washington State. The agency also administers laws andregulations regarding such programs as solid fuel burning devices, asbestos abatement, and open burning. ORCAA's jurisdiction: Clallam, Grays Harbor, Jefferson, Mason, Pacific and Thurston Counties.
Founded: 1968
Phil Johnson, Chairman

1400 People for Puget Sound
1402 3rd Avenue
Suite 1600
Seattle, WA 98101
206-631-2600
Fax: 206-622-8113
E-mail: peopleforpugetsound@wecprotects.org
http://www.pugetsound.org

People for Puget Sound is a regional citizen's organization founded in 1991 to educate and involve ordinary - and extraordinary - people in protecting and restoring the land and waters of Puget Sound. People for Puget Sound's programsare based on partnership and collaborations, scientific credibility, creative use of communications and technology, and a hands-on-style. People for Puget Sound publishes a quarterly newsletter, and many scientific publications.
Founded: 1991
Kerry Cechovic, Program Director
Rein Attemann, Advocacy Manager

1401 Rivers Council of Washington
509 10th Avenue E
Seattle, WA 98102
206-568-1380
Fax: 206-568-1381
E-mail: RIVERSWA@BRIadoon.com
http://www.riverscouncil.org

The Pacific Northwest's oldest river conservation non-profit advocating the protection of free-flowing rivers for recreation, fisheries, and responsible water use.
Denis Hayes, President/CEO

1402 Sea Shepherd
PO Box 2616
Friday Harbor, WA 98250
360-370-5650
Fax: 360-370-5651
E-mail: info@seashepherd.org
http://www.seashepherd.org

An international non-profit, marine wildlife conservation organization whose mission is to end the destruction of habitat and slaughter of wildlife in the world's oceans in order to conserve and protect ecosystems and species.
Founded: 1977
Marnie Gaede, President

1403 Sierra Club: Cascade Chapter
180 Nickerson Street
Suite 202
Seattle, WA 98109
206-378-0114
Fax. 206-378-0034
E-mail: cascade.chapter@sierraclub.org
http://cascade.sierraclub.org

The Sierra Club is the nation's oldest, largest, and most influential grassroots environmental organization. The Cascade Chapter is its voice for most of Washington State. Inspired by nature, we work together to protect our communitiesand the planet.
Margie V Cleve, Chairman
Ken Gersten, Vice Chairman

1404 Solar Washington
PO Box 3832
Seattle, WA 98124
206-618-3620
E-mail: info@solarwashington.org
http://www.solarwashington.org

A private not-tor-profit 501(c)3 association of solar energy equipment manufacturers, system integrators, distributors, dealers, designers, consultants, students, and interested people
.
Dave Kozin, President

1405 Student Conservation Association Northwest
1265 S Main Street
Suite 210
Seattle, WA 98144
206-324-4649
Fax: 206-324-4998
E-mail: webmaster@thesca.org
http://www.thesca.org/

SCA is a national organization with regional offices in Seattle, Oakland, Pittsburg, Washington DC and headquartered in Charlestown NH. Our mission is to build the next generation of conservation leaders and inspire lifelongstewardship of our environment and communities by engaging young people in hands-on service to the land. We offer a wide range of internships and crew based programs for ages 16 years and up.
Founded: 1957
Dale M Penny, President/CEO
Jay A Satz, Vice President

1406 Washington Association of Conservation Districts
185 Beebe Road
Goldendale, WA 98620
509-773-5065
Fax: 509-773-5600
E-mail: wacd@ncia.com
http://www.wacd.org

A non-profit organization representing Washington's 48 Conservation Districts, whos mission is to advance the purposes of Conservation Districts and their constituents by providing leadership, information, and representation.
David Guenther, President

1407 Washington Environmental Council
1402 Third Avenue
Suite 1400
Seattle, WA 98101
206-631-2600
800-561-8294
Fax: 206-622-8113
E-mail: wec@wecprotects.org
http://www.wecprotects.org

Protects what Washingtonians care about- our land and water, fish, and wildlife, and our special way of life. We engage the public and decision makers to improve and enforce protections for the health and well-being of our communities.
Founded: 1967
Jay Manning, President

1408 Washington Public Interest Research Group
1402 Third Avenue
Suite 715
Seattle, WA 98101
206-568-2854
800-213-7383
Fax: 206-568-2858
E-mail: washpirg@pirg.org
http://www.washpirg.org

When consumers are cheated or the voices of ordinary citizens are drowned out by special interest lobbyists, WashPIRG speaks up and takes action.
Steve Blackledge, Regional Director

1409 Washington Recreation and Park Association
PO Box 8416
Lacey, WA 98509
360-459-9396
888-459-0009
Fax: 360-459-4160
E-mail: wrpa@seanet.com
http://www.wrpatoday.org

A not-for-profit professional and public interest organization which is dedicated to enhancing and promoting parks, recreation and arts pursuits in Washington State.
Jessi Bon, President

1410 Washington Refuse and Recycling Association
4160 6th Avenue SE
Suite 205
Lacey, WA 98503
360-943-8859
866-788-9772
Fax: 360-357-6958
E-mail: office@wrra.org
http://www.wrra.org

Represents Washington's diverse and multifaceted solid waste handling industry, providing its members with general legal support, educational seminars, workshops, and representation before regulatory agencies and the Legislature.
Jay Alexander, President
Mark Wash, Vice-President

1411 Washington Toxics Coalition
4649 Sunnyside Avenue N
Suite 540
Seattle, WA 98103
206-632-1545
800-844-7233
Fax: 206-632-8661
E-mail: info@watoxics.org
http://www.watoxics.org

Washington Toxics Coalition protects public health and the environment by eliminating toxic pollution. WTC promotes alternatives, advocates policies, empowers communities, and educates people to create a healthy environment.
Founded: 1981
Jesseca Brand, President
Laurie Valeriano, Executive Director

1412 Washington Wilderness Coalition
305 North
83rd Street
Seattle, WA 98103
206-633-1992
800-627-0062
Fax: 206-633-1996
E-mail: info@wawild.org
http://www.wawild.org

Mission is to preserve and restore wild areas of Washington State throuh citizen empowerment, support for grassroots community groups and advocacy and public education.
Founded: 1979
Roger Mellem, President
Doug North, Vice President

1413 Washington Wildlife Federation
PO Box 1656
Bellevue, WA 98009
206-769-5627
E-mail: info@washingtonwildlife.org
http://www.washingtonwildlife.org

To preserve, enhance, and perpetuate Washington's fish, wildlife and habitat through education and conservation programs.
Ronni McGlenn, President

West Virginia

1414 American Lung Association of West Virginia
American Lung Association
2102 Kanawha Blvd
East
Charleston, WV 25311
304-342-6600
800-LUN- USA
Fax: 304-342-6096
E-mail: cfields@lunginfo.org
http://www.lunginfo.org

The mission of the American Lung Association is to prevent lung disease and promote lung health.
Founded: 1904
Sara Crickenberger, Executive Director
Chantal Fields, Assistant Executive Director

1415 American Society of Landscape Architects: West Virginia Chapter
5088 Washington Street West
2nd Floor
Cross Lanes, WV 25313
304-769-0821
Fax: 304-769-0822
E-mail: tschoolcraft@mbakercorp.com
http://www.wvasla.org

A professional society representing members of the landscape architecture profession throughout the state of West Virginia.
Peter J Williams, President
Laura L. Cox, Secretary

1416 Sierra Club: West Virginia Chapter
PO Box 4142
Morgantown, WV 26504-4142
E-mail: jimscon@gmail.com
http://westvirginia.sierraclub.org
Jim Sconyers, Chair
Gary Nelson, Vice Chair

1417 West Virginia Bureau for Public Health
West Virginia Departmwent of Health and Human Reso
One Davis Square
Suite 100 East
Charleston, WV 25301
304-558-0684
Fax: 304-558-1130
E-mail: DHHRSecretary@wv.gov
http://www.wvdhhr.org

Organizational activities not directed specifically toward children are education, regulation and research.
Chris Curtis, Commisioner
Ronald Forren, Deputy Commisioner

1418 West Virginia Forestry Association
PO Box 718
Ripley, WV 25271
304-372-1955
888-372-9663
Fax: 304-372-1957
E-mail: wvfa@wvadventures.net
http://www.wvfa.org

The West Virginia Forestry Association is a non-profit organization funded by its membership. Our members include individuals and businesses involved in forest management, timber production and wood product manufacturing. Our membersare concerned with protecting the environment, as well as enhancing the future of West Virginia's forests through multiple-use management.
Richard Waybright, Executive Director

1419 West Virginia Highlands Conservancy
HC 64
Box 281
Hillsboro, WV 24946
304-653-4277
E-mail: blittle@citynet.net
http://www.wvhighlands.org

One of the state's oldest environmental activist organizations. A coalition of recreational users of the West Virginia Highlands

came together to address a whole host of environmental threats to our state.
Founded: 1967
Hugh Rogers, President
Peter Shoenfeld, Senior Vice President

1420 West Virginia Woodland Owners Association
PO Box 443 304-382-5307
Nitro, WV 25143 Fax: 304-594-3648
E-mail: Emurriner@aol.com
http://www.woaofwv.org

A nonprofit membership organization started and continues to be operated exclusively by independent West Virginia woodland owners.
Ed Murriner, Secretary/Treasurer

Wisconsin

1421 American Society of Landscape Architects: Wisconsin Chapter
PO Box 851 202-898-2444
Madison, WI 53701 Fax: 202-898-1185
E-mail: wiasla@wiasla.com
http://www.wiasla.com

The Wisconsin state chapter supports professional development, visibility and network working opportunities.
Christa Wollenzien, President
Jay Gehler, President-Elect

1422 Botanical Club of Wisconsin
Wisconsin Academy of Science, Arts, & Letters
430 Lincoln Drive 608-262-2792
Room 251 http://wisplants.uwsp.edu/
Madison, WI 53706
The Botanical Club serves the interests of amateurs and professionals, toward the common goal of learning more about our state's diverse vegitation.
Thomas Eddy, President
Theodore Cochrane, Secretary

1423 Central Wisconsin Environmental Station (CWES)
10186 County Road MM 715-346-2937
Amherst Junction, WI 54407 Fax: 715-346-2493
E-mail: sjohnson@uwsp.edu
http://www.uwsp.edu/cnr/cwes/

Mission is to foster in adults and youth the appreciation, understanding, skill development, and motivation needed to help them build a sustainable balance between the environment, economy, and community.
Founded: 1975
Scott Johnson, Director

1424 Citizens for Animals: Resources and Environment
PO Box 18772 414-466-1250
Milwaukee, WI 53218
Debi Zweifel, Director

1425 Midwest Renewable Energy Association
7558 Deer Road 715-592-6595
Custer, WI 54423 Fax: 715-592-6596
E-mail: info@the-mrea.org
http://www.the-mrea.org

A non profit organization promoting renewable energy, energy efficiency, and sustainable living through education and demonstration. There are over 3200 active international members representing 39 states and 3 foreign countries.
Founded: 1990
Nick Hylla, Executive Director
Julie Brazeau, Instructor Development Coord

1426 River Alliance of Wisconsin
306 E Wilson 608-257-2424
Suite 2W Fax: 608-260-9799
Madison, WI 53703 E-mail: info@wisconsinrivers.org
http://www.wisconsinrivers.org

Mission is to advocate for the protection, enhancement and restoration of Wisconsin's rivers and watersheds.
Jake Barnes, Treasurer

1427 Sierra Club: John Muir Chapter
222 S Hamilton Street 608-256-0565
Suite 1 Fax: 608-256-4562
Madison, WI 53703 E-mail: john.muir.chapter@sierraclub.org
http://wisconsin.sierraclub.org

Preserve and protect the natural environment by empowering citizens, especially democratically based grassroots organizations with charitable resources to further the cause of environmental protection, the vehicle through which TheSierra Club Foundation generally fulfills its charitable mission.
Shahla M Werner, Director
Jacinda Tessmann, Coordinator

1428 Sixteenth Street Community Health Center
1337 South Cesar 414-672-1353
E Chavez Drive Fax: 414-672-9190
Milwaukee, WI 53204 http://www.sschc.org
The mission of the Sixteenth Street Community Health Center is to improve the health and well-being of Milwaukee's Near South Side residents by providing quality, family-based health care, health education and social services, freefrom linguistic, cultural and economic barriers.
Founded: 1969
Rick Walters, President
Tom Gazzana, Vice President

1429 Trees for Tomorrow Natural Resources Educational Center
519 Sheridan Street 715-479-6456
PO Box 609 Fax: 715-479-2318
Eagle River, WI 54521 E-mail: learning@treesfortomorrow.com
http://www.treesfortomorrow.com

Accredited natural resource specialty school. Hosts workshops for middle/high school students during the school year. Workshops emphasize conservation, proper land management and environmental basics.
Founded: 1944
Maggie Bishop, Executive Director
Cheryl Todea, Seasonal Naturalist Coord.

1430 Upper Mississippi River Conservation Committee
W 6442 Highway 35 608-783-8432
Bay City, WI 54650 E-mail: UpperMississippiRiver@fws.gov
http://www.mississippi-river.com
An organization of natural resource managers from IL, IA, MN, MO, and WI, created to promote a continuing cooperation between conservation agencies on the Upper Mississippi River. This is accomplished through workshops, publicationsand annual meetings.
Founded: 1943
Scott Yess, UMRCC Coordinator

1431 Wildlife Society
PO Box 863 608-221-6344
Madison, WI 53701-863 Fax: 608-221-6353
E-mail: jlnack@wisc.edu
http://www.wildlife.org/Wisconsin/home

A nonprofit scientific and educational organization that serves professionals such as government agencies, academia, industry, and non-government organizations in all areas related to the conservation of wildlife and natural resources management.
Tami Ryan, President
Scott Craven, President-Elect

1432 Wisconsin Association for Environmental Education
800 Reserve Street 715-346-2796
110 TNR Fax: 715-346-3835
Stevens Point, WI 54481 E-mail: waee@uwsp.edu
http://www.uwsp.edu/cnr/waee/

A non-profit organization that sponsors conferences, workshops, and gatherings to promote professional growth and networking opportunities.
Founded: 1975
Katie Boseo, Board Member

1433 **Wisconsin Association of Lakes**
4513 Vernon Boulevard
Suite 101
Madison, WI 53705
608-661-4313
800-542-5253
E-mail: info@wisconsinlakes.org
http://www.wisconsinlakes.org

The Wisconsin Association of Lakes is the only statewide non-profit organization working exclusively to protect and enhance the quality of Wisconsin's 15,000 lakes.
Karen Von Huene, Executive Director

1434 **Wisconsin Land and Water Conservation Association**
702 East Johnson Street
Madison, WI 53703-1533
608-441-2677
Fax: 608-441-2676
E-mail: jim@wlwca.org
http://www.wlwca.org

Mission: To assist county Land Conservation Committees and Departments with the protection, enhancement and sustainable use of Wisconsin's natural resources and to represent them through education and governmental interaction.
Jim VandenBrook, Executive Director
Kirsten Moore, Office Manager

1435 **Wisconsin Society for Ornithology**
7239 N
Barnett Lane
Fox Point, WI 53217
414-416-3272
E-mail: WSO@WSOBirds.org
http://www.wsobirds.org

Emphasizes all of the many aspects of birding and to support the research and habitat protection necessary to preserve Wisconsin's birdlife.
Founded: 1939
Carl Schwartz, President
Paul Jakoubek, Web Administrator

1436 **Wisconsin Wildlife Federation**
242 Keoller Avenue
Oshkosh, WI 54901
412-235-9136
Fax: 414-235-6030
E-mail: wiwf@execpc.com
http://www.wiwf.org

Made up of hunters, fishers, trappers, and others that are actively engaged in the outdoors. Recognizes the importance of protecting fish and wildlife habitat.
George Meyer, Executive Director
Jennifer Evans, Business Manager

1437 **Wisconsin Woodland Owners Association**
PO Box 285
Stevens Point, WI 54481
715-346-4798
800-838-9472
Fax: 715-346-4821
E-mail: wwoa@uwsp.edu
http://www.wisconsinwoodlands.org

The Wisconsin Woodland Owners Association, a nonprofit educational organization, was established in 1979 to advance the interests of woodland owners and the cause of forestry; develop public appreciation for the value of Wisconsin'swoodlands and their importance in the economy and overall welfare of the state; foster and encourage wise use and management of Wisconsin's woodlands for timber production, wildlife habitat and recreation; and to educate those interested in managingthe woodlands.
Founded: 1979
Chuck Wagner, President
Jan L Lehrer, Vice President

Wyoming

1438 **Jackson Hole Conservation Alliance**
685 S Cache
PO Box 2728
Jackson, WY 83001
307-733-9417
Fax: 307-733-9008
E-mail: info@jhalliance.org
http://www.jhalliance.org

An organization dedicated to responsible land stewardship in Jackson Hole, Wyoming to ensure that human activities are in harmony with the area's irreplaceable wildlife, scenery and other natural resources.
Founded: 1979
Trevor Stevenson, Executive Director
Gail Fustos, Finance Manager

1439 **Nature Conservancy: Wyoming Chapter**
Nature Conservancy
258 Main Street
Suite 200
Lander, WY 82520
307-332-2971
Fax: 307-332-2974
E-mail: pplatt@tnc.org
http://www.nature.org

The leading conservation organization working around the world to protect ecologically important lands and waters for nature and people.
Founded: 1950
Andrea Erickson, State Director
Paula Hunker, Associate State Director

1440 **Powder River Basin Resource Council**
934 North Main Sreet
Sheridan, WY 82801
307-672-5809
Fax: 307-672-5800
E-mail: info@powderriverbasin.org
http://www.powderriverbasin.org

Committed to the preservation and enrichment of Wyoming's agricultural heritage and rural lifestyle; the conservation of Wyomings unique land, mineral, water and clean air resources, consistent with responsible use of those resourcesto sustain the vitality of present and future generations; the education and empowerment of Wyoming's citizens to raise a coherent voice in decisions. They are the only group in Wyoming that addresses both agricultural and conservation issues.
John Fenton, Chairman
Bob LeResche, Vice Chairman

1441 **Sierra Club: Wyoming Chapter**
PO Box 1736
Laramie, WY 82072
307-742-0056
Fax: 307-460-8046
E-mail: wyomingchapter@gmail.com
http://www.wyoming.sierraclub.org

To advance the preservation and protection of the natural environment by empowering the citizenry, especially democratically-based grassroots organizations, with charitable resources to further the cause of environmental protection.The vehicle through which The Sierra Club Foundation generally fulfills its charitable mission.
Steve Thomas, Regional Director

1442 **Western Association of Fish and Wildlife Agencies**
522 Notre Dame Court
Cheyenne, WY 82009
307-638-1470
Fax: 307-638-1470
E-mail: larry.kruckenberg@wyo.gov
http://www.wafwa.org

WAFWA is a strong advocate of the rights of states and provinces to manage fish and wildlife within their borders. The association has been a key organization in promoting the principles of sound resource management and the building ofpartnerships at the regional, national, and international levels in order to enhance wildlife conservation efforts and the protection of associated habitats and the public interest.
Paul Conry, President
Stephen Barton, Treasurer

1443 **Wyoming Association of Conservation Districts**
517 E 19th Street
Cheyenne, WY 82001
307-632-5716
Fax: 307-638-4099
E-mail: simsshaun@yahoo.com
http://www.conservewy.com

Mission is to provide leadership for the conservation of Wyoming's soil and water resources, promotes the controll of soil erosion, promotes and protects the quality of Wyomings's waters, reduce siltation of stream channels andreservoirs, promote wise use of Wyoming's water, and all other natural resources, preserve and enhance wildlife habitat, protect the tax base and promote the health, safety and general welfare of the citzens of the state through a responsibleconservation ethic.
Founded: 1945
Shaun Sims, President
Jack Berger, Vice President

1444 Wyoming Native Plant Society
1000 East University Avenue
Laramie, WY 82071
307-766-3023
Fax: 307-766-3026
E-mail: wyndd@uwyo.edu
http://uwadmnweb.uwyo.edu/wyndd/wnps/info.asp?p=3182

Goals are to encourage the appreciation and conservation of the native flora and plant communities of Wyoming through education, research, and communication.

Founded: 1981
Lynn Moore, President
Brian Elliott, Vice President

1445 Wyoming Wildlife Federation
PO Box 1312
Lander, WY 82520
307-335-8633
800-786-5434
Fax: 307-335-8690
E-mail: joybannon@wyomingwildlife.org
http://www.wyomingwildlife.org

The Wyoming Wildlife Federation, established in 1937, is Wyomings oldest and largest conservation group advocating sportsmen and sportswomen. The Federation's mission is to work for hunters, anglers and other wildlife enthusiasts toprotect and enhance habitat; propetuate quality hunting and fishing; protect citizens rights to use public lands and waters; and promote ethical hunting and fishing.

Founded: 1937
Steve Kilpatrick, Executive Director
Joy Bannon, Field Director

Awards & Honors

Environmental

1446 **Adirondack Council Conservationist of the Year**
103 Hand Avenue
Suite 3
Elizabethtown, NY 12932
518-873-2240
877-873-2240
Fax: 518-873-6675
E-mail: info@adirondackcouncil.org
http://www.adirondackcouncil.org

This is awarded to the individual or organization who has provided the greatest contribution towards protecting the health of Adirondack Park. The award is presented each year at the Council's Forever WildÆDay, and winners receive aspecailly commissioned, museum-quality, hand-carved common loon in recognition of their achievements.

John F Sheehan, Communications Director
Brian Houseal, Executive Director

1447 **Aerospace Medical Association**
320 S Henry Street
Alexandria, VA 22314
703-739-2240
Fax: 703-739-9652
E-mail: rrayman@asma.org
http://www.asma.org

AsMA is dedicated to uniting the world's professionals in aviation, space and environmental medicine: advancing the frontiers of aerospace medicine by dissemination of knowledge throughout industry, the general public, and governmentalagencies worldwide. Ensuring the highest level of safety, health and performance of those involved in aerospace, AsMA is recognized as the international authority in aerospace medicine.

Russell Rayman, Executive Director

1448 **Air Force Association**
1501 Lee Highway
Arlington, VA 22209
703-247-5800
800-727-3337
Fax: 703-247-5853
E-mail: service@afa.org
http://www.afa.org

The Air Force Association's mission is to advocate aerospace power and a strong national defense; to support the United States Air Force and Air Force Family; and to promote aerospace education to the American people.

Kathy Hartness, Industry Relations

1449 **Air and Waste Management Association**
1 Gateway Center
3rd Floor
Pittsburgh, PA 15222
412-232-3444
Fax: 412-232-3450
E-mail: info@awma.org
http://www.awma.org/

The Air and Waste Management Association is a nonprofit, nonpartisan professional organization that provides training, information and networking opportunites to thousands of environmental professionals in 65 countries.

Adrianne Carolla, Secretary

1450 **American Association of Engineering Societies**
6522 Meadowridge Rd
Suite 101
Elkridge, MD 21075
202-296-2237
Fax: 202-296-1151
E-mail: info@aaes.org
http://www.aaes.org

Multidisciplinary organization dedicated to advancing the knowledge, understanding and practice of engineering in the public interest. Its members represent the mainstream of US engineering-affecting over 1,000,000 engineers inindustry, government and education. Through its councils, commissions, committees and task forces, the AAES addresses questions relating to the engineering profession.

William Koffel, Executive Director

1451 **American Chemical Society**
American Chemical Society
1155 16th Street NW
Washington, DC 20036
800-227-5558
Fax: 202-776-8258
E-mail: webmaster@acs.org
http://www.chemistry.org

The American Chemical Society is a self-governed individual membership organization that consists of more than 158,000 members in the field of chemistry. The organizations provides a broad range of opportunities for peer intereactionand career development, regardless of professional or scientific interests.

Catherine T. Hunt, President

1452 **American Conference of Governmental Industrial Hygienists**
1330 Kemper Meadow Drive
Cincinnati, OH 45240
513-742-6163
Fax: 513-742-3355
E-mail: mail@acgih.org
http://www.acgih.org

The American Conference of Governmental Industrial Hygeienists (ACGIH) is a member-based organization and community of professionals that advances worker health and safety through education and the development and dissemination ofscientific and technical knowledge.

Beverly S Cohen, Chair
Lawrence M Gibbs, Vice Chair

1453 **American Forest and Paper Association**
111 Nineteenth Street, NW
Suite 800
Washington, DC 20036
202-463-2700
800-878-8878
E-mail: info@afandpa.org
http://http://afandpa.org

The American Forest and Paper Association (AF&PA) is the national trade association of the forest, pulp, paperboard wood products industry. We represent member companies engaged i ngrowning, harvesting and processing wood and woodfiber, manufacturing pulp, paper and paperboard products from both virgin and recycled fiber, and producing engineered and traditional wood products.

1454 **American Institute of Chemical Engineers**
3 Park Avenue
New York, NY 10016
212-591-8100
800-242-4363
Fax: 212-591-8888
E-mail: xpress@aiche.org
http://www.aiche.org

Founded in 1908, a professional association of more than 50,000 members that provides leadership in advancing the chemical engineering profession. Fosters and disseminates chemical engineering knowledge, supports the professional andpersonal growth of its members, and applies the expertise of its members to address societal needs through the world.

Scott Berger, Director
Bette Lawler, Sr. Director, Operations

1455 **American Institute of Mining, Metallurgical and Petroleum Engineers**
3 Park Avenue
New York, NY 10016
212-419-7676
Fax: 212-419-7671
E-mail: aimeny@aimeny.org
http://www.idis.com/aime

Organized and operated exclusively to advance, record and disseminate significant knowledge of engineering and the arts and sciences involved in the production and use of minerals, metals, energy sources and materials for the benefitof humankind, both directly as AIME and through Member Services.

Nellie Guernsey, Executive Director

1456 **American Nuclear Society**
555 North Kensington Ave.
La Grange Park, IL 60526
708-352-6611
800-323-3044
Fax: 708-352-0499
E-mail: nucleus@ans.org
http://www.ans.org

The American Nuclear Society is a not-for-profit, international, scientific and educational organization. It was established by a group of individuals who recognized the need to unify the professional activities within the diversefields of nuclear science and technology.

Harry Bradley, Executive Direcotr

1457 **American Society of Civil Engineers**
1801 Alexander Bell Drive 703-295-6300
Reston, VA 20191 800-548-2723
Fax: 703-295-6222
http://www.asce.org

Founded in 1852, the American Society of Civil Engineers represents more than 137,500 members of the civil engineering profession worldwide, and is America's oldest national engineering society. ASCE's vision is to position engineersas global leaders building a better quality of life.

William Marcuson, President

1458 **American Society of Heating, Refrigerating and Air-Conditioning (ASHRAE)**
1791 Tullie Circle NE 404-636-8400
Atlanta, GA 30329 Fax: 404-321-5478
E-mail: ashrae@ashrae.org
http://www.ASHRAE.org

ASHRAE, founded in 1894, is an international organization of some 50,000 persons. ASHRAE fulfills its mission of advancing heating, ventilation, air conditioning and refrigeration to serve humanity and promote a sustainable worldthrough reserach, standards writing, publishing and continuing education.

Jeff Littleton, Executive Vice President

1459 **American Sportfishing Association**
225 Reinekers Lane 703-519-9691
Suite 420 Fax: 703-519-1872
Alexandria, VA 22314 E-mail: info@asafishing.org
http://www.asafishing.org

The American Sportfishing Association is the sportfishing industry's trade association, committed to looking out for the interests of the entire sportfishing community. We give the industry a unified voice, speaking out on behalf ofsportfishing and boating industries, state and federal natural resource agencies, conservation organizations, angler advocacy groups and outdoor journalists when emerging laws and policies could significantly affect sportfishing business orsportfishing itself

Mike Nussman, President/CEO
Gordon Robertson, VP

1460 **American Water Resources Association**
4 West Federal Street 540-687-8390
PO Box 1626 Fax: 540-687-8395
Middleburg, VA 20118 E-mail: terry@awra.org
http://www.awra.org

Founded in 1964, the American Water Resources Association is a non-profit professional association dedicated to the advancement of men and women in water resources management, research, and education. AWRA's membership ismultidisciplinary; its diversity is its hallmark. It is the professional home of a wide variety of water resources experts including engineers, educators, foresters, biologists, ecologists, geographers, managers, regulators, hydrologists andattorneys.

Kenneth D Reid, Executive VP
Terry Meyer, Marketing Director

1461 **Association for Conservation Information**
Montana Department of Fish, Wildlife and Parks
1420 E 6th Street 406-444-4038
PO Box 200701 Fax: 406-444-4952
Helena, MT 59620 E-mail: raasheim@mt.gov
http://http://fwp.mt.gov

ACI, the Association for Conservation Information, is a non-profit association of information and education professionals representing state, federal and Canadian agencies and private conservation organizations. ACI memberprofessionals play a major role in providing natural resource, environmental, wildlife and other information and education to the public through a variety of means, many of which are continental in scope.

Ron Aasheim, Administrator

1462 **Association of Conservation Engineers**
2901 w. Truman Boulevard 573-751-4115
PO Box 180 Fax: 573-751-4467
Jefferson City, MO 65109 http://www.conservation.state.mo.us

Organization of conservation engineers and technicians who are working to conserve and improve our nation's natural heritage. Brings together engineers and allied personnel employed by conservation and recreation agencies andconsultants who have a community of specialized interests in the areas of fish, wildlife, parks, forests and related conservation/recreation fields. Members pool experience and information pertaining to conservation engineering to make naturalresources more accessible.

Anita B Gorman, Chairman
Lowell Mohler, Vice-Chairman

1463 **Association of Consulting Foresters of America**
312 Montgomery Street 703-548-0990
Suite 208 Fax: 703-548-6395
Alexandria, VA 22314 E-mail: director@acf-foresters.org
http://www.acf-foresters.org

To protect the public welfare and property in the practice of forestry, to raise the professional standards and work of ACF Consultants and all other consulting foresters. To develop and expand the services of ACF Consultants.

Lynn C Wilson, Executive Director

1464 **Audubon Naturalist Society of Central Atlantic**
8940 Jones Mill Road 301-652-9188
Chevy Chase, MD 20815 Fax: 301-951-7179
E-mail: contact@audubonnaturalist.com
http://www.audubonnaturalist.com

The Audubon Naturalist Society is an independent environmental education and conservation organization with over 10,000 members in the Washington DC area. The society offers a wide variety of natural history classes and campaigns forthe protection and renewal of the Mid-Atlantic regions natural resources.

Neal Fitzpatrick, Executive Director
Anne Cottingham, Board President

1465 **Audubon Society of New Hampshire**
3 Silk Farm Road 603-224-9909
Concord, NH 03301 Fax: 603-226-0902
E-mail: asnh@nhaudubon.org
http://www.nhaudubon.org

The Audubon Society of New Hampshire, a nonprofit statewide membership organization, is dedicated to the conservation of wildlife and habitat throughout the state. Independent of the National Audubon Society, ASNH has offered programsin wildlife conservation, land protection, environmental policy and environmental education since 1914.

Partricia Casey, Human Resource Manager

1466 **Audubon of Florida: Center for Birds of Prey**
1101 Audubon Way 407-644-0190
Maitland, FL 32751 Fax: 407-644-8940
http://www.audubonofflorida.org

To conserve, protect and restore Florida's natural resources and to create a conservation ethic among all Floridians. The mission is to conserve and restore natural ecosystems, focusing on birds and other wildlife for the benefit ofhumanity and the earth's biological diversity. The Center for Birds of Prey is dedicated to promoting a stewardship ethic towards Florida's birds of prey and their habitats through medical rehabilitation, interactive education and practical research.

Katie Warner, Center Administrator

1467 **Big Thicket Conservation Association**
PO Box 198 409-892-8976
Saratoga, TX 77585 http://www.btatx.org
Dr. Bruce Drury, President

1468 **Botanical Society of America**
PO Box 299
St. Louis, MO 63166
314-577-9566
Fax: 314-577-9515
E-mail: wdahl@botany.org
http://www.botany.org

Promote botany, the field of basic science dealing with the study and inquiry into the form, function, diversity, reproduction, evolution, and uses of plants and their interactions within the biosphere.

Bill Dahl, Executive Director

1469 **Chicago Community Trust**
111 East Wacker Drive
Suite 1400
Chicago, IL 60601
312-616-8000
Fax: 312-616-7955
E-mail: info@cct.org
http://www.cct.org

Terry Mazany, President/CEO
Greg White, Strategy & Operations VP

1470 **Connecticut River Watershed Council**
15 Bank Row
Greenfield, MA 01301
413-772-2020
Fax: 413-772-2090
E-mail: cgwyther@ctriver.org
http://www.ctriver.org

The Connecticut River Watershed Council (CRWC) is the only broad-based citizen advocate for the environmental well-being of the entire Connecticut River. Our primary mission is to promote improvement of water quality and therestoration, conservation, wise development and use of the natural resources of the Connecticut River watershed.

Chelsea Gwyther, Executive Director

1471 **Ecological Society of America**
1990 M St NW
Suite 700
Washington, DC 20036
202-833-8773
Fax: 202-833-8775
E-mail: esahq@esa.org
http://www.esa.org

To promote ecological science by improving communication among ecologists; raise the public's level of awareness of the importance of ecological science; increase the resources available for the conduct of ecological science; andensure the appropriate use of ecological science in environmental decision making by enhancing communication between the ecological community and policy-makers.

Alison Power, President
Katherine S McCarter, Executive Director

1472 **Federal Aviation Administration**
Office of Public Affairs
800 Independence Avenue SW
Washington, DC 20591
202-267-3883
Fax: 202-267-5047
http://www.faa.gov

The major roles of the Federal Aviation Administration (a part of the Department of Transportation) include regulation, development, and research in the areas of civil aviation, civil aeronautics, and U.S. commercial spacetransportation.

Marion C Blakey, Administrator
Robert A Sturgell, Deputy Administrator

1473 **Federation of Fly Fishers**
215 E. Lewis
Livingston, MT 59047
406-222-9369
Fax: 406-222-5823
E-mail: van@fedflyfishers.org
http://www.fedflyfishers.org

The Federation of Fly Fishers seeks to cultivate and advance the art science and sport of flyfishing as the most sporting and enjoyable method of angling and the way of fishing most consistent with the preservation and use of game fishresources; to be the voice for organized fly fishing; to promote conservation of recreational resources; to facilitate and improve the knowledge of fly fishing; and to elevate the standard of integrity, honor and courtesy of anglers.

RP van Gytenbeek, Chief Executive Officer
Bob Wiltshire, Chief Operating Officer

1474 **Frank A Chambers Award**
Air and Waste Management Association
One Gateway Center, 3rd Floor
420 Fort Duquesne Boulevard
Pittsburgh, PA 15222
412-232-3444
800-270-3444
Fax: 412-232-3450
http://www.awma.org

Award for outstanding achievement in the science and art of air pollution control. It requires accomplishment of a technical nature on the part of the recipient which is considered to be a major contribution to the science and art ofair pollution control, the merit of which has been widely recognized by persons in the field.

Steve Wafalosky

1475 **German Marshall Fund of the United States**
1744 R Street NW
Washington, DC 20009
202-745-3950
Fax: 202-265-1662
E-mail: info@gmfus.org
http://www.gmfus.org

To stimulate the exchange of ideas and promote cooperation between the United States and Europe in the spirit of the postwar Marshall Plan. GMF was created in 1972 by a gift from the German people as a permanent memorial to MarshallPlan aid.

Craig Kennedy, President

1476 **Global Tomorrow Coalition**
Capital Research Center
1513 16th Street NW
Washington, DC 20036
202-483-6900
Fax: 202-483-6990
E-mail: contact@capitalresearch.org
http://www.capitalresearch.org/gw

Green Watch is an online database and information clearinghouse providing factual information on over 500 nonprofit environmental groups. This free service identifies the location, leadership and membership of each profiled group.Green Watch also produces timely news reports and analyses of the environmental movement.

Terrence Scanlon, President

1477 **Golden Gate Audubon Society**
2530 San Pablo Avenue
Suite G
Berkeley, CA 94702
510-843-2222
Fax: 510-843-5351
E-mail: ggas@goldengateaudubon.org
http://www.goldengateaudubon.org

A conservation and education organization that has birds as its key component. We seek to protect and enjoy wildlife and their natural habitat in San Francisco and East Bay through interaction between our members and the community.

Mark Welther, Executive Director

1478 **Goldman Environmental Foundation**
211 Lincoln Blvd
San Francisco, CA 94129
415-345-6330
Fax: 415-345-9686
E-mail: info@goldmanprize.org
http://www.goldmanprize.org

Goldman Environmental Prizes are awarded for sustained and important efforts to preserve the natural environment, including, but not limited to:Æprotecting endangered ecosystems and species, combatting destructive development projects,promoting sustainability, influencing environmental policies and striving for environmental justice.

1479 **Great Lakes Commission**
2805 S Industrial Highway
Suite 100
Ann Arbor, MI 48104
734-971-9135
Fax: 734-971-9150
E-mail: eschmidt@glc.org
http://www.glc.org

Binational agency that promotes the orderly, integrated and comprehensive development, use and conservation of the water and related natural resources of the Great Lakes basin and St Lawrence River.

Tim A. Eder, Executive Director

1480 **Honorary Membership**
Air and Waste Management

1 Gateway Center, 3rd Floor
420 Fort Duquesne Blvd
Pittsburgh, PA 15222
412-232-3444
800-270-3444
Fax: 412-232-3450
E-mail: info@awma.org
http://www.awma.org

May be conferred upon persons who have attained eminence in some field related to the mission and objectives of the Association who have rendered valuable service to the Association.
Steve Wafalosky, Business Contact

1481 **Institute of Environmental Sciences and Technology**
Arlington Place One
2340 S Arlington Heights Rd, Suite 100
Arlington Heights, IL 60005
847-255-1561
Fax: 847-255-1699
E-mail: iest@iest.org
http://www.iest.org

An international professional society that serves the environmental sciences in the areas of contamination control in electronics manufacturing and pharmaceutical processes, design, test and evaluation of commercial and militaryequipment and product reliability issues.
Julie Kendrick, Executive Director
Kristin Thryselius, Publication Sales Coor

1482 **International Desalination Association**
PO Box 387
Topsfield, MA 01983
978-887-0410
Fax: 978-887-0411
E-mail: info@idadesal.org
http://www.idadesal.org

IDA is committed to the development and promotion of the appropriate use of desalination and desalination technology worldwide. We endeavor to carry out these goals by encouraging research and development, exchanging, promotingcommunication and disseminating information.
Jose Antonio Medina, President
Lisa R Henthorne, First Vice President

1483 **International Studies Association**
University of South Carolina
817 Henderson Street
Columbia, SC 29208
803-777-3109
Fax: 803-777-8255
E-mail: mgross@sc.edu
http://www.cas.sc.edu/poli

Melissa Gross, Business Manager
Pamela Mauldin, Faculty Coordinator

1484 **International Wildlife Film Festival: Media Center**
718 S Higgins Avenue
Missoula, MT 59801
406-728-9380
Fax: 406-728-2881
E-mail: iwff@wildlifefilms.org
http://www.wildlifefilms.org

Goal is to be the preeminent wildlife film, television and media organization, showcasing the world's best wildlife films and television programs, providing educational resources and events seminars, workshops, field classes, filmtours and many hands-on activities, that emphasize the most up-to-date, factual and ethical scienced based information. Our mission—-to promote awareness, knowledge and understanding of wildlife, habitat, people and nature through excellent film,television and media.
Janet Rose, Executive Director

1485 **Irrigation Association**
6540 Arlington Boulevard
Falls Church, VA 22042
703-536-7080
Fax: 703-536-7019
E-mail: webmaster@irrigation.org
http://www.irrigation.org

To improve the products and practices used to manage water resources and to held shape the worldwide business environment of the irrigation industry.
Karen Koenig, Certification Manager

1486 **John Burroughs Association**
15 West 77th Street
New York, NY 10024
212-769-5169
E-mail: breslof@amnh.org
http://http://research.amnh.org/burroughs

Each year a medal is awarded to the author of a distinguished book of natural history, a list of exceptional national history books for young readers is selected. and an outstanding nature essay is identified.
Robert Abrams, Director
Lisa Breslof, Secretary

1487 **Keep America Beautiful**
1010 Washington Boulevard
Stamford, CT 06901
203-323-8987
Fax: 203-325-9199
E-mail: info@kab.org
http://www.kab.org

Nonprofit organization whose network of local, statewide and international affiliate progams educates individuals about litter prevention and ways to reduce, reuse, recycle and properly manage wase materials.
G Raymon Empson, President

1488 **Keep North Carolina Beautiful**
1503 Mail Service Center
Raleigh, NC 27699
919-733-3109
877-dot-4you
Fax: 919-733-9980
http://www.ncdot.org

North Carolina Keep America Beautiful is a nonprofit public education organization dedicated to enhancing the natural beauty of North Carolina communities, improving waste handling practices and empowering individuals to take greaterresponsibility for improving community environments.

1489 **Lawrence K Cecil Award**
American Institute of Chemical Engineers
3 Park Avenue
New York, NY 10016
212-591-8100
800-242-4363
Fax: 212-591-8888
E-mail: awards@aiche.org
http://www.aiche.org

Recognizes an individual's outstanding chemical engineering contribution and achievement in the preservation or improvement of the environment.
Larry Evans, President

1490 **Lyman A Ripperton Award**
Air and Waste Management Association
One Gateway Center, 3rd Floor
420 Fort Duquesne Boulevard
Pittsburgh, PA 15222
412-232-3444
Fax: 412-232-3450
E-mail: info@awma.org
http://www.awma.org

Awarded for distinguished achievement as an educator in some field of air pollution control. Awarded to an individual, who by precept and example, has inspired students to achieve excellence in all their professional and socialendeavors.
Antoon Van Der Vooren, President

1491 **NSF International**
789 N Disboro Road
PO Box 130140
Ann Arbor, MI 48113
734-769-8010
800-nsf-mark
Fax: 734-769-0109
E-mail: info@nsf.org
http://www.nsf.org

NSF International, The Public Health and Safety Company, is an independent, not-for-profit organization providing a wide range of services around the world. For more than 55 years, NSF has been committed to public health, safety andprotection of the enviroment.
Robert Ferguson, Vice President
Tom Bruursema, General Manager

1492 **National Association for Environmental Education**
PO Box 400
Troy, OH 45373
937-698-6493
Fax: 937-335-5623
The National Association for Environmental Education is a network of professionals, students and volunteers working in the field of environmental education throughout North America and in over 55 countries around the world. NAAEE takesa cooperative, nonconfrontational, scientifically-based approach to promoting education about environmental issues.
Joseph Baust, President
Martha Monroe, President Elect

1493 National Association of Conservation Districts
Service Center
612 West Main Street
League City, TX 77574
281-332-3402
Fax: 281-332-5259
E-mail: beth-mason@nacdnet.org
http://www.nacdnet.org/news/awards/index.phtml

The association's annual Awards Program recognizes individuals and organizations for outstanding work and leadership in soil and water conservation. Awards include: NACD Friend of Conservation; Distinguished Service; President's;Excellence in Communications; District Excellence; and Collaborative Conservation.
Krysta Harden, CEO
Beth Mason, Awards Contact

1494 National Audubon Society
National Audubon Society
700 Broadway
New York, NY 10003
212-979-3000
Fax: 212-979-3188
E-mail: webmaster@audubon.org
http://www.audubon.org

The mission of the National Audubon Society is to conserve and restore natural ecosystems, focusing on birds and other wildlife for the benefit of humanity and the earth's biological diversity. Founded in 1905, the National AudubonSociety is named for John James Audubon, famed orithologist, exployer, and wildlife artist.
Jess Morton, Contact

1495 National Bison Association
The National Bison Association
8690 Wolff Ct
Suite 200
Westminster, CO 80031
303-292-2833
Fax: 303-659-3739
http://www.bisoncentral.com
Dave Carter, Executive Director

1496 National Environmental Training Association
5320 N 16th Street
Suite 114
Phoenix, AZ 85018
602-956-6099
Fax: 602-956-0399
http://ehs-training.org

The National Environmental Training Assoication, is a nonprofit international organization of enviromental, health and safety, other technical training professionals. Activities centeral to NETA's educational services include itssupport for trainer networking, professional development and competency certification for its members, EH&S training information and programs for industry, and development of training competency standards.
Charles L Richardson, Executive Director

1497 National Ocean Industries Association
National Ocean Industries Association
1120 G Street NW
Suite 900
Washington, DC 20005
202-347-6900
Fax: 202-347-8650
E-mail: mkearns@noia.org
http://www.noia.org

The National Ocean Industries Assoication, founded in 1972 with 35 members, represents all facets of the domestic offshore and related industries. Today, our more than 300 member companies are dedicated to the development of offshoreoil and natural gas for the coninued growth and secrity of the United States. NOIA members are engaged in many business activities, in addition to those listed below, including enviromental safeguards, equipment supply, gas transmission,naviogation,ect.

1498 National Press Club
National Press Club
529 14th Street NW
Washington, DC 20045
202-662-7500
E-mail: info@press.org
http://www.press.org

Professional organization of reporters, writers and newspeople employed by newspapers, wire services, magazines, radio and television stations, and other forms of news media; and former newspeople and associates of newspeople. Sponsorsprofessional, sports, travel and cultural events; book rap sessions with news figures and authors; and newsmaker and luncheon speaker sessions. Houses reference library and archives. Offers computer training. Publishes a weekly newsletter.
Jerry Zremski, President

1499 National Recreation and Park Association
National Recreation And Park Association
22377 Belmont Ridge Road
Ashburn, VA 20148
703-858-0784
Fax: 703-858-0794
E-mail: info@nrpa.org
http://www.nrpa.org

The mission of the National Recreation and Park Association is to a advance parks, recreation and environmental conservation efforts that enhance the quality of life for all people.
Craig Baker, Exposition Manager
Krista Barnes, Senior Director

1500 National Recycling Coalition
National Recycling Coalition
805 15th Street Nw
Suite 425
Washington, DC 20005
202-789-1430
Fax: 202-789-1431
E-mail: info@nrc-recycle.org
http://www.nrc-recycle.org

NRC is a not-for-profit organization dedicated to the advancement and improvement of recycling, source reduction, composting, and reuse by providing technical information, education, training, outreach, and advocacy services to itsmembers in order to conserve resources and benefits the environment.
Kate Krebs, Executive Director
Anjian Nicolaidis, Deputy Director

1501 National Water Resources Association
National Water Resources Association
3800 N Fairfax Drive
Suite 4
Arlington, VA 22203
703-524-1544
Fax: 703-524-1548
E-mail: nwra@nwra.org
http://www.nwra.org/

The National Water Resources Association is a nonprofit federation of state organizations whose membership includes rural water districts, municipal water entities, commerical companies and individuals. As an Association we areconcerned with the appropriate management, conservation, and use of water and land resources on a national scope.

1502 National Wild Turkey Federation
770 Augusta Road
PO Box 530
Edgefield, SC 29824
803-637-3106
800-THE-NWTF
Fax: 803-637-0034
E-mail: nwtf@nwtf.net
http://www.nwtf.org/

The NWTF, an international nonprofit conservation and education organization dedicated to conserving wild turkeys and preserving hunting traditions. Growth and progress define the NWTF as it has expanded from 1,300 members in 1973 tonearly a half million today.
Tammy Bristow Sapp, President Communications

1503 National Wildlife Federation
11100 Wildlife Center Drive
Reston, VA 20190
800-822-9919
http://www.nwf.org

The National Wildlife Federation inspires Americans to protect wildlife for our children's future. They represent the power and commitment of over five million members and supporters joined by affiliated wildlife organizationsthroughout the states and territories. They channel the energy of thousands of volunteers from all walks of life to take action because they care about wildlife.
Larry J Schweiger, President/CEO

1504 Natural Resources Defense Council
40 West 20th Street
New York, NY 10011
212-727-2700
Fax: 212-727-1773
E-mail: nrdcinfo@nrdc.org
http://www.nrdc.org

Mission: To safeguard the Earth: its people, its plants and animals, and natural systems on which all life depends.
Frances Beinecke, President
Peter Lehner, Executive Director

1505 Nature Conservancy
4245 N Fairfax Drive
Suite 100
Arlington, VA 22203
800-628-6860
E-mail: webmaster@tnc.org
http://www.nature.org

The Nature Conservancy is a leading international, nonprofit organization dedicated to rpeserving the diversity of life on Earth. The mission of The Nature Conservancy is to preserve teh plants, animals and natural communities thatrepresent the diversity of life on Earth by protecting the lands and waters they need to survive.

1506 **New England Wildflower Society**
180 Hemenway Road
Framingham, MA 01701
508-877-7630
Fax: 508-877-3658
E-mail: information@newenglandwild.org
http://www.newenglandwild.org

New England Wild Flower Society is a recognized leader in native plant conservation. Founded in 1900, the Society is the oldest plant conservation organization in the US. Its purpose is to promote the conservation of temperate NorthAmerican plants through key programs-conservation and research, education, horticulture and habitat preservation. They publish two magazines annually, a seed catalog, nursey catalog, brochures and pamphlets about native plant conservation andhorticulture

Debbi Edelstein, Executive Director
Francis H Clark, Chair, Board of Trustees

1507 **New York Botanical Garden**
200th Street & Kazimiroff Boulevard
Bronx, NY 10458
718-817-8700
Fax: 718-562-8474
http://www.nybg.org

Founded in 1891, the Garden is one of the world's great collections of plants, the region's leading educational center for gardening and horticulture, and an international center for plant research. The New York Botanical Garden is anadvocate for teh plant kingdom.
Wilson Nolen, Chairman
Gregory Long, President

1508 **Outdoor Writers Association of America**
121 Hickory Street
Suite 1
Missoula, MT 59801
406-728-7434
800-692-2477
Fax: 406-728-7445
E-mail: krhoades@owaa.org
http://www.owaa.org

The mission of Outdoor Writers Association of America is to improve the professional skills of our members, set the highest ethical and communications standards, encourage public enjoyment and conservation of natural resources, and bementors for the next generation of professional outdoor communicators.
Kevin Rhoades, Executive Director

1509 **Ozark Society**
63 Robinwood Drive
Little Rock, AR 72227
501-219-4293
E-mail: alice209ok@yahoo.com
http://www.ozarksociety.net

The Ozark Society, was founded in 1962 by Dr. Neil Compton of BEntonville, an Ozark native, and group of associates for the immediate purpose of saving the Buffalo River from dams proposed by the US Army Corps of Engineers. Societyfounders, working with Sen. JW Fullbright, helped get the National Park Service to survey the Buffalo River area and then began to campiagn for the creation of the Buffalo National River as an alternative to the dams.
Alice Andrews, President

1510 **Pennsylvania Association of Environmental Professionals**
174 Crestview Drive
Bellefonte, PA 16823
814-355-2467
Fax: 814-355-2452
E-mail: info@paep.org
http://www.paep.org

A nonpolitical interdisciplinary organization of individuals working in environmental management, planning, impact assessment, environmental protection, compliance, research, engineering, design and education.
Jeff Prawdzik, President
Jason Minnich, Vice President

1511 **Sea Grant Association**
University Of Maine
5784 York Complex
Orono, ME 04469
207-581-1435
Fax: 207-581-1426
E-mail: panderson@maine.edu
http://www.sga.seagrant.org

The Sea Grant Association (SGA) is a non-profit organization dedicated to furthering the Sea Grant program concept. SGA provides the mechanism for academic institutions to coordinate their activities, to set program priorities at boththe regional and national level, and to proved a unified voice for the institutions on issues of importance to the oceans and coasts.
Paul S Anderson, President

1512 **Sierra Club**
85 Second Street
2nd Floor
San Francisco, CA 94105
415-977-5500
Fax: 415-977-5799
E-mail: information@sierraclub.org
http://www.sierraclub.org

To advance the preservation and protection of the natural environment by empowering the citizenry, especially democratically-based grassroots organizations, with charitable resources to further the cause of environmental protection.The vehicle through which The Sierra Club Foundation generally fulfills its charitable mission.
Lisa Renstrom, President

1513 **Society of American Foresters**
5400 Grosvenor Lane
Bethesda, MD 20814
301-897-8720
866-897-8720
Fax: 301-897-3690
E-mail: safweb@safnet.org
http://www.safnet.org

The mission of the Society of American Foresters is to advance the science, education, technology, and practice of forestry; to enhance the competency of its members; to establish professional excellence; and, to use the knowledge,skills, and conservation ethic of the profession to ensure the continued health and use of forest ecosystems and the present and future availability of forest resources to benefit society.

Michael T Goergen, Jr, Executive VP/CEO
Carol McKernon, Member Services Manager

1514 **Society of American Travel Writers**
7044 South 13th Street
Oak Creek, WI 53154
414-908-4949
Fax: 414-768-8001
E-mail: satw@satw.org
http://www.satw.org

SATW is a tax-exempt professional association whose purpose is to promote responsible journalism, provide professional support and development for our members. and encourage the conservation and preservation of travel resourcesworldwide.

1515 **Society of Petroleum Engineers**
PO Box 833836
Richardson, TX 75083
972-952-9393
Fax: 972-952-9434
E-mail: spedal@spe.org
http://www.spe.org

Eve Sprunt, President

1516 **Soil and Water Conservation Society**
945 Sw Ankeny Road
Ankeny, IA 50023
515-289-2331
Fax: 515-289-1227
E-mail: swcs@swcs.org
http://www.swcs.org/

Foster the science and the art of soil, water and related natural resource management to achieve sustainability. To promote and practice an ethic recognizing the interdependence of the people in the environment.
Deborah Cavanaugh-Grant, President

1517 **Solar Energy Industries Association**
805 15th Street NW
Suite 510
Washington, DC 20005
202-682-0556
Fax: 202-628-7779
E-mail: info@seia.org
http://www.seia.org/

SEIA's primary mission is to expand the use of solar technologies in the global marketplace. National members combined with

chapter members in 22 states exceed 500 compines providing solar thermal and solar electric products andservices.
Chris O'Brien, Chairman
Jeffrey D Wolfe, Division Chair

1518 TWS Awards
5410 Grosvenor Lane 301-897-9770
Suite 200 Fax: 301-530-2471
Bethesda, MD 20814-2144 E-mail: yanin@wildlife.org
http://http://joomla.wildlife.org

The Wildlife Society's Awards Program honors individuals and groups who have made notable contributions to wildlife conservation. With more than a dozen awards in all, visit thier website for full details and nomination information.

1519 Trout Unlimited
1300 North 17th Street
Suite 500 703-522-0200
Arlington, VA 22209 800-834-2419
Fax: 703-284-9400
E-mail: trout@tu.org
http://www.tu.org

Mission: To conserve, protect and restore North America's trout and salmon fisheries and their watersheds. We accomplish this mission on local, state and national levels with an extensive and dedicated volunteer network.
Charles Gauvin, President/CEO
Steve Moyer, Vice President

1520 US Army Corps of Engineers
20 Massachusetts Avenue NW 202-761-0011
Washington, DC 20314 E-mail: webmaster@usace.army.mil
http://www.usace.army.mil/

Our mission is to provide quality, responsive engineering services to the nation including: planning, desiging, building and operating water resources and other civila works projects.

1521 US Department of Energy
1000 Independence Avenue SW 800-dia-ldoe
Washington, DC 20585 Fax: 202-586-4403
http://www.energy.gov

The Department of ENergy's mission is to advance the national, economic and energy security of the US; to promote scientific and technological innovation; and to ensure the environmental cleanup of the national nuclear weapons complex.
Samuel W Bodman, Secretary of Energy

1522 US Department of the Interior
1849 C Street NW 202-208-3100
Washington, DC 20240 E-mail: webteam@ios.doi.gov
http://www.doi.gov

1523 US Environmental Protection Agency
Ariel Rios Building 800-438-2474
1200 Pennsylvania Ave Nw http://www.epa.gov
Washington, DC 20460

The mission of the EPA is to protect human health and the environment.

1524 Underwater Society of America
PO Box 628 650-583-8492
Daly City, CA 94017 Fax: 408-294-3496
http://www.underwater-society.org/

The Underwater Society of America was founded in 1959 by the existing skin-diving councils; it was composed of and represented all divers in North America. It is the public diving organization of the United States. It is controlled byits Executive committee, board of directors and delegates of the member councils and clubs meeting annually.
Carol Rose, President

1525 Washington Journalism Center
Po Box 15239 202-296-8455
Washington, DC 20003 Fax: 808-588-365
E-mail: terrymichael@wcpj.org
http://www.wcpj.org

Terry Michael, Executive Director

1526 Water Environment Federation
601 Wythe Street 800-666-0206
Alexandria, VA 22314 Fax: 703-684-2492
E-mail: webfeedback@wef.org
http://www.wef.org

Founded in 1928, the Water Environment Federation (WEF) is a not-for-profit technical and educational organization with members from varied disciplines who work toward the WEF vision of preservation and enhancement of the global waterenvironment. The WEF network includes more than 100,000 water quality professionals from 77 member associations in 31 countries.
William J Bertera, Executive Director

1527 Western Forestry and Conservation Association
4033 SW Canyon Road 503-226-4562
Portland, OR 97221 Fax: 503-226-2515
E-mail: richard@westernforestry.org
http://www.westernforestry.org

Offers continuing education workshops and seminars for professional foresters.

1528 Whooping Crane Conservation Association
715 Earl Drive 337-234-6339
Lawrenceburg, TN 38464 http://www.whoopingcrane.com

The mission is to advance conservation, protection and propagation of the Whooping Crane population, to prevent its extinction, to establish and maintain a captive management program for the perpetuation of the species. We collect anddisseminate knowledge of this species; and advocate and encourage public appreciation and understanding of the Whooping Crane's educational, scientific and economic values.

1529 Wilderness Society
1615 M Street NW 202-833-2300
Washington, DC 20036 800-THE-WILD
E-mail: member@tws.org
http://www.wilderness.org

Deliver to future generations an unspoiled legacy of wild places, with all the precious values they hold: Biological diversity; clean air and water; towering forests, rushing rivers, and sage-sweet, silent deserts.
Brenda Davis, Chair
Doug Walker, Vice Chair

1530 Willowbrook Wildlife Haven Preservation
National Wildlife Rehabilitation Association
2625 Clearwater Road 320-230-9920
Suite 110 Fax: 320-230-3077
St. Cloud, MN 56301 E-mail: nwra@nwrawildlife.org
http://www.nwrawildlife.org

The National Wildlife Rehabilitators Association is a nonprofit international membership organization committed to promoting and improving the integrity and professionalism of wildlife rehabilitation and contributing to thepreservation of natural ecosystems.
Lessie Davis, President

1531 World Environment Center
734 15th Street NW 202-312-1370
Suite 720 Fax: 202-682-1682
Washington, DC 20005 E-mail: info@wec.org
http://www.wec.org

The World Environment Center is an independent, global non-prfot, non-advocacy organization that advances sustainable development worldwide through the business practices of member companies, and in partnerships with governments,multi-lateral and private sector organizations, universities, and other stake holders.

Terry F Yosie, President & CEO
Gwen Davidow, Dir Global Corporate Program

1532 World Wildlife Fund
1250 24th Street NW
Po Box 97180 202-293-4800
Washington, DC 20090 E-mail: membership@wwfus.org
http://www.worldwildlife.org/

World Wildlife Fund is dedicated to protecting the world's wildlife and wildlands. The largest privately supported international

conservation organization in the world, WWF has more than 1 million members in the US alone. Since itsinception in 1961, WWF has invested in over 13,100 projects in 157 countries.
Carter S Roberts, President

Conferences & Trade Shows

Environmental

1533 **Air and Waste Management Association Annual Conference and Exhibition**
1 Gateway Center, 3rd Floor
420 Fort Duquesne Boulevard
Pittsburgh, PA 15222
412-232-3444
800-270-3444
Fax: 412-232-3450
E-mail: info@awma.org
http://www.awma.org
Environmental professionals from all sectors of the economy including colleges, universities, natural resource manufacturing and process industries, consultants, local state, provincial, regional and federal governments, construction,utilities industries.
Edith M Ardiente, President
Richard C Scherr, Secretary

1534 **American Academy of Environmental Medicine Conference**
7701 East Kellogg
Suite 625
Wichita, KS 67207
316-684-5500
Fax: 316-684-5709
E-mail: administrator@aaem.com
http://www.aaem.com
Aims to support physicians and other professionals in serving the public through education about the interaction between humans and their environment, and to promote optimal health through prevention and safe, effective treatment ofthe causes, not the illness.

35+ booths with 200 attendees and 35+ exhibits
James W Willoughby II, President
James F Coy, President Elect

1535 **American Board of Industrial Hygiene Professional Conference**
American Board of Industrial Hygiene
6015 West St Joseph
Suite 102
Lansing, MI 48917
517-321-2638
Fax: 517-321-4624
E-mail: abih@abih.org
http://www.abih.org
Industrial hygiene certification organization. Certified industrial hygienist is offered based on education, experience and examination.
Lynn O'Donnell CIH, Executive Director

1536 **American Conference of Governmental Industrial Hygienists**
1330 Kemper Meadow Drive
Cincinnati, OH 45240
513-742-6163
Fax: 513-742-3355
E-mail: mail@acgih.org
http://www.acgih.org
Advances occupational and environmental health.
3,000 Members
90 booths
Jimmy L Perkins, Chair
A Anthony Rizzuto, Executive Director

1537 **American Industrial Hygiene Association Conference and Exposition**
2700 Prosperity Avenue
Suite 250
Fairfax, VA 22031
703-849-8888
Fax: 703-207-3561
E-mail: infonet@aiha.org
http://www.aiha.org
AIHA promotes, protects and enhances industrial hygienists and other occupational health, safety and environmental professionals in their efforts to improve the health and well-being of workers, the community and the environment.
Kim Bacon, Assistant Manager
Carol Tobin, Director

1538 **American Solar Energy Society Conference**
American Solar Energy Society
2400 Central Avenue
Suite A
Boulder, CO 80301
303-443-3130
Fax: 303-443-3212
E-mail: ases@ases.org
http://www.ases.org
the american solar energy society conference (ases) is the united states section of the international solar energy society. ASES is a non profit organization dedicated to the development and adoption of renewal energy in all forms.
Bradley D. Collins, Executive Director

1539 **American Water Resources Association Conference**
4 West Federal Street
PO Box 1626
Middleburg, VA 20118
540-687-8390
Fax: 540-687-8395
E-mail: terry@awra.org
http://www.awra.org
Founded in 1964, the American Water Resources Association is a non-profit professional association dedicated to the advancement of men and women in water resources management, research and education.
Kenneth D Reid, Executive VP
Terry Meyer, Marketing Director

1540 **Arkansas Association of Conservation Districts Annual Conference**
101 East Capitol
Suite 350
Little Rock, AR 72201
501-682-2915
Fax: 501-682-3991
E-mail: debbiepinreal@aol.com
http://www.aracd.org
Affiliated with the National Association of Conservation Districts. Membership is $25.00 per year for individuals and $1,200.00 per year for organizations and companies.

November
Debbie Moreland, Program Administrator

1541 **Atlantic States Marine Fisheries Commission Annual Meeting**
1444 I Street NW
6th Floor
Washington, DC 20005
202-289-6400
Fax: 202-289-6051
E-mail: info@asmfc.org
http://www.asmfc.org
The Atlantic States Marine Fisheries Commission was formed by the 15 Atlantic coast states in 1942 in recognition that fish do not adhere to political boundaries. The Commission serves as a deliberative body, coordinating theconservation and management of the states shared near shore fishery resources-marine, shell, and anadromous-for sustainable use.
John V O'Shea, Executive Director
George D Lapointe, Chair

1542 **Children's Environmental Health: Research, Practice, Prevention and Policy**
110 Maryland Avenue Northeast
Suite 505
Washington, DC 20002
202-543-4033
Fax: 202-543-8797
E-mail: cehn@cehn.org
http://www.cehn.org
Children's Environmental Health Network is a national non profit organization focused on environmental health. The work of the work focuses on promoting pediatric research, prevention and practice
Nsedu Obot Witherspoon, Executive Director
Joanne Perodin, Program Coordinator

1543 **Coastal Society Conference**
PO Box 3590
Williamsburg, VA 23187
757-565-0999
Fax: 703-933-1596
E-mail: coastalsoc@aol.com
http://www.thecoastalsociety.org
The Coastal Society is an organization of private sector, academic, and government professionals and students dedicated to actively addressing emerging coastal issues by fostering dialogue, forging partnerships, and promotingcommunication and education.
Judy Tucker, Executive Director

1544 **Colorado Water Congress Annual Meeting**
1580 Logan Street 303-837-0812
Suite 400 E-mail: cwc@cowatercongress.org
Denver, CO 80203 http://www.cowatercongress.org
Protects and conserves Colorado's water resources by means of advocacy and education.

January
350 attendees and 9 exhibits
Doug Kemper, Executive Director

1545 **Connecticut Forest and Park Association Annual Meeting**
16 Meriden Road 860-346-2372
Rockfall, CT 06481 Fax: 860-347-7463
E-mail: info@ctwoodlands.org
http://www.ctwoodlands.org
An organization for forest and wildlife conservation. Develops outdoor recreation and natural resources. Provides forest management, construction of hiking trails and consultation in the areas of forestry and environment.

Spring
Richard Whitehouse, President
Gordon Anderson, VP

1546 **ESTECH**
Institute of Environmental Sciences & Technology
Arlington Place One, 2340 S. 847-981-0100
Arlington Heights Rd. Suite 100 Fax: 847-981-4130
Arlington Heights, IL 60005 E-mail: iest@iest.org
http://www.iest.org
An international professional society that serves the environmental sciences in the areas of contamination control in electronics manufacturing and pharmaceutical processes, design, test and evaluation of commercial and militaryequipment and product reliability issues.

April
50 booths with 500 attendees
Corrie Roesslein, Managing Director
Roberta Burrows, Deputy Executive Director

1547 **Environmental Technology Expo**
Association of Energy Engineers
4025 Pleasantdale Road 770-447-5083
Suite 420 Fax: 770-446-3969
Atlanta, GA 30340 E-mail: whit@aeecenter.org
http://www.aeecenter.org
AEE is a source of information in the field of energy efficiency, utility deregulation, facility management, plant engineering, and environmental compliance. Outreach programs include technical seminars, conferences, books, joblistings and certification programs.
Ruth Whitlock, Executive Administrator

1548 **Federation of Environmental Technologists**
9451 N 107th Street 414-354-0070
Milwaukee, WI 53224 Fax: 414-354-0073
E-mail: info@fetinc.org
http://www.fetinc.org
A nonprofit organization formed to assist industry in interpretation of and compliance with environmental regulations. Membership is open to all industries, municipalities, organizations and individuals concerned about environmentalregulations. Currently there are approximately 1000 members and 125 patron companies.

March
200 attendees and 70 exhibits
Barbara Hurula, Executive Director

1549 **Forestry Conservation Communications Association Annual Meeting**
Fcca
PO Box 3217 717-338-1505
Gettysburg, PA 17325 Fax: 717-334-5656
E-mail: nfc@fcca-usa.org
http://www.fcca-usa.org
The FCCA is a national organization. Its main function is to assist federal, state and local governments in public safety two-way radio operations by locating suitable frequencies within specified operating areas, recommending theirassignment to the FCC for licensing, and protecting them once licensed.
Ralph Haller, Executive Director

1550 **Global Warming International Conference and Expo**
Po Box 50303 630-910-1551
Palo Alto, CA 94303 Fax: 630-910-1561
http://www.globalwarming.net
The GWIC is the international body disseminating information on global warming science and policy, serving both governmental,and non-governmental organizations and industries in more than 145 countries. It sponsors unbiased researchsupporting the understanding of global warming and its mitigation.
Sinyan Shen

1551 **GlobalCon**
Association of Energy Engineers
4025 Pleasantdale Road 404-761-0509
Suite 420 Fax: 770-446-3969
Atlanta, GA 30340 E-mail: info@aeecenter.org
http://www.globalconevent.com
Energy/environmental technological equipment.
Ruth Bennett, Information Services Dir.

1552 **Greenprints: Sustainable Communities by Design**
Southface Energy Institute
241 Pine Street Northeast 404-872-3549
Atlanta, GA 30308 Fax: 404-872-5009
E-mail: info@southface.org
http://www.southface.org
Southface promotes sustainable homes, workplaces and communities through education, research, advocacy and technical assistance.Greenprints is a conference and trade show produced by the Southface Energy Institute.

March
100 booths with 1200 attendees
Dave Boles, Controller

1553 **HydroVision**
HCI Publications
410 Archibald Street 816-931-1311
Kansas City, MO 64111 Fax: 816-931-2015
E-mail: info@hcipub.com
http://www.hcipub.com
Serves the hydroelectric industry.

1554 **Institute of Scrap Recycling Industries Convention**
1615 L Street Northwest 202-662-8500
Suite 600 Fax: 202-626-0900
Washington, DC 20036 E-mail: robinwiener@isri.org
http://www.isri.org
Equipment for the recycling industries.
Robin Weiner, President
Marion White, Mailroom Supervisor

1555 **International Association for Energy Economics Conference**
International Association for Energy Economics
28790 Chagrin Boulevard 216-464-5365
Suite 350 Fax: 216-464-2737
Cleveland, OH 44122 E-mail: iaee@iaee.org
http://www.iaee.org
The IAEE is a nonprofit professional organization that provides a forum for the exchange of ideas and experiences among energy professionals. The conference attracts delegates governmental, corporate and academic energydecision-makers.
David L Williams, Executive Director

1556 **International Conference on Solid Waste**
Widener University, Civil Engineering

One University Place
Chester, PA 19013
610-499-4042
Fax: 610-499-4461
E-mail: solid.waste@widener.edu
http://www.widener.edu/solid.waste

An annual conference on solid waste technology and management. Over 150 speakers from 40 countries present their work. Proceedings available.

March
Ronald L Mersky, Chair

1557 Maryland Recyclers Coalition Annual Conference
Maryland Recyclers Coalition
Po Box 1046
Laurel, MD 20725
888-496-3196
Fax: 301-238-4579
E-mail: recycle@marylandrecyclers.org
http://www.marylandrecyclers.org

MRC's mission is to promote sustainable reduction, reuse and recycling of materials otherwise destined for disposal and promote and increase buying products made with recycled material content.

June
Peter Houstle, Executive Director

1558 Massachusetts Association of Conservation Commissions Conference
10 Juniper Road
Belmont, MA 02478
617-489-3930
Fax: 617-489-3935
E-mail: staff@maccweb.org
http://www.maccweb.org

We host the MACC Annual Environmental Conference, the largest such event in New England, with over 40 workshops and nearly 50 exhibitors.

March
1100 attendees and 50 exhibits
Sally Zielinski PhD, Board President
Linda Mack, Executive Director

1559 Massachusetts Water Pollution Control Association Annual Conference
PO Box 221
Groveland, MA 01834
978-374-0170
Fax: 978-374-0170
E-mail: mwpca1965@verizon.net
http://www.mwpca.org

September
John Connor, Secretary/Treasurer

1560 Michigan Association of Conservation Districts Annual Meeting
Po Box 99
Cadillac, MI 49601
231-876-0328
Fax: 231-876-0372
E-mail: macd@macd.org
http://www.macd.org

The Michigan Association of Conservation Districts is a non-governmental, non-profit organization, established to represent and provide services to Michigan's 80 Conservation Districts. The Association represents its members at thestate level by working with legislators, cooperating agencies, and special interest groups whose programs affect the care and management of Michigan's natural resources, especially on private lands.

November
Teresa Salveta, Michigan Coordinator

1561 Michigan Forest Association Annual Meeting
6120 South Clinton Trail
Eaton Rapids, MI 48827
517-663-3423
Fax: 517-663-3423
http://www.michiganforests.com

Mission: To promote good management on all forest land, to educate our members about good forest practices and stewardship of the land, and to inform the general public about forestry issues and the benefits of good forest management.

Summer
William Botti, Executive Director

1562 Minnesota Association of Soil and Water Conservation Districts Annual Meeting
790 Cleveland Avenue S
Suite 201
St. Paul, MN 55116
651-690-9028
Fax: 651-690-9065
http://www.maswcd.org

MASWCD is a nonprofit organization which exists to provide leadership and a common voice for Minnesota's soil and water conservation districts and to maintain a positive, results-oriented relationship with rule making agencies,partners and legislators; expanding education opportunities for the districts so they may carry out effective conservation programs.

December
Ken Pederson, President
Steve Sunderland, Vice President

1563 Montana Association of Conservation Districts Annual Meeting
501 North Sanders
Helena, MT 59601
406-443-5711
Fax: 406-443-0174
E-mail: mail@macdnet.org
http://www.macdnet.org

Montana's 58 Conservation Districts utilize locally-led and largely non-regulatory approaches to successfully address general natural resource issues. CD's have a decades-long history of conserving our state's resources by helpinglocal people match their needs with technical and financial resources, thereby getting good conservation practices on the ground to benefit all of Montanans.

November
Sarah Carlson, Executive Director

1564 Montana Water Environment Association Annual Meeting
516 N Park Street
Suite A
Helena, MT 59601
406-449-7913
Fax: 406-449-6350

Spring

1565 NEHA Annual Education Conference and Exhibition
National Environmental Health Association
720 South Colorado Boulevard
Suite 1000 N
Denver, CO 80246
303-756-9090
Fax: 303-691-9490
E-mail: staff@neha.org
http://www.neha.org

A revealing look at how the Environmental Health Profession is Evolving

June
100 exhibits
Nelson Fabian, Executive Director
Larry Marcum, Manager

1566 NESEA BuildingEnergy Conference
50 Miles Street
Greenfield, MA 01301
413-774-6051
Fax: 413-774-6053
E-mail: nesea@nesea.org
http://www.nesea.org

Held in Boston every March, this conference is the oldest and largest regional buuilding energy and renewable energy conference and trade show for practitioners in the Northeast. Over 4,000 people passed through the doors of the 2009event to take advantage of the high-level educational sessions and top quality exhibits.

March
4000 attendees and 150 exhibits
Arianna Alexsandra Grindrod, Education Director
Jenny Spencer, Trade Show Manager, BE Conf.

1567 National Association Civilian Conservation Corps Alumni
16 Hancock Avenue
Saint Louis, MO 63125
314-487-8666
E-mail: naccca@aol.com
http://www.cccalumni.org

The NACCCA was established as a non-profit organization in 1977 in California. The NACCCA offers annual national reunions, and a scholarship to a descendent of a NACCCA member.

10 booths
Gene Morris, Civilian Records

1568 National Association of Environmental Professionals

100 North 20th Street
4th Floor
Philadelphia, PA 19103
215-564-3484
Fax: 215-564-2175
http://www.naep.org

NAEP is a multidisciplinary association dedicated to the advancement of environmental professionals in the US and abroad, and a forum for state-of-the-art information on environmental planning, research and management. A network ofprofessional contacts and a resource for structured career development, this organization is a strong proponent of ethics and the highest standards of practice in the environmental professions.
Ron Deverman, President
Paul Looney, Vice President

1569 National Conference of Local Environmental Health Administrators

University of Washington
Dept Enviro Health, Box 357234
Seattle, WA 98195
206-616-2097
Fax: 206-543-8123
E-mail: ctreser@u.washington.edu
http://www.ncleha.org

The NCLEHA's purpose is to provide a forum for local administrators to share common concerns and solutions to mutual problems, and to provide a professional organization for environmental health administrators, focused on the issuesand problems of local environmental health programs.
Dave Riggs, Secretary

1570 National Environmental Balancing Bureau Meeting

National Environmental Balancing Bureau
8575 Grovemont Circle
Gaithersburg, MD 20877
301-977-3698
Fax: 301-977-9589
E-mail: barry@neb.org
http://www.nebb.org

The NEBB is a nonprofit organization founded by contractors in the heating, ventilating and air conditioning (HVAC) industry. NEBB exists to help architects, engineers, building owners and contractors produce great buildings with HVACsystems that perform in ways they have visualized and designed.

1571 National Environmental Health Association Annual Education Conference

National Environmental Health Association
720 South Colorado Boulevard
Suite 1000 N
Denver, CO 80246
303-756-9090
Fax: 303-691-9490
E-mail: staff@neha.org
http://www.neha.org

The NEHA AEC and Exhibition is a six-day educational event consisting of nine different environmental health and protection conferences and highlighting a two-day exhibition. It is the only conference that emcompasses all areas ofenvironmental health and protection, including, but not limited to: food protection, onsite wastewater, chemical and bioterrorism preparedness, indoor air quality, hazardous waste, and drinking water.

Late June-Early July
120 booths with 1300 attendees
Larry Marcum, Manager
Nelson Fabian, Executive Director

1572 National Environmental, Safety and Health Training Association

PO Box 10321
Phoenix, AZ 85064-0321
602-956-6099
Fax: 602-956-6399
E-mail: neshta@neshta.org
http://http://neshta.org

The National Environmental, Safety and Health Training Association is a non-profit international society for environmental, safety, health and other technical training and adult education professionals. NESHTA promotes trainercompetency through training and education standards, voluntary certification, and peer networking.

Charles L. Richardson, Executive Director
Suzanne M. Lanctot, Membership Services

1573 National Real Estate Environmental Conference

National Society of Environmental Consultants
PO Box 12528
San Antonio, TX 78212
210-225-2897
800-486-3676
Fax: 956-225-8450

Environmentally responsible management of real estate.

1574 National Recycling Congress Show

805 15th Street Nw
Suite 425
Washington, DC 20005
202-789-1430
Fax: 202-789-1431
E-mail: info@nrc-recycle.org
http://www.nrc-recycle.org

Founded in 1978, the National Recycling Coalition, Inc. provides technical education, disseminates public information on selected recycling issues, shapes public and private policy on recycling and operates programs that encouragerecycling markets and economic development.
Kate Krebs, Executive Director

1575 National Solar Energy Conference

2400 Central Avenue
Suite A
Boulder, CO 80301
303-443-4308
Fax: 303-442-3212
E-mail: pmcfadden@ases.org
http://www.ases.org

The American Solar Energy Society (ASES) presents the Conference along with Green Energy Ohio. The event combines a premiere technical conference, plenary and forum sessions, a Renewable Energy Products and Services exhibit, workshops,tours and special events of interest to professionals and consumers.

750 attendees and 75-100 exhibits
Pam McFadden, Registration/Sales

1576 National Water Resources Association Annual Conference

3800 North Fairfax Drive
Suite 4
Arlington, VA 22203
703-524-1544
Fax: 703-524-1548
E-mail: nwra@nwra.org
http://www.nwra.org

Conservation of water resources in the 17 western reclamation states.

1577 Nebraska Association of Resources Districts Annual Meeting

601 South 12th Street
Suite 201
Lincoln, NE 68508
402-471-7670
Fax: 402-471-7677
E-mail: nard@nrdnet.org
http://www.nrdnet.org

Our mission is to assist NRDs in a coordinated effort to accomplish collectively what may not be accomplished individually to conserve, sustain, and improve our natural resources and environment.

September
Dean E Edson, Executive Director
Jeanne Dryburgh, Office Manager

1578 New England Enviro Expo

Zweigwhite
330 North Wabash
Suite 3201
Chicago, IL 60611
312-628-5870
Fax: 312-628-5878
E-mail: info@zweigwhite.com
http://www.enviroexpo.com

Environmental products/services for industrial, municipal, and government uses.

May
400 booths with 5000 attendees
Dick Ryan, President
Fred White, Executive Vice President

1579 **New England Water Environment Association Annual Meeting**
NEWEA
10 Tower Office Park
Suite 601
Woburn, MA 01801
781-939-0908
Fax: 781-939-0907
E-mail: mail@newea.org
http://www.newea.org

We are a regional member association of the Water Environmental Federation. We provide technical and education for the waste water industry.

150+ booths with 1500 attendees
Erin Mosley, President

1580 **New Hampshire Association of Conservation Commissions Annual Meeting**
54 Portsmouth Street
Concord, NH 03301
603-224-7867
Fax: 603-228-0423
E-mail: info@nhacc.org
http://www.nhacc.org

The New Hampshire Association of Conservation Commissions is a private, non-profit association of municipal conservation commissions. Its purpose is to foster conservation and appropriate use of New Hampshire's natural resources byproviding assistance to conservation commissions, facilitating communication and cooperation among commissions, and helping to create a climate in which commissions can be successful.

November
Carol K Andrews, Executive Director

1581 **New Jersey Society for Environmental Economic Development Annual Conference**
222 West State Street
Trenton, NJ 08608
609-695-3481
Fax: 609-695-0151
http://www.njslom.org

October
William G. Dressel, Executive Director

1582 **New Jersey Water Environment Association Conference**
PO Box 1212
Fair Lawn, NJ 07410
201-296-0021
Fax: 201-296-0031
http://www.njwea.org

The New Jersey Water Environment Association is a nonprofit educational organization dedicated to preserving and enhancing the water environment.
Joseph Bonaccorso, President

1583 **New Mexico Association of Soil and Water Conservation Annual Conference**
New Mexico Association Of Conservation Districts
163 Trail Canyon Road
Carlsbad, NM 88220
505-981-2400
Fax: 505-981-2422
E-mail: conserve@hughes.net
http://http://www.nm.nacdnet.org

The mission of NMACD is to facilitate conservation of the natural resources in New Mexico by providing opportunities and quality support to local conservation districts through representation and leadership.

Fall
Debbie Hughes, Executive Director

1584 **New York Water Environment Association Semi-Annual Conferences**
Nywea
525 Plum Street
Suite 102
Syracuse, NY 13204
315-422-7811
Fax: 315-422-3851
E-mail: pcr@nywea.org
http://www.nywea.org

The New York Water Environment Association is a nonprofit educational association dedicated to the development and dissemination of information concerning water quality management and the nature, collection, treatment, and disposal ofwastewater. Founded in 1929, the Association has over 2,500 members. The NYWEA is a member association of the Water Environment Federation.

Winter and Summer
Patricia Cerro-Reehil, Executive Director

1585 **North American Lake Management Society International Symposium**
4513 Vernon Boulevard, Suite 103
PO Box 5443
Madison, WI 53703
608-233-2836
Fax: 608-233-3186
E-mail: dbrown@nalms.org
http://www.nalms.org

The North American Lake Management Society's mission is to forge partnerships among citizens, scientists and professionals to foster the management and protection of lakes and reservoirs for today and tomorrow.

October and Novembe
100 booths with 850 attendees and 50 exhibits
Darcy Brown, Administrative Assistant

1586 **North Carolina Association of Soil and Water Conservation Districts Annual Conference**
Po Box 27943
Raleigh, NC 27611
919-733-2302
E-mail: bridget.munger@ncmail.net
http://www.ncaswcd.org

The association is an indepented, nonpartisan conservation organization created in 1944 to represent the interests of the 96 local soil and water conservation districts and the 492 district supervisors who direct their local district'sconservation programs.

January
Don Rawls, President

1587 **North Dakota Association of Soil Conservation Districts Annual Conference**
Lincoln Oaks Nursurey
3310 University Drive
Bismarck, ND 58504
701-223-8575
Fax: 701-223-1291
E-mail: lincolnoaks@btinet.net
http://www.lincolnoakes.com

November

1588 **Northeast Recycling Council Conference**
139 Main Street
Suite 401
Brattleboro, VT 05301
802-254-3636
Fax: 802-254-5870
E-mail: patty@nerc.org
http://www.nerc.org

NERC's mission is to leverage the strengths and resources of its member states to advance an environmentally stable economy in the Northeast by promoting source reduction, recycling, and the purchasing of environmentally preferableproducts and services.

March and October
Moon Morgan, Office Manager
Patty Dillon, Manager Of Toxics

1589 **Northeast Resource Recovery Association Annual Conference**
2101 Dover Road
Epsom, NH 03234
603-736-4401
Fax: 603-736-4402
E-mail: info@nrra.net
http://www.recyclewithus.org

The Northeast Resource Recovery Association is a pro-active nonprofit working with its membership to make their recycling programs strong, efficient, and financially successful by providing cooperative marketing, cooperativepurchasing, education and networking opportunities; developing innovative recycling programs; creating sustainable alternatives to reduce the volume and toxicity of the waste, and educating and informing local officials about recycling and solidwaste issues.

June
Rick Cooper, President
Paula Dow, Executive Director

1590 Pacific Fishery Management Council Conferences
7700 Northeast Ambassador Place
Suite 101
Portland, OR 97220
503-820-2280
866-806-7204
Fax: 503-820-2299
E-mail: john.coon@noaa.gov
http://www.pcouncil.org

The Pacific Council has developed fishery management plans for salmon, groundfish and coastal species in the US Exclusive Economic Zone off the coast of Washington, Oregon and California, and recommends Pacific halibut harvestregulations to the International Pacific Halibut Commission.

5x year
Donald McIsaac, Executive Director
John Coon, Deputy Director

1591 Parks and Trails Council of Minnesota Annual Meeting
275 E 4th Street
Suite 250
Saint Paul, MN 55101
651-726-2457
800-944-0707
Fax: 651-726-2458
E-mail: info@parksandtrails.org
http://www.parksandtrails.org

Mission: To acquire, protect and enhance critical lands for the public's enjoyment now and in the future.

March
Judith Erickson, Government Relations
Beth Coleman, Executive Director

1592 Plant and Facilities Expo
Association of Energy Engineers
4025 Pleasantdale Road
Suite 420
Atlanta, GA 30340
404-761-0509
Fax: 770-446-3969
E-mail: info@aeecenter.org
http://www.aeecenter.org

Occupational health/safety systems.
Ruth Bennett, Information Services Dir.

1593 Renewable Energy Roundup & Green Living Fair
PO Box 9507
Austin, TX 78766
512-345-5446
800-465-5049
E-mail: info@txses.org
http://www.txses.org; www.theroundup.org

Organized by the Texas Solar Energy Society and Texas Renewable Energy Industries Association featuring solutions to global warming such as rainwater harvesting, green and sustainable building, alternative transporation, and energyconservation.

September
Natalie Marquis, Executive Director
Russel Smith, Event Coordinator

1594 Solar Cookers International World Conference
1919 21st Street
Suite 101
Sacramento, CA 95814
916-444-6616
Fax: 916-444-5379
E-mail: sbci@igc.apc.org

Equipment for solar cooking and pasteurization of drinking water.

1595 South Dakota Association of Conservation Districts Conference
PO Box 275
Pierre, SD 57501
605-895-4099
Fax: 605-895-9424
http://www.sdconservation.org

September
Angela Ehlers, Executive Director

1596 South Dakota Environmental Health Association Annual Conference
State Department of Health
600 East Capitol Avenue
Pierre, SD 57501
605-773-3361
800-738-2301
E-mail: DOH.INFO@state.sd.us
http://http://doh.sd.gov

April
Doneen Hollingsworth, Secretary of Health

1597 Southeastern Association of Fish and Wildlife Agencies Annual Meeting
8005 Freshwater Farms Road
Tallahassee, FL 32308
850-893-1204
Fax: 850-893-6204
E-mail: seafwa@aol.com
http://www.seafwa.org

The SEAFWA conducts an annual conference each fall to provide a forum for presentation of information and exchange of ideas regarding the management and protection of fish and wildlife resources throughout the nation but with emphasison the southeast.

October/November
Robert M. Brantly, Executive Secretary

1598 Take it Back
Raymond Communications
5111 Berwyn Road
Suite 115
College Park, MD 20740
301-345-4237
Fax: 301-345-4768
E-mail: bruce@raymond.com
http://www.raymond.com

Top recycling experts and practical sessions.

250 attendees
Bruce Popka, Vice President

1599 Texas Environmental Health Association Annual Education Conference
PO Box 10
Leesburg, TX 75451
903-572-7278
Fax: 903-572 4193
E-mail: ginger.shaffer@myteha.org
http://www.myteha.org

The mission of TEHA is to work for the betterment of the health and welfare of people through the improvement of the environment.

March
Margie N Earl, President
Ginger Shaffer, Executive Secretary

1600 Texas Water Conservation Association Annual Conference
221 E 9th Street
Suite 206
Austin, TX 78701
512-472-7216
Fax: 512-472-0537
E-mail: goodson@twca.org
http://www.twca.org

March
Leroy Goodson, Contact
Dean Robbins, Contact

1601 Utah Association of Conservation Districts Annual Conference
1860 N 100 East
Logan, UT 84341
435-753-6029
Fax: 435-755-2117
E-mail: amber.beck@ut.nacdnet.net
http://http://uacd.org

The Utah Association of Conservation Districts is a nonprofit corporation representing Utah's 38 soil conservation districts. By working with landowners, organizations and government, the conservation districts work through voluntary,incentive-based programs to protect soil, water quality and other natural resources.

November
Gordon Younker, Executive Vice President
Susan Stillion, Executive Assistant

1602 **Virginia Association of Soil and Water Conservation Districts Annual Conference**
7308 Hanover Green Drive
Suite 100
Mechanicsville, VA 23111
804-559-0324
Fax: 804-559-0325
E-mail: info@vaswcd.org
http://www.vaswcd.org

The Virginia Association of Soil and Water Conservation Districts (VASWCD) is a private nonprofit association of 47 soil and water conservation districts in Virginia. It is a voluntary, nongovernmental association of Virginia'sdistricts that provides and promotes leadership in the conservation of natural resources through stewardship and education programs.

December
Wilkie WO Chaffin PhD, President

1603 **Virginia Forestry Association Annual Conference**
3308 Augusta Avenue
Richmond, VA 23230
804-278-8733
E-mail: vafa@verizon.net
http://www.vaforestry.org

VFA promotes stewardship and wise use of the Commonwealth's forest resources for the economic and environmental benefits of all Virginians. Membership consists of forest landowners, forest product businesses, forestry professionals,and a variety of individuals and groups who are concerned about the future and well-being of Virginia's forest resources.

Late Spring
Patrick Gottschalk, Secretary of Commerce

1604 **WEFTEC Show**
Water Environment Federation
601 Wythe Street
Alexandria, VA 22314
800-666-0206
Fax: 703-684-2492
E-mail: csc@wef.org
http://www.wef.org

North America's largest annual water quality conference and exposition. Covers a wide spectrum of critical water quality issues.

Fall
16,000 attendees and 800+ exhibits
Tom Wolfe, Director of Advertising

1605 **Waste Expo**
Environmental Industries Association
4301 Connecticut Avenue NW
Suite 300
Washington, DC 20008
202-244-4700
Fax: 202-966-4818
http://www.envasns.org

Waste/recycling equipment and technology.
Bruce Parker, President

1606 **WasteExpo**
11 Riverbend Drive S
Stamford, CT 06907
203-358-9900
800-559-0620
Fax: 203-358-5816
E-mail: laura.magliola@penton.com
http://www.wasteexpo.com

WasteExpo is the largest tradeshow in North America serving the $43 billion solid waste and recycling industries.

11,500 attendees and 450 exhibits
Laura Magliola, Marketing Manager

1607 **West Virginia Forestry Association**
PO Box 718
Ripley, WV 25271
304-372-1955
888-372-9663
Fax: 304-372-1957
E-mail: wvfa@wvadventures.net
http://www.wvfa.org

The West Virginia Forestry Association is a non-profit organization funded by its membership. Our members include individuals and businesses involved in forest management, timber production and wood product manufacturing. Our membersare concerned with protecting the environment, as well as enhancing the future of West Virginia's forests through multiple-use management.

Summer
Richard Waybright, Executive Director

1608 **Western Association of Fish and Wildlife Agencies Annual Meeting**
5400 Bishop Blvd
Cheyenne, WY 82006
307-777-4569
Fax: 307-777-4699
http://www.wafwa.org

July
Larry Kruckenberg, Secretary

1609 **Western Forestry and Conservation Association Conference**
4033 Canyon Road SW
Portland, OR 97221
503-226-4562
Fax: 503-226-2515
E-mail: richard@westernforestry.org
http://www.westernforestry.org

Offers continuing education workshops and seminars for professional foresters throughout the west.

January/February

1610 **Western Society of Naturalists Annual Meeting**
San Diego State University Department Of Biology
5500 Campanile Drive
San Diego, CA 92182
818-677-3256
Fax: 818-677-2034
http://www.wsn-online.org

Members include researchers, educators, academics and others with an interest in the area's biology, particularly its marine life. Membership is $15.00 per year for individuals and $7.00 for students.
Mark Carr, President

1611 **Wildlife Habitat Council Annual Symposium**
Wildlife Habitat Council
8737 Colesville Road
Suite 800
Silver Spring, MD 20910
301-588-8994
Fax: 301-588-4629
E-mail: whc@wildlifehc.org
http://www.wildlifehc.org

The Wildlife Habitat Council is a nonprofit, group of corporations, conservation organizations, and individuals dedicated to restoring and enhancing wildlife habitat.
Emer OBroin, Chairman
Lawrence A Selzer, Vice Chairman

1612 **Wildlife Society Annual Conference**
Wildlife Society
5410 Grosvenor Lane
Suite 200
Bethesda, MD 20814
301-897-9770
Fax: 301-530-2471
E-mail: tws@wildlife.org
http://www.wildlife.org

Annual conference of wildlife professionals, organized by the Wildlife Society.

September
50 booths with 1400 attendees
Michael Hutchins, Executive Director/CEO
Darryl Walter, Dir Membership/Mktg/Conf

1613 **Wisconsin Association for Environmental Education Annual Conference**
8 Nelson Hall
University of Wisconsin
Stevens Point, WI 54481
715-346-2796
Fax: 715-346-3835
E-mail: waee@uwsp.edu
http://www.uwsp.edu/waee

WAEE is a statewide non-profit organization composed of people interested in learning about and helping others learn about environmental issues. Our goal is to promote responsible environmental action through education in the classroomand in the community.

Fall
Cassie Bauer, Student Representative

1614 Wisconsin Land and Water Conservation Association Annual Conference

702 East Johnson Street
Madison, WI 53703
608-441-2677
Fax: 608-441-2676
E-mail: julian@wlwca.org
http://www.wlwca.org

Mission: To assist county Land Conservation Committees and Departments with the protection, enhancement and sustainable use of Wisconsin's natural resources and to represent them through education and governmental interaction.

December
Julian Zelazny, Executive Director

1615 Wisconsin Woodland Owners Association Annual Conference

PO Box 285
Stevens Point, WI 54481
715-346-4798
E-mail: nbozek@uwsp.edu
http://www.wisconsinwoodlands.org

The Wisconsin Woodland Owners Association, a nonprofit educational organization, was established in 1979 to advance the interests of woodland owners and the cause of forestry; develop public appreciation for the value of Wisconsin'swoodlands and their importance in the economy and overall welfare of the state; foster and encourage wise use and management of Wisconsin's woodlands for timber production, wildlife habitat and recreation; and to educate those interested in managingthe woodlands.

October
William J. Horvath, Director

1616 World Energy Engineering Congress

Association of Energy Engineers
4025 Pleasantdale Road
Suite 420
Atlanta, GA 30340
770-447-5083
Fax: 770-446-3969
E-mail: info@aeecenter.org
http://www.aeecenter.org

Equipment and services.
Ruth Bennett, Information Services Dir.

Consultants

Environmental

1617 **3D/International**
1900 West Loop South
Suite 400
Houston, TX 77027
713-871-7000
Fax: 713-871-7171
E-mail: contact@3di.com
http://www.3di.com

Enrvironmental compliance and consulting services

John Murph, PE, President/CEO
Gary Boyd, AIA, Executive VP

1618 **AAA Lead Consultants and Inspections**
1307 West 6th Street
Suite 134
Corona, CA 92882
951-582-9071
Fax: 951-582-9073
E-mail: aaalead@sbcglobal.net
http://www.aaalead.net/index.html/

Offers quality consulting, inspections, monitoring and project design for lead based paint.

Michael Cohn, CEO

1619 **AB2MT Consultants**
9400 South Dadeland Boulevard
Suite 370
Miami, FL 33156
305-670-1011
Fax: 305-670-1016
E-mail: ab2mt@aol.com

Environmental and engineering consulting.
Paula H Church, President

1620 **ABS Consulting**
16855 Northchase Dr
Houston, TX 77060
281-673-2800
Fax: 281-673-2950
E-mail: info@absconsulting.com
http://www.plg.com

ABS Consulting provides rational engineering, science and technology-based solutions that blend effective management controls, state-of-the-art engineering analyses, practical loss-control measures and innovative risk-transfer options.
David Weinstein, President/CEO

1621 **ACC Environmental Consultants**
7977 Capwell Drive
Suite 100
Oakland, CA 94621
510-638-8400
800-525-8838
Fax: 510-638-8404
E-mail: general@accenv.com
http://www.accenv.com

An employee owned environmental and energy consulting firm. Helps companies and public agencies throughout California identify and manage environmental hazards, comply with their OSHA and EPA requirements.
James Wilson, President/CEO
Tim Fallin, Vice President/CEO

1622 **ACRT Environmental Specialists**
1333 Home Avenue
Akron, OH 44310
330-945-7500
800-622-2562
Fax: 330-945-7200
E-mail: askacrt@acrtinc.com
http://www.acrtinc.com

Appraisal, Research and Training is an international consulting service and training organization in the utility and urban forestry, arboricultural, environmental, natural resource and horticultural services.
Michael B. Weidner, President & CEO
Todd Jones, COO

1623 **ADS LLC**
1300 Meridian Street
Suite 3000
Huntsville, AL 35801
800-633-7246
Fax: 256-430-6633
E-mail: adssales@idexcorp.com
http://www.adsenv.com

ADS LLC develops and provides technology-based hardware and software products and services for the water, wastewater, gas, and hydroelectric industries through three divisions, ADS environmental services, hydra-stop and Accusonictechnologies. ADS pioneered the industry's first flow monitoring hardware and software products over 32 years ago, and today continues to provide the highest quality products and services to its clients.

Karl Boone, President
Joseph Goustin, Cheif Financial Officer

1624 **AECOS**
45-939 Kamehameha Highway
Suite 104
Kaneohe, HI 96744
808-234-7770
Fax: 808-234-7775
E-mail: aecos@aecos.com
http://www.aecos.com

Environmental counseling firm providing the services of scientists and facilities in the environmental sciences to clients throughout the Pacific area. Specializes in aquatic (both fresh water and marine) biology and water quality,with practiced expertise in analytical chemistry, oceanography, water pollution, and marine and fresh water ecology.
Eric B. Guinther, President
Susan Burr, Environmental Scientist

1625 **AF Meyer and Associates**
9060 Meadowood Street
Baton Rouge, LA 70815
225-925-0630
Fax: 225-928-7848
E-mail: afmal@webtv.net
http://www.erols.com/afma

Environmental consulting firm.
AF Meyer, President

1626 **AKT Peerless Environmental Services**
22725 Orchard Lake Road
Farmington, MI 48336
248-615-1333
Fax: 248-615-1334
http://old.aktpeerless.com

Providing environmental services to facilitate real estate transfer, development, and redevelopment. Services include phase I ESA, subsurface investigation, remediation, Brownfield's redevelopment, Brownfield's financial incentives.
Tony R. Anthony, Principal

1627 **AM Kinney**
2900 Vernon Place
Cincinnati, OH 45219
513-421-2265
800-AMK-3682
Fax: 513-281-1123
E-mail: nielseng@amkinney.com
http://www.amkinney.com

Provides creative and cost effective solutions in the planning, design and delivery of clients' projects.
George Finch, President

1628 **ANA-Lab Corporation**
11105 Shady Trail
#123
Dallas, TX 75229
972-837-9412
Fax: 972-837-9412
E-mail: corp@ana-lab.com
http://www.ana-lab.com

Environmental laboratory. Offers ICP-MS which allows Ana-Lab to offer improved turn around time, reduce costs, and achieve better quantitation of regulated parameters. Tests are performed by methods specified by the EPA. Specializes inenvironmental chemistry.

C H Whiteside, President
Bill Peery, Jr., Executive Vice President

1629 **APEC-AM Environmental Consultants**
2525 Northwest Expressway
Suite 301D
Oklahoma City, OK 73112
405-840-9327
Fax: 405-840-9328
E-mail: apecapec@msn.com

Environmental assessment
Charlie Bowlin, Principal
Saleem Nizami, Principal

1630 **ARCADIS**
630 Plaza Drive
Suite 200
Highlands Ranch, CO 80129
720-344-3500
866-AUS-7373
Fax: 720-344-3535
E-mail: AUSInternet@arcadis-us.com
http://www.arcadis-us.com
A leading, global, knowledge-driven service provider. Active in the fields of infrastructure, environment and buildings. Feasibility studies, design, engineering, project management, implementation and facility management, plusrelated legal and financial services.
Gary Coates, CEO
Pete Dyke, CFO

1631 **ATC Associates**
600 W. Cummings Park
Suite 5450
Woburn, MA 01801
781-932-9400
Fax: 781-952-6211
http://www.atcassociates.com
Environmental consulting firm with 1,600 experts in 65 offices throughout the United States, including engineers, scientists, technicians, and regulatory specialists.
Pam O'Deen, Business Development
Bobby Toups, President

1632 **ATC Associates: Omaha**
11117 Mockingbird Dr
Omaha, NE 68137
402-697-9747
800-873-5532
Fax: 402-697-9170
http://www.atcassociates.com
Environmental and worker exposure consulting firm for EPA and OSHA compliance.
Bobby Toups, President

1633 **ATS-Chester Engineers**
260 Airside Drive
Moon Township, PA 15108
412-809-6600
Fax: 412-809-6611
http://www.atsengineers.com
Provides services in waste water treatment and air pollution control.
Robert Agbede, President

1634 **Aarcher**
910 Commerce Road
Annapolis, MD 21401
410-897-9100
Fax: 410-897-9104
E-mail: cschwartz@aarcherinc.com
http://www.aarcherinc.com
Aarcher is a small business providing environmental management, assessment and planning services nationwide from its headquarters and regional offices. Aarcher provides environmental compliance audits; NEPA analysis and documentation;natural and cultural resource management planning; site assessment and investigation; plans and permits; and environmental liability assessment and control. Our consulting services are guided by a comprehensive understanding of current environmentalregulations.
Craig J Schwartz, President

1635 **Abacus Environmental**
3440 Fordham Road
Dallas, TX 75216
214-363-0099
Fax: 214-363-3919
E-mail: donweek@jx.netcom.com
http://www.abacusae.com
Full service environmental and occupational safety and health consulting firm. Services include project management, indoor air quality and industrial hygiene, asbestos and lead project management, expert witness testimony and allaspects of workplace safety. Goals are to help reduce client's operating costs, minimize liability for environmental and occupational safety reguations, guidelines, and requirements.
Donald M Weekes Jr, President

1636 **Abco Engineering Corporation**
6901 South Yosemite Street
Suite 205
Centennial, CO 80112
303-220-8220
Fax: 303-796-0810
E-mail: info@abco-corp.com
http://www.abco-corp.com
Provides a full spectrum of engineering and environmental services pertaining to both new construction and existing buildings, including Property Condition Assessment Reports, Phase I Environmental Assessments, Quality Control Reportsand other technical support services related to buildings and building systems including feasibility reports, construction observation and cost eliminating.
Joe Johnson, Director
Michael R Dannecker, Director

1637 **Abonmarche Environmental**
95 West Main Street
PO Box 1088
Benton Harbor, MI 49022
269-927-2295
Fax: 269-927-1017
E-mail: aci@abonmarche.com
http://www.abonmarche.com
Full-service architectural, engineering, land surveying and planning firm.

1638 **AccuTech Environmental Services**
43 West Front Street
Rear Suite
Keyport, NJ 07735
732-739-6444
800-644-ISRA
Fax: 732-739-0451
E-mail: info@accutechenvironmental.com
http://www.accutechenvironmental.com
Aims to meet the environmental consulting needs generated by New Jersey's Environmental Cleanup Responsibility Act by preparing and managing complete environmental sampling and cleanup programs.
Harry Moscatello, President
Nicholas Huszar, Senior Project Manager

1639 **Accutest Laboratories**
2235 US Highway 130
Dayton, NJ 08810
732-329-0200
Fax: 732-329-3499
E-mail: infonj@accutest.com
http://www.accutest.com
Privately held, independent testing laboratory delivering legally defensible data, providing a full range of environmental analytical services to industrial, engineering/consulting and government clients throughout the United States.Operating from coordinated laboratories in New Jersey, Massachusetts, Florida and Texas, resources include a staff of over 200, five million dollars worth of laboratory instrumentation and equipment, and more than 80,000 square feet of laboratoryspace.

1640 **Acheron Engineering Services**
147 Main Street
Newport, ME 04953
207-368-5700
Fax: 207-368-5120
E-mail: WBall@AcheronEngineering.com
http://www.acheronengineering.com
Provides solutions to the most challenging engineering, environmental and geologic issues.
William B Ball, President
Kirk Ball, Engineering Field Technician

1641 **Activated Carbon Services**
409 Meade Drive
Coraopolis, PA 15108
724-457 6576
800-367-2587
Fax: 724-457-1214
E-mail: Henry@pacslabs.com
http://www.pacslabs.com
Training courses and conferences. Provides short courses in spectrocopy, chomatography, quality, safety, environmental, and management. Provides professional manuals and software products. Provides laboratory testing and consultingservices. Company also goes by the following names: Activated Carbon Services, PACS Testing and Consulting, PACS Courses and Conferences. PACS provides: Testing, Training, R & D Conferences, and software for activated carbon users.
Henry G Nowicki PhD/MBA, President
Barbara Sherman, Manager of Operations

1642 **Acumen Industrial Hygiene**
1032 Irving Street
#922
San Francisco, CA 94122
415-242-6060
Fax: 415-242-6006
E-mail: info@acumen-ih.com
http://www.acumen-ih.com
Industrial hygiene consultation.
Paul M. Spillane, Principal

1643 **Advanced Chemistry Labs**
3039 Amwiler Road
Suite 100
Atlanta, GA 30360
770-409-1444
Fax: 770-409-1844
E-mail: acl@acl-labs.net
http://www.advancedchemistrylabs.com

Environmental teststing laboratory.

John Andros, Technical Director

1644 **Advanced Resources International**
4501 Fairfax Drive
Suite 910
Arlington, VA 22203
703-528-8420
Fax: 703-528-0439
E-mail: ari-info@adv-res.com
http://www.adv-res.com

Independent consulting firm focused on providing technical services to the international energy industry.

Vello A Kuuskraa, President
Jonathan R. Kelafant, Senior Vice President

1645 **Advanced Waste Management Systems**
6430 Hixson Pike
PO Box 100
Hixson, TN 37343
423-843-2206
Fax: 423-843-2310
E-mail: info@awm.net
http://www.awm.net/

Provides a wide range of environmental and engineering services to domestic and international clients, including governments, corporations, and provate citizens.

Richard Ellis PhD, CEO
James Mullican, PE, President

1646 **Aerosol Monitoring and Analysis**
1331 A Ashton Road
PO Box 646
Hanover, MD 21076
410-684-3327
E-mail: amalab@aol.com
http://www.amaconsulting.com

Aerosol Monitoring & Analysis, provides Industrial Hygiene, Environmental and Health & Safety to government agencies, institutions, building owners, property managers, architects and engineers.

1647 **Aguirre Engineers**
13276 E Fremont Place
PO Box 3814
Englewood, CO 80112
303-799-8378
Fax: 303-799-8392
E-mail: infoteam@aquirre1.com

Aguirre Engineers is an environmental engineering firm based in Englewwod, CO. Over the past 20 years we have augmented our service offering, from a commercial geotechnical leader, into providing full-scale government contractingservices for radioactive and hazardous waste remediation. The continued growth or our company throughout the years is a solid indicator of high-quality performance and client satisfaction.

1648 **Air Consulting and EngineeringSolutions**
5615 Northwest Central Dr
Suite C109
Houston, TX 77092
713-690-2237
E-mail: info@aces-llc.com
http://aces-llc.com

Air Consulting and Engineers, provides air pollution testing services utilizing United States Environmental Protection Agency. The company was founded in April 1984 to provide prefessional source emission testing and engineering, andair permitting to industries located in Florida and throughout the world.

R. M. Pat Patrick, President
Jim Corbat, Vice President

1649 **Air Sciences**
1301 Washington Avenue
Suite 200
Golden, CO 80401
303-988-2960
Fax: 303-988-2968
E-mail: air@airsci.com
http://www.airsci.com

Air Sciences was founded in the Denver-metro area in 1980 with the purpose of providing superior air pollution consulting services. Air Sciences attained this goal and presently enjoys a unique reputation as a firm that provides bothindustry and government a high quality service in air quality consulting. Our future is focused on emerging disciplines in the air quality arena driven by new air quality standards and regional haze regulations. Air Sciences is an employee ownedfirm.

Ronald Babbit, Electronics Engineer

1650 **Aires Consulting Group**
1550 Hubbard Avenue
Batavia, IL 60510
630-879-3006
800-247-3799
Fax: 630-879-3014
E-mail: info@airesconsulting.com
http://www.airesconsulting.com

National full-service industrial hygiene, environmental and occupational health consulting firm. Assists clients in the control of liability through the application of risk management principals.

Rich Rapacki, VP
Kevin Bannon, Marketing Director

1651 **Airtek Environmental Corporation**
39-37, 29th Street
Long Island City
New York, NY 11101
718-937-3720
Fax: 718-937-3721
E-mail: info@airtekenv.com
http://www.airtekenv.com

Environmental investigation and mangement professionals specializing in multi-jurisdictional regulatory climates.

Mike S Zouak, President

1652 **Alan Plummer Associates, Inc.**
1320 South University Drive
Suite 300
Fort Worth, TX 76107
817-806-1700
Fax: 817-870-2536
E-mail: aplummer@apaienv.com
http://www.apaienv.com

Civil and environmental engineering consulting.

Alan R. Tucker, President
Julie Lippe, Marketing Coordinator

1653 **All 4 Inc**
2393 Kimberton Road
PO Box 299
Kimberton, PA 19442
610-933-5246
Fax: 610-933-5127
E-mail: jegan@all4inc.com
http://www.all4inc.biz

An environmental consulting company specializing in air quality services, primarily assisting clients with complex air permitting, modeling, continuous monitoring, and regulation compliance.

John Egan, Principal Consultant
Dan Holland, Principal Consultant

1654 **Allee, King, Rosen and Fleming**
440 Park Avenue South
7th Floor
New York, NY 10016
212-696-0670
800-899-2573
Fax: 212-779-9721
E-mail: nycinfo@akrf.com
http://www.akrf.com

Environmental consulting firm.

Debra C Allee, AICP, Founder
Edward A Applebome, ITE, President/CEO

1655 **Allied Engineers**
PO Box 2760
San Ramon, CA 94583
925-867-4646
Fax: 925-867-4474
E-mail: info@alliedengineersinc.com
http://www.alliedengineersinc.com

Consulting services in wastewater and industrial waste, including emissions testing.

Robert Dawyat, President

1656 **Allstate Power Vac**
928 East Hazelwood Avenue
Rahway, NJ 07065
732-815-0220
800-876-9699
Fax: 732-815-9892
http://www.aspvac.com

Industrial and environmental waste management.

1657 **Allwest Environmental**
530 Howard Street
Suite 300
San Francisco, CA 94105
415-391-2510
Fax: 714-541-5303
E-mail: info@allwest1.com
http://www.allwest1.com

Practical, business-oriented consulting firm specializing in Environmental and Engineering Due Diligence offering expertise to the real estate industry. Helps clients to understand and manage

potential environmental and buildingliabilites, and to advocate their interests through the discovery and mitigation process.
Marc Cunningham, President
Chris Marinescu, Vice President

1658 Alpha-Omega Environmental Services
933 Northwest 31 Avenue
Pompano Beach, FL 33069
954-969-5906
866-969-6653
Fax: 954-969-5232
E-mail: dave@aomegagroup.com
http://www.aomegagroup.com

Environmental engineering consulting

1659 Alternative Resources
1732 Main Street
Concord, MA 01742
978-371-2054
Fax: 978-371-7269
E-mail: info@alt-res.com
http://www.alt-res.com

Alternative Resources is an independent consulting firm providing management, engineering, environmental, economic and financial advisory in the fields of water and wastewater treatment, solid waste management, residuals management,environmental compliance, and energy production.
Gretchen Karlson, Personnel

1660 Ambient Engineering
PO Box 556
Concord, MA 01742
978-369-8188
888-262-6232
Fax: 978-369-8380
E-mail: info@ambient-engineering.com
http://ambient-engineering.com

An environmental engineering and consulting firm incorporated in 1994. We provide environmental, site civil engineering and regulatory compliance services with a focus on the six New England states.

T J Stevenson, PhD, President
Kenneth Pyzocha, PE, Vice President

1661 American Archaeology Group LLC
208 West Second Street
Lampasas, TX 76550
512-556-4100
Fax: 512-556-3373
E-mail: info@american-archaeology.com
http://www.american-archaeology.com

Professional archeological firm that hand;es state and federal permitting on projects.

Michael R. Bradle, President

1662 American Engineering Testing
550 Cleveland Avenue North
St Paul, MN 55114
651-659-9001
800-972-6364
Fax: 651-659-1379
E-mail: rkaiser@amengtest.com
http://www.amengtest.com

America's people, technology, innovation and quality commited to fulfilling client tequirements.
Robert A Kaiser, VP

1663 American Services Associates
18154 41st Place SE
Issaquah, WA 98027
425-641-5130
Fax: 425-641-5138
E-mail: airsampler@aol.com
http://www.asaearth.com

Consultants in emission testing, permitting, emission control system design, training and continuous emission moniters (CEMs). Producer of video training programs on E{A emission sampling methods in CD and VHS formats. Offices are inIssaquah, Washington.
Wes Snowden, President
John Vareski, Vice President

1664 Andco Environmental Processes
415 Commerce Drive
Amherst, NY 14228
716-691-2100
Fax: 716-691-2880
E-mail: Andco@Localnet.com

Manufacturers of waste disposal treatment systems.
Jack I Reich, Sales Manager

1665 Andersen 2000 Inc/Crown Andersen
1015 Tyrone Road
Suite 410
Tyrone, GA 30290
770-486-2000
800-241-5424
Fax: 770-487-5066
E-mail: tom.vanremmen@and2k.com
http://www.crownandersen.com

Supplying World Industry with Incineration and Air Pollution Control Systems

1666 Anderson Consulting Group
PO Box 407
Downingtown, PA 19335
610-918-7461
Fax: 610-918-9469
E-mail: info@andersonconsultinggroup.com
http://www.andersonconsultinggroup.com

Anderson Consulting Group has helped companies and publics agencies manage their project development risk, drive down construction cost, and improve schedules. Anderson Consulting Group's environmental and geotechnical services areuniquely designed to address client objectives. Our engineering solutions have earned engineering leadership and innovation awards.

1667 Apollo Energy Systems
4100 North Powerline Road
Building D3
Pompano Beach, FL 33073
954-969-7755
Fax: 954-969-7788
http://www.electricauto.com
Products and services includes lead cobalt batteries, alkaline fuel cells, power plants and EV programs.
Robert Aronsson, Director/CEO
Sonny Spoden, Director/CFO

1668 Applied Ecological Services, Inc.
17921 Smith Road
PO Box 256
Brodhead, WI 53520
608-897-8641
Fax: 608-897-8486
E-mail: Info@AppliedEco.com
http://www.appliedeco.com

AES is a broad-based ecological consulting, contracting and restoration firm providing services to foundations, government units, corporations, and commercial/residential developers nationwide. Our staff consultants consisting of amultidisciplinary team of geologists, hydrologists, ecologists, botanists, wildlife biologists, wetland scientists, landscape architects, and prairie and ecosystem restoration specialists manage over 100 projects a year.

Steven I Apfelbaum, Chairman
David W Aslesen, BS, Environment Specialist

1669 Applied Geoscience and Engineering
150-C Love Road
Reading, PA 19607
610-777-5027
Fax: 610-777-4276
E-mail: office@appliedgeoscience.com
http://www.appliedgeoscience.com

Environmental engineering, site assessments, and testing services through subcontractors.
M. Ayub Iqbal, Ph.D, P.E., President

1670 Applied Marine Ecology
658 NE 70th St.
Miami, FL 33145
305-757-0018
Fax: 305-759-3999
Marine ecology research firm.
Anitra Thorhaug, President
Andrew Oerke, CEO

1671 Applied Science Associates
55 Village Square Drive
South Kingston, RI 02879
401-789-6224
Fax: 401-789-1932
E-mail: asa@asascience.com
http://www.asascience.com

A global science and technology solutions company. Through consulting, environmental modeling, and application development, ASA helps a diverse range of clients in government, industry, and academia investigate their issues of concernand obtain functional answers.

Eoin Howlett, CEO
J Craig Swanson, Senior Principal

1672 **Aqua Sierra**
9094 US Highway 285
Morrison, CO 80465
303-697-5486
800-524-FISH
Fax: 303-697-5069
E-mail: info@aqua-sierra.com
http://www.aqua-sierra.com

Aqua Sierra is a complete company servicing fisheries, aquaculture, water quality, wastewater, and database management interest. Aqua Sierra can assure an efficient, effective cost-conscious approach to managing aquatic resources bycombining a broad base of experience in all aspects of fisheries, aquatic ecology, and water quality management.

Bill Logan, President

1673 **Aqua Survey**
469 Point Breeze Road
Flemington, NJ 08822
908-788-8700
Fax: 908-788-9165
E-mail: Mail@AquaSurvey.com
http://www.aquasurvey.com

Aqua Survey is a full service ecotoxicology company founded in 1975. Aqua Survey provides laboratory testing, field sampling and consulting services to a wide variety of clients throughout the world including many of the largest UScorporations, internationally reconized environmental consulting firms, and the public sector.

Kenneth R Hayes, President

1674 **Aqualogic**
30 Devine Street
North Haven, CT 06473
203-248-8959
800-989-8959
Fax: 203-288-4308
E-mail: rheller@aqualogic.com
http://www.aqualogic.com

Industrial Wastewater Treatment Systems and Chemical Recovery Systems.

Dick Heller, Sales Engineer

1675 **Arcadis**
630 Plaza Drive
Suite 200
Highlands Ranch, CO 80129
720-344-3500
800-225-8419
Fax: 720-344-3535
E-mail: AUSInternet@arcadis-us.com
http://www.arcadis-us.com

Complete environmental services and remediation.

Alan Hurley, Area Manager
Gary Coates, CEO

1676 **Architectural Energy Corporation**
2540 Frontier Avenue
Suite 100
Boulder, CO 80301
303-444-4149
800-450-4454
Fax: 303-444-4304
E-mail: info@archenergy.com
http://www.archenergy.com

Michael J Holtz, FAIA, President

1677 **Arctech**
14100 Park Meadow Drive
Suite 210
Chantilly, VA 20151
703-222-0280
Fax: 703-222-0299
E-mail: info@arctech.com
http://www.arctech.com

Arctech a diverse American Corporation is providing cost-effective solutions for energy, environmental, and agriculture market sectors. Arctech group through 25 years of experience in energy, energetics, environment and agriculture,has created holistic solutions in these interrelated market sectors. The enterpreneurial scientist and engineers at Arctech have pioneered the use of our vast resources of coal to make coal-derived humic acid products.

Daman S Walia, President/CEO
Madhu Walia, Administration Director

1678 **Ardea Consulting**
10 1st Street
Woodland, CA 95695
530-669-1645
Fax: 530-669-1674
E-mail: birdtox1@ardeacon.com
http://www.ardeacon.com

Ardea Consulting provides avian and wildlife toxicology guidance to engineering and environmental firms, government agencies, business and non-governmental organizations.

Joseph P Sullivan PhD, Sr. Consultant

1679 **Argus/King Environmental Limited**
7271 Wurzbach
Suite 202
San Antonio, TX 78240
210-493-2560
800-698-6018
Fax: 210-342-9027

Industrial hygiene and indoor air quality management. Mold and bacteria sampling, asbestos and lead testing and forensic.

Robert W Miller, CIH
Henry King, Consultant

1680 **Arro Consulting**
108 W. Airport Road
Lititz, PA 17543
717-569-7021
800-229-6009
Fax: 717-560-0577
E-mail: info@thearrogroup.com
http://www.thearrogroup.com

Environmental engineering.

GM Brown, President
Darrell L. Becker, P.E., Vice President

1681 **Arro Laboratory**
PO Box 686
Caton Farm Road
Joliet, IL 60434
815-727-5436
Fax: 815-740-3234
E-mail: info@arrolab.com
http://www.arrolab.com

Testing and analysis laboratory specializing in resource conservation and recovery act sampling. Research results published in confidential reports to clients.

1682 **Artemel and Associates**
218 North Lee Street
Suite 316
Alexandria, VA 22314
703-683-3838
Fax: 703-836-1370
E-mail: aiusa@artemel.com
http://www.artemel.com

Artemel & Associates is the technical arm of the Artemel Group of companies, with planning, engineering and analytical capabilities. The firm's ares of professinal expertise directly complement Artemel International's areas ofspecialization. Artemel & Associates has been serving clients since 1984, and has benn credited with a variety of successful technical accomplishments both in the United States and around the globe.

Engin Artemel, President

1683 **Ascension Technology**
107 Catamount Drive
Milton, VT 05468
802-893-6657
800-321-6596
Fax: 802-893-6659
E-mail: ascension@ascension-tech.com
http://www.ascension-tech.com

Manufactures motion tracking equipment and provides a full year's warranty, free telephonic support, and on-site support.

Edward C Kern Jr, President

1684 **Associates in Rural Development**
159 Bank Street
Suite 300
Burlington, VT 05401
802-658-3890
Fax: 802-658-4247
E-mail: ard@ardinc.com
http://www.ardinc.com

ARD was founded in 1977 as a Vermont corporation. Vermont's reputation for leadership in environmental affairs and its heritage of local participatory government embody ARD's ideals. Services include: watershed management,resource/sector assessments, EIA, urban environmental magagement, policy and action planning, natural resource assessment and evaluation, NR-based enterprise development, biodiversity conservation and finance, integrated water resource planning andmanagement.

George Burrill, President
Jim Talbot, Sr. VP

1685 Astbury Environmental Engineering
5757 West 74th Street 317-472-0999
Indianapolis, IN 46278 Fax: 317-472-0993
E-mail: info@aeeindy.com
http://www.astburyenviro.com

Astbury Environmental Engineering is a privately owned Indianapolis company that provides a full range of environmental services that include invironemntal management, site investigation and corrective action, health and safety, aircompliance, solid and hazardous waste management, and wastewater.
Steve Wilcox, President/CEO
Fred Nichols, VP, Business Development

1686 Astorino Branch Environmental
227 For Pitt Boulevard 412-765-1700
Pittsburg, PA 15222 800-518-0464
Fax: 412-765-1711
E-mail: marketing@ldastorino.com

Astorino Companies is an architectural, engineering and environmental consulting firm headquartered in downtown Pittsburg, PA.
Louis Astorino, President & CEO

1687 Athena Environmental Sciences
1450 S Rolling Road 410-455-6319
Baltimore, MD 21227 888-892-8408
Fax: 410-455-1155
E-mail: athenaes@athenaenvironmental.com
http://www.athenaes.com

Designs and develops novel products that represent environmentally responsible and economically sound solutions to environmental problems. Contract services are provided to clients for product development. Products developed includethe company's own Spill Pill (TM), a proprietary cleaning agent for petroleum contamination on concrete and other building surfaces, Bilge Tech, Inc.'s Bilge Pill (TM), a cleaning agent for removing oil and dirt buildup in boat bilges, and expertisein biotechnology.
Sheldon Broedel PhD, CEO

1688 Atkins Environmental HELP
PO Box 222320 661-260-2260
Santa Clarita, CA 91322 800-750-0622
Fax: 661-253-3555
E-mail: info@atkinsenvironmental.com
http://www.atkinsenvironmental.com

Environmental, health and safety compliance. Support services.
BJ Atkins, President

1689 Atlantic Testing Laboratories
6431 US Highway 11 315-386-4578
Canton, NY 13617 Fax: 315-386-1012
E-mail: info@AtlanticTesting.com
http://www.atlantictesting.com

ATL is a full-service engineering support firm offering environmental services, subsurface investigations, geoprobe services, water-based investigations, geotechnical engineering, construction materials testing and engineering, specialinspection services, pavement engineering, nondestructive testing, and surveying from our ten offices. The firm currently has extensive capabilities in the areas of underground and aboveground storage tank testing and management and other relatedareas.

Marijean B. Remington, Chief Executive Officer
James J. Kuhn, PE, President

1690 Atlas Environmental Engineering
3185 Airway Avenue 714-890-7129
Suite D-1 Fax: 714-890-7149
Costa Mesa, CA 92626 E-mail: info@aeei.com
http://www.aeei.com

Atlas Environmental Engineering provides very cost effective site assessments, investigations, corrective and remedial action plans and risk-based corrective action for low risk sites, along with groundwater monitoring, sampling, freeproduct removal activities and reporting. We also provide complete groundwater and soil remediation and cleanup activities, including all necessary equipment. Our goal is to provide clients with site closure in a minimal time period.
Karl H Kerner, VP

1691 Ayres Associates
3433 Oakwood Hills Parkway 715-834-3161
PO Box 1590 800-666-3103
Eau Claire, WI 54701 Fax: 715-831-7500
E-mail: Contact@AyresAssociates.com
http://www.ayresassociates.com

Ayres Associates is a multi-specialty architectural/engineering consulting firm that has assisted public and private clients since 1959. Our staff of approximately 330 people provides services in transportation, civil, structural,water resources, levee and river engineering; planning; architecture; environmental science; energy corridors; surveying; geospatial services; and geographic information systems (GIS).

Thomas Pulse, President
Sue Leith, PG, Manager, Marketing

1692 BBS Corporation
1103 Schrock Road 614-888-3100
Suite 400 Fax: 614-888-0043
Columbus, OH 43229 E-mail: email@bbsengineers.com
http://www.bbsengineers.com

A full service multi-disciplinary engineering firm specializing in the planning, design and construction administration of water and wastewater treatment, distribution and collection systems. Other services include data conversion anddatabase design for geographical information systems projects.
Edward Vance, Chairman

1693 BCI Engineers and Scientists
2000 East Edgewood Drive, Suite 215 863-667-2345
Lakeland, FL 33803 Fax: 877-550-4224
E-mail: info@bcieng.com
http://www.bcieng.com

BCI was founded in the early 1970s by former MIT professor, Dr. L.G. Bromwell. At that time, the majority of our clients were in the phosphate and Geotechnical industry. Since its beginning, BCI has grown into a multidisciplinary firmwith over 100 employees. We are proud to offer our valued clients a diverse team of professionals with a unique and complimentary blend of expertise. Our unusual blend of experience allows us to develop solutions to complex engineering andenvironmental challenges.
Richard M Powers, President

1694 BE and K/Terranext
155 South Madison Street 303-399-6148
Suite 311 Fax: 303-399-6146
Denver, CO 80209 E-mail: kmartin@terranext.net
http://www.terranext.net

We have been nationally recognized for excellence in environmental services since 1985. The goal of management is to develop and execute appropriate solutions to complex issues and act as strong advocates for our clients.
Kim Martin, President

1695 BHE Environmental
11733 Chesterdale Road 513-326-1500
Cincinnati, OH 45246 Fax: 513-326-1550
E-mail: jbruck@bheenvironmental.com
http://www.bheenv.com

BHE's mission is to provide a full range of environmental consulting and remediation services that set the standard for quality and responsibility. We strive to serve the total needs of clients and to create a challenging andsupportive work environment for our employees.
John M. Bruck, PE, President

1696 BRC Acoustics and Technology Consulting
1932 First Avenue 206-270-8910
Suite 303 800-843-4524
Seattle, WA 98101 Fax: 206-270-8690
E-mail: brc@brcacoustics.com
http://www.brcacoustics.com

A Seattle-based acoustical and technology consulting firm providing diverse services to public and private clients throughout the United States. Services include architectural and mechanical acoustics, vibration measurement andanalysis, multimedia system design, noise monitoring, acoustical modeling, and noise contour mapping for environmental noise projects.
Daniel C Bruck PhD, President
Roger Andrews, General Manager

1697 **Bac-Ground**
3216 Georgetown 713-664-8452
Houston, TX 77005 Fax: 713-664-2629
E-mail: ebaca@bac-ground.com
http://www.bac-ground.com

Environmental consultant
Ernesto Baca

1698 **Badger Laboratories and Engineering Company**
501 West Bell Street 920-729-1100
Neenah, WI 54986 800-776-7196
Fax: 920-729-4945
E-mail: information@badgerlabs.com
http://www.badgerlabs.com

Badger Laboratories and Engineering provides customers with analytical, engineering and technical services focusing on the environmental field.
Richard Larson, President
Jeff Wagner, Laboratory Services

1699 **Baltec Associates**
69 Fields Lane 845-279-7448
Brewster, NY 10509 Fax: 845-279-7467
E-mail: info@baltecusa.com
http://www.baltecusa.com

Baltec Associates is an international environmental consulting firm specializing in groundwater and soil remediation. We offers professional expertise and technical services for environmental management and planning, assessment,engineering, and remediation projects around the world.

1700 **Barco Enterprises**
11200 Pulaski Highway 800-832-7538
White Marsh, MD 21162 Fax: 410-335-0790
E-mail: barco.enterprises@verizon.net
http://www.barcoenterprises.com

Hazardous materials handling

1701 **Barer Engineering**
199 Main Street 518-236-7070
Suite 600 800-878-2806
Burlington, VT 05401 Fax: 518-236-5796
E-mail: info@barer.com
http://www.barer.com

Environmental engineering; pollution control

1702 **Baron Consulting Company**
181 Research Dr 203-874-5678
PO Box 3337 Fax: 203-874-7863
Milford, CT 06460 E-mail: analyze@baronconsulting.com
http://www.baronconsulting.com

Chemical, environmental and biological testing firm. Analytical also.
Harry Agahigian, Technical Director
Barbara Obert, Lab Manager

1703 **Barr Engineering Company**
3005 Boardwalk Street 734-922-4400
Suite 100 800-632-2277
Ann Arbor, MI 48108 Fax: 734-922-4401
E-mail: askbarr@barr.com
http://www.barr.com

Barr provides engineering, environmental, and information technology services to clients across the nation and around the world. We were incorporated as an employee-owned firm in 1966 and trace our orgins back to the early 1900s.Today, our more than 300 engineers, scientists, and technical support staff in Minnesota, Michigan, and Missouri work with clients in numerous industries, as well as at all levels of government.
Steve Kapeller, Senior Environmental Enginee
David Hibbs, Senior Civil Engineer

1704 **Batta Environmental Associates**
6 Garfield Way 302-737-3376
Newark, DE 19713 800-543-4807
Fax: 302-737-5764
E-mail: bcbatta@battaenv.com
http://www.battaenv.com

BATTA was establihed in 1982 and is a Deleware Corporation registered to conduct work in the states of the Mid-Atlantic Region. BATTA has the in-house expertise in the scientific disciplines of geology, hydrogeology, civil andenvironmental engineering, chemistry, toxicology, health and safety, project design and construction management to adequately perform work without the use of outside consultants.
Naresh C Batta, President/CEO
Neeraj K Batta, Vice President

1705 **Baxter and Woodman**
8678 Ridgefield Road 815-459-1260
Crystal Lake, IL 60012 Fax: 815-455-0450
E-mail: info@baxterwoodman.com
http://www.baxterwoodman.com

Municipal waste, water, transportation, control systems, and mapping services. Our mission statement is: we will be the leader in consulting engineering based on our reputation for trust, integrity, and client service.
Darrel R Gavle, PE, DEE, President/CEO
Steve A Larson, PE, DEE, VP

1706 **Baystate Environmental Consultants, Inc**
296 North Main Street 413-525-3822
East Longmeadow, MA 01028 Fax: 413-525-8348
E-mail: ccarranza@b-e-c.com
http://www.b-e-c.com

BEC offers a wide range of civil engineering, water resources and environmental expertise. BEC was incorporated in 1972 and specializes in lake and pond restoration services, environmental assessment under MEPA/NEPA and wetlandscience. The staff at BEC is exceptionally diverse, having had formal training and long-term experience in multi-disiplinary projects involving site development options, conceptual layout planning, enivronmental permitting and civil engineeringservices.
Carlos Carranza, President

1707 **Beak Consultants**
4600 Northgate Boulevard 916-565-7929
Suite 215 Fax: 916-565-7900
Sacramento, CA 95834
Beak provides a fully integrated approach to environmental planning, assessment and problem solving. Our professional and technical specialists include ecologists, environmental auditors, risk assessors, geochemists, ecotoxicologists,contaminant hydrogeologists, modellers and environmental engineers. We integrate these specialties to provide our clients with a broad range of services.
Rick Swift
Amy Stuhr

1708 **Beals and Thomas**
144 Turnpike Road 508-366-0560
Southborough, MA 01772 Fax: 508-366-4391
E-mail: info@btiweb.com
http://www.btiweb.com

Beals and Thomas is a multidisciplinary consulting firm providing services to support the development and conservation of land and water resources throughout New England and the northeastern United States. Founded in 1984, BTI islocated in Southborough MA. Our mission is to advocate and assist in the attainment of our clients' project goals. We strive to provide creative and solution-oriented land eplanning and design services that are balanced with an environmental ethic.
George G Preble, President
Daniel M Feeney, Principal

1709 Bear West Company
8 East Broadway
Suite 300
Salt Lake City, UT 84111
801-364-0525
801-694-4279
E-mail: bswaney@logansimpson.com
http://www.bearwest.com

Consultants on envionmental issues
Ralph Becker, President
Buck Swaney, Senior Planner

1710 Beaumont Environmental Systems
108 Lintel Drive
McMurray, PA 15317
724-941-1743
Fax: 561-382-6455
http://www.besmp.com

Beaumont company provides Particulate and Gaseous Air Pollution Control Equipment, Systems and Services for Power Generation, Waste Incineration, Utility, Steel, Mining, Cement, Foundry and Pulp and Paper Industries. They design andfurnish systems that include Fabric Filters, Electrostatic Precipitators, Wet Scubbers, Semi Dry Scrubbers and Evaporative Cooloers along with the other necessary systems components.
Will Goss, President

1711 Becher-Hoppe Associates
330 Fourth Street
Wausau, WI 54403
715-845-8000
800-845-8009
Fax: 715-845-8008
E-mail: mailbox@becherhoppe.com
http://www.becherhoppe.com

Becher-Hoppe Associates is a firm of consulting engineers, architects, scientists, real estate specialists and surveyors. We provide a spectrum of professional services to governmental, industry and the private sector for airport,highway, municipal, facilities maintainance, water/wastewater, solid waste and environmental projects. From our location in central Wisconsin, we provide upper Midwest clients with neighborly promptness and efficiency.
Randy W Van Natta, PE, President
Phil Valitchka, Business Development

1712 Benchmark Environmental Consultants
5307 E. Mockingbird Lane
Suite 650
Dallas, TX 75206
214-363-5996
Fax: 214-363-5994
E-mail: info@benchmarkenviro.com
http://www.benchmarkenviro.com

A progressive environmental consulting firm which specialized in solving environmental problems by using a practical business and technical approach.

Kelly Walker, Founder

1713 Bendix Environmental Research
1950 Addison Street
Suite 202
Berkeley, CA 94704
415-861-8484
Fax: 510-845-8484
http://home.earthlink.net/~bendix/

Specializes in toxicology, hazardous materials management, and preparation of environmental documents, or appropriate parts of environmental documents dealing with hazardous materials. Provides expert witness serrvices and litigationresearch and support for toxic tort cases, including workplace and environmental exposures and chemical cancer causation.

Dr Selina Bendix, President
Gilbert G Bendix, Vice President

1714 Beta Associates
858 Fearrington Post
Pittsboro, NC 27312
919-545-0481
Fax: 919-545-0481
E-mail: BetaBob@BetaAssociates.com
http://www.betaassociates.com/

A professional project management organization which provides complete problem analysis, feasibility study and design services. These include specification and construction management for control and monitoring systems.

1715 Better Management Corporation of Ohio
41738 Esterly Drive
PO Box 130
Columbiana, OH 44408
330-482-9028
800-445-7887
Fax: 330-482-9242
E-mail: bmc@bmcohio.com
http://www.bmcohio.com

A focus of providing transportation and disposal services of baled, compacted and loose municipal solid waste as well as C&D material to both public and private waste transfer station companies located mainly along the East Coast fromMaine to Florida.
Jerry Stoneburner, President/CEO
Paul Wilson, Vice President

1716 Beyaz and Patel
800 South Broadway
Suite 200
Walnut Creek, CA 94596
925-934-0707
888-431-0707
Fax: 925-934-0318
E-mail: info@beyazpatel.com
http://www.beyazpatel.com

Structural engineering firm specializing in the structural design and construction management of public works infrastructure projects.
Yogesh B Patel, President
Subhash Patel, VP

1717 Bhate Associates
1608 13th Avenue South
Suite 300
Birmingham, AL 35205
205-918-4000
800-806-4001
Fax: 205-918-4050
E-mail: kgallant@bhate.com
http://www.bhate.com

Consulting environmental engineers
Kathleen Gallant, CPA, Human Resources Director
Jay D. Carter, Principal

1718 Bioengineering Group
18 Commercial Street
Salem, MA 01970
970-740-0096
Fax: 978-740-0097
E-mail: mail@bioengineering.com
http://www.bioengineering.com

Provides a full range of consulting services in the field of bioengineering for erosion control, water quality, habitat restoration and stormwater management.
Wendy Goldsmith, President/CEO

1719 Bioenvironmental Associates
4117 Sumter Square
Fort Collins, CO 80525
970-227-0771
Fax: 970-481-8386
http://www.toolcity.net/~richreen/Bio.htm

Management plans, environmental permitting and compliance monitoring. We specialize in biological inventories for threated and endangered species.
Rex E Thomas PhD, Principal

1720 Biological Frontiers Institute
PO Box 313
Sonoma, CA 95476
707-996-2863
http://www.zoogenetics.com

Genetics, preservation of endangered species
Fred T Shultz, President

1721 Biological Monitoring
1800 Kraft Drive
Suite 101
Blacksburg, VA 24060
540-953-2821
877-953-2821
Fax: 540-951-1481
E-mail: bmi@biomon.com
http://www.biomon.com/

Environmental consulting group

1722 Biological Research Associates
3910 US Highway 301 N
Suite 180
Tampa, FL 33619
813-664-4500
Fax: 813-664-0440
E-mail: callahan@BiologicalResearch.com
http://www.biolresearch.com/

BRA professionals act as proponents of our clients' interest, helping them through the maze of environmental regulations.
Richard Callahan, CEO
J Steve Godley, President

1723 **Biospec Products**
PO Box 788
Bartlesville, OK 74005
918-336-3363
800-617-3363
Fax: 918-336-6060
E-mail: info@biospec.com
http://www.biospec.com

Laboratory scientific equipment.

Tim Hopkins, President
Jeff Anderson, Manager

1724 **Bison Engineering**
1400 11th Avenue
Helena, MT 59601
406-442-5768
Fax: 406-449-6653
E-mail: hrobbins@bison-eng.com
http://www.bison-eng.com

Bison Engineering, Inc. is a full-service environmental consulting firm with extensive experience in air quality permitting, air emissions testing and ambient air monitoring. Our knowledge of the water quality regulatory environmentis substantial and expanding. We also provide an array of other environmental services through our staff and associates to complement our air and water quality expertise.

Harold W Robbins, President
Jeffrey T Chaffee, Vice President

1725 **Bjaam Environmental**
472 Elm Ridge Avenue
PO Box 523
Canal Futon, OH 44614
330-854-5300
800-666-5331
Fax: 330-854-5340
E-mail: info@realtimeboss.com
http://www.riskassessment.com/

Provide one source for reliable, affordable environmental consulting and contracting services, as well as industrial wastewater pre-treatment systems and service

1726 **Black and Veatch Engineers: Architects**
11401 Lamar Avenue
Overland Park, KS 66211
913-458-2000
Fax: 913-458-2934
E-mail: info@bv.com
http://www.bv.com

Len C Rodman, President/CEO
O.H Oskvig, Executive Director

1727 **Blasland, Bouck and Lee**
6723 Towpath Road
PO Box 66
Syracuse, NY 13214
315-446-9120
Fax: 315-449-0017
E-mail: info@bbl-inc.com
http://www.bbl-inc.com/bblinc/

Hazardous waste, environmental compliance, air quality; engineering, solid waste, water, wastewater engineering

Umberto Milletti, Founder/CEO

1728 **Block Environmental Services**
2451 Estand Way
Pleasant Hill, CA 94523
925-682-7200
800-682-7255
Fax: 925-686-0399
E-mail: dblock@blockenviron.com
http://www.blockenviron.com

A environmental consulting firm specializing in indoor air quality and toxicology. We are a Certified Aquatic Bioassay Laboratory.

Ronald Block, President
David Block, Vice President

1729 **Boelter and Yates**
1300 Higgins Road
Suite 301
Park Ridge, IL 60068
847-692-4700
Fax: 847-692-3127
E-mail: info@boelter-yates.com
http://www.boelter-yates.com/

Provide environmental engineering, occupational health and safety management, design engineering, and consulting services.

Fred Boelter, Chairperson
Thomas Kowalski, President/CEO

1730 **Bollyky Associates Inc.**
31 Strawberry Hill Avenue
Stamford, CT 06902
203-967-4223
Fax: 203-967-4845
E-mail: ljbbai@bai-ozone.com
http://www.bai-ozone.com

Engineering firm specializing in Ozone technology, water and wastewater treatment, treatability studies.

L Joseph Bollyky, President
Thomas Kleiber, Office Manager

1731 **Bottom Line Consulting**
27248 Twin Pond Road
Lake Barrington, IL 06010
847-381-0597
Fax: 847-381-0598
E-mail: info@cpabottomline.com

Plastics recycling.

John Fearncombe, President

1732 **Braun Intertec Corporation**
11001 Hampshire Avenue South
Minneapolis, MN 55438
952-995-2000
800-279-6100
Fax: 952-995-2020
E-mail: info@braunintertec.com
http://www.braunintertec.com

An engineering firm providing consulting, management and testing services to clients in the commercial, industrial and residential real estate, institutional, retail, financial and government markets.

Jon A Carlson, CEO
Robert J Janssen, President

1733 **Bregman and Company**
5272 River Road
Suite 550
Bethesda, MD 20816
301-652-4818
Fax: 301-652-4819
E-mail: bob@bregmanandcompany.com
http://www.brinkenv.com

Environmental consulting firm.

Robert Edell, President/CEO

1734 **Brinkerhoff Environmental Services**
1805 Atlantic Avenue
Manasquan, NJ 08736
732-223-2225
800-246-7358
Fax: 732-223-3666
E-mail: lbrinkerhoff@brinkenv.com
http://www.brinkenv.com

Groundwater remediation, environmental site assessments and sensitive area mapping; hazardous material management.

Laura A Brinkerhoff, President
Doug Harm, Vice President

1735 **Brooks Laboratories**
9 Issac Street
Norwalk, CT 06850
203-853-9792
800-843-1631
Fax: 203-853-0273
E-mail: brooklabs@aol.com
http://www.brookslabs.com

Consulting and testing air, soil and water for contamination. Accident and disease prevention.

Michael Zubarev, President
Kalonji Diyoka, VP

1736 **Brown, Vence and Associates**
115 Sansome Street
Suite 800
San Francisco, CA 94104
415-434-0900
Fax: 415-956-6220
http://www.brownvence.com

Waste management energy consulting firm.

1737 **Buck, Seifert and Jost**
65 Oak Street
PO Box 415
Norwood, NJ 07648
201-767-3111
877-867-1071
Fax: 201-767-3178
E-mail: bsjinc@bsjinc.com
http://www.bsjinc.com

Consultancy for the water and wastewater industries.

Ronald von Autenried, PE, President
Guido von Autenried, PE, Director/Chief Engineer

1738 **Burk-Kleinpeter**
4176 Canal Street
New Orleans, LA 70119
504-486-5901
Fax: 504-488-1714
E-mail: mjackson@bkiusa.com
http://www.bkiusa.com

A full service firm bringing together resources from our Engineering, Architecture, Planning and Environmental Science Divisions. Our Divisions, which may function independently also work as a team, providing our clients withassistance from the first conceptual idea through final construction. We also provide services through our professional support groups which include landscape architecture, construction management and inspection, graphic design, aerial photographyand marketing.
J. W.''Bill'' Giardina, Jr., PE, Executive Vice President

1739 **Burns and McDonnell**
9400 Ward Parkway
Kansas City, MO 64114
816-333-9400
Fax: 816-333-3690
E-mail: busdev@burnsmcd.com
http://www.burnsmcd.com/index.html

A multidisciplinary engineering, architectural, construction and environmental service firm. More than 2,900 engineers, architects, scientists and other specialists plan, design and build quality projects around the world.
Greg Graves, Chairman & CEO
Joe Brooks, Director of Corporate Market

1740 **C&H Environmental**
224 Stiger Street
PO Box 188
Hackettstown, NJ 07840
908-852-4855
Fax: 908-852-5275
http://www.candhenvironmental.com

Environmental consulting firm.
John H Crow, PhD, Principal
Timir B Hore, PhD, Principal

1741 **CA Rich**
17 DuPont Street
Plainview, NY 11803
516-576-8844
Fax: 516-576-0093
E-mail: info@carichinc.com
http://www.carichinc.com

An independently owned, private consulting firm providing targeted, solution oriented hydrogeologic and environmental engineering services. Assists in the conception, development, design, implementation, documentation and defense ofsite evaluations and remedial action.
Charles A Rich, Founder/President
Richard J Izzo, Associate

1742 **CBA Environmental Services**
57 Park Lane
Hegins, PA 17938
570-682-8742
Fax: 570-682-8915
E-mail: info@cbaenvironmental.com
http://www.cbaenvironmental.com

Provides environmental solutions from general plant maintenance and cleaning to large-scale soil remediation projects.
Bruce L Bruso, Principal

1743 **CDS Laboratories**
75 Suttle Street
PO Box 2605
Durango, CO 81302
303-247-4220
800-553-6266
Fax: 303-247-4227

Specializes in analytical analysis and testing, consulting, QA, environmental, and dyes.

1744 **CEDA**
3519 Old Red Trail
PO Box 787
Mandan, ND 58554
701-663-0307
Fax:701-667-2090

Provides services in hazardous waste, spill response, and asbestos abatement.
WF Mowatt, President

1745 **CIH Environmental**
1044 Victory Circle
Reading, PA 19605
610-372-6692
Fax: 610-372-0862
E-mail: cihenv@fast.net
http://www.cihenv.com

Provides services in indoor air quality and industrial hygiene and mold/bacterial contaminations.
James E Detwiler, President

1746 **CIH Services**
7148 Creekside Lane
Indianapolis, IN 46250
317-797-7768
Fax: 317-913-1895
E-mail: cihservices@juno.com
http://www.cih-services.com

Services in indoor air quality.
John Beltz, Contact

1747 **CII Engineered Systems**
6767 Forrest Hill Avenue
Richmond, VA 23225
804-320-1405
800-768-2545
Fax: 804-320-9625
E-mail: cii.richmond@ciiservice.com
http://www.ciiservice.com

Services in energy conservation.
Dorothy Thacker, Chairman
Robert Ranson, President

1748 **CK Environmental**
1020 Turnpike Street
#8
Canton, MA 02021
781-828-5200
888-253-0303
Fax: 781-828-5380
E-mail: info@ckenvironmental.com
http://www.ckenvironmental.com

Serivces in regulatory compliance.
Kevin Kelley, Sales Manager

1749 **CRB Geological and Environmental Services**
8744 SW 133rd Street
Miami, FL 33176
305-447-9777
Fax: 305-567-2853
E-mail: blivieri@crbgeo.net
http://www.crbgeo.net/

Environmental consulting.
Frederick R Baddour, President

1750 **CTE Engineers**
303 East Wacker Drive
Suite 600
Chicago, IL 60601
312-938-0300
Fax: 312-938-1109
E-mail: tony.bouchard@cte.aecom.com
http://www.cte-eng.com

Consulting services in the use of computers and electronics to solve pollution problems.
Tony Bouchard, Environmental Services
Carl Mahr, Environmental Services

1751 **CTI and Associates, Inc**
51331 W Pontiac Trail
Wixom, MI 48393
248-486-5100
800-284-8632
Fax: 248-486-5050
http://www.cticompanies.com

Environmental engineering firm.
Morgan Subbarayan, President

1752 **CTL Environmental Services**
24404 South Vermont Avenue
Suite 307
Harbor City, CA 90710
800-777-0605
Fax: 310-530-0792
E-mail: info@ctles.com
http://www.ctles.com

Industrial hygiene and safety, asbestos/lead based paint surveys, environmental site assessments, risk mangement, indoor air quality, radon testing and mold investigation.

1753 **CZR**
2151 Alternate A1A South
Suite 2000
Jupiter, FL 33477
561-747-7455
Fax: 561-747-7576
E-mail: czrinc@czr-inc.com
http://www.czr-inc.com/czrwilm

Environmental impact studies, wetlands delineation, threatened species surveys, environmental resource permitting.

Samuel E Wiley, Vice President

1754 Cabe Associates
144 South Governors Avenue
PO Box 877
Dover, DE 19904
302-674-9280
800-542-7979
Fax: 302-674-1099
E-mail: jpj@cabe.com
http://www.cabe.com

Environmental and pollution control.
Lee J. Beetschen, President

1755 California Environmental
1001 Street
P.O. Box 2815
Sacramento, CA 95812
818-991-1542
Fax: 818-991-0793
Industrial safety and hygiene.
Michael R Tiffany, CIH

1756 California Geo-Systems
1545 Victory Boulevard
2nd Floor
Glendale, CA 91201
818-500-9533
Fax: 818-500-0134
E-mail: geosys@pacebell.net
http://www.geosys1.com

Geotechnical environmental services.
Vince Carnegie, President
Rachel Fischer, Sr. Environmental Geologist

1757 Cambridge Environmental
50 Hampshire Street
Cambridge, MA 02139
617-452-6000
Fax: 617-452-6000
E-mail: info@cambridgeenvironmental.com
http://www.cambridgeenvironmental.com

Consulting and research firm that assesses and helps to minimize risks to health and the environment.
Laura Green, President
Teri Myers Ph.D, Senior Engineer

1758 Camiros Limited
411 South Wells
Suite 400
Chicago, IL 60607
312-922-9211
Fax: 312-922-9689
E-mail: sbland@camiros.com
http://www.camiros.com

Camiros is an active proponent of Sustainable Growth as well as other environmentally sensitive aspects of urban planning and design. In particular, the firm has drafted land use plans and zoning ordinances that pay careful attentionto environmental issues.
Adam Rosa, AICP, Senior Associate
Pam Thompson, Office Manager

1759 Camo Pollution Control
1610 State Route 376
Wappingers Falls, NY 12590
845-463-7310
Environmental consultants.
Michael Tremper, Vice President

1760 Camtech
4550 McKnight Road
Suite 210
Pittsburg, PA 15237
412-931-1210
Fax: 412-931-1304
Environmental consulting.

1761 Canin Associates
500 Delaney Avenue
Suite 404
Orlando, FL 32801
407-422-4040
Fax: 407-425-7427
E-mail: mcanin@canin.com
http://www.canin.com
Environmental services.
Greg Witherspoon, Business Development
Myrna Canin, VP

1762 Cape Environmental Management
500 Pinnacle Court
Suite 100
Norcross, GA 30071
770-908-7200
800-488-4372
Fax: 770-908-7219
http://www.capeenv.com

Environmental consulting firm.
Fernando Rios, President

1763 Capital Environmental Enterprises
2244 Profit Drive
Indianapolis, IN 46239
317-240-8085
888-376-4315
Fax: 317-241-4180
E-mail: info@capitalenvironmentalenterprises.com
http://www.capitalenvironmentalenterprises.com
Environmental consulting.

1764 Cardinal Environmental
3303 Paine Avenue
Sheboygan, WI 53081
920-459-2500
800-413-7225
Fax: 920-459-2503
E-mail: info@cardinalenvironmental.com
http://www.cardinalenvironmental.com
Environmental consulting/analytical laboratory.

Scott A Hanson, President

1765 Carpenter Environmental Associates
307 Museum Village Road
Monroe, NY 10950
845-781-4844
Fax: 845-782-5591
E-mail: mail@cea-enviro.com
http://www.ceaenviro.com/

Environmental engineering and assessment services, including wastewater and storm water management, wetlands and ecological investigations, site assessments, environmental compliance and contingency planning, permitting services, andlitigation support.

Kim Bell Hosea, President
Ralph E Huddleston, Jr., Senior Vice President

1766 Carr Research Laboratory
17 Waban Street
Wellesley, MA 02482
781-235-3132
E-mail: info@carr-research-lab.com
http://www.carr-research.lab.com

Environmental consulting research laboratory providing these services: hydrology, wetlands, lakes, oceanography, water pollution, geology, and environmental engineering.

Jerome B Carr, PhD, President
Deseng Wang, PhD, PE, Dir Engineering Services

1767 Catlin Engineers and Scientists
220 Old Dairy Road
PO Box 10279
Wilmington, NC 28405
910-452-5861
Fax: 910-452-7563
E-mail: info@catlinusa.com
http://www.catlinusa.com

Specializes in providing quality service in the fields of environmental, civil, and geotechnical engineering. Services include soil and ground water remediation, wastewater treatment system design, public infrastructure,environmentally secure landfills, and safe, clean, water supplies.
Richard Catlin, President

1768 Center for Energy and Environmental Analysis Oak Ridge Laboratory
Energy and Environmental Analysis
PO Box 2008
Oak Ridge, TN 37831
865-576-4160
Fax: 865-574-4415
E-mail: sdb@ornl.gov
http://www.ornl.gov

In the Center for Energy and Environmental Analysis, a part of the Energy Division at Oak Ridge National Laboratory, we provide our customers with analysis of energy and environmental issues of local, regional, national, and globalimportance so as to

provide decision makers with information on which to base major policy, program, and project decisions.
Dr. Michael O Lerner, President

1769 Central States Environmental Services
1079 Copple Road
Centralia, IL 62801
618-532-4784
Fax: 618-532-5615
Environmental clean-up contractor.
Elvin Copple, President

1770 Challenge Environmental Systems Inc
2270 Worth Lane
Suite D
Springdale, AR 72764
479-927-1008
Fax: 479-927-1000
E-mail: kent@challenge-sys.com
http://www.challenge-sys.com
Challenge Environmental Systems Inc manufactures environmental equipment for respiration monitoring on wastewater processes, soil remediation, and composting.
Mark L Kuss, President/Founder

1771 Chapman Environmental Control
PO Box 288
Osceola, IN 46561
800-675-8706
Air pollution control.
Frank X Chapman, President

1772 Chelsea Group
89 Awawa Rd
PO Box 68
Maunaloa, HI 96770
808-552-0233
800-626-6722
Fax: 630-729-3189
E-mail: pturner@chelsea-grp.com
http://www.chelsea-grp.com
Specializes in strategic, technical, and marketing consulting to major corporations for enhanced positioning of products and services relating to the indoor environment.
George Benda, Senior Principal
David Munn, PE, Principal

1773 Chemical Data Management Systems
6516 Trinity Court
Suite 201
Dublin, CA 94568
925-551-7300
800-735-1761
Fax: 925-829-3885
E-mail: info@cdms.com
http://www.cdms.com
Provides a full range of hazardous material and OSHA regulatory compliance services to industries using hazardous materials, including implementing compliance programs, submitting necessary reports to all regulatory agencies, andproviding a full range of training services to industry, agencies, and industrial groups.

1774 Chicago Chem Consultants Corporation
14 North Peoria Street
Suite 2C
Chicago, IL 60607
312-226-2436
Fax: 312-226-8886
E-mail: info@chichem.com
http://www.chichem.com
Provides innovative, technologically sophisticated, cost-effective, and risk protective environmental and engineering services.
Jeffrey P Perl, President
Stanley Yoslov, Senior Associate

1775 Cigna Loss Control Services
900 Cottage Grove Road
Bloomfield, CT 06002
800-997-1654
http://www.cigna.com
Provides services in the field of industrial hygiene.
David Cordani, President/CEO
Lisa Bacus, Executive Vice President

1776 Clayton Group Services
45525 Grand River Avenue
Suite 200
Novi, MI 48374
248-344-2661
Fax: 248-344-2656
E-mail: info@claytongrp.com
http://www.claytongrp.com
A full service environmental, occupational health and safety, and laboratory services consulting firm serving both public and private clients.
Lisa Barnes, PE CIH, Sr VP/COO
MJ Haught, Marketing Director

1777 Clean Air Engineering
500 West Wood Street
Palatine, IL 60067
800-553-5511
800-627-0033
Fax: 847-991-3385
E-mail: contact@cleanair.com
http://www.cleanair.com
Environmentally consulting and permitting, process engineering, equipment rental and manufacture, measurement and analytical services.
Allen Kephart, Vice President
Jim Pollack, Director of Sales

1778 Clean Environments
10803 Gulfdale
Suite 210
San Antonio, TX 78216
210-349-7242
800-299-7242
Fax: 210-349-1132
E-mail: sales@cleanenvironments.com
http://www.cleanenvironments.com
Environmental consulting firm.

1779 Clean Technologies
2700 Kirkwood Hwy
Newark, DE 19711
302-999-0924
Fax: 302-999-0925
Environmental engineering firm.
Deborah A Buniski, President

1780 Clean World Engineering
1737 S Naperville Road
Suite 200
Wheaton, IL 60187
630-260-0200
800-761-9603
Fax: 630-260-0797
E-mail: cwe@clean-world.com
http://www.clean-world.com
A woman-owned environmental engineering firm established in 1985. They specialize in meeting the needs of small businesses to FORTUNE 500 companies to large government agencies. They develop practical and cost-efficient soulutions toincreasingly stringent and complex environmental reguations.
Rita Kapur, President/CEO

1781 Coastal Lawyer
173 E Blithedale Avenue
Suite 3
Mill Valley, CA 94941
415-383-3715
Fax: 415-383-3718
E-mail: del@greendogcampaigns.com
Consultation for environmental causes and initiatives. Legal representation, public relations and campaign consulting.
Dotty E LeMieux, Principal

1782 Coastal Planning and Engineering
2481 Northwest Boca Raton Boulevard
Boca Raton, FL 33431
561-391-8102
Fax: 561-391-9116
E-mail: mail@coastalplanning.net
http://www.coastalplanning.net
Environmental consulting firm providing services in coastal engineering, coastal planning, coastal surveying, environmental science, and regulatory permitting.

1783 Cohen Group
3 Waters Park Drive
Suite 226
San Mateo, CA 94403
650-349-9737
Fax: 650-349-3378
E-mail: admin@thecohengroup.com
http://www.thecohengroup.com
Provides a complete range of environmental health and safety services to business and government including indoor air quality, asbestos, respiratory protection, and industrial hygiene safety.
Joel M Cohen, President
Tim Bormann, Vice President

1784 Cohrssen Environmental
3450 Sacremento St
San Francisco, CA 94123
415-775-1105
Industrial hygiene services.
Barbara Cohrssen, Principal Executive

1785 **Columbia Analytical Services**
1317 South 13th Avenue
Kelso, WA 98626
360-577-7222
800-695-7222
Fax: 360-636-1068
http://www.caslab.com
Areas of expertise and services include environmental testing of air, water, soil, hazardous waste, sediments and tissues; process and quality control testing; analytical method development; sampling and mobile laboratory services; andconsulting and data management services.

Stephen W Vincent, President/CEO
Ed Wilson, Employee Representative

1786 **Combustion Unlimited**
PO Box 8856
Philadelphia, PA 19117
215-537-0871
Fax: 215-884-3074
Engineering consulting services in air pollution control and combustion.

John F Straitz III, President

1787 **Committee for Environmentally Effective Packaging**
601 13th Street NW
Suite 900S
Washington, DC 20005
202-783-5594
Fax: 203-783-5595
http://www.epa.gov/epaoswer
Monitors legislation and regulations affecting packaging in the food service industry and educates decision makers on packaging.

1788 **Commonwealth Engineering and Technology CET Engineering Services**
1240 North Mountain Road
Harrisburg, PA 17112
717-541-0622
Fax: 717-541-8004
E-mail: contact@cet-inc.com
http://www.cet-inc.com
Pollution control utilizing the ability of Geographic Informaiton Systems as an analytical tool to be used to analyze water and wastewater systems.

Jeffrey Wendle, President

1789 **Community Conservation Consultants Howlers Forever**
50542 One Quiet Lane
Gays Mills, WI 54631
608-735-4717
Fax: 512-519-8494
E-mail: cc@communityconservation.org
http://www.communityconservation.org
Works together with local rural people to aid in the protection of their wildlife and forests. Projects undertaken have mainly been in India, Belize and Wisconsin with an emphasis on primates and other species. Additional projects areevolving in Madagascar, Costa Rica and other countries.

Robert Horwich, Director
Ashley M Morga, Projects Coordinator

1790 **Compass Environmental**
1751 McCollum Parkway
Kennesaw, GA 30144
770-499-7127
Fax: 770-423-7402
E-mail: staff@compassenv.com
http://www.compassenv.com
Asbestos indoor air quality and industrial hygiene services. Established as an alternative to large companies that are typically structured to provide routine testing and consulting services.
Eva M Ewing, Vice President
William M Ewing, President

1791 **Comprehensive Environmental**
21 Depot Street
Merrimack, NH 03054
603-424-8444
800-725-2550
Fax: 603-424-8441
E-mail: webmaster@ceiengineers.com
http://www.ceiengineers.com
Provides water, wastewater and hazardous waste services with a mission to protect the client, public health and the environment, to be client advocates, to build trust, and to provide objectivity.
Eileen Pannetier, President

1792 **Comprehensive Environmental Strategies**
11950 Rocky Brook Court
Manassas, VA 20112
703-791-7700
Fax: 703-368-6821
Asbestos, indoor air quality, industriel hygiene services.
Reginald B Simmons, Principal Executive

1793 **Conestoga-Rovers and Associates**
2055 Niagra Falls Boulevard
Suite 3
Niagra Falls, NY 14304
716-297-6150
Fax: 716-297-2265
E-mail: info@cra.com
http://www.craworld.com
Family of companies that provide a full-service engineering, environmental, construction and information technology services worldwide.

Frank A Rovers, Principal Executive

1794 **Consertech Group**
5885 Rickenbacker Road
Commerce, CA 90040
323-867-9044
Fax: 323-867-9045
E-mail: bob@conservtechgroup.com
http://www.conservtechgroup.com
Pollution control systems, site assessment, waste problems, water and waste systems.

Robert J MacDonald, President/CEO

1795 **Consultox**
PO Box 51928
New Orleans, LA 70151
504-529-7500
800-566-2301
Fax: 504-926-0638
E-mail: info@consultox.com
http://www.consultox.com
Toxicology consulting firm.

Richard A Parent, President

1796 **Continental Shelf Associates**
8502 SW Kansas Eve
Stuart, FL 34997
772-219-3000
E-mail: csa@conshelf.com
http://www.conshelf.com
Environmental consulting firm.
Kevin Peterson, President/CEO

1797 **Converse Consultants**
222 East Huntington Drive
Suite 211
Monrovia, CA 91016
626-930-1200
Fax: 626-930-1280
E-mail: corporate@converseconsultants.com
http://www.converseconsultants.com
Environmental consulting and engineering firm with offices throughout the United States.

Hashmi S E Quazi, Chairman
William H Chu, Senior Vice President

1798 **Cook Flatt and Strobel Engineers**
2930 SW Woodside Drive
Topeka, KS 66614
785-272-4706
Fax: 785-272-4736
E-mail: cfsengr@cfse.com
http://www.cfse.com
Environmental engineering.

Robert Chambers, President
Sabin Yanez, Senior Vice President

1799 **Cornerstone Environmental, Health and Safety**
880 Lennox Court
Zionsville, IN 46077
317-733-2637
800-285-2568
Fax: 317-577-2481
E-mail: info@corner-enviro.com
http://www.corner-enviro.com
Environmental, health, and safety services.
Jill Para, Contact

1800 Corporate Environmental Advisors
127 Hartwell Street
Suite 2
West Boylston, MA 01583
508-835-8822
800-358-7960
Fax: 508-835-8812
http://www.cea-inc.com
Environmental engineering and consulting firm.
Deborah N Migridichian, CEO

1801 Cox Environmental Engineering
82 Dresser Hill Road
Charlton, MA 01507
508-248-5185
Fax: 508-248-5003
Environmental engineering consulting.

1802 Crouse & Company
4000 Hempfield Plaza Boulevard
Suite 914
Greensburgh, PA 15601
724-838-8200
Fax: 724-832-3627
E-mail: info@keystonerenewable.com
http://www.crouse.com
Natural resources management company dedicated to ushering traditional engineering and natural sciences consulting services into the age of modern information technology.
A Jacob Crouse, President
Samuel T Crouse, Vice President

1803 Cultural Resource Consultants International Archaeology & Ecology
PO Box 315
Chappell Hill, TX 77426
979-530-0333
http://www.culturalresource.com
Historic land use and environmentally sensitive projects.
Robert B d'Aigle, Owner
Nataliya Hryshechko, Laboratory Services Director

1804 Curt B Beck Consulting
408 W Kingsmill Street
PO Box 2442
Pampa, TX 79065
806-665-9281
Fax: 806-665-1965
E-mail: curtbbeck@cableone.net
Pollution control services.
Curt B Beck, Owner

1805 Custom Environmental Services
233 Forest Drive
Santa Barbara, CA 93117
805-968-2112
Fax: 805-968-2137
E-mail: rosalie@custom-env.com
http://www.custom-env.com
Small environmental consulting business offering services that help individuals and companies of all sizes comply with environmental laws, including the Clean Air Act, Clean Water Act, and Medical Waste Management Act.
Rosalie A Skefich, Founder

1806 D'Appolonia
275 Center Road
Monroeville, PA 15146
412-856-9440
Fax: 412-856-9535
E-mail: info@dappolonia.com
http://www.dappolonia.com
Provides engineering, scientific and construction management services for projects involving large civil works and special earth/structure interaction issues.

1807 D/E3
18234 S Miles Road
Suite 44
Cleveland, OH 44128
216-663-1500
Fax: 216-663-1501
Environmental impact statements, corrective process, pollution abatement, hazardous waste, radon and asbestos hazards.
Harold N Danto, President

1808 DPRA
200 Research Drive
Manhattan, KS 66503
785-539-3565
Fax: 785-539-5353
E-mail: info@dpra.com
http://www.dpra.com
Environmental, economic, regulatory and technical research company. Research results published by information services.
Richard Seltzer, President

1809 DW Ryckman and Associates: REACT Environmental Engineers
1120 South 6th Street
St. Louis, MO 63104
314-678-1398
800-325-1398
Fax: 314-678-6610
E-mail: stewart-ryckman@react-env.com
http://www.react-env.com
D.W. Ryckman & Associates, Inc dba REACT Environmental Engineers, was founded in 1975 to provide rapid response and remediation services for environmental and hazardous contamination problems.
SE Ryckman, President

1810 Datanet Engineering
11416 Reisterstown Road
Owings Mills, MD 21117
410-654-1800
888-896-7133
Fax: 410-654-3711
E-mail: info@datanetengineering.com
http://www.datanetengineering.com
Fuel systems repairs maintenance and installation are also provided
John V Cignatta PhD PE, President

1811 DeVany Industrial Consultants
14507 NW 19th Avenue
Vancouver, WA 98685
360-546-0999
Fax: 360-546-0777
E-mail: mdevany@earthlink.net
Strive to provide a full range of safety and industrial hygiene services customized for your particular environment.

1812 Dennis Breedlove and Associates
330 West Canton Avenue
Winter Park, FL 32789
407-677-1882
800-304-1882
Fax: 407-657-7008
Environmental and natural resources consulting firm.

1813 Detail Associates: Environmental Engineering
300 Grand Avenue
Englewood, NJ 07631
201-569-6708
Fax: 201-569-4378
E-mail: dainfo@daienviro.com
http://www.daienviro.com
Asbestos management programs. Indoor air quality. Analytical services. Lead surveys. Phase I, II and III environmental audits.

1814 Donald Friedlander
1091 Willowbrook Road
Staten Island, NY 10314
718-698-7545

1815 Dunn Corporation
316 Douglass Street
2nd Floor
Brooklyn, NY 11217
718-388-9407
Fax: 718-388-0638
E-mail: info@dunndev.com
http://www.dunndev.com

1816 ENSR Consulting and Engineering
2 Technology Park Drive
Westford, MA 01886
978-589-3000
800-722-2440
Fax: 978-589-3100
http://www.ensr.com
Provides consulting, engineering, remediation, and related services to industrial and commercial companies, municipalities, and regulated government agencies throughout the United States, Europe, Latina America, and Asia.
Robert C Weber, President/CEO

1817 ENTRIX
5252 Westchester
Suite 250
Houston, TX 77005
800-368-7511
Fax: 713-666-5227
E-mail: webmaster@entrix.com
http://www.entrix.com

Provides environmental and natural resource management consulting
Todd Williams, President
Richard Firth, Executive VP

1818 ENVIRON Corporation
4350 N Fairfax Drive
Arlington, VA 22203
703-516-2300
Fax: 703-516-2345
http://www.environcorp.com
Health and environmental sciences consultants.
Steve Washburn, CEO

1819 ESS Group
401 Wampanoag Trail
Suite 400
East Providence, RI 02915
401-434-5560
Fax: 401-434-8158
E-mail: info@essgroup.com
http://www.essgroup.com
Environmental Science Services is an multi-disciplinary environmental consulting and engineering firm with offices located in Wellesley, Massachusetts and Providence, Rhode Island. ESS was established in 1979, and has experiencedsteady growth and market diversification to become a recognized leader in the environmental consulting and engineering services business.
Charles J Natale, Jr., President/CEO

1820 ETS
1401 Municipal Road Northwest
Roanoke, VA 24012
540-265-0004
Fax: 540-265-0131
E-mail: jmck@esti-inc.com
http://www.ets.org
ETS is a full-service environmental consulting and training firm specializing in air emissions control, measurement, engineering and consulting services.
John McKenna, Contact
Jack Mycock, Contact

1821 Earth Science Associates
4300 Long Beach Blvd
Suite 310
Long Beach, CA 90807
562-428-3181
Fax: 562-428-3186
E-mail: contactESA@earthsci.com
http://www.earthsci.com
Earth Science Associates is a consultancy serving the international oil and gas industry. ESA specializes in resource assessment, economic evaluation and risk studies and the development of custom geographic information systems. Oiland gas companies use our assessment studies in evaluating the geologic potential of prospects, plays and basins.

1822 Earth Science Associates (ESA Consultants)
PO Box 12067
Knoxville, TN 37912
800-467-6380
E-mail: esa@halos.com
http://www.halos.com

1823 EcoLogic Systems
7977 Capwell Drive
Suite 150
Oakland, CA 94621
510-635-7400
800-223-0609
Fax: 510-634-7402
http://www.ecologicsystems.com
The developer of leading suite of hazardous material management and environmental health and safety compliance software.
Geoff James, Business Development

1824 Ecology and Environment
368 Pleasant View Drive
Lancaster, NY 14086
716-684-8060
Fax: 716-684-0844
E-mail: info@ene.com
http://www.ene.com
Ecology and Environment is a multidisciplinary environmental science and engineering company with more than 25 offices in the US and offices and partners in more than 35 countries. We are a world leader in providing environmentalconsulting services and litigation support.
Dr Bruce Alberts, President
Cheryl Karpowicz, VP

1825 Ed Caicedo Engineers & Consultants
PO Box 22256
Lexington, KY 40522
859-259-0042
E-mail: info@eciengineers.com
http://www.eciengineers.com
We are a Kentucky-based Consulting Engineering firm which provides professional and technical services to the public and private sectors. These services cover all facets of the construction process, including the preparation offeasibility studies, conceptual designs, environmental impact studies, cost-effectiveness analysis, final project design, construction administration, operation and maintenance management.
Eduardo Caicedo, President
William H Meadows, Principal Engineer

1826 Elinor Schwartz
318 South Abingdon Street
Arlington, VA 22204
703-920-5389
Fax: 703-920-5402
E-mail: es@elinorschwartz.com
Representing state agencies and providing research on natural resources, energy and environmental issues.
Elinor Schwartz, Washington Representative

1827 EnSafe
5724 Summer Trees Drive
Memphis, TN 38134
901-372-7962
800-588-7962
Fax: 901-372-2454
http://www.ensafe.com
Services include implementation of occupational health and safety programs, worker's compensation programs, and environmental management systems for clients ranging from large corporations to small businesses to decrease accidentfrequency and accident costs.
Phillip G Coop, President/CEO
Michael Wood, Vice President/CFO

1828 Energy Technology Consultants
2020 E 1st Street
Santa Ana, CA 92705
714-835-6886
Fax: 714-667-7147

1829 EnviroTest Laboratories
315 Fillerton Avenue
Newbrugh, NY 12550
845-562-0890
Fax: 845-562-0841
E-mail: info@envirotestlab.com
http://www.envirotestlaboratories.com
Test soil and water.
Scott Morris, President

1830 Envirocorp
6925 Portwest Drive
110
Houston, TX 77024
713-880-4640
800-535-4105
Fax: 713-880-3248
E-mail: pfh@subsurfacegroup.com
http://www.envirocorpinc.com
Envirocorp, Inc. is a consultant firm with over 25 years of expereonce around the world involving site assessments and remediations. Envirocorp's expertise includes UST removals and remediations, hazardous waste reporting,environmental audits, oil & gas property assessments, and asbestos inspection. Envirocorp has offices in South Bend, Indiana; Baton Rouge, Louisiana and its's corporate office in Houston, Texas.

Peter Keck, Senior Project Manager

1831 Environmental Compliance Consulting
PO Box 11417
Green Bay, WI 54307
920-434-6380
888-ECC-INOW
Environmental assessments.

1832 Environmental Consultants
391 Newman Avenue
Clarksville, IN 47129
812-282-8481
Fax: 812-282-8554
Environmental consulting firm.
Robert E Fuchs, President

1833 **Environmental Resource Associates**
16341 Table Mountain Parkway 303-431-8454
Golden, CO 80403 800-372-0122
Fax: 303-421-0159
E-mail: info@eraqc.com
http://www.eraqc.com

1834 **Environmental Resources Management**
3352 128th Avenue 616-399-3500
Holland, MI 49424 Fax: 616-399-3777
http://www.erm.com

Robin Bidwell, Executive Chair

1835 **Environmental Risk Limited**
120 Mountain Avenue 860-242-9933
Bloomfield, CT 06002 Fax: 860-243-9055
E-mail: info@erl.com
http://www.erl.com

Environmental consulting and engineering firm offers environmental permitting and compliance assistance, site investigation and remediation services, air quality impact analyses, pollution prevention planning, aquatic toxicitylaboratory, hazardous waste management and chemical accident prevention program assistance.
Mitchell M. Wurmbrand, C.C.M., Principal

1836 **Environmental Risk Management**
3109 N McColl Road 956-686-6569
PO Box 3213 800-880-9582
McAllen, TX 78502 Fax: 956-668-7227
E-mail: office@enrisk.com
http://www.enrisk.com

Provides experienced environmental consulting to South Texas. Services includes Phase I, II and III environmental site assessments, leaking petroleum storage tank assessments and project management, asbestos inspections and managementplans, remedial services and non process waste management.
Mark Barron, President

1837 **Environmental Science Associates**
550 Kearney St 415-896-5900
Suite 800 Fax: 415-896-0332
San Francisco, CA 94108 E-mail: mabell@esassoc.com
http://www.esassoc.com

Environmental Science Associates is an environmental consulting firm committed to helping clients meet the environmental challenges of tommorrow today.
Gary Oates, President
Brian Boxer, Vice President

1838 **Environmental Strategies Corporation**
1528 Walnut Street 215-731-4200
Suite 500 Fax: 215-731-4207
Philadelphia, PA 19102 E-mail: info@envirostrat.com
http://www.envirostrat.com

ECS is a complete environmental consulting, management, and engineering firm specializing in identifying potential or actual environmental liabilities and preventing or remediating them.
Lorna M Velardi, President
Samuel S Joshi, Director

1839 **Environmental Testing and Consulting**
2790 Whitten Road 901-213-2400
Memphis, TN 38133 800-264-4522
Fax: 901-213-2440
E-mail: nathan.pera@etcmemphis.com
http://www.etcmemphis.com

Environmental laboratory
Nathan Pera, President

1840 **Enviroplan Consulting**
81 Two Bridges Road 973-575-2555
Fairfield, NJ 07004 Fax: 973-575-6617
E-mail: contact@enviroplan.com
http://www.enviroplan.com/

An air pollution company with 14 offices throughout the United States. Specialize in three areas: air pollution consulting including greenhouse gas emmissions, inventory development and mitigation; ambient air quality and meterologicalmonitoring programs; and wind resource analyses

Howard Ellis, Contact

1841 **Epcon Industrial Systems NV, Ltd**
17777 I-45 South 936-273-3300
Conroe, TX 77385 800-447-7872
Fax: 936-273-4600
E-mail: epcon@epconlp.com
http://www.epconlp.com

Provides a broad line of technology advanced, yet user friendly air pollution control products, finishing systems and heat processing equipment.

1842 **Foothill Engineering Consultants**
18590 Hwy 49 303-278-0622
Plymouth, CA 95669 Fax: 303-278-0624
E-mail: sales@foothillmc.com
http://www.foothillmc.com

Offers services in environmental studies and design, decontamination and decommissioning support, mining services, radiological engineering, waste management, civil engineering, waste management, water resources planning andengineering, and cultural, natural, and physical resources evaluation.
Darrin Punceles

1843 **Franklin D Aldrich MD, PhD**
1094 Quince Avenue 303-443-2316
Boulder, CO 80304 Fax: 303-938-9420
E-mail: w1@fa@hotmail.com
Environmental/ clinical toxicology and consulting.

1844 **GBMC & Associates**
219 Brown Lane 501-847-7077
Bryant, AK 72022 Fax: 501-847-7943
E-mail: vblubaugh@gbmcassoc.com
http://www.gbmcassoc.com

GBMC & Associates are a consulting firm providing strategic environmental services to industrial clients and air permitting support, water quality and toxicity studies, storm water management, environmental program development andreporting.
Vince Blubaugh, Principal/Sr Project Mgr
Chuck Campbell, Senior Engineer

1845 **GEO/Plan Associates**
30 Mann Street 617-740-1340
Hingham, MA 02043 Fax: 617-740-1340

Michu Tcheng, Partner
Peter Rosen, Partner

1846 **Gabbard Environmental Services**
7611 Hope Farm Road 260-493-2982
Fort Wayne, IN 46815 Fax: 219-493-4043
E-mail: wdgabbard@aol.com
http://www.gabbardenviromentalservices.com

Consulting services for environmental affairs such as permitting, compliance, plans and programs.
William D Gabbard, President

1847 **Galson Corporation**
6601 Kirkville Road 315-432-0506
East Syracuse, NY 13057 800-950-0506
Fax: 315-437-0509
http://www.galsonlabs.com

Environmental consulting and engineering and analytical services, specializing in the air management of indoor and outdoor environments.
Philip Rooney, Executive Staff

1848 **Geo-Marine Technology**
725 W Alder Street 406-721-1599
Suite 12 Fax: 406-926-1379
Missoula, MT 59802 E-mail: pam@geomarinetech.com
http://www.geomarinetech.com

Provides geological, geophysical, and hydrographic survey consultancy services to offshore oil and gas industries, offshore survey industries, and governments.

1849 GeoResearch
7806 MacArthur Boulevard 301-229-8111
Cabin John, MD 20818 Fax: 301-229-7980
http://www.georesearch.com
Provides grography-related services from forestry to telecommunications, real-time mobile interactive geographic technologies and databases.

1850 Geomet Technologies
20251 Century Boulevard 301-428-9898
Suite 300 800-296-9898
Germantown, MD 20874 Fax: 301-428-9482
E-mail: salesinfo@geomet.com
http://www.geomet.com
Provides consultant, technical, and material evaluation services in the areas of personal protective systems, indoor and ambient air quality, energy, chemical testing, and environmental services to government agencies, private andcommercial clients.
Peter J Cooper, Vice President

1851 Geospec
17912 Sotile Drive 225-753-8811
Baton Rouge, LA 70809 877-503-5618
Fax: 225-753-8877
E-mail: info@geospec-llc.com
http://www.geospec-llc.com
Geophysical services. Gound penetrating radar, EM, conductivity and resistivity surveys to detect and identify potential environmental hazards or contamination. Borehole and excavation utility clearance.

1852 Gradient Corporation
20 University Road
Cambridge, MA 02138 617-395-5000
Fax: 617-395-5001
E-mail: info@gradientcorp.com
http://www.gradientcorp.com
A consulting firm with nationally recognized specialities in risk and environmental sciences.
Teresa S Bowers, President

1853 Granville Composite Products Corporation
600 Round House Road 717-247-2879
Lewistown, PA 17044 800-350-4660
Fax: 412-291-3291
E-mail: infosales@granville.cc
http://www.granville.cc
Plastic recycling. Molder of recycled pastics.

1854 Great Lakes Educational Consultants
400 Central Avenue 847-441-8911
Suite 200 Fax: 847-881-0724
Northfield, IL 60093 E-mail: rjonaiti@kresanet.org
http://www.greatlakesconsult.com
A consulting firm which develops safety/security/emergency plans to protect the educational/business environment including buildings, grounds, personnel and students. We conduct a hazard analysis to determine planning requirements andprovide a proposal for your consideration.
Gwynne Hales, President

1855 Greeley-Polhemus Group
105 South High Street 215-692-2224
West Chester, PA 19382 Fax: 215-692-4052
Specializes in providing consulting services to the United States Army Corps of Engineers and to non-Federal local sponsors of proposed Federal projects. Provides services in the areas of project planning, economics, finance,institutional strategy development, and environmental studies related to flood control, land uses, recreation, water supply, and navigation.

1856 Groundwater Technology
100 River Ridge Drive 781-769-7600
Suite 300 800-635-0053
Norwood, MA 02062 Fax: 781-769-7992
Groundwater Technology has been a leader in the development and application of advanced technologies for environmental restoration of contaminated sites. One of the largest environmental consulting, engineering and remediation firms.GTI is widely recognized for its innovative, bioremedial technology for rapid cleanup of soil and groundwater, both above-ground and in situ.

1857 HC Nutting, A Terracon Company
611 Lunken Park Drive 513-321-5816
Cincinnati, OH 45226 Fax: 513-321-0294
E-mail: cincinnati@hcnutting.com
http://www.hcnutting.com
Materials tesing company, geotechnical and environmental engineering firm.
Jack Scott, President

1858 HE Cramer Company
8249 Shangrila Circle 801-561-4964
Sandy, UT 84094 Fax: 801-561-4964
E-mail: checo1@qwest.net
H.E. Cramer Company does air pollution consulting, computer software development, and environmental consulting. Research results are published in project reports and professional journals.
Jay R Bjorklund, President

1859 HYGIENETICS Environmental Services
432 Columbia Street 617-621-0363
Suite 16A Fax: 617-621-1609
Cambridge, MA 02141 http://www.hygienetics.com
Hygienetics provides comprehensive analysis, design, and program management services to a diverse group of private sector customers. Primary areas of expertise include environmental site assessments for property transaction, soil andgroundwater investigation and remediation, air resource management, industrial hygiene and asbestos/lead management.
Carmen Pombiero, General Information Contact

1860 Harold I Zeliger PhD
1270 Sacandaga Road 518-882-6800
West Charlton, NY 12010 Fax: 518-882-6926
E-mail: hiz@zeliger.com
http://www.zeliger.com
Areas of expertise include occupational and environmental exposure to toxic chemicals, hazard communication, chemical formulating and processing impact and toxic waste.
Dr Harold I Zeliger, Principal

1861 Hart Crowser, Inc.
1700 Westlake Avenue North 206-324-9530
Suite 200 Fax: 206-328-5581
Seattle, WA 98109 E-mail: corporate@terracon.com
http://www.hartcrowser.com
Hart Crowser, Inc. provides a full range of services from initial site studies through regulatory permitting design, and construction. They integrate these services as required for each project, They know what kind of information isimportant, how to collect it and apply it to te selection of viable solutions, and how actions are perceived by regulatory agencies and the public. Consequently, they design an approach that is practical, cost-effective, and client-oriented.
Mike Bailey, CEO
David Winter, Vice President

1862 Hasbrouck Geophysics
12 Woodside Drive 928-778-6320
Prescott, AZ 86305 Fax: 928-778-6320
E-mail: jim@hasgeo.com
http://www.hasgeo.com

Over 30 years experience in all major surface, airbone, and bore-hole geophisical methods plus strong geological background.
Jim Hasbrouck, Principal

1863 **HazMat Environmental Group**
60 Commerce Drive
Buffalo, NY 14218
716-827-7200
Fax: 716-827-7217
E-mail: jwhite@hazmatinc.com
http://www.hazmatinc.com
Transportation services - specializing in hazardous materials and hazardous waste transportation.

1864 **Heritage Environmental Services**
3719 W. 96th St.
Indianapolis, IN 46268
317-334-2300
877-436-8778
Fax: 800-860-3199
E-mail: webmaster@heritage-enviro.com
http://www.heritage-enviro.com
Provides environmental management, integrated environment remediation services, product recovery and recycling services, waste services, analytical services, consulting and engineering services, and plant and industrial services.
Mike Karpinski, Quality Manager

1865 **Hermann Associates**
117 Church Road
Winnetka, IL 60093
Fax: 847-446-7640

1866 **Huff and Huff**
915 Harger Road
Suite 330
Oak Brooke, IL 60523
630-684-9100
Fax: 630-684-9120
E-mail: Mwunderlich@huffnhuff.com
http://www.huffnhuff.com
Multi-diciplined firm providing environmental, civil, and chemical engineering and consulting services.
James Huff, PE
Richard Trzupek

1867 **Hydrogeologic**
11107 Sunset Hills Road
Suite 400
Reston, VA 20190
703-478-5186
Fax: 703-471-4180
http://www.hgl.com
Gary Mayer, Vice President

1868 **In-Flight Radiation Protection Services**
211 E 70th Street
Suite 12G
New York, NY 10021
212-288-7201
E-mail: robbarish@aol.com
http://robbarish.tripod.com
Our mission is to educate flight crew members and business frequent flyers about the risks of cosmic radiation exposure during air travel.

1869 **Integrated Chemistries Inc.**
Po Box 10558
White Bear Lake, MN 55110
651-426-3224
Fax: 651-426-3114
E-mail: info@integratedchemistries.com
http://www.integratedchemistries.com
Environmental management.
Jim Nash, President

1870 **Integrated Environmental Management**
9040 Executive Park Drive
Suite 205
Knoxville, TN 37923
865-531-9140
Fax: 865-531-9130
IEM is a women-owned small business that provides strategic consulting and services in the areas of radiation, radioactivity, and the environment.

1871 **International Certification Accreditation Board**
PO Box 2099
Glenview, IL 60025
847-724-6631
Fax: 847-724-4223
E-mail: icab@icab-certify.org
http://www.icab-usa.org
A legally recognized, nonprofit, accreditation organization. Established in 2000, ICAB accredits credentialing programs of environmental, safety, medical, pharaceutical, information technology, educational, industrial and trainingorganizations.
Christopher Young, Executive Director

1872 **Interpoll Laboratories**
4500 Ball Road NE
Circle Pines, MN 55014
763-786-6020
Fax: 763-786-7854
E-mail: interpoll@interpoll-labs.com
http://www.interpoll-labs.com
Dan Despen, President
Timothy MacDonald, Manager Field Services

1873 **JJ Keller and Associates**
3003 Breezewood Lane
Neenah, WI 54957
877-564-2333
800-727-7516
E-mail: sales@jjkeller.com
http://www.jjkeller.com
Regulatory compliance, best practices, and training for environmental, safety, and transportation issues.
James J Keller, President

1874 **Jack J Bulloff**
8140 Township Line Road
Indianapolis, IN 46260
317-824-0014
E-mail: jbulloff@ind.net
Environmental consultant
Jack J Bulloff

1875 **James Anderson and Associates**
2123 University Park Drive
Suite 130
Okemos, MI 48864
517-349-8066
Fax: 517-349-7870
E-mail: info@jaa-hlp.cpm
http://www.safe-at-work.com
A leading worldwide provider of noise control, sound exposure, and hearing loss prevention services for the industry.
Lee D Hagev, Executive VP

1876 **James W Sewall Company**
136 Center Street
PO Box 433
Old Town, ME 04468
207-827-4456
800-648-4202
Fax: 207-827-3641
E-mail: info@jws.com
http://www.jws.com
Founded in 1880, Sewall provides comphrehensive services in forestry appraisal and inventory, aerial imagery, GIS consulting and engineering. Sewall's expertise in GIS project implementation is supported by 50 years' experience inaerial photography and photogrammetry and 30 years' experience in data conversion, database design and application development.
Scott E Graham, PE, Vice President
Aaron Shaw, PE, Project Manager

1877 **John Zink Company**
11920 East Apache
Tulsa, OK 74116
918-234-1800
800-421-9242
Fax: 918-234-2700
E-mail: info@johnzink.com
http://www.johnzink.com
John Zink offers technologically advanced equipment and systems for the clean and efficient combustion of fossil fuels and for the removal of contaminants from process affluents entering the atmosphere.
Bill Hermann, Global Marketing Director

1878 **Kemstar Corporation**
3456 Wade Street
Los Angeles, CA 90066
310-390-0180
Fax: 310-391-8143

1879 **Kimre Inc**
16201 Southwest 95 Avenue
Suite 303
Miami, FL 33157
305-233-4249
Fax: 305-233-8687
E-mail: sales@kimre.com
http://www.kimre.com

Technology provides superior air pollution control particulate/mist elimination: Mist Eliminators, Phase Separation, Scrubbers, Mass Transfer, Engineered clog-resistant interlaced mesh (large surface area/void spaces) providesoptimized efficiency using selected filaments/arrangements.

George C Pedersen, CEO
Frederick H Mueller, Sales Manager

1880 **LA Weaver Company**
308 E Jones Street
Releigh, NC 27601
919-832-6242
Fax: 919-831-1130
E-mail: aweaver1@bellsouth.net
http://www.laweaverco.com

Occupational and Environmental safety consulting services.
Al Weaver, President

1881 **LSI Adapt Engineering**
10000 Alliance Road
Cincinnati, OH 45242
513-793-3200
http://www.lsiadapt.com

Consulting and engineering firm specializing in petroleum engineering, geotechnical and environmental issues. Team of professional engineers, licensed environmental site assessors, hydrogeologiststs and geotechnical engineers offer avariety of strengths and services to clients.

Robert J Ready, Chairman/CEO
Scott D Ready, President

1882 **Landau Associates**
10 N Post Street
Suite 218
Spokane, WA 99201
509-327-9737
Fax: 509-327-9691
E-mail: information@landauinc.com
http://www.landauinc.com

Provided environmental and geotechnical services on nearly 2,000 projects for more than 500 private and public clients in the Pacific Northwest and western US since we opened our doors in 1982. A valued resource in waterfrontdevelopment for public and private ports, also expanded beyond the waterfront to serve clients in some of the best known industries, municipal government, and site development.

Jay Bower, President/CEO
Steve Johnston, Principal

1883 **Law Environmental**
3200 Town Point Drive NW
#100
Kennesaw, GA 30144
770-421-3400
Fax: 770-421-3486

1884 **Lawler, Matusky and Skelly Engineers**
1 Blue Hill Plaza
Pearl River, NY 10965
845-735-8300
Fax: 845-735-7466
E-mail: cnevel@lmseng.com
http://www.lmseng.com

Environmental engineering and consulting firm. Research results published in client reports and professional journals.
Abood Karim A, Vice President

1885 **Lenox Institute of Water Technology**
101 Yokun Avenue
PO Box 1639
Lenox, MA 01240
413-637-3025
Fax: 413-637-3362

Provides services in the area of municipal and industrial water and wastewater treatment systems.
Charles L Smith, Executive VP

1886 **Les A Cartier and Associates**
191 Main Street
PO Box 559
Candia, NH 03034
603-483-2180
800-639-7703
Fax: 603-483-8986

Environmental service company; Health and Safety Course in their Hazardous Materials Management Series
Leslie A Cartier, President

1887 **Louis Berger Group**
412 Mount Kemble Avenue
Morristown, NJ 07960
973-407-1000
E-mail: ctompkins@louisberger.com
http://www.louisberger.com

Offers professional services in the areas of civil, structural, mechanical, electrical and environmental engineering; program management; planning; environmental sciences; cultural resources; information services; economics; policy andmanagement analysis; and construction management and support.
Larry D. Walker, President
Fredric S. Berger, Chairman

1888 **Louis Defilippi**
208 Edgewood Lane
Palatine, IL 60067
847-925-8524
E-mail: defilip1@flash.net

We offer consulting services in three broad areas: industrial biotechnology, bioprocessing, and proteomics; environmental and regulatory compliance; biotechnology and applied engineering for the microbiological treatment of hazardouswaste. We are especially valuable when you don't really need a full time in-house expert, but need someone to take an important load off your shoulders, to review your processes and procedures, or just to get things moving faster, on an as-neededbasis.

Dr. Louis DeFilippi, President

1889 **Marc Boogay Consulting Engineer**
253 Main Street
Vista, CA 92084
760-407-4000
Fax: 760-407-4004
E-mail: boogay@sdnc.quik.com
http://www.boogay.com

Marc Boogay and staff have completed more than 600 site assessments. This work has include all varieties of developed and undeveloped properties. Projects have range from Phase I investigations through sampling surveys, remediationdesigns, abatement monitoring, risk assessment, and expert witness testimony. Projects have benn conducted in several states, meeting standards of government agencies as well as many leading/investment institutions.
Marc Boogay, PE, Principal
Todd Jacquay, Soils Engineer

1890 **McVehil-Monnett Associates**
44 Inverness Drive East
Building C
Englewood, CO 80112
303-790-1332
Fax: 303-790-7820
http://www.mcvehil-monnett.com

MMA is a experienced consulting firm of atmospheric scientists, engineers and environmental specialists providing air quality and environmental management system (EMS) services worldwide. Serves the mining, oil and gas, electric powerand manufacturin industries, as well as government agencies and engineering and law firms. Leader in air quality permitting, modeling, monitoring and litigation supoort services as well as environmental management and planning services.

William R Monnett, President
George McVehil, Principal

1891 **Mercury Technology Services**
2633 Viking Way
Richmond, VC V6V-3B6
281-255-3775
Fax: 281-357-0721
E-mail: smw@htech.com
http://www.mercuryts.com

Specialists in solving problems related to mercury pollution and contamination. MTS provides technical services to companies having metals contamination and expert testimony on mercury pollution and remediation.
Lee Varseveld, General Manager & Secretary

1892 **Meteorological Evaluation Services Company**
165 Broadway
Amityville, NY 11701
631-691-3395
Fax: 631-691-3550
http://www.mesamity.com

Consultants in Applied Meteorology, Air Quality and the Environment.

1893 Miceli Kulik Williams and Associates
39 Park Avenue
Rutherford, NJ 07070
201-933-7809
Fax: 201-933-8702
E-mail: info@mkwla.com
http://www.mkwla.com
Offers complete services covering the various aspects of landscape architecture, site planning, and urban design. Present scope of work includes neighborhood rehabilitation, housing and community development, park, recreational andopen space planning, landscape architecture, impact assessment, educational, municipal, commercial and industrial commissions. Project involvement extends throughout the Eastern States.

1894 Michael Baker Corporation
Airside Business Park
100 Airside Drive
Moon Township, PA 15108
412-269-6300
800-553-1153
E-mail: CorpCom@mbakercorp.com
http://www.mbakercorp.com
Michael Baker Corporation provides engineering and operations and maintenance services for its clients' most complex challenges worldwide. The firm's primary practice areas are aviation, environmental, facilities, geospatialinformation technologies, linear utilities, transportation, water/wastewater, and oil & gas. With approximately 4,500 employees in over 400 offices across the U.S. and internationally, Baker is focused on providing services that span the completelife cycle of infrastucture.
David Higie, VP Corporate Communications

1895 Michael Brandman Associates
220 Commerce
Suite 200
Irvine, CA 92602
714-508-4100
888-826 5814
Fax: 714-508-4110
http://www.brandman.com
Michael Brandman Associates is a comprehensive environmental planning services firm specializing in environmental documentation, planning, and natural resources management.
Justin Holt, General Manager
Robert Francisco, President

1896 Micro-Bac
3200 North Interstate Highway 35
Round Rock, TX 78681
512-310-9000
877-559-1800
Fax: 512-310-8800
E-mail: mail@micro-bac.com
http://www.micro-bac.com
Delvelops and manufactures biological products for remediation of contaminated substances; reduction of waste and odor in food processing, agriculture, and sewage; and control of paraffin in oil production.

1897 Midstream Farm
20004 Sterling Creek Lane
Rockville, VA 23146
804-749-8720
804-317 0777
http://www.usaclem.com
Clement Mesavage Jr, Proprietor

1898 Mostardi Platt Environmental
888 Industrial Drive
Elmhurst, IL 60126
630-993-2100
Fax: 630-993-9017
http://www.mostardiplattenv.com
Mostardi Platt Environmental-your full service environmental management partner. Offers innovative solutions and strategies to assist our clients comply with environmental, health and safety regulations and develop environmentalprograms that save long-term costs. We understand our clients need the best possible compliance options. We evaluate a wide variety of technical and economic concerns and work with our clients to establish the best path towards compliance.
Joseph J Macak III, President
Robert A Gere, Engineering Consultant

1899 NTH Consultants
41780 6 Mile Rd.
Northville, MI 48168
248-553-6300
800-736-6842
Fax: 248-324-5179
E-mail: paspalding@nthconsultants.com
http://www.nthconsultants.com
NTH Consultants has provided consulting engineering services to clients throughout the United States since 1968. Headquartered in Farmington Hills, MI, NTH has maintained an office in downtown Detroit since 1980, a regional,full-service office in Exton, PA and offices in Lansing and Grand Rapids, MI since 1992.
Jerome C Neyer, Chairman

1900 National Environment Management Group
PO Box 5131
River Forest, IL 60305
708-771-7350
Fax: 312-733-2478
Environmental consulting.
Jack Hughes, Chairman

1901 National Environmental
1019 W Manchester Boulevard
Suite 102
Inglewood, CA 90301
310-645-4516
800-870-1719
Fax: 310-645-0148
E-mail: customerservice@natlenviro.com
Training school. Training in use of lead, asbestos and hzardous materials.
James McFarland, President
David P Fuller, VP

1902 National Institute for Urban Wildlife
10921 Trotting Ridge Way
Columbia, MD 21044
301-596-3311
Promotes the preservation of wildlife in urban settings, providing support to individuals and organizations invloved in maintaining a place for wildlife in expanding American cities and suburbs. The Institute conducts researchexploring the relationship between humans and wildlife in these habitats, publicizes urban wildlife management methods, and raises public awareness of the value of wildlife in city settings. The Institute also provides consulting services.

1903 National Sanitation Foundation
789 North Dixboro Road
PO Box 130140
Ann Arbor, MI 48113
734-769-8010
800 NSF MARK
Fax: 734-769-0109
E-mail: info@nsf.org
http://www.nsf.org
NSF International, The Public Health and Safety Company, is an independent, not for profit organization providing a wide range of services around the world. For more than 55 years, NSF has been committes to public health, safety andprotection of the environment.
Lori Bestervelt, Sr. Vice President
Kevan P. Lawlor, President/CEO

1904 National Society of Environmental Consultants
303 West Cypress Street
PO Box 12528
San Antonio, TX 78212
210-271-0781
800-486-3676
Fax: 210-225-8450
E-mail: jmd@lincoln-grad.org
http://nsec.lincoln-grad.org/
The mission is to encourage an awareness of environmental risk and the regulations regarding their impact on real property value, to advocate reponsible use and development of real estate resources in harmony with the environment, toelevate the competency of the membership through information and education and to promote the development of ethics and standards of professional practice for the speciality of environmental consultants
Gary T Deane, Executive Director

1905 Natural Resources Consulting Engineers
131 Lincoln Avenue
Suite 300
Fort Collins, CO 80524
970-224-1851
Fax: 970-224-1885
E-mail: office@nrce.com
http://www.nrce.com

Water supply investigations. Native American water rights expert witness testimony.

1906 Network Environmental Systems
1141 Sibley Street
Folsom, CA 95630
800-637-2384
Fax: 916-353-2375
E-mail: office@nesglobal.net
http://www.nesglobal.net
Network Environmental Systems was incorporated in 1988 to privide high quality professional industrial hygiene and environmental management services through customer service excellence.
Jerry Bucklin, President/CEO
Donald Rothenbaum, Senior Vice President

1907 Ninyo and Moore
5710 Ruffin Road
San Diego, CA 92123
858-576-1000
Fax: 858-576-9600
E-mail: nminquiries@ninyoandmoore.com
http://www.ninyoandmoore.com
As a leading geotechnical and environmental scieces engineering and consulting firm, Ninyo & Moore provides specialized services to clients in both public and private sectors.
Avram Ninyo, Principal Engineer

1908 Nordlund and Associates
813 East Ludington Avenue
Ludington, MI 49431
231-843-3485
Fax: 231-843-7676
E-mail: Nordlund@T-one.net
http://www.nordlundandassociates.com
Water systems, wastewater treatment, sanitary landfills and hydrogeological studies.
Holly A. Mulherin, P.E., President
James T. Nordlund, Jr., P.E., Vice President

1909 Normandeau Associates
25 Nashua Road
Bedford, NH 03110
603-472-5191
Fax: 603-472-7052
E-mail: marketing@normandeau.com
http://www.normandeau.com
Normandeau Associates is an employee owned natural resources management consulting and testing services firm that provides: permit assistance, water quality studies, aquatic and terrestrial ecology, environmental impact assessments,property transfer site assessments, wetlands services, contamination studies and biological laboratory services.
Pamela Hall, President
Peter Kinner, Senior VP

1910 Norton Associates
46 Leland Road
Norfolk, MA 02056
508-528-3357
774-244-1248
Fax: 508-758-4759
E-mail: norton@designofmachinery.com
http://www.designofmachinery.com
Professor Norton and his associates have been providing engineering consulting services since 1970. Areas of expertise include: cam design and analysis, linkage design and analysis, street analysis, vibrations in machinery, dynamicsignal analysis, machinery monitoring, and machine dynamic analysis. We also can provide short courses and seminars on site in cam design, dynamic signal analysis and machinery vibrations.
Robert L Norton, President

1911 NuChemCo
5765-F Burke Centre Parkway
#149
Burke, VA 22015
703-548-3200
800-682-4362
Fax: 703-978-0642
E-mail: info@nuchemco.com
http://www.nuchemco.com
Neil B Jurinski
Joseph B Jurinski

1912 OCCU-TECH
4151 N. Mulberry Drive
Suite 275
Kansas City, MO 64116
816-231-5580
800-950-1953
Fax: 816-231-5641
E-mail: service@occutec.com
http://www.occutec.com
OCCU-TECH is a leading safety, health and environmental services company. From OSHA to EPA issues, safety assessments to program development, asbestos inspections to environmental management, our expertise has been relied on for over16 years.

1913 Oak Creek
60 Oak Creek
Buxton, ME 04093
207-776-0861
Fax: 207-929-6374
E-mail: jssmith@oak-creek.net
http://www.oak-creek.net
James S Smith Jr, PhD, President/Toxicologist
Brad House, Senior Scientist

1914 Occupational Health and Safety Management
117 La Farge
Louisville, CO 80027
303-665-8528
Fax: 303-673-0785
Industrial hygiene/safety consulting.
Mary Ann Heaney

1915 Occupational Safety and Health Consultants
12000 6th Street East
Saint Petersburg, FL 33706
727-345-1552
Fax: 727-363-8151
E-mail: oshc@oshc.com
http://www.oshc.com
Air pollution control/industrial hygiene.

1916 Occupational and Environmental Health Consultiing Services
6877 Bonillo Dr
Las Vegas, NV 89103
630-325-2083
Fax: 630-325-2098
E-mail: bobb@safety-epa.com
http://www.safety-epa.com
A full service regulatory, safety, industrial hygiene, and environmental engineering consulting firm. Specialize in assisting all sizes of companies and corporations. Clients include very small businesses up to Fortune 100corporations.
Bob Brandys PhD,MPH,PE,CIH, President

1917 Occusafe
6508 Duffield Drive
Dallas, TX 75248
214-662-6005
E-mail: occusafe@occusafeinc.com
http://www.occusafe.net
OCUSAFE is a full service consulting firm specializing in assistance to management in the areas of occupational safety, industrial hygiene, and environment.

1918 Ocean City Research
50 Tennessee Avenue
Ocean City, NJ 08226
609-399-2417
Fax: 609-399-5233
E-mail: jrepp@corrpro.com
http://www.corrpro.com
Ocean City Research Corporation, incorporated in 1963, is a wholly owned subsidiary of Corrpro Companies, Collectively, the Corrpro affiliated companies represent the largest, independent consulting corrosion engineering organizationin the world.
J Peter Ault, PE

1919 Omega Waste Management
957 Colusa Street
PO Box 495
Corning, CA 96021
530-824-1890
A consulting firm, whose unique and innovative approach to waste removal and recycling has made it one of the largest volume purchasers of waste services in the nation.

1920 Owen Engineering and Management Consultants
5353 West Dartmouth Avenue
Suite 402
Denver, CO 80227
530-677-5286
Fax: 303-969-9394
Water/Wastewater design systems.
Webster J Owen, President

1921 **PACE Analytical Services**
1700 Elm Street
Minneapolis, MN 55414
612-607-1700
Fax: 612-607-6444
E-mail: info@pacelabs.com
http://www.pacelabs.com
Provider of air, water, soil and environmental testing services.
Sarah Cherney, Senior General Manager
Jeff Smith, Senior Account Executive

1922 **PAR Environmental**
1906 21st Street
Sacramento, CA 95811
916-739-8356
Fax: 916-739-0626
E-mail: mlmaniery@aol.com
http://www.paraenvironmental.com
PAR Environmantal Services mission is to provide technical reports on time, within budget, and with meticulous attention to detail.
Mary L Maniery, CEO

1923 **PBR HAWAII**
1001 Bishop Street, ASB Tower
Suite 650
Honolulu, HI 96813
808-521-5631
Fax: 808-523-1402
E-mail: sysadmin@pbrhawaii.com
http://www.pbrhawaii.com
Consulting services in environmental studies,permitting land planning and landscape architecture and graphic design.
Thomas S Witten ASLA, President
Frank Brandt Falsa, Chairman

1924 **PBS Environmental Building Consultants**
4412 SW Corbett Ave
Portland, OR 97239
503-248-1939
888-371-7891
Fax: 866-727-0140
http://www.pbsenv.com
PBS specializes in program development, identification, assessment, testing and corrective action consultation in the areas of: Environmental Engineering, Geotechnical Engineering, Hazardous Materials Management, Industrial HygieneServices, Natural Resources Studies, Training and Laboratory.
Guy Noal, President
Ron Petti, Principal/CEO

1925 **PE LaMoreaux and Associates**
PO Box 2310
Tuscaloosa, AL 35401
205-752-5543
Fax: 205-752-4043
E-mail: info@pela.com
http://www.pela.com
For over three decades, PELA's integration of qualified personnel, up-to-date technology, and sound management has established PELA as an international leader in the environmental consulting field. PELA's expertise in hydrogeology,geotechnical analysis, design and construction management, remediation, computer graphics and models, and permitting can get your project on two feet quicker than you might think.
James Jim La Moreaux, Chairman Of Board
James M Lee, President

1926 **PEER Consultants**
888 17th Street N. W.
Suite 850
Washington, DC 20006
202-478-2060
Fax: 202-478-2050
E-mail: peercpc@peercpc.com
http://www.peercpc.com
For nearly a quarter of a century, PEER Consultants has provided civil, sanitary, and environmental engineering consulting services for public and private sector clients nationwide.
Lilia Abron, President
C. Davis Venn, Vice President/Chief Enginee

1927 **Pacific Soils Engineering**
10653 Progress Way
Cypress, CA 90630
714-220-0770
Fax: 714-220-9589
Services include: Geotechnical Services, Laboratory Testing, Field Observation and Testing, Consultation and Review of Geotechnical Reports.
Daniel Martinez, President

1928 **Parish and Weiner Inc**
297 Knollwood Road
Suite 315
White Plains, NY 10607
914-997-7200
Fax: 914-997-7201
E-mail: pwm@verizon.net
Consulting firm which prepares environmental impact studies, traffic studies, zoning and site plan studies for private developers, non-profit organizations, governmental entities. Also provide expert consultation to lawyers forlitigation and hearings.
Nat Parish, President

1929 **Pavia-Byrne Engineering Corporation**
7443 Obyx St.
New Orleans, LA 70184
504-288-8406
Fax: 504-283-4090
Provides services for environmental control and water treatment including definition, process development, and start up services.
Edgar H Pavia, President

1930 **Perry-Carrington Engineering Corporation**
214 West Second Street
Marshfield, WI 54449
715-384-2133
Fax: 715-384-9797
E-mail: 2perryear@temet.com
http://www.msa-ps.com
Water pollution control systems.
Gill Hnatz, President

1931 **Petra Environmental**
10550 North 6th Avenue
Merrill, WI 54452
715-536-7870
800-458-3772
Fax: 715-536-7890
E-mail: info@petraenvironmental.net
http://www.petraenvironmental.net
PETRA Environmental Consultants, is an environmental engineering firm specializing in environmental compliance, hydrogeological investigations, and environmental assessments.
David Trois, Vice President/ General Mana
Mark Glendenning, CEO

1932 **Phase One**
23282 Mill Creek Drive
Suite 160
Laguna Hills, CA 92653
714-669-8055
800-524-8877
Fax: 714-669-8025
E-mail: info@phasei.com
http://www.phasei.com
A focused environmental consulting practice that specializes in real property assessments for any type of property transfer, leasing development, special uses, and/or financing purposes. Founded in response to the business community'sneed for affordable, standardized and consistently high quality assessment reports that provide recommendations for sound real estate decisions.
Eric D Kieselbach, President/CEO

1933 **Planning Resources**
402 W Liberty Drive
Wheaton, IL 60187
630-668-3788
Fax: 630-668-4125
E-mail: webmaster@planres.com
http://www.planres.com
Land use and environmental planning.
Keven Graham, COO/ Director

1934 **Post, Buckley, Schuh and Jernigan**
2001 Northwest 107th Avenue
Miami, FL 33172
305-592-7275
Fax: 305-599-3809
PBS&J was founded in 1960 by four respected engineers who joined forces to help develop Florida's first planned community. Their tenacity in meeting production schedules, commitment to client service, and ability to provide innovativesolutions to difficult challenges quickly earned our firm a reputation for excellence and laid the foundation for future grouth.
Todd J Kenner, President

1935 **Presnell Associates**
1046 East Chestnut Street
Louisville, KY 40204
502-719-7900
E-mail: presnell@thepoint.net
http://www.qk4.com
The professional practice of Prenell encompasses a variety of services directly related to preserving the environment, including

potable water system planning and design, municipal and industrial wastewater treatment, solid wastemanagement, landfill siting, asbestos management, contamination screening assessments, indoos air quality, and lead paint abatement.
David Smith, President/CEO

1936 Priester and Associates
1345 Garner Lane
Suite 105
Columbia, SC 29210
803-798-4377
877-798-4377
Fax: 803-798-4378
E-mail: priester@conterra.com
Provides personalized environmental services ranging from short-term consulting to extensive remediation and management activities.
LE Priester, President

1937 Process Applications
2627 Redwing Road
Suite 340
Fort Collins, CO 80526
215-493-9361
Fax: 970-223-5786
E-mail: info@palpaperchem.com
http://www.palpaperchem.com
Environmental engineering consultants.
Bob A Hegg, President

1938 Professional Analytical and Consulting Services (PACS)
409 Meade Drive
Coraopolis, PA 15108
724-457-6576
800-367-2587
Fax: 724-457-1214
E-mail: web@pacslabs.com
http://www.pacslabs.com
Training courses and conferences. Provides short courses in spectrocopy, chomatography, quality, safety, environmental, and management. Provides professional manuals and software products. Provides laboratory testing and consultingservices. Company also goes by the following names: Activated Carbon Services, PACS Testing and Consulting, PACS Courses and Conferences. PACS provides: Testing, Training, R & D Conferences, and software for activated carbon users.
Henry G Nowicki PhD/MBA, President
Barbara Sherman, Manager of Operations

1939 Psomas and Associates
1500 Lowa Avenue
Suite 210
Riverside, CA 92507
951-787-8421
E-mail: info@psomas.com
http://www.psomas.com
Psomas is a leading consulting engineering firm offering services in land development, water and natural resources, transportaion, public works, survey and information systems to public and private sector clients.
George Psomas, Chairman

1940 QORE
4201 Pleasant Hill Road Northwest
Suite A
Duluth, GA 30096
770-232-0235
877-767-3462
Fax: 770-232-0238
E-mail: corporate@qore.net
http://www.qore.net
Consultants in property science, in fields of geology, geotechnical and environmental engineering.
Richard D Heckel, PE, President
Ed Heustess, Chief Financial Officer

1941 RDG Geoscience and Engineering
10360 Sapp Brothers Drive
Omaha, NE 68138
402-894-2678
888-260-0893
Fax: 402-894-9043
E-mail: info@rdgge.com
http://www.rdgge.com
Is an earth science and engineering consulting firm that has completed over 1200 projects throughout the mid-west and mountain west of US.
Jon Gross, President
Robert Kalinski, Vice President

1942 RGA Environmental
1466 66th Street
Emeryville, CA 94608
510-547-7771
800-776-5696
Fax: 510-547-1983
E-mail: rga@rgaenv.com
http://www.rgaenv.com
Founded in 1985, RGA Environmental is a specialty consultant in the environmental sciences. Our mission is to provide high-quality environmental engineering, health & safety consulting services to meet the special needs of our clients.
Steven C Rosas, COO, Director of Business

1943 RMT
1212 Deming Way
Suite 200
Madison, WI 53717
608-831-4444
800-283-3443
Fax: 608-831-3334
E-mail: info@rmtinc.com
http://www.rmtinc.com
Serves industrial compaines throughout the world who value environmental and engineering solutions that improve productivity and profitability. RMT's diversified staff of over 550 engineers, scientists and technicians takesresponsibility for managing environmental issues so clients can concentrate on their core business.
Paul M. Daily, CEO
John Kennedy, President

1944 RMT Inc.
1212 Deming Way
Suite 200
Madison, WI 53717
608-831-4444
800-283-3443
Fax: 608-831-3334
E-mail: info@rmtinc.com
http://www.rmtinc.com
RMT delivers environmental engineering health and safety and construction solutions that help industrial companies solve complex problems while improving their bottom line.
Paul M. Daily, CEO
John Kennedy, President

1945 Raterman Group
9000 Crow Canyon Road
Suite 364
Danville, CA 94506
866-545-0111
Fax: 925-555-1233
E-mail: susan@ratermangroup.com
http://www.ratermangroup.com
Industrial hygiene and environmental assessments.
Susan M Raterman, President

1946 Reclamation Services Unlimited
701 Temple Street
Central City, KY 42330
270-754-3976
Fax: 270-754-4374
Environmental consulting services.
Sue Poole Cardwell, President

1947 Redniss and Mead
22 1st Street
Stamford, CT 06905
203-327-0500
800-404-2060
Fax: 203-357-1118
E-mail: a.mead@rednissmead.com
http://www.rednissmead.com
Redniss & Mead, Inc. provides land surveying, civil engineering and land planning services.
Aubrey E Mead, Jr., PE, VP
Raymond L Redniss, PLS, Senior Vice President

1948 Refuse Management Systems
99 Tulip Avenue
#303
Floral Park, NY 11001
516-354-1212
800-346-5926
Fax: 516-354-2434
E-mail: enviroeq@ix.netcom.com
Environmental consultants.
Harvey Podolsky, President

1949 Regional Services Corporation
3200 Sycamore Court
Suite 2B
Columbus, IN 47203
812-372-9511
Fax: 812-372-9520
Solid waste disposal.
Mark Richards, President

1950 **Regulatory Management**
6190 Lehman Drive
Suite 106
Colorado Springs, CO 80918
719-531-6883
Fax: 719-599-4410
E-mail: maxlab@usa.net
Environmental consulting group.
James T Egan, President

1951 **Resource Applications**
9291 Old Keene Mill Road
Burke, VA 22015
703-644-0401
Fax: 703-644-0404
Hazardous waste management, pollution prevention/site remediation.
Damons G Barber, President & CEO

1952 **Resource Concepts**
340 North Minnesota Street
Carson City, NV 89703
775-883-1600
Fax: 775-883-1656
E-mail: john@rci-nv.com
http://www.rci-nv.com
RCI has years of experience and demonstrated accomplisjment working with environmentally sensitive projects. Combining technical abilities and excellent working relationships with regulatory agencies results in highly effective projectplanning and permitting services.
Bruce R Scott, Principal
John McLain, Principal

1953 **Resource Decisions**
931 Diamond Street
San Francisco, CA 94114
415-282-5330
http://www.resourcedecisions.net
Assisting clients to evaluate trade-offs which foster the wise allocation of resources is primary mission of Resource Decisions. To accomplish this mission we apply a wide range of economic and decision-making tools.
Marvin Feldman, PhD, Principal

1954 **Resource Management**
625 Chapin Road
Chapin, SC 29036
803-345-0200
Fax: 803-345-6520
E-mail: resourc9@winusa.com
Hazardous waste management.
Don Dicus, President

1955 **Resource Technology Corporation (RTC)**
2931 Soldier Springs Road
PO Box 1346
Laramie, WY 82070
307-742-5452
800-576-5690
Fax: 307-745-7936
E-mail: rtc@sial.com
http://www.rt-corp.com
They offer Laboratory Proficiency Testing for drinking water, waste water and USEPA RCCRA Program. Certified analytical standards and Certified Reference Materials.

1956 **Respec Engineering**
3824 Jet Drive
Rapid City, SD 57703
605-394-6400
877-737-7321
http://www.respec.com
Since our founding in 1969, RESPEC has remained committed to its original purpose of providing clients with high-quality technical and advisory services.

1957 **Reston Consulting Group (RCG)**
462 Herndon Parkway
Suite 203
Herndon, VA 20170
703-834-1155
Fax: 703-834-3086
E-mail: info@rcg.com
http://www.rcg.com
Rosemarie Franz, Director

1958 **Rich Tech**
2410 Devonshire Drive
Rockford, IL 61107
815-229-1122
Fax: 815-229-1525
Water pollution control.
Gail Rivitts, President
Rich Rivitts, Vice President

1959 **Rizzo Associates**
16 Serra Street
Corte Madera, CA 94925
415-290-1670
Fax: 866-220-6889
http://www.rizzoassociates.com
A leading engineering, transportation, and environmental engineering firm. We work with you throughout the development process to reslove the challenges that arise in planning, permitting, design, and construction phases of complexprojects.
James Rizzo, Founder

1960 **Robert B Balter Company**
18 Music Fair Road
Owings Mills, MD 21117
410-363-1555
Fax: 410-363-8073
E-mail: mknowles@balterco.com
http://www.balterco.com
Environmental consultation.
Michael F. Knowles, Marketing Director

1961 **Rockwood Environmental Services Corporation**
50 Kearney Road
Needham, MA 02494
781-449-8740
Fax: 781-449-8741
E-mail: bwhite@rockwood-enviro.com
http://www.rockwood-enviro.com
Rockwood specializes in solving the problems of hazardous waste management and disposal for New England generators. By shipping wastes directly to ultimate disposal sites on a regular basis, Rockwood reduces current disposal costs andreduces long-term liability exposure.
William A White III, President

1962 **Rodriguez, Villacorta and Weiss**
8765 Springs Cypress
Suite L#177
Spring, TX 77379
281-379-4005
E-mail: mbrooks@rvw.net
http://rvw.net/
Our mission is to provide cost-effective and thorough work product for claims services and loss control. Maximum integration of all in-house and affiliated expertise will guarantee prompt ser vice, nurturing strong client relationshipsbased on dependability, trust and competence.
Richard Rodriguez, Principal Associate

1963 **Roux Associates**
209 Shafter Street
Islandia, NY 11749
631-232-2600
800-322-Roux
Fax: 631-232-9898
E-mail: sales@rouxinc.com
http://www.rouxinc.com
Environmental Consulting and Management.
Steve Sadiker, Vice President

1964 **SLC Consultants/Constructors**
295 Mill Street
Lockport, NY 14094
716-433-0776
800-932-0157
Fax: 716-433-0802

1965 **Safina**
953 N Plum Grove Road
Suite A-1
Schaumburg, IL 60173
847-605-8319
Fax: 847-956-8619
Environmental due diligence.
Sanjiv Pillai, General Manager

1966 **Schneider Instrument Company**
8115 Camargo Road
Cincinnati, OH 45243
513-561-6803
Fax: 513-527-4375
E-mail: schneidxcompany@aol.com
G L Schneider, Vice President

1967 **Schoell and Madson**
14800 28th Ave N
Suite 140
Minneapolis, MN 55447
763-746-1600
Fax: 763-746-1699
E-mail: mail@schoellmadson.com
http://www.schoellmadson.com
We are dedicated to creatively serving our clients by meeting or exceeding their needs in a responsive and cost-effective manner

while providing an interesting and rewarding experience for our employees.

1968 SciComm
7735 Old Georgetown Road
12th Floor
Bethesda, MD 20814
301-652-1900
E-mail: info@scicomm.com
http://www.scicomm.com
A professional services firm specializing in communications, engineering, environmental, and information management services. Organized to carry out the interest, expertise, and vision of co-founder Laura Chen and Dan Lewis.
Laura Chen, President

1969 SevernTrent Laboratories
4101 Shuffel Drive NW
North Canton, OH 44720
866-785-5227
E-mail: webmaster@testamericainc.com
http://www.stl-inc.com
The two compaines merged as Wadsworth/Alert Laboratories in early 1980's and the core business focused on environmental testing, with a specialization in on-site and emergency response projects. Mobile Labs were placed as far north asMichigan, and south to Florida, east to New York, and west to Missouri.
James Hyman, CEO

1970 Shaw Environmental
2103 Research Forest Drive
The Woodland, TX 77380
832-513-1000
E-mail: general@shawgrp.com
http://www.shawgrp.com
Hazardous waste remediation.
Ron Prann, Division Manager

1971 Shell Engineering and Associates
2403 West Ash Street
Columbia, MO 65203
573-445-0106
Fax: 573-445-0137
E-mail: Charles@shellengr.com
http://www.shellengr.com
Shell Engineering provides services firm specializing in communications, engineering, environmental monitoring and engineering. Shell Engineering has completed hundreds of projects since 1975 throughout the United States, Canada.Centeral America, South America, Asia and Africa.
Harvey D Shell, CEO/Chairman
Charles A Shell, President

1972 Sierra Geological and Environmental Consultants
91 South Main Street
PO Box 136
Kent City, MI 49330
800-769-7437
Fax: 616-678-5149
E-mail: info@sierraconsultants.net
http://www.sierraconsultants.net
A full service environmental consulting firm providing assassment, investigation, and cleanup services throughout Michigan and the Great Lakes States.

1973 Slakey and Associates
375 Village Square
PO Box 944
Orinda, CA 94563
925-254-4164
Fax: 925-254-0679
Consulting, civil, mechanical, environmental engineers with 40 years experience in indoor air quality, air pollution control. Design of systems and equipment for collection abatement of fugitive and source missions of dusts, odor andfumes. Industrial clients only.
Philip Slakey, President

1974 Slosky & Company
303 E 17th Avenue
Suite 1080
Denver, CO 80203
303-825-1911
Fax: 303-892-3882
E-mail: Lslosky@slosky.com
http://www.slosky.com
Full service environmental consulting firm.
Leonard Slosky, President

1975 Snyder Research Company
330Twin Dolphin Drive
Suite # 101
Redwood City, CA 94065
408-414-5950
Fax: 408-275-6219
E-mail: info@sdforum.org
http://www.sdforum.org

1976 Staunton-Chow Engineers
5 Pen Plaza,
23rd Floor
New York, NY 10001
212-683-8865
Fax: 212-695-6307
http://www.stauntonchow.com
Known widely as small premiere multidisciplined engineering/architectural consulting firm providing professional services for new construction, repair, alterations, and maintenance for nearly 50 years.
Kin Chow, President

1977 Strata Environmental Services
110 Perimeter Park
Suite E
Knoxville, TN 37922
865-539-2077
Fax: 865-539-3970
E-mail: info@strataenv.com
http://www.strataenv.com
Founded to provide consulting services in geosciences, engineering, air quality, water quality, regulatory compliance, and environmental due diligence.
Charles W. Ferst, CEO

1978 TECHRAD Environmental Services
4619 North Santa Fe Avenue
Oklahoma City, OK 73118
405-528-7016
800-375-7016
Fax: 405-528-3346
Analytical laboratory, environmental site assessments, underground storage tank management and remediation, industrial hygiene, stormwater and hazardous waste management, asbestos consulting and analysis and regulatory compliance.
Edward M Wall, President/CEO

1979 THP
100 E Eighth Street
Cincinnati, OH 45202
533-241-3222
Fax: 513-241-2981
http://www.thpltd.com
Engineering traffic and engineering planning consulting firm.
E James Miller, President

1980 Technos
10430 Northwest 31st Terrace
Miami, FL 33172
305-718-9594
Fax: 305-718-9621
E-mail: info@technos-inc.com
http://www.technos-inc.com
A geologic and geophysical consulting firm specializing in subsurface site characterization for geotechnical, environmental, and groundwater projects.
Lynn Yuhr, President
Ron Kaufmann, VP

1981 Terryn Barill
301 N Harrison
Suite 484
Princeton, NJ 08540
800-718-6690
Fax: 609-243-8703
E-mail: terryn1@mail.com
http://www.terryn.com
Audits/assessments, training, implementation and facilitation.

1982 Tetra Tech
3475 East Foothill Boulevard
Pasadena, CA 91107
626-351-4664
Fax: 626-351-5291
E-mail: info@tetratech.com
http://www.tetratech.com
We provide comprehensive resource management , infraestructure and communications services, including, research and development, applied science, management consulting, engineering and architectural design, construction management, andoperation and maintenance.
Dan L. Batrack, President/CEO
Steven M. Burdick, CFO, Tresurer & Executive VP

1983 **Theil Consulting**
1136 South Fort Thomas Avenue 859-781-2651
Fort Thomas, KY 41075 Fax: 859-781-2356
E-mail: larry@theilair.com
http://www.theilair.com

Experts in industrial process exhausts—especially submicron particles created by heat or other high energy in a process.
Greg Theil, Technical Director
Larry Olson, Sales Manager

1984 **Titan Corp. Ship and Aviation Engineering Group**
11955 Freedom Drive 703-434-4000
Reston, VA 20190 Fax: 703-434-5075
E-mail: corpcomm@titan.com
http://www.titan.com

TITAN provides a wide range of engineering and environmental services. Experience includes ISO 14001 and ISO 9000 series and its implementation, pollution prevention planning, hazardous materials/waste management, database management.
Gene W Ray, Chairman of the Board
Lawrence J Delaney, VP of Operations

1985 **Tradet Laboratories**
8 Industrial Park Drive 304-233-9060
Wheeling, WV 26003 Fax: 304-233-9063
E-mail: info@tra-det.com
http://www.tra-det.com

Coal, analytical and environmental services.
G William Kald, President

1986 **Transviron**
1624 York Road 410-321-6961
Lutherville, MD 21093 Fax: 410-494-9321

1987 **Trinity Consultants**
12770 Merit Drive 972-661-8100
Suite 900 800-229-6655
Dallas, TX 75251 Fax: 972-385-9203
E-mail: information@trinityconsultants.com
http://www.trinityconsultants.com

An environmental consulting company that assists industrial facilities with issues related to regulatory compliance and environmental management. Founded in 1974, this nationwide firm has particular expertise in air quality issues. Trinity also sells environmental software and professional education. T3, a Trinity Consultants Company, provides EH&S management information systems (EMIS) implementation and integration services.

Jay Hofmann, President/CEO
Jack McEnaney, CFO

1988 **Troppe Environmental Consulting**
24 N. High Street 330-375-1900
Akron, OH 44308 Fax: 330-375-1904

Provides level I and level II assessments, water and oil testing, and amtm standards.
Fred Troppe, President

1989 **Versar**
6850 Versar Center 703-750-3000
Springfield, VA 22151 800-283-7727
Fax: 703-642-6807
E-mail: info@versar.com
http://www.versar.com

Versar is a public-held, international professional services firm that applies technology, science, and management skills to enhance its customers' performance.
Anthony L Otten, CEO

1990 **Water and Air Research**
6821 SW Archer Road 352-372-1500
Gainesville, FL 32608 800-242-4927
Fax: 352-378-1500
E-mail: services@waterandair.com
http://www.waterandair.com

Mission is to be an international environmental consulting firm that achieves extraordinary results by partnering with clients that to make informed and responsible decisions regarding the environment.

William C Zegel, President
William Kinser, Director/Manager

1991 **Weavertown Group Optimal Technologies**
2 Dorrington Road 724-746-4850
Carnegie, PA 15106 800-746-4850
Fax: 724-746-9024
E-mail: optimal@optimaltech.com
http://www.weavertown.com

We are an environmental engineering and consulting firm.
Dawn Fuchs, President

1992 **Wenck Associates**
1800 Pioneer Creek Center 763-479-4200
PO Box 249 800-472-2232
Maple Plain, MN 55359 Fax: 763-479-4242
E-mail: wenckmp@wenck.com
http://www.wenck.com

Our mission is to provide our customers strategic advice and technical excellence.

1993 **Weston Solutions, Inc**
1400 Weston Way 610-701-3000
Box 2653 800-7WE-STON
West Chester, PA 19380 Fax: 610-701-3186
E-mail: info@westonsolutions.com
http://www.westonsolutions.com

Weston is a leading infrastructure redevelopment services firm delivering integrated environmental engineering solutions to industry and government worldwide. With an emphasis on creating lasting economic value for its clients, thecompany provides services in site remediation, redevelopment, infrastructure operations and knowledge management.
George Mackenzie, Chairman
William L. Robertson, CEO/President

1994 **Zapata Engineering, Blackhawk Division**
6302 Fairview Road 704-358-8240
Suite 600 888 529 7213
Charlotte, NC 28210 Fax: 704-358-8342
E-mail: zapata@zapatainc.com
http://www.blackhawkgeo.com

High quality geophysical contracting and consulting services over the full spectrum of geophysical technologies, and to apply the geophysical technologies to several cross-cutting areas of engineering and exploration.
Manuel L. Zapata, P.E., President

Environmental Health

Associations

1995 **Acadia Environmental Society**
626 Old Students' Union Building
Wolfville, Nova Scotia B4P-2R6
902-585-2149
Fax: 902-542-3901
E-mail: aes@acadiau.ca

Provides resources on environmental issues. The Society's goal is to encourage and help the Acadia community to adopt and maintain environmentally sound and sustainable practices.
Hillary Barter, Coordinator

1996 **Acid Rain Foundation**
1410 Varsity Drive
Raleigh, NC 27606
919-828-9443
Fax: 919-515-3593
Dr. Harriett S Stubbs, Executive Director

1997 **Action on Smoking and Health**
701 4th St. NW
Washington, DC 20001
202-659-4310
Fax: 202-289-7166
E-mail: info@ash.org
http://ash.org

Organized to use the power of the law to protect the rights of nonsmokers. Emphasis is placed on legal efforts to protect nonsmokers and to get courts to support the rights of nonsmokers. Also conducts educational and awarenesscampaigns regarding the problem of smoking and the rights of nonsmokers.
Laurent Huber, Executive Director

1998 **Advanced Foods & Materials Network**
150 Research Lane
Suite 310
Guelph ON N1G-4T2
519-822-6253
Fax: 519-824-8453
E-mail: info@afmcanada.ca
http://www.afmnet.ca

Canada's front line of research and development in the area of advanced foods and bio-materials, including new, low-cost antibiotics, improved frozen food quality, and fast healing wound dressings.
Dr. Larry Milligan, Chairman
Rickey Yada, Scientific Director

1999 **Agency for Toxic Substances and Disease Registry**
4770 Buford Highway NE
Atlanta, GA 30341
800-232-4636
Fax: 888-232-6348
E-mail: cdcinfo@cdc.gov
http://www.atsdr.cdc.gov

The mission of the agency is to prevent exposure and adverse human health effects and diminished quality of life associated with exposure to hazardous substances from waste sites, unplanned releases, and other sources of pollutionpresent in the enviroment. ATSDR is an operating division of the US Department of Health and Human Services. It divids its activities between those related to a particular site and those related to a specific hazardous substance.
Julie L. Gerberding, MD, MPH, Administrator
Howard Frumkin, MD, DrPH, Director

2000 **Air and Waste Management Association**
1 Gateway Center, 3rd Floor
420 Fort Duquesne
Pittsburgh, PA 15222
412-232-3444
800-270-3444
Fax: 412-232-3450
E-mail: info@awma.org
http://www.awma.org

The Air & Waste Management Association (A&WMA) is a nonprofit, nonpartisan professional organization that provides training, information, and networking opportunities to thousands of environmental professionals in 65 countries.
Sara Head, President
Jim Powell, Executive Director

2001 **Alliance for Acid Rain Control and Energy Policy**
444 N Capitol Street
Suite 602
Washington, DC 20001
202-624-5475
Fax: 202-508-3829

2002 **Alternatives for Community and Environment**
2181 Washington Street
Suite 301
Roxbury, MA 02119
617-442-3343
Fax: 617-442-2425
E-mail: info@ace-ej.org
http://www.ace-ej.org

ACE is a community-based, nonprofit, environmental justice, law and education center. ACE works in partnership with community groups from low income communities and communities of color to help them address their environmental andenvironmental heath issues by providing free legal, educational and organizing services.
Kalila Barnett, Executive Director
Eugene B Benson, Program Director

2003 **American Academy of Environmental Medicine**
6505 E. Central Avenue
#296
Wichita, KS 67206
316-684-5500
Fax: 316-684-5709
E-mail: administrator@aaemonline.org
http://www.aaem.com

The Academy is interested in expanding the knowledge of interactions between human individuals and their environment, as these may be demonstrated to be reflected in their total health. The Academy is comprised primarily of medicalprofessionals who sponsor publications, seminars and courses. A newsletter and journal are among the organization's publications.
Amy L. Dean, President
De Rodgers Fox, Executive Director

2004 **American Association for the Support of Ecological Initiatives**
150 Coleman Road
Middletown, CT 06457
860-346-2967
Fax: 860-347-8459
E-mail: Wwasch@wesleyan.edu
http://http://www.wesleyan.edu/aasei

AASEI is a US 501 nonprofit organization which suports international environmental initiatives in Russian Nature Reserves. In cooperation sith Russia and foreign scientists, students, and universities, AASEI organizes scientificresearch projects, academic internships, work camps, environmental exchanges, and eco-tourism. Our aim is to provide practical support to Russina Reserves, expand opportunities for international scientific research, and promote internationalunderstanding.
Brendan Sweeney, President/Founder
Stephanie Hitztaler, Executive Director

2005 **American Association of Poison Control Centers**
515 King Street
Suite 510
Alexandria, VA 22314
703-894-1858
800-222-1222
Fax: 703-683-2812
E-mail: info@aapcc.org
http://www.aapcc.org

A non-profit national organization that represents the poison control centers of the United States and the interests of poison prevention and treatment of poisoning.

Debbie Carr, M Ed., Executive Director

2006 **American Board of Environmental Medicine**
65 Wehrle Drive
Buffalo, NY 14225
716-833-2213
Fax: 716-833-2244
http://www.americanboardofenvironmentalmedicine.org

To establish and maintain the educational and testing criteria for board certification to ensure optimal standard and quality of the environmental physician.
Dr. Phil Ranhein, President

2007 **American Board of Industrial Hygiene**
6015 W St Joseph Highway
Suite 102
Lansing, MI 48917
517-321-2638
Fax: 517-321-4624
E-mail: abih@abih.org
http://www.abih.org

Premier organization for certifying professionals in the practice of industrial hygiene. Responsible for ensuring high-quality cer-

tification application and examination processes, certifcation maintenance and ethics governance andenforcement.
Lynn O'Donnell, CIH, Executive Director
Mark Finn, Chairman

2008 American Cancer Society
PO Box 22718
Oklahoma, OK 73123
800-227-2345
http://www.cancer.org
The American Cancer Society is the nationwide, community-based, voluntary health organization dedicated to eliminating cancer as a major health problem by preventing cancer, saving lives, and diminishing suffering from cancer throughresearch, education, advocacy and service.
John R Seffrin PhD, CEO

2009 American College of Occupational and Environmental Medicine
25 NW Point Blvd
Suite 700
Elk Grove Village, IL 60007
847-818-1800
Fax: 847-818-9266
E-mail: mdreger@acoem.org
http://www.acoem.org
Made up of physicians in industry, government, academia, private practice and the military, who promote the health of workers through preventive medicine, clinical care, research and education.
Julie Hofman, Director of Finance
Barry S. Eisenberg, Executive Director

2010 American Conference of Governmental Industrial Hygienists
1330 Kemper Meadow Drive
Cincinnati, OH 45240
513-742-6163
Fax: 513-742-3355
E-mail: mail@acgih.org
http://www.acgih.org
The American Conference of Governmental Industrial Hygeienists (ACGIH) is a member-based organization and community of professionals that advances worker health and sattey through education and the development and dissemination ofscientific and technical knowledge.
90 pages Magazine
Robert F. Herrick, Chair
A. Anthony Rizzuto, Executive Director

2011 American Council on Science and Health
1995 Broadway
Suite 202
New York, NY 10023
212-362-7044
866-905-2694
Fax: 212-362-4919
E-mail: acsh@acsh.org
http://www.acsh.org
A consumer education consortium concerned with issues related to food, nutrition, chemicals, pharmaceuticals, lifestyle, the environment and health.
Elizabeth M Whelan, President
Gilbert Ross MD, Medical/Executive Director

2012 American Indian Environmental Office
1200 Pennsylvania Avenue NW
Washington, DC 20460
202-564-0303
Fax: 202-564-0298
E-mail: tribal.portal@epa.gov.
http://www.epa.gov/indian
Coordinates the US environmental Protection Agency-wide effort to strengthen public health and environmental protection in Indian Country, with a special emphasis on building Tribal capacity to administer their own environmentalprograms.
Joann Chase, Director

2013 American Industrial Hygiene Association
3141 Fairview Park Dr.
Suite 777
Falls Church, VA 22042
703-849-8888
Fax: 703-207-3561
E-mail: infonet@aiha.org
http://www.aiha.org
To promote the highest quality of occupational and environmental health and safety within the workplace and the community through advocacy and the provision of services and tools to enhance the professional practice of our members.
Peter J O'Neil, Executive Director
Barbara J. Dawson, President

2014 American Institute of Biological Sciences
1900Campus Commons Drive
Suite 200
Reston, VA 20191
703-674-2500
Fax: 703-674-2509
E-mail: rogrady@aibs.org
http://www.aibs.org
AIBS facilities communication and interactions among biologists, biological societies, and biological disciplines in order to serve and advance the interests of organismal and integrative biology in the broader scientific community andother components of society on issues related to research, education, and public policy.
Dr. Richard O'Grady, Executive Director
Sheri Potter, Manager

2015 American Lung Association
61 Broadway
6th Floor
New York, NY 10006
212-315-8700
http://www.lungusa.org
The American Lung Association has been fighting lung disease in all its forms with emphasis on environmental health, asthma, and tobacco control. The work continues as they strive to make breathing easier for everyone througheducation, community service, advocacy and research programs.
Stephen J Nolasn Esq, President

2016 American Medical Association
515 N State Street
Chicago, IL 60654
312-464-5000
800-621-8335
Fax: 312-464-4184
http://www.ama-assn.org
Mission: To promote the art and science of medicine and the betterment of public health.
Jmaes L. Madara, CEO/Executive Vice President

2017 American Public Health Association
800 I Street NW
Washington, DC 20001
202-777-2742
Fax: 202-777-2534
E-mail: comments@apha.org
http://www.apha.org
Aims to protect all Americans and their communities from preventable, serious health threats and strives to assure community-based health promotion and disease prevention activities and preventive health services are universallyaccessible in the United States.
Georges C Benjamin, Executive Director
Celeste Barnes, Finance & System Controller

2018 American Society for Microbiology
1752 N Street NW
Washington, DC 20036
202-737-3600
Fax: 202-942-9333
E-mail: service@asmusa.org
http://www.asm.org
A scientific society of individuals interested inthe microbiological sciences. The mission is to advance microbiological sciences through the pursuit of scientific knowledge and dissemination of the results of fundamental and appliedresearch.
43,000 Members
Jeffery F. Miller, President
Joseph M. Campos, Secretary

2019 American Society of Safety Engineers
1800 East Oakton Street
Des Plaines, IL 60018
847-699-2929
Fax: 847-768-3434
E-mail: customerservice@asse.org
http://www.asse.org
ASSE is a global association providing professional development and representation for those engaged in the practice of safety, health and environmental issues. Provides services to the private and public sectors to protect people,property and the environment.
James R. Thornton, Chairman
David L. Heidorn, Manager of Gov't Affairs

2020 **Appalachian States Low-Level Radioactive Waste Commission**
Pennsylvania DEP/BRP
400 Market Street, 13th Floor
Harrisburg, PA 17101
717-783-2300
E-mail: kmcginty@state.pa.us
http://www.dep.state.pa.us

The commission was ratified by Maryland, Delaware, Pennsylvania and West Virginia to assure intertstate cooperation for the proper packaging and transportation of low-level radioactive waste. Pennsylvania is the host state and handlesthe administrative duties of the commission at this time.

Tom Corbett, Governor
Chris Abruzzo, Acting Secretary

2021 **Asbestos Information Association of North America**
PO Box 2227
Arlington, VA 22202
703-560-2980
Fax: 703-560-2981
E-mail: aiabjpigg@aol.com

The Asbestos Information Association/North America was founded in 1970 to represent the interest of the asbestos industry and to collect and disseminate information about asbestos and asbestos products, with emphasis on safety, health,and environmental issues. The Association appears before Federal regulatory bodies and works with Government agencies to develop and implement standards for worker protection.

Bob Pigg, President

2022 **Asian Pacific Environmental Network**
310 8th Street
Suite 309
Oakland, CA 94607
510-834-8920
Fax: 510-834-8926
E-mail: info@apen4ej.org
http://www.apen4ej.org

The Asian Pacific Environmental Network (APEN) empowers low-income Asian Pacific Islander (API) communities to take action on environmental and social justice issues. APEN builds organizations in dis-empowered API communities todevelop lasting capacity of the community to achieve solutions to problems affecting people's lives.

Roger Kim, Executive Director
Rachel Shigekane, Board Secretary

2023 **Association for Environmental Health and Sciences**
150 Fearing Street
Amherst, MA 01002
413-549-5170
Fax: 413-549-0579
http://www.aehs.com

The Association for Environmental Health and Sciences (AEHS) was created to facilitate communication and foster cooperation among professionals concerned with the challenge of soil protection and cleanup.

Paul Kostecki, Executive Director
Marc A Nascarella, Managing Ed/Conference Coor

2024 **Association of American Pesticide Control Officials**
PO Box 466
Milford, DE 19963
302-422-8152
Fax: 302-422-2435
E-mail: Info@aapco.org
http://www.aapco.org

Organization formed to provide a rational forum and representation for state pesticide control officials in the development, implementation, and communication of parties and programs related to the sale, transport, application anddisposal of pesticide.

Jeff Comstock, President
Tim Drake, President-Elect

2025 **Association of Battery Recyclers**
PO Box 290286
Tampa, FL 33687
813-626-6151
Fax: 813-622-8388
E-mail: info@batteryrecyclers.com
http://www.batteryrecyclers.com

The Association of Battery Recyclers is a non-profit trade association. ABR strives to keep its members abreast on environmental and health matters and also provides a means for communication with government officials on issuesaffecting the lead recycling industry.

Joyce Morales, Contact

2026 **Association of State and Territorial Health Officials**
2231 Crystal Drive
Suite 450
Arlington, VA 22202
202-371-9090
Fax: 571-527-3189
E-mail: pjarris@astho.org
http://www.astho.org

Dedicated to formulating and influencing sound public health policy, and to assuring excellence in state-based public health practice.

Paul E Jarris MD, Executive Director
Lisa Junker, Communication Director

2027 **Asthma and Allergy Foundation of America**
8201 Corporate Drive
Suite 1000
Landover, MD 20785
202-466-7643
800-727-8462
Fax: 202-466-8940
E-mail: info@aafa.org
http://www.aafa.org

AAFA provides practical information, community based services and support through a national network of chapters and support groups. AAFA develops health education, organizes state and national advocacy efforts and funds research tofind better treatments and cures.

William Mclin, M. Ed., President
Jacqui Vok, Programs & Services Director

2028 **Beyond Pesticides**
701 E Street SE
Suite 200
Washington, DC 20003
202-543-5450
Fax: 202-543-4791
E-mail: info@beyondpesticides.org
http://www.beyondpesticides.org

Beyond Pesticides works with allies in protecting public health and the environment to lead the transition to a world free of toxic pesticides.

Routt Reigart, M.D., President
Jay Feldman, Executive Director

2029 **Bio Integral Resource Center**
PO Box 7414
Berkeley, CA 94707
510-524-2567
Fax: 510-524-1758
E-mail: birc@igc.org
http://www.birc.org

The goal of the Bio Integral Resources Center is to reduce pesticide use by educating the public about effective, less toxic alternatives for pest problems.

Dr. William Quarles, Executive Director

2030 **Bison World**
National Bison Association
8690 Wolff Ct
Suite 200
Westminster, CO 80031
303-292-2833
Fax: 303-845-9081
E-mail: info@bisoncentral.com
http://www.bisoncentral.com

An organization of bison producers dedicated to awareness of the healthy properties of bison meat and bison production.

Dave Carter, Executive Director

2031 **Center for Health, Environment and Justice Library**
150 S Washington Street, Ste 300
PO Box 6806
Falls Church, VA 22040-6806
703-237-2249
Fax: 703-237-8389
E-mail: chej@chej.org
http://www.chej.org

The Center for Health, Environment and Justice works to build healthy communities, with social justice, economic well-being, and democratic governance. We believe this can happen when individuals from communities have the power to playan integral role in promoting human health and environmental integrity. Our role is to provide the tools to build strong, healthy communities where people can live, work, learn, play and pray.

Lois Marie Gibbs, Executive Director

2032 **Center for Science in the Public Interest**
1220 L St. N. W.
Suite 300
Washington, DC 20005
202-332-9110
Fax: 202-265-4954
E-mail: cspi@cspinet.org
http://www.cspinet.org

Mission: To provide useful, objective information to the public and policymakers and to conduct research on food, alcohol,

health, the environment, and other issues related to science and technology; to represent the citizen'sinterests before regulatory, judicial and legislative bodies on food, alcohol, health, the environment, and other issues; and to ensure that science and technology are used for the public good and to encourage scientists to engage in public-interestactivities.
Michael F. Jacobson, Executive Director
Don Allen, Director of Finance

2033 Center for the Evaluation of Risks to Human Reproduction
110 Maryland Avenue NE
Suite 402
Washington, DC 20002
202-543-4033
Fax: 202-543-8797
E-mail: cehn@cehn.org
http://http://cerhr.niehs.nih.gov

The Center's mission includes the following: to provide timely and unbiased, scientifically sound assessments of reproductive health hazards associated with human exposure to naturally occurring and man-made chemicals; to make theseassessments readily available to the public, to state and federal agencies and to the scientific community; and to build an electronic resource for providing, or directing one to, information of public interest concerning human reproductive health.
Dr. Michael D Shelby

2034 Centers for Disease Control & Prevention
National Center for Environmental Health
1600 Clifton Road
Atlanta, GA 30333
800-232-4636
Fax: 800-232-6348
http://www.cdc.gov/nceh

To provide national leadership, through science and service, to promote health and quality of life by preventing and controlling disease and death resulting from interactions between people and their environment.
Dr. Tom Frieden, Director

2035 Chemical Injury Information Network
PO Box 301
White Sulphur Springs, MT 59645
406-547-2255
Fax: 406-547-2455
E-mail: chemicalinjury@ciin.org
http://www.ciin.org

Nonprofit tax-exempt support and advocacy organization run by the chemically injured for the benefit of the chemically injured. CIIN serves an international membership, and focuses primarily on eductaion, credible multiple sensitivityresearch and the empowerment of the chemically injured.

Cinthia Wilson, Executive Director
Al Gore, Vice President

2036 Chlorine Institute
1300 Wilson Boulevard
Suite 525
Arlington, VA 22209
703-894-4140
Fax: 703-894-4130
http://www.chlorineinstitute.org

Exists to support the chlor-alkali industry and serve the public by fostering continuous improvements to safety and the protection of human health and the environment connected with the production, distribution and use of chlorine,sodium and potassium hydoroxides, and sodium hypochlorite; and the distribution and use of hydrogen chloride.

Robyn Kinsley, Director
Anna Belousovitch, Project Coordinator

2037 Columbia Analytical Services
10450 Stancliff Road
Suite 210
Houston, TX 77099
360-577-7222
800-695-7222
Fax: 360-425-9096
http://www.caslab.com

Areas of expertise and services include environmental testing of air, water, soil, hazardous waste, sediments and tissues; process and quality control testing; analytical method development; sampling and mobile laboratory services; andconsulting and data management services.

Nerolie Withnall, Chairman
Greg Kilmister, Managing Director/ CEO

2038 Commonweal
PO Box 316
Bolinas, CA 94924
415-868-0970
Fax: 415-868-2230
E-mail: commonweal@commonweal.org
http://www.commonweal.org

A health and environment research institute that conducts programs that contribute to human and ecosystem health. The Commonweal Health and Environment Program focuses on environmental contaminants.

Michael Lerner, President
Waz Thomas, General Manager

2039 Communities for a Better Environment
1904 Franklin Street
Suite 600
Oakland, CA 94612
510-302-0430
Fax: 510-302-0437
E-mail: cbeca@mail.com
http://www.cbecal.org

Mission: To achieve environmental health and justice by building grassroots power in and with communities of color and working-class communities.
Bill Gallegos, Executive Director
Rev. Daniel Buford, Board Vice President

2040 Community-Based Hazard Management Program
George Perkins Marsh Institute
Clark University
950 Main Street
Worcester, MA 01610
508-793-7711
E-mail: otaylor@clarku.edu
http://www.clarku.edu

The Community-Based Hazardous Management Program (formerly the Childhood Cancer Research Institute) is engaged in capacity building in communities affected by nuclear weapons production and testing and also specializes in radiationhealth risk assessment and management.
Davis Baird, Vice President

2041 Corporate Accountability International
10 Milk Street
Suite 610
Boston, MA 02108
617-695-2525
800-688-8797
Fax: 617-695-2626
E-mail: info@stopcorporateabuse.org
http://www.stopcorporateabuse.org

For more than 30 years, Corporate Accountability International has successfully challenged corporations like GE, NestlS, and Philip Morris to halt abusive practices that threaten public health, the environment and our democracy. Todayour campaigns challenge the dangerous practices of some of the world's most powerful industries.

Kelle Louaillier, Executive Director
Nick Guroff, Communications Director

2042 Council of State and Territorial Epidemiologists (CSTE)
2872 Woodcock Boulevard
Suite 250
Atlanta, GA 30341
770-458-3811
Fax: 770-458-8516
http://www.cste.org

CSTE promotes the effective use of epidemiologic data to guide public health practice and improve health. CSTE accomplishes this by supporting the use of effective public health surveillance and good epidemiologic practice throughtraining, capacity development, and peer consultation, developing standards for practice, and advocating for resources and scientifically based policy.
Tim Jones, President
Jeff Engel, Executive Director

2043 Dangerous Goods Advisory Council
1100 H Street NW
Suite 740
Washington, DC 20005
202-289-4550
Fax: 202-289-4074
E-mail: info@dgac.org
http://www.hmac.org

HMAC promotes improvement in the safe transportation of hazardous materials/dangerous goods globally by: providing education, assistance, and information to the private and public sectors; through our unique status with regulatorybodies; and the adversity and technical strengths of our membership.
Vaughn Arthur, President
Alan I Roberts, Vice President

2044 **Earth Regeneration Society**
1442A Walnut Street
57
Berkeley, CA 94709
510-527-9716
E-mail: alden@earthregenerationsociety.org
http://http://www.newenergymovement.org/
The Earth Regeneration Society does research and education on climate change, ozone, and pollution, and calls for full employment and full social support based on surival programs and national and international networking.
Alden Bryant, President

2045 **EarthSave International**
20555 Devonshire St.
Suite 105
Chatsworth, CA 91311
415-234-0829
Fax: 818-337-1957
E-mail: info@earthsave.org
http://www.earthsave.org
Educates people on the powerful effects that our food choices have on the environment, our health, and all life on Earth, and supports people in moving toward a plant-based diet. Founded by John Robbins, author of Diet for a NewAmerica.
Patricia Carney, Executive Director

2046 **Environmental Defense Fund**
1875 Connecticut Avenue
Suite 600
Washington, DC 20009
212-505-2100
Fax: 212-505-2375
E-mail: members@edf.org
http://www.edf.org
Dedicated to protecting the environmental rights of all people, including future generations. Among these rights are clean air, clean water, healthy, nourishing food and a flourishing ecosystem. Advocates solutions based on science,even when it leads in unfamiliar directions. Works to create solutions that win lasting political, economic and social support because they are bipartisan, efficient and fair.

Fred Krupp, President
Diane Regas, Senior VP Programs

2047 **Environmental Hazards Management Institute**
10 New Market Road
Durham, NH 03821
603-868-1496
800-558-3464
Fax: 603-868-1547
E-mail: info@ehmi.org
http://www.ehmi.org
An independent, nonprofit organization dedicated to understanding enhancement and preservation of our environment. A catalyst for informed environmental decision making by gathering, refining, and disseminating objective information toall stakeholders with emphasis on the role played by individuals and communities of individuals.

Alan John Borner, Chief Executitve Officer

2048 **Environmental Health Coalition**
2727 Hoover Avenue
Suite 202
National City, CA 91950
619-474-0220
Fax: 619-474-1210
E-mail: ehc@environmentalhealth.org
http://www.environmentalhealth.org
One of the oldest and most effective grassroots organizations in the US, using social change strategies to achive environmental and social justice. We believe that justice is accomplished by empowered communities acting together tomake social change. We organize and advocate to protect public health and the environment threatened by toxic pollution. EHC supports broad efforts that create a just society which foster a healthy and sustainable quality of life.
Diane Takvorian, Executive Director
Leticia Ayala, Associate Director

2049 **Environmental Health Education Center**
655 West Lombard Street
Room 665
Baltimore, MD 21201
410-706-1849
Fax: 410-706-0295
http://www.envirn.umaryland.edu
Mission: Supporting nursing professionals seeking accurate, timely and credible scientific information on environmental health and nursing. The ultimate goal is to prevent environmental disease by increasing the numbers of nursingprofessionals who can recognize environmental etiologies and risk factors of disease, promote health through risk reduction and control strategies and empower individuals, families and communities through partnering, advocacy and education.
Nsedu Obot Witherspoon, MPH, Executive Director
Kristie Trousdale, MPH, Program Associate

2050 **Environmental Health Network**
PO Box 1155
Larkspur, CA 94977
415-541-5075
http://www.ehnca.org
Nonprofit, volunteer organization, whose main goal is to promote public awareness of environmental sensitivities and causative factors. EHN's focus is on issues of access and developments relating to the health and welfare of theenvironmentally sensitive.
Janet Harmon, Manager

2051 **Environmental Health Strategy Center**
565 Congress St.
Suite 204
Portland, ME 04101
207-699-5795
E-mail: info@preventharm.org
http://www.preventharm.org
The Environmental Health Strategy Center works to protect human health by reducing exposure to toxic chemicals, expanding the use of safer alternatives, and building partnerships that focus on the environment as a public healthpriority.
Michael Belliveau, Executive Director
Jenny Rottman, Managing Director

2052 **Environmental Information Association**
6935 Wisconsin Avenue
Suite 306
Chevy Chase, MD 20815
301-961-4999
888-343-4342
Fax: 301-961-3094
E-mail: info@eia-usa.org
http://www.eia-usa.org
A nonprofit organization dedicated to providing environmental information to individuals, members, and industry. They specialize in the dissemination of information about the abatement of asbestos and lead based paint, and about safetyand health issues, analytical issues and environmental site assessments.
Brent Kynoch, Managing Director
Kelly Rutt, Development/Communications

2053 **Environmental Justice Resource Center**
223 James P. Brawley Drive SW
Atlanta, GA 30314
404-880-6911
Fax: 404-880-6909
E-mail: ejrc@cau.edu
http://www.ejrc.cau.edu
Since 1994, a research, policy and information clearinghouse on issues related to environmental justice, race and the environment, civil rights, facility siting, land use planning, brownfields, transportation equity, suburban sprawland Smart Growth. The overall goal of the center is to assist, support, train and educate people of color, students, professionals and grassroots community leaders with the goal of facilitating their inclusion into the mainstream of environmentaldecision-making.
Robert D Bullard PhD, Director

2054 **Environmental Mutagen Society**
1821 Michael Faraday Drive
Suite 300
Reston, VA 20190
703-438-8220
Fax: 703-438-3113
E-mail: EMGSHQ@emgs-us.org
http://www.ems-us.org
The Environmental Mutagen Society is the primary scientific society fostering research on the basic mechanisms of mutagensis as well as on the application of this knowledge in the field of genetic toxicology. EMS has seven corescientific content areas.
Mats Ljungman, President
Suzanne M. Morris, Secretary

2055 **Environmental Resource Center**
471 Washington Ave. N
PO Box 819
Ketchum, ID 83340
208-726-4333
Fax: 208-726-1531
E-mail: molly@ercsv.org
http://www.ercsv.org
An oraganization offering environmental education for the community.
Molly G. Goodyear, Executive Director
Allison Marks, Program Director

2056 **Environmental Resource Management (ERM)**
2211 Rimland Drive
Suite 210
Washington, BE 98226
360-647-3900
Fax: 360-312-4183
http://www.erm.com
ERM works around the world with the private sector assessing how their business is likely to be impacted by environmental and social issues, new regulations, consumer concerns and supply chain issues and help companies developappropriate policies and management systems to manage these business risks.
John Alexander, Chief Executive
David Mcarthur, CEO

2057 **Environmental Safety**
1700 North Moore Street
Suite 2000 (20th Floor)
Arlington, VA 22209
703-527-8300
Fax: 703-527-8383
E-mail: info@ashoka.org
http://www.ashoka.org
Ashoka's mission is to shape a citizen sector that is entrepreneurial, productive and globally integrated, and to develop the profession of social entrepreneurship around the world. Ashoka identifies and invests in leading socialentrepreneurs-extraordinary individuals and unprecedented ideas for change in their communities-supporting the individual, idea and institution through all phases of their career. Once elected to Ashoka, Fellows benefit from being part of the globalfellowship for life.
Dr. Iman Bibars, Regional Director
Romanus Berg, CIO

2058 **Environmental Working Group**
1436 U Street Northwest
Suite 100
Washington, DC 20009
202-667-6982
Fax: 202-232-2592
http://www.ewg.org
Mission: To use the power of public information to protect public health and the environment
Ken Cook, President
Heather White, Executive Director

2059 **Environmental and Occupational Health Science Institute**
Rutgers University
170 Frelinghuysen Road
Piscataway, NJ 08854
848-445-0200
E-mail: webmaster@eohsi.rutgers.edu
http://www.eohsi.rutgers.edu
Environmental and Occupational Health Sciences Institute sponsors research, education and service programs in a setting that fosters interaction among experts in environmental health, toxicology, occupational health, exposureassessment, public policy and health education. The Institute also serves as an unbiased source of expertise about environmental problems for communities, employers and government in all areas of occupational and environmental health, toxicology andrisk assessment.
Howard Kipen, M.D, MPH, Associate Director
Kenneth Reuhl PhD, Interim Director

2060 **Food Safety and Inspection Service**
Food Safety Education Office
1400 Independence Avenue SW
Washington, DC 20250
402-344-5000
Fax: 402-344-5005
E-mail: fsis.webmaster@usda.gov
http://www.fsis.usda.gov
The Food Safety and Inspection Services (FSIS) is the public health agency in the U.S. Department of Agriculture responsible for ensuring that the nation's commercial supply of meat, poultry, and egg products is safe, wholesome, andcorrectly labeled and packaged.
Alfred V. Almanza, Administrator

2061 **Food and Drug Administration**
US Department of Health and Human Services
10903 New Hampshire Eve
Silver Spring, MD 20993
301-575-0156
888-463-6332
Fax: 301-796-8240
http://www.fda.gov
The FDA is responsible for protecting the public health by assuring the safety, efficacy, and security of human and veterinary drugs, biological products, medical devices, our nation's food supply, cosmetics, and products that emitradiation.
Margaret Hamburg, MD, Commissioner

2062 **Friends of the River**
1418 20th Street
Suite 100
Sacramento, CA 95811
916-442-3155
888-464-2477
Fax: 916-442-3396
E-mail: info@friendsoftheriver.org
http://www.friendsoftheriver.org
Friends of the River educates, organizes, and advocates to protect and restore California rivers, streams, and watersheds.
Bob Center, Executive Director
Ron Stork, Policy Director

2063 **Halogenated Solvents Industry Alliance**
1530 Wilson Boulevard
Suite 690
Arlington, VA 22209
703-875-0683
Fax: 703-875-0675
E-mail: info@hsia.org
http://www.hsia.org
The mission is to present the interests of users and producers of chlorinated solvents. To promote the continued safe use of these products and to promote the use of sound science in assessing their potential health effects.

Steven Risotto, Executive Director

2064 **Hazardous Waste Resource Center Environmental Technology Council**
1112 16th Street NW
Suite 420
Washington, DC 20036
202-783-0870
Fax: 202-737-2038
E-mail: mail@etc.org
http://www.etc.org
The Environmental Technology Council (ETC) is a trade association of commercial firms that recycle, treat and dispose of industrial and hazardous wastes; and firms involved in cleanup of contaminated sites.
David R Case, Executive Director
Scott Slesunger, VP Goverment Affairs

2065 **Holistic Management International**
5941 Jefferson St. NE
Suite B
Albuquerque, NM 87109
505-842-5252
Fax: 505-843-7900
E-mail: hmi@holisticmanagement.org
http://www.holisticmanagement.org
Enhance the efficiency, natural health, productivity and profitability of their land; increase natural annual profits; provide a framework for family, owners, managers, foreman, communal agriculturalists and other ranch/farmstakeholders to work together toward a common future; and enable development agencies working with marginalized farmers or pastoral people to break the cycle of food and water insecurity.

Peter Holter, CEO
Tracy Favre, Sr Director Contract Sales

2066 **Human Ecology Action League (HEAL)**
PO Box 509
Stockbridge, GA 30281
770-389-4519
Fax: 770-389-4520
E-mail: HEALNatnl@aol.com
http://www.healnatl.org
The Human Ecology Action League Inc (HEAL) is a nonprofit organization founded in 1977 to serve those whose health has been adversely affected by environment exposures; to provide information to those who are concerned about the healtheffects of chemicals; and to alert the general public about the potential dangers of chemicals. Referrals to local HEAL chapters and other support groups are available from the League.
John Heal, Contact

2067 **INFORM**
PO Box 320403
Brooklyn, NY 11232
212-361-2400
Fax: 212-361-2412
E-mail: ramsey@informinc.org
http://www.informinc.org
Dedicated to educating the public about the effects of human activity on the environment and public health. The goal is to empower citizens, businesses and government to adopt practices and policies that will sustain our planet forfuture generations.
Virginia Ramsey, President
Jon Parks, Co-Chair

2068 **Institute for Agriculture and Trade Policy**
2105 First Avenue South
Minneapolis, MN 55404
612-870-0453
Fax: 612-870-4846
http://www.iatp.org

The mission of the Institute for Agriculture and Trade Policy is to foster socially, economically and environmentally sustainable rural communities and regions.
Harriet Barlow, Board Chair
Becky Glass, Board Secretary-Treasurer

2069 **Institute of Hazardous Materials Management**
11900 Parklawn Drive
Suite 450
Rockville, MD 20852
301-984-8969
Fax: 301-984-1516
E-mail: ihmminfo@ihmm.org
http://www.ihmm.org

Mission is to provide recognition for professionals engaged in the managment and engineering control of hazardous materials who have attained the required level of education, experience and competence; foster continued professionaldevelopment of Certified Hazardous Materials Managers (CHMM).
John H Frick, PhD, CHMM, Executive Director
Betty Fishman, Assistant Executive Director

2070 **Laotian Organizing Project**
310 8th Street
Suite 309
Oakland, CA 94607
510-834-8920
Fax: 510-834-8926
E-mail: apen@apen4ej.org
http://www.apen4ej.org

The Laotian Organization Project (LOP), a project of the Asian Pacific Environmental Network, is a membership-based organization of Laotian residents in Richmond and San Pablo, California. LOP works to bring people from the Laotiancommunity together to identify problems, develop solutions, and take action for a more healthy, safe, and just community.
Roger Kim, Executive Director
Mario Lugay, Chair

2071 **MCS Referral and Resources**
618 Wyndhurst Avenue #2
Baltimore, MD 21210
410-889-6666
Fax: 410-889-4944
E-mail: adonnay@mcsrr.org
http://www.mcsrr.org

The mission of MCS Refferal and Resources is to further the diagnosis, treatment, accomodation and prevention of multiple chemical sensitivity (MCS) disorders.
Dr. Anne McCampbell

2072 **Midwest Center for Environmental Science and Public Policy**
One East Hazelwood Drive
Champaign, IL 61820
800-407-0261
E-mail: glrppr@istc.illinois.edu
http://www.glrppr.org

A professional organization dedicated to promoting information exchange and networking to P2 professionals in the Great Lakes regions of the United States and Canada
Bob Iverson, Contact

2073 **Mount Sinai School of Medicine: Division of Environmental Health Science**
Department of Community and Preventive Medicine
Gustave Levy Place
Box 1057
New York, NY 10029
212-241-6500
Fax: 212-241-6696
http://www.mssm.edu/cpm

The Division's ultimate goal is the protection of the public's health by understanding, elucidating and preventing diseases that arise from environmental exposures.
Philip J Landrigan M.D., Chair

2074 **National Alliance for Hispanic Health**
1501 16th Street NW
Washington, DC 20036
202-387-5000
Fax: 202-797-4353
E-mail: alliance@hispanichealth.org
http://www.hispanichealth.org

The mission of the National Alliance for Hispanic Health is to improve the health and well-being of Hispanics. Issues covered include the full range of health and human services issues, including environmental health.
Augustine C. Baca, M.P.A., Chairperson
Lourdes B Garbanati, Ph.D., M.P.H., Vice Chair

2075 **National Association of City and County Health Officials**
1100 17th Street NW
2nd Floor
Washington, DC 20036
202-783-5550
Fax: 202-783-1583
E-mail: info@naccho.org
http://www.naccho.org

The National Assoication of County and City Health Officials is a nonprofit, membership organization serving all 3,000 local health departments nationwide. NACCHO is dedicated to improving the health of people and communities byassuring an effective local public health system. As the Voice of local public health officials at the national level, NACCHO is able to promote the local perspective on national health programs and policies.
Terry Allan, President

2076 **National Association of Noise Control Officials**
53 Cubberly Road
West Windsor, NJ 08550-3400
609-586-2684
Fax: 609-799-2616
http://www.arcat.com

The association consists of employees of the federal and state governments, consultants, scientists, and students concerned with acoustical control in the environment. It now has about 70 members.

Edward J DiPolzere, Executive Director

2077 **National Association of Physicians for the Environment**
6410 Rockledge Drive
Suite 412
Bethesda, MD 20817
307-571-9790
Fax: 301-530-8910
E-mail: nape@napenet.org

The National Association of Physicians for the Environment works to involve physicians and other health care professionals, particularly through their geographic and medical specialty organizations, to deal with the impact ofpollutants on organs and systems of the human body.
Betty Farley, Executive Assistant

2078 **National Association of School Nurses**
1100 Wayne Avenue
Suite 925
Silver Spring, MD 20910
240-821-1130
866-627-6767
Fax: 301-585-1791
E-mail: nasn@nasn.org
http://www.nasn.org

The mission of The National Association of School Nurses is to advance the practice of school nursing and provide leadership in the delivery of quality health programs to school communities.
Amy Garcia, Executive Director

2079 **National Cancer Institute**
National Institutes of Health
BG 9609 MSC 9760
9609 Medical Centre Drive
Bethesda, MD 20892
301-496-6641
800-422-6237
Fax: 301-496-0846
E-mail: ncipressofficers@mail.nih.gov
http://www.cancer.gov

Leads the Nation's fight against cancer by supporting and conducting ground-breaking research in cancer biology, causation, prevention, detection, treatment and survivorship.
John E Niederhuber, Director
Joseph V. Simone, MD, Chairman

2080 **National Capital Poison Center**
3201 New Mexico Avenue NW
Suite 310
Washington, DC 20016
202-362-3867
800-222-1222
Fax: 202-362-8377
E-mail: pc@poison.org
http://www.poison.org

This mission of the Poison Center is to prevent poisonings, save lives, and limit injury from poisoning. In addition, the Center decreases health care costs of poisoning cases. The Center provides

24-hour telephone guidance, teachingmaterials, and professional education.

2081 National Center for Disease Control and Prevention
1600 Clifton Road 404-639-3311
Atlanta, GA 30333 800-232-4636
http://www.cdc.gov

Mission: To promote health and quality of life by preventing and controlling disease, injury, and disability.
Lynn Austin, Chief of Staff

2082 National Center for Environmental Health Strategies
1100 Rural Avenue 856-429-5358
Voorhees, NJ 08043 Fax: 856-816-8820
E-mail: marylamielle@ncehs.org
http://www.ncehs.org/

Fosters the development of creative solutions to environmental health problems with a focus on indoor air quality, chemical sensitivites and environmental disabilities.
Mary Lamielle, Executive Director

2083 National Center for Healthy Housing
10320 Little Patuxent Parkway 410-992-0712
Suite 500 877-312-3046
Columbia, MD 21044 Fax: 443-539-4150
E-mail: rmorley@centerforhealthyhousing.org
http://www.centerforhealthyhousing.org

Formerly known as the National Center for Lead-Safe Housing, it devcops and promotes practical methods to protect children from environmental health hazards in homes while preserving affordable housing.
Rebecca L Morley, Executive Director
Jonathan W Wilson, Deputy Director

2084 National Conference of Local Environmental Health Administrators
University of Washington
Department of Environmental Health 206-616-2097
Box 357234 Fax: 206 543 8123
Seattle, WA 98195 E-mail: ctreser@u.washington.edu
http://depts.washington.edu/clehaweb

The NCLEHA's purpose is to provide a forum for local administrators to share common concerns and solutions to mutual problems, and to provide a professional organization for environmental health administrators, focused on the issuesand problems of local environmental health programs.
Keith L Krinn, Chair
Charles D Treser, Treasurer

2085 National Conference of State Legislatures
7700 E First Place 303-364-7700
Denver, CO 80230 Fax: 303-364-7800
http://www.ncsl.org

The National Conference of State Legislatures serves the legislators and staffs of the nation's 50 states and its commonwealths and territories. NCSL is a bipartisan organization with three objectives: to improve the quality andeffectiveness of state legislatures; to foster interstate communications and cooperation; and to ensure states a strong cohesive voice in the federal system.

William T Pound, Executive Director

2086 National Education Association Health Information Network
1201 16th Street NW 202-822-7570
Suite 216 800-718-8387
Washington, DC 20036 Fax: 202-822-7775
E-mail: info@neahin.org
http://www.neahin.org

The National Education Association Health Information Network believes that sound public education must begin with school employees and students who are healthy and free of preventable diseases and supported with information, materialsand training opportunities that reaffirm these values.
Jerald Newberry, Executive Director
Annelise Cohon, Program Coordinator

2087 National Environmental Coalition of Native Americans
PO Box 988 918-342-3041
Claremore, OK 74018 E-mail: noteno_84@hotmail.com
http://necona.indigenousnative.org

Nonprofit organization formed to educate Indians and Non-Indians about the health dangers of radioactivity and the transport of nuclear waste on America's rails and roads. Networks with environmentalists to develop grassrootscounter-movement to the efforts of the nuclear industry and develop Tribal nuclear free zones across the nation.
Grace Thorpe, President

2088 National Environmental Health Association (NEHA)
720 S Colorado Boulevard 303-756-9090
Suite 1000-N Fax: 303-691-9490
Denver, CO 80246 E-mail: staff@NEHA.org
http://www.neha.org

NEHA is the only national association that represents all of environmental health and protection from terrorism and all-hazards preparedness, to food safety and protection and on site wastewater systems. Over 4500 members and theprofession are served by the association through its Journal of Environmental Health, Annual Education Conference and Exhibition credentialing programs, research and development activities and other services.

Nelson Fabian, Executive Director
Chris Fabian, Senior Manager

2089 National Environmental Health Science and Protection Accreditation Council
4500 9th Avenue NE 206-522 5272
Suite 394 Fax: 206-985-9805
Seattle, WA 98105 E-mail: ehacinfo@aehap.org
http://www.ehacoffice.org

The National Environmental Health Science and Protection Accreditation Council promotes a high quality education for persons studying environmental health science and protection; promotes commonality in coverage of basic concepts ofenvironmental health science and protection education; and promotes undergraduate curricula of a quality and content compatible with admission prerequisites of graduate programs in environmental health science and protection.
Yalonda Sinde, Executive Director

2090 National Environmental Trust
1200 18th Street NW 202-887-8800
5th Floor Fax: 202-887-8877
Washington, DC 20036 E-mail: cdelany@net.org
http://www.environet.org

Manages comprehensive media and public policy campaigns around national environmental issues.
Kymberly Escobar, Director

2091 National Institute for Global Environmental Change
University of California, Davis
2850 Spafford Street 530-757-3350
Suite A Fax: 530-756-6499
Davis, CA 95618 E-mail: nigec@ucdavis.edu
http://nigec.ucdavis.edu

Mission: To assist the nation in its response to human-induced climate and environmental change.
Lawrence B Coleman, Interim National Director

2092 National Institute of Environmental Health Sciences
111 T.W. Alexander Drive 919-541-3201
Research Triangle Park, NC 27709 Fax: 919-541-2260
E-mail: birnbaumls@niehs.nih.gov
http://www.niehs.nih.gov

The mission of the National Institute of Environmental Health Sciences is to reduce the burden of environmentally associated diseases and dysfunctions.
Linda S. Birnbaum, Ph.D, Director
Richard Woychik, Deputy Director

2093 National Oceanic & Atmospheric Administration
1401 Constitution Avenue NW
Room 5128
Washington, DC 20230
202-482-6090
800-638-8972
Fax: 202-482-3154
E-mail: d.james.baker@noaa.gov
http://www.noaa.gov

Describes and predicts changes in the Earth's environment and conserves and wisely manages the nation's coastal and marine resources. Goals and objectives include advance short-term warning and forecast services.
Conrad C Lautenbacher Jr, NOAA Administrator

2094 National Pesticide Information Center Oregon State University
333 Weniger Hall
Corvallis, OR 97331
800-858-7378
Fax: 541-737-0761
E-mail: npic@ace.orst.edu
http://http://npic.orst.edu

Provides objective, science-based information about a wide variety of pesticide-related topics, including: pesticide product information, information on the recognition and management of pesticide poisonings, toxicology andenvironmental chemistry. Highly trained specialists can also provide referrals for the following: investigation of pesticide incidents, emergency treatment information, safety information, health and environmental effects, and clean-up and disposalprocedures.
Dave Stone, Director

2095 National Religious Partnership for the Environment
49 South Pleasant Street
Suite 301
Amherst, MA 01002
413-253-1515
Fax: 413-253-1414
E-mail: nrpe@nrpe.org
http://www.nrpe.org

The mission of the National Religious Partnership for the Environment is to permanently integrate issues of environmental sustainability and justice across all aspects of organized religious life.
Paul Gorman, Executive Director

2096 National Safety Council
Environmental Health Center
1025 Connecticut Avenue NW
Suite 1210
Washington, DC 20036
202-293-2270
Fax: 202-567-5704
E-mail: info@nsc.org
http://www.nsc.org

The Mission of the Environmental Health Center is to foster improved public understanding of significant health risk and challenges facing modern society. This goal reinforces the National Safety Council's commitment to increased andmore effective citizen involvement in safety, health and environmental decision-making.
Jeffrey Shavelson, Policy Analyst

2097 Natural Resources Defense Council
40 West 20th Street
New York, NY 10011
212-727-2700
Fax: 212-727-1773
E-mail: nrdcinfo@nrdc.org
http://www.nrdc.org

Mission: To safeguard the Earth: its people, its plants and animals, and natural systems on which all life depends.
Frances Beinecke, President
Peter Lehner, Executive Director

2098 Navy Environmental Health Center
620 John Paul Jones Circle
Suite 1100
Portsmouth, VA 23708
757-953-0700
Fax: 757-953-0999
http://www.-nehc.med.navy.mil

Ensures Navy and Marine Corps readiness through leadership in prevention of disease and promotion of health.
Captain David Hiland, Commanding Officer

2099 Navy and Marine Corps Public Health Center
620 John Paul Jones Circle
Suite 1100
Portsmouth, VA 23708
757-953-0700
E-mail: ask-nmcphc@med.navy.mil
http://www-nehc.med.navy.mil

The Navy and Marine Corps center for public health services that provides leadership and expertise to ensure mission readiness through disease prevention and health promotion in support of the National Military Strategy.
CAPT Bruce A Cohen MC USN, Commanding Officer
CAPT Mike Henderson MSC USN, Executive Officer

2100 Noise Pollution Clearinghouse
PO Box 1137
Montpelier, VT 05601
888-200-8332
E-mail: webmaster@nonoise.org
http://www.nonoise.org

The Noise Pollution Clearinghouse is a nonprofit organization with extensive online noise related resources. The mission is to create more civil cities and more natural rural and wilderness areas by reducing noise pollution and itssources.

2101 North American Association for Environmental Education
2000 P Street NW
Suite 540
Washington, DC 20036
202-419-0412
Fax: 202-419-0415
E-mail: brian@naaee.org
http://www.naaee.org

A professional association for environmental education that promotes excellence in environmental education and serves environmental educators for the purpose of achieving environmental literacy in order for present and futuregenerations to benefit from a safe and health environment and a better quality of life.
Judy Braus, Executive Director
Christiane Maertens, Deputy Director

2102 Northwest Coalition for Alternatives to Pesticides
PO Box 1393
Eugene, OR 97440
541-344-5044
Fax: 541-344-6923
E-mail: info@pesticide.org
http://www.pesticide.org

The Northwest Coalition for Alternatives to Pesticides protects the health of people and the environment by advancing alternatives to pesticides.
Tony Brand, President
Kim Leval, Executive Director

2103 Novozymes North America Inc
77 Perry Chapel Church Road
Franklinton, NC 27525
919-494-3000
Fax: 919-494-3450
E-mail: enzymesna@novozymes.com
http://www.novozymes.com/en

Novozymes is the biotech bases world leader in enzymes and microorganisms. Using nature's own technologies, they continuously expand the frontiers of biological solutions to improve industrial performance everywhere.
Henrik Gurtler, CEO

2104 Occupational Safety and Health Administration: US Department of Labor
Office of Administrative Services
200 Constitution Avenue NW
Room N-310
Washington, DC 20210
202-693-1999
800-321-6742
http://www.osha.gov

Mission: To assure the safety and health of America's workers by setting and enforcing standards; providing training, outreach, and education; establishing partnerships; and encouraging continual improvement in workplace safety andhealth.

2105 Pesticide Action Network North America
1611 Telegraph Avenue
Suite 1200
Oakland, CA 94612
510-788-9020
E-mail: panna@panna.org
http://www.panna.org

Pesticide Action Network North American advocates the adoption of ecologically sound practices in place of hazardous pestices in place of pesticide use. PANNA works with more than 100 affiliated oragnizations in Canada, Mexico and US,as well as with Pesticide Action Network partners around the world to demand that development agencies and governments redirect support from pesticides to safe alternatives.
Judy Hatcher, Executive Director
Matt Belli, Development Assistant

2106 **Physicians for Social Responsibility**
1111 14th St., NW
Suite 700
Washington, DC 20005
202-667-4260
Fax: 202-667-4201
E-mail: psrnatl@psr.org
http://www.psr.org

A non-profit advocacy organization that is the medical and public health voice for policies to prevent nuclear war and proliferation and to slow, stop and reverse global warming and toxic degradation of the environment.
Catherine Thomasson MD, Executive Director

2107 **Public Citizen**
1600 20th Street NW
Washington, DC 20009
202-588-1000
http://www.citizen.org
Founded by Ralph Nader in 1971, Public Citizen is the consumer's eyes in Washington. With the support of more than 15,000 people like you, we fight for safer drugs and medical devices, cleaner and safer energy sources, a cleanerenvironment, fair trade and a more open and democratic government.
Robert Weissman, President
Margrete S Rangnes, Executive Vice President

2108 **Rachel Carson Center for Natural Resources**
Churchill High School
1850 Bailey Hill Road
Eugene, OR 97405
541-687-3421
E-mail: haberman@4j.lane.edu
http://schools.4j.lane.edu/carson/
Offers an alternative to the traditional high school curriculum, providing students with experience, knowledge, and skills that relate to the natural environment.
Helen Haberman, Environmental Instructor
Tim Whitley, Director

2109 **Rachel Carson Council**
PO Box 10779
Silver Spring, MD 20914
301-593-7507
E-mail: rccouncil@aol.com
http://www.rachelcarsoncouncil.org
Independent nonprofit scientific organization dedicated to protecting the environment against toxic and chemical threats, particularly those of pesticides.
Dr. Diana Post, President

2110 **Rene Dubos Center**
The Rene Dubos Center
279 Bronxville Road
Bronxville, NY 10708
914-337-1636
Fax: 914-771-5206
E-mail: dubos@mindspring.com
http://www.dubos.org
The Rene Dubos Center for Human Environments is a non-profit education and research organization focused on the social and humanistic aspects of environmental problems.
Ruth A Eblen, President

2111 **Rodale Institute**
611 Siegfriedale Road
Kutztown, PA 19530
610-683-1400
Fax: 610-683-8548
E-mail: info@rodaleinst.org
http://www.rodaleinstitute.org
The Institute offers creative opportunities and solutions that contribute to regenerating environmental and human health worldwide. Their mission statement is clear: The Rodale Institute works worldwide to achieve a regenerative foodsystem that improves environmental and human health.
Tim LaSalle, President

2112 **Safer Pest Control Project**
4611 North Ravenswood Avenue
Suite 107
Chicago, IL 60640
773-878-7378
Fax: 773-878-8250
E-mail: general@spcpweb.org
http://spcpweb.org
Dedicated to reducing the health risks and environmental impacts of pesticides and promoting safer alternatives in Illinois.
Ann Alexander, President
Ruth Kerzee, Executive Director

2113 **Second Nature Inc.**
Consortium for Environmental Education in Medicine
18 Tremont Street
Suite 308
Boston, MA 02108
617-722-0036
Fax: 320-451-1612
E-mail: info@secondnature.org
http://www.secondnature.org
Dedicated to advancing our quality of life by demostrating the close links between human health and the environment. The center's goal is to make the relationship of environment to human health an integral part of medical education.
David Hales, President
Steve Tremble, Vice President

2114 **Silicones Environmental, Health and Safety Council of North America**
700 2nd Street NE
Washington, DC 20002
202-249-7000
Fax: 202-249-6100
E-mail: sehsc@americanchemistry.com
http://www.sehsc.com
An organization of North America silicone chemical producers and importers. It promotes the safe use of silicones through product stewardship and environmental, health and safety research. It focuses on coordinating research andsubmitting it for peer review through independent advisory boards and publication of peer-reviewed literature.
Karluss Thomas, Executive Director

2115 **Society for Occupational and Environmental Health**
1010 Vermont Ave. NW
#513
Washington, DC 20005
202-347-4976
Fax: 202-347-4950
E-mail: kkirkland@aoec.org
http://www.soeh.org
Provides a neutral forum where occupational safety and health and environmental issues can be discussed and resolved. Actively seeks to improve the quality of both working and living places.
Katherine H Kirkland, Executive Director

2116 **Society of Environmental Toxicology and Chemistry**
SETAC N America Office
229 South Baylen Street
2nd Floor
Pensacola, FL 32502
850-469-1500
Fax: 850-469-9778
E-mail: setac@setac.org
http://www.setac.org
Mission: To support the development of principles and practices for protection, enhancement and management of sustainable environmental quality and ecosystem integrity.
Greg Schiefer, Executive Director
Jason Anderson, IT Manager

2117 **Synthetic Organic Chemical Manufacturers Association**
1850 M Street NW
Suite 700
Washington, DC 20036
202-721-4100
Fax: 202-296-8120
E-mail: info@socma.com
http://www.socma.com
A trade association that serves the specialty, batch and custom chemical industry. SOCMA member companies make the products and refine the raw materials that make our standard of living possible; from pharmaceuticals to cosmetics,soaps to plastics, and all manner of industrial and construction products. SOCMA promotes innovative, safe and environmentally responsible operations, which are internationally competitive and contribute to a healthy, productive economy.
Joseph Acker, President
Diane McMahon, Director Business Operations

2118 **Teratology Society**
1821 Michael Faraday Drive
Suite 300
Reston, VA 20190
703-438-3104
Fax: 703-483-3113
E-mail: tshq@teratology.org
http://www.teratology.org
A multidisciplinary scientific society founded in 1960, the members of which study the causes and biological processes leading to abnormal development and birth defects at the fundamental and clinical level, and appropriate measuresfor prevention.
Elaine M Faustman, President
Thomas B Knudson, Vice President

2119 Toxicology Information Response Center
1060 Commerce Park
MS 6480
Oak Ridge, TN 37830
865-576-1746
Fax: 865-574-9888
E-mail: slusherkg@ornl.gov
http://www.ornl.gov/TechResources/tirc/hmepg.html

TIRC provides customer search services to both scientific and public communities as a convenient and efficient way to obtain comprehensive scientific information on any subject of interest.

Kim Slusher, Administrator

2120 US Consumer Product Safety Commission
10388 Bayside Drive
Claiborne, MD 21624
703-307-3260
800-638-2772
Fax: 703-782-1620
E-mail: info@cpsc.gov
http://www.cpsc.gov

An independent federal regulatory agency. Helps keep American families safe by reducing the risk of injury or death from consumer products.

John C Scott, President
Carrie-Gould Kabler, Director of Community Reach

2121 US Nuclear Regulatory Commission
One White Flint North
11555 Rockville Pike
Rockville, MD 20852
301-415-7000
800-368-5642
Fax: 301-415-5575
E-mail: pdr@nrc.gov
http://www.nrc.gov

Ensures adequate protection of the public health and safety, the common defense and security, and the environment in the use of nuclear materials in the United States.

Dale E Klein, Chairman
Peter B Lyons, Commissioner

2122 US Public Interest Research Group
218 D Street SE
1st Floor
Washington, DC 20003
202-546-9707
Fax: 202-546-2461
http://www.pirg.org

Mission: To deliver persistent, result-oriented public interest activism that protects our environment, encourages a fair, sustainable economy, and fosters responsive, democratic government.

Andre Delattre, Executive Director
Steve Blackledge, Deputy Director

2123 US-Mexico Border Health Association
211 N. Florence
Suite101
El Paso, TX 79901
915-532-1006
866-785-9867
Fax: 915-833-7840
E-mail: bhc@borderhealth.org
http://www.borderhealth.org

Promotes public and individual health along the United States-Mexico border through reciprocal technical cooperation.

Rebeca Ramos, Interim Executive Director

2124 Water Environment Federation
601 Wythe Street
Alexandria, VA 22314
703-684-2400
800-666-0206
Fax: 703-684-2492
E-mail: csc@wef.org
http://www.wef.org

Nonprofit international membership organization that develops and disseminates technical information on the nature, collection, treatment and disposal of domestic and industrial wastewater.

Janet Blatt, Director
Mincaiee Brown, Executive Director

2125 Western Occupational and Environmental Medical Association
575 Market Street
Suite 2125
San Francisco, CA 94105
415-764-4918
Fax: 415-764-4915
E-mail: woema@hp-assoc.com
http://www.woema.org

The mission is to represent and be a resource to members in the profession and practice of occupational and environmental medicine and to enhance their efforts to promote and improve health in the workplace and the community.

Shannon Jamieson, Executive Director
Walter S Newman, Jr. MD, Chairman

2126 White Lung Association
PO Box 1483
Baltimore, MD 21203
410-243-5864
Fax: 410-243-5234
E-mail: jfite@whitelung.org
http://www.whitelung.org

National nonprofit organization dedicated to the education of the public to the hazards of asbestos exposure. Has developed programs of public education and consults with victims of asbestos exposure, school boards, building owners,government agencies and others interested in identifying asbestos hazards and developing control programs.

James Fite, Executive Director

Pediatric Health: Associations

2127 Academic Pediatric Association
6728 Old McLean Village Drive
McLean, VA 22101
703-556-9222
Fax: 703-556-8729
E-mail: info@academicpeds.org
http://www.academicpeds.org

The mission of the APA is to foster the health and well-being of children and their families by: promoting health services, education and research in general pediatrics; affecting public and governmental policies regarding issues vitalto child health and to education and research in general pediatrics; and supporting the professional growth and development of faculty in general pediatrics.

David Keller, MD, President
Mark Schuster, MD, Ph.D, President Elect

2128 Allergy and Asthma Network: Mothers of Asthmatics
8201 Greensboro Drive
Suite 300
McLean, VA 22102
800-878-4403
Fax: 703-288-5271
http://www.aanma.org

Our mission is to eliminate suffering and death due to asthma and allergies through education, advocacy, community outreach and research.

Nancy Sander, President
Mary McGowan, Executive Director

2129 American Academy of Pediatrics: Committee on Environment Health
141 NW Point Boulevard
Elk Grove Villiage, IL 60007
847-434-4000
800-433-9016
Fax: 847-434-8000
http://www.aap.org

The AAP is commited to the attainment of optimal physical, mental and social health for all infants, children, and young adults. This mission will be accomplished by engaging in the following activities: professional education,advocacy for children and youth, advocacy for pediatricians, public education, membership service and research.

Jay E Berkelhamer, President

2130 American Federation of Teachers
555 New Jersey Avenue NW
Washington, DC 20001
202-879-4400
Fax: 202-879-4597
http://www.aft.org

The American Federation of Teachers is a union that represents K-12 teachers and other school employees, health care professionals and public employees. The union considers itself an advocacy organization for children and the public.

Edward J McElroy, President

2131 Association of Maternal and Child Health Program
2030 M Street
Suite 350
Washington, DC 20036
202-775-0436
Fax: 202-775-0061
http://www.amchp.org

AMCHP accomplishes its mission through the active participation of its members and vital partnerships with government agen-

cies, families and advocates, health care purchasers and providers, academic and research professionals, andothers at the national, state and local levels.
Millie Jones, President
Sam B. Cooper III, President Elect

2132 Childhood Lead Poisoning Prevention Program
Ohio Department of Health
246 N High Street
Columbus, OH 43215
614-728-9454
Fax: 614-728-6793
E-mail: BCFHS@odh.ohio.gov
http://www.odh.state.oh.us

The mission of Ohio's Childhood Lead Poisoning Prevention Program is to eliminate childhood lead poisoning through screening, environmental inspection, abatement, education and case management.
Alvin D Jackson, Director

2133 Children's Defense Fund
25 E Street NW
Washington, DC 20001
800-233-1200
E-mail: cdfinfo@childrensdefense.org
http://www.childrensdefense.org

Mission: To ensure every child a healthy start, a head start, a fair start, a safe start, and a moral start in life and successful passage to adulthood with the help of caring families and communities.
Marian Wright Edelman, President

2134 Children's Environmental Health Network
110 Maryland Avenue NE
Suite 402
Washington, DC 20002
202-543-4033
Fax: 202-543-8797
E-mail: cehn@cehn.org
http://www.cehn.org/

Mission is to promote a healthy environment and to protect the fetus and child from environmental hazards. Three areas of concentration for the Network are education, research and policy. Network's goals are: to promote the developmentof sound public health and child-focused national policy; to stimulate prevention-oriented research; to educate health professionals, policymakers and community members in preventive strategies; and to elevate public awareness of environmentalhazards to children.
Nsedu Obot Witherspoon, Executive Director
Cynthia Bearer, M.D., Ph.D. Chair

2135 Coalition for Clean Air
800 Wilshire Blvd.
Suite 1010
Los Angelos, CA 90017
213-223-6860
Fax: 213-223-6862
E-mail: air@ccair.org
http://www.coalitionforcleanair.org

The Coalition for Clean Air is committed to restoring clean, healthy air to all of California and strengthening the environmental movement by promoting broad-based community involvement, advocating responsible public policy andproviding technical expertise.
Joseph K Lyou, Ph.D, President & CEO
Nicholas Burant, Office Manager

2136 Genesis Fund/National Birth Defects Center: Pregnancy Environmental Hotline
1347 Main Street
Second Floor
Waltham, MA 02451
781-890-4282
800-322-5014
Fax: 781-487-2361
E-mail: info@thegenesisfund.org
http://www.thegenesisfund.org

General information service that provides information regarding exposure to environmental factors during pregnancy and the effects on the developing fetus.
Erica D Agostino, Executive Director

2137 Healthy Child Healthy World
11872 La Grange Avenue
2nd Floor
Los Angeles, CA 90025
310-820-2030
Fax: 310-820-2070
E-mail: info@healthychild.org
http://www.healthychild.org

Healthy Child Healthy World is dedicated to protecting the health and well being of children from harmful environmental exposures. We educate parents, support protective policies, and engage communities to make responsible decisions,simple everyday choices, and well-informed lifestyle improvements to create healthy environments where children and families can flourish.
Rachel Lincoln Sarnoff, Executive Director
Mandy Geisler, Project Manager

2138 Healthy Mothers, Healthy Babies
4401 Ford Avenue
Suite 300
Alexandria, VA 22302
703-837-4792
Fax: 703-664-0485
E-mail: info@hmhb.org
http://www.hmhb.org

Healthy Mothers, Healthy Babies is a coalition of national, state and local providers, advocates and administrators concerned about health of pregnant women, infants and families. The coalition serves as a forum for informationexchange and as a catalyst to encourage collaborative partnerships amoung its members and colleagues.
Janice Frey-Angel, CEO
Andrea Goodman, Program Manager

2139 Healthy Schools Network
773 Madison Avenue
Albany, NY 12208
518-462-0632
202-543-7555
Fax: 518-462-0433
E-mail: info@fhealthyschools.org
http://www.healthyschools.org

HSN is a nationally recognized state-based advocate for the protection of children's environmental health in schools. Engages in research, education, outreach, technical assistance and coalition building to create schols that areenvironmentally responsible to children, and to their communities. Publishes a quarterly newsletter and maintains an Information Clearinghouse and Referral Service.

John Shaw, President
Claire Barnett, Executive Director

2140 Institute of Medicine: Board on Children, Youth and Families
500 Fifth Street, NW
Washington, DC 20001
202-334-1935
Fax: 202-334-3829
E-mail: bocyf@nas.edu
http://www.bocyf.org

The Board on Children, Youth and Families addresses a variety of policy-relevant issues related to the health and development, of children, youth and families. It does so by convening experts to weigh in on matters from the perspectiveof the behavioral, social, and health sciences. The Board operates under the National Research Council and the Institute of Medicine of the National Academics.
Kimber Bogard, Director
Wendy Keenan, Program Associate

2141 Kids for Saving Earth Worldwide
37955 Bridge Road
North Branch, MN 55056
763-559-1234
Fax: 651-674-5005
E-mail: kse@kidsforsavingearth.org
http://www.kidsforsavingearth.org/

To help protect the Earth through kids and adults. To educate and inspire them to participate in Earth-saving actions.
Tessa Hill, President and Director

2142 Kids for a Clean Environment
PO Box 158254
Nashville, TN 37215
615-331-7381
Fax: 615-333-9879
E-mail: kidsface@mindspring.com
http://www.kidsface.org

Mission: To provide information on environmental issues to children, to encourage and facilitate youth's involvement with effective environmental action and to recognize those efforts which result in the improvement of nature.
Melissa Poe, Founder

2143 March of Dimes Birth Defects Foundation
1275 Mamaroneck Avenue
White Plains, NY 10605
914-997-4488
http://www.modimes.org

The mission of the March of Dimes Birth Defects Foundation is to improve the health of babies by preventing birth defects and re-

ducing infant mortality. The March of Dimes carries out the mission through research, community service,education and advocacy.
Ann Umemoto, Associate Director

2144 **Montefiore Medical Center Lead Poisoning Prevention Program**
111 E 210th Street
Bronx, NY 10467
718-920-5016
Fax: 718-920-4377
The Montefiore Lead Poisoning Prevention Program addresses all aspects of childhood lead poisoning from diagnosis and treatment to education and research. Their mission is to treat lead-poisoned children and their families and toeducate families at risk, other medical providers and local, state and national legislators and policy makers.
Nancy Redkey, Project Coordinator

2145 **National Institute of Child Health and Human Development**
Po Box 3006
Rockville, MD 20847
800-370-2943
888-320-6942
Fax: 866-760-5947
E-mail: NICHDinformationresourcecenter@mail.nih.gov
http://www.nichd.nih.gov
National Institute of Child Health and Human Development supports and conducts basic, clinical and epidemiological research on the reproductive, neurobiological, developmental and behavioral processes that determine and maintain thehealth of children, adults, families and populations.
Duane Alexander, Director
John N. Kennedy, President

2146 **National Parent Teachers Association**
1250 N. Pitt Street
Alexandria, VA 22314
703-518-1200
800-307-4782
Fax: 703-836-0942
E-mail: info@pta.org
http://www.pta.org
The mission of the National PTA is to support and speak on behalf of children and youth in the school, in the community and before governmental bodies and other organizations; to assist parents in developing the skills they need toraise and protect their children and to encourage parent and public involvement in the public schools.
Otha Thorton, President
Eric Hargis, Executive Director

2147 **Office of Children's Health Protection**
US Environmental Protection Agency
Ariel Rios Building
1200 Pennsylvania Avenue NW
Washington, DC 20460
202-564-2188
Fax: 202-564-2733
http://www.epa.gov
The mission of the Office of Children's Health Protection is to make the protection of children's health a fundamental goal of public health and environmental protection in the United States.
Joanne Rodman, Associate Director

2148 **Oklahoma Childhood Lead Poisioning PreventionProgram**
Oklahoma Department of Health
1000 Northeast 10th Street
Room 711
Oklahoma, OK 73117
405-271-5600
800-522-0203
Fax: 405-271-4971
E-mail: oklppp@health.ok.gov
http://lpp.health.ok.gov
Mission: To reduce blood lead levels to below a level of concern in all Oklahomans.

Pediatric Health: Publications

2149 **Child Health and the Environment**
Oxford University Press
198 Madison Avenue
New York, NY 10016
212-726-6000
Fax: 919-677-1303
http://www.oup-usa.org
Focus on environmental threats to child health. The first three chapters provide overviews of key children's environmental health issues as well as the role of environmental epidemiology and risk assessment in child health protection.Later chapters address the health affects of metal, PCBs, dioxins, pesticides, hormonally active agents, radiation, indoor and outdoor air pollution, and water contaminants.
416 pages
ISBN: 0-195135-59-8
Donald T Wigle, Author

2150 **Children's Defense Fund**
25 E Street NW
Washington, DC 20001
202-628-8787
800-233-1200
E-mail: cdfinfo@childrensdefense.org
http://www.childrensdefense.org
Mission: To ensure every child a healthy start, a head start, a fair start, a safe start, and a moral start in life and successful passage to adulthood with the help of caring families and communities.
Marian Wright Edelman, President

2151 **Handbook of Pediatric Environmental Health**
American Academy of Pediatrics
141 NW Point Boulevard
Elk Grove Village, IL 60007
847-434-4000
800-433-9016
Fax: 847-434-8000
http://www.aap.org
The AAP is committed to the attainment of optimal physical, mental and social health for all infants, children, and young adults. This mission will be accomplished by engaging in the following activities: professional education,advocacy for children and youth, advocacy for pediatricians, public education, membership service and research.
723 pages
ISBN: 1-581100-29-9
Thomas K. McInerny, President
Errol R. Alden, Executive Director

2152 **Handle with Care: Children and Environmental Carcinogens**
Natural Resources Defense Council
40 West 20th Street
New York, NY 10011
212-727-2700
Fax: 212-727-1773
E-mail: nrdcinfo@nrdc.org
http://www.nrdc.org
Mission: To safeguard the Earth: its people, its plants and animals, and the natural systems on which all life depends.
50 pages
Francis Beinecke, President
Peter Lehner, Executive Director

2153 **Kids Count Data Book: State Profiles of Child Well-Being**
701 St. Paul Street
Baltimore, MD 21202
410-547-6600
Fax: 410-547-6624
E-mail: webmail@aecf.org
http://www.aecf.org/kidscount
Kids Count is national and state-by-state effort to provide makers and citizens with benchmarks of child well-being. It includes variables such as percentage of low birth-weight babies, child death rates, percentage of childern inpoverty, and percentage of children without health insurance.
Annie E. Casey, Founder

2154 **Pesticides and the Immune System: Public Health Risks**
10 G Street NE
Suite 800
Washington, DC 20002
202-729-7600
Fax: 202-729-7610
E-mail: lauralee@wri.org
http://www.wri.org
Brings together for the frist time an extensive body of experimental and epidemiological research from around the world documenting the the effects of widely used pesticides on the immune system and the attendent health risks. In sodoing, it documents that pesticide-related health risks are much more serious than

genrally known, especially in developing countries where exposure is widespread and infectious diseases take a heavy toll.
100 pages
ISBN: 1-569730-87-3
Andrew Steer, President & CEO
Manish Bapna, Executive Vice President

2155 **Resource Guide on Children's Environmental Health**
600 Grant Street
Suite 800
Denver, CO 80203
303-861-5165
Fax: 303-861-5315
E-mail: info@cchn.org
http://www.cchn.org

The Children's Environmental Health Network has developed the Resource Guide on Children's Environmental Health to assist community leaders, policy makers, health and environmental specialists, members of the advocacy community andmedia, and the general public in identifying and accessing key resources in childern's environmental health.
Annette Kowal, CEO
Kitty Bailey, COO

Environmental Law

Associations

2156 Atlantic States Legal Foundation
658 West Onondaga Street
Syracuse, NY 13204
315-475-1170
Fax: 315-475-6719
E-mail: atlantic.states@aslf.org
http://www.aslf.org

Atlantic States Legal Foundation was established in 1982 to provide legal, technical, and organizational assistance on environment issues to citizen organizations (NGOs), individuals, local governments, and others.

Samuel H Sage, President
Robin Chanay, Chair

2157 Business & Legals Reports
100 Winners Circle
Suite 300
Brentwood, TN 37027
860-510-0100
800-727-5257
Fax: 860-510-7220
E-mail: service@blr.com
http://www.blr.com

Provides essential tools for safety and environmental compliance and training needs.
Guy Crossley, Chief Operating Officer
Keating Ed, Chief Content Officer

2158 Center for Community Action and Environmental Justice
PO Box 33124
Riverside, CA 92519
951-360-8451
Fax: 951-360-5950
E-mail: graciela.l@ccaej.org
http://www.ccaej.org

The Center for Community Action and Environmental Justice serves as a resource center for community groups working on environmental justice issues.
Teresa Flores-Lopez, President
Wendy Eads, President-Elect

2159 Center for Health, Environment and Justice Library
150 S Washington Street, Ste 300
PO Box 6806
Falls Church, VA 22040-6806
703-237-2249
Fax: 703-237-8389
E-mail: chej@chej.org
http://www.chej.org

The Center for Health, Environment and Justice works to build healthy communities, with social justice, economic well-being, and democratic governance. We believe this can happen when individuals from communities have the power to playan integral role in promoting human health and environmental integrity. Our role is to provide the tools to build strong, healthy communities where people can live, work, learn, play and pray.

Lois Marie Gibbs, Executive Director

2160 Center for International Environmental Law
1350 Connecticut Avenue NW
Suite 1100
Washington, DC 20036
202-785-8700
Fax: 202-785-8701
E-mail: info@ciel.org
http://www.ciel.org

The Center for International Environmental Law (CIEL) is a nonprofit organization working to use international law and institutions to protect the environment, promote human health, and ensure a just and sustainable society. We providea wide range of services including legal counsel, policy research, analysis, advocacy, education, training, and capacity building.
Carroll Muffett, President
Cameron Aishton, Administrator

2161 Center for Investigative Reporting
2927 Newbury Street
Suite A
Berkeley, CA 94703
510-809-3160
Fax: 510-849-1813
E-mail: center@cironline.org
http://www.muckraker.org

The only independent, nonprofit organization in the country dedicated to investigative reporting in the public interest on a broad range of issues.
Tom Goldstein, President
Christa Scharfenberg, Acting Executive Director

2162 Communities for a Better Environment
1904 Franklin Street
Suite 600
Oakland, CA 94612
510-302-0430
Fax: 510-302-0437
E-mail: cbeca@mail.com
http://www.cbecal.org

Mission: To achieve environmental health and justice by building grassroots power in and with communities of color and working-class communities.
Gideon Kravoc, Board President
Rev. Daniel Buford, Board Vice President

2163 Community Environmental Council
26 West Anapamu Street
2nd Floor
Santa Barbara, CA 93101
805-963-0583
Fax: 805-962-9080
E-mail: cecadmin@cecmail.org
http://www.cecsb.org

The Community Environmental Council is a nonprofit environmental organization headquartered in Santa Barbara, California. Our community involvement includes managing two recycling centers, a household hazardous waste facility, anurban farm, and three community gardens as well as the environmental education program Art From Scrap. In addition CEC provides research, technical assistance and education on local and statewide land use planning, and solid waste and integrated pestmanagement.
Marilyn Parke, CFO
Dave Davis, Executive Director

2164 Community Rights Counsel
1301 Connecticut Avenue NW
Suite 502
Washington, DC 20036
202-296-6889
Fax: 202-296-6895
E-mail: crc@communityrights.org
http://www.communityrights.org

A nonprofit public interest law firm that was formed in 1997 to assist communities in protecting their health and welfare by regulating permissible land uses, and that provides strategic assistance to state and local governmentattorneys in defending land use laws.
Douglas T Kendall, Founder/Executive Director
Timothy J Dowling, Chief Counsel

2165 Conservation Law Foundation
62 Summer Street
Boston, MA 02110
617-350-0990
Fax: 617-350-4030
E-mail: info@clf.org
http://www.clf.org

A nonprofit, member-supported organization that works to solve the environmental problems that threaten the people, natural resources and communities of New England. CLF's advocates use law, economics and science to design andimplement strategies that conserve natural resources, protect public health and promote vital communities in our region.

John Kassel, President
Priscilla Brooks, Vice President

2166 Earthjustice
50 California Street
Suite 500
San Francisco, CA 94112
415-217-2000
800-584-6460
Fax: 415-217-2040
E-mail: info@earthjustice.org
http://www.earthjustice.org

Nonprofit public interest law firm dedicated to protecting the magnificent places, natural resources, and wildlife of this earth and to defending the right of all people to a healthy environment. It enforces and strengthensenvironmental laws on behalf of hundreds of organizations and communities.
Trip Van Noppen, President
Bruce Neighbor, Vice President

2167 **Environmental Defense Fund**
257 Park Avenue South 212-505-2100
17th Floor 800-684-3322
New York, NY 10010 Fax: 212-505-2375
E-mail: members@edf.org
http://www.edf.org

Dedicated to protecting the environmental rights of all people, including future generations. Among these rights are clean air, clean water, healthy, nourishing food and a flourishing ecosystem. Advocates solutions based on science,even when it leads in unfamiliar directions. Works to create solutions that win lasting political, economic and social support because they are bipartisan, efficient and fair

Fred Krupp, President
David Yarnold, Executive Director

2168 **Environmental Law Alliance Worldwide**
1877 Garden Avenue 541-687-8454
Eugene, OR 97403 Fax: 541-687-0535
E-mail: elawus@elaw.org
http://www.elaw.org

E-LAW advocates serve low income communities around the world, helping citizens strengthen and enforce laws to protect communities from toxic pollution and environmental degradation.

Bern Johnson, Executive Director
Lori Maddox, Associate Director

2169 **Environmental Law Institute**
2000 L Street NW 202-939-3800
Suite 620 Fax: 202-939-3868
Washington, DC 20036 E-mail: law@eli.org
http://www.eli.org

Community Education and Training Program provides citizens and grassroots groups with information on environmental law and policy that can help them participate effectively in the decisions that impact public health and the environmentin their communities. Program's activities have included training courses on right to know laws and a series of workshops in demystifying the law, which focus on using the tools of public participation to address issues ranging from hazardous wasteto land use.

John Cruden, President
Alexandra Dapol Dunn, Executive Director

2170 **Environmental Law and Policy Center of the Midwest**
35 E Wacker Drive 312-673-6500
Suite 1600 Fax: 312-795-3730
Chicago, IL 60601 E-mail: elpc@elpc.org
http://www.elpc.org

Howard A. Learner, President/Executive Director
Nancy Loeb, Chair

2171 **Environmental Support Center**
1500 Massachusetts Avenue NW 202-331-9700
Suite 25 Fax: 202-331-8592
Washington, DC 20005 E-mail: envirosupport@hotmail.com
http://www.envsc.org/

The mission of the Environmental Support Center is to promote the quality of the natural environment, human health, and community sustainability by increasing the organizational effectiveness of local, state, and regional organizationsworking on environmental issues and for environmental justice. To be eligible for assistance, your organization must be a local, state or regional nonprofit organization with a portion of its resources devoted to environmental issues.

Judy Hatcher, Interim Co-Director
Yudi Kidokoro, Chair

2172 **Federation of Environmental Technologists**
W 175 N 11081 Stonewood Dr 262-437-1700
Suite 203 Fax: 262-437-1702
Germantown, WI 53022 E-mail: info@fetinc.org
http://www.fetinc.org

A nonprofit organization formed to assist industry in interpretation of and compliance with environmental regulations. Membership is open to all industries, municipalities, organizations and individuals concerned about environmentalregulations. Currently there are approximately 1000 members and 125 patron companies.

Barbara Hurula, Executive Director
Dan Brady, Board Chair

2173 **Greenpeace**
702 H Street NW 202-462-1177
Suite 300 800-326-0959
Washington, DC 20001 E-mail: info@WDC.greenpeace.org
http://www.Greenpeaceusa.org

Greenpeace is an independent campaigning organization which uses non-violent creative confrontation to expose global environmental problems, and to force solutions that are essential to a green and peaceful future.

Phil Radford, Executive Director
David Barre, Communication Director

2174 **Harvard Environmental Law Society**
Harvard Law School
Wasserstein Hall 617-495-3125
1585 Massachusetts Avenue E-mail: els@mail.law.harvard.edu
Cambridge, MA 02138 http://www.law.harvard.edu/students/orgs/els

The Harvard Environmental Law Society was founded by three Harvard Law students who perceived a pressing need for the Law School, and the law in general, to respond more effectively to the nation's environmental problems. To this end,they created an organization that was committed to preparing students to creatively and intelligently use the law in the service of the environment.

Alexa Shasteen, President
Alec Harris, Treasurer

2175 **Humane Society Legislative Fund**
2100 L Street NW 202-676-2314
Suite 310 866-720-2676
Washington, DC 20037 E-mail: humanesociety@hslf.org
http://www.hslf.org

Humane Society Legislative Fund (HSLF) is a social welfare organization. HSLF works to pass animal protection laws at the state and federal level, to educate the public about animal protection issues, and to support humane candidatesfor office.

Michael Markarian, President
Wayne Pacelle, Executive Vice President

2176 **LandWatch Monterey County**
PO Box 1876 831-759-2824
Salinas, CA 93902 Fax: 831-759-2825
E-mail: landwatch@mclw.org
http://www.landwatch.org

LandWatch is a nonprofit membership organization, founded in 1997. LandWatch works to promote and inspire sound land use legislation at the city, country, and regional lands, through grassroots community action.

Chris Fitz, President
Amy White, Executive Director

2177 **League of Conservation Voters**
1920 L Street NW 202-785-8683
Suite 800 Fax: 202-835-0491
Washington, DC 20036 http://www.lcv.org

Works to create a Congress more responsive to your environmental concerns. As the nonpartisan political voice for over nine million members of environmental and conservation groups, LCV is the only national environmental organizationdedicated full-time to educating citizens about the environmental voting records of Members of Congress.

Gene Karpinski, President
Bill Roberts, Chair

2178 **League of Women Voters of the United States**
1730 M Street NW 202-429-1965
Suite 1000 Fax: 202-429-0854
Washington, DC 20036-4508 E-mail: lwv@lwv.org
http://www.lwv.org

The League of Women Voters, a nonpartisan political organization, encourages the informed and active participation of citizens

in government, works to increase understanding of major public policy issues and influences public policythrough education and advocacy.
Elisabeth MacNamara, President
Nancy E. Tate, Executive Director

2179 Legacy International
1020 Legacy Drive
Bedford, VA 24523
540-297-5982
Fax: 540-297-1860
E-mail: mail@legacyintl.org
http://www.legacyintl.org
Creates environments where people can address personal, community, and global needs while developing skills and effective responses to change. Whether working with youths, corporate leaders, educational professionals, entrepreneurs, orindividuals on opposing sides of a conflict, our goal is the same. Programs provide experiences, skills, and strategies that enable people to build better lives for themselves and others around them.
J E Rash, President
Shanti Thompson, VP/Director of Training

2180 National Association of Conservation Districts League City Office
509 Capitol Ct NE
Washington, DC 20002
202-547-6223
Fax: 202-547-6450
http://www.nacdnet.org
To serve conservation districts by providing national leadership and a unified voice for natural resource conservation.
David Guenther, President
Dave Vogel, Executive Director

2181 Natural Resources Defense Council
40 West 20th Street
New York, NY 10011
212-727-2700
Fax: 212-727-1773
E-mail: nrdcinfo@nrdc.org
http://www.nrdc.org
Mission: To safeguard the Earth: its people, its plants and animals, and natural systems on which all life depends.
Frances Beinecke, President
Peter Lehner, Executive Director

2182 Natural Resources Law Center
University of Colorado
2450 Kittredge Loop Road
Boulder, CO 80309
303-492-8047
E-mail: lawadmin@colorado.edu
http://www.colorado.edu/Law/research/gwc
Mission: Promote sustainability in the rapidly changing American West by informing and influencing natural resources policies, and decisions.
Mark Squillace, Director
Heidi Horten, Special Asst. to the Dir.

2183 New Mexico Environmental Law Center
1405 Luisa Street
Suite 5
Santa Fe, NM 87505
505-989-9022
Fax: 505-989-3769
E-mail: nmelc@nmelc.org
http://www.nmenvirolaw.org
The New Mexico Environmental Law Center works to protect New Mexico's communities and their environments through public education, legislative initiatives, administrative negotiations and litigation.
Douglas Meiklejohn, Executive Director
Shelbie Knox, Development Officer

2184 Southern Environmental Law Center
201 W Main Street
Suite 14
Charlottesville, VA 22902
434-977-4090
Fax: 434-977-1483
E-mail: selcva@selcva.org
http://www.southernenvironment.org
Dedicated to protecting the natural resources of Alabama, Georgia, North Carolina, South Carolina, Tennessee and Virginia. Works with more than 100 partner groups to safeguard southern forests, wetlands, coastal resources, rivers, airand water quality, wildlife habitat and rural landscapes through policy reform, public education, and direct legal action.
Frederick S Middleton III, President
Rick Middleton, Executive Director

2185 Stanford Environmental Law Society
559 Nathan Abbott Way
Stanford, CA 94305-8610
650-723-4421
E-mail: davidb4@stanford.edu
http://elj.stanford.edu/
Provides students with a unique set of opportunities to tap into structured programs or to create and pursue their own projects. Both organizations complement the Stanford Environmental and Natural Reources Law and Policy Program.
Zachary Fabish, Co-President
Craig Segall, Co-President

2186 Student Environmental Action Coalition
PO Box 31909
Philadelphia, PA 19104
215-222-4711
E-mail: webteam@seac.org
http://www.seac.org
Student and youth run national network of progressive organizations and individuals whose aim is to uproot environmental injustices through action and education. Works to create progressive social change on both the local and globallevels.
Matt Reitmann, Working Comte Coordinator

2187 US Public Interest Research Group
218 D Street SE
1st Floor
Washington, DC 20003
202-546-9707
Fax: 202-546-2461
E-mail: webmaster@pirg.org
http://www.uspirg.org
Mission: To deliver persistent, result-oriented public interest activism that protects our environment, encourages a fair, sustainable economy, and fosters responsive, democratic government.
Douglas H Phelps, President
Andre Delattre, Executive Director

2188 Western Environmental Law Center
1216 Lincoln Street
Eugene, OR 97401
541-485-2471
Fax: 541-485-2457
E-mail: info@westernlaw.org
http://www.westernlaw.org
The Western Environmental Law Center is a non-profit public interest law firm that works to protect and restore western wildlands and advocates for healthy environments on behalf of communities throughout the West.
Corrie Yackulic, President
Lori Maddox, Vice President

Publications

2189 A Guide to Environmental Law in Washington DC
Environmental Law Institute
2000 L Street NW
Suite 620
Washington, DC 20036
202-939-3800
Fax: 202-939-3868
E-mail: law@eli.org
http://www.eli.org
Community Education and Training Program provides citizens and grassroots groups with information on environmental law and policy that can help them participate effectively in the decisions that impact public health and the environmentin their communities. Program's activities have included training courses on right-to-know laws and a series of workshops in demystifying the law, which focus on using the tools of public participation to address issues ranging from hazardous wasteto land use.
John Cruden, President
Alexandra Dapol Dunn, Executive Director

2190 Buying Green: Federal Purchasing Practices and the Environment
Government Printing Office
732 North Capitol Street NW
Washington, DC 20401
202-512-0000
E-mail: www.gpo.gov
William H Turri, COO
Robert C Tapella, Cheif of Staff

2191 Clean Water Act Twenty Years Later
Island Press
2000 M Street NW
Suite 650
Washington, DC 20036
202-232-7933
Fax: 202-234-1328
E-mail: info@islandpress.org
http://www.islandpress.org

333 pages
ISBN: 1-559632-65-8
Richard W Alder; Jessica C Landman; Diane Cameron, Author
Charles C. Savitt, President
David Miller, Senior Vice President

2192 Comparative Environmental Law and Regulation
Oceana Publications, Inc
198 Madison Avenue
New York, NY 10016
800-334-4249
Fax: 212-726-6476
E-mail: oxfordonline@oup.com
http://www.oceanalaw.com

Key environmental laws, regulations and implementation systems and agencies of 37 countries from around the world.
2 vol pages Semi-Annual
ISBN: 0-379012-51-0
Nicholas A Robinson, Editor

2193 Environmental Defense Fund
257 Park Avenue South
17th Floor
New York, NY 10010
212-505-2100
800-684-3322
Fax: 212-505-2375
E-mail: members@edf.org
http://www.edf.org

Dedicated to protecting the environmental rights of all people, including future generations. Among these rights are clean air, clean water, healthy nourishing food and a flourishing ecosystem. Advocates solutions based on science,even when it leads in unfamiliar directions. Works to create solutions that win lasting political, economic and social support because they are bipartisan, efficient and fair.

Fred Krupp, President
David Yarnold, Executive Director

2194 Environmental Defense Newsletter
257 Park Avenue South
17th Floor
New York, NY 10010
212-505-2100
800-684-3322
Fax: 212-505-2375
E-mail: members@edf.org
http://www.edf.org

Dedicated to protecting the environmental rights of all people, including future generations. Among these rights are clean air, clean water, healthy, nourishing food and a flourishing ecosystem. The solutions we advocate will be basedon science, even when it leads in unfamiliar directions. We will work to create solutions that win lasting political, economic and social support because they are bipartisan, efficient and fair.

Fred Krupp, President
David Yarnold, Executive Director

2195 Environmental Law and Compliance Methods
Oceana Publications, Inc
198 Madison Avenue
New York, NY 10016
800-334-4249
Fax: 212-726-6476
http://www.oceanalaw.com

Presents practical information tailored to professionals responsible for day-to-day compliance with the environmental laws of the US.
678 pages One Time
ISBN: 0-379214-26-1
Edward E Shea, Author

2196 Environmental Politics and Policy
Congressional Quarterly Press
1255 22nd Street NW
Suite 400
Washington, DC 20037
202-729-1800
366 pages
ISBN: 1-568028-78-4
Walker A Rosenbaum, Author

2197 Environmental Regulatory Glossary
Government Institutes
4 Research Place
Suite 200
Rockville, MD 20850
301-921-2300
Fax: 301-921-0373
623 pages
Thomas F P Sullivan, Author

2198 How Wet is a Wetland?: The Impacts of the Proposed Revisions to the Federal Wetlands Manual
Environmental Defense Fund
257 Park Avenue South
17th Floor
New York, NY 10010
212-505-2100
Fax: 212-505-2375
E-mail: members@edf.org
http://www.edf.org

To prevent environmentally induced harm to human populations.

Fred Krupp, President
David Yarnold, Executive Director

2199 Insider's Guide to Environmental Negotiation
Lewis Publishers
PO Box 72264
Albany, GA 31708
229-432-1762
E-mail: tlewis@lewispub.com
http://www.lewispub.com

242 pages
ISBN: 0-873715-09-8
Dale M Gorczynski, Author

2200 International Environmental Policy: From the Twentieth to the Twenty-First Century
Duke University Press
905 W Main Street, Ste 18-B
Durham, NC 27701
919-688-5134
888-651-0122
Fax: 919-688-2615
E-mail: orders@dukepress.edu
http://www.dukepress.com
496 pages
Ken Wissoker, Editor in Chief
Courtney Berger, Assistant Editor

2201 Making Development Sustainable: Redefining Institutions, Policy, and Economics
Island Press
2000 M Street NW
Suite 650
Washington, DC 20036
202-232-7933
Fax: 202-234-1328
E-mail: info@islandpress.org
http://www.islandpress.org

362 pages
ISBN: 1-559632-13-5
Johan Holmberg, Author
Charles C. Savitt, President
David Miller, Senior Vice President

2202 Managing Planet Earth: Perspectives on Population, Ecology and the Law
Greenwood Publishing Group
88 Post Road W
Westport, CT 06881
203-226-3571
800-225-5800
http://www.greenwood.com

184 pages
ISBN: 0-897892-16-X
Miguel A Santos, Author

2203 **Natural Resources Policy and Law: Trends and Directions**
Island Press; Natural Resources Law Center
2000 M Street NW
Suite 650
Washington, DC 20036
202-232-7933
Fax: 202-234-1328
E-mail: info@islandpress.org
http://www.islandpress.org

255 pages
ISBN: 1-559632-46-1
Lawrence J MacDonnell; Sarah F Bates, Author
Charles C. Savitt, President
David Miller, Senior Vice President

2204 **New Mexico Environmental Law Center: Green Fire Report**
1405 Luisa Street
Suite 5
Santa Fe, NM 87505
505-989-9022
Fax: 505-989-3769
E-mail: nmelc@nmelc.org
http://www.nmenvirolaw.org

A publication from the organization dedicated to protecting New Mexico's natural environment and communities from pollution and degradation. Over 80 percent of our clients are indigenous Native American or Hispanic and low income.Cases often include mining issues, growth impacts, water protection, air pollution, public lands protection or indigenous land claims. The organization is supported by grants from foundations, contributions from individuals and fees.
12 pages Quarterly
Douglas Meiklejohn, Executive Director
Shelbie Knox, Development Officer

2205 **Oversight of Implementation of the Clean Air Act Amendments of 1990**
Government Printing Office
1616 P Street NW
Washington, DC 20036
202-328-5000
Fax: 202-512-2104
E-mail: contactcenter@gpo.gov
http://www.rff.org

ISBN: 0-160388-26-0

2206 **People for the Ethical Treatment of Animals**
501 Front Street
Norfolk, VA 23510
757-622-7382
Fax: 757-622-0457
E-mail: info@peta.org
http://www.peta.org

People for the Ethical Treatment of Animals, with more than seven hundred members, is the largest animal rights organization in the world. Founded in 1980, PETA is dedicated to establishing and protecting the rights of all animals.PETA operates under the simple principle that animals are not ours to eat, wear, experiment on, or use for entertainment.
Kathy Guillermo, Senior Vice President, Labor
Tracy Reiman, Executive Vice President

2207 **Renewable Resource Policy: The Legal-Institutional Foundation**
Island Press
2000 M Street NW
Suite 650
Washington, DC 20036
202-232-7933
Fax: 202-234-1328
E-mail: info@islandpress.org
http://www.islandpress.org

572 pages
ISBN: 1-559632-25-9
Charles C. Savitt, President
David Miller, Senior Vice President

2208 **Saving All the Parts: Reconciling Economics and the Endangered Species Act**
Island Press
2000 M Street NW
Suite 650
Washington, DC 20036
202-232-7933
Fax: 202-234-1328
E-mail: info@islandpress.org
http://www.islandpress.org

280 pages
ISBN: 1-559632-02-X
Rocky Barker, Author
Charles C. Savitt, President
David Miller, Senior Vice President

2209 **Searching Out the Headwaters: Change and Rediscovery in Western Policy**
Island Press
2000 M Street NW
Suite 650
Washington, DC 20036
202-232-7933
Fax: 202-234-1328
E-mail: info@islandpress.org
http://www.islandpress.org

253 pages
ISBN: 1-559632-17-8
Sarah F Bates, et al, Author
Charles C. Savitt, President
David Miller, Senior Vice President

2210 **Setting National Priorities: Policy for the Nineties**
Brookings Institution
1775 Massachusetts Ave., NW
Washington, DC 20036
202-797-6000
800-275-1447
Fax: 202-797-6004
http://www.brookings.edu

Strobe Talbott, President
John N. Thorton, Chairman

2211 **Trade and the Environment: Law, Economics and Policy**
Island Press
2000 M Street NW
Suite 650
Washington, DC 20036
202-232-7933
Fax: 202-234-1328
E-mail: info@islandpress.org
http://www.islandpress.org

333 pages
ISBN: 1-559632-67-4
Charles C. Savitt, President
David Miller, Senior Vice President

2212 **Understanding Environmental Administration and Law**
Island Press
2000 M Street NW
Suite 650
Washington, DC 20036
202-232-7933
Fax: 202-234-1328
E-mail: info@islandpress.org
http://www.islandpress.org

239 pages
ISBN: 1-559634-74-X
Susan J Buck, Author
Charles C. Savitt, President
David Miller, Senior Vice President

Financial Resources

Foundations & Charities

2213 AMETEK Foundation
1100 Cassatt Road
PO Box 1764
Berwyn, PA 19312
610-647-2121
800-473-1286
Fax: 215-323-9337
E-mail: webmaster@ametek.com
http://www.ametek.com

The AMETEK Foundation-the charitable arm of AMETEK Inc., a global manufacturer of electronic insturments and electric motors, has long supported efforts to improve early childhood literacy in schools and libraries near its plants andfacilities.
Robert W Yannarell, Assistant Secretary

2214 ARCO Foundation
515 South Flower Street
Los Angeles, CA 90071
213-486-3342
The foundation awards education grants both on the national and regional level. Education programs that are national in scope are funded through the headquarters located in Los Angeles. Regional grants are made to nonprofitorganizations in states where ARCO has facilities and personnel.
Russell Sakaguchi, Program Officer

2215 Abelard Foundation
2530 San Pable Avenue
Suite B
Berkeley, CA 94702
510-644-1904
A family foundation with a 40 year history of progressive funding. The foundation is committed to supporting grassroots social change organizations which engage in community organizing.
Leah Brumer, Executive Director

2216 Acid Rain Foundation
1410 Varsity Drive
Raleigh, NC 27606
919-828-9443
Fax: 919-515-3593
Designed to significantly reduce emissions responsible for acid deposition.
Dr. Harriet S Stubbs, Executive Director

2217 Acorn Foundation
2530 San Pablo Avenue
Suite B
Berkeley, CA 94702
510-644-1904
Environmental issues, bio-diversity, health issues related to environmental hazards.
Leah Brummer, Executive Director

2218 African Wildlife Foundation
1400 Sixteenth Street, NW
Suite 120
Washington, DC 20036
202-939-3333
888-494-5354
Fax: 202-939-3332
E-mail: africanwildlife@awf.org
http://www.awf.org

The African Wildlife Foundation, together with the people of Africa, work to ensure the wildlife and wild lands of Africa will endure forever. The AFW is the leading international conservation organization focused soley on Africa. Webelieve that protecting Africa's wildlife and wild landscapes is the key to the future prosperity of Africa and its people.
Patrick Bregin, CEO
Jeff Chrisfield, CFO

2219 Amax Foundation
200 Park Avenue
New York, NY 10166
212-856-4250
Sonja Michaud, President

2220 American Association of Petroleum Geologists Foundation
Po Box 979
Tulsa, OK 74101
918-584-2555
Fax: 918-560-2665
E-mail: info@aapg.org
http://www.aapg.org

News for explorationists of oil, gas and minerals as well as for geologists with environmental and water well concerns.

David Curtiss, Executive Director
Regina Gill, Administration Manager

2221 American Electric Power
1 Riverside Plaza
Columbus, OH 43215
614-716-1000
E-mail: corpcomm@aep.com
http://www.aep.com

One of the largest electric utilities in the United States, delivering electricity to more then 5 million customers in 11 states. AEP ranks among the nations largest generators of electricity, owning more then 38,000 megawatts ofgenerating capacity in the US.
Nick Akins, President & CEO
Robert P. Powers, Executive Vice President

2222 American Rivers
1101 14th Street NW
Suite 1400
Washington, DC 20005
202-347-7550
877-347-7550
Fax: 202-347-9240
E-mail: outreach@americanrivers.org
http://www.americanrivers.org

Support and donations for the protection and restoration of America's rivers for the benefit of people, fish and wildlife.

William Robert (Bob) Irvin, President
Sandra Adams, Senior VP Advertising

2223 Amoco Foundation
200 East Randolph Drive
Chicago, IL 60601
312-856-6306
E-mail: foundation@amoco.com
http://www.amoco.com

The BP Amoco awards grants for education, primarily in the field of science and engineering, as well as community organizations in BP Amoco communities.
Patricia Wright, Executive Director

2224 Andrew W. Mellon Foundation
140 East 62nd Street
New York, NY 10065
212-838-8400
Fax: 212-888-4172
http://www.mellon.org

The foundation concentrates most of its grantmaking in a few areas. Institutions and programs receiving support are often leaders in fields of Foundation activity, but they may also be promising newcomers, or in a position todemonstrate new ways of overcoming obstacles to achieve program goals.
Earl Lewis, President
John E. Hull, Financial Vice President

2225 Asthma and Allergy Foundation of America
8201 Corporate Drive
Suite 1000
Landover, MD 20785
202-466-7643
800-727-8462
Fax: 202-466-8940
E-mail: info@aafa.org
http://www.aafa.org

Dedicated to improving the quality of life for people with asthma and allergies through education, advocacy and research.

William McLin, President & CEO

2226 Atherton Family Foundation
827 Fort Street Mall
Honolulu, HI 96813
808-566-5524
Fax: 808-521-6286
E-mail: foundations@hcf-hawaii.org
http://www.athertonfamilyfoundation.org

The Atherton Family Foundation is now one of the largest endowed grantmaking private resource in the State of Hawaii, devoted exclusively to the support of charutabe activities. It perpetuates the philanthropic commitment expressedduring the

lifetime of Juliette M. Atherton and Frank C. Atherton, and of the family who have followed them.
Judith M. Dawson, President
Frank C. Atherton, Vice President & Treasurer

2227 Audubon Naturalist Society of the Central Atlantic States
8940 Jones Mill Road
Chevy Chase, MD 20815
301-652-9188
Fax: 301-951-7179
E-mail: contact@audubonnaturalist.org
http://www.audubonnaturalist.org

The Audubon Naturalist Society is an independent environmental education and conservation organization with over 10,000 members in the Washington DC area. The society offers a wide variety of natural history classes and campaigns forprotection and renewal of the Mid-Atlantic regions natural resources.
Neal Fitzpatrick, Executive Director
Kathy Rushing, President

2228 BP America
501 Westlake Park Boulevard
Houston, TX 77079
281-366-2000
E-mail: bpconsum@bp.com
http://www.bp.com

The purpose is to provide products that satisfy human needs, fuel progress and economic growth and to maintain and invest in a sustainable environment.
Dr. Brian Gilvary, CFO
Bernard Looney, COO, Production

2229 Baltimore Gas & Electric Foundation
PO Box 1475
Baltimore, MD 21203
410-265-4100
800-685-0123
Fax: 410-234-7123
E-mail: corporate.communications@bge.com
http://www.bge.com

The mission is to safely, economically, reliably, and profitably deliver gas and electricity to our customers. The vision is to be a recognized leader in energy delivery by enhancing our customer's quality of life, our shareholdersvalue, and our team's well being.
Kenneth W. DeFontes Jr, President & CEO
Carim V. Khouzami, Senior Vice President

2230 Bauman Foundation
2040 S Street, NW
Washington, DC 20009
202-328-2040
Fax: 202-328-2003
http://www.baumanfoundation.org

The Bauman Foundation was funded by the estate of Lionel R. Bauman, a New York City lawyer and businessman. He was a partner in the real estate development firm of Eugene M. Grant & Co. The foundation is managed by Lionel's daughter.Patricia Bauman.
Patricia Bauman, President
Gary D. Bass, Executive Director

2231 Bay and Paul Foundations, The
17 West 94th Street
New York, NY 10025
212-663-1115
Fax: 212-932-0316
E-mail: info@bayandpaulfoundations.org
http://www.bayandpaulfoundations.org

The Bay and Paul Foundations Inc. was formed in January 2005 by the merger of 2 foundations. The Bay Foundation and the Josephine Bay Paul and C. Michael Paul Foundation.
Robert W Ashton, Executive Director
Frederick Bay, President & CEO

2232 Blandin Foundation
100 North Pokegama Avenue
Grand Rapids, MI 55744
218-326-0523
877-882-2257
Fax: 218-327-1949
http://www.blandinfoundation.org

Blandin Foundation is focused on the economic viability of rural Minnesota communities, as part of our mission to help strengthen rural Minnesota and the Grand Rapids area, our home.
Paul M Olson, President

2233 Boise Cascade Corporation
1111 West Jefferson Street
Suite 300
Boise, ID 83728
208-384-6161
Fax: 208-384-7189
E-mail: bcweb@bc.com
http://www.bc.com

As we focus on delivering the best return for our investors, we can be trusted to do what we say and take responsibility for our actions, which we base on values and principles.
Duane McDougall, Chairman
Thomas Carlile, CEO

2234 Cape Branch Foundation
5 Independence Way
Princeton, NJ 08540
609-987-0300
Fax: 609-452-1024

A private foundation which provides grant support for higher education, museums, and land conservation in the New Jersey area. There are no grants to individuals.
Dorothy Frank, Partner

2235 Cargill Foundation
PO Box 9300
Minneapolis, MN 55440
952-742-2546
Fax: 952-742-7224
http://www.cargill.com

Cargill is an international provider of food, agricultural and risk management products and services. With 158,000 employees in 66 countries, the company is committed to using its knoweldge and experience to collaborate with customersto help them succeed.
Gregory R. Page, Chairtman & CEO
David W MacLennan, President, COO & CFO

2236 Caribbean Conservation Corporation
4424 NW 13th Street
Suite B-11
Gainesville, FL 32609
352-373-6441
800-678-7853
Fax: 352-375-2449
E-mail: stc@conserveturtles.org
http://www.conserveturtles.org

Caribbean Conservation Corporation is a nonprofit membership organization based in Gainesville. CCC was the first marine turtle conservation organization in the world, and has more than 40 years of experience in national andinternational sea turtle conservation, research and educational endeavors.
David Godfrey, Executive Director
Laura Forte, President

2237 Carolyn Foundation
818 W 46th Street
Suite 203
Minneapolis, MN 55419
612-596-3266
612-596-3279
Fax: 612-339-1951
E-mail: berdahl@carolynfoundation.org
http://www.carolynfoundation.org

The Carolyn Foundation is a small general foundation. Please check out our website www.carolynfoundation.org for the most up-to-date information regarding funding priorities, guidelines and application process.

Becky Erdahl, Executive Director
Kristen Cullen, Foundation Administrator

2238 Caterpillar Foundation
100 Northeast Adams Street
Peoria, IL 61629
309-675-1000
http://www.caterpillar.com

Provides funding and support from a corporate perspective. Formed in 1952, the Foundation has distributed almost $200 million to support education, health and human services, and civic, cultural, and environmental causes.
Doug Oberhalman, Chairman & CEO
Edward J Scott, Treasurer

2239 Charles Engelhard Foundation
645 5th Avenue
7th Floor
New York, NY 10022
212-935-2430

Provides funding to a wide range of causes including education, medical research, cultural institutions, and wildlife conservation.
Elaine Catterall, Secretary

2240 Chesapeake Bay Foundation
6 Herndon Avenue
Annapolis, MD 21403
410-268-8816
Fax: 410-268-6687
E-mail: chesapeake@cbf.org
http://www.cbf.org

The only independent organization dedicated soley to restoring and protecting the Chesapeake Bay and its tributary rivers.
William C Baker, President
Vollie Melson, Vice President, Development

2241 Chevron Corporation
6001 Bollinger Canyon Road
San Ramon, CA 94583
925-842-1000
E-mail: chevweb@chevron.com
http://www.chevron.com

As a global enterprise that is highly competitive across all energy sectors, Chevron brings together a wealth of talent, shared values and a strong commitment to developing vital energy resources worldwide.
Skip Rhodes, Mgr. Corporate Contributions

2242 Clean Water Action
1444 Eye Street NW
Suite 400
Washington, DC 20005
202-895-0420
Fax: 202-895-0438
E-mail: cwa@cleanwater.org
http://www.cleanwateraction.org

Clean Water Action is a national organization of diverse people and groups working together for clean water, protecting health, creating jobs and making democracy work.

Bob Wendelgass, Executive Director
Robert Wendelgass, President & CEO

2243 Collins Foundation
1618 SW 1st Avenue
Suite 505
Portland, OR 97201
503-227-7171
E-mail: information@collinsfoundation.org
http://www.collinsfoundation.org

An independent private foundation, exists to improve, enrich and give greater expression to the religious, educational, cultural, and scientific endeavors in the state of Oregon and to assist in improving the quality of life in thestate.
Truman W. Collins Jr., President
Cynthia G Adams, Executive Vice President

2244 Compton Foundation
101 Montgomery Street
Suite 850
San Francisco, CA 94104
415-391-9001
Fax: 415-391-9005
E-mail: info@comptonfoundation.org
http://www.comptonfoundation.org

Seeks to foster human and ecological security by addressing contemporary threats to these inalienable rights. We support responsible stewardship that respects the rights of future generations to a balanced and healthy ecology, bothpersonal and global, allowing for the full richness of human experience.
Ellen Friedman, Executive Director
Rebecca DiDomenico, President

2245 Conservation International
2011 Crystal Drive
Suite 500
Arlington, VA 22202
703-341-2400
800-429-5660
Fax: 202-887-5188
http://www.conservation.org

Our mission is to conserve the Earth's living natural heritage, our global biodiversity, and to demonstrate that human societies are able to live harmoniously with nature.
Peter A Seligmann, Chairman of the Board

2246 Conservation Treaty Support Fund
3705 Cardiff Road
Chevy Chase, MD 20815
301-654-3150
800-654-3150
Fax: 301-652-6390
E-mail: ctsf@conservationtreaty.org
http://www.conservationtreaty.org

CTSF's mission is to support the major inter-governmental treaties which conserve wild natural resrouces and habitat for their own sake and the benefit of the people. These includ the Endangered Species Convention and the InternationalWetlands Convention. CTSF raises support for treaty projects from indivduals, corporations, foundations and government agencies. It also develops educational and informational materials including videos and the CITES Endangered Species Book.
1986 pages
George A Furness Jr, President

2247 Conservation and Research Foundation
PO Box 909
Shelburne, VT 05482
913-268-0076
Fax: 913-268-0076
E-mail: mwetzel@kc3ol.dynip.com
http://www.conservationandresearchfoundation.org
Dr Mary Wetzel, President
Philip M Lintilhac, Secretary

2248 Cooper Industries Foundation
PO Box 4446
Houston, TX 77210
713-209-8400
Fax: 713-209-8982
E-mail: info@cooperindustries.com
http://www.cooperindustries.com

Cooper was primarily a one-market company, manufactguring power and compression equipment for the transmission of natural gas. Eventually broadening its product lines to include petroleum and industrial equipment, electrical powerequipment, automotive products tools and hardware.
Alexander M Cutler, Chairman & CEO
Kenneth F Davis, President, Vehicle Group

2249 Cricket Foundation
Exchange Place
Suite 2200
Boston, MA 02109
617-570-1130
Fax: 617-523-1231
Dedicated to improving the quality of life
George W Butterworth III, Counsel

2250 Curtis and Edith Munson Foundation
1990 M Street, NW
Suite 250
Washington, DC 20036
202-887 8992
Fax: 202-887-8987
E-mail: info@munsonfdn.org
http://www.munsonfdn.org

Over the past 15 years, we have emphasized partnerships, collaborations, and seed funding for new projects and organizations within the framework of our programs as defined by our guidelines.
C Wolcott Henry III, President
Angel Braestrup, Executive Director

2251 Deer Creek Foundation
720 Olive Street
Suite 1975
St. Louis, MO 63101
314-241-3228
E-mail: bharvey@dcsfoundation.org
http://dcsfoundation.org
Projects should focus on the preservation and advancement of majority rule in our society, including the protection of basic rights
Mary Stake Hawker, Administrator
Brian Harvey, President

2252 Defenders of Wildlife
1130 17th Street NW
Washington, DC 20036
202-682-9400
800-915-6789
Fax: 202-682-1331
E-mail: defenders@mail.defenders.org
http://www.defenders.org

Dedicated to the protection of all native wild animals and plants in their natural communities. Focus is placed on what scientists consider two of the most serious environmental threats to the planet: the accelerating rate ofextinction of species and the associated loss of biological diversity, and habitat alteration and destruction. Long known for leadership on endangered species issues.
Jamie Rappaport Clark, President & CEO

2253 Digital Equipment Corporation
111 Powder Mill Road
Unit B14
Maynard, MA 01754
508-493-5111
Fax: 508-493-8780
http://www.digitalcentury.com
A leading worldwide supplier of networked computer systems, software and services. Its products serve a variety of applications, such as scientific analysis, industrial control, time-sharing, commercial data processing, graphic arts,word processing, office

automation, health care, instrumentation, engineering, and simulation.
Jane Hamel, Mgr. Corporate Contributions

2254 **Dunspaugh-Dalton Foundation**
1500 San Remo Avenue 305-668-4192
Suite 103 Fax: 305-668-4247
Coral Gables, FL 33146 E-mail: ddf@dunspaughdalton.org
http://www.dunspaughdalton.com
Supports educational, social, medical and cultural institutions in Florida, California and North Carolina.
Sarah Lane Bonner, President
Aexina H Lane, Vice President

2255 **Earth Share**
7735 Old Georgetown Road 240-333-0300
Suite 900 800-875-3863
Bethesda, MD 20814 Fax: 240-333-0301
E-mail: info@earthshare.org
http://www.earthshare.org
A nationwide network of America's leading non-profit environmental and conservation organizations, works to promote environmental education and charitable giving through workplace giving campaigns.
Marci Reed, Executive Director
Steven Kravitz, CFO

2256 **Earth Society Foundation**
238 E 58th Street 212-832-3659
Suite 2400 Fax: 212-826-6213
New York, NY 10022 E-mail: earthsociety1@hotmail.com
http://earthsocietyfoundation.org
Started the original Earth Day, which is devoted to peace, justice and the care of earth. It invites everyone to think and act as trustees of earth.
Mary Carlin, Secretary
Helen Garland, Chairperson

2257 **Echoing Green**
494 Eighth Ave 212-689-1165
2nd Floor Fax: 212-689-9010
New York, NY 10001 E-mail: info@echoinggreen.org
http://www.echoinggreen.org
Echoing Green is a global science venture fund that provides seed funding and support to visionary leaders with bold new ideas for social change.
Cheryl Dorsey, President
David C Hodgson, Chairman

2258 **Edward John Noble Foundation**
Po Box 954 203-438-5690
Ridgefield, CT 06877
EJ Noble Smith, Executive Director

2259 **Energy Foundation**
301 Battery Street 415-561-6700
5th Floor Fax: 415-561-6709
San Francisco, CA 94111 E-mail: energyfund@ef.org
http://www.ef.org
The Energy Foundation is a partnership of major donors interested in solving the world's energy problems. Our mission is to advance energy efficiency and renewable energy-new components of a clean energy future.
Hal Harvey, Executive Director
Eric Heitz, President

2260 **Environmental Law Institute**
2000 L Street NW 202-939-3800
Suite 620 Fax: 202-939-3868
Washington, DC 20036 E-mail: law@eli.org
http://www.eli.org
Provides information services, advice, publications, training courses, seminars, research programs and policy recommendations to engage and empower environmental leaders the world over.
John Cruden, President
Alexandra Dapol Dunn, Executive Director

2261 **Exxon Education Foundation**
225 E John W Carpenter Freeway 972-444-1000
Room 1429 http://www.exxon.com
Irving, TX 75062
It is ExxonMobil's longstanding belief that education is the key to progress, development and economic growth, and we are committed to being a responsible partner in the communities where we operate.
Leonard Fleischer, Mgr. Corporate Contributions

2262 **First Hawaiian Foundation**
999 S Bishop Street 808-525-7000
29th Floor http://www.fhb.com
Honolulu, HI 96813
First Hawaiian Foundation is the charitable arm of First Hawaiian Bank. The foundation funds educational opportunities, access to health care, services for children and youth, human service needs, and the many ways that the arts enrichour lives.
Herbert E Wolff, Secretary

2263 **First Interstate Bank of Nevada Foundation**
PO Box 11007 775-784-3844
Reno, NV 89520
Kevin Day, President

2264 **FishAmerica Foundation**
1001 North Fairfax St. 703-519-9691
Suite 501 Fax: 703-519-1872
Alexandria, VA 22314 E-mail: fishamerica@asafishing.org
http://www.fishamerica.org
Unites the sportfishing industry with conservation groups, government natural resource agencies, corporations, and charitable foundations to invest in fish and habitat conservation and research across the country.
Jeff Marble, Chairman
Patrick Egan, Grants Manager

2265 **FishAmerica Foundation.**
Grant Guidelines
1001 North Fairfax St. 703-519-9691
Suite 501 Fax: 703-519-1872
Alexandria, VA 22314 E-mail: fishamerica@asafishing.org
http://www.fishamerica.org
The FishAmerica Foundation provides funding for local, hands-on projects to enhance fish populations, restore fisheries habitat, improve water quality, and advancing fisheries research in North America; thereby increasing theopportunity for sportfishing success.
Jeff Marble, Chairman
Patrick Egan, Grants Manager

2266 **Frank Weeden Foundation**
747 Third Avenue 212-888-1672
34th Floor Fax: 212-888-1354
New York, NY 10017 E-mail: info@weedenfoundation.org
http://www.weedenfoundation.org
From its inception in 1963, the Foundation embraced the protection of biodiversity as its main priority.
Norman Weeden, Ph.d., President
Don A. Weeden, Executive Director

2267 **Friends of the Earth Foundation**
1100 15th Street NW 202-783-7400
11th Floor 877-843-8687
Washington, DC 20005 Fax: 202-783-0444
E-mail: foe@foe.org
http://www.foe.org
Defends the environment and champions a healthy and just world.
Erich Pica, President

2268 **Frost Foundation**
511 Armijo 505-986-0208
Suite A E-mail: info@frostfound.org
Santa Fe, NM 87501 http://www.frostfound.org
Created to be operated exclusively for educational, charitable and religious purposes. The foundation possesses all powers,

rights, privileges, capacities and immunities which non profit corporations are authorized to possess.
Mary Amelia Whited-Howell, President
Philip B. Howell, Executive Vice President

2269 Fund for Animals
200 West 57th Street 212-246-2096
New York, NY 10019 866-720-2676
Fax: 212-246-2633
E-mail: info@fundforanimals.org
http://www.fundforanimals.org/about/
The Fund for Animals was founded in 1967 by author/humanitarian Cleveland Amory to speak for those who can't. In 2005, The Fund for Animals merged with The Humane Society of the United States, to avoid duplication of program andincrease strength and coordination in the areas of legislation, litigation, humane education and disaster relief.
Marian Probst, Chair

2270 Fund for Preservation of Wildlife and Natural Areas
Boston Safe Deposit and Trust Company
1 Boston Place 617-722-7340
Boston, MA 02108 Fax: 617-722-7129
Accounting services for mutual fund companies.
Sylvia Salas, Director

2271 George B Storer Foundation
PO Box 1270 307-326-8308
Saratoga, WY 82331
Provides support for higher education and social services, especially for the blind, youth organizations, conservation, hospitals, and cultural programs.
Peter Storer, President

2272 Georgia Pacific Foundation
133 Peachtree Street NE 404-652-4000
Atlanta, GA 30303 http://www.gp.com
Invests in educational efforts that empower youth, and provide workers with job readiness training. We also invest in scholarships and technical programs that give workers the skills necessary for today's workplace.
Curley M Dossman, President

2273 Geraldine R. Dodge Foundation
14 Maple Avenue 973-540-8442
Suite 400 Fax: 973-540-1211
Morristown, NJ 07960 E-mail: info@grdodge.org
http://www.grdodge.org
The mission of the Geraldine R. Dodge Foundation is to support and encourage those educational, cultural, social and environmental values that contribute to making our society more humaine and our world more liveable.
Barbara Fulton Moran, Forner Executive Director
Martin J Farawell, Program Director

2274 Greensward Foundation
Po Box 610 Lenox Hill Station E-mail: info@greenswardsparks.org
New York, NY 10021 http://www.echonyc.com
The Greensward Foundation, through its local branches, celebrates and suppports our communities's public parks. We are non-profit. We receive no public funding, subsisting entirely on private grants and member contributions.
Robert M Makla, Director

2275 HKH Foundation
275 Madison Avenue 212-682-7522
33rd Floor http://hkhfoundation.org
New York, NY 10016
Gives a major portion of its funding to the Adirondack Historical Association. Additional funding is distributed to the disarmament and prevention of war, civil liberties and human rights, and environmental protection.
Harriet Barlow, Adv.

2276 Helen Clay Frick Foundation
7227 Reynolds Street 412-371-0600
PO Box 86190
Pittsburgh, PA 15208
Devoted to the interpretation of the life and times of Henry Clay Frick.
DeCoursey E McIntosh, Executive Director

2277 Henry L and Consuelo S Wenger Foundation
100 Renaissance Center 313-567-1212
Detroit, MI 48226
Shelly Raines, Principal Manager

2278 Hoffman-La Roche Foundation
340 Kingsland Street 973-235-5000
Nutley, NJ 07110 http://www.rocheusa.com
Hoffman-La Roche is the US prescription drug unit of the Roche Group, one of the world's leading research-oriented health care groups with core businesses in pharmaceuticals and diagnostics.
Rosemary Bruner, Administrative Director

2279 INFORM
PO Box 320403 212-361-2400
Brooklyn, NY 11232 Fax: 212-361-2412
http://www.informinc.org
INFORM is an independent research organization that examines the effects of business practices on the environment and on human health. Our goal is to identify ways of doing business that ensure environmentally sustainable economicgrowth. Our reports are used by government, industry, and environmental leaders around the world.
Verginia Ramsey, President
Jon Parks, Co Chair

2280 International Primate Protection League
PO Box 776 843-871-2280
Summerville, SC 29484 Fax: 843-871-7988
E-mail: info@ippl.org
http://www.ippl.org
An organization that works worldwide for the conservation and protection of apes and monkeys.
Dr Shirley McGreal, Executive Director
Barbara Allison, Office Manager

2281 International Wildlife Coalition
634 N Falmouth Highway 508-457-1898
Box 388 Fax: 508-457-1898
North Falmouth, MA 02556 E-mail: iwchq@iwc.org
http://www.iwc.org
A federally recognized, non-profit tax-exempt charitable organization. The Coalition is dedicated to public education, research, resuce, rehabilitation, litigation, legislation and international treaty negotiations concerning globalwildlife and natural habitat protection issues.
Daniel J Morast, President

2282 International Wildlife Conservation Society
Grants Management Association
2300 Southern Boulevard 718-220-5100
Bronx, NY 10460 http://www.wcs.org
Saves wildlife and wetlands. We do so through careful science, international conservation, education, and the management of the world's largest system of urban wildlife parks, led by the flagship Bronx Zoo.
Ward W Woods, Chair of the Board
Christian Samper, President & CEO

2283 Jessie Smith Noyes Foundation
6 E 39th Street 212-684-6577
12th Floor Fax: 212-689-6549
New York, NY 10016 E-mail: noyes@noyes.org
http://www.noyes.org

Promotes a sustainable and just social and natural system by supporting grassroots organizations and movements committed to this goal.

Victor DeLuca, President
Margaret Segall, Administration Director

2284 **John D and Catherine T MacArthur Foundation**
140 S Dearborn Street 312-726-8000
Suite 1100 Fax: 312-920-6258
Chicago, IL 60603 E-mail: 4answers@macfound.org
http://www.macfound.org
A private independent grantmaking institution dedicated to helping groups and individuals foster lasting improvement in the human condition.

Robert L Galluci, President

2285 **Jules and Doris Stein Foundation**
PO Box 30
Beverly Hills, CA 90213 323-276-2101
Founded the Jules Stein Eyes Institute at UCLA in the 1960's. Founded as a multidisciplinary center for vision science.
Linda L Valliant, Secretary

2286 **Kangaroo Protection Foundation**
1900 L Street NW
Suite 526 202-452-1100
Washington, DC 20036
Marian Newman, Program Director

2287 **Keep America Beautiful**
1010 Washington Boulevard 203-659-3000
Stamford, CT 06901 Fax: 203-659-3001
E-mail: info@kab.org
http://www.kab.org
Nonprofit organization whose network of local, statewide and international affiliate programs educates individuals about litter prevention and ways to reduce, reuse, recycle and properly manage waste materials. Through partnershipsand strategic alliances with citizens, businesses and government, Keep America Beautiful's programs motivate millions of volunteers annually to clean up, beautify and improve their neighborhoods, thereby creating healthier and safer communityenvironments.
Becky Lyons, COO
Susan Burkhardt, Senior Director, Affiliate M

2288 **Kraft General Foods Foundation**
Kraft Court
Unit 2W 877-535-5666
800-543-5335
Glenview, IL 60025 http://www.kraftfoods.com
Based on the values of innovation, quality, safety, respect, integrtity and openness. These values are what we stand for, the standard of conduct we hold ourselves to and our commitment to the people who work with us, invest in us andpurchase our products.
Pamela Hollie, Dir. Corporate Contributions

2289 **Kroger Company Foundation**
1014 Vine Street 513-762-4443
PO Box 1199 866-221-4141
Cincinnati, OH 45202 http://www.kroger.com
Spans many states with store formats that include grocery and multi-department store, convenience stores and mall jewelry stores. We operate under nearly 2 dozen banners, all of which share the same belief in building strong local tiesand brand loyalty with our customers.
Paul Bernish, VP/Secretary

2290 **Liz Claiborne Foundation**
1441 Broadway Avenue E-mail: corporate.secretary@liz.com
New York, NY 10018 http://www.lizclaiborneinc.com/foundation/default.asp
Established to serve as the Company's center for charitable activiteis. Works to meet the needs of the communities where the major facilities of Liz Claiborne, Inc. are located. Projects focus primarily on helping disadvantaged womengain their self-sufficiency through job training and microenterprise development. The Foundation also provides ongoing support to many artistic and cultural institutions which enhance the livability of our communities.

Paul R Charron, Chairman of the Board/CEO
Angela J Ahrendts, Executive Vice President

2291 **Liz Claiborne and Art Ortenberg Foundation**
650 5th Avenue 212-333-2536
15th Floor Fax: 212-956-3531
New York, NY 10019 E-mail: lcaof@fcc.net
http://www.lcaof.org
The Foundation has 2 primary program interests: mitigation of conflict between the land and resources needs of local communities and conservation of biological diversity in rural landscapes outside of parks and reserves; implementationof relevant, field based scientific, technical and practical training programs for local people. The Foundation typically funds modest, carefully designed field activities-primarily in developing countries and the Northern Rockies.
James Murtaugh, Director
Jeffery T Olson, Director

2292 **Louis and Anne Abrons Foundation**
437 Madison Avenue 212-756-3376
New York, NY 10017
Richard Abrons, President and Director

2293 **Louisiana Land and Exploration Company**
PO Box 60350 504-566-6500
New Orleans, LA 70160
One of the largest independent oil and gas exploration compaines in the United States. It operates a crude oil refinery and conducts exploration and production operations in the United States and selected foreign countries.
Karen A Overson, Contributions Coordinator

2294 **MNC Financial Foundation**
10 Light Street 301-244-5000
PO Box 987-MS251001
Baltimore, MD 21203
Geeorge BP Ward Jr, Secretary/Treasurer
Alfred Lerner, Chairman

2295 **Mark and Catherine Winkler Foundation**
4900 Seminary Road 703-998-0400
Alexandria, VA 22311 Fax: 703-578-7899
Lynne Ball, Executive Director

2296 **Mars Foundation**
2156 Vail Avenue 515-480-6610
Williams, IA 50271 E-mail: wcande@q.com
http://www.multiple-sclerosis-mf.org
The mission of the MARS foundation is to be committed to finding a cure for multiple sclerosis by funding medical research.
Roger G Best, Secretary

2297 **Marshall and Ilsley Foundation**
770 North Water Street 414-765-7835
Milwaukee, WI 53201 http://www.micorp.com
Provides comprehensive financial products and services and unparalleled customer service to personal, business, corporate and institutional customers nationwide.
Diana L Sebion, Secretary

2298 **Mary Reynolds Babcock Foundation**
2920 Reynolda Village 336-748-9222
Winston-Salem, NC 27106 Fax: 336-777-0095
E-mail: info@mrbr.org
http://www.mrbf.org
Our mission is to help people and places to move out of poverty and achieve greater social and economic justice.
Gayle Williams, Executive Director
Sandra Mikush, Assistant Director

2299 Max McGraw Wildlife Foundation
PO Box 9
Dundee, IL 60118
847-741-8000
Fax: 847-741-8157
E-mail: mcgrawwild@AOL.COM
http://www.mcgrawwildlife.org

The foundation's mission: education, research, and land management. Currently, the Foundation is invovled in over 15 research and land management projects through the Chicago region, including participation in the Chicago Wildernessinitiative. Situated on 1,225 acres, the Foundation property is managed by professional land management staff.
Stanley W Koenig, Executive Director
John Thompson, Director Research

2300 Max and Victoria Dreyfus Foundation
2233 Wisconsin Avenue NW
Suite 414
Washington, DC 20007
202-337-3300
Fax: 202-337-3302
E-mail: info@mvdreyfusfoundation.org
http://www.mvdreyfusfoundation.org
A leading figure in the music publishing business, the Foundation's grantmaking supports organizations in the arts, education, health care, hospitals, social services, civic affairs, and religion.
Lucy Gioia, Administrative Assistant

2301 May Stores Foundation
611 Olive Street
St. Louis, MO 63101
314-342-6300
Fax: 314-342-4461
http://www.maycompany.com
James Abrams, VP Corporate Communications

2302 McIntosh Foundation
15840 Meadows Wood Drive
Wellington, FL 33414
202 338 8055
Fax: 202-234-0745
E-mail: mcf@aol.com
The McIntosh foundation began in 1949 who founded the Great Atlantic & Pacific Tea Company...later renamed A&P
Michael A McIntosh, President
Hunter H. McIntosh, Director

2303 Nathan Cummings Foundation
475 Tenth Avenue
Fourteenth Floor
New York, NY 10018
212-787-7300
Fax: 212-787-7377
E-mail: contact@nathancummings.org
http://http://www.nathancummings.org
The Nathan Cummings Foundation is rooted in the Jewish tradition and committed to democratic values and social justice, including fairness, diversity, and community. They seek to build a socially and economically just society thatvalues nature and protects the ecological balance for future generations; promotes humane health care; and fosters arts and cultures that enriches communities.
Simon Greer, President/CEO
Taina McField, Program Officer

2304 National Arbor Day Foundation
100 Arbor Avenue
Nebraska City, NE 68410
402-474-5655
888-448-7337
Fax: 402-474-0820
E-mail: info@arborday.org
http://www.arborday.org
A nonprofit educational, environmental organization that helps people plant and care for trees. We are committed to tree-planting and environmental stewardsip. Newsletter free with $10.00 annual membership.
8 pages Bi-Monthly
John Rosenow, President
Gary Brienzo, Info. Coordinator

2305 National Audubon Society
225 Varick Street
New York, NY 10014
212-979-3000
Fax: 212-979-3188
E-mail: jbianchi@audubon.org
http://www.audubon.org
The mission of the National Audubon Society is to conserve and restore natural ecosystems, focusing on birds and other wildlife for the benefit of humanity and the earth's biological diversity. Founded in 1905, the National AudubonSociety is named for John James Audubon, famed orinthologist, exployer, and wildlife artist.
John Flicker, President

2306 National Fish and Wildlife Foundation
1133 Fifteenth St.
Suite 1100
Washington, DC 20005
202-857-0166
Fax: 202-857-0162
http://www.nfwf.org
Sustains, restores and enhances the Nation's fish, wildlife, plants, and habitats.
Jeff Trandahl, Executive Director/CEO

2307 National Forest Foundation
Fort Missoula Road
Building 27, Suite 3
Missoula, MT 59804
406-542-2805
Fax: 406-542-2810
E-mail: bpossiel@nationalforests.org
http://www.nationalforests.org

The official nonprofit partner of the USDA Forest Service. To accept and administer private contributions, undertaking activities that further the purposes for which the National Forest System was established and conductingeducational, technical, and other activities that support the multiple use, research, and forestry programs administered by the Forest Service.
Bill Possiel, President
David Bell, Chief Operating Officer

2308 National Geographic Society Education Foundation
1145 17th Street NW
Washington, DC 20036
202-857-7310
Fax: 202-429-5701
E-mail: foundation@ngs.org
http://education.nationalgeographic.com

The mission is to motivate and enable each new generation to become geographically literate.
John M. Fahey, Jr.., Chairman
Patrick F. Noonan, Vice Chairman

2309 National Parks Conservation Association
777 6th Street
Suite 700
Washington, DC 20001
202-223-6722
Fax: 202-454-3333
E-mail: npca@npca.org
http://www.npca.org

Mission is to protect and enhance America's National Parks for present and future generations.
Thomas F. Secunda, Chairman
James Nations, Vice President

2310 National Wildlife Federation
11100 Wildlife Center Drive
Reston, VA 20190
202-797-6800
800-822-9919
Fax: 202-797-6646
http://www.nwf.org

The National Wildlife Federation is the largest member-supported conservation group, uniting individuals, organizations, businesses and government to protect wildlife, wild places and the environment.
Larry J Schweiger, President/CEO

2311 Nature Conservancy
4245 North Fairfax Drive
Suite 100
Arlington, VA 22203
703-841-5300
Fax: 703-841-1283
http://www.nature.org
The mission is to preserve plants, animals and natural communities that represent the diversity of life on Earth by protecting the lands and waters they need to survive.
John C Sawhill, President

2312 New England Biolabs Foundation
240 Country Road
Ipswich, MA 01938
978-998-7990
Fax: 978-356-3250
E-mail: info@nebf.org
http://www.nebf.org

NEBF funds grass roots organizations in developing countries that focus on environmental issues and education.

2313 New York Times Company Foundation
620 Eighth Avenue
New York, NY 10018
212-556-1234
Fax: 212-556-3690
http://www.nytco.com

Strongly committed to protecting the environment in all of the many communities in which it operates.
Abbe Serphos, Executive Director
Eileen M. Murphy, Vice President

2314 New-Land Foundation
1114 Avenue of the Americans
46th Floor
New York, NY 10036
212-479-6162
Fax: 212-841-6275

Seeks to foster positive change throughout the global community through its grant making.
Robert Wolf, President

2315 Norcross Wildlife Foundation
250 W 88th Street
New York, NY 10024
212-362-4831
Fax: 212-812-4299
E-mail: norcross_wf_po@prodigy.net
http://www.norcrossws.org

A place of refuge where all wildlife is encouraged not just to survive but also to proliferate naturally, and where certain species, now threatened with extinction, may again attain more normal distribution and benefit the public bytheir survival.
Richard Reagan, President
Karen Outlaw, Executive Director

2316 Northwest Area Foundation
60 Plato Boulevard E
Suite 400
St. Paul, MN 55107
651-224-9635
Fax: 651-225-3881
E-mail: info@nwaf.org
http://www.nwaf.org

Committed to helping communities reduce poverty for the long term.
Kevin Walker, President/CEO

2317 Oliver S and Jennie R Donaldson Charitable Trust
US Trust Company of New York
114 W 47th Street
New York, NY 10036
212-852-3683
Fax: 212-852-3377

Philantropic organization working to promote social change that contributes to a more just, sustainable and peaceful world.
Anne L Smith-Ganey, Secretary

2318 Overbrook Foundation
122 East 42nd Street
Suite 2500
New York, NY 10168
212-661-8710
Fax: 212-661-8664
E-mail: contact@overbrookfoundation.org
http://www.overbrook.org

The Overbrook Foundation strives to improve the lives of people by supporting projects that protect human and civil rights, advance the self-sufficiencey and well being of individuals and their communities, and conserve the naturalenvironment.
Stephen A. Foster, President & CEO

2319 Pacific Whale Foundation
101 N Kihei Road
Suite 25
Kihei, HI 96753
808-879-8811
800-942-5311
Fax: 808-879-2615
http://www.pacificwhale.org

Mission is to promote appreciation, understanding and protection of whales, dolphins, coral reefs and our plantet's oceans. We accomplish this by educating the public from a scientific perspective about the marine environment. Wesupport and conduct responsible marine research and address marine conservation issues in Hawaii and the Pacific. Through educational ecotours, we model and promote sound ecotourism practices and responsible wildlife watching.
Greg Kaufman, Executive Director

2320 Patrick and Anna Cudahy Fund
333 N. Michigan Avenue
Suite 510
Chicago, IL 60601
312-422-1442
Fax: 312-641-5736
E-mail: laurenkrieg@cudahyfund.org
http://cudahyfund.org

Types of support: general/operating support; continuing support; annual campaigns; building/renovation; equipment; program development; seed money; technical assistance; matching funds.
Lauren Krieg, Executive Director

2321 Pew Charitable Trusts
One Commerce Square
2005 Market Street Suite 1800
Philadelphia, PA 19103
215-575-9050
Fax: 215-575-4939
E-mail: info@pewtrusts.org
http://www.pewtrusts.org

Driven by the power of knowledge to solve today's most challenging problems. Pew applies a rigorous, analytical approach to improve public policy, inform the public and stimulate civic life.
Rebecca W. Rimel, President/CEO

2322 Providence Journal Charitable Foundation
75 Fountain Street
Providence, RI 02902
401-277-7000
http://www.providencejournal.com

Focuses on offering local and regional news, information, advertising and interactive opportunities for our audience.
Phil Kukielski, Managing Editor
John Kostrzewa, Business Editor

2323 RARE Center for Tropical Bird Conservation
1529 Walnut Street
Philadelphia, PA 19102
215-568-0420

Works globally to equip people in the world's most threatened natural areas with the tools and motivation they need to care for their natural resources.
John Guarnaccia, Executive Director

2324 Rainforest Action Network
425 Bush Street
Suite 300
San Francisco, CA 94108
415-398-4404
Fax: 415-398-2732
E-mail: answers@ran.org
http://www.ran.org

Rainforest Action Network works to protect the Earth's rainforests and support the rights of their inhabitants through education, grassroots organizing and non-violent direct action.
James D. Gollin, President
Randal Hayes, Founder

2325 Rainforest Alliance
233 Broadway
28th Floor
New York, NY 10279
212-677-1900
888-693-2784
Fax: 212-677-2187
E-mail: info@ra.org

Works to conserve biodiversity and ensure sustainable livelihoods by transforming land-use practices, business practices and consumer behavior.
Daniel R Katz, Chairman
Roger Deromedi, Vice Chairman

2326 Raytheon Company
870 Winter Street
Waltham, MA 02451
781-552-3000
http://www.raytheon.com

Raytheon is a technology leader specializing in defense, homeland security, and other government markets throughout the world.
William H. Swanson, Chairman/CEO
Thomas A. Kennedy, Executive Vice President/ CO

2327 Richard Lounsberry Foundation
1020 19th Street NW
Suite LL60
Washington, DC 20036
202-872-8080
Fax: 202-872-9292
E-mail: foundation@rlounsbery.org
http://http://rlounsbery.org

Aims to enhance national strengths in science and technology through support programs in the areas of science and technology components of key US policy issues, elementary and secondary science and math education, historical studiesand contemporary assessments of key trends in the physical and biomedical sciences and start up assistance for establishing the infrastructure of research projects.
David M. Abshire, President
William Happer, Vice President

2328 Rockefeller Brothers Foundation
475 Riverside Drive
Suite 900
New York, NY 10115
212-812-4200
Fax: 212-812-4299
E-mail: communications@rbf.org
http://www.rbf.org

A philantrophic organization working to promote social change that contributes to a more just, sustainable and peaceful world. The Fund's programs are intended to develop leaders, strenghten institutions, engage citizens, buildcommunity, and foster partnerships that include government, business, and civil society.

Stephen Heintz, President

2329 Rockefeller Family Fund
475 Riverside Drive
Suite 900
New York, NY 10115
212-812-4252
Fax: 212-812-4299
http://www.rffund.org

For thirty years, the Rockefeller Family Fund has worked at the cutting edge of advocacy in such areas as environmental protection, advancing the economic rights of women, and holding public and private institutions accountable fortheir actions.

Peter G Case, President
David Kaiser, Vice President

2330 Safari Club International Foundation
4800 West Gates Pass Road
Tucson, AZ 85745
520-620-1220
800-377-5399
Fax: 520-622-1205
http://www.safariclub.org/

Safari Club Internation Foundation is a charitable organization that funds and manages worldwide programs dedicated to wildlife conservation, outdoor education and humanitarian services.

Craig L. Kauffman, President
Larry B Higgins, Vice President

2331 Samuel Roberts Noble Foundation
2510 Sam Noble Parkway
Ardmore, OK 73401
508-223-5810
Fax: 508-224-6217
http://www.noble.org

One of the largest international offshore drilling contractors in the world.

Bill Buckner, President/CEO
Jill Wallace, VP/CFO

2332 Save the Redwoods League
114 Sansome Street
Room 1200
San Francisco, CA 94104
415-362-2352
888-836-0005
Fax: 415-362-7017
E-mail: info@savetheredwoods.org
http://www.savetheredwoods.org

Guided by their science-based master plan to save redwoods throughout their natural ranges, the Leagues purchases priority pieces of land and donates or sells the property to government agencies for protection as parks and reserves.The league funds restoration, supports research to expand knowledge of redwood forest dynamics, and educates the public about redwoods and their ecosystems, in order to reconnect people with the peace and beauty of these wonders of the natural world.

James Larson, President
Melinda Thomas, Vice President

2333 Scherman Foundation
16 E 52nd Street
Suite #601
New York, NY 10022
212-832-3086
Fax: 212-838-0154
E-mail: mpratt@scherman.org
http://www.scherman.org

The giving program of the Foundation emphasizes long-term general support, reflecting the director's commitment to sustained support for current grantees, and the belief that strong nonprofit leaders who are closest to the issues canbest decide on the most effective use of grant funds.

Mr Mike Pratt, President

2334 Sequoia Foundation
1250 Pacific Avenue
Suite 870
Tacoma, WA 98402
253-627-1634
Fax: 253-627-6249
E-mail: grants@grantmakerconsultants.com
http://www.sequoiafound.org

A private non-profit organization dedicated to the identification and reduction of environmental threats to public health. We seek to support the efforts of local, state, national-and international-public health agencies in promotingand implimenting effective public health policy. This mission is achieved through research collaborations with local, state, federal, and international agencies, community-based organizations, and hospitals and universities.

John S. Petterson Ph.D., Executive Director
Pam Petree, Contracts Manager

2335 Sierra Club Foundation
85 Second Street
Suite 750
San Francisco, CA 94105
415-995-1780
Fax: 415-995-1791
E-mail: foundation@sierraclub.org
http://www.sierraclubfoundation.org

To advance the preservation and protection of the natural environment by empowering the citizenry, especially democratically-based grassroots organizations, with charitable resources to further the cause of environmental protection.The vehicle through which The Sierra Club Foundation generally fulfills its charitable mission.

Peter Martin, Executive Director

2336 Social Justice Fund NW
1904 Third Avenue
Suite 806
Seattle, WA 98101
206-624-4081
Fax: 206-382-2640
E-mail: info@socialjusticefund.org
http://www.socialjusticefund.org

Progressive foundation dedicated to creating a more just society. Funds grass-roots community-based organizations in Idoho, Montana, Wyoming, Washington, and Oregon.

Zeke Spier, Executive Director
Keegan Flaherty, Secretary

2337 Switzer Foundation New Hampshire Charitable Foundation
Po Box 293
Belfast, ME 04915
207-338-5654
800-464-6641
Fax: 603-225-1700
E-mail: info@nhcf.org

Identifies and nurtures environmental leaders who have the ability and determination to make a significant impact, and supports initiatives that will have direct and measurable results to improve environmental quality.

Judith Burrows, Director Student Aid

2338 Texaco Foundation
2000 Westchester Avenue
White Plains, NY 10650
914-701-0320
http://www.texaco.com

The foundation focuses on early childhood education in math and science through its Early Notes (music) program and its Touch Science program, which supports scientific discovery through hands-on learning.

Maria Mike-Mayer, Secretary

2339 Threshold Foundation
Po Box 29903
San Francisco, CA 94129
415-561-6400
Fax: 415-561-6401
E-mail: threshold@tides.org
http://www.thresholdfoundation.org

A progressive foundation and a community of individuals united through wealth, mobilizing money, people and power to create a more just, joyful and sustainable world.

Jodie Evans, President
Craig Harwood, Secretary

2340 Times Mirror Foundation
202 W First Street
Los Angeles, CA 90012
213-237-3945
Fax: 213-237-2116
http://www.timesmirrorfoundation.org

The Times Mirror Foundation, an affiliate of Tribune Company, is dedicated to supporting nonprofit organizations that measur-

ably improve the quality of life in communities we serve. The Foundation focuses its support on programs thatimprove the quality of journalism, education and literacy, strengthen the fabric of the community, and enhance cultural appreciation and understanding.
Cassandra Malry, Treasurer

2341 Tinker Foundation Inc
55 E 59th Street
New York, NY 10022
212-421-6858
Fax: 212-223-3326
E-mail: tinker@tinker.org
http://www.foundationcenter.org/grantmaker/tinker
Endeavors to promote better understanding among the peoples of the US, Latin America, and Iberia. In the environmental policy program area, grants are awarded to to 501(c)(3) or equivalent organizations for projects addressingresource-based economic activities and for improving the formulation of effective environmental governance.
Renate Rennie, Chairman/President
Alan Stoga, Secretary

2342 Town Creek Foundation
121 N West Street
Easton, MD 21601
410-763-8171
Fax: 410-763-8172
E-mail: info@towncreekfdn.org
http://www.towncreekfdn.org
A private philanthropic foundation dedicated to a sustainable environment
Stuart Clarke, Executive Director
Jennifer Stanley, President

2343 TreePeople
12601 Mulholland Drive
Beverly Hills, CA 90210
818-753-4600
Fax: 818-753-4635
E-mail: info@treepeople.org
http://www.treepeople.org
A nonprofit organization that has been serving the Los Angeles area for over three decades. Simply put, our work is about helping nature heal our cities.
Tom Hansen, Executive Director

2344 Trout Unlimited
1300 North 17th Street
Suite 500
Arlington, VA 22209
703-522-0200
800-834-2419
Fax: 703-284-9400
E-mail: trout@tu.org
http://www.tu.org
Mission: To conserve, protect and restore North America's trout and salmon fisheries and their watersheds. We accomplish this mission on local, state and national levels with an extensive and dedicated volunteer network.
Chris Wood, President/CEO
Steve Moyer, Vice President

2345 True North Foundation
508 Westwood Drive
Fort Collins, CO 80524
970-223-5285
Fax: 970-495-0892
Committed to preventing damage to the natural systems, water, air, and land on which all life depends.
Kerry K Anderson, President

2346 Turner Foundation
133 Luckie Street NW
2nd Floor
Atlanta, GA 30303
404-681-9900
Fax: 404-681-0172
http://www.turnerfoundation.org
This Foundation is committed to preventing damage to the natural systems, water, air and land, on which all life depends.
Micheal Finley, President/Treasurer
Rutherford Seydel, Secretary

2347 US-Japan Foundation
145 East 32nd Street
New York, NY 10016
212-481-8753
Fax: 212-481-8762
E-mail: info@us-jf.org
http://www.us-jf.org
Committed to promoting stronger ties between Americans and Japanese by supporting projects that foster mutual knowledge and education, deepen understanding, create effective channels of communication, and address common concerns in anincreasingly interdependent world.
James W. Lintott, Chairman
George R. Packard, President

2348 USF and G Foundation
100 Light Street
Baltimore, MD 21202
410-685-3047

2349 Union of Concerned Scientists
2 Brattle Square
Cambridge, MA 02138
617-547-5552
Fax: 617-864-9405
E-mail: ucs@ucsusa.org
http://www.ucsusa.org
The Union of Scientists is the leading science-based nonprofit organization working for a healthy environment and a safer world. Since 1969. we've used rigorous scientific analysis, innovative policy development, and tenacious citizenadvocacy to advance practical solutions for the environment.
James J. McCarthy, Chair
Peter A. Bradford, Vice Chair

2350 Unitarian Universalist Veatch Program at Shelter Rock
48 Shelter Rock Road
Manhasset, NY 11030
516-627-6576
Fax: 516-627-6596
E-mail: jan@veatch.org
http://www.uucsr.org
Supports Unitarian Universalist organizations that foster the growth and development of the denomination and that increase the involvement of Unitarian Universalists in social action and non-denominational organizations whose goalsreflect UU principles.
Ned Wight, Executive Director

2351 Victoria Foundation
31 Mulberry Street
5th Floor
Newark, NJ 07102
973-792-9200
Fax: 973-792-1300
E-mail: info@victoriafoundation.org
http://www.victoriafoundation.org
A private grantmaking institution. Since the early 1960's the Foundation's trustees have targeted giving to programs that impact the cycle of poverty in Newark, New Jersey.
Kevin Shanley, President/Treasurer
Margaret H. Parker, Vice President

2352 Vidda Foundation
250 West 57th Street
Suite 1928
New York, NY 10107
212-696-4052
Fax: 212-889-7791
http://www.vidda.org
The Vidda Foundation is a private non-operating foundation interested in supporting programs that will have lasting impact in the areas of conservation, education, healthcare, human services, and the arts.
Gerald E Rupp, Chairman

2353 Virginia Environmental Endowment
Three James Center
1051 East Cary Street
PO Box 790
Richmond, VA 23206
804-644-5000
E-mail: info@vee.org
http://www.freenet.vcu.edu/vee
Mission is to improve the quality of the environment by using its capital to encourage all sectors to work together to prevent pollution, conserve natural resources, and promote environmental literacy.
Gerald P McCarthy, Executive Director

2354 W Alton Jones Foundation
232 East High Street
Charlottesville, VA 22902
804-295-2134
Fax: 804-295-1648
E-mail: earth@wajones.org
http://www.wajones.org

Helps to fund hundreds of environmental groups.
Dr. JP Meyers, Director

2355 Wallace Genetic Foundation
4910 Massachusetts Avenue NW
Suite 221
Washington, DC 20016
202-966-2932
http://www.wallacegenetic.org
Committed to funding a variety of interests including agricultural research, preservation of farmland, ecology, conservation and sustainable development.
John D Murray, President
David W Douglas, Vice President, Treasurer

2356 Wilderness Society
1615 M Street NW
Washington, DC 20036
202-833-2300
800-843-9453
E-mail: action@tws.org
http://www.wilderness.org

Deliver to future generations an unspoiled legacy of wild places, with all the precious values they hold: Biological diversity; clean air and water; towering forests, rushing rivers, and sage-sweet, silent deserts.
Brenda Davis, Chair
Doug Walker, Vice Chair

2357 Wildlife Preservation Trust International
3400 West Girard Avenue
Philadelphia, PA 19104
215-222-3636
Fax: 215-222-2191
Empowers local conservation scientists worldwide to protect nature and safeguard ecosystem and human health.

Dr. Mary Pearl

2358 William Bingham Foundation
20305 Center Ridge Road
Suite 629
Cleveland, OH 44116
216-344-5200
E-mail: info@wbinghamfoundation.org
http://wbinghamfoundation.org
Supports organizations in in education, science, health and human services and the arts.
Laura H Gilbertson, Chief Administrator
Daniel L Horn, Secretary

2359 William H Donner Foundation
60 East 42nd Street
Suite 1560
New York, NY 10165
212-949-0404
Fax: 212-949-6022
http://donner.org
When we build let us...build forever. Let it not be for present delight nor for present alone. Let it be such work as our descendants will thank us for.
Timothy E Donner, President
Cristina Winsor, Vice President

2360 William Penn Foundation
Two Logan Square 11th Floor
100 North 18th Street
Philadelphia, PA 19103
215-988-1830
Fax: 215-988-1823
E-mail: grants@williampennfoundation.org
http://www.williampennfoundation.org
To improve the quality of life in the greater Philadelphia region through efforts that foster rich cultural expression, strenghten children's futures, and deepen connections to nature and community. In partnerships with others, we workto advance a vital, just and caring community.
Helen Davis, Interim President
Bergen , Director

2361 William and Flora Hewlett Foundation
2121 Sand Hill Road
Menlo Park, CA 94025
650-234-4500
Fax: 650-234-4501
http://www.hewlett.org
The Foundation concentrates its resources on activities in education, environment, global development, performing arts and population. In addition, the Foundation has programs that make grants to advance the field of philanthropy, andto support disadvantaged communities in the San Francisco Bay Area.
Walter B. Hewlett, Chairman
Larry D Kramer, President

2362 Winston Foundation for World Peace
2040 S Street, NW
Washington, DC 20009
202-483-4215
Fax: 202-483-4219
E-mail: winstonfoun@igc.apc.org

John H. Adams, Director

2363 Wisconsin Energy Corporation Foundation
231 W. Michigan St.
Milwaukee, WI 53203
414-221-2345
Fax: 414-221-2554
http://www.wisconsinenergy.com
Wisconsin Energy's principal business is providng electric and natural gas service to customers across Wisconsin and the Upper Peninsula of Michigan.
David L Hughes, Assistant Treasurer
Gale E Klappa, Chairman, President & CEO

2364 World Parks Endowment
1616 Place Street NW
Suite 200
Washington, DC 20036
202-939-3808
Fax: 202-939-3868
E-mail: worldparks@worldparks.org
http://www.worldlandtrust.org
The World Parks Endowment provides the opportunity to buy rainforest land and establish new protected areas that conserve rainforests and other sites of high biodiversity value. Our projects target lands that conserve rare orendangered species, and are low price, so the minimum amount of the funds protect high priority areas.
Daniel Katz, President

2365 World Research Foundation
41 Bell Rock Plaza
Sedona, AZ 86351
928-284-3300
Fax: 928-284-3530
E-mail: info@wrf.org
http://www.wrf.org

The purpose of the foundation is to locate, gather, codify, evaluate, classify and disseminate information dealing with health and the environment. All countries are contacted to collect the best information in an unbiased, neutral andindependent manner.
LaVerne Boeckmann, Vice President/Founder

2366 World Resources Institute
10 G Street, NW
Suite 800
Washington, DC 20002
202-729-7600
Fax: 202-729-7610
http://www.wri.org
An independent nonprofit organization with a staff of more than 100 scientists, economists, policy experts, business analysts, statistic analysisis, mapmakers and communicators working to protect the Earth and improve people's lives.Our four goals are: protect the Earth's living systems, increase access to information, create sustainable enterprise and opportunity and reverse global warming.
Andrew Steer, President & CEO

2367 World Society for the Protection of Animals
450 Seventh Avenue
31st Floor
New York, NY 10123
646-783-2200
800-883-9772
Fax: 212-564-4250
E-mail: wspa@wspausa.org
http://www.wspa-usa.org or www.wspa-internationa.org
The world's largest alliance of animal welfare organization whose vision is a world where animal welfare matters and animal cruelty ends. We strive to bring about change from grassroots to government levels to benefit animals. WSPAsupports and develops high-profile campaigns, scientifically-backed projects and innovative education initiatives. Its work is recognized by the United Nations and Council of Europe.

Annie Lieberman, USA Executive Director
John Bowen, President

2368 **World Wildlife Fund**
1250 24th Street NW 202-293-4800
Washington, DC 20037 Fax: 202-293-9211
http://www.worldwildlife.org

The largest multinational conservation organization in the world, WWF works in 100 countries and is supported by 1.2 million members in the United States and close to 5 million globally.
Jennifer A Zadwick, Program Information Coord.
Carter Roberts, President & CEO

2369 **Xerces Society**
628 NE Broadway 503-232-6639
Suite 200 855-232-6639
Portland, OR 97232 Fax: 503-233-6794
E-mail: info@xerces.org
http://www.xerces.org

Works with farmers, land managers, golf course staff, public agencies, and gardners to promote the conservation and recovery of native pollinator insects and their habitat.
Scott Hoffman Black, Executive Director

Scholarships

2370 **AGI Minority Geoscience Scholarship**
American Geological Institute
4220 King Street 703-379-2480
Alexandria, VA 22302 800-336-4764
Fax: 703-379-7563
E-mail: pleahy@agiweb.org
http://www.agiweb.org

Provides information services, serves as a voice of shared interests in our profession, plays a major role in strengthening geoscience education, and strives to increase public understanding of the vital role in geosciences play insociety's use of resources and interaction with the environment.
Patrick Leahy, Executive Director
Ann E. Benbow, Education, Outreach Director

2371 **Abundant Life Seed Foundation**
930 Lawrence Street 425-385-5660
PO Box 772 Fax: 360-385-7455
Port Townsend, WA 98368 E-mail: abundant@olypen.com
http://www.abundantlifeseed.org

A nonprofit organization dedicated to the preservation of rare, heirloom and native seeds. ALSF grows and distributes open-pollinated seeds and offers them for sale in an annual catalog. Seeds are also sent to people in need throughthe World Seed Fund. ALSF teaches seed saving through workshops, appreticeships and school programs.
Matthew Dillon, Executive Director
Elsa Golts, Board President

2372 **Alexander Hollaender Distinguished Postdoctoral Fellowships**
PO Box 117 865-576-3146
Oak Ridge, TN 37831 Fax: 865-241-2923
E-mail: communications@orise.orau.gov
http://www.orau.gov/orise/contacts.htm

Prepares and distributes program literature to universities and laboratories across the country, accepts application, convenes a panel to make award recommendation, and issues stipend checks.
Andy Page, Director
Dan Standley, Director

2373 **American Association for the Advancement of Science**
1200 New York Avenue NW 202-326-6400
Washington, DC 20005 Fax: 202-289-4950
http://www.aaas.org

An international non-profit organization dedicated to advancing science around the world by serving as an educator, leader, spokesperson and professional association.
Philip A Sharp, President
William Press, Chairman

2374 **American Geophysical Union Member Programs Division**
2000 Florida Avenue NW 202-462-6900
Washington, DC 20009 800-966-2481
Fax: 202-328-0566
E-mail: service@agu.org
http://about.agu.org

Organized to represent the US in the International Research Council's International Union Of Geodesy and Geophysics and to serve as the National Research Council Committee on Geophysics.
Carol Finn, President
Christine McEntee, Executive Director

2375 **American Indian Science and Engineering Society**
2305 Renard SE Suite 200 505-765-1052
PO Box 9828 Fax: 505-765-5608
Albuquerque, NM 87119 E-mail: info@aises.org
http://www.aises.org

The mission is to increase substantially the representation of American Indian and Alaskan Natives in engineering, science and other related technology disciplines.
Sarah Echohawk, CEO
Shirley LaCourse, Business Development Officer

2376 **American Museum of Natural History**
Central Park West at 79th Street 212-769-5606
New York, NY 10024 Fax: 212-769-5427
http://www.amnh.org

Mission is to discover, interpret, and disseminate-through scientific research and education, knowledge about human cultures, the natural world, and the universe.
Lewis W Bernard, Chairman
Ellen V Futter, President

2377 **American Nuclear Society**
555 North Kensington Avenue 708-352-6611
La Grange Park, IL 60526 800-323-3044
Fax: 708-352-0499
http://www.ans.org

Not-for-profit, international, scientific and educational organization. Established by a group of individuals who recognized the need to unify the professional activities within the diverse fields of nuclear science and technology.
Robert C Fine, Executive Director
Susan Gallier, Editor

2378 **American Society of Naturalists**
Queens College - CUNY
Department of Biology 718-997-3426
Flushing, NY 11367 http://www.amnat.org

Purpose is to advance and to diffuse knowledge of organic evolution and other broad biological principals so as to enhance the conceptual unification of the biological sciences.
Dolph Schluter, President

2379 **American Sport Fishing Association**
1001 North Fairfax St. 703-519-9691
Suite 501 Fax: 703-519-1872
Alexandria, VA 22314 E-mail: info@asafishing.org
http://www.asafishing.org

Unites more then 650 members of the sportfishing and boating industries with state fish and wildlife agencies, federal land and water management agencies, conservation organizations, angler advocacy groups and outdoor journalists. Wesafeguard and promote the enduring social, economic and conservation values of sportfishing.
Mike Nussman, President And CEO
Gordon Robertson, Vice President

2380 **Apple Computer Earth Grants: Community Affairs Department**
1 Infinite Loop 408-996-1010
Cupertino, CA 95014 800-692-7753
http://www.apple.com
Beverly Long, Program Manager

2381 **Beldon Fund**
99 Madison Avenue 212-616-5600
8th Floor 800-591-9595
New York, NY 10016 Fax: 212-616-5656
E-mail: beldoninfo@yahoo.com
http://www.beldon.org

Mission is by supporting effective, nonprofit, advocacy organizations, the Beldon Fund seeks to build a national consensus to achieve and sustain a healthy planet.
Ruth Henning, Executive Director

2382 **Beldon II Fund: Old Kent Bank and Trust Company**
Old Kent Bank 616-771-5326
300 Old Kent Bank Building
Grand Rapids, MI 49503
John R Hunting, President and Director

2383 **Charles A. and Anne Morrow Lindbergh Foundation**
PO Box 11429 763-576-1596
Bainbridge Island, WA 98110 Fax: 763-576-1664
E-mail: info@lindberghfoundation.org
http://www.lindberghfoundation.org

Each year, the Charles A. and Anne Morrow Lindbergh Foundation provides grants to men and women whose individual initiative and work in a wide spectrum of disciplines furthers the Lindbergh's vision of a balance between the advance oftechnology and the perservation of the natural/human environment.

Alun Nichols, President
Yolanka Wulff, Executive Director

2384 **Cousteau Society**
732 Eden Way North 212-532-2588
Suite E, # 707 800-441-4395
Chesapeake, VA 23320 Fax: 757-722-8185
E-mail: communication@cousteau.org
http://www.cousteau.org

Mission is to educate people to understand, to love and to protect the water systems of the planet, marine and fresh water, for the wellbeing of future generations.

Francine Cousteau, President

2385 **DRB Communications**
1234 Summer Street 800-323-1550
Stamford, CT 06905 Fax: 203-324-7175
Robyn DeWolf

2386 **Delmar Publishers Scholarship**
National FAA Foundation
6060 FFA Drive 317-802-6060
PO Box 68960 Fax: 317-802-6061
Indianapolis, IN 46268
Carrie Powers, Contact

2387 **Du Pont de Nemours and Company**
1007 Market Street 302-774-2036
Room 8065 800-441-7515
Wilmington, DE 19898 E-mail: info@dupont.com
http://www.dupont.com

Creating sustainable solutions essential to a better, safer, healthier, life for people everywhere.
Peter C Morrow, Mgr. Corporate Contributions

2388 **Earth Island Institute-Brower Youth Awards**
2150 Allston Way 510-859-9100
Suite 460 Fax: 510-859-9091
Berkeley, CA 94704 E-mail: bya@earthisland.org
http://www.earthisland.org

Incubates and supports over 30 projects working on environmental issues worldwide. Publishes quarterly Earth Island Journal. Project support programs help aspiring and veteran activists alike put ideas into action. Youth programincreases the visibility, effectiveness and influence of youth leadership in the environmental movement, inspiring other young people to work for the Earth.

John A Knox, Executive Dir Operations
Christina Monzer, Program Coordinator

2389 **Environmental Defense Fund**
257 Park Avenue South 212-505-2100
17th Floor 800-684-3322
New York, NY 10010 Fax: 212-505-2375
E-mail: members@edf.org
http://www.edf.org

Dedicated to protecting the environmental rights of all people, including future generations. Among these rights are clean air, clean water, healthy, nourishing food and a flourishing ecosystem. Advocates solutions based on science,even when it leads in unfamiliar directions. Works to create solutions that win lasting political, economic and social support because they are bipartisan, efficient and fair.

Fred Krupp, President
David Yarnold, Executive Director

2390 **Environmental Grantmakers Association**
475 Riverside Drive 212-812-4310
Suite 960 Fax: 212-812-4311
New York, NY 10115 http://ega.org

Mission is to help member organizations become more effective environmental grantmakers through information sharing, collaboration and networking.
Tracy Austin, Executive Director
Heidi Binko, Associate Director

2391 **Environmental Protection Agency: Grants Administration Division**
Grants Operation Branch 202-260-5260
401 M Street SW
Washington, DC 20460

Programs include air and water pollution controll, toxic substances, pesticides, and drinking water regulation, wetlands protection, hazardous waste management, hazardous waste site cleanup and some regulation of radioactive materials.

2392 **Environmental and Engineering Fellowship**
American Association for the Advancement
1333 H Street NW 202-326-6600
Washington, DC 20005 Fax: 202-289-4950

Aimed at postdoctoral to midcareer professionals from any discipline of science, engineering or any relevant interdisciplinary fields.

2393 **Financial Support for Graduate Work**
Women's Seamen's Friend Society of Connecticut
300 Boston Post Road 800-342-5864
West Haven, CT 06516 http://www.newhaven.edu/academics/10844/

Restricted to Connecticut residents who are students at state maritime schools, or Connecticut residents majoring in Marine Sciences at any college or university or residents of any state majoring in Marine Sciences at a Connecticutcollege or university.

2394 **Ford Motor Company Fund**
Bronx Zoo 212-573-5000
43rd Street Fax: 212-351-3677
New York, NY 10017 http://www.fordfound.com

Ford Motor Company Fund is a not-for-profit corporation organized in 1949. Made possible by Ford Motor Company profits, Ford Motor Company Fund supports initiatives and institutions that enhance and improve opportunities for those wholive in the communities where Ford Motor Company operates.
Luis Ubinas, President

2395 **Forest History Society**
701 William Vickers Avenue 919-682-9319
Durham, NC 27701 Fax: 919-682-2349
E-mail: coakes@duke.edu
http://www.foresthistory.org

The Forest History Society is a non-profit educational institution that links the past to the future by identifying, collecting, preserving, interpreting, and disseminating information on the history of people, forests, and theirrelated resources.

Cheryl Oakes, Librarian
Steven Anderson, President

2396 Garden Club of America
14 East 60th Street
3rd Floor
New York, NY 10022
212-753-8287
Fax: 212-753-0134
E-mail: gca@gcamerica.org
http://www.gcamerica.org

Purpose is to stimulate the knowledge and love of gardening, to share the advantages of association by means of educational meetings, conferences, correspondence and publications, and to restore, improve, and protect the quality of theenvironment through educational programs and action in the fields of conservation and civic improvement.
Katherine Astor, Honorary Member
Anne Butler, Receptionist

2397 Georgia M. Hellberg Memorial Scholarships
National Future Federation of America
6060 FFA Drive
PO Box 68960
Indianapolis, IN 46268
317-802-6060
Fax: 317-802-6061
E-mail: webmaster@ffa.org
http://www.ffa.org

Steve A. Brown, Advisor
Sherene R. Donaldson, Executive Secretary

2398 German Marshall Fund of the United States
1744 R Street NW
Washington, DC 20009
202-683-2650
Fax: 202-265-1662
E-mail: info@gmfus.org
http://www.gmfus.org

A nonpartisan American public policy and grantmaking institution dedicated to promoting greater cooperation and understanding between the United States and Europe.
Craig Kennedy, President

2399 Great Lakes Protection Fund
1560 Sherman Avenue
Suite 880
Evanston, IL 60201
847-425-8150
Fax: 847-424-9832
E-mail: info@glpf.org
http://www.glpf.org

A private non profit organization formed by the Govenors of the Great Lakes States. It is a permanent environmental endowdment that supports collaborative actions to improve the health of the Great Lakes ecosystem.

Russell Van Herik, Executive Director
J. David Rankin, Program Director

2400 Hawk Mountain Sanctuary Association
1700 Hawk Mountain Road
Kempton, PA 19529
610-756-6961
Fax: 610-756-4468
E-mail: info@hawkmountain.org
http://www.hawkmountain.org/contact/contact-us~form.aspx

Mission is to conserve birds of prey worldwide by providing leadership in raptor conservation science and education, and my maintaining Hawk Mountain Sanctuary as a model observation, research and education facility.
Wendy Mclean, Chairman
Peter Bennett, Vice Chairman

2401 Hazardous Waste Reduction Loan Program
California Department of Commerce
1001 I Street
PO Box 4025
Sacramento, CA 95812
916-341-6181
E-mail: grants@ciwmb.ca.gov
http://www.ciwmb.ca.gov

Loans assist small business to redude waste generation or to reduce the hazardous properties of waste generated. Proceeds can only be used to finance hazardous waste equipment acquistion, installation and processes.
Merri Stevenson

2402 Heller Charitable and Educational Fund
244 California Street
San Francisco, CA 94111
415-434-3160
Fax: 415-434-3807

Mission is to protect and improve the quality of life through support of programs in the environment, human health, education, and the arts.
Ruth B Heller, Correspondence Secretary

2403 JM Kaplan Fund
261 Madison Avenue
19th Floor
New York, NY 10016
212-767-0630
Fax: 212-767-0639
E-mail: info@jmkfund.org
http://www.jmkfund.org/index.html

Support for the arts, the environment, human rights, and a robust civil society. New interests emerged in programs to support New York City neighborhoods parks and libraries as well as historic preservation and municipal design work inLower Manhattan.
Peter Davidson, Chairman
Conn Nugent, Executive Director

2404 Jessie Ball duPont Religious, Charitable and Educational Fund
1 Independent Drive
Suite 1400
Jacksonville, FL 32202
904-353-0890
800-252-3452
Fax: 904-353-3870
E-mail: contactus@dupontfund.org
http://www.dupontfund.org

A private grantmaking foundation limited in its giving to approximately 330 eligible organizations to which Mrs. duPont personnally contributed to in a five year period 1960-1964. The duPont fund accomplishes its mission by workingcreatively with these organizations and their partners.

Sherry Magill, PhD, President
Davena Sawyer, Exec. Asst to President

2405 Johnson's Wax Fund
1525 Howe Street
Racine, WI 53403
800-494-4855
http://www.scjohnsonwax.com

Through the SC Johnson Fund, in the US, we donate, on average, 5% pre-tax profits every year to increase local and global well-being. Our contributions are targeted to advancing the three legs of sustainability: economic vitality,social progress, and a healthy environmnet.

2406 Joint Oceanographic Institutions
1201 New York Avenue NW
Suite 400
Washington, DC 20005
202-232-3900
Fax: 202-265-4409
E-mail: info@joiscience.org
http://www.joiscience.org

A consortium of 20 premier oceanographic research institutions that serves the US scientific community through management of large scale, global research programs in the fields of marine geology and geophysics and oceanography.
Steven Bohlen, President
Amy Castner, Executive Program Associate

2407 LSB Leakey Foundation
1003B O'Reilly Avenue
San Francisco, CA 94129
415-561-4646
Fax: 415-561-4647
E-mail: info@leakeyfoundation.org
http://www.leakeyfoundation.org/

The mission of the Leakey Foundation is to increase scientific knowledge and public understanding of human origins and evolution.
Sharal Camisa, Managing Director
Paddy Moore, Program Officer

2408 MJ Murdock Charitable Trust
703 Broadway
Suite 710
Vancouver, WA 98660
360-694-8415
Fax: 360-649-1819
http://www.murdock-trust.org

The mission is to enrich the quality of life in the Pacific Northwest by providing grants organizations that seek to strenghten the region's educational and cultural base in creative and sustainable ways.
Steve Moore, Executive Director

2409 **Mary Flagler Cary Charitable Trust**
122 East 42nd Street
Room 3505
New York, NY 10168
212-953-7700
Fax: 212-953-7720
http://www.carytrust.org/
The Trust was established as a testamentary, charitable trust by the will of the late Mary Flagler Cary. The trustees have worked to use the assets of the Trust to carry forward Mrs. Cary's interests, and to elaborate on them in lightof new circumstances and needs. A major part of the Trust's assets continue to be devoted to special commitments relating to the origins of the Trust, especially the Institute of Ecosystem Studies at the Mary Flagler Cary Arboretum in Millbrook, NewYork.

2410 **Maryland Sea Grant**
University of Maryland
4321 Hardwick Road
Suite 300
College Park, MD 20740
301-405-7500
Fax: 301-314-5870
E-mail: moser@mdsg.umd.edu
http://www.mdsg.umd.edu
Supports innovative marine research and education, with a special focus on the Chesapeake Bay.
Dr Fredrika Moser, Director

2411 **National Academy of Sciences**
500 Fifth Street, NW
Washington, DC 20001
202-334-2000
Fax: 202-334-2158
http://www.nasonline.org
The National Academy of Sciences (NAS) is an honorific society of distinguished scholars engaged in scientific and engineering research, dedicated to the furtherance of science and technology and to their use for the general welfare.
Ralph J. Cicerone, President
Diane Griffin, Vice President

2412 **National Center for Atmospheric Research**
PO Box 3000
Boulder, CO 80307
303-497-1601
Fax: 303-497-1314
http://www.ncar.ucar.edu/
NCAR provides the university research and teaching community with tools such as aircraft and radar to observe the atmosphere and with the technology and assistance to interpret and use these observations, including supercomputeraccess, computer models, and user support.
Maura Hagan, Interim Director

2413 **National Environmental Health Association NEHA/AAS Scholarships**
720 S Colorado Boulevard
Suite 1000-N
Denver, CO 80246
303-756-9090
Fax: 303-691-9490
E-mail: staff@neha.org
http://www.neha.org
Mission is to advance the environmental health and protection professional for the purpose of providing a healthful environment for all.
Elizabeth Landeen, Assistant Manager

2414 **Needmor Fund**
42 South Saint Clair Street
Toledo, OH 43604
419-255-5560
Fax: 419-255-5561
E-mail: moreinfo@needmorfund.org
http://www.needmorfund.org/
Mission is to work with others to bring about social justice. The Needmor Fund supposrt people who work together to change the social, economic or politcal conditions which bar their access to participation in a democratic society.
Abby Staranahan, Chair
Ken Rolling, Vice Chair

2415 **Nixon Griffis Fund for Zoological Research: New York Zoological Society**
Bronx Zoo
185th Street & Southern Boulevard
Bronx, NY 10460
212-220-5152
Fax: 212-220-7114
Supports research in zoology, conservation, and marine science. Grants lilmited to $3,000. Grants made four times a year. Applications reviewed by selected US zoo personnel.
John Behler, Contact

2416 **North American Loon Fund Grants**
PO Box 329
Holderness, NH 03245
603-528-4711
800-462-5666
The North American Loon Fund's mission is to promote the preservation of loons and their lake habitats through research, public education, and the involvement of people who share their lakes with loons.
Linda O'Bara, Director

2417 **Oak Ridge Institute Science & Engineering Education Division**
MC100-44
PO Box 117
Oak Ridge, TN 37831
865-576-3146
Fax: 865-241-2923
E-mail: communications@orau.org
http://www.orau.org
Strive to advance scientific research and education by creating mutually beneficial collaborative partnerships involving academe, government, and industry.
Jamey Kennedy, Vice President

2418 **Oklahoma State University**
499 Cordell South
Stillwater, OK 74078
405-744-5721
Fax: 405-744-6758
E-mail: rebekah.scrogum@okstate.edu
http://www.fpst.okstate.edu
The major fields of study include biological science, botany, cell and molecular biology, conservation sciences, medical technology, microbiology, physiology, and zoology.
Burns Hargis, President
Rebekah Scrogum, Administrative Support Speci

2419 **Resources for the Future**
1616 P Street NW
Washington, DC 20036
202-328-5000
Fax: 202-939-3460
E-mail: info@rff.org
http://www.rff.org
RFF is a nonprofit and nonpartisan organization, or think tank, that conducts independent research-rooted primarily in economics and other social sciences-on environmental, energy, climate change and natural resource issues. Itsresearch scope comprises programs in nations around the world.

Philip R. Sharp, President
Lawrence H. Linden, Treasurer

2420 **The Center for Environmental Biotechnology at the University of Tennessee at Knoxville**
1416 Circle Drive, 676 Dabney Hall
Knoxville, TN 37996
865-974-8080
Fax: 865-974-8086
E-mail: cebweb@utk.edu
http://www.ceb.utk.edu
One of the nations oldest and largest university-based multidisciplinary researchunits devoted to environmental analysis. The CEB is a leader in the development of whole cell bioluminescent bioreporters for the detection of organicand inorganic pollutants including environmental endocrine disruptors and toxicants.
Gary S Sayler, Professor & Director
Lee Barham, Research Assistant

2421 **University of Colorado: Boulder**
Campus Box 216
Boulder, CO 80309
303-492-1143
Fax: 303-492-1149
http://www.colorado.edu
Recognized as one of the outstanding public universities in the United States. The Boulder campus has 5 colleges and 4 schools, offering 3,400 courses in about 150 areas of study.
Dr. Robert Sievers, Director

2422 **WERC Undergraduate Fellowships**
New Mexico State University
Box 30001, MSC WERC
Las Cruces, NM 88003
505-646-2038
800-523-5996
Fax: 505-646-4149
E-mail: iee@nmsu.edu
http://www.werc.net
WERC a consortium for environmental education and technology development. The consortium's mission is to develop the hu-

man resources and technologies needed to address environmental issues.
Abbas Ghassemi, Director
Barbara Valdez, Program Coordinator

2423 Water Environment Federation
601 Wythe Street
Alexandria, VA 22314
703-684-2400
800-666-0206
E-mail: inquiry@wef.org
http://www.wef.org
Founded in 1928, the Water Environment Federation (WEF) is a not-for-profit technical and educational organization with members from varied disciplines who work toward the WEF vision of preservation and enhancement of the global waterenvironment. The WEF network includes more than 100,000 water quality professionals from 77 member associations in 31 countries.
Cordell Samuels, President
Sandra Ralston, President Elect

2424 Weston Institute
1400 Weston Way
Po Box 2653
West Chester, PA 19380
610-701-3000
800-7WE-STON
Fax: 610-701-3186
E-mail: contactweston@westonsolutions.com
http://www.westonsolutions.com
A leading environmental and redevelopment firm focused on restoring efficiency to your essential resources: air, land, water, people, and facilities. We can help you develop solutions that maximize resource value and turn environmentalresponsibility into economic growth.
William L. Roberston, President/CEO

2425 Wildlife Conservation Society
Bronx Zoo
2300 Southern Blvd
Bronx, NY 10460
718-220-5100
Fax: 718-365-3694
http://www.wcs.org
The Wildlife Conservation Society saves wildlife and wild lands. We do so through careful science, internation conservation, education, and the management of the world's largest system of urban wildlife parks, led by the flagship BronxZoo. Together, these activities change individual attitudes toward nature and help people imagine wildlife and humans living in sustainable interaction on both a local and a global scale.
Ward W Woods, Chair
Antonia M. Grumbach, Vice Chair

2426 Women's Seamen's Friend Society of Connecticut
291 Whitney Avenue
Suite 403
New Haven, CT 06511
203-777-2165
Fax: 203-777-5774
E-mail: wsfsofct@earthlink.net
http://www.aie.org/scholarships/detail.cfm?id=11622
C. Marshall Davidson, Executive Director

2427 Yale Institute for Biospheric Studies (YIBS)
21 Sachem Street
PO Box 208105
New Haven, CT 06520
203-432-9856
Fax: 203-432-9927
E-mail: roserita.riccitelli@yale.edu
http://www.yale.edu/yibs
The Yale Institute for Biospheric Studies (YIBS) serves as a principal focus for Yale University's research and training efforts in the environmental sciences, and is committed to the teaching of environmental studies to futuregenerations. It provides physical and intellectual centers for research and education that address fundamental questions that will inform the ability to generate solutions to the biosphere's most critical environmental solutions.

Rose Rita Riccitelli, Assistant Director
Oswald Schmitz, Director

Government Agencies & Programs

Federal

2428 **Advisory Committee on Nuclear Waste**
US Nuclear Regulatory Commission
Office Of Public Affairs
Washington, DC 20555
301-415-8200
800-368-5642
Fax: 301-415-5575
E-mail: ram2@nrc.gov
http://www.nrc.gov

Allison M. Macfarlane, Chairman

2429 **Advisory Council on Historic Preservation**
1100 Pennsylvania Avenue NW
202-606-8503
Suite 803, Old Post Office Building
E-mail: achp@achp.gov
Washington, DC 20004
http://www.achp.gov

Mission: To promote the preservation, enhancement, and productive use of our Nation's historic resources, and advise the President and Congress on national historic preservation policy.
John M. Fowler, Executive Director
Valerie Hauser, Director

2430 **Advisory Panel for Ecology**
National Science Foundation
4201 Wilson Boulevard
703-292-5111
Arlington, VA 22230
Fax: 703-292-5090
E-mail: info@nsf.gov
http://www.nsf.gov

To promote the progress of science; to advance the national health, prosperity, and welfare; to secure the national defense.
Dr. Cora B. Murrell, Acting Director

2431 **Agency for Toxic Substances and Disease Registry**
Centers for Disease Control and Prevention
4770 Buford Highway NE
800-232-4636
Atlanta, GA 30341
E-mail: ATSDRIC@cdc.gov
http://www.atsdr.cdc.gov/

This agency provides leadership and direction to programs and activities designed to protect both the public and workers from exposure or adverse health effects of hazardous substances in storage sites or released in fires, explosions,or transportation accidents. The agency also collects, maintains, analyzes and disseminates information relating to serious diseases, mortality and human exposure to toxic or hazardous substances.

2432 **Air and Radiation Research Committee**
Environmental Protection Agency
1200 Pennsylvania Avenue NW
202-564-7400
Washington, DC 20760
866-411-4372
Fax: 202-501-0826
http://www.epa.gov/air

Stephen L Johnson, Administrator
Marcus Peacock, Deputy Administrator

2433 **American Farmland Trust**
1200 18th Street NW
202-331-7300
Suite 800
Fax: 202-659-8339
Washington, DC 20036
E-mail: info@farmland.org
http://www.farmland.org

Mission: To stop the loss of productive farmland and to promote farming practices that lead to a healthy environment.
Jon Scholl, President
William Cohan, Treasurer

2434 **American Indian Environmental Office**
1200 Pennsylvania Avenue NW
202-564-0303
Washington, DC 20460
Fax: 202-564-0298
http://www.epa.gov/indian/

Coordinates the US environmental Protection Agency-wide effort to strengthen public health and environmental protection in Indian Country, with a special emphasis on building Tribal capacity to administer their own environmentalprograms.
Carol Jorgensen, Director
Christopher Hoff, Acting Deputy Director

2435 **Animal and Plant Health Inspection Service Protection Quarantine**
1400 Independence Avenue SW
202-720-5601
Whitten Building, Room 302-E
Fax: 202-690-0472
Washington, DC 20250
E-mail: aelder@aphis.usda.gov
http://www.aphis.usda.gov

Mission: To protect the health and value of American agriculture and natural resources.
Alfred Elder, Deputy Administrator

2436 **Antarctica Project and Southern Ocean Coalition**
1630 Connecticut Avenue NW
202-234-2480
3rd Floor
Fax: 202-387-4823
Washington, DC 20009
E-mail: secretariat@asoc.org
http://www.asoc.org

Concerned with educating the public about environmental problems in the arctic regions. Conducts research pertaining to Antarctica.
Gerry Leape, Chair
Denise Boyd, Vice Chair

2437 **Aquatic Nuisance Species Task Force**
4401 N Fairfax Drive
703-358-1796
Suite 840
Fax: 703-358-1800
Arlington, VA 22203
E-mail: david_britton@fws.gov
http://www.anstaskforce.gov/taskforce.php

An intergovernmental organization dedicated to preventing and controlling aquatic nuisance species. The task forec consists of 10 federal agency reps and 12 ex-officio members
Mamie Parker, Co-Chairman
Scott Nawsham, Executive Secretary

2438 **Argonne National Laboratory**
9700 S Cass Avenue
630-252-2000
Argonne, IL 60439
http://www.anl.gov/

One of the US Department of Energy's largest research centers.

2439 **Army Corps of Engineers**
441 G Street NW
202-761-0011
Washington, DC 20314
E-mail: hq-publicaffairs@usace.army.mil
http://www.usace.army.mil

The Army Corps of Engineers serves as the Army's real property manager; manages and executes civil works programs, including research and development, planning, design, construction, operation and maintenance and real estate activitiesrelated to rivers, harbors and waterways; administers laws for protection and preservation of navigable waters and related resources such as wetlands, and assists in recovery from natural disasters.
Thomas P. Bostick, Commander/Chief Engineers
Todd T. Semonite, Deputy Commander/Deputy Chie

2440 **Aspen Institute**
One Dupont Circle NW
202-736-5800
Suite 700
Fax: 202-467-0790
Washington, DC 20036
http://www.aspeninst.org

A forum that addresses critical environmental issues. Interests include energy, the environment and economics. Partner institutes located in Japan, Italy, Germany and France.
Walter Isaacson, President/CEO
Jane Wales, Vice President

2441 **Atlantic States Marine Fisheries Commission**
1050 North Highland Street
703-842-0740
Suite 200A-N
Fax: 703-842-0741
Arlington, VA 22201
E-mail: tberger@asmfc.org
http://www.asmfc.org

The Atlantic States Marine Fisheries Commission was formed by the 15 Atlantic coast states in 1942 in recognition that fish do not adhere to political boundaries. The Commission serves as a deliberative body, coordinating theconservation and management of

the states shared near shore fishery resources-marine, shell, and anadromous-for sustainable use.
Robert E. Beal, Executive Director
Tina L Berger, Public Affairs/Resource Spcl

2442 **Blue Mountain Natural Resource Institute Advisory Board**
US Department of Agriculture
1400 Independence Avenue SW
Room 240W
Washington, DC 20250
202-205-8333
http://www.fs.fed.us
Charles R Hilty, Management Office

2443 **Bureau of Economic Analysis**
Economics and Statistics Administration
1441 L Street NW
Washington, DC 20230
202-606-9900
Fax: 202-606-5311
E-mail: john.landefeld@bea.doc.gov
http://www.bea.gov
Mission: To promote a better understanding of the US economy by providing the most timely, relevant, and accurate economic accounts data in an objective and cost-effective manner.
Steve Landefeld, Director

2444 **Bureau of Land Management, Land & Renewable Resources**
1849 C Street NW
Room 5665
Washington, DC 20240
202-208-3801
Fax: 202-208-3049
E-mail: director@blm.gov
http://www.blm.gov
The mission of the Bureau of Land Management is to sustain the health, diversity, and productivity of the public lands for the use and enjoyment of present and future generations. Offers environmental education, news about theactivities of the Bureau, events, and regulations. In addition, there is information about ALMRS (Automated Land and Management Record System). This is an information system that contains more than one billion land and mineral records.
Neil Kornze, Deputy Director
Jamie Connell, Acting Deputy Director

2445 **Bureau of Oceans International Environmental & Scientific Affairs**
US Department of State
2201 C Street NW
Washington, DC 20520
202-647-4000
http://www.state.gov
OES coordinates US international oceans, environmental and health policy, integrating US domestic concerns with geopolitical concerns. OES promotes the full range of US interests in the oceans to advance our national security,facilitate commerce, manage fish resources, foster scientific understanding and protect the marine environment through bilateral, regional and multilateral fora.
John F. Kerry, Secretary of State

2446 **Center for Disease Control and Prevention**
National Center for Environmental Health
1600 Clifton Road
Atlanta, GA 30333
404-639-0385
800-232-4636
http://www.cdc.gov
To provide national leadership, through science and service, to promote health and quality of life by preventing and controlling disease and death resulting from interactions between people and their environment.

2447 **Center for Environmental Finance: Environmental Finance Center Network (EFC)**
Environmental Protection Agency
1200 Pennsylvania Ave (2710A)
Washington, DC 20460
202-564-1151
Fax: 202-564-1714
E-mail: ocfoinfo@epa.gov
http://www.epa.gov/efinpage/
Part of the EPA's EFP, the EFC is a network of 9 university-based programs in eight EPA regions.
Diane Thompson, Chief of Staff

2448 **Centers for Disease Control and Prevention**
1600 Clifton Road NE
Atlanta, GA 30333
404-639-0385
800-232-4636
http://www.cdc.gov
The Centers for Disease Control and Prevention protect the public health of the nation by providing leadership and direction in the prevention and control of diseases and other preventable conditions, and responding to public healthemergencies.
Julie Gerberding, Director
William Gimson, Chief Operating Officer

2449 **Chemical, Bioengineering, Environmental & Transport Systems**
National Science Foundation
4201 Wilson Boulevard
Arlington, VA 22230
703-292-5111
http://www.eng.nsf.gov/bes/
CBET supports research and education in the rapidly evolving fields of bioengineering and environmental engineering and in areas that involve the transformation and/or transport of matter and energy by chemical, thermal, or mechanicalmeans.
Dr. Cora Marrett, Acting Director
Martha A. Rubenstein, CFO

2450 **Chesapeake Bay Critical Areas Commission**
1804 W Street
Suite 100
Annapolis, MD 21401
410-260-3460
Fax: 410-974-5338
http://www.dnr.state.md.us/criticalarea/
Develops criteria used by local jurisdictions to develop individual Critical Area programs and amend local comprehensive plans, zoning ordinances and subdivision regulations. Programs are designed to address the unique characteristicsand needs of each county and municipality and together they represent a comprehensive land use strategy for preserving and protecting Maryland's most important natural resource, the Chesapeake Bay.
Kerrie Gallo, Natural Resources Planner
LeeAnne Chandler, Science Advisor

2451 **Chief of Engineers Environmental Advisory Board**
441 G Street NW
Washington, DC 20314
202-761-0008
Fax: 202-761-1683
E-mail: hq-publicaffairs@usace.army.mil
http://www.usace.army.mil
Serves the Armed Forces and the Nation by providing vital engineering services and capabilities, as a public service, across the full spectrum of operations; from peace to war; in support of national interests.
Thomas P. Bostick, Commander/Chief of Engineers

2452 **Civil Division: Consumer Litigation Office**
950 Pennsylvania Avenue NW
Washington, DC 20530
202-514-2000
E-mail: askdoj@usdoj.gov
http://www.usdoj.gov/civil/home.html
The Civil Division's Office of Consumer Litigation is responsible for criminal and civil litigation and related matters arising under a variety of federal statutes administered by its client agencies that protect public health andsafety.
Eugene M Thirolf, Director

2453 **Clean Air Scientific Advisory Committee**
US Environmental Protection Agency
Ariel Rios Building
1200 Pennsylvania Avenue NW
Washington, DC 20460
202-564-2188
http://www.epa.gov
The Clean Air Scientific Advisory Committee (CASAC) has a statutorily mandated responsibility to review and offer scientific advice on the air quality criteria and regulatory documents which form the basis for the National Ambient AirQuality Standards (NAAQS), which are currently lead, particulate matter (PM), ozone and other photochemical oxidants (O3), carbon monoxide (CO), nitrogen oxides (NOx) and sulfur oxides (SOx).
Joanne Rodman, Associate Director

2454 **Coast Guard**
2100 2nd Street SW
Washington, DC 20593
202-267-2229
http://www.uscg.mil
Its core roles are to protect the public, the environment, and US ecomonic and security interests in any maritime region in which

those interests may be at risk, including international waters and America's coasts, ports, and inlandwaterways.
Admiral Robert Papp, Jr, Commandant
Admiral John P. Currier, Vice Commandant

2455 Coastal States Organization
444 N Capitol Street NW
Hall of the States, Suite 638
Washington, DC 20001
202-508-3860
Fax: 202-508-3843
E-mail: cso@coastalstates.org
http://www.coastalstate.org

Mission: To support the shared vision of the coastal states, commonwealths and territories for the protection, conservation, responsible use and sustainable economic development of the nation's coastal and ocean resources.
Mary Munson, Executive Director

2456 Committee on Agriculture, Nutrition, and Forestry
Russell Senate Office Building
Room SR-328A
Washington, DC 20510
202-224-2035
Fax: 202-224-1725
http://agriculture.senate.gov

Tom Vilsack, Agriculture Secretary

2457 Committee on Appropriations
The Capitol Building
Room S-128
Washington, DC 20510
202-224-7363
http://appropriations.senate.gov
Barbara Mikulski, Chairwoman
Richard Shelby, Vice Chairman

2458 Committee on Commerce
Committee on Energy and Commerce
2125 Rayburn House Office Building
Washington, DC 20515
202-225-2927
Fax: 202-225-1919
E-mail: commerce@mail.house.gov
http://www.house.gov/commerce

Fred Upton, Chair
Marsha Blackburn, Vice Chair

2459 Committee on Commerce, Science, and Transportation
508 Dirksen Senate Office Building
Washington, DC 20510
202-224-0411
E-mail: webmaster@commerce.senate.gov
http://commerce.senate.gov
John D. Rockefeller, Chair
John Thune, Ranking Member

2460 Committee on Energy and Natural Resources
304 Dirksen Senate Building
Washington, DC 20510
202-224-4971
Fax: 202-224-6163
E-mail: committee@energy.senate.gov
http://energy.senate.gov

Ron Wyden, Chair
Lisa Murkowski, Ranking Member

2461 Committee on Environment and Public Works Republicans
Senate Dirksen Office Building
Room 410
Washington, DC 20510
202-224-8832
http://epw.senate.gov
Barbara Boxer, Chair

2462 Committee on Government Reform and Oversight
2157 Rayburn House Office Building
Washington, DC 20515
202-225-5074
Fax: 202-225-3974
http://www.house.gov/reform/

Rep. Darrell E. Issa, Chair

2463 Committee on Natural Resources
US House of Representatives
1324 Longworth House Office Bldg.
Washington, DC 20515
202-225-2761
Fax: 202-225-5929
http://resourcescommittee.house.gov

Doc Hastings, Chair

2464 Committee on Science and Technology
2321 Rayburn House Office Building
Washington, DC 20515
202-225-6371
Fax: 202-226-0113
http://science.house.gov

Lamar Smith, Chair

2465 Committee on Small Business and Entrepreneurship: US Senate
428A Russell Senate Office Building
Washington, DC 20510
202-224-5175
Fax: 202-224-5619
http://sbc.senate.gov

Mary L. Landrieu, Chair

2466 Committee on Small Business: House of Representatives
Small Business Committee
2361 Rayburn House Office Bldg.
Washington, DC 20515
202-225-5821
Fax: 202-226-5276
E-mail: smbiz@mail.house.gov
http://www.house.gov/smbiz/

Sam Graves, Chair

2467 Committee on Transportation and Infrastructure
2165 Rayburn House Office Building
Washington, DC 20515
202-225-9446
Fax: 202-225-6782
http://transportation.house.gov

Bill Shuster, Chair

2468 Community Greens
1700 N Moore Street
Suite 2000
Arlington, VA 22209
703-527-8300
Fax: 703-527-8383
E-mail: info@ashoka.org
http://www.communitygreens.org

Mission: To catalyze the development of shared green spaces inside residential blocks in cities across the United States.
Kate Herrod, Director

2469 Cooperative Forestry Research Advisory Council
Department of Agriculture
Cooperative State Research Service
Washington, DC 20250
202-720-4318
http://www.csrees.usda.gov
Peter A Muscato

2470 Council on Environmental Quality
722 Jackson Place, Northwest
Washington, DC 20503
202-395-5750
Fax: 202-456-6546
http://www.whitehouse.gov/administration/eop/ceq/

Formulates and recommends national environmental policies.

Nancy Sutley, Chair

2471 Dangerous Goods Advisory Council
1100 H Street, Northwest
Suite 740
Washington, DC 20005
202-289-4550
Fax: 202-289-4074
E-mail: info@dgac.org
http://www.dgac.org

DGAC is an international, nonprofit, educational organization that promotes safety in the transportation of hazardous materials and dangerous goods, including hazardous substances and hazardous wastes.

Vaughn Arthur, President
Alan I Roberts, Vice President

2472 Department of Agriculture
USDA Forest Service
PO Box 96090
Washington, DC 20090
202-205-1657
E-mail: zbowden@fs.fed.us
http://www.fs.fed.us

2473 Department of Agriculture: Research Department, Forest Environment Research
USDA Forest Service, Research
PO Box 96090
Washington, DC 20090
202-205-1657
E-mail: zbowden@fs.fed.us
http://www.fs.fed.us/research
Ann M Bartuska, Deputy Chief
James Reaves, Associate Deputy Chief

2474 **Department of Agriculture: Forest Inventory, Economics**
Research Department
USDA Forest Service, Research
PO Box 96090
Washington, DC 20090
202-205-1657
E-mail: zbowden@fs.fed.us
http://www.fs.fed.us/research
Ann M Bartuska, Deputy Chief
James Reaves, Associate Deputy Chief

2475 **Department of Agriculture: Forest Service Public Affairs**
Sidney R Yates Federal Building
1400 Independence Avenue SW
Washington, DC 20250
202-205-8333
E-mail: webmaster@fs.fed.us
http://www.fs.fed.us

2476 **Department of Agriculture: National Forest Watershed and Soil Resource**
1400 Independence Avenue SW
Washington, DC 20250
202-205-1657
E-mail: zbowden@fs.fed.us
http://www.fs.fed.us/spf/

2477 **Department of Agriculture: Natural Resources State and Private Forestry Division**
1400 Independence Avenue SW
Washington, DC 20250
202-205-1657
E-mail: zbowden@fs.fed.us
http://www.fs.fed.us/spf

Links forestry and conservation with people from the inner city to the rural countryside. Connects people to resources, ideas and to one another so we can all care for the forests and sustain our communities.
Jim Hubbard, Deputy Chief
Robin Thompson, Associate Deputy Chief

2478 **Department of Agriculture: Research**
1400 Independence Avenue SW
Washington, DC 20250
800-832-1355
E-mail: zbowden@fs.fed.us
http://www.fs.fed.us/research

Jim Reaves, Deputy Chief
James Reaves, Associate Deputy Chief

2479 **Department of Agriculture: Research Department Fire Sciences Program**
1400 Independence Avenue SW
Washington, DC 20250
202-205-1706
http://www.fs.fed.us/recreation

2480 **Department of Agriculture: State & Private Forestry**
1400 Independence Avenue SW
Washington, DC 20250
800-832-1355
E-mail: webmaster@fs.fed.us
http://www.fs.fed.us/spf/

2481 **Department of Commerce: National Oceanic & Atmospheric Administration**
1401 Constitution Avenue NW
Room 5128
Washington, DC 20230
202-482-6090
Fax: 202-482-3154
http://www.noaa.gov
Dr. Kathryn Sullivan, Secretary of Commerce
Lois J. Schiffer, General Counsel

2482 **Department of Commerce: National Marine**
1315 E West Highway
Silver Spring, MD 20910
301-713-2379
Fax: 301-713-2385
http://www.nmfs.noaa.gov

Mission: Stewardship of living marine resources through science-based conservation and management and the promotion of healthy ecosystems.
Samuel D. Rauch III, Assistant Administrator

2483 **Department of Commerce: National Ocean Service**
Office of Ocean Resources Conservation/Assessment
1305 East-West Highway
Silver Spring, MD 20910
301-713-3066
Fax: 301-713-4389
E-mail: nos.info@noaa.gov
http://www.oceanservice.noaa.gov

The National Ocean Service works to observe, understand, and manage our nation's coastal and marine resources.
Holly A. Bamford, Ph.D., Assistant Administrator

2484 **Department of Energy: Office of NEPA Policy and Compliance**
1000 Independence Avenue SW
EH-42
Washington, DC 20585
202-586-4600
800-472-2756
Fax: 202-586-7031
E-mail: denise.freeman@eh.doe.gov
http://www.eh.doe.gov/nepa

This office serves as the contact point for NEPA matters for the US Department of Energy.
Carol M Borgstrom, Director
Lettie Wormley, Secretary

2485 **Department of Energy: Transportation and Alternative Fuels**
1000 Independence Avenue SW
Washington, DC 20585
202-586-8302
Fax: 202-586-9811
E-mail: john.garbak@hq.doe.gov
http://www1.eere.energy.gov

David Danielson, Assistant Secretary
Mike Carr, Principal Deputy Assistant

2486 **Department of Justice: Environment and Natural Resources Division**
950 Pennsylvania Avenue NW
Washington, DC 20530
202-514-2000
E-mail: askdoj@usdoj.gov
http://www.usdoj.gov/enrd

Eric H. Holder, Jr., Attorney General

2487 **Department of Justice: Environment and Resources, Environmental Defense**
PO Box 7415
Ben Franklin Station
Washington, DC 20044
202-514-2701
Fax: 202-514-0557
http://www.justice.gov/enrd/ENRD
Andrew Collier, Executive Director

2488 **Department of State: Bureau of Economic and Business**
2201 C Street NW Room 3529
Washington, DC 20520
202-647-1498
Fax: 202-647-8758
Earl Anthony Wayne, Assistant Secretary

2489 **Department of State: Bureau of Oceans and International Environmental and Scientific Affair**
2201 C Street NW Room 7831
Washington, DC 20520
202-647-2232
Fax: 202-647-0217
http://www.state.gov/g/oes

Mission: We advance sustainable development internationally through leadership in oceans, environment, science and health.
Claudia McMurray, Assistant Secretary

2490 **Department of State: Ocean and Fisheries Affairs**
US Department of State
Office of Marine Conservation
2201 C Street NW, Room 5806
Washington, DC 20520
202-647-2335
Fax: 202-736-7350
http://www.foia.state.gov/records.asp
David Hogan, Deputy Director

2491 **Department of State: Office of Ecology, Health, and Conservation**
2201 C Street NW
OES/ETC, Room 4333
Washington, DC 20520
202-647-2418
Fax: 202-736-7351
http://www.state.gov/g/oes
Paul Blakeburn, Director

2492 **Department of State: Office of Global Change**
Office of Global Change
OES/EGC, US Department State
Washington, DC 20520
202-647-4069
Fax: 202-647-0191
http://www.state.gov/e/oes/climate/
Christo Artusio, Foreign Affairs Officer

2493 **Department of Transportation: Office of Marine Safety, Security & Environmental**
U.S. Coast Guard

1200 New Jersey Avenue, SE
Washington, DC 20590
202-366-5807
Fax: 202-267-4839
E-mail: webmaster.marad@dot.gov
http://www.marad.dot.gov/environment_safety_landing_page/environmen

It plays a key role in asserting the need for consistent, uniform international laws and policies

Paul Jaenichen, Deputy Maritime Admin.
Franklin Parker, Chief Counsel

2494 **Department of Transportation: Office of Pipeline Safety**
1200 New Jersey Avenue
SE East Building 2nd Floor
Washington, DC 20590
202-366-4433
Fax: 202-366-3666
E-mail: phmsa.administrator@dot.gov
http://www.phmsa.dot.gov/pipeline

Mission: To protect people and the environment from the risks of hazardous materials transportation

Cynthia L. Quarterman, Administrator
Timothy P. Butters, Deputy Administrator

2495 **Department of the Interior**
1849 C Street Northwest
Washington, DC 20240
202-208-3100
E-mail: feedback@ios.doi.gov
http://www.doi.gov

Mission: To protect and provide access to our Nation's natural and cultural heritage and honor our trust responsibilities to Indian Tribes and our commitments to island communities.

Sally Jewell, Secretary
Lynn Scarlett, Deputy Secretary

2496 **Department of the Interior, U.S. Fish & Wildlife Service**
1849 C Street NW
Room 3331
Washington, DC 20240-0001
202-208-4646
800-344-9453
Fax: 202-208 6916
http://www.fws.gov

Mission: Working with others, to conserve, protect and enhance fish, wildlife, and plants and their habitats for the continuing benefit of the American people.

Sally Jewell, Secretary

2497 **Department of the Interior: National Parks Service**
1849 C Street Northwest
Washington, DC 20240
202-208-3818
http://www.nps.gov

Mission: The National Park Service preserves unimpaired the natural and cultural resources and values of the national park system for the enjoyment, education, and inspiration of this and future generations. The Park Service cooperateswith partners to extend the benefits of natural and cultural resource conservation and outdoor recreation throughout this country and the world.

Jonathan Jarvis, Director
Peggy O'Dell, Deputy Director

2498 **Department of the Interior: Bureau of Land Management**
1849 C Street Northwest
Room 5665
Washington, DC 20240
202-208-3801
Fax: 202-208-5242
E-mail: director@blm.gov
http://www.blm.gov

Mission: To sustain the health, diversity, and productivity of America's public lands for the use and enjoyment of present and future generations

Jamie Connell, Acting Deputy Director
Janet Lin, Chief of Staff

2499 **Department of the Interior: Division of Parks and Wildlife**
Office of the Solicitor
1849 C Street NW Room 6557
Washington, DC 20240
202-208-4344
Fax: 202-208-3877
E-mail: jason.earwood@sol.doi.gov
http://www.doi.gov/solicitor/divisions.html

Mission: To provides legal counsel on matters regarding the administration of programs and activities of the National Park Service, the Fish and Wildlife Service, the biological research functions of the Geological Survey

Hilary Tompkins, Solicitor

2500 **Department of the Interior: National Resources Department**
National Park Service
Interior Main Interior Building
1849 C Street NW, Room 3127
Washington, DC 20240
202-208-5391
Fax: 202-208-4620
E-mail: gmachlis@uidaho.edu

Mission: To manage the Department's technical and policy reviews of the environmental and natural resource aspects of non-Interior projects and proposals.

F Eugene Hester, Associatate Director

2501 **Department of the Interior: Office of the Solicitor**
Division of Land and Water
1849 C Street NW, MS 6412
Washington, DC 20240
202-208-4423
Fax: 202-219-1792
http://www.doi.gov/solicitor

Mission: To provide legal counsel and representation to the Secretary, the Assistant Secretaries, and the Bureau Directors.

Hilary Tompkins, Solicitor

2502 **Department of the Interior: Soil, Water & Air**
Land and Renewable Rangeland Resources Division
20 M Street SE
WO280
Washington, DC 20003
202-912-7137
Fax: 202-912-7182
E-mail: laford@blm.gov
http://www.blm.gov/wo/st/en/prog/more/soil2.html

Larisa Ford, Leader

2503 **Department of the Interior: Water and Science, Water Resources Division**
Water Resources Division
12201 Sunrise Valley Drive
Reston, VA 20192
703-648-4460
E-mail: usgsnews@usgs.gov
http://www.water.usgs.gov

Provides reliable, impartial, timely information to understand the water resources of the United States.

Bill Werkhelser, Associate Director
Anne-Berry Wade, Public Affairs Officer

2504 **Department of the Interior: Water and Science Bureau of Reclamation**
1849 C Street NW
Washington, DC 20240
202-513-0501
Fax: 202-513-0309
http://www.usbr.gov

To manage, develop, and protect water and related resources in an environmentally and economically sound manner in the interest of the American public.

Michael L Connor, Commissioner
Robert Quint, Chief of Staff

2505 **Department of the Interior: Wild Horses and Burros**
Land and Renewable Resources
1620 L Street NW Room 204
Washington, DC 20036
202-653-5258
866-468-7826
E-mail: wildhorse@blm.gov
http://www.blm.gov/wo/st/en/prog/whbprogram.html

The BLM protects, manages, and controls wild horses and burros under the authority of the Wild Free-Roaming Horses and Burros Act of 1971 to ensure that healthy herds thrive on healthy rangelands.

June Sewing, Director

2506 **Dept. of Agriculture: National Forest Watershed and Hydrology**
14th Street SW Building 201
3rd Floor
Washington, DC 20250
202-205-0886

2507 **Dialogue Committee on Phosphoric Acid Product Consensus and Dispute Resolution**
Environmental Protection Agency
400 M Street SW
Washington, DC 20460
202-260-5495
Deborah Dalton

2508 EPA: Office of Solid Waste, Municipal & Industrial Solid Waste
401 M Street SW Room M2105 202-564-4711
Washington, DC 20460 Fax: 703-308-8686
E-mail: levy.steve@epamail.epa.gov
http://www.epa.gov
Bob Perciasepe, Administrator

2509 Emission Standards Office
National Air Pollution Control Techniques
1200 Pennsylvania Avenue, NW 202-564-1682
Washington, DC 20460 Fax: 919-541-0072
http://www.epa.gov/otaq
The Emission Standards Division (ESD) is responsible for establishing emission standards and managing federal programs for nationawide control of hazardous and criteria pollutant emissions from stationary sources. The Division developsand implements emission standards for hazardous and criteria air pollutants, new source performance standards, control technique guidelines, hazardous waste standards, alternative control techniques documents, and guidance for implementing standards.
Bruce C Jordon, Designated Federal Officer
Christopher Grundler, Director

2510 Environment and Natural Resources: Environmental Crimes Section
Department of Justice
PO Box 7415
202-514-2701
Ben Franklin Station Fax: 202-514-4231
Washington, DC 20044 E-mail: webcontentmgr.enrd@usdoj.gov
http://www.usdoj.gov/enrd
To bring criminal cases against individuals and organizations that break the laws that protect our nation's ecological and wildlife resources

2511 Environmental Change and Security Program: Woodrow Wilson International Center for Scholars
1300 Pennsylvania Avenue NW 202-691-4000
Washington, DC 20004-3027 E-mail: ecsp@wwic.si.edu
http://www.wilsoncenter.org/ecsp
The ECSP provides specialists and interested individuals with a road-map to the myriad conceptions, activities and policy initiatives related to environment, population and security. The project pursues three basic activities:gathering information on related international academic and policy initiatives; organizing meetings of experts and public seminars; and publishing the ECSP Report, The China Environment Series and related papers.ECSP explores a wide range ofenvironment related issues.

Roger-Mark De Souza, Director
Geoffrey D. Dabelko, Senior Advisor

2512 Environmental Financial Advisory Board (EFAB)
US EPA, Office of Enterprise Technology & Innovat.
Environmental Finance Program (Mail 202-564-1151
Code) 2731R 1200 Pennsylvania Ave. NW Fax: 202-564-1714
Washington, DC 20460 E-mail: ocfoinfo@epa.gov
http://www.epa.gov/efinpage/efab.htm
The EFAB provides advice to the Environmental Protection Agency's Administrator and Program Offices around the financial aspects of environmental protection. They are a federally chartered advisory committee operating under the FederalAdvisory Committee Act.

Maryann Froehlich, CFO
David Bloom, Deputy CFO

2513 Environmental Health Sciences Review Committee
Division of Extramural Research and Training
PO Box 12233 919-541-3289
Research Triangle Park, NC 27709 Fax: 919-541-2503
E-mail: bass@niehs.nih.gov
http://www.niehs.nih.gov/dert/home.htm
SRB is responsible for the initial scientific and technical merit review of grant applications and contract proposals submitted to the NIH
J. Patrick Mastin, Ph.D., Deputy Director
Janice Allen, Scientific Review Officer

2514 Environmental Management
US Department of Energy 202-586-7709
1000 Independence Ave SW, Room 5A-014 800-342-5363
Washington, DC 20585 Fax: 202-586-4403
E-mail: em.webcontentmanager@em.doe.gov
http://www.em.doe.gov
The Assistant Secretary for EM provides program policy guidance, manages the assessment and cleanup of departmental inactive waste sites and facilities in compliance with federal, state legal and regulatory requirements. The AS alsodirects a program of safe and effective waste management operations, develops and implements an aggressive applied waste research and development program to provide innovative environmental technologies to yield permanent and cost-effective disposalsolutions.
David G. Huizenga, Senior Advisor

2515 Environmental Management Advisory Board
1000 Independence Avenue SW 202-586-7709
Room 180671 Fax: 202-586-0293
Washington, DC 20585 E-mail: em.webcontentmanager@em.doe.gov
http://www.em.doe.gov
The mission of the Environmental Management Advisory Board is to provide advice, information and recommendations to the Assistant Secretary for Environmental Management regarding environmental restoration and waste management issues.
James Ajello, Chair
Dennis P Ferrigno, Vice Chair

2516 Environmental Protection Agency
Ariel Rios Building 202-272-0167
1200 Pennsylvania Avenue NW E-mail: aaoarm@epa.gov
Washington, DC 20460 http://www.epa.gov
EPA's mission is to protect human health and to safeguard the natural environment- air, awter and land- upon which life depends. For 30 years, EPA has been working for a cleaner, healthier environment for the American people.
Bob Perciasepe, Administrator
Craig E. Hooks, Assistant Administrator

2517 Environmental Protection Agency Air & Radiation
Office of Radiation
Ariel Rios Building 202-564-7404
1200 Pennsylvania Avenue NW 866-411-4372
Washington, DC 20460 Fax: 202-501-0986
E-mail: oar_comments@epa.gov
http://www.epa.gov/air
Mission: Lead the US and the world in protecting human health and the environment.
Gina McCarthy, Assistant Administrator
Janet McCabe, Deputy Assistant Admin.

2518 Environmental Protection Agency Climate Change Division
Ariel Rios Building 202-343-9990
1200 Pennsylvania Avenue E-mail: climatechange@epa.gov
Washington, DC 20460 http://www.epa.gov
EPA's Climate Change Division works to assess and address global climate change and the associated risks to human health and the environment.
Bob Perciasepe, Administrator
Diane Thompson, Chief of Staff

2519 Environmental Protection Agency Ground Water and Drinking Water
Ariel Rios Building 202-564-3750
1200 Pennsylvania Avenue 800-426-4791
Washington, DC 20460 Fax: 202-564-3753
http://www.water.epa.gov/drink/index.cfm
Mission: To protect public health by ensuring safe drinking water and protecting ground water.
Cynthia Dougherty, Director
Nanci Gelb, Deputy Director

2520 Environmental Protection Agency Resource Conservation and Recovery Act
Ariel Rios Building 202-260-4808
1200 Pennsylvania Avenue Fax: 202-260-1400
Washington, DC 20460 http://www.epa.gov

RCRA gave EPA the authority to control hazardous waste from the cradle-to-grave. This includes the generation, transportation, treatment, storage, and disposal of hazardous waste.
Bob Perciasepe, Administrator
Diane Thompson, Chief of Staff

2521 Environmental Protection Agency: Indoor Air Division
Office of Radiation
Ariel Rios Building 202-564-2313
1200 Pennsylvania Avenue NW E-mail: indoorair@epa.gov
Washington, DC 20460 http://www.epa.gov
Mission: To protect the public and the environment from the risks of radiation and indoor air pollution.
Elizabeth Cotsworth, Director

2522 Environmental Protection Agency: Office of Pollution Prevention & Toxics
Pollution Prevention Division
Ariel Rios Building 202-564-3810
1200 Pennsylvania Avenue NW http://www.epa.gov/oppt
Washington, DC 20460
To manage programs under the Toxic Substances Control Act
Wendy Cleland-Hamnett, Director
Barbara Cunningham, Deputy Director

2523 Environmental Protection Agency: Water
Environmental Protection Agency
Ariel Rios Building 202-272-0167
1200 Pennsylvania Avenue NW http://www.water.epa.gov
Washington, DC 20004
Benjamin Grumbles, Assistant Administror
Michael H Shapiro, Deputy Asst Administrator

2524 Federal Aviation Administration
800 Independence Avenue, SW 866-835-5322
Washington, DC 20591 http://www.faa.gov
Mission: To provide the safest, most efficient aerospace system in the world.
Michael P. Huerta, Administrator
Michael G. Whitaker, Deputy Administrator

2525 Federal Energy Regulatory Commission
888 1st Street NE 202-502-6088
Room 11A-1 866-208-3372
Washington, DC 20426 E-mail: customer@ferc.gov
http://www.ferc.gov
FERC is an independent commission within the department which has retained many of the functions of the Federal Power Commission, such as setting rates and charges for the transporation and scale of natural gas and for the transmissionand sale of electricity and the licensing of hydroelectric power projects. In addition, the commission establishes rates or charges for the transportation of oil by pipeline, as well as the valuation of such pipelines.
Jon Wellinghoff, Chair
James Pederson, Chief of Staff

2526 Federal Highway Administration
1200 New Jersey Avenue SE 202-366-4000
Washington, DC 20590 E-mail: web.master@fhwa.dot.gov
http://www.fhwa.dot.gov
Mission: Enhancing mobility through innovation, leadership, and public service.
Victor M. Mendez, Adiministrator
Gregory G. Nadeau, Deputy Administrator

2527 Federal Railroad Administration
1200 New Jersey Avenue, SE 202-493-6000
Washington, DC 20590 E-mail: webmaster@fra.dot.gov
http://www.fra.dot.gov
Office of Acquisition and Grants Services is a centralized procurement Office that negotiates, awards, and administers contracts, purchases grants, and cooperative agreemnts in support of the Federal Railroad Administration. The Officeprocures supplies, services, research development, architecture-engineering, information technology and services, and other requirements related to FRA's mission.
Joseph H Boardman, Administrator
Karen Hedlund, Deputy Administrator

2528 Federal Task Force on Environmental Education
Office of Environmental Education Code 111
1849 C Street NW 202-452-5078
Washington, DC 20240 Fax: 202-452-5199
http://www.epa.gov/enviroed/FTFmemws.html
The Federal Task Force on Environmental Education facilities communication and collaboration among federal agencies and departments that have common interests in supporting and implementing EE programs. The task force places emphasison supporting joint interagency EE projects that leverage both federal and non-federal dollars.
Kathleen MacKinnon

2529 Federal Transit Administration
US Department of Transportation
1200 New Jersey Avenue SE 202-366-4043
4th & 5th Floor, East Building 866-377-8642
Washington, DC 20590 E-mail: fta.webmaster@dot.gov
http://www.fta.dot.gov
Peter M. Rogoff, Administrator
Therese W. McMillan, Deputy Administrator

2530 Food Safety and Inspection Service
Technical Service Center
Edward Zorinsky Federal Building 16 402-344-5000
Suite 260 800-233-3935
Omaha, NE 68102-5908 Fax: 402-344-5005
E-mail: fsis.webmaster@usda.gov
http://www.fsis.usda.gov
The Food Safety and Inspection Service (FSIS) is thepublic health agency in the U.S. Department of Agriculture responsible for ensuring that the nation's commercial supply of meat, poultry, and egg products is safe, wholesome, andcorrectly labeled and packaged.
Laura Hulsey, Director
Alfred V Almanza, Administrator

2531 Food and Drug Administration
US Department of Health and Human Services
10903 New Hampshire Avenue 301-827-3666
Silver Spring, MD 20993 888-463-6332
Fax: 301-443-4915
http://www.cfsan.fda.gov
Mission: Responsible for protecting the public health by assuring the safety, efficacy, and security of human and veterinary drugs, biological products, medical devices, our nation's food supply, cosmetics, and products that emitradiation. The FDA is also responsible for advancing the public health by helping to speed innovations that make medicines and foods more effective, safer, and more affordable.

2532 General Services Administration
1275 First Street, NE 202-501-1231
Washington, DC 20417 866-606-8220
Fax: 202-501-1300
E-mail: fbo.support@gsa.gov
http://www.gsa.gov
Our mission is to provide other federal agencies the workspace, products, services, technology, and policy they need to accomplish their missions. The mission statement contained in our Strategic Plan reflects our recognition that wemust provide Federal agencies with the highest quality service at a competitive cost.
Daniel M. Tangherlini, Administrator
Susan F. Brita, Deputy Administrator

2533 Global Learning and Observations to Benefit the Environment
UCAR-The GLOBE Program 800-858-9947
PO Box 3000 Fax: 970-491-8768
Boulder, CO 80307 E-mail: help@globe.gov
http://www.globe.gov

Mission: To promote the teaching and learning of science, enhance environmental literacy and stewardship, and promote scientific discovery.

Edward Geary, Director
Teresa Kennedy, Deputy Director

2534 House Committee on Agriculture
1301 Longworth House Office Bldg 202-225-2171
Washington, DC 20515 Fax: 202-225-0917
E-mail: agrepublicanpress@mail.house.gov
http://www.agriculture.house.gov

Frank D. Lucas, Chairman
Bob Goodlatte, Vice Chairman

2535 House Committee on Foreign Affairs
2170 Rayburn House Office Building 202-225-5021
Washington, DC 20515 Fax: 202-226-7269
http://www.foreignaffairs.house.gov

Our Committee is charged with overseeing US foreign policy programs and agencies. We manage legislation regarding foreign policy, State Department management, foreign assistance, trade promotion, export controls, foreign arms sales,student exchanges, international broadcasting and many other issues.
Ed Royce, Chairman
Christopher H. Smith, Member

2536 House Committee on Transportation and Infrastructure
2165 Rayburn House Office Bldg 202-225-9446
Washington, DC 20515 Fax: 202-225-6782
http://www.transportation.house.gov

Bill Shuster, Chair
Chris Bertram, Staff Director

2537 Installation Management
600 Army Pentagon 703-693-3233
Room 1E668 866-335-2769
Washington, DC 20310 Fax: 703-693-3507
E-mail: help@us.army.mil
http://www.army.mil

This office is responsible for policy and oversight of construction, utilization, improvement, alteration, maintenance, repair and disposal of real estate and facilities.

2538 Inter-American Foundation
1331 Pennsylvania Ave. NW, 202-360-4530
Suite 1200 Fax: 703-306-4365
Washington, DC 20004 E-mail: inquiries@iaf.gov
http://www.iaf.gov

The Inter-American Foundation (IAF) is an independent foreign assistance agency of the United States government, working to promote equitable, responsive, and participatory self-help development in Latin America and the Caribbean.
Robert N. Kaplan, President
Thomas J. Dodd, Vice Chairman

2539 International Joint Commission
2000 L Street, NW 202-736-9024
Suite 615 Fax: 202-632-2007
Washington, DC 20440 E-mail: lawsonc@washington.ijc.org
http://www.ijc.org

Mission: Prevents and resolves disputes between the United States and Canada, and pursues the common good of both countries as an independent and objective advisor to the two governments.

Charles A. Lawson, Secretary
Frank Bevacqua, Public Information Officer

2540 Land and Minerals Management
1849 C Street NW 202-208-6474
Washington, DC 20240 Fax: 202-208-3144
E-mail: boemrearchive@boemre.gov
http://www.bsee.gov/www.boem.gov

Tommy Beaudreau, Director
Walter Cruickshank, Deputy Director

2541 Land and Minerals Office of Surface Mining Reclamation & Enforcement
Department of the Interior
1951 Constitution Avenue NW 202-208-2565
Washington, DC 20240 E-mail: getinfo@osmre.gov
http://www.osmre.gov

Our mission is to carry out the requirments of the Surface Mining Control and Reclamation Act in cooperation with States and Tribes. Our primary objectives are to ensure that coal mines are operated in a manner that protects citizensand the environment during mining and assures that the land is restored to beneficial use following mining, and to mitigate the effects of past mining byaggressively pursuing reclamation of abandoned coal mines.
Joseph Pizarchik, Director
Michele Altemus, Chief of Staff

2542 Management and Budget Office: Natural Resources, Energy and Science
725 17th Street, NW 202-395-4561
Washington, DC 20503 Fax: 202-395-4639
http://www.whitehouse.gov/omb

This division of the Management and Budget Office assists the President by clearing and coordinating advice on proposed legislation and by making recommendations as to presidential action on legislative enactments related to naturalresources, energy and science.
Rob Portman, Director
Stephen McMillin, Deputy Director

2543 Manpower, Reserve Affairs, Installations and Environment
Environment, Safety and Occupational Health
1665 Air Force Pentagon 703-697-9297
Washington, DC 20330 Fax: 703-614-2884
http://www.af.mil

This office provides guidance, direction, and oversight for the department on all matters pertaining to the environment, safety, and occupational health.

2544 Marine Mammal Commission
4340 East West Highway
Suite 700 301-504-0087
Bethesda, MD 20814 Fax: 301-504-0099
E-mail: mmc@mmc.gov
http://www.mmc.gov

Developing, reviewing and making recommendations on domestic and international actions and policies with respect to marine mammal protection, conservation and with carrying out a research program. Primary objective is to ensure thatfederal programs are being administered in ways that maintain the health and stability of marine ecosystems and do not disadvantage marine mammal populations or species.
Daryl J. Boness, Chairman
Rebecca Lent, Executive Director

2545 Maritime Administration
Maritime Administration (MARAD)
Southeast Federal Center 202-366-5807
1200 New Jersey Avenue SE 800-996-2723
Washington, DC 20590 E-mail: webmaster.marad@dot.gov
http://www.marad.dot.gov

Mission: To improve and strengthen the US marine transportation system-including infrastructure, industry and labor-to meet the economic and security needs of the Nation.
Paul Jaenichen, Deputy Maritime Admin.
Franklin Parker, Chief Counsel

2546 Migratory Bird Conservation Commission
4401 N Fairfax Drive 703-358-1716
Suite 622 Fax: 703-358-2223
Arlington, VA 22203 E-mail: mbcc@fws.gov
http://www.fws.gov/refuges/realty/mbcc.html

The Migratory Bird Conservation Commission (MBCC) is responsible for considering and approving for acquistion areas of migratory bird habitat (other than waterfowl production areas) that have been submitted by regional offices andrecommended by the Secretary. The MBCC is composed of representatives from the Legislative and Executive Branches of government, fixes the price at which such areas may be purchased or rented, and meets three times a year.

Ken Salazar, Chair

2547 Migratory Bird Regulations Committee Office of Migratory Bird Management
4401 N Fairfax Drive
MBSP 4107
Arlington, VA 22203
703-358-1714
Fax: 703-358-2217
E-mail: brian_a_millsap@fws.gov
http://policy.fws.gov/723fw2.html

The Service Regulations Committee will review information provided to it each year on regulatory issues and submit recommendations to the Director. In this regard, the committe receives guidance fromt he office of Migratory BirdManagement, the Division of Law Enforcement, and from the Regional migratory Bird Coordinators. In addition, Flyway Consultants, from the four Flyway Councils, may provide technical data and certain advice as limited by memoranda of understanding.
Krista Holloway, Contact

2548 Mine Safety and Health Administration
1100 Wilson Boulevard
21st Floor
Arlington, VA 22209
202-693-9400
Fax: 202-693-9401
http://www.msha.gov

The mission of the Mine Safety and Health Administration is to administer the provisions of the Federal Mine Safety and Health Act of 1977 and to enforce compliance with mandatory safety and health standards as means to eliminate fatalaccidents; to reduce the frequency and severity of nonfatal accidents; to minimize health hazards; and to promote improved safety and health conditions in the Nation's mines. MSHA carries out the mandates of the Mine Act at all mining and mineralprocessing areas.
Joseph A, Main, Assistant Secretary

2549 NOAA Sanctuaries and Reserves Management Divisions
Department of Commerce
NOAA's National Marine Sanctuaries
1305 E West Highway, 11th Floor
Silver Spring, MD 20910
301-713-3125
Fax: 301-713-0404
E mail: sanctuaries@noaa.gov
http://www.sanctuaries.nos.noaa.gov

Mission: To serve as the trustee for the nation's system of marine protected areas, to conserve, protect and enhance their biodiversity, ecological integrity and cultural legacy.

2550 National Aeronautics and Space Administration
NASA
NASA Headquarters
Suite 5K39
Washington, DC 20546
202-358-0000
Fax: 202-358-4338
E-mail: public-inquiries@hq.nasa.gov
http://www.nasa.gov

Research includes a variety of global environmental conditions.
Charles F. Bolden, Administrator
Lori B. Garver, Deputy Administrator

2551 National Cancer Institute: Cancer Epidemiology and Genetics Division
9609 Medical Center Drive
MSC 9776
Rockville, MD 20892
240-276-7150
800-422-6237
E-mail: ncicontactdceg@mail.nih.gov.
http://www.dceg.cancer.gov/about

The National Cancer Institute expands existing scientific knowledge on cancer cause and prevention as well as on the diagnosis, treatment, and rehabilitation of cancer patients. This division conducts research on cancer epdiemiologyand genetics.
Margaret A. Tucker, Director
Joseph F. Fraumeni, Jr., MD, Senior Investigator and Advi

2552 National Center for Health Statistics
Nat. Cen. for Health Stats. Division of Data Serv.
3311 Toledo Road
Room 5419
Hyattsville, MD 20782
800-232-4636
E-mail: nchsquery@cdc.gov
http://www.cdc.gov/nchs/

The mission of the National Center for Health Statistics (NCHS) is to provide statistical information that will guide actions and policies to improve the health of the American people. As the Nation's principal health statisticsagency, NCHS leads the way with accurate, relevant, and timely data.
Edward Sondik, Director
Jennifer H. Madans, Co-Acting Deputy Director

2553 National Climatic Data Center
Federal Building
151 Patton Avenue
Asheville, NC 28801
828-271-4800
Fax: 828-271-4876
E-mail: ncdc.orders@noaa.gov
http://www.ncdc.noaa.gov

Mission: To manage the Nation's resource of global climatological in-situ and remotely sensed data and information to promote global environmental stewardship; to describe, monitor and assess the climate; and to support efforts topredict changes in the Earth's environment.
Thomas R Karl, Director
M, Tanner, Deputy Director

2554 National Council on Radiation Protection and Measurements
7910 Woodmont Avenue
Suite 400
Bethesda, MD 20814-3095
301-657-2652
800-229-2652
Fax: 301-907-8768
E-mail: ncrp@ncrponline.org
http://www.ncrponline.org

The National Council on Radiation Protection and Measurements (NCRP) seeks to formulate and widely disseminate information, guidance and recommendations on radiation protection and measurements which represent the consensus of leadingscientific thinking.
John D. Boice, President
James R. Cassata, Executive Director

2555 National Environmental Justice Advisory Council
401 M Street Southwest (MC 2201A)
Washington, DC 20460
202-564-2515
800-962-6215
Fax: 202-501-0740
E-mail: environmental-justice-epa@epamail.epa.gov
http://www.epa.gov/compliance/environmentaljustice/nejac/index.html

A federal advisory committee established by charter to provide independent advice, consultation and recommendations to the Administrator of the US Environmental Protection Agency on matters related to environmental justice.
Richard Moore, Chair

2556 National Environmental Satellite Data & Information Service
National Oceanic and Atmospheric Administration
1335 East-West Highway
SSMC1, 8th Floor
Silver Spring, MD 20910
301-713-3578
Fax: 301-713-1249
E-mail: ohn.leslie@noaa.gov
http://www.nesdis.noaa.gov

The National Environmental Satellite, Data and Information Service operates a national environmental satellite system. It acquires, stores and disseminates worldwide environmental data through its data centers.
Mary Ellen Kicza, Assistant Administrator
Charles Baker, Deputy Assistant Admin.

2557 National Health Information Center (NHIC)
US Department of Health and Human Services
PO Box 1133
Washington, DC 20013
301-565-4167
800-336-4797
Fax: 301-984-4256
E-mail: info@nhic.org
http://www.health.gov/nhic

A health information referral line. NHIC links consumers and health professionals who have health questions and organizations best able to provide reliable health information. Maintains an online directory of more than than 1600 healthorganizations that can provide provide information. They include Federal and State agenices, voluntary a professional associations and universities. The database is accessible to the public through the healthfinder web site.
Rachel Langston, Information Services Manager

2558 National Institute for Occupational Safety and Health
395 E Street SW, Suite 9200
Patriots Plaza Building
Washington, DC 20201
202-245-0625
800-232-4636
Fax: 513-533-8347
E-mail: nioshwebmaster@cdc.gov
http://www.cdc.gov/niosh

To ensure safe and healthful working conditions for all working people, occupational safety and health standards are developed, and research and other activities are carried out, through the National Institute for Occupational Safetyand Health.
John Howard, Director
Frank J Hearl, Chief of Staff

2559 National Institute of Environmental Health Sciences
111 T.W. Alexander Drive
Research Triangle Park, NC 27709
919-541-3345
Fax: 301-480-2978
E-mail: webcenter@niehs.nih.gov
http://www.niehs.nih.gov

Environmental research.
Linda S. Birnbaum, Director
Richard Woychik, Deputy Director

2560 National Institutes of Health
9000 Rockville Pike
Bethesda, MD 20892
301-496-4000
E-mail: nihinfo@od.nih.gov
http://www.nih.gov

The National Institutes of Health conducts, supports and promotes biomedical research to improve the health of the American people by increasing the understanding of processes underlying human health, disability and disease. Theinstitutes advance knowledge concerning the health effects of interactions between humans and the environment.
Francis S. Collins, Director
Raynard Kington, Deputy Director

2561 National Lead Information Center
422 South Clinton Avenue
Rochester, NY 14620
800-424-5323
Fax: 585-232-3111
E-mail: leadinfo@epa.gov
http://www.epa.gov/lead/pubs/nlic.htm

Provides the general public and professionals with information about lead hazards and their prevention.
Bob Perciasepe, Administrator
Diane Thompson, Chief of Staff

2562 National Marine Fisheries Service
National Oceanic & Atmospheric Administration
1315 East West Highway
Silver Spring, MD 20910
202-482-6090
Fax: 202-482-3154
E-mail: roland.schmitten@noaa.gov
http://www.nmfs.noaa.gov

NMFS conducts an integrated program of management, research and services for the protection and rational use of living marine resources. It also is responsible for the protection of marine mammals.
Samuel D. Rauch III, Assistant Administrator

2563 National Oceanic & Atmospheric Administration
1401 Constitution Avenue, NW
Room 5128
Washington, DC 20230
202-482-6090
Fax: 202-482-3154
E-mail: webmaster@noaa.gov;
http://www.rdc.noaa.gov

The Administration's mission is to explore, map, and chart the global ocean and its living resources and to manage, use, and conserve those resources; to describe, monitor, and predict conditions in the atmosphere, ocean, sun, andspace environment; to issue warnings against impending destructive natural events; to assess the consequences of inadvertent environmental modification over several scales of time, and to manage and disseminate long-term environmental information.
Dr. Kathryn Sullivan, Administrator
David M. Kennedy, Undersecretary

2564 National Organic Standards Board Agricultural Marketing Service
USDA/AMS
1400 Independence Avenue SW
Washington, DC 20250
202-720-3252
Fax: 202-205-7808
E-mail: amsadministratoroffice@ams.usda.gov
http://www.ams.usda.gov/nop

To facilitate the competitive and efficient marketing of agricultural products
Anne L. Alonzo, Administrator
Julie S Weisman, Vice Chair

2565 National Park Service: Fish, Wildlife and Parks
National Park Service
1849 C Street NW
PO Box 37127
Washington, DC 20240
202-208-4621
Fax: 202-208-7889
E-mail: nps_director@nps.gov
http://www.nps.gov

The National Park Service preserves unimpaired the natural and cultural resources and values of the national park system for the enjoyment, education, and inspiration of this and future generations. The Park Service cooperates withpartners to extend the benefits of natural and cultural resource conservation and outdoor recreation throughout this country and the world.

2566 National Petroleum Council
1625 K Street NW
Suite 600
Washington, DC 20006
202-393-6100
Fax: 202-331-8539
E-mail: info@npc.org
http://www.npc.org

The purpose of the NPC is solely to represent the views of the oil and natural gas industries in advising, informing, and making recommendations to the Secretary of Energy with respect to any matter relating to oil and natural gas, orto the oil and gas industries submitted to it or approved by the Secretary. The NPC does not concern itself with trade practices, nor does it engage in any of the usual trade association activities.
Samuel W Bodman, Secretary
Carla Scali Byrd, Information Coordinator

2567 National Science Foundation
4201 Wilson Boulevard
Arlington, VA 22230
703-292-5111
800-877-8339
E-mail: info@nsf.gov
http://www.nsf.gov

It is the National Science Foundation's mission to promote the progress of science; to advance the national health, prosperity, and welfare; and to secure the national defense.
Cora Marrett, Director
Lawrence Rudolph, General Counsel

2568 National Science Foundation Office of Polar Programs
4201 Wilson Boulevard
Room 755 S
Arlington, VA 22230
703-292-8030
Fax: 703-292-9081
http://www.nsf.gov/od/opp/

OPP shares in the vision and goals expressed in NSF's strategic plan: enable world leadership in science and engineering; promote discovery, dissemination and employment of new knowledge; and support excellence in science, mathematicalengineering and technology education. Polar research and the associated logistics activities make a recognized and visible contribution to these goals.
Kelly Kenison Falkner, Director
Susanne M. LaFratta-Decker, Deputy Director

2569 National Water Supply Improvement Association
PO Box 102
St. Leonard, MD 20685
301-855-1173
Fax: 410-586-2844
Jack C Jorgensen, Executive Director

2570 Natural Resources Conservation Service
1400 Independence Ave., SW 202-720-7246
Room 5105-A Fax: 202-720-7690
Washington, DC 20250 E-mail: elisa.ohalloran@wdc.usda.gov
http://www.nrcs.usda.gov

Provides leadership in a partnership effort to help people conserve, maintain and improve our natural resources and environment. NRCS is the technical delivery arm of USDA and provides conservation information, incentive programs andtechnical assistance at the state and county levels. Contact the Conservation Communications Staff.
Jason Weller, Chief
Thomas Christensen, Associate Chief

2571 Naval Sea Systems Command
1333 Isaac Hull Avenue SE 202-781-0000
Washington Navy Yard, DC 20376 Fax: 202-781-4713
http://www.navsea.navy.mil

The Naval Sea Systems Command provides material support to the Navy and Marine Corps, and for mobilization purposes to the Department of Defense and Department of Transportation, for ships, submarines, and other sea platforms,shipboard combat systems and components, other surface and undersea warfare and weapons systems, and ordinance expendables not specifically assigned to other system commands.

2572 Navy Environmental Health Center
620 John Paul Jones Circle 757-953-0700
Suite 1100 Fax: 757-953-0999
Portsmouth, VA 23708 http://www-nehc.med.navy.mil
Mission: The Navy and Marine Corps center for public health services. We provide leadership and expertise to ensure mission readiness through disease prevention and health promotion in support of the National Military Strategy.
Captain William Stover, Commanding Officer
Captain John B Burgess, Executive Officer

2573 New Forests Project
1025 Vermont Avenue, NW 202-547-3800
7th Floor Fax: 202-546-4784
Washington, DC 20005 E-mail: etoledo@newforests.org
http://www.newforestsproject.com

The New Forest Project strives to protect, conserve and enhance the health of the Earth's ecosystems along with the people depending on them, by supporting integrated grassroots efforts in agroforestry, reforestation, protection ofwatersheds, water and sanitation and renewable energy initiatives.
Erick Toledo, Director

2574 Nuclear Materials, Safety, Safeguards & Operations
Nuclear Regulatory Commission
One White Flint N Building 301-415-7000
11555 Rockville Pike 800-368-5642
Rockville, MD 20852 http://www.nrc.gov
The Division of Industrial and medical Nuclear safety within the Office of Nuclear Materials Safety and safeguards at the NRC has the responsibility for NRC's principal rulemaking and guidance development, licensing, inspection, eventresponse and regulatory activities for material licensed under the Atomic Energy Act of 1954, as amended, to ensure safety and quality associated with the possession, processing, and handling of nuclear material.
Catherine Haney, Director
Scott Moore, Deputy Director

2575 Occupational Safety and Health Administration: US Department of Labor
Office of Administrative Services
200 Constitution Avenue NW 202-693-1999
Room N-310 800-321-6742
Washington, DC 20210 http://www.osha.gov
OSHA's mission is to send every worker home whole and healthy every day. Since the agency was created in 1971, workplace fatalities have been cut in half and occupational injury and illness rates have declined 40 percent. At the sametime, US employment has nearly doubled from 56 million workers at 3.5 million worksites to 105 milion workers at nearly 6.9 million sites.
David Michaels, Assistant Secretary

2576 Oceanic and Atmospheric Research Office
National Oceanic and Atmospheric Administration
1315 E West Highway 301-713-2458
Room 11627 http://www.oar.noaa.gov
Silver Spring, MD 20910
The Office of Oceanic and Atmospheric Research is where much of the work is done that results in better weather forecasts, longer warning lead times for natural disasters, new products from the sea, and greater understanding of ourclimate, atmosphere, and oceans.
Robert Detrick, Assistant Administrator
Steven Fine, Deputy Asst Administrator

2577 Office of Civil Water Enforcement Division
Environmental Protection Agency
US Env. Protect. Agency, Water Enf. 202-564-2240
1200 Pennsylvania Avenue Fax: 202-564-0018
Washington, DC 20460 http://www.epa.gov
Bob Perciasepe, Administrator
Diane Thompson, Chief of Staff

2578 Office of Research & Engineering Hazardous Materials
National Transportation Safety Board
490 L'Enfant Plaza East SW 202-314-6000
Room 5131 http://www.ntsb.gov
Washington, DC 20594
Independently Advancing Transportation Safet
Deborah A. P. Hersman, Chairman
Christopher A. Hart, Vice Chairman

2579 Office of Solid Waste Management & Emergency Response
1200 Pennsylvania Avenue NW 202-566-0200
Washington, DC 20460 http://www.epa.gov/swerrims
Develops guidelines and standards for the land disposal of hazardous wastes and for underground storage tanks. Furnishes techincal assistance in the development, management and operation of solids waste activities and analyzes therecovery of useful energy from solid waste. The Office has undertaken the development and implementatin of a program to respond to abandoned and active hazardous waste sites and accidental release as well as the encouragement of new technology.
Mathy Stanislaus, Assistant Administrator
Barry Breen, Deputy Assistant Admin.

2580 Office of Surface Mining
1951 Constitution Avenue NW 202-208-2565
Washington, DC 20240 E-mail: getinfo@osmre.gov
http://www.osmre.gov
Aids in maintaining proper safety precautions during coal reclamation.
Joseph Pizarchik, Director
Michele Altemus, Chief of Staff

2581 Office of Surface Mining Reclamation & Enforcement
US Department of the Interior
1951 Constitution Avenue NW 202-208-2565
Washington, DC 20240 E-mail: getinfo@osmre.gov
http://www.osmre.gov

The Office of Surface Mining is the bureau of the US Department of the Interior with responsability, in cooperation with the state and indian Tribes, to protect citizens and the environment during coal mining and reclamation, and toreclaim mines abandoned before 1977.
Joseph Pizarchik, Director
Michele Altemus, Chief of Staff

2582 Office of the Chief Economist
Jamie L Whitten Federal Building 202-720-5447
Room 112-A http://www.usda.gov/oce
Washington, DC 20250
The Office of the Chief Economist advises the Secretary on the economic implications of policies and programs affecting the US food and fiber systems and rural areas. The Chief Economist co-

ordinates, reviews, and approves theDepartment's commodity and farm sector forecast.
Joseph W. Glauber, Chief Economist
Robert Johansson, Deputy Chief Economist

2583 Office of the Executive Clerk
17th Street & Pennsylvania Ave NW 202-456-2226
Washington, DC 20500 Fax: 202-456-2569
http://www.whitehouse.gov
This office provides information on when a bill was signed or vetoed, the dates of presidential messages, executive orders, and dates of other presidential actions.
George T Saunders, Executive Clerk

2584 Office of the General Counsel
Mail Stop 3650 202-282-9822
Washington, DC 20528 Fax: 202-282-9186
E-mail: ogc@dhs.gov
http://www.ogc.doc.gov
The Office of the General Counsel provides legal services for all programs, operations and activities of the department.
John Sandweg, General Counsel
Geovette E Washington, Deputy General Counsel

2585 Office of the Secretary of Energy
1000 Independence Avenue SW 202-586-5000
Forrestal Building, Room 7A-257 Fax: 202-586-4403
Washington, DC 20585 E-mail: the.secretary@hq.doe.gov
http://www.doe.gov
The Secretary of Energy provides the framework for a comprehensive and balanced national energy plan through the coordination and administration of the energy functions of the federal government.
Ernest Moniz, Secretary
Daniel B. Poneman, Deputy Secretary

2586 Office of the Secretary of Health and Human Services
200 Independence Avenue SW 202-619-0257
Hubert H Humphery Building http://www.hhs.gov
Washington, DC 20201
The Secretary of Health and Human Services advises the President on health, welfare, and income security plans, policies, and programs of the federal government.
Kathleen Sebelius, Secretary
Bill Corr, Deputy Secretary

2587 Office of the Secretary of the Interior
1849 C Street NW 202-208-3100
Interior Building, Room 6156 E-mail: feedback@ios.doi.gov
Washington, DC 20240 http://www.doi.gov
The Secretary of the Interior is responsible for the administration of over 500 million acres of federal land, and holds in trust approximately 50 million acres of land, mostly Indian reservations; the conservation and development ofmineral and water resources; the conservation, development, and utilization of fish and wildlife resources; the coordination of federal and state recreational programs; the preservation and administration of the nation's scenic and historic areas.
Sally Jewell, Secretary of the Interior
P Lynn Scarlett, Deputy Secretary

2588 Office of the Solicitor
1849 C Street NW 202-208-4423
Interior Building, Room 6352 Fax: 202-219-1792
Washington, DC 20240 E-mail: feedback@ios.doi.gov
http://www.doi.gov/solicitor
Mission: To provide legal counsel and representation to the Secretary, the Assistant Secretaries, and the Bureau Directors.
Hilary Tompkins, Solicitor

2589 Office of the US Trade Representative
600 17th Street NW 202-395-4549
Washington, DC 20508 http://www.ustr.gov
This division of the Office of the US Trade Representative is responsible for the direction of all trade negotiations and the formulation of trade policy for the United States as related to the environment and natural resources.
Miriam Sapiro, Ambassador
Michael Punke, Ambassador

2590 Peace Corps
1111 20th Street NW 202-692-2100
Washington, DC 20526 855-855-1961
http://www.peacecorps.gov
The goal of the Peace Corps is to help people of interested countries in meeting their need for trained men and women, to promote a better understanding of Americans on the part of peolple served and to help promote a betterunderstanding of other peoples on the part of Americans.
Carrie Hessler-Radelet, Deputy Director
Josephine Olsen, Deputy Director

2591 Research, Education and Economics
1400 Independence Avenue SW 202-720-5923
Room 214W Whitten Building Fax: 202-690-2842
Washington, DC 20250-01E-mail: carolyne.foster@osec.usda.gov
http://www.ree.usda.gov
Mission: Federal leadership responsibility for the discovery of knowledge spanning the biological, physical, and social sciences, and involving agricultural research, economic analysis, statistics, outreach, and higher education.
Cathie Woteki, Under Secretary
Ann Bartuska, Deputy Under Secretary

2592 Research, Education, and Economics National Agricultural Statistics Service
1400 Independence Avenue SW 800-727-9540
S Building, Room 4117 E-mail: nass@nass.usda.gov
Washington, DC 20250 http://www.nass.usda.gov
Mission: Provides timely, accurate, and useful statistics in service to US agriculture.
Cynthia Z. F Clark, Administrator
Joseph T. Reilly, Assoiciate Administrator

2593 Risk Assessment and Cost Benefit Analysis Office
Office of the Chief Economist
1400 Independence Avenue SW 202-720-8022
S Building, Room 4032 E-mail: jlohr@oce.usda.gov
Washington, DC 20250 http://www.usda.gov/oce/risk_assessment
ORACBA's primary role is to ensure that major regulations proposed by USDA are based on sound scientific and economic analysis.
Linda Abbott, Director
Mark R. Powell, Risk Scientist

2594 Rural Utilities Service
1400 Independence Avenue SW 202-690-1533
S Building, Room 5151 Fax: 202-690-0500
Washington, DC 20250-701 E-mail: webmaster@rus.usda.gov
http://www.usda.gov/rus
Modern utilities came to rural America through some of the most successful goverment initiatives in American history, carried out through the USDA working with rural cooperatives, nonprofit associations, public bodies, and for-profitutilities. Today, they carry on this tradition helping rural utilities expand and keep their technology up to date, helping establish new and vital services such as distance learning and telemedicine.
James M Andrew, Administrator
Curtis M Anderson, Deputy Administrator

2595 Saint Lawrence Seaway Development Corporation
US Department of Transportation
1200 New Jersey Avenue SE 202-366-0091
Suite W32-300 800-785-2779
Washington, DC 20590 Fax: 202-366-7147
E-mail: info@sls.dot.gov
http://www.seaway.dot.gov
Saint Lawrence Seaway Development Corporation operates and maintains the Great Lakes/St. Lawrence System, which encompasses the St. Lawrence River and the five Great lakes.
Collister Johnson Jr, Administrator
Craig H Middlebrook, Deputy Administrator

2596 Science Advisory Board Environmental Protection Agency
401 M Street SW
Room 1145
Washington, DC 20460
202-382-4126
E-mail: sab@epa.gov
http://www.epa.gov/sab

The SAB was established by Congress to provide independent scientific and engineering advice to the EPA Administrator on the technical basis for EPA regulations. Expressed in terms of the current parlance of the risk assessment/riskmanagement paradigm of decision making, they deal with risk assessment issues and only that portion of risk management that deals strictly with the technical issues associated with various contorol options.

2597 Science and Technology Policy Office
Eisenhower Executive Office Bldg
1650 Pennsylvania Avenue
Washington, DC 20504
202-456-4444
Fax: 202-456-6021
E-mail: info@ostp.gov
http://www.ostp.gov

The Science and Technology Policy Office serves as a source of scientific, engineering, and technological analysis and judgement for the President with respect to major policies, plans, and programs of the federal government. Incarrying out this mission, the office advises the President of scientific and technological considerations involved in areas of national concern, including the economy, national security, health, foreign relations, and the environment.
Rick Siger, Chief of Staff
Ted Wackler, Deputy Chief of Staff

2598 Senate Committee on Appropriations
The Capitol S-128
Washington, DC 20510
202-224-7363
http://www.appropriations.senate.gov
Barbara A. Mikulski, Chair
Richard Shelby, Vice Chair

2599 Senate Committee on Energy and Natural Resources
304 Dirksen Senate Building
Washington, DC 20510
202-224-4971
Fax: 202-224-6163
http://www.energy.senate.gov
Ron Wyden, Chair
Lisa Murkowski, Ranking Member

2600 Senate Committee on Foreign Relations
446 Dirksen Senate Office Builing
Washington, DC 20510-6225
202-224-4651
Fax: 202-224-3612
E-mail: senator@biden.senate.gov
http://www.foreign.senate.gov

No foreign policy can be sustained without the informed consent of the American people. Our government works best when citizens care enough to become involved.
Rob Menendez, Chairman
Bob Corker, Ranking Member

2601 Smithsonian Tropical Research Institute
Smithsonian Institution Research Department
1100 Jefferson Drive
Suite 3123
Washington, DC 20013-7012
202-633-4700
Fax: 202-786-2557
http://www.stri.org
Ira Rubinoff, Director
Georgina de Alba, Associate Director

2602 Take Pride in America Advisory Board Department of the Interior
1849 C Street NW
Washington, DC 20240
202-208-3100
E-mail: webteam@ios.doi.gov
http://www.doi.gov

The purposes of the program include the following: 1-to establish and maintain a public awareness campaign in cooperation with public and private organizations and individuals; 2- To conduct a national awards program to honor thoseindividuals and entities which, in the opinion of the Secretary of the Interior, have distinguished themselves in the above mentioned activities.
Sally Jewell, Secretary of the Interior
David J. Hayes, Deputy Secretary

2603 Technology Administration: National Institute of Standards & Technology
Technology Policy Office
1000 Bureau Drive
Gaithersburg, MD 20899
301-975-4500
E-mail: inquiries@nist.gov
http://www.nist.gov

The National Institute of Standards and Technology assists industry in the development of technology needed to improve product quality, modernize manufacturing processes, ensure product reliability, and facilitate rapidcommercialization of products based on new scientific discoveries. NIST's primary mission is to promote US economic growth by working with industry to develop and apply technology, measurements, and standards.
William A Jeffrey, Director
James Turner, Deputy Director

2604 US Agency for International Development Information Center
Ronald Reagan Building
Washington, DC 20523
202-712-4810
Fax: 202-216-3524
E-mail: pinquiries@usaid.gov
http://www.usaid.gov

Aids in the development of urban environmental programs, forest conservation teams, watershed management and promotes improved pollution control.
Rajiv Shah, Administrator
Donald Steinberg, Deputy Administrator

2605 US Consumer Product Safety Commission
4330 E West Highway
Bethesda, MD 20814
301-504-7923
800-638-2772
Fax: 301-504-0124
http://www.cpsc.gov

An independent federal regulatory agency. Helps keep American families safe by reducing the risk of injury or death from consumer products.
Inez Moore Tenenbaum, Chair
Robert S. Adler, Commissioner

2606 US Customs & Border Protection
1300 Pennsylvania Avenue NW
Washington, DC 20229
202- 32- 800
877-227-5511
http://www.cbp.gov

Mission: Safeguard the American homeland at and beyond our borders.
W Ralph Basham, Commissioner
Deborah J Spero, Deputy Commissioner

2607 US Department of Agriculture
1400 Independence Avenue SW
Washington, DC 20250
202-720-8732
http://www.usda.gov

USDA Mission: Enhance the quality of life for the American people by supporting production of agriculture: ensuring a safe, affordable, nutritious, and accessible food supply; caring for agricultural, forest, and range lands;supporting sound development of rural communities; providing economic opportunities for farm and rural residents; expanding global markets for agricultural and forest products and services; and working to reduce hunger in America and throughout theworld.
Tom Vilsack, Secretary
Michael T. Scuse, Deputy Secretary

2608 US Department of Education
400 Maryland Avenue SW
Washington, DC 20202
202-401-1576
800-872-5327
Fax: 202-401-0689
http://www.ed.gov

Mission: To strengthen the Federal commitment to assuring access to equal educational opportunity for every individual; improve the coordination of Federal education programs; improve the management of Federal education activities; andincrease the accountability of Federal education programs to the President, the Congress, and the public

2609 US Department of Housing and Urban Development
451 7th Street SW
Washington, DC 20410
202-708-1112
800-333-4636
http://www.hud.gov

To create strong, sustainable, inclusive communities and quality affordable homes for all
Shaun Donovan, Secretary
Maurice Jones, Deputy Secretary

2610 US Department of Housing and Urban Development
Office of Lead Hazard Control
451 7th Street SW 202-708-1112
Washington, DC 20410 800-333-4636
Fax: 202-755-1000
http://www.hud.gov/lea/leahome.html
The office works to ensue that hazard controls are conducted in the safest, most cost-effective and efficient way possible to preserve our nation's stock of affordable housing while still ensuring that our children are properlyprotected.
Shaun Donovan, Secretary
Maurice Jones, Deputy Secretary

2611 US Department of Labor
200 Consititution Avenue NW 202-208-3100
Washington, DC 20210 E-mail: feedback@ios.doi.gov
http://www.doi.gov
The Secretary of the Interior is responsible for the administration of over 500 million acres of federal land, and holds in trust approximately 50 million acres of land, mostly Indian reservations; the conservation and development ofmineral and water resources; the conservation, development, and utilization of fish and wildlife resources; the coordination of federal and state recreational programs; the preservation and administration of the nation's scenic and historic areas.
Sally Jewell, Secretary of the Interior
P Lynn Scarlett, Deputy Secretary

2612 US Department of Treasury
1500 Pennsylvania Avenue NW 202-622-2000
Washington, DC 20220 Fax: 202-622-6415
http://www.ustreas.gov
Maintain a strong economy and create economic and job opportunities by promoting the conditions that enable economic growth and stability at home and abroad, strengthen national security by combating threats and protecting theintegrity of the financial system, and manage the U.S. Government's finances and resources effectively
Jacob J. Lew, Secretary
Neal Wolin, Deputy Secretary

2613 US Department of the Army: Office of Public Affairs
1500 Army Pentagon 703-693-0677
Washington, DC 20310 http://www.army.mil
Mission: Public Affairs fulfills the Army's obligation to keep the American people and the Army informed, and helps to establish the conditions that lead to confidence in America's Army and its readiness to conduct operations inpeacetime, conflict and war.
John McHugh, Secretary
Joseph W. Westphal, Undersecretary

2614 US Environmental Protection Agency
Ariel Rios Building 202-272-0167
1200 Pennsylvania Avenue NW E-mail: aaoarm@epa.gov
Washington, DC 20460 http://www.epa.gov
EPA's mission is to protect human health and to safeguard the natural environment- air, awter and land- upon which life depends. For 30 years, EPA has been working for a cleaner, healthier environment for the American people.
Bob Perciasepe, Administrator
Craig E. Hooks, Assistant Administrator

2615 US Environmental Protection Agency Office of Children's Health Protection
1200 Pennsylvania Avenue NW 202-564-2188
Mail Code 1107A, Room 2512 Ariel Rios N Fax: 202-564-2733
Washington, DC 20004 http://www.epa.gov/children
The mission of this office is to make the protection of children's environmental health a fundamental goal of public health and environmental protection in the US.
Melanie Marty, Chair

2616 US Environmental Protection Agency: Clean Air Markets Division
1200 Pennsylvania Avenue NW 202-233-9150
Mail Code 6204J http://www.epa.gov/airmarkets
Washington, DC 20460
Mission: To improve human health and the natural environment through the skillful design, operation, and evaluation of cap and trade and other innovative programs that cost-effectively lower harmful air emissions and their deposition.
Jeb Stenhouse, Chief
Rey Forte, Chief

2617 US Environmental Protection Agency: Office of Air and Radiation
1200 Pennsylvania Avenue NW 866-411-4372
Washington, DC 20760 E-mail: oar_comments@epa.gov
http://www.epa.gov/oar/
Protects human health and the environment by preventing air pollution and exposure to radiation through effective management of public and private resources.
Gina McCarthy, Assistant Administrator
Janet McCabe, Deputy Assistant Admin.

2618 US Environmental Protection Agency: Office of Environmental Justice
1200 Pennsylvania Avenue NW 202-564-2515
Washington, DC 20460 800-962-6215
Fax: 202-501-0740
E-mail: environmental-justice-epa@epamail.epa.org
http://www.epa.gov/compliance/environmentaljustice/index.html
Serves as a focal point for ensuring that communities comprised mainly of people of color or low income receive protection under environmental laws.
Victoria J. Robinson, Contact

2619 US Forest Service
U.S. Dept. of Agriculture
1400 Independence Avenue SW 202-205-8333
Washington, DC 20250-0003 800-832-1355
E-mail: webmaster@fs.fed.us
http://www.fs.fed.us.
Manages National Forests and Grasslands. Provides assistance to private forest operators.
Thomas Tidwell, Chief
Mary Wagner, Associate Chief

2620 US Geological Survey: National Wetlands Research Center
700 Cajundome Boulevard 337-266-8500
Lafayette, LA 70506 Fax: 337-266-8513
E-mail: nwrcinfo@usgs.gov
http://www.nwrc.usgs.gov
To develop and disseminate scientific information needed for understanding the ecology and values of our nation's wetlands and for managing and restoring wetland habitats and associated plant and animal communtities.
Phil Turnipseed, Director

2621 US Nuclear Regulatory Commission
Reference Librarian 301-415-7000
Public Document Room (01F-13) 800-368-5642
Washington, DC 20555 E-mail: pdr@nrc.gov
http://www.nrc.gov
Mission: To regulate the nation's civilian use of byproduct, source, and special nuclear materials to ensure adequate protection of public health and safety, to promote the common defense and security, and to protect the environment.
Catherine Haney, Director
Scott Moore, Deputy Director

2622 United States Department of the Army US Army Corps of Engineers
441 G Street NW 202-761-0011
Washington, DC 20314-1000 http://www.usace.army.mil
Design and constructs military projects for the Army, Air Force, civil works and water resources development projects for coastal

communities. Conducts military Real Estate transactions, is responsible for Emergency Operationsinvolving national emergency and natural disaster, and regulates development in navigable waters, and placement of fill material in waters and wetlands.

Thomas P. Bostick, Commanding General
Todd T. Semonite, Deputy Commanding General

Alabama

2623 Agriculture and Industries Department
Pesticide Laboratory
1445 Federal Drive 334-240-7171
Montgomery, AL 36107 800-642-7761
http://www.agi.stste.al.us/

Mission: To provide timely, fair and expert regulatory control over product, business entities, movement, and application of goods and services for which applicable state and federal law exists and strive to protect and provide serviceto Alabama consumers.

Ron Sparks, Commissioner
Douglas Rigney, Deputy Commissioner

2624 Alabama Cooperative Extension System
224 Duncan Hall Annex 334-844-5270
Auburn University, AL 36849 Fax: 334-844-5276
E-mail: webmaster@aces.edu
http://www.aces.edu

Operates as the primary outreach organization for the land-grant function of Alabama A&M University and Auburn University. Identifies statewide educational needs, audiences, and optimal educational programs that are delivered through anetwork of public and private partners supported by county, state, and federal governments.

Paul Waddy, Extension Coordinator

2625 Alabama Department of Environmental Management
1400 Coliseum Boulevard 334-271-7700
PO Box 301463 Fax: 334-271-7950
Montgomery, AL 36110-2400E-mail: webmaster@adem.state.al.us
http://www.adem.state.al.us

Alabama Department of Environmental Management is the state agency responsible for the adoption and fair enforcement of rules and regulations set to protect and improve the quality of Alabama's environment and the health of all itscitizens. Monitor environmental conditions in Alabama and recommend changes in state law or revise regulations as needed to respond appropriately to changing environmental conditions.

H. Lanier Brown, Chairman
W.Scott Phillips, Vice Chairman

2626 Alabama Forestry Commission
513 Madison Avenue 334-240-9300
Montgomery, AL 36104 Fax: 334-240-9390
http://www.forestry.state.al.us

Mission: To serve Alabama by protecting and sustaining our forest resources using professionally applied stewardship principles and education. We will ensure Alabama's forests contribute to abundant timber and wildlife, clean air andwater, and a healthy economy.

Tommy Thompson, Chair
Salem Saloom, Vice Chairman

2627 Conservation and Natural Resources Department
64 North Union Street 334-242-3486
Suite 468 Fax: 334-242-0999
Montgomery, AL 36130 http://www.outdooralabama.com

N.Gunter Guy Jr., Commissioner
Curtis Jones, Deputy Commissioner

2628 EPA: National Air and Radiation Environmental Laboratory
540 S Morris Avenue 334-270-3400
Montgomery, AL 36115-2600 Fax: 334-270-3454
E-mail: petko.charles@epa.gov
http://www.epa.gov/narel/

The National Air and Radiation Environmental Laboratory is a comprehensive environmental laboratory, and provides services to a wide range of clients, including other EPA offices, Federal agencies, and, in somes cases, the privatesector. The mission is the commitment to developing and applying the most advanced methods for measuring environmental radioactivity and evaluating its risk to the public.

John Griggs, Director
Michael S. Clark, Deputy Director

2629 Geological Survey of Alabama, Agency of the State of Alabama
University of Alabama
420 Hackberry Lane 205-349-2852
Tuscaloosa, AL 35401 Fax: 205-349-2861
E-mail: webmaster@ogb.state.al.us
http://www.gsa.state.al.us

To survey and investigate the mineral, energy, water, and biological resources of the state, to maintain adequate geological, topographic, hydrologic, and biologic databases, and to prepare maps and reports on the state's naturalresources to encourage the safe and prudent development of Alabama's natural resources while providing for the safety, health and well-being of all Americans.

James Griggs, Director
Charles Pearson, Director

Alaska

2630 Alaska Cooperative Fish and Wildlife Research Unit
University of Alaska
209 Irving 1 907-474-7661
PO Box 757020 Fax: 907-474-7872
Fairbanks, AK 99775-7020 E-mail: uaf-iab-akcfwru@alaska.edu
http://www.akcfwru.uaf.edu

The Alaska Unit is a part of a nationwide program created to foster college-level research and graduate student training in support of science-based management of fish and wildlife, and their habitats. The Unit exists by cooperativeagreement between the AK Department of Fish and Game, University of Alaska Fairbanks, US Geological Survey, Wildlife Management Institute, and US Fish and Wildlife Service. The Unit is staffed by 5 USGS scientists, who are also research faculty.

Kathleen Pearse, Administrative Assistant

2631 Alaska Department of Fish and Game
PO Box 115526 907-465-4100
1255 W. 8th Street http://www.adfg.state.ak.us
Juneau, AK 99811-5526

Aims to manage, protect, maintain and improve the fish, game and aquatic plant resources of Alaska. The primary goals are to ensure that Alaska's renwable fish and wildlife resources and their habitats are conserved and managed on thesustained yield prinicpal, and the use of development of these resources are in the best interest of the economy and well-being of the people of the state.

Cora Campbell, Commissioner
Sunny Haight, Director

2632 Alaska Department of Public Safety
5700 E Tudor Road 907-269-5511
Anchorage, AK 99507 http://www.dps.state.ak.us

Provides functions relative to the protection of life, property and wildlife resources.

Joseph A. Masters, Commissioner
Terry Vrabec, Deputy Commissioner

2633 Alaska Division of Forestry: Central Office
550 W 7th Avenue
Suite 1450
Anchorage, AK 99501
907-269-8463
Fax: 907-269-8931
http://www.dnr.state.ak.us/forestry
Mission: To develop, conserve, and enhance Alaska's forests to provide a sustainable supply of forest resources for Alaskans.
Chris Maisch, State Forester
Dean Brown, Deputy State Forester

2634 Alaska Division of Forestry: Coastal Region Office
2417 Tongass Ave
Suite 213
Ketchikan, AK 99901
907-225-3070
Fax: 907-247-3070
http://www.dnr.state.ak.us/forestry
Mission: To develop, conserve, and enhance Alaska's forests to provide a sustainable supply of forest resources for Alaskans.
Chris Maisch, State Forester
Dean Brown, Deputy State Forester

2635 Alaska Division of Forestry: Delta Area Office
Mi. 267.5 Richardson Highway
PO Box 1149
Delta Junction, AK 99737
907-895-4225
Fax: 907-895-2125
http://www.dnr.state.ak.us/forestry
Mission: To develop, conserve, and enhance Alaska's forests to provide a sustainable supply of forest resources for Alaskans.
Chris Maisch, State Forester
Dean Brown, Deputy State Forester

2636 Alaska Division of Forestry: Fairbanks Area Office
3700 Airport Way
Fairbanks, AK 99709-4699
907-451-2600
Fax: 907-458-6895
http://www.dnr.state.ak.us/forestry
Mission: To develop, conserve, and enhance Alaska's forests to provide a sustainable supply of forest resources for Alaskans.
Chris Maisch, State Forester
Dean Brown, Deputy State Forester

2637 Alaska Division of Forestry: Kenai/Kodiak Area Office
42499 Sterling Highway
Soldotna, AK 99669
907-260-4200
Fax: 907-260-4205
http://www.dnr.state.ak.us/forestry
Mission: To develop, conserve, and enhance Alaska's forests to provide a sustainable supply of forest resources for Alaskans.
Chris Maisch, State Forester
Dean Brown, Deputy State Forester

2638 Alaska Division of Forestry: Mat-Su/Southwest Area Office
101 Airport Road
Palmer, AK 99645
907-761-6300
Fax: 907-761-6319
http://www.dnr.state.ak.us/forestry
Mission: To develop, conserve, and enhance Alaska's forests to provide a sustainable supply of forest resources for Alaskans.
Chris Maisch, State Forester
Dean Brown, Deputy State Forester

2639 Alaska Division of Forestry: Northern Region Office
3700 Airport Way
Fairbanks, AK 99709-4699
907-451-2670
Fax: 907-451-2690
http://www.dnr.state.ak.us/forestry
Mission: To develop, conserve, and enhance Alaska's forests to provide a sustainable supply of forest resources for Alaskans.
Chris Maisch, State Forester
Dean Brown, Deputy State Forester

2640 Alaska Division of Forestry: State Forester's Office
550 W 7th Avenue
Suite 1450
Anchorage, AK 99501
907-451-8463
Fax: 907-451-8931
http://www.dnr.state.ak.us/forestry
Mission: To develop, conserve, and enhance Alaska's forests to provide a sustainable supply of forest resources for Alaskans.
Chris Maisch, State Forester
Dean Brown, Deputy State Forester

2641 Alaska Division of Forestry: Tok Area Office
Mile 123 Glenn Highway
PO Box 10
Tok, AK 99780
907-883-1400
Fax: 907-883-5135
http://www.dnr.state.ak.us/forestry
Mission: To develop, conserve, and enhance Alaska's forests to provide a sustainable supply of forest resources for Alaskans.
Chris Maisch, State Forester
Dean Brown, Deputy State Forester

2642 Alaska Division of Forestry: Valdez/Copper River Area Office
Mile 110 Richardson Highway
Box 185
Glennallen, AK 99588
907-822-5534
Fax: 907-822-8600
http://www.dnr.state.ak.us/forestry
Mission: To develop, conserve, and enhance Alaska's forests to provide a sustainable supply of forest resources for Alaskans.
Chris Maisch, State Forester
Dean Brown, Deputy State Forester

2643 Alaska Health Project
218 E 4th Avenue
Anchorage, AK 99501
907-276-2864
Fax: 907-279-3089
E-mail: akhlthproj@aol.com
http://www.ahelp.org/projects/Detail.aspx?id=3
Provides information to professionals and the general public about occupational safety and health, hazardous materials management and waste reduction at work and in the community
Carl Hild, Executive Director

2644 Alaska Oil and Gas Conservation Commission
333 W 7th Avenue
Suite 100
Anchorage, AK 99501
907-279-1433
Fax: 907-276-7542
E-mail: aogcc.customer.svc@alaska.gov
http://www.doa.alaska.gov/ogc/
Protecting the oil and gas of Alaska.
Dan Seamount, Commissioner
John Norman, Commissioner

2645 Alaska Resource Advisory Council
Bureau of Land Management
222 W 7th Avenue
Suite 13
Anchorage, AK 99513
907-271-5555
Fax: 907-271-3684
http://www.blm.gov/ak/advisory.html
A statewide resource advisory council that advises BLM on land management issues for 80 million acres of federal public lands in Alaska. Membership is comprised of representatives from industry, conservation, recreation, Alaska Nativeorganizations, an elected offical, and the public at large. The council meets three times a year.
Thomas P Lonnie, BLM/AK State Director
Sharon Wilson, Alaska RAC Coordinator

2646 Anchorage Office: Alaska Department of Environmental Conservation
555 Cordova Street
Anchorage, AK 99501-2617
907-269-7633
Fax: 907-269-7648
E-mail: Betty.Schorr@alaska.gov
http://www.dec.state.ak.us
The people and industries that operate in our state have both the corporate conscience and the technical ability to work with us on constuctive solutions to basic environmental management and public health issues. We anticipate,collaborate, negotiate, educate and communicate to address the most important environmental and public health risks to Alaska and Alaskans. Investigation, legislation, regulation and litigation are available tools, but not the first tools of choice.
Larry Hartig, Commissioner

2647 Cooperative Extension Service: University of Alaska Fairbanks
308 Tanana Loop
Room 101
Fairbanks, AK 99775-6180
907-474-5211
Fax: 907-474-2631
E-mail: cesweb@alaska.edu
http://www.uaf.edu/coop-ext
Mission: To interpret and extend relevant research-based knowledge in an understandable and usable form; and to encourage the application of this knowledge to solve the problems and meet the challenges that face the people of Alaska;and, to bring the concerns of the community back to the university.
Pete Pinney, Interim Director

2648 Fairbanks Office: Alaska Department of Environmental Conservation
610 University Avenue 907-451-2100
Fairbanks, AK 99709-3643 Fax: 907-451-2362
http://www.dec.state.ak.us
Nancy Sonafrank, Program Manager

2649 Juneau Office: Alaska Department of Environmental Conservation
410 Willoughby Avenue 907-465-5066
Suite 303 Fax: 907-465-5070
Juneau, AK 99811-1800 http://www.dec.state.ak.us
Larry Hartig, Commissioner

2650 Kenai Office: Alaska Department of Environmental Conservation
43335 Kalifornsky Beach Road 907-262-5210
Suite 11, Red Diamond Center Fax: 907-262-2294
Soldotna, AK 99669 http://www.dec.state.ak.us
Kristin Ryan, Director

2651 Kodiak Office: Alaska Department of Environmental Conservation
PO Box 515 907-486-3350
Kodiak, AK 99615 Fax: 907-486-5032
http://www.dec.state.ak.us
Kristin Ryan, Director

2652 Natural Resources Department Public Affairs Information Office
550 West 7th Avenue 907-269-8400
Suite 1260 Fax: 907-269-8901
Anchorage, AK 99501-3557 http://www.dnr.state.ak.us
Kathy Johnson, Manager

2653 Palmer Office: Alaska Department of Environmental Conservation
500 S Alaska Street 907-747-3236
Suite A http://www.dec.state.ak.us
Palmer, AK 99645

2654 Sitka Office: Alaska Department of Environmental Conservation
901 Halibut Point Road 907-747-8614
Suite 3 Fax: 907-747-7419
Sitka, AK 99835-7106 http://www.dec.state.ak.us
Kristin Ryan, Director

2655 Subsistance Resource Commission Cape Krusenstern National Monument
National Park Service
PO Box 1029 907-442-3890
Kotzebue, AK 99752 Fax: 907-442-8316
http://www.nps.gov/cakr
Frank Hays, Superintendent

2656 Subsistence Resource Gates of the Artic National Park
National Park Service
National Park Service-Fairbanks HQ 907-457-5752
4175 Geist Road Fax: 907-455-0601
Fairbanks, AK 99709 http://www.nps.gov/gaar
Susan Holly, Administrative Assistant

2657 United States Department of the Army: US Army Corps of Engineers
441 G Street NW 202-761-0011
Washington, DC 20314-1000 http://www.usace.army.mil
Design and constructs military projects for the Army, Air Force, civil works and water resources development projects for coastal communities. Conducts military Real Estate transactions, is responsible for Emergency Operationsinvolving national emergency and natural disaster, and regulates development in navigable waters, and placement of fill material in waters and wetlands.
Thomas P. Bostick, Commanding General
Todd T. Semonite, Deputy Commanding General

Arizona

2658 Arizona Department of Agriculture: Animal Services Division
1688 West Adams Street 602-542-4373
Phoenix, AZ 85007 http://www.azda.gov/ASD/asd.htm
Mission: Protect consumers from contagious and infectious disease in livestock, poultry, commercially raised fish, meat, milk, and eggs; enforce laws concerning the movement, sale, importation, transport, slaughter, and theft oflivestock.
Donald Butler, Director

2659 Arizona Department of Environmental Quality
1110 West Washington Street 602-771-2300
Phoenix, AZ 85007 800-234-5677
http://www.azdeq.gov/index.html
The Arizona Department of Environmental Quality was established in 1987 to preserve, protect and enhance the environmental and public health through the maintenance of air, land and water resources. The department oversees compliancewith state and federal environmental regulations and works with industry and local governments.
Henry R. Darwin, Director
Misael Cabrera, Deputy Director

2660 Arizona Game & Fish Department
5000 W. Carefree Highway 602-942-3000
Phoenix, AZ 85086-5000 http://www.gf.state.az.us
Aims to conserve, enhance and restore Arizona's diverse wildlife resources and habitats through aggressive protection and management programs, and to provide wildlife resources and safe watercraft and off-highway vehicle recreation forthe enjoyment, appreciation, and use by present and future generations.
Larry D. Voyles, Director
Ty Gray, Deputy Director

2661 Arizona Game & Fish Department: Region I
2878 East White Mountain Blvd 928-367-4281
Pinetop, AZ 85935
Aims to conserve, enhance and restore Arizona's diverse wildlife resources and habitats through aggressive protection and management programs, and to provide wildlife resources and safe watercraft and off-highway vehicle recreation forthe enjoyment, appreciation, and use by present and future generations.
Larry D. Voyles, Director
Ty Gray

2662 Arizona Game & Fish Department: Region II
3500 South Lake Mary Road 928-774-5045
Flagstaff, AZ 86001
Aims to conserve, enhance and restore Arizona's diverse wildlife resources and habitats through aggressive protection and management programs, and to provide wildlife resources and safe watercraft and off-highway vehicle recreation forthe enjoyment, appreciation, and use by present and future generations.
Larry D. Voyles, Director
Ty Gray

2663 Arizona Game & Fish Department: Region III
5325 North Stockton Hill Road 928-692-7700
Kingman, AZ 86409
Aims to conserve, enhance and restore Arizona's diverse wildlife resources and habitats through aggressive protection and management programs, and to provide wildlife resources and safe watercraft and off-highway vehicle recreation forthe enjoyment, appreciation, and use by present and future generations.
Larry D. Voyles, Director
Ty Gray

2664 Arizona Game & Fish Department: Region IV
9140 East 28th Street
Yuma, AZ 85365
928-342-0091
Aims to conserve, enhance and restore Arizona's diverse wildlife resources and habitats through aggressive protection and management programs, and to provide wildlife resources and safe watercraft and off-highway vehicle recreation forthe enjoyment, appreciation, and use by present and future generations.
Larry D. Voyles, Director
Ty Gray

2665 Arizona Game & Fish Department: Region V
555 North Greasewood Road
Tucson, AZ 85745
520-628-5376
Aims to conserve, enhance and restore Arizona's diverse wildlife resources and habitats through aggressive protection and management programs, and to provide wildlife resources and safe watercraft and off-highway vehicle recreation forthe enjoyment, appreciation, and use by present and future generations.
Larry D. Voyles, Director
Ty Gray

2666 Arizona Game & Fish Department: Region VI
7200 East University
Mesa, AZ 85207
480-981-9400
Aims to conserve, enhance and restore Arizona's diverse wildlife resources and habitats through aggressive protection and management programs, and to provide wildlife resources and safe watercraft and off-highway vehicle recreation forthe enjoyment, appreciation, and use by present and future generations.
Larry D. Voyles, Director
Ty Gray

2667 Arizona Geological Survey
416 W Congress Street
Suite 100
Tucson, AZ 85701-1381
520-770-3500
Fax: 520-770-3505
E-mail: web@azgs.az.gov
http://www.azgs.state.az.us
Our mission is to inform and advise the public about the geologic character of Arizona in order to foster understanding and prudent development of the State's land, water, mineral and energy resources.
M Lee Allison, Director
Cindy Castro, Fiscal Services Specialist

2668 Arizona State Parks
1300 West Washington
Phoenix, AZ 85007
602-542-4174
800-285-3703
Fax: 602-542-4188
E-mail: feedback@pr.state.az.us
http://www.pr.state.az.us
Walter D. Armer Jr., Chair
Bryan Martyn, Executive Director

2669 Arizona Strip District-US Department of Interior Bureau of Land Management
345 E Riverside Drive
St George, UT 84790-6714
435-688-3200
Fax: 435-688-3528
http://www.blm.gov/az/st/en/fo/arizona_strip_field.html
Manages nearly 2 million acres in northwestern Arizona, including the Vermilion Cliffs National Monument.
Scott Florence, District Manager
Becky Hammond, Acting Field Manager

2670 Environmental and Analytical Chemistry Laboratory
Arizona Department of Health
250 North 17th Avenue
Phoenix, AZ 85007
602-542-1188
Fax: 602-542-0760
E-mail: piowebmaster@azdhs.gov
http://www.azdhs.gov
State public health laboratory both in chemistry and microbiology. Supports investigations into environmental contamination by analyzing water, soil, air, hazardous materials, food and miscellaneous items for the presence of hazardousand toxic chemicals. Microbiology tests for pathogens and/or indicator organisms.
Will Humble, Director

2671 Gila Box Riparian National Conservation Area BLM Safford District Office
711 14th Avenue
Safford, AZ 85546
928-348-4400
Fax: 928-348-4450
http://www.az.blm.gov
There are more than 14 million acres of public lands in Arizona that people have put in our trust. It's an awesome responsiblity, and one that we take very seriously. We don't try to do it alone. Every day, we work with people to helpmake sure we are doing what is right for Arizona's envrionment, wildlife, culture, and history... for the people who rely upon the land to earn a living or to manufacture the things which make our lives a little easier...and most importantly, forArizona's future.
Tim Shannon, District Manager
Scott Cooke, Field Manager

2672 Phoenix District Advisory Council: BLM
21605 North 7th Avenue
Phoenix, AZ 85027
623-580-5500
Fax: 623-580-5580
http://www.az.blm.gov
Manages public lands and resources in central Arizona, and supports related statewide initiatives and functions to sustain their health, diversity and productivity while providing for customer service and meeting public demandresulting from the expanding Phoenix metropolitan area and growth of adjoining communities.
Mary D'Aversa, District Manager
Rem Hawes, Field Manager

Arkansas

2673 Arkansas Department of Parks and Tourism
One Capitol Mall
Little Rock, AR 72201
501-682-7777
http://www.arkansas.com
To provide optimum quality state park recreation facilities conveniently located and in sufficient quantity to meet the needs of all state citizens and visitors
Richard W. Davis, Executive Director

2674 Arkansas Fish and Game Commission
2 Natural Resources Drive
Little Rock, AR 72205
501-223-6300
800-364-4263
E-mail: askAGFC@agfc.state.ar.us
http://www.agfc.com
The Arkansas Game and Fish Commission plays an important role in keeping The Natural State true to its name.
Ronald Pierce, Commissioner
Ty Patterson, Commissioner

2675 Arkansas Natural Heritage Commission
1500 Tower Building
323 Center Street
Little Rock, AR 72201
501-324-9619
Fax: 501-324-9618
E-mail: arkansas@naturalheritage.org
http://www.naturalheritage.org
Mission: To identify and protect remaining high-quality natural communities and maintain information on the distribution and status of rare species that live within the state.
Mark Karnes, Chairman
Robert Bevis, Vice Chairman

2676 Arkansas State Plant Board
1 Natural Resources Drive
Little Rock, AR 72205
501-225-1598
Fax: 501-219-1697
E-mail: info@aspb.ar.gov
http://www.plantboard.org
Mission: To protect and serve the citizens of Arkansas and the agricultural and business communities by providing information and unbiased enforcement of laws and regulations thus ensuring quality products and services.
Darryl Little, Director

2677 Department of Environmental Quality
5301 Northshore Drive
North Little Rock, AR 72118-5317
501-682-0744
http://www.adeq.state.ar.us
Mission: To protect, enhance and restore the natural environment for the well-being of Arkansas.
Teresa Marks, Director

California

2678 American Cetacean Society
PO Box 1391
San Pedro, CA 90733-1391
310-548-6279
Fax: 310-548-6950
E-mail: acsoffice@acsonline.org
http://www.acsonline.org

A non profit organization that is the oldest whale conservation group in the world. Founded to protect whales, dolphins, porpoises, and their habitats through public education, research grants, and conservation actions.

Diane Glim, President
Barbara Bennett, Secretary

2679 California Department of Education Office of Environmental Education
1430 North Street
Suite 5602
Sacramento, CA 95814
916-319-0800
http://www.cde.ca.gov
Mission: Guiding principles, goals, and objectives of the California Department of Education.
Tom Torlakson, Superintendent
Richard Zeiger, Chief Deputy Superintendent

2680 California Department of Fish and Game
1416 9th Street
12th Floor
Sacramento, CA 95814
916-445-0411
E-mail: Webmaster@wildlife.ca.gov
http://www.dfg.ca.gov
Manages California's diverse fish, wildlife, and plant resources, and the habitats upon which they depend, for their ecological values and for their use and enjoyment by the public.
Charlton H. Bonham, Director
Thomas Gibson, General Counsel

2681 California Department of Water Resources
1416-9th Street
Room 1104-1
Sacramento, CA 95814
916-653-5791
Fax: 916-653-3310
http://www.dwr.water.ca.gov
Mission. To manage the water resources of California in cooperation with other agencies, to benefit the State's people, and to protect, restore, and enhance the natural and human environments.
Mark W. Cowin, Director
Dale K. Hoffman-Floerke, Deputy Director

2682 California Desert District Advisory Council Bureau of Land Management
California State Office
22835 Calle San Juan De Los Lagos
Moreno Valley, CA 92553
951-697-5200
Fax: 951-697-5299
http://www.ca.blm.gov
Mission: To protect the natural, historic, recreation and economic riches, and scenic beauty of the California Desert.

2683 California Environmental Protection Agency
PO Box 2815
Sacramento, CA 95812-2815
916-323-2514
E-mail: cepacomm@calepa.ca.gov
http://www.calepa.ca.gov
Mission: To restore, protect and enhance the environment, to ensure the public health, environmental quality and economic vitality.
Matthew Rodriquez, Secretary
Gordon Burns, Undersecretary

2684 California Institute of Public Affairs
PO Box 99
Claremont, CA 91711
909-621-9018
E-mail: Mail@InterEnvironment.org
http://www.interenvironment.org
A forum for policy dialogue and research on California and international environmental issues. Publishes the online World Directory of Environmental Organizations.
Thaddeus C Trzyna, President
Michael Paparian, Deputy Treasurer

2685 California Pollution Control Financing Authority
915 Capitol Mall, Room 457
Sacramento, CA 95814
916-654-5610
Fax: 916-657-4821
E-mail: cpcfa@treasurer.ca.gov
http://www.treasurer.ca.gov/cpcfa

Bill Lockyer, Chairman
Renee Webster-Hawkins, Executive Director

2686 Department of Agriculture: Forest Service, Pacific Southwest Region
1323 Club Drive
Vallejo, CA 94592-1110
707-562-8737
Fax: 707-562-9130
E-mail: Mailroom R5@fs.fed.us
http://www.fs.fed.us/r5

Randy Moore, Regional Forester
Barnie Gyant, Deputy Regional Forester

2687 Energy Commission
1516 9th Street
MS-29
Sacramento, CA 95814-5512
916-654-4287
http://www.energy.ca.gov
Promoting Efficiency and Conservation, Supporting Cutting-Edge Research, and Developing Our Renewable Energy Resources
Robert B. Weisenmiller, Ph.D., Chair
Karen Douglas, Commissioner

2688 Environmental Protection Agency Region IX
75 Hawthorne Street
San Francisco, CA 94105
415-947-8000
866-EPA-WEST
http://www.epa.gov/region09/
Region 9 covers Arizona, California, Hawaii, Nevada, the Pacific Islands subject to US law, and approximately 140 Tribal Nations. We work together with state, local, and tribal governments in the region to carry out the nationsenvironmental laws.
Wayne Nastri, Regional Administrator

2689 Environmental Protection Office: Hazard Identification
Environmental Health Hazard Assessment Office
1001 Street
Sacramento, CA 95814
916-445-6900
Fax: 916-323-8803
E-mail: P65Public.comments@oehha.ca.gov
http://www.oehha.ca.gov/prop65/hazard_ident/092812HID.html
The mission of the Office of Environmental Health Hazard Assessment (OEHHA) is to protect and enhance public health and the environment by objective scientific evaluation of risks posed by hazardous substances.
Cynthia Oshita, Contact

2690 Environmental Protection Office: Toxic Substance Control Department
1001 Street
PO Box 806
Sacramento, CA 95812
916-323-9723
Fax: 916-323-3215
E-mail: webcoord@dtsc.ca.gov
http://www.dtsc.ca.gov
The Department's mission is to restore, protect and enhance the environment, to ensure public health, environmental quality and economic vitality by regulating hazardous waste, conducting and overseeing cleanups, and developing andpromoting pollution prevention.
Deborah O. Raphael, Director
Miriam Ingenito, Deputy Director

2691 Golden Gate National Recreation Area
Fort Mason
Building 201
San Francisco, CA 94123-22
415-561-4700
http://www.nps.gov/goga
The Golden Gate National Recreation Area (GGNRA) is the largest urban national park in the world. The total park area is 74,000 acres of land and water. Approximately 28 miles of coastline line within its boundaries. It is nearly twoand one-half times the size of San Francisco.
Frank Dean, General Superintendent
Aaron Roth, Deputy Superintendent

2692 Inter-American Tropical Tuna Commission
8601 La Jolla Shores Drive 858-546-7100
La Jolla, CA 92037-1508 Fax: 858-546-7133
E-mail: webmaster@iattc.org
http://www.iattc.org/homeeng.htm
The IATTC, established by international convention in 1950, is responsible for the conservation and management of fisheries for tunas and other species taken by tuna-fishing vessels in the eastern Pacific Ocean. The IATTC also hassignificant responsibilities for the implementation of the International Dolphin Conservation Program (IDCP), and provides the Secretariat for that program.
Guillermo Compean, Director
Richard B. Deriso, Chief Scientist

2693 Klamath Fishery Management Council US Fish & Wildlife Service
1829 South Oregon Street 530-842-5763
Yreka, CA 96097 Fax: 530-842-4517
E-mail: yreka@fws.gov
http://www.fws.gov/yreka/kfmc.htm
To manage harvests and ensure continued viable populations of anadromous fish in the Klamath Basin
Phil Detrich, Supervisor

2694 Native American Heritage Commission
915 Capitol Mall 916-653-4082
Room 364 Fax: 916-657-5390
Sacramento, CA 95814 E-mail: nahc@pacbell.net
http://www.nahc.ca.gov
The mission of the Native American Heritage Comm. is to provide protection to Native American burials from vandalism and inadvertent destruction, provide a procedure for the notification of most likely descendents regarding thediscovery of Native American human remains and associated grave goods, bring legal action to prevent severe and irreparable damage to sacred shrines, ceremonial sites, sanctified cemeteries and place of worship on pub. property, and maintain aninventory of sacred places.

Cynthia Gomez, Executive Secretary
James Ramos, Chair

2695 Pesticide Regulation, Environmental Monitoring and Pesticide Management
1001 I Street 916-445-4300
PO Box 4015 Fax: 916-324-1452
Sacramento, CA 95812-4015 http://www.cdpr.ca.gov
Mission: Protect human health and the environment by regulating pesticide sales and use, and by fostering reduced-risk pest management.
Rudy Artau, Branch Chief
Charles Andrews, Associate Director

2696 Resources Agency: California Coastal Commission
45 Fremont Street 415-904-5250
Suite 2000 Fax: 415-904-5400
San Francisco, CA 94105 http://www.coastal.ca.gov
Mission: To protect, conserve, restore, and enhance environmental and human-based resources of the California coast and ocean for environmentally sustainable and prudent use by current and future generations.
Mary K. Shallenberger, Chair
Steve Kinsey, Vice Chairman

2697 Resources Agency: California Conservation Corps
1719 24th Street 916-341-3100
Sacramento, CA 95816 800-952-5627
Fax: 916-323-8922
http://www.ccc.ca.gov
Engages young men and women in meaningful work, public service educational activities that assist them in becoming more responsible citizens, while protecting and enhancing California's environment, human resources and communities.
David Muraki, Director
Jeffrey Schwarzchild, Chief Counsel

2698 Resources Agency: State Coastal Conservancy
1330 Broadway 510-286-1015
13th Floor Fax: 510-286-0470
Oakland, CA 94612-2530 E-mail: dwayman@scc.ca.gov
http://www.scc.ca.gov
The Coastal Conservancy acts with others to preserve, protect and restore the resources of the California Coast.
Quarterly Magazine
Samuel Schuchat, Executive Officer
Mary Small, Deputy Executive Officer

2699 Southwestern Low-Level Radioactive Waste Commission
1731 Howe Ave #611 916-448-2390
Sacramento, CA 95825 Fax: 916-720-0144
E-mail: kathydavis@swllrwcc.org
http://www.swllrwcc.org
The Southwestern Low-Level Radioactive Waste Commission is the governing body for the Southwestern Low-Level Radioactive Waste Disposal Compact, consisting of Arizona, California, North Dakota, and South Dakota. Created by public law100-712 in 1988, its key duties include controlling the importation and exportation of low-level waste into and out of the region. The Commission has no authority over disposal facility siting, but can make recommendations and comments to ensure safedisposal.

Kathy A David, Executive Director

2700 United States Department of Agriculture Research Education and Economics
800 Buchanan Street 510-559-6060
Albany, CA 94710 Fax: 510-559-5779
http://www.ree.usda.gov
Mission: Dedicated to the creation of a safe, sustainable, competitive US food and fiber system and strong, healthy communities, families, and youth through integrated research, analysis and education.
John King, Director
Cathie Woteki, Undersecretary

Colorado

2701 Bureau of Land Management
Department of the Interior
2815 H Road 970-244-3000
Grand Junction, CO 81506 Fax: 970-244-3083
http://www.blm.gov/co/st/en.html
Manages 8.3 million acres of public lands in Colorado. These lands are managed for a multitude of uses including, but not limited to, recreation, mining, wildlife habitat and grazing. Along with these 8.3 million acres, BLM oversees27.3 million subsurface acres for mineral development.
Catherine Robertson, Field Manager

2702 Bureau of Land Management: Little Snake Field Office
Little Snake Field Office 970-826-5000
455 Emerson Street Fax: 970-526-5002
Craig, CO 81625 E-mail: swiser@blm.gov
http://www.blm.gov

Encompasses 4.2 million acres of federal, state and private lands in Moffat, Routt, and Rio Blanco counties.
Wendy Reynolds, Field Manager

2703 Canon City District Advisory Council
Royal Gorge Field Office 719-269-8500
3028 East Main Street Fax: 719-269-8599
Canon City, CO 81212 http://www.co.blm.gov/ccdo/canon.htm
This office administers over 680,000 surface acres of public land along the Front Range and 6.8 million sub-surface acres

2704 Cheyenne Mountain Zoological Park
4250 Cheyenne Mountain Zoo Road 719-633-9925
Colorado Springs, CO 80906 Fax: 719-633-2254
E-mail: info@cmzoo.org
http://www.cmzoo.org

Mission: To foster an appreciation and respect for all living things. Actifely provide survival assistance for species in peril. Provide a high quality recreational experience. Be source of pride and economic strength.
Erica Meyer, PR Manager

2705 Colorado Department of Agriculture
700 Kipling Street 303-239-4100
Suite 4000 Fax: 303-239-4125
Lakewood, CO 80215 http://www.colorado.gov/ag
Mission: To strengthen and advance Colorado's agriculture industry; ensure a safe, high quality, and sustainable food supply; and protect consumers, the environment, and natural resources.
John R Stulp, Commisioner

2706 Colorado Department of Natural Resources
1313 Sherman Street 303-866-3311
Room 718 800-536-5308
Denver, CO 80203 Fax: 303-866-2115
E-mail: dnr.edoassist@state.co.us
http://www.dnr.state.co.us
Mike King, Executive Director
Bob Randall, Deputy Director

2707 Colorado Department of Natural Resources: Division of Water Resources
1313 Sherman Street 303-866-3581
Room 818 Fax: 303-866-3589
Denver, CO 80203 E-mail: firstname.lastname@state.co.us
http://www.water.state.co.us
The Colorado Division of Water Resources is an agency of the State of Colorado, Department of Natural Resources, operating under the direction of specific state stautes, court decrees, and interstate compacts. The DWR is empowered toadminister all surface and ground water rights throughout the state and ensure that the doctrine of prior appropriation is enforced.
Dick Wolfe, State Engineer
Scott Cuthbertson, Assistant State Engineer

2708 Colorado Department of Public Health Environment Consumer Protection Division
4300 Cherry Creek Drive South 303-692-3620
Denver, CO 80246 Fax: 303-753-6809
http://www.cdphe.state.co.us/cp
The Consumer Protection Division assumes the responsiblity for protecting Colorado residents and visitors by prevention of a wide array of health hazards.

2709 Colorado Department of Public Health and Environment
4300 Cherry Creek Drive South 303-692-2000
Denver, CO 80246 800-886-7689
http://www.cdphe.state.co.us
Mission: Committed to protecting and preserving the health and environment of the people of Colorado.
James B Martin, Executive Director

2710 Colorado River Basin Salinity Control Program
US Bureau of Land Reclamation
125 S State Street 801-524-3753
Room 7311 Fax: 801-524-3847
Salt Lake City, UT 84138-1147 E-mail: kjacobson@usbr.gov
http://www.usbr.gov
The Colorado River and its tributaries provide municipal and industrial water to about 27 million people and irrigation to nearly four million acres of land in the US. The river also serves about 2.3 million people and 500,000 acres inMexico. The threat of salinity is a major concern in both the US and Mexico. Salinity affects agricultural, municipal and industrial water users. We work to control the salinity of the Colorado river and thereby to protect the land and people.
Kib Jacobson, Program Manager
Brad Parry, Program Coordinator

2711 Colorado State Forest Service
Colorado State University
5060 Campus Delivery 970-491-8660
Fort Collins, CO 80523-5060 Fax: 970-491-8645
E-mail: CSFS_FortCollins@mail.colostate.edu
http://www.csfs.colostate.edu
Mission: To provide for the stewardship of forest resources and to reduce related risks to life, property and the environment for the benefit of present and future generations.
Boyd Lebeda, District Forester

2712 Environmental Protection Agency Region VIII (CO, MT, ND, SD, UT, WY)
1595 Wynkoop Street 303-312-6312
Denver, CO 80202-1129 800-227-8917
http://www.epa.gov/region8/
To restore and protect the ecological integrity of the mountains, plains and deserts and to protect the health of their inhabitants.
Shaun McGrath, Regional Administrator

2713 Governors Office of Energy, Management and Conservation: Colorado
225 E 16th Avenue 303-866-2100
Suite 650 800-632-6662
Denver, CO 80203 Fax: 303-866-2930
E-mail: geo@state.co.us
http://www.state.co.us/oemc
Supports cost-effective programs, grants and partnerships that benefit Colorado's economic and natural environment.

2714 Minerals Management Service/Minerals Revenue Management
PO Box 25165 303-231-3162
Denver, CO 80225 http://www.mms.gov
Mission: To manage the ocean energy and mineral resources on the Outer Continental Shelf and Federal and Indian mineral revenues to enhance public and trust benefits, promote responsible use and realize fair value.
Randall B Luthi, Director

2715 Natural Resources Department: Air Quality Division
Department of the Interior
PO Box 25287 303-969-2070
Denver, CO 80225-287 Fax: 303-969-2822
E-mail: christine_shaver@nps.gov
http://www.nature.nps.gov/air/who/npsStaff.cfm
To protect air quality and resources affected by air pollution under the NPS Organic Act and the Clean Air Act
Carol McCoy, Division Chief
Chris Havermann, Office Manager

2716 Natural Resources Department: Oil & Gas Conservation Commission
1120 Lincoln Street Suite 801 303-894-2100
Denver, CO 80203 Fax: 303-894-2109
E-mail: dnr_dnr.ogcc@state.co.us
http://www.cogcc.state.co.us
To foster the responsible development of Colorado's oil and gas natural resources
M. Lepore, Director
J. Missey, Executive Assistant

2717 Natural Resources Department: Wildlife Division
6060 Broadway 303-291-7227
Denver, CO 80216 http://www.wildlife.state.co.us
Manages the state's 960 wildlife species. Regulates hunting and fishing activities by issuing licenses and enforcing regulations. Conducts research to improve wildlife management activities, provides technical assistance to private andother land owners concerning wildlife and habitat management and develops programs to protect and recover threatened and endangered species.
Mark B Konishi, Acting Director

2718 Office of Surface Mining Reclamation & Enforcement
1999 Broadway 303-293-5000
Suite 3320 Fax: 303-844-1546
Denver, CO 80202-3050 http://www.wrcc.osmre.gov/
Al Klein, Regional Director
Jeffrey Fleischman, Field Manager

2719 **Rocky Mountain Low-Level Radioactive Waste Board**
303 E. 17th Street
Suite 1080
Denver, CO 80203-1264
303-825-1912
Fax: 303-892-3882
E-mail: sreynolds@rmllwb.us
http://www.rmllwb.us

Gary Baughman, Director
Leonard C. Slosky, Executive Director

2720 **United States Forest Service: United States Department of Agriculture**
740 Simms Street
Golden, CO 80401
303-275-5350
http://www.fs.fed.us/r2
Dan Jiron, Regional Forester

Connecticut

2721 **Connecticut Department of Agriculture**
165 Capitol Avenue
Hartford, CT 06106
860-713-2500
Fax: 860-713-2514
E-mail: ctdeptag@po.state.ct.us
http://www.ct.gov/doag/site/default.asp
Steven K Reviczky, Commissioner

2722 **Connecticut Department of Environmental Protection**
Department of Environmental Protection
79 Elm Street
Hartford, CT 06106
860-424-3000
E-mail: dep.webmaster@po.state.ct.us
http://www.ct.gov/deep/site/default.asp
Mission: To conserve, improve and protect the natural resources and environment of the State of Connecticut in such a manner as to encourage the social and economic development of Connecticut while preserving the natural environmentand the life forms it supports in a delicate, interrelated and complex balance, to the end that the state may fulfill its responsibility as trustee of the environment for present and future generations.
Daniel C. Esty, Commissioner

2723 **Connecticut Department of Public Health**
410 Capitol Avenue
PO Box 340308
Hartford, CT 06134
860-509-8000
http://www.ct.gov/dph/site/default.asp
Has long recognized the adverse public health impact of environmental sources of lead in many of Connecticut's childern. Established dedicated staff to evaluate these environmental sources and began funding local programs in the1970's. The Childhood Lead Posioning Prevention Program has continued to be active in addressing this issue by implementing additional state and community programs, especially in towns that have been identified as high risk.
Jewell Mullen, Commissioner
Norma Gyle, Deputy Commissioner

District of Columbia

2724 **District of Columbia State Extension Services**
4200 Connecticut Avenue
Building 352, Suite 322
Washington, DC 20008
202-274-7115
Fax: 202-274-7130

Delaware

2725 **Delaware Association of Conservation Districts**
PO Box 242
Dover, DE 19903-242
302-739-9921
Fax: 302-739-6724
E-mail: Martha.Pileggi@state.de.us
http://www.nacdnet.org/about/districts/directory/de.phtml
Coordinates the three state conservation districts.
Wendy Baker, President
Robert Emerson, Vice President

2726 **Delaware Cooperative Extension**
University of Delaware
531 South College Avenue
113 Townsend Hall
Newark, DE 19716-2103
302-831-2504
Fax: 302-831-6758
E-mail: mrodgers@udel.edu
http://www.extension.udel.edu

Contact person Janice A Seitz's title is Associate Dean for Extension and Outreach Director of Extension College of Agriculture and Natural Resources.
Michelle Rogers, Director
Alice Moore, Administrative Assistant

2727 **Delaware Department of Agriculture**
2320 S DuPont Highway
Dover, DE 19901
302-698-4500
800-282-8685
http://dda.delaware.gov
As part of the state government, the department's mission is to sustain and promote the viability of food, fiber and agricultural industries in Delaware through quality services that protect and enhance the environment, health andwelfare of the general public.
Ed Kee, Secretary
E. Austin Short, Deputy Secretary

2728 **Delaware Department of Natural Resources and Environmental Control**
DNREC
89 Kings Highway
Dover, DE 19901
302-739-9000
Fax: 302-739-6242
http://www.dnrec.state.de.us
Protects and manages the state's vital natural resources, protects public health and safety, provides quality outdoor recreation, and serves and educates the citizens of the First State about the wise use, conservation and enhancementof Delaware's environment.

Collin O'Mara, Secretary

2729 **Delaware Sea Grant Program**
University of Delaware
Newark, DE 19716
302-831-8083
E-mail: marinecom@udel.edu
http://www.ocean.udel.edu/seagrant
Using Technology, Innovation, and Cooperation to Tackle Coastal Challenges

Nancy Targett, Director
Jennifer Adkins, Executive Director

2730 **Mid-Atlantic Fishery Management Council**
800 North State Street
Suite 201
Dover, DE 19901
302-674-2331
Fax: 302-674-5399
E-mail: contact@mafmc.org
http://www.mafmc.org
The Mid-Atlantic Fishery Management Council is responsible for management of fisheries in federal waters which occur predominantly off the mid-Atlantic coast.

Richard B. Robins, Chairman
Lee Anderson, Vice Chairman

2731 **United States Department of the Interior United States Fish and Wildlife Service**
Delaware Bay Estuary Project
2610 Whitehall Neck Road
Smyrna, DE 19977
302-653-9152
Fax: 302-653-9421
E-mail: R5ES_DPEP@fws.gov
http://www.fws.gov/delawarebay/
Delaware Bay Estate Project is a field office of the US Fish & Wildlife service's coastal program.
Gregory Breese, Project Leader

Florida

2732 **Department of Commerce National Oceanic & Atlantic Oceanographic & Meteorological Laboratory**
4301 Rickenbacker Causeway 305-361-4420
Miami, FL 33149 Fax: 305-361-4449
E-mail: webmaster@aoml.noaa.gov
http://www.aoml.noaa.gov
Robert M Atlas, Director
Alan P. Leonardi, Deputy Director

2733 **Fish & Wildlife Conservation Commission**
620 South Meridian Street 850-488-4676
Tallahassee, FL 32399 http://www.stste.fl.us/fwc
Mission: Managing fish and wildlife resources for their long-term well-being and the benefit of the people.
Rodney Barreto, Chair

2734 **Florida Department of Agriculture & Consumer Service**
The Capitol, Pl 10 850-488-3022
400 South Monroe Street Fax: 850-488-7585
Tallahassee, FL 32399-800 http://www.freshfromflorida.com
Mission: To safeguard the public and support Florida's agriculture economy by: ensuring the safety and wholesomeness of food and other consumer products through inspection and testing programs; protecting consumers from unfair anddeceptive business practices and providing consumer information; assisting Florida's farmers and agriculture industries with the production and promotion of agriculture products; and conserving and protecting the state's agriculture and naturalresources.
Adam H. Putnam, Commissioner

2735 **Florida Department of Environmental Protection**
3900 Commonwealth Boulevard 850-245-2118
M.S. 49 Fax: 850-245-2128
Tallahassee, FL 32399 E-mail: citizensservices@dep.state.flu.us
http://www.dep.state.fl.us
Mission: To promote the efficient and effective operation of the Agency consistent with its Administratice and statutory reponsibilities.
Rick Scott, Governor
Herschel Vinyard, Jr., Secretary

2736 **Florida State Department of Health**
2585 Merchants Row Blvd 850-245-4444
Tallahassee, FL 32399 http://www.doh.state.fl.us
Mission: To promote and protect the health and safety of all people in Florida through the delivery of quality public health services and the promotion of health care standards.
J. Martin Stubblefield, Deputy Secretary
Kim Barnhill, Chief of Staff

2737 **Gulf of Mexico Fishery Management Council**
2203 North Lois Avenue 813-348-1630
Suite 1100 888-833-1844
Tampa, FL 33607 Fax: 813-348-1711
E-mail: info@gulfcouncil.org
http://www.gulfcouncil.org
The Gulf of Mexico Fishery management Council is one of eight regional Fishery Management Councils which were established by the Fishery conservation and Management Act in 1976 (now called the Magnuson-Stevens Fishery Conservation andMagnuson Act). The Council prepares fishery plans which are designed to manage fishery resources from where state waters end to the 200 mile limit of the Gulf of mexico.
Wayne E Swingle, Executive Director
Rick Leard, Deputy Executive Director

2738 **Lee County Parks & Recreation**
3410 Palm Beach Boulevard 239-533-7275
Fort Myers, FL 33916 Fax: 239-485-2300
E-mail: LeeParks@leegov.com
http://www.leeparks.org/
Our mission is to provide safe, clean and functional Parks & Recreation facilities; to provide programs and services that add to the quality of life for all Lee County residents and visitors; to enhance tourism through special eventsand attractions. We are committed to fulfilling this mission through visionary leadership, individual dedication and the trustworthy use of available resources.
David W. Harner II, Director
Dana Kasler, Deputy Director

2739 **Natural Resources Department: Recreation & Parks Division**
3900 Commonwealth Boulevard 850-245-2157
Tallahassee, FL 32399 http://www.dep.state.fl.us/parks
Mission: To provide resource-based recreation while preserving, interpreting and restoring natural and cultural resources. Our goal is to help create a sense of place by showing park visitors the best of Florida's diverse natural andcultural heritage sites.
Donald V. Forgione, Director

2740 **Southwest Florida Water Management District**
2379 Broad Street 352-796-7211
Brookville, FL 34604-6899 800-423-1476
Fax: 352-754-6885
http://www.watermatters.org
Manages the water and water-related resources within its boundaries. Maintains balance between the water needs of current and future users while protecting and maintaining the natural systems that provide the District with its existingand future water supply. The Conservation Projects Section, in the Resource Conservation and Development Department, is reponsible for managing water conservation, reclaimed water and other alternative source projects, and estimating future waterdemands.
Carlos Beruff, Chairman
Michael A. Babb, Vice Chairman

Georgia

2741 **Board of Scientific Counselors: Agency for Toxic Substance and Disease Registry**
4770 Buford Hwy NE 404-562-1788
Atlanta, GA 30341 800-232-4636
Fax: 404-562-1790
E-mail: ATSDRIC@cdc.gov
http://www.atsdr.cdc.gov
Serves the public by using the best science, taking responsive public health actions, and providing trusted health information to prevent harmful exposures and diseases related to toxic substances

Robin Ikeda, Director
Thomas Sinks, Deputy Director

2742 **Georgia Department of Agriculture**
19 Martin Luther King Jr Drive SW 404-656-3600
Atlanta, GA 30334 800-282-5852
E-mail: tirvin@agr.state.ga.us
http://www.agr.georgia.gov
Mission: To provide excellence in services and regulatory functions, to protect and promote agriculture and consumer interests, and to ensure an abundance of safe food and fiber for Georgia, America and the world by usingstate-of-the-art technology and a professional workforce.
Gary W. Black, Commissioner
James Sutton, Chief Administration Officer

2743 **Georgia Department of Education**
205 Jesse Hill Jr. Drive SE 404-656-2800
Atlanta, GA 30334 Fax: 404-651-8737
E-mail: askdoe@gadoe.org
http://www.doe.k12.ga.us
To function as a service oriented and policy driven agency that meets the needs of local school systems as they go about the business of preparing all students for college or a career in a safe and drug free environment where we ensurethat no chils is left behind.
Joel Thorton, Chief of Staff
Mike Buck, Chief Academic Officer

2744 Georgia Department of Natural Resources: Historic Preservation Division
254 Washington Street, SW
Ground Level
Atlanta, GA 30334
404-656-2840
Fax: 404-651-8739
E-mail: ray luce@dnr.state.ga.us
http://www.georgiashpo.org

To promote the preservation and use of historic places for a better Georgia.
Ray Luce, Director

2745 Georgia Department of Natural Resources: Pollution Prevention Assistance Division
7 Martin Luther King Jr Drive
Suite 450
Atlantic, GA 30334
404-651-5120
800-685-2443
Fax: 404-651-5130
E-mail: info@gasustainability.org
http://www.gasustainability.org

Lauren Travis, Program Manager
David Gipson, Assistant Director

2746 Georgia Sea Grant College Program
University of Georgia
220 Marine Science Building
Athens, GA 30602
706-542-6009
Fax: 706-542-3652
http://www.georgiaseagrant.uga.edu

Goal is to better understand the complex interactions between the physical, chemical, biological and geological processes that are manifested in the area where land and sea come together, and to make that knowledge available and usefulto Georgia's citizens. Sea Grant strives to deepen our understanding of coastal and estuarine ecology, the critical role of fresh water interaction and to expand our knowledge of action beyond the marshes and estuaries and into the life of the riversand streams.
Charles Hopkinson, Director
David Bryant, Assistant Director

2747 National Center for Environmental Health
4770 Buford Highway NE
Mail Stop F-29
Atlanta, GA 30341
770-488-7030
888-232-6789
Fax: 770-488-7042
E-mail: ncehinfo@cehod1.em.cdc.gov
http://www.cdc.gov/nceh

Mission: Plans, directs, and coordinates a national program to maintain and improve the health of the American people by promoting a healthy environment and by preventing premature death and avoidable illness and disability caused bynon-infectious, non-occupational and related factors.
Robin Ikeda, Director

2748 Natural Resource Department
2 Martin Luther King Jr Drive SE
Suite 1252 East Tower
Atlanta, GA 30334
404-656-3500
http://www.state.ga.us/dnr/

The mission of the Department of Natural Resources is to sustain, enhance, protect and conserve Georgia's natural, historic and cultural resources for present and future generations, while recognizing the importance of promoting thedevelopment of commerce and industry that utilize sound environmental practices.
Noel Holcomb, Commissioner

2749 Natural Resources Department: Air Protection
4244 International Parkway
Suite 120
Atlanta, GA 30354
404-363-7000
Fax: 404-363-7100
E-mail: james.capp@dnr.state.ga.us
http://www.georgiaair.org

The Air Protection Branch helps provide Georgia's citizens with clean air and works closely with other branches of Georgia's Environmental Protection Division to assure compliance with environmental laws so that, in addition to clearair, we have clean water, healthy lives and productive land.
James A Capp, Branch Chief

2750 Natural Resources Department: Coastal Resources Division
1 Conservation Way
Brunswick, GA 31520
912-264-7218
Fax: 912-262-3143
http://www.coastalgadnr.org

Spud Woodward, Director
Brad Jane, Ecological Services Chief

2751 Natural Resources Department: Environmental Protection Division
2 Martin Luther King Jr Drive
Suite 1152 East Tower
Atlanta, GA 30334
404-657-5947
888-373-5947
http://www.gaepd.org

Provides Georgia's citizens with clean air, clean water, healthy lives and productive land by assuring compliance with environmental laws and by assisting others to do their part for a better environment.
Carol Couch, Director

2752 United States Department of the Army US Army Corps of Engineers
US Army Engineer Distric
100 W Oglethorpe Ave
Savannah, GA 31401
912-652-5279
E-mail: cesas-cco@usace.army.mil
http://www.sas.usace.army.mil

Mission: To provide quality, responsive engineering services to the nation including: planning, designing, building and operating water resources and other civil works projects; designing and managing the construction of militaryfacilities for the Army and Air Force; and providing design and construction management support for other defense and federal agencies.
Jeffrey M. Hall, District Commander
Ronald L Johnson, Deputy Commander

2753 Wassaw National Wildlife Refuge
1000 Business Center Drive
Suite 10
Savannah, GA 31405
912-832-4608
E-mail: savannahcoastal@fws.gov
http://www.fws.gov/wassaw

The most primitive of Georgia's barrier islands, the 10,053 acre refuge, includes beaches with rolling dunes, live oak and slash pine woodlands, and vast salt marshes. The island supports rookeries for egrets and herons, and a varietyof leading birds are abundant in the summer months. Wassaw also provides prime nesting habitat for the loggerhead seaturtles. Refuge visitors may enjoy recreational activities such as birdwatching, beachocombing, hiking, and general nature studies.
Jane Griess, Project Leader
Kimberley Hayes, Refuge Manager

Hawaii

2754 Agriculture Department
1428 South King Street
Honolulu, HI 96814
808-973-9560
E-mail: hdoainfo@exec.state.hi.vs
http://www.hawaiiag.gov/hdoa/

Sandra Lee Kunimoto, Chair

2755 College of Tropical Agriculture and Human Resources
University of Hawaii
3050 Maile Way
Gilmore 202
Honolulu, HI 96822
808-956-8131
Fax: 808-956-9105
http://www.ctahr.hawaii.edu/site/

Mission: Committed to the preparation of students and all citizens of Hawaii for life in the global community through research and educational programs supporting tropical agriculture systems that foster viable communities, adiversified economy, and a healthy environment.
Maria Gallo, Dean/Director
Robyn Chow-Hoy, Assistant

2756 **Department of Land and Natural Resources Division of Water Resource Management**
1151 Punchbowl Street
Room 227
Honolulu, HI 96813
808-587-0214
Fax: 808-587-0219
E-mail: dlnr.cwrm@hawaii.gov
http://www.hawaii.gov/dlnr/cwrm

William M. Tam, Deputy Director
William J. Aila, Chair

2757 **Environmental Center**
University of Hawaii
2500 Dole Street
Krauss Annex 19
Honolulu, HI 96822
808-956-7361
Fax: 808-956-3980
E-mail: envctr@hawaii.edu
http://www.hawaii.edu/envctr

The Center's three areas of focus are education, research and service. The education function of the Center includes the administration of the Environmental Studies Major Equivalent and Certificate program. It fulfills its researchfunction by identifying and addressing environmentally related research needs, particularly those pertinent to Hawaii. The service function primarily involves the coordination and transfer of technical information from the University community togovernment agencies.
Charlotte Kato, Secretary

2758 **Hawaii Department of Agriculture**
1428 South King Street
Honolulu, HI 96814
808-973-9560
http://www.hawaii.gov/hdoa

Contains devisions such as: Administrative; Animal Industry; Marketing; Measurement Standards; and Plant Industry. Carries out programs to conserve, develop and utilize the agricultural resources of the state. Enforces laws, andformulates and enforces rules and regulation to further control the management of these resources.
Sandra Lee Kunimoto, Chairperson

2759 **Hawaii Institute of Marine Biology University of Hawaii**
PO Box 1346
Kane'ohe, HI 96744
808-236-7401
Fax: 808-236-7443
http://www.hawaii.edu/HIMB

Jo-Ann C Leong, Director

2760 **Health Department: Environmental Quality Control**
235 S Beretania Street
Room 702
Honolulu, HI 96813
808-586-4185
Fax: 808-586-4186
E-mail: oeqc@doh.hawaii.gov
http://hawaii.gov/health/environmental/oeqc/index/html

The office is tasked to implement Chapter 343, Hawaii Revised Statues and Title 11, Chapter 200. This is a systematic process to ensure consideration is given to the environmental consequences of actions proposed within our state. Thereview process offers many opportunities to prevent environmental degradation and protect human communities through decreased citizen involvement and informed decision making.
Gary L. Hooser, Director

2761 **State of Hawaii: Department of Land andNatural Resources**
Kalanimoku Building
1151 Punchbowl Street
Honolulu, HI 96813
808-587-0400
Fax: 808-587-0390
E-mail: dlnr@hawaii.gov
http://www.hawaii.gov/dlnr

State agency.
William J Aila Jr, Chairperson

2762 **Water Resources Research Center University of Hawaii**
2540 Dole Street
Holmes Hall 283
Honolulu, HI 96822
808-956-7847
Fax: 808-956-5044
E-mail: wrrc@hawaii.edu
http://www.wrrc.hawaii.edu

The Water Resources Research Center was organized under the federal Water Resources Research Act of 1964. The Center is supported by university funds, external grants, contracts and a small annual federal grant. WRRC faculty coverthe areas of engineering, hydrology, microbiology, ecology, economics and zoology. Cooperating faculty come from numerous other disciplines. WRRC is open to consideration of any question related to water supply or water quality.

James Moncur, Director

Idaho

2763 **Idaho Association of Soil Conservation Districts**
9173 W. Barnes Drive
Ste c
Boise, ID 83709
208-685-6989
Fax: 208-376-6858
E-mail: kent.foster@agri.idaho.gov
http://www.iascd.org

Provides action at the local level for promoting wise and beneficial conservation of natural resources with emphasis on soil and water.

J Kent Foster, Executive Director

2764 **Idaho Cooperative Extension**
1000 West Hubbard
Suite 145
Coeur D'Alene, ID 83814
208-292-2522
Fax: 208-292-2535
http://www.uidaho.edu/extension/

2765 **Idaho Department of Environmental Quality: Pocatello Regional Office**
444 Hospital Way #300
Pocatello, ID 83201
208-236-6160
888-655-6160
Fax: 208-236-6168
http://www.state.id.us/deq

Mission: To protect human health and preserve the quality of Idaho's air, land, and water for use and enjoyment today and in the future.
Toni Hardesty, Director

2766 **Idaho Department of Environmental Quality: State Office**
1410 North Hilton
Boise, ID 83706
208-373-0502
Fax: 208-373-0417
http://www.deq.idaho.gov

Mission: To protect human health and preserve the quality of Idaho's air, land, and water for use and enjoyment today and in the future.
Toni Hardesty, Director

2767 **Idaho Department of Environmental Quality: Idaho Falls Regional Office**
900 N Skyline
Suite B
Idaho Falls, ID 83402
208-528-2650
800-232-4635
Fax: 208-528-2695
http://www.state.id.us/deq

Mission: To protect human health and preserve the quality of Idaho's air, land, and water for use and enjoyment today and in the future.
Toni Hardesty, Director

2768 **Idaho Department of Fish & Game: Clearwater Region**
3316 16th Street
Lewiston, ID 83501
208-799-5010
Fax: 208-799-5012
http://wwwfishandgame.idaho.gov

Mission: All wildlife, including all wild animals, wild birds, and fish, within the state of Idaho, is hereby declared to be the property of the state of Idaho.
Virgil Moore, Director
James Unsworth, Deputy Director

2769 **Idaho Department of Fish & Game: Headquarters**
600 S Walnut Street
PO Box 25
Boise, ID 83707
208-334-3700
Fax: 208-334-2114
http://www.fishandgame.idaho.gov

Mission: All wildlife, including all wild animals, wild birds, and fish, within the state of Idaho, is hereby declared to be the property of the state of Idaho.
Virgil Moore, Director
James Unsworth, Deputy Director

2770 Idaho Department of Fish & Game: Magic Valley Region
319 South 417 East
Jerome, ID 83338
208-324-4359
Fax: 208-324-1160
http://www.fishandgame.idaho.gov
Mission: All wildlife including all wild animals, wild birds, and fish, within the state of Idaho, is hereby declared to be the property of the state of Idaho.
Virgil Moore, Director
James Unsworth, Deputy Director

2771 Idaho Department of Fish & Game: McCall
555 Deinhard Lane
McCall, ID 83638
208-634-8137
Fax: 208-634-4320
http://www.fishandgame.idaho.gov
Mission: All wildlife, including all wild animals, wild birds, and fish, within the state of Idaho, is hereby declared to be the property of the state of Idaho.
Virgil Moore, Director
James Unsworth, Deputy Director

2772 Idaho Department of Fish & Game: Panhandle Region
2885 West Kathleen Avenue
Coeur d'Alene, ID 83815
208-769-1414
Fax: 208-769-1418
http://www.fishandgame.idaho.gov
Mission: All wildlife, including all wild animals, wild birds, and fish, within the state of Idaho, is hereby declared to be the property of the state of Idaho.
Virgil Moore, Director
James Unsworth, Deputy Director

2773 Idaho Department of Fish & Game: Salmon Region
99 Highway 93 N
PO Box 1336
Salmon, ID 83467
208-756-2271
Fax: 208-756-6274
http://www.fishandgame.idaho.gov
Mission: All wildlife, including all wild animals, wild birds, and fish, within the state of Idaho, is hereby declared to be the property of the state of Idaho.
Virgil Moore, Director
James Unsworth, Deputy Director

2774 Idaho Department of Fish & Game: Southeast Region
1345 Barton Road
Pocatello, ID 83204
208-232-4703
Fax: 208-233-6430
http://www.fishandgame.idaho.gov
Mission: All wildlife, including all wild animals, wild birds, and fish, within the state of Idaho, is hereby declared to be the property of the state of Idaho.
Virgil Moore, Director
James Unsworth, Deputy Director

2775 Idaho Department of Fish & Game: Southwest Region
3101 S Powerline Road
Nampa, ID 83686
208-465-8465
Fax: 208-465-8467
http://www.fishandgame.idaho.gov
Mission: All wildlife, including all wild animals, wild birds, and fish, within the state of Idaho, is hereby declared to be the property of the state of Idaho.
Virgil Moore, Director
James Unsworth, Deputy Director

2776 Idaho Department of Fish & Game: Upper Snake Region
4279 Commerce Circle
Idaho Falls, ID 83401
208-525-7290
Fax: 208-523-7604
http://www.fishandgame.idaho.gov
Mission: All wildlife, including all wild animals, wild birds, and fish, within the state of Idaho, is hereby decalred to be the property of the state of Idaho.
Virgil Moore, Director
James Unsworth, Deputy Director

2777 Idaho Department of Lands
300 N 6th Street, Suite 103
Po Box 83720
Boise, ID 83720-0050
208-334-0200
Fax: 208-334-3698
E-mail: public_records_request@idl.idaho.gov
http://www.idl.idaho.gov
Mission: To manage endowment trust lands to maximize long-term financial returns to the benficiary institutions and provide protection to Idaho's natural resources.
George Bacon, Director
Kathy Opp, Deputy Director

2778 Idaho Department of State Parks and Recreation
PO Box 83720
Boise, ID 83720
208-334-4199
Fax: 208-334-5232
http://www.idahoparks.org
Manages 27 state parks. We also run the registration program for snowmobiles, boats and off-highway vehicles. Money from registrations and other sources goes to develop and maintain trails, facilities and programs statewide for thepeople who use those vehicles.
Robert L Meinen, Director

2779 Idaho Department of Water Resources
322 E Front Street
Boise, ID 83720
208-287-4800
Fax: 208-287-6700
E-mail: IDWRInfo@idwr.idaho.gov
http://www.idwr.idaho.gov/about/
Working for a controlled development and wise management of Idaho's resources. Documents and reports on topics of public interest such as drought, salmon, wilderness and the Snake River Basin.
David R Tuthill Jr, Director

2780 Idaho Geological Survey
University of Idaho
Morrill Hall
3rd Floor
Moscow, ID 83844
208-885-7991
Fax: 208-885-5826
E-mail: igs@uidaho.edu
http://www.idahogeology.org
Roy M Breckenridge, Director
Kurt L Othberg, Director

2781 Idaho State Department of Agriculture
2270 Old Penitentiary Road
Boise, ID 83712
208-332-8500
Fax: 208-334-2170
E-mail: info@agri.idaho.gov
http://www.agri.idaho.gov
Celia R Gould, Director
Brian Oakey, Deputy Director

2782 Lands Department: Soil Conservation Commission
Po Box 790
Boise, ID 83701
208-332-8650
http://www.scc.state.id.us/scc_facts.htm
Responsibilities of the Commission are: organize Districts and provide assistance, coordination, information and training to Disrict supervisors; ensure that Districts function legally and properly as local subdivisions of stategovernment; administer general funds appropriated by the Idaho Legislature to Districts so they can install resource conservation practices and provide technical assistance personnel to Districts administering water quality projects and conductingsoil surveys.
Jerry Nicolescu, Administrator

2783 United States Department of the Interior Bureau of Land Management
3948 Development Avenue
Boise, ID 83705
208-384-3300
Fax: 208-384-3493
http://www.blm.gov

Illinois

2784 Association of Illinois Soil and Water Conservation Districts
4285 North Walnut Street 217-744-3414
Springfield, IL 62707 Fax: 217-744-3420
E-mail: sherry.finn@aiswcd.org
http://www.aiswcd.org

To foster and promote charitable and educational purposes designed to further the principles of soil conservation and stewardship, water conservation and energy conservation. Provides, conducts and sponsors programs to aidindividuals, groups, organizations, government bodies, association and all entities in combating soil erosion and energy water waste.

Lonnie Wilson, President
Tom Beyers, Vice President

2785 Construction Engineering Research Laboratory
US Army Engineer Research and Development Center
PO Box 9005 217-352-6511
Champaign, IL 61826 800-USA-CERL
E-mail: Dana.L.Finney@erdc.usace.mil
http://www.cecer.army.mil

CERL conducts research to support sustainable military installations. Research is directed toward increasing the Army's ability to more efficiently construct, operate and maintain its installations and ensure environmental quality andsafety at a reduced life-cycle cost. Excellent facilities support the Army's training, readiness, mobilization and sustainability missions.
Ilker Adiguzel, Director

2786 Department of Natural Resources: Division of Education
Illinois Department of Natural Resources
One Natural Resources Way 217-524-4126
Springfield, IL 62702 E-mail: dnr.teachkids@illinois.gov
http://www.dnr.state.il.us/education/index.htm

Responsible for the development and dissemination of educational programs and materials and for training in their use. The website provides contests for students, loan materials, education materials, and grant information, in additionto graduate program information, podcasts and workshops. Overall, an excellent resource for education professionals, parents, and students.
Valerie Keener, Administrator

2787 Environmental Protection Agency Bureau of Water
Water Bureau
4500 South Sixth Street Road 312-814-8199
Springfield, IL 62706 http://www.epa.state.il.us/water

Mission: To ensure that Illinois' rivers, streams and lakes will support all uses for which they are designated including protection of aquatic life, recreation and drinking water supplies; ensure that every illinois Public Watersystem will provide water that is consistently safe to drink; and protect Illinois' groundwater resource for designated drinking water and other beneficial uses.
Lisa Bonnett, Director
Elmo Dowd, Associate Director

2788 Environmental Protection Agency: Region 5
77 West Jackson Boulevard 312-353-2000
Chicago, IL 60604-3590 800-621-8431
http://www.epa.gov/region5
Susan Hedman, Region Administrator

2789 Illinois Conservation Foundation
One Natural Resources Way 217-785-2003
Springfield, IL 62702 Fax: 217-785-8405
E-mail: www.ilcf.org/contact_us/
http://www.ilcf.org

Established by law, the ILCF is a volunteer group with a 13-member Board, chaired by the Director of the IL Dept of Natural Resources. The role of the ILCF and its partners is to preserve and enhance our precious natural resources bysupporting and fostering ecological, educational, and recreational programs for the benefit of all citizens of Illinois and for future generations.

Marc Miller, Director

2790 Illinois Department of Agriculture Bureau of Land and Water Resources
PO Box 19281 217-782-2172
Springfield, IL 62794 Fax: 217-785-4505
http://www.agr.state.il.us

Charles A Hartke, Director

2791 Illinois Department of Transportation
2300 S Dirksen Parkway 217-782-7820
Springfield, IL 62764-1 E-mail: Monseurmj@nt.dot.state.il.us
http://www.dot.state.il.us

Provides cost-effective, safe and efficient transportation for the people who live, work, visit and do business in Illinois, and ensures that the system supports the state's economic growth.
Ann L Schneider, Director
Vincent E Rangel, Deputy Director

2792 Illinois Nature Preserves Commission
One Natural Resources Way 217-785-8686
Springfield, IL 62702 Fax: 217-785-2438
E-mail: kelly.neal@illinois.gov
http://www.dnr.state.il.us/inpc

To assist private and public landowners in protecting high quality natral areas and habitats of endangered and threatened species in perpetuity, through voluntary dedication or registration of such lands into the Illinois NaturePreserves Systems. Offering programs in Defence, Protection, and Stewardship.
David L. Thomas, Chair
Donald R. Dann, Vice Chairman

2793 United States Department of the Army US Army Corps of Engineers
US Army Engineer District
Clock Tower Building 309-794-5729
PO Box 2004 Fax: 309-794-5793
Rock Island, IL 61204 http://www.usace.army.mil
Thomas Bostick, Commanding General
Todd T. Semonite, Deputy Commanding General

Indiana

2794 Indiana Department of Natural Resources
402 West Washington Street 317-232-4020
Indianapolis, IN 46204 Fax: 317-232-8036
http://www.ai.org/dnr

Protects, enhances, preserves, and wisely uses natural, cultural, and recreational resources for the benefit of Indiana's citizens through professional leadership, management and education.
Robert E Carter, Director
Todd Tande, Deputy Director

2795 Indiana State Department of Agriculture, Soil Conservation
101 West Ohio 317-232-8770
Suite 1200 Fax: 317-232-1362
Indianapolis, IN 46204 http://www.in.gov/isda

Mission: To facilitate the protection and enhancement of Indiana's land and water.
Jerod Chew, Director

2796 Indiana State Department of Health
2 N Meridan Street 317-233-1325
Indianapolis, IN 46204 E-mail: gwilson@isdh.state.in.us
http://www.state.in.us/isdh

Mission: To support Indiana's economic prosperity and quality of life by promoting, protecting and providing for the health of Hoosiers in their communities.
Judith A Monroe, State Health Commissioner
Mary L Hill, Deputy State Health Commiss.

2797 **Natural Resources Department: Fish & Wildlife**
402 West Washington Street RMW273 317-232-4080
Indianapolis, IN 46204 Fax: 317-232-8150
E-mail: dfw@dnr.in.gov
http://www.in.gov/dnr/fishwild
Mission: To professionally manage Indiana's fish and wildlife for present and future generations, balancing ecological, recreational, and economic benefits.

Iowa

2798 **Iowa Association of County Conservation Boards**
405 SW 3rd Street 515-963-9582
Suite 1 Fax: 515-963-9582
Ankeny, IA 50023 E-mail: iaccb@ecity.net
http://www.ecity.net/iaccb
IACCB is a nonprofit organization assisting member county conservation boards in areas of board member education, public relations and legislation. The association's main purposes are to promote the objectives and supplement theactivities of conservation boards, exchange information, assist boards and members in program development and provide a unified voice in the legislature. IACCB is governed by a nine-member board elected by member counties.

2799 **Iowa Department of Agriculture, and Land Stewardship Division of Soil Conservation**
502 E 9th 515-281-5851
Wallace State Office Building Fax: 515-281-6170
Des Moines, IA 50319 http://www.iowaagriculture.org
The Division of Soil Conservation is responsible for state leadership in the protection and management of soil, water and mineral resources, assisting soil and water conservation districts and private landowners to meet theiragricultural and environmental protection needs.
Chuck Gipp, Director
Karen Fynaardt, Administrative Assistant

2800 **Iowa Department of Natural Resources Administrative Services Division**
502 E 9th Street 515-281-5918
Wallace Office Building Fax: 515-281-8895
Des Moines, IA 50319 http://www.iowadnr.com
Aims to manage, protect, conserve and develop Iowa's natural resources in cooperation with other public and private organizations and individuals, so that the quality of life for Iowans is significantly enhanced by the use, enjoymentand understanding of those resources.

2801 **Iowa State Extension Services**
1032 Wallace Road Office Building 515-294-6192
Ames, IA 55011 Fax: 515-294-4715
E-mail: jlpease@iastate.edu
http://www.extension.iastate.edu/
Dr James L Pease, Specialist

2802 **Natural Resource Department**
502 E 9th Street 515-281-5385
Des Moines, IA 50319 Fax: 515-281-8895
http://www.iowadnr.com
Mission: To conserve and enhance our natural resources in cooperation with individuals and organizations to improve the quality of life for Iowans and ensure a legacy for future generations.
Richard Leopold, Director
Liz Christiansen, Deputy Director

Kansas

2803 **Emporia Research and Survey Office Kansas Department of Wildlife & Parks**
1830 Merchant
PO Box 1525 620-342-0658
1830 Merchant E-mail: randys@wp.state.ks.us
Emporia, KS 66801-1525 http://www.kdwp.state.ks.us
Randy Doll, Commissioner
Robert J. Wilson, Commissioner

2804 **Environmental Protection Agency: Region 7, Air & Toxics Division**
901 North 5th Street 913-551-7003
Lenexa, KS 66219 Fax: 913-551-7066
http://www.epa.gov/region7/
Responsible for management of programs for air, hazardous waste, toxic substances, radiation and pollution prevention in Iowa, Kansa, Missouri and Nebraska as required by the following legistlation: The Clean Air Act, The ResourceConservation and Recovery Act, the Toxic Substances Control Act and the Emergency planning and Community Right-to Know Act.
Patrick Bustos, Director
Hattie Thomas, Deputy Director

2805 **Health & Environment Department: Air & Radiation**
1000 SW Jackson 785-296-1593
Suite 310 Fax: 785-296-8464
Topeka, KS 66612 E-mail: jmitchell@kdheks.gov
http://www.kdheks.gov/bar
Mission: To protect the public from the harmful effects of radiation and air pollution and conserve the natural resources of the state by preventing damage to the environment from releases of radioactive materials or air contaminants.
Rick Bruneti, Director

2806 **Health & Environment Department: EnvironmentDivision**
1000 SW Jackson Street 785-296-1535
Suite 400 Fax: 785-296-8464
Topeka, KS 66612 E-mail: jmitchell@kdheks.gov
http://www.kdheks.gov/environment
The mission of the Division of Environment is the protection of the public health and environment. The division conducts regulatory programs involving public water supplies, industrial discharges, wastewater treatment systems, solidswaste landfills, hazardous waste, air emissions, radioactive materials, asbestos removal, refined petroleum storage tanks and other sources which impact the environment.
John Michtell, Director

2807 **Health & Environment Department: Waste Management**
1000 SW Jackson 785-296-1600
Suite 320 Fax: 785-296-8909
Topeka, KS 66612 http://www.kdheks.gov/waste
Regulates landfills, HHW, Hazardous Waste Permitting, Solid Waste Permitting, Public Outreach, Illegal Dumps.
Bill Bider, Director

2808 **Kansas Cooperative Fish & Wildlife Research Unit**
Kansas State University
205 Leasure Hall 785-532-6070
Manhattan, KS 66506 Fax: 785-532-7159
E-mail: kscfwru@ksu.edu
http://www.k-state.edu/kscfwru
Unit Research contributes to understanding ecological systems within the Great Plains. Unit staff, collaborators, and graduate students conduct research with both natural and altered systems, particularly those impacted by agriculture.Unit projects investigate ways to maintain a rich diversity of endemic wild animals and habitats while meeting the needs of people. The Unit focuses on projects that involve graduate students, and the research needs of cooperators are given priority.
David Haukos, Leader
Jack Cully Jr, Assistant Leader

2809 **Kansas Corporation Commission Conservation Division**
Finney State Office Building 316-337-6200
130 S Market, Room 2078 Fax: 316-337-6211
Wichita, KS 67202 http://www.kcc.state.ks.us

State of Kansas oilfield regulatory agency. The KCC is responsible for the preservation of Kansas' hydro and carbo resources, protection of corrullative right and the prevention and remediation of oil field pollution.
Mark Seivers, Chair
Thomas Wright, Commissioner

2810 Kansas Department of Health & Environment
1000 SW Jackson Street
Topeka, KS 66612
785-296-1500
Fax: 785-368-6368
E-mail: info@kdhe.state.ks.us
http://www.kdhe.state.ks.us

An organization dedicated to optimizing the promotion and protection of the health of Kansas through efficient and effective public health programs and services and through preservation, protection and remediation of natural resourcesof the environment.
Robert Moser, Secretary
Aaron Dunkel, Deputy Secretary

2811 Kansas Department of Wildlife & Parks Region 2
300 SW Wanamaker Road
Topeka, KS 66606
785-273-6740
Fax: 785-273-6757
http://www.kdwp.state.ks.us

Manages and promotes the wildlife and natural resources of Kansas. Administered by a secetary of Wildlife and Parks and is advised by a seven-member Wildlife and Parks Commission.
Randy Doll, Commissioner
Robert J. Wilson, Commissioner

2812 Kansas Department of Wildlife & Parks Region 3
1001 McArtor Drive
Dodge City, KS 67801-6024
620-227-8609
Fax: 620-227-8600
http://www.kdwp.state.ks.us

Randy Doll, Commissioner
Robert J. Wilson, Commissioner

2813 Kansas Department of Wildlife & Parks Region 4
6232 E 29th Street N
Wichita, KS 67220
316-683-8069
http://www.kdwp.state.ks.us
Randy Doll, Commissioner
Robert J. Wilson, Commissioner

2814 Kansas Department of Wildlife & Parks Region 5
1500 W 7th Street
Po Box 777
Chanute, KS 66720
620-431-0380
Fax: 620-431-0381
http://www.kdwp.state.ks.us
This region is made up of 18 counties in the southeastern corner of the state. This area is dominated by the Osage Questas physiographic region, which is characterized by rolling grasslands, limestone bluffs, and heavily timberedbottomlands.
Randy Doll, Commissioner
Robert J. Wilson, Commissioner

2815 Kansas Department of Wildlife and Parks
512 SE 25th Avenue
Pratt, KS 67124
620-672 5911
Fax: 620-672-2972
http://www.kdwp.state.ks.us

Randy Doll, Commissioner
Robert J. Wilson, Commissioner

2816 Kansas Geological Survey
University of Kansas
1930 Constant Avenue
Lawrence, KS 66047-3724
785-864-3965
Fax: 785-864-5317
E-mail: webadmin@kgs.ku.edu
http://www.kgs.ku.edu
Conducts geological studies and research and collects, correlates, preserves and disseminates information leading to a better understanding of the geology of Kansas, with special emphasis on nautral resources of economic value, waterquality and quantity and geologic hazards. This information is published in books and maps both technical and educational and also provides computer programs and data bases derived from geologic investigations.

Rex C. Buchanan, Director & State Geologist

2817 Kansas Health & Environmental Laboratories
6700 SW Topeka Blvd
Building 740
Topeka, KS 66619-1401
785-296-6603
Fax: 785-296-1641
http://www.kdhe.state.ks.us/labs
Provides timely and accurate analytical information for public health benefit in Kansas and assures the quality of statewide laboratory sevices though certification and improvement programs.
Leo Hanning, Interim Director

2818 Kansas Water Office
901 S Kansas Avenue
Topeka, KS 66612
785-296-3185
888-526-9283
Fax: 785-296-0878
E-mail: kwo-info@kwo.ks.gov
http://www.kwo.org
Works to achieve proactive solutions for resource issues of the state and to ensure good quality water to meet the needs of the people and the environment of Kansas. Evaluates and develops public policies, coordinating the waterresource operations of agencies at all levels of government.
Tracy Streeter, Director
Earl Lewis, Assistant Director

2819 Pratt Operations Office Kansas Department of Wildlife & Parks
512 SE 25th Avenue
Pratt, KS 67124
620-672-5911
E-mail: kenb@wp.state.ks.us
http://www.kdwp.state.ks.us

Randy Doll, Commissioner
Robert J. Wilson, Commissioner

Kentucky

2820 Attorney General's Office Civil and Environmental Law Division
700 Capitol Avenue
Capitol Building, Suite 118
Frankfort, KY 40601
502-696-5300
http://ag.ky.gov/civil/uninsured.htm
Jack Conway, Attorney General
Margaret Everson, Asst Deputy Attorney General

2821 Department for Energy Development & Independence
500 Mero Street
12th Floor Capital Plaza Tower
Frankfort, KY 40601
502-564-7192
Fax: 502-564-7484
E-mail: amanda.cook@ky.gov
http://www.energy.ky.gov

Provides leadership to maximize the benefits of energy effeciency and alternate energy through awareness, technology development, energy preparedness and new partnerships and resources.
John Davies, Deputy Commissioner

2822 Department for Environmental Protection
300 Fair Oaks Lane
Frankfort, KY 40601
502-564-0323
Fax: 502-564-4245
E-mail: envhelp@ky.gov
http://www.dep.ky.gov
Mission: To protect and enhance Kentucky's environment. This mission is important because it has a direct impact on Kentucky's public health, our citizens' safety and the quality of Kentucky's valuable natural resources-ourenvironment.
Robert W Logan, Commisioner

2823 Division of Mine Reclamation and Enforcement
Two Hudson Hollow Road
Frankfort, KY 40601
502-564-2340
Fax: 502-564-5848
E-mail: j.hamon@ky.gov
http://www.dmre.ky.gov

The Division of Mine Reclamation and Enforcement is responsible for inspecting all surface and underground coal mining permits in the state to assure compliance with the 1977 Federal Surface Mining Control Act. The DMRE is alsoresponsible for regulating and enforcing the surface mining reclamation laws for non-coal mining sites in the state, including limestone, sand, gravel, clay, shale and the surface effects of dredging river sand and gravel.

2824 **Economic Development Cabinet: Community Development Department Brokerage Division**
Old Capitol Annex 502-564-7140
300 West Broadway 800-626-2930
Frankfort, KY 40601 Fax: 502-564-3256
http://www.thinkkentucky.com

Responsible for encouraging job creation and retention, and new investment in the state
Larry Hayes, Secretary
Hollie Spade, Chief of Staff

2825 **Environmental Protection Department: Waste Management Division**
200 Fair Oaks Lane 502-564-6716
4th Floor Fax: 502-564-4049
Frankfort, KY 40601 E-mail: waste@ky.gov
http://www.waste.ky.gov

Mission: To protect human health and the environment by minimizing adverse impacts on all citizens of the commonwealth through the development and implementation of fair, equitable and effective waste management programs.
Anthony Hatton, Director
Tim Hubbard, Assistant Director

2826 **Environmental Protection Department: Water Division**
200 Fair Oaks Lane 502-564-3410
4th Floor Fax: 502-564-0111
Frankfort, KY 40601 E-mail: water@ky.gov
http://www.water.ky.gov

To manage, protect and enhance the quality of the Commonwealth's water resources for present and future generations through voluntary, regulatory and educational programs
David Morgan, Director
Sandy Gruzesky, Assistant Director

2827 **Fish and Wildlife Resources Department: Fisheries Division**
1 Sportsman's Lane 502-564-3596
Frankfort, KY 40601 800-858-1549
Fax: 502-564-6501
E-mail: info.center@ky.gov
http://www.fw.ky.gov

Mission: To conserve and enhance fish and wildlife resources and provide opportunity for hunting, fishing, trapping, boating and other wildlife related activities.
John Gassett, Commissioner
Benjy T Kinman, Fisheries Director

2828 **Kentucky Department for Public Health**
275 E Main Street 502-564-5497
Franfort, KY 40621 800-372-2973
Fax: 502-564-9523
http://www.chfs.ky.gov/dph

Stephanie Mayfield Gibson, Commissioner

2829 **Kentucky Environmental and Public Protection Cabinet**
500 Metro Street 502-564-3350
Capital Plaza Tower, 5th Floor Fax: 502-564-3354
Frankfort, KY 40601 E-mail: environment@ky.gov
http://www.environment.ky.gov

Provides a safe, clean environment in the Commonwealth, while working with business and industry to help ensure adequate jobs and a strong economy.
Teresa J Hill, Secretary

2830 **Kentucky State Cooperative Extension Services**
University of Kentucky
S-107 Agricultural Science Bldg N 859-257-4302
Lexington, KY 40546-91 Fax: 859-257-3501
E-mail: darlene.mylin@uky.edu
http://www.ca.uky.edu/ces

Jimmy Henning, Director
Gary Palmer, Assistant Director

2831 **Kentucky State Nature Preserves Commission**
801 Schenkel Lane 502-573-2886
Frankfort, KY 40601 Fax: 502-573-2355
E-mail: naturepreserves@ky.gov
http://www.naturepreserves.ky.gov

Aims to protect Kentucky's natural heritage by identifying, acquiring and managing natural areas that represent the best known occurrences of rare native species and natural communities and working together to protect biologicaldiversity.
Don Dott, Director

2832 **Natural Resources Department: Conservation Division**
375 Versailles Road 502-573-3080
Frankfort, KY 40601 Fax: 502-573-1692
E-mail: Angie.Wingfield@ky.gov
http://www.conservation.ky.gov

Assists Kentucky's local conservation districts in the development and implementation of sound soil and water conservation programs to manage, enhance, and promote the wise use of the Commonwealth's natural resources.
Stephen A Coleman, Director

2833 **Natural Resources Department: Division of Forestry**
627 Comanche Trail 502-564-4496
Frankfort, KY 40601 Fax: 502-564-6553
E-mail: gwen.holt@ky.gov
http://www.forestry.ky.gov

Diana Olszowy, Contact

2834 **Natural Resources and Environment Protection Cabinet: Environmental Quality Commission**
500 Mero Street 502-564-2674
Capital Plaza Tower E-mail: eqc@ky.gov
Frankfort, KY 40601 http://www.eqc.ky.gov
To serve as an advisory board to the governor and other state officials on environmental matters
Mark Grisham, Chairman
Steve Coleman, Vice Chairman

2835 **Tourism Cabinet: Parks Department**
2400 Capital Plaza Tower 22nd Floor 502-564-4930
500 Metro Street 800-225-8747
Frankfort, KY 40601 http://www.kentuckytourism.com/stateparks
Mike Mangeot, Commissioner
Hank Phillips, Deputy Commissioner

Louisiana

2836 **Agriculture & Forestry: Soil & Water Conservation**
Louisiana Department of Agriculture and Forestry
PO Box 3554 225-922-1269
Baton Rouge, LA 70821-3554 Fax: 225-922-2577
http://www.ldaf.state.la.us

To sustain and conserve water quality and soil stability on croplands, woodlands, grasslands, wetlands and waterways of Louisiana
Mike Strain, Commissioner
Brad Spicer, Assistant Commissioner

2837 **Culture, Recreation and Tourism**
PO Box 94361 225-342-8115
Baton Rouge, LA 70802 Fax: 225-342-3207
E-mail: ltgov@crt.la.gov
http://www.crt.state.la.us

Desire, W. Honor,, Undersecretary
Shirley S Johnson, Executive Assistant

2838 **Department of Natural Resources: Office of Mineral Resources**
PO Box 2827 225-342-4615
Baton Rouge, LA 70821-2827 Fax: 225-342-4527
E-mail: OMR@dnr.state.la.us.us
http://www.dnr.louisiana.gov/MIN/

Provides staff support to the State Mineral Board in granting and administering leases on state-owned lands and waterbottoms for

the production and development of minerals, primarily oil and gas, for the purpose of optimizing revenueto the state from the royalties, bonuses and rentals generated therefrom.
Stacey Talley, Deputy Assistant Secretary

2839 **Louisana Department of Natural Resources**
PO Box 94396 225-342-4500
Baton Rouge, LA 70804 Fax: 225-342-5861
http://www.dnr.state.la.us
To preserve and enhance the nonrenewable natural resources of the state, consisting of land, water, oil, gas, and other minerals, through conservation, regulation, management and development to ensure that the state of Louisianarealizes appropriate economic benefit from its asset base
Stephen Chustz, Secretary
Lori LeBlanc, Deputy Secretary

2840 **Louisiana Cooperative Extension Services**
PO Box 25100 225-578-6083
Baton Rouge, LA 70894 Fax: 225-578-4225
http://www.lsuagcenter.com/
To provide the people of Louisiana with research-based educational information that will improve their lives and economic well-being
Bill Richardson, Chancellor

2841 **Louisiana Department of Natural Resources Office of Coastal Restoration and Management**
625 N 4th Street 225-342-7591
Baton Rouge, LA 70802 800-267-4019
Fax: 225-342-9439
E-mail: dnr.la.gov/coastal
http://www.dnr.louisiana.gov/crm
Develops, implements and monitors costal vegetated wetland restoration, creation and conservation measures. Preforms engineering, planning and monitoring functions essential to successful development and implementation of wetlandconservation and restoration plans and projects as directed by the Costal Wetlands Conservation and Restoration Plan.
Keith Lowell, Acting Assistant Secretary

2842 **Natural Resources: Conservation Office**
617 N 3rd Street 225-342-5540
PO Box 94275 Fax: 225-342-3705
Baton Rouge, LA 70804 http://www.dnr.louisiana.gov
Regulatory oil and gas agency, State of Louisiana.
James H Welsh, Commissioner of Conservation
Gary P Ross, Asst. Commissioner, Conserva

2843 **Natural Resources: Injection & Mining Division**
PO Box 94275 225-342-5515
Baton Rouge, LA 70804 Fax: 225-342-3094
E-mail: Injection-Mining@la.gov
http://www.dnr.louisiana.gov
Has the responsibility for implementation of major environmental programs statutorily charged to the Office of Conservation. Administers a regulatory and permit program to protect underground sources of drinking water fromendangerment; is responsible for regulating exploration, development and surface mining operations for coal and lignite; and protection of state and private lands.
Joseph S Ball Jr, Director
Laurence Bland, Assistant Director

Maine

2844 **Maine Cooperative Fish & Wildlife Research Unit**
University of Maine
USGS Biological ResourcesDiscipline 207-581-2862
5755 Nutting Hall Fax: 207-581-2858
Orono, ME 04469 http://www.wle.umaine.edu
Mission: To facilitate and strengthen professional education and training of fisheries and wildlife scientists; carry out research programs of aquatic, mammalian, and avian organisms and their habitats; and disseminate research resultsthrough the appropriate media, especially peer-review scientific articles.
Dr Cyndy Loftin, Leader

2845 **Maine Department of Environmental Protection: Augusta**
17 State House Station 207-287-7688
28 Tyson Drive 800-452-1942
Augusta, ME 04333-17 Fax: 207-287-7826
http://www.maine.gov/dep
Responsible for environmental protection and regulation in the state of Maine. Engages in a wide range of activities, makes reccomendations to the Legistlature regarding measures to minimize and eliminate environmental pollution,grants licenses, initiates enforcement actions, and provides information and technical assistance.
Robert A. Foley, Chair
Alvin K. Ahlers, Director

2846 **Maine Department of Conservation**
22 State House Station 207-287-2211
Augusta, ME 04333 Fax: 207-287-2400
http://www.maine.gov/doc
To oversee the management, development and protection of some of Maine's most special places: 17 million acres of forest land, 10.4 million acres of unorganized territory, 48 parks and historic sites and more than 590,000 acres ofpublic-reserved and non-reserved land
Bill Beardsley, Commissioner

2847 **Maine Department of Conservation: Ashland Regional Office**
45 Radar Road 207-435-7963
Ashland, ME 04732 Fax: 207-435-7184
http://www.maine.gov/doc
To oversee the management, development and protection of some of Maine's most special places: 17 million acres of forest land, 10.4 million acres of unorganized territory, 48 parks and historic sites and more than 590,000 acres ofpublic-reserved and non-reserved land
Don Cote, Compliance Investigator
Billie J. MacLean, Regional Representative

2848 **Maine Department of Conservation: Bangor Regional Office**
106 Hogan Road 207-941-4014
BMHI Complex Fax: 207-941-4222
Bangor, ME 04401 http://www.maine.gov/doc
To oversee the management, development and protection of some of Maine's most special places: 17 million acres of forest land, 10.4 million acres of unorganized territory, 48 parks and historic sites and more than 590,000 acres ofpublic-reserved and non-reserved land

2849 **Maine Department of Conservation: Bolton Hill Regional Office**
2870 North Belfast Avenue 207-624-3700
Augusta, ME 04330 Fax: 207-287-8534
http://www.maine.gov/doc
To oversee the management, development and protection of some of Maine's most special places: 17 million acres of forest land, 10.4 million acres of unorganized territory, 48 parks and historic sites and more than 590,000 acres ofpublic-reserved and non-reserved land

2850 **Maine Department of Conservation: Bureau of Parks & Lands**
22 State House Station 207-287-3821
2nd & 1st Floors Fax: 207-287-3823
Augusta, ME 04333 http://www.maine.gov/doc
To oversee the management, development and protection of some of Maine's most special places: 17 million acres of forest land, 10.4 million acres of unorganized territory, 48 parks and historic sites and more than 590,000 acres ofpublic-reserved and non-reserved land

2851 Maine Department of Conservation: Entomology Laboratory
50 Hospital Street
Augusta, ME 04330
207-287-2431
Fax: 207-287-2432
http://www.maine.gov/doc
To oversee the management, development and protection of some of Maine's most special places: 17 million acres of forest land, 10.4 million acres of unorganized territory, 48 parks and historic sites and more than 590,000 acres ofpublic-reserved and non-reserved land

2852 Maine Department of Conservation: Farmington Regional Office
25 Maine Street
PO Box 327
Farmington, ME 04938
207-778-8231
Fax: 207-778-5932
http://www.maine.gov/doc
To oversee the management, development and protection of some of Maine's most special places: 17 million acres of forest land, 10.4 million acres of unorganized territory, 48 parks and historic sites and more than 590,000 acres ofpublic-reserved and non-reserved land

2853 Maine Department of Conservation: Greenville Regional Office
Lake View Drive
PO Box 1107
Greenville, ME 04441-1107
207-695-2466
Fax: 207-695-2380
http://www.maine.gov/doc
To oversee the management, development and protection of some of Maine's most special places: 17 million acres of forest land, 10.4 million acres of unorganized territory, 48 parks and historic sites and more than 590,000 acres ofpublic-reserved and non-reserved land
Keith Smith, Regional Representative

2854 Maine Department of Conservation: Hallowell Regional Office
Winthrop Street
Stevens Complex
Hallowell, ME 04330
207-624-6080
Fax: 207-624-6081
http://www.maine.gov/doc
To oversee the management, development and protection of some of Maine's most special places: 17 million acres of forest land, 10.4 million acres of unorganized territory, 48 parks and historic sites and more than 590,000 acres ofpublic-reserved and non-reserved land

2855 Maine Department of Conservation: Jonesboro Regional Office
Route 1A
PO Box 130
Jonesboro, ME 04648
207-434-2627
Fax: 207-434-2624
http://www.maine.gov/doc
To oversee the management, development and protection of some of Maine's most special places: 17 million acres of forest land, 10.4 million acres of unorganized territory, 48 parks and historic sites and more than 590,000 acres ofpublic-reserved and non-reserved land

2856 Maine Department of Conservation: Land Use Regulation Commission
22 State House Station
4th Floor
Augusta, ME 04333
207-287-2631
Fax: 207-287-7439
http://www.maine.gov/doc
The Maine Land Use Regulation Commission meets monthly in various locations throughout the state to discuss jurisdiction-related issues and to act upon pending cases.

2857 Maine Department of Conservation: Millinocket Regional Office
191 Main Street
East Millinocket, ME 04430
207-746-2244
Fax: 207-746-2243
http://www.maine.gov/doc
To oversee the management, development and protection of some of Maine's most special places: 17 million acres of forest land, 10.4 million acres of unorganized territory, 48 parks and historic sites and more than 590,000 acres ofpublic-reserved and non-reserved land
Marc Russell, Regional Representative

2858 Maine Department of Conservation: Old Town Regional Office
Airport Road
PO Box 415
Old Town, ME 04468
207-827-1818
Fax: 207-827-6295
http://www.maine.gov/doc
To oversee the management, development and protection of some of Maine's most special places: 17 million acres of forest land, 10.4 million acres of unorganized territory, 48 parks and historic sites and more than 590,000 acres ofpublic-reserved and non-reserved land

2859 Maine Department of Conservation: Rangeley Regional Office
133 Fyfe Road
PO Box 307
West Farmington, ME 04992
207-670-7493
Fax: 207-864-5252
http://www.maine.gov/doc
To oversee the management, development and protection of some of Maine's most special places: 17 million acres of forest land, 10.4 million acres of unorganized territory, 48 parks and historic sites and more than 590,000 acres ofpublic-reserved and non-reserved land
Sara Brusila, Regional Representative

2860 Maine Department of Environmental Protection: Presque Isle
1235 Central Drive
Skyway Park
Presque Isle, ME 04769
207-764-0477
888-769-1053
Fax: 207-760-3143
http://www.maine.gov/dep

2861 Maine Department of Environmental Protection: Portland
312 Canco Road
Portland, ME 04103
207-822-6300
888-769-1036
Fax: 207-822-6303
http://www.maine.gov/dep
Robert A. Foley, Chair
Alvin K. Ahlers, Director

2862 Maine Inland Fisheries & Wildlife Department
284 State Street Station 41SHS
41 State House Station
Augusta, ME 04333-42
207-287-8000
Fax: 207-287-6395
E-mail: ifw.webmaster@maine.gov
http://www.maine.gov/ifw
The Department of Inland Fisheries & Wildlife was established to ensure that all species of wildlife and aquatic resources in the State of Maine are maintained and perpetuated for their intrinsic and ecological values, for theireconomic contribution, and for their recreational, scientific and educational use by the people of the State. The Department is also responsible for the establishment and enforcement of rules and regulations.
Chandler E. Woodcock, Commissioner
Andrea Erskine, Deputy Commissioner

2863 Maine Natural Areas Program
93 State House Station
Augusta, ME 04333-93
207-287-8044
Fax: 207-287-8040
E-mail: maine.nap@maine.gov
http://www.maine.gov/doc/nrimc/mnap/
Mission: To ensure the maintenance of Maine's natural heritage for the benefit of present and future generations. MNAP facilitates informed decision-making in development planning, conservation, and natural resources management. TheProgram's success relies upon using consistent and objective methods to collect, organize, and interpret information.
Molly Docherty, Director

2864 Maine Sea Grant College Program
University of Maine
5784 York Complex
The University of Maine
Orono, ME 04469-5784
207-581-1435
Fax: 207-581-1426
E-mail: umseagrant@maine.edu
http://www.seagrant.umaine.edu
Paul Anderson, Director
Beth Bisson, Assistant Director

2865 Northeastern Forest Fire Protection Compact
P.O. Box 6192
21 Parmenter Terrace
China Village, ME 04926
207-968-3782
Fax: 207-968-3782
E-mail: info@nffpc.org
http://www.nffpc.org

The mandate of the Northeastern Forest Fire Protection Commission is to provide the means for its member states and provinces to cope with fires that might be beyond the capabilities of a singler member through infromation, technologyand resources sharing activities.
Tom Parent, Executive Director

2866 University of Maine Cooperative Extension Forestry & Wildlife Office
5755 Nutting Hall
Room 105
Orono, ME 04469
207-581-2892
Fax: 207-581-3466
http://www.umext.maine.edu/
Catherine Elliott, Wildlife Specialist
Les Hyde, Extension Educator

Massachusetts

2867 Connecticut River Salmon Association
103 E Plumtree Road
Sunderland, MA 01375
413-548-8002
860-644-0159
Fax: 413-548-9746
E-mail: info@ctriversalmon.org
http://www.ctriversalmon.org

To support the effort to restore Atlantic salmon in the Connecticut River basin. An invitation is extended to explore the site to learn more about our organization and the work being done to reestablish a species that had been extinctin this region since about 1800.
Robert A. Jones, President
Richard G. Bell, Vice President

2868 Department of Agricultural Resources
251 Causeway Street
Suite 500
Boston, MA 02114
617-626-1700
Fax: 617-626-1850
E-mail: dwebber@state.ma.us
http://www.mass.gov/agr/animalhealth/index.htm

The Bureau of Animal Health focuses its efforts on ensuring the health and safety of the Commonwealth's domestic animals. Through diligent inspection, examination, licensing, quarantine, and enforcement of laws, regulations and ordersand the provision of technical assistance the Bureau promotes the welfare of companion and food-producing animals in Massachusetts.

2869 Department of Environmental Protection
One Winter Street
Boston, MA 02108
617-292-5500
Fax: 617-556-1049
http://www.mass.gov/dep

The Department of Environmental Protection is the state agency responsible for ensuring clean air and water, the safe management of toxics and hazards, the recycling of solid and hazardous wastes, the timely cleanup of hazardous wastesites and spills, and the preservation of wetlands and coastal resources.
Arleen O'Donnell, Acting Commissioner

2870 Department of Fish & Game
251 Causeway Street
Suite 400
Boston, MA 02114
617-626-1500
Fax: 617-626-1505
http://www.mass.gov/dfwele

The Department of Fish & Game works to preserve the state's natural resources and people's right to conservation of those resources, as protected by Article 97 of the Massachusetts Constitution. To carry out this mission, theDepartment exercises responsibility over the Commonwealth's marine and freshwater fisheries, wildlife species, plants, and natural communities, as well as the habitats that support them.
Mary B Griffin, Commissioner

2871 EPA: Region 1, Air Management Division
5 Post Office Square
Suite 100
Boston, MA 02019-3912
617-918-1111
888-372-7341
Fax: 617-918-1112
http://www.epa.gov/region1

The mission of the US Environmental Protection Agency is to protect human health and to safeguard the natural environment- air, water and land- upon which life depends.
H. Curtis Spalding, Region Administrator

2872 Environmental Affairs Bureau of Markets
251 Causeway Street
Suite 500
Boston, MA 02114
617-626-1750
Fax: 617-626-1850
http://www.massdfa.org/agricult.html

2873 Environmental Affairs: Hazardous Waste Facilities Site Safety Council
100 Cambridge Street
Boston, MA 02202
617-727-6629

2874 Environmental Protection Agency Region 1 (CT, ME, MA, NH, RI, VT)
5 Post Office Square
Suite 100
Boston, MA 02019-3912
617-918-1111
888-372-7341
Fax: 617-918-1112
http://www.epa.gov/region1

The mission of the US Environmental Protection Agency is to protect human health and to safeguard the natural environment- air, water and land- upon which life depends.
H. Curtis Spalding, Region Administrator

2875 Executive Office of Energy & Environmental Affairs
Executive Office of Environmental Affairs
100 Cambridge Street
Suite 900
Boston, MA 02114
617-626-1000
Fax: 617-626-1181
E-mail: env.internet@state.ma.us
http://www.mass.gov/envir/eoea.htm

Richard K. Sullivan, Secretary
Kathleen Baskin, Director of Water Policy

2876 Massachusetts Highway Department
10 Park Plaza
Suite 4160
Boston, MA 02116
857-368-4636
877-623-6846
Fax: 857-368-0601
E-mail: feedback@mhd.state.ma.us
http://www.massdot.state.ma.us/highway/Main.aspx

To deliver excellent customer service to people who travel in the Commonwealth, and provide our nation's safest and most reliable transportation system in a way that strengthens our economy and quality of life
Luisa Paiewonsky, Commissioner

2877 New England Interstate Water Pollution Control Commission
650 Suffolk Street
Suite 410
Lowell, MA 01854
978-323-7929
Fax: 978-323-7919
E-mail: mail@neiwpcc.org
http://www.neiwpcc.org

The New England Interstate Water Pollution Control Commission, a nonprofit interstate agency established by an Act of Congress, serves and assist its members states individually and collectively by providing coordination, publiceducation, training and leadership in the management and protection of water quality in the New England Region and New York.
Peter LaFlamme, Chair
Yvonne Bolton, Vice Chairman

2878 United States Department of the Army US Army Corps of Engineers
696 Virginia Road
Concord, MA 01742
978-318-8220
Fax: 978-318-8821
http://www.usace.army.mil

Thomas Bostick, Commanding General
Todd T. Semonite, Deputy Commanding General

2879 Waquoit Bay National Estuarine Research Reserve
131 Waquoit Highway
PO Box 3092
Waquoit, MA 02536
508-457-0495
Fax: 617-727-5537
http://www.waquoitbayreserve.org

In 1979, The Commonwealth of Massachusetts designated Waquoit Bay as an Area of Critical Environment Concern (ACEC) in recognition of its significant natural resources. The designation provides a state-wide umbrella of protection

andoversight under the exisiting regulations of different state agencies which include higher standards of protection for ACEC's. The Waquoit Bay ACEC includes parts of the Bay proper. Although the ACEC covers 2522 acres, including Washburn Island andSouth Cape Beach.
Alison Leschen, Reserve Manager
Sheri Proft, Fiscal Administrator

Maryland

2880 Chesapeake Bay Executive Council
Chesapeake Bay Program Office — 410-267-5700
410 Severn Avenue, Suite 109 — 800-908-7229
Annapolis, MD 21403 — Fax: 410-267-5777
http://www.chesapeakebay.net/exec.htm
The Chesapeake Bay Executive Council establishes the policy direction for the restoration and protection of the Chesapeake Bay and its living resources. A series of Directives, Agreements, and Amendments signed by the ExecutiveCouncil set goals and guide policy for the Bay restoration. The Council meets annually.
Nicholas DiPasquale, Chairman
Greg Barranco, Coordinator

2881 Interstate Commission on the Potomac River Basin
51 Monroe Street — 301-984-1908
Suite PE-08 — Fax: 301-984-5841
Rockville, MD 20850 — E-mail: info@icprb.org
http://www.potomacriver.org
The Interstate Commission on the Potomac River Basin is an interstate compact agency established to help protect the Potomac River and its 14,670-square-mile watershed. Its mission is to enhance, protect, and conserve the water andassociated land resources of the Potomac River and its tributaries through regional and interstate cooperation.
Carlton Haywood, Executive Director
Bo Park, Administrative Officer

2882 Maryland Department of Agriculture
50 Harry S Truman Parkway — 410-841-5700
Annapolis, MD 21401 — 800-492-5590
Fax: 410-841-5914
http://www.mda.state.md.us
Established on the basis of agriculture's growing importance and impact to the economy of the state. Many activities are regulatory in nature, others are assigned to a category of public service and some are educational or promotionalin scope. All are intended to provide the maximum protection possible for the consumer as well as promote the economic well-being of farmers, food and fiber processors and businesses engage in agricultural related operations.
Earl F Hance, Secretary

2883 Maryland Department of Agriculture: State Soil Conservation Committee
50 Harry S Truman Parkway — 410-841-5863
Annapolis, MD 21401 — Fax: 410-841-5736
http://www.mda.state.md.us
Bill Giese, Chair
Charles Rice, Vice Chairman

2884 Maryland Department of Health and Mental Hygiene
201 W Preston Street — 410-767-6500
Baltimore, MD 21201 — 877-463-3464
Fax: 410-767-6489
E-mail: dhmh.healthmd@maryland.gov
http://www.dhmh.state.md.us/
The Maryland Department of Health and Mental Hygiene's mission is to protect and promote health and prevent disease and injury. This is accomplished through the provision of population-based health services and core public health;assessment, assurance and policy development.
Joshua M. Sharfstein, Secretary

2885 Maryland Department of the Environment: Water Management Field Office
160 South Water Street — 301-689-1486
Frostburg, MD 21532 — Fax: 301-689-6543
E-mail: mdecambr@intercom.net
http://www.mde.state.md.us
To restore and maintain the quality of the State's ground and surface waters, protect wetland habitats throughout the State, and manage the utilization of Maryland's mineral resources.
Scott Boylan, Program Chief

2886 Maryland Department of the Environment/Water Management: Nontidal Wetlands & Waterways
District Court/Multi Service Bldg — 410-713-3685
201 Baptist Street, Suite 22 — Fax: 410-713-3686
Salisbury, MD 21801 — E-mail: salisb@shore.intercom.net
http://www.mde.state.md.us
Steve Dawson, Manager

2887 Maryland Department of the Environment: Air & Radiation Management Field Office
201 Baptist Street — 410-713-3680
Suite 15 — Fax: 410-713-3681
Salisbury, MD 21801 — E-mail: awilliams@mde.state.md.us
http://www.mde.state.md.us
Jay Bozman, Manager

2888 Maryland Department of the Environment: Air and Radiation Management Main Field Office
160 South Water Street — 301-689-5756
Frostburg, MD 21532 — Fax: 301-689-6544
E-mail: frostbur@hereintown.net
http://www.mde.state.md.us
Cathy Singer, Manager

2889 Maryland Department of the Environment: Field Operations Office
416 Chinquapin Round Road — 443-482-2700
Annapolis, MD 21401 — http://www.mde.state.md.us
John Steinfort, Manager

2890 Maryland Department of the Environment: Main Office
1800 Washington Blvd — 410-537-3000
Baltimore, MD 21230 — 800-633-6101
E-mail: mdeprf@olg.com
http://www.mde.state.md.us
To protect and restore the quality of Maryland's air, land, and water resources, while fostering economic development, healthy and safe communities, and quality environmental education for the benefit of the environment, public health,and future generations.
Robert Summers, Secretary
David Costello, Deputy Secretary

2891 Maryland National Capital Park & Planning Commission
6611 Kenilworth Avenue — 301-454-1740
Riverdale, MD 20737 — Fax: 301-454-1750
E-mail: mcp-infocounter@mncppc-mc.org
http://www.mncppc.org
Is a bi-county agency empowered by the State of Maryland to acquire, develop, maintain and administer a regional system of parks withing Montgomery and Prince George's Counties, and to prepare and administer a general plan for thephysical development of the two counties.
Patricia Barney, Executive Director
Joseph Zimmerman, Secretary-Treasurer's Office

2892 NOAA Chesapeake Bay Office
410 Severn Avenue — 410-267-5660
Chesapeake Bay Office — Fax: 410-267-5666
Annapolis, MD 21403 — http://noaa.chesapeakebay.net
NOAA Chesapeake Bay Office works to help protect and restore the Chesapeake Bay through its programs in fisheries management, habitat restoration, coastal observations, and education, and represents NOAA in the Chesapeake Bay Program.

Michigan

2893 Great Lakes Environmental Research Laboratory
4840 S. State Rd
Ann Arbor, MI 48108-9719
734-741-2235
Fax: 734-741-2055
http://www.glerl.noaa.gov

Conducts integrated, interdisciplinary environmental research in support of resource management and environmental services in coastal and estuarine waters with a special emphasis on the Great Lakes. Laboratory performs field,analytical, and laboratory investigations to improve understanding and prediction of coastal and estarine processes and the interdependencies with the atmosphere and sediments.
Marie C. Colton, Director
John Bratton, Deputy Director

2894 Great Lakes Fishery Commission
2100 Commonwealth Boulevard
Suite 100
Ann Arbor, MI 48105
734-662-3209
Fax: 734-741-2010
E-mail: info@glfc.org
http://www.glfc.org

The Great Lakes Fishery Commision was established by the Convention on Great Lakes Fisheries between Canada and the US in 1955. It has two major responsibilities: to develop coordinated programs of research on the Great Lakes and, onthe basis of the findings, to recommend measures which will permit the maximum sustained productivity in stocks of fish of common concern; and to formulate and implement a program to eradicate or minimize sea lamprey populations in the Great Lakes.
Michael Hansen, Chairman
David Ullrich, Commissioner

2895 Michigan Department of Community Health
Capitol View Building
201 Townsend Street
Lansing, MI 48913
517-373-3740
800-649-3777
Fax: 517-335-8509
http://www.michigan.gov/mdch

A state agency which continually and diligently endeavors to prevent disease, prolong life and promote the public health
James K. Haveman, Director
Angela Awrey, Deputy Director/ COO

2896 Michigan Department of Environmental Quality
525 W Allegan Street, 6th Floor
PO Box 30473
Lansing, MI 48909-7973
517-373-7917
800 662 9278
http://www.michigan.gov/deq

Promotes wise management of Michigan's air, land, and water resources to support a sustainable environment, healthy communities, and vibrant economy
Dan Wyant, Director
Jim Kasprzak, State Bureau Administrator

2897 Michigan Department of Natural Resources
PO Box 30028
Lansing, MI 48909
517-241-7427
Fax: 517-241-7428
E-mail: dnr-wld-webpages@state.mi.us
http://www.michigan.gov/dnr

Committed to the conservation, protection, management, use and enjoyment of the state's natural and cultural resources for current and future generations
Keith Creagh, Director
Dennis Knapp, Chief of Staff

2898 Michigan State University Extension
Agriculture Hall
Room 108
East Lansing, MI 48824
517-355-2308
Fax: 517-355-6473
http://www.msue.msu.edu/msue/

Michigan State University Extension helps people improve their lives through an educational process that applies knowledge to critical issues, needs and opportunities.
Thomas G Coon, Director
Stephen B. Lovejoy, Associate Director

2899 Natural Resources: Wildlife Division
PO Box 30444
Lansing, MI 48909-7944
517-373-1263
Fax: 517-373-1547
http://www.michigan.gov/dnr

Committed to the conservation, protection, management, use and enjoyment of the state's natural and cultural resources for current and future generations
Keith Creagh, Director
Terry Minzey, Regional Supervisor

Minnesota

2900 Minnesota Board of Water & Soil Resources
520 Lafayette Road North
St Paul, MN 55155
651-296-3767
Fax: 651-297-5615
E-mail: BWSR.webmaster@state.mn.us
http://www.bwsr.state.mn.us

The Minnesota Board of Water and Soil Resources assists local governments to manage and conserve their irreplaceable water and soil resources.
Brian Napstad, Chairman of the Board
Tom Loveall, Co-Commissioner

2901 Minnesota Department of Agriculture
625 Robert Street North
St Paul, MN 55155-2538
651-201-6000
800-967-2474
Fax: 651-297-5522
E-mail: mda.info@state.mn.us
http://www.mda.state.mn.us

The MDA's mission is to work toward a diverse ag industry that is profitable as well as environmentally sound; to protect the public health safety regarding food and ag products; and to ensure orderly commerce in agricultural and foodproducts. We have two major branches of the department to accomplish this mission: regulatory divisions and non-regulatory divisions.
Dave Frederickson, Commissioner
Jim Boerboom, Deputy Commissioner

2902 Minnesota Department of Natural Resources
500 Lafayette Road
Box 21
St. Paul, MN 55155-4040
651-296-6157
888-646-6367
Fax: 651-297-4946
E-mail: info@dnr.state.mn.us
http://www.dnr.state.mn.us

The DNR vision hinges on the concept of sustainability. To DNR, sustainability means protecting and restoring the natural environment while enhancing economic opportunity and community well-being. DNR endorsed ecosystem-basedmanagement as its method to achieve sustainability goals. Sustainability addresses three related elements: the environment, the economy and the community. The goal is to maintain all three elements in a healthy state indefinitely.
Tom Landwehr, Commissioner
Bob Meier, Policy/Government Relations

2903 Minnesota Environmental Quality Board
520 Lafayette Road North
St Paul, MN 55155
651-757-2014
Fax: 651-296-6334
E-mail: eqb@mnplan.state.mn.us
http://www.eqb.state.mn.us

The mission of the Environmental Quality Board is to lead Minnesota environmental policy by responding to key issues, providing appropriate review and coordination, serving as a public forum and developing long-range strategies toenhance Minnesota's environmental quality. The Environmental Quality Board consists of 10 state agency commissioners or directors and five citizen members. It was established by the Minnesota Legislature in 1973.
Bob Patton, Executive Director
Dave Frederickson, Chair

2904 Minnesota Pollution Control Agency
520 Lafayette Road North
St. Paul, MN 55155-4194
651-296-6300
800-657-3864
Fax: 651-296-7923
http://www.pca.state.mn.us

Established in 1967 to protect Minnesota's environment through monitoring environmental quality and enforcing environmental regulations.
John Linc Stine, Commissioner
Michelle Beeman, Deputy Commissioner

2905 Minnesota Pollution Control Agency: Duluth
525 S Lake Avenue
Suite 400
Duluth, MN 55802
218-723-4660
800-657-3864
Fax: 218-723-4727
http://www.pca.state.mn.us

MPCA staff at Duluth and the other six agency offices: identify environmental problems through testing, monitoring, inspections and research; develop environmental priorities; set standards and propose rules to protect people and theenvironment; develop permits; provide technical assistance; respond to emergencies and encourage pollution prevention and sustainability.
Suzanne Hanson, Manager

2906 Minnesota Sea Grant College Program
University of Minnesota
144 Chester Park
31 W College Street
Duluth, MN 55812
218-726-8106
Fax: 218-726-6556
E-mail: seagr@d.umn.edu
http://www.seagrant.umn.edu

Minnesota Sea Grant is dedicated to providing the tools and technology for responsible management and policy decisions to maintain and enhance Lake Superior and Minnesota's inland aquatic economies and resources. We involveuniversities, federal and state agencies, the public and industry in a partnership to understand the complex nature of the multidisciplinary problems facing us, and then help in the development of the infrastructure necessary for innovativesolutions.
Jeffrey Gunderson, Acting Director
Judy Zomerfelt, Executive Secretary

2907 United States Department of the Army US Army Corps of Engineers
190 5th Street East
Suite 401
St. Paul, MN 55101-1638
651-290-5200
Fax: 651-290-5752
http://www.usace.army.mil

Deliver vital public and military engineering services; partnering in peace and war to strengthen our Nation's security, energize the economy and reduce risks from disasters
Thomas P. Bostick, Commanding General
Todd T. Semonite, Deputy Commanding General

Mississippi

2908 Gulf Coast Research Laboratory
703 E Beach Drive
Ocean Springs, MS 39564
228-872-4200
Fax: 228-872-4204
http://www.usm.edu/gcrl

Operates centers of excellence and national research and development programs in fisheries, geospatial technologies, marine aquaculture, environmental assessment and marine toxicology
Eric N. Powell, Director
Dr Jeffrey M Lotz, Chair

2909 Mississippi Alabama Sea Grant Consortium
703 East Beach Drive
Ocean Springs, MS 39564
228-818-8836
Fax: 228-818-8841
E-mail: swanndl@auburn.edu
http://www.masgc.org

A federal state partnership that is dedicated to activities that foster the conservation and sustainable development of coastal and marine resources in Mississippi and Alabama.

Dr La Don Swann, Director
Stephen Sempier, Deputy Director

2910 Mississippi Department Agriculture & Commerce
121 North Jefferson Street
Jackson, MS 39201
601-359-1100
Fax: 601-354-6290
E-mail: WebMaster@mdac.ms.gov
http://www.mdac.state.ms.us/Index.asp

The mission of the Mississippi Department of Agriculture and Commerce is to regulate and promote agricultural-related businesses within the state and to promote Mississippi's products throughout both the state and the rest of the worldfor the benefit of all Mississippi citizens.
Cindy Hyde-Smith, Commissioner

2911 Mississippi Department of Environmental Quality
PO Box 2261
Jackson, MS 39225
601-961-5171
888-786-0661
E-mail: charles-chisolm@deq.state.ms.us
http://www.deq.state.ms.us

Mission: To safeguard the health, safety, and welfare of present and future generations of Mississippians by conserving and improving our environment and fostering wise economic growth through focused research and responsibleregulation.
Trudy D Fisher, Executive Director
Martha Dairymple, Chairman

2912 Mississippi Department of Wildlife, Fisheries and Parks
1505 Eastover Drive
Jackson, MS 39211
601-432-2400
http://www.mdwfp.com

It is the mission of the Mississippi Department of Wildlife, Fisheries and Parks to conserve and enhance Mississippi's natural resources, to provide continuing outdoor recreational opportunities, to maintain the ecological integrityand aesthetic quality of the resources and to ensure socioeconomic and educational opportunities for present and future generations.
Jerry Munro, Chairman
Sam Polles, Executive Director

2913 Mississippi Forestry Commission
660 North Street
Suite 300
Jackson, MS 39202
601-359-1386
Fax: 601-359-1349
http://www.mfc.ms.gov

Mission: To provide active leadership in forest protection, forest management, forest inventory and effective forest information distribution, necessary for Mississippi's sustainable forset-based economy.
Floyd Hobbs, Chairman
Joseph E. Pettigrew, Vice Chair

2914 Mississippi State Department of Health Bureau of Child/Adolescent Health
PO Box 1700
Jackson, MS 39215
601-576-7464
866-453-4948
http://www.msdh.state.ms.us

The Mississippi Department of Health's mission is to promote and protect the health of the citizens of Missippi. Geographic focus: Missippi other organizational activies, not directed specifically toward children; advocacy, directservice delivery, education, organizing, regulation, social services
Sam Valentine, Director

2915 United States Department of the Army US Army Corps of Engineers
4155 Clay Street
Vicksburg, MS 39180
601-631-5972
http://www.usace.army.mil

Deliver vital public and military engineering services; partnering in peace and war to strengthen our Nation's security, energize the economy and reduce risks from disasters
Thomas P. Bostick, Commanding General
Todd T. Semonite, Deputy Commanding General

Missouri

2916 **Missouri Conservation Department**
3500 East Gans Road
Columbia, MO 65201
573-815-7901
Fax: 573-815-7902
http://mdc.mo.gov

2917 **Missouri Department of Natural Resources**
PO Box 176
Jefferson City, MO 65102
573-751-3443
800-361-4827
Fax: 573-751-7627
E-mail: contact@dnr.mo.gov
http://www.dnr.mo.gov

The Department of Natural Resources preserves, protects and enhances Missouri's natural, cultural and energy resources and works to inspire their enjoyment and responsible use for present and future generations. Our staff work toensure that our state enjoys clean air to breathe, clean water for drinking and recreation and land that sustains a diversity of life.
Sara Parker Pauley, Director

2918 **Natural Resources Department: Air Pollution Control**
PO Box 176
Jefferson City, MO 65102
573-751-4817
800-334-6946
Fax: 573-751-8656
E-mail: cleanair@dnr.mo.gov
http://www.dnr.mo.gov

Mission: To maintain the purity of Missouri's air to protect the health, general welfare and property of the people
Jack Baker, Chairman
Gary Pendergrass, Vice Chair

2919 **Natural Resources Department: Energy Center**
PO Box 176
Jefferson City, MO 65102
573-751-3443
800-361-4827
Fax: 573-751-6860
E-mail: energy@dnr.mo.gov
http://www.dnr.mo.gov

A nonregulatory state agency that works to protect the environment and stimulate the economy through energy efficiency and renewable energy resources and technologies.

2920 **Natural Resources Department: Environmental Improvement and Energy Resources Authority**
PO Box 744
Jefferson City, MO 65102
573-751-4919
Fax: 573-635-3486
E-mail: eiera@dnr.mo.gov
http://www.dnr.mo.gov

A quasi-governmental agency that serves as the financing arm for the Missouri Department of Natural Resources.
Deron Cherry, Director
Andy Dalton, Director

2921 **United States Department of the Army US Army Corps of Engineers**
US Army Engineer District
601 E 12th Street
Room 736
Kansas City, MO 64106
816-389-3486
http://www.usace.army.mil

Deliver vital public and military engineering services; partnering in peace and war to strengthen our Nation's security, energize the economy and reduce risks from disasters
Thomas P. Bostick, Commanding General
Todd T. Semonite, Deputy Commanding General

Montana

2922 **Butte District Advisory Council**
106 N Parkmont
Butte, MT 59702
406-533-7600
Fax: 406-533-7660
E-mail: mt_butte_fo@blm.gov
http://www.mt.blm.gov/bdo/

Jamie Conell, State Director
Theresa Hanley, Deputy State Director

2923 **Crown of the Continent Research Learning Center - Glacier National Park**
PO Box 128
West Glacier, MT 59936
406-888-7800
Fax: 406-888-7808
E-mail: tara_carolin@nps.gov
http://www.nps.gov/glac/naturescience/ccrlc/htm

Designed to increase the effectiveness and communication of research and science results in national parks through facilitating the use of parks for scientific inquiry, supporting science-informed decision making, communicating therelevance of and providing access to knowledge gained through scientific research, and promoting science literacy and resource stewardship
Tara Carolin, Director
Melissa Sladek, Science Comm Specialist

2924 **Environmental Quality Council**
State Capitol, Room 171
PO Box 201704
Helena, MT 59620-1704
406-444-3742
Fax: 406-444-3971
E-mail: teverts@mt.gov
http://www.leg.mt.gov/lepo.asp

The EQC is a state legislative committee create by the 1971 Montana Environmental Policy Act. As outlined in MEPA, the EQC'S purpose is to encourage conditions under which people can coexist with nature in productive harmony. TheCouncil fulfills this purpose by assisting the Legislature in the development of natural resource and environmental policy, by conducting studies on related issues and by serving in an advisory capacity to the state's natural resource programs.

Jim Keane, Chairman
Duane Ankney

2925 **Lewiston District Advisory Council Bureau of Land Management**
920 Northeast Main Street
PO Box 1160
Lewistown, MT 59457
406-538-1900
Fax: 406-538-1904
http://www.blm.gov.mt

Manages approximately 750,300 surface acres of public land scattered across eight counties in central Montana

2926 **Montana Department of Agriculture**
302 North Roberts
Helena, MT 59620-0201
406-444-3144
Fax: 406-444-5409
E-mail: agr@mt.us
http://www.agr.mt.gov

Mission: To protect producers and consumers and to enhance and develop agriculture and allied industries.
Ron de Yong, Acting Director

2927 **Montana Natural Heritage Program**
1515 East 6th Avenue
Helena, MT 59620-1800
406-444-5354
Fax: 406-444-0266
E-mail: mtnhp@mt.gov
http://www.mtnhp.org

The Montana Natural Heritage Program is the state's source for information on the status and distribution of our native animals and plants, emphasizing species of concern and high quality habitats such as wetlands.
Allan Cox, Lead Program Manager
Darlene Patzer, Finance/Grants Administrator

2928 **Natural Resources & Conservation Department**
1625 11th Avenue
Helena, MT 59601
406-444-2074
Fax: 406-444-2684
http://www.dnrc.mt.gov

To help ensure that Montana's land and water resources provide benefits for present and future generations
John Tubbs, Director

Nebraska

2929 Central Interstate Low-Level Radioactive Waste Commission
PO Box 4770
Lincoln, NE 68504-770
402-476-8247
Fax: 402-476-8205
E-mail: rita@cillrwcc.org
http://www.cillrwcc.org
Rita Houskie, Administrator

2930 Department of Agriculture: Natural Resources Conservation Service
National Soil Survey Center
100 Centennial Mall N Room 152
Lincoln, NE 68508-3866
402-437-5499
Fax: 402-437-5336
http://www.soils.usda.gov
Developing and maintaining soil survey data and information systems; assistance in planning regional work planning conferences; liaison to NCSS Regional Agriculture Experiment Station Soil Survey Committees; and technical coordinationat the national level
Jonathan W. Hempel, Director
Linda M. Bouc, Administrative Assistant

2931 Department of Natural Resources
301 Centennial Mall S
PO Box 94676
Lincoln, NE 68509
402-471-2363
Fax: 402-471-2900
http://www.dnr.ne.gov
State Natural Resources Agency
Ann Saloman Bleed, Director
Brian P Dunnigan, Deputy Director

2932 Nebraska Department of Agriculture
301 Centennial Mall S
PO Box 94947
Lincoln, NE 68509-4947
402-471-2341
Fax: 402-471-6876
E-mail: agr.webmaster@nebraska.gov
http://www.agr.ne.gov
Regulatory state agency.

Greg Ibach, Director
Bobbie Kriz-Wickham, Assistant Director

2933 Nebraska Department of Environmental Quality
1200 N Street Suite 400
PO Box 98922
Lincoln, NE 68509
402-471-2186
Fax: 402-471-2909
E-mail: MoreInfo@NDEQ.state.NE.US
http://www.deq.state.ne.us
Mission: To protect the quality of Nebraska's environment-our air, land, and water resources. Enforce regulations and provide assistance.

2934 Nebraska Ethanol Board
301 Centennial Mall S
PO Box 94922
Lincoln, NE 68509
402-471-2941
Fax: 402-471-2470
E-mail: info@ne-ethanol.org
http://www.ne-ethanol.org
The Nebraska Ethanol Board assists ethanol producers with programs and strategies for marketing ethanol and related co-products. The Board supports organizations and policies that advocate the increased use of ethanol fuels, andadministers public information, education and ethanol research projects. The Board also assists companies and organizations in the development of ethanol production facilities in Nebraska.

Todd C Sneller, Administrator
Steve Sorum, Project Manager

2935 Nebraska Game & Parks Commission: Fisheries Division
2200 N 33rd Street
PO Box 30370
Lincoln, NE 68503
402-471-5552
Fax: 402-471-4992
E-mail: Donna.Waller@nebraska.gov
http://www.outdoornebraska.ne.gov
Mission: Stewardship of the state's fish, wildlife, park, and outdoor recreation resources in the best long-term interests of the people and those resources
James Douglas, Director
Tim McCoy, Deputy Director

2936 Nebraska Games & Parks Commission
2200 North 33rd Street
Lincoln, NE 68503
402-471-0641
E-mail: webmaster@ngpc.ne.gov
http://www.outdoornebraska.ne.gov
Mission: Stewardship of the state's fish, wildlife, park, and outdoor recreation resources in the best long-term interests of the people and those resources
James Douglas, Director
Tim McCoy, Deputy Director

2937 Nebraska Games & Parks: Wildlife Division
2200 N 33rd Street
PO Box 30370
Lincoln, NE 68503
402-471-5410
Fax: 402-471-4992
E-mail: jim.douglas@nebraska.gov
http://www.outdoornebraska.gov
Mission: Stewardship of the state's fish, wildlife, park, and outdoor recreation resources in the best long-term interests of the people and those resources
James Douglas, Director
Tim McCoy, Deputy Director

2938 United States Department of the Army US Army Corps of Engineers
US Army Engineer District
215 N 17th Street
Omaha, NE 68102-4978
402-995-2417
Fax: 402-221-4626
http://www.usace.army.mil
Deliver vital public and military engineering services; partnering in peace and war to strengthen our Nation's security, energize the economy and reduce risks from disasters
Thomas P. Bostick, Commanding General
Todd T. Semonite, Deputy Commanding General

Nevada

2939 Bureau of Land Management
Department of the Interior
HC 33 Box 33500
Ely, NV 89301
775-289-1800
Fax: 775-289-1910
http://www.blm.gov/nv/st/en/fo/ely_field_office.html

2940 Carson City Field Office Advisory Council
Bureau of Land Management
5665 Morgan Mill Road
Carson City, NV 89701
775-885-6000
Fax: 775-885-6147
http://www.blm.gov/nv/st/en/fo/carson_city_field.html
A Federal Land Management Agency.

2941 Conservation and Natural Resources Department
Wildlife Division, Conservation Education
901 South Stewart Street
Suite1003
Carson City, NV 89701
775-684-2700
Fax: 775-684-2715
E-mail: ndowinfo@govmail.state.nv.us
http://www.dcnr.nv.gov
The Department of Conservation and Natural Resources (DCNR) is responsible for the establishment and administration of goals, objectives and priorities for the preservation of the State's natural resources.
Leo Drozdoff, Director
Kay Scherer, Deputy Director

2942 Conservation and Natural Resources: Water Resources Division
901 South Stewart Street
Suite 2002
Carson City, NV 89701
775-684-2800
Fax: 775-684-2811
E-mail: hricci@wr.state.nv.us
http://www.water.nv.gov

To conserve, protect, manage and enhance the State's water resources for Nevada's citizens through the appropriation and reallocation of the public waters
Jason King, State Engineer
Tracy Taylor, Deputy

2943 **Department of the Interior: Bureau of Reclamation**
Lower Colorado Regional Office
PO Box 61470
Boulder City, NV 89006
702-293-8000
Fax: 702-293-8418
http://cdiac.esd.ornl.gov/
Manage a number of environmental managment programs related to the lower Colorado River.
Jayne Harkins, Deputy Regional Director

2944 **Las Vegas Bureau of Land Management**
4701 N Torrey Pines Drive
Las Vegas, NV 89130
702-515-5000
http://www.nv.blm.gov
The Bureau of Land Management's mission is to help sustain the health, diversity and productivity of public lands so they can be used and enjoyed by both present and future generations.

2945 **Nevada Bureau of Mines & Geology**
University of Nevada
Mail Stop 178
Reno, NV 89557
775-784-6691
Fax: 775-784-1709
E-mail: nbmg@unr.edu
http://www.nbmg.unr.edu
Research and public service unit of the University of Nevada and is the state geological survey
James E. Faulds, Director/State Geologist

2946 **Nevada Department of Wildlife**
1100 Valley Road
Reno, NV 89512
775-688-1500
Fax: 775-688-1207
http://www.ndow.org
Responsible for the restoration and management of fish and wildlife resources, and the promotion of boating safety on Nevada's waters
Tony Wasley, Director
Rich Haskins, Deputy Director

2947 **Nevada Natural Heritage Program**
901 South Stewart Street
Suite 5002
Carson City, NV 89701
775-684-2900
Fax: 775-684-2909
http://www.heritage.nv.gov
The mission is to develop and maintain a cost effective central information source and inventory of locations, biology, and status of all threatened, endangered, rare and at-risk plants and animals in Nevada.
Jennifer Newmark, Administrator
Jessica Sanders, Office Manager

2948 **Tahoe Regional Planning Agency (TRPA) Advisory Planning Commission**
128 Market Street
Stateline, NV 89449
775-588-4547
Fax: 775-588-4527
E-mail: trpa@trpa.org
http://www.trpa.org
The TRPA leads the cooperative effort to preserve, restore and enhance the natural and human environment of the Lake Tahoe Region. The Code of Ordinances regulates, among other things, land use, density, rate of growth, land coverage,excavation and scenic impacts. These regulations are designed to bring the region into compliance with the threshold standards established for water quality, air quality, soil conservation, wildlife habitat, vegetation, noise, recreation and scenicresources.

New Hampshire

2949 **New Hampshire Department of Environmental Services**
29 Hazen Drive
PO Box 95
Concord, NH 03302-0095
603-271-3503
Fax: 603-271-2867
http://www.des.state.nh.us
Mission: To help sustain a high quality of life for all citizens by protecting and restoring the environment and public health in New Hampshire.
Tom Burack, Commissioner
Vicki V. Quiram, Assistant Commissioner

2950 **New Hampshire Fish and Game Department**
11 Hazen Drive
Concord, NH 03301
603-271-3421
Fax: 603-271-1438
E-mail: info@wildlife.nh.gov
http://www.wildnh.com
As the guardian of the states fish, wildlife and marine resources, the department works with the public to: conserve, manage and protect these resources and their habitats; inform and advise the public about these resources; providethe public with opportunities to use and appreciate these resources.
Gelnn Normandeau, Executive Director
Tanya L Haskell, Administrative Assistant

2951 **New Hampshire State Conservation Committee**
PO Box 3907
Concord, NH 03302
603-271-1092
http://www.nh.gov/scc
Coordinates the work of the ten county conservation districts in the state of New Hampshire.
Jim Raynes, Chairman

2952 **Resources & Development Council: State Planning**
Department of Resources & Economic Development
172 Pembroke Road
P.O. Box 1856
Concord, NH 03302-1856
603-271-2411
Fax: 603-271-2629
E-mail: sboucher@dred.state.nh.us
http://www.dred.state.nh.us
Promoting the principles of smart growth at the state, regional, and local levels through the municipal and regional planning assistance program
Meredith Hatfield, Director
Michele Zydel, Administrative Secretary

2953 **University of New Hampshire Cooperative Extension**
Taylor Hall
59 College Road
Durham, NH 03824
603-862-1520
Fax: 603-862-1585
E-mail: webinfo@unh.edu
http://www.extension.unh.edu
The University of New Hampshire Cooperative Extension provides New Hampshire citizens with research-based education and information, enhancing their ability to make informed decisions that strengthen youth, families and communities,sustain natural resources, and improve the economy.
John Pike, Dean/Director
Lisa Townson, Assistant Director

New Jersey

2954 **New Jersey Department of Agriculture**
PO Box 330
Trenton, NJ 08625
609-292-3976
Fax: 609-292-3978
http://www.nj.gov/agriculture
The New Jersey Department of Agriculture is an agency which oversees programs that serve virutally all New Jersey citizens. A major priority of the NJDA is to promote, protect and serve the Garden State's diverse agriculture andagribusiness industries.
Douglas H. Fisher, Secretary

2955 **New Jersey Department of Environmental Protection**
401 E State Street
7th Floor, E Wing
Trenton, NJ 08625
609-777-3373
866-337-5669
Fax: 609-292-7695
http://www.nj.gov/dep/
A state department dedicated to protecting New Jersey's air, land, water and natural resources.
Bob Martin, Commissioner
Irene Kropp, Deputy Commissioner

2956 New Jersey Department of Environmental Protection: Site Remediation Program
401 E State Street
PO Box 420
Trenton, NJ 08625-0420
609-292-1250
Fax: 609-777-1914
http://www.state.nj.us/dep/srp
Kenneth Kloo, Director
David Sweeney, Assistant Commissioner

2957 New Jersey Division of Fish & Wildlife
501 E State Street, 3rd Fl
PO Box 420
Trenton, NJ 08625-0420
609-292-2965
Fax: 609-292-8207
http://www.njfishandwildlife.com
Our mission is to protect and manage the state's fish and wildlife to maximize their long-term biological, recreation and economic values for all New Jerseyans.
David Chanda, Director
Larry Herrighty, Assistant Director of Operat

2958 New Jersey Geological Survey
PO Box 420
Mail Code:29-01
Trenton, NJ 08625-0420
609-292-1185
Fax: 609-633-1004
E-mail: njgsweb@dep.state.nj.us
http://www.njgeology.org
State agency that maps, interprets and provides geoscience information to the public on geology and ground water resources.
Karl Muessig, State Geologist

2959 New Jersey Pinelands Commission
PO Box 7
15 Springfield Road
New Lisbon, NJ 08064
609-894-7300
Fax: 609-894-7330
E-mail: info@njpines.state.nj.us
http://www.state.nj.us/pinelands/
Mission: To preserve, protect, and enhance the natural and cultural resourcse of the Pinelands National Reserve, and to encourage compatible economic and other human activities consistent with that purpose.
Mark S. Lohbauer, Chairman
Nancy Wittenberg, Executive Director

New Mexico

2960 Albuquerque Bureau of Land Management
435 Montano Road NE
Albuquerque, NM 87107-4935
505-761-8700
Fax: 505-761-8911
http://www.nm.blm.gov
Ed Singleton, District Manager
Ernest J Chavez, Assistant District Manager

2961 Attorney General
Environmental Enforcement
PO Drawer 1508
Santa Fe, NM 87504-1508
505-827-6000
Fax: 505-827-5826
http://www.ago.state.nm.us
Gary King, Attorney General

2962 Energy, Minerals & Natural Resources: Energy Conservation & Management Division
1220 South Street
Francis Drive
Santa Fe, NM 87505
505-476-3310
http://www.emnrd.state.nm.us/ecmd/
Encourages efficient energy use in New Mexico by offerin programs and information for state agencies, companies and induviduals.
Louise N. Martinez, Director

2963 Energy, Minerals and Natural Resources Department
1220 S St. Francis Drive
Santa Fe, NM 87505
505-476-3200
Fax: 505-476-3220
http://www.emnrd.state.nm.us
Mission is to provide leadership in the protection, conservation, management and responsible use of New Mexico's natural resources.
David Martin, Cabinet Secretary
Brett F. Woods, Deputy Cabinet Secretary

2964 New Mexico Bureau of Geology & Mineral Resources
801 Leroy Place
Socorro, NM 87801-4796
505-835-5420
Fax: 505-835-6333
E-mail: scholle1@nmt.edu
http://www.geoinfo.nmt.edu
A service and research division of the New Mexico Institute of Mining and Technology. Acts as the geological survey of New Mexico.
Paul Bauer, Principal Geologist, Assoc.
Bruce Allen, Field Geologist

2965 New Mexico Cooperative Fish & Wildlife Research Unit
New Mexico University MSC 4901
PO Box 30003
Las Cruces, NM 88003
505-646-6053
Fax: 505-646-1281
http://www.swregap.nmsu.edu/info.htm
The New Mexico Research Unit conducts, research on problems of mutual concern to cooperators; graduate academic training; technical assistance in fish and wildlife management; and conservation education through publications, lectures,and demonstrations.
Colleen Caldwell, Leader
Louis Bender, Assistant Unit Leader

2966 New Mexico Department of Game & Fish
PO Box 25112
Santa Fe, NM 87504
505-476-8000
888-248-6866
E-mail: ispa@state.nm.us
http://www.wildlife.state.nm.us
To conserve, regulate, propagate and protect the wildlife and fish within the state of New Mexico using a flexible management system that ensures sustainable use for public food supply, recreation and safety; and to provide foroff-highway motor vehicle recreation that recognizes cultural, historic, and resource values while ensuring public safety
Jim Lane, Director
Alexa Sandoval, Chief

2967 New Mexico Environment Department
1190 St. Francis Drive
Suite N4050
Santa Fe, NM 87505
505-827-2855
800-219-6157
http://www.nmenv.state.nm.us
The New Mexico Environment Department's mission is to provide the highest quality of life throughout the state by promoting a safe, clean, and productive environment.
Ryan Flynn, Cabinet Secretary
Butch Tongate, Deputy Secretary

2968 New Mexico Soil & Water Conservation Commission
MSC APR PO Box 30005
Las Cruces, NM 88003
505-646-2642
Fax: 505-646-1540
E-mail: acoleman@nmda.nmsu.edu
http://www.nmacd.org/state-agencies
Serves as the state entity providing guidance and policy direction to the local Soil and Water Conservation Districts
Jose Varela-Lopez, Chairman

2969 Roswell District Advisory Council: Bureau of Land Management
2909 W 2nd Street
Roswell, NM 88201-2019
505-627-0272
Fax: 505-627-0276
http://www.nm.blm.gov/rfo/index.htm
Larry Ashley, Engine Module Leader

2970 United States Department of the Interior: United States Fish and Wildlife Service
500 Gold Avenue SW
Albuquerque, NM 87102
505-248-6911
E-mail: RDTuggle@fws.gov
http://www.fws.gov/southwest/
Mission: To work with others, to conserve, protect and enhance fish, wildlife, and plants and their habitats for the continuing benefit of the American people.
Benjamin Tuggle, Director

New York

2971 Adirondack Park Agency
1133 NYS Route 86 518-891-4050
PO Box 99 Fax: 518-891-3938
Ray Brook, NY 12977 http://www.apa.state.ny.us
Mission: To protect the public and private resources of the Park through the exercise of the powers and duties provided by law.
Leilani Ulrich, Chair
Richard Booth, Commissioner

2972 Department of Environmental Conservation
625 Broadway 518-402-8545
Albany, NY 12233-0001 800-847-7332
Fax: 518-402-8541
E-mail: dpaeweb@gw.dec.state.ny.us
http://www.dec.ny.gov
Mission: To conserve, improve, and protect New York State's natural resources and environment, and control water, land and air pollution, in order to enhance the health, safety and welfare of the people of the state and their overalleconomic and social well being.
Joe Martens, Commissioner
Marc Gerstman, Executive Dep Commissioner

2973 Department of Environmental Conservation: Division of Air Resources
625 Broadway 518-402-8452
Albany, NY 12233-3250 E-mail: DARWeb@gw.dec.state.ny.us
http://www.dec.ny.gov/about/644.html
Maintains and improves New York State air quality through research, permitting and enforcement.
Jared Snyder, Assistant Commissioner

2974 Department of Environmental Conservation: Division of Mineral Resources
625 Broadway 518-402-8076
3rd Floor Fax: 518-402-8060
Albany, NY 12233-6500 E-mail: dmninfo@gw.dec.state.ny.us
http://www.dec.ny.gov/about/636.html
The Division of Mineral Resources is responsible for ensuring the environmentally sound, economic development of New York's non-renewable energy and mineral resources for the benefit of current and future generations. To carry out thismission, we regulate the extraction of oil and gas, and require the reclamation of land after mining.
Bradley J. Field, Director
Kathleen F. Sanford, Assistant Director

2975 New York Cooperative Fish & Wildlife Research Unit
Cornell University, Fernow Hall 607-255-2839
Natural Resources Department Fax: 607-255-1895
Ithaca, NY 14853-3001 E-mail: dnrcru-mailbox@cornell.edu
http://www.coopunits.org/New_York/index.html
Pays particular attention to the resource problems and issues of the Northeastern States with New York as its focal point

William Fisher, Unit Leader
Mitchell Eaton, Assistant Leader

2976 New York Department of Health
Corning Tower 518-402-7500
Empire State Plaza Fax: 518-402-7509
Albany, NY 12237 http://www.health.state.ny.us
Working together and committed to excellence, we protect and promote the health of New Yorkers through prevention, science and the assurance of quality health care delivery.
Nirav R. Shah, Commissioner

2977 New York State Office of Parks, Recreation and Historic Preservation
Empire State Plaza 518-474-0456
Agency Building 1 http://www.nysparks.com
Albany, NY 12238
The agency operates 168 parks offering a wide variety of recreational, cultural and education activities, and 35 state historic sites; sponsors boating and snowmobiling, nature study and outreach programs; manages grant programs forboating and snowmobiling enforcement and aid to zoos, botanical gardens, aquariums; and administers funds for federal historical preservation and parks programs, the Environmental Protection Fund and the 1996 Clean Water/Clean Air Bond act.
Rose Harvey, Commissioner

2978 New York State Soil and Water Conservation Committee
10B Airline Drive 518-457-3738
Albany, NY 12235 Fax: 518-457-3412
E-mail: virginia.weston@agriculture.ny.gov
http://www.nys-soilandwater.org
The New York State Soil and Water Conservation Committee is composed of voting and advisory members who represent a wide range of agricultural, environmental and other interests. The Committee operates through a network of partnershipsbetween state, federal and local agencies, as well as citizen interests and the private sector. The mission of the Committee is to develop and oversee and agricultural nonpoint source water quality program for New York State.
Michael Latham, Director
Brian Steinmuller, Assistant Director

2979 Tug Hill Tomorrow Land Trust
PO Box 6063 315-779-8240
Watertown, NY 13601 Fax: 315-782-6192
E-mail: thtomorr@northnet.org
http://www.tughilltomorrowlandtrust.org
A regional, private, nonprofit founded by a group of Tug Hill residents to serve the region of 2,100 square miles serving portions of Jefferson, Lewis, Oneida & Oswego Counties. The mission is two-fold: increase awareness andappreciation of the Tug Hill Rgion through education; and to help retain the forest, farm, recreation, and wild land of the region through voluntary, private land protection efforts.

Bob Quinn, Chairman
George Bibbins, Vice Chair

2980 United States Department of the Army US Army Corps of Engineers
1776 Niagara Street 716-879-4410
Buffalo, NY 14207-3199 http://www.lrb.usace.army.mil
Delivers world class engineering solutions to the Great Lakes Region, the Army, and the Nation in order to ensure national security, environmental sustainability, water resource management, and emergency assistance during peace and war
LTC Owen J. Beaudoin, Commander and District Engin
MAJ Michael A. Busby, Deputy Commander

North Carolina

2981 Carnivore Preservation Trust
1940 Hanks Chapel Road 919-542-4684
Pittsboro, NC 27312 Fax: 919-542-4454
E-mail: info@cptigers.org
http://www.cptigers.org
Is a wildlife sanctuary, offering unique opportunities to learn about these animals and their critical importance to our quality of life on Earth.
Pam Fulk, Executive Director
Amanda Byrne, IT Administrator

2982 Department of Agriculture & Consumer Services
2 West Edenton Street 919-707-3000
Raleigh, NC 27601 http://www.ncagr.com
Mission: To improve the state of agriculture in North Carolina by providing services to farmers and agribusinesses, and to serve the citizens of North Carolina by providing services and enforcing laws to protect consumers.
Steve Troxler, Commissioner

2983 **North Carolina Board of Science and Technology**
301 North Wilmington Street 919-715-0303
1326 Mail Service Center Fax: 919-733-8356
Raleigh, NC 27699-1326 E-mail: tguffey@nccommerce.com
http://www.ncscienceandtechnology.com
Encourages, promotes, and supports scientific, engineering, and industrial research applications in North Carolina.
John Hardin, Executive Director
Trudy Guffey, Executive Assistant

2984 **North Carolina Department of Environment and Natural Resources**
1601 Mail Service Center 919-733-4984
Raleigh, NC 27699-1601 877-623-6748
Fax: 919-715-3060
http://www.enr.state.nc.us
John E. Skvarla, III, Secretary
Lacy Presnell, General Counsel

2985 **United States Department of the Army US Army Corps of Engineers**
69 Darlington Avenue 910-251-4626
PO Box 1890 910-251-4185
Wilmington, NC 28403 http://www.saw.usace.army.mil
Provides quality planning, design, construction, and operations products and services to meet the needs of civilian and military customers.
Colonel Steven Baker, Commander
Lieutenant Colo King, Deputy Commander

North Dakota

2986 **Dakotas Resource Advisory Council: Department of the Interior**
Bureau of Land Management
99 23rd Avenue West 701-227-7700
Suite A Fax: 701-227-7701
Dickinson, ND 58601 http://www.blm.gov
The Dakotas Council currently has 15 members. It is structured to provide a balance of membership by area of expertise, training, and experience. It consists of five individuals in each of three categories.

2987 **ND Game and Fish Department**
100 N Bismarck Expressway 701-328-6300
Bismarck, ND 58501-5095 Fax: 701-328-6352
E-mail: ndgf@nd.gov
http://www.gf.nd.gov
To protect, conserve and enhance fish and wildlife populations and their habitats for sustained public consumptive and nonconsumptive use.
Terry Steinwood, Director
Duane DeKrey, Deputy Director

2988 **North Dakota Forest Service**
307 First Street E 701-228-5422
Bottineau, ND 58318-1100 Fax: 701-228-5448
E-mail: forest@nd.gov
http://www.nd.gov/forest
The ND Forest Service administers forestry programs statewide. The agency operates a nursery at Towner specializing in the production of conifer tree stock. The nursery is the sole supplier of evergreen seedlings in North Dakota.Technial assistance relating to the management of private forest lands, state forest lands, urban and community forests, tree planting and wildland fire protection is provided by the agency. The ND Forest Service also owns and manages app. 13,278acres of state lands.

Larry Kotchman, State Forester
Kathy Wyman, Administrative Assistant

2989 **North Dakota Parks and Recreation Department**
1600 E Century Ave. 701-328-5357
Suite 3 Fax: 701-328-5363
Bismarck, ND 58503 E-mail: parkrec@state.nd.us
http://www.ndparks.com
The state government agency charged with managing North Dakota's state parks and recreation areas; the state's nature preserves and natural area programs; motorized and non-motorized trail programs; recreational grants and state-widerecreation planning; and state scenic byways program.

Douglass A Prchal, Director
Dorothy Streyle, Coordinator

Ohio

2990 **Division of Environmental Services**
Ohio EPA
8955 East Main Street 614-644-4247
Reynoldsburg, OH 43068 Fax: 614-644-4272
http://www.epa.state.oh.us/des
The Division of Environmental Services provides biological and chemical data and technical assistance to other divisions within Ohio EPA, state and local agencies, and private entities in order to help monitor and protect human healthand the environment to ensure a high quality of life in Ohio.
Steve Roberts, Quality Assurance Supervisor

2991 **Environmental Protection Agency: Ohio Division of Surface Water**
50 West Town Street 614-644-2001
Suite 700 Fax: 614-644-2745
Columbus, OH 43215 http://www.epa.state.oh.us/dsw
To protect, enhance and restore all waters of the state for the health, safety and welfare of present and future generations. We accomplish this mission by monitoring the aquatic environment, permitting, enforcing environmental laws,using and refining scientifically sound methods and regulations, planning, coordinating, educating, providing technical assistance and encouraging pollution prevention practices.
George Elmaraghy, Division Chief
Brian Hall, Assistant Chief

2992 **Lead Poisoning Prevention Program**
Ohio Department of Health
246 N High Street 614-466-5332
Columbus, OH 43215 877-532-3723
Fax: 614-728-6793
E-mail: lead@odh.ohio.gov
http://www.odh.state.oh.us/data
The Lead Poisoning Prevention Program ensures the public receives safe and proper lead abatement, detection, and analytical services by requiring those services be conducted according to federal and state regulations, and by trainedand licensed personnel.
Chris Alexander, Program Supervisor
Pam Blais, Environmental Supervisor

2993 **Ohio Department of Natural Resources Division of Geological Survey**
2045 Morse Rd 614-265-6576
Bldg C Fax: 614-447-1918
Columbus, OH 43229-6693 E-mail: geo.survey@dnr.state.oh.us
http://www.ohiodnr.com/geosurvey
Provides geologic information and services for responsible management of Ohio's natural resources. Geologic maps, reports and data files developed by the division can be used by individuals, educators, industry, business andgovernment.

Thomas J. Serenko, Division Chief
Mike P. Angle, Assistant Chief

2994 **Ohio Environmental Protection Agency**
50 West Town Street
Suite 700
Columbus, OH 43215
614-644-2782
Fax: 614-644-2329
E-mail: request@www.epa.state.oh.us
http://www.epa.state.oh.us

Mission: To protect the environment and public health by ensuring compliance with environmental laws and demonstrating leadership in environmental stewardship.
Scott J. Nally, Director
Laura Factor, Assistant Director

2995 **Ohio River Valley Water Sanitation Commission**
5735 Kellogg Avenue
Cincinnati, OH 45230
513-231-7719
Fax: 513-231-7761
E-mail: info@orsanco.org
http://www.orsanco.org

ORSANCO operates programs to improve water quality in the Ohio River and its tributaries, including: setting waste water discharge standards; performing biological assessment; monitoring for the chemical and physical properties of thewaterways; and conducting special surveys and studies. Also coordinates emergency response activities for spills or accidental discharges to the river and promotes public participating programs.
Kenneth Komoroski, Chairman
Toby Frevert, Vice-Chairman

2996 **Ohio Water Development Authority**
480 South High Street
Columbus, OH 43215
614-466-5822
Fax: 614-644-9964
http://www.owda.org

Provides financial assistance for environmental infrastructure from the sale of municipal revenue bonds through loans to local governments in Ohio and issuing Industrial Revenue Bonds for qualified projects. The vision of OWDA is tocontinue to provide assistance for environmental infrastructure by being responsive to the needs of local government agencies, enhancing the provision of financial and technical assistance and developing new financial assistance products for theprivate sector.

James P. Joyce, Chairman
Steve Grossman, Executive Director

Oklahoma

2997 **Oklahoma Department of Environmental Quality**
PO Box 1677
Oklahoma City, OK 73101-1677
405-702-0100
800-869-1400
Fax: 405-702-1001
http://www.deq.state.ok.us

Administers environmental laws considering both the economy of today and the environment of tomorrow.

2998 **Oklahoma Department of Health**
1000 Northeast 10th Street
Oklahoma, OK 73117
405 271-5600
800-522-0203
Fax: 405-271-6199
http://www.health.state.ok.us

The Oklahoma State Department of Health is to protect and promote the health of citizens of Oklahoma and to prevent disease and injury, and to assure the conditions by which our citizens can be healthy.
Terry L. Cline, Commissioner

2999 **Salt Plains National Wildlife Refuge**
Route 1 Box 76
Jet, OK 73749
580-626-4794
Fax: 580-626-4793
E-mail: fw2_rw_saltplains@fws.gov
http://saltplains.fws.gov

Provide quality habitat for migratory waterfowl
Debbie Pike, Park Ranger

3000 **Water Quality Division**
5225 N Shurtel
Oklahoma City, OK 73118
405-702-8100
800-869-1400
Fax: 405-810-1046
http://www.deq.state.ok.us/WQDNew

Larry Edmison, Director

Oregon

3001 **Burns District: Bureau of Land Management**
Department of the Interior
28910 Highway 20 West
Hines, OR 97738
541-573-4400
E-mail: BLM_OR_BU_Mail@blm.gov=
http://www.blm.gov/or/districts/burns

Dana Shuford, Manager
Melissa Towers, Administrative Officer

3002 **Department of Transportation**
355 Capitol St. NE
Salem, OR 97301-3871
888-275-6368
Fax: 503-986-3432
http://www.oregon.gov/odot

Mission: To provide a safe, efficient transportation system that supports economic opportunity and livable communities for Oregonians.
Pat Egan, Chairman
David Lohman, Commissioner

3003 **Eugene District: Bureau of Land Management**
Department of the Interior
PO Box 10226
Eugene, OR 97440
541-683-6600
888-442-3061
Fax: 541-683-6981
E-mail: OR_Eugene_Mail@blm.gov
http://www.blm.gov/or/districts/eugene

The Eugene District manages several ecosystems ranging from coastal inlands to dense Douglas-fir, hemlock, and cedar forests. The wide variation in the lands managed by the District offers the perfect compromise between the urban parksin the cities and the high elevation recreation opportunities in the adjacent Willamette, Siuslaw and Umpqua National Forest.
Ginnie Grilley, Manager

3004 **Klamath River Compact Commission**
280 Main Street
Klamath Falls, OR 97601-6331
541-882-4436
Created by the Klamath River Compact in 1957, KRCC is a three member commission whose purpose, with respect to the water of the Klamath River Basin, is to faciliate and promote the orderly, integrated, and comprehensive developement,use, conservation and control of water for development of lands by irrigation, protection of fish and wildlife, domestic and industrial use, hydropower, navigation, and flood protection.

3005 **Lakeview District: Bureau of Land Management**
Department of the Interior
1301 South G Street
Lakeview, OR 97630
541-947-2177
Fax: 541-947-6399
E-mail: BLM_OR_LV_Mailbox@blm.gov
http://www.blm.gov/or/districts/lakeview

3006 **Medford District: Bureau of Land Management**
3040 Biddle Road
Medford, OR 97504
541-618-2200
E-mail: BLM_OR_MD_Mail@blm.gov
http://www.blm.gov/or/districts/medford

The Bureau of Land Management's Medford District oversees approximately 862,000 acres of scattered public lands between the Cascade and Siskiyou mountain ranges and from the Oregon/California border to Canyon Creek and southern DouglasCounty. This large land base is divided into four Resource Areas: Ashland, Butte Falls, Grants Pass and Glendale.

3007 Oregon Department of Environmental Quality
811 SW Sixth Avenue
Portland, OR 97204-1390
503-229-5696
800-452-4011
Fax: 503-229-6124
E-mail: deq.info@deq.state.or.us
http://www.oregon.gov/deq

Mission: To be a leader in restoring, maintaining and enhancing the quality of Oregon's air, land and water.

Dick Pederson, Director
Joni Hammond, Deputy Director

3008 Oregon Department of Fish and Wildlife
3406 Cherry Avenue NE
Salem, OR 97303
503-947-6000
800-720-6339
E-mail: odfw.info@state.or.us
http://www.dfw.state.or.us

Commissioners formulate general state programs and policies concerning management and conservation of fish wildlife resources and establishes seasons, methods and bag limits for recreational and commercial take.

Roy Elicker, Director
David Lane, Deputy Administrator-Informa

3009 Oregon Department of Forestry
2600 State Street
Salem, OR 97310
503-945-7200
800-437-4490
Fax: 503-945-7212
http://www.odf.state.or.us

Mission: To serve the people of Oregon by protecting, managing, and promoting stewardship of Oregon's forests to enhance environmental, economic, and community sustainability.

Doug Decker, State Forester
Paul Bell, Deputy State Forester

3010 Oregon Department of Land Conservation and Development
635 Capitol Street NE
Suite 150
Salem, OR 97301-2540
503-373-0050
Fax: 503-378-5518
http://www.lcd.state.or.us

Mission: Support all of our partners in creating and implementing comprehensive plans that reflect and balance the statewide planning goals, the vision of citizens, and the interests of local, state, federal and tribal governments.

Jim Rue, Director
Caroline Maclaren, Deputy Director

3011 Oregon Water Resource Department
725 Summer Street Northeast
Suite A
Salem, OR 97301
503-986-0900
Fax: 503-986-0904
E-mail: webmaster@wrd.state.or.us
http://www.wrd.state.or.us

Mission: To serve the public by practicing and promoting responsible water management through two key goals: to directly address Oregon's water supply needs; and to restore and protect streamflows and watersheds in order to ensure thelong-term sustainability of Oregon's ecosystems, economy, and quality of life.

Phillip C Ward, Director
Brenda Bateman, Public Information Officer

3012 Prineville District: Bureau of Land Management
Department of the Interior
3050 NE Third Street
Prineville, OR 97754
541-416-6700
Fax: 541-416-6798
E-mail: BLM_OR_PR_Mail@blm.gov
http://www.blm.gov/or/districts/prineville

Debbie Henderson-Norton, Manager
Steve Robertson, Associate Manager

3013 Roseburg District: Bureau of Land Management
Department of the Interior
777 NW Garden Valley Boulevard
Roseburg, OR 97471
541-440-4930
Fax: 541-440-4948
E-mail: BLM_OR_RB_Mail@blm.gov
http://www.blm.gov/or/districts/roseburg

Public lands of the Roseburg District, located in southwestern Oregon, contain some of the most productive forests in the world. An important mainstay of the local economy, which acquires timber from both private and federal lands inthe region. The district is criss-crossed with streams and rivers that support sport fishing. With Interstate 5 running through the middle of the district, and east-west state highways connecting Crater Lake to the Pacfic coast, the district drawsmany tourists.

3014 Salem District: Bureau of Land Management
Department of the Interior
1717 Fabry Road Southeast
Salem, OR 97306
503-375-5646
Fax: 503-375-5622
E-mail: BLM_OR_SA_Mail@blm.gov
http://www.blm.gov/or/districts/salem

BLM Mission: to sustain the health, diversity and productivity of the public lands for the use and enjoyment of present and future generations. Salem District manages 400,000 acres scattered across 13 counties. Seventy three percent ofOregon's population live within the boundries of this district. Their major focus is an ecosystem management approach involving many different disciplines. Salem employs 200 full-time employees working in forestry, land surveying, wildlife biology,hydrology, etc.

Aaron Horton, Manager
Don Hollenkamp, Associate Manager

3015 United States Department of the Army: US Army Corps of Engineers
US Army Engineer Division
PO Box 2946
Portland, OR 97208
503-808-5150

3016 Vale District: Bureau of Land Management
Department of the Interior
100 Oregon Street
Vale, OR 97918
541-473-3144
Fax: 541-473-6213
E-mail: BLM_OR_VL_Mail@blm.gov
http://www.blm.gov/or/districts/vale

The Vale District of the Bureau of Land Management manages 4.9 million acres of public land in eastern Oregon. The mission of the BLM is to sustain the health, diversity, and productivity of the public lands for the use and enjoymentof present and future generations.

Dave Henderson, Manager
Larry Frazier, Associate Manager

Pennsylvania

3017 Allegheny National Forest
US Forest Service
4 Farm Colony Road
Warren, PA 16365
814-723-5150
Fax: 814-726-1465
E-mail: r9_allegheny_nf@fs.fed.us
http://www.fs.fed.us/r9/allegheny

An organization dedicated to providing advice for development of the corridor management plan for the northern section of the Allegheny River that has been designated as a National Wild and Scenic River.

Erin Connelly, Forest Supervisor

3018 Childhood Lead Poisoning Prevention Program
Pennsylvania Department of Health
PO Box 90
Harrisburg, PA 17108
717-783-8451
Fax: 717-772-0323

The mission of the Pennsylvania Department of Health, Childhood Lead Poisoning Prevention Program is to make the citizens of the Commonwealth aware of the dangers of lead poisoning and to reduce the number of children who becomelead-poisoned.

3019 Citizens Advisory Council
Pennsylvania Department Environmental Protection
13th Floor, RCSOB
PO Box 8459
Harrisburg, PA 17105-8549
717-787-4527
Fax: 717-787-2878
E-mail: mahughes@pa.gov
http://www.depweb.state.pa.us/cac

Advises the Department of Environmental Protection, the Governor and the General Assembly on environmental issues and the work of the Department.

Susan Wilson, Executive Director
Joyce Hatala, Chair

3020 Department of the Interior: National Parks
200 Chestnut Street 215-597-7013
5th Floor Fax: 215-597-8015
Philadelphia, PA 19106 http://www.nps.gov
Dennis Reidenbach, Regional Director

3021 Environmental Protection Agency: Region III
1650 Arch Street 215-814-5000
Philadelphia, PA 19103-2029 800-438-2474
http://www.epa.gov/region03
Region III is responsible for federal environmental programs in Delaware, Maryland, Pennsylvania, Virginia, West Virginia and District of Columbia. Programs include air and water pollution control; toxic substances, pesticides, anddrinking water regulation; wetlands protection; hazardous waste management, hazardous waste dump site cleanup; and some aspects of radioactive materials regulation.
Shawn M. Garvin, Administrator

3022 Lacawac Sanctuary Foundation
94 Sanctuary Road 570-689-9494
Lake Ariel, PA 18436 Fax: 570-689-2017
E-mail: info@lacawac.org
http://www.lacawac.org
A nature preserve and historic site in northeastern PA's Pocono Mountains. The main function is the protection of its natural areas and historic buildings, including the pristine glacial Lake Lacawac. Research space is available forvisiting researchers, and participants in the Pocono Comparative Lakes Program.
Bob Sadoski, Executive Director
Lesley Knoll, Director of Research and Edu

3023 Pennsylvania Department of Conservation and Natural Resources
Rachel Carson State Office Building 717-787-2869
400 Market Street, PO Box 8767 Fax: 717-772-9106
Harrisburg, PA 17105-8767 E-mail: ra-askdcnr@state.pa.us
http://www.dcnr.state.pa.us
Mission: To maintain, improve and preserve state parks; to manage state forest lands to assure their long-term health, sustainability and economic use; to provide information on Pennsylvania's ecological and geological resources; andto administer grant and technical assistance programs that will benefit rivers conservation, trails and greenways, local recreation, regional heritage conservation and environmental education programs across Pennsylvania.
Ellen Ferretti, Secretary
Jennifer Stepulitis, Executive Secretary

3024 Pennsylvania Fish & Boat Commission: Northeast Region
5566 Main Road 570-477-5717
Sweet Valley, PA 18656 Fax: 570-477-3221
E-mail: ra-needureach@pa.gov
http://www.fishandboat.com
Mission: To protect, conserve, and enhance the Commonwealth's aquatic resources and provide fishing and boating opportunities.
Steven M. Ketterer, President
G. Warren Elliott, Vice-President

3025 Pennsylvania Forest Stewardship Program
PO Box 8552 717-787-2106
Harrisburg, PA 17105
Forest stewardship is a US Forest Service program with the goal of helping private landowners manage their lands for various objectives. Landowners participating in the Forest Stewardship Program work with a private forestry consultantto depelop a customized plan for their land and objetives. Studies show that landowners that work with professionals and follow their customized plan are more likely to engage in practices that sustain forest values.

3026 Pennsylvania Game Commission
2001 Elmerton Avenue 717-787-4250
Harrisburg, PA 17110 Fax: 717-772-0542
http://www.pgc.state.pa.us
The Pennsylvania Game Commission has the specific responsibility of acting as steward of the Commonwealth's wild birds and wild animals for the benefit of present and future generations. In carrying out this state constitutionalmandate, the Pennsylvania Game Commission will: Protect, conserve and manage the diversity of wildlife and their habitats; Provide wildlife related education, services, and recreational opportunities for both consumptive and non-consumptive uses ofwildlife.
Thomas Boop, President
Roxane Palone, Vice President

3027 Susquehanna River Basin Commission
1721 N Front Street 717-238-0423
Harrisburg, PA 17102 Fax: 717-238-2436
E-mail: srbc@srbc.net
http://www.srbc.net
The responsibility of SRBC is to enhance public welfare through comprehensive planning, water supply allocation & management of the water resources of the Susquehanna River Basin. The SRBC works to reduce damages caused by floods;provide for the reasonable & sustained development & use of surface & ground water for municipal, agricultural, recreational, commercial & industrial purposes; protect & restore fisheries, wetlands & aquatic habitat; protect water quality & instreamuses.
Paul O Swartz, Executive Director
Thomas W. Beauduy, Deputy Executive Director

3028 United States Department of the Army US Army Corps of Engineers
US Army Engineer District
1000 Liberty Avenue 412-395-7500
Pittsburgh, PA 15222-4186 Fax: 412-644-2811
http://www.usace.army.mil
Michael P Crall, District Engineer
Peter A Stelnig, Deputy District Engineer

Rhode Island

3029 Division of Parks and Recreation
2321 Hartford Avenue 401-222-2632
Johnston, RI 02919 Fax: 401-934-6010
E-mail: riparks@earthlink.net
http://www.riparks.com
The objective of the Division of Parks & Recreation is to provide all Rhode Island Residents and Visitors the opportunity to enjoy a diverse mix of well-maintained, scenic, safe, accessible areas and facilities within our park systemand to offer a variety of outdoor recreational opportunities and programming which may benefit and enhance our Quality of Life.

3030 Environmental Management: Division of Fish and Wildlife
4808 Tower Hill Road 401-789-3094
Wakefield, RI 02879 Fax: 401-783-4460
http://www.state.ri.us/dems/programs/
Agency manages the fish and wildlife resources of the State of Rhode Island inluding marine fisheries. The division has 60 employees and is located in 4 stations statwide.

Michael Lapisky, Chief

3031 Rhode Island Department of Environmental Management
235 Promenade Street 401-222-6800
Providence, RI 02908 http://www.dem.ri.gov
We are committed to preserving the quality of Rhode Island's environment, maintaining and safety of its residents and protecting

the natural systems upon which life depends. Together with many partners, we offer assistance toindividuals, business and municipalities, conduct research, find solutions, and enforce laws created to protect the environment.
W Michael Sullivan, Director

3032 Rhode Island Department of Evironmental Management: Forest Environment
1037 Hartford Pike 401-647-4389
North Scituate, RI 02857 Fax: 401-647-3590
http://www.dem.ri.gov/programs.bnaters/forest/index.htm
Coordinates a statewide forest fire protection plan, provides forest fire protection on state lands, assists rural volunteer fire departments, and develops forest and wildlife management plans for private landowners who choose tomanage their property in ways that will protect these resources on their land. The program promotes public understanding of environmental conservation, enforces Department rules and regulations on DEM lands.
Catherine Sparks, Chief

3033 Rhode Island Water Resources Board
1 Capitol Hill 401-574-8400
3rd Floor Fax: 401-574-8401
Providence, RI 02908 http://www.wrb.state.ri.us
An executive agency of state government charged with managingther proper development, utilization and conservation of water resources. The primary responsibility is to ensure that sufficient water supply is available for present andfuture generations, apportioning available water to all areas of the state.
Daniel W Varin, Chairman
Juan Mariscal, General Manager

South Carolina

3034 Blackbeard Island National Wildlife Refuge
694 Beech Hill Lane 843-784-2468
Hardeeville, SC 29927 Fax: 843-784-2465
E-mail: savannahcoastal@fws.gov
http://www.fws.gov/blackbeardisland
This Georgia barrier island's 5,618 acres includes maritime forest, saltmarsh, freshwater marsh, and beach habitat, 3,000 of which has been set aside as National wilderness of variety of recreational activities are availableyear-round, including wildlife observation, birdwatching, hiking and beachcombing.
Jane Griess, Project Leader
Kimberley Hayes, Refuge Manager

3035 Department of Interior: South Carolina Fish and Wildlife
Clemson University
261 Lehotsky Hall 864-656-2432
Clemson, SC 29634 Fax: 864-656-1350
E-mail: southeast@fws.gov
http://www.fws.gov/southeast
Cindy Dohner, Regional Director

3036 Department of Parks, Recreation and Tourism
1205 Pendleton Street 803-734-1700
Edgar A Brown Building 866-224-9339
Columbia, SC 29201 http://www.scprt.com
Mission: To learn more about our purpose, mission, and vision.
Pam Benjamin, Director of Human Resources

3037 Office of Environmental Laboratory Certification
PO Box 72 803-896-0970
State Park, SC 29147 Fax: 803-896-0850
http://www.scdhec.net/envserv/html
We offer certification to any environmental laboratory wishing to analyze samples for South Carolina's Department of Health and Environmental Control [DHEC]. This scope of certification covers the Safe Drinking Water Act (SDWA), theClean Water Act (NPDES), and solid & hazardous wastes including RCRA and CERCLA requirements (SW846 methodologies).

3038 South Atlantic Fishery Management Council
4055 Faber Place Drive 843-571-4366
Suite 201 Fax: 843-769-4520
North Charleston, SC 29405 E-mail: safmc@safmc.net
http://www.safmc.net
The South Atlantic Fishery Management Council is headquartered in Charleston, SC, and is responsible for the conservation and management of fish stocks within the 200-mile limit of the Atlantic off the coasts of North Carolina, SouthCarolina, Georgia, and east florida to Key West.
David M. Cupka, Chairman
Ben C. Hartig, Vice Chairman

3039 South Carolina Department of Health and Environmental Control
2600 Bull Street 803-898-3432
Columbia, SC 29201 http://www.scdhec.net
Mission: We promote and protect the health of the public and the environment.

3040 South Carolina Department of Natural Resources
1000 Assembly Street 803-734-4007
Rembert C Dennis Building Fax: 803-734-4300
Columbia, SC 29201 http://www.dnr.state.sc.us
Mission: To serve as the principal advocate for and steward of South Carolina's natural resources.
Alvin A. Taylor, Director
D. Carmichael Jr., Special Assistant to the Dir

3041 South Carolina Forestry Commission
5500 Broad River Road 803-896-8800
Columbia, SC 29212 Fax: 803-798-8097
E-mail: scfc@forestry.state.sc.us
http://www.trees.sc.gov
The mission of the Forestry Commission is to protect, promote, enhance and nurture the forest lands of South Carolina in a manner consistent with achieving the greatest good for its citizens. Responsibilities extend to all forestlands, both rural and urban, and to all associated forest values and amenities including, but not limited to: timber, wildlife, water quality, air quality, soil protection, recreation and aesthetics.
Henry E Kodama, State Forester
Tom Patton, Deputy State Forester

3042 United States Department of the Army US Army Corps of Engineers
69A Hagood Avenue 843-329-8000
Charleston, SC 29403 Fax: 843-329-2332
E-mail: CESAC-PAO@usace.army.mil
http://www.sac.usace.army.mil
The Charleston District (USACE), South Atlantic Division serves the citizens of South Carolina, the Region, and the Nation by providing quality water resources, value engineering/value management, environmental, and international andinteragency projects and services.
Lt. Col. Edward Chamberlayne, Commander
Maj. John O'Brien, Deputy Commander

South Dakota

3043 Attorney General's Office
1302 East Highway 14 605-773-3215
Suite 1 Fax: 605-773-4106
Pierre, SD 57501-8501 E-mail: atghelp@state.sd.us
http://www.atg.sd.gov
The Natural Resources Division of the South Dakota Attorney General's Office provides specialized legal counsel to state agencies in environmental, agricultural, financial, Indian law and natural resource matters. It focuses on (1)state boards and agencies which issue environmental, water, and agricultural permits and the lease of state mineral lands; (2) environmental litigation before boards and agencies and in the courts; and (3) jurisdictional disputes.
Marty J. Jackley, Attorney General

3044 **Department of Environment & Natural Resources**
523 E Capitol Avenue
Pierre, SD 57501
605-773-3151
Fax: 605-773-6035
E-mail: denrinternet@state.sd.us
http://www.state.sd.us/denr/denr.html

Our mission is to provide environmental and natural resources assessment, financial assistance, and regulation in a customer service manner that protects the public health, conserves natural resources, preserves the environment andpromotes economic development.

Steven M. Pirner, Secretary of the Department

3045 **Department of Wildlife and Fisheries Sciences**
South Dakota State University
Box 2140b
Brookings, SD 57007
605-688-6121
Fax: 605-688-4515
E-mail: terri.symens@sdstate.edu
http://www.sdstate.edu/nrm/

David Willis, Department Head
Nels Troelstrup, Assistant Department Head

3046 **South Dakota Department of Game, Fish & Parks**
523 E Capitol Avenue
Pierre, SD 57501
605-773-3485
Fax: 605-773-5842
E-mail: wildinfo@state.sd.us
http://www.gfp.sd.gov

The purpose of the Department of Game, Fish and Parks is to perpetuate, conserve, manage, protect and enhance South Dakota's wildlife resources, parks and outdoor recreational opportunities for the use, benefit and enjoyment of thepeople of this state and its visitors, and to give the highest priority to the welfare of this states's wildlife and parks, and their environment, in planning and decisions.

Susie Knippling, Chairwoman
John Cooper, Vice Chair

3047 **South Dakota Department of Health**
600 E Capitol Avenue
Pierre, SD 57501-2536
605-773-3361
800-738-2301
E-mail: DOH.info@state.sd.us
http://www.state.sd.us/doh

Mission: To prevent disease and promote health, ensure access to needed, high-quality health care, and to efficiently manage public health resources.

Doneen Hollingsworth, Secretary
Joan Adam, Division Director, Administr

3048 **South Dakota State Extension Services**
South Dakota State University
Box 2207D
Brookings, SD 57007
605-688-4792
Fax: 605-688-6733
http://www.sdstate.edu/sdsuextension/index.cfm

Extension serves the people of South Dakota by helping them apply unbiased, scientific knowledge to improve their lives. Extension also offers educational information, programs, and services in response to local issues and needs.

Barry Dunn, Extension Director
Karla Trautman, Associate Director

Tennessee

3049 **Carbon Dioxide Information Analysis Center**
Oak Ridge National Laboratory
Building 2040
Bethel Valley Road, PO Box 2008
Oak Ridge, TN 37831-6290
865-574-0390
Fax: 865-574-2232
E-mail: cdiac@ornl.gov
http://www.cdiac.esd.ornl.gov

The primary global-change data and information analysis center of the US Department of Energy. Responds to data and information requests from users from all over the world who are concerned with the greenhouse effect and global climatechange.

Tom Boden, Director
Fredia Glenn, Executive Administrative Ass

3050 **Obed Wild & Scenic River**
PO Box 429
Wartburg, TN 37887
423-346-6294
Fax: 423-346-3362
E-mail: rebecca_schapansky@nps.gov
http://www.nps.gov/obed/

Approximately 45 miles of wild and scenic river are comprised of the Obed River, Clear Creek, Daddy's Creek and Emory River. These water courses have cut rugged gorges leaving exciting whitewater gorges with bluffs as high as 500 feetabove the water.

Niki Stephanie Nicholas, Superintendent
Barbara Olmstead, Administrative Officer

3051 **Tennessee Department of Agriculture**
Ellington Agricultural Center
Melrose Station, PO Box 40627
Nashville, TN 37204
615-837-5103
Fax: 615-837-5333
E-mail: TN.Agriculture@TN.gov
http://www.tennessee.gov/agriculture

Mission: To serve the citizens of Tennessee by promoting wise uses of our agriculture and forest resources, developing economic opportunities, and ensuring safe and dependable food and fiber.

Julius Johnson, Commissioner
Jai Templeton, Deputy Commissioner

3052 **Tennessee Department of Environment and Conservation**
401 Church Street
L&C Annex, 1st Floor
Nashville, TN 37243
615-532-0109
888-891-8332
E-mail: ask.TDEC@tn.gov
http://www.state.tn.us/environment

Safeguarding the health and safety of Tennessee citizens from environmental hazards

Robert J. Martineau, Jr., Commissioner
Shari Meghreblian, Deputy Commissioner

3053 **Tennessee Valley Authority**
400 W Summit Hill Drive
Knoxville, TN 37902-1499
865-632-2101
E-mail: tvainfo@tva.com
http://www.tva.gov

TVA generates prosperity in the Tennessee Valley by promoting economic development, supplying low-cost, reliable power and supporting a thriving river system.

Bill Johnson, President/CEO
Janet Hernin, Executive Vice President

3054 **United States Army Engineer District: Memphis**
167 N Main Street
Memphis, TN 38103
901-544-3222
800-317-4156
E-mail: MemphisPAO@usace.army.mil
http://www.mvm.usace.army.mil

Provides flood control, navigation, environmental stewardship, emergency operations, and other authorized civil works to benefit the region and the Nation.

Col. Vernie L. Reichling, Jr., Commander
Lt. Col. Thomas Patton, Deputy Commander

3055 **University of Tennessee Extension**
2621 Morgan Circle
121 Morgan Hall
Knoxville, TN 37996
865-974-7114
Fax: 865-974-1068
E-mail: tlcross@utk.edu
http://www.utextension.tennessee.edu

Statewide educational organization that brings research-based information about agriculture, family and consumer sciences, and resource development to the people of Tennessee where they live and work.

Tim L. Cross, Dean
Shirley W. Hastings, Deputy Dean

3056 **Wildlife Resources Agency**
PO Box 41489
Nashville, TN 37204
615-781-6500
Fax: 615-741-4606
E-mail: melinda.raymond@tn.gov
http://www.state.tn.us/twra

The Tennessee Wildlife Resources Agency develops, manages and maintains sound programs of hunting, fishing, trapping, boating, and other wildlife related outdoor recreational activities.

Ed Carter, Executive Director

3057 Wildlife Resources Agency: Fisheries Management Division
PO Box 40747
Nashville, TN 37204
615-781-6575
Fax: 615-781-6667
http://www.state.tn.us/twra

Ed Carter, Executive Director

Texas

3058 Attorney General of Texas Natural Resources Division (NRD)
300 W 15th Street
PO Box 12548
Austin, TX 78711-2548
512-463-2100
Fax: 512-475-2994
http://www.oag.state.tx.us

The NRD represents the enviromental and energy agencies of the State of Texas in court. NRD's primary activity is the prosecution of lawsuits, referred by state agencies, that involve violations of the state's enviromental and naturalresources protection laws. NRD also defends permits issued by agencies uder those laws and defends challenges to the statues and regulations themselves.NRD also has primary enforcement responsibility for protecting the public's access to Texasbeaches.

Greg Abbott, Attorney General

3059 Bureau of Economic Geology
University of Texas at Austin
University Station
Box X
Austin, TX 78713-8924
512-471-1534
888-839-4365
Fax: 512-471-0140
E-mail: begmail@beg.utexas.edu
http://www.beg.utexas.edu

The Bureau provides wide-ranging advisory, technical, informational, and research-based services to industries, nonprofit organizations, and Federal, State, and local agencies.

Scott W Tinker, Director
Jay Kipper, Associate Director

3060 Chihuahuan Desert Research Institute
PO Box 905
Fort Davis, TX 79734
432-364-2499
Fax: 432-364-2686
http://www.cdri.org

Conducts research on the Chihuahuan Desert.

Thomas Bruner, Executive Director Interim
Jack Burgess, Director

3061 Environmental Protection Agency: Region VI
1445 Ross Avenue
Suite 1200
Dallas, TX 75202
214-665-2760
800-887-6063
http://www.epa.gov/region06

Region 6 encompasses the ecologically, demographically and economically diverse of states of Arkansas, Louisiana, New Mexico, Oklahoma and Texas. The regional vision is to meet the environmental needs of a changing world.

Ron Curry, Regional Administrator
Larry Starfield, Deputy Administrator

3062 Guadalupe: Blanco River Authority
933 E Court Street
Seguin, TX 78155
830-379-5822
Fax: 830-379-9718
E-mail: comments@gbra.org
http://www.gbra.org

Aims to conserve and protect the water resources of the Guadalupe River basin and make them available for beneficial use. Services include water and wastewater treatment, water quality testing, the management of water rights anddelivery of stored water, the production of electricity from seven hydroelectric plants and engineering design support.

W.E West Jr., General Manager
James Murphy, Executive Manager

3063 Parks & Wildlife: Public Lands Division
4200 Smith School Road
Austin, TX 78744
512-389-4800
800-792-1112
Fax: 512-389-4960
http://www.tpwd.state.tx.us

In 1963 the Parks Board merged with the game and Fish Commission to form the Texas Parks and Wildlife Department. The merger created the Parks Division, currently the Public Lands Division. In 1967 park acquisition and developmentincreased with the passage of a $75 million parks bond authorization and the dedication of a portion of the state's cigarette tax to the development of state and local parks.

Carter Smith, Executive Director
Joe Carter, Internal Affairs

3064 Parks & Wildlife: Resource Protection Division
4200 Smith School Road
Austin, TX 78744
512-389-4864
http://www.tpwd.state.tx.us

The Resource Protection Division protects Tezas fich, wildlife, plant and mineral resources from degradation or depletion. The division investigates any environmental contamination that may cause loss of fish or wildlife. It providesinformation and recommendations to other government agencies and participates in administrative and judicial proceedings concerning pollution incidents, development, development projects and other actions that may affect fish and wildlife.

Carter Smith, Executive Director
Joe Carter, Internal Affairs

3065 Pecos River Commission
PO Box 969
Marfa, TX 79843
432-729-3225
Fax: 432-729-3224
E-mail: tatecattle@sbcglobal.net
http://www.tceq.state.tx.us

The Pecos River Compact Commission administers the Pecos River Compact to ensure that Texas receives its equitable share of quality water from the Pecos River and its tributaries as appointed by the Compact. The Compact includes thestates of New Mexico and Texas.

Frederic Tate, Commissioner

3066 Rio Grande Compact Commission
401 East Franklin Avenue
Ste. 560
El Paso, TX 79901
915-834-7075
Fax: 915-834-7080
E-mail: pgordon@gordonmottpc.com
http://www.tceq.state.tx.us

The Rio Grande Compact Commission administers the Rio Grande Compact to ensure that Texas receives its equitable share of quality water from the Rio Grande and its tributaries as appointed by the Compact. The Compact includes thestates of Colorado, New Mexico, and Texas.

Patrick R Gordon, Commisioner

3067 Sabine River Compact Commission
PO Box 556
Mauriceville, TX 77626
409-988-9428
E-mail: gary.gagnon@att.net
http://www.tceq.state.tx.us

The Sabine River Compact Commission administers the Sabine River Compact to ensure that Texas receives its equitable share of quality water from the Sabine River and its tributaries as apportioned by the Compact. The Compact includesthe states of Texas and Louisiana.

Gary E Gagnon, Commissioner
Jerry F. Gipson, Commissioner

3068 Texas Animal Health Commission
2105 Kramer Lane
Austin, TX 78758
512-719-0700
800-550-8242
Fax: 512-719-0719
http://www.tahc.state.tx.us

TAHC works to keep pests from reoccurring as major livestock health hazards. Ultimately, the TAHC mission and role is the assurance of marketability and mobility of Texas livestock. TAHC works to sustain and continue to make a vitalcontribution to a wholesome and abundant supply of meat, eggs, and dairy products at affordable costs.

Dee Ellis, Executive Director
Gene Snelson, General Counsel

3069 Texas Cooperative Extension
Jack K Williams Administration Bldg 979-845-7800
Room 112, 7101 TAMU Fax: 979-845-9542
College Station, TX 77843 E-mail: tce@tamu.edu
http://texasextension.tamu.edu
Edward G Smith, Director

3070 Texas Department of Agriculture
PO Box 12847 512-463-7476
Austin, TX 78711-2847 800-835-5832
Fax: 888-223-8861
E-mail: Customer.Relations@TexasAgriculture.gov
http://www.texasagriculture.gov
TDA's mission is to partner with all Texans to make Texas the nation's leader in agriculture, fortify our economy, empower rural communities, promote healthy lifestyles, and cultivate winning strategies for rural, suburban and urbanTexas through exceptional service and the common threads of agriculture in our daily lives
Todd Staples, Commissioner
Drew DeBerry, Deputy Commissioner

3071 Texas Department of Health
1100 W 49th Street 512-776-7111
Austin, TX 78756-3199 888-963-7111
Fax: 512-458-7686
E-mail: web.master@dshs.state.tx.us
http://www.tdh.state.tx.us
The Texas Department of Health is the state government agency charged with protecting and promoting the health of the public.
David L. Lakey, Commissioner
Kirk Cole, Associate Commissioner

3072 Texas Forest Service
301 Tarrow 979-458-6606
Suite 364 Fax: 979-458-6610
College Station, TX 77840 http://texasforestservice.tamu.edu
The mission is to provide statewide leadership and professional assistance to assure the states's forest, tree and related natural resources are wisely used, nurtured, protected and perpetuated for the benefit of all Texans.
James Hull, Director

3073 Texas Natural Resource Conservation Commission
12100 Park 35 Circle 512-239-1000
Austin, TX 78753 Fax: 512-239-4430
http://www.tnrcc.state.tx.us
The Texas Natural Resource Conservation Commission strives to keep our state's human and natural resources consistent with sustainable economic development. Our goal is clean air, clean water and the safe management of waste.

3074 Texas Parks & Wildlife Department
4200 Smith School Road 512-389-4800
Austin, TX 78744 800-792-1112
Fax: 512-389-4814
E-mail: webcomments@tpwd.state.tx.us
http://www.tpwd.state.tx.us
Mission: To manage and conserve the natural and cultural resources of Texas and to provide hunting, fishing and outdoor recreation opportunities for the use and enjoyment of present and future generations.
Carter Smith, Executive Director
Joe Carter, Internal Affairs

3075 Texas State Soil and Water Conservation Board (TSSWCB)
4311 South 31st Street 254-773-2250
Suite 125 800-792-3485
Temple, TX 76502 Fax: 254-773-3311
http://www.tsswcb.state.tx.us
The state agency that administers Texas' soil and water conservation laws and coordinates conservation and nonpoint source pollution abatement programs through the State. The Board is composed of 7 members, 2 Governor appointed and 5landowners, from across Texas, and is the lead state agency for planning, management, and abatement of agricultural and silvicultural (forestry) nonpoint source pollution, and administers the Texas Brush Control Program. There are regional officesthroughout Texas.
Marty H. Graham, Chairman
Scott Buckles, Vice-Chairman

3076 United States Department of the Army: US Army Corps of Engineers
819 Taylor Street 817-886-1306
Fort Worth, TX 76102-0300 http://www.usace.army.mil
Christopher W Martin, Commander

Utah

3077 Cedar City District: Bureau of Land Management
Department of the Interior
176 East D.L. Sargent Drive 435-865-3000
Cedar City, UT 84721 Fax: 435-865-3053
E-mail: utccmail@blm.gov
http://www.blm.gov/ut/st/en/fo/cedar_city.html
Responsible for administering about 2.1 million acres of public lands located in Iron and Beaver counties in southwestern Utah
Todd S Christiansen, Field Manager

3078 Colorado River Basin Salinity Control Advisory Council: Upper Colorado Region
US Bureau of Reclamation
125 S State Street 801-524-3774
Room 6107 Fax: 801-524-3856
Salt Lake City, UT 84138 http://www.usbr.gov/uc
Rick Gold, Director

3079 Moab District: Bureau of Land Management
Department of the Interior
82 East Dogwood 435-259-2100
Moab, UT 84532 Fax: 435-259-2106
http://www.blm.gov/ut/st/en/fo/moab.html
The BLM is committed to providing the highest possible level of access to its facilities, programs, services, and activities on the public lands for persons with disabilities
Maggie Wyatt, Manager

3080 Richfield Field Office: Bureau of Land Management
Department of the Interior
150 E 900 N 435-896-1500
Richfield, UT 84701 Fax: 435-896-1550
E-mail: utrfmail@blm.gov
http://www.blm.gov/ut/st/en/fo/richfield.html
Cornell Christensen, Manager

3081 Salt Lake District: Bureau of Land Management
Department of the Interior
2370 South 2300 West 801-977-4300
Salt Lake City, UT http://www.blm.gov/ut/st/en/fo/salt_lake.html
The BLM administers public lands within a framework of numerous laws. The most comprehensive of these is the Federal Land Policy and Management Act of 1976. All Bureau policies, procedures and management actions must be consistent withFLPMA and the other laws that govern use of the public lands. It is their mission to sustain the health, diversity and productivity of the public lands for the use and enjoyment of present and future generations.
Glenn Carpenter, Manager

3082 Upper Colorado River Commission
355 S 400 E Street 801-531-1150
Salt Lake City, UT 84111-2969 Fax: 801-531-9750
E-mail: dostler@ucrcommission.com
http://www.usbr.gov/uc/rm/amp/amwg/amwgbioALT_ostler.html
The Upper Colorado River Commission is an interstate compact administration agency created by the Upper Colorado River Basin Compact of 1948. Since its inception, the Commission (made up of Commissioners appointed by the Governor ofeach Upper Division State and one appointed by the President of the United States) has actively participated in the development, utilization

and conservation of the water resources of the Colorado River Basin.
Don Ostler, Executive Director

3083 Utah Department of Agriculture and Food
350 N Redwood Road — 801-538-7100
Salt Lake City, UT 84114-6500 — Fax: 801-538-7126
E-mail: agriculture@utah.gov
http://www.ag.utah.gov
Leonard M. Blackham, Commissioner
Kyle Stephens, Deputy Commissioner

3084 Utah Geological Survey
1594 W North Temple, Suite 3110 — 801-537-3300
PO Box 146100 — Fax: 801-537-3400
Salt Lake City, UT 84114-6100 — http://www.geology.utah.gov
The Utah Geological Survey is an applied scientific agency that creates, interprets and provides information about Utah's geologic environment, resources and hazards to promote safe, beneficial and wise use of land.
Bill Loughlin, Chair
Mark D. Bunnell, Co-Chair

3085 Utah Natural Resources: Water Resources Section
1594 W North Temple, Room 310 — 801-538-7230
Salt Lake City, UT 84116 — Fax: 801-538-7229
http://www.water.utah.gov
Mission: Plan, conserve, develop and protect Utah's water resources.
Michael R. Styler, Executive Director
Joseph Paulick, Chairman

3086 Utah Natural Resources: Wildlife Resource Division
1594 W N Temple, Suite 2110 — 801-538-4700
Salt Lake City, UT 84116 — Fax: 801-538-4745
http://www.wildlife.utah.gov
Mission: To serve the people of Utah as trustee and guardian of the state's wildlife and to ensure its future and values through management, protection, conservation and education.

3087 Utah State Department of Natural Resources: Division of Forestry, Fire, & State Lands
1594 W North Temple, Suite 3520 — 801-538-5555
PO Box 145703 — Fax: 801-533-4111
Salt Lake City, UT 84114-5703 — http://www.ffsl.utah.gov
The Division of Forestry, Fire & State Lands manages, sustains and strengthens Utah's forests, rangelands, sovereign lands and watersheds for its citizens and visitors
Dick Buehler, State Forester/Director
Brian Cottam, Deputy Director

3088 Vernal District: Bureau of Land Management
Department of the Interior
170 South 500 East — 435-781-4423
Vernal, UT 84078 — Fax: 435-781-4410
E-mail: BLM_UT_Vernal_Comments@blm.gov
http://www.ut.blm.gov/vernal/index.html
Bill Stringer, Manager

Vermont

3089 Department of Forests, Parks, and Recreation
103 South Main Street — 802-241-3670
Waterbury, VT 05671 — Fax: 802-244-1481
http://www.vtfpr.org
Mission: To practice and encourage high quality stewardship of Vermont's environment by: monitoring and maintaining the health, integrity and diversity of important species, natural communities, and ecological processes; managingforests for sustainable use; providing and promoting opportunities for compatible outdoor recreation; and furnishing related information, education, and service.
Michael C. Snyder, Commissioner
Tracy Zeno, Executive Assistant

3090 Vermont Agency of Agriculture, Food and Markets
116 State Street — 802-828-2430
Montpelier, VT 05620-2901 — E-mail: AGR.Helpdesk@state.vt.us
http://www.vermontagriculture.com
To facilitate, support and encourage the growth and viability of agriculture while protecting the working landscape, human health, animal health, plant health, consumers and the environment
Chuck Ross, Secretary
Jolinda LaClair, Deputy Secretary

3091 Vermont Agency of Natural Resources
1 National Life Drive, Davis 2 — 802-828-1294
Montpelier, VT 05620-3901 — Fax: 802-244-1102
http://www.anr.state.vt.us
To draw from and build upon Vermonters' shared ethic of responsibility for our natural environment, an ethic that encompasses a sense of place, community and quality of life, and understanding that we are an integral part of theenvironment and that we must all be responsible stewards for this and future generations
Deb Markowitz, Secretary

3092 Vermont Department of Health
108 Cherry Street — 802-863-7200
PO Box 70 — 800-464-4343
Burlington, VT 05402 — Fax: 802-865-7754
http://www.healthvermont.gov
The Vermont Department of Health, the state's public health agency, works to protect and improve the health of our population through core public health functions. Core public health functions are those activities that lay thegroundwork for healthy communities.
Harry Chen MD, Commissioner

Virginia

3093 Commerce and Trade: Mines, Minerals and Energy Department
Depart. Mines, Minerals & Energy — 804-692-3200
9th St Office Bldg, 202 North 9th Street — Fax: 804-692-3200
Richmond, VA 23219 — http://www.mme.state.va.us/
Mission: To enhance the development and conservation of energy and mineral resources in a safe and environmentally sound manner in order to support a more productive economy in Virginia.
George P. Willis, Director

3094 Conservation & Development of Public Beaches Board
Virginia Department of Conservation & Recreation
600 E. Main St., 24th Floor — 804-786-2064
Richmond, VA 23219 — E-mail: pco@dcr.virginia.gov
http://www.dcr.state.va.us/sw/pubbeach.htm
Helps localities maintain and improve public beaches to enhance recreation for Virginia's citizens and visitors
Mark E. Smith, Chair
W. Bruce Wingo, Vice-Chairman

3095 Department of Conservation & Recreation: Division of Dam Safety
600 E. Main St., 24th Floor — 804-371-6095
Richmond, VA 23219 — Fax: 804-786-0536
E-mail: pco@dcr.virginia.gov
http://www.dcr.virginia.gov
The program's purpose is to provide for safe design, construction, operation and maintenance of dams to protect public safety.
Mark E. Smith, Chair
W. Bruce Wingo, Vice-Chairman

3096 Division of Mineral Resources
900 Natural Resources Drive — 804-951-6341
Ste. 400 — Fax: 804-951-6366
Charlottesville, VA 22903 — E-mail: DgmrInfo@dmme.virginia.gov.
http://www.dmme.virginia.gov
Mission: To enhance the development and conservation of energy and mineral resources in a safe and environmentally sound manner to support a more productive economy in Virginia. DMR gen-

erates, collects, complies, and evaluates geologicdata, creates and publishes geologic maps and report, works cooperatively with other state and federal agencies, and is the primary source of information on geology, minerla and energy resources, and geologic hazards for both the mineral and energyindustries.
Ed Erb, Director

3097 Division of State Parks
Virginia Department of Conservation & Recreation
600 E. Main St., 24th Floor
Richmond, VA 23219
804-692-0403
800-933-7275
Fax: 804-786-9294
E-mail: pco@dcr.virginia.gov
http://www.dcr.virginia.gov

3098 Secretary of Commerce and Trade
PO Box 1475
Richmond, VA 23218
804-786-7831
Fax: 804-371-0250
E-mail: mdd@mme.state.va.us
http://www.commerce.virginia.gov
The secretayr of Commerce and Trade oversees the economic, community, and workforce development of the Commonwealth. Each of the 13 Commerce and Trade agencies actively contributes to the Commonwealth's economic strength and highquality of life.
Jim Cheng, Sec of Commerce & Trade
Carry Roth, Deputy Secretary

3099 US Geological Survey
12201 Sunrise Valley Drive
Reston, VA 20192
703-648-4000
http://va.water.usgs.gov
Mission: The Unites States Geological Survey serves the Nation by providing reliable scientific information to describe and understand the Earth; minimize loss of life and property from natural disasters; manage water, biological,energy, and mineral resources; and enhance and protect our quality of life.
Mark D Myers, Director
Bob Doyle, Deputy Director

3100 Virginia Cooperative Fish & Wildlife Research Unit
Virginia Polytechnic Institute & State Unversity
106 Cheatham Hall
Blacksburg, VA 24061
540-231-4934
E-mail: vacfwru@listserve.vt.edu
http://www.coopunits.org
A field station of the US Geological Survey, dedicated to research and management of fish and wildlife resources in Virginia and surrounding states. Expertise includes freshwater fish and mollusks and large game mammals. The unitincludes 3 research scientists.
Ken Williams, Chief
Jim Fleming, Supervisor

3101 Virginia Department of Environmental Quality
629 E Main Street
PO Box 1105
Richmond, VA 23218
804-698-4000
800-592-5482
Fax: 804-698-4500
E-mail: vanaturally@deq.virginia.gov
http://www.deq.virginia.gov
Virginia's regulatory state agency for air, water waste management and coastal resources. The department is also the coordinating clearinghouse for environmental education and information; and maintains the state's gateway.
David K Paylor, Director

3102 Virginia Department of Game & Inland Fisheries: Wildlife Division
4010 West Broad Street
Richmond, VA 23230
804-367-9588
Fax: 804-367-9147
E-mail: dgifweb@dgif.virginia.gov
http://www.dgif.state.va.us

3103 Virginia Department of Game & Inland Fisheries Fisheries Division
4010 West Broad Street
Richmond, VA 23230
804-367-8704
Fax: 804-367-9147
E-mail: dgifweb@dgif.virginia.gov
http://www.dgif.state.va.us

3104 Virginia Department of Game and Inland Fisheries
4010 West Broad Street
PO Box 11104
Richmond, VA 23230
804-367-1000
Fax: 804-364-9147
E-mail: dgifweb@dgif.virginia.gov
http://www.dgif.state.va.us
To manage Virginia's wildlife and inland fish to maintain optimum population of all species to serve the needs of the commonwealth; to provide opportunity for all to enjoy wildlife, inland fish, boating and related outdoor recreation;to promote safety for persons and property in connection with boating, hunting and fishing.
J Carlton Courter III, Director

3105 Virginia Department of Health Commissioners Office
1500 East Main Street Suite 214
Richmond, VA 23219
804-786-3561
Fax: 804-786-4616
http://www.vdh.state.va.us
Cynthia C. Romero, Commissioner

3106 Virginia Department of Mines, Minerals & Energy: Division of Mined Land Reclamation
3405 Mountain Empire Road
Big Stone Gap, VA 24219
276-523-8100
Fax: 276-523-8148
E-mail: dmlrinfo@dmme.virginia.gov
http://www.dmme.virginia.gov
Responsible for ensuring the reclamation of land affected by surface and underground coal mining activity
Randy Casey, Director

3107 Virginia Department of Mines, Minerals and Energy: Division of Mineral Resources
900 Natural Resources Drive
Ste. 400
Charlottesville, VA 22903
804-951-6341
Fax: 804-951-6366
E-mail: DgmrInfo@dmme.virginia.gov.
http://www.dmme.virginia.gov
Mission: To enhance the development and conservation of energy and mineral resources in a safe and environementally sound manner to support a more productive economy in Virginia.

3108 Virginia Museum of Natural History
21 Starling Avenue
Martinsville, VA 24112
276-634-4141
Fax: 276-634-4199
http://www.vmnh.net
We are a state museum of natural history with research scientists in marine biology, vertebrate and invertebrate paleontology, archaeology, earth sciences, entomology, and mammalogy. Creates education programs, exhibits, and fieldtrips focused on natural history and environmental issues. Its publishing division specializes in works by natural scientists and environmental educators in the US and abroad. Writing, editorial, and design services available for books, reports, textbooks, etc..
Joe Keiper, Executive Director
Gloria Niblett, Director of Administration

3109 Virginia Sea Grant Program
1208 Greate Road
PO Box 1346
Gloucester Point, VA 23062
804-684-7530
E-mail: rickards@virginia.edu
http://www.virginia.edu
Virginia Sea Grant facilitates research, educational, and outreach activities promoting sustainable management of marine resources.
William DuPaul, Interim Director
Cynthia L Suchman, Assistant Director

Washington

3110 Department of Commerce: Pacific Marine Environmental Laboratory
7600 Sand Point Way NE
Seattle, WA 98115
206-526-6239
Fax: 206-526-6815
http://www.pmel.noaa.gov
PMEL carries out interdisciplinary scientific investigations in oceanography and atmospheric science.
Christopher Sabine, Director
Dan Simon, Associate Director

3111 Department of Fish and Wildlife
1111 Washington Street SE 360-902-2200
Olympia, WA 98501
Fax: 360-902-2947
http://www.wdfw.wa.gov
To preserve, protect and perpetuate fish, wildlife and ecosystems while providing sustainable fish and wildlife recreational and commercial opportunities
Phil Anderson, Director

3112 Environmental Protection Agency: Region 10 Environmental Services
1200 6th Avenue 206-553-1200
Seattle, WA 98101 800-424-4372
Fax: 206-553-1809
E-mail: epa-seattle@epa.gov
http://www.epa.gov/r10earth
Dennis Mclerran, Regional Administrator

3113 Julia Butler Hansen Refuge for the Columbian White-Tailed Deer
PO Box 566
Cathlamet, WA 98612 360-795-3915
Fax: 360-795-0803
http://www.pacific.fws.gov/refuges/field/WA_julia.htm
Offers critical habitat for the endangered Columbian white-tailed deer. The refuge also provides a wintering area for tundra swans, Canada geese, mallards, American wigeon and pintails. Deer and elk are easily observed and photographedfrom the country road that circles the mainland portion of the refuge. Evenings and mornings are the best time to spot animals. Open year-round. No fees charged.

3114 Washington Cooperative Fish & Wildlife Research Unit
University of Washington
Box 355020 206-543-6475
Seattle, WA 98195 E-mail: washcoop@u.washington.edu
http://www.coopunits.org
Chris Grue, Unit Leader
David Beauchamp, Assistant Unit Leader

3115 Washington Department of Ecology
300 Desmond Drive 360-407-6000
Lacey, WA 98503 Fax: 360-459-6007
http://www.ecy.wa.gov
The mission is to protect, preserve and enhance Washington's environment and to promote the wise management of our air, land and water.
Maia D. Bellon, Director

3116 Washington Department of Fish & Wildlife: Fish and Wildlife Commission
600 Capitol Way N 360-902-2267
Olympia, WA 98501-1091 Fax: 360-902-2448
E-mail: commission@dfw.wa.gov
http://www.wdfw.wa.gov/commission
The Fish and Wildlife Commission's primary role is to establish policy and direction for fish and wildlife species and their habitats in Washington and to monitor the Department's implementation of the goals, policies and objectivesestablished by the Commission. The Commission also classifies wildlife and establishes the basic rules and regulations governing the time, place, manner, and methods used to harvest or enjoy fish and wildlife.
Miranda Wecker, Chair
Bradley Smith, Vice Chair

3117 Washington Department of Fish & Wildlife: Habitat Program
600 Capitol Way N 360-902-2534
Olympia, WA 98501 Fax: 360-902-2946
E-mail: habitatprogram@dfw.wa.gov
http://www.wdfw.wa.gov
Includes Maps and Digital Info Requests.
Phil Anderson, Director

3118 Washington Department of Natural Resources: Southeast Region
713 Bowers Road 509-925-8510
Ellensburg, WA 98926-9301 Fax: 509-925-8522
E-mail: southeast.region@dnr.wa.gov
http://www.dnr.wa.gov
In partnership with citizens and governments, the Washington State DNR provides innovative leadership and expertise to ensure environmental protection, public safety, perpetual funding for schools and communities, and a rich quality oflife
Peter Goldmark, Commissioner

3119 Washington Dept. of Natural Resources: Northwest Division
919 North Township Street 360-856-3500
Sedro Woolley, WA 98284-9384 Fax: 360-856-2150
E-mail: northwest.region@dnr.wa.gov
http://www.dnr.wa.gov
In partnership with citizens and governments, the Washington State DNR provides innovative leadership and expertise to ensure environmental protection, public safety, perpetual funding for schools and communities, and a rich quality oflife
Peter Goldmark, Commissioner

3120 Washington Dept. of Natural Resources: South Puget Sound Region
950 Farman Avenue North 360-825-1631
Enumclaw, WA 98022-9282 Fax: 360-825-1672
E-mail: southpuget.region@dnr.wa.gov
http://www.dnr.wa.gov
In partnership with citizens and governments, the Washington State DNR provides innovative leadership and expertise to ensure environmental protection, public safety, perpetual funding for schools and communities, and a rich quality oflife
Peter Goldmark, Commissioner

3121 Washington Sea Grant Program
University of Washington
3716 Brooklyn Avenue NE 206-543-6600
Seattle, WA 98105-6716 Fax: 206-685-0380
E-mail: seagrant@uw.edu
http://www.wsg.washington.edu/
Mission: Washington Sea Grant serves communities, industries and the people of Washington state, the Pacific Northwest and the nation through research, education and outreach by: identifying and addressing important marine issues;providing better tools for management of the marine environment and use of its resources; and initiating and supporting strategic partnerships within the marine community.
Penelope D Dalton, Director
Raechel Waters, Associate Director

3122 Washington State Parks & Recreation Commission: Eastern Region
7150 Cleanwater Drive SW
PO Box 42650 360-902-8844
Olympia, WA 98504 E-mail: infocent@parks.wa.gov
http://www.parks.wa.gov
The Washington State Parks and Recreation Commission aquires, operates, enhances and protects a diverse system of recreational, cultural, historical, and natural sites. The Commission fosters outdoor recreation and education statewideto provide enjoyment and enrichment for all and a valued legacy to future generations.
Rex Derr, Director
Judy Johnson, Deputy Director

West Virginia

3123 Capitol Conservation District
418 Goff Mountain Road 304-759-0736
Suite 102 Fax: 304-776-5326
Cross Lanes, WV 25313 E-mail: ccd@wvca.us
http://www.wvca.us
Walt Helmick, Commissioner
Daniel J. Robinson, Commissioner

3124 Gauley River National Recreation Area Advisory National Park Service
PO Box 246
Glen Jean, WV 25846
304-465-0508
Fax: 304-465-0591
E-mail: katy_miller@nps.gov
http://www.nps.gov/gar www.nps.gov/neri www.nps.gov/blue

Located in the southern West Virginia, New River Gorge National River was established in 1978 to conserve and protect 53 miles of the New River as a free-flowing waterway. This unit of the National Park System encompasses over 70,000acres of land along the New River between the towns of Hinton and Fayetteville. New River Gorge National River and Bluestone National Scenic River are both managed by our same office in Glen Jean, WV.
Lorrie Sprague, Public Information Officer

3125 West Virginia Cooperative Fish & Wildlife Research Unit USGS
322 Percival Hall West Virginia Un
PO Box 6125
Morgantown, WV 26506-6125
304-293-3794
Fax: 304-293-4826
E-mail: wvcoop@wvu.edu
http://www.coopunits.org

Patricia Mazik, Unit Leader Fisheries
Petra Wood, Assistant Leader Wildlife

3126 West Virginia Department of Environmental Protection
WV Dpt of Environmental Protection
1356 Hansford Street
Charleston, WV 25301
304-926-3647
Fax: 304-926-3637
http://www.wvdep.org

3127 West Virginia Division of Natural Resources
324 4th Avenue
South Charleston, WV 25303
304-558-2754
Fax: 304-558-2768
http://www.wvdnr.gov

Frank Jezioro, Director
Harry F Price, Executive Secretary

3128 West Virginia Geological & Economic Survey
1 Mont Chateau Road
Morgantown, WV 26508-8079
304-594-2331
Fax: 304-594-2575
E-mail: info@geosrv.wvnet.edu
http://www.wvgs.wvnet.edu

Michael Hohn, Director/State Geologist

Wisconsin

3129 Great Lakes Indian Fish and Wildlife Commission
PO Box 9
Odanah, WI 54861
715-682-6619
Fax: 715-682-9294
http://www.glifwc.org

Mission: To help ensure significant, off-reservation harvests while protecting the resources for generations to come.

James Zorn, Executive Administrator
Gerald DePerry, Deputy Administrator

3130 Natural Resources Department
PO Box 7921
Madison, WI 53707-7921
608-266-2621
Fax: 608-261-4380
http://www.dnr.wi.gov

Mission: To protect and enhance our natural resources; to provide a healthy, sustainable environment; to ensure the right of all people; to work with people; and to consider the future and generations to follow.
P Scott Hassett, Secretary

3131 Wisconsin Cooperative Fishery Research Unit
University of Wisconsin
College of Natural Resources
Stevens Point, WI 54481
715-346-2178
Fax: 715-346-3624
E-mail: coopfish@uwsp.edu
http://www.uwsp.edu/cnr/wicfru

3132 Wisconsin Department of Agriculture Trade & Cosumer Protection: Land & Water Resources Bureau
2811 Agriculture Drive
PO Box 8911
Madison, WI 53708
608-224-5012
Fax: 608-224-4615
http://www.datcp.state.wi.us
Ben Brancel, Secretary

3133 Wisconsin Geological & Natural History Survey
University of Wisconsin Extension
3817 Mineral Point Road
Madison, WI 53705
608-262-1705
Fax: 608-262-8086
http://www.wisconsingeologicalsurvey.org

Mission: The survey conducts earth-science surveys, field studies, and research. We provide objective scientific information about the geology, mineral resources, water resources, soil, and biology of Wisconsin. We collect, interpret,disseminate, and archive natural resource information. We communicate the results of our activities through publications, technical talks, and responses to inquiries from the public.
William G. Batten, State Geologist & Director

3134 Wisconsin State Extension Services Community Natural Resources & Economic Development
University of Wisconsin Extension
432 N Lake Street
Madison, WI 53706
608-263-2781
Fax: 606-262-9166
http://www.uwex.edu/ces/

Rick Klemme, Dean

Wyoming

3135 Casper District: Bureau of Land Management
Department of the Interior
2987 Prospector Drive
Casper, WY 82604
307-261-7600
Fax: 307-261-7587
E-mail: casper_wymail@blm.gov
http://www.blm.gov/Director/fo_map/casper_fo.lhtml

3136 Environmental Quality Department
122 W 25th Street
Herschler Building
Cheyenne, WY 82002
307-777-7937
Fax: 307-777-7682
E-mail: keith.guille@wyo.gov
http://www.deq.state.wy.us

DEQ contributes to Wyoming's quality of life through a combination of monitoring, permitting, inspection, enforcement and restoration/remediation activities which protect, conserve and enhance the environment while supportingresponsible stewardship of our state's resources.
Todd Parfitt, Director

3137 Rock Springs Field Office: Bureau of Land Management
Department of the Interior
280 Highway 191 N
Rock Springs, WY 82901
307-352-0256
Fax: 307-352-0329
http://www.wy.blm.gov

BLM's Rock Springs Field Office is a federal agency in the USA that manages over 3.6 million acres of public land surface and 3.5 million acres of public sub-surface minerals in the southwestern part of the great State of Wyoming. Forthese public lands, BLM administers a variety of programs including mineral exploration and development, wildlife habitat, outdoor recreation, wild horses, lifestock grazing and historic trails.

3138 Wyoming Board of Land Commissioners
Herschler Building 3W
122 West 25th Street
Cheyenne, WY 82002
307-777-7331
Fax: 307-777-5400
E-mail: slfmail@wyo.gov
http://www.lands.state.wy.us

Jason Crowder, Assistant Director
Russ Noel, Assistant Director

3139 **Wyoming Cooperative Fish and Wildlife Research Unit**
University of Wyoming
Biological Sciences Building 307-766-5415
Box 3166 Fax: 307-766-5400
Laramie, WY 82071 http://www.wyocoopunit.org/index.php/test/
Unit conducts fish and wildlife research for the state of Wyoming conservation, fish department and federal agencies.
Matthew K. Kauffman, Leader

3140 **Wyoming State Forestry Division**
5500 Bishop Blvd 307-777-7586
Cheyenne, WY 82002-0060 Fax: 307-777-5986
E-mail: forestry@wyo.gov
http://www.lands.state.wy.us
The Forestry Division's general reposnsibility and objectives are to promote and assist the multiple use management and protection of Wyoming's 270,000 acres of state and 1.9 million acres of private forest lands; to provide forestryassistance and information to landowners, industry, communities and public agencies; and to help provide rural, range, and forest land fire protection, equipment and training.
Bill Crasper, State Forester
Dan Perko, Deputy State Forester

3141 **Wyoming State Geological Survey**
PO Box 1347 307-766-2286
Laramie, WY 82073 Fax: 307-766-2605
E-mail: wsgs-info@uwyo.edu
http://www.wsgs.uwyo.edu
The Wyoming State Geological Survey's mission is to promote the beneficial and environmentally sound use of Wyoming's vast geologic, mineral, and energy resources while helping to protect the public from geologic hazards.

Thomas Drean, Director
Kathy Olson, Administrative Officer

Alabama: US Forests, Parks, Refuges

3142 **Bon Secour National Wildlife Refuge**
12295 State Highway 180 251-540-7720
Gulf Shores, AL 36542 Fax: 251-540-7301
E-mail: bonsecour@fws.gov
http://bonsecour.fws.gov/index_files/slide0001.htm
Gulf Shores offer nature enthusiasts much to explore. The Bon Secour NWR, which lies just 6 miles west of Gulf Shores, caters equally to the angler, the hiker and the birder. The refuge encourages guests to enjoy a leisurely hikethrough the grounds or a fishing excursion on the 40-acre fresh water Gator Lake. Pack a picnic lunch and your binoculars, park your blanket on one of the many secluded beaches and savor the scenery. Call 1-866-SEA TURTLE to report sea turtleactivity.

3143 **Choctaw National Wildlife Refuge**
PO Box 150 251-843-5238
Gilbertown, AL 36908 Fax: 251-843-2568
E-mail: choctaw@fws.gov
http://www.fws.gov/choctaw
The objectives of the Refuge are: to manage habitat for wintering waterfowl, maintain habitat and provide protection for threatened and endangered species, manage wood duck nest boxes and brood rearing habitat, maintain wildlifediversity, manage forest to be productive bottomland hardwoods, and to provide wildlife dependent recreation.

Robert Dailey, Manager

3144 **Little River Canyon National Preserve**
4322 Little River Trail NE 256-845-9605
Ste.100 Fax: 256-997-9129
Fort Payne, AL 35967 E-mail: LIRI_Superintendent@nps.gov
http://www.nps.gov/liri
Little River flows for most of its length atop Lookout Mountain in northeast Alabama. The river and canyon systems are spectacular Appalachian Plateau landscapes any season of the year. Forested uplands, waterfalls, canyon rims andbluffs, stream riffles and pools, boulders and sandstone cliffs offer settings for a variety of recreational activities. Natural resources and cultural heritage come together to tell the story of the preserve, a special place in the SouthernAppalachians.

3145 **Wheeler National Wildlife Refuge Complex**
2700 Refuge Headquarters Road 256-353-7243
Decatur, AL 35603 Fax: 256-340-9728
E-mail: wheeler@fws.gov
http://www.fws.gov/wheeler/
The 35,000 acre wildlife refuge was established in 1938 The refuge is located between Decatur and Huntsville in the Tennessee River Valley of northern Alabama.
Dwight Cooley, Project Leader

3146 **William B Bankhead National Forest**
Bankhead Ranger District 205-489-5111
PO Box 278 Fax: 205-489-3427
Double Springs, AL 35553
http://www.forestcamping.com/dow/southern/bankinfo.htm
The William B Bankhead national Forest covers 180,000 acres in Franklin, Winston and Lawrence counties. Within the forest are the 26,000 acre Sipsey Wilkderness and the Sipsey Wild and Scenic River, offering 61.4 miles of seasonalcanoeing.

Alaska: US Forests, Parks, Refuges

3147 **Alagnak Wild River Katmai National Park**
PO Box 245 907-246-3305
King Salmon, AK 99613 Fax: 907-246-2116
http://www.nps.gov/alag
The Alagnak river offers 69 miles of outstanding white-water floating. The river is also noted for abundant wildlife and sport fishing for five species of salmon.

3148 **Alaska Maritime National Wildlife Refuge**
95 Sterling Highway 907-235-6546
Suite 1 Fax: 907-235-7783
Homer, AK 99603 E-mail: alaskamaritime@fws.gov
http://alaska.fws.gov/nwr/akmar/index.htm
To administer a national network of lands and waters for the conservation management and where appropiate, restoration of the fish, wildlife, and plant resources and their habitats within the US for the benefit of present and futuregeneration of Americans.

3149 **Alaska Peninsula National Wildlife Refuge**
PO Box 277 907-246-3339
King Salmon, AK 99613 Fax: 907-246-6696
http://www.gorp.com/gorp/resource/us_nwr/ak_ak_pe.htm

3150 **Becharof National Wildlife Refuge**
PO Box 277 907-246-3339
MS 545 Fax: 907-246-6696
King Salmon, AK 99613 E-mail: becharof@fws.gov
http://becharof.fws.gov

Daryle Lons, Manager

3151 **Chugach National Forest**
161 East 1st Avenue 907-743-9500
Door 8 Fax: 907-743-9476
Anchorage, AK 99503 http://www.fs.fed.us/r10/chugach

3152 **Denali National Park and Preserve**
PO Box 9 907-683-2294
Denali Park, AK 99755-0009 Fax: 907-683-9612
E-mail: denali_info@nps.gov
http://www.nps.gov/dena

3153 **Innoko National Wildlife Refuge**
PO Box 69 907-524-3251
MS 549 888-601-7970
McGrath, AK 99627 Fax: 907-524-3141
E-mail: innoko@fws.gov
http://innoko.fws.gov

The Innoko National Wildlife Refuge was established December 2, 1980, with the passage of the Alaska National Interest Lands Conservation Act. This 3.85 million acre refuge supports a large nesting waterfowl population, and is wellpopulated with moose, bear, and other animals, as well as a variety of game birds and neotropical bird species and is a relatively flat plain covering much of the drainage area of the Innoko and Iditarod rivers. The vegetation of the reguse is atransition zone.
William H Schaff, Manager

3154 Izembek National Wildlife Refuge
Box 127
MS 515
Cold Bay, AK 99571
907-532-2445
877-837-6332
Fax: 907-532-2549
E-mail: izembek@fws.gov
http://izembec.fws.gov
Established to conserve fish, wildlife and habitats in their natural diversity including, waterfowl, shorebirds, other migratory birds, brown bears and salmon; to fulfill treaty obligations; to provide the opportunity for continuedsubsistence uses by local residents consistent with the purposes previously mentioned; and to ensure necessary water quality and quantity.
Nancy Hoffman, Wildlife Refuge Manager

3155 Kanuti National Wildlife Refuge
101 12th Avenue
MS 555 Room 262
Fairbanks, AK 99701
907-456-0329
877-220-1853
Fax: 907-456-0506
E-mail: kanuti_refuge@fws.gov
http://www.kanuti.fws.gov
Mike Spindler, Manager

3156 Katmai National Park and Preserve
PO Box 7
King Salmon, AK 99613
907-246-3305
Fax: 907-246-2116
http://www.nps.gov/katm

3157 Kenai Fjords National Park
PO Box 1727
Seward, AK 99664
907-422-0500
Fax: 907-422-0571
http://www.nps.gov/kefj
This park encompasses over 600,000 acres of wild coastal Alaska. The Harding Icefield dominates most of the park. This 300-square mile bowl of ice spills out into numerous glaciers at its edges. Tidewater glaciers and the amazingmarine wildlife of the park can be viewed from boat or air. Humpback whales, orca, many species of sea birds, Steller sea lions and other marine wildlife come here because of the rich variety of foods. Sea birds and sea lions also raise their youngon the rocky sites.

3158 Kenai National Wildlife Refuge
PO Box 2139
Soldotna, AK 99669
907-262-7021
Fax: 907-487-2144
http://www.gorp.com/gorp/resource/us_nwr/ak_kenai.htm

3159 Kobuk Valley National Park
PO Box 1029
Kotzebue, AK 99752
907-442-3890
Fax: 907-442-8316
E-mail: NWAK_superintendant@nps.gov
http://www.nps.gov/kova
Mission: Cooperative stewardship for the conservation and understanding of natural and cultural resources in Northwest Alaska.

3160 Kodiak National Wildlife Refuge
1390 Buskin River Road
MS 559
Kodiak, AK 99615
907-487-2600
888-408-3514
Fax: 907-487-2144
E-mail: kodiak@fws.gov
http://www.kodiak.fws.gov
Kodiak National Wildlife Refuge was established to conserve Kodiak brown bears, salmon, sea otters, sea lions, other marine mammals, and migratory birds; to fulfill treaty obligations; to provide for continued subsistence uses; and toensure necessary water quanlity and quantity.
Gary Wheeler, Manager
Jason Osles, Park Ranger

3161 Koyukuk and Nowitna National Wildlife Refuge
101 Front Street
PO Box 287
Galena, AK 99741-0287
907-656-1231
800-656-1231
Fax: 907-656-1708
E-mail: r7kynwr@fws.gov
http://www.koyukuk.fws.gov
Approximately 200 miles west of Fairbanks, the refuge lies within a solar basin encircled by rolling hills capped by alpine tundra. The Nowitna River, a nationally designated Wild River, bisects the refuge and forms a broad meanderingfloodplain. The river passes through a scenic 15 mile canyon with peaks up to 2,100 feet.
Kenton Moos, Manager

3162 Lake Clark National Park and Preserve
240 West 5th Avenue
Suite 236
Anchorage, AK 99501
907-644-3626
Fax: 907-644-3810
E-mail: jeelan_eastlack@nmps.gov
http://www.nps.gov/lacl
Lake Clark National Park and Preserve was created to protect scenic beauty, populations of fish and wildlife, watersheds essential for red salmon, and the traditional lifestyle of local residents.
Dick Proenneke, Wilderness Steward

3163 Selawik National Wildlife Refuge
160 2nd Avenue
PO Box 270
Kotzebue, AK 99752
907-442-3799
800-492-8848
Fax: 907-442-3124
E-mail: selawik@fws.gov
http://www.fws.gov/refuge/Selawik/contact.html
Selawik National Wildlife Refuge was established to conserve the Western Arctic caribou herd, waterfowl, shorebirds, other migratory birds, salmon, and sheefish; to fulfill treaty obligations; to provide for continued subsistence uses;and to ensure necessary water quality and quantity.
LeeAnne Ayres, Manager
Tina Moran, Deputy Refuge Manager

3164 Tetlin National Wildlife Refuge
PO Box 779
Tok, AK 99780
907-883-5312
Fax: 907-883-5747
E-mail: tetlin@fws.gov
http://www.tetlin.fws.gov
Ryan Mollnow, Refuge Manager
Greg Risdahl, Deputy Refuge Manager

3165 Togiak National Wildlife Refuge
PO Box 270
MS 569
Dillingham, AK 99576
907-842-1063
800-817-2538
Fax: 907-842-5402
E-mail: togiak@fws.gov
http://www.togiak.fws.gov
Established to conserve fish and wildlife populations and habitats in their natural diversity including salmon, marine birds, mammals, migrating birds and large mammals, to fulfill international treaty obligations; to provide forcontinued subsistence uses; and to ensure necessary water quality and quantity.
Paul Liedberg, Manager

3166 Tongass National Forest: Chatham Area
204 Siginaka Way
Sitka, AK 99835-7316
907-747-6671
Fax: 907-747-4331
http://www.fs.fed.us/r10/tongass
The Tongass National Forest is a forest of islands and trees and rain. It also abounds in animals and birds and fish, with unsurpassed scenery. It's a place where eagles are commonplace, most every road is a deer crossing, and bearsuse the trails too. The spirituality and scenery demands respect.
Fred Salinas, Forest Supervisor

3167 Tongass National Forest: Ketchikan Area
Federal Building
648 Mission Street
Ketchikan, AK 99901
907-225-3101
Fax: 907-228-6215
http://www.fs.fed.us/r10/tongass
The Tongass National Forest is a forest of islands and trees and rain. It also abounds in animals and birds and fish, with unsurpassed scenery. It's a place where eagles are commonplace, most

every road is a deer crossing, and bearsuse the trails too. The Tongass is a wild place, where the natural world is a strong presence that nurtures spirituality and materially demands respect.

3168 Tongass National Forest: Stikine Area
123 Scow Bay Loop Road
PO Box 309
Petersburg, AK 99833-0309
907-772-3841
Fax: 907-772-5895
http://www.fs.fed.us/r10/tongass

The Tongass National Forest is a forest of islands and trees and rain. It also abounds in animals and birds and fish, with unsurpassed scenery. It's a place where eagles are commonplace, most every road is a deer crossing, and bearsuse the trails too. The Tongass is a wild place, where the natural world is a strong presence that nurtures spirituality and materially demands respect.

3169 Yukon Delta National Wildlife Refuge
807 Chief Eddie Hoffman Road
PO Box 346 MS 535
Bethel, AK 99559
907-543-3151
Fax: 907-543-4413
E-mail: yukondelta@fws.gov
http://www.yukondelta.fws.gov

Yukon Delta National Wildlife Refuge was established to conserce shorebirds, seabirds, whistling swans, emperor, white-fronted and Canada geese, black brant and other migratory birds, salmon, muskox, and marine mammals; to fulfilltreaty obligations; to provide for continued subsistence uses; and to ensure necessary water quality and quantity.
Michael Rearden, Manager

3170 Yukon Flats National Wildlife Refuge
101 12th Avenue
Room 264 MS 575
Fairbanks, AK 99701
907-456-0440
800-531-0676
Fax: 907-456-0447
E-mail: yukonflats@fws.gov
http://www.yukonflats.fws.gov

Located about 100 air miles north of Fairbanks, encompassing about 12 million acres along the Yukon River. In the spring, millions of migrating birds converge on the refuge. With its 40,000 lakes and other wetlands, it has one of thehighest waterfowl nesting densities in North America for ducks, geese, sandhill cranes, loons, grebes and songbirds. Each year, the Yukon Flats is a major contributor to the migrations that occur along the North American flyways.
Robert Jess, Refuge Manager
Wennona Brown, Deputy Refuge Manager

3171 Yukon-Charley Rivers National Preserve
PO Box 167
Eagle, AK 99738
907-547-2233
Fax: 907-547-2247
E-mail: yuch_eagle_cheifofoperation
http://www.nps.gov/yuch

Arizona: US Forests, Parks, Refuges

3172 Apache-Sitgreaves National Forest
PO Box 640
Springerville, AZ 85938
928-333-4301
Fax: 928-333-5966
http://www.fs.fed.us/r3/asnf

Taking care of the land while making the forest resources available to all shareholders. Resources include: high quality water, wilderness, and outdoor recreation; quality habitat for many plants and animals; wood for paper, homes, andhundreds of other uses; forage for wildlife and livestock; a source of minerals.
Chris Knopp, Forests Supervisor
Pam Baltimore, Public Affairs Officer

3173 Bill Williams River National Wildlife Refuge
60911 Highway 95
Parker, AZ 85344
928-667-4144
Fax: 928-667-3402
E-mail: dick_gilbert@fws.gov
http://www.billwilliamsriver.org

Bill Williams River National Wildlife Refuge is located along the Bill Williams River in La Paz and Mojave Counties, Arizona, with the river as the dividing line between the two counties. The refuge was established in 1941 as part ofHavasu NWR as mitigation for the Boulder and Parker Dam projects. In 1993, the two refuges were seperated and the Bill W Unit became the Bill Williams River NWR.

Larry Voyles, Member
Dave Weedman, Member

3174 Buenos Aires National Wildlife Refuge
PO Box 109
Sasabe, AZ 85633
520-823-4251
Fax: 520-823-4247
http://southwest.fws.gov/refuges/arizona/buenosaires

3175 Cabeza Prieta National Wildlife Refuge
1611 N 2nd Avenue
Ajo, AZ 85321
520-387-6483
Fax: 520-387-5359
E-mail: cabezaprieta@fws.gov
http://www.fws.gov/southwest/refuges/arizona/cabeza.htm
Roger Di Rosa, Manager

3176 Chiricahua National Monument
12856 East Rhyolite Creek Road
Wilcox, AZ 85643
520-824-3560
Fax: 520-824-3421
http://www.nps.gov/chir

The monument is mecca for hikers and birders. At the intersection of the Chiricahuan and Sonoran deserts, and the southern Rocky Mountains and northern Sierra Madre in Mexico, Chiricahua plants and animals represents one of the premierareas for biological diversity in the northern hemisphere.

3177 Coconino National Forest
1824 South Thompson Street
Flagstaff, AZ 86001
928-527-3600
Fax: 928-527-3620
http://www.fs.fed.us/r3/coconino/

The Coconino National Forest is one of the most diverse National Forests in the country with landscapes ranging from the famous Red Rocks of Sedona to Ponderosa Pine Forests, to alpine tundra

3178 Coronado National Forest
300 W Congress Street
Tucson, AZ 85701
520-388-8300
http://www.fs.fed.us/r3/coronado

The Coronado National Forest covers 1,780,000 acres of southeastern Arizona and southwestern New Mexico. Elevations range from 3,000 feet to 10,720 feet in 12 widely scattered mountain ranges or sky islands that rise dramatically fromthe desert floor, supporting plant communities as biologically diverse as those encountered on a trip from Mexico to Canada. The views are spectacular from these mountains, and visitors may experience all four seasons during a single day's journey.
Jim Upchurch, Forest Supervisor

3179 Glen Canyon National Recreation Area
Glen Canyon NRA
PO Box 1507
Page, AZ 86040
928-608-6200
Fax: 928-608-6259
E-mail: GLCA_CHVC@nps.gov
http://www.nps.gov/glca

Glen Canyon National Recreation Area offers unparalleled opportunities for water-based & backcountry recreation. The recreation area stretches for hundreds of miles from Lees Ferry in Arizona to the Orange Cliffs of southern Utah,encompassing scenic vistas, geologic wonders, and a panorama of human history. Additionally, the controversy surrounding the construction of Glen Cayon Dam and the creation of Lake Powell contributed to the birth of modern day environmental movement.

3180 Grand Canyon National Park
PO Box 129
Grand Canyon, AZ 86023
928-638-7888
Fax: 928-638-7797
http://www.nps.gov/grca

3181 Imperial National Wildlife Refuge
PO Box 72217
Yuma, AZ 85365
928-783-3371
Fax: 928-783-0652
E-mail: FW2_RW_Imperial@fws.gov
http://www.fws.gov/southwest/refuges/arizona/imperial/index

Imperial National Wildlife Refuge protects wildlife habitat along 30 miles of the lower Colorado River in Arizona and California, including the last unchannelized section before the river enters Mexico.
Elaine Johnson, Manager

3182 Kaibab National Forest
800 South Sixth Street
Williams, AZ 86046
928-635-8200
Fax: 928-635-8208
http://www.fs.fed.us/r3/kai/

3183 Kofa National Wildlife Refuge
356 West 1st Street
Yuma, AZ 85364
928-783-7861
E-mail: FW2_RW_Kofa@fws.gov
http://www.gorp.away.com/gorp/resource/us_nwr/az_kofa.htm

3184 Organ Pipe Cactus National Monument
10 Organ Pipe Drive
Ajo, AZ 85321
520-387-6849
E-mail: orpi_information@nps.gov
http://www.nps.gov/orpi

Organ Pipe Cactus National Monument celebrates the life and landscape of the Sonoran Desert. Here, in this desert wilderness of plants and animals and dramatic mountains and plains scenery, you can drive a lonely road, hike abackcountry trail, camp beneath a clear desert sky, or just soak in the warmth and beauty of Southwest.

3185 Petrified Forest National Park
PO Box 2217
Petrified Forest, AZ 86028
928-524-6228
Fax: 928-524-3567
E-mail: PEFO_superintendant@nps.gov
http://www.nps.gov/pefo

Petrified Forest is a surprising land of scenic wonders and fascinating science. The park is located in northeast Arizona and features one of the world's largest and most colorful concentrations of petrified wood. Also included in thopark's 93,533 acres are the multihued badlands of the Chinle Formation known as the Painted Desert, historic structures, archeological sites and displays of 225 millio-year-old fossils.

3186 Prescott National Forest
344 S Cortez Street
Prescott, AZ 86303
928-443-8000
http://www.fs.fed.us/r3/prescott

This involves taking care of the land while making the forest resources available to all shareholders. Resources include high quality water, wilderness and outdoor recreation; quality habitat for many plants and animals; wood forpaper, homes and hundreds of other uses; forage for wildlife and livestock; and minerals.

3187 Saguaro National Park
3693 S Old Spanish Trail
Tuscon, AZ 85730-5601
520-733-5153
Fax: 520-733-5183
E-mail: mailto:sagu_information@nps.gov
http://www.nps.gov/sagu

This unique desert is home to the most recognizable cactus in the world, the majestic saguaro. Visitors of all ages are fascinated and enchanted by these desert gaints, especially their many interesting and complex interrelationshipswith other desert life. With the average life span of 150 years, a mature saguaro may grow to the height of 50 feet and weigh over 10 tons.

3188 San Bernardino/Leslie Canyon National Refuge
PO Box 3509
Douglas, AZ 85607
520-364-2104
Fax: 520-364-2130
http://www.fws.gov/southwest/refuges/arizona/sanbernardino.htm
Bill Radke, Manager

3189 Sunset Crater Volcano National Monument
6400 N. Hwy 89
Flagstaff, AZ 86004
928-526-0502
Fax: 928-714-0565
http://www.nps.gov/sucr

Welcome to the Flagstaff Area National Monuments! There is something for everyone: prehistoic cliff dwellings at Walnut Canyon, the mountain scenery and geology of Sunset Crater Volcano, and the painted desert landscape and masonrypueblos of Wupatki National Monument. Here at Sunset Crater Volcano, amid lava and cinders, one can imagine a landscape still hot to the touch. Imagine the thoughts of the prehistoric people who lived here when the eruption occured.

3190 Tonto National Forest
2324 East McDowell Road
Phoenix, AZ 85006
602-225-5200
Fax: 602-225-5295
http://www.fs.fed.us/r3/tonto

The Tonto National Forest occupies about 2.8 million acres which generally lie northeast of Phoenix, Ariz., to the Mogollon Rim and east to the San Carlos and Fort Apache Indain Reservations. The west side approximately interstate 17which stretches north of Phoenix to Flagstaff. The lower elevations are of the Sonoran Desert type while the northern portion of the Forest is generally Pinon, Juniper, and Ponderosa Pine types.

3191 Walnut Canyon National Monument
6400 N. Hwy 89
Flagstaff, AZ 86004
928-526-1157
Fax: 928-526-4259
http://www.nps.gov/waca

Hike down into Walnut Canyon and walk in the footsteps of people who lived here over 900 years ago. Built under limestone overhangs, these dwellings were occupied from about 1100 to 1250. Look down into the canyon and imagine the creekrunning through. Visualize a woman hiking up from the bottom with a pot of water on her back. Imagine the men on the rim farming corn or hunting deer. Think of a cold winter night with your family huddled around the fire.

3192 Wupatki National Monument
25137 N Wupatki Loop
Flagstaff, AZ 86004
928-679-2365
Fax: 928-679-2349
http://www.nps.gov

Wupatki, comprised of big skies, open grassland, and desert scrub, with Painted Desert to the east and San Francisco Peaks to the west. A visit to this beautiful landscape will remind you what life was like in this region 900 yearsago.
Chuck Sypher, District Ranger

Arkansas: US Forests, Parks, Refuges

3193 Bald Knob National Wildlife Refuge
1439 Coal Chute Road
Bald Knob, AR 72010
501-724-2458
Fax: 501-724-2460
E-mail: robert_alexander@fws.gov
http://www.fws.gov/baldknob

The refuge facts established in 1993 has 14,800 acres and the location is in White County, Ar approximately two miles south of Bald Knob, AR on Coal Chute Road. It provides habitat for migratory waterfowl and other birds. And also forendangered species recreational and environmental education opportunities.
Robert Alexander, Manager

3194 Buffalo National River
402 N Walnut
Suite 136
Harrison, AR 72601
870-365-2700
Fax: 870-365-2701
E-mail: buff_information@nps.gov
http://www.nps.gov/buff

One of the few remaining unpolluted, free-flowing rivers in the lower 48 states offering both swift-running and placid stretches. The river encompasses 135 miles of the 150 mile long river. It begins as a trickle in the BostonMountains 15 miles above the park boundary. Following what is likely an ancient riverbed, the Buffalo cuts its way through massive limestone bluffs traveling eastward throug the Ozarks and into the Whtie River.

3195 Felsenthal National Wildlife Refuge
5531 Highway 82 West
Crossett, AR 71635
870-364-3167
Fax: 870-364-3757
E-mail: felsenthal@fws.gov
http://www.fws.gov/felsenthal

65,000 acre national wildlife refuge with abuntant water resources - 15,000 acres, and vast bottomland hardwood forest that rises to the pine uplands.
Bernard J Petersen, Project Leader

3196 Greers Ferry National Fish Hatchery
349 Hatchery Road
Heber Springs, AR 72543
501-362-3615
Fax: 501-362-4007
E-mail: greersferry@fws.gov
http://www.fws.gov/greersferry

Through self-guided tours at the hatchery, visitors can observe techniques of trout production, view information exhibits in the aquarium, and see trout in the outdoor raceways. Adjacent to the hatchery, visitors can camp at JFK Parkand trout fish the Little

Red River. Nearby, the US Army Corps of Engineers has a visitor center, two mini-hiking trails and an overlook of Greers Ferry Dam. Greers Ferry Lake on the other side of the dam offers camping, swimming, fishing and otherwater sports.
Sherri Shoults, Hatchery Manager

3197 Holla Bend National Wildlife Refuge
10448 Holla Bend Road 479-229-4300
Dardanelle, AR 72834 Fax: 479-229-4302
E-mail: hollabend@fws.gov
http://www.fws.gov/HollaBend
Part of a system of over 475 national wildlife refuges located across the country. Administered by US Fish and Wildlife Service, this system of refuges, the finest in the world, protects important habitat needed to provide a home for awide variety of wildlife. These refuges also provide the public with valuable opportunities to see and learn about wildlife and to enjoy outdoor activities such as hunting and fishing. Holla Bend's main purpose is to provide a winter home for ducksand geese.

Durwin Carter, Manager

3198 Hot Springs National Park
101 Reserve Street 501-620-6715
Hot Springs, AR 71901 Fax: 501-624-3458
E-mail: HOSP_Interpretation@nps.gov
http://www.nps.gov/hosp
The park protects eight historic bathhouses with the former luxurious Fordyce Bathhouse housing the park visitor center. The entire Bathhouse Row area is national Historic Landmark District that contains the grandest collection ofbathhouses of its kind in North America. By protecting the 47 hot springs and their watershed, the National Park Service continues to provide visitors with historic leisure activities such as hiking, picnicking and scenic drives.

Josie Fernandez, Superintendent
Mardi Arce, Deputy Superintendent

3199 Ouachita National Forest
Federal Building 501-321-5202
PO Box 1270 Fax: 501-321-5305
Hot Springs, AR 71902 http://www.fs.fed.us/r8/ouachita
Mission: To sustain the ecological health and productivity of lands and waters entrusted to our care and provide for human uses compatible with that goal. We understand that our greatest asset is the land, our greatest strength is ourworkforce, and our greatest challenge is achieving public understanding, trust, and confidence in all that we do.

3200 Overflow National Wildlife Refuge
3858 Highway 8 East 870-473-2869
Parkdale, AR 71661 Fax: 870-473-5191
http://southeast.fws.gov/Overflow/index.html
Refuge objectives are to: provide a diversity of habitat types for migratory waterfowl and other birds; provide habitat and protection for the delisted bald eagle; provide opportunities for environmental and ecological research;provide a variety of recreational opportunities consistent with primary wildlife objectives; and expand the public's understanding of and appreciation for the environment with special emphasis on natural resources.

Lake Lewis, Manager

3201 Ozark-St. Francis National Forest
605 W Main Street 479-964-7200
Russleville, AR 72801 http://www.fs.fed.us/oonf/ozark
The Ozark-St. Francis National Forests are really two separate Forests with many differences. They are distinct in their own topographical, geological, biological, cultural and social differences, yet each makes up a part of theoverall National Forest system.
Judi Henry, Forest Supervisor

3202 Pond Creek National Wildlife Refuge
1958 Central Road 870-289-2126
Lockesburg, AR 71846 Fax: 870-289-2127
http://www.fws.gov/southeast/PondCreek
Pond Creek National Wildlife Refuge plans to: protect the area's wetland and bottomland hardwood hbitat for natural diversity of wildlife; provide habitat for neo-tropical migratory birds; provide wintering habitat for migratorywaterfowl; provide breeding and nesting habitat for wood ducks; and to provide opportunities for compatible public outdoor recreation.

Paul Gideon, Manager

3203 Wapanocca National Wildlife Refuge
178 Hammond Avenue Highway 42 East 870-343-2595
PO Box 279 Fax: 870-343-2416
Turrell, AR 72384 E-mail: bill_peterson@fws.gov
http://www.fws.gov/wapanocca/
The 5,484 acre refuge is an important stopover for waterfowl traveling the Mississippi Flyway and for songbirds as they migrate to and from Central and South America. The refuge is open to limited small and big game hunting. Auto tourroutes offers excellent wildlife observation, photography and hiking opportunities. An observation platform is located on the east side of the 600 acre Wapanocca Lake.

Bill Peterson, Refuge Manager

3204 White River National Wildlife Refuge
57 South CC Camp Road 870-282-8200
PO Box 205 Fax: 870-282-8234
St Charles, AR 72140 E-mail: whiteriver@fws.gov
http://www.fws.gov/whiteriver
Refuge objectives are to provide: optimum habitat for migratory birds; habitat and protection for endangered species: a natural diversity of wildlife common to the White River bottoms; opportunities and facilities for wildlife orientedrecreation and environmental education; cooperation with other water and land managing agencies and private interests to foster proper management of the White River Basin's resources; and preservation of appropriate wooded areas in their naturalcondition.
Keith Weaver, Project Leader

California: US Forests, Parks, Refuges

3205 Angeles National Forest
701 North Santa Anita Avenue 626-574-1613
Arcadia, CA 91006 Fax: 626-574-5207
http://www.fs.fed.us/r5/angeles
The Angeles National Forest covers 650,000 acres and is the backyard playground to the huge metropolitan area of Los Angeles. The Los Angeles National Forest manages the watersheds eithin its boundaries to provide valuable water tosouthern California and to protect surrounding communities from catastrophics floods.
Tom Contreras, Forest Supervisor

3206 Bear Valley National Wildlife Refuge
4009 Hill Rd 916-667-2231
Tulelake, CA 96134 Fax: 916-667-3299
E-mail: ron_cole@fws.gov
http://www.fws.gov
Refuge was established to protect a major winter night roost site for bald egales. The acquisition program was completed in 1991. Klamath Basin hosts the largest wintering popluation of blad eagles in the contiguous United States, withnumbers some years approaching 1,000. Refuge serves as one of serveral eagle roots in the Basin. It consists of large stands of old-growth tinmber, which protects the birds at night from the harsh winter weather.
Ron Cole, Refuge Manager

3207 Bitter Creek National Wildlife Refuge
Hopper Mountain NWR 805-644-5185
Po Box 5839 Fax: 805-644-1732
Ventura, CA 93005 http://www.hoppermountain.fws.gov/bitterck

The primary wildlife traditional feeding and roosting habitat for the California condor. Also provides habitat for the San Joaquin kit fox, golden eagle, Southern bald eagle and American peregrine falcon. 14,000 contiguous acres,mostly annual grasslands with some juniper and scrub oak with grass understory. Public use is severely limited because of the sensitive situation of the California condor. The refuge can be viewed from the Cerro Noroeste Road.
Dan Tappe, Refuge Manager

3208 **Blue Ridge National Wildlife Refuge**
Kern NWR 805-644-5185
PO Box 5839 http://www.hoppermountain.fws.gov/blueridge
Ventura, CA 93005
Primary wildlife area is a traditional summer roosting site for the endangered Califorina condor. The habitat includes 897 acres of rugged mountains, rock outcroppings, chaparral and coniferous trees. The refuge is closed to publicaccess due to the sensitivity of California condors and its isolation and difficulty in access.
Dan Tappe, Refuge Manager

3209 **Castle Rock National Wildlife Refuge**
Humboldt Bay NWR 707-733-5406
PO Box 576 Fax: 707-733-1946
Loleta, CA 95551 http://www.gorp.com
The Refuge is a 14-acre offshore rock with steep cliffs and sparse vegetation. It was established in 1981 to protect an important migration staging area of the threatened Aleutian Canada goose. Over 21,000 of these roost on the island,which contains the second largest seabird breeding colony in California. Haul-out for a variety of marine mammals, including California sea lion, Stellar sea lion and northern elephant seal. Not open to the public, but wildlife can be observed fromshore.

3210 **Channel Islands National Park**
1901 Spinnaker Drive 805-658-5730
Ventura, CA 93001 Fax: 805-658-5799
E-mail: chis_interpretation@nps.gov
http://www.nps.gov/chis/siteindex.htm
Encompasses five of the eight California Channel Islands and their ocean environment, preserving and protecting a wealth of natural and cultural resources. Marine life ranges from microscopic plankton to the blue whale, the largestanimal to live on Earth. Archeological and cultural resources span a period of more than 10,000 years of human habitation.

3211 **Clear Lake National Wildlife Refuge**
Klamath Basin NWR Complex 916-667-2231
Route 1 Box 74 Fax: 916-667-3299
Tulelake, CA 96134 http://klamathbasinrefuges.fws.gov
Clear Lake National Wildlife Refuge plans to: maintain habitat for endangered, threatened and sensitive species; provide and enhance habitat for fall and spring migrant waterfowl; protect native habitats and wildlife representativeofthe natural biological diversity of the Klamath Basin; integrate the maintenance of productive wetland habitats and sustainable agriculture; and to provide high quality wildlife-dependent visitor services.

3212 **Cleveland National Forest**
10845 Rancho Bernardo Road 858-673-6180
Suite 200 Fax: 858-673-6192
San Diego, CA 92127 http://www.fs.fed.us/r5/cleveland

3213 **Coachella Valley National Wildlife Refuge**
906 W Siclair Road 760-348-5278
PO Box 120 Fax: 760-348-7245
Calipatria, CA 92233 E-mail: christian_schoneman@fws.gov
http://www.fws.gov
Contains 13,000 acres consisting of palm oasis woodlands, perennial desert pools and blow-sand habitat. This habitat is critical for the Coachella Valley fringe-toed lizard (Uma inornata) and flat-tailed horned lizard. These threatenedspecies are restricted to the refuge dune system and a few other small areas. Also has the state's second largest grove of native fan palms and the Coachella milk-vetch, a species of special concern.
Christian Schoneman, Project Leader

3214 **Death Valley National Park**
PO Box 579 760-786-3200
Death Valley, CA 92328 Fax: 760-786-3246
E-mail: deva_superintendant@nps.gov
http://www.nps.gov/deva/index.htm
Death Valley National Park has more than 3.3 million acres of spectacular desert scenery, interesting and rare desert wildlife, complex geology, undisturbed wilderness and sites of historical and cultural interest. The National ParkService is dedicated to the protection and preservation of this park's unique resources for everyone to enjoy now and for future generations.

3215 **Delevan National Wildlife Refuge**
Sacramento NWR Complex 530-934-2801
752 County Road 99W Fax: 530-934-7814
Willows, CA 95988 http://www.fws.gov/sacramentovalleyrefuges
Delevan NWR is part of the Sacramento NWR Complex and is located in the Sacramento Valley of north-central California. The refuge consists of nearly 5,800 acres comprised of seasonal marsh, permanent ponds, watergrass and uplands inColusa County.

3216 **Devil's Postpile National Monument**
PO Box 3999 760-934-2289
Mammoth Lakes, CA 93546 Fax: 760-934-4780
http://www.nps.gov/depo
The geologic formation that is the Postpile is the world's finest example of unusual columnar basalt. Its columns of lava, with their four to seven sides, display of honeycomb pattern of order and harmony. Another jewel in the Monumentis the San Joaquin River.

3217 **Eldorado National Forest**
100 Forni Road 530-622-5061
Placeville, CA 95667 Fax: 530-621-5297
http://www.fs.fed.us/r5/eldorado
Situated near the California gold discovery site on the American River at Coloma, this forest still boast numerous gold-bearing rivers and streams.Fishing opportunities are abundant. Only 34 miles of waterways are stocked, theremainder contain resident trout. Winter sports are cross country ski, sonowmobile and snowshoe. Backcountry exploration takes place year round in the Desolation and Mokelumme wildernesses.
Kathy Hardy, Forest Supervisor

3218 **Ellicott Slough National Wildlife Refuge**
San Andreas Rd 510-792-0222
Watsonville, CA 94560 E-mail: sfbaynwrc@fws.gov
http://www.fws.gov

3219 **Havasu National Wildlife Refuge**
317 Mesquite Ave 760-326-3853
Needles, CA 92363 Fax: 760-326-5745
E-mail: linda_l_miller@fws.gov
http://www.fws.gov/southwest/refuges/arizona/havasu
Benjamin Tuggle, Regional Director

3220 **Hopper Mountain National Wildlife Refuge**
PO Box 5839 805-644-5185
Ventura, CA 93005 Fax: 805-644-1732
E-mail: hoppermountain@fws.gov
http://www.fws.gov/hoppermountain
The area is a traditional feeding site for the endangered California condor. Condors use the area frequently from October through May. A variety of other birds occur during migration and year round. The habitat includes 2,471 acres ofgrassland, chaparral and coastal sage scrub. There is a small, 350 acre area of intact California black walnut groves, some of the last remaining in southern California.
Dan Tappe, Refuge Manager

3221 **Inyo National Forest**
351 Pacu Lane 760-873-2400
Suite 200 http://www.r5.fs.fed.us/inyo/
Bishop, CA 93514
The Inyo National Forest is a unique and special area of public land located along the aestern edge of California and Sierra Ne-

vada. Extending 165 miles along the California/Nevada border between Los Angeles and Reno, the Inyo Nationalforest includes 1.9 million acres of pristine lakes, fragile meadows, winding streams, rugged Sierra Nevada peaks, and arid Great Baisn Mountains. Elevations range frome 4,000 to 14,495 feet, providing diverse habitats that support vegetationpatterns ranging.

3222 Joshua Tree National Park

74485 National Park Drive 760-367-5500
Twentynine Palms, CA 92277-3597 Fax: 760-367-6392
E-mail: JOTR_info@nps.gov
http://www.nps.gov/jotr

Joshua Tree National Park's 794,000 acres span the transition between the Mojave and Colorado deserts of Southern California. Proclaimed a National Monument in 1936 and a Biosphere Reserve in 1984, Joshua Tree was designated a NationalPark In 1994. The area possesses a rich human history and a pristine natural environment.

3223 Kern National Wildlife Refuge

PO Box 670 661-725-2767
Delano, CA 93216-0670 Fax: 661-725-6041
http://www.natureali.org/KNWR.htm

David Hardt, Manager

3224 Kings Canyon National Park

Sequoia & Kings Canyon National Park
47050 Generals Highway 559-565-3341
Three Rivers, CA 93271 Fax: 559-565-3730
http://www.kingscanyon.areaparks.com

Kings Canyon National Park, located in California's Sierra Nevada Mountains, is a park most famous for its pristine stands of Giant Sequoia trees. Visitors explore Grant Grove along a network of easy trails. For the more adventurous,longer trails including those in the remote Kings Canyon Backcountry provide a greater challenge.

3225 Klamath Basin National Wildlife Refuges

4009 Hill Road 530-667-2231
Tulelake, CA 96134 Fax: 530-667-8337
E-mail: r8kbwebmaster@fws.gov
http://http://klamathbasinrefuges.fws.gov

The Klamath Basin National Wildlife Refuges Complex consists of six refuges in Northern California and Southern Oregon. The refuges support the largest concentration of migratory water fowl on the west coast and the largest winteringnumbers of bald eagles in the lower 48 states.

Ron Cole, Refuge Manager
Greg Austin, Assistant Refuge Manager

3226 Klamath National Forest

1312 Fairlane Road
Yreka, CA 96097 530-842-6131
http://www.fs.fed.us/r5/klamath

The Klamath National Forest covers an area of 1,700,000 acres located in Siskiyou County, Northern California and Jackson County, Oregon. The forest comprises some five wilderness areas, Marble Mountain, Russian Wilderness Area,Trinity Alps, Red Buttes Wilderness Area and Siskiyou Wilderness Area.

Peg Boland, Forest Supervisor
Patricia A Grantham, Deputy Forest Supervisor

3227 Lake Tahoe Basin Management Unit

35 College Drive 530-543-2600
S Lake Tahoe, CA 96150 Fax: 530-573-2693
http://www.fs.fed.us/r5/ltbmu/

Majestic sceenery and diverse recreation oppotunities draw millions of visitors to the Lake Tahoe Basin annually. Changing colors throughout the year afford a brilliant backdrop to the many available activities in all seasons. TheBasin is home to a rich diversity of plants and animals that can be viewed during walks at interpertive sites and on many forest trails.

3228 Lassen National Forest

2550 Riverside Drive 530-257-2151
Susanville, CA 96130 http://www.fs.fed.us/r5/lassen

Lassen National Forest lies at the heart of a fascinating part of California, a crossroads of people and nature. This is where the Sierra Nevada, the Cascades, the Modoc Plateau and the Great Basin meet. Within Lassen National Forest,you can explore a lava tube or the land of Ishi, the last survivor of the Yahi Tana Native American tribe: watch prong-horn antelope glide across sage flats; drive four-wheel trails into granite country appointed with sapphire lakes or discoverwildflowers on foot.

3229 Lava Beds National Monument

1 Indian Well Headquarters 530-667-8100
Tulelake, CA 96134 Fax: 530-667-2737
E-mail: LABE_SUperintendent@nps.gov
http://www.nps.gov/labe

Volcanic eruptions on the Medicine Lake shield volcano have created an incredibly rugged landscape punctuated by cinder cones, lava flows, spatter cones, lava tube caves and pit craters. During the Modoc War of 1872-1873, the ModocIndains used these tortuous lava flows to their advantage. Under the leadership of Captain Jack, the Modocs took refuge in Captain Jack's Stronghold, a natural lava fortress.

3230 Los Padres National Forest

6755 Hollister Avenue 805-968-6640
Suite 150 http://www.fs.fed.us/r5/lospadres
Goleta, CA 93117

Los Padres National Forest encompasses nearly 2 million acres of the central coastal mountains of California.

Ken Heffner, Forest Supervisor
Ann Garland, Deputy Forest Supervisor

3231 Lower Klamath National Wildlife Refuge

Hill Road, Route 1 530-667-2231
Box 74 http://klamathbasinrefuges.fws.gov
Tulelake, CA 96134

The objectives of the refuge are to: maintain habitat for endangered, threatened and sensitive species; provide and enhance habitat for fall and spring migrant waterfowl; protect native habitats and wildlife representative of thenatural biological diversity of the Klamath Basin; integrate the maintenance of productive wetland habitats and sustainable agriculture; provide high quality wildlife-dependent visitor services.

3232 Mendocino National Forest

825 North Humboldt Avenue 530-934-3316
Willows, CA 95988 E-mail: mailroom_r5_mendocino@fs.fed.us
http://www.fs.fed.us/r5/mendocino

The Mendocino national Forest was set aside by President Roosevelt in 1907. It was frist named the Stony Creek Reserve and then the Stony Creek National Forest. It was later named the California National Forest and in 1932 became theMendocino National Forest. The MNF straddles the eastern spur of the Coastal Mountain Range in northernwestern Califonia, just a three hour drive north of San Francisco and Sacramento.

Tom Contreras, Forest Supervisor

3233 Modoc National Forest

800 West 12th Street 530-233-5811
Alturas, CA 96101 Fax: 530-233-8709
http://www.fs.fed.us/r5/modoc

A land of contrasts and unspoiled vaction-hideaway settings. Nestled in the extreme northeastern corner of California, The Modoc National Forest is 140 miles east of Redding on Highway 299, and 169 miles north of Reno, Nevada, viahighway 395. The Modoc National Forest features several mountain areas. The Warner Mountains, on its east, are the western edge of Great Basin Province, the Medicine Lake Highlands, to northwest, are a couthern spur of the Cascade Range.

Stanley G Sylva, Forest Supervisor

3234 Modoc National Wildlife Refuge

PO Box 1610 530-233-3572
Alturas, CA 96101-1610 Fax: 530-233-4143
E-mail: modoc@fws.gov
http://www.modoc.fws.gov

A 7,000+ acre refuge established to manage and protect migratory waterfowl.

Steve Clay, Refuge Manager
Sean Cross, Assistant Refuge Manager

3235 **Pinnacles National Monument**
5000 Highway 146 831-389-4485
Paicines, CA 95043 Fax: 831-389-4489
http://www.nps.gov/pinn
Rising out of the chaparral-covered Gabilan Mountains, east of central California's Salinas Valley, are the spectacular remains of an ancient volcano. Massive monoliths, spires, sheer-walled canyons and talus passages define millionsof years of erosion, faulting and tectonic plate movement is reowned for the beauty and variety of its spring wildflowers. Hiking, rock climbing, picnicing and sildlife observation can be enjoyed throughout the year.

3236 **Pixley National Wildlife Refuge**
Kern NWR 661-725-2767
Po Box 670 http://www.fws.gov
Delano, CA 93216
Pixley national Wildlife Refuge provides for the endangered San Joaquin kit fox, Tipton kangaroo rat, and blunt-nosed leopard lizard.

3237 **Plumas National Forest**
159 Lawrence Street 530-283-2050
Quincy, CA 95971-6025 Fax: 530-283-7746
http://www.fs.fed.us/r5/plumas
The Plumas National Forest has fresh conifer forests, rugged cayons, crystal clear lakes, grassy meadows, trout filled streams and brilliant star-filled skies. Located where the Sierra Nevada and Cascade Mountain ranges meet, thisforest has more than 100 lakes, 1,000 miles of rivers and streams, and over a million acres of National Forest.
Alice Carlton, Forest Supervisor

3238 **Redwood National Park**
1111 2nd Street 707-464-6101
Crescent City, CA 95531 Fax: 707-464-1812
http://www.nps.gov/redw
The world's tallest living trees can found along the northern California coast. Of the coast redwood forests still around today, almost one half of them can be found within the projected boundaries of Redwood National and State Parks.In 1994, the National Park Service and the Califonia State Parks joined forces to manage four parks: Redwood National, Jebediah Smith, Del Norte Coast, and Prairie Creek Redwoods State Parks collectively known as Redwood National and State Parks.

3239 **Sacramento National Wildlife Refuge Complex**
752 County Road 99 West 530-934-2801
Willows, CA 95988 Fax: 530-934-7814
E-mail: sacramentovalleyrefuges@fws.gov
http://sacramentovalleyrefuges.fws.gov
The Complex consists of five national wildlife refuges and three wildlife management areas that comprise over 35,000 acres of wetlands and uplands in the Sacramento Valley of California. In addition there are over 30,000 acres ofconservation easements in the Complex. The refuges and easements serve as resting and feeding areas for nearly half the migratory birds on the Pacific Flyway.

3240 **Salinas River National Wildlife Refuge**
PO Box 524 510-792-0222
Newark, CA 94560 http://www.fws.gov
367 acres of diverse habitats including ocean, beach, dunes, grassland, river, lagoon, and salt marsh.

3241 **San Bernardino National Forest**
602 South Tippecanoe Avenue 909-382-2600
San Bernardino, CA 92408 http://www.fs.fed.us/r5/sanbernardino
In the San Bernardino Mountains, the forest service has developed an extensive network of campgrounds and dozens of picnic areas for families and groups who want to enjoy a day in the mountains. The forest offers camping, picnicking,fishing, boating, swimming, hiking, horseback riding and more. During the winter, visitors come to the forest to cross-contry and down ski, snowboard and snowmobile.
Jeanne Wade Evans, Forest Supervisor
Max Copenhagen, Deputy Forest Supervisor

3242 **San Francisco Bay National Wildlife Refuge Complex**
9500 Thornton Avenue 510-792-0222
Newark, CA 94560 E-mail: sfbaynwrc@fws.gov
http://www.fws.gov/sfbayrefuges
The San Francisco Bay National Refuge Complex is a collection of seven National Wildlife Refuges administered by the US Fish and Wildlife Service-Antioch Dunes National Wildlife Refuge, Don Edwards San Francisco Bay National Wildliferefuge, Ellicott Slough National Wildlife Refuge, Farallon National Wildlife Refuge, Marin Islands National Wildlife Refuge, Salinas River National Wildlife Refuge, and San Pablo National Wildlife Refuge.

3243 **San Luis National Wildlife Refuge**
PO Box 2176 209-826-3508
Los Banos, CA 93635 Fax: 209-826-1445
http://http://www.fws.gov/sanluis
Mission: Working with others, to conserve, protect and enhance fish, wildlife, and plants and their habitats for the continuing benefit of the American people.

3244 **San Pablo Bay National Wildlife Refuge**
7715 Lakeville Highway 707-769-4200
Petaluma, CA 94954 http://www.pickleweed.org
San Pablo Bay National Wildlife Refuge protects and preserves habitat critical to the survival of the endangered California clapper rail and salt marsh harvest mouse. The Refuge and surrounding San Pablo Bay area also provide winteringhabitat for millions of shorebirds and thousands of waterfowl, including the largest wintering population of canvasbacks on the west coast.
Jerry Karr, President
B K Cooper, Vice President

3245 **Santa Monica Mountains National Recreation**
401 West Hillcrest Drive 805-370-2301
Thousand Oaks, CA 91360 Fax: 805-370-2351
http://www.nps.gov/samo
Santa Monica Mountains rise above Los Angeles, widen to meet the curve of Santa Monica Bay and reach their highest peaks facing the ocean, forming a beautiful and multi-faceted landscape. Santa Monica Mountains National Recreation Areais a cooperative effort that joins federal, state and local park agencies with private preserves and landowners to protect the natural and cultural resources of this transverse mountain range and seashore.

3246 **Sequoia National Forest**
1839 South Newcomb Street 559-784-1500
Porterville, CA 93257 Fax: 559-781-4744
http://www.fs.fed.us/r5/sequoia
The Sequoia National Forest is at the southern tip of the Sierra Nevada range. Its highest point is 12,432 foot Florence Peak in the Golden Trout Wilderness. The forest has five wildernesses, a scenic byway and four wild and scenicrivers. About 10,000 cows graze on the forest land. Camping, water sports, hiking, downhill and cross-country skiing and horseback riding are amoung the forest's many recreational activities.

3247 **Shasta-Trinity National Forest**
3644 Avtech Parkway 530-226-2500
Redding, CA 96002 Fax: 530-226-2470
http://www.fs.fed.us/r5/shastatrinity
J Sharon Heywood, Forest Supervisor

3248 **Sierra National Forest**
1600 Tollhouse Road 559-297-0706
Clovis, CA 93611 E-mail: dkohut@fs.fed.us
http://www.fs.fed.us/r5/sierra
Edward C Cole, Forest Supervisor

3249 **Six Rivers National Forest**
1330 Bayshore Way 707-442-1721
Eureka, CA 95501 Fax: 707-442-9242
http://www.fs.fed.us/r5/sixrivers
Six Rivers National Forest lies east of Redwood State and National Parks in northwestern California, and stretches southward from the Oregon border for about 140 miles.
Tyrone Kelley, Forest Supervisor
Will Metz, Deputy Forest Supervisor

3250 **Sonny Bono Salton Sea National Wildlife Refuge Complex**
906 W Sinclair Road
Calipatria, CA 92233
760-348-5278
http://saltonsea.fws.gov
The Refuge is composed of two disjunctive units, separated by 18 miles of private lands. Each unit contains managed wetland habitat, agricultural fields, and tree rows. The courses of the New and Alamo rivers run through the Refuge,providing freshwater inflow to the Salton Sea.

3251 **Stanislaus National Forest**
19777 Greenley Road
Sonora, CA 95370
209-532-3671
Fax: 209-533-1890
http://www.fs.fed.us/r5/stanislaus
The Stanislaus National Forest, created on February 22, 1897, is among the oldest of the National Forests. It is named for the Stanislaus River whose headwaters rise within Forest boundaries. The Spanish explorer Gabriel Moraga namedthe river Our Lady of Guadalupe during an 1806 expedition. Later, the river was renamed in honor of Estanislao, an Indian leader.

3252 **Sutter National Wildlife Refuge**
Sacramento NWR Complex
752 County Road 99W
Willows, CA 95988
530-934-2801
Fax: 530-934-7814
http://www.fws.gov

3253 **Tahoe National Forest**
631 Coyote Street
Nevada City, CA 95959
530-265-4531
http://www.fs.fed.us/r5/tahoe/
The Tahoe National Forest straddles the crest of the Sierra Nevada mountains in northern California, and encompasses a vast territory, from the golden foothills on the western slope to the high peaks of the Sierra crest.

3254 **Tijuana Slough National Wildlife Refuge**
Tijuana River NERR
301 Caspian Way
Imperial Beach, CA 91932
619-575-2704
Fax: 619-575-6913
http://www.fws.gov
Established in 1980 to conserve and protect endangered and threatened fish, wildlife and plant species. Conservation of the light-footed clapper rail was the primary impetus for the creation of the refuge. The refuge is part of alarger unit called the Tijuana River National Estuarine Research Reserve, which is administered by the National Oceanographic and Atmospheric Administration.

3255 **Tule Lake National Wildlife Refuge**
4009 Hill Road
Tulelake, CA 96134
530-667-2231
Fax: 530-667-3299
http://www.fws.gov/klamathbasinrefuges/tulelake/tulelake.html
The objectives of Tule Lake are to: maintain habitat for endangered, threatened and sensitive species; provide and enhance habitat for fall and spring migrant waterfowl; protect native habitats and wildlife representative of thenatural biological diversity of the Klamath Basin; integrate the maintenance of productive wetland habitats and sustainable agriculture; and ensure that the refuge agricultural practices confirm to the principles of integrated pest management.

3256 **Yosemite National Park**
PO Box 577
Yosemite National Park, CA 95389
209-372-0200
http://www.nps.gov
Yosemite National Park embraces a spectacular tract of mountain- and-valley scenery in the Sierra Nevada, which was set aside as a national park in 1890. The park harbors a grand collection of waterfalls, meadows, and forests thatinclude groves of giant sequoias, the world's largest living things. Highlights of the park include Yosemite Valley, and its high cliffs and waterfalls;Wawona's history center and historic hotel; the Mariposa Grove, which contains hundreds of ancientgiant sequoias.

Colorado: US Forests, Parks, Refuges

3257 **Alamosa/Monte Vista/ Baca National Wildlife Refuge Complex**
9383 El Rancho Lane
Alamosa, CO 81101
719-589-4021
Fax: 719-587-0595
E-mail: alamosa@fws.gov
http://alamosa.fws.gov
The Valley extends over 100 miles from north to south and 50 miles from east to west, with dwarfing mountains in three directions. The surrounding mountains feed the arid valley with precious surface water, as well as replenish anexpansive underground reservoir. This liquid wealth has made two National Wildlife Refuges possible in the San Luis Valley: Alamosa and Monte Vista.

3258 **Arapaho National Wildlife Refuge**
953 JC Rd 32
Walden, CO 80480
970-723-8202
Fax: 970-723-8528
E-mail: arapaho@fws.gov
http://arapaho.fws.gov
Arapaho National Wildlife Refuge supports diverse wildlife habitats including sagebrush grassland uplands, grassland meadows, willow riparian areas, wetlands and mixed conifer and aspen woodland. This refuge is one in a system of over500 National Wildlife Refuges, a network of lands set aside and managed specifically for wildlife. It is administered by the US Fish and Wildlife Service.

3259 **Browns Park National Wildlife Refuge**
1318 Highway 318
Maybell, CO 81640
970-365-3613
Fax: 970-365-3614
E-mail: brownspark@fws.gov
http://www.brownspark.fws.gov
The primary purpose of Browns Park Refuge is to provide high quality nesting and migration habitat for the Great Basin Canada Goose, ducks and other migratory birds. Before Flaming Gorge Dam was constructed in 1962, the Green Riverflooded annually, creating excellent waterfowl nesting, feeding and resting marshes in the backwater sloughs and old stream meanders. The dam stopped the flooding, eliminating much of this waterfowl habitat.

3260 **Colorado National Monument**
Fruita, CO 81521
970-858-3617
Fax: 970-858-0372
E-mail: COLM_Info@nps.gov
http://www.nps.gov/colm
Colorado National Monument consists of geological features including: towering red sandstone monoliths, deep sheer-walled canyons and a variety of wildlife.

3261 **Curecanti National Recreation Area**
102 Elk Creek
Gunnison, CO 81230
970-641-2337
Fax: 970-641-3127
E-mail: CURE_Vis_Mail@nps.gov
http://www.nps.gov/cure
Three reservoirs, named for corresponding dams on the Gunnison River, form the heart of Curecanti National Recreation Area; Blue Mesa Reservoir, Morrow Point Reservoir and the Crystal Reservoir.

3262 **Dinosaur National Monument**
4545 East Highway 40
Dinosaur, CO 81610
970-374-3000
Fax: 970-374-3003
http://www.nps.gov/dino
Dinosaur Monument protects a large deposit of fossil dinosaur bones that lived millons of years ago.

3263 **Florissant Fossil Beds National Monument**
PO Box 185
Florissant, CO 80816
719-748-3253
Fax: 719-748-3164
E-mail: FLFO_Information@nps.gov
http://www.nps.gov/flfo
Huge petrified redwoods and incredibly detailed fossils of ancient insects and plants reveal a very different Colorado of long

ago. A lake formed in the valley and the fine-grained sediments at its bottom became the final resting-placefor thousands of insects and plants. These sediments compacted into layers of shale and preserved the delicated details of these organisms as fossils.

3264 Great Sand Dunes National Park & Preserve
11999 Highway 150
Mosca, CO 81146
719-378-6399
Fax: 719-378-6310
http://www.nps.gov/grsa

These dunes are the tallest in North America, rising 750 feet from the valley floor. The dunes are home to some unique and spectacular species of flora and fauna. Besides a large variety of birds, there are quite a few species ofmammals that visit or reside within the dunes. Few reptiles are found here due to the high altitude.

3265 Rio Grande National Forest
1803 W US Highway 160
Monte Vista, CO 81144
719-852-5941
http://www.fs.fed.us/r2/riogrande

The Rio Grande National Forest is 1.86 million acres located in southwestern Colorado and remains one of the true undiscovered jewels of Colorado. The Continental Divide runs for 236 miles along most of the western border of theForest. The Forest present myraid ecosystems; from 7600-ft alpine desert to over 14,300-ft in the majestic Sangre de Cristo Wilderness on the eastern side.

3266 Rocky Mountain National Park
1000 Highway 36
Estes Park, CO 80517
970-586-1206
Fax: 970-586-1256
E-mail: ROMO_informatin@nps.gov
http://www.nps.gov/romo

3267 San Juan National Forest
15 Burnett Court
Durango, CO 81301
970-247-4874
Fax: 970-385-1243
http://www.fs.fed.us/r2/sanjuan

San Jaun National Forest, a region of forested mountains, 14,000-foot peaks, scenic roads, geological wonders, hisoric and prehistoric communities, and a narrow-gauge railroad.

Mark Stiles, Forest Supervisor
Howard Sargent, Deputy Forest Supervisor

3268 White River National Forest
900 Grand Avenue
PO Box 948
Glenwood Springs, CO 81602
970-945-2521
Fax: 970-945-3266
http://www.fs.fed.us/r2/whiteriver

The two and one quarter million acre White River National Forest is located in the heart of the Colorado Rocky Mountains, approximately two to four hours west of Denver on Interstate 70. The scenic beauty of the area, along with ampledeveloped and undeveloped recreation opportunities on the forest, accounts for the fact the White River consistently ranks as one of the top five Forests nationwide for total recreation use.

Connecticut: US Forests, Parks, Refuges

3269 Stewart B McKinney National Wildlife Refuge
733 Old Clinton Road
Westbrook, CT 06498
860-399-2513
Fax: 860-399-2515
E-mail: r5rw_sbmnwr@fws.mail.gov
http://www.fws.gov/northeast/mckinney

Delaware: US Forests, Parks, Refuges

3270 Bombay Hook National Wildlife Refuge
2591 Whitehall Neck Road
Smyrna, DE 19977
302-653-6872
E-mail: fw5rw_bhnwr@fws.gov
http://bombayhook.fws.gov

Stretching about eight miles along Delaware Bay and covering nearly 16,000 acres, Bombay Hook NWR was established as a refuge for migratory waterfowl. Today, the Refuge provides habitat for a diversity of wildlife. The refuge offersauto tours, walking trails, observation towers, and interpretive displays for the visiting public.

3271 Prime Hook National Wildlife Refuge
11978 Turkle Pond Road
Milton, DE 19968
302-684-8419
Fax: 302-684-8504
E-mail: FW5RW_PHNWR@fws.gov
http://primehook.fws.gov

The Prime Hook National Wlidlife Refuge spans about 10,000 acres along the western Delaware Bay. The marshes of the refuge are ideal habitat for thousands of migrating ducks, geese, and shorebirds. The refuge is also home to woodlandand grassland birds, reptiles, amphibians, and mammals, including the endangered Delmarva Peninsula Fox Squirrel. Avid photographers can enjoy the beauty of wildlife from a photography blind and wheel-chair accessible observation platform.

District of Columbia: US Forests, Parks, Refuges

3272 Battleground National Cemetery
6625 Georgia Avenue, NW
Washington, DC 20240
202-426-6924
Fax: 202-426-1845
http://www.nps.gov/cwdw/btcemet.htm

Battleground National Cemetery, located at 6625 Georgia Avenue NW, was established shortly after the Battle of Fort Stevens in the summer of 1864. The battle, which lasted two days (July 11-12, 1864) marked the defeat of General JubalA Early's Confederate campaign to launch an offensive action against the poorly defended Nation's Capital. Near the entrance are monuments commemorating those units which fought at Fort Stevens.

Florida: US Forests, Parks, Refuges

3273 Arthur R Marshall Loxahatchee National Wildlife Refuge
10216 Lee Road
Boynton Beach, FL 33437
561-734-8303
http://www.fws.gov/loxahatchee

Welcome to the Arthur R. Marshall Loxahatchee National Wildlife Refuge, the last northernmost portion of the unique Everglades. With over 221 square miles of Everglades habitat, A.R.M. Loxahatchee National Wildlife Refuge is home tothe American alligator and the endangered Everglades snail kite. In any given year, as many as 257 species of birds may use the refuge's diverse wetland habitats.

3274 Big Cypress National Preserve
33100 Tamiami Trail East
Ochopee, FL 34141
239-695-1201
Fax: 239-695-3901
E-mail: bob_degross@nps.gov
http://www.nps.gov/bicy

The 729,000 acre Big Cypress National Preserve was set aside to ensure the preservation, conservation, and protection of the natural scenic, floral and faunal, and recreational values of the Big Cypress Watershed. The importance ofthis watershed to the Everglades National Park was a major consideration for its establishment. The name Big Cypress refers to the large size of this area. Vast expanses of cypress strands span this unique landscape.

3275 Biscayne National Park
9700 SW 328 Street
Homestead, FL 33033
305-230-7275
Fax: 305-230-1190
E-mail: BISC_Information@nps.gov
http://www.nps.gov/bisc

Turquoise waters, emerald islands and fish-bejeweled reefs make Biscayne National Park a paradise for wildlife-watching, snorkeling, diving, boating, fishing and other activities. Within the park boundaries are the longest stretch ofmangrove forest left on Florida's east coast, the clear shallow waters of Biscayne Bay, over 40 of the northernmost Florida Keys, and a spectacular living coral reef. Superimposed on all of this natural beauty is 10,000 years of human history.

3276 Canaveral National Seashore
212 South Washington Avenue
Titusville, FL 32796
321-267-1110
Fax: 321-264-2906
E-mail: cana_resource_management@nps.gov
http://www.nbbd.com/godo/cns/

Canaveral National Seashore is a step into the past, protection for the present and a doorway into the future. The 100 Native American Archeological sites that are within our boundaries are evidence of past generations of people thatlived here. Canaveral National Seashore covers 57,000 acres and is the longest stretch (24 miles) of undeveloped beach on Florida's east coast. Fourteen endangered species make their home within Canaveral's boundaries.
Carol Clark, Superintendent

3277 Chassahowitzka National Wildlife Refuge Complex
1502 SE Kings Bay Drive
Crystal River, FL 34429
352-563-2088
Fax: 352-795-7961
E-mail: chassahowitzka@fws.gov
http://chassahowitzka.fws.gov

A complex of 5 National Wildlife Refuges on the Gulf Coast of Florida including Crystal River NWR. Established in 1983 for the protection of the endangered West Indian manatee. Office hours are from 7:30 AM to 4:00 PM Monday thruFriday. The office is also open Saturdays and Sundays during the winter months (November 15 - March 31) please call the office at 352-563-2088 for more information.
James Kraus, Manager

3278 Dry Torgus National Park & Everglades National Park
40001 State Road 9336
Homestead, FL 33034
305-242-7700
Fax: 305-242-7711
E-mail: drto_information@nps.gov
http://www.nps.gov/drto

Recognized for its near-pristine natural resources including sea grass beds, fisheries, and sea turtle and nesting habit. The area also lays claim to a rich cultural heritage with a diverse array of themes. Fort Jefferson, on GardenKey, is the park's central cultural feature and one of the largest 19th century American masonry coastal forts.
Dan Kimball, Superintendent
Keith Whisenant, Deputy Superintendent

3279 Egmont Key National Wildlife Refuge
1502 SE Kings Bay Drive
Crystal River, FL 34429
352-563-2088
Fax: 352-795-7961
http://www.fws.gov/egmontkey

This barrier island refuge is approximately 350 acres and was established to provide nesting, feeding and resting habitat for brown pelicans and other migratory birds. The combined resources of the US Fish and Wildlife Service andFlorida Park Service provide protection for Egmont Key and its wildlife, as well as an enjoyable experience for the visitor.
James Kraus, Manager

3280 Everglades National Park
40001 State Road 9336
Homestead, FL 33034
305-242-7700
Fax: 305-242-7711
E-mail: EVER_Information@nps.gov
http://www.nps.gov/ever

The largest subtropical wilderness in the United States, boasts rare and endangered species. It has been designated a World Heritage Site, international Biosphere Reserve, and Wetland of International Importance, significant to allpeople of the world.
Dan Kimball, Superintendent
Keith Whisenant, Deputy Superintendent

3281 Florida Panther National Wildlife Refuge
3860 Tollgate Boulevard
Suite 300
Naples, FL 34114
239-353-8442
Fax: 239-353-8640
E-mail: floridapanther@fws.gov
http://www.fws.gov/floridapanther

Mission: To conserve and manage lands and waters in concert with other agency efforts within the Big Cypress Watershed, primarily for the Florida Panther, other endangered and threatened species, natural diversity, and culturalresources for the benefit of the American people.
Layne Hamilton, Manager

3282 Hobe Sound National Wildlife Refuge and Nature Center
PO Box 645
Hobe Sound, FL 33475
772-546-6141
Fax: 772-545-7572
E-mail: hobesound@fws.gov
http://www.fws.gov/hobesound

Refuge objectives are to: maintain and restore diverse habitats designed to achieve refuge purposes and wildlife population objectives; maintain viable diverse populations of native flora and fauna consistent with sound biologicalprinciples; manage natural and cultural resources through land protection and partnership; and develop and implement wildlife dependent recreation and environmental education that leads to enjoyable recreation experiences and a greater understandingof resources.
Margo Stahl, Refuge Manager
Debbie Fritz-Quincy, Nature Center Director

3283 JN Darling National Wildlife Refuge
1 Wildlife Drive
Sanibel, FL 33957
239-472-1100
Fax: 239-472-4061
E-mail: dingdarling@fws.gov
http://www.fws.gov/dingdarling

The refuge on Sanibel Island is a subtropical barrier island in the Gulf of Mexico hemmed by mangrove trees, shallow bays and white sandy beaches. The 6,300-acre refuge is connected to the mainland by a three-mile causeway. Named in1967 for Jay Norwood (Ding) Darling, an editorial cartoonist, pioneer conservationist and originator of the federal Duck Stamp Program. Darling, who was the first director of what is now the US Fish and Wildlife Service, wintered on neighboringCaptiva Island.
Robert Jess, Manager

3284 Lake Woodruff National Wildlife Refuge
2045 Mud Lake Road
DeLeon Springs, FL 32130
904-985-4673
Fax: 904-985-0926
E-mail: lakewoodruff@fws.gov
http://www.fws.gov/lakewoodruff

Encompasses two large lakes offering sights of diverse habitats and a variety of wildlife. Fishing and boating are the primary recreational activities.
Harold Morrow, Project Leader

3285 National Key Deer Refuge
179 Key Deer Blvd
Big Pine Key Plaza
Big Pine Key, FL 33043
305-872-2239
Fax: 305-872-2154
E-mail: keydeer@fws.gov
http://nationalkeydeer.fws.gov

Refuge objectives are: to protect and preserve Key deer and other wildlife resources in the Florida Keys; to conserve endangered and threatened fish, wildlife and plants; to provide habitat and protection for migratory birds; and toprovide opportunities for environmental education and public viewing of refuge wildlife and habitats.
Anne Morkill, Manager

3286 Pelican Island National Wildlife Refuge
1339 20th Street
Vero Beach, FL 32960
772-562-3909
Fax: 772-299-3101
E-mail: pelicanisland@fws.gov
http://www.fws.gov/pelicanisland

Charlie Pelizza, Refuge Manager
Nick Wirwa, Refuge Manager

3287 St. Marks National Wildlife Refuge
1255 Lighthouse Road
St Marks, FL 32355
850-925-6121
E-mail: saintmarks@fws.gov
http://www.fws.gov/saintmarks

Saint Marks National Wildlife Refuge is in Wakulla, Jefferson and Taylor counties along the Gulf coast of north Florida. The refuge is approximately 25 miles south of Tallahassee. The refuge encompasses 65,000 acres of divided tidalflats; and freshwater impoundments harbor a large variety of wildlife, including 434 verebrate species, excluding fish. Over quarter million vistors enjoy a variety of outdoor recreation opportunities annually.

3288 St. Vincent National Wildlife Refuge
PO Box 447 850-653-8808
Apalachicola, FL 32329 Fax: 850-653-9893
E-mail: saintvincent@fws.gov
http://www.fws.gov/saintvincent

The historic St Vincent National Wildlife Refuge is a large barrier island, four miles wide and nine miles long. It was inhabited as early as 240A.D. and is known to have been visited by Franciscan friars in the early 1600s. Over itshistory, private landowners developed the island into a preserve housing Asian and African wildlife and an assortment in between. The US Fish and Wildlife Service purchased the island in 1968 bringing an end to the exotic jungle.

Monica Harris, Manager

3289 Timucuan Ecological & Historic Preserve
12713 Fort Caroline Road 904-221-5568
Jacksonville, FL 32225 Fax: 904-221-5248
http://www.nps.gov/timu

The 46,000 acre Timucan Ecological and Historic Preserve was established to protect one of the last unspoiled coastal wetlands on the Atlantic Coast and to preserve historic and prehistoric sites within the area. The estuarineecosystem includes aslt marsh, coastal dunes, hardwood hammock, as well as salt, fresh, and brackish waters, all rich in native vegetation and animal life.

Barbara Goodman, Superintendent

Georgia: US Forests, Parks, Refuges

3290 Chattahoochee-Oconee National Forest
1755 Cleveland Highway 770-297-3000
Gainesville, GA 30501 Fax: 770-297-3011
http://www.fs.fed.us/conf

Together, these forest offer more than ten wilderness areas, six beaches, and thousands of acres of lakes and stream. The forest is real draw for history buffs, who can get absorbed in tracing events such as the Trail of Tears and manya Civil War battle.

3291 Cumberland Island National Seashore
PO Box 806 912-882-4336
Saint Marys, GA 31558 Fax: 912-882-6284
http://www.nps.gov/cuis

Cumberland Island is 17.5 miles long and totals 36,415 acres of which 16,850 are marsh, mud flats, and todal crreks. Well know for its sea turtles, abundant shore bierds, dune fields, maritime forest, salt marshes, and historicstructures.

3292 Okefenokee National Wildlife Refuge
Route 2 Box 3330 912-496-7836
Folkston, GA 31537 http://www.fws.gov/okefenokee

Okefenokee NWR was established in 1937 to preserve the 438,000 acre Okefenokee Swamp. Presently the refuge encompasses approximately 396,000 acres of which 353,000 are designated as Wilderness. Habitats include open wet prairies,cypress forests, scrub-shrub, oak hammocks and longleaf pine forests. The prosperity and survival of the swamp, and the species dependent on it, is directly tied with maintaining the integrity of complex ecological processes, including hydrology andfire.

3293 Piedmont National Wildlife Refuge
718 Juliette Road 478-986-5441
Hillsboro, GA 31038 Fax: 478-986-9646
E-mail: piedmont@fws.gov
http://www.fws.gov/piedmont

35,000 acre national wildlife refuge with hiking trails, gravel roads throughout, wildlife drive, hunting and fishing opportunities, bird watching.

3294 Pinckney Island National Wild Refuge
Savannah Coastal Refuges
1000 Business Center Drive 912-652-4415
Suite 10 Fax: 912-652-4385
Savannah, GA 31405 http://www.fws.gov/pinckneyisland

A group of islands and small hammocks, the 4,053-acre refuge includes a variety of land types: saltmarsh, forestland, brushland, fallow fields and freshwater ponds. Pinckney, the largest of the refuge islands, is 3.8 miles long and1.75 miles across at its greatest width. Boaters who navigate the refuge's estuarine waters may view shore and wading birds, including the endangered wood stork, that feeds on mudflats, oysterbeds and shores.

3295 Savannah National Wildlife Refuge
1000 Business Center Drive 912-652-4415
Suite 10 Fax: 912-652-4385
Savannah, GA 31405 E-mail: savannacoastal@fws.gov
http://www.fws.gov/savannah

Refuge objectives are to provide: a refuge and feeding ground for native birds and wild animals; habitat and protection for threatened and endangered plants and animals; habitat and sanctuary for migratory birds consistent with theobjectives of the Atlantic Flyway; habitats for other species of indigenous wildlife and fishery resources; management of furbearers, deer and other upland animals; and opportunities for environmental education, interpretation and recreation for thevisiting public.

Hawaii: US Forests, Parks, Refuges

3296 Haleakala National Park
PO Box 369 808-572-4400
Makawao, HI 96768 http://www.nps.gov/hale

The Park preserves the outstanding volcanic landscape of the upper slopes of Haleakala on the island of Maui and protects the unique and fragile ecosystems of Kipahulu Valley, the scenic pools along Oheo gulch, and many rare andendangered species. Haleakala National Park was designated an International Biosphere Reserve.

3297 Hawaii Volcanoes National Park
PO Box 52 808-985-6000
Hawaii National Park, HI 96718 Fax: 808-985-6004
http://www.nps.gov/havo

Established in 1916, this 333,000 acre National Park encompasses coastal lava plains, rain forests and deserts. It preserves and protects active volcanoes, rare and endangered plants and animals, and Hawaiian archeological sites.

3298 Huleia National Wildlife Refuge: Kauai
PO Box 1128 808-828-1413
Kilauea Fax: 808-828-6634
Kauai, HI 96754 E-mail: shannon_smith@fws.gov
http://www.gorp.com

Located on the southeast side of Kauai, lies adjacent to the famous Menehune Fish Pond, a registered National Historic Landmark. The Huleia Refuge is approximately 241 acres of wetlands which provides habitat for five endangeredHawaiian waterbirds.

Shannon Smith, Refuge Manager
Mike Mitchell, Deputy Refuge Manager

3299 James Campbell National Wildlife Refuge
Oahu Refuge Complex 808-637-6330
66-590 Kam Highway, Rm 2C Fax: 808-637-3578
Haleiwa, HI 96712 E-mail: sylvia_pelissa@fws.gov
http://www.fws.gov/pacificislands/wnwr/ojamesnwr.html

James Campbell NWR lies at the northernmost tip of Oahu near the community of Kahuku and serves as a strategic landfall for native and migratory birds coming from as far away as Alaska, Siberia, and Asia. The specific purpose of theRefuge is to provide habitat for Hawaii's four endemic, endangered waterbirds and other native wildlife, as well as migratory waterfowl and shorebirds. A total of 102 bird species have been documented on the Refuge since its creation.

Sylvia R Pelizza, Manager

3300 **Kauai National Wildlife Refuge Complex**
PO Box 1128 808-828-1413
Kilauea, HI 96754 Fax: 808-828-1414
http://www.fws.gov/pacificislands/wnwr/kauainwrindex.html
Kauai is also known as the Garden Isle for its lush vegetation and spectacular waterfalls. It is the oldest of the Hawaiian islands chain and is approximately 553 square miles in size. The Kauai National Wildlife Refuge Complexconsists of Kilauea Point, Hanalei, and Huleia National Wildlife Refuges.

3301 **Kealia Pond National Wildlife Refuge**
Maui Refuge Complex 808-875-1582
PO Box 1042 Fax: 808-875-2945
Kihei, HI 96753 http://www.fws.gov/pacificislands
Glynnis Nakai, Manager

3302 **Kilauea Point National Wildlife Refuge**
PO Box 1128 808-828-1413
Kilauea, HI 96754 Fax: 808-828-1414
http://www.fws.gov/pacificislands/wnwr/kkilaueanwr.html
This National Wildlife Refuge provides nesting habitat for seabirds; notably red-footed boobies, Laysan albatross and wedge-tailed shearwaters. The Refuge is also home to the historic Kilauea Point Lighthouse and native marine coastalplant communities. In winter, the 180 foot high precipice provides an ideal site for viewing humpback whales in offshore waters.
Mike Hawkes, Refuge Manager

3303 **Oahu National Wildlife Refuge Complex**
66-590 Kamehameha Highway 808-637-6330
Room 2C Fax: 808-637-3578
Haleiwa, HI 96712 http://www.fws.gov/pacificislands
Sylvia Pelizza, Manager

3304 **Pearl Harbor National Wildlife Refuge**
66-590 Kamehameha Highway 808-637-6330
Room 2C Fax: 808-637-3578
Haleiwa, HI 96712 http://www.fws.gov/pacificislands
Sylvia Pelizza, Manager

Idaho: US Forests, Parks, Refuges

3305 **Bear Lake National Wildlife Refuge**
PO Box 9 208-847-1757
Montpelier, ID 83254 Fax: 208-847-1319
E-mail: annette_deknijf@fws.gov
http://www.fws.gov/pacific/refuges/field/ID_Bearlk.htm
18,000 acres of marsh and uplands north of Bear Lake proper. Approx 7 miles south of Montpelier. White-faced ibis, Franklin's gulls, sandhill cranes, lots of ducks, Canada geese, Trumpeter swans.
Annette deKnijf, Refuge Manager

3306 **Boise National Forest**
1249 S Vinnell Way 208-373-4100
Boise, ID 83709 E-mail: r4_boise_info@fs.fed.us
http://wwwfs.fed.us/r4/boise
The predominantly Ponderosa pine and Douglas fir ecosystem provides homes for fish and wildlife; fiber for wood and paper products; forage for cows and sheep; precious metals for industrial and personal use; and an unlimited menu ofyear round opportunities. The Boise National Forest also contains a number of unique sites, including the Experimental Forest, the Lucky Peak Nursery and Bogus Basin Ski Area.

3307 **Camas National Wildlife Refuge Southeast Idaho Refuge Complex**
2150 E 2350 N 208-662-5423
Hamer, ID 83425 http://www.fws.gov/pacific/refuges
Cama NWR is 36 miles north of Idaho Falls in southeast Idaho, in the Cama Creek floodplain. Elevation is 4,800 feet. About half of its acreage consists of lakes, ponds and marshlands; the remainder is grass sagebrush uplands, meadowsand farm fields. Camas Creek flows for 8 miles through the length of the refuge and is the source of water for many of the lakes and ponds. Tall cottonwood trees along the creek attract a wide variety of songbirds.

3308 **Caribou-Targhee National Forest**
1405 Hollipark Drive 208-524-7500
Idaho Falls, ID 83401 E-mail: jjbennett@fs.fed.us
http://www.fs.fed.us/r4/caribou-targhee
The Caribou National Forest was created to help preserve wilderness land in an area marked by mining activity and westward migration. The forest now covers more than 1 million acres in southeast Idaho, with small portions in Utah andWyoming. Several north-south mountain ranges of the Overthrust Belt dominate the landscape. Caribou National Park offers a wide variety of outdoor activities, including camping, hiking, fishing, climbing, skiing and horseback riding.
Larry Timchak, Supervisor
Lynn Ballard, Public Affairs

3309 **Clearwater National Forest**
12730 Highway 12 208-476-4541
Orofino, ID 83544 Fax: 208-476-8329
E-mail: elozar@fs.fed.us.com
http://www.fs.fed.us/r1/clearwater/
The Clearwater National Forest covers 1.8 million acres from the jagged peaks of the Bitterroot Mountains in the east to the river canyons and rolling hills of the Palouse Prairie in the west. The North Fork of the Clearwater & theLochsa rivers provide miles of tumbling white water interspersed with quiet pools for migratory and resident fish. The mountains provide habitat for elk, moose, whitetail & mule deer, gray wolf, cougar, mountain goats, and many smaller mammals.
Tom Reilly, Forest Supervisor
Kimberly Nelson, Public Affairs

3310 **Craters of the Moon National Monument & Preserve**
PO Box 29 208-527-3257
Arco, ID 83213 Fax: 208-527-3073
http://www.nps.gov/crmo
A sea of lava flows with scattered islands of cinder cones and sagebrush characterizes this wierd and scenic landscape known as Craters of the Moon. Craters of the Moon National Monument and Preserve contains three young lava fieldscovering almost half a million acres. These remarkably well preserved volcanic features resulted from geologic events that appear to have happened yesterday and will likely continue tomorrow.

3311 **Deer Flat National Wildlife Refuge**
13751 Upper Embankment Road 208-467-9278
Nampa, ID 83686 Fax: 208-467-1019
E-mail: deerflat@fws.gov
http://deerflat.fws.gov
One of the nation's oldest refuges. It includes the Lake Lowell sector and the Snake River Islands sector. The refuge provides a mix of wildlife habitats, including open waters, wetland edges around the lake, sagebrush uplands,grasslands and riparian forests. More than 250 birds and 30 mammals have been seen on the refuge, providing excellent wildlife observation and photography opportunities.

3312 **Grays Lake National Wildlife Refuge**
74 Grays Lake Road 208-574-2755
Wayan, ID 83285 http://www.fws.gov/pacific/refuges
Twenty-seven miles north of Soda Springs in southeast Idaho, the refuge lies in a high mountain valley at 6,400 feet. Grays Lake is actually a large, shallow marsh with dense vegetation and little open water. Most of the marshvegetation is bulrush and cattail. Adjacent lands are primarily wet meadows and grasslands.

3313 **Idaho Panhandle National Forest**
3815 Schreiber Way 208-765-7223
Coeur d'Alene, ID 83815 Fax: 208-765-7307
http://www.fs.fed.us/ipnf

3314 **Kootenai National Wildlife Refuge**
287 Westside Rd
Bonners Ferry, ID 83805
208-267-3888
Fax: 208-267-5570
E-mail: tammie_coon@fws.gov
http://kootenai.fws.gov/
The 2,774 acre refuge is located in the northern panhandle of Idaho, and serves as a resting and feeding area for migratory birds.

3315 **Minidoka National Wildlife Refuge**
961 E Minidoka Dam
Rupert, ID 83350
208-436-3589
http://www.fws.gov/pacific/refuges
Lying 12 miles northeast of Rupert in the Snake River Valley in south-central Idaho, the refuge extends upstream about 25 miles from the Minidoka Dam along both shores of the Snake River and includes all of Lake Walcott. Over half therefuge is open water, with some small marsh area.

3316 **Nez Perce National Forest**
1005 Highway 13
Grangeville, ID 83530
208-983-1950
Fax: 208-983-4099
http://www.fs.fed.us/r1/nezperce
The Forest is best known for its wild character. Nearly half of the Forest is designated wilderness. It also sports two rivers popular with thrill-seeking floaters-the Selway and the Salmon.
Jane Cottrell, Forest Supervisor

3317 **Payette National Forest**
800 W Lakeside Avenue
McCall, ID 83638
208-634-0700
E-mail: webmaster@fs.fed.us
http://www.fs.fed.us/r4/payette
Payette National Forest spans over 2.3 million acres of some of west central Idaho's most beautiful and diverse country. In one day you can travel from hot desert grasslands through cool conifer forests to snow-capped peaks. Thespectacular land is bordered by two of the deepest canyons in North America— the Salmon River Canyon On the north and Hells Canyon of the Sake River on the west. To the east lies 2.4 million-acre the largest Congressionally designated wilderness inthe lower 48 states.
Suzanne Rainville, Forest Supervisor

3318 **Sawtooth National Forest**
2647 Kimberly Road E
Twin Falls, ID 83301
208-737-3200
http://www.fs.fed.us/r4/sawtooth
The Sawtooth National Forest encompasses 2.1 million acres of some of the nation's most magnificent country. Managed and protected by the US Department of Agriculture's Forest Service, the Sawtooth National Forest is working, producingforest that has been providing goods and services to the American people since its establishment in 1905.
Jane Kollmeyer, Forest Supervisor

3319 **Southeast Idaho National Wildlife Refuge Complex**
4425 Burley Drive
Suite A
Chubbuck, ID 83202
208-237-6615
http://www.fws.gov/pacific/refuges/field/ID_SEID.htm

Illinois: US Forests, Parks, Refuges

3320 **Mark Twain National Wildlife Refuge Complex**
1704 N 24th Street
Quincy, IL 62301
217-224-8580
E-mail: Dick_Steinbach@fws.gov
http://midwest.fws.gov/marktwain
Administrative office over five refuges; Port Louisa NWR, Great River NWR, Clarence Common NWR, Two Rivers NWR, and Middle Mississippi River NWR.
Richard Steinbach, Manager

3321 **Shawnee National Forest**
50 Highway 145 South
Harrisburg, IL 62946
618-253-7114
800-699-6637
Fax: 618-253-1060
http://www.fs.fed.us/r9/forests/shawnee
The Shawnee National Forest lies in the rough, unglaciated areas known as the Illinois Ozark and Shawnee Hills. The geology is spectacular and divergent, with numerous stone bluffs and overlooks transcending to lowland areas.
Rebecca Banker, Public Affairs

3322 **Upper Mississippi River National Wildlife & Fish Refuge: Savanna District**
Riverview Road
Thomson, IL 61285
815-273-2732
Fax: 815-273-2960
http://www.fws.gov/midwest/uppermississippiriver
The Upper Mississippi River National Wildlife and Fish Refuge covers nearly 240,000 acres and extends along 281 miles of the Mississippi River. This Refuge is home to a diverse collection of wildlife, including bald eagles, great blueherons, sandhill cranes and spectacular concentrations of waterfowl. Local residents and visitors enjoy a wide array of opportunties throughout the year such as fishing, hunting, wildlife observation, photography, interpretation and environmentaleducation.

Ed Britton, District Manager
Pam Steinhaus, Visitor Service Manager

Indiana: US Forests, Parks, Refuges

3323 **Indiana Dunes National Lakeshore**
1100 N Mineral Springs Road
Porter, IN 46304
219-926-7561
http://www.nps.gov/indu
Indiana Dunes National Lakeshore, authorized by Congress in 1996, is located approximately 50 miles southeast of Chicago, Illinois in the counties of Lake, Porter and LaPorte in Northwest Indiana. The national lakeshore runs for nearly25 miles along southern Lake Michigan, bordered by Michigan City, Indiana on the east and Gary on the west. The park contains approximately 15,000 acres, 2,182 of which are located in Indiana Dunes State Park managed by the Indiana Department ofNatural Resources.

Iowa: US Forests, Parks, Refuges

3324 **DeSoto National Wildlife Refuge**
1434 316th Lane
Missouri Valley, IA 51555
712-642-4121
Fax: 712-642-2877
E-mail: Larry_Klimek@fws.gov
http://www.fws.gov/midwest/desoto
DeSoto Refuge is located along the Missouri River, 25 miles north of Omaha, NE. Popular activities include fishing, picnicking, mushroom-picking, hiking, boating, and wildlife observation. Peak viewing of 500,000 waterfowl inmid-November. The DeSoto Visitor Center houses over 200,000 artifacts from the 1860's steamboat Bertrand.

Larry Klimek, Refuge Manager
Mindy Sheets, Assistant Refuge Manager

3325 **McGregor District Upper: Mississippi River National Wildlife & Fish Refuge**
PO Box 460
McGregor, IA 52157
563-873-3423
Fax: 563-873-3803
E-mail: uppermississippiriver@fws.gov
http://www.fws.gov/midwest/uppermississippiriver

T Yager, Manager

Kansas: US Forests, Parks, Refuges

3326 **Kirwin National Wildlife Refuge**
702 East Xavier Road
Kirwin, KS 67644
785-543-6673
http://www.fws.gov/kirwin
Craig Mowry, Manager
Diane Stockman, Administrative Assistant

Kentucky: US Forests, Parks, Refuges

3327 **Daniel Boone National Forest**
1700 Bypass Road 859-745-3100
Winchester, KY 40391 Fax: 859-744-1568
http://www.fs.fed.us/r8/boone
The mission is to achive quality land management under the sustainable multiple-use management concept to meer the diverse need of people.

3328 **Mammoth Cave National Park**
1 Mammoth Cave Parkway 270-758-2180
PO Box 7 E-mail: MACA_Park_information@nps.gov
Mammoth Cave, KY 42259 http://www.nps.gov/maca
Established to preserve the cave system, including Mammoth Cave, the scenic river valleys of the Green and Nolin Rivers, and a section of the hilly country of south central Kentucky. This is the longest recorded cave system in theworld with more than 360 miles explored and mapped. Established July 1, 1941. Designated a World Heritage Site October 27, 1981. Designated a Biosphere Reserve in 1990.
Patrick Reed, Superintendent
Bruce Powell, Deputy Superintendent

Louisiana: US Forests, Parks, Refuges

3329 **Atchafalaya National Wildlife Refuge**
PO Box 127 318-566-2251
Krotz Springs, LA 70750 http://www.fws.gov/atchafalaya
The State of Louisiana's Sherburne Wildlife Management Area is located in the upper third of the Atchafalaya River Basin between Interstate Highway 10 and US Highway 190. It covers approximately 11,780 acres and was established in 1983by the Louisiana Department of Wildlife and Fisheries. The area supervisor's headquaters is located east of Krotz Springs, Louisiana, on LA 975 approximately three miles south of US Highway 190.

3330 **Cameron Prairie National Wildlife Refuge**
1428 Highway 27 337-598-2216
Bell City, LA 70630 Fax: 337-598-2492
E-mail: cameronprairie@fws.gov
http://www.fws.gov/cameronprairie/index.html
The refuge contains 9,621 acres of fresh marsh, coastal prairie and old rice fields. East Cove Unit of the refuge contains 14,927 acres of brackish and salt marsh. Seasonal visitors include the Peregrine falcon, alligators, whitetailed deer, wading and shorebirds, ducks and geese and various migratory birds.
Glen Harris, Manager

3331 **Catahoula National Wildlife Refuge**
PO Drawer Z 318-992-5261
Rhinehart, LA 71363 Fax: 318-992-6023
E-mail: catahoula@fws.gov
http://catahoula.fws.gov
The objectives of the refuge are: to provide wintering habitat for migratory waterfowl consistent with Mississippi Flyway objectives; to provide habitat and protection for endangered species; preserve bottomland hardwoods and providehabitat necessary for wildlife diversity; provide opportunities for environmental education, interpretation and wildlife oriented recreation.
Greg Harper, Manager

3332 **D'Arbonne National Wildlife Refuge**
11372 Highway 143 318-726-4400
Farmerville, LA 71363 Fax: 318-726-4667
E-mail: northlarefuges@fws.gov
http://www.fws.gov/darbonne
The Refuge provides habitat for a diversity of migratory birds and resident wildlife species, provides habitat and protection for endangered species such as the bald eagle, wood stork and red-cockaded woodpecker and providesopportunities for wildlife-oriented recreation, environmental education and interpretation.

Kelby Ouchley, Manager

3333 **Kisatchie National Forest**
2500 Shreveport Highway 318-473-7160
Pineville, LA 71360 E-mail: www.fs.fed.us/r8/kisatchie
The Kisatchie National Forest has a lot to offer vistors, such as 355 miles of trails for hiking, camping, mountain biking, horseback riding, ORV riding. Other recreational opportunites include four lakes, an 8700 acre Wilderness anddozens of caming sites. The forest also provides opportunities to hunt and fish.

3334 **Lacassine National Wildlife Refuge**
209 Nature Road 337-774-5923
Lake Arthur, LA 70549 Fax: 337-774-9913
E-mail: lacassine@fws.gov
http://www.fws.gov/swlarefugecomplex/lacassine
The nearly 35,000 acre refuge is mostly freshwater marsh habitat. It preserves one of the major wintering grounds for waterfowl in the US. Wintering populations of ducks and geese at Lacassine are among the largest in the NationalWildlife Refuge System. Portions of the refuge are open year-round from one hour before sunrise until one hour after sunset. Please consult refuge brochures or contact the refuge office for more details. A vicinity map and refuge map are available.
Larry Narcisse, Manager

3335 **Sabine National Wildlife Refuge**
3000 Holly Beach Highway 337-762-3816
Hackberry, LA 70645 Fax: 337-762-3780
E-mail: sabine@fws.gov
http://www.fws.gov/sabine/
The objectives of the refuge is to provide habitat for migratory waterfowl and other birds, to preserve and enhance coastal marshes for fish and wildlife, and to provide outdoor recreation and environmental education for the public.
Don Voros, Project Manager
Terence Delaine, Refuge Manager

Maine: US Forests, Parks, Refuges

3336 **Acadia National Park**
PO Box 177 207-288-8800
Bar Harbor, ME 04609 Fax: 208-288-8813
E-mail: Acadia_Information@nps.gov
http://www.nps.gov/acad/faqs.htm
The purpose of the commission is to consult with the Secretary of the Interior, or his designee, on matters relating to the management and development of the park, including but not liited to the acquisition of lands and interests inlands and termination of rights of use and occupancy.

3337 **Sunkhaze Meadows National Wildlife Refuge**
1168 Main Street 207-827-6138
Old Town, ME 04468 Fax: 207-827-6099
E-mail: info@sunkhaze.org
http://www.sunkhaze.org
Sunkhaze Meadows NWR was established to protect a large peat bog and its associated wildlife. There are three divisions of the refuge, totalling 11,772 acres. The areas are open to wildlife-dependent recreation.

Maryland: US Forests, Parks, Refuges

3338 **Antietam National Battlefield**
PO Box 158 301-432-5124
Sharpsburg, MD 21782 Fax: 301-432-4590
http://www.nps.gov/anti

3339 **Assateague Island National Seashore**
7206 National Seashore Lane 410-641-1441
Berlin, MD 21811 Fax: 410-641-1099
http://www.nps.gov/asis/home.htm

Natural resource management and environmental education related to coastal resources in general and Assateague Island in particular.
Trish Kicklighter, Superintendent

3340 **Patuxent Research Refuge**
10901 Scarlet Tanager Loop 301-497-5580
Laurel, MD 20708 Fax: 301-497-5515
http://www.fws.gov/northeast/patuxent/index.htm
One of over 500 refuges in the National Wildlife Refuge System, a network of lands and waters specifically for the protection of wildlife and wildlife habitat.
Brad Knudsen, Project Leader/Manager

Massachusetts: US Forests, Parks, Refuges

3341 **Boston National Historical Park**
Charleston Navy Yard 617-242-5642
Boston, MA 02129 Fax: 617-242-6006
http://www.nps.gov/bost
Boston National Historical Park tells the story of the events that led to the American Revolution and the Navy that kept the nation strong.

3342 **Cape Cod National Seashore**
99 Marconi Station Site Road 508-349-3785
Wellfleet, MA 02667 Fax: 508-349-9052
E-mail: CACO_Superintendent@nps.gov
http://www.nps.gov/caco/home.html
Cape Cod National Seashore comprises 43,604 acres of shoreline and upland landscape features, including a forty-mile long stretch of pristine sandy beach, dozens of clear, deep, freshwater kettle ponds, and upland scenes that depictevidence of how people have used the land. A variety of historic structures are within the boundary of the Seashore, including lighthouses, a lifesaving station, and numerous Cape Cod style houses.

3343 **Great Meadows National Wildlife Refuge**
73 Weir Hill Road 978-443-4661
Sudbury, MA 01776 Fax: 978-443-2898
http://www.fws.gov/northeast/greatmeadows
The Sudbury office serves as the headquarters for the eight refuge Eastern Massachusetts National Wildlife Refuge Complex. Public use opportunities are available at a number of the complex's refuges.
Libby Herland, Complex Manager

3344 **Silvio O Conte National Fish & Wildlife Refuge**
52 Avenue A 413-863-0209
Turners Falls, MA 01376 Fax: 413-863-3070
E-mail: boardman@k12.oit.umass.edu
http://www.fws.gov/r5soc
The Connecticut River Watershed, 7.2 million acres in four states, is larger and more heavily populated than areas usually considered when creating a refuge. The refuge's purposes are also much broader than usual. The new scientificand social challenge of protecting natural diversity cannot be met by land acquistion alone. The refuge's primary action is to involve people of the watershed, especially landowners and land managers, in environmental education programs andcooperative management.

Michigan: US Forests, Parks, Refuges

3345 **Hiawatha National Forest**
2727 North Lincoln Road 906-786-4062
Escanaba, MI 49829 Fax: 906-789-3311
http://www.fs.fed.us/r9/forests/hiawatha
Located in the central and easter Upper Peninsula of Michigan, the firest affords visitors access to white sand, scenic beaches and relatively undeveloped shorelines along three of Americas's Inland Seas, Lake Superior, Michigan andHuron.

3346 **Huron-Manistee National Forest**
1755 S Mitchell Street 231-775-2421
Cadillac, MI 49601 800-821-6263
Fax: 231-775-5551
http://www.fs.fed.us/r9/hmnf/
The Huron-Manistee National Forest comprise almost a million acres of public lands extending across the northern lower peninsula of Michigan. The Huron-Manistee national Forest provide recreation opportunities for visitors, habitat forfish and wildlife, and resources for local industry.

3347 **Ottawa National Forest**
E6248 US Highway 2 906-932-1330
Ironwood, MI 49938 Fax: 906-932-0122
http://www.fs.fed.us/r9/ottawa
The almost one million acres of the Ottawa National Forest are located in the western Upper Peninsula of Michigan. It extends from the south shore of Lake Superior down to Wisconsin and the Nicolet National Forest. The area is rich inwildlife viewing opportunities; topography in the northern portion is the most dramatic with breathtaking views of rolling hills dotted with lakes, rivers and spectacular waterfalls.

3348 **Pictured Rocks National Lakeshore**
N8391 Sand Point Road 906-387-2607
PO Box 40 Fax: 906-387-4025
Munising, MI 49862 http://www.nps.gov/piro/home.htm
Multicolored sandstone cliffs, beaches, and dunes, waterfalls, inland lakes, wildlife and the forest of Lake Superior shoreline beckon visitors to explore this 73,000+ acre park. Attractions include a lighthouse and former Coast Guardlife-saving stations along with old farmsteads and orchards. The park is a four season recreational destination where hiking, camping, hunting, nature study, and winter activities abound.

3349 **Seney National Wildlife Refuge**
1674 Refuge Entrance Road 906-586-9851
Seney, MI 49883 Fax: 906-586-3800
E-mail: seney@fws.gov
http://www.fws.gov/midwest/seney
Seney National Wildlife Refuge was established as a refuge and breeding ground for migratory birds and other wildlife. Today, Seney supports a variety of wildlife, including protected and reintroduced species. Bald eagles, commonloons, and trumpeter swans are regularly seen during the summer months, especially June and July, when they are raising their young.
Mark Vaniman, Manager
Greg McClellan, Deputy Manager

3350 **Shiawassee National Wildlife Refuge**
6975 Mower Road 989-777-5930
Saginaw, MI 48601 Fax: 989-777-9200
E-mail: shiawassee@fws.gov
http://www.fws.gov/midwest/shiawassee
The refuge is comprised of over 9400 acres of wetlands, uplands, and bottomland hardwood forests. Four rivers flow through. Over 12 miles of hiking trails, bank fishing sites, and two photography blinds are available. Environmentaleducation progrms are offered at Green Point Environmental Learning Center in Saginaw.
Steve Kahl, Manager
Ed DeVries, Assistant Manager

3351 **Sleeping Bear Dunes National Lakeshore**
9922 Front Street 231-326-5134
Empire, MI 49630 Fax: 231-326-5382
http://www.nps.gov/slbe
Sleeping Bear Dunes National Lakeshore encompasses a 60 km stretch of Lake Michigan's eastern coastline, as well as North and South Manitou Islands. The park was established primarily for its outstanding natural features, includingforests, beaches, dune formations and ancient glacial phenomena. The Lakeshore also contains many cultural features including an 1871 lighthouse, three former Life-Saving Service (Coast Guard) Stations and an extensive rural historic farm district.

Minnesota: US Forests, Parks, Refuges

3352 Agassiz National Wildlife Refuge
22996 290th Street Northeast 218-449-4115
Middle River, MN 56737 Fax: 218-449-3241
E-mail: agassiz@fws.gov
http://midwest.fws.gov/agassiz/
The National Refuge provides resting, nesting and feeding habitat for waterfowl and other migratory birds. Agassiz NWR is designated a Globally Important Bird Area by the American Bird Conservancy. It protects endangered and threatenedspecies. It also provides for biodiversity, public opportunities for outdoor recreation and environmental education.
Margaret Anderson, Manager

3353 Big Stone National Wildlife Refuge
44843 County Road 19 320-273-2191
Odessa, MN 56276 Fax: 320-273-2231
E-mail: BigStone@fws.gov
http://midwest.fws.gov/bigstone
Fig Stone NWR is one of more than 545 National Wildlife Refuges administered as part of the National Wildlife Refuge System by the US Fish and Wildlife Service. The Refuge now overlays 11,585.8 acres of the Minnesota River Valley inwestern Minnesota. A unique visual and geological feature of the Refuge is the red, lichen covered granite outcrops for which the Refuge was named. The Refuge offers an auto tour route, nature trails, wildlife observation, hunting and fishingopportunities.
Alice Hanley, Manager

3354 Chippewa National Forest
200 Ash Avenue Northwest 218-335-8600
Cass Lake, MN 56633 http://www.fs.fed.us/r9/chippewa/
The Chippewa was the first National Forest established east of the Mississippi. The Forest boundary encompasses 1.6 millon, of which over 666,618 acres are managed by the USDA Forest Service. Aspen, birch, pines, balsam fir and maplesblanket the uplands. Water is abundant, with over 1300 lakes, 923 miles of rivers and streams, and 400,000 acres of wetlands.
Robert M Harper, Forest Supervisor

3355 Crane Meadows National Wildlife Refuge
19502 Iris Road 320-632-1575
Little Falls, MN 56345 Fax: 320-632-5471
E-mail: cranemeadows@fws.gov
http://www.fws.gov/midwest/CraneMeadows
Crane Meadows National Wildlife Refuge was established in 1992 to preserve a large, natural wetland complex. The refuge is located in central Minnesota and serves as an important stop for many species of migrating birds.

3356 Detroit Lakes Wetland Management District
26624 N Tower Road 218-847-4431
Detroit Lakes, MN 56501 Fax: 218-847-4156
E-mail: DetroitLakes@fws.gov
http://www.fws.gov/Midwest.detroitlakes/
The district covers approximately 6000 square miles. From east to west, these are: the Red River Valley floodplain, the glacial moraine/prairie pothole region, and the hardwood/coniferous forest. Land acquisition and managementefforts are focused in the prairie pothole region of the WMD, with a goal of providing habitat for nesting waterfowl.

Scott Kahan, Manager

3357 Mille Lacs National Wildlife Refuge
36289 State Highway 65 218-768-2402
McGregor, MN 55760 Fax: 218-768-3040
E-mail: millelacs@fws.gov
http://midwest.fws.gov/millelacs
Comprised of two small islands in Mille Lacs Lake in central Minnesota. The islands are boulder and gravel outcrops for colonial nesting birds including common terns and ring-billed gulls.

Walt Ford, Manager

3358 Minnesota Valley National Wildlife Refuge
3815 American Blvd East 612-854-5900
Bloomington, MN 55425 Fax: 612-725-3279
E-mail: minnesotavalley@fws.gov
http://www.fws.gov/midwest/MinnesotaValley
Mission: To restore and manage the ecological communities of the Lower Minnesota River Valley and its watershed while providing environmental education and wildlife dependent recreation.
Thomas Larson, Manager

3359 Rice Lake National Wildlife Refuge
36289 State Highway 65 218-768-2402
McGregor, MN 55760 Fax: 218-768-3040
E-mail: ricelakes@fws.gov
http://www.fws.gov/midwest/RiceLake
Walt Ford, Manager

3360 Rydell National Wildlife Refuge
17788 349th Street Southeast 218-687-2229
Erskine, MN 56535 Fax: 218-687-2225
E-mail: dave_bennett@fws.gov
http://www.fws.gov/midwesty/rydell
Dave Bennett, Manager

3361 Sherburne National Wildlife Refuge
17076 293rd Avenue 763-389-3323
Zimmerman, MN 55398 Fax: 763-389-3493
E-mail: sherburne@fws.gov
http://www.fws.gov/midwest/sherburne/index.htm
Mission: To represent a diverse biological community characteristic of the transition zone between tallgrass prairie and forest.

3362 Superior National Forest
8901 Grand Avenue Place 218-626-4300
Duluth, MN 55808 Fax: 218-626-4398
E-mail: r9 superior NF@fs.fed.us
http://www.fs.fed.us/r9/forests/superior
Located in northeastern tip of Minnesota, the Superior National Forest stretches 150 miles along the US-Canadian border, encompassing 3.85 million acres. This hilly deep pine forest is home to moose, wolves, black bears, loons andmigratory birds. More than 2,250 miles of stream flow within the forest, including the renowned Boundary Waters Canoe Area, where you can canoe, portage and camp in the spirit of the French Canadian voyagers of 200 years ago.

Jim Sanders, Forest Supervisor

3363 Tamarac National Wildlife Refuge
35704 County Highway 26 218-847-2641
Rochert, MN 56578 Fax: 218-847-9141
http://www.fws.gov/midwest/tamarac
Established in 1938, Tamarac Refuge is dedicated to providing a breeding ground and sanctuary for migratory birds and other wildlife. Situated at a unique transitional zone where hardwood forest, boreal forest and tallgrass prairiemeets. Tamarac provides boundless opportunities for visitors to observe wildlife in their natural surroundings. Spring and fall migrations of songbirds and waterfowl can be spectacular. Their visitor center offers interpretive displays and programs.

3364 Voyageurs National Park
3131 Highway 53 218-283-9821
International Falls, MN 56649 Fax: 218-285-7407
http://www.nps.gov/voya
The park lies in the southern part of the Canadian Shield, representing some of the oldest exposed rock formations in the world. This bedrock has been shaped and carved by at least four periods of glaciation. The topography of the parkis rugged and varied; rolling hills are interspersed between bogs, beaver ponds, swamps, islands, small lakes and four large lakes.

3365 Winona District National Wildlife Refuge Upper Mississippi River National Wildlife and Fish
51 E 4th Street 507-452-4232
Winona, MN 55987 Fax: 507-452-0851
http://www.fws.gov/midwest/uppermississippiriver

Refuge objectives are to: protect and preserve one of America's premier fish and wildlife areas; provide habitat for migratory birds, fish, plants and resident wildlife; protect and enhance habitat for endangered species; provideinterpretation, environmental education and wildlife-oriented recreational public use opportunities; and conserve a diversity of plant life.
Don Hultman, Manager

Mississippi: US Forests, Parks, Refuges

3366 **Bienville National Forest**
3473 Highway 35 S 601-469-3811
Forest, MS 39074 http://www.fs.fed.us/r8/mississippi/bienville
The forest offers camping, picnicking, swimming, hiking, fishing and historic sites. Bienville boasts the largest known cluster of old growth pine forest in Mississippi in the 180-acre Bienville Pines Scenic Area. Here visitors canwander among towering loblolly and shortleaf pines, many more than two centuries old. The 23-mile Shockaloe Horse Trail, a national recreation trail, starts near the town of Forest.

3367 **Mississippi Sandhill Crane National Wildlife Refuge**
7200 Crane Lane 228-497-6322
Gautier, MS 39553 Fax: 228-497-5407
E-mail: mississippisandhillcrane@fws.gov
http://www.fws.gov/mississippisandhillcrane
The Refuge is located in southeast Mississippi in Jackson County a few miles north of the Gulf of Mexico. This 20,000 acre refuge was established in 1975 to protect the endangered Mississippi Sandhill Cranes and the wet pine savannahabitat they prefer. Visitor Center hours Tues-Sat 9-3, featuring exhibits, informational videos, and a walking trail - where you can view carnivorous plants. Free entry.
Ted Rentmeister, Refuge Manager
Douglas Hunt, Refuge Manager

3368 **Noxubee National Wildlife Refuge**
2970 Bluff Lake Road 662-323-5548
Brooksville, MS 39739 Fax: 662-323-6390
E-mail: noxubee@fws.gov
http://noxubee.fws.gov
Established in 1940 to protect and enhance habitat for the conservation of migratory birds, endangered species and other wildlife. The recreational and educational opportunities provided on the refuge help the public experience natureand learn how sound management ensures that future generations continue to enjoy fish and wildlife and their habitats.

3369 **Panther Swamp National Wildlife Refuge**
13695 River Road 662-746-5060
Yazoo City, MS 39194 Fax: 662-746-5055
E-mail: Bo_Sloan@fws.gov
http://pantherswamp.fws.gov/index.html
Refuge objectives are: to provide resting, nesting and feeding habitat for waterfowl and other migratory birds; to provide habitat for resident wildlife; to protect endangered and threatened species; and to provide public useopportunities for outdoor recreation and environmental education.
Bo Sloan, Refuge Manager

Missouri: US Forests, Parks, Refuges

3370 **Mark Twain National Forest**
401 Fairgrounds Road 573-364-4621
Rollo, MO 65401 Fax: 573-364-6844
http://www.fs.fed.us/r9/forests/marktwain
The Mark Twain National forest is located in southern and centeral Missouri, and extends from the St Francois Mountains in the southeast to glades in the southwest, from the southwest, from the prairie lands the Missouri River to thenation's most ancient mountains in the south.

3371 **Mingo National Wildlife Refuge**
24279 State Highway 51 573-222-3589
Puxico, MO 63960 Fax: 573-222-6343
E-mail: mingo@fws.gov
http://www.fws.gov/midwest/mingo
Established as a resting and wintering area for migratory waterfowl and other birds. The 21,592-acre Refuge contains approximately 15,000 acres of bottomland hardwood forest, 3,500 acres of marsh and water, 506 acres of cropland, 704acres of seasonally flooded impoundments, and 474 acres of grassy openings.

3372 **Ozark National Scenic Riverways**
404 Watercress Drive 573-323-4236
PO Box 490 Fax: 573-323-4140
Van Buren, MO 63965 E-mail: ozar_superintendent@nps.gov
http://www.nps.gov/ozar
Missouri's largest National Park and America's first to preserve a free flowing river in its wild state. Covers some 80,000 acres along 134 miles of the Current and Jacks Fork Rivers. Staff provide elementary level environmentaleducation programs on natural history, with an emphasis on karst and water issues. Publishes More Than Skin Deep, a Teacher's Guide to Caves and Groundwater, a curriculum guide suitable for grades K-12.

3373 **Swan Lake National Wildlife Refuge**
16194 Swan Lake Avenue 660-856-3323
Sumner, MO 64681 Fax: 660-856-3687
E-mail: john_benson@fws.gov
http://www.fws.gov/midwest/swanlake
Steve Whitson, Project Director

Montana: US Forests, Parks, Refuges

3374 **Beaverhead-Deerlodge National Forest**
420 Barrett Street 406-683-3900
Dillon, MT 59725 http://www.fs.fed.us/r1/bdnf
Bruce Ramsey, Forest Supervisor
Thomas D Osen, District Ranger

3375 **Benton Lake National Wildlife Refuge**
922 Bootlegger Trail 406-727-7400
Great Falls, MT 59404 Fax: 406-727-7432
http://www.fws.gov/bentonlake
Kathleen Burchett, Project Leader
Robert F Johnson Jr, Deputy Manager

3376 **Bighorn Canyon National Recreation Area**
5 Avenue B 406-666-2412
PO Box 7458 Fax: 406-666-2415
Fort Smith, MT 59035 http://www.nps.gov/bica
This dam, named after the famous Crow chairman Robert Yellowtail, harnessed the waters of the Bighorn River and turned this variable stream into a magnificent lake. The Afterbay Lake below the Yellowtail Dam is a good spot for troutfishing and wildlife viewing for ducks, geese and other animals. The Bighorn River below the Afterbay Dam is a world class trout fishing area. Bighorn Canyon National Recreation Area boasts breath-takign scenery, countless varieties of wildlife.

3377 **Bitterroot National Forest**
1801 N First Street 406-363-7100
Hamilton, MT 59840 Fax: 406-363-7106
E-mail: rl_bitterroot_comments@fs.fed.us
http://www.fs.fed.us/rl/bitterroot/
The 1.6 million acre Bitterroot National Forest, in west central Montana and east central Idaho, is part of the Norther Rocky Mountains. National Forest land begins above the foothills of the Bitterroot River Valley in two mountainranges—the Bitterroot Mountains on the west and the Sapphire Mountains on the east side of the valley.

3378 **Bowdoin National Wildlife Refuge: Refuge Manager**
194 Bowdoin Auto Tour Road 406-654-2863
Malta, MT 59538 Fax: 406-654-2866
E-mail: bowdoin@fws.gov
http://www.fws.gov/bowdoin

Bowdoin National Wildlife Refuge was established in 1936 as a migratory bird refuge. It is located in the short and mixed greens prairie region of North-central Montana and encompasses 15,551 acres.

3379 **Custer National Forest**
1310 Main Street 406-657-6200
Billings, MT 59105 Fax: 406-657-6222
http://www.fs.fed.us/r1/custer/

The Custer national Forest is made up of 1.2 million acres of high alpine mountain country, and small pockets of timbered buttes and grasslands scattered across two states, Montana and South Dakota.

Mary C Erickson, Acting Forest Supervisor
Chris C Worth, Deputy Forest Supervisor

3380 **Flathead National Forest**
1935 3rd Avenue E 406-758-5200
Kalispell, MT 59901 Fax: 406-758-5363
http://www.fs.fed.us/r1/flathead/

The 2.3 million-acre Flathead national Forest is bordered by Canada to the north, Glacier National Park to the north and east and Clark National Forest to the east, the Lolo national Forest to the south, and the Kootenai NationalForest to the west.

3381 **Gallatin National Forest**
PO Box 130 406-587-6701
Bozeman, MT 59771 http://www.fs.fed.us/r1/gallatin

3382 **Helena National Forest**
2880 Skyway Drive 406-449-5201
Helena, MT 59602 Fax: 406-449-5436
http://www.fs.fed.us/r1/helena/

The Helena National Forest offers close to one million acres of diverse landscapes and wildland opportunities. Located in west central Montana, the Helena National Forest boasts some of the most vivid glimpses into the past of thishistorically rich area.

3383 **Kootenai National Forest**
31374 Highway 2 West 406-293-6211
Libby, MT 59923 Fax: 406-283-7709
http://www.fs.fed.us/r1/kootenai

The Kootenai National Forest, conataining 2.2 million acres, is located in the extreme northwest corner of Montana, Bordered on the north by Canada and on the west by Idaho. Of the total acres, 50,384 are in the state of Idaho. Accessinto the forest is available from US highways 2 and 93, and Montana State Highways 37, 56, 200, and 508.

Paul Bradford, Forest Supervisor

3384 **Lee Metcalf National Wildlife Refuge**
4567 Wildfowl Lane 406-777-5552
Stevensville, MT 59870 Fax: 406-777-2489
http://www.leemetcalf.fws.gov

Mission is to manage habitat for a diversity of wildlife species with emphasis on migratory birds and endangered and threatened species.

3385 **Lewis & Clark National Forest**
1101 15th Street N 406-791-7700
Great Falls, MT 59405 http://www.fs.usda.gov/lcnf

The 1.8 million acres of the Lewis and clark National Forest are scatteered into seven separate mountain ranges. The Forest is situated i west central Montana. The boundaries spread eastward from the rugged, mountainous ContinentalDivide onto the plains. When looking at a map, the National Forest System lands appear as islands of forest within oceans of prairie. Because of its wide-ranging land pattern, the forest is separated into two divisions: the Rocky Mountain and theJefferson.

3386 **Lolo National Forest**
Building 24-A Fort Missoula 406-329-3750
Missoula, MT 59804 http://www.fs.fed.us/r1/lolo

Of the 15 National Forests in the Northern Region of the USDA Forest Service, the Lolo National Forest is estimated to be the third largest. It is located in western Montana. Several major tributaries to the Clark Fork River of theColumbia River Basin flow through the Forest. Its 2.1 million acres of diverse and spectacular mountainous country extend into seven counties.

Debbie Austin, Forest Supervisor
Paul Matter, District Ranger

3387 **Medicine Lake National Wildlife Refuge Complex**
223 North Shore Road 406-789-2305
Medicine Lake, MT 59247 Fax: 406-789-2350
E-mail: medicinelake@fws.gov
http://www.fws.gov/medicinelake

Medicine Lake National Wildlife Refuge is located on the heavily glaciated rolling plains of northeaster Montana, between Missouri River and the Canadian Border.

3388 **National Bison Range National Wildlife Refuge**
58355 Bisons Range Road 406-644-2211
Moiese, MT 59824 Fax: 406-644-2211
http://www.fws.gov/bisonrange/nbr

Jeff King, Project Leader
Bob Rebarchik, Deputy Project leader

3389 **Red Rocks Lakes National Wildlife Refuge**
27650B South Valley Road 406-276-3536
Lima, MT 59739 Fax: 406-276-3538
E-mail: redrocks@fws.gov
http://www.fws.gov/redrocks

Primarily a high elevation mountain wetland-riparian area. Red Rock Creek flows through the upper end of the Centennial Valley, within which the Refuge lies, creating the impressive Upper Red Rock Lake, River Marsh and Lower Red RockLake marshlands. The rugged Centennial Mountains border the Refuge on the south, catching the snows of winter that replenish the Refuge's lakes and marshes.

Nebraska: US Forests, Parks, Refuges

3390 **Crescent Lake National Wildlife Refuge**
10630 Road 181 308-762-4893
Ellsworth, NE 69340 Fax: 308-762-7606
E-mail: crescentlake@fws.gov
http://www.fws.gov/crescentlake/CrescentLake/

Located in the panhandle of Western Nebraska, Crescent Lake consists of 45,818 acres of rolling sandhills interspersed with numberous shallow wetlands and lakes. Plant and animal species call Crescent Lake home, while visitors canparticipate in a variety of public use activities.

3391 **Fort Niobrara National Wildlife Refuge**
Fort Niobrara/Valentine NWR Complex
HC 14, Box 67 402-376-3789
Valentine, NE 69201 Fax: 402-376-3217
E-mail: fortniobrara@fws.gov
http://www.fws.gov/fortniobrara

National Wildlife Refuge Complex includes Fort Niobrara NWR, Valentine NWR and Seier NWR. Complex lands include riverine, riparian, marshland, hand prairie, and sandhills prairie habitats.

Steven A Hicks, Project Leader

3392 **Nebraska & Samuel R McKelvie National Forest**
125 N Main Street 308-432-0300
Chadron, NE 69337 E-mail: nnf_info@fs.fed.us
http://www.fs.fed.us/r2/nebraska

There is an unusual combination of the native ponderosa pine forest of the Nebraska and Samuel R. McKelvie National Forests and mixed grass prairies on the Buffalo Gap, Fort Pierre, and Oglala National Grasslands

Jane Darnell, Supervisor
Stephen Lenzo, Deputy Supervisor

Nevada: US Forests, Parks, Refuges

3393 **Anaho Island National Wildlife Refuge**
Stillwater Wildlife Management
9604 Auction Road
PO Box 1236
Fallon, NV 89406
775-423-5128
E-mail: stillwater@fws.gov
http://www.fws.gov/stillwater/anaho_refuge
Primary wildlife Anaho Island has one of the largest white pelican nesting colonies in North America, as well as cormorant, great blue heron and gull nesting colonies. An island in Pyramid Lake in Great Basin. Closed to public entry toprotect wildlife. Contact refuge manager for information.

3394 **Ash Meadows National Wildlife Refuge**
610 Springs Meadows Road
Amargosa Valley, NV 89020
775-372-5435
Fax: 775-372-5436
E-mail: Daniel_Balduini@fws.gov
http://www.fws.gov/refuge/ash_meadows/
Refuge staff are responsible for managing the 22,117 acre refuge, most of which is spring-fed wetland and alkaline desert upland The refuge area habitat for at least 24 plants and animals found nowhere else in the world. Four fishesand one plant are currently listed as endangered. Species found on the refuge include numerous endemic species, the greatest concentration in the US and the second greatest in all of North America.

Sharon McKelvey, Manager

3395 **Desert National Wildlife Refuge Complex**
HCR 38, Box 700
Las Vegas, NV 89124
702-879-6110
http://www.fws.gov/desertcomplex
Established in 1936 for perpetuating the desert bighorn sheep. Two threatened, and twenty-nine species of concern can be found at the refuge. Wildlife observation is one of the most popular refuge activities. Big game hunting is very limited, but also very popular. Bird watching is another popular activity. A growing program provides additional opportunities and students are able to earn college credits through an internship at the refuge.

3396 **Great Basin National Park**
100 Great Basin National Park
Baker, NV 89311
775-234-7331
Fax: 775-234-7269
http://www.nps.gov/grba
Great Basin National Park includes streams, lakes, alpine plants, abundant wildlife, a variety of forest types including groves of ancient bristlecone pines, and numerous limestone caverns, including beatiful Lehman Caves.

3397 **Humboldt-Toiyabe National Forest**
1200 Franklin Way
Sparks, NV 89431
775-331-6444
Fax: 775-355-5399
http://www.fs.fed.us/r4/htnf
The Humboldt-Toiyabe National Forest encompasses all of Nevada and the far Eastern edge of California. The Humboldt-Toiyabe is the largest forest in the lower 48 states.
Bill Dunkelberger, Forest Supervisor
Jack Isaacs, Deputy Forest Supervisor

3398 **Lake Mead National Recreation Area (NRA)**
601 Nevada Way
Boulder City, NV 89005
702-293-8990
Fax: 702-293-8936
E-mail: LAME_Interpretation@nps.gov
http://www.nps.gov/lame
Lake Mead NRA, which includes Lake Mohave, offers a wealth of things to do and places to go year-round. Its huge lakes cater to boaters, swimmers, sunbathers and fishermen while its desert rewards hikers, wildlife photographers androadside sightseers. Three of America's four desert ecosystems: the Mojave, the Great Basin and the Sonoran Desert meet in here. As a result, this seemingly barren area contains a surprising variety of plants animals, some of which may be foundnowhere else.

3399 **Moapa Valley National Wildlife Refuge**
4701 N Torrey Pines Drive
Las Vegas, NV 89130
702-515-5450
Fax: 702-515-5460
http://www.fws.gov/desertcomplex/moapavalley
To secure habitat for the endangered Moapa dace, a small fish commonly found throughout the headwaters of the Muddy River system

Amy Lavoie, Refuge Manager

3400 **Pahranagat National Wildlife Refuge**
PO Box 510
Alamo, NV 89001
775-725-3417
Fax: 775-725-3389
E-mail: amy_lavoie@fws.gov
http://www.fws.gov/refuge/Pahranagat/
Refuge staff are responsible for managing the 5,380 acre refuge, a mixture of desert, open water, native grass meadows, cropland and marsh. The refuge provides habitat for migratory birds of the Pacific Flyway and several speciesabound at this desert oasis. Wildlife observation is one of the most popular refuge activities. Waterfowl and small game hunting are also very popular, as is bird watching. A growing program provides additional opportunities, including internshipsfor college students.

Amy Lavoie, Refuge Manager
Annji Greenwood, Deputy Refuge Manager

New Hampshire: US Forests, Parks, Refuges

3401 **Lake Umbagog National Wildlife Refuge**
PO Box 240
2756 Dam Road
Errol, NH 03579
603-482-3415
Fax: 603-482-3308
E-mail: lakeumbagog@fws.gov
http://www.fws.gov/northeast/lakeumbagog/
Northern Forest refuge of New Hampshire and Maine provides long-term conservation of important wetland/upland habitats for wildlife, migratory birds and protected species.

3402 **White Mountain National Forest**
71 White Mountain Drive
Campton, NH 03223
603-536-6100
Fax: 603-528-8783
http://www.fs.fed.us/r9/forests/white_mountain
The White Mountain National Forest is located in northern New Hampshire and southwestern Maine, and lies within Carroll, Coos, and Grafton Counties in New Hampshire, and Oxford County in Maine.
Tom Wagner, Forest Supervisor

New Jersey: US Forests, Parks, Refuges

3403 **Cape May National Wildlife Refuge**
24 Kimbles Beach Road
Cape May Courthouse, NJ 08210
609-463-0994
Fax: 609-463-1667
E-mail: capemay@fws.gov
http://www.fws.gov/northeast/capemay/

3404 **Great Swamp National Wildlife Refuge**
241 Pleasant Plains Road
Basking Ridge, NJ 07920
973-425-1222
Fax: 973-425-7309
E-mail: greatswamp@fws.gov
http://www.fws.gov/northeast/greatswamp
Swamp woodland, hardwood ridges, cattail marsh and grassland are typical of this approximately 7,800 acre refuge. The Swamp contains many large old oak and beach trees, stands of mountain laurel, mosses, ferns and species of many otherplants of both Northern and Southern botanical zones.
William Koch, Refuge Manager
Steve Henry, Deputy Refuge Manager

New Mexico: US Forests, Parks, Refuges

3405 **Bitter Lake National Wildlife Refuge**
4200 East Pine Lodge Road 505-622-6755
Roswell, NM 88201 Fax: 505-623-9039
E-mail: steve_alvarez@fws.gov
http://www.fws.gov/refuge/bitter_lake/
Native grasses, sand dunes, brushy bottomlands, seven lakes and a red-rimmed plateau make up Bitter Lake National Wildlife Refuge, winter home for thousands of migratory birds. The Lakes on the refuge were formed within the ancientriver beds of the Pecos River. These lakes store about 1,000 acres of water at their highest levels, while nearby marshland, mudflats and the Pecos Rriver provide an additional 24,500 acres of habitat.
Floyd Truetken, Refuge Manager

3406 **Bosque del Apache National Wildlife Refuge**
1001 Highway 1 505-835-1828
San Antonio, NM 87832 Fax: 505-835-0314
E-mail: fw2_rw_bosque_del_apache@fws.gov
http://www.fws.gov/southwest/refuges/newmex/bosque/
Bosque del Apache NWR is located in south-central New Mexico, along the Rio Grande in the northern reach of the Chihuahuan Desert. Habitats include cottonwood forests, seasonally managed wetlands, farm fields, saltgrass meadows, anddesert uplands. The refuge features large concentrations of sandhill cranes, light geese, and migrating waterfowl in fall and winter, shorebirds and songbirds travel through in spring and fall, and hummingbirds are abundant in summer.

3407 **Capulin Volcano National Monument National Park Service**
46 Volcano Rd. 505-278-2201
Capulin, NM 88414 Fax: 505-278-2211
http://www.nps.gov/cavo
Capulin Volcano is long extinct, and today the forested slopes provide habitat for mule deer, wild turkey, black bear and other wildlife. Abundant displays of wildflowers bloom on the mountain each summer. A two mile paved roadspiraling to the volcano rim makes Capulin Volcano one of the most accessible volcanos in the world. Trails leading around the rim allow exploration of this classic cinder cone.
, Superintendent, Park Ranger

3408 **Carlsbad Caverns National Park**
3225 National Parks Highway 505-785-2232
Carlsbad, NM 88220 Fax: 505-785-2133
E-mail: cave_park_information@nps.gov
http://www.nps.gov/cave
Established to preserve Carlsbad Cavern and numerous other caves within a Permian-age fossil reef, the park contains over 100 known caves, including Lechuguilla Cave-the nation's deepest limestone cave and third longest. CarlsbadCavern, with one of the world's largest underground chambers and countless formations, is highly accessible, with a variety of tours offered year-round.
John Benjamin, Superintendent
Chuck Barat, Deputy Superintendent

3409 **Carson National Park**
208 Cruz Alta Road 505-758-6200
Taos, NM 87571 Fax: 505-758-6213
E-mail: mailroom_r3_carson@fs.fed.us
http://www.fs.usda.gov/carson
Some of the finest mountain scenery in the southwest is found in the 1.5 million acres covered by the Carson National Forest. Elevations rise from 6,000 feet to 13,161 feet. The scenic Sangre de Cristo Mountains include Wheeler Peak,the highest peak in New Mexico.

3410 **Cibola National Forest**
2113 Osuna Road Northeast Suite A 505-346-3900
Albuquerque, NM 87113 Fax: 505-346-3901
http://www.fs.fed.us/r3/cibola
Cibola, pronounced See'-bo-lah, is thought to be the original Zuni Indian name for their group of pueblos or tribal lands. Later, the Spanish interpreted the word to mean, buffalo. Valued for its recreation opportunities, naturalbeauty, timber, watersheds, water, forage, and wilderness resources, the forest is managed to give the American people the greatest benefits that can be produced on a permanent basis.
Elaine Kohrman, Forest Supervisor
Ruth Sutton, Public Affairs

3411 **El Malpais National Monument**
123 E Roosevelt Avenue 505-876-2783
201 E Roosevelt Fax: 505-285-5661
Grants, NM 87020 E-mail: Leslie_DeLong@nps.gov
http://www.nps.gov/elma/
This monument preserves 114,277 acres of which 109,260 acres are federal and 5,017 acres are private. Volcanic features such as lava flows, cinder cones, pressure ridges and complex lava tube systems dominate the landscape. Sandstonebluffs and mesas border the eastern side, providing to vast wilderness.
Douglas E Eury

3412 **Las Vegas National Wildlife Refuge**
Route 1 Box 399 505-425-3581
Las Vegas, NM 87701 http://www.gorp.com
8,672 acres consisting of native grassland, cropland, marshes, ponds, forested canyons, and streams.
Joe B Rodriguez, Manager

3413 **Lincoln National Forest**
3463 Las Palomas Rd. 575-434-7200
Alamogordo, NM 88310 Fax: 575-434-7218
http://www.fs.fed.us/r3/lincoln/
The Lincoln consists of three ranger districts: Sacramento, Smokey Bear and Guadalupe
Travis Moseley, Forest Supervisor
Karla Eldridge, Administrative Officer

3414 **Maxwell National Wildlife Refuge**
PO Box 276 575-375-2331
Maxwell, NM 87728 Fax: 575-375-2331
E-mail: fw2_rw_maxwell@fws.gov
http://www.fws.gov/refuge/maxwell/
At an altitude of 6,050 feet, the refuge is made up of more than 3,000 acres of gently rolling prairie, playa lakes and farmland for waterfowl. Rangeland and reclaimed farmland on the refuge are made up of a variety of grassesincluding blue grama, galleta, sand dropseed, threeawn and buffalo grass, as well as fourwing saltbush and cactus. Several lakes provide approximately 700 acres of roosting and feeding habitat for waterfowl. Supports waterfowl nesting and is alsobeneficial to shore birds.
Leann Wilkins, Refuge Manager

3415 **San Andres National Wildlife Refuge**
5686 Santa Gertrudis Dr. 505-382-5047
Las Cruces, NM 88012 Fax: 505-382-5454
E-mail: lorie_hardin@fws.gov
http://www.fws.gov/southwest/refuges/newmex/sanandres/index.html
Refuge not open to the public due to its location within the boundaries of U.S. Department of Army, White Sands Missile Range. Primary emphasis has been focused on restoring a remnant population of desert bighorn sheet (OvisCanadensis Mexicana)
Kevin Cobble, Refuge Manager

3416 **Sevilleta National Wildlife Refuge**
PO Box 1248 505-864-4021
Socorro, NM 87801 Fax: 505-864-7761
E-mail: Jeannine_Kimble@fws.gov
http://www.fws.gov/refuge/sevilleta/
Home to over 1200 species of plants, 89 species of mammals, 225 species of birds and 15 species of amphibians. More commonly seen species include mule deer, coyotes, pronghorns, red-tailed hawks, northern harriers, western diamondbackrattlesnakes, roadrunners, sandhill cranes and many different types of waterfowl and migrating shorebirds. Bobcats, elk, bighorn sheep and an occasional mountain lion also roam the hillsides.
Kathy Granillo, Manager
Renee Robichaud, Deputy Refuge Manager

3417 **White Sands National Monument**
PO Box 1086 505-479-6124
Holloman Air Force Base, NM 88330 Fax: 505-479-4333
E-mail: whsa_interpretation@nps.gov
http://www.nps.gov/whsa/
White Sands National Mounment preserves a major portion of this gypsum dune field, along with the plants and animals that have successfully adapted to this constantly changing environment.
Dennis L Ditmanson

New York: US Forests, Parks, Refuges

3418 **Fire Island National Seashore**
120 Laurel Street 631-687-4750
Patchogue, NY 11772-3596 Fax: 631-289-4898
E-mail: fiis_interpretation@nps.gov
http://www.nps.gov/fiis/
There are 32 miles of sandy beaches and saltwater marshes, a sunken forest of 300 year old holly trees, hiking trails, a wilderness area and many other sites on the Fire Island National Seashore.
Michael T Reynolds, Superintendent
K Christopher Soller, Superintendent

3419 **Gateway National Recreation Area**
210 New York Avenue 718-354-4606
Staten Island, NY 10305 Fax: 718-354-4764
E-mail: carole_silano@nps.gov
http://www.nps.gov/gate/
Gateway NRA is a 26,000 acre recreation area located in the heart of the New York metropolitan area. The park extends through three New York City boroughs and into northern New Jersey. Parks sites offer a variety of recreationopportunities, along with a chance to explore many significant cultural resources.
Kevin Buckley, Supt

3420 **Iroquois National Wildlife Refuge**
1101 Casey Road 585-948-5445
Basom, NY 14013 Fax: 585-948-9538
E-mail: iroquois@fws.gov
http://www.fws.gov/refuge/iroquois/
Iroquois National Wildlife Refuge lies within the rural township of Alabama, New York, midway between Buffalo and Rochester. Part of what the locals call the Alabama Swamps, its 10,818 acres of freshwater marshes, and hardwood swampsbounded by woods, forest, pastures and wet meadows, serve the habitat needs of many animals as a major stopover for migrating birds and as a year-round residence.
Robert Lamayr, Refuge Manager

3421 **Montezuma National Wildlife Refuge**
3395 Routes 5 & 20 East 315-568-5987
Seneca Falls, NY 13148 Fax: 315-568-8835
E-mail: andrea_vanbeusichem@fws.gov
http://www.fws.gov/r5mnwr
Montezuma is the premiere refuge in New York State. View bald eagles year-round. Spring and fall bring tens of thousands of migrating ducks and geese. View Shaebirds in early spring and late summer. May and June are great for warblerwatching. Volunteer opportunities available Spring- Fall.
Tom Jasikoff, Manager
Andrea VanBeusichem, Visitor Services Manager

3422 **Seatuck National Wildlife Refuge: Long Island National Wildlife Refuge Complex**
340 Smith Road 631-286-0485
Shirley, NY 11967 Fax: 516-581-2003
E-mail: R5RW_STKNWR@fws.gov
http://www.fws.gov/northeast/longislandrefuges/seatuck.html
Located along the southern shore of Long Island, the Refuge consists of half salt marsh and half freshwater wetlands, ponds and sparsely wooded areas. It is part of the larger Great South Bay, which is a significant coastal habitat formigrating birds. Limited recreation includes viewing wildlife and bird watching.
Charles Stenvall, Manager

3423 **Target Rock National Wildlife Refuge Long Island National Wildlife Refuge Complex**
340 Smith Road 631-286-0485
Shirley, NY 11967 Fax: 516-286-4003
http://www.fws.gov/northeast/targetrock/
The refuge was established in 1967. It consists of mixed upland forest, a half mile of rocky beach, a brackish and several vernal ponds. The offshore, beach and pond habitats provide foraging areas for piping plover, winteringwaterfowl and fish species.

North Carolina: US Forests, Parks, Refuges

3424 **Alligator River National Wildlife Refuge**
PO Box 1969 252-473-1131
Manteo, NC 27954 Fax: 252-473-1668
E-mail: alligatorriver@fws.gov
http://http://www.fws.gov/alligatorriver
Provide habitat and protection for endangered species such as red wolves, red-cockaded woodpeckers, and American alligators
Mike Bryant, Refuge Manager
Scott Lanier, Deputy Refuge Manager

3425 **Cape Hatteras National Seashore**
1401 National Park Drive 252-473-2111
Manteo, NC 27954 Fax: 252-473-2595
E-mail: CAHA_Information@nps.gov
http://www.nps.gov/caha/
A thin broken strand of islands curves out into the Atlantic Ocean and then back again in a sheltering embrace of North Carolina's mainland coast and its offshore sounds. These are the Outer Banks of North Carolina. Today their longstretches of beach, sand dunes, marshes and woodlands are set aside as Cape Hatteras National Seashore.
Lawrence A Belli, Superintendent

3426 **Cape Lookout National Seashore**
131 Charles Street 252-728-2250
Harkers Island, NC 28531 Fax: 252-728-2160
E-mail: CALO_information@nps.gov
http://www.nps.gov/calo
The seashore is a 56 mile long section of the Outer Banks of North Carolina running from Ocracoke Inlet on the northeast to Beafort Inlet on the southeast. The four undeveloped barrier island, make up the seashore- North Core Banks,South Core Banks, Middle Core Banks and Shackleford Banks- may seem barren and isolated but they offer many natural and historical features that can make a visit very rewarding.
Robert A Vogel, Superintendent
Donna O Tiptor, Administrative Officer

3427 **Cedar Island National Wildlife Refuge**
85 Mattamuskeet Road 252-926-4021
Swan Quarter, NC 27885 Fax: 252-926-1743
E-mail: mattamuskeet@fws.gov
http://www.fws.gov/cedarisland/
Provide habitat and protection for endangered species such as American alligators and brown pelicans
Peter Campbell, Refuge Manager
Jerry Fringeli, Deputy Refuge Manager

3428 **Currituck National Wildlife Refuge**
Mackay Island NWR 919-429-3100
PO Box 39 Fax: 919-429-3185
Knotts Island, NC 27950-0039 http://www.gorp.com
The purpose of the Refuge is to preserve and protect a portion of the Outer Banks habitat for wintering waterfowl, endangered species, other migratory birds, and native wildlife

3429 Mattamuskeet National Wildlife Refuge
Route 1
Box N-2
Swan Quarter, NC 27885
919-926-4021
E-mail: r4rw_nc.mtk@fws.gov
http://www.gorp.com
Located in eastern North Carolina in Hyde County, the Mattamuskeet Refuge consists of more than 50,000 acres of water, marsh, timber and crop lands. The refuge's most significant feature is lake Mattamuskeet, the largest natural lakein North Carolina. The lake is 18 miles long and five to 6 miles wide, encompassing approximately 40,000 acres, but averages 2 feet in depth.
Don Temple, Manager

3430 Nantahala National Forest
160-A Zillicoa Street
Asheville, NC 28802
828-257-4200
Fax: 828-257-4263
The National Forests of North Carolina include four national forests covering 1.2 million acres from the mountains to the sea. The Nantahala is located in the Appalachians of southwest North Carolina. The Nantahala is the largest ofthe four forests, totaling 528,541 acres. The Nantahala sits adjacent to Great Smokey Mountains National Park.

3431 Pea Island River National Wildlife Refuge
PO Box 1969
Manteo, NC 27954
252-473-1131
Fax: 252-473-1668
E-mail: alligatorriver@fws.gov
http://http://www.fws.gov/peaisland
Provide nesting, resting, and wintering habitat for migratory birds, including the greater snow geese and other migratory waterfowl, shorebirds, wading birds, raptors, and neotropical migrants
Mike Bryant, Refuge Manager
Scott Lanier, Deputy Refuge Manager

3432 Pee Dee National Wildlife Refuge
5770 U.S. Hwy. 52 North
Wadesboro, NC 28170
704-694-4424
Fax: 704-694-6570
E-mail: fw4_rw_pee_dee@fws.gov
http://www.fws.gov/peedee/
Refuge objectives are to: provide habitat for migratory waterfowl and song birds; to provide habitat and protection for an endangered species, the red-cockaded woodpecker; to provide recreation, environmental education andinterpretation for the public; to engage in dynamic partnering.
J.D Bricken, Refuge Manager
Greg Walmsley, Assistant Refuge Manager

3433 Pocosin Lakes National Wildlife Refuge
205 South Ludington Dr
PO Box 329
Columbia, NC 27925
252-796-3004
Fax: 252-796-3010
E-mail: pocosinlakes@fws.gov
http://www.fws.gov/pocosinlakes/
The 112,000 acre refuge was established to protect and ehnhance a unique habitat called a pocosin and contains a variety of wildlife including endangered species such as the red wolf, bald eagle, peregrine falcon and red-cockadedwoodpecker as well as natural vegetation and scenic areas.

Howard Philips, Refuge Manager
David Kitts, Deputy Manager

3434 Roanoke River National Wildlife Refuge
114 W Water Street
PO Box 430
Windsor, NC 27983
252-794-3808
Fax: 252-794-3780
E-mail: roanokeriver@fws.gov
http://www.fws.gov/roanokeriver/
Refuge objectives are: to provide habitat for migratory waterfowl, neo-tropical migrants and other birds; to provide migrating, spawning and nursery habitat for anadromous fish; (i.e. blueback herring, alewife, hickory shad and stripedbass); to enhance and protect forested wetlands consisting of bottomland hardwoods and swamps; to protect and manage for endangered and threatened wildlife; and to provide recreation and environmental education for the public

Matt Connolly, Refuge Manager
Jean Richer, Biologist

3435 Swanquarter National Wildlife Refuge
85 Mattamuskeet Road
Swan Quarter, NC 27885
252-926-4021
Fax: 252-926-1743
E-mail: mattamuskeet@fws.gov
http://www.fws.gov/swanquarter/
Provide habitat for endangered species such as bald eagles, peregrine falcons, and American alligators.
Peter Campbell, Refuge Manager
Jerry Fringeli, Deputy Refuge Manager

North Dakota: US Forests, Parks, Refuges

3436 Crosby Wetland Management District
10100 Hwy 42 NW
Crosby, ND 58730
701-965-6488
E-mail: crosbywetlands@fws.gov
http://www.fws.gov/lostwood/crosby.htm
Previously a part of the Des Lacs NWR Complex, the Crosby WMD includes of 17,000 acres of Waterfowl Production Areas (WPAs), numerous grassland and wetland easment contracts, and the 3,219 acre Lake Zahl NWR.
Tim K Kessler, WMD Manager

3437 Des Lacs National Wildlife Refuge
42000 520th Street NW
Kenmare, ND 58746
701-385-4046
Fax: 701-385-3214
E-mail: deslacs@fws.gov
http://www.deslacs.fws.gov/
Previously a part of the old Des Lacs NWR complex, the Des Lacs NWR is a smaller parcel that is home to wildlife and water fowl. The Lakes no longer encompass the the wetlands that are part of Crosby Wetlands district.

3438 Devils Lake Wetland Management District
Devils Lake WMD
PO Box 908
Devils Lake, ND 58301
701-662-8611
Fax: 701-662-8612
E-mail: DevilsLake@fws.gov
http://www.devilslake.fws.gov
Located in the heart of the Prairie Pothole Region of the US. The northeastern North Dakota counties of Towner, Cavalier, Pembina, Benson, Ramsey, Walsh, Nelson and Grand Forks are included in the District. Managed by the US Fish andWildlife Service, the district provides wetland areas needed by waterfowl in the spring and summer for nesting and feeding. Hundreds of thousands of waterfowl also use these wetlands in the spring and fall for feeding and resting during longmigratory flights.
Roger Hollevoet, Project Leader
Jim Alfonso, Deputy Project leader

3439 Lake Ilo National Wildlife Refuge
489 102 Avenue SW
Dunn Center, ND 58626
701-548-8110
Fax: 701-548-8108
E-mail: lakeilo@fws.gov
http://www.fws.gov/lakeilo
Located near the center of Dunn County in west central North Dakota, the refuge habitat is made up of native prairie, planted grasslands and wetlands. The uplands are characterized by gently sloping hills and terraces with creeks andan occasional slough. The average rainfall of 16.8 inches supports a prairie environment with a climate of hot dry summers, occasional thunderstorms and cold winters.
Kory Richardson, Refuge Manager

3440 Long Lake National Wildlife Refuge
12000 353rd Street 56
Moffit, ND 58560
701-387-4397
Fax: 701-387-4767
E-mail: r6rw-llk@fws.gov
http://www.longlake.fws.gov
The Refuge is about 18 miles long and contains 22,300 acres. The Refuge attracts a diversity and abundance of animals and waterfowl, both resident and migratory. Over 200 species of birds use the Refuge for breeding, rearing theiryoung and as a migratory stop. Long Lake Refuge is open for birdwatching, fishing, photography, boating, hiking and regulated hunting.

3441 **Lostwood National Wildlife Refuge**
8315 Highway 8 701-848-2722
Kenmare, ND 58746-9046 Fax: 701-848-2702
E-mail: Lostwood@fws.gov
http://www.fws.gov/lostwood/lostwoodnwr.htm

Lies in the highly productive pothole region that produces more ducks than any other region in the lower 48 states. The refuge is a land of rolling hills mantled in short-grass and mixed with grass prairie interspersed with numerouswetlands. Established to preserve a unique wildlife habitat, Lostwood is an important link in our nation's system of more than 410 wildlife refuges.

3442 **Theodore Roosevelt National Park**
Box 7 701-623-4730
Medora, ND 58645-0007 Fax: 701-623-4840
E-mail: susan_recce@nps.gov
http://www.nps.gov/thro/

Here in the North Dakota badlands, where many of his personal concerns first gave rise to his later environmental efforts, Roosevelt is remembered with a national park that bears his name and honors the memory of this greatconservationist. Theodore Roosevelt NAtional Park is colorful North Dakota badlands and is home to a variety of plants and animals, including bison, prairie dogs, and elk.

Ohio: US Forests, Parks, Refuges

3443 **Cuyahoga Valley National Park**
15610 Vaughn Road 216-524-1497
Brecksville, OH 44141 800-445-9667
Fax: 440-546-5989
E-mail: cuva_canal_visitor_center@nps.gov
http://www.nps.gov/cuva or www.dayinthevalley.com

Cuyahoga Valley National Park protects 33,000 acres along the Cuyahoga River between Cleveland and Akron, Ohio. Managed by the National Park Service, CVNP combines cultural, historical, recreational and natural activities in onesetting. Visitors can hike, bike, birdwatch, golf, fish, ski, ride Cuyahoga Valley Scenic Railroad, explore the history of the Ohio and Erie Canal on a 20 mile section of the Towpath Trail, and attend national park ranger-guided programs, concerts,art exhibits and more.

Mary Pat Doorley, Media contact

3444 **Ottawa National Wildlife Refuge**
14000 W State Route 2 419-898-0014
Oak Harbor, OH 43449 Fax: 419-898-7895
E-mail: ottawa@fws.gov
http://www.fws.gov/midwest/ottawa/

Refuge objectives are: to restore optimum acreage to a natural floodplain condition; to improve and restore wetland habitat, to improve fishery and wildlife resources, to provide for biodiversity; and to provide public opportunitiesfor outdoor recreation and environmental education.

Dan Frisk, Refuge Manager

Oklahoma: US Forests, Parks, Refuges

3445 **Deep Fork National Wildlife Refuge**
PO Box 816 918-652-0456
Okmulgee, OK 74447 Fax: 918-652-3427
E-mail: lori_jones@fws.gov
http://www.fws.gov/southwest/refuges/oklahoma/deep%20fork/

Protecting important wetlands along the Deep Fork River, Deep Fork National Wildlife Refuge in eastern Oklahoma is a newcomer to the National Wildlife Refuge System. Established in 1993, the 9,000 acre refuge is subject to flooding atleast once a year. This flooding results in excellent conditions for waterfowl, including mallard, blue-winged teal, shoveler, pintail and wood ducks.

Darrin B Unruh, Manager

3446 **Little River National Wildlife Refuge**
PO Box 340 405-584-6211
Broken Bow, OK 74728 Fax: 405-584-2034
http://www.gorp.com

13,000 acres of bottomland hardwoods within the floodplain of Little River.

Berlin A Heck, Manager

3447 **Oklahoma Bat Caves National Wildlife Refuge**
Route 1 Box 18-A 918-773-5251
Vian, OK 74962 Fax: 918-773-5252
http://www.gorp.com

The endangered status of wildlife species and the delicate (and hazardous) nature of the habitat precludes any recreational use. Approved studies can be done under proper supervision.

3448 **Optima National Wildlife Refuge**
20834 east 940 Road 580-664-2205
Butler, OK 73625 Fax: 580-664-2206
E-mail: washita@fws.gov
http://www.fws.gov/southwest/refuges/oklahoma/optima/

Located in the middle of the Oklahoma panhandle, the 4,333-acre refuge is made up of grasslands and wooded bottomland on the Coldwater Creek arm of the Army Corps of Engineers Optima Reservoir Project.

Daniel Moss, Refuge Manager

3449 **Sequoyah National Wildlife Refuge**
Route 1 Box 18 A 918-773-5251
Vian, OK 74962-9304 Fax: 918-773-5598
E-mail: chad_ford@fws.gov
http://http://southwest.fws.gov/refuges/oklahoma/sequoy.html

Sequoyah National Wildlife Refuge is home to wildlife as unique as the bald eagle and as elusive as the bobcat

Jeff Haas, Refuge Manager
Scott Gilje, Assistant Refuge Manager

3450 **US Fish & Wildlife Service Tishomingo National Wildlife Refuge**
12000 S Refuge Road 580-371-2402
Tishomingo, OK 73460 Fax: 580-371-9312
E-mail: fw2_rw_tishomingo@fws.gov
http://http://southwest.fws.gov/refuges/oklahoma/tishomingo

The 16,464-acre Refuge lies at the upper Washita arm of Lake Texoma and is administered for the benefit of migratory waterfowl in the Central Flyway. It offers a variety of aquatic habitats for wildlife. The murky water of theCumberland Pool provides abundant nutrients for innumerable microscopic plants and animals. Seasonally flooded flats and willow shallows lying at the Pool's edge also provide excellent wildlife habitat.

Kris Patton, Refuge Manager

3451 **Washita National Wildlife Refuge**
Route 1 Box 685 405-664-2205
Butler, OK 73625 E-mail: r2rw_wa@fws.gov
http://www.gorp.com

Provides habitat for migrating/wintering waterfowl. Endangered species managed include the bald eagle, whooping crane, and interior least tern.

Jon M Brock, Manager

Oregon: US Forests, Parks, Refuges

3452 **Ankeny National Wildlife Refuge**
Western Oregon NWR Complex 503-327-2444
2301 Wintel Road Fax: 541-757-4450
Jefferson, OR 97352 http://www.gorp.com

Refuge's primary management goal is to provide vital wintering habitat for dusky Canada geese. The refuge includes flat to gently rolling land near the confluence of the Willamette and Santiam rivers. The refuge's fertile farmedfields, hedgerows, forests, and wetlands provide a variety of wildlife habitats. the refuge is open to limited opportunites for wildlife-oriented education and recreation. Ducks, geese, and swans are commonly seen in refuge fields and ponds throughthe fall and winter.

3453 Bandon Marsh National Wildlife Refuge
Oregon Coast NWR Complex 541-867-4550
2127 SE Marine Science Drive http://www.gorp.com
Newport, OR 97365

3454 Baskett Slough National Wildlife Refuge
Western Oregon NWR Complex 503-757-7236
26208 Finley Refuge Road http://www.gorp.com
Corvallis, OR 97333
Includes 2,492 acres typical of Willamette Vallley's irrigated hillsides, oak-covered knolls and grass fields. Wetlands include Morgan Lake and Baskett Slough. The refuge's objective is the protection and management of winteringhabitat for dusky Canada geese. Several species of waterfowl, herons, hawks, quail , shorebirds, mourning doves, woodpeckers and a variety of songbirds frequent the area, as well as mammals, amphibians and reptiles. Recreation includes observation,study and photography.
Richard Guadagno, Manager

3455 Cape Meares National Wildlife Refuge
Western Oregon NWR Complex 503-757-7236
26208 Finley Refuge Road http://www.gorp.com
Corvallis, OR 97333

3456 Cold Springs National Wildlife Refuge
PO Box 239 541-992-3232
Umatilla, OR 97882 E-mail: gary_hagedorn@fws.gov
http://www.gorp.com
Cold Springs NWR lies in sharp contrast with the arid desert surroundings of northeastern Oregon. The refuge, a tree-lined reservoir, lies 7 miles east of the agricultural community of Hermiston. The variety of refuge habitats attractsan abundance of wildlife. Cold Springs supports peak populations of over 45,000 winter waterfowl comprised mainly of mallards and Canada geese.

3457 Columbia River Gorge National Scenic Area
902 Wasco Avenue 541-386-2333
Waucoma Center, Suite 200 http://www.fs.fed.us/r6/columbia/
Hood River, OR 97031
The Columbia River Gorge is a espaectacular river canyon cutting the only sea-level route through the Cascade Mountain Range. It's 80 miles long and to 4,00 feet deep with the north canyon walls in Washington State and the south canyonwalls in Oregon State.

3458 Crater Lake National Park
Highway 62 541-594-3000
PO Box 7 Fax: 541-594-3010
Crater Lake, OR 97604 http://www.nps.gov/crla/home.html
During the summer, visitors may navigate the Rim Drive around the lake, enjoy boat tours, stay in the historic Crater Lake Lodge Camp or hike some of the park's various trails. The winter brings some of the heaviest snowfall in thecountry, averaging 533 inches per year. Although park facilities mostly close for the snow season, visitors may view the lake during fair weather, enjoy cross-country skiing, and participate in weekend snowshoe hikes.
Dave Morris, Supt

3459 Deschutes National Forest
63095 Deschutes Market Road 541-383-5300
Bend, OR 97701 Fax: 541-383-5531
http://www.fs.usda.gov/centraloregon
Scenic backdrop of volcanic attraction, evergreen forest, mountain lakes, caves, desert areas and alpine meadows.

3460 Fremont Winema National Forest
1300 S G Street 541-947-2151
Lakeview, OR 97630 Fax: 541-947-6399
http://www.fs.usda.gov/fremont-winema
Located in Oregon's Outback, the forest provides the self reliant recreationist the opportunity to discover nature in a rustic environment.

3461 Malheur National Forest
431 Patterson Bridge Road 541-575-1731
PO Box 909 E-mail: jtrosclair02@fs.fed.us
John Day, OR 97845 http://www.fs.usda.gov/malheur/
The 1,460,000 acre Malheur National Forest is located in the blue Mountains of Eastern Oregon. The diverse and beautiful scenery of the forest includes high desert grasslands, sage and juniper, pine, fir and other tree species, and thehidden gem of alpine lakes and meadows. Elevations vary from about 4000feet (1200 meters) to the 9038 foot (2754 meters) top Strawberry Mountain. The Strawberry Mountain range extends east to west through the center of the forest.
Bonnie J Wood, Forest Supervisor

3462 Malheur National Wildlife Refuge
36391 Sodhouse Lane 541-493-2612
Princeton, OR 97721 Fax: 541-493-2405
E-mail: tim_bodeen@fws.gov
http://www.fws.gov/malheur
Tim Bodeen, Manager

3463 McKay Creek National Wildlife Refuge
Umatilla NWR Complex 503-922-3232
PO Box 239 http://www.gorp.com
Umatilla, OR 97882

3464 Mount Hood National Forest
16400 Champion Way 503-668-1700
Sandy, OR 97055 Fax: 503-668-1641
http://www.fs.usda.gov/mthood/
Located 20 miles east of the city of Portland and the northern Willamette River valley, Mt Hood National Forest extends south from the strikingly beautiful Columbia River Gorge across more than sixty miles of forested mountains, lakesand streams to OlAllie Scienic Area, a high lake basin under the slopes of Mt Jefferson. Our many visitors enjoy fishing, caming, boating and hiking in the summer, hunting in the fall, skiing and other snow sports in the winter.

3465 National Park Service: John Day Fossil Beds National Monument
32651 Highway 19 541-987-2333
Kimberly, OR 97845-9701 Fax: 541-987-2336
E-mail: joda_interpretation@nps.gov
http://www.nps.gov/joda
Within the heavily eroded volcanic deposits of the scenic John Day Fossil Basin is a great diversity of well-preserved plant and animal fossils. This remarkably complete record spans more than 40 of the 65 million years of the CenozoicEra (the Age of Mammals). The monument was established in 1975.
John Fiedor, Chief Visitor Services

3466 Ochoco National Forest
3160 NE 3rd Street 541-416-6500
Prineville, OR 97754 Fax: 541-416-6695
http://www.fs.fed.us/r6/centraloregon
With a total of almost 1,500 square miles, the Ochoco National Forest is endowed with vast natural resources, scenic grandeur and tremendous recreation opportunities. People are drawn to the Ochoco for its majestic ponderosa pinestands, picturesque rimrock vantage points, deep canyons, unique geologic formations, abundant wildlife and plentiful sunshine.

3467 Oregon Caves National Monument
19000 Caves Highway 541-592-2100
Cave Junction, OR 97523 Fax: 541-592-3981
http://www.nps.gov/orca
Oregan Caves National Monument is small in size, 480 acres, but rich in diversity. Above ground, the monument encompasses a remnant old-growth coniferous forest. It harbors a fantastic array of plants, and a Douglas-fir tree with thewildest known girth in Oregon. Three hiking trails access this forest. Below ground is an active marble cave created by natural forces over hundreds of thousands of years in one of the world's most diverse geologic realms.

Vicki Snitzler, Superintendent

3468 Oregon Coastal Refuges
2127 SE OSU Drive
Newport, OR 97365
541-867-4550
Fax: 541-867-4551
http://www.gorp.com
575 acres of rocks and islands located offshore along the length of the Oregon coast. Most of the refuge is included in the Oregon Islands Wilderness.
Nancy Morrissey, Manager

3469 Oregon Islands National Wildlife Refuge
c/o Oregon Coast NWR Complex
2127 SE Marine Science Drive
Newport, OR 97365
541-867-4550
http://www.gorp.com
575 acres of rocks and islands located offshore along the length of the Oregon coast. Most of the refuge is included in the Oregon Islands Wilderness.

3470 Rogue River National Forest
3040 Biddle Road
Medford, OR 97504
541-858-2200
Fax: 541-858-2220
http://www.fs.fed.us/r6/rogue
Rob MacWhorter, Forest Supervisor
Tracy Tophooven, Deputy Forest Supervisor

3471 Sheldon National Wildlife Refuge
US Fish and Wildlife Service- Pacific Region
PO Box 111
18 South G
Lakeview, OR 97630
503-947-3315
Fax: 503-947-4414
http://www.fws.gov/sheldonhartmtn/sheldon/
Provide habitat for pronghorn antelope, the primary species, and populations of native secondary species (e.g., mule deer, sage-grouse, and song birds) in such numbers as may be necessary to maintain a balanced wildlife population
Brian Day, Manager

3472 Siskiyou National Forest
2164 Northeast Spaulding Avenue
Grants Pass, OR 97526
541-471-6500
Fax: 541-471-6514
http://www.fs.usda.gov/rogue-siskiyou/
The Siskiyou National Forest embodies the most complex soils, geology, landscape, and plant communities in the Pacific Northwest. World-class rivers, biological diversity, fisheries, and complex watersheds rank the Siskiyou high in theNation as an outstanding resource.
Roy Bergstrom, District Ranger

3473 Siuslaw National Forest
3200 SW Jefferson Way
Corvallis, OR 97331
541-750-7000
Fax: 541-750-7234
http://www.fs.usda.gov/siuslaw
The Siuslaw National Forest encompasses one of the most productive and diverse landscapes in the world from fertile soils, which support tall stands of Douglas fir, western hemlock and Sitka spruce forests laced with miles of riversand streams, to miles of open sand dunes. These rich settings from habitats for a broad array of plants and animals and provide endless opportunities for learning.
Jerry Ingersoll, Forest Supervisor

3474 Three Arch Rocks National Wildlife Refuge
Western Oregon NWR Complex
26208 Finley Refuge Road
Corvallis, OR 97333
503-757-7236
http://www.gorp.com
Large numbers of nesting common murres, tufted puffins, and Brandt's and pelagic cormorants use the area. Northern and California seal lions and harbor seals.

3475 Umatilla National Forest
72510 Coyote Road
Pendleton, OR 97801
541-278-3716
http://www.fs.usda.gov/umatilla
The Umatilla National Forest, located in the Blue Mountains of southeast Wasington and northeast Oregon, covers 1.4 million acres of diverse landscapes and plant communities. The forest has some mountainous terrain, but most of theforest consists of v-shaped valleys separated by narrow ridges or plateaus.
Kevin Martin, Forest Supervisor

3476 Umpqua National Forest
2900 NW Stewart Parkway
PO Box 1008
Roseburg, OR 97471
541-957-3200
Fax: 541-957-3495
E-mail: jcaplan@fs.fed.us
http://www.fs.usda.gov/umpqua/
The Umpqua National Forest covers nearly one million acres and is located in the western slopes of the Cascades in Southwest Oregon. The forest encommpasses a diverse area of rugged peaks, high rolling meadows, sparkling rivers andlakes and deep canyons producing a wealth of water resources, timber, forage, minerals, wildlife and outdoor recreation opportunities.
Kelly Miller, Information Assistant

3477 Wallowa-Whitman National Forest
1500 Dewey Avenue
PO Bos 907
Baker, OR 97814
541-523-6391
Fax: 541-523-1315
http://www.fs.usda.gov/wallowa-whitman/
The Wallowa-Whitman National Forest contains 2.3 million acres ranging in elevation from 875 feet in Hells Canyon, to 9845 feet in the Eagle Cap Wilderness. Our varied forests are managed as sustainable ecosystems providing cleanwater, wildlife habitat and valuable forest products. For things to do and places to be, the Wallowa-Whitman is the setting for a variety of year-round recreation. You are welcome at the Wallowa-Whitman National Forest.

3478 William L Finley National Wildlife Refuge
26208 Finley Refuge Road
Corvallis, OR 97333
503-757-7236
http://www.gorp.com
Primary objective for the refuge is the protection and management of wintering habitat for dusky Canada geese. In addition to geese, other migratory and resident animals use refuge lands

3479 Winema National Forest
2819 Dahlia Street
Klamath Falls, OR 97601
541-883-6714
Fax: 541-883-6709
http://www.fs.usda.gov/fremont-winema
The 1.1 million acre Winema National Forest lies on the eastern slopes of the Cascade Mountain Range in South Central Oregon, an area noted for its year-round sunshine. The Forest borders Crater Lake National Park near the crest of theCascades and stretches eastward into the Klamath River Basin. Near the floor of the Basin the Forest gives way to vast marshes and meadows assoicated with Upper Klamath Lake and the Williamson River.

Pennsylvania: US Forests, Parks, Refuges

3480 Allegheny National Forest
4 Farm Colony Road
Warren, PA 16365
814-723-5150
Fax: 814 726 1465
E-mail: r9_allegheny_nf@fs.fed.us
http://www.fs.usda.gov/allegheny/
An organization dedicated to providing advice for development of the corridor management plan for the northern section of the Allegheny River that has been designated as a National Wild and Scenic River.
Erin Connelly, Forest Supervisor

3481 Delaware National Scenic River: Delaware Water Gap National Recreation Area
Delaware Water Gap National Recreation Area
HQ River Road - Route 209
Bushkill, PA 18324
570-588-2435
Fax: 570-588-2780
E-mail: dewa_interpretation@nps
http://www.nationalparksgallery.com/

3482 Erie National Wildlife Refuge
11296 Wood Duck Lane
Guys Mills, PA 16327
814-789-3585
Fax: 814-789-2909
http://www.fws.gov/refuge/erie/
A haven for migratory birds consisting of two divisions: the Sugar Lake Division and the Seneca Division. Refuge management objectives include: providing waterfowl and other migratory birds with nesting, feeding, brooding, and restinghabitat; providing habitat to support a diversity of other wildlife species;

and enhancing opportunities for wildlife-oriented public recreation and environmental education.

Patty Nagel, Deputy Refuge Manager

3483 Gettysburg National Military Park
1195 Baltimore Pike, Suite 100 717-334-1124
Gettysburg, PA 17325-2804 Fax: 717-334-1891
E-mail: gett_superintendant@nps.gov
http://www.nps.gov/gett/index.htm

A unit of the national park service preserving 6000 acres of Gettysburg battlefield, and the Soldiers' National Cemetery, site of Lincoln's Gettysburg Address.

3484 John Heinz National Wildlife Refuge at Tinicum
8601 Lindbergh Boulevard 215-365-3118
Philadelphia, PA 19153 Fax: 215-365-2846
E-mail: JohnHeinzNWR@fws.gov
http://www.fws.gov/heinz/index.html

The John Heinz National Wildlife Refuge at Tinicum is administered by the Department of Interior's U.S. Fish and Wildlife Service and is located in Philadelphia and Delaware Counties, Pennsylvania. The refuge protects the last 200acres of freshwater tidal marsh in Pennsylvania. The refuge has become a resting and feeding area for more than 20 species of birds, 80 of which nest here. Fox, deer, muskrat, turtles, fish, frogs and a wide variety of wildflowers and plants callthe refuge home.

3485 Upper Delaware Scenic & Recreational River
274 River Road 570-729-7134
Beach Lake, PA 18405 Fax: 570-729-8565
http://www.nps.gov/upde

As a part of the National Wild and Scenic Rivers System, upper Delaware Scenic and Recreational River stretches 73.4 miles (118.3 km) along the New York/Pennsylvania border. The longest free flowing river in the Northeast, it includesriffles and Class I and II rapids between placid pools eddies. Public fishing and boating accesses are provided, although most land along the river is privately owned. Wintering bald eagles are among the wildlife that may be seen here.

Dave Forney, Superintendent
Michael Reubet, Chief Resource Management

Rhode Island: US Forests, Parks, Refuges

3486 Rhode Island National Wildlife Refuge Complex
3769 D Old Post Road 401-364-0170
PO Box 307 Fax: 401-364-0170
Charlestown, RI 02813 E-mail: fw5rw_rinwr@fws.gov
http://www.fws.gov/northeast/ri.htm

Charles Vandemoer, Complex Refuge Manager
Gary M Andres, Deputy Refuge Manager

South Carolina: US Forests, Parks, Refuges

3487 Ace Basin National Wildlife Refuge
PO Box 848 843-889-3084
Hollywood, SC 29449 Fax: 843-889-3282
http://www.fws.gov/acebasin/

The Ace Basin National Wildlife Refuge was established in 1990 to assist in preserving the nationally significant wildlife and related habitats within the 350,000-acre Ashepoo, Combahee and South Edisto (ACE) rivers basin. The wetlandshabitat of the area has been preserved during the last several centuries through careful management by private landowners. An antebellum mansion that survived the Civil War now serves in part as office space for the refuge.

Jane Griess, Refuge Manager

3488 Cape Romain National Wildlife Refuge
5801 Highway 17 North 843-928-3264
Awendaw, SC 29429 Fax: 843-928-3803
E-mail: caperomain@fws.gov
http://www.fws.gov/caperomain/

Refuge objectives are to: provide habitat for waterfowl, shorebirds, wading birds and resident species; provide habitat and management of endangered and threatened species; provide protection of Class I Wilderness Area; and provideenvironmental education and recreation for the public.

Sarah Dawsey, Refuge Manager
Raye Nilius, Project Leader

3489 Carolina Sandhills National Wildlife Refuge
Route 2 Box 330 803-335-8401
McBee, SC 29101 Fax: 803-335-8406
http://www.gorp.com

Richard P Ingram, Manager

3490 Francis Marion-Sumter National Forest
4931 Broad River Road 803-561-4000
Columbia, SC 29212 Fax: 803-561-4004
http://www.fs.fed.us/r8/fms/

Headquaters in the capital city of Columbia, both forests are managed for many uses; including timber and wood production, watershed protection and improvement, habitat for wildlife and fish species, wilderness area management,minerals leasing and outdoor recreation.

Paul Bradley, Forest Supervisor

3491 Santee National Wildlife Refuge
2125 Fort Watson Road 803-478-2217
Summerton, SC 29148 Fax: 803-478-2314
E-mail: santee@fws.gov
http://www.fws.gov/santee

Wildlife viewing opportunities available at the refuge on hiking, biking, canoeing/kayaking, and driving trails. A refuge visitor center is open Tuesday thru Saturday from 8-4. Located off of I-95 at exit 102 in Summerton, SC, SanteeNational Wildlife offers something for everybody.

Marc Epstein, Refuge Manager
Christopher Spivey, Refuge Officer

South Dakota: US Forests, Parks, Refuges

3492 Badlands National Park
PO Box 6 605-433-5361
Interior, SD 57750 Fax: 605-433-5404
http://www.nps.gov/badl/

Consists of acres of sharply eroded buttes, pinnacles and spires blended with the largest protected mixed grass prarie in the US. The Badlands Wilderness Area covers 64,000 acres and is the site of the reintroduction of theblack-footed ferret, the most endangered land mammal in North America. The Stronghold Unit is co-managed with the Oglala Sioux Tribe and includes site of 1890s Glost Dances. Over 11,000 years of human history pale to the ages old paleontologicalresources.

William R Supernaugh, Superintendent

3493 Black Hills National Forest
1019 N. 5th Street 605-673-9200
Custer, SD 57730 Fax: 605-673-9350
E-mail: r2_blackhills_webinfo@fs.fed.us
http://www.fs.fed.us/r2/blackhills/

Eleven reservoirs, 30 campgrounds, 2 scenic byways, 1300 miles of streams, 13,000 acres of wilderness, 353 miles of trails, and much more. The forest is managed for multiple use so don't be surprised to see mining, logging, cattlegrazing, and summer homes on your travel.

3494 Huron Wetland Management District
200 4th Street SW 605-352-5894
Federal Building, Room 309 Fax: 605-352-6709
Huron, SD 57350 E-mail: huronwetlands@fws.gov
http://www.fws.gov/huronwetlands/

The public lands of the HWMD, called Waterfowl Production Areas, are part of the National Wildlife Refuge System. The refuges and WPAs are vitally important to wildlife and people. They provide food, water, cover and space for hundredsof species of birds, mammals, reptiles, amphibians, fish and plants. Managed to benefit endangered species, migratory birds and other wildlife and provide places to learn about and enjoy wildlife. HWMD's mission is to preserve wetlands and managehabitat.
harris Hoisted, Project Leader

3495 Jewel Cave National Monument
11149 U.S. Highway 16 605-673-8300
Building B12 Fax: 605-673-8301
Custer, SD 57730 E-mail: mailto:JECA_Interpretation@nps.gov
http://www.nps.gov/jeca/

With more than 125 miles sureyed, jewel cave is recognized as the third longest cave in the world. Airflow within its passages indicates a vast area yet to be explored. Cave tours provide opportunities for viewing this pristine cavesystem and its wide varitey of speleothems including stalactites, stalagmites, draperies, frostwork, flowstone, boxwork and hydromagnesite balloons. The cave is an important hibernaculum for several species of bats.
Kate Cannon, Superintendent

3496 Sand Lake National Wildlife Refuge
39650 Sand Lake Drive 605-885-6320
Columbia, SD 57433 Fax: 605-885-6333
E-mail: sandlake@fws.gov
http://www.fws.gov/sandlake/

Sand Lake Refuge is haven for wildlife and those who enjoy it. Home to more than 266 species of birds, 40 mammal species and a variety of fish, reptiles and amphibians, this 22,000 acre refuge is a mosaic of wildlife and the wildplaces they need. Sand Lake is also a very popular recreation spot. Wildlife observation, fishing, hunting, photography, interpretation and environmental education are all popular activities at the refuge.

3497 Wind Cave National Park
26611 US Highway 385 605-745-4600
Hot Springs, SD 57747 Fax: 605-745-4207
http://www.nps.gov/wica

One of the world's longest and most complex caves lies beneath the 28,295 acres of rolling, mixed grass prairie ecosystems of Wind Cave National Park. The park is home to a large variety of prairie wildlife such as bison, pronghornantelope and prairie dogs. The cave is famous for the rare cave formation called boxwork.

Vidal Davila, Park Superintendent

Tennessee: US Forests, Parks, Refuges

3498 Big South Fork National River Recreation Area
4564 Leatherwood Road 423-569-9778
Onieda, TN 37841 Fax: 423-569-5505
http://www.nps.gov/biso/

The free-flowing Big South Fork of the Cumberland River and its tributaries pass through 90 miles of scenic gorges and valleys containing a wide range of natural and historic features. The area offers a broad range of recreationalopportunities including camping, whitewater rafting, kayaking, canoeing, hiking, horseback riding, mountain biking, hunting and fishing, The US Army Corps of Engineers, with its experience in managing river basins, was charged with land acquisition,planning and deve
William K Dickinson, Superintendent

3499 Cherokee National Forest
2800 N Ocoee Street NW 423-476-9700
Po Box 2010 Fax: 423-476-9721
Cleveland, TN 37312-5374 http://www.fs.usda.gov/cherokee

The Cherokee is steeped in colorful history and rich in the grandeur of the Appalachian Mountains. The forest is separated into two sections by Great Smoky Mountains Park and shares other boundaries with national forest in Georgia,North Carolina and Virginia.
Tom Speaks, Forest Supervisor

3500 Chickasaw National Wildlife Refuge
1505 Sand Bluff Road 731-635-7621
Ripley, TN 38063 Fax: 731-635-0178
E-mail: fw4_rw_chickasaw.fws.gov
http://www.fws.gov/chickasaw/

Established to provide essentail habitat for migratory birds in the Lower Mississippi Valley. The refuge supports a variety of wildlife. Visitors can see large numbers of migratory wasterfowl in the winter. Neotropical migratory birdsand shorebirds are a common site yearround. The refuge is open to hunting and fishing-special regulations apply. Please contact the refuge manager for current regulations.
Bryan Woodward, Refuge Manager

3501 Cross Creeks National Wildlife Refuge
643 Wildlife Road 931-232-7477
Dover, TN 37058 Fax: 931-232-5958
E-mail: crosscreeks@fws.gov
http://www.fws.gov/crosscreeks/

Its primary purpose is to provide feeding and resting habitat for migratory birds with an emphasis placed on providing habitat for wintering waterfowl.
Vicki C Grafe, Manager

3502 Great Smokey Mountains National Park
107 Park Headquarters Road 865-436-1200
Gatlinburg, TN 37738 Fax: 865-436-1220
E-mail: grsm_smokies_information@nps.gov
http://www.nps.gov/grsm

The national park, in the state of North Carolina is world renowned for the diversity of its plant and animal resources, the beauty of its ancient mountains, the quality of its remnants of Southern Appalachian mountain culture, and thedepth and integrity of the wilderness sanctuary within its boundaries, it is one the largest protected areas in the east.
Randall R Pope, Supt

3503 Hatchie National Wildlife Refuge
4172 Highway 76 South 901-772-0501
Brownsville, TN 38012-8322 Fax: 901-772-7839
E-mail: r4rw_tn.htc@fws.gov
http://www.gorp.com

The dominant habitat type is 9,400 acres of seasonally flooded bottomland hardwoods. Other habitats include 400 acres of upland forest; 534 acres of open water, including 9 oxbow lakes; and 1,100 acres of agricultural areas managed ascropland, moist soil and old field habitats.
Marvin L Nichols, Manager

3504 Lower Hatchie National Wildlife Refuge
1505 Sand Bluff Road 901-635-7621
Ripley, TN 38063 Fax: 901-635-7621
E-mail: r4rw_tn.rlf@fws.gov
http://www.fws.gov/lowerhatchie/

The Refuge's primary purposes are to be a sanctuary for migratory birds and to preserve a representative portion of the fast vanishing bottomland hardwood forests as habitat for wintering waterfowl and other migratory birds.

3505 Reelfoot National Wildlife Refuge
4343 Highway 157 901-538-2481
Union City, TN 38261 Fax: 901-538-9760
E-mail: r4rw_tn.rlf@fws.gov
http://www.gorp.com

Reelfoot Lake is approximately 13,000 acres and provides numerous recreational opportunities including sport fishing and hunting.
Randy Cook, Manager

3506 Tennessee National Wildlife Refuge
PO Box 849
Paris, TN 38242
901-642-2091
Fax: 901-644-3351
E-mail: r4rw_tn.tns@fws.gov
http://www.gorp.com

The refuge provides habitat for more than 226 species of birds, 47 species of mammals, 90 species of reptiles and amphibians and 109 species of fish.
John Taylor, Manager

Texas: US Forests, Parks, Refuges

3507 Alibates Flint Quarries National Monument: Lake Meredith National Recreation Area
PO Box 1460
Fritch, TX 79036
806-857-3151
Fax: 806-857-2319
http://www.nps.gov/alfl

ALIBATES: The only national monument in Texas. Preserves over 700 archeological sites. The monument can only be viewed by ranger-led guided tours. LAKE MEREDITH: A 45,000 acre recreation area that includes a 10,000 acre reservoirwhere visitors can enjoy water and land recreational activities such as hunting, fishing, boating, horseback riding, off-road vehicles, jetskies and the like.
Karren Brown, Supt

3508 Amistad National Recreation Area
4121 Veterans Blvd.
Del Rio, TX 78840
830-775-7491
Fax: 830-778-9248
E-mail: interpretation@nps.gov
http://www.amistad.areaparks.com

Situated on the United States-Mexico border, is know primarily for excellent year round, water-based recreation including: fishing , boating, swimming, suba diving. Also provides opportunities for picnicking, camping and hinting. Thereservoir, at the confluence of the Rio Grande, Devils and Pecos rivers, was created by Amistad Dam in 1969, This area is reach in technology and rock art, and contains a wide variety of plant and animal life.
Alan W. Cox, Supt

3509 Angelina National Forest
2221 N. Raguet St
Lufkin, TX 75904
936-639-8501
Fax: 936-639-8588
E-mail: mailroom_r8_texas@fs.fed.us
http://www.fs.usda.gov/detail/texas/about-forest/districts/?cid=fsw

The Angelina National Forest is located in the heart of Texas. The reservoir, a 114,500 acre lake on the Angelina River is noted for its fishing, boating and water skiing.

3510 Big Bend National Park
PO Box 129
Big Bend National Park, TX 79834
915-477-2251
Fax: 915-477-1175
http://www.nps.gov/bibe/

The Big Bend National Park is situated on the boundary with Mexico along the Rio Grande. It is a place where countries and cultures meet, also a place that merges natural environments, from desert to mountains. It's a place where southmeets north and east meets west, creating a great diversity of plants and animals. The park covers over 801,000 acres of west Texas in the place where the Rio Grande makes a sharp turn - the Big Bend.
Robert Arnberger, Supt

3511 Big Thicket National Preserve
6044 FM 420
Kountze, TX 77625
409-951-6800
Fax: 409-951-6714
E-mail: BITH_Administration@nps.gov
http://www.nps.gov/bith

The Preserve consists of nine land units and six water corridors encompassing more than 97,000 acres. Big Thicket was the first Preserve in the National Park System and protects and area of rich biological diversity. A convergence ofecosystems occured here during the last Ice Age. It brought together, in one geographical location, the eastern hardwood forests, the Gulf coastal plains and the midwest praries.
Ronald Switzer, Supt

3512 Grulla National Wildlife Refuge
Muleshoe NWR
PO Box 549
Muleshoe, TX 79347
806-946-3341
Fax: 806-946-3317
E-mail: fw2_rw_muleshoe@fws.gov
http://www.fws.gov/southwest/refuges/newmex/grulla/index.html

Located in Roosevelt County, New Mexico, near the small town of Arch, approximately 25 miles northwest of Muleshoe National Wildlife Refuge. Grulla NWR, which is managed by the staff at Muleshoe NWR, has 3,236 acres, more than 2,000 ofwhich make up the saline lake bed of Salt Lake. The rest of the refuge is grassland. When the lake holds sufficient water, Grulla NWR is a wintering area for lesser sandhill cranes. Ring-necked pheasant, scaled quail and lesser prairie chickens maybe seen.
Jude Smith, Refuge Manager

3513 Guadalupe Mountains National Park
400 Pine Canyon Drive
Salt Flat, TX 79847-9400
915-828-3251
Fax: 915-828-3269
E-mail: GUMO_Superintendent@nps.gov
http://www.nps.gov/gumo

This mountain mass contains portions of the world's most extensive and significant Permian limestone fossil reef, earth fault peaks, unusual flora and fauna. Guadalupe Peak, highest point in Texas at 8,749 feet.
John Lujan, Superintendent
Fred Armstrong, Chief of Resource Management

3514 Hagerman National Wildlife Refuge
6465 Refuge Road
Sherman, TX 75092
903-786-2826
Fax: 903-786-3327
E-mail: gayle_ellis@fws.gov
http://www.fws.gov/refuge/hagerman/

Hagerman NWR lies on the Big Mineral Arm of Lake Texoma, on the Red River between Oklahoma and Texas. Established in 1946, the refuge includes 3,000 acres of marsh and water and 8,000 acres of upland and farmland. During fall, winterand spring, the marshes and waters are in constant use by migrating and wintering waterfowl.
Kathy Whaley, Manager

3515 Padre Island National Seashore
PO Box 181300
Corpus Christi, TX 78480-1300
361-949-8068
Fax: 361-949-8023
http://www.nps.gov/pais

Encompassing 130,434 acres, the longest remaining undeveloped stretch of barrier island in the world, and offers a wide variety of flora and fauna as well as recreation.

3516 Santa Ana National Wildlife Refuge
3325 Green Jay
Box 202A
Alamo, TX 78516
956-784-7500
Fax: 956-787-8338
E-mail: christine_donald@fws.gov
http://www.fws.gov/refuge/santa_ana/

The 2,088 acre refuge along the banks of the lower Rio Grande was established in 1943 for the protection of migratory birds. Considered the jewel of the refuge system, this essential island of thorn forest habitat is host or home tonearly 400 different types of birds and a myriad of other species, including the indigo snake, malachite butterfly and the endangered ocelot. Provides habitat for thousands of migrating birds and about one half of all butterfly species found in NorthAmerica.
Jeff Howland, Refuge Manager

Utah: US Forests, Parks, Refuges

3517 **Arches National Park**
PO Box 907 435-719-2299
Moab, UT 84532-0907 Fax: 435-719-2300
E-mail: archinfo@nps.gov
http://www.nps.gov/arch/

Arches National Park preserves over two thousand natural sandstone arches and a variety of other unique geological resources. The extraordinary features of the park are highlighted by a striking environment of contrasting colors,landforms and textures. Administered by Canyonlands National Park
] pages
Laura Jess, Supt

3518 **Ashley National Forest**
PO Box 279 435-784-3445
Manila, UT 84046 Fax: 435-781-5295
http://www.fs.usda.gov/ashley

Remarkable features include Kings Peak (highest peak in Utah), Flaming Gorge National Recreation Area, Flaming Gorge-Uintas National Scenic Byway, The Green River Corridor
Rowdy Muir, District Ranger

3519 **Bear River Migratory Bird Refuge**
58 S 435-723-5887
Brigham City, UT 84302 Fax: 435-723-8873
E-mail: bearriver@fws.gov
http://www.fws.gov/refuge/bear river migratory bird refuge/

To date, close to 1 million cubic yards of earth has been moved to restore and enhance the refuge. Forty-seven primary water control structures have been restored along with over forty-seven miles of dikes. Through volunteer efforts,debris has been removed from the old headquaters site and a new pavilion, restroom, demonstration pond, and kiosk have been built on the site. The 12-mile auto tour route has been reopened to the public.
Alan K Trout, Manager

3520 **Bryce Canyon National Park**
PO Box 640201 435-834-5322
Bryce Canyon, UT 84764-0201 Fax: 435-834-4102
http://www.nps.gov/brca

Consists of 37,277 acres of scenic colorful rock formations and desert wonderland. Bryce Canyon National Park is named for one of a series of horseshoe-shaped amphitheaters carved from the eastern edge of the Paunsaugunt Plateau insouthern Utah. Erosion has shaped colorful Claron limestones, sandstones and mudstones into thousands of spires, fins, pinnacles and mazes. Collectively called hoodoos, these unique formations are whimsically arranged and tinted with colors toonumerous to name.

Craig C Axtell

3521 **Canyonlands National Park**
2282 S West Resource Boulevard 435-719-2313
Moab, UT 84532 Fax: 435-719-2300
E-mail: canyinfo@nps.gov
http://www.nps.gov/cany/index.htm

Canyonlands National Park preserves a stunning landscape of sedimentary sandstones eroded into countless canyons, mesas and buttes by the Colorado River and its tributaries. Largely undeveloped, the park is a popular backcountrydestination and scientific research site.

3522 **Capitol Reef National Park**
HC 70 Box 15 435-425-3791
Torrey, UT 84775-9602 Fax: 435-425-3026
E-mail: care_administration@nps.gov
http://www.capitol.reef.national-park.com

The Waterpocket Fold, a 100 mile long wrinkle in the earth's know as a monoclide, extends from nearby Thousand Lakes Mountain to the Colorado River. Capitol Reef National Park was established to protect this grand and colorful geologicfeature, as well as the unique historical and cultural history found in the area.
Albert J Hendricks, Supt

3523 **Cedar Breaks National Monument**
2390 W Highway 56 435-586-9451
Suite 11 Fax: 435-586-3813
Cedar City, UT 84720 http://www.nps.gov/cebr/
Millons of years of sedimentation, uplift and erosion continue to create a deep canyon of rock walls, fins, spires and columms, that spans some three miles, and over 2,000 feet deep. The rim of the canyon is over 10,000 feet above sealevel, and is forested with islands of Englemann spruce, subalpine fir and aspen: separated by broad meadows of brillant summertime wild flowers.
Denny Davies, Supt
Ateve Robinson, Chief Ranger

3524 **Dixie National Forest**
1789 N Wedgewood Ln 435-865-3700
Cedar City, UT 84720 Fax: 435-865-3791
http://www.fs.usda.gov/dixie

The Dixie is located adjacent to three National Parks, Bryce Canyon, Zion and Capitol Reef.The red sandstone formations of Red Canyon rival those of Bryce Canyon National park. From the top of Powell Point, it is possible to see farinto three different states. Boulder Mountain and the many different lakes provide opportunities for hiking, fishing and viewing outstanding scenery.
Mary Wagner, Forest Supervisor

3525 **Fish Springs National Wildlife Refuge**
PO Box 568 435-693-3122
Dugway, UT 84022 Fax: 435-693-9933
http://www.fws.gov/fishsprings/

Located at the southern end of the Great Salt Lake Desert in western Utah, Fish Springs National Wildlife Refuge encompasses 17,992 acres between two small mountain ranges. Five major springs and several lesser springs and seeps flowfrom a faultline at the base of the eastern front of the Fish Springs Mountain Range, These warm, saline springs provide virtually all of the water for the Refuge's 10,000-acre marsh system.
Jerry Bana, Manager

3526 **Fishlake National Forest**
115 E 900 N 435-896-9233
Richfield, UT 84701 Fax: 435-896-9347
http://www.fs.fed.us/r4/fishlake/
The Fishlake National Forest in central Utah features majestic stands of aspen encircling open mountain meadows that are lush with a diverse community of forbs and grasses. The mountains of the Fishlake are a source of water for manyof the neighboring communities and agricultural valleys in the region. Hunting, fishing and OHV use are among the most popular forms of recreation enjoyed by forest visitors.
Allen Rowley, Forest Supervisor

3527 **Natural Bridges National Monument**
HC 60 435-692-1234
Box 1 Fax: 435-692-1111
Lake Powell, UT 84533 E-mail: nabrinfo@nps.gov
http://www.nps.gov/nabr

Natural Bridges protects some of the finest examples of ancient stone architecture in the southwest. The monument is located in the southeast Utah on a pinyon-juniper covered mesa bisected by deep canyons of Permian age Ceder MesaSandstone. Where meandering streams cut through the cayon walls, three natural bridges formed: Kachina, Owachomo and Sipapu.

Coralee S Hays, Superintendent

3528 **Ouray National Wildlife Refuge**
266 West 100 North #2
Vernal, UT 84078
801-789-0351
Fax: 801-789-4805
http://www.gorp.com

Gary Montoya, Manager

3529 **Timpanogos Cave National Monument**
Rural Route 3 Box 200
American Fork, UT 84003
801-756-5239
Fax: 801-756-5661
http://www.nps.gov/tica

Timpanogos Cave Natioanl Monument sits high in the Wasatch Mountains. The cave system consists of three spectacularly decorated caverns. Each cavern has unique colors and formations. Helicitites and anthodites are just a few of themany dazzling formations to be found in the many chambers. As visitors climb to the cavern entrance, on a hike gaining over 1,000 feet in elevation, they are offered incredible views of American Fork Canyon.

Dennis Davis, Superintendent

3530 **Uinta National Forest**
88 W 100 N
Provo, UT 84601
801-342-5100
Fax: 801-342-5144
E-mail: uwc-info@fs.fed.us
http://www.fs.usda.gov/uwcnf

The Uinta National Forest ranges from high western desert at Vernon to lofty mountain peaks such as Mount Nebo (elevation 11,877 feet, the highest peak in the Wasatch Range) and Mount Timpanogos (elevation 11,750 feet). The forestcontains three wilderness areas: the Lone Peak, the Mount Timpanogos and the Mount Nebo Wildernesses. The Forest surrounds the Timpanogos Cave National Mounment.

Peter Karp, Forest Supervisor

3531 **Wasatch-Cache National Forest**
3285 East 3300 South
Salt Lake City, UT 84109
801-466-6411
Fax: 801-524-3172
E-mail: uwc-info@fs.fed.us
http://www.fs.usda.gov/uwcnf

Wasatch-Cache National Forest lands are located in three major areas: the northern and western slopes of the Uinta Mountains. The Wasatch Front from Lone Peak north to the Idaho border including the Wasatch, Monte cristo, and BearRiver Ranges. The Stansbury Range, in the Great Basin.

Tom Tidwell, Forest Supervisor

3532 **Zion National Park**
Star Route 9
Springdale, UT 84767-1099
435-772-3256
Fax: 435-772-3426
E-mail: zion_park_information@nps.gov
http://www.nps.gov/zion

Protected within Zion National Park's 229 square miles (593.1 km) is a spectacular cliff-and-cayon landscape and wilderness full of the unexpected including the world's largest arch -Kolob Arch- with a span that measures 310 feet(94.5m). Wildlife such as mule deer, golden eagles, and mountain lions also inhabit the park. Mukuntuweap National Monument proclaimed July 31, 1909; incorporated in Zion National Monument March 18, 1918; established as national park Nov. 19, 1919.

Ron Terry, Public Information Officer

Vermont: US Forests, Parks, Refuges

3533 **Green Mountains & Finger Lakes National Forest**
231 North Main Street
Rutland, VT 05701
802-747-6700
Fax: 802-747-6766
http://www.fs.usda.gov/greenmountain

3534 **Missisquoi National Wildlife Refuge**
29 Tabor Road
Swanton, VT 05488
802-868-4781
Fax: 802-868-2379
E-mail: missisquoi@fws.gov
http://www.fws.gov/northeast/missisquoi/

The 6,592-acre refuge includes most of the Missisquoi River delta where it flows into Missisquoi Bay. The refuge consists of quiet waters and wetlands which attract large flocks of migratory birds.

Mark Sweeny, Manager

Virginia: US Forests, Parks, Refuges

3535 **George Washington National Forest**
5162 Valleypointe Parkway
PO Box 233
Roanoke, VA 24019
540-265-5100
Fax: 540-265-5145
http://www.fs.usda.gov/gwj

Outstanding hiking trails, campsites, fishing and canoeing are the hallmarks of George Washington Forest in Virginia and West Virginia, part of the George Washington and Jefferson National Forest.

3536 **Jefferson National Forest**
5162 Valleypointe Parkway
Roanoke, VA 24019
540-265-5100
888-265-0019
http://www.fs.usda.gov/gwj

The Jefferson National Forest is prize Appalachia country: tumbling waterfalls, rare wildflowers, vividly colored hills and Virginia's highest peak. Jefferson National Forest spreads 690,000 acres of hardwood and conifer forest acrosswest-central Virginia, West Virgina and Kentucky, including the ridge province of the Blue Ridge mountains.

3537 **Mason Neck National Wildlife Refuge**
12638 Darby Brooke Ct.
Woodbridge, VA 22192
703-490-4979
http://www.fws.gov/refuge/mason_neck/

The refuge, the Mason Neck State Park, the Northern Virginia Park Authority, the Gunston Hall Plantation and the Virginia Department of Game and Inland Fisheries are cooperating in the management of their combined 5,000+ acres on theMason Neck peninsula. This cooperation provides a wide variety of recreational activities while protecting natural resources. The primary objective of the refuge is to protect essential nesting, feeding and roosting habitat for bald eagles.

J Frederick Milton, Manager

3538 **Shenandoah National Park**
3655 US Highway 211 East
Luray, VA 22835
540-999-3500
Fax: 540-999-3601
http://www.nps.gov/shen/index.htm

Shenandoah National park lies astride a beautiful section of the blue rige mountains, which from the eastern rampart of the Appalachian Mountains between Pennsylvania and Georgia. The Shenandoah River flows through the valley to thewest, with Massanutten Mountain, 40 miles long, standing between the river's north and south forks. The rolling Piedmont country lies to the east of the park. Skyline Drive, a 105- mile road that winds along the crest of the mountainsthrough thelength of the park.

William Wade, Supt

Washington: US Forests, Parks, Refuges

3539 **Colville National Forest**
765 South Main Street
Coleville, WA 99114
509-684-7000
Fax: 509-684-7280
http://www.fs.usda.gov/colville

The Colville National Forest encompasses over one million acres in northeastern Washington. The Sherman Pass National Scenic Byway leads through a portion of the Forest, with camping, fishing, hiking, picnicking, mountain biking,cross-country skiing, sonowmobiling and other recreational activities. 49 Degrees North, a full service ski resort, is located east of Chewelah, about one hour north of Spokane. The Salmo-Prist Wilderness Area sits in the northeast corner of theforest.

3540 **Conboy Lake National Wildlife Refuge**
PO Box 5
Glenwood, WA 98619
509-546-8300
Fax: 509-364-3667
E-mail: mcriver@fws.gov
http://www.fws.gov/refuge/conboy_lake/

Located in the northwest corner of Klickitat County, Washington, the refuge was established primarily for waterfowl. The broad range of habitat diversity provides for a broad diversity of resident wildlife species.
Harold E Cole, Manager

3541 Gifford Pinchot National Forest
10600 N.E. 51st Circle 360-891-5000
Vancouver, WA 98682 Fax: 360-891-5045
http://www.fs.fed.us/gpnf/
The Gifford Pinchot National Forst is one of the oldest National Forests in the United States. Include as part of The Mount Rainier Forest Reserve in 1897, this area was set aside as the columbia National Forest in 1908, and renamedthe Gifford Pinchot National Forest in 1949. The Forest, located in southwest Washington State, now contains 1,312,000 acres and includes the 110,000- acre Mount St. Helens National Volcanic Mounument established by congress in 1982.

3542 Lewis & Clark National Wildlife Refuge
Julia Butler Hansen NWR 206-795-3915
PO Box 566 http://www.gorp.com
Cathlamet, WA 98612

3543 McNary National Wildlife Refuge
64 Maple Road 509-546-8300
PO Box 544 Fax: 509-546-8303
Burbank, WA 99323 E-mail: mcriver@fws.gov
http://www.fws.gov/mcnary/
A resting and feeding area for up to 100,000 migrating waterfowl. It includes 3,629 acres of water and marsh, croplands, grasslands, trees and shrubs.
Robyn Thorson, Regional Manager
Richard Hannon, Deputy Regional Manager

3544 Mount Baker-Snoqualmie National Forests
2930 Wetmore Avenue 425-783-6000
Suite 3A 800-627-0062
Everett, WA 98201 http://www.fs.usda.gov/mbs
An urban forest, extending over 140 miles along the western slopes of the Cascade Mountains from the Canadian border to Mount Rainier National Park.
Jennifer Eberlien, Forest Supervisor

3545 Mount Rainier National Park
Tahoma Woods, Star Route 253-569-2211
Ashford, WA 98304 Fax: 360-569-2170
E-mail: MORAInfo@nps.gov
http://www.nps.gov/mora/
Established in 1899. 235,625 acres (97% is designated Wilderness). Includes mount Rainier (14,410'), an active volcano encased in over 35 square miles of snow and ice. The park contains outstanding examples of old growth forests andsubalpine meadows. Designated a National Historic landmark District in 1997 as a showcase for the NPS Rustic style architecture of the 1920s and 1930s.
William Briggle, Supt

3546 North Cascades National Park Service Complex
810 State Route 20 360-854-7200
Sedro-Woolley, WA 98284 Fax: 360-856-1934
E-mail: NOCA_Interpretation@nps.gov
http://www.nps.gov/noca

3547 Okanogan National Forest
1240 S 2nd Avenue 509-826-3275
PO Box 950 Fax: 509-826-3789
Okanogan, WA 98840 http://www.fs.usda.gov/okawen/
There is a variety of country from craggy peaks to rolling meadows, to rich old growth forest and classic groves of ponderosa pine. We're called the Sunny Okanogan and for good reason: summers here are hot and dry, and our winters arefamous for brilliant clear skies and plenty of snow.

3548 Okanogan and Wenatchee National Forests Headquarters
215 Melody Lane 509-664-9200
Wenatchee, WA 98801 Fax: 509-664-9280
http://www.fs.fed.us/r6/wenatchee/forest/formain.htm
The 2.2 million acre Wenatchee National Forest extends about 135 miles along the east side of the crest of the Cascade Mountains in Washington State. This National Forest is most noted for its wide range of recreation opportunities.There truly is something for everyone who likes to have fun in the outdoors.
Rebecca Heath, Forest Supervisor

3549 Olympic National Forest
1835 Black Lake Boulevard SW 360-956-2402
Olympia, WA 98512 http://www.fs.fed.us/r6/olympic
The National Forests are part of America's great outdoors and are public lands. They are managed for the multiple uses of recreation, wildlife, timber, gazing, mining, oil and gas, watershed and wilderness. The Olympic National Forestis over 632,000 acres in size and is divided into two Ranger Districts: Hood Canal and Pacific.

3550 Olympic National Park
600 East Park Avenue 360-565-3000
Port Angeles, WA 98362 Fax: 360-565-3015
E-mail: olym_visitor_center@nps.gov
Often referred to as three parks in one, Olympic National Park encompasses three distinctly different ecosystems-rugged glacier capped mountains, over 73 miles of wild Pacific coast and magnificent mountains are still largely pristinein character and are Olympic's gift to you.
Karen Gustin, Superintendent

3551 Ross Lake National Recreation Area North Cascades National Park
810 State Route 20 360-854-7200
Sedro Woolley, WA 98284 Fax: 360-856-1934
E-mail: mailto:NOCA_Interp@nps.gov
http://www.nps.gov/rola
The most accessible part of the North Cascades National Park Service Complex. Is also the corridor for scenic Washington State Route 20, the North Cascades Highway, and includes three reserviors.

3552 Toppenish National Wildlife Refuge
State Route 97 509-546-8300
Toppenish, WA 98948 800-344-9453
E-mail: mcriver@fws.gov
http://www.fws.gov/refuge/toppenish/
An important migration and wintering area for waterfowl in the Yakima Valley of eastern Washington. Wetland impoundments along Toppenish Creek provide natural foods for wintering mallards and other ducks. Ducks and other water birdsbreed in the wetland impoundments during the summer. Native shrub-steppe communities and riparian areas along Toppenish and Snake creeks provide habitat for many other species of birds. The refuge has active hunting and wildlife-viewing programs.
George J Fenn, Manager

3553 Umatilla National Wildlife Refuge
Mid-Columbian River Refuges
64 Maple Street 509-546-8300
Burbank, WA 99323 Fax: 509-546-8303
E-mail: mcriver@fws.gov
http://www.fws.gov/mcriver/
The refuge is a varied mix of open water, sloughs, shallow marsh, seasonal wetlands, cropland, islands, and shrub-steppe upland habitats
Morris C LeFever, Manager

3554 Willapa National Wildlife Refuge
3888 State Route 101 206-484-3482
Ilwaco, WA 98624 E-mail: willapa@fws.gov
http://www.fws.gov/willapa/
Located on Willapa Bay in Pacific County, the southernmost coastal county in Washington. The upland forest varies in successional stages from recently logged areas to a unique rem-

nant of virgin, coastal cedar-hemlock forest home todeer, bear, elk, grouse, beaver and numerous songbirds and small mammals.
James A Hidy, Manager

West Virginia: US Forests, Parks, Refuges

3555 **Monongahela National Forest**
200 Sycamore Street
Elkins, WV 26241
304-636-1800
Fax: 304-636-1875
http://www.fs.usda.gov/mnf

The Monongahela National Forest was established following passage of the 1911 Weeks Act. This act authorized the purchase of land for long-term watershed protection and natural resource management following massive cutting of theEastern forests in the late 1800's and at the turn of the century.

3556 **Ohio River Islands National Wildlife Refuge**
3982 Waverly Road
Williamstown, WV 26187
304-375-2923
Fax: 304-422-0754
E-mail: fw5rw_ohrinwr@fws.gov
http://www.fws.gov/refuge/ohio_river_islands/

The refuge extends 362 river miles from Shippingport, Pennsylvania to Manchester, Ohio along one of the nation's busiest waterways. Ohio River Islands and their back channels have long been recognized for high quality fish andwildlife, recreation, scientific and natural heritage values.
Jerry L Wilson, Manager

Wisconsin: US Forests, Parks, Refuges

3557 **Apostle Islands National Lakeshore**
415 Washington Street
Route 1, Box 4
Bayfield, WI 54814
715-779-3397
Fax: 715-779-3049
E-mail: APIS_Webmaster@nps.gov
http://www.nps.gov/apis/index.htm

The national lakeshore includes 21 islands and 12 miles of mainland Lake Superior shoreline, featuring pristine stretches of sand beach, spectacular sea caves, remnant old growth forests, resident bald eagles and black bears and thelargest collection of lighthouses anywhere in the National Park System.
Robert J Krumenaker, Superintendant

3558 **Chequamegon National Forest**
1170 4th Avenue S
Park Falls, WI 54552
715-762-2461
Fax: 715-762-5179
http://www.fs.usda.gov/cnnf

Shaped principally by glacial action some 10,000 years ago, the forest offers a variety of hiking, ATV, and cross-country ski trails at different levels of difficulty. These campgrounds are located on either a lake or a river and offerfishing and boating.

3559 **Ice Age National Scientific Reserve**
PO Box 7921
Madison, WI 53707
608-266-2183
Fax: 608-267-7474
E-mail: brigit.brown@dnr.state.wi.us

This first national scientific reserve contains nationally significant features of continental glaciation. State parks in the area are open to the public.
Tom Gilbert, Supt

3560 **Nicolet National Forest**
500 Hanson Lake Road
Rhinelander, WI 54501
715-362-1300
Fax: 715-362-1359
http://www.fs.usda.gov/cnnf

Located in Wisconsin's Northwoods where towering pine and hardwood forests are interspersed with hundreds of crystal clear lakes and streams, the Nicolet offers you many opportunities to enjoy the outdoors. Within a day's drive of theChicago, Milwaukee, St. Paul and Minneapolis metropolitan areas, the forest is a place where urban dwellers can truly get away from it all in the scenic beauty of the northwoods.

3561 **St Croix National Scenic Riverway**
401 N Hamilton Street
St Croix Falls, WI 54024
715-483-3284
Fax: 715-483-3288
http://www.nps.gov/sacn/index.htm

The St. Croix National Scenic Riverway is home to the endangered Higgins Eye and Winged Mapleleaf mussels, bald eagles, gray wolves, and the prehistoric paddlefish. The 252 miles of Riverway provide numerous recreational opportunitiesfor boaters, canoeists, kayakers and others.

Tom Bradley, Superintendent
Ron Erickson, Education Team Manager

Wyoming: US Forests, Parks, Refuges

3562 **Bighorn National Forest**
2013 Eastside 2nd Street
Sheridan, WY 82801
307-674-2600
Fax: 307-674-2668
http://www.fs.usda.gov/bighorn

The forest has 32 campgrounds, 14 picnic areas, 2 visitor centers, 2 ski areas, 7 lodges, 2 recreation lakes, 3 scenic byways and over 1500 miles of trails. The Bighorn National Forest is 80 miles long and 30 miles wide. The mostcommon tree is the lodgepole pine. The Bighorn River, flowing along the west side of the forest was first named by American Indians due to the great herds of bighorn sheep at its mouth.
Bill Bass, Forest Supervisor

3563 **Bridger-Teton National Forest**
340 N Cache-Forest Service Bldg
PO Box 1888
Jackson, WY 83001
307-739-5500
Fax: 307-739-5010
E-mail: r4_b-t_info@fs.fed.us
http://www.fs.fed.us/btnf/

With it's 3.4 million acres, it is the second largest National Forest outside Alaska. Included are more than 1.2 million acres of wilderness in the Bridger, Gros Ventre, and Teton Wildernesses. The Bridger-Teton is a land of variedrecreational opportunities, beautiful vistas, and abundant wildlife. Its crystal blue skies are puctuated by awesome mountain ranges which include the Gros Ventre, Teton, Salt River, Wind River, and Wyoming Mountain Ranges.
Jacque Buchanan, Forest Supervisor
Pamela Bode, Resources Staff Officer

3564 **Devils Tower National Monument**
PO Box 10
Devils Tower, WY 82714-0010
307-467-5283
Fax: 307-467-5350
E-mail: deto_interpretation@nps.gov
http://www.nps.gov/deto/home.html

This unit of the National Park Service protects the nearly vertical monolith known as Devil's Tower. The rolling hills of this 1347 acre park are covered with pine forests, deciduous woodlands, and prairie grasslands. Known byseveral northern plains tribes as Bear Lodge, it is sacred to many American Indians. Devil's Tower was proclaimed in September, 1906 as the nation's first national monument by President Theodore Roosevelt.

Dorothy FireCloud, Superintendent

3565 **Fossil Butte National Monument**
PO Box 592
Kemmerer, WY 83101
307-877-4455
Fax: 307-877-4457
E-mail: FOBU_Superintendent@nps.gov
http://www.nps.gov/fobu

Located in southwest Wyoming, Fossil Butte National Monument represents one of the richest fossil localities in the world. Fifty million-year-old fish, insects, birds, reptiles, and plants are nearly perfectly preserved in limestone.
David E McGinnis, Superintendent
Marcia Fagnant, Park Ranger

3566 **Grand Teton National Park**
PO Box 170
Moose, WY 83012-0170
307-739-3300
Fax: 307-739-3438
E-mail: GRTE_info@nps.gov
http://www.nps.gov/grte

Established in 1929 and enlarged in 1950 to protect a rugged, awe-inspiring mountain range with numerous piedmont lakes nestled amoung its flanks, and a wide sagebrush-covered valley called Jackson Hole. Administered by the NationalPark Service under the Department of the Interior, Grand Teton is one of 384 units within the national park system. It encompasses approximately 310,000 acres or 485 square miles of northwestern Wyoming, just south of Yellowstone National Park.

Mary Gibson Scott, Supt

3567 Medicine Bow National Forest

2468 Jackson Street
Laramie, WY 82070
307-745-2300
Fax: 307-745-2398
http://www.fs.fed.us/r2/mbr/about/districts/laramie.shtml/

The Medicine Bow National Forest dates back to May 22, 1902, with the establishment of the Medicine Bow Forest Reserve by President Theodore Roosevelt. In 1929, the former Hayden National Forest along the Continental Divide wasformerly a War Department target and maneuver reservation under joint administration by the Forest Service and the War Department. In 1959, the area formerly used by the military was added to the Medicine Bow National Forest.

3568 National Elk Refuge

PO Box 510
Jackson, WY 83001
307-733-9212
Fax: 307-733-9729
E-mail: nationalelkrefuge@fws.gov
http://nationalelkrefuge.fws.gov/

More than 7,500 elk make the winter range of National Elk Refuge their home from October until May. Adjacent to the north side of Jackson, Wyoming, the 25,000-acre refuge includes nearly 1600 acres of open water and marsh lands, 47different mammals and nearly 175 species of birds.

Mike Hedrick, Manager

3569 Seedskadee National Wildlife Refuge

PO Box 700
Green River, WY 82935
307-875-2187
Fax: 307 875 4425
E-mail: Seedskadee@fws.gov
http://www.seedskadee.fws.gov

Fishery resource is managed cooperatively with the state G&F and includes a special regulations area to promote catch and release fishing for trophy trout (brown, Snake River cutthroat and rainbow trout). Refuge lands are rich inhistorical and cultural resources as the area was utilized by nomadic Indian tribes, fur trappers, early pioneers and travelers heading for the better life of California and Oregon. Many of the old campsites, river crossings and early structuresstill exist.

3570 Shoshone National Forest

808 Meadow Lane
Cody, WY 82414
307-527-6241
Fax: 307-578-1212
http://www.fs.usda.gov/shoshone

The Shoshone consists of 2.4 million acres of varied terrain ranging from sagebrush flats to rugged mountain peaks and includes portions of the Absaroka, Wind River, and Beartooth Mountain Ranges. Elevations on the Shoshone range from4,600 feet at the mouth of the spectacular Clarks Fork Canyon to 13,804 feet on ganneett Peak, Wyoming's highest point. Geologists delightedly call the Shoshone's varied topography an open book.

Joe Alexander, Forest Supervisor

3571 Yellowstone National Park

PO Box 168
Yellowstone National Park, WY 82190-0168
307-344-7381
Fax: 307-344-2014
E-mail: yell_visitor_services@nps.gov
http://www.nps.gov

Established on March 1, 1872, Yellowstone National Park is the first and oldest national park in the world. Preserved within Yellowstone are Old Faithful Geyser and some 10,000 hot springs and geysers, the majority of the plant'stotal. These geothermal wonders are evidence of one of the world's largest active volcanoes; its last eruption created a crater or caldera that spans almost half of the park.

Suzanne Lewis, Superintendent

Publications

Directories & Handbooks: Air & Climate

3572 **Acid Rain**
Watts, Franklin
90 Sherman Turnpike 203-797-3500
Danbury, CT 06816 800-621-1115
Fax: 203-797-3657
Lists over 4,000 citations, with abstracts, to the worldwide literature on the sources of acid rain and its effects on the environment.

3573 **Weather America**
Grey House Publishing
4919 Route 22 518-789-8700
Amenia, NY 12501 800-562-2139
Fax: 845-373-6390
E-mail: books@greyhouse.com
http://www.greyhouse.com
Provides extensive climatological data for over 4,000 national and cooperative weather stations throughout the US. Includes a new major storms section and a nationwide ranking section that provides rankings for maximum and minimumtemperatures, precipitation, snowfall, fog, humidity and wind speed. Each of 50 state sections contains a city index for locating the nearest weather station to the city/county being researched and a narrative description of the state's climaticconditions.
Publication Date: 2010 2,013 pages
ISBN: 1-891482-29-7
Leslie Mackenzie, Publisher
David Garoogian, Editor

Directories & Handbooks: Business

3574 **American Caves**
American Caves Conservation Association
119 E Main Street 270-786-1466
PO Box 409 Fax: 270-786-1467
Horse Cave, KY 42749 E-mail: debraheavers@caven.org
http://www.cavern.org
A bi-annual membership publication. Published by the American Caves Conservation Association and available by subscription to nonmembers.
David Foster, Executive Director/Author
Debra Heavers, Editor

3575 **Associations Canada**
Grey House Publishing Canada
555 Richmond Street West 416-644-6479
2nd Floor 866-433-4739
Toronto, Ontario M5V 3B1 Fax: 416-644-1904
E-mail: info@greyhouse.ca
http://www.greyhouse.ca
Annual directory of Canadian associations and environmental groups including industry, commerical and professional organizations.
Publication Date: 2011 1200 pages
Bryon Moore, General Manager

3576 **Business and the Environment: A Resource Guide**
Island Press
1718 Connecticut Avenue NW 202-232-7933
Suite 300 800-828-1302
Washington, DC 20009 Fax: 202-234-1328
E-mail: info@islandpress.org
http://www.islandpress.org
Includes more than 1,000 references to material from scholarly journals, government agencies, case clearing-houses, research organizations, trade magazines and the popular press. It was the most current (1992) listing of research onself-monitoring and compliance programs and environmental performance strategies for corporate competitiveness.
Publication Date: 1992 382 pages
ISBN: 1-559631-59-7
Barbara Dean, Executive Editor
Jonathan Cobb, Executive Editor

3577 **California Certified Organic Farmers: Membership Directory**
2155 Delaware Ave. 831-423-2263
Suite 150 Fax: 831-423-4528
Santa Cruz, CA 95060 E-mail: ccof@ccof.org
http://www.ccof.org
Annual
Brian Leahy, Executive Director
Helge Hellberg, Marketing Director

3578 **Directory of Environmental Information Sources**
Government Institutes
4 Research Place 301-907-1000
Suite 200A Fax: 301-921-2362
Rockville, MD 20850
Over 1,400 federal and state government agencies, professional and scientific organizations and trade associations are profiled.
322 pages

3579 **Directory of New York City Environmental Organizations**
Council on the Environment of New York City
51 Chambers Street 212-788-7900
Room 228 Fax: 212-788-7913
New York, NY 10007 E-mail: conyc@cenyc.org
http://www.cenyc.org
Promotes environmental awareness and solutions to environmental problems.

3580 **Directory of Professional Services**
Professional Services Institute
1730 Rhode Island Avenue NW 202-659-4613
Suite 1000 800-424-2869
Washington, DC 20036 Fax: 202-775-5917

3581 **Directory of Socially Responsible Investments**
Funding Exchange
666 Broadway 212-529-5300
Suite 500 Fax: 212-982-9272
New York, NY 10012 E-mail: mailto:%20FEXEXC@aol.com
http://www.udc.edu/index-b.htm
Network of 15 community foundations around the country with a national office in New York City. Staff at the national office are responsible for three main program areas: grantmaking, donor programs and member fund services.

3582 **EPA Information Resources Directory**
National Technical Information Service
5285 Port Royal Road 703-605-6000
Springfield, VA 22161 http://www.ntis.gov
Supports the nation's economic growth and job creation by providing access to information that stimulates innovation and discovery. NTIS accomplishes this mission through two major programs: information collection and dissemination tothe public and production and other services to federal agencies.

3583 **EnviroSafety Directory**
IEI Publishing Division
1635 W Alabama St 713-529-1616
Houston, TX 77006 800-654-1480
Fax: 281-529-0936
E-mail: iei@mail.infohwy.com
http://www.oilonline.com
Approximately 6,000 environmental services, state agencies and EPA/Superfund sites within the EPA regions 4, 6 and 9.
James W Self, Editor
Janis Johnson, Managing Editor

3584 **Environment: Books by Small Presses of the General Society of Mechanics & Tradesmen**
Small Press Center

20 West 44th Street
New York, NY 10036
212-764-7021
Fax: 212-840-2046
E-mail: smallpress@aol.com
http://www.smallpress.org

Publication Date: 1992 250 pages
ISBN: 0-962276-93-6
Paula Matta, Author

3585 Environmental Address Book: The Environment's Greatest Champions and Worst Offenders
Perigee Books
200 Madison Avenue
New York, NY 10016
212-951-8400
http://www.penguinputnam.com

3586 Fibre Market News: Paper Recycling Markets Directory
Recycling Media Group GIE Publishers
4012 Bridge Avenue
Cleveland, OH 44113
216-961-4130
800-456-0707
Fax: 216-961-0364

A list of over 2,000 dealers, brokers, packers and graders of paper stock in the US and Canada.
Dan Sandoval, Internet/Senior Editor
Jim Keefe, Group Publisher

3587 Greenpeace Guide to Anti-Environmental Organizations
Odonian Press
PO Box 776
Berkeley, CA 94701
510-486-0313
800-326-0959
Fax: 415-512-8699

Corporations, foundations and public relations firms determined to be anti-environmental despite their attempts to project the green image.
Publication Date: 1993 111 pages
ISBN: 1-878825-05-3
Carl Deal, Author

3588 Guide to Curriculum Planning in Environmental Education
125 S Webster Street
PO Box 7841
Madison, WI 53707
608-266-2188
800-441-4563
Fax: 608-267-9110
E-mail: sandi.mcnamer@dpi.state.wi.us
http://www.dpi.state.wi.us/pubsales

Provides a direction in planning a comprehensive environmental education program based on perceptual awareness knowledge, environmental ethics, citizen action skills and citizen action experience.
Publication Date: 1994 167 pages Book
Sandi McNamer, Publications Director

3589 Handbook on Air Filtration
IEST
2340 S. Arlington Heights Road
Suite 100
Arlington Heights, IL 60005
847-981-0100
Fax: 847-981-4130
E-mail: iest@iest.org
http://www.iest.org

Covers a broad range of applications for users who require removal of airborn particulate contamination for maximum air cleanliness.

ISBN: 1-877862-60-6
Julie Kendrick, Executive Director

3590 Harbinger File
Harbinger Communications, Inc
5 N Union Street
Elgin, IL 60123
847-622-0905
800-320-7206
Fax: 847-622-0830
E-mail: info@harbingeronline.com
http://www.harbingeronline.com

3591 National Environmental Data Referral Service
US National Environmental Data Referral Service
1825 Connecticut Avenue NW
Washington, DC 20235
202-606-4089

More than 22,200 data resources that have available data on climatology and meteorology, ecology and pollution, geography, geophysics and geology, hydrology and limnology, oceanography and transmissions from remote sensing satellites.

3592 National Environmental Organizations
US Environmental Directories
PO Box 65156
St Paul, MN 55165

3593 New Jersey Environmental Directory
Youth Environmental Society
PO Box 441
Cranbury, NJ 08512
609-655-8030

Environmental education and leadership programs for high school students in New Jersey.

3594 Opportunities in Environmental Careers
VGM Career Books
4255 W Touphy Avenue
Lincolnwood, IL 60646
847-679-5500
800-323-4900
Fax: 847-679-2494

Odom Fanning, Author

3595 Research Services Directory
Grey House Publishing
4919 Route 22
Amenia, NY 12501
518-789-8700
800-562-2139
Fax: 845-373-6390
E-mail: books@greyhouse.com
http://www.greyhouse.com

Provides access to well over 8,000 corporate and independent commercial research firms and laboratories offering contract services for hands on, basic or applied research in environmental and other areas. Provides the company's nameand addresses, as well as a company description and research and technical fields served.
Publication Date: 2003 1,200 pages
ISBN: 1-891482-30-0
Leslie Mackenzie, Publisher
Richard Gottlieb, Editor

3596 State Environmental Agencies on the Internet
Government Institutes
4 Research Place
Suite 200A
Rockville, MD 20850
301-907-1000
Fax: 301-921-2362
http://www.govinst.com

Provides a concise profile of each state agency's requirements and resources-including hard-to-find online laws, rules, and regulations-in one quick-reference guide.

3597 Water Environment & Technology Buyer's Guide and Yearbook
Water Environment Federation
601 Wythe Street
Alexandria, VA 22314
800-666-0206
Fax: 703-684-2492
E-mail: webfeedback@wef.org
http://www.wef.org

Founded in 1928, the Water Environment Federation (WEF) is a not for profit technical and educational organization with members from varied disciplines who work toward the WEF vision of preservation and enhancement of the global waterenvironment. The WEF network includes water quality professionals from 76 Member Associations in 30 countries.
William J Bertera, Executive Director

3598 World Directory of Environmental Organizations Online
California Institute of Public Affairs
PO Box 189040
Sacramento, CA 95818
916-442-2472
http://www.interenvironment.org

A guide to governmental and nongovernmental organizations and programs concerned with protecting the earth's resources. It also covers national and international organizations throughout the world. Only available online.

Directories & Handbooks: Design & Architecture

3599 **Directory of International Periodicals and Newsletters on Built Environments**
Van Nostrand Reinhold

More than 1,400 international periodicals and newsletters that cover architectural design and the building industry and the aspects of the environment that deal with the industry are covered.
Publication Date: 1992 175 pages
ISBN: 0-442230-03-6
Frances C Gretes, Author

Directories & Handbooks: Disaster Peparedness & Response

3600 **Association of State Floodplain Managers**
Association of State Floodplain Managers
2809 Fish Hatchery Road
Suite 204
Madison, WI 53713
608-274-0123
Fax: 608-274-0696
E-mail: asfpm@floods.org
http://www.floods.org

A complete name/address/phone listing for all key floodplain managers in the nation, comprehensive summary of ASFPM's activities of past year and planned future directions, key federal agency programs, much more. Free to currentmembers.
Diane Watson, Editor

3601 **EI Environmental Services Directory Online**
Environmental Information Limited
PO Box 390266
Edina, MN 55439
952-831-2473
Fax: 952-831-6550
E-mail: ei@enviro-information.com
http://www.envirobiz.com

The most comprehensive, largest directory of environmental services in the United States. Coverage includes asbestos & lead abatement, consulting, laboratories, transportation, industrial cleaning, municipal solid waste facilities,hazardous waste facilities, indsutrial waste facilities, well drilling, soil boring, drum reconditioning, spill response, and remediation services.
Cary Perket

3602 **Floodplain Management: State & Local Programs**
Association of State Floodplain Managers
2809 Fish Hatchery Road
Madison, WI 53713
608-274-0123
Fax: 608-274-0696
E-mail: asfpm@floods.org
http://www.floods.org

The most comprehensive source assembled to date, this report summarizes and analyzes various state and local programs and activities.
Publication Date: 2005

3603 **Hazardous Materials Regulations Guide**
JJ Keller
3003 West Breezewood Lane
PO Box 368
Neenah, WI 54957
920-722-2848
877-564-2333
Fax: 800-727-7516
E-mail: sales@jjkeller.com
http://www.jjkeller.com

A complete reference guide of hazardous materials regulations.
May/Novemeber
ISBN: 0-934674-94-9
Tom Ziebell, Editor

3604 **Institute of Chemical Waste Management Directory of Hazardous Waste Treatment**
National Solid Wastes Management Assn.
4301 Connecticut Ave.
Suite 1000
Washington, DC 20008
202-244-4700
800-424-2869
Fax: 202-966-4824
http://www.nswma.org

3605 **Pesticide Directory: A Guide to Producers and Products, Regulators, and Researchers**
Thomson Publications
Box 9335
Fresno, CA 93791
559-266-2964
Fax: 559-266-0189
http://www.agbook.com

This directory is for the person who needs to know anything about the US pesticide industry. It includes basic manufacturers and formulators along with their products, key personnel, managers, district/regional offices and otherpertinent information. Other sections include Universities, State Extension Centers, USDA, EPA, National Organizations, US Forest Service, Poison Control Centers and much more.
Publication Date: 1987 153 pages Biannual
ISBN: 0-913702-45-5
WT Thomson, Author
Susan Heflin, President/Owner

3606 **SEEK**
520 Lafayette Rd N.
St. Paul, MN 55155
651-215-0256
888-668-3224
E-mail: seek@moea.state.mn.us
http://www.seek.state.mn.us/comment.cfm

Minnesotas's interactive directory of environmetal education resources.

3607 **The Homeland Security Directory**
Grey House Publishing
4919 Route 22
Amenia, NY 12510
518-789-8700
800-562-2139
Fax: 518-789-0556
E-mail: books@greyhouse.com
http://www.greyhouse.com

A comprehensive, annual resource for national, state and local officials responsible for homeland security along with manufacturers of homeland security products and services.
Publication Date: 2011 900 pages
Leslie Mackenzie, Publisher
Jessica Moody, Marketing Director

3608 **Tracking Toxic Wastes in CA: A Guide to Federal and State Government Information Sources**
INFORM
120 Wall Street
14th Floor
New York, NY 10005
212-361-2400
Fax: 212-361-2412
http://www.informinc.org/INFORM.html

Directories & Handbooks: Energy & Transportation

3609 **Alternative Energy Network Online**
Environmental Information Networks
119 South Fairfax Street
Alexandria, VA 22314
703-683-0774
Fax: 703-683-3893
E-mail: sales@eintoday.com
http://www.eintoday.com

Reports on news of all energy sources designed as alternatives to conventional fossil fuels, including wind, solar and alcohol fuels.

3610 **Current Alternative Energy Research and Development in Illinois**
Department of Energy & Natural Resources
325 W Adams
Room 300
Springfield, IL 62704
217-785-2800
800-252-8955
Fax: 217-785-2618

3611 **Department of Energy Annual Procurement and Financial Assistance Report**
US Department of Energy

Mail Stop 142 800-342-5303
Washington, DC 20585 Fax: 202-586-4403
Offers a list of universities, research centers and laboratories that represent the Department of Energy.

3612 **Directory of Solar-Terrestrial Physics Monitoring Stations**
Air Force Geophysics Laboratory
Department of Defense 781-377-3977
Hanscom Air Force Base, MA 01731 Fax: 781-377-4498

3613 **Energy Science and Technology**
US Department of Energy
1 Science Gov Way 865-576-1188
Oak Ridge, TN 37830 Fax: 865-576-2865
E-mail: ISTIWebmaster@osti.gov
http://www.osti.gov/resource.html
To collect, preserve, disseminate, and leverage the scientific and technical information (STI) resources of the Department of Energy to provide access to national and global STI for use by DOE, the scientific research community,academia, US industry, and the public to expand the knowledge base of science and technology.

3614 **Energy Statistics Spreadsheets**
Institute of Gas Technology
3424 S State St 312-842-4100
Chicago, IL 60616 Fax: 773-567-5209
The coverage of this database encompasses worldwide energy industry statistics, including production, consumption, reserves, imports and prices.

3615 **Interstate Oil Compact Commission and State Oil and Gas Agencies Directory**
Interstate Oil & Gas Compact Commission
2101 N. Lincoln Blvd. 405-521-2302
Oklahoma City, OK 73105 800-822-4015
Fax: 405-521-3099
E-mail: iogcc@iogcc.state.ok.us
http://www.iogcc.oklaosf.state.ok.us
A directory of members and in the back is a list of state oil and gas agencies

3616 **Women's Council on Energy and the Environment Membership Directory**
PO Box 33211 703-351-7850
Washington, DC 20033 Fax: 202-478-2098
E-mail: info@wcee.org
http://www.wcee.org
Offers valuable information on over 800 members representing consulting firms, private industry and the environmental community.
Publication Date: 1980
Clare Piercy, Executive Director
JoAnne Scribner, Deputy Executive Director

Directories & Handbooks: Environmental Engineering

3617 **Association of Conservation Engineers: Membership Directory**
Engineering Section Alabama Dept. of Conservation
573-522-2323
Fax: 573-522-2324
E-mail: mihalg@mail.conservation.state.mo.us
http://www.conservation.state.mo.us/engineering/ace

3618 **Energy Engineering: Directory of Software for Energy Managers and Engineers**
Fairmont Press
700 Indian Trail 770-925-9388
Liburn, GA 30047 Fax: 770-381-9865
E-mail: linda@fairmontpress.com
http://www.fairmontpress.com
Directory of services and supplies to the industry.
Publication Date: 1904 80 pages Bimonthly
ISSN: 0199-8895
Wayne C Turner, Author
Wayne C Turner, Editor

3619 **NEPA Lessons Learned**
Office of NEPA Policy & Compliance
1000 Independence Avenue SW 202-586-4600
EH-42 800-472-2756
Washington, DC 20585 Fax: 202-586-7031
E-mail: denise.freeman@eh.doe.gov
http://www.eh.doe.gov/nepa
Publication Date: 1994 Quarterly
Carol M Borgstrom, Director

3620 **Pollution Abstracts**
Cambridge Scientific Abstracts
7200 Wisconsin Avenue 301-961-6700
Suite 601 800-843-7751
Bethesda, MD 20814 Fax: 301-961-6720
E-mail: sales@csa.com
http://www.csa.com
This database provides fast access to the environmental information necessary to resolve day to day problems, ensure ongoing compliance, and handle emergency situations more effectively.
James P McGinty, President
Ted Caris, Publisher

Directories & Handbooks: Environmental Health

3621 **American Academy of Environmental Medicine Directory**
American Academy of Environmental Medicine
7701 E Kellogg 316-684-5500
Suite 625 Fax: 316-684-5709
Wichita, KS 67207 E-mail: administrator@aaem.com
http://www.aaem.com
To suppoprt physicians and other professionals in serving the public through education about the interaction between humans and their environment. Also to promote optimal health through prevention, and safe and effective treatment ofthe causes, not the illness.
Dee Rogers, Contact

3622 **Canadian Environmental Resource Guide**
Grey House Publishing Canada
555 Richmond Street West 416-644-6479
2nd Floor 866-433-4739
Toronto, Ontario M5V 3B1 Fax: 416-644-1904
E-mail: info@greyhouse.ca
http://www.greyhouse.ca
Annual directory — Canada's most complete reference of environmental associations and organizations, government regulators and purchasing groups, product and service companies and special libraries.
Publication Date: 2011 1200 pages
Bryon Moore, General Manager

3623 **Directory of NEHA Credentialed Professionals**
720 S Colorado Boulevard 303-756-9090
Suite 1000-N Fax: 303-691-9490
Denver, CO 80246 E-mail: staff@neha.org
http://www.neha.org
This is a directory of all NEHA credentialed professionals. It is available to NEHA credentialed professionals only.
Catalog 569

3624 **Ecosystem Change and Public Health: A Global Perspective**
Johns Hopkins University Press

2715 N Charles Street 410-516-6900
Baltimore, MD 21218 800-537-5487
Fax: 410-516-6968
http://www.press.jhu.edu/books

The strength of the John Hopkins University Press' publications in medicine is in part a reflection of the university and medical institution's excellence and long term tradition of exceptional research and clinical care. Joan Aron'sEcosystem Change and Public Health is the first textbook devoted to this emerging field. The book covers such topics as global climate change, stratospheric ozone depletion, water resources management, ecology and infectious disease. Paperback

Publication Date: 2001 526 pages
ISBN: 0-801865-82-4
Joan Aron, Author
Joan Aron, Editor
Jonathan Pratz, Editor

3625 Environmental Encyclopedia
Thomson Gale
27500 Drake Road 248-699-4253
Farmington Hills, MI 48331 800-877-4253
Fax: 800-414-5043
http://www.galegroup.com

Consisting of nearly 1,300 signed articles and term definitions. The encyclopedia provides in-depth, worldwide coverage of environmental issues. Each article written in a nontechnical style and provides current status, analysis andsuggests solutions whenever possible.

Publication Date: 2002 2000 pages
ISBN: 0-787654-86-8
Virginia Regish, Contact

3626 Environmental Guidebook: A Selective Guide to Environmental Organizations and Related Entities
Environmental Frontlines
PO Box 43 650-323-8452
Menlo Park, CA 94026 E-mail: info@envirofront.org
http://www.envirofront.org

Designed to serve as an essential reference book profiling nearly 500 national organizations and other entities actively engaged in environmental issues in the US and beyond.

312 pages
ISBN: 0-972068-50-3
Jeff Staudinger, Author

3627 Environmental Key Contacts and Information Sources
Government Institutes
4 Research Place
Suite 200A 301-907-9100
Fax: 301-921-2362
Rockville, MD 20850 http://www.govinst.com

An updated and revised compilation of Government Institutes' two previous directories, this reference contains more than 400 pages of contact information for more than 2,700 federal, state, and local environmental agencies andorganizations. This directory also includes contacts for information concerning environmental protection, hazardous waste materials, clean water and air, environmental assessment and management, pesticides, pollution control, recycling, naturalresources and conservation.

Publication Date: 1998 424 pages
ISBN: 0-865876-39-8
Charlene Ikonomou and Diane Pacchione, Author

3628 Pesticide Directory: A Guide to Producers and Products, Regulators, and Researchers
Thomson Publications
Box 9335 559-266-2964
Fresno, CA 93791 Fax: 559-266-0189
http://www.agbook.com

This directory is for the person who needs to know anything about the US pesticide industry. It includes basic manufacturers and formulators along with their products, key personnel, managers, district/regional offices and otherpertinent information. Other sections include Universities, State Extension Centers, USDA, EPA, National Organizations, US Forest Service, Poison Control Centers and much more.

Publication Date: 1987 153 pages Biannual
ISBN: 0-913702-45-5
WT Thomson, Author
Susan Heflin, President/Owner

Directories & Handbooks: Habitat Preservation & Land Use

3629 Alliance for Wildlife Rehabilitation and Education Wildlife Care Directory
1912 Harbor Boulevard 949-722-0606
Costa Mesa, CA 92627

3630 Biodiversity Action Network
1630 Connecticut Avenue 202-547-8902
3rd Floor Fax: 202-265-0222
Washington, DC 20009 http://www.bionet-us.org

An information exchange network launched by the Center for International Environmental Law.

3631 Conservation Directory 2004: The Guide to Worldwide Environmental Organizations
National Wildlife Federation
11100 Wild Life Center Drive 800-822-9919
Reston, VA 20190 http://www.nwf.org/conservationDirectory/

Your guide to thousands of environmental non-profit, education, commercial, and government groups operating across the planet.

Robin Assa, Sales Assistant

3632 County Conservation Board Outdoor Adventure Guide
Iowa Association of County Conservation Boards
405 SW 3rd Street 515-963-9582
Suite 1 Fax: 515-963-9582
Ankeny, IA 50021 E-mail: iaccb@ecity.net
http://http://george.ecity.net/iaccb/guide.htm

Includes a map of each county with the area to be shaded in or a pinpoint of the location, and has information on cabin rentals, camping, shelters, playgrounds, swimming, fishing, boating, boat rental, sports and fields, hunting,nature centers, praires, historic sites, wildlife exhibits and more.

184 pages
Don Brazelton, Contact

3633 DOCKET
US Environmental Protection Agency
US EPA Region 3 215-814-2993
1650 Arch Street (3PM52) Fax: 215-814-5102
Philadelphia, PA 19103 E-mail: teller.lawrence@epa.gov
http://www.epa.gov

This database offers the complete text of summaries of all justice cases filed by the US Department of Justice on behalf of the US Environmental Protection Agency.

3634 Directory of Resource Recovery Projects and Services
Institute of Resource Recovery
1730 Rhode Island Avenue NW 202-659-4613
Suite 1000 Fax: 202-775-5917
Washington, DC 20036

3635 Ecology Abstracts
Cambridge Scientific Abstracts
7200 Wisconsin Avenue 301-961-6700
Suite 601 800-843-7751
Bethesda, MD 20814 Fax: 301-961-6720
E-mail: sales@csa.com
http://www.csa.com

This large database updated continuously, offers over 150,000 citations, with abstracts, to the worldwide literature available on ecology and the environment.

James P McGinty, President
Theodore Caris, Publisher

3636 Environmental Bibliography
International Academy at Santa Barbara
5385 Hollister Avenue
#210
Santa Barbara, CA 93111
805-683-8889
Fax: 805-965-6071
E-mail: info@iasb.org
http://www.iasb.org

Over 615,000 citations are offered in this database, aimed at scientific, technical and popular periodical literature dealing with the environment.

ISSN: 1053-1440

3637 Environmental Concerns: Directory of the Environmental Industry in Colorado
Business Research Division-Univ. of Colorado
420 UCB
Boulder, CO 80309-0420
303-492-8227
Fax: 303-492-3620
http://leeds.colorado.edu/brd

Approximately 1,300 private businesses, government organizations and corporations in Colorado that contribute to environmental protection and rehabilitation.

ISBN: 1-883226-02-3
Gin Hayden, Editor
Sean Shepherd, Editor

3638 Environmental Guide to the Internet
Government Institutes
4 Research Place
Suite 200A
Rockville, MD 20850
301-907-9100
Fax: 301-921-2362
http://www.govinst.com

Provides information for the best sites in the internet dealing with the preservation and protection of the environment, ecology, and conservation and offers over 320 new listings and addresses. Writin for environmental consultants,industry professionals, researchers, lawyers, educators, and students, contains the top 1,200 environmental internet resources, including, newletters and journals, and world wide web sites
Publication Date: 1997 384 pages
ISBN: 0-865875-78-2
Carol Briggs-Erickson and Toni Murphy, Author

3639 Environmental Guidebook: A Selective Guide to Environmental Organizations and Related Entities
Environmental Frontlines
PO Box 43
Menlo Park, CA 94026
650-323-8452
E-mail: info@envirofront.org
http://www.envirofront.org

Designed to serve as an essential reference book profiling nearly 500 national organizations and other entities actively engaged in environmental issues in the US and beyond.
312 pages
ISBN: 0-972068-50-3
Jeff Staudinger, Author

3640 Helping Out in the Outdoors: A Directory of Volunteer Opportunities on Public Lands
American Hiking Society
1422 Fenwick Lane
Silver Spring, MD 20910
301-565-6704
Fax: 301-565-6714
E-mail: info@americanhiking.org
http://www.americanhiking.org

Mary Margaret Sloan, President

3641 Hospitality Directory
Human Ecology Action League (HEAL)
PO Box 29629
Atlanta, GA 30359
404-248-1898
Fax: 404-248-0162
E-mail: HEALNatnl@aol.com
http://members.aol.com/HEALNatnl/index.html

Nonprofit organization founded in 1977 to serve those whose health has been adversely affected by environment exposures; to provide information to those who are concerned about the health effects of chemicals; and to alert the generalpublic about the potential dangers of chemicals.
Katherine P Collier, Contact

3642 Human Ecology Action League Directory
Human Ecology Action League
PO Box 29629
Atlanta, GA 30359
404-248-1898
Fax: 404-248-0162
E-mail: HEALNatnl@aol.com
http://members.aol.com/HEALNatnl/index.html

The Human Ecology Action League Inc (HEAL) is a nonprofit organization founded in 1977 to serve those whose health has been affected by environmental exposures; to provide information to those who are concerned about the health effectsof chemicals; and to alert the general public about the potential dangers of chemicals. Referrals to local HEAL chapters and other support groups are available from the League.
Katherine P Collier, Contact

3643 Hummingbird Connection
6560 Highway 179
Suite 204
Sedona, AZ 86351
928-284-2251
800-529-3699
E-mail: info@hummingbird.org
http://www.hummingbirdsociety.org

Published by the Hummingbird Society.
Publication Date: 1992 16 pages Quarterly
ISSN: 1097-3427
H Ross Hawkins, Author/Editor

3644 International Society of Tropical Foresters: Membership Directory
5400 Grosvenor Lane
Bethesda, MD 20814
301-897-8720
Fax: 301-897-3690
E-mail: istfi@igc.apc.org

The International Society of Tropical Foresters, Inc. (ISTF) is a nonprofit organization committed to the protection, wise management and rational use of the world's tropical forests. Established in 1950, ISTF was reactivated in 1979.It has about 1500 members in more than 100 countries. Financial support comes from membership dues, donations and grants. ISTF sponsors meetings, promotes chapters in other countries, maintains a web site and has chapters at universities.
Warren T Doolittle, President

3645 Journal of Wildlife Rehabilitation
International Wildlife Rehabilitation Council
PO Box 8187
San Jose, CA 95155
408-271-2685
Fax: 408-271-9285
E-mail: office@iwrc-online.org
http://www.iwrc-online.org

A peer reviewed scientific journal that has served as a primary reference for wildlife rehabilitators and others involved in the care and conservation of wildlife. Features articles, columns and reviews, with topics ranging from allaspects of wildlife care to administration, fundraising, education programs, case studies, environmental issues, legalities, ethics and more. And is also a benefit of membership to IWRC.
Publication Date: 1978 40 pages Quarterly
Jennifer Gursu, Executive Director

3646 LEXIS Environmental Law Library
Lexis Nexis Group
PO Box 933
Dayton, OH 45401
937-865-6800
800-227-9597
Fax: 937-865-6909
http://www.lexis-nexis.com

This database contains decisions related to environmental law from the Supreme Court and other legislative bodies.

3647 Learning About Our Place
311 Curtis Street
Jamestown, NY 14701
716-665-2473
800-758-6841
Fax: 716-665-3794
E-mail: mail@rtpi.org
http://www.rtpi.org

47 lesson plans that connect learning to nature and the outdoors
15-30 pages Quarterly
Jim Berry, President

3648 Managed Area Basic Record
The Nature Conservancy

4245 N. Fairfax Drive 804-295-6106
Suite 100 Fax: 804-979-0370
Arlington, VA 22203 E-mail: cmullen@tnc.org
http://http://nature.org

3649 Minienvironments
IEST
2340 S. Arlington Heights Road 847-981-0100
Suite 100 Fax: 847-981-4130
Arlington Heights, IL 60005 E-mail: iest@iest.org
http://www.iest.org

The purpose of this document is to provide a framework for describing minienvironments for microelectronics and similar applications.
Publication Date: 2002 28 pages
ISBN: 1-877862-83-5
Julie Kendrick, Executive Director

3650 Morrison Environmental Directory
PO Box 2312 316-262-0100
Wichita, KS 67201

ISSN: 1060-488

3651 National Directory of Conservation Land Trusts
Land Trust Alliance
1660 L St. NW 202-638-4725
Suite 1100 Fax: 202-638-4730
Washington, DC 20036 E-mail: info@lta.org
http://www.lta.org

More than 1,200 nonprofit land conservation organizations at the local and regional levels are profiled.
210 pages

3652 New York State Department of Environmental Conservation Personnel Directory: Internet Only
NYS Department of Environmental Conservation
625 Broadway 518-402-8013
Albany, NY 12233 Fax: 518-402-9036
E-mail: dinnelson@gw.dec.state.ny.us
http://www.dec.state.ny.us

Internet only, this directory includes DEC's executive management and division directors. Executive managers are appointed by the Governor to carry out the policies of the state. Division directors have direct management responsibilityfor the department's programs.
Mary A Kadlecek, Chief Internet Publications

3653 Nonprofit Sample and Core Repositories Open to the Public in the United States
Branch of Sedimentary Processes
MS 939 Federal Center 303-236-5760
Denver, CO 80225 Fax: 303-236-0459
Walter E Dean, Contact

3654 Range and Land Management Handbook
Wyoming Association of Conservation Districts
517 E 19th Street 307-632-5716
Cheyenne, WY 82001 Fax: 307-638-4099
http://www.conservewy.com

This publication is intended for people from all walks of life who want to gain an appreciation of rangelands. This publication is also an introduction to the various fields of range management.
Annual

3655 Takings Litigation Handbook: Defending Takings Challenges to Land Use Regulations
American Legal Publishing Corporation
432 Walnut Street 800-445-5588
Suite 1200 Fax: 513-763-3562
Cincinnati, OH 45202 E-mail: customerservice@amlegal.com
http://www.amlegal.com

No government attorney, land use planner or other local official can effectively protect their community from harmful land use without a working knowledge of takings law. Developers and other landowners increasingly are attempting touse takings litigation, or the mere threat of takings litigation, to convince government agencies to relax or abandon vital protections for our neighborhoods and natural environment.
Publication Date: 2000 404 pages
Kendall, Dowling and Schwartz, Author
Douglas Kendall, Executive Director

3656 Trout Unlimited Chapter and Council Handbook
Trout Unlimited
1300 North 17th Street 703-522-0200
Suite 500 Fax: 703-284-9400
Arlington, VA 22209 E-mail: trout@tu.org
http://www.tu.org

Charles Gauvin, President/CEO
Kenneth Mendez, Executive VP/COO

3657 Turtle Help Network
New York Turtle and Tortoise Society
PO Box 878 212-459-4803
Orange, NJ 07051

3658 Wilson Journal of Ornithology
OSNA
5400 Bosque Blvd 254-399-9636
Suite 680 E-mail: business@osnabirds.org
Waco, TX 76710 http://www.ummz.umich.edu/birds/wos/index.html

Scholarly journal consisting of articles on bird studies, orinthological news, reviews of new bird books and related subjects.
Quarterly
Dr Doris J Watt, President
John A Smallwood, Secretary

3659 Wisconsin Department of Public Instruction
125 S Webster Street 608-266-2188
PO Box 7841 800-441-4563
Madison, WI 53707 Fax: 608-267-9110
E-mail: sandi.mcnamer@dpi.state.wi.us
http://www.dpi.state.wi.us/pubsales

State education department publisher of K-12 curriculum planning guides in 25 subject areas including environmental education and science.
Sandi McNamer, Publications Director

Directories & Handbooks: Recycling & Pollution Prevention

3660 A Glossary of Terms and Definitions Relating to Contamination Control
IEST
5005 Newport Drive 847-255-1561
Suite 506 Fax: 847-255-1699
Rolling Meadows, IL 60008 E-mail: iest@iest.org
http://www.iest.org

A publication from the Institute of Environmental Science and Technology.
Publication Date: 1995 32 pages
ISBN: 1-877862-28-2
Julie Kendrick, Executive Director

3661 American Recycling Market Directory: Reference Manual
Recycling Data Management Corp.
PO Box 577 315-471-0707
Ogdensburg, NY 13669 800-267-0707
Fax: 613-471-3258

Comprehensive directory/reference manual to materials recycling markets. Helps individuals locate buyers and sellers of recyclable materials on a regional basis throughout North America. Contains 20,000 cross-referenced company andagency listings. Sections include: scrap metals, waste paper, paper mills, auto dismantlers, demolition, glass, oil, rubber and textiles recyclers, recycling centers, MRF's composting, equipment and consulting services, industry references UBC specsand more.

3662 Analysis of the Stockholm Convention on Persistent Organic Pollutants
Oceana Publications, Inc
198 Madison Ave
New York, NY 10016
800-334-4249
Fax: 212-726-6476
E-mail: oxfordonline@oup.com
http://www.oceanalaw.com

This book analyzes the Stockholm Convention on Persistent Organic Pollutants. Prepared under the auspices of the UN Environment Programme Chemical Division.
Publication Date: 2003 200 pages One Time
ISBN: 0-379215-06-3
Mario Antonio Olsen, Author

3663 Criteria Pollutant Point Source Directory
North American Water Office
3394 Lake Elmo Ave
Lake Elmo, MN 55042
651-770-3861
Fax: 651-770-3976
E-mail: gwillc@mtn.org
http://http://www.nawo.org

3664 Directory of Municipal Solid Waste Management Facilities
The Institute of Solid Waste Disposal
1730 Rhode Island Avenue NW
Suite 1000
Washington, DC 20036
202-659-4613
Fax: 202-296-7915

3665 EI Environmental Services Directory
Environmental Information Networks
8525 Arjons Drive
Suite H
San Diego, CA 92126
858-695-0050
Fax: 952-831-6550
E-mail: ei@mr.net
http://www.envirobiz.com

Waste-handling facilities, transportation and spill response firms, laboratories and the broad scope of environmental services. Online versions are also available.

ISSN: 1053-475N
Cary Perket

3666 Environmental Encyclopedia
Thomson Gale
27500 Drake Road
Farmington Hills, MI 48331
248-699-4253
800-877-4253
Fax: 800-414-5043
http://www.galegroup.com

Consisting of nearly 1,300 signed articles and definitions. The encyclopedia provides in depth, worldwide coverage of environmental issues. Each article written in a non technical style and provides current status, analysis andsuggests solutions whenever possible.
Publication Date: 2002 2000 pages
ISBN: 0-787654-86-8
Virginia Regish, Contact

3667 Environmental Guide to the Internet
Government Institutes
4 Research Place
Suite 200A
Rockville, MD 20850
301-907-9100
Fax: 301-921-2362
http://www.govinst.com

Provides information for the best sites on the internet dealing with the preservation and protection of the environment, ecology, and conservation and offers over 320 new listings and addresses. Writin for environmental consultants,industry professionals, researchers, lawyers, educators, and students, contains the top 1,200 environmental internet resources, including, newletters and journals, and world wide web sites
Publication Date: 1997 384 pages
ISBN: 0-865875-78-2
Carol Briggs-Erickson and Toni Murphy, Author

3668 Environmental Guidebook: A Selective Guide to Environmental Organizations and Related Entities
Environmental Frontlines
PO Box 43
Menlo Park, CA 94026
650-323-8452
E-mail: info@envirofront.org
http://www.envirofront.org

Designed to serve as an essential reference book profiling nearly 500 national organizations and other entities actively engaged in environmental issues in the US and beyond.
312 pages
ISBN: 0-972068-50-3
Jeff Staudinger, Author

3669 Fibre Market News: Paper Recycling Markets Directory
Recycling Media Group GIE Publishers
4012 Bridge Avenue
Cleveland, OH 44113
216-961-4130
800-456-0707
Fax: 216-961-0364

A list of over 2,000 dealers, brokers, packers and graders of paper stock in the US and Canada.
Dan Sandoval, Editor

3670 Hazardous Materials Regulations Guide
JJ Keller
3003 West Breezewood Lane
PO Box 368
Neenah, WI 54957
877-564-2333
Fax: 800-727-7516
E-mail: sales@jjkeller.com
http://www.jjkeller.com

A complete reference guide of hazardous materials regulations.
May/November
ISBN: 0-934674-94-9
Tom Ziebell, Editor

3671 How-To: 1,400 Best Books on Doing Almost Everything
R.R. Bowker Company
630 Central Ave.
New Providence, NJ 07974
908-286-1090
888-269-5372
E-mail: info@bowker.com
http://www.bowker.com/bowkerweb/

3672 Institute of Chemical Waste Management Directory of Hazardous Waste Treatment and Disposal
National Solid Wastes Management Assn
4301 Connecticut Avenue NW
Suite 300
Washington, DC 20008
202-244-4700
Fax: 202-966-4824
http://www.nswma.org

3673 International Handbook of Pollution Control
Greenwood Publishing Group
88 Post Road W
Westport, CT 06881
203-226-3571
E-mail: webmaster@greenwood.com
http://www.greenwood.com

Publication Date: 1989 482 pages
ISBN: 0-313240-17-5
Edward J Kormondy, Author

3674 List of Water Pollution Control Administrators
Assn. of State and Interstate Water Pollution Con.
1221 Connecticut Ave. NW
2nd Floor
Washington, DC 20036
202-898-0905
Fax: 202-898-0929
E-mail: admin1@aswipca.org
http://www.asiwpca.org

Roberta Savage, Executive Director
Linda Eichmiller, Deputy Director

3675 Nebraska Recycling Resource Directory
Nebraska Dept of Environmental Quality
1200 N Street Suite 400
PO Box 98922
Lincoln, NE 68509
402-471-2186
877-253-2603
Fax: 402-471-2909
E-mail: MoreInfo@nebraska.gov
http://www.deq.state.ne.us

Publication Date: 1986 139 pages Bi-Annually
Steve Danahy, Unit Supervisor

3676 **Pesticide Directory: A Guide to Producers and Products, Regulators, and Researchers**
Thomson Publications
Box 9335 559-266-2964
Fresno, CA 93791 Fax: 559-266-0189
http://www.agbook.com

This directory is for the person who needs to know anything about the US pesticide industry. It includes basic manufacturers and formulators along with their products, key personnel, managers, district/regional offices and otherpertinent information. Other sections include Universities, State Extension Centers, USDA, EPA, National Organizations, US Forest Service, Poison Control Centers and much more.

Publication Date: 1987 153 pages Biannual
ISBN: 0-913702-45-5
WT Thomson, Author
Susan Heflin, President/Owner

3677 **Pollution Abstracts**
Cambridge Scientific Abstracts
7200 Wisconsin Avenue 301-961-6700
Suite 601 800-843-7751
Bethesda, MD 20814 Fax: 301-961-6720
E-mail: sales@csa.com
http://www.csa.com

This database provides fast access to the environmental information necessary to resolve day to day problems, ensure ongoing compliance, and handle emergency situations more effectively.

James P McGinty, President
Ted Caris, Publisher

3678 **Product Cleanliness Levels and Contamination Control Program**
IEST
5005 Newport Drive 847-255-1561
Suite 506 Fax: 847-255-1699
Rolling Meadows, IL 60008 E-mail: iest@iest.org
http://www.iest.org

Intended to provide a basis for specifying product cleanliness levels and contamination control program requirments with emphasis on contaminants that affect product performance.

Publication Date: 2002 20 pages
ISBN: 1-877862-82-7
Julie Kendrick, Executive Director

3679 **Recycling Related Newsletters, Publications And Periodicals**
Continnuus
PO Box 416 303-575-5676
Denver, CO 80201 Fax: 970-292-2136

3680 **Recycling Today: Recycling Products & Services Buyers Guide**
Recycling Today GIE Publishers
4020 Kinross Lakes Parkway 216-961-4130
#201 800-456-0707
Richfield, OH 44286 Fax: 216-961-0364
E-mail: jkeefe@gie.net
http://www.recyclingtoday.com

Directory of services and supplies to the industry.

Dan Sandoval, Internet/Senior Editor
James Keefe, Group Publisher

3681 **Scholastic Environmental Atlas of the United States**
Scholastic
730 Broadway 212-505-3000
New York, NY 10003 E-mail: uwpress@washinton.edu
http://www.washington.edu/uwpress/

3682 **Tracking Toxic Wastes in CA: A Guide to Federal and State Government Information Sources**
INFORM
5 Hanover Square 212-361-2400
Floor 19 Fax: 212-361-2412
New York, NY 10004 http://www.informinc.org

3683 **Waste Age: Resource Recovery Acitivities Update Issue**
National Solid Wastes Management Assn.
1730 Rhode Island Avenue NW 202-659-4613
Suite 1000
Washington, DC 20036

3684 **Waste Age: Waste Industry Buyer Guide**
National Solid Wastes Management
1730 Rhode Island Avenue NW 202-659-4613
Suite 1000 800-424-2869
Washington, DC 20036 Fax: 202-659-0925

3685 **Wastes to Resources: Appropriate Technologies for Sewage Treatment and Conversion**
National Center for Appropriate Techology
3040 Continental Drive 406-494-4572
Butte, MT 59701 800-275-6228
Fax: 406-494-2905
E-mail: info@ncat.org
http://www.ncat.org

Kathy Hadley, Executive Director

Directories & Handbooks: Sustainable Development

3686 **Solar Energy Resource Guide/SERG**
NorCal Solar
PO Box 3008 530-852-0354
Berkeley, CA 94703 E-mail: info@norcalsolar.org
http://www.norcalsolar.org

Articles and resources on solar electric, solar thermal, financial analysis, etc. Also a guidebook for education on the workings and intstallation of solar technology.

96 pages
Claudia Wentworth, President
Liz Merry, Program Manager

Directories & Handbooks: Travel & Tourism

3687 **Access America: An Atlas and Guide to the National Parks for Visitors with Disabilities**
Northern Cartographic
4050 Williston Road 802-860-2886
South Burlington, VT 05403 Fax: 802-865-4912
E-mail: info@ncarto.com
http://www.ncarto.com

Publication Date: 1988
ISBN: 0-944187-00-5

3688 **Audubon Society Field Guide to the Natural Places of the Northeast**
National Audubon Society
700 Broadway 212-979-3000
New York, NY 10003 Fax: 212-979-3188
http://www.audubon.org

3689 **Complete Guide to America's National Parks: The Official Visitor's Guide**
National Park Foundation
11 Dupont Circle NW 202-238-4200
Suite 600 800-285-2448
Washington, DC 20036 Fax: 202-234-3103
E-mail: ask-npf@nationalparks.org

3690 **Field Guide to American Windmills**
University of Oklahoma Press
2800 Venture Drive 405-325-2000
Norman, OK 73069 800-627-7377
Fax: 405-364-5798

This guide to America's windmills is both a complete general history of turbine wheel mills and an identification guide to the 112 most common models, which still dot landscapes today.
Publication Date: 1985 528 pages
T Lindsay Baker, Author

3691 Guide to the National Wildlife Refuges
Macmillan Publishing Company
National Wildlife Guide 212-832-2101
590 Madison Avenue http://www.nationalwildlifeguide.com
New York, NY 10022
More than 500 National Wildlife Refuges and satellite refuges are listed.
684 pages

3692 National Parks Visitor Facilities and Services
Conference of National Park Concessioners
PO Box 29041 480-967-6006
Phoenix, AZ 85038 http://www.nps.gov/legacy/business.html
Within the parks, private businesses provide accommodations and services for visitors under concession contracts.
Rex G Maughan, Chairman

3693 National Parks: National Park Campgrounds Issue
National Parks Conservation Association
1300 19th Street Northwest 800-628-7275
Suite 300 Fax: 202-659-0650
Washington, DC 20036 E-mail: npca@npca.org
http://www.npca.org
To safeguard the scenic beauty, wildlife, and historical and cultural treasures of the largest and most diverse park system in the world.
Thomas C Kiernan, President
Tom Martin, Executive Vice President

3694 National Wildlife Refuges: A Visitor's Guide
Fish and Wildlife Services, Interior Department
1849 C Street NW 703-358-2043
Washington, DC 20242 E-mail: webteam@ios.doi.gov
http://www.fws.gov
Contains a map showing national wildlife refuges that provide recrational and educational opportunities. Provides tips for visiting national wildlife refuges. Also list refuges in all 50 States, Puerto Rico and the Virgin Islans, withthe best wildlife viewing season and the features of each refuge.
ISBN: 0-160617-00-6

3695 Nature Center Directory
Wisconsin Association for Environmental Education
8 Nelson Hall 715-346-2796
University of Wisconsin-Stevens Point Fax: 715-346-3835
Stevens Point, WI 54481 E-mail: waee@uwsp.edu
http://www.uwsp.edu/waee
Annual

3696 Rails-to-Trails Magazine
1100 17th Street NW 202-331-9696
10th Floor Fax: 202-331-9680
Washington, DC 20036 E-mail: railtrails@railtrails.org
http://www.railtotrails.org
Official magazine of the Rails-to-Trails Conservancy (RTC). The RTC is a national nonprofit organization dedicated to creating a nationwide network of trails from former rail lines and connecting corridors. It does not own or manageany rail trails.
Keith Laughlin, President
Jeff Ciabotti, VP Trail Development

3697 Recreation Sites in Southwestern National Forests
USDA Forest Service
Public Affairs Office 505-842-3292
333 Broadway Blvd SE Fax: 505-842-3106
Albuquerque, NM 87102 http://www.fs.fed.us/r3
Listings for all recreation sites for Arizona and New Mexico.
72 pages
Corbin Newman, Regional Forester

3698 Sierra Club Guide to the Natural Areas of California
Sierra Club
85 2nd Street 415-977-5500
2nd Floor Fax: 415-977-5799
San Francisco, CA 94105 E-mail: information@sierraclub.org
http://www.sierraclub.org
Revised and updated, this comprehensive guide makes more than 200 wilderness areas in California, including many lesser known natural areas, accessible to the outdoor enthusiast.
Publication Date: 1997 352 pages
ISBN: 0-871568-50-0
John Perry and Jane Greverus Perry, Author

3699 Thermal Springs of Wyoming
Wyoming State Geological Survey
PO Box 1347 307-766-2286
Laramie, WY 82073 Fax: 307-766-2605
E-mail: wsgs-info@uwyo.edu
http://www.wsgs.uwyo.edu
Ronald C Surdam, Agency Director
Richard W Jones, Editor

3700 Traveler's Guide to the Smoky Mountains Region
Harvard Common Press
535 Albany Street 617-423-5803
Boston, MA 02118 Fax: 619-695-9794
E-mail: orders@harvardcommonpress.com
http://www.harvardcommonpress.com
Features museums, events of the South Appalachians of Tennessee, North Carolilna, Virginia and Georgia
Publication Date: 1985 288 pages
ISBN: 0-916782-64-6
Valerie Cimino, Executive Editor
Christine Alaimo, Associate Publisher

3701 Wild Places & Open Spaces Map
Division of Fish and Wildlife
PO Box 400 609-292-9450
Trenton, NJ 08625 Fax: 609-984-1414
http://www.njfishandwildlife.com
Designed similar to a road map, offers the outdoors person a welath of information on locating and exploring New Jersey's open spaces in compact and easy to read format. Showcasing a full color map of New Jersey, with more than 700,000acres of public open space.
Carol Nash, Customer Service

Directories & Handbooks: Water Resources

3702 Citizen's Directory for Water Quality Abuses
Izaak Walton League of America
707 Conservation Lane 301-548-0150
Gaithersburg, MD 20878 800-453-5463
Fax: 301-548-0146
E-mail: general@iwla.org
http://www.iwla.org
Paul Hansen, Executive Director

3703 Coordination Directory of State and Federal Agency Water Resources Officials: Missouri Basin
Department of Water Resources
5231 South 19th Street 402-471-2363
Lincoln, NE 68512 http://ne.water.usgs.gov

3704 How Wet is a Wetland?: The Impacts of the Proposed Revisions to the Federal Wetlands Manual
Environmental Defense Fund

257 Park Avenue South 212-505-2100
New York, NY 10010 800-684-3322
Fax: 212-505-0892
E-mail: media@environmentaldefense.org
http://www.environmentaldefense.org

Publication Date: 1992
Fred Krupp, President

3705 Hydro Review: Industry Source Book Issue
HCI Publications
410 Archibald Street 816-931-1311
Kansas City, MO 64111 Fax: 816-931-2015
E-mail: info@hcipub.com
http://www.hcipub.com

List of over 800 manufacturers and suppliers of products and services to the hydroelectric industry in the US and Canada.
January
Carl Vansant, Editor-In-Chief

3706 List of Water Pollution Control Administrators
Assn. of State and Interstate Water Pollution Con.
1221 Connecticut Ave. NW 202-898-0905
2nd Floor Fax: 202-898-0929
Washington, DC 20036 E-mail: admin1@aswipca.org
http://www.asiwpca.org

Roberta Savage, Executive Director
Linda Eichmiller, Deputy Director

3707 Water Environment & Technology Buyer's Guide and Yearbook
Water Environment Federation
601 Wythe Street 703-684-2400
Alexandria, VA 22314 800-666-0206
Fax: 703-684-2492
E-mail: webfeedback@wef.org
http://www.wef.org

Founded in 1928, the Water Environment Foundation (WEF) is a not for profit technical and educational organization with members from varied disiplines who work toward the WEF vision of preservation and enhancement of the globalwaterenvironment. The WEF network includes water quality professionals from 76 Member Associations in 30 countries.
William J Bertera, Executive Director

Periodicals: Air & Climate

3708 Air/Water Pollution Report
Business Publishers
PO Box 17592 301-589-5103
Baltimore, MD 21297 800-274-6737
Fax: 301-589-8493
E-mail: custserv@bpines.com
http://www.bpinews.com

Regulatory activities and governmental legislation and litigation are covered in this pulication.
Publication Date: 1963 Monthly
Leonard Eiserer, Publisher

3709 Bulletin of the American Meteorological Society
45 Beacon Street 617-227-2425
Boston, MA 02108 Fax: 617-742-8718
E-mail: amsinfo@ametsoc.org
http://www.ametsoc.org

The American Meteorological Society promotes the development and dissemination of information and education on the atmospheric and related oceanic and hydrologic sciences and the advancement of their professional applications.
Publication Date: 1919 Monthly
Ronald D McPherson, Executive Director

3710 Climate Institute: Climate Alert
Coping with Climate Change
1785 Massachusetts Avenue NW 202-547-0104
Washington, DC 20036 Fax: 202-547-0111
E-mail: info@climate.org
http://www.climate.org

The Climate Institute works to protect the balance between climate and life on earth by facilitating dialogue among scientists, policy makers, business executives and citizens. In all its efforts, the institute strives to be a sourceof objective, reliable information.
Publication Date: 1988 8-12 pages Quarterly
ISSN: 1071-3271
John Topping, President

3711 Earth Share of Georgia Newsletter
1447 Peachtree Street 404-873-3173
Suite 214 Fax: 404-873-3135
Atlanta, GA 30309 E-mail: info@earthsharega.org
http://www.earthsharega.org

Nonprofit federation of local, national and global environmental groups addressing the critical environmental issues. ESGA raises funds for these groups through workplace giving campaigns, special events and individual contributions.
Publication Date: 1992 Bi-Monthly
Madeline Reamy, Executive Director

3712 Environmental Policy Alert
Inside Washington Publishers
1225 South Clark Street 703-416-8500
Suite 1400 800-424-9068
Arlington, VA 22202 Fax: 703-416-8543
E-mail: iwp@iwpnews.com
http://www.iwpnews.com

Addresses the legislative news and provides reports on the federal environmental policy process.
Publication Date: 1980
Paul Finger, Publisher

3713 Journal of the Air Pollution Control Association
Air Pollution Control Association
420 Fort Duquesne 412-232-3444
Boulevard #3
Pittsburgh, PA 15222
A comprehensive journal offering information to the environment and conservation industry.

3714 Journal of the Air and Waste Management Association
Air and Waste Management Association
420 Fort Duquesne Blvd. 412-232-3444
Pittsburgh, PA 15222 800-270-3444
Fax: 412-232-3450
E-mail: info@awma.org
http://www.awma.org

Published for the working environmental professional and carries peer-reviewed technical papers on a variety of topics form control technology to science.
Publication Date: 1951 Monthly
Maura Moktar, Managing Editor

3715 Population Reference Bureau: Household Transportation Use and Urban Pollution
1875 Connecticut Avenue NW 202-483-1100
Suite 520 800-877-9881
Washington, DC 20009 Fax: 202-328-3937
E-mail: popref@prb.org
http://www.prb.org

Publication Date: 1929
Peter Donaldson, President
Mary Mederios Kent, Editor

3716 Population Reference Bureau: Population & Environment Dynamics
1875 Connecticut Avenue NW 202-483-1100
Suite 520 800-877-9881
Washington, DC 20009 Fax: 202-328-3937
E-mail: popref@prb.org
http://www.prb.org

PRB publishes the quarterly Population Bulletin, the annual World Population Data Sheet, and PRB Reports on America, as well as specialized publications covering population and public

policy issues in the U.S. and abroad, particularlyin developing countries.
Publication Date: 1929
Peter Donaldson, President
Mary Mederios Kent, Editor

3717 **Population Reference Bureau: Water**
1875 Connecticut Avenue NW 202-483-1100
Suite 520 800-877-9887
Washington, DC 20009 Fax: 202-328-3937
E-mail: popref@prb.org
http://www.prb.org

Publication Date: 1929
Peter Donaldson, President
Mary Mederios Kent, Editor

3718 **Trinity Consultants Air Issues Review**
12770 Merit Drive 972-661-8100
Suite 900 800-229-6655
Dallas, TX 75251 Fax: 972-385-9203
E-mail: information@trinityconsultants.com
http://www.trinityconsultants.com
An environmental consulting company that assists industrial facilities with issues related to regulatory compliance and environmental management. Founded in 1974, this nationwide firm has particular expertise in air quality issues.Trinity also sells environmental software and professional education. T3, a Trinity Consultants Company, provides EH&S management information systems (EMIS) implementation and integration services.
Publication Date: 1990 8 pages Quarterly
John Hofmann, VP
Patrick Delamater, VP

3719 **Weather & Climate Report**
Nautilus Press
1054 National Press Building 202-347-6643
Washington, DC 20043
Reports on federal actions which impact weather, climate research and global changes in climate.
Monthly
ISSN: 0730-8256
John R Botzum, Editor

3720 **World Resource Review**
SUPCON International
PO Box 50303 630-910-1551
Palo Alto, CA 94303 Fax: 630-910-1561
E-mail: syshen@megsinet.net
http://www.globalwarming.net
For business and government readers, provides expert worldwide reviews of global warming and extreme events in relation to the management of natural, mineral and material resources. Subjects include global warming impacts onagriculture, energy, and infrastructure, monitoring of changes in resources using remote sensing, actions of national and international bodies, global carbon budget, greenhouse budget and more.
Publication Date: 1990 Quarterly
ISSN: 1042-8011
Dr. Sinya Shen, Production Manager

3721 **World Watch**
Worldwatch Institute
1776 Massachusetts Avenue NW 202-452-1999
Washington, DC 20036 Fax: 202-296-7365
E-mail: worldwatch@worldwatch.org
http://www.worldwatch.org
Magazine on global environmental issues.
Publication Date: 1975 40 pages
ISSN: 0896-0615
Ed Ayres, Author
Lester Brown, Founding Publisher
Lisa Mastny, Senior Editor

Periodicals: Business

3722 **AFE Journal**
8160 Corporate Park Drive 513-489-2473
Suite 125 Fax: 513-247-7422
Cincinnati, OH 45242 E-mail: mail@afe.org
http://www.afe.org
AFE Journal is a bimonthly publication from the Association for Facilities Engineering.
48 pages Bimonthly
ISSN: 1088-5900
Gabriella Jacobs, Author
Gabriella Jacobs, Editor

3723 **ALBC News**
American Livestock Breeds Conservancy
PO Box 477 919-542-5704
Pittsboro, NC 27312 Fax: 919-545-0022
E-mail: albc@albc-usa.org
http://www.albc-usa.org
ALBC News is a bi-monthly newsletter published by the American Livestock Breeds Conservancy.
Publication Date: 1987 20 pages Bi-Monthly
ISSN: 1064-1599
Cindy Rubel, Author
Cindy Rubel, Editor

3724 **Abstracts of Presentations**
Wildlife Society
5410 Grosvenor Lane 301-897-9770
Suite 200 Fax: 301-530-2471
Bethesda, MD 20814 E-mail: tws@wildlife.org
http://www.wildlife.org
A yearly publication of the Wildlife Society.
Publication Date: 1994 300 pages Yearly
Gene Pozniak, Production Editor

3725 **Advisor**
Great Lakes Commission
Eisenhower Corporate Park 734-665-9135
2805 South Industrial Hwy, Suite 100 Fax: 734-971-9150
Ann Arbor, MI 48104 E-mail: glc@great-lakes.net
http://www.glc.org
Covers economic and environmental issues of the Great Lakes region with a special focus on activities of the Great Lakes Commission.
Publication Date: 1955 12 pages Bi-Monthly
Julie Wagemakers, Production Manager

3726 **Agribusiness Fieldman**
Western Agricultural Publishing Company
4969 E Clinton Way 559-252-7000
Suite 104 Fax: 559-252-7387
Fresno, CA 93727
Aimed at keeping the professional agriculture consultant posted on changes in the agricultural-chemical industry. Provides news about pests and control measures for all segments of the agricultural-chemical industry.
Paul Baltimore, Publisher
Margi Katz, Editor

3727 **American Environmental Laboratory**
International Scientific Communications
PO Box 870 203-926-9300
Shelton, CT 06484 Fax: 203-926-9310
E-mail: iscpubs@iscpubs.com
http://www.iscpubs.com
Laboratory activities, new equipment, and analysis and collection of samples are the main topics.
Bi-Monthly
Brian Howard, Publisher/Editor-in-Chief

3728 **Annual Newsletter and Report**
The Peregrine Fund

5668 W Flying Hawk Lane
Boise, ID 83709
208-362-3716
Fax: 208-362-2376
E-mail: tpf@peregrinefund.org
http://www.peregrinefund.org

Yearly publication from The Peregrine Fund. Free with $25 membership fee.
Publication Date: 1970 Yearly
William Burnham, Author
Dr William Burnham, President

3729 Bison World
National Bison Association
8690 Wolff Ct.
Suite 200
Westminster, CO 80031
303-292-2833
Fax: 303-659-3739
E-mail: info@bisoncentral.com
http://www.bisoncentral.com

Published by the NBA, an organization of bison producers dedicated to awareness of the healthy properties of bison meat and bison production.
Publication Date: 1975 100 pages Quarterly
Sam Albrecht, Publisher
Laurie Dineen, Editor

3730 Business and the Environment
Cutter Information Corporation
37 Broadway
Suite 1
Arlington, MA 02474
781-648-8700
800-888-8939
Fax: 781-648-1950
E-mail: service@cutter.com
http://www.cutter.com

Environmental investment trends, deals and market developments.
Karen Fine Coburn, Publisher
Kathleen Victory, Editor

3731 CAC Annual Reports
Citizens Advisory Council
13th Floor, RCSOB
PO Box 8459
Harrisburg, PA 17105
717-787-4527
Fax: 717-787-2878
E-mail: mioff.stephanie@state.pa.us
http://www.cacdep.state.pa.us

Publisher by the Citizens Advisory Council.
Publication Date: 1977 20-40 pages Annual
Susan Wilson, Executive Director
Stephanie Mioff, Administrative Assistant

3732 Chemosphere
Pergamon Press
660 White Plains Road
Tarrytown, NY 10591
914-524-9200
Fax: 914-592-3625
Related to environmental affairs. Accepts advertising.
100 pages
T Stephen, Editor
Rosemarie Fazzolari, Advertising

3733 Connecticut Sea Grant
1080 Shennecossett Road
Groton, CT 06340
860-405-9128
Fax: 860-405-9109
http://www.seagrant.uconn.edu

Based at the University of Connecticut, CT Sea Grant is part of the National Sea Grant network, whose mission is the conservation and wise use of coastal and marine resources through research, education and outreach.
Peg Van Patten, Communications Director

3734 Earth First! Journal
PO Box 3023
Tucson, AZ 85702
520-620-6900
Fax: 413-254-0057
E-mail: collective@earthfirstjournal.org
http://www.earthfirstjournal.org/

Earth First! Journal was founded in 1979 in response to a lethargic, compromising and increasingly corporate environmental community. Earth First! takes a decidedly different tack toward environmental issues. We believe in using allthe tools in the toolbox, ranging from grassroots organizing and involvement in the legal process to civil disobedience and monkeywrenching.
Publication Date: 1979 64 pages Bimonthly
ISSN: 1055-8411

3735 Earth Island Journal
Earth Island Institute
2150 Allston Way
Suite 460
Berkeley, CA 94704-1375
415-788-3666
Fax: 415-788-7324
E-mail: editor@earthisland.org
http://www.earthisland.org

Publication from the Earth Island Institute - cutting-edge news, analysis and commentary on vital international environmental news.
Publication Date: 1987 64 pages Quarterly
ISSN: 1041-0406
Audrey Webb, Editor
Jason Mark, Editor

3736 Economic Opportunity Report
Business Publishers
PO Box 17592
Baltimore, MD 21297
301-587-6300
800-274-6737
Fax: 301-587-4530
E-mail: custserv@bpinews.com
http://www.bpinews.com

Antipoverty news coverage and analysis which gives insight into developments that affect social programs.
Publication Date: 1963
Leonard A Eiserer, Publisher
Beth Early, Operations Director

3737 Environmental Business Journal
ZweigWhite
321 Commonwealth Road
Suite 101
Wayland, MA 01778
508-651-1559
800-466-6275
Fax: 800-842-1560
E-mail: info@zweigwhite.com
http://www.environmentalbusinessjournal.com

EBJ is the leading business newsletter for the environmental industry, providing competive strategies, new business opportunities, and up-to-date market trends and data. Now published by ZweigWhite, the EBJ comes out every month.
Publication Date: 1988 16+ pages Monthly
, President

3738 Environmental Compliance Update
High Tech Publishing Company
PO Box 1275
Amherst, MA 01004
413-534-4500
Identifies and analyzes the issues and business and economic impact of environmental compliance laws and regulations. Monitors the relevant changes due to legislation, court decisions, private rulings and technology.
Lori Reilly, Editor

3739 Environmental News
CA Business Publications
PO Box 3359
Fort Worth, TX 76113
817-924-5301
Fax: 817-922-8893
E-mail: txenv@aol.com

Follows the progress of public environmental stock companies, provides updates on environmental contract opportunities, news of international environmental opportunities, and profiles innovative new companies.
Carolyn Ashford, Publisher/Editor

3740 Environmental Packaging
Thompson Publishing Group
1725 K Street NW
Suite 700
Washington, DC 20006
202-872-4000
800-677-3789
Fax: 202-739-9578
http://www.thompson.com

A newletter aimed at the environmental regulatory specialist, product development managers, purchasing managers, legal counsel and package designers covering state-by-state regulations and the FCA guidelines and enforcement.
Publication Date: 1972
Daphne Musselwhite, Publisher

3741 Florida Forests Magazine
Florida Forestry Association

PO Box 1696 850-222-5646
Tallahassee, FL 32302 Fax: 850-222-6179
E-mail: info@forestfla.org
http://www.floridaforest.org

A publication of the Florida Forestry Association.
Publication Date: 1997 26-32 pages Quarterly
J Doran, Executive VP

3742 George Miksch Sutton Avian Research Center Sutton Newsletter
PO Box 2007 918-336-7778
Bartlesville, OK 74005 Fax: 918-336-7783
E-mail: gmsarc@aol.com
http://www.suttoncenter.org

Newsletter published by George Miksch Sutton Avian Research Center.
Publication Date: 1990 8-10 pages Semiannual
Steve Sherrod, Executive Director
Alan Jenkins, Assistant Director

3743 Green Business Letter
Tilden Press
6 Hillwood Place 202-332-1700
Oakland, CA 94610 Fax: 202-332-3028
E-mail: gbl@greenbiz.com
http://www.greenbiz.com

Hands-on journal for environmentally conscious companies, covering management strategies, facilities management, personnel policies and procurement with environmental consciousness. Emphasis on products, resources and how-toinformation.
8 pages
ISSN: 1056-490X
Joel Makower, Editor

3744 In Business: The Magazine for Sustainable Enterprises and Communities
JG Press, Inc
419 State Avenue 610-967-4135
Emmaus, PA 18049 E-mail: advert@jgpress.com
http://www.jgpress.com

Jerome Goldstein, Editor

3745 International Environment Reporter
Bureau of National Affairs
1231 25th Street NW 202-452-4200
Washington, DC 20037 800-372-1033
Fax: 202-822-8092
http://www.bna.com

A four-binder information and reference service covering international environmental law and developing policy in the major industrial nations.
William A Beltz, Publisher

3746 International Environmental Systems Update
BSI Management Systems
12110 Sunset Hills Road 703-437-9000
Suite 200 800-862-4977
Reston, VA 20190 Fax: 703-435-7979
E-mail: solutions@bsiamercas.com
http://www.bsiamericas.com

Provides accurate, up-to-date and useful information for environmental professionals around the globe. Monthly publication brings current environmental events into the limelight, dissecting complex issues, helping hundreds oforganizations improve their environmental and business preformance.
Publication Date: 1994 24 pages Monthly
ISSN: 1079-0837
Marcus Darby, Publisher

3747 McCoy's RCRA Unraveled
McCoy & Associates
12596 West Bayaud Avenue 303-526-2674
Suite 210 Fax: 303-526-5471
Lakewood, CO 80228 E-mail: info@mccoyseminars.com
http://www.understandRCRA.com

This book addresses the most troublesome areas in 40 CFR Parts 261 and 262 of the federal regulations. Our engineers have researched every scrap of guidance EPA has ever issued on these troublesome topics, studied the Federal Registerpreamble language, and talked to thousands of people who attented our RCRA seminars and shared their real-world experiences. It includes a keyword index with more than 1,300 entries, 200 probing examples from EPA's own guidance documents and ahelpful acronym list.
Publication Date: 2005 828 pages Yearly
Paul Gallagher, President
Nancy Pribble, Marketing Manager

3748 NFPA Journal
One Batterymarch Park 617-770-3000
Quincy, MA 02169 Fax: 617-770-0700
E-mail: nfpa@nfpa.org
http://www.nfpa.org

A bi-monthly journal published by the National Fire Protection Association.
Bi-Monthly

3749 NSS News
National Speleological Society
2813 Cave Avenue 256-852-1300
Huntsville, AL 35810 Fax: 256-851-9241
E-mail: nss@caves.org
http://www.caves.org

Published by the National Speleological Society.
Publication Date: 1942 Monthly
ISSN: 0027-7010
Dave Bunnell, Editor

3750 Newsleaf
4949 Tealtown Road 513-831-1711
Milford, OH 45150 Fax: 513-831-8052
E-mail: cnc@cincynature.org
http://www.cincynature.org

Newsleaf is a quarterly publication for Cincinatti Nature Center members. This publication provides informative articles that teach readers about native flora and fauna.
Publication Date: 1965 20-24 pages Quarterly
Rhonda Barnes-Kloth, Communications Manager

3751 Proceedings of the Desert Fishes Council
Desert Fishes Council
PO Box 337 760-872-8751
Bishop, CA 93515 http://www.desertfishes.org
Yearly publication from Desert Fishes Council.
Publication Date: 1969 Yearly
ISSN: 1068-0381
E P Pister, Executive Secretary

3752 Proceedings of the Southeastern Association of Fish and Wildlife Agencies
8005 Freshwater Farms Road 850-893-1204
Tallahassee, FL 32308 Fax: 850-893-6204
E-mail: SEAFWA@aol.com
http://www.seafwa.org

Proceedings of the SEAFWA - an annual publication.
Publication Date: 1947 4-900 pages Yearly
Robert M Brantly, Executive Secretary

3753 Pumper
COLE Publishing
1720 Maple Lake Dam Road 715-546-3346
PO Box 220 800-257-7222
Three Lakes, WI 54562 Fax: 715-546-3786
E-mail: info@pumper.com
http://www.pumper.com

Emphasis on companies, individuals and industry events while focusing on customer service, environmental issues and employment trends.
Publication Date: 1947
Ken Lowther, Editor

3754 Regulatory Update
Arkansas Environmental Federation
1400 W Markham Street 501-374-0263
Suite 302 Fax: 501-374-8752
Little Rock, AR 72201 http://www.environmentark.org

The AEF focuses on practical, common-sense laws and regulations based on sound science; a teamwork approach to compliance; waste minimization and pollution prevention. The AEF enables information to be exchanged on a daily basisbetween its members, government regulators, and policy makers.
Publication Date: 1967 Semi-Annual
Randy Thurman, Executive Director

3755 Risk Policy Report
Inside Washington Publishers
1225 South Clark Street
Suite 1400
Arlington, VA 22202
703-416-8500
800-424-9068
E-mail: iwp@iwpnews.com
http://www.iwnews.com

Contains analysis, great perspectives, industry news, policymaking profiles and a calendar of events.
Monthly
David P Clarke, Publisher/Editor

3756 Semillero
731 8th Street SE
Washington, DC 20003
202-547-3800
Fax: 202-546-4784
E-mail: etoledo@newforestsproject.com
http://www.newforestsproject.com

Our electronic publication has more than 2500 subscribers in the US and Latin America. It provides useful information and references to specific resources regarding agro-forestry, rural development and grant information.
Publication Date: 1982
Erick Toledo and Catalina Serna, Author
Erick Toledo, Director

Periodicals: Design & Architecture

3757 LICA News
Land Improvement Contractors of America
3080 Ogden Avenue
Suite 300
Lisle, IL 60532
630-548-1984
Fax: 630-548-9189
E-mail: nlica@aol.com
http://www.licanational.com

Official publication of Land Improvement Contractors of America.
Gerald J Biuso Sr, Executive VP
Eileen Levy, Publisher

3758 MSW Management
Forester Communications
PO Box 3100
Santa Barbara, CA 93130
805-682-1300
Fax: 805-682-0200
E-mail: erosion@ix.netcom.com
http://www.mswmanagement.com

Provides general news on facility construction, financing, new equipment and revenue issues.
Publication Date: 1991 7 Times Yearly
Daniel Waldman, Publisher

Periodicals: Disaster Preparedness & Response

3759 Hazard Technology
EIS International
555 Herndon Parkway
Herndon, VA 20170
703-478-9808
Fax: 703-787-6720

Application of technology to the field of emergency and environmental management to save lives and protect property.
James W Morentz PhD, Publisher
Leslie Atkin, Managing Editor

3760 Hazardous Materials Newsletter
Hazardous Materials Publishing
243 West Main Street
Kutztown, PA 19530
610-683-6721
Fax: 610-683-3171
E-mail: lheffner@hazmat-tsp.com
http://www.hazmatpublishing.com

Focuses on response to and control of hazardous materials emergencies. Particularly appropriate tools, equipment, materials, methods, procedures, strategies and lessons learned. Addresses leak, fore and spill control for incidentcommanders and experienced responders, including incident clauses, prevention and remedial actions; decisionmaking; scene management; control and containment; response teams; and product identification and hazards.
12 pages

3761 Natural Hazards Observer
Natural Hazards Center
University of Colorado
482 UCB
Boulder, CO 80309
303-492-6818
Fax: 303-492-2151
E-mail: hazctr@colorado.edu
http://www.colorado.edu/hazards

A periodical of the Natural Hazards Center that covers current disaster issues; new international, national, and local disaster management, mitigation, and education programs; hazards research; political and policy developments; newinformation sources and Web sites; upcoming conference; and recent publications
Bi Monthly
Dan Whipple, Editor
Kathleen Tierney, Director

Periodicals: Energy & Transportation

3762 AERO SunTimes
Alternative Energy Resources Organization
432 N Last Chance Gulch
Helena, MT 59601
406-443-7272
Fax: 406-442-9120
E-mail: aero@aeromt.org

The SunTimes is the newsletter for AERO. The organization is a statewide grassroots group whose members work together to strengthen communities through promoting sustainable agriculture, local food production and citizen-based SmartGrowth community planning.
Publication Date: 1978 4-24 pages Quarterly
ISSN: 1046-0993
Kiki Hubbard, Editor
Jean Duncan, Editor

3763 Butane-Propane News
Butane-Propane News, Inc
PO Box 660698
Arcadia, CA 91066
626-357-2168
800-214-4386
Fax: 626-303-2854
E-mail: arey@bpnews.com
http://www.bpnews.com

Offers information to professionals that are involved in the distribution, production, shipping and sales of butane and propane in the US and internationally. $32 for US one year subscription; $60 for international one yearsubscription.
Publication Date: 1939 48-96 pages Monthly
ISSN: 0007-7259
Ann Rey, Editor/Director

3764 Cars of Tomorrow
Northeast Sustainable Energy Association
50 Miles Street
Greenfield, MA 01301
413-774-6051
Fax: 413-774-6053
E-mail: nesea@nesea.org
http://www.nesea.org

Offers a look at the energy options of vehicles of the future.
Curriculum
David Barclay, Executive Director
Arianna Alexsandra Grindrod, Education Director

3765 E&P Environment
Pasha Publications
1600 Wilson Boulevard
Suite 600
Arlington, VA 22209
703-528-1244
800-424-2908
Fax: 703-528-1253

Reports on environmental regulations, advances in technology and litigation aimed specifically at the exploration and production segments of the oil and gas industry.
Harry Baisden, Group Publisher
Michael Hopps, Editor

3766 Energy Engineering
Association of Energy Engineers
4025 Pleasantdale Road
Suite 420
Atlanta, GA 30340
770-447-5083
Fax: 770-446-3969
E-mail: webmaster@aeecenter.org
http://www.aeecenter.org

Engineering solutions to cost efficiency problems and mechanical contractors who design, specify, install, maintain, and purchase non-residential heating, ventilating, air conditioning and refrigeration equipment and components.
Wayne Turner, Editor-in-Chief

3767 Energy Journal
International Association for Energy Economics
28790 Chagrin Boulevard
Suite 350
Cleveland, OH 44122
216-464-5365
Fax: 216-464-2737
E-mail: iaee@iaee.org
http://www.iaee.org

Promotes the advancement and dissemination of new knowledge on energy matters and related topics. Topics include: transportation, electricity markets, environmental issues, natural gas topics, and carbon emissions reduction.
Publication Date: 1980 200 pages Quarterly
David L Williams, Executive Director

3768 Getting Around Clean & Green
Northeast Sustainable Energy Association
50 Miles Street
Greenfield, MA 01301
413-774-6051
Fax: 413-774-6053
E-mail: nesea@nesea.org
http://www.nesea.org

This interdisciplinary science/social studies curriculum allows students to explore the transportation and environmental issues in their own lives. Activities cover: transportation systems, health impacts, environmental andtransportation histories, carpooling, and mass transit.
90 pages Curriculum
David Barclay, Executive Director
Arianna Alexsandra Grindrod, Education Director

3769 Getting Around Without Gasoline
Northeast Sustainable Energy Association
50 Miles Street
Greenfield, MA 01301
413-774-6051
Fax: 413-774-6053
E-mail: nesea@nesea.org
http://www.nesea.org

An interdisciplinary unit that explores the feasibility of getting around without using gasoline. Students can conduct various activities to compare powering vehicles with gasoline versus electricity.
60 pages S & H Only
David Barclay, Executive Director
Arianna Alexsandra Grindrod, Education Director

3770 Heliographs
Illinois Solar Energy Association
PO Box 634
Wheaton, IL 60189
630-260-0424
E-mail: info@illinoissolar.org
http://www.illinoissolar.org

Publication Date: 1975 12 pages Quarterly

3771 IAEE Membership Directory
International Association for Energy Economics
28790 Chagrin Boulevard
Suite 350
Cleveland, OH 44122
216-464-5365
Fax: 216-464-2737
E-mail: iaee@iaee.org
http://www.iaee.org

One of the three periodicals put out by the International Association for Energy Economics (IAEE). It lists members contact information and affiliation and general association information. Also available online.
Annual
David L Williams, Executive Director

3772 IAEE Newsletter
International Association for Energy Economics
28790 Chagrin Boulevard
Suite 350
Cleveland, OH 44122
216-464-5365
Fax: 216-464-2737
E-mail: iaee@iaee.org
http://www.iaee.org

Association information including: upcoming events, conferences, special reports, affiliate activities, and chapter news.
Quarterly
David L Williams, Executive Director

3773 International Journal of Hydrogen Energy
5783 SW 40 Street
#303
Miami, FL 33155
305-284-4666
Fax: 305-284-4792
E-mail: info@iahe.org
http://www.iahe.org

A monthly publication serving to inform scientists and the public of advances made in hydrogen energy research and development.
Publication Date: 1976 120 pages Monthly
ISSN: 0360-3199
T Nejat Veziroglu, Author
T Neja Veziroglu, Editor-in-Chief

3774 Midwest Renewable Energy Association Newsletter
7558 Deer Road
Custer, WI 54423
715-592-6595
Fax: 715-592-6596
E-mail: info@the-mrea.org
http://www.the-mrea.org

ReNews includes articles on energy issues, book reviews, case studies, and other general information about renewable energy.
Quarterly
Tehri Parker, Executive Director

3775 Northeast Sun
Northeast Sustainable Energy Association
50 Miles Street
Greenfield, MA 01301
413-774-6051
Fax: 413-774-6053
E-mail: nesea@nesea.org
http://www.nesea.org

Promotes responsible use of energy for a stronger economy and cleaner environment. Northeast Sun is a bi-annual Spring and Fall publication that includes articles by leading authorities on sustainable energy practices, energyefficiency and renewable energy, and each Fall issue includes the Sustainable Green Pages Directory of engery professionals in the Northeast. Subscription is free with membership.
Bi-Annual
David Barclay, Executive Director
Arianna Alexsandra Grindrod, Education Director

3776 Nuclear Monitor
Nuclear Information & Resource Services
1424 16th Street NW
Suite 404
Washington, DC 20036
202-328-0002
Fax: 202-462-2183
E-mail: nirsnet@nirs.org
http://www.nirs.org

Nuclear power, radioactive waste and sustainable energy news for environmental activities, state and local officials and investment communities.
12 pages Monthly
Michael Mariotte, Editor

3777 Nuclear Waste News
Business Publishers
8737 Colesville Road
PO Box 17592
Baltimore, MD 21297
301-589-5103
800-274-6737
Fax: 301-589-8493
E-mail: custserv@bpinews.com
http://www.bpinews.com

Worldwide coverage of the nuclear waste management industry, including waste generation, radiological environmental remediation, packaging, transport, processing and disposal.
Weekly
Leonard A Eiserer, Publisher
Beth Early, Associate Publisher

3778 **Radwaste Magazine**
American Nuclear Society
555 North Kensington Avenue
LaGrange Park, IL 60526
708-352-6611
800-323-3044
Fax: 708-352-0499
E-mail: radwaste@ans.org
http://www.ans.org

Addresses issues in all fields of radioactive waste management, removal, handling, disposal, treatment, cleanup and environmental restoration.
6x per Year
Nancy Zacha, Publisher

3779 **ReNews**
Midwest Renewable Energy Association
PO Box 249
Amherst, WI 54406
715-592-6595
Fax: 715-592-6596
E-mail: info@the-mrea.org
http://www.the-mrea.org

ReNews is a quarterly newsletter that includes articles on energy issues, book reviews, case studies, and other general information about renewable energy.
Quarterly

3780 **Solar Energy**
Elsevier Science
360 Park Avenue South
11th Floor
New York, NY 10010
212-989-5800
Fax: 212-633-3990
E-mail: usinfo-f@elsevier.com
http://www.elsevier.com

John A Duffie, Editor

3781 **Solar Energy Report**
PO Box 782
Rio Vista, CA 94571
949-837-7430
Fax: 949-709-8043
http://www.calseia.org
Bi-Monthly

3782 **Solar Reflector**
Texas Solar Energy Society
PO Box 1447
Austin, TX 78767
512-326-3391
800-465-5049
Fax: 512-444-0333
E-mail: info@txses.org
http://www.txses.org

A Texas Solar Energy Society publication. Promotes the wise use of sustainable and non-polluting resources.
Quarterly
Natalie Marquis, Executive Director

3783 **Solar Today**
American Solar Energy Society
2400 Central Avenue
Suite A
Boulder, CO 80301
303-443-3130
Fax: 303-443-3212
E-mail: ases@ases.org
http://www.ases.org
Provides information and case histories and reviews of a variety of renewable energy technologies, including solar, wind, biomass and geothermal.
Donna McClane, Publications

3784 **Sustainable Green Pages Directory**
Northeast Sustainable Energy Association
50 Miles Street
Greenfield, MA 01301
413-774-6051
Fax: 413-774-6053
E-mail: nesea@nesea.org
http://www.nesea.org
The SPG Directory lists over 30 categories of sustainable energy professionals working throughout the Northeast, including architects, engineers, builders, energy auditors, consultants and renewable energy installers and manufacturers.It is the largest directory of its kind and the only one that targets the Northeastern USA. Published in the Northeast Sun magazine and onlines.
September Annual
David Barclay, Executive Director
Arianna Alexandra Grindrod, Education Director

Periodicals: Environmental Engineering

3785 **Air and Waste Management Association's Magazine for Environmental Managers**
Air and Waste Management Association
One Gateway Center
420 Fort Duquesne Blvd., 3rd Floor
Pittsburgh, PA 15222
412-232-3444
800-270-3444
Fax: 412-232-3450
E-mail: info@awma.org
http://www.awma.org

A magazine that contains sections of Washington and Canadian reports, a calendar of events, government affairs, news focus, campus research, business briefs, district control news, porfessional development programs, professionalservices and other issues facing the environmental professionals.
Todd Zahniser, Publisher/Editor

3786 **Asbestos & Lead Abatement Report**
Business Publishers
PO Box 17592
Baltimore, MD 21297
301-589-5103
800-274-6737
Fax: 301-589-8493
E-mail: bpinews@bpinews.com
http://www.bpinews.com

Tracks the major legal, legislative, regulatory, business and technological developments in the asbestos and lead abatement industries.
Weekly
Leonard A Eiserer, Publisher
Beth Early, Associate Publisher

3787 **Curt B Beck Consulting Engineer: Newsletter**
408 W Kingsmill Street
PO Box 2442
Pampa, TX 79006
806-665-9281
888-665-9281
Fax: 806-665-1965
E-mail: curtbbeck@cableone.net
http://www.pan-tex.net/usr/b/beck

Pollution control services.
Publication Date: 1984 Monthly
Curt B Beck, Owner

3788 **Defense Cleanup**
Business Publishers
PO Box 17592
Baltimore, MD 21297
301-587-6300
800-274-6737
Fax: 301-587-4530
E-mail: bpinews@bpinews.com
http://www.bpinews.com

Covers the latest news and analysis of defense cleanup activity. Including base remediation and closure, contract awards and site cleanups.
Weekly
Leonard A Eiserer, Publisher
Beth Early, Associate Publisher

3789 **EI Digest**
Environmental Information
PO Box 390266
Edina, MN 55439
952-831-2473
Fax: 952-831-6550
E-mail: ei@enviro-information.com
http://www.envirobiz.com
Contains market studies of commercial hazardous waste management companies with in-depth analysis of trends in policy, regulations, technology and business.
Publication Date: 1983
ISSN: 1042-251X
Cary Perket, Editor

3790 **Environment**
Helen Dwight Reid Educational Foundation

1319 18th Street NW
Washington, DC 20036
202-296-6267
800-365-9753
Fax: 202-296-5149
E-mail: subscribe@heldref.org
http://www.heldref.org

Provides environment professionals and concerned citizens with authoritative yet accessible articles that provide critical analysis of environmental science and policy issues, book recommendations, commentaries, news briefs and reviewson environmental websites and major governmental and institutional reports.
Publication Date: 1958 48 pages Monthly
ISSN: 0013-9157
Douglas Kirkpatrick, Executive Director
Barbara T Richman, Managing Editor

3791 Environment 21

Florida Environments Publishing
4010 Newberry Road
#F
Gainesville, FL 32607
352-373-1401
Fax: 352-373-1405
E-mail: info@enviroworld.com
http://www.enviroworld.com

Regulations, wildlife, hazard waste/materials, ground/surface/drinking water and other issues concerning Florida's environment are emphasized in this publication for the environmental management team.
Dave Newport, Publisher

3792 Environmental Engineer Magazine

American Academy of Environmental Engineers
130 Holiday Court
Suite 100
Annapolis, MD 21401
410-266-3311
Fax: 410-266-7653
E-mail: info@aaee.net
http://www.aaee.net

Official magazine of the American Academy of Environmental Engineers. It addresses issues and practice with: updates on legal developments affecting environmental engineering, documentation of the profession's heritage, articles onenvironmental policy, and profiles of leading environmental engineers.
Quarterly
Lawrence C Pencak, Executive Director
Yolanda Y Moulden, Production Manager

3793 Environmental Engineering Science

Mary Ann Liebert
140 Huguenot Street
3rd Floor
New Rochelle, NY 10801
914-740-2100
800-MLI-EBER
Fax: 914-740-2101
E-mail: info@liebertpub.com
http://www.liebertpub.com

The focus is on pollution control of the suface, ground, and drinking water, and highlight research news and product developments that aid in the fight against pollution.
Bi-Monthly
ISSN: 1092-8758
Mary Ann Liebert, Publisher
Dumpnico Grosso PhD, Editor-in-Chief

3794 Environmental Manager

Air and Waste Management Association
420 Fort Duquesne Blvd
3rd Floor
Pittsburgh, PA 15222
412-232-3444
800-270-3444
Fax: 412-232-3450
E-mail: info@awma.org
http://www.awma.org

Features timely articles on business, regulatory, and technical issues of interest to the environmental industry.
Tim Keener, Editor
Lisa Bucher, Managing Editor

3795 Environmental and Energy Study Institute

122 C Street NW
Suite 630
Washington, DC 20001
202-628-1400
Fax: 202-628-1825
E-mail: eesi@eesi.org
http://www.eesi.org

A nonprofit organization dedicated to promoting environmentally sustainable societies. EESI believes meeting this goal requires transitions to social and economic patterns that sustain people, the environment and the natural resourcesupon which present and future generations depend. EESI produces credible, timely information and innovative public policy initiatives that lead to these transitions. These products take the form of publications, briefings, work shops and taskforces.
Publication Date: 1984
Carol Werner, Executive Director

3796 Federation of Environmental Technologists

9451 N 107th Street
Milwaukee, WI 53224
414-354-0070
Fax: 414-354-0073
E-mail: info@fetinc.org
http://www.fetinc.org

A nonprofit organization formed to assist industry in interpretation of and compliance with environmental regulations. Membership is open to all industries, municipalities, organizations and individuals concerned about environmentalregulations. Currently there are approximately 1000 members and 125 patron companies.
Publication Date: 1982 Monthly
Barbara Hurula, Executive Director

3797 Food Protection Trends

International Association for Food Protection
6200 Aurora Avenue
Suite 200W
Des Moines, IA 50322
515-276-3344
800-369-6337
Fax: 515-276-8655
E-mail: info@foodprotection.org
http://www.foodprotection.org

Published as the general membership publication by the International Association for Food Protection, each issue contains refereed articles on applied research, applications of current technology and general interest subjects for foodsafety professionals. Regular features include industry and association news, an industry related product section and a calendar of meetings, seminars and workshops.Updates of government regulations and sanitary design is also featured. All membersreceive FPT.
Publication Date: 1981 80+ pages Monthly
ISSN: 1043-3546
David W Tharp, Executive Director
Lisa K Hovey, Managing Editor

3798 Hazardous Materials Intelligence Report

World Information Systems
129 Mount Auburn
Cambridge, MA 02238
617-491-5100
Fax: 617-492-3312

Provides news analysis on environmental business, hazardous materials, waste management, pollution prevention and control. Covers regulations, legislation and court decisions, new technology, contract opportunities and awards andconference notices.
Richard S Golob, Publisher
Roger B Wilson Jr, Editor

3799 Hazmat Transport News

Business Publishers
PO Box 17592
Baltimore, MD 21297
301-587-6300
800-274-6737
Fax: 301-587-4530
E-mail: bpinews@bpinews.com
http://www.bpinews.com

Reports on the regulatory, enforcement, legislative and litigation developments affecting hazardous materials transportation.
Monthly
Leonard A Eiserer, Publisher
Beth Early, Associate Publisher

3800 Integrated Waste Management

McGraw Hill
PO Box 182604
Columbus, OH 43272
877-833-5524
Fax: 614-759-3749
http://www.mcgraw-hill.com

Articles geared toward integration of solid waste management.
8 pages
Kevin Hamilton, Publisher

3801 International Journal of Phytoremediation

Taylor & Francis Inc

325 Chestnut Street 413-549-5170
Suite 800 Fax: 413-549-0579
Philadelphia, PA 19106 http://www.aehs.com
An official journal of the Association for Environmental Health and Sciences (AEHS). Dedicated to current laboratory and field research on how to use plant systems to remediate contaminated environments.
6 Issues Yr
ISSN: 1522-6514
Jason White, Managing Editor

3802 Iowa Academy of Science Journal
Iowa Academy of Science
UNI - 175 Baker Hall 319-273-2021
2607 Campus Street Fax: 319-273-2807
Cedar Falls, IA 50614-0508 E-mail: iascience@uni.edu
http://www.iacad.org
Quarterly

Craig Johnson, Executive Director

3803 Journal of Environmental Engineering
American Society of Civil Engineers
1801 Alexander Bell Drive 703-295-6300
Reston, VA 20191 Fax: 703-295-6211
E-mail: onlinejls@asce.org
http://http://pubs.asce.org/journals/environmental
The journal of Environmental Engineering presents a collection of broad interdisciplinary information on the practice and status of research in environmental engineering science, systems engineering, and sanitation.
Publication Date: 1875
Raymond A Ferrara, Editor
Melissa Junior, Director, Journals

3804 Journal of Environmental Quality
American Society of Agronomy
677 S Segoe Road 608-273-8080
Madison, WI 53711 Fax: 608-273-2021
http://www.agronomy.org
Written for university, government and industry scientists interested in the impacts of environmental perturbations on the biological and physical sciences. Domestic member price: $50 (Int'l $103); Domestic non-member price: $650(Int'l $703).
Bi-Monthly
Dennis Corwin, Editor
Susan Ernst, Managing Editor

3805 Journal of Environmental and Engineering Geophysics: JEEG
1720 South Bellaire Street 303-531-7517
Suite 110 Fax: 303-820-3844
Denver, CO 80222 E-mail: staff@eegs.org
http://www.eegs.org
A peer reviewed journal of the EEGS made available to members and a variety of libraries.
Publication Date: 1992 Quarterly
ISSN: 1083-1363
Kathie Barstnar, Executive Director
Janet Simms, Editor

3806 Journal of IEST
Institute of Environmental Sciences & Technology
2340 S. Arlington Heights Rd 847-981-0100
Suite 100 Fax: 847-981-4130
Arlingotn Heights, IL 60005 E-mail: iest@iest.org
http://www.iest.org
An annual journal published by the Institute of Environmental Sciences & Technology.
Publication Date: 1957 185 pages Annual
ISSN: 1098-4321
Charles W Berndt, VP Communications

3807 Kennedy-Jenks Consultants: Alert Newsletter
303 Second Street 415-243-2150
Suite 300 S Fax: 415-896-0999
San Francisco, CA 94107 http://www.kennedyjenks.com
Environmental engineering consulting company.
Publication Date: 1990 6 pages 3 times/year
Gordon Morris, Graphics Services Manager
Rena Chin, Editor

3808 Kennedy-Jenks Consultants: Spotlights
303 Second Street 415-243-2150
Suite 300 S Fax: 415-896-0999
San Francisco, CA 94107 http://www.kennedyjenks.com
Environmental engineering consulting company.
Publication Date: 1981 12 pages 3 times/year
Gordon Morris, Graphics Services Manager
Rena Chin, Editor

3809 Lead Detection & Abatement Contractor
IAQ Publications
7920 Norfolk Avenue 301-913-0115
Suite 900 Fax: 301-913-0119
Bethesda, MD 20814 E-mail: iaqpubs@aol.com
http://www.iaqpubs.com
Feature articles include new on legislation, operational and safety issues that affect the removal of lead and lead by-products from paint, water, soil, and air.
Susan Valenti, Editor

3810 Leading Edge
Society of Exploration Geophysicists
8801 South Yale Avenue 918-497-5500
Tulsa, OK 74137 Fax: 918-497-5557
E-mail: jlawnick@seg.org
http://www.seg.org
Addresses a broad spectrum of topics related to applied geophysics. Material immediately accessible to a broad audience.
Publication Date: 1930 116 pages
ISSN: 1070-485X
Dean Clark, Editor
Linda Holeman, Associate Editor

3811 McCoy's CAA Unraveled
McCoy & Associates
12595 W Bayaud AvenueRoad 303-526-2674
Suite 210 Fax: 303-526-5471
Lakewood, CO 80228 E-mail: info@mccoyseminars.com
http://www.understandRCRA.com

414 pages

3812 McCoy's RCRA Reference
McCoy & Associates
12595 W Bayaud AvenueRoad 303-526-2674
Suite 210 Fax: 303-526-5471
Lakewood, CO 80228 E-mail: info@mccoyseminars.com
http://www.understandRCRA.com

1190 pages

3813 Medical Waste News
Business Publishers
PO Box 17592 301-589-5103
Baltimore, MD 21297 800-274-6737
Fax: 301-589-8493
E-mail: custserv@bpinews.com
http://www.bpinews.com
Reports on the rapidly evolving legislative and regulatory actions in medical waste management. Includes coverage of incineration, laboratory wastes, infection control, liability and legal issues and waste transport.
Publication Date: 1963
Leonard A Eiserer, Publisher
Beth Early, Operations Director

3814 New York State Conservationist
NYS Department of Environmental Conservation
625 Broadway 518-402-8047
2nd Floor 800-678-6399
Albany, NY 12233 Fax: 518-402-9036
E-mail: dinnelson@gw.dec.state.ny.us
http://www.dec.state.ny.us/

An informative and entertaining full-color bi-monthly magazine featuring New York State's natural resources and peoples' enjoyment of those resources.
Bi-Monthly
ISSN: 0010-650X
David Nelson, Editor

3815 Noise Control Engineering Journal
Institute of Noise Control Engineering
PO Box 17592 515-294-6142
Baltimore, MD 21297 Fax: 515-294-3528
E-mail: ibo@inceusa.org
http://www.inceusa.org
The technical publication of the Institute of Noise Control Engineering. It contains technical articles on all aspects of noise control engineering.
Bi-Monthly
ISSN: 0736-2501
Joseph M Cuschieri, Executive Director
Courtney Burroughs, Editor in Chief

3816 Noise Regulation Report
Business Publishers
PO Box 17592 301-589-5103
Baltimore, MD 21297 800-274-6737
Fax: 301-589-8493
E-mail: custserv@bpinews.com
http://www.bpinews.com
Exclusive coverage of airport, highway, occupational and open space noise, noise control and mitigation issues.
Publication Date: 1963
Leonard A Eiserer, Publisher
Beth Early, Operations Director

3817 Plumbing Standards
American Society of Sanitary Engineering
901 Canterbury 440-835-3040
Suite A Fax: 440-835-3488
Westlake, OH 44145 E-mail: info@asse-plumbing.org
http://www.asse-plumbing.org
Disseminates industry-wide technical information on standards, updates, water, wastewater, plumbing design, and other topics related to the water industry.
Shannon M Corcoran, Executive Director
Megan Bryant, Managing Editor

3818 Pollution Engineering
Cahners Business Information
2000 Clearwater Drive 630-320-7000
Oak Brook, IL 60523 Fax: 630-288-8282
http://www.pollutionengineering.com
Serves the field of pollution control in manufacturing industries, utilities, consulting engineers and constructors. Also serves government agencies including administration of federal, state and local environmental programs.
ISSN: 0032-3640
Barbara Olsen, Publisher
Roy Bigham, Managing Editor

3819 RMT Newsletter
744 Heartland Trail 608-831-4444
PO Box 8923 800-283-3443
Madison, WI 53717 Fax: 608-831-3334
E-mail: info@rmtinc.com
http://www.rmtinc.com
Global engineering and management consulting firm that develops environmental solutions for industry. With a 600 person staff and 20 offices throughout the US and Europe helping clients sustain the environment while meeting theirbusiness objectives. Engineers, scientists and construction managers can take a project from conception through successful completion. Expertise includes air, water and waste permitting, remediation, hazardous/solid waste management, air pollutioncontrol and more.
8 pages Quarterly
Jodi Burmester, Marketing Communications

3820 SPAC Newsletter
Soil and Plant Analysis Council
300 Speedway Cirlce 402-476-0300
Suite 2 Fax: 402-476-0302
Lincoln, NE 68502 E-mail: bvaughan@ogsource.com
http://www.spcouncil.com
Quarterly newsletter.
Quarterly
Mark Flock, President
Bryon Vaughan, Secretary/Treasurer

3821 Sludge
Business Publishers
PO Box 17592 301-589-5103
Baltimore, MD 21297 800-274-6737
Fax: 301-589-8493
E-mail: custserv@bpinews.com
http://www.bpinews.com
Premier insider guide to the biosolids industry. Follows developments in and management of beneficial use and wastewater residuals, with practical information about industrial sludge, incineration, special wastes, permits andlandfills.
BiWeekly
Leonard A Eiserer, Publisher
Beth Early, Operations Director

3822 Soil & Sediment Contamination:An International Journal
Taylor & Francis Inc
325 Chestnut Street 413-549-5170
Suite 800 Fax: 413-549-0579
Philadelphia, PA 19106 http://www.achs.com
An official journal of the Association for Environmental Health and Sciences (AEHS). An internationally peer-reviewed publication that focuses on sediment and soil contamination.
Bi Monthly
ISSN: 1532-0383
James Dragun, Editor-in-Chief
Paul Kostecki, Managing Editor

3823 Solid Waste Report
Business Publishers
PO Box 17592 301-589-5103
Baltimore, MD 21297 800-274-6737
Fax: 301-589-8493
E-mail: custserv@bpinews.com
http://www.bpinews.com
Comprehensive news and analysis of legislation, regulation and litigation in solid waste management. Regularly features federal rules, congressional actions, state updates and business trends.
Weekly
Leonard A Eiserer, Publisher
Beth Early, Associate Publisher

3824 Waste News
Crain Communications
1725 Merriman Road 330-836-9180
#300 Fax: 330-836-1692
Akron, OH 44313 E-mail: editorial@wastenews.com
http://www.wastenews.com
Editorial content focuses on waste management and recycling issues, primarily how businesses deal with the waste they generate. Covers waste management service providers, legistlative and regulatory environmental issues, emergingtechnologies, municipal recycling and waste issues, commodity market price, mergers, aquisitions and expansions.
Publication Date: 1995 Bi-Weekly
ISSN: 1091-699
Allan Gerlat, Editor
Brennan Lafferty, Managing Editor

3825 Widener University: International Conference on Solid Waste Proceedings
One University Place 610-499-4042
Chester, PA 19013 Fax: 610-499-4461
E-mail: solid.waste@widener.edu
http://www.widener.edu/solid.waste

Publication of the annual conference on solid waste technology and management. Over 100 speakers from 35 countries present their work. Proceedings available.
Publication Date: 1983 Quarterly
ISSN: 1088-1697
Ronald L Mersky, Editor
Iraj Zandi, Founder

Periodicals: Environmental Health

3826 **American College of Toxicology**
9650 Rockville Pike 301-571-1840
Bethesda, MD 20814 Fax: 301-571-1852
E-mail: ekagan@actox.org
http://www.actox.org

The American College of Toxicology is a 501-0-3 nonprofit organization. It is not a degree-granting organization. The American College of Toxicology is dedicated to providing an interactive forum for the advancement and exchange oftoxicologic information between industry, goverment, and academia. There is an annual meeting in November each year. The ACT publiches a journal, International Journal of Toxicology on a bi-monthly basis.

ISSN: 1091-5818
Carol L Lemire, Executive Director
Eve Gamzu Kagan, Assistant Executive Director

3827 **American Journal of Public Health**
American Public Health Association
800 I Street NW 202-777-2742
Washington, DC 20001 888-320-2742
Fax: 202-777-2533
E-mail: ellen.meyer@apha.org
http://www.apha.org

Peer-reviewed journal of the American Public Health Association (APHA) for public health workers and academics. Its emphasis is on research and practioners experiences.
12 Issues/Yr
Ellen Meyer, Director Publications
Nancy Johnson, Executive Editor

3828 **Applied and Environmental Microbiology**
American Society for Microbiology
1752 N Street NW 202-737-3600
Washington, DC 20036 Fax: 202-942-9333
E-mail: oed@asmusa.org
http://www.asm.org

Contains current significant research in industrial microbiology, microbial ecology, biotechnology, public health microbiology and food microbiology.
Samuel Kaplan, Chairman Publications Board
Linda M Illig, Director Journals

3829 **Asbestos & Lead Abatement Report**
Business Publishers
PO Box 17592 301-589-5103
Baltimore, MD 21297 800-274-6737
Fax: 301-589-8493
E-mail: custserv@bpinews.com
http://www.bpinews.com

Contains articles on regulation compliance, environmental trends and business opportunities.
Leonard A Eiserer, Publisher

3830 **Aviation, Space and Environmental Medicine**
Aerospace Medical Association
320 S Henry Street 703-739-2240
Alexandria, VA 22314 Fax: 703-739-9652
E-mail: pday@asma.org
http://www.asma.org

Provides contact with physicians, life scientists, bioengineers, and medical specialists working in both basic medical research and in its clinical applications.
Publication Date: 1929 962 pages Monthly
ISSN: 0095-6562
Sarah A Nunneley MD, Author
Sarah A Nunneley, Editor-in-Chief
Sarah A Pierce-Rubio, Editor Assistant

3831 **Bio Integral Resource Center: Common Sense Pest Control**
PO Box 7414 510-524-2567
Berkeley, CA 94707 Fax: 510-524-1758
E-mail: birc@igc.org
http://www.birc.org

Features least toxic solutions to pest problems of the home and garden. Those who are chemically sensitive and looking for alternatives may find what they need in the Quarterly.
Publication Date: 1984 24 pages Quarterly
ISSN: 8756-7881
Dr. William Quarles, Executive Director

3832 **Bio Integral Resource Center: IPM Practitioner**
PO Box 7414 510-524-2567
Berkeley, CA 94707 Fax: 510-524-1758
E-mail: birc@igc.org
http://www.birc.org

Focuses on management alternatives for pests such as insects, mites, ticks, vertebrates, weeds and plant pathogens.
Publication Date: 1979 24 pages 10 Times a Year
ISSN: 0738-969x
Dr. William Quarles, Executive Director

3833 **Center for Statistical Ecology & Environmental Statistics: Environmental & Ecological Statistics**
Kluwer Academic Publishers
Pennsylvania State University 814-865-9442
421 Thomas Building, Dept of Statistics Fax: 814-865-1278
University Park, PA 16802 E-mail: gpp@stat.psu.edu
http://www.stat.psu.edu/~gpp

The Center is the first of its kind in the world and enjoys national and international reputation. They have an ongoing program of research that integrates statistics, ecology and the environment. The emphasis is on the environment andcollaborative research, training and exposition on improving the quantification and communication of man's impact on the environment. Major interest also lies in statistical investigations of the impact of the environment on man. Contact them forfull listings.
Publication Date: 1984 110 pages Quarterly
ISSN: 1352-8505
Ganapati P Patil, Editor-in-Chief

3834 **EH&S Software News Online**
Donley Technology
220 Garfield Avenue 804-224-9427
PO Box 152 Fax: 804-224-7958
Colonial Beach, VA 22443 E-mail: donleytech@donleytech.com
http://www.donleytech.com

Reports on news and upgraded software products, database, and on-line systems from commercial developers and government resources.
Quarterly
John Donley, Editor
Elizabeth Donley, Managing Editor/Publisher

3835 **Enterprise Software: Essential EH&S**
Essential Technologies
1401 Rockville Pike 301-284-3000
#500 Fax: 301-284-3001
Rockville, MD 20852 E-mail: info@essentech.com
http://www.essential-technologies.com

Integrated solutions for emissions management, hazard communication, compliance management, occupational health and safety and contingency management.
James Morentz, Publisher

3836 **Environmental Connections**
Connecticut College

270 Mohegan Avenue 860-439-5417
Box 5293 Fax: 860-439-2418
New London, CT 06320 E-mail: ccbes@conncoll.edu
http://www.ccbes.conncoll.edu

Publication Date: 1998 10 pages 2 times per year
Robert Askins, Director
Diane Whitelaw, Assistant Director

3837 Environmental Dimensions
Trine Publishers
28 Kilbarry Crescent 613-749-3735
Ottawa, Ontario K1K Fax: 613-749-6807
E-mail: trine@istar.ca
http://www.envirodim.com

Provides the environmental professionals with news and information on current environmental health issues, solution, and hazards, as well as examining governmental policies, legal news and Canada's environmental preformance.
22 times per year
Roland Blassnig, Editor

3838 Environmental Health Letter
Business Publishers
PO Box 17592 301-589-5103
Baltimore, MD 21297 800-274-6737
Fax: 301-589-8493
E-mail: custserv@bpinews.com
http://www.bpinews.com

Comprehensive coverage of the latest policies and ground-breaking research that explores the potential links between environmental factors and human health.
8 pages
Leonard A Eiserer, Publisher
Beth Early, Operations Director

3839 Environmental Health perspectives
National Inst. of Environmental Health Sciences
C/O Blogar & Partners 919-653-2581
14600 Weston Parkway, Suite 300 866-541-3841
Cary, NC 27513 Fax: 919-678-8696
E-mail: ehponline@niehs.nih.gov
http://www.ehponline.org

Annual subscription.
224 pages Monthly
Hugh Tilson, Editor-in-Chief
Karen A Warren, Business Manager

3840 Florida Journal of Environmental Health
Florida Environmental Health Association
5101 Ortega Blvd 904-384-0838
Jacksonville, FL 32210 E-mail: Scexedir@aol.com
http://www.feha.org

Promotes public health by means of advanced environmental control.
Quarterly
ISSN: 0897-1823
Lu Grimm, Editor
Jennifer M Willimas, Executive Director

3841 Healthy Schools Network Newsletter
773 Madison Avenue 518-462-0632
Albany, NY 12208 Fax: 518-462-0433
E-mail: info@healthyschools.rog
http://www.healthyschools.org

HSN is a nationally recognized state-based advocate for the protection of children's environmental health in schools. Engages in research, education, outreach, technical assistance and coalition building to create schols that areenvironmentally responsible to children, and to their communities. Publishes a quarterly newsletter and maintains an Information Clearinghouse and Referral Service.
Quarterly
Claire L Barnett, Executive Director

3842 Human Ecology Action League Magazine
2250 N Druid Hills Road NE 404-248-1898
Atlanta, GA 30329 Fax: 404-248-0162
E-mail: HEALNatnl@aol.com
http://members.aol.com/HEALNatnl/index/html

The Human Ecology Action League Inc (HEAL) is a nonprofit organization founded in 1977 to serve those whose health has been adversely affected by environment exposures; to provide information to those who are concerned about the healtheffects of chemicals; and to alert the general public about the potential dangers of chemicals. Referrals to local HEAL chapters and other support groups are available from the League.
Publication Date: 1977 35 pages Quarterly
ISSN: 8755-7878
Diane Thomas, Editor

3843 Indoor Environment Review
IAQ Publications
7920 Norfolk Avenue 301-913-0115
Suite 900 Fax: 301-913-0119
Bethesda, MD 20814 E-mail: iaqpubs@aol.com
http://www.iaqpubs.com

New technology, research and legislation concerning all indoor air and water quality issues.
Robert Morrow, Editor

3844 Industrial Health and Hazards Update
InfoTeam
PO Box 15640 954-473-9560
Plantation, FL 33318 Fax: 954-473-0544
E-mail: infoteamma@aol.com

Covers occupational safety, health hazards, and disease; mitigation and control of hazardous situations; waste recycling and treatment.
20 pages
Dr. David Allen, Associate Editor

3845 Journal of Environmental Health
National Environmental Health Association
720 S Colorado Boulevard 303-756-9090
Suite 1000-N Fax: 303-691-9490
Denver, CO 80246 E-mail: staff@neha.org
http://www.neha.org

A practical journal containing information on a variety of environmental health issues.
Publication Date: 1937 70-76 pages 10 Times a Year
ISSN: 0022-0892
Nelson E Fabain, Executive Director
Julie Collins, Content Editor

3846 Journal of Medical Entomology
Journal of Entomology
10001 Derekwood Lane 301-731-4535
Suite 100 Fax: 301-731-4538
Lanham, MD 20706 E-mail: esa@entsoc.org
http://www.entsoc.org

Contributions report on all phases of medical entomology and medical acarology, including the systematics and biology of insects, acarines, and other arthropods of public health and veterinary significance.
John Edman, Editor-in-Chief

3847 Journal of Pesticide Reform
PO Box 1393 541-344-5044
Eugene, OR 97440 Fax: 541-344-6923
E-mail: info@pesticide.org
http://www.pesticide.org

Pesticide factsheets, alternatives factsheets for common pest problems, and helpful information on how to take action for change are featured in this journal. Each issue also includes updates on NCAP's work, news on pesticide issues,and reviews of books and videos.
Publication Date: 1984 24 pages Quarterly
Caroline Cox, Editor
Norma Grier, Executive Director

3848 Nation's Health, The
American Public Health Association

800 I Street NW 202-777-2742
Washington, DC 20001 888-320-2742
Fax: 202-777-2533
E-mail: ellen.meyer@apha.org
http://www.apha.org

Monthly newspaper of the American Public Health Association (APHA). It focuses on the latest public health news that public health professionals need to know such as food safety, racial and ethnic disparities, patients' rights,environmental issues, and health screening.

10 Issues/Yr
Ellen Meyer, Director Publications
Michele Late, Executive Editor

3849 National Institute of Environmental Health Sciences Journal
111 T.W. Alexander Drive 919-496-2433
Research Triangle Park, NC 27709 Fax: 919-496-8276
E-mail: olden@NIEHS.nih.gov
http://www.niehs.nih.gov

The National Institute of Environmental Health Sciences is the principal federal agency for basic biomedical research on the health effects of environmental agents. It is the headquarters for the National Toxicology Program whichcoordinates toxicology studies within the Department of Health and Human Services.

Publication Date: 1972 150 pages Monthly
ISSN: 0091-6765
Kenneth Olden PhD, Director

3850 Natural Resources Council of America: Environmental Resource Handbook
Universal Reference Publications
1616 P Street 202-232-6631
NW Suite 340 Fax: 240-465-0467
Washington, DC 20036 http://www.NaturalResourcesCouncil.org

Environmental Resource Handbook updates.

4 pages
Laura Seal, Membership Coordinator

3851 Natural Resources Council of America: Conservation Voice
1616 P Street 202-232-6631
NW Suite 340 Fax: 240-465-0467
Washington, DC 20036 http://www.naturalresourcescouncil.org

Charts the news, events, and personnel that shape the face of the conservation movement and includes the quarterly supplemental publication NEPA news.

Publication Date: 1958 6-8 pages Bi-Monthly
Andrea Yank, Executive Director

3852 Natural Resources Council of America: NEPA News
1616 P Street 202-232-6631
NW Suite 340 Fax: 240-465-0467
Washington, DC 20036 http://www.naturalresourcescouncil.org

Publication Date: 1994 8 pages Quarterly
Andrea Yank, Executive Director

Periodicals: Gaming & Hunting

3853 American Bass Association Newsletter
402 N Prospect Avenue 310-376-1026
Redondo Beach, CA 90277 Fax: 310-376-5072
E-mail: feedback@americanbass.com
http://www.americanbass.com

Publication Date: 1989 24 pages Quarterly
Craig Sutherland, Editor

3854 IPPL News
PO Box 776 843-871-2280
Summerville, SC 29484 Fax: 843-871-7988
E-mail: info@ippl.org
http://www.ippl.org

Educates readers in more than 50 countries about action that can be taken to protect primates.

Publication Date: 1974 32 pages 3 Times a Year
ISSN: 1040-3027
Dr Shirley McGreal, Chairperson
Marjorie Doggett, Secretary

3855 International Game Fish Association Newsletter
300 Gulf Stream Way 954-927-2628
Dania Beach, FL 33004 Fax: 954-924-4299
E-mail: hq@igfa.org
http://www.igfa.org

Founded as record-keeper and to maintain fishing rules. Today, emphasis is on conservation and education. Newsletters published are World Record Game Fish, annually and The International Angler, bi-monthly.

Bi-Monhtly
Rob Kramer, President

3856 JAKES Magazine
Wild Turkey Center 803-637-3106
PO Box 530 800-THE-NWTF
Edgefield, SC 29824 Fax: 803-637-0034
E-mail: nwtf@nwtf.net
http://www.nwtf.org

JAKES (Juniors Acquiring Knowledge, Ethics and Sportsmanship) is a magazine which provides fun and educational articles focusing on young hunters, outdoor activities, the environment and other items of interest to readers 17 years oldand younger. Free with membership.

Quarterly
Matt Lindler, Editor

3857 Mid-Atlantic Fishery Management Council Newsletter
300 S New Street 302-674-2331
Federal Building, Room 2115 877-446-2362
Dover, DE 19904 Fax: 302-674-5399
http://www.mafmc.org

Publication Date: 1998 8 pages Quarterly
Daniel T Furlong, Executive Director

3858 Turkey Call
770 Augusta Road 803-637-3106
PO Box 530 800-THE-NWTF
Edgefield, SC 29824 Fax: 803-637-0034
E-mail: nwtf@nwtf.net
http://www.nwtf.org

A magazine for turkey hunting enthusiasts, provides articles to help you improve your hunting skills and learn how to enhance your land for wildlife. Free with membership.

Bi-Monthly
Doug Howlett, Editor

3859 Wheelin' Sportsmen
770 Augusta Road 803-637-3106
PO Box 530 800-THE-NWTF
Edgefield, SC 29824 Fax: 803-637-0034
E-mail: nwtf@nwtf.net
http://www.nwtf.org

Magazine for all disabled people and their able-bodied partners who are interested in the outdoors, especially recreational shooting, hunting and fishing. Free with membership.

Quarterly
Karen Roop, Editor

3860 Women in the Outdoors
770 Augusta Road 803-637-3106
PO Box 530 800-THE-NWTF
Edgefield, SC 29824 Fax: 803-637-0034
E-mail: nwtf@nwtf.net
http://www.nwtf.org

Magazine that delivers features on a variety of outdoor topics of interest to the novice and experienced outdoorswoman. Free with membership.

Quarterly
Karen Roop, Editor

Periodicals: Habitat Preservation & Land Use

3861 ANJEC Report
Association/New Jersey Environmental Commissions
PO Box 157
Mendham, NJ 07945
973-539-7547
Fax: 973-539-7713
E-mail: info@anjec.org
http://www.anjec.org

Nonprofit organization promoting public interest in natural resorce protection and supporting municipal environmental commissions throughout New Jersey.
Publication Date: 1970 32 pages Quarterly
Sandy Batty, Executive Director

3862 Afield
4705 University Drive
Suite 290
Durham, NC 27707
919-403-8558
Fax: 919-403-0379
E-mail: northcarolina@tnc.org
http://www.nature.org/northcarolina

Published by The Nature Conservancy, saving the last great places of North Carolina.
Quarterly Newsletter
Katherine Skinner, Executive Director

3863 Aldo Leopold Foundation: The Leopold Outdoor
E13701 Levee Road
Baraboo, WI 53913
608-355-0279
Fax: 608-356-7309
E-mail: mail@aldoleopold.org
http://www.aldoleopold.org

A nonprofit organization founded in 1982, works to promote the philosophy of Aldo Leopold and the land ethic he so eloquently defined in his writing. The foundation actively integrates programs on land stewardship, environmentaleducation and scientific research to promote care of natural resources and have an ethical relationship between people and land.
Publication Date: 1999 8 pages Quarterly
Steve Swenson, Ecologist
Buddy Huffaker, Executive Director

3864 American Association for Advancement of Science: Animal Keeper's Forum
1200 New York Avenue Northwest
Washington, DC 20005
202-326-6400
Fax: 202-289-4985
E-mail: webster@aaas.org
http://www.aaas.org

The American Association for the Advancement of Science is the world's largest general science and publisher of the peer-reviewed journal. With more than 138,000 members and 275, AAAS serves as an authoritative source for informationon the latest developments in science and bridges gaps among scientists, policy- makers and the public to advance science and science education.
Publication Date: 1947 54 pages Monthly
ISSN: 0164-9531
Alan Leshner, Executive Director

3865 American Birding Association: Birding
4945 N Street
Suite 200
Colorado Springs, CO 80919
719-578-9703
800-850-2473
Fax: 719-578-1480
E-mail: member@aba.org
http://www.aba.org

The American Birding Association represents the interests of birdwatchers in various arenas, and helps birders increase their knowledge, skills, and enjoyment of birding. ABA also contributes to bird conservation by linking the skillsof its members to on-the-ground projects. ABA promotes field-birding skills through meetings, workshops, equipment, and guided involvement in birding, promoting national and international birders networks and publications.
Publication Date: 1972 8 pages Bi Monthly
Rob Robinson, Executive Director

3866 American Birding Association: Winging It
4945 N. 30th St.
Suite 200
Colorado Springs, CO 80919
719-578-9703
800-850-2473
Fax: 719-578-1480
E-mail: member@aba.org
http://www.americanbirding.org

The American Birding Association represents the interests of birdwatchers in various arenas, and helps birders increase their knowledge, skills, and enjoyment of birding. ABA also contributes to bird conservation by linking the skillsof its members to on-the-ground projects. ABA promotes field-birding skills through meetings, workshops, equipment, and guided involvement in birding, promoting national and international birders networks and publications.
Publication Date: 1989 24 pages Bi Monthly
Steve Runnels, Executive Director
Rick Wright, Editor

3867 American Entomologist
Journal of Entomology
10001 Derekwood Lane
Suite 100
Lanham, MD 20706
301-731-4535
Fax: 301-731-4538
E-mail: esa@entsoc.org
http://www.entsoc.org

American Entomologist is a quarterly, general interest entomology magazine written for both scientists and nonscientists. It publishes colorful, illustrated feature articles, peer-reviewed scientific reports, provocative and humorouscolumns, letters, book reviews, and obituaries.
Publication Date: 1955 64 pages Quarterly
ISSN: 1046-2821
Gene Kristky, Editor-in-Chief

3868 American Forests Magazine
PO Box 2000
Washington, DC 20013
202-955-4500
800 368 5748
Fax: 202-955-4588
E-mail: info@amfor.org
http://www.americanforests.org

Published by American Forests, the oldest national citizens conservation organization in the US.
Quarterly
Gerald Gray, VP Forest Policy Center
Deborah Gangloff, Executive Director

3869 Annals of the Entomological Society of America
Journal of Entomology
10001 Derekwood Lane
Suite 100
Lanham, MD 20706
301-731-4535
Fax: 301-731-4538
E-mail: esa@entsoc.org
http://www.entsoc.org

Contributions report on the basic aspects of the biology of anthropods and are divided into categories by subject matter; systematics; ecology and population biology; arthropods in relation to plant disease; conservation biology andbiodiversity; physiology, biochemistry, and toxicology; morphology, history, and fine sructure; genetics and behavior.
Bi-Monthly
Joe B Keiper, Editor-in-Chief

3870 Annual Review of Entomology
Annual Reviews
10001 Derekwood Lane
Suite 100
Lanham, MD 20706
301-731-4535
Fax: 301-731-4538
E-mail: esa@entsoc.org
http://www.entsoc.org

This is published in Januray and made available through ESA on a regular subscription basis. The series occupies a special place within the field of entomology. Authoritative critical reviews by eminent scientists provide a valuableresource for students, teachers, and researchers: specialists and nonspecialists.
Yearly
Alan Kahan, Director Communications

3871 Appalachian Mountain Club
Appalachian Mountain Club Books

5 Joy Street 617-523-0655
Boston, MA 02108 800-262-4455
Fax: 617-523-0722
E-mail: information@outdoors.org
http://www.outdoors.org

The AMC, founded in 1876, promotes the protection, enjoyment, and wise use of the mountains, rivers and trails of the Northeast. We encourage people to enjoy and protect the natural world because we believe that successful conservationdepends on this experience. The AMC publishes an award-winning magazine and more than 60 guide books to the Northeast.
Andrew Falender, Executive Director
Clair O'Connell, Director Development

3872 Arthropod Management Tests
Journal of Entomology
10001 Derekwood Lane 301-731-4535
Suite 100 Fax: 301-731-4538
Lanham, MD 20706 E-mail: esa@entsoc.org
http://www.entsoc.org

This is published in late spring. The purpose is to promote timely dissemination of information on preliminary and routine screening tests on management of arthropods, both beneficial and harmful. Pest management methods tested andreported may include the use of chemical pesticides as well as other materials or agents, such as insect growth regulators, pheromones, natural enemies for biological control, or pest-resistant plants/animals. Reports are based on tests conducted byreseachers.
Yearly
David L Kerns, Editor-in-Chief

3873 Biodiversity Institute Newsletter
University of Kansas
Dyche Hall
Lawrence, KS 66045 785-864-4540
Fax: 785-864-5335

A comprehensive research, graduate education and public service institution dedicated to biodiversity science and collections. Collections of more than 7 million plant and animal specimens, with particular strengths in neotropicalamphibians, great plains, flora, bees and antarctic plant fossils.
Publication Date: 1978 6 pages Quarterly
Dr Leonard Krishtalka, Director

3874 Blowhole
3625 Brigantine Boulevard 609-266-0538
PO Box 773 Fax: 609-266-6300
Brigantine, NJ 08203 E-mail: mmsc@verizon.net
http://marinemammalstrandingcenter.org

A quarterly newsletter published by the Marine Mammal Stranding Center.
Publication Date: 1978 8 pages Quarterly
Robert C Schoelkopf, Director
Sheila M Dean, Co-Director

3875 Carolina Bird Club
6325 Falls of the Neuse Road 910-791-5726
STE 9 PMB 150 Fax: 910-791-7228
Raleigh, NC 27615 E-mail: hq@carolinabirdclub.org
http://www.carolinabirdclub.org

A nonprofit educational and scientific association, open to anyone interested in the study and conservation of wildlife, particularly birds. Meets each winter, spring and fall. Meeting sites are selected to give participants anopportunity to see many different kinds of birds. Guided field trips, informative programs and business sessions are combined for an exciting weekend of meeting with people who share an enthusiasm and concern for birds.
Publication Date: 1937 Quarterly
ISSN: 0009-1987
Dana Harris, HQ Secretary
Ken Fiala, Editor

3876 Coalition for Education in the Outdoors
2217 Professional Studies Building 607-753-4971
SUNY Cortland Fax: 607-753-5982
Cortland, NY 13045 E-mail: info@outdooredcoalition.org
http://www.outdooredcoalition.org

A network of organizations, business, institutions, centers, agencies, and associations linked and communicating in support of the broad purpose of education in, for, and about the outdoors. Takes a board view of outdoor education andseeks not to duplicate or compete with the work of organizations, but to provide services not easily performed by other groups.
Publication Date: 1987 48-52 pages Bi-Annual
ISSN: 1065-5204
Charles Yaple, Executive Director

3877 College of Tropical Agriculture and Human Resources: Impact Report
University of Hawaii
3050 Maile Way 808-956-7056
Gilmore 119 Fax: 808-956-5966
Honolulu, HI 96822 E-mail: ocs@ctahr.hawaii.edu
http://www.ctahr.hawaii.edu

The vision of the college is to be the premier resource for tropical agricultural systems and resource management in the Asia-Pacific region. Its mission outlines a commitment to the preparation of students and all citizens of Hawaiifor life in a global community through research and education programs supporting tropical agricultural systems that foster viable communities, a diversified economy and a healthy environment.
Annual
Andrew G Hashimoto, Dean/Director

3878 Connecticut Woodlands
Middlefield 860-346-2372
16 Meriden Road Fax: 860-347-7463
Rockfall, CT 06481 E-mail: conn.forest.assoc@snet.net
http://www.ctwoodlands.org

Quarterly publication of the Connecticut Forest and Park Association, an organization for forest and wildlife conservation. Develops outdoor recreation and natural resources. Provides forest management, construction of hiking trailsand consultation in the areas of forestry and environment.
Quarterly
Chris Woodside, Editor

3879 Conservancy of Southwest Florida
Eye On The Issues
1450 Merrihue Drive 232-262-0304
Naples, FL 34102 Fax: 232-262-0672
E-mail: info@conservancy.org
http://www.conservancy.org

8 pages Quarterly
Kathy Prosser, President/CEO
Sheila Etalamaki, Director Finance

3880 Conservation & Natural Resources: Water Resources Division, Nevada Wildlife Almanac
901 S. Stewart Street 775-681-2800
Suite 2002 Fax: 775-684-2811
Carson City, NV 89701 E-mail: hricci@wr.state.nv.us
http://ndwr.state.nv.us

Publication Date: 1996 12 pages Twice/year
Hugh Ricci, State Engineer

3881 Conservation Commission News
New Hampshire Association of Conservation Comm.
54 Portsmouth Street 603-224-7867
Concord, NH 03301 E-mail: info@nhacc.org
http://www.nhacc.org

Encourage conservation and appropriate use of New Hampshire's natural resources by providing assistance to New Hampshire's municipal conservation commissions and by facilitating communication among commissions and between commissionsand other public and private agencies involved in conservation.
8 pages
Marjory Swope, Publisher

3882 Conservation Communique
Wyoming Association of Conservation Districts
517 East 19th Street 307-632-5716
Cheyenne, WY 82001 Fax: 307-638-4099
http://www.conservewy.com

Quarterly
Kelly Brown, Editor

3883 Conservation Conversation
Montana Association of Conservation Districts
PO Box 99
Cadillac, MI 49601
231-876-0328
Fax: 231-876-0372
E-mail: macd@macd.org
http://www.macd.org
Quarterly

3884 Conservation Leader
Utah Association of Conservation Districts
1860 North 100 East
Logan, UT 84341
435-753-6029
Fax: 435-755-2117
Quarterly

3885 Conservation Notes: New England Wildflower Society
180 Hemenway Road
Framingham, MA 01701
508-877-7630
508-877-6553
Fax: 508-877-3658
E-mail: information@newenglandwild.org
http://www.newenglandwild.org

36 pages Yearly
Debbi Edelstein, Executive Director
Frances Clark, Chair, Board of Trustees

3886 Conservation Partner
Arkansas Association of Conservation Districts
101 E Capitol
Suite 350
Little Rock, AR 72201
501-682-2915
Fax: 501-682-3991
http://www.aracd.org
Quarterly
Debbie Moreland, Program Administrator

3887 Conservation Visions
Nebraska Association of Resources Districts
601 S 12th Street
Suite 201
Lincoln, NE 68508
402-471-7670
Fax: 402-471-7677
E-mail: nard@nrdnet.org
http://www.nrdnet.org
Bi-Monthly
Dean E Edson, Executive Director

3888 Conservogram
Soil and Water Conservation Society
945 Southwest Ankeny Road
Ankeny, IA 50023
515-289-2331
Fax: 515-289-1227
E-mail: pubs@swcs.org
http://www.swcs.org

Published for the professionals in the natural resource fields, and contains highlights on the news and ideas in the preservation of natural resources.
Monthly
Suzi Case, Editor

3889 Consultant
Assoc of Consulting Foresters of America, Inc
312 Montgomery Street
Suite 208
Alexandria, VA 22314
703-548-0990
888-540-8733
Fax: 703-548-6395
E-mail: director@acf-foresters.org
http://www.acf-foresters.org

Publication from Association of Consulting Foresters of America, Inc.
Publication Date: 1948
Lynn C Wilson, Executive Director

3890 Cornell Lab of Ornithology: Birdscope
Birdscope
159 Sapsucker Woods Road
Ithaca, NY 14850
607-254-2451
Fax: 607-254-2415
E-mail: cornellbirds@cornell.edu
http://www.birds.cornell.edu

Quarterly,Newsletter
Miyoko Chu, Communications Director

3891 Cornell Lab of Ornithology: Living Bird
Birdscope
159 Sapsucker Woods Road
Ithaca, NY 14850
607-254-2475
Fax: 607-254-2415
E-mail: cornellbirds@cornell.edu
http://www.birds.cornell.edu

Quarterly, Magazine
Miyoko Chu, Communications Director

3892 Department of Natural Resources
301 Centennial Mall South
PO Box 94676
Lincoln, NE 68509
402-471-2363
Fax: 402-471-2900
E-mail: webmaster@dnr.state.ne.us
http://www.dnr.state.ne

Quarterly
Roger K Patterson, Director

3893 District Connection Newsletter
North Carolina Assoc. of Soil/Water Cons. Dist.
1614 Mail Service Center
Raleigh, NC 27699
919-733-2302
Fax: 919-715-3559
http://www.enr.state.nc.us\DSWC

Monthly
David Williams, Acting Director

3894 E Magazine
Doug Moss
28 Knight St
Norwalk, CT 06851
203-854-5559
Fax: 203-866-0602
E-mail: jessica@emagazine.com
http://www.emagazine.com

A comprehensive magazine dealing with environmental issues and national conservation concerns.
Publication Date: 1990 64 pages Bimonthly
Doug Moss, Publisher/Executive Director

3895 ESA Newsletter
Journal of Entomology
10001 Derekwood Lane
Suite 100
Lanham, MD 20706
301-731-4535
Fax: 301-731-4538
E-mail: esa@entsoc.org
http://www.entsoc.org

ESA Newsletter is a monthly publication presenting timely information of interest to ESA members. In addition to feature articles, it contains meeting announcements, society business, listing of employment oppurtunities, notice ofgrants and awards, member profiles, and branch and section news.
Monthly
Lisa Spurlock, Editor

3896 Eagle Nature Foundation Ltd: Bald Eagle News
Bald Eagle News
300 E Hickory
Apple River, IL 61001
815-594-2306
Fax: 815-594-2305
E-mail: eaglenature.tni@juno.com
http://eaglenature.com

A quarterly publication from the Eagle Nature Foundation.
Publication Date: 1992 20 pages Quarterly
Terrence N Ingram, Executive Director

3897 Earth Steward
Michigan Association of Conservation Districts
3001 Coolidge Road
Suite 250
East Lansing, MI 48823-6362
517-324-4421
Fax: 517-324-4435
E-mail: macd@macd.org
http://www.macd.org

Quarterly membership newsletter
Quarterly
Mike Lawless, President MACD State Council
Lori Phalen, Executive Director

3898 Ecosphere
Forum International
91 Gregory Lane
Suite 21
Pleasant Hill, CA 94523
925-997-1864
800-252-4475
Fax: 925-946-1500
E-mail: fti@foruminternational.com
http://www.foruminternational.com

Accepts advertising. The first ever environmental/ecological magazine. It is dedicated to the interrelations of man in nature and

a balanced approach of its biological, economic, socio-political and spiritual components. Since 1965.
Publication Date: 1965 16-48 pages Bi Monthly
Dr. Nicolas Hetzer, Production Manager
J McCormack, Circulation Director

3899 Elm Leaves
Elm Research Institute
11 Kit Street
Keene, NH 03431
603-358-6198
800-367-3567
Fax: 603-358-6305
E-mail: libertyelm@webryders.com
http://www.libertyelm.com

A semi annual publication published by the Elm Research Institute. Free with membership.
Publication Date: 1967 4-9 pages Semi-Annually
John Hansel, Editor/Executive Director
Yvonne Spalthoff, Assistant Director

3900 Environmental Concern: The Wonders of Wetlands, an Educators Guide
POW-The Planning of Wetlands
201 Boundary Lane
PO Box P
St Michaels, MD 21663
410-745-9620
Fax: 410-745-3517
E-mail: order@wetland.org
http://www.wetland.org

Since its founding in 1972, EC has been specializing in consulting, planning design, education services, construction services and research related to all aspects of wetlands. As wetlands and contiguous upland forests and meadows areinteracting ecosystems EC specializes in consulting, planning, design, and project supervision services for such upland ecosystem constructions and restorations for the purpose of wetland buffers, reforestation, wildlife habitat and critical areas ofpreservation.
Publication Date: 1995 Quarterly
ISSN: 1095-2063
Suzanne Pittengar Slear, President

3901 Environmental Entomology
Journal of Entomology
10001 Derekwood Lane
Suite 100
Lanham, MD 20706
301-731-4535
Fax: 301-731-4538
E-mail: esa@entsoc.org
http://www.entsoc.org

Contributions report on the interaction of insects with biological, chemical, and physiological and chemical ecology (abiotic effects, pheromonea, effects of miscellaneous pollutants), community/ecosystem ecology (trophic-levelsstudies, associations), population ecology (mating, reproduction, movement, behavior, parasitism, predation, microbial ecology, insect-plant relations), pest management and sampling (integrated pest management, sampling, distribution), and biologicalcontrol.
Bi-Monthly
E Alan Cameron, Editor-in-Chief

3902 Everglades Reporter
Friends of the Everglades
7800 Red Road
Suite 215K
South Miami, FL 33143
305-669-0858
Fax: 305-669-4108
E-mail: info@everglades.org
http://www.everglades.org

Protecting the Everglades. A bi-annual publication from Friends of the Everglades.
Publication Date: 1971 8 pages Quarterly
David Reiner, President

3903 Fisheries
American Fisheries Society
5410 Grosvenor Lane
Bethesda, MD 20814
301-897-8616
Fax: 307-897-8096
E-mail: main@fisheries.org
http://www.fisheries.org

Peer-reviewed articles that address contemporary issues and problems, techniques, philosophies and other areas of interest to the general fisheries profession. Monthly features include letters, meeting notices, book listings andreviews, environmental essays and organization profiles.
Kristin Merriman-Clarke, Editor

3904 Fisheries Focus: Atlantic
Atlantic States Marine Fisheries Commission
1444 I Street Northwest
6th Floor
Washington, DC 20005
202-289-6400
Fax: 202-289-6051
E-mail: comments@asmfc.org
http://www.asmfc.org

12 pages Monthly
John V O'Shea, Executive Director
Tina L Berger, Public Affairs/Resource Spec

3905 Forest History Society
701 William Vickers Avenue
Durham, NC 27701
919-682-9319
Fax: 919-682-2349
E-mail: coakes@duke.edu
http://www.foresthistory.org

The Forest History Society is a non-profit educational institution that links the past to the future by identifying, collecting, preserving, interpreting, and disseminating information on the history of people, forests, and theirrelated resources.
Publication Date: 1946
Cheryl Oakes, Librarian
Steven Anderson, President

3906 Forest Voice
Native Forest Council
PO Box 2190
Eugene, OR 97402
541-688-2600
Fax: 541-461-2156
E-mail: info@forestcouncil.org
http://www.forestcouncil.org

Quarterly publication from Native Forest Council.
Publication Date: 1989 16 pages Quarterly
ISSN: 1069-2002
Timothy Hermach, President

3907 Forestry Source
Society of American Foresters
5400 Grosvenor Lane
Bethesda, MD 20814
301-897-8720
866-897-8720
Fax: 301-897-3690
E-mail: safweb@safnet.org
http://www.safnet.org

Tabloid newsletter covering important information regarding critical issues in forestry research and technology, legislative updates and news about SAF programs and activities on a national and local level.
20 pages Monthly
Matt Walls, Editor

3908 Game & Fish Commission Wildlife Management Division Newsletter
2 Natural Resources Drive
Little Rock, AR 72205
501-223-6300
800-364-4263
Fax: 501-223-6452
http://www.agfc.com

Dedicated to managing wildlife in the state of Arkansas.
Publication Date: 1920 33-35 pages 5x year
Doyle Shook, Chief

3909 Golden Gate Audubon Society
2530 San Pablo Avenue
Suite G
Berkeley, CA 94702
510-843-2222
Fax: 510-843-5351
E-mail: ggas@goldengateaudubon.org
http://www.goldengateaudubon.org

Monthly publication from Golden Gate Audubon Society. Published 10 times yearly.
Publication Date: 1917 12 pages Monthly
ISSN: 0164-971x
Mark Welther, Executive Director

3910 Great Plains Native Plant Society Newsletter
PO Box 641
Hot Springs, SD 57747
605-745-3397
Fax: 605-745-3397
E-mail: cascade@gwtc.net

The Society's mission is to engage in scientific research regarding plants of the Great Plains of North America; to disseminate this knowledge through the creation of one or more educational botanical garders of such flora, featuringbut not limited to Barr's discoveries; and to engage any educational activities which may

further public familiarity with the plants of the Great Plains, their uses and enjoyment.
Publication Date: 1984 4-8 pages Intermittant
Cynthia Reed, President

3911 Green Space
New York Parks and Conservation Association
29 Elk Street 518-434-1583
Albany, NY 12207 Fax: 518-427-0067
E-mail: ptny@ptny.org
http://www.nypca.org
Semi-Annual
Robin Dropkin, Executive Director

3912 Habitat Hotline
Atlantic States Marine Fisheries Commission
1444 I Street Northwest 202-289-6400
6th Floor Fax: 202-289-6051
Washington, DC 20005 E-mail: info@asmfc.org
http://www.asmfc.org
6 pages Quarterly
John V O'Shea, Executive Director
Tina L Berger, Public Affairs/Resource Spec

3913 Illinois Audubon Society
PO Box 2547 217-544-BIRD
Springfield, IL 62708 Fax: 217-544-7433
E-mail: ias@illinoisaudubon.org
http://www.illinoisaudubon.org
A membership organization dedicated to the preservation of Illinois Wildlife and the habitats which support them. Has sanctuaries, conservation education and land acquisition programs and publishes quarterly magazines and newsletters.
Publication Date: 1916 28 pages Quarterly
ISSN: 1061-9801

3914 Illinois Environmental Council: IEC Bulletin
107 W Cook Street 217-544-5954
Suite E Fax: 217-544-5958
Springfield, IL 62704 E-mail: iec@ilenviro.org
http://www.ilenviro.org
The IEC is a coalition of over 70 environmental, conservation and health groups.
Bi Monthly
Jonathan Goldman, Executive Director
Jennifer Sublett, Outreach Coordinator

3915 In Brief
223 S King Street 808-599-2436
Suite 400 Fax: 808-521-6841
Honolulu, HI 96813 E-mail: eajushi@earthjustice.org
http://www.earthjustice.org
Newsletter of Earthjustice, a nonprofit public interest law firm dedicated to protecting the magnificent places, natural resources and wildlife of this earth and to defending the right of all people to a healthy environment. We bringabout far-reaching change by enforcing and strengthening environmental laws on behalf of hundreds of organizations and communities.
Quarterly
Douglas Hannold, Managing Attorney

3916 Iowa Cooperative Fish & Wildlife Research Unit: Annual Report
Iowa State University
Science Hall II 515-294-3056
Ames, IA 50011 Fax: 515-294-5468
Publication Date: 1932 50 pages Annual

3917 Iowa Native Plant Society Newsletter
Iowa State University
Botany Department 515-294-9499
Ames, IA 50011 Fax: 515-294-1337
E-mail: dlewis@iastate.edu
An organization of amateur and professional botanists and native plant enthusiasts who are interested in the scientific, educational and cultural aspects, as well as the preservation and conservation of the native plants of Iowa. TheSociety was organized in 1995 to create a forum where plant enthusiasts, gardners and professional botanists could exchange ideas and coordinate activities such as field trips, work shops, and restoration of natural areas.
Publication Date: 1995 12 pages 3/4 times X year
Tom Rosburg, President
Deb Lewis, Contact Person

3918 Journal of Caves & Karst Studies
National Speleological Society
2813 Cave Avenue 256-852-1300
Huntsville, AL 35810 Fax: 256-851-9241
E-mail: nss@caves.org
http://www.caves.org
A quarterly journal published by the National Speleological Society.
Quarterly
ISSN: 1090-6924
Stephanie Searles, Operations Manager
Dave Bunnell, Editor

3919 Journal of Economic Entomology
Journal of Entomology
10001 Derekwood Lane 301-731-4535
Suite 100 Fax: 301-731-4538
Lanham, MD 20706 E-mail: esa@entsoc.org
http://www.entsoc.org
Contributions report on the economic significance of insects and are divided into categories by subject matter: apiculture and social insects; arthropods in relation to plant disease, biological and microbial disease; ecology andbehavior; ecotoxicology; extension; field and forage crops; forest entomology; horticultural entomology; household and structural insects; insecticide resistance and resistance management; medical entomology; plant resistance; sampling andbiostatistics.
Bi-Monthly
John T Trumble, Editor-in-Chief

3920 Land Use Law Report
Business Publishers
PO Box 17592 301-587-6300
Baltimore, MD 21297 800-274-6737
Fax: 301-587-4530
E-mail: custserv@bpinews.com
http://www.bpinews.com
Provides timely news on court decisions, legislation and regulations that impact today's most pressing land-use policy planning and legal issues.
Biweekly
James D Lawlor, Author
Adam Goldstein, Publisher
James D Lawlor, Editor

3921 Land and Water Magazine
Land and Water
320 A Street 515-576-3191
Fort Dodge, IA 50501 Fax: 515-576-2606
E-mail: landandwater@frontiernet.net
http://www.landandwater.com
Edited for contractors, engineers, architects, government officials and those working in the field of natural resource management and restoration from idea stage through project completion and maintenance.
Publication Date: 1974 72 pages Bimonthly
ISSN: 0192-9453
Amy Dencklau, Publisher/Editor

3922 Leaves Newsletter
Michigan Forest Association
6120 S. Clinton Trail 517-663-3423
Eaton Rapids, MI 48827 E-mail: mfa@i-star.com
http://www.michiganforests.com
A monthly publication from the Michigan Forest Association.
Monthly
McClain B Smith Jr, Executive Director

3923 MACC Newsletter
Alba Press

10 Juniper Road 617-489-3930
Belmont, MA 02478 Fax: 617-489-3935
E-mail: staff@maccweb.org
http://www.maccweb.org

Published six times a year, each issue features carefully chosen technical and interpreative articles, updates on government actions and policies, notices of workshops and meetings, publications, listings and a professional directory.

16 pages Bi-Monthly
Lindsay Martucci, Editor

3924 **Michigan Forests Magazine**
Michigan Forest Association
1558 Barrington 734-665-8279
Ann Arbor, MI 48103 Fax: 734-913-9167
E-mail: mfa@i-star.com
http://www.michiganforests.com

A quarterly magazine published by the Michigan Forest Association.

Quarterly
McClain B Smith Jr, Executive Director

3925 **Minnesota Plant Press**
Minnesota Native Plant Society
220 Biological Science Center E-mail: president@mnnps.org
1445 Gortner Avenue http://www.mnnps.org
Saint Paul, MN 55108

A nonprofit organization dedicated to the conservation of the native plants of Minnesota through public education and advocacy. Offered are monthly meetings, field trips, symposia and a regular newsletter.

4 per year
Jason Husveth, President
Gerry Drewry, Editor

3926 **Monitor**
Florida Defenders of the Environment
4424 NW 13 Street 352-378-8465
Suite C-8 Fax: 352-377-0869
Gainesville, FL 32609 E-mail: fde@fladefenders.org
http://www.fladefenders.org

Newsletter of Florida Defenders of the Environment, one of the oldest and most accomplished conservation organizations in Florida with a network of scientists, economists and other professionals dedicated to preserving and protectingthe state's natural resources. FDE's top priority is currently the restoration of a 16-mile stretch of the Ocklawaha River and its 9,000-acre floodplain forest by removal of Rodman Dam- the last vestige of the Cross-Florida Barge Canal.

Publication Date: 1982 6-8 pages Bi-Annually
Nick Williams, Executive Director

3927 **Montana Land Reliance Newsletter**
324 Fuller Avenue 406-443-7027
PO Box 355 Fax: 406-443-7061
Helena, MT 59624 E-mail: info@mtlandreliance.org
http://www.mtlandreliance.org

Montana's only private, statewide land trust, an apolitical, nonprofit corporation. Our mission is to provide permanent protection for private lands that are ecologically significant for agricultural production, fish and wildlifehabitat and scenic open space. We publish a newsletter twice per year.

8 pages Spring/Fall
Jay Erickson, Managing Director
Rock Ringling, Managing Director

3928 **NACD News & Views**
National Association of Conservation Districts
509 Capitol Court, NE 202-547-6223
Washington, DC 20002 Fax: 202-547-6450
http://www.nacdnet.org

Newsletter of the nonprofit organization that represents the nation's 3,000 conservation districts and 17,000 men and women who serve on their governing boards. Conservation districts, local units of government established under statelaw to carry out natural resource management programs at the local level, work with more than 2.5 million cooperating landowners and operators to help them amange and protect land and water resources on nearly 98% of the private lands in the UnitedStates.

Publication Date: 1952 8 pages Bi-Monthly
Maxine Mathis, Production Manager

3929 **National Gardener Magazine**
National Garden Clubs, Inc
4401 Magnolia Avenue 314-776-7574
St Louis, MO 63110 800-550-6007
Fax: 314-776-5108
E-mail: headquarters@gardenclub.org
http://www.gardenclub.org

National Garden Clubs, Inc publishes The National Gardener Magazinequarterly.

Publication Date: 1970 48 pages Quarterly
ISSN: 0027-9331
Susan Davidson, Author
Susan Davidson, Editor

3930 **National Grange Newsletter**
1616 H Street Northwest 202-628-3507
Washington, DC 20006 888-447-2643
Fax: 202-347-1091
E-mail: rweiss@nationalgrange.org
http://www.nationalgrange.org

The Grange is a family based community organization with a special interest in agriculture and rural america as well as in legislative efforts regarding these issues.

6 pages Bi-Monthly
William Steele, President
Richard Weiss, COO

3931 **National Recreation and Park Association, (NRPA): Parks & Recreation Magazine**
Parks and Recreation Magazine
22377 Belmont Ridge Road 703-858-0784
Ashburn, VA 20148 Fax: 703-858-0794
E-mail: info@nrpa.org
http://www.nrpa.org

The NRPA, headquartered in Ashburn Virginia, is a national nonprofit organization devoted to advancing park, recreation and conservation efforts that enhance the quality of life for all Americans. The Association works to extendsocial, health, cultural and economic benefits of parks and recreation, through its network of 23,000 recreation and park professionals and civic leaders. NRPA encourages recreation initiatives for youth in high-risk environments.

100 pages Monthly
ISSN: 0031-2215
John Thorner, Executive Director
Rachel Roberts, Editor

3932 **National Wildlife Magazine**
National Wildlife Federation
11100 Wildlife Center Drive 800-822-9919
Reston, VA 20190 http://www.nwf.org

The official member magazine of the National Wildlife Federation.

6 Issues/Yr
Larry J Schweiger, President/CEO
Mark Wexler, Editorial Director

3933 **National Woodlands Magazine**
National Woodland Owners Association
374 Maple Avenue E 703-255-2700
Suite 310 800-476-8733
Vienna, VA 22180 Fax: 703-281-9200
E-mail: argow@nwoa.net
http://www.nationalwoodlands.org

Provides timely information about forestry and forest practices with news from Washington, DC and state capitals. Written for non-industrial, private woodland owners. Includes state landowner association news.

28 pages Quarterly
Keith A Argow, Publisher
Eric Johnson, Editor

3934 Natural Resources Department: Fish & Wildlife Newsletter
402 West Washington Street RMW273 317-232-4080
Indianapolis, IN 46204 Fax: 317-232-8150
http://www.state.in.us/dnr/fishwild/index.htm
Publication Date: 1985 12 pages Quarterly

3935 Nature Conservancy: Nebraska Chapter Newsletter
402-342-0282
1025 Leavenworth Street
Omaha, NE 68102 Fax: 402-342-0474
E-mail: nebraska@tnc.org
http://nature.org

The mission of the Nature Conservancy is to preserve the plants, animals and natural communities that represent the diversity of life on Earth by protecting the lands and waters they need to survive.
Publication Date: 1987 12 pages Quarterly
Jill Jeffrey, Donor Relations Manager

3936 Nature's Voice, The DNS Online Newsletter
Delaware Nature Society
PO Box 700 302-239-2334
Hockessin, DE 19707 Fax: 302-239-2473
E-mail: dnsinfo@delawarenaturesociety.org
http://www.delawarenaturesociety.org
Now only available online, the newsletter offers trail information, nature center updates and programs, volunteer opportunities and more about what's happening in the outdoors of Delaware.
Michael Riska, Executive Director

3937 New England WildFlower: New England Wildflower Society
180 Hemenway Road 508-877-7630
Framingham, MA 01701 Fax: 508-877-3658
E-mail: information@newenglandwild.org
http://www.newenglandwild.org
36 pages Twice a Year
Debbi Edelstein, Executive Director
Frances Clark, Chair, Board of Trustees

3938 New Jersey Environmental Lobby News
204 W State Street 609-396-3774
Trenton, NJ 08608 Fax: 609-396-4521
E-mail: njelcurtis@aol.org
http://www.njenvironment.org
Quarterly publication from New Jersey Environmental Lobby.
Publication Date: 1971 8 pages Quarterly
ISSN: 1535-2021
Anne Poole, President
Marie A Curtis, Executive Director

3939 North Dakota Association of Soil Conservation Districts Newsletter
3310 University Drive 701-223-8518
Bismarck, ND 58504 Fax: 701-223-1291
E-mail: gpuppe@tic.bisman.com
http://www.ndascd.org

Quarterly
Gary Puppe, Executive VP

3940 Outdoors Unlimited
121 Hickory Street 406-728-7434
Suite 1 Fax: 406-728-7445
Missoula, MT 59801 E-mail: owaa@montana.com
http://www.owaa.org
Magazine of the Outdoor Writers Association of America. Membership fees are $175.00 (individual), $325.00 (supporting), $40.00 (student)
Publication Date: 1962 35 pages Monthly
Kevin Rhoades, Executive Director

3941 Pacific Fishery Management Council Newsletter
7700 NE Ambassador Place 503-820-2280
Suite 200 866-806-7204
Portland, OR 97220 Fax: 503-820-2299
E-mail: Donald.McIsaac@noaa.gov
http://www.pcouncil.org
24 pages 5x Year
Donald McIsaac, Executive Director
John Coon, Deputy Director

3942 Parks and Trails Council of Minnesota: Newsletter
275 E 4th Street 651-726-2457
Suite 250 800-944-0707
Saint Paul, MN 55101 Fax: 651-726-2458
E-mail: info@parksandtrails.org
http://www.parksandtrails.org
Mission: To acquire, protect and enhance critical lands for the public's enjoyment now and in the future.
Quarterly
Judith Erickson, Government Relations
Beth Coleman, Executive Director

3943 Powder River Basin Resource Council: Powder River Breaks Newsletter
934 North Main 307-672-5809
Sheridan, WY 82801 Fax: 307-672-5800
E-mail: resources@powderriverbasin.org
http://www.powderriverbasin.org
Committed to the preservation and enrichment of Wyoming's agricultural heritage and rural lifestyle; the conservation of Wyomings unique land, mineral, water and clean air resources, consistent with responsible use of those resourcesto sustain the vitality of present and future generations; the education and empowerment of Wyoming's citizens to raise a coherent voice in decisions. They are the only group in Wyoming that addresses both agricultural and conservation issues.
Publication Date: 1973 8-12 pages 6x year
Jillian Malone, Editor
Stephanie Avey, Assistant Editor

3944 Prairie Naturalist Magazine
600 Park Street 785-628-4214
Department of Biological Sciences Fax: 316-341-5607
Hays, KS 67601 E-mail: efinck@fhsu.edu
http://www.fhsu.edu
Published by the North Dakota Natural Science Society, a regional organization with interests in the natural history of grasslands and the Great Plains.
Publication Date: 1968 260 pages Quarterly
ISSN: 0091-0376
Elmer J Finck, Editor

3945 Reef Line
Reef Relief Environmental Center
PO Box 430 305-294-3100
Key West, FL 33041 Fax: 305-293-9515
E-mail: info@reefrelief.org
http://www.reefrelief.org
Reef Line is a quarterly publication from Reef Relief.
Publication Date: 1986 16 pages Quarterly
Michael Blades, Project Director
DeeVon Quirdo, Executive Director

3946 SWOAM News
Small Woodland Owners Association of Maine
153 Hospital Street 207-626-0005
PO Box 836 877-467-9626
Augusta, ME 04332 Fax: 207-626-7992
E-mail: info@swoam.com
http://www.swoam.com

Monthly
Tom Doak, Executive Director

3947 Save San Francisco Bay Association: Watershed Newsletter
350 Frank H Ogawa Plaza
Suite 900
Oakland, CA 94612
510-452-9261
Fax: 510-452-9266
E-mail: SAVEBAY@savesfbay.org
http://www.savesfbay.org

Save the Bay has worked for over 40 years to protect the San Francisco Bay-Delta from pollution, fill, shoreline destruction and fresh water diversion. We have launched a century of renewal to restore bay fish and wildlife, reclaimtidal wetlands and make the bay safe and accessible to all.
8-10 pages 3-4 times/year
David Lewis, Executive Director

3948 Scenic America Newsletter
Scenic America
1250 Eye Street NW
Suite 750
Washington, DC 20005
202-638-1839
Fax: 202-638-3171
E-mail: tracy@scenic.org
http://www.scenic.org

12 pages 3 Times Per Year
Mary Tracy, President
Peggy Lint, Office Manager

3949 Shore and Beach
5460 Beaujolais Lane
Fort Myers, FL 33919
239-489-2616
Fax: 239-489-9917
E-mail: ExDir@asbpa.org
http://www.asbpa.org

A quarterly publication from the American Shore and Beach Preservation Association.
24 pages Quarterly
ISSN: 0037-4237
Ken Gooderham, Executive Director/Editor
Kate Gooderham, Executive Director/Editor

3950 Sierra Club, NJ Chapter: The Jersey Sierran
139 W Hanover Street
Trenton, NJ 08618
609-656-7612
Fax: 609-656-7618
E-mail: webmaster@sierraactivist.org
http://www.sierraactivist.org

The Sierra Club is our country's oldest and most effective grassroots environmental organization. Hikes and outings are scheduled throughout the year. We are dedicated to fighting sprawl and over-development.
Publication Date: 1992 14 pages Quarterly
Jeff Tittle, Director
Dennis Schvejda, Conservation Coordinator

3951 Sierra Club: Pennsylvania Chapter Newsletter
600 North 2nd Street
Suite 300A
Harrisburg, PA 17101
717-232-0101
Fax: 717-238-6330
E-mail: sierraclub.pa@paonline.com
http://www.sierraclub.org/chapter/pa/

The Pennsylvania chapter includes 11 local Sierra Club groups. Emphasis is on state environmental policy advocacy, outings, education and local environmental protection efforts.
18 pages Quarterly
Jeff Schmidt, Sr. Chapter Director

3952 Southern Appalachian Botanical Society: Gastanea
Newberry College
2100 College Street
Newberry, SC 29108
803-321-5257
Fax: 803-321-5636
E-mail: chorn@newberry.edu
http://www.newberrynet.com/sabs/

This is a professional organization for those interested in botanical research, especially in the areas of ecology, floristics and systematics. To this end, we publish a journal, CASTANEA, and a newsletter, CHINQUAPIN.
Publication Date: 1936 350 pages Quarterly
ISSN: 0008-7475
Michael E Held, PhD, President
Charles Horn, Treasurer

3953 Terrain Magazine
2530 San Pablo Avenue
Berkeley, CA 94702
510-548-2220
Fax: 510-548-2240
E-mail: info@ecologycenter.org
http://www.ecologycenter.org

A quarterly magazine published by the Ecology Center of Berkeley, CA.
Publication Date: 1971 39 pages Quarterly
ISSN: 1526-8322
Linnea Due, Editor-in-Chief

3954 Tidbits Newsletter
Minnesota Association/Soil and Water Cons. Dist.
790 Cleveland Avenue S
Suite 216
St. Paul, MN 55075
651-690-9028
Fax: 651-690-9065
E-mail: leann.buck@maswcd.org
http://www.maswcd.org

Quarterly
Le Ann Buck, Executive Director
Sheila Vanney, Editor

3955 Tide
Coastal Conservation Association
4801 Woodway Drive
Houston, TX 77056
713-626-4234
800-201-FISH
E-mail: ccantl@joincca.org

TIDE is the official bimonthly magazine of the Coastal Conservation Association. It has received local, state and national acclaim for writing, photography and layout and currently boasts a circulation of more than 70,000. TIDE isavailable only to members of the Coastal Conservation Association.

3956 Upper Mississippi River Conservation Committee Newsletter
4469 48th Avenue Court
Rock Island, IL 61201
309-793-5800
Fax: 309-793-5804
E-mail: umrcc@mississippi-river.com/umrcc
http://mississippi-river.com/umrcc

A bimonthly newsletter published by the Upper Mississippi River Conservation Committee.
10 pages Bi monthly
Mike McGhee, Chairman

3957 Urban Land Magazine
Urban Land Institute
1025 Thomas Jefferson Street NW
Suite 500 W
Washington, DC 20007
202-624-7000
800-321-5011
Fax: 202-624-7140
http://www.uli.org

Nonprofit research and education organization dedicated to improving land use policy and development practice. Publishes a monthly magazine, several quarterly publications and books. Topics relate to real estate development includinggovernment sensitive development, smart growth, sustainable development and city parks.
Monthly
Kristina Kessler, Chief Editor

3958 Utah Geological Survey: Survey Notes
1594 W N Temple Suite 3110
PO Box 146100
Salt Lake City, UT 84114
801-537-3300
Fax: 801-537-3400
http://www.ugs.state.ut.us

The Utah Geological Survey is an applied scientific agency that creates, interprets and provides information about Utah's geologic environment, resources and hazards to promote safe, beneficial and wise use of land. This is theirpublication, which is issued three times yearly.
Publication Date: 1964 3 Times Yearly
ISSN: 1061-7930
Richard Allis, Director

3959 Virginia Forests Magazine
Virginia Forestry Association
3808 Augusta Avenue
Richmond, VA 23255
804-278-8733
Fax: 804-320-1447
E-mail: vafa@erols.com
http://www.vaforestry.org

Quarterly magazine published by the Virginia Forestry Association.
Quarterly
Paul Howe, VFA Executive Vice President

3960 WAEE Bulletin
Wisconsin Association for Environmental Education
8 Nelson Hall
University of Wisconsin
Stevens Point, WI 54481
715-346-2796
E-mail: waee@uwsp.edu
Quarterly
Carol Weston, Administrative Assistant

3961 West Virginia Forestry Association Newsletter
PO Box 718
Ripley, WV 25271
304-372-1955
888-372-9663
Fax: 304-372-1957
E-mail: wvfa@wvadventures.net
http://www.wvfa.org
Monthly
Richard Waybright, Executive Director

3962 Western Pennsylvania Conservancy Newsletter
209 4th Avenue
Pittsburgh, PA 15222
412-288-2777
866-JOI-NWPC
Fax: 412-281-1792
E-mail: wpc@paconserve.org
http://www.paconserve.org
WPC, working together to save the places we care about, protects natural lands, promotes healthy and attractive communities, and preserves Fallingwater, Frank Lloyd Wright's masterwork in Mill Run, which was entrusted to theConservancy in 1963. Since its inception in 1932, the Conservancy has protected more than 280,000 acres of natural lands in Pennsylvania. We continue to work to secure lands of ecological significance that frequently offer recreational and scenicvalues.
16 pages Quarterly
Larry Schweiger, President

3963 Western Proceedings Newsletter
Western Association of Fish and Wildlife Agencies
5400 Bishop Boulevard
Cheyenne, WY 82006
307-777-4569
Fax: 307-777-4699
E-mail: ikruck@state.wy.us
Annual

3964 Western Society of Naturalists: Newsletter
San Diego State University Biology Department
5500 Campanile Street
San Diego, CA 92182
818-677-3256
Fax: 818-677-2034
http://www.wsn-online.org
Mark Carr, President
Ralph Larson, President Elect

3965 Wetlands in the United States
American Ground Water Trust
50 Pleasant Street Ste 2
Concord, NH 03301
603-228-5444
Fax: 603-228-6557
E-mail: trustinfo@agwt.org
http://www.agwt.org
15 pages Quarterly
Andrew Stone, Director

3966 Whalewatcher
PO Box 1391
San Pedro, CA 90733
310-548-6279
Fax: 310-548-6950
E-mail: info@acsonline.org
http://www.acsonline.org
A bi-annual publication from the American Cetacean Society. Cost included with membership fees.
Publication Date: 1967 30 pages Bi-Annual
Diane Alps, Administrative Assistant

3967 Wilderness Education Association
900 E 7th Street
Bloomington, IN 47405
812-855-4095
Fax: 812-855-8697
E-mail: wea@indiana.edu
http://www.weainfo.org/
Publication Date: 1976 4-6 pages 3 Times Per Year

3968 Wildfowl Trust of North America: Newsletter
Wildfowl Trust of North America
600 Discovery Lane
PO Box 519
Grasonville, MD 21638
410-827-6694
Fax: 410-827-6713
E-mail: cbec@cbec-wtna.org
http://www.cbec-wtna.org
Published by the Wildfowl Trust of North America.
Publication Date: 1995 8 pages Qaurterly
Judy Wink, Executive Director
Sharyn B Harlow, Executive Admin. Assistant

3969 Wildlife Law News Quarterly and Weekly Alerts
University of New Mexico School of Law
MSC 11 6060rd NE
One University of New Mexico
Albuquerque, NM 87131
505-277-5006
Fax: 505-277-7064
E-mail: musgrave@unm.edu
http://wildlifenews.unm.edu
A quarterly publication from the New Mexico Center for Wildlife Law.
Publication Date: 1993 16 pages Quarterly
ISSN: 1085-7338
R Musgrave, Editor
D Macke, Editor

3970 Wildlife Society Bulletin
Wildlife Society
5410 Grosvenor Lane
Suite 200
Bethesda, MD 20814
301-897-9770
Fax: 301-530-2471
E-mail: tws@wildlife.org
http://www.wildlife.org
A quarterly publication from the Wildlife Society.
Publication Date: 1973 Quarterly
ISSN: 0091-7648
Warren Ballard, Editor

3971 Woodland Management Newsletter
Wisconsin Woodland Owners Association
PO Box 285
Stevens Point, WI 54481
715-346-4798
Fax: 715-346-4821
E-mail: nbozek@uwsp.edu
http://www.wisconsinwoodlands.org
Quarterly
Tim Eisele, Editor

3972 Woodland Report
National Woodland Owners Association
374 Maple Avenue E
Suite 310
Vienna, VA 22180
703-255-2700
800-476-8733
Fax: 703-281-9200
E-mail: argow@nwoa.net
http://www.nationalwoodlands.org
Provides timely information about forestry and forest practices with news from Washington, DC and state capitals. Written for non-industrial, private woodland owners. Includes state landowner association news.
2 pages
Keith A Argow, Publisher
Eric Johnson, Editor

3973 World Wildlife Fund: US Focus
1250 24th Street NW
Suite 500
Washington, DC 20037
202-293-4800
http://www.worldwildlife.org
WWF projects.
8 pages
Pat Sullivan, Publisher

Periodicals: Recycling & Pollution Prevention

3974 AARA Newsletter
Arizona Automotive Recyclers Association
1030 E Baseline Rd
#105-1025
Tempe, AZ 85283
480-609-3999
E-mail: admin@aara.com
http://www.aara.com

Quarterly newsletter of the AARA, a select group of recyclers providing quality recycled parts for the benefit of our customers, communities and environment. There are 90 member companies. AARA is affiliated with the AutomotiveDismantlers and Recyclers Association.
Quarterly
Mike Pierson Jr, President
Layla Ressler, Vice President

3975 Air/Water Pollution Report
Business Publishers
8737 Colesville Road
10th Floor
Silver Spring, MD 20910
301-589-5103
800-274-6737
Fax: 301-589-8493
E-mail: custserv@bpinews.com
http://www.bpinews.com

Provides comprehensive coverage of economic, political, legislative, regulatory and domestic and international implications of air and water pollution.
Weekly
Leonard A Eiserer, Publisher
Beth Early, Associate Publisher

3976 American Waste Digest
Carasue Moody
226 King Street
Pottstown, PA 19464
610-326-9480
800-442-4215
Fax: 610-326-9752
E-mail: awd@americanwastedigest.com
http://www.americanwastedigest.com

Provides reviews on new products, profiles on sucessful waste removal businesses, and provides discussion on legislation on municipal regulations on recycling.
100 pages Monthly
Carasue Moody, Publisher/Editor

3977 BNA's Environmental Compliance Bulletin
Bureau of National Affairs
1231 25th Street NW
Washington, DC 20037
202-452-4200
800-372-1033
Fax: 202-452-5331
http://www.bna.com

Cover the water and air pollution, waste management and regulatory updates, as well as a summary of selected regulatory actions and a list of key environmental compliance dates.
Kevin Fepherston, Managing Editor

3978 Bio-Integral Resource Center: IPM Practitioner
PO Box 7414
Berkeley, CA 94707
510-524-2567
Fax: 510-524-1758
E-mail: birc@igc.org
http://www.birc.org

The goal of the Bio Integral Resources Center is to reduce pesticide use by educating the public about effective, least-toxic alternatives for pest problems.
Publication Date: 1979 6-12 pages
ISSN: 0738-968x
Dr. William Quarles, Executive Director

3979 C&D Recycler
Gie Publishing
4012 Bridge Avenue
Cleveland, OH 44113
216-961-4130
800-456-0707
Fax: 216-961-0364
E-mail: btaylor@gie.net
http://www.cdrecycler.com

Brian Taylor, Editor

3980 Common Sense Pest Control Quarterly
PO Box 7414
Berkeley, CA 94707
510-524-2567
Fax: 510-524-1758
E-mail: birc@igc.org
http://www.birc.org

A quarterly publication published by the Bio Integral Resource Center
Publication Date: 1984 24 pages Quarterly
ISSN: 8756-7881
Dr. William Quarles, Executive Director

3981 Composting News
McEntee Media Corporation
9815 Hazelwood Avenue
Cleveland, OH 44149
440-238-6603
Fax: 440-238-6712
E-mail: ken@recycle.cc
http://www.recycle.cc

New composting projects, research, regulations and legislation, as well as the latest news in the composting industry.
Publication Date: 1992 Monthly
Ken McEntee, Publisher

3982 Daily Environment Report
Bureau of National Affairs
1231 25th Street NW
Washington, DC 20037
202-452-4200
800-372-1033
Fax: 202-822-8092
http://www.bna.com

A 40-page daily report providing comprehensive, in-depth coverage of national and international environmental news. Each issue contains summaries of the top news stories, articles, and in-brief items, and a journal of meetings, agencyactivities, hearings and legal proceedings. Coverage includes air and water pollution, hazardous substances, and hazardous waste, solid waste, oil spills, gas drilling, pollution prevention, impact statements and budget matters.
40 pages
ISSN: 1060-2976
William A Beltz, Publisher

3983 E-Scrap News
Resource Recycling
PO Box 42270
Portland, OR 97242
503-233-1305
Fax: 503-233-1356
E-mail: info@resource-recycling.com
http://www.resource-recycling.com

64 pages
ISSN: 0744-4710
Justin Gast, Editor

3984 Earth Preservers
PO Box 6
Westfield, NJ 07091
908-654-9293
E-mail: earthpreservers@att.net
http://www.earthpreserves.com

Award winning monthly environmental newspaper for school children aged 7 to 15.
4 pages
Bill Paul, Publisher

3985 Environment Reporter
Bureau of National Affairs
1231 25th Street NW
Washington, DC 20037
202-452-4200
800-372-1033
Fax: 202-822-8092
http://www.bna.com

A weekly notification and reference service covering the full-spectrum of legislative, administrative, judicial, industrial and technological developments affecting pollution control and environmental protection.

ISSN: 0013-9211
William A Beltz, Publisher
Patricia Spencer, Managing Editor

3986 Environmental Engineering Science
Mary Ann Liebert

140 Huguenot Street
3rd Floor
New Rochelle, NY 10801
914-740-2100
800-MLI-EBER
Fax: 914-740-2101
E-mail: info@liebertpub.com
http://www.liebertpub.com

The focus is on pollution control of the suface, ground, and drinking water, and highlight research news and product developments that aid in the fight against pollution.
Bi-Monthly
ISSN: 1092-8758
Mary Ann Liebert, Publisher
Dumpnico Grosso PhD, Editor-in-Chief

3987 Environmental Notice
235 S Beretania Street
Room 702
Honolulu, HI 96813
808-586-4185
Fax: 808-586-4186
E-mail: oeqc@doh.hawaii.gov
http://hawaii.gov/health/environemtnal/oeqc/index/html

A bi-monthly publication from the Health Department Environmental Quality Control division.
Publication Date: 1978 24 pages Bi monthly
Kathy Kealoha, Director

3988 Environmental Regulation
State Capitals Newsletters
PO Box 7376
Alexandria, VA 22307
703-768-9600
Fax: 703-768-9690
E-mail: newsletters@statecapitals.com
http://www.statecapitals.com

Weekly news from the state capitals keeps you informed on state programs, recycling, wetlands, ground water protection, beach renourishment, land management, greenspace laws, brownfields, livestock regulation, wilderness preservation,urban sprawl and solid waste.
Publication Date: 1946 4-10 pages Newsletter 48x/Yr
ISSN: 1061-9682
Ellen Klein, Editor

3989 Environmental Regulatory Advisor
JJ Keller
3003 W Breezewood Lane
PO Box 368
Neenah, WI 54957
877-564-2333
Fax: 800-727-7516
E-mail: sales@jjkeller.com
http://www.jjkeller.com

Covers developments at the EPA.
12 pages
ISSN: 1056-3164
Tom Ziebell, Editor

3990 Environmental Science and Technology
American Chemical Society
1155 16th Street NW
Washington, DC 20036
800-221-5558
Fax: 202-872-4615
E-mail: help@acs.org
http://www.acs.org

Articles on pollution control, waste treatment, climate changes and various other environmental interests.
110 pages Semi-Monthly
Bruce Poorman, Ad Manager
Steve Cole, Managing Editor

3991 Environmental Systems Corporation Newsletter
200 Tech Center Drive
Knoxville, TN 37912
865-688-7900
Fax: 865-687-8977
E-mail: esccorp@envirosys.com
http://www.envirosys.com

Data acquisition and reporting systems for electric power producers and industrial sources, ESC is the leading supplier of CEM and ambient data systems in the US Newsletter is free.
Publication Date: 1994 4 pages Quarterly
Steve Drevik, Sr. Marketing Manager

3992 Environmental Times
Environmental Assessment Association
1224 N Nokomis NE
Alexandria, MN 56308
320-763-4320
Fax: 320-763-9290
E-mail: eaa@iami.org
http://www.iami.org/eaa.cfm

This publication contains environmental conferences and expos, industry trends, federal regulations related to the environment and industry assessments.
Robert Johnson, Publisher/Editor

3993 From the Ground Up
Ecology Center
117 Division Street
Ann Arbor, MI 48104
734-761-3186
Fax: 734-663-2414
E-mail: info@crocenter.org
http://www.crocenter.org

Progressive environmental news from southeast Michigan.
32 pages
Michael Garfield, Editor

3994 Full Circle
Northeast Resource Recovery Association
PO Box 721
Concord, NH 03302
603-798-5777
Fax: 603-798-5744
E-mail: nrra@tds.net
http://www.recyclewithus.org

Bi-Monthly
Elizabeth Bedard, Executive Director

3995 Hauler
Hauler Magazine
166 South Main Street
PO Box 508
New Hope, PA 18938
215-997-3622
Fax: 215-997-3623
E-mail: mag@thehauler.com
http://www.thehauler.com

This magazine serves as an advertising guide to new products in the waste management, recycling, and environmental industries.
Publication Date: 1978 Monthly
Thomas N Smith, Publisher/Editor

3996 HazMat Management
Business Information Group
1450 Don Mills Road
Don Mills, Ontario M3B
416-442-2223
888-702-1111
Fax: 416-442-2917
E-mail: sales@hazmatmag.com
http://www.hazmatmag.com

Solutions for the environment.
Publication Date: 1989 Bi-Annual
ISSN: 0843-9303
Thea Papadakis, Publisher
Connie Vitello, Editor

3997 Hazardous Waste News
Business Publishers
PO Box 17592
Baltimore, MD 21297
301-589-5103
800-274-6737
Fax: 301-589-8493
E-mail: custserv@bpinews.com
http://www.bpinews.com

Comprehensive federal, state and local coverage of legislation and regulation affecting all aspects of the hazardous waste industry including Superfund, Resource Conservation and Recovery Act, US EPA, incineration, land disposal andmore.
8 pages
Leonard A Eiserer, Publisher
Beth Early, Operations Director

3998 Hazardous Waste/Superfund Week
Business Publishers
PO Box 17592lle Road
Baltimore, MD 21297
301-589-5103
800-274-6737
Fax: 301-589-8493
E-mail: custserv@bpinews.com
http://www.bpinews.com

Provides comprehensive coverage on hazardous waste disposal and cleanup, behind-the-scenes coverage of congressional action, EPA initiatives, Superfund sites, regulatory changes, court cases, enforcement news, contract opportunities,new technologies, research findings and business developments.
Weekly
Leonard A Eiserer, Publisher
Beth Early, Associate Publisher

3999 Hazmat Transportation News
Bureau of National Affairs
1801 S. Bell Street
Arlington, VA 22202
800-372-1033
Fax: 202-822-8092
http://www.bna.com

A two-binder service containing the full-text of rules and regulations governing shipment of hazardous material by rail, air, ship, highway and pipeline, including DOT's Hazardous Materials Tables and EPA's rules for its hazardouswaste tracking system.
Stan Pond, Managing Editor

4000 Inside EPA
Inside Washington Publishers
1225 South Clark Street
Suite 1400
Arlington, VA 22202
703-416-8500
Fax: 703-415-8543
E-mail: iwp@iwpnews.com
http://www.iwpnews.com

Gives timely information on all facets of waste, water, air, and other environmental regulatory programs.
Publication Date: 1980 Weekly
Al Sosenko, Publisher

4001 Institute of Scrap Recycling Industries
1615 L Street NW
Suite 600
Washington, DC 20036
202-662-8500
Fax: 202-626-0900
E-mail: kentkiser@scrap.org
http://www.isri.org

Publication Date: 1988 148 pages Bi monthly
ISSN: 0036-9527
Frank Cozzi, President
Kent Kiser, Publisher/Editor-in-Chief

4002 Journal of Environmental Education
Heldref Publications
1319 18th Street NW
Washington, DC 20036
202-296-6267
Fax: 202-296-5149
E-mail: webmaster@heldref.org
http://www.heldref.org

The issues featured are case studies, environmental philosophy and policy discussions, new research evaluations and information on environmental education.
Douglas Kirkpatrick, Publisher/Executive Director

4003 KIND News
National Assn for Humane & Environmental Education
67 Norwich Essex Turnpike
East Haddam, CT 06423
860-434-8666
Fax: 860-434-6282
E-mail: nahee@nahee.org
http://www.nahee.org

Classroom newspaper for kids in grades K-6. It features articles, puzzles and celebrity interviews that teach children the value of showing kindness and respect to animals, the environment, and one another.
Publication Date: 1985 4 pages 9 per year
William DeRosa, Executive Director
Dorothy Weller, Director Outreach & Fulf.

4004 Legislative Bulletin
Arkansas Environmental Federation
1400 W Markham Street
Suite 302
Little Rock, AR 72201
501-374-0263
Fax: 501-374-8752
http://www.environmentark.org
Publication Date: 1967
Randy Thurman, Executive Director

4005 Minnesota Pollution Control Agency Minnesota Environment Magazine
520 Lafayette Road North
St. Paul, MN 55155
651-296-6300
800-657-3864
Fax: 651-296-7923
E-mail: vicki.schindeldecker@pca.state.mn.us
http://www.pca.state.mn.us

Established in 1967 to protect Minnesota's environment through monitoring environmental quality and enforcing environmental regulations.
Publication Date: 2000 16-20 pages Quarterly
Paul Eger, Comm./Chair Citizens' Board

4006 Northeast Recycling Council Bulletin
139 Main Street
Suite 401
Brattleboro, VT 05301
802-254-3636
Fax: 802-254-5870
E-mail: info@nerc.org
http://www.nerc.org

Monthly
Lynn Rubinstein, Executive Director

4007 Northeast Recycling Council News
139 Main Street
Suite 401
Brattleboro, VT 05301
802-254-3636
Fax: 802-254-5870
E-mail: info@nerc.org
http://www.nerc.org

3x Year
Lynn Rubenstein, Executive Director

4008 Oregon Refuse and Recycling Association Newsletter
PO Box 2186
Salem, OR 97308
503-588-1837
800-527-7624
Fax: 503-399-7784
E-mail: orrainfo@orra.net
http://www.orra.net

Monthly
Max Brittingham, Executive Director
Kristin Mitchell, Editor

4009 Plastics Recycling Update
Resource Recycling
PO Box 42270
Portland, OR 97242
503-233-1305
Fax: 503-233-1356
E-mail: subscriptions@resource-recycling.com
http://www.resource-recycling.com

Monthly
Justin Gast, Managing Editor
Mary Lynch, Circulation

4010 Pollution Equipment News
Rimbach Publishing
8650 Babcock Boulevard
Pittsburgh, PA 15237
412-364-5366
800-245-3182
Fax: 412-369-9720
E-mail: info@rimbach.com
http://www.rimbach.com

Provides information to those responsible for selecting products and services for air, water, wastewater and hazardous waste pollution abatement.
Publication Date: 1967 64 pages Bi-Monthly
ISSN: 0032-3659
Raquel Rimbach, Editor
Norberta Rimbach, Publisher/President

4011 Pollution Prevention News
US EPA
1200 Pennsylvania Avenue, NW
Washington, DC 20460
202-272-0167
Fax: 202-260-2219
http://www.epa.gov

Articles include recent information on source reduction and sustainable technologies in industry, transportation, consumer, agriculture, energy, and the international sector.
Maureen Eichelberger, Editor

4012 Recharger Magazine
Recharger Magazine
1050 East Flamingo Road
Suite N237
Las Vegas, NV 89119
702-438-5557
Fax: 702-873-9671
E-mail: info@rechargermag.com
http://www.rechargermag.com

Information including articles that cover business and marketing, technical updates, association and industry news, and company profiles. On the remanufactured imaging supplies industry, related features focus on the importance ofrecycling, government legislation, and product comparisons. Annual trade event in Las Vegas.
Publication Date: 1989 300+ pages Monthly
ISSN: 1053-7503
Julie Kerrane, Author
Phyllis Gurgevich, Publisher
Amy Turner, Managing Editor

4013 Recycled News
Maryland Recyclers Coalition
PO Box 1046
Laurel, MD 20725
888-496-3196
Fax: 301-238-4579
E-mail: info@marylandrecyclers.org
http://www.marylandrecyclers.org

2 pages Bi-Monthly
Jackie King, Executive Director

4014 Recycling Laws International
Raymond Communications
5111 Berwin Road
Suite 115
College Park, MD 20740
301-345-4237
Fax: 301-345-4768
E-mail: circulation@raymond.com
http://www.raymond.com

Covers recycling, takeback and green labeling policy for business in 38 countries. Available online.
Publication Date: 1995 Bi-Monthly
Bruce Popka, Vice President

4015 Recycling Markets
NV Business Publishers Corporation
43 Main Street
Avon by the Sea, NJ 07717
732-502-0500
Fax: 732-502-9606
E-mail: jcurley@nvpublications.com
http://www.nvpublications.com

Contains profiles on recycling mills, as well as large users and generators of recycled materials for the broker, dealers and processors of paper stock, scrap metal, plastics and glass.
Jim Curley, Editor
Anna Dutko Rowley, Managing Editor

4016 Recycling Product News
Baum Publications
201-2323 Boundary Road
Vancouver, Can, BC V5M
604-291-9900
Fax: 604-291-1906
E-mail: webadmin@baumpub.com
http://www.baumpub.com

Published for the recycling center operators and other waste mangers, articles discuss technology and new products.
Engelbert J Baum, Publisher
Keith Barker, Editor

4017 Recycling Today
GIE Media
4020 Kinross Lakes Parkway
#201
Richfield, OH 44286
800-456-0707
Fax: 216-925-5022
E-mail: dtoto@gie.net
http://www.recyclingtoday.com

Published for the secondary commodity processing/recycling market.
James R Keefe, Group Publisher
Brian Taylor, Editor

4018 Resource Recovery Report
5313 38th Street NW
PO Box 3356
Warrenton, VA 20188
540-347-4500
800-627-8913
Fax: 540-348-4540
E-mail: rwill@coordgrp.com
http://www.coordgrp.com

Covers all alternatives to landfills, i.e., recycling, energy recovery, composting in North America, Government, industry, associations, universities, etc. are included.
12 pages
Richard Will, Production Manager

4019 Resource Recycling Magazine
Resource Recycling
PO Box 42270
Portland, OR 97242
503-233-1305
Fax: 503-233-1356
E-mail: info@resource-recycling.com
http://www.resource-recycling.com

Monthly
Justin Gast, Managing Editor
Mary Lynch, Circulation

4020 Reuse/Recycle Newsletter
Technomic Publishing Company
PO Box 3535
Lancaster, PA 17601
717-291-5609
800-233-9936
Fax: 717-295-4538
E-mail: aflannery@techpub.com
http://www.techpub.com

Provides news and information on important developments in both industrial and municipal recycling, and focuses on large-scale post-consumer, post-commercial, and post-industrial waste recycling.
8 pages
ISSN: 0048-7457
Susan E Selke, Author
Amy Flannery, Marketing

4021 Scrap
Institute of Scrap Recycling Industries
1615 L Street NW
Suite 600
Washington, DC 20036
202-662-8500
Fax: 202-626-0945
E-mail: ellenross@scrap.org
http://www.scrap.org

Serves the scrap processing and recycling industry. Subscription: $32.95 (US), $38.95 (Canada/Mexico) & $104.95 (all other international)
Bi-Monthly
Kent Kiser, Publisher/Editor-in-Chief
Ellen Ross, Production Director

4022 Solid Waste & Recycling
Southam Environment Group
1450 Don Mills Road
Don Mills, Ontario M3B
416-442-5600
800-387-0273
Fax: 416-510-5130
E-mail: bobrien@solidwastemag.com
http://www.solidwastemag.com

Published to emphasize on municipal and commercial aspects of collection, handling, transportation, hauling, disposal and treatment of solid waste , including incineration, recycling and landfill technology.
Brad O'Brien, Publisher
Guy Crittenden, Editor-in-Chief

4023 Solid Waste Report
Business Publishers
PO Box 17592
Baltimore, MD 21297
301 589 5103
800-274-6737
Fax: 301-589-8493
E-mail: custserv@bpinews.com
http://www.bpinews.com

Comprehensive news and analysis of legislation, regulation and litigation in solid waste management including resource recovery, recycling, collection and disposal. Regularly features international news, state updates and businesstrends.
Bi-Weekly
Leonard A Eiserer, Publisher
Beth Early, Operations Director

4024 State Recycling Laws Update
Raymond Communications
5111 Berwin Road
Suite 115
College Park, MD 20740
301-345-4237
Fax: 301-345-4768
E-mail: michele@raymond.com
http://www.raymond.com

Provides coverage of recycling legislation affecting business, as well as the outlook on future legislation across the US and Canada.
Bruce Popka, Vice President

4025 Waste Age
Environmental Industry Associations
4301 Connecticut Avenue NW
#300
Washington, DC 20008
202-244-4700
800-424-2869
Fax: 202-966-4868
E-mail: ptom@primediabusiness.com
http://www.wasteage.com

Contents focus on new system technologies, recycling, resource recovery and sanitary landfills with regular features on updates in the status of government regulations, new products, guides, com-

pany profiles, exclusive surveyinformation, legislative implications and news.
Patricia-Anne Tom, Editor
Stephen Ursery, Managing Editor

4026 Waste Age's Recycling Times
Environmental Industry Associations
4301 Connecticut Avenue NW 202-244-4700
#300 800-424-2869
Washington, DC 20008 Fax: 202-966-4868
E-mail: ptom@primediabusiness.com
http://www.wasteage.com

Features municipalities, recycling goals and rates, program innovations, waste habits, and new materials being recycled.
Patricia-Anne Tom, Editor
Stephen Ursery, Managing Editor

4027 Waste Handling Equipment News
Lee Publications
6113 State Highway 5 518-673-3237
PO Box 121 800-218-5586
Palatine Bridge, NY 13428 Fax: 518-673-2381
E-mail: rbrown@leepub.com
http://www.leepub.com

Dicusses the latest developments in woodwaste, C&D, scrapmetal, concrete, asphalt, recycling and composting with the emphasis on equipment.
Publication Date: 1993 50 pages Monthly
Coyle Rockwell, Author
Holly Reiser, Editor
Richard Brown, Production Coordinator

4028 Waste Recovery Report
Icon/Information Concepts
211 S 45th Street 215-349-6500
Philadelphia, PA 19104 Fax: 215-349-6502
E-mail: wasterec@aol.com
http://www.icodat.com

Contains information on waste-to-energy, recycling, composting and other technologies.
Publication Date: 1975 6 pages Monthly
ISSN: 0889-0072
Alan Krigman, Publisher/Editor

Periodicals: Sustainable Development

4029 AERO SunTimes
Alternative Energy Resources Organization
432 N Last Chance Gulch 406-443-7272
Helena, MT 59601 Fax: 406-442-9120
E-mail: aero@aeromt.org

The SunTimes is the newsletter for AERO. The organization is a statewide grassroots group whose members work together to strengthen communities through promoting sustainable agriculture, local food production and citizen-based SmartGrowth community planning.
Publication Date: 1978 4-24 pages Quarterly
ISSN: 1046-0993
Kiki Hubbard, Editor
Jean Duncan, Editor

4030 California Association of Resource Conservation Districts- CCP News
801 K Street 916-457-7094
Suite 1415 Fax: 916-457-7934
Sacramento, CA 93101 http://www.carcd.org
Quarterly
Patrick Truman, President
Brian Leahy, Executive Director

4031 Californians for Population Stabilization: CAPS News
1129 State Street 805-564-6626
Suite 3-D Fax: 805-564-6636
Santa Barbara, CA 93101 E-mail: info@capsweb.org
http://www.capsweb.org

A nonprofit, public interest organization that works to protect California's environment and quality of life by turning the tide of population growth.
Publication Date: 1986 8 pages 3x year
Diana Hull PhD, President
Ben Zuckerman PhD, Vice President

4032 Cultivar
Center for Agoecology
1156 High Street 831-459-2506
Santa Cruz, CA 95064 Fax: 831-459-2867
http://www.agroecology.org

Publication Date: 1985 9-12 pages Bi-Yearly
Steven Gliessman, Professor Agroecology
Martha Brown, Editor

4033 Ecosphere
Forum International
91 Gregory Lane 800-252-4475
Suite 21 Fax: 925-946-1500
Pleasant Hill, CA 94523 E-mail: fti@foruminternational.com
http://www.foruminternational.com

Accepts advertising. The first ever environmental/ecological magazine. It is dedicated to the interrelations of man in nature and a balanced approach of its biological, economic, socio-political and spiritual components. Since 1965.
Publication Date: 1965 16-48 pages Bi-monthly
Dr. Nicolas Hetzer, Production Manager
J McCormack, Circulation Director

4034 EnviroNews
600 Forbes Avenue 412-396-6000
331 Fisher Hall 800-456-0590
Pittsburgh, PA 15282 Fax: 412-396-4092
E-mail: bembic@duq.edu
http://www.science.duq.edu

Educating environmental professionals for the twenty-first century is the focus of the Duquesne University Environmental Science and Management (ESM) Masters Degree Program. The program grew out of the perceived need to combine depthof knowledge in environmental science with a comprehensive understanding of the business, legal and policy implications surrounding environmental issues.
4 pages Semester Newsletter
Sonia Bembic, Program Advisor

4035 Environmental News
Arkansas Environmental Federation
1400 W Markham Street 501-374-0263
Suite 302 Fax: 501-374-8752
Little Rock, AR 72201 E-mail: rthurman@environmentark.org
http://www.environmentark.org

Randy Thurman, Executive Director

4036 Forest Magazine
Forest Service Employees for Environmental Ethics
PO Box 11615 541-484-2692
Eugene, OR 97440 Fax: 541-484-3004
E-mail: fseee@fseee.org
http://www.fseee.org

FSEEE is the largest forest watchdog organization in the nation. Since 1989, FSEEE has defended the rights and responsibilities of brave scientists and resource professionals working to assure the long-term health and vitality of ournational forests. FSEEE publishes Forest Magazine quarterly to educate the public on forest issues.
Publication Date: 1989 50 pages Bi-Monthly
ISSN: 1534-9284
Andy Stahl, Executive Director
Patricia Marshall, Editor

4037 Forest Service Employees for Environmental Ethics
PO Box 11615 541-484-2692
Eugene, OR 97440 Fax: 541-484-3004
E-mail: fseee@fseee.org
http://www.fseee.org

FSEEE is the largest forest watchdog organization in the nation. Since 1989, FSEEE has defended the rights and responsibilities

of brave scientists and resource professionals working to assure the long-term health and vitality of ournational forests. FSEEE publishes Forest Magazine quarterly to educate the public on forest issues.
Andy Stahl, Executive Director

4038 Greens/Green Party USA Green Politics Green Politics
PO Box 1134 978-682-4353
Lawrence, MA 01842 866-GRE-ENS2
Fax: 978-682-4318
E-mail: gpusa@greens.org
http://www.greenparty.org
Is a national non-profit membership organization dedicated to advancing the Green Ten Key Values as a guiding force in American society and politics.
12 pages Quarterly
Don Fitz, Editor

4039 International Boreal Forest Newsletter
Institute for World Resource Research
PO Box 50303 630-910-1551
Palo Alto, CA 94303 Fax: 630-910-1561
http://www.globalwarming.net
Covers all phases of developments in forestry and reforestation of northern nations including the US, Canada, Russia, Sweden, Finland, Norway, China, Japan and others. Its goal is to increase the worldwide understanding of theecological and economic roles of the northern forest regions of the world.
Dr. Yuan Lee, Editor-in-Chief
BJ Jefferson, Advertising/Sales

4040 International Society of Tropical Foresters: ISTF Notices
5400 Grosvenor Lane 301-897-8720
Bethesda, MD 20814 Fax: 301-897-3690
E-mail: istfi@igc.apc.org
The International Society of Tropical Foresters, Inc. (ISTF) is a nonprofit organization committed to the protection, wise management and rational use of the world's tropical forests. Established in 1950, ISTF was reactivated in 1979.It has about 1500 members in more than 100 countries. Financial support comes from membership dues, donations and grants. ISTF sponsors meetings, promotes chapters in other countries, maintains a web site and has chapters at universities.
Warren T Doolittle, President

4041 Jackson Hole Conservation Alliance: Alliance News
PO Box 2728 307-733-9417
Jackson, WY 83001 Fax: 307-733-9008
E-mail: info@jhalliance.org
http://www.jhalliance.org
An organization dedicated to responsible land stewardship in Jackson Hole, Wyoming to ensure that human activities are in harmony with the area's irreplaceable wildlife, scenery and other natural resources.
20 pages Quarterly

Cindy Harger, Managing Director

4042 Leopold Letter
Leopold Center for Sustainable Agriculture
209 Curtiss Hall 515-294-3711
Ames, IA 50011 Fax: 515-294-9696
E-mail: leocenter@iastate.edu
http://www.leopold.iastate.edu
To inform diverse audiences about Leopold Center programs and activities; to encourage increased interest in and use of sustainable farming practicies; and to stimulate public discussion about sustainable agriculture in Iowa.
Publication Date: 1987 12 pages Quarterly
ISSN: 1065-2116
Jerry DeWitt, Director
Laura Miller, Editor

4043 Minnesota Department of Agriculture: MDA Quarterly
625 Robert St. N. 651-201-6000
St Paul, MN 55155 800-967-2474
Fax: 651-297-5522
E-mail: webinfo@mda.state.mn.us
http://www.mda.state.mn.us
The MDA's mission is to work toward a diverse ag industry that is profitable as well as environmentally sound; to protect the public health safety regarding food and ag products; and to ensure orderly commerce in agricultural and foodproducts. We have two major branches of the department to accomplish this mission: regulatory divisions and non-regulatory divisions.
Publication Date: 2000
Gene Hugoson, Commissioner
Michael Schommer, Editor

4044 Mountain Research and Development
PO Box 1978 530-752-8330
Davis, CA 95617 http://www.mrd-journal.org/about_mrd.htm
The leading journal specifically devoted to the world's mountains. It has been published since 1981 and has established itself as a renowned international publication containing well-researched, peer-reviewed scientific articles byauthors from around the world.
Professor Hans Hurni, Editor-in-Chief

4045 Northeast Sun
Northeast Sustainable Energy Association
50 Miles Street 413-774-6051
Greenfield, MA 01301 Fax: 413-774-6053
E-mail: nesea@nesea.org
http://www.nesea.org
Promotes responsible use of energy for a stronger economy and cleaner environment. Northeast Sun is a bi-annual Spring and Fall publication that includes articles by leading authorities on sustainable energy practices, energyefficiency and renewable energy, and each Fall issue includes the Sustainable Green Pages Directory of engery professionals in the Northeast. Subscription is free with membership.
Bi-Annual
David Barclay, Executive Director
Arianna Alexsandra Grindrod, Education Director

4046 Pinchot Letter
1616 P Street NW 202-797-6580
Suite 100 Fax: 202-797-6583
Washington, DC 20036 E-mail: pinchot@pinchot.org
http://www.pinchot.org
A tri-annual newsletter published by the Pinchot Institute for Conservation, an independent nonprofit organization that works collaboratively with all Americans-from federal and state policymakers to citizens in rural communities-tostrengthen forest conservation by advancing sustainable forest management, developing conservation leaders and providing science-based solutions to natural resource issues.
Publication Date: 1995 20 pages Tri-Annual
Dr V Alaric Sample, President

4047 Population Institute Newsletter
107 2nd Street NE 202-544-3300
Suite 207 188-787-0038
Washington, DC 20002 Fax: 202-544-0068
E-mail: web@populationinstitute.org
http://www.populationinstitute.org
The Population Institute is the World's largest independent nonprofit, educational organization dedicated exclusively to achieving a more equitable balance between the worlds population, environment, and resources. Established in 1969,the Institute, with members in 172 countries, is headquartered on Capitol Hill in Washington DC. The Institute uses a variety of resources and programs to bring its concerns about the consequences of rapid poulation growth to the forefront of thenational agenda.
Publication Date: 1988 8 pages Bi-Monthly
Werner Fornos, President
Hal Burdett, Executive Editor

4048 **Population Reference Bureau: World Population Data Sheet**
1875 Connecticut Avenue NW
Suite 520
Washington, DC 20009
202-483-1100
800-877-9881
Fax: 202-328-3937
E-mail: popref@prb.org
http://www.prb.org

Up-to-date demographic data and estimates for all the countries and major regions of the world.

William P Butz, President/CEO

4049 **Reporter**
Population Connection
2120 L Street NW
Suite 500
Washington, DC 20037
202-332-2200
Fax: 202-332-2302
E-mail: info@popconnect.org
http://www.popconnect.org

Looks at the connections between overpopulation and the environment around the world and features reports from our activists on Capitol Hill Days 2005. This publication is included in your $25.00 memberhsip fee.

Publication Date: 1972 24 pages Quarterly
ISSN: 0199-0071
John Seager, President/CEO
Mara Nelson Grynavinski, Editor

4050 **Resource Development Newsletter**
University of Tennessee
PO Box 1071
Knoxville, TN 37901
865-974-7448
Fax: 423-974-7448

Community development information.

4 pages
Dr Alan Barefield, Publisher

4051 **Restoration Ecology Magazine**
Blackwell Science
350 Main Street
Malden, MA 02148
781-388-8200
Fax: 781-388-8210
http://www.blackwellpublishing.com

Provides the most recent developments in the ecological and biological restoration field for both the fundamental and practical implications of restorations.

Richard Hobbs, Editor

4052 **Society of American Foresters Information Center Newsletter**
5400 Grosvenor Lane
Bethesda, MD 20814
301-897-8720
Fax: 301-897-3690
E-mail: safweb@safnet.org
http://www.safnet.org

An organization that represents the forestry profession in the United States. Its mission is to advance the science, education, technology and practice of forestry.

Publication Date: 1996 24 pages Monthly
Michael T Goergen, Jr, EVP/CEO

4053 **Solar Energy Magazine**
Elsevier Science
360 Park Avenue S
11th Floor
New York, NY 10010
212-989-5800
Fax: 212-633-3680
E-mail: usinfo-f@elseview.com
http://www.elseview.com

Devoted exclusively to the science and technology of solar energy applications.

Publication Date: 1957
ISSN: 0380-92X
D Yogi Goswami, Editor-in-Chief

4054 **Solar Energy Report**
California Solar Energy Industries Association
PO Box 782
Rio Vista, CA 94571
916-747-6987
Fax: 707-374-4767
E-mail: info@calseia.org
http://www.calseia.org

Bi-Monthly
Les Nelson, President

4055 **Southface Journal of Sustainable Building**
Southface Energy Institute
241 Pine Street NE
Atlanta, GA 30308
404-872-3549
Fax: 404-872-5009
E-mail: info@southface.org
http://www.southface.org

Contains articles on numerous sustainable building topics. Free to members and available online.

Publication Date: 1978 24 pages Quarterly
Dennis Creech, Executive Director/Editor

4056 **Sustainable Green Pages Directory**
Northeast Sustainable Energy Association
50 Miles Street
Greenfield, MA 01301
413-774-6051
Fax: 413-774-6053
E-mail: nesea@nesea.org
http://www.nesea.org

The SPG Directory lists over 30 categories of sustainable energy professionals working throughout the Northeast, including architects, engineers, builders, energy auditors, consultants and renewable energy installers and manufacturers.It is the largest directory of its kind and the only one that targets the Northeastern USA. Published in the Northeast Sun magazine and online.

September Annual
David Barclay, Executive Director
Arianna Alexsandra Grindrod, Education Director

4057 **Tall Timbers Research Station: Bulletin Series**
13093 Henry Beadel Drive
Tallahassee, FL 32312
850-893-4153
Fax: 850-668-7781
E-mail: rose@ttrs.org
http://www.talltimbers.org

Dedicated to protecting wildlands and preserving natural habitats. Promotes public education on the importance of natural disturbances to the environment and the subsequent need for wildlife and land management. Conducts fire ecologyresearch and other biological research programs through the Tall Timbers Research Station. Operates museum.

Publication Date: 1962
ISSN: 0496-7631
Lane Green, Executive Director
R Todd Engstrom, Editor

4058 **Tall Timbers Research Station: Fire Ecology Conference Proceedings**
13093 Henry Beadel Drive
Tallahassee, FL 32312
850-893-4153
Fax: 850-668-7781
E-mail: rose@ttrs.org
http://www.talltimbers.org

Dedicated to protecting wildlands and preserving natural habitats. Promotes public education on the importance of natural disturbances to the environment and the subsequent need for wildlife and land management. Conducts fire ecologyresearch and other biological research programs through the Tall Timbers Research Station. Operates museum.

Publication Date: 1962
ISSN: 0082-1527
Lane Green, Executive Director
R Todd Engstrom, Editor

4059 **Tall Timbers Research Station: Game Bird Seminar Proceedings**
13093 Henry Beadel Drive
Tallahassee, FL 32312
850-893-4153
Fax: 850-668-7781
E-mail: rose@ttrs.org
http://www.talltimbers.org

Dedicated to protecting wildlands and preserving natural habitats. Promotes public education on the importance of natural disturbances to the environment and the subsequent need for wildlife and land management. Conducts fire ecologyresearch and other biological research programs through the Tall Timbers Research Station. Operates museum.

Publication Date: 1980
ISSN: 1087-4372
Lane Green, Executive Director
R Todd Engstrom, Editor

4060 **Tall Timbers Research Station: Miscellaneous Series**
13093 Henry Beadel Drive 850-893-4153
Tallahassee, FL 32312 Fax: 850-668-7781
E-mail: rose@ttrs.org
http://www.talltimbers.org

Dedicated to protecting wildlands and preserving natural habitats. Promotes public education on the importance of natural disturbances to the environment and the subsequent need for wildlife and land management. Conducts fire ecologyresearch and other biological research programs through the Tall Timbers Research Station. Operates museum.
Publication Date: 1961
ISSN: 0494-764x
Lane Green, Executive Director
R Todd Engstrom, Editor

4061 **Totally Tree-Mendous Activities**
Northeast Sustainable Energy Association
50 Miles Street 413-774-6051
Greenfield, MA 01301 Fax: 413-774-6053
E-mail: nesea@nesea.org
http://www.nesea.org

Resource for teachers and parents that offers creative and fun tree-based projects for students.
40 pages
David Barclay, Executive Director
Arianna Alexsandra Grindrod, Education Director

4062 **Woodland Steward**
Massachusetts Forestry Association
270 Jackson Street 413-323-7326
Belchertown, MA 01007 Fax: 413-323-9594
This publication is full of information about Massachusett's forest and ways that landowners can manage their woodlands to achieve their goals in an environmentally sustainable manner. Free with membership.
Bi-Monthly
Gregory Cox, Executive Director

4063 **Worldwatch Institute: State of the World**
1776 Massachusetts Avenue NW 202-452-1999
Washington, DC 20036 Fax: 202-296-7365
E-mail: worldwatch@worldwatch.org
http://www.worldwatch.org

The most authoritative go-to resource for those who understand the importance of nuturing a safe, sane and healthy global environment through both policy and action.
Annual
ISBN: 0-393326-66-7
Christopher Flavin, President
Tom Prugh, Editor

4064 **Worldwatch Institute: Vital Signs**
1776 Massachusetts Avenue NW 202-452-1999
Suite 800 Fax: 202-296-7365
Washington, DC 20036 http://www.worldwatch.org
Provides comprehensive, user-friendly information on key trends and includes tables and graphs that help readers access the developments that are changing their lives for better or for worse.
Annual
ISBN: 0-393326-89-6
Christopher Flavin, President
Tom Prugh, Editor

4065 **Worldwatch Institute: World Watch**
1776 Massachusetts Avenue NW 202-452-1999
Suite 800 Fax: 202-296-7365
Washington, DC 20036 http://www.worldwatch.org
The Worldwatch Institute is an independent, nonprofit environmental research organization in Washington DC. Its mission is to foster a sustainable society in which human needs are met in ways that do not threaten the health of thenatural environment or future generations. To this end, this Institute conducts interdisciplinary research on emerging global issues, the results of which are published and disseminated to decision-makers and the media.
Bi-Monthly
Christopher Flavin, President
Tom Prugh, Editor

4066 **Worldwatch Institute: Worldwatch Papers**
1776 Massachusetts Avenue NW 202-452-1999
Suite 800 Fax: 202-296-7365
Washington, DC 20036 http://www.worldwatch.org
Provides cutting-edge analysis on an environmental topic that is making - or is about to make - headlines worldwide.
50-70 pages 5x times year
Christopher Flavin, President
Tom Prugh, Editor

Periodicals: Travel & Tourism

4067 **New York State Parks, Recreation and Historic Preservation**
Empire State Plaza 518-474-0456
Agency Building 1 Fax: 518-486-2924
Albany, NY 12238 http://www.nysparks.com
Publishes New York State Boat Launching Guide, Camping/Cabin Reservation Info, Snowmobiling Guide and Preservation Magazine.
Bernadette Castro, Commissioner

4068 **Noxubee National Wildlife Refuge Newsletter**
2970 Bluff Lake Road 662-323-5548
Brooksville, MS 39739 Fax: 662-323-6390
E-mail: noxubee@fws.gov
http://http://www.fws.gov/noxubee/

Noxubee National Wildlife Refuge was established in 1940 to protect and enhance habitat for the conservation of migratory birds, endangered species and other wildlife. The recreational and educational opportunities provided on therefuge help the public experience nature and learn how sound management ensures that future generations continue to enjoy fish and wildlife and their habitats.
2 pages Bi-Annual
Andrea Duncan, Editor

4069 **Parks and Recreation Magazine**
National Recreation and Park Association
22377 Belmont Ridge Road 703-858-0784
Ashburn, VA 20148 Fax: 703-858-0794
E-mail: info@nrpa.org
http://www.activeparks.comornrpa.org

Informs, motivates and inspires professionals, civic leaders and citizens to elevate the value of parks and recreation as a public service.
Monthly
John Thorner, Exectutive Director
Rachel Roberts, Editor

4070 **Potomac Appalachian**
118 Park Street SE 703-242-0693
Vienna, VA 22180 Fax: 703-242-0968
E-mail: info@patc.net
http://www.patc.net

Published by the Potomac Appalachian Trail Club, which through volunteer efforts, education and advocacy, acquires, maintains and protects the trail and lands of the Appalachian Trail, other trails and related facilities in theMid-Atlantic Region for the enjoyment of present and future hikers. PATC publishes hiking guides, maps and history books of the Appalachian Trail and other trails in our area of responsibility. The monthly newsletter is sent to members and uponrequest. Free to members.
16-20 pages Monthly
ISSN: 098 -8154
Thomas R Johnson, President

Periodicals: Water Resources

4071 **Air Water Pollution Report's Environment Week**
Business Publishers

PO Box 17592 301-589-5103
Baltimore, MD 21297 800-274-6737
Fax: 301-589-8493
E-mail: custserv@bpinews.com
http://www.bpinews.com

Provides a balanced, insightful update on the week's most important environmental news from Washington, DC.

Leonard A Eiserer, Publisher
David Goeller, Editor

4072 Air/Water Pollution Report
Business Publishers
PO Box 17592 301-589-5103
Baltimore, MD 21297 800-274-6737
Fax: 301-589-8493
E-mail: custserv@bpinews.com
http://www.bpinews.com

Regulatory activities and governmental legislation, in addition to litigation are covered in this pulication.

Leonard A Eiserer, Publisher
David Goeller, Editor

4073 America's Priceless Groundwater
American Ground Water Trust
50 Pleasant Street Ste 2 603-228-5444
Concord, NH 03301 Fax: 603-228-6557
E-mail: trustinfo@agwt.org
http://www.agwt.org

15 pages Quarterly
Andrew Stone, Director

4074 American Fisheries Society: Water Quality Matters
324 25th Street 801-625-5358
Ogden, UT 84401 Fax: 801-625-5756
E-mail: glampman@fs.fed.us

8 pages 1-2 per year
Georgina Lampman, President
Gregg Lomincky, Editor

4075 American Water Resources Association: Journal of the American Water Resources Association
PO Box 1626 540-687-8390
Middleburg, VA 20118 Fax: 540-687-8395
E-mail: terry@awra.org
http://www.awra.org

AWRA is a nonprofit, scientific educational association for individuals and organizations involved in all aspects of water resources. Its goal is to advance multidisciplinary water resources management and research through itsconferences, publications, technical commettees, state sections and student chapters.

Publication Date: 1964 Bi-Monthly
ISSN: 1093-474X
Kenneth D Reid, Executive VP
Terry Meyer, Marketing Director

4076 American Water Resources Association: Water Resources IMPACT
PO Box 1626 540-687-8390
Middleburg, VA 20118 Fax: 540-687-8395
E-mail: terry@awra.org
http://www.awra.org

AWRA is a nonprofit, scientific educational association for individuals and organizations involved in all aspects of water resources. Its goal is to advance multidisciplinary water resources management and research through itsconferences, publications, technical commettees, state sections and student chapters.

Bi-Monthly
ISSN: 1093-474X
Kenneth D Reid, Executive VP
Terry Meyer, Marketing Director

4077 Arsenic and Groud Water Home
American Ground Water Trust
50 Pleasant Street Ste 2 603-228-5444
Concord, NH 03301 Fax: 603-228-6557
E-mail: trustinfo@agwt.org
http://www.agwt.org

15 pages Quarterly
Andrew Stone, Director

4078 Bacteria and Water Wells
American Ground Water Trust
50 Pleasant Street Ste2 603-228-5444
Concord, NH 03301 Fax: 603-228-6557
E-mail: trustinfo@agwt.org
http://www.agwt.org

15 pages Quarterly
Andrew Stone, Director

4079 Blue Planet Magazine
The Ocean Conservancy
2029 K Street 202-429-5609
Washington, DC 20006 800-519-1541
Fax: 202-429-0056
E-mail: info@oceanconservancy.org
http://www.oceanconservancy.org

To educate peoeple about ocean issues; inspire readers with the beauty and wonder of oceans; encourage dedication to appreciating and protecting marine resources; and enlist new volunteers in the ocean community. Free with membershipfee of $25.00

46 pages Quarterly
Roger Rufe,Jr, President/CEO
Sara Bennington, Editor

4080 Clean Water Network: CWN Status Water Report
Spills and Kills
1200 New York Avenue, NW 202-289-2421
Suite 400 Fax: 202-289-1060
Washington, DC 20005 E-mail: info@cwn.org
http://www.cwn.org

A nonprofit network of over 1,000 organizations that deal with clean water issues covered by the Clean Water Act. Our member organizations consist of a variety of organizations representing environmentalists, family farmers, recreationanglers, commercial fishermen, surfers, boaters, faith communities, labor unions and civic associates. We publish a monthly newsletter and various reports.

8-12 pages Monthly
Katherine Smitherman, Executive Director

4081 Clean Water Report Newsletter
Business Publishers
PO Box 17592 301-589-5103
Baltimore, MD 21297 800-274-6737
Fax: 301-589-8493
E-mail: custserv@bpinews.com
http://www.bpinews.com

Follows the latest news from the EPA, Congress, the states, the courts, and private industry. A key information source for environmental professionals, covering the important issues of ground and drinking water, wastewater treatment,wetlands, drought, coastal protection, non-point source pollution, agrichemical contamination and more.

8 pages Bi-Weekly
ISSN: 0009-8620
Leonard A Eiserer, Publisher
Louise Harris, Editor

4082 Clearwaters Magazine
New York Water Environment Association
525 Plum Street 315-422-7811
Suite 102 Fax: 315-422-3851
Syracuse, NY 13204 E-mail: pcr@nywea.org
http://www.nywea.org

Published by The New York Water Environment Association, a nonprofit educational association dedicated to the development and dissemination of information concerning water quality management and the nature, collection, treatment, anddisposal of wastewater. Founded in 1929, the Association has over 2,500

members. The NYWEA is a member association of the Water Environment Federation.
Quarterly
Patricia Cerro-Reehil, Executive Director
Robert D Hennigan, Executive Editor

4083 Colorado Department of Natural Resources: Division of Water Resources: StreamLines
1313 Sherman Street 303-866-3581
Room 818 Fax: 303-866-3589
Denver, CO 80203 http://www.water.state.co.us
The Colorado Division of Water Resources is an agency of the State of Colorado, Department of Natural Resources, operating under the direction of specific state staute s, court decrees, and interstate compacts. The DWR is empowered toadminister all surface and ground water rights throughout the state and ensure that the doctrine of prior appropiation is enforced.
Publication Date: 1988 4-8 pages Quarterly
Hal D Simpson, Director Water Resources
Russell George, Executive Director

4084 Colorado Water Rights
1580 Logan Street 303-837-0812
#400 Fax: 303-837-1607
Denver, CO 80203 E-mail: cwc@cowatercongress.org
http://www.cowatercongress.org
This newsletter helps the Colorado Water Congress protect and conserve Colorado's water resouces by educating its readers.
Publication Date: 1982 4-16 pages Quarterly
Doug Kemper, Executive Director

4085 Confluence
Texas Water Conservation Association
221 E 9th Street http://www.twca.org
Suite 206
Austin, TX 78701
The official newsletter of the Texas Water Conservation Association. For those interested in water issues from river authorities to industrial concerns.
Quarterly

4086 Domestic Water Treatment for Homeowners
American Ground Water Trust
50 Pleasant Street Ste 2 603-228-5444
Concord, NH 03301 Fax: 603-228-6557
E-mail: trustinfo@agwt.org
http://www.agwt.org
15 pages Quarterly
Andrew Stone, Director

4087 Environmental Policy Alert
Inside Washington Publishers
1225 South Clark Street 703-416-8500
Suite 1400 800-424-9068
Arlington, VA 22202 Fax: 703-416-8543
E-mail: iwp@iwpnews.com
http://www.iwpnews.com
Is a reliable resource for all regulatory, congressional and litigation developments in air quality, waste cleanup, clean water and other environmental quality issues. Also provides a special focus on efforts to reinvent environmentalpolicies.
Publication Date: 1984 Bi-Weekly
Jeremy Bernstein, Editor

4088 Georgia Water and Pollution Control Association: Operator
2121 New Market Parkway 770-618-8690
Suite 144 Fax: 770-618-8695
Marietta, GA 30067 E-mail: info@gwpca.org
http://www.gawponline.org
The GW+PCA is dedicated to education, dissemination of technical and scientific information, increased public understanding and promotion of sound public laws and programs in the water resources and related environmental fields.Founded in 1932.
Publication Date: 1970 56-68 pages Quarterly
Jack C Dozier, PE, Executive Director

4089 Georgia Water and Pollution Control Association: News & Notes
2121 New Market Parkway 770-618-8690
Suite 144 Fax: 770-618-8695
Marietta, GA 30067 E-mail: info@gwpca.org
http://www.gawponline.org
The GW+PCA is dedicated to education, dissemination of technical and scientific information, increased public understanding and promotion of sound public laws and programs in the water resources and related environmental fields.Founded in 1932.
Publication Date: 1970 20-28 pages Monthly
Jack C Dozier, PE, Executive Director

4090 Groundwater: A Course of Wonder
American Ground Water Trust
50 Pleasant Street Ste 2 603-228-5444
Concord, NH 03301 Fax: 603-228-6557
E-mail: trustinfo@agwt.org
http://www.agwt.org
15 pages Quarterly
Andrew Stone, Director

4091 Gulf of Mexico Science
Dauphin Island Sea Lab
101 Bienville Boulevard 251-861-2141
Dauphin Island, AL 36528 Fax: 251-861-4646
http://www.disl.org
Journal devoted to disemminating knowledge of the Gulf of Mexico and adjacent areas. Appropriate topics of consideration for publication include all areas of marine science.
2x Year
ISSN: 1087-688X
Carolyn Wood, Assistant Editor

4092 International Desalination and Water Reuse Quarterly
Lineal Publishing Company
306 Eagle Dr 561-451-9429
Jupiter, FL 33477 Fax: 561-451-9435
Disseminates technical information, reviews and analyzes regional developments in the field, as well as new products and processes. The publication provides, on a continuing basis, a major vehicle in which to promote desalination andwater reuse technologies, equipment, and design to potential users.
Irv Lineal, Publisher

4093 Journal of Soil and Water Conservation
Soil & Water Conservation Society
945 SW Ankeny Road 515-289-2331
Ankeny, IA 50023 Fax: 515-289-1227
E-mail: swcs@swcs.org
http://www.swcs.org
Publication includes a variety of conservation subjects, as well as international conservation issues.
Craig Cox, Executive Director
Deb Happe, Editor/Communications Dir

4094 Journal of the American Shore and Beach Preservation Association
American Shore & Beach Preservation Association
5460 Beaujolais Lane 239-489-2616
Fort Myers, FL 33919 Fax: 239-489-9917
E-mail: exdir@asbpa.org
http://www.asbpa.org
Peer-reviewed journal of the ASBPA. It provides sound, interesting technical information concerning shores and beaches of the nation and worldwide.
24 pages Quarterly
ISSN: 0037-4237
Kate & Ken Gooderham, Editors
Dr Beth Sciaudone, Managing Editor

4095 Journal of the New England Water Environment
New England Water Environment Association
10 Tower Office Park 781-939-0908
Suite 601 Fax: 781-939-0907
Woburn, MA 01801 E-mail: mail@newea.org
http://www.newea.org

Bi-annual publication from New England Water Environment Association.
Publication Date: 1929 150 pages Bi-Annual
ISSN: 1077-3002
Susan Landon, Journal/Publications Dir

4096 Journal of the North American Benthological Society
North American Benthological Society
PO Box 7065
Lawrence, KS 66044
E-mail: amorin@outtawa.ca
http://www.benthos.org
The society is an international scientific organization that promotes better understanding of biotic communities of lake and stream bottoms and their role in aquatic ecosystems. The journal includes articles that promote the furtherunderstanding of benthic communities and helps members to keep current on interests.
Quarterly
ISSN: 0887-3593
N LeRoy Poff, President

4097 Mass Waters
Massachusetts Water Pollution Control Association
PO Box 221
Groveland, MA 01834
978-374-0170
Fax: 978-521-4083
E-mail: mwpca1965@verizon.net
http://www.mwpca.org
Quarterly
John Connor, Secretary/Treasurer

4098 Mono Lake Committee Newsletter
Corner of Hwy 395 & 3rd Street
PO Box 29
Lee Vining, CA 93541
760-647-6595
Fax: 760-647-6377
E-mail: info@monolake.org
http://www.monolake.org
Nonprofit citizen's group dedicated to: protecting and restoring the Mono Basin ecosystem; educating the public about Mono Lake and the impacts on the environment of excessive water use; promoting cooperative solutions that protectMono Lake and meet real water needs without transferring environmental problems to other areas.
Publication Date: 1978 28 pages Quarterly
Geoffrey McQuilkin, Executive Director
Arya Degenhardt, Editor

4099 Montana Environmental Training Center Newsletter
Hagener Science Center
Rm #110
MSU-Northern
Havre, MT 59501
406-265-3763
Fax: 406-265-3750
E-mail: boylej@msun.edu
http://www.msun.edu/grants/metc/gary.asp
METC is a cooperative effort between Montana State University-Northern and the Montana Department of Environmental Quality. Basic, advance training, and continuing education in the areas of water and wastewater operation, maintenance,safety, process control, cross connection and backflow prevention along with courses in basic water science and watershed awareness define the training activities of METC. A newsletter and Training Announcement are published quarterly.
Quarterly
Jan Boyle, Director

4100 Montana Environmental Training Center Training Announcement
Hagener Science Center
Rm #110
MSU-Northern
Havre, MT 59501
406-265-3763
Fax: 406-265-3750
E-mail: boylej@msun.edu
http://www.msun.edu/grants/metc/gary.asp
METC is a cooperative effort between Montana State University-Northern and the Montana Department of Environmental Quality. Basic, advance training, and continuing education in the areas of water and wastewater operation, maintenance,safety, process control, cross connection and backflow prevention along with courses in basic water science and watershed awareness define the training activities of METC. A newsletter and Training Announcement are published quarterly.
Quarterly
Jan Boyle, Director

4101 Montana Water Environment Association: Newsletter
516 N Park Street
Suite A
Helena, MT 59601
406-449-7913
Fax: 406-449-6350
Semi-Annual
Carl Anderson, President

4102 New Mexico Rural Water Association Newsletter
3413 Carlisle Boulevard NE
Albuquerque, NM 87110
505-884-1031
800-819-9893
Fax: 505-884-1032
E-mail: contact @nmrwa.org
http://www.nmrwa.org
To provide top quality, responsive technical assistance and training for rural water and wastewater systems in New Mexico.
Quarterly
Matthew Holmes, Executive Director
Robert Matthews, Co-Editor

4103 New York Water Environment Association Clearwaters
525 Plum Street
Suite 102
Syracuse, NY 13204
315-422-7811
Fax: 315-422-3851
E-mail: pcr@nywea.org
http://www.nywea.org
Contains articles on environmental issues, regulatory changes, technological advances as well as, updates on members and activities.
50 pages Quarterly
Patricia Cerro-Reehil, Executive Director
Hope Dodge, Editor

4104 Oregon Water Resources Congress Newsletter
1201 Court Street NE
Salem, OR 97301
503-363-0121
Fax: 503-371-4926
E-mail: owrc@owrc.org
http://www.owrc.org
Is to promote the protection and use of water rights and the wise stewardship of water resources.
Quarterly
Anita Winkler, Executive Director
Carol Zielinski, Editor

4105 Ozark National Scenic Riverways
Ozark National Scenic Riverways
PO Box 490
Van Buren, MO 63965
573-323-4236
Fax: 573-323-4140
E-mail: ozar_superintendent@nps.gov
http://www.nps.gov/ozar
Missouri's largest National Park and America's first to preserve a free flowing river in its wild state. Covers some 80,000 acres along 134 miles of the Current and Jacks Fork Rivers. Staff provide elementary level environmentaleducation programs on natural history, with an emphasis on karst and water issues. Publishes More Than Skin Deep, a Teacher's Guide to Caves and Groundwater, a curriculum guide suitable for grades K-12.
Publication Date: 1964 Annual
Noel Poe, Superintendent

4106 Pacific Rivers Council: Freeflow
PO Box 10798
Eugene, OR 97440
541-345-0119
Fax: 541-345-0710
E-mail: info@pacrivers.org
http://www.pacrivers.org
Promoting the protection and restoration of rivers, their watersheds, and native aquatic species.
Quarterly
David Bayles, Executive Director
Holly Spencer, Editor

4107 Pipeline
National Environmental Services Center
NRCCE Building, Evandale Drive
PO Box 6064
Morgantown, WV 26506
304-293-4191
800-624-8301
Fax: 304-293-3161
E-mail: nsfc_orders@mail.nesc.wvu.edu
http://www.nsfc.wvu.edu

Newsletter of the National Small Flows Clearinghouse, a non-profit national source of information about small flows technologies-those systems that have fewer than one million gallons of wastewater flowing through them per day-rangingfrom individual septic systems to small sewage treatment plants. Free to US residents.

Publication Date: 1990 8 pages Quarterly
ISSN: 1060-0043
Dr Gerald Iwan, Director
Jen Hause, Engineering Scientist

4108 Puerto Rico Water Resources and Environmental Research Institute Newsletter

University of Puerto Rico
College of Engineering 787-833-0300
PO Box 9040 Fax: 787-832-0119
Mayaguez, PR 00681 E-mail: PRWRERI@uprm.edu
http://www.ece.uprm.edu/rumhp/prwrri

Its objectives are to: conduct research aimed at resolving local and national water resources problems; train scientists and engineers through hands-on participation in research; and to facilitate the incorporation of research resultsin the knowledge base of water resources professionals.

Publication Date: 1990 4 pages Quarterly/thru Email
Jose R Cedeno, Associate Director

4109 Runoff Rundown

Center for Watershed Protection
8390 Main Street 410-461-8323
Second Floor Fax: 410-461-8324
Ellicott City, MD 21043 E-mail: center@cwp.org
http://www.cwp.org or www.stormwatercenter.net

Electronic newsletter published by the Center for Watershed Protection, a nonprofit 501(c)3 organization dedicated to finding new ways to protect and restore our nation's streams, lakes, rivers and estuaries. The center publishesnumerous technical publications on all aspects of watershed protection, including stormwater management, watershed planning and better site design.

Publication Date: 2000 Quarterly
Hye Yeong Kwon, Executive Director
Lauren Lasher, Editor

4110 Save San Francisco Bay Association: Watershed Newsletter

350 Frank H Ogawa Plaza 510-452-9261
Suite 900 Fax: 510-452-9266
Oakland, CA 94612 E-mail: SAVEBAY@savesfbay.org
http://www.savesfbay.org

Save the Bay has worked for over 40 years to protect the San Francisco Bay-Delta from pollution, fill, shoreline destruction and fresh water diversion. We have launched a century of renewal to restore bay fish and wildlife, reclaimtidal wetlands and make the bay safe and accessible to all.

8-10 pages 3-4 times/year
David Lewis, Executive Director
Paul Revier, Editor

4111 Small Flow Quarterly

NRCCE Building, Evandale Drive 304-293-4191
PO Box 6064 800-624-8301
Morgantown, WV 26506 Fax: 304-293-3161
E-mail: nsfc_orders@mail.nesc.wvu.edu
http://www.nsfc.wvu.edu

Magazine of the National Small Flows Clearinghouse, a non-profit national source of information about small flows technologies-those systems that have fewer than one million gallons of wastewater flowing through them per day-rangingfrom individual septic systems to small sewage treatment plants. Free to US residents.

Publication Date: 2000 50 pages Quarterly
ISSN: 1528-6827
Dr Gerald Iwan, Director
Jen Hause, Engineering Scientist

4112 South Carolina Sea Grant Consortium

287 Meeting Street 843-727-2078
Charleston, SC 29401 Fax: 843-727-2080
http://www.scseagrant.org

A state agency that supports coastal and marine research, education, outreach, and one technical assistance program that fosters sustainable economic development and resource conservation. The consortium represents eight university andstate research organizations and induces a number of information products on coastal and marine resource topics.

Publication Date: 1982 16 pages
M Richard DeVoe, Executive Director

4113 TCS Bulletin

PO Box 25408 703-768-1599
Alexandria, VA 22313 Fax: 703-768-1596
E-mail: coastalsoc@aol.com
http://www.thecoastalsociety.org

Organization of private sector, academic, government professionals and students dedicated to actively addressing emerging coastal issues by fostering dialogue, forging partnerships and promoting communication and education. Thispublication covers issues of aquaculture-related law and coastal management research.

Publication Date: 1975 24 pages Yearly
Paul Ticco, President
John Duff, Editor

4114 Tide

Coastal Conservation Association
6919 Portwest 713-626-4234
Suite 100 800-201-FISH
Houston, TX 77024 E-mail: ccantl@joincca.org
http://www.joincca.org

TIDE is the official bimonthly magazine of the Coastal Conservation Association. It has received local, state and national acclaim for writing, photography and layout and currently boasts a circulation of more than 70,000. TIDE isavailable only to members of the Coastal Conservation Association.

Bi-Monthly
Pat Murray, Executive Director
Ted Venker, Editor

4115 Utah Watershed Review

Utah Association of Conservation Districts
1860 North 100 East 435-753-6029
Logan, UT 84341 Fax: 435-755-2117
http://www.uacd.org

Provides information about what's new in Utah and watershed volunteer work and management.

Bi-Monthly
Gordon Younker, EVP
Jack Wilbur, Editor

4116 Water & Wastes Digest

Scranton Gillette Communications
3030 W. Salt Creek Lane 847-391-1000
Suite 201 Fax: 847-390-0408
Arlington Heights, IL 60005 http://www.scrantongillette.com

This serves readers in the water and/or wastewater industries. These people work for municipalities, in industry, or as engineers. They design, specify, buy, operate and maintain equipment, chemicals, software and wastewater treatmentservices.

128 pages
ISSN: 0043-1181
Dennis Martyka, Publisher
Tim Gregorski, Editorial Director

4117 Water Conservation in Your Home

American Ground Water Trust
50 Pleasant Street Ste 2 603-228-5444
Concord, NH 03301 Fax: 603-228-6557
E-mail: trustinfo@agwt.org
http://www.agwt.org

15 pages Quarterly
Andrew Stone, Director

4118 Water Quality Products

Scranton Gillette Communications
3030 W. Salt Creek Lane 847-391-1000
Suite 201 Fax: 847-390-0408
Arlington Heights, IL 60005 http://www.scrantongillette.com

Provides balanced editorial content including developments in water conditioning, filtration and disinfection for residential, commercial and industrial systems.
68 pages
ISSN: 1092-0978
Dennis Martyka, Publisher
Tracy Fabre, Editor

4119 Water Resource Center: Minnegram
University of Minnesota
173 McNeal 1985 Buford Avenue 612-624-9282
St Paul, MN 55108 Fax: 612-625-1263
Fax: '
E-mail: ander045@umn.edu
http://www.wrc.coafes.umn.edu
Four University water programs, Extension Water Quality Program, Center for Hydrocultural Impacts on Water Quality, Water Resources Research Center and Water Resources Science Graduate Program make up the Water Resources Center. Thecenter sponsors and coordinates programs in research, graduate education, outreach and service to address water resource management issues.
Publication Date: 1986 Quarterly
Jim Anderson, Co-Director
Debra Swackhamer, Co-Director

4120 WaterMatters
Southwest Florida Water Management District
2379 Broad Street 352-796-7211
Brookville, FL 34604 Fax: 352-754-6885
http://www.watermatters.org
Newletter of the Southwest Florida Water Management District, which manages the water and water-related resources within its boundaries. Maintains balance between the water needs of current and future users while protecting andmaintaining the natural systems that provide the District with its existing and future water supply. The Conservation Projects Section, is reponsible for managing water conservation, reclaimed water, other alternative source projects, and estimatingfuture water demands.
2 pages Monthly
Dave Moore, Executive Director
Rebecca Bray, Editor

Books: Air & Climate

4121 Air Pollution Control and the German Experience: Lessons for the United States
Center for Clean Air Policy
750 1st Street NE 202-408-9260
Suite 940 Fax: 202-408-8896
Washington, DC 20002 E-mail: communications@ccap.org
http://www.ccap.org

4122 Caring for Our Air
Enslow Publishers, Inc
40 Industrial Road, Dept. F61 908-771-9400
PO Box 398 800-398-2504
Berkeley Heights, NJ 07922 Fax: 908-771-0925
E-mail: customerservice@enslow.com
http://www.enslow.com
Publication Date: 1976

4123 Center for Resource Economics
1718 Connecticut Avenue NW 202-232-7933
Suite 300 Fax: 202-234-1328
Wasington, DC 20009 E-mail: info@islandpress.org
http://www.islandpress.org
Works to educate the public about global environmental issues. Methods include publishing literature on environmental concerns.

4124 Confronting Climate Change: Strategies for Energy Research and Development
National Academy Press
500 5th Street NW 202-334-3313
Lockbox 285 888-624-8373
Washington, DC 20055 Fax: 202-334-2451
http://www.nap.edu
Publication Date: 1990 144 pages
ISBN: 0-309043-47-6

4125 Fight Global Warming: 29 Things You Can Do
Environmental Defense Fund
257 Park Avenue South 212-505-2100
17th Floor 800-684-3322
New York, NY 10010 Fax: 212-505-2375
E-mail: members@edf.org
http://www.edf.org
Fred Krupp, President
David Yarnold, Executive Director

4126 Fundamentals of Stack Gas Dispersion
Milton R. Beychok Consulting
1126 Colony Plaza 949-718-1360
Newport Beach, CA 92660 Fax: 949-718-1360
E-mail: mbeychok@air-dispersion.com
http://www.air-dispertion.com
The most comprehensive single-source reference book on dispertion modeling of continuous buoyant pollution plumes.
Milton R Beychok, Principal

4127 Healing the Planet: Strategies for Resolving the Environmental Crisis
Addison-Wesley Publishing Company
75 Arlington Street 617-848-7500
Suite 300 http://www.aw.com
Boston, MA 02116

4128 Indoor Air Quality: Design Guide Book
Fairmont Press
700 Indian Trail 770-925-9388
Liburn, GA 30047 Fax: 770-381-9865
E-mail: linda@fairmontpress.com
http://www.fairmontpress.com

4129 Ozone Depletion and Climate Change: Constructing a Global Response
SUNY Press
194 Washington Ave 518-472-5000
Suite 305 800-666-2211
Albany, NY 12210 Fax: 518-472-5038
E-mail: info@sunypress.edu
http://www.sunypress.edu
Available in both soft and hardcover, this book offers solutions that address climate change from a global viewpoint.
Publication Date: 2005 276 pages
Matthew J Hoffman, Author

4130 Politics of Air Pollution: Urban Growth, Ecological Modernization, and Symbolic Inclusion
SUNY Press
194 Washington Ave 518-472-5000
Suite 305 800-666-2211
Albany, NY 12210 Fax: 518-472-5038
E-mail: info@sunypress.edu
http://www.sunypress.edu
Available in both soft and hardcover, this title addresses the relationship between urban growth and pollution.
Publication Date: 2005 152 pages
George A Gonzalez, Author

4131 To Breath Free: Eastern Europe's Environmental Crisis
John Hopkins University Press
3400 N Charles Street 410-516-6900
Baltimore, MD 21218 800-537-5487
http://www.jhubookis.com
Adam Glazer, Promotions Manager

Books: Business

4132 Environmental Career Guide: Job Opportunities with the Earth in Mind
J Wiley & Sons
605 3rd Avenue
6th Floor
New York, NY 10158
212-850-6000
Fax: 212-850-6088
http://www.wiley.com
Publication Date: 1991 208 pages
ISBN: 0-471534-13-7
Nicholas Basta, Author

4133 Environmental Disputes: Community Involvement in Conflict Resolution
Island Press
PO Box 7
Covelo, CA 95428
707-983-6432
800-828-1302
Fax: 707-983-6414
A book published by Island Press which helps citizen groups, business and government understand how Envionmental Dispute Settlement-a set of procedures for settling disputes over environmental policies without litigation-can work forthem.
Publication Date: 1990 295 pages
ISBN: 0-933280-74-2
James E Crowfoot, Julia Wondolleck, Author

4134 Globalization and the Environment: Greening Global Political Economy
SUNY Press
194 Washington Ave
Suite 305
Albany, NY 12210
518-472-5000
800-666-2211
Fax: 518-472-5038
E-mail: info@sunypress.edu
http://www.sunypress.edu
Also in hardcover, 40.00.
Publication Date: 2004 175 pages
Gabriela Kutting, Author

4135 Shopping for a Better Environment: Brand Name Guide to Environmentally Responsible Shopping
Meadowbrook Press
5451 Smetana Drive
Minnetonka, MN 55343
800-338-2232
Fax: 952-930-1940
E-mail: info@meadowbrookpress.com
http://www.meadowbrookpress.com

Books: Design & Architecture

4136 Designing Healthy Cities
Krieger Publishing Co.
PO Box 9542
Melbourne, FL 32902
321-724-9542
800-724-0025
Fax: 321-951-3671
E-mail: info@krieger-publishing.com
http://www.krieger-publishing.com
Krieger Publishing Company produces quality books in various fields of interest. We have an extensive Natural Science listing.
Publication Date: 1998 158 pages
ISBN: 0-894649-27-2
Cheryl Stanton, Advertising

4137 Indoor Air Quality: Design Guide Book
Fairmont Press
700 Indian Trail
Liburn, GA 30047
770-925-9388
Fax: 770-381-9865
E-mail: linda@fairmountpress.com
http://www.fairmontpress.com

Books: Disaster Preparedness & Response

4138 Acceptable Risk?: Making Decisions in a Toxic Environment
University of California Press
2120 Berkeley Way
Berkeley, CA 94704
510-642-4247
Fax: 510-643-7127
E-mail: askucp@ucpress.edu
http://www.ucpress.edu

4139 Borrowed Earth, Borrowed Time: Healing America's Chemical Wounds
Plenum Publishers
233 Spring Street
New York, NY 10013
212-460-1500
Fax: 212-460-1575
http://www.plenum.com
Publication Date: 1991

Books: Energy & Transportation

4140 Coming Clean: Breaking America's Addiction to Oil And Coal
Sierra Club Books
85 Second Street
2nd Floor
San Francisco, CA 94105
415-977-5500
Fax: 415-977-5799
http://www.sieraaclub.org/books/
As Americans awaken to their addiction to oil and coal, we want to take action towards a cleaner path. This title provides the road map, showing how we can promote real solutions, and collectively pressure government and corporationsto change their energy priorities.
256 pages
Michael Brune, Author

4141 Confronting Climate Change: Strategies for Energy Research and Development
National Academy Press
500 5th Street NW
Washington, DC 20055
202-334-3313
888-624-8373
Fax: 202-334-2451
http://www.nap.edu
Publication Date: 1990 144 pages
ISBN: 0-309043-47-6

4142 Energy & Environmental Strategies for the 1990's
Fairmont Press
700 Indian Tr.
Lilburn, GA 30047
770-925-9388
Fax: 770-381-9865
E-mail: linda@fairmontpress.com
http://www.fairmontpress.com

4143 Energy Management and Conservation
National Conference of State Legislatures
7700 E First Place
Denver, CO 80230
303-364-7700
Fax: 303-364-7800
http://www.ncsl.org

4144 Getting Around Clean & Green
Northeast Sustainable Energy Association
50 Miles Street
Greenfield, MA 01301
413-774-6051
Fax: 413-774-6053
E-mail: nesea@nesea.org
http://www.nesea.org
This interdisciplinary science/social studies curriculum allows students to explore the transportation and environmental issues in their own lives. Activities cover: transportation systems, health impacts, environmental andtransportation histories, carpooling, and mass transit.
90 pages Curriculum
David Barclay, Executive Director
Arianna Alexsandra Grindrod, Education Director

4145 Getting Around Without Gasoline
Northeast Sustainable Energy Association

50 Miles Street
Greenfield, MA 01301
413-774-6051
Fax: 413-774-6053
E-mail: nesea@nesea.org
http://www.nesea.org

An interdisciplinary unit that explores the feasibility of getting around without using gasoline. Students can conduct various activities to compare powering vehicles with gasoline versus electricity.

60 pages S & H Only
David Barclay, Executive Director
Arianna Alexander Gridrod, Education Director

4146 Global Science: Energy, Resources, Environment
Kendall-Hunt Publishing Company
4050 Westmark Drive
PO Box 1840
Dubuque, IA 52004
319-589-1000
800-772-9165
http://www.kendallhunt.com

4147 Oil, Globalization, and the War for the Arctic Refuge
SUNY Press
194 Washington Ave
Suite 305
Albany, NY 12210
518-472-5000
800-666-2211
Fax: 518-472-5038
E-mail: info@sunypress.edu
http://www.sunypress.edu

Also in hardcover, 71.50.
Publication Date: 2006 227 pages
David M Stanlea, Author

4148 Transporting Atlanta: The Mode of Mobility Under Construction
SUNY Press
194 Washington Ave
Suite 305
Albany, NY 12210
518-472-5000
800-666-2211
Fax: 518-472-5038
E-mail: info@sunypress.edu
http://www.sunypress.edu

Publication Date: 2009 220 pages
Miriam Konrad, Author

Books: Environmental Engineering

4149 Principles of Environmental Science and Technology
Elsevier Science Publishers
360 Park Avenue South
New York, NY 10010
212-989-5800
Fax: 212-633-3990
http://www.elsevier.com

Books: Environmental Health

4150 Ecologue: The Environmental Catalogue and Consumer's Guide for a Safe Earth
Prentice Hall Press (Simon & Schuster Division)
1 Gulf & Western Plaza
New York, NY 10023
212-373-8500
800-223-1360
http://www.prenhall.com

Books: Gaming & Hunting

4151 Better Trout Habitat: A Guide to Stream Restoration
Island Press
1718 Connecticut Avenue NW
Suite 300
Washington, DC 20009
202-232-7933
Fax: 202-234-1328
E-mail: info@islandpress.org
http://www.islandpress.org

Books: Habitat Preservation & Land Use

4152 50 Simple Things Kids Can Do to Save the Earth
Andrews and McMeel
4520 Main Street
Suite 700
Kansas City, MO 64111
816-932-6700
Fax: 816-932-6706

4153 Access EPA: Clearinghouses and Hotlines
National Technical Information Service
5285 Port Royal Road
Springfield, VA 22161
703-487-4650
E-mail: info@ntis.gov
http://www.ntis.gov

Publication Date: 1991 57 pages

4154 Access EPA: Library and Information Services
National Technical Information Service
5285 Port Royal Road
Springfield, VA 22161
703-487-4650
E-mail: info@ntis.gov
http://www.ntis.gov

Publication Date: 1990 110 pages

4155 After Earth Day: Continuing the Conservation Effort
University of North Texas Press
PO Box 311336
Denton, TX 76203
940-565-2142
800-826-8911
Fax: 940-565-4590
E-mail: rchrisman@unt.edu
http://www.unt.edu/untpress

Publication Date: 1992 241 pages
ISBN: 1-574414-44-0
Karen DeVinney, Managing Editor

4156 Agatha's Feather Bed: Not Just Another Wild Goose Story
Peachtree Publishers
1700 Chattahoochee Avenue
Atlanta, GA 30318
404-876-8761
Fax: 404-875-2578
E-mail: hello@peachtree-online.com
http://www.peachtree-online.com

32 pages
ISBN: 1-561450-08-1

4157 America in the 21st Century: Environmental Concerns
Population Reference Bureau
1707 H Street NW
Suite 200
Washington, DC 20006
202-530-5810
800-877-9881
Fax: 202-328-3937
E-mail: popref@prb.org
http://www.prb.org; www.popplanet.org

4158 Ancient Ones: The World of the Old-Growth Douglas Fir
Sierra Club Books
85 2nd Street
2nd Floor
San Francisco, CA 94105
415-977-5500
Fax: 415-977-5799
http://www.sierraclub.org/books/

A children's book that offers insight on one of the oldest species of trees.

32 pages
ISBN: 0-871566-82-6
Barbara Bash, Author
Suzanne Head, Editor
Robert Heinzman, Editor

4159 Association of State Wetland Managers Symposium
Association of State Wetland Managers
2 Basin Road
Windham, ME 04062
207-892-3399
Fax: 207-892-3089
E-mail: aswm@aswm.org
http://www.aswm.org

Jeanne Christie, Executive Director
Jon Kusler, Associate Director

4160 At Odds with Progress: Americans and Conservation
University of Arizona Press

355 S Euclid Avenue
Suite 103
Tucson, AZ 85719
520-621-1441
Fax: 520-621-8899
http://www.uapress.arizona.edu
Publication Date: 1991 255 pages
ISBN: 0-816509-17-4
Bret Wallach, Author

4161 Balancing on the Brink of Extinction
Island Press
1718 Connecticut Avenue NW
Suite 300
Washington, DC 20009
202-232-7933
Fax: 202-232-1328
E-mail: info@islandpress.org
http://www.islandpress.org

Publication Date: 1991 329 pages
Kathryn A Kohm, Author

4162 Beyond the Beauty Strip: Saving What's Left of Our Forests
Tilbury House Publishers
2 Mechanic Street
Suite 3
Gardiner, ME 04345
207-582-1899
Fax: 202-582-8227
E-mail: tilbury@tilburyhouse.com
http://www.tilburyhouse.com

4163 Biodiversity and Ecosystem Function
Springer-Verlag
233 Spring Street
New York, NY 10013
212-460-1500
800-777-4643
Fax: 212-460-1575
E-mail: service-ny@springer-sbm.com
http://www.springeronline.com

Publication Date: 1994 528 pages

4164 Bioremediation
McGraw-Hill
1221 Avenue of the Americas
New York, NY 10020
212-512-2000
800-722-4726
http://www.magraw-hill.com

4165 Bluebird Bibliography
North American Bluebird Society
PO Box 43
Miamiville, OH 45147
812-988-1876
Fax: 330-359-5455
E-mail: info@nabluebirdsociety.org
http://www.nabluebirdsociety.org

4166 Butterflies of Delmarva
Delware Nature Society and Tidewater Publishers
PO Box 700
Hockessin, DE 19707
301-239-2334
Fax: 302-239-2473
E-mail: e-mail@dnashland.org
http://www.delawarenaturesociety.org

The result of the author's lifelong interest in the 61 adult butterfly species that naturally occur on the Delmarva Peninsula, this field guide clearly identifies the adult, larva and pulpa stages, discusses the differences in colorand wing patterns between sexes, as well as the habitat, range, and food sources of each species. 132 full-color photographs illustrate the text. Includes general butterfly information, and how to attrract them to your garden. Paperback
Publication Date: 1998 138 pages 2nd Edition
ISBN: 0-870334-53-0
Dr. Elton N Woodbury, Author

4167 Clean Sites Annual Report
Clean Sites
46161 West Lake Drive
Suite 230-B
Potomac Falls, VA 20165
703-519-2140
Fax: 703-519-2141
E-mail: cses@cleansites.com
http://www.cleansites.com

We apply sound project management principles, real-world experience, and cost control measures to find creative solutions to environmental remediation and land reuse problems.
Douglas Ammon, Contact

4168 Connections: Linking Population and the Environment Teaching Kit
Population Reference Bureau
1875 Connecticut Avenue NW
Suite 520
Washington, DC 20009
202-483-1100
800-877-9881
Fax: 202-328-3937
E-mail: popref@prb.org
http://www.prb.org

4169 Conservation and Research Foundation Five Year Report
Conservation and Research Foundation
PO Box 909
Shelburne, VT 05482
913-268-0076
Fax: 913-268-0076
Publication from Conservation and Research Foundation which is published every five years and distributed to contributors. This publication is also available upon request.
Publication Date: 1998 43 pages
Dr Mary Wetzel, President

4170 Decade of Destruction: The Crusade to Save the Amazon Rain Forest
Henry Holt and Company
175 Fifth Avenue
New York, NY 10010
646-307-5095
Fax: 212-633-0748
E-mail: publicity@hholt.com
http://www.henryholt.com

215 pages
Adrian Cowell, Author

4171 Discordant Harmonies: A New Ecology for the Twenty-first Century
Oxford University Press
198 Madison Avenue
New York, NY 10016
212-679-7300
Fax: 212-725-2972
http://www.oup.co.uk

Publication Date: 1992 254 pages
ISBN: 0-195074-69-6
Daniel B Botkin, Author

4172 Earth Keeping
Zondervan Publishing House
5300 Patterson Avenue SE
Grand Rapids, MI 49530
616-698-6900
Fax: 616-698-3439
http://www.zondervan.com

4173 Earthright
Prima Publishing & Communications
PO Box 1260BK
Rocklin, CA 95677
916-786-0426
800-632-8676
Fax: 916-632-4405
http://www.primapublishing.com

4174 Ecology of Greenways: Design and Function of Linear Conservation
University of Minnesota Press
111 Third Avenue South
Suite 290
Minneapolis, MN 55401
612-627-1970
800-388-3863
Fax: 612-627-1980
E-mail: lfreeman@epx.cis.umn.edu
http://www.upress.umn.edu

Publication Date: 1994 238 pages
ISBN: 0-816621-57-8
Daniel S Smith, Paul Cawood Hellmund, Author

4175 **Eli's Songs**
MacMillan Publishing Company
866 3rd Avenue 212-702-2000
New York, NY 10022 800-257-5755
http://www.macmillian.com

4176 **Endangered Kingdom: The Struggle to Save America's Wildlife**
John Wiley & Sons
605 3rd Avenue 212-850-6890
New York, NY 10158 800-825-7550
Fax: 212-850-8800
http://www.wiley.co.uk

Publication Date: 1991 241 pages
ISBN: 0-471528-22-6
Roger L DiSilvestro, Author

4177 **Environment in Peril**
Smithsonian Institution Press
SI Building, Room 153, MRC 010 202-633-1000
PO Box 37012 800-782-4612
Washington, DC 20013 Fax: 202-633-5285
E-mail: info@si.edu
http://www.si.edu

4178 **Environmental Concern in Florida and the Nation**
University of Florida Press
15 NW 15th Street 352-392-1351
Gainesville, FL 32611 800-226-3822
Fax: 352-392-7302
http://www.upf.com

Publication Date: 1997 144 pages
ISBN: 0-813010-56-X
Lance Dehaven-Smith, Author

4179 **Environmental Concern: A Comprehensive Review of Wetlands Assessment Producers**
POW-The Planning of Wetlands
201 Boundary Lane 410-745-9620
PO Box P Fax: 410-745-3517
St Michaels, MD 21663 E-mail: order@wetland.org
http://www.wetland.org

Since its founding in 1972, EC has been specializing in consulting, planning design, education services, construction services and research related to all aspects of wetlands. As wetlands and contiguous upland forests and meadows areinteracting ecosystems EC specializes in consulting, planning, design, and project supervision services for such upland ecosystem constructions and restorations for the purpose of wetland buffers, reforestation, wildlife habitat and critical areas ofpreservation.
Publication Date: 1999 Quarterly
ISBN: 1-883226-04-x
Suzanne Pitenger Slear, President

4180 **Environmental Concern: Evaluation for Planned Wetlands**
POW-The Planning of Wetlands
201 Boundary Lane 410-745-9620
PO Box P Fax: 410-745-3517
St Michaels, MD 21663 E-mail: order@wetland.org
http://www.wetland.org

Since its founding in 1972, EC has been specializing in consulting, planning design, education services, construction services and research related to all aspects of wetlands. As wetlands and contiguous upland forests and meadows areinteracting ecosystems EC specializes in consulting, planning, design, and project supervision services for such upland ecosystem constructions and restorations for the purpose of wetland buffers, reforestation, wildlife habitat and critical areas ofpreservation.
Publication Date: 1994 Quarterly
ISBN: 1-883226-03-1
Suzanne Pittenger Slear, President

4181 **Environmental Concern: The Wonders of Wetlands**
POW-The Planning of Wetlands
201 Boundary Lane 410-745-9620
PO Box P Fax: 410-745-3517
St Michaels, MD 21663 E-mail: order@wetland.org
http://www.wetland.org

Since its founding in 1972, EC has been specializing in consulting, planning design, education services, construction services and research related to all aspects of wetlands. As wetlands and contiguous upland forests and meadows areinteracting ecosystems EC specializes in consulting, planning, design, and project supervision services for such upland ecosystem constructions and restorations for the purpose of wetland buffers, reforestation, wildlife habitat and critical areas ofpreservation.
Publication Date: 1995
ISBN: 1-888631-00-7
Suzanne Pittenger Slear, President

4182 **Environmental Crisis: Opposing Viewpoints**
Greenhaven Press
PO Box 289009 858-485-9549
San Diego, CA 92128 800-231-5163
Fax: 800-550-5448
E-mail: info@grennhaven.com
http://www.greenhaven.com

4183 **Environmental Profiles: A Global Guide to Projects and People**
Garland Publishing
717 5th Avenue 212-751-7447
25th Floor Fax: 212-308-9399
New York, NY 10022 http://www.garlandpub.com
Publication Date: 1993 1112 pages
ISBN: 0-815300-63-8

4184 **Friends of the Earth Foundation Annual Report**
Friends of the Earth Found.
218 D Street SE 202-544-2600
Washington, DC 20003 Fax: 202-543-4710
http://www.oceanic-society.org

4185 **Future Primitive**
University of North Texas Press
PO Box 311336 940-565-2142
Denton, TX 76203 800-826-8911
Fax: 940-565-4590
E-mail: rchrisman@unt.edu
http://www.unt.edu/untpress
Publication Date: 1996 223 pages
ISBN: 1-574410-07-5
Ronald Chrisman, Director
Karen DeVinney, Managing Editor

4186 **Going Green: A Kid's Handbook to Saving the Planet**
Puffin Books
375 Hudson Street 212-366-2403
New York, NY 10014 http://www.puffin.co.uk
Out of print—limited availability.
Publication Date: 1990
ISBN: 0-140345-97-3

4187 **Guide to Spring Wildflower Areas**
Minnesota Native Plant Society
1520 St. Olaf Avenue 507-786-2222
Northfield, MN 55057 E-mail: MNPS@HotPOP.com
http://www.stolaf.edu

Updated its guide to over 40 wildflower sites in the Twin Cities area. The guide contains a description and location for each.
4 per year

4188 **Guide to Urban Wildlife Management**
National Institute for Urban Wildlife
10921 Trotting Ridge Way 301-596-3311
Columbia, MD 21044

4189 **Information Please Environmental Almanac**
Houghton Mifflin Company

222 Berkeley Street
30th Floor
Boston, MA 02116
617-725-5000
http://www.hmco.com
Publication Date: 1992 704 pages
ISBN: 0-395637-67-8

4190 **International Protection of the Environment**
Oceana Publications, Inc
198 Madison Avenue
New York, NY 10016
800-334-4249
Fax: 212-726-6476
E-mail: info@oceanalaw.com
http://www.oceanalaw.com
This set provides the documents which form the framework of softlaw administrative instruments for the implementation of international environment treaties under Agenda 21.
Publication Date: 1995 7 vol pages Bi-Monthly
ISBN: 0-379102-95-1
Nicholas A Robinson & Wolfgang Burhenne, Author

4191 **International Society for Endangered Cats**
3070 Riverside Drive Suite 160
Columbus, OH 43221
614-487-8760
Fax: 614-487-8769
Publication Date: 1990 237 pages
ISBN: 0-816019-44-4
Bill Simpson, President
Patricia Currie, Executive Director

4192 **Just A Dream**
Houghton Mifflin Company
Beacon Street
30th Floor
Boston, MA 02108
617-725-5000

4193 **Krieger Publishing Company: Wildlife Habitat Management of Wetlands**
Krieger Publishing Co.
PO Box 9542
Melbourne, FL 32902
321-724-9542
800-724-0025
Fax: 321-951-3671
E-mail: info@krieger-publishing.com
http://www.krieger-publishing.com
Krieger Publishing Company produces quality books in various fields of interest. We have an extensive Natural Science listing.
Publication Date: 1992 572 pages
ISBN: 1-575240-89-0
Cheryl Stanton, Advertising

4194 **Krieger Publishing Company: Wildlife Habitat Management of Forestlands/Rangelands/Farmlands**
Krieger Publishing Co.
PO Box 9542
Melbourne, FL 32902
321-724-9542
800-724-0025
Fax: 321-951-3671
E-mail: info@krieger-publishing.com
http://www.krieger-publishing.com
Krieger Publishing Company produces quality books in various fields of interest. We have an extensive Natural Science listing.
Publication Date: 1994 868 pages
ISBN: 1-575240-93-9
Cheryl Stanton, Advertising

4195 **Last Extinction**
MIT Press
5 Cambridge Center
Cambridge, MA 02142
617-253-5646
Fax: 617-258-6779
Today there is a new and more widespread awareness of what some consider to be the great tragedy of our time - organisms which took many thousands or even millions of years to evolve are being snuffed out permanently owing to humanactivity.
Publication Date: 1993
Les Kaufman, Kenneth Mallory, Author

4196 **Mastering Nepa: A Step-By-Step Approach**
Solano Press
PO Box 773
Point Arena, CA 95468
800-931-9373
Fax: 707-884-4109
http://www.solano.com
Publication Date: 1993 250 pages
ISBN: 0-923956-14-x
Ronald E Bass, Albert I Herson, Author

4197 **National Wildlife Rehabilitators Association Annual Report**
National Wildlife Rehabilitators Association
14 N 7th Avenue
St Cloud, MN 56303
320-259-4086
Fax: 320-259-4086
E-mail: nwra@nwrawildlife.org
http://www.nwrawildlife.org

4198 **Nature and the American: Three Centuries of Changing Attitudes**
Unviersity of Nebraska Press
1111 Lincoln Mall
Lincoln, NE 68588
402-472-3581
http://www.nebraskapress.unl.edu

4199 **Ordinance Information Packet**
Scenic America
1634 I Street NW
Suite 510
Washington, DC 20006
202-638-0550
Fax: 202-638-3171
http://www.scenic.org

4200 **Ozone Diplomacy: New Directions in Safeguarding the Planet**
Harvard University Press
79 Garden Street
Cambridge, MA 02138
617-495-2600
Fax: 617-495-5898
E-mail: botref@oeb.harvard.edu
http://www.hup.harvard.edu
Offers an insider's view of the politics, economics, science and diplomacy involved in creating the precedent-setting treaty to protect the Earth: the 1987 Montreal Protocol on Substances That Deplete the Ozone Layer.
Richard Elliot Benedick, Author

4201 **Practical Guide to Environmental Management**
1616 P Street NW
Suite 200
Washington, DC 20036
202-939-3800
Fax: 202-939-3868

4202 **Preserving the World Ecology**
H W Wilson Company
950 University Avenue
Bronx, NY 10452
718-588-8400
Fax: 718-588-6365
http://www.hwwilson.com

4203 **Protecting Our Environment: Lessons from the European Union**
SUNY Press
194 Washington Ave
Suite 305
Albany, NY 12210
518-472-5000
800-666-2211
Fax: 518-472-5038
E-mail: info@sunypress.edu
http://www.sunypress.edu
Available in both hard and soft cover, this title deals with the environment as a global issue.
Publication Date: 2005 204 pages
Janet R Hunter, Zachary A Smith, Author

4204 **Quill's Adventures in Grozzieland**
John Muir Publications
PO Box 613
Santa Fe, NM 87504
505-982-4078
800-888-7504
Fax: 505-988-1680

4205 **RARE Center for Tropical Conservation Annual Report**
Rare Center for Tropical Conservation

1616 Walnut Street
Suite 911
Philadelphia, PA 19103
215-735-3510
Fax: 215-735-3615
http://www.rarecenter.org

4206 **Resource Conservation and Management**
Wadsworth Publishing Company
10 Davis Drive
Belmont, CA 94002
415-595-2350
Fax: 415-637-7544
http://www.wadsworth.com

4207 **Revolution for Nature: From the Environment to the Connatural World**
University of North Texas Press
PO Box 311336
Denton, TX 76203
940-565-2142
800-826-8911
Fax: 940-565-4590
E-mail: rchrisman@unt.edu
http://www.unt.edu/untpress

145 pages
ISBN: 1-574417-0X-
Ronald Chrisman, Director
Karen DeVinney, Managing Editor

4208 **Saving Sterling Forest: The Epic Struggle to Preserve New York's Highlands**
SUNY Press
194 Washington Ave
Suite 305
Albany, NY 12210
518-472-5000
800-666-2211
Fax: 518-472-5038
E-mail: info@sunypress.edu
http://www.sunypress.edu

Also in hardcover, 59.50.
Publication Date: 2007 216 pages
Ann Botshon, Author

4209 **Seed Listing**
Native Seeds/SEARCH
526 N. Fourth Avenue
Tucson, AZ 85705
520-622-5561
Fax: 520-622-5591
http://www.nativeseeds.org

4210 **Statement of Policy and Practices forProtection of Wetlands**
National Wildlife Fed. Corporate Conservation Coun
1400 16th Street NW
Washington, DC 20036
202-797-6870
Fax: 202-797-6871

4211 **Student Conservation Association Northwest: Lightly on the Land**
1265 S Main Street
Suite 210
Seattle, WA 98144
206-324-4649
Fax: 206-324-4998
http://www.sca-inc.org

SCA is a national organization with regional offices in Seattle, Oakland, Pittsburg, Washington DC and headquartered in Charlestown NH. Our mission is to build the next generation of conservation leaders and inspire lifelongstewardship of our environment and communities by engaging young people in hands-on service to the land. We offer a wide range of internships and crew based programs for ages 16 years and up.
Publication Date: 1996 267 pages
ISBN: 0-898869-91-7
Su Thieds, Director of Regional Progams

4212 **Transactions of Annual North American Wildlife and Natural Resources Conference**
Wildlife Management
1101 14th Street NW
Suite 801
Washington, DC 20005
202-371-1808
Fax: 202-408-5059

4213 **Urban Wildlife Manager's Notebook**
National Institute for Urban Wildlife
10921 Trotting Ridge Way
Columbia, MD 21044
301-596-3311

4214 **Wetlands Protection: The Role of Economics**
Environmental Law Institute
1616 P Street NW
Suite 200
Washington, DC 20036
202-939-3800
Fax: 202-939-3868

4215 **Wilderness Society Annual Report**
1615 M Street NW
Washington, DC 20036
202-833-2300
800-THE-WILD
E-mail: member@tws.org
http://www.wilderness.org

Deliver to future generations an unspoiled legacy of wild places, with all the precious values they hold: Biological diversity; clean air and water; towering forests, rushing rivers, and sage-sweet, silent deserts.
Brenda Davis, Chair
Doug Walker, Vice Chair

4216 **Wildlife Conservation in Metropolitan Environments**
National Institute for Urban Wildlife
10921 Trotting Ridge Way
Columbia, MD 21044
301-596-3311

4217 **Wildlife Habitat Relationships in Forested Ecosystems**
Timber Press
133 SW 2nd Avenue
Suite 450
Portland, OR 97204
503-227-2878
Fax: 503-227-3070
http://www.timber-press.com

Available by special order.
Publication Date: 1997
David R Patton, Author

4218 **Wildlife Research and Management in the National Parks**
University of Illinois Press
1325 S Oak Street
Champaign, IL 61820
217-333-0950
Fax: 217-244-8082
http://www.press.uillinois.edu

Publication Date: 1992 240 pages
ISBN: 0-252018-24-9
Gerald R Wright, Author

4219 **Wildlife-Habitat Relationships: Concepts and Applications**
University of Wisconsin Press
114 N Murray Street
Madison, WI 53715
608-262-8782

Anyone working with wildlife must be concerned with its habitat identification, measurement and analysis. Wildlife-Habitat Relationships goes beyond introductory wildlife biology texts and specialized studies of single species toprovide a broad but advanced understanding of habitat relationships applicable to all terrestrial species.
Publication Date: 1998 416 pages
ISBN: 0-299156-40-0
Michael L Morrison, Bruce G Marcot, Author

Books: Recycling & Pollution Prevention

4220 **An Ontology of Trash: The Disposable and Its Problematic Nature**
SUNY Press
194 Washington Ave
Suite 305
Albany, NY 12210
518-472-5000
800-666-2211
Fax: 518-472-5038
E-mail: info@sunypress.edu
http://www.sunypress.edu

Also in hardcover, 65.00.
Publication Date: 2008 238 pages
Greg Kennedy, Author

4221 **Aunt Ipp's Museum of Junk**
HarperCollins
10 E 53rd Street
New York, NY 10022
212-207-7000
800-424-6234
Fax: 212-207-7433
http://www.harpercollins.com

4222 **Beyond 40 Percent: Record-Setting Recycling and Composting Programs**
Island Press
1718 Connecticut Avenue NW
Suite 300
Washington, DC 20009
202-232-7933
Fax: 202-234-1328
E-mail: info@islandpress.org
http://www.islandpress.org

Publication Date: 1991 280 pages
ISBN: 1-559630-73-6

4223 **Borrowed Earth, Borrowed Time: Healing America's Chemical Wounds**
Plenum Publishers
233 Spring Street
New York, NY 10013
212-460-1500
Fax: 212-460-1575
http://www.plenum.com

Publication Date: 1991

4224 **Caring for Our Air**
Enslow Publishers
40 Industrial Road, Dept. F61
PO Box 398
Berkeley Heights, NJ 07922
800-398-2504
Fax: 908-964-4116
http://www.enslow.com

4225 **Community Recycling: System Design to Management**
Prentice Hall
Route 9W
Englewood Cliffs, NJ 07632
201-592-2000
800-947-7700
E-mail: orders@prenhall.com
http://www.prenhall.com

A guide for getting into the growing business of community recycling, for those with little or no previous experience with the technical details of recycling. Discusses marketing, management, equipment, profit comparisons of variousprocessing methods and legal considerations.
Publication Date: 1992 240 pages
ISBN: 0-131557-89-0
Nyles V Reinfeld, Carl M Layman, Author

4226 **Garbage and Recycling**
Kingfisher Publications
http://www.kingfisherpub.com

Publication Date: 1995 32 pages
ISBN: 1-856976-15-7
Rosie Harlow, Sally Morgan, Author

4227 **Hey Mr. Green: Sierra Magazine's Answer Guy Tackles Your Toughest Green Living Questions**
Sierra Club Books
85 Second Street
2nd Floor
San Francisco, CA 94105
415-977-5500
Fax: 415-977-5799
http://www.sierraclub.org/books

When is the right time to replace an old refridgerator? Is it more environmentally correct to buy your beer in bottles or cans? And is it okay to knit a sweater with acrylic (pertoleum-based) yarn? Bob Schildgen has been Mr. Green inSierra Magazine for several years now, providing fact-backed replies to reader's questions. Well organized, funny, and supremely useful, this title offers green-living tips for everyday.
Publication Date: 2009 224 pages
ISBN: 1-578051-43-4
Bob Schildgen, Author

4228 **How On Earth Do We Recycle Glass?**
Millbrook Press
2 Old New Milford Road
PO Box 335
Brookfield, CT 06804
203-740-2220
800-462-4703
Fax: 203-740-2526
http://www.millbrookpress.com

4229 **Let's Talk Trash: The Kids' Book About Recycling**
Waterfront Books
85 Crescent Road
Burlington, VT 05401
802-658-7477
http://www.waterfrontsbooks.com

4230 **Plastic: America's Packaging Dilemma**
Island Press
1718 Connecticut Avenue NW
Suite 300
Washington, DC 20009
202-232-7933
Fax: 202-234-1328
E-mail: info@islandpress.org
http://www.islandpress.org

4231 **Pollution Knows No Frontiers**
Paragon House of Publishers
1925 Oakcrest Avenue
Suite 7
St. Paul, MN 55113
651-644-3087
Fax: 651-644-0997
E-mail: paragon@paragonhouse.com
http://www.paragonhouse.com

4232 **Recycle!: A Handbook for Kids**
Little, Brown & Company
1271 Avenue of the Americas
New York, NY 10020
800-759-0190
Fax: 212-522-0885
http://www.twbookmark.com

Publication Date: 1996 32 pages
Gail Gibbons, Editor

4233 **Recycling Paper: From Fiber to Finished Product**
TAPPI Press
15 Technology Parkway South
Norcross, GA 30092
770-446-1400
Fax: 770-446-6947
http://www.tappi.org

4234 **Reducing Toxics**
Island Press
1718 Connecticut Avenue NW
Suite 300
Washington, DC 20009
202-232-7933
Fax: 202-234-1328
E-mail: info@islandpress.org
http://www.islandpress.org

Publication Date: 1995 460 pages
Robert Gottlieb, Editor

Books: Sustainable Development

4235 **Biodiversity Prospecting: Using Genetic Resources for Sustainable Development**
World Resources Institute
10 G Street NE
Suite 800
Washington, DC 20002
202-729-7600
Fax: 202-729-7610
http://www.wri.org

4236 **Building Sustainable Communities: An Environmental Guide for Local Government**
Global Cities Project
2926 Philmore Street
San Francisco, CA 94123
415-775-0791
http://www.globalcities.org

4237 **Center for Ecoliteracy**
2528 San Peblo Avenue
Berkeley, CA 94702
510-845-4595
Fax: 510-845-1439
E-mail: info@ecoliteracy.org
http://www.ecoliteracy.org

The Center for Ecoliteracy is dedicated to fostering a profound understanding of the natural world, grounded in direct experience that leads to sustainable patterns of living.
Publication Date: 2000 90 pages Paperback
ISBN: 0-967565-23-5
Zenobia Barlow, Executive Director

4238 Constructing Sustainable Development
SUNY Press
194 Washington Avenue
Suite 305
Albany, NY 12210
518-472-5000
800-666-2211
Fax: 518-472-5038
Publication Date: 2000 188 pages
Neil E Harrison, Author

4239 Ecological Literacy: Educating Our Children for a Sustainable World
Sierra Club Books
85 Second Street
2nd Floor
San Francisco, CA 94105
415-977-5500
Fax: 415-977-5799
http://www.sierraclub.org/books
256 pages
ISBN: 1-578051-53-3
Michael K Stone and Zenobia Barlow, Author

4240 Environmental Defense Annual Report
Environmental Defense
257 Park Avenue South
17th Floor
New York, NY 10010
212-505-2100
800-684-3322
Fax: 212-505-2375
E-mail: members@edf.org
http://www.edf.org
Environmental Defense believes that a sustainable environment will require economic and social systems that are equitable and just.
Fred Krupp, President
David Yarnold, Executive Director

4241 Environmental Integration: Our Common Challenge
SUNY Press
194 Washington Ave
Suite 305
Albany, NY 12210
518-472-5000
800-666-2211
Fax: 518-472-5038
E-mail: info@sunypress.edu
http://www.sunypress.edu
Also in hardcover, 85.00.
Publication Date: 2009 290 pages
Ton Buhrs, Author

4242 Environmental Policy Making: Assessing the Use of Alternative Policy Instruments
SUNY Press
194 Washington Ave
Suite 305
Albany, NY 12210
518-472-5000
800-666-2211
Fax: 518-472-5038
E-mail: info@sunypress.edu
http://www.sunypress.edu
Also in hardcover, 85.00.
Publication Date: 2005 276 pages
Michael T Hatch, Author

4243 Environmental Profiles: A Global Guide to Projects and People
Garland Publishing
717 5th Avenue
25th Floor
New York, NY 10022
212-751-7447
Fax: 212-308-9399
http://www.garlandpub.com
Publication Date: 1993 1112 pages
ISBN: 0-815300-63-8

4244 Global Environment
Jones and Bartlett Publishers
40 Tall Pine Drive
Sudbury, MA 01776
800-832-0034
Fax: 978-443-8000
E-mail: info@jbpub.com
http://www.jbpub.com

4245 Gnat is Older than Man: Global Environment and Human Agenda
Princeton University Press
41 William Street
Princeton, NJ 08540
609-258-4900
800-777-4726
Fax: 609-258-6305
http://www.pup.princeton.edu

4246 Implementation of Environmental Policies in Developing Countries
SUNY Press
194 Washington Ave
Suite 305
Albany, NY 12210
518-472-5000
800-666-2211
Fax: 518-472-5038
E-mail: info@sunypress.edu
http://www.sunypress.edu
A Case of Protected Areas and Tourism in Brazil. Also in hardcover, 50.00.
Publication Date: 2008 150 pages
Jose Antonio Puppim de Oliveira, Author

4247 Managing Sustainable Development
Earthscan Publications
8-12 Camden High Street
London
207-387-8558
Fax: 207-387-8998
Publication Date: 2001 304 pages
Michael Carley, Editor

4248 Practice of Sustainable Development
Urban Land Institute
1025 Thomas Jefferson Street NW
Suite 500 W
Washington, DC 20007
202-624-7000
Fax: 202-624-7140
E-mail: customerservice@uli.org
http://www.uli.org
Publication Date: 2000 160 pages
ISBN: 0-874208-31-9
Douglas R Porter, Author

4249 Sustainable Planning and Development
WIT Press
978-667-5841
Fax: 978-667-7582
E-mail: salesUSA@witpress.com
http://www.witpress.com
Publication Date: 2003 1048 pages
ISBN: 1-853129-85-2
Linda Ouellette, Customer Service Manager

4250 The Incompleat Eco-Philosopher:Essay from the Edges of Environmental Ethics
SUNY Press
194 Washington Ave
Suite 305
Albany, NY 12210
518-472-5000
800-666-2211
Fax: 518-472-5038
E-mail: info@sunypress.edu
http://www.sunypress.edu
Also in hardcover for 65.50
Publication Date: 2009 210 pages
Anthony Weston, Author

4251 Urban Sprawl, Global Warming, and the Empire of Capital
SUNY Press
194 Washington Ave
Suite 305
Albany, NY 12210
518-472-5000
800-666-2211
Fax: 518-472-5038
E-mail: info@sunypress.edu
http://www.sunypress.edu

Also in hardcover, 60.00.
Publication Date: 2009 170 pages
George A Gonzalez, Author

4252 Who Gets What? Domestic Influences on International Negotiations Allocating Shared Resources
SUNY Press
194 Washington Ave
Suite 305
Albany, NY 12210
518-472-5000
800-666-2211
Fax: 518-472-5038
E-mail: info@sunypress.edu
http://www.sunypress.edu

Also in hardcover, 60.00.
Publication Date: 2008 192 pages
Aslaug Asgeirsdottir, Author

4253 Worldwatch Paper 101: Discarding the Throwaway Society
Worldwatch Intitutes
1776 Massachusetts Ave. NW
Washington, DC 20036
202-452-1999
Fax: 202-296-7365
http://www.worldwatch.org

Books: Travel & Tourism

4254 Appalachian Mountain Club
Appalachian Mountain Club Books
5 Joy Street
Boston, MA 02108
617-523-0636
800-262-4455
Fax: 617-523-0722
E-mail: information@outdoors.org
http://www.outdoors.org

The AMC, founded in 1876, promotes the protection, enjoyment, and wise use of the mountains, rivers and trails of the Northeast. We encourage people to enjoy and protect the natural world because we believe that successful conservationdepends on this experience. The AMC publishes an award-winning magazine and more than 60 guide books to the Northeast.
Andrew Falender, Executive Director
Chase O'Connell, Director Development

4255 Prospect Park Handbook
Greensward Found
Lenox Hill Station
PO Box 610
New York, NY 10021
212-473-6283
http://www.greenswardparks.org

Books: Water Resources

4256 And Two if By Sea: Fighting the Attack on America's Coasts
Coast Alliance
202-546-9609

This book is the benchmark in the effort to save the coasts.
Publication Date: 1986

4257 Comparative Health Effects Assessment of Drinking Water Treatment Technologies
Government Institutes Division
16855 Northchase Drive
Houston, TX 77060
281-673-2800
http://www.govinst.com

The report evaluates the public health impact of the most widespread drinking water treatment technologies, with particular emphasis on disinfection.
Publication Date: 1988 20 pages

4258 Dying Oceans
Gareth Stevens, Inc
PO Box 360140
Strongsville, OH 44136
414-332-3520
800-542-2595
Fax: 414-332-3567
http://www.garethstevens.com

Publication Date: 1991
ISBN: 0-836804-76-7

4259 Freshwater Resources and Interstate Cooperation: Strategies to Mitigate an Environmental Risk
SUNY Press
194 Washington Ave
Suite 305
Albany, NY 12210
518-472-5000
800-666-2211
Fax: 518-472-5038
E-mail: info@sunypress.edu
http://www.sunypress.edu

Also in hardcover, 60.00.
Publication Date: 2008 184 pages
Frederick D Gordon, Author

4260 Living Waters: Reading the Rivers of the Lower Great Lakes
SUNY Press
194 Washington Ave
Suite 305
Albany, NY 12210
518-472-5000
800-666-2211
Fax: 518-472-5038
E-mail: info@sunypress.edu
http://www.sunypress.edu

Also in hardcover for 45.00
Publication Date: 2009 213 pages
Margaret Wooster, Author

4261 Managing Troubled Water: The Role of Marine Environmental Monitoring
Duke University Press
905 W Main Street
Suite 18B
Durham, NC 27701
919-687-3600
Fax: 919-688-4574
http://www.dukepress.edu
Publication Date: 1990

4262 Turning the Tide: Saving the Chesapeake Bay
Island Press
1718 Connecticut Avenue NW
Suite 300
Washington, DC 20009
707-983-6432
800-828-1302
E-mail: info@islandpress.org
http://www.islandpress.org

The Chesapeake Bay is one of the most productive and important ecosystems on earth, and as such is a model for other estuaries facing the demands of commerce, tourism, transportation, recreation and other uses. Turning the Tidepresents a comprehensive look at two decades of efforts to save the bay, outlining which methods have worked and which have not.
Publication Date: 2003 352 pages
ISBN: 1-559635-48-7
Tom Horton, Author

4263 Using Common Sense to Protect the Coasts: The Need to Expand Coastal Barrier Resources
Coast Alliance
PO Box 505
Sandy Hook, NJ 07732
732-872-0111
E-mail: coast@coastalliance.org
http://www.coastalliance.org

This report gives a common sense approach to protecting coastal areas from unwise development that would benefit American taxpayers.
Publication Date: 1990

Library Collections

4264 3M: 201 Technical Library
3M Center
St. Paul, MN 55133
651-575-1300
Fax: 651-736-3940
http://www.3M.com

High-tech library that manages its collection with 3M digital identification.

4265 **Acres International Library**
100 Sylvan Parkway 716-689-3737
Amherst, NY 14228 Fax: 716-689-3749
E-mail: amherst@acres.com
http://www.acres.com
Serves clients in the hydroelectric power, highways and bridges, mining, heavy industrial, civil/geotechnical and environmental and hazardous waste sectors.
Marion D'Amboise, Librarian

4266 **Alaska Department of Fish and Game Habitat Library**
333 Raspberry Road 907-267-2314
Anchorage, AK 99518 Fax: 907-349-1723
Celia Rozen, Contact

4267 **Alaska Resources Library and Information Services**
ARLIS Suite 111 Library Building 907-272-7547
3211 Providence Drive Fax: 907-786-7652
Anchorage, AK 99508 E-mail: reference@arlis.org
http://www.arlis.org
ARLIS is the mother lode of Alaska resources information. ARLIS has served as the central library for rresource information supporting management of 235 million acres of federal and 100 million acres of state and water resourcesthroughout Alaska.
Publication Date: 1997
Carrie Holba, Reference Services Coord

4268 **American Academy of Pediatrics**
141 NW Point Boulevard 847-434-4000
PO Box 747 Fax: 847-434-8000
Elk Grove Village, IL 60007 http://www.aap.org
Dedicated to the health of all children.

4269 **American Water Works Association**
6666 W Quincy Avenue 303-794-7711
Denver, CO 80235 Fax: 303-347-0804
http://www.awwa.org
Dedicated to the promotion of public health and welfare in the provision of drinking water of unquestionable quality and sufficient quantity. AWWA must be proactive and effective in advancing the technology, science, management andgovernment policies relative to the stewardship of water.
Jack W Hoffbuhr, Executive Director

4270 **Aquatic Research Institute: Aquatic Sciences and Technology Archive**
2242 Davis Court 510-782-4058
Hayward, CA 94545 Fax: 510-784-0945
Library and data base in aquatic sciences and technologies also research faculty in aquatic sciences.
V Parker, Archv

4271 **Arizona State Energy Office Information Center**
3800 N Central 602-280-1402
Suite 1200 Fax: 602-280-1445
Phoenix, AZ 85012 E-mail: energy@azcommerce.com
Maxine Robertson, Assistant Director

4272 **Arizona State University Architecture and Environmental Design Library**
College of Architecture and Environmental Design
4300 480-965-6400
Tempe, AZ 85287 Fax: 480-727-6965
E-mail: deborah.koshinsky@asu.edu
http://www.asu.edu/caed/AEDlibrary
Deborah H Koshinsky, Director

4273 **Arkansas Energy Office Library**
1 State Capitol Mall 501-682-1370
Little Rock, AR 72201 Fax: 501-682-2703
E-mail: cbenson@1800arkansas.com

4274 **Atmospheric Sciences Model Division Library**
US Environmental Protection Agency
79 TW Alexander Drive 919-541-4536
4201 Building, Room 308 Fax: 919-541-1379
Research Triangle Park, NC 27711 http://www.epa.gov
Serves the NOAA Division assigned to support the EPA National Exposure Laboratory and Office of Air Quality Planning and Standards. The major field of interest is the meteorological aspects of air pollution, including numerical andphysical model development and application.
Evelyn M Poole-Kober, Tech. Pubns.

4275 **Belle W Baruch Institute for Marine Biology and Coastal Research Library**
607 EWS Building 803-777-5288
Columbia, SC 29208 Fax: 803-777-3935

4276 **Bickelhaupt Arboretum Education Center**
340 S 14th Street 319-242-4771
Clinton, IA 52742

4277 **Brown University Center for Environmental Studies Library**
135 Angel Street 401-863-3449
Box 1943 Fax: 401-863-3503
Providence, RI 02912 E-mail: envstudies@brown.edu
http://www.envstudies.brown.edu
The Center for Environmental Studies at Brown University was established with the primary aim of educating individuals to solve challenging environmental problems both at the local and global levels. It also works directly to improvehuman well-being and environmental quality through community, city, and state partnerships in service and research.
J Timmons Roberts, Program Director

4278 **Burroughs Audubon Center and Library**
Burroughs Audubon Society
21905 SW Woods Chapel Road 816-795-8177
Independence, MO 64050

4279 **CH2M Hill**
Corvallis Regional Office Library
80112 541-752-4271
http://www.ch2m.com
The firm's solutions keep sustainability always in mind, along with government regulations, environmental concerns, maintenance requirements, and public perceptions. A team of experts brings the knowledge gained from a wide range ofprojects around the world, rigourous attention to detail, and a capability to create innovative solutions that are also models for the industry.
Shirley Fisher, COO

4280 **California Energy Commission Library**
1516 9th Street 916-654-4292
MS 10 Fax: 916-654-4046
Sacramento, CA 95814 E-mail: library@energy.state.ca.us
http://www.energy.ca.gov/library.index.html
The state's central repository for information on all forms of energy. The collection consists of more than 22,000 titles on energy policy, energy conservation, energy consumption, electric utilities, environmental issues, petroleum,natural gas, solar, wind, biomass, nuclear power and related subjects. The Library serves Energy Commission staff, California state government agencies, the Legislature and its staff, and members of the public.
Karen Kasuba n, Librarian

4281 **California State Resources Agency Library**
1416 9th Street 916-653-2225
Room 117 Fax: 916-653-1856
Sacramento, CA 95814
Contains books, documents and subscriptions on topics including: flood control; natural resources (in California); endangered species (in California); soil conservation; water; water pollution; water quality; water resources;conservation and water supply.

4282 **Center for Coastal Fisheries and Habitat Research: Rice Library**
101 Pivers Island Road 252-728-8713
Beaufort, NC 28516 Fax: 252-838-0809
E-mail: patti.marraro@noaa.gov
http://www8.nos.noaa.gov/ricelibrary
Ensures the delivery of scientific, technical, and legistlative information to library users including NOAA staff, general public, academia, industry, and governmental agencies. Houses comprehensive coverage of marine fisheries,fisheries statistics, habitat restoration, mapping and remote sensing, marine chemistry, pollution and toxicology, living marine resources, protected species, and oceanography.
Patti M Marraro, Technical Info Specialist

4283 **Center for Health, Environment and Justice Library**
150 S Washington Street, Ste 300 703-237-2249
PO Box 6806 Fax: 703-237-8389
Falls Church, VA 22040-6806 E-mail: chej@chej.org
http://www.chej.org
Works to build healthy communities, with social justice, economic well-being, and democratic governance. We believe this can happen when individuals from communities have the power to play an integral role in promoting human health andenvironmental integrity. Our role is to provide the tools to build strong, healthy communities where people can live, work, learn, play and pray.
Lois Marie Gibbs, Executive Director

4284 **Clinton River Watershed Council Library**
101 Main Street 248-601-0606
Suite 100 Fax: 248-601-1280
Rochester, MI 48307 http://www.crwc.org

4285 **Colorado River Board of California**
770 Fairmont Avenue 818-500-1625
Suite 100 Fax: 818-543-4685
Glendale, CA 91203 E-mail: crb@crb.ca.gov
http://www.crb.ca.gov

4286 **Columbia River Inter-Tribal Fish Commission**
StreamNet Library
729 NE Oregon Street 503-736-3581
Suite 190 Fax: 503-731-1260
Portland, OR 97232 E-mail: fishlib@critfc.org
http://www.fishlib.org
Serving the scientific and environmental community of the Pacific Northwest, The StreamNet Library works in cooperation with the region's fish and wildlife recovery efforts. The library provides access to technical information on theColumbia Basin fisheries, ecosystem and other relevant subjects for states in the Pacfic Northwest. The library collections emphasize less commonly available grey literature, such as consultant's reports, state documents and nonprofit organizations'reports.
Lenora Oftedahl, Librarian
Todd Hannon, Assistant Librarian

4287 **DER Research Library**
Pennsylvania Department of Environmental Resources
Box 8458 717-787-9647
Harrisburg, PA 17105 Fax: 717-772-0288

4288 **Dawes Arboretum Library**
7770 Jacksontown Road SE 740-323-2355
Newark, OH 43056 800-44D-AWES
Fax: 740-323-4058
http://www.dawesarb.org

4289 **Delaware River Basin Commission Library**
25 State Police Drive 609-883-9500
Box 7360 Fax: 609-883-9522
West Trenton, NJ 08628 http://www.drbc.net
The Commission is a federal/interstate agency responsible for managing the water resources at the Delaware River Basin.
Carol R Collier, Executive Director
Clarke Rupert, Communications Director

4290 **Division of Water Resources Library**
Kansas Department of Agriculture
109 SW 9th Street 785-296-3717
2nd Floor Fax: 785-296-1176
Topeka, KS 66612

4291 **Duke University Biology: Forestry Library**
Duke University
Perkins Library 919-660-5880
Durham, NC 27708 Fax: 919-684-2855
http://www.lib.duke.edu
David M Talbert

4292 **Earthworm Recycling Information Center**
35 Medford Street 617-628-1844
Somerville, MA 02143 Fax: 617-628-2773
John Perkins, Contact

4293 **Eastern States Office Library**
US Bureau of Land Management
7450 Boston Boulevard 703-440-1561
Springfield, VA 22153 Fax: 703-440-1599
Terry Lewis, Contact

4294 **Eastern Technical Associates Library**
PO Box 1009 919-878-3188
Garner, NC 27529 Fax: 919-872-5199
E-mail: tomrose@eta-is-opacity.com
http://www.eta-is-opacity.com
Environmental consulting firm. Research results published in government reports.
Publication Date: 1979
Thomas H Rose, President

4295 **Ecology Center Library**
2530 San Pablo Avenue 510-548-2220
Berkeley, CA 94702 Fax: 510-548-2240
E-mail: info@ecologycenter.org
http://www.ecologycenter.org.

4296 **Environment and Natural Resources Branch Library**
US Department of Justice
One Congress Street 617-918-1807
Suite 1100 Fax: 617-918-1810
Boston, MA 02114 E-mail: friedman.fred@epa.gov
http://www.eoa.gov
Research library for Solid Wasteto conduct research and answer questions in the subject fields of nonhazarodus solid waste and recycling.
Leola Decker, Librarian

4297 **Environmental Action Coalition Library: Resource Center**
625 Broadway 212-677-1601
2nd Floor Fax: 212-505-8613
New York, NY 10012 http://www.enviro-action.org
Paul Berizzi, Executive Director

4298 **Environmental Coalition on Nuclear Power Library**
433 Orlando Avenue 814-237-3900
State College, PA 16803 Fax: 814-237-3900
Dr Judith Johnsrud, Executive Officer

4299 **Environmental Contracting Center Library**
ENSR Consulting and Engineering
Box 2105 970-493-8878
Fort Collins, CO 80522 800-722-2440
E-mail: faq/default.asp
http://www.ensr.com
Beth Mullan, Librarian

4300 **Environmental Research Associates Library**
PO Box 219 610-449-7400
Villanova, PA 19085 Fax: 610-449-7404

Research and consulting ecologists and testing firm. Research results published in professional journals. Research results for private clients.
Publication Date: 1970
M H Levin PhD, Director

4301 Federated Conservationists of Westchester County (FCWC) Office Resource Library
78 N Broadway 914-422-4053
White Plains, NY 10603 Fax: 914-289-0539
E-mail: info@fcwc.org
http://www.fcwc.org

4302 Fish and Wildlife Reference Service
5430 Grosvenor Lane 301-492-6403
Suite 110 800-582-3421
Bethesda, MD 20814 Fax: 301-564-4059
To provide policy guidance regarding the operation and use of the Fish and Wildlife Reference Service.
Paul E Wilson, Project Manager

4303 Florida Conservation Foundation
1191 Orange Avenue 407-644-5377
Winter Park, FL 32789

4304 Forest History Society Library and Archives
701 William Vickers Avenue 919-682-9319
Durham, NC 27701 Fax: 919-682-2349
E-mail: coakes@duke.edu
http://www.foresthistory.org
The Forest History Society is a non-profit educational institution that links the past to the future by identifying, collecting, preserving, interpreting, and disseminating information on the history of people, forests, and theirrelated resources.
Publication Date: 1946
Cheryl Oakes, Librarian
Steven Anderson, President

4305 Galveston District Library
US Army Corps of Engineers
Box 1229 409-766-3196
Galveston, TX 77553 Fax: 409-766-3905
E-mail: clark.bartee@usace.army.mil
http://www.swg.usace.army.mil/library.htm
Clark Bartee

4306 Georgia State Forestry Commission Library
PO Box 819 912-751-3480
Macon, GA 31202 Fax: 912-751-3465
Fred Allen, Director

4307 Glen Helen Association Library
405 Corry Street 937-767-7375
Yellow Springs, OH 45387

4308 Great Lakes Environmental Research Laboratory
2205 Commonwealth Boulevard 734-741-2235
Ann Arbor, MI 48105 Fax: 734-741-2055
http://www.glerl.com
Conducts integrated interdiciplinary environmental research in support of resource management and environmental services in costal and esturine water with special emphasis on the Great Lakes.

4309 Huxley College of Environmental Studies
Western Washington University 360-650-3000
Bellingham, WA 98225 E-mail: huxley@cc.wwu.edu
One of the oldest environmental studies colleges in the nation. Innovative and indisciplinary academic programs reflect a broad view of the physical, biological, social and cultural world.
Hailey Outzs, Coordinater

4310 Illinois State Water Survey Library
208 Water Survey Research Center 217-244-5459
2204 Griffith Drive Fax: 217-333-6540
Champaign, IL 61820 E-mail: library@sws.uiuc.edu
http://www.sws.uiuc.edu/chief
The Illinois State Water Survey, a division of the office of Scientific Research and Analysis of the Illinois Department of Natural Resources and affiliated with the University of Illinois, is the primary agency in Illinois concernedwith water and atmosheric resources.
Patricia G Morse, Librarian

4311 Institute of Ecosystem Studies
65 Sharon Turnpike 845-677-5343
Box AB Fax: 845-677-5976
Millbrook, NY 12545 E-mail: Cadwalladerj@ecostudies.org
http://www.ecostudies.org
Ecology research and education institution; independent; international.
Jill Cadwallader, Public Information Officer

4312 International Academy at Santa Barbara Library
800 Garden Street 805-965-5010
Suite D Fax: 805-965-6071
Santa Barbara, CA 93101
Susan J Shaffer, Office Manager

4313 International Game Fish Association
300 Gulf Stream Way 954-927-2628
Dania Beach, FL 33004 Fax: 954-924-4299
E-mail: hq@igfa.org
http://www.igfa.org
Founded as record-keeper and to maintain fishing rules. Today, emphasis is on conservation and education. Encourages youngsters to enter the sport and maintains a huge library on the subject of fishing. Has a network of well over 300representatives around the world, many of whom are conservation leaders in their communities.
Rob Kramer, President

4314 Interstate Oil and Gas Compact Commission Library
900 NE 23rd Street 405-525-3556
Box 53127 Fax: 405-525-3592
Oklahoma City, OK 73152 E-mail: iogcc@iogcc.state.ok.us
http://www.iogcc.oklaosf.state.ok.us
W Timothy Dowd, Executive Director

4315 Lake Michigan Federation
17 N State Street 312-939-0838
Suite 1390 Fax: 312-939-2708
Chicago, IL 60602 E-mail: chicago@greatlakes.org
http://www.lakemichigan.org
Works to restore fish and wildlife habitat, conserve land and water, and eliminate pollution in the watershed of America's largest lake. We achieve these through education, research, law, science, economics and strategic partnerships.

4316 Lionael A Walford Library
74 Magruder Road 732-872-3035
Highlands, NJ 07732 Fax: 732-872-3088
Claire L Steimle, Librarian

4317 Los Angeles County Sanitation District Technical Library
PO Box 4998 562-699-7411
Whittier, CA 90607 Fax: 562-699-5422
http://www.lacsd.org

4318 Louisiana Department of Environmental Quality Information Resource Center
7290 Bluebonnet Boulevard 225-765-0169
2nd Floor Fax: 225-765-0222
Baton Rouge, LA 70810 E-mail: pattyb@deq.state.la.us
To promote a healthy environment by providing a specialized environmental library to meet the informational and educational needs of the DEQ employees and the citizens of Louisiana.
Patty Birkett, Tech. Librarian

4319 Marine Environmental Sciences Consortium
Dauphin Island Sea Lab
101 Bienville Boulevard 251-861-2141
Dauphin Island, AL 36528 Fax: 251-861-4646
http://www.disl.org

Carolyn Wood, Assistant Editor

4320 Massachusetts Audubon Society's Berkshire Wildelife Sanctuaries
Pleasant Valley Wildlife Sanctuary
472 W Mountain Road 413-637-0320
Lenox, MA 01240 Fax: 413-637-0499
E-mail: berkshires@massaudubon.org
http://www.massaudubon.org

The Massachusetts Audubon Society is an environmental organization with emphases in conservation, advocacy and education. The advocacy effort is statewide and features a legislative team in Boston.
Publication Date: 1896
Rene Laubach, Sanctuary Director

4321 Minneapolis Public Library and Information Center
Technology and Science Department
300 Nicolet Mall 612-372-6570
Minneapolis, MN 55401 Fax: 312-372-6546
The varied collection in the Technology/Science/Government Documents department runs from agriculture to zoology, computers to cooking, engineering to handicrafts, medicine to motorcycle repair to military science. Special resourcesinclude a complete US Patent and Trademark collection and the CASSIS Patent Trademark Databases, a collection of US industrial standards, including publications from ANSI (American National Standards Institutes).

4322 Minnesota Department of Natural Resources DNR Library
500 Lafayette Road 651-297-4929
Box 21 Fax: 651-297-4946
St. Paul, MN 55155 E-mail: dnr.library@state.mn.us
15,000 titles on natural resource subjects available on interlibrary loan.
Jo Ann Musumeci, Librarian

4323 Minnesota Department of Trade and Economic Development Library
500 Metro Square 651-296-8902
121 7th Place E Fax: 651-296-1290
St. Paul, MN 55101
Pat Fenton, Sr. Librarian

4324 Minot State University Bottineau Library
105 Simrall Boulevard 701-228-5454
Bottineau, ND 58318 Fax: 701-228-5468
http://www.misu-b.nodak.edu

Jan Wysocki, Library Director

4325 Mississippi Department of Environmental Quality Library
PO Box 20307 601-961-5024
Jackson, MS 39289 Fax: 601-354-6965
E-mail: ronnie_sanders@deq.state.ms.us
http://www.deq.state.ms.ud

Geology and environmental reference library. Holdings in geosciences, hydrology, pollution control, paleontology, petroleum geology, land and water resources. Special collections; Topographic maps, United States, State andInternational Geoloical survey publications.
Ronnie Sanders, Librarian

4326 Missouri Department of Natural Resources Geological Survey & Resource Assessment Division
Box 250 573-368-2101
Rolla, MO 65401 Fax: 573-368-2111
Mimi Garstang, Director/State Geologist

4327 National Audubon Society: Aullwood Audubon Center and Farm Library
1000 Aullwood Road 937-890-7360
Dayton, OH 45414 Fax: 937-890-2382
E-mail: aullwood@gemair.com
Known as the Miami Valley's first educational farm, here visitors will discover a variety of native grasses and flowers, 300 year old oak trees and threatened bird species.

4328 National Institute for Urban Wildlife Library
10921 Trotting Ridge Way 301-596-3311
Columbia, MD 21004 http://www.webdirectory.com/wildlife/
Louise E Dove, Wildlife Biology

4329 Native Americans for a Clean Environment Resource Office
Box 1671 918-458-4322
Tahlequah, OK 74465 Fax: 918-458-0322
NACE is to raise the consciousness of Indian people and the general public about environment hazards, with an emphasis on the nuclear industry.
Lance Hughes, Executive Director

4330 Nature Conservancy Long Island Chapter
Uplands Farm Environmental Center
250 Lawrence Hill Road 516-367-3225
Cold Spring Harbor, NY 11724 Fax: 516-367-4715

4331 Nebraska Natural Resources Commission Planning Library
301 Centennial Mall S 402-471-2081
Box 94876 Fax: 402-471-3132
Lincoln, NE 68509 E-mail: mosaic@nrcdec.nrc.state.ne.us
http://www.nrc.state.ne.us/

4332 New England Coalition on Nuclear Pollution Library
PO Box 545 802-257-0336
Brattleboro, VT 05302 E-mail: energy@necnp.org
http://www.necnp.org

4333 New England Governors' Conference Reference Library
76 Summer Street 617 423 6900
Boston, MA 02110 Fax: 617 423 7327
E-mail: info@negc.org
http://www.negc.org

4334 Occupational Safety and Health Library
1111 3rd Avenue 206-553-5930
Suite 715 Fax: 206-553-6499
Seattle, WA 98101

4335 Ohio Environmental Protection Agency Library
122 South Front Street 614-644-3024
Columbus, OH 43215 Fax: 614-728-9500
http://www.epa.state.oh.us

Ruth Ann Evans, Librarian

4336 Peninsula Conservation Foundation Library of the Environment
3921 E Bayshore Road 650-962-9876
Palo Alto, CA 94303 Fax: 650-962-8234

4337 People, Food and Land Foundation Library
35751 Oak Springs 559-855-3710
Tollhouse, CA 93667 E-mail: sunmt@sunmt.org
http://www.sunmt.org

4338 Rainforest Action Network Library
221 Pine Street 415-398-4404
Suite 500 Fax: 415-398-2732
San Francisco, CA 94104 E-mail: rainforest @ran.org
Rainforest Action Network works to protect the Earth's rainforests and support the rights of their inhabitants through education, grassroots organizing and non-violent direct action.
Michael Brune, Executive Director

4339 **Region 2 Library**
US Environmental Protection Agency
290 Broadway 212-637-3185
16th Floor Fax: 212-637-3086
New York, NY 10007 http://www.epa.gov/region02/library
Is a research and reference library for use by EPA staff, EPA contractors, other government agencies, and the public. The library contains or has access to scientific and technical materials in paper and electronic media related to awide variety of environmental issues, with and emphasis on EPA's Region 2.
Eveline M Goodman, Head Librarian

4340 **Region 9 Library**
US Environmental Protection Agency
75 Hawthorne Street 13th Floor 415-774-1510
San Francisco, CA 94105 Fax: 415-744-1474
E-mail: libaray-reg9@epa.gov
http://www.epa.gov/region9/library
Deborra Samuels, Head Librarian & Coordinator

4341 **Rob and Bessie Welder Wildlife Foundation Library**
Walker Wildlife Foundation 361-364-2643
PO Box 1400 Fax: 361-364-2650
Sinton, TX 78387 E-mail: welderwf@aol.com
http://www.members.aol.com/welderwf/welderhome
Private, nonprofit operation foundation which conducts research and education in wildlife management and related fields. Funds graduate fellowships and conducts its reserach and education program on its 7,800 acre wildlife refuge inthe surrounding South Texas region and throughout the United States.
Dr. D Lynn Drawe, Director
Vandra Davis, Librarian

4342 **Schuylkill Center for Environmental Education**
8480 Hagy's Mill Road 215-482-7300
Philadelphia, PA 19128 Fax: 215-482-8158
http://www.schuylkillcenter.org
Karin James, Resource Librarian

4343 **Society of American Foresters Information Center**
5400 Grosvenor Lane 301-897-8720
Bethesda, MD 20814 Fax: 301-897-3690
http://www.safnet.org
An organization that represents the forestry profession in the United States. Its mission is to advance the science, education, technology and practice of forestry.
Jeff Ghannam, Director Media Relations

4344 **Solartherm Library**
1315 Apple Avenue 301-587-8686
Silver Spring, MD 20910 Fax: 301-587-8688
http://www.solartherm.com

4345 **Solid Waste Association of North America**
1100 Wayne Avenue 800-467-9262
Suite 700 Fax: 301-589-7068
Silver Spring, MD 20910 E-mail: info@swana.org
http://www.swana.org
Nonprofit trade association designed to serve the municipal solid waste industry in cutting-edge informational and technilogical practices.
Dr John Skinner, Executive Director

4346 **Southeast Fisheries Laboratory Library**
75 Virginia Beach Drive 305-361-4229
Miami, FL 33149 Fax: 305-361-4499

4347 **Southwest Research and Information Center**
105 Stanford SE 505-262-1862
PO Box 4524 Fax: 505-262-1864
Albuquerque, NM 87106 E-mail: sricdon@earthlink.net
http://www.sric.org
SRIC exists to provide timely, accurate information to the public on matters that affect the environment, human health, and communities in order to protect natural resources, promote citizen participation, and ensure environmental andsocial justice now and for future generations.
Dan Hancock, Administrator
Annette Aguayo, Information Specialist

4348 **St Paul Plant Pathology Library**
395 Borlaug Hall 612-625-9777
St Paul Campus
St Paul, MN 55108
Subject oriented library, specializing in plant diseases, plant virology, mycology, mycotoxicology and the effects of air pollution on vegetation. The collection contains approximately 8000 volumes of books, periodicals and PlantPathology theses. Over 50 current periodicals are recieved.

4349 **St. Paul Forestry Library**
University of Minnesota
B-50 Skok Hall 612-624-3222
2003 Upper Buford Circle Fax: 612-624-3733
St. Paul, MN 55108 E-mail: heroL228@umn.edu
http://http://forestry.lib.umn.edu
Houses a general collection of books, journals, government documents, maps, and pamphlets relating to the subjects of forestry, forest products, outdoor recreation, range management, and remote sensing. There is also a small generalrefernce section. Also compiles and maintains four databases focused on aspects of forestry: Social Sciences in Forestry, Urban Forestry, Tropical Conservation and Development, Trails Planning Construction and Maintenance Planning.
Philip Herold, Librarian

4350 **State University of New York**
College of Environmental Science and Forestry
Environamental Science and Forestry 315-470-6715
Syracuse, NY 13210 Fax: 315-470-6512
E-mail: spweiter@esf.edu
http://www.esf.edu/moonlib
Moon Library supports the SUNY College of Environmental Science and Forestry where students major in Engineering, Chemistry, Biology, Landscape Architecture, Forest Resources Management and Environmental Studies.
Stephen Weiter, Director/College Libraries

4351 **Staten Island Institute of Arts and Sciences**
William T Davis Education Center
75 Stuyvesant Place 718-987-6233
State Island, NY 10301 Fax: 718-273-5683
Patricia Salmon, Curator of History

4352 **Texas Water Commission Library**
PO Box 13087 512-463-7834
Austin, TX 78711

4353 **Turner, Collie and Braden Library**
Box 130089 713-267-2826
Houston, TX 77219 Fax: 713-780-0838
E-mail: rushbrookd@tcbhou.com
http://www.tcbhou.com
David Rushbrook, Librarian
Renee Miller, Library Assistant

4354 **US Bureau of Land Management**
California State Office
2135 Butano Drive 916-978-4400
Sacramento, CA 95825 Fax: 916-978-4305
It is the mission of the Bureau of Land management to sustain the health, diversity and productivity of the public lands for the use an employment of present and future generations.

4355 **US Bureau of Land Management Library**
Denver Federal Center Building 50 303-236-6648
Box 25047 Fax: 303-236-4810
Denver, CO 80225 E-mail: blm_library@blm.gov
http://www.blm.gov/nstc/library/library.html
The BLM Library serves the information and research needs of BLM personnel. The library also serves as the point of contract for bureau publications and information with other federal agen-

cies and the public. The collection covers allaspects of land management and natural resources.
Barbara Campbell, Director

4356 US Department of Agriculture: National Agricultural Library, Water Quality Info Center
10301 Baltimore Boulevard 301-504-6077
Beltsville, MD 20705 Fax: 301-504-7098
E-mail: wqic@nal.usda.gov/wqic
http://www.nal.usda.gov/wqic
Collects, organizes and communicates the scientific findings, educational methologies and public policy issues related to water and agriculture.
Joseph R Makuch, Coord. WQIC

4357 US Geological Survey: Great Lakes Science Center
1451 Green Road 734-994-3331
Ann Arbor, MI 48105 Fax: 734-994-8780
E-mail: GS-B-GLSC-Webmaster@usgs.gov
http://www.glsc.usgs.gov
The USGS Great Lakes Science Center exists to meet the Nation's need for scientific information for restoring, enhancing, managing, and protecting living resources and their habitats in the Great Lakes. The center is headquartered inAnn Arbor, Michigan, and has biological research stations and vessels located throughout the Great Lakes basin.
Russell Strach, Center Director
Jacqueline F Savino, Deputy Center Director

4358 US Geological Survey: National Wetlands Research Center
700 Cajundome Boulevard 337-266-8692
Lafayette, LA 70506 Fax: 337-266-8841
E-mail: nwrclibrary@usgs.gov
http://www.nwrc.usgs.gov/library
The National Wetlands Research Center is a source and clearinghouse of science information about wetlands in the United States and the world for fellow agencies, private entities, academia, and the public at large. Staff members obtainand provide this information by performing original scientific research and developing research results into literature and technological tools. They then disseminate that information through a variety of means.

4359 US Geological Survey: Upper Midwest Environmental Sciences Center Library
2630 Fanta Reed Road 608-781-6215
La Crosse, WI 54603 Fax: 608-783-6066
A federal library with technical holdings mainly in aquatic sciences, bird and amphibean materials.
Kathy Mannstedt, Librarian

4360 US Geological Survey: Water Resources Division Library
375 S Euclid Avenue 520-670-6201
Tucson, AZ 85719

4361 Unexpected Wildlife Refuge Library
110 Unexpected Road 856-697-3541
Newfield, NJ 08344 http://www.animalplace.org

4362 University of California
1 Shields Avenue 530-752-1011
Davis, CA 95616

4363 University of Florida Coastal Engineering Archives
209 Yon Hall 352-392-2710
Gainesville, FL 32611 Fax: 352-392-2710
E-mail: Twedell@coastal.ufl.edu
Helen Twedell, Archivist
Kimberly Hunt, Sr. Library Technical Asst

4364 University of Hawaii at Manoa Water Resources Center
2540 Dole Street 808-956-7847
Homes Hall 283 Fax: 808-956-5044
Honolulu, HI 96822 E-mail: morav@hawaii.edu
http://www.wrrc.hawaii.edu
Coordinates and conducts research to identify, characterize and quantify water/environmental related problems in the state of Hawaii. Based on the research WRRC makes recommendations to all agencies and organizations withresponsibilities to manage the water/ environmental resources in Hawaii.
Phillip Morakik, Technology Transfer Spec
James Moncur, Director

4365 University of Illinois at Chicago
Energy Resource Center
851 S Morgan Street 312-996-4490
12th Floor Fax: 312-996-5420
Chicago, IL 60607 E-mail: rsanka1@uic.edu
http://h008.erc.uic.edu/welcome.htm
The Energy Resources center is an interdiciplinary public service, research, and special projects organization dedicated to improving energy efficiency and the environment. Conducts studies in the fields of energy and environment andprovides industry, utilities, government agencies and the public with assistance, information, and advice on new technologies, public policy, and professional development training.
James Hartnett, Director

4366 University of Maryland: Center for Environmental Science Chesapeake Biological Lab
1 Willams Street 410-326-7287
Box 38 Fax: 410-326-7302
Solomons, MD 20688 http://www.cbl.umces.edu
Kathleen A Heil, Librarian

4367 University of Montana Wilderness Institute Library
Forestry Building 406-243-5361
Room 207 Fax: 406-243-4845
Missoula, MT 59812 E-mail: wi@forestry.umt.edu
http://www.forestry.umt.edu/wi

4368 Vermont Institute of Natural Sciences Library
27023 Church Hill Road 802-457-2779
Woodstock, VT 05091 Fax: 802-457-2779

4369 Voices from the Earth
Box 4524 505-262-1862
Albuquerque, NM 87106 E-mail: sricdon@earthlink.net
http://www.sric.org
SRIC exists to provide timely, accurate information to the public on matters that affect the environment, human health, and communities in order to protect natural resources, promote citizen participation, and ensure environmental andsocial justice now and for future generations.
Dan Hancock, Administrator
Annette Aguayo, Information Specialist

4370 Wasserman Public Affairs Library
University of Texas at Austin
General Libraries 512-495-4400
Sid Richardson Hall 3243 Fax: 512-495-4347
Austin, TX 78712 E-mail: pal@lib.utexas.edu
http://www.lib.utexas.edu/pal
Stephen Littrell, Head Librarian

4371 Western Ecology Division Library
US Environmental Protection Agency
200 SW 35th Street 541-754-4731
Corvallis, OR 97333 Fax: 541-754-4799
E-mail: obrien.mary@epa.gov
http://www.epa.gov/libraries/wed/html
Publication Date: 1966
Kathy Martin, Program Analyst
Mary O'Brien, Librarian

4372 Wildlife Management Institute Library
1101 14th Street NW 202-371-1808
Suite 725 Fax: 202-408-5059
Washington, DC 20005
Richard E McCabe, Sec./Dir., Pubns.

4373 **Wisconsin Department of Natural Resources Library**
Box 7921 608-266-8933
Madison, WI 53707 Fax: 608-266-5226
Contains books, journals, and EPA reports on air pollution, geology, hazardous waste, natural resources management, recycling, soil pollution, solid waste, toxic substances, waste minimization, wastewater, water pollution, andwetlands.
Erin Matiszik, Librarian

4374 **Wisconsin's Water Library at UW Madison**
University of Wisconsin
1975 Willow Drive, Floor 2 608-262-3069
Madison, WI 53706 Fax: 608-262-0591
E-mail: AskWater@aqua.wisc.edu
http://www.aqua.wisc.edu/waterlibrary
Wisconsin's Water Library is a collection of materials that cover all major topics in water resources, but is particularly strong in Wisconsin and Great Lakes water issues, groundwater protection, wetlands issues, and the impacts ofagricultural chemicals. The collection consists of over 31,000 hard copy and microfiche documents, over 35 journals and 130 newsletters.
Anne K Moser, Special Librarian

4375 **Yale University School of Forestry and Environmental Studies Library**
205 Prospect Street 203-432-5132
New Haven, CT 06511 Fax: 203-432-5942
http://www.library.yale.edu/scilib/forestl.html
A part of the Yale University Library System, the library serves the resource needs of the graduate students and faculty of Yale's 100 year old school of Forestry and Environmental Studies.
Carla Heister, Librarian

Publishers

4376 **Academic Press: New York**
Academic Press
15 E 26th Street 212-592-1000
15th Floor E-mail: ap@acad.com
New York, NY 10010 http://customerservice.apnet.com

4377 **Adison Wesley Longman**
Pearson
26 Prince Andrew Place 905-853-7888
Toronto ONT M3C-2T8 800-563-9196
Fax: 800-263-7733
E-mail: webinfo.pubcanada@pearson.com
http://pearson.com
One integrated and diverse company offering learning resources on an extraordinary level. Pearson has an estblished reputation for producing market-leading educational products and services as well as a comprehensive range ofbest-selling consumer, environmental technical and professional titles.

4378 **Blackwell Publishers**
Blackwell Publishers
350 Main Street 781-388-8200
Malden, MA 02148 Fax: 781-388-8210
Blackwell Publishers are dedicated to serving the global academic community. We recognize that publishing is about making connections. Knowledge is not constrained by national or liguistic boundries. Many academics are engaged in bothteaching and research. Our readers are often our authors as well. We develop books for students which take account of the latest research and we aim to make the journals we publish as acessible as possible.

4379 **Boxwood Press**
183 Ocean View Boulevard 408-375-9110
Pacific Grove, CA 93950 Fax: 408-375-0430
E-mail: boxwood@boxwoodpress.com
Publishes significant titles in the areas of Natural History, Area Studies, General Sciences and Local and Special Interest. Founded in 1952, it first published lab manuals, then expanded to include a variety of mainly biologicaltitles.

4380 **CABI Publishing**
CAB International 617-395-4056
875 Massachusetts Ave, 7th Floor 800-552-3083
Cambridge, MA 02139 Fax: 617-354-6875
E-mail: cabi-nao@cabi.org
http://www.cabi.org
CABI publishing is a leading international, nonprofit publisher in applied life sciences, including animal science, nutrition, integrated crop management and forestry. Our products have a global reputation for quality, relevance andauthority, and are used in over 100 countries. Our long-established print publishing activities include a substantial book and reference work list, and an expanding primary and review journal program.

4381 **CRC Press**
CRC Press
2000 NW Corporate Boulevard 561-994-0555
Boca Raton, FL 33431 800-272-7737
Fax: 800-374-3401
http://www.crcpress.com
CRC Press LLC is recognized as a leader in scientific, medical, environmental science, engineering, business, technical, mathamatical, and statistics publishing. CRC Press LLC publishes books, journals, newsletters and databases.Customers have access to publications through individual purchases, bookstores, libraries and on-line acess at www.crcpress.com

4382 **Chelsea Green Publishing Company**
85 N Main Street 802-295-6300
PO Box 428 800-639-4099
White River Junction, VT 05001 Fax: 802-295-6444
E-mail: publicity@chelseagreen.com
http://www.chelseagreen.com
Chelsea Green publishes information that helps us lead pleasurable lives on a planet where human activities are in harmony and balance with nature.Free catolog listing over 250 titles on sustainable living, innovative shelter andorganic gardening.
Alice Blackmer, Publicity Director

4383 **DK Publishing**
DK Publishing
95 Madison Avenue 212-213-4800
New York, NY 10016 Fax: 212-213-5240
Dorling Kindersley is an international publishing company specialising in the creation of high quality, illustrated information books, interactive software, TV programs and online resources for childern and adults. Founded in London1974, DK now has offices in the UK, USA, Australia, South Africa, India France, Germany and Russia.
Publication Date: 1974

4384 **Elsevier Science**
Elsevier Sciences
655 Avenue of the Americas 212-633-3730
New York, NY 10010 Fax: 212-633-3680
E-mail: usinfo-f@elsevier.com
Our focus will be entirely on scientific, technical and medical publishing. Together we can offer customers choice across our portfolio, with outstanding platforms for the delivery of electronic services and a high level of investmentto ensure the development of leading electronic products.

4385 **Environmental Working Group**
1436 U Street 202-667-6982
Suite 100 http://www.ewg.org
Washington, DC 20009
The Environmental Working Group is a leading content provider for public interest groups and concerned citizens who are campaigning to protect the environment. Offers reports, articles, technical assistance and the development ofcomputer databases and Internet resources.
Ken Cook, President

4386 **Global and Environmental Education Resources**
Global Change Research Information

Suite 250 1717 202-223-6262
Pennsylvania Ave NW Fax: 202-223-3065
Washington, DC 20006 E-mail: information@gcrio.org
http://www.gcrio.org/edu.html

Multidisciplinary and international in scope, this collection of resources was selected for its relevance to global change and environmental education. Included is a wide range of resources in a variety of formats for educators andstudents at all levels (K-12 and higher education), librarians, citizens and community groups.

4387 **Grey House Publishing**
4919 Route 22 518-789-8700
Amenia, NY 12501 800-562-2139
Fax: 845-373-6390
E-mail: books@greyhouse.com
http://www.greyhouse.com

Directories, handbooks and reference works for public, high school and academic libraries and the business and health communities. Publishes environmental directories for US and Canadian markets.
Leslie Mackenzie, Publisher
Richard Gottlieb, Editor

4388 **Grey House Publishing Canada**
555 Richmond Street West 416-644-6479
2nd Floor 866-433-4739
Toronto, Ontario M5V 3B1 Fax: 416-644-1904
E-mail: info@micromedia.ca
http://www.micromedia.ca

Canada's largest developer, publisher and distributor of value-added reference information for the academic, library, government and corporate markets. Our mission is to be Canada's one stop shop for information products and services.We license content from media, government and other sources and organize, abstract and compile this content into databases. Through a combination of technology expertise and a full service approach, our solutions provide access to a wide range ofinformation.
Bryon Moore, General Manager

4389 **Institute for Food and Development Policy**
398 60th Street 510-654-4400
Oakland, CA 94618 Fax: 510-654-4551
E-mail: foodfirst@foodfirst.org
http://www.foodfirst.org

Publishes books on poverty, agriculture and development, also backgrounders, policy briefs and development reports.
Publication Date: 1975
Eric Holt-GimŠNez, Executive Director

4390 **Island Press**
Distribution Center
PO Box 7 707-983-6432
Covelo, CA 95428 800-828-1302
Fax: 707-983-6414
E-mail: service@islandpress.com
http://www.islandpress.com

Mission-oriented nonprofit publisher organized in 1984 to help meet the need for accessible, solutions-oriented information through a unique approach that addresses the multidisciplinary nature of environmental problems. Our program isdesigned to translate technical information from a range of disciplines into a book format that is accessible and informative to citizen activists, educators, students and professionals involved in the study or management of environmental problems.
Bernice Hiatt, Customer Service

4391 **It's Academic**
29 West 35th Street 212-216-7800
New York, NY 10001 Fax: 212-564-7854

A tool for teachers who use Routledge books in their classes. To aid in finding the books best suited for your needs, we offer: pages which highlight books designed specifically for your courses, a list of conferences at which wedisplay our books, journal information, a forum for instructors to send us their comments, supplements available on line and a subject search menu.

4392 **Kluwer Academic Publishers**
101 Philip Drive 781-871-6600
Assinippi Park Fax: 781-871-6528
Norwell, MA 02061

A sector of the Wolters Kluwer publishing group. Operates world-wide from offices in Dordrecht, Boston, New York and London. All over the world, scientists and professionals hold our publications in high esteem.

4393 **Krieger Publishing Company**
Krieger Publishing Co.
PO Box 9542 321-724-9542
Melbourne, FL 32902 800-724-0025
Fax: 321-951-3671
E-mail: info@krieger-publishing.com
http://www.krieger-publishing.com

Krieger Publishing Company produces quality books in various fields of interest. We have an extensive Natural Science listing.
Cheryl Stanton, Advertising

4394 **MIT Press**
55 Hayward Street 617-253-5646
Cambridge, MA 02142 Fax: 617-258-6779
http://mitpress.mit.edu

The only university press in the US whose list is based in science and technology. Our environment list is strong in policy and the social sciences. We are committed to the edges and frontiers of the world - to exploring new fields andnew modes of inquiry. We publish about 200 new books a year and over 40 journals including Global Environmental Politics. We have a long-term commitment to both design excellence and the efficient and creative use of new technologies.
Clay Morgan, Senior Acquisition Editor

4395 **McGraw-Hill Education**
The McGraw Hill Companies
1221 Avenue of the Americas 212-512-2000
40th Floor Fax: 212-512-6111
New York, NY 10020

A global leader in educational materials and professional information, with offices in more than 30 countries and publications in more than 40 languages, we develop products that influence people's lives from preschool through career.The scope of our operations, the quality of our editorial product and the pace at which we are developing new media to fulfill our customers' information requirements are increasing.

4396 **National Information Service Corporation**
NISC USA, Wyman Towers 410-243-0797
3100 St. Paul Street Fax: 410-243-0982
Baltimore, MD 21218

Publishes information products for access through BiblioLine, our Web search service, or on CD-ROM. Some of our abstract and index services are available in print. NISC's bibliographic and full-text databases cover a wide range oftopics in the natural and social sciences, arts and humanities. Some titles provide comprehensive coverage of particular geographic regions, such as Latin America, Africa, South-East Asia or the Arctic and Antarctic.

4397 **O'Reilly & Associates**
101 Morris Street 800-998-9938
Sebastopol, CA 95472 Fax: 707-829-0104

Premier information source for leading-edge computer technologies. We offer the knowledge of experts through our books, conferences and web sites. Our books, known for their animals on the covers, occupy a treasured place on theshelves of developers building the next generation of software. Conferences and summits bring innovators together to shape the ideas that spark new industries. From the Internet to the web, Linux, Open Source and peer-to-peer networking, we puttechnologies on the map.

4398 **Random House**
1540 Broadway 212-782-9000
New York, NY 10036 Fax: 212-302-7985

The world's largest English-language general trade book publisher. It is a division of the Bertelsmann Book Group of Bertelsmann AG, one of the foremost media companies in the world.

4399 Simon & Schuster
1230 Avenue of the Americas 212-698-7000
New York, NY 10020 Fax: 212-698-2359
E-mail: ken.riel@simonandschuster.com.
Ken Riel

4400 Springer-Verlag New York
175 Fifth Avenue 212-460-1500
New York, NY 10010 Fax: 212-473-6272
Founded in 1964 and maintained its position last year as the Springer Group's largest foreign subsidiary. In 1999, 426 new titles were released. In addition, 50 journals were published, most of them available in electronic form as wellas via the Springer information system LINK. The number of license agreements in the North American market has increased fivefold due to the increasing demand for this leading Online Library.

4401 Virginia Museum of Natural History
1001 Douglas Avenue 540-666-8600
Martinsville, VA 24112 Fax: 540-632-6487
http://www.vmnh.org
Our publishing division specializes in works by natural scientists and environmental educators in the US and abroad. Writing, editorial, and design services available for books, reports, manuals, text books, presentations, fieldguides.
24 pages Quarterly
ISSN: 1085-5084
Susan Felker, Managing Editor\Outreach

4402 WW Norton & Company
500 5th Avenue 212-354-5500
New York, NY 10110 Fax: 212-869-0856
The oldest and largest publishing house owned wholly by its employees, strives to carry out the imperative of its founder to publish books of long-term value in the areas of fiction, nonfiction and poetry. The roots of the company dateback to 1923, when William Warder Norton and his wife, M.D. Herter Norton, began publishing lectures delivered at the People's Institute, the adult education division of New York City's Cooper Union.

4403 Wiley North America
605 3rd Avenue 212-850-6000
New York, NY 10158 Fax: 212-850-6088
The company was founded in 1807, during the Jefferson presidency. In the early years, Wiley was best known for the works of Washington Irving, Edgar Allen Poe, Herman Melville and other 19th century American literary giants. By theturn of the century, Wiley was established as a leading publisher of scientific and technical information.

Research Centers

Corporate & Commercial Centers

4404 **AAA & Associates**
28 West Adams
Suite 1511
Detroit, MI 48226
313-961-4122
Fax: 313-588-6232
Katherine Banicki, President

4405 **AB Gurda Company**
6061 Whitnall Way
Hales Corners, WI 53130
414-529-3116
Environmental testing and analysis firm.

4406 **ABC Research Corporation**
3437 SW 24th Avenue
Gainesville, FL 32607
352-372-0436
866-233-5883
Fax: 352-378-6483
E-mail: info@abcr.com
http://www.abcr.com
Research and analysis laboratory. Research results published in scientific journals.
Dr William L Brown, President
Dr Peter Bodnaruck, VP

4407 **ACRES Research**
6621 W Ridgeway Avenue
Cedar Falls, IA 50613
319-277-6661
Fax: 319 266-7569
E-mail: acresres@aol.com
http://www.acresresearch.com
Environmental research and testing.
Bert Schou PhD, President

4408 **ACZ Laboratories, Inc**
2773 Downhill Drive
Steamboat Springs, CO 80487
970-879-6590
800-334-5493
Fax: 815-301-3857
E-mail: sales@acz.com
http://www.acz.com
A full service environmental analytical lab with inorganic, organic and radiochemical capabilities. We perform analysis on a wide variety of matrices including water, wastewater, waste, soil, plant and animal tissue as well as fishtissue.
Sue Webber, Project Manager
Tony Antalek, Project Manager

4409 **ADA Technologies**
8100 Shaffer Parkway
Suite 130
Littleton, CO 80127-4107
303-792-5615
800-232-0296
Fax: 303-792-5633
E-mail: ada@adatech.com
http://www.adatech.com
Product development and testing of environmental technologies.
James P. Budimlya, President & CEO
Russell Farmer, Executive Vice President

4410 **AECOM**
10 Iverness Center Parkway
Suite 120
Birmingham, AL 35242
205-980-0054
800-722-2440
Fax: 205-980-1509
E-mail: askenvironment@aecom.com
http://www.aecom.com
AECOM is a global provider of environmental and energy development services to industry and government. As a full-service environmental firm, AECOM's professionals provide clients with consulting, engineering, remediation, and relatedservices from over 24 countries.
John Dionisio, Chairman & CEO
Michael S. Burke, President

4411 **AER**
131 Hartwell Avenue
Lexington, MA 02421
781-761-2288
Fax: 781-761-2299
E-mail: ross@aer.com
http://www.aer.com
Ron Isaacs, CEO
Guy Seeley, Executive Vice President

4412 **AMA Analytical Services**
4475 Forbes Boulevard
Lanham, MD 20706
301-459-2640
800-346-0961
Fax: 301-459-2643
E-mail: info@amalab.com
http://www.amalab.com
Environmental research. Asbestos, lead and explosives analysis.
David P Hood, CEO

4413 **ANA-Lab Corporation**
2600 Dudley Road
PO Box 9000
Kilgore, TX 75663
903-984-0551
Fax: 903-984-5914
E-mail: corp@ana-lab.com
http://www.ana-lab.com
Environmental laboratory. Offers ICP-MS which allows Ana-Lab to offer improved turn around time, reduce costs, and achieve better quantitation of regulated parameters. Tests are performed by methods specified by the EPA. Specializes inenvironmental chemistry.
C H Whiteside, President
Bill Peery, Jr., SVP/COO

4414 **APC Lab**
13760 Manolia Avenue
Chino, CA 91710
909-590-1828
Fax: 909-590-1498
E-mail: apcl@apclab.com
Environmental and industrial testing laboratory. Research results published in journals and conference reports.
Irene Huang, Public Relations

4415 **APS Technology**
7 Laser Lane
Wallingford, CT 06492
860-613-4450
Fax: 203-284-7428
E-mail: contact@aps-tech.com
http://www.aps-tech.com
Product development, conceptual design, engineering, prototype manufacture and test analysis.
William E Turner, President
Denis Bigin, VP

4416 **ARDL**
400 Aviation Drive
Mount Vernon, IL 62864
618-244-3235
Fax: 618-244-1149
Environmental sampling and testing laboratory; Research Development Engineering. Alternate Name: Applied Research and Development Laboratories, Inc.
Larry Gibbons PhD, President
Don Gillespie, Marketing Manager

4417 **ASW Environmental Consultants**
20 N Plains Industrial Road
PO Box 495
Wallingford, CT 06492
203-265-0509
Fax: 203-265-1476
Jason J Sarojak, PE

4418 **ATC Associates**
7988 Centerpoint Drive
Suite 100
Indianapolis, IN 46256
317-849-4990
877-282-4756
Fax: 317-849-4278
http://www.atcassociates.com
Technical engineering research and environmental consulting firm.
Bobby Toupes, President

4419 **ATC Environmental**
720 E Benson Road
Sioux Falls, SD 57103
605-338-0555
Donald Beck

4420 ATL
2921 N. 30th Avenue
Phoenix, AZ 85017-5402
602-241-1097
Fax: 602-277-1306
E-mail: tatafcr@ATL-quality.com
http://www.atl-quality.com
Technical engineering evaluation firm. Research results published in test summaries and project reports.
Frank C Rivera, President
David P Hayes, VP

4421 AW Research Laboratories
16326 Airport Road
Brainerd, MN 56401
218-829-7974
Fax: 218-829-1316
http://www.awlab.com
A.W. Research Laboratories, Inc. (AWRL) provides environmental consulting services and water quality analysis. AWRL specializes in the use of remote sensing techniques for lake analysis and management.
Alan W Cibuzar, CEO

4422 AZTEC Laboratories
6402 Stadium Drive
PO Box 7953
Kansas City, MO 64129
816-921-3922
Data collection and analysis, systems design and product development firm.

4423 Aaron Environmental
189 Atwater Street
Plantsville, CT 06479
860-276-1201
800-372-2766
Fax: 860-276-1233
E-mail: info@aaronenvironmental.com
http://www.aaronenvironmental.com
Joyce Kogut, President
Mike Bolegh, Business Manager

4424 Accurate Engineering Laboratories
4831 S. Whipple Ave.
Chicago, IL 60632
773- 52- 310
Fax: 773-384-8681
http://www.accu-labs.com
Environmental engineering laboratory.
Noel Buczkowski, President

4425 Accutest Laboratories
2235 Route 130 S
Building B
Dayton, NJ 08810
732-329-0200
Fax: 732-329-3499
http://www.accutest.com
Environmental testing firm.
Phillip B. Rooney, Chairman & CEO
Gene Malloy, President & COO

4426 Acts Testing Labs
25 Anderson Rd
Buffalo, NY 14228
716-505-3300
Fax: 716-505-3301
Global consumer products testing organization providing quality assurance testing, inspections and consulting services.
Tom Fatta, Contact

4427 Adelaide Associates
7 Holland Avenue
White Plains, NY 10603
914-949-3109
Fax: 914-949-8103
E-mail: adelaide@bestweb.net
Environmental health consulting and testing firm. Additional offices: White Plains, NY, Poughkeepsie, NY and Perth Amboy, NJ.
Ron Birlinski, CEO

4428 Adelaide Environmental Health Associates
113 Court Street
Binghamton, NY 13901
607-722-6839
Fax: 607-771-0752
http://www.adelaidellc.com
Stephanie A. Soter, President
John W. Soter, Vice President

4429 Adirondack Environmental Services
314 N Pearl Street
Albany, NY 12207
518-434-4546
800-848-4983
Fax: 518-434-0891
E-mail: aes@adirondackenvironmental.com
http://www.adirondackenvironmental.com
Analytical medical laboratory.

4430 Adirondack Lakes Survey Corporation
Route 86
PO Box 296
Ray Brook, NY 12977
518-897-1354
Fax: 518-897-1364
E-mail: info@adirondacklakessurvey.org
http://www.adirondacklakessurvey.org
Determines the extent and magnitude of acidification of lakes and ponds in the Adironack region.

4431 Advance Pump and Filter Company
10 Calef Highway
Lee, NH 03824
603-868-3212
800-863-3212
Fax: 603-868-3230
E-mail: info@advanceh2o.com
http://www.advanceh2o.com
Services include water treatment, submersible pumps, jet pumps, water tanks, sewage and sump systems.
Cathleen Pleadwell, Business Manager

4432 Advanced Terra Testing
833 Parfet Street
Unit A
Lakewood, CO 80215
303-232-8308
888-859-8378
Fax: 303-232-1579
E-mail: info@terratesting.com
http://www.terratesting.com
Geotechnical and geosynthetic testing firm.
Chris Wienecke, Co-Owner
Duke C. Wilson, Co-Owner

4433 AeroVironment
181 West Huntington Drive
Suite 202
Monrovia, CA 91016
626-357-9983
Fax: 626-359-9628
E-mail: info@avinc.com
http://www.aerovironment.com
Research, service and consulting firm specializing in the environment, alternative energy and aerodynamic design. Research results published in project reports and technical journals.
Tim Conver, CEO
Jikun Kim, CFO

4434 Aerosol Monitoring & Analysis
1331 Ashton Road
Hanover, MD 21076
410-684-3327
Fax: 410-684-3384
http://www.amatraining.com
Environmental services firm.

4435 Agvise Laboratories
604 Highway 15 West
PO Box 510
Northwood, ND 58267
701-587-6010
Fax: 701-587-6013
E-mail: agvise@polarcomm.com
http://www.agvise.com
Applied and product research in environmental applications.
Bob Deutsch, President
Bob Wallace, CEO/CFO

4436 Alan Plummer and Associates
1320 South University Drive
Suite 300
Fort Worth, TX 76107-5737
817-806-1700
Fax: 817-870-2536
http://www.apaienv.com
Civil and environmental engineering consulting.
Alan H Plummer Jr, President

4437 Alar Engineering Corporation
9651 West 196th Street
Mokena, IL 60448
708-479-6100
Fax: 708-479-9059
Alex Doncer, President

4438 Alden Research Laboratory
30 Shrewsbury Street 508-829-6000
Holden, MA 01520 Fax: 508-829-5939
E-mail: info@aldenlab.com
http://www.aldenlab.com

Hydraulic engineering firm solving air and water flow problems using physical and CFD models and field testing, for areas such as fish passage/protection systems, free surface and closed conduit flow, pump/turbine performance,hydraulic structures, environmental hydraulics, fluid equipment, 3D air flow, and flow meter calibration.
Stuart A. Cain, President
David K. Anderson, Vice President

4439 Allied Laboratories
716 North Iowa 630-279-0390
Villa Park, IL 60181 Fax: 630-279-3114

Irving I Domsky, Director

4440 Alloway Testing
1101 N Cole Street 419-223-1362
Lima, OH 45805 800-436-1243
Fax: 419-227-3792
http://www.alloway.com

Environmental sampling and analysis laboratory.
John R Hoffman, President
Lana Jackson, Labrotary Manager

4441 Alpha Manufacturing Company
100 Old Barnwell Road 803-739-4500
PO Box 2809 Fax: 803-739-0517
West Columbia, SC 29170 E-mail: mail@alphamfg.com
http://www.alphamfg.com

Physical testing of environmental testing and repair services, and instrument design.
Patricia O. Young, President & CEO
Dean Young, General Manager

4442 Alton Geoscience
21 Technology Drive 949-753-0101
Irvine, CA 92618 Fax: 949-753-0111
http://www.trcsolutions.com

Environmental remediation and consulting firm.
Jenny Rue, Public Relations
Larry Farrington, Contact

4443 Amalgamated Technologies
13901 N 73rd Street 480-991-2901
Suite 208
Scottsdale, AZ 85260

Firm providing metals and materials development, processing and testing.
Roy E Beal, President

4444 American Environmental Network
9151 Rumsey Road 410-730-8525
Suite 150 Fax: 410-997-2586
Columbia, MD 21045
Paul Jackson, Marketing Manager

4445 American Testing Laboratory
11 Industrial Road 201-489-8573
Pequannock, NJ 07440 800-488-4951
Fax: 201-489-9365
E-mail: info@mytestlab.com
http://www.americantestinglaboratory.com

Multidisciplinary testing laboratory offering a wide range of confidential testing services including environmental simulations (humidity, high/low temperature extremes).
Daniel Narbone, Manager

4446 American Waste Processing
2100 West Madison Street 708-681-3999
Maywood, IL 60153 800-841-6900
Fax: 708-681-3583
E-mail: american@american-waste.com
http://www.american.waste.com

Non-hazardous waste management, disposal/transfer, station/recycling, roll off containers.

William Vajdik, President

4447 Analab
630 Heron Drive 856-467-4555
PO Box 336 800-262-5229
Bridgeport, NJ 08014 Fax: 856-467-1212
E-mail: info@analab1.com
http://www.analab1.com

Compliance lab services for EMC/EMI, safety and ESD.
Jason Smith, Director/Manager

4448 Analyte Laboratories
2121 Cedar Circle Drive 410-747-3844
Catonsville, MD 21228 Fax: 410-747-4007

4449 Analytical Laboratories and Consulting
361 West 5th Avenue
Eugene, OR 97401 541-485-8404
Fax: 541-484-5995

Rory E White, Sr. Analyst

4450 Analytical Process Laboratories
8222 W Calumet Road 414-355-3909
Milwaukee, WI 53223 800-236-3909
Fax: 414-355-3099
http://www.apl-inc.net

Materials analysis laboratory and environmental engineering.
Jitendra Shah, President
Tarla Shah, Vice President

4451 Analytical Resources
4611 S 134th Place 206-695-6200
Tukwila, WA 98168-3240 Fax: 206 695 6201
http://www.arilabs.com

Environmental testing and analysis laboratory.
Mark Weidner, President
Stephanie Lucas, Project Manager

4452 Analytical Services
110 Technology Parkway 770-734-4200
Nocross, GA 30092 800-ASI-7227
Fax: 770-734-4201
http://www.asi-lab.com

Environmental testing and analysis firm.

G Wyn Jones, President

4453 Anametrix
1961 Concourse Drive 408-432-8192
Suite E Fax: 408-432-8198
San Jose, CA 95131-1708
Doug Robbins, President

4454 AndCare
PO Box 14566 Parkway 919-544-8220
Research Triangle Park, NC 27709 Fax: 919-544-9808

Development and commercialization of low cost, simple to use diagnostic devices and tests for medical, environmental, and laboratory markets.

Dr. Steven Wagner, PhD, President

4455 Anderson Engineering Consultants
10205 W Rockwood Road 501-455-4545
Little Rock, AR 72204 Fax: 501-455-4552
http://www.aecigeo.com

Firm providing engineering, inspection, and testing services specializing in geotechnology and materials, and environmental sciences. Services include site studies, soil testing, engineering surveys, specification evaluation, andfailure investigation.

4456 **Andrea Aromatics**
PO Box 3091
Princeton, NJ 08543
609-695-7710
Fax: 609-392-8914
E-mail: orders@andreaaromatics.com
http://www.andreaaromatics.com

Natural essential oils, fragrances, deodorants, odor neutralizers.

Michael D'Andrea, VP
Richard D'Andrea, President

4457 **Anlab**
1910 S Street
Sacramento, CA 95814
916-447-2946

4458 **Anteon Corporation**
3211 Jermantown Road
Suite 200
Fairfax, VA 22030-2201
703-246-0200
Fax: 703-246-0797
http://www.anteon.com
Joseph M. Kampf, CEO

4459 **Applied Biomathematics**
100 N Country Road
Setauket, NY 11733
631-751-4350
Fax: 631-751-3435
E-mail: admin@ramas.com
http://www.ramas.com

Environmental and ecological software development firm.
Lev Ginzburg, President

4460 **Applied Coastal Research & Engineering**
766 Falmouth Road
Suite A-1
Mashpee, MA 02649
508-539-3737
Fax: 508-539-3739
E-mail: info@appliedcoastal.com
http://www.appliedcoastal.com

Environmental analysis.
Mark Bynes PhD, President
John S. Ramsey, Senior Coastal Engineer

4461 **Applied Technical Services**
1049 Triad Court
Marietta, GA 30066
770-423-1400
888-287-5227
Fax: 770-514-3299
http://www.atslab.com

Environmental, chemical, and mechanical testing and consulting company.
Jim F Hill, President

4462 **Aquatec Chemical International**
408 Auburn Avenue
Pontiac, MI 48342
313-334-4747
Douglas Schwartz, President

4463 **Architectural Energy Corporation**
2540 Frontier Avenue
Suite 100
Boulder, CO 80301
303-444-4149
800-450-4454
Fax: 303-444-4304
E-mail: info@archenergy.com
http://www.archenergy.com

Energy, daylighting and sustainable design and analysis; LEED certification services; building commissioning, energy auditing and diagnostic testing; home energy rating software (RFOM/Rate); commercial energy analysis software(VisualDOE); and data acquisition equipment.

Michael J Holtz, FAIA, President

4464 **Ardaman & Associates**
8008 S Orange Avenue
Orlando, FL 32809
407-855-3860
800-683-SOIL
Fax: 407-859-8121
E-mail: mmongeau@ardaman.com
http://www.ardaman.com

Geotechnical, environmental and materials consultants.
Mark L Mongeau PE, Vice President

4465 **Arete Associates**
9301 Corbin Avenue
Northridge, CA 91324
818-88-220
Fax: 818-885-2210
E-mail: info@arete.com
http://www.arete.com

Environmental research.
John Mclean, President & CEO
David Kane, Vice President

4466 **Aroostook Testing & Consulting Laboratory**
160 Airport Drive
Presque Isle, ME 04769
207-762-5771
Fax: 207-764-8123
E-mail: atclabs@ainop.com
http://www.aroostooktesting.com

Toxiological and environmental laboratory.

G Noel Currie III, President

4467 **Arro**
Caton Farm Road
PO Box 686
Joliet, IL 60434
815-727-5436
Fax: 815-740-3234

Robert J Rolih, President

4468 **Artesian Laboratories**
630 Churchmans Road
Newark, DE 19702
302-266-9121
Fax: 302-454-8720
Environmental sampling and testing laboratory. Research results published in methods reports to clients.

4469 **Association of Ecosystem Research Centers**
730 11th Street NW
Washington, DC 20001
202-628-1500
Fax: 202-628-1509
E-mail: aerc@culter.colorado.edu
http://www.ecosystemresearch.org

Brings together 39 US research programs in universities and private, state and federal laboratories that conduct research, provide training and analyze policy at the ecosystem level of environmental science and natural resources management. Although AERC is an association of professional scientists rather than environmental activists, its goals and interest complement those of conservation organizations.
John A. Arnone III, President
Lucinda Johnson, Secretary

4470 **Astro-Chem Services**
4102 2nd Avenue W
PO Box 972
Williston, ND 58802
701-572-7355
800-568-6614
Fax: 701-774-3907
E-mail: info@astrochemlab.com
http://www.astrochemlab.com

A modern analytical laboratory that specializes in the in the petroleum and agricultural industry

David Zander, President
Bruce Kyllo, Lab Manager

4471 **Astro-Pure Water Purifiers**
1441 SW 1st Way
Deerfield Beach, FL 33441
954-422-8966
Fax: 954-422-8966
Manufacturers complete line of water treatment equipment, purifiers, De Calcifiers, R.O., V.V., iron filters, chemical feed equipment. Sizes for portable, point of use, central commercial and industrial. Manufacturers and privatelabels counter top units.

RL Stefl, President

4472 **Atlantic Testing Laboratories**
6431 US Highway 11
PO Box 29
Canton, NY 13617
315-386-4578
Fax: 315-386-1012
E-mail: atl-test@northweb.com
http://www.atlantictest.com

ATL is a full service engineering support firm offering environmental services, subsurface investigations, geoprobe services, water-based investigations, geotechnical engineering, construction materials testing and engineering, specialinspection services, pavement engineering, non-destructive testing, and surveying from ten office sites. The firm currently has extensive capabilities in the areas of underground and above-ground storage tank testing and management, and relatedareas.

Marijean B. Remington, CEO
James J. Kuhn, President

4473 Atlas Weathering Services Group
45601 N 47th Avenue
Phoenix, AZ 85087
623-465-7356
800-255-3738
Fax: 623-465-9409
E-mail: atlas.info@ametek.com
http://www.atlaswsg.com
Technical research firm specializing in environmental testing. Research results published in reports to clients and in archival journals.
Jack Martin, President

4474 Atmospheric & Environmental Research
131 Hartwell Avenue
Lexington, MA 02421
781-761-2288
Fax: 781-761-2299
E-mail: aer@aer.com
http://www.aer.com
Firm providing research, consulting, and assessment on atmospheric chemistry, meteorology, climate, and air quality.
Ron Isaacs, President & CEO
Guy Ceeley, Executive Vice President

4475 Axiom Laboratories
24 Tobey Road
Bloomfield, CT 06002
860-242-6291
Fax: 860-286-0634
E-mail: mackeyw@worldnet.att.net
Environmental and materials analytical testing services.
William AG Macke, President

4476 B&P Laboratories
5635 Delridge Way SW
Seattle, WA 98106
206-937-3644
Fax: 206-937-1348
E-mail: mail@bplabs.net
http://www.bplabs.net
Environmental testing and chemical laboratory water analyses (ICP);Mercury analyzer sulfates, fluorides, chlorides (DIONEX); cyandes (CONTES); storm waters; fats, oil & grease (FOG); Karl Fischer corrosion testing; process solutions
Victor Broto, President

4477 BC Analytical
4100 Atlas Court
Bakersfield, CA 93308
661-327-4911
Fax: 661-327-1918
http://www.bclabs.com
Lab capabilities include diversified sample matrices for drinkg waters, ground water monitoring and waste acceptance. Diversified analytical methods include general chemistry and field services including field analysis, sampling andcourier service.
Carolyn Jackson, President
Richard Eglin, Vice President

4478 BC Laboratories
4100 Atlas Court
Bakersfield, CA 93308
661-327-4911
Fax: 661-327-1918
http://www.bclabs.com
Chemical analysis and environmental monitoring of hazardous waste. Research results published in project reports.
Carolyn Jackson, President
Richard Eglin, Vice President

4479 BC Research
200 Granville Street
Suite 1800
Vancouver, BC V6C1S
604-224-4331
Fax: 604-224-0540
E-mail: info@bcri.ca
http://www.bcri.ca
Research results published in scientific journals and trade magazines.
Clive Brereton, President
Kevin Dodds, CFO

4480 BCI Engineers & Scientists
2000 Edgewood Drive
Suite 215
Lakeland, FL 33807
863-667-2345
877-550-4224
Fax: 863-667-2262
http://www.bcieng.com
Environmental and civil engineering, geotechnical processes, and chemical research and development firm.
Rick Powers, President/CEO
Wendy Lee, Chief Financial Officer

4481 BCM Engineers
920 Germantown Pike
Suite 200
Plymouth Meeting, PA 19462
610-313-3100
Fax: 610-313-3151
http://www.atcassociates.com
Services include environmental, geotechnical and materials, remedial design, industrial hygiene and hazardous management planning.
Bobby Toups, Chief Executive Officer
Albert Petersen, Authority Engineer

4482 Babcock & Wilcox Company
13024 Ballantyne Corporate Place
Suite 700
Charlotte, NC 22827
704-625-4900
Fax: 704-625-4910
http://www.babcock.com
Deliver innovative technologies and solutions to fulfill the needs of our customers
E.James Ferland, President
Jenny L. Apker, Vice President

4483 Badger Laboratories & Engineering Company
501 West Bell Street
Neenah, WI 54956
920-729-1100
800-776-7196
Fax: 920-729-4945
E-mail: information@badgerlabs.com
http://www.badgerlabs.com
Stephen Taylor, President

4484 Baird Scientific
532 Oak Street
Carthage, MO 64836
417-358-5567
Gary Baird, President/Owner

4485 Baker Environmental
420 Rouser Road
Coraopolis, PA 15108
412-269-6000
Fax: 412-269-2534
Environmental engineering company.
Andrew P Paja, President

4486 Baker-Shiflett
5701 East Loop 820 South
Fort Worth, TX 76119
817-478-8254
Fax: 817-478-8874
Larry Gardner, Administrative Manager

4487 Barnebey & Sutcliffe Corporation
835 North Cassady Avenue
PO Box 2526
Columbus, OH 43216
614-258-9501
Fax: 614-258-0222
http://www.bscairfiltration.com
Unparalleled technical assistance in selection of the most cost-effective activated carbon for the application
Amanda L Fisher, Marketing Coordinator

4488 Barton & Loguidice
290 Elwood Davis Road
Box 3107
Syracuse, NY 13220
315-457-5200
800-724-1070
Fax: 315-451-0052
E-mail: info@BartonandLoguidice.com
http://www.BartonandLoguidice.com
Since 1961,Barton and Loguidice, P.C. has assisted a wide variety of clients in meeting their engineering requirements. As a full service, multi-disciplinary firm, B and L has the expertise and capacity to perform a wide array of highquality engineering ser-

vices including bridge and highway, facilities, water, wastewater, environmental, and solid waste engineering. The firm continues to serve as an engineering services leader in Upstate New York.
Scott Chenet, Contact

4489 Baxter and Woodman
8678 Ridgefield Road 815-459-1260
Crystal Lake, IL 60012 Fax: 815-455-0450
E-mail: info@baxterwoodman.com
http://www.baxterwoodman.com
Environmental engineering firm.

4490 Bell Evaluation Laboratory
17300 Mercury Drive 281-488-3701
Houston, TX 77058 Fax: 281-488-8543
E-mail: bellabs@bellabs.com
http://www.bellabs.com
Coating testing and evaluation firm.
Robert T Bell, Contact

4491 Belle W Baruch Institute for Marine Biology and Coastal Research
607 EWS Building 803-777-5288
Columbia, SC 29208 Fax: 803-777-3935
http://www.links.baruch.sc.edu
Conducts basic and applied research in marine and coastal environments.
Jim Morris, Director
Margaret Bergin, Business Manager

4492 Beltran Associates
1133 East 35th Street 718-338-3311
Brooklyn, NY 11210 Fax: 718-253-9028
E-mail: info@beltrantechnologies.com
http://www.beltrantechnologies.com
A leader in advanced gas cleaning and air pollution control for a broad spectrum of industrial processes and emission requirements. Our reputation is based on 50 years of successful research, development and problem solving leading tomore than 1000 installations worldwide.
Mike Beltran, President
Swapan Mitra, Sales Manager

4493 Benchmark Analytics
4777 Saucon Creek Road 610-974-8100
Center Valley, PA 18034-9004 Fax: 610-974-8104
E-mail: f.adamsky@benchmarkanalyticslabs.com
http://www.benchmarkanalyticslabs.com
Benchmark Analytics is an independent analytical testing laboratory. Benchmark analyzes many types of samples including drinking water, wastewater and soil in addition to testing food, mold, sludge, soot, air samples and industrialproducts.
Fiona Adamsky, General Manager

4494 Bendix Environmental Research
1950 Addison Street 415-861-8484
Suite 202 Fax: 510-845-8484
Berkeley, CA 94704 http://www.home.earthlink.net/~bendix/#A1
Specializes in toxicology, hazardous materials management, and preparation of environmental documents, or appropriate parts of environmental documents dealing with hazardous materials
Selina Bendix, PhD, President
Gilbert G. Bendix, Vice President

4495 Bhate Environmental Associates
5115 Maryland Way 615-377-0725
Brentwood, TN 37027 Fax: 615-661-4226
http://www.bhate.com
Environmental consulting.

4496 Bio-Chem Analysts Inc
4940 North Memorial Pkwy 256-859-2161
PO Box 3270 Fax: 256-859-9222
Huntsville, AL 35810
Environmental testing of water, wastewater, air, soil, and hazardous waste.
Vijay Thakore, President

4497 Bio-Science Research Institute
4813 Cheyenne Way 909-628-3007
Chino, CA 91710 Fax: 909-590-8948
Independent environmental testing laboratory.

4498 Bio/West
1063 West 1400 North 435-752-4202
Logan, UT 84321-2291 Fax: 435-752-0507
http://www.bio-west.com
Using scientific principles, making sound resource decisions, and providing context-sensitive solutions for more than 35 years
Darren Oslen, President
Ed Oborny, Vice President

4499 Biological Research Associates
3910 N US Highway 301 813-664-4500
Suite 180 Fax: 813-664-0440
Tampa, FL 33619
Environmental research and consulting firm.

4500 Biomarine
16 E Main Street 978-281-0222
PO Box 1153 Fax: 978-283-6296
Gloucester, MA 01930 E-mail: biomarine@verizon.net
http://www.biomarinelab.com
Provides water and seafood analysis and consulting for the public, private companies and government.
Jim Groleau, Laboratory Director
John Marletta, Vice President

4501 Bionetics Corporation Analytical Laboratories
20 Research Drive 757-865-0880
Hampton, VA 23666 Fax: 757-865-8014
Joseph A Stern, President

4502 Bioscience
966 Postal Road 484-245-5232
Suite 200 800-627-3069
Allentown, PA 18109 Fax: 484-245-5236
E-mail: bioscience@bioscienceinc.com
http://www.bioscienceinc.com
Specialized microbes for wastewater and hazardous waste, biological treatment. BOD and COD monitoring instruments and test kits for water and wastewater analysis.
Thomas G Zitrides, President
Richard Bleam, Director of Technical Svc.

4503 Biospherics
12051 Indian Creek Court 301-419-3900
Beltsville, MD 20705 Fax: 301-210-4909
Gilbert V Levin, PhD, President

4504 Black Rock Test Lab
5 Eastgate Plaza 304-296-8347
Morgantown, WV 26501

4505 BlazeTech Corporation
29B Montvale Ave 781-759-0700
Woburn, MA 01801 Fax: 781-759-0703
E-mail: office@blazetech.com
http://www.blazetech.com
An engineering consulting firm specializing in fire, explosion, environmental safety and homeland defense. They have developed specialized software for the chemical, petroleum, aerospace and power industries: ADORA, BLAZETANK andothers.
Albert Moussa, President

4506 Bollyky Associates Inc
31 Strawberry Hill Avenue
Stamford, CT 06902
203-967-4223
Fax: 203-967-4845
E-mail: ljbbai@bai-ozone.com
http://www.bai-ozone.com

Engineering firm specializing in Ozone technology, water and wastewater treatment, treatability studies.

L Joseph Bollyky, President
Thomas Kleiber, Office Manager

4507 Bolt Technology Corporation
4 Duke Place
Norwalk, CT 06854
203-853-0700
Fax: 203-854-9601
E-mail: John.Andros@Bolt-Technology.com
http://www.bolt-technology.com/

Raymond M Soto, President
Joseph Espeso, Sr. VP/Finance/CEO

4508 Braun Intertec Corporation
11001 Hampshire Avenue South
Minneapolis, MN 55438
952-995-2000
800-279-6100
Fax: 952-995-2020
E-mail: info@braunintertec.com
http://www.braunintertec.com

Full-service engineering, environmental and infrastructure consulting and testing organization.

Robert J Janssen PE, President
John A. Carlson, CEO

4509 Braun Intertec Northwest
11001 Hampshire Avenue S
Minneapolis, MN 55438
952-995-2000
800-279-6100
Fax: 952-995-2020
E-mail: info@braunintertec.com
http://www.braunintertec.com

Testing and quality control monitoring laboratory specializing in construction inspections, materials testing, soils engineering and geological services.

Robert J Janssen PE, President
John A. Carlson, CEO

4510 Briggs Associates
2300 Holcomb Bridge Road
Suite 103, #366
Roswell, GA 30076
770-993-4559
Fax: 781-871-7982
E-mail: briggscentral@briggsassociates.org
http://www.briggsassociates.org

Environmental engineering and testing facility.

Meet David Kimmel, President/COO
Meet Al Blackwelder, COO

4511 Brighton Analytical
2105 Pless Drive
Brighton, MI 48114
810-229-7575
Fax: 810-229-8650
E-mail: bai-brighton@sbcglobal.net
http://www.brightonanalytical.net

J Shawn Letwin, Laboratory Director

4512 Brooks Companies
3900 Essex Ln
Suite 555
Houston, TX 77027
713-337-2222
866-454-1900
Fax: 713-337-2239
http://www.brookecompanies.com

Margaret Y Brooks PhD, President

4513 Brooks Laboratories
9 Isaac Street
Norwalk, CT 06850
203-853-9792
800-843-1631
Fax: 203-853-0273
E-mail: info@brooksenviro.com
http://www.brookenviro.com

Consulting and testing air, soil and water for contamination. Accident and disease prevention.

Michael Zubarev, President
Kalonji Diyoka, VP

4514 Brotcke Engineering Company
750 Merus Court
PO Box 1168
Fenton, MO 63026-2028
636-343-3029
800-969-3029
Fax: 636-343-3773
E-mail: info@bwp-inc.com
http://www.brotcke.com

Professional engineering firm that provides well drilling and pump services.

Paul Brotcke, President

4515 Buchart-Horn
445 W Philadelphia Street
York, PA 17401-3383
717-852-1400
800-274-2224
E-mail: ckinney@bh-ba.com
http://www.bh-ba.com

This company provides environmental engineering, consulting, civil engineering, facility design and planning as well as laboratory and testing services.

Brian S. Funkhouser, President/CEO
Charles L. Kinney, Regional Manager

4516 Burt Hill Kosar Rittelmann Associates
400 Morgan Center
101 East Diamond Street
Butler, PA 16001
724-285-4761
Fax: 724-285-6815
E-mail: john.brock@burthill.com
http://www.burthill.com

John Brock, Chief Operating Office/Vice
Michael Carter, Principal

4517 Business Health Environmental Lab
33 E 7th Street
300 Doctors Building
Covington, KY 41011
859-431-6224
Fax: 859-431-6228

Dan Moos, President

4518 C L Technology Division of Microbac Lab
101 Bellevue Road
Suite 301
Pittsburgh, PA 15229-2132
412-459-1060
Fax: 866-515-4668
E-mail: microbac_info@microbac.com
http://www.microbac.com

Research and development laboratory specializing in analysis and testing. Services include: air quality; environmental testing, consulting and analysis; nutraceutical testing and analysis; consumer products testing; food producttesting; fuel and manufactured products testing.

J Trevor Boyce, Chairman/CEO
James Nokes, President

4519 CDS Laboratories
122 Cary Hall
Buffalo, NY 14214
716-829-2797
Fax: 716-829-3979
E-mail: cdsdept@buffalo.edu
http://www.cdswebserver.med.buffalo.edu

Carol M. Altman, Sr. Administrative Asst
MaryAnn L. Doscocz, Department Administrator

4520 CENSOL
582 Hawthorne
L9T-4N8
Milton, ON L9T4N
416-219-6950
Fax: 905-878-8775
E-mail: contactme@censol.ca
http://www.laughton.ca

Environmental consulting and testing firm. Research results published in technical association papers.

4521 CET Environmental Services
7032 South Revere Parkway
Englewood, CO 80112
720-875-9115
Fax: 720-875-9114
http://www.cetenvironmental.com

Provides environmental consulting, engineering, remediation & construction servies. There are three primary segments: Industrial services, environmental remediation & government. programs.

Steven H Davis, President & CEO
Dale W Bleck, CFO

4522 CONSAD Research Corporation
211 North Whitfield Street
Suite 250
Pittsburgh, PA 15206
412-363-5500
Fax: 412-363-5509
E-mail: info@consad.com
http://www.consad.com

Social science research and consulting firm. Research results published in journals and project and government reports.
Wilbur A Steger, President
Frederick H Rueter, VP

4523 CPAC
One Fuller Way
Great Bend, KS 67530
585-382-3223
800-522-0499
Fax: 620-793-4523
E-mail: info@fuller.com
http://www.fuller.com

CPAC, Inc. manages holdings in two industries: Cleaning and Personal Care and Imaging. The Fuller Brands segment develops, manufactures, and markets over 2799 branded and private lavel products for commercial cleaning, householdcleaning, and personal care. CPAC Imaging manufactures, packages, and distrubtes branded and private label chemicals for photographic, health care, and graphic arts markets as well as associated imaging equipment and silver refining services.
Thomas N Hendrickson, President

4524 Cascadia Research
218 1/2 W 4th Avenue
Olympia, WA 98501
360-943-7325
800-747-7329
E-mail: calambokidis@cascadiaresearch.org
http://www.cascadiaresearch.org

Nonprofit tax-exempt scientific and educational organization founded to conduct research needed to manage and protect threatened marine mammals.

4525 Cedar Grove Environmental Laboratories
100 Gallagherville Road
Downingtown, PA 19335
610-269-6977
Fax: 610-269-6965
http://www.cgelab.com

Environmental analysis firm serving agriculture and industry.

4526 Ceimic Corporation
10 Dean Knauss Drive
Narragansett, RI 02882
401-782-8900
Fax: 401-782-8905
http://www.ceimic.com

Environmental testing for water and soil.
Margaret Marple, Marketing
John McGarry, President

4527 Center for Solid & Hazardous Waste Management
1929 Stadium Road Nuclear Science
Bldg 634, Room No. 528
Gainesville, FL 32611
352-392-6264
Fax: 352-846-0183
E-mail: rogersrd@ufl.edu
http://www.hinkleycenter.org

The center serves the citizens of Florida by providing leadership in the field of waste management research and by supporting the Florida Department of Environmental Protection in its mission to preserve and protect the state's naturalresources.
David Jee, Chairman
Sumpter H. Barker, President

4528 Center for Technology, Policy & Industrial Development
77 Massachusetts Avenue
Building E38-600
Cambridge, MA 02139-4307
617-324-7103
Fax: 617-258-7845
E-mail: ssrcinfo@mit.edu
http://www.ssrc.mit.edu

Environmental research.
Deborah Nightingale, Director
Nicolene Hengen, Assistant Director for Strat

4529 Central Virginia Laboratories and Consultants
3109 Odd Fellows Road
PO Box 10938
Lynchburg, VA 24506
804-847-2852
Fax: 804-847-2830
Adrian K Mood, President

4530 Century West Engineering Corporation
5331 SW Macadam Ave
Suite 207
Portland, OR 97239
541-322-8962
Fax: 509-624-0355
http://www.centurywest.com

4531 Chas. T Main: Environmental Division
Prudential Center
Boston, MA 02199
617-262-3200
Fax: 781-401-2575

Environmental consulting firm specializing in site assessments, surveys, and tests and analysis.

4532 Chemical Resource Processing
2525 Battleground Road
PO Box 1914
Deer Park, TX 77536
281-930-2525
Fax: 281-930-2535

Environmental consulting and chemical processing firm.

4533 Chemical Waste Disposal Corporation
4214 19th Avenue
Astoria, NY 11105
718-274-3339
Fax: 718-726-7917

Environmental waste disposal and consulting company.

4534 Chemir Analytical Services
2672 Metro Boulevard
Maryland Heights, MO 63043
314-291-6620
800-659-7659
Fax: 314-291-6630
E-mail: info@chemir.com
http://www.chemir.com

Provides a wide range of chemical analysis and chemical testing services. Experienced at solving difficult problems including product failure analysis, materials identification, plastic testing or reverse engineering. An independenttesting lab with scientists that can provide litigation support such as expert witness testimony in intellectual property or products liability cases.
Dr Shri Thanedar, President

4535 Chesner Engineering
38 West Park Avenue
Suite 200
Long Beach, NY 11561
516-431-4031
Fax: 516-717-2621
E-mail: cemail@chesnerengineering.com
http://www.chesnerengineering.com

Civil, environmental, and waste management firm that provides professional services to industry and government. Specializes in the areas of waste and by-product material recycling and stabliization, marine and dredge environmentalmanagement, risk assessment and environmental modeling, environmental database program development, remedial site investigations and cleanup management, and water and wastewater treatment.
Warren Chesner, President

4536 Chihuahuan Desert Research Institute
43869 SH 118
PO Box 905
Fort Davis, TX 79734
432-364-2499
Fax: 432-364-2686
E-mail: mforeman@cdri.org
http://www.cdri.org

Conducts research on the Chihuahuan Desert.
Thomas Bruner, President
Martha Hansen, VP

4537 ChromatoChem
2837 Fort Missoula Road
Missoula, MT 59801
406-728-5897
Fax: 406-728-5924
http://www.cfpub.epa.gov

Biotechnology firm. Research results published in proposals to the Environmental Protection Agency.
Bob Perciasepe, Administrator
Arthur A. Elkins, Jr. Inspector General

4538 Chyun Associates
267 Wall Street
Princeton, NJ 08540
609-924-5151

4539 Clark Engineering Corporation
621 Lilac Drive N
Minneapolis, MN 55422-4609
763-545-9196
877-246-9196
E-mail: ccasperson@clark-eng.com
http://www.clark-eng.com

Stephen E Clark, President
Doughlas Fell, Executive VP/CEO

4540 Clark's Industrial Hygiene and Environmental Laboratory
1801 Route 51 S
Building 9
Jefferson Hills, PA 15025
412-387-1001
888-325-8517
Fax: 412-387-1027
E-mail: info@clarktesting.com
http://www.clarktesting.com

General industrial hygiene consulting and field services laboratory that provides support to the environmental efforts of industry, both light and heavy, refineries, power industry, aluminum, steel and environmental consulting firms.Maintains AIHA (American Industrial Hygiene Association) accreditation for asbestos (PLM and PCM), metals, organic solvents, diffusive samplers and silica.

Paul Heffernan, CEO
Lee Rogers, Quality Assurance Manager

4541 Clean Air Engineering
500 West Wood Street
Palatine, IL 60067
847-991-3300
800-627-0033
Fax: 847-991-3385
E-mail: contact@cleanair.com
http://www.cleanair.com

Environmentally consulting and permitting, process engineering, equipment rental and manufacture, measurement and analytical services.

Allen Kephart, Vice President
Jim Pollack, Director of Sales

4542 Clean Harbors
42 Longwater Drive
PO Box 9149
Norwell, MA 02061-9149
781-792-5000
800-615-8265
Fax: 781-282-0058
http://www.cleanharbors.com

Environmental consulting firm specializing in soil analysis, site assessments, and water sample testing

4543 Clean Water Systems
2322 Marina Drive
Klamath Falls, OR 97601-146
541-882-9993
Fax: 541-882-9994
E-mail: info@cleanwatersysintl.com
http://www.cleanwatersysintl.com

Environmental research firm. Designs, develops and manufactures ultra-violet electronic water purification units and systems and electronic measuring systems. The Company has developed lines of proprietary electronic monitoring andcontrol systems and electronic ballast.

Charles Romary, President

4544 Coastal Resources
25 Old Solomons Island Road
Annapolis, MD 24101
410-956-9000
Fax: 410-956-0566
E-mail: coastal@coastal-resources.net
http://www.coastal-resources.net

Environmental impact assessments and nontidal wetlands identification expert testimony. Also conducts field investigations for a broad range of natural resources including soils, wetlands, streams, water quality, forests, wildlife,habitats and rare, threatened and endangered species.

Betsy M Weinkam, President/Enviro Biologist
Chuck Weinkam, Sr Environmental Scientist

4545 Colorado Analytical
240 S Main Avenue
PO Box 507
Brighton, CO 80601
303-659-2313
Fax: 303-659-2315
E-mail: info@coloradolab.com
http://www.coloradolab.com

Agricultural consulting and testing laboratory. Research results published in project reports and test summaries.

4546 Colorado Research Associates
PO Box 9027
Bellevue, WA 98009-3027
425-556-9055
Fax: 425-556-9099
E-mail: info@nwra.com
http://www.nwra.com

Environmental research.

Donald Delisi, Founder/Chairman/Executive V
Tim Dunkerton, VP

4547 Columbus Instruments International
950 N Hague Avenue
Columbus, OH 43204
614-276-0861
800-669-5011
Fax: 614-276-0529
E-mail: sales@colinst.com
http://www.colinst.com

Manufacturer of biomedical and environmental research equipment which includes respirometers and gas analysis monitoring systems.

Jan Czekdjewski, President
Ken Kober, Sales Manager

4548 Columbus Water and Chemical Testing Laboratory
4628 Indianola Avenue
Columbus, OH 43214
614-262-4372

4549 Commonwealth Technology
1263 E. New Circle Road
Lexington, KY 40505
859-294-3911
800-755-5672
Fax: 859-276-4374
E-mail: fyi@ctienv.com
http://www.commonwealthtechnology.com

Environmental engineering and analysis firm.

4550 CompuChem Environmental Corporation
501 Madison Avenue
Cary, NC 27513
919-379-4100
800-833-5097
Fax: 919-379-4050
E-mail: markross@compuchemlabs.com
http://www.compuchemlabs.com

Environmental testing laboratory.

Kenneth Grzybowski, Vice President
Mark Ross, VP of Sales & Marketing

4551 Conjun Laboratories
9283 Highway 15
Isom, KY 41824
606-633-8027

4552 Conservation Foundation
1919 M Street NW
Suite 600
Washington, DC 20036
202-912-1000
Fax: 202-912-0765
http://www.conservation.org

Conducts research and develops knowledge and techniques to improve the quality of the environment.

Peter A. Seligmann, Chairman of the Board
Rob Walton, Chairman of Executive Commit

4553 Consumer Testing Laboratories
1840 Argentia Road
Missssauga, ON L5N1P
905-812-7783
Fax: 905-812-3271
E-mail: canada@consumertesting.com
http://www.consumertesting.com

Research in textiles, safety wear.

Stewart Satter, President

4554 Container Testing Laboratory
P.O. Box 60508
Santa Barbara, CA 93106
805-683-5825
Fax: 805-683-5625
E-mail: sales@containertechnology.com
http://www.containertechnology.com

Independent third party testing laboratory.

Anton Cotaj, Laboratory Director/Manager

4555 Conti Testing Laboratories
3190 Industrial Blvd 412-833-7766
PO Box 174 Fax: 412-854-0373
Bethel Park, PA 15102 E-mail: contilab@verizon.net
http://www.contitesting.com
Analytical commerical laboratory, fuel analysis (coal, coke, alternative fuels), metals, ore barge gauging, customize analysis.
Patricia A Otroba, President
Timothy Otrobe, CEO

4556 Continental Systems
7870 Deering Avenue 818-340-3217
Canoga Park, CA 91304 Fax: 818-340-2405
Environmental laboratory specializing in soil and water analysis.
Janis Butler, President

4557 Controlled Environment Corporation
Gorham Industrial Park 207-854-9126
29 Sanford Drive 800-569-5444
Gorham, ME 04038 Fax: 207-854-4357
E-mail: ceec@ceecusa.com
http://www.ceecusa.com
Firm providing research, design, and development services relating to clean rooms and contamination control.
Matthew F Pec, President

4558 Controls for Environmental Pollution
1925 Rosina Street 505-982-9841
Box 5351 800-545-2188
Santa Fe, NM 87502 Fax: 505-982-9289
James J Mueller, President

4559 Converse Consultants
622 State Route 10 West 973-428-0934
Whippany, NJ 07981 Fax: 973-428-0713
E-mail: whippany@converseconsultants.com
http://www.converseconsultants.com
Applied and product research in environmental studies.
Hashmi S.E. Quazi, Chairman/Regional Manager
Ruben L. Romero, CFO

4560 Copper State Analytical Lab
1050 Spire Drive Suite I 928-443-5227
Prescott, AZ 86305 Fax: 928-443-5277
E-mail: info@prescottlab.com
http://www.prescottlab.com
Hazardous waste characterization, organic and inorganic waste oil characterization, waste water analysis, potable water analysis, microbiology, general waters and soil chemistry.
D.A. Shah, President
Andrew Shah, Lab Manager

4561 Corning
1 Riverfront Plaza 607-974-9000
Corning, NY 14831 Fax: 607-974-8091
E-mail: Inquiries@corning.com
http://www.corning.com
Wendell P. Weeks, Chairman/CEO
James B. Flaws, Vice Chair/CFO

4562 Corrosion Testing Laboratories
60 Blue Hen Drive 302-454-8200
Newark, DE 19713 Fax: 302-454-8204
E-mail: web@corrosionlab.net
http://www.corrosionlab.com
Corrosion testing laboratory. Research results published in technical journals and conference proceedings.
Randy Nixon, President/Senior Consultant
Bradley D. Krantz, Vice President

4563 Coshocton Environmental Testing Service
709 Main Street 740-622-3328
Coshocton, OH 43812 800-870-6570
Fax: 740-622-3368
E-mail: cets1@hotmail.com
http://www.cets1.com
Environmental testing service.

4564 Crane Environmental
2650 Eisenhower Avenue 610-631-7700
Bldg 100A 800-828-2447
Trooper, PA 19403 Fax: 610-631-6800
http://www.craneenv.com
Industrial water treatment equipment.

4565 Crosby & Overton
1610 W 17th Street 562-432-5445
Long Beach, CA 90813 800-827-6729
Fax: 562-436-7540
http://www.crosbyoverton.com
Fully permitted RCRA Part B TSD facility located in Southern California. The Facility can process both bulk and drummed waste, including lab-packs. Crosby & Overton can process a wide variety of D,F,K,P and U listed RCRA waste.
Bob Ritter, Sales Manager
Michelle Dalot, Sales

4566 Curtis & Tompkins
2323 5th Street 510-486-0900
Berkeley, CA 94710 Fax: 510-486-0532
http://www.curtisandtompkins.com
C Bruce Godfrey, President
Maggie Chan, CFO

4567 Cutter Environment
37 Broadway 781-648-8700
Suite 1 800-964-8702
Arlington, MA 02474 Fax: 781-648-8707
E-mail: consortium@cutter.com
http://www.cutter.com
Environmental research.
Karen Coburn, President
Karen Fine Coburn, CEO

4568 Cyberchron Corporation
2700 Route 9 845-265-3700
PO Box 160 Fax: 845-265-3752
Cold Spring, NY 10516 http://www.cyberchron.com
Computer manufacturing firm specializing in the development of computers designed to withstand extreme travel, environmental, and work conditions.

4569 Cyrus Rice Consulting Group
1200 Fourth Avenue 412-269-2468
Coraopolis, PA 15108 Fax: 412-375-7507
E-mail: support@cyrusrice.com
http://www.cyrusrice.com
Al Owens, VP

4570 DE3
2800 Woods Hollow Road 608-274-4330
Madison, WI 53711 800-356-9526
Fax: 608-277-2516
E-mail: custserv@promega.com
http://www.worldwide.promega.com
Environmental engineering research and testing firm.
Harold N Danto, President

4571 DLZ Laboratories - Cleveland
1000 Rockefeller Building 216-771-1090
614 W Superior Avenue 800-336-5352
Cleveland, OH 44113 Fax: 216-771-0334
E-mail: dlzroundabouts.com
http://www.dlz.com OR www.dlzcorporation.com
DLZ, a minority-owned business enterprise, is a full-service, multidisciplinary professional corporation that provides complete architectural, engineering, and environmental services to both the public and private sectors. Researchstudies are published in professional journals and project reports.
Vikram Rajadhyaksha, Chairman
Bill Sampson, Marketing Director

4572 DLZ Laboratories - Columbus/Corporate
6121 Huntley Road 614-888-0040
Columbus, OH 43229 800-336-5352
Fax: 614-436-0161
E-mail: dlzroundabouts.com
http://www.dlz.com OR www.dlzcorporation.com
DLZ, a minority-owned business enterprise, is a full-service, multidisciplinary professional corporation that provides complete architectural, engineering, and environmental services to both the public and private sectors. Researchstudies are published in professional journals and project reports.
Vikram Rajadhyaksha, Chairman
Bill Sampson, Marketing Director

4573 DLZ Laboratories - Cuyahoga Falls
2162 Front Street 330-923-0401
Cuyahoga Falls, OH 44221 800-336-5352
Fax: 330-928-1029
E-mail: dlzroundabouts.com
http://www.dlz.com OR www.dlzcorporation.com
DLZ, a minority-owned business enterprise, is a full-service, multidisciplinary professional corporation that provides complete architectural, engineering, and environmental services to both the public and private sectors. Researchstudies are published in professional journals and project reports.
Vikram Rajadhyaksha, Chairman
Bill Sampson, Marketing Director

4574 DOWL HKM
1041 B Street 907-562-2000
Anchorage, AK 99503 Fax: 907-563-3953
http://www.dowlhkm.com
Serves clients' needs in the areas of environmental planning, National Environmental Policy Act (NEPA) documentation, permitting, engineering and public involvement. Environmental studies and analyses include wetland delineation andfunction and values assessment, vegetation mapping, GIS mapping and analysis, environmental site assessment, air and noise impact analysis. Section 106 consultation, hydrology studies, and secondary and cumulative impact analysis.

Stewart G. Osgood, President
Steven K. Noble, Vice President

4575 DPRA
200 Research Drive 785-539-3565
Manhattan, KS 66503 Fax: 785-539-5353
http://www.dpra.com
Environmental, economic, regulatory and technical research company. Research results published by information services.
Richard Seltzer, President

4576 DW Ryckman and Associates REACT Environmental Engineers
1120 S 6th Street 314-678-1398
St. Louis, MO 63104-3628 800-325-1398
Fax: 314-678-6610
E-mail: stewart_ryckman@react-env.com
http://www.react-env.com
D.W. Ryckman & Associates, Inc., d.b.a. REACT Environmental Engineers, was founded in 1975 to provide rapid response and remediation services for environmental and hazardous contamination problems.

SE Ryckman, President

4577 Daily Analytical Laboratories
1621 West Candletree Drive 309-692-5252
Peoria, IL 61614 Fax: 309-692-0488
http://www.web.extension.illinois.edu
Kurt Stepping, Chief Chemist

4578 Dan Raviv Associates
57 E Willow Street 973-564-6006
Millburn, NJ 07041 Fax: 973-564-6442
E-mail: ddrai@ix.netcom.com
http://www.danraviv.com
Environmental consulting firm specializing in environmental impact studies, waste management, site assessment and litigation support.
Dan D Raviv PhD, President
John J Trela PhD, Director/Manager

4579 Danaher Corporation
2200 Pennsylvania Avenue NW 202-828-0850
Washington, DC 20037 Fax: 202-828-0860
http://www.danaher.com
Development of process and environmental controls, tools and components.
H. Lawrence Culp, President/CEO
Daniel L. Comas, Executive VP/CFO

4580 Datachem Laboratories
960 W Levoy Drive 801-266-7700
Salt Lake City, UT 84123 Fax: 801-268-9992
http://www.alsglobal.com
Analytical laboratory provides lab analysis of soil, water, air and asbestos samples.
Brent Stephens, VP/Laboratory Director

4581 Davis Research
23801 Calabasas Rd. 662-332-1943
Suite 1036 Fax: 662-332-0081
Calabasas, CA 91302-1595 E-mail: info@davisresearch.com
http://www.davisresearch.com
Agricultural, food and environmental testing and research firm.
R G Davis, President
Diane Barnham, Director/Manager

4582 Dellavalle Laboratory
1910 W McKinley Avenue 818-591-2408
Suite 110 800-228-9896
Fresno, CA 93728 Fax: 818-591-2488
http://www.dellavallelab.com
Agricultural laboatory analyzes plant, soil, manure and water (ag, domestic, wastewater). Certified Professional Soil Scientists/Agronomists/Crop Advisors and others provide consultation on nutrient and fertilizer management, cropfeasibility, regulatory compliance, troubleshooting and related areas.

Hugh A Rathbun, President
Bill Davis, CEO

4583 Douglass Environmental Services
8649 Bash Street 317-595-9108
Indianapolis, IN 46256 Fax: 317-822-8362
Environmental engineering and testing firm.

4584 Duke Solutions
1 Winthrop Square 617-482-8228
Boston, MA 02110 Fax: 617-482-3784

4585 Dynamac Corporation
CSS-Dynamac, 10301 Democracy Lane 703-691-4612
Suite 300 800-888-4612
Fairfax, VA 22030 Fax: 703-691-4615
E-mail: ibaumel@dynamac.com
http://www.css-dynamac.com
A scientific research, engineering, and information technology company, conducting state of the art field and laboratory research, and providing scientific and technical support to federal and state environmental programs.
Jolanda Janczewski, Chairman
Dianne N. Janczewski, CEO

4586 E&A Environmental Consultants
11629 Central Street 781-344-6446
Stoughton, MA 02072 Fax: 781-575-8915
E-mail: EAEnviron@aol.com
http://http://members.aol.com/eaenviron/index.html
An environmental consulting firm, E&A provides waste management solutions through the utilization of alternative and innovative management and treatment techniques. E&A has developed expertise in all aspects of composting and organicwaste utiliza-

tion. Research results are published in presentations, journals, and newsletters.
Eliot Epstein PhD, Ch. Environmental Scientist
Charles M Alix PE, Senior Engineer

4587 E&S Environmental Chemistry
PO Box 609 541-758-5777
Corvallis, OR 97339-609 Fax: 541-758-4413
http://www.esenvironmental.com
Environmental research.
Tim Sullivan, President
Jayne Charles, Office Manager

4588 EA Engineering Science and Technology
225 Schilling Circle 410-584-7000
Suite 400 Fax: 410-771-1625
Hunt Valley, MD 21031 E-mail: info@eaest.com
http://www.eaest.com
Ian D. MacFarlane, President
Jaffrey Harman, VP

4589 EADS Group
1126 8th Avenue 814-944-5035
Altoona, PA 16602 800-626-0904
Fax: 814-944-4862
E-mail: ibelsel@eadsgroup.com
http://www.eadsgroup.com
The EADS Group has experienced personnel that provide environmental risk assessments and site investigations, wetlands delineation and mitigation, and all related permitting. The scope of services covers terrestrial and aquaticecology, water resources, threatened and endangered species, vegetation and wetlands, soils and geology, air quality, noise, hazardous waste, socioeconomics and land use. The EADS Group has five offices in Pennsylvania and one in Maryland.
Dennis M Stidinger, President
Steve Sesack, P.E.

4590 EAI Corporation
1308 Continental Drive 410-676-1449
Suite J Fax: 410-671-7241
Abingdon, MD 21009 E-mail: info@eaicorp.com
http://www.eaicorp.com
Environmental engineering and scientific firm. Research results published in private reports to clients.
Charles Speranzella, President
Tom Albro, VP

4591 EMCO Testing & Engineering
PO Box 266 860-886-0697
Taftville, CT 06380 Fax: 860-886-0697
E-mail: emco@99main.com
Water treatment and environmental research and consulting, including: storm water pollution prevention; well water contamination investigation; property contamination investigation; solar energy application to commercial andresidential buildings.
Dr Ernie Cohen, President/R&D

4592 EMCON Alaska
201 E 56th Avenue 907-562-3452
Suite 300 Fax: 907-563-2814
Anchorage, AK 99518
Environmental engineering firm.

4593 EMMES Corporation
401 North Washington Street 301-251-1161
Suite 700 Fax: 301-251-1355
Rockville, MD 20850 E-mail: info@emmes.com
http://www.emmes.com
Firm providing medical data management and statistical support services. Research results published in scientific literature.
Don Stablein, President
Anne Laindblad, Executive VP

4594 EMS Laboratories, Inc.
117 W Bellevue Drive 626-568-4065
Pasadena, CA 91105-2503 800-675-5777
Fax: 626-796-5282
E-mail: contact@emslabs.com
http://www.emslabs.com
Environmental testing lab services. Asbestos/Lead/,I.H. testing. Fully accredited AIHA lab for metal waste characterization.
Bernadine Kolk, President
Anthony Kolk, CEO

4595 EN-CAS Analytical Laboratories
2359 Farrington Point Drive 336-785-3252
Winston-Salem, NC 27107 Fax: 336-785-3262
E-mail: info@en-cas.com
http://www.en-cas.com
Chemical and environmental testing and analysis company.

4596 ENSR Consulting and Engineering
1601 Prospect Parkway 970-493-8878
Fort Collins, CO 80525 Fax: 970-493-0213
Environmental engineering and consulting firm.
Will Wright, Director/Manager

4597 ENSR-Anchorage
1835 S Bragaw Street 907-561-5700
Suite 490 800-662-7232
Anchorage, AK 99508-3439 Fax: 907-273-4555
E-mail: AECOMInvestorRelations@aecom.com
http://www.ensr.aecom.com
ENSR is a global provider of environmental and energy development services to industry and government. As a full-service environmental firm, ENSR's professionals provide clients with consulting, engineering, remediation, and relatedservices from over 15 countries.
John M. Dionisio, Chairman/CEO
Daniel R. Tishman, VP

4598 ENSR-Billings
207 North Broadway 406-652-7481
Suite 315 800-662-7232
Billings, MT 59101 Fax: 406-652-7485
E-mail: AECOMInvestorRelations@aecom.com
http://www.ensr.aecom.com
ENSR is a global provider of environmental and energy development services to industry and government. As a full-service environmental firm, ENSR's professionals provide clients with consulting, engineering, remediation, and relatedservices from over 15 countries.
John M. Dionisio, Chairman/CEO
Daniel R. Tishman, VP

4599 ENSR-Carmel
4030 Vincennes Road 317-297-6200
Suite 250 800-662-7232
Indianapolis, IN 46268 Fax: 317-293-4295
E-mail: AECOMInvestorRelations@aecom.com
http://www.ensr.aecom.com
ENSR is a global provider of environmental and energy development services to industry and government. As a full-service environmental firm, ENSR's professionals provide clients with consulting, engineering, remediation, and relatedservices from over 15 countries.
John M. Dionisio, Chairman/CEO
Daniel R. Tishman, VP

4600 ENSR-Chicago
303 East Wacker Drive 312-373-7700
Suite 1400 800-662-7232
Chicago, IL 60601 Fax: 312-373-6800
E-mail: AECOMInvestorRelations@aecom.com
http://www.ensr.aecom.com
ENSR is a global provider of environmental and energy development services to industry and government. As a full-service environmental firm, ENSR's professionals provide clients with

consulting, engineering, remediation, and relatedservices from over 15 countries.
John M. Dionisio, Chairman/CEO
Daniel R. Tishman, VP

4601 ENSR-Columbia (MD)
8320 Guilford Road 410-884-9280
Suite L 800-662-7232
Columbia, MD 21046 Fax: 410-884-9271
E-mail: AECOMInvestorRelations@aecom.com
http://www.ensr.aecom.com
ENSR is a global provider of environmental and energy development services to industry and government. As a full-service environmental firm, ENSR's professionals provide clients with consulting, engineering, remediation, and relatedservices from over 15 countries.
John M. Dionisio, Chairman/CEO
Daniel R. Tishman, VP

4602 ENSR-Fort Collins
1601 Prospect Parkway 970-493-8878
Fort Collins, CO 80525-9769 800-662-7232
Fax: 970-493-0213
E-mail: AECOMInvestorRelations@aecom.com
http://www.ensr.aecom.com
ENSR is a global provider of environmental and energy development services to industry and government. As a full-service environmental firm, ENSR's professionals provide clients with consulting, engineering, remediation, and relatedservices from over 15 countries.
John M. Dionisio, Chairman/CEO
Daniel R. Tishman, VP

4603 ENSR-Harvard
325 Ayer Road 978-772-2345
Harvard, MA 01451 800-662-7232
Fax: 978-772-4956
E-mail: AECOMInvestorRelations@aecom.com
http://www.ensr.aecom.com
ENSR is a global provider of environmental and energy development services to industry and government. As a full-service environmental firm, ENSR's professionals provide clients with consulting, engineering, remediation, and relatedservices from over 15 countries.
John M. Dionisio, Chairman/CEO
Daniel R. Tishman, VP

4604 ENSR-Kalamazoo
645 Griswold Street 313-237-8500
Suite 1300 800-662-7232
Detroit, MI 48226 Fax: 313-237-8500
E-mail: AECOMInvestorRelations@aecom.com
http://www.ensr.aecom.com
ENSR is a global provider of environmental and energy development services to industry and government. As a full-service environmental firm, ENSR's professionals provide clients with consulting, engineering, remediation, and relatedservices from over 15 countries.
John M. Dionisio, Chairman/CEO
Daniel R. Tishman, VP

4605 ENSR-Minneapolis
332 Minnesota Street 763-852-4200
Suite E1000 800-662-7232
St Paul, MN 55101-1957 Fax: 763-473-0400
E-mail: AECOMInvestorRelations@aecom.com
http://www.ensr.aecom.com
ENSR is a global provider of environmental and energy development services to industry and government. As a full-service environmental firm, ENSR's professionals provide clients with consulting, engineering, remediation, and relatedservices from over 15 countries.
John M. Dionisio, Chairman/CEO
Daniel R. Tishman, VP

4606 ENSR-New Orleans
1555 Poydras Street 504-592-3559
Suite 1860 800-662-7232
New Orleans, LA 70112 Fax: 504-522-2085
E-mail: AECOMInvestorRelations@aecom.com
http://www.ensr.aecom.com
ENSR is a global provider of environmental and energy development services to industry and government. As a full-service environmental firm, ENSR's professionals provide clients with consulting, engineering, remediation, and relatedservices from over 15 countries.
John M. Dionisio, Chairman/CEO
Daniel R. Tishman, VP

4607 ENSR-Norcross
2 Sun Court at Technology Park 770-441-2364
Suite 200 800-662-7232
Norcross, GA 30092 Fax: 678-966-0751
E-mail: AECOMInvestorRelations@aecom.com
http://www.ensr.aecom.com
ENSR is a global provider of environmental and energy development services to industry and government. As a full-service environmental firm, ENSR's professionals provide clients with consulting, engineering, remediation, and relatedservices from over 15 countries.
John M. Dionisio, Chairman/CEO
Daniel R. Tishman, VP

4608 ENSR-Portland (ME)
500 Southborough Drive 207-775-2800
South Portland, ME 04101-3209 800-662-7232
Fax: 207-775-4820
E-mail: AECOMInvestorRelations@aecom.com
http://www.ensr.aecom.com
ENSR is a global provider of environmental and energy development services to industry and government. As a full-service environmental firm, ENSR's professionals provide clients with consulting, engineering, remediation, and relatedservices from over 15 countries.
John M. Dionisio, Chairman/CEO
Daniel R. Tishman, VP

4609 ENSR-Sacramento
10461 Old Placerville Road 916-361-6400
Suite 170 800-662-7232
Sacramento, CA 95827 Fax: 916-361-6401
E-mail: AECOMInvestorRelations@aecom.com
http://www.ensr.aecom.com
ENSR is a global provider of environmental and energy development services to industry and government. As a full-service environmental firm, ENSR's professionals provide clients with consulting, engineering, remediation, and relatedservices from over 15 countries.
John M. Dionisio, Chairman/CEO
Daniel R. Tishman, VP

4610 ENSR-Shawnee Mission
6400 Glenwood Street 913-362-8444
Suite 105 800-662-7232
Shawnee Mission, KS 66202 Fax: 913-362-1044
E-mail: AECOMInvestorRelations@aecom.com
http://www.ensr.aecom.com
ENSR is a global provider of environmental and energy development services to industry and government. As a full-service environmental firm, ENSR's professionals provide clients with consulting, engineering, remediation, and relatedservices from over 15 countries.
John M. Dionisio, Chairman/CEO
Daniel R. Tishman, VP

4611 ENSR-St Petersburg
10210 Highland Manor Drive 813-630-2500
Suite 350 800-662-7232
Tampa, FL 33610 Fax: 813-621-2300
E-mail: AECOMInvestorRelations@aecom.com
http://www.ensr.aecom.com
ENSR is a global provider of environmental and energy development services to industry and government. As a full-service envi-

ronmental firm, ENSR's professionals provide clients with consulting, engineering, remediation, and relatedservices from over 15 countries.
John M. Dionisio, Chairman/CEO
Daniel R. Tishman, VP

4612 ENSR-Stamford
500 Enterprise Drive 860-263-5800
Suite 1A 800-662-7232
Rocky Hill, CT 06067 Fax: 860-263-5777
E-mail: AECOMInvestorRelations@aecom.com
http://www.ensr.aecom.com
ENSR is a global provider of environmental and energy development services to industry and government. As a full-service environmental firm, ENSR's professionals provide clients with consulting, engineering, remediation, and relatedservices from over 15 countries.
John M. Dionisio, Chairman/CEO
Daniel R. Tishman, VP

4613 ENTRIX
5252 Westchester Street 713-666-6223
Suite 250 800-368-7511
Houston, TX 77005 Fax: 713-666-5227
http://www.entrix.com
Provides environmental and natural resource management engineering
Todd Williams, CEO/President
Richard Firth, Executive VP

4614 ENVIRO Tech Services
910 54th Avenue 970-346-3900
Suite 230 800-369-3878
Greeley, CO 80634 Fax: 785-827-8765
http://www.envirotechservices.com
Roger Knoph, President/CEO
Kevin Whyrick, CFO

4615 ESA Laboratories
Laboratories, 22 Alpha Road 978-250-7150
Chelmsford, MA 01824 Fax: 978-250-7171
Environmental and biological testing laboratory.

4616 ESS Group, Inc.
100 Fifth Avenue 781-419-7696
5th Floor Fax: 781-622-2612
Waltham, MA 02451 E-mail: info@essgroup.com
http://www.essgroup.com
The ESS team of scientists, engineers, and regulatory specialists provides a comprehensive range of services related to energy facility development, land and waterfront development, water resource management and ecology, and industrialpermitting and compliance.
Charles Natale, President/CEO
Christopher Rein, Senior Vice President

4617 ETS
1401 Municipal Road NW 540-265-0004
Roanoke, VA 24012-1309 Fax: 540-265-0131
E-mail: jmck@etsi-inc.com
http://www.etsi-inc.com
Research results published by The Environmental Protection Agency, Department of Energy, and Air Pollution Control Association in papers and government reports. ETS is a full-service environmental consulting and training firmspecializing in air emissions control, measurement, engineering and consulting services.
John McKenna, CEO
Terry Williamson

4618 ETTI Engineers and Consultants
1000 Rand Road 847-526-1606
Unit 210 Fax: 847-526-7443
Wauconda, IL 60084 E-mail: solutions@ettinc.com
http://www.ettinc.com
Engineering research and testing laboratory specializing in construction services and environmental needs. Research results published in project reports and test summaries.
Wes Scott, President

4619 Eaglebrook Environmental Laboratories
1152 Junction Avenue 219-322-0450
Schererville, IN 46375 Fax: 219-322-0440
Environmental testing service.

4620 Earth Dimensions
1091 Jamison Road 716-655-1717
Elma, NY 14059 Fax: 716-655-2915
Geotechnical soil investigations and wetland delineations.
Don Owens, President
Brian Bartron, Geologist/Drilling Manager

4621 Earth Regeneration Society
1442A Walnut Street 510-426-4621
Number 57 Fax: 510-849-0183
Berkeley, CA 94709 E-mail: software@imaja.com
http://www.imaja.com
The Earth Regeneration Society does research and education on climate change, ozone, and pollution, and calls for full employment and full social support based on surival programs and national and international networking.
Alden Bryant, President

4622 Earth Tech
4135 Technology Parkway 920-458-8711
PO Box 1067 Fax: 920-458-0537
Sheboygan, WI 53083 http://www.aecom.com
Specializes in the planning, design, and construction management and observation of environmental and infrastructure projects including water/wastewater; solid, hazardous and process waste facilities; environmental restoration;transportation; and architecture. The company's staff size, multiple office locations and comprehensive mix of expertise and experience combined iwht an in-depth knowledge of technical and regulatory issues, provide our clients with a valuableresource for solutions.
Diane Creel, President

4623 Earth Technology Corporation
300 Oceangate 562-951-2000
Suite 700 Fax: 562-951-2100
Long Beach, CA 90802 http://www.earthtech.com/
Alan P. Krusi, President

4624 Earthwatch International
114 Western Ave 978-461-0081
Boston, MA 02134 800-776-0188
Fax: 978-461-2332
E-mail: info@earthwatch.org
http://www.earthwatch.org
Engages people worldwide in scientific research and education to promote the understanding and action necessary for a sustainable environment.
Alexandra (Alix Goelet, Co-Chair
Merril L. Magowan, Co-Chair

4625 East Texas Testing Laboratory
1717 E Erwin Street 903-595-4421
Tyler, TX 75702 Fax: 903-595-6113
E-mail: ettlinc@ettlinc.com
http://www.ettlinc.com
Engineering research and testing laboratory specializing in construction services and environmental needs. Research results published in project reports and test summaries.
Darrell Flatt, President
Thomas R. McLemore, CFO

4626 Eastern Technical Associates
PO Box 1009 919-878-3188
Garner, NC 27529 Fax: 919-872-5199
E-mail: tomrose@eta-is-opacity.com
http://www.eta-is-opacity.com

Environmental consulting firm services of which include visible emissions training & certification. Research results published in government reports.

Thomas H Rose, President/Co-Founder
Willie S Lee, Co-Founder

4627 Eberline Analytical, Lionville Laboratory
264 Welsh Pool Road
Exton, PA 19341
610-280-3060
800-841-5487
Fax: 610-280-3041
E-mail: info@eberlineservices.com
http://www.eberlineservices.com

Analytical, consulting, and field services offer broad capabilities in: radiological characterization and analyses; environmental chemical analyses; hazardous, radioactive, and mixed waste management; and environmental, safety, andhealth management.

Carter Nulton, Laboratory Manager
William F Niemeyer, Business Development Manager

4628 Eberline Services - Albuquerque
7021 Pan American Freeway NE
Albuquerque, NM 87109-4238
505-262-2694
877-477-8989
Fax: 505-262-2698
E-mail: info@eberlineservices.com
http://www.eberlineservices.com

Provides analytical, consulting and field services, offering broad capabilities in radiological characterization and analysis; hazaradous, radioactive, and mixed waste management; and environmental, safety, and health management. Inaddition, Eberline Services provides onsite staff and services for site characterization and remediation, decontamination and decommissioning, waste management, and facility operations.

Leva Jensen, Laboratory Manager
William F Niemeyer, Project Manager

4629 Eberline Services - Los Alamos
183 Central Park Square
Los Almos, NM 87544
505-262-2694
877-477-8989
Fax: 505-262-2698
E-mail: info@eberlineservices.com
http://www.eberlineservices.com

Provides analytical, consulting and field services, offering broad capabilities in radiological characterizaion and analysis; hazaradous, radioactive, and mixed waste management; and environmental, safety, and health management. Inaddition, Eberline Services provides onsite staff and services for site characterization and remediation, decontamination and decommissioning, waste management, and facility operations.

Leva Jensen, Laboratory Manager
William F Niemeyer, Project Manager

4630 Eberline Services - Oak Ridge
601 Scarboro Road
Oak Ridge, TN 37830-7371
865-481-0683
877-477-8989
Fax: 865-483-4621
E-mail: info@eberlineservices.com
http://www.eberlineservices.com

Provides analytical, consulting and field services, offering broad capabilities in radiological characterizaion and analysis; hazaradous, radioactive, and mixed waste management; and environmental, safety, and health management. Inaddition, Eberline Services provides onsite staff and services for site characterization and remediation, decontamination and decommissioning, waste management, and facility operations.

Leva Jensen, Laboratory Manager
William F Niemeyer, Project Manager

4631 Eberline Services - Richland
3200 George Washington Way
Richland, WA 99352
509-420-0841
877-477-8989
Fax: 505-262-2698
E-mail: info@eberlineservices.com
http://www.eberlineservices.com

Provides analytical, consulting and field services, offering broad capabilities in radiological characterizaion and analysis; hazaradous, radioactive, and mixed waste management; and environmental, safety, and health management. Inaddition, Eberline Services provides onsite staff and services for site characterization and remediation, decontamination and decommissioning, waste management, and facility operations.

Leva Jensen, Laboratory Manager
William F Niemeyer, Project Manager

4632 Eberline Services - Richmond
2030 Wright Avenue
Richmond, CA 94804-3849
510-235-2633
800-841-5487
Fax: 510-235-0438
E-mail: info@eberlineservices.com
http://www.eberlineservices.com

Analytical, consulting, and field services offer broad capabilities in: radiological characterization and analysis; hazardous, radioactive, and mixed waste management; and environmental, safety, and health management.

Leva Jensen, Laboratory Manager
William F Niemeyer, Program Manager

4633 Eco-Analysts
1420 S. Blaine
Suite 14
Moscow, ID 83843
208-882-2588
Fax: 208-883-4288
E-mail: eco@ecoanalysts.com
http://www.ecoanalysts.com

Specializes in Aquatic Taxonomy and Bioassessment. An independent environmental consulting firm located in Moscow, Idaho. Experienced in the identification of freshwater organisms; macroinvertebrates, periphyton, plankton, and fish.Offer aquatic bioassessment and biological monitoring services.

Gary Lester, President/CEO
Scott Lindstrom, CFO

4634 EcoTest Laboratories
575 Broadhollow Rd
Melville, NY 11747
631-694-3040
Fax: 631-422-3770
E-mail: tpowell@II2M.com
http://www.h2mlabs.com

Environmental testing laboratory.

Tom Powell, VP Technical Operations
Jen Aracri, Project Manager

4635 Ecological Engineering Associates
508 Boston Post Road
PO Box 415
Weston, MA 02493-3
978-369-9440
Fax: 508-748-9740
E-mail: info@ecological-engineering.com
http://www.ecological-engineering.com

Bruce Strong, Operations Manager

4636 Ecology and Environment
Buffalo Corporate Center
368 Pleasant View Drive
Lancaster, NY 14086
716-684-8060
Fax: 716-684-0844
E-mail: info@ene.com
http://www.ene.com

E and E is a multidisciplinary environmental science and engineering company with more than 25 offices in the US and offices and partners in more than 35 countries. We are a world leader in providing environmental consulting servicesand litigation support.

Kevin Neumaier, President/CEO
Ronald J Skare, Sr. VP Marketing/Sales

4637 Economists
2121 K Street, NW
Suite 1100
Washington, DC 20037
202-223-4700
Fax: 202-296-7138
E-mail: info@ei.com
http://www.ei.com

Firm providing economic analysis and public policy evaluation, with emphasis on private antitrust litigation, communications regulation, and the Environment.

Bruce M Owen, President
Henry B. McFarland, VP

4638 Ecotope
4056 9th Avenue NE 206-322-3753
Seattle, WA 98105 Fax: 206-325-7270
http://www.ecotope.com
Energy efficiency research, architecture, and engineering.
David Baylon, President
Jonathan Heller, Principal/Lead Mechanical En

4639 Eder Associates
480 Forest Avenue 516-671-8440
Locust Valley, NY 11560 Fax: 516-671-3349
Environmental engineering and consulting firm.
Leonard J Eden, President

4640 Eichleay Corporation of Illinois
11919 S Avenue O 773-731-7010
Chicago, IL 60617
Environmental consulting firm.

4641 El Dorado Engineering
2964 W 4700 South 801-966-8288
Suite 109 Fax: 801-966-8499
Salt Lake City, UT 84118 E-mail: eldorado50@aol.com
Environmental applications.
Ralph W Haye, President

4642 Electron Microprobe Laboratory Bilby Research Center
Northern Arizona University 928-523-9565
PO Box 6013 Fax: 928-523-7290
Flagstaff, AZ 86011 E-mail: james.wittke@nau.edu
http://www4.nau.edu
The primary goal at the Bilby Research Center is to promote research across the Northern Arizona University campus. Research support services include professional editing; imaging services include illustration, photography, andvideography; and website design.
James H Wittke, Director
Marcelle Coder, Project Director

4643 Elm Research Institute
11 Kit Street 603-358-6198
Keene, NH 03431 800-367-3567
Fax: 603-358-6305
E-mail: libertytreesociety@gmail.com
http://www.libertytreesociety.org
A nonprofit organization dedicated to the restoration and preservation of the American Elm. Provides disease-resistant American Liberty Elms to municipalities, colleges and volunteer nonprofit groups for public planting. Distributionof Elm Fungicide for treatment of Dutch Elm Disease.

John Hansel, Executive Director
Yvonne Spalthoff, Assistant Director

4644 Emcon Baker-Shiflett
5701 E Loop S 817-478-8254
Fort Worth, TX 76119 Fax: 817-478-8874
Consulting engineers providing research services to the construction industry.
Larry Gardner, Contact

4645 Endyne Labs
160 James Brown Drive 802-879-4333
Williston, VT 05495 Fax: 802-879-7103
E-mail: info@endynelabs.com
http://www.endynelabs.com
Endyne Labs is a full-service environmental testing laboratory that specializes in the analysis of organic, inorganic, metals and microbiological contaminants in a variety of matrices including drinking water, wastewater, soil,hazardous waste and air.
Harry B Locker PhD, President

4646 Energetics
7067 Columbia Gateway Drive 410-290-0370
Columbia, MD 21046 Fax: 410-290-0377
E-mail: webmaster@energetics.com
http://www.energetics.com
Environmental engineering firm.
Nancy Margolis, President
Christopher Kelley, VP

4647 Energy & Environmental Technology
400 Perimeter Center Terrace NE 770-558-1205
Suite 105 E-mail: Jaye@EandETech.com
Atlanta, GA 30346 http://www.eandetech.com
Environmental research.
Jack Locke, President
Russel Jones, VP

4648 Energy Conversion Devices
2956 Waterview Drive 248-293-0440
Rochester Hills, MI 48309 800-528-0617
Fax: 248-844-1214
http://www.ovonic.com
Maintained a strong core competence in materials research and advanced product development throughout its forty plus year history. The company protects the results of these efforts through an extensive patent collection.

Stanford Ovshinsky, President/CTO
Iris Ovshinsky, Vice President

4649 Energy Laboratories
400 West Boxelder Road 307-686-7175
Gillette, WY 82718 866-686-7175
Fax: 307-682-4625
E-mail: casper@energylab.com
http://www.energylab.com
Environmental data collection, testing and analysis firm.
Tracey Archer, Project Manager
Alyson Degnan, Project Manager

4650 Energy and Environmental Analysis
9300 Lee Highway 703-934-3603
Fairfax, VA 22031-1207 800-532-4783
Fax: 703-934-3740
E-mail: info@icfi.com
http://www.icfi.com
Consulting firm offering technical, analytical, and managerial services in the energy/environmental field.
Sudhakar Kesavan, Chairman/CEO
John Wasson, President/COO

4651 Engineering & Environmental Management Group
11251 Roger Bacon Drive 703-318-4522
Reston, VA 20910 Fax: 703-318-4729
Environmental applications.

4652 Engineering Analysis
715 Arcadia Circle 256-533-9391
Huntsville, AL 35801 Fax: 256-533-9325
E-mail: eai@mindspring.com
http://eai.home.mindspring.com
Environmental and safety research and analysis organization. Research results published in client and technical reports and professional journals.
Frank B Tatom, President
Theodore (Ted) Sumrall, Consultant

4653 Entek Environmental & Technical Services
3 Agway Drive 518-269-3170
Rensselaer, NY 12144 800-888-9200
Fax: 518-283-4031
E-mail: uhlig@entek-env.com
http://www.entek-env.com/

Environmental consulting and engineering firm.
Patrick J McDonough, Director/Manager

4654 Entropy
PO Box 90067 919-781-3550
Raleigh, NC 27675 800-486-3550
Fax: 919-787-8442
E-mail: sales@entropyinc.com
http://www.entropyinc.com

Provides air emission testing services.
Robert Drew, President

4655 Enviro Dynamics
1340 Old Chain Bridge Road
Suite 300
Mc Lean, VA 22101
703-760-0023
Fax: 703-760-9382
E-mail: ian@2edi.com
http://www.2edi.com

Occupational and environmental health analysis and consulting firm.
William J Keanet, President

4656 Enviro Systems
1 Lafayette Road
PO Box 778
Hampton, NH 03842
603-926-3345
Fax: 603-926-3521
E-mail: pkarbe@envirosystems.com
http://www.envirosystems.com

Environmental compliance testing services, specializing in analytical chemistry and environmental toxicity testing with fresh and salt water, soil and sediment.

Petra Karbe, VP Marketing

4657 Enviro-Bio-Tech
4693 19th St. Court East
Bradenton, FL 34203
941-757-2591
800-314-6263
Fax: 941-757-2592
E-mail: info@environmentalbiotech.com
http://www.environmentalbiotech.com

Chemical analysis firm.
Harpal Singh, President

4658 Enviro-Lab
45-10 Court Square
Long Island City, NY 11101
718-392-0185
Fax: 718-392-8654
E-mail: info@envirolab.com
http://http://www.envirolab.com

Environmental Toxicology Laboratory (ETL) is a research, development and testing laboratory; concentrating its efforts on new approaches to toxicity testing. The mission of ETL is the further advancement of the Tetramitis Assay aswell as the promotion and commercialization of the test.

Dr. Robert L Jaffe, Ph.D, Director of Lab. Science

4659 Enviro-Sciences
781 Route 15 South
Hopatcong, NJ 07849
973-398-8183
Fax: 973-398-8037
E-mail: info@enviro-sciences.com
http://www.enviro-sciences.com

Environmental sciences firm.
Irving D Cohen, CEO
Glenn Lechner, Marketing Manager

4660 EnviroAnalytical
286 Mask Island Drive
Barry's Bay, ON K0J 1
613-756-0101
800-427-8591
Fax: 613-756-0909
E-mail: info@enviro-analytical.com
http://www.enviro-analytical.com

Environmental compliance analysis, R&D, personnel training and analytical method development.
Dr S Sethi, Job Director

4661 Enviroclean Technology
5201 Blue Lagoon Drive, 8th Floor
Miami, FL 33126
305-267-6667
Fax: 305-267-1117
E-mail: bill lorenz@erm.com
http://www.erm.com

Environmental laboratory service company.
John Alexander, CEO
David McArthur, Regional CEO

4662 Envirodyne Engineers
303 E Wacker Drive
Suite 600
Chicago, IL 60601
312-938-0300
Fax: 312-938-1109

Environmental science research firm.

4663 Environ Laboratories
9725 Girard Avenue S
Minneapolis, MN 55431
952-888-7795
800-826-3710
Fax: 952-888-6345
http://www.environlab.com

Laboratory providing environmental and physical testing of products and materials to commercial and military specifications.
Alan G Thompson, President

4664 Environment Associates
9604 Variel Avenue
Chatsworth, CA 91311
818-709-0568
800-354-1522
Fax: 818-709-8914
E-mail: Andrews@Eatest.com
http://www.eatest.com

Provides a full spectrum of environmental test services to Aerospace, Military and commercial manufacturers including temperature, humidity, altitude, thermal vacuum, shock, vibration, corrosive atmosphere, a DSCC approved connectortest lab, hydraulic and pneumatic test capabilities, flow testing firewall testing, EMMI/EMC testing and more. Services also include test procedure development formal test reports, certification and test fixture modifications and adaptations.

William Spaulding, President
Andrew Spaulding, Sales

4665 Environment/One Corporation
2773 Balltown Road
Niskayuna, NY 12309
518-346-6161
Fax: 518-346-6188
E-mail: eone@eone.com
http://www.eone.com

Environmental analysis and instrumentation firm. Research results published in technical journals.

George A. Fursheim, Communications Director

4666 Environmental Acoustical Research
PO Box 18888
Boulder, CO 80308
303-447-2619
800-525-2690
Fax: 303-447-2637
E-mail: info@earinc.com
http://www.earinc.com

Specialized hearing protection and enhancement systems.
Garry G. Gordon, President/Audiologist
Andrew Gordon, Lab/Marketing Director

4667 Environmental Analysis
3278 N Highway 67
Florissant, MO 63033
314-921-4488
Fax: 314-921-4494

Environmental analytical laboratory.
R M Ferris, President

4668 Environmental Analytical Laboratory
95 Beaver Street
Waltham, MA 02453
781-893-8330
Fax: 781-893-4414
E-mail: Info@hubtesting.net
http://www.hubtesting.net

Environmental testing services company specializing in asbestos consulting and analysis, waste water, soils and surveys. Also mold remediation and screening.

Frederick Boyle, President

4669 Environmental Audits
11327 W. Lincoln Ave.
West Allis, WI 53227
414-226-5563
Fax: 414-231-9374
E-mail: info@environmentalaudits.net
http://www.environmentalaudits.net

Consulting firm specializing in environmental science.

John R Ruetz, President

4670 Environmental Chemical
1240 Bayshore Highway
Burlingame, CA 94010
650-347-1555
Fax: 650-347-8789
http://www.ecc.net

Research and testing firm.

4671 **Environmental Consultants**
391 Newman Avenue 812-282-8481
Clarksville, IN 47129 Fax: 812-282-8554
Environmental consulting firm.
Robert E Fuchs, President

4672 **Environmental Consulting Laboratories**
1005 Boston Post Road 203-245-0568
Madison, CT 06443 800-246-9624
E-mail: eclinc@aol.com
Environmental testing and consulting firm.

4673 **Environmental Consulting Laboratories, Inc.**
1005 Boston Post Road 203-245-0568
Madison, CT 06443 800-246-9624
Fax: 203-318-0830
E-mail: eclinc@aol.com
Environmental testing and consulting firm. Specializing in Micro Biology and aquatic tixicity.
David Barris, President/Lab Director

4674 **Environmental Control**
622 Truman Street NE 505-232-7700
Albuquerque, NM 87110 Fax: 505-232-0942
http://www.environmentcontrol.com
Environmental consulting and analytical laboratory. Research results published in project reports and test summaries.
Reid Warner, Owner
James J Meuller, President

4675 **Environmental Control Laboratories**
38818 Talyor Industrial Parkway 440-353-3700
North Ridgeville, OH 44039 800-962-0118
Fax: 440-353-3773
E-mail: eclabs@compuserve.com
E.C. Labs does environmental testing, such as: waste water, soil, asbestos, remediation and constrution projects.
Ron Schiedel, Marketing Manager
Phyllis Conley, Lab Manager

4676 **Environmental Data Resources**
440 Wheelers Farms Road 203-783-0300
Milford, CT 06461 800-352-0050
Fax: 800-231-6802
http://www.edrnet.com
Applied and product research in environmental applications.
Rob Barber, CEO
Jon Walker, Executive VP

4677 **Environmental Elements Corporation**
333 West Camden St. 410-333-1560
Suite 500 877-637-8234
Batlimore, MD 21201 Fax: 410-333-1888
E-mail: msa@mdstad.com
http://www.EEC1.com
Environmental Elements Corporation, the leading supplier of air pollution control systems for over 50 years, designs, installs, and maintains electrostatic precipitators, fabric filters, gas, and particulate scrubbing andAmmonia-on-Demand (AOD) Systems. EEC technologies enable customers in a broad range of power and generation, pulp, and paper, waste-to-energy, rock products, metals and petrochemical industries to operate their facilities in compliance withparticulate and gaseous emissions.
Robert L. McKinney, Chairman
Alison L. Asti, Executive Director

4678 **Environmental Health Sciences Research Laboratory**
127 New Market Street 504-394-2233
PO Box 379 Fax: 504-394-7982
Belle Chasse, LA 70037

4679 **Environmental Innovations**
9600 West Flag Avenue 414-358-7760
Milwaukee, WI 53225 Fax: 414-358-7770
Environmental engineering and consulting firm.

4680 **Environmental Laboratories**
1 United Nations Plaza 212-963-6010
Room DC-1-1155 Fax: 917-367-4046
New York, NY 10017 E-mail: iaeany@un.org
http://www.iaea.org
Yukiya Amano, Director General
Janice Dunn Lee, Head, Dept of Management

4681 **Environmental Management: Guthrie**
5200 N.E. Highway 33 405-282-8510
PO Box 700 800-510-8510
Guthrie, OK 73044 Fax: 405-282-8533
http://www.emiok.com
Full service environmental firm provides emergency response remediation routine waste management for hazardous and non hazardous materials and consulting. The firm owns the transportation and remediation equipment along with providinga full technical staff.
Terry Bobo, President
Keeton Hill, Health and Safety Officer

4682 **Environmental Management: Waltham**
95 Beaver Street 781-893-8330
Waltham, MA 02453 Fax: 781-893-4414
E-mail: Info@hubtesting.net
http://www.hubtesting.net
Environmental testing services, consulting services, environmental abatement services, water quality/chemical testing, asbestos remediation monitoring and inspections, mold testing/mold remediation, industrial hygiene services.
Susan Boyle, Vice President

4683 **Environmental Measurements**
2660 California Street 415-567-8089
San Francisco, CA 94115 Fax: 415-398-7664
E-mail: sales@langan.net
http://http://lpi.langan.net

4684 **Environmental Monitoring Laboratory**
59 N Plains Industrial Road 203-284-0555
Suite A Fax: 203-284-2064
Wallingford, CT 06492
Laboratory providing environmental chemistry services including analysis, bioassays, product efficacy and research and development in the areas of water and wastewater, agricultural chemicals, protective coatings, petroleum products,metals and chemicals.
Jan D Dunn PhD, Director/Manager

4685 **Environmental Quality Protection Systems Company**
5150 Keele Street 601-961-5650
Jackson, MS 39206 Fax: 601-354-6612
Environmental engineering and science firm.

4686 **Environmental Research Associates**
16341 Table Mountain Parkway 303-421-0122
Golden, CO 80403 800-372-0122
Fax: 303-421-0159
E-mail: info@eraqc.com
http://www.eraqc.com
Research and consulting ecologists and testing firm. Research results published in professional journals. Research results for private clients.
M H Levin PhD, Director

4687 **Environmental Resource Associates**
16341 Table Mountain Parkway 303-421-0122
Golden, CO 80403 800-372-0122
Fax: 303-421-0159
E-mail: info@eraqc.com
http://www.eraqc.com
Engineering consultant.

4688 **Environmental Risk Limited**
120 Mountain Avenue
Bloomfield, CT 06002
860-242-9933
Fax: 860-243-9055
E-mail: info@erl.com
http://www.erl.com
Environmental consulting and engineering firm offers environmental permitting and compliance assistance, site investigation and remediation services, air quality impact analyses, pollution prevention planning, aquatic toxicitylaboratory, hazardous waste management and chemical accident prevention program assistance.
Gordon T Brookman, President

4689 **Environmental Risk: Clifton Division**
1373 Broad Street
Suite 301
Clifton, NJ 07013
973-773-8322
Fax: 973-243-9055
Environmental engineering and consulting services.

4690 **Environmental Science & Engineering**
1200 E. California Blvd
MC 131-24
Pasadena, CA 91125-2400
626-795-6070
Fax: 626-795-6028
E-mail: miuragps.caltech.edu
http://www.ese.caltech.edu
Comprehensive environmental and engineering consulting firm.
Jean-Lou Chameau, President
Elizabeth Boyd, Academic Assistant

4691 **Environmental Services International**
6404 Maccorkle Avenue
Saint Albans, WV 25177
301 768 2233
Fax: 304-768-9988
E-mail: esi@citynet.net
Consulting, engineering, and analytical firm. Research results published in reports to clients.

4692 **Environmental Systems Corporation**
10801 N Mopac Bldg 1-200
Austin, TX 78759
512-250-7900
Fax: 512-258-5836
E-mail: support@envirosys.com
http://www.envirosys.com
Data acquisition and reporting systems for electric power producers and industrial sources, ESC is the leading supplier of CEM and ambient data systems in the US.
Jack R. Missimer, President
Jeff Rabenteine, VP

4693 **Environmental Technical Services**
834 Castle Ridge Road
Austin, TX 78746
512-327-6672
Fax: 512-327-1974
http://www.wetlands.com/
Firm conducts sewer rehabilitation and tank testing.

4694 **Environmental Testing Services**
95 Beaver Street
Waltham, MA 02453
781-893-8330
Fax: 781-893-4414
E-mail: Info@hubtesting.net
http://www.hubtesting.net
Environmental testing services company specializing in asbestos consulting and analysis, waste water, soils and surveys. Also mold remediation and screening.
Frederick Boyle, President

4695 **Environmental Testing and Consulting**
2790 Whitten Road
Memphis, TN 38133
901-213-2400
800-264-4522
Fax: 901-213-2440
http://www.etcmemphis.com
Environmental testing service. Research results published in proprietary reports.
Linda Harper, Environmental Sales

4696 **Environmental Working Group**
1436 U St. NW
Suite 100
Washington, DC 20009
202-667-6982
Fax: 202-232-2592
http://www.ewg.org
Cutting-edge research on health and the environment.
David Baker, Founder/Executive Director
Drummond Pike, Chair/Director

4697 **Enviropro**
9765 Eton Avenue
Chatsworth, CA 91311
818-998-7197
Fax: 818-998-7258
Environmental engineering services. Spcialize in: Site investigation/remediation; Real Estate transfers: Phase I and II assessments; feasibility studies; clean-up of contaminated property, soil and groundwater; Methane gasinvestigations.
Zvia Uziel, President
Dr Michael Uziel, Director/Manager

4698 **Enviroscan Inc**
1051 Columbia Avenue
Lancaster, PA 17603
717-396-8922
Fax: 717-396-8746
E-mail: email@enviroscan.com
http://www.enviroscan.com
Specializes in non-intrusive, non-deestructive land marine and borhole geophysics for engineers, environmental consultants, architects, industry, government and others. Geophysics is the earth science equivalent of medical radiology,and is used to locate subsurface objects such as utilities, underground storage tanks, drums, bedrock depths, sinkholes, contaminant plumes, fractures, graves, downed aircraft(in oceans, lakes) and submerged items.
Felicia Kegel Bechtel, President
Geoffrey T. Stankiewicz, Vice President

4699 **Envisage Environmental**
PO Box 152
Richfield, OH 44286
440-526-0990
Fax: 440-526-8555
Environmental engineering firm

4700 **Eppley Laboratory**
12 Sheffield Avenue
PO Box 419
Newport, RI 02840
401-847-1020
Fax: 401-847-1031
E-mail: info@eppleylab.com
http://www.eppleylab.com
Produces radiometer, pyranometers, pyrheliometers and pyrgeometers that measure solar and terrestrial radiation.
George L Kirk, President

4701 **Era Laboratories**
4730 Oneota Street
Duluth, MN 55807-2719
218-727-6380
800-727-6380
Fax: 218-727-3049
E-mail: info@eralabs.com
http://www.eralabs.com
Environmental laboratory serving the agricultural industry through chemical analysis and sampling.
Robert D Manuson, President

4702 **Ernaco**
3740 Capulet Terr.
Silver Spring, MD 20906
301-598-5025
Firm offers biomedical, health and environmental research services.
Dr Muriel M Lippman, President

4703 **Eureka Laboratories**
4701 S. Whipple Street
Chicago, IL 60632
773-847-9672
Fax: 773-847-9675
Shao-Pin Yo, Laboratory Director

4704 **Eustis Engineering Services, LLC**
3011 28th Street
Metairie, LA 70002
504-834-0157
800-966-0157
Fax: 504-834-0354
E-mail: info@eustiseng.com
http://www.eustiseng.com
Geotechnical firm performing complete investigations, dynamic pile testing, cone penetrometer testing, CQC and materials testing and environmental services.
William W Gwyn, President
John R Eustis, Executive Vice President

4705 Evans Cooling Systems
1 Mountain Rd
Suffield, CT 06078
860-668-1114
Fax: 860-668-2757
E-mail: tech@evanscooling.com
http://www.evanscooling.com
Environmental applications.
J. Thomas Light, President/CEO
Edward L. Coyle, VP/COO

4706 Everglades Laboratories
1602 Clare Avenue
West Palm Beach, FL 33401
561-833-4200
Fax: 561-833-7280
E-mail: info@evergladeslabs.com
http://www.evergladeslabs.com/
Dr. Ben Martin, Director

4707 Excel Environmental Resources
111 North Center Drive
New Brunswick, NJ 08902
732-545-9525
800-810-3923
Fax: 732-545-9425
E-mail: info@excelenv.com
http://www.excelenv.com
Environmental research.
Laura J. Dodge, President
Ron Harwood, Executive VP

4708 First Coast Environmental Laboratory
8818 Arlington Expressway
Jacksonville, FL 32211
904-725-4847
Fax: 904-725-2215
Analytical laboratory.
Adolph W Wollitz, Director/Manager

4709 Fishbeck, Thompson, Carr & Huber, Inc.
1515 Arboretum Drive, SE
Grand Rapids, MI 49546
616-575-3824
Fax: 616-464-3993
E-mail: info@ftch.com
http://www.ftch.com
Environmental consulting and engineering firm.

James A. Susan, P.E., President
Kenneth G. Wiley, CPG, Vice President

4710 Flowers Chemical Laboratories
481 Newburyport Avenue
PO Box 150597
Altamonte Springs, FL 32701
407-339-5984
800-669-5227
Fax: 407-260-6110
E-mail: jeff@flowerslabs.com
http://www.flowerslabs.com
Analytical consulting firm. Research results published in reports to clients. Displays report in a pdf or html format.

Dr Jefferson Flowers, President

4711 Forensic Engineering
1439 Legion Road
Burlington, ON L7S1T
905-632-3040
800-263-6351
Fax: 905-632-2131
E-mail: forensic@forensiceng.ca
http://www.forensiceng.ca

Joe M Beard, President

4712 Fredericktowne Labs
3020 Ventrie Court
PO Box 245
Myersville, MD 21778
301-293-3340
800-332-3340
Fax: 301-293-2366
E-mail: info@Fredericktownelabs.com
http://www.Fredericktownelabs.com
Environmental testing lab performing analyses on drinking water, waste water and natural waters for microbiological, inorganic, metal and organic contaminants. State certified laboratory. State certified sample collectors.Consulting services.

Mary Miller, PhD, Laboratory Director
Kathy Ryan, Special Projects Coordinator

4713 Free-Col Laboratories: A Division of Modern Industries
11618 Cotton Road
Meadville, PA 16335
814-724-6242
Fax: 814-333-1466
E-mail: johnp@modernind.com
http://www.modernind.com
Full service environmental laboratory - drinking water, waste water, solid waste, industrial hygiene testing; materials testing & engineering; non-destructive testing; mechanical testing; chemical analysis; failure analysis;consulting.
John Paraska, Director

4714 Froehling & Robertson
3015 Dumbarton Road
Richmond, VA 23228
804-264-2701
Fax: 804-264-0782
http://www.fandr.com
Environmental and construction materials testing lab.
Bob Hill, Branch Manager
Scott Sutton, Business Development

4715 FuelCell Energy
3 Great Pasture Road
Danbury, CT 06813
203-825-6000
E-mail: dferenz@fce.com
http://www.fce.com
Developer and manufacturer of clean and efficient electric power generators. Products are designed for distributed generation users including schools, data centers, hospitals, buildings, waste water treatment plants and othercommercial and industrial applications.
Chip Bottone, President/CEO
Michael Bishop, Sr. VP/CFO/Treasurer

4716 Fugro McClelland
6100 Hillcroft
Houston, TX 77081
713-369-5600
Fax: 512-444-3996
http://www.fugrogeoconsulting.com
Environmental, geotechnical, marine geoscience and environmental engineering firm.
Frank Marshall, President

4717 G&E Engineering
P.O. Box 3592
Olympic Valley, CA 96146-3592
405-840-0301
Fax: 405-840-4307
E-mail: eidinger@earthlink.net
http://www.geengineeringsystems.com

Environmental impact assessment firm.
Richard Adams, President
John Eidinger

4718 GE Osmonics: GE Water Technologies
4636 Somerton Road
Trevose, PA 19053
952-933-2277
866-439-2837
Fax: 952-933-0141
E-mail: anthony.kobilnyk@ge.com
http://www.gewater.com
Water and process technologies from GE Osmonics provide water, wastewater and process systems solutions.

Jeffrey R Immelt, Chairman/CEO
Heiner Markhoff, President/CEO

4719 GEO Plan Associates
30 Mann Street
Hingham, MA 02043-1316
781-740-1340
Fax: 781-740-1340
E-mail: geoplanassoc@gmail.com
Scientific and technical consulting, environmental planning and analysis firm. Experienced in coastal and shallow marine geology, land-use planning, and transportation.

Peter S Rosen PhD, Partner
Michu Tcheng, Partner

4720 GEO-CENTERS
4805 Westway Park Blvd.
Houston, TX 77041
281-443-8150
Fax: 281-443-8010
E-mail: mmohr@geocenter.com
http://www.geocenter.com

Provider of WMD homeland security preparedness services and products with major strengths in chemical and biological research.
Sukhie Hyare, President
John Asma, VP of Marketing

4721 GKY and Associates
4229 Lafayette Ctr Dr 703-870-7000
Suite 1850 Fax: 703-870-7039
Chantilly, VA 21051 E-mail: sstein@gky.com
http://www.gky.com
Civil and environmental systems engineering consulting organization. Research results published in project reports, government publications, and professional journals.
Stuart Stein, President
Brett Martin, VP

4722 GL Applied Research
142 Hawley Street 847-223-2220
PO Box 187 Fax: 847-223-2287
Grayslake, IL 60030 E-mail: glapplied@glappliedresearch.com
http://www.glappliedresearch.com
Analytical and process control instrumentation development and manufacture; photometric analyzers.
Edgar Watson Jr, President

4723 GSEE
599 Waldron Road 615-793-7547
La Vergne, TN 37086 Fax: 615-793-5070
E-mail: gsee@gseeinc.com
http://www.gseeinc.com
GSEE provides environmental engineering and technical services for municipal, industrial and governmental clientele as well as other engineering consultants and manufacturers throughout the United States and abroad. GSEE offersexisting plant evaluations, process engineering, detail engineering, and operations training.
Wendy Ingram, Lab Director

4724 GZA GeoEnvironmental
One Edgewater Drive 781-278-3700
Norwood, MA 02062 Fax: 781-278-5701
E-mail: info@gza.com
http://www.gza.com
Geotechnical and geohydrological testing and analysis firm.
William R Beloff, President/CEO
Joseph P Hehir, CFO

4725 Gabriel Laboratories
1421 North Elston 773-486-2123
Chicago, IL 60642 Fax: 773-486-0004
E-mail: gabriel@gabrielenvironmental.com
http://www.gabrielenvironmental.com
John Polich, President
Danuta Panek, VP

4726 Galson Laboratories
6601 Kirkville Road 315-432-5227
PO Box 369 888-432-5227
East Syracuse, NY 13057 Fax: 315-437-0509
E-mail: pweaver@galsonlabs.com
http://www.galsonlabs.com
Environmental industrial hygiene and biological testing service.
Philip Rooney, Chairman
Joe Unangst, President/CEO

4727 Gas Technology Institute
1700 S Mount Prospect Road 847-768-0500
Des Plaines, IL 60018 Fax: 847-768-0501
E-mail: info@gastechnology.org
http://www.gastechnology.org
Energy and environmental research.
David Carroll, President/CEO
Ronald Snedic, VP

4728 Gaynes Labs
9708 Industrial Drive 708-223-6655
Bridgeview, IL 60455 Fax: 708-233-6985
E-mail: Gayneslabs@aol.com
http://www.internetresults.com/gaynes/
Research laboratories. Research results published in confidential test summaries and project reports. Services include environmental testing, atmospheric simulations, frequency vibration testing, temperature and humidity simulationtesting.
Philip Ross, Material Testing Manager

4729 General Engineering Labs
2040 Savage Road 843-556-8171
PO Box 30712 Fax: 843-766-1178
Charleston, SC 29417 E-mail: grm@gel.com
http://www.gel.com
Environmental testing lab.
James M. Stelling, President/CEO
Douglas E. Earnest, CFO

4730 General Oil Company/GOC-Waste Compliance Services
35796 Veronica Street 734-266-6500
PO Box 1204 800-323-9905
Livonia, MI 48150 Fax: 734-266-6400
E-mail: twesterdale@generaloilco.com
http://www.generaloilco.com
Waste Compliance Services (WCS) is an analytical laboratory, serving the industrial community. WCS services a broad client base that includes manufacturing industries, environmental consultants, independent contractors, andindividuals. Services include effluent management programs (permit negotiation and management, sampling, self monitoring reports and waste treatment assistance) and analytical testing services.
Timothy A Westerdale, President/CEO
Adam Westerdale, VP/Chief Operating Officer

4731 General Sciences Corporation
205 Schoolhouse Rd. 215-723-8588
Souderton, PA 18964 Fax: 215-723-8875
http://www.general-sciences.com
Consulting and research firm specializing in environmental sciences.
Jeffrey Chen, President

4732 General Systems Division
1025 West Nursery Road 410-636-8700
Suite 120 Fax: 410-636-8708
Linthicum Heights, MD 21090 http://www.nct-active.com
Environmental studies.
Michael Parella, President

4733 Geo Environmental Technologies
103 E. Lemon Ave. 310-732-4825
Suite 212 Fax: 401-751-8613
Monrovia, CA 91016 http://www.geoenvironment-technologies.com
Environmental testing and consulting company.
Jeff Couture, Contact Person

4734 Geo-Con
400 Penn Center Boulevard 412-856-7700
Suite 503 Fax: 412-373-3357
Pittsburgh, PA 15235 E-mail: lmartin@geocon.net
http://www.geocon.net
Environmental services firm provides soil remediation by mixing soil with chemicals designed to eliminate the contaminants.
James Brannigan, VP of Opertaions
Loren Martin, Business Development Manager

4735 GeoPotential
22323 E Wild Fern Lane 503-622-0154
Brightwood, OR 97011 Fax: 503-492-4404
E-mail: geopotential@aol.com
http://www.members.aol.com/resiii/geomain.htm
GeoPotential provides subsurface mapping surveys to locate underground objects such as underground storage tanks, utilities,

geology, etc. They use geophysical methods consisting of ground penetrating radar, magnetics,electromagnetics and gravity.

Ralph Soule, President

4736 Geological Sciences & Laboratories
3133 N Main Street 606-439-3373
Hazard, KY 41701

4737 Geomatrix
210 East High Street 732-579-8283
Bound Brook, NJ 08805 Fax: 732-579-8305
E-mail: info@geosoftinc.com
http://www.geosoftinc.com
Environmental engineering and consulting firm.

4738 Geomet Technologies
20251 Century Boulevard 301-428-9898
Suite 300 800-296-9898
Germantown, MD 20874 Fax: 301-428-9482
E-mail: salesinfo@geomet.com
http://www.geomet.com

Robert L Durfee, President

4739 Geophex
605 Mercury Street 919-839-8515
Raleigh, NC 27603 Fax: 919-839-8528
E-mail: info@geophex.com
http://www.geophex.com
Environmental services firm.
IJ Won, President

4740 George Miksch Sutton Avian Research Center
PO Box 2007 918-336-7778
PO Box 2007 Fax: 918-336-7783
Bartlesville, OK 74005-2007 E-mail: gmsarc@aol.com
http://www.suttoncenter.org
Finding cooperative conservation solutions for birds and the natural world through science and education.

George Kamp, Chairman
Lee Holcombe, President

4741 Geotechnical and Materials Testing
693 Plymouth Ave NE 616-456-5469
Grand Rapids, MI 49505 800-968-8378
Fax: 616-456-5784
http://www.mtc-test.com
Environmental engineering and consulting firm.
Ahmed N Elrefai, President

4742 Gerhart Laboratories
Route 219 814-634-0820
Garrett, PA 15542
Environmental testing laboratory.
Michael Gerhart, President

4743 Giblin Associates
PO Box 6172 707-528-3078
Santa Rosa, CA 95406 Fax: 707-528-2837
Environmental and geotechnical engineering firm.
Jere A Giblin, President

4744 Global Geochemistry Corporation
Station A 902-453-0061
PO Box 9469 Fax: 902-453-0061
Halifax, NS B3K5S http://www.global-geoenergy.com
Consulting firm in the fields of geochemistry and environmental sciences. Research results published by the firm's scientists in journals.
Prasanta Mukhopadhyay, President

4745 Globetrotters Engineering Corporation
300 S Wacker Drive 312-922-6400
Suite 400 Fax: 312-922-2953
Chicago, IL 60606 E-mail: marketing@gec-group.com
http://www.gec-group.com

Niranjan S Shah, Chair
James Kotzamanis, Director of Human Resources

4746 GoodKind & O'Dea
31 Saint James Avenue 617-695-3400
Suite 1601 Fax: 617-695-3310
Boston, MA 02116
Architectural and engineering consulting firm.
David K Blake, Contact

4747 Gordon & Associates
1 Gateway Center 617-227-2707
Suite 312 Fax: 617-916-9218
Newton, MA 02458 E-mail: jsanders@gordonassociates.com
http://www.gordonassociates.com
Environmental consulting firm specializing in waste residuals.

Howard J. Gordon, President
Robert S. Kamanitz, Sr. VP

4748 Gordon Piatt Energy Group
7811 Baumgart Road 800-848-8197
Evansville, IN 47725 800-848-8197
Fax: 812-867-8197
E-mail: sales@ciciboilers.com
http://www.gordonpiattparts.com

Jim Salomon, President

4749 Grand Junction Laboratories
435 North Avenue 970-242-7618
Grand Junction, CO 81501 Fax: 970-243-7235

Brian Bauer, Director

4750 Greeley-Polhemus Group
1310 Birmingham Road 610-793-9440
West Chester, PA 19382
Environmental engineering and economic analysis firm.

4751 Ground Technology
14227 Fern Drive 281-597-8866
Houston, TX 77079 Fax: 281-597-8308
E-mail: ground@groundtechinc.com
http://www.groundtechinc.com

A multi-disciplinary engineering firm specializing in environmental services, geotechnical engineering, and construction materials and inspection services. GTI is a woman owned business enterprise as well as minority/disadvantagedenterprise certified by TxDOT, METRO, the State of Texas, and City of Houston, HISD, and the Houston Minority Business Council.

Ruma Acharya, President

4752 Groundwater Specialists
3806 Telluride Place 303-494-8122
Boulder, CO 80305 Fax: 303-494-5443
E-mail: gws@qwest.net
Groundwater exploration; dewatering; waterwell design; mitigation of high groundwater problems.

William H Bellis, Hydrologist

4753 Gruen, Gruen & Associates
595 Market Street 415-433-7598
Suite 1180 Fax: 415-989-4224
San Francisco, CA 94105 http://www.ggassoc.com
Nina J Gruen, Principle Sociologist
Claude Gruen, Principal Economist

4754 **Guanterra Environmental Services**
1721 S Grand Avenue 714-258-8610
Santa Ana, CA 92705 Fax: 714-258-0921
Chemical analysis technical and consulting research firm. Research results published in project reports and professional journals.

4755 **Guardian Systems**
1108 Ashville Road NE 205-699-6647
PO Box 190 866-729-7211
Leeds, AL 35094 Fax: 205-699-3882
E-mail: awilliams@gsilab.com
http://www.gsilab.com
Laboratory division provides a full range of analysis for inorganic, organicand physical testing of drinking water, wastewater, groundwater sediments, sludge, waste materials and soils. Industrial Hygiene division provides equipmentand analysis to meet OSHA requirements. Bio-Assay division can accommodate Aquatic Toxicity monitoring requirement.

Linda Miller, President
Gerald Miller, CEO

4756 **Gulf Coast Analytical Laboratories**
7979 GSRI Avenue 225-769-4900
Baton Rouge, LA 70820 Fax: 225-767-5717
E-mail: edg@gcal.com
http://www.gcal.com
Environmental and industrial testing laboratory

Ed Gallagher, Sales Director

4757 **Gutierrez, Smouse, Wilmut and Associates**
11117 Shady Trl 972-620-1255
Dallas, TX 75229 Fax: 972-620-8028
Environmental engineering consulting firm. Research results published in project reports and technical journals.
Charles G Wilmut, President

4758 **H John Heinz III Center for Science**
900 17th Street NW 202-737-6307
Suite 700 Fax: 202-737-6410
Washington, DC 20006 E-mail: info@heinzctr.org
http://www.heinzctr.org
The Center is a nonpartisan, nonprofit institute dedicated to improving the scientific and economic foundation for environmental policy through nmultisectoral collaboration. The Heinz Center fosters collaboration among industry,environmental organizations, academia, and all levels of government in each of its program areas.

John Peterson Myers, Chair/CEO
Teresa Heinz, Vice Chair

4759 **H2M Group: Holzmacherm McLendon & Murrell**
575 Broad Hollow Road 631-694-3040
Melville, NY 11747-5076 Fax: 631-694-4122
E-mail: labs@h2m.com
http://www.h2mlabs.com
Engineers, hydrogeologists, geologists and scientists strive to balance society's dynamic industrial and commercial growth with appropriate development and conservation of natural and man-made resources.

John J Molloy, President
Joann M. Slavin, Sr. VP

4760 **HC Nutting, A Terracon Company**
611 Lunken Park Drive 513-321-5816
Cincinnati, OH 45226 800-593-7777
Fax: 513-321-0294
E-mail: corporate@terracon.com
http://www.terracon.com
A materials testing company, geotechnical and environmental engineering firm.
Jack Scott, President
Jim Cahill, CEO

4761 **HTS**
416 Pickering Street 713-692-8373
Houston, TX 77091
Ron Langston, President

4762 **HWS Consulting Group**
PO Box 80358 402-479-2200
Lincoln, NE 68501 Fax: 402-479-2276
James Linderholm, President

4763 **Hach Company**
Box 389 970-669-3050
Loveland, CO 80539-389 800-227-4224
Fax: 970-669-2932
E-mail: techhelp@hach.com
http://www.hach.com

Bruce Hach, President

4764 **Haley & Aldrich**
465 Medford St. 617-886-7400
Suite 2200 Fax: 619-285-7169
Boston, MA 02129 E-mail: info@haleyaldrich.com
http://www.haleyaldrich.com
Haley & Aldrich provides leading edge underground engineering and environmental consulting services, nationally and internationally. The staff encompass a wide range of disciplines, offering their clients integrated solutions.Environmental services include corrective action; environmental management, health and safety consulting; and environmental site assessment/due diligence.

Lawrence Smith, President/CEO

4765 **Halliburton Company**
3000 N. Sam Houston Pkwy E. 281-871-4000
Houston, TX 77032 Fax: 214-978-2611
http://www.halliburton.com
One of the world's largest providers of products and services to the oil and gas industries.

Milton Carroll, Chairman
David J. Lesar, Chairman of the Board

4766 **Hamilton Research, Ltd.**
80 Grove Street 914-631-9194
Tarrytown, NY 10591 Fax: 914-631-6134
E-mail: rwh@rwhamilton.com
Hamilton Research is a consulting firm specializing in environmental physiology. Our focus is mainly on exposure of people to pressures less and greater than atmospheric, and involves dealing with different breathing gases, especiallyhigh and low levels of oxygen, and the consequences of changes in pressure, especially decompression. Another important area of interest is hyperbaric oxygen therapy.

R W Hamilton, President

4767 **Hampton Roads Testing Laboratories**
611 Howmet Drive 757-826-5310
Hampton, VA 23661
Independent third party testing laboratory. Performs sampling and analysis in accordance with the required ASTM or ISO Standards.

4768 **Handex Environmental Recovery**
500 Campus Drive 732-536-8500
PO Box 451 Fax: 732-536-7751
Morganville, NJ 07751
Environmental management and analysis firm.
CL Smith, CEO

4769 **Hart Crowser**
1700 Westlake Avenue North 206-328-5581
Suite 200 Fax: 206-324-9530
Seattle, WA 98109-6212 E-mail: rick.moore@hartcrowser.com
http://www.hartcrowser.com

Hart Crowser, Inc. provides a full range of services from initial site studies through regulatory permitting, design, and construction. They integrate thses services as required by each project. They know what kind of information isimportant, how to collect it and apply it to the selection of viable solutions, and how actions are perceived by regulatory agencies and the public. Consequently, they design an appraoch that is practical, cost-effective, and client-oriented.

Mike Bailey, CEO
William Abercrombie, Sr. Principal

4770 Hatch Mott MacDonald
PO Box 1008 973-379-3400
27 Bleeker Street 800-832-3272
Millburn, NJ 07041 Fax: 973-376-1072
E-mail: info@hatchmott.com
http://www.hatchmott.com

Hatch Mott MacDonald is a client-focused consulting firm providing planning, investigation, design and management capabilities in engineering disciplines and environmental sciences. Areas of expertise include industrial wastewater,site utilities engineering, hazardous and solid waste management and environmental site assessments.

Nicholas DeNichilo, President/CEO
Dennis Suler, Executive VP

4771 Hatcher-Sayre
905 Southlake Boulevard 804-794-0216
Richmond, VA 23236 Fax: 804-379-8934
Environmental consulting and engineering services firm.

4772 Havens & Emerson
700 Bond Court Building 216-621-2407
1300 E 9th Street Fax: 216-621-4972
Cleveland, OH 44114
Environmental engineering firm.
Gary Siegel, President/CEO

4773 Hayden Environmental Group
561 Congress Park Drive 937-438-3010
Dayton, OH 45459 Fax: 937-438-3020
E-mail: hayden@heg.com
http://www.heg.com

Testing, sampling, and analysis service.
Phillip L. Hayden, Principal
Michael G. Mariscalco, Principal

4774 Hayes, Seay, Mattern & Mattern
PO Box 13446 540-857-3100
Roanoke, VA 24034 Fax: 540-857-3296
Troy S Kincer, PE, Principal Associate
Guy E Slagle, PE, LS, Vice President

4775 HazMat Environmental Group
60 Commerce Drive 716-827-7200
Buffalo, NY 14218-1040 Fax: 716-827-7217
http://www.hazmatinc.com
Transportation services - specializing in hazardous materials and hazardous waste transportation.

Ricky F Wickham, General Manager of Operation

4776 Henry Souther Laboratories
24 Tobey Road 860-242-6291
Bloomfield, CT 06002 Fax: 860-286-0634

Richard J Lombardi, VP

4777 Heritage Laboratories
560 North Rogers Road 913-764-1045
Olathe, KS 66062 Fax: 913-764-3372
http://www.heritagelabs.net
Environmental testing laboratory.

4778 Heritage Remediation Engineering
4925 Heller Street 502-473-0638
Louisville, KY 40218 Fax: 502-459-4988
Environemtal management and remediation company.

4779 Hess Environmental Services
6057 Executive Centre Drive 901-377-9139
Suite 6 Fax: 901-377-9150
Memphis, TN 38134 E-mail: HES@hessenv.com
http://www.hessenv.com
Hess Environmental Services, Inc. (HES) is an environmental consulting/engineering firm. Their primary activities are: Indoor air quality (IAQ) (Mold and Bacterial) Investigations; Title V Air and Other Permit Applications; Phase I,II, III Property Assessments; Remedial Investigations, Audits, Enviromental Health and Safety, Storm Water, Wastewater, Air Monitoring, Asbestos Inspection and Sampling.

Connie Hess, President
Gary Siebenschuh, VP

4780 Hidell-Eyster Technical Services
PO Box 325 781-749-8040
Accord, MA 02018 Fax: 781-749-2304
E-mail: Info@hidelleyster.com
http://www.hidelleyster.com
Environmental and bottled water assessment and consulting company.
Henry R Hidell, Founder/Chairman
Carroll S. Keim, President/CEO

4781 Hillmann Environmental Company
1600 Route 22 East 908-688-7800
Suite 107 Fax: 908-686-2636
Union, NJ 07083 http://www.hillmannconsulting.com
Christopher Hillmann, Founder
Joseph Hillmann, Executive VP

4782 Honeywell Technology Center
3660 Technology Drive 480-353-3020
Minneapolis, MN 55418 877-841-2840
Fax: 612-951-7438
E-mail: info@htc.honeywell.com
http://www.honeywell.com
Parent holding company with numerous high-tech units involved in environmental, energy, computer hardware and industrial automation research and development.

4783 Hoosier Microbiological Laboratory
912 West McGalliard 765-288-1124
Muncie, IN 47303 Fax: 765-288-8378
Donald A Hendrickson, Owner

4784 Horner & Shifrin
5200 Oakland Avenue 314-531-4321
Saint Louis, MO 63110-1490 Fax: 314-531-6966
http://www.hornershifrin.com
Civil, structural, and environmental engineering firm.

Duane L. Siegfried, President
Gino E.B. Bernardez, VP

4785 Houston Advanced Research Center
4800 Research Forest Drive 281-367-1348
The Woodlands, TX 77381 Fax: 281-363-7914
E-mail: webmaster@harc.edu
http://www.harc.edu

Environmental studies

John R. Butler, Chairman
Elizabeth Lyons Ghrist, President

4786 **Humphrey Energy Enterprises**
One Beacon Street 617-720-5222
Suite 2320 Fax: 617-720-5507
Boston, MA 02108 E-mail: info@humphreyenterprises.com
http://www.humphreyenterprises.com

John W. Humphrey, Chairman/Principal
James Humphrey, CEO/Principal

4787 **Huntingdon Engineering & Environmental**
1940 Orange Tree Lane 909-793-2691
Redlands, CA 92374 Fax: 909-793-1704
http://www.dell.com/outlet

Offers the following service(s): Environmental remediation, engineering services, environmental consultant, environmental research, petroleum, mining, and chemical engineers and sanitary engineers.

4788 **Hydro Science Laboratories**
320 West Water Street 732-349-9692
P.O. Box 4978 800-624-3100
Toms River, NJ 08754 Fax: 732-349-9729
E-mail: info@HydroscienceInc.com
http://www.hydroscienceinc.com

Environmental testing and analysis laboratory.
Robert Salt, Director of Business Dvlpmt

4789 **Hydro-logic**
1927 North 1275 Road 785-550-6474
Eudora, KS 66025 Fax: 785-542-3971
E-mail: info@hydro-logic.com
http://www.hydro-logic.com

Offers professional environmental services, specializing in hydraulic soil and groundwater sampling. Maintains a multidisiplinary team of geologists, hydrologists, chemists, and regulatory compliance specialists.
Thomas Barr, President

4790 **Hydrocomp**
13 Jenkins Court 603-868-3344
Suite 200 Fax: 603-868-3366
Durham, NH 03824 E-mail: info@hydrocompinc.com
http://www.hydrocompinc.com

Jill Aaron, Owner
Donald MacPherson, Owner

4791 **Hydrologic**
370 Encinal Street 888-426-5644
Suite 150 888-426-5644
Santa Cruz, CA 95060 Fax: 831-336-9840
E-mail: andrea@hydrologicsystems.com
http://www.hydrologicsystems.com

Environmental laboratory services firm.
Richard Gellert, President
Rebekah Penrod, Accounting Manager

4792 **IAS Laboratories Inter Ag Services**
2515 E University Drive 602-273-7248
Phoenix, AZ 85034 Fax: 602-275-3836
E-mail: caw@iaslabs.com
http://www.iaslabs.com

IAS is an international agricultural laboratory and research facility serving that provides a variety of environmental services including: soil fertility and water suitability testing; ASTM, AASHTO, ADOT & CDOT testing; quality controltesting for the fertilizer industry; and plant tissue, petiole and soil analysis for agriculture and farmers.
Paul J Eberhardt PhD, President
Sheri K McLane, Laboratory Manager

4793 **IC Laboratories**
3253 Grapevine St. 951-681-4422
Mira Loma, CA 91752 Fax: 951-681-4404
E-mail: iclabs@iclabs.net
http://www.iclabs.net

Firm providing qualitative and quantitative materials analysis through X-ray diffraction. Studies focus on powders, metals, fibers, and clays, including analysis of crystallinity, thin films, environmental dusts, geological materials,and fabrics. Also provides limited research and development and consulting.

4794 **ICS Radiation Technologies**
8416 Florence Avenue 562-923-1837
Suite 207 Fax: 562-923-3609
Downey, CA 90240 E-mail: mike@icsrad.com
http://www.icsrad.com

Testing, engineering and consulting firm specializing in radiation effects in semiconductor devices.
Dr Michael K Gauthier, President

4795 **IHI Environmental**
4685 S. Ash Ave. 480-897-8200
Suite H-4 Fax: 480-897-1133
Temple, AZ 85282 E-mail: ihi@ihi-env.com
http://www.ihi-env.com/

William T. Hopkins, Chairman
Donald E. Marano, President

4796 **INFORM**
5 Hanover Street 212-361-2400
14th Floor Fax: 212-361-2412
New York, NY 10004 E-mail: inform@informinc.org
http://www.informinc.org

INFORM is an independent research organization that examines the effects of business practices on the environment and on human health. Our goal is to identify ways of doing business that ensure environmentally sustainable economicgrowth. Our reports are used by government, industry, and environmental leaders around the world.
Joanna Underwood, President

4797 **Ike Yen Associates**
867 Marymount Lane 714-621-2302
Claremont, CA 91711

4798 **Image**
4525 Kingston Street 303-371-3338
Denver, CO 80239 Fax: 303-371-3299

Biochemistry and environmental research firm. Research results published in professional journals.

4799 **ImmuCell Corporation**
56 Evergreen Drive 207-878-2770
Portland, ME 04103 Fax: 207-878-2117
E-mail: info@immucell.com
http://www.immucell.com

Biotechnology testing kits, animal health products and environment water testing.
Michael F Brigham, President

4800 **Industrial Laboratories**
4046 Youngfield Street 303-287-9691
Wheat Ridge, CO 80033 800-456-5288
Fax: 303-287-0964
E-mail: kinman@industriallabs.net
http://www.industriallabs.net

Provides quality laboratory analysis and consultation. ICP Mineral Analysis.

Petra Hartmann, President
Lisle Goeldner, Controller

4801 **Informatics Division of Bio-Rad**
Two Penn Center Plaza 267-322-6931
Suite 800 888-524-6723
Philadelphia, PA 19102-1737 Fax: 267-322-6932
E-mail: informatics.usa@bio-rad.com
http://www.bio-rad.com

Richard Shaps, Division Manager

4802 **Innovative Biotechnologies International**
335 Lang Boulevard 716-773-4232
Grand Island, NY 14702 Fax: 716-773-4257
E-mail: info@ibi.cc
http://www.ibi.cc

Manufacturing technology of biosensing technology.

4803 Inprimis
500 West Cypress Creek Road 954-556-4020
Suite 1 Fax: 954-556-4031
Fort Lauderdale, FL 33309 E-mail: info@ener1.com
http://www.inprimis.com/
Provides hardware and software technology, communications solutions that enbale data transmission, connectivity of devices, and access to applications and information via the Internet, personal computers, and/or server-basedenvironments. Also designs, manufactures, markets, and supports quality, innovative products that have a cost, performance, and time-to-market advantage.
Kevin P. Fitzgerald, Chairman/CEO
Ronald N. Stewart, Executive VP

4804 Institute for Alternative Agriculture
9200 Edmonston Road 301-441-8777
Suite 117 Fax: 301-220-0164
Greenbelt, MD 20770 E-mail: hawiaa@access.digex.net
The Wallace Institute advances this goal by providing the leadership, and policy research and analysis necessary to influence national agriculturalpolicy. It is a contributing member of a growing national alternaative agriculturenetwork, and works directly with government agencies, educational and research institutions, producer groups, farmers, scientists, advocates, and other organizations that provide agricultural research, education, and information services.
Dr. I Garth Youngberg, Executive Director

4805 Institute for Applied Research
103 W. Lockwood 314-968-9625
Suite 200 E-mail: contact@iarstl.org
St. Louis, MO 63119 http://www.iarstl.org

4806 Institute for Environmental Education
16 Upton Drive 978-658-5272
Wilmington, MA 01887 800-823-6239
Fax: 978-658-5435
E-mail: sales@ieetrains.com
http://www.ieetrains.com
IEE is New England's largest environmental training provider with over 57 classes in Asbestos, OSHA, Lead-paint and Environmental Health and Safety.
Martin Wood, President
Roy Teresky, VP Marketing

4807 Integral System
5200 Philadelphia Way 443-539-5330
Suite A Fax: 301-577-1982
Lanham, MD 20706 http://www.integ.com
Custom computer systems for satellite control; environmental monitoring.

4808 Inter-Mountain Laboratories
1673 Terra Avenue 307-672-8945
Sheridan, WY 82801 Fax: 307-672-6053
E-mail: ebrandjord@imlinc.com
http://www.intermountainlabs.com
Provides high-quality analytical, engineering and field services to industry and governmental agencies.
Duane Madsen, President
Eric Brandjord, Business Development

4809 International Asbestos Testing Laboratories
9000 Commerce Parkway 856-231-9449
Suite B 877-428-4285
Mount Laurel, NJ 08054 Fax: 856-231-9818
E-mail: info@iatl.com
http://www.iatl.com
An environmental laboratory specializing in asbestos, lead and mold analysis. Provides environmental laboratory services to environmental consultants, engineers, building owners and govt. agencies throughout the US, Canada and othercountries. Accredited by numerous agencies including the National Voluntary Laboratory Accreditation Program (NVLAP) and the American Industrial Hygiene Association (AIHA).
Eric M. Snyder, President
Shirley Clark, Business Development

4810 International Maritime, Inc
1250 24th Street N.W. 202-333-8501
Suite 350 Fax: 202-318-8114
Washington, DC 20037 E-mail: imaassoc@msn.com
http://www.imastudies.com
James R. McCaul, Founder

4811 International Science and Technology Institute
1820 North Fort Myer Drive 703-807-2080
Suite 600 Fax: 703-807-1126
Arlington, VA 22209 E-mail: isti@istiinc.com
http://www.istiinc.com
Provides technical assistance in project design, implementation, and evaluation; database development and maintenance; institutional and human resource development; policy and economic analysis, methodological research and analysis;strategic planning; and workshop and conference design and organization.
BK Wesley Copeland, Vice Chair

4812 International Society of Chemical Ecology
University of California
Department of Entomology 909-787-5821
Riverside, CA 92521 Fax: 909-787-3086
E-mail: jocelyn.millar@ucr.edu
http://www.isce.ucr.edu/Society/
ISCE is organized specifically to promote the understanding of interactions between organisms and their environment. Research areas include the chemistry, biochemistry and function of natural products, their importance at all levels ofecological organization, their evolutionary origin and their practical application.
John Hildebrand, President

4813 Interpoll Laboratories
4500 Ball Road NE 763-786-6020
Circle Pines, MN 55014 Fax: 763-786-7854
E-mail: interpoll@interpoll-labs.com
http://www.interpoll-labs.com
Interpoll is a full service environmental laboratory with a multidisciplinary staff. They provide their clients with responsive and accurate solutions to their environmental needs. Interpoll offers a full range of environmentaltesting services including stationary source testing, laboratory analysis, groundwater monitoring, ambient air monitoring and pharmaceutical analysis.
Dan Despen, President
Timothy MacDonald, Manager Field Services

4814 Invensys Climate Controls
191 East North Avneue 630-260-3400
Carol Stream, IL 60188 http://www.invensyscontrols.com
Formely the Robertshaw Controls Company. Founded after a successfully designing and manufacturing a line of top quality smoke alarms for the residential smoke alarm market.

4815 J Dallon and Associates
16 Fox Hollow Road 201-825-4574
Ramsey, NJ 07446
Research and consulting firm specializing in hortoculture.
Dr Joseph Dallon Jr, President

4816 J Phillip Keathley: Agricultural Services Division
25330 Ruess Avenue 209-599-2800
Ripon, CA 95366
Dr. J Phillip Keathley, President

4817 JABA
2766 North Country Club Road 520-327-7440
Tucson, AZ 85716 Fax: 520-327-7450
E-mail: info@jaba.com
http://www.jaba.com

Mining exploration and environmental analysis firm.
James A Briscoe, President

4818 JH Kleinfelder & Associates
4670 Willow Road
Suite 100
Pleasanton, CA 94588
925-484-1700
Fax: 925-484-5838
http://www.kleinfelder.com
Geotechnical and environmental Engineering firm.
William C. Siegel, President
Michael P. Kesler, COO

4819 JH Stuard Associates
22 Tanglewood Drive
Woodstock, VT 05091
802-878-5171
Environmental Consulting firm.
Joe Shockcor, President

4820 JK Research Associates
86 Gold Hill Road
Breckenridge, CO 80424
970-453-1760

4821 JL Rogers & Callcott Engineers
PO Box 5655
Greenville, SC 29606-5655
864-232-1556
Fax: 864-233-9058
E-mail: rogers.callcott@rogersandcallcott.com
http://www.rogersandcallcott.com
Environmental engineering research firm.

4822 JM Best
119 S College Street
Washington, PA 15301
724-222-2102
Performs geologic, economic and engineering evaluations for oil and gas well drilling. Also provides completion operations, environmental studies, map preparations and investigative studies.

4823 JR Henderson Labs
123 Seaman Avenue
Beachwood, NJ 08722
732-341-1211
Fax: 732-505-1658
http://www.jrhendersonlabs.com
Environmental laboratory.
Elmer Hemphill, President

4824 JWS Delavau Company
10101 Roosevelt Blvd
Philadelphia, PA 19154-2105
215-671-1400
Fax: 215-671-1401
http://www.delavau.com
International environmental and technical company.
David L Sokol, President

4825 James R Reed and Associates
770 Pilot House Drive
Newport News, VA 23606
757-873-4703
800-873-4703
Fax: 757-873-1498
E-mail: claiborne@jrreed.com
http://www.jrreed.com
Full service environmental testing facility offering quality analysis and reliable technical services to industry, local and federal government, engineers and private citizens. Areas of expertise include organic and inorganic chemicalanalyses, microbiological testing, and aquatic toxicity monitoring. Certificationto include NELAC Certification for the State of Virginia.
Han Ping Huang, President
Elaine Claiborne, Laboratory Director

4826 James W Bunger and Associates
PO Box 520037
Salt Lake City, UT 84152-37
801-975-1456
Fax: 801-975-1530
E-mail: about@jwba.com
http://www.jwba.com
Energy research and development firm specializing in environmental and oil remediation.
James W. Bunger, President/CEO
Donald E. Cogswell, Process Development

4827 Jane Goodall Institute for Wildlife Research, Education and Conservation
1595 Spring Hill Rd
Suite 550
Vienna, VA 22182
703-682-9220
800-99C-HIMP
Fax: 703-682-9312
http://www.janegoodall.org
A tax-exempt, nonprofit corporation, founded in 1977 focusing on Jane Goodall.
Jane Goodall, Founder
Donald Kendall, Co-Chair

4828 John D MacArthur Agro Ecology Research Center
300 Buck Island Ranch Road
Lake Placid, FL 33852
863-699-0242
Fax: 863-699-2217
E-mail: maerc@archbold-station.org
http://www.maerc.org
The MacArthur Agro Ecology Research Center at Buck Island Ranch is dedicated to a mission of long-term research, education and outreach related to the ecological and social value of subtropical grazing lands. The Center is at a 10,300acre cattle ranch on a long-term lease to Archbold Biological Station from the John D and Catherine T MacArthur Foundation. Provides researchers the opportunity to evaluate the relationship between economic and ecological factors and how these changeover time.
Betsey Boughton, Director
O'Gene L. Lollis, Ranch Manager

4829 Johnson Company
100 State Street
Suite 600
Montpelier, VT 05602
802-229-4600
Fax: 802-229-5876
E-mail: info@jcomail.com
http://www.johnsonco.com
Environmental science and engineering consulting
Chris M Crandell, President
Michael R Moore, VP

4830 Johnson Controls
5757 N Green Bay Avenue
Milwaukee, WI 53201
414-524-1200
Fax: 414-228-2446
http://www.johnsoncontrols.com
Research in environmental controls.
Dennis Archer, Chairman/CEO
Natalie A. Black, Sr. VP

4831 Johnson Research Center
University of Alabama at Huntsville
Huntsville, AL 35899
256-890-6343
Fax: 256-890-6848
Environmental research.
Dr. Michael Eley, CEO

4832 Jones & Henry Laboratories
2567 Tracy Road
Northwood, OH 43619
419-666-0411
Fax: 419-666-1657
E-mail: jhlabs@glasscity.net
http://www.jhlaboratories.com
Environmental sampling and testing laboratory.
Fred W Doering, President
David Collins, Marketing Manager

4833 Joyce Environmental Consultants
1604 Ownby Lane
Richmond, VA 23220
804-355-4520
Fax: 804-355-4282
E-mail: info@joyceengineering.com
http://www.joyceengineering.com
Connie Morrison, VP

4834 KAI Technologies
16 Marin Way
Stratham, NH 03885
603-778-1888
Fax: 603-778-0700
E-mail: info@kaitechnologies.com
http://www.kaitechnologies.com
Applied and product research in the environment.
Bruce L. Cliff, Director

4835 KCM
3475 East Foothill Boulevard 626-351-4664
Pasadena, CA 91107-6024 Fax: 626-351-5291
E-mail: info@tetratech.com
http://www.tetratech.com
Applied and product research in the environment.
Dan L. Batrack, Chairman/President/CEO
Steven M. Burdick, Executive VP

4836 KE Sorrells Research Associates
8100 National Drive 501-562-8139
Little Rock, AR 72209-4839 800-331-8139
Fax: 501-562-7025
E-mail: kesorrells@comcast.net
http://www.sorrellsresearch.com
Analytical chemistry and applied research company providing consulting services in water technology and stream ecology.
KE Sorrells, President
Cecil Sorrells, CEO

4837 KLM Engineering
3394 Lake Elmo Avenue N 651-773-5111
PO Box 897 888-959-5111
Lake Elmo, MN 55042 Fax: 651-773-5222
E-mail: jkollmer@klmengineering.com
http://www.klmengineering.com
Structural engineering and inspection firm specializing in the industry of steel and concrete plate structures.
Jack R Kollmer, President/Principal
Shawn A Mulhern, Vice President-Sales/Mktg.

4838 Kag Laboratories International
2323 Jackson Street 920-426-2222
Oshkosh, WI 54901 800-356-6045
Fax: 920-273-6128
E-mail: akkhwaja@aol.com
http://www.kaglab.com/
An independent agricultural testing and consulting laboratory. Professional scientific services for agriculture, soil, feed, plant, water and other fields. Total farm management services including high value crops such as cranberry,stevia, blueberry, ginseng, strawberry, herbs, etc. Consultation and recommendation to increase net yield. Available for contractual applied research for all agribusiness industries in Wisconsin, North America and world-wide.
Dr. Akhtar Khwaja, President
Ruma Roy, Vice President/Chemist

4839 Kansas City Testing Laboratory
1308 Adams Street 913-321-8100
Kansas City, KS 66103 Fax: 913-321-8181
http://www.kctesting.com
Consulting engineering firm employed in geotechnical, materials, and environmental engineering. Research results published in Project reports.
Elisabeth DeCoursey, President/Co-Owner
Scott Martens, VP/Co-Owner

4840 Kar Laboratories
4425 Manchester Road 269-381-9666
Kalamazoo, MI 49001 Fax: 269-381-9698
E-mail: info@karlabs.com
http://www.karlabs.com
Environmental testing laboratory, wastewater, drinking water, hay waste, soil and air.
William Rauch, President
Jayne Rauch, Marketing Manager

4841 Kemper Research Foundation
122 Main Street 513-249-2489
Milford, OH 45150
Richard Kemper, Director

4842 Kemron Environmental Services
2343-A State Route 821 740-373-4308
Marietta, OH 45750 Fax: 740-376-2536
E-mail: mzumbro@kemron.com
http://www.kemron.com
Environmental testing and analysis firm.
Juan J. Gutierrez, President/CEO
John Dwyer, Executive VP

4843 Kennedy-Jenks Consultants
303 Second Street 415-243-2150
Suite 300 Fax: 415-896-0999
San Francisco, CA 94107 E-mail: info@kennedyjenks.com
http://www.kennedyjenks.com
Environmental engineering consulting company.
Lynn Takaichi, Chair
Keith London, President/CEO

4844 Kentucky Resource Laboratory
Highway 421 606-598-2605
Manchester, KY 40962 Fax: 606-598-1544
Environmental testing firm.
Roy Rice, President

4845 Kenvirons
452 Versailles Road 502-695-4357
Frankfort, KY 40601 Fax: 502-695-4363
E-mail: rrussell@kenvirons.com
http://kenvirons.com
A multi-disciplined environmental and civil engineering firm. Offers engineering services in a range of areas to include water and wastewater related studies and system design, dam design, hydrological studies, environmentalassessments, air and water quality studies, urban and industrial planning, solid waste management, energy-environment interface, computer technology and laboratory services.
Randall Russell, President
Douglas Griffin, Chair

4846 Keystone Labs
600 East 17th Street South 800-858-5227
Suite B 800-858-5227
Newton, IA 50208 Fax: 641-792-7989
http://www.keystonelabs.com
Keystone Laboroatories, Inc. is a full service environmental laboratory committeed to providing the highest quality services at competitive prives.
Jodi King, President
Jerry Dawson, Manager

4847 Kinnetic Laboratories
307 Washington Street 831-457-3950
Santa Cruz, CA 95060 Fax: 831-426-0405
E-mail: kkronsch@kinneticlabs.com
http://www.kineticlabs.com
Environmental marine, physical, toxicological, water quality, biological research and scientific consulting and services.
Mary Lee Kinney, President
Mark Savoie, VP

4848 Kleinfelder
981 Garcia Avenue 925-427-6477
Suite A Fax: 925-427-6478
Pittsburg, CA 94565 http://www.kleinfelder.com
Laboratories testing.
William C. Siegel, President
Michael P. Kesler, COO

4849 Konheim & Ketcham
175 Pacific Street 718-330-0550
Brooklyn, NY 11201 Fax: 718-330-0582
E-mail: csk@konheimketcham.com
http://www.konheimketcham.com
Environmental and transportation planning.
Carolyn S Konheim, President
Brian T. Ketcham, Executive VP

4850 Kraim Environmental Engineering Services
11437 Etiwanda Avenue 818-363-0952
Northridge, CA 91326 Fax: 818-363-0492
E-mail: luftmench@msn.com

Environmental engineering firm.

Jerry Kraim, President

4851 Kramer & Associates
4501 Bogan Avenue NE 505-881-0243
Suite A1 800-281-1400
Albuquerque, NM 87109 Fax: 505-881-7738
E-mail: eservice@kramerandassociates.com
http://www.kramerandassociates.com

Environmental monitoring firm. Research results published in conference proceedings.

Lyn Kramer, MD/Partner
Gary Kramer, Contact

4852 Ktech Corporation
10800 Gibson S E 505-998-5830
Albuquerque, NM 87123 Fax: 505-998-5848
E-mail: rswanson@ktech.com
http://www.ktech.com/corporate/history.cfm

Ktech Corporation, an employee-owned company based in Albuquerque, New Mexico, is dedicated to providing outstanding technical support services, sound scientific and engineering work, and proven management expertise to a wide varietyof government and industry clients.

Steven E Downie, President
Robert E Swanson, VP/Chief Operations Officer

4853 LaBella Associates P.C.
300 State Street 585-454-6110
Suite 201 Fax: 585-454-3066
Rochester, NY 14614 E-mail: labweb@labellapc.com
http://www.labellapc.com

Civil and environmental engineering firm.

Salvatore A. LaBella, Founder
Robert Healy, President

4854 LaQue Center for Corrosion Technology
521 Fort Fisher Blvd, North 910-256-2271
Kure Beach, NC 28449 Fax: 910-256-9816
E-mail: info@laque.com
http://www.laque.com

Corrosion technology firm. Research results published in trade journals and presented at technical association meetings.

W T Raines, President
D G Melton, VP

4855 Laboratory Corporation of America Holdings
1904 Alexander Drive 919-572-6900
Research Triangle Park, NC 27709 800-533-0567
http://www.labcorp.com

4856 Laboratory Services Division of Consumers Energy
135 W Trail Street 517-788-2238
Jackson, MI 49201 Fax: 517-788-1104
E-mail: naserafin@cmsenergy.com
http://www.laboratoryservices.com

Laboratory Services is a full-service testing laboratory. Services include: calibration, nondestructive testing, metallurgy, materials testing and chemistry. They are A2LA accredited (ISO/IEC 17025)-request scope-and 10CFR50 AppendixB authorized.

Nick Serafin, Marketing Manager

4857 Lancaster Laboratories
2425 New Holland Pike 717-656-2300
Lancaster, PA 17601 Fax: 717-656-2681
E-mail: pha@lancasterlabs.com
http://www.lancasterlabs.com

Premier contract testing laboratory serving environmental, pharmaceutical and biophamaceutical clients worldwide. Offers a broad range of high quality analytical services in full compliance with EPA and FDA regulations and clientrequirements.

Gilles Martin, Chairman
Valerie Hanote, Board Member

4858 Lancy Environmental
181 Thorn Hill Road 724-772-0044
Warrendale, PA 15086 Fax: 724-772-1360
Gerald Rogers, President

4859 Land Management Decisions
3048 Research Drive 814-231-1248
State College, PA 16801 Fax: 814-231-1253
Dr. Dale E Baker, President

4860 Land Management Group Inc
3805 Wrightsville Avenue 910-452-0001
Suite 15 Fax: 910-452-0060
Wilmington, NC 28403 E-mail: rbrant@LMGroup.net
http://www.lmgroup.net

LMG provides environmental servicesin the following discplines: wetland delineations and permitting; soil mapping and waste water suitability studies; phase I & II environmental site assiessments; EA and EIS land use and ecologicalstudies; wetland mitigations; and coastal management (CAMA) permitting assistance.

Robert I. Moul, Founder/President
Craig Turner, VP

4861 Land Research Management
1300 N Congress Avenue 561-686-2481
Suite C Fax: 561-684-8709
West Palm Beach, FL 33409 E-mail: lrmi@bellsouth.net

Land planning and zoning. environmental assessments and market analysis firm. Research results published in reports.

Kevin McGinley, President

4862 Lark Enterprises
2665 Ellwood Road 724-658-5676
New Castle, PA 16101 Fax: 508-943-8833
E-mail: rjlark@aol.com
http://www.larkenterprises.org

Environmental research.
Justin Bruce, President
Roger Zallon, VP

4863 Laticrete International
1 Laticrete Park N 203-393-0010
91 Amity Road Fax: 203-393-1684
Bethany, CT 06524-3423 http://www.laticrete.com

Firm providing chemical, mechanical, and environmental simulation testing of concrete and aggregrate building materials.
Henry M. Rothberg, Chairman/Founder
David A. Rothberg, Chairman/CEO

4864 Law & Company of Wilmington
1711 Castle Street 910-762-7082
Wilmington, NC 28403 Fax: 910-762-8785

Richard W Spivey, President

4865 Lawler, Matusky and Skelly Engineers
1 Blue Hill Plaza 845-735-8300
Pearl River, NY 10965 Fax: 845-735-7466
E-mail: cnevel@lmseng.com
http://www.lmseng.com

We anticipate the environmental and engineering needs of our clients and contribute to their success by providing creative solutions.
Christy Nevel, Director Marketing

4866 Lawrence Berkeley Laboratory: Structural Biology Division
1 Cyclotron Road 510-486-4311
Mail Stop 3-0226 Fax: 510-486-6059
Berkeley, CA 94720 http://www.lbl.gov/sbdiv/

4867 Lawrence G Spielvogel
21506 Valley Forge Circle 610-783-6350
King of Prussia, PA 19406 Fax: 610-783-6349
A consulting engineer who specializes in energy management and procurement and problem solving in buildings.
Lawrence G Spielvogel, President

4868 Ledoux and Company
359 Alfred Avenue 201-837-7160
Teaneck, NJ 07666-5755 Fax: 201-837-1235
E-mail: Bruce@ledoux.com
http://www.ledoux.com

A.R. Ledoux, Founder
LA Ledoux, President

4869 Lee Wilson and Associates
105 Cienega Street 505-988-9811
Santa Fe, NM 87501 Fax: 505-986-0092
Environmental consulting firm. Research results published in project reports.
Lee Wilson, President

4870 Leighton & Associates
17781 Cowan Street 949-250-1421
Irvine, CA 92614 Fax: 949-250-1114
http://www.leightongeo.com
Geotechnical and environmental engineering firm.
F. Beach Leighton, Founder
Bruce Clark, Contact

4871 Life Science Resources
Post Office Box 379 808-553-3211
Hoolehua, HI 96729 800-543-3211
Fax: 808-553-5033
E-mail: Support@LifescienceResources.com
http://www.lifescienceresources.com
Biomedical and environmental sciences research firm.

4872 Life Systems
916-C Old Liverpool Road 315-378-4338
Liverpool, NY 13088 Fax: 315-299-5090
E-mail: info@lifesysteminternational.com
http://www.lifesysteminternational.com
Environmental engineering research and consulting organization. Research results published In project reports and in technical journals.
R Wynveen, President

4873 Los Alamos Technical Associates
6501 Americas Parkway NE 505-884-3800
Suite 200 800-952-5282
Albuquerque, NM 87110 Fax: 505-880-3560
E-mail: info@lata.com
http://www.lata.com

Environmental studies.
Phil Reinig, Chairman/CEO
Bob Kingsbury, President/COO

4874 Louisville Testing Laboratory
1401 West Chestnut Street 502-584-5914
Louisville, KY 40203 Fax: 502-584-5914
Kenneth Smith Jr, President

4875 Lowry Systems
146 South Street 800-434-9080
Blue Hill, ME 04614 Fax: 207-374-3503
E-mail: info@lowryh2o.com
http://www.lowryh2o.com

Environmental research.
Sylvia Lowry, President

4876 Lycott Environmental Inc
600 Charlton Street 508-765-0101
Southbridge, MA 01550 800-462-8211
Fax: 508-765-1352
E-mail: lycottine@aol.com
http://www.lycott.com
Environmental science and ecological planning consultant and research firm. Research results published in project reports.
Lee D Lyman, President

4877 Lyle Environmental Management
1507 Chambers Road 614-488-1022
Columbus, OH 43212 Fax: 614-488-1198
Chemical research and consulting service.

4878 Lyle Laboratories
1507 Chambers Road 614-488-1022
Columbus, OH 43212 Fax: 614-488-1198
E-mail: manager@lylelabs.com
http://www.lylelabs.com

Dr. Thomas Eggers, Director

4879 Lynntech
2501 Earl Rudder Freeway South 979-764-2200
Suite 100 Fax: 979-764-2343
College Station, TX 77845 E-mail: requests@lynntech.com
http://www.lynntech.com
Oliver J Murphy, President

4880 MBA Labs
340 South 66th Street 713-928-2701
Houston, TX 77261 800-472-1485
Fax: 281-292-7492
E-mail: mbalabs@mbalabs.com
http://www.mbalabs.com
Independently owned and operated since 1968, mba Labs serves industry, government agencies and private citizens in Houston, the continental US and even across the globe. Conform to standards established by the EPA, the TNRCC and meetthe equivalent of ISO 9000 requirements for laboratories through their accreditation by NELAC.

Herman J Kresse

4881 MBA Polymers
500 West Ohio Avenue 510-231-9031
Richmond, CA 94804 Fax: 510-231-0302
E-mail: info@mbapolymers.com
http://www.mbapolymers.com/
Environmental research.
Mike Biddle, Founder/President
Nigel Hunton, CEO

4882 MBC Applied Environmental Sciences
3000 Redhill Avenue 714-850-4830
Costa Mesa, CA 92626 Fax: 714-850-4840
E-mail: info@mbcnet.net
http://www.mbcnet.net
Environmenatl consultants since 1969. Specializing in marine biology and ecology, oceanography, EIR, EIS, EA, toxicity testing, technical meetings, expert witnesses. MBE/DBE certified.
Shane Beck, President
Charles T. Mitchell, VP

4883 MWH Global
380 Interlocken Crescent 303-533-1900
Suite 200 Fax: 303-533-1901
Broomfield, CO 80021 E-mail: webinfo@mwhglobal.com
http://www.mwhglobal.com
MWH, globally driving the wet infrastructure sector, is leading the world in results-oriented management services, technical engineering, construction services and solutions to create a better world. The wet infrastructure sectorencompasses a full range of water related projects and programs from water supply, treatment and storage, dams, water management for the natural resources

industry and coastal restoration to renewable power and environmental services.

Joseph D. Adams, President
Paul F. Boulos, President

4884 **MWH Laboratories**
750 Royal Oaks Drive 626-386-1100
Suite 100 800-566-5227
Monrovia, CA 91016 Fax: 626-386-1101
E-mail: mwhlabs@mwhglobal.com
http://www.mwhlabs.com
Environmental testing laboratory that provides water and wastewater analyses including: drinking water synthetic organic and volatile organic tests; recycled water tests; organic disinfection byproduct and precursor analyses; inorganicdisinfection byproducts and precursors; inorganic tests including a complete suite of metals to low-reporting levels; microbiological analyses ; and radiochemical analyses.

Andrew Eaton Ph.D, Technical Director
Ed Wilson, Laboratory Director

4885 **Mabbett & Associates: Environmental Consultants and Engineers**
5 Alfred Circle 781-275-6050
Bedford, MA 01730 800-877-6050
Fax: 781-275-5651
E-mail: info@mabbett.com
http://www.mabbett.com
Mabbett & Associates (M&A) provides multi-disciplinary environmental, health and safety services to manufacturing and commercial industry, institutions and public agencies. M&A's services include pollution prevention and wasteminimization, site assessment and remediation, environmental pollution control, environmental management systems and auditing, training and occupational safety and health.

Arthur N Mabbett, President
Paul D. Stelnberg, Sr. VP

4886 **Mack Laboratories**
1163 Nicole Court 909-394-9007
Glendora, CA 91740 Fax: 909-394-9411
E-mail: info@macklabs.com
http://www.macklabs.com

4887 **Magma-Seal**
10116 Aspen Street 512-836-4936
Austin, TX 78758 Fax: 512-836-4936
E-mail: tkdw39a@prodigy.com
Develops materials (plastic and rubber) to withstand severe environmental conditions.
Earl Dumitro, President

4888 **Malcolm Pirnie**
630 Plaza Drive 720-344-3500
Suite 200 800-478-6870
Highlands Ranch, CO 80129 Fax: 720-344-3535
E-mail: AUSInternet@arcadis-us.com
http://www.pirnie.com
Provides environmental engineering, science and consulting services to over 3,000 public and private clients.
Paul L Busch, PhD, President
Gary Coates, CEO

4889 **Maryland Spectral Services**
1500 Caton Center Drive 410-247-7600
Suite G Fax: 410-247-7602
Baltimore, MD 21227 E-mail: labman@mdspectral.com
http://www.mdspectral.com
Samuel Hamner, VP

4890 **Massachusetts Technological Lab**
330 Pleasant Street 617-484-7314
Belmont, MA 02178 E-mail: masstechlab@juno.com
Applies research in the following areas: telecommunications and Internet.
Dr Ta-Ming Fang, President

4891 **Mateson Chemical Corporation**
1025 E Montgomery Avenue 215-423-3200
Philadelphia, PA 19125 Fax: 215-423-1164
http://www.matesonchemical.com
Environmental, toxic, materials, hazerdous waste research.

4892 **Mayhew Environmental Training Associates (META)**
PO Box 786 785-842-6382
Lawrence, KS 66044 800-444-6382
Fax: 785-842-6993
E-mail: salesmeta@cs.com
http://www.metaworld.org
Environmental testing lab offering site assessments.
Thomas Bradford Mayhew, President

4893 **McCoy & McCoy Laboratories**
825 Industrial Road 270-821-7375
Madisonville, KY 42431 Fax: 270-444-6572
http://www.mccoylabs.com
Environmental assessment laboratory.
Mercia Cocke, Account Collections
Mike Baumgardner, Laboratory Operations

4894 **McIlvaine Company**
191 Waukegan Road 847-784-0012
Suite 208 Fax: 847-784-0061
Northfield, IL 60093 E-mail: editor@mcilvainecompany.com
http://www.mcilvainecompany.com
Environmental research and consulting firm. Research results published in manuals updated by newsletters and abstracts.
Robert W McIlvaine, President
Marilyn McIlvaine, Marketing Manager

4895 **McLaren-Hart**
3039 Kilgore Road 916-638-3696
Rancho Cordova, CA 95670 Fax: 916-638-6840
http://www.mclaren-hart.com
Environmental research.

4896 **McNamee Advanced Technology**
3135 S State Street 734-665-5553
Suite 301 Fax: 734-665-2570
Ann Arbor, MI 48108
Environmental engineering firm, offering environmental consulting and environmental testing services.

4897 **McVehil-Monnett Associates**
44 Inverness Drive E 303-790-1332
Suite C Fax: 303-790-7820
Englewood, CO 80112 http://www.mcvehil-monnett.com
Experienced consulting firm of atmospheric scientsits, engineers and environmental specialists providing air quality and environmental management system (EMS) services worldwide. Serves the mining, oil and gas, electric power andmanufacturing industries as well as government agencies and engineering and law firms.

William R Monnett, President/CEO
George McVehil, Principal

4898 **McWhorter and Associates**
33 Bull Street 912-234-8891
Suite 500 Fax: 912-234-8892
Savannah, GA 31401-9419 E-mail: info@tankcarrobot.com
http://www.mcwhorterassoc.com

Thomas McWhorter, President

4899 **Mega Engineering**
10800 Lockwood Drive 301-681-4778
Silver Spring, MD 20901 Fax: 301-681-5683

Richard E Dame, PE

4900 **Membrane Technology & Research Corporate Headquarters**
39630 Eureka Drive
Newark, CA 94560
650-328-2228
Fax: 650-328-6580
E-mail: sales@mtrinc.com
http://www.mtrinc.com

Supplier of membrane-based hydrocarbon recovery systems natural gas treatment systems and hydrogen recovery systems. Company capabilities include membrane and module manufacturing, process and system design, project engineering andcommissioning services.

Dr. Hans Wijmans, President
Nick Wynn, Commercial Operations

4901 **Merck & Company**
One Merck Drive
PO Box 100
Whitehouse Station, NJ 08889-100
908-423-1000
Fax: 732-594-3810
http://www.merck.com

Kenneth C. Frazier, Chairman/President/CEO
Leslie A. Brun, Chairman/CEO

4902 **Merrimack Engineering Services**
66 Park Street
Andover, MA 01810
978-475-3555
Fax: 978-475-1448
E-mail: merreng@aol.com
http://www.merrimackengineering.com

Research of all forms of environmental studies.
Stephen Stapinski, President

4903 **Metro Services Laboratories**
6309 Fern Valley Pass
Louisville, KY 40228
502-964-0865
Fax: 502-241-4347

Environmental testing laboratory offering air, water and soil testing services.

4904 **Michael Baker Jr: Civil and Water Division**
100 Airside Drive
Moon Township, PA 15108
412-269-6300
800-553-1153
Fax: 724-495-4017
E-mail: hchakrav@mbakercorp.com
http://www.mbakercorp.com

4905 **Michael Baker Jr: Environmental Division**
165 South Union Boulevard
Suite 200
Lakewood, CO 80228
720-514-1100
Fax: 720-514-1120
http://www.mbakercorp.com
Andrew P Pajak, President

4906 **Mickle, Wagner & Coleman**
3434 Country Club Avenue
PO Box 1507
Fort Smith, AR 72903
479-649-8484
Fax: 479-649-8486
E-mail: info@mwc-engr.com
http://www.mwc-engr.com/

Provides civil and environmental engineering services, offering clients a broad range of plan designs and development capabilities from water, sewer, and drainage to streets, bridges, and dams, airports, recreational facilities, andresidential subdivisions.
Patrick J Mickle, PE, Chief Engineer

4907 **Microseeps, Inc**
220 William Pitt Way
Pittsburgh, PA 15238
412-826-5245
800-659-2887
Fax: 412-826-3433
E-mail: info@microseeps.com
http://www.microseeps.com

A full service, NELAP certified environmental laboratory which specializes in the evaluation of groundwater geochemistry for use in in-situ remediation processes.

Robert J Pirkle, President
Thomas W Hill, Sr. VP

4908 **Microspec Analytical**
3352 128th Avenue
Holland, MI 49424
616-399-6070
Fax: 616-399-6185
E-mail: info@mspec.com
http://www.mspec.com

Environmental research and resting firm. Research results published in journals and client reports.
Tom Beamish, President

4909 **Midwest Environmental Assistance Center**
6561 N Seeley Avenue
Chicago, IL 60645
773-973-4850
Fax: 773-973-4851
E-mail: meac2@aol.com

Noise pollution research firm.
Howard R Schechter, President

4910 **Midwest Laboratories, Inc.**
13611 B Street
Omaha, NE 68144
402-334-7770
Fax: 402-334-9121
E-mail: pohlman@midwestlabs.com
http://www.midwestlabs.com

Midwest Laboratories, Inc. offers analytical services to agriculture, industry and municipal entities throughout the US and Canada. Using wet chemistry methods, they have the capability of testing soil, water, feed, food, plants,fertilizers and residues. Their quality assurance program (QA/QC) provides consistent production of reliable data with high accuracy and precision.

Ken Pohlman, President
John DeBoer, VP

4911 **Midwest Research Institute**
425 Volker Boulevard
Kansas City, MO 64110-2241
816-753-7600
Fax: 816-753-8420
E-mail: bduncan@mriresearch.org
http://www.mriresearch.org

Midwest Research Institute is an independent, not-for-profit organization that performs contract research for clients in business, industry and government. MRI conducts programs in the areas of environment, health, engineering,technology development and energy research.
Thomas M. Sack, President/CEO
Dan E. Arvizu, Executive VP

4912 **MikroPul Environmental Systems Division of Beacon Industrial Group**
17 Wachung Avenue
Chatham, NJ 07928
973-635-1115
800-892-7278
Fax: 973-635-0678
E-mail: info@mikropul.com
http://www.mikropul.com

Established in 1929, MikroPul is a manufacturer of dust control and product recovery products, from small unit collectors to complete engineered systems, for industrial applications worldwide.
Lacy Hayes, President/Beacon Ind Group
Richard Bearse, Chairman/Beacon Ind Group

4913 **Miller Engineers**
PO Box 422
Manlius, NY 13104
315-682-0028
Fax: 920-458-0369
E-mail: DougMiller@MillerEngineers.com
http://www.millerengineers.com

Civil and environmental engineering firm.
Roger G Miller, President

4914 **Minnesota Valley Testing Laboratories**
1126 N Front Street
New Ulm, MN 56073
507-354-8517
800-782-3557
Fax: 507-359-1231
E-mail: crc@mvtl.com
http://www.mvtl.com

Independent bacteriological and chemical analysis firm, with services in environmental, agricultural, and energy fields. Research results published in project reports.
Jerry Balbach, President
Thomas R. Berg, CEO

4915 Mirage Systems
PO Box 820
DeLand, FL 32721
386-740-9222
Fax: 386-740-9444
E-mail: info@miragesys.com
http://www.miragesys.com
Environmental research.
Robert S Ziernicki, President

4916 Montgomery Watson Mining Group
380 Interlocken Crescent
Suite 200
Broomfield, CO 80021
303-533-1900
Fax: 303-533-1901
http://www.mwhglobal.com
Mine engineering and environmental services firm.
Joseph D. Adams, President
David G. Barnes, CFO

4917 Mycotech
100 Commons Road
Ste 7354
Dripping Springs, TX 78620
406-782-2386
800-272-3716
Fax: 406-782-9912
E-mail: mbi@mycotechbiological.com
http://www.mycotechbiological.com
Clifford Bradley, Director R&D

4918 Myra L Frank & Associates
811 W 7th Street
Suite 800
Los Angeles, CA 90017
213-627-5376
Fax: 213-627-6853
E-mail: fwilliams@myrafrank.com
http://www.myrafrank.com
Environmental impact analysis firm. Architectural historic surveys.
Florence Williams

4919 Mystic Air Quality Consultants
1204 North Road
Route 117
Groton, CT 06340
860-449-8903
800-247-7746
Fax: 860-449-8860
E-mail: maqc2@aol.com
http://www.mysticair.com
Indoor air quality and industrial hygiene services.
Chris Eident, CEO

4920 NET Pacific
3qb ODC International Plaza
Bldg 219 salcedo St. Legaspi Village
Makati City, PH 01229
632-893-9306
Fax: 632-812-4852
http://www.netpacific.net

4921 National Institute for Urban Wildlife
10921 Trotting Ridge Way
Columbia, MD 21044
301-596-3311
Promotes the preservation of wildlife in urban settings, providing support to individuals and organizations invloved in maintaining a place for wildlife in expanding American cities and suburbs. The Institute conducts researchexploring the relationship between humans and wildlife in these habitats, publicizes urban wildlife management methods, and raises public awareness of the value of wildlife in city settings. The Institute also provides consulting services.

4922 National Loss Control Service Corporation
1 Kemper Drive
Long Grove, IL 60049
847-320-2488
Fax: 847-320-4331
Environmental science laboratory.
Joan Wronski, Laboratory Manager

4923 National Oceanic & Atmospheric Administration
1401 Constitution Avenue, NW
Room 5128
Washington, DC 20230
301-713-0836
http://www.noaa.gov
Earth system research including climate, weather, and atmospheric chemistry, space weather research and forecasts.
Edward Horton, CAO
Andrea Pawley, Chief of Staff

4924 National Renewable Energy Laboratory/NREL
15013 Denver West Parkway
Golden, CO 80401
303-275-3000
Fax: 303-275-4053
E-mail: public_affairs@nrel.gov
http://www.nrel.gov
The National Renewable Energy Laboratory/NREL began operating in 1977 as the Solar Energy Research Institute. It was designated a national laboratory of the U.S. Department of Energy (DOE) in September 1991 and its name changed toNREL. NREL develops renewable energy and energy efficiency technologies and practices, advances related science and engineering, and transfers knowledge and innovations to address the nation's energy and environmental goals.
Dan Arvizu, Director
William Glover, Deputy Lab Director

4925 Neilson Research Corporation
245 South Grape Street
Medford, OR 97501
541-770-5678
800-600-5227
Fax: 541-770-2901
E-mail: clientservices@nrclabs.com
http://www.nrclabs.com
Provides analytical services to support environmental projects including testing of drinking water, wastewater, ground and surface water, foods soils, sediments, sludges, filters, air, and hazardous waste samples.
John WT Neils, CEO

4926 Neponset Valley Engineering Company
378 Page Street
Suite 10
Stoughton, MA 02072
781-297-7040
Fax: 781-297-7050
Environmental engineering analysis and consulting firm.

4927 New England Testing Laboratory
1254 Douglas Avenue
North Providence, RI 02904
888-863-8522
888-863-8522
Fax: 401-354-8951
E-mail: rich.warila@newenglandtesting.com
http://www.newenglandtesting.com
Richard Warila, VP
Mark Bishop, VP Operations

4928 New York Testing Laboratories
375 Rabro Drive
Hauppage, NY 11788
631-761-5555
800-281-3329
Fax: 718-657-3902
E-mail: jhicks@mtllab.com
http://www.mtllab.net
Consulting on a range of disciplines including environmental.
Charles Realmuto, Director Marketing

4929 Newport Electronics
2229 South Yale Street
Santa Ana, CA 92704-4401
714-540-4914
800-639-7678
Fax: 203-968-7311
E-mail: info@newportus.com
http://www.newportus.com
Manufacturer of industrial and environmental instrumentation including signal conditioners, digital panel meters, PID controllers and temperature sensors.
Milton Hollander, President

4930 Nobis Engineering
18 Chenell Drive
Concord, NH 03301
603-224-4182
Fax: 603-224-2507
http://www.nobisengineering.com
Environmental engineering consulting firm.

4931 Normandeau Associates
1019B Cherokee Avenue, Northwest
Aiken, SC 29801
803-644-6262
Fax: 803-644-6965
E-mail: marketing@normandeau.com
http://www.normandeau.com
Jean Eidson
Rick Simmons

4932 North American Environmental Services
2848 Banwick Road 614-487-1109
Columbus, OH 43232 Fax: 614-291-8682
http://www.northamericanenviro.com
Environmental science research firm.
D Craig Kissock, President

4933 Northeast Test Consultants
587 Spring Street 207-854-3939
Westbrook, ME 04092-3918 Fax: 207-854-3658
E-mail: info@netest.com
http://www.netest.com
Asbestos and lead testing/industrial hygiene.

Stephen Broadhead, Laboratory Manager

4934 Northern Lights Institute
210 N Higgins #326 406-721-7415
PO Box 8084 Fax: 406-721-7415
Missoula, MT 59807
Donald Snow, Program Director

4935 Nuclear Consulting Services
7000 Huntley Road 614-846-5710
Columbus, OH 43229 Fax: 614-431-0858
Joseph C Enneking, VP

4936 O'Brien & Gere Engineers
Box 4873 315-956-6100
Syracuse, NY 13221-4873 Fax: 315-463-7554
http://www.obg.com

R. Leland Davis, President
Timothy J. Barry, Sr. VP

4937 OA Laboratories and Research, Inc.
4717 North Shadeland Avenue 317-639-2626
Indianapolis, IN 46202-2628 Fax: 317-377-1924
E-mail: oalabs@dajanigroup.com
http://www.oalabsandresearch.com
OA Laboratories and Research, Inc. serves customers in Indiana and throughout the United States by meeting their Analytical needs.

Usama H. Dajani, President/CEO
Lisa K. Mesalam, Executive Secretary/Office M

4938 Oak Ridge Institute for Science and Education
1299 Bethel Valley Road 865-241-5947
Bldg SC-200 Fax: 865-576-5576
Oak Ridge, TN 37830 E-mail: communications@orau.org
http://www.orau.org

Andy Page, President/CEO
Eric Abelquist, Executive VP

4939 Occupational Health Conservation
5118 N 56th Street 813-626-8156
Tampa, FL 33610 800-229-8156
Fax: 813-623-6702
Environmental impact assessment firm.
James F Rizk, President

4940 Occusafe
1209 Tool Drive 337-365-6595
New Lberia, LA 70560 888-261-8925
Fax: 630-941-3865
E-mail: info@occusafe-inc.com
http://www.occusafe-inc.com
Employee safety, industrial hygiene and environmental consulting firm.
Bryan Aucoin, President
Travis Martin, Sr. VP

4941 Ogden Environment & Energy Services Company
4455 Brookfield Corporate Drive 703-488-3700
Suite 100 Fax: 703-488-3701
Chantilly, VA 20151
Environmental engineering and consulting company.
J Mark Elliot, President

4942 Ogden Environment & Energy Services Company
5510 Morehouse Drive 858-458-9044
San Diego, CA 92121 Fax: 858-458-0943
Scientific and environmental engineering; analytical chemistry.
Mike Nienberg, Executive VP

4943 Oil-Dri Corporation of America
410 N Michigan Avenue 312-321-1515
Suite 400 800-645-3747
Chicago, IL 60611 Fax: 312-321-1271
E-mail: info@oildri.com
http://www.oildri.com

Absorbents for consumers, industrial, agricultural, environmental and fluid purification.
Reagan Culbertson, Investor Relations Manager

4944 Olver
1116 S Main Street 540-552-5548
Blacksburg, VA 24060 Fax: 540-552-5577
E-mail: info@olver.com
http://www.olver.com

Engineering research and consulting firm specializing in environmental design and analysis. Research results published in project reports.

4945 Omega Thermal Technologies
21 Elbo Lane 610-572-2332
Mount Laurel, NJ 08054 Fax: 610-664-1258
E-mail: contact@ottusa.com
http://www.ottusa.com

Technology consultants, designers and constructors offering technical expertise and hardware design for thermal processing and environmental studies.
Kenneth W Hladun, President
Peter V. Hewka, VP

4946 Oneil M Banks
336 S Main Street 410-879-4676
Suite 2D Fax: 410-836-8685
Bel Air, MD 21014
Industrial and environmental hygiene and toxicology consulting company.

4947 Online Environs
201 Broadway 617-577-0202
Suite 7 Fax: 617-577-0772
Cambridge, MA 02139 http://www.environs.com
Telecommunications and Internet research.
Anrew Yu, President

4948 Operational Technology Corporation
4100 NW Loop 410 Street 210-731-0000
Suite 230 800-677-8072
San Antonio, TX 78229 Fax: 210-731-0008
E-mail: info@otcorp.com
http://www.otcorp.com
Employment research firm providing information technologies, computer sales and service and environmental services.
John Fernandez, CEO

4949 Orlando Laboratories
820 Humphries Avenue 407-896-6645
Orlando, FL 32814 Fax: 407-898-6588
Independent environmental testing and analysis laboratory.

4950 Ostergaard Acoustical Associates
200 Executive Drive 973-731-7002
Suite 350 Fax: 973-731-6680
West Orange, NJ 07052 E-mail: info@acousticalconsultant.com
http://www.acousticalconsultant.com
Environmental, acoustic and noise control testing and analysis firm. Research results published in project reports.

R Kring Herbert, Principal
Edward M. Clark, Principal

4951 Ozark Environmental Laboratories
PO Box 806 573-364-8900
Rolla, MO 65402 Fax: 573-341-2040
Firm providing construction materials testing on soils, aggregates, and asphaltic and portland cement concrete; water and wastewater physical and chemical analysis; and quality control studies encompassing physical measurements andchemical analysis.

4952 P&P Laboratories
2025 Woodlynne Avenue 856-962-6188
Oaklyn, NJ 08107
Environmental testing and chemical toxicology laboratory.

4953 PACE
100 Marshall Drive 724-772-0610
Warrendale, PA 15086 Fax: 724-772-1686
Environmental testing and analysis firm.

4954 PACE Analytical Services
1700 Elm Street 612-607-0151
Suite 200 Fax: 612-607-6444
Minneapolis, MN 55414 E-mail: nathan.cklund@pacelabs.com
http://www.pacelabs.com
Provider of air, water, soil and environmental testing services.
Steve A Vanderboom, CEO
Gabe LeBrun, VP/CFO

4955 PACE Environmental Products
5240 W Coplay Road 610-262-3818
Whitehall, PA 18052 800-303-4532
Fax: 610-262-4445
E-mail: sales@paceems.com
http://www.paceems.com
Manufacturer and Integrator of continuous emissions monitoring systems (EMS). Regulatory, process, and certification stack testing. In-shop analyzer repair, CEMS field service. Parts, sales, rentals, repairs and service.
Damian Gaiotti, Sales Manager

4956 PACE Resources, Incorporated
40 S Richland Avenue 717-852-1300
York, PA 17404 800-711-8075
Fax: 717-852-1301
E-mail: pace40@aol.com
This company is the parent of units involved in environmental engineering and consulting, civil engineering, architectural planning, data processing, printing and other services.
Russell E Horn, Jr, President

4957 PARS Environmental
500 Horizon Drive 609-890-7277
Suite 540 800-959-1119
Robbinsville, NJ 08691 Fax: 609-890-9116
E-mail: info@parsenviro.com
http://www.parsenviro.com
Environmental consulting company.
HS Gill, President

4958 PCCI
300 N Lee Street 703-684-2060
Suite 201 Fax: 703-684-5343
Alexandria, VA 22314 E-mail: use form on website
http://www.pccii.com
Provides sensible solutions to difficult engineering and environmental problems in coastal, ocean and inland environments. Specialties include: environmental compliance; all hazards emergency response planning, trainings, drills andexercises; and marine engineering.
Robert W Urban, President
John Kupersmith, VP

4959 PDC Laboratories
2231 West Altorser Drive 309-692-9688
Peoria, IL 61615 Fax: 309-692-9689
http://www.pdcarea.com
Environmental laboratory performs air sample analysis, soil analysis, and potential toxic waste analysis.

4960 PE LaMoreaux & Associates
PO Box 2310 205-752-5543
Tuscaloosa, AL 35403 Fax: 205-752-4043
E-mail: info@pela.com
http://www.pela.com
Consulting hydrologists, geologists, engineers, and environmental scientists. Research results published in brochures, pamphlets, news releases, speeches, seminars, studies, and reports.
James ""Mike"" Lee, President/CEO
Dr. Bashir Memon, Executive VP

4961 PEI Associates
11499 Chester Road 513-782-4700
Suite 200 Fax: 513-782-4807
Cincinnati, OH 45246
Environmental consulting firm. Research results published in government publications.

4962 PELA
PO Box 2310 205-752-5543
Tuscaloosa, AL 35403 Fax: 205-752-4043
E-mail: info@pela.com
http://www.pela.com
For over three decades, PELA's integration of qualified personnel, up to date technology, and sound management has established PELA as an international leader in the environmental consulting field. PELA's expertise in hydrology,geotechnical analysis, design and construction management, remediation, computer graphics and models, and permitting can get your project on the two feet quicker than you might think.
James ""Mike"" Lee, President/CEO
Dr. Bashir Memon, Executive VP

4963 PRC Environmental Management
233 N Michigan Avenue 312-938-0300
Suite 1621 Fax: 312-931-1109
Chicago, IL 60601
Robert Banosten, VP

4964 PRD Tech
1776 Mentor Avenue 513-731-1800
Suite 400-A Fax: 513-984-5710
Cincinnati, OH 45212 E-mail: prdbiofilter@aol.com
http://www.prdtechinc.com
Biological and chemical research and commercial technology development firm, serving primarily the baking, brewing, and other food industry segments with their environmental control needs - odor and volatile organic compound (VOC)control applications.
Ramesh Melarkode, President

4965 PSC Environmental Services
2337 N. Penn Road 215-822-2676
Hatfield, PA 19440 800-292-2510
Fax: 215-997-1315
http://www.pscnow.com
Environmental services
Bruce Roberson, President/CEO
Jeffrey Stocks, Sr. VP/CFO

4966 PSI
1901 South Meyers Road 630-691-1587
Suite 400 800-548-7901
Oakbrook Terrace, IL 60181 Fax: 630-691-1587
E-mail: info@psiusa.com
http://www.psiusa.com
Distinguished as a leader in environmental consulting, geotechnical engineering, and construction testing services, PSI is nationally recognized in several disciplines, including: construction services, materials testing, roofconsulting and asbestos management.

4967 Pace
2400 Cumberland Drive 219-464-2389
Valparaiso, IN 46383 Fax: 219-462-2953

Environmental testing laboratory.
Les Arnold, President

4968 Pace Laboratory
9893 Brewers Court 301-490-9860
Laurel, MD 20723 http://www.pacelab.edu
Environmental testing laboratory.
Eric Holinger
Steve Marquez

4969 Pace New Jersey
284 Raritan Center Parkway 973-257-9300
Edison, NJ 08837 Fax: 973-257-0777
Environmental analytical laboratory and data management firm.

4970 Pacific Gamefish Research Foundation
47-381 Kealakehe Parkway 808-329-6105
PO Box 4800 Fax: 808-329-1148
Kailua Kona, HI 96740

4971 Pacific Northwest National Lab
902 Battelle Boulevard 509-375-2121
PO Box 999 888-375-7665
Richland, WA 99352 Fax: 509-375-2491
E-mail: inquiry@pnl.gov
http://www.pnl.gov
Contract research and development for the government environmental restoration, energy, national security and health.
Mike Kluse, Lab Director
Steve Ashby, Deputy Director

4972 Pacific Northwest Research Institute
720 Broadway 206-726-1200
Seattle, WA 98122 800-745-1527
Fax: 206-726-1206
E-mail: info@pndri.org
http://www.pnri.org
Established as Pacific Northwest Research Foundation in 1956 by Dr. William B Hutchinson, Sr. as the first private nonprofit biomedical and clinical research institute in the Northwest. As founder and first director, Dr. Hutchinson'sprimary objective was to provide a facility for basic and clinical research dedicated to the improvement of patient care. Sponsors basic science efforts in biochemistry, molecular biology and immunology as they pertain to the clinical areas of cancerand diabetes.
Doug Shaw, Chair
Ardythe Johnson, Vice Chair

4973 Pacific Nuclear
2525 West 10th St. 925-706-8300
Antioch, CA 94509-9111 800-706-3395
Fax: 925-706-8396
http://www.pacificnucleartechnology.com

4974 Package Research Laboratory
41 Pine Street 973-627-4405
Rockaway, NJ 07866 Fax: 973-627-4407
E-mail: info@package-testing.com
http://www.package-testing.com
Packaged product testing facility. Research results published in reports, videos and pictures. Custom tests designed. DOT/UN certification on hazardous materials. Extreme environment testing. Pallet load and pallet merchandizingtesting. Design and packaging development, consulting, package analysis, project management, and vendor audits.
David Dixon, VP
Brian Berg, R&D

4975 Pan American Laboratories
4099 Highway 190 east Service 985-893-4097
Covington, LA 70433 Fax: 985-893-6195
E-mail: pamlab@pamlab.com
http://www.pamlab.com/
Pharmaceutical manufacturer.
Samuel Camp, Chairman
Kenny Ladner, President

4976 Pan Earth Designs
16525 103rd Street SE 360-458-9173
Suite A Fax: 360-458-9123
Yelm, WA 98597
Environmental research firm.

4977 Par Environmental Services
1906 21st Street 916-739-8356
PO Box 160756 Fax: 916-739-0626
Sacramento, CA 95816-756 E-mail: mlmaniery@yahoo.com
http://www.parenvironmental.com
Environmental research firm.
Mary L. Maniery, President

4978 Parsons Engineering Science
100 W Walnut Street 626-440-2000
Pasadena, CA 91124 Fax: 626-440-2630
E-mail: erin.kuhlman@parsons.com
http://www.parsons.com
Environmental engineering testing and consulting company with expertise in advanced wastewater treatment.
Mark K. Holdsworth, Co-Founder
Kenneth C. Dahlberg, Chairman

4979 Penniman & Browne
3015 Dumbarton Road 804-264-2701
Richmond, VA 23228 Fax: 804-264-0782
E-mail: clientservices@pandbinc.com
http://www.pandbinc.com
Independent testing laboratory whose mission is to provide excellent client service with its scope of both engineering and chemical services.
Hans V Steer, Client Services Manager

4980 Peoria Disposal Company
2231 West Altorfer Drive 309-692-9688
Peoria, IL 61615 Fax: 309-688-0881
http://www.pdclab.com
Environmental services firm, especially hazardous waste testing.

4981 Pharmaco LSR
Mettlers Road 732-873-2550
Box 2360 Fax: 732-873-3992
East Millstone, NJ 08875
Dr. Geoffrey K Hogan, President

4982 Philip Environmental Services
210 W Sand Bank Road 618-281-7173
PO Box 230 Fax: 618-281-5120
Columbia, IL 62236 http://www.philipinc.com
Environmental research and analysis firm.
Jenny Penland, President

4983 Physical Sciences
20 New England Business Center 978-689-0003
Andover, MA 01810-1077 Fax: 978-689-3232
E-mail: contact@psicorp.com
http://www.psicorp.com
PSI focuses on providing contract research and development services in a variety of technical areas to both government and commercial customers. Our interests range from basic research to technology development, with an emphasis onapplied research.
George Caledonia, Chairman
David Green, President/CEO

4984 Pittsburgh Mineral & Environmental Technology
700 5th Avenue 724-843-5000
New Brighton, PA 15066-1837 Fax: 724-843-5353
E-mail: pmet@pmet-inc.com
http://www.pmet-inc.com
A full service company specializing in metals and mineral processing, coal ash utilization, waste stream management, and precision analysis. Also develops technologies dedicated to waste

minimibation, treatment, and conversion tosafe,usable, profitable products.

Thomas E Weyand, President
William F Sutton, EVP

4985 Planning Concepts
1920 E. Northland Avenue 920-730-3333
Appleton, WI 54911 800-798-5722
Fax: 920-731-7401
E-mail: cindy@planningconcepts.net
http://www.planningconcepts.net

Environmental impact assessment firm.
Richard Gasman, President
Randall Schmitz, VP

4986 Planning Design & Research Engineers
2000 Lindell Avenue 615-298-2065
Nashville, TN 37203-5509 Fax: 615-269-4119
E-mail: ttichenor@pdre.net
http://www.PDRE.net

Environmental engineers, asbestos, lead paint design, testing underground tanks, hazardous waste projects, Phase I and II site assessments.

Teresa Tichenor, Office Manager

4987 Planning Resources
402 W Liberty Drive 630-668-3788
Wheaton, IL 60187 Fax: 630-668-4125
E-mail: webmaster@planres.com
http://www.planres.com

Land use and environmental planning.
Lan R Richart, President
Pamela J Richart, VP

4988 Plant Research Technologies
525 Del Rey Avenue Unit C 408-245-4423
PO Box 6008 Fax: 408-245-8043
Sunnyvale, CA 94086
Contact research organization which provides agricultural and analytical applied services.
Basil Burke PhD, President

4989 Plasma Science & Fusion Center
77 Massachusetts Avenue 617-253-8100
NW 16 Fax: 617-253-0570
Cambridge, MA 02139 E-mail: info@psfc.mit.edu
http://www.psfc.mit.edu
Plasma science and technology and plasma fusion energy research.
Miklos Porkolab, Director/Manager
Carol Arlington, Director

4990 Polaroid Corporation
549 Technology Square 617-577-2000
Cambridge, MA 02139 Fax: 617-577-5618
http://www.polaroid.com

4991 Polyengineering
1935 Headland Avenue 334-793-4700
PO Box 837 888-793-4700
Dothan, AL 36302 Fax: 334-793-9015
E-mail: info@polyengineering.com
http://www.polyengineering.com
Offers a broad range of professional engineering and architectural services as well as financial services and administrative support.

Max A. Mobley, Chairman/President
Glenn D. Stephens, Sr. VP

4992 Polytechnic
3740 W Morse Avenue 847-677-0450
Lincolnwood, IL 60712 Fax: 847-677-0480

4993 Porter Consultants
4400 Old William Penn Highway 412-380-7500
Suite 200 Fax: 412-380-6899
Monroeville, PA 15146 E-mail: info@porteres.com
http://www.porter-consulting.com
Executive recruiting firm specializing in national and international placement of Sales, Marketing, Management, Executive-level, and Technical Support professionals within a wide rang of industries including High Tech, Exhibit.Telecommunications, Medical, and Pharmaceutical.
William Porter, Founder/President
Art Floro, Sr.VP/Executive Recruiter

4994 Powell Labs Limited
1915 Aliceanna Street 410-558-3540
Baltimore, MD 21231
Provides services in the specialty fields of metallurgical investigations, failure analysis, metal overheating and corrosion failures, remaining life assessments of high temperature components, identification of casting andmanufacturing defects, microbiological investigations, alloy identification, cycle water, cooling water, drinking water, high purity water, industrial process water, waste water, water and stream formed deposits, field examinations and training.

4995 Precision Environmental
180 Canada Larga Road 805-500-3713
Ventura, CA 93001 800-375-7786
Fax: 805-648-6999
http://www.precisionenv.com

Precision Environmental, Inc. was founded at Stanford University with the purpose of providing quality environmental contracting services to clients with asbestos contamination problems. State licensed and registered.

4996 Princeton Energy Resources International
1700 Rockville Pike 301-881-0650
Suite 550 Fax: 301-230-1232
Rockville, MD 20852 http://www.perihq.com
Engineering and consulting firm: engineering and environmental technology, environmental management and global climate change issues, economic research, aviation economics, and human factors
Adolfo Menendez, Chairman/CEO
Nicholas P. Cheremisinoff, VP

4997 Priorities Institute
3233 Vallejo Street 303-477-3792
#3B Fax: 303-838-8105
Denver, CO 80211 E-mail: mail@priorities.org
http://www.priorities.org
Nonprofit, educational research organization that explores issues of critical importance that are not adequately researched by existing educational, media, research, governmental or other organizations.
Logan Perkins, Director/Founder

4998 Professional Service Industries
1211 W. Cambridge Circle Drive 913-310-1600
Kansas City, KS 66103 800-548-7901
Fax: 913-310-1601
http://www.psiusa.com

Elizabeth Noakes, Department Manager

4999 Professional Service Industries Laboratory
4106 NW Riverside Drive 816-741-9466
Riverside, MO 64150 Fax: 816-587-2996
Engineering test laboratory.
Stephen Fitzer, President

5000 Professional Service Industries/Jammal & Associates Division
1675 Lee Road 407-645-5560
Winter Park, FL 32789 Fax: 407-645-1320
William N Phillips, Executive VP

5001 Q-Lab
1005 SW 18th Avenue 305-245-5600
PO Box 349490 Fax: 305-245-5656
Homestead, FL 33034-1725 E-mail: q-lab@q-lab.com
http://www.q-panel.com
Firm providing environmental simulation testing.
George Grossman, Founder
Doug Grossman, President

5002 QC
1205 Industrial Highway 215-355-3900
Southampton, PA 18966 Fax: 215-355-7231
Environmental testing lab.

5003 Quantum Environmental
167 Little Lake Drive 734-930-2600
Ann Arbor, MI 48104 Fax: 734-930-2798
E-mail: info@quantumenvironmental.com
http://www.quantumenvironmental.com
Environmental remediation firm.

5004 R&R Visual
1828 W Olson Road 574-224-5426
Rochester, IN 46975 800-656-4225
Fax: 574-223-7953
E-mail: info@rapidview.com
http://www.rapidview.com
Developing and providing unique inspection solutions to the nuclear, petrochemical, industrial and municipal sewer industries.
Rex Robinson, President
Kris Robinson, VP

5005 RE/SPEC
3824 Jet Drive 605-394-6400
Rapid City, SD 57703-4757 877-737-7321
Fax: 605-394-6456
http://www.respec.com
Tom Zeller, VP Finance
Daniel B. Adams, Sr. Project Manager

5006 RETEC Group/ENSR-Seattle
710 Second Avenue 206-624-9349
Suite 1000 Fax: 206-624-2839
Seattle, WA 98104 E-mail: askensr@ensr.aecom.com
http://www.aecom.com
The RETEC Group/ENSR is an environmental management consulting and engineering firm that solves complex problems throughout the three main stages of the business life cycle-from new asset development to ongoing operations to finalasset disposition and restoration. RETEC develops integrated solutions logically aligned to optimize these business needs-financially, operationally, environmentally-ultimately, creating healthier businesses. RETEC merged with ENSR in February 2007.
John M. Dionisio, Chairman/CEO
Richard G. Newman, Chairman, Emirates

5007 RMC Corporation Laboratories
214 W Main Plaza 417-256-1101
West Plains, MO 65775 Fax: 417-256-1103
Environmental waste studies. Research results published in journals.
Joseph Cooke, President
Dr R Soundararajan, Director R&D

5008 RMT
1212 Deming Way 608-831-4444
Suite 200 800-283-3443
Madison, WI 53717 Fax: 608-831-3334
E-mail: info@rmtinc.com
http://www.rmtinc.com
Global engineering and management consulting firm that develops environmental solutions for industry. With a 600 person staff and 20 offices throughout the US and Europe helping clients sustain the environment while meeting theirbusiness objectives. Engineers, scientists and construction managers take a project from conception through successful completion. Expertise includes air, water and waste permitting, remediation, hazardous/solid waste management, air pollutioncontrol and more.
John Kennedy, President
Katherine Martin, VP

5009 RV Fitzsimmons & Associates
1860 Arthur Road 630-231-0680
West Chicago, IL 60185 Fax: 630-957-4394
E-mail: rajan@therightstuff.com
http://www.therightstuff.com
Environmental testing and consulting firm.
Robert Fitzsimmons, President

5010 Radian Corporation
1601 Market Street 512-244-0100
Philadelphia, PA 19103 877-723-4261
Fax: 512-388-0966
http://www.radian.biz
Environmental science and industrial safety research and consulting firm. Research results published in project reports and in professional journals.
David J. Beilder, President
Teresa Bryce Bazemore, President

5011 Ralph Stone and Company
10954 Santa Monica Boulevard 310-478-1501
Los Angeles, CA 90025 800-813-9613
Fax: 310-478-7359
E-mail: rstoneco@aol.com
http://www.ralphstoneco.com
Environmental - Phase 1&2; Remediation; Geology
Richard Kahle, President
James Rowlands, VP

5012 Ramco
3150 Brunswick Pike 609-620-4800
Suite 130 800-472-6261
Lawrenceville, NJ 08648 Fax: 609-620-4860
http://www.ramco.com
P R Venketrama Raja, Vice Chairman
Virender Aggarwal, CEO

5013 Raytheon Company
870 Winter Street 781-522-3000
Waltham, MA 02451 Fax: 781-522-3001
E-mail: cjkovalsky@raytheon.com
http://www.raytheon.com
An environmental testing firm, one of Raytheon's unique testing resources is the Andover Environmental Test Laboratory (ETL), a full-service, state-of-the-art facility. ETL specializes in performing static, dynamic (vibration, shock,and acceleration) and climatic test procedures, as well as comprehensive failure analysis studies.
William H Swanson, Chairman/CEO
Thomas M. Culligan, Sr. VP

5014 Recon Environmental Corporation
1927 5th Avenue 619-308-9333
San Diego, CA 92101-2358 Fax: 619-308-9334
http://www.recon-us.com
Environmental engineering, consulting, and laboratory services. Research results published in project reports and government publications.
Robert MacAller, President
Bobbi Herdes, Private Team Leader

5015 Recon Systems
5815 Willowdale Ave. SE 330-484-8444
Waynesburg, OH 44688 Fax: 330-484-8555
http://www.reconsystems.com
Dr. Norman J Weinstein, President

5016 Recra Environmental
10 Hazelwood Drive 800-527-3272
Suite 110 Fax: 716-691-2617
Amherst, NY 14228-2298 http://www.clu-in.org

Research and development chemical and environmental measurement information.

Kenneth Kinecki, Technology Developer Contact

5017 Reed and Associates
269 Germantown Bend Cove 847-718-0101
Cordova, TN 38018 Fax: 847-718-0202
http://www.myreedhome.com
Environmental testing laboratory.

5018 Reid, Quebe, Allison, Wilcox & Associates
4755 Kingsway Drive 317-255-6060
Suite 400 Fax: 317-255-8354
Indianapolis, IN 46205
Architectural and environmental engineering research firm.
J Edward Doyle, President

5019 Reliance Laboratories
2001 Young Court 304-842-5285
Racine, WI 53404 800-634-6155
Fax: 304-842-5351
E-mail: neil_czarnecki@reliancelaboratories.com
http://www.reliancelaboratories.com

William F Kirk Jr, President

5020 Remtech
110 12th Street NW 205-682-7900
Suite E 106 Fax: 205-682-7953
Birmingham, AL 35203
Systems design and engineering firm specializing in energy and environmental control applications. Research results published in project reports and are presented in papers at conferences.
Gene Fuller, President

5021 Research Planning
1121 Park Street 803-256-7322
PO Box 328 Fax: 803-254-6445
Columbia, SC 29202 E-mail: info@mail.researchplanning.com
http://www.researchplanning.com
Scientific consulting firm specializing in the environment and natural resource assessment. Extensive experience in field surveys, EIS, spatial data analysis, and international work in Central America, West Africa and the Middle East.Research results published in professional journals, proceedings, and project reports. Woman-owned, small business concern.
Miles O. Hayes, Chairman
Jacqueline Michel, President

5022 Resource Technologies Corporation
248 E Calder Way 877-489-0199
Suite 300 877-489-0199
State College, PA 16801 Fax: 814-237-1769
E-mail: april@resourcetec.com
http://www.resourcetec.com
An independent research, development and technical services firm located in central Pennsylvania. Specializes in appraisal and assessment services, information system development, assessment appeals and digitalmapping, web basedapplications, geotechnical services, environmental and ecological analysis and planning and management services.
Jeffrey R Stern, President
Ronald W Stingelin, Contact

5023 Resources for the Future
1616 P Street NW 202-328-5000
Suite 600 Fax: 202-939-3460
Washington, DC 20036 E-mail: info@rff.org
http://www.rff.org
RFF is a nonprofit and nonpartisan think tank located in Washington DC that conducts independent research-rooted primarily in economics and other social sciences on environmental and natural resource issues. RFF was founded in 1952.

W. Bowman Cutter, Chair
John M. Deutch, Vice Chair

5024 Responsive Management
130 Fraklin Street 540-432-1888
Harrisonburg, VA 22801 Fax: 540-432-1892
E-mail: mark@responsivemanagement.com
http://www.responsivemanagement.com
Responsive Management is a Virginia-based public opinion polling and survey research firm specializing in fisheries, wildlife, natural resource, outdoor recreation and environmental issues.
Mark Damian Duda, Executive Director
Steven J. Bissell, Qualitative Research Analyst

5025 Revet Environmental and Analytical Lab
181 Cedar Hill Street 508-460-7600
Marlborough, MA 01752 Fax: 508-460-7777
Environmental analysis and consulting laboratory.
V Taylor, President

5026 Ricerca Biosciences LLC
7528 Auburn Road 440-357-3300
Concord, OH 44077 888-742-3722
Fax: 440-354-6276
E-mail: info@ricerca.com
http://www.ricerca.com
Ricerca, a premier solution provider, offers expertise in both biology and chemistry to enable life sciences companies to fully leverage integrated, cost-effective, best practices approach to lead optimization and drug development.Services include in-vitro/in-vivo ADME, pharmacology, toxicology, medicinal, process, analytical chemistry, cGMP API scale-up production, regulatory support.

Michael E. Placke, President
Lawrence R. Lima, VP

5027 Rich Technology
PO Box 4886 803-523-3415
Glen Allen, VA 23058 Fax: 815-229-1525
http://www.richtech.com
Environmental engineering research firm.
Dan Garfi, Chairman
Mark Wensell, Vice Chairman

5028 Riviana Foods: RVR Package Testing Center
1702 Taylor Street 713-861-8221
Houston, TX 77007 Fax: 713-861-9939
Lejo C Brana, Director Packaging

5029 Robert Bosch Corporation
32104 State Road 2 574-237-2100
New Carlisle, IN 46552 Fax: 219-654-8755
Controlled-road environmental testing of automotive components for passenger cars, trucks, buses, tractor-trailers and off-road vehicles; certification to federal brake commission and fuel economy requirements.

5030 Robert D Niehaus
140 E Carrillo Street 805-962-0611
Santa Barbara, CA 93101 Fax: 805-962-0097
http://www.rdniehaus.com
Socioeconomic and environmental planning organization. Research results published in reports.
Robert Niehaus, President/Principal Economis
Robert McCleary, Executive VP

5031 Rone Engineers
8908 Ambassador Row 214-630-9745
Dallas, TX 75247 Fax: 214-630-9819
http://www.roneengineers.com
Provider of Geotechnical, Construction Materials Testing and Environmental Consulting services throughout Texas and the Southwest.
Richard K. Leigh, President
Mark D. Gray, VP

5032 Roux Associates
209 Shafter Street 631-232-2600
Islandia, NY 11749 800-322-ROUX
Fax: 631-232-9898
E-mail: sales@rouxinc.com
http://www.rouxinc.com
Environmental Consulting and Management.

Paul Roux, Chairman
Doug Swanson, President/CEO

5033 Rummel, Klepper & Kahl
81 Mosher Street 410-728-2900
Baltimore, MD 21217 800-787-3755
Fax: 410-728-2992
http://www.rkkengineers.com
Civil, site, transpotation, environmental, structural engineering services.

5034 S-F Analytical Laboratories
2345 South 170th Street 262-754-5300
New Berlin, WI 53151 800-300-6700
Fax: 262-754-5310
E-mail: dkliber@sflabs.com
http://www.sflabs.com
Environmental and materials testing laboratory.

David L Kliber, President/CEO

5035 SCS Engineers
3900 Kilroy Airport Way 562-426-9544
Suite 100 Fax: 562-427-0805
Long Beach, CA 90806-6816 E-mail: service@scsengineers.com
http://www.scsengineers.com
Delivers economically and environmentally sound solutions for solid waste management and site remediation projects throughout the world. Provides engineering, construction, and contract operations services to private and public sectorclients through a network of more than 40 offices and 500 professional staff working in the US and abroad.

Bob Stearns, Founder/Chairman
Jim Walsh, President/CEO

5036 SGI International
1200 Prospect Street 858-551-1090
Suite 325 Fax: 858-551-0247
La Jolla, CA 92037 E-mail: info@sgiinternational.com
http://www.sgiinternational.com
Environmental applications.
Michael L Rose, President

5037 SGS Environmental Services Inc
201 Route 17 North 201-508-3000
Rutherford, NJ 07070 Fax: 201-508-3183
E-mail: julie.shumway@sgs.com
http://www.sgsgroup.us.com
Environmental laboratory services.

Chris Kirk, CEO
Julie Shumway, Business Development

5038 SHB AGRA
3232 W Virginia Avenue 602-995-3916
Phoenix, AZ 85009 Fax: 602-995-3921
Geotechnical and environmental research firm.

5039 SP Engineering
45 Congress Street, Building 4 978-745-4569
PO Box 848, Shetland Park Fax: 978-745-4881
Salem, MA 01970 E-mail: brucepoolesp@aol.com
http://www.spengineeringinc.com
SP Engineering specializes in all areas of environmental compliance. Services include testing for chemical or bacterial contamination of well water and assessments for the presence of petroleum products or hazardous waste, in additionto performing environmental audits insuring owners that all the tenants in their industrial complexes are in compliance with government regulations relative to hazardous waste disposal.

Bruce Poole, Executive Director

5040 SPECTROGRAM Corporation
287 Boston Post Road 203-318-0535
Madison, CT 06443 Fax: 203-318-0535
E-mail: spectrogram@msn.com
http://www.spectrogram.com
Research, development and manufacturing firm which produces analytical instrumentation and systems in the fields of analytical chemistry (environmental) and elastomeric physical testing (rubber and plastics). Also offers a line ofproducts, each of which is involved in on-line environmental monitoring for the detection of an accidental release of petroleum products (oil spills).

HR Gram, President/CEO

5041 STL Denver
4955 Yarrow Street 303-736-0100
Arvada, CO 80002 800-572-8958
Fax: 303-431-7171
Testing and analysis services.

5042 STS Consultants
750 Corporate Woods Parkway 847-279-2500
Vernon Hills, IL 60061 800-859-7871
Fax: 847-279-2510
http://stsltd.com
Consulting engineering firm offering an integrated package of services in geotechnical engineering, waste management, environmental management, and construction technology.
Thomas W Wolf, CEO

5043 STS Consultants
111 Pfingsten Road 630-272-6520
Northbrook, IL 60062 Fax: 847-498-2721

Mike Russell, President

5044 Saint Louis Testing Laboratories
2810 Clark Avenue 314-531-8080
Saint Louis, MO 63103 Fax: 314-531-8085
E-mail: testlab@labinc.com
http://www.labinc.com/
Research and testing laboratory specializing in chemical, metallurgical, nondestructive and environmental testing and field services. Research results published in project reports.

W Trowbridge, President

5045 Samtest
3730 James Savage Road 989-496-3610
Midland, MI 48642 Fax: 989-496-3190
Geotechnical and environmental services firm.

5046 Sari Sommarstrom
PO Box 219 530-467-5783
Etna, CA 96027 Fax: 530-467-3623
E-mail: sari@sisqtel.net

5047 Savannah Laboratories
PO Box 13548 912-354-7854
Savannah, GA 31416 Fax: 912-352-0165
Environmental and biological research and testing laboratory with expertise in fish farming technology.

5048 Scitest
1110 E. Collins Blvd. 972-479-1300
Suite 130 Fax: 972-479-1301
Richardson, TX 75081 E-mail: info@scitest.com
http://www.scitest.com
Environmental testing and analysis laboratory.
Roderick J Lamothe, President

5049 Separation Systems Technology
100 Nightingale Ln 850-932-1433
Gulf Breeze, FL 32561 Fax: 850-934-8642
E-mail: office@separationsystems.com
http://www.separationsystems.com
Environmental research.
Robert L Riley, President

5050 Shannon & Wilson
400 N 34th Street 206-632-8020
PO Box 300303 Fax: 206-695-6777
Seattle, WA 98103 E-mail: info-seattle@shanwil.com
http://www.shannonwilson.com
Environmental research.

5051 Sheladia Associates
15825 Shady Grove Road 301-590-3939
Suite 100 Fax: 301-948-7174
Rockville, MD 20850 http://www.sheladia.com
Consulting firm specializing in environmental studies. Research results published in research reports for the government.
A Moytayek, President

5052 Shell Engineering and Associates
2403 West Ash 573-445-0106
Columbia, MO 65203 Fax: 573-445-0137
E-mail: charles@shellengr.com
http://www.shellengr.com
Harvey D Shell, Founder/Chairman/CEO
Charles Shell, President

5053 Sherry Laboratories
2417 West Pinhook Road 337-235-0483
Lafayette, LA 70508 800-737-2378
Fax: 337-233-6540
http://www.sherrylabs.com
Analytical environmental laboratory.
Mel Burnell, President

5054 Shive-Hattery Engineers & Architects
316 2nd Street SE 319-362-0313
Suite 500 800-798-0313
Cedar Rapids, IA 52406-1599 Fax: 319-362-2883
E-mail: shiveco@shive-hattery.com
http://www.shive-hattery.com
Donald P Hattery, Chairman

5055 Siebe Appliance Controls
2809 Emerywood Parkway 804-756-6500
Richmond, VA 23294 Fax: 804-756-6563
Automatic temperature, environmental, electronic appliance, heating, cooling and gas safety controls and valves; thermostats and oven burners.

5056 Siemens Water Technologies
10 Technology Drive 978-614-7156
Lowell, MA 01851 800-224-9474
Fax: 978-934-9499
E-mail: mary.grenier@siemens.com
http://www.water.siemens.com
Products and services includes: environmental devices and controls; system troubleshooting/diagnostics; system startup; instrumentation calibration and commissioning, and radio topographic path analysis.
Ursula Boehm, VP
Reudiger Knauf, VP

5057 Simpson Electric Company
520 Simpson Ave. 715-588-3311
PO Box 99 Fax: 715-588-3326
Lac Du Flambeau, WI 54538 http://www.simpsonelectric.com
Analog and digital panel meters, meter relays, controllers, volt-ohm-milliammeters, scopes and industrial and environmental test instruments.

5058 Skinner and Sherman Laboratories
1st Avenue 781-890-7200
Waltham, MA 02451 Fax: 781-890-7003

5059 Smith & Mahoney
540 Broadway 518-463-4107
PO 22047 Fax: 518-463-3823
Albany, NY 12201
Michael W McNarney, President

5060 Snell Environmental Group
1425 Keystone Avenue 517-393-6800
PO Box 22127 800-336-5352
Lansing, MI 48911 Fax: 517-272-7390
E-mail: seg-adm@ix.netcom.com
http://www.dlzcorp.com
Consulting structural engineers.
Vikram (Raj) Rajadhyaksha, Chairman
John O'Mallia, President

5061 Soil Engineering Testing/SET
2401 West 66th Street 612-353-5770
Richfield, MN 55423 Fax: 651-760-4312
E-mail: labinfo@soilengineeringtesting.com
http://www.soilengineeringtesting.com/
A comprehensive soil mechanics laboratory facility for engineering disciplines, environmental and hydrological applications. Scope of services includes: water content; unit mass; liquid limit; sieve analysis; specific gravity; pH;organic content; unconfined compression; and expansion index.
Slade Olson, President
John Whelan, VP

5062 Solar Testing Laboratories
1125 Valley Belt Road 216-741-7007
Cleveland, OH 44131 Fax: 216-741-7011
E-mail: stl@solartestinglabs.com
http://www.stlohio.com
Geotechnical, environmental engineering, materials testing, and construction inspection laboratory. Services include environ mental site assessments, assisting in the selection and coordination of the work of remediation contractors,asbestos inspection and abatement supervision, micro purgegroundwater sampling, sediment control inspection, landfill closure quality assurance, radiological assessments, U.S.T. closures and RCRA closures and facility investigation.
George J Ata PE, President

5063 Southeastern Engineering & Testing Laboratories
4761 SW 51st Street 954-584-4322
Davie, FL 33314 Fax: 954-584-4338
E-mail: jack@seetl.com
http://www.seetl.com
Geotechnical and environmental engineering consulting firm and construction materials engineering laboratory.
Jack Krouskroup, Director

5064 Southern Petroleum Laboratory/SPL
8850 Interchange Drive 713-660-0901
PO Box 20807 877-SPL-LABS
Houston, TX 77054 Fax: 713-660-8975
E-mail: HRBrown@spl-inc.com
http://www.spl-inc.com
SPL provides technical and analytical services to the oil and gas industry including environmental and hydrocarbon analytical services as well as field (gas & liquid measurement) services.
Christopher Brown, President
Steve Grenda, CEO

5065 Southern Research Institute COBRA Training Facility Center for Domestic Preparedness
61 Responder Drive 256-847-2515
PO Box 5129 Fax: 256-847-2525
Anniston, AL 35211 E-mail: secrist@southernresearch.org
http://www.southernresearch.org
Southern Research Institute is an independent research corporation with established capabilities in pharmaceutical discovery

and development, engineering, chemical and biological defense, environmental and energy-related sciences.Research is conducted through contracts and grants with government and commerical clients.
John A Secrist III PhD, President/CEO
Tommy Hurn, Facilities Director

5066 Southern Research Institute Corporate Office: Life Sciences/Environment/Energy
2000 Ninth Avenue S 205-581-2000
PO Box 55305 800-967-6774
Birmingham, AL 35255 Fax: 205-581-2726
E-mail: secrist@southernresearch.org
http://www.southernresearch.org
Southern Research Institute is an independent research corporation with established capabilities in pharmaceutical discovery and development, engineering, chemical and biological defense, environmental and energy-related sciences.Research is conducted through contracts and grants with government and commerical clients.
John A Secrist III PhD, President/CEO
David A. Rutledge, Chief Financial Officer

5067 Southern Research Institute: Carbon To LiquidsDevelopment Center
Highway 25 North 205-670-5068
PO Box 1069 800-967-6774
Wilsonville, AL 35186 Fax: 205-670-5843
E-mail: secrist@southernresearch.org
http://www.southernresearch.org
Southern Research Institute is an independent research corporation with established capabilities in pharmaceutical discovery and development, engineering, chemical and biological defense, environmental and energy-related sciences.Research is conducted through contracts and grants with government and commerical clients.
John A Secrist III PhD, President/CEO
David A. Rutledge, Chief Financial Officer

5068 Southern Research Institute: Chemical Defense Training Facility-Missouri
5201 International Drive 919-282-1050
Durham, CA 27712 800-967-6774
Fax: 573-596-0722
E-mail: secrist@southernresearch.org
http://www.southernresearch.org
Southern Research Institute is an independent research corporation with established capabilities in pharmaceutical discovery and development, engineering, chemical and biological defense, environmental and energy-related sciences.Research is conducted through contracts and grants with government and commerical clients.
John A Secrist III PhD, President/CEO
David A. Rutledge, Chief Financial Officer

5069 Southern Research Institute: Engineering Research Center
757 Tom Martin Drive 205-581-2000
Birmingham, AL 35211 800-967-6774
Fax: 205-581-2726
E-mail: secrist@southernresearch.org
http://www.southernresearch.org
Southern Research Institute is an independent research corporation with established capabilities in pharmaceutical discovery and development, engineering, chemical and biological defense, environmental and energy-related sciences.Research is conducted through contracts and grants with government and commerical clients.
John A Secrist III PhD, President/CEO
David A. Rutledge, Chief Financial Officer

5070 Southern Research Institute: Environment & Energy Research
994 Ellington Field 256-726-9334
Houston, AL 35805 Fax: 256-726-9340
E-mail: secrist@southernresearch.org
http://www.southernresearch.org
Southern Research Institute is an independent research corporation with established capabilities in pharmaceutical discovery and development, engineering, chemical and biological defense, environmental and energy-related sciences.Research is conducted through contracts and grants with government and commerical clients.
John A Secrist III PhD, President/CEO
David A. Rutledge, Chief Financial Officer

5071 Southern Research Institute: Infectious Disease Research Facility
431 Aviation Way 301-694-3232
Frederick, MD 21701 Fax: 301-694-7223
E-mail: secrist@southernresearch.org
http://www.southernresearch.org
Southern Research Institute is an independent research corporation with established capabilities in pharmaceutical discovery and development, engineering, chemical and biological defense, environmental and energy-related sciences.Research is conducted through contracts and grants with government and commerical clients.
John A Secrist III PhD, lab Director-Austin
David A. Rutledge, Chief Financial Officer

5072 Southern Research Institute: Power Systems Development Facility
PO Box 1069 205-670-5068
Highway 25 N Fax: 205-670-5843
Wilsonville, AL 35186 E-mail: secrist@southernresearch.org
http://www.southernresearch.org
Southern Research Institute is an independent research corporation with established capabilities in pharmaceutical discovery and development, engineering, chemical and biological defense, environmental and energy-related sciences.Research is conducted through contracts and grants with government and commerical clients.
John A Secrist III PhD, President/CEO
David A. Rutledge, Chief Financial Officer

5073 Southern Testing & Research Laboratories
317 Covered Bridge Road 252-237-4175
Catersville, GA 30120 Fax: 252-237-9341
http://www.southerntesting.com
Full-service laboratory with over 75 chemists, microbiologists and support personnel that provides personalized service to clients. Capabilities include pharmaceutical, foods and feeds, environmental, industrial hygiene, agriculturaland microbiological sciences. Laboratory is FDA-inspected GLP/cGMP laboratory utilizing AOAC, USP, EPA, USDA, AACC, AOCS, ISO, client and in-house validated methods.
Robert Dermer, Managing Director
Walter Hogg, Business Development

5074 Spears Professional Environmental & Archeological Research Services
13858 S Highway 170 479-839-3663
West Fork, AR 72774 Fax: 479-839-2575
E-mail: SPEARSC@aol.com
Archeological research service. The company conducts cultural resources studies including background studies for Environmental Impact Studies, archeological surveys, significance testing, and data recovery/excavation. Large multi-yearprojects have included cultural resources surveys for timber sales and studies for proposed interstates and utilities.
Carol S Spears, President/Owner

5075 Spectrochem Laboratories
545 Commerce Street 201-337-4774
Franklin Lakes, NJ 07417 Fax: 201-337-1255
http://www.spectrochem.in
Research and development firm specializing in environmental sciences and inorganic chemistry. Research results published in proceedings at technical conferences.
Irene Van Dren, President

5076 Spectrum Sciences & Software
91 Hill Avenue NW 850-796-0909
Fort Walton Beach, FL 32548 Fax: 850-244-9560
E-mail: lcars@specsci.com OR ir@spectrumholdingscorp.com
http://www.specsci.com

An environmental research firm, Spectrum provides diversified capabilities of a large business in a number of advanced technologies. Services include all the disciplines and technologies relevant to operations and maintenance; computerand system sciences; manufacturing; comprehensive planning and environmental assessment technology; and system design testing and evaluation.

Jeremy Maines, Information Technology
Dwight Howard, VP Business Development

5077 Spotts, Stevens and McCoy
1047 North Park Road 610-621-2000
Reading, PA 19610-307 Fax: 610-621-2001
E-mail: information@ssmgroup.com
http://www.ssmgroup.com

An engineering and consulting firm, serving business, industry, and government, SSM provides consulting services in the areas of environmental health and safety, regulatory compliance and training. In addition, SSM provides costeffective, well-engineered solutions to environmental health and safety issues facing facility owners in industry, education, healthcare and local government.

Eileen Kaley, Marketing Director

5078 Standard Testing and Engineering - Corporate
3400 Lincoln Boulevard 405-528-0541
Oklahoma City, OK 73105-5493 800-725-0541
Fax: 405-528-0559
E-mail: bburris@stantest.com
http://www.stantest.com

Standard Testing and Engineering Company was founded in 1951 as a professional engineering firm specializing in materials testing and engineering for the construction and manufacturing industries. Standard Testing also providesenvironmental services such as groundwater studies. Standard Testing's capabilities include a wide variety of specialties such as environmental engineering, and industrial hygiene.

Charles B Burris PE, Engineer/Director

5079 Standard Testing and Engineering - Enid
902 Trails West Loop 580-725-3130
Enid, OK 73703-6336 800-725-3130
Fax: 580-237-3211
E-mail: bburris@stantest.com
http://www.stantest.com

Standard Testing and Engineering Company was founded in 1951 as a professional engineering firm specializing in materials testing and engineering for the construction and manufacturing industries. Standard Testing also providesenvironmental services such as groundwater studies. Standard Testing's capabilities include a wide variety of specialties such as environmental engineering, and industrial hygiene.

G Beckman, Engineer

5080 Standard Testing and Engineering - Lawton
900 Southeast Second 580-353-0872
""J"" Ave. 800-725-0872
Lawton, OK 73501-2481 Fax: 580-353-1263
E-mail: bburris@stantest.com
http://www.stantest.com

Standard Testing and Engineering Company was founded in 1951 as a professional engineering firm specializing in materials testing and engineering for the construction and manufacturing industries. Standard Testing also providesenvironmental services such as groundwater studies. Standard Testing's capabilities include a wide variety of specialties such as environmental engineering, and industrial hygiene.

K Wayman, Engineer

5081 Standard Testing and Engineering - Oklahoma City Environmental Services Division
4300 N Lincoln Boulevard 405-424-8378
Oklahoma, OK 73105-5106 800-725-8378
Fax: 405-424-8129
E-mail: bburris@stantest.com
http://www.stantest.com

Standard Testing and Engineering Company was founded in 1951 as a professional engineering firm specializing in materials testing and engineering for the construction and manufacturing industries. Standard Testing also providesenvironmental services such as groundwater studies. Standard Testing's capabilities include a wide variety of specialties such as environmental engineering, and industrial hygiene.

S Baber, Engineer

5082 Standard Testing and Engineering - Tulsa
10816 E. Newton St. 918-439-9539
Suite 110 800-725-4592
Tulsa, OK 74116 Fax: 918-437-0853
E-mail: bburris@stantest.com
http://www.stantest.com

Standard Testing and Engineering Company was founded in 1951 as a professional engineering firm specializing in materials testing and engineering for the construction and manufacturing industries. Standard Testing also providesenvironmental services such as groundwater studies. Standard Testing's capabilities include a wide variety of specialties such as environmental engineering, and industrial hygiene.

M Hunter, Engineer

5083 Stanford Technology Corporation
57 Poplar Street 203-348-4080
PO Box 2100D 866-717-7363
Glenbrook, CT 06906 Fax: 203 327 5225
E-mail: stctestlab@aol.com
http://www.stanfordtechnology.com

High technology research firm. Research results published in confidential project reports.

Charles C Cullari, President
Gerald T Ciccone, VP

5084 Stantec Consulting Services
4875 Riverside Drive 478-474-6100
Macon, GA 31210 Fax: 478-474-8933
E-mail: media@stantec.com
http://www.stantec.com

Stantec, founded in 1954, provides professional design and consulting services in planning, engineering, architecture, surveying, economics, and project management. Stantec supports public and private sector clients in a diverse rangeof markets in the infrastructure and facilities sector at every stage, from initial concept and financial feasibility to project completion and beyond.

Tony Franceschini, President/CEO
Jay Averill, Communications/Media

5085 Steven Winter Associates - New York NY
307 7th Avenue 212-564-5800
Suite 1701 Fax: 212-741-8673
New York, NY 10001 E-mail: swa@swinter.com
http://www.swinter.com

New York client base includes City, State, and Federal agencies, and owners of a wide array of buildings from small residential to well-known sustainable buildings, such as Battery Park City, 4 Times Square, AOL/Time Warner and HearstHeadquarters. SWA is working with many developers, architects, engineers, and building scientists to help deliver higher performance buildings throughout the NYC metropolitan area and in the surrounding region.

Steven Winter, President

5086 Steven Winter Associates - Norwalk CT
61 Washington Street 203-857-0200
Norwalk, CT 06854 Fax: 203-852-0741
E-mail: swa@swinter.com
http://www.swinter.com

Founded in 1972, Steven Winter Associates, Inc. (SWA) provides a variety of services including: building system assessment, green materials and product specifications, LEED assessments and certification, green building commissioning,accessibility conformance, energy auditing capabilities, builder/operator training, preparation of green guidelines, HVAC troubleshooting, indooor air quality analysis and testing, solar and PV design engineering.

Steven Winter, President

5087 Steven Winter Associates - Washington DC
1616 H Street NW 202-628-6100
Suite 900 Fax: 202-393-5043
Washington, DC 20006 E-mail: swadc@swinter.com
http://www.swinter.com

Located just a few blocks from the White House in the historic downtown section, SWA/DC focuses on technology transfer, buildings-related policy analysis, information dissemination, media outreach & publishing, association management,classroom and web-based training, and buildings research work on behalf of U.S. DOE, HUD, EPA, and the national energy laboratories. SWA/DC also provides logistical support to HUD's Office of Native American Programs (ONAP).
Steven Winter, President

5088 Stone Environmental
535 Stone Cutters Way 802-229-4541
Montpelier, VT 05602 800-959-9987
Fax: 802-229-5417
E-mail: sei@stone-env.com
http://www.stone-env.com

Environmental consulting services and technologies that include: environmental planning and documentation; environmental compliance; waste management; environmental spatial analysis; remediation. Scientific disciplines include: civilengineering; environmental engineering and chemistry; forest biology; hydrogeology; geology; soil science; and geographic information systems.
Christopher Stone, President
David Healy, Vice President

5089 Stork Heron Testing Laboratories
1200 Westinghouse Boulevard 704-588-1131
Suite A 888-786-7555
Charlotte, NC 28273 Fax: 704-588-5412
E-mail: info.charlotte@element.com
http://www.element.com

Analysis and testing laboratory offering environmental control services including mechanical, metallurgical, and chemical analysis in addition to materials testing, nondestructive testing, failure analysis and product evaluation.
Charles Noall, President/CEO
Jo Wetz, Executive VP/CFO

5090 Stork Southwestern Laboratories
222 Cavalcade Street 713-692-9151
PO Box 8768 888-786-7555
Houston, TX 77009 Fax: 713-696-6307
E-mail: info.houston@element.com
http://www.element.com

Analysis and testing laboratory offering environmental control services including materials testing; nondestructive testing; polymer testing and polymeric materials testing; electrical and thermal testing; failure analysis;construction materials testing and engineering; product evaluation; surface testing, and air emissions.
Charles Noall, President/CEO
Jo Wetz, Executive VP/CFO

5091 Suburban Laboratories
4140 Litt Drive 708-544-3260
Hillside, IL 60162 800-783-5227
Fax: 708-544-8587
E-mail: Info@suburbanlabs.com
http://www.suburbanlabs.com

Environmental laboratory providing chemical, chromatographic, and spectrographic analysis of biological materials, including water and groundwater, soil, and hazardous materials for priority pollutants, metals, and pesticide residues.
Dan Galeher, VP of sales & Service
Shane Clarke, Business Development Manager

5092 Sunsearch
PO Box 590 203-453-6591
393A Soundview Road 800-338-0258
Guilford, CT 06437 Fax: 203-458-9011
E-mail: ebarber@sunsearchinc.com
http://www.sunsearchinc.com

Designs, installs and services solar energy systems. Additional services includes: feasibility studies; inspections or assessments of existing systems; repair and redesign of existing systems; service agreements and evaluation ofcomplex systems.

Everett M Barber Jr, President

5093 Systech Environmental Corporation
3085 Woodman Drive 937-643-1240
Suite 300 800-888-8011
Dayton, OH 45420 Fax: 937-643-1203
E-mail: Erica.Hawk@lafarge-na.com
http://www.go2systech.com

Provider of alternative fuels to cement kilns.
Erica Hawk, Corporate Mktg Specialist

5094 TAKA Asbestos Analytical Services
PO Box 208 631-261-2117
Greenlawn, NY 11740 Fax: 631-261-2120

TAKA provides environmental consultation, testing and analytical services for the assessment and detection of onsite asbestos materials. The president and owner of TAKA, Dr. Thomas A. Kubic, has extensive experience with forensicmicroscopy and advanced techniques in sampling and evaluation of airborne asbestos particles using Polarized Light Microscopy.
Thomas A Kubic PhD/MS/JD/FABC, President/Owner

5095 TRAC Laboratories
16969 North Texas Ave. 281-461-7886
Suite 300 Fax: 940-566-2698
Webster, TX 77598 E-mail: info@traclabs.com
http://www.traclabs.com

Provide multi-disciplinary problem-solving approaches to environmental and public health issues.
David Kortenkamp, President/CEO
Bryn Wolfe, Director of Communication

5096 TRC Environmental Corporation-Alexandria
8550 United Plaza Blvd. 225-216-7483
Suite 502 Fax: 225-216-0732
Baton Rouge, LA 70809 E-mail: cobrien@trcsolutions.com
http://www.trcsolutions.com

A provider of engineering, financial, risk management and construction services to large industrial and government customers throughout the United States, TRC provides customer focused solutions in three primary markets: environmental,energy and infrastructure. Environmental services include project development, resolving legacy environmental issues, ensuring compliance for continuing operations, and identifing and mitigating future environmental risks.

Christopher P Vincze, Chairman/CEO
Richard H. Grogan, Chairman of Talisman Managem

5097 TRC Environmental Corporation-Atlanta
4155 Shackleford Road. 770-270-1192
Norcross, GA 30093 Fax: 770-270-1392
E-mail: cobrien@trcsolutions.com
http://www.trcsolutions.com

A provider of engineering, financial, risk management and construction services to large industrial and government customers throughout the United States, TRC provides customer focused solutions in three primary markets: environmental,energy and infrastructure. Environmental services include project development, resolving legacy environmental issues, ensuring compliance for continuing operations, and identifing and mitigating future environmental risks.

Christopher P Vincze, Chairman/CEO
Richard H. Grogan, Chairman of Talisman Managem

5098 TRC Environmental Corporation-Augusta
249 Western Avenue 207-621-7000
Augusta, ME 04330 Fax: 207-621-7001
E-mail: cobrien@trcsolutions.com
http://www.trcsolutions.com

A provider of engineering, financial, risk management and construction services to large industrial and government customers throughout the United States, TRC provides customer focused solutions in three primary markets: environmental,energy and infrastructure. Environmental services include project development, resolving legacy environmental issues, ensuring compliance for continuing operations, and identifing and mitigating future environmental risks.

Christopher P Vincze, Chairman/CEO
Richard H. Grogan, Chairman of Talisman Managem

5099 TRC Environmental Corporation-Boston
2 Liberty Square 617-350-3444
6th Floor Fax: 617-350-3443
Boston, MA 02109 E-mail: cobrien@trcsolutions.com
http://www.trcsolutions.com

A provider of engineering, financial, risk management and construction services to large industrial and government customers throughout the United States, TRC provides customer focused solutions in three primary markets: environmental,energy and infrastructure. Environmental services include project development, resolving legacy environmental issues, ensuring compliance for continuing operations, and identifing and mitigating future environmental risks.

Christopher P Vincze, Chairman/CEO
Richard H. Grogan, Chairman of Talisman Managem

5100 TRC Environmental Corporation-Bridgeport
500 Bic Drive 203-876-1453
Suite 103 Fax: 203-876-1486
Milford, CT 06461 E-mail: cobrien@trcsolutions.com
http://www.trcsolutions.com

A provider of engineering, financial, risk management and construction services to large industrial and government customers throughout the United States, TRC provides customer focused solutions in three primary markets: environmental,energy and infrastructure. Environmental services include project development, resolving legacy environmental issues, ensuring compliance for continuing operations, and identifing and mitigating future environmental risks.

Christopher P Vincze, Chairman/CEO
Richard H. Grogan, Chairman of Talisman Managem

5101 TRC Environmental Corporation-Chicago
230 West Monroe Street 312-578-0870
Suite 2370 Fax: 312-578-0877
Chicago, IL 60606 E-mail: cobrien@trcsolutions.com
http://www.trcsolutions.com

A provider of engineering, financial, risk management and construction services to large industrial and government customers throughout the United States, TRC provides customer focused solutions in three primary markets: environmental,energy and infrastructure. Environmental services include project development, resolving legacy environmental issues, ensuring compliance for continuing operations, and identifing and mitigating future environmental risks.

Christopher P Vincze, Chairman/CEO
Richard H. Grogan, Chairman of Talisman Managem

5102 TRC Environmental Corporation-Ellicott City
4425 Forbes Blvd 301-306-6981
Lanham, MD 20706 Fax: 301-306-6986
E-mail: cobrien@trcsolutions.com
http://www.trcsolutions.com

A provider of engineering, financial, risk management and construction services to large industrial and government customers throughout the United States, TRC provides customer focused solutions in three primary markets: environmental,energy and infrastructure. Environmental services include project development, resolving legacy environmental issues, ensuring compliance for continuing operations, and identifing and mitigating future environmental risks.

Christopher P Vincze, Chairman/CEO
Richard H. Grogan, Chairman of Talisman Managem

5103 TRC Environmental Corporation-Henderson
1009 Whitney Ranch Drive 702-248-6415
Henderson, NV 89014 Fax: 702-248-0626
E-mail: cobrien@trcsolutions.com
http://www.trcsolutions.com

A provider of engineering, financial, risk management and construction services to large industrial and government customers throughout the United States, TRC provides customer focused solutions in three primary markets: environmental,energy and infrastructure. Environmental services include project development, resolving legacy environmental issues, ensuring compliance for continuing operations, and identifing and mitigating future environmental risks.

Christopher P Vincze, Chairman/CEO
Richard H. Grogan, Chairman of Talisman Managem

5104 TRC Environmental Corporation-Honolulu
677 Ala Moana Boulevard 808-728-4111
Suite 920 Fax: 808-638-5649
Honolulu, HI 96813 E-mail: cobrien@trcsolutions.com
http://www.trcsolutions.com

A provider of engineering, financial, risk management and construction services to large industrial and government customers throughout the United States, TRC provides customer focused solutions in three primary markets: environmental,energy and infrastructure. Environmental services include project development, resolving legacy environmental issues, ensuring compliance for continuing operations, and identifing and mitigating future environmental risks.

Christopher P Vincze, Chairman/CEO
Richard H. Grogan, Chairman of Talisman Managem

5105 TRC Environmental Corporation-Indianapolis
1301 Corporate Center Drive 651-686-0700
Suite 177 Fax: 651-686-4434
Eagan, MN 55121 E-mail: cobrien@trcsolutions.com
http://www.trcsolutions.com

A provider of engineering, financial, risk management and construction services to large industrial and government customers throughout the United States, TRC provides customer focused solutions in three primary markets: environmental,energy and infrastructure. Environmental services include project development, resolving legacy environmental issues, ensuring compliance for continuing operations, and identifing and mitigating future environmental risks.

Christopher P Vincze, Chairman/CEO
Richard H. Grogan, Chairman of Talisman Managem

5106 TRC Environmental Corporation-Irvine
123 Technology Drive 949-727-9336
Irvine, CA 92618 Fax: 949-727-7399
E-mail: dzarider@trcsolutions.com
http://www.trcsolutions.com

A provider of engineering, financial, risk management and construction services to large industrial and government customers throughout the United States, TRC provides customer focused solutions in three primary markets: environmental,energy and infrastructure. Environmental services include project development, resolving legacy environmental issues, ensuring compliance for continuing operations, and identifing and mitigating future environmental risks.

Christopher P Vincze, Chairman/CEO
Richard H. Grogan, Chairman of Talisman Managem

5107 TRC Environmental Corporation-Jackson
1540 Eisenhower Place 734-971-7080
Ann Arbor, MI 48108 Fax: 734-971-9022
E-mail: cobrien@trcsolutions.com
http://www.trcsolutions.com

A provider of engineering, financial, risk management and construction services to large industrial and government customers throughout the United States, TRC provides customer focused solutions in three primary markets: environmental,energy and infrastructure. Environmental services include project development, resolving legacy environmental issues, ensuring compliance for continuing operations, and identifing and mitigating future environmental risks.

Christopher P Vincze, Chairman/CEO
Richard H. Grogan, Chairman of Talisman Managem

5108 TRC Environmental Corporation-Kansas City
Livestock Exchange Building 816-474-1500
1600 Genessee Street, Suite 416 Fax: 816-474-1853
Kansas City, MO 64102 E-mail: cobrien@trcsolutions.com
http://www.trcsolutions.com

A provider of engineering, financial, risk management and construction services to large industrial and government customers throughout the United States, TRC provides customer focused solutions in three primary markets: environmental,energy and infrastructure. Environmental services include project development, resolving legacy environmental issues, ensuring compliance for continuing operations, and identifing and mitigating future environmental risks.

Christopher P Vincze, Chairman/CEO
Richard H. Grogan, Chairman of Talisman Managem

5109 TRC Environmental Corporation-Lexington
670 Morrison Road 614-655-5360
Suite 220 Fax: 614-866-4359
Guhanna, OH 43230 E-mail: cobrien@trcsolutions.com
http://www.trcsolutions.com

A provider of engineering, financial, risk management and construction services to large industrial and government customers throughout the United States, TRC provides customer focused solutions in three primary markets: environmental,energy and infrastructure. Environmental services include project development, resolving legacy environmental issues, ensuring compliance for continuing operations, and identifing and mitigating future environmental risks.

Christopher P Vincze, Chairman/CEO
Richard H. Grogan, Chairman of Talisman Managem

5110 TRC Environmental Corporation-Littleton
19 Old Town Square 970-419-4364
Suite 238 Fax: 303-792-0122
Fort Collins, CO 80524 E-mail: cobrien@trcsolutions.com
http://www.trcsolutions.com

A provider of engineering, financial, risk management and construction services to large industrial and government customers throughout the United States, TRC provides customer focused solutions in three primary markets: environmental,energy and infrastructure. Environmental services include project development, resolving legacy environmental issues, ensuring compliance for continuing operations, and identifing and mitigating future environmental risks.

Christopher P Vincze, Chairman/CEO
Richard H. Grogan, Chairman of Talisman Managem

5111 TRC Environmental Corporation-Lowell
650 Suffolk Street 978-970-5600
Lowell, MA 01854 Fax: 978-453-1995
E-mail: gharkness@trcsolutions.com
http://www.trcsolutions.com

A provider of engineering, financial, risk management and construction services to large industrial and government customers throughout the United States, TRC provides customer focused solutions in three primary markets: environmental,energy and infrastructure. Environmental services include project development, resolving legacy environmental issues, ensuring compliance for continuing operations, and identifing and mitigating future environmental risks.

Christopher P Vincze, Chairman/CEO
Richard H. Grogan, Chairman of Talisman Managem

5112 TRC Environmental Corporation-Phoenix
650 Suffolk Street 978-970-5600
Lowell, MA 01854 Fax: 978-453-1995
E-mail: gharkness@trcsolutions.com
http://www.trcsolutions.com

A provider of engineering, financial, risk management and construction services to large industrial and government customers throughout the United States, TRC provides customer focused solutions in three primary markets: environmental,energy and infrastructure. Environmental services include project development, resolving legacy environmental issues, ensuring compliance for continuing operations, and identifing and mitigating future environmental risks.

Christopher P Vincze, Chairman/CEO
Richard H. Grogan, Chairman of Talisman Managem

5113 TRC Environmental Corporation-Princeton
Research Park 609-497-1379
322 Wall Street Fax: 609-497-1879
Princeton, NJ 08540 E-mail: cobrien@trcsolutions.com
http://www.trcsolutions.com

A provider of engineering, financial, risk management and construction services to large industrial and government customers throughout the United States, TRC provides customer focused solutions in three primary markets: environmental,energy and infrastructure. Environmental services include project development, resolving legacy environmental issues, ensuring compliance for continuing operations, and identifing and mitigating future environmental risks.

Christopher P Vincze, Chairman/CEO
Richard H. Grogan, Chairman of Talisman Managem

5114 TRC Environmental Corporation-San Francisco
101 2nd St #300 415-644-3000
San Francisco, CA 94105 Fax: 415-541-9378
E-mail: cobrien@trcsolutions.com
http://www.trcsolutions.com

A provider of engineering, financial, risk management and construction services to large industrial and government customers throughout the United States, TRC provides customer focused solutions in three primary markets: environmental,energy and infrastructure. Environmental services include project development, resolving legacy environmental issues, ensuring compliance for continuing operations, and identifing and mitigating future environmental risks.

Christopher P Vincze, Chairman/CEO
Richard H. Grogan, Chairman of Talisman Managem

5115 TRC Environmental Corporation-West Palm Beach
1665 Palm Beach Lakes Boulevard 561-681-3494
Suite 720 Fax: 561-681-3496
West Palm Beach, FL 33401 E-mail: cobrien@trcsolutions.com
http://www.trcsolutions.com

A provider of engineering, financial, risk management and construction services to large industrial and government customers throughout the United States, TRC provides customer focused solutions in three primary markets: environmental,energy and infrastructure. Environmental services include project development, resolving legacy environmental issues, ensuring compliance for continuing operations, and identifing and mitigating future environmental risks.

Christopher P Vincze, Chairman/CEO
Richard H. Grogan, Chairman of Talisman Managem

5116 TRC Environmental Corporation-Windsor
21 Griffin Road North 860-298-9692
Windsor, CT 06095 Fax: 860-298-6399
E-mail: czoephel@trcsolutions.com
http://www.trcsolutions.com

A provider of engineering, financial, risk management and construction services to large industrial and government customers throughout the United States, TRC provides customer focused solutions in three primary markets: environmental,energy and infrastructure. Environmental services include project development, resolving legacy environmental issues, ensuring compliance for continuing operations, and identifing and mitigating future environmental risks.

Christopher P Vincze, Chairman/CEO
Richard H. Grogan, Chairman of Talisman Managem

5117 TRC Garrow Associates
3772 Pleasantdale Road 770-270-1192
Suite 200 Fax: 770-270-1392
Atlanta, GA 30340 E-mail: bgarrow@trcgarrow.com
http://www.trcgarrow.com

TRC Garrow Associates provides business consulting services focusing on environmental analysis, planning and development.
Barbara Garrow, President

5118 Talos Technology Consulting
3336 Fern Hollow Place 703-715-3500
Suite 100 Fax: 703-715-0109
Herndon, VA 20171 E-mail: information@talos.com
http://www.talos.com

An environmental computer company, Talos works with businesses and government organizations to help them capitalize upon emerging technologies and achieve their organizational objectives. Talos professionals perform strategic planning;requirements analysis; design documentation; software trade surveying; system security planning; cost-benefit analysis; and surveys of technology markets.
Scott Little, Strategic Development
Rob Smith, Chief Technology Officer

5119 Taylor Engineering
10151 Deerwood Park Blvd. 904-731-7040
Bldg. 300, Suite 300 Fax: 904-731-9847
Jacksonville, FL 32256 E-mail: marketing@taylorengineering.com
http://www.taylorengineering.com

Services in coastal engineering consulting, dredging and dredged material management, hydrology and hydraulics, environmental services, and construction support services.

Terrence Hall P.E., President

5120 Tellus Institute
11 Arlington Street 617-266-5400
Boston, MA 02116-3411 Fax: 617-266-8303
E-mail: info@tellus.org
http://www.tellus.org

Environmental research and strategic development firm. Services include: analyzing energy systems and environmental impacts; evaluating policies for transition to efficient and renewable energy technology; formulating strategies formitigating and adapting to climate change; evaluating long-term solutions that balance competing freshwater needs for basic services; and developing methods to support comprehensive river basin assessment.
Paul D Raskin PhD, President
David McAnulty, Administrative Director

5121 TestAmerica-Austin
14050 Summit Drive 512-244-0855
Suite A100 Fax: 512-244-0160
Austin, TX 78728 E-mail: webmaster@testamericainc.com
http://www.testamericainc.com

Environmental engineering research and consulting firm. Testing capabilities include chemical, physical and biological analyses of a variety of matrices, including aqueous, solid, drinking water, waste, tissue, air and saline/estuarinesamples. Specialty capabilities include air toxics testing, mixed waste testing, tissue preparation and analysis, aquatic toxicology, dioxin/furan testing and microscopy.
James E. Hyman, President/CEO
James Miller, VP National Accounts & Progr

5122 TestAmerica-Buffalo
25 Kraft Ave. 518-438-8140
Albany, NY 12205 Fax: 518-438-8150
E-mail: webmaster@testamericainc.com
http://www.testamericainc.com

Environmental engineering research and consulting firm. Testing capabilities include chemical, physical and biological analyses of a variety of matrices, including aqueous, solid, drinking water, waste, tissue, air and saline/estuarinesamples. Specialty capabilities include air toxics testing, mixed waste testing, tissue preparation and analysis, aquatic toxicology, dioxin/furan testing and microscopy.
James E. Hyman, President/CEO
James Miller, VP National Accounts & Progr

5123 TestAmerica-Burlington
30 Community Drive 802-660-1990
Suite 11 Fax: 802-660-1919
South Burlington, VT 05403 E-mail: webmaster@testamericainc.com
http://www.testamericainc.com

Environmental engineering research and consulting firm. Testing capabilities include chemical, physical and biological analyses of a variety of matrices, including aqueous, solid, drinking water, waste, tissue, air and saline/estuarinesamples. Specialty capabilities include air toxics testing, mixed waste testing, tissue preparation and analysis, aquatic toxicology, dioxin/furan testing and microscopy.
James E. Hyman, President/CEO
James Miller, VP National Accounts & Progr

5124 TestAmerica-Chicago
2417 Bond Street 708-534-5200
University Park, IL 60484 Fax: 708-534-5211
E-mail: webmaster@testamericainc.com
http://www.testamericainc.com

Environmental engineering research and consulting firm. Testing capabilities include chemical, physical and biological analyses of a variety of matrices, including aqueous, solid, drinking water, waste, tissue, air and saline/estuarinesamples. Specialty capabilities include air toxics testing, mixed waste testing, tissue preparation and analysis, aquatic toxicology, dioxin/furan testing and microscopy.
James E. Hyman, President/CEO
James Miller, VP National Accounts & Progr

5125 TestAmerica-Connecticut
19 Old Kings Highway South 203-244-1142
Suite 100 Fax: 203-929-8142
Darien, CT 06820 E-mail: webmaster@testamericainc.com
http://www.testamericainc.com

Environmental engineering research and consulting firm. Testing capabilities include chemical, physical and biological analyses of a variety of matrices, including aqueous, solid, drinking water, waste, tissue, air and saline/estuarinesamples. Specialty capabilities include air toxics testing, mixed waste testing, tissue preparation and analysis, aquatic toxicology, dioxin/furan testing and microscopy.
James E. Hyman, President/CEO
James Miller, VP National Accounts & Progr

5126 TestAmerica-Corpus Christi
1733 N Padre Island Drive 361-289-2673
Corpus Christi, TX 78408 Fax: 361-289-2471
E-mail: webmaster@testamericainc.com
http://www.testamericainc.com
Environmental engineering research and consulting firm. Testing capabilities include chemical, physical and biological analyses of a variety of matrices, including aqueous, solid, drinking water, waste, tissue, air and saline/estuarinesamples. Specialty capabilities include air toxics testing, mixed waste testing, tissue preparation and analysis, aquatic toxicology, dioxin/furan testing and microscopy.
James E. Hyman, President/CEO
James Miller, VP National Accounts & Progr

5127 TestAmerica-Denver
4955 Yarrow Street 303-736-0100
Arvada, CO 80002 Fax: 303-431-7171
E-mail: webmaster@testamericainc.com
http://www.testamericainc.com
Environmental engineering research and consulting firm. Testing capabilities include chemical, physical and biological analyses of a variety of matrices, including aqueous, solid, drinking water, waste, tissue, air and saline/estuarinesamples. Specialty capabilities include air toxics testing, mixed waste testing, tissue preparation and analysis, aquatic toxicology, dioxin/furan testing and microscopy.
James E. Hyman, President/CEO
James Miller, VP National Accounts & Progr

5128 TestAmerica-Edison
3000 Lincoln Drive East 856-334-1030
Suite A Fax: 732-549-3679
Marlton, NJ 08053 E-mail: webmaster@testamericainc.com
http://www.testamericainc.com
Environmental engineering research and consulting firm. Testing capabilities include chemical, physical and biological analyses of a variety of matrices, including aqueous, solid, drinking water, waste, tissue, air and saline/estuarinesamples. Specialty capabilities include air toxics testing, mixed waste testing, tissue preparation and analysis, aquatic toxicology, dioxin/furan testing and microscopy.
James E. Hyman, President/CEO
James Miller, VP National Accounts & Progr

5129 TestAmerica-Houston
6310 Rothway Street 713-690-4444
Houston, TX 77040 Fax: 713-690-5646
E-mail: webmaster@testamericainc.com
http://www.testamericainc.com
Environmental engineering research and consulting firm. Testing capabilities include chemical, physical and biological analyses of a variety of matrices, including aqueous, solid, drinking water, waste, tissue, air and saline/estuarinesamples. Specialty capabilities include air toxics testing, mixed waste testing, tissue preparation and analysis, aquatic toxicology, dioxin/furan testing and microscopy.
James E. Hyman, President/CEO
James Miller, VP National Accounts & Progr

5130 TestAmerica-Knoxville
2960 Foster Creighton Drive 615-726-0177
Nashville, TN 37204 Fax: 615-726-3404
E-mail: webmaster@testamericainc.com
http://www.testamericainc.com
Environmental engineering research and consulting firm. Testing capabilities include chemical, physical and biological analyses of a variety of matrices, including aqueous, solid, drinking water, waste, tissue, air and saline/estuarinesamples. Specialty capabilities include air toxics testing, mixed waste testing, tissue preparation and analysis, aquatic toxicology, dioxin/furan testing and microscopy.
James E. Hyman, President/CEO
James Miller, VP National Accounts & Progr

5131 TestAmerica-Los Angeles
17461 Derian Ave. 949-261-1022
Suite 100 Fax: 949-260-3299
Irvine, CA 92614 E-mail: webmaster@testamericainc.com
http://www.testamericainc.com
Environmental engineering research and consulting firm. Testing capabilities include chemical, physical and biological analyses of a variety of matrices, including aqueous, solid, drinking water, waste, tissue, air and saline/estuarinesamples. Specialty capabilities include air toxics testing, mixed waste testing, tissue preparation and analysis, aquatic toxicology, dioxin/furan testing and microscopy.
James E. Hyman, President/CEO
James Miller, VP National Accounts & Progr

5132 TestAmerica-Mobile
1870 W. Prince Road 520-807-3801
Suite 59 Fax: 251-666-6696
Tucson, AZ 85705 E-mail: webmaster@testamericainc.com
http://www.testamericainc.com
Environmental engineering research and consulting firm. Testing capabilities include chemical, physical and biological analyses of a variety of matrices, including aqueous, solid, drinking water, waste, tissue, air and saline/estuarinesamples. Specialty capabilities include air toxics testing, mixed waste testing, tissue preparation and analysis, aquatic toxicology, dioxin/furan testing and microscopy.
James E. Hyman, President/CEO
James Miller, VP National Accounts & Progr

5133 TestAmerica-New Orleans
6113 Benefit Dr 225-755-8200
Baton Rouge, LA 70809 Fax: 225-755-3080
E-mail: webmaster@testamericainc.com
http://www.testamericainc.com
Environmental engineering research and consulting firm. Testing capabilities include chemical, physical and biological analyses of a variety of matrices, including aqueous, solid, drinking water, waste, tissue, air and saline/estuarinesamples. Specialty capabilities include air toxics testing, mixed waste testing, tissue preparation and analysis, aquatic toxicology, dioxin/furan testing and microscopy.
James E. Hyman, President/CEO
James Miller, VP National Accounts & Progr

5134 TestAmerica-North Canton
4738 Gateway Circle 937-294-6856
Dayton, OH 45440 800-572-9839
Fax: 937-499-1249
E-mail: webmaster@testamericainc.com
http://www.testamericainc.com
Environmental engineering research and consulting firm. Testing capabilities include chemical, physical and biological analyses of a variety of matrices, including aqueous, solid, drinking water, waste, tissue, air and saline/estuarinesamples. Specialty capabilities include air toxics testing, mixed waste testing, tissue preparation and analysis, aquatic toxicology, dioxin/furan testing and microscopy.
James E. Hyman, President/CEO
James Miller, VP National Accounts & Progr

5135 TestAmerica-Orlando
8010 Sunport Drive 407-851-2560
Suite 116 800-851-2560
Orlando, FL 32809 Fax: 407-856-0886
E-mail: webmaster@testamericainc.com
http://www.testamericainc.com
Environmental engineering research and consulting firm. Testing capabilities include chemical, physical and biological analyses of a variety of matrices, including aqueous, solid, drinking water, waste, tissue, air and saline/estuarinesamples. Specialty capabilities include air toxics testing, mixed waste testing, tissue preparation and analysis, aquatic toxicology, dioxin/furan testing and microscopy.
James E. Hyman, President/CEO
James Miller, VP National Accounts & Progr

5136 **TestAmerica-Pensacola**
6301 NW 5th Way 954-809-5580
Suite 2850 Fax: 954-776-8485
Ft. Lauderdale, FL 33309 E-mail: webmaster@testamericainc.com
http://www.testamericainc.com
Environmental engineering research and consulting firm. Testing capabilities include chemical, physical and biological analyses of a variety of matrices, including aqueous, solid, drinking water, waste, tissue, air and saline/estuarinesamples. Specialty capabilities include air toxics testing, mixed waste testing, tissue preparation and analysis, aquatic toxicology, dioxin/furan testing and microscopy.
James E. Hyman, President/CEO
James Miller, VP National Accounts & Progr

5137 **TestAmerica-Phoenix / Aerotech Environmental Laboratories**
4645 East Cotton Center Blvd 602-437-3340
Building 3, Suite 189 866-772-5227
Phoenix, AZ 85040 Fax: 602-454-9303
E-mail: webmaster@testamericainc.com
http://www.testamericainc.com
Environmental engineering research and consulting firm. Testing capabilities include chemical, physical and biological analyses of a variety of matrices, including aqueous, solid, drinking water, waste, tissue, air and saline/estuarinesamples. Specialty capabilities include air toxics testing, mixed waste testing, tissue preparation and analysis, aquatic toxicology, dioxin/furan testing and microscopy.
James E. Hyman, President/CEO
James Miller, VP National Accounts & Progr

5138 **TestAmerica-Pittsburgh**
301 Alpha Drive 412-963-7058
RIDC Park Fax: 412-963-2468
Pittsburgh, PA 15238 E-mail: webmaster@testamericainc.com
http://www.testamericainc.com
Environmental engineering research and consulting firm. Testing capabilities include chemical, physical and biological analyses of a variety of matrices, including aqueous, solid, drinking water, waste, tissue, air and saline/estuarinesamples. Specialty capabilities include air toxics testing, mixed waste testing, tissue preparation and analysis, aquatic toxicology, dioxin/furan testing and microscopy.
James E. Hyman, President/CEO
James Miller, VP National Accounts & Progr

5139 **TestAmerica-Richland**
2800 George Washington Way 509-375-3131
Richland, WA 99354 Fax: 509-375-5590
E-mail: webmaster@testamericainc.com
http://www.testamericainc.com
Environmental engineering research and consulting firm. Testing capabilities include chemical, physical and biological analyses of a variety of matrices, including aqueous, solid, drinking water, waste, tissue, air and saline/estuarinesamples. Specialty capabilities include air toxics testing, mixed waste testing, tissue preparation and analysis, aquatic toxicology, dioxin/furan testing and microscopy.
James E. Hyman, President/CEO
James Miller, VP National Accounts & Progr

5140 **TestAmerica-San Francisco**
1220 Quarry Lane 925-484-1919
Pleasanton, CA 94566 Fax: 925-600-3002
E-mail: webmaster@testamericainc.com
http://www.testamericainc.com
Environmental engineering research and consulting firm. Testing capabilities include chemical, physical and biological analyses of a variety of matrices, including aqueous, solid, drinking water, waste, tissue, air and saline/estuarinesamples. Specialty capabilities include air toxics testing, mixed waste testing, tissue preparation and analysis, aquatic toxicology, dioxin/furan testing and microscopy.
James E. Hyman, President/CEO
James Miller, VP National Accounts & Progr

5141 **TestAmerica-Savannah**
5102 LaRoche Avenue 912-354-7858
Savannah, GA 31404 Fax: 912-352-0165
E-mail: webmaster@testamericainc.com
http://www.testamericainc.com
Environmental engineering research and consulting firm. Testing capabilities include chemical, physical and biological analyses of a variety of matrices, including aqueous, solid, drinking water, waste, tissue, air and saline/estuarinesamples. Specialty capabilities include air toxics testing, mixed waste testing, tissue preparation and analysis, aquatic toxicology, dioxin/furan testing and microscopy.
James E. Hyman, President/CEO
James Miller, VP National Accounts & Progr

5142 **TestAmerica-St Louis**
13715 Rider Trail North 314-298-8566
Earth City, MO 63045 Fax: 314-298-8757
E-mail: webmaster@testamericainc.com
http://www.testamericainc.com
Environmental engineering research and consulting firm. Testing capabilities include chemical, physical and biological analyses of a variety of matrices, including aqueous, solid, drinking water, waste, tissue, air and saline/estuarinesamples. Specialty capabilities include air toxics testing, mixed waste testing, tissue preparation and analysis, aquatic toxicology, dioxin/furan testing and microscopy.
James E. Hyman, President/CEO
James Miller, VP National Accounts & Progr

5143 **TestAmerica-Tacoma**
5755 8th Street E 253-922-2310
Tacoma, WA 98424 Fax: 253-922-5047
E-mail: webmaster@testamericainc.com
http://www.testamericainc.com
Environmental engineering research and consulting firm. Testing capabilities include chemical, physical and biological analyses of a variety of matrices, including aqueous, solid, drinking water, waste, tissue, air and saline/estuarinesamples. Specialty capabilities include air toxics testing, mixed waste testing, tissue preparation and analysis, aquatic toxicology, dioxin/furan testing and microscopy.
James E. Hyman, President/CEO
James Miller, VP National Accounts & Progr

5144 **TestAmerica-Tallahassee**
2846 Industrial Plaza Drive 850-878-3994
Suite 100 Fax: 850-878-9504
Tallahassee, FL 32301 E-mail: webmaster@testamericainc.com
http://www.testamericainc.com
Environmental engineering research and consulting firm. Testing capabilities include chemical, physical and biological analyses of a variety of matrices, including aqueous, solid, drinking water, waste, tissue, air and saline/estuarinesamples. Specialty capabilities include air toxics testing, mixed waste testing, tissue preparation and analysis, aquatic toxicology, dioxin/furan testing and microscopy.
James E. Hyman, President/CEO
James Miller, VP National Accounts & Progr

5145 **TestAmerica-Tampa**
6712 Benjamin Road 813-885-7427
Suite 100 Fax: 813-885-7049
Tampa, FL 33634 E-mail: webmaster@testamericainc.com
http://www.testamericainc.com
Environmental engineering research and consulting firm. Testing capabilities include chemical, physical and biological analyses of a variety of matrices, including aqueous, solid, drinking water, waste, tissue, air and saline/estuarinesamples. Specialty capabilities include air toxics testing, mixed waste testing, tissue preparation and analysis, aquatic toxicology, dioxin/furan testing and microscopy.
James E. Hyman, President/CEO
James Miller, VP National Accounts & Progr

5146 TestAmerica-Valparaiso
2400 Cumberland Drive 219-464-2389
Valparaiso, IN 46383 800-688-6522
Fax: 219-462-2953
E-mail: webmaster@testamericainc.com
http://www.testamericainc.com
Environmental engineering research and consulting firm. Testing capabilities include chemical, physical and biological analyses of a variety of matrices, including aqueous, solid, drinking water, waste, tissue, air and saline/estuarinesamples. Specialty capabilities include air toxics testing, mixed waste testing, tissue preparation and analysis, aquatic toxicology, dioxin/furan testing and microscopy.
James E. Hyman, President/CEO
James Miller, VP National Accounts & Progr

5147 TestAmerica-West Sacramento
880 Riverside Parkway 916-373-5600
West Sacramento, CA 95605 Fax: 916-372-1059
E-mail: webmaster@testamericainc.com
http://www.testamericainc.com
Environmental engineering research and consulting firm. Testing capabilities include chemical, physical and biological analyses of a variety of matrices, including aqueous, solid, drinking water, waste, tissue, air and saline/estuarinesamples. Specialty capabilities include air toxics testing, mixed waste testing, tissue preparation and analysis, aquatic toxicology, dioxin/furan testing and microscopy.
James E. Hyman, President/CEO
James Miller, VP National Accounts & Progr

5148 TestAmerica-Westfield
53 Southampton Road 413-572-4000
Westfield, MA 01085 Fax: 413-572-3707
E-mail: webmaster@testamericainc.com
http://www.testamericainc.com
Environmental engineering research and consulting firm. Testing capabilities include chemical, physical and biological analyses of a variety of matrices, including aqueous, solid, drinking water, waste, tissue, air and saline/estuarinesamples. Specialty capabilities include air toxics testing, mixed waste testing, tissue preparation and analysis, aquatic toxicology, dioxin/furan testing and microscopy.
James E. Hyman, President/CEO
James Miller, VP National Accounts & Progr

5149 Testing & Inspection Services, Inc.
Thornton Laboratories
1145 E Cass Street 813-223-9702
PO Box 2880 Fax: 813-223-9332
Tampa, FL 33602 E-mail: steve.fickett@thorntonlab.com
http://www.thorntonlab.com
Environmental & fertilizer sampling and testing laboratory and general analytical testing lab.
Stephen B. Fickett, President
Hugh B. Rodriques, COO/VP lab Operations

5150 Testing Engineers & Consultants (TEC) - AnnArbor
3985 Varsity Drive 734-971-0030
Ann Arbor, MI 48108 Fax: 734-971-3721
E-mail: tec@tectest.com
http://www.tectest.com
TEC specializes in environmental and geotechnical engineering, materials testing, roof systems management, facility asset management, and indoor air quality. Environmental services include: baseline assessments; contaminationassessments; expert testimony; feasibility studies; hazardous materials surveys; and hyrogeological/groundwater investigations.
John Banicki, Founder/Chairman
Katherine Banicki, President

5151 Testing Engineers & Consultants (TEC) - Detroit
601 W Fort Street 313-837-8464
Suite 440 800-835-2654
Detroit, MI 48226 Fax: 313-837-1305
E-mail: tec@tectest.com
http://www.tectest.com
TEC specializes in environmental and geotechnical engineering, materials testing, roof systems management, facility asset management, and indoor air quality. Environmental services include: baseline assessments; contaminationassessments; expert testimony; feasibility studies; hazardous materials surveys; and hyrogeological/groundwater investigations.
John Banicki, Founder/Chairman
Katherine Banicki, President

5152 Testing Engineers & Consultants (TEC) - Troy
1343 Rochester Road 248-588-6200
Troy, MI 48083 Fax: 248-588-6232
E-mail: tec@tectest.com
http://www.tectest.com
TEC specializes in environmental and geotechnical engineering, materials testing, roof systems management, facility asset management, and indoor air quality. Environmental services include: baseline assessments; contaminationassessments; expert testimony; feasibility studies; hazardous materials surveys; and hyrogeological/groundwater investigations.
John Banicki, Founder/Chairman
Katherine Banicki, President

5153 Tetra Tech - Christiana DE
240 Continental Drive 302-738-7551
Suite 200 800-462-0910
Newark, DE 19713 Fax: 302-454-5980
http://www.tetratech.com
Tetra Tech is a provider of specialized management consulting and technical services in resource management, infrastructure and communication. The company's clients include a diverse base of public and private sector organizationsserviced through more than 330 offices located in the US and internationally. Tetra Tech's services include research and development, applied science and technology, engineering design, program management, construction management, and operations andmaintenance.
Dan L. Batrack, Chairman/CEO
Steven M. Burdick, Executive VP

5154 Tetra Tech - Pasadena CA/Corporate
3475 E Foothill Boulevard 626-351-4664
3rd Floor Fax: 626-351-5291
Pasadena, CA 91107 http://www.tetratech.com
Tetra Tech is a provider of specialized management consulting and technical services in resource management, infrastructure and communication. The company's clients include a diverse base of public and private sector organizationsserviced through more than 200 offices located in the US and internationally. Tetra Tech's services include research and development, applied science and technology, engineering design, program management, construction management, and operations andmaintenance.
Sam W Box, President
Dan L Batrack, CEO/COO

5155 Thermo Fisher Scientific
81 Wyman Street 781-622-1000
Waltham, MA 02454 800-678-5599
Fax: 781-622-1207
E-mail: lori.gorski@thermo.com
http://www.thermofisher.com
Provides a wide range of products, services and solutions for research, analysis, discovery and diagnostics using advanced technologies ranging from mass spectrometry and elemental analysis to chromatography, molecular spectroscopy,and microanalysis.

Additional services includes automated systems and technologies from standalone robots to complete liquid handling systems.

Marc N. Casper, President/CEO
Lori Gorski, Media Relations

5156 ThermoEnergy Corporation
10 New Bond Street 508-854-1628
Worcester, MA 01606 Fax: 508-854-1753
E-mail: technology@thermoenergy.com
http://www.thermoenergy.com

ThermoEnergy Corporation is an integrated technologies company seeking to develop and commercialize patented water treatment and clean energy technologies. Products and services solutions include removing nitrogen from wastewaterstreams, converting sewage sludge to a renewable high-energy fuel, and enabling the conversion of coal and other hydrocarbon fuels into energy with zero air emissions.
James F. Wood, Chairman/President/CEO
Gregory M. Landegger, VP/COO/CFO

5157 Thermotron Industries
291 Kollen Park Drive 616-393-4580
Holland, MI 49423 Fax: 616-392-5643
E-mail: info@thermotron.com
http://www.thermotron.com

Manufacturers and suppliers of environmental testing, test system integration, screening, simulation equipment, and vibration equipment for transportation and screening test requirements. Additional services includes integrated testingsolutions with Research & Development and Total Quality Control to help insure product reliability and performance.
Mark Lamers, Technical Manager
Kevin Ewing, Marketing/Sales Manager

5158 Thompson Engineering
2970 Cottage Hill Road 251-666-2443
Suite 190 Fax: 251-666-6422
Mobile, AL 36606 E-mail: info@thompsonengineering.com
http://www.thompsonengineering.com

A multi disciplined engineering design, environmental consulting, construction management, construction inspection and materials testing firm. The Environmental Division is comprised of a diverse team of professionals with significantknowledge and experience in environmental compliance and permitting, audits and assessments, engineering design, and monitoring and supervision of remedial activities.

Henry R. Seawell III, Chairman
John H. Baker III, President

5159 Tighe & Bond
4 Barlows Landing Road 508-564-7285
Unit 15 Fax: 413-562-5317
Pocasset, MA 02559 E-mail: info@tighebond.com
http://www.tighebond.com

Tighe & Bond provides engineering and consulting services to a wide variety of clients, from some of the largest municipalities in the country to small, privately-held businesses. Areas of expertise includes water supply, wastewatermanagement, buildings, roadways, environmental permitting, remediation, health and safety training.
David E. Pinsky, President
Jeffrey P Bibeau, Environmental Manager

5160 Timber Products Inspection - Conyers
1641 Sigman Road 770-922-8000
Conyers, GA 30012 Fax: 770-922-1290
E-mail: info@tpinspection.com
http://www.tpinspection.com

Timber Products Inspection, Inc. (TP) is an independent inspection, testing and consulting company with expertise in all phases of the wood products industry. TP provides quality auditing services in the areas of sawmilling, drying,component fabrication as well as value added processes such as pressure treating and gluing.
Jay Moore, Executive VP
David Conner, VP of Eastern Operations

5161 Timber Products Inspection - Vancouver
105 SE 124th Avenue 360-449-3138
Vancouver, WA 98684 Fax: 360-449-3953
E-mail: info@tpinspection.com
http://www.tpinspection.com

Timber Products Inspection, Inc. (TP) is an independent inspection, testing and consulting company with expertise in all phases of the wood products industry. TP provides quality auditing services in the areas of sawmilling, drying,component fabrication as well as value added processes such as pressure treating and gluing.

Jay Moore, Executive VP
David Conner, VP of Eastern Operations

5162 Tox Scan
42 Hangar Way 831-724-4522
Watsonville, CA 95076 Fax: 831-761-5449
E-mail: dlewis@toxscan.com
http://www.toxscan.com

Environmental bioassay and bioacoumulation testing.

David B. Lewis, Director

5163 Transviron
1624 York Road 410-321-6961
Lutherville, MD 21093 Fax: 410-949-9321
E-mail: Transviron@comcast.net
http://www.transviron.com

Civil and environmental engineering firm. Technical consulting services includes: water supply and distribution; storm water management; highways and bridges; hazardous waste management; water and wastewater treatment plant operationsand construction management; wastewater collection and treatment.
Charles S. Bao, President
Michelle Ireland, Marketing Coordinator

5164 Tri-State Laboratories
2870 Salt Springs Road 330-797-8844
Youngstown, OH 44509 800-523-0347
Fax: 330-797-3264
E-mail: trislabs@aol.com
http://www.tristatelabs.net

Environmental testing laboratory services of which include: asbestos testing; field services; forensic analysis and court testimony; hazardous waste analysis; inorganics/wet chemistry, metals, and organic analysis.

A Bari Lateef PhD, CEO
Wendy Hanna, COO

5165 Turner Laboratories
2445 North Coyote Drive 520-882-5880
Suite 104 Fax: 520-882-9788
Tucson, AZ 85745 E-mail: sales@turnerlabs.com
http://www.turnerlabs.com

Turner Laboratories is an advanced, full-service environmental testing laboratory specializing in providing a wide range of analytical services including: inorganic, organic, wet chemistry and microbiological testing on soils/solids,drinking water, wastewater and groundwater.

Nancy D Turner, President
Michael McGovern, Executive VP

5166 URS
600 Montgomery Street 415-774-2700
26th Floor 888-877-7752
San Francisco, CA 94111-2728 Fax: 415-398-1905
E-mail: media_contact@urs.com
http://www.urscorp.com

An environmental analysis and comprehensive engineering service firm, URS provides a full range of planning, design, program and construction management services to a wide variety of private and public sector clients. URS hasapproximately 30,000 em-

ployees in a network of more than 370 offices and contract-specific job sites in 20 countries.
Martin M Koffel, Chairman/CEO
Thomas W Biship, VP/Strategic Development

5167 US Public Interest Research Group
44 Winter Street 617-747-4370
4th Floor Fax: 617-292-8057
Boston, MA 02108 E-mail: info@uspirg.org
http://www.uspirg.org
US PIRG is an advocate for the public interest. We uncover threats to public health and well-being and fight to end them, using the time-tested tools of investigative research, media exposes, grassroots organizing, advocacy andlitigation.
Douglas H Phelps, President/Chairman
Andre Delattre, Executive Director

5168 US Public Interest Research Group - Washington
218 D Street SE 202-546-9707
1st Floor Fax: 202-546-2461
Washington, DC 20003 E-mail: uspirg@pirg.org
http://www.uspirg.org
US PIRG is an advocate for the public interest. We uncover threats to public health and well-being and fight to end them, using the time-tested tools of investigative research, media exposes, grassroots organizing, advocacy andlitigation.
Douglas H Phelps, President/Chairman
Andre Delattre, Executive Director

5169 USDA Forest Service: Pacific Southwest Research Station
800 Buchanan Street 510-559-6300
West Annex Building Fax: 510-559-6440
Albany, CA 94710-11 E-mail: psw_webmaster@fs.fed.us
http://www.fs.fed.us/psw/
A Governmental Research Organization specializing in research on forest ecosystems, including fire, watersheds, forest genetics and diversity, wildlife, forest diseases, and urban forestry.
Jim Baldwin, Project Manager
Marilyn Hartley, Communications Director

5170 Umpqua Research Company
125 Volunteer Way 541-863-7770
PO Box 609 Fax: 541-863-7775
Myrtle Creek, OR 97457 E-mail: info@urcmail.net
http://www.urc.cc
UMPQUA Research Company (URC), founded in 1973 by David F. Putnam and Gerald V. Colombo, offers technical services in four primary areas: Drinking Water and Environmental Analysis; Air and Water Purification Related EngineeringServices (including NASA Flight Hardware); Research & Development; and Materials Testing. The staff includes chemical, electrical, and mechanical engineers, chemists, physicists, and biological scientists.
William F Michalek PE, President
James R. Akse, VP

5171 United Environmental Services
86 Hillside Drive 570-788-8180
Drums, PA 18222 Fax: 856-227-6578
E-mail: Mamrakv ues@aol.com
http://www.unitedenvironmental.com
An environmental testing and analysis firm providing a full range of construction, remedial and maintenance services at landfills, commercial and industrial sites, including Brownfield re-development projects.
Rod Sterner, VP
Walter Meck, CEO

5172 Universal Environmental Technologies
87 Technology Way 603-883-9312
Nashua, NH 03060 Fax: 603-883-9314
E-mail: info@u-e-t.net
http://www.u-e-t.net
An environmental research firm, Universal Environmental Technologies specializes in the design, fabrication and installation of integrated groundwater and soil remediation systems that are used on retail petroleum sites, industrialmanufacturing sites, EPA Superfund sites and U.S. military bases.
Sharon McMillin, VP/Remedial Services

5173 Upstate Laboratories
6034 Corporate Drive 315-437-0255
East Syracuse, NY 13057 Fax: 315-437-1209
E-mail: AScala@Upstatelabs.com
http://www.enalytic.com
Testing laboratory specializing in environmental and organic/synthetic analysis. Services include certification and air quality (mycology).
Anthony J Scala, President/CEO/Chemist
Corey Niland, Quality Assurance & Control

5174 Vara International: Division of Calgon Corporation
400 Calgon Carbon Drive 412-787-6700
Pittsburgh, PA 15205 800-4CA-BON
Fax: 412-787-6676
E-mail: info@calgoncarbon-us.com
http://www.calgoncarbon.com
An environmental and industrial process research firm, Vara International is a global manufacturer and supplier of granular activated carbon, innovative treatment systems, value added technologies and services for optimizing productionprocesses and safely purifying the environment.
Randall S. Dearth, President/CEO
Robert P. O'Brien, EVP/Chief Operating Officer

5175 Versar
6850 Versar Center 703-750-3000
PO Box 1549 800-283-7727
Springfield, VA 22151 Fax: 703-642-6825
E-mail: info@versar.com
http://www.versar.com
Engineering and environmental research organization. Research results published in project reports, government publications, books, articles, and technical reports.
Amoretta M. Hoeber, President
Anthony L. Otten, CEO

5176 Vista Leak Detection
755 N Mary Avenue 408-830-3300
Sunnyvale, CA 94085 Fax: 408-830-3399
E-mail: info@VistaLD.com
http://www.vistaleakdetection.com
Vista Research provides leak detection products and services to airport, oil industry and military clients for ensuring the integrity of underground/aboveground pipeline and tank systems.
William W Pickett, VP/Operations
Cody Freeman, Contracts Administrator

5177 Volumetric Techniques, Ltd. / VTEQE
317 Bernice Drive 631-472-4848
Bayport, NY 11705 Fax: 631-472-4991
E-mail: vteqe@msn.com
http://http://vteqeltd.com/137.html
Full service environmental engineering organization, VTEQE specializes in all aspects of the environmental services industry, including assessments (ESA Phase 1,2), site engineering, investigations/reports, remediation/cleanupstrategies, Phase 3, and bottled water facility licensing dealing with contaminated water, groundwater, soil, also engineering design, construction management, and full revitalization management.
Sander Sternig, President/CEO/Chairman
Benito San Pedro, Professional Engineer

5178 WERC: Consortium for Environmental Education & Technology Development
New Mexico State University
PO Box 30001 575-646-2038
Las Cruces, NM 88003-8001 800-523-5996
Fax: 505-646-5474
E-mail: iee@nmsu.edu
http://www.ieenmsu.com

A consortium focusing on environmental education and technology development. The consortium's mission is to develop the human resources and technologies needed to address environmental issues. WERC's program aims to achieveenvironmental excellence through education, public outreach and technology development and deployment.
Abbas Ghassemi PhD, Executive Director
Patricia Pines, Administrative Asst.

5179 Waid & Associates - Austin/Corporate
10800 Pecan Park Blvd 512-255-9999
Suite 300 Fax: 512-255-8780
Austin, TX 78750 E-mail: information@waid.com
http://www.waid.com
Waid & Associates is an engineering and environmental services firm that specializes in air quality services, particularly emissions control, permits, and compliance. Additional services include wastewater/waste management andenvironmental information management systems.
Jay R Hoover PE, President/Principal Engineer
Sara A. Hutson, Principal Engineer

5180 Waid & Associates - Houston
2600 South Shore Blvd. 281-333-9990
Suite 300 Fax: 512-255-8780
League City, TX 77573 E-mail: information@waid.com
http://www.waid.com
Waid & Associates is an engineering and environmental services firm that specializes in air quality services, particularly emissions control, permits, and compliance. Additional services include wastewater/waste management andenvironmental information management systems.
Jay R Hoover PE, President/Principal Engineer
Sara A. Hutson, Principal Engineer

5181 Waid & Associates - Permian Basin
24 Smith Road 432-682-9999
Suite 304 Fax: 432-682-7774
Midland, TX 79705 E-mail: information@waid.com
http://www.waid.com
Waid & Associates is an engineering and environmental services firm that specializes in air quality services, particularly emissions control, permits, and compliance. Additional services include wastewater/waste management andenvironmental information management systems.
Jay R Hoover PE, President/Principal Engineer
Sara A. Hutson, Principal Engineer

5182 Waste Water Engineers
210 Coy Court 248-236-9800
Oxford, MI 48371 Fax: 248-236-9870
E-mail: casec@wastewatereng.com
http://www.wastewatereng.com
Environmental science research consultant. Research results published in project reports. Environmental civil engineering consultant.
Thomas H Patton Jr, President

5183 Water and Air Research
6821 SW Archer Road 352-372-1500
Gainesville, FL 32608 800-242-4927
Fax: 352-378-1500
E-mail: lmosura-bliss@waterandair.com
http://www.waterandair.com
Environmental research and consulting firm. Research results published in client reports.
William C Zegel, President
Connie Bieber, Director/Manager

5184 Watkins Environmental Sciences
PO Box 6655 315-446-4763
Syracuse, NY 13217 Fax: 315-446-4764
E-mail: awatkins3@gmail.com
http://www.watkinsenvironmental.com
Environmental assessments, septic system designs, residential water sampling and testing services, home inspections, radon, foundation designs & inspections.
Andrew A Watkins PE, President

5185 Weather Services Corporation
131A Great Road 781-275-8860
Bedford, MA 01730 Fax: 781-271-0178
Michael Leavitt, President

5186 West Coast Analytical Service
9240 Santa Fe Springs Road 562-948-2225
Santa Fe Springs, CA 90670 Fax: 562-948-5850
http://www.wcaslab.com
DJ Northington, PhD, President
Eric Lindsay, General Manager

5187 West Michigan Testing
815 E Ludington Avenue 231-843-3353
Ludington, MI 49431 Fax: 231-843-7676
We provide soil borings, geotechnical services, environmental assessments, construction materials testing and asbestos inspection.
James T Nordlund Jr, Vice President

5188 West More Mechanical Testing and Research
221 Westmoreland Drive 724-537-3131
PO Box 388 Fax: 724-537-3151
Youngstown, PA 15696 E-mail: admin@wmtr.com
http://www.wmtr.com
James Dague, Laboratory Manager

5189 Western Environmental Services
913 N Foster Road 307-234-5511
Casper, WY 82601 800-545-5711
Fax: 307-234-8324
E-mail: aroylance@testair.com
http://www.testair.com
Air emission testing.
James Meador, Founder/Project Manager
Alan Roylance, President

5190 Western Michigan Environmental Services
1007 Lake Drive 616-451-3051
Grand rapids, MI 49505 Fax: 616-451-3054
http://www.wmeac.org
Julie Parks, President
David Rein, VP

5191 Westinghouse Electric Company
1000 Westinghouse Drive 412-244-2000
Suite 572A 888-943-8442
Cranberry Township, PA 16066 Fax: 412-642-4985
http://www.westinghousenuclear.com
Danny Roderick, President/Chief Executive Of
David A. Howell, Sr. VP

5192 Westinghouse Remediation Services
675 Park N Boulevard 404-298-7101
Suite F-100 Fax: 404-296-9752
Clarkston, GA 30021
Environmental remediation firm.

5193 Weston Solutions, Inc
1400 Weston Way 610-701-3000
Box 2653 800-7WE-STON
West Chester, PA 19380 Fax: 610-701-3186
E-mail: info@westonsolutions.com
http://www.westonsolutions.com
Weston is a leading infrastructure redevelopment services firm delivering integrated environmental engineering solutions to industry and government worldwide. With an emphasis on creating lasting economic value for its clients, thecompany provides ser-

vices in site remediation, redevelopment, infrastructure operations and knowledge management.
William L. Robertson, President/Chief Executive Of
Vincent A. Laino, Sr. VP/CFO

5194 Whibco
87 East Commerce Street 856-455-9200
Bridgeton, NJ 08302 Fax: 856-455-9009
http://www.whibco.com
Andrew R Strelczyk, Director Quality Control

5195 Wik Associates
PO Box 230 302-322-2558
New Castle, DE 19720 Fax: 302-322-8921
Environmental testing and analysis firm.

5196 William T Lorenz & Company
3541 Norwegian Hollow Road 608-935-9285
Dodgeville, WI 53533 Fax: 608-935-2010
Environmental and water resources marketing, consulting, and product research firm.

5197 William W Walker Jr
1127 Lowell Road 978-369-8061
Concord, MA 01742-5522 Fax: 978-369-8061
E-mail: wwwalker@wwwalker.net
http://www.wwwalker.net
William W Walker, Jr, Environmental Engineer

5198 Woods End Research Laboratory
290 Belgrade Rd 207-293-2457
PO Box 297 800-451-0337
Mount Vernon, ME 04352 Fax: 207-293-2488
E-mail: info@woodsend.org
http://www.woodsend.org
Compost analysis; bioremediation design; solvita test kits for soil and compost. Quality Seal of Approval Program for Compost Products.
William Brinton, President

5199 World Resources Company
1600 Anderson Road 703-734-9800
Suite 200 Fax: 703-790-7245
Mc Lean, VA 22102 E-mail: corporate@wrcusa.net
http://www.worldresourcescompany.com
World Resources Company (WRC) is a highly specialized environmental risk management company that designs, implements and manages recycling activities and provides environmental services for non-ferrous metal industries nationally andinternationally. This support includes regulatory, environmental, transportation, production, and all other aspects of business inherent to recycling services.
Peter T Halpin, CEO

5200 Yellowstone Environmental Science
65-1116 Hoku'ula Rd. 808-885-4194
PO Box 2709 Fax: 808-885-4114
Kamuela, HI 96743 E-mail: yes@yestech.com
http://www.yestech.com
Mary M Hunter, President
Robert M. Hunter, Director

5201 Yes Technologies
65-1116 Hoku'ula Rd. 808-885-4194
PO Box 2709 Fax: 808-885-4114
Kamuela, HI 96743 E-mail: yes@yestech.com
http://www.yestech.com
Environmental and public health research and development. Patent consulting.
Mary M Hunter, President
Robert M. Hunter, Director

5202 Zimpro Environmental
301 West Military Road 715-359-7211
Rothschild, WI 54474 Fax: 715-355-3219
William Copa, VP Technical Services

5203 Zurn Industries
1801 Pittsburgh Avenue 855-663-9876
Erie, PA 16502 800-997-3876
Fax: 919-775-3541
E-mail: sean.martin@zurn.com
http://www.zurn.com
Environmental systems including air, land, thermal and water; energy systems including steam and heat; mechanical systems.
Sean Martin, VP Marketing & Sales
Michael Boone, General Manager

University Centers

5204 Adirondack Ecological Center
SUNY College of Environmental Science & Forestry
1 Forestry Drive 315-470-6500
Syracuse, NY 13210 Fax: 518-582-2181
E-mail: aechwf@esf.edu
http://www.esf.edu
Provides the organizational framework for research, instructional, and public service activities thoughout the Adriondack region.
Vita DeMarchi, Chair
Matthew J. Marko, Vice Chair

5205 Agricultural Research and Development Center
University of Nebraska
1071 County Road G 402-624-8000
Ithaca, NE 68033 Fax: 402-624-8010
E-mail: ardc@unl.edu
http://ardc.unl.edu
Serves as the primary site for field based reseach with 5,000 acres of row crops and 5,000 domestic farm animals used for teaching and research.
Mark Schroeder, Director
Ruby Urban, Asst. Director

5206 Akron Center for Environmental Studies
University of Akron
215 Crouse Hall 330-972-5389
Akron, OH 44325-4102 Fax: 330-972-7611
E-mail: ids@uakron.edu
http://www.uakron.edu
Richard W. Poque, Chair
Ralph J. Palmisano, Vice Chair

5207 Albrook Hydraulics Laboratory
Washington State University
PO Box 641227 509-335-3564
Pullman, WA 99164 Fax: 509-335-7632
E-mail: rhh@wsu.edu
http://www.wsu.edu
Research laboratory capable of performing projects with physically scaled hydraulic models. 15,000 square feet of floor space, discharge capacity up to 70 cubic feet per second, modern instrumentaion and shop facilities.
Elson S. Floyd, President
Daniel Bernardo, Vice President

5208 Alternative Energy Institute
Texas A&M University 806-656-2296
PO Box 248 WT Fax: 806-656-2733
Canyon, TX 79016 E-mail: aeimail@wtamu.edu
http://www.windenergy.org
Byungik Chang, Director
Ken Starcher, Associate Director

5209 American Petroleum Institute University
1220 L Street NW 202-682-8000
Washington, DC 20005-4070 Fax: 202-682-8232
E-mail: training@api.org
http://www.api-u.org
API, through its university, provides training materials to help those in the oil and natural gas business meet regulatory requirements and industry standards. It works with the National Science Teachers Association and othereducational groups to impart sci-

entific literacy and develop critical thinking skills in the classroom.
Jack N. Gerard, President/CEO

5210 American Society of Primatologists
University of Washington
PO Box 357330 206-543-0440
Seattle, WA 98195 Fax: 206-685-0305
http://www.asp.org
Conducts research on primates.

5211 Applied Energy Research Laboratory
North Carolina State University 919-515-5236
Raleigh, NC 27695 http://www.mae.ncsu.edu/centers/aerl/
Dr. John A Edwards, Director

5212 Aquatic Research Laboratory
Lake Superior State University
650 W Easterday Avenue 906-635-1949
Sault Sainte Marie, MI 49783 888-800-LSSU
Fax: 906-635-2266
Administered through the college of Arts and Sciences.
Prof Alex Litvinov, Director

5213 Architecture Research Laboratory
University of Arizona
College of Architecture 520-621-6751
Tucson, AZ 85721 Fax: 520-621-8700
E-mail: Whampton@ccit.arizona.edu
http://www.architectureresearchlab.com
Provides assistance in the areas of education, applied research and public service.
Alexandra Fenton, Co-Founder
Michael S Bergin, Co-Founder

5214 Biological Reserve
Denison University 740-587-6261
Granville, OH 43023 E-mail: stocker@denison.edu
http://webby.cc.denison.edu/biology/bioreserve/DUBR.shml
Enhances the education of students in Biology and the Environmental Sciences by providing opportunities for field studies.
Dr. John E Fauth, Contact

5215 Caesar Kleberg Wildlife Research Institute
Texas A&M University
700 University Boulevard 361-595-3922
MSC 218 Fax: 361-593-3924
Kingsville, TX 78363 E-mail: ckwri@tamuk.com
http://www.ckwri.tamuk.edu
Facilitates complex wildlife-related research studies. Includes modern high-tech facilities, specially designed wildlife pens, and rangeland tracts.
Rebecca Trant, Administrative Officer
Yolanda Ballard, Office Manager

5216 California Sea Grant College Program
University of California
9500 Gilman Drive 858-534-4440
Deptartment 0232 Fax: 858-534-2231
La Jolla, CA 92093-232 E-mail: jeckman@ucsd.edu
http://www.csgc.ucsd.edu
James E. Eckman, Director
Shauna Oh, Associate Director

5217 Cedar Creek Natural History Area
University of Minnesota
2660 Fawn Lake Drive NE 763-434-5131
Bethel, MN 55005 Fax: 763-434-7361
Twenty-two hundred hectare experimental ecological reserve.

5218 Center for Applied Energy Research
University of Kentucky
2540 Research Park Drive 859-257-0305
Lexington, KY 40511-8479 Fax: 859-257-0220
E-mail: rodney.andrews@uky.edu
http://www.caer.uky.edu
An applied research and development center with an international reputation, focusing on the optimal use of Kentucky's energy resources for the benefit of its people.
Rodney Andrews, Director
Don Challman, Associate Director

5219 Center for Applied Environmental Research
University of Michigan
130 Mumford Hall 810-767-7373
Columbia, MO 65211 Fax: 573-884-2199
E-mail: BarnettC@missouri.edu
http://www.cares.missouri.ed
Chris Barnett, Co-Director
Chris Fulcher, Co-Director

5220 Center for Aquatic Research and Resource Management
Florida State University
319 Stadium Drive 850-644-3700
Tallahassee, FL 32306-4295 Fax: 850-645-8447
E-mail: livingston@bio.fsu.edu
http://www.bio.fsu.edu/carrma.htm
Conducts research designed to answer aquatic resource-management questions posed by government agencies and private concerns. Research is conducted in lakes, rivers, and near-shore coastal systems throughout the southeastern UnitedStates with a multi-disciplinary approach to topics such as light, nutrients, primary productivity, fate and effects of storm water pollutants, sediment-water interactions, community assemblages of fish and invertebrates in various habitats andtrophic dynamics.
Dr. Robert J Livingston, Director

5221 Center for Cave and Karst Studies
Western Kentucky University
1906 College Heights Blvd. #31066 270-745-0111
Bowling Green, KY 42101-3576 Fax: 270-745-3961
E-mail: wku@wku.edu
http://www.wku.edu
Promotes research on all aspects of cave and karst studies with emphasis upon solving environmental problems associated with karst.
Gary A. Ransdell, President
Dr. Phillip W. Bale, Regent

5222 Center for Crops Utilization Research
Iowa State University of Science & Technology
1041 Food Sciences Building 515-294-0160
Iowa State University Fax: 515-294-6261
Ames, IA 50011 E-mail: ccur@iastate.edu
http://www.ccur.iastate.edu
Incorporates various aspects of new product and product research, applications development, and technology transfer. Activities focus on developing technologies for producing food and industrial products from agricultural materials,developing agricultural substitutes for petrochemicals, and exploring and modifying the functional properties of crop-derived materials.
Dr. Lawrence A Johnson, Director
Peggy Best, Admin Specialist

5223 Center for Earth & Environmental Science
SUNY Plattsburgh
723 West Michigan Street 317-274-7154
SL 118 877-554-1041
Indianapolis, IN 46202 Fax: 317-274-7966
E-mail: cees@iupui.edu
http://www.cees.iupui.edu
Undergraduate degree programs in environmental science, geology, planning and geography, with special emphasis on watershed science, remote sensing and geographic information systems, and aquatic and terrestrial ecology. The center isone of the oldest and largest environmental programs in the US, with 16 full-time interdisciplinary faculty and diverse field sites.
Dr. Pamela A. Martin, Director
Robert C. Barr, Research Scientist

5224 Center for Environmental Communications (CEC)
Rutgers University

31 Pine Street 732-932-1966
New Brunswick, NJ 08901 Fax: 732-932-9544
E-mail: cec@aesop.rutgers.edu

The CEC, located on the Cook College Campus, brings together university investigators to provide a social science perspective to environmental problem solving. CEC has gained international recognition for responding to environmentalcommunication dilemmas with research, training, and public service. Established in 1986, CEC is now jointly sponsored by the New Jersey Agricultural Experiment Station and the Edward J. Bloustein School of Planning and Public Policy.

Caron Chess, Director

5225 Center for Environmental Health Sciences
Massachusetts Institute of Technology
77 Massachusetts Avenue 617-253-1000
Building 16-743 Fax: 617-258-9344
Cambridge, MA 02139-4307 http://web.mit.edu
L. Rafael Reif, President
Israel Ruiz, Executive VP

5226 Center for Environmental Medicine Asthma & Lung Biology
University of North Carolina
554 Human Studies Facility 919-962-0126
CB# 7310, 104 Mason Farm Road 866-962-4457
Chapel Hill, NC 27599-7310 Fax: 919-966-9863
E-mail: slshaw@med.unc.edu
http://www.med.unc.edu

The CEMALB are a group of investigators with diverse research interests that include cardiopulmonary medicine, immunology, lung physiology, cell biology, cell and molecular immunology, molecular toxicology and epidemiology. We conductresearch studies involving human volunteers that are aimed at understanding the negative health effects of air pollution on the lung and heart.

Philip A Bromberg, MD, Scientific Director
David B Peden, MD, MS, Center Director

5227 Center for Environmental Research Education
SUNY Buffalo
1300 Elmwood Avenue 716-878-4329
Upton Hall, Room 314 Fax: 716-878-6644
Buffalo, NY 14222 E-mail: zolnowsa@buffalostate.edu
http://www.buffalostate.edu
Marsha D. Jackson, President
Father Robert J Pecoraro, VP

5228 Center for Environmental Studies
Williams College
Hopkins Hall, 880 Main Street 413-597-3131
Williamstown, MA 01267 Fax: 413-597-3489
http://www.williams.edu

Provides students with the opportunity to learn how environmental issues are interconnected with many traditional fields of study. Offered as a concentration, the program encourages students to become well grounded in a single field bypersuing a major in a traditional discipline or department, while focusing several of their elective courses on the interdisciplinary study of the environment.

Karen Merrill, Director
Sarah Gardner, Associate Director

5229 Center for Environmental Toxicology and Technology
Colorado State University 970-491-7051
1601 Campus Delivery Fax: 970-491-8304
Fort Collins, CO 80523-1601 E-mail: dvmadmissions@colostate.edu
http://www.csu-cvmbs.colostate.edu
Mark Stetter, Dean
Chris Haase, Asst. to Dean

5230 Center for Field Biology
Austin Pay State University
PO Box 4718 931-221-7019
Clarksville, TN 37044 Fax: 931-221-6372
E-mail: fieldbiology@apsu.edu
http://www.apsu.edu/field_biology

The Center of Excellence for Field Biology at Austin Peay State University brings together scholars and students from various biological disciplines to conduct research on topics in field biology and ecology, including toxicology,population and community ecology, and the ecology and biology of rare, threatened and endangered species. Major research efforts have focused on the ecology and biology of the flora and fauna of the Land Between the Lakes.

Dr. Andrew N Barrass, Director
Dr. Steve Hamilton, Director

5231 Center for Global & Regional Environmental Research
University of Iowa
424 IATL 319-335-3333
Iowa City, IA 52242 Fax: 319-335-3337
E-mail: jfrank@cgrer.uiowa.edu
http://www.cgrer.uiowa.edu
Greg Carmichael, Co-Director
Jerry Schnoor, Co-Director

5232 Center for Global Change Science (MIT)
Massachusetts Institute of Technology
77 Massachusetts Avenue 617-253-4902
Room 54-1312 Fax: 617-253-0354
Cambridge, MA 02139-4307 E-mail: cgcs@mit.edu
http://www.cgcs.mit.edu

Addresses long-standing scientific problems whose solution is necessary for accurate prediction of changes in the global environment. The CGCS is interdisciplinary and interdepartmental, and builds on research and educational programsin earth sciences and engineering. The Center is also involved in substantial cooperative efforts focused on climate modeling, and on climate-policy research.

Michael Richard, Personnel Administrator
Robens Joseph, Financial Officer

5233 Center for Groundwater Research (CGR)
Oregon Health & Science University
20000 NW Walker Road 503-748-1070
Beaverton, OR 97006-8921 Fax: 503-748-1273
E-mail: info@ebs.ogi.edu
http://www.cgr.ebs.ogi.edu

The CGR coordinates a range of projects relating to the transport and fate of contaminants in soils and groundwater. The scope of the Center includes: the development of new sampling and site characterization techniques; thedevelopment of new analytical techniques; and other improved groundwater remediation techniques.

Richard L. Johnson, Director
Dr. James Pankow, Professor

5234 Center for Hazardous Substance Research
Kansas State University 785-532-6519
Ward Hall 104 Fax: 785-532-5985
Manhattan, KS 66506-2502 E-mail: chsr@k-state.edu
http://www.engg.ksu.edu/CHSR

Dr. Larry E. Erickson, Director
Blase A. Leven, Associate Director

5235 Center for International Development Research
Duke University
PO Box 8500 613-236-6163
Ottawa, ON K1G3H Fax: 613-238-7230
E-mail: info@idrc.ca
http://www.idrc.ca

Denis Desautels, Chairperson
Jean Label, President

5236 Center for International Food and Agricultural Policy
University of Minnesota

University of Minnesota 612-625-8713
332 Classroom Office Bldg, 1994 Buford A Fax: 612-625-6245
St. Paul, MN 55108-6040 E-mail: cifap@umn.edu
http://www.cifap.umn.edu

With its interdisciplinary approach, CIFAP uses its research and education activities to increase international understanding about food, agriculture, nutrition, natural and human resources, and the environment, and to positivelyaffect the policies of both developed and developing countries.

C Ford Runge, Director
Terry Roe, Professor of Applied Economi

5237 **Center for Lake Superior Ecosystem Research**
Michigan Technological University
1400 Townsend Drive 906-487-2769
Houghton, MI 49931 E-mail: wkerfoot@mtu.edu
http://www.mtu.edu/level3/centers.html

An interdisiplinary center with goals to promote and strengthen ecological research and graduate programs at MTU through developing and applying technological advances to ecological problems, to advocate an ecosystem perspective forstudying aquatic and terrestrial portions of the Lake Superior watershed and to become a resource center for basic information on watershed and lake properties.

5238 **Center for Marine Biology**
University of New Hampshire
85 Adams Point Road 603-862-2175
Durham, NH 03824 Fax: 603-862-1101
E-mail: ray.grizzle@unh.edu
http://http://marine.unh.edu/jacksonlab.htm

The Center for Marine Biology (CMB) fosters excellence in marine biological research and education. Its primary goals are to strengthen and focus research and graduate education in modern marine biology and to encourage the developmentof high-quality undergraduate programs in all aspects of marine biology. The center helps faculty members compete for external grant funds and fosters coordination of marine research efforts, both with the life sciences and in other disciplines.

Ray Grizzle, Research Scientist

5239 **Center for Population Biology**
University of California
One Shields Avenue 530-752-1274
2320 Storer Hall Fax: 530-752-1449
Davis, CA 95616 http://www.cpb.ucdavis.edu

Founded in 1989, the Center for Population Biology unites UC Davis' population biologists. The center's membership comprises graduate students enrolled in the http://www-eve.ucdavis.edu/popbio.htm, graduate students interested inpopulation biology who are earning their degrees in graduate programs such as ecology or entomology, postdoctoral researchers, from nine academic departments and sections, 17 of whom have faculty appointments in the division.

John J. Stachowicz, Director
Theresa Garcia, Graduate Group Coordinator

5240 **Center for Resource Policy Studies**
University of Wisconsin
1450 Linden Drive 608-262-8254
Room 240
Madison, WI 53706

The Center for Resource Policy Studies and Programs uses interdisciplinary research, teaching and extension efforts to analyze resource policies and development programs. This center gives particular emphasis to the social scienceaspects of natural resource policy issues.

5241 **Center for Statistical Ecology & Environmental Statistics**
Pennsylvania State University
Dept of Statistics 814-865-9442
421 Thomas Building Fax: 814-865-1278
University Park, PA 16802 E-mail: gpp@stat.psu.edu
http://www.stat.psu.edu/~gpp/aims_scope.htm

The Center is the first of its kind in the world and enjoys national and international reputation. They have an ongoing program of research that integrates statistics, ecology and the environment. The emphasis is on the environment andcollaborative research, training and exposition on improving the quantification and communication of man's impact on the environment. Major interest also lies in statistical investigations of the impact of the environment on man.

Ganapati P Patil, Director

5242 **Center for Streamside Studies**
University of Washington
Box 352100 206-543-6920
Seattle, WA 98195 Fax: 206-543-3254
http://dept.washington.edu/cssuw/

The mission of the Center for Streamside Studies is to provide scientific information necessary for the resolution of management issues related to the production and protection of forest, fish, wildlife, and water resources associatedwith the streams and rivers in the Pacific Northwest.

Robert J Naiman, Director

5243 **Center for Tropical Agriculture**
University of Florida
Km 17, Recta Cali-Palmira 650-833-6625
Apartado A,reo 6713 Fax: 650-833-6626
Cali, CO AA671 E-mail: ciat@cgiar.org
http://www.ciat.cgiar.org

Enhances research and education on tropical agriculture between University of Florida and tropical countries.

Wanda Collins, Board Chair
Geoffrey Hawtin, Vice Chair

5244 **Center for Water Resources and Environmental Research (CWRER)**
The City College of New York
160 Convent Avenue 212-650-7000
New York, NY 10031 E-mail: rk@ce.eng.ccny.cuny.edu
http://www.ccny.cuny.edu

The Center investigates pollution movement, surface water and groundwater cleanup, wetland preservation, watershed management, hydraulics and hydrology of natural flow systems, ecology preservation and the technical and sociopoliticaloutcomes.

Dr. Lisa Staiano-Coico, President
Dr. Maurizio Trevisan, Provost

5245 **Center for the Management, Utilization and Protection of Water Resources**
Tennessee Technological University
1 William L Jones Dr 931-372-3101
Box 5033 800-255-8881
Cookeville, TN 38505 Fax: 931-372-6346
E-mail: dgeorge@tntech.edu
http://www.tntech.edu/wrc

The Center for the Management, Utilization and Protection of Water Resources at Tennessee Technological University is dedicated to the vision of enhancing environmental education through research. Using interdisciplinary teams ofresearchers, the Center focuses its work in the core areas of environmental resource management and protection, environmental hazards, and environmental information.

Philip Oldham, President
Mark Stephens, Interim Provost

5246 **Clean Energy Research Institute**
University of Miami
4202 East Fowler Avenue 813-974-7322
Mail Stop ENB118 Fax: 813-974-2050
Tampa, FL 33620 E-mail: stefanak@eng.usf.edu
http://www.cerc.eng.usf.edu

Acts as the focal point of energy and environmental related activities in the College of Engineering. Its goals are to conduct research and to generate research proposals to investigate energy and environmental problems; to organizeseminars, workshops and conferences using researchers within and without the University; to assemble, compile, publish and disseminate information

on every aspect of energy and environmental problems; and to cooperate with other organs of theUniversity.
Elias (Lee) Stefanakos, Director
Yogi D. Goswami, Director

5247 Cobbs Creek Community Environment Educational Center (CCCEEC)
700 Cobbs Creek Parkway 215-685-1900
63rd & Catharine Streets Fax: 215-764-1586
Philadelphia, PA 19143 E-mail: cobbscreekinfo@gmail.com
http://www.cobbscreekcenter.org

CCCEEC is designated to institutionalize the practice of Urban Environmental Education. Their mission is to preserve the quality for residents living in the Cobbs Creek area of Philadelphia through the establishment of a center foreducating and informing people about the issues affecting their environment.
Carole Williams-Green, Founder
Sharon Williams-Losier, President

5248 College of Forest Resources
University of Washington
College of Forest Resources 206-543-2730
PO Box 352100 Fax: 206-685-0790
Seattle, WA 98195-2100 E-mail: sefsuw@u.washington.edu
http://www.cfr.washington.edu

The University of Washington College of Forest Resources is dedicated to generating and disseminating knowledge for the stewardship of natural and managed environments and the sustainable use of their products and services throughteaching, research and outreach.
Beverly Anderson, Administrator
Tom DeLuca, Director

5249 Colorado Cooperative Fish & Wildlife Research Unit
Colorado State University
1474 Campus Delivery 970-491-5396
Fort Collins, CO 80523-1474 Fax: 970-491-1413
http://www.warnercnr.colostate.edu

The Colorado Cooperative Wildlife Research Unit was founded in 1947, and the Colorado Cooperative Fishery Research Unit was established in 1963. The two Units were combined in 1984 into the Colorado Cooperative Fish and WildlifeResearch Unit. This unit is staffed, supported, and coordinated by the Colorado Division of Wildlife, Colorado State University, the United States Geological Survey , and the Wildlife Management Insisitute.
David Anderson, Program Director/Chief Scien
Denise Culver, Research Associate

5250 Cooperative Fish & Wildlife Research Unit
University of Missouri
Colorado State University 970-491-5020
1474 Campus Delivery Fax: 970-491-5091
Fort Collins, CO 80523-1474 http://www.warnercnr.colostate.edu
David Anderson, Program Director
Carroll Bjork, Illustrator I

5251 Cornell Waste Management Institute
Department of Crop and Soil Science 607-255-1187
817 Bradfield Hall Fax: 607-255-8207
Ithaca, NY 14853 E-mail: cwmi@cornell.edu
http://cwmi.css.cornell.edu

Conduct applied research and outreach focused on composting and land application of sewage sludges.

Lauri Wellin, Administrative Assistant
Jean Bonhotal, Director

5252 ERI Earth Research Institute
University of California
6832 Ellison Hall 805-893-4885
University of California Fax: 805-893-2578
Santa Barbara, CA 93106-3060 E-mail: webmaster@eri.ucsb.edu
http://www.eri.ucsb.edu

Purpose is to increase our understanding of the geological processes and evolution of the earth's crust and lithosphere, and the impact these processes have on society.
Susannah Porter, Director
David Siegel, Director

5253 Eagle Lake Biological Field Station
California State University
Department of Biology Sciences 530-898-5356
California State University Fax: 530-898-5060
Chico, CA 95929-515 E-mail: rbogiatto@oavax.csuchico.edu
http://www.csuchico.edu

The Eagle Lake Biological Field Station, located 26 miles northwest of Susanville in Lassen County, California is a ten building facility on the eastern shore of Eagle Lake. The field station is administered by California StateUniversity, Chico and the CSUC Foundation with support from the University of California Natural Reserve System and UC Davis. The ELBFS is open to any individual or group whose purpose is primarily academic and whose activities are consistent withthe isolation.
Raymond J Bogiatto, Director
Jeffrey Bell, Chair, Biology

5254 Earth Science & Observation Center
University of Colorado Boulder
University of Colorado at Boulder 303-492-5086
216 UCB Fax: 303-492-1149
Boulder, CO 80309-216 E-mail: lornay.hansen@colorado.edu
http://www.cires.colorado.edu/esoc

We advance scientific and societal understanding of the Earth System based on innovative remote sensing research. Through our research, we provide fundamental insights into how the Earth system functions, how it is changing, and whatthose changes mean for life on earth, for the benefit of human kind.
Dr Waleed Abdalati, Director
Lornay Hansen, Administration

5255 Ecology Center
2530 San Pablo Avenue 510-548-2220
Suite H Fax: 510-548-2240
Berkeley, CA 94702 E-mail: store@ecologycenter.org
http://www.ecologycenter.org

The Utah State University Ecology Center is an administrative structure in the University that supports and coordinates ecological research and graduate education in the science of ecology, and provides professional information andadvice for decision makers considering actions that affect the environment.
Raquel Pinderhughes, President
Becca Prager, Secretary

5256 Energy Resources Center
Univeristy of Illinois at Chicago
The University of Illinois at Chica 312-996-4490
MC 156, 1309 South Halsted Street, 2nd F Fax: 312-996-5620
Chicago, IL 60607 E-mail: erc@uic.edu
http://www.erc.uic.edu

The Center is a University of Illinois at Chicago interdiciplinary research and public service organization. It was established in 1973 by the University's Board of Trustees to conduct studies in the field of energy and to providelocal, state and federal governments and the public with current information on energy technology and policy.
John J. Cuttica, Director
Henry C. Kurth, Associate Director

5257 Energy, Environment & Resource Center
University of Tennesee at Knoxville
University of Tennessee, Knoxville 865-974-8080
676 Dabney Hall Fax: 865-974-8086
Knoxville, TN 37996-1605 E-mail: cebweb@utk.edu
http://www.ceb.utk.edu

Gary S Sayler, Founding Director
Sabine Nabenfuehr, Administrative Assistant

5258 Environmental & Water Resources Engineering Area
Texas A&M University

Civil Engineering Department 979-845-3011
301 E. Dean Keeton St. Stop C1700 Fax: 979-862-1542
Austin, TX 78712 E-mail: krose@mail.utexas.edu
http://www.ce.utexas.edu

David Allens, Chair
Neal Armstrong, Vice Provost

5259 Environmental Center
University of Hawaii
2500 Dole Street 808-956-7361
Krauss Annex 19 Fax: 808-956-3980
Honolulu, HI 96822 E-mail: envctr@hawaii.edu
http://www.hawaii.edu/envctr

The Center's three areas of focus are education, research and service. The education function of the Center includes the administration of the Environmental Studies Major Equivalent and Certificate program. It fulfills its researchfunction by identifying and addressing environmentally related research needs, particularly those pertinent to Hawaii. The service function primarily involves the coordination and transfer of technical information from the University community togovernment agencies.
Charlotte Kato, Secretary
Chittaranjan Ray, Director

5260 Environmental Chemistry and Technology Program
University of Wisconsin at Madison
680 N Park Street 608-263-3264
Room 122 Fax: 608-262-0454
Madison, WI 53706-1481 E-mail: mcpossin@wisc.edu
http://www.engr.wisc.edu

Marc A. Anderson, Professor and Chair
Anders W. Andren, Professor Research

5261 Environmental Exposure Laboratory
University of California
1000 Veterans Avenue 310-825-2739
Rehabilitation Center, Room A163
Los Angeles, CA 90024
Dr. Henry Gong Jr, Director

5262 Environmental Human Toxicology
University of Florida
Bldg 471 Mowry Road 352-294-4514
PO Box 110885 Fax: 352-392-4707
Gainesville, FL 32611 http://www.toxicology.vetmed.ufl.edu
The Center serves as an interface between basic research and its applications for evaluation of human health and environmental risk. The research and teaching activities of the Center provide a resource to identify and reduce riskassociated with environmental pollution, food contamination, and workplace hazards. The center provides a forum for the discussion of specific and general problems concerning the potential adverse human health effects associated with chemicalexposure.
Dr. Stephen Roberts, Director
Dr. Steve Roberts, Director

5263 Environmental Institue and Water Resources Research Institute
Auburn University
1090 South Donahue Drive 334-844-4132
Auburn, AL 36849 Fax: 334-844-4462
E-mail: hatchlu@auburn.edu
http://www.awrri.auburn.edu

Samuel Fowler, Director
Dr Upton Hatch, Director

5264 Environmental Institute of Houston
University ofg Houston
University of Houston-Clear Lake 281-283-3950
2700 Bay Area Blvd., MC 540, North Offic Fax: 281-283-3953
Houston, TX 77058-1098 E-mail: eih@uhcl.edu
http://www.eih.uhcl.edu
The mission of EIH is to help people in the Houston region participate more effectively in environmental improvement. Information and technology will be obtained and disseminated from research supported by EIH in critical areasincluding pollution prevention, natural resource conservation, public policy and societal issues. EIH will seek to expand balanced environmental education based on objective scholarship to empower the community to make sound decisions onenvironmental issues.
Sheila Brown, Board Member
Alecya Gallaway, Board Member

5265 Environmental Remote Sensing Center
University of Wisconsin
1225 W Dayton Street 608-263-3251
Floor 12 Fax: 608-262-5964
Madison, WI 53706 E-mail: sventura@wisc.edu
http://www.ersc.ssec.wisc.edu

A university research center focused on application of remote sensing and attending geospatial technologies in government, business and science. Particular heritage in the application of remote sensing in natural resource managementand environmental monitoring. A NASA-sponsored Affiliated Research Center.
Prof Thomas Lillesand, Director

5266 Environmental Research Institute
University of Idaho
Student Union Building 208-885-6111
PO Box 444264 888-8UI-DAHO
Moscow, ID 83844-4264 Fax: 208-885-9119
E-mail: info@uidaho.edu
http://www.uidaho.edu
The faculty, associated with the institute, perform multidisciplinary research in environmental molecular ecology, restoration of contaminated soils and waters, and microbial genomics related to environmental processes.
Douglas D. Baker, Provost/Executive VP
Ken Edmunds, President, State Board of Ed

5267 Environmental Resource Center
San Jose Southern University
101 Center Pointe Drive 919-469-1585
Cary, NC 27513-5706 800 537 2372
Fax: 919-342-0807
E-mail: service@ercweb.com
http://www.ercweb.com

The Environmental Resource Center is a nonprofit information and outreach organization within the Environmental Studes department at San Jose Southern University, serving the San Jose community since 1971.
Annemarie Vallesteros, Executive Director

5268 Environmental Science & Engineering Program
Clarkson University
1200 E California Blvd. MC 131-24 626-395-6070
Pasadena, CA 91125 Fax: 626-795-6028
E-mail: miur@gps.caltech.edu
http://www.esc.caltech.edu

Paul Wennberg, Executive Officer
Andrew Thompson, Option Representative

5269 Environmental Studies Institute
University of Pennsylvania
The University of Texas at Austin 512-471-5847
1 University Station C9000 Fax: 512-232-1913
Austin, TX 78712 E-mail: banner@jsg.utexas.edu
http://www.esi.utexas.edu
The Institute for Environmental Studies is dedicated to improving the understanding of key scientific, economic, and political issues that underlie environmental problems and their management. The mission of the Institute is to bringscholars together from across the University in order to promote collaborations in education and research endeavors in the area of environmental issues. These collaborative endeavors span basic and applied sciences, engineering and the social andhuman sciences.
Jay L. Banner, Director
Nina Schenck, Financial Analyst

5270 Environmental Systems Application Center
Indiana University
107 S Indiana Avenue 812-855-4848
Bloomington, IN 47405
The goals of the Center are to promote excellence in environmental science research and to foster increased interdisciplinary collaboration among environmental science faculty on the Indiana University-Bloomington campus. The Centerhas no degree pro-

grams. The Center can be listed as an affiliation of the associated faculty in publications and in correspondence.

5271 Environmental Systems Engineering Institute
University of Central Florida
University of Central Florida 407-823-2841
4000 Central Florida Boulevard Fax: 407-823-3315
Orlando, FL 32816-2450 http://www.cece.ucf.edu
Dr. Essam Radwan, Interim Chair
Necati Catbas, Deptt Assoc. Chairman

5272 Environmental Toxicology Center
University of Wisconsin
1300 University Avenue 608-263-4580
1530 MSC Fax: 608-262-5245
Madison, WI 53706 http://www.metc.med.wisc.edu
Environmental Toxicology is the study of the adverse effects on individual life forms and ecosystems of environmental agents (chemical, physcial, biological) whether of natural origin or released through human activity, and origins andcontrol of these harmful agents.
Christopher A. Bradfield, Director
Prof. Colin R Jefcoate, Director

5273 Environmental and Occupational Health Science Institute
Rutgers University
170 Frelinghuysen Road 848-445-0202
PO Box 1179 Fax: 732-445-0131
Piscataway, NJ 08854 E-mail: webmaster@eohsi.rutgers.edu
http://www.eohsi.rutgers.edu
The major objectives of the institute are to: improve understanding of the impact of environmental chemicals on human health; to find ways to quantify and prevent exposure to hazardous substances; and develop methods to identify andtreat people adversely affected by environmental agents. Devises approaches for educating the public about the relative risks from chemical exposure. Trains professionals to accomplish these tasks.
Kenneth Reuhl, Interim Director
Howard Kipen, Assoc Director

5274 Feed and Fertilizer Laboratory
Louisiana State University
Department Agriculture and Forestry 208-332-8500
PO Box 790 Fax: 208-334-2170
Boise, ID 83701-790 E-mail: info@agri.idaho.gov
http://www.agri.idaho.gov
Celia R. Gould, Director
Brian J. Oakey, Deputy Director

5275 Field Station & Ecological Reserves
University of Kansas
The University of Kansas 785-864-2700
1450 Jayhawk Blvd. Fax: 785-864-5093
Lawrence, KS 66045 http://www.kufs.ku.edu
The KSR is dedicated to field-based environmental reseach and education. KSR is located within the transition zone (ecotone) between the eastern deciduous forest and tallgrass prairie biomes. The 3,000 acres of diverse native andmanaged habitats, experimental systems, support facilities, and longterm databases are used to undertake an outstanding array of scholarly activities. Environmental stewardship is a stong emphasis as high-quality natural areas are preserved for thefuture.
Bernadette Gray-Little, University Chancellor
Jeffrey Vitter, Executive Vice Chancellor

5276 Fitch Natural History Reservation
University of Kansas
Kansas Biological Survey 785-864-1500
2101 Constant Avenue Fax: 785-864-1534
Lawrence, KS 66047 http://www.kufs.ku.edu
Bernadette Gray-Little, University Chancellor
Jeffrey Vitter, Executive Vice Chancellor

5277 Florida Cooperative Fish and Wildlife Research Unit
University of Florida
University of Florida 352-846-0534
Bldg. 810, McCarty Annex A, PO Box 11048Fax: 352-846-0841
Gainesville, FL 32611-485 E-mail: mghale@ufl.edu
http://www.wec.ufl.edu
The Cooperative Research Unit has three facets to its mission: education—Cooperative Unit scientists teach university courses at the graduate level, provide academic guidence to graduate students, and serve on academic committees;research—Cooperative Unit scientists conduct research that is designed to meet the information needs expressed by unit cooperators; technical Assistance— unit provides technical assistance and training to State and federal personnel and othernatural resources.
Dr. Wiley M Kitchens, Leader
M. gay Hale, Admin Asst.

5278 Florida Museum of Natural History
University of Florida
Dickinson Hall, 1659 Museum Road 352-392-1721
PO Box 117800 Fax: 352-392-8783
Gainesville, FL 32611-7800 E-mail: gdshaak@flmnh.ufl.edu
http://www.flmnh.ufl.edu
The Florida Museum of Natural History, on the University of Florida Campus, is one of the leading university natural history museums in the nation. With over 30 million specimens and artifacts in its permanent collections, it is thelargest collection-based museum in the southeastern US. The museum was established by the Legislature in 1917 at the University of Florida where it functions in a dual capacity as the official state museum of Florida and the University Museum.
Dr Douglas S Jones, Director
Dr Beverly Sensbach, Associate Director

5279 Formaldehyde Institute
1330 Connecticut Avenue NW 202-833-2131
Washington, DC 20036 Fax: 202-659-1699
http://www.ainc.org
John F Murray, Executive Director

5280 Gannett Energy Laboratory
Florida Institute of Technology
PO Box 67100 717-763-7211
Harrisburg, PA 17106-7100 800-233-1055
http://www.gannettfleming.com
William M. Stout, Chairman/CEO
Robert M. Scaer, Vice Chairman

5281 Global Change & Environmental Quality Program
University of Colorado
University of Colorado at Boulder 303-492-1411
Campus Box 214 Fax: 303-492-1414
Boulder, CO 80309 E-mail: bob.sievers@colorado.edu
http://www.colorado.edu
In addition to addressing CU's overall objectives, the Global Change and Environmental Quality Program is pursuing three main goals; studying environmental issues at the local level, including the cleanup and restoration of toxicsites, such as Rocky Flats, the Rocky Mountain Arsenal, and mine tailing sites; waste treatment and water quality; and land use.
Bob Sievers, Director
Rosella Chavez, Admin Asst.

5282 Graduate Program in Community and Regional Planning
University of Texas
Main Building 512-471-0134
Austin, TX 78701 Fax: 512-471-0716
The CRP provides its graduates with the theoretical foundations, specific skills and practical experience to succeed in professional planning and related policy careers. They strive to create a diverse student body and program and arecommitted to building a professional planning community that rese,bles those where graduates will work. The program has a strong focus on sustainable development processes and practices. Finding paths that balance growth with improved environmentalperformance.
Jane Shaughness, Graduate Admissions Coor.

5283 **Great Lakes Coastal Research Laboratory**
Purdue University
School of Civil Engineering 765-494-4600
West Lafayette, IN 47907

5284 **Great Lakes/Mid-Atlantic Hazardous Substance Research Center**
University of Michigan
One Potomac Yard (South Building) 734-763-2274
2777 South Crystal Drive http://www.epa.gov
Arlington, VA 22202
The mission of the Great Lakes Mid- Atlanic Center for Hazardous Substances Research is to foster and support integrated, intersdiciplinary, and collaborative efforts that advance the science and technology of hazardous substancemanagement to benefit human and environmental health and well-being.
Diane Thompson, Chief of Staff
Arvin Ganesan, Assoc. Administrator

5285 **Great Plains: Rocky Mountain Hazardous Substance Research Center**
Kansas State University
Kansas State University 785-532-6519
104 Ward Hall 800-798-7796
Manhattan, KS 66506-2502 Fax: 785-532-5985
E-mail: hsrc@ksu.edu
http://www.engg.ksu.edu/HSRC
Conducts research and transfers technology on hazardous substance management, and remediation of contaminated soil and water.
Dr. Larry Erickson, Center Director
Dr. Richard B. Hayter, Technology Transfer & Traini

5286 **Greenley Memorial Research Center**
University of Missouri
Greenley Memorial Center 660-739-4410
Randall Smoot, Box 126 Fax: 660-739-4500
Novelty, MO 63460 E-mail: smootr@missouri.edu
http://www.aes.missouri.edu
Randall Smoot, Director
Kelly Nelson, Research Agronomist

5287 **HT Peters Aquatic Biology Laboratory**
Sattgast 230 218-755-2920
1500 Birchmont Drive NE #27 800-475-2001
Bemidji, MN 56601-2699 Fax: 218-755-4107
E-mail: dcloutman@bemidjistate.edu
http://www.bemidjistate.edu
Dr. Richard Hansen, President
Bill Maki, VP

5288 **Harry Reid Center for Environmental Studies**
University of Las Vegas
4505 Maryland Parkway 702-895-3382
Box 454009 Fax: 702-895-3094
Las Vegas, NV 89154-4009 E-mail: oliver.hemmers@unlv.edu
http://www.hrc.nevada.edu
The HRC was started in 1981 under UNLV's Marjorie Barrick Museum of Natural History. HRC currently includes 65 staff members and a 65,000 square foot building with four laboratories.
Dr. Oliver A. Hemmers, Executive Director
Leisa Baldwin-Rodriguez, Finance Director

5289 **Hawaii Cooperative Fishery Research Unit**
University of Hawaii at Manoa
2538 The Mall 808-956-8350
Honolulu, HI 96822-2279 Fax: 808-956-4238
E-mail: kkhardin@hawaii.edu
http://www.coopunits.org
Alan Friedlander, Asst Unit Leader
Kim Harding, University Staff

5290 **Hawaii Undersea Research Laboratory**
University of Hawaii at Manoa
1000 Pope Road 808-956-6335
Marine Science Building (MSB) 303 Fax: 808-956-9772
Honolulu, HI 96822 E-mail: HURLinfo@hawaii.edu
http://www.soest.hawaii.edu
One of six research centers funded by NOAA's National Undersea Research Program. HURL operates two 2000-meter Pisces submersibles and a remotely operated vehicle. Research projects include fisheries research, geology and biology of thedeepsea around the Hawaiian Islands.
Diane Apau, Admin Officer
Karynne Chong Morgan, Admin Officer

5291 **Henry S Conrad Environmental Research Area**
1210 Grinnell College 641-269-4000
Grinnell, IA 50112-1690 Fax: 641-269-4984
E-mail: bakermar@grinnell.edu
http://www.grinell.edu
Paula V. Smith, Vp Academic Affairs
Retta Kelley, Administrative Asst. II

5292 **Highlands Biological Station**
University of North Carolina
265 N Sixth Street 828-526-2602
PO Box 580 Fax: 828-526-2797
Highlands, NC 28741 E-mail: hbs@email.wcu.edu
http://www.highlandsbiological.org
The Station is an interinstitutional center of the University of North Carolina and includes the Highlands Nature Center and Botanical Gardens, as well as the Biological Laboratory. Our mission, for more than 75 years has been tofoster education and research focused on the rich natural heritage of the Highlands Plateau.
Dr. James T. Costa, Executive Director
Dr. Thomas Martin, Director

5293 **Hudsonia**
30 Campus Rd 845-758-7053
PO Box 5000 Fax: 845-758-7033
Annandale, NY 12504-5000 E-mail: kiviat@bard.edu
http://www.hudsonia.org
Since 1981 Hudsonia has conducted environmental research, education, training and technical assistance to protect the Hudson River Valley's natural heritage. Nonpartisan and non-ideological, Hudsonia serves as a neutral voice in thechallenging process of land conservation.
Judith L. Schneyer, Administrative Director
Erik Kiviat, Executive Director

5294 **Huntsman Environmental Research Center**
C/O Biological Engineering Departme 435-797-1418
4105 Old Main Hill Fax: 435-797-1248
Logan, UT 84322-4105 E-mail: herc@usu.edu
http://www.herc.usu.edu
The establishement of the Hunts man Environmental Research Center recognized the fundamental interdependence of the health of man and the health of the environment. The HERC's mission is to engage in research in the key areas ofrecycling, degradability, improvement of air and water quality and conservation of trees. The center purpose is to solve environmental problems and to provide realistic and comprehensive research solutions for our environment.
Stan L. Albrecht, President
Raymond T. Coward, Executive VP

5295 **INFORM**
PO Box 320403 212-361-2400
Brooklyn, NY 11232 Fax: 212-361-2412
http://www.informinc.org
INFORM is an independent research organization that examines the effects of business practices on the environment and on human health. Our goal is to identify ways of doing business that ensure environmentally sustainable economicgrowth. Our reports are used by government, industry, and environmental leaders around the world.
Jon Parks, Co-Chair
Marina Belesis-Casoria, Co-Chair

5296 Idaho Cooperative Fish & Wildlife Research Unit
University of Idaho
Student Union Building 208-885-6111
PO Box 444264 888-8UI-DAHO
Moscow, ID 83844-4264 Fax: 208-885-9119
E-mail: info@uidaho.edu
http://www.uidaho.edu
The faculty, associated with the institute, perform multidisciplinary research in environmental molecular ecology, restoration of contaminated soils and waters, and microbial genomics related to environmental processes.

Douglas D. Baker, Provost/Executive VP
Ken Edmunds, President, State Board of Ed

5297 Institute for Biopsychological Studies of Color, Light, Radiation, Health
San Jose State University
One Washington Square 408-924-1000
Psychology Department Fax: 408-924-1018
San Jose, CA 95192 http://www.sjsu.edu
Shawn Bibb, VP for Finance & Administrat
Ellen Junn, Provost/VP for Academic Affa

5298 Institute for Ecological Infrastructure Engineering
Losuisiana State University
College of Engineering 225-578-1399
102 ELAB Fax: 225-578-8662
Baton Rouge, LA 70803 E-mail: eielab@eiel.lsu.edu
http://www.eiel.lsu.edu
Institute for Ecological Infrastructure Engineering integrates engineering with science (physical, chemical, life & social) for the co-development of society and nature (ecosystems).
Lily A Rusch, Director

5299 Institute for Environmental Science
University of Texas at Dallas
Arlington Place One 847-981-0100
2340 South Arlington Heights Road, Suite Fax: 847-981-4130
Arlington, IL 60005-4510 E-mail: information@iest.org
http://www.iest.org
Greg Winn, President
John Weaver, Fiscal VP

5300 Institute for Lake Superior Research
University of Minnesota
University of Wisconsin-Superior 715-394-8101
Belknap & Catlin, PO Box 2000 E-mail: relations@uwsuper.edu
Superior, WI 54880 http://www.uwsuper.edu
Janet Hanson, Vice Chancellor
Jeff Kahler, Budget & Policy Analyst

5301 Institute for Regional and Community Studies
Western Illinois University 309-298-1566
Tillman Hall 413B
Macomb, IL 61455

5302 Institute for Urban Ports and Harbors
School of Marine and Atmospheric Sciences
Stony Brook University 631-632-8700
Endeavor Hall, Room 145 Fax: 631-632-8820
Stony Brook, NY 11794-5000 E-mail: Minghua.Zhang@stonybrook.edu
http://www.somas.stonybrook.edu
Minghua Zhang, Dean/Director
R. Lawrence Swanson, Associate Dean

5303 Institute of Analytical and Environmental Chemistry
University of New Haven
300 Boston Post Road 203-932-7171
West Haven, CT 06516 800-342-5864
http://www.newhaven.edu
Steven H. Kaplan, President
Lourdes Alvarez, Dean

5304 Institute of Chemical Toxicology
Wayne State University
2727 2nd Avenue 313-577-0100
Room 4000 Fax: 313-577-0082
Detroit, MI 48201 http://www.wayne.edu

5305 Institute of Ecology
University of California
1 Shields Avenue Davis 530-752-1011
Davis, CA 95616 Fax: 530-752-3350
E-mail: aking@ucdavis.edu
http://www.ucdavis.edu
Linda P.B. Katehi, Chancellor
Ralph Hexter, Provost/Executive Vice Chanc

5306 Interdisciplinary Center for Aeronomy & Other Atmospheric Sciences
University of Florida
317, Bryant Space Science Center 352-392-2001
PO Box 112050 Fax: 352-392-2003
Gainesville, FL 32611-2050 E-mail: aesgreen@ufl.edu
http://www.plaza.ulf.edu
Prof. Alex ES Green, Director

5307 Iowa Cooperative Fish & Wildlife Research Unit
Iowa State University
NREM-ICFWRU 515-294-3056
339 Science II Fax: 515-294-5468
Ames, IA 50011-3221 E-mail: coppunit@iastate.edu
http://www.cfwru.iastate.edu
The Iowa landscape and economy are dominated by production agriculture. Game and non-game wildlife species inhabiting the state are influenced by the destruction, degradation and frgamentation of wetland, prairie, and forest habitatscaused by intensified agricultural practices. This Unit is designed to identify, and emaphsize these effects through research and education programs.
Jessica Bell, Administrative Specialist
Dr. Erwin E. Klaas, Professor

5308 Iowa Waste Reduction Center
University of Northern Iowa
113, BCS Building 319-273-8905
University of Northern Iowa 800-422-3109
Cedar Falls, IA 50614 Fax: 319-273-6582
E-mail: publicrelations@iwrc.org
http://www.iwrc.org
A service of the University of Northern Iowa, it provides free and confidential environmental regulatory assistance to Iowa small businesses. The IWRC has also developed two products available to the painting and coating industry:LaserPaint and VirtualPaint.
Dan Nickey, Sr. Program Manager
Jim Olson, Associate Director

5309 James H Barrow Field Station
Hiram College Biological Station 330-527-2141
Garrettsville, OH 44231 Fax: 330-527-3187
The James H Barrow Field Station was established in 1967 to provide Hiram College students the opportunity to supplement classroom activities with hands-on learning experiences. Over the Last 32 years the Station has grown anddeveloped into an active research and educational facility that not only echances the College's science and environmental studies programs, but also provides a means for the general public to increase their understanding and appreciation of Ohio'snatural history.

5310 John F Kennedy School of Government Environmental and Natural Resources Program
Harvard University
79 John F Kennedy Street 617-495-1351
Cambridge, MA 02138 Fax: 617-495-1635
E-mail: enrp@ksg.harvard.edu
http://http://bcsia.ksg.harvard.edu/?program+ENRP
Henry Lee, Director

5311 Juneau Center School of Fisheries & Ocean Sciences
University of Alaska Fairbanks

17101 Point Lena Loop Rd 907-796-5441
UAF Fisheries Division Fax: 907-796-5447
Juneau, AK 99801-8344 E-mail: fisheries@uaf.edu
http://www.sfos.uaf.edu

JCSFOS has the primary responsibility within the University for education, research and public service in support of fisheries related areas of oceanography, marine biology and limnology with emphasis on Alaskan waters and the Arctic.The school's goal is to maintain and develop the broad expertise among its faculty and students needed to contribute to the wise use of Alaska's natural resources.

Dr. Michael Castellini, Dean/Professor
Keith Criddle, Director

5312 Kresge Center for Environmental Health
Harvard University
677 Huntington Avenue 617-732-1272
Boston, MA 02115 E-mail: brain@hsph.harvard.edu
http://www.hsph.harvard.edu

The Kresge Center serves as the focus for research and training activities in environmental health at the Harvard School of Public Health and elsewhere in the University. The Center was established in 1958 to promote interactions amongbiological scientists, physical scientists and engineers working on environmental problems of human health concern.

Julio Frenk, Dean
Michael Kan, Executive Dean for Administr

5313 Laboratory for Energy and the Environment
Massachusetts Institute of Technology
Massachusetts Institute of Technolo 617-258-8891
77 Massachusetts Avenue, E19-307 Fax: 617-253-8013
Cambridge, MA 02139-4307 E-mail: thill@mit.edu
http://www.mitei.mit.edu

The LFEE at the Massachusetts Institute of Technology brings together collaborating faculty and staff in 13 departments to address the complex interrelationships between energy and the environment, and other global environmentalchallenges.

Prof. Robert C. Armstrong, Director
Prof. Angela M. Belcher, Professor

5314 Leopold Center for Sustainable Agriculture
Leopold Center for Sustainable Agri 515-294-3711
209 Curtiss Hall - Iowa State University Fax: 515-294-9696
Ames, IA 50011-1050 E-mail: leocenter@iastate.edu
http://www.leopold.iastate.edu

The center was created by the 1987 Iowa Ground Water Protection Act with a three fold mission: 1) to identify and reduce adverse environmental impacts of farming practices, 2) develop profitable farming systems that conserve naturalresources, and 3) create educational programs with the ISU Extension Service. The center opertes a competitive grant program and supports several muti-desciplinary research teams and initatives. It is named after internationally acclaimed and Iowaborn Aldo Leopold.

William Ehm, Chair
Keith Summerville, Vice Chairman

5315 Living Marine Resources Institute
Stony Brook University 631-632-6000
Stony Brook, NY 11794 Fax: 631-632-9441
E-mail: Loreen.Brandes@stonybrook.edu
http://www.stonybrook.edu

LIMRI is one of several specialized institutes subsumed within the Marine Sciences Research Center of Stony Brook University. LIMRI's program of research includes investigations on marine fisheries, harmful algal blooms, marine law &policy, and aquaculture. The Institute operates the Flax Pond Marine Laboratory, a seaside, seawater-equipped facility for experimental work, located 5 miles north of the main campus on a tidal pond adjacent to Long Island Sound.

Samuel L. Stanley, President
William Arens, Vice Provost

5316 Long-Term Ecological Research Project
University of Colorado
1 University of New Mexico 505-277-2649
Albuquerque, NM 87131 Fax: 303-492-0434
E-mail: tech-support@lternet.edu
http://www.lternet.edu

Scott Collins, Chair
Bob Waide, Executive Director

5317 Louisiana Sea Grant College Program
Louisiana State University
Sea Grant Building 225-578-6564
Baton Rouge, LA 70803 Fax: 225-578-6331
http://www.laseagrant.org

Works to promote stewardship of the state's coastal resources through a combination of research, education and outreach programs critical to the cultural, economic, and environmental health of Louisiana's coastal zone. Part of theNational Sea Grant Program, it is one of 32 programs located in coastal, Great Lakes, and Puerto Rican coast areas.

Robert R. Twilley, Executive Director
Ronald E. Becker, Associate Director

5318 MIT Sea Grant College Program
Massachusetts Institute of Technology
77 Massachusettes Ave. 617-253-7131
E 38-300 Fax: 617-258-5730
Cambridge, MA 02139 E-mail: chrys@mit.edu
http://www.seagrant.mit.edu

Chrys Chryssostomidis, Director
Stefano Brizzolara, Asst Director

5319 Marine Science Institute
University of Texas
The University of Texas 361-749-6741
750 Channel View Drive Fax: 361-749-6777
Port Aransas, TX 78373 http://www.utmsi.utexas.edu

The Marine Institute is an organized research unit of The University of Texas at Austin. Institute scientists are engaged in both multi-investigator, multi-disciplinary studies and individual research projects in the local area andthroughout the world. Many of these projects are combinations of field and laboratory investigations. The Institute receives an operating budget annually that is based on a two-year advanced budget approval by the state legislature.

Edward J. Buskey, Interim Chair
G. Joan Holt, Interim Director

5320 Marine and Freshwater Biomedical Sciences Center
University of Miami
4600 Rickenbacker Cswy 305-421-4609
East Grosvenor Bldg., #E211, E213 888-232-8635
Miami, FL 33149 Fax: 305-421-4833
E-mail: lfleming@med.miami.edu
http://www.yyy.rsmas.miami.edu

The Environmental Health Science Center is an integral part of the University, with 20 faculty postdoctoral fellows and outreach personnel. Supported by the US government our research focus is on human health applications for diseaseprevention. Research includes neurotoxicology, potent marine metabolites present in seafood, environmental intoxicants, fisheries models for hepatic metabolism and development of sentinel species for xenobiotic evaluation. Courses, conferences,seminars, outreach.

Lora E. Fleming, Co Director Investigator
Sharon L. Smith, Co Director Investigator

5321 Massachusetts Cooperative Fish & Wildlife Unit
University of Massachusetts
Holdsworth Natural Resources Center 413-545-0398
PO Box 34220 Fax: 413-545-4358
Amherst, MA 01003-4220 E-mail: sdestef@eco.umass.edu
http://www.coopunits.org

Stephen DeStefano, Unit Leader
Allison Roy, Asst. Unit Leader

5322 Masschusetts Water Resources Research Center
University of Massachusetts

Blaisdell House
113 Grinnell Way
Amherst, MA 01003
413-545-5531
Fax: 413-253-1309
E-mail: wrrc@cns.umass.edu
http://www.wrrc.umass.edu

The Center has three objectives: 1) to develop, through research, new technology and more efficient methods for resolving local, state and national water resources problems; 2) to train water scientists and engineers through on-the-jobparticipation in water resources research and outreach; 3) to facilitate water research coordination and the application of research results by means of information dissemination, technology transfer and outreach.

Paula Rees, Director
Marie-Fran‡oise Hatte, Assoc. Director

5323 **Millar Wilson Laboratory for Chemical Research**
Jacksonville University
2800 University Boulevard N
Jacksonville, FL 32211
904-744-3950
Fax: 904-744-0101
E-mail: Lsonnen@ju.edu
http://www.dept.ju.edu

5324 **Mining and Mineral Resources Research Center**
205 Particle Science & Technology
Gainesville, FL 32611
352-846-1194
Fax: 352-846-1196
E-mail: info@perc.ufl.edu
http://www.perc.ufl.edu/mrrc

Brij M. Moudgil, Director
B. Koopman, Affiliated Faculty

5325 **Mississippi Cooperative Fish & Wildlife Research Unit**
Mississippi State University
Mail Stop 9691
Mississippi State, MS 39762
662-325-2643
Fax: 662-325-8795
http://www.coopunits.org

Hal Schramm, Unit Leader
Leandro Miranda, Asst. Unit Leader

5326 **Mississippi State Chemical Laboratory**
Mississippi State University
PO Box CR
Mississippi State, MS 39762
662-325-2323
Fax: 662-325-1618
http://www.msstate.edu

Mark E. Keenum, President
Jerome A. Gilbert, Provost/Executive Vice Presi

5327 **Montana Cooperative Fishery Research Unit**
Montana St University Dept Ecology
100 Culbertson Hall, PO Box 172000
Bozeman, MT 59717-2000
406-994-2672
Fax: 406-994-7479
E-mail: wdemay@montana.edu
http://www.montana.edu

Dr. Robert G White, Leader
Wanda DeMay, Manager

5328 **Monterey Bay Watershed Project**
California State University
100 Campus Center
Watershed Institute Building 42
Seaside, CA 93955-8001
831-582-3689
Fax: 831-582-5114
E-mail: laura_lienk@csumb.edu
http://www.watershed.csumb.edu

The Watershed Institute is a direct action, community based coalition of researchers, restoration ecologists, educators, students, planners and area volunteers dedicated to restoring the watersheds of the Monterey Bay region throughrestoration, education and research. Their policy is to work with state and federal agencies, private landowners and local planners to gain access to critical lands. Institute staff are involved in local land and water planning.

Laura Lee Lienk, Co-Director
Doug Smith, Co-Director/Professor

5329 **Museum of Zoology**
University of Massachusetts
Zoology Department
Amherst, MA 01003
413-545-2287
E-mail: web@admin.umass.edu
http://www.umass.edu

Kumble R. Subbaswamy, Chancellor
James V. Staros, Provost/Vice Chancellor

5330 **National Center for Ground Water Research**
University of Oklahoma
660 Parrington Oval
Norman, OK 73019
405-325-0311
Fax: 405-325-7596
E-mail: canter@ou.edu

Dr Larry Canter, Director

5331 **National Center for Vehicle Emissions Control & Safety**
Colorado State University
1584 Campus Delivery
Fort Collins, CO 80523
970-491-7240
Fax: 970-491-7801
E-mail: ncvecs@cahs.colostate.edu
http://www.colostate.edu

NCVECS is a nationally and internationally recognized university based research and training center devoted to motor vehicle emission issues. NCVECS primarily assists states with research and training related to their local vehicleinspection program. In addition, research is conducted on OBDII systems, alternative fuels and diesel vehicle issues.

Dr Lenora Bohren, Director
Joe Beebe, Automotive Emissions Testing

5332 **National Institute for Global Environmental Change: South Central Regional Center**
Tulane University
605 Lindy Boogs Center
New Orleans, LA 70118
504-865-5250
Fax: 504-865-6745
E-mail: nigec@tulane.edu
http://www.nigec.tulane.edu

Dr Stathis Michaelides, Professor
Valentina M. Tournier, Regional Assistant

5333 **National Mine Land Reclamation Center: Eastern Region**
State University of Pennsylvania
106 Land & Water Resources Building
University Park, PA 16802
814-863-0291
Fax: 814-865-3378
E-mail: ajm2@psu.edu
http://www.wvmdtaskforce.com

Ben Greene, Chairman/President
Buddy Beach, VP

5334 **National Mine Land Reclamation Center: Midwest Region**
Southern Illinois University
1201 W Gregory
Carbondale, IL 62901
618-453-2496
Fax: 217-333-8816
http://www.wvmdtaskforce.com

Ben Greene, Chairman/President
Buddy Beach, VP

5335 **National Mine Land Reclamation Center: Western Region**
Highway 6 S
Mandan, ND 58554
701-777-5217
E-mail: jsolc@eerc.und.nodak.edu
http://www.wvmdtaskforce.com

Ben Greene, Chairman/President
Buddy Beach, VP

5336 **National Park Service Cooperative Unit: Athens**
University of Georgia
Institute of Ecology
Athens, GA 30602
706-542-8301

Dr. Stephen Cover-Shabica, Contact

5337 **National Research Center for Coal and Energy (NRCCE)**
West Virginia University
PO Box 6064
Morgantown, WV 26506
304-293-4974
Fax: 304-293-3749
E-mail: Paul.Ziemkiewicz@mail.wvu.edu
http://www.wvwri.org

A research and training center at West Virginia University, advances innovations for energy and the environment by working with research faculty across WVU and with other university, government, and private sector researchersnationwide. The center is organized into a variety of multidisciplinary programs, centers, and institutes focusing on topics such as clean energy production, energy distribution, energy efficiency, alternative fuels, watershed restorationandpreservation.

Paul F. Ziemkiewicz, PhD, Director
Tamara F. Vandivort, Associate Director

5338 Natural Energy Laboratory of Hawaii Authority
73-4460 Queen Kaahumanu Hwy. #101 808-327-9585
Kailua Kona, HI 96740-2637 Fax: 808-327-9586
E-mail: inquires@nelha.org
http://www.nelha.org

NELHA, an agency of the State of Hawaii, operates facilities at Keahole Point on Hawaii Island that pump ashore cold deep and warm surface seawater for commercial and research tenants from the private and public sectors. Tenantsutilize the seawater and NELHA's high sunlight and consistant temperatures in a wide range of aquaculture and energy projects.

Ron Baird, CEO

5339 New Hampshire Sea Grant College Program
University of New Hampshire
Kingman Farm Unit 603-862-1234
Main Street Fax: 603-743-3997
Durham, NH 03824 E-mail: steve.adams@unh.edu
http://www.seagrant.unh.edu

A component of the National Sea Grant College Program, NH Sea Grant works toward the conservation, wise use and development of marine resources in the state and region.
Mark W. Huddleston, President
John Aber, Provost

5340 New York Cooperative Fish & Wildlife Research Unit
Cornell University
211 Fernow Hall 607-255-2839
Ithaca, NY 14853-3001 Fax: 607-255-1895
E-mail: meaton@usgs.gov
http://www.coopunits.org/New_York

William Fisher, Unit Leader
Mitchell Eaton, Asst. Unit Leader

5341 New York State Water Resources Institute
Cornell University
204A Rice Hall 607-255-5941
Ithaca, NY 14853 Fax: 607-255-5945
E-mail: sjr4@cornell.edu
http://www.wri.eas.cornell.edu

Susan J. Riha, Director
Brian G. Rahm, Post Doctoral Associate

5342 Northwoods Field Station
Hiram College
PO Box 67 330-569-3211
Hiram, OH 44234 800-362-5280
http://www.hiram.edu

Thomas V. Chema, President
Gay Cull Addicott, President

5343 Occupational & Environmental Health Laboratory
University of North Alabama
2206 East Mall 604-822-2772
Vancouver, BC V6T1Z Fax: 604-822-4994
E-mail: mha.program@ubc.ca
http://www.spph.ubc.ca

Dr. David Patrick, Director
Cecilia Gruber, Asst. Director

5344 Ocean & Coastal Policy Center
University of California
Woolley-5134 805-893-8393
Santa Barbara, CA 93106 Fax: 805-893-8062
E-mail: mcginnis@lifesci.ucsb.edu
http://www.ocpc.msi.ucsb.edu

Dr. Michael Vincent, Conratct

5345 Ocean Engineering Center
Massachusetts Institute of Technolo 617-253-9344
77 Massachusetts Avenue, Room 5-228 Fax: 603-862-0241
Cambridge, MA 02139 E-mail: oe@mit.edu
http://www.oe.mit.edu

Geoff Fox, Administrative Assistant II
Mary Mullowney, Administrative Assistant II

5346 Oceanic Institute
Makapuu Point 808-259-3102
41-202 Kalanianaole Highway Fax: 808-259-5971
Waimanalo, HI 96795 E-mail: oi@oceanicinstitute.org
http://www.oceanicinstitute.org

Oceanic Institute is a not-for-profit organization dedicated to research, development and transfer of oceanographic, marine Environmental, and aquaculture technologies. Oceanic Institute is a world leader in conducting appliedresearch in aquaculture production and marine resource conservation. Its mission is to develop and transfer environmentally responsible technologies to increase aquatic food production while promoting the sustainable use of ocean resources.

Dr. Geoffrey Bannister, Chairman
James A. Ajello, Board Of Trustees

5347 Oregon Cooperative Fishery Research Unit
Oregon State University
Oregon State University 541-737-1000
104 Nash Hall Fax: 541-737-3590
Corvallis, OR 97331 E-mail: OSU.Provost@oregonstate.edu
http://www.oregonstate.edu

Dr. Edward J. Ray, President
Sabah U. Randhawa, Provost

5348 Oregon Cooperative Park Studies Unit
Oregon State University
3200 Jefferson Way 541-737-2056
Corvallis, OR 97331 E-mail: starkeye@ccmail.orst.edu
http://www.cof.orst.edu/
Dr Edward E Starkey, Codirector

5349 Oregon Sea Grant College Program
Oregon State University
1600 SW Western Blvd 541-737-2714
Suite 350 Fax: 541-737-7958
Corvallis, OR 97333 http://www.seagrant.oregonstate.edu
Stephen B Brandt, Director
Joe Cone, Assistant Director

5350 Pennsylvania Cooperative Fish & Wildlife Research Unit
Pennsylvania State University
117 Forest Resources Bldg 814-865-7541
University Park, PA 16802 Fax: 814-865-3725
E-mail: klc2@psu.edu
http://www.ecosystems.psu.edu

Michael G. Messina, Head/Professor
Linda Spangler, Manager

5351 Permaculture Gap Mountain
9 Old County Road 603-532-6877
Jaffrey, NH 03452

5352 Pesticide Research Center
Michigan State University
Michigan State University 517-432-6200
426 Auditorium Rd, Board of Trustees Roo 800-500-1554
East Lansing, MI 48824-1046 E-mail: beekman@msu.edu
http://www.msu.edu

Joel I. Ferguson, Chairperson
Bill Beekman, VP/Secretary

5353 Planning Institute
University of Southern California

Von KleinSmid Center 351
Los Angeles, CA 90089
213-740-2311
Fax: 213-740-1801
E-mail: sppd@usc.edu
http://www.usc.edu

Wallis Annenberg, Chairman
C.L. Max Nikias, President

5354 Program for International Collaboration in Agroecology
University of California Santa Cruz
MS: PICA
1156 High Street
Santa Cruz, CA 95064
831-459-4051
Fax: 831-459-2867
E-mail: gliess@ucsc.edu
http://www.agroecology.org

Researches, develops, and advances sustainable food and agricultural systems that are environmentally sound, economically viable, socially responsible, nonexploitive, and that serve as a foundation for future generations. A specialfocus on promoting an international network of training programs in agroecology.

Stephen R. Gliessman, Professor of Agroecology
Vivan Vadakan, PICA Program Manager

5355 Program in Freshwater Biology
University of Mississippi
University of Mississippi
P.O. Box 1848
University, MS 38677
662-915-2787
Fax: 662-915-5144
E-mail: biology@olemiss.edu
http://www.olemiss.edu

Dr. James Kushlan, Chairman
Daniel W. Jones, Chancellor

5356 Randolph G Pack Environmental Institute
One Forestry Drive
107 Marshall Hall
Syracuse, NY 13210
315-470-6500
Fax: 315-470-6915
E-mail: envsty@esf.edu
http://www.esf.edu

The Institute seeks to advance scholoarly and popular knowledge of key contemporary issues related to environmental policy and regulartion. It focuses on how democratic public decisions affecting the natural environment are made,concentrating on such topics as public participation, environmental equity, and sustainable development.

Vita DeMarchi, Chair
Cornelius B. Murphy, President

5357 Rare and/or Endangered Species Research Center
215 Mitchell Street
Florence, AL 35630
256-760-4429

5358 Red Butte Garden and Arboretum
300 Wakara Way
Salt Lake City, UT 84108
801-585-0556
http://www.redbuttegarden.org
Carter Livingston, Chair
David Gee, Vice Chair

5359 Remote Sensing/Geographic Information Systems Facility
Geography Building
673 Auditorium Road
East Lansing, MI 48824
517-353-7195
Fax: 517-353-1821
E-mail: info@rsgis.msu.edu
http://www.rsgis.msu.edu

Dr Susan Berta, Interim Chairperson
Justin Booth, Director

5360 Renew America
1200 18th Street Northwest
Suite 1100
Washington, DC 20036
202-721-1545
Fax: 202-467-5780
E-mail: info@renewamerica.com
http://www.renewamerica.com

Stephen Stone, President
Matt C. Abbott, Columnist

5361 Research Triangle Institute
3040 Cornwallis Road
PO Box 12194
Research Triangle Park, NC 27709-2194
919-541-6000
Fax: 919-541-7155
E-mail: listen@rti.org
http://www.rti.org

Clients around the world rely on RTI to conduct innovative, multidisciplinary research to meet their R and D challenges. RTI's staff of more then 1,850 people represents a diverse set of technical capabilities in health and medicine,environmental protection, technology commercialization, decision support systems and education and training.
William M. Moore, Chair
Richard H. Brodhead, President

5362 Resources for the Future
1616 P Street Northwest
Suite 600
Washington, DC 20036
202-328-5000
Fax: 202-939-3460
E-mail: info@rff.org
http://www.rff.org

RFF is a nonprofit and nonpartisan think tank located in Washington DC that conducts independent research-rooted primarily in economics and other social sciences on environmental and natural resource issues. RFF was founded in 1952.

W. Bowman Cutter, Chair
John M. Deutch, Vice Chair

5363 Resources for the Future: Energy & Natural Resources Division
1616 P Street, Northwest
Suite 600
Washington, DC 20036
202-328-5000
Fax: 202-939-3460
E-mail: info@rff.org
http://www.rff.org

W. Bowman Cutter, Chair
John M. Deutch, Vice Chair

5364 Resources for the Future: Quality of the Environment Division
1616 P Street, Northwest
Suite 600
Washington, DC 20036
202-328-5000
Fax: 202-939-3460
E-mail: info@rff.org
http://www.rff.org

W. Bowman Cutter, Chair
John M. Deutch, Vice Chair

5365 River Studies Center
University of Wisconsin
University of Wisconsin-La Crosse
1725 State Street
La Crosse, WI 54601
608-785-8000
Fax: 608-785-6460
http://www.uwlax.edu
Dr. Mark Sandheinrich, Center Director
Dr. Roger Haro, Asst. Center Director

5366 Robert J Bernard Biological Field Station
1400 N Amherst Avenue
Claremont, CA 91711
909-398-1751
E-mail: wallace.meyer@pomona.edu
http://www.bfs.claremont.edu/

Robert J. Bernard
Dr. Wallace Meyer III, Director

5367 Rocky Mountain Biological Laboratory
PO Box 519
Crested Butte, CO 81224
970-349-7231
Fax: 970-349-7481
E-mail: admin@rmbl.org
http://www.rmbl.org

High-altitude field station whose principal purpose is to provide quality research and teaching facilities for biologists and biology students of all diciplines who can benefit personally and intellectually from studying at thislocation. An important further purpose of the Laboratory is to promote the understanding and protection of the high altitude ecosystems of Colorado and the watershed of the Gunnison River through through the professional activities of its members.

Scott Wissinger, President
Carol M. Johnson, VP

5368 Rocky Mountain Mineral Law Foundation
9191 Sheridan Boulevard #203 303-321-8100
Westminster, CO 80031 Fax: 303-321-7657
E-mail: info@rmmlf.org
http://www.rmmlf.org

Paul J. Schlauch, President's Fund
Stevia Walther, Executive Director

5369 Romberg Tiburon Centers
San Francisco State University
3152 Paradise Drive 415-338-6063
PO Box 855 Fax: 415-435-7120
Tiburon, CA 94920 E-mail: jviale@sfsu.edu
http://www.rtc.sfsu.edu

Annelies Atchley, Owner/Artist
Sheldon Axler, Dean

5370 Roosevelt Wildlife Station
1 Forestry Drive 315-470-6764
405 Illick Hall Fax: 315-470-6934
Syracuse, NY 13210 E-mail: jpgibbs@syr.edu
http://www.esf.ed

Dr. James P. Gibbs, Director
Dr. Jacqueline Frair, Associate Director

5371 Salt Institute
700 N. Fairfax St 703-549-4648
Suite 600 Fax: 703-548-2194
Alexandria, VA 22314-2040 E-mail: info@saltinstitute.org
http://www.saltinstitute.org

The Salt Institute is an international trade association of salt producers. It has information about the environmental impacts of salt production and use.

Lori Roman, President
Morton Satin, VP

5372 School for Field Studies
100 Cummings Center 978-741-3567
Suite 534-G 800-989-4435
Beverly, MA 01915 Fax: 978-922-3835
E-mail: ereid@fieldstudies.org
http://www.fieldstudies.org

Students conduct hands on, community-focused environmental field work around the world. Addresses critical environmental issues including preserving entire ecosystems or individual species, balancing economic development andconservation, and finding ways to manage and maintain wildlife, marine and agricultural resources.

James A. Cramer, President
Priscilla Deck, Development

5373 School of Marine Affairs (SMA)
University of Washington
University of Washington 206-543-7004
3707 Brooklyn Avenue NE Fax: 206-543-1417
Seattle, WA 98105-6715 E-mail: uwsmea@uw.edu
http://www.depts.washington.edu

SMA is a masters-level, professional school within the University of Washington specializing in the interdisciplinary teaching and research on contemporary coastal and ocean resources, environmental and developmental problems.

Suanty Kaghan, Admin Specialist
Tiffany Dion, Program Advisor

5374 Science and Public Policy
Rockefeller University 212-327-8000
1230 York Avenue, Box 234 Fax: 212-327-7519
New York, NY 10065 http://www.rockefeller.edu

David Rockefeller, Honorary Chair
Russel L. Carson, Chair

5375 Seatuck Foundation: Seatuck Research Program
Seatuck Environmental Association 631-581-6908
PO Box 31 E-mail: staff@seatuck.org
Islip, NY 11751 http://www.seatuck.org

Tom Moldovan, President
Cindy Mullin, VP

5376 Society for Ecological Restoration
1017 O Street NW 202-299-9518
Washington, DC 20001 Fax: 520-622-5491
E-mail: info@ser.org
http://www.ser.org

Steve Whisent, Chair
Cara R. Nelson, Vice Chair

5377 Society for the Application of Free Energy
1315 Apple Avenue 301-587-8686
Silver Spring, MD 20910 Fax: 301-587-8688
E-mail: uv@uvbi.com
http://www.solarthem.com

5378 Soil and Water Research
4115 Gourrier Avenue 225-757-7726
Baton Rouge, LA 70808 Fax: 225-757-7728
http://mse.ars.usda.gov/la/btn/swr/

Mission is to characterize and quantify the transport and fate of agrochemicals in high water table soils, develop integrated soil, water, and agrochemical management systems that provide profitable yields and improve water table soilsin the humid, warm temperature areas of the US and develop improved soil and water management systems and operational procedures that enhance crop production conditions and increase the efficiency of conducting farming operationsin a timely manner.

Dr. James Fouss, Research Leader

5379 Solar Energy Group
University of Chicago
1835 E 6th Street 480-884-1603
Suite 24 Fax: 480-884-1888
Tempe, AZ 85281 E-mail: solareg@gmail.com
http://www.solarengineeringgroup.com

5380 Solar Energy and Energy Conversion Laboratory
University of Florida
Dept. of Mechanical and Aerospace E 352-392-0812
PO Box 6300 Fax: 352-392-1071
Gainesville, FL 32611-6300 E-mail: execdirector@asme.org
http://www.asme.org

Has uniquely influenced the development of solar energy and renewable energy conversion systems all over the world through its research, education and training. Has pioneered research in many areas of solar energy, energy conversionand conservation. The lab has been designated as an ASME National Landmark.

Marc Goldsmith, President
Madiha Kotb, President-Elect Nominee

5381 South Carolina Agromedicine Program
Medical University of South Carolin 843-792-2211
179 Ashley Avenue, Colcock Hall 800-922-5250
Charleston, SC 29425 Fax: 843-792-4702
E-mail: Simpsowm@musc.edu
http://www.musc.edu

Information, consultation, referral service for professional and lay persons involved in or in contact with agriculture or agricultural products.

Raymond G. Greenberg, President
Dr. Mark Sothmann, VP for Academic Affairs/Prov

5382 South Carolina Sea Grant Consortium
287 Meeting Street 843-953-2078
Charleston, SC 29401 Fax: 843-953-2080
http://www.scseagrant.org

A state agency that supports coastal and marine research, education, outreach, one technical assistance program that foster sustainable economic development and resource conservation. The consortium represents eight university andstate research organi-

zations and induces a number of information products on coastal and marine resource topics.
16 pages
M Richard DeVoie, Executive Director

5383 Southern California Pacific Coastal Water Research Project
3535 Harbor Blvd 714-755-3200
Suite 110 Fax: 714-755-3299
Costa Mesa, CA 92626 http://www.sccwrp.org
SCCWRP is a joint powers agency focusing on marine environmental research. Ajoint powers agency is one that is formed when several government agencies have a common mission that can be better addressed by pooling resources andknowledge. In our case, the common mission is to gather the necessary scientific information so that our member agencies can effectively and cost-efficiently protect the Southern California marine environment.
Dr. Stephen Weisberg, Executive Director
Ken Schiff, Deputy Director

5384 Southwest Consortium on Plant Genetics & Water Resources
New Mexico State University 575-646-0111
Box 3GL E-mail: admissions@nmsu.edu
Las Cruces, NM 88003 http://www.nmsu.edu
Dr. John D Kemp, Chairman
Garrey Carruthers, President

5385 Strom Thurmond Institute of Government & Public Affairs, Regional Development Group
Clemson University 864-656-4700
Clemson, SC 29634 http://www.sti.clemson.edu
Jeffrey S. Allen, Director
Carolyn Benson, Administrative Analyst

5386 Stroud Water Research Center
970 Spencer Road 610-268-2153
Avondale, PA 19311 Fax: 610-268-0490
E-mail: webmaster@stroudcenter.org
http://www.stroudcenter.org
The Stroud Water Research Center seeks to understand streams and rivers and to use the knowledge gained from its research to promote environmental stewardship and resolve freshwater challenges throughout the world.
Bernard W. Sweeney, President/Director/Sr. Resea
David B. Arscott, VP

5387 Sustainable Agriculture Research & Education Program
ASI at UC Davis
1 Shields Avenue 530-752-3915
Davis, CA 95616 Fax: 530-752-2829
E-mail: asi@ucdavis.edu
http://www.sarep.ucdavis.edu

Tom Tomich, Director
Bev Ransom, Program Manager

5388 Tennessee Cooperative Fishery Research Unit
Tennessee Technological University
Biology Department 931-372-3094
PO Box 5114 Fax: 931-372-6257
Cookeville, TN 38505 E-mail: jim_layzer@tntech.edu
http://www.tntech.edu

Betty Harris
Kendall Moles

5389 Texas Center for Policy Studies
707 Rio Grande 512-474-0811
Suite 200 Fax: 512-474-7846
Austin, TX 78701 http://www.texascenter.org
David Hall, Chair/Board Member
Cyrus Reed, Treasurer/Board Member

5390 Texas Water Resources Institute
500 Research Parkway A110 979-845-1851
2260 TAMU Fax: 979-845-0662
College Station, TX 77843-2260 E-mail: twri@tamu.edu
http://www.twri.tamu.edu
Roel Lopez, Interim Director
Kevin Wagner, Assoc. Director

5391 The Natural History Museum & Biodiversity Research Center
University of Kansas
Dyche Hall 785-864-4540
1345 Jayhawk Boulevard Fax: 785-864-5335
Lawrence, KS 66045-7593 E-mail: naturalhistory@ku.edu
http://www.naturelhistory.ku.edu
At the UK Natural History Museum & Biodiversity Research Center, they study the life of the planet for the benefit of the earth and its inhabitants. They document the diverse life of the earth, uncover its patters and document theresearch in order to better understand the natural environments, enhance power to predict environmental phenomena, and provide knowledge for natural resource management. Their ability to discover, document and disseminate their research leads thenation.
Dr. Leanord Krishtalka, Director-Admin
Linda Trueb, Assoc. Director

5392 Throckmorton-Purdue Agricultural Center
8343 US231 Southy 765-538-3422
US 231 Fax: 765-538-3423
Lafayette, IN 47909-9049 E-mail: jayyoung@purdue.edu
http://www.ag.purdue.edu
Karen Plaut, Assoc Dean/Director
Marshall A. Martin, Sr. Assoc. Director

5393 Toxic Chemicals Laboratory
Cornell University
Cornell University, Tower Road 607-255-4538
New York State College of Agriculture
Ithaca, NY 14853

5394 US Forest Service: Wildlife Habitat & Silviculture Laboratory
USDA Forest Service, Southern Resea 936-569-7981
506 Hayter Street Fax: 936-569-9681
Nacogdoches, TX 75965 http://www.srs.fs.usda.gov
We assess impacts of forest management practices on wildlife populations and their habitats and provide guide lines to land managers for improving their management to accommodate wildlife.
Cory K. Adams, Wildlife Biologist
Gina Franke, Support Services Specialist

5395 USDA Forest Service: Northern Research Station
11 Campus Blvd. 610-557-4017
Suite 200 Fax: 517-355-5121
Newtown Square, PA 19073 E-mail: rhaack@fs.fed.us
http://www.nrs.fs.fed.us
Dr. Robert Haack, Research Entonologist
Deb Dietzman, Services Group Leader

5396 USDA Forest Service: Rocky Mountain Research Station
240 West Prospect 970-498-1100
Fort Collins, CO 80526 Fax: 970-295-5927
http://www.fs.fed.us
We seek to be an unbiased source of scientific information; provide tools that consider the multidisciplinary nature of natural resource decisions and recognize that resource managers need scientific information that is integrated anddeveloped for application. Research results are made available through a variety of technical reports, seminars, demonstrations, exhibits and personal consultations. These help resource managers and planners balance economic and environmental demandsworldwide.
Cloetta Schroeder, AD Operations
Angela Baca, Director

5397 UVA Institute for Environmental Negotiation
University of Virginia

The Institute for Environmental Neg 434-924-1970
PO Box 400179 Fax: 434-924-0231
Charlottesville, VA 22904-4179 E-mail: ed7k@virginia.edu
http://www.virginia.edu/ien

The Institute for Environmental Negotiation is committed to building a sustainable future for Virginia's communities and beyond by: bringing people together to develop sustainable solutions; providing people with learning opportunitiesto be creative and collaborative leaders; and building understanding of best collaborative practices.

Dr E Franklin Dukes, Director
Tanya Denckla Cobb, Associate Director

5398 University Forest
University of Missouri
2600 Bay Area Boulevard 281-286-5959
Houston, TX 77058 Fax: 281-286-2095
E-mail: info@universityforestUHCL.com
http://www.universityforestuhcl.com
Lawrance Samaranayake, Manager
Steven Fance, Maintenance Assistant

5399 VT Forest Resource Center and Arboretum
University of Tennessee
901 S Illinois Avenue 865-483-3571
Oak Ridge, TN 37830 Fax: 865-483-3572
E-mail: utforest@utk.edu
http://www.forestry.tennessee.edu

The UT Forestry Experiment Station mission is to:(1) provide the land and supporting resources necessary for conducting modern and effective forestry, wildlife, and associated social, biological and ecological research programs;(2)demonstrate the application of optimal forest and wildlife management technologies; and (3) assist with transfer of new technology to forest land owners and industries.

Kevin P. Hoyt, Center Director
Lynne Lucas, Administrative Specialist I

5400 Vantuna Research Group
Moore Laboratory of Zoology
Occidental College 323-259-2500
1600 Campus Road Fax: 323-259-2958
Los Angeles, CA 90041 http://www.oxy.edu
John S Stephens, Director

5401 Virginia Center for Coal & Energy Research
Virginia Tech 540-231-5038
Mail Code 0411 Fax: 540-231-4078
Blacksburg, VA 24061 E-mail: vccer@vt.edu
http://www.energy.vt.edu

Created by an Act of the VA General Assembly in 1977 as a study, research, information and resource facility for the commonwealth of VA, and is located at VA Tech. The mission involves four primary functions: research in energy andcoal related issues of interest to the Commonweatlth; coordination of coal and energy research at VA Tech; dissemination of coal and energy data to users in the Commonwealth; examination of socio-economic implications and environmental impacts ofcoal and energy.

K. Scott Keim, President
Scott Kreutzer, VP

5402 Washington Cooperative Fishery Research Unit
University of Washington
Box 355020 206-543-6475
Seattle, WA 98195-5020 http://www.depts.washington.edu
Dr. Christian Grue, Unit Leader
Dr. Glenn VanBlaricom, Asst. Unit Leader

5403 Waste Management Education & Research Consortium
New Mexico State University
Box 30001, MSC WERC 505-646-2038
Las Cruces, NM 88003 800-523-5996
Fax: 505-646-4149
E-mail: bdelrio@nmsu.edu
http://www.werc.net

A key component of WERC is higher education degree programs. To support this component, WERC administers a Fellowship Program at each academic partner institution. The primary objective for the WERC Fellowship program is to helpstudents develop a program which will lead to environmental related career opportunities upon graduation.

Barbara Valdez, Program Facilitator

5404 Waste Management Research & Education Institute
University of Tennessee
The EERC & the University of Tennes 865-974-1000
676 Dabney Hall Fax: 865-974-8086
Knoxville, TN 37996 E-mail: ceb@utk.edu
http://www.eerc.ra.utk.edu
Jack N. Barkenbus, Executive Director
Kim Davis, Asst. Director

5405 Water Quality Laboratory
Western Wyoming Community College 307-382-1662
PO Box 428 http://www.wwcc.cc.wy.us/
Rock Springs, WY 82901
Craig Thompson, Director

5406 Water Resource Center
University of Minnesota
173 McNeal Hall 612-624-9282
1985 Buford Avenue Fax: 612-625-1263
St Paul, MN 55108 E-mail: umwrc@umn.edu
http://www.wrc.umn.edu

The center coordinatoes research, education and extension programs on water resource issues. Administrative responsibility for Water Resource Sciences Graduate Program. Is the Water Resources Institute for Minnesota.

Faye Sleeper, Co-Director
Deborah L. Swackhamer, Co Director

5407 Water Resources Institute
University of Wisconsin
1975 Willow Drive 608-262-0905
Floor 2 Fax: 608-262-0591
Madison, WI 53706-1103 E-mail: hurley@aqua.wisc.edu
http://www.wri.wisc.edu

The University of Wisconsin Water Resources Institute's primary mission is to plan, develop and coordinate research programs that address present and emerging water-and land-related issues. It has developed a broadly based statewideprogram of basic and applied research that has effectively confronted a spectrum of societal concerns. It is one of 54 institutes or centers located at the Land Grant College in each state.

James Hurley, Director
Terri Liebmann, Assistant Director/Accountin

5408 Water Resources Research Institute at Kent University
Kent State University
230 Research One Bldg 330-672-2529
PO Box 5190 Fax: 330-672-4834
Kent, OH 44242 E-mail: rheath@kent.edu
http://http://dept.kent.edu/wrri

The institute fosters a broad-based approach to the evaluation and analysis of environmental problems related to water use. WRRI is a resouce for citizens, governmental agencies and policy makers, providing reliable scientificinformation on which to base decisions related to the wise use and management of water and land management, water policy decisions and environmental conservation.

Dr. Robert T Heath, Director
Dr. Joseph Otiz, Assistant Director

5409 Water Resources Research of the University of North Carolina
North Carolina State University
1575 Varsity Drive, Module 7 919-515-2815
NCSU Campus Box 7912 Fax: 919-515-2839
Raleigh, NC 27695-7912 E-mail: water_resources@ncsu.edu
http://www.ncsu.edu

One of 54 state water institutes authorized to administer and promote federal/state partnerships in research and information transfer on water-related issues. Identifies and supports research needed to help solve water quality andwater resources problems in NC. Publishes peer-reviewed reports on completed research projects. Sponsors educational seminars and conferences and provides public information on water issues through publication of a newsletter.

Susan White, Director
David Genereux, Associate Director

5410 Water Testing Laboratory
Morehead State University
Box 804
Morehead, KY 40351
606-783-2961
http://www.morehead-st.edu
Rita Wright, Contact

5411 Weather Analysis Center
University of Michigan
Space Research Building
2455 Hayward Street
Ann Arbor, MI 48109
734-936-0482
Fax: 734-763-0437
E-mail: dbaker@umich.edu
http://www.aoss.engin.umich.edu

Atmospheric, planetary and space science engineering.
Dr Dennis Baker, Director

5412 West Virginia Water Research Institute
West Virginia University
Room 202 NRCCE
Box 6064
Morgantown, WV 26506
304-293-4974
Fax: 304-293-7822
E-mail: pziemkie@wvu.edu
http://www.wvwri.org

The West Virginia Water Research Institute (WVWRI) has served as a statewide vehicle for performing research related to water issues. WVWRI serves as the coordinating body for the following programs: the National Mine Land ReclamationCenter, Appalachian Clean Streams Initiatve, Acid Drainage Technology Initiative, Northern WV Brownfields Assistant Center, Hydrogeology Research Center, State Water Institutes, and more.

Paul F. Ziemkiewicz, PhD, Director
Tamara F. Vandivort, Assoc. Director

5413 Western Research Farm
36515 Highway 34 E
Castana, IA 51010
712-885-2802
E-mail: wroush@iastate.edu
Wayne B Roush, Ag Specialist

5414 Wetland Biogeochemistry Institute
University of Florida
106 Newell Hall, Box 110510
Gainesville, FL 32611
352-392-1803
Fax: 225-388-6423
http://www.soils.ifas.ufl.edu
William H Patrick Jr, Director
K. Ramesh Reddy

5415 Wilderness Institute: University of Montana
School of Forestry
Missola, MT 59812
406-243-5361
800-462-8636
Fax: 406-243-4845
E-mail: wi@cfc.umt.edu
http://www.cfc.umt.edu

Mission is to further understand wilderness and its stewardship through education, outreach, and scholarship. Activity is guided by the philosophy that wildlands are increasingly significant, ecologically and socially, and educateddialogue about the role of wild places in our nation's future should be promoted. Engaged in undergraduate education, graduate student research, the dissemination of wilderness information and the promotion of scholarship on wilderness issues.
Wayne Freimund, Director
Natalie Dawson, Associate Director

5416 Wilderness Research Center
University of Idaho
College of Natural Resources
Room 18a
Moscow, ID 83844-1139
208-885-7911
Fax: 208-885-6226
E-mail: wrc@uidaho.edu
http://www.webpages.uidaho.ed

The mission of the WRC is to study the human dimensions of wilderness ecosystems. The WRC conducts research and teaches courses on the use of wilderness for personal growth, therapy, education, and leadership development.
Steve Hollenhorst, Ph.D, Director
Lilly Steinhorst, Administrative Assistant

5417 Wisconsin Applied Water Pollution Research Consortium: University of Wisconsin-Madison
University of Wisconsin
3232 Engineering Hall
1415 Engineering Drive
Madison, WI 53706-1691
608-263-7773
Fax: 608-262-5199
E-mail: harringt@engr.wisc.edu
http://www.engr.wisc.edu

This consortium seeks effective and economical solutions to water supply problems and pollution control in Wisconsin. It conducts innovative practical research that cannot be carried out effectively by individual organizations.
Gregory W. Harrington, Director

5418 Wisconsin Rural Development Center
USDA Rural Development-WI
5417 Clem's Way
Stevens Point, WI 54482
715-345-7600
800-670-6553
Fax: 715-345-7669
E-mail: RD.Webmaster@wi.usda.gov
http://www.rurdev.usda.gov/wi
Stan Gruszynski, State Director

5419 Wisconsin Sea Grant Institute
University of Wisconsin
1975 Williw Drive
Floor 2
Madison, WI 53706-1103
608-262-0905
Fax: 608-262-0591
E-mail: hurley@aqua.wisc.edu
http://www.seagrant.wisc.edu

The University of Wisconsin Sea Grant Institute is a statewide program of basic and applied research, education, and technology transfer dedicated to the wise stewardship and sustainable use of Great Lakes and ocean resources. It ispart of a national network of 30 university-based programs.

James Hurley, Director
Songyan Jiang, Administrative Assistant

5420 Yale Institute for Biospheric Studies (YIBS)
21 Sachem Street
PO Box 208105
New Haven, CT 06520-8105
203-432-9856
Fax: 203-432-9927
E-mail: roserita.riccitelli@yale.edu
http://www.yale.edu/yibs

Rose Rita Riccitelli, Assistant Director
LaToya Sealy, Administrative Assistant

Educational Resources & Programs

Universities

5421 **Academy for Educational Development**
Center for Environmental Strategies
1825 Connecticut Avenue NW 202-884-8000
Washington, DC 20009 Fax: 202-884-8400
E-mail: web@aed.org
http://www.fhi360.org
Develops sustainable solutions to global environmental protection and natural resource management problems through individual and institutional behavior change, education, training and communication strategies. Efforts are driven by astrong commitment to improve or maintain environmental quality as well as the quality of life for diverse communities and groups through the provision of technical assistance, guided practice and capacity building support.
Edward Russell, Chair
Willard Cates, President

5422 **Allegheny College**
Environmental Science/Studies
520 North Main Street 814-332-3100
Meadville, PA 16335 E-mail: info@allegheny.edu
http://www.allegheny.edu
Offers the study of interrelationships between human activities and the environment. Two major programs: 1) Environmental Science. Core courses include biology, chemistry, geology, and mathematics. Upper level courses synthesize,integrate and apply basic sciences toward solving real environmental problems; 2) Environmental Studies. Objective is to study the concept of sustainability in an integrated way.
Barbara D. Riess, Chairperson
Richard J Cook, President

5423 **Antioch College**
Glen Helen Outoor Education Center
1075 State Route 343 937-319-6082
1 Morgan Place Fax: 937-767-6655
Yellow Springs, OH 4538 /E-mail: rjaramillo@antioch-college.edu
http://www.antiochcollege.org
Training in residential naturalist instruction for upper elementary aged students. Classes and field experience in outdoor education methods and natural history. Care for hawk or owl in Raptor Center.
Mark Roosevelt, President
Hassan Rahmanian, VP

5424 **Antioch University/New England**
Environmental Studies
40 Avon Street 800-553-8920
Keene, NH 03431-3516 Fax: 603-357-0718
E-mail: admissions@antiochne.edu
http://www.antiochne.edu
For those committed to scholarly excellence and wish to design, implement and evaluate research regarding crucial environmental issues. The PhD program cultivates a dynamic learning community of environmental practioners who addresscomplex regional, national, and global issues responsibly, creatively, and compassionately.
Polly Chandler, Chair
David Caruso, President

5425 **Antioch University/Seattle**
Center for Creative Change
2326 Sixth Avenue 206-441-5352
Seattle, WA 98121 E-mail: osmythe@antiochsea.edu/
http://www.antiochsea.edu
Approches environmental concerns by emphasizing social science perspectives and natural science literacy. The program is part of the Center for Creative Change, an integrated professional studies center.
Cassandra Manuelito-Kerkvliet, Ph.D, President
Brigid Mercer, VP

5426 **Arkansas Tech University**
Wildlife Conservation Program
1605 Coliseum Drive 479-968-0389
Suite 141 800-582-6953
Russellville, AR 72801 E-mail: sdonnell@atu.edu
http://www.atu.edu
A two-year preparatory program in Wildlife Conservation with an outlined Wildlife Curriculum was developed at Arkansas Tech University in 1956. Two years later, plans were made to elevate this program to a four-year program. During the1959-1960 academic year, a full slate of courses was developed that provided the foudation for degree that specialized in fisheries and wildlife management.
Shauna Donnell, Vice President

5427 **Auburn University**
Environmental Institute
1090 South Donahue Drive 334-844-4132
Auburn, AL 36849 Fax: 334-844-4462
E-mail: kochafr@auburn.edu
http://www.auei.auburn.edu
Serves faculty, governments, and the general public in a coordinating role to bring together teams to develop acceptable and economically feasible means of enhancing the environmental quality of the state and nation.
Frances Kochan, Chair
M. Kay Stone, Academic Program Assistant

5428 **Ball State University**
Natural Resources and Environmental Management
2000 West University 765-289-1241
Muncie, IN 47306 800-382-8540
Fax: 765-285-2606
E-mail: nrem@bsu.edu
http://www.bsu.edu/nrem
The Natural Resources and Environmental Management Department enhances scientific competence and prepares students for a variety of environmental careers. Programs focus on air, energy, land, parks, recreation, soil, waste management,and water and emergency management.

James Eflin, Chairperson

5429 **Bard College**
Environmental and Urban Studies
PO Box 5000 845-758-6822
Annandale-on-Hudson, NY 12504 5000 http://www.bard.edu
This program focuses on both the lived and built environments. Its goal is to involve students in empirically-based studies that bridge the divisions between natural and artificial, given and created. This approach is designed to buildon the transformations within a range of social and natual sciences, ranging from systems theory to envirornmental toxicology.
Sanjib Baruah, Director
Felicia Keesing, Professor

5430 **Bemidji State University**
Center for Environmental, Earth & Space Studies
1500 Birchmont Drive NE 218-755-2001
Bemidji, MN 56601-2699 800-475-2001
Fax: 218-755-4048
E-mail: fchang@bemidjistate.edu
http://www.bemidjistate.edu/
The Center for Environmental, Earth and Space Studies (CEESS) offer a unique variety of interdisciplinary degree programs. Degrees in Environmental Studies include both B.S. and M.S., and a B.S. or B.A. with geology minor is alsoavailable. Students in the CEESS program are concerned with both the technological problems and social apects of enviromental issues.

Dr. Richard Hanson, President
Paul Lindseth, Director

5431 **Bradley University**
Geological Sciences Program

1501 West Bradley Avenue 309-676-7611
Peoria, IL 61625 800-447-6460
E-mail: admissions@bradley.edu
http://www.admissions.bradley.edu

Aims to develop an awareness of the Earth as a dynamic and unified system in time and space. Curriculum is preparatory for careers in geology, engineering geology, geophysics, hydrogeology, oceanography or secondary Earth scienceteaching.

Joanne K. Glasser, President
Dr. David Glassman, Provost/VP

5432 Brooklyn College
Environmental Studies
PO Box 8102 718-951-4159
Pittsburgh, PA 15217 Fax: 718-951-4546
E-mail: yklein@brooklyn.cuny.edu
http://www.envirolink.org

Program is aimed at educating students to be fluent in social and physical sciences as related to the environment. In addition, the program draws from other courses in humanities, social sciences, mathematics, and sciences. Thisinterdisciplanary approach is designed to introduce the field of environmental studies and to apply this knowledge to various careers.

Yehuda Klein, Deputy Director

5433 Brown University
Center for Environmental Studies
135 Angel Street 401-863-3449
Box 1943 Fax: 401-863-3503
Providence, RI 02912 E-mail: janet_blume@brown.edu
http://www.envstudies.brown.edu

The Center for Environmental Studies at Brown University was established with the primary aim of educating individuals to solve challenging environmental problems both at the local and global levels. It also works directly to improvehuman well-being and environmental quality through community, city, and state partnerships in service and research.

Janet Blume, Interim Director
Jeanne Loewenstein, Administrative Manager

5434 California Polytechnic State University
Institute for City & Regional Planning
California Polytechnic State Univer 805-756-1315
San Luis Obispo, CA 93407-283 Fax: 805-756-1340
E-mail: crp@calopoly.edu
http://www.planning.calpoly.edu

Developed to coordinate interdisciplinary projects and research relating to the management of watersheds, urban areas, marine environments and related natural and human resources. The Institute offers specialists in various areas suchas biological science, business administation, city and regional planning, civil and environmental engineering, economics, geology, landscape architecture, natural resources management, political science and soil science.

Hemalata C. Dandekar, Department Head
Kathy Lehmkuhl, Administrative Support Coord

5435 California State University/Fullerton
Environmental Studies
PO Box 34080 714-278-2011
Fullerton, CA 92834-9480 E-mail: arwebmaster@fullerton.edu
http://www.fullerton.edu

The Environmental Studies program is an interdisciplinary program that broadens environmental knowledge and awareness. It's designed to prepare students as professionals in the environmental field by providing an opportunity to learnapplicable skills and to develop an appropriate body of knowledge.

Mildred Garcia, President
Stephen G. Garcia, Interim VP

5436 California State University/Seaside
Capstone Project Program
100 Campus Center 831-582-3689
Building 42 E-mail: laura_lienk@csumb.edu
Seaside, CA 93955-8001 http://www.watershed.csumb.edu

Capstone Projects encompass a broad array of student interests, primarily within the programs of Earth Systems Science and Policy. A Capstone Project is similar to a senior thesis project at other universites, and showcases mastery ofESSP skills. They follow a set of outcome based, interdisciplinary criteria used to measure the competence of participants.

Laura Lee Lienk, Co-Director
Doug Smith, Co-Director

5437 California University of Pennsylvania
Biological & Environmental Sciences
250 University Avenue 724-938-4000
California, PA 15419 E-mail: pavtis@cup.edu
http://www.calu.edu

Department includes intensive scientific curricula that prepare students for graduate work in the biological and environmental sciences and career work in related areas.

Guido M. Pichini, Chairman
Geraldine M. Jones, Interim President

5438 Carnegie Mellon University
Civil and Environmental Engineering Program
5000 Forbes Avenue 412-268-2940
119 Porter Hall Fax: 412-268-7813
Pittsburgh, PA 15213 E-mail: webmaster@ce.cmu.edu
http://www.ce.cmu.edu

A major function of the Environmental Institute is to enable Carnegie Mellon to play a leadership role in developing educational programs on environmental issues. These include initiatives at both undergraduate and graduate levels.

Irving Oppenheim, Interim Department Head
Deborah Lange, Executive Director

5439 Clark University
Environmental Science & Policy
950 Main Street 508-793-7711
Worcester, MA 01610 E-mail: idce@clarku.edu
http://www.clarku.edu/

An interdisciplinary approach that emphasizes policy questions involving the environment and use and misuse of science and technology. Its goal is to enable individuals to deal with technical and environmental issues in social andpolitical areas. Topics addresses deal with urgent and important issues, including assessment and management of environmental risks to humans and ecosystems, capacity for sustainable development in third world countriie, and integrated watershedmanagement.

David P. Angel, President
Davis Baird, Provost/VP for Academic Affa

5440 Clemson University
Environmental Engineering and Earth Sciences
Clemson University 864-656-3311
Clemson, SC 29634 http://www.clemson.edu

Programs in the environmental field focus on environmental process engineering, hydrogeology, environmental health physics and radiochemistry, environmental chemistry and sustainable systems.

Esin Gulari, Dean

5441 Colby-Sawyer College
Community & Environmental Studies
541 Main Street 603-526-3000
New London, NH 03257 E-mail: kslover@colby-sawyer.edu
http://www.colby-sawyer.edu

Bachelor of Science degree in Community and Environmental Studies. A minor in CES is also available.

Thomas C. Csatari, Chair
Thomas C. Galligan, President

5442 College of Natural Resources
Conservation Management Institute
1900 Kraft Drive 540-231-7348
Suite 250 Fax: 540-231-7019
Blacksburg, VA 24061 E-mail: CMIinfo@vt.edu
http://www.cmi.vt.edu

Offers multi-disciplinary research that addresses conservation management effectiveness throughout the world. Faculty from far reaching research institutions work collaboratively on projects ranging from endangered species propagationto natural resource-based satellite imagery interpretation.

Scott D Klopfer, Director
Ginger E Hicks, Program Administrator

5443 **College of William and Mary**
Center for Conservation Biology
PO Box 1346 804-684-7000
1375 Greate Road Fax: 804-684-7097
Gloucester Point, VA 23062-1346 E-mail: wmaster@vims.edu
http://www.vims.edu/

The Center for Conservation Biology is an organization dedicated to discovering innovative solutions to environmental problems that are both scientifically sound and practical within today's social context. It has been a leader inconservation issues throughout the mid-Atlantic region with a philosophy that uses a general systems approach to locate critical information needs and to plot a deliberate course of action to reach goals.

John T. Wells, Dean And Director
Jennifer Latour, CFO/CAO

5444 **Colorado Mountain College**
Natural Resource Management Program
802 Grand Avenue 970-945-8691
Glenwood Springs, CO 81601 800-621-8559
Fax: 970-947-8324
E-mail: servicedesk@coloradomtn.edu
http://www.coloradomtn.edu

The Natural Resource Management program grew out of the Environmental Technology, which was one of the most well established programs of its kind in the country. It specializes in helping students graduate with entry-level skills in avariety of environmental fields, while combining aquatic and terrestrial resource management. Students are trained in career fields of environmental site assessment, hydrology, soil science, environmental law and others.

Renee Kuharski, Asst. VP
Jan Dean, Executive Administrative Ass

5445 **Colorado School of Mines**
Environmental Engineering & Applied Science
1500 Illinois Street 303-273-3000
Golden, CO 80401 800-446-9488
http://www.mines.edu

This public research university devoted to engineering and applied science, offers a curriculum and research program that is geared toward responsible stewardship of the earth and its resources. It has broad expertise in resourceexploration, extration, production and utilization. The programs at Mines are central to balancing resource availability with environmental protection.

James Spaanstra, Chairman
Richard Truly, Vice Chairman

5446 **Colorado State University**
College of Natural Resouses
101 Natural Resources Building 970-491-6675
Campus Delivery 1401 Fax: 970-491-0279
Fort Collins, CO 80523-1401 http://www.warnercnr.colostate.edu

The College of Natural Resources is one of the most comprehensive environment and natural resources programs in the nation. With four departments and eight undergraduate majors, 9 minors and 13 concentrations, students address the mostcurrent issues in environment and natural resources, including endangered species, water quality, biological diversity, parks forests and wildlife management, recreation and environmental and ecosystem sciences.

Joyce Berry, Dean
Scott Webb, Director of Development

5447 **Columbia University**
Public Admin in Environmental Science & Policy
116th and Broadway 212-854-1754
New York, NY 10027 http://www.columbia.edu

The program is designed to train sophisticated public managers and policymakers who apply innovative, system-based thinking to environmental issues. It emphasizes practical skills and is enriched by ecological and plantatary science.

Lee C. Bollinger, President
Robert Kasdin, Sr. Executive VP

5448 **Connecticut College**
Goodwin Niering Center for Conservation Biology
270 Mohegan Avenue 860-447-1911
Box 5293 Fax: 860-439-5277
New London, CT 6320 E-mail: goodwin-nieringcenter@conncoll.edu
http://www.conncoll.edu

A comprehensive, interdisciplinary program aimed at understanding contemporary ecological challenges. Its Certificate Program offers students the opportunity to blend thier interest in the environment with a non-science major and is ofparticular interest to those planning careers in environmental policy, law, economies or education.

Ulysses B. Hammond, VP for Administration
Glenn Dreyer, Executive Director

5449 **Conservation Leadership School**
117 Forest Resources Building 814-865-7541
University Park, PA 16802 877-778-2937
Fax: 814-865-3725
E-mail: mgm20@psu.edu
http://www.ecosystems.psu.edu

A one-week residential program for high school students to learn about the world around them through exploration and hands-on activities. The classroom includes over 700 acres of forest, fields, wetlands, and streams, and learningabout the environment includes having fun, meeting new friends and learning leadership skills.

Michael G. Messina, Head/Professor
Linda Spangler, Manager

5450 **Cornell University**
Center for the Environment
Day Hall Lobby 607-254-4636
Cornell University Fax: 607-254-6225
Ithaca, NY 14853 E-mail: info@cornell.edu
http://www.cornell.edu

Offers opportunities for graduate study in the ecology, management, and policy of fishery, forest, wetland, wildlife, and other environmental resources. There also are opportunities to focus on conservation biology, agroforestry,environmetnal change, and conservation and sustainable development.

David J. Skorton, President
Kent Fuchs, Provost

5451 **Dartmouth College**
Department of Earth Sciences
Dartmouth College 603-646-1110
Hanover, NH 03755 E-mail: cantact@dartmouth.edu
http://www.dartmouth.edu/

Offers opportunities for learning and research in all major disciplines devoted to the study of the earth, including its structure and development, the oceans and atmosphere, weather and climate. Teaching and research at a moreadvanced level emphasize watershed processes, environmental biogeochemistry, geophysics and mechanics, sedimentology, paleontology, economic geology, end remote sensing of the earth from aircraft and satellites.

Philip J. Hanlon '77, President
Martin N. Wybourne, Interim Provost/Vice Provost

5452 **Delaware Valley College**
Agronomy & Environmental Science
700 East Butler Avenue 215-345-1500
Doylestown, PA 18901 800-233-5825
E-mail: webmaster@delval.edu
http://www.delval.edu

The Department of Agronomy and Environmental Science offers courses designed to give a broad, workable background in the plant, soil, turf or environmental sciences. Focusing on the environmental issues facing society today, thesecourses provide the knowledge and training necessary to be successful in the field or to move on to the graduate level.

Dorothy Prisco, Vice President

5453 Drake University
Environmental Science & Policy Program
2507 University Avenue 515-271-2011
Olin Hall 800-443-7253
Des Moines, IA 50311-4505 Fax: 515-271-3702
E-mail: thomas.rosburg@drake.edu
http://www.drake.edu

Environmental Science and Policy Program is an interdisciplinary program that awards BS and BA degrees in both Environmental Science and Environmental Policy.

Larry Zimpleman, Chairman/President/CEO
David Maxwell, President

5454 Duke University/Marine Laboratory
Nicholas School of the Environment
Marine Laboratory 252-504-7502
135 Duke Marine Lab Road Fax: 252-504-7648
Beaufort, NC 28516-9721 E-mail: hnearing@duke.edu
http://www.nicholas.duke.edu/marinelab

The Laboratory is a campus of Duke University and a unit within the Nicholas School of the Environment. The mission is education, research, and service to understand marine systems, including the human component, and to developapproaches for marine conservation and restoration.

Belinda Williford, Administrator
Cindy Van Dover, Director

5455 Duquesne University
Environmental Science & Management Program
600 Forbes Avenue 412-396-6000
Pittsburgh, PA 15282 E-mail: admissions@dug.edu
http://www.duq.edu

Educating environmental professionals for the twenty-first century is the focus of this program, which grew out of the need to combine depth of knowledge in environmental science with a comprehensive understanding of the business,legal and policy implications surrounding environmental issues.
Charles J. Dougherty, President
Linda Drago, VP for Legal Affairs & Gener

5456 Eastern Illinois University
Aquatic and Fisheries Program
600 Lincoln Avenue 217-581-5000
Charleston, IL 61920 877-581-2348
E-mail: admissions@eiu.edu
http://www.eiu.edu

Offers aquatic ecology, fisheries biology, and physiological ecology. Specific areas of concentration include community analysis of stream fishes, life history and demographics of fish, bioenergetics of development and life historyphenomena, and lipid storage and utilization patterns of fish.
William L. Perry, President
Blair M. Lord, Provost

5457 Eastern Michigan University
Kresge Environmental Education Center
202 Welch Hall 734-487-1849
Ypsilanti, MI 48197 800-468-6368
Fax: 734-487-6559
E-mail: tkasper@emich.edu
http://www.emich.edu

The Kresge Environmental Education Center is located in Mayfield, about six miles north east of the city of Lapeer. The main buildings are located on Fish Lake Road in the middle of the center's 240 acres. These 240 acres sit next to7,000 acres of state land.
Francine Parker, Chair
Mike Morris, Vice Chair

5458 Eastern Nazarene College
Eastern Environmental Program
23 East Elm Avenue 617-745-3000
Quincy, MA 02170 800-88E-NC88
Fax: 617-745-3907
E-mail: jonathan.e.twining@enc.edu
http://www.enc.edu

Cross-disciplinary program which provides for students strong pereparation in the several scientific disciplines involved in the study of environmental issues. The program is jointly sponsored by the Department of Biology andChemistry in order to provide the appropriate basis in all the sciences for students wishing to pursue environmental careers or graduate school.
Elizabeth Buckley, Chair
Dr. Corlis McGee, President

5459 Fairleigh Dickinson University
Environmental Studies/System Science
College at Florham 973-443-8500
285 Madison Avenue Fax: 973-443-8921
Madison, NJ 07940 http://www.fdu.edu

This program offers students a wide variety of 18 concentrations, including envionmental chemistry, environmental risk assessment, water treatment, environmental planning, groundwater hydrology, environmental remediation, soil science,land-use planning and air pollution.
Patrick J. Zenner, Chair
Sheldon Drucker, President

5460 Ferrum College
Environmental Science
PO Box 1000 540-365-2121
Ferrum, VA 24088 800-868-9797
Fax: 540-365-4203
E-mail: webmaster@ferrum.edu
http://www.ferrum.edu

Offers programs in environmental science that includes informationon air pollutant deposition in the Great Lakes and the formulation of membrances for ion-selective electrodes. The program also includes participation in a water qualitymonitoring project on Smith Mountain Lake that uses a geographical information system to model soil loss in its watershed.
Samuel L. Lionberger, Chair
Jennifer L. Braaten, President

5461 Field Station & Ecological Reserves
University of Kansas
C/O Kansas Biological Survey 785-864-1500
2101 Constant Avenue Fax: 785-864-1534
Lawrence, KS 66047 http://www.ksr.ku.edu

The KSR is dedicated to field-based environmental reseach and education. KSR is located within the transition zone (ecotone) between the eastern deciduous forest and tallgrass prairie biomes. The 3,000 acres of diverse native andmanaged habitats, experimental systems, support facilities, and longterm databases are used to undertake an outstanding array of scholarly activities. Environmental stewardship is a stong emphasis as high-quality natural areas are preserved for thefuture.
Bernadette Gray-Little, Chancellor
Jeffrey Vitter, Executive Vice Chancellor/Pr

5462 Florida State University
Environmental Studies
600 W. College Avenue 850-644-2525
Tallahassee, FL 32306 Fax: 850-644-9936
E-mail: admissions@admin.fsu.edu
http://www.fsu.edu

Offers the study of environmental issues as they relate to geological phenomena, which include volcanic and earthquake hazards, resource and land- use planning, air and water pollution, waste disposal, glaciation and sea-level change,landslides, flooding, shoreline erosion, and global change issues.
Eric J. Barron, President
Dr. Garnett S. Stokes, Provost

5463 George Washington University
International Environmental Policy & Management
2121 1st Street NW 202-994-1000
Washington, DC 20052 E-mail: hmerchnt@awu.edu
http://www.gwu.edu/

Offers a program on International Environmental Policy and Management and Marketing Management, held in various locations around the world
Steven Knapp, President
Steven R. Lerman, Provost

5464 Georgetown University
Environmental Studies
37th O Streets NW
Washington, DC 20057
202-687-0100
E-mail: webmaster@georgetown.edu
http://www.georgetown.edu

Environmental Studies is an interdisciplinary program designed to allow an undergraduate of the college majoring in any discipline to focus on environmental issues. Environmental Studies provides a framework for the study offundamental mechanisms of ecosystems and human interaction with the Earth. Environmental studies encompasses the humanities, social sciences and natural sciences as they relate to environmental questions.

Dr. John J. DeGioia, President
Chris Augostini, Sr. VP/COO

5465 Hocking College
Environmental Restoration Technology Program
3301 Hocking Parkway
Nelsonville, OH 45764
740-753-3591
877-462-5464
Fax: 740-753-7065
E-mail: admissions@hocking.edu
http://www.hocking.edu

Growing concern for the environment has increased the need for technicians qualified in the restoration of environmentally unstable land, water, and air. Hocking College's Environmental Restoration technology prepares students for thatchallenge.

Tammy Andrews

5466 Idaho State University
Geochemistry & Hydrogeology Program
921 South Eighth Avenue
Pocatello, ID 83209
208-282-0211
E-mail: webmaster@isu.edu
http://www.isu.edu/

Emphasizes environmental geochemistry and hydrogeology. This specialty is ideal in southern Idaho where problems of nuclear and toxic waste clean-up at the Idaho National Environmental Engineering Laboratory will require study andgenerate research monies for years to come.

Robert A. Wharton, Provost And Vice President

5467 Indiana State University
Department of Ecology & Organismal Biology
200 North Seventh Street
Terre Haute, IN 47809-1902
812-237-4000
800-468-6478
Fax: 812-237-8525
E-mail: rlfaq@isugw.indstate.edu
http://www.indstate.edu/

This department conducts research in the areas of ecology, evolution, and conservation. The M.S. and Ph.D degrees garnered in state-of-the-art laboratories and local field stations enable students to conduct innovative research andplay significant roles as well-trained evnironmentists.

Dr. Daniel J. Bradley, President
David Campbell, Secretary

5468 Iowa State University
Environmental Studies Program
100 Enrollment Services Center
Ames, IA 50011-2011
515-294-5836
800-262-3810
Fax: 515-294-2592
E-mail: contact@iastate.edu
http://www.iastate.edu

The Environmental Studies Program deals with the relationship between humans and nature, or between humans and natural systems. The curriculum is designed to give students an understanding of regional and global environmental issuesand an appreciation of different perspectives regarding these issues. Courses are provided for both students pursuing careers related to the environment and those with an interest in environmental issues.

5469 Johns Hopkins University
Department of Geography/Environmental Engineering
Wyman Park Building, 4th Floor
3400 N Charles Street
Baltimore, MD 21218
410-516-4050
E-mail: engineeringinfo@jhu.edu
http://www.jhu.edu/

Concerned with understanding the nature and dynamics of ecosystems, engineered systems, and societies. Offers a broad range of graduate programs including the natural, social and engineering sciences.

Ronald J. Daniels, President
Jonathan A. Bagger, Interim Provost/Sr. VP for A

5470 Kansas State University
Department of Agricultural Economics
342 Waters Hall
Manhattan, KS 66506
785-532-6011
Fax: 785-532-6897
E-mail: k-state@k-state.edu
http://www.k-state.edu

The Department of Agricultural Economics has a rich tradition of services to agriculture and related fields. The department has a history of succes in its land-grant mission, teaching, research, and extension outreach, maintaininglarge and diverse programs in undergraduate and graduate instruction, as well as research and extension outreach.

Kirk H Schulz, President
Dana Hastings, Administrative Assistant

5471 Keene State College
Environmental Studies
229 Main Street
Keene, NH 03435
800-572-1909
E-mail: agagnon@keene.edu
http://www.keene.edu

Environmental Studies is an interdisciplinary program comprised of courses in Biology, Chemistry, Economics, Geography, Geology, and Political Science. Two concentration options are Environmental Policy and Environmental Science, bothof which will prepare students for a wide range of environment-related career opportunities.

Dr. Jay V. Kahn, President
Barbara A. Hall, Administrative Assistant

5472 Lake Erie College
Environmental Management Program
391 West Washington Street
Painesville, OH 44077
440-296-1856
800-533-4996
Fax: 440-375-7005
E-mail: webmaster@lec.edu
http://www.lakeerie.edu

Interdisciplinary major, grounded in the sciences and liberal arts,designed for those who want to pursue career paths utilizing environmental science in decision making. Courses include environmental management, biology, chemistry,mathamatics and business. Program is designed to help students build a solid knolwledge base in regional and global environmental issues

Elizabeth Abraham, Owner/CEO
Michael T. Victor, President

5473 Louisiana State University
Environmental Sciences Program
1271 Energy, Coast and Environment Building
Baton Rouge, LA 70803
225-578-9421
Fax: 225-578-4286
E-mail: cstrom4@lsu.edu
http://www.environmental.lsu.edu

Environmental Sciences program is designed to provide a broad-based graduate education to prepare students for careers in industrial, government, and academia. The program builds on a strong undergraduate background in the sciences.

Larry Rouse, Chair/Assoc. Professor
Edward Laws, Interim Chair

5474 Louisiana Tech University
Wildlife Conservation Program
305 Wisteria Street
PO Box 10197
Ruston, LA 71272
318-257-4287
E-mail: ANSmail@ans.latech.edu
http://www.ans.latech.edu/

The Wildlife Conservation degree program meets the certification requirements of the Wildlife Society, and graduates may apply for certification as an Associate Wildlife Biologist.

James D. Liberatos, Dean
Betty T. Jensen, Administrative Assistant

5475 Miami University
Institute of Environmental Sciences
Campus Avenue Building
301 S. Campus Ave.
Oxford, OH 45056-3434
513-529-2531
E-mail: admission@muohio.edu
http://www.muohio.edu/

Offers a masters degree in Environmental Science. This interdisciplinary program stresses problem solving and community service, and provides practical experience in many potential areas of concentration, preparing students for avariety of practical careers in public and private sector jobs.

David C. Hodge, President
Bobby Gempesaw, Provost

5476 **Michigan Technological University**
Applied Technology & Environmental Science
1400 Townsend Drive 906-487-1885
Houghton, MI 49931-1295 800-966-3764
Fax: 906-487-2915
E-mail: forest@mtu.edu
http://www.mtu.edu

A degree in Applied Ecology and Environmental Sciences prepares students to address complex environmental problems posed by the use of natural resources. Students learn how to protect the integrity of ecosystems and help assure thatnatural resources will be managed wisely for generations of sustainable use.
Dr. Dale R. Tahtinen, VP for Governmental Relation
Daniel D. Greenlee, Treasurer

5477 **Middlebury College**
Environmental Studies
121a South Main Street 802-443-5000
Middlebury, VT 05753 Fax: 802-443-2060
E-mail: admissions@middlebury.edu
http://www.middlebury.edu

Explores the relationship between humans and their environment. Students pursuing the ES major work in a variety of disciplines, including biology, chemistry, economics, geography, geology, literature, the performing arts, philosophy,political science, religion and sociology.
Ronald D. Liebowitz, President
Susan Campbell, VP for Planning & Assessment

5478 **Montana State University**
Montana Environmental Training Center
2100 16th Avenue South 406-265-3730
Great Falls, MT 59405 800-662-6132
E-mail: webmaster@msun.edu
http://www.msun.edu/

A cooperative effort between Montana State University/Northern and the Montana Department of Environmental Quality. Offers basic, advance training, and continuing education in the areas of water and wastewater operation, maintenance,safety, process control, cross connection and backflow prevention along with courses in basic water science and watershed awareness. A newsletter and Training Announcement are published quarterly.
Dr. James Limbaugh, Chancellor
Marianne Hamilton, Administrative Assistant

5479 **New Mexico State University**
Department of Geological Sciences
Box 30001 575-646-2708
MSC 3AB Fax: 575-646-1056
Las Cruces, NM 88003 E-mail: geology@nmsu.edu
http://www.nmsu.edu/~geology

Offers both undergraduate and graduate study leading to advanced degrees in geological science. Advanced training qualifies students for employment in such branches of geological science as mining, petroleum, environmental andengineering geology, government service or for further graduate study. The education experience may include sedimentology, geochemistry, volcanology, stratigraphy, geotectonics and paleontology.
Lee Hubbard, Administrative Department
Dr. Nancy S. McMillan, Department Head

5480 **North Dakota State University**
Department of Biological Sciences
PO Box 6050 701-231-7087
Fargo, ND 58108-6050 Fax: 701-231-7149
http://www.ndsu.nodak.edu

Department offers undergraduate and graduate degrees in biological disciplines, including environmental and conservation sciences.

Dean Bresciani, President
Barb Pederson, Executive Assistant

5481 **Northeastern Illinois University**
International Center for Tropical Ecology
5500 N St. Louis 773-583-4050
Chicago, IL 60625-4699 Fax: 773-442-4900
E-mail: admrec@neiu.edu
http://www.neiu.edu

The International Center for Tropical Ecology provides a focal point for interdisciplinary research and graduate education in all aspects of the conservation of tropical ecosystems. The Center, formed in collaboration with the MissouriBotanical Garden, supports a network in the United States of students, scientists, and conservationists from tropical countries to study issues related to biodiversity conservation.

Sharon Hahs, President
Richard J. helldobler, Provost/VP for Academic Affa

5482 **Northern Arizona University**
Environmental Sciences
South San Francisco Street 928-523-9011
Flagstaff, AZ 86011 Fax: 928-523-6023
E-mail: distance.programs@nau.edu
http://www.nau.edu/

Designed to offer students a technically rigorous foundation and broad exposure to the environmental science. The core courses in environmental sciences are interdisciplinary, and team taught by scientists with different backgroundsand specialties, providing multiple perspectives and rich learning experiences.
John D. Haeger, President
Tom Acker, Professor of Mechanical Engi

5483 **Northern Michigan University**
Environmental Studies
1401 Presque Isle Avenue 906-227-1000
Marquette, MI 49855-5301 Fax: 906-227-2249
http://www.nmu.edu

Research focuses on the Upper Peninsula environment, ethnic groups, economy, politics, folklore and literature.
L. Garnet Lewis, Chair
Richard M. Popp, Vice Chair

5484 **Northland College**
Environmental Studies
1411 Ellis Avenue S 715-682-1699
Ashland, WI 54806 800-753-1840
Fax: 715-682-1308
E-mail: info@northland.edu
http://www.northland.edu

Offers a comprehensive range of environmental programs that integrate traditional study with a keen eye toward problem-solving and environmental impact.
Karen Halbersleben, President
Rick Fairbanks, Provost

5485 **Ohio State University**
School of Environment and Natural Resources
2021 Coffey Road 614-292-2265
210 Kottman Hall Fax: 614-292-7432
Columbus, OH 43210 E-mail: geise.1@osu.edu
http://www.senr.osu.edu

Focuses on the science and management of natural resources and the environment. A variety of integrated undergraduate programs of study provide the foundation to a variety of career paths dealing with natural resources and theenvironment. Graduates are employed as environmental and ecosystem scientists; forest, wildlife and fisheries reserchers and biologists; environmental educators, communicators and naturalists; and park, forest, and wildlife managers.
Olivia Ameredes, Fiscal Manager
Jennifer Donovan, Office Associate

5486 Oklahoma State University
Environmental Science Program
Stillwater, OK 74078
405-744-5000
E-mail: osu-it@okstate.edu
http://www.it.okstate.edu

Environmental Science Program is designed to broaden the scope of scientific and technological study through a multidisciplinary approach encompassing social and legal aspects of environmental concerns and based on ecologicalfoundations.
Darlene Hightower, CIO
Michael Shuttic, Compliance Officer

5487 Oregon State University
Environmental Sciences
Corvallis, OR 97331
541-737-1000
Fax: 541-737-3590
E-mail: OSU.Provost@oregonstate.edu
http://www.oregonstate.edu

Offers programs that are central to the mission of the university, which includes wise use of natural resources. Recognized as a Land, Sea, and Space Grant institution, OSU has exceptional strength in many of the disciplines that arerequired to provide a high-quality interdisciplinary education for future environmental scientists.
Dr. Edward J. Ray, President
Sabah U. Randhawa, Provost

5488 Pennsylvania State University
Center for Statistical Ecology
323 Thomas Building
814-865-1348
University Park, PA 16802
Fax: 814-863-7114
E-mail: b2a@stat.psu.edu
http://www.stat.psu.edu

This ground-breaking program enjoys national and international recognition. With an ongoing program of research that integrates statistics, ecology and the environment, the emphasis is on the environment and collaborative research,training and exposition on improving the quantification and communication of human impact on the environment. Studies also include statistical investigations of the impact of the environment on man.
Bonnie Cain, Financial Secretary
Barbara Freed, Administrative Assistant

5489 Portland State University
Environmental Sciences & Resources Program
PO Box 751
503-725-3000
Portland, OR 97207
Fax: 503-725-4882
E-mail: psuinfo@pdx.edu
http://www.pdx.edu

Environmental studies are central to the mission of Portland State University, which serves the state's major urban center. The Environmental Sciences and Resources program offers both under graduate and graduate degrees.
Win Wiewel, President
John Reuter, Program Director

5490 Prescott College
Department of Environmental Studies
220 Grove Avenue
877-350-2100
Prescott, AZ 86301
Fax: 928-776-5242
E-mail: admissions@prescott.edu
http://www.prescott.edu/

Prescott College is a private liberal arts collage offering a resident BA and limited residency BA, MA, and PhD. Small groups of students work actively on real-world projects with faculty who are leaders in the field of environmentalstudies. Offers dynamic and active laboratories for students and gives them the opportunity to be on the cutting edge of environmental and sustainabilty research.
Paul Burkhardt, President/Ececutive VP
Frank Cardamone, Provost

5491 Purdue University
Natural Resources & Environmental Science
3440 Lilly Hall
765-494-4786
915 W State Street
888-398-4636
West Lafayette, IN 47907-1284
Fax: 765-496-2926
E-mail: nres@purdue.edu
http://www.ag.purdue.edu

An interdisciplinary program at the Purdue School of Agriculture designed to prepare students to work with environmental problems which impact our basic natural resources, specifically land, air and water. Faculty from all departmentsin the school contribute to the curriculum. NRES is a flexible program which allows students, working closely with an academic advisor, to develop their personal curriculum to meet individual career goals.
Dr John Graveel, Director/Professor of Agrono
Jane Wiercioch, Program Coordinator

5492 Rensselaer Polytechnic Institute
Lally School of Management and Technology
110 8th Street
518-276-2812
Pittsburgh Building
E-mail: lally-dean-l@lists.rpi.edu
Troy, NY 12180
http://www.lallyschool.rpi.edu

Committed to integrating green business strategy throughout all management curriculum. An MBA with an Environmental Management and Policy Concentration is truly designed as an interdisciplinary degree, enabling graduates to work intraditional business settings with the knowledge and skill to help these businesses realize environmental, health and safety strategy.
Thomas Begley, Dean
Chaina Porter, Administrative Coordinator

5493 Rice University
Urban & Environmental Policy Program
6100 Main
713-348-7423
PO Box 1892
800-527-OWLS
Huston, TX 77251
E-mail: admi@rice.edu
http://www.rice.edu

This program is designed to introduce students to how environmental policies are developed and how science and engineering issues are included in effective policy.
David W. Leebron, President
David K. Vassar, Sr. Asst. to the President

5494 Roger Williams University
Center for Environmental Development
One Old Ferry Road
401-253-1040
Bristol, RI 02809
800-458-7144
Fax: 401-254-3310
E-mail: mdg@alpha.rwu.edu
http://www.rwu.edu/

Undergraduate program in marine biology combining chemistry, biology, physics, and mathmatics. Designed to keep and develop interest in the sciences by using field research and laboratory experimentation.
Rodney A. Butler, Chairman
Donald J. Farish, President

5495 SUNY/Cortland
Coalition for Education in the Outdoors
Park Center
607-753-4971
PO Box 2000
Fax: 607-753-5982
Cortland, NY 13045-900E-mail: outdoored@outdooredcoalition.org
http://www.outdooredcoalition.org

A nonprofit network of outdoor and environmental education centers, nature centers, conservation and recreation organizations, outdoor education and experimental education associations, public and private schools and fish and wildlifeagencies. All those involved in the coalition share the desire to support and encourage environmental and outdoor education and its goals.
Erik J. Bitterbaum, President
Mark Prus, Provost

5496 SUNY/Fredonia
Environmental Sciences
280 Central Avenue
716-673-3111
Fredonia, NY 14063
800-252-1212
Fax: 716-673-3249
E-mail: admissions@fredonia.edu
http://www.fredonia.edu/

Rigorous, interdisciplinary program in environmental science with 68 semester hours of core courses in mathematics, biology, chemistry, environmental sciences, and geosciences. Students are prepared to pursue graduate studies,professional certifications, or employment in the private or public sector.

Ginny Horvath, President
Mrs. Denise Szalkowski, Assistant to the President

5497 **SUNY/Plattsburgh**
Environmental Science
101 Broad Street 518-564-2000
Plattsburgh, NY 12901 E-mail: franzida@plattsburg.edu
http://www.plattsburg.edu

One of the largest and most established environmental science programs in the US, with 20 interdisciplinary faculty and nearly 300 majors among five degree programs. Opportunities for hands-on work and practical experience are providedby close proximity to the Adirondack Mountains State Forest Preserve, Plattsburgh's location on the banks of Lake Champlain, and affiliations with the Miner Agricultural Research Institute and more.
John Ettling, President
Dr. James Liszka, Provost

5498 **SUNY/Syracuse**
College of Environmental Science & Forestry
One Forestry Drive 315-470-6500
106 Bray Hall 800-777-7373
Syracuse, NY 13210 Fax: 315-470-6933
E-mail: esfinfo@esf.edu
http://www.esf.edu

As part of its education mission, SUNY offers an accredited engineering undergraduate program in Forest Engineering and graduate programs at both the masters and doctoral levels. The Faculty also conducts research and public serviceprograms that study how a variety of events affect our environment.
Vita DeMarchi, Chair
Matthew J. Marko, Vice Chair

5499 **School for Field Studies**
Environmental Field Studies
100 Cummings Center 978-741-3567
Suite 534-G 800-989-4418
Beverly, MA 01915 Fax: 978-922-3835
E-mail: sfs@fieldstudies.org
http://www.fieldstudies.org

Teaches students to address critical environmental problems using an interdisciplinary experimental approach to education.
Terry Andreas, Chairman
James A. Cramer, President

5500 **Slippery Rock University**
Environmental Geosciences
1 Morrow Way 724-738-2015
Slippery Rock, PA 16057 800-929-4778
Fax: 724-738-2913
E-mail: asktherock@sru.edu
http://www.sru.edu/

Prepares students for ocupations with industrial laboratories concerned with air, water and soil pollution control, engineering firms that study industrial pollution and prepare environmental impact statements, and state and federalagencies charged with monitoring the environment.
James Hathaway, Chair
Michael May, Director of Admissions

5501 **Sonoma State University**
Environmental Studies & Planning Program
1801 E Cotati Avenue 707-664-2880
Rohnert Park, CA 94928-3609 Fax: 707-644-4060
E-mail: cynthia.jowers@sonoma.edu
http://www.sonoma.edu

Founded as an interdisciplinary program during a period of growing environmental concern. The department has evolved and matured, now stressing the development of a global prespective by synthesizing knowledge from a variety ofscientific and academic disciplines, the acquisition of specific professional skills through a focused course of study, and the application of knowledge and skills through effective strategies for environmental management.

Dr. Ruben Arminana, President
Andrew Rogerson, Provost/VP for Academic Affa

5502 **Southern Connecticut State University**
Environmental Education Program
501 Crescent Avenue 203-392-7278
Jennings Hall, Room 342 888-500-SCSU
New Haven, CT 06515 Fax: 203-392-6614
E-mail: information@southernct.edu
http://www.southernct.edu

This program focuses on practicality and application of theory bringing about environmental change through educational processes. The objective is to prepare well informed people who are dedicated to improving environmental conditions.
Cheryl J Norton, President
Susan Cusato, Chair Department of Science

5503 **Southern Oregon University**
Environmental Education Program
1250 Siskiyou Boulevard 541-552-6600
Siskiyou Environmental Center 800-482-7672
Ashland, OR 97520 Fax: 541-552-6614
E-mail: presidentsoffice@sou.edu
http://www.sou.edu/

Designed to promote a better understanding of the environment and environmental issues, including an awarenesss and knowledge of biodiversity and ecosystem complexity. Seeks to prepare students for active roles in education and socialchange related to resolution of environmental problems and conflicts affecting present and future generations.
Mary Cullinan, President
James M. Klein, Provost/VP for Academic Affa

5504 **St. Lawrence University**
Environmental Studies
23 Romoda Drive 315-229-5011
Canton, NY 13617 800-285-1856
E-mail: icania@stlawu.edu
http://www.stlawu.edu

Programs offer ten options for combining environmental studies with traditional disciplines (eg. biology, economics) plus B.A. program in Environmental Studies.
Ms. Jacquelyn M Bouchard, President
Ms. Dayle B. Burgess, Assistant to the President

5505 **Stanford University**
Center for Environmental Studies
Building - MC 4205 650-736-8688
473 Via Ortega Fax: 650-725-3402
Stanford, CA 94305 E-mail: environment@stanford.edu
http://www.woods.stanford.edu

Focuses on significant environmental problems and draws methods and analyses from multiple diciplines.
Luis Tam, Assosciate Director
Debbie Drake Dunne, ExecutiveDirector

5506 **Sterling College**
Center for Northern Studies
Sterling College Admissions 802-586-7711
PO Box 72 800-648-3591
Craftsbury Common, VT 05827 Fax: 802-586-2596
E-mail: admissions@sterlingcollege.edu
http://www.sterlingcollege.edu

Center for Northern Studies is part of a small, undergraduate teaching and research institution located in Wolcott, Vermont. Its program is interdisciplinary in nature, integrating social and natural sciences, humanities and resourceissues in the Circumpolar North.

Matthew Allen Derr, President
Melissa Fisher '00, COO

5507 **Tennessee Technological University**
Bioenvironmental Sciences

1 William L Jones Dr 931-372-3101
Cookeville, TN 38505 800-255-8881
E-mail: visit@tntech.edu
http://www.tntech.edu

Prepares graduates for high-level careers in various areas of biology and bioenvironmentl sciences.
Philip Oldham, President
Mark Stephens, Interim Provost/VP for Acade

5508 Texas A & M University
Center for Natural Resource Information Technology
113 Administration Building 979-845-1060
College Station, TX 77843 Fax: 409-845-6430
E-mail: admissions@tamu.edu
http://www.tamu.edu

Serves as a point of contact for external organizations seeking cooperative efforts to assemble and disseminate information, create information technologies, and research critical natural resource concepts. The center strives tofacilitate technology transfer through training of end users and establishing necessary information infrastructures.
R. Bowen Loftin '71, President
Dr. Karan L. Watson, Provost/Executive VP for Aca

5509 Texas Christian University
Environmental Science Program
PO Box 298830 817-257-7270
Fort Worth, TX 76129 Fax: 817-257-7789
E-mail: m.slattery@tcu.edu
http://www.ensc.tcu.edu

A program helping students to understand the connection between science and the earth.
Michael C. Slattery, Director
R. Nowell Donovan, Provost/Vice Chancellor for

5510 Treasure Valley Community College
Biology Department
650 College Boulevard 541-881-TVCC
Ontario, OR 97914 888-987-8822
Fax: 541-881-2721
E-mail: rfindley@tvcc.cc
http://www.tvcc.cc

Offers several courses for those seeking careers in natural resource management including range management, wildland fire management, and forest management.
Dana M. Young, President
Randy Griffin, VP of Administrative Service

5511 Tulane University
Environmental Health & Sciences
6823 St. Charles Avenue 504-865-5000
New Orleans, LA 70118 800-873-9283
Fax: 504-862-8715
E-mail: website@tulane.edu
http://www.tulane.edu

Environmental Health Sciences offers several graduate degree programs, including Public Health and Science. Graduates will be prepared to meet the needs of public health professionals such as environmental health and health officers,as well as undertake responsible positions in government, industrial facilities, research, or edutional institutions.
Scott S. Cowen, President
Yvette M. Jones, Executive VP

5512 University of Arizona
Soutywest Environmental Health Sciences Center
1501 Campbell Avenue 520-626-4555
PO Box 245018 Fax: 602-827-2074
Tucson, AZ 85721 E-mail: admissions@arizona.edu
http://www.arizona.edu

This center serves as a platform to promote the study of health effects of environmental agents. The SWEHSC promotes interdisciplinary research collaborations driven by cutting-edge technologies. Research in the SWEHSC is focused onmechanisms of action of environmetnal agents in living systems.
Ann Weaver Hart, President
Keith A. Joiner, Vice Provost

5513 University of California/Berkeley
Environmental Management Program
1995 University Avenue 510-642-4111
Suite 110 E-mail: info@unex.berkeley.edu
Berkeley, CA 94704-7000 http://www.unex.berkeley.edu/
The Environmental Management Program prepares students to take on significant leadership roles in the environmental community.
Diana Wu, Acting Dean
Ted Huang, CFO

5514 University of California/Los Angeles
Geoscience Engineering
1147 Murphy Hall 310-825-3101
Box 951436 Fax: 310-206-1206
Los Angeles, CA 90095 E-mail: ugadm@saonet.ucla.edu
http://www.ulca.edu
Programs study the principles of, and offer pracitcums in, soil mechanics and foundation engineering in light of geologic conditions, recognition, prediction, and control or abatement of subsidence, landslides, earthquakes, and othergeologic aspects of urban planning and subsurface disposal of liquids and solid wastes.
Mark G. Yudof, President
Marsha Kelman, Secretary

5515 University of California/Santa Barbara
Bren School of Environmental Studies
Bren Hall 805-893-2968
Room 4312 Fax: 805-893-8686
Santa Barbara, CA 93106-4160 E-mail: esprogram@es.ucsb.edu
http://www.es.ucsb.edu
Program provides students with the scholarly background and intellectual skills necessary to understand complex environmental problems and formulate decisions that are environmentally sound. Academic process is interdisciplinary drawing upon not only environmental science faculty, but also the resources of a variety of related departments and disciplines.

Dr. Joshua P. Schimel, Chair
Cheryl Hutton, Financial Manager

5516 University of California/Santa Cruz
Environmental Studies
1156 Hight Street 831-459-2634
Santa Cruz, CA 95064 E-mail: env@ucsc.edu
http://www.envs.ucsc.edu

Offers programs that prepare students to make significant contributions in the various fields of environmental study, whether pursing a career with private or non-profit institutions.
George Blumenthal, Chancellor
Alison Galloway, Provost/Executive Vice Chanc

5517 University of Colorado
Environmental Engineering Program
Regent Administrative Center 125 303-492-8908
552 UCB E-mail: apply@colorado.edu
Boulder, CO 80309 http://www.colorado.edu
Environmental Engineering Progam in the Department of Civil, Environmental, and Architectural Engineering at the University of Colorado in Boulder welcomes students, alumni, and colleagues in environmental engineering with aninvitation to explore areas of environmental emphasis, B.S., M.S., and Ph.D programs, research, and facilities.
Philip P. DiStefano, Chancellor
Bob Sievers, Director

5518 University of Florida
College of Natural Resources & Environment
103 Black Hall 352-392-9230
PO Box 116455 Fax: 352-392-9748
Gainesville, FL 32611 E-mail: kbray@ufl.edu
http://www.snre.ufl.edu
Science based, multidisciplinary and academically rigorous, the College of Natural Resources & Environment has students and a curriculum that includes 200 courses taught in 56 departments of

other colleges. The 290 affiliate facultyhave their primary appointments in discipline-centered departments of other colleges.
Jack Payne, Chair
Joseph Glover, Provost/Sr. VP for Academic

5519 **University of Florida/Gainesville**
School of Forest Resources and Conservation
118 Newins-Ziegler Hall 352-392-3261
PO Box 110410 Fax: 352-392-1707
Gainesville, FL 32611 http://www.ufl.edu
Offers baccalaureate (BSFRC) and graduate (PhD, MS, MFRC, MFAS, incl. a joint JD with the College of Law and a co-major with Dept of Statistics) degree programs; conducts fundamental and applied research; and provides public servicethrough extension programs. Programs include forestry, geomatics, fisheries, and aquatic sciences, natural resource economics, management, and policy, as well as related programs in natural resource education, ecotourism, and agroforestry.
C. David Brown, II, Chair
Christopher T. Corr, Executive VP

5520 **University of Georgia**
Savannah River Ecology Laboratory
Drawer E 803-725-2472
Aiken, SC 29802 Fax: 803-725-3309
http://www.srel.edu
Our goal is to attract collaborating scientists from across the DOE complex and the nation for collaborative work at the interface of fundamental and applied environmental research. We strive to improve the management of contaminatedstites. The staff and facilities of AACES are available to researchers in environmental science and engineering and to practitoneers from industry, government, academia and private foundations.
Olin E. Rhodes, Director
John Seaman, Assistant Director

5521 **University of Hawaii/Manoa**
Oceanography & Global Environmental Sciences
1000 Pope Road 808-956-7633
MSB 205 Fax: 808-956-9225
Honolulu, HI 96822 E-mail: ocean@soest.hawaii.edu
http://www.soest.hawaii.edu
Bachelor of Science degree in Global Environmental Science offered through the Department of Oceanography, University of Hawaii at Manoa.

Jane Schoonmaker, Undergraduate Chair

5522 **University of Idaho**
College of Natural Resources
709 S. Deakin Street 208-885-6111
Moscow, ID 83844 Fax: 208-885-5534
E-mail: info@uidaho.edu
http://www.uidaho.edu
Consists of 5 departments which together form a comprehensive educational program on the study and management of natural resources. Each department has several degree options to provide students with a flexible curriculum for theirdegree. We educate resource professionals with truly integrated resource management skills using innovative instructional programs. Our education occurs in a residential setting and provides a balance between theoretical and pratical experiences.
Ken Edmunds, President
Donald L. Burnett, Interim President

5523 **University of Illinois/Springfield**
Environmental Studies
One University Plaza 217-206-6600
MS UHB 1080 888-977-4847
Springfield, IL 62703 E-mail: admissions@uis.edu
http://www.uis.edu/
Goal of the environmental studies program is to enhance society's ability to create an environmentally acceptable future. Program faculty with diverse backgrounds in social and natural sciences and humanities are committed todeveloping interdisciplinary approaches to environmental problem solving. The primary objective is to educate citizens and professionals who are aware of environmental issues and their origins, causes, effects, and resolutions.
Harry J. Berman, Provost/Vice Chancellor

5524 **University of Illinois/Urbana**
Department of Natural Resources and Environment
1102 South Goodwin Avenue 217-333-2770
W-503 Turner Hall Fax: 217-244-3219
Urbana, IL 61801 E-mail: nres@illinois.edu
http://www.nres.illinois.ed
Establishes and implements research and educational programs that enhance environmental stewardship in the management and use of natural, agricultural, and urban systems in a socially responsible manner.
Bruce Branham, Associate Prof/Interim Head
Crystal E. Bartanen, Program Administrative Assis

5525 **University of Iowa**
MacBride Raptor Project
100 CRWC E230 319-335-9293
Iowa City, IA 52242 Fax: 319-335-6655
E-mail: rec-services@uiowa.edu
http://www.recserv.uiowa.edu
Jointly sponsored by the University of Iowa and Kirkwood Community College, the project has two main facilities. Classes are held at the educational display facility and rehabilitation flight cage at the Macbride Nature RecreationalArea, and at the Raptor Clinic and educational display at KCC. The project is dedicated to the preservation of birds of prey and their habitats through rehabilitation of injured raptors, public education programs and raptor reseach.
Mark J. Braun, Interim VP for strategic Com
David Drake, Sr. Associate

5526 **University of Maine**
Environmental Studies
23 University Street 207-834-7500
Fort Kent, ME 04743 888-879-8635
Fax: 207-834-7466
E-mail: umfkadm@maine.edu
http://www.umfk.maine.edu
Offers a broad knowledge of the natural and social sciences, with the ability to focus of an area of personal interest. Students learn to critically identify environmental problems, collect and interpret data, communicate complexenvironmental issues, and explore creative solutions, while working closely with an interdisciplinary group of faculty with expertise in biology, chemistry, forestry, the social sciences and the humanities.
Steven Selva, Professor

5527 **University of Maryland**
Environmental Policy Programs
2101 Van Munching Hall 301-405-1000
College Park, MD 20742 Fax: 301-403-4675
E-mail: jbanders@umd.edu
http://www.umd.edu
This part-time degree program is intented for highly ambitious mid-career professionals who are ready to advance within the field, understand the importance and value of a professional degree and able to attend one or two classes perweek for two years. A minimum of 5 years of policy related work experience is required. For-profit, nonprofit and public sector work will be considered. A minimum udergraduate GPA of 3.0 is required.
Wallace D. Loh, President
Mary Ann Rankin, Provost

5528 **University of Maryland/Baltimore**
Environmental Science Studies
1000 Hilltop Circle 410-455-2274
Baltimore, MD 21250 800-UMB-C4US
Fax: 410-455-1094
E-mail: adnmissions@umbc.edu
http://www.umbc.edu
The goal of the MEES program is to train students with career interests in environmental science involving terrestrial, freshwater, marine, or estuarine systems. The program is university-wide and interdisciplinary, allowing studentsto use facilities and interact

with all faculty in order to plan a program best suited to their particular interests.

Freeman A. Hrabowski, III, President
Patrice McDermott, Vice Provost

5529 University of Maryland/College Park
Environmental Chemistry
0107 Chemistry Building 301-405-1788
College Park, MD 20742-4454 Fax: 301-314-9121
E-mail: chem-web@umd.edu
http://www.chem.umd.edu

The combined Chemistry and Biochemistry Departments offers specialized training at the graduate level in environmental chemistry. In addition to course work in traditional chemistry subjects, students in this specialty take specificenvironmental courses and do research under the guidance of faculty members specializing in this area.

Michael Doyle, Professor & Chair
Herman Ammon, Associate Chair/Professor

5530 University of Miami
Rosenstiel School of Marine & Atmospheric Science
4600 Rickenbacker Causeway 305-421-4000
Miami, FL 33149-1098 Fax: 305-421-4711
E-mail: dean@rsmas.miami.edu
http://www.rsmas.miami.edu/

Established as the Marine Laboratory of the University of Miami. It has grown from its modest beginnings in a boathouse to one of the nations leading institutions for oceanographic research and education.

Ron Avissar, Dean
Ramon Alfonso, Director

5531 University of Minnesota/St. Paul
College of Agriculatural & Environmental Sciences
240 Williamson Hall 612-625-2008
231 Pillsbury Drive S.E. 800-752-1000
Minneapolis, MN 55455-213 Fax: 612-626-1693
E-mail: spccc@umn.edu
http://www1.umn.edu

The programs offered through this college are designed to prepare students for work in a variety of environmental disciplines, specifically those that relate to the agriculture industry

Karen Kaler, President
Karen Hanson, Provost/Sr. VP for Academic

5532 University of Montana
Environmetal Studies
32 Campus Drive 406-243-0211
Missoula, MT 59812 E-mail: david.micus@umontana.edu
http://www.umt.edu

Interdisciplinary graduate and undergraduate program in environmental studies.

Royce C. Engstrom, President
Perry J. Brown, Provost/Sr. VP for Academic

5533 University of Nebraska
Environmental Studies Program
1400 R Street 402-472-7211
Lincoln, NE 68588 E-mail: hperlman1@unl.edu
http://www.unl.edu

The Environmental Studies Program is designed to serve a variety of students concerned about environmental issues and change. The program provides a thorough, holistic view of the environment and human-environmental interaction and thetechnical skills for active participation in an environmental career.

Harvey Perlman, Chancellor

5534 University of Nevada/Las Vegas
Department of Civil & Environmental Engineering
4505 S Maryland Parkway 702-895-3701
Box 454015 Fax: 702-895-3936
Las Vegas, NV 89154-4015 E-mail: ce-info@ce.unlv.edu
http://www.unlv.edu

Department of Civil and Environmental Engineering offers programs leading to a Master of Science in Engineering and Doctor of Philosophy, with concentration in six areas: environmental engineering; fluid mechanics and hydraulics;geotechnical engineering; structural engineering; construction engineering; and transportation systems.

Donald Hayes, Chair/Professor
Allen Sampson, Sr Development Tech

5535 University of Nevada/Reno
Civil & Environmental Engineering
1664 N. Virginia Street 775-784-1110
Reno, NV 89557-208 866-2NE-ADA
Fax: 775-784-4466
E-mail: vdadams@unr.neveda.edu
http://www.unr.edu

Offers an educational program in environmental engineering. Environmental engineers have taken an increasingly important role in the application on engineering and scientific principles to protect and preserve human health andenvironment. The curriculum is designed with the goal of providing each student with the necessary fundamentals and background in engineering science and design to address many different challenges.

Dr Manos Maragakis, Dean
Dr Indira Chatterjee, Professor/Assoc. Dean

5536 University of New Haven
Environmental Science
300 Boston Post Road 203-932-7319
Westhaven, CT 06516 800-342-5864
E-mail: adminfo@newhaven.edu
http://www.newhaven.edu

The bachelor of science program in environmental science is designed to give students a strong foundation in the fudamental sciences, including biology, chemistry, physics, and geology, and how they relate to our environmentalconcerns.

Steven H. Kaplan, President
Lourdes Alvarez, Dean

5537 University of North Carolina/Chapel Hill
Environmental Science & Studies
153A Country Club Road 919-966-3621
Jackson Hall Fax: 919-962-3045
Chapel Hill, NC 27514 E-mail: unchelp@admissions.unc.edu
http://www.admissions.unc.edu

The Environmental Science and Studies program leads to degrees in Environmental Science or Environmental Studies. Students investigate the relationship between the environment and society, focusing on environmental management, law andbusiness. The programs combines traditional classroom teaching with extensive use of interdisciplinary, team-based field projects, internships, study abroad and research.

Holden Thorp, Chancellor
Jim Dean, Provost

5538 University of Oregon
Environmental Studies
5223 University of Oregon 541-346-2549
Eugene, OR 97403-5223 Fax: 541-346-6056
E-mail: adickman@uoregon.edu
http://www.envs.uoregon.edu

Environmental Studies crosses the boundaries of traditional disciplines, challenging faculty and students to look at the relationship between humans and their environment from a new perspective. They are dedicated to gaining greaterunderstanding of the natural world from an ecological perspective; devising policy and behavior that address contemporary environmental problems; and promoting a rethinking of basic cultural premises, ways of structuring knowledge and the rootmetaphors of society.

Alan Dickman, Program Director
RaDonna Aymong, Office Manager

5539 University of Pennsylvania
Natural Resource Conservation Program
3451 Walnut Street 215-898-5000
Philadelphia, PA 19104 E-mail: webmaster@upenn.edu
http://www.upenn.edu

The mission of our department is to bring the time perspective of the Earth scientist/historian to bear on contemporary problems of natural resource conservation and environmental quality.
Dr. Amy Gutmann, President
Vincent Price, Provost

5540 University of Pittsburgh
Department of Geology & Planetary Science
4107 O'Hara Street 412-624-8780
200 SRCC Building Fax: 412-624-3914
Pittsburgh, PA 15260-3332 E-mail: mookie@pitt.edu
http://www.geology.pitt.edu

Equips students with an understanding of earth systems and the impact of humans on the biosphere, atmosphere and hydrosphere. Courses in the natural and social sciences, humanities, and schools of law, business, and public healthprovide a comprehensive, interdisciplinary background in environmental issues and public policy.
Patricia DeMarco, Executive Director
K. Christopher Beard, Head of Section

5541 University of Redlands
Environmental Studies
1200 E Colton Avenue 909-793-2121
PO Box 3080 Fax: 909-793-2029
Redlands, CA 92373 E-mail: kerry_robles@redlands.edu
http://www.redlands.edu

Designed to promote a new way of thinking and acting about our relationship to the world, including graduating students who are environmentally literate, sensitive to competing demands and conflicting values of each issue and finally,and have the creativity, confidence and conviction to begin effecting change.
Dr. Ralph W. Kuncl, President
Bradley N. Adams '93, Managing Director

5542 University of South Carolina
Belle Baruch Institute of Marine Costalsciences
Gambrell Hall 803-777-7161
Room 251 Fax: 803-777-4532
Columbia, SC 29208 E-mail: bergin.sc.edu
http://www.cas.sc.edu

Environmental research and programs are focused on estuarine systems and their associated watersheds. More than 160 investigators representing 30 academic institutes and agencies are affiliated with over 100 projects. The lab providessupport for undergraduate classes, graduate students, and senior scientists. Long-term environmental monitoring, training programs and outreach activities are sponsored by the North-inlet-Winyah Bay National Estuarine research reserve.

Dr. Roger Sawyer, Executive Dean
Dr. Anne Bezuidenhout, Sr. Associate Dean

5543 University of Southern California
Environmental Sciences, Policy/Engineering Program
University Park Campus 213-740-2311
Hancock Building, Room 232 http://www.usc.edu
Los Angeles, CA 90089

This multidisciplinary doctoral training program is funded by the National Science Foundation, and prepares students to confront, analyze and resolve the challenges posed by problems of urban sustainablilty. Engineering SustainableCities is high on the list of goals of the program, which allows students to transcend disciplines, and conduct policy-relevant research on major environmental problems.
C.L. Max Nikias, President
Elizabeth Garrett, Provost/Sr. VP for Academic

5544 University of Southern Mississippi
Environmental Science Program
118 College Drive 601-266-4748
Building #5018 Fax: 601-266-5797
Hattiesburg, MS 39406-1 E-mail: admissions@usm.edu
http://www.usm.edu

The Environmental Science concentration focuses on industrial problems related to the working environment, pollution control, and safety. Courses address major industrial issues, including environmental impact statements, industrialhygiene and environmental laws and regulations.
Frank Moore, Chair
Angela Williams, Administrative Assistant

5545 University of Tennessee
Geoscience Program
University Street 731-881-7000
Martin, TN 38238 800-829-utm1
Fax: 901-587-7029
E-mail: admitme@utm.edu
http://www.utm.edu

This program focuses on the application of geology to the interaction between man and the environment. Topics include geohazards, chemical and nuclear contamination of soils and water, remediation of environmental problems andgovernmental environmental agencies and laws.
Tom Rakes, Chancellor
Nancy Yarbrough, Interim Vice Chancellor

5546 University of Virginia
Department of Environmental Sciences
291 McCormick Road 434-924-7761
PO Box 400123 Fax: 434-982-2137
Charlottesville, VA 22904-4123 E-mail: ralph@virginia.edu
http://www.evsc.virginia.edu

Offers instruction and research opportunities in Ecology, Geosciences, Hydrology, and Atmospheric Sciences. The research endeavors of both faculty and graduate students, whether disciplinary or interdisciplinary, deal largely withproblems of fundamental scientific interest and with applied sciences, management or policy making.
Allen Cindy, Asst to Dept/Chair/Clark
Pam Hoover, Administrative Support Speci

5547 University of Washington
Environmental Science
18115 Campus Way NE 425-352-5000
Bothell, WA 98011-8246 425.352.5303
Fax: 425-352-5303
E-mail: info@uwb.edu
http://www.uwb.edu

Primary goal of this program is to train a new generation of interdisciplinary scientists who are able to work in both the public and private sectors to address some of the pressing environmental issues that face our society.
Kenyon S. Chan, Chancellor
Marilyn Cox, Vice Chancellor

5548 University of West Florida
Environmental Studies
11000 University Parkway 850-474-2000
Pensacola, FL 32514 Fax: 850-474-3131
E-mail: web@uwf.edu
http://www.uwf.edu

The program in Environmental Studies consists of a multi-disciplinary approach that combines natural science and resource management. Students learn to analyze physical and socioeconomic environments and to reach decisions concerningenvironmental use and protection. It offers a core curriculum that is designed to provide the student with a solid foundation in earth and life sciences, as well as in modern methods and techniques.
Lewis Bear, Chair
Judy Bense, President

5549 University of Wisconsin/Green Bay
Environmental Science
2420 Nicolet Drive 920-465-2000
Green Bay, WI 54311 E-mail: uwgb@uwgb.edu
http://www.uwgb.edu

This program is interdisciplinary, emphasizing an integrated approach to knowledge in the field. Because the study of the environmental science major is grounded in the natural sciences and mathematics, the curriculum includes a socialscience component, enabling students to gain an understanding of environmen-

tal economic and policy issues. Field experiences, internships and practicums are emphasized.
Thomas K. Harden, Chancellor
Julia E. Wallace, Provost/Vice Chancellor for

5550 University of Wisconsin/Madison
Environmental Monitoring Program
212 Agricultural Hall 608-261-1432
1450 Linden Drive Fax: 608-265-9534
Madison, WI 53706 E-mail: waes@cals.wisc.edu
http://www.cals.wisc.edu/waes
Remote sensing and geographic information systems offer sophisticated and powerful tools for monitoring the environment on large geographic scales over time. Students in the Environmental Monitoring Program learn to employ thesetechnologies in fields of their choice, from forestry to urban planning to environmental engineering.
Kathryn VandenBosch, Dean/Director
Angela Seitler, Assistant Director

5551 University of Wisconsin/Stevens Point
Environmental Task Force Progeam
2100 Main Street 715-346-0123
Stevens Point, WI 54481-3897 Fax: 715-346-2561
E-mail: webmaster@uwsp.edu
http://www.uwsp.edu/
This program involves two water chemistry labs which tests for organics and inorganics. This is staffed by five full time workers, plus a part time faculty director, and about 40 students are hired and/or trained each year. Samplingis performed with state-of-the-art field sampling and laboratory analytical equipment nutrients, pesticides, polynuclear aromatic hydrocarbons, polychlorinated biphenyls, and volatile organic compounds.

Bernie L. Patterson, Chancellor
Greg Summers, Provost/Vice Chancellor

5552 University of the South
Environmental Studies
735 University Avenue 931-598-1000
Sewanee, TN 37383 800-522-2234
Fax: 931-598-1667
E-mail: collegeadmission@sewanee.edu
http://www.sewanee.edu
Brings together students, faculty, and staff from thirteen academic departments to study, discuss, and research environmental issues at local, national, and international scales. The program's goal is to expose students to a variety ofviewpoints concerning environmental issues, and to offer the interdisciplinary tools they need to become environmental problem solvers before they graduate from Sewanee.

John McCardell, Vice Chancellor
John Swallow, Provost

5553 Utah State University
Berryman Institute
Wildland Resources Department 435-797-0242
5230 Old Main Hill Fax: 435-797-3796
Logan, UT 84322 http://www.berrymaninstitute.org
The Berryman Institute is a functional component of the Department of Wildland Resources and the College of Natural Resources. Its faculty members hold academics appointments in various departments throughout Utah State University andother universities. This multidisciplinary approach is calculated to speed the discovery and development of innovative methods to solve human wildlife conflict.
Dr. Terry A. Messmer, Director
Lana Barr, Assistant to the Director

5554 Vanderbilt University
Vanderbilt Center for Environmental Management
2301 Vanderbilt Place 615-322-5000
Nashville, TN 37235 Fax: 615-343-7177
E-mail: mark.a.cohen@vanderbilt.edu
http://www.vanderbilt.edu
VCEMS provides guidance and support for the interdisciplinary study of environmental issues. The Center brings faculty and students together from various disciplines for collaborative study and research on topics such as environmentalrisk assessment, management and communication, policy analysis, civil and criminal liability, environmentally conscious manufacturing and technology management, and global environmental studies.
Nicholas S. Zeppos, Chancellor
Dr. Mark Cohen, Co-Director

5555 Vermont Law School
Environmental Law Center
164 Chelsea Street 802-831-1000
PO Box 96 800-227-1395
South Royalton, VT 05068 http://www.vermontlaw.edu
The Environmental Law Center administers three different degrees in Environmental Law, each adaptable to career objectives in both public and private sectors. The school's mission is to educate for stewardship, to teach an awareness ofunderlining environmental issues and values, to provide a solid knowledge of environmental law and to develop skills to administer and improve policies.
J. Scott Cameron, Chair
Margaret Martin Barry, Professor of Law/Associate D

5556 Virginia Polytechnic Institute
Environmental Science
965 Prices Fork Road 540-231-6267
Blackburg, VA 24061 Fax: 540-231-3242
E-mail: vtadmiss@vt.edu
http://www.vt.edu
This program deals with crop production, soil utilization, and environmental stewardship. Its professionals are concerned with helping to feed the world and protect the environment, and include women and men who work to grow crucialcommodities, improve water quality, develop environmentally acceptable methods for protecting crops from pests, and advise municipalities on use of the land resource.
Steven C Hodges, Department Head

5557 Virginia Tech
Environmental Science
112 Burruss Hall 540-231-6272
Blacksburg, VA 24061 Fax: 540-231-3431
E-mail: studentaffairs@vt.edu
http://www.vt.edu
Provides a B.S. degree for environmental professionals needed in the private and public sector and by nonprofit organizations. Built on a rigorous interdisciplinary curriculum that stresses the basic sciences, environmentaltechnologies, soils, and analytical skills. Graduates are in high demand in the environmental arena.

Patty Perillo, VP for Student Affairs
Frank Shushok, Associate VP

5558 Warren Wilson College
Natural & Social Sciences
Warren Wilson College 828-298-3325
PO Box 9000 Fax: 828-299-4841
Asheville, NC 28815 E-mail: pfeiffer@warren-wilson.edu
http://www.warren-wilson.edu
Combines rigorous courses in the natural and social sciences with abundant natural resources near the classrooom. Courses and work crews give students a balance of theory, first hand knowledge and field experience. Successful programsmost often result when students, with the help of an advisor, begin planning course work and indentifying goals during their first year.
William Sanborn Pfeiffer, President

5559 Washington State University
Environmental Science
PO Box 641067 509-335-3009
Pullman, WA 99164-1067 Fax: 509-335-3700
E-mail: sees@wsu.edu
http://www.sees.wsu.edu
The students in this diverse program are encouraged to specialize in their specific interest, including agricultural ecology, biological science, environmental education, environmental quality (air and water), natural resourcemanagement, systems, environmental/land use planning or hazardous waste management.
Elson Floyd, President
Stephen Bollens, Director

5560 West Virginia University
Environmental Geosciences Program
1168 Agricultural Sciences Building 304-293-4006
PO Box 6108 Fax: 304-293-7337
Morgantown, WV 26506-6108 http://www.davis.wvu.edu

The Environmental Geosciences program features an interdisciplinary approach to environmental issues. Graduates will be well prepared to face the environmental challenges, whether in government or in the corporate world.

Dan Robison, Dean
Dennis K. Smith, Assoc. Dean

5561 Western Montana College
Environmental Sciences Program
710 S Atlantic Street 406-683-7331
Dillon, MT 59725 877-683-7331
Fax: 406-683-7331
E-mail: admissions@umwestern.edu
http://www.umwestern.edu

The mission of the environmental sciences programs is to provide students with an in-depth understanding of the natural processes which create and shape our environment. Students will become informed, critical thinkers capable ofscientifically evaluating complex issues involving the environment. Student development will occur through interdisciplinary, field-based research projects that have societal relevance.

Roxanne Engellant, Foundation Director
Kelly Allen, Administrative Assistant

5562 Williams College
Center for Environmental Studies
Hopkins Hall 413-597-3131
880 Main Street Fax: 412-597-3489
Williamstown, MA 01267 E-mail: szepke@williams.edu
http://www.williams.edu

The Environmental Studies program provides students with tools, ideas, and opportunities to engage constructively with the environmental and social issues brought about by changes in population, economic activity, and values. Theenvironmental studies program is interdisciplinary and broad, including the coditions of inner-city poverty as well as the magnificent scenery of wildlands, encompassing the view of planet earth from near space as well as from culturalanthropologists.

Hank Art, Director

5563 Yale University
Office of Public Affairs
265 Church Street 203-432-1345
Suite 901 Fax: 203-432-1323
New Haven, CT 06511 E-mail: undergraduate.admission@yale.edu
http://www.yale.edu

Our mission is to provide the leadership and knowledge needed to restore and sustain both the health of the biosphere and the well-being of its people. Believing that human enterprise can and must be conducted in harmony with theenvironment, we are committed to using natural resources in ways that sustain both resources and ourselves. Solving environmental problems must incorporate human values and motivations and a deep respect for both human and natural communities.

Richard Charles Levin, President

Workshops & Camps

5564 A Closer Look at Plant Life
Educational Images
PO Box 3456 607-732-1090
Westside Station 800-527-4264
Elmira, NY 14905-456 Fax: 607-732-1183
E-mail: edimages@edimages.com
http://www.educationalimages.com

Access a wealth of information on every major group of vascular and nonvascular plants. Includes details on plant microanatomy; external and internal structures; life cycles; and processes such as growth transpiration andphotosynthesis.

Charles R Belinky, Ph.D, CEO

5565 A Closer Look at Pondlife - CD-ROM
Educational Images
PO Box 3456 607-732-1090
Westside Station 800-527-4264
Elmira, NY 14905-456 Fax: 607-732-1183
E-mail: edimages@edimages.com
http://www.educationalimages.com

Through the wonders of close-up photography, this unique CD-ROM brings students face-to-face with the inner workings of a freshwater pond, the myriad creatures and plants that reside there, and the dynamic interactions that go onbeneath the surface. This disk features a library of reference information, images, illustrations, clip art, video clips and more!

Charles R Belinky, Ph.D, CEO

5566 Abbott's Mill Nature Center
Delaware Nature Society
3511 Barley Mill Road 302-239-2334
PO Box 700 Fax: 302-239-2473
Hockessin, DE 19707 E-mail: dnsinfo@delawarenaturesociety.org
http://www.delawarenaturesociety.org

Abbott's Mill Nature Center features education programs for families, school classes and public groups, walking trails through fields, pine woods and streams, and a historic, fully-operating gristmill.

Peter H. Flint, President
Sharon Struthers, VP

5567 Air and Waste Management Association
One Gateway Center 3rd Floor 412-232-3444
420 Fort Duquesne Blvd. Fax: 412-232-3450
Pittsburg, PA 15222 E-mail: info@awma.org
http://www.awma.org

The Air & Waste Management Association is a non profit, nonpatism professional organization that provides training, information, and networking opportunities to 12,000 environmental professionals in 65 countries. The Association'sgoals are to stengthen the environmental professionals in critical environmental decision making to benefit society.

Sara Head, President
Michael Miller, President Elect

5568 American Museum of Natural History
Center for Biodiversity and Conservation
Central Park West 212-769-5100
79th Street Fax: 212-769-5427
New York, NY 10024-5192 E-mail: biodiversity@amnh.org
http://www.amnh.org

Conducts research and field projects based on information provided by Museum departments.

Lewis W. Bernard, Chairman
Ellen V. Futter, President

5569 Animal Tracks and Signs
Educational Images
PO Box 3456 607-732-1090
Westside Station 800-527-4264
Elmira, NY 14905-456 Fax: 607-732-1183
E-mail: edimages@edimages.com
http://www.educationalimages.com

Presents various animal tracks and signs throughout the seasons, and provides useful information about the special characteristics and natural history of the animals that left the signs. Footprints, scratch marks, nesting places,wallows, scats and signs of food gathering are all detailed. Coverage includes deer, fox, porcupine, rabbit, bear, mink, otter, owl, woodpecker, killdeer, wild turkey, sapsucker and grouse.

Charles R Belinky, Ph.D, CEO

5570 Annotated Invertebrate Clipart CD-ROM
Educational Images
PO Box 3456 607-732-1090
Westside Station 800-527-4264
Elmira, NY 14905-456 Fax: 607-732-1183
E-mail: edimages@edimages.com
http://www.educationalimages.com

780 colorful graphics of invertebrates from protists through urochordates, supported by extensive written annotations in addition to traditional labels. Includes presentation graphics and page after page of supplemental information onclassification, anatomy, evolution, development, reproduction, etc.

Charles R Belinky, Ph.D, CEO

5571 Annotated Vertebrate Clipart CD-ROM
Educational Images
PO Box 3456 607-732-1090
Westside Station 800-527-4264
Elmira, NY 14905-456 Fax: 607-732-1183
E-mail: edimages@edimages.com
http://www.educationalimages.com

792 colorful graphics of vertebrates from urochordates and tunicates through mammals, supported by extensive written annotations in addition to traditional labels. Includes presentation graphics and page after page of supplementalinformation on classification, organ systems, anatomy, evolution, development, reproduction, etc.

Charles R Belinky, Ph.D, CEO

5572 Argonne National Laboratory
9700 S Cass Avenue 630-252-2000
Argonne, IL 60439 E-mail: dep_webmaster@anl.gov
http://www.anl.gov/

We focus on four broad strategic environmental areas under which specific programs and projects are conducted. Our staff of over 100 multidisciplinary professionals are organized in a matrix fashion to undertake programs and projectswith technical managers and staff from seven sections, each specializing in specific technical disciplines.

Robert J. Zimmer, Chairman
Eric D. Isaacs, President

5573 Ashland Nature Center
Delaware Nature Society
3511 Barley Mill Road 302-239-2334
PO Box 700 Fax: 302-239-2473
Hockessin, DE 19707 E-mail: dnsinfo@delawarenaturesociety.org
http://www.delawarenaturesociety.org

Open year round, seven days a week, Ashland is headquarters of the Delaware Nature Society. Ashland Nature Center offers self-guided nature trails traversing 81 acres of rolling terrain, through meadows, woodlands, and marshes.Programs for all ages are offered, including schools and groups.

Peter H. Flint, President
Sharon Struthers, VP

5574 Aspen Global Change Institute
104 Midland Ave 970-925-7376
Suite 205 Fax: 970-925-7097
Rasalt, CO 81621 E-mail: agcimail@agci.org
http://www.agci.org

A Colorado nonprofit dedicated to furthering the understanding of Earth systems through interdisciplinary science meetings, publications, and educational programs about global environmental change.

Dr. Martin Hoffert, Chairman
John Katzenberger, President

5575 Association for Environmental Health and Sciences
150 Fearing Street 413-549-5170
Amherst, MA 01002 Fax: 413-549-0579
E-mail: info@aehs.com
http://www.aehs.com

Created to facilitate communication and foster cooperation among professionals concerned with the challenge of soil protection and cleanup. Experience over the past decades has revealed the need for a consistent and reliable networkfor the exchange of information derived from multiple sources and disciplines among people who, because of different disciplinary affiliations and interests, may not have easy access to significant portions of the information map.

Paul Kostecki, Executive Director

5576 Audubon Expedition Institute
29 Everett Street 617-868-9600
Cambridge, MA 02138 800-999-1959
E-mail: info@lesley.edu
http://www.lesley.edu/

Students challenge themselves and their assumptions through experimental learning and direct contact with social, natural, historical and urban environments. Subjects are studied and integrated through real life experiences.

Donald Perrin, Chair

5577 Bio-Integral Resource Center
PO Box 7414 510-524-2567
Berkeley, CA 94707 Fax: 510-524-1758
E-mail: birc@igc.org
http://www.birc.org

The goal of the Bio Integral Resources Center is to reduce pesticide use by educating the public about effective, least-toxic alternatives for pest problems.

Dr. William Quarles, Executive Director

5578 Biosystems and Agricultural Engineering
Univerity of Kentucky
128 C.E Barnhart Building 859 257 3000
University of Kentucky Fax: 859-257-5671
Lexington, KY 40546-276 E-mail: gates@bae.uky.edu
http://www.bae.uky.edu/

Biosystems and Agricultural Engineering provides an essential link between the biological sciences and the engineering profession. The linkage is necessary for the development of food and fiber production and processing systems whichpreserves our natural resources base.

Dr. Sue E. Nokes, Chair
Dr. Czarena Crofcheck, Director of Undergraduate St

5579 Bishop Resource Area
3000 E. Line St. 760-873-4344
Bishop, CA 93514 Fax: 760-873-7830
E-mail: wmrcinfo@ucla.edu
http://www.wmrs.edu

The Bishop Resource Area has facilitated aerial photo interpretation and remote sensing programs in local schools through corporate and public partnerships. The program incorporates aerial photo interpretation, its relationship tomapping and land use history.

Antony Orme, Director
Glen MacDonald, Director

5580 Bog Ecology
Educational Images
PO Box 3456 607-732-1090
Westside Station 800-527-4264
Elmira, NY 14905-456 Fax: 607-732-1183
E-mail: edimages@edimages.com
http://www.educationalimages.com

A comprehensive program that explores the origin and formation of bogs, common plants and animals, and compares bogs to other types of wetlands. Bog succession is illustrated by use of diagrams and photographs. 74 frames and guide.

Charles R Belinky, Ph.D, CEO

5581 Camp Fire USA
1100 Walnut Street 816-285-2010
Suite 1900 800-669-6884
Kansas City, MO 64106-2197 Fax: 816-285-9444
E-mail: info@campfireusa.org
http://www.campfireusa.org

Not-for-profit, youth development organization, Camp Fire USA provides fun, coeducational programs for approximately 650,000 youth from birth to age 21. Helps boys and girls learn and play side by side in comfortable, informalsettings.

Ms. Elizabeth Darling, President/CEO
Richard Goldfarb, Sr. VP

5582 Camp Habitat Northern Alaska Environmental Center
830 College Road 907-452-5021
Fairbanks, AK 99701-1535 Fax: 907-452-3100
E-mail: info@northern.org
http://www.northern.org

Camp Habitat is a nature education program for young people ages 4-17 sponsored by the Northern Alaska Environmental Center, Friends of Creamer's Field, and Alaska Department of Fish & Game. The mission of Camp Habitat is to provideyoung people with guided explorations of their natural surroundings through interactive, hands-on activities. Skilled instructors and resource specialists lead small groups through new outdoor activities focusing on the habitats of Interior Alaska.

Jon Miller, President
Carol Norton, Treasurer

5583 Center for Environmental Research and Conservation
1200 Amsterdam Avenue 212-854-8179
New York, NY 10027-5557 Fax: 212-854-8188
E-mail: eices@columbia.edu
http://www.cerc.columbia.edu

CERC, a consortium of five education and research institutions, was created in response to critical environmental concerns facing the Earth. Within the next fifty years human influence will affect every place on the planet. That impactwill almost certainly result in species extinctions, ecosystem degradation and a loss of the benefits those species and ecosystems provide to people.
Shahid Naeem, Director
Alexandra Varga, Deputy Director

5584 Center for Geography and Environmental Education
311 Conference Center Building 865-974-4251
University of Tennessee Fax: 865-974-1838
Knoxville, TN 37996 E-mail: mckeowni@utk.edu
http://eerc.ra.utk.edu/CGEE.html

A research and outreach center at the University of Tennessee. The CGEE focuses on environmental and geography education contributions to education for sustainable development. CGEE is responsible for the Tennessee Solid WasteEducation Project.

Dr. Rosalyn McKeown-Ice, Director

5585 Center for Mathematical Services
4202 East Fowler Avenue 813-974-2011
Adm 147 Fax: 974-974-2700
Tampa, FL 33620 E-mail: uco@admin.usf.edu
http://www.usf.edu

Mission is to help prepare students of all levels to effectively use mathematics as a tool to analyze situations and resolve problems. In the field of mathematical sciences it serves as an interface for the University with thesecondary schools in the area served by the University of South Florida. By means of this interface special programs in the mathematics, science, and engineering are offered at the University of South Florida for secondary students.
Ralph Wilcox, Provost/VP
Dr. Dwayne Smith, Sr. Vice Provost

5586 Cetacean Society International
PO Box 953 203-770-8615
Georgetown, CT 06829 Fax: 860-561-0187
E-mail: rossiter@csiwhalesalive.org
http://www.csiwhalesalive.org

All volunteer, nonprofit conservation, educational and research organization to benefit whales, dolphins, porpoises and the marine environment. Promotes education and conservation programs, including whale and dolphin watching, andnoninvasive, benign research. Advocates for laws and treaties to prevent commercial whaling, habitat destruction and other harmful or destructive human interactions. CSI's world goal is to minimize cetacean killing and captures and to enhance publicawareness.
William W Rossiter, President
Brent Hall, VP

5587 Chicago Botanic Garden
1000 Lake Cook Road 847-835-5440
Glencoe, IL 60022 http://www.chicagobotanic.org

The Chicago Horticultural Society has been promoting gardens and gardening since 1890. Generations of Chicagoans have been touched by the Society's flower shows, victory gardens, horticultural lectures and more. The mission encompassesthree important components: collections, programs and research. A living museum, the Chicago Botanic Garden serves both a public and a scientific community.
Robert F. Finke, Chair
John L. Howard, Vice Chair/Secretary

5588 Clean Ocean Action
18 Hartshorne Drive 732-872-0111
Suite 2 Fax: 732-872-8041
Highlands, NJ 07732 E-mail: info@cleanoceanaction.org
http://www.cleanoceanaction.org

Clean Ocean Action is a broad-based coalition of over 150 conservation, community, diving, fishing, environmental, surfing, women's and business groups that works to improve and protect the waters off the New York and New Jersey coast.

Cindy Zipf, Executive Director
Mary-Beth Thompson, Operations Director

5589 Cleaner and Greener Environment
PO Box 5425 608-280-0255
Madison, WI 53705-425 877-977-9277
Fax: 608-255-7202
E-mail: info@cleanerandgreener.org
http://www.cleanerandgreener.org

Cleaner and Greener Environment is a program of Leonardo Academy, a 501 environmental nonprofit organization. Leonardo Academy reports reductions in emissions, and promotes the development of markets for the emission reductions thatresult from energy efficiency, renewable energy, and other emission reduction action.

5590 Climate Change Program
Dade County Dept. of Env. Res. Mgm. 305-372-6825
701 NW 1st Court Fax: 305-372-6954
Miami, FL 33136 E-mail: dermp2@itd.metro-dade.com

Receives monies from sources such as fees from pollution prevention events, grants, allocations, appropriations and workshop fees. These funds are then used in developing, promoting and conducting environmental workshops, expositions,symposia, conferences and other forms of public information for the purpose of educating industry, government and the public about pollution prevention.
Nichole Hefty, Coordinator

5591 Coastal Resources Center
University of Rhode Island
220 South Ferry Road 401-874-6224
Narragansett, RI 02882 Fax: 401-874-6920
E-mail: info@crc.uri.edu
http://www.crc.uri.edu

Mobilizes governments, business and communities around the world to work together as stewards of coastal ecosystems. With partners we strive to define and achieve the health, equitable allocation of wealth, and sustainable intensitiesof human activity at the transition between the land and sea.
Brian Crawford, Director
Lesley Squillante, Asst. Director

5592 Comet Halley: Once in a Lifetime!
Educational Images
PO Box 3456 607-732-1090
Westside Station 800-527-4264
Elmira, NY 14905-456 Fax: 607-732-1183
E-mail: edimages@edimages.com
http://www.educationalimages.com

Particularly relevant because of the recent appearance of Hale-Bopp, this program presents the reactions to comets in ancient, historic and relatively modern times, press coverage of the 1910 Halley return, superstitions and beliefs,current scientific knowledge and research, and much more.

Charles R Belinky, Ph.D, CEO

5593 **Cooch-Dayett Mills**
Delaware Nature Society
PO Box 700 302-239-2334
Hockessin, DE 19707 Fax: 302-239-2473
E-mail: dnsinfo@delawarenaturesociety.org
http://www.delawarenaturesociety.org

Programming provided by the delaware nature society features environmental education and natural history for families, classes, groups and the public. The historic roller mills, along with natural features of the site, become theclassroom.

Peter H. Flint, President
Sharon Struthers, VP

5594 **Cooperative Institute for Research in Environmental Sciences: K-12 and Public Outreach**
University of Colorado
CIRES Bldg., Rm. 318 303-492-1143
Boulder, CO 80309-216 Fax: 303-492-1149
E-mail: info@cires.colorado.edu
http://www.cires.colorado.edu/education/outreach

We educate people about Earth and environmental science issues that are relevant to our everyday lives, through outreach to the public and to the K-12 education community.

Waleed Abdalati, Director
William M. Lewis, Jr., Assoc. Director

5595 **Coverdale Farm**
Delaware Nature Society
PO Box 700 302-239-2334
Hockessin, DE 19707 Fax: 302-239-2473
E-mail: dnsinfo@delawarenaturesociety.org
http://www.delawarenaturesociety.org

School students and guests of all ages participate in seasonal programs, learning about the farm cycle of life and humans' dependence on soil, water, plants and animals for survival.

Peter H. Flint, President
Sharon Struthers, VP

5596 **Deep Portage Conservation Reserve**
2197 Nature Center Drive NW 218-682-2325
Hackensack, MN 56452 888-280-9908
Fax: 218-682-3121
E-mail: portage@uslink.net
http://www.deep-portage.org

Deep Portage serves schools, groups, organizations, research teams, area residents and visitor with resident environmental education programs, weekly classes, interpretive programs, wildflower garden displays, land use demonstrations,summer youth camps and recreation opportunities of birding, hiking, hunting and skiing.

Dale Yerger, Executive Director
Molly Malecek, Assistant Director

5597 **Department of Energy and Geo-Environmental Engineering**
116 Deike Building 814-865-6546
University Park, PA 16802 Fax: 814-863-7708
E-mail: contact@ems.psu.edu
http://www.ems.psu.edu

Through education, research and service, EGEE aspires to insure that socisty is provided with an affordable supply of energy and minerals, concomitant with protecting the environment.

William E. Easterling, Dean
Larry Achterberg, Director of Business & Opera

5598 **DuPont Environmental Education Center**
Delaware Nature Society
PO Box 700 302-239-2334
Hockessin, DE 19707 Fax: 302-239-2473
E-mail: dnsinfo@delawarenaturesociety.org
http://www.delawarenaturesociety.org

Programming provided by the delaware nature society features environmental education and natural history for families, classes, groups and the public. The historic roller mills, along with natural features of the site, become theclassroom.

Peter H. Flint, President
Sharon Struthers, VP

5599 **Earth Day Network**
1616 P Street NW 202-518-0044
Suite 340 Fax: 202-518-8794
Washington, DC 20036 E-mail: buchanan@earthday.org
http://www.earthday.net

This nonprofit network was created to be a vehicle for increased awareness & responsibility through the promotion of Earth Day. Offers workshops.

Denis Hayes, Board Chair/President/CEO
Gerald Torres, Vice Chair

5600 **Earth Force**
2555 W 34th Avenue 303-433-2956
Denver, CO 80211 Fax: 888-899-5324
E-mail: earthforce@earthforce.org
http://www.earthforce.org

Earth Force offers educators innovatove programs and resources. The young graduates of these programs create lasting solutions to environmental problems in their communities. Earth Force's goal is to help youth become environmentalproblem solvers.

James Macgregor, Chairman
Chris Chopyak, President

5601 **Ecological & Environmental Learning Services**
46 Back Bone Hill Road 732-577-5599
Clarksburg, NJ 08510 800-206-6672
Fax: 732-577-5598

Ecological & Environmental Learning Services provides K-12 education consulting for teacher professional development, curriculum development and education programs and assemblies. EELS has the expertise and experience to providesolutions for enhancing the academic excellence of students in the following areas: Science (particularly in science research); Ecology; Environmental Science; and Environmental Education.

5602 **Ecology and Environmental Sciences**
5782 Winslow Hall 207-581-1561
Room 305 877-486-2364
Orono, ME 04469 E-mail: mark.anderson@umit.maine.edu
http://www.umaine.edu

Faculty from five different academic departments, covering biological, physical and social sciences, work together to offer a broad educational experience for our students. Since these faculty have active research programs, studentsnot only get access to the most up-to-date information, but also get employment opportunities in their fields of study during the academic year and the summer months.

Paul W. Ferguson, President

5603 **Economic Development/Marketing California Environmental Business Council**
UC Extention 408-748-2170
3120 De La Cruz Fax: 408-748-2189
Santa Clara, CA 95054 E-mail: br1027@aol.com

The CEBC is a nonprofit trade and business assoication that promotes and assists California's environmental technology and services industry at the state, national, and international levels. Founded in 1994, the CEBC currently has morethan 100 member compines and other organizations throughout the state that represent all segments of the environmental industry.

5604 **Energy Thinking for Massachusetts**
Northeast Sustainable Energy Association
50 Miles Street 413-774-6051
Greenfield, MA 01301 Fax: 413-774-6053
E-mail: nesea@nesea.org
http://www.nesea.org

CD
Caitiona Cooke, Chair
Michael Bruss, Secretary

5605 **Energy Thinking for Pennsylvania**
Northeast Sustainable Energy Association

50 Miles Street
Greenfield, MA 01301
413-774-6051
Fax: 413-774-6053
E-mail: nesea@nesea.org
http://www.nesea.org
CD
Caitiona Cooke, Chair
Michael Bruss, Secretary

5606 Environmental Data Resources
440 Wheelers Farms Road
Milford, CT 06461
203-783-0300
800-352-0050
Fax: 800-231-6802
E-mail: resinfo@edrnet.com
http://www.edrnet.com
Applied and product research in environmental applications.
Jon Walker, Executive VP
Rob Barber, CEO

5607 Environmental Education Council of Ohio
PO Box 1004
Lancaster, OH 43130-1004
740-653-2649
800-992-6682
Fax: 330-823-8531
E-mail: director@eeco-online.org
http://www.eeco.wildapricot.org
EECO believes that: we are all learners interacting with others in lifelong process, education is vital for individuals to reach their full potential as members of our global community, a healthy and sustainable environment isessential to the survival of the planet. It is the mission of EECO to lead in facilitating and promoting environmental education which nurtures knowledge, attitudes and behaviors that foster global stewardship.
Joyce Meredith, President
Denise Natoli Brooks, VP

5608 Environmental Education K-12
PO Box 2057
Lake Placid, FL 33862
863-465-2571
Fax: 863-699-1927
E-mail: archbold@archbold-station.org
http://arcbold-station.org
Archbold Biological Station provides environmental education programs to help people af all ages discover and understand the unique and endangered Florida scrib. Several programs for children Grades K-12 are offered each year. Theprogram goals are; promote a sound foundation in ecological principles, nurture a sense of stewardship for Florida scrub habitat, demostrate the value of scientific research, and develop a deeper understanding of the importance of natural habitatsfor investigation.
Dr. Hilary Swain, Executive Director

5609 Environmental Forum of Marin
PO Box 151546
San Rafael, CA 94915
415-484-8336
E-mail: forum@MarinEFM.org
http://www.marinefm.org
Dedicated to protecting and enhancing the environment by educating its members and the Marin citizenry on environmental issues. In futherance of this goal, the Environmental Forum of Marin conducts annual training programs onenvironmental matters, provides continuing education for its members and public, and supports citizen action to influence environmental decision-making and public policy.
Sarah Kelley, President
Pat Nelson, Secretary

5610 Environmental Law Institute
2000 L Street, NW
Suite 620
Washington, DC 20036
202-939-3800
Fax: 202-939-3868
E-mail: law@eli.org
http://www.eli.org
Edward L. Strohbehn Jr., Chairman
John Cruden, President

5611 Environmental Resources
700 W Virginia Street
Suite 601
Milwaukee, WI 53204
414-289-9505
Fax: 414-289-9552
http://www.erm.com/en/locations/USA
Owner and co-founder of Moraine Multimedia, and Environmental Resources developes continuing education programs.
Shawn Doherty, Global Commercial Director
David McArthur, Regional CEO

5612 Environmental Sciences
900 University Ave.
Riverside, CA 92521
951-827-1012
Fax: 951-827-3993
E-mail: enviro@eas.slu.edu
http://www.envisci.ucr.edu
Environmental Sciences is concerned with the near-surface realm of Earth and the way humans interact with that environment. Environmental scientist are concerned with water availability and equal, waste disposal, the use of Earth'slimited resources, and natural hazards such as earthquakes, landslides, and floods. Environmental scientists use the principles of geology, physics, chemistry, and biology to understand these phenomena and solve environmental problems.
Jennifer Reising, Chair Support for Earth Scie
Janice Leslie, FAO

5613 Exploring Animal Life - CD-ROM
Educational Images
PO Box 3456
Westside Station
Elmira, NY 14905-456
607-732-1090
800-527-4264
Fax: 607-732-1183
E-mail: edimages@edimages.com
http://www.educationalimages.com
A curriculum oriented presentation and an instant encyclopedia, filled with superb photographs, informative text, exciting video clips, printable diagrams and illustrations, and lab activities. Provides a fascinating survey of themajor divisions of animal life and their characteristics: sponges, molluscs, insects, arthropods, fish, reptiles, birds and mammals are fully presented in the order in which you teach them.
Charles R Belinky, Ph.D, CEO

5614 Exploring Environmental Science Topics
Educational Images
PO Box 3456
Westside Station
Elmira, NY 14905-456
607-732-1090
800-527-4264
Fax: 607-732-1183
E-mail: edimages@edimages.com
http://www.educationalimages.com
Provides a curriculum oriented presentation, an instant encyclopedia, superb photographs, video clips, informative text, printable diagrams & illustrations, & lab activities. This program offers a fascinating survey of environmentaltopics & concerns such as the environmental costs of energy; acid rain; energy flow and the greenhouse effect; oil spills; tundra, chaparral, desert, grassland and forest biomes; the hydrological cycle and water pollution; and the recycling elementsin the biosphere.
CD-Rom
Charles R Belinky, Ph.D, CEO

5615 Exploring Freshwater Communities
Educational Images
PO Box 3456
Westside Station
Elmira, NY 14905-456
607-732-1090
800-527-4264
Fax: 607-732-1183
E-mail: edimages@edimages.com
http://www.educationalimages.com
A complete resource for studying freshwater biomes. It provides a fascinating survey of the ecology of swamps, bogs, marshes, wetlands, streams, ponds, lakes and the Everglades. There is even an introduction to fish restoration andwater pollution.
CD-Rom
Charles R Belinky, Ph.D, CEO

5616 Five Winds International
199 Woolwich Street
Guelph, ON N1H3V
613-722-6629
Fax: 613-722-0574
E-mail: info@fivewinds.com
http://www.fivewinds.com

Five Winds helps companies and organizations understand sustainability to improve their performance and succeed in the marketplace.
Kevin Brady, Founder/Sr. Associate
Jim Fava, Founder/Sr. Director

5617 Fossil Rim Wildlife Center
2155 County Road 2008 254-897-2960
PO Box 2189 888-775-6742
Glen Rose, TX 76043 Fax: 254-897-3785
E-mail: vistor-services@fossilrim.org
http://www.fossilrim.org

Fossil Rim Wildlife Center is dedicated to conservation of species in peril, scientific research, training of professionals, creative management of natural resources, and impactful public education. Through these activities we providea diversity of compelling learning experiences which invoke positive change in the way people think, feel and act environmentally. Also provides scenic drives and lodgings for visitors, and is open all seasons.
Billie Kinnard, Marketing/PR Director
Lisa Roberts, Membership Director

5618 GLOBE
Mailstop T28H 800-858-9947
Moffett Field, CA 94035 Fax: 650-604-1913
E-mail: help@globe.gov
http://www.globe.gov

GLOBE is a worldwide hands on, primary and secondary school based science and education program.

5619 Glacier Institute
137 Main Street 406-755-1211
PO Box 1887 Fax: 406-755-7154
Kalispell, MT 59903 E-mail: register@glacierinstitute.org
http://www.glacierinstitute.org

The Glacier Institute serves adults and children as an educational leader in the Crown of the Continent ecosystem with Glacier National Park at its center. Emphasizing field based learning experiences, the Institute provides anobjective and science based understanding of the area's ecology and its interaction with people. Through this non advocacy approach to outdoor education, participants can be better prepared to make informed and constructive decisions which impactthis & other ecosystems.
Joyce Baltz, Executive Director
Hallie M. Brown, Office Administrator

5620 Global Nest
Michigan State University
281 State Route 79 732-333-5848
Suite 208 Fax: 732-333-5946
Morganville, NJ 07751 E-mail: info@globalnest.com
http://www.globalnest.com

The Global Nest constitutes an international association of scientists, technologists, engineers and other interested groups involved in all scientific and technological aspects of the environment as well as in application techniquesaiming at the development of sustainable solutions. Its main target is to support and assist the dissemination of information regarding the most contemporary methods for improving quality of life through the development and application oftechnologies.

5621 Gore Range Natural Science School
318 Walking Mountains Lane 970-827-9725
PO Box 9469 Fax: 970-827-9730
Avon, CO 81620 E-mail: science@gorerange.org
http://www.gorerange.org

Offers summer day and overnight programs for students in 3rd grade up. During the academic school year GRNSS provides integrated field science education to local and visiting schools. Its mission is to raise environmental awareness andinspire stewardship of the Eagle River watershed.
Phil Brodsky, Chair
Pat Tierney, Vice Chair

5622 Groundwater Foundation
The Groundwater Foundation
5561 S 48th Street 402-434-2740
Suite 215 800-858-4844
Lincoln, NE 68516 Fax: 402-434-2742
E-mail: info@groundwater.org
http://www.groundwater.org

the groundwater foundation is a non profit organization, that is dedicated to informing the public about one of our greatest hidden resources, groundwater since 1985 our program and publications presents the benefits everyone recievesfrom groundwater,and the risks that threaten groundwater quality. we make learning about ground water fun and understandable for kids and adults alike.
James Burks, Chair
Jay Beaumont, Vice Chair

5623 Hazardous Chemicals: Handle With Care
Educational Images
PO Box 3456 607-732-1090
Westside Station 800-527-4264
Elmira, NY 14905-456 Fax: 607-732-1183
E-mail: edimages@edimages.com
http://www.educationalimages.com

Shows the importance of hazardous chemicals in our daily lives and problems caused by ignorance, mistakes, accidents and occasionally, recklessness in their use. Four case studies show how toxic chemicals were introduced into theenvironment causing serious health and environmental effects. Video, 56 page guide with lesson plans, projects, reproducible handouts.
Charles R Belinky, CEO

5624 Hidden Villa
26870 Moody Road 650-949-8650
Los Altos Hills, CA 94022 Fax: 650-948-4159
E-mail: info@hiddenvilla.org
http://www.hiddenvilla.org

A non-profit 1600 acre organic farm and wilderness preserve serving approx. 50,000 visitors. Programs and offerings include: Hidden Villa Environmental Education Program, Summer Camp, a resident intern program, Community SupportedAgriculture, a Hostel for domestic and international travelers, meeting/retreat rental space, Community Programs and eight miles of hiking trails and picnic areas.
Richard Peers, Chair
Martin Neiman, Treasurer

5625 Ice Age Relicts: Living Glaciers and Signs of Ancient Ice Sheets
Educational Images
PO Box 3456 607-732-1090
Westside Station 800-527-4264
Elmira, NY 14905-456 Fax: 607-732-1183
E-mail: edimages@edimages.com
http://www.educationalimages.com

Glaciers, living relicts of the ice age, are still important today. They hold much of the earth's fresh water, sculpted much of North America, and promise an early return to finish their work. Provides a coherent picture of howglaciers work, and what they did. 26 page guide. Video or filmstrips.
Charles R Belinky, Ph.D, CEO

5626 International Center for Earth Concerns
Centennial Valley, MT 805-649-3535
Fax: 805-649-1757
E-mail: earthconcerns@earthconcerns.org
http://www.earthconcerns.org

Dedicated to providing for public use, a world class botanic garden, outdoor learning-ecology center and a 50-passenger all-electric floating classroom on Lake Casitas. These facilities are used to promote a better understanding ofman's place in the environment, as well as to help develop a sense of respect, responsibility and compassion for animals and nature.
John Hoyt, Founding President
John Taft, Chairman

5627 Invertebrate Animal Videos
Educational Images

PO Box 3456
Westside Station
Elmira, NY 14905-456
607-732-1090
800-527-4264
Fax: 607-732-1183
E-mail: edimages@edimages.com
http://www.educationalimages.com

Four part series. Each a 40-minute multimedia presentation with easy going narration and hundreds of interactive links. Part I: sponges, anemones, corals and flatworms. Part II: molluscs, segmented worms and minor phyla. Part III:the insects. Part IV: noninsect arthropods and echinoderms.
Charles R Belinky, Ph.D, CEO

5628 Jones & Stokes
11820 Northup Way
Suite E300
Bellevue, WA 98005
425-822-1077
Fax: 425-822-1079

An employee-owned company, Jones & Stokes is the best consulting source for integrated environmental planning and natural resources management services in the western United States.
Grant Bailey

5629 Killer Whales: Lords of the Sea
Educational Images
PO Boc 3456
Westside Station
Elmira, NY 14905-456
607-732-1090
800-527-4264
Fax: 607-732-1183
E-mail: edimages@edimages.com
http://www.educationalimages.com

Separates facts from myth about these majestic, maligned and usually misrepresented scagoing mammals: both wild and captive killer whales, their mental and physical powers, their feeding and reproductive behavior, physiology,sociology and echolocation. Information on other cetaceans is presented for comparison and better understanding. Provides scientific information and reports on ongoing research.
Charles R Belinky, Ph.D, CEO

5630 Legacy International
1020 Legacy Drive
Bedford, VA 24523
540-297-5982
Fax: 540-297-1860
E-mail: mail@legacyintl.org
http://www.legacyintl.org

Creates environments where people can address personal, community, and global needs while developing skills and effective responses to change.Whether working with youths, corporate leaders, educational professionals, entrepreneurs, orindividuals on opposing sides of a conflict, our goal is the same. Programs provide experiences, skills, and strategies that enable people to build better lives for themselves and others around them.
JE Rash, President/Founder
Shanti Thompson, VP

5631 Lesley/Audubon Environmental Education Programs
Lesley University
29 Everett Street
Cambridge, MA 02138
617-868-9600
E-mail: info@lesley.edu
http://www.lesley.edu

In partership with Audubon Expedition Institute in Belfast, Lesley University offers a Bachelor of Science degree in Environmental Studies, a Master of Science degree in Environmental Education and a Master of Science in EcologicalTeaching and Learning. Students travel throughout the US earning academic credit and gaining first-hand experience of environmental issues.
Donald Perrin, Chair

5632 Let's Grow Houseplants
Educational Images
Po Box 3456
Westside Station
Elmira, NY 14905-456
607-732-1090
800-527-4264
Fax: 607-732-1183
E-mail: edimages@edimages.com
http://www.educationalimages.com

Details different kinds of plants and their needs, when to water, selection, how to start from seeds and cuttings, how to make inexpensive pots, etc. Perfect to initiate an elementary classroom gardening project. 74 frames and guide.For elementary and preschool.
Charles R Belinky, Ph.D, CEO

5633 Lost Valley Educational Center
81868 Lost Valley Lane
Dexter, OR 97431
541-937-3351
E-mail: info@lostvalley.org
http://www.lostvalley.org

Offers a wide variety of programs, including residential interships, educational workshops that emphasize hands on, experiential learning and personal/spiritual growth workshops. The Center also provides a supportive and nourishingplace to hold individuals and organizations who share our vision for an environmentally sound, pollution free world to hold conferences, retreats and workshops.
Dianne Brause, Co-Founder

5634 MacKenzie Environmental Education Center
Wisconsin Department of Natural Resources
W7303 County Road CS & Q
Poynette, WI 53955
608-635-8105
Fax: 608-635-2743
E-mail: info@naturenet.com
http://www.mackenziecenter.com

Located only 20 miles north of Madison, the MacKenzie Center offers a wide array of outdoor experiences. Five themed nature trails, prairie restorations, picnic area, nature study, three museums and a wildlife exhibit containing liveanimals that are native to Wisconsin, are here to help you gain a better understanding of our natural resources.
Ruth Ann Lee, Director
Derek A. Duane, Maintenance

5635 Marine Biological Laboratory
7 Mbl Street
Woods Hole, MA 02543
508-548-3705
Fax: 508-457-1924
E-mail: mdonovan@mbl.edu
http://www.mbl.edu

For more than a century, scientists from around the world have been gathering in Woods Hole. The best students from the best universities, the brightest young faculty, the most succesful scientists working at the pinnacle of theprofession, an unmatched collection of researchers and educators congregates every year in the seaside village whose name has become synonimous with science.
John W. Rowe, Chairman
William I. Huyett, Vice Chair

5636 Microscopic Pond
Educational Images
PO Box 3456
Westside Station
Elmira, NY 14905-456
607-732-1090
800-527-4264
Fax: 607-732-1183
E-mail: edimages@edimages.com
http://www.educationalimages.com

Introduces students to both the micrscopic plant and animal life of a pond. Various groups of algae are discussed and illustrated, including desmids, Pediastrum, Pithophora, Spyrogyra, Volvox, Nostac, calothrix, Bacillariophyseae,Dinophyseae, and amoebas (includeing Amoeba proteus), Arcella, the testaceans, and many others. With only a few exceptions, all of the organisms in this program were photographed live.
Charles R Belinky, Ph.D, CEO

5637 Mote Environmental Services
1600 Ken Thompson Parkway
Sarasota, FL 34236
941-388-4441
800-691-6683
http://www.mote.org

Mote Environmental Services offers consulting services focused on marine and coastal issues, where our expertise is strongest. We provide superior, results-oriented investigations and management planning service within our areas oftechnical and policy specialty. MESI is a wholly owned subsidiary of Mote Marine Laboratory, an independent, nonprofit research and public education institution dedicated to excellence in marine and environmental sciences.
Eugene Beckstein, Chairman
G. Lowe Morrison, Vice Chairman

5638 National Environmental Health Association (NEHA)
720 South Colorado Boulevard 303-756-9090
Suite 1000-N 866-956-2258
Denver, CO 80246 Fax: 303-691-9490
E-mail: staff@neha.org
http://www.neha.org

NEHA is the only national association that represents all of environmental health and protection from terrorism and all-hazards preparedness, to food safety and protection and onsite wastewater systems. Over 4500 members and theprofession are served by the association through its Journal of Environmental Health, Annual Educational Conference & Exhibition, credentialing programs, research and development activities and other services.

Brian Collins, President
Alicia Enriquez Collins, President-Elect

5639 National Institute of Environmental Health Sciences
111 TW Alexander Drive 919-541-3345
PO Box 12233 Fax: 919-541-4395
Research Tri Pk, NC 27709 E-mail: webcenter@niehs.nih.gov
http://www.niehs.nih.gov

The National Institute of Environmental Health Sciences is the principal federal agency for basic biomedical research on the health effects of environmental agents. It is the headquarters for the National Toxicology Program whichcoordinates toxicology studies within the Department of Health and Human Services.

Linda S. Birnbaum, Director
Richard Woychik, Deputy Director

5640 National PTA: Environmental Project
1250 N. Pitt Street Alexandria 703-518-1200
Alexandria, VA 22314 800-307-4782
Fax: 703-836-0942
E-mail: info@pta.org
http://www.pta.org

The mission of the National PTA is to support and speak on behalf of children and youth in the school, in the community and before governmental bodies and other organizations; to assist parents in developing the skills they need toraise and protect their children and to encourage parent and public involvement in the public schools. Engages in advocacy and education, including workshops and lobbying.

Betsy Landers, President
Otha Thornton, President-Elect

5641 Natural Resources Conservation and Management
Lexindton Convention And Visitors Bureau
301 East Vine Street 859-244-7706
Lexington, KY 40507 800-845-3959
E-mail: lexadmin@visitlex.com

As a trained professional, you will have a variety of challenging employment opportunities in public agencies and industry to contribute to sustained productivity and equality of all of our natural resources. In addition, some studentsfind that the Natural Resource Conservation and Management program satisfies their desire for a career in environmental education or environmental journalism.

David Lord, President

5642 Nielsen Environmental Field School
9600 Achenbach Canyon Road 575-532-5535
Las Cruces, NM 88011 Fax: 575-532-5978
E-mail: info@envirofieldschool.com
http://www.envirofieldschool.com

In 1990, the Nielsen Environmental Field School was created in reponse to a demand from the environmental industry for practically oriented, hands-on environmental field training.

David M. Nielsen, Co-Founder
Gillian L. Nielsen, Co-Founder

5643 Northwest Environmental Education Council
Northwest Environmental Education Council
650 S. Orcas Street 206-762-1976
Suite 220 Fax: 206-762-1979
Seattle, WA 98108 E-mail: emcwayne@nweec.org
http://www.nweec.org

The Northwest Environmental Education Council increases environmental awareness, appreciation and stewardship by providing environmental education and science training opportunities for youth and adults.

Tasya Gray, President
Lief Horwitz, Vice President

5644 Northwest Interpretive Association
Northwest Interpretive Association
164 South Jackson Street 206-220-4140
Seattle, WA 98104 877-874-6775
http://www.nwpubliclands.com

Works with public and management agencies to operate educational bookstores. Our mission is to provide visitors with information they need to learn about the nature and natural history of public lands so they can make wise choicesabout the lands use, preservation and protection. We accomplish our mission by selling educational and interpretive materials directly to visitors as well as returning net proceeds to the site where they were guaranteed to help fund other programs.

Mark Lester, Chair

5645 Office of Energy and Environmental Industries
International Trade Administraction 202-482-5225
14th and Constitution Avenue, NW, Room 4 800-usa-trad
Washington, DC 20230 Fax: 202-482-5665
http://www.ita.doc.gov/td/energy/index.htm

The Office of Energy and Environmental Industries (OEEI) is the principal resource and key contact point within the US Department of Commerce for American environmental technology companies. OEEI's goal is to facilitate and increaseexports of environmental technologuies-goods and services-by providing support and guidance to US exporters.

Adam O'Malley, Office Director
Man Cho, Team Leader, Energy

5646 Perkiomen Watershed Conservancy
1 Skippack Pike 610-287-9383
Schwenksville, PA 19473 Fax: 610-287-9237
E-mail: pwc@perkiomenwatershed.org
http://www.perkiomenwatershed.org/

A nonprofit organization founded in 1964 by local citizens that works to protect the watershed of the Perkiomen Creek and its tributaries. This is accomplished through environmental education, conservation programs and watershedstewardship activities.

Crystal Gilchrist, Executive Director
Trudy Phillips, Director for Env Education

5647 Primary Ecological Succession
Educational Images
PO Box 3456 607-732-1090
Westside Station 800-527-4264
Elmira, NY 14905-456 Fax: 607-732-1183
E-mail: edimages@edimages.com
http://www.educationalimages.com

An illustrated explanation of basic concepts of primary succession: the pioneer community; tolerant vs. intolerant species; stabilization; stratification and the climax community. Concise overview followed by classic, specificexamples of succession - on bare rock, on the sand dunes of Lake Michigan, on the outer banks of North Carolina - all explored in detail. 72 frames and guide.

Charles R Belinky, Ph.D, CEO

5648 Project Oceanology
University Of Connecticut
Avery Point Campus 860-445-9007
1084 Shennecossett Road 800-364-8472
Groton, CT 06340 Fax: 860-449-8008
E-mail: projecto@oceanology.org
http://www.oceanology.org

Project Oceanology is owned and operated by Interdistrict Committee for Project Oceanology and association of 25 educational institutions in Massachusetts, Rodhe Island, Connecticut and

New York. Members of this associations includepublic school districts, private schools, states university, public and private colleges, a maritime museum and an aquarium. The project is governed by an assembly of delegates representing the member institutions.
Thaxter Tewksbury, Director
Lauren Rader, Chief Instructor

5649 Project WILD
5555 Morningside Drive 713-520-1936
Suite 212 Fax: 713-520-8008
Houston, TX 77005 E-mail: info@councilforee.org
http://www.projectwild.org

Project WILD is one of the most widely-used conservation and environmental education programs among educators of students in kindergarten through high school. Project WILD is based on the premise that young people and educators have avital interest in learning about natural world.
Mark LeFebre, Senior Program Manager
Josetta Hawthorne, Executive Director

5650 Resource-Use Education Council
The Virginia Natural Resources Education Guide
PO Box 11104 804-698-4442
Richmond, VA 23230 Fax: 804-698-4522
E-mail: jkcomfort@deg.virginia.gov
http://www.virginianaturally.org

In the mid 1950s, representatives from Virginia and federal natural resource agencies, along with professors in the colleges of education and resource management, came together as the Virginia Resource Use Education Council. For 35years, the VRUEC sponsored a summer conservation course for teachers at four of Virginia's colleges.
Ann Regn, Chairman

5651 Risk Management Internet Services
Managerial Technologies Corporation
2400 East Main Street 630-221-9116
Suite 103- 319 Fax: 312-602-4935
St Charles, IL 60174 E-mail: info@rmis.com
http://rmis.com

Dedicated to bringing risk management related professions together with the consultants, developers and providers who service them.

5652 Ross & Associates Environmental Consulting,Ltd
1218 Third Avenue 206-447-1805
Suite 1207 Fax: 206-447-0956
Seattle, WA 98101 E-mail: rossmail@ross-assoc.com
http://www.ross-assoc.com

Ross and Associates environmental consulting, is a small group of highly motivated professionals committed to helping environmental and natural resources agencies improve management programs and achieve better environmental results.
Rob Greenwood, Principal
Tim Larson, Principal

5653 SEEK
520 Lafayette Rd. N. 651-757-2700
St. Paul, MN 55155-4194 800-857-3864
E-mail: seek.pca@state.mn.us
http://www.seek.state.mn.us

The SEEK directory works as a clearinghouse for all types of environmental education resources, from articles to lesson plans, from performances to displays, and many more. These resources come a variety of organizations throughoutMinnesota, including schools and colleges, government agencies, libraries and businesses.
Lee Ann Landstrom, Chair
Karen Balmer, Board of Teaching

5654 Sacramento River Discovery Center
1000 Sale Lane 530-527-1196
Red Bluff, CA 96080 Fax: 530-527-1312
E-mail: lgreen@tehama.k12.ca.us
http://www.srdc.tehama.k12.ca.us

The mission of the Sacramento River Discovery Center is to educate the public's school programs. Teacher professional development, camping, rafting and tourist events are available.
Lupe Green, Executive Director
Anna Draper, Program Manager

5655 Save the Dolphins Project Earth Island Institute
2150 Allston Way 510-859-9100
Suite 460 Fax: 510-859-9091
Berkeley, CA 94704-1375 E-mail: johnknox@earthisland.org
http://www.earthisland.org
Martha Davis, President
Kenneth Brower, VP

5656 Schlitz Audubon Nature Center
1111 E Brown Deer Road 414-352-2880
Milwaukee, WI 53217 Fax: 414-352-6091
E-mail: smanning@sanc.org
http://www.schlitzauduboncenter.com

A unique urban area of green just 15 minutes north of downtown Milwaukee, we are located along the shore of Lake Michigan. Escape from the world of concrete to hike seven miles of trails, walk along the beach and feel far away from thecity or view forests and wildlife from the 60-foot observation tower. Remember to bring your binoculars, you never know what you may want to take a closer look at while visiting the Center.
Margarete R. Harvey, President
Stuart D. Findlay, Treasurer

5657 School of Public & Environmental Affairs
Indiana University
1315 East Tenth Street 812-855-4848
Bloomington, IN 47405 800-765-7755
E-mail: gassibey@ium.edu
http://www.spea.indiana.edu

The School of Public Environmental Affairs offer environmental science summer programs to high school students and middle/high school teachers who want answers to environmental questions.
Michael McRobbie, President
Mary Anna Weber, VP

5658 Science House
909 Capability Drive 919-515-6118
Suite 1200 Fax: 919-515-7545
Raleigh, NC 27606 E-mail: science_house@ncsu.edu
http://www.thesciencehouse.org

The activities of The Science House is itself a partership of facultu and stuff from science and education departments across the NC State campus, and collaborates with many other k-12 support organization in North Carolina.

5659 Seacamp Association, Inc
Newfound Harbor Marine Institute
1300 Big Pine Avenue 305-872-2331
Big Pine Key, FL 33043 877-SEA-AMP
Fax: 305-872-2555
E-mail: info@seacamp.org
http://www.seacamp.org

To create awareness of the complex and fragile marine world and to foster critical thinking and informed decision making about man's use of natural resources. One of the few organizations in the US providing experiential education inmarine studies to students aged 8 to 21 years.
Irene Hooper, President
Betty Rein, VP

5660 Setting Up a Small Aquarium
Educational Images
PO Box 3456 607-732-1090
Westside Station 800-527-4264
Elmira, NY 14905-456 Fax: 607-732-1183
E-mail: edimages@edimages.com
http://www.educationalimages.com

Details the exact procedure to be followed in setting up either a marine or freshwater aquarium successfully. Methods are scientifically sound, well documented, and up-to-date.
Charles R Belinky, Ph.D, CEO

5661 Sierra Club
85 Second Street 415-977-5500
2nd Floor Fax: 415-977-5797
San Francisco, CA 94105 E-mail: information@sierraclub.org
http://www.sierraclub.org
Aims to explore, enjoy, and protect the wild places of the earth, to practice and promote the responsible use of the earth's ecosystems and resources, to educate and enlist humanity to protect and restore the quality of the naturaland human environment, and to use all lawful means to carry out these objectives.
John Miur, Founder
Robbie Cox, President

5662 Smithsonian Environmental Research Center
Po Box 28 443-482-2200
647 Contees Wharf Road Fax: 443-482-2380
Edgewater, MD 21037-28 E-mail: hollyj@si.edu
http://www.serc.si.edu
The Smithsonian Environmental Research Center advances stewardship of the biosphere through interdisciplinary research and educational outreach. SERC's scientists study a variety of interconnected ecosystems at the Center's primaryresearch site here in Maryland, and at affiliated sites around the world.
Suzanne H. Woolsey, Chairperson
V.K. Holtzendorf, VP

5663 Society of Environmental Toxicology and Chemistry
SETAC N America Office
229 South Baylen Street 850-469-1500
2nd Floor Fax: 850-469-9778
Pensacola, FL 32502 E-mail: setac@setac.org
http://www.setac.org
The Society of Environmental Toxicology and Chemistry provides a forum for the examination of environmental issues by environmental professionals from industry, academia, government, and public-interest groups.
Patrick D. Guiney, President
Kurt J. Maier, VP

5664 Southwest Environmental Health Sciences: Community Outreach and Education Program
University Of Arizona College Of Pharmacy
Room 244 520-626-5594
Po Box 210207 Fax: 520-626-6944
Tucson, AZ 85721-20E-mail: swehsc-info@pharmacy.arizona..edu
http://www.coep.pharmacy.arizona.edu
The COEP goals are to review, develop, and disseminate quality environmental health science curricula. Develop and host K-12 teacher training workshops, communicate with the general public about local and common environmental healthscience concerns, share research results from SWEHSC investigators with the COEP target audiences.
Marti Lindsey, Director
Stephanie Nardei, Information Specialist

5665 Spiders in Perspective: Their Webs, Ways and Worth
Educational Images
PO Box 3456 607-732-1090
Elmira, NY 14905 800-527-4264
Fax: 607-732-1183
Comprehensive coverage of the nature of spiders, their diversity of structures, and their remarkable behavior patterns. Presents the unique world of creatures you may have ignored before, but probably never will again. Coverslocomotion, the various perceptual senses, silk production, camouflage and mimicry, webs, hunting, predation by wasps, kleptoparasitism, courtship and reproduction, population densities, impact on humans, etc. 2 parts, 76 & 78 frames. Video, slidesor filmstrip.

Charles R Belinky, Ph.D., CEO

5666 Student Conservation Association
Po Box 550 603-543-1700
689 River Road Fax: 603-543-1828
Charlestown, NH 03603 E-mail: internships@thesca.org
http://www.thesca.org
America's largest and oldest provider of conservation service opportunities, outdoor education and career training for youth. SCA is building the next generation of conservation leaders and inspire lifelong stewardship of ourenvironment and communities.
Dale Penny, President/CEO
Valrie Bailey, Executive VP/Chaief of Staff

5667 The Groundwater Foundation
5561 S 48th Street 402-434-2740
Suite 215 800-858-4844
Lincoln, NE 68516 Fax: 402-434-2742
E-mail: info@groundwater.org
http://www.groundwater.org
The Groundwater Foundation is a nonprofit organization that is dedicated to informing the public about one of our greatest hidden resources, groundwater. Since 1985, our programs and publications present the benefits everyone receivesfrom groundwater and the risks that threaten groundwater quality. We make learning about groundwater fun and understandable for kids and adults alike.

James Burks, Chair
Jay Beaumont, Vice Chair

5668 The Nelson Institute for Environmental Studies
UW Madison, 550 N Park Street 608-262-7996
70 Science Hall Fax: 608-262-2273
Madison, WI 53706-1491 E-mail: nelson@mailplus.wisc.edu
http://www.nelson.wisc.edu
Few institutions can match the University of Wisconsin-Madison's expertise in environmental studies. Literally hundreds of professors teach and conduct research in environmentally related subjects ranging from agriculture to zoology.Their scholarship and achievement are widely recognized. In dozens of academic fields, the university is consistently rated the nation's best and most prolific.
Janet Silbernagel, Program Chairs, Conservation
Jess Gilbert, Program Chairs, Culture, His

5669 Thorne Ecological Institute
1466 N 63rd Street 303-499-3647
PO Box 19107 Fax: 720-565-3873
Boulder, CO 80308 E-mail: info@thornenature.org
http://www.thornenature.org
Offers hands-on environmental education for young people along the Front Range of Colorado.
Melissa Amold, Chair
Mike Moelter, Vice Chair

5670 Trees for Tomorrow
519 Sheridan Street 715-479-6456
PO Box 609 800-838-9472
Eagle River, WI 54521 Fax: 715-479-2318
E-mail: learning@treesfortomorrow.com
http://www.treesfortomorrow.com
Private, nonprofit natural resource education school that uses a combination of field studies and classroom presentations to teach conservation values, as well as demonstrate the benefits of modern resource management.

Maggie Bishop, Executive Director
Sheri Buller, Assistant Director

5671 Triumvirate Environmental
200 Inner Belt Road 800-966-9282
Somerville, MA 02143 Fax: 617-628-8099
E-mail: contactus@triumvirate.com
http://www.triumvirate.com
Triumvirate Environmental is a full-service environmental management firm headquartered in eastern Massachusetts. Serving the environmental and hazardous waste needs of clients throughout the northeast in the areas of biotechnology andpharmaceuticals, education, health care, metal platers and

finishers, manufacturing, and utilities, Triumvirate Environmental is the industry leader in personalized service.

5672 Tropical Forest Foundation
2121 Eisenhower Avenue 703-518-8834
Suite 200 Fax: 703-518-8974
Alexandria, VA 22314 E-mail: tff@tropicalforestfoundation.org
http://www.tropicalforestfoundation.org

A non-profit educational institution dedicated to the conservation of tropical forests through sustainable forestry. Its Board of Directors includes representatives from industry, government, science, academia and conservation.

Shawn Draper, Chairman
Steve Tourek, President

5673 US Environmental Protection Agency: Great Lakes National Program Office
77 West Jackson Boulevard 312-353-2117
G-17 800-621-8431
Chicago, IL 60604-3511 Fax: 312-886-6869
http://www.epa.gov/greatlakes

The focus for the State of the Lakes Ecosystem Conference (SOLEC) 1996 is the nearshore zone of the Great Lakes. Nearshore ecosystems are complex and dynamic with many measurable parameters. The nearshore area is extremely important tooverall ecosystem function. It is the most productive zone within each of the Great Lakes and is the area most affected by human activity. Nearshore zones include embayments, tributaries and tributary mouths, marshes and other wetlands, and dunes.

5674 Water Resources Management
550 N Park Street 608-265-5296
122 Science Hall Fax: 608-262-0014
Madison, WI 53706-1491 E-mail: nelsongrad@mailplus.wisc.edu
http://www.nelson.wisc.edu

The program addresses the complex, interdisciplinary aspects of managing resources by helping students integrate the biological and phisical sciences with engineering and law and the social sciences. The workshop provides anopportunity for students to work outside of the textbook environment and tackle a rea-world problem.

Eileen Hanneman, Sr. Administrative Program S
Carol Enseki, Department Administrator

5675 Wilderness Education Association
2150 N 107th Street 206-367-8704
Suite 205 800-572-3015
Seattle, WA 98133 Fax: 206-367-8777
E-mail: nationaloffice@weainfo.org
http://www.weainfo.org

Mike McGowan, President
Ricky Haro, VP

5676 Windows on the Wild
World Wildlife Fund
1250 24th Street Northwest 202-293-4800
Po Box 97180 800-225-5993
Washington, DC 20037 Fax: 202-293-9211
http://www.windowsonthewild.com

Provides educators with interdisciplinary curriculum materials and training programs. By using biodiversity as its organizing theme, WOW provides students with a unique window for exploring a range of topics including science,economics, social studies, language arts, geography and civics.

Jennifer A Zadwick, Program Information Coord.

5677 World Resources Institute
10 G Street, NE 202-729-7600
Suite 800 Fax: 202-729-7610
Washington, DC 20002 http://www.wri.org

WRI provides information, ideas, and solutions to global environmental problems. Our mission is to move human society to live in ways that protect the environment for current and future generations, with programs that meet globalchallenges by using knowledge to catalyze public and private action. Goals include safeguarding earth's climate from further harm, protecting the ecosystems, and reducing the use of materials and generation of wastes in the production of goods andservices.

James Gustave Speth, Founder/Trustee
James A. Harmon, Chairman

5678 Young Entomologists Society
6907 West Grand River Avenue 517-886-0630
Lansing, MI 48906 Fax: 517-886-0630
E-mail: yesbugs@aol.com
http://www.members.@aol.com/YESbugs/mainmenu.html

To provide young people with a combination of programs, publications, and educational materials that enrich their insect and spider studies through dynamic, innovative, and enjoyable learning experience.

Gary Dunn, Director Of Education

Industry Web Sites

Environmental

5679 **ABS Consulting Training Services**
http://www.absconsulting.com/svc_training.cfm
Government Institutes Division provides continuing education and practical information on government regulatory topics. We recognize that you face unique challenges presented by the ever-increasing number of new regulations and theresulting rapid evolution of new technologies.

5680 **Academy of Natural Sciences**
http://www.acnatsci.org
Our mission is to create the basis for a healthy and sustainable planet through exploration, research and education.

5681 **ActiveSet.org**
http://www.activeset.org
ActiveSet.org was created for the benefit of professionals involved with all aspects of environmental air quality testing, monitoring and management. Environmental Managers can easily research and contact emissions testing firms,services and products either by state, region, or using the site's built-in search engine. Facility owners and managers use ActiveSet.org's free online request for proposals form to reach stack testing firms all over the country for their nextproject.

5682 **Adirondack Council**
http://www.adirondackcouncil.org
The Adirondack Council is a nonprofit environmental group working to protect the open space resources of New York's six million acre Adirondack Park and to help sustain the natural and human communities of the region. It monitorsdevelopment on private lands and ensures the mandated constitutional protection of public lands.

5683 **Advanced Recovery**
http://www.advancedrecovery.com
Advanced Recovery, based in New Jersey, is involved in the recycling industry. They promote the proper disposal of all scrap, but are particularly interested in the disposal of electronic equipment, such as computer monitors consistingof lead.

5684 **Advanced Technologies And Practices**
http://www.advancedbuildings.org
A building professional's guide to more than 90 environmentally-appropriate technologies and practices. Architects, engineers and buildings managers can improve the energy and resource efficiency of commercial, industrial andmulti-unit residential buildings through the use of the technologies and practices described in this web site.

5685 **Advanced Technology Environmental Education Center**
http://www.ateec.org
ATEEC's mission is the advancement of environmental technology education through curriculum development, professional development and program improvement in the nation's community colleges and high schools. ATEEC is funded by theNational Science Foundation and is a partnership of the Hazardous Materials Training and Research Institute, the National Partnership for Environmental Technology Education, and the University of Northern Iowa.

5686 **African Environmental Research and Consulting Group**
http://www.africanenviro.org
The AERCG is a US nonprofit organization with offices in Africa and Western countries. The group focuses on improving the quality of life, mitigating environmental hazards and the protection of human health in Africa. They are involvedin promoting sustainable development in African communities, their site contains information about their efforts.

5687 **Agency for Toxic Substances and Disease Registry**
http://www.atsdr.cdc.gov/
The mission of the Agency for Toxic Substances and Disease Registry, as an agency of the US Department of Health and Human Services, is to prevent exposure and adverse human health effects and diminished quality of life associated withexposure to hazardous substances from waste sites, unplanned releases and other sources of pollution present in the environment.

5688 **Agriculture Network Information Center**
http://www.agnic.org
The Agriculture Network Information Center is a voluntary alliance of the National Agricultural Library, land-grant universities and other agricultural organizations in cooperation with citizen groups and government agencies. AgNICfocuses on providing agricultural information in electronic format over the World Wide Web via the Internet.

5689 **Air Force Center for Environmental Excellence**
http://www.afcee.brooks.af.mil
The Air Force Center for Environmental Excellence provides our customers with a complete range of world class enviromental, architectural and landscape design, planning and construction management services and products.

5690 **Air and Waste Management Association**
http://www.awma.org
The Air and Waste Management Association is a nonprofit, nonpartisan professional organization that provides training, information and networking opportunities to thousands of environmental professionals in 65 countries.

5691 **Alabama Department of Environmental Management**
http://www.adem.state.al.us
Provides environmental stewardship through the implementation of authorized environmental statutes, advocating statutory change as needed.

5692 **Alaska Chilkat Bald Eagle Preserve**
http://www.dnr.state.ak.us/parks/units/eagleprv.htm
The Alaska Chilkat Bald Eagle Preserve was created by the State of Alaska in June 1982. The Preserve was established to protect and perpetuate the world's largest concentration of bald eagles and their critical habitat. It alsosustains and protects the natural salmon runs.

5693 **Alfred Wegener Institute for Polar and Marine Research**
http://www.awi-bremerhaven.de/index-e.html
Polar and Marine research are central themes of Global system and Environmental Science. The Alfred Wegener Institute conducts research in the Arctic, the Antarctic and at temperate latitudes. It coordinates Polar research in Germanyand provides both the necessary equipment and the essential logistic back up for polar expeditions. Website is in the German language.

5694 **Alliance for Environmental Technology**
http://www.aet.org
The Alliance for Environmental Technology is an international association of chemical manufacturers and forest products companies dedicated to improving the environmental performance of the pulp and paper industry. AET supports the useof Elemental Chlorine-Free technology based on chlorine dioxide.

5695 **American Academy of Environmental Engineers**
http://www.aaee.net
The American Academy of Environmental Engineers is dedicated to excellence in the practice of environmental engineering to ensure the public health, safety and welfare to enable humankind to co-exist in harmony with nature.

5696 **American Chemical Society**
http://www.chemistry.org/portal/a/c/s/1/home.html
The mission is to promote the public perception and understanding of chemistry and the chemical sciences through public outreach programs and public awareness campaigns; involve the Society's more than 163,000 member's in improving thepublic's perception of chemistry.

5697 American Conference of Governmental Industrial Hygienists
http://www.acgih.org/home.htm
Member-based organization and community of professionals that advances worker health and safety through education and the development and dissemination of scientific and technical knowledge.

5698 American Council for an Energy-Efficient Economy
http://www.aceee.org
The American Council for an Energy-Efficient Economy is a nonprofit organization dedicated to advancing energy efficiency as a means of promoting both economic prosperity and environmental protection.

5699 American Farmland Trust
http://www.farmland.org
American Farmland Trust is a private nonprofit organization founded in 1980 to protect our nation's farmland. AFT works to stop the loss of productive farmland and to promote farming practices that lead to a healthy environment.

5700 American Forests
http://www.americanforests.org
American Forests is a world leader in planting trees for environmental restoration, a pioneer in the science and practice of urban forestry and a primary communicator of the benefits of trees and forests.

5701 American Geophysical Union
http://earth.agu.org
AGU's mission is to promote the scientific study of Earth and its environment in space and to disseminate the results to the public, to promote cooperation among scientific organizations involved in geophysics and related disciplinesand to initiate and participate in geophysical research programs.

5702 American Hydrogen Association
http://www.clean-air.org
The Mission of AHA is to facilitate achievements of prosperity without pollution and to close the information gap between researchers, industry and the public, drawing on world-wide developments concerning hydrogen, solar, wind, hydro,ocean and biomass resource materials, energy conversion, wealth-addition economics and the environment.

5703 American Rivers
http://www.americanrivers.org
American Rivers is a national nonprofit conservation organization dedicated to protecting and restoring America's rivers and to fostering a river stewardship ethic.

5704 American Solar Energy Society
http://www.ases.org
The American Solar Energy Society is a national organization dedicated to advancing the use of solar energy for the benefit of US citizens and the global environment. ASES promotes the widespread near-term and long-term use of solarenergy.

5705 Ames Laboratory: Environment Technology Department
http://www.etd.ameslab.gov
The Ames Laboratory's Environmental & Protection Sciences Program is playing an important role in the US Department of Energy's initiative to cleanup hazardous waste, responding to remediation problems that need faster, safer, betteror cheaper technological solutions. You'll find information here about those technologies, the scientists behind them and our efforts to move these technologies into the marketplace.

5706 Antarctic and Southern Ocean Coalition
http://www.asoc.org
The Antartic Project is the Secretariat of the Antartic and Southern Ocean Coalition which contains nearly 230 organizations in 49 countries and leads the national and international campaigns to protect the biological diversity andpristine wilderness of Antartica, including its oceans and marine life. We work for passage of strong measures which protect the marine ecosystem from the harmful effects of overfishing, and work to ensure that the integrity of the land and animalsis maintained.

5707 Argonne National Laboratory
http://www.anl.gov
Argonne National Laboratory is one of the US Department of Energy's largest research centers. It is also the nation's first national laboratory, chartered in 1946.

5708 Arizona Geological Survey
http://www.azgs.state.az.us/
To inform and advise the public about the geologic character of Arizona in order to foster understanding and prudent development of the State's land, water, mineral and energy resources.

5709 Arkansas Natural Heritage Commission
http://www.naturalheritage.org
The Arkansas Natural Heritage Commission (ANHC) is responsible for maintaining the most up-to-date and comprehensive source of information concerning the rare plant and animal species, and high-quality natural communities of Arkansas.Systematic analysis of this natural heritage data can be used to identify locations that hold exceptional importance for the state's natural diversity, but that lack formal protection.

5710 Asia-Pacific Centre for Environmental Law
http://http://law.nus.edu.sg/apcel
APCEL was established in response to the need for capacity-building in environmental legal education and the need for promotion of awareness in environmental issues. It is currently working closely with IUCN's Commission onEnvironmental Law.

5711 Association of Energy Engineers
http://www.aeecenter.org
A nonprofit professional society which promotes the scientific and educational interests of those engaged in the energy industry and fosters action for sustainable development.

5712 Association of State Flood Plain Managers
http://www.floods.org/home/default.asp
Promotes common interest in flood damage abatement, supports environmental protection for floodplain areas, provides education on floodplain management practices and policy and urges incorporating multi-objective management, approachesto solve local flooding problems.

5713 Associations of University Leaders for a Sustainable Future
http://www.ulsf.org
The mission of the Association of University Leaders for Sustainable Future is to make sustainability a major focus of teaching, research, operations and outreach at colleges and universities worldwide. ULSF pursues this missionthrough advocacy, education, research, assessment, membership support and international partnerships to advance education for sustainability.

5714 Atlantic Salmon Federation
http://www.asf.ca
The Atlantic Salmon Federation is an international nonprofit organization which promotes the conservation and wise management of the wild Atlantic salmon and its environment.

5715 Australian Cooperative Research Centres
http://www.crc.gov.au/Information/default.aspx
The Cooperative Research Centers, generally known as CRCs, bring together researchers from universities, CSIRO and other government laboratories and private industry or public sector agencies in long-term collaborative arrangementswhich support research and development and education activities that achieve real outcomes of national economic and social significance.

5716 Australian Oceanographic Data Centre
http://www.aodc.gov.au/about.html
The mission of the Australian Oceanographic Data Centre is to acquire, manage and distribute oceanographic information and provide specialist oceanographic advice to; enable the Australian Defence Force to exploit the above and belowwater physical op-

erating environments for strategic, operational and tactical advantage meet national and international obligations to manage oceanographic information.

5717 Bat Conservation International
http://www.batcon.org
The mission of Bat Conservation International is to protect and restore bats and their habitats worldwide.

5718 Battelle Seattle Research Center
http://www.seattle.battelle.org/
Battelle Memorial Institute is a multidimensional organization dedicated to making the future better for everyone. Although that may sound a bit grand, it really is Battelle's mission. From 1929 to the present, putting innovation andtechnology to practical use has been our goal.

5719 Bellona Foundation
http://www.bellona.no
Bellona Foundation on the web brings you news and background on important environmental issues.

5720 Benton Foundation
http://www.benton.org/
Since 1981, the Foundation has worked to articulate a public interest vision for the digital age and to demonstrate the value of communications for solving social problems. Through its projects, the foundation bridges the worlds ofphilanthropy, public policy and community action to promote the use of digital media to engage, equip and connect people for social change.

5721 Best Manufacturing Practices Center of Excellence
http://www.bmpcoc.org
The Office of Naval Research's Best Manufacturing Practices Program is a unique, innovative technology transfer effort that improves the competitiveness of the US industrial base both here and abroad. The main goal at BMP is toincrease the quality, reliability and maintainability of goods produced by American firms.

5722 Biocatalysis/Biodegradation Database
http://www.umbbd.ahc.umn.edu/
This database contains information on microbial biocatalytic reations and biodegradation pathways for primarily xenobiotic, chemical compounds. The goal of the UM-BBD is to provide information on microbial enzyme catalyzed reactionsthat are important for biotechnology.

5723 Bioelectromagnetics Society
http://www.bioelectromagnetics.org/
The Bioeletromagnetics Society was established in 1978 as an independent organization of biological and physical scientists, physicians and engineers interested in the interactions of non-ionizing radiation with biological systems.BEMS is incorporated as a nonprofit organization in the District of Columbia and is registered with the Internal Revenue Service as a educational and training organization.

5724 Birding on the Web
http://www.birder.com
Birding is the most extensive section of this site. You will find checklists which span the globe, birding Hot Spots, and rare bird alert phone numbers. In the Backyard Birders section you can also find information on seeds to attractbirds, building bird houses, and links to home pages of other bird watchers.

5725 British Atmospheric Data Centre
http://www.badc.rl.ac.uk/
The role of the BADC is to assist UK atmosperic researchers to locate, access and interpret atmospheric data to ensure the long-term integrity of atmospheric data produced by NERC projects. The BADC has substantial data holdings of itsown and also provides information and links to data held by other data centres.

5726 Brookhaven National Laboratory
http://www.bnl.gov/world/Default.asp
The department of Energy's Brookhaven National Laboratory conducts research in physical, biomedical and environmental sciences, as well as in energy technologies. Brookhaven also builds and operates major facilities available touniversity, industrial and government scientists.

5727 Brown is Green
http://www.brown.edu/Departments/Brown_Is_Green/
The listserv dicussion lists provide for some good conservation, conjecture and occasional facts and figures, but are not reliable sources of information for students, faculty and staff working on campus environmental programs. The WebServer is our attempt at making current information on Brown's and other University campus' environmental programs freely available over the internet.

5728 Bureau of International Recycling
http://www.bir.org
BIR is an international trade federation representing the world's recycling industry, covering in particular ferrous and non-ferrous metals, paper and textiles. Plastics, rubber, tires and glass are also studied and traded by some BIRmembers.

5729 Bureau of Reclamation
http://www.usbr.gov
The mission of the Bureau of Reclamation is to manage, develop and protect water and related resources in an environmentally and economically sound manner in the interest of the American public.

5730 Bureau of Transportation Statistics
http://www.bts.gov
The 1991 Intermodal Surface Transportation Efficiency Act established the Bureau of Transportation Statistics for data collection, analysis and reporting and to ensure the most cost-effective use of transportation-monitoring resources.We strive to increase public awareness of the nation's transportation system and its implications and improve the transportation knowledge base of decision makers.

5731 Business & Legal Reports
http://www.blr.com/
Business & Legal Reports has been helping employers avoid legal problems for 25 years. Human Resources, Compensation, Environmental and Safe managers know that they can count on our compliance and training products to keep them out oftrouble. BLR's attorneys are constantly researching federal and state legislation, best practices, industry trends and impending changes that can affect your organization.

5732 California Conservation Corps
http://www.ccc.ca.gov/cccweb/index.htm
The CCC is the oldest, largest and longest-running youth conservation corps in the world! Nearly 90,000 young men and women have worked more than 50 million hours to protect and enhance California's environment and communities and haveprovided six million hours of assistance with emergencies like fires, floods and earthquakes. We're proud of our accomplishments and hope you are too!

5733 California Energy Commission
http://www.energy.ca.gov
The California Energy Commission is the state's primary energy policy and planning agency. It was created by the Legislature in 1974 and located in Sacramento.

5734 California Environmental Protection Agency
http://www.calepa.ca.gov
The mission of the Cailfornia Environmental Protection Agency is to restore, protect and enhance the environment, to ensure public health, environmental quality and economic vitality.

5735 California Environmental Resources Evaluation System (CERES)
http://http://resources.ca.gov/
The goal of CERES is to improve environmental analysis and planning by integrating natural and cultural resource information from multiple contributors and by making it available and useful to wide variety of users. CERES collects andintegrates data and information and distributes it via the World Wide Web.

5736 **California League of Conservation Voters**
http://www.ecovote.org/
The California League of Conservation Voters is the nation's largest and oldest state political action organization for the environment. Founded in 1972, the League mobilizes California voters to support environmentally responsiblecandidates and issues and serves as a watchdog to hold elected officials accountable for their environmental votes.

5737 **California Resources Agency**
http://http://resources.ca.gov/
The California Resources Agency is responsible for the conservation, enhancement and management of California's natural and cultural resources, including land, water, wildlife, parks, minerals and historic sites. The Agency is composedof departments, boards, conservations, commissions and programs.

5738 **Canadian Chlorine Chemistry Council**
http://www.cfour.org/cms/
To facilitate dialogue and promote coordinated action in Canada among key stakeholders in order to bring about a balanced view of chlorine chemistry to enable society to make informed, science based decisions on issues involvingchlorine.

5739 **Canadian Council of Ministers of the Environment (CCME)**
http://www.ccme.ca
CCME works to promote cooperation on and coordination of interjurisdictional issues such as waste management, air pollution and toxic chemicals. CCME members propose nationally-consistent environmental standards and objectives so as toachieve a high level of environmental quality across the country.

5740 **Canadian Environmental Assessment Agency**
http://www.ceaa.gc.ca/index_e.htm
To provide Canadians with high quality environmental assessments that contribute to informed decision-making in support of sustainable development.

5741 **Canadian Institute for Environmental Law and Policy (CIELAP)**
http://www.cielap.org
To provide leadership in the research and development of environmental law and policy that promotes the public interest and principles of sustainability.

5742 **Carbon Dioxide Information Analysis Center (CDIAC)**
http://www.cdiac.esd.ornl.gov/home.html
CDIAC responds to data and information requests from users all over the world who are concerned with the greenhouse effect and global climate change. CDIAC's data holdings include records of the concentrations of carbon dioxide andother radioactively active gases in the atmosphere.

5743 **Carnegie Institute of Technology, Department of Civil & Environmental Engineering**
http://www.ce.cmu.edu
Carnegie Mellon's Department of Civil and Environmental Engineering is a part of the engineering college, Carnegie Institute of Technology. The department maintains a commitment to excellence and innovation in education and research.

5744 **Center for Disease Control**
http://www.cdc.gov
To promote health and quality of life by preventing and controlling disease, injury and disability. CDC seeks to accomplish its mission by working with partners throughout the nation and world to monitor health, detect and investigatehealth problems, conduct research to enhance prevention, develop and advocate sound public health policies, implement prevention strategies, promote healthy behaviors, foster safe and healthful environments and provide leadership and training.

5745 **Center for Environmental Biotechnology**
http:////www.ceb.utk.edu/
The Center for Environmental Biotechnology at the University of Tennessee, Knoxville was established in 1986 to foster a multidisciplinary approach for training the next generation of environmental scientists and solving environmentalproblems through biotechnology.

5746 **Center for Environmental Citizenship**
http://www.envirocitizen.org/
The Center for Environmental Citizenship is a national nonpartisan 501 organization. We were founded by young activists in 1992 to encourage college students to be environmental citizens. CEC is dedicated to educating, training andorganizing a diverse national network of young leaders to protect the environment.

5747 **Center for Environmental Design Research College of Environmental Design**
http://www.cedr.berkeley.edu/
The Center for Environmental Design Research is an Organized Research Unit of the University of California at Berkeley. The Center's mission is to encourage research in environmental planning and design, in order to increase thefactual content of design decisions and to promote systematic approaches to design decision making.

5748 **Center for Health Effects of Environmental Contamination**
http:////www.cheec.uiowa.edu/
The University of Iowa Center for Health Effects of Environmental Contamination supports and conducts research to identify, measure and prevent adverse health outcomes related to exposure to environmental toxins. CHEEC organizes andparticipates in educational and outreach programs, provides environmental health expertise to local, state and federal entities and serves as a resource to Iowans in the field of environmental health.

5749 **Center for International Earth Science Information Network (CIESIN)**
http://www.ciesin.org
CIESIN works at the intersection of the social, natural and information services, specializing in on-line data and information management, spatial data integration and training and interdisciplinary research related to humaninteractions in the environment.

5750 **Center for International Environmental Law**
http://www.ciel.org
The Center for International Environmental Law is a public interest nonprofit environmental law firm founded in 1989 to strengthen international and comparative environmental law and policy around the world. CIEL provides a full rangeof environmental legal services in both international and comparative national law.

5751 **Center for Plant Conservation**
http://www.centerforplantconservation.org/
The CPC is a consortium of 28 American botanical gardens and arboreta whose mission is to conserve and restore the rare native plants of the US. To meet this end, they are involved in plant conservation, research and education. Thissite includes information about the National Collection of Endangered Plants which is maintained by the group.

5752 **Center for Renewable Energy and Sustainable Technology**
http://www.crest.org
CREST's goal is to accelerate the use of renewable energy by providing credible information, insightful analysis and innovative strategies amid changing energy markets and mounting environmental needs. The combined CREST organizationboasts a strong platform for research, publication and dissemination of timely information regarding sustainable energy.

5753 **Central European Environmental Data Request Facility**
http://www.cedar.at/sitemap/htm
CEDAR was created to provide computing and Internetworking facilities to support international data exchange with the Central and Eastern European environmental community. Focusing at first on mainly Central and Eastern Europeancountries, CE-

DAR's activities expanded quickly to an audience all over the world.

5754 Centre for the Analysis and Dissemination of Demonstrated Energy Technologies
http://www.caddet.org

A unique source of global information on proven commercial applications covering the full range of energy-saving technologies.

5755 Cetacean Society International
http://csiwhalesalive.org/

CSI is all volunteer nonprofit conservation, education and research organization based in the USA, with volunteer representatives in 26 countries around the world. The goal of the Cetacean Society International is to achieve on aglobal basis the optimum utilization of cetacean resources through benign utilization and the elimination of all killing and captive display of whales, dolphins, and porpoises. Our ultimate aim is peaceful coexistence and mutual enrichment for humansand cetaceans.

5756 Chanslor Wetlands Wildlife Project
http://www.sonomawetlands.org

Chanslor Wetlands Wildlife Project protects 250 acres of crucial habitat adjoining the historic fishing community of Bodega Bay just 1.25 hours north of San Francisco. Dedicated in 1973, the Chanslor Wetlands encompasses a rarebrackish marsh as well as freshwater marshes, vernal pools and ponds bordered by Salmon Creek.

5757 Charles Darwin Research Station
http://www.darwinfoundation.org/

Our mission is to conduct scientific research and environmental education about conservation and natural resource management in the Galapagos archipelago and its surrounding Marine Reserve. Scientific research and monitoring projectsare conducted at the CDRS in conjunction and cooperation with our chief partner, the Galapagos National Park Service, which functions as the principal government authority in charge of conservation and natural resource issues in the Galapagos.

5758 Chemical Industry Institute of Toxicology
http://www.ciit.org

Founded in 1974, CIT is a nonprofit toxicology research institute dedicated to providing an improved scientific basis for understanding and assessing the potential adverse effects of chemicals, pharmaceuticals and consumer products onhuman health.

5759 Chicago Wilderness
http://www.chiwild.org

The lands stretching south and west from the shores of Lake Michigan hold one of North America's great metropolises. More than nine million people live in northwestern Indiana, northeastern Illinois and southeastern Wisconsin. Livingamong them, on islands of green, are thousands of species of native plants and animals-species that make up some of the rarest natural communities on earth. We call these communities and the lands and waters that are their homes Chicago Wilderness.

5760 Children of the Green Earth
707-839-5013
866-983-2784
E-mail: mail@childrenofthegreenearth.com
http://www.childrenofthegreenearth.com

Children of the Green Earth is committed to offering quality, organic, earth friendly products for children of all ages. From grandmothers to babies, we've got something for everyone. All of our products are ethical, bothenvironmentally and socially, meaning only organically grown products and all of the work involved in making the products is sweat shop and child labor free.

5761 China Council for International Cooperation on Environment and Development
http://www.iisd.org/trade/cciced/

The China Council for International Cooperation on Environment & Development will continue to act as a bridge between China and other countries in cooperation on environment and development by introducing useful experiences of othercountries to China and communicating to the world the determination and aspiration of the Chinese Government and people for sustainable development.

5762 Chlorine Chemistry Council
http://www.c3.org

The Chlorine Chemistry Council, a business council of the American Chemistry Council, is a national trade association based in Arlington, VA representing the manufacturers and users of chlorine and chlorine-related products. Chlorineis widely used as a disease-fighting disinfection agent, as a basic component in pharmaceuticals and a myriad other products that are essential to modern life.

5763 City Farmer
http://www.cityfarmer.org/

Our nonprofit society promotes urban food production and environmental conservation from a small office in downtown Vancouver, British Columbia and from our demonstration food garden in nearby Kitsilano, a residential neighborhood.

5764 Climate Change and Human Health
http://www.jhu.edu/~climate/

The Climate Change and Human Health Integrated Assessment Web provodes recent and relevant information about the potential impacts of climate change through integrated assessment.

5765 Coastal Conservation Association
http://www.joincca.org

CCA is a national organization dedicated to the conservation and preservation of marine resources.

5766 Code of Federal Regulations
http://www.gpoaccess.gov/cfr/

The Code of Federal Regulations is a codification of the general and permanent rules published in the Federal Register by the Executive departments and agencies of the Federal Government.

5767 Colorado Department of Natural Resources
http://www.dnr.state.co.us/index.asp

The Colorado Department of Natural Resources was created to develop, protect and enhance Colorado natural resources for the use and enjoyment of the state's present and future residents, as well as for visitors to the state.

5768 Colorado School of Mines
http://www.mines.edu/index_js.shtml

The Colorado School of Mines shall be a specialized baccalaureate and graduate research institution with high admission standards. The Colorado School of Mines shall have a unique mission in energy, mineral and materials science andengineering and associated engineering and science fields.

5769 Columbia Earth Institute: Columbia University
http://www.earthinstitute.columbia.edu

The Earth Institute at Columbia University is the world's leading academic center for the integrated study of Earth, its environment and society. The Earth Institute builds upon excellence in the core disciplines-earth sciences,biological sciences, engineering sciences, social sciences and health sciences-and stresses cross-disciplinary approaches to complex problems.

5770 Connecticut Department of Environmental Protection
http://http://dep.state.ct.us/

The mission of the Department of Environmental Protection is to conserve, improve and protect the natural resources and environment of the State of Connecticut while preserving the natural environment and the life forms it supports ina delicate, interrelated and complex balance, to the end that the state may fulfill its responsibility as trustee of the environment for present and future generations.

5771 Conservation Fund
http://www.conservationfund.org

Works with private and public agencies and organizations to protect wildlife habitats, historic sites and parks.

5772 Conservation International
http://www.conservation.org

Our mission is to conserve the Earth's living natural heritage, our global biodiversity, and to demonstrate that human societies are able to live harmoniously with nature.

5773 Conservation Treaty Support Fund

http://www.conservationtreaty.org

The unique mission of the Conservation Treaty Support Fund is to support major inter governmental treaties which conserve wild natural resources for their own sake and the benefit of people. The fund believes these undertakings havethe best potential for global conservation, because they stem from the will of the nations of the world, are premised on the goal of sustaining living natural resources and have created a framework for effective conservation supported by manyagencies.

5774 Consortium on Green Design and Manufacturing (CGDM)

http://http://cgdm.berkeley.edu/

The Consortium on Green Design and Manfacturing (CGDM) is an interdisciplinary research initiative at the University of California, Berkeley and an industry/government/university partnership to develop linkages between manufacturingand design and their environmental effects and to integrate engineering information, management practices and government policy-making.

5775 Consultative Group on International Agricultural Research (CGIAR)

http://www.cgiar.org

To contribute to food security and poverty eradication in developing countries through research, partnerships, capacity building and policy support. Promotes sustainable agricultural development based on the environmentally soundmanagement of natural resources.

5776 Coral Health and Monitoring Program (CHAMP)

http://coral.aoml.noaa.gov

The mission of the Coral Health and Monitoring Program is to provide services to help improve and sustain coral reef health throughout the world.

5777 Coral Reef Alliance

http://www.coral.org

The Coral Reef Alliance (CORAL) is a member supported, nonprofit organization dedicated to keeping coral reefs alive around the world. Coral reefs are one of nature's most magnificent creations, filled with thousands of unique andvaluable plants and animals. CORAL works with marine park managers, businesses and communities to help increase their capacity to protect their local coral reefs.

5778 Cornell University Center for the Environment

http://www.cfe.cornell.edu

The Cornell Center for the Environment is committed to research, teaching and outreach focused on environmental issues, with the goals of enhancing the quality of life, encouraging economic vitality and promoting the conservation ofnatural resources for sustainable future.

5779 Council for Agricultural Science & Technology (CAST)

http://www.cast-science.org/

CAST is a nonprofit organization composed of scientific societies and many individual, student, company, nonprofit and associate society members. CAST's Board of Directors is composed of representatives of the scientific societies andindividual members as well as an Executive Committee. CAST assembles, interprets and communicates science based information regionally, nationally and internationally on food, fiber, agricultural, natural resources and related environmental issues tostakeholders.

5780 Council on Environmental Quality (CEQ)

http://ceq.eh.doe.gov or www.whitehouse.gov/CEQ/

The Council on Environmental Quality coordinates federal environmental efforts and works closely with agenices and other White House offices in the development of environmental policies and initiatives.

5781 Coweeta LTER Site

http://coweeta.ecology.uga.edu/

The program was developed to support research of ecological phenomena that occur on time scales of decades or centuries, periods of time normally investigated with research support from National Science Foundation.

5782 CropLife Canada

http://www.cropro.org/

To support sustainable agriculture in Canada, in cooperation with others, by building trust and appreciation for plant life science technologies.

5783 Declining Amphibian Populations Task Force

http://www.open.ac.uk/daptf/

Established in 1991, the DAPTF consists of a network of over 3,000 scientists and conservationists belonging to national and regional working groups which now cover more than 90 countries around the world. The mission of the DAPTF isto determine the nature, extent and causes of declines of amphibians throughout the world and to promote means by which declines can be halted or reversed.

5784 Defenders of Wildlife

http://www.defenders.org

Dedicated to the protection of all native wild animals and plants in their natural communities. Focus is placed on what scientists consider two of the most serious environmental threats to the planet: the accelerating rate ofextinction of species and the associated loss of biological diversity, and habitat alteration and destruction. Long known for leadership on endangered species issues.

5785 Defense Technical Information Center (DTIC)

http://www.dtic.mil

To improve the productivity of those who use scientific and technical information to accomplish a Defense mission objective, DTIC manages 13 Information Analysis Centers staffed by experienced information specialists, scientists andengineers who help customers locate, analyze and use scientific and technical information in a specialized subject area.

5786 Delaware Department of Natural Resources and Environmental Control

DNREC

http://www.dnrec.state.de.us

Delaware Department Of Natural Resources and Environmental Control's mission is to protect Delaware's environment for future generations.

5787 Department of Conservation

http://www.conservation.state.mo.us

The mission is to protect and manage the fish, forest and wildlife resources of the state; to serve the public and facilitate their participation in resource management activities; to provide opportunity for all citizens to use, enjoyand learn about fish, forest and wildlife resources.

5788 Department of Energy

http://www.doe.gov/engine/content.do

The Department of Energy's mission is to foster a secure and reliable energy system that is environmentally and economically sustainable, to be a responsible steward of the nation's nuclear weapons, to cleanup our own facilities and tosupport continued US leadership in science and technology.

5789 Department of the Interior

http://www.doi.gov

The Interior Department has had a wide range of responsibilities enstrusted to it: the construction of the national capital's water system, the colonization of freed slaves in Haiti, exploration of western wilderness, oversight of theDistrict of Columbia jail, regulation of territorial governments, management of hospitals and universities, management of public parks, the basic responsibilities for Indians, public lands, patents and pensions.

5790 DiveWeb

http://www.sandiegodiving.com/resources/links/items/277.html

DiveWeb is the original comprehensive online resource for information about commerical diving, ROV, marine technology, offshore/telecommunications and inland/coastal underwater industries.

5791 EDIE: Environmental Data Interactive Exchange
http://www.edie.net
EDIE is a free, personalized, interactive news, information and communications service for water, waste and environmental professionals around the world. With comprehensive independent coverage, powerful search facilities, e-mailalerts and discussion forums, EDIE provides a one-stop-shop for the exchange of specialized information on the Web.

5792 EE-Link (Environmental Education-Link)
http://http://eelink.net/pages/EE-Link+Introduction
EE-Link is a participant in the Environmental Education and Training Partnership of the North American Association for Environmental Education.

5793 Earth Day Network
http://www.earthday.net/
Earth Day Network is the nonprofit coordinating body of worldwide Earth Day activities. Our goal is to promote a healthy environment and a peaceful, just, sustainable world by sending environmental awareness through educationalmaterials and publications and by organizing events, activities and annual campaigns. Our network includes more than 5,000 organizations in 184 countries.

5794 Earth Observing System Amazon Project
http://boto.ocean.washington.edu/eos/
This project is a NASA Earth Observing System Interdisciplinary Investigation. The purpose of this research project is to understand the biogeochemistry, hydrology and sedimentation of the Amazon River and its drainage basin.

5795 Earth Preservers
http://www.earthpreservers.com
The web site for the environmental newspaper for kids and adults. Features of environmental work being done by kids all over the world. Contains articles and interesting facts.

5796 Earth Resources Laboratory at MIT
http://http://eaps.mit.edu/erl/
The Earth Resources Laboratory, formed in 1982, brings together faculty, staff and students dedicated to research in applied geophysics that will further our understanding of the Earth, its resources and the environment.

5797 EarthVote.com
http://www.earthvote.com
Twenty-four hour global resource for domestic and global environmental and social issues. Input your own voting topic or vote on current issues.

5798 Earthlink
http://www.earthlink.org.au/earthlink/listings.php
Earthlink is dedicated to creating a just sustainable world by harnessing economic power for positive change. Earthlink is designed to educate and encourage people to use their spending and investing power to bring about increasedsocial justice and environmental responsibility.

5799 Earthwatch Institute
http://www.earthwatch.org
The mission of the Earthwatch Institute is to promote sustainable conservation of our natural resources and cultural heritage by creating partnerships between scientists, educators and the general public.

5800 EcoEarth
http://www.ecoearth.info
Empowering the environmental sustainability movement, EcoEarth provides a landslide of environmental news postings and information, updated daily. Search, blog and network capabilities.

5801 EcoTradeNet
http://www.ecosecretariat.org/ECOTradeNet/index.htm
This Site provides trade information in respect of Member States of the Economic Cooperation Organziation. It's objective is not only to facilitate intra-regional trade cooperation but also provide relevant and updated information tothe prospective trader from outside the ECO region.

5802 Ecologia
http://www.ecologia.org
Ecologia is a private nonprofit organization providing information, training and technical support for grassroots environmental groups. Ecologia offers technical and humanitarian assistance to individuals and organizations working tosolve ecological problems at the local, regional, national and global levels.

5803 Ecology Action Centre
http://www.ecologyaction.ca
The Ecology Action Centre has been an active advocate protecting the environment since 1972. The Centre's earliest projects included recycling, composting and energy conservation and these are now widely recognized environmentalissues.

5804 Edison Electric Institute
http://www.eei.org/
Edison Electric Institute is the association of US shareholder owned electric compaines, international affiliates and industry associates worldwide. Our US members serve over 90 percent of all customers served by the shareholder ownedsegment of the industry.

5805 Edwards Aquifer Research and Data Center
http://www.eardc.txstate.edu/
The Edwards Aquifer Research and Data Center was established in 1979 by special funding for Southwest Texas State University to provide a public service in the study, understanding and use of the very fragile natural resource known asthe Edwards Aquifer.

5806 Electric Power Research Institute (EPRI)
http://http://my.epri.com/portal/server.pt
EPRI is a nonprofit organization committed to providing science and technology-based solutions of indispensable value to our global energy customers. To carry out our mission, we manage a far-reaching program of scientific research,technology development and product implementation.

5807 Elsevier Science Tables of Contents
http://www.elsevier.com/wps/find/homepage.cws_home
Elsevier Science has become the undisputed market leader in the publication and dissemination of literature covering the broad spectrum of scientific endeavors.

5808 Endangered Species Recovery Program
http://http://esrp.csustan.edu/
The Endangered Species Recovery Program's mission is to facilitate endangered species recovery and resolve conservation conflicts through scientifically based recovery planning and implementation.

5809 Energy & Environmental Research Center (EERC)
http://www.eerc.und.nodak.edu/
The EERC is dedicated to moving promising technologies out of the laboratory and into the marketplace to produce energy cleanly and efficiently, minimizing enviromental impacts and conserving precious natural resources.

5810 Energy Ideas Clearinghouse
http://www.energyideas.org/
EnergyIdeas is the most comprehensive technical resource that Northwest businesses, industy, government and utilities use to implement energy technologies and practices.

5811 Energy Technology Data Exchange
http://www.etde.org/
ETDE through its member countries provides an extensive bibliographic database announcing published energy research and technology information.

5812 **Enviro Village**
http://www.envirovillage.com
Indoor air quality and environment resource

5813 **Enviroene**
http://http://es.epa.gov/
Provides users with pollution prevention/cleaner production solutions, compliance and enforcement assistance information and innovative technology and policy options.

5814 **Enviro-Access**
http://www.enviroaccess.ca
Enviro-Access is a business partner investing in the development of environmental technologies by supplying companies in the environemtal sector with the professional services required during the various steps of bringing theirproducts and services to the market-place.

5815 **EnviroOne.com**
http://enviroone.com
EnviroOne.com is your one stop center for everything environmental. We have created propriety technology that combines a vast array of resources, timely content, innovative tools and e-commerce functionality that closes the loop onsearching for information and having the ability to immediately act upon that information.

5816 **Envirolink Library**
http://library.envirolink.org/start.html
EnviroLink is a nonprofit organization, a grassroots online community that unites hundreds of organizations and volunteers around the world with millions of people in more than 150 countries. EnviroLink is dedicated to providingcomprehensive, up-to-date environmental information and news. We recognize that our technologies are just tools, and that the solutions to our ecological challenges lie within our communities and their connection to the Earth itself.

5817 **Envirolink Network**
http://envirolink.org
EnviroLink is a nonprofit organization, a grassroots online community that unites hundreds of organizations and volunteers around the world with millions of people in more than 150 countries. EnviroLink is dedicated to providingcomprehensive, up-to-date environmental information and news. We recognize that our technologies are just tools, and that the solutions to our ecological challenges lie within our communities and their connection to the Earth itself.

5818 **Environment Council UK**
http://www.the-environment-council.org.uk/
The Environment Council is an independent UK charity which brings together people from all sectors of business, non-governmental organizations, government and the community to develop long term solutions to environmental issues.

5819 **Environment in Asia**
http://www.asianenviro.com/
AsianEnviro is a collaboration between AET Ltd and ERM Japan. This site draws on the established regional networks of environmental professionals in both organizations to deliver targeted environmental business intelligence. Pleasenote that translation is necessary to view this page.

5820 **Environmental Alliance for Senior Involvement**
http://www.easi.org/links.html
The mission of the Environmental Alliance for Senior Involvement is to build, promote and utilize the environmental ethic, expertise and commitment of older persons to expand citizen involvement in protecting and caring for ourenvironment for present and future generations.

5821 **Environmental Assessment Association**
http://www.iami.org/eaa.html
The Environmental Assessment Association is an international organization dedicated to providing members with information and education in the Real Estate Industry in respect to Environmentaal Inspections, Testing and HazardousMaterial Removal.

5822 **Environmental Change Network (ECN)**
http://www.ecn.ac.uk/
To establish and maintain a selected network of sites within the UK from which to obtain comparable long-term datasets through the monitoring of range of variables identified as being of major environmental importance.

5823 **Environmental Compliance Assistance Center**
http://www.epa.gov/compliance/
The purpose of this site is to bring complicated environmental laws and regulations into everyday language that the normal business person can understand, and to give that person associated information on educational opportunities.

5824 **Environmental Contaminants Encyclopedia**
http://www.nature.nps.gov/hazardssafety/toxic/index.cfm
This product differs from existing databases in that it has an environmental toxicology emphasis and it summarizes information on these issues into a single, easily searchable source.

5825 **Environmental Defense**
http://www.environmentaldefense.org/home.cfm
Environmental Defense is dedicated to protecting the environmental rights of all people, including future generations. Among these rights are clean air, clean water, healthy, nourishing food and flourishing ecosystem.

5826 **Environmental Measurements Laboratory**
http://www.eml.st.dhs.gov/
EML's current mission is to conduct scientific investigations and develop technologies related to environmental restoration, site and facility characterization and environmental surveillance and monitoring.

5827 **Environmental News Network**
http://www.enn.com/
Since 1993, the Environmental News Network has been working to educate the world about environmental issues facing our Earth. We began as a monthly print publication called Environmental News Briefing, and two years later discoveredthe Internet as an effective means of reaching a broader, more diverse audience.

5828 **Environmental Organization Web Directory**
http://www.webdirectory.com/
Our goal is simple: we strive to make it easy for people from around the world to find your web page.

5829 **Environmental Protection**
http://www.eponline.com
Website dedicated to pollution and waste treatment solutions for environmental professionals.

5830 **Environmental Protection Agency, US**
http://www.epa.gov/
The mission of the United States Environmental Protection Agency is to protect human health and to safeguard the natural environment air, water, and land upon which life depends.

5831 **Environmental Research Institute of Michigan-Altarum**
http://www.altarum.org/
ERIM promotes sustainable societal wellbeing by helping our customers employ new knowledge and decision support tools to solve complex systems problems in the healthcare, national security and energy, environment and transportationsectors.

5832 **Environmental Resource Center**
http://www.ercweb.com
Environmental Resource Center is a full-service environmental consulting firm that has been serving the needs of private industry and government for over seventeen years with the highest standards of quality at a competitive price.

5833 **Environmental Resources Information Network/ Environment Australia Online**

http://kaos.erin.gov.au

ERIN, the Environmental Resources Information Network, provides environmental information for policy developers and decision makers. ERIN is a National facility, using the latest computing technology to provide access to a vastreservoir of information on the Australian environment, and the analytical tools to interpret it.

5834 **Environmental Resources Management**

http://www.erm.com

Environmental Resources Management has well-established reputation as one of the world's largest providers of environmental management consulting services. We have 25 year's experience working with both the public and private sectorsacross a broad spectrum of industries.

5835 **Environmental Simulations**

http://www.groundwatermodels.com

Our mission is to provide our software clients with superior and technical support. To provide cost-effective in house training courses, state-of-the-art groundwater modeling services and high quality independent hydrogeologicalconsulting.

5836 **Environmental Treaties and Resource Indicators**

http://sedac.ciesin.columbia.edu/entri/

ENTRI, a database of searchable treaties and resource indicators, is provided by the CIESIN organization with the assistance of many other groups. They use nine specific issue areas to search the database.

5837 **Environmental Working Group**

http://www.ewg.org

The Environmental Working Group is a leading content provider for public interest groups and concerned citizens who are campaigning to protect the environment.

5838 **Environmental and Societal Impacts Groups**

http://www.isse.ucar.edu/

ESIG studies environmental change and responses to such change inorder to gain insights into how decision makers, from individuals to governements to international coalitions, might better understand and cope with impacts associatedwith the complex relationship of the atmosphere, environment, and society.

5839 **Essential Information**

http://www.essential.org/about.html

Founded by Ralph Nader. A nonprofit, tax-exempt organization. We are involved in a variety of projects to encourage citizens to become active and engaged in their communities. We provide provocative information to the public onimportant topics neglected by the mass media and policy makers. Publishes a monthly magazine, books and reports, sponsors investigative journalism conferences, provides writers with grants to persue investigations and operates information clearinghouses.

5840 **European Centre for Nature Conservation**

http://www.ecnc.nl

ECNC actively promotes, by bringing the gap between science and policy, the conservation of nature and especially of biodiversity in Europe, because of their intrinsic values and their relevance to economy and European culture; therebyECNC seeks the integration of nature conservation considerations into other policies.

5841 **European Forest Institute (EFI)**

http://www.efi.fi

EFI's mission is to promote, conduct and co-operate in research of forests, forestry and forest products at the pan-European level; and to make the results of the research known to all interested parties, notably in the areas of policyformulation and implementation, in order to promote the conservation and sustainable management of forests in Europe.

5842 **Everglades Digital Library**

http://everglades.fiu.edu/

The Everglades Information Network is a program of library and information services in support of research, restoration, and resource management of the south Florida environment. The EIN serves researchers, resource managers,educators, students, researchers, decision makers, and concerned citizens both within south Florida and around the world.

5843 **Federal Emergency Management Agency FEMA**

http://www.fema.gov/

Advising on building codes and flood plain management, teaching people how to get through a disaster, helping equip local and state emergency preparedness, the range of FEMA's activities is broad indeed.

5844 **Federal Geographic Data Committee**

http://www.fgdc.gov/

The Federal Geographic Data Committee is a 19 member interagency committee composed of representatives from the Executive Office of the President, Cabinet-level and independent agencies. The FGDC is developing the National Spatial DataInfrasturcture (NSDI) in cooperation with organizations from State, local and tribal governments, the academic community, and the private sector.

5845 **Fedworld Information Network**

http://www.fedworld.gov

We here at FedWorld have enjoyed thinking outside the box to offer multiple distribution channels to disseminate information to the public and to the Federal Government. The modes of access, the variety of documents available, and thetechnological expertise at FedWorld are expanding with technology.

5846 **Finnish Forest Research Institute: METLA**

http://www.metla.fi

The Finnish Forest Research Institute builds the future of the forest sector through research. METLA social task is to promote through research economically, ecologically and socially sustainable management and utilization of theforests.

5847 **Fish and Wildlife Information Exchange Homepage**

http://www.cmiweb.org/fwie/fwie.html

The FWIE is a technical assistance center and information clearinghouse for fish, wildlife, and land management agencies and organizations. The FWIE also assists with the planning, development, implementation, and maintenance ofinformation management and delivery systems.

5848 **Florida Center for Environmental Studies**

http://www.ces.fau.edu

The Mission of the Center is to collect, analyze, and promote the use of scientifically-sound information concerning tropical and subtropical freshwater ecosystems.

5849 **Florida Cooperative Extension Service**

http://www.wec.ufl.edu/extension

Part of the mission of the Florida Cooperative Extension Service is to disseminate and provide access to science-based information that will contribute to the solution of natural resource problems of concern to the people of Florida.Wildlife Extension specialists in the Department of Wildlife Ecology and Conservation serve , advice, and develop educational programs for Florida citizens in conjunction with county extension agents and other state , county and local organizations.

5850 **Florida Department of Environmental Protection**

http://www.dep.state.fl.us

The mission of the Department of Environmental Protection is: More Protection, Less Process. The Department accomplishes its mission in a manner that provides stewardship of Florida's ecosystems so that the State's unique quality oflife may be preserved for present and future generations.

5851 **Forest History Society**

http://www.lib.duke.edu/forest

The Forest History Society is a non-profit educational institution that links the past to the future by identifying, collecting, preserving, interpreting, and disseminating information on the history of people, forests, and theirrelated resources.

5852 Forest Service Employees for Environmental Ethics
http://www.fseee.org/
Forest Service Employess for Environmental Ethics is a 501 nonprofit organization. Our mission is to forge a socially responsible value system for the Forest Service based on a land ethic that ensures ecologically and economicallysustainable resource management.

5853 Friends of the Earth International
http://www.foei.org/
Friends of the Earth International is a worldwide federation of national environmental organizations. This federation aims to: protect the earth against futher deterioration and repair damage inflicted upon the environment by humanactivities and negligence; preserve the earth's ecological, cultural and ethic diversity.

5854 GAP (Gap Analysis Program) National
http://www.gap.uidaho.edu/
The mission of the GAP Analysis Program is to provide regional assessments of the conservation status of native vertebrate species and natural land cover types and to facilitate the application of this information to land managementactivities.

5855 GLOBE Program
http://www.globe.gov
GLOBE is a worldwide hands-on, primary and secondary school based science and education program.

5856 Galapagos Coalition
http://www.law.emory.edu/PI/GALAPAGOS/
The Galapagos Coalition is a group of biologists, other scientists, and lawyers with expertise in environemntal and international law, many of whom have done research in the Galapagos and all of whom are interested in the understandingthe relationship between the conservation of the Galapagos and human activities.

5857 General Accounting Office
http://www.gao.gov
The General Accounting Office is the audit, evalution and investigative arm of Congress. GAO exists to support the congress in meeting its Constitutional responsibilities and to help improve the performance and ensure accountability ofthe federal government for the American people. GAO examines the use of public funds, evaluates federal programs and activities and provides analysis, options, recommendations and other assistance to help the Congress make effective oversite, policyand funding.

5858 Geohydrodynamics and Environmental Research
http://modbg.oce.ulg.ac.be/
The general objective of the MODB is to deliver advanced data products to mediterranean research projects supported by the MAST programme of the European Union. All products are however freely distributed to the whole scientificcommunity.

5859 Georgia Department of Natural Resources
http://www.gadnr.org/
The mission of the Department of Natural Resources is to sustain, enhance, protect and conserve Georgia's natural, historic and cultural resources for present and future generations, while recognizing the importance of promoting thedevelopment of commerce and industry that utilize sound environmental practices.

5860 Geotechnical and Geoenvironmental Software Directory
http://www.ggsd.com/ggsd/index.cfm
This site contains a summary of links to sites describing software used for seepage/groundwater flow modeling.

5861 Germinal Project
http://http://lasig.epfl.ch/projets/germinal/Germinal.html
GERMINAL is an interdissiplinary project established by the institutes of the Department of Rural Engineeing and by the directorship of the Swiss Federal Institute of Technology at Lausanne. Its goal is the development of a global,integrated approach for land use planning and environmental management based on the use of Geographic Information Systems.

5862 Global Change Master Directory (GCMD)
http://gcmd.gsfc.nasa.gov/
The mission of the Global Change Master Directory is to assist the scientific community in the discovery of and linkage to Earth science data, as well as to provide data holders a means to advertise their data to the Earth ScienceCommunity.

5863 Global Change Research Information Office
http://gcrio.org
The US Global Change Research Information Office provides access to data and information on global change research, adaption/mitigation strategies and technologies, and global change-related educational resources on behalf of thevarious US Federal Agenices and Organizations that are involved in the US Global Change Research Program

5864 Global Ecovillage Network
http://http://gen.ecovillage.org/
GEN's main aim is to support and encourage the evolution of sustainable settlements across the world through: Internal and External Communications services; facilitating information exchange and flow about ecovillages anddemonstrations sites.

5865 Global Environmental Options (GEO)
http://www.genonetwork.org
GEO was created to bring attention to the impact that buildings and planning have on the environment and biodiversity. To reduce these impacts, GEO develops integrated high performance green building stragies for professionals andother decision makers worldwide, coordinating hands-on building and planningprojects that showcase green design.

5866 Global Network of Environment & Technology
http://www.gnet.org/
GNET provides worldwide access to timely information on environmental news, products and services, marketing opportunities, contracts, government programs, policy and law, and business assitance resources via the World Wide Web.

5867 Global Research Information Database (GRID)
http://www.grida.no/
GRID-Arendal provides environmental information, communications and capacity buildings services for information management and assessment. Established to strengthen the United Nations through its Environmental Program, our focus is tomake credible, science-based knowledge understandable to the public and to decision making for sustainable development.

5868 Great Lakes Fishery Commission
2100 Commonwealth Boulevard 734-662-3209
Ann Arbor, MI 48105 Fax: 734-741-2010
http://www.glfc.org
To develop coordinated programs of research on the Great Lakes, and, on the basis of the findings, to recommend measures which will permit the maximum sustained productivity in stocks of fish of common concern.

5869 Great Lakes Information Network (GLIN)
http://www.great-lakes.net
The Great Lakes Information Network is an partnership that provides one place to find information relating to the binational Great Lakes-St Lawrence region of North America. GLIN offers a wealth of data and information about theregion's environment, economy, tourism, education and more.

5870 Green Mountain Institute for Environmental Democracy
http://www.gmied.org
The Green Mountain Institute for Environmental Democracy seeks to reinvigorate the essential connections among the public, government and information necessary for effective improvements in environmental quality.

5871 Green Seal
http://www.greenseal.org
Green Seal is the independent nonprofit organization dedicated to protecting the environment by promoting the manufacture and sale of enviromentally responsible consumer products. It sets environmental standards and awards a Green Sealof Approval to products that cause less harm to the environment than other similar products.

5872 Green University Initiative
http://www.gwu.edu/~greenu/
The George Washington Green University Initiative began as a grassroot movement to implement sustainable practices into all aspects of life at GW. At Green University we work towards ecosystem protection, incorporating environmentaljustice into daily activities and decisions.

5873 Greenbelt Alliance
http://www.greenbelt.org/
Our mission is to make the San Francisco Bay Area a better place to live by protecting the region's Greenbelt and improving the livability of its cities and towns. Scince 1958 we have worked in partnership with diverse coalitions onpublic policy development, advocacy and education.

5874 Greenhouse Gas Technology Information Exchange GREENTIE
http://www.greentie.org
IEA GREENTIE is an international information network that distributes details of suppliers whose technologies help to reduce greenhouse gas emissions. GREENTIE also provides information on leading international organizations and IEAprograms whose R&D and information activities center around clean energy technologies.

5875 Ground-Water Remediation Technologies Analysis Center
http://www.gwrtac.org
The Groundwater Remediation Technologies Analysis Center compiles, analyzes and disseminates information on innovative ground-water remediation technologies. GWRTAC prepares reports by technical teams selectively chosen from ConcurrentTechnologies Corporation, the University of Pittsburgh and other supporting institutions, also maintaining an active outreach program.

5876 Harbor Branch Oceanographic Institution
http://www.hboi.edu
Harbor Branch Oceanographic Institution is dedicated to exploring the world's oceans, integrating the science and technology of the sea with the needs of humankind.

5877 Harvard Forest
http://http://harvardforest.fas.harvard.edu/
Through the years researchers at the Forest have focused on silviculture and forest management, soils and the development of forest site concepts, the biology of temperate and tropical trees, forest ecology and economics and ecosystemdynamics.

5878 Hawaii Biological Survey
http://http://hbs.bishopmuseum.org/hbs1.html
It was created to locate, identify and evaluate all native and non-native species of flora and fauna within the State and maintain the reference collections of that flora and fauna for a wide range of uses.

5879 Hawaiian Ecosystems at Risk (HEAR)
http://www.hear.org
The mission of the Hawaiian Ecosystem at Risk project is to promote technology, methods and information to decision-makers, resource managers and the general public to aid in the fight against harmful alien species in Hawaii and thePacific Basin.

5880 Hawkwatch International
http://www.hawkwatch.org/
Our mission is to protect hawks, eagles, other birds of prey and their environment through research, education, and conservation.

5881 Hazardous Substance Research Centers
http://www.hsrc.org
Hazardous Substance Research Center is a national organization that carries out an active program of basic and applied research, technology transfer and training. Our activities are conducted regionally by five multi-universitycenters, which focus on different aspects of hazardous substance management.

5882 Hazardous Waste Clean-Up Information (CLU-IN)
http://www.clu-in.com
Providing information about innovative treatment and site characterization technologies while acting as a forum for all waste remediation stakeholders.

5883 Headwaters Science Center
http://www.hscbemidji.org/
Headwaters Science Center is dedicated to science education and environmental awareness. It features hands-on exhibits, a live animal collection and special events and science-related programs and demonstrations.

5884 Heartwood
http://www.heartwood.org/
An association of groups, individuals and businesses dedicated to the health and well being of the native forest of the Central Hardwood region and its interdependent plant, animal and human communities.

5885 Holland Island Preservation Foundation
http://www.intercom.net/local/holland/index.html
Our goal is to stabilize and preserve this beautiful island, not only for the people that once lived there, but also for the wildlife that thrives there still. With modern tools and techniques, this fragile ecosystem can be saved fromultimate destruction.

5886 Horned Lizard Conservation Society (HLCS)
http://www.hornedlizards.com
The Texas Chapter of the Horned Lizard Conservation Society (HLCS) is devoted to discovering why the Texas Horned Lizard has declined in numbers so dramatically in recent years and what can be done to reverse the process.

5887 Houston Audubon Society
http://www.houstonaudubon.org/
The Houston Audubon Society works for the thoughtful conservation of the earth's natural resources by educating people to the value of the natural world; protecting, preserving and enhancing wildlife habitat and encouraging the passageof legislation to protect the environemnt.

5888 Howl: The PAWS Wildlife Center
http://www.paws.org/wildlife/index.htm
The PAWS Wildlife Center is a world reowned wildlife rehabilitation facility. Formerly known as HOWL, the PAWS Wildlife Center receives over 5,000 injured or displaced wild animals every year. The center houses and rehabilitateswildanimals, and prepares them for eventual release back into the wild.

5889 IFAW: International Fund for Animal Welfare
http://www.ifaw.org
IFAW's mission is to improve the welfare of wild and domestic animals throughout the world by reducing commercial exploitation of animals in distress. We seek to motivate the public to prevent cruelty to animals and promote animalwelfare and conservation policies that advance the well-being of both animals and people.

5890 IISDnet: International Institute for Sustainable Development
http://www.iisd.org/
Our mission is to champion innovation, enabling societies to live sustainably.

5891 Illinois Recycling Association
http://www.illinoisrecycles.org/
The Illinois Recycling Association's mission is to encourage the responsible use of resources by promoting waste reduction, re-use and recycling.

5892 Indiana Department of Natural Resources
http://www.in.gov/dnr/
The mission of the Indiana Department of Natural Resources is to protect, enhance, preserve and wisely use natural, cultural and recreational resources for the benefit of Indiana's citizens through professional leadership, managementand education.

5893 Information Center for the Environment (ICE)
http://ice.ucdavis.edu/
The Foundation wishes to participate actively in all activities and efforts to protection, preservation and exploitation of mangrove ecosystem for the prosperity of all people.

5894 Inland Seas Education Association
http://www.schoolship.org/
Inland Seas Education Association is a nonprofit organization whose mission is to provide a floating classroom where people of all ages can gain first-hand training and experience in the Great Lakes ecosystem. The knowledge gainedthrough these experiences will provide the leadership, understanding and commitment needed for the long-term stewardship of the Great Lakes.

5895 International Association for Energy Economics
http://www.iaee.org
The International Association for Energy Economics provides a forum for the exchange of ideas, experience and issues among professionals interested in energy economics. Its scope is worldwide, as are its members who come from diversebackgrounds-corporate, academic, scientific and government.

5896 International Association for Environmental Hydrology
http://www.hydroweb.com
Worldwide association of environmental hydrologists dedicated to the protection and cleanup of fresh water resources.

5897 International Canopy Network (ICAN)
http://www.evergreen.edu/ican/
The International Canopy Network is devoted to facilitating the continuing interaction of people concerned with forest canopies and forest ecosystems around the world. ICAN is a nonprofit organization supported by a global community ofscientists, conservation advocates, canopy educators and environmental professionals. The organization is funded by subscriber dues, donations and grants.

5898 International Centre for Gas Technology Information
http://www.gtionline.org/
Offers gas technology decisionmakers a competitive information edge; affording immediate connection with the world's natural gas technology leaders; and by allowing easy access to provider services and equipment that serve the naturalgas industry.

5899 International Council for the Exploration of the Sea(ICES)
http://www.ices.dk/ocean/
ICES is a leading forum for the promotion, coordination and gas dissemination of research on the physical, chemical and biological systems in the North Atlantic and advice on human impact on its environment, in particular fisherieseffects in the Northeast Atlantic.

5900 International Crane Foundation
http://www.savingcranes.org/
The International Crane Foundation works worldwide to conserve cranes and the wetland and grasslands communities on which they depend. ICF is dedicated to providing experience, knowledge, and inspiration to involve people in resolvingthreats to these ecosystems.

5901 International Energy Agency Solar Heating and Cooling Programme
http://www.iea-shc.org
The Solar Heating and Cooling Programme was one of the frist IEA Implementing Agreements to be established. Since 1977, its 21 members have collaborating to advance active solar, passive solar and photovoltaic technologies and theirapplication in buildings.

5902 International Geosphere-Biosphere Programme
http://www.igbp.kva.se
Our scientific objective is to describe and understand the interactive physical, chemical and biological processes that regulate the total Earth System, the unique environment that it provides for life, the changes that are occurringin this system, and the manner in which they are influenced by human actions.

5903 International Ground Source Heat Pump Association(IGSHPA)
http://www.igshpa.okstate.edu/default.htm
As an organization, IGSHPA pursues these goals: Supporting GHP industry research and development; promoting the GHP-related current events internationally. Developing and distuting internationally recognized training materials.

5904 International Institute for Industrial Environmental Economics
http://www.iiiee.lu.se/
The mission of the Institute is to the international advancement of sustainable development by conducting at the forefront of issues pretaining to cleaner production, and to educate present and future decision makers within all sectorsof society in the formulation and implemantation of preventive environmental strategies. The Institute is founded on the firm conviction that a preventive approach to environmental problems is necessary for the perpetuation of life on this planet.

5905 International Marine Mammal Association
http://www.imma.org
The International Marine Mammal Association is a non profit organization dedicated to promoting the conservation of marine mammals and their habitats worldwide, through research and education.

5906 International Otter Survival Fund
http://www.otter.org/
The International Otter Survival Fund is a global organization working to conserve all 13 species of otter by helping to support scientists and other workers in practical conservation, education, research and rescue and rehabilitation.

5907 International Primate Protection League (IPPL)
http://www.ippl.org
The International Primate Protection League was funded in 1973, and since this time has been working continuously for the well-being of primates.

5908 International Research Institute for Climate Prediction
http://www.ir.columbia.edu/climate/cid/
The vision for the IRI is that of an innovative science institution working to accelerate the ability of societies worldwide to cope with climate fluctuations, especially those that cause devastating impacts on humans and theenvironment, thereby reaping the benefits of decades of research on the predictability of El Nino-Southern Oscillation phenomenon and other climate variations.

5909 International Rivers Network
http://www.irn.org/index.html
IRN's mission is to halt and reverse the degradation of river systems; to support local communities in protecting and restoring the well-being of the people, cultures and ecosystems that depend on rivers; to promote sustainable,environmentally sound alternatives to damming and channeling rivers.

5910 International Satellite Land Surface Climatology Project (ISLSCP)
http://www.gewex.org
ISLSCP Objective is to demosnstrate the type of surface and near-surface satellite measurements that are relevant to climate and global change studies. Develop and improve algorithms for the interpretation of satellite measurements ofland-surface features.

5911 **International Snow Leopard Trust**
http://www.snowleopard.org
The International Snow Leopard Trust is dedicated to the conservation of the endangered snow leopard and its mountain ecosystem through a balanced approach that considers the needs of the people and the environment.

5912 **International Society for Ecological Modelling (ISEM)**
http://www.isemna.org
The International Society for Ecological Modelling promotes the international exchange of ideas, scientific results, and general knowledge in the area of the application of systems analysis and simulation in ecology and naturalresource management.

5913 **International Society for Environmental Ethics**
http://www.cep.unt.edu
ISEE now maintains this website, which includes the largest bibliography in the world on environmental ethics, over 7,000 entries. Newsletters over the last ten years also available here, and by consulting these a full historicalrecord may be obtained.

5914 **International Society of Arboriculture**
http://www.isa-arbor.com
The mission is through research, technology, and education promote the professional practice of arboriculture and foster a greater public awareness of the benefits of trees.

5915 **International Solar Energy Society**
http://www.ises.org/
The mission is to encourage the use and acceptance of Renewable Energy technologies; to realise a global community of industry, individuals and institutions in support of renewable energy and to create a structure to facillatecooperation and exchange.

5916 **International Union of Forestry Research Organizations (IUFRO)**
http://www.iufro.org
IUFRO is a nonprofit, non-governmental international network of forest scientists. Its objective are to promote international cooperation in forestry and forest products research. IUFRO's activities are organized primarily through its268 specialized Units in 8 technical Divisions.

5917 **International Wildlife Coalition**
http://www.iwc.org
The International Wildlife Coalition is a federally recognized, nonprofit taxexempt charitable organization. Founded in 1984, the Coalition is dedicated to public education, research, rescue, rebilitation, litigation and internationaltreaty negotiations concerning global wildlife and natural habitat protection issues.

5918 **International Wolf Center**
http://www.wolf.org
The mission of the International Wolf Center is profoundly simple. We support the survival of the wolf around thr world by teaching about its life, its association with other species and dynamic relationships to humans.

5919 **International Year of the Ocean -1998**
http://www.yoto98.noaa.gov
The overall objective is to focus and reinforce the attention of the public, governments and decision makers at large on the importance of the oceans and the marine environment as resources for sustainable development.

5920 **Iowa Department of Natural Resources**
http://www.iowadnr.com
The department's mission is to manage, protect, conserve, and develop Iowa's natural reources in cooperation with other public and private organizations and individuals, so that the quality of life for Iowans is significantly enchancedby the use, enjoyment and understanding of those resources.

5921 **Irish Peatland Conservation Council**
http://www.ipcc.ie
The Irish Peatland Conservation Council is an independent conservation charity. We were established in 1982 to campaign for the conservation of a representative sample of living intact Irish bogs and peatlands and we need your support.

5922 **Island Wildlife Natural Care Centre**
http://www.islandstrust.bc.ca
Its mission is to function in a twofold manner. Frist, by rehabilitating North American wildlife, including marine mammals, with emphasis on alternative, non-toxic, non-invasive treatments. Second, educationally, by furtheringknowledge of treatments available to professionals in the field, and by educationg the public on both rehabilitation and the interaction of man and wild animals.

5923 **Izaak Walton League**
http://www.iwla.org
The mission is to conserve, maintain, protect and restore the soil, forest, water and other natural resources of the United States and other lands; to promote means and opportunities for education of the public with respect to suchresources and their enjoyment and wholesome utilization.

5924 **Jane Goodall Institute**
http://www.janegoodall.org/
The Jane Goodall Institute advances the power of individuals to take informed and compassionate action to improve the environment of all living things.

5925 **Jefferson Land Trust**
http://www.saveland.org
Jefferson Land Trust is a private, nonprofit, grass-roots organization with a mission to conserve property and natural resources. Landowners may work with a Land Trust when they wish to permanently protect the ecological, scenic,historic, or recreational qualities of land they own from inappropriate development.

5926 **John M Judy Environmental Education Consortium**
http://www.utm.edu/departments/ed/cece/john.html
The purpose of the Consortium is to promote and enhance environmental education through systemic change toward infusing a collective environmental consciousness and individual environmental ethic into the learning and teaching process.

5927 **Joint Center for Energy Management (JCEM)**
http://bechtel.colorado.edu/Graduate Programs/Jcem/jcemmain.html
The Joint Center for Energy Management is a research center in the Department of Civil, Environmental, and Architectural Engineering at the University of Colorado at Boulder. It is dedicated to excellence in energy-related research,development, education, and technical assistance.

5928 **Journey North**
http://www.learner.org/jnorth/index.html
Journey North engages students in a global study of wildlife migration and seasonal change. K-12 students share their own field observations with classmates across North America. Widely considered a best-practices model for education,we are the nation's citizen science project for children.

5929 **Kansas Environmental Almanac**
http://www.idir.net/-chsjones/
Kansas is a magnificent place. We owe it to ourselves, to earlier generations and those yet to come, to take good care of our home. With that goal in mind, the Kansas Environmental Almanac will collect and house information pertainingto the Kansas environment and its protection.

5930 **Kentucky Department of Fish and Wildlife Resources**
http://www.kdfwr.state.ky.us/
We are stewards of Kentucky's fish and wildlife resources and their habitats. We manage for the perpetuation of these resources and their use by present and future generations. Through partnerships, we will enhance wildlife diversityand promote sustainable use, including hunting, fishing, boating and other nature-related recreation.

5931 **Kentucky Water Resources Research Institute**
http://www.uky.edu/WaterResources/

The institute mission is to stimulate water resources and water-related environmental research. To assist and stimulate academic units in the conduct of undergraduate and graduate education in water resources and water-relatedenvironmental issues.

5932 Kola Ecogeochemistry
http://www.ngu.no/kola

The primary aims are to map the extent of contamination by inorganic elements in various media around industrial centres. To map the content of raionuclides in topsoil throughout the Project area and to shed light on the process anddynamics of trace element cycling in catchments.

5933 LIFE
http://life.csu.edu.au/

Founded in 1992, the LIFE Site is Australia's frist information service on the World Wide Web. The main focus is on biological information, especially the environment and biodiversity.

5934 LTER (US Long-Term Ecological Research)
http://www.lternet.edu

The mission of the LTER Network is to facilitate and conduct ecological research through: Understanding ecological pheonmena over long temporal and large spatial scales. Creating a legacy of well-designed and documented long-termexperiments and observations for future generations.

5935 Lake Pontchartrain Basin Foundation
http://www.saveourlake.org

The Lake Pontchartrain Basin Foundation, a membership-basede citizens organization, is the public's independent voice dedicated to restoring and preserving the Lake Pontchartrain Basin.

5936 Land Conservancy of San Luis Obispo County
http://www.special-places.org/

Take pride in our active approach to land conservation. Pursues the protection of open space through land aquisition, conservation easements, restoration, and stewardship.

5937 Land Trust Alliance
http://www.lta.org

Founded in 1982, the Land Trust Alliance is the national leader of the private land conservation movement, promoting voluntary land conservation across the country and providing resources, leadership and training to the nation's 1,200plus nonprofit, grassroots land trusts, helping them to protect important open spaces.

5938 League of Conservation Voters
http://www.lcv.org

The League of Conservation Voters works to create a Congress more responsive to your environmental concerns. As the nonpartisan political voice for over nine million members of environmental and conservation groups LCV is the onlynational environmental organization dedicated full-time to educating citizens about the environmental voting records of Members of Congress.

5939 Learning about Backyard Birds
http://www.birdfeeding.org

Free resource material from the National Birdfeeding Society, including background and guidance for instructors and facilitators as well as project materials for group use.

5940 Leave No Trace
http://www.leavenotrace.com

The mission of the Leave No Trace program is to promote and inspire responsible outdoor recreation through education, research, and partnership. The program is managed by LNT, a nonprofit organization located in Boulder, Colorado.

5941 Living on Earth
http://www.loe.org

Living on Earth with Steve Curwood is the weekly environmental news and information program distributed by National Public Radio.

5942 Lloyd Center for Environment Studies
http://www.thelloydcenter.org

The Lloyd Center for Environmental Studies is a nonprofit organization that provides education programs and conducts research to develop a scientific and public understanding of coastal, estaurine, and watershed environments insoutheastern New England.

5943 Louisiana Department of Agriculture & Forestry
http://www.ldaf.state.la.us

The Louisiana Department of Agriculture & Forestry was created in accordance with the provisions of Article IV, Section 10 of the Constitution of Louisiana. The commissioner of agriculture and forestry heads the department andexercises all functions of the state relating to the promotion, protection, and advancement of agriculture and forestry, expert research and educational functions expressly allocated by the constitution or by law to other state agencies.

5944 Louisiana Energy & Environmental Resources & Information Center
http://www.leeric.lsu.edu/

A primary LEERIC objective is to serve information needs of LSU's faculty, staff, and researchers. LEERIC also provides energy and environmental educational programs for consumers and non-college educators and students.

5945 Lower Rio Grande Ecosystem Initiative
http://www.cerc.usgs.gov/lrgrei/lrgrei.htm

The Lower Rio Grande Ecosystem Initiative was established by the Biological Division of the USGS to address research and information needs pertinent to the biotic resources of the river and its adjacent terrestrial habitats.

5946 Macaw Landing Foundation
http://www.macawlanding.org/

The foundation is operated solely by volunteers, which allows us to spend all the donated money entirely on Macaws. The Foundation is dedicated to preservation of Macaws.

5947 Maine Department of Conservation
http://www.state.me.us/doc/

Created in 1973, the Department of Conservation's Mission is to benefit the citizens, landowners, and users of the state's natural resources by promoting and performing stewardship and ensuring responsible balanced use of Marine'sland, forest, water, and mineral resources.

5948 Maine Department of Inland Fisheries & Wildlife
http://www.state.me.us/ifw

Conserves, protects, and enhances the inland fisheries and wildlife resources and promotes efficiency in program management through employee involvement, intitiative, innovation, and teamwork.

5949 Mangrove Replenishment Initiative
http://www.mangrove.org

The Mangrove Replenishment Initiative began as a local project along the central east coast of Florida; however, in the last few years it has contributed to wide range of habitat creation and restoration programs that are internationalin scope.

5950 Manomet Center for Conservation Science
http://www.manomet.org

Manomet's mission is to conserve natural resources for the benefit of wildlife and human populations. Through research and collaboration, Manomet builds science-based, cooperative solutions to environmental problems.

5951 Marine Environmental Research Institute
http://www.downeast.net

The Marine Environmental Research Institute is a 501 nonprofit charitable organization dedicated to scientific research and education on the impacts of pollution on marine life, and to protecting the health and biodiversity of themarine environment for furture generations.

5952 Marine Mammal Center
http://www.tmmc.org
We recognize our interdependence with marine mammals, their improtance as sentinels of the ocean environment, and our responsibility to use our awareness, compassion and intelligence to ensure their survival and the conservation oftheir habitat.

5953 Marine Technology Society
http://www.mtsociety.org
Our mission is to disseminate marine science and technical knowledge, to promote and support education for marine scientists, engineers and technicians, advance the development of tools and procedures required to explore, study andfurther the responsible and sustainable use of the oceans. Provide servicesthat create a broader understanding of the relevance of marine sciences to other technologies, arts and human affairs.

5954 Maryland Department of Natural Resources
http://www.dnr.state.md.us
The Maryland Department of Natural Resources is the state agency which overseas the management and wise use of the living and natural resources of the Chesapeake Bay and its tributaries. The resources of Maryland portion of thewatershed include its state forests and parks, fisheries, wildlife and the recreation of citizens.

5955 Maryland Forests Association
http://www.mdforests.org
Incorporated in 1976, the Maryland Forests Association is a nonprofit 501 citizens organization whose membership includes more than 500 individuals and companies from throughout Maryland and the tri state area.

5956 Massachusetts Department of Fisheries, Wildlife and Environmental Law Enforcement
http://www.state.ma.us/dfwele
Massachusetts state agency responsible for the management and conservation of the state's fisheries and wildlife, including rare and endangered species.

5957 Medomak Valley Land Trust
http://www.medomakvalley.org
The Medomak Valley Land Trust is a local, private nonprofit oragnization edstablished in 1991 to preserve the natural, recreational, scenic and productive values of the Medomak River watershed. Our goals are to foster a regionalperspective of the watershed and to encourage valley residents to work together to ensure that the resources they value will remain for future generations.

5958 Messinger Woods Wildlife Care and Education Center
http://www.wildlifecare.org
The mission is to promote community awareness, education and instruction, involvement, understanding, appreciation, and acceptance of our wildlife in order to conserve it. To co-exist and protect each other, our natural surroundings,and all the inhabitants of our earth by education & example.

5959 Michigan Department of Environment Quality
http://www.michigan.gov/deq
Our mission is to drive improvements in environmental quality for the protection of public health and natural resources to benefit current and future generations. This will be accomplished through effective administration of agencyprograms, providing for the use of innovative strategies, while helping to foster a strong and sustainable economy.

5960 Michigan Department of Natural Resources
http://www.michigan.gov/dnr
The Department of Natural Resources is responsible for the stewardship of Michigan's natural resources and for the provision of outdoor recreational opportunities; a role is has relished sonce creation of the original ConservationDepartment in 1921.

5961 Michigan Environmental Science Board
http://www.michigan.gov/mesb
The MESB is an independent state egency established to provide scientific and technical advice to the Governor of Michigan and to state departments, on matters affecting the protection and management of Michigan's environmental andnatural resources.

5962 Michigan Forest Association
http://www.michiganforests.com
The mission of the Michigan Forest Association is to promote good management on all forest land, to educate our members about good forest practices and stewardship of the land. To inform the general public about forestry issues and thebenefits of good forest management.

5963 Michigan United Conservation Clubs
http://www.mucc.org
MUCC is the largest statewide conservation in the nation. The mission of Uniting Citizens to Conserve Michigan's Natural Resources and Protect our outdoor heritage. MUCC works to conserve Michigan's wildlife, fisheries, waters, forest,air, and soils by providing information, education and advocacy.

5964 Midwest Renewable Energy Association (MREA)
http://www.the-mrea.org
The Midwest Renewable Energy Association is a nonprofit network for sharing ideas, resources, and information with individuals, business, and communities to promote a sustainable future through renewable energy and energy efficiency.

5965 Milton Keynes Wildlife Hospital
http://mkweb.co.uk/
We are one of the few establishments in the UK to be licensed by the Department of the Environment to care for certain species of birds. A purely voluntary organization and rely solely on donations from the public and local companiesin order to keep the hospital open.

5966 Mineral Policy Center
http://www.mineralpolicy.org
Mineral Policy Center is a nonprofit environmental organization dedicated to protecting communities and the environment by preventing the environmental impacts associated with irresponsible mining and mineral development, and bycleaning up pollution caused by past mining.

5967 Minnesota Department of Natural Resources
http://www.dnr.state.mn.us
The DNR vision hinges on the concept of sustainability. Protecting and restoring the natural environment while enhancing economic opportunity and community well-being. DNR endorsed ecosystem-based management as its methods to achievesustainability, and uses the concept of ecosystems integrity as a benchmark to measure progress toward sustainability goals. The goal is to maintain environment, econony and the community in a healthy state indefinitely.

5968 Minnesota Pollution Control Agency
http://www.pca.state.mn.us
This site includes a great deal of information on air, water, and waste pollution in Minnesota. It also contains data on regulations and permits, clean-up techniques, prevention, publications, and programs to protect Minnesota'senvironment. The MPCA site has a calender of events, information for childern, news releases, training opportunities, and conference information.

5969 Minnesotans for An Energy-Efficient Economy(ME3)
http://www.me3.org
ME3 is a coalition working to improve the quality of life, the environment and the economy of Minnesota by promoting energy efficiency and the sound use of renewable energy. Through a program research, public education, and theintervention in the decision making process. ME3 seeks to develop and build consensus for energy vision that will ensure the well being of future generations.

5970 Missouri Audubon Council
http://www.audubon.org/chapter/mo
The Audubon Society's mission is to conserve and restore natural ecosystems, focusing on birds and other wildlife for the benefit of

humanity and earth's biological diversity. The purpose of the Missouri Audubon Council is to representthe interests of the 14 chapters of the National Audubon Society on a state level.

5971 Missouri Department of Conservation
http://www.conservation.state.mo.us
The mission of the Missouri Department of Conservation is to protect and manage the fish, forest, and wildlife resources of the state, to serve the public and facilitate their participation in resources management activities, toprovide opportunity fos all citizens to use, enjoy, and learn about fish, forest and wildlife resources.

5972 Missouri Prairie Foundation
http://www.moprairie.org
The Missouri Praire Foundation mission is to preserve the Greater Praire Chicken. To restore the vegetative and faunal balance to the grassland ecosystem, not just to one species, even through the praire chicken is on the verge ofextirpation from Missouri.

5973 Mmarie
http://www.kuleuven.ac.be/mmarie
The general objectives of MMARIE are to create an interdisciplinary forum for the exchange of information and experience, related to projects carried out by the participants, and to facilitate collaboration between the partners.

5974 Monarch Watch
http://www.monarchwatch.org
Our goals are to further science education, particularly in primary and secondary school systems, to promote the conservation of Monarch butterflies; and to invlove thousands of students and adults in a cooperative study of theMonarch's spectacular fall migration.

5975 Mountain Lion Foundation
http://www.mountainlion.org
The Mountain Lion Foudation is a nonprofit conservation and education organization dedicated to protecting the mountain lion, its wild habitat, and the wildlif that shares that habitat. The foundation is dedicated to the propositionthat much can be done to preserve the cougar as a viable species and that the success of this effort can assure the survival of other species.

5976 NEMO: Oceanographic Data Server
http://nemo.ucsd.edu
Nemo is a collection of data useful for physical oceanographers here at Scripps Institutions of Oceanography.

5977 NIREX
http://www.nda.gov.uk/
NIREX, with the agreement of the Government, to examine safe, environmental and economic aspects of deep geological disposal of radioactive waste. We deal with intermediate level waste, which accounts for the majority of radioactivewaste currently in storage, and also with some low-level waste.

5978 NOAA (National Oceanic and Atmospheric Administration)
http://www.noaa.gov
NOAA's mission is to describe and predict changes in the Earth's environment, and conserve and wisely manage the Nation's coastal and marine resources. NOAA's strategy consist of seven interrelated Strategic Goals for environmentassessment,, predictions and stewardship.

5979 Napa County Resource Conservation
http://www.naparcd.org
Napa County Resource Conservation mission is to encourage and assist acceptance of individual responsibility for watershed management; the goals are enhacement of wildlife habitat, reduction of soil erosion, protection and enhacementof water quality, and promotion of land stewardship and sustainable agriculture.

5980 National Agricultural Pest Information System
http://www.ceris.purdue.edu
NAPIS is the database for the Cooperative Agricultural Pest Survey and is maintained by the Center for Environmental and Regulatory Information Systems (CERIS). This site contains pest information, the NAPIS User Guide, the CAPSProgram Guidebook, and the APHIS Environmental Manual. There is also a list of government certified nurseries.

5981 National Arborist Association
http://www.natlarb.com
NAA is a trade association of commercial tree care firms that develops that safety and education programs, satndards of tree care practice, and management information for arboriculture firms around the world.

5982 National Association for Environmental Management
http://www.naem.org
Dedicated to advancing the profession of environmental management and supports the professional corporate and facility environmental manager.

5983 National Association for Pet Container Resources
http://www.napcor.com
The National Association for Pet Container Resources is the trade association for the PET plastic industry in the United States and Canada. Its mission is to facilitate PET plastic recycling and to promote the usage of PET packaging.

5984 National Association of Conservation Districts
http://www.nacdnet.org
Thier mission is to serve conservation districts by providing national leadership and a unified voice for natural resource conservation. The association works with landowners, organizations and agency partners in the district helpingto protect the soil, water, forest wildlife and other resources.

5985 National Association of Environmental Professionals
http://www.naep.org
NAEP is a multi-disciplinary association dedicated to the advancement of persons in the environmental profession in the US and abroad; a forum for state of the art information on environmental planning, research and management; anetwork of professional contacts and exchange on information among colleagues in industry, government, academic, and the private sector.

5986 National Association of State Foresters
http://www.stateforesters.org
State Foresters provide management assistance and protection services for over-two-thirds of the nation's forests.

5987 National Audubon Society
http://www.audubon.org
The mission of the National Audubon Society is to conserve and restor natural ecosystems, focusing on birds and other wildlife for the benefit of humanity and the earth's biological diversity.

5988 National Center for Atmospheric Research
http://www.ncar.ucar.edu
NCAR's mission to plan, organize, and conduct atmospheric and related research programs in collaboration with the universities and other institutions, to provide state of the art research tools and facilities to the atmosphericsciences community, to support and enhance university atmospheric science education, and to facilitate the transfer of technology to both the public and private sectors.

5989 National Center for Ecological Analysis and Synthesis
http://www.nceas.ucsb.edu/
The mission is to advance the state of ecological knowledge through the search for general patterns and principles, to organize and synthesize ecological information in a manner useful to researchers, resource managers, and policymakers addressing important environmental issues.

5990 National Energy Foundation
http://www.nef1.org
A nonprofit educational organization dedicated to the development, dissemination and implementation of supplemental educa-

tional materials and programs primarily related to energy, water, natural resources, science, conservation and theenvironment.

5991 **National Energy Technology Laboratory**
http://www.alrc.doe.gov
Our mission is to provide stewardship for the Nation's mineral resources by conserving materials produced from minerals.

5992 **National Environmental Health Association(NEHA)**
CO http://www.neha.org
NEHA is the only national association that represents all of environmental health and protection from terrorism and all-hazards preparedness, to food safety and protection and onsite wastewater systems

5993 **National Estuary Program**
http://www.epa.gov/nep/
The National Estuary Program was established in 1987 by amendments to Clean Water to identify, restore, and protect nationally significant estuaries of the United States. NEP targets a broad range of issues and engages localcommunities in the process. The program focuses not just on improving water quality in an estuary, but on maintaining the integrity of the whole systems-its chemical, physical and biological properties, as well as its economic, recreational, andaesthetic values.

5994 **National Ground Water Association**
http://www.ngwa.org/
Providing and protecting the world's ground water resource. Enhance the skills and credibility of all ground water professionals, develop and exchange industry knowledge and promote the ground water industry and understanding ofground water resources.

5995 **National Institute for Environmental Studies**
http://www.nies.go.jp/index.html
The National Institute for Environmental Studies was established in 1974 at Tsukuba Science City, about 60 kilometers northeast of Tokyo, as the main research branch of the Environment Agency of the Government of Japan. NIES is thesole national institute for comprehensive research in the environmental sciences.

5996 **National Institute of Environmental Health Science (NIEHS)**
http://www.niehs.nih.gov/
The mission is to reduce the burden of human illness and dysfunction from environmental causes by understanding each of these elements and how they interrelate. The NIEHS achives its mission through multidisciplinary biomedicalresearch programs, prevention and intervention efforts, and communication strategies that encompass training, education, technology transfer, and community outreach.

5997 **National Library for the Environment**
http://www.cnie.org/nle
The National Library for the Environment is a universal, timely, easy to use,single point entry to quality environmental data and information for the use of all participants in the environmental enterprise. This online library icludesdirectories of academic environmental programs, journals, funding sources, meetings, job opportunities, news sources, laws and treaties, reports, reference materials, and more.

5998 **National Oceanic and Atmospheric Administration**
http://www.noaa.gov
NOAA mission is to describe and predict changes in the Earth's environment, and conserve and wisely manage the Nation's coastal and marine resources.

5999 **National Outdoor Leadership School**
http://www.nols.edu/
Over the past 35 years NOLS has become the leader in wilderness education. NOLS is now the largest backcountry permit holder in the United States and runs courses on four continents. NOLS has gone from 100 students in 1965 toapproximately 3,070 students in 1999. As NOLS enters the 21st century, it remainscommited to the quality of courses and programs that it offers, as well as to the wilderness environment that serves as our classroom.

6000 **National Park and Conservation Association**
http://www.npca.org/
The National Parks & Conservation Association has been the sole voice of the American people in the fight to safeguard the scenic beauty, wildlife, and historical and cultural treasures of the largest and most diverse park system inthe world.

6001 **National Pollutant Inventory**
http://www.npi.gov.au
Provides Australians with free access to information on the types and amounts of pollutants being emitted in their community.

6002 **National Pollution Prevention Center for Higher Education (NPPC)**
http://www.css.snre.umich.edu/
The National Pollutant Release Inventory was established under the Canadian Environmental Protection Act, to provide information on the type and quality of pollutantas being released into Canada's environment. The inventory is anationwide, publicly accessible database of releases and transfers of 178 specified substances to air, water and land.

6003 **National Renewable Energy Laboratory (NREL)**
http://www.nrel.gov/
As the nation's leading center for renewable energy research, NREL is developing new energy technologies to benefit both the environment and the economy.

6004 **National Sea Grant Library**
http://nsgd.gso.uri.edu
The National Sea Grant Library was established as an archive and lending library for Sea Grant funded documents. These documents cover a wide variety of subjects, including oceanography, marine education, aquaculture, fisheries,limonology, coastal zone management, marine recreation and law. NSGL staff lends documents all over the world to aid scientists, teachers, students, fishermen and many other individuals in their reseacrh and studies.

6005 **National Society for Clean Air**
http://www.nsca.org.uk
NCSA is a nonprofit group made up of organizations and individuals who promote clean air through the reduction of air, water, and land pollution, noise and other contaminats, while having due regard for other aspects of theenvironment. The society exmines environmental policy issues from air quality perspective and aims to place them in a broader social and economic context.

6006 **National Wildlife Health Center**
http://www.aphis.usda.gov.ws.nwrc
The National Wildlife Health Center's mission is to improve information, technical assistance, and research on national and international wildlife health issues. To fulfill the NWHC mission, the Center monitors disease and assesses theimpact od disease on wildlife populations; defines ecological relationships leading to occurrence of disease; transfers technology for disease prevention and control; and provides guidance, training and on site assistance for reducing wildlifelosses.

6007 **National Wildlife Rehabilitators Association**
http://www.nwrawildlife.org
The National Wildlife Rehabilitation Association is a nonprofit international membership organization committed to promoting and improving the integrity and professionalism of wildlife rehabilitation and contributing to thepreservation of natural ecosystems.

6008 **National Woodland Owners Association**
http://www.woodlandowners.org
An independent landowners group with the purpose of developing policy, legislation and representation at the national level, and providing educational and networking opportunities to landowners throught the country. There are currently35 state partner organizations.

6009 **Native Americans and the Environment**
http://www.cnie.org/NAE

The mission is to educate the public on environmental problems in Native American Communities; to explore the values and historical experiences that Native Americans bring to bear on environmental issues and to promote conservationmeasures that respect Native American land and resource rights.

6010 **Native Forest Council**

http://www.forestcouncil.org

The mission is to provide visionary leadership and to ensure the integrity of public land ecosystems, without compromising people or forests.

6011 **Native Forest Network**

http://www.native forest.org/

The Native Forest Network's mission is to protect the world's remaining native forest by they temperature or otherwise, to ensure they can survive, flourish and maintain their evolutionary potential.

6012 **Natural Energy Laboratory of Hawaii**

E-mail: inquires@nelha.org
http://www.nelha.org

NELHA mangers comprehensive environmental monitoring of seawater. This site describes the participants in this program and the projects in which they are involved. NELHA's goal is to help businesses utilize Hawaii's natural resources.Information available here includes water quality data, NELHA's Seawater Delivery System information, Ocean Thermal Energy Converstion material, and bibliographical information.
Thomas H Daniel, Scientific Manager

6013 **Natural Environmental Research Council**

http://www.nerc.ac.uk/

The mission is to promote and support, by any means, high quality basic, strategic and applied research, survey, long-term environmental monitoring and related postgraduate training in terrestrial, marine and freshwater biology andEarth, atmospheric, hydrological, oceanographic and polar sciences and Earth observation. To provide advice on, dieeminate knowledge and promote public understanding of the fields aforesaid.

6014 **Natural Resources Canada**

http://www.nrcan-rncan.gc.ca

Advanced Forest Technologies Program purpose is to develop new approaches in the areas of remote sensing, geographic information systems, artifical intelligence, expert systems and decision support systems to: assist the resource andenvironmental manager with integrated resource planning; provide the land manager with tools for sustainable development.

6015 **Natural Resources Defense Council**

http://www.nrdc.org

Works to safeguard the Earth: its people, its plants and animals, and natural systems on which all life depends.

6016 **Nature Conservancy**

http://www.tnc.org/

The mission of The Nature Conservancy is to preserve the plants, animals and natural communities that represent the diversity of life on Earth by protecting the lands and waters they need to survive.

6017 **Nature Conservancy of Texas**

http://www.tnc.org/texas/

The Nature Conservancy of Texas conserves habitat for native wildlife, using science based research and a cooperative approach to protect the animals and plants that represent Texas' precious natural heritage.

6018 **Nature Node**

http://www.naturenode.com

Online community celebrating the diversity of life on our planet. It is a place to build a virtual community of like-minded individuals.

6019 **Nature Saskatchewan**

http://www.naturesask.ca

Our mission is to promote appreciation and understanding of our natural environment through education, and through conservation and research, to protec and preserve natural ecosystems and their biodiversity.

6020 **NatureNet**

http://naturenet.net/index.html

NatureNet is a voluntary enterprise to provide a good resource for practical nature conservation and countryside management on the Web. Based in UK, and most of the information available on Naturenet relates to the UK, particularyEngland.

6021 **New England Wild Flower Society**

http://www.newfs.org

The New England Wild Flower Society is the oldest plant conservation organization in the United States, promoting the conservation of temperature North American plants through key programs.

6022 **New England Wildlife Center**

http://www.newildlife.com

The New England Wildlife Center is a native wildlife preservation, rehabilitation , animal habitat and environmetal protection, educational organization. We afford humane care to native and naturalized wild animals through our wildlifemedicine hospital. We conduct no research on patients. The center is a nonprofit environmental native habitat protection and preservation organization.

6023 **New Forest Project**

http://www.newforestsproject.com/

To protect conserve, and enhance the health of the Earth's ecosystems by supporting integrated grassrrots efforts to maintain and rebuild the world's forest through the promotion of agroforestry, reforestation, the protection ofwatersheds, and the initiation of renewable energy products.

6024 **New Hampshire Department of Environmental Sciences (DES)**

http://www.des.state.nh.us/

The mission of the Department of Environmental Services is to protect, maintain and anhance environmental quality public health in New Hampshire.

6025 **New Hampshire Fish and Game Department**

http://www.wildlife.state.nh.us/

The mission is to conserve, manage and protect these resources and their habitats; inform and educate the public about these resources and provide the public with opportunities to use and appreciate these resources.

6026 **New Jersey Department of Environmental Protection**

http://www.state.nj.us/dep/

The mission is to assist the residents of New Jersey in preserving, retoring, sustaining, protecting and enhancing the environment to ensure the integration of high environmental quality, public health and economic vitality.

6027 **New Jersey Division of Fish, Game and Wildlife**

http://www.state.nj.us/dep/fgw/

The mission of the Divison of Fish, Game, and Wildlife is to protect and manage the State's fish and wildlife resources to maximize their long term economic, recreational and biological values for the citizens of New Jersey.

6028 **New Mexico Wilderness Alliance**

http://www.nmwild.org

The New Mexico Wilderness Allince is dedicated to the protection, restoration, and rewilding of New Mexico's Wilderness areas. We focus on forward-looking measures to develop an active and educates Wilderness constituency throughoutthe state.

6029 **New Mexico Wildlife Association**

http://www.wildlifewest.org

The New Mexico Wildlife Association is a nonprofit corporation dedicated to yhe preservation of the rich heritage of native New Mexico wildlife and its habitat through education, scientific research, and the sponsorship of wildlifepark.

6030 **New York Association for Reduction, Reuse and Recycling**
http://www.ny.sar3.org/
The mission is to provide state-wide leadership on waste reduction, reuse and recycling issues and practices.

6031 **New York State Department of Environmental Conservation**
http://www.dec.state.ny.us
The mission of the department is to conserve, improve, and protect its natural resources and environment, and control water, land and air ollution, in order to enhance the health, safety and welfare of the peolple of the state andtheir overall economic and social well being.

6032 **North American Commission for Environmental Cooperation**
http://www.cec.org
The Commission for Environmental Cooperation is an international organization created by Canada, Mexico and the US under the North American Agreement on Environmental Cooperation. The CEC was established to address regionalenvironmental concerns, help prevent potential trade and environmental conflicts and to promote the effective enforcement of environmental law.

6033 **North American Lake Management Society**
http://www.nalms.org
Members are academics, lake managers and others interested in furthering the understanding of lake ecology.

6034 **North Carolina Coastal Federation**
http://www.nccoast.org/
NNCF is a nonprofit tax exempt organization which seeks to protect and restore the states's coastal environment, culture and economy through citizen involvement in the management of coastal resources.

6035 **North Carolina Department of Environment and Natural Resources**
http://www.enr.state.nc.us
The mission is to lead stewardship agency for preservation and protection of North Carolina's outstanding natural resources. The organization administers regulatory programs designed to protect air quality, water quality, and thepublic's health.

6036 **North Cascades Conservation Council**
http://www.northcascades.org
The NCCC keeps government officials, environmental organizations, and the general public informed about issues affecting the Greater North Cascade Ecosystem. Action is pursued through legislative, legal, and public participationchannels to protect the lands, waters, plants and wildlife.

6037 **Northeast Advanced Vehicle Consortium**
http://www.navc.org/home.html
The Northeast Advanced Vehicle Consortium is a nonprofit association of private and public sector firms and agencies workimg together to promote advanced vehicle technologies in the Northeast US. NAVC is now the principal multi-state,nonprofit funding mechanism for advanced transportation research, technology development and demostration in the region.

6038 **Northeast Sustainable Energy Association**
http://www.nesea.org
NESEA is a regional membership organization comprised of engineers, educators, builders, students, energy experts, environmental activists, transportation planners, architects, and other citizens interested in responsible energy use.The goal is to bring clean electricity, green transportation, and healthy, efficient buildings into everyday use in order to strengthen the economy and improve the environment.

6039 **Northern Prairie Wildlife Research Center**
http://www.npwrc.usgs.gov/
Our mission is to develop research information on the quantitative requirements for sustainable wildlife populations. To design and conduct studies of numbers and distribution of flora and fauna including identification of changeresulting from habitat loss and modification. To disseminate the latest in technical information and research findings such that interested audiences benefit to the maximum extent possible.

6040 **Ocean Voice International**
http://www.ovi.ca/
Ocean Voice International is a nonprofit membership based marine environmental organization.

6041 **Oceania Project**
http://nornet.nor.com.au/
The Oceania Project mission is to promote awareness and co-operation to instigate and maintain the process of rehabilitation, preservation and conservation of Cetacea and the Oceans; the promotion and undertaking of scientific researchof Cetacea and the Oceans for the benefit of the community. To provide environmentally sensitive Ocean platforms for non-manipulative research, education and experiential programmes of Cetacea and the Oceans using sensitive vessels.

6042 **Oceanic Resource Foundation**
http://www.orf.org/
The Oceanic Resource Foundation is a nonprofit, scientific researchorganization dedicated to the preservation of the global marine environment and marine biological diversity.

6043 **Office of Energy Efficiency**
http://oee.nrcan.gc.ca/
The office of Energy Efficiency, Canada's centre of excellence for energy efficiency and alternative fuels information, is pplaying a dynamic leadership role in helping Canadians save millions of dollars in energy cost while addressingthe challenges of climate change.

6044 **Office of Protected Resources**
http://www.nmfs.noaa.gov/pr/
The Office of Protected Resources provides program oversight, national policy direction and guidance on the conservation of those marine mammals and endangered species, and their habitats, under the jurisdiction of the Secretary ofCommerce; develops national guidelines and policies for relevant protected resources programs, and provides oversight, advice and guidance on scientific aspects of managing protected species and marine protected areas.

6045 **Ohio Environmental Protection Agency**
http://www.epa.state.oh.us
The Ohio EPA has authority to implement laws and regulations regarding air and water quality standards; solid hazardous and infectious waste disposal standards; quality planning, supervision of sewage treatment and public drinkingwater supplies; and cleanup of unregulated hazardous waste sites. The Ohio EPA cooperates with government and private agencies, manages some federally funded pollution control projects, obtains technical and laboratory services, investigateenvironment problems, etc.

6046 **Ohio Wildlife Center**
http://www.ohiowildlifecenter.org/
The Ohio Wildlife Center is a nonprofit educational organization that promotes increased appreciation and understanding of the natural environment, with particular emphasis on wildlife. OWC is supported by individuals from all walks oflife who wish to improve their own understanding of native wild species and local wildlife issues.

6047 **Oklahoma Department of Wildlife Conservation**
http://www.wildlifedepartment.com
The mission is to manage Oklahoma's wildlife resources and habitat to provide scientific, educational, aesthetic, economic and recreational benefits for present and future generations of hunters, anglers and others who appreciatewildlife.

6048 **Ontario Environment Network**
http://www.oen.ca
The Ontario Environment Network is a nonprofit, nongovernmental network serving Ontario's environmental nonprofit, nongovernmental community. The OEN seeks to increase

awareness of these organizations and encourage discussions aboutmeans to protect the environment.

6049 Organization of American States: Department of Regional Development and Environment

http://www.oas.org

Conducts technical cooperation and training programs to assist the member States in their efforts to preserve natural resources. It works with the countries on planning sustainable development, managing the environment and preparinginvestment programs and projects.

6050 PureZone

http://www.purezone.com

PureZone is a group effort among manufacturers, suppliers, and installers of Heating and Ventilating systems designed to maximize the quality of aour air in our buildings.

6051 Rachel Carson Council

http://www.rachelcarsoncouncil.com

A clearinghouse and library with information at both scientific and layperson levels on pesticides related issues. Rachel Carson Council develops its knowledge from literature searches and conservations with experts. It then providesanswers to the public and also products various publications clarifying pestcide dangers and bringing alternative pest controls to the public's attention.

6052 Renewable Fuels Association

http://www.ethanolrfa.org

Members are companies and individuals involved in the production and use of ethanol. Ethanol is sold nationwide as a high-octane fuel that delivers improved vehicle performance while reducing emissions and improving air quality.

6053 Renewable Natural Resources Foundation

http://www.rnrf.org

Consortium of professional and scientific organizations with an interest in natural rsources. Established to advance sciences and education in renewable natural resources; promote the application of sound scientific practices inmanaging and conserving renewable natural resources; foster coordination and cooperation among professional, scientific and educational organizations having leadership responsibilities for renewable natural resources; and develop a Renewable NaturalResources Center.

6054 Society for Conservation Biology (SCB)

http://www.conbio.org/

The mission of the Center for Conservation Biology Network is to help develop the technical means for the protection, maintenance and restoration of life on this planet-its species, its ecological and evolutionary processes and itsparticular and total environment; to help raise awareness, educate and encourage personal involvement of the public and academics alike.

6055 Steel Recycling Institute

http://www.recycle-steel.org

Promotes steel recycling and works to forge a coalition of steelmakers, can manufacturers, legislators, government officials, solid waste managers, business and consumer groups.

6056 Student Conservation Association

http://www.sca-inc.org

To build the next generation of conservation leaders and inspire lifelong stewardship of our environment and communities by engaging young people in hands on service to the land.

6057 Synthetic Organic Chemical Manufacturers Association

http://www.socma.com

A trade association that serves the specialty, batch and custom chemical industry. SOCMA member companies make the products and refine the raw materials that make our standard of living possible; from pharmaceuticals to cosmetics,soaps to plastics, and all manner of industrial and construction products. SOCMA promotes innovative, safe and environmentally responsible operations, which are internationally competitive and contribute to a healthy, productive economy.

6058 TechKnow

http://www.techknow.org

TechKnow is an interactive database that is available over the Internet. The database is a springboard for people interested in Environmentally Sustainable technologies. Originally, TechKnow only contained environmental remediationtechnologies but has now branched off to other forms of sustainable technologies. One of the main goals of the database is to remain current and topical.

6059 The Environment Directory

http://www.webdirectory.com

Includes agriculture, animals, arts, business, databases, design, disasters, education, employment, energy, forestry, general environmental interest, government, health, land conservation, parks and recreation, pollution, products andservices, publications, recycling, science, social science, sustainable development, transportation, usenet newsgroups, vegetarianism, water resources, weather and wildlife.

6060 US Environmental Protection Agency: Environmental Monitoring and Assessment Program

http://www.epa.gov

A research program to develop the tools necessary to monitor and assess the status and trends of national ecological resources.

6061 United States Geological Survey: National Earthquake Information Centre

http://www.earthquake.usgs.gov

Determine location and size of all destructive eartquakes worldwide and immediatly disseminate this information to concerned national and agencies, scientistsm, and the general public

6062 Vertical Net

http://www.verticalnet.com

Vertical Net is the Internet's leading bussines e-commerce enabler, providing ent to end e-commerce salutions that are targeted at district business segments through two strategic business units- Vertical Markets and Vertical NetSolutions. While both units focus on a core area of eexpertise, each also leverages the strengths, resources and experience of the other.

6063 Wisconsin Sea Grant Program

http://www.seagrant.wisc.edu

Wisconsin Sea grant is a statewide program of basic and applied research, education, and outreach and technology transfer dedicated to the stewardship and sustainable use of the nation's Great Lakes and ocean resources.

6064 World Data Centre: National Geophysical Data Centre

http://www.ngdc.noaa.gov

Data management in the broadest sense. Play an integral role in the nation's research into the environment, and at the same time provide public domain data to a wide group of users.

6065 World Fish Center

http://www.worldfishcenter.org/

Our mission is to promote sustainable development and use of living aquatics based on environmentally sound management.

6066 World Women in Environment and Development Organization

http://www.wedo.org

International advocacy organization that seeks to increase the power of women worldwide as policymakers at all levels in governments, institutions and forums to achive economic and social justice, healthy and peaceful planet, and humanrights for all.

Online Databases & Clearinghouses

Environmental

6067 Air Risk Information Support Center Hotline
US Office of Air Quality Planning & Standards
Mail Drop 13 919-541-0888
Research Triangle Park, NC 27711 Fax: 919-541-1818
Holly Reid, Co-chair

6068 Alternative Treatment Technology Information Center
4 Research Place 301-670-6294
Suite 210 Fax: 301-670-3815
Rockville, MD 20850
Gary Turner, System Operator

6069 Asbestos Ombudsman Clearinghouse Hotline
401 M Street SW 703-305-5938
A-149 C 800-368-5888
Washington, DC 20460 Fax: 703-305-6462
Karen V Brown, Ombudsman

6070 Bureau of Explosives Hotline
50 F Street NW 202-639-2222
Washington, DC 20001 Fax: 412-741-0609
http://www.aar.org/aarhome.nsf

6071 CQS Health and Environmental
43 Boynton Street 617-522-3466
South 2R http://www.cqs.com
Boston, MA 02130
Jonathan Campbell, Health Consultant

6072 Carbon Dioxide Information Analysis Center
Environmental Services Division
Oak Ridge National Lab Bldg 1000 865-574-0390
PO Box 2008 Fax: 865-574-2232
Oak Ridge, TN 37831
RI Vanhook, Dir. Opns. & User Servs. Mgr

6073 Center for Environmental Research Information
ORD Research Information Unit
26 West Martin Luther King Drive 513-569-7562
MS G-72
Cincinnati, OH 45268
Dorothy Williams, Executive Officer

6074 Center for Environmental and Regulatory Information Systems
Purdue University
1231 Cumberland Avenue 317-494-7309
Suite A Fax: 317-494-9727
West Layfayette, IN 47906 http://www.ceris.purdue.edu/ceris
Eileen Luke, Director

6075 Center for Health, Environment and Justice
PO Box 6806 703-237-2249
Falls Church, VA 22040
The Center for Heath, Environment and Justice trains and assists local people to fight for justice, become empowered to protect their communities from environmental threats and build strong locally controlled organizations. CHEJconnects these strong local groups with each other to build a movement from the bottom up.
Lois Marie Gibbs, Executive Director

6076 Center for Sustainable Systems
University of Michigan
440 Church Street 734-764-1412
Dana Building Fax: 734-647-5841
Ann Arbor, MI 48109-1041 E-mail: css.info@umich.edu
http://http://css.snre.umich.edu
CSS advances concepts of sustainability through interdisciplinary research and education. Collaborates with diverse stakeholders to develop and apply life cycle based models and sustainability metrics for systems that meet societalneeds. Promotes tools and knowledge that support the design, evaluation, and improvement of complex systems.

Jonathan W Bulkley, Co-Director
Gregory A Keoleian, Co-Director

6077 Chemtrec Center
1300 Wilson Boulevard 800-CMA-8200
Arlington, VA 22209 Fax: 703-741-6037

6078 Chemtrec Hotline
2501 M Street NW 800-764-9563
Washington, DC 20037

6079 Clean Ocean Action
18 Hartshorne Drive 732-872-0111
Sandy Hook, NJ 07732 Fax: 732-872-8041
E-mail: SandyHook@cleanoceanaction.org
http://www.cleanoceanaction.org
Clean Ocean Action is a broad-based coalition of over 150 conservation, community, diving, fishing, environmental, surfing, women's and business groups that works to improve and protect the waters off the New York and New Jersey coast.

Cindy Zipf, Executive Director
Mary-Beth Thompson, Operations Director

6080 Clean-Up Information Bulletin Board System
US EPA Technology Innovation Office
401 M Street 301-589-8368
OS-10W Fax: 301-589-8487
Washington, DC 20460
Beth Ann Kyle, System Operator

6081 Congressional Clearinghouse on the Future
H2-555 House Annex 2 202-226-3434
Washington, DC 20515

6082 Conservation Locator
NYS Department of Environmental Conservation
625 Broadway 518-402-8013
2nd Floor Fax: 518-402-9036
Albany, NY 12233 http://www.dec.state.ny.us/website/locator
A web-based index of current DEC publications, with listings by subject, links to publications available on the web and directions for obtainig copies of print-only publications.
Helen Paruolo, EnCon Program Assistant

6083 Consumer Energy Council of America
2000 L Street NW 202-659-0404
Suite 802 Fax: 202-659-0407
Washington, DC 20036 E-mail: outreach@cecarf.org
http://www.cecarf.org
A senior public interest organization in the US focused on the energy, telecommunications and other network industries that provide essential services to consumers.

Ellen Berman, President
Peggy Welsch, Senior VP

6084 Consumer Product Safety Commission Hotline
Office of the Secretary 800-638-2882
Washington, DC 20207

6085 Control Technology Center
Emission Standards Division
US EPA, MD 13 919-541-0800
Research Triangle Park, NC 27709 Fax: 919-541-0072
Bob Blaszczak, ESD/ QAQPS

6086 EPA Model Clearinghouse
Office of Air Quality Planning 919-541-5683
Research Triangle Park, NC 27711 Fax: 919-541-2464
Dean A Wilson

6087 EPA Public Information Center
US EPA
401 M Street 202-260-7751
PM- 211B
Washington, DC 20460

6088 EPCRA (SARA Title III) Hotline
US EPA
401 M Street SW 202-479-2449
OS120 800-535-0202
Washington, DC 20460 Fax: 703-412-3333

6089 Electronic Bulletin Board System
US EPA
26 West Martin Luther King Drive 513-569-7358
Cincinnati, OH 800-258-9605
Fax: 513-569-7585
Charles W Guion

6090 Emergency Planning and Community Right-to-Know Information Hotline
Booz, Allen & Hamilton
1725 Jefferson Davis Highway 703-920-8977
Arlington, VA 22202 800-535-0202
Fax: 703-486-3333
Dan Kovacs, Contractor

6091 Emission Factor Clearinghouse
US EPA
MD-14 919-541-1000
Research Triangle Park, NC 27709 Fax: 919-541-0684
Dennis Shipman

6092 Environmental Financing Information Network
US EPA
EFN, WH-547 202-564-4994
401 M Street, East Tower, Room 1117 Fax: 202-565-2694
Washington, DC 20460
June Lobit

6093 Green Committees of Correspondence Clearinghouse
PO Box 30208 816-931-9366
Kansas City, MO 64112
Amy Belanger, Coordinator

6094 Green Lights Program
Bruce Company
1850 K Street 290 202-775-6650
Washington, DC 20006 Fax: 202-775-6680
Maria Theesen

6095 Hazardous Waste Ombudsman Program
US EPA
401 M Street SW 202-260-9361
OS-130, Room SE 315 800-262-7937
Washington, DC 20460 Fax: 202-260-8929
http://www.epa.gov/earth100/records/000154.html
Bob Knox, Headquarters Contact

6096 Indoor Air Quality Information Center
1200 Pennsylvania Avenue NW 202-343-9370
Washington, DC 20460 800-438-4318
Fax: 202-343-2394
E-mail: iaqinfo@aol.com
http://www.epa.gov/iaq/iaqinfo.html
Susan Dolgin

6097 Inspector General Hotline
US EPA
1200 Pennsylvania Avenue NW 800-424-4000
Washington, DC 20460 Fax: 202-260-6976
Ed Maddox

6098 International Ground Water Modeling Center
Colorado School of Mines 303-273-3103
Golden, CO 80401 Fax: 303-273-3278
Paul van der Hijde, Director

6099 Kentucky Partners State Waste Reduction Center
University of Louisville
Ernst Hall 502-588-7260
Room 312
Louisville, KY 40292
Joyce St. Clair, Executive Director

6100 Methods Information Communications Exchange
11251 Roger Bacon Drive 703-676-4690
Reston, VA 20190 Fax: 703-318-4646
E-mail: mice@cpmx.saic.com
http://www.epa.gov/sw-846/mice.htm
Ray Anderson, Contractor

6101 Minority Energy Information Clearinghouse
Office of Minority Economic Impact/US Energy Dept.
100 Independence Ave SW 202-586-8698
Forrestal Building, Room 5B-110 800-543-2325
Washington, DC 20585
Effie A Young, Officer

6102 Montana Natural Resource Information System
Montana State Library
1515 East 6th Avenue 406-444-3115
Helena, MT 59620 Fax: 406-444-5612
E-mail: msl.state.mt.us
Alan Cox

6103 National Air Toxics Information Clearinghouse
US EPA
Mail Drop 13 919-541-3586
Office of Air Quality and Standards Fax: 919-541-7674
Research Triangle Park, NC 27709
Vasu Kilaru, Database Administrator

6104 National Capital Poison Center
Georgetown Univertisy Hospital
3201 New Mexico Avenue 202-362-3867
Suite 310
Washington, DC 20016

6105 National Center for Biotechnology Information
National Library of Medicine 301-496-2475
Building 38A, Room 8N805 Fax: 301-480-9241
Bethseda, MD 20894 E-mail: info@ncbi.nlm.nih.gov
http://www.ncbi.nlm.nih.gov

The National center for Biotechnology Information creates public databases, conducts research in computational biology, develops software tools for analyzing genome data, and dissemanates biomedical information, all for the betterunderstanding of molecular processes affecting human health and disease.

6106 National Ground Water Information Center
601 Dempsey Road 800-551-7379
Westerville, OH 43081 800-242-4965
Fax: 614-898-7786
Kevin McCray, Assistant Executive Director

6107 National Pesticide Information Retrieval System
1231 Cumberland Avenue 317-494-7309
Suite A Fax: 317-494-9727
West Lafayette, IN 4706
Virginia Walters

6108 National Pesticide Telecommunications Network
Preventive Medicine & Community Health
Texas Tech University 806-858-7378
Sciences Center 800-858-PEST
Lubbock, TX 79430 Fax: 806-743-3094
Frank L Davido

6109 National Radon Hotline
National Safety Concil
1025 Connecticut Avenue NW 202-293-2270
#1200 800-767-7236
Washington, DC 20036 Fax: 202-293-0032
E-mail: airqual@nsc.org
http://www.nsu.org/issues/radon/index.htm

Provides information on radon and other indoor air quality issues through various toll-free hotlines and publications.
Kristin Marstiller, Senior Program Manager

6110 National Renewable Energy Laboratory
Technical Inquiry Service
1617 Cole Boulevard 303-275-4099
Golden, CO 80401
Steve Rubin, Manager

6111 National Response Center
US Coast Guard
2100 2nd Street SW 202-267-2675
Room 2611 800-424-8802
Washington, DC 20593 Fax: 202-267-2181
Commander David Beach

6112 National Small Flows Clearinghouse
West Virginia University
NRCCE Building, Evandale Drive 304-293-4191
PO Box 6064 800-624-8301
Morgantown, WV 26506 Fax: 304-293-3161
E-mail: nsfc_orders@mail.nesc.wvu.edu
http://www.nsfc.wvu.edu
Nonprofit national source of information about small flows technologies-those systems that have fewer than one million gallons of wastewater flowing through them per day-ranging from individual septic systems to small sewage treatmentplants. Offers more than 450 free and low-cost educational products, a toll-free technical assistance hotline, five computer databases, two free publications and an online discussion group.
Peter Casey, NSFC Program Coordinator
Jen Hause, NSFC Engineering Scientist

6113 New York State Department of Environmental Conservation
625 Broadway 518-402-8013
Pollution Prevention Unit
Albany, NY 12233
John E Iannotti, PE

6114 Northeast Multi-Media Pollution Prevention
Northeast Waste Management Officials Association
85 Merrimac Street 617-367-8558
Boston, MA 02114
Terri Goldberg, Program Manager

6115 Nuclear Information and Resource Service
6930 Carroll Avenue 301-270-6477
Suite 340 Fax: 301-270-4291
Tacoma Park, MD 20912 E-mail: nirsnet@nirs.org
http://www.nirs.org
NIRS is the information and networking center for citizens and environmental organizations concerned about nuclear power, radioactive waste, radiation, and sustainable energy issues.
Michael Mariotte, Executive Director

6116 OTS Chemical Assessment Desk
401 M Street SW 202-260-3583
(TS-778)
Washington, DC 20460
Terry O'Bryan, Executive Officer

6117 Pesticide Action Network North America
49 Powell Street 415-981-1771
Suite 500 Fax: 415-981-1991
San Francisco, CA 94102
Kathryn Gilje, Executive Director

6118 Powder River Basin Resource Council
Energy Convertation Education Committee
23 North Scott 307-672-5809
Sheridan, WY 82801
Jill Morrision, Organizer

6119 Public Information Center
US EPA
401 M Street SW 202-260-7751
PM-211B
Washington, DC 20460
Alison Cook, Director

6120 RACT/BACT/LAER Clearinghouse
Office of Air Quality Planning
Emissions Standards Division 919-541-0800
MD-13 Fax: 919-541-0072
Research Triangle Park, NC 27709
Bob Blaszczak, ESD

6121 Rachel Carson Council
8940 Jones Mill Road 301-652-1877
Chevy Chase, MD 20815
Dr. Diana Post, Executive Director

6122 Records of Decision System Hotline
Computer Sciences Corporation
401 M Street SW 202-260-3770
Room L101
Washington, DC 20460
Thomas Batts

6123 Risk Communication Hotline
US EPA
401 M Street SW 202-260-5606
W Tower, Room 425 Fax: 202-260-9757
Washington, DC 20460
Ernestine Thomas

6124 Small Business Ombudsman Clearinghouse
1200 Pennsylvania Avenue NW 202-566-2075
Washington, DC 20460 800-368-5888
Fax: 202-566-1505
E-mail: rogers.joanb@epa.gov
http://www.epa.gov/sbo OR www.smallbiz-envirweb.org
Also: Hotline US EPA Office of Small Business Programs, Asbestos and Small Business Ombudsman Program. The EPA Asbestos and Small Business Ombusdman (ASBO) helps the EPA responsibly protect the environment and human health througheconomic and compliance assistance services to small businesses.
Joan B Rogers, ASBO Ombudsman

6125 Solid Waste Information Clearinghouse and Hotline
1100 Wayne Avenue, Suite 700 800-467-9262
PO Box 7219 Fax: 301-589-7068
Silver Spring, MD 20907 E-mail: tvondeak@swana.org
http://www.swana.org
Todd von Deak, Dir Marketing/Member Service

6126 Stratospheric Ozone Information Hotline
US Environmental Protection Agency
1200 Pennsylvania Avenue NW 202-343-9210
Washington, DC 20460 800-296-1996
Fax: 202-343-2363
E-mail: miles.louise@epa.gov
http://www.epa.gov/ozone

6127 Sustainable Buildings Industry Council
1112 16th Street NW 202-628-7400
Suite 240 Fax: 202-393-5043
Washington, DC 20036 E-mail: SBIC@SBICouncil.org
http://www.sbicouncil.org
Helen English, Executive Director

6128 TNN Bulletin Board System
Office of Air Quality Planning
Standards Tech Transfer Network 919-541-5616
Research Triangle Park, NC 27709 Fax: 919-541-0824
Hersch Rorex, System Manager

6129 TSCA Assistance Information Service Hotline
Environmental Assistance Division
1200 Pennsylvania Avenue NW 202-554-1404
Mail Code 74080 Fax: 202-554-5603
Washington, DC 20460 E-mail: tsca-hotline@epamail.epa.gov

The information service furnishes TSCA regulation information to the chemical industry, labor and trade organization, environmental groups and the general public. Technical as well as general information is available.
John Alter, Primary EPA

6130 Toxicology Information Response Center
Oak Ridge National Laboratory
1060 Commerce Park 865-574-4160
MS-6480 Fax: 865-574-0595
Oak Ridge, TN 37831 http://www.ornl.gov
Thomas Mason, Director

6131 Toxnet
6707 Democracy Boulevard http://toxnet.nlm.nih.gov
2 Democracy Plaza, Suite 510
Bethesda, MD 20892
TOXNET offers a high quality database, some scientifically peer-reviewed, in an easy to use interface, and includes links to additional sources of dat related toxicology and environmental health. An array of information to inform thepublic and the scientific community about environmental hazards. TOXNET is a product of the National Library of Medicine's Toxicology and Environmental Infromation Program.

6132 US Global Change Data and Information System
61 Route 9w 914-365-8930
PO Box 1000 Fax: 914-365-8922
Palisades, NY 10964 http://globalchange.gov

6133 Waste Exchange Clearinghouse
University of Michigan
400 Ann Street NW 616-363-3262
Number 201-A
Grand Rapids, MI 49504
Jeffery L Duphin

6134 Wastewater Treatment Information Exhange
National Small Flows Clearinghouse
West Virginia University 800-624-8301
PO Box 6064 Fax: 304-293-3161
Morgantown, WV 56506
Loukis Kissonergis

6135 Wetlands Protection Hotline
Geological Resource Consultants
1555 Wilson Boulevard 703-527-5190
Suite 500 800-832-7828
Arlington, VA 22209
John Ruffing

6136 White Lung Association
PO Box 1483 410-243-5864
Baltimore, MD 21203 Fax: 410-243-5892
James Fite, Executive Director

6137 Wisconsin Energy Information Clearinghouse
Wisconsin Division of Energy
101 East Wilson Street 608-266-8234
Madison, WI 53702 Fax: 608-267-6931
E-mail: heat@wisconsin.gov
http://www.doa.state.wi.us/energy/
The Division of Energy Services administers the Wisconsin Home Energy Assistance Program, the Wisconsin Weatherization Program, and the Lead Hazard Reduction Program.
Judy Ziewacz, State Energy Office Director

Videos

Environmental

6138 Acid Rain: A North American Challenge
National Film Board of Canada
1123 Broadway
Suite 307
New York, NY 10010
212-629-8890
Fax: 212-629-8502
E-mail: j.sirabella@nfb.ca
http://www.nfb.ca
Summarizes what we know today about the causes and effect of the menace of acid rain.

6139 Adventures of the Little Koala & Friends
Family Home Entertaiment
15400 Sherman Way
PO Box 10124
Van Nuys, CA 91410
818-908-0303
http://www.familyhome ent.com

6140 Air Pollution: A First Film
2349 Chaffee Drive
St Louis, MO 63146
314-569-0211

6141 Alaska: Outrage at Valdez
Cousteau Collection Volume 1
Facets Media
1517 Fullerton Aveune
Chicago, IL 60614
773-281-4114
http://www.centerstage.net/film/cinemas/

6142 Black Waters
Green Mountain Post Films
PO Box 229
Turner Falls, MA 01376
413-863-4754
Fax: 413-863-8248
E-mail: info@gmpfilms.com
http://www.gmpfilms.com

6143 Bog Ecology
Educational Images
PO Box 3456
Elmira, NY 14905
607-732-1090
800-527-4264
Fax: 607-732-1183
E mail: info@edimages.com
http://www.educationalimages.com
Charles R Belinky PhD, CEO

6144 Captain Planet & the Planeteers: Toxic Terror
Turner Home Entertainment Company
1 CNN N Tower
12th Floor
Atlanta, GA 30348
404-827-1700
http://www.turner.com

6145 Carnivores
Walt Disney Home Video
500 S Buena Vista Street
Burbank, CA 91521
818-562-3560
http://www.disneyvideos.com

6146 Chelyabinsk: The Most Contaminated Spot on the Planet
Filmakers Library
124 E 40th Street
New York, NY 10016
212-808-4980
Fax: 212-808-4983
E-mail: info@filmakers.com
http://www.filmakers.com
The story of the Chelyabinsk atomic weapons complex, including a 1957 explosion, 1967 storm that spread radioactive dust, and the dumping of radioactive waste into a water-supply river.
Linda Gottesman, Co-President

6147 Chemical Kids
Filmakers Library
124 E 40th Street
New York, NY 10016
212-808-4980
Fax: 212-808-4983
E-mail: info@filmakers.com
http://www.filmakers.com
Alarming facts about man-made chemicals in food and water, especially how children are the most affected.
Linda Gottesman, Co-President

6148 Children of Chernobyl
Filmakers Library
124 E 40th Street
New York, NY 10016
212-808-4980
Fax: 212-808-4983
E-mail: info@filmakers.com
http://www.filmakers.com
Reveals the tragedy at Chernobyl through exclusive archival film and eyewitness accounts — deception and cover-up on a grand scale.
Linda Gottesman, Co-President

6149 City of the Future
University of California
2176 Shattuck Avenue
Media Center
Berkeley, CA 94704
510-642-0460
http://www.berkley.edu

6150 Clouds of Doubt
Electronics Arts Intermix
536 Braodway
9th Floor
New York, NY 10012
212-966-4605
http://www.eci.org

6151 Cocos Island: Treasure Island
ESPN Home Video
ESPN Plaza
Bristol, CT 06010
860-585-2000
http://www.espn.com

6152 Coral Cities of the Caribbean
Nancy Sefton/Triton Productions
Earthwise Media
PO Box 1223
Poulsbo, WA 98370
360-271-1584
Fax: 360-394-2168
E-mail: info@earthwisevideos.com
http://www.earthwisevideos.com
Journey the coral reefs of the Caribbean with the fishes and invertebrates that reside in these coral cities.
Nancy Sefton, Creative Director
Wes Nicholson, Technical Director

6153 Designing the Environment
NETCHE
1800 N 33rd Street
Lincoln, NE 68503
402-472-3611
Fax: 402-472-1785
E-mail: netche@unl.edu
http://www.netdb.unl.edu/netchevideo

6154 Disappearance of the Great Rainforest
Arthur Mokin Productions
PO Box 1866
Santa Rosa, CA 95402
707-542-4868
800-238-4868

6155 Dolphin
Media Guild
PO Box 910534
San Diego, CA 92191
858-755-9191
Fax: 858-755-4931

6156 Earth Summit: What Next?
EcuFilm
810 12th Avenue S
Nashville, TN 37203
615-242-6277
800-251-4091
http://www.ecufilm.com

6157 Earth at Risk Environmental Series
Library Video Company
PO Box 580
Wunnewood, PA 19096
610-645-4000
800-843-3620
Fax: 610-645-4040
E-mail: comments@libraryvideo.com
http://www.libraryvideo.com

6158 Earth's Physical Resources
Media Guild
PO Box 910534
San Diego, CA 92191
858-755-9191
Fax: 858-755-4931

6159 Earthwise Media
PO Box 1223
Poulsbo, WA 98370
360-271-1584
Fax: 360-394-2168
E-mail: info@earthwisevideos.com
http://www.earthwisevideos.com
Production company specializing in environmental educational videos, multi-media presentations and computer aided learning tools.
Wes Nicholson, Technical Director

6160 Ecological Realities: Natural Laws at Work
University of California
2176 Shattuck Avenue
Berkeley, CA 94704
510-642-0460

6161 Educational Images
PO Box 3456
Elmira, NY 14905
607-732-1090
800-527-4264
Fax: 607-732-1183
E-mail: info@edimages.com
http://www.educationalimages.com
Produces educational CD ROMs, slide sets and videos on ecology, geology, aquatic life and related biological science and medical topics, plus stock photos for digital and print.
Charles R Belinky PhD, CEO

6162 Effluents of Affluence
University of Michigan
Film Video Library
919 S University Avenue, Room 207
Ann Arbor, MI 48109
734-764-5360
Fax: 734-764-6849
E-mail: ful.office@umich.edu
http://www.lib.umich.edu

6163 Elephant Boy
HBO Home Video
1114 6th Avenue
New York, NY 10036
212-512-7400
http://www.hbohomevideo.com

6164 Empire of the Red Bear
Discovery Home Entertainmnet
7700 Wisconsin Avenue
Bethesda, MD 20814
301-986-1999
E-mail: letters@discovery.com
http://www.discovery.com

6165 Endangered Species: Massasauga Rattler and Bog Turtle
Educational Images
PO Box 3456
Elmira, NY 14905
607-732-1090
800-527-4264
Fax: 607-732-1183
E-mail: info@edimages.com
http://www.educationalimages.com
Charles R Belinky PhD, CEO

6166 Enemies of the Oak
Carolina Biological Supply Company
2700 York Road
Burlington, NC 27215
919-584-0381
800-334-5551
E-mail: carolina@carolina.com
http://www.carolina.com

6167 Energetics of Life
The Media Guild
PO Box 910534
San Diego, CA 92191
858-755-9191
Fax: 858-755-4931

6168 Energy Now
Educational Images
PO Box 3456
Elmira, NY 14905
607-732-1090
800-527-4264
Fax: 607-732-1183
E-mail: info@edimages.com
http://www.educationalimages.com
Charles R Belinky PhD, CEO

6169 Energy to Go Around
The Media Guild
PO Box 910534
San Diego, CA 92191
858-755-9191
Fax: 858-755-4931

6170 Energy: The Alternatives
The Media Guild
PO Box 910534
San Diego, CA 92191
858-755-9191
Fax: 858-755-4931

6171 Everglades Region: An Ecological Study
The Media Guild
PO Box 910534
San Diego, CA 92191
858-755-9191
Fax: 858-755-4931

6172 Exploring the Forest
Alfred Higgins Productions
6350 Laurel Canyon Boulevard
North Hollywood, CA 91606
818-762-3300
Fax: 818-762-8223
http://www.alfredhigginsprod.com

6173 Fascinating World of Forestry
Educational Images
PO Box 3456
Elmira, NY 14905
607-732-1090
800-527-4264
Fax: 607-732-1183
E-mail: info@edimages.com
http://www.educationalimages.com
Charles R Belinky PhD, CEO

6174 Flag: The Story of the White White-Tailed Deer
Educational Images
PO Box 3456
Elmira, NY 14905
607-732-1090
800-527-4264
Fax: 607-732-1183
E-mail: info@edimages.com
http://www.educationalimages.com
Charles R Belinky PhD, CEO

6175 Florida Bay and the Everglades
Educational Images
PO Box 3456
Elmira, NY 14905
607-732-1090
800-527-4264
Fax: 607-732-1183
E-mail: info@edimages.com
http://www.educationalimages.com
Charles R Belinky PhD, CEO

6176 Food from the Rainforest
The Media Guild
PO Box 910534
San Diego, CA 92191
858-755-9191
Fax: 858-755-4931

6177 Forms of Energy
Educational Images
PO Box 3456
Elmira, NY 14905
607-732-1090
800-527-4264
Fax: 607-732-1183
E-mail: info@edimages.com
http://www.educationalimages.com
Charles R Belinky PhD, CEO

6178 Freshwater and Saltwater Marshes
Educational Images
PO Box 3456
Elmira, NY 14905
607-732-1090
800-527-4264
Fax: 607-732-1183
E-mail: info@edimages.com
http://www.educationalimages.com
Charles R Belinky PhD, CEO

6179 GPN Educationl Media
1407 Fleet Street
Baltimore, MD 21231
800-228-4630
Fax: 800-306-2330
E-mail: inquiry@shopgpn.com
http://www.shopgpn.com

Produces educational media - video, CD-ROM, DVD, Internet-for-16. Free previews available on line and on video.

Jen Haus, VP Marketing

6180 Great American Woodlots
Cornell University
8 Business & Technology Park
Ithaca, NY 14850
607-255-2091
607-255-9946
http://www.cornell.edu

6181 Green TV
1125 Hayes Street
San Francisco, CA 94117
415-255-4797
Fax: 415-255-4664
E-mail: fgreen@greentv.org
http://www.greentv.org

Video production company that combines environmental journalism with dramatic wildlife and natural history footage.
Frank Green, Owner/President

6182 Guardians of the Cliff: The Peregrine Falcon Story
Educational Images
PO Box 3456
Elmira, NY 14905
607-732-1090
800 527-4264
Fax: 607-732-1183
E-mail: info@edimages.com
http://www.educationalimages.com

Charles R Belinky PhD, CEO

6183 Happy Campers with Miss Shirley & Friends
Kids Express
1106 South Truckee Way
Aurora, CO 80017
888-492-5437
E-mail: missshirleybowers@msn.com
http://www.kids-express.com

6184 I Walk in the Desert
Educational Images
PO Box 3456
Elmira, NY 14905
607-732-1090
800-527-4264
Fax: 607-732-1183
E-mail: info@edimages.com
http://www.educationalimages.com

Charles R Belinky PhD, CEO

6185 Joe Albert's Fox Hunt
Education Development Center
55 Chapel Street
Newton, MA 02160
617-969-7100
800-225-4276
E-mail: www@edc.org
http://www.edc.org

6186 John Muir
Educational Images
PO Box 3456
Elmira, NY 14905
607-732-1090
800-527-4264
Fax: 607-732-1183
E-mail: info@edimages.com
http://www.educationalimages.com

Charles R Belinky PhD, CEO

6187 Legacy of an Oil Spill
Media Guild
PO Box 910534
San Diego, CA 92191
858-755-9191
800-886-9191
Fax: 858-755-4931
E-mail: info@mediaguild.com
http://www.mediaguild.com

Documenting the 1989 oil spill into Alaska's Prince William Sound which damaged 1,000 miles of shoreline and killed hundreds of thousands of wildlife. This video looks at the long-term effects of the spill on several species.
Ruth Pipitone

6188 Life on a Rocky Shore
Earthwise Media
PO Box 1223
Poulsbo, WA 98370
360-271-1584
Fax: 360-394-2168
E-mail: info@earthwisevideos.com
http://www.earthwisevideos.com

An introduction to the plants and animals of the Pacific Northwest's rich Intertidal Zone. The self-paced presentation uses 100 photos, video clips and graphics to illustrate the story of life in the Zone. Learn about the tides, changing bands of life, and adaptation of life in the Zone. Discusses marine biology and includes teacher's guide for grades 6-12, with review, vocabulary and quizzes.

Wes Nicholson, Technical Director & Owner

6189 Manatees: A Living Resource
Educational Images
PO Box 3456
Elmira, NY 14905
607-732-1090
800-527-4264
Fax: 607-732-1183
E-mail: info@edimages.com
http://www.educationalimages.com

Charles R Belinky PhD, CEO

6190 Mitzi A Da Si: A Visit to Yellowstone National Park
Educational Images
PO Box 3456
Elmira, NY 14905
607-732-1090
800-527-4264
Fax: 607-732-1183
E-mail: info@edimages.com
http://www.educationalimages.com

Charles R Belinky PhD, CEO

6191 Modeling Photosynthesis
Media Guild
PO Box 910534
San Diego, CA 92191
858-755-9191
Fax: 858-755-4931

6192 Our Precious Environment
Educational Images
PO Box 3456
Elmira, NY 14905
607-732-1090
800-527-4264
Fax: 607-732-1183
E-mail: info@edimages.com
http://www.educationalimages.com

Charles R Belinky PhD, CEO

6193 RMC Medical Inc
3019 Darnell Road
Philadephia, PA 19154
215-824-4100
800-332-0672
Fax: 215-824-1371
E-mail: rmcmedical@cs.com
http://www.rmcmedical.com

Manufacturer of decontamination emergency response equipment.

Lois White, Sales/Marketing Manager

6194 Rainbows in the Sea: A Guide to Earth's Coral Reefs
Earthwise Media
PO Box 1323
Poulsbo, WA 98370
360-271-1584
Fax: 360-394-2168
E-mail: info@earthwisevideos.com
http://www.earthwisevideos.com

Showcases the wide variety of colorful fish and invertebrates living in coral reefs, how they form and what they need to blossom. Includes teacher's guide and recommended by the National Science Teachers Association.
28 minutes
Wes Nicholson, Technical Director

6195 Return of the Dragon
Educational Images
PO Box 3456
Elmira, NY 14905
607-732-1090
800-527-4264
Fax: 607-732-1183
E-mail: info@edimages.com
http://www.educationalimages.com

Charles R Belinky PhD, CEO

6196 Salt Marshes-A Special Resource
Educational Images

PO Box 3456
Elmira, NY 14905
607-732-1090
800-527-4264
Fax: 607-732-1183
E-mail: info@edimages.com
http://www.educationalimages.com

Charles R Belinky PhD, CEO

6197 Sand Dune Ecology and Formation
Educational Images
PO Box 3456
Elmira, NY 14905
607-732-1090
800-527-4264
Fax: 607-732-1183
E-mail: info@edimages.com
http://www.educationalimages.com

Charles R Belinky PhD, CEO

6198 Seals
Media Guild
PO Box 910534
San Diego, CA 92191
858-755-9191
Fax: 858-755-4931

6199 Song of the Salish Sea: A Natural History of Northwest Waters
Earthwise Media
PO Box 1323
Poulsbo, WA 98370
360-271-1584
Fax: 360-394-2168
E-mail: info@earthwisevideos.com
http://www.earthwisevideos.com

Examines the fragile habitats that make up the Strait of Georgia, Strait of Juan de Fuca and Puget Sound. Includes teacher's guide, Puget Sound Beach Guide, Kids for Puget Sound Passport, and curriculums for grades 6-12.
45 minutes
Wes Nicholson, Technical Director

6200 Survey of Environment
Educational Images
PO Box 3456
Elmira, NY 14905
607-732-1090
800-527-4264
Fax: 607-732-1183
E-mail: info@edimages.com
http://www.educationalimages.com

Charles R Belinky PhD, CEO

6201 The World Between the Tides: A Guide to Pacific Rocky Shores
Earthwise Media
PO Box 1323
Poulsbo, WA 98370
360-271-1584
Fax: 360-394-2168
E-mail: info@earthwisevideos.com
http://www.earthwisevideos.com

A narrated journey along the intertidal area that examines harsh conditions, and how animals and plants have adapted. Received the National Communicator Award of Distinction and praise from the NW Aquatic & Marine Educators. Includesteacher's guide.
23 minutes
Wes Nicholson, Technical Director

6202 Tropical Rainforest
The Media Guild
PO Box 910534
San Diego, CA 92191
858-755-9191
Fax: 858-755-4931

6203 Tropical Rainforests Under Fire
Educational Images
PO Box 3456
Elmira, NY 14905
607-732-1090
800-527-4264
Fax: 607-732-1183
E-mail: info@edimages.com
http://www.educationalimages.com

Charles R Belinky PhD, CEO

6204 Warm-Blooded Sea Mammals of the Deep
Cousteau Odyssey Volume 10
Warner Home Video
4000 Warner Boulevard
Burbank, CA 91522
818-954-6000
http://www.store.warnervideo.com

6205 Warming Warning
Media Guild
PO Box 910534
San Diego, CA 92191
858-755-9191
Fax: 858-755-4931

6206 Water Resources Videos
Educational Images
PO Box 3456
Elmira, NY 14905
607-732-1090
800-527-4264
Fax: 607-732-1183
E-mail: info@edimages.com
http://www.educationalimages.com

Charles R Belinky PhD, CEO

6207 Watershed: Canada's Threatened Rainforest
Media Guild
PO Box 910534
San Diego, CA 92191
858-755-9191
800-886-9191
Fax: 858-755-4931
E-mail: info@mediaguild.com
http://www.mediaguild.com

Chronicles the expedition to the Pacific Coast's rainforest, including environmental issues, complex ecosystems, and efforts of conservationists.
Ruth Pipitone

6208 Wetlands: Development, Progress, Environmental Protection under Changing Law
American Law Institute
4025 Chestnut Street
Philadelphia, PA 19104
215-243-1600
800-CLE-NEWS
Fax: 215-243-1664
E-mail: jmendicino@ali.org
http://www.ali.org

6209 Whales
Cousteau Undersea World Volume 10
Churchill Media
12210 Nebraska Avenue
Los Angeles, CA 90025
310-207-6600
Fax: 310-207-1330

6210 Wilderness Video
New Nature In Motion: Yellowstone, Yosemite, Etc.
PO Box 3150
Ashland, OR 97520
541-488-9363
Fax: 541-488-9363
E-mail: Bob@Wildernessvideo.com
http://www.wildernessvideo.com

Collection of high definition stock footage, including nature, national parks, and cities.

Bob Glusic, Owner

6211 Windrifters: The Bald Eagle Story
Educational Images
PO Box 3456
Elmira, NY 14905
607-732-1090
800-527-4264
Fax: 607-732-1183
E-mail: info@edimages.com
http://www.educationalimages.com

Charles R Belinky PhD, CEO

Green Product Catalogs

General

6212 **Acorn Designs**
5066 Mott Evans Road
Trumansburg, NY 14886
800-299-3997
Fax: 607-387-5609
E-mail: info@acorndesigns.org
http://www.acorndesigns.org

Totes and other items with wildlife and nature themes; high post-consumer recycled paper; images from nature as note cards and journals; organic cotton tees. Art and images represent the works of over 30 artists.
Steve Sierigk, Owner

6213 **Alexandra Avery Purely Natural Body Care**
4717 SE Belmont Street
Portland, OR 97215
503-236-5926
800-669-1863
Fax: 503-234-7272
E-mail: aavery42@earthlink.net

100% natural and cruelty free aromatherapy products for face and body care.
Alexandra Avery, President

6214 **American Resources Group**
374 Maple Avenue
Suite 310
Vienna, VA 22180
703-255-2700
Fax: 703-281-9200
E-mail: info@american-resources.org
http://www.american-resources.org

Provides a listing of resources and links for environmental research centers, associations and consulting engineers.
Keith A Argow PhD, President

6215 **Artistic Video**
87 Tyler Avenue
Sound Beach, NY 11789
631-744-5999
888-982-4244
Fax: 631-744-5993
E-mail: bobklien@movementsofmagic.com
http://www.movementsofmagic.com

Instructional videos and DVDs on health and fitness, alternative healing, children's programs about animals, free interactive section with articles, discussion forums, video clips, classes, instructions, Tai-Chi and other nature oriented cultures and practices.
Bob Klein, President

6216 **BDM Holdings**
7915 Jones Branch Drive
McLean, VA 22102
703-848-5000
Bennie Dibona, VP Engineering/Environment

6217 **Balance of Nature**
Unviersity of Chicago Press
1427 East 60th Street
Chicago, IL 60637
773-702-7700
Fax: 773-702-9756
http://www.press.chicago.edu

6218 **Bio-Sun Systems**
RR 2 Box 134A
Millerton, PA 16936
570-527-2200
800-847-8840
Fax: 570-537-6200
E-mail: biosun@npacc.net
http://www.bio-sun.com

Composting toilets and modular restrooms.
Donna White, President
Al White, VP

6219 **Cotton Clouds**
5176 S 14th Avenue
Safford, AZ 85546
520-428-7000
Fax: 520-428-6630
E-mail: cottonclouds@az.org

Yarn, patterns, books, video's, kit for weaving crochet, knitting and spinning.

6220 **Earth Options**
Solar Electric Engineering
117 Morris Street
Sebastopol, CA 95472
707-824-4150
882-198-1986
Fax: 707-542-4358
http://882-198-1986

Environmental retail products.

6221 **Earth Science**
PO Box 1925
Corona, CA 91718
909-371-7565
800-222-6720
Fax: 909-371-0509
http://800-222-6720

All-natural, environmentally sound skin and hair care products.
Kristine Schoenauer, President

6222 **Eco-Store**
2441 Edgewater Drive
Orlando, FL 32804
407-426-9949
800-556-9949
Fax: 407-649-3148
E-mail: beth@eco-store.com
http://800-556-9949

Environmental home products, gifts, etc.

6223 **Ecology Store**
6928 Queens Boulevard
Flushing, NY 11377
718-446-4444
800-548-9660
Fax: 718-446-9860
http://800-548-9660

Range of environmental products.

6224 **Energy Efficient Environments**
2119 Inverness Lane
Glen View, IL 60025
847-475-3005
800-336-3749
E-mail: info@eeenvironments.com
http://www.eeenvironments.com

Efficient and earth-friendly devices for energy, water and light use.

6225 **Environment Friendly Papers**
Cherry Paper
13520 Liberty Avenue
Jamaica, NY 11419
718-297-3000
Fax: 718-297-2986
E-mail: cherryop@AOL.com

100% recycled gift stationary, with original designs depicting flora and fauna of South Africa and environmental themes.

6226 **Erlander's Natural Products**
Nature's Department Store
2279 Lake Avenue
Altadena, CA 91001
626-797-7004
800-562-8873
Fax: 626-798-2663
E-mail: erlander@webtv.net
http://800-562-8873

Natural olive oil-wine soap; bar and liquid roach killer from herbs, organic red zinfandel wine, 100% organic cotton pillows and mattresses, jewelry - semi-precious and costume, washing compound/non-detergent, sodium sesqui carbonate.
Leatrice Erlander, Co-Owner
Stig Erlander, Co-Owner

6227 **GAIA Clean Earth Products**
PO Box 1906
York, PA 17405
717-840-1638
800-726-5496
Fax: 800-726-5496
E-mail: gaia@blazenet.net
http://800-726-5496

Environmentally-compatible products.
Brian N Hartman, President

6228 **Greenpeace**
564 Mission Street Box 416
San Francisco, CA 94105
510-538-7842
800-326-0959
Fax: 202-462-4517
E-mail: greenpeace@npgear.com
http://800-326-0959

Environmentally and socially responsible apparel, accessories and gifts.

6229 Jason Natural Cosmetics
8468 Warern Drive
Culver City, CA 90232
877-JAS-ON01
Fax: 310-838-9274
E-mail: jnp@jason-natural.com
http://877-JAS-ON01

All natural cosmetics.
Jeffrey Light, President

6230 Look Alive!
Rice Lake Products
100 27th Street NE
Minot, ND 58703
701-857-6357
800-998-7450
Fax: 701-857-6300
E-mail: ricelake@dalotah.com
http://800-998-7450

Environmentally safe movement devices for hunting decoys, as well as bird and pest deterring owls for home garden, boats and businesses.
Virgil Farstad, President

6231 Real Goods
Real Goods Solar
833 West South Boulder Road
Louisville, CO 80027
800-919-2400
http://www.realgoods.com
Source for simple living products designed to balance with a conscious lifestyle. Offers products that reduce energy consumption, from solar panels and wind turbines to complete solar power systems.

6232 Real Goods Trading Company
PO Box 8507
Ukiah, CA 95482
707-744-2100
800-347-0070
Fax: 707-468-9394
http://800-347-0070
Recycled papers, environmental gifts and household goods.

6233 Second Renaissance Books
17 George Washington Plaza
Gaylordsville, CT 06755
800-729-6149
Fax: 860-355-7160
E-mail: inquiries@secondrenaissance.com
http://800-729-6149

Editorially selected books and audio tapes. Complete selection of writing and letters by Ayn Rand.

6234 Sparky Boy Enterprises
1512 Gold Avenue
Bozeman, MT 59715
406-587-5891
800-289-6656
Fax: 406-587-0223
E-mail: ecostoke@mcn.net
http://800-289-6656

Natural products for the home, lawn and garden.
Wayne Vinje, President

6235 Sunrise Lane Products
780 Greenwich Street
New York, NY 10014
212-243-4745
Environmentally safe and cruelty-free products for home and personal care.
Rossella Mocerino, President

6236 The Green Catalog
Advertising Specialty Institute
http://www.asicentral.som

Features products that are friendly to the enviroment, designed to inspire social responsibility.

6237 The Green Life
The Green Life Store
2409 Main Street
Santa Monica, CA 90405
310-392-4702
E-mail: info@thegreenlife.com
http://www.thegreenlifecostore.com

Green products that are the most ecologically friendly available, for home & garden, bed & bath, children, cleaning, office, and pets.
Scott O'Brien, Owner

6238 Williams Distributors
1801 S Cardinal Lane
New Berlin, WI 53151
262-597-9865
All natural products; nutrition, health, home care and personal care, plus water purification systems.
GL Williams, President

SECTION TWO:

STATISTICS
&
RANKINGS

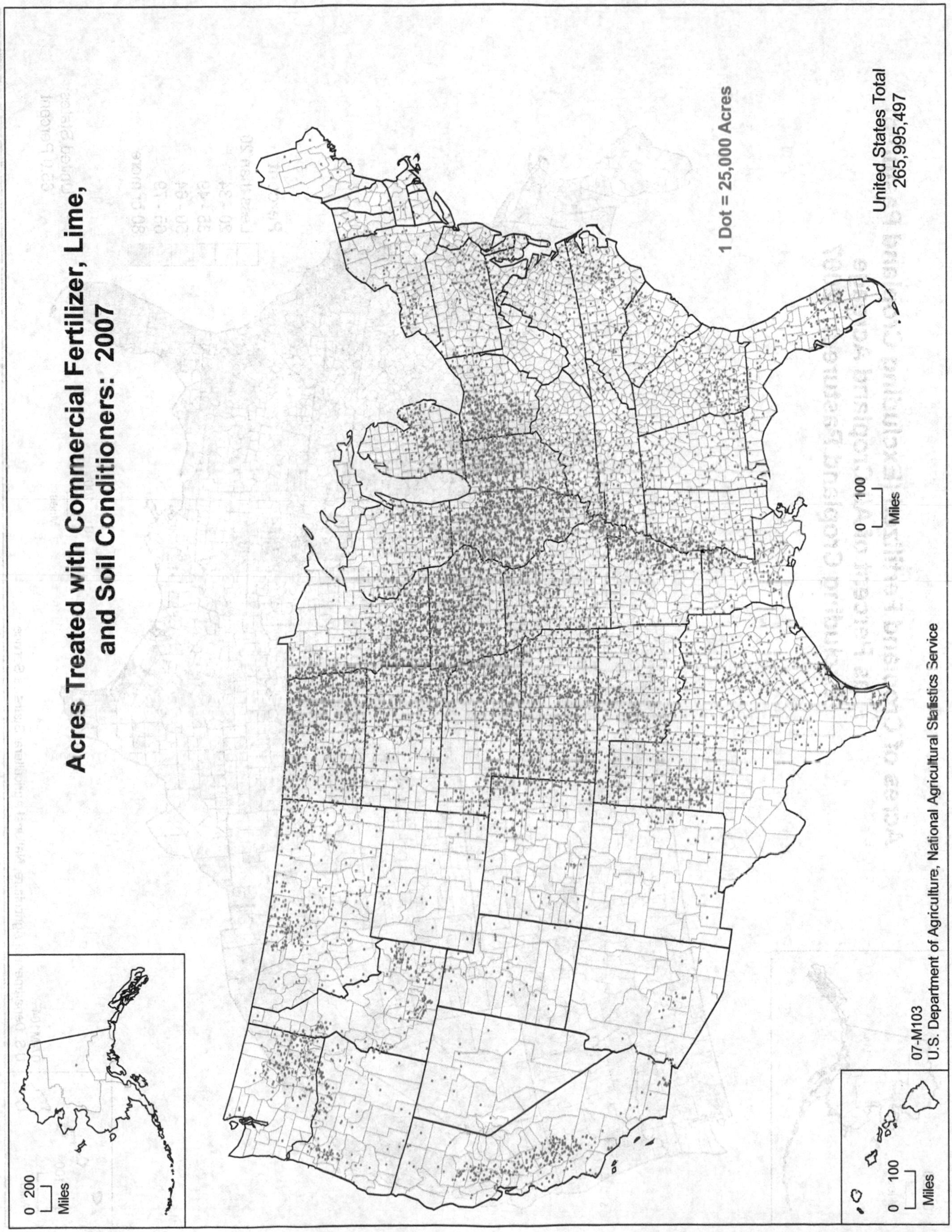
Acres Treated with Commercial Fertilizer, Lime, and Soil Conditioners: 2007
1 Dot = 25,000 Acres
United States Total
265,995,497
0 100
Miles
0 200
Miles
0 100
Miles
07-M103
U.S. Department of Agriculture, National Agricultural Statistics Service

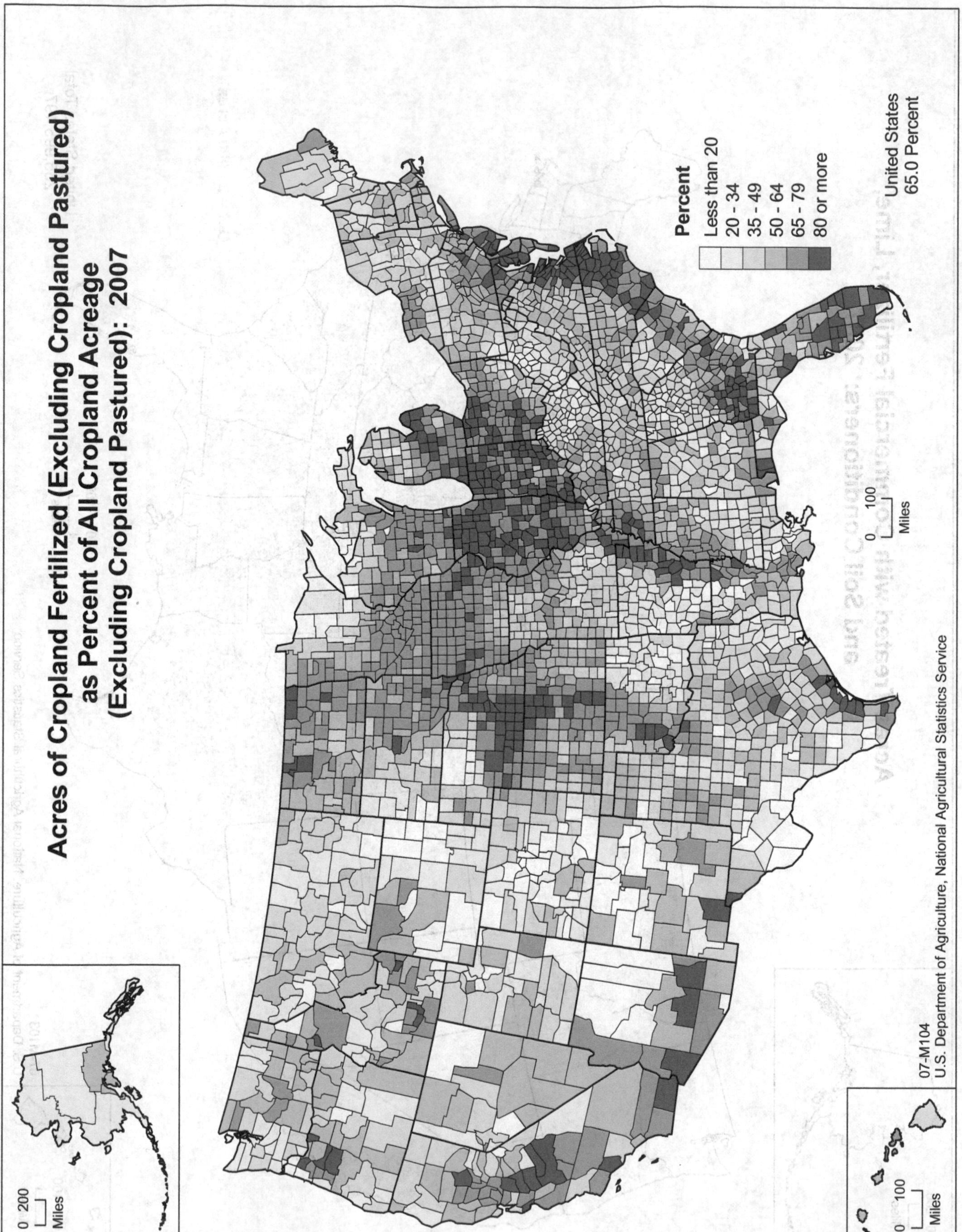
Acres of Cropland Fertilized (Excluding Cropland Pastured)
as Percent of All Cropland Acreage
(Excluding Cropland Pastured): 2007
Percent
Less than 20
20 - 34
35 - 49
50 - 64
65 - 79
80 or more
United States
65.0 Percent
0 100
Miles
0 200
Miles
0 100
Miles
07-M104
U.S. Department of Agriculture, National Agricultural Statistics Service

2007 Census of Agriculture

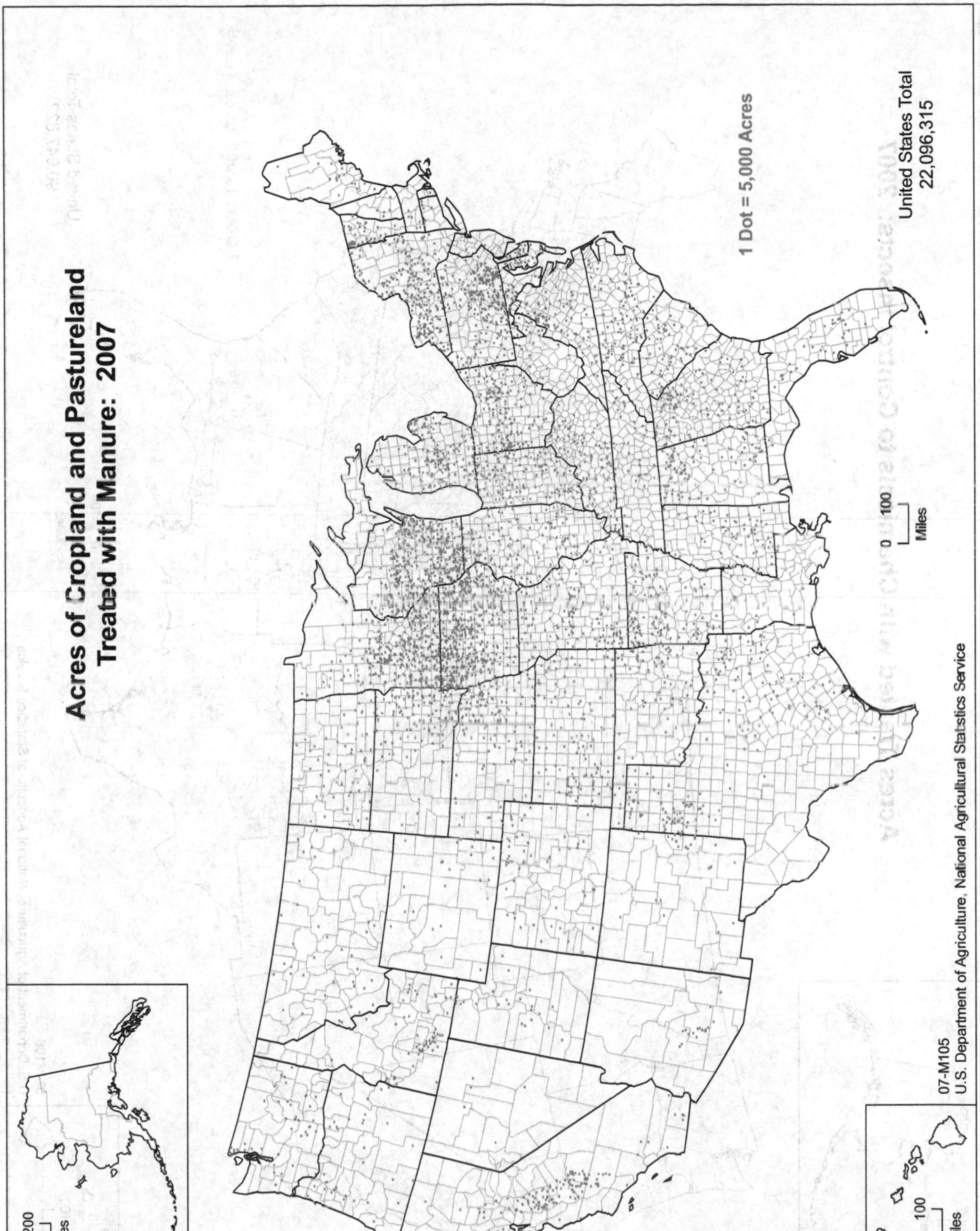

2007 Census of Agriculture

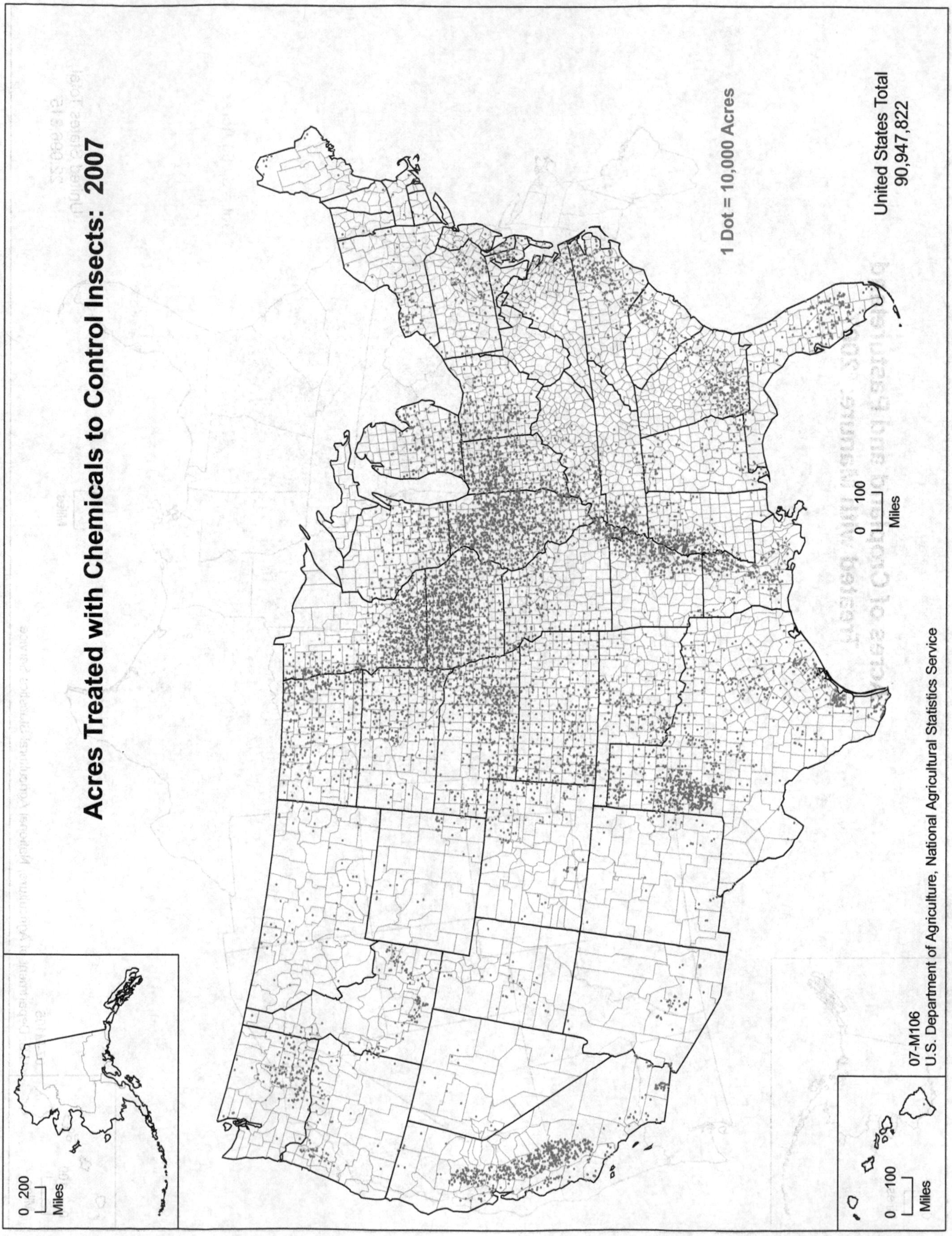

2007 Census of Agriculture

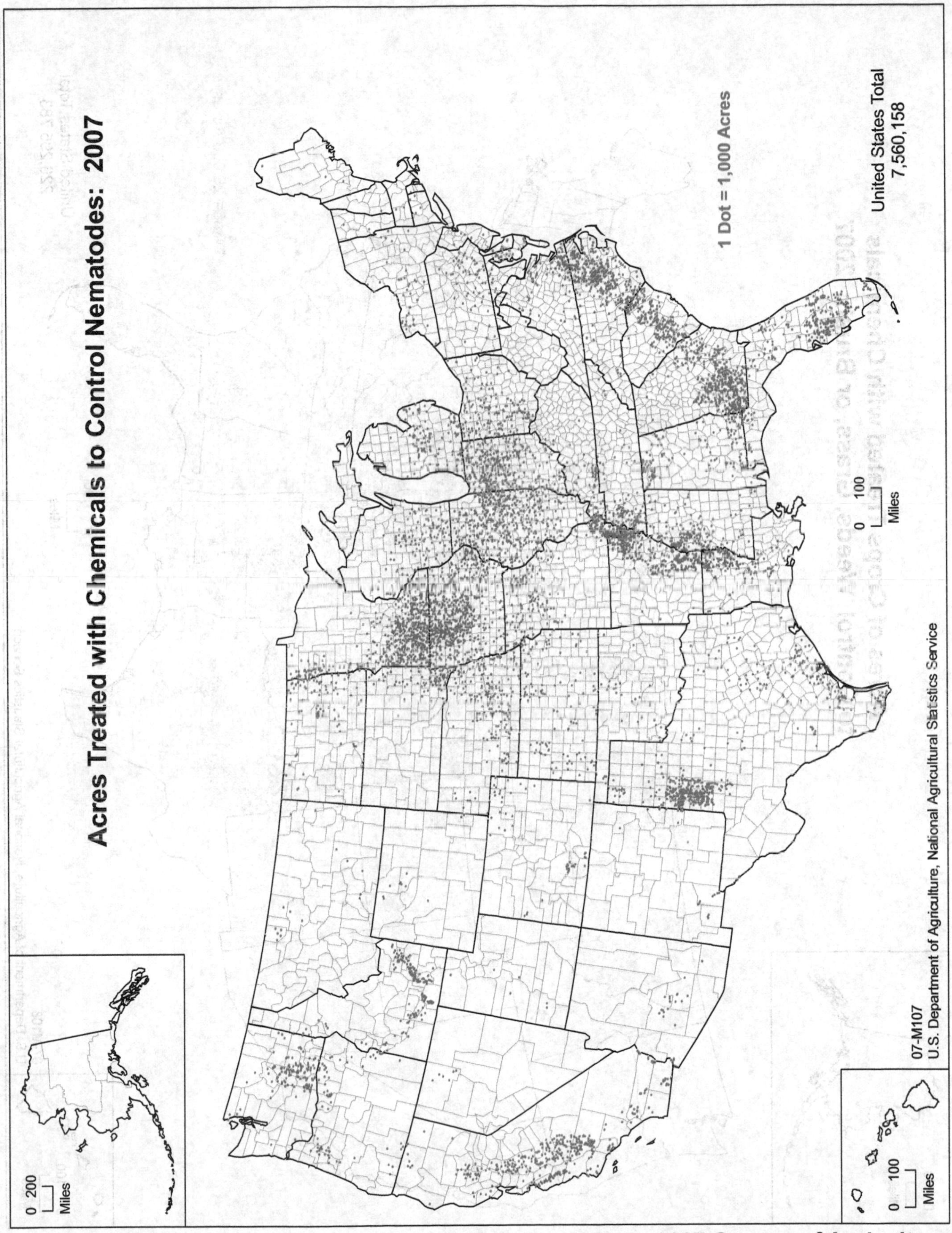

2007 Census of Agriculture

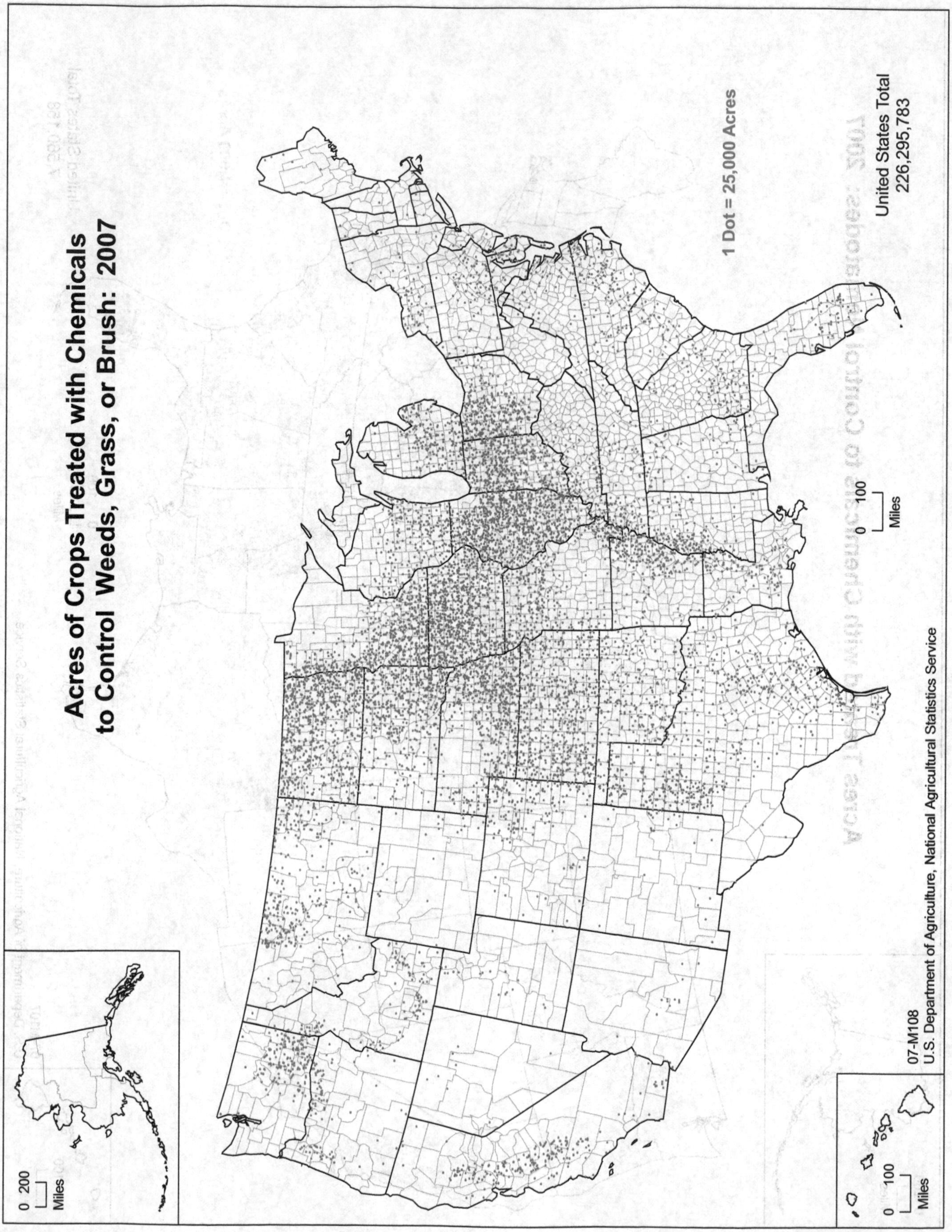

2007 Census of Agriculture

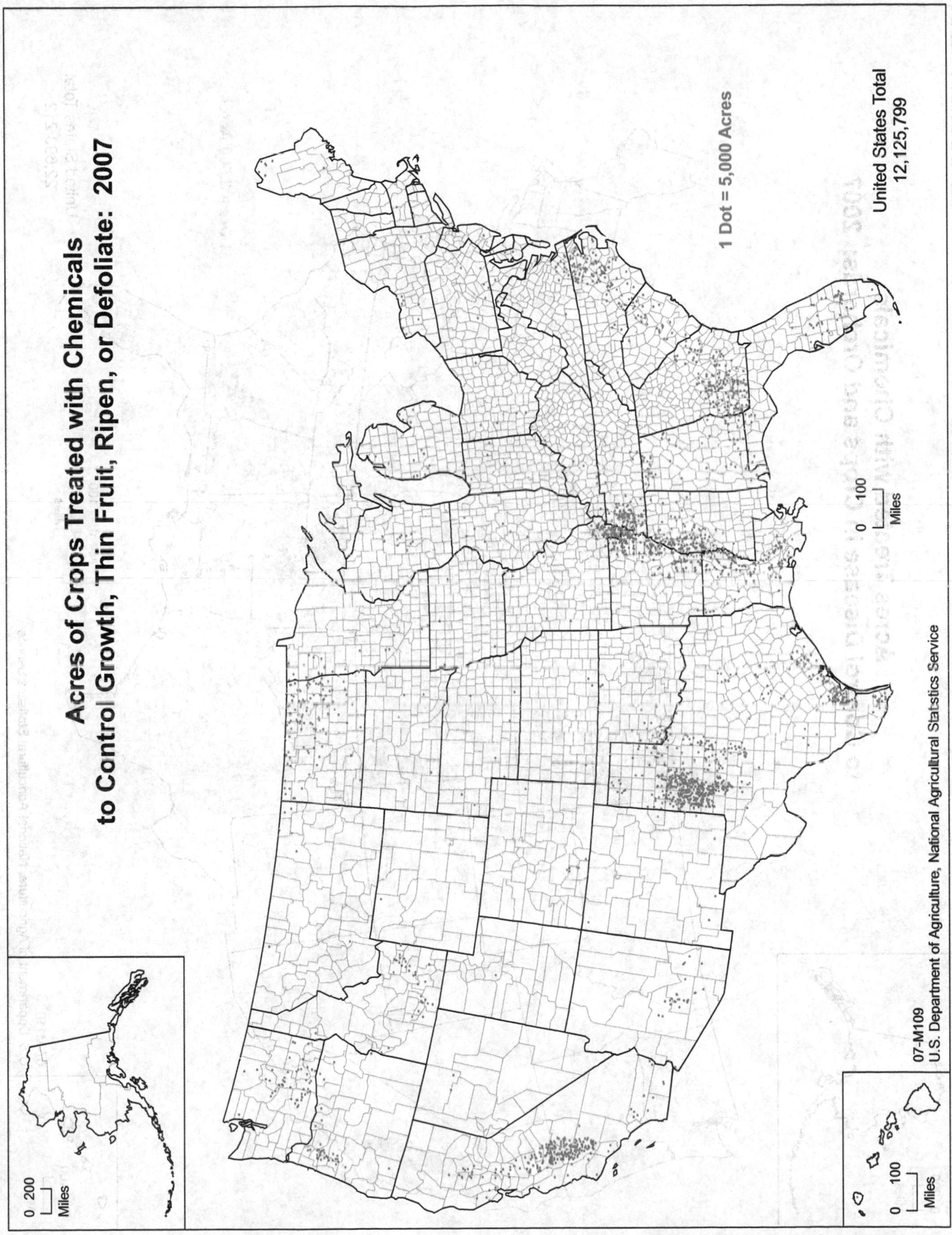
Acres of Crops Treated with Chemicals
to Control Growth, Thin Fruit, Ripen, or Defoliate: 2007
1 Dot = 5,000 Acres
United States Total
12,125,799
0 100
Miles
0 200
Miles
0 100
Miles
07-M109
U.S. Department of Agriculture, National Agricultural Statistics Service

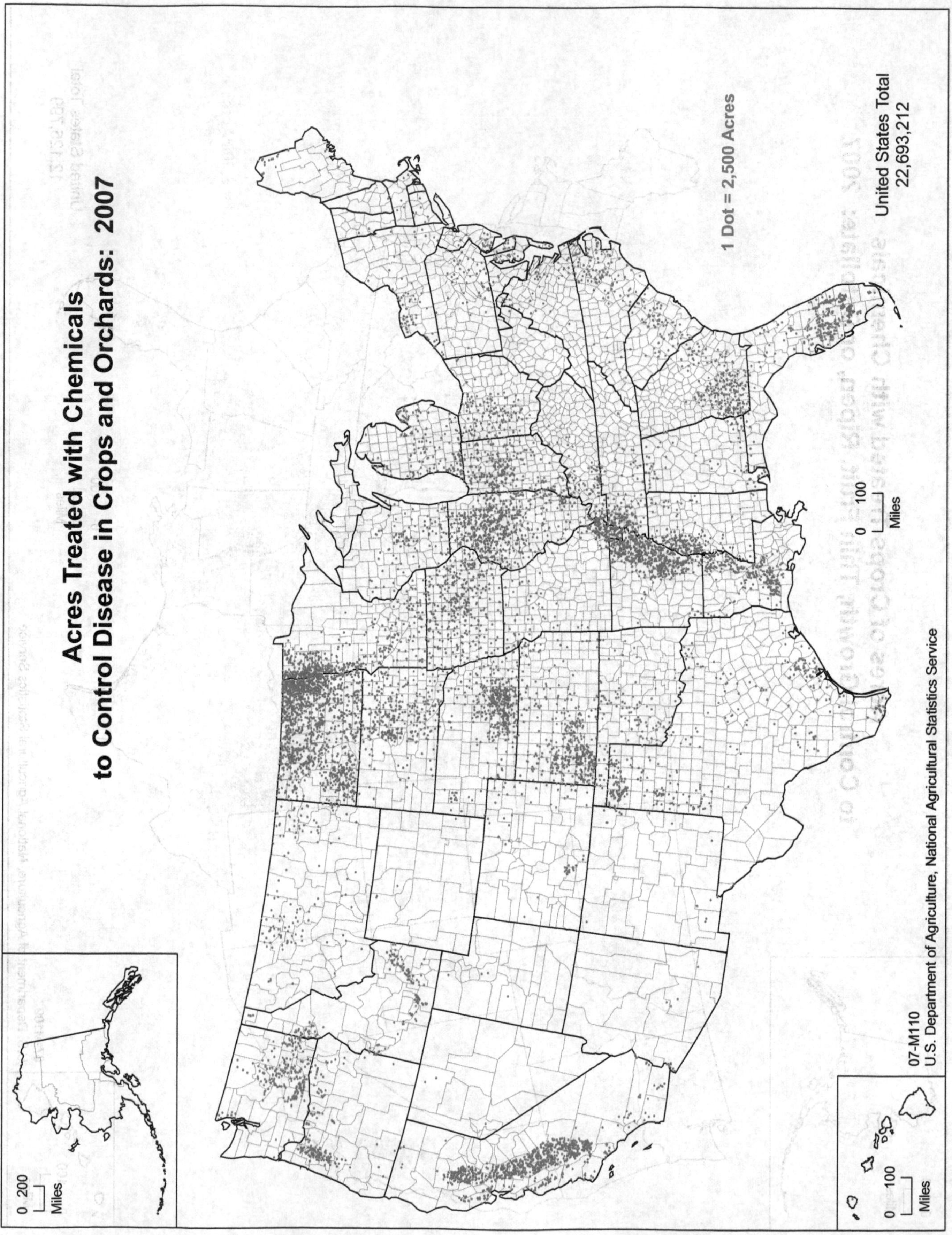

2007 Census of Agriculture

Air Quality Index Report, 2012

Metropolitan Statistical Area	Days with AQI Data	Number of Days when Air Quality was...				AQI Statistics		Number of Days when AQI Pollutant was...					
		Good	Moderate	Unhealthy for Sensitive Groups	Unhealthy or Very Unhealthy	Max	Median	CO	NO_2	O_3	SO_2	$PM_{2.5}$	PM_{10}
Aberdeen, SD	123	104	19	0	0	77	28	0	0	0	0	109	14
Aberdeen, WA	366	348	18	0	0	81	20	0	0	0	0	366	0
Adjuntas, PR	77	74	3	0	0	66	18	0	0	0	0	77	0
Adrian, MI	245	164	67	12	2	161	45	0	0	173	0	72	0
Akron, OH	366	271	94	1	0	140	38.5	21	0	155	108	82	0
Albany, GA	360	254	104	2	0	124	38	0	0	0	0	359	1
Albany-Lebanon, OR	366	319	47	0	0	91	23	0	0	0	0	366	0
Albany-Schenectady-Troy, NY	366	301	63	2	0	119	36.5	0	0	249	0	117	0
Albuquerque, NM	366	141	210	12	3	291	56	0	2	192	0	135	37
Alexandria, LA	362	177	185	0	0	88	52	0	0	0	0	362	0
Allegan, MI	240	163	51	23	3	169	41	0	0	172	0	68	0
Allentown-Bethlehem-Easton, PA-NJ	366	172	186	8	0	149	51.5	0	7	81	11	267	0
Altoona, PA	366	216	142	8	0	137	45	0	0	124	10	230	2
Amarillo, TX	366	281	83	2	0	114	42	0	0	321	0	45	0
Americus, GA	243	232	11	0	0	80	35	0	0	243	0	0	0
Ames, IA	214	193	21	0	0	71	38.5	0	0	214	0	0	0
Anchorage, AK	366	255	106	5	0	127	33	4	0	124	0	176	62
Anderson, IN	352	222	128	2	0	127	45	0	0	128	0	224	0
Anderson, SC	226	210	14	2	0	137	36	0	0	226	0	0	0
Ann Arbor, MI	364	292	56	16	0	140	36.5	0	0	314	0	50	0
Appleton, WI	366	257	102	6	1	150	41	0	0	100	0	200	0
Ardmore, OK	350	195	149	6	0	122	47	0	0	140	0	210	0
Arkadelphia, AR	347	328	18	1	0	111	32	0	0	347	0	0	0
Asheville, NC	366	271	92	3	0	124	44	0	0	161	0	205	0
Ashtabula, OH	366	323	37	5	1	154	29	0	0	210	156	0	0
Athens, OH	55	44	11	0	0	68	34	0	0	0	0	55	0
Athens, TN	366	337	26	3	0	112	14.5	0	142	0	119	100	5
Athens-Clarke County, GA	366	262	99	4	1	153	42	0	0	104	0	262	0
Atlanta-Sandy Springs-Marietta, GA	366	114	233	16	3	203	58	0	5	100	0	261	0
Atlantic City, NJ	362	309	49	4	0	129	36	0	0	254	0	108	0
Augusta-Richmond County, GA-SC	366	238	124	4	0	127	44	0	0	85	0	281	0
Augusta-Waterville, ME	311	299	12	0	0	79	29	0	80	192	8	31	0
Austin-Round Rock, TX	366	263	99	4	0	147	41.5	0	3	189	0	174	0
Bakersfield, CA	366	87	166	96	17	179	74	0	3	217	0	139	7
Baltimore-Towson, MD	366	177	169	18	2	185	52	0	9	157	0	200	0
Bangor, ME	366	337	29	0	0	72	33	0	0	208	0	156	2
Baraboo, WI	365	282	80	3	0	127	38	0	0	175	0	185	5
Barnstable Town, MA	213	191	16	6	0	140	36	0	0	213	0	0	0
Baton Rouge, LA	366	174	179	13	0	135	51.5	0	5	138	7	213	3
Bay City, MI	119	97	22	0	0	85	27	0	0	0	0	119	0
Beaumont-Port Arthur, TX	366	240	114	11	1	192	45	0	3	147	21	195	0
Beaver Dam, WI	366	255	105	5	1	154	42	0	0	215	0	150	1
Beckley, WV	121	102	19	0	0	64	33	0	0	0	0	121	0
Bellingham, WA	344	339	5	0	0	80	21.5	0	0	114	0	230	0
Bend, OR	366	320	28	1	17	546	33	0	0	127	0	239	0
Bennington, VT	358	338	20	0	0	93	31	0	0	320	0	38	0
Berlin, NH-VT	366	326	40	0	0	93	41	0	0	366	0	0	0
Billings, MT	366	309	54	3	0	125	25	0	0	0	155	211	0
Birmingham-Hoover, AL	366	161	195	10	0	147	52	0	0	97	9	257	3
Bishop, CA	366	228	115	9	14	3812	45	0	0	265	0	12	89
Bismarck, ND	366	337	29	0	0	68	34	0	27	185	5	134	15
Blacksburg-Christiansburg-Radford, VA	350	332	18	0	0	100	37	0	0	350	0	0	0
Bloomington, IN	358	256	91	11	0	134	42	0	0	145	0	213	0

Metropolitan Statistical Area	Days with AQI Data	Number of Days when Air Quality was... Good	Moderate	Unhealthy for Sensitive Groups	Unhealthy or Very Unhealthy	AQI Statistics Max	Median	Number of Days when AQI Pollutant was... CO	NO_2	O_3	SO_2	$PM_{2.5}$	PM_{10}
Bloomington-Normal, IL	362	283	73	6	0	111	38	0	0	316	0	46	0
Boise City-Nampa, ID	366	289	70	4	3	215	37	2	20	186	1	61	96
Boone, NC	120	111	9	0	0	66	32	0	0	0	0	120	0
Boston-Cambridge-Quincy, MA-NH	366	224	136	5	1	160	47	0	18	90	2	255	1
Boulder, CO	363	255	103	5	0	147	42	0	0	337	0	24	2
Bowling Green, KY	366	279	78	9	0	137	41	0	0	267	0	99	0
Bozeman, MT	366	305	53	8	0	138	25	2	25	0	0	339	0
Bradenton-Sarasota-Venice, FL	366	272	93	1	0	101	42	0	0	150	0	216	0
Brainerd, MN	360	320	40	0	0	98	33	0	0	184	0	176	0
Branson, MO	214	181	31	2	0	104	40.5	0	0	214	0	0	0
Bremerton-Silverdale, WA	317	300	17	0	0	68	19	0	0	0	0	317	0
Bridgeport-Stamford-Norwalk, CT	366	257	84	24	1	154	42	0	19	162	0	184	1
Brigham City, UT	366	264	100	2	0	106	43	0	0	290	0	76	0
Brookings, SD	366	310	56	0	0	97	36	0	0	251	0	59	56
Brownsville-Harlingen, TX	366	272	94	0	0	85	41	0	0	113	0	239	14
Brunswick, GA	364	360	4	0	0	87	28	0	0	218	97	41	8
Buffalo-Niagara Falls, NY	366	225	133	8	0	145	44	0	3	132	0	231	0
Burlington, NC	361	294	67	0	0	88	37	0	0	0	0	361	0
Burlington-South Burlington, VT	366	341	25	0	0	84	33.5	0	8	309	0	49	0
Butte-Silver Bow, MT	363	257	93	8	5	174	31	0	0	0	0	291	72
Cadillac, MI	366	316	43	7	0	122	35	0	1	339	0	26	0
Cambridge, MD	366	304	50	11	1	195	36	3	0	295	2	66	0
Canon City, CO	57	56	1	0	0	54	15	0	0	0	0	0	57
Canton-Massillon, OH	366	192	168	5	1	166	49	5	0	126	0	235	0
Cape Coral-Fort Myers, FL	366	328	38	0	0	97	36	0	0	213	0	151	2
Carlsbad-Artesia, NM	353	274	75	3	1	155	41	0	0	326	0	27	0
Carson City, NV	211	161	50	0	0	97	44	0	0	211	0	0	0
Casper, WY	366	345	20	1	0	103	30	0	84	174	55	45	8
Cedar Rapids, IA	366	227	138	1	0	104	44	0	0	132	4	229	1
Centralia, WA	366	342	24	0	0	69	21	0	0	0	0	366	0
Chambersburg, PA	274	245	29	0	0	100	36	0	0	274	0	0	0
Champaign-Urbana, IL	366	296	66	4	0	114	37	0	0	303	1	62	0
Charleston, WV	366	273	91	2	0	116	40	0	0	167	77	91	31
Charleston-North Charleston, SC	366	239	126	1	0	134	43	0	5	55	0	306	0
Charlotte-Gastonia-Concord, NC-SC	366	230	125	10	1	190	47	0	1	145	0	220	0
Charlottesville, VA	366	309	56	1	0	101	36	0	0	142	0	224	0
Chattanooga, TN-GA	352	194	150	8	0	137	48	0	0	126	0	226	0
Cheyenne, WY	366	291	75	0	0	93	42	0	5	325	0	36	0
Chicago-Naperville-Joliet, IL-IN-WI	366	53	266	37	10	190	64	0	25	60	36	225	20
Chico, CA	366	259	102	5	0	111	41.5	0	8	334	0	24	0
Cincinnati-Middletown, OH-KY-IN	366	115	208	39	4	179	58	0	0	109	54	198	5
Clarksburg, WV	115	85	30	0	0	85	38	0	0	0	0	115	0
Clarksville, TN-KY	366	206	154	6	0	135	47	0	0	176	38	152	0
Clearlake, CA	366	355	10	1	0	119	32	0	0	362	0	4	0
Cleveland, MS	360	248	108	4	0	109	42	0	0	97	0	263	0
Cleveland, TN	366	362	4	0	0	71	9	0	186	0	128	0	52
Cleveland-Elyria-Mentor, OH	366	108	199	54	5	182	62	9	1	76	95	170	15
Clinton, IA	366	143	218	5	0	106	55	0	0	55	6	305	0
Coeur dAlene, ID	0	0	0	0	0	0	0	0	0	0	0	0	0
Colorado Springs, CO	366	254	108	4	0	109	44	0	0	354	0	10	2
Columbia, MO	214	166	42	6	0	124	42	0	0	214	0	0	0
Columbia, SC	366	226	137	3	0	105	47	0	1	95	10	260	0
Columbia, TN	112	97	15	0	0	64	34	0	0	0	0	112	0
Columbus, GA-AL	366	252	113	1	0	104	42	0	0	105	0	260	1
Columbus, OH	366	217	135	13	1	177	47	0	0	156	0	207	3
Concord, NH	366	322	43	1	0	102	30	0	0	145	97	124	0

Metropolitan Statistical Area	Days with AQI Data	Number of Days when Air Quality was... Good	Moderate	Unhealthy for Sensitive Groups	Unhealthy or Very Unhealthy	AQI Statistics Max	Median	Number of Days when AQI Pollutant was... CO	NO_2	O_3	SO_2	$PM_{2.5}$	PM_{10}
Cookeville, TN	108	89	19	0	0	63	34	0	0	0	0	108	0
Coos Bay, OR	276	272	3	1	0	143	17.5	0	0	0	0	276	0
Corning, NY	366	339	27	0	0	84	31	0	0	317	0	49	0
Corpus Christi, TX	366	279	82	5	0	130	39	0	0	185	3	177	1
Corsicana, TX	366	293	71	2	0	135	39.5	0	0	202	9	155	0
Corvallis, OR	355	333	22	0	0	65	16	0	0	0	0	355	0
Crescent City, CA	58	58	0	0	0	32	11	0	0	0	0	0	58
Culpeper, VA	54	54	0	0	0	30	12.5	0	0	0	0	0	54
Dallas-Fort Worth-Arlington, TX	366	146	184	32	4	187	54	0	13	154	0	198	1
Dalton, GA	245	222	22	1	0	101	40	0	0	245	0	0	0
Daphne-Fairhope-Foley, AL	285	244	41	0	0	97	36	0	0	195	0	90	0
Davenport-Moline-Rock Island, IA-IL	366	146	217	3	0	134	55	0	0	59	0	228	79
Dayton, OH	366	255	96	14	1	151	41	1	0	287	3	75	0
Decatur, AL	285	238	44	3	0	109	38	0	0	203	0	82	0
Decatur, IL	366	235	127	4	0	106	44	0	0	151	11	204	0
Deltona-Daytona Beach-Ormond Beach, FL	366	316	50	0	0	87	37	0	0	159	0	207	0
Deming, NM	366	283	76	3	4	994	43	0	2	324	0	0	40
Denver-Aurora, CO	366	135	205	23	3	164	56	0	108	196	6	42	14
Des Moines-West Des Moines, IA	366	253	113	0	0	93	43	0	6	121	0	238	1
Detroit-Warren-Livonia, MI	366	130	198	35	3	200	58	0	13	70	99	137	47
Dickinson, ND	366	363	3	0	0	59	31	0	0	269	77	20	0
Dodge City, KS	366	365	1	0	0	94	12	0	0	0	0	0	366
Dothan, AL	285	253	32	0	0	80	36	0	0	198	0	87	0
Douglas, GA	60	48	12	0	0	60	34.5	0	0	0	0	60	0
Dover, DE	343	260	68	14	1	156	39	0	0	241	0	102	0
DuBois, PA	354	322	31	1	0	140	32	0	0	354	0	0	0
Duluth, MN-WI	366	325	40	1	0	104	34	0	0	263	0	98	5
Durango, CO	366	276	90	0	0	93	44	0	3	360	0	0	3
Durham, NC	365	298	62	5	0	127	38	0	0	137	0	228	0
Dyersburg, TN	115	91	24	0	0	73	35	0	0	0	0	115	0
Eagle Pass, TX	266	214	52	0	0	84	33	0	0	0	0	266	0
East Liverpool-Salem, OH	366	365	1	0	0	67	6	0	0	0	310	0	56
East Stroudsburg, PA	366	283	83	0	0	93	37	0	0	206	0	160	0
Eau Claire, WI	307	251	56	0	0	100	38	0	0	196	0	109	2
Effingham, IL	196	152	42	2	0	142	42	0	0	196	0	0	0
El Centro, CA	366	196	147	20	3	274	48	4	74	205	0	67	16
El Dorado, AR	366	325	39	1	1	200	5	0	0	0	254	112	0
Elizabethtown, KY	310	223	83	4	0	137	41	0	0	149	0	161	0
Elkhart-Goshen, IN	362	206	151	4	1	190	46	0	0	106	0	256	0
Elko, NV	357	334	23	0	0	83	22	0	0	0	0	0	357
Ellensburg, WA	358	288	53	11	6	278	21	0	0	0	0	358	0
Elmira, NY	361	345	16	0	0	100	31	0	0	356	5	0	0
El Paso, TX	366	126	226	10	4	643	55	0	24	114	0	209	19
Erie, PA	366	221	134	10	1	159	45	0	1	148	0	217	0
Eugene-Springfield, OR	366	267	92	7	0	149	36	0	0	100	0	266	0
Eureka-Arcata-Fortuna, CA	366	316	50	0	0	72	33	0	0	182	0	184	0
Evanston, WY	366	305	61	0	0	100	41	0	0	347	0	0	19
Evansville, IN-KY	366	167	181	18	0	140	52	3	1	127	20	215	0
Fairbanks, AK	366	234	91	24	17	222	38	0	0	124	8	212	22
Fairmont, WV	122	80	42	0	0	84	40	0	0	0	0	122	0
Fajardo, PR	335	310	25	0	0	69	20	0	0	0	0	19	316
Fallon, NV	211	211	0	0	0	47	30	0	0	211	0	0	0
Fargo, ND-MN	366	302	64	0	0	91	37	0	3	165	0	173	25
Farmington, NM	366	256	110	0	0	97	44	0	22	329	1	8	6
Fayetteville, NC	366	294	70	2	0	122	40	0	0	137	3	226	0
Fayetteville-Springdale-Rogers, AR-MO	366	293	68	5	0	127	39	0	0	321	0	45	0

Metropolitan Statistical Area	Days with AQI Data	Number of Days when Air Quality was...				AQI Statistics		Number of Days when AQI Pollutant was...					
		Good	Moderate	Unhealthy for Sensitive Groups	Unhealthy or Very Unhealthy	Max	Median	CO	NO_2	O_3	SO_2	$PM_{2.5}$	PM_{10}
Fernley, NV	214	171	42	1	0	101	43	0	0	214	0	0	0
Flagstaff, AZ	364	304	58	2	0	111	42	0	0	359	0	3	2
Flint, MI	242	178	50	14	0	147	40	0	0	175	0	67	0
Florence, SC	309	270	37	2	0	122	36	0	0	215	0	94	0
Florence-Muscle Shoals, AL	285	242	41	2	0	114	38	0	0	203	0	82	0
Fond du Lac, WI	209	168	35	5	1	166	37	0	0	209	0	0	0
Fort Collins-Loveland, CO	366	214	127	25	0	147	47	0	0	351	0	12	3
Fort Madison-Keokuk, IA-MO	111	72	39	0	0	81	40	0	0	0	0	111	0
Fort Payne, AL	366	315	51	0	0	100	37	0	0	312	0	54	0
Fort Smith, AR-OK	364	284	73	7	0	132	38	0	44	223	0	70	27
Fort Walton Beach-Crestview-Destin, FL	366	355	11	0	0	71	31	0	0	366	0	0	0
Fort Wayne, IN	366	127	232	6	1	154	55	5	0	60	0	301	0
Fresno, CA	366	87	175	88	16	201	75	0	1	203	0	160	2
Gadsden, AL	280	242	38	0	0	71	37	0	0	187	0	93	0
Gaffney, SC	239	200	37	2	0	104	41	0	0	239	0	0	0
Gainesville, FL	366	336	27	1	2	157	34	0	0	216	0	150	0
Gainesville, GA	328	210	118	0	0	75	45	0	0	0	0	328	0
Gallup, NM	263	263	0	0	0	39	14	0	0	0	0	0	263
Gardnerville Ranchos, NV	105	102	3	0	0	77	9	105	0	0	0	0	0
Georgetown, SC	343	343	0	0	0	47	17	0	0	0	0	0	343
Gettysburg, PA	366	229	134	3	0	146	44	0	1	172	0	193	0
Gillette, WY	366	153	205	7	1	152	54	0	6	125	8	16	211
Goldsboro, NC	341	277	64	0	0	80	37	0	0	0	0	341	0
Granbury, TX	353	314	31	8	0	116	36	0	0	353	0	0	0
Grand Island, NE	119	103	16	0	0	71	30	0	0	0	0	119	0
Grand Junction, CO	366	285	80	1	0	111	43	0	0	328	0	22	16
Grand Rapids-Wyoming, MI	366	291	60	15	0	135	35	2	0	294	0	70	0
Grants Pass, OR	366	317	49	0	0	77	23	0	0	0	0	366	0
Great Falls, MT	360	299	58	3	0	132	32	0	0	0	0	360	0
Greeley, CO	366	248	111	7	0	137	43	7	0	320	0	39	0
Green Bay, WI	366	254	94	17	1	154	40	0	0	151	33	182	0
Greensboro-High Point, NC	364	278	81	5	0	129	41	0	0	146	0	218	0
Greenville, NC	254	225	28	0	1	151	36	0	0	180	0	74	0
Greenville-Mauldin-Easley, SC	366	245	120	1	0	111	45	0	10	135	0	218	3
Grenada, MS	115	87	28	0	0	85	36	0	0	0	0	115	0
Guayama, PR	317	303	14	0	0	70	3	0	0	0	195	49	73
Gulfport-Biloxi, MS	364	269	93	2	0	114	39	0	0	105	0	259	0
Hagerstown-Martinsburg, MD-WV	363	216	143	4	0	127	45	0	0	137	0	226	0
Hammond, LA	114	94	20	0	0	74	33.5	0	0	0	0	114	0
Hanford-Corcoran, CA	366	134	190	38	4	155	60.5	0	1	185	0	149	31
Harriman, TN	366	142	224	0	0	88	53	0	0	0	0	365	1
Harrisburg-Carlisle, PA	366	182	175	9	0	114	51	0	0	111	0	255	0
Harrison, AR	366	321	43	2	0	114	37.5	0	0	366	0	0	0
Harrisonburg, VA	356	310	46	0	0	100	33	0	110	165	5	76	0
Hartford-West Hartford-East Hartford, CT	366	235	115	15	1	156	44	0	4	123	0	239	0
Hattiesburg, MS	301	205	96	0	0	73	41	0	0	0	0	301	0
Helena, MT	366	270	88	7	1	172	37	0	0	187	0	179	0
Helena-West Helena, AR	59	46	13	0	0	63	36	0	0	0	0	59	0
Hickory-Lenoir-Morganton, NC	365	267	97	1	0	109	43	0	0	137	0	228	0
Hilo, HI	366	1	28	117	220	322	168	0	0	0	357	9	0
Hobbs, NM	363	330	32	1	0	117	35	0	24	206	0	132	1
Holland-Grand Haven, MI	366	297	57	12	0	137	32	0	0	172	122	72	0
Homosassa Springs, FL	109	104	5	0	0	85	25	0	0	0	0	109	0
Honolulu, HI	366	334	32	0	0	75	33	0	0	78	3	282	3
Hot Springs, AR	122	87	35	0	0	74	43	0	0	0	0	122	0
Houma-Bayou Cane-Thibodaux, LA	361	294	64	3	0	111	37	0	0	234	0	127	0

Metropolitan Statistical Area	Days with AQI Data	Number of Days when Air Quality was... Good	Moderate	Unhealthy for Sensitive Groups	Unhealthy or Very Unhealthy	AQI Statistics Max	Median	Number of Days when AQI Pollutant was... CO	NO_2	O_3	SO_2	$PM_{2.5}$	PM_{10}
Houston-Sugar Land-Baytown, TX	366	139	193	30	4	209	54	0	15	104	0	235	12
Huntington, IN	181	161	19	1	0	106	38	0	0	181	0	0	0
Huntington-Ashland, WV-KY-OH	366	255	105	6	0	137	42.5	0	20	165	7	164	10
Huntsville, AL	338	280	54	4	0	122	40	0	0	207	0	77	54
Idaho Falls, ID	0	0	0	0	0	0	0	0	0	0	0	0	0
Indiana, PA	366	286	62	18	0	132	38.5	0	0	283	83	0	0
Indianapolis-Carmel, IN	366	91	246	27	2	161	61	0	0	86	46	234	0
Iowa City, IA	366	204	162	0	0	90	46	0	0	0	0	366	0
Ithaca, NY	359	329	30	0	0	100	34	0	0	359	0	0	0
Jackson, MS	366	245	120	1	0	132	44	0	0	70	0	296	0
Jackson, TN	119	95	24	0	0	84	36	0	0	0	0	119	0
Jackson, WY-ID	345	297	47	1	0	110	42	0	0	319	0	22	4
Jacksonville, FL	366	290	71	4	1	165	39	0	1	163	36	163	3
Jamestown-Dunkirk-Fredonia, NY	366	311	44	10	1	172	36	0	0	329	8	29	0
Janesville, WI	193	145	42	6	0	119	42	0	0	193	0	0	0
Jasper, IN	357	277	63	15	2	161	17	0	0	0	246	111	0
Jefferson City, MO	214	161	50	3	0	119	41.5	0	0	214	0	0	0
Johnstown, PA	366	211	153	2	0	135	47	0	3	99	23	234	7
Joplin, MO	327	241	72	14	0	134	38	0	0	194	0	0	133
Juneau, AK	362	322	39	1	0	117	21	0	0	0	0	356	6
Kahului-Wailuku, HI	337	322	15	0	0	64	25	0	0	0	0	337	0
Kalamazoo-Portage, MI	244	173	58	12	1	166	42	0	0	171	0	73	0
Kalispell, MT	366	300	66	0	0	94	36	0	0	194	0	139	33
Kansas City, MO-KS	366	83	211	68	4	180	62	0	4	102	86	170	4
Kapaa, HI	366	340	25	1	0	107	27	14	5	0	35	312	0
Keene, NH	366	288	77	1	0	104	34	0	0	226	0	140	0
Kennewick-Richland-Pasco, WA	366	317	48	1	0	104	23	0	0	0	0	326	40
Killeen-Temple-Fort Hood, TX	300	321	40	5	0	129	36	0	0	366	0	0	0
Kingsport-Bristol-Bristol, TN-VA	366	122	106	126	12	200	74	0	28	64	254	20	0
Kingston, NY	363	346	17	0	0	87	33	0	0	360	3	0	0
Kingsville, TX	328	262	66	0	0	88	35	0	0	0	0	328	0
Kinston, NC	277	252	24	1	0	119	35	0	0	206	0	71	0
Klamath Falls, OR	359	252	98	8	1	152	30	0	0	0	0	359	0
Knoxville, TN	366	193	162	9	2	203	49	0	0	177	0	172	17
Kokomo, IN	11	8	3	0	0	58	33	0	0	0	0	11	0
Laconia, NH	210	197	13	0	0	80	33.5	0	0	175	0	35	0
La Crosse, WI-MN	318	237	81	0	0	96	40	0	0	156	0	162	0
Lafayette, IN	364	128	233	3	0	132	55	0	0	49	0	315	0
Lafayette, LA	366	242	123	1	0	109	43	0	0	116	0	248	2
La Grande, OR	364	308	54	2	0	121	26	0	0	0	0	363	1
Lake Charles, LA	366	273	92	1	0	114	40	0	0	153	16	197	0
Lake City, FL	366	326	39	0	1	153	34	0	0	235	0	131	0
Lake Havasu City-Kingman, AZ	212	207	4	1	0	116	19	0	0	0	0	14	198
Lakeland, FL	366	302	61	3	0	129	39	0	0	147	0	219	0
Lancaster, PA	366	158	193	14	1	154	54	0	3	95	0	268	0
Lansing-East Lansing, MI	362	295	58	9	0	142	35	0	30	282	1	49	0
Laramie, WY	365	239	124	2	0	125	47	0	0	265	0	9	91
Laredo, TX	346	245	100	1	0	103	41	0	0	41	0	300	5
Las Cruces, NM	366	111	229	15	11	1635	59	0	6	137	0	135	88
Las Vegas-Paradise, NV	366	134	203	27	2	180	57	0	13	242	0	101	10
Laurel, MS	115	75	40	0	0	91	43	0	0	0	0	115	0
Lawrenceburg, TN	117	95	22	0	0	65	35	0	0	0	0	117	0
Lawton, OK	364	232	128	4	0	127	45	0	0	185	0	179	0
Lebanon, NH-VT	366	332	34	0	0	80	33	0	0	261	0	105	0
Lebanon, PA	366	182	176	8	0	114	51	0	0	112	0	254	0
Lewiston, ID-WA	366	274	82	5	5	188	29.5	0	0	0	0	366	0

Metropolitan Statistical Area	Days with AQI Data	Number of Days when Air Quality was...				AQI Statistics		Number of Days when AQI Pollutant was...					
		Good	Moderate	Unhealthy for Sensitive Groups	Unhealthy or Very Unhealthy	Max	Median	CO	NO_2	O_3	SO_2	$PM_{2.5}$	PM_{10}
Lewiston-Auburn, ME	363	323	40	0	0	80	32	0	0	129	0	232	2
Lexington, NE	61	50	11	0	0	73	26	0	0	0	0	0	61
Lexington-Fayette, KY	366	232	127	7	0	127	44	0	11	118	2	234	1
Lima, OH	366	286	67	13	0	145	34	0	0	204	129	33	0
Lincoln, NE	287	262	25	0	0	80	36	24	0	188	0	75	0
Lincolnton, NC	214	179	31	4	0	129	42	0	0	214	0	0	0
Little Rock-North Little Rock-Conway, AR	366	156	200	10	0	124	52	0	12	92	0	262	0
Logan, UT-ID	366	248	114	4	0	125	45	0	30	167	0	169	0
Longview, TX	364	321	39	4	0	119	34	0	1	347	16	0	0
Longview, WA	351	332	19	0	0	70	20	0	0	0	0	351	0
Los Angeles-Long Beach-Santa Ana, CA	366	33	226	97	10	192	79	0	21	143	0	200	2
Louisville/Jefferson County, KY-IN	366	121	200	40	5	185	57	0	3	93	53	217	0
Lubbock, TX	278	231	45	2	0	113	35	0	0	0	0	278	0
Lumberton, NC	122	102	20	0	0	77	33.5	0	0	0	0	122	0
Lynchburg, VA	115	102	13	0	0	65	30	0	0	0	0	115	0
Macon, GA	366	225	139	2	0	122	46	0	0	78	2	286	0
Madera, CA	366	110	198	54	4	174	61	0	0	165	0	188	13
Madison, WI	355	237	116	2	0	129	43	0	0	174	0	181	0
Malone, NY	366	363	2	1	0	113	10	0	138	175	53	0	0
Manchester-Nashua, NH	366	327	36	3	0	124	35	1	0	324	0	41	0
Manhattan, KS	361	309	44	8	0	129	36	0	0	361	0	0	0
Manitowoc, WI	195	158	27	9	1	151	35	0	0	195	0	0	0
Marshall, MN	364	301	63	0	0	87	36	0	0	162	0	202	0
Marshall, TX	366	258	106	2	0	111	42	0	0	153	0	213	0
Mason City, IA	356	344	12	0	0	66	19	0	0	0	0	0	356
Mayaguez, PR	115	103	12	0	0	72	20	0	0	0	0	115	0
McAlester, OK	366	205	156	5	0	122	48	0	0	160	0	206	0
McAllen-Edinburg-Mission, TX	366	266	100	0	0	81	40.5	0	0	99	0	265	2
Medford, OR	366	249	116	1	0	110	42	0	0	147	0	219	0
Memphis, TN-MS-AR	366	205	141	19	1	204	48.5	0	4	135	0	227	0
Merced, CA	366	193	154	19	0	138	49.5	0	1	232	0	131	2
Meridian, MS	366	255	111	0	0	76	42	0	0	46	0	320	0
Miami, OK	365	247	113	5	0	137	44	0	0	125	0	235	5
Miami-Fort Lauderdale-Pompano Beach, FL	366	247	117	2	0	136	43	0	4	83	0	279	0
Michigan City-La Porte, IN	366	294	54	13	5	202	33	0	0	167	128	71	0
Middlesborough, KY	259	207	50	2	0	111	43	0	0	225	0	34	0
Milwaukee-Waukesha-West Allis, WI	366	172	168	24	2	166	52	0	7	123	0	236	0
Minneapolis-St. Paul-Bloomington, MN-WI	366	218	143	4	1	159	46	0	16	107	1	221	21
Missoula, MT	366	101	218	32	15	178	60	0	0	39	0	325	2
Mobile, AL	284	247	36	1	0	106	35	0	0	208	0	73	3
Modesto, CA	366	138	169	55	4	177	58	0	3	179	0	183	1
Monroe, LA	366	175	191	0	0	91	51	0	0	33	0	333	0
Monroe, MI	124	87	36	1	0	105	40.5	0	0	0	0	124	0
Montgomery, AL	280	227	52	1	0	102	40	0	0	188	0	92	0
Morehead City, NC	283	280	3	0	0	67	31	0	0	283	0	0	0
Morgantown, WV	366	311	54	1	0	124	33	0	0	189	101	76	0
Morristown, TN	245	192	48	3	2	190	42	0	0	245	0	0	0
Moscow, ID	347	314	27	2	4	173	12	0	0	0	0	347	0
Moses Lake, WA	365	331	34	0	0	95	22	0	0	0	0	365	0
Mount Vernon, IL	232	155	67	10	0	140	45	0	0	204	0	28	0
Mount Vernon, OH	214	173	40	0	1	156	42	0	0	214	0	0	0
Mount Vernon-Anacortes, WA	366	363	3	0	0	56	27	0	90	193	0	83	0
Muncie, IN	242	175	64	3	0	114	43	0	0	166	0	76	0
Muscatine, IA	366	170	163	26	7	200	52	0	0	0	78	287	1
Muskegon-Norton Shores, MI	242	174	44	23	1	169	39	0	0	173	0	69	0
Muskogee, OK	334	304	29	1	0	103	27	0	0	0	53	0	281

Metropolitan Statistical Area	Days with AQI Data	Number of Days when Air Quality was... Good	Moderate	Unhealthy for Sensitive Groups	Unhealthy or Very Unhealthy	AQI Statistics Max	Median	Number of Days when AQI Pollutant was... CO	NO_2	O_3	SO_2	$PM_{2.5}$	PM_{10}
Napa, CA	366	277	89	0	0	84	36	0	7	182	0	177	0
Naples-Marco Island, FL	366	330	36	0	0	84	35	0	0	167	0	199	0
Nashville-Murfreesboro-Franklin, TN	366	190	153	22	1	161	49	0	7	123	1	235	0
New Castle, IN	119	88	31	0	0	73	35	0	0	0	0	119	0
New Castle, PA	366	325	36	5	0	129	32	2	0	292	10	0	62
New Haven-Milford, CT	366	216	134	14	2	161	46.5	0	5	122	2	237	0
New Orleans-Metairie-Kenner, LA	362	143	175	37	7	174	55	0	3	84	90	184	1
New Philadelphia-Dover, OH	293	289	4	0	0	81	11	0	0	0	293	0	0
New York-Northern New Jersey, NY-NJ-PA	366	130	214	22	0	150	55	0	38	113	4	208	3
Niles-Benton Harbor, MI	244	174	51	16	3	195	41	0	0	175	0	69	0
Nogales, AZ	337	229	107	1	0	108	41	0	0	0	0	25	312
Norwich-New London, CT	340	242	90	7	1	172	41	0	0	130	0	210	0
Ocala, FL	366	311	55	0	0	77	37	0	0	122	0	244	0
Odessa, TX	366	307	59	0	0	79	37	0	0	0	0	366	0
Ogden-Clearfield, UT	366	224	136	5	1	163	47	0	55	171	0	138	2
Oklahoma City, OK	366	172	171	23	0	140	52	0	23	170	0	171	2
Olympia, WA	361	303	54	3	1	153	30	0	0	129	0	232	0
Omaha-Council Bluffs, NE-IA	366	124	228	14	0	123	57	0	0	71	27	118	150
Orlando-Kissimmee, FL	366	314	51	1	0	116	38	0	0	193	0	172	1
Ottawa-Streator, IL	362	362	0	0	0	37	1	0	0	0	362	0	0
Owensboro, KY	366	256	95	14	1	164	42	0	16	176	8	166	0
Oxnard-Thousand Oaks-Ventura, CA	366	173	176	17	0	129	52	0	3	190	0	172	1
Paducah, KY-IL	366	254	96	13	3	179	42	0	18	200	4	143	1
Pahrump, NV	366	341	24	1	0	107	19	0	0	0	0	0	366
Palatka, FL	366	362	4	0	0	72	17	0	0	0	33	0	333
Palm Bay-Melbourne-Titusville, FL	366	316	47	3	0	117	38	0	0	196	0	170	0
Palm Coast, FL	362	351	11	0	0	97	32	0	0	362	0	0	0
Panama City-Lynn Haven, FL	366	318	48	0	0	92	36	0	0	183	0	183	0
Parkersburg-Marietta-Vienna, WV-OH	366	285	77	4	0	124	37	0	0	189	106	71	0
Pascagoula, MS	363	315	46	2	0	101	33	0	83	217	11	52	0
Payson, AZ	366	65	157	120	24	200	89	0	0	67	261	0	38
Pendleton-Hermiston, OR	365	300	65	0	0	93	36	0	0	137	0	228	0
Pensacola-Ferry Pass-Brent, FL	366	271	95	0	0	100	40	0	0	157	1	208	0
Peoria, IL	366	179	156	27	4	200	51	0	0	128	84	154	0
Philadelphia-Camden-Wilm., PA-NJ-DE-MD	366	64	275	25	2	154	61	0	3	65	1	295	2
Phoenix Lake-Cedar Ridge, CA	366	276	87	3	0	114	38	0	0	366	0	0	0
Phoenix-Mesa-Scottsdale, AZ	366	31	241	78	16	594	78.5	0	14	87	0	45	220
Pittsburgh, PA	366	79	228	55	4	200	62	0	2	60	65	238	1
Pittsfield, MA	348	242	106	0	0	97	42	0	0	104	0	244	0
Platteville, WI	362	292	70	0	0	92	32	0	0	0	0	362	0
Pocatello, ID	366	231	128	5	2	162	43	0	0	0	142	181	43
Ponca City, OK	363	227	126	10	0	135	45	0	0	167	58	138	0
Ponce, PR	357	330	27	0	0	72	22	78	0	0	0	30	249
Port Angeles, WA	366	310	56	0	0	81	36	0	0	159	0	207	0
Portland-South Portland-Biddeford, ME	366	306	56	4	0	116	36	0	29	216	0	120	0
Portland-Vancouver-Beaverton, OR-WA	366	276	88	2	0	117	36	0	1	178	0	187	0
Port St. Lucie, FL	366	318	47	1	0	104	38	0	0	184	0	182	0
Portsmouth, OH	366	332	34	0	0	69	20	0	0	0	22	114	230
Poughkeepsie-Newburgh-Middletown, NY	366	309	55	2	0	101	36	0	0	218	0	148	0
Prescott, AZ	266	226	40	0	0	97	42	0	0	245	0	19	2
Price, UT	364	278	84	2	0	108	42	0	31	333	0	0	0
Prineville, OR	360	282	76	2	0	105	24.5	0	0	0	0	360	0
Providence-New Bedford-Fall River, RI-MA	366	248	104	13	1	154	44	0	5	168	23	170	0
Provo-Orem, UT	366	221	140	5	0	132	47	0	72	188	0	103	3
Pueblo, CO	133	127	6	0	0	80	24	0	0	0	0	89	44
Pullman, WA	366	331	31	2	2	155	19	0	0	0	0	366	0

Metropolitan Statistical Area	Days with AQI Data	Number of Days when Air Quality was... Good	Moderate	Unhealthy for Sensitive Groups	Unhealthy or Very Unhealthy	AQI Statistics Max	Median	Number of Days when AQI Pollutant was... CO	NO_2	O_3	SO_2	$PM_{2.5}$	PM_{10}
Quincy, IL-MO	364	327	35	2	0	127	33	0	0	338	0	26	0
Racine, WI	189	139	30	19	1	151	38	0	0	189	0	0	0
Raleigh-Cary, NC	366	262	99	4	1	151	42.5	0	0	155	0	211	0
Rapid City, SD	366	278	88	0	0	90	42	0	4	209	0	53	100
Reading, PA	366	187	173	6	0	122	50	0	1	130	0	235	0
Red Bluff, CA	366	229	128	9	0	124	43	0	0	268	0	98	0
Redding, CA	366	309	54	3	0	114	40	0	0	357	0	9	0
Red Wing, MN	227	214	13	0	0	74	35	0	0	227	0	0	0
Reno-Sparks, NV	366	192	170	4	0	138	49	0	24	231	0	90	21
Richmond, IN	361	360	1	0	0	91	6	0	0	0	361	0	0
Richmond, VA	366	276	78	11	1	154	42	0	52	161	4	149	0
Richmond-Berea, KY	119	96	23	0	0	67	33	0	0	0	0	119	0
Riverside-San Bernardino-Ontario, CA	366	22	190	120	34	233	91.5	0	9	159	0	160	38
Riverton, WY	366	290	75	1	0	117	43	0	3	327	0	22	14
Roanoke, VA	366	273	92	1	0	104	41	0	11	122	0	233	0
Rochester, MN	359	275	84	0	0	97	38	0	0	161	0	198	0
Rochester, NY	366	304	59	3	0	127	36	0	0	222	0	144	0
Rockford, IL	366	309	56	1	0	122	34	1	0	308	0	57	0
Rockland, ME	180	173	7	0	0	80	31	0	0	180	0	0	0
Rock Springs, WY	366	269	90	6	1	284	44	0	4	277	11	16	58
Rocky Mount, NC	360	299	60	1	0	137	37	0	0	106	0	254	0
Rome, GA	366	48	315	3	0	139	64	0	0	0	9	357	0
Roseburg, OR	362	341	21	0	0	69	19	0	0	0	0	362	0
Russellville, AR	57	49	8	0	0	66	34	0	0	0	0	57	0
Rutland, VT	366	340	26	0	0	95	18	7	239	0	10	110	0
Sacramento—Arden-Arcade—Roseville, CA	366	179	136	45	6	177	51	0	16	272	0	77	1
St. Cloud, MN	366	299	66	1	0	105	36	0	0	138	0	228	0
St. George, UT	351	276	72	3	0	111	42	0	6	326	0	19	0
St. Joseph, MO-KS	363	204	156	3	0	127	47	0	0	139	0	208	16
St. Louis, MO-IL	366	60	209	78	19	257	68	0	5	76	79	177	29
St. Marys, PA	364	337	25	2	0	132	34	0	0	364	0	0	0
Salem, OR	364	314	50	0	0	77	28	0	0	134	0	230	0
Salinas, CA	366	333	33	0	0	72	35	1	5	206	0	117	37
Salisbury, NC	366	258	99	8	1	190	43	0	0	187	0	179	0
Salt Lake City, UT	366	204	150	12	0	145	48.5	0	53	178	2	113	20
San Antonio, TX	366	241	117	8	0	137	45	0	2	165	0	199	0
San Diego-Carlsbad-San Marcos, CA	366	74	270	21	1	165	61.5	0	19	95	0	220	32
San Francisco-Oakland-Fremont, CA	366	231	130	5	0	137	45	0	38	138	1	189	0
San Jose-Sunnyvale-Santa Clara, CA	366	240	122	4	0	111	45	0	6	186	0	173	1
San Juan-Caguas-Guaynabo, PR	366	291	75	0	0	83	38	6	162	35	9	30	124
San Luis Obispo-Paso Robles, CA	366	189	163	14	0	129	50	0	0	228	0	111	27
Santa Barbara-Santa Maria-Goleta, CA	366	269	95	2	0	114	44	0	2	233	4	127	0
Santa Cruz-Watsonville, CA	365	358	7	0	0	87	32	0	0	263	0	102	0
Santa Fe, NM	366	310	56	0	0	93	42	0	0	359	0	7	0
Santa Rosa-Petaluma, CA	366	307	59	0	0	80	35	0	8	177	0	181	0
Sault Ste. Marie, MI	272	231	35	6	0	122	33	0	0	142	0	130	0
Savannah, GA	366	236	122	8	0	124	43	0	0	61	78	227	0
Scottsbluff, NE	237	196	40	0	1	161	43	0	0	173	0	64	0
Scranton—Wilkes-Barre, PA	366	274	89	3	0	114	38	0	11	201	0	153	1
Seaford, DE	366	307	45	13	1	174	36	0	2	328	0	36	0
Seattle-Tacoma-Bellevue, WA	366	239	118	8	1	156	42	0	0	108	0	258	0
Sebastian-Vero Beach, FL	362	350	12	0	0	90	34	0	0	362	0	0	0
Sebring, FL	364	357	7	0	0	67	31	0	0	364	0	0	0
Seneca, SC	325	311	14	0	0	80	29	0	0	196	129	0	0
Sevierville, TN	366	294	69	3	0	129	42	0	0	366	0	0	0
Seymour, IN	152	143	8	1	0	101	37.5	0	0	152	0	0	0

Metropolitan Statistical Area	Days with AQI Data	Number of Days when Air Quality was... Good	Moderate	Unhealthy for Sensitive Groups	Unhealthy or Very Unhealthy	AQI Statistics Max	Median	Number of Days when AQI Pollutant was... CO	NO_2	O_3	SO_2	$PM_{2.5}$	PM_{10}
Sheboygan, WI	198	147	28	20	3	166	38	0	0	198	0	0	0
Shelton, WA	366	320	45	1	0	116	24.5	0	0	0	0	366	0
Sheridan, WY	358	330	28	0	0	78	21	0	0	0	0	113	245
Show Low, AZ	366	298	67	1	0	106	42	0	0	362	0	0	4
Shreveport-Bossier City, LA	366	247	116	2	1	176	43	0	0	181	0	182	3
Sierra Vista-Douglas, AZ	358	273	83	2	0	120	44	0	0	330	0	3	25
Silver City, NM	366	354	12	0	0	67	37	0	0	366	0	0	0
Silverthorne, CO	123	119	4	0	0	64	12	0	0	0	0	0	123
Sioux City, IA-NE-SD	366	227	136	3	0	111	45	0	15	133	4	193	21
Sioux Falls, SD	366	261	104	0	1	170	40	0	21	224	0	109	12
Somerset, KY	277	235	39	3	0	111	39	0	0	210	0	67	0
Somerset, PA	334	314	19	1	0	116	33	0	0	334	0	0	0
South Bend-Mishawaka, IN-MI	366	183	168	13	2	201	50.5	0	12	95	0	259	0
Spartanburg, SC	365	249	114	2	0	124	45	0	0	106	0	259	0
Spokane, WA	366	283	81	2	0	112	38	2	0	110	0	249	5
Springfield, IL	366	292	68	6	0	114	36.5	1	0	307	1	57	0
Springfield, MA	366	242	118	6	0	122	42	0	12	151	0	203	0
Springfield, MO	366	211	148	7	0	124	48	0	0	135	45	186	0
Springfield, OH	366	271	90	5	0	147	39	0	0	190	102	74	0
State College, PA	366	214	147	5	0	134	40	0	0	137	1	228	0
Stockton, CA	366	161	182	21	2	156	53	0	5	167	0	190	4
Summerville, GA	265	245	20	0	0	93	36	0	0	245	0	0	20
Syracuse, NY	366	328	36	2	0	111	33	0	0	334	0	32	0
Tahlequah, OK	286	222	58	6	0	116	40	0	0	286	0	0	0
Talladega-Sylacauga, AL	116	82	34	0	0	77	42	0	0	0	0	116	0
Tallahassee, FL	366	278	84	4	0	147	39	0	0	139	0	227	0
Tampa-St. Petersburg-Clearwater, FL	366	246	107	13	0	132	45	0	0	122	23	221	0
Taos, NM	366	365	1	0	0	54	17	0	0	0	0	343	23
Terre Haute, IN	366	178	171	17	0	134	51	0	0	78	60	227	1
Texarkana, TX-Texarkana, AR	59	37	22	0	0	77	46	0	0	0	0	59	0
The Dalles, OR	365	337	28	0	0	73	20	0	0	0	0	365	0
Thomasville-Lexington, NC	360	237	123	0	0	80	43	0	0	0	0	360	0
Toledo, OH	335	238	82	15	0	150	41	0	0	174	0	71	90
Topeka, KS	366	287	71	8	0	124	37.5	0	0	305	0	45	16
Torrington, CT	364	305	56	3	0	109	37	0	0	248	0	116	0
Traverse City, MI	183	143	27	13	0	122	39	0	0	183	0	0	0
Trenton-Ewing, NJ	366	264	91	11	0	119	41	0	0	228	0	138	0
Truckee-Grass Valley, CA	366	264	92	10	0	140	38.5	0	0	349	0	17	0
Tucson, AZ	366	223	141	2	0	143	47	0	19	201	0	17	129
Tulsa, OK	366	146	191	27	2	177	54	0	2	152	44	161	7
Tupelo, MS	345	244	100	1	0	116	42	0	0	95	0	250	0
Tuscaloosa, AL	283	257	26	0	0	77	34	0	0	185	0	98	0
Twin Falls, ID	355	318	34	2	1	155	21	0	0	0	0	355	0
Tyler, TX	366	319	43	4	0	122	36	0	0	366	0	0	0
Ukiah, CA	270	239	31	0	0	77	31.5	0	0	147	0	115	8
Utica-Rome, NY	366	301	65	0	0	93	37	0	0	230	0	136	0
Valdosta, GA	345	167	176	2	0	132	51	0	0	0	0	345	0
Vallejo-Fairfield, CA	366	276	88	2	0	116	38.5	0	10	203	0	153	0
Vernal, UT	366	233	126	6	1	163	47	0	13	292	0	56	5
Victoria, TX	359	350	9	0	0	84	28	0	0	359	0	0	0
Vincennes, IN	360	295	57	8	0	114	35	0	0	360	0	0	0
Vineland-Millville-Bridgeton, NJ	340	277	53	10	0	140	37	0	0	256	0	84	0
Virginia Bch-Norfolk-Newport News, VA-NC	366	291	71	3	1	164	41	0	12	144	22	188	0
Visalia-Porterville, CA	366	107	150	101	8	169	72.5	0	1	227	0	136	2
Wabash, IN	364	304	54	6	0	145	34	0	0	364	0	0	0
Waco, TX	366	310	53	3	0	129	36	0	9	257	1	99	0

Metropolitan Statistical Area	Days with AQI Data	Number of Days when Air Quality was... Good	Moderate	Unhealthy for Sensitive Groups	Unhealthy or Very Unhealthy	AQI Statistics Max	Median	Number of Days when AQI Pollutant was... CO	NO_2	O_3	SO_2	$PM_{2.5}$	PM_{10}
Walla Walla, WA	363	327	36	0	0	92	18	0	0	0	0	363	0
Walterboro, SC	366	289	74	3	0	122	40	0	0	68	0	298	0
Warner Robins, GA	330	217	112	1	0	142	43	0	0	0	0	330	0
Warren, PA	366	314	46	6	0	128	10	0	0	0	366	0	0
Washington, IN	353	331	15	7	0	133	6	0	0	0	353	0	0
Washington, NC	358	358	0	0	0	40	1	0	0	0	358	0	0
Washington-Arlington-Alex., DC-VA-MD-WV	366	118	224	21	3	190	56.5	0	20	125	0	221	0
Washington Court House, OH, AR	357	309	44	3	1	174	34	0	0	357	0	0	0
Waterloo-Cedar Falls, IA	366	233	133	0	0	98	45	0	0	136	0	230	0
Watertown, SD	357	240	117	0	0	91	42	0	0	0	0	311	46
Watertown-Fort Atkinson, WI	196	151	41	4	0	142	40	0	0	196	0	0	0
Watertown-Fort Drum, NY	366	341	20	5	0	116	30	0	0	366	0	0	0
Wausau, WI	223	204	19	0	0	87	37	0	0	223	0	0	0
Weirton-Steubenville, WV-OH	366	148	193	24	1	167	55	0	0	87	61	217	1
Wenatchee, WA	366	260	81	10	15	347	31	0	0	0	0	366	0
Wheeling, WV-OH	366	156	207	3	0	129	53	0	0	85	39	242	0
Whitewater, WI	193	148	40	5	0	150	41	0	0	193	0	0	0
Wichita, KS	366	237	114	14	1	156	43	2	46	235	0	47	36
Wichita Falls, TX	335	317	18	0	0	72	28	0	0	0	0	335	0
Williamsport, PA	350	327	23	0	0	93	31	0	0	344	0	0	6
Willimantic, CT	362	340	20	2	0	122	31	0	0	362	0	0	0
Williston, ND	366	292	61	9	4	200	11	0	0	0	366	0	0
Wilmington, NC	366	322	43	1	0	104	34	0	0	147	33	186	0
Wilmington, OH	214	152	54	7	1	161	45	0	0	214	0	0	0
Winchester, VA-WV	361	259	101	1	0	101	41	0	0	136	0	225	0
Winston-Salem, NC	366	257	103	6	0	150	42	0	15	152	0	199	0
Worcester, MA	366	291	74	1	0	142	38	0	44	162	0	159	1
Yakima, WA	366	243	115	3	5	170	36	0	0	0	0	366	0
Yauco, PR	77	71	6	0	0	67	17	0	0	0	0	77	0
York-Hanover, PA	366	191	167	8	0	142	49	0	7	134	2	223	0
Youngstown-Warren-Boardman, OH-PA	366	168	184	13	1	161	52	0	0	126	12	227	1
Yuba City, CA	366	268	90	8	0	124	42	0	26	263	0	75	2
Yuma, AZ	366	259	90	16	1	160	44	0	0	172	0	13	181

Notes: *Dashes indicates data was not available; The Air Quality Index (AQI) is an index for reporting daily air quality. It tells you how clean or polluted your air is, and what associated health concerns you should be aware of. The AQI focuses on health effects that can happen within a few hours or days after breathing polluted air. EPA uses the AQI for six major air pollutants regulated by the Clean Air Act: CO (carbon monoxide), NO (nitrogen dioxide), O (ground-level ozone), SO (sulfur dioxide), PM (particulate matter 10 - particles with diameters of 10 micrometers or less), PM (particulate matter 2.5 - particles with diameters of 2.5 micrometers or less). For each of these pollutants, EPA has established national air quality standards to protect against harmful health effects.*

The AQI runs from 0 to 500. The higher the AQI value, the greater the level of air pollution and the greater the health danger. For example, an AQI value of 50 represents good air quality and little potential to affect public health, while an AQI value over 300 represents hazardous air quality. An AQI value of 100 generally corresponds to the national air quality standard for the pollutant, which is the level EPA has set to protect public health. So, AQI values below 100 are generally thought of as satisfactory. When AQI values are above 100, air quality is considered to be unhealthy-at first for certain sensitive groups of people, then for everyone as AQI values get higher. Each category corresponds to a different level of health concern. For example, when the AQI for a pollutant is between 51 and 100, the health concern is "Moderate." Here are the six levels of health concern and what they mean:

- *"Good" The AQI value for your community is between 0 and 50. Air quality is considered satisfactory and air pollution poses little or no risk.*
- *"Moderate" The AQI for your community is between 51 and 100. Air quality is acceptable; however, for some pollutants there may be a moderate health concern for a very small number of individuals. For example, people who are unusually sensitive to ozone may experience respiratory symptoms.*
- *"Unhealthy for Sensitive Groups" Certain groups of people are particularly sensitive to the harmful effects of certain air pollutants. This means they are likely to be affected at lower levels than the general public. For example, children and adults who are active outdoors and people with respiratory disease are at greater risk from exposure to ozone, while people with heart disease are at greater risk from carbon monoxide. Some people may be sensitive to more than one pollutant. When AQI values are between 101 and 150, members of sensitive groups may experience health effects. The general public is not likely to be affected when the AQI is in this range.*
- *"Unhealthy" AQI values are between 151 and 200. Everyone may begin to experience health effects. Members of sensitive groups may experience more serious health effects.*
- *"Very Unhealthy" AQI values between 201 and 300 trigger a health alert, meaning everyone may experience more serious health effects.*
- *"Hazardous" AQI values over 300 trigger health warnings of emergency conditions. The entire population is more likely to be affected.*

Source: *U.S. Environmental Protection Agency, Office of Air and Radiation, Air Quality Index Report, 2012*

Brownfields Prevalence: Number of Sites and Estimated Acreage, 1993/2010

City	State	Est. Brownfield Sites in 1993	Est. Brownfield Sites in 2010	Est. Avg. Size of Brownfield Sites in 1993 (Acres)	Est. Avg. Size of Brownfield Sites in 2010 (Acres)
Akron	Ohio	3	6	6	8
Alameda	California	250	270	0.15	0.2
Allentown	Pennsylvania	20	10	7	7
Arlington	Texas	*	1650	*	*
Arlington Heights	Illinois	*	*	*	*
Asheville	North Carolina	300	300	2	2
Atlanta	Georgia	*	164	*	9.3
Babylon	New York	*	350	*	0.24
Baltimore	Maryland	1000	1000	*	*
Bartlett	Illinois	4	1	1	0.5
Bessemer	Alabama	40	30	10	8
Biloxi	Mississippi	9	20	5.5	5
Binghamton	New York	23	21	5	5
Boston	Massachusetts	1250	1400	0.25	0.25
Bridgeport	Connecticut	500	450	3	3
Camden	New Jersey	500	485	3	3
Cape Coral	Florida	*	*	*	*
Carson	California	*	217	*	4.5
Charleston	South Carolina	75	100	10	5
Chattanooga	Tennessee	*	*	*	*
Chicago Heights	Illinois	52	30	1.5	2.5
Cincinnati	Ohio	*	15	*	28.116
Clearwater	Florida	*	244	*	1.5
Clovis	New Mexico	1	1	1	1
Columbia	South Carolina	11	35	1	1
Columbus	Ohio	18	28	30	10
Dallas	Texas	*	*	*	*
Dayton	Ohio	*	30	*	10
Dearborn	Michigan	*	20	*	50
Denton	Texas	*	*	*	*
Dubuque	Iowa	*	38	*	3
Durham	North Carolina	*	*	*	*
Elizabeth	New Jersey	*	160	*	1.5
Evansville	Indiana	350	300	1.5	1
Fayetteville	North Carolina	100	125	250	300
Florence	Alabama	*	20	*	5
Fort Myers	Florida	*	50	*	0.93
Fresno	California	*	*	*	*
Frisco	Texas	*	*	*	*
Glendale Heights	Illinois	2	2	1	1
Gloucester	Massachusetts	*	*	*	*
Grand Rapids	Michigan	*	*	*	1
Green Bay	Wisconsin	31	15	*	1.5
Greensboro	North Carolina	*	30	*	2
Gulfport	Mississippi	2000	1709	*	6.8
Hagerstown	Maryland	36	33	*	*
Hartford	Connecticut	20	35	5	3.5
Hoffman Estates	Illinois	*	*	*	*
Honolulu	Hawaii	*	*	*	*
Houston	Texas	1000	2000	*	3
Huntsville	Alabama	*	*	*	*
Indianapolis	Indiana	*	1617	*	4.03
Irvine	California	*	*	*	*
Isabela	Puerto Rico	4	4	15	15
Jackson	Mississippi	*	250	*	0.57
Kalamazoo	Michigan	200	340	2.5	2.5
Kansas City	Kansas	*	*	*	*
Lakeland	Florida	1	2	85	*
Las Vegas	Nevada	3	2	69	57.5
Lewiston	Maine	18	11	*	*
Louisville	Kentucky	*	67	*	8
Memphis	Tennessee	23	149	*	23
Miami Beach	Florida	*	1	*	2.83

Milwaukee	Wisconsin	400	300	2	1
Monroe	Louisiana	9	8	3	2.5
Naugatuck	Connecticut	15	10	50	150
New Orleans	Louisiana	500	450	1	1
Niagara Falls	New York	1750	1750	1.5	1.5
North Chicago	Illinois	*	*	*	*
North Little Rock	Arkansas	50	50	1	1
North Miami	Florida	*	0	*	*
Norwalk	Connecticut	*	261	*	0.5
Orland Park	Illinois	*	1	*	20
Palm Beach Gardens	Florida	*	0	*	*
Pawtucket	Rhode Island	90	88	0.5	0.5
Pembroke Pines	Florida	*	*	*	*
Piscataway	New Jersey	5	8	7	7
Portland	Oregon	*	515	*	2.8
Racine	Wisconsin	*	300	*	*
Radnor	Pennsylvania	*	*	*	*
Saint Louis	Missouri	*	304	*	0.3
Saint Paul	Minnesota	225	200	40	10
San Juan	Puerto Rico	*	130	*	5
Sanford	North Carolina	60	28	12	4.2
Shreveport	Louisiana	*	460	*	5
Somerville	Massachusetts	750	500	0.5	0.5
Southgate	Michigan	*	1	*	*
Syracuse	New York	*	163	*	8.2
Tacoma	Washington	*	322	*	0.25
Tallahassee	Florida	*	1	*	3
Toa Baja	Puerto Rico	*	1	*	0.33
Tucson	Arizona	*	5200	*	*
Vista	California	*	250	*	1
Waco	Texas	*	100	*	3
Warren	Ohio	5	5	7	7
West Palm Beach	Florida	*	4236	*	1
Wilson	North Carolina	*	75	*	2
York	Pennsylvania	121	70	0.526	0.573
Zanesville	Ohio	*	*	*	*
99 Respondents		*Est. Brownfield Sites in 1993*	*Est. Brownfield Sites in 2010*		
Totals		11,824	29,624		

Source: The U.S. Conference of Mayors, Recycling America's Land: A National Report on Brownfields Redevelopment (1993-2010), November 2010, Volume IX

Brownfields Redeveloped Since 1993: Number of Sites and Estimated Acreage

City	State	Since 1993, Sites redeveloped	Since 1993, Acres Developed	In Progress Sites	In Progress Acres
Akron	Ohio	12	60	5	50
Alameda	California	10	2	2	2
Allentown	Pennsylvania	10	62	4	31
Arlington	Texas	35	380	6	10
Arlington Heights	Illinois	*	*	*	*
Asheville	North Carolina	1	3	3	14
Atlanta	Georgia	*	*	15	266
Babylon	New York	*	*	20	*
Baltimore	Maryland	45	*	5	40
Bartlett	Illinois	3	10	1	0.5
Biloxi	Mississippi	*	*	*	*
Binghamton	New York	2	35	*	*
Boston	Massachusetts	*	*	1	2.43
Bridgeport	Connecticut	50	150	15	95
Camden	New Jersey	15	20	3	37
Cape Coral	Florida	*	*	*	*
Carson	California	*	*	3	162
Charleston	South Carolina	6	50	200	800
Chattanooga	Tennessee	*	*	*	*
Chicago Heights	Illinois	2	11	1	8
Cincinnati	Ohio	5	31	5	139
Bessemer	Alabama	10	200	2	25
Clearwater	Florida	15	30	10	18
Clovis	New Mexico	1	1	1	1
Columbia	South Carolina	46	46	35	35
Columbus	Ohio	19	200	7	100
Dallas	Texas	53	1046	5	55
Dayton	Ohio	10	150	3	130
Dearborn	Michigan	9	100	2	75
Denton	Texas	*	*	1	2
Dubuque	Iowa	3	80	4	85
Durham	North Carolina	*	*	*	*
Elizabeth	New Jersey	12	190	9	30
Evansville	Indiana	8	75	3	18
Fayetteville	North Carolina	1	15	1	100
Florence	Alabama	*	*	2	25
Fort Myers	Florida	5	19	*	*
Fresno	California	*	*	1	3
Frisco	Texas	*	*	*	*
Glendale Heights	Illinois	1	1	*	*
Gloucester	Massachusetts	*	*	2	4
Grand Rapids	Michigan	90	280.55	10	10
Green Bay	Wisconsin	*	*	3	10
Greensboro	North Carolina	*	*	1	10
Gulfport	Mississippi	*	*	*	*
Hagerstown	Maryland	5	*	*	*
Hartford	Connecticut	*	*	10	30
Hoffman Estates	Illinois	*	*	*	*
Honolulu	Hawaii	*	*	1	2
Houston	Texas	68	1914.57	39	682

Huntsville	Alabama	*	*	*	*
Indianapolis	Indiana	44	200	35	140
Irvine	California	*	*	*	*
Isabela	Puerto Rico	*	*	*	*
Jackson	Mississippi	*	45	20	80
Kalamazoo	Michigan	30	103	16	133.94
Kansas City	Kansas	*	*	*	*
Lakeland	Florida	1	1	*	*
Las Vegas	Nevada	2	11.5	2	57.5
Lewiston	Maine	4	21	4	6.5
Louisville	Kentucky	24	*	11	*
Memphis	Tennessee	20	*	4	*
Miami Beach	Florida	1	2.83	*	*
Milwaukee	Wisconsin	90	200	40	100
Monroe	Louisiana	1	5	1	5
Naugatuck	Connecticut	5	10	3	8
New Orleans	Louisiana	28	52	5	6
Niagara Falls	New York	3	200	3	100
North Chicago	Illinois	1	2	1	40
North Little Rock	Arkansas	10	10	3	180
North Miami	Florida	*	*	*	*
Norwalk	Connecticut	*	*	4	10
Orland Park	Illinois	*	*	1	20
Palm Beach Gardens	Florida	*	*	*	*
Pawtucket	Rhode Island	1	1	3	10
Pembroke Pines	Florida	*	*	*	*
Piscataway	New Jersey	1	1	*	*
Portland	Oregon	*	*	*	*
Racine	Wisconsin	3	11	2	20
Radnor	Pennsylvania	*	*	*	*
Saint Louis	Missouri	30	*	79	*
Saint Paul	Minnesota	25	625	8	80
San Juan	Puerto Rico	*	*	130	5
Sanford	North Carolina	32	84	2	6
Shreveport	Louisiana	42	228	5	28
Somerville	Massachusetts	25	40	20	100
Southgate	Michigan	*	*	*	*
Syracuse	New York	4	160	30	393
Tacoma	Washington	3	5	3	6
Tallahassee	Florida	1	2.5	2	6
Toa Baja	Puerto Rico	*	*	1	0.33
Tucson	Arizona	25	*	12	*
Vista	California	2	2	*	*
Waco	Texas	*	*	1	5
Warren	Ohio	*	*	2	10
West Palm Beach	Florida	*	25	10	3.05
Wilson	North Carolina	*	*	*	*
York	Pennsylvania	*	*	2	12
Zanesville	Ohio	*	*	1	4.33
99 Respondents		**Sites redeveloped since 1993**	**Acres developed since 1993**	**Sites in progress**	**Acres in progress**
Totals		1,010.00	7,209.95	907.00	4,682.58

Source: The U.S. Conference of Mayors, Recycling America's Land: A National Report on Brownfields Redevelopment (1993-2010), November 2010, Volume IX

Estimated Annual Tax Revenue Gains from Brownfields Redevelopment

City	State	Est. Annual Tax Revenue Gained Conservative	Est. Annual Tax Revenue Gained Optimistic	Est. Annual Tax Revenue Gained Actual Since '93
Akron	Ohio	*	*	*
Alameda	California	$550,000.00	$950,000.00	*
Allentown	Pennsylvania	$150,000.00	$250,000.00	$500,000.00
Arlington	Texas	*	*	*
Arlington Heights	Illinois	*	*	*
Asheville	North Carolina	$1,000,000.00	$2,000,000.00	$500,000.00
Atlanta	Georgia	$4,614,000.00	$23,070,000.00	*
Babylon	New York	$5,000,000.00	$8,000,000.00	*
Baltimore	Maryland	*	*	*
Bartlett	Illinois	$35,000.00	$50,000.00	$1,360,000.00
Bessemer	Alabama	$5,000,000.00	$20,000,000.00	*
Biloxi	Mississippi	*	*	*
Binghamton	New York	*	*	*
Boston	Massachusetts	$7,000,000.00	$10,000,000.00	*
Bridgeport	Connecticut	$20,000,000.00	$50,000,000.00	*
Camden	New Jersey	$54,359,000.00	$71,253,000.00	*
Cape Coral	Florida	*	*	*
Carson	California	*	*	*
Charleston	South Carolina	$50,000,000.00	$25,000,000.00	*
Chattanooga	Tennessee	*	*	*
Chicago Heights	Illinois	*	*	*
Cincinnati	Ohio	*	*	*
Clearwater	Florida	$2,500,000.00	$5,000,000.00	*
Clovis	New Mexico	$100,000.00	$100,000.00	*
Columbia	South Carolina	$63,700,000.00	$100,000,000.00	$12,500,000.00
Columbus	Ohio	$15,000,000.00	$15,000,000.00	$175,000,000.00
Dallas	Texas	$5,000,000.00	$10,000,000.00	*
Dayton	Ohio	$1,000,000.00	$3,000,000.00	*
Dearborn	Michigan	$100,000,000.00	$140,000,000.00	*
Denton	Texas	*	*	*
Dubuque	Iowa	$4,000,000.00	$8,000,000.00	$4,106,500.00
Durham	North Carolina	*	*	*
Elizabeth	New Jersey	$30,000,000.00	$45,000,000.00	$6,600,000.00
Evansville	Indiana	*	*	*
Fayetteville	North Carolina	$250,000.00	$1,000,000.00	*
Florence	Alabama	*	*	*
Fort Myers	Florida	*	*	*
Fresno	California	*	*	*
Frisco	Texas	*	*	*
Glendale Heights	Illinois	$50,000.00	$100,000.00	*
Gloucester	Massachusetts	$3,000,000.00	$12,000,000.00	*
Grand Rapids	Michigan	$2,533,998.00	$4,500,000.00	$7,380,170.00
Green Bay	Wisconsin	*	*	*
Greensboro	North Carolina	$250,000.00	$250,000.00	*
Gulfport	Mississippi	$5,000,000.00	$10,000,000.00	*
Hagerstown	Maryland	*	*	*
Hartford	Connecticut	$500,000.00	$2,000,000.00	*
Hoffman Estates	Illinois	*	*	*
Honolulu	Hawaii	*	*	*
Houston	Texas	*	*	*
Huntsville	Alabama	*	*	*
Indianapolis	Indiana	$11,500,000.00	$20,000,000.00	*
Irvine	California	*	*	*
Isabela	Puerto Rico	$5,000,000.00	$7,000,000.00	$10,000,000.00
Jackson	Mississippi	$125,000.00	$200,000.00	$50,000.00
Kalamazoo	Michigan	$16,000,000.00	$30,000,000.00	$4,538,583.00

Kansas City	Kansas	*	*	*
Lakeland	Florida	$15,000.00	$35,000.00	*
Las Vegas	Nevada	$16,000,000.00	$28,182,000.00	$2,163,250.00
Lewiston	Maine	$252,000,000.00	$317,000,000.00	$718,000.00
Louisville	Kentucky	$67,250.00	$80,700.00	*
Memphis	Tennessee	$8,000,000.00	$25,000,000.00	*
Miami Beach	Florida	*	*	*
Milwaukee	Wisconsin	$50,000,000.00	$100,000,000.00	$17,000,000.00
Monroe	Louisiana	*	*	*
Naugatuck	Connecticut	$500,000.00	$1,000,000.00	*
New Orleans	Louisiana	$5,000,000.00	$20,000,000.00	$1,500,000.00
Niagara Falls	New York	*	*	*
North Chicago	Illinois	$30,000.00	$50,000.00	*
North Little Rock	Arkansas	*	*	$2,000,000.00
North Miami	Florida	*	*	*
Norwalk	Connecticut	*	*	*
Orland Park	Illinois	*	*	*
Palm Beach Gardens	Florida	*	*	*
Pawtucket	Rhode Island	*	*	*
Pembroke Pines	Florida	*	*	*
Piscataway	New Jersey	*	*	*
Portland	Oregon	*	*	*
Racine	Wisconsin	*	$1,197,057.00	*
Radnor	Pennsylvania	*	*	*
Saint Louis	Missouri	*	*	*
Saint Paul	Minnesota	$8,000,000.00	$10,000,000.00	$5,900,000.00
San Juan	Puerto Rico	$1,600,000.00	$2,400,000.00	*
Sanford	North Carolina	$40,000.00	$400,000.00	*
Shreveport	Louisiana	*	*	*
Somerville	Massachusetts	$106,000,000.00	$120,000,000.00	*
Southgate	Michigan	*	*	*
Syracuse	New York	$9,587,119.50	$38,348,478.00	$56,224,371.00
Tacoma	Washington	*	*	*
Tallahassee	Florida	$1,000,000.00	$3,000,000.00	$593,260.00
Toa Baja	Puerto Rico	*	*	*
Tucson	Arizona	*	*	*
Vista	California	*	*	*
Waco	Texas	*	*	*
Warren	Ohio	*	*	*
West Palm Beach	Florida	*	*	*
Wilson	North Carolina	$200,000.00	$500,000.00	*
York	Pennsylvania	$500,000.00	$2,000,000.00	*
Zanesville	Ohio	*	*	*
Total Respondents: 99		*Est. Annual Tax Revenue Gained Conservative* *$871,206,367.50*	*Est. Annual Tax Revenue Gained Optimistic* *$1,291,966,235.00*	*Est. Annual Tax Revenue Gained Actual Since '93* *$308,634,134.00*

Source: The U.S. Conference of Mayors, Recycling America's Land: A National Report on Brownfields Redevelopment (1993-2010), November 2010, Volume IX

Indicator B1

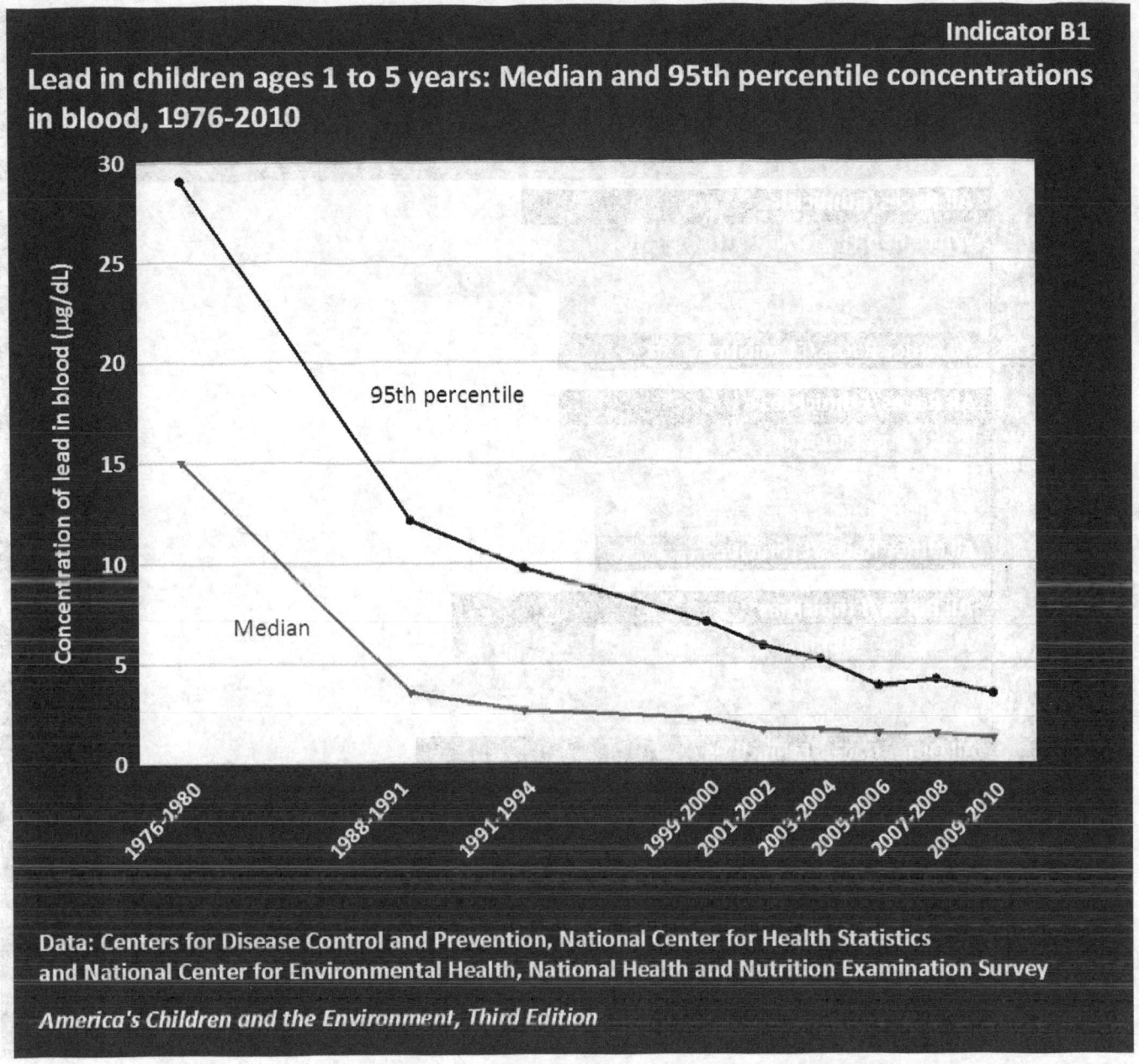

Lead in children ages 1 to 5 years: Median and 95th percentile concentrations in blood, 1976-2010

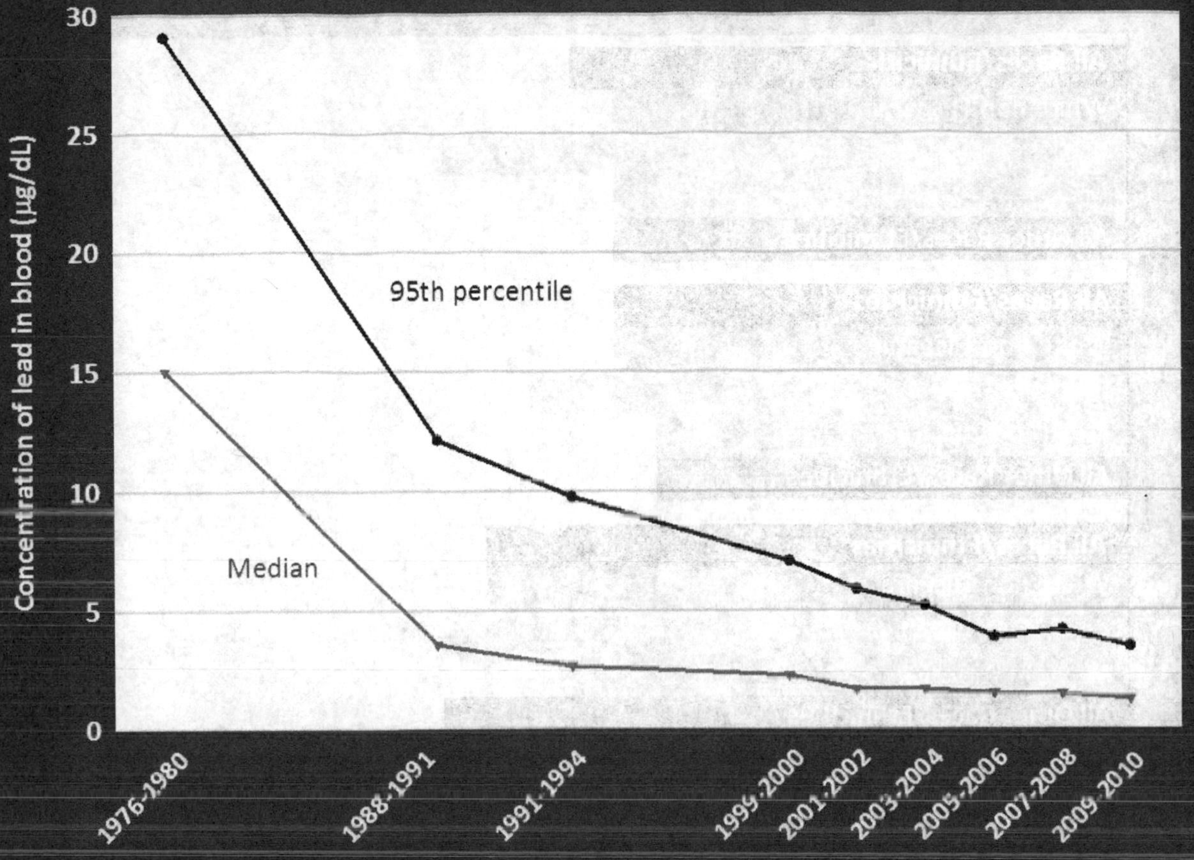

Data: Centers for Disease Control and Prevention, National Center for Health Statistics and National Center for Environmental Health, National Health and Nutrition Examination Survey

America's Children and the Environment, Third Edition

Indicator B2

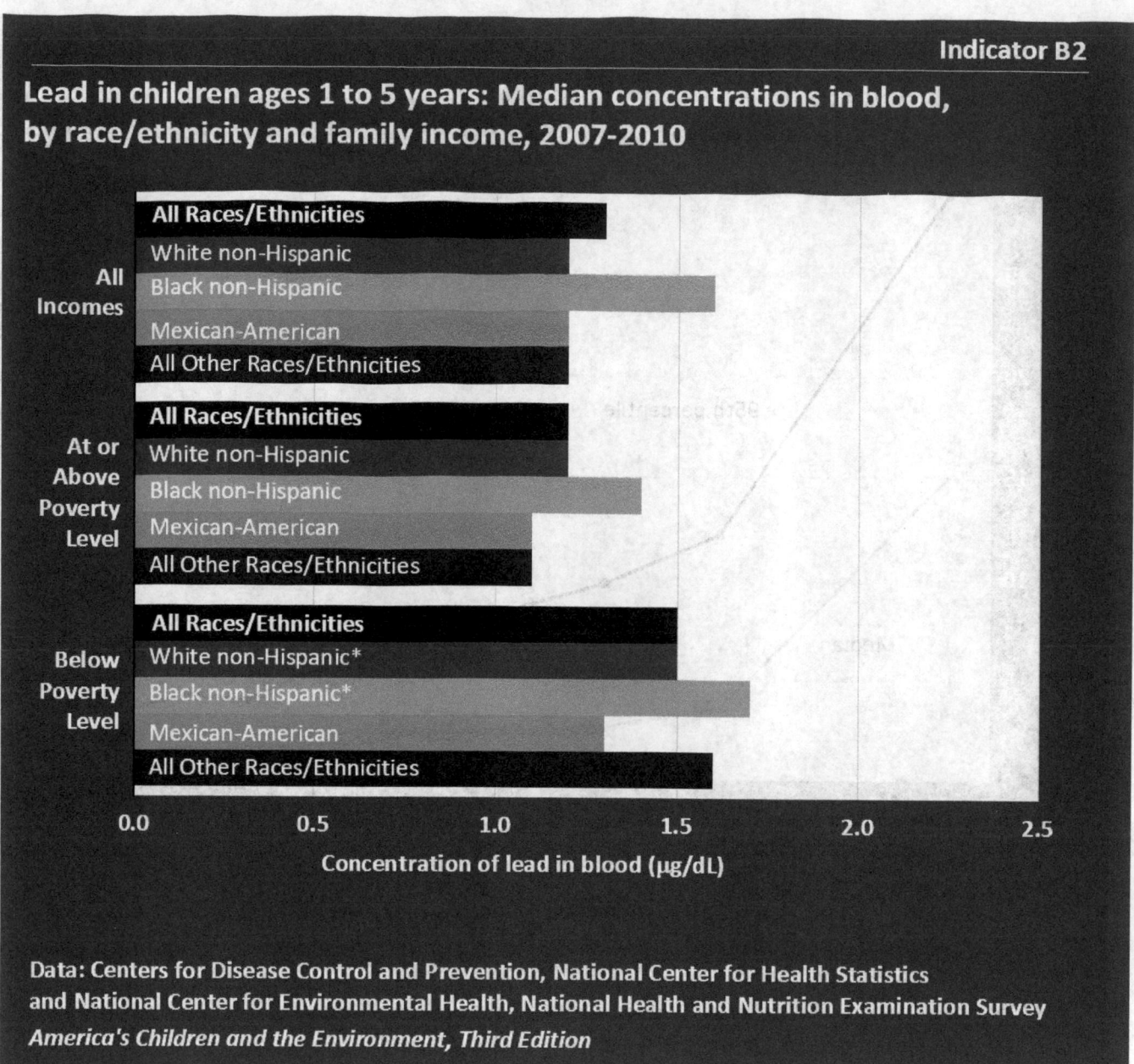

Lead in children ages 1 to 5 years: Median concentrations in blood, by race/ethnicity and family income, 2007-2010

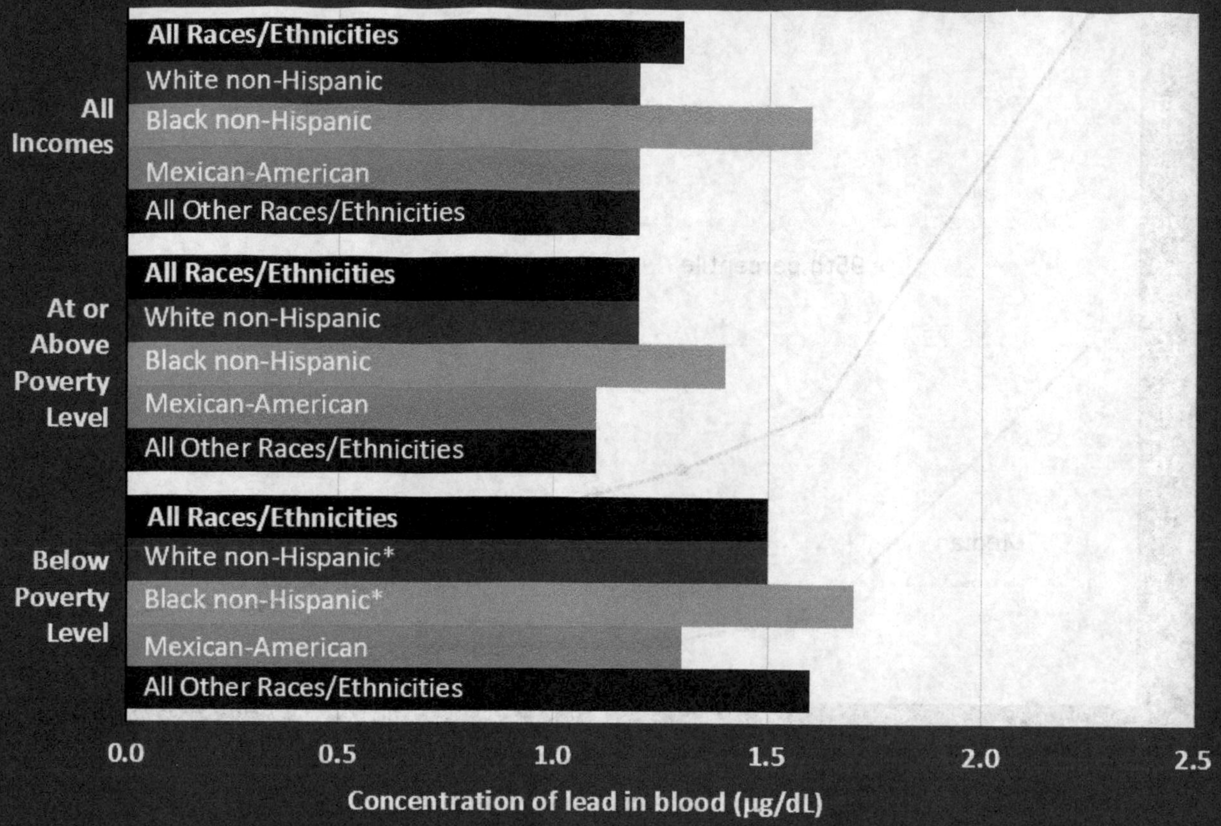

Data: Centers for Disease Control and Prevention, National Center for Health Statistics and National Center for Environmental Health, National Health and Nutrition Examination Survey

America's Children and the Environment, Third Edition

Indicator B3

Mercury in women ages 16 to 49 years: Median and 95th percentile concentrations in blood, 1999-2010

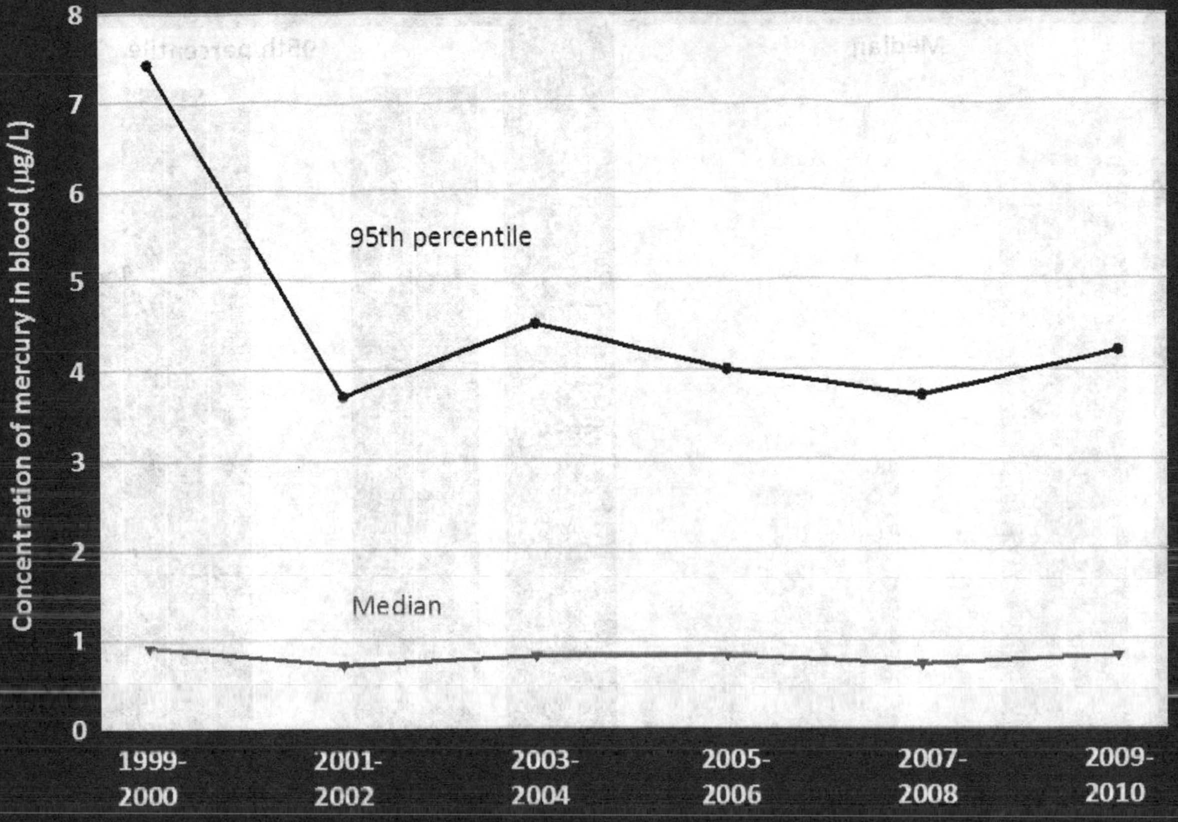

Data: Centers for Disease Control and Prevention, National Center for Health Statistics and National Center for Environmental Health, National Health and Nutrition Examination Survey

Note: To reflect exposures to women who are pregnant or may become pregnant, the estimates are adjusted for the probability (by age and race/ethnicity) that a woman gives birth.

America's Children and the Environment, Third Edition

Indicator B4

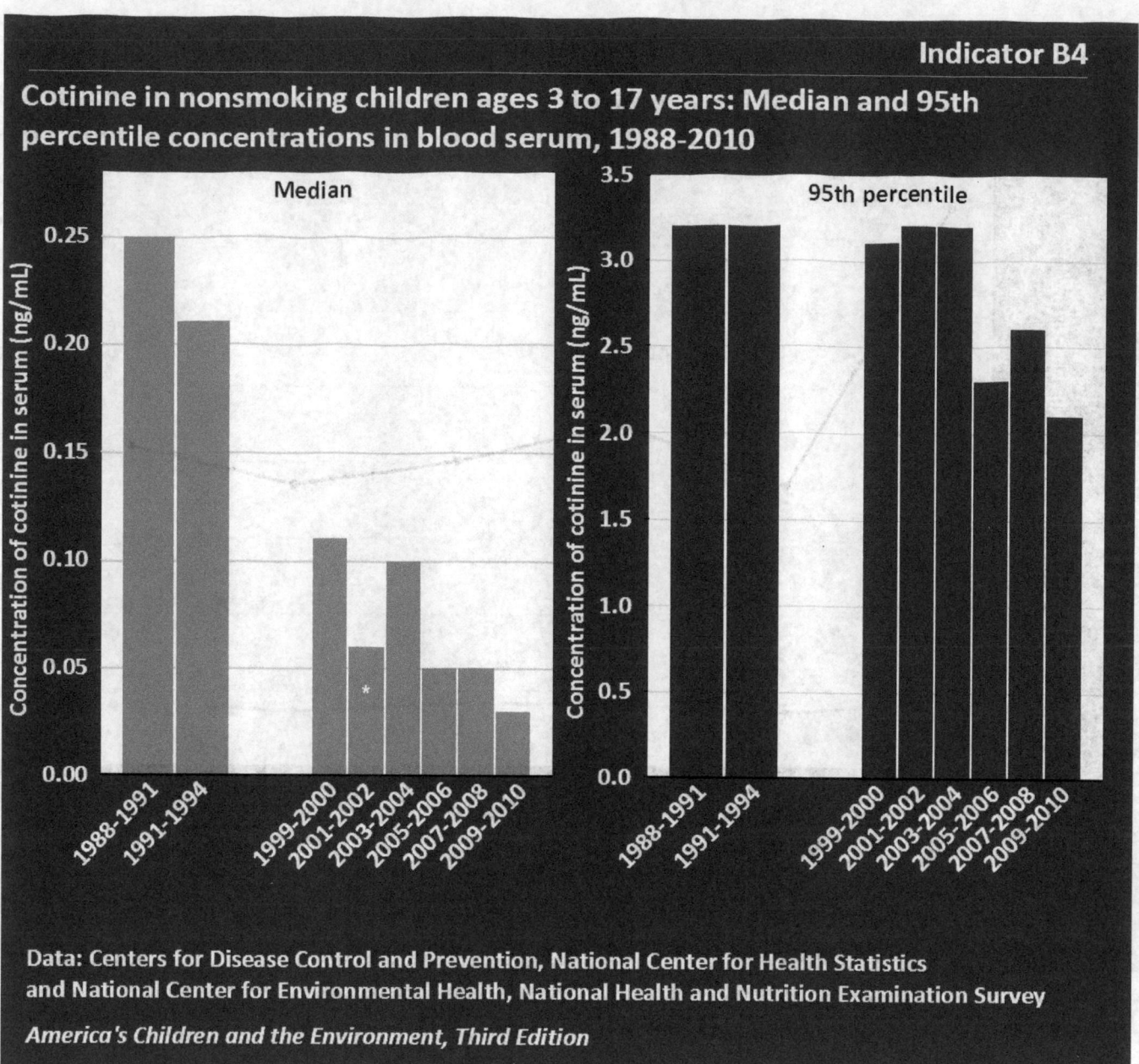

Cotinine in nonsmoking children ages 3 to 17 years: Median and 95th percentile concentrations in blood serum, 1988-2010

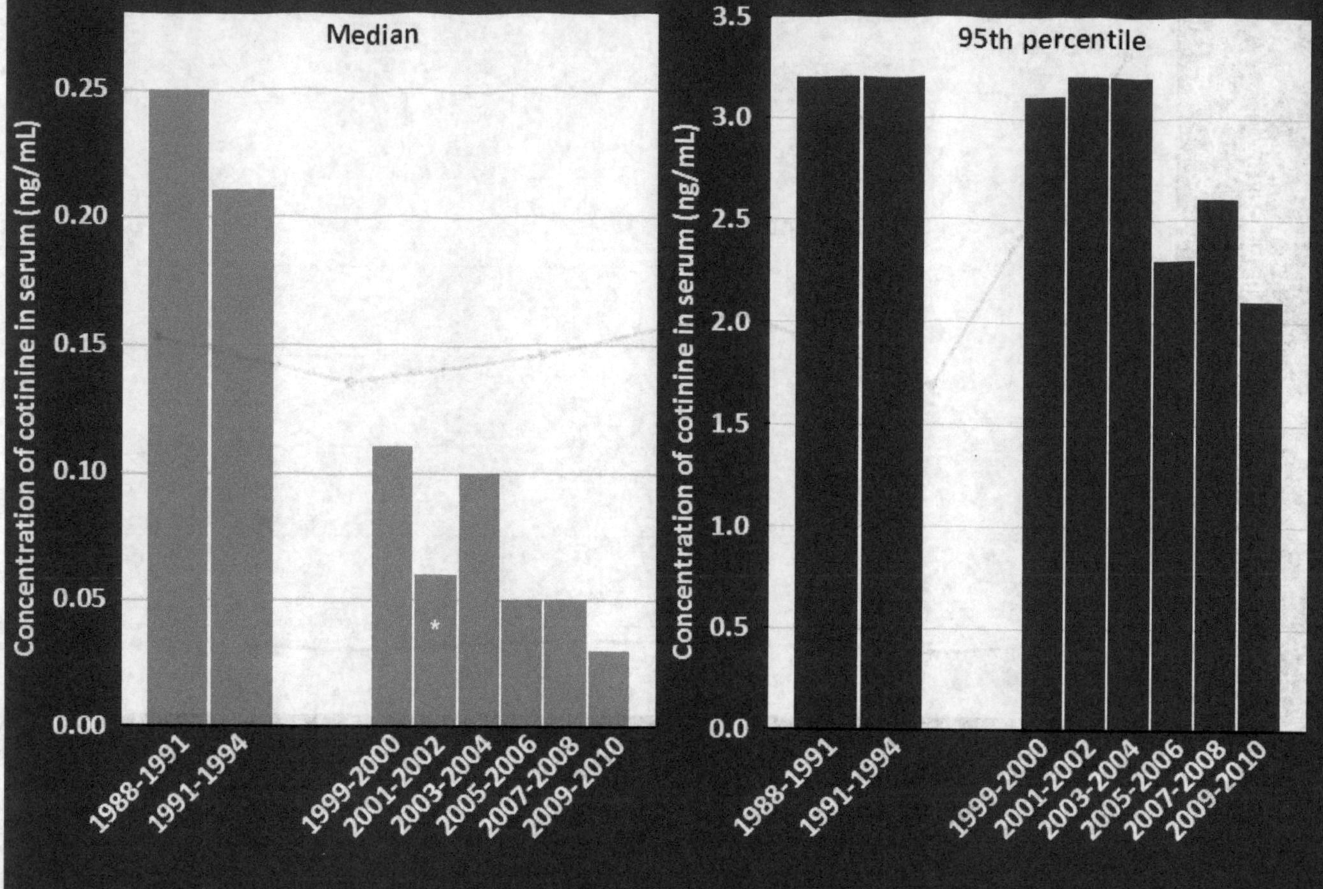

Data: Centers for Disease Control and Prevention, National Center for Health Statistics and National Center for Environmental Health, National Health and Nutrition Examination Survey

America's Children and the Environment, Third Edition

Indicator B5

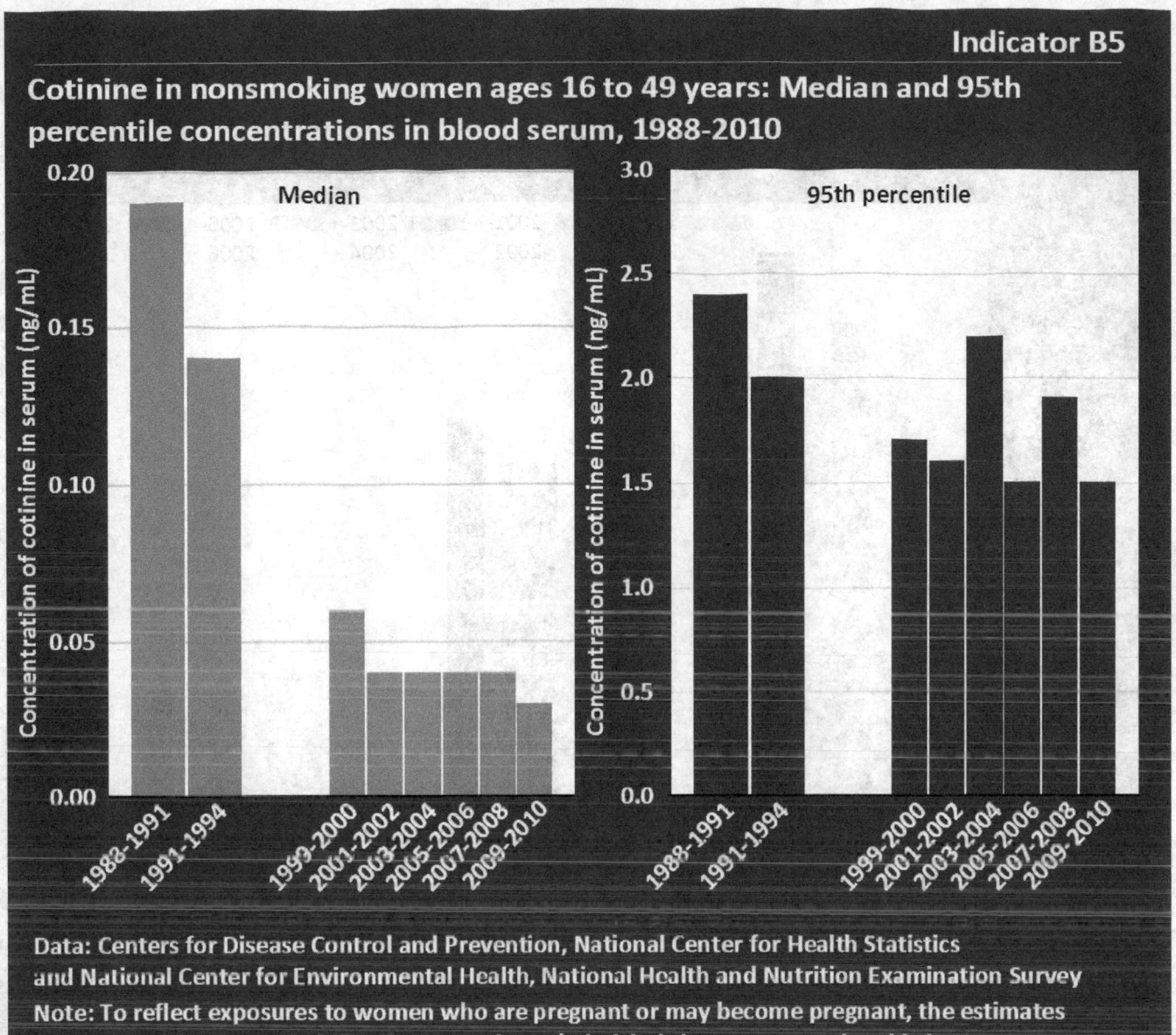

Cotinine in nonsmoking women ages 16 to 49 years: Median and 95th percentile concentrations in blood serum, 1988-2010

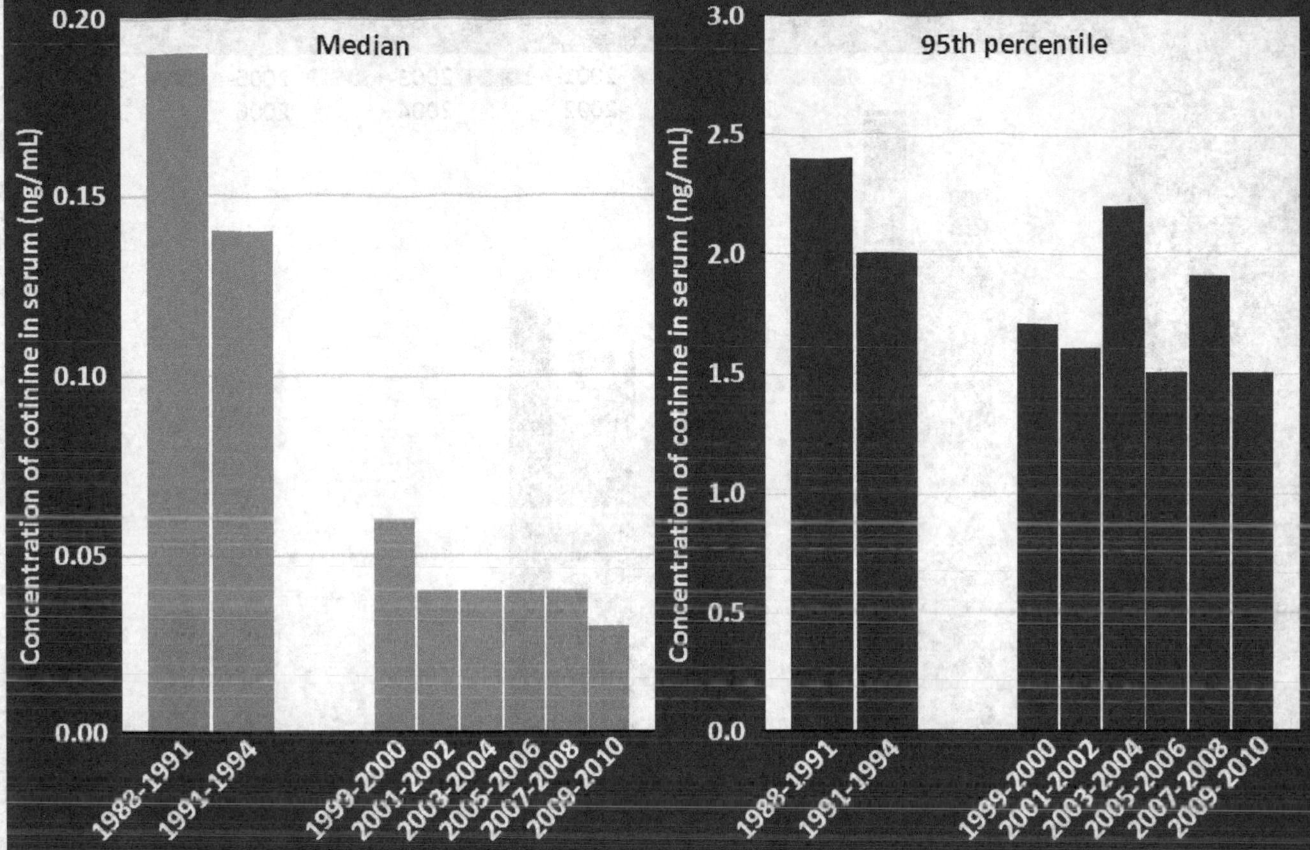

Data: Centers for Disease Control and Prevention, National Center for Health Statistics and National Center for Environmental Health, National Health and Nutrition Examination Survey

Note: To reflect exposures to women who are pregnant or may become pregnant, the estimates are adjusted for the probability (by age and race/ethnicity) that a woman gives birth.

America's Children and the Environment, Third Edition

Indicator B9

Phthalate metabolites in women ages 16 to 49 years: Median concentrations in urine, 1999-2008

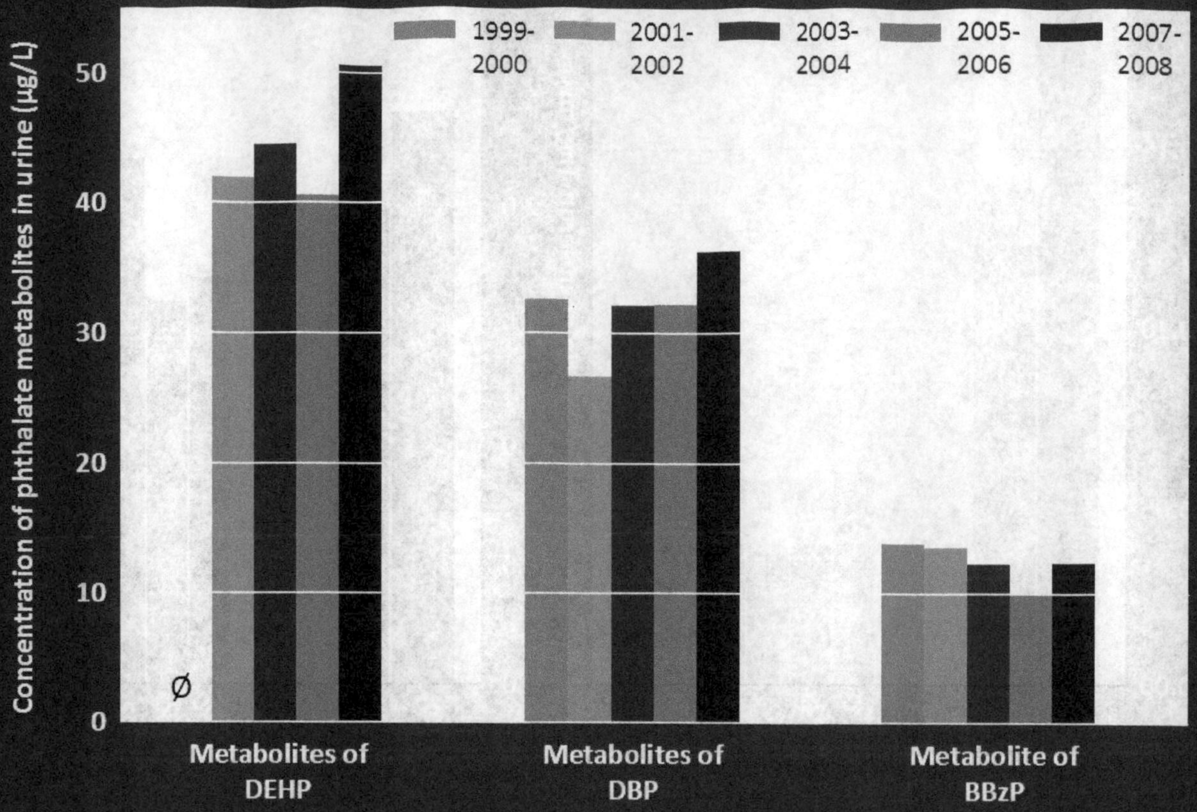

Data: Centers for Disease Control and Prevention, National Center for Health Statistics and National Center for Environmental Health, National Health and Nutrition Examination Survey

Note: To reflect exposures to women who are pregnant or may become pregnant, the estimates are adjusted for the probability (by age and race/ethnicity) that a woman gives birth.

America's Children and the Environment, Third Edition

Indicator B11

Bisphenol A in women ages 16 to 49 years: Median and 95th percentile concentrations in urine, 2003-2010

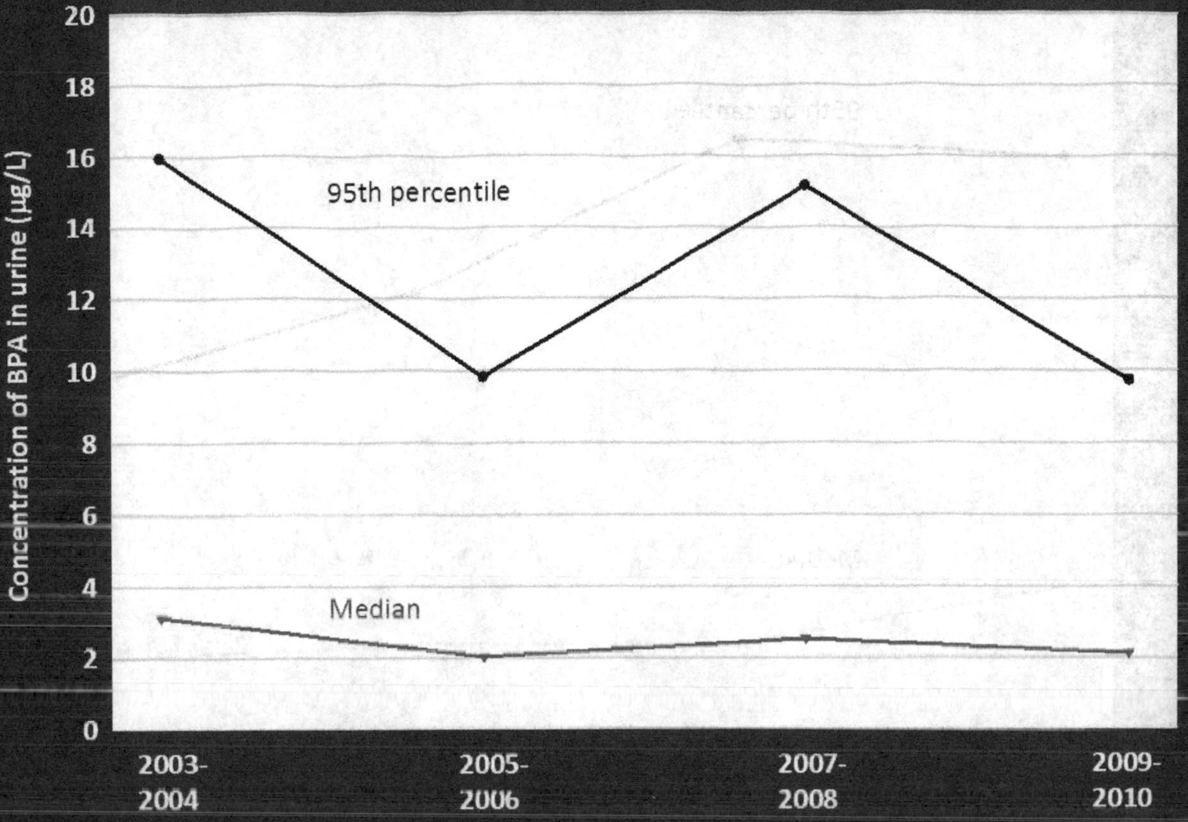

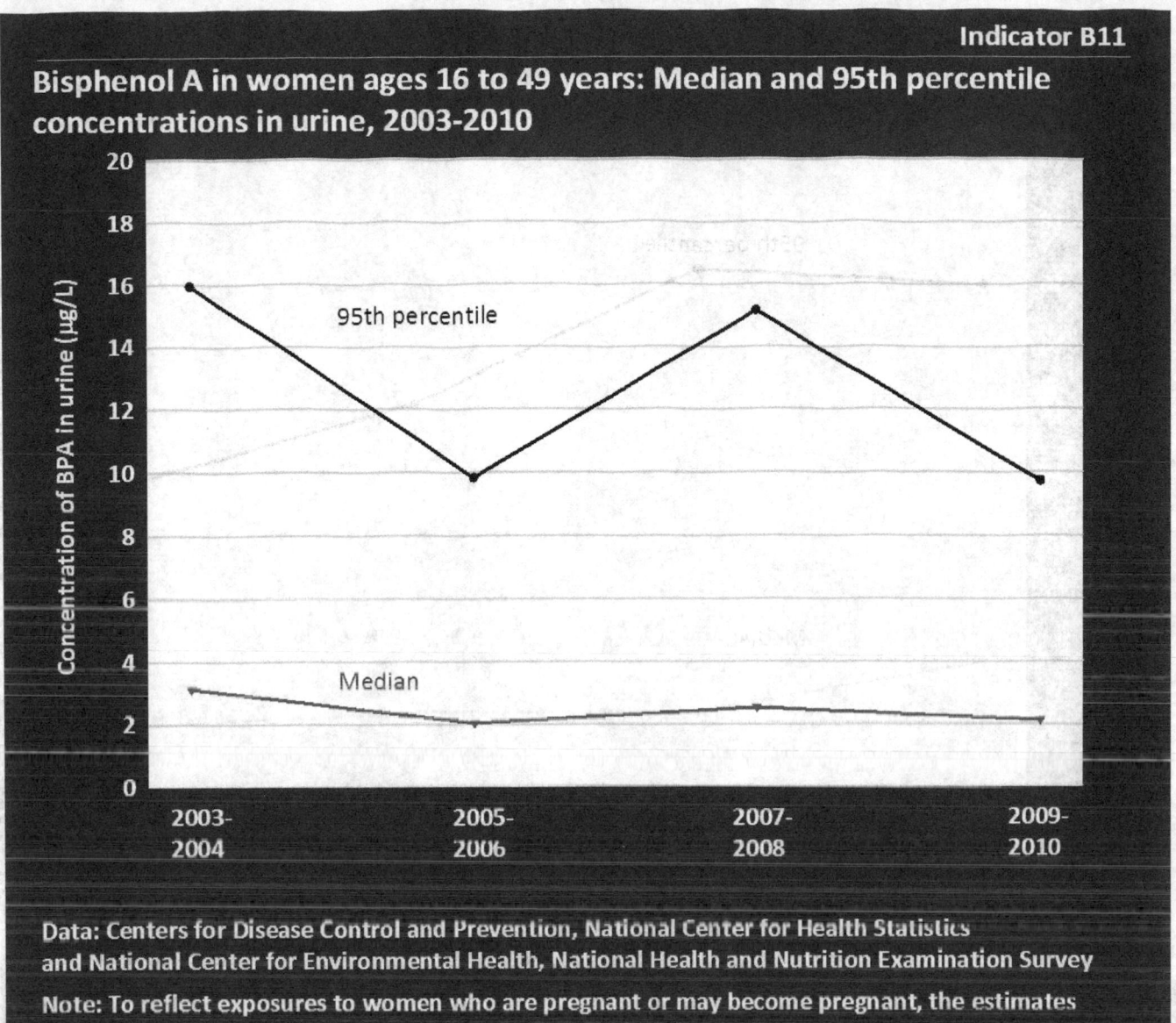

Data: Centers for Disease Control and Prevention, National Center for Health Statistics and National Center for Environmental Health, National Health and Nutrition Examination Survey

Note: To reflect exposures to women who are pregnant or may become pregnant, the estimates are adjusted for the probability (by age and race/ethnicity) that a woman gives birth.

America's Children and the Environment, Third Edition

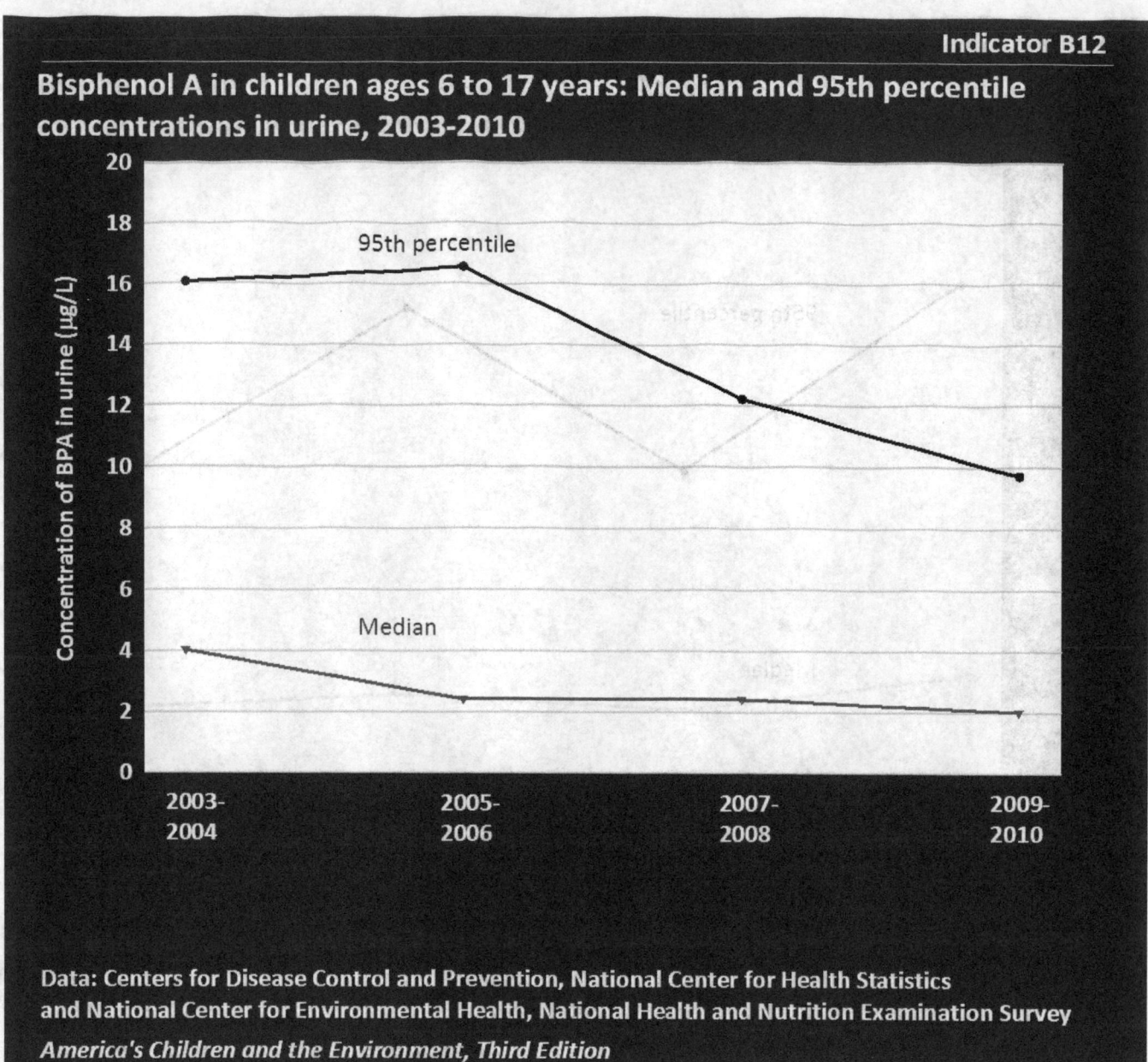

Indicator B12

Bisphenol A in children ages 6 to 17 years: Median and 95th percentile concentrations in urine, 2003-2010

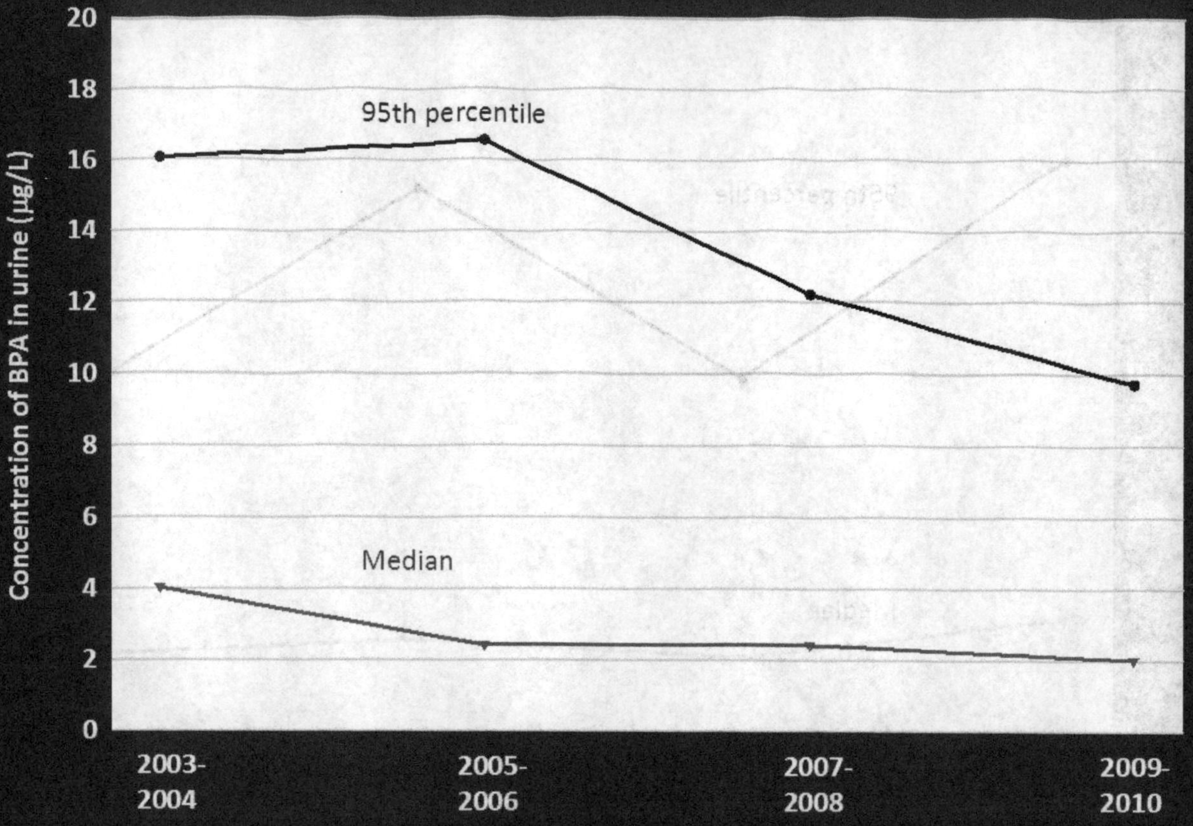

Data: Centers for Disease Control and Prevention, National Center for Health Statistics and National Center for Environmental Health, National Health and Nutrition Examination Survey

America's Children and the Environment, Third Edition

Indicator B13

Perchlorate in women ages 16 to 49 years: Median and 95th percentile concentrations in urine, 2001-2008

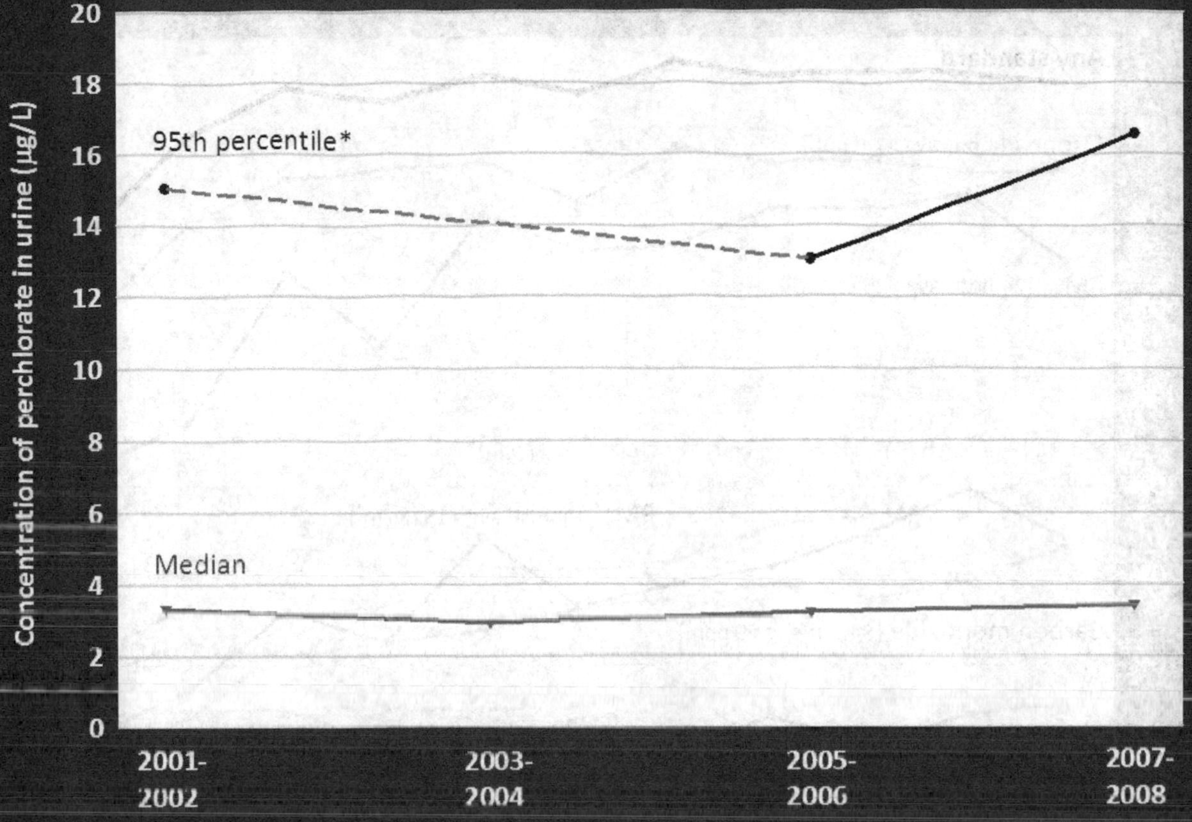

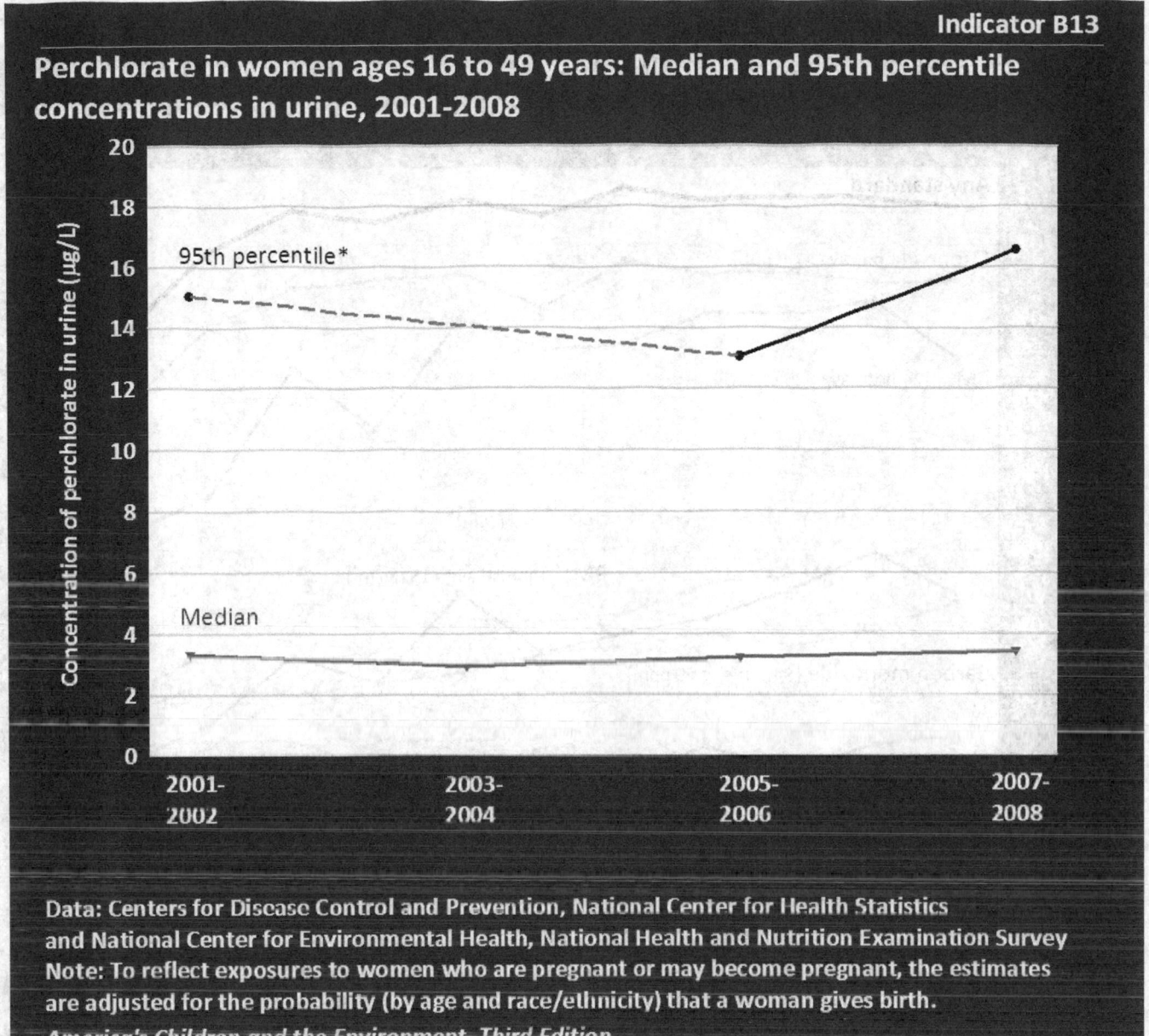

Data: Centers for Disease Control and Prevention, National Center for Health Statistics and National Center for Environmental Health, National Health and Nutrition Examination Survey

Note: To reflect exposures to women who are pregnant or may become pregnant, the estimates are adjusted for the probability (by age and race/ethnicity) that a woman gives birth.

America's Children and the Environment, Third Edition

Indicator E1

Percentage of children ages 0 to 17 years living in counties with pollutant concentrations above the levels of the current air quality standards, 1999-2009

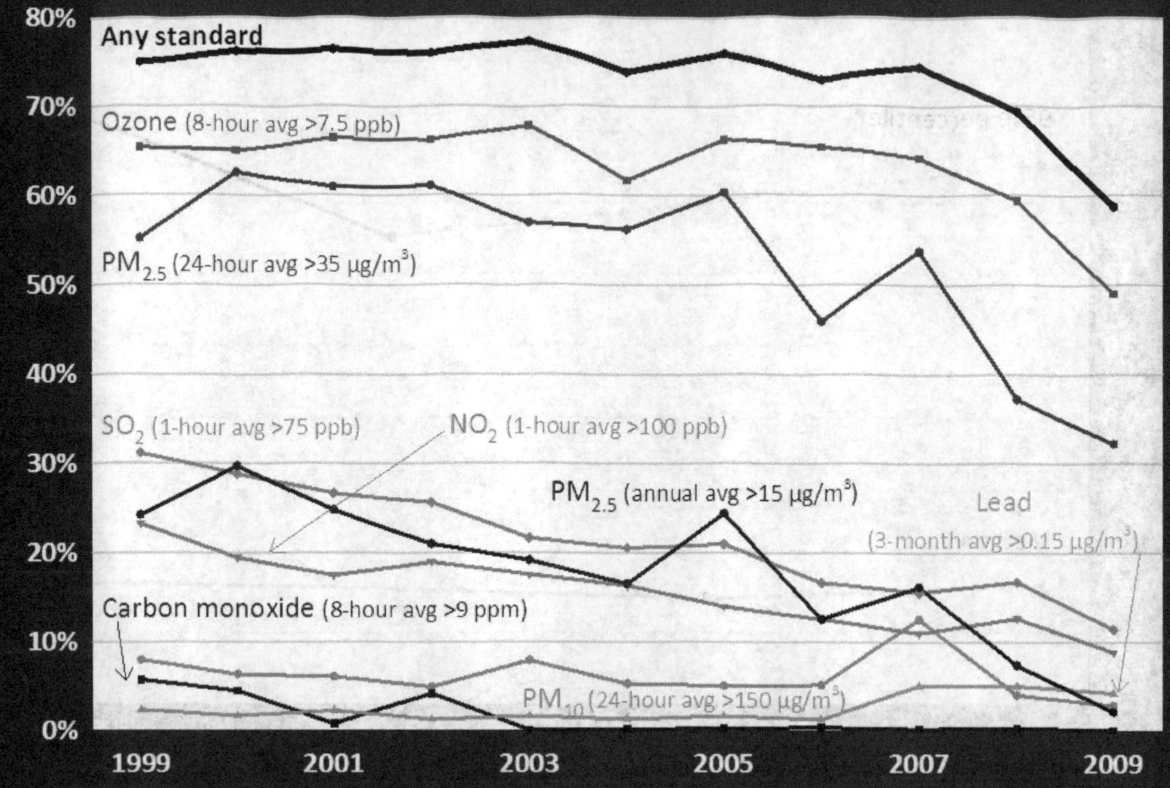

Data: U.S. Environmental Protection Agency, Office of Air and Radiation, Air Quality System

Note: EPA periodically reviews air quality standards and may change them based on updated scientific findings. Measuring concentrations above the level of a standard is not equivalent to violating the standard. The level of a standard may be exceeded on multiple days before the exceedance is considered a violation of the standard. See text for additional discussion.

America's Children and the Environment, Third Edition

Indicator E2

Percentage of children ages 0 to 17 years living in counties with 8-hour ozone and 24-hour $PM_{2.5}$ concentrations above the levels of air quality standards, by frequency of occurrence, 2009

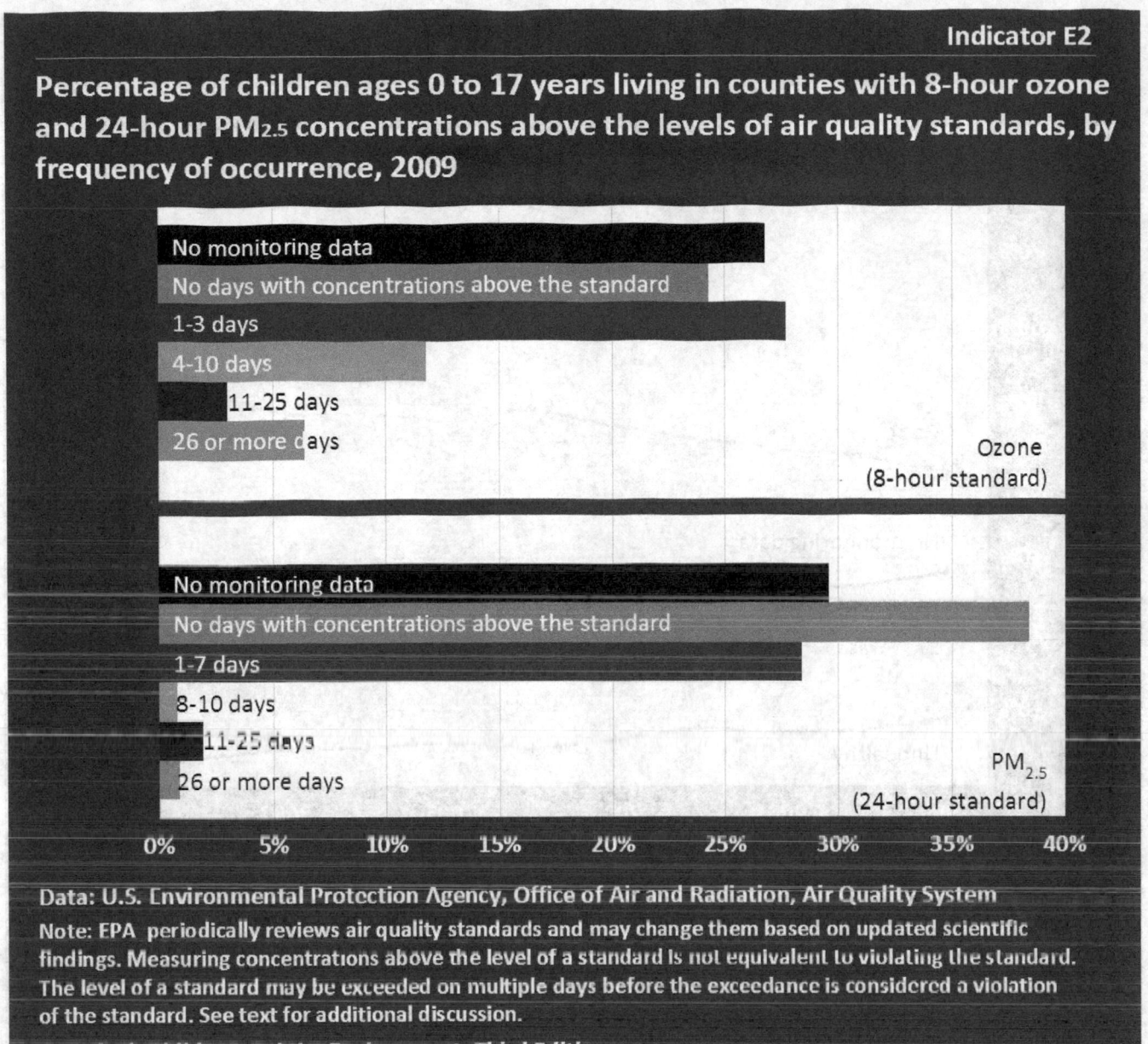

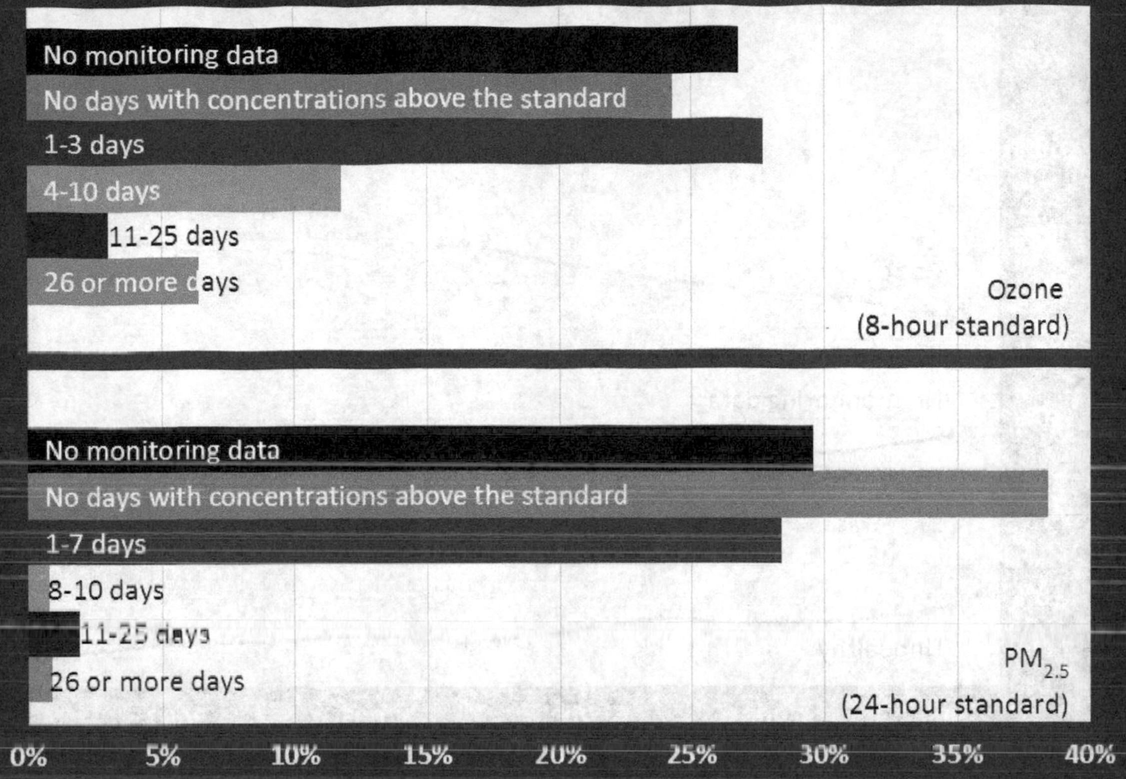

Data: U.S. Environmental Protection Agency, Office of Air and Radiation, Air Quality System

Note: EPA periodically reviews air quality standards and may change them based on updated scientific findings. Measuring concentrations above the level of a standard is not equivalent to violating the standard. The level of a standard may be exceeded on multiple days before the exceedance is considered a violation of the standard. See text for additional discussion.

America's Children and the Environment, Third Edition

Indicator E3

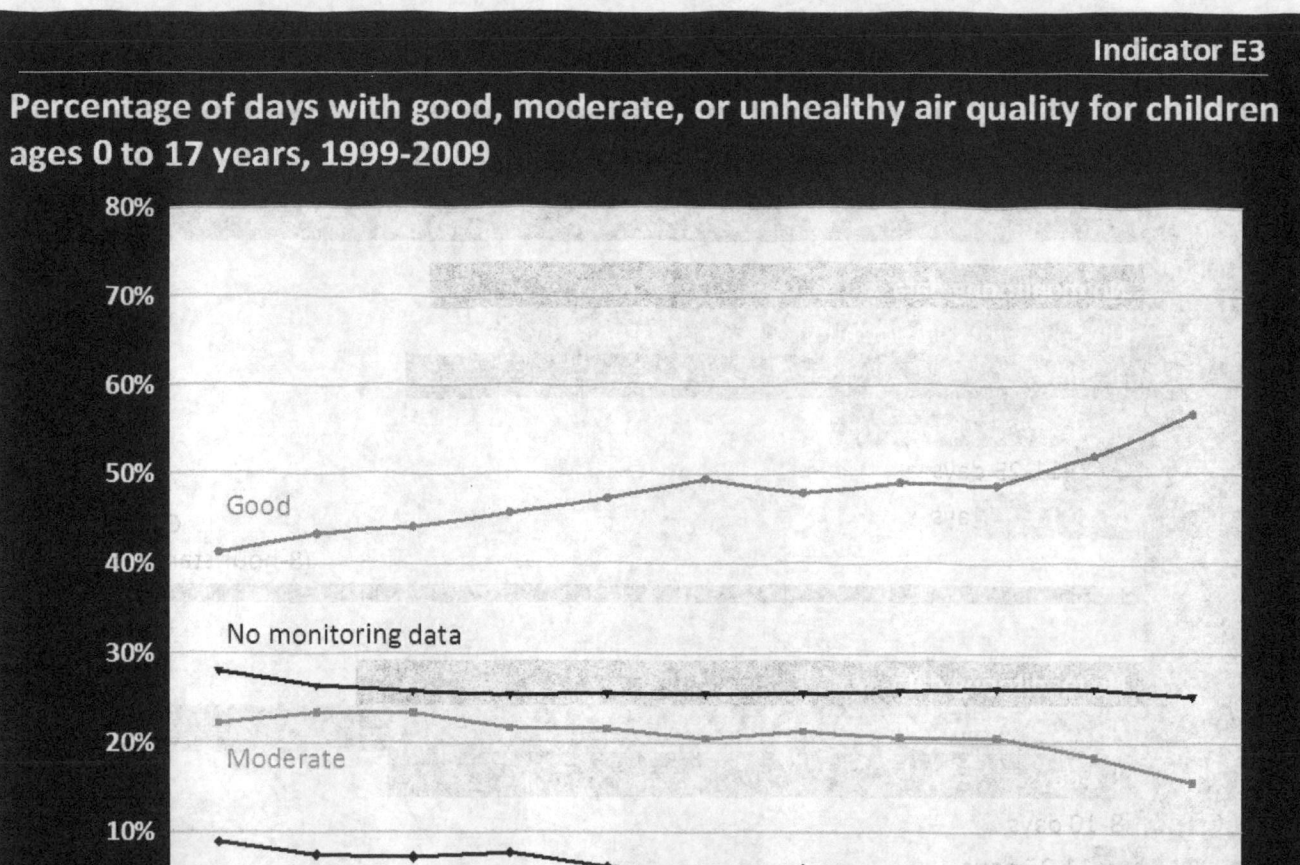

Percentage of days with good, moderate, or unhealthy air quality for children ages 0 to 17 years, 1999-2009

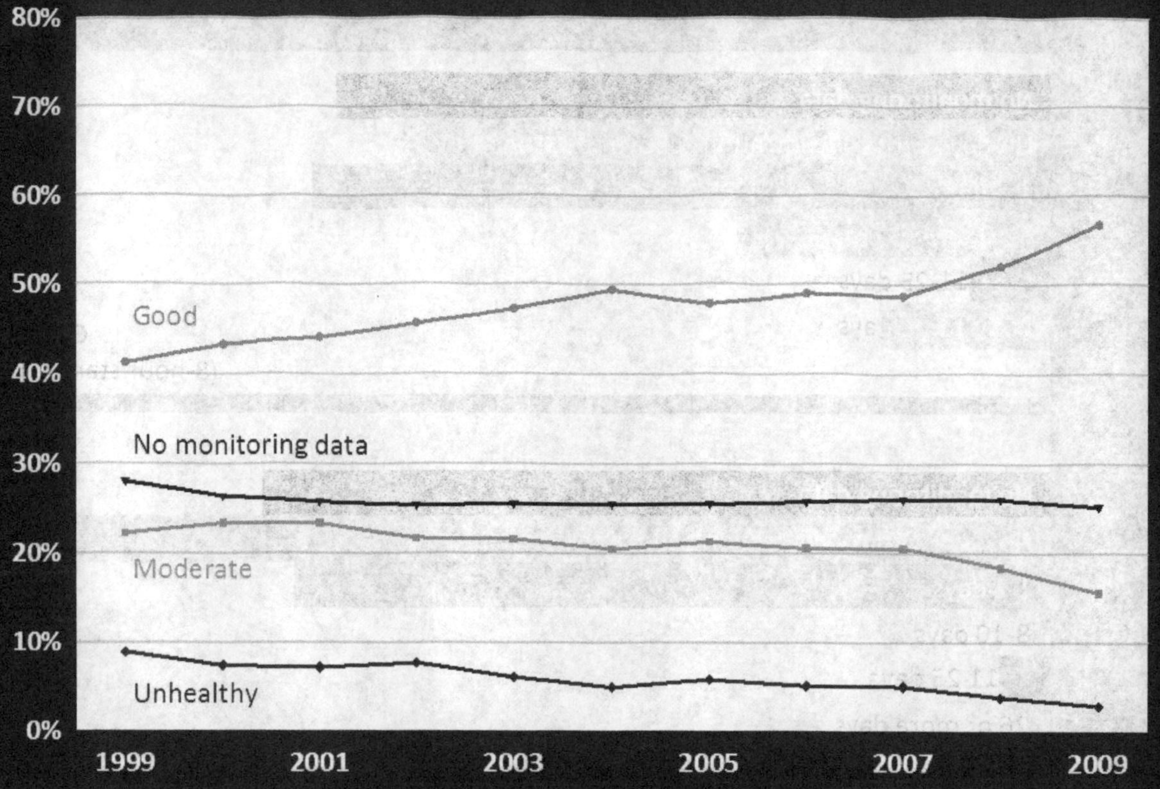

Data: U.S. Environmental Protection Agency, Office of Air and Radiation, Air Quality System

Note: Good, moderate, and unhealthy air quality are defined using EPA's Air Quality Index (AQI). The health information that supports EPA's periodic reviews of the air quality standards informs decisions on the AQI breakpoints and may change based on updated scientific findings. See text for additional discussion.

America's Children and the Environment, Third Edition

Indicator E5

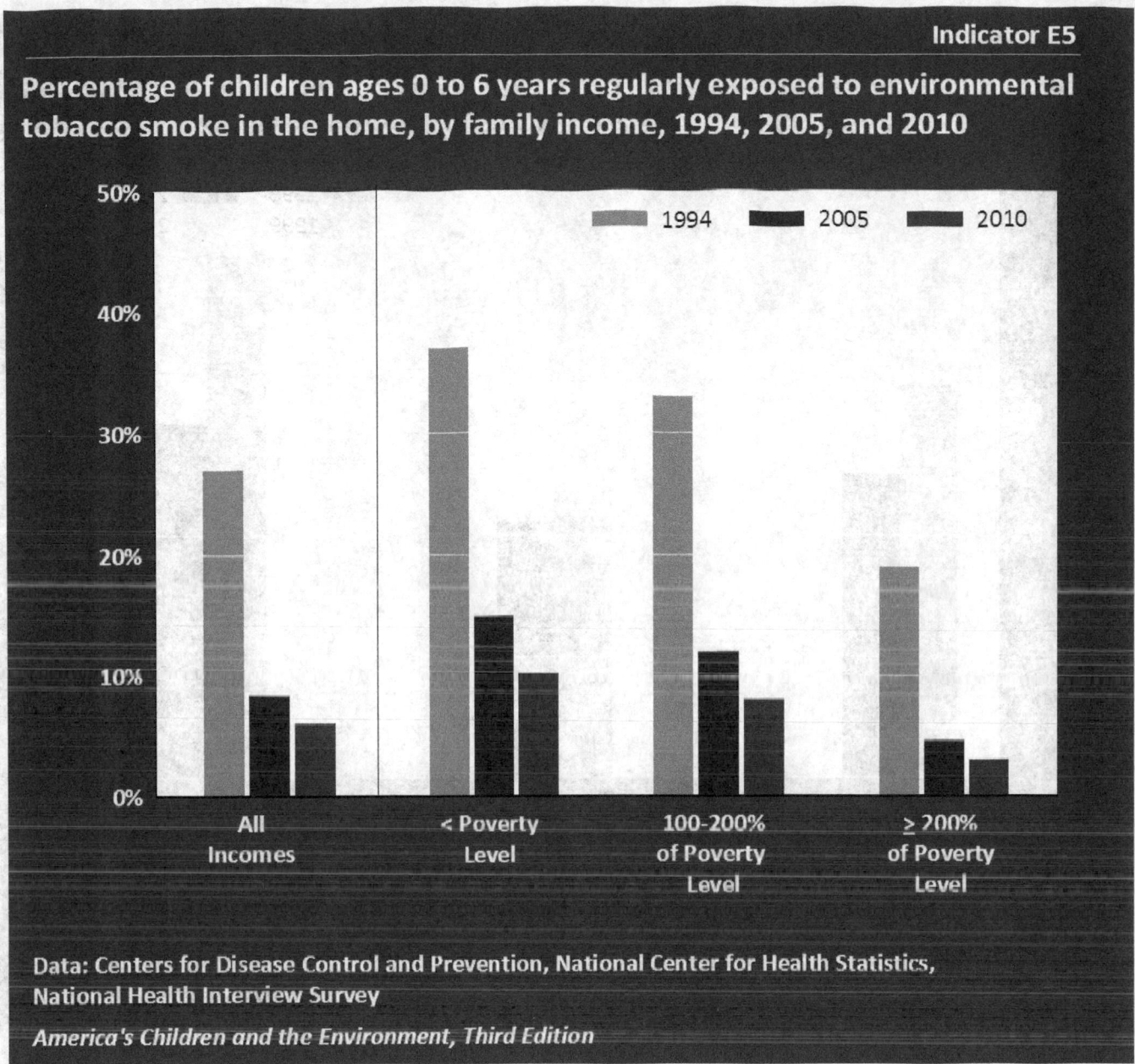

Percentage of children ages 0 to 6 years regularly exposed to environmental tobacco smoke in the home, by family income, 1994, 2005, and 2010

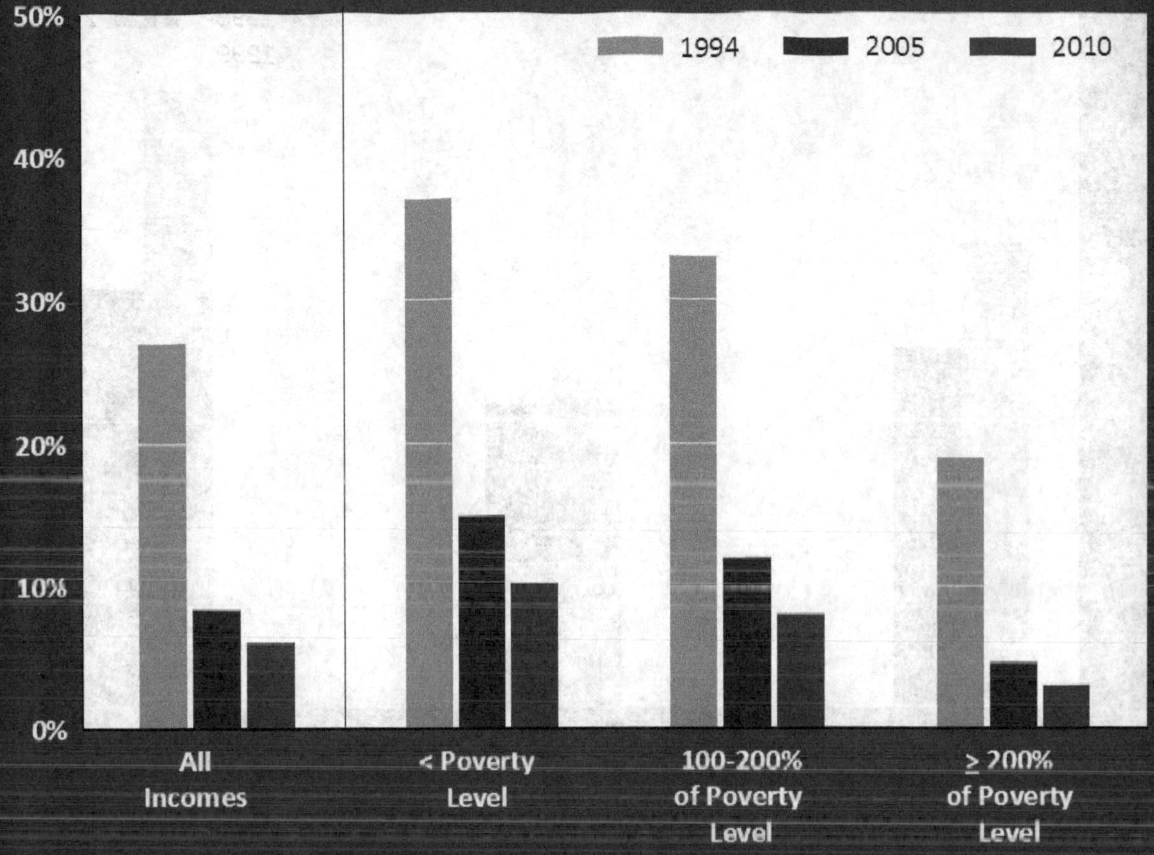

Data: Centers for Disease Control and Prevention, National Center for Health Statistics, National Health Interview Survey

America's Children and the Environment, Third Edition

Indicator E6

Percentage of children ages 0 to 5 years living in homes with interior lead hazards, 1998-1999 and 2005-2006

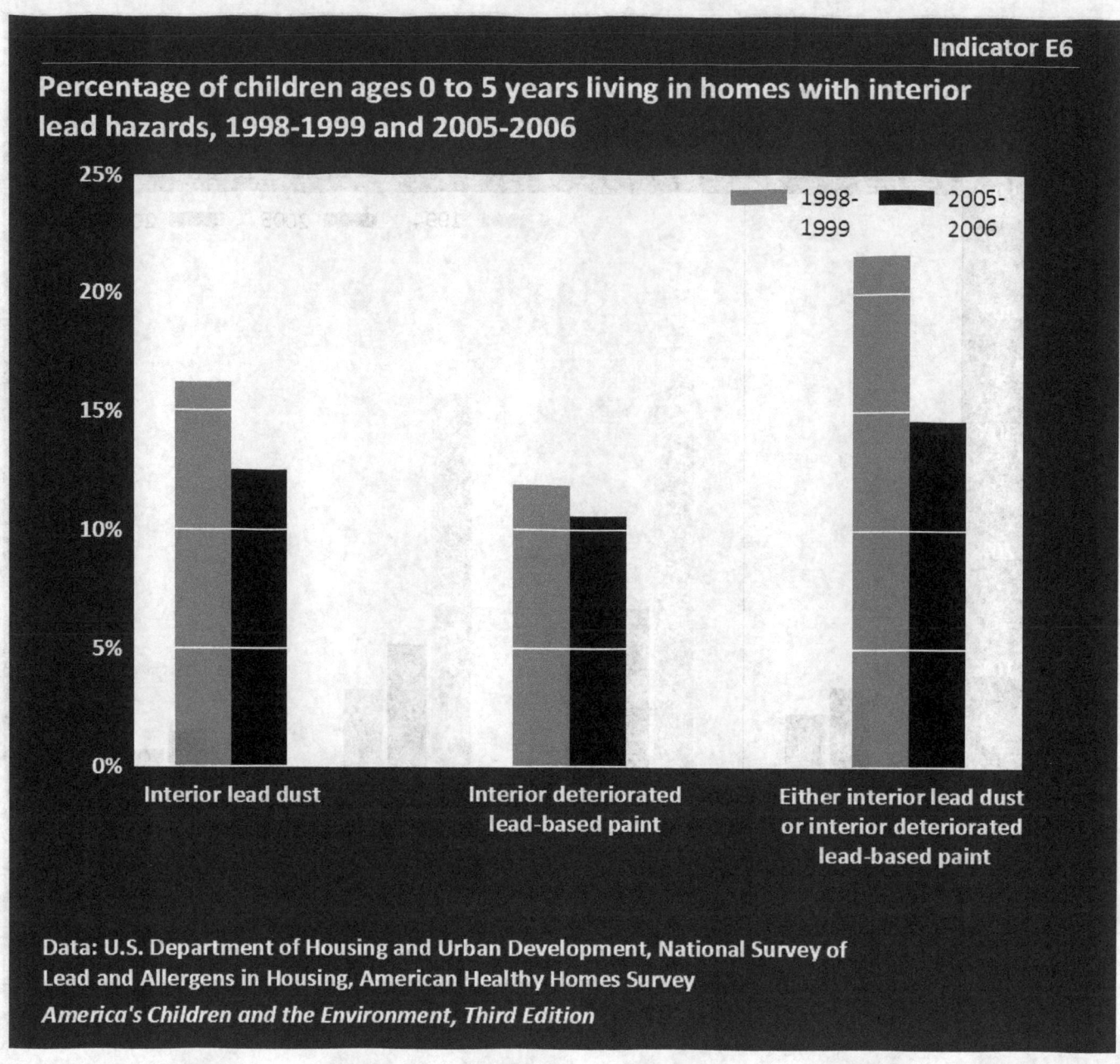

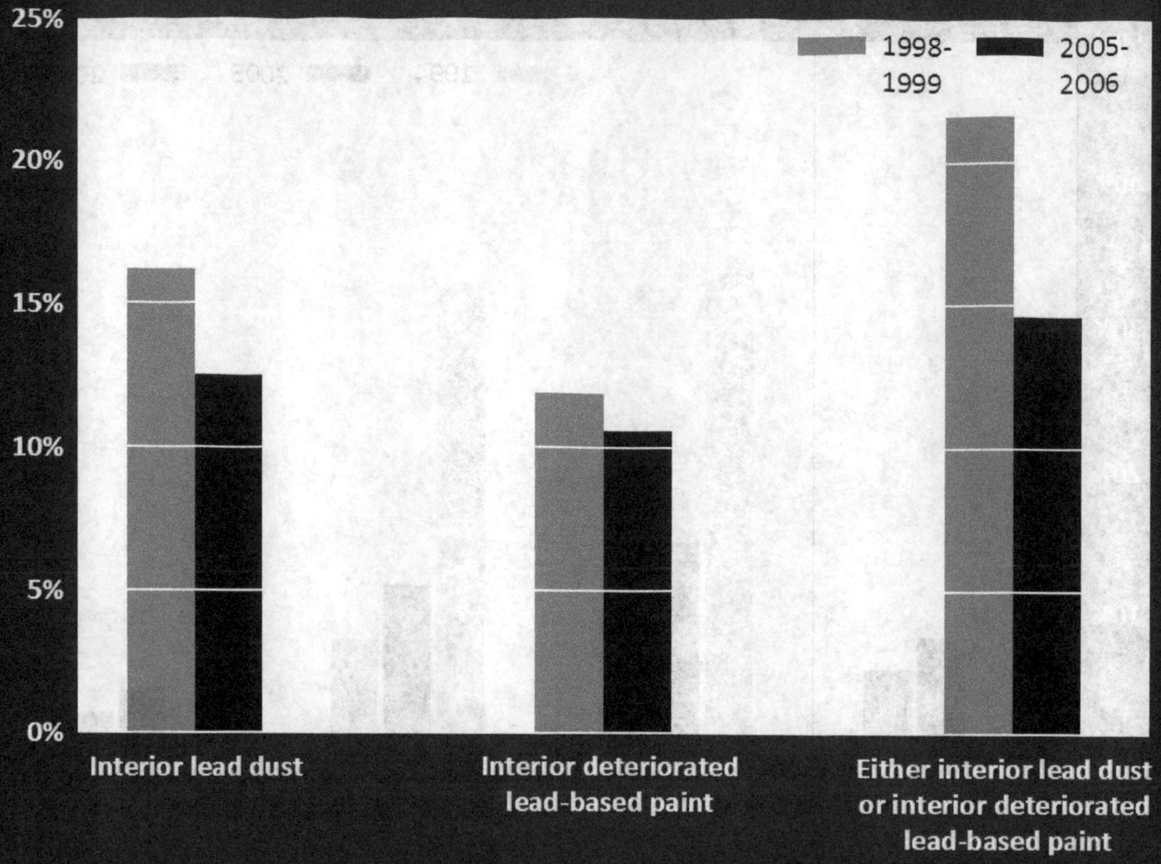

Data: U.S. Department of Housing and Urban Development, National Survey of Lead and Allergens in Housing, American Healthy Homes Survey

America's Children and the Environment, Third Edition

Indicator E7

Estimated percentage of children ages 0 to 17 years served by community water systems that did not meet all applicable health-based drinking water standards, 1993-2009

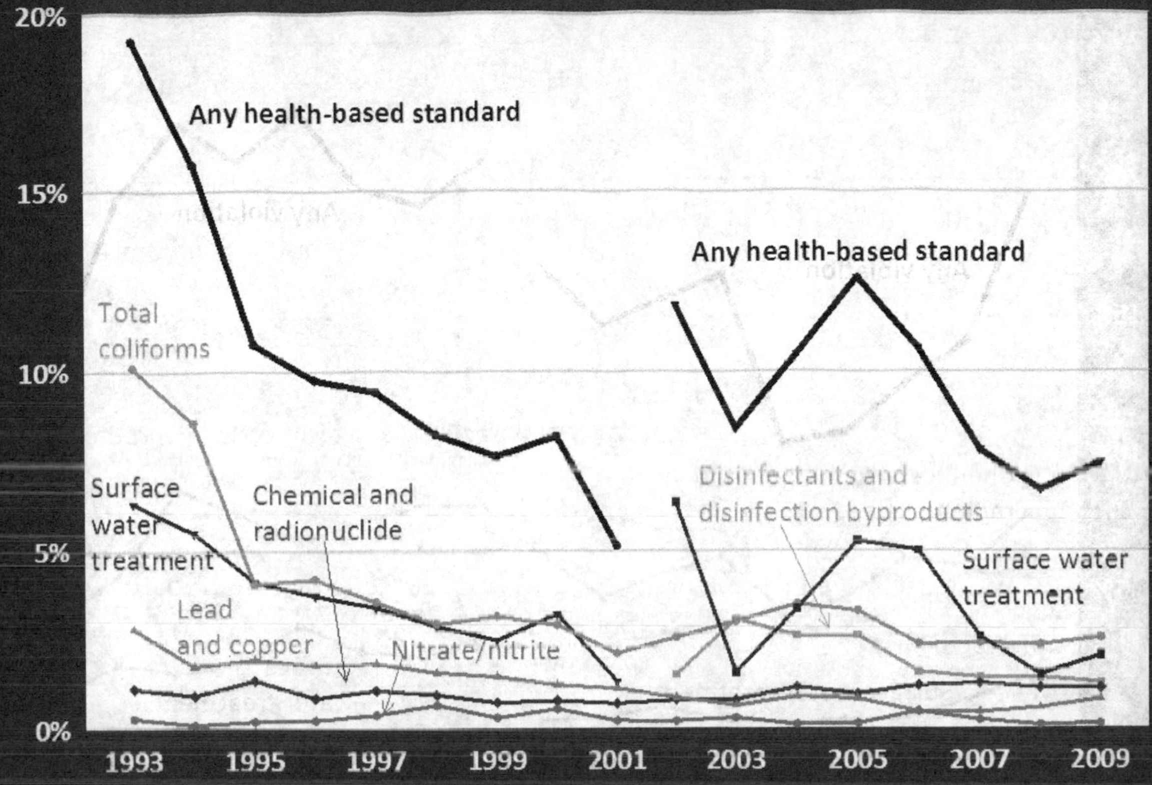

Data: U.S. Environmental Protection Agency, Office of Water, Safe Drinking Water Information System, Federal Version

Note: Breaks in lines for "Any health-based standard" and "Surface water treatment" reflect substantial regulatory changes implemented in 2002.

America's Children and the Environment, Third Edition

Indicator E8

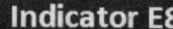

Estimated percentage of children ages 0 to 17 years served by community water systems with violations of drinking water monitoring and reporting requirements, 1993-2009

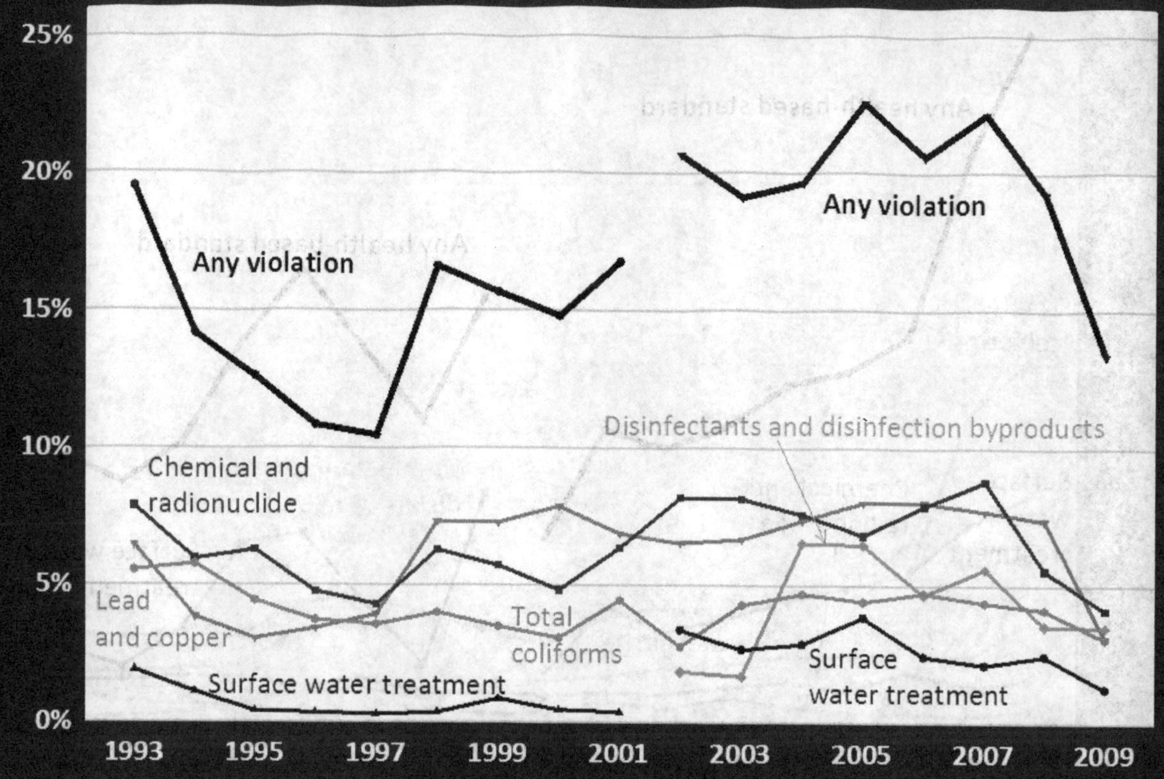

Data: U.S. Environmental Protection Agency, Office of Water, Safe Drinking Water Information System, Federal Version

Note: Breaks in lines for "Any violation" and "Surface water treatment" reflect substantial regulatory changes implemented in 2002.

America's Children and the Environment, Third Edition

Indicator E9

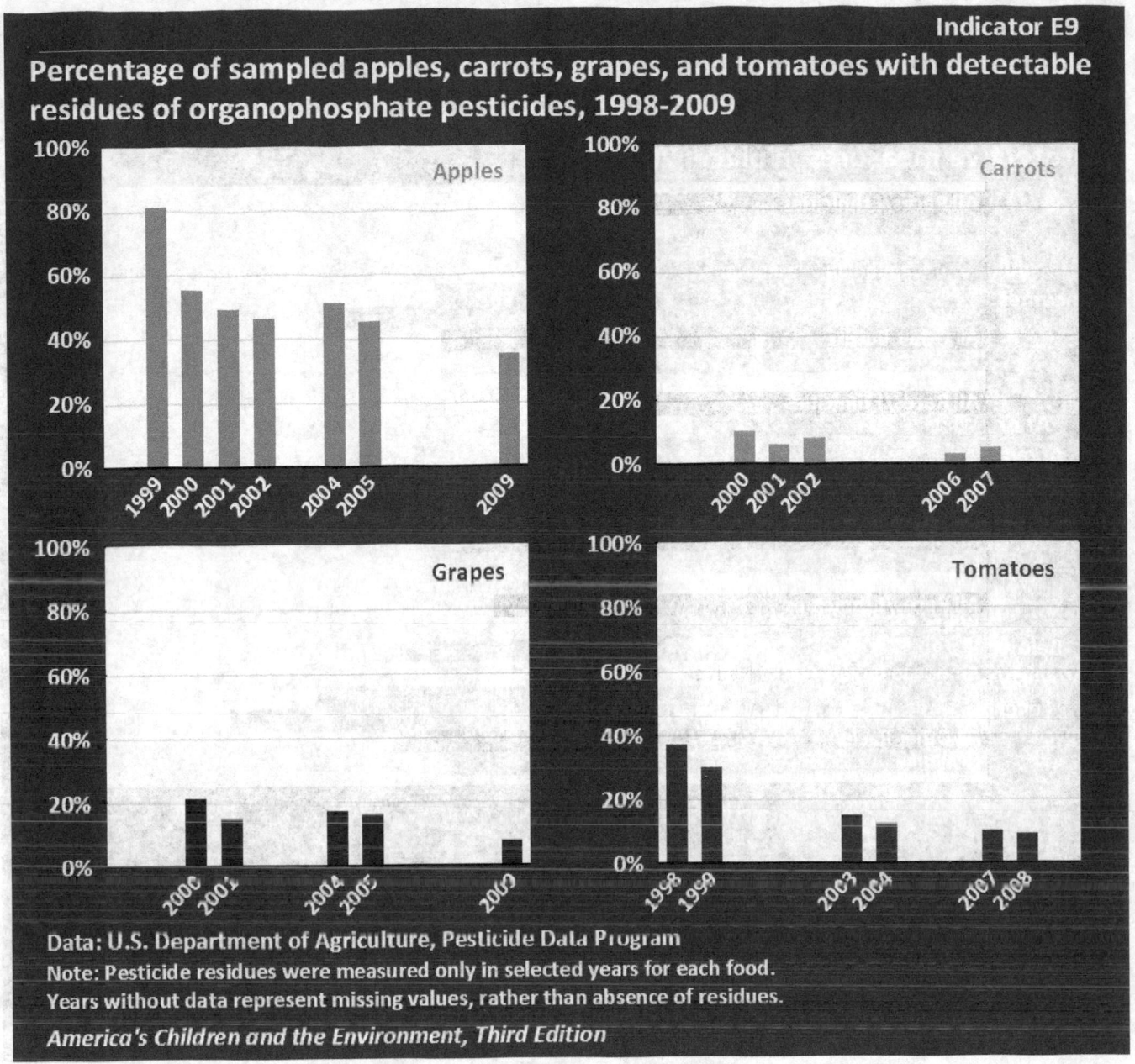

Percentage of sampled apples, carrots, grapes, and tomatoes with detectable residues of organophosphate pesticides, 1998-2009

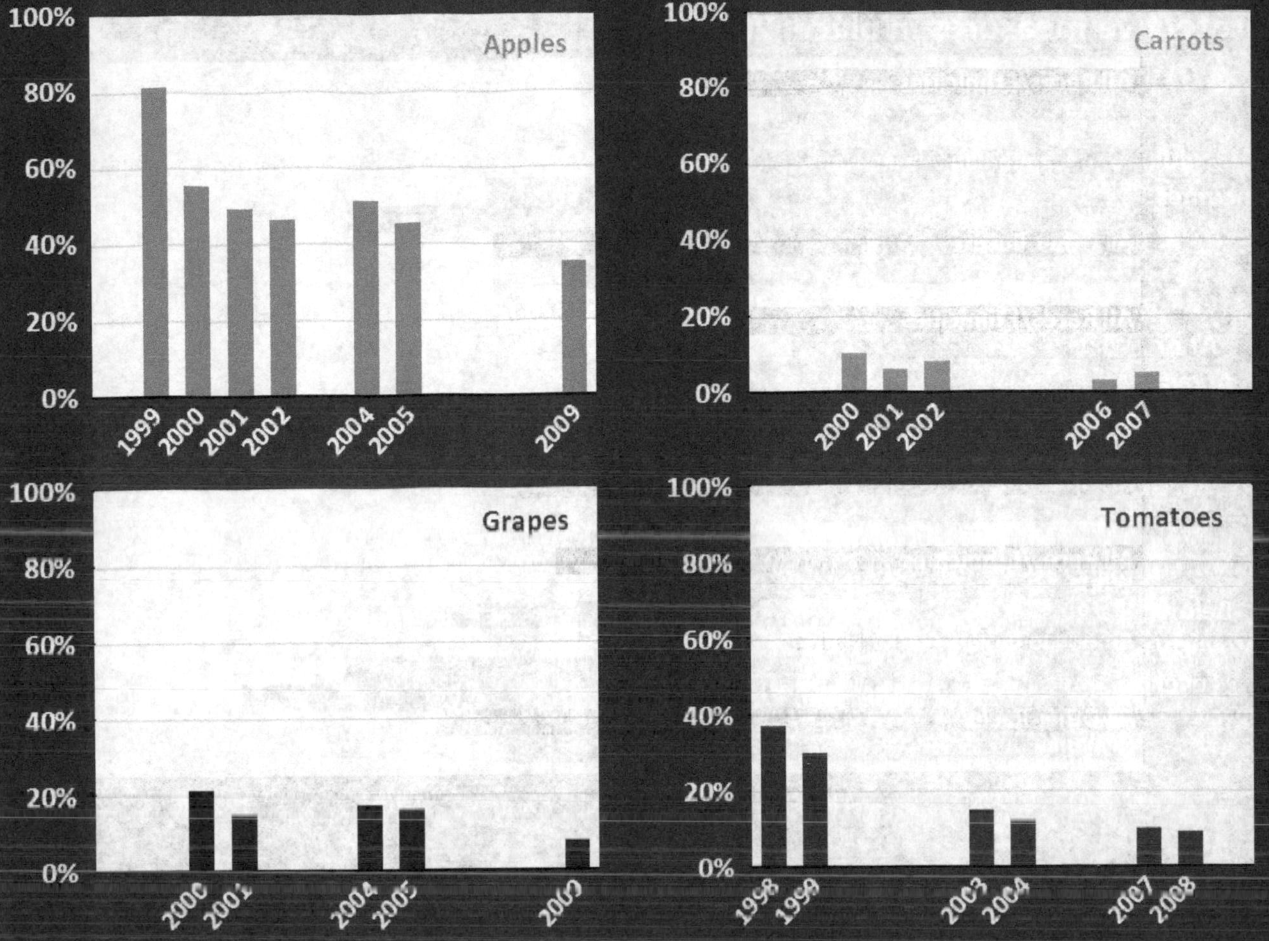

Data: U.S. Department of Agriculture, Pesticide Data Program

Note: Pesticide residues were measured only in selected years for each food.

Years without data represent missing values, rather than absence of residues.

America's Children and the Environment, Third Edition

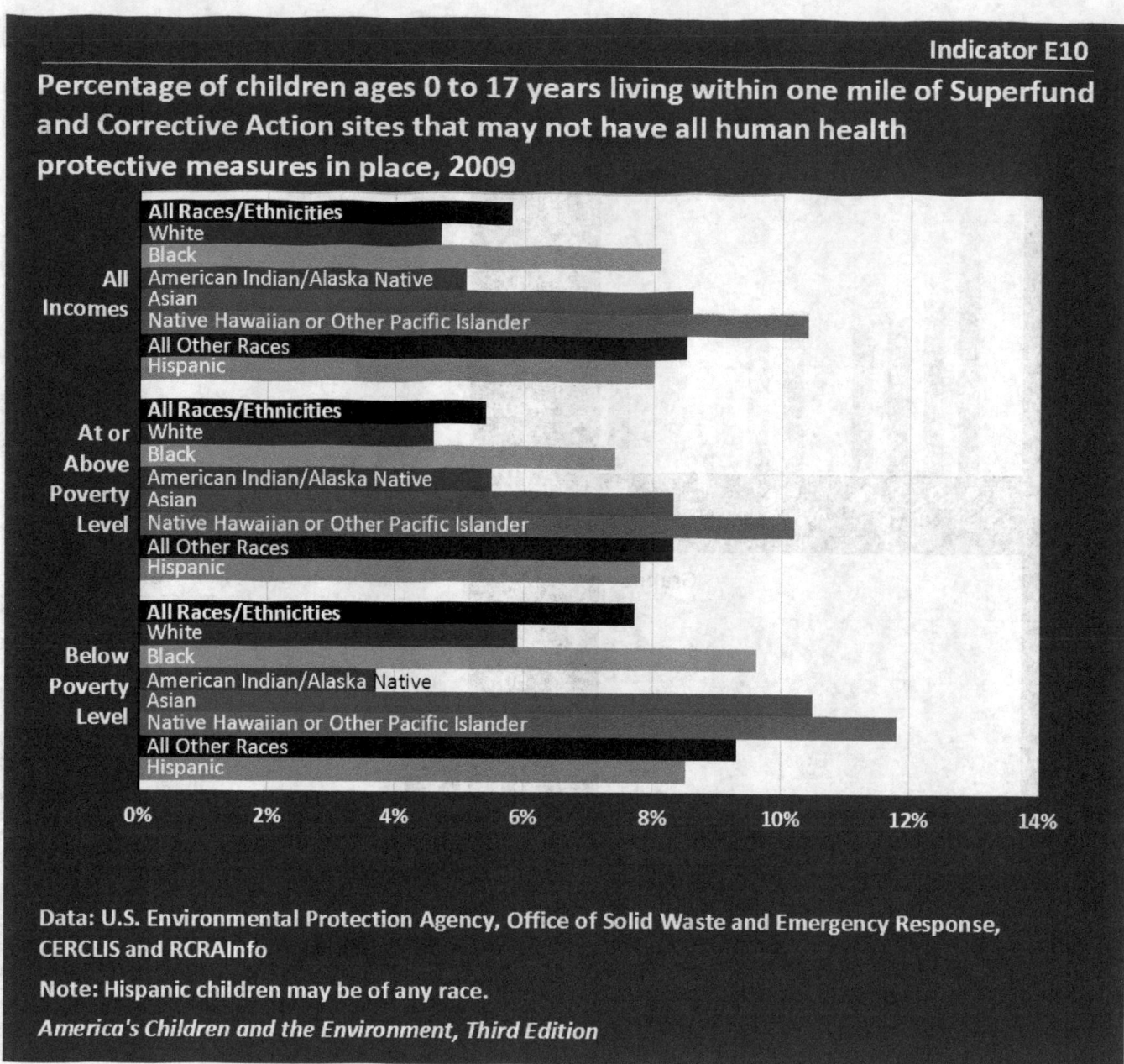

Indicator E10

Percentage of children ages 0 to 17 years living within one mile of Superfund and Corrective Action sites that may not have all human health protective measures in place, 2009

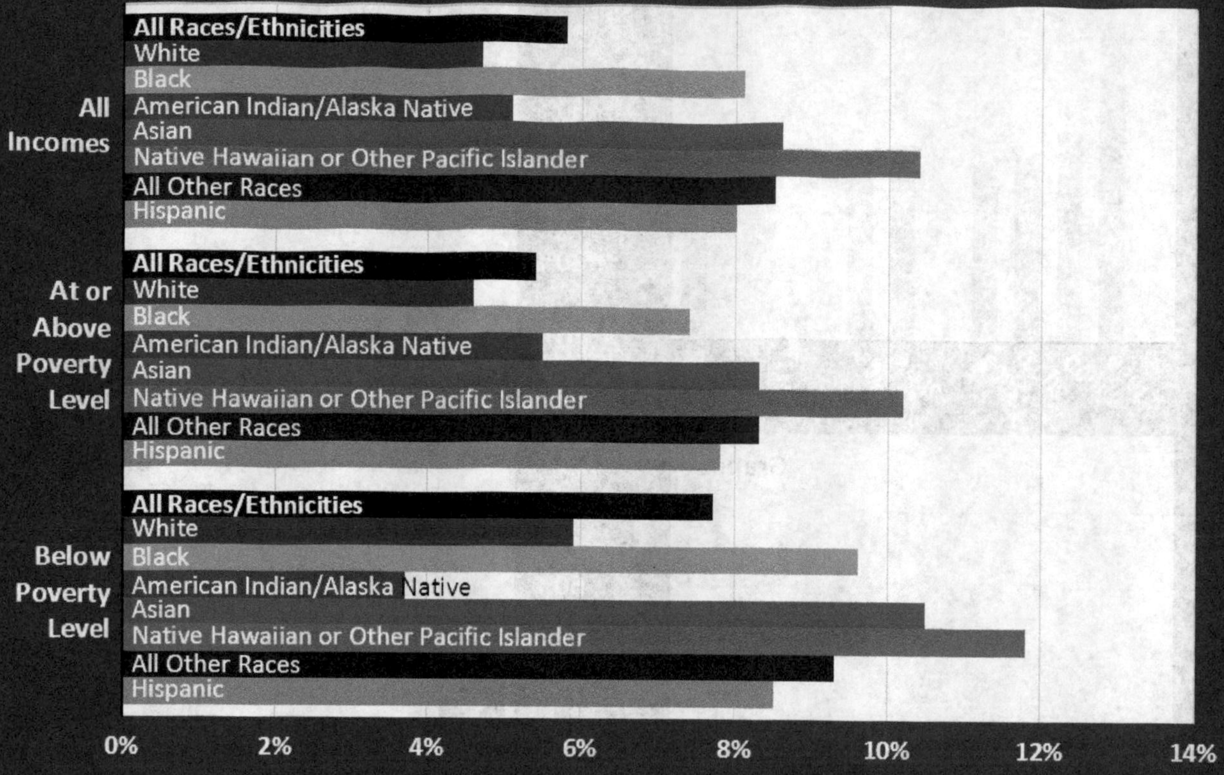

Data: U.S. Environmental Protection Agency, Office of Solid Waste and Emergency Response, CERCLIS and RCRAInfo

Note: Hispanic children may be of any race.

America's Children and the Environment, Third Edition

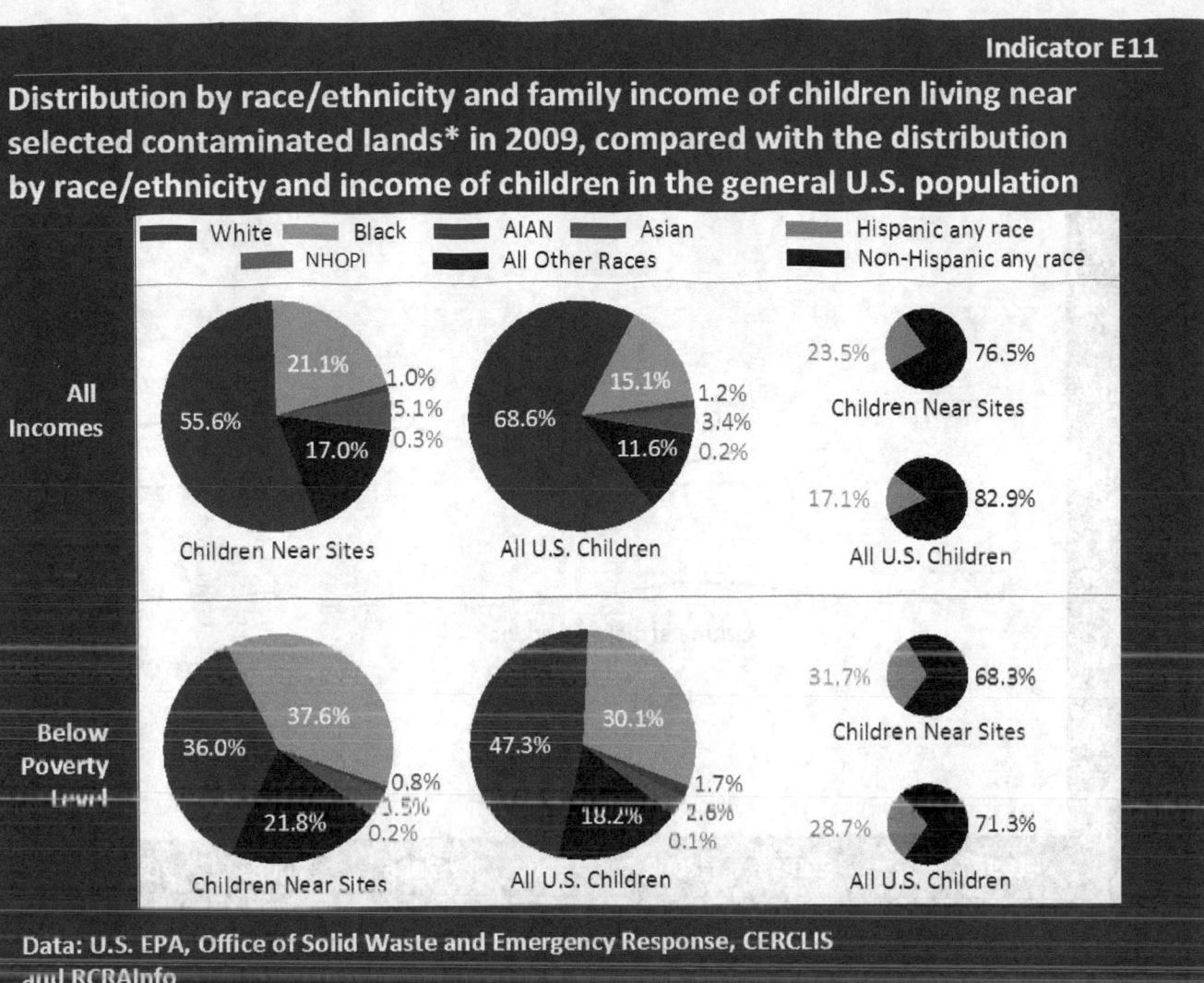

Indicator E11

Distribution by race/ethnicity and family income of children living near selected contaminated lands* in 2009, compared with the distribution by race/ethnicity and income of children in the general U.S. population

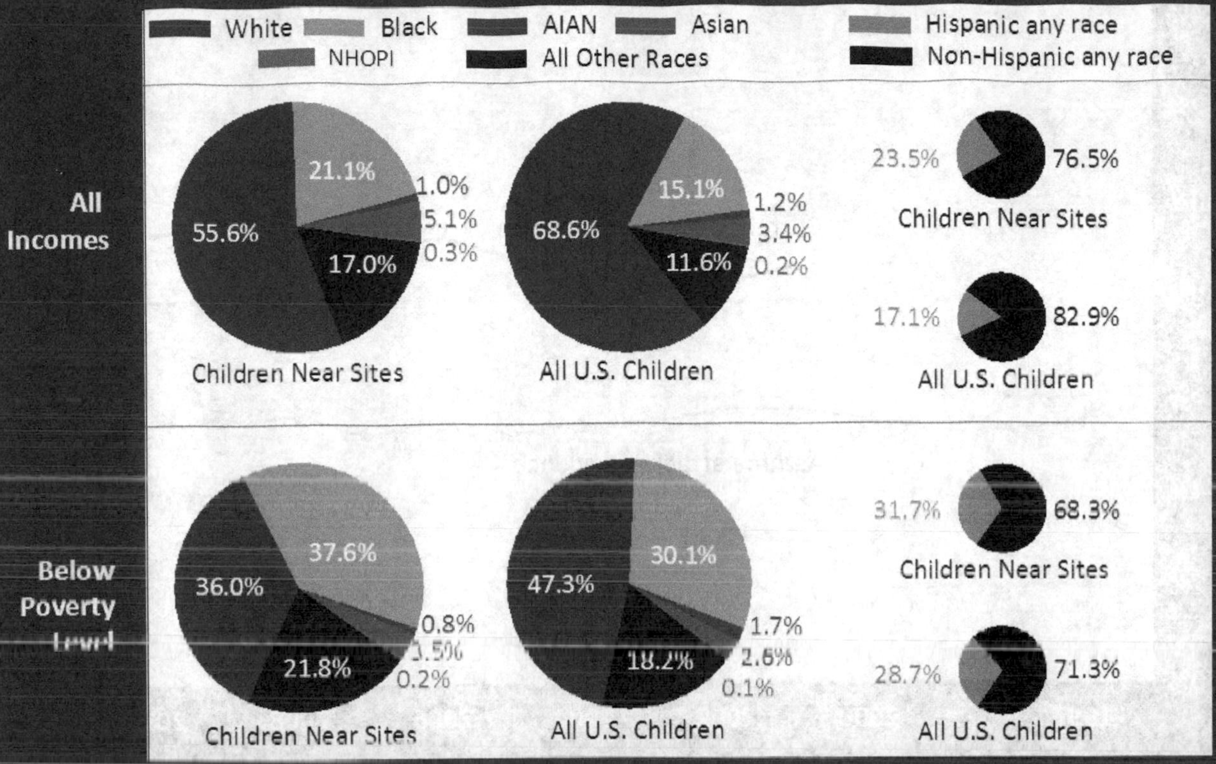

Data: U.S. EPA, Office of Solid Waste and Emergency Response, CERCLIS and RCRAInfo

Note: AIAN = American Indian/Alaska Native. NHOPI = Native Hawaiian or Other Pacific Islander. Hispanic children may be of any race.

* Within one mile of Superfund and Corrective Action sites that may not have all human health protective measures in place.

America's Children and the Environment, Third Edition

Indicator H1

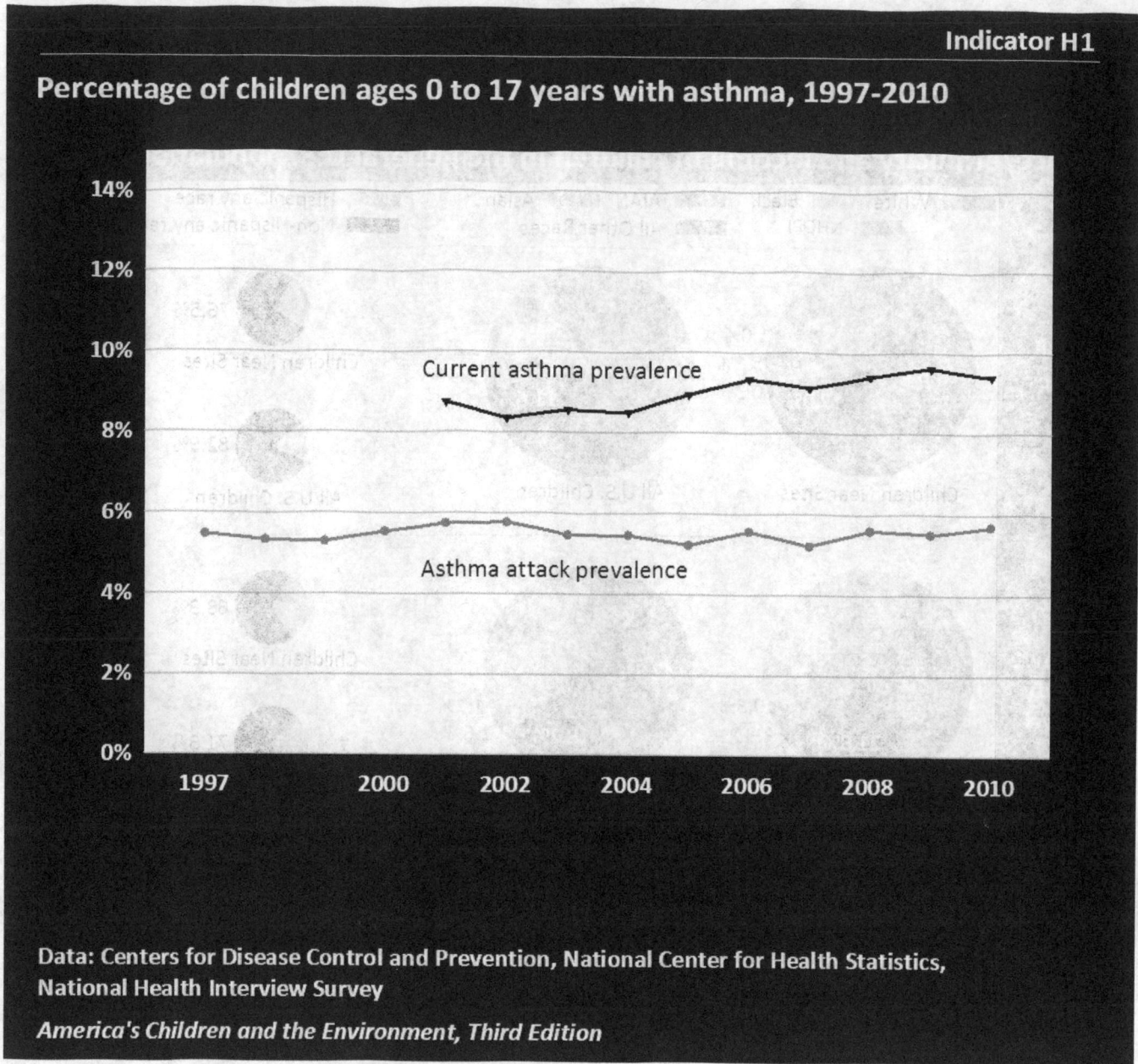

Percentage of children ages 0 to 17 years with asthma, 1997-2010

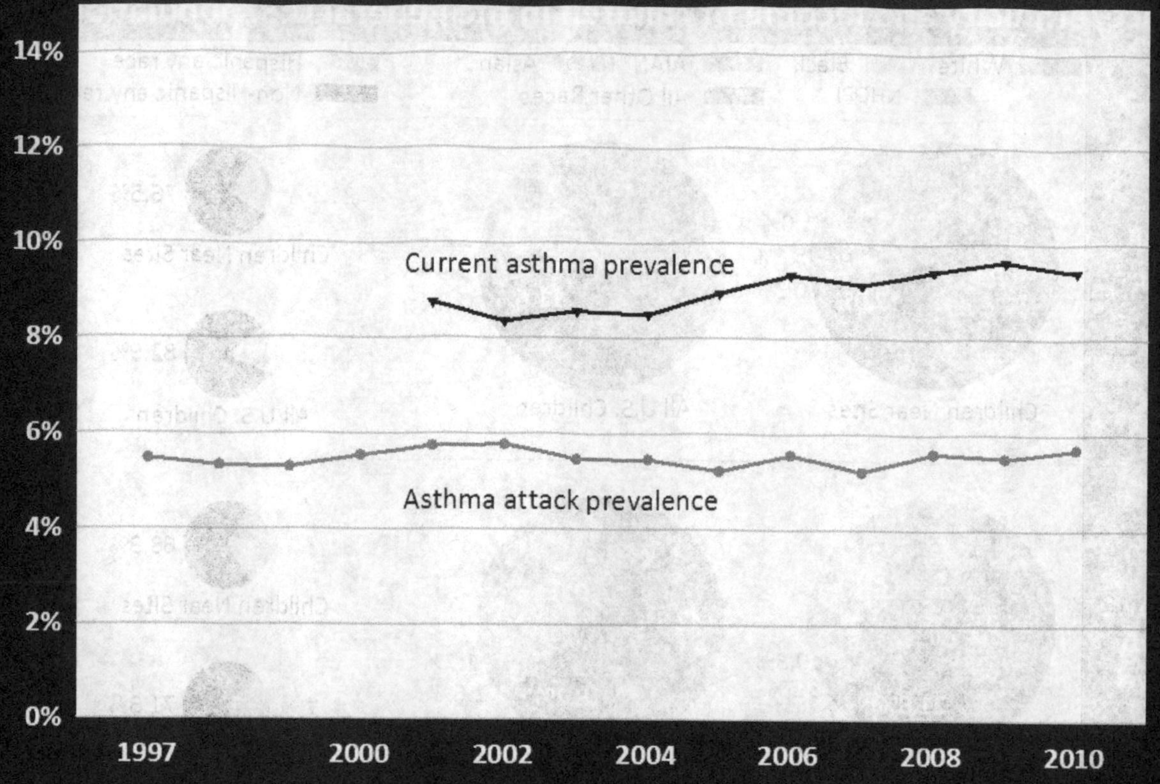

Data: Centers for Disease Control and Prevention, National Center for Health Statistics, National Health Interview Survey

America's Children and the Environment, Third Edition

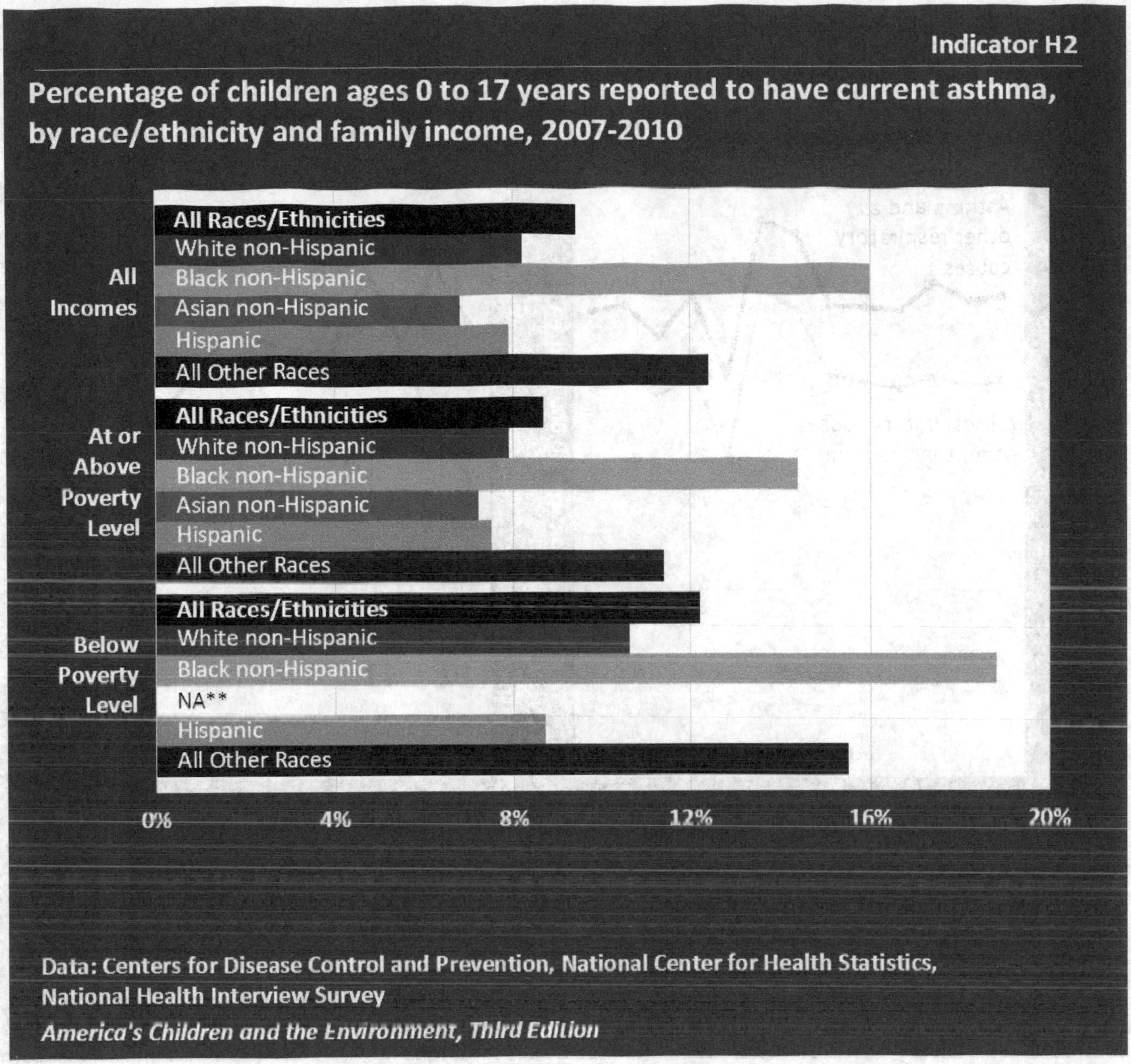
Indicator H2
Percentage of children ages 0 to 17 years reported to have current asthma, by race/ethnicity and family income, 2007-2010
All Incomes
At or Above Poverty Level
Below Poverty Level
All Races/Ethnicities
White non-Hispanic
Black non-Hispanic
Asian non-Hispanic
Hispanic
All Other Races
NA**
0%
4%
8%
12%
16%
20%
Data: Centers for Disease Control and Prevention, National Center for Health Statistics, National Health Interview Survey
America's Children and the Environment, Third Edition

Indicator H3

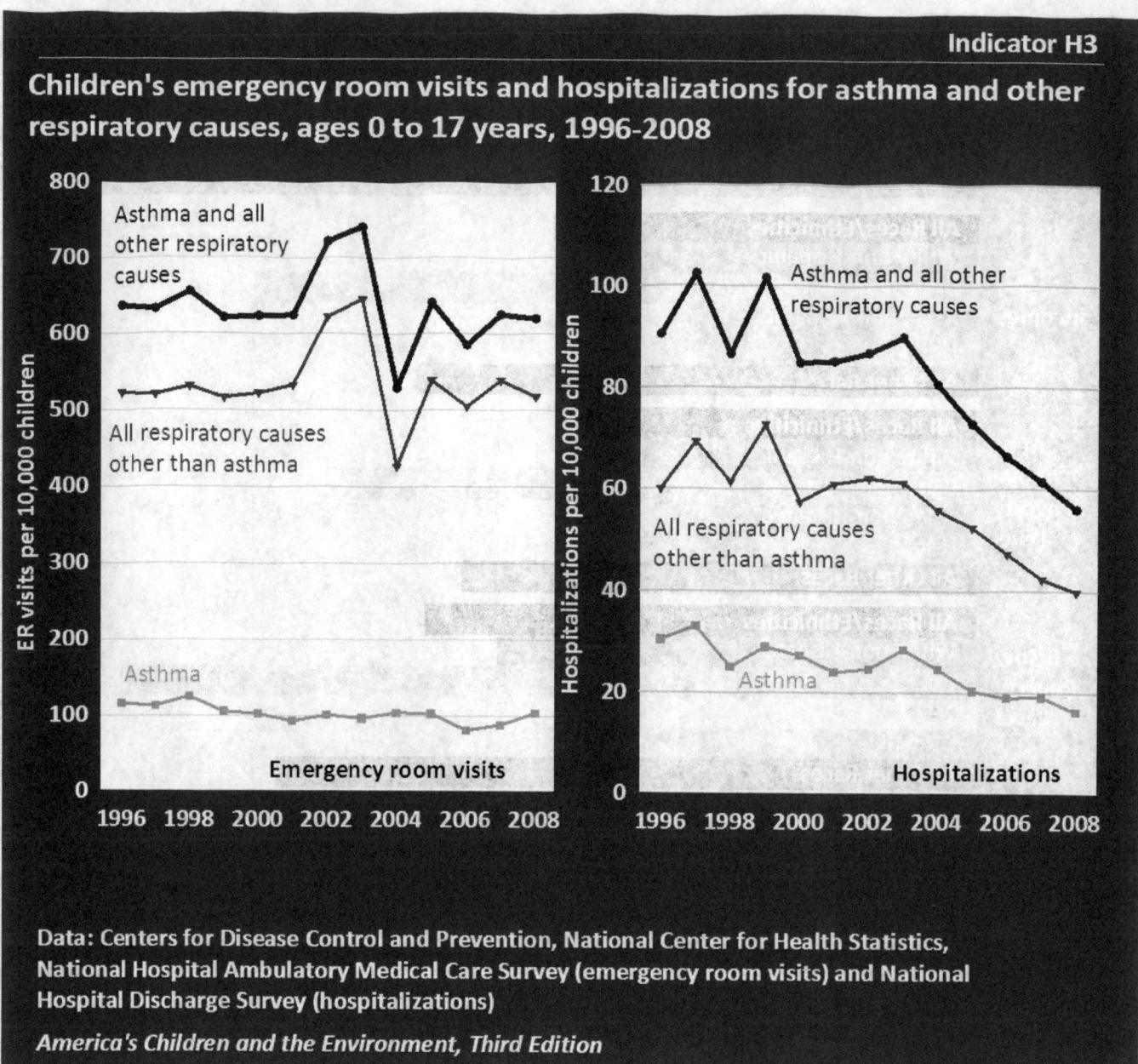

Children's emergency room visits and hospitalizations for asthma and other respiratory causes, ages 0 to 17 years, 1996-2008

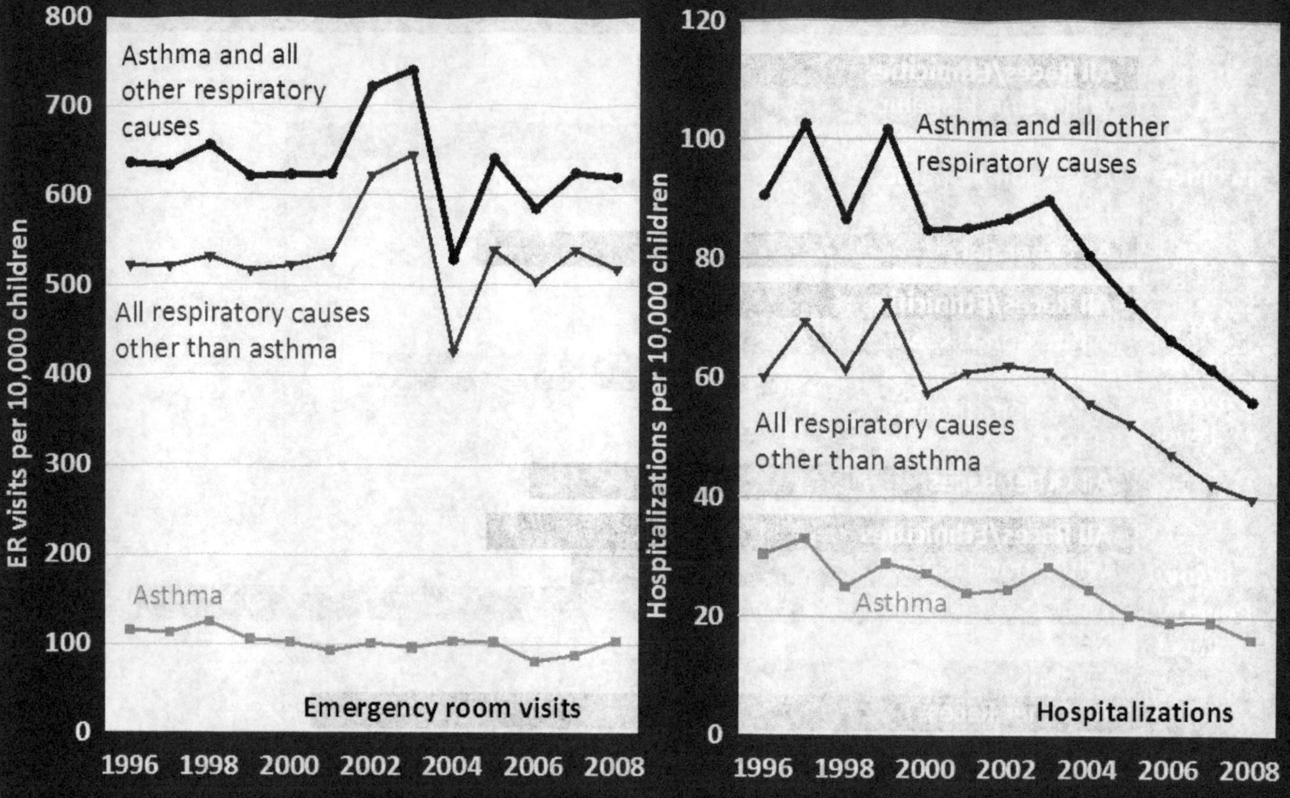

Data: Centers for Disease Control and Prevention, National Center for Health Statistics, National Hospital Ambulatory Medical Care Survey (emergency room visits) and National Hospital Discharge Survey (hospitalizations)

America's Children and the Environment, Third Edition

Indicator H4

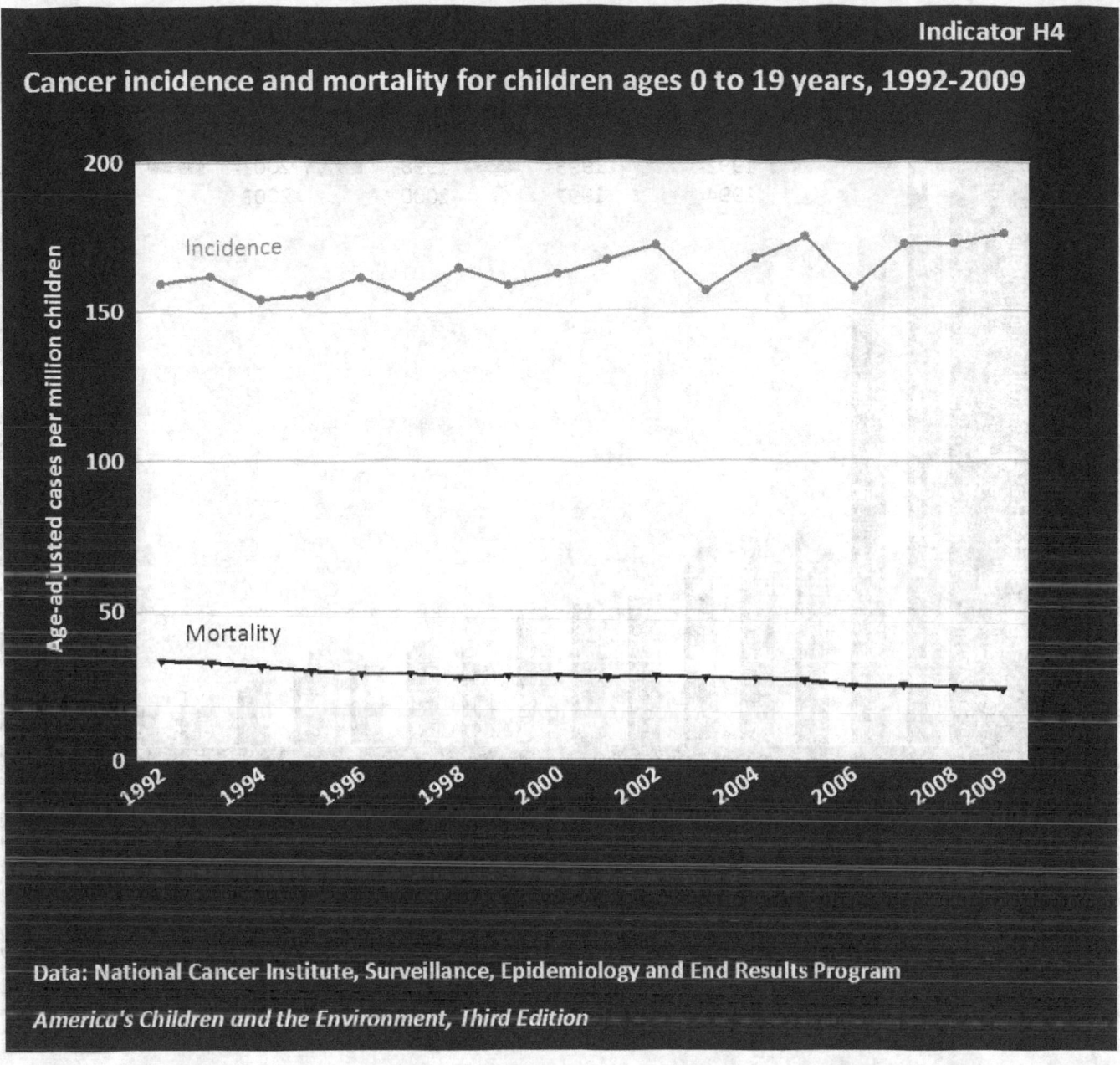

Cancer incidence and mortality for children ages 0 to 19 years, 1992-2009

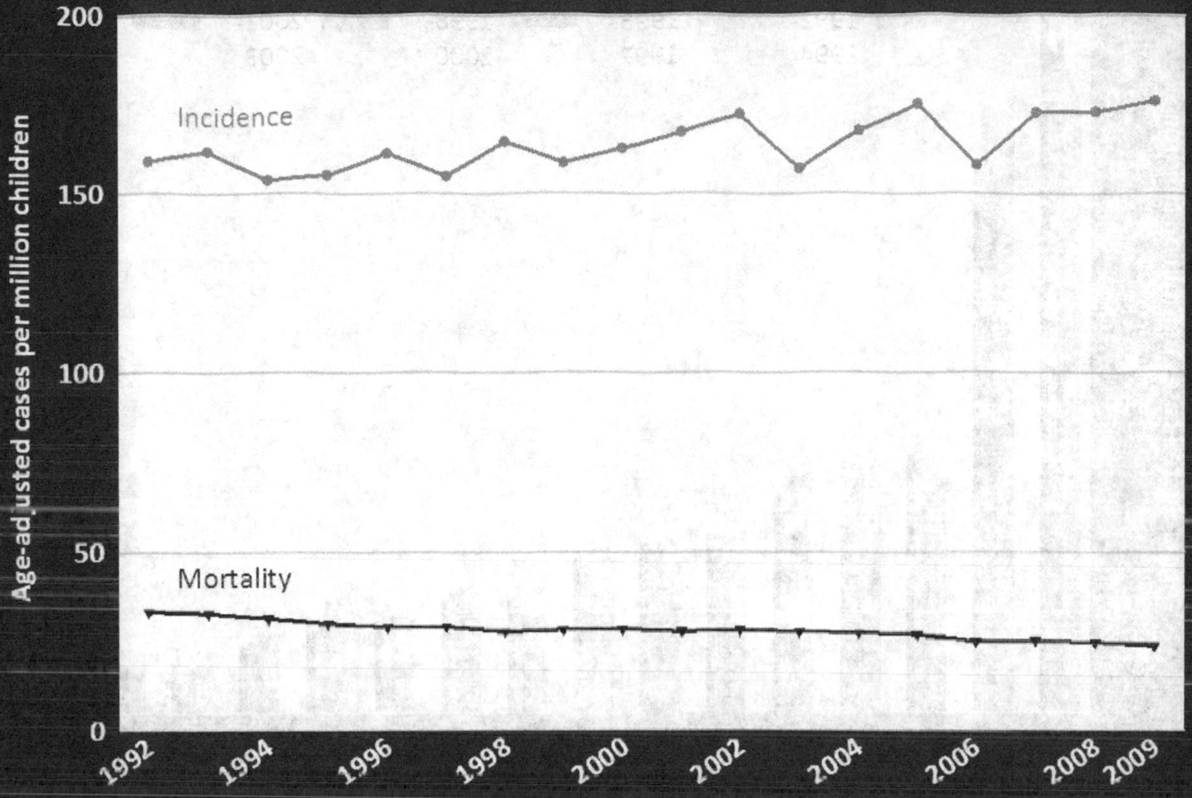

Data: National Cancer Institute, Surveillance, Epidemiology and End Results Program

America's Children and the Environment, Third Edition

Indicator H5

Cancer incidence for children ages 0 to 19 years, by type, 1992-2006

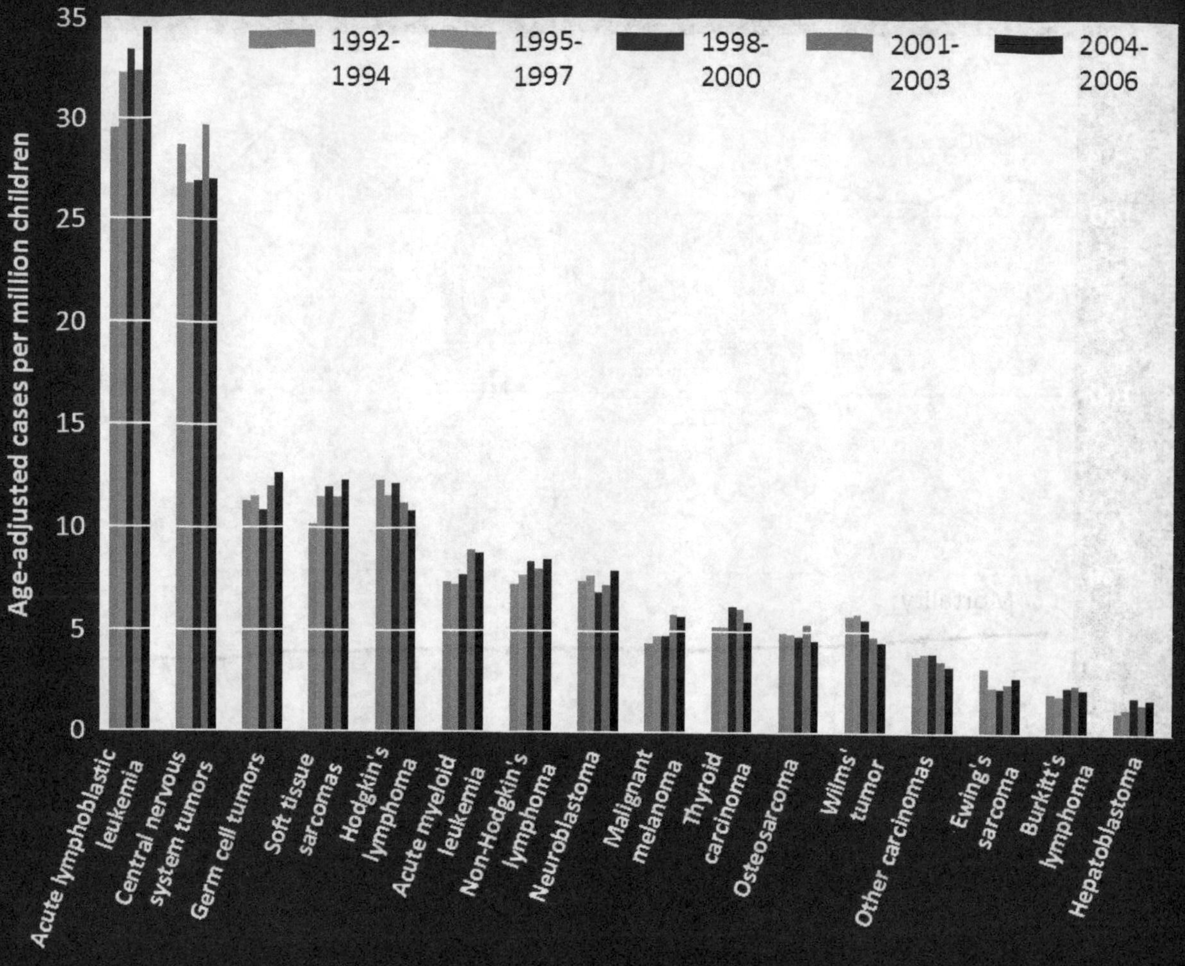

Data: National Cancer Institute, Surveilliance, Epidemiology, and End Results Program

America's Children and the Environment, Third Edition

Indicator H6

Percentage of children ages 5 to 17 years reported to have attention-deficit/hyperactivity disorder, by sex, 1997-2010

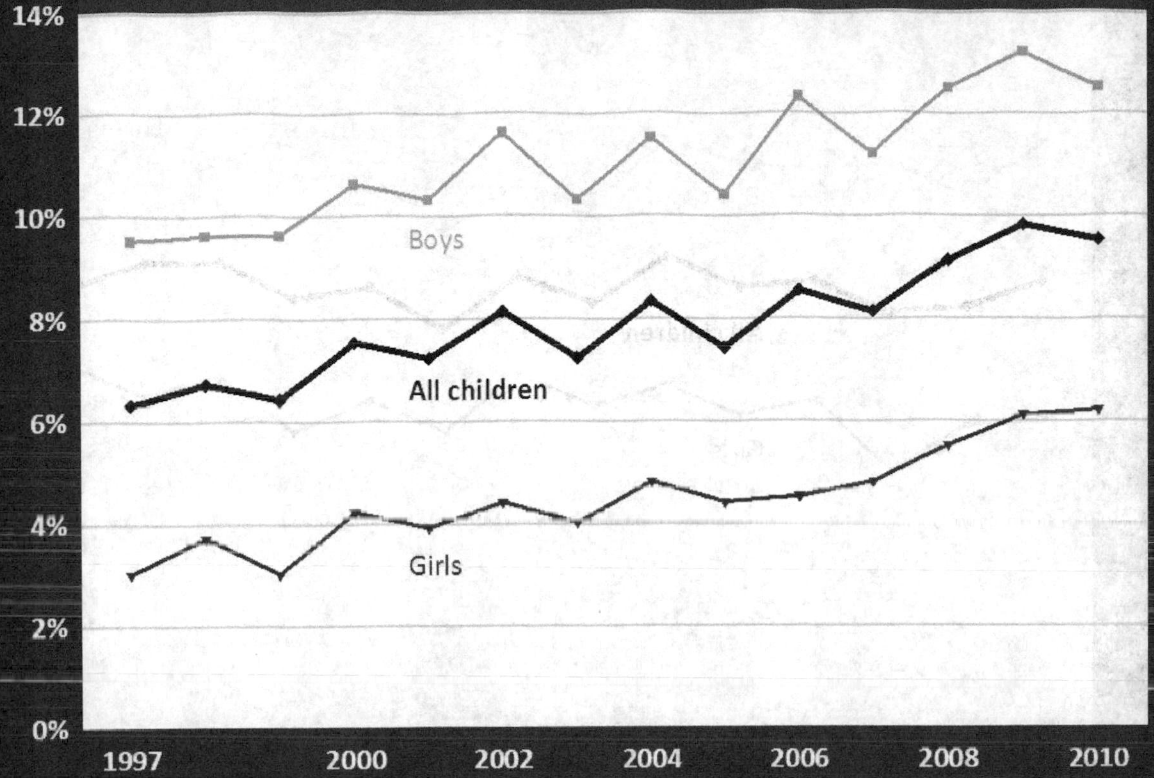

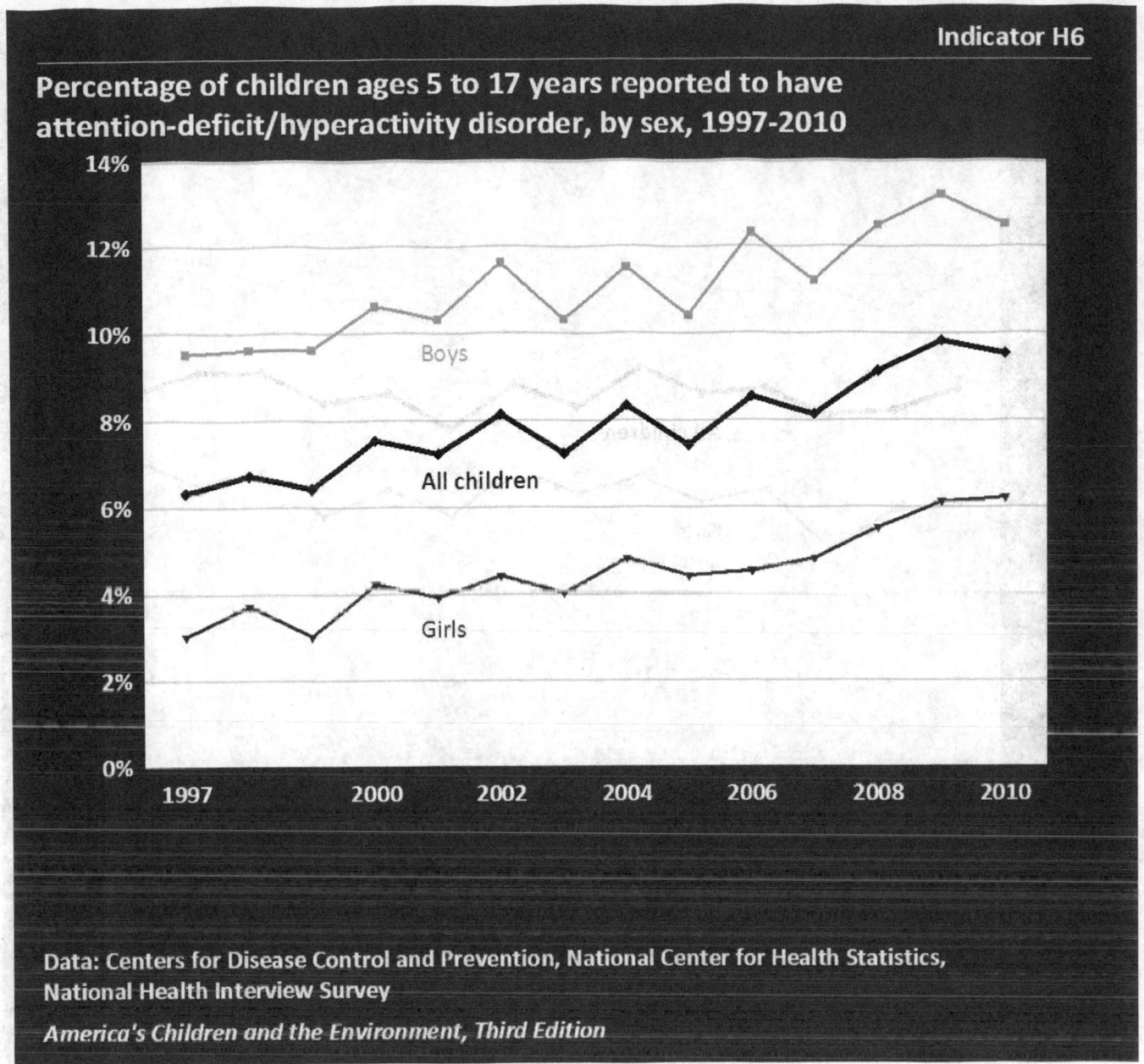

Data: Centers for Disease Control and Prevention, National Center for Health Statistics, National Health Interview Survey

America's Children and the Environment, Third Edition

Indicator H7

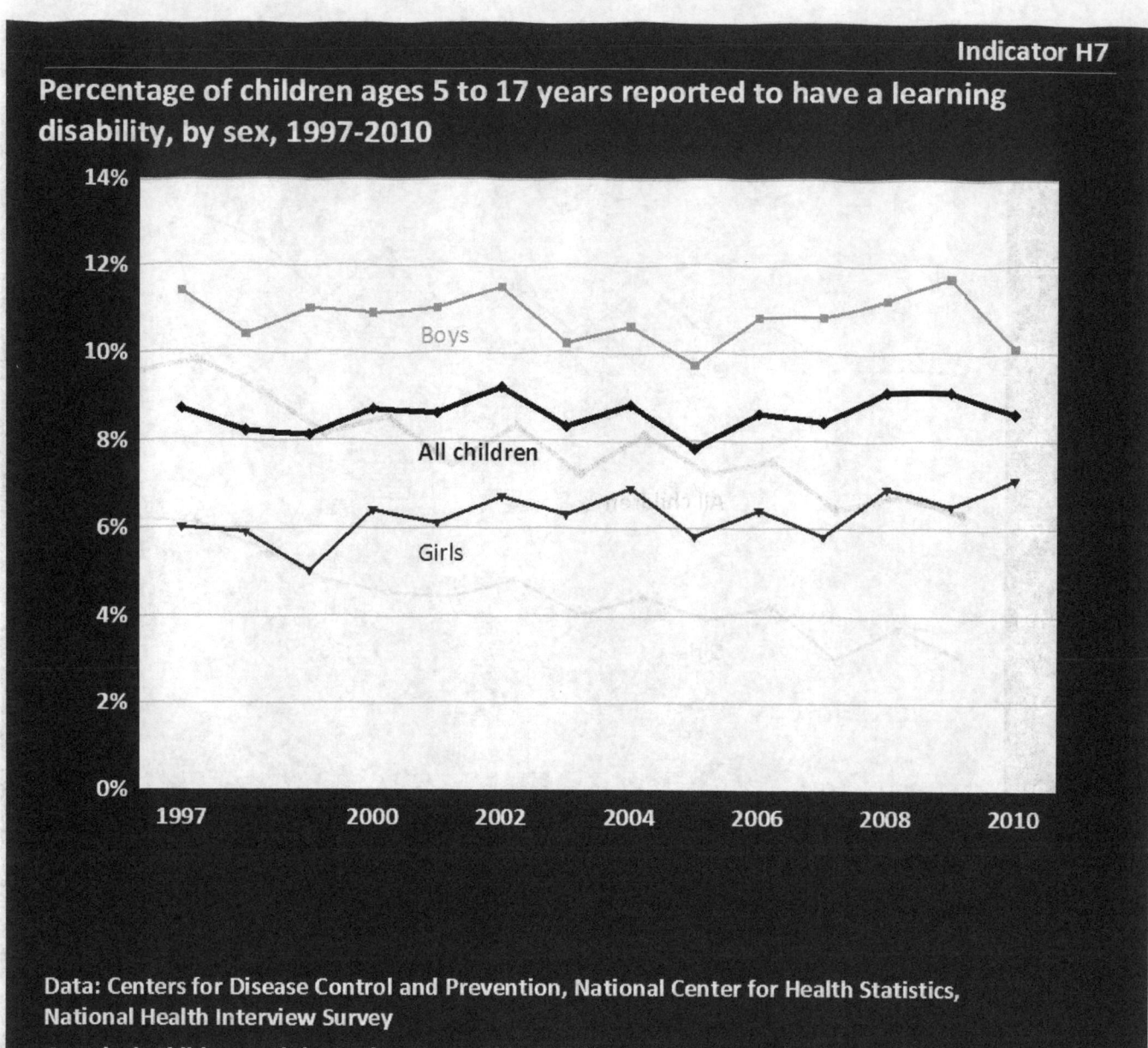

Percentage of children ages 5 to 17 years reported to have a learning disability, by sex, 1997-2010

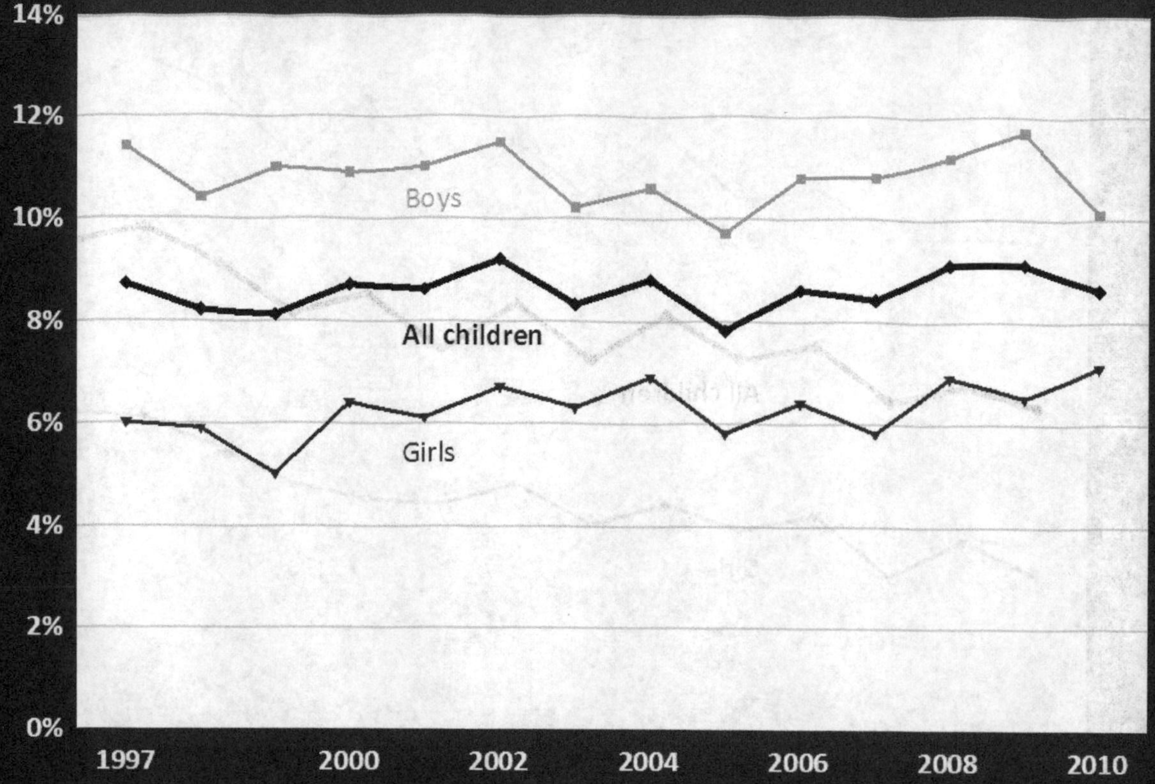

Data: Centers for Disease Control and Prevention, National Center for Health Statistics, National Health Interview Survey

America's Children and the Environment, Third Edition

Indicator H8

Percentage of children ages 5 to 17 years reported to have autism, 1997-2010

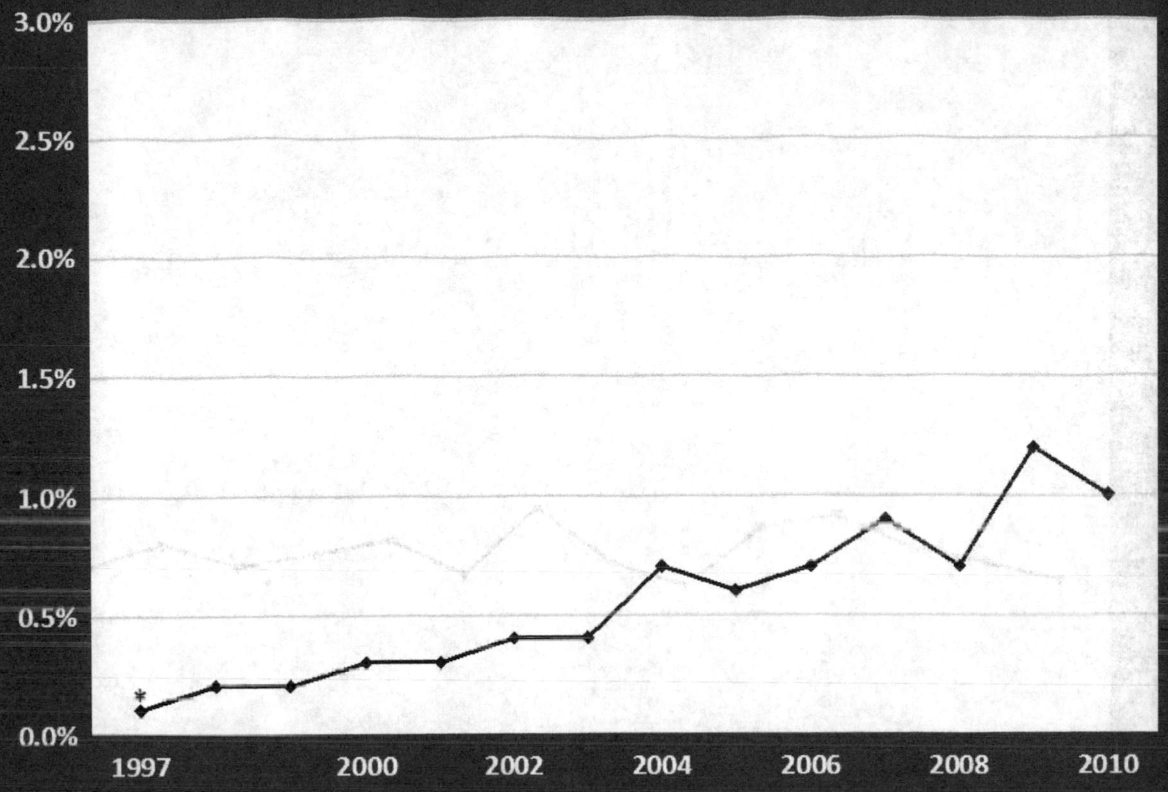

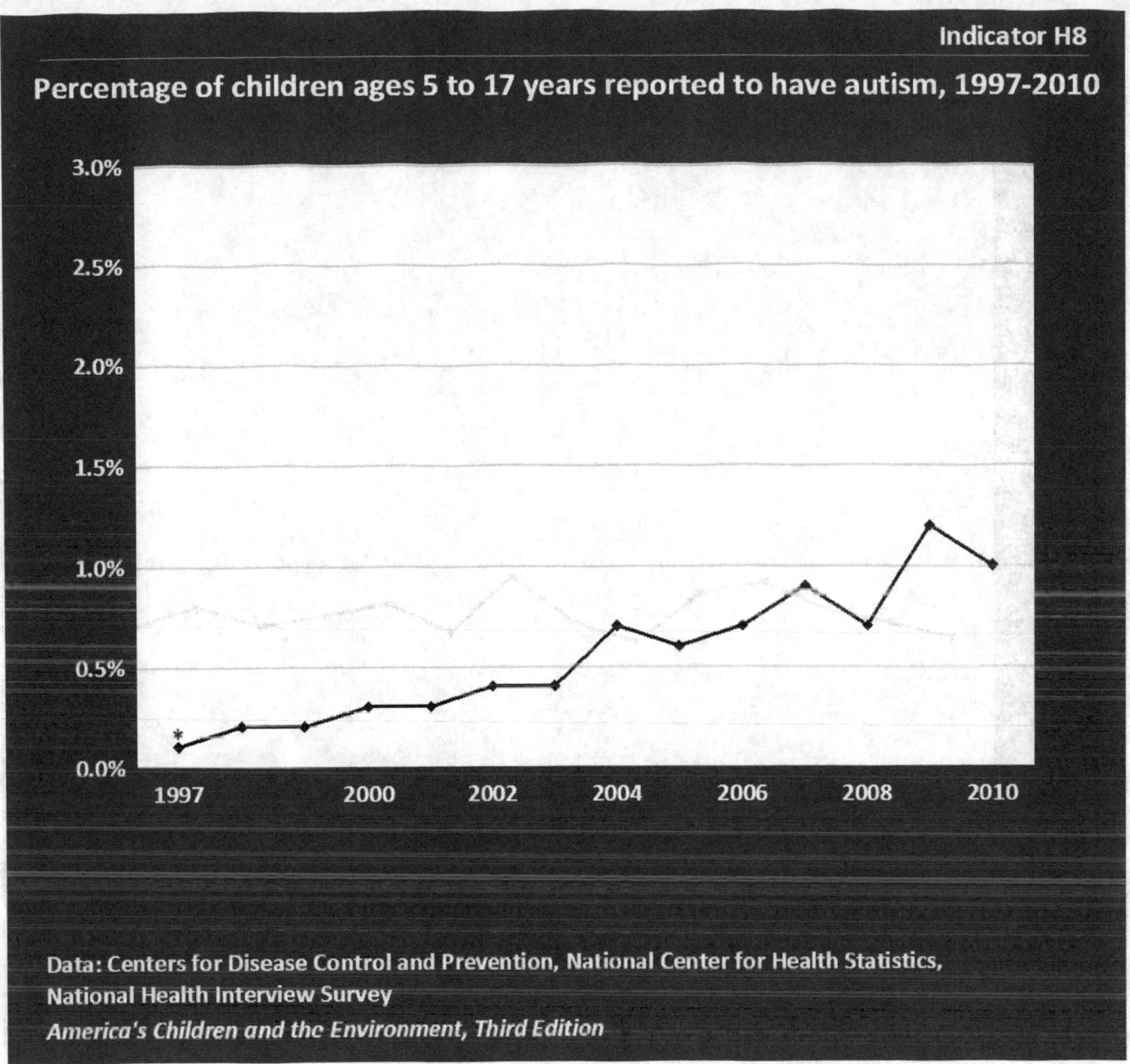

Data: Centers for Disease Control and Prevention, National Center for Health Statistics, National Health Interview Survey

America's Children and the Environment, Third Edition

Indicator H9

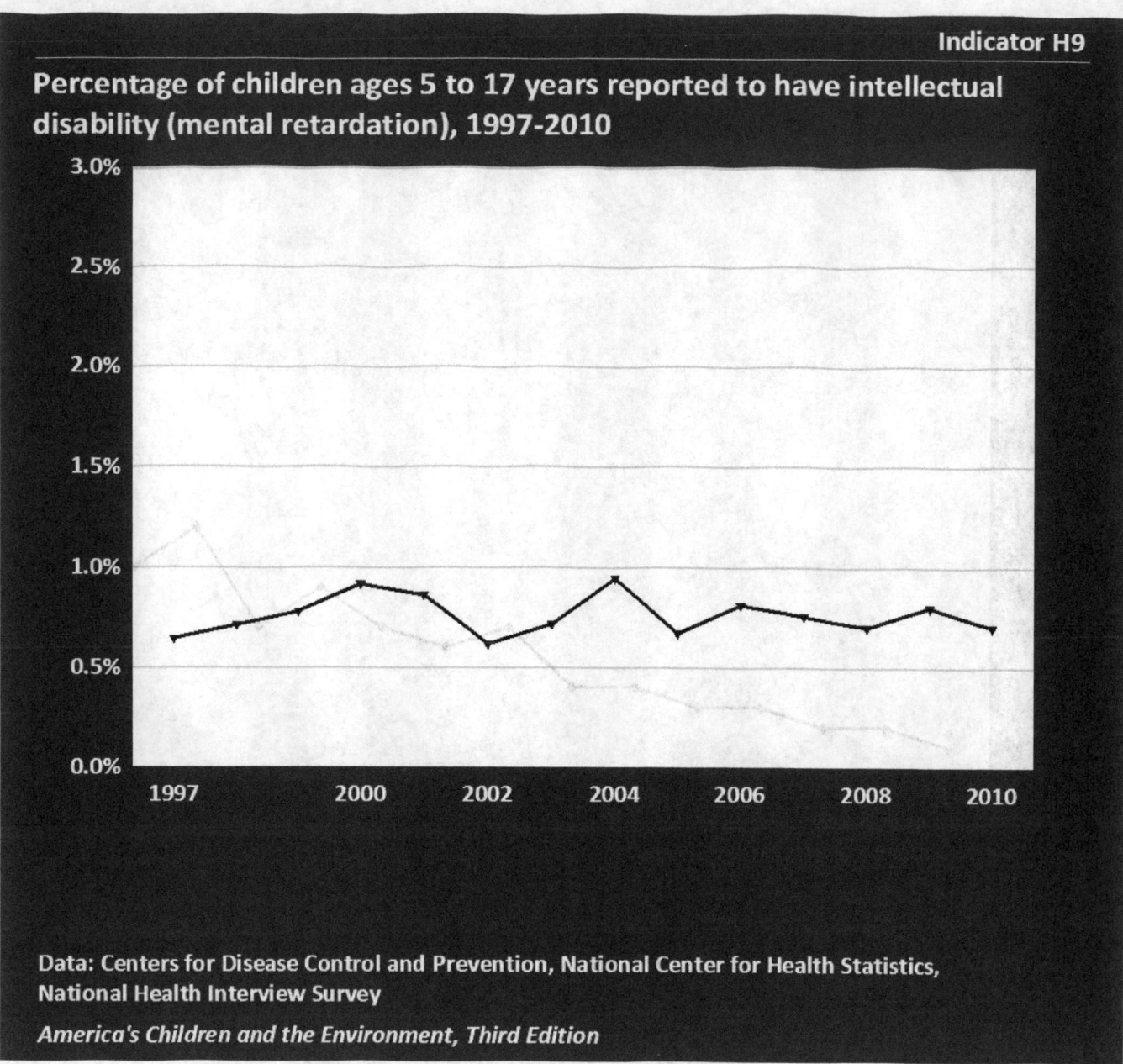

Percentage of children ages 5 to 17 years reported to have intellectual disability (mental retardation), 1997-2010

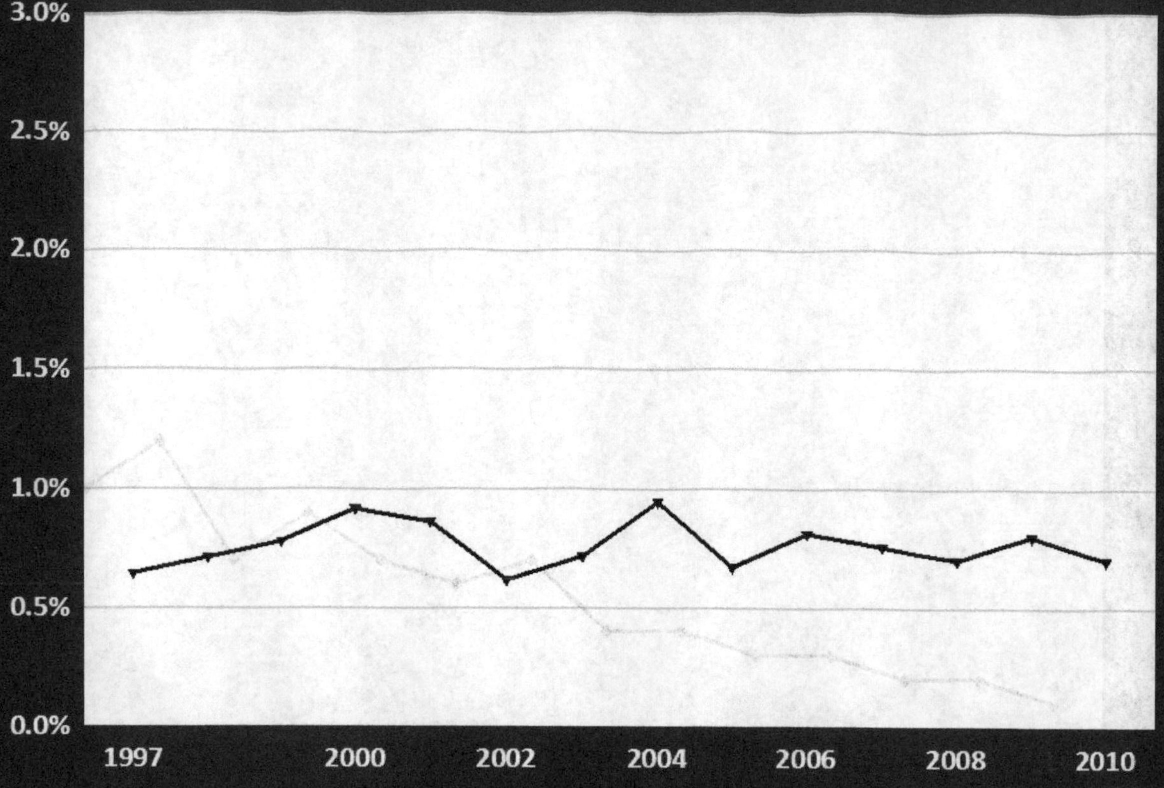

Data: Centers for Disease Control and Prevention, National Center for Health Statistics, National Health Interview Survey

America's Children and the Environment, Third Edition

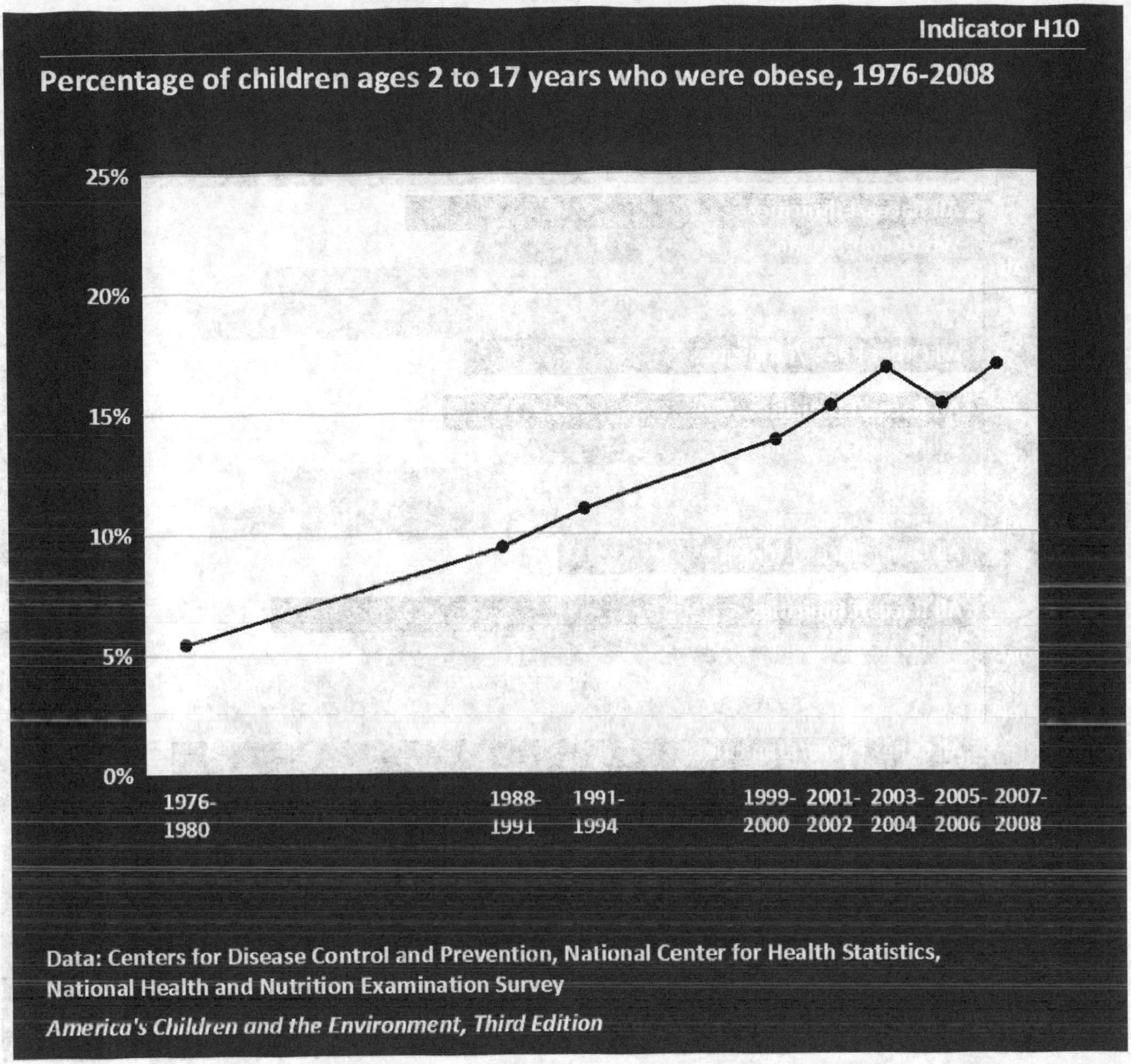
Indicator H10
Percentage of children ages 2 to 17 years who were obese, 1976-2008
25%
20%
15%
10%
5%
0%
1976-1980
1988-1991
1991-1994
1999-2000
2001-2002
2003-2004
2005-2006
2007-2008
Data: Centers for Disease Control and Prevention, National Center for Health Statistics, National Health and Nutrition Examination Survey
America's Children and the Environment, Third Edition

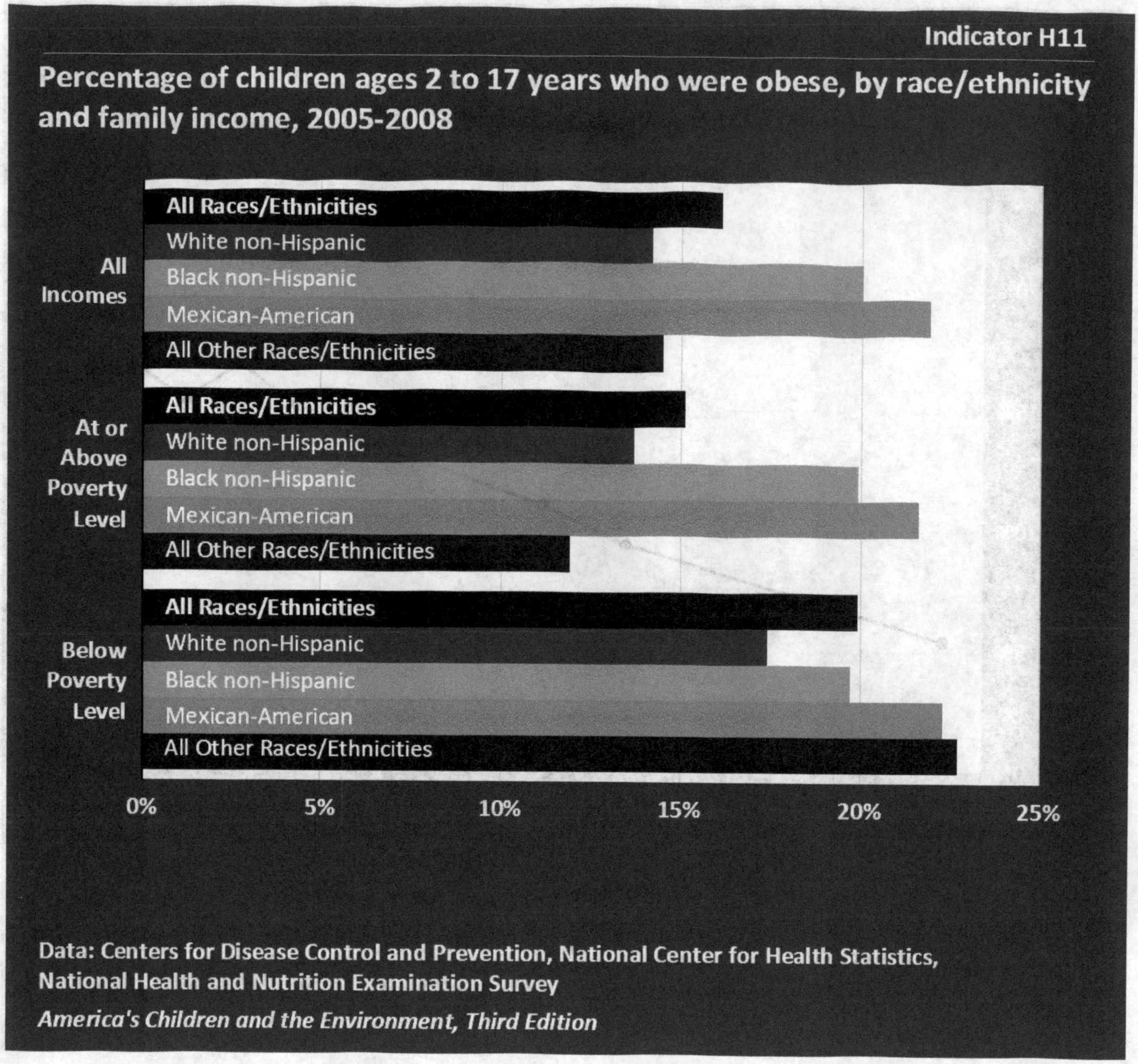
Indicator H11
Percentage of children ages 2 to 17 years who were obese, by race/ethnicity and family income, 2005-2008
All Incomes
At or Above Poverty Level
Below Poverty Level
All Races/Ethnicities
White non-Hispanic
Black non-Hispanic
Mexican-American
All Other Races/Ethnicities
0%
5%
10%
15%
20%
25%
Data: Centers for Disease Control and Prevention, National Center for Health Statistics, National Health and Nutrition Examination Survey
America's Children and the Environment, Third Edition

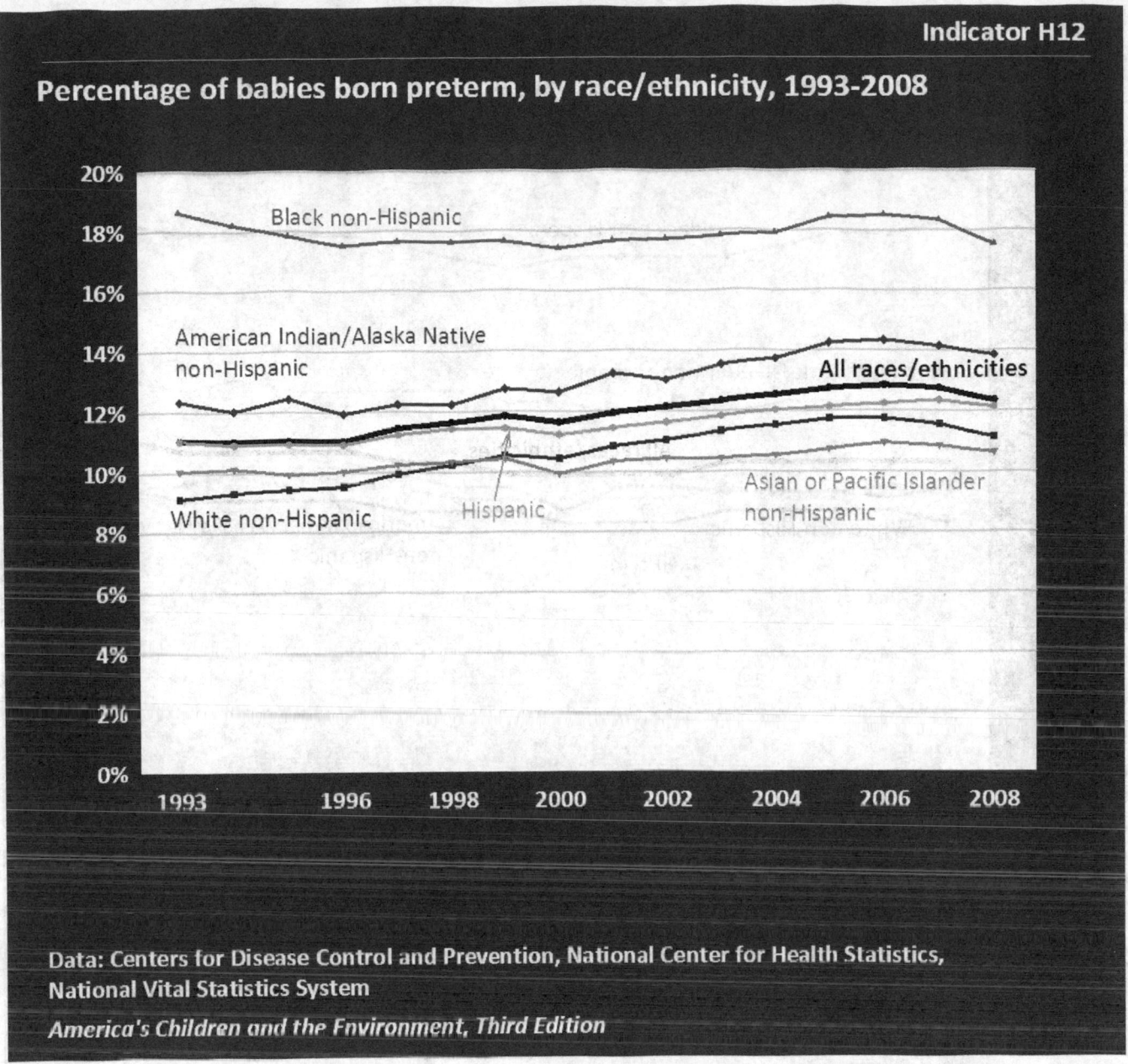

Indicator H12

Percentage of babies born preterm, by race/ethnicity, 1993-2008

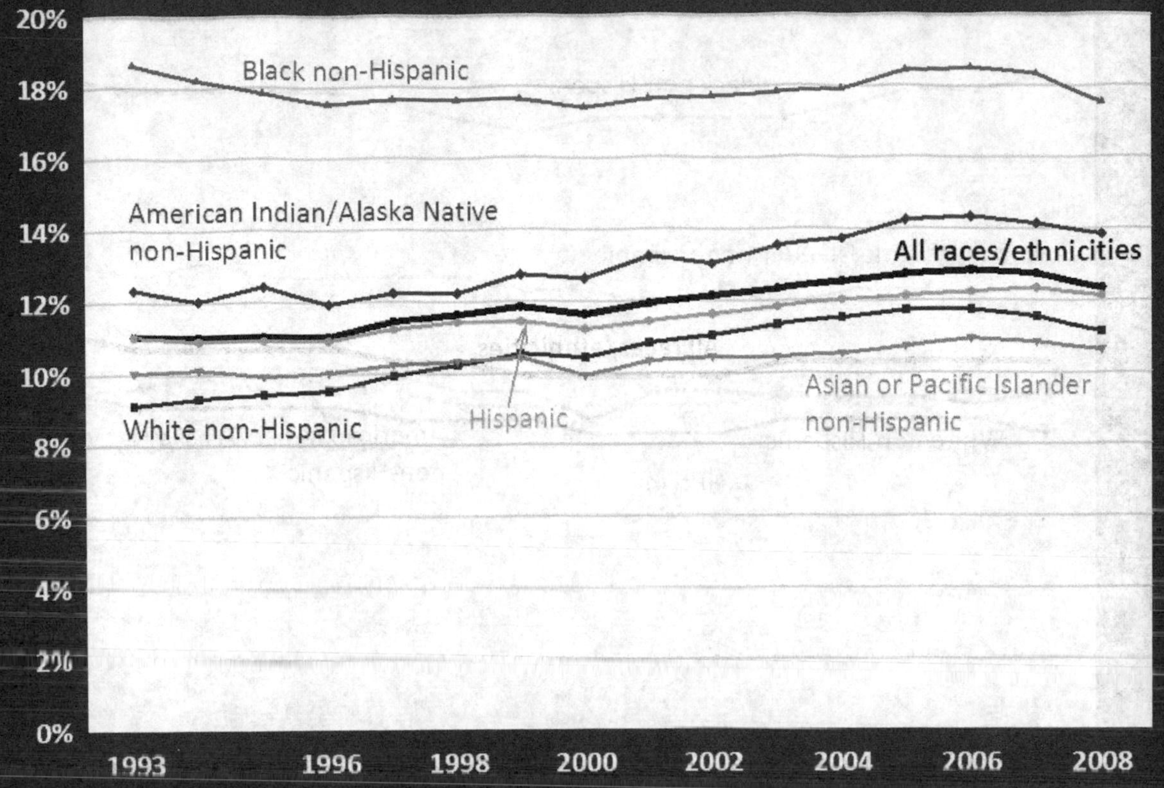

Data: Centers for Disease Control and Prevention, National Center for Health Statistics, National Vital Statistics System

America's Children and the Environment, Third Edition

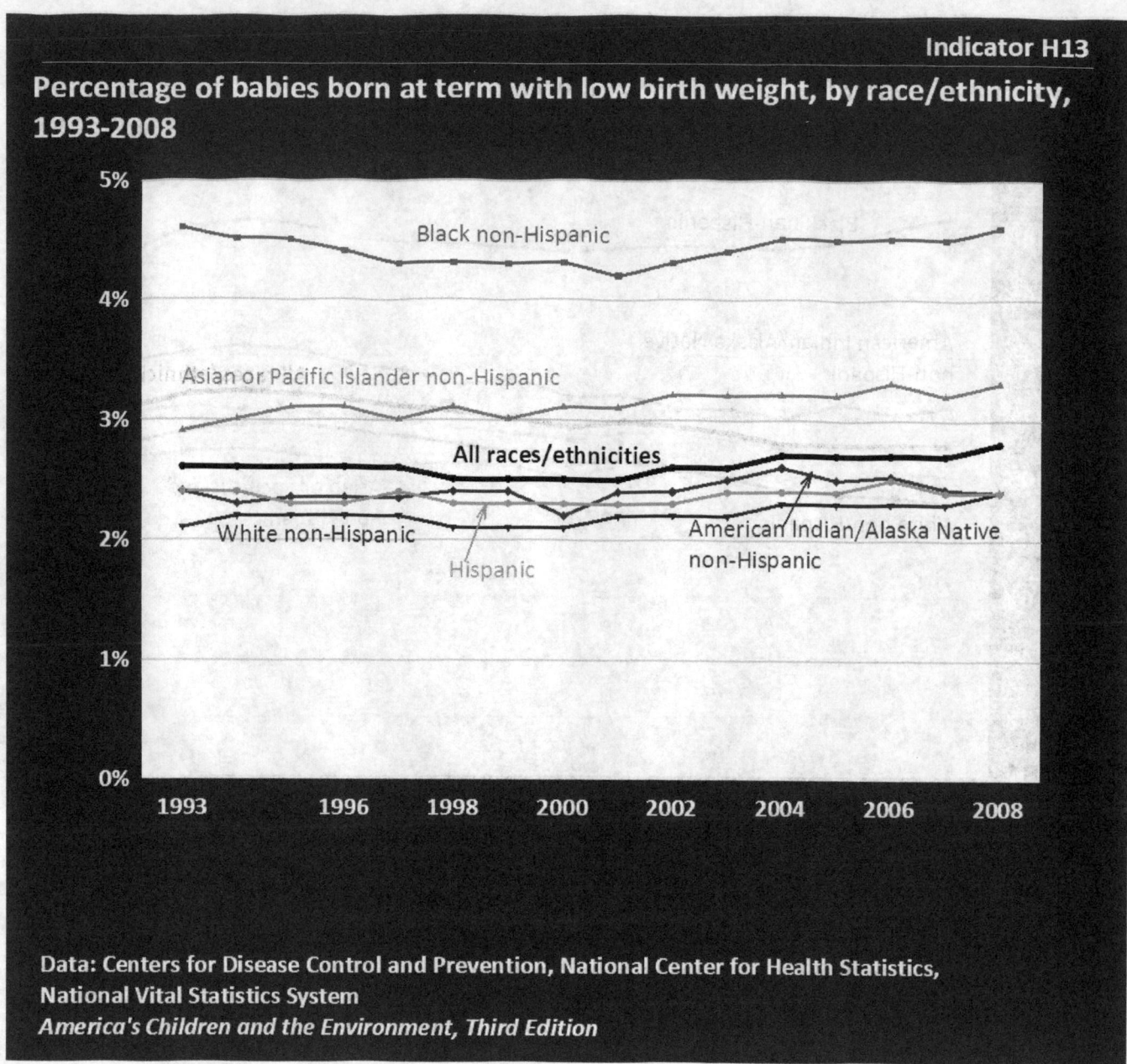

Indicator H13

Percentage of babies born at term with low birth weight, by race/ethnicity, 1993-2008

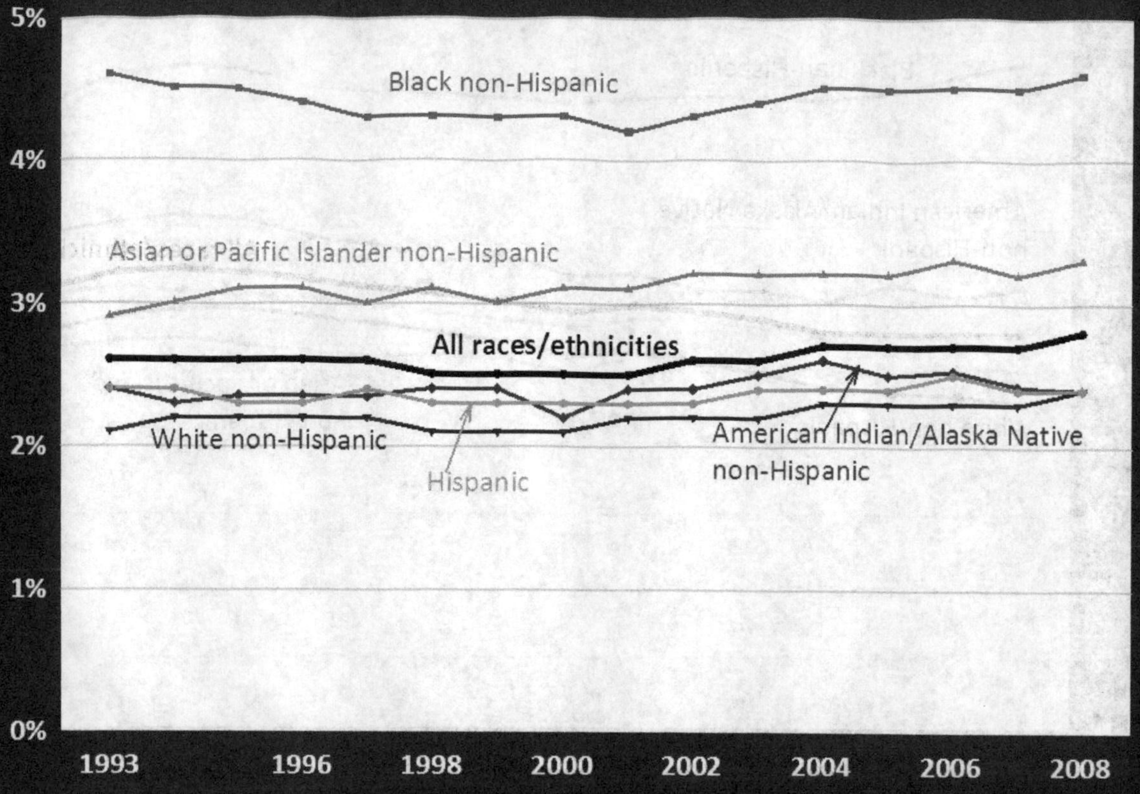

Data: Centers for Disease Control and Prevention, National Center for Health Statistics, National Vital Statistics System

America's Children and the Environment, Third Edition

The table below shows the number of active, current CWS, NTNCWS, TNCWS and aggregate total water systems for each state. Also shown is the total number of systems per state with ground water and surface water as their source and the number and percent of CWS systems per state that experienced at least one health-based violation during the reporting period. Data are for active water systems, from the SDWIS/Fed third quarter FY2011 inventory tables.

		Water System Type				Source of Water				CWS's with Reported Health-Based Violations	
		CWS	NTNCWS	TNCWS	Total	Ground	Surface	Unknown	Total	Systems	Percent
AK	Systems	437	256	864	1,557	1,292	264	1	1,557	84	5%
	Population	609,959	61,838	106,123	777,920	356,482	420,850	588	777,920	43,083	6%
AL	Systems	529	23	59	611	370	241	0	611	22	4%
	Population	5,516,594	14,734	6,332	5,553,660	1,551,946	3,985,714	0	5,553,660	112,911	2%
AR	Systems	710	35	362	1,107	681	426	0	1,107	101	9%
	Population	2,709,389	9,072	20,483	2,738,944	903,736	1,835,208	0	2,738,944	298,226	11%
AZ	Systems	780	204	586	1,570	1,502	68	0	1,570	95	6%
	Population	6,225,100	121,495	117,028	6,463,623	2,817,951	3,645,672	0	6,463,623	182,815	3%
CA	Systems	3,055	1,513	3,196	7,764	6,413	1,307	44	7,764	312	4%
	Population	40,960,545	389,720	855,324	42,205,589	7,113,070	35,087,714	4,805	42,205,589	1,142,978	3%
CO	Systems	877	178	998	2,053	1,509	544	0	2,053	74	4%
	Population	5,386,406	76,286	247,953	5,710,645	713,710	4,996,935	0	5,710,645	381,948	7%
CT	Systems	545	586	1,459	2,590	2,508	78	4	2,590	69	3%
	Population	2,703,626	114,185	59,662	2,837,473	429,541	2,441,492	6,440	2,837,473	35,624	1%
DC	Systems	5	1	0	6	0	6	0	6	0	0%
	Population	606,730	370		607,100	0	607,100	0	607,100	0	0%
DE	Systems	216	82	195	493	486	7	0	493	18	4%
	Population	899,801	22,324	53,982	976,107	489,327	486,780	0	976,107	221,726	23%

Source: *U.S. EPA, Drinking Water and Ground Water Statistics, Fiscal Year 2011*

		Water System Type				Source of Water				CWS's with Reported Health-Based Violations	
		CWS	NTNCWS	TNCWS	Total	Ground	Surface	Unknown	Total	Systems	Percent
FL	Systems	1,735	883	2,989	5,607	5,533	74	0	5,607	117	2%
	Population	19,221,968	241,415	257,744	19,721,127	15,774,819	3,946,308	0	19,721,127	691,902	4%
GA	Systems	1,776	192	462	2,430	2,194	236	0	2,430	69	3%
	Population	8,432,935	64,432	75,888	8,573,255	1,816,835	6,756,420	0	8,573,255	229,087	1%
HI	Systems	111	17	2	130	118	12	0	130	3	2%
	Population	1,472,544	11,425	375	1,484,344	1,319,270	165,074	0	1,484,344	7,927	1%
IA	Systems	1,127	135	655	1,917	1,766	151	0	1,917	60	3%
	Population	2,742,242	48,095	76,655	2,866,992	1,549,191	1,317,801	0	2,866,992	178,689	6%
ID	Systems	745	225	986	1,956	1,872	84	0	1,956	129	7%
	Population	1,100,437	52,366	99,611	1,252,414	987,898	264,516	0	1,252,414	137,279	11%
IL	Systems	1,751	419	3,426	5,596	4,838	758	0	5,596	78	1%
	Population	12,128,970	135,391	344,924	12,609,285	3,623,164	8,986,121	0	12,609,285	409,426	3%
IN	Systems	813	573	2,822	4,208	4,090	118	0	4,208	58	1%
	Population	4,870,296	195,358	383,646	5,449,300	2,966,457	2,482,843	0	5,449,300	173,345	3%
KS	Systems	887	45	90	1,022	650	372	0	1,022	109	11%
	Population	2,676,572	21,296	4,266	2,702,134	762,026	1,940,108	0	2,702,134	280,898	10%
KY	Systems	402	21	39	462	141	321	0	462	55	12%
	Population	4,441,302	11,025	4,895	4,457,222	395,869	4,061,353	0	4,457,222	509,432	11%
LA	Systems	1,049	144	210	1,403	1,307	96	0	1,403	74	5%
	Population	4,921,528	56,471	47,876	5,025,875	2,990,524	2,035,351	0	5,025,875	436,031	9%
MA	Systems	538	273	999	1,810	1,577	227	6	1,810	95	5%
	Population	9,320,228	74,560	170,687	9,565,475	1,849,024	7,716,266	185	9,565,475	896,940	9%

Source: *U.S. EPA, Drinking Water and Ground Water Statistics, Fiscal Year 2011*

		Water System Type				Source of Water				CWS's with Reported Health-Based Violations	
		CWS	NTNCWS	TNCWS	Total	Ground	Surface	Unknown	Total	Systems	Percent
MD	Systems	476	562	2,466	3,504	3,400	101	2	3,504	32	1%
	Population	5,194,297	161,140	267,388	5,622,825	1,046,753	4,574,371	1,701	5,622,825	69,099	1%
ME	Systems	378	346	1,149	1,873	1,798	75	0	1,873	46	2%
	Population	664,022	66,076	183,241	913,339	464,427	448,912	0	913,339	76,254	8%
MI	Systems	1,397	1,374	8,475	11,246	10,937	309	0	11,246	79	1%
	Population	7,615,948	326,679	1,014,416	8,957,043	3,014,780	5,942,263	0	8,957,043	256,492	3%
MN	Systems	961	502	5,655	7,118	6,998	120	0	7,118	51	1%
	Population	4,262,862	76,460	535,380	4,874,702	3,460,120	1,414,582	0	4,874,702	162,314	3%
MO	Systems	1,475	224	1,084	2,783	2,549	234	0	2,783	187	7%
	Population	5,171,609	71,769	115,984	5,359,362	2,045,596	3,313,766	0	5,359,362	347,553	6%
MS	Systems	1,107	82	74	1,263	1,248	13	2	1,263	55	4%
	Population	3,152,385	74,531	11,551	3,238,467	2,989,901	247,851	715	3,238,467	249,304	8%
MT	Systems	698	262	1,143	2,103	1,881	222	0	2,103	83	4%
	Population	713,698	81,987	172,974	968,659	559,822	408,837	0	968,659	66,503	7%
NC	Systems	2,081	405	3,606	6,092	5,648	444	0	6,092	195	3%
	Population	7,622,946	113,479	315,869	8,052,294	1,968,393	6,083,901	0	8,052,294	324,873	4%
ND	Systems	332	28	182	542	411	131	0	542	14	3%
	Population	581,311	4,153	19,936	605,400	276,106	329,294	0	605,400	16,528	3%
NE	Systems	589	160	574	1,323	1,247	76	0	1,323	144	11%
	Population	1,479,705	49,711	52,220	1,581,636	751,818	829,818	0	1,581,636	160,528	10%
NH	Systems	705	435	1,287	2,427	2,368	59	0	2,427	107	4%
	Population	855,402	92,312	220,800	1,168,514	638,786	529,728	0	1,168,514	93,070	8%

Source: *U.S. EPA, Drinking Water and Ground Water Statistics, Fiscal Year 2011*

		Water System Type				Source of Water				CWS's with Reported Health-Based Violations	
		CWS	NTNCWS	TNCWS	Total	Ground	Surface	Unknown	Total	Systems	Percent
NJ	Systems	612	776	2,503	3,891	3,748	143	0	3,891	67	2%
	Population	8,998,715	352,412	428,677	9,779,804	3,422,805	6,356,999	0	9,779,804	1,459,099	15%
NM	Systems	600	152	440	1,192	1,126	66	0	1,192	113	9%
	Population	1,810,927	50,807	75,950	1,937,684	1,049,799	887,885	0	1,937,684	156,487	8%
NV	Systems	211	109	241	561	524	37	0	561	43	8%
	Population	2,557,680	42,140	21,592	2,621,412	294,822	2,326,590	0	2,621,412	66,693	3%
NY	Systems	2,466	748	5,774	8,988	7,865	1,112	11	8,988	217	2%
	Population	17,828,851	308,553	2,826,924	20,964,328	4,925,090	16,038,874	364	20,964,328	953,787	5%
OH	Systems	1,240	731	2,913	4,884	4,563	321	0	4,884	73	1%
	Population	10,411,689	213,288	404,088	11,029,065	3,386,152	7,642,913	0	11,029,065	326,423	3%
OK	Systems	1,105	105	459	1,669	906	763	0	1,669	161	10%
	Population	3,567,235	20,664	36,751	3,624,650	683,197	2,941,453	0	3,624,650	765,011	21%
OR	Systems	875	334	1,396	2,605	2,299	305	1	2,605	147	6%
	Population	3,374,323	70,222	200,723	3,645,650	800,545	2,844,648	75	3,645,650	182,433	5%
PA	Systems	2,061	1,215	5,949	9,225	8,628	591	6	9,225	145	2%
	Population	10,744,868	492,105	756,148	11,993,121	2,530,047	9,462,887	187	11,993,121	2,264,708	19%
RI	Systems	89	79	317	485	456	29	0	485	13	3%
	Population	989,055	29,787	55,550	1,074,392	224,892	849,500	0	1,074,392	74,608	7%
SC	Systems	600	121	721	1,442	1,099	343	0	1,442	28	2%
	Population	3,822,295	44,046	41,395	3,907,736	595,713	3,312,023	0	3,907,736	47,687	1%
SD	Systems	456	24	164	644	500	144	0	644	82	13%
	Population	719,433	8,468	23,103	751,004	316,491	434,513	0	751,004	45,639	6%

Source: *U.S. EPA, Drinking Water and Ground Water Statistics, Fiscal Year 2011*

		Water System Type				Source of Water				CWS's with Reported Health-Based Violations	
		CWS	NTNCWS	TNCWS	Total	Ground	Surface	Unknown	Total	Systems	Percent
TN	Systems	485	46	360	891	524	353	0	891	6	1%
	Population	6,329,778	25,802	56,982	6,412,562	1,471,473	4,941,089	0	6,412,562	44,195	1%
TX	Systems	4,721	898	1,345	6,964	5,560	1,399	5	6,964	386	6%
	Population	25,062,602	509,897	275,817	25,848,316	6,051,176	19,796,769	371	25,848,316	2,090,770	8%
UT	Systems	465	67	481	1,013	870	143	0	1,013	43	4%
	Population	2,728,314	28,050	78,508	2,834,872	821,207	2,013,665	0	2,834,872	148,091	5%
VA	Systems	1,169	544	1,074	2,787	2,395	392	0	2,787	116	4%
	Population	6,607,284	314,872	167,892	7,090,048	751,035	6,339,013	0	7,090,048	196,866	3%
VT	Systems	439	242	682	1,363	1,247	116	0	1,363	69	5%
	Population	446,339	44,173	97,799	588,311	315,300	273,011	0	588,311	69,198	12%
WA	Systems	2,291	349	1,707	4,347	4,073	272	2	4,347	39	1%
	Population	6,418,929	156,358	402,820	6,983,048	3,194,928	3,787,818	262	6,983,048	13,812	0%
WI	Systems	1,070	856	9,539	11,465	11,409	56	0	11,465	84	1%
	Population	4,015,261	208,017	719,637	4,942,915	3,086,928	1,855,987	0	4,942,915	259,586	5%
WV	Systems	492	121	429	1,042	710	332	0	1,042	24	2%
	Population	1,509,947	39,502	31,183	1,580,632	303,110	1,277,522	0	1,580,632	63,240	4%
WY	Systems	313	90	392	795	653	142	0	795	25	3%
	Population	449,992	22,662	74,623	547,277	198,125	349,152	0	547,277	15,896	3%
Total Systems		**50,047**	**17,792**	**82,980**	**150,819**	**136,487**	**14,248**	**84**	**150,819**	**4,496**	**3%**
Total Population		**292,659,815**	**5,821,980**	**12,619,375**	**311,101,170**	**100,050,217**	**211,035,260**	**15,693**	**311,101,170**	**17,436,620**	**6%**

Source: *U.S. EPA, Drinking Water and Ground Water Statistics, Fiscal Year 2011*

Percentage of Community Water Systems Meeting Health-based Standards

The Government Performance and Results Act (GPRA) of 1993 requires federal executive agencies to develop long-term Strategic Plans defining general goals and objectives for their programs. Under the act, agencies must also develop Annual Performance Plans that describe the goals for their program activities and publish an Annual Performance Report showing actual results compared against the performance goals.

Under its Annual Performance Plan, strategic objective 2.1: Protect Public Health, sub-objective 2.1.1: Water Safe to Drink, EPA set a goal of 91 percent of the population served by community water systems will receive drinking water that meets all applicable health-based drinking water standards through approaches that include effective treatment and source water protection. The table below shows the performance results as a national aggregate and broken-out by EPA Region.[1]

		EPA Region									
	National	1	2	3	4	5	6	7	8	9	10
2011	93.2%	91%	84%	89%	96%	96%	91%	92%	94%	97%	97%
2010	92.2%	91%	83%	97%	94%	93%	91%	82%	93%	96%	92%
2009	92.1%	92%	79%	90%	94%	95%	90%	94%	96%	97%	96%
2008	92.0%	91%	82%	90%	94%	95%	89%	83%	96%	98%	96%
2007	91.5%	92%	76%	95%	93%	93%	92%	93%	97%	95%	92%
2006	89.4%	92%	61%	93%	93%	92%	88%	91%	96%	98%	95%
2005	88.5%	92%	55%	93%	93%	94%	88%	91%	95%	95%	95%
2004	90.0%	93%	80%	85%	93%	96%	92%	91%	92%	86%	93%
2003	89.6%	89%	54%	95%	93%	95%	93%	93%	92%	98%	93%
2002	93.6%	88%	81%	98%	96%	94%	93%	95%	97%	99%	91%
2001	90.8%	65%	77%	98%	95%	92%	96%	90%	94%	97%	83%
2000	90.7%	62%	76%	97%	95%	95%	96%	95%	94%	94%	83%
1999	90.5%	75%	61%	98%	95%	95%	95%	95%	94%	97%	94%
1998	89.0%	64%	60%	97%	95%	95%	95%	94%	93%	95%	89%
1997	86.5%	62%	55%	97%	93%	92%	93%	95%	91%	95%	74%
1996	85.6%	60%	53%	92%	93%	92%	94%	95%	93%	91%	74%
1995	83.8%	57%	52%	91%	92%	92%	88%	95%	90%	88%	75%
1994	83.0%	57%	87%	87%	90%	88%	87%	94%	91%	90%	87%
1993	78.8%	60%	85%	85%	90%	77%	92%	93%	92%	69%	85%
		CT, ME, MA, NH, RI, VT	NJ, NY, PR, VI	DE, DC, MD, PA, VA, WV	AL, FL, GA, KY, MS, NC, SC, TN	IL, IN, MI, MN, OH, WI	AR, LA, NM, OK TX	IA, KS, MO, NE	CO, MT, ND, SD, UT, WY	AZ, CA, HI, NV, AS, GU, MP, PW	AK, ID, OR, WA

[1] 2005 Baseline: 89 percent of population; note that year-to-year performance is expected to change over time as new standards take effect.)

Source: *U.S. EPA, Drinking Water and Ground Water Statistics, Fiscal Year 2011*

Notice: These measures are based on violations reported by states to the EPA Safe Drinking Water Information System/Fed (SDWIS/Fed). EPA is aware of inaccuracies and underreporting of some data to this system and is working with the states to improve the quality of the data.

Community Water Systems (CWS) Violations

This section presents three tables showing reported violations experienced by CWS broken out by the number of violations, number of systems in violation and the population in violation (based on the retail population served). Sources for these data are as follows:

Fiscal Year	SDWIS/Fed Data Source
2011	FY2011 Quarter 3
2010	FY2010 Quarter 3
2009	FY2009 Quarter 3
2008	FY2008 Quarter 3
2007	FY2007 Quarter 3
2006	FY2006 Quarter 3
2005	FY2005 Quarter 4, except for Chemical Monitoring/Reporting violations which are from FY2006 Quarter 1
2004	FY2004 Quarter 4 frozen tables, except for Chemical Monitoring/Reporting violations which are from FY2005 Quarter 1
2003	FY2003 Quarter 4 frozen tables, except for Chemical Monitoring/Reporting violations which are from FY2004 Quarter 1

Please note that totals for the number of systems in violation and for population affected should be lower than the sum in each row as some systems will have incurred more than one type of violation. Compliance information since FY2003 includes new Disinfectant Byproducts (DBP) and Interim Enhanced Surface Water Treatment Rule (IESWTR) rules.

CWS Violations Reported Nationally by Fiscal Year

The following tables show the number of CWS violations by type, number of those systems in violation, and the population affected by fiscal year.

Violation Totals by Fiscal Year

	Violation Type					
FY	MCL	MRDL	TT	M/R	Other	Total
2011	8,522	4	1,992	76,031	22,618	**109,167**
2010	9,052	4	2,348	42,677	21,776	**75,857**
2009	9,971	5	2,392	60,823	20,941	**94,132**
2008	9,883	5	2,647	103,064	20,774	**136,373**
2007	9,410	5	3,056	61,316	23,299	**97,086**
2006	9,076	7	2,790	57,117	19,245	**88,235**
2005	9,360	4	3,036	109,167	18,414	**139,981**
2004	5,340	6	2,168	87,393	14,459	**109,366**
2003	4,688	1	2,299	58,675	12,671	**78,334**

Source: *U.S. EPA, Drinking Water and Ground Water Statistics, Fiscal Year 2011*

Systems in Violation by Fiscal Year

			Violation Type			
FY	MCL	MRDL	TT	M/R	Other	Total*
2011	4,010	4	1,263	17,519	8,416	**18,421**
2010	4,092	3	1,411	11,118	7,807	**18,663**
2009	4,451	3	1,401	13,403	8,546	**20,684**
2008	4,553	5	1,506	13,084	8,631	**20,797**
2007	4,412	4	1,648	12,619	10,429	**21,544**
2006	4,371	3	1,538	13,071	9,600	**21,618**
2005	4,383	4	1,625	14,291	10,258	**22,772**
2004	3,419	4	1,409	13,551	8,947	**21,055**
2003	3,042	1	1,458	12,819	8,109	**20,280**

Population Affected by Fiscal Year

			Violation Type			
FY	MCL	MRDL	TT	M/R	Other	Total*
2011	14,915,599	54,128	8,105,335	60,653,341	18,305,917	**70,959,083**
2010	14,064,004	4,388	10,539,506	50,775,665	17,476,368	**79,731,863**
2009	15,918,279	29,763	10,643,904	50,360,756	20,077,807	**78,507,217**
2008	15,841,822	1,021	10,086,935	57,538,783	21,872,736	**83,385,983**
2007	16,105,351	263,875	10,895,825	51,148,667	30,434,294	**87,843,223**
2006	16,221,483	46.344	16,612,762	52,289,555	23,372,794	**83,062,903**
2005	18,951,548	424,859	16,879,450	61,767,844	23,442,800	**90,890,243**
2004	15,018,194	3,617	16,588,301	48,675,006	17,833,120	**76,870,272**
2003	15,438,443	2,250	16,969,087	49,497,572	12,726,332	**80,765,799**

*Totals for the number of systems in violation and for the population affected are lower than the sum in each row because some systems have incurred more than one type of violation.

Source: *U.S. EPA, Drinking Water and Ground Water Statistics, Fiscal Year 2011*

CWS Violations Reported Nationally by System Size

The next three tables present the same information for FY2011 as in the previous section, only with water systems arranged by the following population size categories:

- Very Small 500 or less
- Small 501-3,300
- Medium 3,301-10,000
- Large 10,001-100,000
- Very Large >100,000

Number of Violations

	Violation Type					
	MCL	MRDL	TT	M/R	Other	Total
Very Small	4,791	1	1,232	50,117	17,795	**73,936**
Small	2,379	2	450	17,113	3,382	**23,326**
Medium	856	0	154	5,201	897	**7,108**
Large	475	1	133	3,443	526	**4,578**
Very Large	21	0	23	157	18	**219**

Number of Systems in Violation

	Violation Type					
	MCL	MRDL	TT	M/R	Other	Total*
Very Small	2,185	1	756	7,307	5,131	**11,434**
Small	972	2	291	2,840	1,611	**4,502**
Medium	386	0	92	795	460	**1,415**
Large	275	1	84	553	303	**993**
Very Large	13	0	10	51	16	**77**

Population Affected

	Violation Type					
	MCL	MRDL	TT	M/R	Other	Total*
Very Small	354,602	56	121,990	1,173,293	777,570	**1,828,187**
Small	1,401,995	3,072	618,893	3,897,674	2,209,961	**6,249,402**
Medium	2,286,476	0	521,222	4,569,055	2,657,065	**8,148,439**
Large	6,757,968	51,000	2,205,565	15,338,207	8,232,136	**26,719,084**
Very Large	4,080,953	0	4,849,769	21,630,050	3,762,010	**28,013,971**

*Totals for the number of systems in violation and for the population affected are lower than the sum in each row because some systems have incurred more than one type of violation.

Source: *U.S. EPA, Drinking Water and Ground Water Statistics, Fiscal Year 2011*

NTNCWS Violations Reported by Fiscal Year

This section presents three tables showing reported violations experienced by Non-Transient Non-Community Water Systems (NTNCWS) broken out by the number of violations, number of systems in violation, and the population in violation (based on the retail population served). Sources for these data are as follows:

Fiscal Year	SDWIS/Fed Data Source
2011	FY2011 Quarter 3
2010	FY2010 Quarter 3
2009	FY2009 Quarter 3
2008	FY2008 Quarter 3
2007	FY2007 Quarter 3
2006	FY2006 Quarter 3
2005	FY2005 Quarter 4, except for Chemical Monitoring/Reporting violations which are from FY2006 Quarter 1
2004	FY2004 Quarter 4 frozen tables, except for Chemical Monitoring/Reporting violations which are from FY2005 Quarter 1
2003	FY2003 Quarter 4 frozen tables, except for Chemical Monitoring/Reporting violations which are from FY2004 Quarter 1

Please note that totals for the number of systems in violation and for population affected should be lower than the sum in each row as some systems will have incurred more than one type of violation. Compliance information since FY2003 includes new Disinfectant Byproducts (DBP) and Interim Enhanced Surface Water Treatment Rule (IESWTR) rules.

Number of Violations

	Violation Type					
FY	MCL	MRDL	TT	M/R	Other	Total
2011	1,906		490	30,366	3,213	**35,975**
2010	2,167		670	20,940	3,395	**27,172**
2009	3,882	1	185	14,276	8,516	**22,519**
2008	2,206		766	39,379	3,449	**45,800**
2007	2,141		794	28,581	2,490	**34,006**
2006	1,833		827	27,728	2,063	**32,451**
2005	1,851	1	853	48,276	717	**51,698**
2004	1,348		681	34,097	538	**36,664**
2003	1,383		680	25,588	503	**28,154**

Source: *U.S. EPA, Drinking Water and Ground Water Statistics, Fiscal Year 2011*

Number of Systems in Violation

	Violation Type					
FY	MCL	MRDL	TT	M/R	Other	Total*
2011	1,147		383	6,362	1,224	**7,097**
2010	1,271		508	4,331	1,208	**7,318**
2009	3,882	1	185	14,276	8,516	**22,519**
2008	1,326		536	5,178	1,227	**6,870**
2007	1,313		539	4,903	1,238	**6,618**
2006	1,198		539	5,143	1,059	**6,590**
2005	1,160	1	550	5,578	491	**6,778**
2004	1,020		474	4,957	356	**5,987**
2003	1,024		495	4,752	317	**5,794**

Population Affected

	Violation Type					
FY	MCL	MRDL	TT	M/R	Other	Total*
2011	323,658		110,452	2,194,604	338,521	**2,284,361**
2010	411,318		141,011	1,415,409	343,874	**2,311,612**
2009	1,289,606	300	37,459	2,434,722	826,580	**3,413,437**
2008	423,663		181,073	1,630,978	343,836	**2,141,033**
2007	398,021		188,740	1,526,926	355,150	**2,083,785**
2006	405,274		170,672	1,670,822	277,538	**2,136,600**
2005	342,398	110	164,644	1,665,415	122,177	**2,035,743**
2004	286,638		130,242	1,401,311	88,003	**1,711,868**
2003	265,927		140,053	1,432,966	85,026	**1,746,697**

*Totals for the number of systems in violation and for the population affected are lower than the sum in each row because some systems have incurred more than one type of violation.

Source: *U.S. EPA, Drinking Water and Ground Water Statistics, Fiscal Year 2011*

TNCWS Violations Reported by Fiscal Year

This section presents three tables showing reported violations experienced by Transient Non-Community Water Systems (TNCWS) broken out by the number of violations, number of systems in violation, and the population in violation (based on the retail population served). Sources for these data are as follows:

Fiscal Year	SDWIS/Fed Data Source
2011	FY2011 Quarter 3
2010	FY2010 Quarter 3
2009	FY2009 Quarter 3
2008	FY2008 Quarter 3
2007	FY2007 Quarter 3
2006	FY2006 Quarter 3
2005	FY2005 Quarter 4, except for Chemical Monitoring/Reporting violations which are from FY2006 Quarter 1
2004	FY2004 Quarter 4 frozen tables, except for Chemical Monitoring/Reporting violations which are from FY2005 Quarter 1
2003	FY2003 Quarter 4 frozen tables, except for Chemical Monitoring/Reporting violations which are from FY2004 Quarter 1

Number of Violations

	Violation Type					
FY	MCL	MRDL	TT	M/R	Other	Total
2011	5,111	0	365	24,189	21,303	**50,968**
2010	5,335	0	338	23,880	27,894	**57,447**
2009	4,969	1	259	24,397	26,422	**56,048**
2008	5,259	0	384	26,589	24,437	**56,669**
2007	5,575	0	435	28,599	22,078	**56,687**
2006	5,264	0	474	29,848	19,010	**54,596**
2005	4,994	0	502	34,880	4,800	**45,176**
2004	5,003	0	415	34,295	3,028	**42,741**
2003	5,063	0	573	33,666	8,640	**47,942**

Source: *U.S. EPA, Drinking Water and Ground Water Statistics, Fiscal Year 2011*

Number of Systems in Violation

	Violation Type					
FY	MCL	MRDL	TT	M/R	Other	Total*
2011	3,957	0	267	15,790	7,926	**25,071**
2010	4,088	0	220	13,843	8,548	**26,699**
2009	3,882	1	185	14,276	8,516	**22,519**
2008	4,068	0	227	14,938	8,159	**22,714**
2007	4,319	0	237	15,626	7,664	**22,996**
2006	4,066	0	211	15,571	6,417	**21,800**
2005	3,961	0	215	17,542	2,284	**21,236**
2004	3,960	0	195	17,314	1,697	**20,653**
2003	4,055	0	245	17,429	3,685	**21,338**

Population Affected

	Violation Type					
FY	MCL	MRDL	TT	M/R	Other	Total*
2011	555,458	0	31,922	1,518,170	755,442	**2,860,992**
2010	490,848	0	38,667	1,669,101	813,174	**3,011,790**
2009	1,289,606	300	37,459	2,434,722	826,580	**3,413,437**
2008	548,776	0	58,580	1,959,479	859,435	**2,900,038**
2007	538,931	0	63,160	1,999,117	731,880	**2,799,528**
2006	1,296,508	0	50,372	2,166,532	642,080	**3,596,226**
2005	541,171	0	86,648	2,260,178	344,411	**2,812,854**
2004	549,164	0	51,915	2,205,971	234,291	**2,705,723**
2003	540,765	0	40,518	2,159,794	340,950	**2,647,611**

*Totals for the number of systems in violation and for the population affected are lower than the sum in each row because some systems have incurred more than one type of violation.

Source: *U.S. EPA, Drinking Water and Ground Water Statistics, Fiscal Year 2011*

MCL, MRDL and TT Violations Reported

All data in these tables are taken from the FY2011 third quarter "frozen" dataset.

Microbial Rules Violations

Microbial rules apply to all water system types.

Total Coliform Rule (TCR)

The TCR applies to all types of water systems.

	Water System Population Size Category					
	Very Small 25-500	Small 501-3,300	Medium 3,301-10,000	Large 10,001-100,000	Very Large >100,000	Total
Number of Violations	7,132	790	285	217	7	8,431
Systems in Violation	5,399	617	237	186	7	6,435
Population Affected	593,805	807,370	1,418,876	4,276,334	2,740,959	9,837,344

Stage 1 Disinfectant Byproducts (Stage 1 DBP)

The Stage 1 DBP rule applies to CWS and NTNCWS that disinfect and to TNCWS that use Chlorine Dioxide (ClO_2) disinfection.

	Water System Population Size Category					
	Very Small 25-500	Small 501-3,300	Medium 3,301-10,000	Large 10,001-100,000	Very Large >100,000	Total
Number of Violations	1,021	1,095	353	129	1	2,599
Systems in Violation	453	367	139	66	1	1,026
Population Affected	78,524	554,389	805,647	1,606,165	137,201	3,181,926

Source: *U.S. EPA, Drinking Water and Ground Water Statistics, Fiscal Year 2011*

Surface Water Treatment Rule (SWTR)
The SWTR applies to all water system types that use surface water as their source.

	Water System Population Size Category					
	Very Small 25-500	Small 501-3,300	Medium 3,301-10,000	Large 10,001-100,000	Very Large >100,000	Total
Number of Violations	622	127	28	12	5	794
Systems in Violation	291	79	21	10	3	404
Population Affected	49,048	99,671	112,283	356,043	2,048,000	2,665,045

Interim Enhanced and Long Term-1 Surface Water Treatment Rule (IE&LT1 SWTR)
The IE&LT1 SWTR applies to all water system types that use surface water as their source.

	Water System Population Size Category					
	Very Small 25-500	Small 501-3,300	Medium 3,301-10,000	Large 10,001-100,000	Very Large >100,000	Total
Number of Violations	123	89	39	61	18	330
Systems in Violation	52	43	22	37	6	160
Population Affected	9,932	69,609	120,992	981,181	2,673,469	3,855,183

Source: *U.S. EPA, Drinking Water and Ground Water Statistics, Fiscal Year 2011*

Organics Rules Violations

These rules apply to CWS and NTNCWS.

Volatile Organic Compounds (VOC)

	Water System Population Size Category					
	Very Small 25-500	Small 501-3,300	Medium 3,301-10,000	Large 10,001-100,000	Very Large >100,000	Total
Number of Violations	30	15	0	6	0	51
Systems in Violation	14	7	0	5	0	26
Population Affected	2,327	6,877	0	207,216	0	216,420

Synthetic Organic Compounds

	Water System Population Size Category					
	Very Small 25-500	Small 501-3,300	Medium 3,301-10,000	Large 10,001-100,000	Very Large >100,000	Total
Number of Violations	30	13	5	0	0	48
Systems in Violation	15	6	2	0	0	23
Population Affected	2,844	6,489	8,653	0	0	17,986

Source: *U.S. EPA, Drinking Water and Ground Water Statistics, Fiscal Year 2011*

Inorganic Compounds (IOCs)

The IOCs rule applies to CWS and NTNCWS.

Nitrate and Nitrite

	Water System Population Size Category					
	Very Small 25-500	Small 501-3,300	Medium 3,301-10,000	Large 10,001-100,000	Very Large >100,000	Total
Number of Violations	559	145	9	6	1	720
Systems in Violation	246	60	4	3	1	314
Population Affected	37,306	72,777	19,501	56,056	114,840	300,480

Arsenic

	Water System Population Size Category					
	Very Small 25-500	Small 501-3,300	Medium 3,301-10,000	Large 10,001-100,000	Very Large >100,000	Total
Number of Violations	1,486	461	166	66	2	2,181
Systems in Violation	578	144	37	23	1	783
Population Affected	82,961	195,034	229,785	635,554	631,253	1,774,587

Source: *U.S. EPA, Drinking Water and Ground Water Statistics, Fiscal Year 2011*

Other Inorganic Compounds

	Water System Population Size Category					
	Very Small 25-500	Small 501-3,300	Medium 3,301-10,000	Large 10,001-100,000	Very Large >100,000	Total
Number of Violations	287	76	47	9	4	423
Systems in Violation	102	29	6	3	1	141
Population Affected	15,660	35,163	37,974	36,439	100,700	225,936

Radionuclides

The radionuclides rule applies to CWS.

	Water System Population Size Category					
	Very Small 25-500	Small 501-3,300	Medium 3,301-10,000	Large 10,001-100,000	Very Large >100,000	Total
Number of Violations	557	232	69	72	6	936
Systems in Violation	188	78	21	10	2	299
Population Affected	31,635	100,188	116,397	250,155	356,000	854,375

Lead and Copper Rule

The lead and copper rule applies to CWS and NTNCWS.

	Water System Population Size Category					
	Very Small 25-500	Small 501-3,300	Medium 3,301-10,000	Large 10,001-100,000	Very Large >100,000	Total
Number of Violations	669	146	30	15	0	860
Systems in Violation	549	124	20	13	0	706
Population Affected	75,957	149,741	104,225	332,542	0	662,465

Source: *U.S. EPA, Drinking Water and Ground Water Statistics, Fiscal Year 2011*

Monitoring Violations Reported

All data in these tables are taken from the FY2010 fourth quarter "frozen" dataset.

Microbial Rules Violations

Microbial rules apply to all water system types.

Total Coliform Rule (TCR)

The TCR applies to all types of water systems.

	Water System Population Size Category					
	Very Small 25-500	Small 501-3,300	Medium 3,301-10,000	Large 10,001-100,000	Very Large >100,000	Total
Number of Violations	23,437	2,117	231	114	14	25,963
Systems in Violation	14,398	1,418	191	104	11	16,122
Population Affected	1,509,201	1,755,514	1,095,327	2,947,297	3,600,019	10,907,358

Stage 1 Disinfectant Byproducts (Stage 1 DBP)

The Stage 1 DBP rule applies to CWS and NTNCWS that disinfect and to TNCWS that use Chlorine Dioxide (ClO_2) disinfection.

	Water System Population Size Category					
	Very Small 25-500	Small 501-3,300	Medium 3,301-10,000	Large 10,001-100,000	Very Large >100,000	Total
Number of Violations	3,386	1,255	312	196	16	5,165
Systems in Violation	1,990	802	205	115	9	3,121
Population Affected	335,839	1,084,694	1,185,559	3,288,044	2,455,289	8,349,425

Source: U.S. EPA, Drinking Water and Ground Water Statistics, Fiscal Year 2011

Surface Water Treatment Rule (SWTR)

The SWTR applies to all water system types that use surface water as their source.

	Water System Population Size Category					
	Very Small 25-500	Small 501-3,300	Medium 3,301-10,000	Large 10,001-100,000	Very Large >100,000	Total
Number of Violations	787	207	72	21	5	1,092
Systems in Violation	269	113	39	19	2	442
Population Affected	45,619	153,318	212,669	490,328	8,120,000	9,021,934

Interim Enhanced and Long Term-1 Surface Water Treatment Rule (IE&LT1 SWTR)

The IE&LT1 SWTR applies to all water system types that use surface water as their source.

	Water System Population Size Category					
	Very Small 25-500	Small 501-3,300	Medium 3,301-10,000	Large 10,001-100,000	Very Large >100,000	Total
Number of Violations	259	140	53	18	4	474
Systems in Violation	105	67	23	12	3	210
Population Affected	18,371	94,517	128,147	356,567	2,134,220	2,731,822

Source: *U.S. EPA, Drinking Water and Ground Water Statistics, Fiscal Year 2011*

Organics Rules Violations

These rules apply to CWS and NTNCWS.

Volatile Organic Compounds (VOC)

	Water System Population Size Category					
	Very Small 25-500	Small 501-3,300	Medium 3,301-10,000	Large 10,001-100,000	Very Large >100,000	Total
Number of Violations	22,882	4,985	1,325	1,161	42	30,395
Systems in Violation	919	196	49	44	2	1,210
Population Affected	125,437	254,344	274,657	1,140,427	400,812	2,195,677

Synthetic Organic Compounds

	Water System Population Size Category					
	Very Small 25-500	Small 501-3,300	Medium 3,301-10,000	Large 10,001-100,000	Very Large >100,000	Total
Number of Violations	20,953	9,229	2,443	1,125	6	33,756
Systems in Violation	894	383	102	66	4	1,449
Population Affected	129,488	475,697	564,393	1,548,902	1,239,927	3,958,407

Source: *U.S. EPA, Drinking Water and Ground Water Statistics, Fiscal Year 2011*

Inorganic Compounds (IOCs)

The IOCs rule applies to CWS and NTNCWS.

Nitrate and Nitrite

	Water System Population Size Category					
	Very Small 25-500	Small 501-3,300	Medium 3,301-10,000	Large 10,001-100,000	Very Large >100,000	Total
Number of Violations	1,454	344	106	57	12	1,973
Systems in Violation	1,106	251	70	39	5	1,471
Population Affected	160,769	326,799	397,185	1,189,255	1,444,002	3,518,010

Arsenic

	Water System Population Size Category					
	Very Small 25-500	Small 501-3,300	Medium 3,301-10,000	Large 10,001-100,000	Very Large >100,000	Total
Number of Violations	974	224	54	38	3	1,293
Systems in Violation	813	181	40	26	2	1,062
Population Affected	112,388	203,550	214,920	603,317	365,045	1,499,220

Source: *U.S. EPA, Drinking Water and Ground Water Statistics, Fiscal Year 2011*

Other Inorganic Compounds

	Water System Population Size Category					
	Very Small 25-500	Small 501-3,300	Medium 3,301-10,000	Large 10,001-100,000	Very Large >100,000	Total
Number of Violations	7,314	1,460	404	287	27	9,492
Systems in Violation	866	202	51	31	6	1,156
Population Affected	121,956	256,182	261,968	828,247	1,182,793	2,651,146

Radionuclides

The radionuclides rule applies to CWS.

	Water System Population Size Category					
	Very Small 25-500	Small 501-3,300	Medium 3,301-10,000	Large 10,001-100,000	Very Large >100,000	Total
Number of Violations	1,157	302	67	123	3	1,652
Systems in Violation	309	85	18	39	2	453
Population Affected	49,147	110,914	102,161	1,076,580	1,537,460	2,876,262

Lead and Copper Rule

The lead and copper rule applies to CWS and NTNCWS.

	Water System Population Size Category					
	Very Small 25-500	Small 501-3,300	Medium 3,301-10,000	Large 10,001-100,000	Very Large >100,000	Total
Number of Violations	7,066	1,617	313	220	20	9,236
Systems in Violation	5,008	1,292	270	181	15	6,766
Population Affected	759,332	1,606,199	1,520,155	4,941,002	3,344,965	12,171,653

Source: *U.S. EPA, Drinking Water and Ground Water Statistics, Fiscal Year 2011*

Average Fluoridation Levels by County

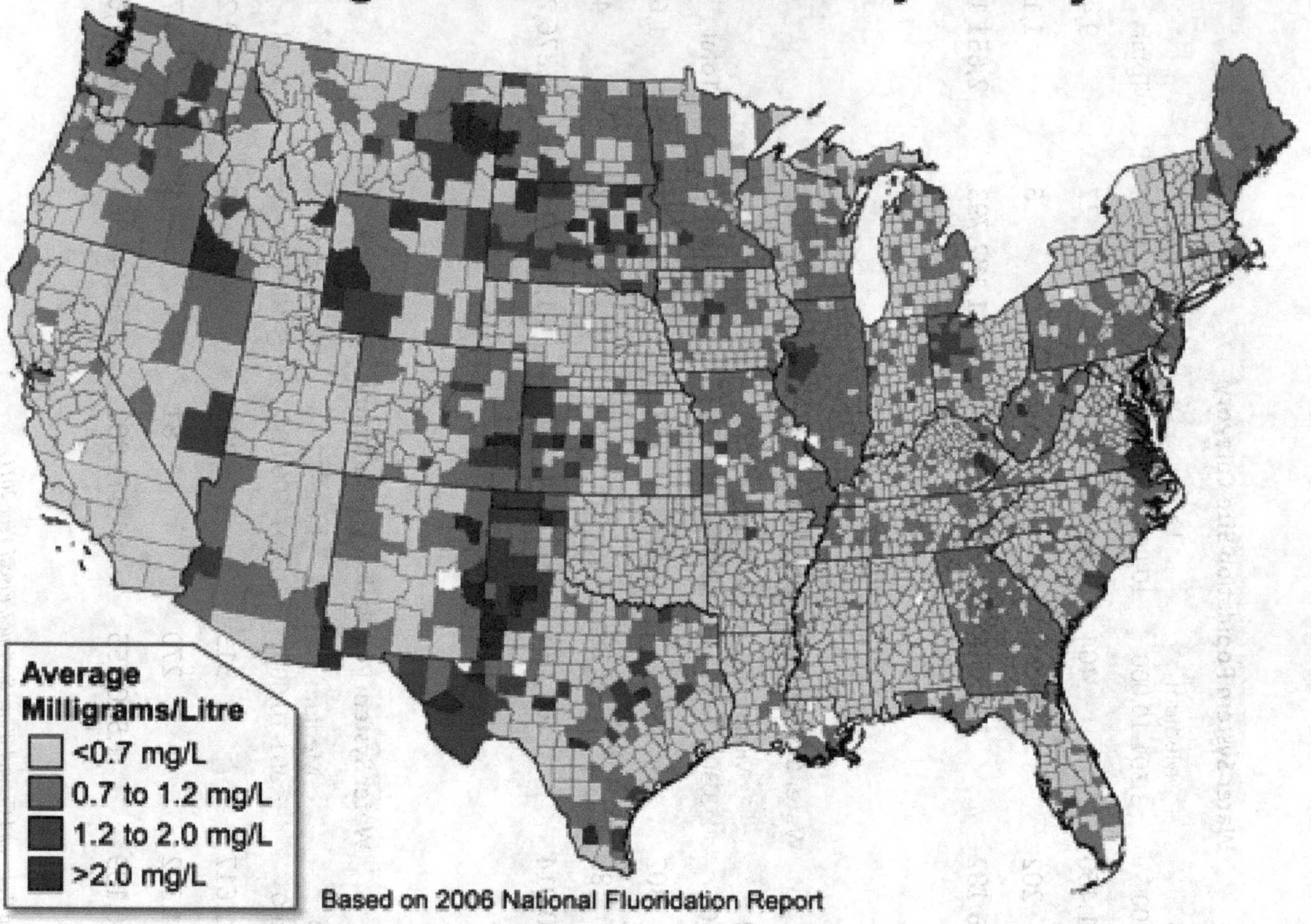

Note: Page last modified: September 17, 2008

Source: Division of Oral Health, National Center for Chronic Disease Prevention and Health Promotion

Delisted Species

Species name	Date species first listed	Date species delisted	Reason delisted
Agave, Arizona (Agave arizonica)	5/18/1984	6/19/2006	Original Data in Error - Not a listable entity
Alligator, American (Alligator mississippiensis)	7/27/1979	6/4/1987	Recovered
Barberry, Truckee (Berberis (=Mahonia) sonnei)	12/6/1979	10/1/2003	Original Data in Error - Taxonomic revision
Bidens, cuneate (Bidens cuneata)	2/17/1984	2/6/1996	Original Data in Error - Taxonomic revision
Broadbill, Guam (Myiagra freycineti)	8/27/1984	2/23/2004	Extinct
Butterfly, Bahama swallowtail (Heraclides andraemon bonhotei)	4/28/1976	8/31/1984	Original Data in Error - Act amendment
Cactus, Lloyd's hedgehog (Echinocereus lloydii)	11/28/1979	6/24/1999	Original Data in Error - Taxonomic revision
Cactus, spineless hedgehog (Echinocereus triglochidiatus var. inermis)	12/7/1979	9/22/1993	Original Data in Error - Not a listable entity
Cinquefoil, Robbins' (Potentilla robbinsiana)	9/17/1980	8/27/2002	Recovered
Cisco, longjaw (Coregonus alpenae)	3/11/1967	9/2/1983	Extinct
Coneflower, Tennessee purple (Echinacea tennesseensis)	7/5/1979	9/2/2011	Recovered
Crocodile, Morelet's (Crocodylus moreletii)	6/2/1970	5/23/2012	Recovered
Daisy, Maguire (Erigeron maguirei)	9/5/1985	2/18/2011	Recovered
Deer, Columbian white-tailed Douglas County DPS (Odocoileus virginianus leucurus)	7/24/2003	7/24/2003	Recovered
Dove, Palau ground (Gallicolumba canifrons)	6/2/1970	9/12/1985	Recovered
Duck, Mexican U.S.A. only (Anas diazi)	3/11/1967	7/25/1978	Original Data in Error - Taxonomic revision
Eagle, bald lower 48 States (Haliaeetus leucocephalus)	3/11/1967	8/8/2007	Recovered
Falcon, American peregrine (Falco peregrinus anatum)	6/2/1970	8/25/1999	Recovered
Falcon, Arctic peregrine (Falco peregrinus tundrius)	6/2/1970	10/5/1994	Recovered
Flycatcher, Palau fantail (Rhipidura lepida)	6/2/1970	9/12/1985	Recovered
Gambusia, Amistad (Gambusia amistadensis)	4/30/1980	12/4/1987	Extinct
Globeberry, Tumamoc (Tumamoca macdougalii)	4/29/1986	6/18/1993	Original Data in Error - New information discovered
Goose, Aleutian Canada (Branta canadensis leucopareia)	3/11/1967	3/20/2001	Recovered
Hedgehog cactus, purple-spined (Echinocereus engelmannii var. purpureus)	10/11/1979	11/27/1989	Original Data in Error - Taxonomic revision
Kangaroo, eastern gray (Macropus giganteus)	12/30/1974	3/9/1995	Recovered
Kangaroo, red (Macropus rufus)	12/30/1974	3/9/1995	Recovered
Kangaroo, western gray (Macropus fuliginosus)	12/30/1974	3/9/1995	Recovered
Mallard, Mariana (Anas oustaleti)	12/8/1977	2/23/2004	Extinct
Milk-vetch, Rydberg (Astragalus perianus)	5/27/1978	9/14/1989	Original Data in Error - New information discovered
Monarch, Tinian (old world flycatcher) (Monarcha takatsukasae)	6/2/1970	9/21/2004	Recovered
Owl, Palau (Pyrroglaux podargina)	6/2/1970	9/12/1985	Recovered
Pearlymussel, Sampson's (Epioblasma sampsoni)	6/14/1976	1/9/1984	Extinct
Pelican, brown except U.S. Atlantic coast, FL, AL (Pelecanus occidentalis)	6/2/1970	12/17/2009	Recovered
Pelican, brown U.S. Atlantic coast, FL, AL (Pelecanus occidentalis)	6/2/1970	2/4/1985	Recovered
Pennyroyal, Mckittrick (Hedeoma apiculatum)	7/13/1982	9/22/1993	Original Data in Error - New information discovered
Pike, blue (Stizostedion vitreum glaucum)	3/11/1967	9/2/1983	Extinct
Pupfish, Tecopa (Cyprinodon nevadensis calidae)	10/13/1970	1/15/1982	Extinct
Pygmy-owl, cactus ferruginous AZ pop. (Glaucidium brasilianum cactorum)	3/10/1997	4/14/2006	Original Data in Error - Not a listable entity
Seal, Caribbean monk (Monachus tropicalis)	4/10/1979	10/28/2008	Extinct & Unlist
Shrew, Dismal Swamp southeastern (Sorex longirostris fisheri)	9/26/1986	2/28/2000	Original Data in Error - New information discovered
Snail, Utah valvata (Valvata utahensis)	12/14/1992	9/24/2010	Original Data in Error - New information discovered
Snake, Concho water (Nerodia paucimaculata)	9/3/1986	11/28/2011	Recovered
Snake, Lake Erie water, subspecies range clarified (Nerodia sipedon insularum)	8/30/1999	9/15/2011	Recovered
Sparrow, Santa Barbara song (Melospiza melodia graminea)	6/4/1973	10/12/1983	Extinct
Sparrow, dusky seaside (Ammodramus maritimus nigrescens)	3/11/1967	12/12/1990	Extinct
Springsnail, Idaho (Pyrgulopsis idahoensis)	12/14/1992	9/5/2007	Original Data in Error - Taxonomic revision
Squirrel, Virginia northern flying, Entire (Glaucomys sabrinus fuscus)	7/31/1985	3/4/2013	Recovered
Sunflower, Eggert's (Helianthus eggertii)	5/22/1997	8/18/2005	Recovered

Species name	Date species first listed	Date species delisted	Reason delisted
Treefrog, pine barrens FL pop.(Hyla andersonii)	12/18/1977	11/22/1983	Original Data in Error - New information discovered
Trout, coastal cutthroat Umpqua R.(Oncorhynchus clarki clarki)	9/13/1996	4/26/2000	Original Data in Error - Taxonomic revision
Turtle, Indian flap-shelled (Lissemys punctata punctata)	6/14/1976	2/29/1984	Original Data in Error - Erroneous data
Whale, gray except where listed (Eschrichtius robustus)	6/16/1994	6/16/1994	Recovered
Wolf, gray MN (Canis lupus)	4/10/1978	1/27/12	Recovered
Wolf, gray Western Great Lakes DPS (Canis lupus)	4/2/2009	12/28/2011	Recovered
Wolf, gray Northern Rocky Mountain DPS (delisted, excepy WY) (Canis lupus)	5/5/2011	5/5/2011	Recovered
Wolf, gray WY, EXPN population (Canis lupus)	5/5/2011	9/30/2012	Recovered
Woolly-star, Hoover's (Eriastrum hooveri)	7/19/1990	10/7/2003	Recovered

Notes: *Data as of August 28, 2013*
Source: *U.S. Fish & Wildlife Service, Threatened and Endangered Species System (TESS)*

Summary of Listed Species, Listed Populations[1] and Recovery Plans[2]

Group	United States[3]		Foreign		Total listings (U.S. and foreign)	U.S. listings with active recovery plans[2]
	Endangered	Threatened	Endangered	Threatened		
Animals						
Amphibians	17	11	8	1	33	17
Arachnids	12	0	0	0	12	12
Birds	78	15	208	16	317	86
Clams	72	12	2	0	86	71
Corals	0	2	0	0	2	0
Crustaceans	20	3	0	0	23	18
Fishes	84	70	11	1	166	102
Insects	57	10	4	0	71	40
Mammals	69	16	256	20	361	62
Reptiles	14	22	70	20	126	35
Snails	33	13	1	0	47	30
Animal Subtotal	456	174	560	58	1,248	473
Plants						
Conifers and Cycads	2	1	0	2	5	3
Ferns and Allies	28	2	0	0	30	26
Flowering Plants	669	150	1	0	820	641
Lichens	2	0	0	0	2	2
Plant Subtotal	701	153	1	2	857	672
Grand Total	1,157	327	561	60	2,105	1,145

Notes: *Data as of August 28, 2013; (1) A listing has an E or a T in the "status" column of the tables in 50 CFR 17.11(h) or 50 CFR 17.12(h) (the "List of Endangered and Threatened Wildlife and Plants"). 18 animal species (11 in the U.S.3 and 7 Foreign) are counted more than once in the above table, primarily because these animals have distinct population segments (each with its own individual listing status); (2) There are a total of 594 distinct active (Draft and Final) recovery plans. Some recovery plans cover more than one species, and a few species have separate plans covering different parts of their ranges. This count includes only plans generated by the USFWS (or jointly by the USFWS and NMFS), and only listed species that occur in the United States; (3) United States listings include those populations in which the United States shares jurisdiction with another nation.*

Source: *U.S. Fish & Wildlife Service, Threatened and Endangered Species System (TESS)*

Figure F1. Primary Energy Consumption and Delivered Total Energy, 2010

(Quadrillion Btu)

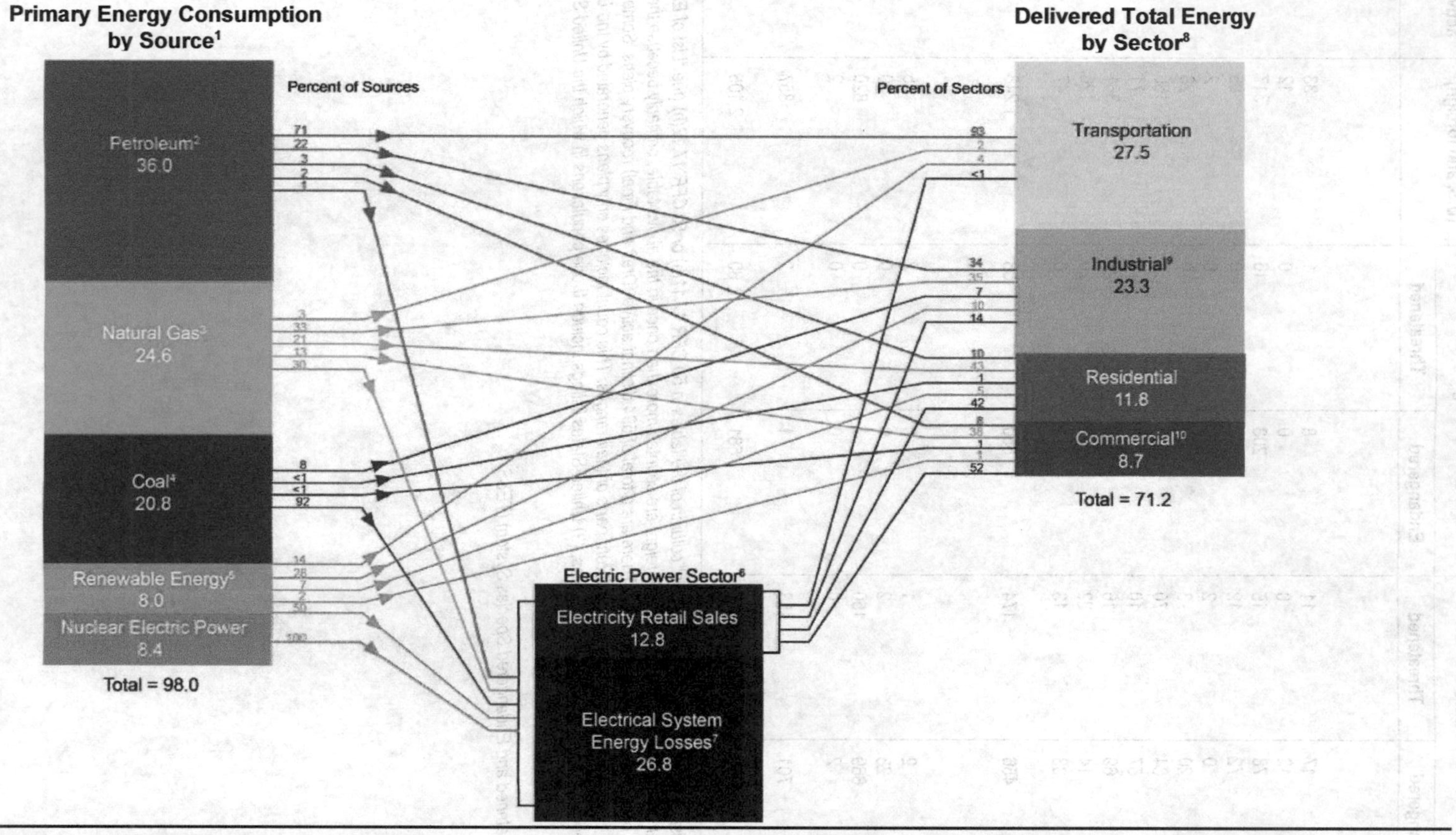

[1] Includes electricity net imports, not shown separately.

[2] Does not include biofuels that have been blended with petroleum–biofuels are included in "Renewable Energy."

[3] Excludes supplemental gaseous fuels.

[4] Includes less than 0.1 quadrillion Btu of coal coke net exports.

[5] Conventional hydroelectric power, geothermal, solar/PV, wind, and biomass.

[6] Electricity-only and combined-heat-and-power (CHP) plants whose primary business is to sell electricity, or electricity and heat, to the public.

[7] Calculated as the primary energy consumed by the electric power sector minus the energy content of electricity retail sales. See Note, "Electrical System Energy Losses," at end of Section 2.

[8] Includes transformation losses other than electrical system energy losses. For example, see notes 9 and 10 on this page.

[9] Includes industrial combined-heat-and-power (CHP) and industrial electricity-only plants.

[10] Includes commercial combined-heat-and-power (CHP) and commercial electricity-only plants.

Note: Sum of components may not equal total due to independent rounding.

Sources: U.S. Energy Information Administration, *Annual Energy Review 2010*, Tables 1.3, 2.1b-f, 10.3, and 10.4.

Source: *U.S. Energy Information Administration, Annual Energy Review 2011*

Figure 1.0 Energy Flow, 2011
(Quadrillion Btu)

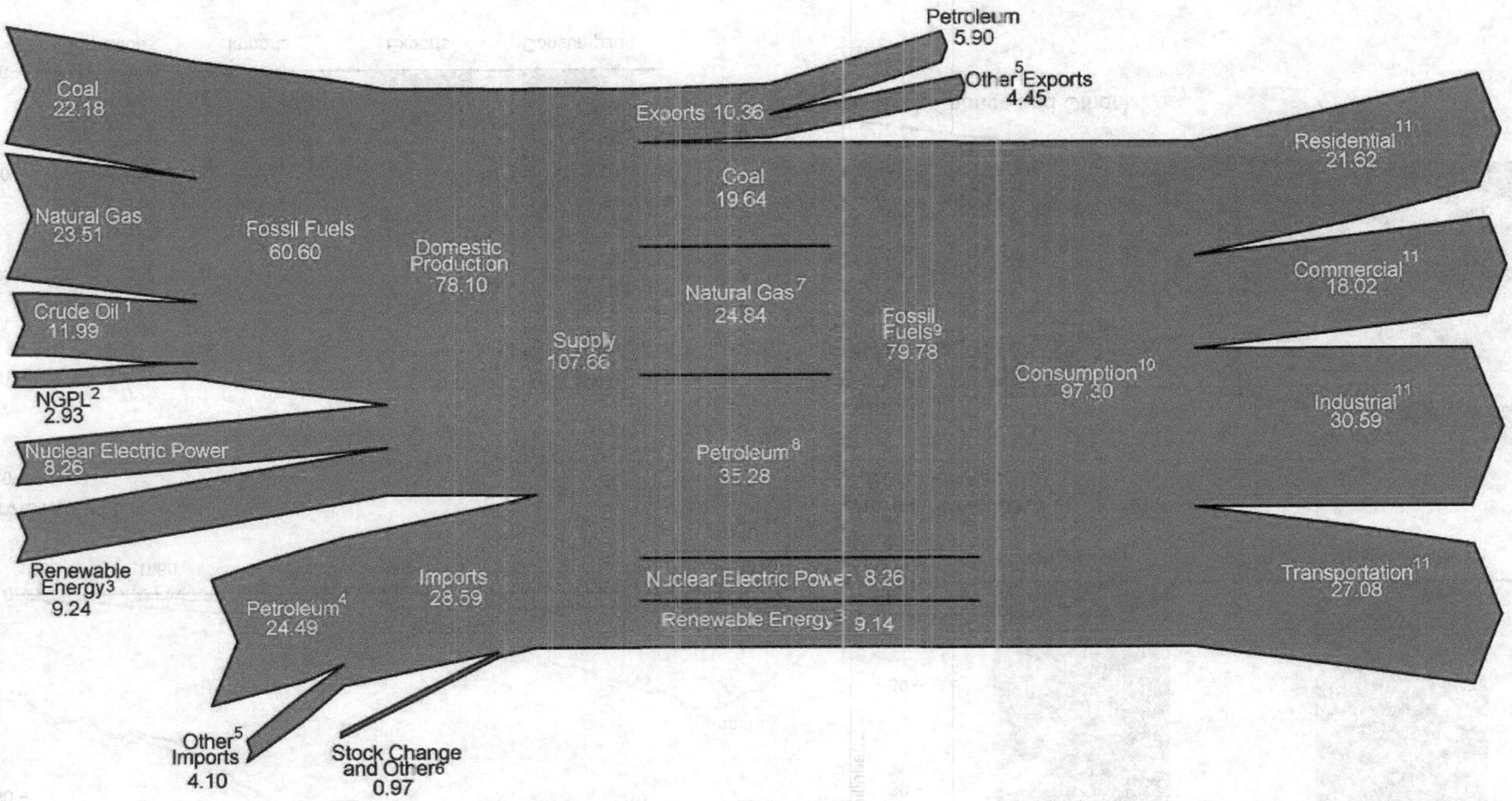

[1] Includes lease condensate.
[2] Natural gas plant liquids.
[3] Conventional hydroelectric power, biomass, geothermal, solar/photovoltaic, and wind.
[4] Crude oil and petroleum products. Includes imports into the Strategic Petroleum Reserve.
[5] Natural gas, coal, coal coke, biofuels, and electricity.
[6] Adjustments, losses, and unaccounted for.
[7] Natural gas only; excludes supplemental gaseous fuels.
[8] Petroleum products, including natural gas plant liquids, and crude oil burned as fuel.
[9] Includes 0.01 quadrillion Btu of coal coke net imports.
[10] Includes 0.13 quadrillion Btu of electricity net imports.
[11] Total energy consumption, which is the sum of primary energy consumption, electricity retail sales, and electrical system energy losses. Losses are allocated to the end-use sectors in proportion to each sector's share of total electricity retail sales. See Note, "Electrical Systems Energy Losses," at end of Section 2.

Notes: • Data are preliminary. • Values are derived from source data prior to rounding for publication. • Totals may not equal sum of components due to independent rounding.

Sources: Tables 1.1, 1.2, 1.3, 1.4, and 2.1a.

Source: *U.S. Energy Information Administration, Annual Energy Review 2011*

Figure 1.1 Primary Energy Overview

Overview, 1949-2011

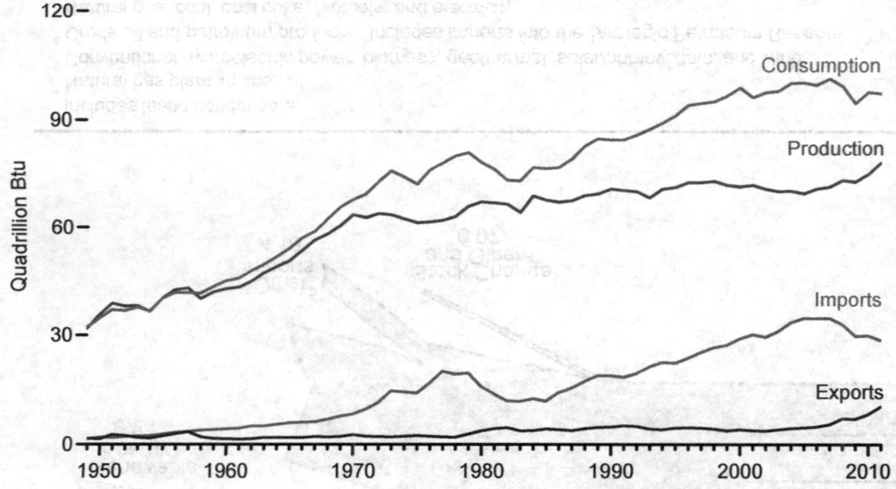

Production and Consumption, 2011

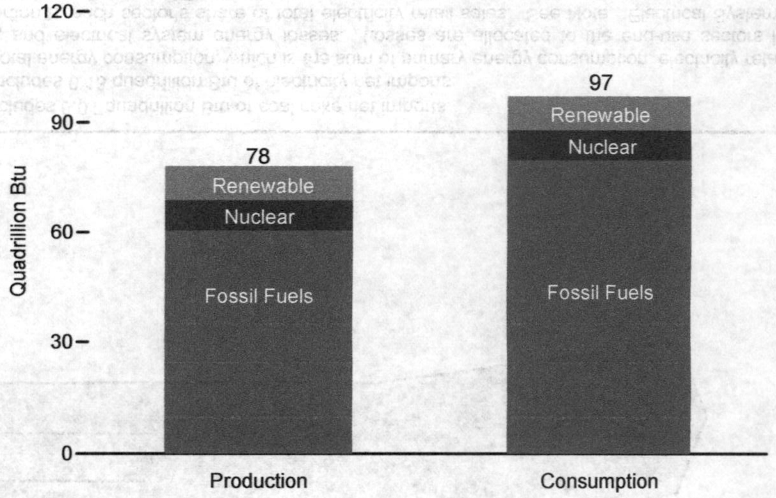

Overview, 2011

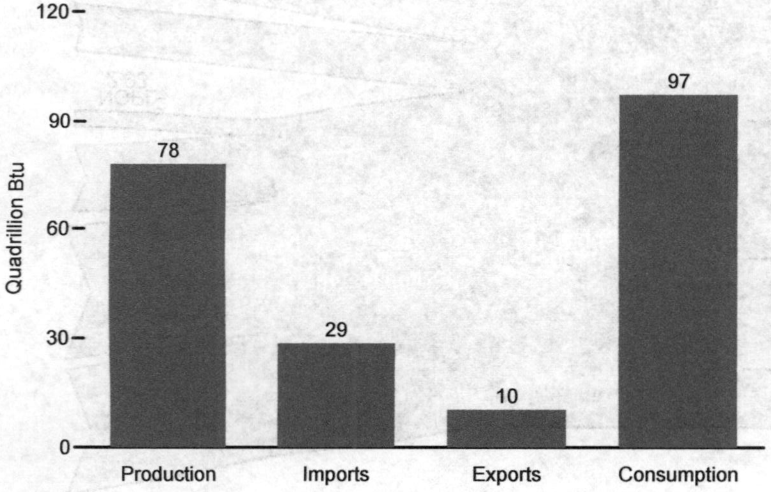

Energy Flow, 2011
(Quadrillion Btu)

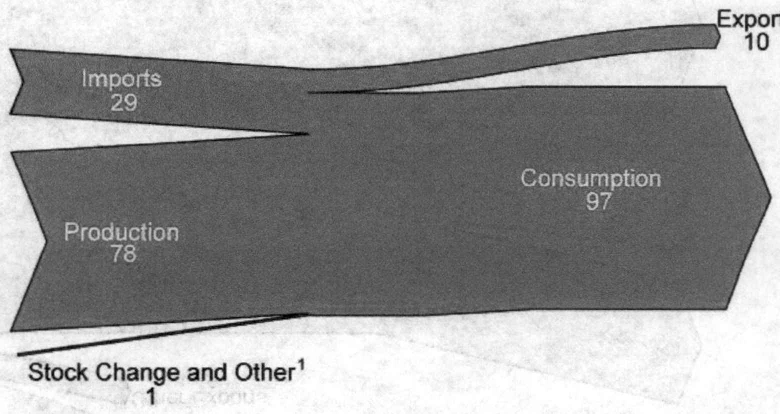

[1] Adjustments, losses, and unaccounted for.

Source: Table 1.1.

Source: *U.S. Energy Information Administration, Annual Energy Review 2011*

Table 1.1 Primary Energy Overview, Selected Years, 1949-2011

(Quadrillion Btu)

Year	Production				Trade					Stock Change and Other [8]	Consumption			
					Imports		Exports		Net Imports [1]					
	Fossil Fuels [2]	Nuclear Electric Power [3]	Renewable Energy [4]	Total	Petroleum [5]	Total [6]	Coal	Total [7]	Total		Fossil Fuels [9]	Nuclear Electric Power [3]	Renewable Energy [4]	Total [10]
1949	28.748	0.000	2.974	31.722	1.427	1.448	0.877	1.592	-0.144	0.403	29.002	0.000	2.974	31.982
1950	32.563	.000	2.978	35.540	1.886	1.913	.786	1.465	.448	-1.372	31.632	.000	2.978	34.616
1955	37.364	.000	2.784	40.148	2.752	2.790	1.465	2.286	.504	-.444	37.410	.000	2.784	40.208
1960	39.869	.006	2.928	42.803	3.999	4.188	1.023	1.477	2.710	-.427	42.137	.006	2.928	45.086
1965	47.235	.043	3.396	50.674	5.402	5.892	1.376	1.829	4.063	-.722	50.577	.043	3.396	54.015
1970	59.186	.239	4.070	63.495	7.470	8.342	1.936	2.632	5.709	-1.367	63.522	.239	4.070	67.838
1975	54.733	1.900	4.687	61.320	12.948	14.032	1.761	2.323	11.709	-1.065	65.357	1.900	4.687	71.965
1976	54.723	2.111	4.727	61.561	15.672	16.760	1.597	2.172	14.588	-.175	69.107	2.111	4.727	75.975
1977	55.101	2.702	4.209	62.012	18.756	19.948	1.442	2.052	17.896	-1.946	70.991	2.702	4.209	77.961
1978	55.074	3.024	5.005	63.104	17.824	19.106	1.078	1.920	17.186	-.339	71.854	3.024	5.005	79.950
1979	58.006	2.776	5.123	65.904	17.933	19.460	1.753	2.855	16.605	-1.650	72.891	2.776	5.123	80.859
1980	59.008	2.739	5.428	67.175	14.658	15.796	2.421	3.695	12.101	-1.210	69.828	2.739	5.428	78.067
1981	58.529	3.008	5.414	66.951	12.639	13.719	2.944	4.307	9.412	-.257	67.571	3.008	5.414	76.106
1982	57.458	3.131	5.980	66.569	10.777	11.861	2.787	4.608	7.253	-.723	63.888	3.131	5.980	73.099
1983	54.416	3.203	6.496	64.114	10.647	11.752	2.045	3.693	8.059	.798	63.152	3.203	6.496	72.971
1984	58.849	3.553	6.438	68.840	11.433	12.471	2.151	3.786	8.685	-.892	66.506	3.553	6.438	76.632
1985	57.539	4.076	6.084	67.698	10.609	11.781	2.438	4.196	7.584	1.110	66.093	4.076	6.084	76.392
1986	56.575	4.380	6.111	67.066	13.201	14.151	2.248	4.021	10.130	-.549	66.033	4.380	6.111	76.647
1987	57.167	4.754	5.622	67.542	14.162	15.398	2.093	3.812	11.586	-.074	68.521	4.754	5.622	79.054
1988	57.875	5.587	5.457	68.919	15.747	17.296	2.499	4.366	12.929	.861	71.557	5.587	5.457	82.709
1989	57.483	5.602	6.235	69.320	17.162	18.766	2.637	4.661	14.105	1.361	72.911	5.602	6.235	84.786
1990	58.560	6.104	6.041	70.705	17.117	18.817	2.772	4.752	14.065	-.284	72.332	6.104	6.041	84.485
1991	57.872	6.422	6.069	70.362	16.348	18.335	2.854	5.141	13.194	.882	71.880	6.422	6.069	84.438
1992	57.655	6.479	5.821	[R]69.956	16.968	19.372	2.682	4.937	14.435	1.392	73.396	6.479	5.821	85.783
1993	55.822	6.410	6.083	68.315	18.510	21.273	1.962	4.258	17.014	2.094	74.836	6.410	6.083	87.424
1994	58.044	6.694	5.988	70.726	19.243	22.390	1.879	4.061	18.329	.037	76.256	6.694	5.988	89.091
1995	57.540	7.075	6.558	71.174	18.881	22.260	2.318	4.511	17.750	2.105	77.259	7.075	6.560	91.029
1996	58.387	7.087	7.012	72.486	20.284	23.702	2.368	4.633	19.069	2.468	79.785	7.087	7.014	94.022
1997	58.857	6.597	7.018	72.472	21.740	25.215	2.193	4.514	20.701	1.429	80.873	6.597	7.016	94.602
1998	59.314	7.068	6.494	72.876	22.908	26.581	2.092	4.299	22.281	-.140	81.369	7.068	6.493	95.018
1999	57.614	7.610	6.517	71.742	23.133	27.252	1.525	3.715	23.537	1.373	82.427	7.610	6.516	96.652
2000	57.366	7.862	6.104	71.332	24.531	28.973	1.528	4.006	24.967	[R]2.515	84.731	7.862	6.106	[R]98.814
2001	58.541	8.029	5.164	71.735	25.398	30.157	1.265	3.771	26.386	-1.953	82.902	8.029	5.163	96.168
2002	[R]56.837	8.145	5.734	[R]70.716	24.674	29.408	1.032	3.669	25.739	[R]1.190	[R]83.699	8.145	5.729	[R]97.645
2003	56.099	7.959	5.982	70.040	26.219	31.061	1.117	4.054	27.007	.931	84.014	7.959	5.983	97.978
2004	55.895	8.222	6.070	70.188	28.197	33.544	1.253	4.434	29.110	[R].864	[R]85.819	8.222	6.082	[R]100.162
2005	55.038	8.161	6.229	[R]69.428	29.248	34.709	1.273	4.560	30.149	[R].705	[R]85.794	8.161	6.242	[R]100.282
2006	55.968	8.215	[R]6.599	[R]70.782	29.169	34.679	1.264	4.872	29.806	[R]-.959	[R]84.702	8.215	[R]6.649	[R]99.629
2007	[R]56.409	8.455	[R]6.509	[R]71.373	28.781	34.703	1.507	5.482	29.221	[R].702	[R]86.211	8.455	[R]6.523	[R]101.296
2008	57.482	8.427	[R]7.202	[R]73.111	27.685	32.992	2.071	7.060	25.932	[R].231	[R]83.549	8.427	[R]7.186	[R]99.275
2009	[R]56.685	8.356	[R]7.616	[R]72.657	25.082	29.706	1.515	6.965	22.741	[R]-.839	[R]78.488	8.356	[R]7.600	[R]94.559
2010	[R]58.235	[R]8.434	[R]8.136	[R]74.806	[R]25.371	[R]29.877	2.101	[R]8.234	[R]21.643	[R]1.273	[R]81.109	[R]8.434	[R]8.090	[R]97.722
2011[P]	60.601	8.259	9.236	78.096	24.491	28.587	2.751	10.356	18.232	.974	79.779	8.259	9.135	97.301

[1] Net imports equal imports minus exports. A minus sign indicates exports are greater than imports.

[2] Coal, natural gas (dry), crude oil, and natural gas plant liquids.

[3] Nuclear electricity net generation (converted to Btu using the nuclear heat rate—see Table A3).

[4] See Tables 10.1–10.2c for notes on series components and estimation; and see Note, "Renewable Energy Production and Consumption," at end of Section 10.

[5] Crude oil and petroleum products. Includes imports into the Strategic Petroleum Reserve.

[6] Also includes natural gas, coal, coal coke, fuel ethanol, biodiesel, and electricity.

[7] Also includes natural gas, petroleum, coal coke, biodiesel, and electricity.

[8] Calculated as consumption and exports minus production and imports. Includes petroleum stock change and adjustments; natural gas net storage withdrawals and balancing item; coal stock change, losses, and unaccounted for; fuel ethanol stock change; and biodiesel stock change and balancing item.

[9] Coal, coal coke net imports, natural gas, and petroleum. For petroleum, product supplied is used as an approximation of petroleum consumption. See Note 1, "Petroleum Products Supplied and Petroleum Consumption," at end of Section 5.

[10] Also includes electricity net imports.

R=Revised. P=Preliminary.

Notes: • See "Primary Energy," "Primary Energy Production," and "Primary Energy Consumption" in Glossary. • Totals may not equal sum of components due to independent rounding.

Web Pages: • See http://www.eia.gov/totalenergy/data/monthly/#summary for updated monthly and annual data. • See http://www.eia.gov/totalenergy/data/annual/#summary for all annual data beginning in 1949.

Sources: Tables 1.2, 1.3, and 1.4.

Source: *U.S. Energy Information Administration, Annual Energy Review 2011*

Figure 1.2 Primary Energy Production by Source

By Source Category, 1949-2011

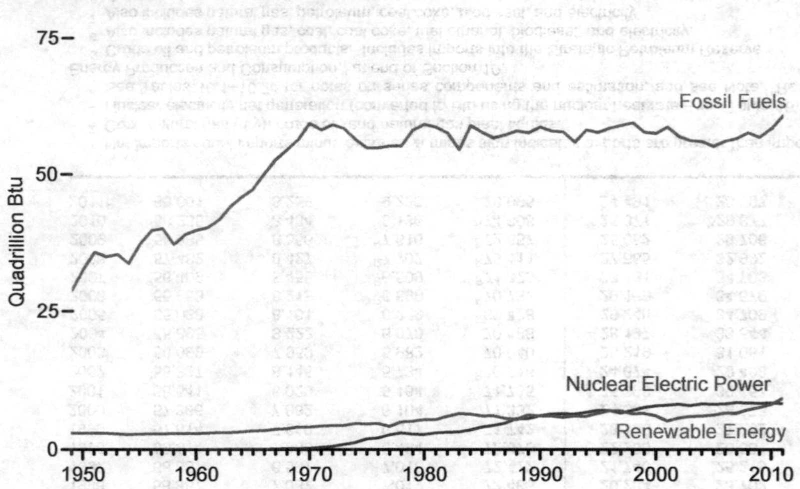

By Source, 2011

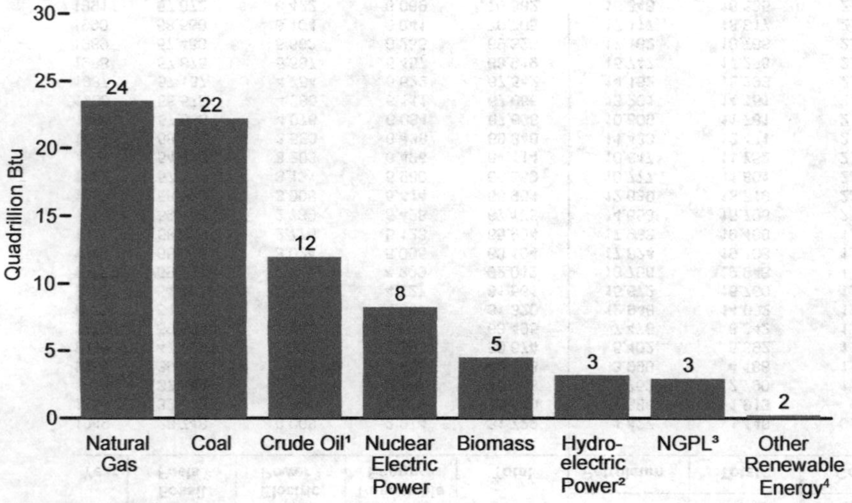

By Source, 1949-2011

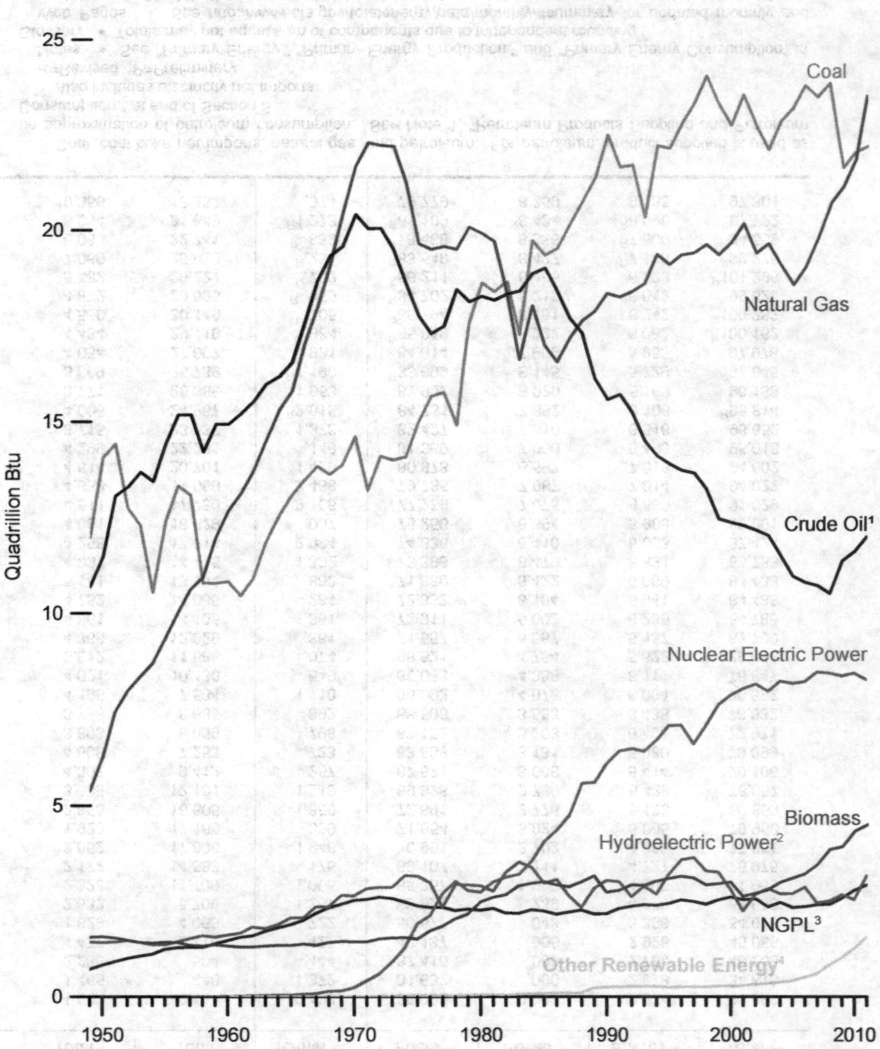

[1] Includes lease condensate.
[2] Conventional hydroelectric power.
[3] Natural gas plant liquids.
[4] Geothermal, solar/photovoltaic, and wind.
Source: Table 1.2.

Source: *U.S. Energy Information Administration, Annual Energy Review 2011*

Table 1.2 Primary Energy Production by Source, Selected Years, 1949-2011

(Quadrillion Btu)

Year	Fossil Fuels					Nuclear Electric Power [5]	Renewable Energy [1]						Total
	Coal [2]	Natural Gas (Dry)	Crude Oil [3]	NGPL [4]	Total		Hydro-electric Power [6]	Geothermal [7]	Solar/PV [8]	Wind [9]	Biomass [10]	Total	
1949	11.974	5.377	10.683	0.714	28.748	0.000	1.425	NA	NA	NA	1.549	2.974	31.722
1950	14.060	6.233	11.447	.823	32.563	.000	1.415	NA	NA	NA	1.562	2.978	35.540
1955	12.370	9.345	14.410	1.240	37.364	.000	1.360	NA	NA	NA	1.424	2.784	40.148
1960	10.817	12.656	14.935	1.461	39.869	.006	1.608	(s)	NA	NA	1.320	2.928	42.803
1965	13.055	15.775	16.521	1.883	47.235	.043	2.059	.002	NA	NA	1.335	3.396	50.674
1970	14.607	21.666	20.401	2.512	59.186	.239	2.634	.006	NA	NA	1.431	4.070	63.495
1975	14.989	19.640	17.729	2.374	54.733	1.900	3.155	.034	NA	NA	1.499	4.687	61.320
1976	15.654	19.480	17.262	2.327	54.723	2.111	2.976	.038	NA	NA	1.713	4.727	61.561
1977	15.755	19.565	17.454	2.327	55.101	2.702	2.333	.037	NA	NA	1.838	4.209	62.012
1978	14.910	19.485	18.434	2.245	55.074	3.024	2.937	.031	NA	NA	2.038	5.005	63.104
1979	17.540	20.076	18.104	2.286	58.006	2.776	2.931	.040	NA	NA	2.152	5.123	65.904
1980	18.598	19.908	18.249	2.254	59.008	2.739	2.900	.053	NA	NA	2.476	5.428	67.175
1981	18.377	19.699	18.146	2.307	58.529	3.008	2.758	.059	NA	NA	2.596	5.414	66.951
1982	18.639	18.319	18.309	2.191	57.458	3.131	3.266	.051	NA	NA	2.663	5.980	66.569
1983	17.247	16.593	18.392	2.184	54.416	3.203	3.527	.064	NA	(s)	2.904	6.496	64.114
1984	19.719	18.008	18.848	2.274	58.849	3.553	3.386	.081	(s)	(s)	2.971	6.438	68.840
1985	19.325	16.980	18.992	2.241	57.539	4.076	2.970	.097	(s)	(s)	3.016	6.084	67.698
1986	19.509	16.541	18.376	2.149	56.575	4.380	3.071	.108	(s)	(s)	2.932	6.111	67.066
1987	20.141	17.136	17.675	2.215	57.167	4.754	2.635	.112	(s)	(s)	2.875	5.622	67.542
1988	20.738	17.599	17.279	2.260	57.875	5.587	2.334	.106	(s)	(s)	3.016	5.457	68.919
1989	[2]21.360	17.847	16.117	2.158	57.483	5.602	2.837	.162	.055	.022	3.159	6.235	69.320
1990	22.488	18.326	15.571	2.175	58.560	6.104	3.046	.171	.059	.029	2.735	6.041	70.705
1991	21.636	18.229	15.701	2.306	57.872	6.422	3.016	.178	.062	.031	2.782	6.069	70.362
1992	21.694	18.375	15.223	2.363	57.655	6.479	2.617	.179	.064	.030	2.932	5.821	R69.956
1993	20.336	18.584	14.494	2.408	55.822	6.410	2.892	.186	.066	.031	2.908	6.083	68.315
1994	22.202	19.348	14.103	2.391	58.044	6.694	2.683	.173	.068	.036	3.028	5.988	70.726
1995	22.130	19.082	13.887	2.442	57.540	7.075	3.205	.152	.069	.033	3.099	6.558	71.174
1996	22.790	19.344	13.723	2.530	58.387	7.087	3.590	.163	.070	.033	3.155	7.012	72.486
1997	23.310	19.394	13.658	2.495	58.857	6.597	3.640	.167	.070	.034	3.108	7.018	72.472
1998	24.045	19.613	13.235	2.420	59.314	7.068	3.297	.168	.069	.031	2.929	6.494	72.876
1999	23.295	19.341	12.451	2.528	57.614	7.610	3.268	.171	.068	.046	2.965	6.517	71.742
2000	22.735	19.662	12.358	2.611	57.366	7.862	2.811	.164	R.066	.057	3.006	6.104	71.332
2001	[2]23.547	20.166	12.282	2.547	58.541	8.029	2.242	.164	.064	.070	2.624	5.164	71.735
2002	22.732	R19.382	12.163	2.559	R56.837	8.145	2.689	.171	.063	.105	2.705	5.734	R70.716
2003	22.094	19.633	12.026	2.346	56.099	7.959	2.825	.175	.062	.115	2.805	5.982	70.040
2004	22.852	19.074	11.503	2.466	55.895	8.222	2.690	.178	.063	.142	2.998	6.070	70.188
2005	23.185	18.556	10.963	2.334	55.038	8.161	2.703	.181	.063	.178	3.104	6.229	R69.428
2006	23.790	19.022	10.801	2.356	55.968	8.215	2.869	.181	.068	.264	R3.216	R6.599	R70.782
2007	23.493	R19.786	10.721	2.409	R56.409	8.455	2.446	.186	.076	.341	R3.461	R6.509	R71.373
2008	23.851	20.703	10.509	2.419	57.482	8.427	2.511	.192	.089	.546	R3.864	R7.202	R73.111
2009	R21.624	R21.139	11.348	2.574	R56.685	8.356	2.669	.200	.098	.721	R3.928	R7.616	R72.657
2010	R22.038	R21.823	R11.593	R2.781	R58.235	R8.434	R2.539	R.208	R.126	R.923	R4.341	R8.136	R74.806
2011P	22.181	23.506	11.986	2.928	60.601	8.259	3.171	.226	.158	1.168	4.511	9.236	78.096

[1] Most data are estimates. See Tables 10.1–10.2c for notes on series components and estimation; and see Note, "Renewable Energy Production and Consumption," at end of Section 10.
[2] Beginning in 1989, includes waste coal supplied. Beginning in 2001, also includes a small amount of refuse recovery. See Table 7.1.
[3] Includes lease condensate.
[4] Natural gas plant liquids.
[5] Nuclear electricity net generation (converted to Btu using the nuclear heat rate—see Table A6).
[6] Conventional hydroelectricity net generation (converted to Btu using the fossil-fuels heat rate—see Table A6).
[7] Geothermal electricity net generation (converted to Btu using the fossil-fuels heat rate—see Table A6), and geothermal heat pump and direct use energy.
[8] Solar thermal and photovoltaic (PV) electricity net generation (converted to Btu using the fossil-fuels heat rate—see Table A6), and solar thermal direct use energy.
[9] Wind electricity net generation (converted to Btu using the fossil-fuels heat rate—see Table A6).
[10] Wood and wood-derived fuels, biomass waste, and total biomass inputs to the production of fuel ethanol and biodiesel.

R=Revised. P=Preliminary. NA=Not available. (s)=Less than 0.0005 quadrillion Btu.

Notes: • See "Primary Energy Production" in Glossary. • Totals may not equal sum of components due to independent rounding.

Web Pages: • See http://www.eia.gov/totalenergy/data/monthly/#summary for updated monthly and annual data. • See http://www.eia.gov/totalenergy/data/annual/#summary for all annual data beginning in 1949.

Sources: Tables 5.1, 6.1, 7.1, 8.2a, 10.1, A2, A4, A5, and A6.

Source: *U.S. Energy Information Administration, Annual Energy Review 2011*

Figure 1.3 Primary Energy Consumption Estimates by Source

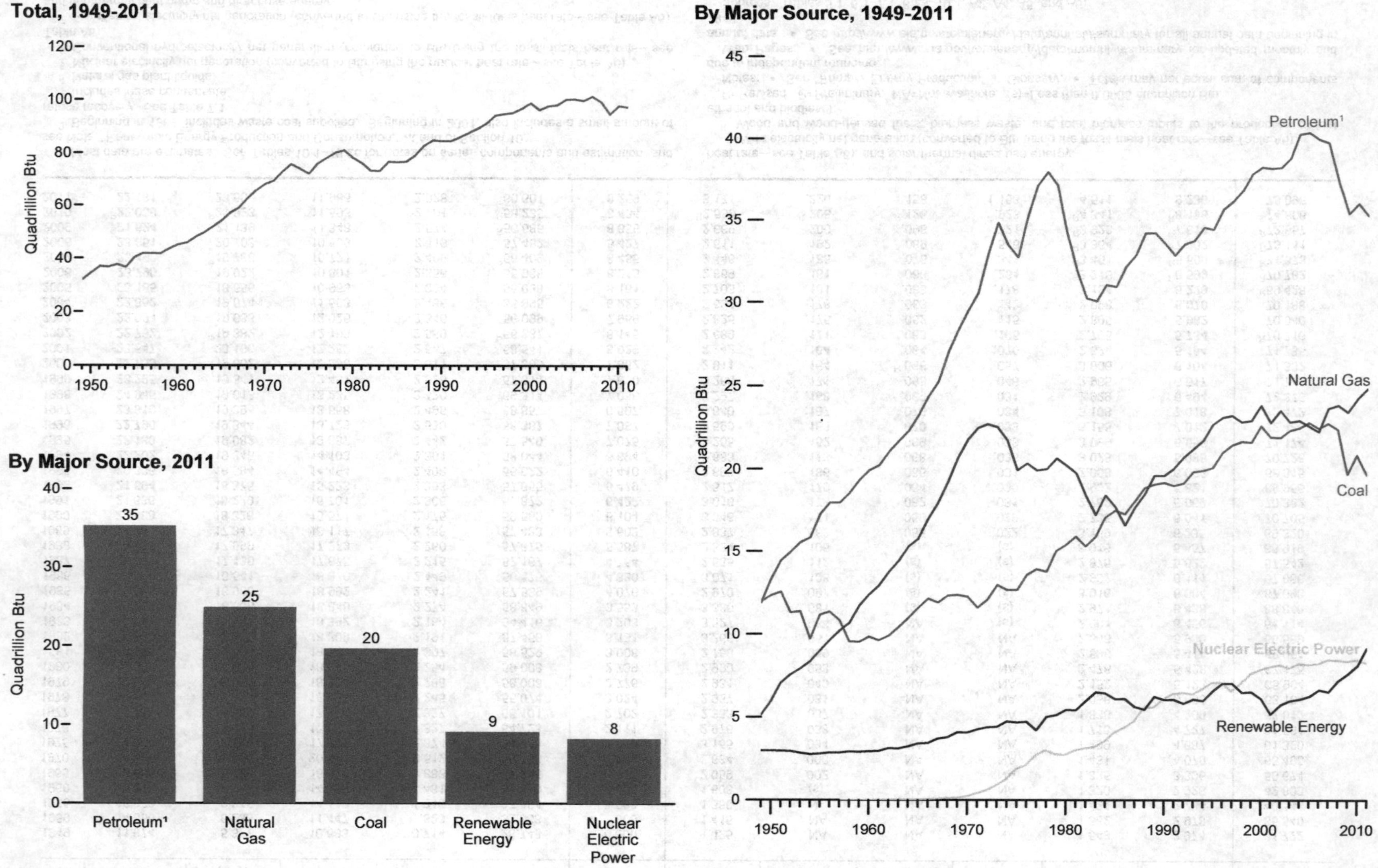

[1] Petroleum products supplied, including natural gas plant liquids and crude oil burned as fuel. Does not include biofuels that have been blended with petroleum—biofuels are included in "Renewable Energy." For petroleum, product supplied is used as an approximation of petroleum consumption. See Note 1, "Petroleum Products Supplied and Petroleum Consumption," at the end of Section 5

Sources: Tables 1.2 and 1.3.

***Source:** U.S. Energy Information Administration, Annual Energy Review 2011*

Table 1.3 Primary Energy Consumption Estimates by Source, Selected Years, 1949-2011

(Quadrillion Btu)

	Fossil Fuels						Renewable Energy [1]						
							Noncombustible [2]						
Year	Coal	Coal Coke Net Imports [3]	Natural Gas [4]	Petroleum [5]	Total	Nuclear Electric Power	Captured Energy [6]	Adjustment for Fossil Fuel Equivalence [6]	Total [6,7]	Biomass [7]	Total	Electricity Net Imports [3]	Total
1949	11.981	-0.007	5.145	11.883	29.002	0.000	0.323	1.101	1.425	1.549	2.974	0.005	31.982
1950	12.347	.001	5.968	13.315	31.632	.000	.344	1.071	1.415	1.562	2.978	.006	34.616
1955	11.167	-.010	8.998	17.255	37.410	.000	.397	.963	1.360	1.424	2.784	.014	40.208
1960	9.838	-.006	12.385	19.919	42.137	.006	.510	1.098	1.608	1.320	2.928	.015	45.086
1965	11.581	-.018	15.769	23.246	50.577	.043	.673	1.388	2.061	1.335	3.396	(s)	54.015
1970	12.265	-.058	21.795	29.521	63.522	.239	.858	1.781	2.639	1.431	4.070	.007	67.838
1975	12.663	.014	19.948	32.732	65.357	1.900	1.045	2.143	3.188	1.499	4.687	.021	71.965
1976	13.584	(s)	20.345	35.178	69.107	2.111	.991	2.022	3.014	1.713	4.727	.029	75.975
1977	13.922	.015	19.931	37.124	70.991	2.702	.775	1.595	2.371	1.838	4.209	.059	77.961
1978	13.766	.125	20.000	37.963	71.854	3.024	.977	1.990	2.968	2.038	5.005	.067	79.950
1979	15.040	.063	20.666	37.122	72.891	2.776	.979	1.992	2.971	2.152	5.123	.069	80.859
1980	15.423	-.035	20.235	34.205	69.828	2.739	.970	1.983	2.953	2.476	5.428	.071	78.067
1981	15.908	-.016	19.747	31.932	67.571	3.008	.920	1.898	2.817	2.596	5.414	.113	76.106
1982	15.322	-.022	18.356	30.232	63.888	3.131	1.082	2.234	3.316	2.663	5.980	.100	73.099
1983	15.894	-.016	17.221	30.052	63.152	3.203	1.165	2.426	3.591	2.904	6.496	.121	72.971
1984	17.071	-.011	18.394	31.053	66.506	3.553	1.133	2.334	3.467	2.971	6.438	.135	76.632
1985	17.478	-.013	17.703	30.925	66.093	4.076	1.002	2.066	3.068	3.016	6.084	.140	76.392
1986	17.260	-.017	16.591	32.198	66.033	4.380	1.038	2.141	3.179	2.932	6.111	.122	76.647
1987	18.008	.009	17.640	32.864	68.521	4.754	.900	1.847	2.747	2.875	5.622	.158	79.054
1988	18.846	.040	18.448	34.223	71.557	5.587	.807	1.634	2.441	3.016	5.457	.108	82.709
1989	19.070	.030	19.602	34.209	72.911	5.602	1.048	2.028	3.076	3.159	6.235	.037	84.786
1990	19.173	.005	19.603	33.552	72.332	6.104	1.128	2.177	3.306	2.735	6.041	.008	84.485
1991	18.992	.010	20.033	32.846	71.880	6.422	1.121	2.166	3.287	2.782	6.069	.067	84.438
1992	19.122	.035	20.714	33.525	73.396	6.479	1.001	1.889	2.890	2.932	5.821	.087	85.783
1993	19.835	.027	21.229	33.745	74.836	6.410	1.100	2.074	3.174	2.908	6.083	.095	87.424
1994	19.909	.058	21.728	34.561	76.256	6.694	1.030	1.930	2.961	3.028	5.988	.153	89.091
1995	20.089	.061	22.671	34.438	77.259	7.075	1.197	2.262	3.459	3.101	6.560	.134	91.029
1996	21.002	.023	23.085	35.675	79.785	7.087	1.325	2.530	3.857	3.157	7.014	.137	94.022
1997	21.445	.046	23.223	36.159	80.873	6.597	1.360	2.550	3.910	3.105	7.016	.116	94.602
1998	21.656	.067	22.830	36.816	81.369	7.068	1.247	2.318	3.565	2.927	6.493	.088	95.018
1999	21.623	.058	22.909	37.838	82.427	7.610	1.240	2.312	3.552	2.963	6.516	.099	96.652
2000	22.580	.065	23.824	38.262	84.731	7.862	1.090	2.008	3.098	3.008	6.106	.115	[R]98.814
2001	21.914	.029	22.773	38.186	82.902	8.029	.893	1.647	2.540	2.622	5.163	.075	96.168
2002	21.904	.061	[R]23.510	38.224	[R]83.699	8.145	1.070	1.959	3.029	2.701	5.729	.072	[R]97.645
2003	22.321	.051	22.831	38.811	84.014	7.959	1.114	2.062	3.176	2.807	5.983	.022	97.978
2004	22.466	.138	[R]22.923	40.292	[R]85.819	8.222	1.103	1.969	3.073	3.010	6.082	.039	[R]100.162
2005	22.797	.044	[R]22.565	40.388	[R]85.794	8.161	1.127	1.998	3.125	[R]3.117	6.242	.085	[R]100.282
2006	22.447	.061	[R]22.239	39.955	[R]84.702	8.215	1.229	2.153	3.382	[R]3.267	[R]6.649	.063	[R]99.629
2007	22.749	.025	[R]23.663	39.774	[R]86.211	8.455	1.125	1.924	3.048	[R]3.474	[R]6.523	.107	[R]101.296
2008	22.385	.041	[R]23.843	37.280	[R]83.549	8.427	1.238	2.099	3.338	[R]3.849	[R]7.186	.112	[R]99.275
2009	19.692	-.024	[R]23.416	35.403	[R]78.488	8.356	1.382	2.306	3.688	[R]3.912	[R]7.600	.116	[R]94.559
2010	[R]20.850	-.006	[R]24.256	[R]36.010	[R]81.109	[R]8.434	[R]1.440	[R]2.355	[R]3.796	[R]4.294	[R]8.090	[R].089	[R]97.722
2011[P]	19.643	.011	24.843	35.283	79.779	8.259	1.785	2.939	4.724	4.411	9.135	.127	97.301

[1] Most data are estimates. See Note, "Renewable Energy Production and Consumption," at end of Section 10.

[2] Conventional hydroelectric power, geothermal, solar thermal, photovoltaic, and wind. See Note 1, "Noncombustible Renewable Energy," at end of section.

[3] Net imports equal imports minus exports. A minus sign indicates exports are greater than imports.

[4] Natural gas only; excludes supplemental gaseous fuels. See Note 1, "Supplemental Gaseous Fuels," at end of Section 6.

[5] Petroleum products supplied, including natural gas plant liquids and crude oil burned as fuel. Does not include biofuels that have been blended with petroleum—biofuels are included in "Biomass." For petroleum, product supplied is used as an approximation of petroleum consumption. See Note 1, "Petroleum Products Supplied and Petroleum Consumption," at end of Section 5.

[6] See Note 1, "Noncombustible Renewable Energy," at end of section.

[7] See Table 10.1 for a breakdown of individual sources.

R=Revised. P=Preliminary. (s)=Less than 0.0005 and greater than -0.0005 quadrillion Btu.

Notes: • See "Primary Energy Consumption" in Glossary. • See Table E1 for estimated energy consumption for 1635–1945. • See Note 3, "Electricity Imports and Exports," at end of Section 8. • Totals may not equal sum of components due to independent rounding.

Web Pages: • See http://www.eia.gov/totalenergy/data/monthly/#summary for updated monthly and annual data. • See http://www.eia.gov/totalenergy/data/annual/#summary for all annual data beginning in 1949.

Sources: Tables 5.12, 6.1, 7.1, 7.8, 8.1, 8.2a, 10.1, 10.3, A4, A5, and A6.

***Source:** U.S. Energy Information Administration, Annual Energy Review 2011*

Figure 1.4 Primary Energy Trade by Source, 1949-2011

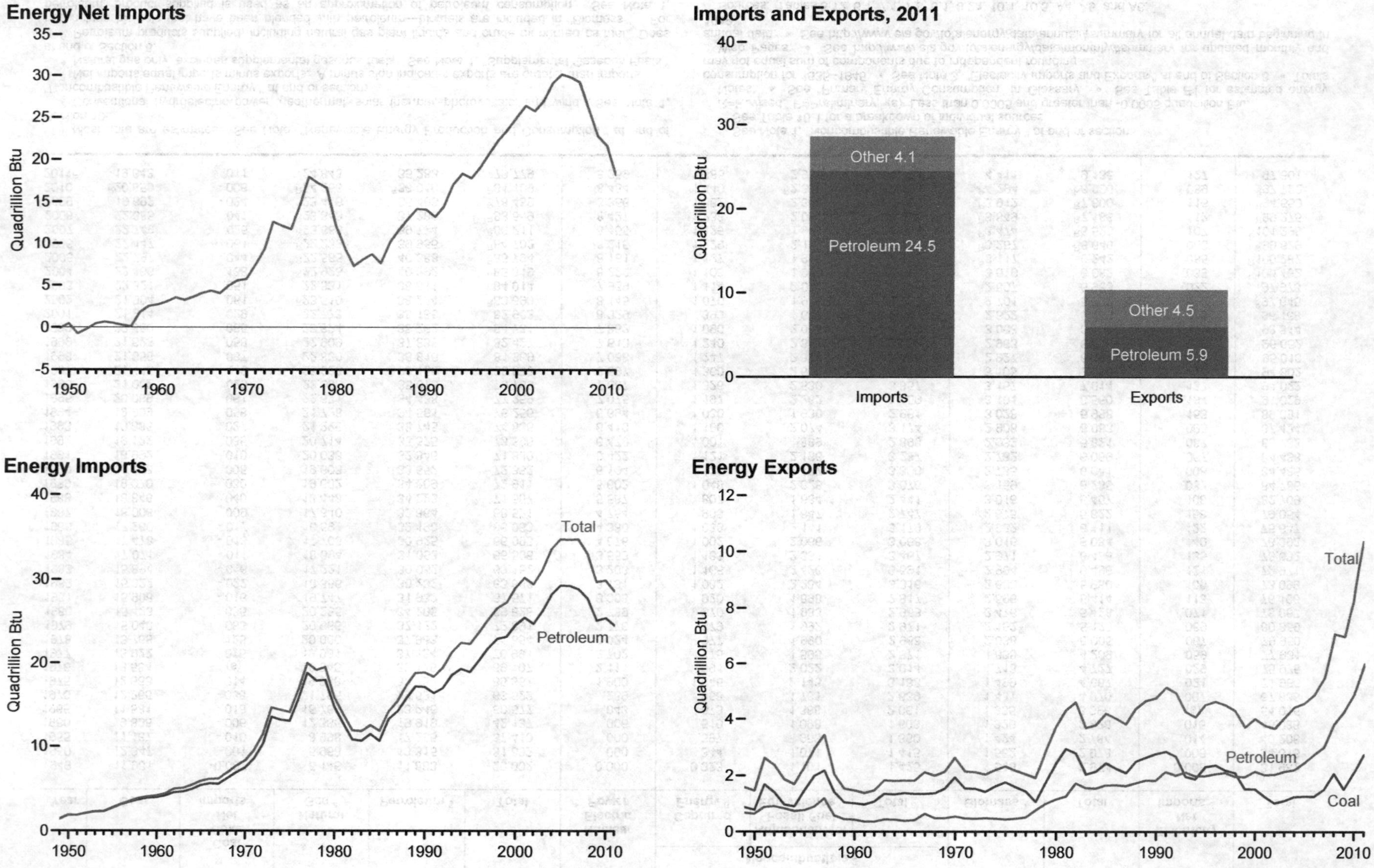

Note: Negative net imports are net exports.

Source: Table 1.4.

Source: *U.S. Energy Information Administration, Annual Energy Review 2011*

Table 1.4 Primary Energy Trade by Source, Selected Years, 1949-2011

(Quadrillion Btu)

	Imports									Exports									Net Imports [1]
				Petroleum									Petroleum						
Year	Coal	Coal Coke	Natural Gas	Crude Oil [2]	Petroleum Products [3]	Total	Bio-fuels [4]	Elec-tricity	Total	Coal	Coal Coke	Natural Gas	Crude Oil [2]	Petroleum Products [3]	Total	Bio-fuels [5]	Elec-tricity	Total	Total
1949	0.008	0.007	0.000	0.915	0.513	1.427	NA	0.006	1.448	0.877	0.014	0.021	0.192	0.488	0.680	NA	0.001	1.592	-0.144
1950	.009	.011	.000	1.056	.830	1.886	NA	.007	1.913	.786	.010	.027	.202	.440	.642	NA	.001	1.465	.448
1955	.008	.003	.011	1.691	1.061	2.752	NA	.016	2.790	1.465	.013	.032	.067	.707	.774	NA	.002	2.286	.504
1960	.007	.003	.161	2.196	1.802	3.999	NA	.018	4.188	1.023	.009	.012	.018	.413	.431	NA	.003	1.477	2.710
1965	.005	.002	.471	2.654	2.748	5.402	NA	.012	5.892	1.376	.021	.027	.006	.386	.392	NA	.013	1.829	4.063
1970	.001	.004	.846	2.814	4.656	7.470	NA	.021	8.342	1.936	.061	.072	.029	.520	.549	NA	.014	2.632	5.709
1975	.024	.045	.978	8.721	4.227	12.948	NA	.038	14.032	1.761	.032	.074	.012	.427	.439	NA	.017	2.323	11.709
1976	.030	.033	.988	11.239	4.434	15.672	NA	.037	16.760	1.597	.033	.066	.017	.452	.469	NA	.008	2.172	14.588
1977	.041	.045	1.037	14.027	4.728	18.756	NA	.069	19.948	1.442	.031	.056	.106	.408	.514	NA	.009	2.052	17.896
1978	.074	.142	.995	13.460	4.364	17.824	NA	.072	19.106	1.078	.017	.053	.335	.432	.767	NA	.005	1.920	17.186
1979	.051	.099	1.300	13.825	4.108	17.933	NA	.077	19.460	1.753	.036	.056	.497	.505	1.002	NA	.007	2.855	16.605
1980	.030	.016	1.006	11.195	3.463	14.658	NA	.085	15.796	2.421	.051	.049	.609	.551	1.160	NA	.014	3.695	12.101
1981	.026	.013	.917	9.336	3.303	12.639	NA	.124	13.779	2.944	.029	.060	.432	.781	1.264	NA	.010	4.307	9.412
1982	.019	.003	.950	7.418	3.360	10.777	NA	.112	11.861	2.787	.025	.052	.500	1.231	1.732	NA	.012	4.608	7.253
1983	.032	.001	.940	7.079	3.568	10.647	NA	.132	11.752	2.045	.016	.055	.348	1.217	1.565	NA	.011	3.693	8.059
1984	.032	.014	.847	7.302	4.131	11.433	NA	.144	12.471	2.151	.026	.055	.384	1.161	1.545	NA	.009	3.786	8.685
1985	.049	.014	.952	6.814	3.796	10.609	NA	.157	11.781	2.438	.028	.056	.432	1.225	1.657	NA	.017	4.196	7.584
1986	.055	.008	.748	9.002	4.199	13.201	NA	.139	14.151	2.248	.025	.062	.326	1.344	1.670	NA	.016	4.021	10.130
1987	.044	.023	.992	10.067	4.095	14.162	NA	.178	15.398	2.093	.014	.055	.319	1.311	1.630	NA	.020	3.812	11.586
1988	.053	.067	1.296	11.027	4.720	15.747	NA	.133	17.296	2.499	.027	.075	.329	1.412	1.741	NA	.024	4.366	12.929
1989	.071	.057	1.387	12.596	4.565	17.162	NA	.089	18.766	2.637	.027	.109	.300	1.536	1.836	NA	.052	4.661	14.105
1990	.067	.019	1.551	12.766	4.351	17.117	NA	.063	18.817	2.772	.014	.087	.230	1.594	1.824	NA	.055	4.752	14.065
1991	.085	.029	1.798	12.553	3.794	16.348	NA	.075	18.335	2.854	.020	.132	.246	1.882	2.128	NA	.008	5.141	13.194
1992	.095	.052	2.161	13.253	3.714	16.968	NA	.096	19.372	2.682	.017	.220	.188	1.819	2.008	NA	.010	4.937	14.435
1993	.205	.053	2.397	14.749	3.760	18.510	.001	.107	21.273	1.962	.026	.142	.208	1.907	2.115	NA	.012	4.258	17.014
1994	.222	.083	2.682	15.340	3.904	19.243	.001	.160	22.390	1.879	.024	.164	.209	1.779	1.988	NA	.007	4.061	18.329
1995	.237	.095	2.901	15.669	3.211	18.881	.001	.146	22.250	2.318	.034	.156	.200	1.791	1.991	NA	.012	4.511	17.750
1996	.203	.063	3.002	16.341	3.943	20.284	.001	.148	23.732	2.368	.040	.155	.233	1.825	2.059	NA	.011	4.633	19.069
1997	.187	.078	3.063	17.876	3.864	21.740	(s)	.147	25.215	2.193	.031	.159	.228	1.872	2.100	NA	.031	4.514	20.701
1998	.218	.095	3.225	18.916	3.992	22.908	(s)	.135	26.531	2.092	.028	.161	.233	1.740	1.972	NA	.047	4.299	22.281
1999	.227	.080	3.664	18.935	4.198	23.133	(s)	.147	27.252	1.525	.022	.164	.250	1.705	1.955	NA	.049	3.715	23.537
2000	.313	.094	3.869	19.783	4.749	24.531	(s)	.166	28.973	1.528	.028	.245	.106	2.048	2.154	NA	.051	4.006	24.967
2001	.495	.063	4.068	20.348	5.051	25.393	.002	.131	30.157	1.265	.033	.377	.043	1.996	2.039	(s)	.056	3.771	26.386
2002	.422	.080	4.104	19.920	4.754	24.674	.002	.125	29.408	1.032	.020	.520	.019	2.023	2.042	(s)	.054	3.669	25.739
2003	.626	.068	4.042	21.060	5.159	26.219	.002	.104	31.061	1.117	.018	.686	.026	2.124	2.151	.001	.082	4.054	27.007
2004	.682	.170	4.365	22.082	6.114	28.197	.013	.117	33.544	1.253	.033	.862	.057	2.151	2.208	.001	.078	4.434	29.110
2005	.762	.088	4.450	22.091	7.157	29.248	.012	.150	34.709	1.273	.043	.735	.067	2.374	2.442	.001	.065	4.560	30.149
2006	.906	.101	4.291	22.085	7.084	29.169	.066	.146	34.679	1.264	.040	.730	.052	2.699	2.751	.004	.083	4.872	29.806
2007	.909	.061	4.723	21.914	6.868	28.781	.054	.175	34.703	1.507	.036	.830	.058	2.949	3.007	.035	.069	5.482	29.221
2008	.855	.089	4.084	21.448	6.237	27.685	.084	.195	32.992	2.071	.049	.972	.061	3.739	3.800	.086	.083	7.060	25.932
2009	.566	.009	3.845	19.699	5.383	25.082	.026	.178	29.706	1.515	.032	1.082	.093	4.147	4.240	.034	.062	6.965	22.741
2010	.484	.030	R3.834	R20.140	R5.231	R25.371	.004	.154	R29.877	2.101	.036	1.147	.088	R4.750	R4.838	R.046	R.065	R8.234	R21.643
2011P	.327	.035	3.540	19.561	4.930	24.491	.016	.178	28.587	2.751	.024	1.521	.100	5.801	5.901	.108	.051	10.356	18.232

[1] Net imports equal imports minus exports. Minus sign indicates exports are greater than imports.

[2] Crude oil and lease condensate. Imports data include imports into the Strategic Petroleum Reserve, which began in 1977.

[3] Petroleum products, unfinished oils, pentanes plus, and gasoline blending components. Does not include biofuels.

[4] Fuel ethanol (minus denaturant) and biodiesel.

[5] Biodiesel only.

R=Revised. P=Preliminary. NA=Not available. (s)=Less than 0.0005 quadrillion Btu.

Notes: • Includes trade between the United States (50 States and the District of Columbia) and its territories and possessions. • See "Primary Energy" in Glossary. • See Note 3, "Electricity Imports and Exports," at end of Section 8. • Totals may not equal sum of components due to independent rounding.

Web Pages: • See http://www.eia.gov/totalenergy/data/monthly/#summary for updated monthly and annual data. • See http://www.eia.gov/totalenergy/data/annual/#summary for all annual data beginning in 1949.

Sources: Tables 5.1b 5.3, 5.5, 6.1, 7.1, 7.8, 8.1, 10.3, 10.4, A2, A3, A4, A5, and A6.

***Source:** U.S. Energy Information Administration: Annual Energy Review 2011*

Figure 1.5 Energy Consumption and Expenditures Indicators Estimates

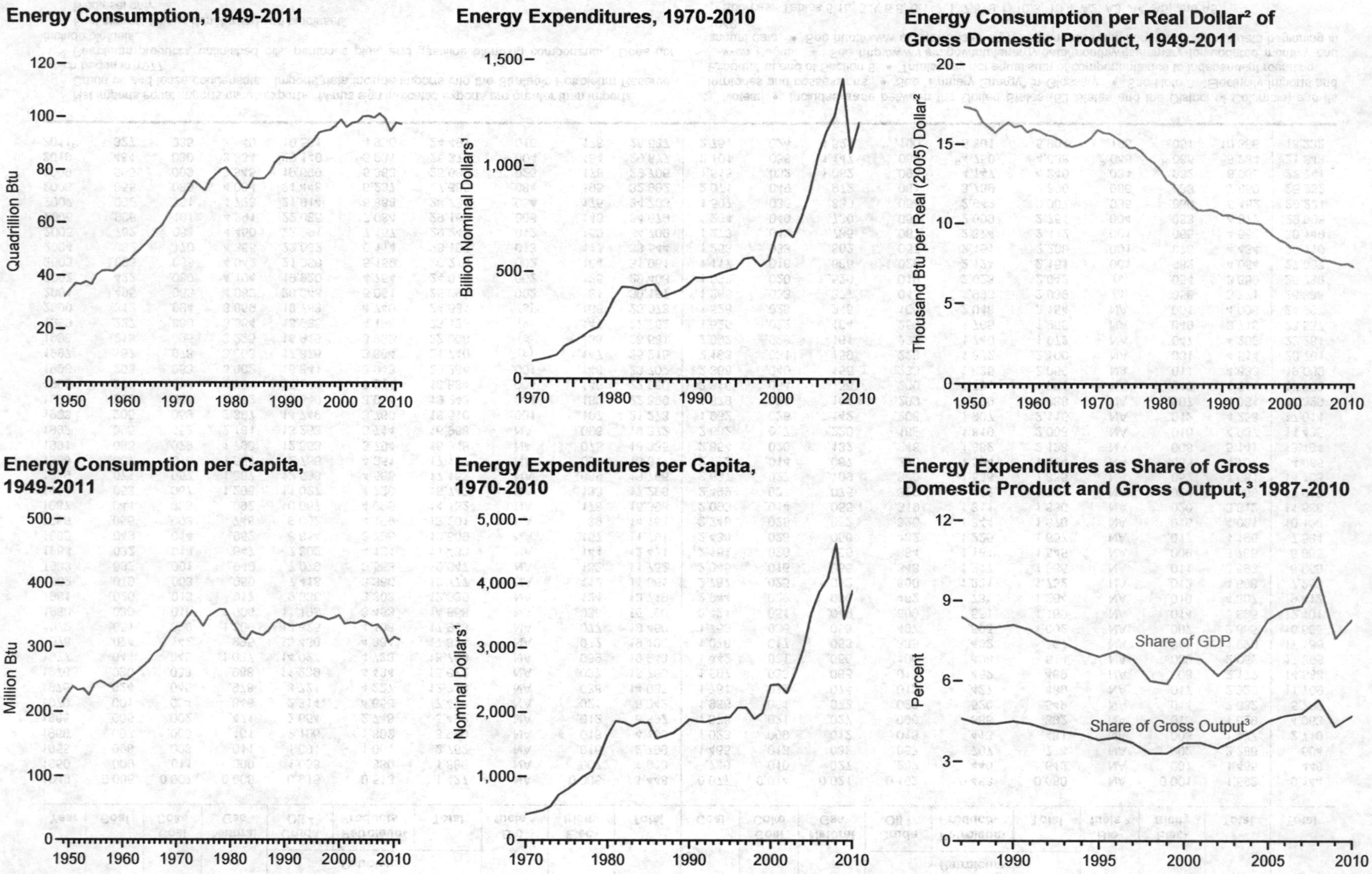

[1] See "Nominal Dollars" in Glossary.

[2] In chained (2005) dollars, calculated by using gross domestic product implicit price deflators in Table D1. See "Chained Dollars" in Glossary.

[3] Gross output is the value of gross domestic product (GDP) plus the value of intermediate inputs used to produce GDP.

Source: Table 1.5.

Source: *U.S. Energy Information Administration, Annual Energy Review 2011*

Table 1.5 Energy Consumption, Expenditures, and Emissions Indicators Estimates, Selected Years, 1949-2011

Year	Energy Consumption	Energy Consumption per Capita	Energy Expenditures [1]	Energy Expenditures [1] per Capita	Gross Output [3]	Energy Expenditures [1] as Share of Gross Output [3]	Gross Domestic Product (GDP)	Energy Expenditures [1] as Share of GDP	Gross Domestic Product (GDP)	Energy Consumption per Real Dollar of GDP	Carbon Dioxide Emissions [2] per Real Dollar of GDP
	Quadrillion Btu	Million Btu	Million Nominal Dollars [4]	Nominal Dollars [4]	Billion Nominal Dollars [4]	Percent	Billion Nominal Dollars [4]	Percent	Billion Real (2005) Dollars [5]	Thousand Btu per Real (2005) Dollar [5]	Metric Tons Carbon Dioxide per Million Real (2005) Dollars [5]
1949	31.982	214	NA	NA	NA	NA	267.2	NA	R1,843.1	R17.35	R1,197
1950	34.616	227	NA	NA	NA	NA	293.7	NA	R2,004.2	R17.27	R1,189
1955	40.208	242	NA	NA	NA	NA	414.7	NA	R2,498.2	R16.09	R1,075
1960	45.086	250	NA	NA	NA	NA	526.4	NA	R2,828.5	R15.94	R1,030
1965	54.015	278	NA	NA	NA	NA	719.1	NA	R3,607.0	R14.98	R960
1970	67.838	331	82,860	404	NA	NA	1,038.3	8.0	R4,266.3	R15.90	R999
1975	71.965	333	R171,837	R796	NA	NA	1,637.7	10.5	R4,875.4	R14.76	R910
1976	75.975	348	R193,896	889	NA	NA	1,824.6	10.6	R5,136.9	R14.79	R916
1977	77.961	354	R220,476	1,001	NA	NA	2,030.1	10.9	R5,373.1	R14.51	R902
1978	79.950	359	R239,255	R1,075	NA	NA	2,293.8	10.4	R5,672.8	R14.09	R863
1979	80.859	359	R297,549	1,322	NA	NA	2,562.2	11.6	R5,850.1	R13.82	R849
1980	78.067	344	R374,347	1,647	NA	NA	2,788.1	13.4	R5,834.0	R13.38	R818
1981	76.106	332	R427,898	R1,865	NA	NA	3,126.8	13.7	R5,982.1	R12.72	R776
1982	73.099	316	R426,479	R1,841	NA	NA	3,253.2	13.1	R5,865.9	R12.46	751
1983	72.971	312	R417,476	R1,786	NA	NA	3,534.6	11.8	R6,130.9	R11.90	R715
1984	76.632	325	R435,195	1,845	NA	NA	3,930.9	11.1	R6,571.5	R11.66	R702
1985	76.392	321	R438,347	1,842	NA	NA	4,217.5	10.4	R6,843.4	R11.16	672
1986	76.647	319	R383,518	1,597	NA	NA	4,460.1	8.6	R7,080.5	R10.83	R651
1987	79.054	326	R396,587	R1,637	8,639.9	4.6	4,736.4	8.4	R7,307.0	R10.82	R652
1988	82.709	338	R410,515	R1,679	9,359.5	4.4	5,100.4	8.0	R7,607.4	R10.87	R655
1989	84.786	344	R437,679	1,773	9,969.6	4.4	5,482.1	8.0	R7,879.2	R10.76	643
1990	84.485	338	R472,653	1,893	10,511.1	4.5	5,800.5	8.1	R8,027.1	10.52	R628
1991	84.438	334	R470,668	1,860	10,676.5	4.4	5,992.1	7.9	R8,008.3	R10.54	R624
1992	85.783	334	R475,644	R1,854	11,242.4	4.2	6,342.3	7.5	R8,280.0	R10.36	615
1993	87.424	336	R491,231	R1,890	11,857.6	4.1	6,667.4	7.4	R8,516.2	R10.27	R609
1994	89.091	339	504,073	1,916	12,647.2	4.0	7,085.2	7.1	R8,863.1	R10.05	593
1995	91.029	342	513,947	1,930	13,451.6	3.8	7,414.7	6.9	R9,086.0	R10.02	R585
1996	94.022	349	559,890	2,078	14,259.9	3.9	7,838.5	7.1	R9,425.8	9.97	R584
1997	94.602	347	566,714	2,079	15,160.5	3.7	8,332.4	6.8	R9,845.9	R9.61	566
1998	95.018	344	525,515	1,905	15,987.4	3.3	8,793.5	6.0	R10,274.7	R9.25	547
1999	96.652	346	R556,379	1,994	17,017.4	3.3	9,353.5	5.9	R10,770.7	8.97	R528
2000	R98.814	350	R685,902	2,431	18,305.7	3.7	9,951.5	6.9	R11,216.4	R8.81	523
2001	96.168	337	694,484	R2,437	18,576.5	3.7	10,286.2	6.8	R11,337.5	8.48	508
2002	R97.645	R339	R662,414	R2,303	18,874.2	3.5	10,642.3	6.2	R11,543.1	8.46	503
2003	97.978	338	754,708	R2,601	19,832.3	3.8	R11,142.2	6.8	R11,836.4	R8.28	495
2004	R100.162	342	R871,097	R2,975	21,267.7	4.1	R11,853.3	7.3	R12,246.9	R8.18	R488
2005	R100.282	339	R1,046,897	R3,543	23,046.9	4.5	R12,623.0	8.3	R12,623.0	R7.94	R475
2006	R99.629	334	R1,159,687	R3,887	24,477.0	4.7	R13,377.2	8.7	R12,958.5	R7.69	R457
2007	R101.296	336	R1,234,282	R4,097	25,819.7	4.8	R14,028.7	8.8	R13,206.4	R7.67	R456
2008	R99.275	326	R1,408,845	R4,633	26,561.9	5.3	R14,291.5	R9.9	R13,161.9	R7.54	R444
2009	R94.559	308	R1,061,220	R3,459	24,568.6	4.3	R13,939.0	R7.6	R12,703.1	R7.44	R427
2010	R97.722	R316	R1,204,827	R3,895	25,811.4	4.7	R14,526.5	R8.3	R13,088.0	R7.47	R429
2011P	97.301	312	NA	NA	NA	NA	15,094.0	NA	13,315.1	7.31	412

1 Expenditures include taxes where data are available.
2 Carbon dioxide emissions from energy consumption. See Table 11.1.
3 Gross output is the value of GDP plus the value of intermediate inputs used to produce GDP.
4 See "Nominal Dollars" in Glossary.
5 In chained (2005) dollars. See "Chained Dollars" in Glossary.
R=Revised. P=Preliminary. NA=Not available.

Web Page: For all data beginning in 1949, see http://www.eia.gov/totalenergy/data/annual/#summary.
Sources: **Energy Consumption:** Table 1.3. **Energy Expenditures:** Table 3.5. **Gross Domestic Product:** Table D1. **Population Data:** Table D1. **Gross Output:** U.S. Department of Commerce, Bureau of Economic Analysis, Gross Domestic Product by Industry Data, Gross Output, All Industries. **Carbon Dioxide Emissions:** Table 11.1. **Other Columns:** Calculated by U.S. Energy Information Administration.

Source: *U.S. Energy Information Administration, Annual Energy Review 2011*

Figure 1.6 State-Level Energy Consumption Estimates and Estimated Consumption per Capita, 2010

Consumption

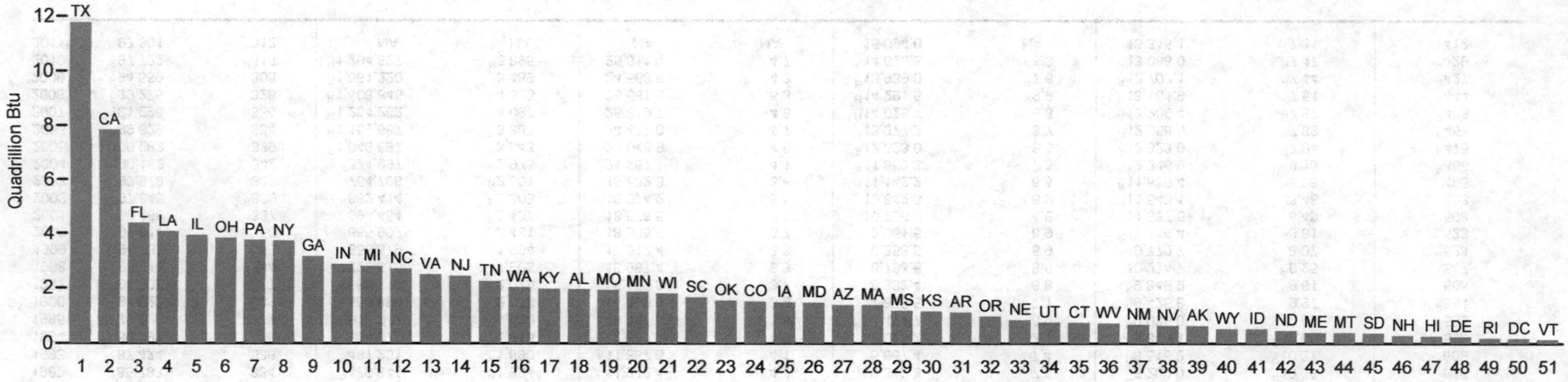

Consumption per Capita

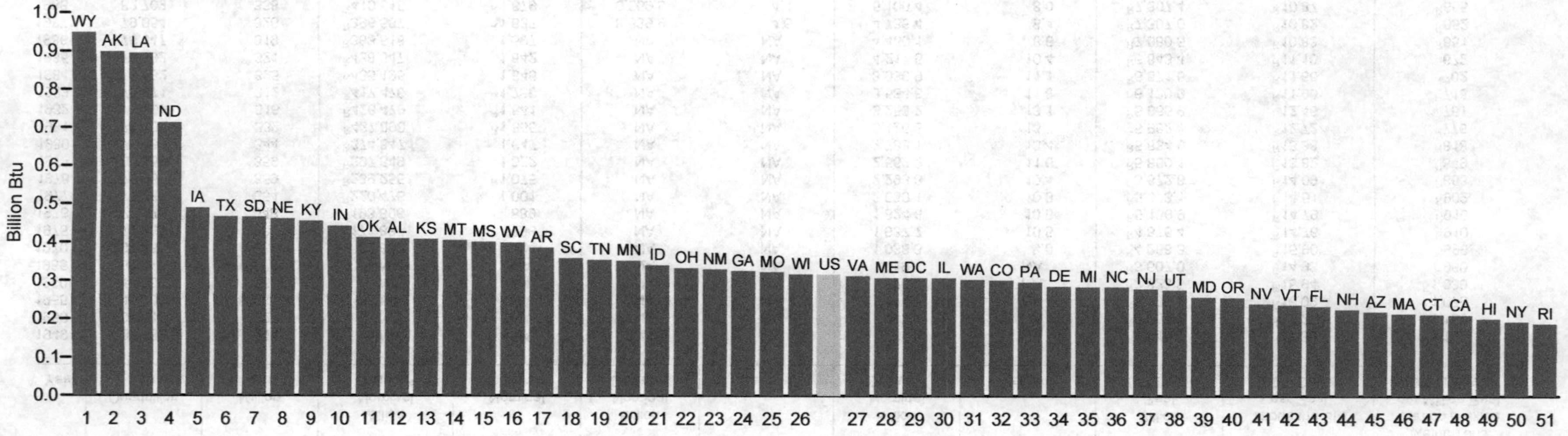

Source: Table 1.6.

Source: *U.S. Energy Information Administration, Annual Energy Review 2011*

Table 1.6 State-Level Energy Consumption, Expenditure, and Price Estimates, 2010

Rank	Consumption		Consumption per Capita		Expenditures [1]		Expenditures [1] per Capita		Prices [1]	
	Trillion Btu		Million Btu		Million Dollars [2]		Dollars [2]		Dollars [2] per Million Btu	
1	Texas	11,769.9	Wyoming	948.1	Texas	137,532	Alaska	8,807	Hawaii	30.75
2	California	7,825.7	Alaska	898.5	California	117,003	Louisiana	8,661	District of Columbia	26.19
3	Florida	4,381.9	Louisiana	894.4	New York	61,619	Wyoming	7,904	Connecticut	25.63
4	Louisiana	4,065.4	North Dakota	712.6	Florida	60,172	North Dakota	6,740	Vermont	24.20
5	Illinois	3,936.7	Iowa	489.3	Pennsylvania	48,701	Texas	5,446	New Hampshire	23.87
6	Ohio	3,833.7	Texas	466.1	Ohio	45,081	Iowa	4,841	Massachusetts	23.32
7	Pennsylvania	3,758.8	South Dakota	464.9	Illinois	44,989	Maine	4,746	Rhode Island	23.12
8	New York	3,728.4	Nebraska	461.1	Louisiana	39,369	South Dakota	4,651	Delaware	22.95
9	Georgia	3,155.7	Kentucky	454.7	New Jersey	37,362	Montana	4,610	New York	22.91
10	Indiana	2,871.1	Indiana	442.3	Georgia	37,338	Kentucky	4,526	Maryland	22.48
11	Michigan	2,798.1	Oklahoma	412.6	Michigan	34,540	Alabama	4,494	Arizona	21.78
12	North Carolina	2,705.2	Alabama	409.5	North Carolina	32,989	Mississippi	4,446	Florida	21.66
13	Virginia	2,502.1	Kansas	407.6	Virginia	29,826	Nebraska	4,421	New Jersey	20.91
14	New Jersey	2,447.5	Montana	405.1	Indiana	27,374	Kansas	4,357	Nevada	20.87
15	Tennessee	2,250.6	Mississippi	400.4	Tennessee	25,153	Vermont	4,344	California	20.66
16	Washington	2,036.5	West Virginia	398.4	Massachusetts	24,512	Oklahoma	4,268	Alaska	20.25
17	Kentucky	1,976.5	Arkansas	385.3	Washington	22,893	West Virginia	4,251	North Carolina	19.98
18	Alabama	1,959.7	South Carolina	358.3	Missouri	22,885	New Jersey	4,246	Pennsylvania	19.56
19	Missouri	1,928.4	Tennessee	354.0	Maryland	21,517	Indiana	4,217	New Mexico	19.40
20	Minnesota	1,867.3	Minnesota	351.6	Alabama	21,507	Hawaii	4,191	Virginia	18.91
21	Wisconsin	1,800.1	Idaho	339.7	Wisconsin	21,483	Arkansas	4,128	Oregon	18.89
22	South Carolina	1,661.6	Ohio	332.3	Minnesota	20,869	South Carolina	4,034	Maine	18.78
23	Oklahoma	1,551.6	New Mexico	329.2	Kentucky	19,675	District of Columbia	4,033	Missouri	18.54
24	Colorado	1,516.9	Georgia	324.9	Arizona	19,374	Delaware	4,019	Tennessee	18.33
25	Iowa	1,492.3	Missouri	321.6	South Carolina	18,705	Connecticut	3,977	South Carolina	18.26
26	Maryland	1,481.1	Wisconsin	316.3	Colorado	16,751	New Hampshire	3,971	Michigan	18.22
27	Arizona	1,399.6	Virginia	311.8	Oklahoma	16,049	Tennessee	3,956	Wisconsin	18.22
28	Massachusetts	1,396.9	Maine	306.8	Iowa	14,766	Minnesota	3,930	Washington	18.11
29	Mississippi	1,189.2	District of Columbia	306.6	Connecticut	14,221	Ohio	3,907	Georgia	17.96
30	Kansas	1,165.3	Illinois	306.5	Mississippi	13,206	Georgia	3,844	Ohio	17.93
31	Arkansas	1,125.6	Washington	302.0	Oregon	12,592	Pennsylvania	3,829	Montana	17.73
32	Oregon	977.1	Colorado	300.5	Kansas	12,457	Missouri	3,817	Kansas	17.72
33	Nebraska	843.8	Pennsylvania	295.6	Arkansas	12,061	Wisconsin	3,774	Mississippi	17.63
34	Utah	763.7	Delaware	284.7	Nevada	9,294	Massachusetts	3,739	Alabama	17.49
35	Connecticut	754.0	Michigan	283.3	Utah	8,332	Maryland	3,719	Texas	17.46
36	West Virginia	738.9	North Carolina	283.0	Nebraska	8,091	Virginia	3,717	Colorado	17.24
37	New Mexico	680.1	New Jersey	278.1	West Virginia	7,882	Idaho	3,622	Illinois	17.17
38	Nevada	646.1	Utah	275.2	New Mexico	7,435	New Mexico	3,599	West Virginia	17.09
39	Alaska	641.7	Maryland	256.0	Maine	6,300	Rhode Island	3,506	South Dakota	16.92
40	Wyoming	535.3	Oregon	254.6	Alaska	6,289	Illinois	3,503	Kentucky	16.89
41	Idaho	533.8	Nevada	238.9	Hawaii	5,714	Michigan	3,497	Minnesota	16.82
42	North Dakota	480.7	Vermont	235.9	Idaho	5,691	North Carolina	3,451	Oklahoma	16.78
43	Maine	407.3	Florida	232.6	New Hampshire	5,229	Nevada	3,437	Arkansas	16.76
44	Montana	401.4	New Hampshire	224.4	Montana	4,568	Washington	3,395	Idaho	16.68
45	South Dakota	379.6	Arizona	218.2	North Dakota	4,547	Colorado	3,319	Utah	16.66
46	New Hampshire	295.5	Massachusetts	213.1	Wyoming	4,462	Oregon	3,281	Nebraska	16.27
47	Hawaii	272.2	Connecticut	210.9	South Dakota	3,798	Florida	3,194	Iowa	15.46
48	Delaware	256.2	California	209.6	Rhode Island	3,690	New York	3,177	Wyoming	15.16
49	Rhode Island	197.2	Hawaii	199.6	Delaware	3,616	California	3,134	Indiana	14.75
50	District of Columbia	185.5	New York	192.2	Vermont	2,719	Arizona	3,021	Louisiana	14.73
51	Vermont	147.6	Rhode Island	187.4	District of Columbia	2,439	Utah	3,002	North Dakota	13.73
	United States	**[3,4]97,710.6**	**United States**	**315.9**	**United States**	**[5]1,204,827**	**United States**	**3,895**	**United States**	**18.73**

[1] Prices and expenditures include taxes where data are available.
[2] Prices are not adjusted for inflation. See "Nominal Dollars" in Glossary.
[3] Includes -6.2 trillion Btu of coal coke net imports, which are not allocated to the States.
[4] The U.S. consumption value in this table does not match those in Tables 1.1 and 1.3 because it 1) does not include biodiesel; and 2) is the sum of State values, which use State average heat contents to convert physical units of coal and natural gas to Btu.
[5] Includes $158 million for coal coke net imports, which are not allocated to the States.

Note: Rankings based on unrounded data.
Web Page: For related information, see http://www.eia.gov/state/seds/seds-data-complete.cfm.
Sources: **Consumption:** U.S. Energy Information Administration (EIA), "State Energy Data 2010: Consumption" (June 2012), Tables C10 and C11. **Expenditures and Prices:** EIA, "State Energy Data 2010: Prices and Expenditures" (June 2012), Table E15. "State Energy Data 2010" includes State-level data by end-use sector and type of energy. Consumption estimates are annual 1960 through 2010, and price and expenditure estimates are annual 1970 through 2010.

Source: *U.S. Energy Information Administration, Annual Energy Review 2011*

Figure 2.0 Primary Energy Consumption by Source and Sector, 2011
(Quadrillion Btu)

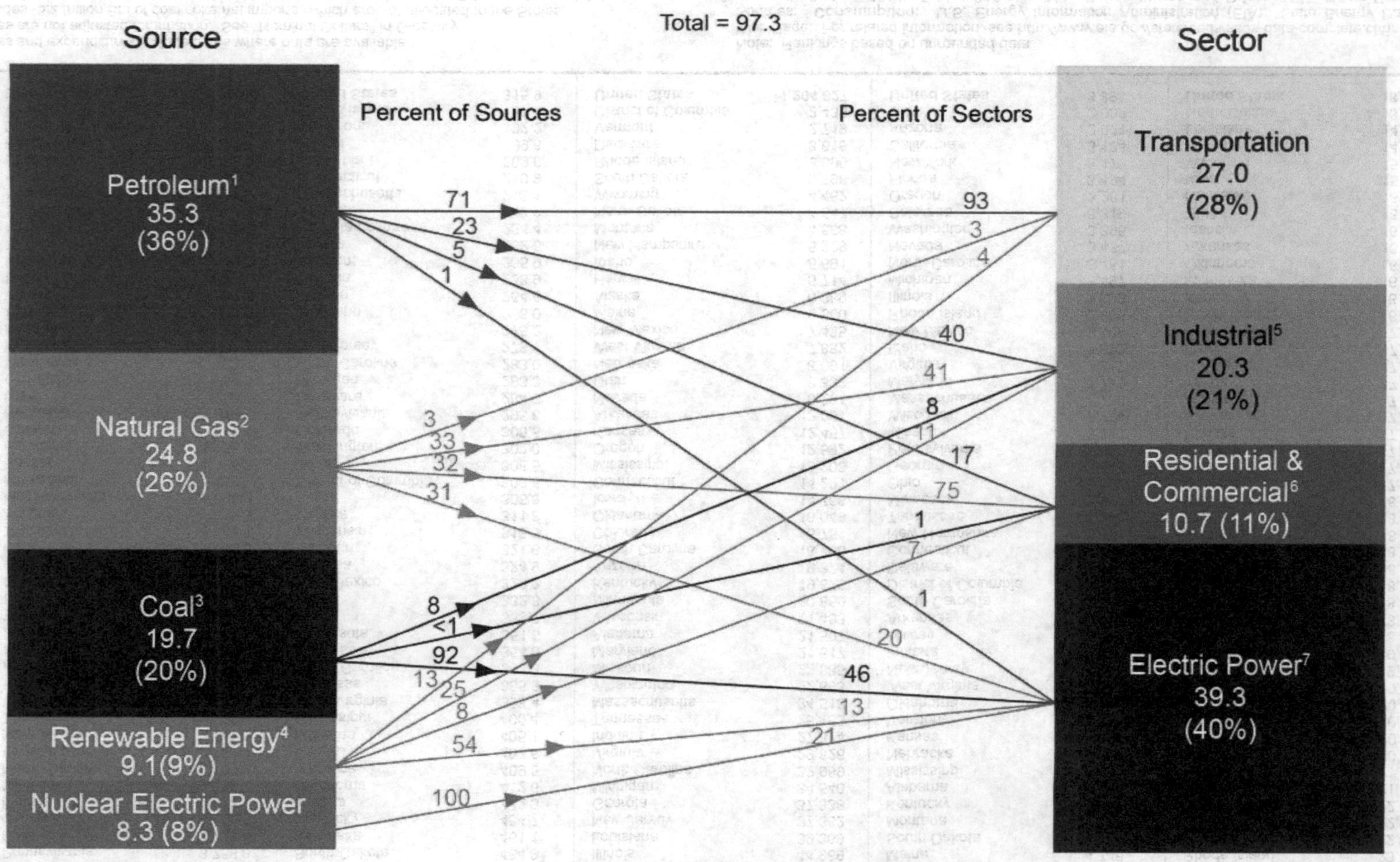

[1] Does not include biofuels that have been blended with petroleum—biofuels are included in "Renewable Energy."

[2] Excludes supplemental gaseous fuels.

[3] Includes less than 0.1 quadrillion Btu of coal coke net imports.

[4] Conventional hydroelectric power, geothermal, solar/photovoltaic, wind, and biomass.

[5] Includes industrial combined-heat-and-power (CHP) and industrial electricity-only plants.

[6] Includes commercial combined-heat-and-power (CHP) and commercial electricity-only plants.

[7] Electricity-only and combined-heat-and-power (CHP) plants whose primary business is to sell electricity, or electricity and heat, to the public. Includes 0.1 quadrillion Btu of electricity net imports not shown under "Source."

Notes: Primary energy in the form that it is first accounted for in a statistical energy balance, before any transformation to secondary or tertiary forms of energy (for example, coal is used to generate electricity). • Sum of components may not equal total due to independent rounding.

Sources: U.S. Energy Information Administration, *Annual Energy Review 2011*, Tables 1.3, 2.1b-2.1f , 10.3, and 10.4.

Source: *U.S. Energy Information Administration, Annual Energy Review 2011*

Figure 2.1a Energy Consumption Estimates by Sector Overview

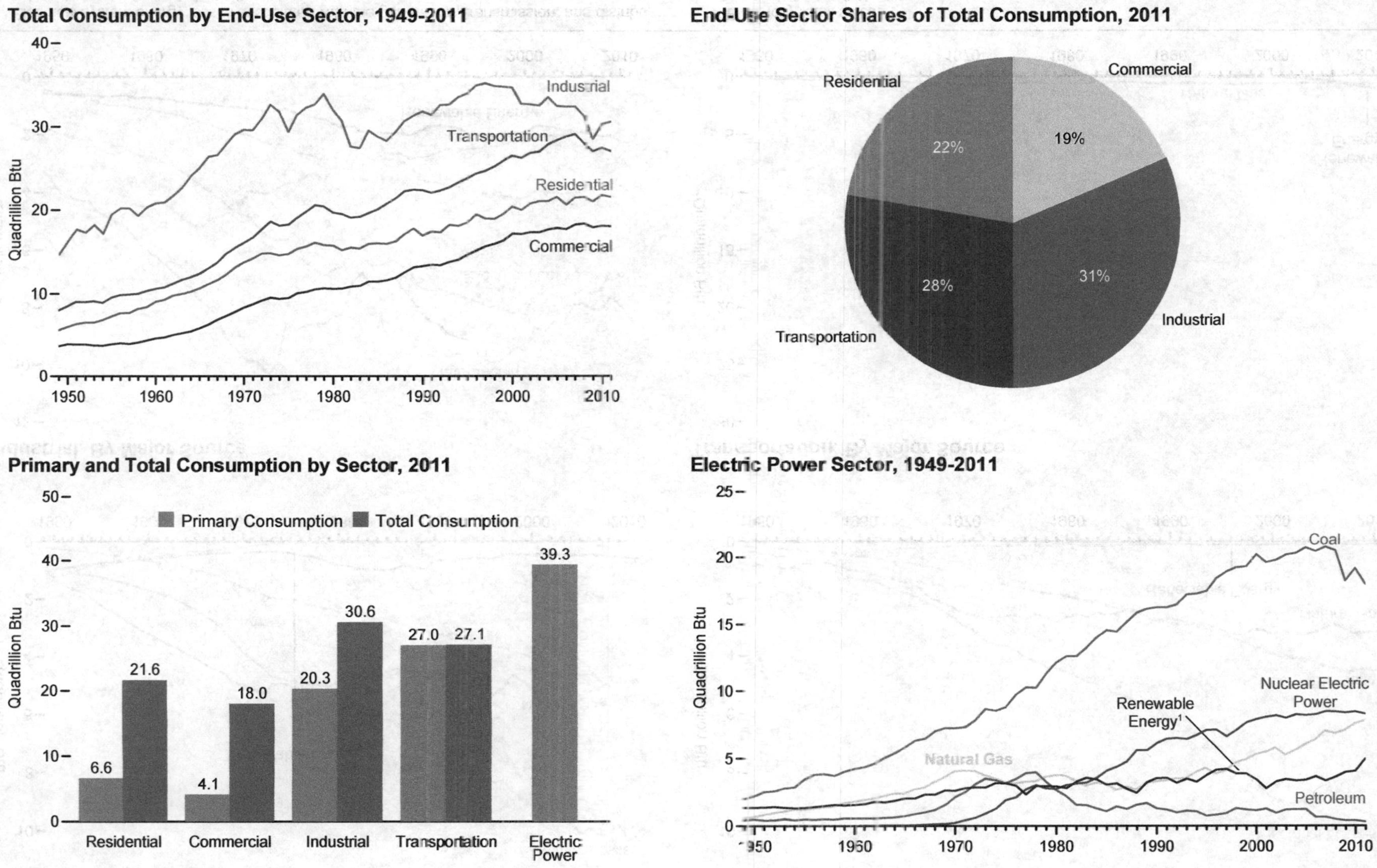

[1] Conventional hydroelectric power, geothermal, solar/photovoltaic, wind, and biomass.

Note: • See "Primary Energy Consumption" in Glossary. • Sum of components may not equal 100 percent due to independent rounding.

Sources: Tables 2.1a and 2.1f.

Source: *U.S. Energy Information Administration, Annual Energy Review 2011*

Figure 2.1b Energy Consumption Estimates by End-Use Sector, 1949-2011

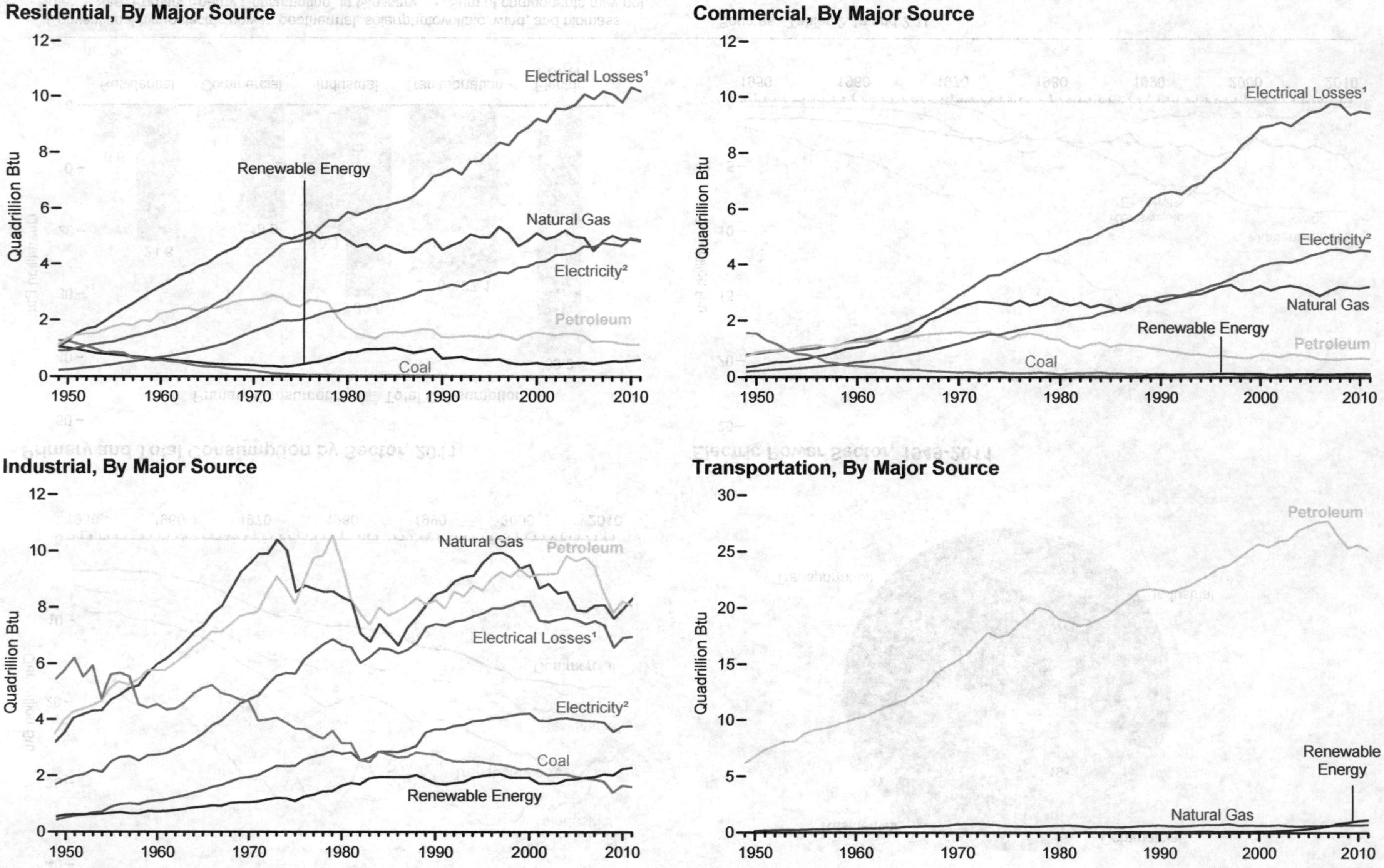

¹ Electrical system energy losses associated with the generation, transmission, and distribution of energy in the form of electricity.

² Electricity retail sales.
Sources: Tables 2.1b–2.1e.

***Source:** U.S. Energy Information Administration, Annual Energy Review 2011*

Table 2.1a Energy Consumption Estimates by Sector, Selected Years, 1949-2011

(Trillion Btu)

Year	End-Use Sectors								Electric Power Sector [3,4]	Balancing Item [7]	Total Primary [8]
	Residential		Commercial [1]		Industrial [2]		Transportation				
	Primary [5]	Total [6]	Primary [5]	Total [6]	Primary [5]	Total [6]	Primary [5]	Total [6]	Primary [5]		
1949	4,460	5,599	2,669	3,669	12,633	14,724	7,880	7,990	4,339	(s)	31,982
1950	4,829	5,989	2,834	3,893	13,890	16,241	8,383	8,492	4,679	(s)	34,616
1955	5,608	7,278	2,561	3,895	16,103	19,485	9,474	9,550	6,461	(s)	40,208
1960	6,651	9,039	2,723	4,609	16,996	20,842	10,560	10,596	8,158	(s)	45,086
1965	7,279	10,639	3,177	5,845	20,148	25,098	12,399	12,432	11,012	(s)	54,015
1970	8,322	13,766	4,237	8,346	22,964	29,628	16,062	16,098	16,253	(s)	67,838
1975	7,990	14,813	4,059	9,492	21,434	29,413	18,210	18,245	20,270	1	71,965
1976	8,391	15,410	4,371	10,063	22,665	31,393	19,067	19,101	21,473	8	75,975
1977	8,194	15,662	4,258	10,208	23,165	32,263	19,786	19,822	22,551	7	77,961
1978	8,260	16,132	4,309	10,512	23,244	32,688	20,583	20,617	23,553	2	79,950
1979	7,919	15,813	4,366	10,648	24,192	33,925	20,437	20,472	23,943	2	80,859
1980	7,439	15,753	4,105	10,578	22,595	32,039	19,659	19,697	24,269	-1	78,067
1981	7,045	15,262	3,837	10,616	21,318	30,712	19,478	19,514	24,425	3	76,106
1982	7,147	15,531	3,864	10,860	19,053	27,614	19,052	19,089	23,979	4	73,099
1983	6,832	15,425	3,840	10,938	18,548	27,428	19,134	19,177	24,614	3	72,971
1984	7,211	15,960	4,001	11,444	20,174	29,570	19,609	19,656	25,635	3	76,632
1985	7,148	16,041	3,732	11,451	19,443	28,816	20,041	20,088	26,032	-4	76,392
1986	6,906	15,975	3,693	11,606	19,078	28,274	20,740	20,789	26,227	3	76,647
1987	6,923	16,263	3,774	11,946	19,953	29,379	21,419	21,469	26,988	-3	79,054
1988	7,357	17,133	3,994	12,578	20,862	30,677	22,267	22,318	28,227	3	82,709
1989	7,567	17,786	4,043	13,193	20,874	31,320	22,424	22,478	[4]29,869	9	84,786
1990	6,557	16,945	3,896	13,320	21,180	31,810	22,366	22,420	30,495	-9	84,485
1991	6,747	17,420	3,945	13,500	20,824	31,399	22,065	22,118	30,856	1	84,438
1992	6,950	17,356	3,991	13,441	21,756	32,571	22,363	22,415	30,723	(s)	85,783
1993	7,146	18,218	3,973	13,820	21,753	32,629	22,715	22,768	31,847	-10	87,424
1994	6,978	18,112	4,016	14,098	22,393	33,521	23,311	23,366	32,399	-6	89,091
1995	6,936	18,519	4,101	14,690	22,719	33,971	23,791	23,846	33,479	3	91,029
1996	R7,467	19,504	4,273	15,172	23,410	34,904	24,383	24,437	34,485	4	94,022
1997	7,033	18,965	4,295	15,681	23,686	35,200	24,695	24,750	34,886	6	94,602
1998	6,413	18,955	4,005	15,968	23,177	34,843	25,201	25,256	36,225	-3	95,018
1999	6,775	19,557	4,053	16,376	22,950	34,764	25,891	25,949	36,976	6	96,652
2000	7,159	20,425	4,278	17,175	22,824	34,664	26,489	26,548	38,062	2	R98,814
2001	6,868	20,042	4,084	17,137	21,794	32,720	26,213	26,275	37,215	-6	96,168
2002	R6,912	R20,791	R4,132	R17,345	R21,799	R32,662	R26,781	R26,842	38,016	5	R97,645
2003	7,211	21,110	4,283	17,343	21,503	32,532	26,920	26,994	38,062	-1	97,978
2004	6,993	21,093	4,232	17,659	R22,412	R33,520	27,817	27,895	38,713	-6	R100,162
2005	6,909	21,626	4,051	R17,857	R21,411	R32,446	28,272	28,353	39,638	(s)	R100,282
2006	R6,168	R20,688	R3,747	R17,711	R21,536	R32,401	28,751	28,830	39,428	(s)	R99,629
2007	R6,598	R21,531	R3,922	R18,255	R21,370	R32,394	R29,029	R29,117	40,377	R-1	R101,296
2008	6,817	21,596	4,073	18,381	R20,480	R31,290	27,925	28,008	39,978	(s)	R99,275
2009	6,619	R21,064	4,061	17,899	R18,813	R28,525	R26,989	R27,071	38,077	(s)	R94,559
2010	R6,603	R21,862	R4,039	R18,078	R20,062	R30,309	R27,384	R27,466	R39,626	R8	R97,722
2011P	6,585	21,619	4,090	18,021	20,291	30,592	26,999	27,079	39,346	-9	97,301

[1] Commercial sector, including commercial combined-heat-and-power (CHP) and commercial electricity-only plants.

[2] Industrial sector, including industrial combined-heat-and-power (CHP) and industrial electricity-only plants.

[3] Electricity-only and combined-heat-and-power (CHP) plants within the NAICS 22 category whose primary business is to sell electricity, or electricity and heat, to the public.

[4] Through 1988, data are for electric utilities only; beginning in 1989, data are for electric utilities and independent power producers.

[5] See "Primary Energy Consumption" in Glossary.

[6] Total energy consumption in the end-use sectors consists of primary energy consumption, electricity retail sales, and electrical system energy losses. See Note, "Electrical System Energy Losses," at end of section.

[7] A balancing item. The sum of primary consumption in the five energy-use sectors equals the sum of total consumption in the four end-use sectors. However, total energy consumption does not equal the sum of the sectoral components due to the use of sector-specific conversion factors for natural gas and coal.

[8] Primary energy consumption total. See Table 1.3.

R=Revised. P=Preliminary. (s)=Less than 0.5 trillion Btu and greater than -0.5 trillion Btu.

Notes: • See Note 2, "Classification of Power Plants Into Energy-Use Sectors," at end of Section 8. • Totals may not equal sum of components due to independent rounding.

Web Pages: • See http://www.eia.gov/totalenergy/data/monthly/#consumption for updated monthly and annual data. • See http://www.eia.gov/totalenergy/data/annual/#consumption for all annual data beginning in 1949.

Sources: Tables 1.3 and 2.1b–2.1f.

Source: *U.S. Energy Information Administration, Annual Energy Review 2011*

Table 2.1b Residential Sector Energy Consumption Estimates, Selected Years, 1949-2011

(Trillion Btu)

Year	Primary Consumption [1]											
	Fossil Fuels				Renewable Energy [2]					Electricity Retail Sales [8]	Electrical System Energy Losses [9]	Total
	Coal	Natural Gas [3]	Petroleum [4]	Total	Geothermal [5]	Solar/PV [6]	Biomass [7]	Total	Total Primary			
1949	1,272	1,027	1,106	3,405	NA	NA	1,055	1,055	4,460	228	911	5,599
1950	1,261	1,240	1,322	3,824	NA	NA	1,006	1,006	4,829	246	913	5,989
1955	867	2,198	1,767	4,833	NA	NA	775	775	5,608	438	1,232	7,278
1960	585	3,212	2,227	6,024	NA	NA	627	627	6,651	687	1,701	9,039
1965	352	4,028	2,432	6,811	NA	NA	468	468	7,279	993	2,367	10,639
1970	209	4,987	2,725	7,922	NA	NA	401	401	8,322	1,591	3,852	13,766
1975	63	5,023	2,479	7,564	NA	NA	425	425	7,990	2,007	4,817	14,813
1976	59	5,147	2,703	7,910	NA	NA	482	482	8,391	2,069	4,950	15,410
1977	57	4,913	2,681	7,652	NA	NA	542	542	8,194	2,202	5,267	15,662
1978	49	4,981	2,607	7,638	NA	NA	622	622	8,260	2,301	5,571	16,132
1979	37	5,055	2,099	7,191	NA	NA	728	728	7,919	2,330	5,564	15,813
1980	31	4,825	1,734	6,589	NA	NA	850	850	7,439	2,448	5,866	15,753
1981	30	4,614	1,531	6,175	NA	NA	870	870	7,045	2,464	5,752	15,262
1982	32	4,711	1,434	6,177	NA	NA	970	970	7,147	2,489	5,895	15,531
1983	31	4,478	1,353	5,862	NA	NA	970	970	6,832	2,562	6,031	15,425
1984	40	4,661	1,531	6,231	NA	NA	980	980	7,211	2,662	6,087	15,960
1985	39	4,534	1,565	6,138	NA	NA	1,010	1,010	7,148	2,709	6,184	16,041
1986	40	4,405	1,541	5,986	NA	NA	920	920	6,906	2,795	6,274	15,975
1987	37	4,420	1,617	6,073	NA	NA	850	850	6,923	2,902	6,438	16,263
1988	37	4,735	1,675	6,447	NA	NA	910	910	7,357	3,046	6,729	17,133
1989	31	4,899	1,660	6,590	5	52	920	977	7,567	3,090	7,129	17,786
1990	31	4,491	1,394	5,916	6	56	580	641	6,557	3,153	7,235	16,945
1991	25	4,667	1,381	6,073	6	57	610	673	6,747	3,260	7,414	17,420
1992	26	4,805	1,414	6,244	6	R60	640	706	6,950	3,193	7,212	17,356
1993	26	5,063	1,439	6,528	7	61	550	618	7,146	3,394	7,677	18,218
1994	21	4,960	1,408	6,389	6	63	520	589	6,978	3,441	7,693	18,112
1995	17	4,954	1,374	6,345	7	64	520	591	6,936	3,557	8,026	18,519
1996	17	5,354	1,484	6,854	7	65	540	612	R7,467	3,694	8,344	19,504
1997	16	5,093	1,422	6,531	8	64	430	502	7,033	3,671	8,261	18,965
1998	12	4,646	1,304	5,962	8	64	380	452	6,413	3,856	8,686	18,955
1999	14	4,835	1,465	6,314	9	63	390	461	6,775	3,906	8,875	19,557
2000	11	5,105	1,554	6,670	9	R61	420	489	7,159	4,069	9,197	20,425
2001	12	4,889	1,529	6,430	9	59	370	438	6,868	4,100	9,074	20,042
2002	12	R4,995	1,457	R6,464	10	57	380	448	R6,912	4,317	9,562	R20,791
2003	12	5,209	1,519	6,741	13	57	400	470	7,211	4,353	9,546	21,110
2004	11	4,981	1,520	6,513	14	57	410	481	6,993	4,408	9,691	21,093
2005	8	4,946	1,451	6,406	16	58	430	504	6,909	4,638	10,079	21,626
2006	6	4,476	1,224	5,706	18	63	R380	R462	R6,168	4,611	9,909	R20,688
2007	8	R4,835	1,254	R6,097	22	70	R410	R502	R6,598	4,750	10,182	R21,531
2008	8	5,010	1,243	6,261	26	80	450	R557	6,817	4,708	10,071	21,596
2009	8	4,883	1,176	6,067	33	89	430	552	6,619	4,656	9,789	R21,064
2010	7	R4,883	R1,142	R6,032	37	R114	420	R571	R6,603	R4,933	R10,326	R21,862
2011P	6	4,830	1,139	5,975	40	140	430	610	6,585	4,858	10,176	21,619

[1] See "Primary Energy Consumption" in Glossary.
[2] Data are estimates. See Table 10.2a for notes on series components.
[3] Natural gas only; excludes the estimated portion of supplemental gaseous fuels. See Note 1, "Supplemental Gaseous Fuels," at end of Section 6.
[4] Based on petroleum product supplied. For petroleum, product supplied is used as an approximation of petroleum consumption. See Note 1, "Petroleum Products Supplied and Petroleum Consumption," at end of Section 5.
[5] Geothermal heat pump and direct use energy.
[6] Solar thermal direct use energy, and photovoltaic (PV) electricity net generation (converted to Btu using the fossil-fuels heat rate—see Table A6). Includes small amounts of distributed solar thermal and PV energy used in the commercial, industrial, and electric power sectors.
[7] Wood and wood-derived fuels.
[8] Electricity retail sales to ultimate customers reported by electric utilities and, beginning in 1996, other energy service providers.
[9] Total losses are calculated as the primary energy consumed by the electric power sector minus the energy content of electricity retail sales. Total losses are allocated to the end-use sectors in proportion to each sector's share of total electricity retail sales. See Note, "Electrical System Energy Losses," at end of section.

R=Revised. P=Preliminary. NA=Not available.

Note: Totals may not equal sum of components due to independent rounding.

Web Pages: • See http://www.eia.gov/totalenergy/data/monthly/#consumption for updated monthly and annual data. • See http://www.eia.gov/totalenergy/data/annual/#consumption for all annual data beginning in 1949.

Sources: Tables 2.1f, 5.14a, 6.5, 7.3, 8.9, 10.2a, A4, A5, and A6.

Source: *U.S. Energy Information Administration, Annual Energy Review 2011*

Table 2.1c Commercial Sector Energy Consumption Estimates, Selected Years, 1949-2011
(Trillion Btu)

	Primary Consumption [1]													
	Fossil Fuels				Renewable Energy [2]									
Year	Coal	Natural Gas [3]	Petroleum [4,5]	Total	Hydroelectric Power [6]	Geothermal [7]	Solar/PV [8]	Wind [9]	Biomass [10]	Total	Total Primary	Electricity Retail Sales [11]	Electrical System Energy Losses [12]	Total
1949	1,554	360	735	2,649	NA	NA	NA	NA	20	20	2,669	200	800	3,669
1950	1,542	401	872	2,815	NA	NA	NA	NA	19	19	2,834	225	834	3,893
1955	801	651	1,095	2,547	NA	NA	NA	NA	15	15	2,561	350	984	3,895
1960	407	1,056	1,248	2,711	NA	NA	NA	NA	12	12	2,723	543	1,344	4,609
1965	265	1,490	1,413	3,168	NA	NA	NA	NA	9	9	3,177	789	1,880	5,845
1970	165	2,473	1,592	4,229	NA	NA	NA	NA	8	8	4,237	1,201	2,908	8,346
1975	147	2,558	1,346	4,051	NA	NA	NA	NA	8	8	4,059	1,598	3,835	9,492
1976	144	2,718	1,500	4,362	NA	NA	NA	NA	9	9	4,371	1,678	4,014	10,063
1977	148	2,548	1,552	4,248	NA	NA	NA	NA	10	10	4,258	1,754	4,196	10,208
1978	165	2,643	1,490	4,297	NA	NA	NA	NA	12	12	4,309	1,813	4,390	10,512
1979	149	2,836	1,367	4,352	NA	NA	NA	NA	14	14	4,366	1,854	4,428	10,648
1980	115	2,651	1,318	4,084	NA	NA	NA	NA	21	21	4,105	1,906	4,567	10,578
1981	137	2,557	1,122	3,816	NA	NA	NA	NA	21	21	3,837	2,033	4,746	10,616
1982	155	2,650	1,037	3,842	NA	NA	NA	NA	22	22	3,864	2,077	4,919	10,860
1983	162	2,486	1,170	3,818	NA	NA	NA	NA	22	22	3,840	2,116	4,982	10,938
1984	169	2,582	1,227	3,978	NA	NA	NA	NA	22	22	4,001	2,264	5,179	11,444
1985	137	2,488	1,083	3,708	NA	NA	NA	NA	24	24	3,732	2,351	5,368	11,451
1986	135	2,367	1,162	3,665	NA	NA	NA	NA	27	27	3,693	2,439	5,475	11,606
1987	125	2,489	1,131	3,745	NA	NA	NA	NA	30	30	3,774	2,539	5,633	11,946
1988	131	2,731	1,099	3,961	NA	NA	NA	NA	33	33	3,994	2,675	5,909	12,578
1989	115	2,785	1,041	3,941	1	3	–	–	99	102	4,043	2,767	6,384	13,193
1990	124	2,682	991	3,798	1	3	–	–	94	98	3,896	2,860	6,564	13,320
1991	116	2,795	935	3,846	1	3	–	–	95	100	3,945	2,918	6,636	13,500
1992	117	2,871	893	3,881	1	3	–	–	105	109	3,991	2,900	6,550	13,441
1993	117	2,923	819	3,859	1	3	–	–	109	114	3,973	3,019	6,828	13,820
1994	118	2,962	825	3,905	1	4	–	–	106	112	4,016	3,116	6,966	14,098
1995	117	3,096	769	3,982	1	5	–	–	113	118	4,101	3,252	7,338	14,690
1996	122	3,226	790	4,138	1	5	–	–	129	135	4,273	3,344	7,555	15,172
1997	129	3,285	743	4,157	1	6	–	–	131	138	4,295	3,503	7,883	15,681
1998	93	3,083	702	3,878	1	7	–	–	118	127	4,005	3,678	8,285	15,968
1999	103	3,115	707	3,925	1	7	–	–	121	129	4,053	3,766	8,557	16,376
2000	92	3,252	807	4,150	1	8	–	–	119	128	4,278	3,956	8,942	17,175
2001	97	3,097	790	3,984	1	8	–	–	92	101	4,084	4,062	8,990	17,137
2002	90	R3,212	726	R4,028	(s)	9	–	–	95	104	R4,132	4,110	9,104	R17,345
2003	82	3,261	827	4,170	1	11	–	–	101	113	4,283	4,090	8,969	17,343
2004	103	3,201	809	4,113	1	12	–	–	105	118	4,232	4,198	9,229	17,659
2005	97	3,073	761	3,932	1	14	–	–	105	R120	4,051	4,351	9,455	R17,857
2006	65	2,902	663	3,629	1	14	–	–	R103	R118	R3,747	4,435	9,529	R17,711
2007	70	R3,085	649	R3,805	1	14	–	–	R103	118	R3,922	4,560	9,773	R18,255
2008	69	3,228	651	3,948	1	15	(s)	–	109	125	4,073	4,558	9,749	18,381
2009	63	3,187	682	3,932	1	17	(s)	(s)	112	129	4,061	4,460	9,378	17,899
2010	R60	R3,164	R685	R3,908	1	19	(s)	(s)	R111	R130	R4,039	R4,539	R9,501	R18,078
2011P	51	3,225	683	3,959	1	20	(s)	(s)	110	131	4,090	4,501	9,429	18,021

1 See "Primary Energy Consumption" in Glossary.
2 Most data are estimates. See Table 10.2a for notes on series components and estimation.
3 Natural gas only; excludes the estimated portion of supplemental gaseous fuels. See Note 1, "Supplemental Gaseous Fuels," at end of Section 6.
4 Based on petroleum product supplied. For petroleum, product supplied is used as an approximation of petroleum consumption. See Note 1, "Petroleum Products Supplied and Petroleum Consumption," at end of Section 5.
5 Does not include biofuels that have been blended with petroleum—biofuels are included in "Biomass."
6 Conventional hydroelectricity net generation (converted to Btu using the fossil-fuels heat rate—see Table A6).
7 Geothermal heat pump and direct use energy.
8 Photovoltaic (PV) electricity net generation (converted to Btu using the fossil-fuels heat rate—see Table A6) at commercial plants with capacity of 1 megawatt or greater.
9 Wind electricity net generation (converted to Btu using the fossil-fuels heat rate—see Table A6).
10 Wood and wood-derived fuels; municipal solid waste from biogenic sources, landfill gas, sludge waste, agricultural byproducts, and other biomass; and fuel ethanol (minus denaturant). Through 2000, also includes non-renewable waste (municipal solid waste from non-biogenic sources, and tire-derived fuels).
11 Electricity retail sales to ultimate customers reported by electric utilities and, beginning in 1996, other energy service providers.
12 Total losses are calculated as the primary energy consumed by the electric power sector minus the energy content of electricity retail sales. Total losses are allocated to the end-use sectors in proportion to each sector's share of total electricity retail sales. See Note, "Electrical System Energy Losses," at end of section.

R=Revised. P=Preliminary. NA=Not available. – =No data reported. (s)=Less than 0.5 trillion Btu.

Notes: • The commercial sector includes commercial combined-heat-and-power (CHP) and commercial electricity-only plants. See Note 2, "Classification of Power Plants Into Energy-Use Sectors," at end of Section 3. • Totals may not equal sum of components due to independent rounding.

Web Pages: • See http://www.eia.gov/totalenergy/data/monthly/#consumption for updated monthly and annual data. • See http://www.eia.gov/totalenergy/data/annual/#consumption for all annual data beginning in 1949.

Sources: Tables 2.1f, 5.14a, 6.5, 7.3, 8.9, 10.2a, A4, A5, and A6.

Source: U.S. Energy Information Administration, Annual Energy Review 2011

Table 2.1d Industrial Sector Energy Consumption Estimates, Selected Years, 1949-2011

(Trillion Btu)

	Primary Consumption [1]														
	Fossil Fuels						Renewable Energy [2]								
Year	Coal	Coal Coke Net Imports	Natural Gas [3]	Petroleum [4,5]	Total	Hydroelectric Power [6]	Geothermal [7]	Solar/PV [8]	Wind [9]	Biomass [10]	Total	Total Primary	Electricity Retail Sales [11]	Electrical System Energy Losses [12]	Total
1949	5,433	-7	3,188	3,475	12,090	76	NA	NA	NA	468	544	12,633	418	1,672	14,724
1950	5,781	1	3,546	3,960	13,288	69	NA	NA	NA	532	602	13,890	500	1,852	16,241
1955	5,620	-10	4,701	5,123	15,434	38	NA	NA	NA	631	669	16,103	887	2,495	19,485
1960	4,543	-6	5,973	5,766	16,277	39	NA	NA	NA	680	719	16,996	1,107	2,739	20,842
1965	5,127	-18	7,339	6,813	19,260	33	NA	NA	NA	855	888	20,148	1,463	3,487	25,098
1970	4,656	-58	9,536	7,776	21,911	34	NA	NA	NA	1,019	1,053	22,964	1,948	4,716	29,628
1975	3,667	14	8,532	8,127	20,339	32	NA	NA	NA	1,063	1,096	21,434	2,346	5,632	29,413
1976	3,661	(s)	8,762	8,990	21,412	33	NA	NA	NA	1,220	1,253	22,665	2,573	6,155	31,393
1977	3,454	15	8,635	9,747	21,851	33	NA	NA	NA	1,281	1,314	23,165	2,682	6,416	32,263
1978	3,314	125	8,539	9,835	21,812	32	NA	NA	NA	1,400	1,432	23,244	2,761	6,683	32,688
1979	3,593	63	8,549	10,548	22,753	34	NA	NA	NA	1,405	1,439	24,192	2,873	6,860	33,925
1980	3,155	-35	8,333	9,509	20,962	33	NA	NA	NA	1,600	1,633	22,595	2,781	6,664	32,039
1981	3,157	-16	8,185	8,265	19,590	33	NA	NA	NA	1,695	1,728	21,318	2,817	6,576	30,712
1982	2,552	-22	7,068	7,772	17,370	33	NA	NA	NA	1,650	1,683	19,053	2,542	6,020	27,614
1983	2,490	-16	6,776	7,390	16,640	33	NA	NA	NA	1,874	1,908	18,548	2,648	6,232	27,428
1984	2,842	-11	7,405	7,987	18,222	33	NA	NA	NA	1,918	1,951	20,174	2,859	6,538	29,570
1985	2,760	-13	7,032	7,714	17,492	33	NA	NA	NA	1,918	1,951	19,443	2,855	6,518	28,816
1986	2,641	-17	6,646	7,860	17,130	33	NA	NA	NA	1,915	1,948	19,078	2,834	6,362	28,274
1987	2,673	9	7,283	8,042	18,006	33	NA	NA	NA	1,914	1,947	19,953	2,928	6,497	29,379
1988	2,828	40	7,655	8,317	18,840	33	NA	NA	NA	1,989	2,022	20,862	3,059	6,757	30,677
1989	2,787	30	8,088	8,098	19,003	28	2	–	–	1,841	1,871	20,874	3,158	7,288	31,320
1990	2,756	5	8,451	8,251	19,463	31	2	–	–	1,684	1,717	21,180	3,226	7,404	31,810
1991	2,601	10	8,572	7,958	19,141	30	2	–	–	1,652	1,684	20,824	3,230	7,345	31,399
1992	2,515	35	8,918	8,552	20,019	31	2	–	–	1,705	1,737	21,756	3,319	7,496	32,571
1993	2,496	27	9,070	8,386	19,980	30	2	–	–	1,741	1,773	21,753	3,334	7,541	32,629
1994	2,510	58	9,126	8,771	20,465	62	3	–	–	1,862	1,927	22,393	3,439	7,689	33,521
1995	2,488	61	9,592	8,586	20,727	55	3	–	–	1,934	1,992	22,719	3,455	7,796	33,971
1996	2,434	23	9,901	9,019	21,377	61	3	–	–	1,969	2,033	23,410	3,527	7,968	34,904
1997	2,395	46	9,933	9,255	21,629	58	3	–	–	1,996	2,057	23,686	3,542	7,972	35,200
1998	2,335	67	9,763	9,082	21,248	55	3	–	–	1,872	1,929	23,177	3,587	8,079	34,843
1999	2,227	58	9,375	9,356	21,016	49	4	–	–	1,882	1,934	22,950	3,611	8,203	34,764
2000	2,256	65	9,500	9,075	20,896	42	4	–	–	1,881	1,928	22,824	3,631	8,208	34,664
2001	2,192	29	8,676	9,178	20,075	33	5	–	–	1,681	1,719	21,794	3,400	7,526	32,720
2002	2,019	61	R8,832	9,168	R20,079	39	5	–	–	1,676	1,720	R21,799	3,379	7,484	R32,662
2003	2,041	51	8,488	9,197	19,777	43	3	–	–	1,679	1,726	21,503	3,454	7,575	32,532
2004	2,047	138	R8,550	9,825	R20,559	33	4	–	–	1,817	1,853	R22,412	3,473	7,635	R33,520
2005	1,954	44	R7,907	9,633	R19,538	32	4	–	–	1,837	1,873	R21,411	3,477	7,557	R32,446
2006	1,914	61	R7,861	9,770	R19,606	29	4	–	–	1,897	1,930	R21,536	3,451	7,415	R32,401
2007	1,865	25	R8,074	9,451	R19,414	16	5	–	–	R1,936	R1,956	R21,370	3,507	7,517	R32,394
2008	1,796	41	R8,083	8,511	R18,431	17	5	–	–	R2,028	R2,049	R20,480	3,444	7,365	R31,290
2009	1,396	-24	7,609	7,816	R16,797	18	4	–	–	R1,994	R2,016	R18,813	3,130	6,582	R28,525
2010	R1,649	-6	R7,959	R8,210	R17,812	16	4	(s)	–	R2,230	R2,250	R20,062	R3,313	R6,934	R30,309
2011P	1,599	11	8,321	8,064	17,995	18	4	(s)	(s)	2,273	2,295	20,291	3,329	6,973	30,592

[1] See "Primary Energy Consumption" in Glossary.
[2] Most data are estimates. See Table 10.2b for notes on series components and estimation.
[3] Natural gas only; excludes the estimated portion of supplemental gaseous fuels. See Note 1, "Supplemental Gaseous Fuels," at end of Section 6.
[4] Based on petroleum product supplied. For petroleum, product supplied is used as an approximation of petroleum consumption. See Note 1, "Petroleum Products Supplied and Petroleum Consumption," at end of Section 5.
[5] Does not include biofuels that have been blended with petroleum—biofuels are included in "Biomass."
[6] Conventional hydroelectricity net generation (converted to Btu using the fossil-fuels heat rate—see Table A6).
[7] Geothermal heat pump and direct use energy.
[8] Photovoltaic (PV) electricity net generation (converted to Btu using the fossil-fuels heat rate—see Table A6) at industrial plants with capacity of 1 megawatt or greater.
[9] Wind electricity net generation (converted to Btu using the fossil-fuels heat rate—see Table A6).
[10] Wood and wood-derived fuels; municipal solid waste from biogenic sources, landfill gas, sludge waste, agricultural byproducts, and other biomass; fuel ethanol (minus denaturant); and losses and co-products from the production of fuel ethanol and biodiesel. Through 2000, also includes non-renewable waste (municipal solid waste from non-biogenic sources, and tire-derived fuels).
[11] Electricity retail sales to ultimate customers reported by electric utilities and, beginning in 1996, other energy service providers.
[12] Total losses are calculated as the primary energy consumed by the electric power sector minus the energy content of electricity retail sales. Total losses are allocated to the end-use sectors in proportion to each sector's share of total electricity retail sales. See Note, "Electrical System Energy Losses," at end of section.

R=Revised. P=Preliminary. NA=Not available. – =No data reported. (s)=Less than +0.5 trillion Btu and greater than -0.5 trillion Btu.

Notes: • The industrial sector includes industrial combined-heat-and-power (CHP) and industrial electricity-only plants. See Note 2, "Classification of Power Plants Into Energy-Use Sectors," at end of Section 8. • Totals may not equal sum of components due to independent rounding.

Web Pages: • See http://www.eia.gov/totalenergy/data/monthly/#consumption for updated monthly and annual data. • See http://www.eia.gov/totalenergy/data/annual/#consumption for all annual data beginning in 1949.

Sources: Tables 2.1f, 5.14b, 6.5, 7.3, 7.8, 8.9, 10.2b, A4, A5, and A6.

Source: *U.S. Energy Information Administration, Annual Energy Review 2011*

Table 2.1e Transportation Sector Energy Consumption Estimates, Selected Years, 1949-2011

(Trillion Btu)

Year	Primary Consumption [1]						Electricity Retail Sales [7]	Electrical System Energy Losses [8]	Total
	Fossil Fuels				Renewable Energy [2]	Total Primary			
	Coal	Natural Gas [3]	Petroleum [4,5]	Total	Biomass [6]				
1949	1,727	NA	6,152	7,880	NA	7,880	22	88	7,990
1950	1,564	130	6,690	8,383	NA	8,383	23	86	8,492
1955	421	254	8,799	9,474	NA	9,474	20	56	9,550
1960	75	359	10,125	10,560	NA	10,560	10	26	10,596
1965	16	517	11,866	12,399	NA	12,399	10	24	12,432
1970	7	745	15,310	16,062	NA	16,062	11	26	16,098
1975	1	595	17,615	18,210	NA	18,210	10	24	18,245
1976	(s)	559	18,508	19,067	NA	19,067	10	24	19,101
1977	(s)	543	19,243	19,786	NA	19,786	10	25	19,822
1978	([9])	539	20,044	20,583	NA	20,583	10	24	20,617
1979	([9])	612	19,825	20,437	NA	20,437	10	24	20,472
1980	([9])	650	19,009	19,659	NA	19,659	11	27	19,697
1981	([9])	658	18,813	19,471	7	19,478	11	25	19,514
1982	([9])	612	18,422	19,034	18	19,052	11	26	19,089
1983	([9])	505	18,595	19,100	34	19,134	13	30	19,177
1984	([9])	545	19,023	19,567	41	19,609	14	33	19,656
1985	([9])	519	19,472	19,992	50	20,041	14	32	20,088
1986	([9])	499	20,183	20,682	57	20,740	15	34	20,789
1987	([9])	535	20,817	21,353	66	21,419	16	35	21,469
1988	([9])	632	21,568	22,199	67	22,267	16	35	22,318
1989	([9])	649	21,707	22,356	68	22,424	16	38	22,478
1990	([9])	680	21,626	22,306	60	22,366	16	37	22,420
1991	([9])	620	21,374	21,995	70	22,065	16	37	22,118
1992	([9])	608	21,675	22,283	80	22,363	16	36	22,415
1993	([9])	645	21,977	22,621	94	22,715	16	37	22,768
1994	([9])	709	22,497	23,206	105	23,311	17	38	23,366
1995	([9])	724	22,955	23,679	112	23,791	17	38	23,846
1996	([9])	737	23,565	24,302	81	24,383	17	38	24,437
1997	([9])	780	23,813	24,593	102	24,695	17	38	24,750
1998	([9])	666	24,422	25,088	113	25,201	17	38	25,256
1999	([9])	675	25,098	25,774	118	25,891	17	40	25,949
2000	([9])	672	25,682	26,354	135	26,489	18	42	26,548
2001	([9])	658	25,412	26,070	142	26,213	20	43	26,275
2002	([9])	R699	25,913	R26,612	170	R26,781	19	42	R26,842
2003	([9])	627	26,063	26,690	230	26,920	23	51	26,994
2004	([9])	602	26,925	27,527	290	27,817	25	54	27,895
2005	([9])	624	27,309	27,933	339	28,272	26	56	28,353
2006	([9])	625	27,651	28,276	475	28,751	25	54	28,830
2007	([9])	R663	27,763	R28,427	602	R29,029	28	60	R29,117
2008	([9])	692	26,407	27,099	826	27,925	26	56	28,008
2009	([9])	R715	25,339	R26,054	R935	R26,989	27	56	R27,071
2010	([9])	R716	R25,595	R26,310	R1,074	R27,384	26	55	R27,466
2011P	([9])	735	25,110	25,845	1,154	26,999	26	54	27,079

1 See "Primary Energy Consumption" in Glossary.

2 Data are estimates. See Table 10.2b for notes on series components.

3 Natural gas only; does not include supplemental gaseous fuels—see Note 1, "Supplemental Gaseous Fuels," at end of Section 6. Data are for natural gas consumed in the operation of pipelines (primarily in compressors) and small amounts consumed as vehicle fuel—see Table 6.5.

4 Based on petroleum product supplied. For petroleum, product supplied is used as an approximation of petroleum consumption. See Note 1, "Petroleum Products Supplied and Petroleum Consumption," at end of Section 5.

5 Does not include biofuels that have been blended with petroleum—biofuels are included in "Biomass."

6 Fuel ethanol (minus denaturant) and biodiesel.

7 Electricity retail sales to ultimate customers reported by electric utilities and, beginning in 1996, other energy service providers.

8 Total losses are calculated as the primary energy consumed by the electric power sector minus the energy content of electricity retail sales. Total losses are allocated to the end-use sectors in proportion to each sector's share of total electricity retail sales. See Note, "Electrical System Energy Losses," at end of section.

9 Beginning in 1978, the small amounts of coal consumed for transportation are reported as industrial sector consumption.

R=Revised. P=Preliminary. NA=Not available. (s)=Less than 0.5 trillion Btu.

Note: Totals may not equal sum of components due to independent rounding.

Web Pages: • See http://www.eia.gov/totalenergy/data/monthly/#consumption for updated monthly and annual data. • See http://www.eia.gov/totalenergy/data/annual/#consumption for all annual data beginning in 1949.

Sources: Tables 2.1f, 5.14c, 6.5, 7.3, 8.9, 10.2b, A4, A5, and A6.

Source: *U.S. Energy Information Administration, Annual Energy Review 2011*

Table 2.1f Electric Power Sector Energy Consumption, Selected Years, 1949-2011

(Trillion Btu)

	Primary Consumption [1]													
	Fossil Fuels					Renewable Energy [2]								
Year	Coal	Natural Gas [3]	Petroleum [4]	Total	Nuclear Electric Power [5]	Hydroelectric Power [6]	Geothermal [7]	Solar/PV [8]	Wind [9]	Biomass [10]	Total	Electricity Net Imports [11]	Total Primary
1949	1,995	569	415	2,979	0	1,349	NA	NA	NA	6	1,355	5	4,339
1950	2,199	651	472	3,322	0	1,346	NA	NA	NA	5	1,351	6	4,679
1955	3,458	1,194	471	5,123	0	1,322	NA	NA	NA	3	1,325	14	6,461
1960	4,228	1,785	553	6,565	6	1,569	(s)	NA	NA	2	1,571	15	8,158
1965	5,821	2,395	722	8,938	43	2,026	2	NA	NA	3	2,031	(s)	11,012
1970	7,227	4,054	2,117	13,399	239	2,600	6	NA	NA	4	2,609	7	16,253
1975	8,786	3,240	3,166	15,191	1,900	3,122	34	NA	NA	2	3,158	21	20,270
1976	9,720	3,152	3,477	16,349	2,111	2,943	38	NA	NA	3	2,983	29	21,473
1977	10,262	3,284	3,901	17,446	2,702	2,301	37	NA	NA	5	2,343	59	22,551
1978	10,238	3,297	3,987	17,522	3,024	2,905	31	NA	NA	3	2,940	67	23,553
1979	11,260	3,613	3,283	18,156	2,776	2,897	40	NA	NA	5	2,942	69	23,943
1980	12,123	3,778	2,634	18,534	2,739	2,867	53	NA	NA	5	2,925	71	24,269
1981	12,583	3,730	2,202	18,516	3,008	2,725	59	NA	NA	4	2,788	113	24,425
1982	12,582	3,312	1,568	17,462	3,131	3,233	51	NA	NA	3	3,286	100	23,979
1983	13,213	2,972	1,544	17,729	3,203	3,494	64	NA	(s)	4	3,562	121	24,614
1984	14,019	3,199	1,286	18,504	3,553	3,353	81	(s)	(s)	9	3,443	135	25,635
1985	14,542	3,135	1,090	18,767	4,076	2,937	97	(s)	(s)	14	3,049	140	26,032
1986	14,444	2,670	1,452	18,566	4,380	3,038	108	(s)	(s)	12	3,158	122	26,227
1987	15,173	2,916	1,257	19,346	4,754	2,602	112	(s)	(s)	15	2,729	158	26,988
1988	15,850	2,693	1,563	20,106	5,587	2,302	106	(s)	(s)	17	2,425	108	28,227
1989[12]	16,137	3,173	1,703	21,013	5,602	2,808	152	3	22	232	3,217	37	29,869
1990	16,261	3,309	1,289	20,859	6,104	3,014	161	4	29	317	3,524	8	30,495
1991	16,250	3,377	1,198	20,825	6,422	2,985	167	5	31	354	3,542	67	30,856
1992	16,466	3,512	991	20,968	6,479	2,586	167	4	30	402	3,189	87	30,723
1993	17,196	3,538	1,124	21,857	6,410	2,861	173	5	31	415	3,484	95	31,847
1994	17,261	3,977	1,059	22,297	6,694	2,620	160	5	36	434	3,255	153	32,399
1995	17,466	4,302	755	22,523	7,075	3,149	138	5	33	422	3,747	134	33,479
1996	18,429	3,862	817	23,109	7,087	3,528	148	5	33	438	4,153	137	34,485
1997	18,905	4,126	927	23,957	6,597	3,581	150	5	34	446	4,216	116	34,886
1998	19,216	4,675	1,306	25,197	7,068	3,241	151	5	31	444	3,872	88	36,225
1999	19,279	4,902	1,211	25,393	7,610	3,218	152	5	46	453	3,874	99	36,976
2000	20,220	5,293	1,144	26,658	7,862	2,768	144	5	57	453	3,427	115	38,062
2001	19,614	5,458	1,277	26,348	8,029	2,209	142	6	70	337	2,763	75	37,215
2002	19,783	5,767	961	26,511	8,145	2,650	147	6	105	380	3,288	72	38,016
2003	20,185	5,246	1,205	26,636	7,959	2,781	148	5	115	397	3,445	22	38,062
2004	20,305	5,595	1,212	27,112	8,222	2,656	148	6	142	388	3,340	39	38,713
2005	20,737	6,015	1,235	27,986	8,161	2,670	147	6	178	406	3,406	85	39,638
2006	20,462	6,375	648	27,485	8,215	2,839	145	5	264	412	3,665	63	39,428
2007	20,808	7,005	657	28,470	8,455	2,430	145	6	341	423	3,345	107	40,377
2008	20,513	6,829	468	27,810	8,427	2,494	146	9	546	435	3,630	112	39,978
2009	18,225	7,022	390	25,638	8,356	2,650	146	9	721	441	3,967	116	38,077
2010	19,133	R7,527	378	R27,039	R8,434	R2,521	R148	R12	R923	R459	R4,064	R89	R39,626
2011P	17,986	7,740	288	26,014	8,259	3,153	163	18	1,168	444	4,945	127	39,346

[1] See "Primary Energy Consumption" in Glossary.

[2] See Table 10.2c for notes on series components.

[3] Natural gas only; excludes the estimated portion of supplemental gaseous fuels. See Note 1, "Supplemental Gaseous Fuels," at end of Section 6.

[4] See Table 5.14c for series components.

[5] Nuclear electricity net generation (converted to Btu using the nuclear heat rate—see Table A6).

[6] Conventional hydroelectricity net generation (converted to Btu using the fossil-fuels heat rate—see Table A6).

[7] Geothermal electricity net generation (converted to Btu using the fossil-fuels heat rate—see Table A6).

[8] Solar thermal and photovoltaic (PV) electricity net generation (converted to Btu using the fossil-fuels heat rate—see Table A6).

[9] Wind electricity net generation (converted to Btu using the fossil-fuels heat rate—see Table A6).

[10] Wood and wood-derived fuels; and municipal solid waste from biogenic sources, landfill gas, sludge waste, agricultural byproducts, and other biomass. Through 2000, also includes non-renewable waste (municipal solid waste from non-biogenic sources, and tire-derived fuels).

[11] Net imports equal imports minus exports.

[12] Through 1988, data are for electric utilities only. Beginning in 1989, data are for electric utilities and independent power producers.

R=Revised. P=Preliminary. NA=Not available. (s)=Less than 0.5 trillion Btu.

Notes: • Data are for fuels consumed to produce electricity and useful thermal output. • The electric power sector comprises electricity-only and combined-heat-and-power (CHP) plants within the NAICS 22 category whose primary business is to sell electricity, or electricity and heat, to the public. • See Note 3, "Electricity Imports and Exports," at end of Section 8. • Totals may not equal sum of components due to independent rounding.

Web Pages: • See http://www.eia.gov/totalenergy/data/monthly/#consumption for updated monthly and annual data. • See http://www.eia.gov/totalenergy/data/annual/#consumption for all annual data beginning in 1949.

Sources: Tables 5.14c, 6.5, 7.3, 8.1, 8.2b, 10.2c, A4, A5, and A6.

Source: *U.S. Energy Information Administration, Annual Energy Review 2011*

Figure 2.4 Household Energy Consumption

Household Energy Consumpton by Census Region, Selected Years, 1978-2009[1]

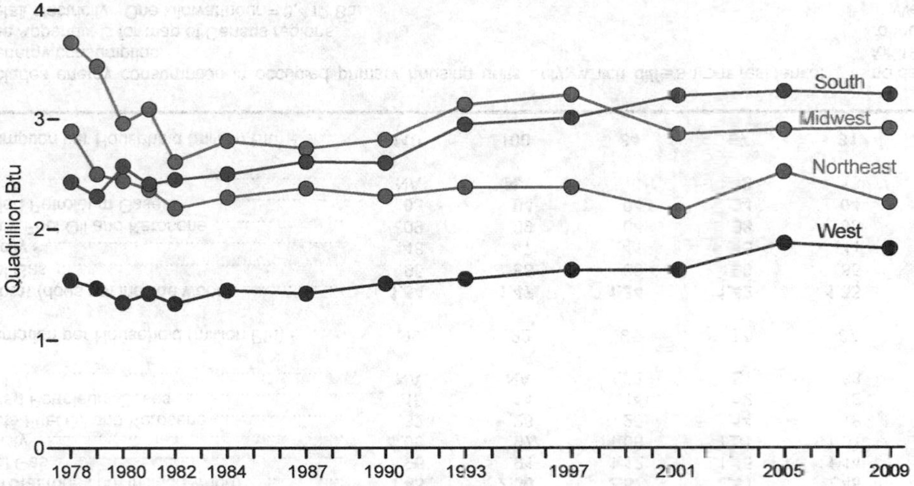

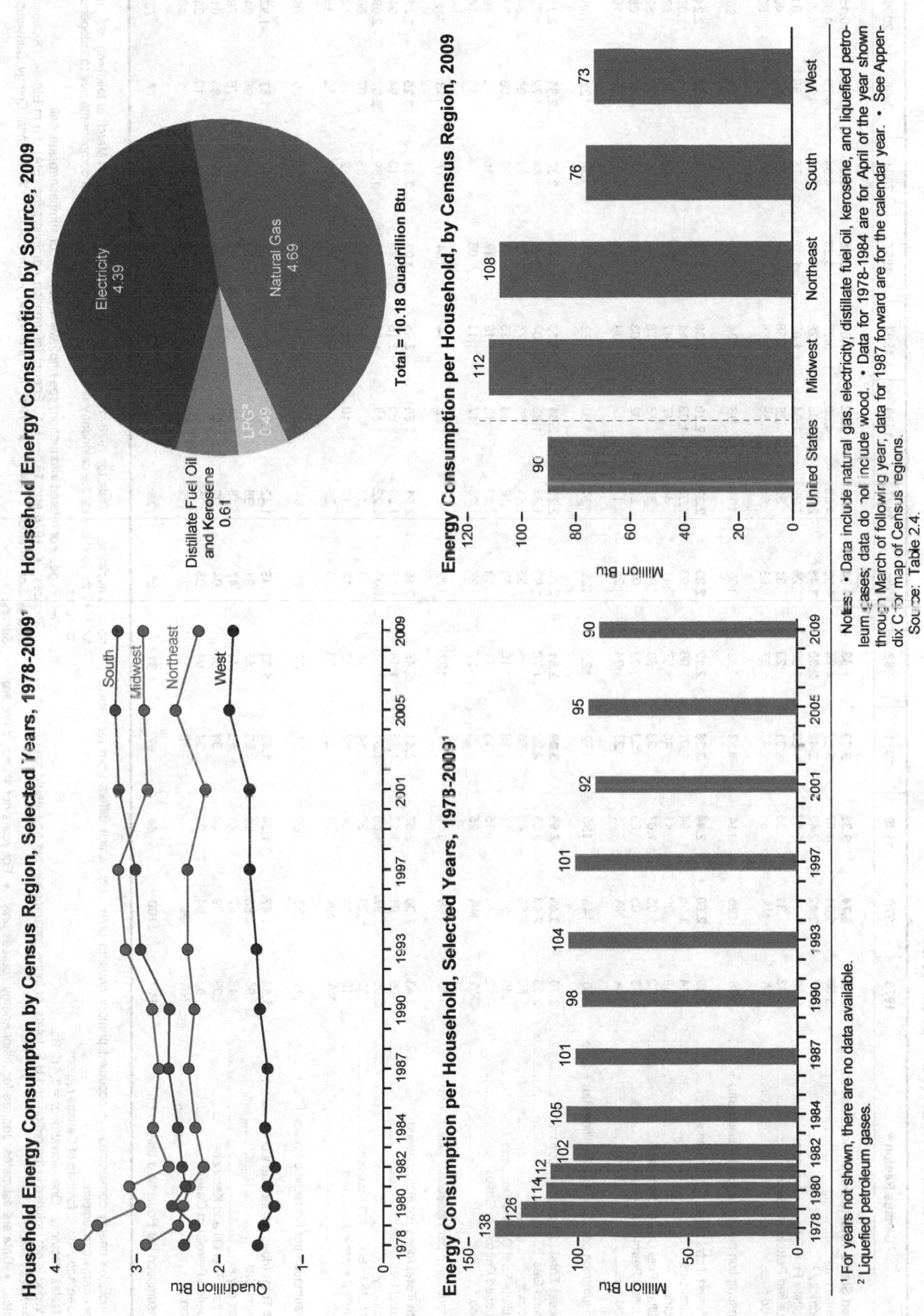

Household Energy Consumption by Source, 2009

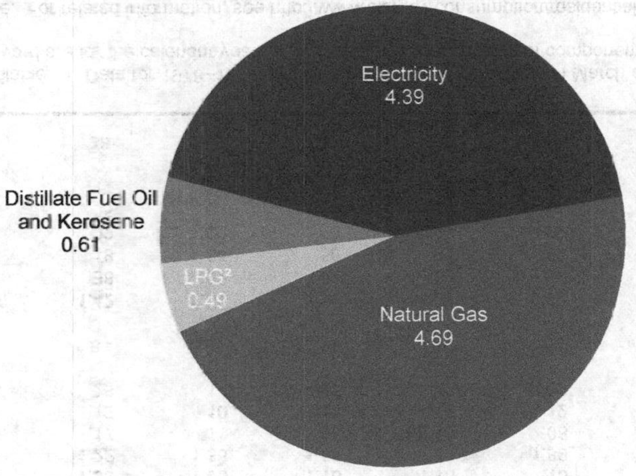

Total = 10.18 Quadrillion Btu

Energy Consumption per Household, Selected Years, 1978-2009[1]

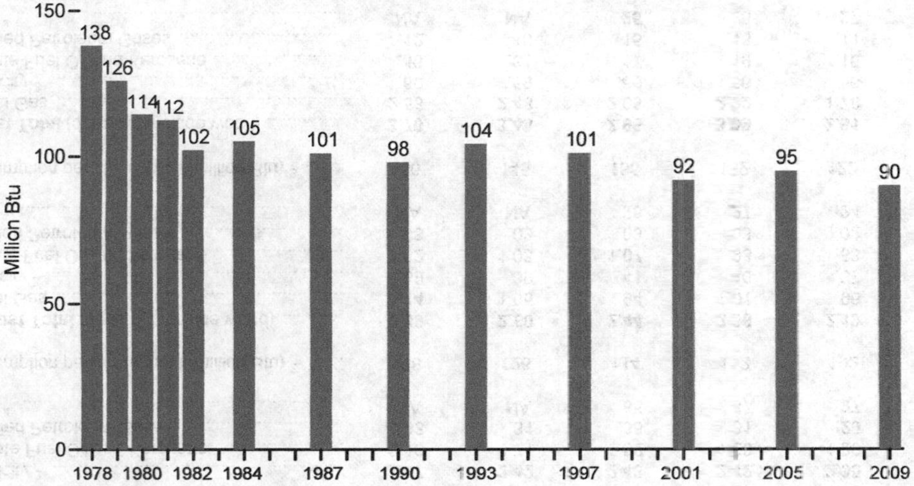

Energy Consumption per Household, by Census Region, 2009

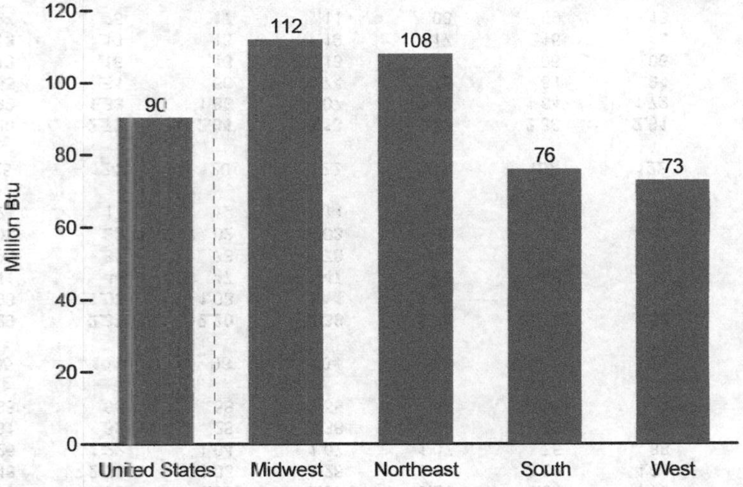

[1] For years not shown, there are no data available.
[2] Liquefied petroleum gases.

Notes: • Data include natural gas, electricity, distillate fuel oil, kerosene, and liquefied petroleum gases; data do not include wood. • Data for 1978-1984 are for April of the year shown through March of following year; data for 1987 forward are for the calendar year. • See Appendix C for map of Census regions.

Source: Table 2.4.

Source: *U.S. Energy Information Administration, Annual Energy Review 2011*

Table 2.4 Household[1] Energy Consumption by Census Region, Selected Years, 1978-2009

(Quadrillion Btu, Except as Noted)

Census Region[2]	1978	1979	1980	1981	1982	1984	1987	1990	1993	1997	2001	2005	2009
United States Total (does not include wood)	**10.56**	**9.74**	**9.32**	**9.29**	**8.58**	**9.04**	**9.13**	**9.22**	**10.01**	**10.25**	**9.86**	**10.55**	**10.18**
Natural Gas	5.58	5.31	4.97	5.27	4.74	4.98	4.83	4.86	5.27	5.28	4.84	4.79	4.69
Electricity[3]	2.47	2.42	2.48	2.42	2.35	2.48	2.76	3.03	3.28	3.54	3.89	4.35	4.39
Distillate Fuel Oil and Kerosene	2.19	1.71	1.52	1.28	1.20	1.26	1.22	1.04	1.07	1.07	.75	.88	.61
Liquefied Petroleum Gases	.33	.31	.35	.31	.29	.31	.32	.28	.38	.36	.38	.52	.49
Wood[4]	NA	NA	.85	.87	.97	.98	.85	.58	.55	.43	.37	.43	.50
Consumption per Household (million Btu)[3]	138	126	114	112	102	105	101	98	104	101	92	95	90
Northeast Total (does not include wood)	**2.89**	**2.50**	**2.44**	**2.36**	**2.19**	**2.29**	**2.37**	**2.30**	**2.38**	**2.38**	**2.16**	**2.52**	**2.24**
Natural Gas	1.14	1.05	.94	1.01	.96	.93	1.03	1.03	1.11	1.03	.98	1.15	1.06
Electricity[3]	.39	.39	.41	.40	.37	.41	.44	.47	.47	.49	.53	.58	.57
Distillate Fuel Oil and Kerosene	1.32	1.03	1.07	.93	.83	.93	.87	.78	.78	.84	.60	.72	.52
Liquefied Petroleum Gases	.03	.03	.03	.03	.02	.03	.02	.02	.03	.03	.05	.07	.08
Wood[4]	NA	NA	.26	.27	.24	.21	.17	.12	.14	.14	.10	.09	.10
Consumption per Household (million Btu)[3]	166	145	138	132	122	125	124	120	122	121	107	122	108
Midwest Total (does not include wood)	**3.70**	**3.48**	**2.96**	**3.09**	**2.61**	**2.80**	**2.73**	**2.81**	**3.13**	**3.22**	**2.86**	**2.91**	**2.91**
Natural Gas	2.53	2.48	2.05	2.22	1.78	1.99	1.83	1.88	2.07	2.20	1.84	1.72	1.75
Electricity[3]	.60	.59	.60	.56	.56	.55	.61	.66	.74	.75	.81	.94	.94
Distillate Fuel Oil and Kerosene	.46	.31	.17	.19	.16	.13	.16	.13	.13	.11	.06	.06	.03
Liquefied Petroleum Gases	.12	.10	.15	.13	.11	.13	.13	.13	.19	.17	.15	.18	.19
Wood[4]	NA	NA	.25	.25	.27	.27	.25	.17	.11	.08	.09	.13	.14
Consumption per Household (million Btu)[3]	180	168	141	146	122	129	123	122	134	134	117	113	112
South Total (does not include wood)	**2.43**	**2.30**	**2.57**	**2.41**	**2.45**	**2.50**	**2.61**	**2.60**	**2.95**	**3.01**	**3.21**	**3.25**	**3.22**
Natural Gas	.96	.91	1.12	1.15	1.14	1.15	1.09	1.03	1.18	1.13	1.13	.94	.94
Electricity[3]	1.00	.97	1.06	1.01	1.01	1.06	1.22	1.36	1.51	1.67	1.89	2.07	2.09
Distillate Fuel Oil and Kerosene	.32	.28	.25	.14	.18	.16	.17	.11	.13	.10	.08	.07	.05
Liquefied Petroleum Gases	.15	.14	.14	.12	.12	.12	.12	.10	.13	.12	.12	.18	.14
Wood[4]	NA	NA	.23	.21	.33	.33	.26	.17	.17	.12	.09	.12	.16
Consumption per Household (million Btu)[3]	99	92	95	87	87	85	84	81	88	84	83	80	76
West Total (does not include wood)	**1.54**	**1.47**	**1.34**	**1.42**	**1.33**	**1.45**	**1.42**	**1.51**	**1.55**	**1.63**	**1.63**	**1.87**	**1.82**
Natural Gas	.95	.88	.86	.90	.85	.91	.88	.92	.91	.93	.90	.98	.94
Electricity[3]	.48	.47	.41	.46	.41	.47	.48	.54	.56	.64	.66	.76	.79
Distillate Fuel Oil and Kerosene	.09	.09	.04	.03	.03	.04	.02	.02	.03	.03	.02	.03	.01
Liquefied Petroleum Gases	.03	.04	.04	.04	.04	.03	.05	.03	.04	.04	.06	.10	.08
Wood[4]	NA	NA	.11	.13	.13	.17	.17	.12	.12	.10	.10	.09	.10
Consumption per Household (million Btu)[3]	110	100	84	87	81	85	78	78	76	75	70	77	73

[1] Includes energy consumption in occupied primary housing units only, which differs from residential sector energy consumption.
[2] See Appendix C for map of Census regions.
[3] Retail electricity. One kilowatthour = 3,412 Btu.
[4] Wood is not included in the region and U.S. totals, or in the consumption-per-household data.
NA=Not available.
Notes: • Data are estimates, and are for major energy sources only. • For years not shown, there are no data available. • Data for 1978–1984 are for April of year shown through March of following year; data for 1987 forward are for the calendar year. • Totals may not equal sum of components due to independent rounding.
Web Page: For related information, see http://www.eia.gov/consumption/residential/.
Sources: • 1978 and 1979—U.S. Energy Information Administration (EIA), Form EIA-84, "Residential Energy Consumption Survey." • 1980 forward—EIA, Form EIA-457, "Residential Energy Consumption Survey."

Source: *U.S. Energy Information Administration, Annual Energy Review 2011*

Figure 2.5 Household Energy Consumption and Expenditures

Household Energy Consumption by End Use, Selected Years, 1978-2005[1]

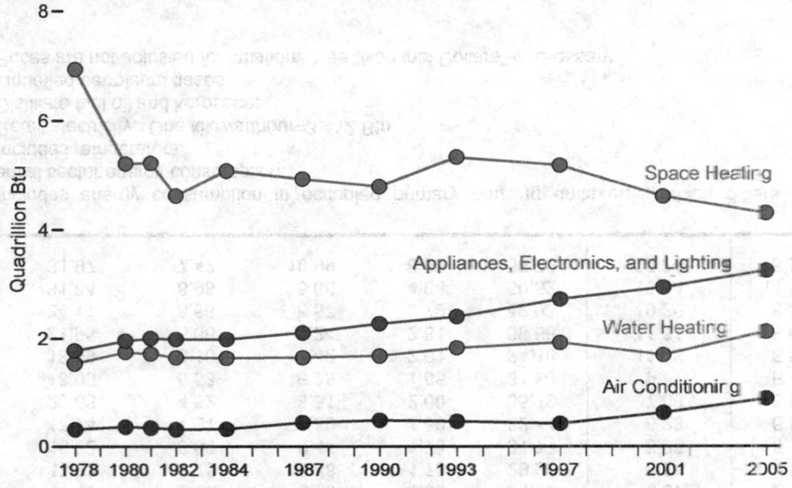

Household Energy Expenditures, Selected Years, 1978-2005[1]

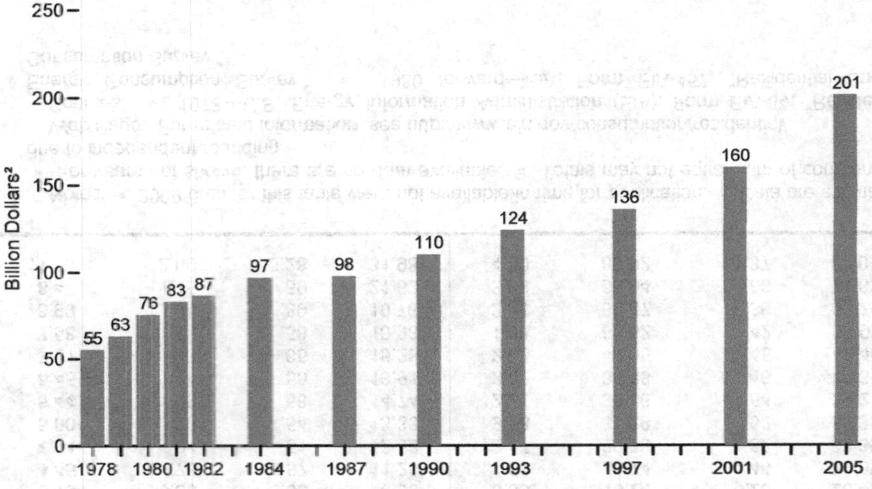

Household Energy Consumption for Space Heating by Fuel 2005

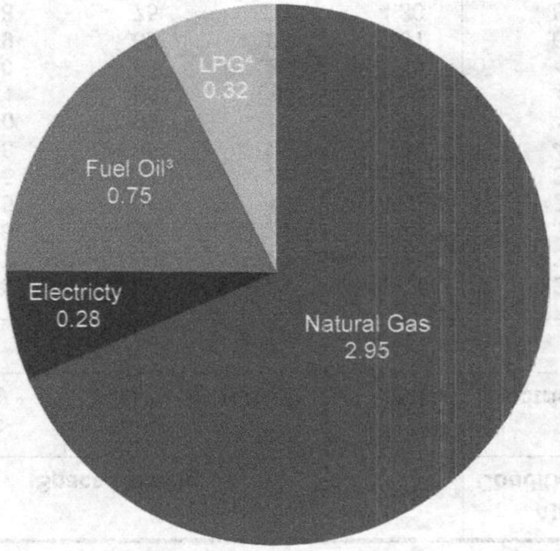

Total = 4.30 Quadrillion Btu

Appliances, Electronics, and Lighting Expenditures, Selected Years, 1978-2005[1]

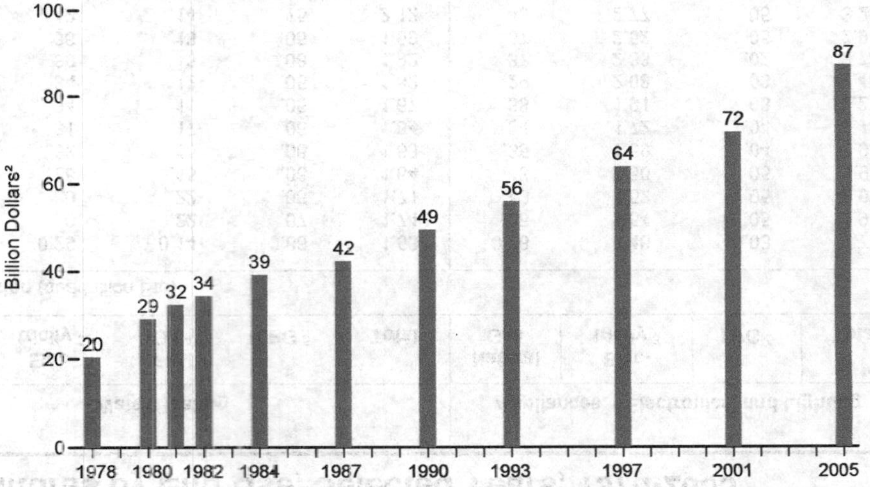

[1] For years not shown, there are no data available.
[2] Prices are not adjusted for inflation. See "Nominal Dollars" in Glossary.
[3] Distillate fuel oil and kerosene.
[4] Liquefied petroleum gases
Source: Table 2.5.

***Source:** U.S. Energy Information Administration, Annual Energy Review 2011*

Table 2.5 Household [1] Energy Consumption and Expenditures by End Use, Selected Years, 1978-2005

Year	Space Heating					Air Conditioning	Water Heating					Appliances, [2] Electronics, and Lighting			
	Natural Gas	Elec-tricity [3]	Fuel Oil [4]	LPG [5]	Total	Electricity [3]	Natural Gas	Elec-tricity [3]	Fuel Oil [4]	LPG [5]	Total	Natural Gas	Elec-tricity [3]	LPG [5]	Total
	Consumption (quadrillion Btu)														
1978	4.26	0.40	2.05	0.23	6.94	0.31	1.04	0.29	0.14	0.06	1.53	0.28	1.46	0.03	1.77
1980	3.41	.27	1.30	.23	5.21	.36	1.15	.30	.22	.07	1.74	.36	1.54	.05	1.95
1981	3.69	.26	1.06	.21	5.22	.34	1.13	.30	.22	.06	1.71	.43	1.52	.05	2.00
1982	3.14	.25	1.04	.19	4.62	.31	1.15	.28	.15	.06	1.64	.43	1.50	.05	1.98
1984	3.51	.25	1.11	.21	5.08	.32	1.10	.32	.15	.06	1.63	.35	1.59	.04	1.98
1987	3.38	.28	1.05	.22	4.93	.44	1.10	.31	.17	.06	1.64	.34	1.72	.04	2.10
1990	3.37	.30	.93	.19	4.79	.48	1.16	.34	.11	.06	1.67	.33	1.91	.03	2.27
1993	3.67	.41	.95	.30	5.33	.46	1.31	.34	.12	.05	1.82	.29	2.08	.03	2.40
1997	3.61	.40	.91	.26	5.18	.42	1.29	.39	.16	.08	1.92	.37	2.33	.02	2.72
2001	3.32	.39	.62	.28	4.61	.62	1.15	.36	.13	.05	1.69	.37	2.52	.05	2.94
2005	2.95	.28	.75	.32	4.30	.88	1.41	.42	.14	.15	2.12	.43	2.77	.05	3.25
	Expenditures (billion nominal dollars [6])														
1978	11.49	3.53	8.06	1.05	24.13	3.97	2.88	3.15	0.56	0.36	6.95	0.93	19.24	0.25	20.42
1980	13.22	3.78	10.48	1.78	29.26	5.84	4.51	4.45	1.76	.57	11.29	1.91	26.74	.44	29.09
1981	16.62	3.93	9.44	1.78	31.77	6.23	5.13	4.94	1.94	.51	12.52	2.17	29.70	.52	32.39
1982	17.74	4.21	8.80	1.69	32.44	6.23	6.51	5.00	1.28	.54	13.33	2.58	31.29	.52	34.39
1984	20.66	4.62	8.51	2.00	35.79	7.06	6.63	6.44	1.09	.58	14.74	2.31	36.36	.54	39.21
1987	18.05	5.53	6.25	1.85	31.68	9.77	6.02	6.45	.94	.50	13.91	2.02	39.83	.46	42.31
1990	18.59	6.16	7.42	2.01	34.18	11.23	6.59	7.21	.83	.65	15.28	2.03	46.95	.48	49.46
1993	21.95	8.66	6.24	2.81	39.66	11.31	8.08	7.58	.74	.58	16.98	1.98	53.52	.42	55.92
1997	24.11	8.56	6.57	2.79	42.03	10.20	8.84	8.99	1.04	.89	19.76	2.86	60.57	.36	63.79
2001	31.84	8.98	5.66	4.04	50.52	15.94	11.31	8.47	1.15	.69	21.62	3.83	66.94	.86	71.63
2005	31.97	7.42	10.99	6.35	56.73	25.26	15.57	11.13	2.00	3.28	31.98	4.80	80.92	1.37	87.09

[1] Includes energy consumption in occupied primary housing units only, which differs from residential sector energy consumption.
[2] Includes refrigerators.
[3] Retail electricity. One kilowatthour=3,412 Btu.
[4] Distillate fuel oil and kerosene.
[5] Liquefied petroleum gases.
[6] Prices are not adjusted for inflation. See "Nominal Dollars" in Glossary.

Notes: • 2009 data for this table were not available in time for publication. • Data are estimates. • For years not shown, there are no data available. • Totals may not equal sum of components due to independent rounding.

Web Page: For related information, see http://www.eia.gov/consumption/residential/.

Sources: • 1978—U.S. Energy Information Administration (EIA), Form EIA-84, "Residential Energy Consumption Survey." • 1980 forward—EIA, Form EIA-457, "Residential Energy Consumption Survey."

Source: *U.S. Energy Information Administration, Annual Energy Review 2011*

Figure 2.6 Household End Uses: Fuel Types, Appliances, and Electronics

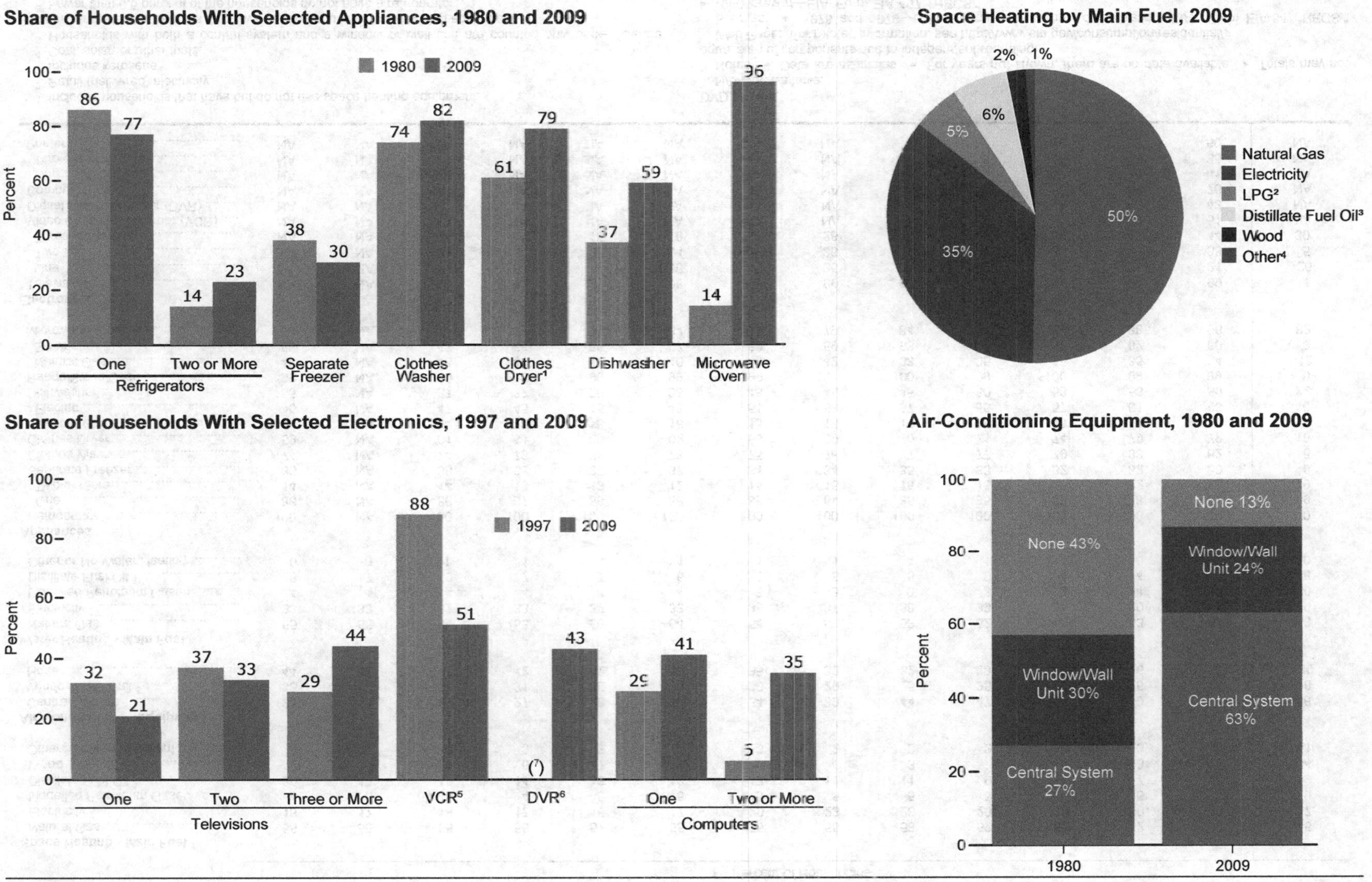

[1] Natural gas and electric.
[2] Liquefied petroleum gases.
[3] Includes kerosene.
[4] Coal, solar, other fuel, or no heating equipment.
[5] Video Cassette Recorder.
[6] Digital Video Recorder.
[7] Not collected in 1997.

Note: Total may not equal sum of components due to independent rounding.
Source: Table 2.6.

Source: *U.S. Energy Information Administration, Annual Energy Review 2011*

Table 2.6 Household End Uses: Fuel Types, Appliances, and Electronics, Selected Years, 1978-2009

Appliance	1978	1979	1980	1981	1982	1984	1987	1990	1993	1997	2001	2005	2009	Change 1980 to 2009
Total Households (millions)	77	78	82	83	84	86	91	94	97	101	107	111	114	32
	Percent of Households													
Space Heating - Main Fuel [1]														
Natural Gas	55	55	55	56	57	55	55	55	53	52	55	52	50	-5
Electricity [2]	16	17	18	17	16	17	20	23	26	29	29	30	35	17
Liquefied Petroleum Gases	4	5	5	4	5	5	5	5	5	5	5	5	5	0
Distillate Fuel Oil [3]	20	17	15	14	13	12	12	11	11	9	7	7	6	-9
Wood	2	4	6	6	7	7	6	4	3	2	2	3	2	-4
Other [4] or No Equipment	3	2	2	3	3	3	3	2	2	2	2	3	1	-1
Air Conditioning - Equipment														
Central System [5]	23	24	27	27	28	30	34	39	44	47	55	59	63	36
Window/Wall Unit [5]	33	31	30	31	30	30	30	29	25	25	23	25	24	-6
None	44	45	43	42	42	40	36	32	32	28	23	16	13	-30
Water Heating - Main Fuel														
Natural Gas	55	55	54	55	56	54	54	53	53	52	54	53	51	-3
Electricity [2]	33	33	32	33	32	33	35	37	38	39	38	39	41	9
Liquefied Petroleum Gases	4	4	4	4	4	4	3	3	3	3	3	4	4	0
Distillate Fuel Oil [3]	8	7	9	7	7	6	6	5	5	5	4	4	3	-6
Other or No Water Heating	0	0	1	1	1	1	1	1	1	1	0	0	1	0
Appliances														
Refrigerator [6]	100	NA	100	100	100	100	100	100	100	100	100	100	100	0
One	86	NA	86	87	86	88	86	84	85	85	83	78	77	-9
Two or More	14	NA	14	13	13	12	14	15	15	15	17	22	23	9
Separate Freezer	35	NA	38	38	37	37	34	34	35	33	32	32	30	-8
Clothes Washer	74	NA	74	73	71	73	75	76	77	77	79	83	82	8
Clothes Dryer	59	NA	61	61	60	62	66	69	70	71	74	79	79	18
Natural Gas	14	NA	14	16	15	16	15	16	14	15	16	17	15	1
Electric	45	NA	47	45	45	46	51	53	57	55	57	61	63	16
Dishwasher	35	NA	37	37	36	38	43	45	45	50	53	58	59	22
Range/Stove/Oven	99	NA	99	100	99	99	99	100	100	99	100	99	99	0
Natural Gas	48	NA	46	46	47	46	43	42	33	35	35	35	34	-12
Electric	53	NA	57	56	56	57	60	59	63	62	62	62	60	3
Microwave Oven	8	NA	14	17	21	34	61	79	84	83	86	88	96	82
Electronics														
Television	NA	NA	98	98	98	98	98	99	99	99	99	99	99	1
One	NA	NA	47	51	49	46	40	35	34	32	27	21	21	-26
Two	NA	NA	38	34	35	34	35	36	36	37	36	35	33	-5
Three or More	NA	NA	14	14	15	18	23	28	28	29	36	43	44	30
Video Cassette Recorder (VCR)	NA	NA	NA	NA	NA	NA	NA	NA	NA	88	[7] 90	80	51	NA
Digital Video Recorder (DVR)	NA	NA	NA	NA	NA	NA	NA	NA	NA	NA	NA	NA	43	NA
Computer	NA	NA	NA	NA	NA	NA	NA	NA	NA	35	56	68	76	NA
One	NA	NA	NA	NA	NA	NA	NA	NA	NA	29	42	45	41	NA
Two or More	NA	NA	NA	NA	NA	NA	NA	NA	NA	6	15	23	35	NA
Printer	NA	NA	NA	NA	NA	NA	NA	NA	5	12	49	59	60	NA

[1] Includes households that have but do not use space heating equipment.
[2] Retail (delivered) electricity.
[3] Includes kerosene.
[4] Coal, solar, or other fuels.
[5] Households with both a central system and a window or wall unit are counted only under "Central System." Includes households that have but do not use air conditioning equipment.
[6] Fewer than 0.5 percent of the households do not have a refrigerator.
[7] The 2001 "Residential Energy Consumption Survey (RECS)" only had one question for VCRs and DVD players.

NA=Not available.

Notes: • Data are estimates. • For years not shown, there are no data available. • Totals may not equal sum of components due to independent rounding.

Web Page: For related information, see http://www.eia.gov/consumption/residential/.

Sources: • 1978 and 1979—U.S. Energy Information Administration (EIA), Form EIA-84, "RECS." • 1980 forward—EIA, Form EIA-457, "RECS."

Source: *U.S. Energy Information Administration, Annual Energy Review 2011*

Figure 2.7 Type of Heating in Occupied Housing Units, 1950 and 2009

By Fuel Type

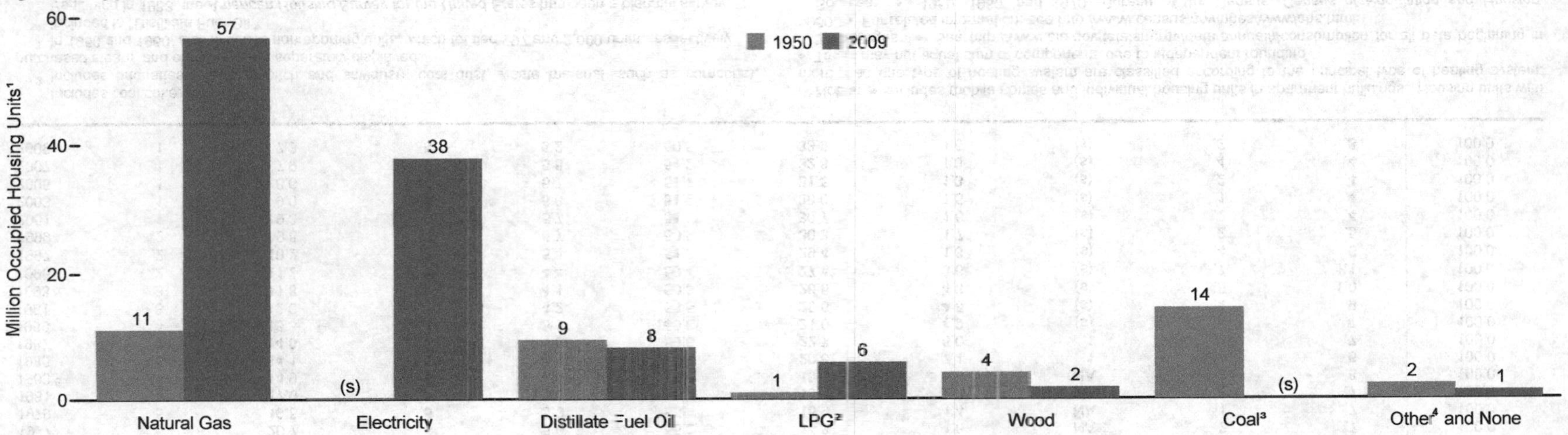

By Fuel Type, Share of Total

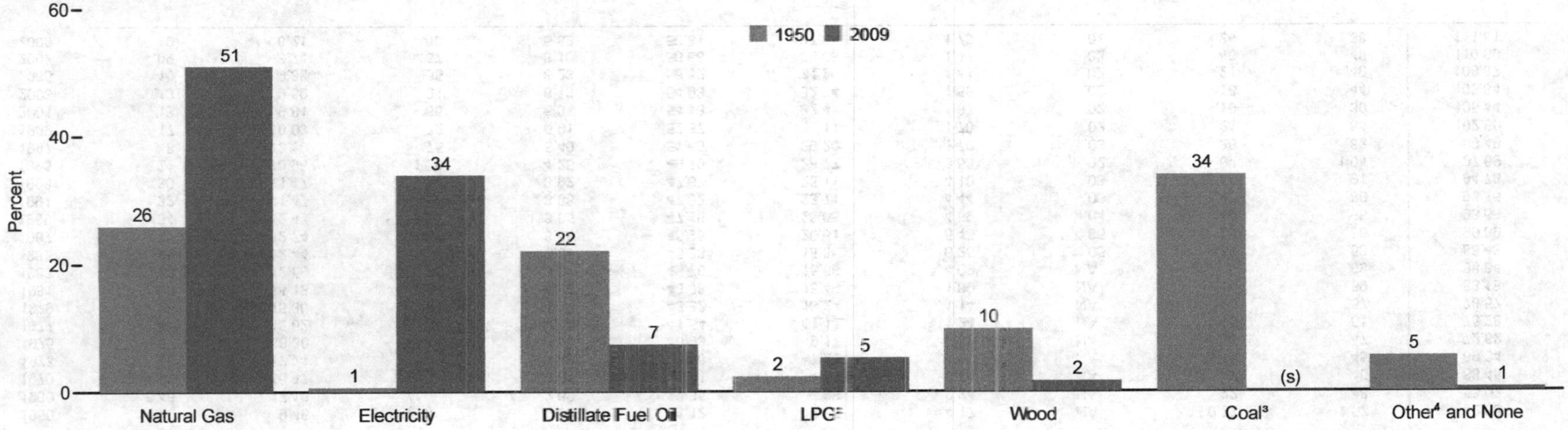

[1] Sum of components do not equal total due to independent rounding.
[2] Liquefied petroleum gases.
[3] Includes coal coke.
[4] Kerosene, solar, and other.
(s)=Less than 0.5.
Source: Table 2.7.

Source: *U.S. Energy Information Administration, Annual Energy Review 2011*

Table 2.7 Type of Heating in Occupied Housing Units, Selected Years, 1950-2009

Year	Coal [1]	Distillate Fuel Oil	Kerosene	Liquefied Petroleum Gases	Natural Gas	Electricity	Wood	Solar	Other [2]	None [3]	Total
					Million Occupied Housing Units						
1950	14.48	9.46	([4])	0.98	11.12	0.28	4.17	NA	0.77	1.57	42.83
1960	6.46	17.16	([4])	2.69	22.85	.93	2.24	NA	.22	.48	53.02
1970	1.82	16.47	([4])	3.81	35.01	4.88	.79	NA	.27	.40	63.45
1973	.80	17.24	([4])	4.42	38.46	7.21	.60	NA	.15	.45	69.34
1975	.57	16.30	([4])	4.15	40.93	9.17	.85	NA	.08	.47	72.52
1977	.45	15.62	.44	4.18	41.54	11.15	1.24	NA	.15	.51	75.28
1979	.36	15.30	.41	4.13	43.32	13.24	1.14	NA	.10	.57	78.57
1981	.36	14.13	.37	4.17	46.08	15.49	1.89	NA	.10	.59	83.18
1983 [5]	.43	12.59	.45	3.87	46.70	15.68	4.09	NA	.16	.68	84.64
1985	.45	12.44	1.06	3.58	45.33	18.36	6.25	.05	.37	.53	88.43
1987	.41	12.74	1.08	3.66	45.96	20.61	5.45	.05	.28	.66	90.89
1989	.34	12.47	1.07	3.66	47.40	23.06	4.59	.04	.40	.66	93.68
1991	.32	11.47	.99	3.88	47.02	23.71	4.44	.03	.41	.86	93.15
1993	.30	11.17	1.02	3.92	47.67	25.11	4.10	.03	.50	.91	94.73
1995	.21	10.98	1.06	4.25	49.20	26.77	3.53	.02	.64	1.04	97.69
1997	.18	10.10	.75	5.40	51.05	29.20	1.79	.03	.36	.62	99.49
1999	.17	10.03	.72	5.91	52.37	31.14	1.70	.02	.21	.54	102.80
2001 [6]	.13	9.81	.65	6.04	54.13	32.41	1.67	.02	.19	.39	105.44
2003	.13	9.50	.64	6.13	54.93	32.34	1.56	.02	.16	.44	105.84
2005	.10	9.38	.55	6.23	56.32	34.26	1.41	.02	.21	.40	108.87
2007	.09	8.74	.57	6.10	56.68	36.08	1.47	.02	.46	.48	110.69
2009	.10	8.21	.60	5.82	56.81	37.85	1.78	.01	.24	.38	111.81
						Percent					
1950	33.8	22.1	([4])	2.3	26.0	0.6	9.7	NA	1.8	3.7	100.0
1960	12.2	32.4	([4])	5.1	43.1	1.8	4.2	NA	.4	.9	100.0
1970	2.9	26.0	([4])	6.0	55.2	7.7	1.3	NA	.4	.6	100.0
1973	1.2	24.9	([4])	6.4	55.5	10.4	.9	NA	.2	.7	100.0
1975	.8	22.5	([4])	5.7	56.4	12.6	1.2	NA	.1	.6	100.0
1977	.6	20.7	.6	5.6	55.2	14.8	1.6	NA	.2	.7	100.0
1979	.5	19.5	.5	5.3	55.1	16.9	1.4	NA	.1	.7	100.0
1981	.4	17.0	.4	5.0	55.4	18.6	2.3	NA	.1	.7	100.0
1983 [5]	.5	14.9	.5	4.6	55.2	18.5	4.8	NA	.2	.8	100.0
1985	.5	14.1	1.2	4.1	51.3	20.8	7.1	.1	.4	.6	100.0
1987	.4	14.0	1.2	4.0	50.6	22.7	6.0	.1	.3	.7	100.0
1989	.4	13.3	1.1	3.9	50.6	24.6	4.9	(s)	.4	.7	100.0
1991	.3	12.3	1.1	4.2	50.5	25.5	4.8	(s)	.4	.9	100.0
1993	.3	11.8	1.1	4.1	50.3	26.5	4.3	(s)	.5	1.0	100.0
1995	.2	11.2	1.1	4.4	50.4	27.4	3.6	(s)	.7	1.1	100.0
1997	.2	10.2	.8	5.4	51.3	29.4	1.8	(s)	.4	.6	100.0
1999	.2	9.8	.7	5.7	50.9	30.3	1.7	(s)	.2	.5	100.0
2001 [6]	.1	9.3	.6	5.7	51.3	30.7	1.6	(s)	.2	.4	100.0
2003	.1	9.0	.6	5.8	51.9	30.6	1.5	(s)	.1	.4	100.0
2005	.1	8.6	.5	5.7	51.7	31.5	1.3	(s)	.2	.4	100.0
2007	.1	7.9	.5	5.5	51.2	32.6	1.3	(s)	.4	.4	100.0
2009	.1	7.3	.5	5.2	50.8	33.9	1.6	(s)	.2	.3	100.0

[1] Includes coal coke.

[2] Includes briquettes (made of pitch and sawdust), coal dust, waste material (such as corncobs), purchased steam, and other fuels not separately displayed.

[3] In 1950 and 1960, also includes nonreporting units, which totaled 997 and 2,000 units, respectively.

[4] Included in "Distillate Fuel Oil."

[5] Beginning in 1983, the *American Housing Survey for the United States* has been a biennial survey.

[6] Beginning in 2001, data are consistent with the 2000 Census. For 2001 data consistent with the 1990 Census, see *American Housing Survey for the United States: 2001.*

NA=Not available. (s)=Less than 0.05 percent.

Notes: • Includes mobile homes and individual housing units in apartment buildings. Housing units with more than one type of heating system are classified according to the principal type of heating system. • Totals may not equal sum of components due to independent rounding.

Web Pages: • See http://www.eia.gov/totalenergy/data/annual/#consumption for all data beginning in 1950. • For related information, see http://www.census.gov/hhes/www/ahs.html.

Sources: • 1950, 1960, and 1970—Bureau of the Census, *Census of Population and Housing.* • 1973-1981—Bureau of the Census, *American Housing Survey for the United States,* annual surveys, Table 2-5. • 1983 forward—Bureau of the Census, *American Housing Survey for the United States,* biennial surveys, Table 2-5.

Source: *U.S. Energy Information Administration, Annual Energy Review 2011*

Figure 2.8 Motor Vehicle Mileage, Fuel Consumption, and Fuel Economy

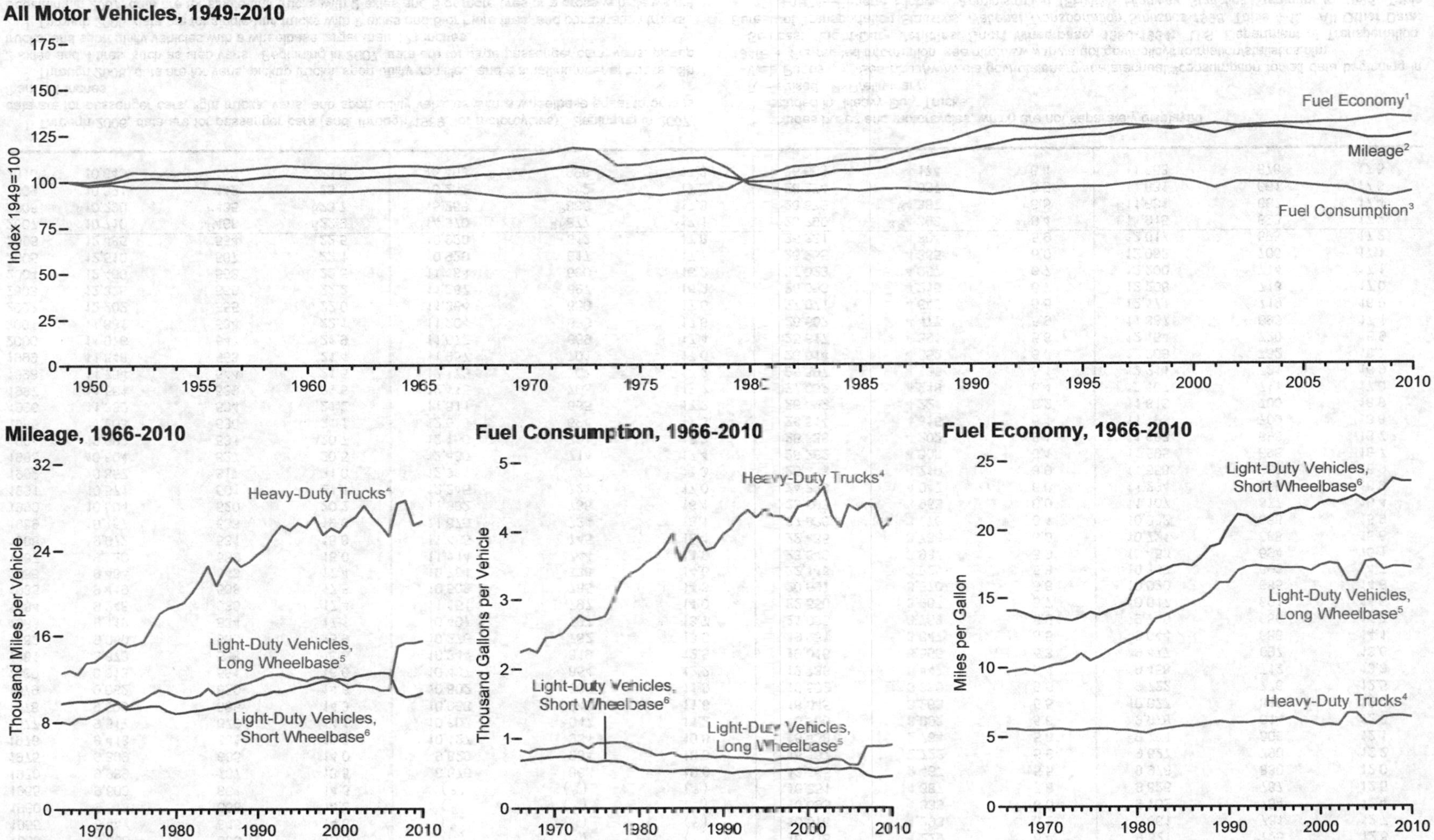

[1] Miles per gallon.
[2] Miles per vehicle.
[3] Gallons per vehicle.
[4] Through 2006, data are for single-unit trucks with 2 axles and 6 or more tires, and combination trucks. Beginning in 2007, data are for single-unit trucks with 2 axles and 6 or more tires or a gross vehicle weight rating exceeding 10,000 pounds, and combination trucks.
[5] Through 2006, data are for vans, pickup trucks, sport utility vehicles, and a small number of trucks with 2 axles and 4 tires, such as step vans. Beginning in 2007, data are for large passenger cars, vans, pickup trucks, and sport utility vehicles with a wheelbase larger than 121 inches.
[6] Through 2006, data are for passenger cars (and, through 1989, for motorcycles). Beginning in 2007, data are for passenger cars, light trucks, vans, and sport utility vehicles with a wheelbase equal to or less than 121 inches.

Source: Table 2.8.

Source: *U.S. Energy Information Administration, Annual Energy Review 2011*

Table 2.8 Motor Vehicle Mileage, Fuel Consumption, and Fuel Economy, Selected Years, 1949-2010

Year	Light-Duty Vehicles, Short Wheelbase [1]			Light-Duty Vehicles, Long Wheelbase [2]			Heavy-Duty Trucks [3]			All Motor Vehicles [4]		
	Mileage	Fuel Consumption	Fuel Economy	Mileage	Fuel Consumption	Fuel Economy	Mileage	Fuel Consumption	Fuel Economy	Mileage	Fuel Consumption	Fuel Economy
	Miles per Vehicle	Gallons per Vehicle	Miles per Gallon	Miles per Vehicle	Gallons per Vehicle	Miles per Gallon	Miles per vehicle	Gallons per vehicle	Miles per Gallon	Miles per Vehicle	Gallons per Vehicle	Miles per Gallon
1949	9,388	627	15.0	(5)	(5)	(5)	9,712	1,080	9.0	9,498	726	13.1
1950	9,060	603	15.0	(5)	(5)	(5)	10,316	1,229	8.4	9,321	725	12.8
1955	9,447	645	14.6	(5)	(5)	(5)	10,576	1,293	8.2	9,661	761	12.7
1960	9,518	668	14.3	(5)	(5)	(5)	10,693	1,333	8.0	9,732	784	12.4
1965	9,603	661	14.5	(5)	(5)	(5)	10,851	1,387	7.8	9,826	787	12.5
1970	9,989	737	13.5	8,676	866	10.0	13,565	2,467	5.5	9,976	830	12.0
1975	9,309	665	14.0	9,829	934	10.5	15,167	2,722	5.6	9,627	790	12.2
1976	9,418	681	13.8	10,127	934	10.8	15,438	2,764	5.6	9,774	806	12.1
1977	9,517	676	14.1	10,607	947	11.2	16,700	3,002	5.6	9,978	814	12.3
1978	9,500	665	14.3	10,968	948	11.6	18,045	3,263	5.5	10,077	816	12.4
1979	9,062	620	14.6	10,802	905	11.9	18,502	3,380	5.5	9,722	776	12.5
1980	8,813	551	16.0	10,437	854	12.2	18,736	3,447	5.4	9,458	712	13.3
1981	8,873	538	16.5	10,244	819	12.5	19,016	3,565	5.3	9,477	697	13.6
1982	9,050	535	16.9	10,276	762	13.5	19,931	3,647	5.5	9,644	686	14.1
1983	9,118	534	17.1	10,497	767	13.7	21,083	3,769	5.6	9,760	686	14.2
1984	9,248	530	17.4	11,151	797	14.0	22,550	3,967	5.7	10,017	691	14.5
1985	9,419	538	17.5	10,506	735	14.3	20,597	3,570	5.8	10,020	685	14.6
1986	9,464	543	17.4	10,764	738	14.6	22,143	3,821	5.8	10,143	692	14.7
1987	9,720	539	18.0	11,114	744	14.9	23,349	3,937	5.9	10,453	694	15.1
1988	9,972	531	18.8	11,465	745	15.4	22,485	3,736	6.0	10,721	688	15.6
1989	10,157	533	19.0	11,676	724	16.1	22,926	3,776	6.1	10,932	688	15.9
1990	10,504	520	20.2	11,902	738	16.1	23,603	3,953	6.0	11,107	677	16.4
1991	10,571	501	21.1	12,245	721	17.0	24,229	4,047	6.0	11,294	669	16.9
1992	10,857	517	21.0	12,381	717	17.3	25,373	4,210	6.0	11,558	683	16.9
1993	10,804	527	20.5	12,430	714	17.4	26,262	4,309	6.1	11,595	693	16.7
1994	10,992	531	20.7	12,156	701	17.3	25,838	4,202	6.1	11,683	698	16.7
1995	11,203	530	21.1	12,018	694	17.3	26,514	4,315	6.1	11,793	700	16.8
1996	11,330	534	21.2	11,811	685	17.2	26,092	4,221	6.2	11,813	700	16.9
1997	11,581	539	21.5	12,115	703	17.2	27,032	4,218	6.4	12,107	711	17.0
1998	11,754	544	21.6	12,173	707	17.2	25,397	4,135	6.1	12,211	721	16.9
1999	11,848	553	21.4	11,957	701	17.0	26,014	4,352	6.0	12,206	732	16.7
2000	11,976	547	21.9	11,672	669	17.4	25,617	4,391	5.8	12,164	720	16.9
2001	11,831	534	22.1	11,204	636	17.6	26,602	4,477	5.9	11,887	695	17.1
2002	12,202	555	22.0	11,364	650	17.5	27,071	4,642	5.8	12,171	719	16.9
2003	12,325	556	22.2	11,287	697	16.2	28,093	4,215	6.7	12,208	718	17.0
2004	12,460	553	22.5	11,184	690	16.2	27,023	4,057	6.7	12,200	714	17.1
2005	12,510	567	22.1	10,920	617	17.7	26,235	4,385	6.0	12,082	706	17.1
2006	12,485	554	22.5	10,920	612	17.8	25,231	4,304	5.9	12,017	698	17.2
2007	[1,R]10,710	[1,R]468	[1,R]22.9	[2,R]14,970	[2,R]877	[2,R]17.1	[3,R]28,290	[3,R]4,398	[3,R]6.4	[R]11,915	693	17.2
2008	[R]10,290	[R]435	[R]23.7	[R]15,256	[R]880	[R]17.3	[R]28,573	[R]4,387	[R]6.5	[R]11,631	667	17.4
2009	10,391	442	23.5	15,252	882	17.3	26,274	4,037	6.5	11,631	661	17.6
2010[P]	10,649	453	23.5	15,463	898	17.2	26,609	4,174	6.4	11,853	678	17.5

[1] Through 2006, data are for passenger cars (and, through 1989, for motorcycles). Beginning in 2007, data are for passenger cars, light trucks, vans, and sport utility vehicles with a wheelbase equal to or less than 121 inches.

[2] Through 2006, data are for vans, pickup trucks, sport utility vehicles, and a small number of trucks with 2 axles and 4 tires, such as step vans. Beginning in 2007, data are for large passenger cars, vans, pickup trucks, and sport utility vehicles with a wheelbase larger than 121 inches.

[3] Through 2006, data are for single-unit trucks with 2 axles and 6 or more tires, and combination trucks. Beginning in 2007, data are for single-unit trucks with 2 axles and 6 or more tires or a gross vehicle weight rating exceeding 10,000 pounds, and combination trucks.

[4] Includes buses and motorcycles, which are not separately displayed.

[5] Included in "Heavy-Duty Trucks."

R=Revised. P=Preliminary.

Web Pages: • See http://www.eia.gov/totalenergy/data/annual/#consumption for all data beginning in 1949. • For related information, see http://www.fhwa.dot.gov/policyinformation/statistics.cfm.

Sources: **Light-Duty Vehicles, Short Wheelbase, 1990-1994:** U.S. Department of Transportation, Bureau of Transportation Statistics, *National Transportation Statistics 1998,* Table 4-13. **All Other Data:** • 1949-1994—Federal Highway Administration (FHWA), *Highway Statistics Summary to 1995,* Table VM-201A. • 1995 forward—FHWA, *Highway Statistics,* annual reports, Table VM-1.

Source: *U.S. Energy Information Administration, Annual Energy Review 2011*

Figure 4.1 Technically Recoverable Crude Oil and Natural Gas Resource Estimates, 2009

Crude Oil and Lease Condensate, Total Technically Recoverable Resources

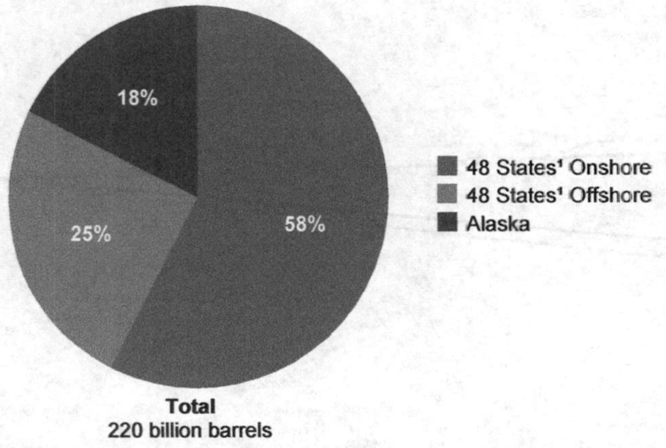

Dry Natural Gas, Total Technically Recoverable Resources

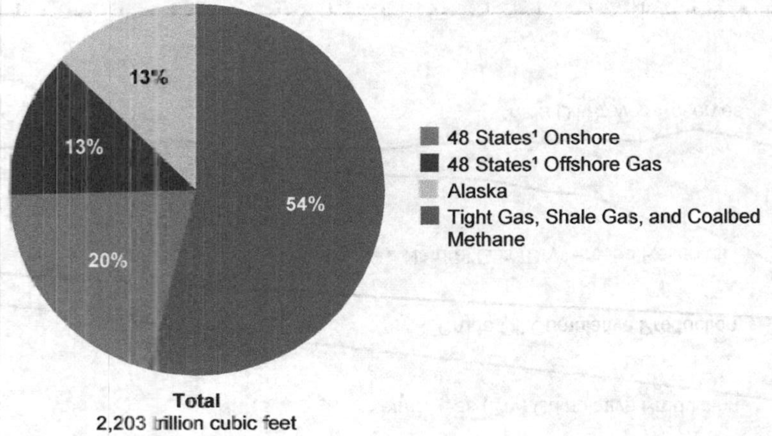

Crude Oil and Lease Condensate by Type

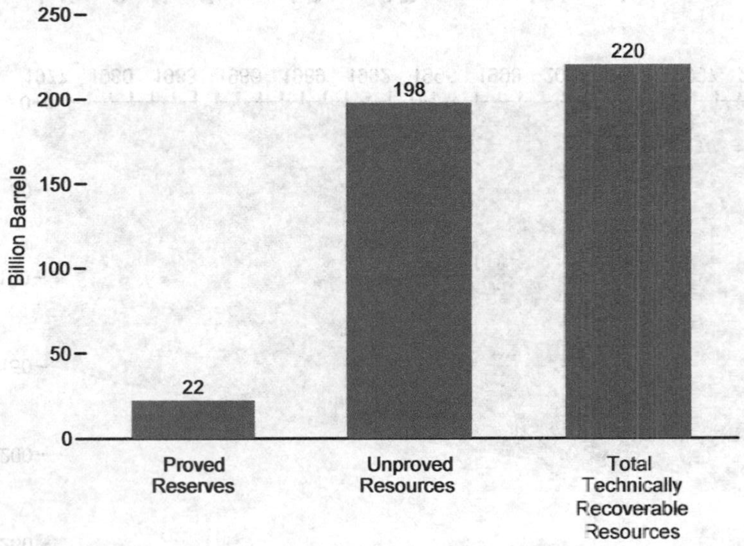

Dry Natural Gas by Type

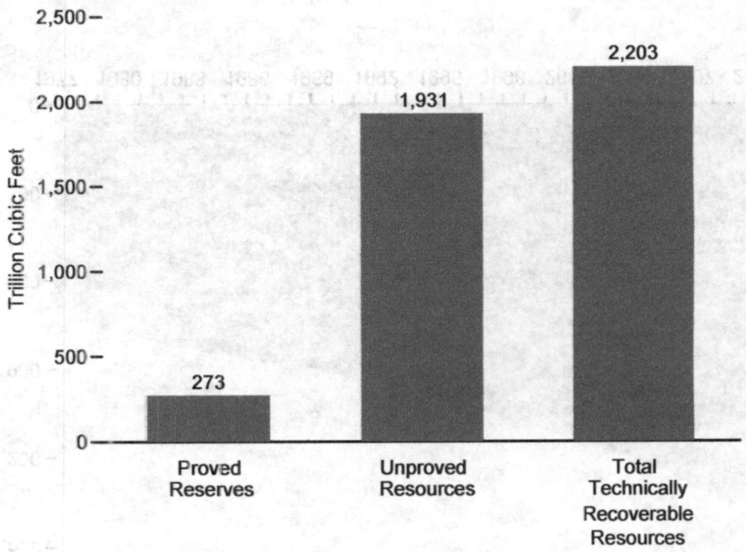

[1] "48 States" is the United States excluding Alaska and Hawaii.
Note: Sum of components may not equal 100 percent due to independent rounding.

Source: Table 4.1.

Source: *U.S. Energy Information Administration, Annual Energy Review 2011*

Figure 4.2 Crude Oil and Natural Gas Cumulative Production and Proved Reserves, 1977-2010

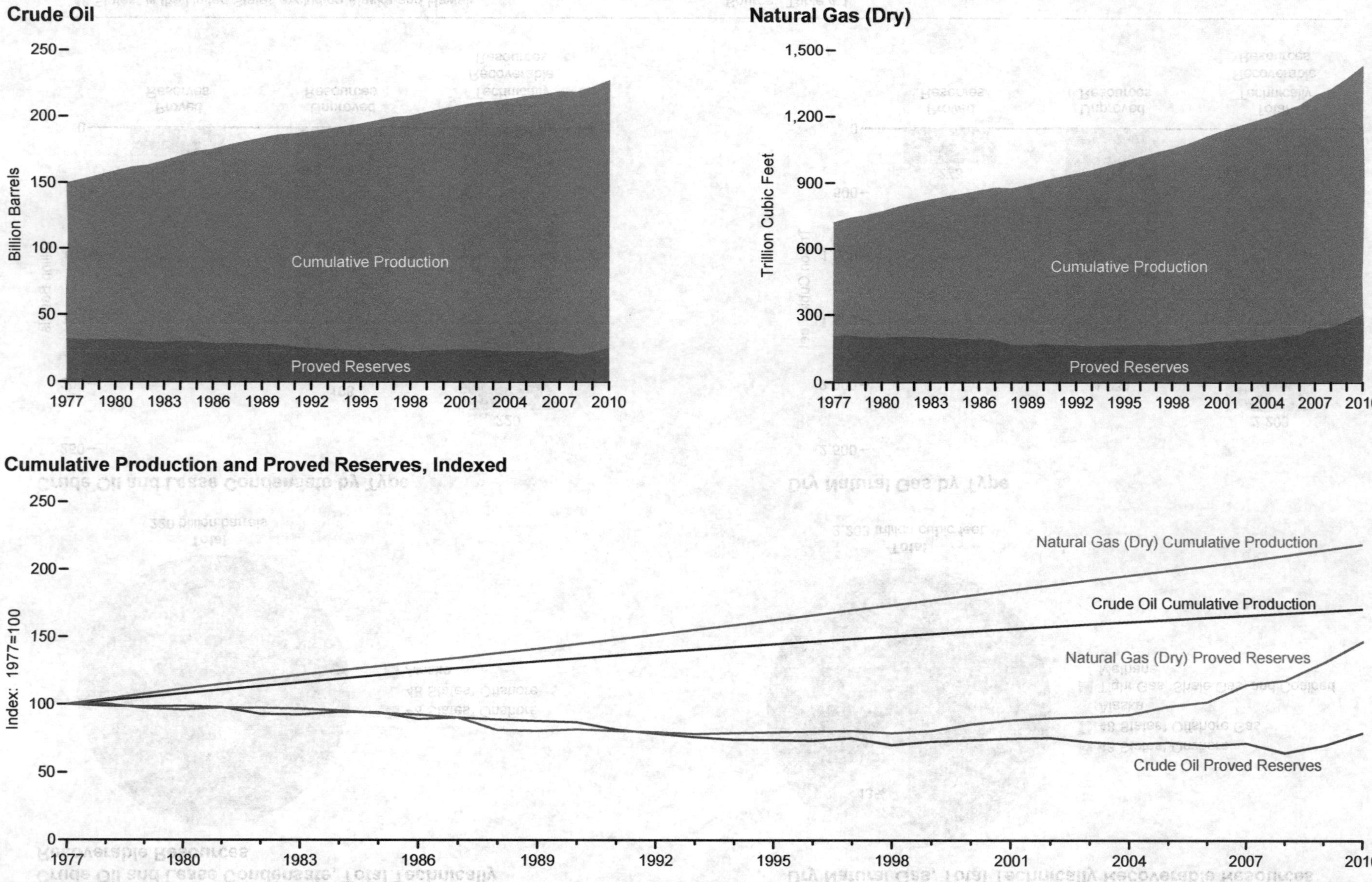

Notes: • Data are at end of year. • Crude oil includes lease condensate.

Source: Table 4.2.

Source: *U.S. Energy Information Administration, Annual Energy Review 2011*

Figure 4.3 Crude Oil, Natural Gas, and Natural Gas Liquids Proved Reserves

Total, 1949-2010

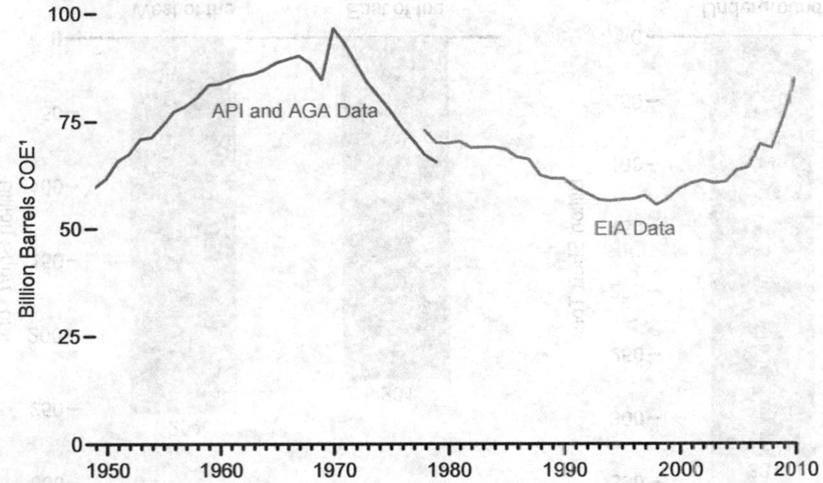

By Type, 2010

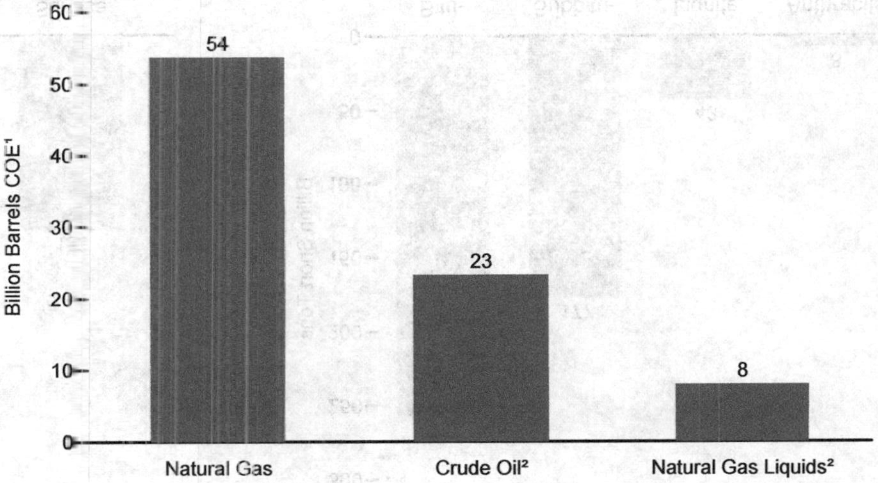

By Type, 1949-2010

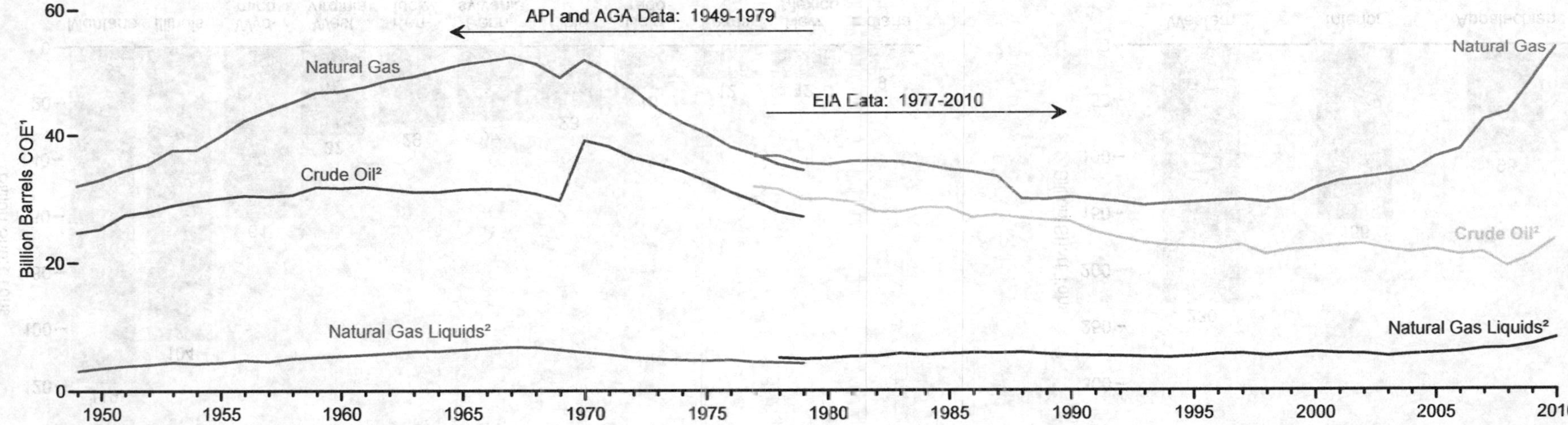

[1] COE=crude oil equivalent.
[2] To the extent that lease condensate is measured or estimated it is included in "Natural Gas Liquids"; otherwise, lease condensate is included in "Crude Oil."

Notes: • Data are at end of year. • API=American Petroleum Institute. AGA=American Gas Association. EIA=U.S. Energy Information Administration.
Source: Table 4.3.

Source: U.S. Energy Information Administration, Annual Energy Review 2011

Figure 4.8 Coal Demonstrated Reserve Base, January 1, 2011

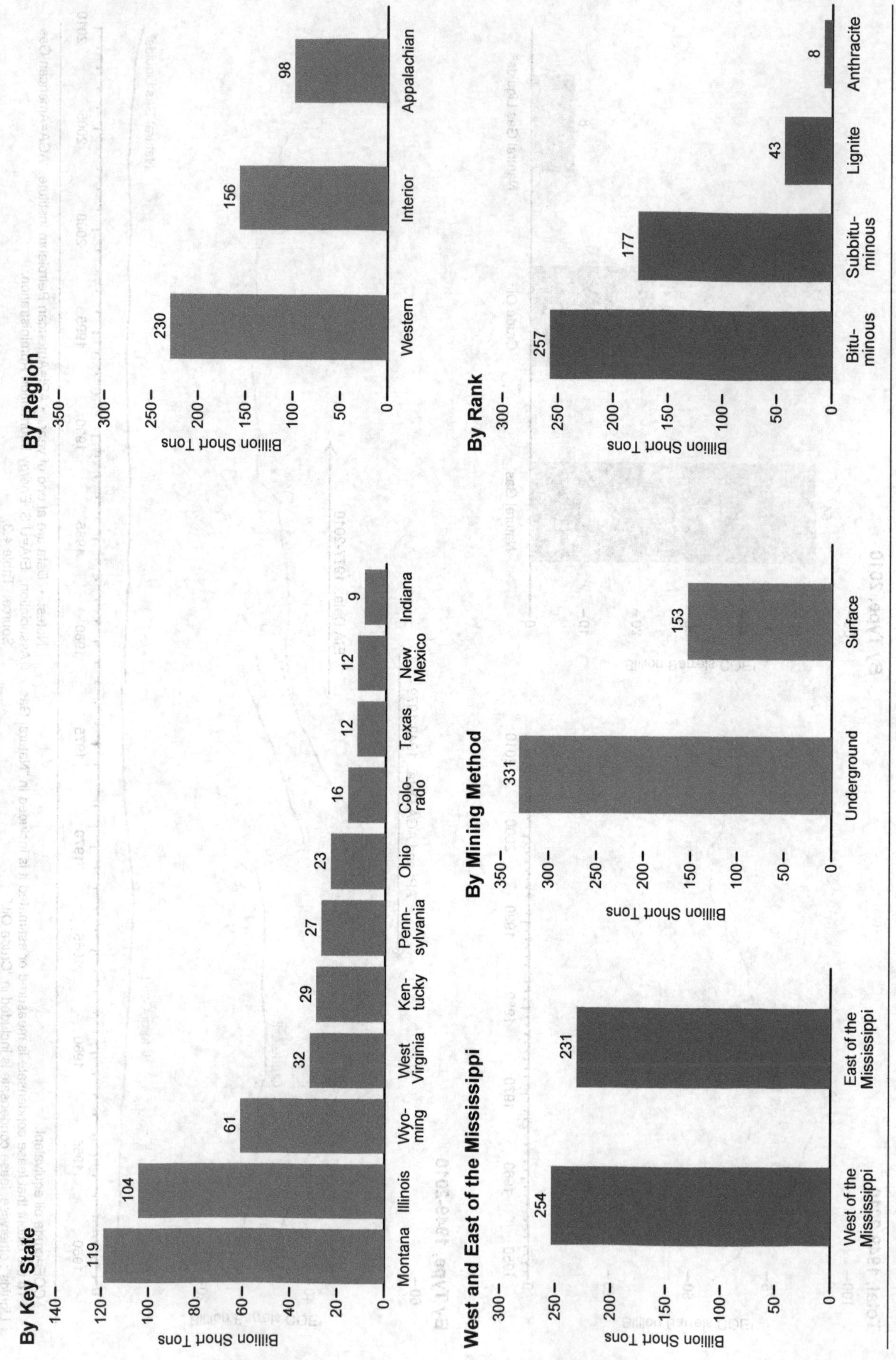

Source: Table 4.8.

Source: *U.S. Energy Information Administration, Annual Energy Review 2011*

Table 4.8 Coal Demonstrated Reserve Base, January 1, 2011

(Billion Short Tons)

Region and State	Anthracite		Bituminous Coal		Subbituminous Coal		Lignite	Total		
	Underground	Surface	Underground	Surface	Underground	Surface	Surface [1]	Underground	Surface	Total
Appalachian	**4.0**	**3.3**	**68.2**	**21.9**	**0.0**	**0.0**	**1.1**	**72.1**	**26.3**	**98.4**
Alabama	.0	.0	.9	2.1	.0	.0	1.1	.9	3.1	4.0
Kentucky, Eastern	.0	.0	.8	9.1	.0	.0	.0	.8	9.1	9.8
Ohio	.0	.0	17.4	5.7	.0	.0	.0	17.4	5.7	23.1
Pennsylvania	3.8	3.3	18.9	.8	.0	.0	.0	22.7	4.2	26.9
Virginia	.1	.0	.9	.5	.0	.0	.0	1.0	.5	1.5
West Virginia	.0	.0	28.3	3.4	.0	.0	.0	28.3	3.4	31.7
Other [2]	.0	.0	1.1	.3	.0	.0	.0	1.1	.3	1.4
Interior	**.1**	**(s)**	**116.6**	**27.1**	**.0**	**.0**	**12.6**	**116.7**	**39.6**	**156.4**
Illinois	.0	.0	87.6	16.5	.0	.0	.0	87.6	16.5	104.2
Indiana	.0	.0	8.6	.6	.0	.0	.0	8.6	.6	9.2
Iowa	.0	.0	1.7	.5	.0	.0	.0	1.7	.5	2.2
Kentucky, Western	.0	.0	15.6	3.6	.0	.0	.0	15.6	3.6	19.2
Missouri	.0	.0	1.5	4.5	.0	.0	.0	1.5	4.5	6.0
Oklahoma	.0	.0	1.2	.3	.0	.0	.0	1.2	.3	1.5
Texas	.0	.0	.0	.0	.0	.0	12.1	.0	12.1	12.1
Other [3]	.1	(s)	.3	1.1	.0	.0	0.4	.4	1.5	1.9
Western	**(s)**	**.0**	**21.2**	**2.3**	**121.2**	**55.9**	**29.2**	**142.4**	**87.4**	**229.7**
Alaska	.0	.0	.6	.1	4.8	.6	(s)	5.4	.7	6.1
Colorado	(s)	.0	7.5	.6	3.7	.0	4.2	11.2	4.8	15.9
Montana	.0	.0	1.4	.0	69.6	32.3	15.8	70.9	48.0	119.0
New Mexico	(s)	.0	2.7	.9	3.4	5.0	.0	6.1	5.9	12.0
North Dakota	.0	.0	.0	.0	.0	.0	8.9	.0	8.9	8.9
Utah	.0	.0	4.9	.3	(s)	.0	.0	4.9	.3	5.2
Washington	.0	.0	.3	.0	1.0	.0	(s)	1.3	(s)	1.3
Wyoming	.0	.0	3.8	.5	38.6	18.1	.0	42.5	18.5	61.0
Other [4]	.0	.0	(s)	.0	(s)	(s)	.4	(s)	.4	.4
U.S. Total	**4.1**	**3.4**	**206.0**	**51.2**	**121.1**	**55.9**	**42.8**	**331.2**	**153.3**	**484.5**
States East of the Mississippi River	4.0	3.3	180.0	42.6	.0	.0	1.1	184.0	47.0	231.0
States West of the Mississippi River	.1	(s)	25.9	8.6	121.1	55.9	41.7	147.2	106.3	253.5

[1] Lignite resources are not mined underground in the United States.
[2] Georgia, Maryland, North Carolina, and Tennessee.
[3] Arkansas, Kansas, Louisiana, and Michigan.
[4] Arizona, Idaho, Oregon, and South Dakota.
(s)=Less than 0.05 billion short tons.

Notes: • See *U.S. Coal Reserves: 1997 Update* on the Web Page for a description of the methodology used to produce these data. • Data represent remaining measured and indicated coal resources, analyzed and on file, meeting minimum seam and depth criteria, and in the ground as of January 1, 2011. These coal resources are not totally recoverable. Net recoverability with current mining technologies ranges from 0 percent (in far northern Alaska) to more than 90 percent. Fifty-four percent of the demonstrated reserve base of coal in the United States is estimated to be recoverable. • Totals may not equal sum of components due to independent rounding.

Web Page: For related information, see http://www.eia.gov/coal/.

Source: U.S. Energy Information Administration, Coal Reserves Database.

Source: *U.S. Energy Information Administration, Annual Energy Review 2011*

Figure 4.9 Uranium Exploration and Development Drilling

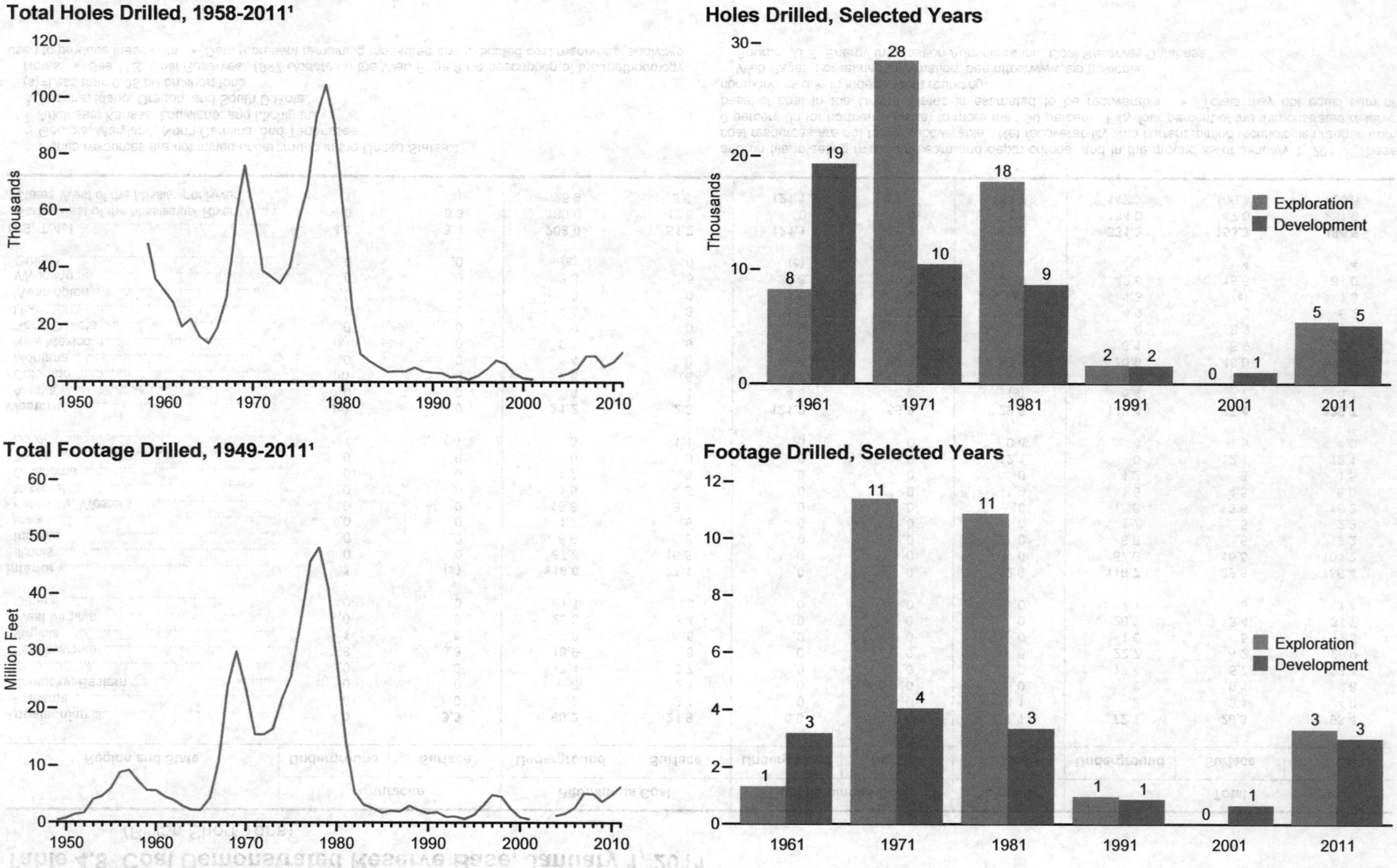

[1] In 2002 and 2003, data are withheld to avoid disclosure.

Source: Table 4.9.

Source: *U.S. Energy Information Administration, Annual Energy Review 2011*

Table 4.9 Uranium Exploration and Development Drilling, Selected Years, 1949-2011

Year	Exploration [1] Holes Drilled (Thousands)	Exploration [1] Footage Drilled (Million Feet)	Development [2] Holes Drilled (Thousands)	Development [2] Footage Drilled (Million Feet)	Total Holes Drilled (Thousands)	Total Footage Drilled (Million Feet)
1949	NA	0.36	NA	0.05	NA	0.41
1950	NA	.57	NA	.21	NA	.78
1955	NA	5.27	NA	.76	NA	6.03
1960	7.34	1.40	24.40	4.21	31.73	5.61
1965	6.23	1.16	7.33	.95	13.56	2.11
1970	43.98	17.98	14.87	5.55	58.85	23.53
1975	34.29	15.69	21.60	9.73	55.89	25.42
1976	40.41	20.36	27.23	14.44	67.64	34.80
1977	62.60	27.96	30.85	17.62	93.45	45.58
1978	75.07	28.95	29.29	19.15	104.35	48.10
1979	60.46	28.07	30.19	13.01	90.65	41.08
1980	39.61	19.60	20.19	8.59	59.80	28.19
1981	17.75	10.87	8.67	3.35	26.42	14.22
1982	6.97	4.23	3.00	1.13	9.97	5.36
1983	4.29	2.09	3.01	1.08	7.30	3.17
1984	4.80	2.26	.72	.29	5.52	2.55
1985	2.88	1.42	.77	.34	3.65	1.76
1986	1.99	1.10	1.85	.97	3.83	2.07
1987	1.82	1.11	1.99	.86	3.81	1.97
1988	2.03	1.28	3.18	1.73	5.21	3.01
1989	2.09	1.43	1.75	.80	3.84	2.23
1990	1.51	.87	1.91	.81	3.42	1.68
1991	1.62	.97	1.57	.87	3.20	1.84
1992	.94	.56	.83	.50	1.77	1.06
1993	.36	.22	1.67	.89	2.02	1.11
1994	.52	.34	.48	.32	1.00	.66
1995	.58	.40	1.73	.95	2.31	1.35
1996	1.12	.88	3.58	2.16	4.70	3.05
1997	1.94	1.33	5.86	3.56	7.79	4.88
1998	1.37	.89	5.23	3.75	6.60	4.64
1999	.27	.18	2.91	2.33	3.18	2.50
2000	W	W	W	W	1.55	1.02
2001	.00	.00	1.02	.66	1.02	.66
2002	W	W	W	W	W	W
2003	NA	NA	NA	NA	W	W
2004	W	W	W	W	2.19	1.25
2005	W	W	W	W	3.14	1.67
2006	1.47	.82	3.43	1.89	4.90	2.71
2007	4.35	2.20	5.00	2.95	9.35	5.15
2008	5.20	2.54	4.16	2.55	9.36	5.09
2009	1.79	1.05	3.89	2.69	5.68	3.74
2010	2.44	1.46	4.77	3.44	7.21	4.90
2011	5.44	3.32	5.16	3.00	10.60	6.33

[1] Includes surface drilling in search of new ore deposits or extensions of known deposits and drilling at the location of a discovery up to the time the company decides sufficient ore reserves are present to justify commercial exploitation.

[2] Includes all surface drilling on an ore deposit to determine more precisely size, grade, and configuration subsequent to the time that commercial exploitation is deemed feasible.

NA=Not available. W=Value withheld to avoid disclosure of individual company data.

Note: Totals may not equal sum of components due to independent rounding.

Web Pages: • See http://www.eia.gov/totalenergy/data/annual/#resources for all data beginning in 1949. • For related information, see http://www.eia.gov/nuclear/.

Sources: • 1949-1981—U.S. Department of Energy, Grand Junction Office, *Statistical Data of the Uranium Industry, January 1, 1983,* Report No. GJO-100 (1983), Table VIII-5. • 1982-2002—U.S. Energy Information Administration (EIA), *Uranium Industry Annual,* annual reports. • 2003-2005—EIA, "Domestic Uranium Production Report," annual reports. • 2006 forward—EIA, "2011 Domestic Uranium Production Report" (May 2012), Table 1.

Source: *U.S. Energy Information Administration, Annual Energy Review 2011*

Figure 4.10 Uranium Reserves, 2008

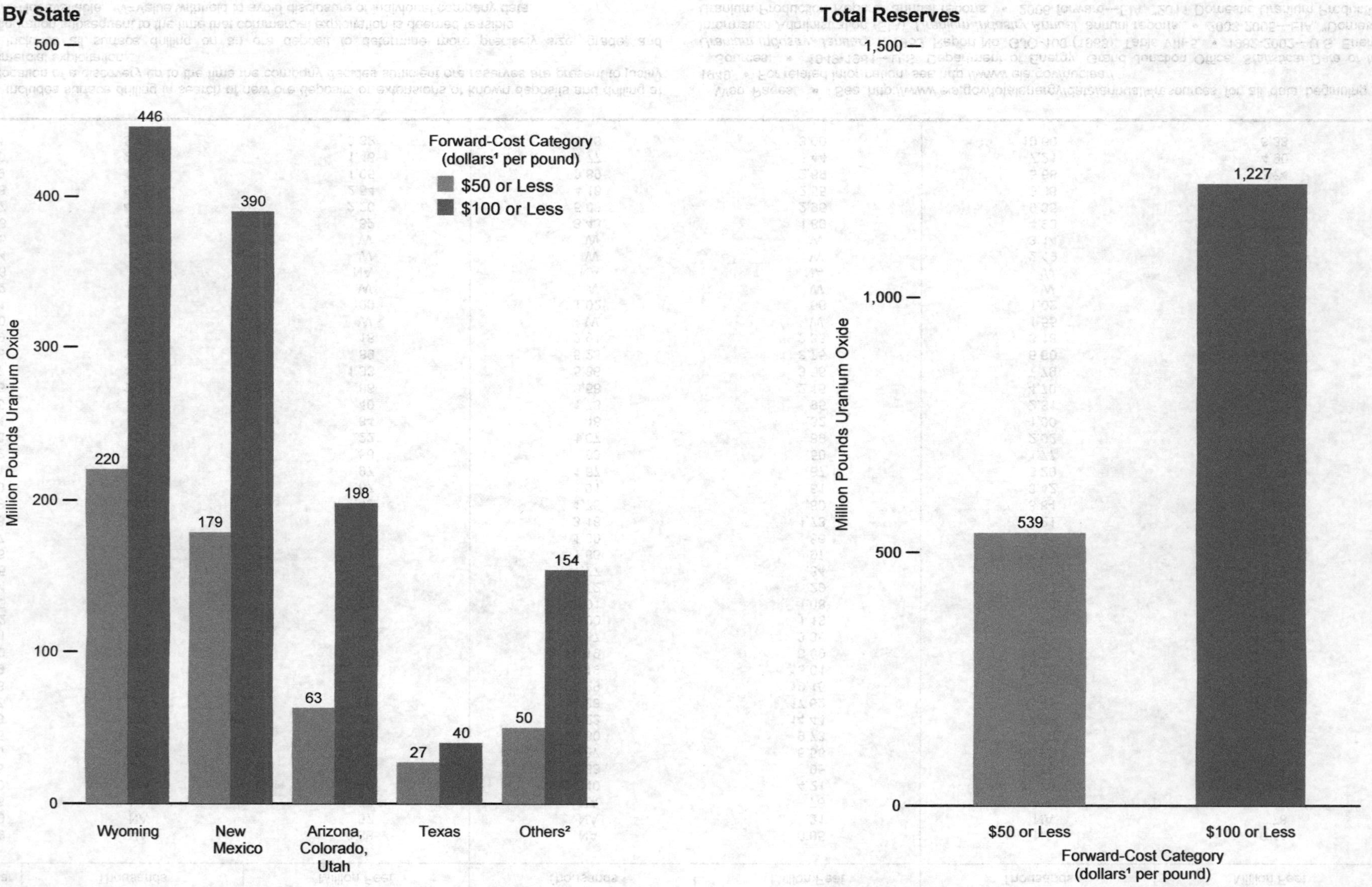

[1] See "Nominal Dollars" in Glossary.
[2] Alaska, California, Idaho, Montana, Nebraska, Nevada, North Dakota, Oregon, South Dakota, Virginia, and Washington.

Notes: • See "Uranium Oxide" in Glossary. • Data are at end of year.
Source: Table 4.10.

Source: *U.S. Energy Information Administration, Annual Energy Review 2011*

Table 4.10 Uranium Reserves,[1] 2008

(Million Pounds Uranium Oxide)

State	Forward-Cost [2] Category (dollars [3] per pound)	
	$50 or Less	$100 or Less
Total	**539**	**1,227**
Wyoming	220	446
New Mexico	179	390
Arizona, Colorado, Utah	63	198
Texas	27	40
Others [4]	50	154

[1] The U.S. Energy Information Administration (EIA) category of uranium reserves is equivalent to the internationally reported category of "Reasonably Assured Resources" (RAR).

[2] Forward costs include the costs for power and fuel, labor, materials, insurance, severance and ad valorem taxes, and applicable administrative costs. Past capital costs are considered "sunk" costs and mining of the individual deposits may or may not return such costs to investors. Sunk costs for such items as exploration and land acquisition are excluded as are the costs for income taxes, profit, and the cost of money. The forward costs used to estimate U.S. uranium ore reserves are independent of the price at which uranium produced from the estimated reserves might be sold in the commercial market. Reserves values in forward-cost categories are cumulative; that is, the quantity at each level of forward cost includes all reserves at the lower cost in that category.

[3] Prices are not adjusted for inflation. See "Nominal Dollars" in Glossary.

[4] Alaska, California, Idaho, Montana, Nebraska, Nevada, North Dakota, Oregon, South Dakota, Virginia, and Washington.

Notes: • Estimates are at end of year. • See "Uranium Oxide" in Glossary. • For updates, see http://www.eia.gov/cneaf/nuclear/page/reserves/ures.html.

Web Page: For related information, see http://www.eia.gov/nuclear/.

Sources: EIA, *U.S. Uranium Reserves Estimates* (July 2010), Table 1.

Source: *U.S. Energy Information Administration, Annual Energy Review 2011*

Figure 4.11 Concentrating Solar Resources

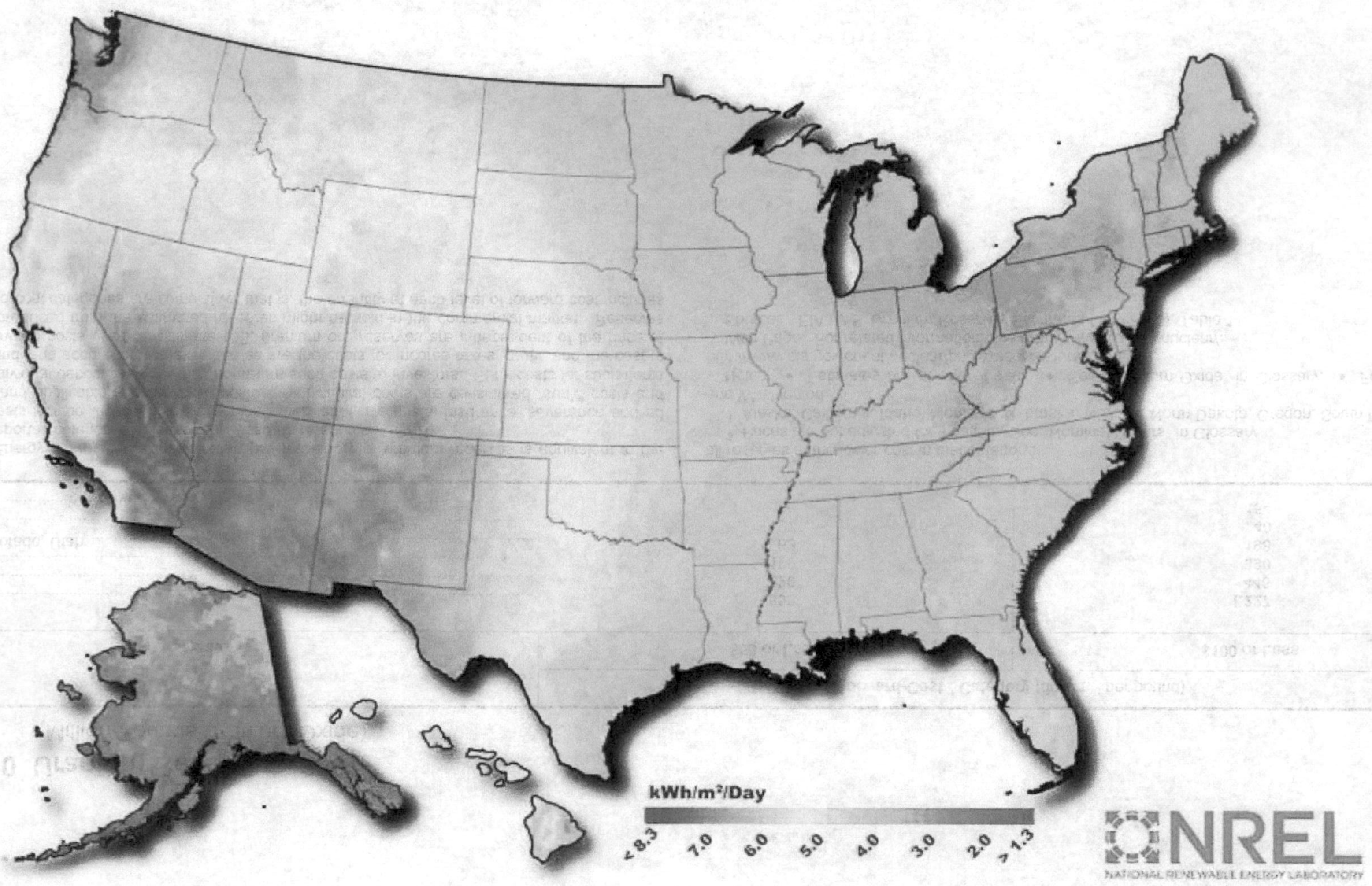

Notes: • Annual average direct normal solar resource data are shown. • kWh/m^2/Day = kilowatthours per square meter per day.

Web Page: For related information, see http://www.nrel.gov/gis/maps.html.

Sources: This map was created by the National Renewable Energy Laboratory for the Department of Energy (October 20, 2008). The data for Hawaii and the 48 contiguous States are a 10-kilometer (km) satellite modeled dataset (SUNY/NREL, 2007) representing data from 1998-2005. The data for Alaska are a 40-km dataset produced by the Climatological Solar Radiation Model (NREL, 2003).

Source: *U.S. Energy Information Administration, Annual Energy Review 2011*

Figure 4.12 Photovoltaic Solar Resources

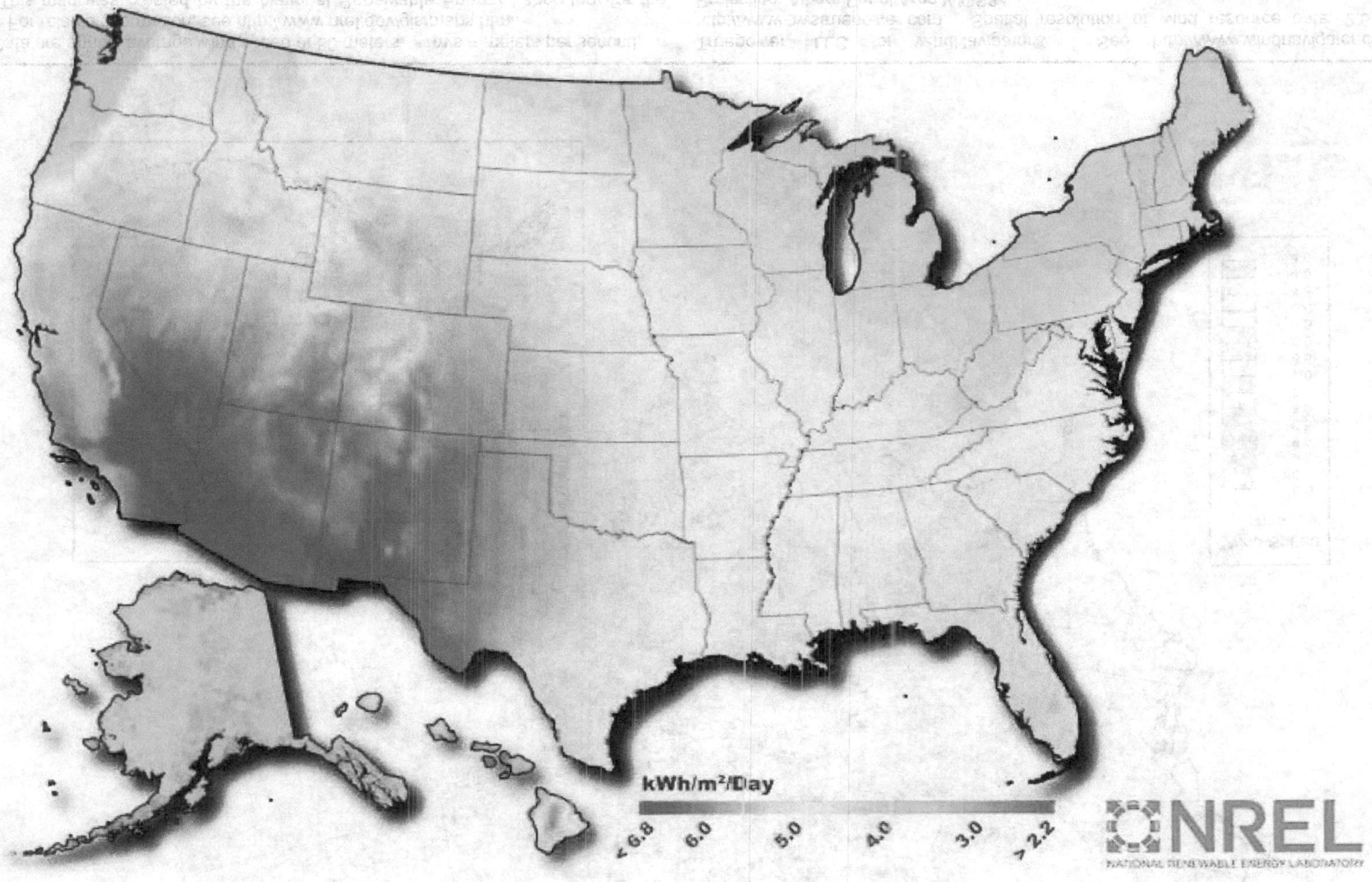

Notes: • Annual average solar resource data are shown for a tilt=latitude collector. • kWh/m²/Day = kilowatthours per square meter per day.

Web Page: For related information, see http://www.nrel.gov/gis/maps.html.

Sources: This map was created by the National Renewable Energy Laboratory for the Department of Energy (October 20, 2008). The data for Hawaii and the 48 contiguous States are a 10-kilometer (km) satellite modeled dataset (SUNY/NREL, 2007) representing data from 1998-2005. The data for Alaska are a 40-km dataset produced by the Climatological Solar Radiation Model (NREL, 2003).

Source: *U.S. Energy Information Administration, Annual Energy Review 2011*

Figure 4.13 Onshore Wind Resources

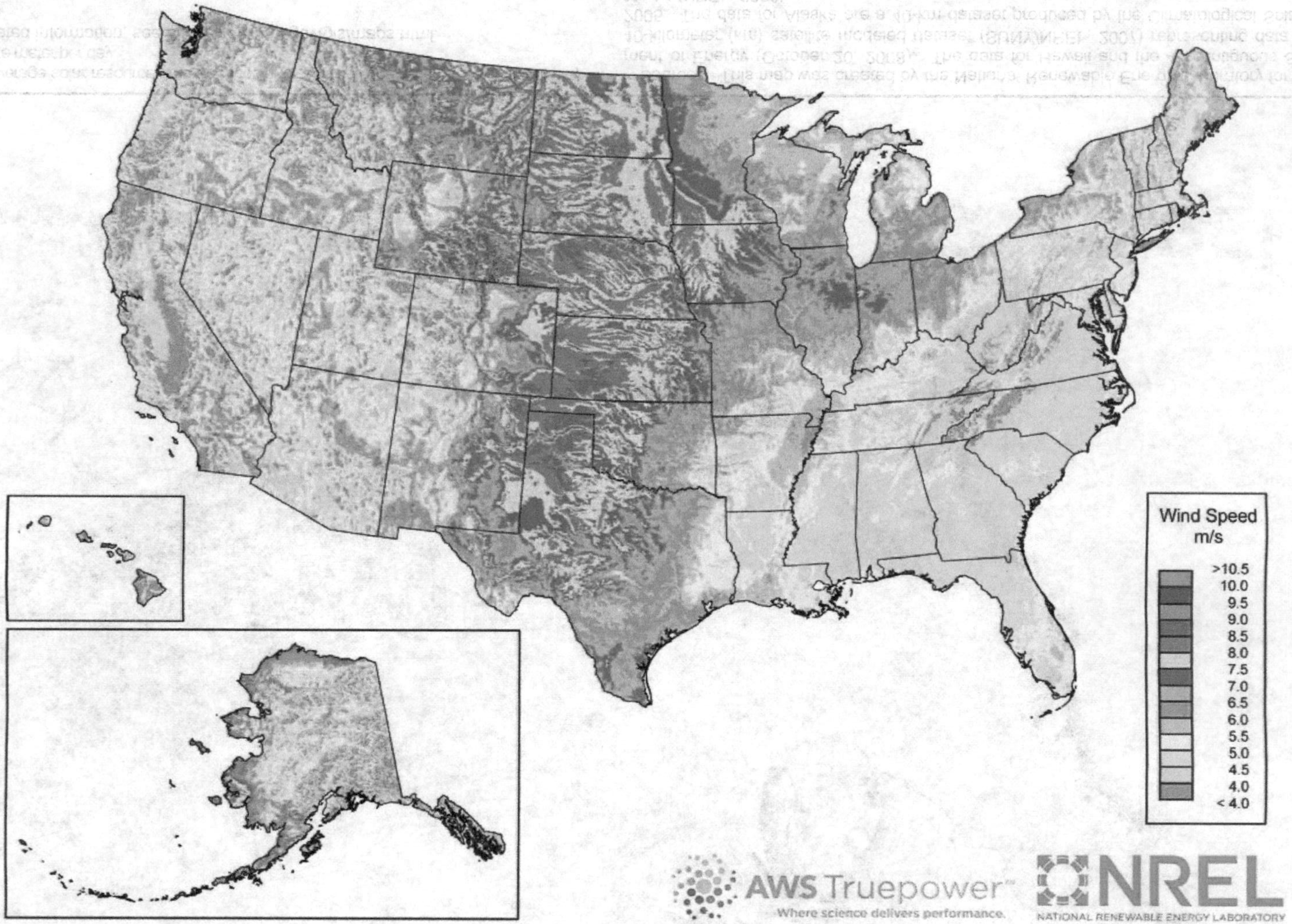

Notes: • Data are annual average wind speed at 80 meters. • m/s = meters per second.
Web Page: For related information, see http://www.nrel.gov/gis/maps.html.
Sources: This map was created by the National Renewable Energy Laboratory for the Department of Energy (April 1, 2011). Wind resource estimates developed by AWS Truepower, LLC for windNavigator®. See http://www.windnavigator.com and http://www.awstruepower.com. Spatial resolution of wind resource data: 2.5 kilometers. Projection: Albers Equal Area WGS84.

Source: *U.S. Energy Information Administration, Annual Energy Review 2011*

Figure 4.14 Offshore Wind Resources

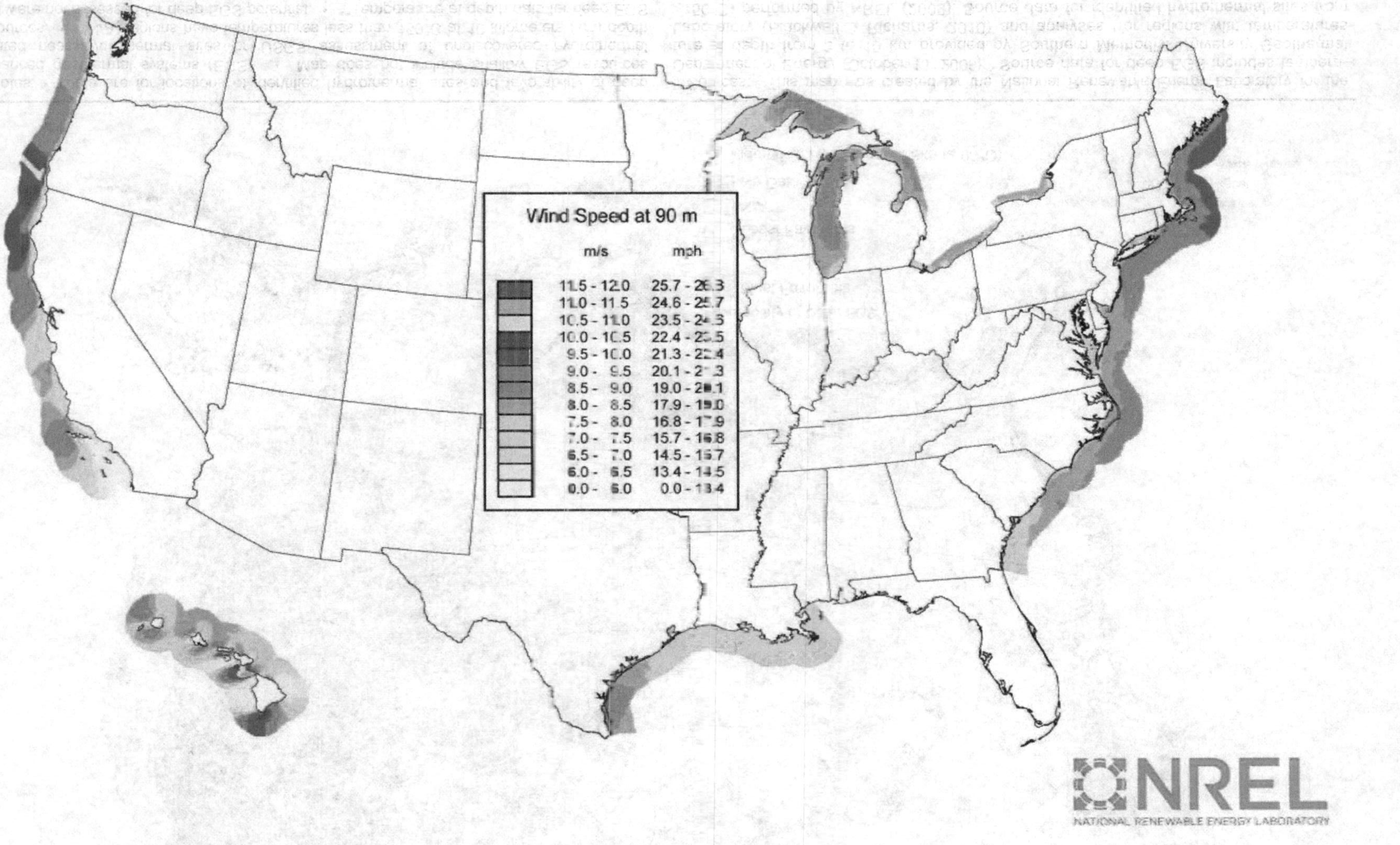

Notes: • Data are annual average wind speed at 90 meters. • m/s = meters per second. • mph = miles per hour.

Web Page: For related information, see http://www.nrel.gov/gis/maps.html.

Source: This map was created by the National Renewable Energy Laboratory for the Department of Energy (January 10, 2011).

Source: *U.S. Energy Information Administration, Annual Energy Review 2011*

Figure 4.15 Geothermal Resources

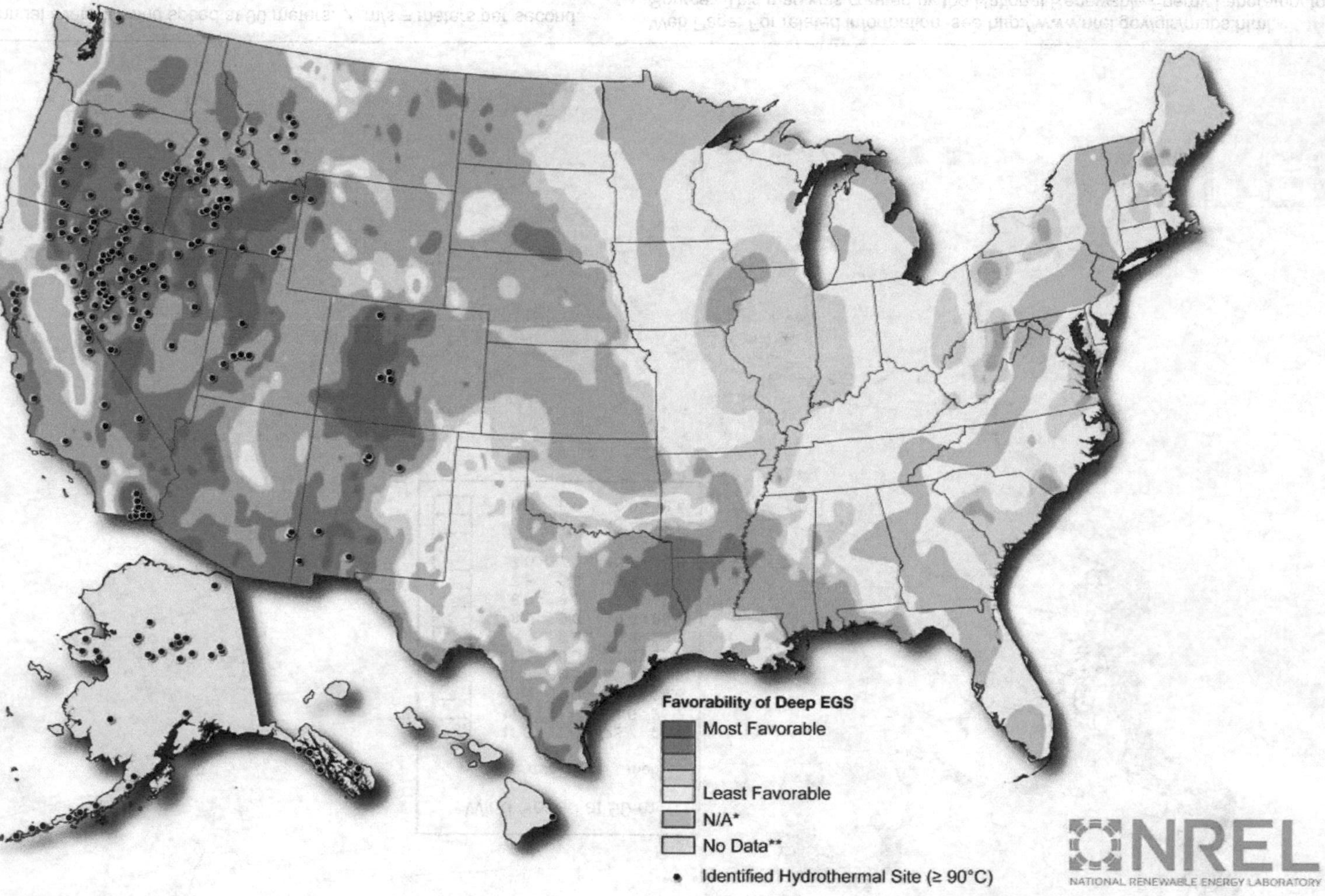

Notes: • Data are for locations of identified hydrothermal sites and favorability of deep enhanced geothermal systems (EGS). • Map does not include shallow EGS resources located near hydrothermal sites or USGS assessment of undiscovered hydrothermal resources. • *"N/A" regions have temperatures less than 150°C at 10 kilometers (km) depth and were not assessed for deep EGS potential. • **Temperature at depth data for deep EGS in Alaska and Hawaii not available.

Web Page: For related information, see http://www.nrel.gov/gis/maps.html.

Sources: This map was created by the National Renewable Energy Laboratory for the Department of Energy (October 13, 2009). Source data for deep EGS includes temperature at depth from 3 to 10 km provided by Southern Methodist University Geothermal Laboratory (Blackwell & Richards, 2010) and analyses (for regions with temperatures ≥150°C) performed by NREL (2009). Source data for identified hydrothermal sites from USGS Assessment of Moderate- and High-Temperature Geothermal Resources of the United States (2008).

Source: *U.S. Energy Information Administration, Annual Energy Review 2011*

Figure 4.16 Biomass Resources

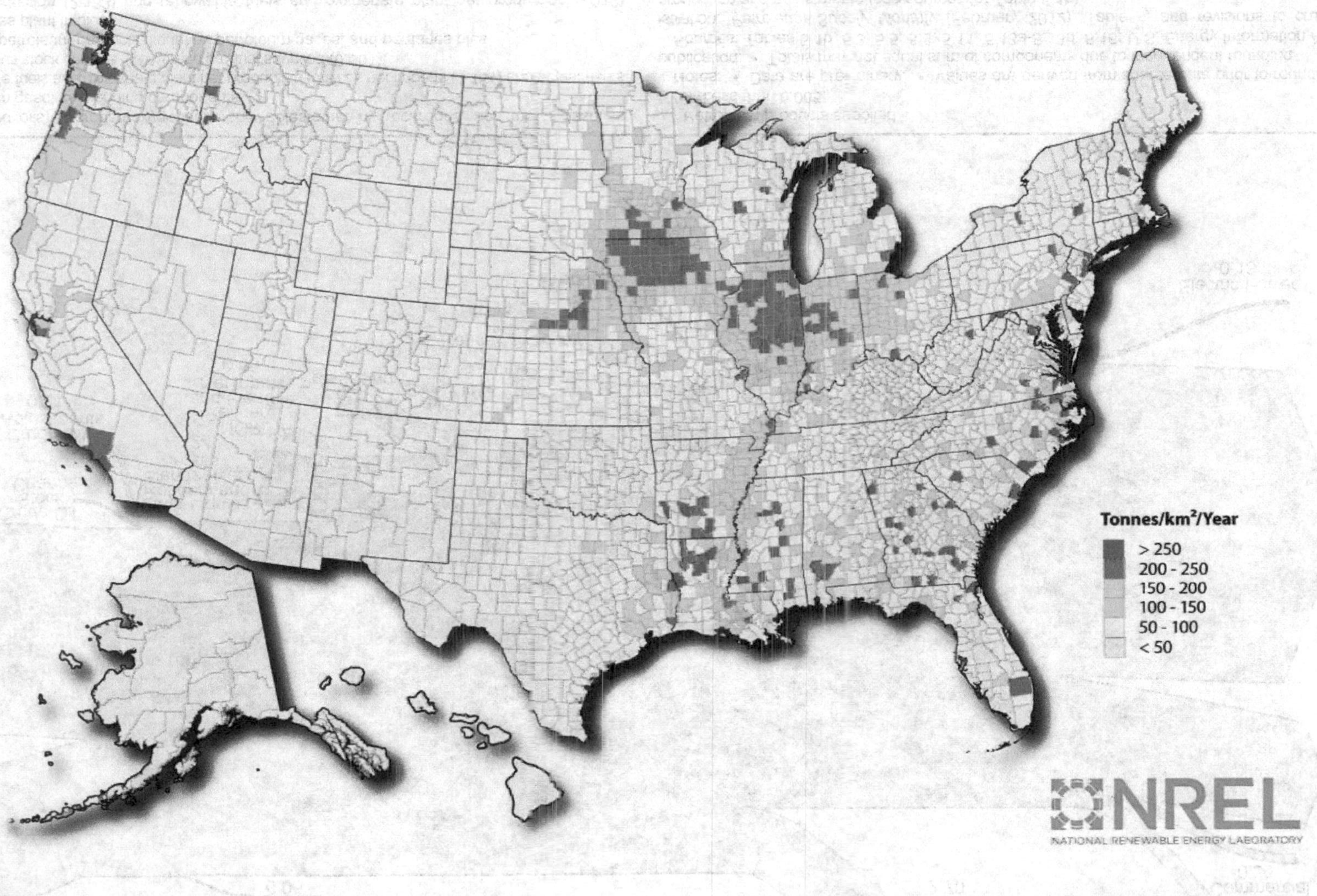

Notes: • Data are for total biomass per square kilometer. • km² = square kilometer. • This study estimates the biomass resources currently available in the United States by county. It includes the following feedstock categories: crop residues (5 year average: 2003-2007), forest and primary mill residues (2007), secondary mill and urban wood waste (2002), methane emissions from landfills (2008), domestic wastewater treatment (2007), and animal manure (2002). For more information on the data development, please refer to http://www.nrel.gov/docs/fy06osti/39181.pdf. Although, the document contains the methodology for the development of an older assessment, the information is applicable to this assessment as well. The difference is only in the data's time period.

Web Page: For related information, see http://www.nrel.gov/gis/maps.html.

Source: This map was created by the National Renewable Energy Laboratory for the Department of Energy (September 23, 2009).

Source: *U.S. Energy Information Administration, Annual Energy Review 2011*

Figure 5.0. Petroleum Flow, 2011
(Million Barrels per Day)

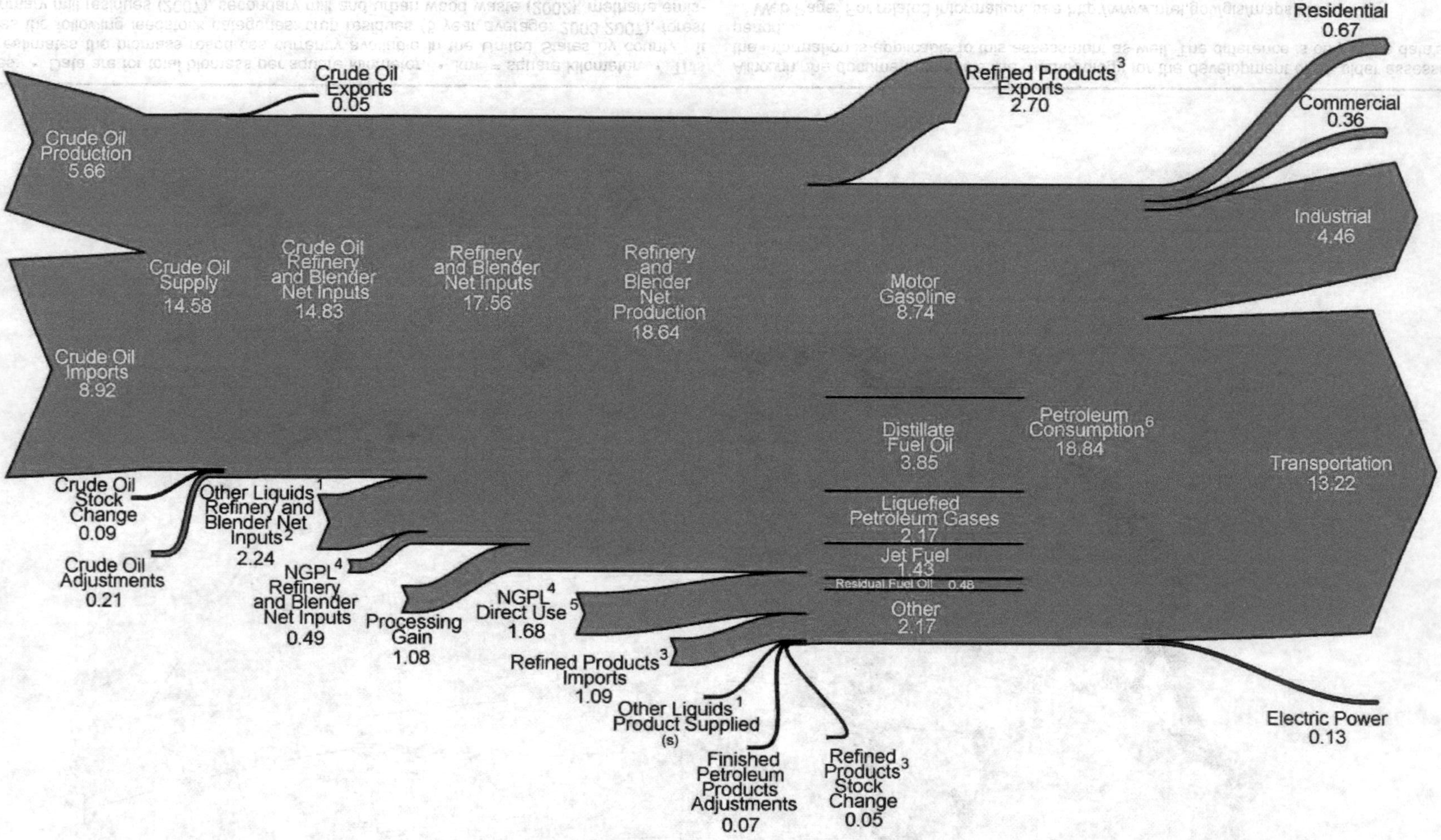

[1] Unfinished oils, hydrogen/oxygenates/renewables/other hydrocarbons, and motor gasoline and aviation gasoline blending components.

[2] Renewable fuels and oxygenate plant net production (0.972), net imports (1.164) and adjustments (0.122) minus stock change (0.019) and product supplied (0.001).

[3] Finished petroleum products, liquefied petroleum gases, and pentanes plus.

[4] Natural gas plant liquids.

[5] Field production (2.183) and renewable fuels and oxygenate plant net production (-.019) minus refinery and blender net inputs (0.489).

[6] Petroleum products supplied.

(s)=Less than 0.005.

Notes: • Data are preliminary. • Values are derived from source data prior to rounding for publication. • Totals may not equal sum of components due to independent rounding.

Sources: Tables 5.1b, 5.3, 5.5, 5.8, 5.11, 5.13a-5.13d, 5.16; U.S. Energy Information Administration, *Petroleum Supply Monthly* (February 2012), Table 4; and revisions to crude oil production and adjustments (see sources for Table 5.1b).

Source: *U.S. Energy Information Administration, Annual Energy Review 2011*

Figure 5.1a Petroleum and Other Liquids Overview

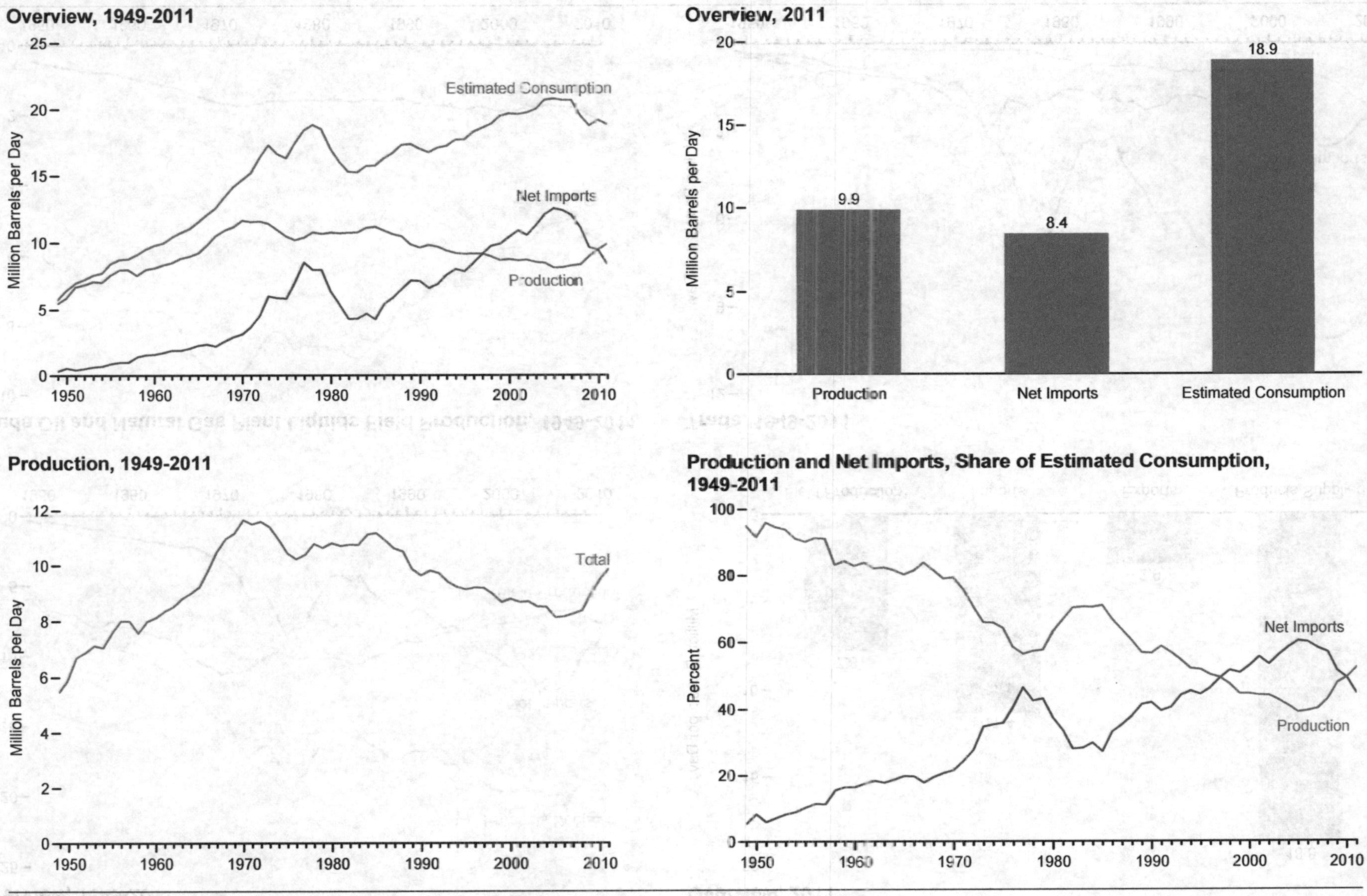

Note: Production includes production of crude oil (including lease condensate), natural gas plant liquids, fuel ethanol (minus denaturant), and biodiesel; and processing gain.

Source: Table 5.1a.

Source: *U.S. Energy Information Administration, Annual Energy Review 2011*

Figure 5.1b Petroleum Overview

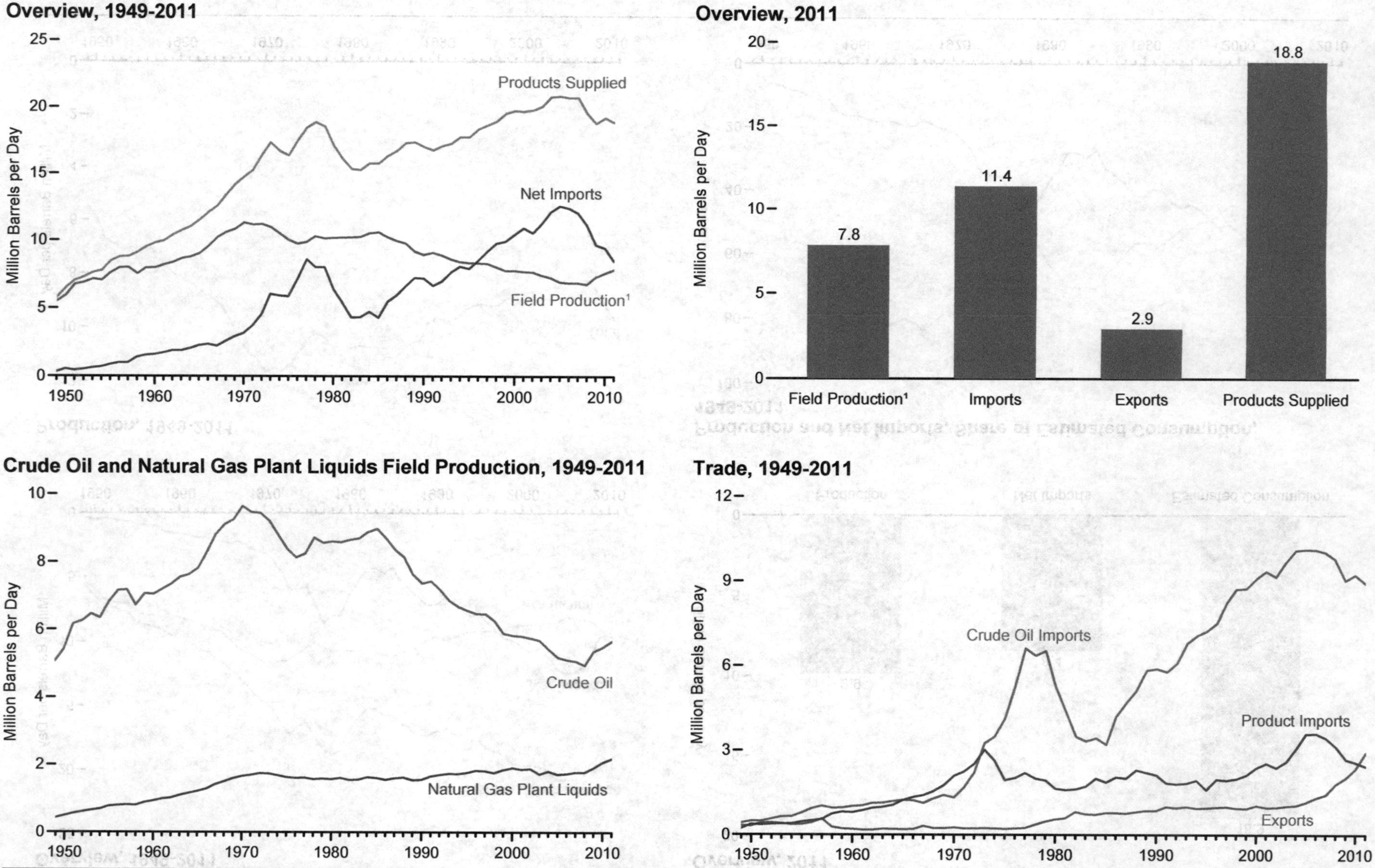

[1] Crude oil and natural gas plant liquids field production.

Sources: Tables 5.1b.and 5.3

Source: *U.S. Energy Information Administration, Annual Energy Review 2011*

Table 5.1a Petroleum and Other Liquids Overview, Selected Years, 1949-2011

Year	Production [1]	Production as Share of Estimated Consumption	Net Imports [2]	Net Imports as Share of Estimated Consumption	Balancing Item [3]	Estimated Consumption [4]
	Thousand Barrels per Day	*Percent*	Thousand Barrels per Day	*Percent*	Thousand Barrels per Day	
1949	5,475	*95.0*	318	*5.5*	-30	5,763
1950	5,908	*91.5*	545	*8.4*	5	6,458
1955	7,611	*90.0*	880	*10.4*	-37	8,455
1960	8,110	*82.8*	1,613	*16.5*	74	9,797
1965	9,234	*80.2*	2,281	*19.8*	-2	11,512
1970	11,656	*79.3*	3,161	*21.5*	-119	14,697
1975	10,467	*64.1*	5,846	*35.8*	8	16,322
1976	10,213	*58.5*	7,090	*40.6*	159	17,461
1977	10,387	*56.4*	8,565	*46.5*	-520	18,431
1978	10,771	*57.2*	8,002	*42.5*	74	18,847
1979	10,662	*57.6*	7,985	*43.1*	-135	18,513
1980	10,767	*63.1*	6,365	*37.3*	-76	17,056
1981	10,693	*66.6*	5,401	*33.6*	-31	16,063
1982	10,744	*70.2*	4,298	*28.1*	268	15,310
1983	10,761	*70.5*	4,312	*28.3*	185	15,258
1984	11,095	*70.4*	4,715	*29.9*	-52	15,758
1985	11,177	*70.9*	4,286	*27.2*	302	15,766
1986	10,893	*66.7*	5,439	*33.3*	-5	16,326
1987	10,636	*63.6*	5,914	*35.4*	168	16,717
1988	10,473	*60.4*	6,587	*38.0*	277	17,336
1989	9,874	*56.8*	7,202	*41.4*	303	17,379
1990	9,645	*56.6*	7,161	*42.0*	230	17,036
1991	9,846	*58.7*	6,626	*39.5*	297	16,769
1992	9,703	*56.8*	6,938	*40.6*	455	17,096
1993	9,422	*54.7*	7,618	*44.2*	195	17,235
1994	9,239	*52.1*	8,054	*45.5*	424	17,716
1995	9,183	*51.8*	7,886	*44.5*	654	17,723
1996	9,194	*50.2*	8,498	*46.4*	616	18,308
1997	9,201	*49.4*	9,158	*49.2*	260	18,619
1998	8,987	*47.5*	9,764	*51.6*	165	18,915
1999	8,711	*44.6*	9,912	*50.8*	894	19,517
2000	8,784	*44.6*	10,419	*52.9*	496	19,699
2001	8,686	*44.2*	10,900	*55.5*	60	19,647
2002	8,720	*44.1*	10,547	*53.4*	493	19,760
2003	8,554	*42.7*	11,238	*56.1*	239	20,031
2004	8,498	*41.0*	12,097	*58.4*	133	20,728
2005	8,140	*39.1*	12,549	*60.3*	114	20,803
2006	8,163	*39.4*	12,391	*59.9*	143	20,697
2007	8,292	*40.1*	12,027	*58.1*	376	20,695
2008	8,364	*42.9*	11,090	*56.9*	51	19,506
2009	R8,981	*47.8*	9,654	*51.4*	154	R18,789
2010	R9,490	R*49.4*	R9,435	*49.2*	R267	R19,192
2011	E9,884	E*52.4*	P8,432	P*44.7*	P561	P18,877

[1] Crude oil (including lease condensate) production; natural gas plant liquids production; and processing gain (refinery and blender net production minus refinery and blender net inputs). Beginning in 1981, also includes fuel ethanol (minus denaturant) production. Beginning in 2001, also includes biodiesel production.

[2] Net imports equal imports minus exports. Includes petroleum (excluding biofuels) net imports. Beginning in 1993, also includes fuel ethanol (minus denaturant) net imports. Beginning in 2001, also includes biodiesel net imports. Beginning in 2009, also includes a small amount of other biofuels (such as bio-jet fuel and bio-ETBE) imports.

[3] Includes petroleum and biofuels stock withdrawals (stock change multiplied by -1); petroleum adjustments; and biodiesel balancing item.

[4] Includes estimated consumption of petroleum. Beginning in 1981, also includes estimated consumption of fuel ethanol minus denaturant. Beginning in 2001, also includes estimated consumption of biodiesel. Techniques used to estimate consumption vary depending on the product. Petroleum product supplied is used as an approximation of petroleum consumption, which is adjusted to exclude biofuels in order to prevent double counting. See Note 1, "Petroleum Products Supplied and Petroleum Consumption," at end of section. Estimated consumption of fuel ethanol minus denaturant in 2011 is calculated as fuel ethanol refinery and blender net inputs minus fuel ethanol adjustments minus the amount of denaturant in fuel ethanol consumed; for other years, see sources in Table 10.3. Estimated consumption of biodiesel in 2011 is calculated as biodiesel production plus biodiesel net imports minus biodiesel stock change; for other years, see sources in Table 10.4.

R=Revised. P=Preliminary. E=Estimate.

Web Pages: • See http://www.eia.gov/totalenergy/data/monthly/#petroleum for updated monthly and annual data. • See http://www.eia.gov/totalenergy/data/annual/#petroleum for all annual data beginning in 1949. • See http://www.eia.gov/petroleum/ and http://www.eia.gov/renewable/ for related information.

Sources: **Production:** Tables 5.1b, 10.3, and 10.4. **Net Imports:** Tables 5.1b, 10.3, and 10.4; and U.S. Energy Information Administration (EIA), *Petroleum Supply Annual (PSA)*, *Petroleum Supply Monthly (PSM)*, and earlier publications—see sources for Table 5.1b. **Balancing Item:** Calculated as estimated consumption minus production and net imports. **Estimated Consumption:** Tables 5.1b, 10.3, and 10.4; and EIA, PSA, PSM, and earlier publications—see sources for Table 5.1b.

Source: *U.S. Energy Information Administration, Annual Energy Review 2011*

Table 5.1b Petroleum Overview, Selected Years, 1949-2011

(Thousand Barrels per Day)

Year	Field Production [1]					Renewable Fuels and Oxygenates [5]	Processing Gain [6]	Trade			Stock Change [8,10]	Adjustments [11]	Petroleum Products Supplied [8]
	Crude Oil [2]			Natural Gas Plant Liquids [4]	Total			Imports [7,8]	Exports	Net Imports [8,9]			
	48 States [3]	Alaska	Total										
1949	5,046	0	5,046	430	5,477	NA	-2	645	327	318	-8	-38	5,763
1950	5,407	0	5,407	499	5,906	NA	2	850	305	545	-56	-51	6,458
1955	6,807	0	6,807	771	7,578	NA	34	1,248	368	880	(s)	-37	8,455
1960	7,034	2	7,035	929	7,965	NA	146	1,815	202	1,613	-83	-8	9,797
1965	7,774	30	7,804	1,210	9,014	NA	220	2,468	187	2,281	-8	-10	11,512
1970	9,408	229	9,637	1,660	11,297	NA	359	3,419	259	3,161	103	-16	14,697
1975	8,183	191	8,375	1,633	10,007	NA	460	6,056	209	5,846	32	41	16,322
1976	7,958	173	8,132	1,604	9,736	NA	477	7,313	223	7,090	-58	101	17,461
1977	7,781	464	8,245	1,618	9,862	NA	524	8,807	243	8,565	548	28	18,431
1978	7,478	1,229	8,707	1,567	10,275	NA	496	8,363	362	8,002	-94	-20	18,847
1979	7,151	1,401	8,552	1,584	10,135	NA	527	8,456	471	7,985	173	38	18,513
1980	6,980	1,617	8,597	1,573	10,170	NA	597	6,909	544	6,365	140	64	17,056
1981	6,962	1,609	8,572	1,609	10,180	NA	508	5,996	595	5,401	160	129	16,058
1982	6,953	1,696	8,649	1,550	10,199	NA	531	5,113	815	4,298	-147	121	15,296
1983	6,974	1,714	8,688	1,559	10,246	NA	488	5,051	739	4,312	-20	165	15,231
1984	7,157	1,722	8,879	1,630	10,509	NA	553	5,437	722	4,715	280	228	15,726
1985	7,146	1,825	8,971	1,609	10,581	NA	557	5,067	781	4,286	-103	200	15,726
1986	6,814	1,867	8,680	1,551	10,231	NA	616	6,224	785	5,439	202	197	16,281
1987	6,387	1,962	8,349	1,595	9,944	NA	639	6,678	764	5,914	41	209	16,665
1988	6,123	2,017	8,140	1,625	9,765	NA	655	7,402	815	6,587	-28	249	17,283
1989	5,739	1,874	7,613	1,546	9,159	NA	661	8,061	859	7,202	-43	260	17,325
1990	5,582	1,773	7,355	1,559	8,914	NA	683	8,018	857	7,161	107	338	16,988
1991	5,618	1,798	7,417	1,659	9,076	NA	715	7,627	1,001	6,626	-10	287	16,714
1992	5,457	1,714	7,171	1,697	8,868	NA	772	7,888	950	6,938	-68	386	17,033
1993	5,264	1,582	6,847	1,736	8,582	NA	766	8,620	1,003	7,618	151	422	17,237
1994	5,103	1,559	6,662	1,727	8,388	NA	768	8,996	942	8,054	15	523	17,718
1995	5,076	1,484	6,560	1,762	8,322	NA	774	8,835	949	7,886	-246	496	17,725
1996	5,071	1,393	6,465	1,830	8,295	NA	837	9,478	981	8,498	-151	528	18,309
1997	5,156	1,296	6,452	1,817	8,269	NA	850	10,162	1,003	9,158	143	487	18,620
1998	5,077	1,175	6,252	1,759	8,011	NA	886	10,708	945	9,764	239	495	18,917
1999	4,832	1,050	5,881	1,850	7,731	NA	886	10,852	940	9,912	-422	567	19,519
2000	4,851	970	5,822	1,911	7,733	NA	948	11,459	1,040	10,419	-69	532	19,701
2001	4,839	963	5,801	1,868	7,670	NA	903	11,871	971	10,900	325	501	19,649
2002	4,761	984	5,746	1,880	7,626	NA	957	11,530	984	10,546	-105	527	19,761
2003	4,706	974	5,681	1,719	7,400	NA	974	12,264	1,027	11,238	56	478	20,034
2004	4,510	908	5,419	1,809	7,228	NA	1,051	13,145	1,048	12,097	209	564	20,731
2005	4,314	864	5,178	1,717	6,895	NA	989	13,714	1,165	12,549	145	513	20,802
2006	4,361	741	5,102	1,739	6,841	NA	994	13,707	1,317	12,390	60	522	20,687
2007	4,342	722	5,064	1,783	6,847	NA	996	13,468	1,433	12,036	-148	653	20,680
2008	4,268	683	4,950	1,784	6,734	NA	993	12,915	1,802	11,114	195	852	19,498
2009	4,715	645	5,361	1,910	7,270	746	979	11,691	2,024	9,667	109	218	18,771
2010	R4,874	R601	R5,476	R2,074	R7,550	R907	R1,068	R11,793	R2,353	R9,441	R49	R264	R19,180
2011	E5,090	E572	E5,662	P2,183	E7,844	P954	P1,085	P11,360	P2,924	P8,436	P-115	P402	P18,835

[1] Crude oil production on leases, and natural gas liquids (liquefied petroleum gases, pentanes plus, and a small amount of finished petroleum products) production at natural gas processing plants. Excludes what was previously classified as "Field Production" of finished motor gasoline, motor gasoline blending components, and other hydrocarbons and oxygenates; these are now included in "Adjustments."

[2] Includes lease condensate.

[3] United States excluding Alaska and Hawaii.

[4] See Table 5.10.

[5] Renewable fuels and oxygenate plant net production.

[6] Refinery and blender net production minus refinery and blender net inputs. See Table 5.8.

[7] Includes crude oil imports for the Strategic Petroleum Reserve, which began in 1977. See Table 5.17.

[8] Beginning in 1993, includes fuel ethanol blended into motor gasoline. Beginning in 2009, also includes biodiesel and other renewable fuels blended into petroleum.

[9] Net imports equal imports minus exports.

[10] A negative value indicates a decrease in stocks and a positive value indicates an increase. Includes crude oil stocks in the Strategic Petroleum Reserve, but excludes distillate fuel oil stocks in the Northeast Heating Oil Reserve. See Table 5.16.

[11] An adjustment for crude oil, finished motor gasoline, motor gasoline blending components, fuel ethanol, and distillate fuel oil. See EIA, *Petroleum Supply Monthly (PSM)*, Appendix B.

R=Revised. P=Preliminary. E=Estimate. NA=Not available. (s)=Less than 500 barrels per day and greater than -500 barrels per day.

Notes: • See Note 1, "Petroleum Products Supplied and Petroleum Consumption," and Note 2, "Changes Affecting Petroleum Production and Product Supplied Statistics," at end of section. • Totals may not equal sum of components due to independent rounding.

Web Pages: • See http://www.eia.gov/totalenergy/data/monthly/#petroleum for updated monthly and annual data. • See http://www.eia.gov/totalenergy/data/annual/#petroleum for all annual data beginning in 1949. • See http://www.eia.gov/petroleum/ for related information.

Sources: • 1949-1975—Bureau of Mines, Mineral Industry Surveys, *Petroleum Statement, Annual*, annual reports. • 1976-1980—U.S. Energy Information Administration (EIA), Energy Data Reports, *Petroleum Statement, Annual*, annual reports. • 1981-2009—EIA, *Petroleum Supply Annual (PSA)*, annual reports. • 2010 and 2011—EIA, PSA, annual report; *Petroleum Supply Monthly*, monthly reports; and revisions to crude oil production, total field production, and adjustments, published in the *Monthly Energy Review* (May 2012), Table 3.1 (based on crude oil production data from: State government agencies; U.S. Department of the Interior, Bureau of Safety and Environmental Enforcement, and predecessor agencies; and Form EIA-182, "Domestic Crude Oil First Purchase Report").

Source: *U.S. Energy Information Administration, Annual Energy Review 2011*

Figure 5.2 Crude Oil Production and Crude Oil Well Productivity, 1954-2011

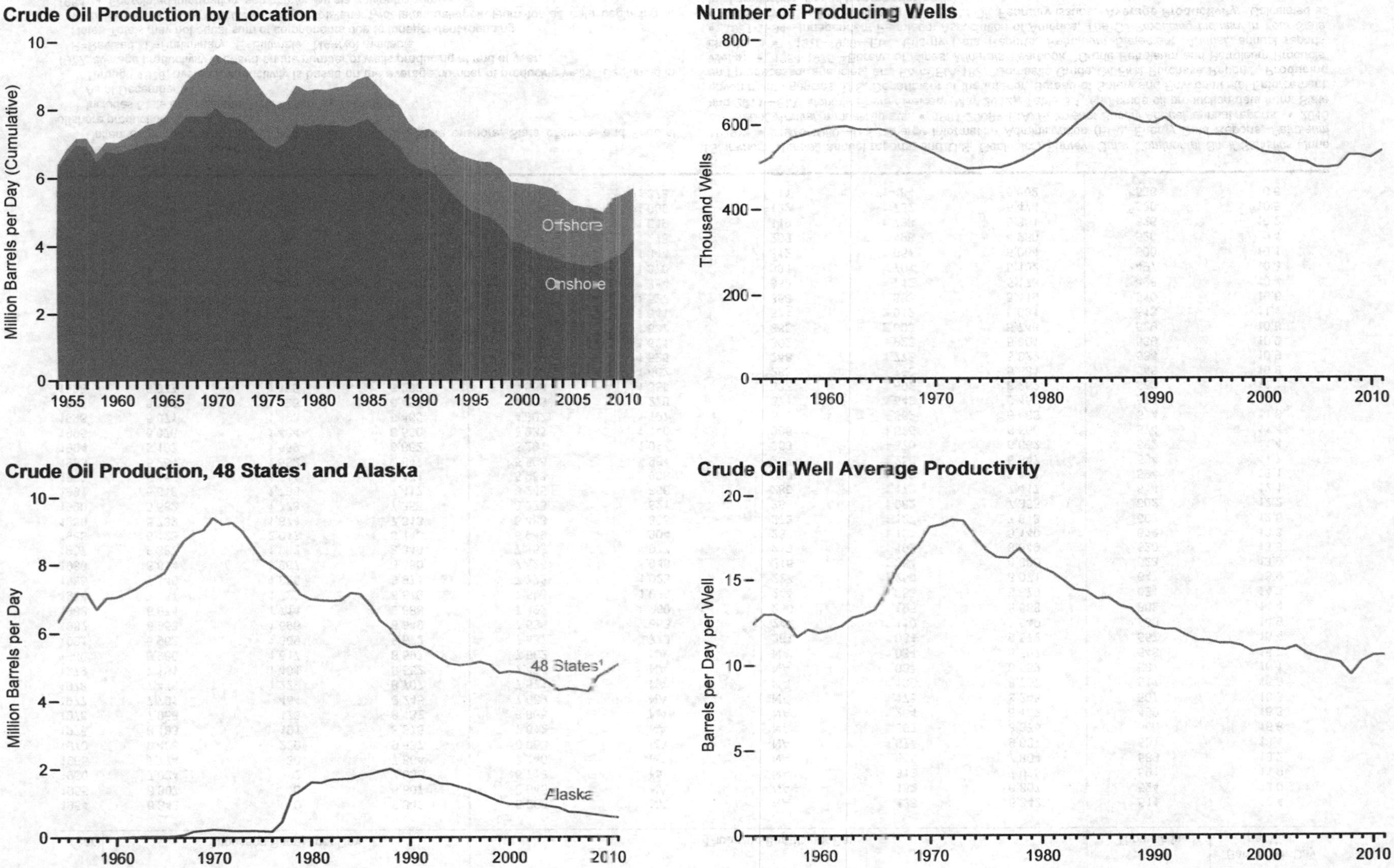

[1] United States excluding Alaska and Hawaii.
Note: Crude oil includes lease condensate.

Source: Table 5.2.

Source: *U.S. Energy Information Administration, Annual Energy Review 2011*

Table 5.2 Crude Oil Production and Crude Oil Well Productivity, Selected Years, 1954-2011

Year	Crude Oil Production								Crude Oil Well[1] Productivity	
					Offshore					
	48 States[2]	Alaska[3]	Total	Onshore	Federal	State	Total	Total	Producing Wells[4]	Average Productivity[5]
	Thousand Barrels per Day			Thousand Barrels per Day					Thousands	Barrels per Day per Well
1954	6,342	0	6,342	6,209	NA	NA	133	6,342	511	12.4
1955	6,807	0	6,807	6,645	NA	NA	162	6,807	524	13.0
1960	7,034	2	7,035	6,716	NA	NA	319	7,035	591	11.9
1965	7,774	30	7,804	7,140	NA	NA	665	7,804	589	13.2
1970	9,408	229	9,637	8,060	NA	NA	1,577	9,637	531	18.1
1975	8,183	191	8,375	7,012	NA	NA	1,362	8,375	500	16.8
1976	7,958	173	8,132	6,868	NA	NA	1,264	8,132	499	16.3
1977	7,781	464	8,245	7,069	NA	NA	1,176	8,245	507	16.3
1978	7,478	1,229	8,707	7,571	NA	NA	1,136	8,707	517	16.8
1979	7,151	1,401	8,552	7,485	NA	NA	1,067	8,552	531	16.1
1980	6,980	1,617	8,597	7,562	NA	NA	1,034	8,597	548	15.7
1981	6,962	1,609	8,572	7,537	773	261	1,034	8,572	557	15.4
1982	6,953	1,696	8,649	7,538	863	247	1,110	8,649	580	14.9
1983	6,974	1,714	8,688	7,492	960	236	1,196	8,688	603	14.4
1984	7,157	1,722	8,879	7,596	1,039	244	1,283	8,879	621	14.3
1985	7,146	1,825	8,971	7,722	1,023	227	1,250	8,971	647	13.9
1986	6,814	1,867	8,680	7,426	1,038	216	1,254	8,680	623	13.9
1987	6,387	1,962	8,349	7,153	977	219	1,196	8,349	620	13.5
1988	6,123	2,017	8,140	6,949	904	287	1,191	8,140	612	13.3
1989	5,739	1,874	7,613	6,486	855	272	1,127	7,613	603	12.6
1990	5,582	1,773	7,355	6,273	821	261	1,082	7,355	602	12.2
1991	5,618	1,798	7,417	6,245	886	286	1,172	7,417	614	12.1
1992	5,457	1,714	7,171	5,953	938	280	1,218	7,171	594	12.1
1993	5,264	1,582	6,847	R5,596	964	287	R1,250	6,847	584	11.7
1994	5,103	1,559	6,662	5,291	1,017	353	1,370	6,662	582	11.4
1995	5,076	1,484	6,560	5,035	1,140	385	1,525	6,560	574	11.4
1996	5,071	1,393	6,465	4,902	1,197	365	1,562	6,465	574	11.3
1997	5,156	1,296	6,452	4,803	1,278	371	1,648	6,452	573	11.3
1998	5,077	1,175	6,252	4,560	1,355	337	1,692	6,252	562	11.1
1999	4,832	1,050	5,881	4,132	1,462	288	1,750	5,881	546	10.8
2000	4,851	970	5,822	4,049	1,525	248	1,773	5,822	534	10.9
2001	4,839	963	5,801	3,879	1,621	302	1,923	5,801	530	10.9
2002	4,761	984	5,746	3,743	1,637	365	2,003	5,746	529	10.9
2003	4,706	974	5,681	3,668	1,641	371	2,012	5,681	513	11.1
2004	4,510	908	5,419	3,536	1,527	356	1,883	5,419	510	10.6
2005	4,314	864	5,178	3,466	1,354	358	1,712	5,178	498	10.4
2006	4,361	741	5,102	3,401	1,370	331	1,701	5,102	497	10.3
2007	4,342	722	5,064	3,407	1,344	312	1,657	5,064	500	10.1
2008	4,268	683	4,950	3,452	1,218	280	1,498	4,950	526	9.4
2009	4,715	645	5,361	3,622	1,619	119	1,738	5,361	526	10.2
2010	R4,874	R601	R5,476	RE3,744	E1,609	E122	RE1,732	R5,476	R520	R10.5
2011	E5,090	E572	E5,662	E4,178	E1,373	E111	E1,484	E5,662	P536	E10.6

1 See "Crude Oil Well" in Glossary.
2 United States excluding Alaska and Hawaii. Includes State onshore, State offshore, and Federal offshore production.
3 Includes State onshore and State offshore production.
4 As of December 31.
5 Through 1976, average productivity is based on the average number of producing wells. Beginning in 1977, average productivity is based on the number of wells producing at end of year.
R=Revised. P=Preliminary. E=Estimate. NA=Not available.
Note: Totals may not equal sum of components due to independent rounding.
Web Pages: • See http://www.eia.gov/totalenergy/data/annual/#petroleum for all data beginning in 1954. • For related information, see http://www.eia.gov/petroleum/.
Sources: **Crude Oil Production:** • 1954-1975—Bureau of Mines, Mineral Industry Surveys, *Petroleum Statement, Annual,* annual reports; and U.S. Geological Survey, *Outer Continental Shelf Statistics* (June 1979). • 1976-1980—U.S. Energy Information Administration (EIA), Energy Data Reports, *Petroleum Statement, Annual,* annual reports. • 1981-2009—EIA, *Petroleum Supply Annual,* annual reports. • 2010 and 2011—EIA, *Monthly Energy Review* (May 2012), Table 3.1; and crude oil production data from: State government agencies; U.S. Department of the Interior, Bureau of Safety and Environmental Enforcement, and predecessor agencies; and Form EIA-182, "Domestic Crude Oil First Purchase Report." **Producing Wells:** • 1954-1975—Bureau of Mines, *Minerals Yearbook,* "Crude Petroleum and Petroleum Products" chapter. • 1976-1980—EIA, Energy Data Reports, *Petroleum Statement, Annual,* annual reports. • 1981-1994—Independent Petroleum Association of America, *The Oil Producing Industry in Your State.* • 1995 forward—Gulf Publishing Co., *World Oil,* February issues. **Average Productivity:** Calculated as total production divided by producing wells.

Source: *U.S. Energy Information Administration, Annual Energy Review 2011*

Figure 5.3 Petroleum Imports by Type

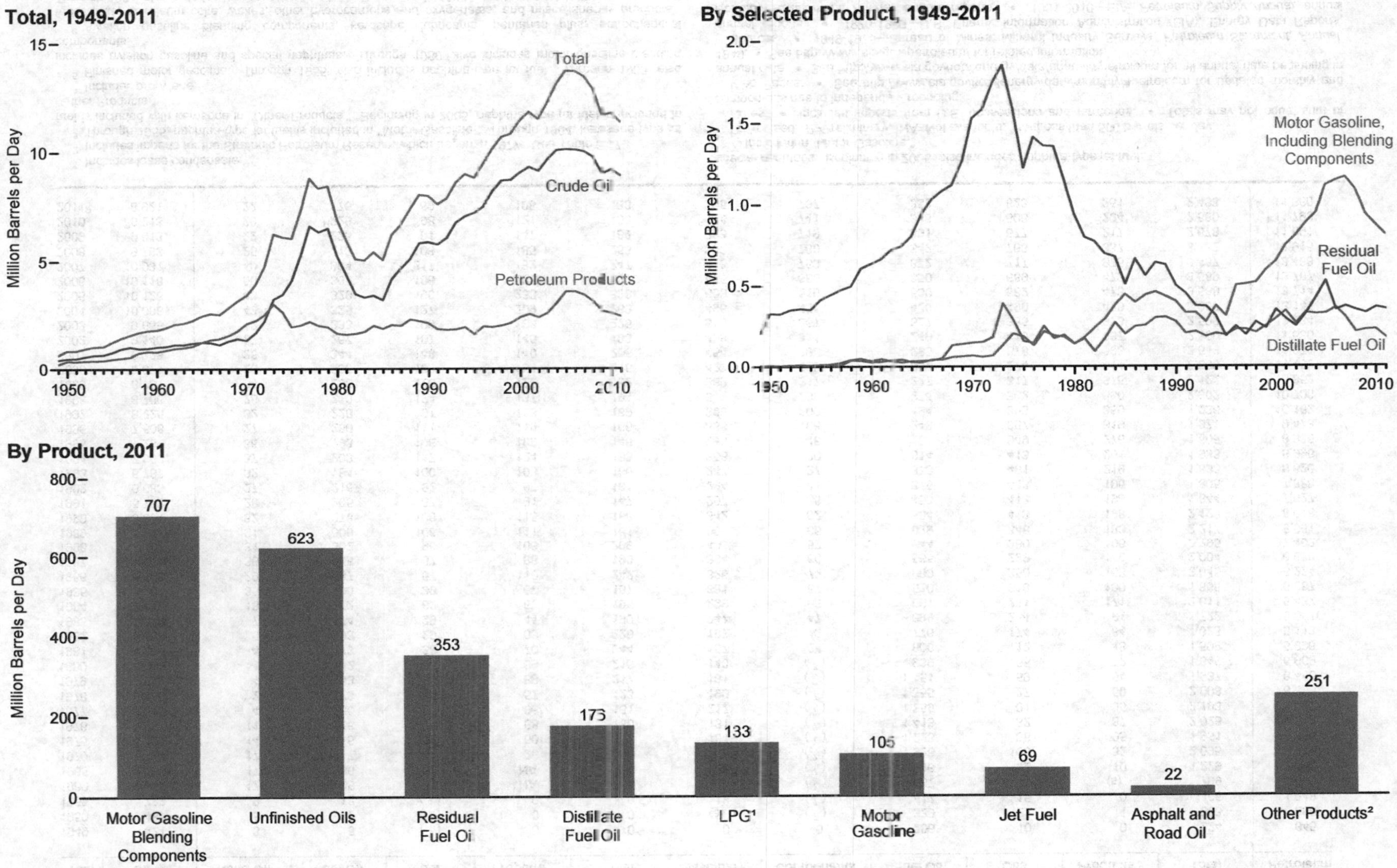

[1] Liquefied petroleum gases.

[2] Aviation gasoline and blending components, kerosene, lubricants, naphtha-type jet fuel, pentanes plus, petrochemical feedstocks, petroleum coke, special naphthas, waxes, other hydrocarbons and oxygenates, and miscellaneous products.

Source: Table 5.3.

Source: *U.S. Energy Information Administration, Annual Energy Review 2011*

Table 5.3 Petroleum Imports by Type, Selected Years, 1949-2011

(Thousand Barrels per Day)

Year	Crude Oil [1,2]	Petroleum Products											Total Petroleum
		Asphalt and Road Oil	Distillate Fuel Oil	Jet Fuel [3]	Liquefied Petroleum Gases		Motor Gasoline [5]	Motor Gasoline Blending Components	Residual Fuel Oil	Unfinished Oils	Other Products [6]	Total	
					Propane [4]	Total							
1949	421	3	5	(3)	0	0	0	0	206	10	0	224	645
1950	487	5	7	(3)	0	0	(s)	(7)	329	21	1	363	850
1955	782	9	12	(3)	0	0	13	(7)	417	15	0	466	1,248
1960	1,015	17	35	34	NA	4	27	(7)	637	45	(s)	799	1,815
1965	1,238	17	36	81	NA	21	28	(7)	946	92	10	1,229	2,468
1970	1,324	17	147	144	26	52	67	(7)	1,528	108	32	2,095	3,419
1975	4,105	14	155	133	60	112	184	(7)	1,223	36	95	1,951	6,056
1976	5,287	11	146	76	68	130	131	(7)	1,413	32	87	2,026	7,313
1977	6,615	4	250	75	86	161	217	(7)	1,359	31	95	2,193	8,807
1978	6,356	2	173	86	57	123	190	(7)	1,355	27	50	2,008	8,363
1979	6,519	4	193	78	88	217	181	(7)	1,151	59	54	1,937	8,456
1980	5,263	4	142	80	69	216	140	(7)	939	55	72	1,646	6,909
1981	4,396	4	173	38	70	244	157	24	800	112	48	1,599	5,996
1982	3,488	5	93	29	63	226	197	42	776	174	84	1,625	5,113
1983	3,329	7	174	29	44	190	247	47	699	234	94	1,722	5,051
1984	3,426	18	272	62	67	195	299	83	681	231	171	2,011	5,437
1985	3,201	35	200	39	67	187	381	67	510	318	130	1,866	5,067
1986	4,178	29	247	57	110	242	326	72	669	250	153	2,045	6,224
1987	4,674	36	255	67	88	190	384	60	565	299	146	2,004	6,678
1988	5,107	31	302	90	106	209	405	57	644	360	196	2,295	7,402
1989	5,843	31	306	106	111	181	369	66	629	348	183	2,217	8,061
1990	5,894	32	278	108	115	188	342	62	504	413	198	2,123	8,018
1991	5,782	28	205	67	91	147	297	36	453	413	198	1,844	7,627
1992	6,083	27	216	82	85	131	294	41	375	443	195	1,805	7,888
1993	6,787	32	184	100	103	160	247	27	373	491	219	1,833	8,620
1994	7,063	37	203	117	124	183	356	20	314	413	291	1,933	8,996
1995	7,230	36	193	106	102	146	265	48	187	349	276	1,605	8,835
1996	7,508	27	230	111	119	166	336	166	248	367	319	1,971	9,478
1997	8,225	32	228	91	113	169	309	200	194	353	360	1,936	10,162
1998	8,706	28	210	124	137	194	311	209	275	302	350	2,002	10,708
1999	8,731	34	250	128	122	182	382	217	237	317	375	2,122	10,852
2000	9,071	28	295	162	161	215	427	223	352	274	414	2,389	11,459
2001	9,328	26	344	148	140	206	454	298	295	378	393	2,543	11,871
2002	9,140	27	267	107	145	183	498	311	249	410	337	2,390	11,530
2003	9,665	12	333	109	168	225	518	367	327	335	373	2,599	12,264
2004	10,088	43	325	127	209	263	496	451	426	490	436	3,057	13,145
2005	10,126	43	329	190	233	328	603	510	530	582	473	3,588	13,714
2006	10,118	50	365	186	228	332	475	669	350	689	473	3,589	13,707
2007	10,031	40	304	217	182	247	413	753	372	717	375	3,437	13,468
2008	9,783	25	213	103	185	253	302	789	349	763	337	3,132	12,915
2009	9,013	22	225	81	147	182	223	719	331	677	217	2,678	11,691
2010	R9,213	20	R228	R98	R121	R153	R134	R741	R366	R606	R234	R2,580	R11,793
2011P	8,921	22	176	69	108	133	105	707	353	623	251	2,438	11,360

[1] Includes lease condensate.

[2] Includes imports for the Strategic Petroleum Reserve, which began in 1977. See Table 5.17.

[3] Through 1955, naphtha-type jet fuel is included in "Motor Gasoline." Through 1964, kerosene-type jet fuel is included with kerosene in "Other Products." Beginning in 2005, naphtha-type jet fuel is included in "Other Products."

[4] Includes propylene.

[5] Finished motor gasoline. Through 1955, also includes naphtha-type jet fuel. Through 1963, also includes aviation gasoline and special naphthas. Through 1980, also includes motor gasoline blending components.

[6] Aviation gasoline blending components, kerosene, lubricants, pentanes plus, petrochemical feedstocks, petroleum coke, waxes, other hydrocarbons and oxygenates, and miscellaneous products. Through 1964, also includes kerosene-type jet fuel. Beginning in 1964, also includes aviation gasoline and special naphthas. Beginning in 2005, also includes naphtha-type jet fuel.

[7] Included in "Motor Gasoline."

R=Revised. P=Preliminary. NA=Not available. (s)=Less than 500 barrels per day.

Notes: • Includes imports from U.S. possessions and territories. • Totals may not equal sum of components due to independent rounding.

Web Pages: • See http://www.eia.gov/totalenergy/data/monthly/#petroleum for updated monthly and annual data. • See http://www.eia.gov/totalenergy/data/annual/#petroleum for all annual data beginning in 1949. • See http://www.eia.gov/petroleum/ for related information.

Sources: • 1949-1975—Bureau of Mines, Mineral Industry Surveys, *Petroleum Statement, Annual*, annual reports. • 1976-1980—U.S. Energy Information Administration (EIA), Energy Data Reports, *Petroleum Statement, Annual*, annual reports. • 1981-2010—EIA, *Petroleum Supply Annual*, annual reports. • 2011—EIA, *Petroleum Supply Monthly* (February 2012).

Source: *U.S. Energy Information Administration, Annual Energy Review 2011*

Figure 5.4 Petroleum Imports by Country of Origin

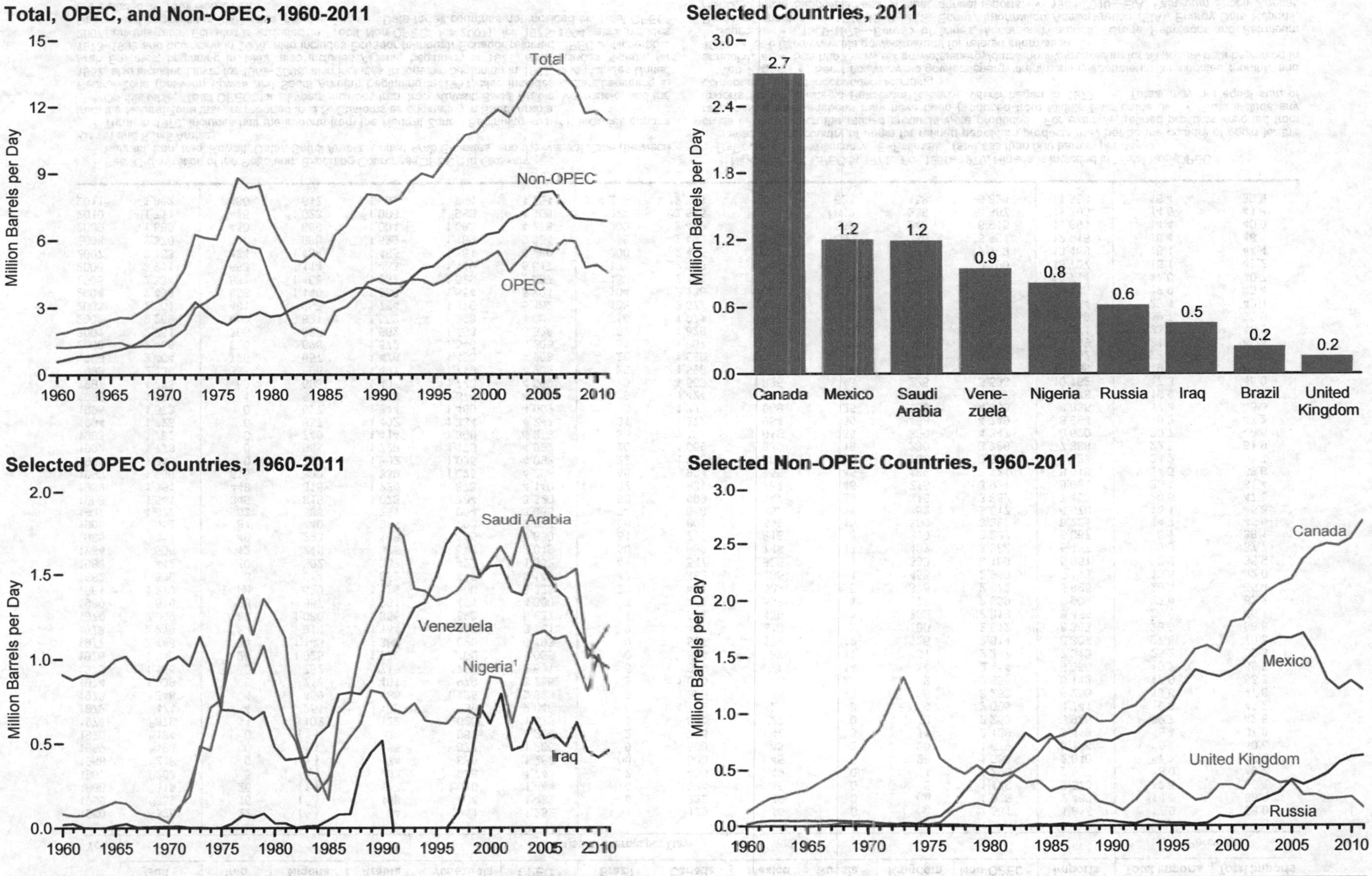

[1] On this graph, imports from Nigeria are shown beginning in 1971, when Nigeria joined OPEC.

Note: OPEC=Organization of the Petroleum Exporting Countries.
Source: Table 5.4.

Source: *U.S. Energy Information Administration, Annual Energy Review 2011*

Table 5.4 Petroleum Imports by Country of Origin, Selected Years, 1960-2011

Year	Selected OPEC[1] Countries: Persian Gulf[2]	Iraq	Nigeria	Saudi Arabia[3]	Venezuela	Total OPEC[4]	Selected Non-OPEC[1] Countries: Brazil	Canada	Mexico	Russia[5]	United Kingdom	Total Non-OPEC[4]	Total Imports	Imports From Persian Gulf[2] as Share of Total Imports	Imports From OPEC[1] as Share of Total Imports
	Thousand Barrels per Day													Percent	
1960	RE326	22	(6)	84	911	1,233	1	120	16	0	(s)	581	1,815	RE17.9	68.0
1965	R359	16	(6)	158	994	1,439	0	323	48	0	(s)	1,029	2,468	R14.5	58.3
1966	R319	26	(6)	147	1,018	1,444	0	384	45	0	6	1,129	2,573	R12.4	56.1
1967	R203	5	(6)	92	938	1,247	2	450	49	0	11	1,290	2,537	R8.0	49.2
1968	R218	0	(6)	74	886	1,287	(s)	506	45	0	28	1,553	2,840	R7.7	45.3
1969	R193	0	(6)	65	875	1,286	0	608	43	2	20	1,879	3,166	R6.1	40.6
1970	R184	0	(6)	30	989	1,294	2	766	42	3	11	2,126	3,419	R5.4	37.8
1971	R379	11	102	128	1,020	1,673	3	857	27	0	10	2,253	3,926	R9.7	42.6
1972	471	4	251	190	959	2,046	5	1,108	21	8	9	2,695	4,741	9.9	43.2
1973	848	4	459	486	1,135	2,993	9	1,325	16	26	15	3,263	6,256	13.6	47.8
1974	1,039	0	713	461	979	3,256	2	1,070	8	20	8	2,856	6,112	17.0	53.3
1975	1,165	2	762	715	702	3,601	5	846	71	14	14	2,454	6,056	19.2	59.5
1976	1,840	26	1,025	1,230	700	5,066	0	599	87	11	31	2,247	7,313	25.2	69.3
1977	2,448	74	1,143	1,380	690	6,193	0	517	179	12	126	2,614	8,807	27.8	70.3
1978	2,219	62	919	1,144	646	5,751	0	467	318	8	180	2,612	8,363	26.5	68.8
1979	2,069	88	1,080	1,356	690	5,637	1	538	439	1	202	2,819	8,456	24.5	66.7
1980	1,519	28	857	1,261	481	4,300	3	455	533	1	176	2,609	6,909	22.0	62.2
1981	1,219	(s)	620	1,129	406	3,323	23	447	522	5	375	2,672	5,996	20.3	55.4
1982	696	3	514	552	412	2,146	47	482	685	1	456	2,968	5,113	13.6	42.0
1983	442	10	302	337	422	1,862	41	547	826	1	382	3,189	5,051	8.8	36.9
1984	506	12	216	325	548	2,049	60	630	748	13	402	3,388	5,437	9.3	37.7
1985	311	46	293	168	605	1,830	61	770	816	8	310	3,237	5,067	6.1	36.1
1986	912	81	440	685	793	2,837	50	807	699	18	350	3,387	6,224	14.7	45.6
1987	1,077	83	535	751	804	3,060	84	848	655	11	352	3,617	6,678	16.1	45.8
1988	1,541	345	618	1,073	794	3,520	98	999	747	29	315	3,882	7,402	20.8	47.6
1989	1,861	449	815	1,224	873	4,140	82	931	767	48	215	3,921	8,061	23.1	51.4
1990	1,966	518	800	1,339	1,025	4,296	49	934	755	45	189	3,721	8,018	24.5	53.6
1991	1,845	0	703	1,802	1,035	4,092	22	1,033	807	29	138	3,535	7,627	24.2	53.7
1992	1,778	0	681	1,720	1,170	4,092	20	1,069	830	18	230	3,796	7,888	22.5	51.9
1993	1,782	0	740	1,414	1,300	4,273	33	1,181	919	55	350	4,347	8,620	20.7	49.6
1994	1,728	0	637	1,402	1,334	4,247	31	1,272	984	30	458	4,749	8,996	19.2	47.2
1995	1,573	0	627	1,344	1,480	4,002	8	1,332	1,068	25	383	4,833	8,835	17.8	45.3
1996	1,604	1	617	1,363	1,676	4,211	9	1,424	1,244	25	308	5,267	9,478	16.9	44.4
1997	1,755	89	698	1,407	1,773	4,569	5	1,563	1,385	13	226	5,593	10,162	17.3	45.0
1998	2,136	336	696	1,491	1,719	4,905	26	1,598	1,351	24	250	5,803	10,708	19.9	45.8
1999	2,464	725	657	1,478	1,493	4,953	26	1,539	1,324	89	365	5,899	10,852	22.7	45.6
2000	2,488	620	896	1,572	1,546	5,203	51	1,807	1,373	72	366	6,257	11,459	21.7	45.4
2001	2,761	795	885	1,662	1,553	5,528	82	1,828	1,440	90	324	6,343	11,871	23.3	46.6
2002	2,269	459	621	1,552	1,398	4,605	116	1,971	1,547	210	478	6,925	11,530	19.7	39.9
2003	2,501	481	867	1,774	1,376	5,162	108	2,072	1,623	254	440	7,103	12,264	20.4	42.1
2004	2,493	656	1,140	1,558	1,554	5,701	104	2,138	1,665	298	380	7,444	13,145	19.0	43.4
2005	2,334	531	1,166	1,537	1,529	5,587	156	2,181	1,662	410	396	8,127	13,714	17.0	40.7
2006	2,211	553	1,114	1,463	1,419	5,517	193	2,353	1,705	369	272	8,190	13,707	16.1	40.2
2007	2,163	484	1,134	1,485	1,361	5,980	200	2,455	1,532	414	277	7,489	13,468	16.1	44.4
2008	2,370	627	988	1,529	1,189	5,954	258	2,493	1,302	465	236	6,961	12,915	18.4	46.1
2009	1,689	450	809	1,004	1,063	4,776	309	2,479	1,210	563	245	6,915	11,691	14.4	40.9
2010	R1,711	R415	R1,023	R1,096	R988	R4,906	R272	R2,535	R1,284	R612	256	R6,887	R11,793	14.5	41.6
2011P	1,862	460	817	1,195	944	4,534	249	2,706	1,205	621	158	6,825	11,360	16.4	39.9

[1] See "Organization of the Petroleum Exporting Countries (OPEC)" in Glossary.
[2] Bahrain, Iran, Iraq, Kuwait, Qatar, Saudi Arabia, United Arab Emirates, and the Neutral Zone (between Kuwait and Saudi Arabia).
[3] Through 1970, includes half the imports from the Neutral Zone. Beginning in 1971, includes imports from the Neutral Zone that are reported to U.S. Customs as originating in Saudi Arabia.
[4] On this table, "Total OPEC" for all years includes Iran, Iraq, Kuwait, Saudi Arabia, Venezuela, and the Neutral Zone (between Kuwait and Saudi Arabia); beginning in 1961, also includes Qatar; beginning in 1962, also includes Libya; for 1962–2008, also includes Indonesia; beginning in 1967, also includes United Arab Emirates; beginning in 1969, also includes Algeria; beginning in 1971, also includes Nigeria; for 1973–1992 and beginning in 2008, also includes Ecuador (although Ecuador rejoined OPEC in November 2007, on this table Ecuador is included in "Total Non-OPEC" for 2007); for 1975–1994, also includes Gabon; and beginning in 2007, also includes Angola. Data for all countries not included in "Total OPEC" are included in "Total Non-OPEC."
[5] Through 1992, may include imports from republics other than Russia in the former U.S.S.R. See "U.S.S.R." in Glossary.
[6] Nigeria joined OPEC in 1971. For 1960–1970, Nigeria is included in "Total Non-OPEC."

R=Revised. P=Preliminary. E=Estimate. (s)=Less than 500 barrels per day.

Notes: • The country of origin for refined petroleum products may not be the country of origin for the crude oil from which the refined products were produced. For example, refined products imported from refineries in the Caribbean may have been produced from Middle East crude oil. • Data include any imports for the Strategic Petroleum Reserve, which began in 1977. • Totals may not equal sum of components due to independent rounding.

Web Pages: • See http://www.eia.gov/totalenergy/data/monthly/#petroleum for updated monthly and annual data. • See http://www.eia.gov/totalenergy/data/annual/#petroleum for all annual data beginning in 1960. • See http://www.eia.gov/petroleum/ for related information.

Sources: • 1960-1975—Bureau of Mines, *Minerals Yearbook,* "Crude Petroleum and Petroleum Products" chapter. • 1976-1980—U.S. Energy Information Administration (EIA), Energy Data Reports, *P.A.D. Districts Supply/Demand, Annual,* annual reports. • 1981-2010—EIA, *Petroleum Supply Annual,* annual reports. • 2011—EIA, *Petroleum Supply Monthly* (February 2012).

Source: *U.S. Energy Information Administration, Annual Energy Review 2011*

Figure 5.5 Petroleum Exports by Type

Total, 1949-2011

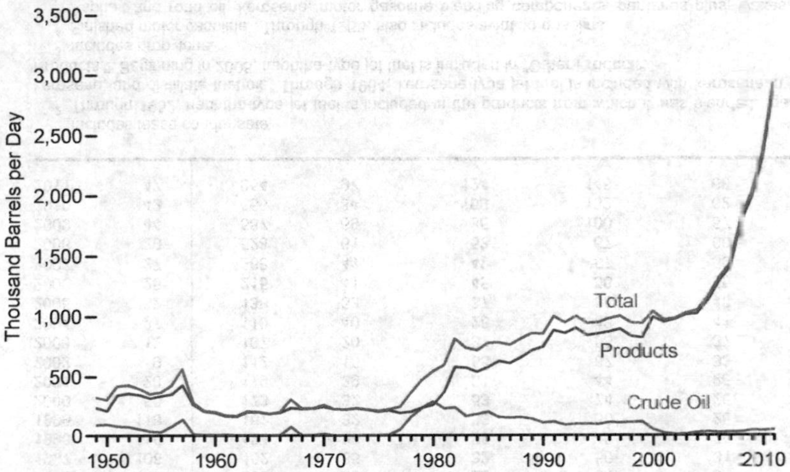

By Selected Product, 1949-2011

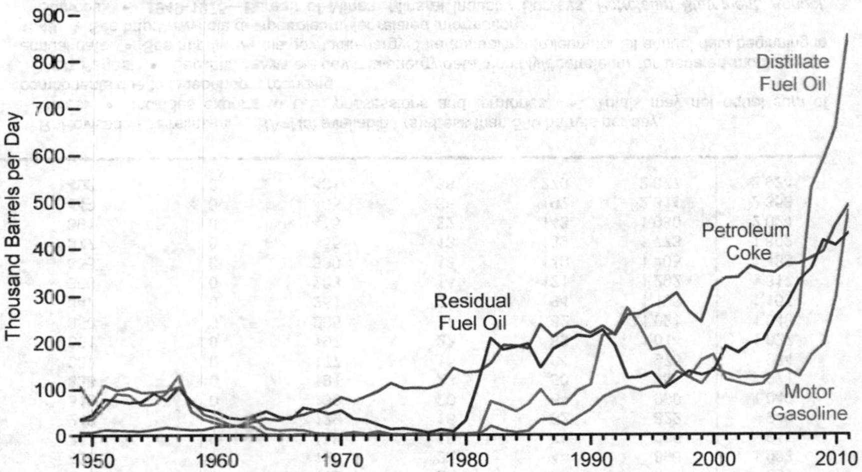

By Product, 2011

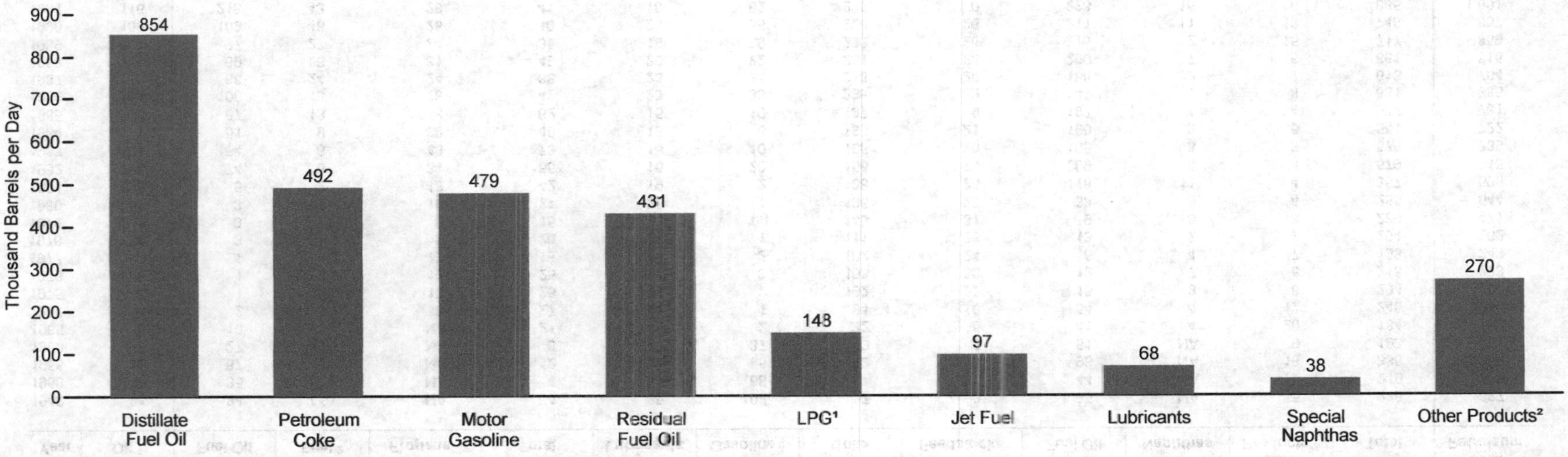

[1] Liquefied petroleum gases.

[2] Asphalt and road oil, aviation gasoline, kerosene, motor gasoline blending components, naphtha-type jet fuel, pentanes plus, waxes, other hydrocarbons and oxygenates, and miscellaneous products.

Source: Table 5.5.

Source: *U.S. Energy Information Administration, Annual Energy Review 2011*

Table 5.5 Petroleum Exports by Type, Selected Years, 1949-2011

(Thousand Barrels per Day)

Year	Crude Oil [1]	Petroleum Products												Total Petroleum
		Distillate Fuel Oil	Jet Fuel [2]	Liquefied Petroleum Gases		Lubricants	Motor Gasoline [4]	Petroleum Coke	Petrochemical Feedstocks	Residual Fuel Oil	Special Naphthas	Other Products [5]	Total	
				Propane [3]	Total									
1949	91	34	([2])	NA	4	35	108	7	0	35	NA	15	236	327
1950	95	35	([2])	NA	4	39	68	7	0	44	NA	12	210	305
1955	32	67	(s)	NA	12	39	95	12	0	93	NA	18	336	368
1960	8	27	(s)	NA	8	43	37	19	0	51	NA	9	193	202
1965	3	10	3	NA	21	45	2	32	5	41	4	20	184	187
1970	14	2	6	6	27	44	1	84	10	54	4	12	245	259
1975	6	1	2	13	26	25	2	102	22	15	3	6	204	209
1976	8	1	2	13	25	26	3	103	30	12	7	6	215	223
1977	50	1	2	10	18	26	2	102	24	6	4	7	193	243
1978	158	3	1	9	20	27	1	111	23	13	2	2	204	362
1979	235	3	1	8	15	23	(s)	146	31	9	5	3	236	471
1980	287	3	1	10	21	23	1	136	29	33	5	4	258	544
1981	228	5	2	18	42	19	2	138	26	118	11	4	367	595
1982	236	74	6	31	65	16	20	156	24	209	5	4	579	815
1983	164	64	6	43	73	16	10	195	20	185	3	3	575	739
1984	181	51	9	30	48	15	6	193	21	190	2	6	541	722
1985	204	67	13	48	62	15	10	187	19	197	1	4	577	781
1986	154	100	18	28	42	23	33	238	22	147	1	8	631	785
1987	151	66	24	24	38	23	35	213	20	186	2	7	613	764
1988	155	69	28	31	49	26	22	231	23	200	7	6	661	815
1989	142	97	27	24	35	19	39	233	26	215	12	15	717	859
1990	109	109	43	28	40	20	55	220	26	211	11	13	748	857
1991	116	215	43	28	41	18	82	235	0	226	15	9	885	1,001
1992	89	219	43	33	49	16	96	216	0	193	14	16	861	950
1993	98	274	59	26	43	19	105	258	0	123	4	20	904	1,003
1994	99	234	20	24	38	22	97	261	0	125	20	26	843	942
1995	95	183	26	38	58	25	104	277	0	136	21	25	855	949
1996	110	190	48	28	51	34	104	285	0	102	21	36	871	981
1997	108	152	35	32	50	31	137	306	0	120	22	44	896	1,003
1998	110	124	26	25	42	25	125	267	0	138	18	70	835	945
1999	118	162	32	33	50	28	111	242	0	129	16	52	822	940
2000	50	173	32	53	74	26	144	319	0	139	20	64	990	1,040
2001	20	119	29	31	44	26	133	336	0	191	23	50	951	971
2002	9	112	15	55	67	33	124	337	0	177	15	94	975	984
2003	12	107	20	37	56	37	125	361	0	197	22	89	1,014	1,027
2004	27	110	40	28	43	41	124	350	0	205	27	82	1,021	1,048
2005	32	138	53	37	53	40	136	347	0	251	21	94	1,133	1,165
2006	25	215	41	45	56	55	142	366	0	283	14	121	1,292	1,317
2007	27	268	41	42	57	59	127	366	0	330	18	140	1,405	1,433
2008	29	528	61	53	67	60	172	377	0	355	13	139	1,773	1,802
2009	44	587	69	85	100	57	195	391	0	415	22	143	1,980	2,024
2010	42	656	84	109	132	62	296	449	0	405	36	R192	R2,311	R2,353
2011P	47	854	97	124	148	68	479	492	0	431	38	270	2,877	2,924

[1] Includes lease condensate.

[2] Through 1952, naphtha-type jet fuel is included in the products from which it was blended: gasoline, kerosene, and distillate fuel oil. Through 1964, kerosene-type jet fuel is included with kerosene in "Other Products." Beginning in 2005, naphtha-type jet fuel is included in "Other Products."

[3] Includes propylene.

[4] Finished motor gasoline. Through 1963, also includes aviation gasoline.

[5] Asphalt and road oil, kerosene, motor gasoline blending components, pentanes plus, waxes, other hydrocarbons and oxygenates, and miscellaneous products. Through 1964, also includes kerosene-type jet fuel. Beginning in 1964, also includes aviation gasoline. Beginning in 2005, also includes naphtha-type jet fuel.

R=Revised. P=Preliminary. NA=Not available. (s)=Less than 500 barrels per day.

Notes: • Includes exports to U.S. possessions and territories. • Totals may not equal sum of components due to independent rounding.

Web Pages: • See http://www.eia.gov/totalenergy/data/monthly/#petroleum for updated monthly and annual data. • See http://www.eia.gov/totalenergy/data/annual/#petroleum for all annual data beginning in 1949. • See http://www.eia.gov/petroleum/ for related information.

Sources: • 1949-1975—Bureau of Mines, Mineral Industry Surveys, *Petroleum Statement, Annual,* annual reports. • 1976-1980—U.S. Energy Information Administration (EIA), Energy Data Reports, *Petroleum Statement, Annual,* annual reports. • 1981-2010—EIA, *Petroleum Supply Annual,* annual reports. • 2011—EIA, *Petroleum Supply Monthly* (February 2012).

Source: *U.S. Energy Information Administration, Annual Energy Review 2011*

Figure 5.6 Petroleum Exports by Country of Destination

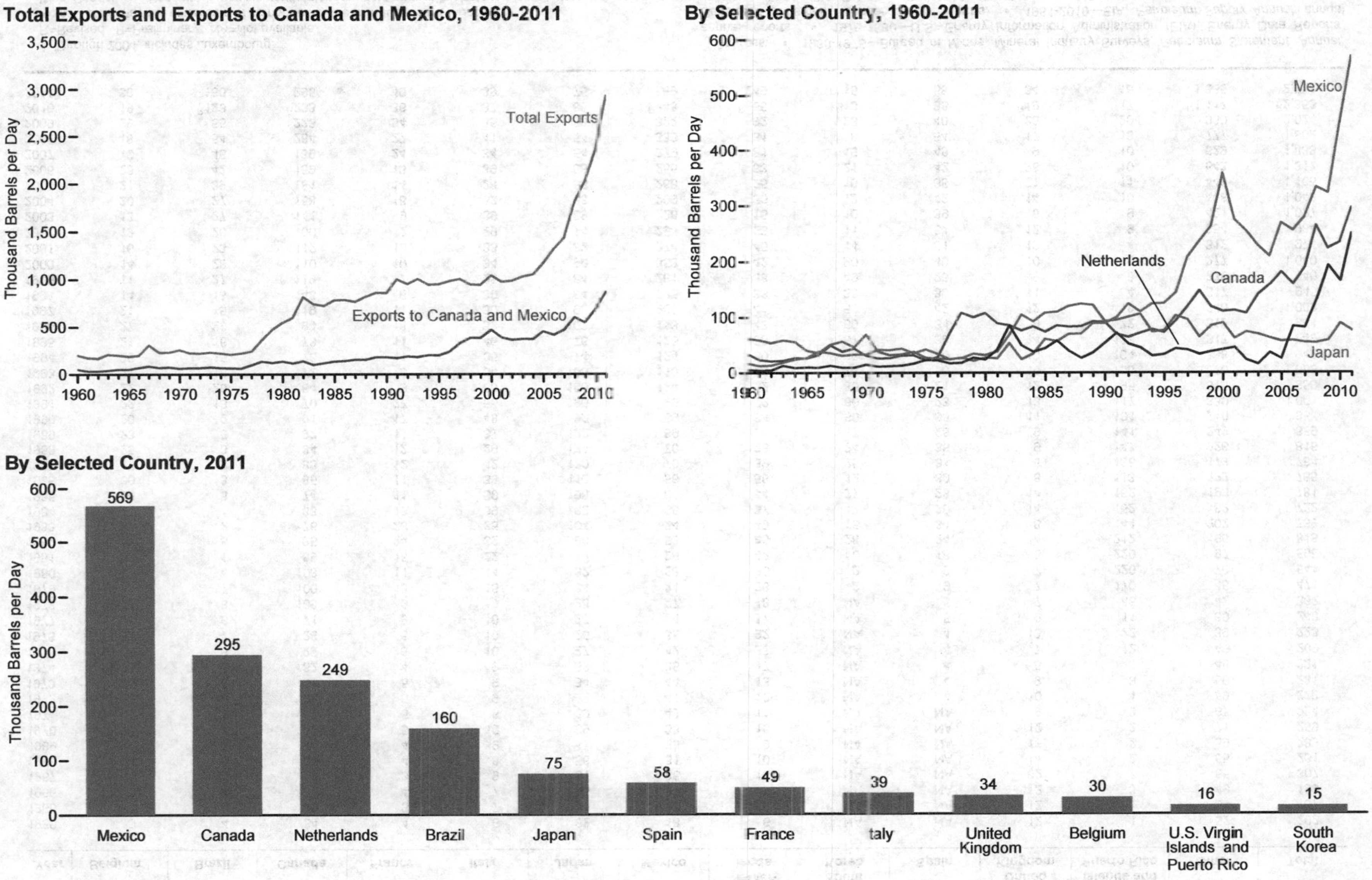

Source: Table 5.6.

Source: *U.S. Energy Information Administration, Annual Energy Review 2011*

Table 5.6 Petroleum Exports by Country of Destination, Selected Years, 1960-2011

(Thousand Barrels per Day)

Year	Belgium [1]	Brazil	Canada	France	Italy	Japan	Mexico	Nether-lands	South Korea	Spain	United Kingdom	U.S. Virgin Islands and Puerto Rico	Other	Total
1960	3	4	34	4	6	62	18	6	NA	NA	12	1	52	202
1965	3	3	26	3	7	40	27	10	NA	NA	12	1	54	187
1966	3	4	32	4	7	36	39	9	NA	NA	12	3	49	198
1967	5	6	50	3	9	51	36	13	NA	NA	62	7	65	307
1968	4	8	39	4	8	56	31	10	NA	NA	14	2	55	231
1969	4	7	44	4	9	47	33	9	NA	NA	13	2	59	233
1970	5	7	31	5	10	69	33	15	NA	NA	12	2	71	259
1971	7	9	26	5	8	39	42	11	NA	NA	9	3	67	224
1972	13	9	26	5	9	32	41	12	NA	4	10	4	59	222
1973	15	8	31	5	9	34	44	13	NA	4	9	3	56	231
1974	13	9	32	4	9	38	35	17	NA	4	6	6	48	221
1975	9	6	22	6	10	27	42	23	NA	4	7	12	40	209
1976	12	7	28	6	10	25	35	22	NA	4	13	22	39	223
1977	16	6	71	9	10	25	24	17	NA	5	9	11	39	243
1978	15	8	108	9	10	26	27	18	NA	5	7	86	42	362
1979	19	7	100	13	15	34	21	28	2	9	7	170	45	471
1980	20	4	108	11	14	32	28	23	2	8	7	220	70	544
1981	12	1	89	15	22	38	26	42	10	18	5	220	97	595
1982	17	8	85	24	32	68	53	85	28	24	14	212	165	815
1983	22	2	76	23	35	104	24	49	15	34	8	144	202	739
1984	21	1	83	18	39	92	35	37	17	29	14	152	182	722
1985	26	3	74	11	30	108	61	44	27	28	14	162	193	781
1986	30	3	85	11	39	110	56	58	12	39	8	113	222	785
1987	17	2	83	12	42	120	70	39	25	31	6	136	179	764
1988	25	3	84	12	29	124	70	26	24	36	9	147	226	815
1989	23	5	92	11	37	122	89	36	17	28	9	141	249	859
1990	20	2	91	17	48	92	89	54	60	33	11	101	240	857
1991	22	13	70	27	55	95	99	72	66	23	13	117	330	1,001
1992	22	20	64	9	38	100	124	52	80	21	12	95	315	950
1993	21	16	72	8	34	105	110	45	74	30	10	108	370	1,003
1994	26	15	78	11	35	74	124	30	66	30	10	104	338	942
1995	21	16	73	11	46	76	125	33	57	38	14	123	317	949
1996	27	29	94	18	32	102	143	43	60	34	9	72	318	981
1997	21	15	119	11	30	95	207	41	50	42	12	18	340	1,003
1998	14	18	148	8	30	64	235	33	33	30	11	4	317	945
1999	11	27	119	7	25	84	261	38	49	26	9	8	276	940
2000	14	28	110	10	34	90	358	42	20	40	10	10	277	1,040
2001	16	23	112	13	33	62	274	45	14	51	13	4	312	971
2002	19	26	106	12	29	74	254	23	11	54	12	9	354	984
2003	13	27	141	9	39	69	228	15	10	39	6	9	421	1,027
2004	20	27	158	18	32	63	209	36	12	42	14	10	408	1,048
2005	21	39	181	14	28	56	268	25	16	35	21	11	449	1,165
2006	23	42	159	13	39	58	255	83	21	42	28	10	543	1,317
2007	13	46	189	24	34	54	279	81	16	48	9	10	629	1,433
2008	18	54	264	27	41	54	333	131	18	54	17	13	777	1,802
2009	29	55	223	34	35	58	322	192	23	40	33	20	960	2,024
2010	19	R123	R233	36	37	88	R448	R165	R13	36	R19	17	R1,117	R2,353
2011P	30	160	295	49	39	75	569	249	15	58	34	16	1,335	2,924

[1] Through 2004, includes Luxembourg.
R=Revised. P=Preliminary. NA=Not available.
Note: Totals may not equal sum of components due to independent rounding.
Web Pages: • See http://www.eia.gov/totalenergy/data/annual/#petroleum for all data beginning in 1960. • For related information, see http://www.eia.gov/petroleum/.

Sources: • 1960-1975—Bureau of Mines, Mineral Industry Surveys, *Petroleum Statement, Annual,* annual reports. • 1976-1980—U.S. Energy Information Administration (EIA), Energy Data Reports, *Petroleum Statement, Annual,* annual reports. • 1981-2010—EIA, *Petroleum Supply Annual,* annual reports. • 2011—EIA, *Petroleum Supply Monthly* (February 2012).

Source: *U.S. Energy Information Administration, Annual Energy Review 2011*

Figure 5.7 Petroleum Net Imports by Country of Origin, 1960-2011

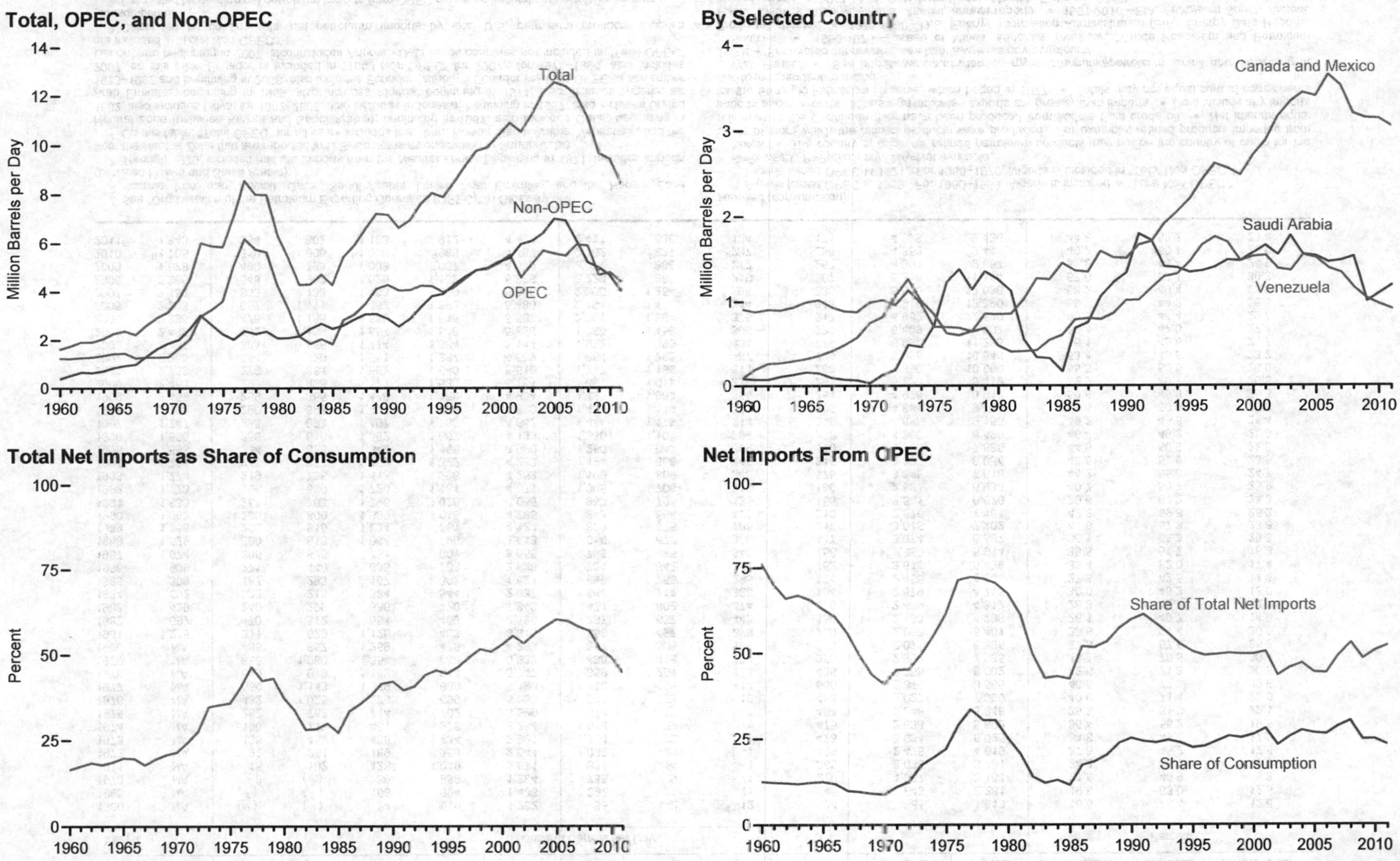

Note: OPEC=Organization of the Petroleum Exporting Countries.

Source: Table 5.7.

Source: *U.S. Energy Information Administration, Annual Energy Review 2011*

Table 5.7 Petroleum Net Imports by Country of Origin, Selected Years, 1960-2011

Year	Persian Gulf [2]	Selected OPEC [1] Countries: Algeria	Nigeria	Saudi Arabia [3]	Venezuela	Total OPEC [4]	Selected Non-OPEC [1] Countries: Canada	Mexico	United Kingdom	U.S. Virgin Islands and Puerto Rico	Total Non-OPEC [4]	Total Net Imports	Total Net Imports as Share of Consumption [5]	Net Imports From OPEC [1]: Share of Total Net Imports [6]	Share of Consumption [7]
	Thousand Barrels per Day												Percent		
1960	NA	(8)	(9)	84	910	1,232	86	-2	-12	34	381	1,613	16.5	76.4	12.6
1965	NA	(8)	(9)	158	994	1,438	297	21	-11	45	843	2,281	19.8	63.0	12.5
1970	NA	8	(9)	30	989	1,294	736	9	-1	270	1,867	3,161	21.5	40.9	8.8
1971	NA	15	102	128	1,019	1,671	831	-14	1	365	2,030	3,701	24.3	45.1	11.0
1972	NA	92	251	189	959	2,044	1,082	-20	-1	428	2,475	4,519	27.6	45.2	12.5
1973	NA	136	459	485	1,134	2,991	1,294	-28	6	426	3,034	6,025	34.8	49.6	17.3
1974	NA	190	713	461	978	3,254	1,038	-27	1	475	2,638	5,892	35.4	55.2	19.5
1975	NA	282	762	714	702	3,599	824	29	7	484	2,248	5,846	35.8	61.6	22.1
1976	NA	432	1,025	1,229	699	5,063	571	53	19	488	2,027	7,090	40.6	71.4	29.0
1977	NA	559	1,143	1,379	689	6,190	446	155	117	560	2,375	8,565	46.5	72.3	33.6
1978	NA	649	919	1,142	644	5,747	359	291	173	436	2,255	8,002	42.5	71.8	30.5
1979	NA	636	1,080	1,354	688	5,633	438	418	196	353	2,352	7,985	43.1	70.5	30.4
1980	NA	488	857	1,259	478	4,293	347	506	169	256	2,071	6,365	37.3	67.5	25.2
1981	1,215	311	620	1,128	403	3,315	358	497	370	169	2,086	5,401	33.6	61.4	20.6
1982	692	170	512	551	409	2,136	397	632	442	154	2,163	4,298	28.1	49.7	14.0
1983	439	240	299	336	420	1,843	471	802	374	178	2,469	4,312	28.3	42.7	12.1
1984	502	323	215	324	544	2,037	547	714	388	184	2,679	4,715	30.0	43.2	13.0
1985	309	187	293	167	602	1,821	696	755	295	114	2,465	4,286	27.3	42.5	11.6
1986	909	271	440	685	788	2,828	721	642	342	152	2,611	5,439	33.4	52.0	17.4
1987	1,074	295	535	751	801	3,055	765	585	346	158	2,859	5,914	35.5	51.7	18.3
1988	1,529	300	618	1,064	790	3,513	916	677	306	117	3,074	6,587	38.1	53.3	20.3
1989	1,858	269	815	1,224	861	4,124	839	678	206	212	3,078	7,202	41.6	57.3	23.8
1990	1,962	280	800	1,339	1,016	4,285	843	666	179	213	2,876	7,161	42.2	59.8	25.2
1991	1,833	253	703	1,796	1,020	4,065	963	707	125	153	2,561	6,626	39.6	61.3	24.3
1992	1,773	196	680	1,720	1,161	4,071	1,005	706	219	180	2,867	6,938	40.7	58.7	23.9
1993	1,774	219	736	1,413	1,296	4,253	1,109	809	340	175	3,365	7,618	44.2	55.8	24.7
1994	1,723	243	637	1,402	1,322	4,233	1,194	860	448	246	3,822	8,054	45.5	52.6	23.9
1995	1,563	234	626	1,343	1,468	3,980	1,260	943	369	170	3,906	7,886	44.5	50.5	22.5
1996	1,596	256	616	1,362	1,667	4,193	1,330	1,101	299	262	4,305	8,498	46.4	49.3	22.9
1997	1,747	285	693	1,407	1,758	4,542	1,444	1,178	214	298	4,616	9,158	49.2	49.6	24.4
1998	2,132	290	693	1,491	1,700	4,880	1,451	1,116	239	305	4,884	9,764	51.6	50.0	25.8
1999	2,459	259	655	1,478	1,480	4,934	1,421	1,063	356	284	4,978	9,912	50.8	49.8	25.3
2000	2,483	225	896	1,571	1,530	5,181	1,697	1,015	356	297	5,238	10,419	52.9	49.7	26.3
2001	2,758	278	884	1,662	1,540	5,510	1,717	1,166	311	268	5,390	10,900	55.5	50.5	28.0
2002	2,265	264	620	1,551	1,387	4,589	1,864	1,292	467	224	5,958	10,546	53.4	43.5	23.2
2003	2,497	381	866	1,774	1,364	5,144	1,932	1,395	434	279	6,094	11,238	56.1	45.8	25.7
2004	2,489	452	1,139	1,557	1,548	5,688	1,980	1,456	366	321	6,409	12,097	58.4	47.0	27.4
2005	2,330	478	1,165	1,536	1,515	5,567	2,001	1,394	375	317	6,982	12,549	60.3	44.4	26.8
2006	2,208	657	1,111	1,462	1,392	5,480	2,194	1,450	244	318	6,910	12,390	59.9	44.2	26.5
2007	2,159	663	1,133	1,483	1,339	5,946	2,266	1,254	268	336	6,090	12,036	58.2	49.4	28.8
2008	2,368	548	982	1,529	1,162	5,899	2,229	969	219	307	5,214	11,114	57.0	53.1	30.3
2009	1,678	490	798	1,003	1,037	4,675	2,257	888	212	257	4,991	9,667	51.5	48.4	24.9
2010	R1,705	R510	R1,006	R1,096	R968	R4,787	R2,302	R837	R237	R236	R4,653	R9,441	R49.2	R50.7	R25.0
2011P	1,843	354	802	1,193	912	4,408	2,411	636	124	171	4,028	8,436	44.8	52.2	23.4

1 See "Organization of the Petroleum Exporting Countries (OPEC)" in Glossary.
2 Bahrain, Iran, Iraq, Kuwait, Qatar, Saudi Arabia, United Arab Emirates, and the Neutral Zone (between Kuwait and Saudi Arabia).
3 Through 1970, includes half the imports from the Neutral Zone. Beginning in 1971, includes imports from the Neutral Zone that are reported to U.S. Customs as originating in Saudi Arabia.
4 On this table, "Total OPEC" for all years includes Iran, Iraq, Kuwait, Saudi Arabia, Venezuela, and the Neutral Zone (between Kuwait and Saudi Arabia); beginning in 1961, also includes Qatar; beginning in 1962, also includes Libya; for 1962–2008, also includes Indonesia; beginning in 1967, also includes United Arab Emirates; beginning in 1969, also includes Algeria; beginning in 1971, also includes Nigeria; for 1973–1992 and beginning in 2008, also includes Ecuador (although Ecuador rejoined OPEC in November 2007, on this table Ecuador is included in "Total Non-OPEC" for 2007); for 1975–1994, also includes Gabon; and beginning in 2007, also includes Angola. Data for all countries not included in "Total OPEC" are included in "Total Non-OPEC."
5 Calculated by dividing total net petroleum imports by total U.S. petroleum products supplied (consumption).
6 Calculated by dividing net petroleum imports from OPEC countries by total net petroleum imports.
7 Calculated by dividing net petroleum imports from OPEC countries by total U.S. petroleum product supplied (consumption).
8 Algeria joined OPEC in 1969. For 1960–1968, Algeria is included in "Total Non-OPEC."
9 Nigeria joined OPEC in 1971. For 1960–1970, Nigeria is included in "Total Non-OPEC."
R=Revised. P=Preliminary. NA=Not available.

Notes: • The country of origin for refined petroleum products may not be the country of origin for the crude oil from which the refined products were produced. For example, refined products imported from refineries in the Caribbean may have been produced from Middle East crude oil. • Net imports equal imports minus exports. Minus sign indicates exports are greater than imports. • Data include any imports for the Strategic Petroleum Reserve, which began in 1977. • Totals may not equal sum of components due to independent rounding.

Web Pages: • See http://www.eia.gov/totalenergy/data/annual/#petroleum for all data beginning in 1960. • For related information, see http://www.eia.gov/petroleum/.

Sources: • 1960-1975—Bureau of Mines, *Minerals Yearbook,* "Crude Petroleum and Petroleum Products" chapter. • 1976-1980—U.S. Energy Information Administration (EIA), Energy Data Reports, *P.A.D. Districts Supply/Demand, Annual,* annual reports. • 1981-2010—EIA, *Petroleum Supply Annual,* annual reports. • 2011—EIA, *Petroleum Supply Monthly* (February 2012).

Source: *U.S. Energy Information Administration, Annual Energy Review 2011*

Figure 5.24 Retail Motor Gasoline and On-Highway Diesel Fuel Prices

Motor Gasoline, All Grades, 1978-2011

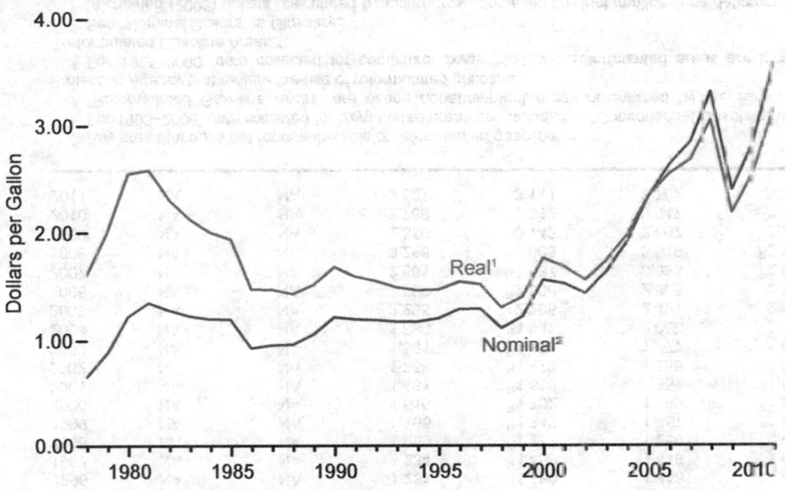

Regular Motor Gasoline by Area Type and On-Highway Diesel Fuel, 2011

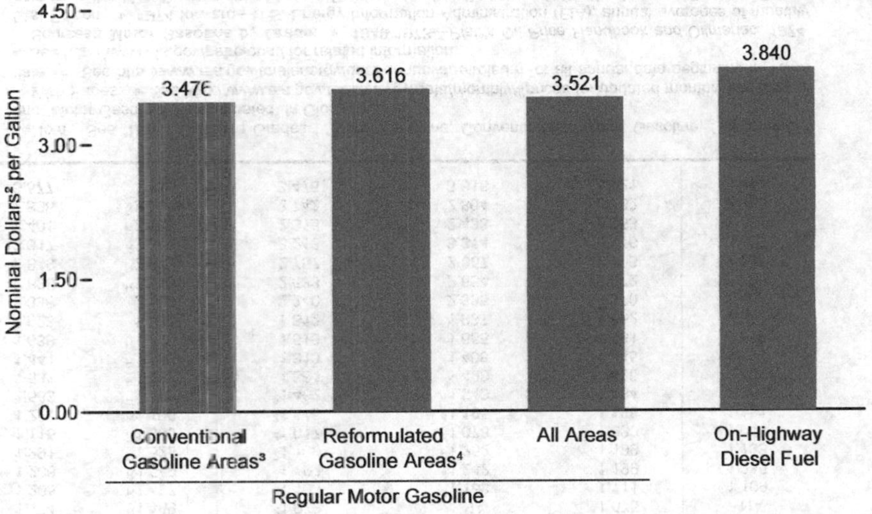

Motor Gasoline by Grade, 1949-2011

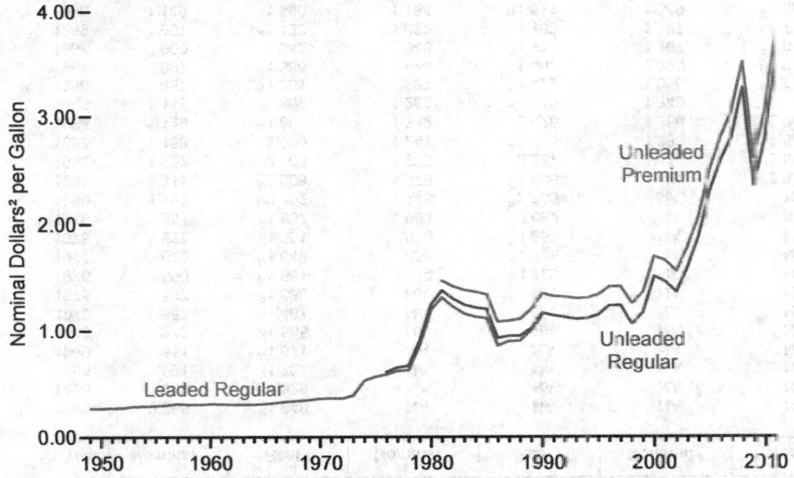

Motor Gasoline Price and Consumption, 1978-2011, Indexed to 1978

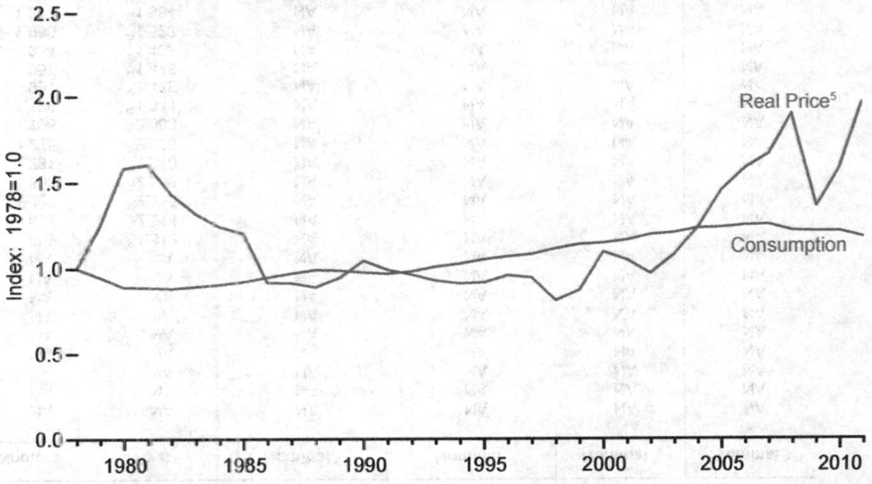

[1] In chained (2005) dollars, calculated by using gross domestic product implicit price deflators in Table D1. See "Chained Dollars" in Glossary.
[2] See "Nominal Dollars" in Glossary.
[3] Any area that does not require the sale of reformulated gasoline.
[4] "Reformulated Gasoline Areas" are ozone nonattainment areas designated by the Environmental Protection Agency that require the use of reformulated gasoline.
[5] All grades, in chained (2005) dollars.

Sources: Tables 5.11 and 5.24.

Source: *U.S. Energy Information Administration, Annual Energy Review 2011*

Table 5.24 Retail Motor Gasoline and On-Highway Diesel Fuel Prices, Selected Years, 1949-2011

(Dollars per Gallon)

Year	Motor Gasoline by Grade								Regular Motor Gasoline by Area Type			On-Highway Diesel Fuel
	Leaded Regular		Unleaded Regular		Unleaded Premium		All Grades		Conventional Gasoline Areas [1,2]	Reformulated Gasoline Areas [3,4]	All Areas	
	Nominal [5]	Real [6]	Nominal [5]	Real [6]	Nominal [5]	Real [6]	Nominal [5]	Real [6]	Nominal [5]	Nominal [5]	Nominal [5]	Nominal [5]
1949	0.268	[R]1.848	NA	NA	NA	NA	NA	NA	NA	NA	NA	NA
1950	.268	[R]1.829	NA	NA	NA	NA	NA	NA	NA	NA	NA	NA
1955	.291	[R]1.753	NA	NA	NA	NA	NA	NA	NA	NA	NA	NA
1960	.311	[R]1.671	NA	NA	NA	NA	NA	NA	NA	NA	NA	NA
1965	.312	[R]1.565	NA	NA	NA	NA	NA	NA	NA	NA	NA	NA
1970	.357	[R]1.467	NA	NA	NA	NA	NA	NA	NA	NA	NA	NA
1975	.567	[R]1.688	NA	NA	NA	NA	NA	NA	NA	NA	NA	NA
1976	.590	[R]1.661	.614	[R]1.729	NA	NA	NA	NA	NA	NA	NA	NA
1977	.622	[R]1.646	.656	[R]1.736	NA	NA	NA	NA	NA	NA	NA	NA
1978	[R].627	[R]1.551	.670	[R]1.657	NA	NA	.652	[R]1.612	NA	NA	NA	NA
1979	.857	[R]1.957	.903	[R]2.062	NA	NA	.882	[R]2.014	NA	NA	NA	NA
1980	1.191	[R]2.492	1.245	[R]2.605	NA	NA	1.221	[R]2.555	NA	NA	NA	NA
1981	1.311	[R]2.508	1.378	[R]2.636	[7]1.470	[7,R]2.812	1.353	[R]2.588	NA	NA	NA	NA
1982	1.222	[R]2.203	1.296	[R]2.337	1.415	[R]2.551	1.281	[R]2.310	NA	NA	NA	NA
1983	[R]1.158	2.009	1.241	[R]2.153	1.383	[R]2.399	1.225	[R]2.125	NA	NA	NA	NA
1984	1.129	[R]1.887	1.212	[R]2.026	1.366	[R]2.284	1.198	[R]2.003	NA	NA	NA	NA
1985	1.115	[R]1.809	1.202	[R]1.950	1.340	[R]2.174	1.196	[R]1.941	NA	NA	NA	NA
1986	.857	[R]1.361	.927	[R]1.472	1.085	[R]1.722	.931	[R]1.478	NA	NA	NA	NA
1987	.897	[R]1.384	.948	[R]1.463	1.093	[R]1.686	.957	[R]1.476	NA	NA	NA	NA
1988	[R].900	1.342	.946	[R]1.411	1.107	[R]1.651	[R].964	1.438	NA	NA	NA	NA
1989	[R].997	[R]1.433	[R]1.022	1.469	1.197	[R]1.720	1.060	[R]1.523	NA	NA	NA	NA
1990	1.149	[R]1.590	1.164	[R]1.611	1.349	[R]1.867	1.217	[R]1.684	NA	NA	NA	NA
1991	NA	NA	1.140	[R]1.524	1.321	[R]1.765	1.196	[R]1.598	1.098	NA	1.098	NA
1992	NA	NA	1.127	[R]1.471	1.316	[R]1.718	1.190	[R]1.554	1.087	NA	1.087	NA
1993	NA	NA	1.108	[R]1.415	1.302	[R]1.663	1.173	[R]1.498	[2]1.067	NA	1.067	NA
1994	NA	NA	1.112	[R]1.391	1.305	[R]1.632	1.174	[R]1.469	[2]1.072	NA	1.075	NA
1995	NA	NA	1.147	[R]1.406	1.336	[R]1.637	1.205	[R]1.477	[2]1.103	[4]1.163	1.111	1.109
1996	NA	NA	1.231	[R]1.480	1.413	[R]1.699	1.288	[R]1.549	[2]1.192	[4]1.242	1.199	1.235
1997	NA	NA	1.234	[R]1.458	1.416	[R]1.673	1.291	[R]1.525	[2]1.189	[4]1.252	1.199	1.198
1998	NA	NA	1.059	[R]1.237	1.250	[R]1.461	1.115	[R]1.303	[2]1.017	[4]1.078	1.030	1.044
1999	NA	NA	1.165	[R]1.342	1.357	[R]1.563	1.221	[R]1.406	[2]1.116	[4]1.195	1.136	1.121
2000	NA	NA	1.510	[R]1.702	1.693	[R]1.908	1.563	[R]1.762	[2]1.462	[4]1.543	1.484	1.491
2001	NA	NA	1.461	[R]1.610	1.657	[R]1.826	1.531	[R]1.687	1.384	1.498	1.420	1.401
2002	NA	NA	1.358	[R]1.473	1.556	[R]1.688	1.441	[R]1.563	1.313	1.408	1.345	1.319
2003	NA	NA	1.591	[R]1.690	1.777	1.888	1.638	[R]1.740	1.516	1.655	1.561	1.509
2004	NA	NA	1.880	[R]1.942	2.068	2.137	1.923	1.987	1.812	1.937	1.852	1.810
2005	NA	NA	2.295	2.295	2.491	2.491	2.338	2.338	2.240	2.335	2.270	2.402
2006	NA	NA	2.589	[R]2.508	2.805	2.717	2.635	[R]2.553	2.533	2.654	2.572	2.705
2007	NA	NA	2.801	[R]2.637	3.033	[R]2.855	2.849	[R]2.682	2.767	2.857	2.796	2.885
2008	NA	NA	3.266	[R]3.008	3.519	[R]3.241	3.317	[R]3.055	3.213	3.314	3.246	3.803
2009	NA	NA	2.350	[R]2.142	2.607	[R]2.376	2.401	[R]2.188	2.315	2.433	2.353	2.467
2010	NA	NA	2.788	[R]2.512	3.047	[R]2.745	2.836	[R]2.555	2.742	2.864	2.782	2.992
2011	NA	NA	3.527	3.111	3.792	3.345	3.577	3.155	3.476	3.616	3.521	3.840

[1] Any area that does not require the sale of reformulated gasoline.
[2] For 1993–2000, data collected for oxygenated areas are included in "Conventional Gasoline Areas."
[3] "Reformulated Gasoline Areas" are ozone nonattainment areas designated by the Environmental Protection Agency that require the use of reformulated gasoline.
[4] For 1995–2000, data collected for combined oxygenated and reformulated areas are included in "Reformulated Gasoline Areas."
[5] See "Nominal Dollars" in Glossary.
[6] In chained (2005) dollars, calculated by using gross domestic product implicit price deflators in Table D1. See "Chained Dollars" in Glossary.
[7] The 1981 average price is based on September through December data only.
R=Revised. NA=Not available.

Note: See "Motor Gasoline Grades," "Motor Gasoline, Conventional," "Motor Gasoline, Oxygenated," and "Motor Gasoline, Reformulated" in Glossary.

Web Pages: • See http://www.eia.gov/totalenergy/data/monthly/#prices for updated monthly and annual data. • See http://www.eia.gov/totalenergy/data/annual/#petroleum for all annual data beginning in 1949. • See http://www.eia.gov/petroleum/ for related information.

Sources: **Motor Gasoline by Grade:** • 1949-1973—*Platt's Oil Price Handbook and Oilmanac, 1974,* 51st Edition. • 1974 forward—U.S. Energy Information Administration (EIA), annual averages of monthly data from the U.S. Department of Labor, Bureau of Labor Statistics, *U.S. City Average Gasoline Prices.* **Regular Motor Gasoline by Area Type:** EIA, weighted annual averages of data from "Weekly U.S. Retail Gasoline Prices, Regular Grade." **On-Highway Diesel Fuel:** EIA, weighted annual averages of data from "Weekly Retail On-Highway Diesel Prices."

Source: *U.S. Energy Information Administration, Annual Energy Review 2011*

Figure 6.0 Natural Gas Flow, 2011
(Trillion Cubic Feet)

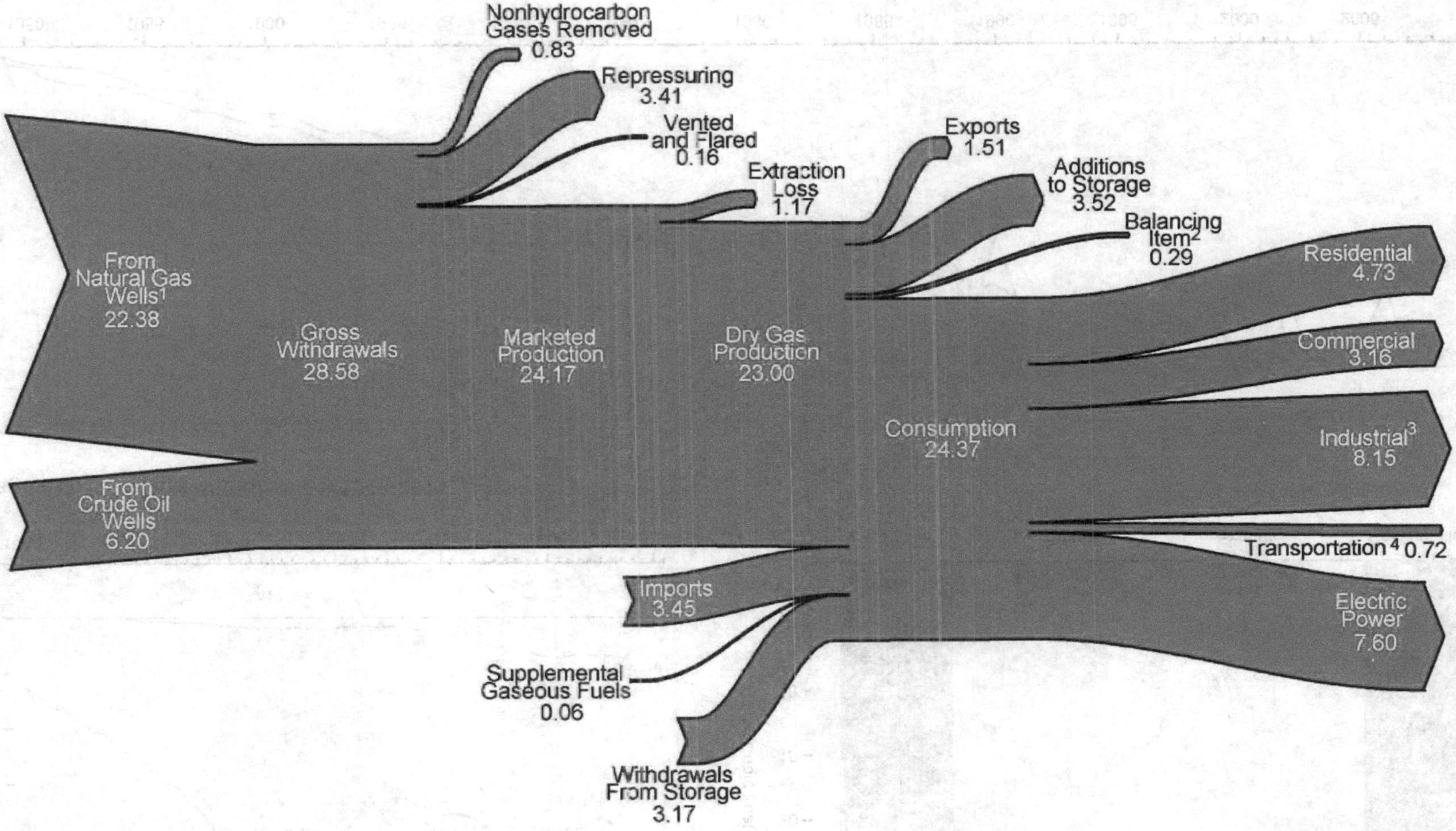

natural gas gross withdrawals from coalbed wells and shale gas wells.
...st and imbalances in data due to differences among data sources.
...t fuel, and other industrial.

[4] Natural gas consumed in the operation of pipelines (primarily in compressors), and as fuel in the delivery of natural gas to consumers; plus a small quantity used as vehicle fuel.

Notes: • Data are preliminary. • Values are derived from source data prior to rounding for publication. • Totals may not equal sum of components due to independent rounding.

Sources: Tables 6.1, 6.2, and 6.5.

Source: *U.S. Energy Information Administration, Annual Energy Review 2011*

gure 6.1 Natural Gas Overview

Overview, 1949-2011

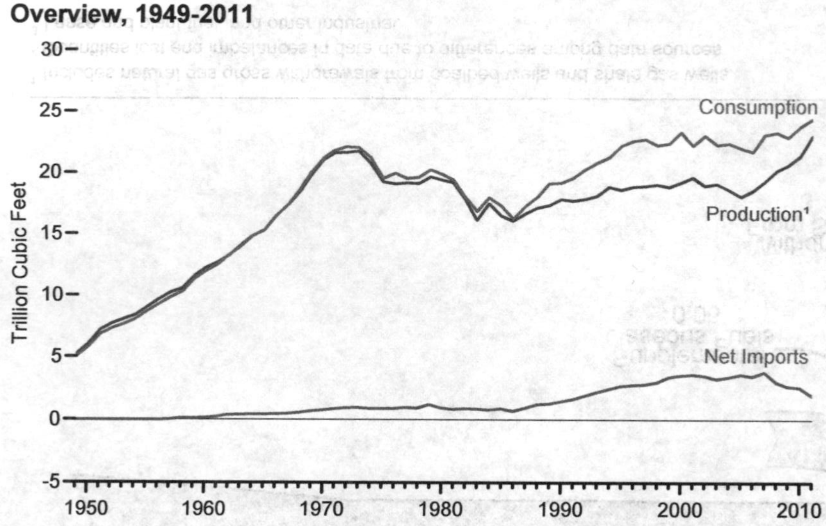

Overview, 2011

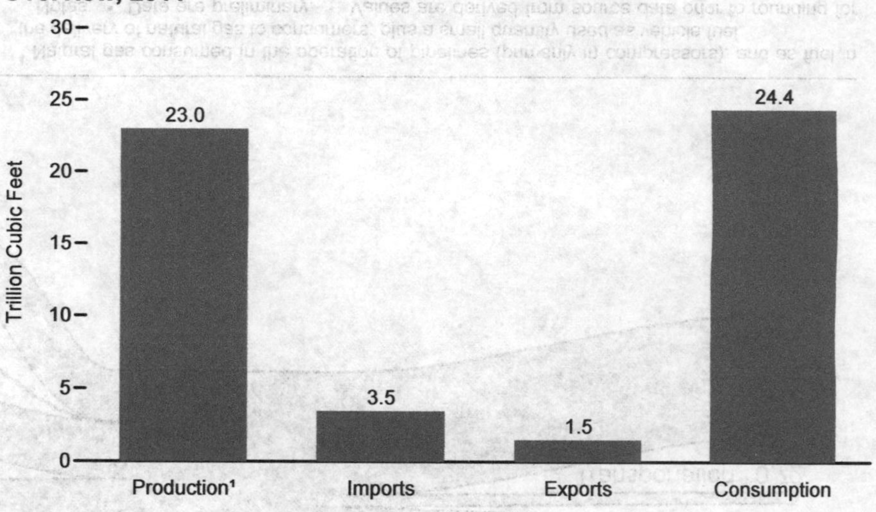

Storage Additions and Withdrawals, 1949-2011

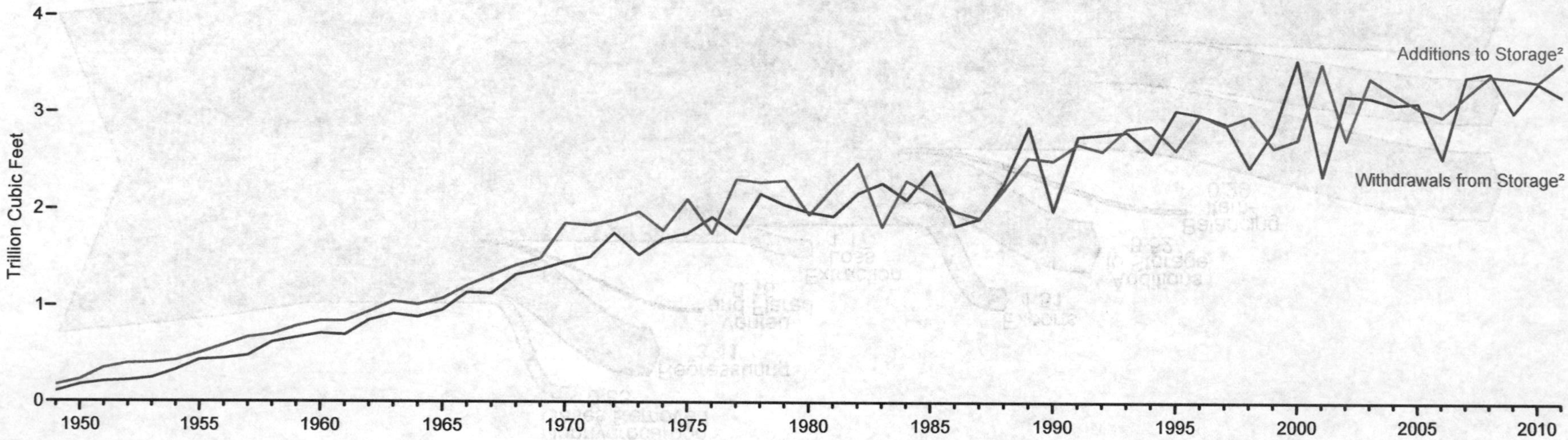

[1] Dry gas.

[2] Underground storage. For 1980-2010, also includes liquefied natural gas in above-ground tanks.

Source: Table 6.1.

***Source:** U.S. Energy Information Administration, Annual Energy Review 2011*

Table 6.1 Natural Gas Overview, Selected Years, 1949-2011

(Billion Cubic Feet)

Year	Dry Gas Production	Supplemental Gaseous Fuels [2]	Trade			Storage [1] Activity			Balancing Item [5]	Consumption [6]
			Imports	Exports	Net Imports [3]	Withdrawals	Additions	Net Withdrawals [4]		
1949	5,195	NA	0	20	-20	106	172	-66	-139	4,971
1950	6,022	NA	0	26	-26	175	230	-54	-175	5,767
1955	9,029	NA	11	31	-20	437	505	-68	-247	8,694
1960	12,228	NA	156	11	144	713	844	-132	-274	11,967
1965	15,286	NA	456	26	430	960	1,078	-118	-319	15,280
1970	21,014	NA	821	70	751	1,459	1,857	-398	-228	21,139
1975	19,236	NA	953	73	880	1,760	2,104	-344	-235	19,538
1976	19,098	NA	964	65	899	1,921	1,756	165	-216	19,946
1977	19,163	NA	1,011	56	955	1,750	2,307	-557	-41	19,521
1978	19,122	NA	966	53	913	2,158	2,278	-120	-287	19,627
1979	19,663	NA	1,253	56	1,198	2,047	2,295	-248	-372	20,241
1980	19,403	155	985	49	936	1,972	1,949	23	-640	19,877
1981	19,181	176	904	59	845	1,930	2,228	-297	-500	19,404
1982	17,820	145	933	52	882	2,164	2,472	-308	-537	18,001
1983	16,094	132	918	55	864	2,270	1,822	447	-703	16,835
1984	17,466	110	843	55	788	2,098	2,295	-197	-217	17,951
1985	16,454	126	950	55	894	2,397	2,163	235	-428	17,281
1986	16,059	113	750	61	689	1,837	1,984	-147	-493	16,221
1987	16,621	101	993	54	939	1,905	1,911	-6	-444	17,211
1988	17,103	101	1,294	74	1,220	2,270	2,211	59	-453	18,030
1989	17,311	107	1,382	107	1,275	2,854	2,528	326	101	[7]19,119
1990	17,810	123	1,532	86	1,447	1,986	2,499	-513	307	[7]19,174
1991	17,698	113	1,773	129	1,644	2,752	2,672	80	27	[7]19,562
1992	17,840	118	2,138	216	1,921	2,772	2,599	173	176	[7]20,228
1993	18,095	119	2,350	140	2,210	2,799	2,835	-36	401	20,790
1994	18,821	111	2,624	162	2,462	2,579	2,865	-286	139	21,247
1995	18,599	110	2,841	154	2,687	3,025	2,610	415	396	22,207
1996	18,854	109	2,937	153	2,784	2,981	2,979	2	860	22,609
1997	18,902	103	2,994	157	2,837	2,894	2,870	24	871	22,737
1998	19,024	102	3,152	159	2,993	2,432	2,961	-530	657	22,246
1999	18,832	98	3,586	163	3,422	2,808	2,636	172	-119	22,405
2000	19,182	90	3,782	244	3,538	3,550	2,721	829	R-306	23,333
2001	19,616	86	3,977	373	3,604	2,344	3,510	-1,166	99	22,239
2002	18,928	68	4,015	516	3,499	3,180	2,713	467	R65	R23,027
2003	19,099	68	3,944	680	3,264	3,161	3,358	-197	44	22,277
2004	18,591	60	4,259	854	3,404	3,088	3,202	-114	R461	R22,403
2005	18,051	64	4,341	729	3,612	3,107	3,055	52	R236	R22,014
2006	18,504	66	4,186	724	3,462	2,527	2,963	-436	R103	R21,699
2007	19,266	63	4,608	822	3,785	3,375	3,183	192	R-203	R23,104
2008	20,159	61	3,984	963	3,021	3,420	3,385	34	R2	R23,277
2009	R20,624	65	3,751	1,072	2,679	3,007	3,362	-355	R-103	R22,910
2010	R21,332	R65	R3,741	R1,137	R2,604	R3,311	R3,324	R-13	R-213	R23,775
2011	E23,000	P61	P3,453	P1,507	P1,946	P3,175	P3,523	P-348	P-290	P24,369

1 Underground storage. For 1980–2010, also includes liquefied natural gas in above-ground tanks.
2 See Note 1, "Supplemental Gaseous Fuels," at end of section.
3 Net imports equal imports minus exports. Minus sign indicates exports are greater than imports.
4 Net withdrawals equal withdrawals minus additions. Minus sign indicates additions are greater than withdrawals.
5 Quantities lost and imbalances in data due to differences among data sources. Since 1980, excludes intransit shipments that cross the U.S.-Canada border (i.e., natural gas delivered to its destination via the other country).
6 See Note 2, "Natural Gas Consumption," at end of section.
7 For 1989–1992, a small amount of consumption at independent power producers may be counted in both "Other Industrial" and "Electric Power Sector" on Table 6.5. See Note 3, "Natural Gas Consumption, 1989–1992," at end of section.
R=Revised. P=Preliminary. E=Estimate. NA=Not available.

Notes: • Beginning with 1965, all volumes are shown on a pressure base of 14.73 p.s.i.a. at 60° F. For prior years, the pressure base was 14.65 p.s.i.a. at 60° F. • Totals may not equal sum of components due to independent rounding.

Web Pages: • See http://www.eia.gov/totalenergy/data/monthly/#naturalgas for updated monthly and annual data. • See http://www.eia.gov/totalenergy/data/annual/#naturalgas for all annual data beginning in 1949. • See http://www.eia.gov/naturalgas/ for related information.

Sources: **Dry Gas Production:** Table 6.2. **Supplemental Gaseous Fuels:** • 1980-2006—U.S. Energy Information Administration (EIA), *Natural Gas Annual (NGA)*, annual reports. • 2007 forward—EIA, *Natural Gas Monthly (NGM)* (March 2012), Table 1. **Trade:** Table 6.3. **Storage Activity:** • 1949-2010—EIA, *NGA*, annual reports. • 2011—EIA, NGM (March 2012), Table 8. **Balancing Item:** Calculated as consumption minus dry gas production, supplemental gaseous fuels, net imports, and net withdrawals. **Consumption:** Table 6.5.

Source: *U.S. Energy Information Administration, Annual Energy Review 2011*

Figure 6.2 Natural Gas Production

Gross Withdrawals and Dry Gas Production, 1949-2011

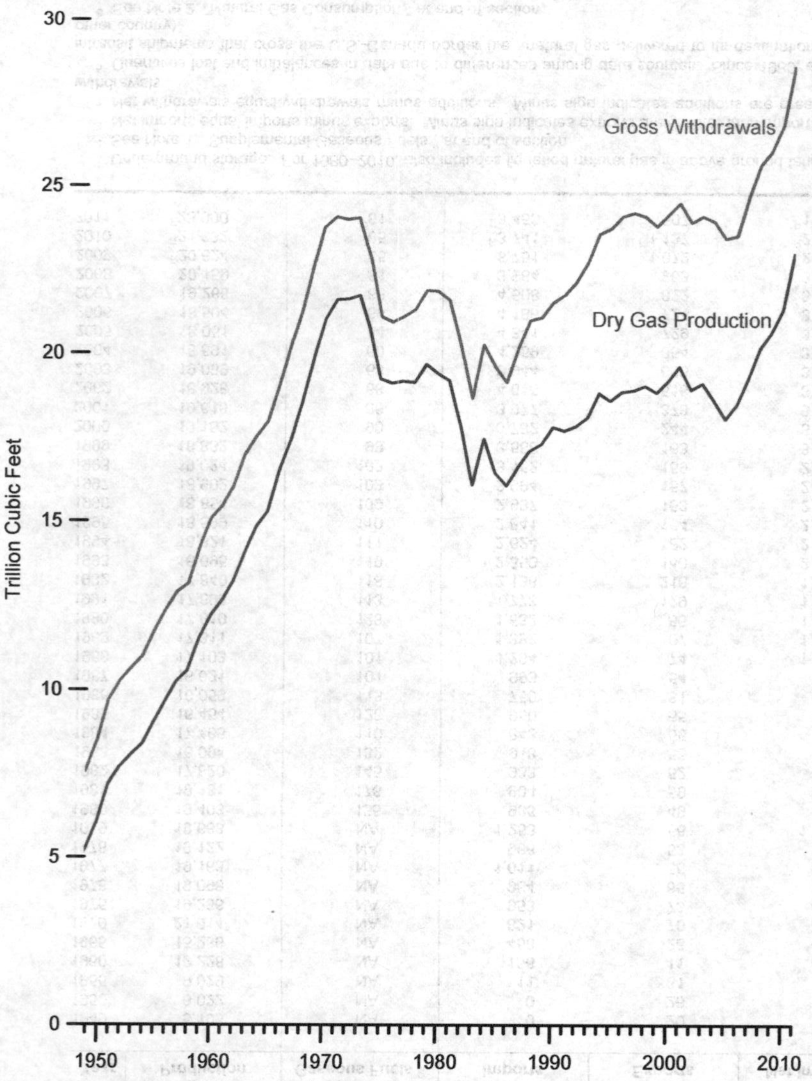

Production Flow, 2011
(Trillion Cubic Feet)

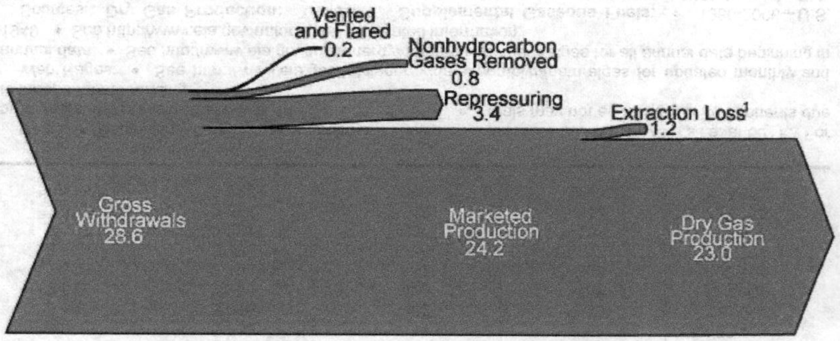

Gross Withdrawals by Well Type, 2011

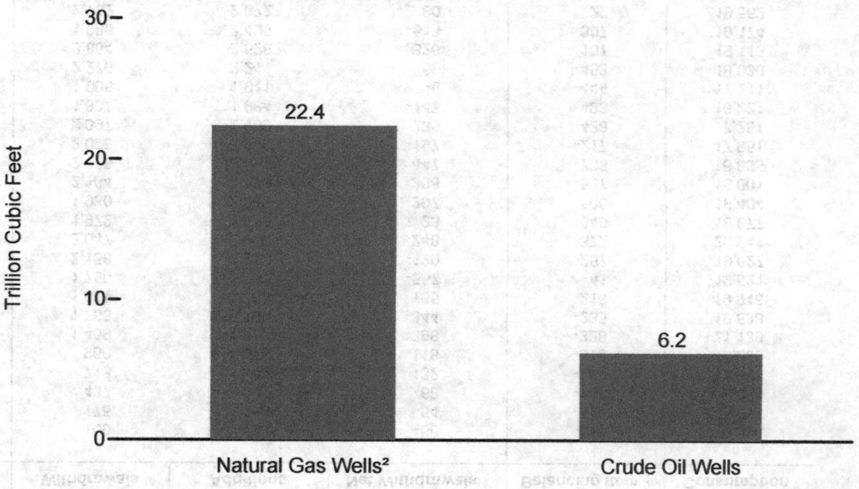

[1] Volume reduction resulting from the removal of natural gas plant liquids, which are transferred to petroleum supply.

[2] Includes natural gas gross withdrawals from coalbed wells and shale gas wells.
Source: Table 6.2.

Source: *U.S. Energy Information Administration, Annual Energy Review 2011*

Table 6.2 Natural Gas Production, Selected Years, 1949-2011

(Billion Cubic Feet)

Year	Natural Gas Gross Withdrawals: Natural Gas Wells	Crude Oil Wells	Coalbed Wells	Shale Gas Wells	Total	Repressuring	Nonhydrocarbon Gases Removed	Vented and Flared	Marketed Production	Extraction Loss [1]	Dry Gas Production
1949	4,986	2,561	NA	NA	7,547	1,273	NA	854	5,420	224	5,195
1950	5,603	2,876	NA	NA	8,480	1,397	NA	801	6,282	260	6,022
1955	7,842	3,878	NA	NA	11,720	1,541	NA	774	9,405	377	9,029
1960	10,853	4,234	NA	NA	15,088	1,754	NA	563	12,771	543	12,228
1965	13,524	4,440	NA	NA	17,963	1,604	NA	319	16,040	753	15,286
1970	18,595	5,192	NA	NA	23,786	1,376	NA	489	21,921	906	21,014
1975	17,380	3,723	NA	NA	21,104	861	NA	134	20,109	872	19,236
1976	17,191	3,753	NA	NA	20,944	859	NA	132	19,952	854	19,098
1977	17,416	3,681	NA	NA	21,097	935	NA	137	20,025	863	19,163
1978	17,394	3,915	NA	NA	21,309	1,181	NA	153	19,974	852	19,122
1979	18,034	3,849	NA	NA	21,883	1,245	NA	167	20,471	808	19,663
1980	17,573	4,297	NA	NA	21,870	1,365	199	125	20,180	777	19,403
1981	17,337	4,251	NA	NA	21,587	1,312	222	98	19,956	775	19,181
1982	15,809	4,463	NA	NA	20,272	1,388	208	93	18,582	762	17,820
1983	14,153	4,506	NA	NA	18,659	1,458	222	95	16,884	790	16,094
1984	15,513	4,754	NA	NA	20,267	1,630	224	108	18,304	838	17,466
1985	14,535	5,071	NA	NA	19,607	1,915	326	95	17,270	816	16,454
1986	14,154	4,977	NA	NA	19,131	1,838	337	98	16,859	800	16,059
1987	14,807	5,333	NA	NA	20,140	2,208	376	124	17,433	812	16,621
1988	15,467	5,532	NA	NA	20,999	2,478	460	143	17,918	816	17,103
1989	15,709	5,366	NA	NA	21,074	2,475	362	142	18,095	785	17,311
1990	16,054	5,469	NA	NA	21,523	2,489	289	150	18,594	784	17,810
1991	16,018	5,732	NA	NA	21,750	2,772	276	170	18,532	835	17,698
1992	16,165	5,967	NA	NA	22,132	2,973	280	168	18,712	872	17,840
1993	16,691	6,035	NA	NA	22,725	3,103	414	227	18,982	886	18,095
1994	17,351	6,230	NA	NA	23,581	3,231	412	228	19,710	889	18,821
1995	17,282	6,462	NA	NA	23,744	3,565	388	284	19,506	908	18,599
1996	17,737	6,376	NA	NA	24,114	3,511	518	272	19,812	958	18,854
1997	17,844	6,369	NA	NA	24,213	3,492	599	256	19,866	964	18,902
1998	17,729	6,380	NA	NA	24,108	3,427	617	103	19,961	938	19,024
1999	17,590	6,233	NA	NA	23,823	3,293	615	110	19,805	973	18,832
2000	17,726	6,448	NA	NA	24,174	3,380	505	91	20,198	1,016	19,182
2001	18,129	6,371	NA	NA	24,501	3,371	463	97	20,570	954	19,616
2002	17,795	6,146	NA	NA	23,941	3,455	502	99	19,885	957	18,928
2003	17,882	6,237	NA	NA	24,119	3,548	499	98	19,974	876	19,099
2004	17,885	6,084	NA	NA	23,970	3,702	654	96	19,517	927	18,591
2005	17,472	5,985	NA	NA	23,457	3,700	711	119	18,927	876	18,051
2006	17,996	5,539	NA	NA	23,535	3,265	731	129	19,410	906	18,504
2007	17,065	5,818	1,780	NA	24,664	3,663	661	143	20,196	930	19,266
2008	15,618	5,747	1,986	2,284	25,636	3,639	719	167	21,112	953	20,159
2009	[R]14,885	[R]5,812	1,977	3,384	[R]26,057	3,522	722	165	[R]21,648	1,024	[R]20,624
2010	[2,R]20,841	[R]5,995	([2])	([2])	[R]26,836	[R]3,432	[R]837	[R]166	[R]22,402	[R]1,070	[R]21,332
2011	[E]22,378	[E]6,199	([2])	([2])	[P]28,576	[E]3,410	[E]831	[E]165	[E]24,170	[P]1,169	[E]23,000

[1] Volume reduction resulting from the removal of natural gas plant liquids, which are transferred to petroleum supply (see Tables 5.1b and 5.10).

[2] Beginning in 2010, natural gas gross withdrawals from coalbed wells and shale gas wells are included in "Natural Gas Wells."

R=Revised. P=Preliminary. E=Estimate. NA=Not available.

Notes: • Beginning with 1965 data, all volumes are shown on a pressure base of 14.73 p.s.i.a. at 60° F. For prior years, the pressure base was 14.65 p.s.i.a. at 60° F. • Totals may not equal sum of components due to independent rounding.

Web Pages: • See http://www.eia.gov/totalenergy/data/monthly/#naturalgas for updated monthly and annual data • See http://www.eia.gov/totalenergy/data/annual/#naturalgas for all annual data beginning in 1949. • See http://www.eia.gov/naturalgas/ for related information.

Sources: **Natural Gas Wells, Crude Oil Wells, Coalbed Wells,** and **Shale Gas Wells:** • 1949-1966—Bureau of Mines, *Minerals Yearbook,* "Natural Gas" chapter. • 1967-2010—U.S. Energy Information Administration (EIA), *Natural Gas Annual (NGA),* annual reports. • 2011—EIA estimates based on previous year's data. **Total Gross Withdrawals, Marketed Production, Extraction Loss,** and **Dry Gas Production:** • 1949-2006—EIA, NGA, annual reports. • 2007 forward—EIA, *Natural Gas Monthly* (March 2012), Table 1. **All Other Data:** • 1949-2010—EIA, NGA, annual reports. • 2011—EIA estimates based on previous year's data.

Source: *U.S. Energy Information Administration, Annual Energy Review 2011*

Figure 6.3 Natural Gas Imports, Exports, and Net Imports

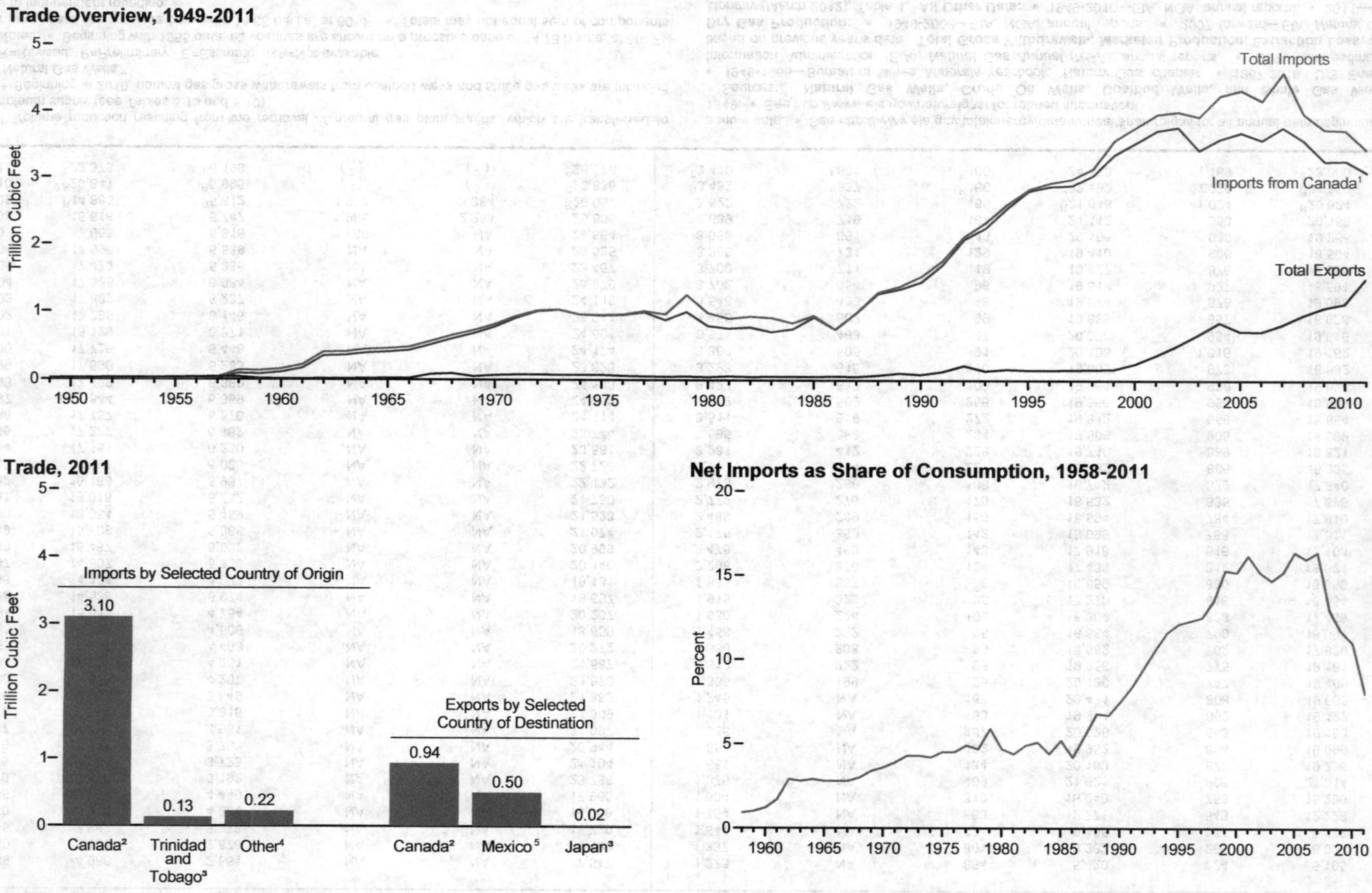

[1] By pipeline, except for very small amounts of liquefied natural gas in 1973, 1977, and 1981.
[2] By pipeline.
[3] As liquefied natural gas.
[4] By pipeline from Mexico, and as liquefied natural gas from Egypt, Nigeria, Norway, Qatar, Peru, and Yemen.
[5] By pipeline, except for very small amounts of liquefied natural gas.
Source: Table 6.3.

Source: *U.S. Energy Information Administration, Annual Energy Review 2011*

Table 6.3 Natural Gas Imports, Exports, and Net Imports, Selected Years, 1949-2011

(Billion Cubic Feet, Except as Noted)

Year	Imports by Country of Origin									Exports by Country of Destination					Net Imports [1]	
	Algeria [2]	Canada [3]	Egypt [2]	Mexico [3]	Nigeria [2]	Qatar [2]	Trinidad and Tobago [2]	Other [2,4]	Total	Canada [3]	Japan [2]	Mexico [3]	Other [2,5]	Total	Total	Percent of U.S. Consumption
1949	0	0	0	0	0	0	0	0	0	(s)	0	20	0	20	-20	([6])
1950	0	0	0	0	0	0	0	0	0	3	0	23	0	26	-26	([6])
1955	0	11	0	(s)	0	0	0	0	11	11	0	20	0	31	-20	([6])
1960	0	109	0	47	0	0	0	0	156	6	0	6	0	11	144	1.2
1965	0	405	0	52	0	0	0	0	456	18	0	8	0	26	430	2.8
1970	1	779	0	41	0	0	0	0	821	11	44	15	0	70	751	3.6
1975	5	948	0	0	0	0	0	0	953	10	53	9	0	73	880	4.5
1976	10	954	0	0	0	0	0	0	964	8	50	7	0	65	899	4.5
1977	11	997	0	2	0	0	0	0	1,011	(s)	52	4	0	56	955	4.9
1978	84	881	0	0	0	0	0	0	966	(s)	48	4	0	53	913	4.7
1979	253	1,001	0	0	0	0	0	0	1,253	(s)	51	4	0	56	1,198	5.9
1980	86	797	0	102	0	0	0	0	985	(s)	45	4	0	49	936	4.7
1981	37	762	0	105	0	0	0	0	904	(s)	56	3	0	59	845	4.4
1982	55	783	0	95	0	0	0	0	933	(s)	50	2	0	52	882	4.9
1983	131	712	0	75	0	0	0	0	918	(s)	53	2	0	55	864	5.1
1984	36	755	0	52	0	0	0	0	843	(s)	53	2	0	55	788	4.4
1985	24	926	0	0	0	0	0	0	950	(s)	53	2	0	55	894	5.2
1986	0	749	0	0	0	0	0	2	750	9	50	2	0	61	689	4.2
1987	0	993	0	0	0	0	0	0	993	3	49	2	0	54	939	5.5
1988	17	1,276	0	0	0	0	0	0	1,294	20	52	2	0	74	1,220	6.8
1989	42	1,339	0	0	0	0	0	0	1,382	38	51	17	0	107	1,275	6.7
1990	84	1,448	0	0	0	0	0	0	1,532	17	53	16	0	86	1,447	7.5
1991	64	1,710	0	0	0	0	0	0	1,773	15	54	60	0	129	1,644	8.4
1992	43	2,094	0	0	0	0	0	0	2,138	68	53	96	0	216	1,921	9.5
1993	82	2,267	0	2	0	0	0	0	2,350	45	56	40	0	140	2,210	10.6
1994	51	2,566	0	7	0	0	0	0	2,624	53	63	47	0	162	2,462	11.6
1995	18	2,816	0	7	0	0	0	0	2,841	28	65	61	0	154	2,687	12.1
1996	35	2,883	0	14	0	0	0	5	2,937	52	68	34	0	153	2,784	12.3
1997	66	2,899	0	17	0	0	0	12	2,994	56	62	38	0	157	2,837	12.5
1998	69	3,052	0	15	0	0	0	17	3,152	40	66	53	0	159	2,993	13.5
1999	76	3,368	0	55	0	20	51	17	3,586	39	64	61	0	163	3,422	15.3
2000	47	3,544	0	12	13	46	99	21	3,782	73	66	106	0	244	3,538	15.2
2001	65	3,729	0	10	38	23	98	14	3,977	167	66	141	0	373	3,604	16.2
2002	27	3,785	0	2	8	35	151	8	4,015	189	63	263	0	516	3,499	15.2
2003	53	3,437	0	0	50	14	378	11	3,944	271	66	343	0	680	3,264	14.7
2004	120	3,607	0	0	12	12	462	46	4,259	395	62	397	0	854	3,404	15.2
2005	97	3,700	73	9	8	3	439	11	4,341	358	65	305	0	729	3,612	16.4
2006	17	3,590	120	13	57	0	389	0	4,186	341	61	322	0	724	3,462	16.0
2007	77	3,783	115	54	95	18	448	18	4,608	482	47	292	2	822	3,785	16.4
2008	0	3,589	55	43	12	3	267	15	3,984	559	39	365	0	963	3,021	13.0
2009	0	3,271	160	28	13	13	236	29	3,751	701	31	338	3	1,072	2,679	11.7
2010	0	R3,280	73	30	42	46	190	81	R3,741	R739	33	333	32	R1,137	R2,604	R11.0
2011P	0	3,102	35	3	2	91	129	92	3,453	937	18	500	52	1,507	1,946	8.0

[1] Net imports equal imports minus exports.

[2] As liquefied natural gas.

[3] By pipeline, except for very small amounts of liquefied natural gas imported from Canada in 1973, 1977, and 1981, and exported to Mexico beginning in 1998.

[4] Australia in 1997–2001 and 2004; Brunei in 2002; Equatorial Guinea in 2007; Indonesia in 1986 and 2000; Malaysia in 1999 and 2002–2005; Norway in 2008 forward; Oman in 2000–2005; Peru in 2010 and 2011; United Arab Emirates in 1996–2000; Yemen in 2010 and 2011; and Other (unassigned) in 2004.

[5] Brazil in 2010 and 2011; Chile in 2011; China in 2011; India in 2010 and 2011; Russia in 2007; South Korea in 2009 forward; Spain in 2010 and 2011; and United Kingdom in 2010 and 2011.

[6] Not meaningful because there were net exports during this year.

R=Revised. P=Preliminary. (s)=Less than 0.5 billion cubic feet.

Note: Totals may not equal sum of components due to independent rounding.

Web Pages: • See http://www.eia.gov/totalenergy/data/monthly/#naturalgas for updated monthly and annual data. • See http://www.eia.gov/totalenergy/data/annual/#naturalgas for all annual data beginning in 1949. • See http://www.eia.gov/naturalgas/ for related information.

Sources: **Percent of U.S. Consumption:** Calculated by dividing natural gas net imports by total natural gas consumption—see Table 6.1. **All Other Data:** • 1949-1954—U.S. Energy Information Administration (EIA) estimates based on Bureau of Mines, Minerals Yearbook, "Natural Gas" chapter. • 1955-1971—EIA, Federal Power Commission, by telephone. • 1972-1987—EIA, Form FPC-14, "Annual Report for Importers and Exporters of Natural Gas." • 1988-2009—EIA, *Natural Gas Annual*, annual reports. • 2010 and 2011—EIA, *Natural Gas Monthly* (March 2012), Tables 4 and 5.

Source: *U.S. Energy Information Administration, Annual Energy Review 2011*

Figure 7.0 Coal Flow, 2011
(Million Short Tons)

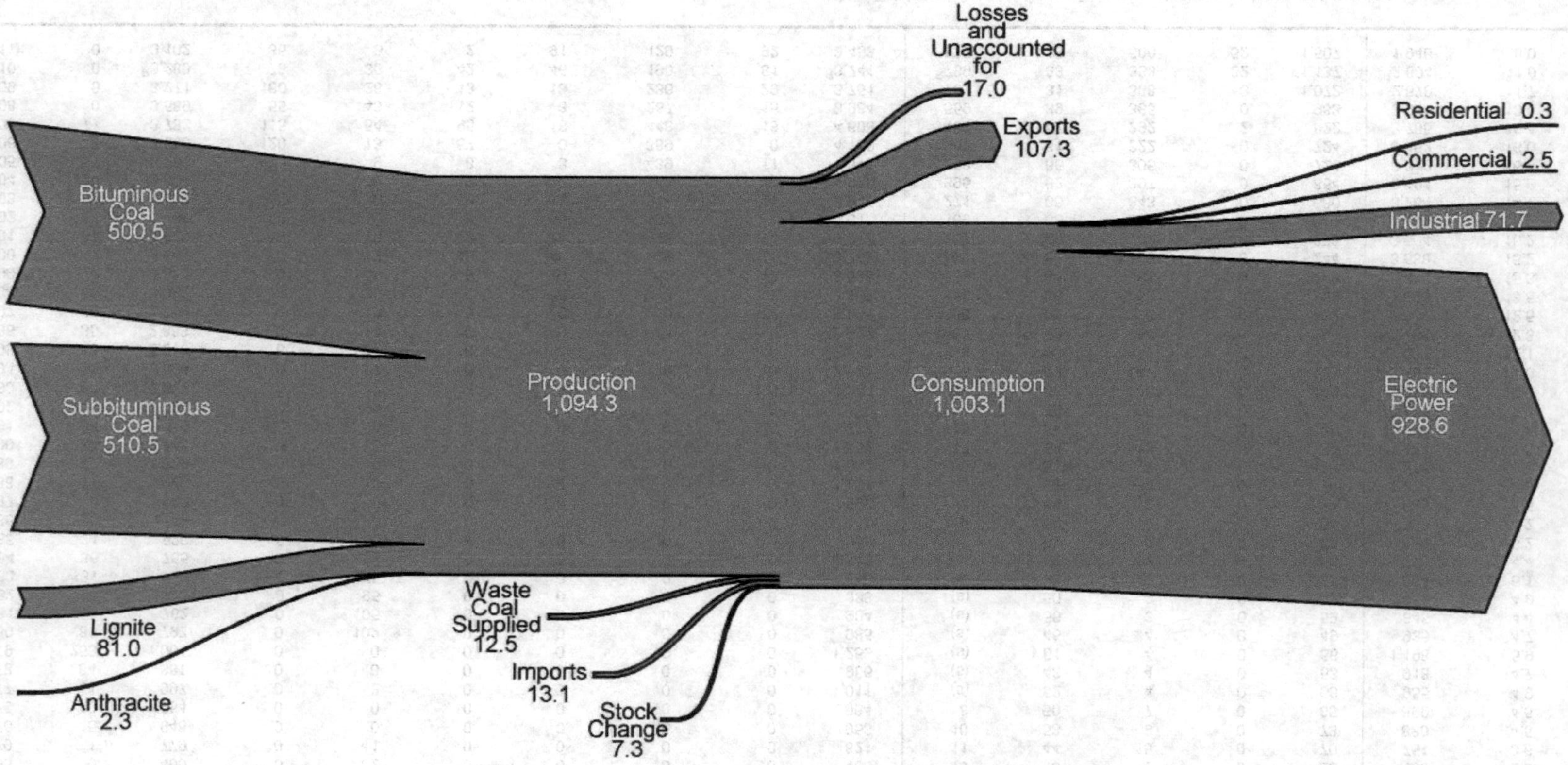

Notes: • Production categories are estimated; all data are preliminary. • Values are derived from source data prior to rounding for publication. • Totals may not equal sum of components due to independent rounding.

Sources: Tables 7.1, 7.2, and 7.3.

***Source:** U.S. Energy Information Administration, Annual Energy Review 2011*

Figure 7.1 Coal Overview

Overview, 1949-2011

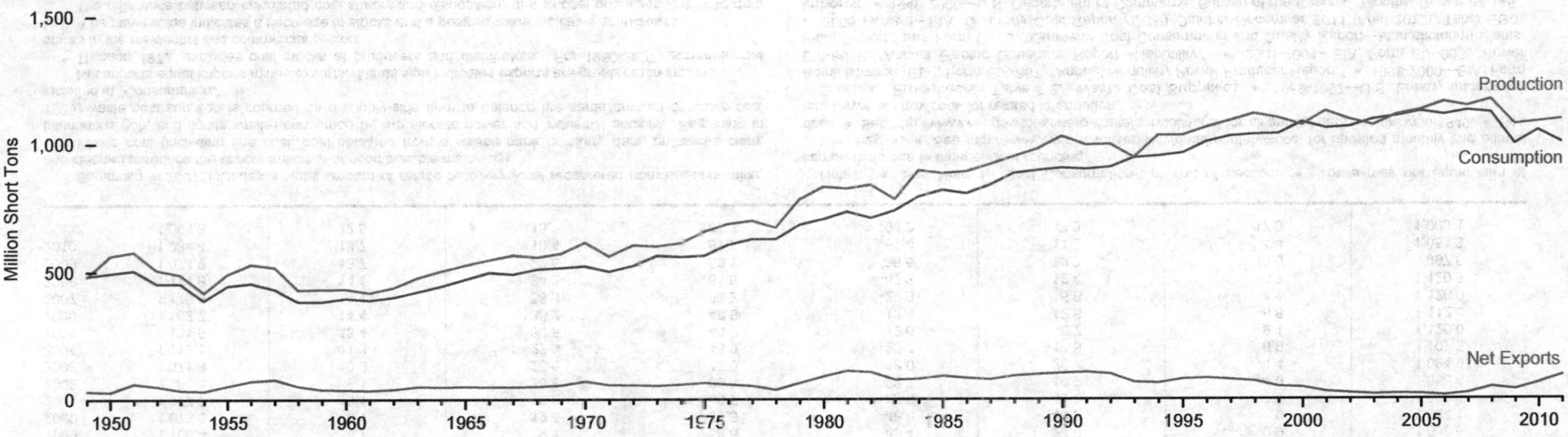

Overview, 2011

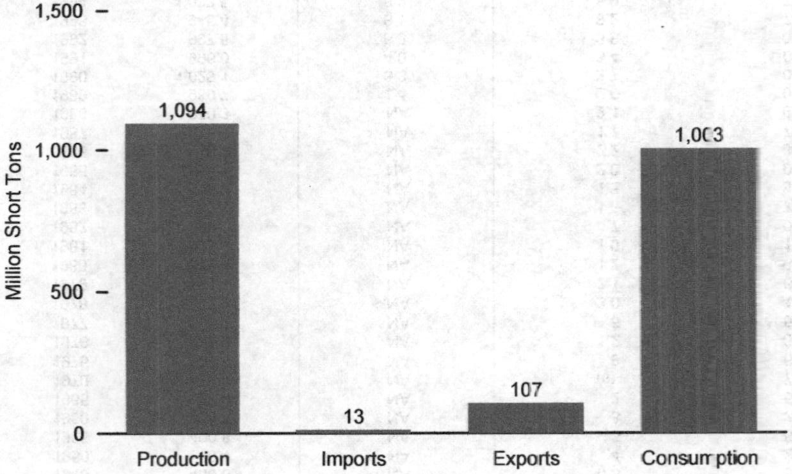

Production as Share of Consumption by Major Source, 1949-2011

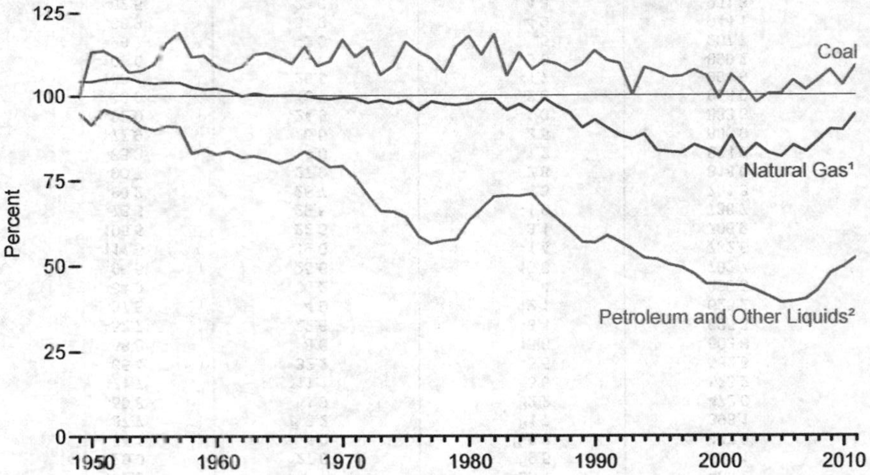

[1] Dry natural gas production as share of natural gas consumption.
[2] Petroleum and other liquids production as share of petroleum and other liquids estimated consumption.

Sources: Tables 5.1a, 6.1, and 7.1.

Source: *U.S. Energy Information Administration, Annual Energy Review 2011*

Table 7.1 Coal Overview, Selected Years, 1949-2011

(Million Short Tons)

Year	Production [1]	Waste Coal Supplied [2]	Trade: Imports	Trade: Exports	Trade: Net Imports [3]	Stock Change [4,5]	Losses and Unaccounted for [6]	Consumption
1949	480.6	NA	0.3	32.8	-32.5	([7])	[7]-35.1	483.2
1950	560.4	NA	.4	29.4	-29.0	[R]27.8	[R]9.5	494.1
1955	490.8	NA	.3	54.4	-54.1	[R]-4.0	[R]-6.3	447.0
1960	434.3	NA	.3	38.0	-37.7	[R]-3.2	[R]1.7	398.1
1965	527.0	NA	.2	51.0	-50.8	[R]1.9	[R]2.2	472.0
1970	612.7	NA	(s)	71.7	-71.7	[R]11.1	[R]6.6	523.2
1975	654.6	NA	.9	66.3	-65.4	32.2	-5.5	562.6
1976	684.9	NA	1.2	60.0	-58.8	8.5	13.8	603.8
1977	697.2	NA	1.6	54.3	-52.7	22.6	-3.4	625.3
1978	670.2	NA	3.0	40.7	-37.8	-4.9	12.1	625.2
1979	781.1	NA	2.1	66.0	-64.0	36.2	.4	680.5
1980	829.7	NA	1.2	91.7	-90.5	25.6	10.8	702.7
1981	823.8	NA	1.0	112.5	-111.5	-19.0	-1.4	732.6
1982	838.1	NA	.7	106.3	-105.5	22.6	3.1	706.9
1983	782.1	NA	1.3	77.8	-76.5	-29.5	-1.6	736.7
1984	895.9	NA	1.3	81.5	-80.2	28.7	-4.3	791.3
1985	883.6	NA	2.0	92.7	-90.7	-27.9	2.8	818.0
1986	890.3	NA	2.2	85.5	-83.3	4.0	-1.2	804.2
1987	918.8	NA	1.7	79.6	-77.9	6.5	-2.5	836.9
1988	950.3	NA	2.1	95.0	-92.9	-24.9	-1.3	883.6
1989	980.7	1.4	2.9	100.8	-98.0	-13.7	2.9	895.0
1990	1,029.1	3.3	2.7	105.8	-103.1	26.5	-1.7	904.5
1991	996.0	4.0	3.4	109.0	-105.6	-.9	-3.9	899.2
1992	997.5	6.3	3.8	102.5	-98.7	-3.0	.5	907.7
1993	945.4	8.1	8.2	74.5	-66.3	-51.9	-4.9	944.1
1994	1,033.5	8.2	8.9	71.4	-62.5	23.6	4.3	951.3
1995	1,033.0	8.6	9.5	88.5	-79.1	-.3	.6	962.1
1996	1,063.9	8.8	8.1	90.5	-82.4	-17.5	1.4	1,006.3
1997	1,089.9	8.1	7.5	83.5	-76.1	-11.3	3.7	1,029.5
1998	1,117.5	8.7	8.7	78.0	-69.3	24.2	-4.4	1,037.1
1999	1,100.4	8.7	9.1	58.5	-49.4	24.0	-2.9	1,038.6
2000	1,073.6	9.1	12.5	58.5	-46.0	-48.3	.9	1,084.1
2001	[1]1,127.7	10.1	19.8	48.7	-28.9	41.6	7.1	1,060.1
2002	1,094.3	9.1	16.9	39.6	-22.7	10.2	4.0	1,066.4
2003	1,071.8	10.0	25.0	43.0	-18.0	-26.7	-4.4	1,094.9
2004	1,112.1	11.3	27.3	48.0	-20.7	-11.5	6.9	1,107.3
2005	1,131.5	13.4	30.5	49.9	-19.5	-9.7	9.1	1,126.0
2006	1,162.7	14.4	36.2	49.6	-13.4	42.6	8.8	1,112.3
2007	1,146.6	14.1	36.3	59.2	-22.8	5.8	4.1	1,128.0
2008	1,171.8	14.1	34.2	81.5	-47.3	12.4	5.7	1,120.5
2009	1,074.9	13.7	22.6	59.1	-36.5	39.7	15.0	997.5
2010	[R]1,084.4	[R]13.7	19.4	81.7	-62.4	[R]-11.2	[R]-4.4	[R]1,051.3
2011[P]	1,094.3	12.5	13.1	107.3	-94.2	-7.3	17.0	1,003.1

[1] Beginning in 2001, includes a small amount of refuse recovery (coal recaptured from a refuse mine, and cleaned to reduce the concentration of noncombustible materials).

[2] Waste coal (including fine coal, coal obtained from a refuse bank or slurry dam, anthracite culm, bituminous gob, and lignite waste) consumed by the electric power and industrial sectors. Beginning in 1989, waste coal supplied is counted as a supply-side item to balance the same amount of waste coal included in "Consumption."

[3] Net imports equal imports minus exports. Minus sign indicates exports are greater than imports.

[4] Through 1972, excludes coal stocks at producers and distributors. For 1980-2007, excludes coal stocks in the residential and commercial sectors.

[5] A negative value indicates a decrease in stocks and a positive value indicates an increase.

[6] The difference between calculated coal supply and disposition, due to coal quantities lost or to data reporting problems.

[7] In 1949, stock change is included in "Losses and Unaccounted for."

R=Revised. P=Preliminary. NA=Not available. (s)=Less than 0.05 million short tons.

Notes: • See Note 1, "Coal Consumption," at end of section. • Totals may not equal sum of components due to independent rounding.

Web Pages: • See http://www.eia.gov/totalenergy/data/monthly/#coal for updated monthly and annual data. • See http://www.eia.gov/totalenergy/data/annual/#coal for all annual data beginning in 1949. • See http://www.eia.gov/coal/ for related information.

Sources: **Production:** Table 7.2. **Waste Coal Supplied:** • 1989-1997—U.S. Energy Information Administration (EIA), Form EIA-867, "Annual Nonutility Power Producer Report." • 1998-2000—EIA, Form EIA-860B, "Annual Electric Generator Report—Nonutility." • 2001-2004—EIA, Form EIA-906, "Power Plant Report," and Form EIA-3, "Quarterly Coal Consumption and Quality Report—Manufacturing Plants. • 2005 forward—EIA, *Quarterly Coal Report (QCR) October-December 2011* (April 2012), Table ES-1. **Imports:** • 1949-2000—U.S. Department of Commerce, Bureau of the Census, "Monthly Report IM 145." • 2001 forward—Table 7.4. **Exports:** Table 7.5. **Stock Change:** Table 7.6. **Losses and Unaccounted for:** Calculated as the sum of production, imports, and waste coal supplied, minus exports, stock change, and consumption. **Consumption:** Table 7.3.

Source: *U.S. Energy Information Administration, Annual Energy Review 2011*

Figure 7.2 Coal Production, 1949-2011

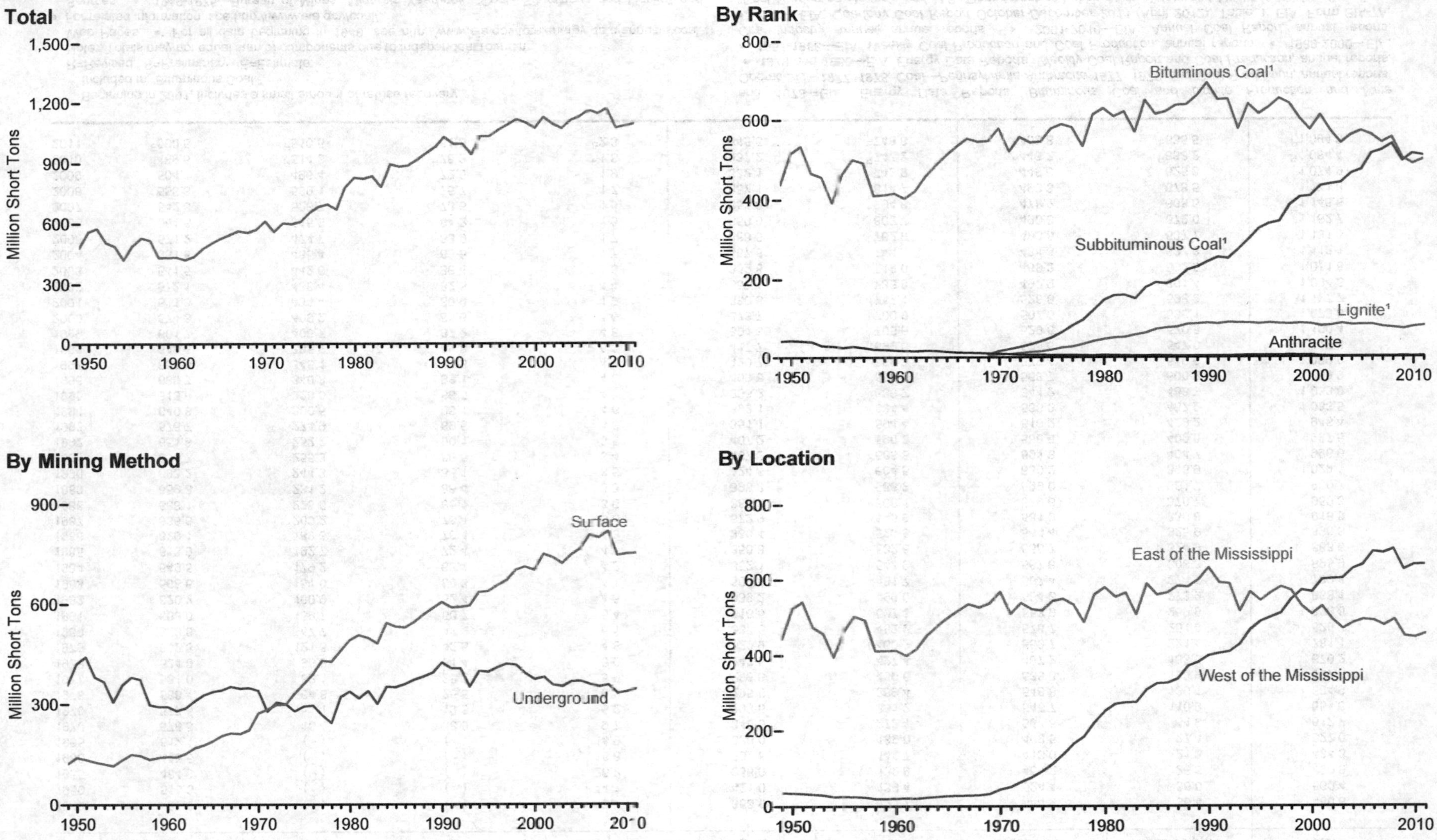

¹ Subbituminous coal and lignite are included in bituminous coal prior to 1969.

Source: Table 7.2.

Source: *U.S. Energy Information Administration, Annual Energy Review 2011*

Table 7.2 Coal Production, Selected Years, 1949-2011

(Million Short Tons)

	Rank				Mining Method		Location		
Year	Bituminous Coal [1]	Subbituminous Coal	Lignite	Anthracite [1]	Underground	Surface [1]	East of the Mississippi [1]	West of the Mississippi [1]	Total [1]
1949	437.9	([2])	([2])	42.7	358.9	121.7	444.2	36.4	480.6
1950	516.3	([2])	([2])	44.1	421.0	139.4	524.4	36.0	560.4
1955	464.6	([2])	([2])	26.2	358.0	132.9	464.2	26.6	490.8
1960	415.5	([2])	([2])	18.8	292.6	141.7	413.0	21.3	434.3
1965	512.1	([2])	([2])	14.9	338.0	189.0	499.5	27.4	527.0
1970	578.5	16.4	8.0	9.7	340.5	272.1	567.8	44.9	612.7
1975	577.5	51.1	19.8	6.2	293.5	361.2	543.7	110.9	654.6
1976	588.4	64.8	25.5	6.2	295.5	389.4	548.8	136.1	684.9
1977	581.0	82.1	28.2	5.9	266.6	430.6	533.3	163.9	697.2
1978	534.0	96.8	34.4	5.0	242.8	427.4	487.2	183.0	670.2
1979	612.3	121.5	42.5	4.8	320.9	460.2	559.7	221.4	781.1
1980	628.8	147.7	47.2	6.1	337.5	492.2	578.7	251.0	829.7
1981	608.0	159.7	50.7	5.4	316.5	507.3	553.9	269.9	823.8
1982	620.2	160.9	52.4	4.6	339.2	499.0	564.3	273.9	838.1
1983	568.6	151.0	58.3	4.1	300.4	481.7	507.4	274.7	782.1
1984	649.5	179.2	63.1	4.2	352.1	543.9	587.6	308.3	895.9
1985	613.9	192.7	72.4	4.7	350.8	532.8	558.7	324.9	883.6
1986	620.1	189.6	76.4	4.3	360.4	529.9	564.4	325.9	890.3
1987	636.6	200.2	78.4	3.6	372.9	545.9	581.9	336.8	918.8
1988	638.1	223.5	85.1	3.6	382.2	568.1	579.6	370.7	950.3
1989	659.8	231.2	86.4	3.3	393.8	586.9	599.0	381.7	980.7
1990	693.2	244.3	88.1	3.5	424.5	604.5	630.2	398.9	1,029.1
1991	650.7	255.3	86.5	3.4	407.2	588.8	591.3	404.7	996.0
1992	651.8	252.2	90.1	3.5	407.2	590.3	588.6	409.0	997.5
1993	576.7	274.9	89.5	4.3	351.1	594.4	516.2	429.2	945.4
1994	640.3	300.5	88.1	4.6	399.1	634.4	566.3	467.2	1,033.5
1995	613.8	328.0	86.5	4.7	396.2	636.7	544.2	488.7	1,033.0
1996	630.7	340.3	88.1	4.8	409.8	654.0	563.7	500.2	1,063.9
1997	653.8	345.1	86.3	4.7	420.7	669.3	579.4	510.6	1,089.9
1998	640.6	385.9	85.8	5.3	417.7	699.8	570.6	547.0	1,117.5
1999	601.7	406.7	87.2	4.8	391.8	708.6	529.6	570.8	1,100.4
2000	574.3	409.2	85.6	4.6	373.7	700.0	507.5	566.1	1,073.6
2001	[1]611.3	434.4	80.0	[1]1.9	380.6	[1]747.1	[1]528.8	[1]598.9	[1]1,127.7
2002	572.1	438.4	82.5	1.4	357.4	736.9	492.9	601.4	1,094.3
2003	541.5	442.6	86.4	1.3	352.8	719.0	469.2	602.5	1,071.8
2004	561.5	465.4	83.5	1.7	367.6	744.5	484.8	627.3	1,112.1
2005	571.2	474.7	83.9	1.7	368.6	762.9	493.8	637.7	1,131.5
2006	561.6	515.3	84.2	1.5	359.0	803.7	490.8	672.0	1,162.7
2007	542.8	523.7	78.6	1.6	351.8	794.8	478.2	668.5	1,146.6
2008	555.3	539.1	75.7	1.7	357.1	814.7	493.3	678.5	1,171.8
2009	504.1	496.4	72.5	1.9	332.1	742.9	449.6	625.3	1,074.9
2010	[R]489.5	[R]514.8	[R]78.2	[R]1.8	[R]337.2	[R]747.2	[R]446.2	[R]638.2	[R]1,084.4
2011	[E]500.5	[E]510.5	[E]81.0	[E]2.3	[E]345.5	[E]748.8	[E]455.8	[E]638.5	[P]1,094.3

[1] Beginning in 2001, includes a small amount of refuse recovery.
[2] Included in "Bituminous Coal."
R=Revised. P=Preliminary. E=Estimate.
Note: Totals may not equal sum of components due to independent rounding.
Web Pages: • For all data beginning in 1949, see http://www.eia.gov/totalenergy/data/annual/#coal. • For related information, see http://www.eia.gov/coal/.
Sources: • 1949-1975—Bureau of Mines, *Minerals Yearbook*, "Coal—Bituminous and Lignite" and "Coal—Pennsylvania Anthracite" chapters. • 1976—U.S. Energy Information Administration (EIA), Energy Data Reports, *Coal—Bituminous and Lignite in 1976* and *Coal—Pennsylvania Anthracite 1976*. • 1977 and 1978—EIA, Energy Data Reports, *Bituminous Coal and Lignite Production and Mine Operations—1977; 1978, Coal—Pennsylvania Anthracite 1977; 1978*, and *Coal Production*, annual reports. • 1979 and 1980—EIA, Energy Data Reports, *Weekly Coal Report* and *Coal Production*, annual reports. • 1981-1988—EIA, *Weekly Coal Production* and *Coal Production*, annual reports. • 1989-2000—EIA, *Coal Industry Annual*, annual reports. • 2001-2010—EIA, *Annual Coal Report*, annual reports. • 2011—EIA, *Quarterly Coal Report October-December 2011* (April 2012), Table 1; EIA, Form EIA-7A, "Coal Production Report"; and U.S. Department of Labor, Mine Safety and Health Administration, Form 7000-2, "Quarterly Mine Employment and Coal Production Report."

Source: *U.S. Energy Information Administration, Annual Energy Review 2011*

Figure 7.3 Coal Consumption by Sector

By Sector, 1949-2011

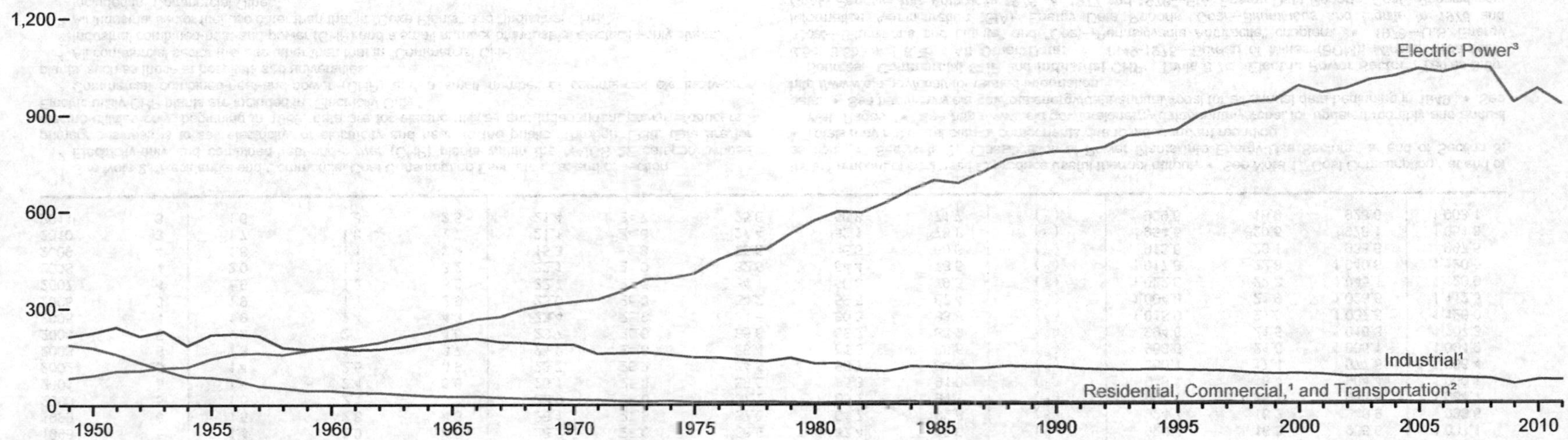

By Sector, 2011

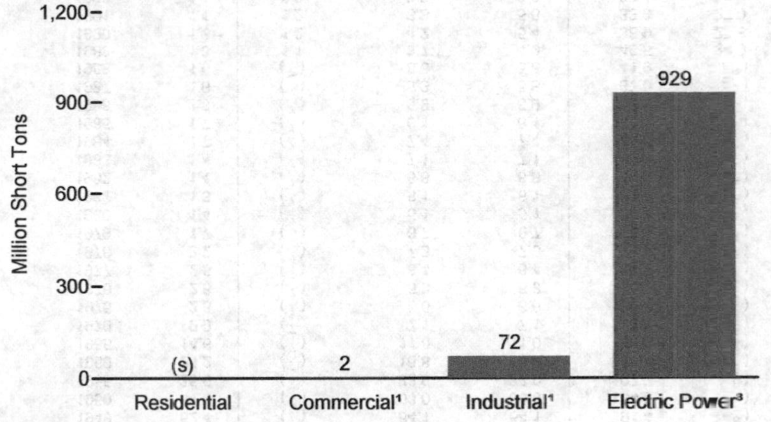

Sector Shares, 1949 and 2011

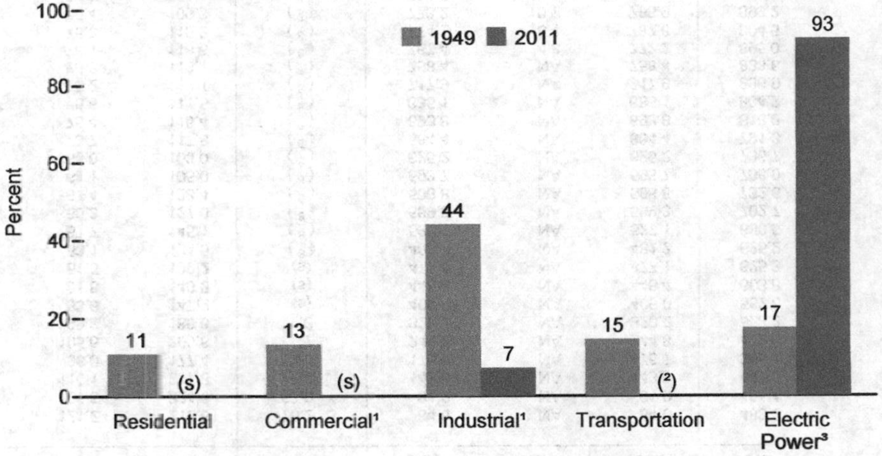

[1] Includes combined-heat-and-power (CHP) plants and a small number of electricity-only plants.

[2] For 1978 forward, small amounts of transportation sector use are included in "Industrial."

[3] Electricity-only and combined-heat-and-power (CHP) plants whose primary business is to sell electricity, or electricity and heat, to the public.

(s)=Less than 0.5.

Source: Table 7.3.

***Source:** U.S. Energy Information Administration, Annual Energy Review 2011*

Table 7.3 Coal Consumption by Sector, Selected Years, 1949-2011

(Million Short Tons)

Year	Residential Sector[1]	Commercial Sector[1]			Industrial Sector					Transportation Sector	Electric Power Sector[2]			Total
		CHP[3]	Other[4]	Total	Coke Plants	Other Industrial			Total		Electricity Only	CHP	Total	
						CHP[5]	Non-CHP[6]	Total						
1949	52.4	(7)	64.1	64.1	91.4	(8)	121.2	121.2	212.6	70.2	84.0	NA	84.0	483.2
1950	51.6	(7)	63.0	63.0	104.0	(8)	120.6	120.6	224.6	63.0	91.9	NA	91.9	494.1
1955	35.6	(7)	32.9	32.9	107.7	(8)	110.1	110.1	217.8	17.0	143.8	NA	143.8	447.0
1960	24.2	(7)	16.8	16.8	81.4	(8)	96.0	96.0	177.4	3.0	176.7	NA	176.7	398.1
1965	14.6	(7)	11.0	11.0	95.3	(8)	105.6	105.6	200.8	.7	244.8	NA	244.8	472.0
1970	9.0	(7)	7.1	7.1	96.5	(8)	90.2	90.2	186.6	.3	320.2	NA	320.2	523.2
1975	2.8	(7)	6.6	6.6	83.6	(8)	63.6	63.6	147.2	(s)	406.0	NA	406.0	562.6
1976	2.6	(7)	6.3	6.3	84.7	(8)	61.8	61.8	146.5	(s)	448.4	NA	448.4	603.8
1977	2.5	(7)	6.4	6.4	77.7	(8)	61.5	61.5	139.2	(s)	477.1	NA	477.1	625.3
1978	2.2	(7)	7.3	7.3	71.4	(8)	63.1	63.1	134.5	(8)	481.2	NA	481.2	625.2
1979	1.7	(7)	6.7	6.7	77.4	(8)	67.7	67.7	145.1	(8)	527.1	NA	527.1	680.5
1980	1.4	(7)	5.1	5.1	66.7	(8)	60.3	60.3	127.0	(8)	569.3	NA	569.3	702.7
1981	1.3	(7)	6.1	6.1	61.0	(8)	67.4	67.4	128.4	(8)	596.8	NA	596.8	732.6
1982	1.4	(7)	6.8	6.8	40.9	(8)	64.1	64.1	105.0	(8)	593.7	NA	593.7	706.9
1983	1.4	(7)	7.1	7.1	37.0	(8)	66.0	66.0	103.0	(8)	625.2	NA	625.2	736.7
1984	1.7	(7)	7.4	7.4	44.0	(8)	73.7	73.7	117.8	(8)	664.4	NA	664.4	791.3
1985	1.7	(7)	6.1	6.1	41.1	(8)	75.4	75.4	116.4	(8)	693.8	NA	693.8	818.0
1986	1.8	(7)	5.9	5.9	35.9	(8)	75.6	75.6	111.5	(8)	685.1	NA	685.1	804.2
1987	1.6	(7)	5.3	5.3	37.0	(8)	75.2	75.2	112.1	(8)	717.9	NA	717.9	836.9
1988	1.6	(7)	5.6	5.6	41.9	(8)	76.3	76.3	118.1	(8)	758.4	NA	758.4	883.6
1989	1.3	1.1	3.7	4.9	40.5	24.9	51.3	76.1	116.6	(8)	767.4	4.8	772.2	895.0
1990	1.3	1.2	4.2	5.4	38.9	27.8	48.5	76.3	115.2	(8)	774.2	8.4	782.6	904.5
1991	1.1	1.2	3.8	5.0	33.9	27.0	48.4	75.4	109.3	(8)	773.2	10.7	783.9	899.2
1992	1.1	1.2	3.9	5.0	32.4	28.2	45.8	74.0	106.4	(8)	781.2	13.9	795.1	907.7
1993	1.1	1.4	3.7	5.1	31.3	28.9	46.0	74.9	106.2	(8)	816.6	15.1	831.6	944.1
1994	.9	1.3	3.8	5.1	31.7	29.7	45.5	75.2	106.9	(8)	821.2	17.1	838.4	951.3
1995	.8	1.4	3.6	5.1	33.0	29.4	43.7	73.1	106.1	(8)	832.9	17.3	850.2	962.1
1996	.7	1.7	3.6	5.3	31.7	29.4	42.3	71.7	103.4	(8)	878.8	18.1	896.9	1,006.3
1997	.7	1.7	4.0	5.8	30.2	29.9	41.7	71.5	101.7	(8)	904.2	17.1	921.4	1,029.5
1998	.5	1.4	2.9	4.3	28.2	28.6	38.9	67.4	95.6	(8)	920.4	16.3	936.6	1,037.1
1999	.6	1.5	2.8	4.3	28.1	27.8	37.0	64.7	92.8	(8)	924.7	16.2	940.9	1,038.6
2000	.5	1.5	2.1	3.7	28.9	28.0	37.2	65.2	94.1	(8)	967.1	18.7	985.8	1,084.1
2001	.5	1.4	2.4	3.9	26.1	25.8	39.5	65.3	91.3	(8)	946.1	18.4	964.4	1,060.1
2002	.5	1.4	2.5	3.9	23.7	26.2	34.5	60.7	84.4	(8)	960.1	17.4	977.5	1,066.4
2003	.6	1.8	1.9	3.7	24.2	24.8	36.4	61.3	85.5	(8)	983.5	21.6	1,005.1	1,094.9
2004	.5	1.9	2.7	4.6	23.7	26.6	35.6	62.2	85.9	(8)	994.8	21.5	1,016.3	1,107.3
2005	.4	1.9	2.4	4.3	23.4	25.9	34.5	60.3	83.8	(8)	1,015.6	21.8	1,037.5	1,126.0
2006	.3	1.9	1.1	2.9	23.0	25.3	34.2	59.5	82.4	(8)	1,004.8	21.9	1,026.6	1,112.3
2007	.4	1.9	1.2	3.2	22.7	22.5	34.1	56.6	79.3	(8)	1,022.8	22.3	1,045.1	1,128.0
2008	.4	2.0	1.1	3.2	22.1	21.9	32.5	54.4	76.5	(8)	1,017.8	22.8	1,040.6	1,120.5
2009	.4	1.8	1.1	2.9	15.3	19.8	25.5	45.3	60.6	(8)	913.6	20.1	933.6	997.5
2010	.3	[R]1.7	1.0	2.7	21.1	[R]24.6	[R]27.4	[R]52.1	[R]73.2	(8)	[R]954.5	[R]20.5	[R]975.1	[R]1,051.3
2011[P]	.3	1.6	.8	2.5	21.4	24.7	25.6	50.3	71.7	(8)	909.6	18.9	928.6	1,003.1

[1] See Note 2, "Residential and Commercial Coal Consumption Estimates," at end of section.

[2] Electricity-only and combined-heat-and-power (CHP) plants within the NAICS 22 category whose primary business is to sell electricity, or electricity and heat, to the public. Through 1988, data are for electric utilities only; beginning in 1989, data are for electric utilities and independent power producers. Electric utility CHP plants are included in "Electricity Only."

[3] Commercial combined-heat-and-power (CHP) and a small number of commercial electricity-only plants, such as those at hospitals and universities.

[4] All commercial sector fuel use other than that in "Commercial CHP."

[5] Industrial combined-heat-and-power (CHP) and a small number of industrial electricity-only plants.

[6] All industrial sector fuel use other than that in "Coke Plants" and "Industrial CHP."

[7] Included in "Commercial Other."

[8] Included in "Industrial Non-CHP."

R=Revised. P=Preliminary. NA=Not available. (s)=Less than 0.05 million short tons.

Notes: • See Tables 8.5a–8.5d for the amount of coal used to produce electricity and Tables 8.6a–8.6c for the amount of coal used to produce useful thermal output. • See Note 1, "Coal Consumption," at end of section. • See Note 2, "Classification of Power Plants Into Energy-Use Sectors," at end of Section 8. • Totals may not equal sum of components due to independent rounding.

Web Pages: • See http://www.eia.gov/totalenergy/data/monthly/#coal for updated monthly and annual data. • See http://www.eia.gov/totalenergy/data/annual/#coal for all annual data beginning in 1949. • See http://www.eia.gov/coal/ for related information.

Sources: **Commercial CHP and Industrial CHP:** Table 8.7c. **Electric Power Sector:** Tables 8.5b, 8.5c, 8.6b, and 8.7b. **All Other Data:** • 1949-1975—Bureau of Mines (BOM), *Minerals Yearbook*, "Coal—Bituminous and Lignite" and "Coal—Pennsylvania Anthracite" chapters. • 1976—U.S. Energy Information Administration (EIA), Energy Data Reports, *Coal—Bituminous and Lignite in 1976* and *Coal—Pennsylvania Anthracite 1976*. • 1977 and 1978—EIA, Energy Data Reports, *Coal—Pennsylvania Anthracite 1977; 1978*, and *Weekly Coal Report*. • 1979 and 1980—EIA, Energy Data Report, *Weekly Coal Report*. • 1981-2004—EIA, *Quarterly Coal Report (QCR) October-December*, quarterly reports. • 2005 forward—EIA, QCR October-December 2011 (April 2012), Table 32.

Source: *U.S. Energy Information Administration, Annual Energy Review 2011*

Figure 7.4 Coal Imports by Country of Origin

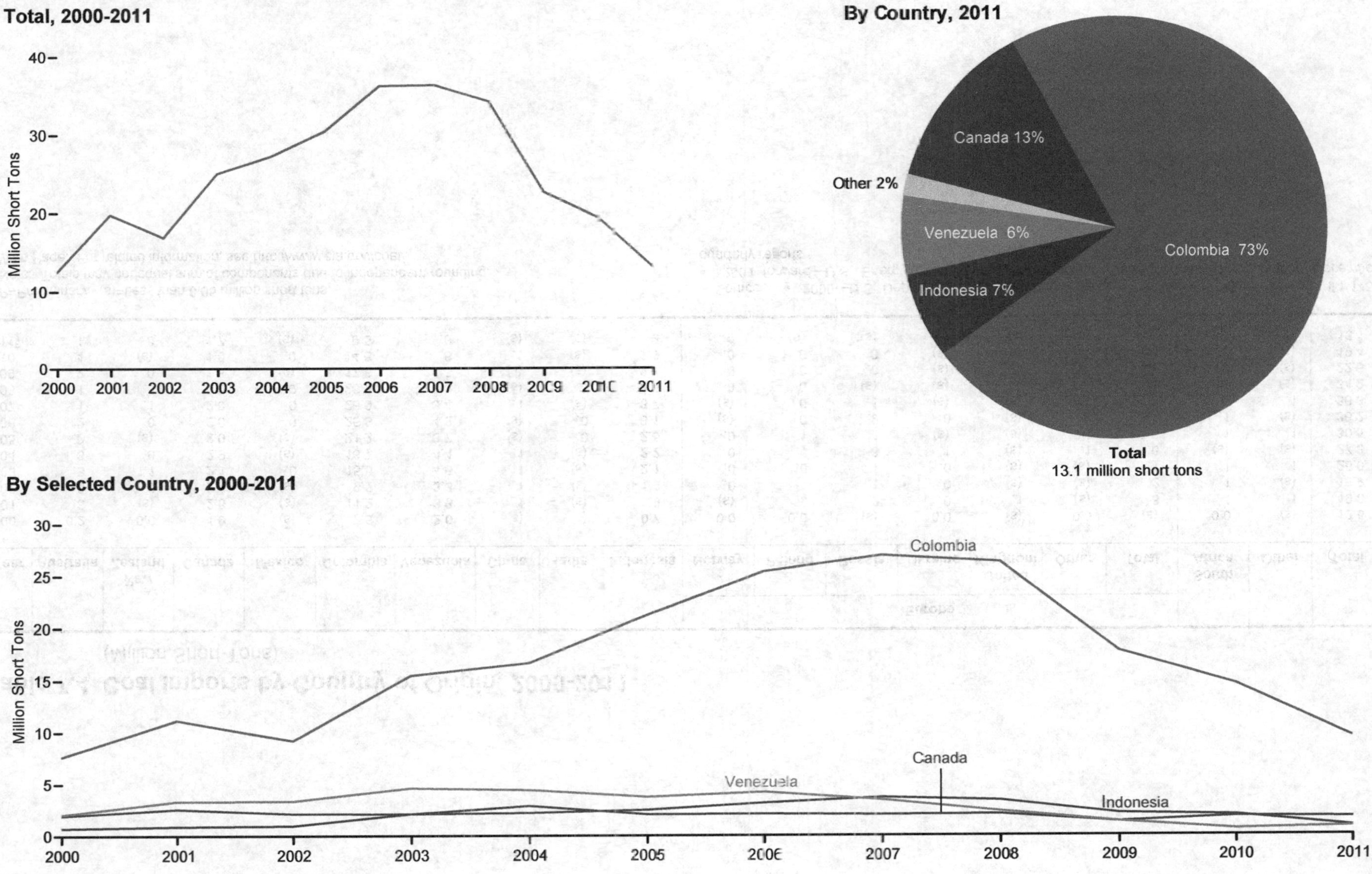

Note: Sum of components may not equal 100 percent due to independent rounding

Source: Table 7.4.

Source: *U.S. Energy Information Administration, Annual Energy Review 2011*

Table 7.4 Coal Imports by Country of Origin, 2000-2011

(Million Short Tons)

Year	Australia	New Zealand	Canada	Mexico	Colombia	Venezuela	China	India	Indonesia	Europe							South Africa	Other	Total
										Norway	Poland	Russia	Ukraine	United Kingdom	Other	Total			
2000	0.2	0.0	1.9	(s)	7.6	2.0	(s)	(s)	0.7	0.0	0.0	(s)	0.0	(s)	0.0	(s)	0.0	(s)	12.5
2001	.3	(s)	2.6	(s)	11.2	3.3	.1	(s)	.9	(s)	.5	.2	.0	.1	(s)	.8	.4	.1	19.8
2002	.8	.0	2.1	(s)	9.2	3.3	.1	(s)	1.0	.0	.1	.1	.0	(s)	(s)	.2	.1	(s)	16.9
2003	.3	.1	2.1	.0	15.5	4.6	.1	(s)	2.1	.0	.0	.1	.0	(s)	(s)	.1	.1	.1	25.0
2004	.3	.0	2.9	(s)	16.7	4.4	.1	(s)	2.2	.0	.1	.3	.1	(s)	.1	.6	(s)	(s)	27.3
2005	.2	(s)	2.0	(s)	21.2	3.7	(s)	.0	2.5	.0	.1	.4	(s)	(s)	.1	.6	.1	.1	30.5
2006	.2	.0	2.0	.0	25.3	4.2	(s)	.0	3.1	(s)	.0	.9	.0	(s)	.2	1.1	.1	(s)	36.2
2007	.1	.1	2.0	.0	26.9	3.4	.1	(s)	3.7	(s)	.0	.1	(s)	(s)	(s)	.2	.0	.1	36.3
2008	.1	.0	2.0	.0	26.3	2.3	(s)	.0	3.4	.0	.0	(s)	(s)	.0	(s)	(s)	(s)	(s)	34.2
2009	.2	.0	1.3	(s)	17.8	1.3	(s)	(s)	2.1	.0	.0	.0	(s)	(s)	(s)	(s)	.0	(s)	22.6
2010	.4	(s)	1.8	.0	14.6	.6	.1	(s)	1.9	.0	.0	.0	(s)	(s)	(s)	(s)	.0	(s)	19.4
2011P	.1	.0	1.7	(s)	9.5	.8	(s)	(s)	.9	.0	(s)	(s)	.1	.0	(s)	.1	(s)	.1	13.1

P=Preliminary. (s)=Less than 0.05 million short tons.
Note: Totals may not equal sum of components due to independent rounding.
Web Page: For related information, see http://www.eia.gov/coal/.

Sources: • 2000—U.S. Department of Commerce, Bureau of the Census, "Monthly Report IM 145."
• 2001 forward—U.S. Energy Information Administration, *Quarterly Coal Report October-December*, quarterly reports.

Source: *U.S. Energy Information Administration, Annual Energy Review 2011*

Figure 7.5 Coal Exports by Country of Destination

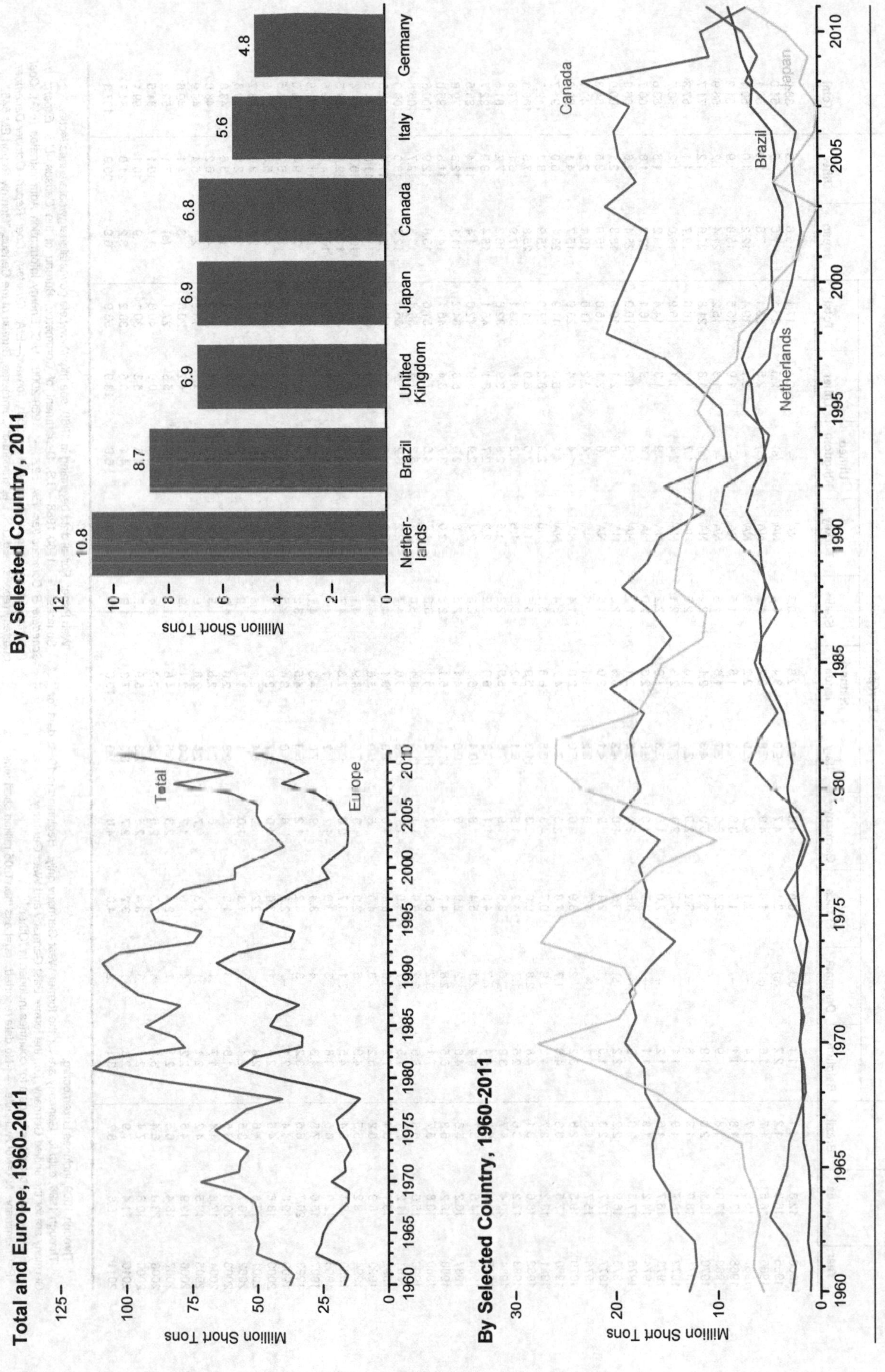

Source: Table 7.5.

Source: U.S. Energy Information Administration, Annual Energy Review 2011

Table 7.5 Coal Exports by Country of Destination, Selected Years, 1960-2011

(Million Short Tons)

Year	Canada	Brazil	Europe: Belgium [1]	Europe: Denmark	Europe: France	Europe: Germany [2]	Europe: Italy	Europe: Nether-lands	Europe: Spain	Europe: Turkey	Europe: United Kingdom	Europe: Other [3]	Europe: Total	Japan	Other [3]	Total
1960	12.8	1.1	1.1	0.1	0.8	4.6	4.9	2.8	0.3	NA	–	2.4	17.1	5.6	1.3	38.0
1965	16.3	1.2	2.2	(s)	2.1	4.7	9.0	3.4	1.4	NA	(s)	2.3	25.1	7.5	.9	51.0
1966	16.5	1.7	1.8	(s)	1.6	4.9	7.8	3.2	1.2	NA	(s)	2.5	23.1	7.8	1.0	50.1
1967	15.8	1.7	1.4	–	2.1	4.7	5.9	2.2	1.0	NA	–	2.1	19.4	12.2	1.0	50.1
1968	17.1	1.8	1.1	–	1.5	3.8	4.3	1.5	1.5	NA	–	1.9	15.5	15.8	.9	51.2
1969	17.3	1.8	.9	–	2.3	3.5	3.7	1.6	1.8	NA	–	1.3	15.2	21.4	1.2	56.9
1970	19.1	2.0	1.9	–	3.6	5.0	4.3	2.1	3.2	NA	(s)	1.8	21.8	27.6	1.2	71.7
1971	18.0	1.9	.8	–	3.2	2.9	2.7	1.6	2.6	NA	1.7	1.1	16.6	19.7	1.1	57.3
1972	18.7	1.9	1.1	–	1.7	2.4	3.7	2.3	2.1	NA	2.4	1.1	16.9	18.0	1.2	56.7
1973	16.7	1.6	1.2	–	2.0	1.6	3.3	1.8	2.2	NA	.9	1.3	14.4	19.2	1.6	53.6
1974	14.2	1.3	1.1	–	2.7	1.5	3.9	2.6	2.0	NA	1.4	.9	16.1	27.3	1.8	60.7
1975	17.3	2.0	.6	–	3.6	2.0	4.5	2.1	2.7	NA	1.9	1.6	19.0	25.4	2.6	66.3
1976	16.9	2.2	2.2	(s)	3.5	1.0	4.2	3.5	2.5	NA	.8	2.1	19.9	18.8	2.1	60.0
1977	17.7	2.3	1.5	.1	2.1	.9	4.1	2.0	1.6	NA	.6	2.1	15.0	15.9	3.5	54.3
1978	15.7	1.5	1.1	–	1.7	.6	3.2	1.1	.8	NA	.4	2.2	11.0	10.1	2.5	40.7
1979	19.5	2.8	3.2	.2	3.9	2.6	5.0	2.0	1.4	NA	1.4	4.4	23.9	15.7	4.1	66.0
1980	17.5	3.3	4.6	1.7	7.8	2.5	7.1	4.7	3.4	NA	4.1	6.0	41.9	23.1	6.0	91.7
1981	18.2	2.7	4.3	3.9	9.7	4.3	10.5	6.8	6.4	.6	2.3	8.2	57.0	25.9	8.7	112.5
1982	18.6	3.1	4.8	2.8	9.0	2.3	11.3	5.9	5.6	1.6	2.0	6.0	51.3	25.8	7.5	106.3
1983	17.2	3.6	2.5	1.7	4.2	1.5	8.1	4.2	3.3	1.6	1.2	4.7	33.1	17.9	6.1	77.8
1984	20.4	4.7	3.9	.6	3.8	.9	7.6	5.5	2.3	1.5	2.9	3.9	32.8	16.3	7.2	81.5
1985	16.4	5.9	4.4	2.2	4.5	1.1	10.3	6.3	3.5	2.2	2.7	8.1	45.1	15.4	9.9	92.7
1986	14.5	5.7	4.4	2.1	5.4	.8	10.4	5.6	2.6	2.4	2.9	5.9	42.6	11.4	11.4	85.5
1987	16.2	5.8	4.6	.9	2.9	.5	9.5	4.1	2.5	.8	2.6	5.8	34.2	11.1	12.3	79.6
1988	19.2	5.3	6.5	2.8	4.3	.7	11.1	5.1	2.5	2.0	3.7	6.4	45.1	14.1	11.3	95.0
1989	16.8	5.7	7.1	3.2	6.5	.7	11.2	6.1	3.3	1.7	4.5	7.2	51.6	13.8	12.9	100.8
1990	15.5	5.8	8.5	3.2	6.9	1.1	11.9	8.4	3.8	2.1	5.2	7.4	58.4	13.3	12.7	105.8
1991	11.2	7.1	7.5	4.7	9.5	1.7	11.3	9.6	4.7	2.2	6.2	8.2	65.5	12.3	13.0	109.0
1992	15.1	6.4	7.2	3.8	8.1	1.0	9.3	9.1	4.5	2.0	5.6	6.6	57.3	12.3	11.4	102.5
1993	8.9	5.2	5.2	.3	4.0	.5	6.9	5.6	4.1	1.6	4.1	5.3	37.6	11.9	11.0	74.5
1994	9.2	5.5	4.9	.5	2.9	.3	7.5	4.9	4.1	1.3	3.4	6.0	35.8	10.2	10.7	71.4
1995	9.4	6.4	4.5	2.1	3.7	2.0	9.1	7.3	4.7	2.0	4.7	8.7	48.6	11.8	12.4	88.5
1996	12.0	6.5	4.6	1.3	3.9	1.1	9.2	7.1	4.1	2.2	6.2	7.7	47.2	10.5	14.2	90.5
1997	15.0	7.5	4.3	.4	3.4	.9	7.0	4.8	4.1	2.1	7.2	7.1	41.3	8.0	11.8	83.5
1998	20.7	6.5	3.2	.3	3.2	1.2	5.3	4.5	3.2	1.6	5.9	5.3	33.8	7.7	9.4	78.0
1999	19.8	4.4	2.1	–	2.5	.6	4.0	3.4	2.5	.8	3.2	3.5	22.5	5.0	6.7	58.5
2000	18.8	4.5	2.9	.1	3.0	1.0	3.7	2.6	2.7	1.8	3.3	3.9	25.0	4.4	5.8	58.5
2001	17.6	4.6	2.8	–	2.2	.9	5.4	2.1	1.6	.9	2.5	2.4	20.8	2.1	3.6	48.7
2002	16.7	3.5	2.4	–	1.3	1.0	3.1	1.7	1.9	.6	1.9	1.8	15.6	1.3	2.6	39.6
2003	20.8	3.5	1.8	.3	1.3	.5	2.8	2.0	1.8	1.1	1.5	2.1	15.1	(s)	3.6	43.0
2004	17.8	4.4	1.7	.1	1.1	.6	2.1	2.5	1.5	1.3	2.0	2.3	15.2	4.4	6.2	48.0
2005	19.5	4.2	2.1	.1	1.3	.7	2.5	2.6	1.9	1.9	1.8	4.1	18.8	2.1	5.4	49.9
2006	19.9	4.5	2.2	.4	1.6	1.7	3.3	2.1	1.6	1.2	2.6	4.2	20.8	.3	4.1	49.6
2007	18.4	6.5	2.1	.1	2.4	2.3	3.5	4.6	1.5	1.4	3.4	5.8	27.1	(s)	7.1	59.2
2008	23.0	6.4	3.1	.4	3.5	2.5	3.2	7.0	2.4	1.9	5.8	10.6	40.3	1.7	10.1	81.5
2009	10.6	7.4	2.7	.3	3.4	2.5	2.3	5.9	1.7	1.4	4.6	5.3	30.1	.9	10.1	59.1
2010	11.4	7.9	2.3	.1	3.2	2.7	3.3	7.3	1.9	2.5	4.4	10.5	38.2	3.2	21.0	81.7
2011P	6.8	8.7	3.1	.2	4.0	4.8	5.6	10.8	1.8	2.9	6.9	13.9	53.9	6.9	30.9	107.3

[1] Through 1999, includes Luxembourg.

[2] Through 1990, data for Germany are for the former West Germany only. Beginning in 1991, data for Germany are for the unified Germany, i.e., the former East Germany and West Germany.

[3] See source publications for data for countries included in "Other."

P=Preliminary. NA=Not Available. – =No data reported. (s)=Less than 0.05 million short tons.

Note: Totals may not equal sum of components due to independent rounding.

Web Page: For all data beginning in 1960, see http://www.eia.gov/totalenergy/data/annual/#coal.

Sources: • 1960-1988—U.S. Department of Commerce, Bureau of the Census, *U.S. Exports by Schedule B Commodities, EM 522.* • 1989-2000—U.S. Energy Information Administration (EIA), *Coal Industry Annual,* annual reports. • 2001 forward—EIA, *Quarterly Coal Report October-December,* quarterly reports; and U.S. Department of Commerce, Bureau of the Census, "Monthly Report EM 545."

Source: *U.S. Energy Information Administration, Annual Energy Review 2011*

Figure 8.0 Electricity Flow, 2011
(Quadrillion Btu)

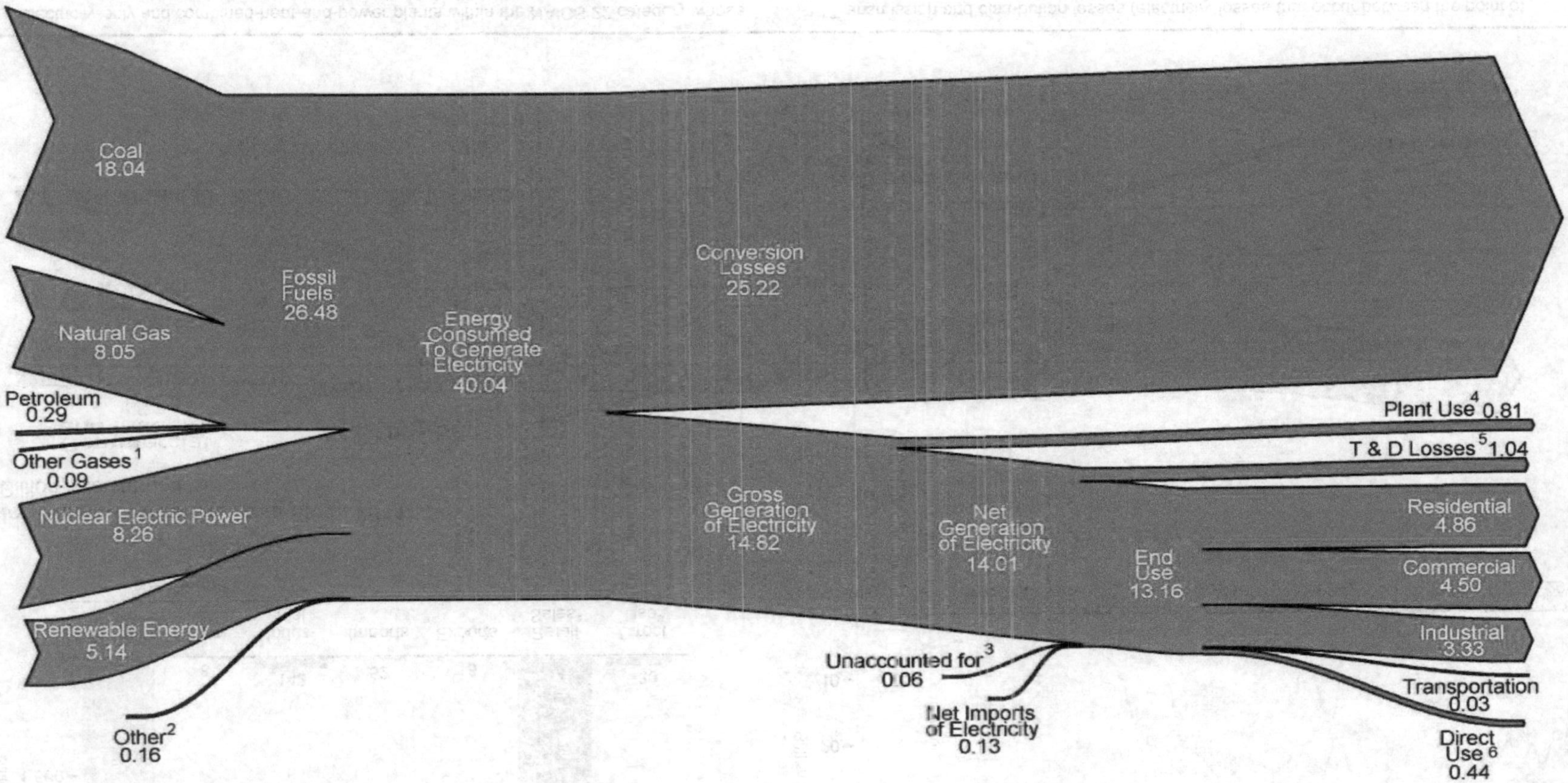

[1] Blast furnace gas, propane gas, and other manufactured and waste gases derived from fossil fuels.

[2] Batteries, chemicals, hydrogen, pitch, purchased steam, sulfur, miscellaneous technologies, and non-renewable waste (municipal solid waste from non-biogenic sources, and tire-derived fuels).

[3] Data collection frame differences and nonsampling error. Derived for the diagram by subtracting the "T & D Losses" estimate from "T & D Losses and Unaccounted for" derived from Table 8.1.

[4] Electric energy used in the operation of power plants.

[5] Transmission and distribution losses (electricity losses that occur between the point of generation and delivery to the customer) are estimated as 7 percent of gross generation.

[6] Use of electricity that is 1) self-generated, 2) produced by either the same entity that consumes the power or an affiliate, and 3) used in direct support of a service or industrial process located within the same facility or group of facilities that house the generating equipment. Direct use is exclusive of station use.

Notes: • Data are preliminary. • See Note, "Electrical System Energy Losses," at the end of Section 2. • Net generation of electricity includes pumped storage facility production minus energy used for pumping. • Values are derived from source data prior to rounding for publication. • Totals may not equal sum of components due to independent rounding.

Sources: Tables 8.1, 8.4a, 8.9, A6 (column 7), and U.S. Energy Information Administration, Form EIA-923, "Power Plant Operations Report."

Source: *U.S. Energy Information Administration, Annual Energy Review 2011*

Figure 8.1 Electricity Overview

Overview, 2011

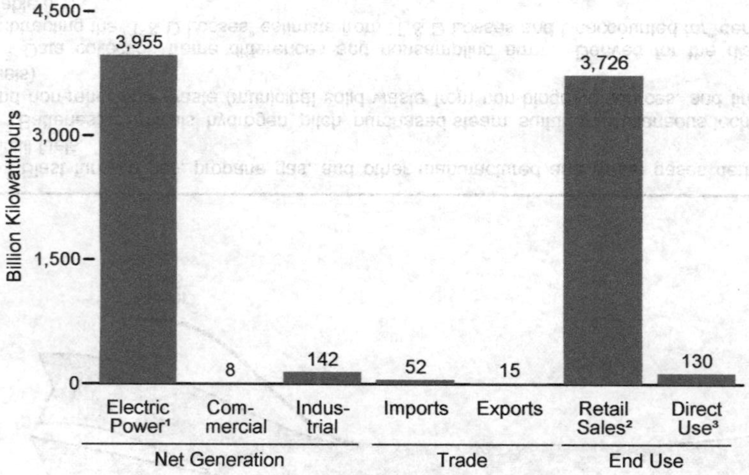

Electricity Trade, 1949-2011

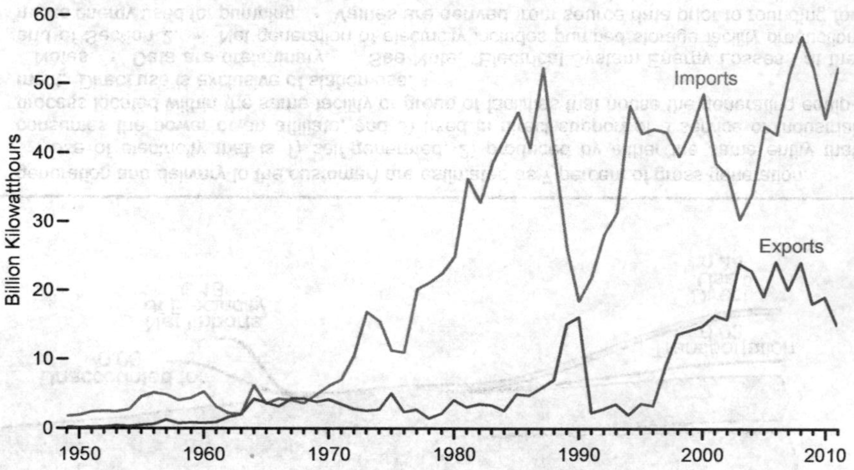

Net-Generation-to-End-Use Flow, 2011
(Billion Kilowatthours)

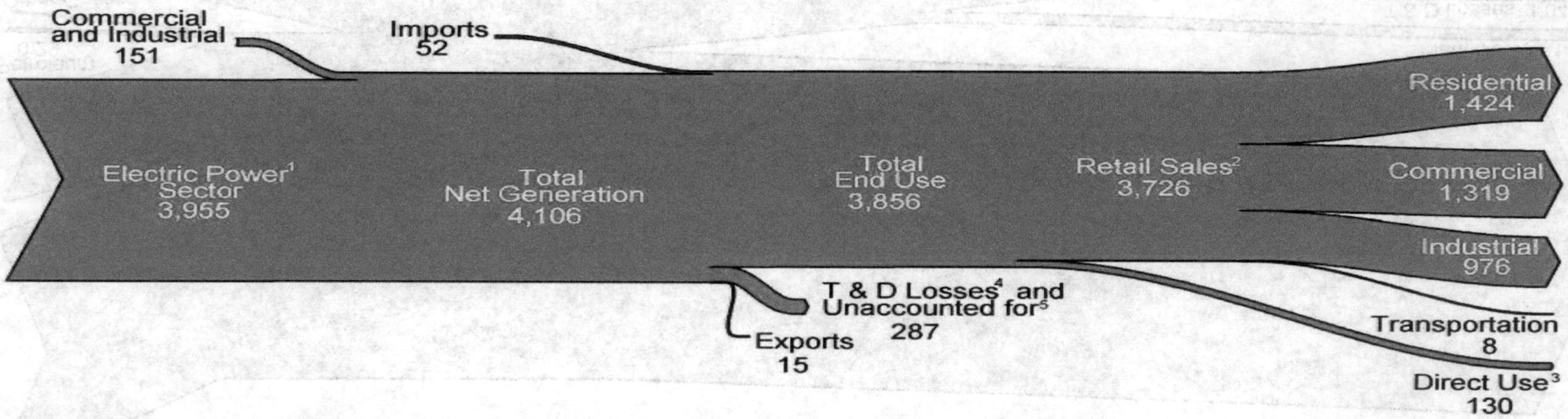

[1] Electricity-only and combined-heat-and-power plants within the NAICS 22 category whose primary business is to sell electricity, or electricity and heat, to the public.
[2] Electricity retail sales to ultimate customers reported by electric utilities and other energy service providers.
[3] See Table 8.1, footnote 8.
[4] Transmission and distribution losses (electricity losses that occur between the point of generation and delivery to the customer). See Note, "Electrical System Energy Losses," at the end of Section 2.
[5] Data collection frame differences and nonsampling error.
Sources: Tables 8.1 and 8.9.

Source: *U.S. Energy Information Administration, Annual Energy Review 2011*

Table 8.1 Electricity Overview, Selected Years, 1949-2011

(Billion Kilowatthours)

Year	Net Generation				Trade					T & D Losses [5] and Unaccounted for [6]	End Use		
					Imports [1]		Exports [1]		Net Imports [1]				
	Electric Power Sector [2]	Commercial Sector [3]	Industrial Sector [4]	Total	From Canada	Total	To Canada	Total	Total		Retail Sales [7]	Direct Use [8]	Total
1949	291	NA	5	296	NA	2	NA	(s)	2	43	255	NA	255
1950	329	NA	5	334	NA	2	NA	(s)	2	44	291	NA	291
1955	547	NA	3	550	NA	5	NA	(s)	4	58	497	NA	497
1960	756	NA	4	759	NA	5	NA	1	5	76	688	NA	688
1965	1,055	NA	3	1,058	NA	4	NA	4	(s)	104	954	NA	954
1970	1,532	NA	3	1,535	NA	6	NA	4	2	145	1,392	NA	1,392
1975	1,918	NA	3	1,921	NA	11	NA	5	6	180	1,747	NA	1,747
1976	2,038	NA	3	2,041	NA	11	NA	2	9	194	1,855	NA	1,855
1977	2,124	NA	3	2,127	NA	20	NA	3	17	197	1,948	NA	1,948
1978	2,206	NA	3	2,209	NA	21	NA	1	20	211	2,018	NA	2,018
1979	2,247	NA	3	2,251	NA	23	NA	2	20	200	2,071	NA	2,071
1980	2,286	NA	3	2,290	NA	25	NA	4	21	216	2,094	NA	2,094
1981	2,295	NA	3	2,298	NA	36	NA	3	33	184	2,147	NA	2,147
1982	2,241	NA	3	2,244	NA	33	NA	4	29	187	2,086	NA	2,086
1983	2,310	NA	3	2,313	NA	39	NA	3	35	198	2,151	NA	2,151
1984	2,416	NA	3	2,419	NA	42	NA	3	40	173	2,286	NA	2,286
1985	2,470	NA	3	2,473	NA	46	NA	5	41	190	2,324	NA	2,324
1986	2,487	NA	3	2,490	NA	41	NA	5	36	158	2,369	NA	2,369
1987	2,572	NA	3	2,575	NA	52	NA	6	46	164	2,457	NA	2,457
1988	2,704	NA	3	2,707	NA	39	NA	7	32	161	2,578	NA	2,578
1989	[2]2,848	4	[4]115	2,967	NA	26	NA	15	11	222	2,647	109	2,756
1990	2,901	6	131	3,038	16	18	16	16	2	203	2,713	125	2,837
1991	2,936	6	133	3,074	20	22	2	2	20	207	2,762	124	2,886
1992	2,934	6	143	3,084	26	28	2	3	25	212	2,763	134	2,897
1993	3,044	7	146	3,197	29	31	3	4	28	224	2,861	139	3,001
1994	3,089	8	151	3,248	45	47	1	2	45	211	2,935	146	3,081
1995	3,194	8	151	3,353	41	43	2	4	39	229	3,013	151	3,164
1996	3,284	9	151	3,444	42	43	2	3	40	231	3,101	153	3,254
1997	3,329	9	154	3,492	43	43	7	9	34	224	3,146	156	3,302
1998	3,457	9	154	3,620	40	40	12	14	26	221	3,264	161	3,425
1999	3,530	9	156	3,695	43	43	13	14	29	240	3,312	172	3,484
2000	3,638	8	157	3,802	49	49	13	15	34	244	3,421	171	3,592
2001	3,580	7	149	3,737	38	39	16	16	22	202	3,394	163	3,557
2002	3,698	7	153	3,858	37	37	15	16	21	248	3,465	166	3,632
2003	3,721	7	155	3,883	29	30	24	24	6	228	3,494	168	3,662
2004	3,808	8	154	3,971	33	34	22	23	11	266	3,547	168	3,716
2005	3,902	8	145	4,055	42	44	19	19	25	269	3,661	150	3,811
2006	3,908	8	148	4,065	42	43	23	24	18	266	3,670	147	3,817
2007	4,005	8	143	4,157	50	51	20	20	31	298	3,765	126	3,890
2008	3,974	8	137	4,119	56	57	24	24	33	287	3,733	132	3,865
2009	3,810	8	132	3,950	51	52	18	18	34	261	3,597	127	3,724
2010	R3,972	R9	R144	R4,125	44	45	R18	19	26	R265	R3,754	R132	R3,886
2011	P3,955	P8	P142	P4,106	P51	P52	P14	P15	P37	P287	P3,726	E130	P3,856

[1] Electricity transmitted across U.S. borders. Net imports equal imports minus exports.

[2] Electricity-only and combined-heat-and-power (CHP) plants within the NAICS 22 category whose primary business is to sell electricity, or electricity and heat, to the public. Through 1988, data are for electric utilities only; beginning in 1989, data are for electric utilities and independent power producers.

[3] Commercial combined-heat-and-power (CHP) and commercial electricity-only plants.

[4] Industrial combined-heat-and-power (CHP) and industrial electricity-only plants. Through 1988, data are for industrial hydroelectric power only.

[5] Transmission and distribution losses (electricity losses that occur between the point of generation and delivery to the customer). See Note, "Electrical System Energy Losses," at end of Section 2.

[6] Data collection frame differences and nonsampling error.

[7] Electricity retail sales to ultimate customers by electric utilities and, beginning in 1996, other energy service providers.

[8] Use of electricity that is 1) self-generated, 2) produced by either the same entity that consumes the power or an affiliate, and 3) used in direct support of a service or industrial process located within the same facility or group of facilities that house the generating equipment. Direct use is exclusive of station use.

R=Revised. P=Preliminary. E=Estimate. NA=Not available. (s)=Less than 0.5 billion kilowatthours.

Notes: • See Note 1, "Coverage of Electricity Statistics," and Note 2, "Classification of Power Plants Into Energy-Use Sectors," at end of section. • Totals may not equal sum of components due to independent rounding.

Web Pages: • See http://www.eia.gov/totalenergy/data/monthly/#electricity for updated monthly and annual data. • See http://www.eia.gov/totalenergy/data/annual/#electricity for all annual data beginning in 1949. • See http://www.eia.gov/electricity/ for related information.

Sources: See end of section.

Source: *U.S. Energy Information Administration, Annual Energy Review 2011*

Figure 8.2a Electricity Net Generation, Total (All Sectors)

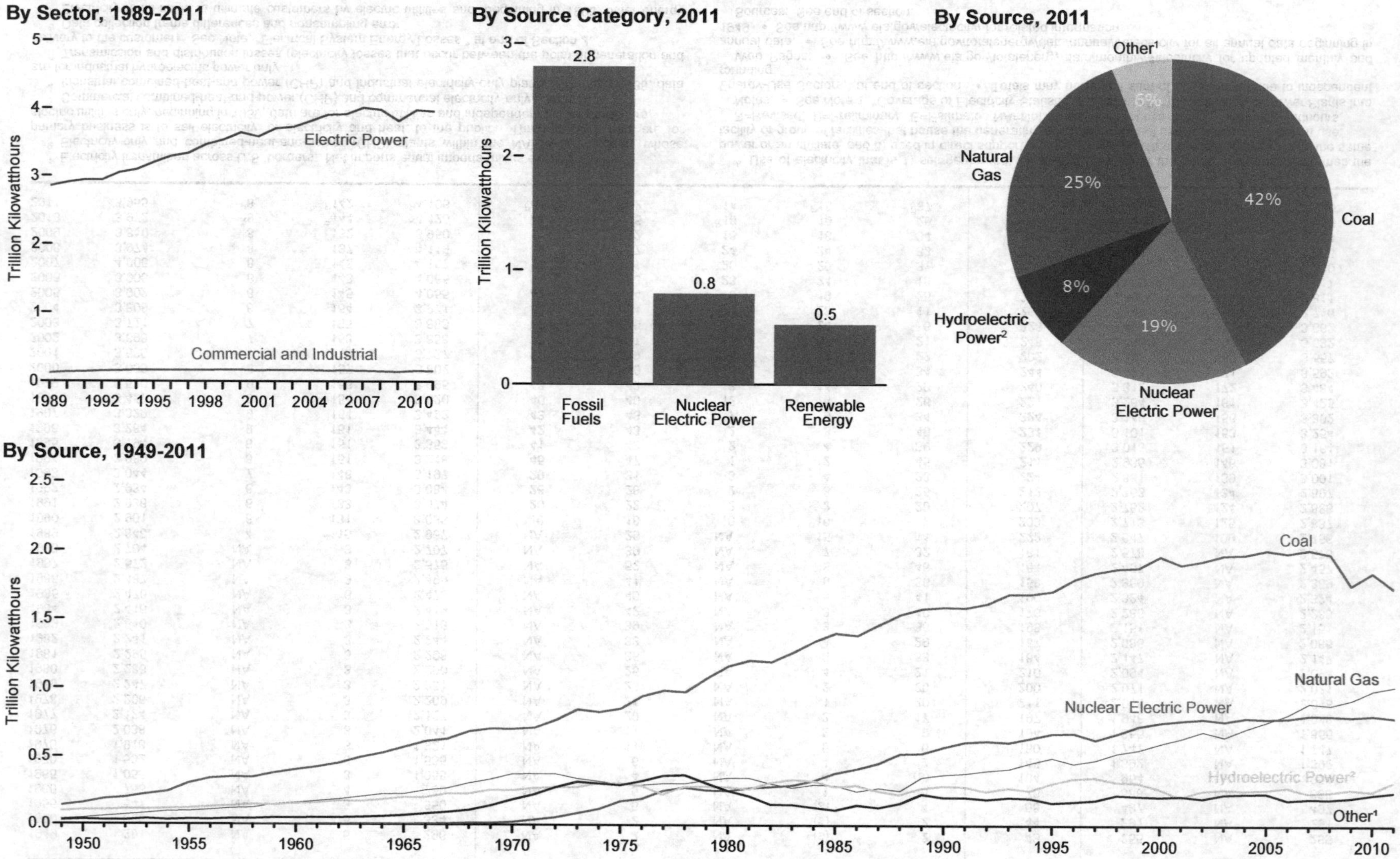

[1] Wind, petroleum, wood, waste, geothermal, other gases, solar thermal and photovoltaic, batteries, chemicals, hydrogen, pitch, purchased steam, sulfur, miscellaneous technologies, and non-renewable waste (municipal solid waste from non-biogenic sources, and tire-derived fuels).

[2] Conventional hydroelectric power and pumped storage.

Note: Sum of components may not equal 100 percent due to independent rounding.

Sources: Tables 8.2a, 8.2b, and 8.2d.

Source: *U.S. Energy Information Administration, Annual Energy Review 2011*

Figure 8.2b Electricity Net Generation by Sector

By Sector, 2011

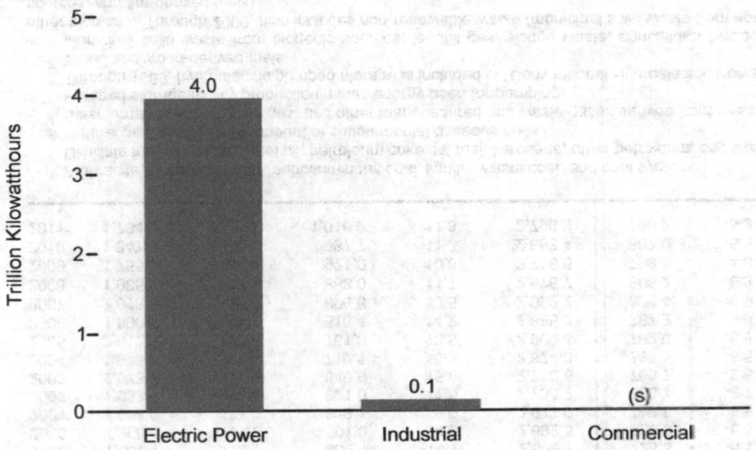

Electric Power Sector by Plant Type, 1989-2011

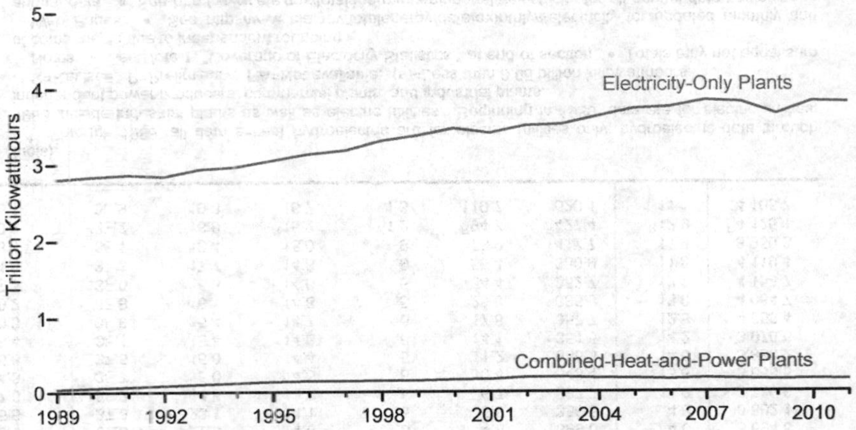

Industrial and Commercial Sectors, 2011

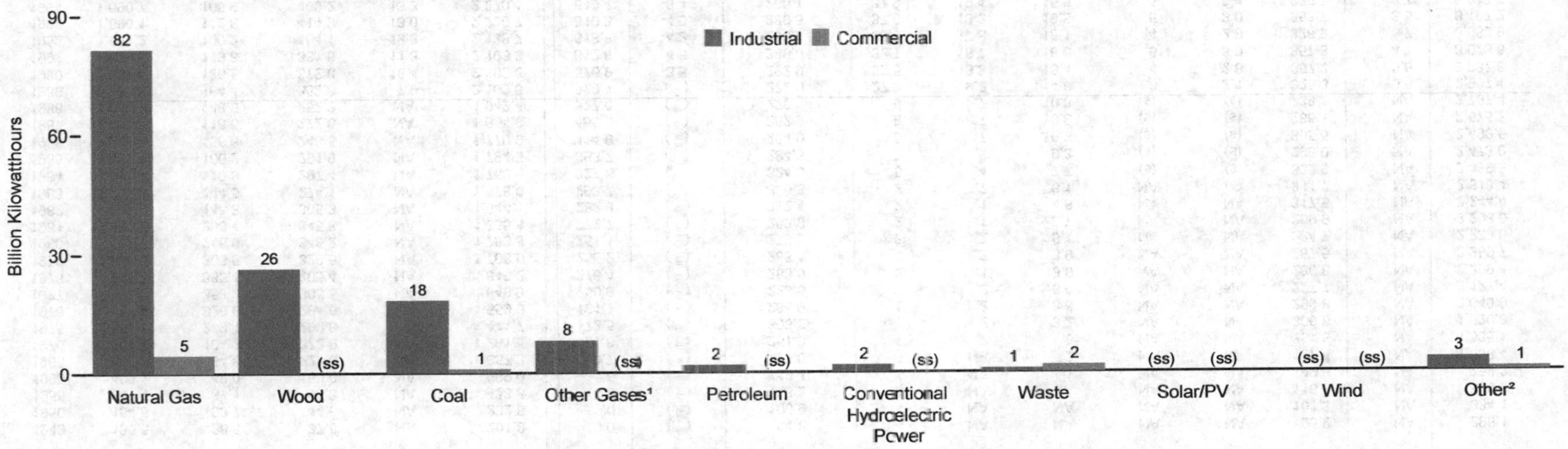

[1] Blast furnace gas, propane gas, and other manufactured and waste gases derived from fossil fuels.

[2] Batteries, chemicals, hydrogen, pitch, purchased steam, sulfur, miscellaneous technologies, and non-renewable waste (municipal solid waste from non-biogenic sources, and tire-derived fuels).

(s) = Less than 0.05 trillion kilowatthours.

(ss) = Less than 0.5 billion kilowatthours.

Sources: Tables 8.2b-8.2d.

Source: *U.S. Energy Information Administration, Annual Energy Review 2011*

Table 8.2a Electricity Net Generation: Total (All Sectors), Selected Years, 1949-2011

(Sum of Tables 8.2b and 8.2d; Billion Kilowatthours)

Year	Fossil Fuels					Nuclear Electric Power	Hydro-electric Pumped Storage [5]	Renewable Energy								Total
	Coal [1]	Petroleum [2]	Natural Gas [3]	Other Gases [4]	Total			Conventional Hydroelectric Power [6]	Biomass: Wood [7]	Biomass: Waste [8]	Geo-thermal	Solar/PV [9]	Wind	Total	Other [10]	
1949	135.5	28.5	37.0	NA	201.0	0.0	(6)	94.8	0.4	NA	NA	NA	NA	95.2	NA	296.1
1950	154.5	33.7	44.6	NA	232.8	.0	(6)	100.9	.4	NA	NA	NA	NA	101.3	NA	334.1
1955	301.4	37.1	95.3	NA	433.8	.0	(6)	116.2	.3	NA	NA	NA	NA	116.5	NA	550.3
1960	403.1	48.0	158.0	NA	609.0	.5	(6)	149.4	.1	NA	(s)	NA	NA	149.6	NA	759.2
1965	570.9	64.8	221.6	NA	857.3	3.7	(6)	197.0	.3	NA	.2	NA	NA	197.4	NA	1,058.4
1970	704.4	184.2	372.9	NA	1,261.5	21.8	(6)	251.0	.1	.2	.5	NA	NA	251.8	NA	1,535.1
1975	852.8	289.1	299.8	NA	1,441.7	172.5	(6)	303.2	(s)	.2	3.2	NA	NA	306.6	NA	1,920.8
1976	944.4	320.0	294.6	NA	1,559.0	191.1	(6)	286.9	.1	.2	3.6	NA	NA	290.8	NA	2,040.9
1977	985.2	358.2	305.5	NA	1,648.9	250.9	(6)	223.6	.3	.2	3.6	NA	NA	227.7	NA	2,127.4
1978	975.7	365.1	305.4	NA	1,646.2	276.4	(6)	283.5	.2	.1	3.0	NA	NA	286.8	NA	2,209.4
1979	1,075.0	303.5	329.5	NA	1,708.0	255.2	(6)	283.1	.3	.2	3.9	NA	NA	287.5	NA	2,250.7
1980	1,161.6	246.0	346.2	NA	1,753.8	251.1	(6)	279.2	.3	.2	5.1	NA	NA	284.7	NA	2,289.6
1981	1,203.2	206.4	345.8	NA	1,755.4	272.7	(6)	263.8	.2	.1	5.7	NA	NA	269.9	NA	2,298.0
1982	1,192.0	146.8	305.3	NA	1,644.1	282.8	(6)	312.4	.2	.1	4.8	NA	NA	317.5	NA	2,244.4
1983	1,259.4	144.5	274.1	NA	1,678.0	293.7	(6)	335.3	.2	.2	6.1	NA	(s)	341.7	NA	2,313.4
1984	1,341.7	119.8	297.4	NA	1,758.9	327.6	(6)	324.3	.5	.4	7.7	(s)	(s)	332.9	NA	2,419.5
1985	1,402.1	100.2	291.9	NA	1,794.3	383.7	(6)	284.3	.7	.6	9.3	(s)	(s)	295.0	NA	2,473.0
1986	1,385.8	136.6	248.5	NA	1,770.9	414.0	(6)	294.0	.5	.7	10.3	(s)	(s)	305.5	NA	2,490.5
1987	1,463.8	118.5	272.6	NA	1,854.9	455.3	(6)	252.9	.8	.7	10.8	(s)	(s)	265.1	NA	2,575.3
1988	1,540.7	148.9	252.8	NA	1,942.4	527.0	(6)	226.1	.9	.7	10.3	(s)	(s)	238.1	NA	2,707.4
1989 [11]	1,583.8	164.4	352.6	7.9	2,108.6	529.4	(6)	272.0	27.2	9.2	14.6	.3	2.1	325.3	3.8	2,967.1
1990	1,594.0	126.5	372.8	10.4	2,103.6	576.9	-3.5	292.9	32.5	13.3	15.4	.4	2.8	357.2	3.6	3,037.8
1991	1,590.6	119.8	381.6	11.3	2,103.3	612.6	-4.5	289.0	33.7	15.7	16.0	.5	3.0	357.8	4.7	3,073.8
1992	1,621.2	100.2	404.1	13.3	2,138.7	618.8	-4.2	253.1	36.5	17.8	16.1	.4	2.9	326.9	3.7	3,083.9
1993	1,690.1	112.8	414.9	13.0	2,230.7	610.3	-4.0	280.5	37.6	18.3	16.8	.5	3.0	356.7	3.5	3,197.2
1994	1,690.7	105.9	460.2	13.3	2,270.1	640.4	-3.4	260.1	37.9	19.1	15.5	.5	3.4	336.7	3.7	3,247.5
1995	1,709.4	74.6	496.1	13.9	2,293.9	673.4	-2.7	310.8	36.5	20.4	13.4	.5	3.2	384.8	4.1	3,353.5
1996	1,795.2	81.4	455.1	14.4	2,346.0	674.7	-3.1	347.2	36.8	20.9	14.3	.5	3.2	423.0	3.6	3,444.2
1997	1,845.0	92.6	479.4	13.4	2,430.3	628.6	-4.0	356.5	36.9	21.7	14.7	.5	3.3	433.6	3.6	3,492.2
1998	1,873.5	128.8	531.3	13.5	2,547.1	673.7	-4.5	323.3	36.3	22.4	14.8	.5	3.0	400.4	3.6	3,620.3
1999	1,881.1	118.1	556.4	14.1	2,569.7	728.3	-6.1	319.5	37.0	22.6	14.8	.5	4.5	399.0	4.0	3,694.8
2000	1,966.3	111.2	601.0	14.0	2,692.5	753.9	-5.5	275.6	37.6	23.1	14.1	.5	5.6	356.5	4.8	3,802.1
2001	1,904.0	124.9	639.1	9.0	2,677.0	768.8	-8.8	217.0	35.2	14.5	13.7	.5	6.7	287.7	11.9	3,736.6
2002	1,933.1	94.6	691.0	11.5	2,730.2	780.1	-8.7	264.3	38.7	15.0	14.5	.6	10.4	343.4	13.5	3,858.5
2003	1,973.7	119.4	649.9	15.6	2,758.6	763.7	-8.5	275.8	37.5	15.8	14.4	.5	11.2	355.3	14.0	3,883.2
2004	1,978.3	121.1	710.1	15.3	2,824.8	788.5	-8.5	268.4	38.1	15.4	14.8	.6	14.1	351.5	14.2	3,970.6
2005	2,012.9	122.2	761.0	13.5	2,909.5	782.0	-6.6	270.3	38.9	15.4	14.7	.6	17.8	357.7	12.8	4,055.4
2006	1,990.5	64.2	816.4	14.2	2,885.3	787.2	-6.6	289.2	38.8	16.1	14.6	.5	26.6	385.8	13.0	4,064.7
2007	2,016.5	65.7	896.6	13.5	2,992.2	806.4	-6.9	247.5	39.0	16.5	14.6	.6	34.4	352.7	12.2	4,156.7
2008	1,985.8	46.2	883.0	11.7	2,926.7	806.2	-6.3	254.8	37.3	17.7	14.8	.9	55.4	380.9	11.8	4,119.4
2009	1,755.9	38.9	921.0	10.6	2,726.5	798.9	-4.6	273.4	36.1	18.4	15.0	.9	73.9	417.7	11.9	3,950.3
2010	R1,847.3	R37.1	R987.7	R11.3	R2,883.4	807.0	R-5.5	R260.2	R37.2	R18.9	R15.2	R1.2	R94.7	R427.4	R12.9	R4,125.1
2011P	1,734.3	28.2	1,016.6	11.3	2,790.3	790.2	-5.9	325.1	36.9	19.8	16.7	1.8	119.7	520.1	11.1	4,105.7

1 Anthracite, bituminous coal, subbituminous coal, lignite, waste coal, and coal synfuel.
2 Distillate fuel oil, residual fuel oil, petroleum coke, jet fuel, kerosene, other petroleum, and waste oil.
3 Natural gas, plus a small amount of supplemental gaseous fuels.
4 Blast furnace gas, propane gas, and other manufactured and waste gases derived from fossil fuels.
5 Pumped storage facility production minus energy used for pumping.
6 Through 1989, hydroelectric pumped storage is included in "Conventional Hydroelectric Power."
7 Wood and wood-derived fuels.
8 Municipal solid waste from biogenic sources, landfill gas, sludge waste, agricultural byproducts, and other biomass. Through 2000, also includes non-renewable waste (municipal solid waste from non-biogenic sources, and tire-derived fuels).
9 Solar thermal and photovoltaic (PV) energy.
10 Batteries, chemicals, hydrogen, pitch, purchased steam, sulfur, miscellaneous technologies, and, beginning in 2001, non-renewable waste (municipal solid waste from non-biogenic sources, and tire-derived fuels).
11 Through 1988, all data except hydroelectric are for electric utilities only; hydroelectric data through 1988 include industrial plants as well as electric utilities. Beginning in 1989, data are for electric utilities, independent power producers, commercial plants, and industrial plants.

R=Revised. P=Preliminary. NA=Not available. (s)=Less than 0.05 billion kilowatthours.

Notes: • See Note 1, "Coverage of Electricity Statistics," at end of section. • Totals may not equal sum of components due to independent rounding.

Web Pages: • See http://www.eia.gov/totalenergy/data/monthly/#electricity for updated monthly and annual data. • See http://www.eia.gov/totalenergy/data/annual/#electricity for all annual data beginning in 1949. • See http://www.eia.gov/electricity/ for related information.

Sources: • 1949-1988—Table 8.2b for electric power sector, and Table 8.1 for industrial sector. • 1989 forward—Tables 8.2b and 8.2d.

Source: *U.S. Energy Information Administration, Annual Energy Review 2011*

Table 8.2b Electricity Net Generation: Electric Power Sector, Selected Years, 1949-2011

(Subset of Table 8.2a; Billion Kilowatthours)

Year	Fossil Fuels					Nuclear Electric Power	Hydro-electric Pumped Storage [5]	Renewable Energy							Other [10]	Total
	Coal [1]	Petroleum [2]	Natural Gas [3]	Other Gases [4]	Total			Conventional Hydroelectric Power [6]	Biomass: Wood [7]	Biomass: Waste [8]	Geo-thermal	Solar/PV [9]	Wind	Total		
1949	135.5	28.5	37.0	NA	201.0	0.0	([6])	89.7	0.4	NA	NA	NA	NA	90.1	NA	291.1
1950	154.5	33.7	44.6	NA	232.8	.0	([6])	95.9	.4	NA	NA	NA	NA	96.3	NA	329.1
1955	301.4	37.1	95.3	NA	433.8	.0	([6])	113.0	.3	NA	NA	NA	NA	113.3	NA	547.0
1960	403.1	48.0	158.0	NA	609.0	.5	([6])	145.8	.1	NA	(s)	NA	NA	146.0	NA	755.5
1965	570.9	64.8	221.6	NA	857.3	3.7	([6])	193.9	.3	NA	.2	NA	NA	194.3	NA	1,055.3
1970	704.4	184.2	372.9	NA	1,261.5	21.8	([6])	247.7	.1	2	.5	NA	NA	248.6	NA	1,531.9
1975	852.8	289.1	299.8	NA	1,441.7	172.5	([6])	300.0	(s)	2	3.2	NA	NA	303.5	NA	1,917.6
1976	944.4	320.0	294.6	NA	1,559.0	191.1	([6])	283.7	.1	2	3.6	NA	NA	287.6	NA	2,037.7
1977	985.2	358.2	305.5	NA	1,648.9	250.9	([6])	220.5	.3	2	3.6	NA	NA	224.5	NA	2,124.3
1978	975.7	365.1	305.4	NA	1,646.2	276.4	([6])	280.4	.2	1	3.0	NA	NA	283.7	NA	2,206.3
1979	1,075.0	303.5	329.5	NA	1,708.0	255.2	([6])	279.8	.3	2	3.9	NA	NA	284.2	NA	2,247.4
1980	1,161.6	246.0	346.2	NA	1,753.8	251.1	([6])	276.0	.3	2	5.1	NA	NA	281.5	NA	2,286.4
1981	1,203.2	206.4	345.8	NA	1,755.4	272.7	([6])	260.7	.2	1	5.7	NA	NA	266.7	NA	2,294.8
1982	1,192.0	146.8	305.3	NA	1,644.1	282.8	([6])	309.2	.2	1	4.8	NA	NA	314.4	NA	2,241.2
1983	1,259.4	144.5	274.1	NA	1,678.0	293.7	([6])	332.1	.2	2	6.1	NA	(s)	338.6	NA	2,310.3
1984	1,341.7	119.8	297.4	NA	1,758.9	327.6	([6])	321.2	.5	4	7.7	(s)	(s)	329.8	NA	2,416.3
1985	1,402.1	100.2	291.9	NA	1,794.3	383.7	([6])	281.1	.7	6	9.3	(s)	(s)	291.9	NA	2,469.8
1986	1,385.8	136.6	248.5	NA	1,770.9	414.0	([6])	290.8	.5	7	10.3	(s)	(s)	302.3	NA	2,487.3
1987	1,463.8	118.5	272.6	NA	1,854.9	455.3	([6])	249.7	.8	7	10.8	(s)	(s)	262.0	NA	2,572.1
1988	1,540.7	148.9	252.8	NA	1,942.4	527.0	([6])	222.9	.9	7	10.3	(s)	(s)	234.9	NA	2,704.3
1989[11]	1,562.4	159.0	297.3	.5	2,019.1	529.4	([6])	269.2	5.6	7.7	14.6	.3	2.1	299.5	.3	2,848.2
1990	1,572.1	118.9	309.5	.6	2,001.1	576.9	-3.5	289.8	7.0	11.5	15.4	.4	2.8	326.9	(s)	2,901.3
1991	1,568.8	112.8	317.8	.7	2,000.1	612.6	-4.5	286.0	7.7	13.9	16.0	.5	3.0	327.0	.4	2,935.6
1992	1,597.7	92.2	334.3	1.2	2,025.4	618.8	-4.2	250.0	8.5	15.9	16.1	.4	2.9	293.9	.5	2,934.4
1993	1,665.5	105.4	342.2	1.0	2,114.1	610.3	-4.0	277.5	9.2	16.2	16.8	.5	3.0	323.2	.4	3,043.9
1994	1,666.3	98.7	385.7	1.1	2,151.7	640.4	-3.4	254.0	9.2	17.0	15.5	.5	3.4	299.7	.2	3,088.7
1995	1,686.1	68.1	419.2	1.9	2,175.3	673.4	-2.7	305.4	7.6	18.0	13.4	.5	3.2	348.0	.2	3,194.2
1996	1,772.0	74.8	378.8	1.3	2,226.9	674.7	-3.1	341.2	8.4	17.8	14.3	.5	3.2	385.4	.2	3,284.1
1997	1,820.8	86.5	399.6	1.5	2,308.4	628.6	-4.0	350.6	8.7	18.5	14.7	.5	3.3	396.3	.1	3,329.4
1998	1,850.2	122.2	449.3	2.3	2,424.0	673.7	-4.5	317.9	8.6	19.2	14.8	.5	3.0	364.0	.2	3,457.4
1999	1,858.6	111.5	473.0	1.6	2,444.8	728.3	-6.1	314.7	9.0	19.5	14.8	.5	4.5	362.9	.1	3,530.0
2000	1,943.1	105.2	518.0	2.0	2,568.3	753.9	-5.5	271.3	8.9	20.3	14.1	.5	5.6	320.7	.1	3,637.5
2001	1,882.8	119.1	554.9	.6	2,557.5	768.8	-8.8	213.7	8.3	12.9	13.7	.5	6.7	256.0	6.5	3,580.1
2002	1,910.6	89.7	607.7	2.0	2,610.0	780.1	-8.7	260.5	9.0	13.1	14.5	.6	10.4	308.0	9.1	3,698.5
2003	1,952.7	113.7	567.3	2.6	2,636.4	763.7	-8.5	271.5	9.5	13.8	14.4	.5	11.2	321.0	8.6	3,721.2
2004	1,957.2	114.7	627.2	3.6	2,702.6	788.5	-8.5	265.1	9.7	13.1	14.8	.6	14.1	317.4	8.3	3,808.4
2005	1,992.1	116.5	683.8	3.8	2,796.1	782.0	-6.6	267.0	10.6	13.0	14.7	.6	17.8	323.7	6.9	3,902.2
2006	1,969.7	59.7	734.4	4.3	2,768.1	787.2	-6.6	286.3	10.3	13.9	14.6	.5	26.6	352.2	7.1	3,908.1
2007	1,998.4	61.3	814.8	4.0	2,878.5	806.4	-6.9	245.8	10.7	14.3	14.6	.6	34.4	320.5	6.8	4,005.3
2008	1,968.8	42.9	802.4	3.2	2,817.3	806.2	-6.3	253.1	10.6	15.4	14.8	.9	55.4	350.2	7.0	3,974.3
2009	1,741.1	35.8	841.0	3.1	2,621.0	798.9	-4.6	271.5	10.7	16.0	15.0	.9	73.9	388.0	6.6	3,809.8
2010	R1,827.7	R34.7	R901.4	R3.0	R2,766.8	807.0	R-5.5	R258.5	R11.4	R16.4	R15.2	R1.2	94.6	R397.3	R6.8	R3,972.4
2011P	1,714.9	26.2	930.6	3.1	2,674.8	790.2	-5.9	323.1	10.5	17.2	16.7	1.8	119.7	489.0	6.9	3,955.1

1 Anthracite, bituminous coal, subbituminous coal, lignite, waste coal, and coal synfuel.
2 Distillate fuel oil, residual fuel oil, petroleum coke, jet fuel, kerosene, other petroleum, and waste oil.
3 Natural gas, plus a small amount of supplemental gaseous fuels.
4 Blast furnace gas, propane gas, and other manufactured and waste gases derived from fossil fuels.
5 Pumped storage facility production minus energy used for pumping.
6 Through 1989, hydroelectric pumped storage is included in "Conventional Hydroelectric Power."
7 Wood and wood-derived fuels.
8 Municipal solid waste from biogenic sources, landfill gas, sludge waste, agricultural byproducts, and other biomass. Through 2000, also includes non-renewable waste (municipal solid waste from non-biogenic sources, and tire-derived fuels).
9 Solar thermal and photovoltaic (PV) energy.
10 Batteries, chemicals, hydrogen, pitch, purchased steam, sulfur, miscellaneous technologies, and, beginning in 2001, non-renewable waste (municipal solid waste from non-biogenic sources, and tire-derived fuels).
11 Through 1988, data are for electric utilities only. Beginning in 1989, data are for electric utilities and independent power producers.
R=Revised. P=Preliminary. NA=Not available. (s)=Less than 0.05 billion kilowatthours.

Notes: • The electric power sector comprises electricity-only and combined-heat-and-power (CHP) plants within the NAICS 22 category whose primary business is to sell electricity, or electricity and heat, to the public. • See Table 8.2d for commercial and industrial CHP and electricity-only data. • See Note 1, "Coverage of Electricity Statistics," and Note 2, "Classification of Power Plants Into Energy-Use Sectors," at end of section. • Totals may not equal sum of components due to independent rounding.

Web Pages: • See http://www.eia.gov/totalenergy/data/monthly/#electricity for updated monthly and annual data. • See http://www.eia.gov/totalenergy/data/annual/#electricity for all annual data beginning in 1949. • See http://www.eia.gov/electricity/ for related information.

Sources: • 1949-September 1977—Federal Power Commission, Form FPC-4, "Monthly Power Plant Report." • October 1977-1981—Federal Energy Regulatory Commission, Form FPC-4, "Monthly Power Plant Report." • 1982-1988—U.S. Energy Information Administration (EIA), Form EIA-759, "Monthly Power Plant Report." • 1989-1997—EIA, Form EIA-759, "Monthly Power Plant Report," and Form EIA-867, "Annual Nonutility Power Producer Report." • 1998-2000—EIA, Form EIA-759, "Monthly Power Plant Report," and Form EIA-860B, "Annual Electric Generator Report—Nonutility." • 2001-2003—EIA, Form EIA-906, "Power Plant Report." • 2004-2007—EIA, Form EIA-906, "Power Plant Report," and Form EIA-920, "Combined Heat and Power Plant Report." • 2008 forward—EIA, Form EIA-923, "Power Plant Operations Report."

***Source:** U.S. Energy Information Administration, Annual Energy Review 2011*

Table 8.2c Electricity Net Generation: Electric Power Sector by Plant Type, Selected Years, 1989-2011

(Breakout of Table 8.2b; Billion Kilowatthours)

Year	Fossil Fuels: Coal [1]	Fossil Fuels: Petroleum [2]	Fossil Fuels: Natural Gas [3]	Fossil Fuels: Other Gases [4]	Fossil Fuels: Total	Nuclear Electric Power	Hydro-electric Pumped Storage [5]	Renewable Energy: Conventional Hydroelectric Power [6]	Renewable Energy: Biomass: Wood [7]	Renewable Energy: Biomass: Waste [8]	Renewable Energy: Geo-thermal	Renewable Energy: Solar/PV [9]	Renewable Energy: Wind	Renewable Energy: Total	Other [10]	Total
Electricity-Only Plants [11]																
1989	1,554.0	158.3	266.9	–	1,979.3	529.4	([6])	269.2	4.2	6.9	14.6	0.3	2.1	297.3	–	2,805.9
1990	1,560.2	117.6	264.7	(s)	1,942.4	576.9	-3.5	289.8	5.6	10.4	15.4	.4	2.8	324.3	–	2,840.0
1995	1,658.0	62.0	317.4	(s)	2,037.4	673.4	-2.7	305.4	5.9	16.3	13.4	.5	3.2	344.7	–	3,052.8
1996	1,742.8	68.5	272.8	(s)	2,084.1	674.7	-3.1	341.2	6.5	16.1	14.3	.5	3.2	381.8	–	3,137.6
1997	1,793.2	80.3	291.1	(s)	2,164.6	628.6	-4.0	350.6	6.5	16.4	14.7	.5	3.3	392.0	–	3,181.3
1998	1,823.0	115.7	335.9	.1	2,274.6	673.7	-4.5	317.9	6.6	17.0	14.8	.5	3.0	359.8	–	3,303.6
1999	1,832.1	104.8	356.6	(s)	2,293.6	728.3	-6.1	314.7	7.3	17.1	14.8	.5	4.5	358.8	–	3,374.6
2000	1,910.6	98.0	399.4	.2	2,408.2	753.9	-5.5	271.3	7.3	17.6	14.1	.5	5.6	316.4	–	3,472.9
2001	1,851.8	113.2	427.0	(s)	2,392.0	768.8	-8.8	213.7	6.6	11.3	13.7	.5	6.7	252.6	5.9	3,410.5
2002	1,881.2	83.3	456.8	.2	2,421.5	780.1	-8.7	260.5	7.3	11.2	14.5	.6	10.4	304.3	7.6	3,504.8
2003	1,915.8	108.5	421.2	.3	2,445.7	763.7	-8.5	271.5	7.4	11.9	14.4	.5	11.2	317.0	7.6	3,525.5
2004	1,921.1	109.4	491.2	.4	2,522.0	788.5	-8.5	265.1	8.1	11.8	14.8	.6	14.1	314.5	7.6	3,624.1
2005	1,955.5	111.2	553.2	(s)	2,619.9	782.0	-6.6	267.0	8.5	11.7	14.7	.6	17.8	320.3	6.2	3,721.8
2006	1,933.7	55.2	618.0	(s)	2,607.0	787.2	-6.6	286.2	8.3	12.5	14.6	.5	26.6	348.7	6.3	3,742.7
2007	1,962.0	56.9	686.3	.1	2,705.3	806.4	-6.9	245.8	8.7	12.9	14.6	.6	34.4	317.1	6.0	3,828.0
2008	1,932.0	39.3	683.3	(s)	2,654.6	806.2	-6.3	253.1	8.6	14.0	14.8	.9	55.4	346.8	6.2	3,807.4
2009	1,711.9	31.9	722.7	.1	2,466.6	798.9	-4.6	271.5	8.5	14.3	15.0	.9	73.9	384.0	5.8	3,650.7
2010	R1,797.5	R32.4	R779.4	.1	R2,609.3	807.0	R-5.5	R258.5	R9.3	R14.7	R15.2	R1.2	94.6	R393.6	6.0	R3,810.3
2011P	1,687.9	24.1	809.2	(s)	2,521.2	790.2	-5.9	323.1	8.5	15.5	16.7	1.8	119.7	485.3	6.1	3,796.9
Combined-Heat-and-Power Plants [12]																
1989	8.4	0.7	30.4	0.5	39.9	–	–	–	1.3	0.9	–	–	–	2.2	0.3	42.3
1990	11.9	1.3	44.8	.6	58.7	–	–	–	1.4	1.1	–	–	–	2.6	(s)	61.3
1995	28.1	6.1	101.7	1.9	137.9	–	–	–	1.7	1.7	–	–	–	3.4	.2	141.5
1996	29.2	6.3	105.9	1.3	142.7	–	–	–	1.9	1.7	–	–	–	3.6	.2	146.6
1997	27.6	6.2	108.5	1.5	143.7	–	–	–	2.2	2.1	–	–	–	4.3	.1	148.1
1998	27.2	6.6	113.4	2.3	149.4	–	–	–	2.0	2.3	–	–	–	4.2	.2	153.8
1999	26.6	6.7	116.4	1.6	151.2	–	–	–	1.7	2.4	–	–	–	4.1	.1	155.4
2000	32.5	7.2	118.6	1.8	160.2	–	–	–	1.6	2.7	–	–	–	4.3	.1	164.6
2001	31.0	6.0	128.0	.6	165.5	–	–	–	1.7	1.7	–	–	–	3.4	.6	169.5
2002	29.4	6.5	150.9	1.7	188.5	–	–	–	1.7	2.0	–	–	–	3.7	1.4	193.7
2003	36.9	5.2	146.1	2.4	190.6	–	–	–	2.1	1.9	–	–	–	4.0	1.1	195.7
2004	36.1	5.3	136.0	3.2	180.6	–	–	–	1.6	1.3	–	–	–	2.9	.7	184.3
2005	36.5	5.3	130.7	3.8	176.2	–	–	(s)	2.1	1.3	–	–	–	3.4	.7	180.4
2006	36.0	4.5	116.4	4.2	161.1	–	–	(s)	2.0	1.4	–	–	–	3.5	.8	165.4
2007	36.4	4.4	128.4	3.9	173.2	–	–	(s)	2.0	1.4	–	–	–	3.5	.7	177.4
2008	36.9	3.6	119.0	3.2	162.7	–	–	(s)	2.0	1.4	–	–	–	3.4	.8	166.9
2009	29.2	3.9	118.3	3.0	154.4	–	–	(s)	2.3	1.7	–	–	–	3.9	.8	159.1
2010	R30.3	R2.3	R122.0	R2.9	R157.5	–	–	R–	R2.1	1.6	–	–	–	R3.8	R.8	R162.0
2011P	26.9	2.1	121.4	3.1	153.6	–	–	–	2.0	1.7	–	–	–	3.7	.9	158.1

1 Anthracite, bituminous coal, subbituminous coal, lignite, waste coal, and coal synfuel.
2 Distillate fuel oil, residual fuel oil, petroleum coke, jet fuel, kerosene, other petroleum, and waste oil.
3 Natural gas, plus a small amount of supplemental gaseous fuels.
4 Blast furnace gas, propane gas, and other manufactured and waste gases derived from fossil fuels.
5 Pumped storage facility production minus energy used for pumping.
6 Through 1989, hydroelectric pumped storage is included in "Conventional Hydroelectric Power."
7 Wood and wood-derived fuels.
8 Municipal solid waste from biogenic sources, landfill gas, sludge waste, agricultural byproducts, and other biomass. Through 2000, also includes non-renewable waste (municipal solid waste from non-biogenic sources, and tire-derived fuels).
9 Solar thermal and photovoltaic (PV) energy.
10 Batteries, chemicals, hydrogen, pitch, purchased steam, sulfur, miscellaneous technologies, and, beginning in 2001, non-renewable waste (municipal solid waste from non-biogenic sources, and tire-derived fuels).
11 Electricity-only plants within the NAICS 22 category whose primary business is to sell electricity to the public. Data also include a small number of electric utility combined-heat-and-power (CHP) plants.
12 Combined-heat-and-power (CHP) plants within the NAICS 22 category whose primary business is to sell electricity and heat to the public. Data do not include electric utility CHP plants—these are included under "Electricity-Only Plants."

R=Revised. P=Preliminary. – =No data reported. (s)=Less than 0.05 billion kilowatthours.

Notes: • See Table 8.2d for commercial and industrial CHP and electricity-only data. • See Note 1, "Coverage of Electricity Statistics," and Note 2, "Classification of Power Plants Into Energy-Use Sectors," at end of section. • Totals may not equal sum of components due to independent rounding.

Web Pages: • See http://www.eia.gov/totalenergy/data/annual/#electricity for all data beginning in 1989. • For related information, see http://www.eia.gov/electricity/.

Sources: • 1989-1997—U.S. Energy Information Administration (EIA), Form EIA-759, "Monthly Power Plant Report," and Form EIA-867, "Annual Nonutility Power Producer Report." • 1998-2000—EIA, Form EIA-759, "Monthly Power Plant Report," and Form EIA-860B, "Annual Electric Generator Report—Nonutility." • 2001-2003—EIA, Form EIA-906, "Power Plant Report." • 2004-2007—EIA, Form EIA-906, "Power Plant Report," and Form EIA-920, "Combined Heat and Power Plant Report." • 2008 forward—EIA, Form EIA-923, "Power Plant Operations Report."

Source: *U.S. Energy Information Administration, Annual Energy Review 2011*

Table 8.2d Electricity Net Generation: Commercial and Industrial Sectors, Selected Years, 1989-2011

(Subset of Table 8.2a; Billion Kilowatthours)

Year	Fossil Fuels					Nuclear Electric Power	Hydro-electric Pumped Storage [5]	Renewable Energy								Total
	Coal [1]	Petroleum [2]	Natural Gas [3]	Other Gases [4]	Total			Conventional Hydroelectric Power	Biomass: Wood [6]	Biomass: Waste [7]	Geo-thermal	Solar/PV [8]	Wind	Total	Other [9]	
Commercial Sector [10]																
1989	0.7	0.6	2.2	0.1	3.6	–	–	0.1	0.1	0.5	–	–	–	0.7	–	4.3
1990	.8	.6	3.3	.1	4.8	–	–	.1	.1	.8	–	–	–	1.1	–	5.8
1995	1.0	.4	5.2	–	6.5	–	–	.1	.1	1.5	–	–	–	1.7	(s)	8.2
1996	1.1	.4	5.2	(s)	6.7	–	–	.1	.1	2.2	–	–	–	2.4	(s)	9.0
1997	1.0	.4	4.7	(s)	6.2	–	–	.1	(s)	2.3	–	–	–	2.5	(s)	8.7
1998	1.0	.4	4.9	(s)	6.3	–	–	.1	(s)	2.3	–	–	–	2.5	–	8.7
1999	1.0	.4	4.6	(s)	6.0	–	–	.1	(s)	2.4	–	–	–	2.5	(s)	8.6
2000	1.1	.4	4.3	(s)	5.8	–	–	.1	(s)	2.0	–	–	–	2.1	(s)	7.9
2001	1.0	.4	4.4	(s)	5.9	–	–	.1	(s)	1.0	–	–	–	1.1	.5	7.4
2002	1.0	.4	4.3	(s)	5.7	–	–	(s)	(s)	1.1	–	–	–	1.1	.6	7.4
2003	1.2	.4	3.9	–	5.5	–	–	.1	(s)	1.3	–	–	–	1.4	.6	7.5
2004	1.3	.5	4.0	–	5.8	–	–	.1	(s)	1.6	–	–	–	1.7	.8	8.3
2005	1.4	.4	4.2	–	6.0	–	–	.1	(s)	1.7	–	–	–	1.8	.8	8.5
2006	1.3	.2	4.4	(s)	5.9	–	–	.1	(s)	1.6	–	–	–	1.7	.8	8.4
2007	1.4	.2	4.3	–	5.8	–	–	.1	(s)	1.6	–	–	–	1.7	.8	8.3
2008	1.3	.1	4.2	–	5.6	–	–	.1	(s)	1.5	–	(s)	–	1.6	.7	7.9
2009	1.1	.2	4.2	–	5.5	–	–	.1	(s)	1.7	–	(s)	(s)	1.8	.8	8.2
2010	1.1	.1	R4.7	R(s)	R6.0	–	–	.1	(s)	1.7	–	(s)	(s)	1.8	.8	R8.6
2011P	1.0	.1	4.5	(s)	5.6	–	–	.1	(s)	1.7	–	(s)	(s)	1.9	.9	8.4
Industrial Sector [11]																
1989	20.7	4.8	53.2	7.3	85.9	–	–	2.7	21.6	0.9	–	–	–	25.2	3.5	114.7
1990	21.1	7.0	60.0	9.6	97.8	–	–	3.0	25.4	.9	–	–	–	29.3	3.6	130.7
1995	22.4	6.0	71.7	11.9	112.1	–	–	5.3	28.9	.9	–	–	–	35.1	3.9	151.0
1996	22.2	6.3	71.0	13.0	112.5	–	–	5.9	28.4	.9	–	–	–	35.2	3.4	151.0
1997	23.2	5.6	75.1	11.8	115.8	–	–	5.7	28.2	.9	–	–	–	34.8	3.5	154.1
1998	22.3	6.2	77.1	11.2	116.8	–	–	5.3	27.7	.9	–	–	–	33.9	3.4	154.1
1999	21.5	6.1	78.8	12.5	118.9	–	–	4.8	28.1	.7	–	–	–	33.5	3.9	156.3
2000	22.1	5.6	78.8	11.9	118.4	–	–	4.1	28.7	.8	–	–	–	33.6	4.7	156.7
2001	20.1	5.3	79.8	8.5	113.6	–	–	3.1	26.9	.6	–	–	–	30.6	4.9	149.2
2002	21.5	4.4	79.0	9.5	114.4	–	–	3.8	29.6	.8	–	–	–	34.3	3.8	152.6
2003	19.8	5.3	78.7	13.0	116.8	–	–	4.2	28.0	.7	–	–	–	32.9	4.8	154.5
2004	19.8	6.0	79.0	11.7	116.4	–	–	3.2	28.4	.8	–	–	–	32.4	5.1	153.9
2005	19.5	5.4	72.9	9.7	107.4	–	–	3.2	28.3	.7	–	–	–	32.2	5.1	144.7
2006	19.5	4.2	77.7	9.9	111.3	–	–	2.9	28.4	.6	–	–	–	31.9	5.1	148.3
2007	16.7	4.2	77.6	9.4	107.9	–	–	1.6	28.3	.6	–	–	–	30.5	4.7	143.1
2008	15.7	3.2	76.4	8.5	103.9	–	–	1.7	26.6	.8	–	–	–	29.1	4.1	137.1
2009	13.7	3.0	75.7	7.6	100.0	–	–	1.9	25.3	.7	–	–	–	27.9	4.5	132.3
2010	18.4	R2.3	R81.6	R8.3	R110.6	–	–	R1.7	R25.7	R.9	–	(s)	–	R28.2	R5.2	R144.1
2011P	18.4	1.8	81.5	8.1	109.9	–	–	1.8	26.4	.9	–	(s)	(s)	29.1	3.3	142.3

[1] Anthracite, bituminous coal, subbituminous coal, lignite, waste coal, and coal synfuel.
[2] Distillate fuel oil, residual fuel oil, petroleum coke, jet fuel, kerosene, other petroleum, and waste oil.
[3] Natural gas, plus a small amount of supplemental gaseous fuels.
[4] Blast furnace gas, propane gas, and other manufactured and waste gases derived from fossil fuels.
[5] Pumped storage facility production minus energy used for pumping.
[6] Wood and wood-derived fuels.
[7] Municipal solid waste from biogenic sources, landfill gas, sludge waste, agricultural byproducts, and other biomass. Through 2000, also includes non-renewable waste (municipal solid waste from non-biogenic sources, and tire-derived fuels).
[8] Solar thermal and photovoltaic (PV) energy.
[9] Batteries, chemicals, hydrogen, pitch, purchased steam, sulfur, miscellaneous technologies, and, beginning in 2001, non-renewable waste (municipal solid waste from non-biogenic sources, and tire-derived fuels).
[10] Commercial combined-heat-and-power (CHP) and commercial electricity-only plants.
[11] Industrial combined-heat-and-power (CHP) and industrial electricity-only plants.

R=Revised. P=Preliminary. – =No data reported. (s)=Less than 0.05 billion kilowatthours.

Notes: • See Tables 8.2b and 8.2c for electric power sector electricity-only and CHP data. • See Note 1, "Coverage of Electricity Statistics," and Note 2, "Classification of Power Plants Into Energy-Use Sectors," at end of section. • Totals may not equal sum of components due to independent rounding.

Web Pages: • See http://www.eia.gov/totalenergy/data/monthly/#electricity for updated monthly and annual data. • See http://www.eia.gov/totalenergy/data/annual/#electricity for all annual data beginning in 1989. • See http://www.eia.gov/electricity/ for related information.

Sources: • 1989-1997—U.S. Energy Information Administration (EIA), Form EIA-867, "Annual Nonutility Power Producer Report." • 1998-2000—EIA, Form EIA-860B, "Annual Electric Generator Report—Nonutility." • 2001-2003—EIA, Form EIA-906, "Power Plant Report." • 2004-2007—EIA, Form EIA-906, "Power Plant Report," and Form EIA-920, "Combined Heat and Power Plant Report." • 2008 forward—EIA, Form EIA-923, "Power Plant Operations Report."

Source: *U.S. Energy Information Administration, Annual Energy Review 2011*

Figure 8.10 Average Retail Prices of Electricity

Total, 1960-2011

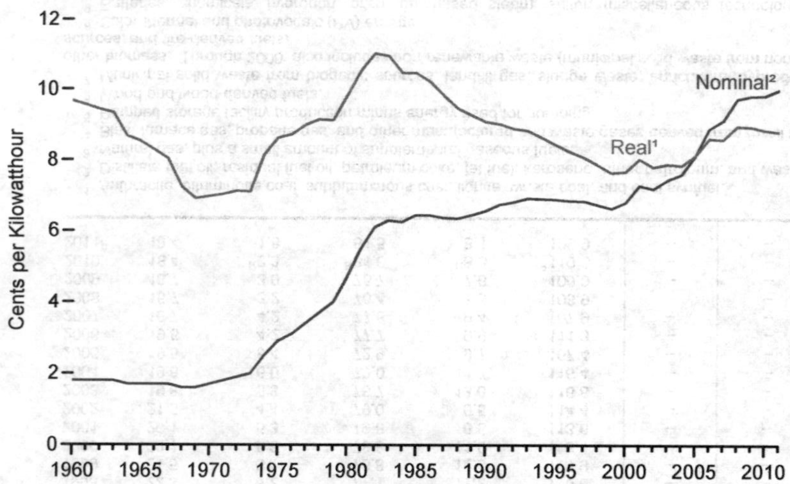

By Sector, 2011

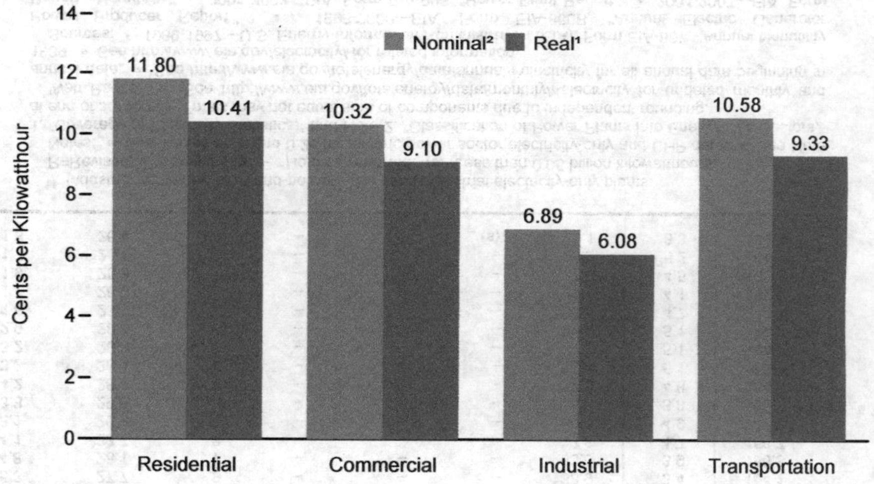

By Sector, Nominal² Prices, 1960-2011

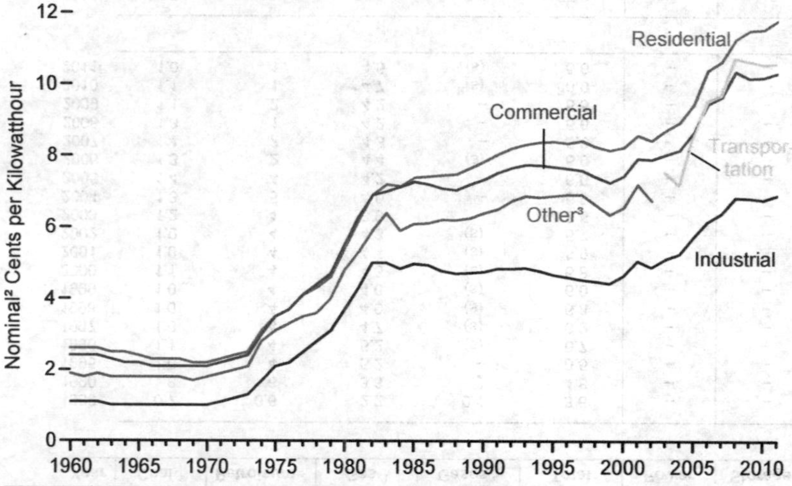

By Sector, Real¹ Prices, 1960-2011

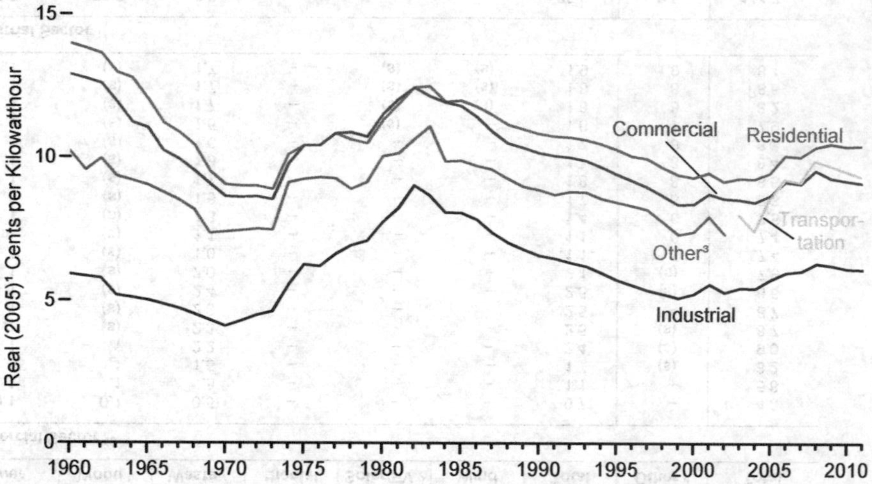

[1] In chained (2005) dollars, calculated by using gross domestic product implicit price deflators in Table D1. See "Chained Dollars" in Glossary.
[2] See "Nominal Price" in Glossary.
[3] Public street and highway lighting, interdepartmental sales, other sales to public authorities, agriculture and irrigation, and transportation including railroads and railways.

Note: Taxes are included.

Source: Table 8.10.

Source: *U.S. Energy Information Administration, Annual Energy Review 2011*

Table 8.10 Average Retail Prices of Electricity, Selected Years, 1960-2011

(Cents per Kilowatthour, Including Taxes)

Year	Residential		Commercial [1]		Industrial [2]		Transportation [3]		Other [4]		Total	
	Nominal [5]	Real [6]	Nominal [5]	Real [6]	Nominal [5]	Real [6]	Nominal [5]	Real [6]	Nominal [5]	Real [6]	Nominal [5]	Real [6]
1960	2.6	14.0	2.4	12.9	1.1	5.9	NA	NA	1.9	10.2	1.8	9.7
1965	2.4	R12.0	2.2	11.0	1.0	5.0	NA	NA	1.8	9.0	1.7	8.5
1966	2.3	11.2	2.1	R10.2	1.0	4.9	NA	NA	1.8	8.8	1.7	8.3
1967	2.3	10.9	2.1	R9.9	1.0	4.7	NA	NA	1.8	8.5	1.7	R8.0
1968	2.3	R10.4	2.1	9.5	1.0	4.5	NA	NA	1.8	8.2	1.6	7.3
1969	2.2	9.5	2.1	9.1	1.0	4.3	NA	NA	1.7	7.4	1.6	6.9
1970	2.2	R9.0	2.1	8.6	1.0	4.1	NA	NA	1.8	7.4	1.7	7.0
1971	2.3	9.0	2.2	8.6	1.1	4.3	NA	NA	1.9	7.4	1.8	R7.0
1972	2.4	9.0	2.3	8.6	1.2	4.5	NA	NA	2.0	7.5	1.9	7.1
1973	2.5	8.9	2.4	8.5	1.3	4.6	NA	NA	2.1	7.5	2.0	7.1
1974	3.1	10.1	3.0	9.8	1.7	5.5	NA	NA	2.8	9.1	2.5	8.2
1975	3.5	10.4	3.5	10.4	2.1	6.3	NA	NA	3.1	9.2	2.9	8.6
1976	3.7	10.4	3.7	10.4	2.2	6.2	NA	NA	3.3	9.3	3.1	8.7
1977	4.1	10.9	4.1	10.9	2.5	6.6	NA	NA	3.5	9.3	3.4	9.0
1978	4.3	10.6	4.4	10.9	2.8	6.9	NA	NA	3.6	8.9	3.7	9.2
1979	4.6	10.5	4.7	10.7	3.1	7.1	NA	NA	4.0	9.1	4.0	9.1
1980	5.4	11.3	5.5	11.5	3.7	R7.7	NA	NA	4.8	R10.0	4.7	9.8
1981	6.2	11.9	6.3	12.1	4.3	8.2	NA	NA	5.3	R10.1	5.5	10.5
1982	6.9	R12.4	6.9	R12.4	5.0	9.0	NA	NA	5.9	R10.6	6.1	11.0
1983	7.2	12.5	7.0	R12.1	5.0	8.7	NA	NA	6.4	11.1	6.3	10.9
1984	7.15	R11.95	7.13	R11.92	4.83	R8.07	NA	NA	5.90	R9.86	6.25	R10.45
1985	7.39	R11.99	7.27	R11.80	4.97	R8.06	NA	NA	6.09	R9.88	6.44	R10.45
1986	7.42	R11.78	7.20	R11.43	4.93	7.83	NA	NA	6.11	R9.70	6.44	R10.22
1987	7.45	R11.49	7.08	R10.92	4.77	R7.36	NA	NA	6.21	R9.58	6.37	R9.83
1988	7.48	R11.16	7.04	R10.50	4.70	R7.01	NA	NA	6.20	R9.25	6.35	R9.47
1989	7.65	11.00	7.20	R10.35	4.72	R6.78	NA	NA	6.25	R8.98	6.45	R9.27
1990	7.83	10.84	7.34	R10.16	4.74	R6.56	NA	NA	6.40	8.86	6.57	R9.09
1991	8.04	10.75	7.53	R10.06	4.83	6.46	NA	NA	6.51	R8.70	6.75	R9.02
1992	8.21	R10.72	7.66	R10.00	4.83	6.31	NA	NA	6.74	R8.80	6.82	R8.90
1993	8.32	R10.63	7.74	9.89	4.85	R6.19	NA	NA	6.88	R8.79	6.93	R8.85
1994	8.38	R10.48	7.73	R9.67	4.77	5.97	NA	NA	6.84	8.56	6.91	R8.64
1995	8.40	R10.29	7.69	R9.42	4.66	R5.71	NA	NA	6.88	R8.43	6.89	R8.44
1996	8.36	R10.05	7.64	R9.19	4.60	R5.53	NA	NA	6.91	R8.31	6.86	R8.25
1997	8.43	R9.96	7.59	R8.97	4.53	R5.35	NA	NA	6.91	8.17	6.85	R8.09
1998	8.26	R9.65	7.41	R8.66	4.48	R5.23	NA	NA	6.63	7.75	6.74	7.88
1999	8.16	9.40	7.26	R8.36	4.43	R5.10	NA	NA	6.35	R7.31	6.64	7.65
2000	8.24	R9.29	7.43	R8.37	4.64	5.23	NA	NA	6.56	R7.39	6.81	7.68
2001	8.58	9.46	7.92	R8.73	5.05	5.57	NA	NA	7.20	7.94	7.29	8.04
2002	8.44	R9.15	7.89	R8.56	4.88	R5.29	NA	NA	6.75	R7.32	7.20	R7.81
2003	8.72	R9.26	8.03	8.53	5.11	5.43	7.54	8.01	– –	– –	7.44	R7.90
2004	8.95	9.25	8.17	8.44	5.25	R5.42	7.18	7.42	– –	– –	7.61	7.86
2005	9.45	9.45	8.67	8.67	5.73	5.73	8.57	8.57	– –	– –	8.14	8.14
2006	10.40	10.07	9.46	9.16	6.16	5.97	9.54	9.24	– –	– –	8.90	8.62
2007	10.65	R10.03	9.65	9.08	6.39	R6.02	9.70	9.13	– –	– –	9.13	8.59
2008	11.26	10.37	10.36	9.54	6.83	6.29	10.74	9.89	– –	– –	9.74	8.97
2009	11.51	R10.49	10.17	R9.27	6.81	6.21	10.65	R9.71	– –	– –	9.82	R8.95
2010	R11.54	R10.40	R10.19	R9.18	R6.77	R6.10	R10.57	R9.52	– –	– –	R9.83	R8.86
2011P	11.80	10.41	10.32	9.10	6.39	6.08	10.58	9.33	– –	– –	9.99	8.81

[1] Commercial sector. For 1960–2002, prices exclude public street and highway lighting, interdepartmental sales, and other sales to public authorities.

[2] Industrial sector. For 1960–2002, prices exclude agriculture and irrigation.

[3] Transportation sector, including railroads and railways.

[4] Public street and highway lighting, interdepartmental sales, other sales to public authorities, agriculture and irrigation, and transportation including railroads and railways.

[5] See "Nominal Price" in Glossary.

[6] In chained (2005) dollars, calculated by using gross domestic product implicit price deflators in Table D1. See "Chained Dollars" in Glossary.

R=Revised. P=Preliminary. NA=Not available. – – =Not applicable.

Notes: • Beginning in 2003, the category "Other" has been replaced by "Transportation," and the categories "Commercial" and "Industrial" have been redefined. • Data represent revenue from electricity retail sales divided by electricity retail sales. • Prices include State and local taxes, energy or demand charges, customer service charges, environmental surcharges, franchise fees, fuel adjustments, and other miscellaneous charges applied to end-use customers during normal billing operations. Prices do not include deferred charges, credits, or other adjustments, such as fuel or revenue from purchased power, from previous reporting periods. • Through 1979, data are for Classes A and B privately owned electric utilities only. (Class A utilities are those with operating revenues of $2.5 million or more; Class B utilities are those with between $1 million and $2.5 million.) For 1980–1982, data are for selected Class A utilities whose electric operating revenues were $100 million or more during the previous year. For 1983, data are for a selected sample of electric utilities. Beginning in 1984, data are for a census of electric utilities. Beginning in 1996, data also include energy service providers selling to retail customers.

Web Pages: • See http://www.eia.gov/totalenergy/data/monthly/#prices for updated monthly and annual data. • See http://www.eia.gov/totalenergy/data/annual/#electricity for all annual data beginning in 1960. • See http://www.eia.gov/electricity/ for related information.

Sources: • 1960-September 1977—Federal Power Commission, Form FPC-5, "Monthly Statement of Electric Operating Revenues and Income." • October 1977-February 1980—Federal Energy Regulatory Commission (FERC), Form FPC-5, "Monthly Statement of Electric Operating Revenues and Income." • March 1980-1982—FERC, Form FERC-5, "Electric Utility Company Monthly Statement." • 1983—U.S. Energy Information Administration (EIA), Form EIA-826, "Electric Utility Company Monthly Statement." • 1984-1996—EIA, Form EIA-861, "Annual Electric Utility Report." • 1997 forward—EIA, *Electric Power Monthly* (February 2012), Table 5.3.

Source: *U.S. Energy Information Administration, Annual Energy Review 2011*

Figure 9.1 Nuclear Generating Units

Operable Units,[1] 1957-2011

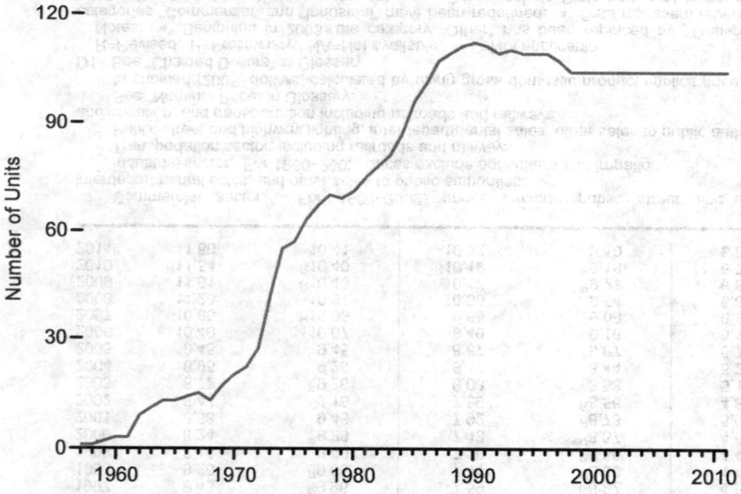

Nuclear Net Summer Capacity Change, 1950-2011

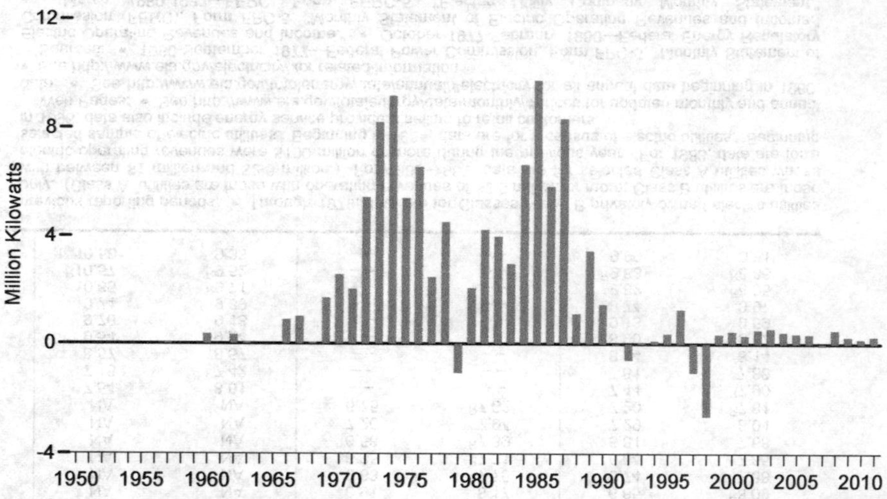

Status of All Nuclear Generating Units, 2011

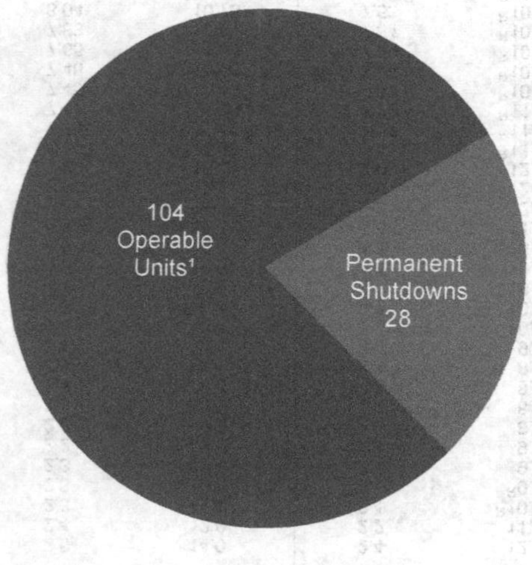

Permanent Shutdowns by Year, 1955-2011

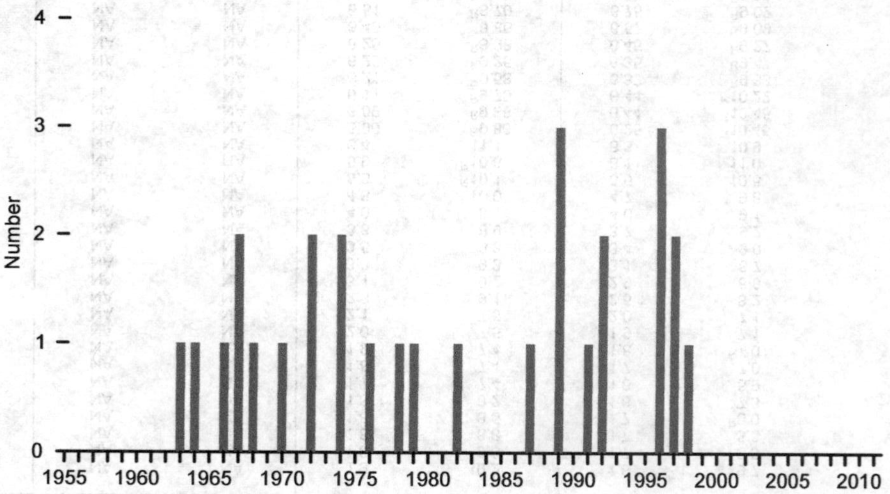

[1] Units holding full-power operating licenses, or equivalent permission to operate, at the end of the year.

Note: Data are at end of year.
Sources: Tables 9.1 and 8.11a.

Source: *U.S. Energy Information Administration, Annual Energy Review 2011*

Table 9.1 Nuclear Generating Units, 1955-2011

Year	Original Licensing Regulations (10 CFR Part 50) [1]			Current Licensing Regulations (10 CFR Part 52) [1]			Permanent Shutdowns	Operable Units [7]
	Construction Permits Issued [2,3]	Low-Power Operating Licenses Issued [3,4]	Full-Power Operating Licenses Issued [3,5]	Early Site Permits Issued [3]	Combined License Applications Received [6]	Combined Licenses Issued [3]		
1955	1	0	0	--	--	--	0	0
1956	3	0	0	--	--	--	0	0
1957	1	1	1	--	--	--	0	1
1958	0	0	0	--	--	--	0	1
1959	3	1	1	--	--	--	0	2
1960	7	1	1	--	--	--	0	3
1961	0	0	0	--	--	--	0	3
1962	1	7	6	--	--	--	0	9
1963	1	3	2	--	--	--	R1	11
1964	3	2	3	--	--	--	1	13
1965	1	0	0	--	--	--	0	13
1966	5	1	2	--	--	--	1	14
1967	14	3	3	--	--	--	2	15
1968	23	0	0	--	--	--	R1	13
1969	7	4	4	--	--	--	0	17
1970	10	4	3	--	--	--	R1	20
1971	4	5	2	--	--	--	0	22
1972	8	6	6	--	--	--	R2	27
1973	14	12	15	--	--	--	0	42
1974	23	14	15	--	--	--	2	55
1975	9	3	2	--	--	--	0	57
1976	9	7	7	--	--	--	1	63
1977	15	4	4	--	--	--	0	67
1978	13	3	4	--	--	--	1	70
1979	2	0	0	--	--	--	1	69
1980	0	5	2	--	--	--	0	71
1981	0	3	4	--	--	--	0	75
1982	0	6	4	--	--	--	1	78
1983	0	3	3	--	--	--	0	81
1984	0	7	6	--	--	--	0	87
1985	0	7	9	--	--	--	0	96
1986	0	7	5	--	--	--	0	101
1987	0	6	8	--	--	--	R1	107
1988	0	1	2	--	--	--	0	109
1989	0	3	4	--	--	--	R3	111
1990	0	1	2	--	--	--	R0	112
1991	0	0	0	--	--	--	1	111
1992	0	0	0	--	--	--	2	109
1993	0	1	1	--	--	--	0	110
1994	0	0	0	--	--	--	R0	109
1995	0	1	0	--	--	--	0	109
1996	0	0	1	--	--	--	R3	109
1997	0	0	0	0	0	0	2	107
1998	0	0	0	0	0	0	R1	104
1999-2006	0	0	0	0	0	0	0	104
2007	0	0	0	3	5	0	0	104
2008	0	0	0	0	R12	0	0	104
2009	0	0	0	1	1	0	0	104
2010	0	0	0	0	0	0	0	104
2011	0	0	0	0	0	0	0	104
Total	177	132	132	4	R18	0	28	--

[1] Data in columns 1–3 are based on the U.S. Nuclear Regulatory Commission (NRC) regulation 10 CFR Part 50. Data in columns 4–6 are based on the NRC regulation 10 CFR Part 52. See Note 1, "Pending Actions on Nuclear Generating Units," at end of section.

[2] Issuance by regulatory authority of a permit, or equivalent permission, to begin construction. Under current licensing regulations, the construction permit is no longer issued separately from the operating license.

[3] Numbers reflect permits or licenses issued in a given year, not extant permits or licenses.

[4] Issuance by regulatory authority of license, or equivalent permission, to conduct testing but not to operate at full power.

[5] Issuance by regulatory authority of full-power operating license, or equivalent permission note that some units receive full-power licenses the same year they receive low-power licenses). Units initially undergo low-power testing prior to commercial operation.

[6] Number of applications received for combined construction and operating licenses, including one that was subsequently withdrawn. Does not represent the total number of reactor units included in the applications. See Note 1, "Pending Actions on Nuclear Generating Units," at end of Section.

[7] Total of nuclear generating units holding full-power licenses, or equivalent permission to operate, at the end of the year (the number of operable units equals the cumulative number of units holding full-power licenses minus the cumulative number of permanent shutdowns).

-- =Not applicable.

Note: See Note 2, "Coverage of Nuclear Energy Statistics," at end of section.

Web Page: For related information, see http://www.eia.gov/nuclear/.

Sources: See end of section.

***Source:** U.S. Energy Information Administration, Annual Energy Review 2011*

Figure 9.2 Nuclear Power Plant Operations

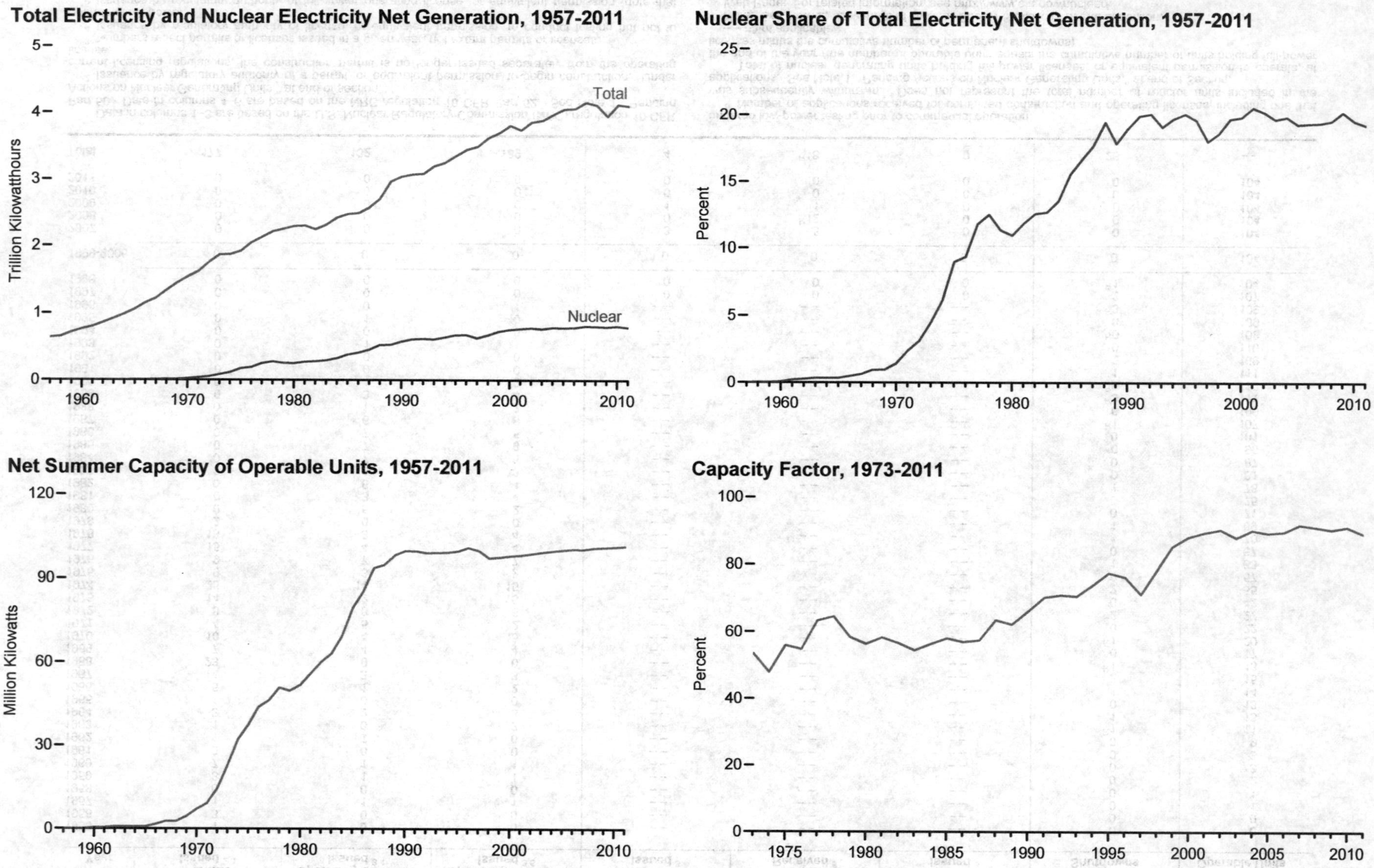

Sources: Tables 8.1 and 9.2.

Source: *U.S. Energy Information Administration, Annual Energy Review 2011*

Table 9.2 Nuclear Power Plant Operations, 1957-2011

Year	Nuclear Electricity Net Generation	Nuclear Share of Total Electricity Net Generation	Net Summer Capacity of Operable Units [1]	Capacity Factor [2]
	Billion Kilowatthours	Percent	Million Kilowatts	Percent
1957	(s)	(s)	0.1	NA
1958	.2	(s)	.1	NA
1959	.2	(s)	.1	NA
1960	.5	.1	.4	NA
1961	1.7	.2	.4	NA
1962	2.3	.3	.7	NA
1963	3.2	.3	.8	NA
1964	3.3	.3	.8	NA
1965	3.7	.3	.8	NA
1966	5.5	.5	1.7	NA
1967	7.7	.6	2.7	NA
1968	12.5	.9	2.7	NA
1969	13.9	1.0	4.4	NA
1970	21.8	1.4	7.0	NA
1971	38.1	2.4	9.0	NA
1972	54.1	3.1	14.5	NA
1973	83.5	4.5	22.7	53.5
1974	114.0	6.1	31.9	47.8
1975	172.5	9.0	37.3	55.9
1976	191.1	9.4	43.8	54.7
1977	250.9	11.8	46.3	63.3
1978	276.4	12.5	50.8	64.5
1979	255.2	11.3	49.7	58.4
1980	251.1	11.0	51.8	56.3
1981	272.7	11.9	56.0	58.2
1982	282.8	12.6	60.0	56.6
1983	293.7	12.7	63.0	54.4
1984	327.6	13.5	69.7	56.3
1985	383.7	15.5	79.4	58.0
1986	414.0	16.6	85.2	56.9
1987	455.3	17.7	93.6	57.4
1988	527.0	19.5	94.7	63.5
1989	529.4	17.8	98.2	62.2
1990	576.9	19.0	99.6	66.0
1991	612.6	19.9	99.6	70.2
1992	618.8	20.1	99.0	70.9
1993	610.3	19.1	99.0	70.5
1994	640.4	19.7	99.1	73.8
1995	673.4	20.1	99.5	77.4
1996	674.7	19.6	100.8	76.2
1997	628.6	18.0	99.7	71.1
1998	673.7	18.6	97.1	78.2
1999	728.3	19.7	97.4	85.3
2000	753.9	19.8	97.9	88.1
2001	768.8	20.6	98.2	89.4
2002	780.1	20.2	98.7	90.3
2003	763.7	19.7	99.2	87.9
2004	788.5	19.9	99.6	90.1
2005	782.0	19.3	100.0	89.3
2006	787.2	19.4	100.3	89.6
2007	806.4	19.4	100.3	91.8
2008	806.2	19.6	100.3	91.1
2009	798.9	20.2	101.0	90.3
2010	807.0	19.6	R101.2	R91.1
2011P	790.2	19.2	101.4	89.1

[1] At end of year. See "Generator Net Summer Capacity" in Glossary.
[2] See "Generator Capacity Factor" in Glossary.
R=Revised. P=Preliminary. NA=Not available. (s)=Less than 0.05.
Note: See Note 2, "Coverage of Nuclear Energy Statistics," at end of section.
Web Pages: • See http://www.eia.gov/totalenergy/data/monthly/#nuclear for updated monthly and annual data. • See http://www.eia.gov/nuclear/ for related information.
Sources: **Nuclear Electricity Net Generation** and **Nuclear Share of Electricity Net Generation:** Table 8.2a. **Net Summer Capacity of Operable Units:** Table 8.11a. **Capacity Factor:** U.S. Energy Information Administration, *Monthly Energy Review* (April 2012), Table 8.1. Annual capacity factors are weighted averages of monthly capacity factors.

Source: *U.S. Energy Information Administration, Annual Energy Review 2011*

Figure 9.3 Uranium Overview

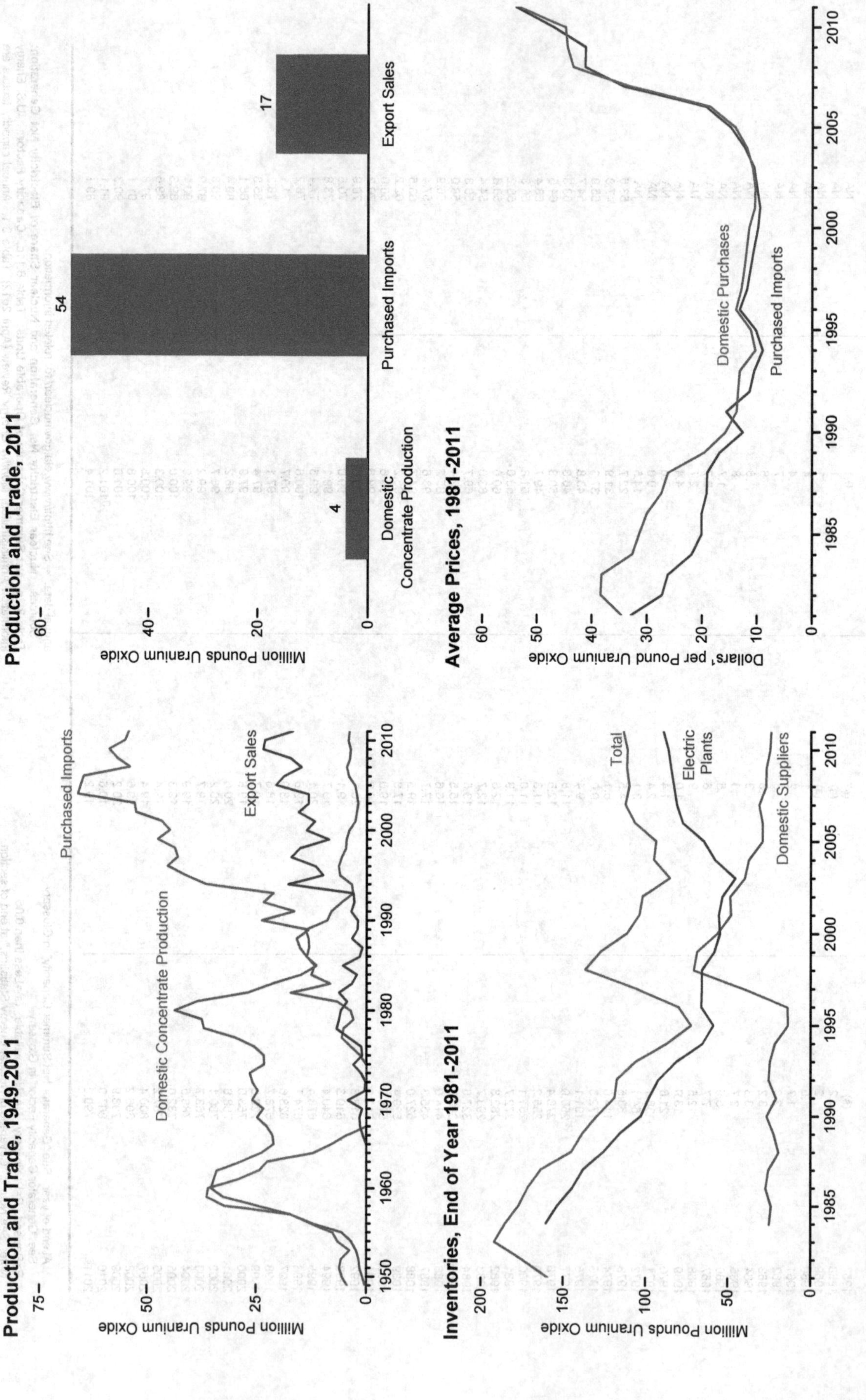

[1] Prices are not adjusted for inflation. See "Nominal Dollars" in Glossary.
Note: See "Uranium Oxide" in Glossary.

Source: Table 9.3.

Source: U.S. Energy Information Administration, Annual Energy Review 2011

Table 9.3 Uranium Overview, Selected Years, 1949-2011

Year	Domestic Concentrate Production [1]	Purchased Imports [2]	Export [2] Sales	Electric Plant Purchases From Domestic Suppliers	Loaded Into U.S. Nuclear Reactors [3]	Inventories: Domestic Suppliers	Inventories: Electric Plants	Inventories: Total	Average Price: Purchased Imports	Average Price: Domestic Purchases
	Million Pounds Uranium Oxide								Dollars [4] per Pound Uranium Oxide	
1949	0.36	4.3	0.0	NA	NA	NA	NA	NA	NA	NA
1950	.92	5.5	.0	NA	NA	NA	NA	NA	NA	NA
1955	5.56	7.6	.0	NA	NA	NA	NA	NA	NA	NA
1960	35.28	36.0	.0	NA	NA	NA	NA	NA	NA	NA
1965	20.88	8.0	.0	NA	NA	NA	NA	NA	NA	NA
1970	25.81	.0	4.2	NA	NA	NA	NA	NA	– –	NA
1975	23.20	1.4	1.0	NA	NA	NA	NA	NA	NA	NA
1976	25.49	3.6	1.2	NA	NA	NA	NA	NA	NA	NA
1977	29.88	5.6	4.0	NA	NA	NA	NA	NA	NA	NA
1978	36.97	5.2	6.8	NA	NA	NA	NA	NA	NA	NA
1979	37.47	3.0	6.2	NA	NA	NA	NA	NA	NA	NA
1980	43.70	3.6	5.8	NA	NA	NA	NA	NA	NA	NA
1981	38.47	6.6	4.4	32.6	NA	NA	NA	159.2	32.90	34.65
1982	26.87	17.1	6.2	27.1	NA	NA	NA	174.8	27.23	38.37
1983	21.16	8.2	3.3	24.2	NA	NA	NA	191.8	26.16	38.21
1984	14.88	12.5	2.2	22.5	NA	25.0	160.2	185.2	21.86	32.65
1985	11.31	11.7	5.3	21.7	NA	23.7	153.2	176.9	20.08	31.43
1986	13.51	13.5	1.6	18.9	NA	27.0	144.1	171.1	20.07	30.01
1987	12.99	15.1	1.0	20.8	NA	25.4	137.8	163.2	19.14	27.37
1988	13.13	15.8	3.3	17.6	NA	19.3	125.5	144.8	19.03	26.15
1989	13.84	13.1	2.1	18.4	NA	22.2	115.8	138.1	16.75	19.56
1990	8.89	23.7	2.0	20.5	NA	26.4	102.7	129.1	12.55	15.70
1991	7.95	16.3	3.5	26.8	34.6	20.7	98.0	118.7	15.55	13.66
1992	5.65	23.3	2.8	23.4	43.0	25.2	92.1	117.3	11.34	13.45
1993	3.06	21.0	3.0	15.5	45.1	24.5	81.2	105.7	10.53	13.14
1994	3.35	36.6	17.7	22.7	40.4	21.5	65.4	86.9	8.95	10.30
1995	6.04	41.3	9.8	22.3	51.1	13.7	58.7	72.5	10.20	11.11
1996	6.32	45.4	11.5	23.7	45.2	13.9	66.1	80.0	13.15	13.81
1997	5.64	43.0	17.0	19.4	43.2	40.4	65.9	106.2	11.81	12.87
1998	4.71	43.7	15.1	21.6	33.2	70.7	65.8	136.5	11.19	12.31
1999	4.61	47.6	8.5	21.4	53.8	68.8	58.3	127.1	10.55	11.88
2000	3.96	44.9	13.6	24.3	51.5	56.5	54.8	111.3	9.84	11.45
2001	2.64	46.7	11.7	27.5	52.7	48.1	55.6	103.8	9.51	10.45
2002	2.34	52.7	15.4	22.7	57.2	48.7	53.5	102.1	10.05	10.35
2003	[5,E] 2.00	53.0	13.2	21.7	62.3	39.9	45.6	85.5	10.59	10.84
2004	2.28	66.1	13.2	28.2	50.1	37.5	57.7	95.2	12.25	11.91
2005	2.69	65.5	20.5	27.3	58.3	29.1	64.7	93.8	14.83	13.98
2006	4.11	64.8	18.7	27.9	51.7	29.1	77.5	106.6	19.31	18.54
2007	4.53	54.1	14.8	18.5	45.5	31.2	81.2	112.4	34.18	33.13
2008	3.90	57.1	17.2	20.4	51.3	27.0	83.0	110.0	41.30	43.43
2009	3.71	58.9	23.5	17.6	49.4	26.8	84.8	111.5	41.23	44.53
2010	4.23	55.3	23.1	16.2	44.3	R 24.7	86.5	R 111.3	47.01	44.88
2011	3.99	54.4	16.7	19.8	P 52.0	P 24.1	P 89.5	P 113.6	54.00	53.41

1 See "Uranium Concentrate" in Glossary.

2 Import quantities through 1970 are reported for fiscal years. Prior to 1968, the Atomic Energy Commission was the sole purchaser of all imported uranium oxide. Trade data prior to 1982 were for transactions conducted by uranium suppliers only. For 1982 forward, transactions by uranium buyers (consumers) have been included. Buyer imports and exports prior to 1982 are believed to be small.

3 Does not include any fuel rods removed from reactors and later reloaded.

4 Prices are not adjusted for inflation. See "Nominal Dollars" in Glossary.

5 Value has been rounded to avoid disclosure of individual company data.

R=Revised. P=Preliminary. E=Estimate. NA=Not available. – – =Not applicable.

Note: See "Uranium Oxide" in Glossary.

Web Pages: • For all data beginning in 1949, see http://www.eia.gov/totalenergy/data/annual/#nuclear. • For related information, see http://www.eia.gov/nuclear/.

Sources: • 1949-1966—U.S. Department of Energy, Grand Junction Office, *Statistical Data of the Uranium Industry*, Report No. GJO-100, annual reports. • 1967-2002—U.S. Energy Information Administration (EIA), *Uranium Industry Annual*, annual reports. • 2003-2006—EIA, "Uranium Marketing Annual Report," annual reports. • 2007 forward—EIA, "2011 Domestic Uranium Production Report" (May 2012), Table 3; EIA, "2011 Uranium Marketing Annual Report" (May 2012), Tables 5, 18, 19, 21, and 22; and EIA, Form EIA-858, "Uranium Marketing Annual Survey."

Source: *U.S. Energy Information Administration, Annual Energy Review 2011*

Figure 10.1 Renewable Energy Consumption by Major Source

Renewable Energy as Share of Total Primary Energy Consumption, 2011

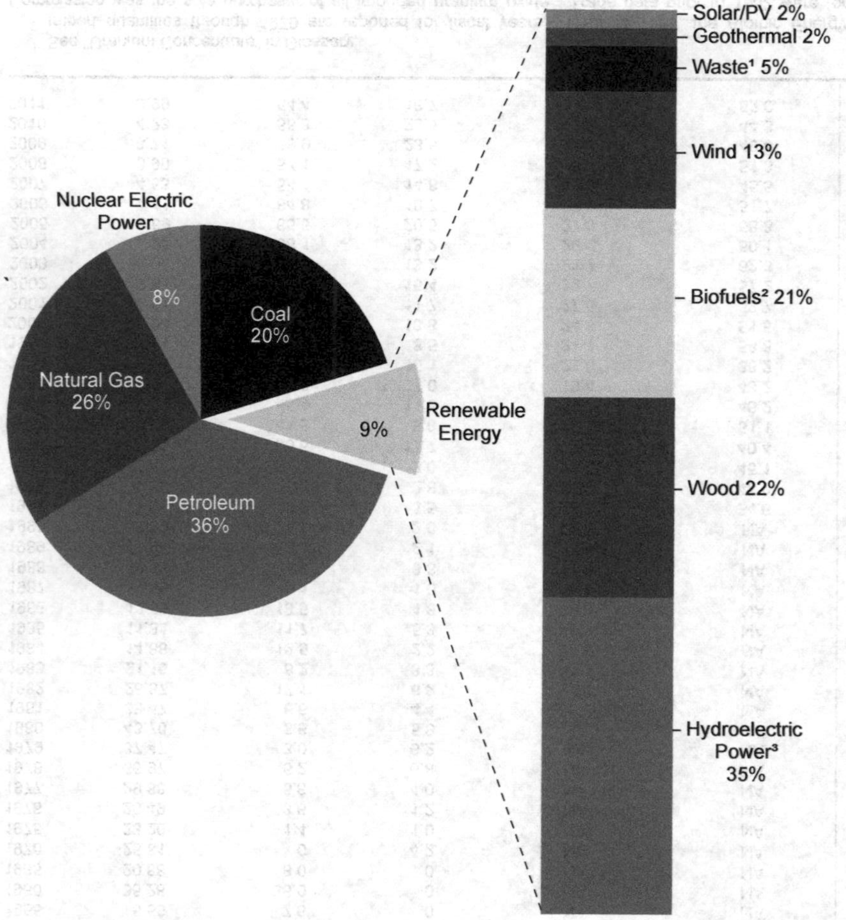

Renewable Energy Consumption by Source, 1949-2011

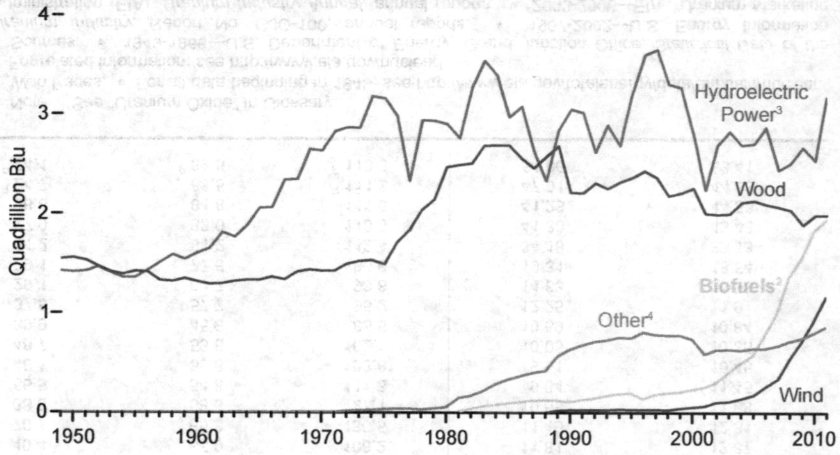

Renewable Energy Consumption by Source, 2011

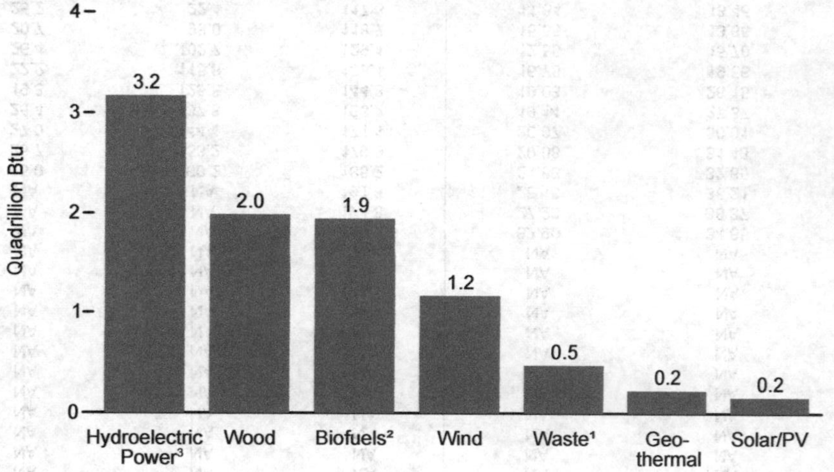

[1] Municipal solid waste from biogenic sources, landfill gas, sludge waste, agricultural byproducts, and other biomass.
[2] Fuel ethanol (minus denaturant) and biodiesel consumption, plus losses and co-products from the production of fuel ethanol and biodiesel.
[3] Conventional hydroelectric power.
[4] Geothermal, solar/PV, and waste.
Notes: Sum of components may not equal 100 percent due to independent rounding.
Sources: Tables 1.3 and 10.1.

Source: *U.S. Energy Information Administration, Annual Energy Review 2011*

Table 10.1 Renewable Energy Production and Consumption by Primary Energy Source, Selected Years, 1949-2011

(Trillion Btu)

	Production[1]			Consumption								
	Biomass		Total Renewable Energy[4]	Hydro-electric Power[5]	Geo-thermal[6]	Solar/PV[7]	Wind[8]	Biomass				Total Renewable Energy
Year	Biofuels[2]	Total[3]						Wood[9]	Waste[10]	Biofuels[11]	Total	
1949	NA	1,549	2,974	1,425	NA	NA	NA	1,549	NA	NA	1,549	2,974
1950	NA	1,562	2,978	1,415	NA	NA	NA	1,562	NA	NA	1,562	2,978
1955	NA	1,424	2,784	1,360	NA	NA	NA	1,424	NA	NA	1,424	2,784
1960	NA	1,320	2,928	1,608	(s)	NA	NA	1,320	NA	NA	1,320	2,928
1965	NA	1,335	3,396	2,059	2	NA	NA	1,335	NA	NA	1,335	3,396
1970	NA	1,431	4,070	2,634	6	NA	NA	1,429	2	NA	1,431	4,070
1975	NA	1,499	4,687	3,155	34	NA	NA	1,497	2	NA	1,499	4,687
1976	NA	1,713	4,727	2,976	38	NA	NA	1,711	2	NA	1,713	4,727
1977	NA	1,838	4,209	2,333	37	NA	NA	1,837	2	NA	1,838	4,209
1978	NA	2,038	5,005	2,937	31	NA	NA	2,036	1	NA	2,038	5,005
1979	NA	2,152	5,123	2,931	40	NA	NA	2,150	2	NA	2,152	5,123
1980	NA	2,476	5,428	2,900	53	NA	NA	2,474	2	NA	2,476	5,428
1981	13	2,596	5,414	2,758	59	NA	NA	2,496	88	13	2,596	5,414
1982	34	2,663	5,980	3,266	51	NA	NA	2,510	119	34	2,663	5,980
1983	63	2,904	6,496	3,527	64	NA	(s)	2,684	157	63	2,904	6,496
1984	77	2,971	6,438	3,386	81	(s)	(s)	2,686	208	77	2,971	6,438
1985	93	3,016	6,084	2,970	97	(s)	(s)	2,687	236	93	3,016	6,084
1986	107	2,932	6,111	3,071	108	(s)	(s)	2,562	263	107	2,932	6,111
1987	123	2,875	5,622	2,635	112	(s)	(s)	2,463	289	123	2,875	5,622
1988	124	3,016	5,457	2,334	106	(s)	(s)	2,577	315	124	3,016	5,457
1989	125	3,159	6,235	2,837	162	55	22	2,680	354	125	3,159	6,235
1990	111	2,735	6,041	3,046	171	59	29	2,216	408	111	2,735	6,041
1991	128	2,782	6,069	3,016	178	62	31	2,214	440	128	2,782	6,069
1992	145	2,932	5,821	2,617	179	64	30	2,313	473	145	2,932	5,821
1993	169	2,908	6,083	2,892	186	66	31	2,260	479	169	2,908	6,083
1994	188	3,028	5,988	2,683	173	68	36	2,324	515	188	3,028	5,988
1995	198	3,099	6,558	3,205	152	69	33	2,370	531	200	3,101	6,560
1996	141	3,155	7,012	3,590	163	70	33	2,437	577	143	3,157	7,014
1997	186	3,108	7,018	3,640	167	70	34	2,371	551	184	3,105	7,016
1998	202	2,929	6,494	3,297	168	69	31	2,184	542	201	2,927	6,493
1999	211	2,965	6,517	3,268	171	68	46	2,214	540	209	2,963	6,516
2000	233	3,006	6,104	2,811	164	R66	57	2,262	511	236	3,008	6,106
2001	254	2,624	5,164	2,242	164	64	70	2,006	364	253	2,622	5,163
2002	308	2,705	5,734	2,689	171	63	105	1,995	402	303	2,701	5,729
2003	402	2,805	5,982	2,825	175	62	115	2,002	401	404	2,807	5,983
2004	487	2,998	6,070	2,690	178	63	142	2,121	389	499	3,010	6,082
2005	564	3,104	6,229	2,703	181	63	178	R2,137	403	577	R3,117	6,242
2006	720	R3,216	R6,599	2,869	181	68	264	R2,099	397	771	R3,267	R6,649
2007	978	R3,461	R6,509	2,446	186	76	341	R2,070	413	991	R3,474	R6,523
2008	1,387	R3,864	R7,202	2,511	192	89	546	R2,040	436	1,372	R3,849	R7,186
2009	R1,584	R3,928	R7,616	2,669	200	98	721	R1,891	R453	R1,568	R3,912	R7,600
2010	R1,884	R4,341	R8,136	R2,539	R208	R126	R923	R1,988	R469	R1,837	R4,294	R8,090
2011P	2,047	4,511	9,236	3,171	226	158	1,168	1,987	477	1,947	4,411	9,135

1 Production equals consumption for all renewable energy sources except biofuels.
2 Total biomass inputs to the production of fuel ethanol and biodiesel.
3 Wood and wood-derived fuels, biomass waste, and total biomass inputs to the production of fuel ethanol and biodiesel.
4 Hydroelectric power, geothermal, solar thermal/photovoltaic, wind, and biomass.
5 Conventional hydroelectricity net generation (converted to Btu using the fossil-fuels heat rate—see Table A6).
6 Geothermal electricity net generation (converted to Btu using the fossil-fuels heat rate—see Table A6), and geothermal heat pump and direct use energy.
7 Solar thermal and photovoltaic (PV) electricity net generation (converted to Btu using the fossil-fuels heat rate—see Table A6), and solar thermal direct use energy.
8 Wind electricity net generation (converted to Btu using the fossil-fuels heat rate—see Table A6).
9 Wood and wood-derived fuels.
10 Municipal solid waste from biogenic sources, landfill gas, sludge waste, agricultural byproducts, and other biomass. Through 2000, also includes non-renewable waste (municipal solid waste from non-biogenic sources, and tire-derived fuels).
11 Fuel ethanol (minus denaturant) and biodiesel consumption, plus losses and co-products from the production of fuel ethanol and biodiesel.

R=Revised. P=Preliminary. NA=Not available. (s)=Less than 0.5 trillion Btu.

Notes: • Most data for the residential, commercial, industrial, and transportation sectors are estimates. See notes and sources for Tables 10.2a and 10.2b. • See Tables 8.2a–8.2d and 8.3a–8.3c for electricity net generation and useful thermal output from renewable energy sources; Tables 8.4a–8.4c, 8.5a–8.5d, 8.6a–8.6c, and 8.7a–8.7c for renewable energy consumption for electricity generation and useful thermal output; and Tables 8.11a–8.11d for renewable energy electric net summer capacity. • See Note, "Renewable Energy Production and Consumption," at end of section. • See Table E1 for estimated renewable energy consumption for 1635–1945. • Totals may not equal sum of components due to independent rounding.

Web Pages: • See http://www.eia.gov/totalenergy/data/monthly/#renewable for updated monthly and annual data. • See http://www.eia.gov/totalenergy/data/annual/#renewable for all annual data beginning in 1949. • See http://www.eia.gov/renewable/ for related information.

Sources: **Biofuels:** Tables 10.3 and 10.4. **All Other Data:** Tables 10.2a–10.2c.

***Source:** U.S. Energy Information Administration, Annual Energy Review 2011*

Figure 10.2a Renewable Energy Consumption: End-Use Sectors, 1989-2011

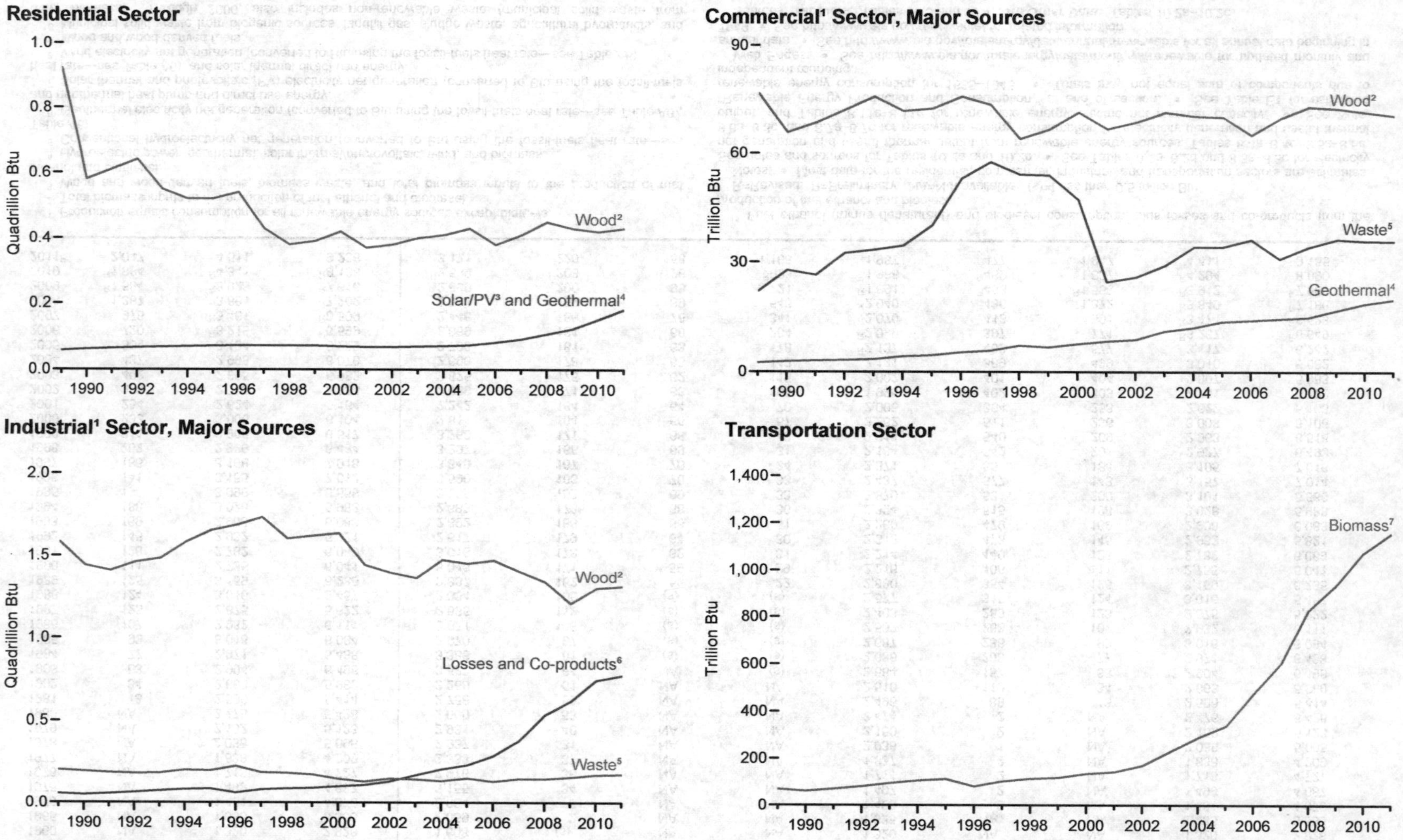

[1] Includes fuel used at combined-heat-and-power (CHP) plants and a small number of electricity-only plants.
[2] Wood and wood-derived fuels.
[3] Solar thermal direct use energy, and photovoltaic (PV) electricity net generation. Includes small amounts of distributed solar thermal and PV energy used in the commercial, industrial, and electric power sectors.
[4] Geothermal heat pump and direct use energy.
[5] Municipal solid waste from biogenic sources, landfill gas, sludge waste, agricultural byproducts, and other biomass. Through 2000, also includes non-renewable waste (municipal solid waste from non-biogenic sources, and tire-derived fuels).
[6] From the production of fuel ethanol and biodiesel.
[7] The fuel ethanol (minus denaturant) portion of motor fuels (such as E10 and E85), and biodiesel. See "Biodiesel" in Glossary.

Note: See related Figures 10.2b and 10.2c.
Sources: Tables 10.2a and 10.2b.

Source: *U.S. Energy Information Administration, Annual Energy Review 2011*

Figure 10.2b Renewable Energy Consumption: End-Use Sectors and Electric Power Sector

End-Use Sectors, 1949-2011

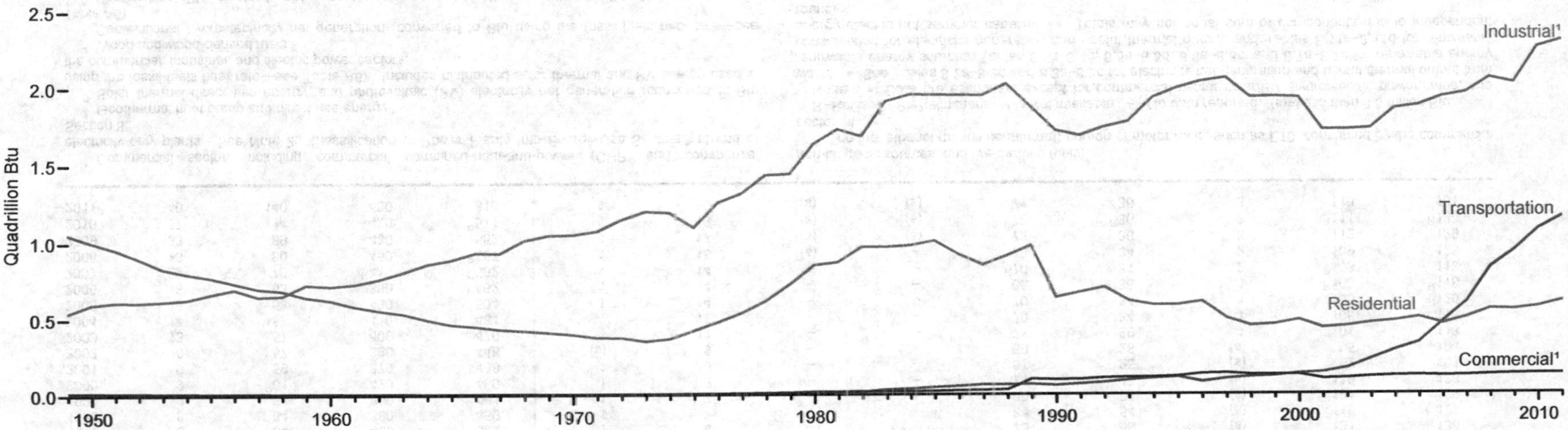

End-Use Sectors and Electric Power Sector, 2011

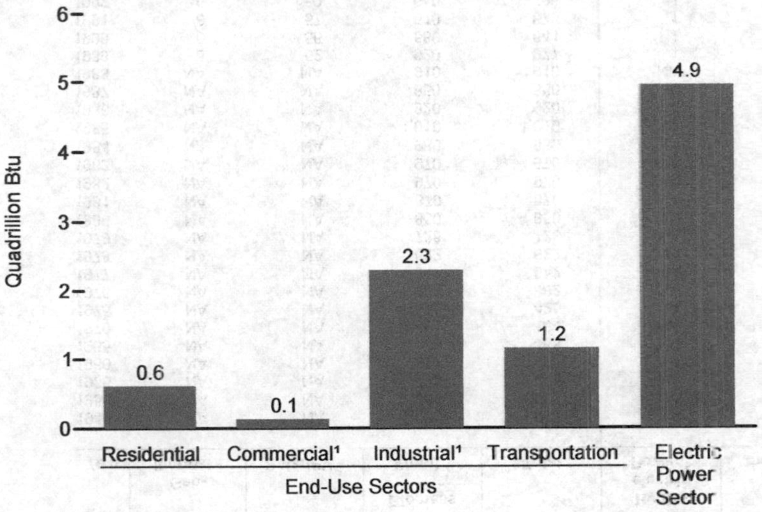

End-Use Sectors and Electric Power Sector Shares of Total Renewable Energy Consumption, 2011

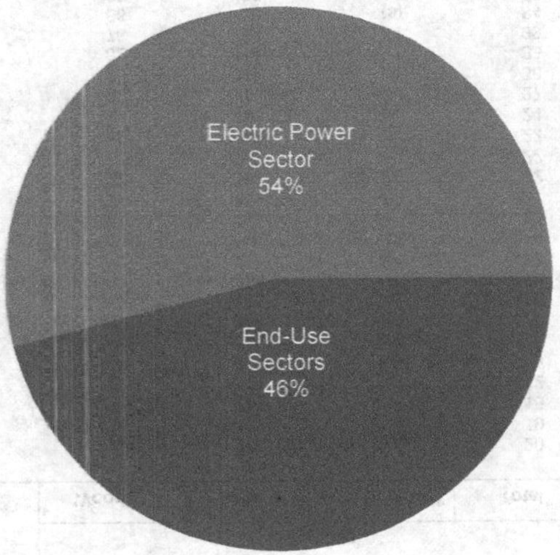

[1] Includes fuel use at combined-heat-and-power (CHP) plants and a small number of electricity-only plants.

Note: See related Figures 10.2a and 10.2c.
Sources: Tables 10.2a-10.2c.

Source: *U.S. Energy Information Administration, Annual Energy Review 2011*

Table 10.2a Renewable Energy Consumption: Residential and Commercial Sectors, Selected Years, 1949-2011

(Trillion Btu)

Year	Residential Sector				Commercial Sector [1]								
	Geo-thermal [2]	Solar/PV [3]	Biomass: Wood [4]	Total	Hydro-electric Power [5]	Geo-thermal [2]	Solar/PV [6]	Wind [7]	Biomass: Wood [4]	Biomass: Waste [8]	Biomass: Fuel Ethanol [9]	Biomass: Total	Total
1949	NA	NA	1,055	1,055	NA	NA	NA	NA	20	NA	NA	20	20
1950	NA	NA	1,006	1,006	NA	NA	NA	NA	19	NA	NA	19	19
1955	NA	NA	775	775	NA	NA	NA	NA	15	NA	NA	15	15
1960	NA	NA	627	627	NA	NA	NA	NA	12	NA	NA	12	12
1965	NA	NA	468	468	NA	NA	NA	NA	9	NA	NA	9	9
1970	NA	NA	401	401	NA	NA	NA	NA	8	NA	NA	8	8
1975	NA	NA	425	425	NA	NA	NA	NA	8	NA	NA	8	8
1976	NA	NA	482	482	NA	NA	NA	NA	9	NA	NA	9	9
1977	NA	NA	542	542	NA	NA	NA	NA	10	NA	NA	10	10
1978	NA	NA	622	622	NA	NA	NA	NA	12	NA	NA	12	12
1979	NA	NA	728	728	NA	NA	NA	NA	14	NA	NA	14	14
1980	NA	NA	850	850	NA	NA	NA	NA	21	NA	NA	21	21
1981	NA	NA	870	870	NA	NA	NA	NA	21	NA	(s)	21	21
1982	NA	NA	970	970	NA	NA	NA	NA	22	NA	(s)	22	22
1983	NA	NA	970	970	NA	NA	NA	NA	22	NA	(s)	22	22
1984	NA	NA	980	980	NA	NA	NA	NA	22	NA	(s)	22	22
1985	NA	NA	1,010	1,010	NA	NA	NA	NA	24	NA	(s)	24	24
1986	NA	NA	920	920	NA	NA	NA	NA	27	NA	(s)	27	27
1987	NA	NA	850	850	NA	NA	NA	NA	29	NA	1	30	30
1988	NA	NA	910	910	NA	NA	NA	NA	32	NA	1	33	33
1989	5	52	920	977	1	3	–	–	76	22	1	99	102
1990	6	56	580	641	1	3	–	–	66	28	(s)	94	98
1991	6	57	610	673	1	3	–	–	68	26	(s)	95	100
1992	6	R60	640	706	1	3	–	–	72	32	(s)	105	109
1993	7	61	550	618	1	3	–	–	76	33	(s)	109	114
1994	6	63	520	589	1	4	–	–	72	35	(s)	106	112
1995	7	64	520	591	1	5	–	–	72	40	(s)	113	118
1996	7	65	540	612	1	5	–	–	76	53	(s)	129	135
1997	8	64	430	502	1	6	–	–	73	58	(s)	131	138
1998	8	64	380	452	1	7	–	–	64	54	(s)	118	127
1999	9	63	390	461	1	7	–	–	67	54	(s)	121	129
2000	9	R61	420	489	1	8	–	–	71	47	(s)	119	128
2001	9	59	370	438	1	8	–	–	67	25	(s)	92	101
2002	10	57	380	448	(s)	9	–	–	69	26	(s)	95	104
2003	13	57	400	470	1	11	–	–	71	29	1	101	113
2004	14	57	410	481	1	12	–	–	70	34	1	105	118
2005	16	58	430	504	1	14	–	–	70	34	1	105	R120
2006	18	63	R380	R462	1	14	–	–	65	36	1	R103	R118
2007	22	70	R410	R502	1	14	–	–	R70	31	2	R103	118
2008	26	80	450	R557	1	15	(s)	–	73	34	2	109	125
2009	33	89	430	552	1	17	(s)	(s)	72	36	3	112	129
2010	37	R114	420	R571	1	19	(s)	(s)	R72	R36	3	R111	R130
2011P	40	140	430	610	1	20	(s)	(s)	71	36	3	110	131

[1] Commercial sector, including commercial combined-heat-and-power (CHP) and commercial electricity-only plants. See Note 2, "Classification of Power Plants Into Energy-Use Sectors," at end of Section 8.

[2] Geothermal heat pump and direct use energy.

[3] Solar thermal direct use energy, and photovoltaic (PV) electricity net generation (converted to Btu using the fossil-fuels heat rate—see Table A6). Includes distributed solar thermal and PV energy used in the commercial, industrial, and electric power sectors.

[4] Wood and wood-derived fuels.

[5] Conventional hydroelectricity net generation (converted to Btu using the fossil-fuels heat rate—see Table A6).

[6] Photovoltaic (PV) electricity net generation (converted to Btu using the fossil-fuels heat rate—see Table A6) at commercial plants with capacity of 1 megawatt or greater.

[7] Wind electricity net generation (converted to Btu using the fossil-fuels heat rate—see Table A6).

[8] Municipal solid waste from biogenic sources, landfill gas, sludge waste, agricultural byproducts, and other biomass. Through 2000, also includes non-renewable waste (municipal solid waste from non-biogenic sources, and tire-derived fuels).

[9] The fuel ethanol (minus denaturant) portion of motor fuels, such as E10, consumed by the commercial sector.

R=Revised. P=Preliminary. NA=Not available. – =No data reported. (s)=Less than 0.5 trillion Btu.

Notes: • Data are estimates, except for commercial sector solar/PV, hydroelectric power, wind, and waste. • See Tables 8.2a–8.2d and 8.3a–8.3c for electricity net generation and useful thermal output from renewable energy sources; Tables 8.4a–8.4c, 8.5a–8.5d, 8.6a–8.6c, and 8.7a–8.7c for renewable energy consumption for electricity generation and useful thermal output; and Tables 8.11a–8.11d for renewable energy electric net summer capacity. • Totals may not equal sum of components due to independent rounding.

Web Pages: • See http://www.eia.gov/totalenergy/data/monthly/#renewable for updated monthly and annual data. • See http://www.eia.gov/totalenergy/data/annual/#renewable for all annual data beginning in 1949. • See http://www.eia.gov/renewable/ for related information.

Sources: See end of section.

***Source:** U.S. Energy Information Administration, Annual Energy Review 2011*

Table 10.2b Renewable Energy Consumption: Industrial and Transportation Sectors, Selected Years, 1949-2011

(Trillion Btu)

	Industrial Sector [1]										Transportation Sector		
					Biomass						Biomass		
Year	Hydro-electric Power [2]	Geo-thermal [3]	Solar/PV [4]	Wind [5]	Wood [6]	Waste [7]	Fuel Ethanol [8]	Losses and Co-products [9]	Total	Total	Fuel Ethanol [10]	Biodiesel	Total
1949	76	NA	NA	NA	468	NA	NA	NA	468	544	NA	NA	NA
1950	69	NA	NA	NA	532	NA	NA	NA	532	602	NA	NA	NA
1955	38	NA	NA	NA	631	NA	NA	NA	631	669	NA	NA	NA
1960	39	NA	NA	NA	680	NA	NA	NA	680	719	NA	NA	NA
1965	33	NA	NA	NA	855	NA	NA	NA	855	888	NA	NA	NA
1970	34	NA	NA	NA	1,019	NA	NA	NA	1,019	1,053	NA	NA	NA
1975	32	NA	NA	NA	1,063	NA	NA	NA	1,063	1,096	NA	NA	NA
1976	33	NA	NA	NA	1,220	NA	NA	NA	1,220	1,253	NA	NA	NA
1977	33	NA	NA	NA	1,281	NA	NA	NA	1,281	1,314	NA	NA	NA
1978	32	NA	NA	NA	1,400	NA	NA	NA	1,400	1,432	NA	NA	NA
1979	34	NA	NA	NA	1,405	NA	NA	NA	1,405	1,439	NA	NA	NA
1980	33	NA	NA	NA	1,600	NA	NA	NA	1,600	1,633	NA	NA	NA
1981	33	NA	NA	NA	1,602	87	(s)	6	1,695	1,728	7	NA	7
1982	33	NA	NA	NA	1,516	118	(s)	16	1,650	1,683	18	NA	18
1983	33	NA	NA	NA	1,690	155	(s)	29	1,874	1,908	34	NA	34
1984	33	NA	NA	NA	1,679	204	1	35	1,918	1,951	41	NA	41
1985	33	NA	NA	NA	1,645	230	1	42	1,918	1,951	50	NA	50
1986	33	NA	NA	NA	1,610	256	1	48	1,915	1,948	57	NA	57
1987	33	NA	NA	NA	1,576	282	1	55	1,914	1,947	66	NA	66
1988	33	NA	NA	NA	1,625	308	1	55	1,989	2,022	67	NA	67
1989	28	2	–	–	1,584	200	1	56	1,841	1,871	68	NA	68
1990	31	2	–	–	1,442	192	1	49	1,684	1,717	60	NA	60
1991	30	2	–	–	1,410	185	1	56	1,652	1,684	70	NA	70
1992	31	2	–	–	1,461	179	1	64	1,705	1,737	80	NA	80
1993	30	2	–	–	1,484	181	1	74	1,741	1,773	94	NA	94
1994	62	3	–	–	1,580	199	1	82	1,862	1,927	105	NA	105
1995	55	3	–	–	1,652	195	2	86	1,934	1,992	112	NA	112
1996	61	3	–	–	1,683	224	1	61	1,969	2,033	81	NA	81
1997	58	3	–	–	1,731	184	1	80	1,996	2,057	102	NA	102
1998	55	3	–	–	1,603	180	1	86	1,872	1,929	113	NA	113
1999	49	4	–	–	1,620	171	1	90	1,882	1,934	118	NA	118
2000	42	4	–	–	1,636	145	1	99	1,881	1,928	135	NA	135
2001	33	5	–	–	1,443	129	3	108	1,681	1,719	141	1	142
2002	39	5	–	–	1,396	146	3	130	1,676	1,720	168	2	170
2003	43	3	–	–	1,363	142	4	159	1,679	1,726	228	2	230
2004	33	4	–	–	1,476	132	6	203	1,817	1,853	286	3	290
2005	32	4	–	–	1,452	148	7	230	1,837	1,873	327	12	339
2006	29	4	–	–	1,472	130	10	285	1,897	1,930	442	33	475
2007	16	5	–	–	R1,405	144	10	377	R1,936	R1,956	557	46	602
2008	17	5	–	–	R1,340	144	12	532	R2,028	R2,049	786	40	826
2009	18	4	–	–	R1,208	R155	13	617	R1,994	R2,016	894	R42	R935
2010	16	4	(s)	–	R1,301	R169	R17	R742	R2,230	R2,250	R1,040	R34	R1,074
2011P	18	4	(s)	(s)	1,311	172	17	772	2,273	2,295	1,042	112	1,154

[1] Industrial sector, including industrial combined-heat-and-power (CHP) and industrial electricity-only plants. See Note 2, "Classification of Power Plants Into Energy-Use Sectors," at end of Section 8.
[2] Conventional hydroelectricity net generation (converted to Btu using the fossil-fuels heat rate—see Table A6).
[3] Geothermal heat pump and direct use energy.
[4] Photovoltaic (PV) electricity net generation (converted to Btu using the fossil-fuels heat rate—see Table A6) at industrial plants with capacity of 1 megawatt or greater.
[5] Wind electricity net generation (converted to Btu using the fossil-fuels heat rate—see Table A6).
[6] Wood and wood-derived fuels.
[7] Municipal solid waste from biogenic sources, landfill gas, sludge waste, agricultural byproducts, and other biomass. Through 2000, also includes non-renewable waste (municipal solid waste from non-biogenic sources, and tire-derived fuels).
[8] The fuel ethanol (minus denaturant) portion of motor fuels, such as E10, consumed by the industrial sector.
[9] Losses and co-products from the production of fuel ethanol and biodiesel. Does not include natural gas, electricity, and other non-biomass energy used in the production of fuel ethanol and biodiesel—these are included in the industrial sector consumption statistics for the appropriate energy source.
[10] The fuel ethanol (minus denaturant) portion of motor fuels, such as E10 and E85, consumed by the transportation sector.

R=Revised. P=Preliminary. NA=Not available. – =No data reported. (s)=Less than 0.5 trillion Btu.

Notes: • Data are estimates, except for industrial sector hydroelectric power in 1949–1978 and 1989 forward, solar/PV, and wind. • See Tables 8.2a–8.2d and 8.3a–8.3c for electricity net generation and useful thermal output from renewable energy sources; Tables 8.4a–8.4c, 8.5a–8.5d, 8.6a–8.6c, and 8.7a–8.7c for renewable energy consumption for electricity generation and useful thermal output; and Tables 8.11a–8.11d for renewable energy electric net summer capacity. • Totals may not equal sum of components due to independent rounding.

Web Pages: • See http://www.eia.gov/totalenergy/data/monthly/#renewable for updated monthly and annual data. • See http://www.eia.gov/totalenergy/data/annual/#renewable for all annual data beginning in 1949. • See http://www.eia.gov/renewable/ for related information.

Sources: See end of section.

Source: *U.S. Energy Information Administration, Annual Energy Review 2011*

Figure 10.2c Renewable Energy Consumption: Electric Power Sector

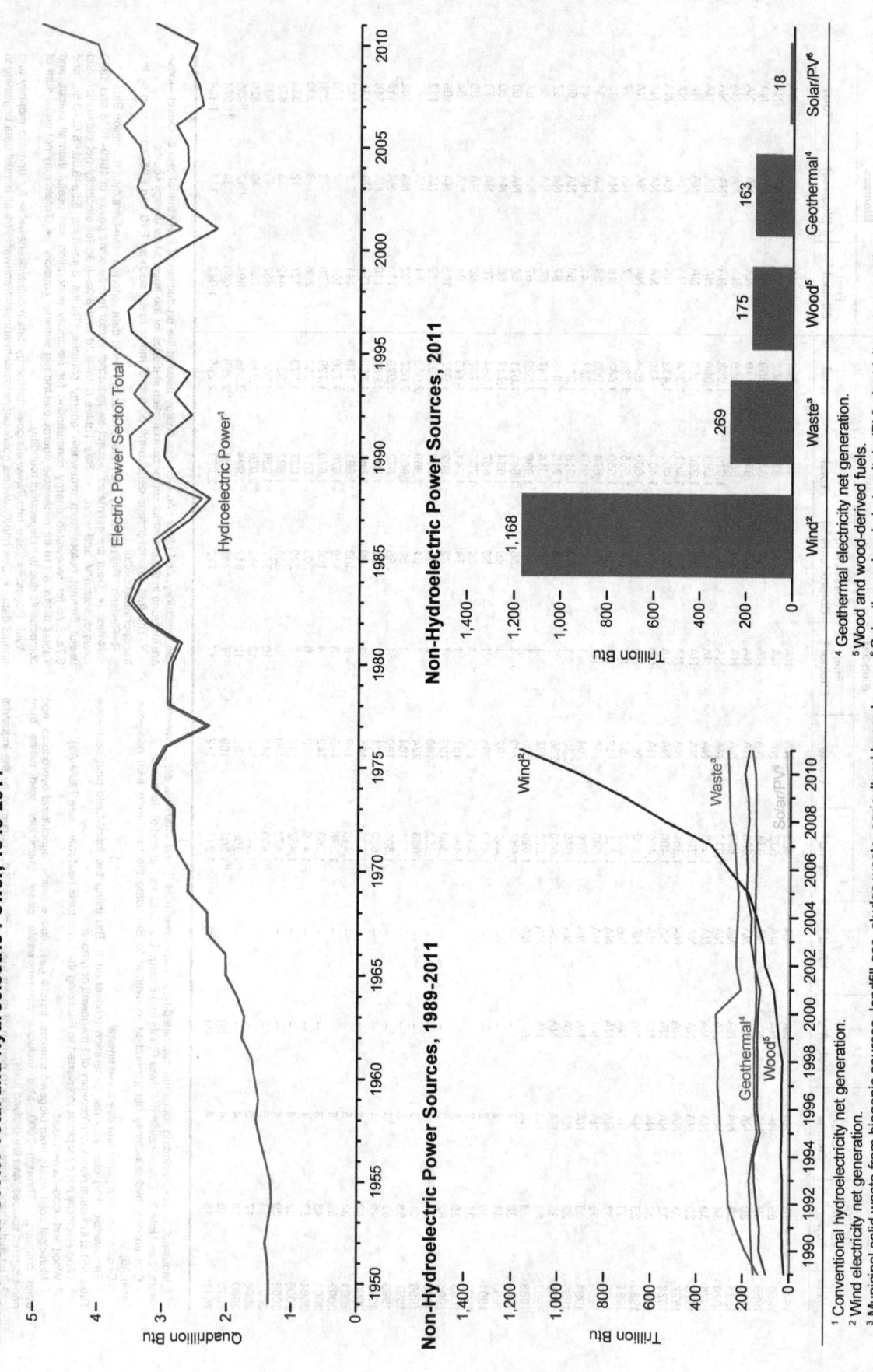

Electric Power Sector Total and Hydroelectric Power, 1949-2011

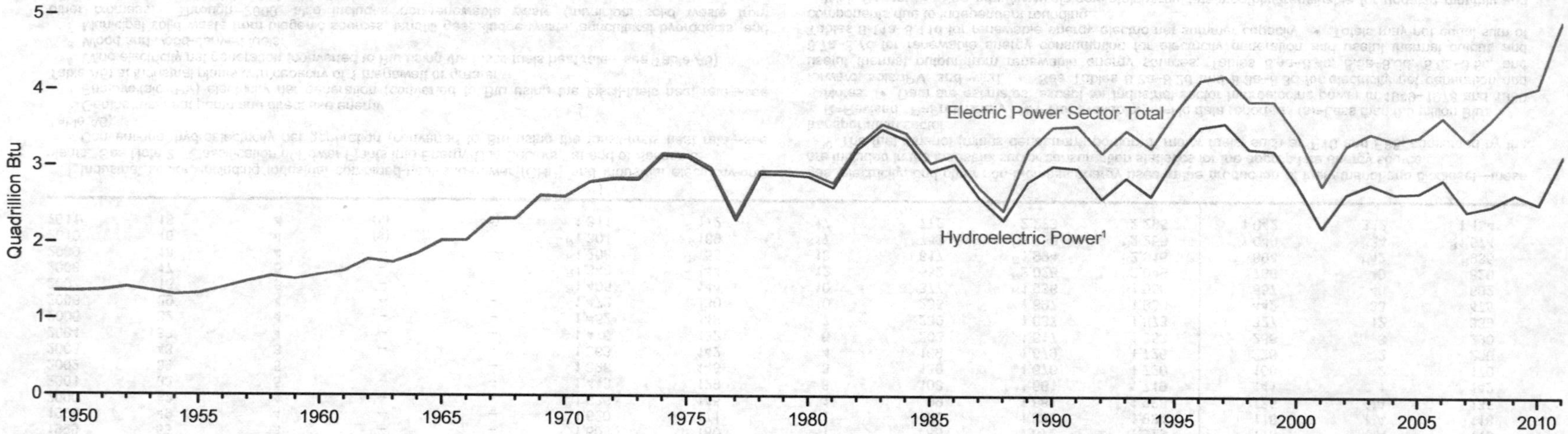

Non-Hydroelectric Power Sources, 1989-2011

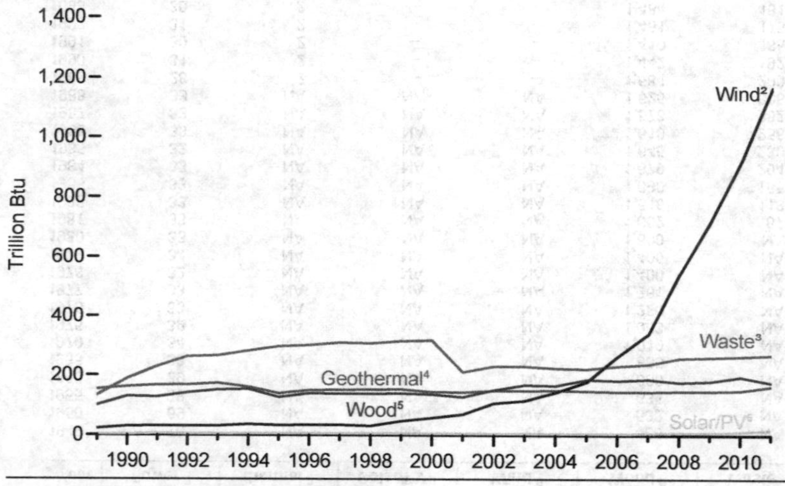

Non-Hydroelectric Power Sources, 2011

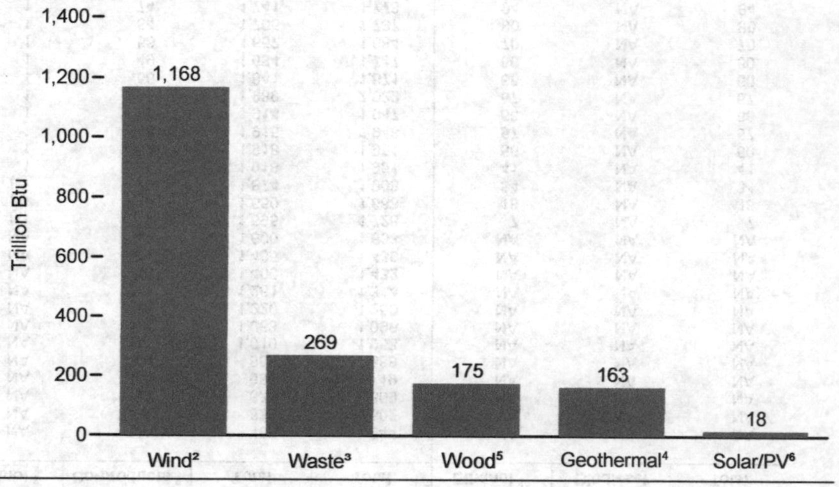

[1] Conventional hydroelectricity net generation.
[2] Wind electricity net generation.
[3] Municipal solid waste from biogenic sources, landfill gas, sludge waste, agricultural byproducts, and other biomass. Through 2000, also includes non-renewable waste (municipal solid waste from non-biogenic sources, and tire-derived fuels).
[4] Geothermal electricity net generation.
[5] Wood and wood-derived fuels.
[6] Solar thermal and photovoltaic (PV) electricity net generation.

Note: See related Figures 10.2a and 10.2b on the end-use sectors.
Source: Table 10.2c.

Source: *U.S. Energy Information Administration, Annual Energy Review 2011*

Table 10.2c Renewable Energy Consumption: Electric Power Sector, Selected Years, 1949-2011

(Trillion Btu)

Year	Hydroelectric Power [1]	Geothermal [2]	Solar/PV [3]	Wind [4]	Biomass: Wood [5]	Biomass: Waste [6]	Biomass: Total	Total
1949	1,349	NA	NA	NA	6	NA	6	1,355
1950	1,346	NA	NA	NA	5	NA	5	1,351
1955	1,322	NA	NA	NA	3	NA	3	1,325
1960	1,569	(s)	NA	NA	2	NA	2	1,571
1965	2,026	2	NA	NA	3	NA	3	2,031
1970	2,600	6	NA	NA	1	2	4	2,609
1975	3,122	34	NA	NA	(s)	2	2	3,158
1976	2,943	38	NA	NA	1	2	3	2,983
1977	2,301	37	NA	NA	3	2	5	2,343
1978	2,905	31	NA	NA	2	1	3	2,940
1979	2,897	40	NA	NA	3	2	5	2,942
1980	2,867	53	NA	NA	3	2	5	2,925
1981	2,725	59	NA	NA	3	1	4	2,788
1982	3,233	51	NA	NA	2	1	3	3,286
1983	3,494	64	NA	(s)	2	2	4	3,562
1984	3,353	81	(s)	(s)	5	4	9	3,443
1985	2,937	97	(s)	(s)	8	7	14	3,049
1986	3,038	108	(s)	(s)	5	7	12	3,158
1987	2,602	112	(s)	(s)	8	7	15	2,729
1988	2,302	106	(s)	(s)	10	8	17	2,425
1989[7]	2,808	152	3	22	100	132	232	3,217
1990	3,014	161	4	29	129	188	317	3,524
1991	2,985	167	5	31	126	229	354	3,542
1992	2,586	167	4	30	140	262	402	3,189
1993	2,861	173	5	31	150	265	415	3,484
1994	2,620	160	5	36	152	282	434	3,255
1995	3,149	138	5	33	125	296	422	3,747
1996	3,528	148	5	33	138	300	438	4,153
1997	3,581	150	5	34	137	309	446	4,216
1998	3,241	151	5	31	137	308	444	3,872
1999	3,218	152	5	46	138	315	453	3,874
2000	2,768	144	5	57	134	318	453	3,427
2001	2,209	142	6	70	126	211	337	2,763
2002	2,650	147	6	105	150	230	380	3,288
2003	2,781	148	5	115	167	230	397	3,445
2004	2,656	148	6	142	165	223	388	3,340
2005	2,670	147	6	178	185	221	406	3,406
2006	2,839	145	5	264	182	231	412	3,665
2007	2,430	145	6	341	186	237	423	3,345
2008	2,494	146	9	546	177	258	435	3,630
2009	2,650	146	9	721	180	261	441	3,967
2010	R2,521	R148	R12	R923	R196	R264	R459	R4,064
2011P	3,153	163	18	1,168	175	269	444	4,945

[1] Conventional hydroelectricity net generation (converted to Btu using the fossil-fuels heat rate—see Table A6).
[2] Geothermal electricity net generation (converted to Btu using the fossil-fuels heat rate—see Table A6).
[3] Solar thermal and photovoltaic (PV) electricity net generation (converted to Btu using the fossil-fuels heat rate—see Table A6).
[4] Wind electricity net generation (converted to Btu using the fossil-fuels heat rate—see Table A6).
[5] Wood and wood-derived fuels.
[6] Municipal solid waste from biogenic sources, landfill gas, sludge waste, agricultural byproducts, and other biomass. Through 2000, also includes non-renewable waste (municipal solid waste from non-biogenic sources, and tire-derived fuels).
[7] Through 1988, data are for electric utilities only. Beginning in 1989, data are for electric utilities and independent power producers.

R=Revised. P=Preliminary. NA=Not available. (s)=Less than 0.5 trillion Btu.

Notes: • The electric power sector comprises electricity-only and combined-heat-and-power (CHP) plants within the NAICS 22 category whose primary business is to sell electricity, or electricity and heat, to the public. • See Tables 8.2a–8.2d and 8.3a–8.3c for electricity net generation and useful thermal output from renewable energy sources; Tables 8.4a–8.4c, 8.5a–8.5d, 8.6a–8.6c, and 8.7a–8.7c for renewable energy consumption for electricity generation and useful thermal output; and Tables 8.11a–8.11d for renewable energy electric net summer capacity. • See Note 3, "Electricity Imports and Exports," at end of Section 8. • Totals may not equal sum of components due to independent rounding.

Web Pages: • See http://www.eia.gov/totalenergy/data/monthly/#renewable for updated monthly and annual data. • See http://www.eia.gov/totalenergy/data/annual/#renewable for all annual data beginning in 1949. • See http://www.eia.gov/renewable/ for related information.

Sources: Tables 8.2b, 3.5c, 8.7b, and A6.

Source: *U.S. Energy Information Administration, Annual Energy Review 2011*

Figure 10.5 Estimated Number of Alternative-Fueled Vehicles in Use and Alternative Fuel Consumption

Vehicles in Use, 1995-2010

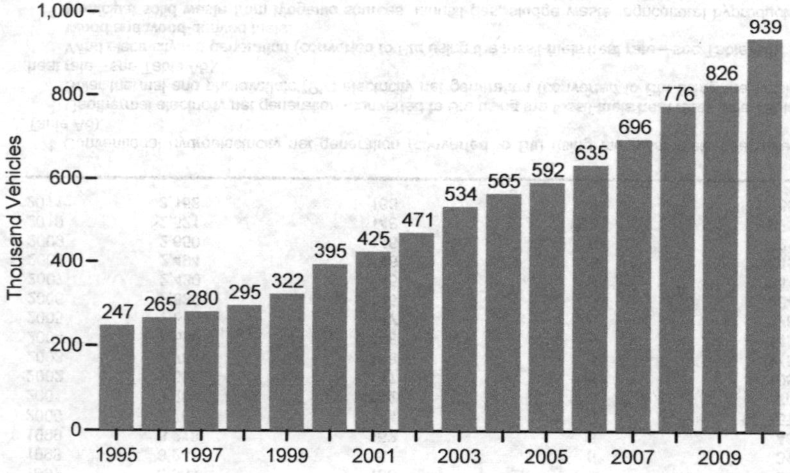

Vehicles in Use by Fuel Type, 2010

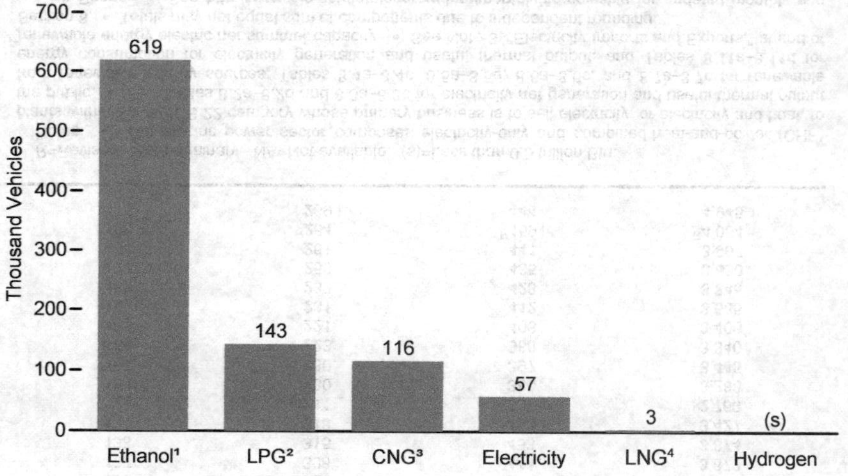

Fuel Consumption,[5] 1995-2010

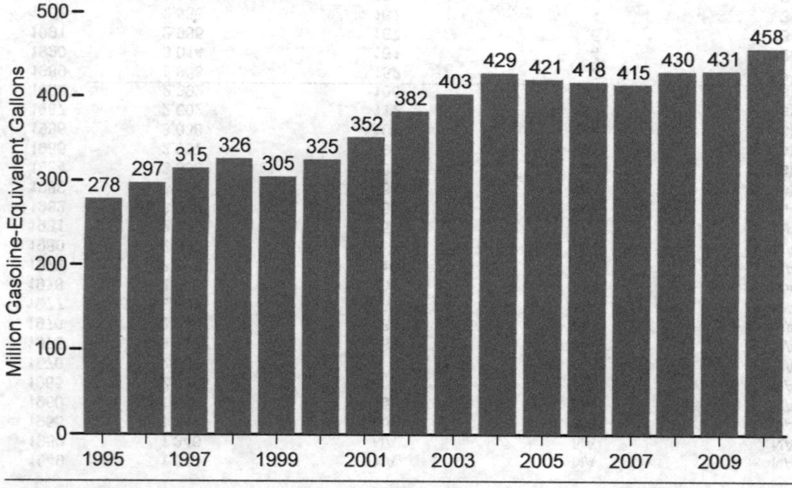

Fuel Consumption by Type, 2010

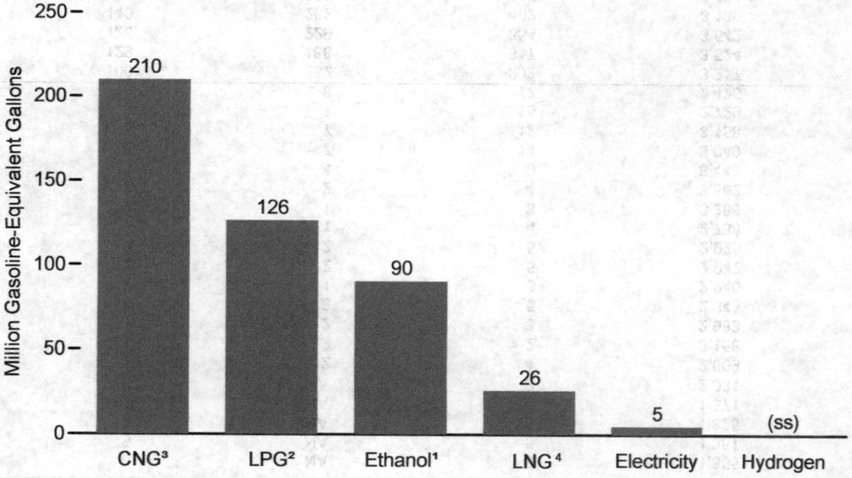

[1] Ethanol, 85 percent (E85). Includes only those E85 vehicles believed to be used as alternative-fueled vehicles, primarily fleet-operated vehicles; excludes other vehicles with E85-fueling capability.

[2] Liquefied petroleum gases.

[3] Compressed natural gas.

[4] Liquefied natural gas.

[5] Excludes oxygenates and biodiesel.

(s)=Fewer than 0.5 thousand vehicles.

(ss)=Less than 0.5 million gasoline-equivalent gallons.

Source: Table 10.5.

Source: *U.S. Energy Information Administration, Annual Energy Review 2011*

Table 10.5 Estimated Number of Alternative-Fueled Vehicles in Use and Fuel Consumption, 1992-2010

Year	Alternative and Replacement Fuels [1]											Oxygenates [2]				
	Liquefied Petroleum Gases	Compressed Natural Gas	Liquefied Natural Gas	Methanol, 85 Percent (M85) [3]	Methanol, Neat (M100) [4]	Ethanol, 85 Percent (E85) [3,5]	Ethanol, 95 Percent (E95) [3]	Electricity [6]	Hydrogen	Other Fuels [7]	Subtotal	Methyl Tertiary Butyl Ether [8]	Ethanol in Gasohol [9]	Total	Biodiesel [10]	Total
	Alternative-Fueled Vehicles in Use [11] (number)															
1992	NA	23,191	90	4,850	404	172	38	1,607	NA	NA	NA	NA	NA	NA	NA	NA
1993	NA	32,714	299	10,263	414	441	27	1,690	NA	NA	NA	NA	NA	NA	NA	NA
1994	NA	41,227	484	15,484	415	605	33	2,224	NA	NA	NA	NA	NA	NA	NA	NA
1995	172,806	50,218	603	18,319	386	1,527	136	2,860	0	0	246,855	NA	NA	NA	NA	NA
1996	175,585	60,144	663	20,265	172	4,536	361	3,280	0	0	265,006	NA	NA	NA	NA	NA
1997	175,679	68,571	813	21,040	172	9,130	347	4,453	0	0	280,205	NA	NA	NA	NA	NA
1998	177,183	78,782	1,172	19,648	200	12,788	14	5,243	0	0	295,030	NA	NA	NA	NA	NA
1999	178,610	91,267	1,681	18,964	198	24,604	14	6,964	0	0	322,302	NA	NA	NA	NA	NA
2000	181,994	100,750	2,090	10,426	0	87,570	4	11,830	0	0	394,664	NA	NA	NA	NA	NA
2001	185,053	111,851	2,576	7,827	0	100,303	0	17,847	0	0	425,457	NA	NA	NA	NA	NA
2002	187,680	120,839	2,708	5,873	0	120,951	0	33,047	0	0	471,098	NA	NA	NA	NA	NA
2003	190,369	114,406	2,640	0	0	179,090	0	47,485	9	0	533,999	NA	NA	NA	NA	NA
2004	182,864	118,532	2,717	0	0	211,800	0	49,536	43	0	565,492	NA	NA	NA	NA	NA
2005	173,795	117,699	2,748	0	0	246,363	0	51,398	119	3	592,125	NA	NA	NA	NA	NA
2006	164,846	116,131	2,798	0	0	297,099	0	53,526	159	3	634,562	NA	NA	NA	NA	NA
2007	158,254	114,391	2,781	0	0	364,384	0	55,730	223	3	695,766	NA	NA	NA	NA	NA
2008	151,049	113,973	3,101	0	0	450,327	0	56,901	313	3	775,667	NA	NA	NA	NA	NA
2009	147,030	114,270	3,176	0	0	504,297	0	57,185	357	3	826,318	NA	NA	NA	NA	NA
2010	143,037	115,863	3,354	0	0	618,505	0	57,462	421	0	938,643	NA	NA	NA	NA	NA
	Fuel Consumption [12] (thousand gasoline-equivalent gallons)															
1992	NA	17,159	598	1,121	2,672	22	87	359	NA	NA	NA	1,175,964	719,408	1,895,372	NA	NA
1993	NA	22,035	1,944	1,671	3,321	49	82	288	NA	NA	NA	2,070,897	779,958	2,850,854	NA	NA
1994	NA	24,643	2,398	2,455	3,347	82	144	430	NA	NA	NA	2,020,455	868,113	2,888,569	NA	NA
1995	233,178	35,865	2,821	2,122	2,255	195	1,021	663	0	0	278,121	2,693,407	934,615	3,628,022	NA	3,906,142
1996	239,648	47,861	3,320	1,862	364	712	2,770	773	0	0	297,310	2,751,955	677,537	3,429,492	NA	3,726,802
1997	238,845	66,495	3,798	1,630	364	1,314	1,166	1,010	0	0	314,621	3,106,745	852,514	3,959,260	NA	4,273,880
1998	241,881	73,859	5,463	1,271	471	1,772	61	1,202	0	0	325,980	2,905,781	912,858	3,818,639	NA	4,144,620
1999	210,247	81,211	5,959	1,126	469	4,019	64	1,524	0	0	304,618	3,405,390	975,255	4,380,645	NA	4,685,263
2000	213,012	88,478	7,423	614	0	12,388	13	3,058	0	0	324,986	3,298,803	1,114,313	4,413,116	6,828	4,744,930
2001	216,319	106,584	9,122	461	0	15,007	0	4,066	0	0	351,558	3,354,949	1,173,323	4,528,272	10,627	4,890,457
2002	223,600	123,081	9,593	354	0	18,250	0	7,274	0	0	382,152	3,122,859	1,450,721	4,573,580	16,824	4,972,556
2003	224,697	133,222	13,503	0	0	26,376	0	5,141	2	0	402,941	2,368,400	1,919,572	4,287,972	14,082	4,704,995
2004	211,883	158,903	20,888	0	0	31,581	0	5,269	8	0	428,532	1,877,300	2,414,167	4,291,467	27,616	4,747,615
2005	188,171	166,878	22,409	0	0	38,074	0	5,219	25	2	420,778	1,654,500	2,756,663	4,411,163	93,281	4,925,222
2006	173,130	172,011	23,474	0	0	44,041	0	5,104	41	2	417,803	435,000	3,729,168	4,164,168	267,623	4,849,594
2007	152,360	178,565	24,594	0	0	54,091	0	5,037	66	2	414,715	0	4,694,304	4,694,304	367,764	5,476,783
2008	147,784	189,358	25,554	0	0	62,464	0	5,050	117	2	430,329	0	6,442,781	6,442,781	324,329	7,197,439
2009	129,631	199,513	25,652	0	0	71,213	0	4,956	140	2	431,107	0	7,343,133	7,343,133	325,102	8,099,342
2010	126,354	210,007	26,072	0	0	90,323	0	4,847	152	0	457,755	0	8,527,431	8,527,431	235,188	9,220,374

[1] See "Alternative Fuel" and "Replacement Fuel" in Glossary.
[2] See "Oxygenates" in Glossary.
[3] Remaining portion is motor gasoline. Consumption data include the motor gasoline portion of the fuel.
[4] One hundred percent methanol.
[5] Includes only those E85 vehicles believed to be used as alternative-fuels vehicles (AFVs), primarily fleet-operated vehicles; excludes other vehicles with E85-fueling capability. In 1997, some vehicle manufacturers began including E85-fueling capability in certain model lines of vehicles. For 2010, the U.S. Energy Information Administration (EIA) estimates that the number of E85 vehicles that are capable of operating on E85, motor gasoline, or both, is about 10 million. Many of these AFVs are sold and used as traditional gasoline-powered vehicles.
[6] Excludes gasoline-electric hybrids.
[7] May include P-Series fuel or any other fuel designated by the Secretary of Energy as an alternative fuel in accordance with the Energy Policy Act of 1995.
[8] In addition to methyl tertiary butyl ether (MTBE), includes a very small amount of other ethers, primarily tertiary amyl methyl ether (TAME) and ethyl tertiary butyl ether (ETBE).
[9] Data do not include the motor gasoline portion of the fuel.
[10] "Biodiesel" may be used as a diesel fuel substitute or diesel fuel additive or extender. See "Biodiesel" in Glossary.
[11] "Vehicles in Use" data represent accumulated acquisitions, less retirements, as of the end of each calendar year; data do not include concept and demonstration vehicles that are not ready for delivery to end users. See "Alternative-Fuel Vehicle" in Glossary.
[12] Fuel consumption quantities are expressed in a common base unit of gasoline-equivalent gallons to allow comparisons of different fuel types. Gasoline-equivalent gallons do not represent gasoline displacement. Gasoline equivalent is computed by dividing the gross heat content of the replacement fuel by the gross heat content of gasoline (using an approximate heat content of 122,619 Btu per gallon) and multiplying the result by the replacement fuel consumption value. See "Heat Content" in Glossary.

NA=Not available.

Note: Totals may not equal sum of components due to independent rounding.

Web Page: For related information, see http://www.eia.gov/renewable/.

Sources: • 1992-1994—Science Applications International Corporation, "Alternative Transportation Fuels and Vehicles Data Development," unpublished final report prepared for the EIA, (McLean, VA, July 1996), and U.S. Department of Energy, Office of Energy Efficiency and Renewable Energy. Data were revised by using gross instead of net heat contents. For a table of gross and net heat contents, see EIA, *Alternatives to Traditional Transportation Fuels: An Overview* (June 1994), Table 22. • 1995-2002—EIA, "Alternatives to Traditional Transportation Fuels 2003 Estimated Data" (February 2004), Tables 1 and 10. Data were revised by using gross instead of net heat contents. • 2003 forward—EIA, Alternative-Fuel Vehicle Interactive Data Viewer (see http://www.eia.gov/renewable/afv/users.cfm#tabs_charts-2 and http://www.eia.gov/renewable/afv/xls/New%20C1%20GEGs.xls); and "Alternatives to Traditional Transportation Fuels," annual reports, Table C1.

Source: *U.S. Energy Information Administration, Annual Energy Review 2011*

Figure 11.1 Carbon Dioxide Emissions From Energy Consumption

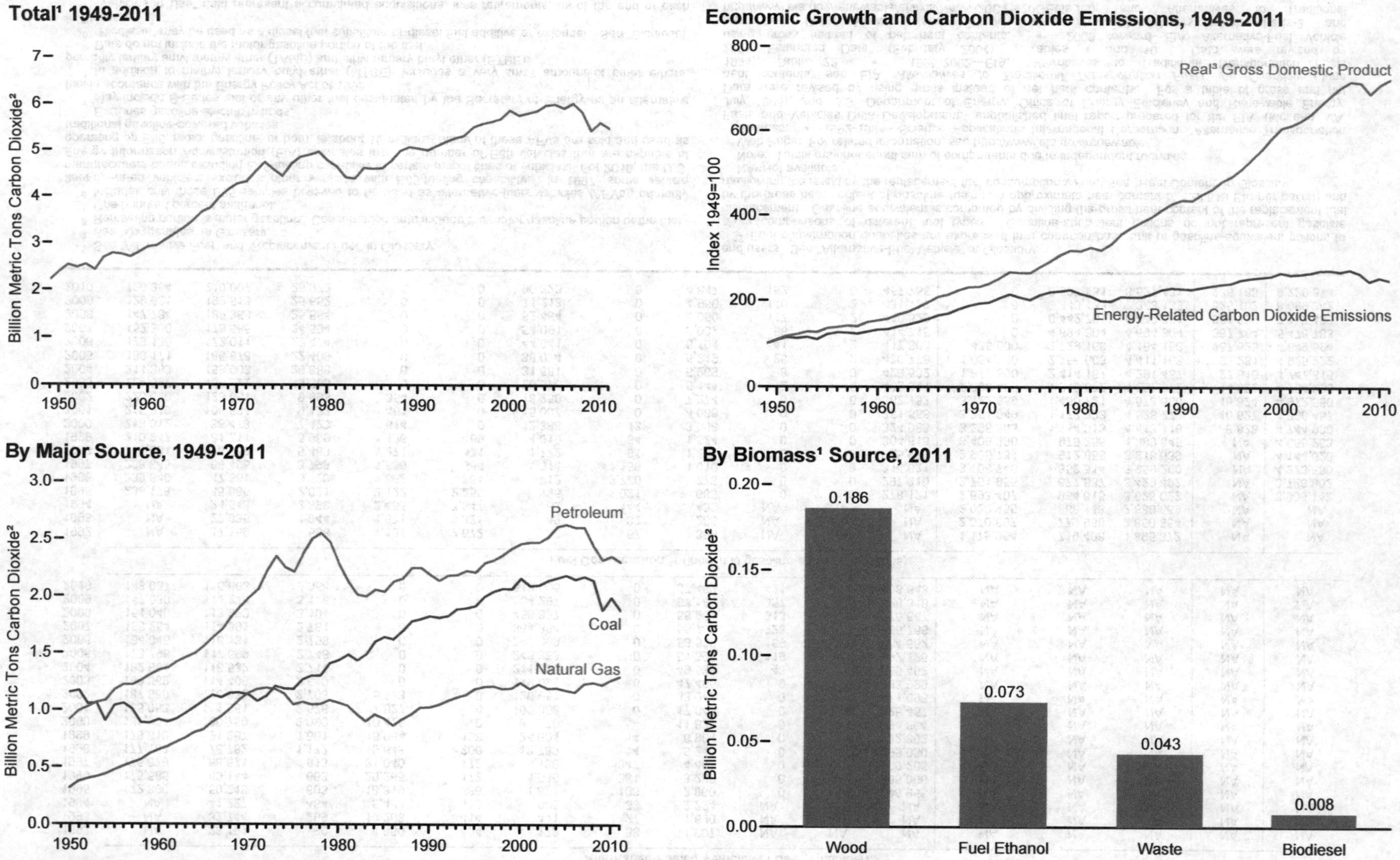

[1] Carbon dioxide emissions from biomass energy consumption are excluded from total emissions. See Note, "Accounting for Carbon Dioxide Emissions From Biomass Energy Combustion," at end of section.

[2] Metric tons of carbon dioxide can be converted to metric tons of carbon equivalent by multiplying by 12/44.

[3] Based on chained (2005) dollars.

Sources: Tables 1.5, 11.1, and 11.2a-11.2e.

***Source:** U.S. Energy Information Administration, Annual Energy Review 2011*

Table 11.1 Carbon Dioxide Emissions From Energy Consumption by Source, Selected Years, 1949-2011

(Million Metric Tons of Carbon Dioxide [1])

			Petroleum												Biomass [2]				
Year	Coal [3]	Natural Gas [4]	Aviation Gasoline	Distillate Fuel Oil [5]	Jet Fuel	Kerosene	LPG [6]	Lubricants	Motor Gasoline [7]	Petroleum Coke	Residual Fuel Oil	Other [8]	Total	Total [2,9]	*Wood* [10]	*Waste* [11]	*Fuel Ethanol* [12]	*Biodiesel*	*Total*
1949	1,118	270	12	140	NA	42	13	7	329	8	244	25	820	2,207	*145*	*NA*	*NA*	*NA*	*145*
1950	1,152	313	14	168	NA	43	16	9	357	8	273	26	918	2,382	*147*	*NA*	*NA*	*NA*	*147*
1955	1,038	472	24	247	21	43	27	10	473	13	274	38	1,175	2,685	*134*	*NA*	*NA*	*NA*	*134*
1960	915	650	21	291	53	41	42	10	543	29	275	45	1,349	2,914	*124*	*NA*	*NA*	*NA*	*124*
1965	1,075	828	15	330	87	40	57	11	627	39	289	65	1,559	3,462	*125*	*NA*	*NA*	*NA*	*125*
1970	1,134	1,144	7	394	141	39	78	11	739	41	396	85	1,983	4,261	*134*	*(s)*	*NA*	*NA*	*134*
1975	1,181	1,047	5	443	146	24	82	11	911	48	443	97	2,209	4,437	*140*	*(s)*	*NA*	*NA*	*141*
1976	1,266	1,068	5	488	144	25	86	13	955	47	506	103	2,372	4,705	*161*	*(s)*	*NA*	*NA*	*161*
1977	1,300	1,046	5	520	152	26	85	13	979	52	553	115	2,500	4,846	*172*	*(s)*	*NA*	*NA*	*172*
1978	1,298	1,050	5	533	154	26	83	14	1,011	50	544	127	2,548	4,896	*191*	*(s)*	*NA*	*NA*	*191*
1979	1,410	1,085	5	514	157	23	95	15	960	48	509	139	2,469	4,964	*202*	*(s)*	*NA*	*NA*	*202*
1980	1,436	1,063	4	446	156	24	87	13	900	46	453	142	2,272	4,770	*232*	*(s)*	*NA*	*NA*	*232*
1981	1,485	1,036	4	439	147	19	85	13	899	48	376	93	2,122	4,642	*234*	*5*	*(s)*	*NA*	*240*
1982	1,433	963	3	415	148	19	85	11	892	49	309	80	2,011	4,406	*235*	*7*	*1*	*NA*	*244*
1983	1,488	901	3	418	153	19	85	12	904	48	255	98	1,995	4,383	*252*	*10*	*2*	*NA*	*264*
1984	1,598	962	3	443	172	17	88	13	914	51	247	106	2,053	4,613	*252*	*13*	*3*	*NA*	*267*
1985	1,638	926	3	445	178	17	86	12	930	55	216	93	2,035	4,600	*252*	*14*	*3*	*NA*	*270*
1986	1,617	866	4	453	191	15	83	12	958	56	255	98	2,125	4,608	*240*	*16*	*4*	*NA*	*260*
1987	1,691	920	3	463	202	14	82	13	932	60	227	106	2,152	4,764	*231*	*18*	*5*	*NA*	*253*
1988	1,775	962	3	487	212	14	83	13	1,003	63	249	119	2,246	4,982	*242*	*19*	*5*	*NA*	*266*
1989	1,795	1,022	3	491	218	13	82	13	1,000	62	246	118	2,246	5,067	*251*	*22*	*5*	*NA*	*278*
1990	1,821	1,025	3	470	223	6	69	13	938	67	220	127	2,187	5,039	*208*	*24*	*4*	*NA*	*237*
1991	1,807	1,047	3	454	215	7	71	12	982	66	207	117	2,134	4,996	*208*	*26*	*5*	*NA*	*239*
1992	1,822	1,082	3	464	213	6	77	12	999	74	196	135	2,180	5,093	*217*	*27*	*6*	*NA*	*250*
1993	1,882	1,110	3	473	215	7	76	12	1,015	76	193	114	2,184	5,185	*212*	*28*	*7*	*NA*	*246*
1994	1,893	1,134	3	492	224	7	79	13	1,022	74	183	124	2,221	5,258	*218*	*29*	*7*	*NA*	*255*
1995	1,913	1,184	3	498	222	8	78	13	1,044	75	152	114	2,207	5,314	*222*	*30*	*8*	*NA*	*260*
1996	1,995	1,205	3	524	232	9	84	12	1,063	78	152	132	2,290	5,501	*229*	*32*	*6*	*NA*	*266*
1997	2,040	1,211	3	534	234	10	85	13	1,075	79	142	138	2,313	5,575	*222*	*30*	*7*	*NA*	*259*
1998	2,064	1,189	2	538	238	12	75	14	1,107	89	158	125	2,358	5,622	*205*	*30*	*8*	*NA*	*242*
1999	2,062	1,192	3	555	245	11	91	14	1,127	93	148	130	2,417	5,682	*208*	*29*	*8*	*NA*	*245*
2000	2,155	1,241	3	580	254	10	102	14	1,135	84	163	117	2,461	5,867	*212*	*27*	*9*	*NA*	*248*
2001	2,088	1,187	2	598	243	11	92	13	1,151	88	145	132	2,473	5,759	*188*	*33*	*10*	*(s)*	*231*
2002	2,095	R1,227	2	587	237	6	98	12	1,183	94	125	127	2,472	R5,806	*187*	*36*	*12*	*(s)*	*235*
2003	2,136	1,191	2	610	231	8	95	11	1,188	94	138	140	2,518	5,857	*188*	*36*	*16*	*(s)*	*240*
2004	2,160	R1,195	2	632	240	10	98	12	1,214	105	155	142	2,609	5,975	*199*	*35*	*20*	*(s)*	*255*
2005	2,182	1,175	2	640	246	10	94	12	1,214	105	164	141	2,628	R5,997	*200*	*37*	*23*	*1*	*261*
2006	2,147	R1,158	2	648	240	8	93	11	1,224	104	122	150	2,603	R5,919	*R197*	*36*	*31*	*2*	*R266*
2007	2,172	R1,233	2	652	238	5	94	12	1,227	98	129	148	2,603	R6,020	*R194*	*37*	*39*	*3*	*R274*
2008	2,139	1,243	2	615	226	2	89	11	1,166	92	111	130	2,444	5,838	*R191*	*40*	*55*	*3*	*289*
2009	1,876	R1,222	2	564	204	3	91	10	1,157	87	91	111	2,320	R5,429	*R177*	*41*	*62*	*3*	*R284*
2010	R1,988	R1,265	2	R590	R210	3	R94	11	R1,146	77	R96	R120	R2,349	R5,612	*186*	*R43*	*R73*	*2*	*304*
2011P	1,874	1,296	2	596	209	2	92	10	1,111	75	86	116	2,299	5,481	*186*	*43*	*73*	*8*	*311*

[1] Metric tons of carbon dioxide can be converted to metric tons of carbon equivalent by multiplying by 12/44.

[2] Carbon dioxide emissions from biomass energy consumption are excluded from total emissions in this table. See Note, "Accounting for Carbon Dioxide Emissions From Biomass Energy Combustion," at end of section.

[3] Includes coal coke net imports.

[4] Natural gas, excluding supplemental gaseous fuels.

[5] Distillate fuel oil, excluding biodiesel.

[6] Liquefied petroleum gases.

[7] Finished motor gasoline, excluding fuel ethanol.

[8] Aviation gasoline blending components, crude oil, motor gasoline blending components, pentanes plus, petrochemical feedstocks, special naphthas, still gas, unfinished oils, waxes, and miscellaneous petroleum products.

[9] Includes electric power sector use of geothermal energy and non-biomass waste. See Table 11.3e.

[10] Wood and wood-derived fuels.

[11] Municipal solid waste from biogenic sources, landfill gas, sludge waste, agricultural byproducts, and other biomass.

[12] Fuel ethanol minus denaturant.

R=Revised. P=Preliminary. NA=Not available. (s)=Less than 0.5 million metric tons of carbon dioxide.

Notes: • Data are estimates for carbon dioxide emissions from energy consumption, including the non-combustion use of fossil fuels. • See "Carbon Dioxide" in Glossary. • Totals may not equal sum of components due to independent rounding.

Web Pages: • See http://www.eia.gov/totalenergy/data/monthly/#environment for updated monthly and annual data. • See http://www.eia.gov/totalenergy/data/annual/#environment for all annual data beginning in 1949. • See http://www.eia.gov/environment/ for related information.

Sources: • 1949-1972—U.S. Energy Information Administration (EIA) estimates based on data in *Annual Energy Review* Tables 2.1b–2.1f, 5.12, 7.3, 7.8, 10.2a–10.2c, and A5. • 1973 forward—EIA, *Monthly Energy Review* (May 2012), Tables 12.1 and 12.7.

Source: *U.S. Energy Information Administration, Annual Energy Review 2011*

Figure 11.2 Carbon Dioxide Emissions From Energy Consumption by Sector, 1949-2011

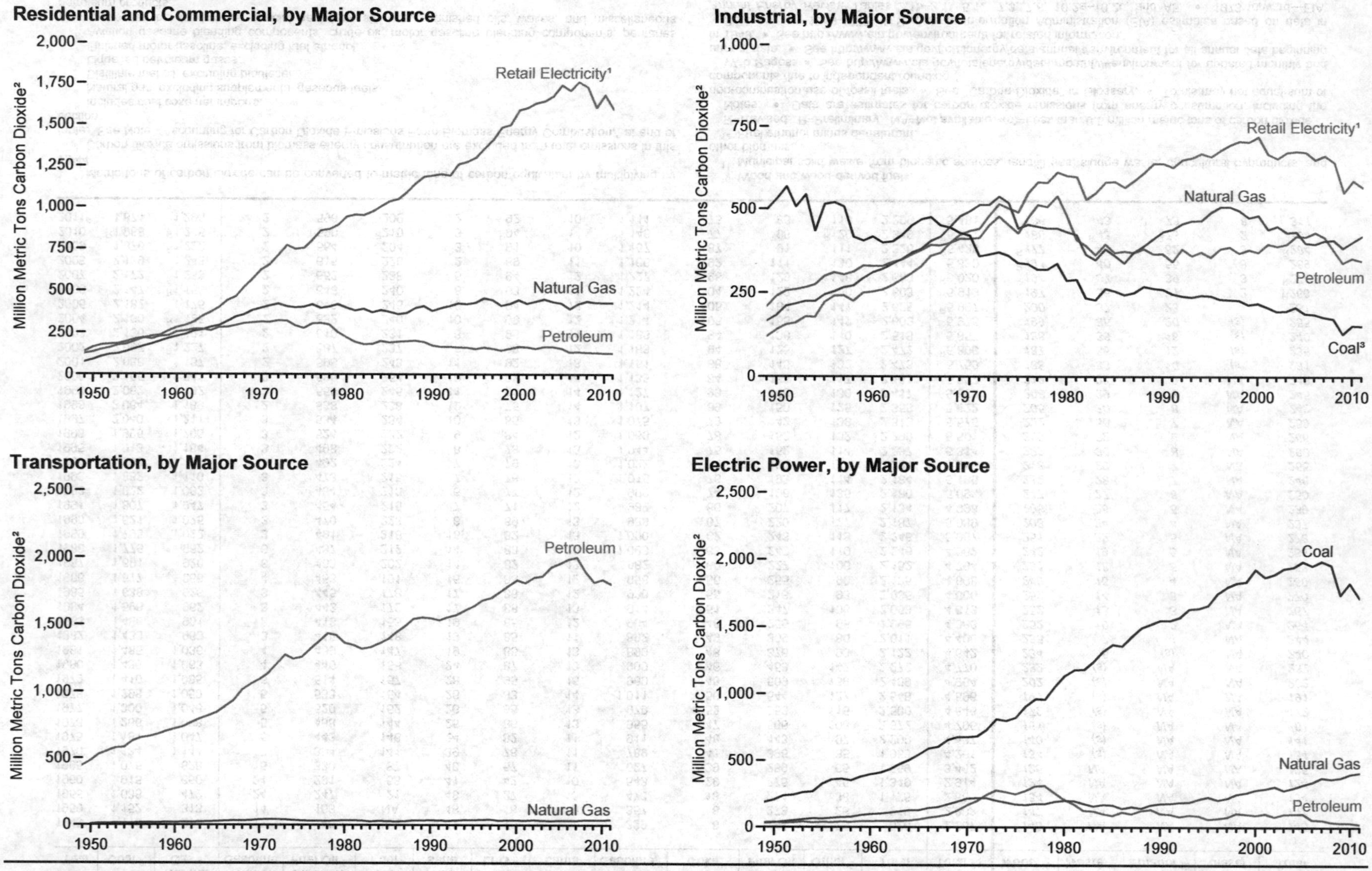

¹ Emissions from energy consumption in the electric power sector are allocated to the end-use sectors in proportion to each sector's share of total electricity retail sales (see Tables 8.9 and 11.2e).

² Metric tons of carbon dioxide can be converted to metric tons of carbon equivalent by multiplying by 12/44.

³ Includes coal coke net imports.

Source: Tables 11.2a-11.2e.

Source: *U.S. Energy Information Administration, Annual Energy Review 2011*

Table 11.2a Carbon Dioxide Emissions From Energy Consumption: Residential Sector, Selected Years, 1949-2011

(Million Metric Tons of Carbon Dioxide [1])

Year	Coal	Natural Gas [3]	Petroleum: Distillate Fuel Oil [4]	Petroleum: Kerosene	Petroleum: Liquefied Petroleum Gases	Petroleum: Total	Retail Electricity [5]	Total [2]	Biomass [2]: Wood [6]	Biomass [2]: Total [6]
1949	121	55	51	21	7	80	66	321	99	99
1950	120	66	61	25	9	95	69	350	94	94
1955	83	117	87	27	13	127	110	436	73	73
1960	56	170	115	26	19	160	156	542	59	59
1965	34	214	125	24	24	174	223	644	44	44
1970	20	265	137	22	35	194	355	833	38	38
1975	6	266	132	12	32	176	419	867	40	40
1976	6	273	145	13	34	192	442	913	45	45
1977	5	261	146	12	33	191	478	935	51	51
1978	5	264	143	11	32	186	484	938	58	58
1979	4	268	119	10	21	150	496	918	68	68
1980	3	256	96	8	20	124	529	911	80	80
1981	3	245	84	6	19	109	522	878	82	82
1982	3	250	77	7	18	102	518	873	91	91
1983	3	238	68	6	22	95	531	867	91	91
1984	4	247	80	12	18	109	542	902	92	92
1985	4	241	80	11	20	111	553	909	95	95
1986	4	234	81	9	19	109	558	905	86	86
1987	4	234	85	9	22	115	581	934	80	80
1988	4	251	87	10	22	119	609	982	85	85
1989	3	260	85	8	24	117	625	1,005	86	86
1990	3	238	72	5	22	98	624	963	54	54
1991	2	248	68	5	24	97	633	980	57	57
1992	2	255	72	5	23	100	624	981	60	60
1993	2	269	71	5	25	101	667	1,040	52	52
1994	2	263	70	5	24	99	668	1,032	49	49
1995	2	263	66	5	25	96	678	1,039	49	49
1996	2	284	68	6	30	104	710	1,099	51	51
1997	2	270	64	7	29	99	719	1,090	40	40
1998	1	247	56	8	27	91	759	1,097	36	36
1999	1	257	61	8	33	102	762	1,122	37	37
2000	1	271	66	7	35	108	805	1,185	39	39
2001	1	259	66	7	33	106	805	1,172	35	35
2002	1	R265	63	4	34	101	835	R1,203	36	36
2003	1	276	66	5	34	106	847	1,230	38	38
2004	1	264	68	6	32	106	856	1,228	38	38
2005	1	262	62	6	32	101	897	1,261	40	40
2006	1	237	52	5	28	85	869	1,192	R36	R36
2007	1	257	53	3	31	87	897	R1,241	R38	R38
2008	1	266	49	2	35	85	878	1,229	42	42
2009	1	259	44	2	35	81	819	1,159	40	40
2010	1	R259	R43	2	R33	R78	R875	R1,212	39	39
2011[P]	1	256	43	1	33	78	827	1,162	40	40

[1] Metric tons of carbon dioxide can be converted to metric tons of carbon equivalent by multiplying by 12/44.

[2] Carbon dioxide emissions from biomass energy consumption are excluded from total emissions in this table. See Note, "Accounting for Carbon Dioxide Emissions From Biomass Energy Combustion," at end of section.

[3] Natural gas, excluding supplemental gaseous fuels.

[4] Distillate fuel oil, excluding biodiesel.

[5] Emissions from energy consumption (for electricity and a small amount of useful thermal output) in the electric power sector are allocated to the end-use sectors in proportion to each sector's share of total electricity retail sales. See Tables 8.9 and 11.2e.

[6] Wood and wood-derived fuels.

R=Revised. P=Preliminary.

Notes: • Data are estimates for carbon dioxide emissions from energy consumption. • See "Carbon Dioxide" in Glossary. • Totals may not equal sum of components due to independent rounding.

Web Pages: • See http://www.eia.gov/totalenergy/data/monthly/#environment for updated monthly and annual data. • See http://www.eia.gov/totalenergy/data/annual/#environment for all annual data beginning in 1949. • See http://www.eia.gov/environment/ for related information.

Sources: • 1949-1972—U.S. Energy Information Administration (EIA) estimates based on data in *Annual Energy Review* Tables 2.1b, 5.14a, 8.9, 10.2a, and 11.2e. • 1973 forward—EIA, *Monthly Energy Review* (May 2012), Tables 12.2 and 12.7.

***Source:** U.S. Energy Information Administration, Annual Energy Review 2011*

Table 11.2b Carbon Dioxide Emissions From Energy Consumption: Commercial Sector, Selected Years, 1949-2011

(Million Metric Tons of Carbon Dioxide [1])

Year	Coal	Natural Gas [3]	Petroleum								Retail Electricity [7]	Total [2]	Biomass [2]			
			Distillate Fuel Oil [4]	Kerosene	LPG [5]	Motor Gasoline [6]	Petroleum Coke	Residual Fuel Oil	Total				*Wood* [8]	*Waste* [9]	*Fuel Ethanol* [10]	*Total*
1949	148	19	16	3	2	7	NA	28	55		58	280	2	NA	NA	2
1950	147	21	19	3	2	7	NA	33	66		63	297	2	NA	NA	2
1955	76	35	28	4	3	9	NA	38	82		88	281	1	NA	NA	1
1960	39	56	36	3	5	5	NA	44	93		124	312	1	NA	NA	1
1965	25	79	39	4	6	5	NA	51	106		177	387	1	NA	NA	1
1970	16	131	43	4	9	6	NA	56	119		268	534	1	NA	NA	1
1975	14	136	43	4	8	6	NA	39	100		333	583	1	NA	NA	1
1976	14	144	48	3	9	7	NA	45	111		358	627	1	NA	NA	1
1977	14	135	49	4	9	7	NA	46	115		380	645	1	NA	NA	1
1978	16	140	49	4	8	8	NA	42	110		381	648	1	NA	NA	1
1979	14	150	43	6	6	7	NA	40	102		395	661	1	NA	NA	1
1980	11	141	38	3	6	8	NA	44	98		412	662	2	NA	NA	2
1981	13	136	33	5	5	7	NA	33	83		431	663	2	NA	(s)	2
1982	15	141	32	2	5	6	NA	31	77		432	665	2	NA	(s)	2
1983	15	132	48	8	6	7	NA	16	85		439	671	2	NA	(s)	2
1984	16	137	54	3	5	8	NA	21	90		461	704	2	NA	(s)	2
1985	13	132	46	2	6	7	NA	18	79		480	704	2	NA	(s)	2
1986	13	126	46	4	6	8	NA	23	85		487	711	3	NA	(s)	3
1987	12	132	44	4	6	8	NA	21	83		509	736	3	NA	(s)	3
1988	12	145	44	2	6	8	NA	21	81		534	772	3	NA	(s)	3
1989	11	148	42	2	7	7	0	18	76		559	794	7	1	(s)	9
1990	12	142	39	1	6	8	0	18	73		566	793	6	2	(s)	8
1991	11	148	38	1	7	6	0	17	68		567	794	6	2	(s)	8
1992	11	152	37	1	7	6	(s)	15	65		567	796	7	2	(s)	9
1993	11	155	36	1	7	2	(s)	14	60		593	819	7	2	(s)	9
1994	11	157	37	1	7	2	(s)	14	60		605	833	7	2	(s)	9
1995	11	164	35	2	7	1	(s)	11	56		620	851	7	2	(s)	9
1996	12	171	35	2	8	2	(s)	11	57		643	883	7	3	(s)	10
1997	12	174	32	2	8	3	(s)	9	54		686	926	7	3	(s)	10
1998	9	164	31	2	7	3	(s)	7	51		724	947	6	3	(s)	9
1999	10	165	32	2	9	2	(s)	6	51		735	960	6	3	(s)	9
2000	9	173	36	2	9	3	(s)	7	58		783	1,022	7	2	(s)	9
2001	9	164	37	2	9	3	(s)	6	57		797	1,027	6	2	(s)	9
2002	9	[R]170	32	1	9	3	(s)	6	52		795	[R]1,026	6	2	(s)	9
2003	8	173	35	1	10	4	(s)	9	59		796	1,036	7	3	(s)	9
2004	10	170	34	1	10	3	(s)	10	58		816	1,054	7	3	(s)	10
2005	9	163	33	2	8	3	(s)	9	55		842	1,069	7	3	(s)	10
2006	6	154	29	1	8	3	(s)	6	48		836	1,043	6	3	(s)	9
2007	7	164	28	1	8	4	(s)	6	47		861	[R]1,078	7	3	(s)	9
2008	7	171	27	(s)	10	3	(s)	6	46		850	1,074	7	3	(s)	10
2009	6	169	30	(s)	9	4	(s)	6	49		785	1,008	7	3	(s)	10
2010	[R]6	[R]168	[R]30	(s)	9	4	(s)	[R]6	[R]49		805	[R]1,027	7	3	(s)	10
2011[P]	5	171	30	(s)	9	4	(s)	6	49		767	992	7	3	(s)	10

[1] Metric tons of carbon dioxide can be converted to metric tons of carbon equivalent by multiplying by 12/44.

[2] Carbon dioxide emissions from biomass energy consumption are excluded from total emissions in this table. See Note, "Accounting for Carbon Dioxide Emissions From Biomass Energy Combustion," at end of section.

[3] Natural gas, excluding supplemental gaseous fuels.

[4] Distillate fuel oil, excluding biodiesel.

[5] Liquefied petroleum gases.

[6] Finished motor gasoline, excluding fuel ethanol.

[7] Emissions from energy consumption (for electricity and a small amount of useful thermal output) in the electric power sector are allocated to the end-use sectors in proportion to each sector's share of total electricity retail sales. See Tables 8.9 and 11.2e.

[8] Wood and wood-derived fuels.

[9] Municipal solid waste from biogenic sources, landfill gas, sludge waste, agricultural byproducts, and other biomass.

[10] Fuel ethanol minus denaturant.

R=Revised. P=Preliminary. NA=Not available. (s)=Less than 0.5 million metric tons of carbon dioxide.

Notes: • Data are estimates for carbon dioxide emissions from energy consumption. • See "Carbon Dioxide" in Glossary. • Totals may not equal sum of components due to independent rounding.

Web Pages: • See http://www.eia.gov/totalenergy/data/monthly/#environment for updated monthly and annual data. • See http://www.eia.gov/totalenergy/data/annual/#environment for all annual data beginning in 1949. • See http://www.eia.gov/environment/ for related information.

Sources: • 1949-1972—U.S. Energy Information Administration (EIA) estimates based on data in *Annual Energy Review* Tables 2.1c, 5.14a, 8.9, 10.2a, and 11.2e. • 1973 forward—EIA, *Monthly Energy Review (MER)* (May 2012), Tables 12.3 and 12.7, and MER data system calculations.

Source: *U.S. Energy Information Administration, Annual Energy Review 2011*

Table 11.2c Carbon Dioxide Emissions From Energy Consumption: Industrial Sector, Selected Years, 1949-2011

(Million Metric Tons of Carbon Dioxide [1])

Year	Coal	Coal Coke Net Imports	Natural Gas [3]	Petroleum: Distillate Fuel Oil [4]	Petroleum: Kero-sene	Petroleum: LPG [5]	Petroleum: Lubri-cants	Petroleum: Motor Gasoline [6]	Petroleum: Petroleum Coke	Petroleum: Residual Fuel Oil	Petroleum: Other [7]	Petroleum: Total	Retail Elec-tricity [8]	Total [2]	Biomass [2]: Wood [9]	Biomass [2]: Waste [10]	Biomass [2]: Fuel Ethanol [11]	Biomass [2]: Total
1949	500	-1	166	41	18	3	3	16	8	95	25	209	120	995	44	NA	NA	44
1950	531	(s)	184	51	20	4	3	18	8	110	26	239	140	1,095	50	NA	NA	50
1955	516	-1	244	72	17	10	4	24	13	122	38	299	222	1,281	59	NA	NA	59
1960	418	-1	310	74	12	17	4	27	29	123	45	329	252	1,308	64	NA	NA	64
1965	471	-2	380	83	12	24	5	24	39	123	65	376	323	1,553	80	NA	NA	80
1970	427	-7	494	89	13	31	6	21	39	126	85	410	434	1,759	96	NA	NA	96
1975	336	2	442	97	9	39	6	16	48	117	97	427	490	1,696	100	NA	NA	100
1976	335	(s)	453	111	9	41	6	15	47	141	103	474	549	1,811	114	NA	NA	114
1977	316	2	447	125	10	40	7	14	52	150	115	513	582	1,860	120	NA	NA	120
1978	304	14	442	127	11	40	7	13	48	133	127	506	580	1,846	131	NA	NA	131
1979	329	7	442	128	13	66	8	11	47	128	139	540	612	1,931	132	NA	NA	132
1980	289	-4	431	96	13	61	7	11	45	105	142	480	601	1,797	150	NA	NA	150
1981	290	-2	422	101	8	58	6	11	47	83	93	408	597	1,715	150	5	(s)	156
1982	235	-2	364	95	10	60	6	10	48	81	80	390	529	1,515	142	7	(s)	149
1983	230	-2	347	83	5	55	6	8	48	61	98	362	549	1,486	159	9	(s)	168
1984	262	-1	380	87	3	62	7	11	50	68	106	394	582	1,617	157	12	(s)	170
1985	256	-2	360	81	3	58	6	15	54	57	93	369	583	1,566	154	14	(s)	168
1986	245	-2	338	84	2	56	6	15	55	57	98	373	566	1,520	151	16	(s)	167
1987	248	1	371	83	2	53	7	15	59	45	106	369	587	1,575	148	17	(s)	165
1988	263	5	389	82	2	54	7	14	61	42	119	381	611	1,648	152	19	(s)	171
1989	259	3	411	83	2	49	7	14	60	31	118	365	638	1,677	149	12	(s)	161
1990	258	1	432	84	1	39	7	13	64	31	127	366	638	1,695	135	12	(s)	147
1991	244	1	439	79	1	39	6	14	63	24	117	342	627	1,653	132	11	(s)	143
1992	235	4	456	81	1	45	6	14	70	28	135	380	649	1,724	137	10	(s)	148
1993	233	3	464	81	1	43	6	13	68	33	114	360	655	1,715	139	11	(s)	150
1994	235	7	465	81	1	46	7	14	67	31	124	371	668	1,745	148	11	(s)	160
1995	233	7	490	82	1	45	7	14	67	24	114	355	659	1,743	155	11	(s)	166
1996	227	3	506	86	1	46	6	14	70	24	132	381	678	1,795	158	12	(s)	170
1997	224	5	506	88	1	48	7	15	68	21	138	386	694	1,815	162	10	(s)	172
1998	219	8	495	88	2	39	7	14	77	16	125	368	706	1,796	150	10	(s)	160
1999	208	7	474	86	1	48	7	11	81	14	130	378	704	1,772	152	9	(s)	161
2000	211	7	481	87	1	56	7	11	74	17	117	370	719	1,788	153	8	(s)	161
2001	204	3	439	95	2	49	6	21	77	14	132	395	667	1,709	135	12	(s)	147
2002	188	7	R448	88	1	54	6	22	76	13	127	388	654	R1,685	131	13	(s)	144
2003	190	6	430	83	2	50	6	23	76	15	140	394	672	1,692	128	13	(s)	141
2004	191	16	R432	88	2	55	6	26	82	17	142	419	675	R1,732	138	12	(s)	151
2005	183	5	398	92	3	51	6	25	80	20	141	417	673	1,675	136	13	(s)	150
2006	179	7	R395	92	2	56	6	26	82	16	150	430	650	R1,662	138	12	1	151
2007	175	3	R405	92	1	54	6	21	80	13	148	415	662	R1,661	R132	13	1	146
2008	168	5	407	93	(s)	42	6	17	76	14	130	377	642	R1,599	126	13	1	140
2009	131	-3	383	80	(s)	46	5	17	73	7	111	339	551	1,401	R113	14	1	R128
2010	R154	-1	R401	R86	R1	R50	6	R19	62	8	R120	R352	R587	R1,494	R122	15	1	139
2011P	150	1	419	88	(s)	48	5	18	62	8	116	345	567	1,482	123	16	1	140

[1] Metric tons of carbon dioxide can be converted to metric tons of carbon equivalent by multiplying by 12/44.

[2] Carbon dioxide emissions from biomass energy consumption are excluded from total emissions in this table. See Note, "Accounting for Carbon Dioxide Emissions From Biomass Energy Combustion," at end of section.

[3] Natural gas, excluding supplemental gaseous fuels.

[4] Distillate fuel oil, excluding biodiesel.

[5] Liquefied petroleum gases.

[6] Finished motor gasoline, excluding fuel ethanol.

[7] Aviation gasoline blending components, crude oil, motor gasoline blending components, pentanes plus, petrochemical feedstocks, special naphthas, still gas, unfinished oils, waxes, and miscellaneous petroleum products.

[8] Emissions from energy consumption (for electricity and a small amount of useful thermal output) in the electric power sector are allocated to the end-use sectors in proportion to each sector's share of total electricity retail sales. See Tables 8.9 and 11.2e.

[9] Wood and wood-derived fuels.

[10] Municipal solid waste from biogenic sources, landfill gas, sludge waste, agricultural byproducts, and other biomass.

[11] Fuel ethanol minus denaturant.

R=Revised. P=Preliminary. NA=Not available. (s)=Less than 0.5 and greater than -0.5 million metric tons of carbon dioxide.

Notes: • Data are estimates for carbon dioxide emissions from energy consumption, including the non-combustion use of fossil fuels. • See "Carbon Dioxide" in Glossary. • Totals may not equal sum of components due to independent rounding.

Web Pages: • See http://www.eia.gov/totalenergy/data/monthly/#environment for updated monthly and annual data. • See http://www.eia.gov/totalenergy/data/annual/#environment for all annual data beginning in 1949. • See http://www.eia.gov/environment/ for related information.

Sources: • 1949-1972—U.S. Energy Information Administration (EIA) estimates based on data in *Annual Energy Review* Tables 2.1d, 5.14b, 8.9, 10.2b, and 11.2e. • 1973 forward—EIA, *Monthly Energy Review (MER)* (May 2012), Tables 12.4 and 12.7, and MER data system calculations.

Source: *U.S. Energy Information Administration, Annual Energy Review 2011*

Table 11.2d Carbon Dioxide Emissions From Energy Consumption: Transportation Sector, Selected Years, 1949-2011

(Million Metric Tons of Carbon Dioxide [1])

			Petroleum										Biomass [2]		
Year	Coal	Natural Gas [3]	Aviation Gasoline	Distillate Fuel Oil [4]	Jet Fuel	LPG [5]	Lubricants	Motor Gasoline [6]	Residual Fuel Oil	Total	Retail Electricity [7]	Total [2]	*Fuel Ethanol* [8]	*Biodiesel*	*Total*
1949	161	NA	12	30	NA	(s)	4	306	91	443	6	611	*NA*	*NA*	*NA*
1950	146	7	14	35	NA	(s)	5	332	95	481	6	640	*NA*	*NA*	*NA*
1955	39	13	24	58	21	1	6	439	80	629	5	687	*NA*	*NA*	*NA*
1960	7	19	21	65	53	1	6	511	66	723	2	751	*NA*	*NA*	*NA*
1965	1	27	15	80	87	2	6	597	61	847	2	878	*NA*	*NA*	*NA*
1970	1	40	7	115	141	3	5	763	60	1,093	2	1,136	*NA*	*NA*	*NA*
1975	(s)	32	5	155	145	3	6	889	56	1,258	2	1,292	*NA*	*NA*	*NA*
1976	(s)	30	5	167	143	3	6	933	65	1,322	2	1,354	*NA*	*NA*	*NA*
1977	(s)	29	5	182	149	3	6	958	72	1,375	2	1,406	*NA*	*NA*	*NA*
1978	([9])	29	5	196	153	3	7	991	78	1,433	2	1,464	*NA*	*NA*	*NA*
1979	([9])	32	5	213	156	1	7	941	97	1,420	2	1,454	*NA*	*NA*	*NA*
1980	([9])	34	4	204	155	1	6	881	110	1,363	2	1,400	*NA*	*NA*	*NA*
1981	([9])	35	4	212	147	2	6	881	96	1,348	2	1,385	*(s)*	*NA*	*(s)*
1982	([9])	32	3	204	148	2	6	876	80	1,319	2	1,354	*1*	*NA*	*1*
1983	([9])	27	3	213	153	3	6	888	65	1,330	3	1,359	*2*	*NA*	*2*
1984	([9])	29	3	216	172	3	6	895	64	1,358	3	1,390	*3*	*NA*	*3*
1985	([9])	28	3	232	178	2	6	908	62	1,391	3	1,421	*3*	*NA*	*3*
1986	([9])	26	4	235	191	2	6	936	69	1,443	3	1,472	*4*	*NA*	*4*
1987	([9])	28	3	244	202	1	6	959	71	1,487	3	1,519	*5*	*NA*	*5*
1988	([9])	34	3	265	212	1	6	981	72	1,542	3	1,579	*5*	*NA*	*5*
1989	([9])	34	3	270	218	1	6	979	77	1,554	3	1,591	*5*	*NA*	*5*
1990	([9])	36	3	268	223	1	7	967	80	1,548	3	1,588	*4*	*NA*	*4*
1991	([9])	33	3	263	215	1	6	962	81	1,532	3	1,568	*5*	*NA*	*5*
1992	([9])	32	3	269	213	1	6	979	84	1,556	3	1,592	*5*	*NA*	*5*
1993	([9])	34	3	278	215	1	6	1,000	71	1,574	3	1,611	*6*	*NA*	*6*
1994	([9])	38	3	295	224	2	6	1,007	70	1,607	3	1,647	*7*	*NA*	*7*
1995	([9])	38	3	307	222	1	6	1,029	72	1,639	3	1,681	*8*	*NA*	*8*
1996	([9])	39	3	327	232	1	6	1,047	67	1,683	3	1,725	*6*	*NA*	*6*
1997	([9])	41	3	342	234	1	6	1,057	56	1,699	3	1,744	*7*	*NA*	*7*
1998	([9])	35	2	352	238	1	7	1,090	53	1,743	3	1,782	*8*	*NA*	*8*
1999	([9])	36	3	366	245	1	7	1,115	52	1,789	3	1,828	*8*	*NA*	*8*
2000	([9])	36	3	378	254	1	7	1,121	70	1,833	4	1,872	*9*	*NA*	*9*
2001	([9])	35	2	387	243	1	6	1,127	46	1,813	4	1,852	*10*	*(s)*	*10*
2002	([9])	37	2	394	237	1	6	1,158	53	1,851	4	1,892	*11*	*(s)*	*12*
2003	([9])	33	2	414	231	1	6	1,161	45	1,861	5	1,899	*16*	*(s)*	*16*
2004	([9])	32	2	434	240	1	6	1,185	58	1,926	5	1,962	*20*	*(s)*	*20*
2005	([9])	33	2	444	246	2	6	1,186	66	1,953	5	1,991	*22*	*1*	*23*
2006	([9])	33	2	469	240	2	5	1,194	71	1,984	5	2,022	*30*	*2*	*33*
2007	([9])	35	2	472	238	1	6	1,201	78	1,999	5	2,040	*38*	*3*	*R41*
2008	([9])	37	2	440	226	3	5	1,146	72	1,895	5	1,937	*54*	*3*	*57*
2009	([9])	R38	2	404	204	2	5	1,137	64	1,818	5	R1,860	*61*	*3*	*64*
2010	([9])	R38	2	R425	R210	2	5	R1,124	R69	R1,836	5	R1,879	*R71*	*2*	*R74*
2011P	([9])	39	2	430	209	2	5	1,089	65	1,802	4	1,845	*71*	*8*	*80*

[1] Metric tons of carbon dioxide can be converted to metric tons of carbon equivalent by multiplying by 12/44.

[2] Carbon dioxide emissions from biomass energy consumption are excluded from total emissions in this table. See Note, "Accounting for Carbon Dioxide Emissions From Biomass Energy Combustion," at end of section.

[3] Natural gas, excluding supplemental gaseous fuels.

[4] Distillate fuel oil, excluding biodiesel.

[5] Liquefied petroleum gases.

[6] Finished motor gasoline, excluding fuel ethanol.

[7] Emissions from energy consumption (for electricity and a small amount of useful thermal output) in the electric power sector are allocated to the end-use sectors in proportion to each sector's share of total electricity retail sales. See Tables 8.9 and 11.2e.

[8] Fuel ethanol minus denaturant.

[9] Beginning in 1978, the small amounts of coal consumed for transportation are reported as industrial sector consumption.

R=Revised. P=Preliminary. NA=Not available. (s)=Less than 0.5 million metric tons of carbon dioxide.

Notes: • Data are estimates for carbon dioxide emissions from energy consumption, including the non-combustion use of fossil fuels. • See "Carbon Dioxide" in Glossary. • Totals may not equal sum of components due to independent rounding.

Web Pages: • See http://www.eia.gov/totalenergy/data/monthly/#environment for updated monthly and annual data. • See http://www.eia.gov/totalenergy/data/annual/#environment for all annual data beginning in 1949. • See http://www.eia.gov/environment/ for related information.

Sources: • 1949-1972—U.S. Energy Information Administration (EIA) estimates based on data in *Annual Energy Review* Tables 2.1e, 5.14c, 8.9, 10.2b, and 11.2e. • 1973 forward—EIA, *Monthly Energy Review (MER)* (May 2012), Tables 12.5 and 12.7, and MER data system calculations.

Source: *U.S. Energy Information Administration, Annual Energy Review 2011*

Table 11.2e Carbon Dioxide Emissions From Energy Consumption: Electric Power Sector, Selected Years, 1949-2011

(Million Metric Tons of Carbon Dioxide [1])

Year	Coal	Natural Gas [3]	Petroleum: Distillate Fuel Oil [4]	Petroleum: Petroleum Coke	Petroleum: Residual Fuel Oil	Petroleum: Total	Geo-thermal	Non-Biomass Waste [5]	Total [2]	Biomass [2]: Wood [6]	Biomass [2]: Waste [7]	Biomass [2]: Total
1949	187	30	2	NA	30	33	NA	NA	250	*1*	*NA*	*1*
1950	206	35	2	NA	35	37	NA	NA	278	*1*	*NA*	*1*
1955	324	63	2	NA	35	37	NA	NA	424	*(s)*	*NA*	*(s)*
1960	396	95	2	NA	42	43	NA	NA	535	*(s)*	*NA*	*(s)*
1965	546	127	2	NA	55	57	NA	NA	730	*(s)*	*NA*	*(s)*
1970	678	215	10	2	154	166	NA	NA	1,059	*(s)*	*(s)*	*(s)*
1975	824	172	17	(s)	231	248	NA	NA	1,244	*(s)*	*(s)*	*(s)*
1976	911	167	18	(s)	255	273	NA	NA	1,351	*(s)*	*(s)*	*(s)*
1977	962	174	21	(s)	285	306	NA	NA	1,442	*(s)*	*(s)*	*(s)*
1978	960	175	20	1	291	313	NA	NA	1,448	*(s)*	*(s)*	*(s)*
1979	1,056	192	13	1	244	258	NA	NA	1,505	*(s)*	*(s)*	*(s)*
1980	1,137	200	12	1	194	207	NA	NA	1,544	*(s)*	*(s)*	*(s)*
1981	1,180	198	9	(s)	163	173	NA	NA	1,551	*(s)*	*(s)*	*(s)*
1982	1,182	176	7	(s)	116	123	NA	NA	1,481	*(s)*	*(s)*	*(s)*
1983	1,242	158	7	1	113	121	NA	NA	1,521	*(s)*	*(s)*	*(s)*
1984	1,318	170	6	1	94	101	NA	NA	1,588	*(s)*	*(s)*	*1*
1985	1,367	166	6	1	79	86	NA	NA	1,619	*1*	*(s)*	*1*
1986	1,357	142	6	1	107	114	NA	NA	1,613	*(s)*	*(s)*	*1*
1987	1,427	155	7	1	91	99	NA	NA	1,680	*1*	*(s)*	*1*
1988	1,492	143	8	1	114	123	NA	NA	1,758	*1*	*(s)*	*1*
1989	1,519	168	11	2	121	134	(s)	4	1,826	*9*	*8*	*17*
1990	1,548	176	7	3	92	102	(s)	6	1,831	*12*	*11*	*23*
1991	1,548	179	6	3	86	95	(s)	7	1,830	*12*	*13*	*25*
1992	1,570	186	5	5	69	79	(s)	8	1,843	*13*	*15*	*28*
1993	1,633	188	6	8	76	90	(s)	9	1,919	*14*	*15*	*29*
1994	1,639	211	9	7	68	84	(s)	9	1,944	*14*	*16*	*30*
1995	1,661	228	8	8	45	61	(s)	10	1,960	*12*	*17*	*28*
1996	1,752	205	8	8	50	66	(s)	10	2,033	*13*	*17*	*30*
1997	1,797	219	8	10	56	75	(s)	10	2,101	*13*	*17*	*30*
1998	1,828	248	10	13	82	105	(s)	10	2,192	*13*	*17*	*30*
1999	1,836	260	10	11	76	97	(s)	10	2,204	*13*	*17*	*30*
2000	1,927	281	13	10	69	91	(s)	10	2,310	*13*	*17*	*29*
2001	1,870	290	12	11	79	102	(s)	11	2,273	*12*	*19*	*31*
2002	1,890	306	9	18	52	79	(s)	13	2,288	*14*	*21*	*35*
2003	1,931	278	12	18	69	98	(s)	11	2,319	*16*	*21*	*37*
2004	1,943	297	8	23	69	100	(s)	11	2,352	*15*	*20*	*36*
2005	1,984	319	8	25	69	102	(s)	11	2,417	*17*	*20*	*37*
2006	1,954	338	5	22	28	56	(s)	12	2,359	*17*	*21*	*38*
2007	1,987	372	7	17	31	55	(s)	11	2,426	*17*	*22*	*39*
2008	1,959	362	5	16	19	40	(s)	12	2,374	*17*	*23*	*40*
2009	1,741	373	5	14	14	34	(s)	11	2,159	*17*	*24*	*41*
2010	1,828	399	6	15	12	33	(s)	11	2,271	*18*	*R24*	*R42*
2011P	1,718	411	5	14	7	25	(s)	11	2,166	*16*	*24*	*41*

[1] Metric tons of carbon dioxide can be converted to metric tons of carbon equivalent by multiplying by 12/44.

[2] Carbon dioxide emissions from biomass energy consumption are excluded from total emissions in this table. See Note, "Accounting for Carbon Dioxide Emissions From Biomass Energy Combustion," at end of section.

[3] Natural gas, excluding supplemental gaseous fuels.

[4] Distillate fuel oil, excluding biodiesel.

[5] Municipal solid waste from non-biogenic sources, and tire-derived fuels.

[6] Wood and wood-derived fuels.

[7] Municipal solid waste from biogenic sources, landfill gas, sludge waste, agricultural byproducts, and other biomass.

R=Revised. P=Preliminary. NA=Not available. (s)=Less than 0.5 million metric tons of carbon dioxide.

Notes: • Data are estimates for carbon dioxide emissions from energy consumption. • See "Carbon Dioxide" in Glossary. • Totals may not equal sum of components due to independent rounding.

Web Pages: • See http://www.eia.gov/totalenergy/data/monthly/#environment for updated monthly and annual data. • See http://www.eia.gov/totalenergy/data/annual/#environment for all annual data beginning in 1949. • See http://www.eia.gov/environment/ for related information.

Sources: • 1949-1972—U.S. Energy Information Administration (EIA) estimates based on data in *Annual Energy Review* Tables 2.1f, 5.14c, and 10.2c. • 1973 forward—EIA, *Monthly Energy Review (MER)* (May 2012), Table 12.6 and MER data system calculations.

Source: *U.S. Energy Information Administration, Annual Energy Review 2011*

Environmental Revenue and Expenditures, by State

State	Revenue ($/per capita)					Current Operational Expenses ($/per capita)					
	NRF[2]	NRO[3]	PR[4]	S[5]	SWM[6]	NRFG[1]	NRF[2]	NRO[3]	PR[4]	S[5]	SWM[6]
Alabama	0.87	2.40	5.84	0.00	1.62	5.41	4.67	38.91	4.93	0.00	0.33
Alaska	1.56	28.28	3.71	0.00	0.00	237.12	117.28	123.73	19.75	0.00	0.00
Arizona	0.00	3.11	2.99	0.00	0.51	9.69	4.36	22.69	7.55	0.00	0.24
Arkansas	1.09	5.88	8.24	0.00	0.00	19.43	3.23	78.74	19.54	0.00	3.60
California	0.22	34.62	2.58	0.00	0.00	6.23	12.99	58.11	9.01	4.71	41.53
Colorado	0.00	3.87	3.51	0.00	0.73	18.01	0.00	29.58	11.35	0.62	0.04
Connecticut	0.16	0.31	1.82	0.00	36.95	6.59	2.78	22.60	3.84	0.00	41.22
Delaware	0.42	1.96	12.40	0.00	71.79	16.65	2.41	64.71	34.97	0.00	40.49
Florida	0.51	3.57	2.25	0.00	1.30	11.70	2.89	40.80	5.57	0.00	7.79
Georgia	0.81	2.56	12.69	0.00	0.00	2.27	5.70	36.96	17.89	1.28	0.12
Hawaii	0.05	13.54	6.82	0.00	0.00	2.39	10.96	47.52	52.64	0.04	0.00
Idaho	34.69	2.12	4.60	0.00	0.00	42.01	22.35	43.16	13.69	0.02	0.00
Illinois	0.00	0.99	0.72	0.00	0.00	7.46	0.11	7.46	5.22	1.76	1.97
Indiana	0.60	6.59	3.48	0.00	0.00	3.28	1.15	38.12	7.19	0.15	0.86
Iowa	0.07	13.63	1.42	0.00	1.45	7.96	1.44	66.83	5.75	0.23	0.67
Kansas	0.00	12.32	1.98	0.00	0.00	10.16	0.00	60.10	9.25	0.85	0.00
Kentucky	0.00	12.05	13.70	0.00	0.00	8.85	3.63	56.97	21.55	0.05	6.44
Louisiana	0.51	59.05	17.04	0.00	0.00	21.32	4.49	87.28	48.39	0.00	0.00
Maine	0.01	10.03	4.39	0.00	12.81	36.88	1.88	83.93	15.45	0.02	0.01
Maryland	0.38	1.90	4.89	19.25	0.03	1.59	1.87	72.51	12.90	18.73	4.17
Massachusetts	0.00	5.98	8.75	59.05	0.00	3.59	0.13	33.61	21.81	27.43	1.43
Michigan	3.24	0.22	0.52	0.00	0.00	6.21	2.69	14.67	7.69	0.00	0.74
Minnesota	4.18	7.44	4.97	0.00	0.00	20.06	9.68	52.56	36.27	0.00	4.06
Mississippi	0.18	15.46	3.11	0.00	0.00	27.99	8.21	51.62	19.92	0.00	0.00
Missouri	0.74	0.99	0.65	0.00	0.29	2.78	1.40	43.94	5.92	0.00	0.39
Montana	15.64	21.18	2.18	0.00	0.07	57.05	33.49	96.52	12.95	2.44	0.90
Nebraska	0.00	17.17	4.41	0.00	0.00	17.86	0.00	91.20	17.04	2.57	6.28
Nevada	1.20	1.53	1.82	0.00	0.00	8.28	4.32	27.07	6.82	0.00	2.48
New Hampshire	0.61	2.66	12.44	1.28	0.34	15.37	3.60	23.75	12.72	0.90	14.60
New Jersey	0.00	0.74	21.60	2.34	3.52	2.65	2.29	46.56	31.42	0.33	4.45
New Mexico	0.00	7.02	2.37	0.00	0.00	13.94	11.77	74.81	28.12	0.00	0.86
New York	0.00	2.29	12.14	0.00	1.30	2.92	1.88	12.52	19.07	0.00	1.59
North Carolina	0.57	3.39	1.06	0.00	0.06	7.80	5.50	35.30	12.75	0.39	1.23
North Dakota	0.81	32.38	4.28	0.00	0.00	41.32	3.86	216.41	22.99	0.00	0.00
Ohio	0.10	1.94	1.48	0.20	0.00	3.59	0.50	23.41	3.65	1.14	2.67
Oklahoma	0.02	3.68	5.63	0.00	0.31	5.96	0.00	41.83	17.37	0.26	0.19
Oregon	22.24	5.25	5.69	0.00	0.00	31.05	25.56	49.74	16.51	0.37	1.59
Pennsylvania	2.46	1.94	2.89	0.00	0.00	9.00	3.73	32.13	14.76	1.10	2.35
Rhode Island	0.05	2.90	5.05	72.10	12.36	5.14	1.03	32.19	5.01	31.93	28.92
South Carolina	1.40	3.74	6.53	0.00	0.00	12.61	3.96	20.67	14.72	0.00	0.00
South Dakota	0.15	15.78	0.94	0.00	0.00	42.13	10.57	86.89	41.33	0.00	0.00
Tennessee	0.08	3.73	5.17	0.00	0.41	10.10	2.61	34.84	12.65	0.00	0.87
Texas	0.00	1.29	1.61	0.01	2.88	6.46	0.89	24.65	4.86	0.28	2.13
Utah	0.26	4.71	0.69	0.00	1.22	17.83	5.03	37.89	13.80	0.00	0.03
Vermont	1.56	1.89	13.05	0.00	0.00	25.19	8.48	88.06	20.35	15.15	10.42
Virginia	0.24	0.02	3.01	0.00	0.00	7.39	3.04	15.21	12.86	3.56	0.36
Washington	30.65	2.56	0.42	0.00	1.40	22.61	11.09	47.52	10.45	0.00	1.52
West Virginia	1.03	10.67	8.91	1.33	0.32	7.62	3.99	85.17	30.38	0.00	4.42
Wisconsin	1.84	10.15	6.96	0.01	0.15	14.58	12.26	46.36	3.79	0.01	1.39
Wyoming	1.73	9.20	2.69	0.00	0.03	110.68	125.92	223.10	50.21	0.00	8.70

Notes: *(1) Natural Resources, Fish & Game; (2) Natural Resources, Forestry; (3) Natural Resources, Other; (4) Parks & Recreation; (5) Sewerage; (6) Solid Waste Management*

Source: *U.S. Census Bureau, State and Local Government Finances, 2011*

Environmental Revenue and Expenditures for U.S Counties with Populations of 100,000+

County	State	Revenue ($/per capita)			Current Operational Expenses ($/per capita)			
		Parks & Recreation	Sewerage	Solid Waste Management	Parks & Recreation	Sewerage	Solid Waste Management	Natural Resources, Other
Ada	ID	0.25	0.00	27.50	1.33	0.00	21.13	8.20
Adams	CO	5.96	0.00	0.89	12.72	0.00	0.45	15.20
Adams	PA	0.00	0.00	0.00	32.58	0.00	1.24	54.44
Aiken	SC	0.27	12.02	11.87	39.88	2.14	32.32	0.26
Alachua	FL	0.00	0.00	31.10	5.32	0.00	61.83	15.32
Alamance	NC	0.21	0.00	22.05	11.50	0.00	14.55	2.08
Alameda	CA	0.00	0.00	0.00	0.45	0.00	0.00	29.04
Albany	NY	21.81	3.98	0.00	20.72	54.05	0.00	0.00
Allegan	MI	1.05	0.00	0.00	3.02	0.00	0.00	5.95
Allegheny	PA	4.71	0.00	0.00	23.31	0.00	0.00	0.23
Allen	IN	15.20	0.00	2.89	20.65	1.91	4.29	0.89
Allen	OH	0.00	53.96	0.00	11.11	38.26	0.00	2.45
Anderson	SC	0.00	17.45	30.66	12.96	13.33	26.06	0.00
Androscoggin	ME	0.00	0.00	0.00	0.00	0.00	0.00	0.00
Anne Arundel	MD	18.20	102.25	91.27	65.24	127.42	90.62	8.31
Anoka	MN	10.81	0.00	19.81	21.40	0.00	17.72	1.79
Arapahoe	CO	0.43	0.00	0.00	23.90	0.00	0.00	0.00
Arlington	VA	38.02	63.27	64.69	109.48	11.93	86.13	56.38
Ashtabula	OH	0.00	24.00	4.05	10.34	16.42	6.54	0.95
Atlantic	NJ	1.77	114.58	112.94	5.32	69.66	94.18	1.92
Baldwin	AL	0.00	0.00	65.94	5.66	0.00	50.03	0.37
Baltimore	MD	4.38	182.65	3.13	41.88	134.66	72.07	24.10
Barnstable	MA	0.00	0.00	0.00	0.00	0.00	0.00	11.65
Bay	FL	1.04	62.78	78.99	9.44	73.99	59.02	23.04
Bay	MI	8.14	34.85	0.00	24.39	25.00	0.00	6.45
Beaufort	SC	4.19	19.84	0.00	23.11	24.56	34.17	0.12
Beaver	PA	0.09	0.00	0.00	7.57	0.00	2.15	0.00
Bell	TX	4.82	0.00	0.00	15.19	0.00	0.02	2.22
Benton	AR	0.00	0.00	0.00	0.00	0.00	0.00	0.00
Benton	WA	0.09	0.00	0.89	3.70	0.00	0.09	4.88
Bergen	NJ	9.48	68.39	9.50	12.63	52.17	19.21	0.00
Berkeley	SC	2.90	150.08	57.93	5.77	67.20	37.23	0.08
Berks	PA	0.00	0.00	1.09	7.09	0.00	2.19	2.50
Bernalillo	NM	1.40	0.00	7.32	17.62	0.68	7.07	0.30
Berrien	MI	3.04	0.00	3.16	5.78	0.00	11.30	23.35
Bexar	TX	0.16	0.00	0.00	1.75	0.00	0.00	6.30
Bibb	GA	0.00	0.00	16.42	3.88	0.00	16.43	1.54
Black Hawk	IA	2.27	1.44	0.00	20.62	0.66	0.00	1.66
Blair	PA	0.00	0.00	1.97	5.98	0.00	2.75	0.45
Blount	TN	0.00	0.00	0.00	0.51	0.00	0.63	2.41
Boone	KY	3.40	0.00	1.13	14.59	0.00	1.13	0.00
Boone	MO	0.00	0.00	0.00	0.40	1.33	0.28	0.10
Bossier	LA	0.00	0.00	0.00	5.28	0.00	0.09	8.10
Boulder	CO	0.65	0.00	21.03	61.32	0.29	18.92	29.59
Brazoria	TX	0.00	0.00	0.00	8.02	0.00	0.13	2.36
Brazos	TX	0.00	0.00	0.16	4.77	0.00	0.39	1.70
Brevard	FL	12.00	0.00	66.62	57.32	0.00	60.57	29.93
Bristol	MA	0.00	0.00	0.00	0.00	0.00	0.00	0.00
Broome	NY	10.04	0.00	43.43	30.22	0.00	36.67	0.34
Broward	FL	8.93	37.62	60.88	38.74	22.48	56.57	9.11
Brown	WI	11.27	0.00	31.87	38.83	0.00	24.04	11.66
Bucks	PA	2.15	0.00	2.26	8.05	0.00	0.39	0.55
Buncombe	NC	3.81	0.00	27.64	11.69	0.00	18.29	1.64
Burlington	NJ	0.03	0.00	42.95	0.54	0.00	26.33	0.33

County	State	Revenue ($/per capita)			Current Operational Expenses ($/per capita)			
		Parks & Recreation	Sewerage	Solid Waste Management	Parks & Recreation	Sewerage	Solid Waste Management	Natural Resources, Other
Butler	OH	0.04	51.38	0.00	0.10	49.47	0.00	1.28
Butler	PA	1.48	0.00	0.00	3.45	0.00	0.50	3.13
Butte	CA	0.00	0.00	30.35	0.25	0.00	24.14	19.63
Cabarrus	NC	6.61	0.00	4.82	13.40	0.00	5.16	4.40
Cache	UT	0.00	0.00	0.00	21.01	0.00	0.00	3.17
Caddo	LA	0.07	3.73	0.00	4.02	2.60	8.73	0.20
Calcasieu	LA	16.54	1.30	0.00	58.44	1.34	29.10	50.83
Calhoun	AL	0.00	0.00	1.99	3.58	0.00	13.49	0.00
Calhoun	MI	0.42	0.00	1.99	11.14	0.00	1.86	6.08
Cambria	PA	0.00	0.00	0.00	7.91	0.00	0.00	12.10
Camden	NJ	0.35	0.00	70.46	4.57	0.00	66.36	0.28
Cameron	TX	10.81	0.00	0.35	8.81	0.00	0.14	0.84
Canadian	OK	0.00	0.00	0.00	0.00	0.00	0.00	3.94
Canyon	ID	0.00	0.00	14.55	0.75	0.00	9.33	0.04
Carroll	GA	8.74	0.00	22.78	22.49	0.00	40.00	1.65
Carroll	MD	10.14	35.19	43.72	23.37	41.69	78.22	127.96
Cass	ND	0.02	0.00	0.00	6.08	0.00	0.00	143.20
Catawba	NC	0.00	1.87	36.32	3.95	1.97	28.27	4.35
Centre	PA	0.00	0.00	0.00	0.28	0.00	2.69	9.91
Champaign	IL	0.00	0.00	0.00	0.00	0.00	0.01	16.86
Charles	MD	17.04	85.37	37.19	90.92	96.17	23.95	29.88
Charleston	SC	0.00	0.00	76.29	4.54	16.98	95.45	0.00
Charlotte	FL	9.85	144.02	109.27	76.02	214.82	115.01	45.76
Chatham	GA	2.38	2.80	5.73	17.21	6.66	11.16	0.17
Chautauqua	NY	0.00	25.37	85.75	4.63	21.79	37.33	0.21
Cherokee	GA	5.13	0.00	11.78	24.77	0.00	1.71	0.00
Chester	PA	0.85	0.00	0.00	16.87	0.00	0.00	25.43
Chesterfield	VA	1.66	108.03	10.54	38.74	58.51	7.02	13.09
Chittenden	VT	0.00	0.00	0.00	0.00	0.00	0.00	0.00
Citrus	FL	3.67	49.32	41.92	10.69	79.92	29.35	28.27
Clackamas	OR	13.15	73.87	1.73	38.32	48.50	8.76	7.23
Clark	IN	2.07	3.60	8.84	0.00	0.34	9.14	1.97
Clark	NV	31.38	68.78	0.00	109.43	33.27	0.00	12.38
Clark	OH	0.00	25.85	6.14	0.00	18.20	8.34	3.12
Clark	WA	9.51	27.73	4.89	18.69	18.63	5.87	6.18
Clay	FL	0.00	0.00	18.71	7.76	0.00	91.31	2.08
Clay	MO	10.65	0.00	0.00	26.12	0.00	0.00	0.00
Clayton	GA	9.03	0.00	7.79	28.35	0.00	13.72	0.69
Clermont	OH	0.00	79.43	1.80	0.00	50.71	3.75	0.00
Cleveland	OK	0.00	0.00	0.00	0.00	0.00	0.00	0.00
Cobb	GA	31.70	102.86	8.70	54.57	88.32	4.03	0.00
Cochise	AZ	0.00	0.00	33.13	0.00	3.08	38.05	0.00
Coconino	AZ	6.23	0.00	9.72	18.43	7.55	13.76	4.34
Collier	FL	19.97	155.95	99.68	101.08	79.15	82.74	30.56
Collin	TX	0.24	0.00	0.00	1.23	0.00	0.00	0.37
Columbia	GA	4.59	120.20	0.34	17.79	42.33	3.54	0.99
Columbiana	OH	0.00	14.91	0.00	0.40	13.28	0.00	0.00
Comal	TX	0.00	0.00	0.00	1.28	0.00	2.97	3.29
Comanche	OK	0.00	0.00	0.00	5.39	0.00	0.00	0.00
Contra Costa	CA	0.00	25.71	1.54	0.00	19.80	0.00	33.08
Cook	IL	11.24	0.00	0.00	29.96	0.00	0.00	0.00
Coweta	GA	3.27	0.00	5.82	17.96	0.00	10.44	1.26
Cowlitz	WA	6.41	87.29	38.80	26.70	32.45	29.19	7.00
Cumberland	ME	0.00	0.00	0.00	0.00	0.00	0.00	0.00
Cumberland	NJ	0.00	0.00	72.79	1.29	0.00	53.12	3.71
Cumberland	NC	5.49	0.00	11.63	30.59	0.43	29.24	1.44

County	State	Revenue ($/per capita)			Current Operational Expenses ($/per capita)			
		Parks & Recreation	Sewerage	Solid Waste Management	Parks & Recreation	Sewerage	Solid Waste Management	Natural Resources, Other
Cumberland	PA	0.00	0.00	0.49	0.57	0.00	1.49	5.76
Cuyahoga	OH	0.00	15.73	1.93	0.00	14.81	1.53	0.05
Dakota	MN	1.96	0.00	17.78	15.55	0.00	18.59	12.37
Dallas	TX	1.17	0.00	0.00	0.97	0.00	0.00	0.00
Dane	WI	18.73	0.00	20.41	30.20	0.00	17.38	4.71
Dauphin	PA	0.00	0.00	3.32	7.68	0.00	4.85	7.30
Davidson	NC	0.41	0.89	25.37	5.35	1.19	27.36	3.11
Davis	UT	0.00	0.00	48.30	12.22	0.00	47.81	7.84
Dekalb	GA	4.20	105.78	94.63	23.57	59.17	48.91	0.09
De Kalb	IL	0.57	0.00	0.00	5.66	0.00	0.00	9.02
Delaware	IN	1.61	2.29	0.00	2.54	3.07	0.00	1.90
Delaware	OH	0.00	81.71	1.32	2.77	52.01	0.49	4.64
Delaware	PA	0.00	0.00	0.00	2.93	0.00	20.88	0.44
Denton	TX	0.00	0.00	0.00	0.57	0.00	0.00	0.60
Deschutes	OR	8.45	0.00	40.63	13.71	0.00	25.85	2.57
Desoto	MS	35.44	0.00	12.40	58.78	0.00	4.33	1.79
Dona Ana	NM	0.00	5.76	0.00	0.34	12.28	9.84	0.00
Dorchester	SC	1.61	74.09	0.00	1.94	35.13	34.99	0.00
Douglas	CO	2.33	0.00	0.17	16.68	0.00	0.20	2.02
Douglas	GA	2.79	0.00	13.90	43.25	0.00	12.24	0.02
Douglas	KS	0.00	0.00	0.00	2.74	0.00	0.00	0.70
Douglas	NE	0.10	0.00	0.00	5.33	0.00	0.50	20.43
Douglas	OR	25.67	0.00	6.76	51.71	0.00	22.75	11.63
Du Page	IL	0.00	20.16	0.00	0.00	17.35	0.00	44.34
Durham	NC	0.00	39.65	5.07	6.52	13.08	7.33	11.56
Dutchess	NY	0.59	0.00	50.72	9.02	0.00	63.60	1.78
Eaton	MI	0.68	0.00	2.50	4.22	0.00	2.56	7.99
Ector	TX	5.06	0.00	0.00	9.08	0.00	0.00	0.92
El Dorado	CA	0.29	0.00	1.15	3.19	0.00	1.15	24.84
El Paso	CO	0.00	0.00	1.21	4.46	0.00	1.44	0.18
El Paso	TX	1.09	0.38	0.30	8.60	0.20	0.32	0.85
Elkhart	IN	0.37	12.64	16.73	12.88	10.01	20.20	0.17
Ellis	TX	0.00	0.00	0.00	0.00	0.00	0.00	1.21
Erie	NY	1.66	6.83	0.00	27.61	36.01	0.00	0.00
Erie	PA	0.00	0.00	0.00	0.00	0.00	0.00	0.00
Escambia	FL	14.71	0.00	39.25	28.76	0.00	39.62	11.65
Essex	NJ	11.36	0.00	58.27	13.89	0.00	47.55	0.00
Etowah	AL	0.00	0.00	0.00	0.22	0.00	2.83	0.00
Fairfax	VA	46.20	168.27	95.98	102.19	98.37	95.07	0.00
Fairfield	OH	0.00	23.43	0.00	0.94	18.34	0.00	2.65
Faulkner	AR	0.00	0.02	0.00	0.64	0.85	0.00	0.35
Fayette	GA	2.25	53.98	1.33	9.94	43.72	1.54	0.97
Fayette	PA	0.00	0.00	0.00	0.82	0.00	0.00	1.71
Florence	SC	3.12	0.00	17.34	15.87	0.00	30.72	0.03
Forsyth	GA	10.30	70.50	7.00	37.36	71.36	3.82	1.89
Forsyth	NC	10.45	0.00	0.00	21.62	0.00	0.00	7.51
Fort Bend	TX	0.23	0.00	0.81	2.65	0.00	0.84	12.03
Franklin	MO	0.00	3.99	0.00	0.00	4.12	0.00	0.16
Franklin	OH	0.00	3.31	0.00	0.21	3.39	0.00	0.00
Franklin	PA	0.00	0.00	0.00	0.36	0.00	0.00	4.19
Frederick	MD	4.48	53.04	105.03	64.99	57.99	79.79	39.98
Fresno	CA	1.51	7.72	10.46	2.63	6.33	12.19	12.07
Fulton	GA	0.62	51.86	0.02	3.28	34.80	1.40	0.61
Galveston	TX	0.86	0.00	0.00	10.55	0.00	0.00	6.25
Gaston	NC	0.69	0.00	24.73	6.22	0.00	26.43	2.97

County	State	Revenue ($/per capita) Parks & Recreation	Revenue Sewerage	Revenue Solid Waste Management	Current Operational Expenses ($/per capita) Parks & Recreation	Current Operational Expenses Sewerage	Current Operational Expenses Solid Waste Management	Natural Resources, Other
Genesee	MI	5.50	0.00	0.00	17.77	0.00	0.57	9.05
Gloucester	NJ	6.45	0.00	70.48	14.81	0.03	60.00	1.38
Grayson	TX	0.00	0.00	0.00	1.38	0.00	0.00	1.75
Greene	MO	0.00	0.00	0.00	0.00	0.09	0.00	0.09
Greene	OH	0.60	97.63	6.96	10.87	43.50	12.14	3.16
Greenville	SC	0.00	17.14	9.66	4.96	14.05	13.82	0.00
Gregg	TX	0.00	0.00	0.00	0.01	0.00	0.00	1.31
Guadalupe	TX	0.00	0.00	0.00	0.00	0.00	0.97	1.68
Guilford	NC	0.00	0.85	0.00	6.25	0.00	2.03	1.61
Gwinnett	GA	4.55	126.33	25.65	44.42	85.37	25.70	0.00
Hall	GA	1.16	2.97	28.50	19.57	3.10	32.96	2.20
Hamilton	IN	10.14	0.00	0.04	18.27	5.58	2.32	3.00
Hamilton	OH	2.42	275.79	0.00	35.25	0.00	0.00	9.40
Hamilton	TN	2.74	0.35	1.14	19.97	0.00	0.47	1.36
Harford	MD	3.70	54.10	43.52	71.06	54.98	58.26	6.12
Harnett	NC	0.07	114.31	37.24	5.48	59.74	31.92	3.02
Harris	TX	0.77	0.00	0.00	1.59	0.00	0.02	21.68
Harrison	MS	0.00	0.00	0.00	14.15	0.00	0.00	2.08
Hawaii	HI	4.80	35.50	35.75	83.06	34.09	118.94	2.54
Hays	TX	0.00	0.00	0.00	9.54	0.00	0.00	0.00
Henderson	NC	1.99	5.89	36.59	13.14	2.30	39.03	13.70
Hendricks	IN	0.00	0.00	0.00	14.47	31.45	0.30	2.42
Hennepin	MN	1.60	0.00	42.38	2.76	0.00	32.91	0.00
Henrico	VA	5.24	139.27	71.85	52.47	78.45	40.58	1.11
Henry	GA	5.07	0.00	0.00	23.55	0.00	0.00	2.12
Hernando	FL	2.64	53.53	43.50	16.15	103.09	11.36	6.74
Hidalgo	TX	0.04	0.00	0.08	4.21	0.00	7.32	30.91
Hillsborough	FL	4.25	0.00	79.56	35.07	0.00	75.87	26.98
Hillsborough	NH	0.00	0.00	0.00	0.00	0.00	0.00	1.23
Hinds	MS	0.00	0.00	0.00	0.31	0.00	9.85	1.15
Horry	SC	2.34	0.00	2.66	20.15	0.00	21.00	15.76
Houston	GA	0.00	20.96	45.70	0.08	16.68	49.89	2.48
Howard	MD	50.84	84.99	69.10	83.10	33.46	50.00	48.75
Hudson	NJ	0.27	0.00	57.57	10.70	0.00	55.01	0.00
Humboldt	CA	2.83	0.00	7.21	3.34	0.00	4.12	8.70
Hunterdon	NJ	15.47	0.00	0.73	19.65	0.00	4.67	3.27
Imperial	CA	0.30	0.00	8.45	3.99	0.17	12.94	19.84
Indian River	FL	22.81	96.47	64.57	75.22	61.97	69.71	5.61
Ingham	MI	4.00	0.00	0.00	24.38	0.00	0.00	16.49
Iredell	NC	1.94	0.00	43.84	7.16	0.00	22.94	2.25
Jackson	MI	9.93	0.00	60.74	8.22	0.00	53.47	13.91
Jackson	MS	4.29	0.00	0.00	28.27	0.00	11.78	3.39
Jackson	MO	7.55	0.31	0.00	25.63	0.40	0.00	0.00
Jackson	OR	11.36	0.00	0.00	40.56	0.00	0.88	15.92
Jasper	MO	0.00	0.00	0.00	0.00	0.00	0.00	0.00
Jefferson	AL	0.00	231.58	1.90	0.43	89.47	2.17	0.00
Jefferson	CO	0.77	0.00	0.00	18.86	0.00	0.51	1.28
Jefferson	MO	0.69	0.00	0.00	4.08	0.00	0.00	0.33
Jefferson	NY	0.00	0.00	17.77	2.91	0.00	20.25	3.60
Jefferson	TX	14.61	0.00	0.00	25.85	0.00	0.04	1.47
Jefferson	LA	9.16	47.42	45.52	58.74	67.58	62.86	73.42
Johnson	IN	0.14	0.00	0.00	7.35	3.06	0.00	2.28
Johnson	IA	0.00	0.00	0.00	8.34	0.00	4.15	5.94
Johnson	KS	26.63	130.59	0.00	53.55	77.88	0.00	8.82
Johnson	TX	0.00	0.00	0.00	1.42	0.00	0.00	0.98
Johnston	NC	0.00	74.33	31.24	1.02	50.62	24.90	2.79

County	State	Revenue ($/per capita)			Current Operational Expenses ($/per capita)			
		Parks & Recreation	Sewerage	Solid Waste Management	Parks & Recreation	Sewerage	Solid Waste Management	Natural Resources, Other
Kalamazoo	MI	2.97	0.00	0.00	12.09	0.00	0.00	1.20
Kanawha	WV	3.97	0.00	0.00	10.03	0.00	0.00	0.00
Kane	IL	0.00	0.00	0.07	0.00	0.00	0.65	12.39
Kankakee	IL	0.00	0.00	0.00	0.00	0.00	0.00	0.73
Kennebec	ME	0.00	0.00	0.00	0.00	0.00	0.00	0.00
Kenosha	WI	16.99	0.00	0.75	28.39	0.00	0.00	20.20
Kent	DE	1.99	86.24	16.33	9.03	56.99	19.01	1.08
Kent	MI	4.77	0.00	63.09	11.86	0.00	54.92	4.46
Kenton	KY	27.05	472.33	0.00	29.80	453.46	0.00	0.57
Kern	CA	2.63	1.34	54.39	13.96	4.05	47.77	7.11
King	WA	3.43	166.82	44.62	35.57	64.86	43.17	24.65
Kings	CA	0.29	0.00	0.00	12.20	0.00	0.00	14.90
Kitsap	WA	3.35	86.67	48.62	15.00	53.20	50.71	4.31
Knox	TN	0.81	0.00	0.00	26.05	0.00	9.92	0.70
Kootenai	ID	0.45	0.09	78.39	2.37	0.00	63.38	7.13
La Crosse	WI	3.52	0.00	82.32	6.91	0.00	80.63	17.96
La Porte	IN	0.75	0.00	0.00	15.56	1.03	21.22	4.08
Lackawanna	PA	0.30	0.00	0.00	11.68	0.00	0.62	1.51
Lake	FL	0.78	0.00	58.89	9.46	0.00	69.06	8.81
Lake	IL	0.00	39.67	0.81	0.00	27.60	3.22	40.78
Lake	IN	14.58	0.09	0.00	20.24	0.56	0.00	1.05
Lake	OH	0.00	67.86	25.60	0.00	42.70	26.70	0.00
Lancaster	NE	0.00	0.00	0.00	5.20	0.00	0.00	3.53
Lancaster	PA	0.78	0.00	0.00	2.65	0.00	0.00	14.79
Lane	OR	2.51	0.00	40.44	6.81	0.00	42.52	8.15
Larimer	CO	16.47	0.00	12.07	29.59	0.00	10.71	10.99
La Salle	IL	0.00	0.00	0.00	3.91	0.00	0.00	0.00
Lebanon	PA	0.00	0.00	0.00	0.00	0.00	0.00	0.00
Lee	AL	0.00	0.00	16.71	0.53	0.00	18.20	0.54
Lee	FL	6.65	69.00	112.10	49.04	26.85	93.94	18.98
Lehigh	PA	3.20	0.00	0.39	5.73	0.00	1.57	2.60
Lenawee	MI	0.00	0.00	1.62	0.33	0.00	0.90	21.01
Leon	FL	0.16	3.43	27.82	14.43	15.91	35.29	29.64
Lexington	SC	0.01	0.00	7.47	0.72	0.00	32.78	4.84
Licking	OH	0.00	16.00	0.06	1.93	12.36	3.03	2.97
Linn	IA	2.70	0.00	0.00	18.52	0.00	0.21	2.39
Linn	OR	18.59	0.00	0.00	17.77	0.00	0.00	3.01
Livingston	MI	0.00	0.00	0.00	0.00	0.00	0.00	0.00
Livingston	LA	5.87	17.21	0.00	15.53	12.15	0.00	26.53
Lorain	OH	0.00	3.92	12.82	0.00	4.51	10.54	0.18
Los Angeles	CA	1.91	5.94	4.40	25.86	5.87	2.93	25.10
Loudoun	VA	47.60	0.00	14.93	100.56	0.72	19.10	0.76
Lowndes	GA	0.00	20.48	12.78	0.00	15.09	9.11	1.31
Lubbock	TX	0.00	0.00	0.00	1.32	0.00	0.00	0.86
Lucas	OH	25.94	15.93	3.67	81.24	10.81	5.00	0.68
Luzerne	PA	0.58	0.00	1.43	0.47	0.00	1.44	25.31
Lycoming	PA	0.00	0.00	111.74	0.09	0.00	99.68	8.68
Macomb	MI	0.22	0.00	0.00	0.37	3.74	0.00	2.88
Macon	IL	0.00	0.00	0.00	0.00	0.00	2.84	0.00
Madera	CA	0.04	0.00	27.73	0.05	0.00	29.13	9.41
Madison	AL	0.25	0.00	30.64	7.96	0.00	27.92	0.00
Madison	IL	0.00	9.86	0.00	3.43	8.85	6.73	20.05
Madison	IN	0.06	0.00	0.00	19.61	6.69	0.00	2.23
Mahoning	OH	0.00	83.64	11.71	0.00	65.87	14.62	0.00
Manatee	FL	17.04	159.44	111.46	62.10	145.02	97.13	28.93
Marathon	WI	4.95	0.00	19.45	24.03	0.00	21.20	5.81

County	State	Revenue ($/per capita) Parks & Recreation	Revenue Sewerage	Revenue Solid Waste Management	Current Operational Expenses ($/per capita) Parks & Recreation	Current Operational Expenses Sewerage	Current Operational Expenses Solid Waste Management	Current Operational Expenses Natural Resources, Other
Maricopa	AZ	1.47	0.00	0.12	2.47	0.52	3.48	9.85
Marin	CA	26.87	48.43	0.00	74.62	33.75	0.00	27.46
Marion	FL	3.07	35.74	7.29	14.16	11.61	26.71	13.25
Marion	OR	0.52	1.14	61.55	1.39	2.20	53.75	1.11
Martin	FL	6.00	81.51	117.54	43.49	49.80	107.12	87.00
Maui	HI	9.91	277.66	98.87	164.38	141.18	111.27	12.30
Mchenry	IL	3.50	0.00	0.00	28.69	0.00	0.00	0.00
Mclean	IL	0.00	0.00	0.00	6.31	0.00	0.00	0.00
Mclennan	TX	0.00	0.00	0.00	0.47	0.00	0.42	1.15
Mecklenburg	NC	2.79	0.00	13.43	29.48	0.00	15.83	3.68
Medina	OH	0.00	72.88	41.22	0.00	73.05	38.28	0.53
Merced	CA	1.23	0.00	35.52	7.66	0.00	24.77	13.66
Mercer	NJ	18.77	0.00	116.35	29.32	0.00	101.43	0.86
Mercer	PA	0.00	0.00	0.00	0.14	0.00	0.00	0.00
Merrimack	NH	0.00	0.00	0.00	0.00	0.00	0.00	4.86
Mesa	CO	0.77	0.35	26.74	12.79	0.72	24.11	1.04
Miami	OH	0.00	22.21	48.11	1.20	18.09	49.48	8.15
Miami-dade	FL	17.61	121.94	106.05	76.29	77.32	88.90	18.04
Middlesex	NJ	5.02	98.98	48.95	13.32	57.63	49.27	0.49
Midland	TX	0.00	0.00	0.00	3.69	0.00	0.00	1.51
Milwaukee	WI	40.96	0.00	0.00	96.37	0.00	0.00	0.00
Minnehaha	SD	0.51	0.00	0.00	8.23	0.00	0.00	2.60
Missoula	MT	9.53	0.00	2.42	15.96	0.00	3.63	22.92
Mobile	AL	0.00	0.00	0.00	6.40	0.00	9.12	0.00
Mohave	AZ	5.59	0.00	6.45	6.29	0.00	9.60	10.41
Monmouth	NJ	11.11	0.00	44.87	29.31	0.00	48.37	0.99
Monroe	IN	1.45	0.14	0.00	15.93	0.00	0.00	1.50
Monroe	MI	0.06	0.00	0.00	3.23	0.00	0.00	4.47
Monroe	NY	3.23	28.38	7.96	17.13	60.12	17.02	0.00
Monroe	PA	0.51	0.00	0.00	18.82	0.00	0.59	27.01
Monterey	CA	13.13	4.70	0.00	27.20	5.15	0.36	51.11
Montgomery	AL	0.00	0.00	0.00	4.01	0.00	0.51	0.00
Montgomery	MD	50.56	134.84	102.29	171.83	76.80	97.55	12.43
Montgomery	OH	0.00	77.83	42.52	2.41	61.63	29.67	4.19
Montgomery	PA	0.30	0.00	0.01	11.10	0.00	0.96	0.00
Montgomery	TN	0.10	0.00	0.00	1.73	0.00	0.68	2.07
Montgomery	TX	0.76	0.00	0.00	2.57	0.00	0.00	1.97
Morgan	AL	0.00	0.00	0.00	8.77	0.00	18.93	0.00
Morris	NJ	29.01	0.00	75.23	55.58	0.00	81.98	0.57
Multnomah	OR	0.00	1.10	0.00	0.00	0.54	0.00	0.35
Muskegon	MI	3.87	69.95	15.73	5.12	56.84	21.20	0.00
Napa	CA	0.00	28.20	0.00	0.01	85.97	0.00	97.94
Nassau	NY	21.07	1.64	0.00	20.62	61.12	0.00	6.49
Navajo	AZ	0.00	0.00	0.00	1.54	0.00	0.00	10.71
New Castle	DE	2.06	123.36	0.00	7.71	115.71	0.00	1.62
New Hanover	NC	0.88	0.00	54.13	27.10	0.00	55.90	2.77
Niagara	NY	2.67	2.06	2.03	19.10	16.54	2.26	2.33
Norfolk	MA	1.52	0.00	0.00	1.28	0.00	0.00	0.00
Northampton	PA	0.09	0.00	0.00	4.66	0.00	0.69	10.59
Nueces	TX	2.25	0.00	0.00	11.62	0.00	0.00	0.68
Oakland	MI	6.47	29.01	0.00	12.42	127.49	0.00	0.73
Ocean	NJ	2.40	0.00	0.00	10.72	0.00	5.85	0.87
Okaloosa	FL	6.17	67.48	40.41	35.31	61.93	42.81	2.36
Oklahoma	OK	0.00	0.00	0.00	0.00	0.00	0.00	0.00
Olmsted	MN	0.00	0.49	114.16	14.34	0.25	84.26	4.56
Oneida	NY	0.00	50.55	0.00	4.27	31.88	0.00	12.55

County	State	Revenue ($/per capita)			Current Operational Expenses ($/per capita)			
		Parks & Recreation	Sewerage	Solid Waste Management	Parks & Recreation	Sewerage	Solid Waste Management	Natural Resources, Other
Onondaga	NY	4.92	125.82	0.00	34.73	104.43	0.00	2.59
Onslow	NC	0.85	0.00	37.41	9.20	0.00	19.66	2.54
Ontario	NY	0.34	27.32	0.00	4.15	20.51	13.77	5.80
Orange	CA	12.94	0.00	34.21	32.23	0.00	30.30	20.12
Orange	FL	35.60	84.46	65.29	24.31	146.21	46.09	19.88
Orange	NY	5.27	13.90	32.21	19.37	18.68	34.23	5.07
Orange	NC	22.11	0.96	76.04	38.59	3.00	76.77	13.25
Osceola	FL	11.04	0.00	18.48	44.07	0.00	48.23	8.38
Oswego	NY	0.04	0.00	60.24	8.98	0.00	48.70	1.38
Ottawa	MI	1.46	40.49	1.24	8.47	25.56	2.90	11.12
Ouachita	LA	0.83	20.72	0.00	6.31	13.21	0.00	0.34
Outagamie	WI	0.45	0.00	54.76	6.03	0.00	76.75	14.55
Palm Beach	FL	12.66	43.84	176.93	46.96	43.13	119.27	29.54
Parker	TX	0.00	0.00	0.00	0.00	0.00	2.35	2.31
Pasco	FL	2.22	96.61	48.28	19.67	119.93	66.90	3.28
Passaic	NJ	2.89	0.00	0.00	5.38	0.00	0.77	0.34
Paulding	GA	2.89	66.85	5.21	14.76	63.99	6.87	3.08
Penobscot	ME	0.00	0.00	0.00	0.00	0.00	0.00	0.27
Peoria	IL	0.00	0.00	1.63	1.00	0.00	1.69	0.00
Pickens	SC	2.58	10.31	0.00	10.02	11.30	27.16	0.50
Pierce	WA	9.99	68.24	3.85	21.64	31.26	5.78	18.01
Pima	AZ	1.52	150.84	3.71	18.95	115.78	5.48	1.28
Pinal	AZ	0.81	0.00	0.00	0.18	0.00	1.18	7.83
Pinellas	FL	4.56	59.02	86.33	17.10	56.09	61.54	16.14
Pitt	NC	0.00	0.00	46.45	0.48	0.00	42.87	3.61
Placer	CA	3.63	36.80	7.64	11.53	30.06	4.86	6.70
Plymouth	MA	0.00	0.00	0.00	0.00	0.00	0.00	0.00
Polk	FL	0.42	0.00	59.39	12.63	0.00	70.89	9.80
Polk	IA	22.49	1.62	0.00	19.35	2.12	1.08	19.41
Portage	OH	0.00	73.70	22.74	0.00	56.81	20.48	0.00
Porter	IN	5.03	0.01	0.00	5.07	2.51	0.00	1.98
Potter	TX	0.00	0.00	0.00	0.41	0.00	0.00	1.34
Prince Georges	MD	14.56	151.76	101.86	207.29	80.17	100.92	1.50
Prince William	VA	31.69	112.97	44.02	58.95	94.36	27.08	0.00
Pueblo	CO	5.17	0.00	0.00	9.56	0.00	0.00	4.07
Pulaski	AR	0.00	0.00	10.17	0.00	0.00	9.87	0.04
Racine	WI	3.13	0.00	0.00	9.77	0.00	0.00	6.21
Ramsey	MN	9.63	0.00	0.00	20.76	0.00	36.04	1.50
Randall	TX	0.00	0.00	0.00	0.00	0.00	0.00	2.59
Randolph	NC	0.00	0.45	15.99	0.49	3.01	21.13	5.40
Rankin	MS	0.00	0.00	26.62	11.04	0.00	27.04	2.27
Rapides	LA	6.31	6.67	0.00	14.96	7.29	0.00	2.29
Rensselaer	NY	0.00	31.53	0.00	2.91	26.88	0.00	0.61
Richland	OH	0.00	20.97	0.00	0.74	11.14	0.00	0.38
Richland	SC	1.35	7.27	58.31	2.65	8.10	60.92	1.77
Riverside	CA	3.51	2.03	25.37	4.74	1.94	22.01	25.85
Robeson	NC	0.23	39.96	48.66	7.58	19.31	32.11	4.29
Rock	WI	0.23	0.00	0.00	4.70	0.00	0.00	5.92
Rock Island	IL	11.40	0.00	0.00	24.83	0.00	0.00	25.49
Rockingham	NH	0.00	0.00	0.00	0.00	0.00	0.00	1.61
Rockland	NY	0.06	2.75	133.07	7.35	59.50	115.20	0.00
Rowan	NC	9.04	0.00	36.52	18.45	0.00	23.46	1.60
Rutherford	TN	0.00	0.00	4.79	1.38	0.00	10.22	3.33
Sacramento	CA	8.85	16.37	47.54	19.88	19.79	38.07	3.22
Saginaw	MI	0.30	0.00	1.50	29.00	0.00	2.55	3.17
Salt Lake	UT	6.30	0.00	13.50	98.30	0.00	11.20	7.46

County	State	Revenue ($/per capita) Parks & Recreation	Sewerage	Solid Waste Management	Current Operational Expenses ($/per capita) Parks & Recreation	Sewerage	Solid Waste Management	Natural Resources, Other
San Bernardino	CA	4.25	3.22	28.63	7.81	1.08	46.80	26.04
San Diego	CA	1.19	6.51	4.17	7.00	5.70	4.17	5.32
San Joaquin	CA	2.22	1.79	28.75	9.18	4.19	22.35	18.55
San Juan	NM	4.85	0.00	0.00	37.76	0.00	25.44	9.38
San Luis Obispo	CA	23.96	1.57	7.22	28.52	0.47	0.60	55.23
San Mateo	CA	1.93	5.83	8.38	12.42	4.56	3.39	7.39
Sandoval	NM	1.29	0.00	17.44	4.17	0.08	20.96	0.00
Sangamon	IL	0.00	0.00	0.00	0.00	0.00	0.00	0.00
Santa Barbara	CA	9.89	17.33	52.23	25.19	11.28	48.94	33.49
Santa Clara	CA	2.35	1.14	0.54	18.49	1.43	0.68	2.13
Santa Cruz	CA	4.78	78.90	60.93	22.19	53.17	47.57	17.83
Santa Fe	NM	0.00	0.86	4.10	4.59	1.88	10.34	2.35
Santa Rosa	FL	1.26	0.00	26.84	6.96	0.01	24.93	10.21
Sarasota	FL	5.28	125.04	45.68	74.73	51.92	84.22	66.64
Saratoga	NY	0.00	56.97	0.00	4.28	34.85	0.00	5.54
Sarpy	NE	1.76	0.49	17.39	10.46	4.48	13.93	1.94
Schenectady	NY	2.34	0.00	0.96	4.93	0.00	2.15	2.06
Schuylkill	PA	0.00	0.00	0.00	3.52	0.00	0.00	36.17
Scott	IA	6.16	0.00	0.00	13.73	0.00	5.51	15.35
Scott	MN	0.00	0.00	0.00	10.16	0.00	0.00	14.71
Sebastian	AR	6.22	0.00	0.00	10.48	0.00	0.00	0.00
Sedgwick	KS	0.43	0.00	2.53	22.57	5.42	2.81	4.48
Seminole	FL	3.09	56.61	28.79	14.18	43.45	57.30	13.51
Shasta	CA	0.00	0.00	18.47	0.68	0.00	7.37	0.00
Shawnee	KS	6.83	0.00	49.59	50.78	0.15	38.76	3.36
Sheboygan	WI	0.01	0.00	0.00	2.84	0.00	0.00	20.61
Shelby	AL	0.00	0.00	19.13	4.42	0.00	16.77	0.00
Shelby	TN	0.53	0.63	0.02	0.88	0.00	0.31	0.58
Skagit	WA	4.70	14.29	71.74	11.98	9.23	73.89	50.14
Smith	TX	0.00	0.00	0.00	0.00	0.00	0.63	1.03
Snohomish	WA	4.17	0.71	63.22	11.65	13.47	46.76	4.55
Solano	CA	1.04	0.00	0.00	3.60	0.00	0.00	0.00
Somerset	NJ	0.00	0.00	1.55	26.91	0.00	10.36	3.20
Sonoma	CA	9.00	39.38	67.51	39.77	28.19	66.82	0.00
Spartanburg	SC	2.69	0.00	28.28	21.85	0.00	18.50	0.00
Spokane	WA	9.67	34.85	0.00	21.27	27.23	2.34	6.38
Spotsylvania	VA	4.67	83.14	1.05	21.37	53.58	32.86	1.22
St Charles	MO	11.30	0.00	0.00	24.34	0.00	0.00	0.25
St Clair	IL	0.00	0.00	0.00	0.00	0.00	0.00	0.00
St Clair	MI	0.52	3.93	24.45	13.52	3.93	24.99	14.63
St Johns	FL	41.83	68.29	93.93	82.72	43.30	87.16	8.58
St Joseph	IN	0.00	0.00	2.62	19.15	3.12	2.62	0.96
St Lawrence	NY	0.00	0.00	33.03	2.38	0.15	37.77	6.61
St Louis	MN	0.00	0.00	29.90	5.12	0.00	32.54	29.81
St Louis	MO	1.71	3.00	1.16	27.54	3.02	2.36	0.14
St Lucie	FL	8.24	14.96	33.62	59.99	12.56	64.63	20.68
St Marys	MD	34.64	66.29	3.83	99.37	33.79	38.58	15.52
St Tammany	LA	7.64	18.05	1.94	27.97	12.03	1.17	22.98
Stafford	VA	11.98	109.69	0.00	51.30	75.43	0.00	1.18
Stanislaus	CA	3.85	0.00	27.06	21.78	0.00	30.95	8.19
Stark	OH	0.00	56.69	0.00	0.01	85.74	0.00	0.00
Stearns	MN	0.00	0.00	3.90	9.07	0.00	3.53	29.66
Strafford	NH	0.00	0.00	0.00	0.00	0.00	0.00	0.00
Suffolk	NY	6.96	18.27	0.00	13.11	34.89	0.00	4.11
Sullivan	TN	1.68	0.00	6.43	1.72	0.00	11.49	1.12
Summit	OH	0.00	69.23	0.00	0.00	51.45	0.00	0.00

County	State	Revenue ($/per capita) Parks & Recreation	Revenue Sewerage	Revenue Solid Waste Management	Current Operational Expenses ($/per capita) Parks & Recreation	Expenses Sewerage	Expenses Solid Waste Management	Expenses Natural Resources, Other
Sumner	TN	0.00	0.00	0.00	0.00	0.00	0.00	2.68
Sumter	SC	7.52	19.38	15.86	26.01	1.72	39.81	0.59
Sussex	DE	0.00	78.81	0.00	0.00	63.22	0.00	0.00
Sussex	NJ	0.00	35.96	71.24	0.19	23.19	52.12	1.07
Tangipahoa	LA	0.00	11.62	25.11	9.36	9.12	48.18	15.30
Tarrant	TX	0.00	0.00	0.00	0.00	0.00	0.00	1.81
Taylor	TX	0.00	0.00	0.00	0.14	0.00	0.00	3.94
Tazewell	IL	0.00	0.00	0.00	0.00	0.00	0.00	0.00
Thurston	WA	2.39	5.10	78.60	4.96	11.16	57.70	6.87
Tippecanoe	IN	1.05	0.00	0.06	6.09	0.82	0.24	3.04
Tom Green	TX	0.07	0.00	0.00	1.76	0.00	0.00	4.09
Tompkins	NY	0.00	0.00	58.76	18.18	0.00	46.96	8.30
Travis	TX	0.37	0.00	0.00	7.95	0.00	0.57	3.92
Trumbull	OH	0.00	57.52	0.00	0.00	53.46	0.00	0.00
Tulare	CA	0.36	0.32	17.74	7.28	0.28	27.88	0.00
Tulsa	OK	3.44	0.00	0.00	15.10	0.00	0.00	1.46
Tuscaloosa	AL	0.00	0.00	0.00	12.33	0.00	0.79	0.00
Ulster	NY	0.58	0.00	79.21	3.86	0.00	74.62	2.04
Union	NJ	10.07	0.00	0.00	18.37	0.00	0.69	0.64
Union	NC	2.80	71.06	17.43	7.38	39.32	19.85	3.39
Utah	UT	2.75	23.39	13.10	4.40	21.59	12.82	0.96
Vanderburgh	IN	6.61	0.00	0.00	18.05	0.96	0.00	1.88
Ventura	CA	3.86	32.19	0.04	4.05	27.66	0.00	48.29
Vigo	IN	0.00	0.45	1.66	21.02	0.11	0.00	4.46
Volusia	FL	6.81	9.38	43.18	49.70	19.60	45.83	12.54
Wake	NC	0.17	0.00	26.03	36.22	0.02	24.11	6.14
Walworth	WI	0.16	0.00	0.68	0.80	0.00	2.78	16.42
Warren	KY	0.35	0.00	0.00	13.87	0.00	2.73	4.76
Warren	NJ	0.00	0.00	64.48	47.85	0.00	47.85	3.36
Warren	OH	0.00	42.57	0.00	0.00	33.70	0.76	0.00
Washington	AR	0.00	0.00	1.56	0.00	0.00	1.71	0.00
Washington	MD	9.81	41.72	43.66	29.91	43.26	55.86	22.36
Washington	MN	0.59	0.00	0.00	9.44	0.00	0.00	0.13
Washington	OR	0.00	195.15	0.00	1.50	96.70	0.00	3.52
Washington	PA	0.00	0.00	0.00	0.93	0.00	0.00	1.49
Washington	TN	0.00	0.00	0.00	0.06	0.00	13.10	2.41
Washington	UT	0.00	15.89	58.86	3.08	14.28	57.37	5.99
Washington	WI	9.85	0.00	0.00	30.89	0.00	1.05	11.15
Washoe	NV	30.33	26.84	0.00	78.39	10.40	0.00	6.87
Washtenaw	MI	9.37	0.00	0.00	37.99	0.00	1.28	7.59
Waukesha	WI	14.35	0.00	3.40	34.37	0.00	6.40	1.37
Wayne	MI	2.98	49.32	0.00	8.91	51.64	0.00	1.27
Wayne	NC	0.00	0.86	30.64	1.67	0.79	24.09	5.50
Wayne	OH	0.00	7.61	0.00	0.00	19.78	0.95	4.77
Webb	TX	0.00	0.00	0.00	1.11	0.88	0.00	0.64
Weber	UT	0.00	0.00	0.00	48.05	0.00	0.03	0.92
Weld	CO	0.00	0.00	4.52	4.54	0.00	0.66	8.87
Westchester	NY	36.66	2.23	21.60	52.02	38.53	58.33	1.33
Westmoreland	PA	0.00	0.00	0.00	7.08	0.00	0.00	4.76
Whatcom	WA	1.67	0.00	3.76	16.21	0.00	4.42	19.43
Wichita	TX	0.00	0.00	0.00	0.00	0.00	0.00	0.78
Will	IL	0.00	0.00	1.51	0.00	0.00	1.13	16.18
Williamson	TN	22.01	0.00	5.19	51.59	0.00	22.16	1.79
Williamson	TX	0.00	0.00	0.00	3.62	0.00	0.14	1.30
Wilson	TN	0.00	0.00	2.54	0.00	0.00	17.95	9.20

County	State	Revenue ($/per capita)			Current Operational Expenses ($/per capita)			
		Parks & Recreation	Sewerage	Solid Waste Management	Parks & Recreation	Sewerage	Solid Waste Management	Natural Resources, Other
Winnebago	IL	7.52	0.00	0.00	5.92	0.00	0.00	14.36
Winnebago	WI	1.62	0.00	39.52	10.17	0.00	78.82	9.99
Wood	OH	0.00	0.00	19.15	2.43	0.00	20.23	4.34
Woodbury	IA	0.00	0.00	0.00	3.58	0.00	1.89	12.91
Wright	MN	0.00	0.00	1.01	9.70	0.00	3.61	3.51
Yakima	WA	0.01	0.52	34.55	0.47	0.48	24.72	13.93
Yavapai	AZ	0.00	0.00	1.54	0.00	0.24	6.09	0.52
Yellowstone	MT	3.26	0.00	3.27	3.49	0.00	3.32	2.32
Yolo	CA	0.66	0.00	38.92	6.34	0.20	40.31	7.87
York	ME	0.00	0.00	0.00	0.00	0.00	0.00	0.00
York	PA	1.06	0.00	0.00	7.11	0.00	0.00	3.68
York	SC	0.87	29.75	23.88	11.23	23.20	31.67	0.00
Yuma	AZ	0.00	0.00	0.00	0.03	4.74	4.66	6.48

Source: *U.S. Census Bureau, State and Local Governments Finances, 2011*

Environmental Revenue and Expenditures for U.S. Cities/Townships with Populations of 50,000+

City	State	Revenue ($/per capita)			Current Operational Expenses ($/per capita)			
		Park & Recreation	Sewerage	Solid Waste Management	Parks & Recreation	Sewerage	Solid Waste Management	Natural Resources, Other
Abilene (city)	TX	5.83	95.53	104.82	52.59	64.15	78.81	0.00
Abington (township)	PA	15.84	159.86	93.29	78.36	144.06	92.10	0.00
Akron (city)	OH	4.84	230.77	0.00	10.17	141.41	0.00	0.00
Albany (city)	GA	16.87	197.60	116.67	118.95	165.79	102.84	0.00
Albany (city)	NY	11.96	0.00	108.97	51.91	0.00	89.31	0.00
Albuquerque (city)	NM	25.08	88.86	112.55	131.96	46.67	82.03	0.12
Alexandria (city)	VA	17.76	240.82	41.95	168.79	160.24	65.84	0.00
Alhambra (city)	CA	28.28	50.68	97.26	71.02	15.69	94.95	0.00
Allen (city)	TX	64.23	114.08	69.74	166.98	30.95	60.67	8.50
Allentown (city)	PA	14.63	122.74	111.37	54.93	104.38	117.26	0.00
Amarillo (city)	TX	21.72	90.79	90.52	81.28	71.30	57.53	0.00
Ames (city)	IA	23.01	105.45	79.23	56.83	96.38	68.84	0.00
Amherst (town)	NY	39.97	0.04	0.48	77.40	101.91	66.37	19.75
Anaheim (city)	CA	103.36	0.00	167.44	143.18	0.00	135.39	0.00
Anchorage (municipality)	AK	20.44	128.39	94.98	116.01	78.34	62.74	0.00
Anderson (city)	IN	5.59	364.21	40.53	27.31	209.94	50.74	0.00
Ann Arbor (city)	MI	30.60	256.74	26.95	100.42	120.96	113.41	0.00
Antioch (city)	CA	16.71	44.24	0.00	41.74	10.00	0.00	0.00
Appleton (city)	WI	16.19	112.29	6.10	55.71	145.00	47.05	10.53
Arlington (city)	TX	32.87	154.11	0.00	82.03	99.39	0.00	0.00
Arlington Heights (village)	IL	4.97	0.00	22.73	5.42	0.00	19.88	0.00
Arvada (city)	CO	92.77	122.17	0.00	204.06	83.78	0.00	0.00
Asheville (city)	NC	61.35	234.56	13.81	156.66	148.73	66.17	9.16
Athens-clarke Co. (unified govt)	GA	6.89	138.54	61.82	58.53	76.29	43.56	1.24
Atlanta (city)	GA	70.41	422.24	123.99	171.79	209.47	81.98	0.00
Auburn (city)	AL	1.39	164.07	58.73	91.49	83.89	58.11	0.00
Augusta-Richmond Co. (cons. govt)	GA	19.75	152.74	151.31	71.65	120.19	121.79	1.20
Aurora (city)	CO	41.10	153.03	0.00	110.25	105.02	0.00	0.00
Aurora (city)	IL	10.61	16.08	9.38	41.76	13.55	9.39	0.00
Austin (city)	TX	33.66	229.51	94.13	104.74	99.45	75.30	53.73
Avondale (city)	AZ	3.38	94.41	63.93	3.74	137.19	51.46	0.00
Babylon (town)	NY	9.68	0.00	84.18	45.96	0.00	216.67	3.66
Bakersfield (city)	CA	3.00	100.01	113.87	73.49	47.28	108.45	0.00
Baldwin Park (city)	CA	0.97	0.00	0.44	51.72	0.00	4.31	0.00
Baltimore (city)	MD	0.11	257.79	8.34	62.53	233.07	116.62	0.00
Baton Rouge-E Baton Rouge (city/par.)	LA	26.19	307.97	165.16	59.80	169.10	151.90	3.51
Battle Creek (city)	MI	44.17	252.24	54.27	107.23	198.22	52.08	0.00
Bayonne (city)	NJ	0.00	132.92	0.00	50.25	101.74	37.65	0.00
Baytown (city)	TX	4.71	205.73	59.40	75.35	95.75	60.46	0.06
Beaumont (city)	TX	9.07	118.20	78.06	63.56	60.83	54.08	0.00
Beaverton (city)	OR	0.00	91.52	0.00	3.00	68.72	0.00	0.00
Bellevue (city)	WA	78.87	478.91	8.95	238.25	283.06	12.08	3.55
Bellingham (city)	WA	7.44	248.51	1.38	118.66	131.43	8.69	0.00
Bend (city)	OR	0.00	214.08	0.00	0.00	89.46	0.00	0.00
Bensalem (township)	PA	46.85	0.00	0.00	144.26	0.00	0.00	0.00
Berkeley (city)	CA	27.61	111.63	299.71	137.13	79.83	329.94	0.00
Berwyn (city)	IL	8.12	44.67	76.72	26.95	47.69	75.30	0.00
Bethlehem (city)	PA	24.13	160.55	22.75	62.39	106.39	61.32	0.59
Billings (city)	MT	4.70	104.82	94.21	42.83	70.23	81.19	0.00
Birmingham (city)	AL	1.85	0.00	0.00	63.94	0.00	77.43	0.00
Bismarck (city)	ND	81.86	103.41	76.97	94.61	106.54	74.81	0.00
Blaine (city)	MN	0.00	100.67	42.86	19.25	31.16	45.82	0.00
Bloomington (city)	IL	71.00	74.08	55.89	204.65	31.89	127.96	0.00
Bloomington (city)	IN	40.73	187.14	11.47	128.45	131.46	23.56	0.00

City	State	Revenue ($/per capita)			Current Operational Expenses ($/per capita)			
		Park & Recreation	Sewerage	Solid Waste Management	Parks & Recreation	Sewerage	Solid Waste Management	Natural Resources, Other
Bloomington (city)	MN	44.13	168.33	10.06	136.73	69.74	13.44	0.00
Blue Springs (city)	MO	39.30	128.03	0.00	70.55	63.49	1.03	0.00
Boca Raton (city)	FL	73.91	197.79	46.62	380.53	172.74	70.24	222.95
Boise (city)	ID	32.32	130.83	114.57	95.07	92.15	115.14	0.19
Bolingbrook (village)	IL	94.65	40.48	0.00	121.99	12.53	65.68	0.00
Bossier (city)	LA	4.11	160.53	70.29	94.45	73.18	57.85	0.00
Boston (city)	MA	0.00	247.46	0.00	25.73	45.20	87.21	2.03
Boulder (city)	CO	66.72	181.68	0.00	319.18	107.50	0.00	15.26
Bowie (city)	MD	31.96	50.43	0.00	107.10	49.23	113.36	0.00
Bowling Green (city)	KY	42.55	141.75	0.00	105.40	131.99	0.60	0.00
Boynton Beach (city)	FL	60.50	272.84	136.30	132.52	185.54	95.74	6.22
Brick (township)	NJ	6.07	229.30	0.16	26.68	109.41	94.68	0.00
Bridgeport (city)	CT	14.82	194.67	0.91	42.28	128.86	49.59	0.00
Bristol (city)	CT	6.66	80.08	23.48	41.50	51.49	90.99	0.00
Bristol (township)	PA	1.26	88.07	0.42	1.69	69.75	95.97	0.00
Brockton (city)	MA	9.54	205.87	80.50	12.21	85.96	76.39	0.46
Broken Arrow (city)	OK	18.30	116.21	54.72	39.51	60.25	42.42	0.00
Brookhaven (town)	NY	7.28	0.00	129.59	35.62	0.13	153.42	0.05
Brookline (town)	MA	19.17	214.13	45.56	48.22	23.34	46.12	3.10
Brooklyn Park (city)	MN	35.55	73.03	14.74	74.44	83.41	14.81	0.00
Broomfield (city/co.)	CO	71.28	106.69	0.00	203.30	83.67	3.42	0.00
Brownsville (city)	TX	6.42	111.35	71.98	48.13	76.67	24.25	0.00
Bryan (city)	TX	21.44	162.33	101.27	53.04	65.58	91.63	0.00
Buena Park (city)	CA	9.47	14.76	33.99	61.70	7.40	34.47	0.00
Buffalo (city)	NY	0.29	205.53	68.65	22.88	133.51	118.61	0.00
Burbank (city)	CA	51.37	144.48	145.51	109.41	87.51	122.86	0.41
Burnsville (city)	MN	37.59	138.94	0.00	95.88	112.13	3.71	10.45
Cambridge (city)	MA	10.31	383.67	0.00	160.66	19.00	50.32	0.74
Camden (city)	NJ	0.00	104.88	0.00	11.60	42.86	66.55	0.00
Canton Charter (township)	MI	49.23	186.35	0.00	119.56	58.52	35.59	0.00
Canton (city)	OH	0.00	182.38	90.53	31.41	113.33	65.45	0.00
Cape Coral (city)	FL	50.06	219.00	0.00	106.43	129.99	0.00	20.96
Carlsbad (city)	CA	71.75	103.97	30.29	183.24	84.45	24.15	0.24
Carmel (city)	IN	100.57	82.83	0.00	46.02	81.36	0.00	0.00
Carrollton (city)	TX	25.21	95.40	65.32	67.37	58.43	54.35	7.26
Carson (city)	CA	25.15	0.00	0.01	170.03	0.00	1.16	0.00
Carson (city)	NV	20.19	122.01	49.25	136.97	88.52	27.90	2.79
Cary (town)	NC	35.00	215.91	49.63	87.26	125.10	39.34	101.79
Casper (city)	WY	84.82	128.99	186.31	151.02	105.70	110.67	0.00
Cedar Rapids (city)	IA	47.87	317.16	199.20	66.08	181.14	181.37	0.01
Centennial (city)	CO	0.00	0.00	0.00	0.78	0.00	0.00	0.00
Champaign (city)	IL	0.00	24.86	3.53	0.00	49.94	5.24	0.00
Chandler (city)	AZ	0.00	133.87	56.23	0.29	66.74	56.93	0.00
Chapel Hill (town)	NC	11.58	32.17	6.08	103.30	15.90	58.78	12.58
Charleston (city)	SC	16.36	59.78	0.00	138.08	0.00	0.00	0.00
Charleston (city)	WV	27.59	348.46	81.17	184.36	255.16	95.68	0.00
Charlotte (city)	NC	0.07	247.92	16.40	13.76	71.50	60.45	5.92
Chattanooga (city)	TN	8.22	376.75	40.58	112.35	324.92	114.75	5.09
Cheektowaga (town)	NY	10.61	4.35	1.61	55.35	109.54	73.73	4.50
Cherry Hill (township)	NJ	0.00	58.16	0.00	7.94	27.41	76.63	0.00
Chesapeake (city)	VA	5.38	109.08	0.00	55.08	36.02	74.29	0.00
Cheyenne (city)	WY	34.83	146.29	215.27	98.07	93.65	91.35	0.00
Chicago (city)	IL	7.12	73.54	0.00	18.41	32.21	52.27	0.25
Chicopee (city)	MA	14.76	189.65	13.98	39.28	83.28	21.47	0.00
Chino (city)	CA	14.59	86.63	162.50	73.54	103.38	156.79	0.00
Chino Hills (city)	CA	15.49	73.84	56.02	42.11	66.50	56.02	0.00

City	State	Revenue ($/per capita)			Current Operational Expenses ($/per capita)			
		Park & Recreation	Sewerage	Solid Waste Management	Parks & Recreation	Sewerage	Solid Waste Management	Natural Resources, Other
Chula Vista (city)	CA	4.73	134.08	6.52	129.54	101.04	4.55	0.00
Cicero (town)	IL	0.00	55.44	43.54	0.00	32.52	22.03	0.00
Cincinnati (city)	OH	34.53	30.04	0.00	109.52	405.36	51.55	0.00
Citrus Heights (city)	CA	0.00	0.00	7.36	0.00	0.00	6.42	0.00
Clarkstown (town)	NY	23.57	0.00	0.07	71.94	12.16	107.59	19.43
Clarksville (city)	TN	10.64	159.96	0.00	43.67	117.23	0.00	0.00
Clay (town)	NY	4.86	0.00	0.00	15.55	13.92	44.93	23.47
Clearwater (city)	FL	69.51	338.11	181.83	221.47	163.05	143.13	104.70
Cleveland (city)	OH	9.90	63.28	8.26	106.42	47.69	64.05	0.00
Clifton (city)	NJ	2.34	106.27	3.71	14.37	0.23	80.10	0.00
Clinton Charter (township)	MI	6.03	176.30	43.35	21.99	49.30	39.97	0.00
Clovis (city)	CA	40.21	161.22	173.82	44.89	71.32	130.95	0.00
College Station (city)	TX	13.87	122.76	76.49	96.25	56.48	62.58	9.54
Colonie (town)	NY	31.49	86.53	115.23	62.49	54.80	45.81	0.21
Colorado Springs (city)	CO	5.49	159.14	0.00	26.75	85.66	0.00	0.00
Colton (city)	CA	3.82	168.98	0.00	30.72	92.17	0.00	0.00
Columbia (city)	MO	37.60	112.71	138.24	110.29	62.50	114.91	0.00
Columbia (city)	SC	4.99	454.21	1.82	83.74	344.47	60.06	13.38
Columbus (city)	OH	13.40	319.55	0.02	131.97	77.10	36.31	0.00
Columbus (consol. govt)	GA	11.70	146.11	50.58	57.56	19.71	53.75	0.74
Compton (city)	CA	1.04	9.55	94.85	52.09	4.91	97.02	0.00
Concord (city)	CA	02.00	149.41	0.00	09.18	138.19	0.00	0.00
Concord (city)	NC	20.60	258.97	1.66	48.10	155.14	102.22	0.00
Conway (city)	AR	14.11	109.15	134.33	35.36	53.78	93.28	0.00
Coon Rapids (city)	MN	37.56	116.55	0.00	64.55	95.35	2.28	0.00
Coral Springs (city)	FL	34.19	74.22	0.00	106.73	69.67	0.17	0.00
Corona (city)	CA	8.29	181.59	45.09	48.89	111.92	47.04	0.00
Corpus Christi (city)	TX	36.85	167.70	104.88	91.65	92.59	77.08	0.00
Corvallis (city)	OR	25.87	199.86	0.00	99.50	145.28	5.34	0.00
Costa Mesa (city)	CA	12.56	0.00	0.00	50.66	0.00	0.00	0.00
Council Bluffs (city)	IA	16.46	86.20	81.07	64.53	159.73	79.22	1.06
Cranston (city)	RI	0.00	234.83	0.00	35.28	188.33	0.00	0.00
Dallas (city)	TX	31.35	100.18	67.07	107.96	00.36	40.40	11.54
Daly (city)	CA	19.16	156.33	4.70	98.59	150.02	0.04	0.00
Danbury (city)	CT	40.71	140.35	0.00	71.58	86.50	3.68	3.54
Davenport (city)	IA	41.16	160.15	46.06	122.15	133.30	47.86	1.64
Davie (town)	FL	0.00	0.00	0.00	46.30	0.00	0.00	0.00
Dayton (city)	OH	22.48	260.64	0.00	47.33	205.91	0.00	0.00
Daytona Beach (city)	FL	129.09	362.23	193.41	211.80	114.91	146.53	87.01
Dearborn (city)	MI	39.97	259.10	0.00	152.50	62.83	50.11	0.00
Dearborn Heights (city)	MI	3.60	149.65	0.00	20.22	70.39	58.07	0.00
Decatur (city)	AL	75.59	205.07	99.20	203.80	122.26	120.50	0.00
Decatur (city)	IL	0.00	27.05	7.59	0.91	14.25	7.32	0.00
Deerfield Beach (city)	FL	25.11	117.88	189.01	73.81	216.60	203.30	66.13
Delray Beach (city)	FL	85.84	0.00	78.83	279.87	0.00	72.57	30.14
Deltona (city)	FL	1.53	60.88	0.00	22.06	80.74	48.41	23.04
Denton (city)	TX	29.75	184.82	162.56	94.78	118.47	131.58	0.00
Denver (city/co.)	CO	77.78	125.57	13.36	184.52	134.83	39.68	0.00
Des Moines (city)	IA	11.04	220.97	53.10	52.75	201.89	51.05	11.85
Des Plaines (city)	IL	0.00	71.77	63.29	0.00	33.26	62.13	0.00
Detroit (city)	MI	2.80	611.18	64.81	31.41	395.23	34.08	2.87
Dothan (city)	AL	36.99	90.72	0.00	124.14	80.81	82.75	0.00
Downey (city)	CA	36.08	13.55	4.28	80.42	12.41	4.58	0.00
Dubuque (city)	IA	23.16	163.07	53.91	115.85	78.02	50.35	5.53
Duluth (city)	MN	155.10	288.22	0.00	223.17	200.66	0.00	0.00
Durham (city)	NC	39.53	214.88	33.55	53.61	108.78	88.73	27.28

City	State	Revenue ($/per capita)			Current Operational Expenses ($/per capita)			
		Park & Recreation	Sewerage	Solid Waste Management	Parks & Recreation	Sewerage	Solid Waste Management	Natural Resources, Other
Eagan (city)	MN	60.76	110.77	0.00	108.68	112.26	0.00	8.04
East Orange (city)	NJ	8.09	90.42	0.00	34.93	72.20	74.70	0.00
Eau Claire (city)	WI	21.89	105.92	1.47	98.77	97.40	1.47	13.83
Eden Prairie (city)	MN	0.00	68.69	0.00	145.24	92.16	54.10	0.00
Edison (township)	NJ	1.22	121.98	2.65	31.06	49.54	15.92	0.00
Edmond (city)	OK	39.01	87.80	91.01	61.51	36.72	58.30	0.00
El Cajon (city)	CA	4.56	115.67	0.00	43.23	138.13	0.00	0.00
El Monte (city)	CA	4.99	0.00	0.00	27.97	0.00	0.00	0.00
El Paso (city)	TX	17.28	78.92	69.26	56.61	42.34	30.75	0.00
Elgin (city)	IL	59.92	48.42	2.41	144.12	16.03	44.15	0.00
Elizabeth (city)	NJ	0.75	149.08	1.92	70.55	93.36	68.32	0.00
Elk Grove (city)	CA	0.00	0.00	82.49	1.27	0.00	69.13	0.00
Elkhart (city)	IN	15.25	177.35	0.00	47.48	111.35	43.18	2.04
Elyria (city)	OH	3.76	189.52	73.33	32.48	183.05	67.46	0.84
Erie (city)	PA	4.22	203.25	66.35	16.42	80.08	37.18	0.00
Escondido (city)	CA	17.96	197.27	0.00	65.94	119.29	0.00	0.00
Eugene (city)	OR	35.42	330.98	0.00	151.45	160.78	11.60	0.55
Evanston (city)	IL	70.15	179.81	32.74	176.88	32.26	62.12	0.00
Evansville (city)	IN	33.82	233.45	39.84	92.74	161.95	44.15	13.23
Everett (city)	WA	44.76	280.04	21.51	127.69	209.21	3.01	7.86
Fairfield (city)	CA	57.74	0.00	0.00	117.83	0.00	0.00	0.00
Fairfield (town)	CT	17.31	89.57	0.00	68.30	77.33	59.20	16.82
Fall River (city)	MA	0.00	211.50	0.00	13.48	91.33	27.72	0.00
Fargo (city)	ND	51.95	121.01	98.69	32.88	63.71	58.84	13.35
Farmington Hills (city)	MI	53.34	123.48	0.00	100.18	42.02	43.89	0.00
Fayetteville (city)	AR	12.48	210.78	121.30	46.11	152.45	114.26	0.00
Fayetteville (city)	NC	4.67	197.26	11.36	59.33	114.59	57.06	5.10
Federal Way (city)	WA	24.42	38.42	3.09	63.27	26.77	4.40	0.00
Fishers (town)	IN	1.38	113.42	0.00	9.52	90.91	0.00	0.00
Flagstaff (city)	AZ	0.00	108.35	182.34	0.00	67.28	163.85	10.37
Flint (city)	MI	5.42	172.19	0.00	46.73	241.92	43.00	0.00
Florissant (city)	MO	33.21	0.00	0.00	104.20	7.27	0.00	0.00
Flower Mound (city)	TX	25.48	133.56	2.01	93.91	108.75	1.11	0.00
Fontana (city)	CA	14.46	64.31	0.00	48.20	62.51	0.00	0.00
Fort Collins (city)	CO	69.09	133.30	0.00	176.94	73.03	0.00	32.25
Fort Lauderdale (city)	FL	42.26	0.00	113.54	199.17	0.00	128.04	65.82
Fort Myers (city)	FL	111.58	474.20	225.67	229.64	444.65	168.87	116.79
Fort Smith (city)	AR	3.50	144.35	153.66	38.48	78.68	121.52	0.00
Fort Wayne (city)	IN	15.64	205.76	38.93	71.05	94.41	34.37	0.00
Fort Worth (city)	TX	8.65	206.53	70.39	57.60	114.04	51.22	0.00
Framingham (town)	MA	1.23	260.09	8.15	37.33	54.03	51.26	1.41
Franklin (city)	TN	0.00	199.18	106.66	50.60	112.81	116.62	0.00
Franklin (township)	NJ	0.00	176.53	0.00	7.66	144.29	10.21	0.00
Frederick (city)	MD	55.14	124.40	0.72	122.06	109.78	53.42	0.00
Fremont (city)	CA	26.84	0.00	23.49	32.81	0.00	24.04	0.15
Fresno (city)	CA	14.49	154.91	125.26	38.51	63.52	105.70	6.17
Frisco (city)	TX	43.98	113.37	77.83	91.16	92.43	70.78	0.00
Fullerton (city)	CA	18.97	46.01	73.33	45.13	18.10	70.97	0.00
Gainesville (city)	FL	9.79	325.80	66.19	81.15	137.59	62.07	0.02
Gaithersburg (city)	MD	53.63	0.00	0.00	138.79	0.00	35.54	0.00
Garden Grove (city)	CA	7.64	86.91	0.00	36.78	70.25	0.00	0.39
Garland (city)	TX	17.19	176.90	107.68	48.95	94.81	66.94	0.00
Gary (city)	IN	3.67	319.87	23.35	28.73	236.59	62.84	0.00
Gastonia (city)	NC	9.37	234.23	23.49	67.33	169.46	79.05	0.00
Gilbert (town)	AZ	12.15	103.99	82.48	46.97	50.04	59.80	0.00
Glendale (city)	AZ	0.00	145.60	200.51	0.00	72.91	82.71	0.00

City	State	Revenue ($/per capita) Park & Recreation	Revenue ($/per capita) Sewerage	Revenue ($/per capita) Solid Waste Management	Current Operational Expenses ($/per capita) Parks & Recreation	Current Operational Expenses ($/per capita) Sewerage	Current Operational Expenses ($/per capita) Solid Waste Management	Current Operational Expenses ($/per capita) Natural Resources, Other
Glendale (city)	CA	15.41	78.96	114.42	91.96	65.24	87.91	0.00
Gloucester (township)	NJ	2.14	96.13	0.00	10.98	51.64	89.95	0.00
Goodyear (city)	AZ	23.99	121.19	88.46	183.21	42.94	71.65	0.00
Grand Forks (city)	ND	66.03	140.05	141.91	31.51	90.54	99.32	0.00
Grand Prairie (city)	TX	47.29	133.29	58.21	104.68	87.45	42.73	0.00
Grand Rapids (city)	MI	12.79	266.59	25.87	35.88	113.26	75.85	0.00
Great Falls (city)	MT	42.17	138.14	54.64	88.13	90.16	50.70	13.23
Greece (town)	NY	2.41	0.89	0.00	14.00	9.54	5.64	5.30
Greeley (city)	CO	19.95	127.28	0.00	146.55	62.07	0.00	0.06
Green Bay (city)	WI	38.93	125.04	0.25	74.26	111.04	76.94	37.34
Greenburgh (town)	NY	19.57	0.00	0.40	85.88	4.16	45.25	0.00
Greensboro (city)	NC	78.57	217.09	68.72	150.38	134.05	128.30	15.73
Greenville (city)	NC	12.96	223.22	63.53	82.60	147.57	65.24	0.00
Greenville (city)	SC	1.63	143.78	0.00	150.99	73.70	0.00	0.00
Greenwich (town)	CT	54.70	0.26	7.01	172.06	66.62	114.92	11.13
Gresham (city)	OR	0.58	201.10	4.49	27.07	117.41	6.14	0.00
Gulfport (city)	MS	0.18	192.87	75.77	110.87	150.38	58.47	0.00
Hamburg (town)	NY	20.22	0.23	0.00	61.49	10.27	2.74	0.18
Hamden (town)	CT	7.87	0.00	0.00	14.52	0.00	0.00	0.00
Hamilton (city)	OH	12.90	199.64	52.55	15.41	72.31	49.41	0.00
Hamilton (township)	NJ	0.90	146.86	0.09	37.85	109.33	56.61	0.00
Hammond (city)	IN	174.01	223.16	62.91	105.90	209.17	70.78	0.00
Hampton (city)	VA	99.72	98.15	128.87	214.07	72.67	104.88	0.00
Hartford (city)	CT	0.46	0.00	0.69	0.76	0.00	25.97	0.00
Haverhill (city)	MA	0.00	132.25	0.00	3.45	85.60	49.64	0.94
Hawthorne (city)	CA	7.79	14.78	0.00	16.75	8.62	0.00	0.00
Hayward (city)	CA	0.00	141.06	0.00	8.31	96.11	3.49	0.36
Hempstead (town)	NY	8.33	0.00	11.45	77.33	0.00	109.15	11.24
Hempstead (village)	NY	0.30	0.00	80.05	47.87	0.50	53.52	0.00
Henderson (city)	NV	38.94	129.57	0.00	190.14	102.06	0.00	2.89
Hesperia (city)	CA	0.00	0.00	0.00	0.00	0.00	0.00	0.00
Hialeah (city)	FL	4.56	124.02	61.96	51.63	85.11	66.98	5.86
High Point (city)	NC	28.58	227.22	80.02	100.25	102.27	115.92	3.37
Hillsboro (city)	OR	23.52	221.73	0.00	143.50	20.71	0.00	0.00
Hoffman Estates (village)	IL	39.73	31.27	19.17	71.18	37.52	21.49	0.00
Hollywood (city)	FL	27.75	323.46	96.87	100.59	195.19	105.78	33.63
Homestead (city)	FL	4.13	114.47	107.45	63.48	138.42	160.08	0.00
Honolulu (city/co.)	HI	26.24	355.59	101.94	90.26	100.12	128.00	0.00
Hoover (city)	AL	14.49	51.09	0.09	93.45	27.13	73.10	0.00
Houston (city)	TX	14.35	206.81	0.93	62.78	65.90	30.04	0.00
Howell (township)	NJ	0.00	119.02	0.00	8.30	93.86	12.82	0.14
Huntington Beach (city)	CA	23.33	56.08	55.75	82.61	27.46	59.70	0.12
Huntington (town)	NY	35.48	4.75	101.73	65.57	20.11	192.58	4.51
Huntsville (city)	AL	45.44	186.10	55.21	117.85	71.09	0.00	3.66
Idaho Falls (city)	ID	39.81	187.11	39.81	125.13	96.32	50.55	0.00
Independence (city)	MO	41.73	146.03	0.00	109.91	140.85	0.00	0.00
Indianapolis (city)	IN	25.07	199.99	18.04	65.34	77.39	48.56	0.30
Indio (city)	CA	11.05	0.00	3.01	52.45	0.00	1.09	0.00
Inglewood (city)	CA	1.62	30.38	106.12	64.45	21.04	98.15	3.52
Iowa (city)	IA	14.66	197.30	121.57	84.55	86.17	110.61	0.00
Irvine (city)	CA	32.97	0.00	0.00	162.04	0.00	0.00	0.00
Irving (city)	TX	7.71	122.07	49.32	126.07	93.64	49.42	20.98
Irvington (township)	NJ	0.00	85.25	0.00	17.64	51.87	43.04	0.00
Islip (town)	NY	23.75	0.00	0.00	36.97	0.00	136.32	1.18
Jackson (city)	MS	10.39	140.64	71.12	68.12	87.96	57.68	0.00
Jackson (city)	TN	45.07	0.00	157.89	135.94	0.00	133.95	0.00

City	State	Revenue ($/per capita)			Current Operational Expenses ($/per capita)			
		Park & Recreation	Sewerage	Solid Waste Management	Parks & Recreation	Sewerage	Solid Waste Management	Natural Resources, Other
Jackson (township)	NJ	0.00	86.24	0.00	3.65	66.98	31.48	0.13
Jacksonville (city)	FL	8.57	216.77	49.60	86.57	92.83	87.90	37.35
Jacksonville (city)	NC	6.84	205.87	38.63	56.24	167.20	71.45	0.07
Janesville (city)	WI	13.87	145.94	90.30	46.61	99.50	109.56	0.00
Jersey (city)	NJ	0.00	182.71	7.32	24.26	53.15	109.03	0.00
Johns Creek (city)	GA	0.53	0.00	0.00	9.85	0.00	0.00	0.00
Johnson (city)	TN	13.52	200.03	181.26	75.69	122.32	162.42	0.00
Joliet (city)	IL	21.37	140.93	82.15	47.32	55.51	77.80	0.00
Jonesboro (city)	AR	1.92	77.71	0.10	29.21	59.13	47.32	0.00
Kalamazoo (city)	MI	23.05	257.83	0.00	50.43	253.87	31.89	10.19
Kansas (city)	MO	19.12	225.60	0.00	137.54	130.33	0.00	0.00
Kenner (city)	LA	6.18	65.97	44.54	68.35	74.17	59.89	0.00
Kennewick (city)	WA	28.40	94.59	0.74	103.37	38.80	0.73	0.00
Kenosha (city)	WI	9.48	97.73	3.34	70.08	104.51	46.81	6.70
Kent (city)	WA	31.78	383.24	0.00	117.25	272.65	0.18	2.20
Kettering (city)	OH	109.36	0.00	0.00	215.96	0.00	0.00	0.00
Killeen (city)	TX	17.96	104.49	106.35	45.62	75.12	79.85	14.04
Kissimmee (city)	FL	18.57	61.63	52.16	88.72	50.77	58.74	0.00
Knoxville (city)	TN	17.05	368.11	4.85	86.65	174.86	56.58	0.00
La Crosse (city)	WI	94.62	125.84	0.53	151.05	114.32	27.14	10.70
Lafayette (city)	IN	18.95	341.72	0.00	80.92	131.41	24.84	0.00
Lafayette (city/parish)	LA	101.49	199.75	99.30	172.91	122.52	92.91	66.55
Lake Charles (city)	LA	27.25	124.47	0.00	96.52	99.38	52.48	0.00
Lake Forest (city)	CA	3.43	0.00	0.00	59.12	0.00	0.39	0.00
Lake Havasu (city)	AZ	19.23	580.33	22.83	107.60	27.85	4.93	0.00
Lakeland (city)	FL	79.44	230.63	132.23	243.54	172.16	113.69	16.32
Lakeville (city)	MN	17.30	74.29	0.00	54.28	66.29	0.00	6.97
Lakewood (city)	CA	12.09	0.00	58.29	136.08	0.00	58.12	0.00
Lakewood (city)	CO	57.99	34.45	0.00	89.12	33.17	0.00	37.39
Lakewood (city)	OH	0.00	114.19	0.00	39.82	75.79	61.36	0.00
Lakewood (township)	NJ	0.00	42.34	0.50	14.47	10.24	55.07	0.00
Lancaster (city)	CA	15.09	0.00	0.00	64.82	0.00	0.00	0.00
Lancaster (city)	PA	3.83	166.03	57.06	50.98	101.35	55.27	0.00
Lansing (city)	MI	45.19	255.53	36.02	123.63	110.38	37.63	0.00
Laredo (city)	TX	2.36	96.25	67.75	44.60	77.54	59.84	0.00
Las Cruces (city)	NM	0.02	116.00	108.17	19.57	70.80	94.28	5.32
Las Vegas (city)	NV	10.86	168.27	0.00	84.84	85.64	9.78	6.46
Lauderhill (city)	FL	1.35	66.83	0.00	49.82	68.55	0.00	92.78
Lawrence (city)	KS	28.01	170.50	117.18	96.80	88.44	98.16	2.20
Lawrence (city)	MA	0.27	116.45	0.00	6.83	5.83	53.09	0.00
Lawton (city)	OK	3.32	123.31	83.22	55.59	61.43	40.88	0.00
Layton (city)	UT	10.70	93.94	37.59	55.90	31.08	17.90	0.00
League (city)	TX	6.45	133.96	35.44	30.31	65.92	32.46	0.00
Lees Summit (city)	MO	33.55	149.22	30.23	74.83	106.50	44.97	0.00
Lewisville (city)	TX	17.80	110.85	34.02	113.76	54.00	1.99	0.00
Lexington-Fayette (urban co. govt)	KY	20.94	159.58	32.32	25.40	96.31	102.73	0.00
Lincoln (city)	NE	23.96	84.00	22.03	31.98	45.15	22.66	0.00
Little Rock (city)	AR	73.47	217.10	83.36	153.09	118.93	55.70	0.00
Livermore (city)	CA	30.59	229.68	2.59	26.64	180.10	5.06	0.00
Livonia (city)	MI	40.82	132.46	0.99	113.89	133.65	122.51	0.00
Lodi (city)	CA	24.74	215.32	0.00	85.28	116.97	0.00	0.00
Long Beach (city)	CA	12.12	35.58	175.68	240.43	29.92	154.71	0.00
Longmont (city)	CO	74.70	135.52	67.30	198.83	92.69	66.95	0.00
Longview (city)	TX	12.17	134.53	58.48	78.70	96.54	47.54	22.68
Lorain (city)	OH	0.00	183.22	0.00	4.76	147.46	0.48	0.00
Los Angeles (city)	CA	38.05	141.34	83.78	83.36	83.34	52.68	0.00

City	State	Revenue ($/per capita)			Current Operational Expenses ($/per capita)			
		Park & Recreation	Sewerage	Solid Waste Management	Parks & Recreation	Sewerage	Solid Waste Management	Natural Resources, Other
Louisville-Jefferson Co. (metro govt)	KY	30.49	0.00	3.17	45.80	0.00	24.48	8.43
Loveland (city)	CO	53.68	164.23	86.29	186.90	109.75	76.03	0.00
Lowell (city)	MA	3.18	143.19	28.09	20.35	75.60	54.15	0.00
Lower Merion (township)	PA	3.68	138.21	107.38	99.59	107.24	103.43	0.00
Lubbock (city)	TX	19.54	116.39	74.22	57.40	63.17	59.44	0.00
Lynchburg (city)	VA	8.19	248.90	10.15	110.07	123.88	8.75	0.28
Lynn (city)	MA	6.72	0.00	0.00	3.40	0.00	52.07	0.02
Macomb (township)	MI	27.65	93.57	0.00	31.36	96.78	0.00	0.00
Macon (city)	GA	6.58	0.00	66.69	83.01	3.28	55.14	0.00
Madison (city)	WI	30.82	100.68	6.79	122.00	32.20	63.90	20.12
Malden (city)	MA	0.00	233.02	20.45	16.20	14.52	44.89	0.08
Manchester (city)	NH	13.32	194.32	0.12	43.52	62.57	16.78	0.00
Manchester (town)	CT	5.99	112.19	102.92	92.62	77.78	106.04	0.00
Manhattan (city)	KS	10.71	119.43	0.00	94.03	68.27	0.00	0.00
Maple Grove (city)	MN	60.02	69.29	18.57	168.76	73.59	19.28	8.95
Marietta (city)	GA	73.35	238.32	61.61	38.57	182.68	74.64	0.00
Mcallen (city)	TX	15.31	100.95	118.17	126.77	57.01	90.17	0.00
Mckinney (city)	TX	6.41	145.59	47.90	56.41	76.73	46.72	2.39
Medford (city)	MA	0.00	234.10	0.00	10.13	19.46	77.72	0.11
Medford (city)	OR	29.60	111.58	0.00	38.75	73.12	0.00	0.00
Melbourne (city)	FL	41.53	215.08	0.00	117.22	199.44	0.00	0.00
Memphis (city)	TN	12.19	189.00	92.00	80.59	86.79	75.66	0.00
Menifee (city)	CA	2.23	0.00	0.00	0.00	0.00	0.00	0.00
Merced (city)	CA	3.52	203.87	142.13	53.41	114.07	129.13	0.19
Meriden (city)	CT	0.33	154.07	0.48	31.81	149.54	26.47	0.00
Meridian (city)	ID	0.00	167.77	0.00	28.19	76.92	0.00	0.00
Mesa (city)	AZ	18.58	139.84	108.59	93.91	45.27	60.44	0.00
Mesquite (city)	TX	11.61	114.87	49.60	98.20	52.18	38.34	4.62
Miami Beach (city)	FL	235.25	536.52	73.82	594.66	351.31	188.19	684.29
Miami (city)	FL	39.76	0.00	61.50	110.14	11.14	49.78	69.68
Miami Gardens (city)	FL	25.90	0.00	0.00	87.17	0.00	0.00	17.58
Middletown (township)	NJ	6.85	140.93	0.00	33.82	112.04	65.99	0.00
Midland (city)	TX	10.80	86.10	80.00	72.44	61.43	60.40	0.00
Midwest (city)	OK	25.31	94.30	81.05	40.79	81.72	55.38	0.00
Milford (city)	CT	7.18	2.24	1.74	23.41	130.27	90.71	0.04
Millcreek (township)	PA	3.20	171.52	0.00	18.65	163.09	0.00	2.82
Milwaukee (city)	WI	8.18	167.76	61.10	0.00	76.17	60.00	7.83
Minneapolis (city)	MN	66.72	227.60	77.47	304.51	33.36	77.61	0.00
Miramar (city)	FL	22.77	152.65	1.47	66.47	68.19	0.00	67.69
Mission Viejo (city)	CA	16.53	0.00	0.00	109.43	0.00	0.00	0.00
Missoula (city)	MT	13.66	99.70	0.00	72.27	58.05	0.00	0.66
Missouri (city)	TX	26.72	24.97	25.18	33.70	23.58	13.52	1.16
Mobile (city)	AL	45.19	271.26	2.16	126.83	191.88	56.32	0.00
Modesto (city)	CA	16.78	196.40	22.25	67.00	124.78	19.04	0.00
Montebello (city)	CA	51.44	0.00	56.14	155.87	0.00	56.14	0.00
Montgomery (city)	AL	20.63	0.00	73.14	136.15	0.00	64.88	0.00
Moore (city)	OK	2.40	100.74	70.42	23.66	66.94	21.21	0.00
Moreno Valley (city)	CA	13.41	0.00	0.00	88.04	0.00	0.00	0.00
Mount Pleasant (town)	SC	32.72	220.20	0.18	74.44	109.43	94.45	6.84
Mount Prospect (village)	IL	0.00	48.26	39.27	5.78	47.11	73.88	0.00
Mount Vernon (city)	NY	1.41	0.00	0.00	70.29	10.21	88.44	0.00
Muncie (city)	IN	8.32	160.52	0.00	23.49	318.50	72.55	0.00
Murfreesboro (city)	TN	30.91	129.87	0.10	89.55	82.92	38.56	0.00
Murrieta (city)	CA	6.45	0.00	0.00	82.92	0.00	0.00	0.00
Nampa (city)	ID	105.58	119.63	85.56	146.45	104.34	90.08	0.00
Naperville (city)	IL	5.24	62.85	0.00	49.94	39.57	43.89	0.00

City	State	Revenue ($/per capita)			Current Operational Expenses ($/per capita)			
		Park & Recreation	Sewerage	Solid Waste Management	Parks & Recreation	Sewerage	Solid Waste Management	Natural Resources, Other
Nashua (city)	NH	1.99	101.57	26.07	34.40	117.89	68.11	14.72
Nashville-Davidson Co. (metro govt)	TN	24.25	186.11	8.11	132.49	94.99	33.03	4.56
National (city)	CA	1.74	126.57	0.00	39.24	116.32	0.00	0.00
New Bedford (city)	MA	6.03	204.25	0.04	11.69	114.79	50.53	2.18
New Braunfels (city)	TX	30.57	163.91	101.40	76.29	87.41	92.15	0.00
New Britain (city)	CT	33.06	99.20	0.00	104.94	81.03	73.46	0.00
New Brunswick (city)	NJ	0.00	197.84	0.00	29.12	25.41	40.88	0.00
New Haven (city)	CT	10.16	0.00	54.85	52.97	0.00	53.58	0.00
New Orleans (city)	LA	102.62	206.47	50.35	176.94	230.33	117.07	0.00
New Rochelle (city)	NY	26.39	0.00	24.10	32.13	30.20	53.81	7.15
New York (city)	NY	7.82	219.91	1.11	94.34	44.12	139.07	0.00
Newark (city)	NJ	0.00	191.78	0.00	38.57	20.36	82.08	0.00
Newport Beach (city)	CA	35.25	39.30	0.00	168.68	29.91	0.00	0.00
Newport News (city)	VA	35.67	136.46	63.61	121.04	113.28	56.03	0.00
Newton (city)	MA	1.79	271.70	0.00	44.36	37.07	71.82	0.81
Niagara Falls (city)	NY	16.00	0.00	0.66	45.56	0.00	67.90	0.00
Norfolk (city)	VA	24.19	148.70	85.19	183.55	77.63	79.04	0.00
Normal (town)	IL	72.18	77.07	20.38	146.33	26.06	36.25	0.00
Norman (city)	OK	15.15	99.85	103.79	59.10	78.08	147.71	0.00
North Bergen (township)	NJ	5.28	210.03	0.00	32.05	217.33	0.00	0.00
North Charleston (city)	SC	3.85	32.74	0.00	42.71	28.88	35.08	0.00
North Hempstead (town)	NY	54.04	5.49	67.09	110.59	43.41	115.57	0.00
North Las Vegas (city)	NV	8.56	178.08	0.00	64.22	78.81	0.00	8.42
North Little Rock (city)	AR	15.95	171.24	10.02	83.46	166.94	66.77	0.00
North Miami (city)	FL	6.48	195.56	115.01	90.53	181.27	84.73	23.22
North Richland Hills (city)	TX	105.54	133.62	0.00	167.69	151.35	0.00	0.05
Norwalk (city)	CA	9.13	0.00	0.00	56.93	0.00	0.00	0.00
Norwalk (city)	CT	111.16	154.83	0.00	142.07	84.85	0.00	0.00
Novi (city)	MI	53.96	145.68	0.00	58.15	133.26	0.00	10.50
O'fallon (city)	MO	38.55	111.16	54.37	78.95	36.83	38.47	5.02
Oak Lawn (village)	IL	0.00	49.18	68.71	2.10	38.83	68.12	0.00
Oakland (city)	CA	7.61	107.05	0.00	80.38	52.73	0.00	3.96
Ocala (city)	FL	32.19	350.55	181.60	122.31	194.37	161.72	0.00
Oceanside (city)	CA	6.24	201.03	138.39	68.86	119.62	123.84	0.00
Odessa (city)	TX	12.95	129.51	98.51	53.07	50.32	82.57	0.00
Ogden (city)	UT	24.75	174.50	58.91	84.89	113.85	52.79	0.00
Oklahoma (city)	OK	45.88	125.40	68.85	148.58	34.45	54.74	0.00
Olathe (city)	KS	12.91	127.61	88.79	13.32	86.39	77.47	0.00
Old Bridge (township)	NJ	11.21	188.99	0.06	27.40	93.15	9.97	0.00
Omaha (city)	NE	20.52	121.77	1.47	63.43	66.32	47.50	37.89
Ontario (city)	CA	3.64	111.12	187.76	63.02	83.51	136.75	1.27
Orange (city)	CA	5.78	0.00	64.19	41.29	0.00	64.79	0.40
Orem (city)	UT	22.21	108.79	35.27	68.23	88.06	36.15	0.00
Orland Park (village)	IL	70.64	86.48	0.00	149.28	58.70	0.00	0.00
Orlando (city)	FL	85.57	231.88	98.96	253.87	278.66	95.48	102.92
Oshkosh (city)	WI	16.77	131.18	4.48	85.35	112.90	33.03	4.09
Overland Park (city)	KS	78.93	20.15	0.00	38.95	17.78	0.00	0.00
Owensboro (city)	KY	29.35	221.09	91.00	76.45	13.76	53.61	0.00
Oxnard (city)	CA	24.51	127.12	227.63	95.59	83.30	197.38	0.00
Oyster Bay (town)	NY	21.01	1.37	29.02	113.28	12.40	210.86	7.80
Palatine (village)	IL	0.00	46.53	64.12	0.00	20.48	61.53	0.00
Palm Bay (city)	FL	2.56	77.57	1.05	34.86	111.82	0.00	2.93
Palm Coast (city)	FL	20.74	140.61	103.14	50.36	122.51	100.44	80.29
Palmdale (city)	CA	10.74	35.63	0.00	59.24	13.29	0.00	0.00
Parma (city)	OH	11.52	0.00	0.00	51.21	0.00	0.00	0.00
Parsippany-troy Hills (township)	NJ	92.70	286.54	45.87	111.67	171.31	60.22	0.00

City	State	Revenue ($/per capita)			Current Operational Expenses ($/per capita)			
		Park & Recreation	Sewerage	Solid Waste Management	Parks & Recreation	Sewerage	Solid Waste Management	Natural Resources, Other
Pasadena (city)	CA	97.38	47.70	100.78	226.28	27.58	93.06	0.00
Pasadena (city)	TX	18.32	94.70	43.69	52.31	67.76	61.35	0.00
Pasco (city)	WA	8.38	159.52	0.00	50.90	69.67	0.00	0.00
Passaic (city)	NJ	0.73	70.25	2.88	13.63	73.14	55.59	0.00
Paterson (city)	NJ	0.00	47.91	3.38	30.39	6.45	73.32	0.00
Pawtucket (city)	RI	0.06	0.00	3.27	25.51	8.81	44.57	0.00
Peabody (city)	MA	37.37	182.08	7.73	60.14	12.64	63.47	0.35
Pearland (city)	TX	7.59	112.23	80.12	52.02	71.18	80.70	0.00
Pembroke Pines (city)	FL	60.99	120.77	0.00	94.78	230.77	0.00	17.65
Pensacola (city)	FL	29.99	0.00	119.41	156.60	0.00	119.95	55.66
Peoria (city)	AZ	42.94	106.71	77.82	109.67	122.12	40.87	0.00
Peoria (city)	IL	0.00	0.00	3.42	22.35	0.00	4.51	0.00
Philadelphia (city)	PA	0.88	188.83	6.54	35.19	125.92	57.11	0.00
Phoenix (city)	AZ	21.39	145.48	99.29	96.88	77.73	62.30	0.63
Piscataway (township)	NJ	0.00	143.92	0.00	23.91	30.08	12.99	0.00
Pittsburg (city)	CA	9.29	68.55	0.00	35.12	19.02	0.00	0.33
Pittsburgh (city)	PA	7.51	0.00	0.00	47.49	0.00	31.39	0.00
Plano (city)	TX	38.13	200.26	55.78	114.93	34.75	54.77	11.37
Plantation (city)	FL	62.53	154.14	2.20	147.61	131.12	6.33	68.87
Pleasanton (city)	CA	95.17	159.38	0.00	282.36	172.60	0.00	0.00
Plymouth (city)	MN	19.65	101.96	5.78	110.36	31.23	14.65	23.70
Plymouth (town)	MA	1.74	97.00	33.97	11.07	40.85	14.85	0.89
Pocatello (city)	ID	20.68	142.44	115.44	55.46	58.69	63.99	15.72
Pomona (city)	CA	1.01	29.16	60.69	22.35	20.56	60.64	0.00
Pompano Beach (city)	FL	42.30	154.94	52.97	100.48	164.12	33.58	127.35
Pontiac (city)	MI	0.15	164.50	13.51	43.27	125.26	65.01	0.00
Port Arthur (city)	TX	0.19	138.11	142.20	49.98	85.40	152.07	0.00
Port Orange (city)	FL	41.63	225.50	140.33	79.99	271.71	136.86	0.00
Port St Lucie (city)	FL	18.25	6.78	0.00	69.88	40.73	0.00	7.40
Portland (city)	ME	30.59	321.52	53.51	96.08	223.54	62.53	0.00
Portland (city)	OR	55.37	418.48	2.88	123.08	180.94	7.89	0.00
Portsmouth (city)	VA	26.90	267.40	146.84	121.64	94.97	133.38	0.00
Providence (city)	RI	4.05	0.00	0.00	19.20	4.08	76.22	0.00
Provo (city)	UT	25.30	63.87	29.81	75.23	27.07	27.97	0.00
Pueblo (city)	CO	21.60	154.14	0.00	60.32	85.98	0.00	0.00
Quincy (city)	MA	0.27	266.38	0.00	23.72	31.98	68.57	0.00
Racine (city)	WI	14.01	171.28	5.87	114.00	180.52	62.59	6.30
Raleigh (city)	NC	48.38	231.71	46.15	151.26	133.46	59.77	1.77
Ramapo (town)	NY	33.56	0.29	6.75	69.92	15.68	28.34	0.00
Rancho Cordova (city)	CA	0.00	0.00	0.00	12.20	0.00	0.00	0.00
Rancho Cucamonga (city)	CA	23.44	2.20	6.12	35.98	0.00	6.57	0.00
Rapid (city)	SD	121.00	139.93	120.48	212.28	70.87	78.01	0.32
Reading (city)	PA	3.08	333.25	26.31	29.04	157.38	89.46	0.00
Redding (city)	CA	10.56	216.92	204.69	74.37	83.96	182.90	0.00
Redondo Beach (city)	CA	25.75	36.90	55.55	84.57	16.15	53.48	0.00
Reno (city)	NV	18.79	195.35	0.00	56.80	123.81	0.00	0.00
Renton (city)	WA	37.05	258.46	168.33	91.64	188.82	137.24	0.00
Revere (city)	MA	0.00	13.58	0.00	4.27	19.53	59.24	0.12
Rialto (city)	CA	9.18	104.27	9.13	29.54	73.65	5.86	0.00
Richardson (city)	TX	48.44	157.70	123.11	138.75	149.52	117.72	0.00
Richmond (city)	CA	4.99	168.04	0.00	66.52	88.11	0.00	0.00
Richmond (city)	VA	9.97	296.24	113.89	89.65	184.57	119.40	0.00
Rio Rancho (city)	NM	14.73	157.22	0.00	58.57	28.48	4.44	3.31
Riverside (city)	CA	7.37	109.74	63.47	58.67	84.88	51.57	0.00
Roanoke (city)	VA	6.92	0.00	21.82	72.91	0.00	60.28	0.00
Rochester (city)	MN	63.16	199.83	0.00	126.45	89.37	0.00	0.00

City	State	Revenue ($/per capita) Park & Recreation	Revenue ($/per capita) Sewerage	Revenue ($/per capita) Solid Waste Management	Current Operational Expenses ($/per capita) Parks & Recreation	Current Operational Expenses ($/per capita) Sewerage	Current Operational Expenses ($/per capita) Solid Waste Management	Current Operational Expenses ($/per capita) Natural Resources, Other
Rochester (city)	NY	10.55	0.00	123.48	67.57	1.84	150.44	0.00
Rochester Hills (city)	MI	46.72	168.87	0.00	146.17	42.50	0.00	0.00
Rock Hill (city)	SC	20.92	270.97	102.16	115.02	232.96	36.17	15.27
Rockford (city)	IL	0.43	0.00	56.05	0.00	3.21	43.11	0.00
Rockville (city)	MD	116.34	115.13	89.50	313.70	113.81	89.37	0.00
Rocky Mount (city)	NC	16.01	263.04	100.28	129.32	188.46	105.52	3.46
Rogers (city)	AR	4.75	185.99	3.81	64.24	68.20	5.74	0.00
Roseville (city)	CA	73.64	284.18	174.12	155.65	138.85	128.50	0.00
Roswell (city)	GA	1.15	1.74	111.17	140.29	9.44	78.12	0.00
Round Rock (city)	TX	26.45	165.24	14.80	71.46	75.58	1.72	0.08
Rowlett (city)	TX	27.53	195.57	79.77	57.62	23.52	53.27	8.63
Royal Oak (city)	MI	19.52	271.93	0.00	64.17	198.88	102.24	0.00
Sacramento (city)	CA	21.84	47.42	137.43	168.42	35.71	101.30	0.00
Saginaw (city)	MI	0.00	419.39	26.42	7.75	259.53	63.06	0.00
Salem (city)	OR	0.00	273.72	0.00	56.44	167.20	0.00	0.00
Salinas (city)	CA	1.07	24.43	0.00	29.84	22.29	0.00	0.00
Salt Lake (city)	UT	42.47	135.50	55.21	91.72	82.66	45.54	0.00
San Angelo (city)	TX	6.32	145.76	9.62	49.81	55.48	7.75	0.00
San Antonio (city)	TX	10.61	188.11	65.34	84.30	107.14	58.96	0.55
San Bernardino (city)	CA	2.85	111.63	116.87	27.04	85.18	97.95	1.25
San Buenaventura (city)	CA	63.26	153.39	0.53	104.66	118.42	8.19	0.00
San Diego (city)	CA	62.98	273.62	38.96	144.81	137.66	32.09	10.44
San Francisco (city/co.)	CA	42.51	279.99	0.00	267.99	160.59	0.00	0.00
San Jose (city)	CA	22.99	177.27	117.23	102.77	118.49	113.00	0.10
San Leandro (city)	CA	25.30	123.34	0.00	75.09	67.37	0.00	0.00
San Marcos (city)	CA	21.08	0.00	0.00	110.22	0.00	0.00	0.00
San Mateo (city)	CA	59.46	232.80	15.01	130.98	171.45	11.18	0.00
San Rafael (city)	CA	89.56	0.00	0.00	162.30	0.00	0.00	0.00
Sandy (city)	UT	31.04	37.16	47.32	71.21	16.03	40.29	0.00
Sandy Springs (city)	GA	8.01	0.00	0.00	54.96	10.36	0.00	0.00
Sanford (city)	FL	7.32	228.88	100.17	79.20	131.19	96.88	73.38
Santa Ana (city)	CA	12.25	15.77	49.97	52.05	9.12	47.27	0.00
Santa Barbara (city)	CA	52.57	166.64	190.79	189.68	151.66	203.26	0.00
Santa Clara (city)	CA	23.38	171.36	147.18	117.71	135.76	138.79	0.00
Santa Clarita (city)	CA	25.10	0.00	1.65	153.81	0.00	2.37	0.00
Santa Fe (city)	NM	54.98	184.32	147.62	253.86	129.06	131.50	35.03
Santa Maria (city)	CA	10.11	65.64	168.63	74.84	37.27	165.08	0.00
Santa Monica (city)	CA	150.04	198.59	243.73	447.57	106.40	239.18	0.00
Santa Rosa (city)	CA	35.85	400.55	0.00	60.58	201.61	0.00	0.69
Savannah (city)	GA	5.46	177.26	147.39	141.61	200.58	169.03	0.00
Schaumburg (village)	IL	5.83	28.74	0.00	30.20	30.29	19.16	0.00
Schenectady (city)	NY	13.50	172.04	57.37	28.52	100.10	61.69	0.00
Scottsdale (city)	AZ	34.81	193.66	96.34	155.37	80.15	70.83	0.00
Scranton (city)	PA	0.68	0.00	55.68	14.77	0.00	45.30	0.00
Seattle (city)	WA	53.48	402.44	215.95	244.75	115.52	197.15	9.25
Shawnee (city)	KS	19.45	0.00	0.00	70.95	24.82	0.00	0.00
Shelby Charter (township)	MI	6.67	86.68	0.00	37.06	16.88	0.00	0.00
Shoreline (city)	WA	24.66	59.03	0.00	77.82	25.45	0.00	4.09
Shreveport (city)	LA	68.05	139.88	54.02	131.36	72.48	100.73	0.00
Simi Valley (city)	CA	0.00	117.61	0.54	4.17	97.19	7.86	0.00
Sioux (city)	IA	14.66	222.69	49.85	155.69	175.22	73.05	0.00
Sioux Falls (city)	SD	7.45	107.75	66.35	104.26	55.85	33.97	0.04
Skokie (village)	IL	19.62	0.00	4.14	29.30	0.00	61.02	0.00
Smithtown (town)	NY	16.38	0.00	139.95	46.88	0.00	149.57	8.68
Somerville (city)	MA	0.00	244.42	0.00	5.97	10.42	71.85	1.56
South Bend (city)	IN	94.53	304.76	47.13	166.19	132.73	41.72	0.00

City	State	Revenue ($/per capita): Park & Recreation	Revenue ($/per capita): Sewerage	Revenue ($/per capita): Solid Waste Management	Current Operational Expenses ($/per capita): Parks & Recreation	Current Operational Expenses ($/per capita): Sewerage	Current Operational Expenses ($/per capita): Solid Waste Management	Current Operational Expenses ($/per capita): Natural Resources, Other
South Gate (city)	CA	9.13	14.04	33.27	42.91	9.99	34.70	0.00
Southampton (town)	NY	45.38	0.00	38.92	154.99	1.73	42.03	0.35
Southfield (city)	MI	26.62	0.00	43.80	123.57	0.00	43.45	0.00
Sparks (city)	NV	28.25	206.45	0.00	65.76	157.65	0.00	0.00
Spokane (city)	WA	32.61	314.40	343.31	75.90	130.07	275.37	0.00
Spokane Valley (city)	WA	2.86	19.41	0.00	25.65	13.69	0.00	0.09
Springdale (city)	AR	11.20	161.37	1.53	32.84	90.69	1.28	0.00
Springfield (city)	IL	0.00	50.31	0.00	0.00	32.46	0.00	0.00
Springfield (city)	MA	11.84	0.00	24.58	76.83	0.00	52.89	0.00
Springfield (city)	MO	54.79	149.06	16.38	190.69	169.21	28.05	4.86
Springfield (city)	OH	0.00	172.09	0.00	0.00	95.47	0.00	6.40
Springfield (city)	OR	0.00	670.64	0.00	0.00	337.64	0.00	0.00
St Charles (city)	MO	33.03	135.80	0.00	116.30	58.55	0.00	0.00
St Clair Shores (city)	MI	50.02	187.78	0.00	65.59	139.40	53.81	0.00
St Cloud (city)	MN	41.25	102.90	46.75	90.09	60.05	37.57	0.00
St George (city)	UT	75.19	150.14	47.52	162.87	98.73	46.75	0.00
St Joseph (city)	MO	24.04	204.83	42.62	77.04	133.22	27.51	0.00
St Louis (city)	MO	0.85	7.88	0.00	69.12	9.10	49.71	0.00
St Paul (city)	MN	35.98	164.60	0.00	185.65	90.61	11.78	0.00
St Peters (city)	MO	112.16	77.15	131.55	196.41	97.38	144.78	0.00
St Petersburg (city)	FL	65.70	197.39	163.05	223.33	161.92	138.46	52.46
Stamford (city)	CT	28.94	156.52	11.94	42.29	91.31	91.00	0.00
Sterling Heights (city)	MI	3.80	113.41	0.00	15.17	19.51	34.31	0.00
Stockton (city)	CA	15.05	165.55	0.00	71.36	132.96	0.00	0.00
Suffolk (city)	VA	9.42	45.66	0.00	51.57	34.94	38.91	0.00
Sugar Land (city)	TX	5.11	177.13	61.66	42.31	81.42	66.98	0.00
Sunnyvale (city)	CA	77.85	173.31	437.53	143.10	100.77	400.43	0.00
Sunrise (city)	FL	13.90	493.94	162.60	121.63	287.58	171.79	32.28
Surprise (city)	AZ	0.00	130.33	56.15	105.41	68.08	43.96	0.00
Syracuse (city)	NY	3.20	42.01	1.01	49.29	43.03	48.00	0.00
Tacoma (city)	WA	9.94	390.87	282.52	50.97	229.91	154.62	2.15
Tallahassee (city)	FL	23.34	275.60	116.88	113.34	184.82	108.37	83.29
Tampa (city)	FL	0.00	257.07	169.00	136.89	229.48	183.81	0.00
Taunton (city)	MA	0.00	136.36	17.59	17.50	71.46	32.48	4.21
Taylor (city)	MI	59.73	103.42	0.00	60.59	31.62	0.00	0.00
Taylorsville (city)	UT	0.00	19.79	0.00	2.18	7.84	0.00	0.00
Temecula (city)	CA	22.04	0.07	0.00	163.98	58.38	0.00	0.00
Tempe (city)	AZ	13.86	204.99	94.79	39.38	100.03	78.22	0.00
Terre Haute (city)	IN	19.91	200.13	1.37	62.52	150.81	11.81	0.03
Thornton (city)	CO	30.66	87.66	39.77	122.10	77.38	34.07	0.00
Thousand Oaks (city)	CA	65.03	153.84	10.43	74.19	99.26	11.17	0.00
Toledo (city)	OH	0.77	206.57	0.00	11.40	155.09	48.35	1.15
Toms River (township)	NJ	34.03	206.13	2.05	35.86	49.75	93.30	0.00
Tonawanda (town)	NY	62.38	89.09	4.44	120.57	148.94	62.56	4.84
Topeka (city)	KS	20.45	238.51	0.00	85.86	126.87	0.00	0.00
Torrance (city)	CA	31.46	10.87	74.71	122.26	9.54	81.18	0.00
Tracy (city)	CA	16.24	129.18	192.14	58.84	80.47	210.70	0.00
Trenton (city)	NJ	0.00	149.80	0.00	19.28	122.68	123.06	0.00
Troy (city)	MI	64.97	147.16	0.00	119.62	14.87	50.75	0.00
Tucson (city)	AZ	19.92	4.66	85.52	108.46	0.00	71.84	0.00
Tulsa (city)	OK	36.79	171.19	55.26	73.20	164.25	54.70	0.00
Tuscaloosa (city)	AL	1.64	263.16	39.35	52.15	67.85	71.65	0.11
Tyler (city)	TX	0.76	90.58	106.49	40.87	76.60	103.35	3.40
Union (city)	NJ	4.51	0.00	5.42	18.55	0.00	101.72	0.00
Union (town)	NY	3.89	8.39	0.00	17.78	16.27	25.27	0.11
Union (township)	NJ	0.00	82.66	0.00	6.81	70.94	77.57	0.00

City	State	Revenue ($/per capita)			Current Operational Expenses ($/per capita)			
		Park & Recreation	Sewerage	Solid Waste Management	Parks & Recreation	Sewerage	Solid Waste Management	Natural Resources, Other
Upper Darby (township)	PA	6.22	67.14	44.24	37.92	89.32	43.43	0.00
Utica (city)	NY	9.24	27.86	0.00	59.68	20.58	36.84	0.00
Vacaville (city)	CA	35.51	273.21	0.00	80.26	241.65	0.00	0.00
Vallejo (city)	CA	0.47	217.29	13.75	1.90	154.18	16.07	0.00
Vancouver (city)	WA	40.78	261.73	4.62	75.16	97.79	9.57	0.00
Victoria (city)	TX	7.16	175.76	65.95	50.95	77.87	48.19	0.00
Victorville (city)	CA	5.44	109.16	132.04	40.46	119.32	120.39	0.00
Vineland (city)	NJ	0.00	148.54	0.00	11.56	128.17	4.22	0.00
Virginia Beach (city)	VA	51.73	161.94	5.30	176.14	114.43	67.41	2.00
Visalia (city)	CA	26.70	153.31	134.97	94.08	81.74	125.20	0.00
Vista (city)	CA	26.66	250.93	5.63	96.26	133.89	0.00	0.00
Waco (city)	TX	39.23	156.59	129.29	145.12	72.53	90.33	0.00
Waltham (city)	MA	8.31	290.56	0.00	21.52	13.28	74.71	1.01
Warner Robins (city)	GA	6.23	93.23	115.01	28.59	54.80	120.23	0.00
Warren (city)	MI	16.63	125.33	0.00	57.35	95.86	56.57	0.00
Warwick (city)	RI	10.73	232.80	0.00	38.07	76.02	25.32	0.00
Washington Dc (city)	DC	42.36	410.31	8.48	237.37	243.16	153.27	55.25
Waterbury (city)	CT	14.60	158.64	1.37	40.12	147.22	53.33	0.00
Waterford Charter (township)	MI	10.64	153.11	0.00	28.76	128.41	0.00	0.00
Waterloo (city)	IA	31.62	196.93	65.14	88.14	95.25	45.84	0.00
Waukegan (city)	IL	0.00	27.90	0.00	0.00	18.18	52.79	0.00
Waukesha (city)	WI	22.51	131.55	0.00	83.95	127.05	40.23	16.11
Wayne (township)	NJ	14.71	159.84	0.00	62.74	157.63	92.88	5.19
West Allis (city)	WI	1.62	100.30	23.82	7.10	86.52	71.63	126.12
West Bloomfield Charter (township)	MI	7.28	143.90	0.00	6.80	123.50	5.70	0.00
West Covina (city)	CA	11.69	0.00	0.00	27.21	0.00	0.00	0.00
West Des Moines (city)	IA	21.87	180.24	30.10	78.22	108.73	30.79	1.27
West Hartford (town)	CT	46.86	0.00	0.00	93.52	0.00	0.00	0.00
West Haven (city)	CT	16.29	131.90	0.61	31.69	87.41	55.85	0.00
West Jordan (city)	UT	0.51	72.79	39.43	25.37	103.25	31.12	0.00
West Palm Beach (city)	FL	30.20	240.27	130.30	184.29	214.16	86.62	50.58
West Valley (city)	UT	35.43	27.18	35.36	88.84	24.03	26.86	0.00
Westland (city)	MI	8.59	148.58	0.00	32.78	131.28	50.31	0.00
Westminster (city)	CA	6.61	0.00	0.00	39.07	0.00	0.00	0.00
Westminster (city)	CO	85.32	132.66	0.00	172.88	66.56	0.00	0.00
Weymouth Town (city)	MA	0.00	276.58	0.00	9.27	20.15	89.15	1.38
Wheaton (city)	IL	0.00	79.97	0.00	10.06	45.28	0.00	0.00
White Plains (city)	NY	19.30	25.01	0.00	136.56	21.62	120.03	0.00
Whittier (city)	CA	28.86	23.15	111.89	99.53	17.85	101.22	0.00
Wichita (city)	KS	10.82	119.74	2.57	65.32	66.02	3.33	15.18
Wichita Falls (city)	TX	20.28	104.44	113.12	65.94	42.13	84.19	0.00
Wilmington (city)	DE	0.83	257.19	0.00	142.26	245.04	95.45	0.00
Wilmington (city)	NC	23.13	66.12	75.45	58.84	37.54	63.92	14.90
Winston-salem (city)	NC	39.52	197.62	54.02	79.67	99.56	113.68	0.57
Woodbridge (township)	NJ	50.05	215.79	3.60	95.82	162.42	84.58	0.00
Woodbury (city)	MN	49.53	114.46	0.00	98.32	88.09	0.00	0.00
Worcester (city)	MA	6.10	178.16	18.25	26.24	138.01	28.62	0.00
Kansas City-Wyandotte Co. (unif. govt)	KS	7.91	155.26	44.96	41.57	111.56	44.06	10.70
Wyoming (city)	MI	3.51	220.48	0.00	64.85	153.64	4.95	0.00
Yakima (city)	WA	13.78	176.97	54.10	42.22	91.93	29.45	19.61
Yonkers (city)	NY	12.65	24.14	0.00	36.51	5.29	103.71	0.00
Yorba Linda (city)	CA	102.62	0.00	80.18	146.51	0.00	79.74	0.06
Youngstown (city)	OH	2.96	272.76	60.52	36.44	258.92	41.29	0.00
Ypsilanti Charter (township)	MI	19.30	0.00	0.00	38.68	0.00	46.81	0.00
Yuma (city)	AZ	32.38	218.88	33.74	119.15	152.37	33.56	0.00

***Source:** U.S. Census Bureau, State and Local Government Finances, 2011*

Trends in Greenhouse Gas Emissions

2.1 Recent Trends in U.S. Greenhouse Gas Emissions and Sinks

In 2011, total U.S. greenhouse gas emissions were 6,702.3 Tg or million metric tons CO_2 Eq. Total U.S. emissions have increased by 8.4 percent from 1990 to 2011, and emissions decreased from 2010 to 2011 by 1.6 percent (108.0 Tg CO_2 Eq.). The decrease from 2010 to 2011 was due to a decrease in the carbon intensity of fuels consumed to generate electricity due to a decrease in coal consumption, with increased natural gas consumption and a significant increase in hydropower used. Additionally, relatively mild winter conditions, especially in the South Atlantic Region of the United States where electricity is an important heating fuel, resulted in an overall decrease in electricity demand in most sectors. Since 1990, U.S. emissions have increased at an average annual rate of 0.4 percent.

Figure 2-1: U.S. Greenhouse Gas Emissions by Gas

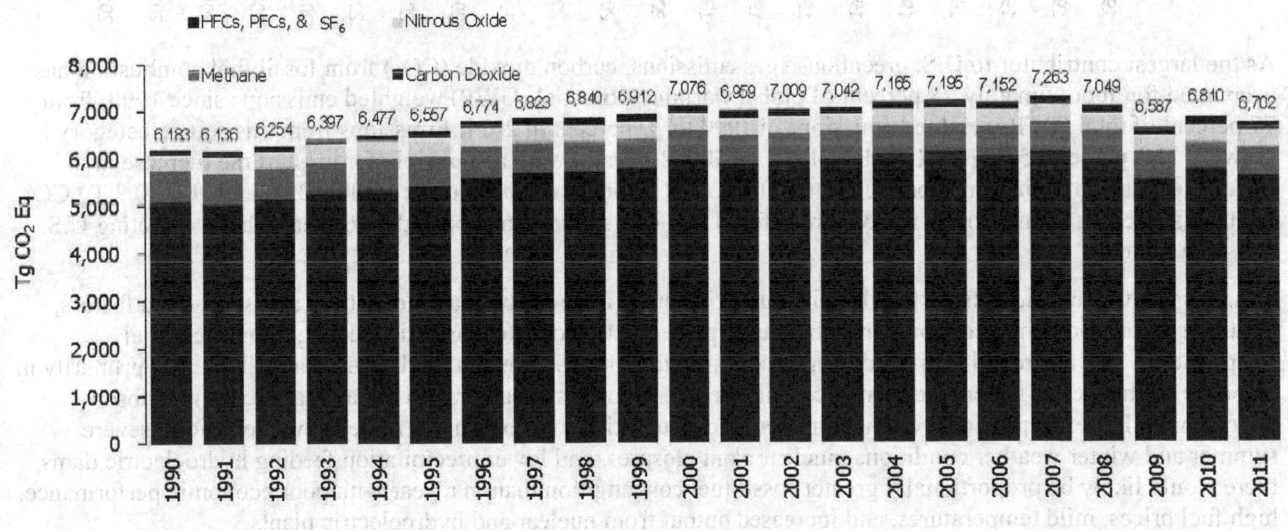

Source: *U.S. EPA, Inventory of U.S. Greenhouse Gas Emissions and Sinks: 1990–2011*

Figure 2-2: Annual Percent Change in U.S. Greenhouse Gas Emissions

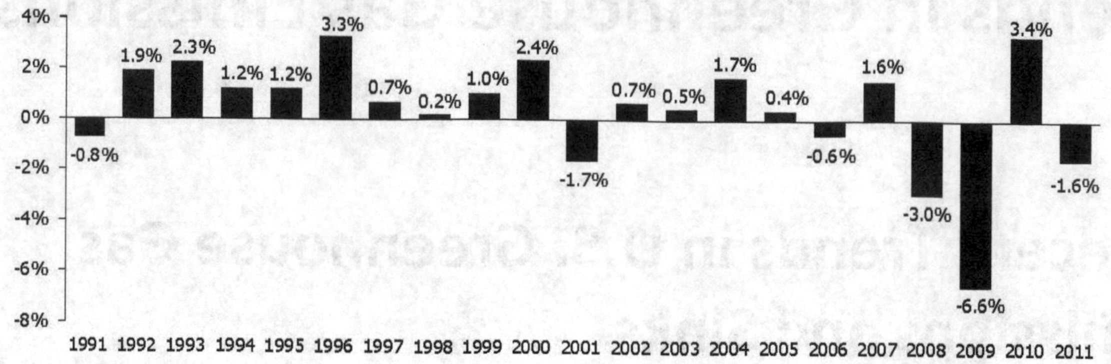

Figure 2-3: Cumulative Change in Annual U.S. Greenhouse Gas Emissions Relative to 1990

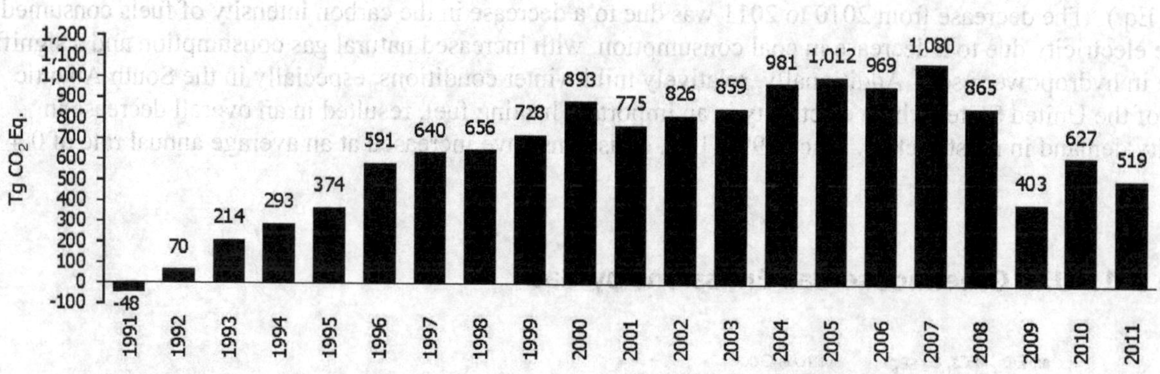

As the largest contributor to U.S. greenhouse gas emissions, carbon dioxide (CO_2) from fossil fuel combustion has accounted for approximately 78 percent of global warming potential (GWP) weighted emissions since 1990, from 77 percent of total GWP-weighted emissions in 1990 to 79 percent in 2011. Emissions from this source category grew by 11.1 percent (528.7 Tg CO_2 Eq.) from 1990 to 2011 and were responsible for most of the increase in national emissions during this period. From 2010 to 2011, these emissions decreased by 2.4 percent (130.9 Tg CO_2 Eq.). Historically, changes in emissions from fossil fuel combustion have been the dominant factor affecting U.S. emission trends.

Changes in CO_2 emissions from fossil fuel combustion are influenced by many long-term and short-term factors, including population and economic growth, energy price fluctuations, technological changes, and seasonal temperatures. On an annual basis, the overall consumption of fossil fuels in the United States fluctuates primarily in response to changes in general economic conditions, energy prices, weather, and the availability of non-fossil alternatives. For example, in a year with increased consumption of goods and services, low fuel prices, severe summer and winter weather conditions, nuclear plant closures, and lower precipitation feeding hydroelectric dams, there would likely be proportionally greater fossil fuel consumption than in a year with poor economic performance, high fuel prices, mild temperatures, and increased output from nuclear and hydroelectric plants.

In the longer-term, energy consumption patterns respond to changes that affect the scale of consumption (e.g., population, number of cars, and size of houses), the efficiency with which energy is used in equipment (e.g., cars, power plants, steel mills, and light bulbs) and behavioral choices (e.g., walking, bicycling, or telecommuting to work instead of driving).

Energy-related CO_2 emissions also depend on the type of fuel or energy consumed and its carbon (C) intensity. Producing a unit of heat or electricity using natural gas instead of coal, for example, can reduce the CO_2 emissions because of the lower C content of natural gas.

A brief discussion of the year to year variability in fuel combustion emissions is provided below, beginning with 2007.

Source: *U.S. EPA, Inventory of U.S. Greenhouse Gas Emissions and Sinks: 1990–2011*

Emissions from fossil fuel combustion decreased from 2007 to 2008. Several factors contributed to this decrease in emissions. An increase in energy prices coupled with the economic downturn led to a decrease in energy demand and a resulting decrease in emissions from 2007 to 2008. In 2008, the price of coal, natural gas, and petroleum used to generate electricity, as well as the price of fuels used for transportation, increased significantly. As a result of this price increase, coal, natural gas, and petroleum consumption used for electricity generation decreased by 1.4 percent, 2.5 percent, and 28.8 percent, respectively. The increase in the cost of fuels to generate electricity translated into an increase in the price of electricity, leading to a decrease in electricity consumption across all sectors except the commercial sector. The increase in transportation fuel prices led to a decrease in vehicle miles traveled (VMT) and a 4.7 percent decrease in transportation fossil fuel combustion emissions from 2007 to 2008. Cooler weather conditions in the summer led to a decrease in cooling degree days by 8.7 percent and a decrease in electricity demand compared to 2007, whereas cooler winter conditions led to a 5.6 percent increase in heating degree days compared to 2007 and a resulting increase in demand for heating fuels. The increased emissions from winter heating energy demand was offset by a decrease in emissions from summer cooling related electricity demand. Lastly, renewable energy consumption for electricity generation increased by 9.5 percent from 2007 to 2008, driven by a significant increase in solar and wind energy consumption (of 17.3 percent and 60.2 percent, respectively).[43] This increase in renewable energy generation contributed to a decrease in the carbon intensity of electricity generation.

From 2008 to 2009, CO_2 from fossil fuel combustion emissions experienced a decrease of 6.6 percent, the greatest decrease of any year over the course of the twenty-year period. Various factors contributed to this decrease in emissions. The continued economic downturn resulted in a 3.1 percent decrease in GDP, and a decrease in energy consumption across all sectors. The economic downturn also impacted total industrial production and manufacturing output, which decreased by 11.4 and 13.8 percent, respectively. In 2009, the price of coal used to generate electricity increased, while the price of natural gas used to generate electricity decreased significantly. As a result, natural gas was used for a greater share of electricity generation in 2009 than 2008, and coal was used for a smaller share. The fuel switching from coal to natural gas and additional electricity generation from other energy sources in 2009, which included a 6.3 percent increase in hydropower generation from the previous year, resulted in a decrease in carbon intensity, and in turn, a decrease in emissions from electricity generation. From 2008 to 2009, industrial sector emissions decreased significantly as a result of a decrease in output from energy-intensive industries of 24.6 percent in nonmetallic mineral and 26.0 percent in primary metal industries. The residential and commercial sectors only experienced minor decreases in emissions as summer and winter weather conditions were less energy-intensive from 2008 to 2009, and the price of electricity only increased slightly. Heating degree days decreased slightly and cooling degree days decreased by 3.8 percent from 2008 to 2009.

From 2009 to 2010, CO_2 emissions from fossil fuel combustion increased by 3.6 percent, which represents one of the largest annual increases in CO_2 emissions from fossil fuel combustion for the twenty one-year period.[44] This increase is primarily due to an increase in economic output 2009 to 2010, where total industrial production and manufacturing output increased by 5.4 and 6.3 percent, respectively (FRB 2011). Carbon dioxide emissions from fossil fuel combustion in the industrial sector increased by 8.0 percent, including increased emissions from the combustion of fuel oil, natural gas and coal. Overall, coal consumption increased by 5.4 percent, the largest increase in coal consumption for the twenty one-year period between 1990 and 2011. In 2010, weather conditions remained fairly constant in the winter and were much hotter in the summer compared to 2009, as heating degree days decreased slightly by 0.7 percent and cooling degree days increased by 18.6 percent to their highest levels in the twenty one-year period. As a result of the more energy-intensive summer weather conditions, electricity sales to the residential and commercial end-use sectors in 2010 increased approximately 6.0 percent and 1.8 percent, respectively.

From 2010 to 2011, CO_2 emissions from fossil fuel combustion decreased by 2.4 percent. This decrease is a result of multiple factors including: (1) a decrease in the carbon intensity of fuels consumed to generate electricity due to a decrease in coal consumption, with increased natural gas consumption and a significant increase in hydropower used; (2) a decrease in transportation-related energy consumption due to higher fuel costs, improvements in fuel efficiency, and a reduction in miles traveled; and (3) relatively mild winter conditions resulting in an overall

[43] Renewable energy, as defined in EIA's energy statistics, includes the following energy sources: hydroelectric power, geothermal energy, biofuels, solar energy, and wind energy.

[44] This increase also represents the largest absolute and percentage increase since 1988 (EIA 2011a).

Source: *U.S. EPA, Inventory of U.S. Greenhouse Gas Emissions and Sinks: 1990–2011*

decrease in energy demand in most sectors. In addition, changing fuel prices played a role in the decreasing emissions. Significant increases in the price of motor gasoline in the transportation sector led to a decrease in energy consumption by 1.1 percent. In addition, an increase in the price of coal and a concurrent decrease in natural gas prices led to a 5.7 percent decrease and a 2.5 percent increase in fuel consumption of these fuels by electric generators. This change in fuel prices also reduced the carbon intensity of fuels used to produce electricity in 2011, further contributing to the decrease in fossil fuel combustion emissions.

Overall, from 1990 to 2011, total emissions of CO_2 increased by 504.0 Tg CO_2 Eq. (9.9 percent), while total emissions of CH_4 decreased by 52.7 Tg CO_2 Eq. (8.2 percent), and total emissions of N_2O increased 12.6 Tg CO_2 Eq. (3.6 percent). During the same period, aggregate weighted emissions of HFCs, PFCs, and SF_6 rose by 55.1 Tg CO_2 Eq. (61.1 percent). Despite being emitted in smaller quantities relative to the other principal greenhouse gases, emissions of HFCs, PFCs, and SF_6 are significant because many of them have extremely high GWPs and, in the cases of PFCs and SF_6, long atmospheric lifetimes. Conversely, U.S. greenhouse gas emissions were partly offset by C sequestration in managed forests, trees in urban areas, agricultural soils, and landfilled yard trimmings. These were estimated to offset 13.5 percent of total emissions in 2011.

Table 2-1 summarizes emissions and sinks from all U.S. anthropogenic sources in weighted units of Tg CO_2 Eq., while unweighted gas emissions and sinks in gigagrams (Gg) are provided in Table 2-2.

Table 2-1: Recent Trends in U.S. Greenhouse Gas Emissions and Sinks (Tg CO_2 Eq.)

Gas/Source	1990	2005	2007	2008	2009	2010	2011
CO_2	**5,108.8**	**6,109.3**	**6,128.6**	**5,944.8**	**5,517.9**	**5,736.4**	**5,612.9**
Fossil Fuel Combustion	4,748.5	5,748.7	5,767.7	5,590.6	5,222.4	5,408.1	5,277.2
Electricity Generation	1,820.8	2,402.1	2,412.8	2,360.9	2,146.4	2,259.2	2,158.5
Transportation	1,494.0	1,891.7	1,904.7	1,816.0	1,749.2	1,763.9	1,745.0
Industrial	848.6	823.4	844.4	802.0	722.6	780.2	773.2
Residential	338.3	357.9	341.6	347.0	337.0	334.6	328.8
Commercial	219.0	223.5	218.9	223.8	223.4	220.6	222.1
U.S. Territories	27.9	50.0	45.2	41.0	43.8	49.6	49.7
Non-Energy Use of Fuels	117.4	142.7	134.9	139.5	124.0	132.8	130.6
Iron and Steel Production & Metallurgical Coke Production	99.8	66.7	71.3	66.8	43.0	55.7	64.3
Natural Gas Systems	37.7	29.9	30.9	32.6	32.2	32.3	32.3
Cement Production	33.3	45.2	44.5	40.5	29.0	30.9	31.6
Lime Production	11.5	14.3	14.6	14.3	11.2	13.1	13.8
Incineration of Waste	8.0	12.5	12.7	11.9	11.7	12.0	12.0
Other Process Uses of Carbonates	4.9	6.3	7.4	5.9	7.6	9.6	9.2
Ammonia Production	13.0	9.2	9.1	7.9	7.9	8.7	8.8
Cropland Remaining Cropland	7.1	7.9	8.2	8.6	7.2	8.4	8.1
Urea Consumption for Non-Agricultural Purposes	3.8	3.7	4.9	4.1	3.4	4.4	4.3
Petrochemical Production	3.4	4.3	4.1	3.6	2.8	3.5	3.5
Aluminum Production	6.8	4.1	4.3	4.5	3.0	2.7	3.3
Soda Ash Production and Consumption	2.8	3.0	2.9	3.0	2.6	2.7	2.7
Titanium Dioxide Production	1.2	1.8	1.9	1.8	1.6	1.8	1.9
Carbon Dioxide Consumption	1.4	1.3	1.9	1.8	1.8	2.2	1.8
Ferroalloy Production	2.2	1.4	1.6	1.6	1.5	1.7	1.7
Glass Production	1.5	1.9	1.5	1.5	1.0	1.5	1.3
Zinc Production	0.6	1.0	1.0	1.2	0.9	1.2	1.3
Phosphoric Acid Production	1.5	1.3	1.2	1.1	1.0	1.1	1.2
Wetlands Remaining Wetlands	1.0	1.1	1.0	1.0	1.1	1.0	0.9
Lead Production	0.5	0.6	0.6	0.5	0.5	0.5	0.5
Petroleum Systems	0.4	0.3	0.3	0.3	0.3	0.3	0.3
Silicon Carbide Production and Consumption	0.4	0.2	0.2	0.2	0.1	0.2	0.2
Land Use, Land-Use Change, and Forestry (Sink)[a]	*(794.5)*	*(997.8)*	*(929.2)*	*(902.6)*	*(882.6)*	*(888.8)*	*(905.0)*
Wood Biomass and Ethanol Consumption[b]	*218.6*	*228.7*	*238.3*	*251.7*	*245.1*	*264.5*	*264.5*
International Bunker Fuels[c]	*103.5*	*113.1*	*115.3*	*114.3*	*106.4*	*117.0*	*111.3*
CH_4	**639.9**	**593.6**	**618.6**	**618.8**	**603.8**	**592.7**	**587.2**
Natural Gas Systems	161.2	159.0	168.4	163.4	150.7	143.6	144.7

Source: *U.S. EPA, Inventory of U.S. Greenhouse Gas Emissions and Sinks: 1990–2011*

Enteric Fermentation	132.7	137.0	141.8	141.4	140.6	139.3	137.4
Landfills	147.8	112.5	111.6	113.6	113.3	106.8	103.0
Coal Mining	84.1	56.9	57.9	67.1	70.3	72.4	63.2
Manure Management	31.5	47.6	52.4	51.5	50.5	51.8	52.0
Petroleum Systems	35.2	29.2	29.8	30.0	30.5	30.8	31.5
Wastewater Treatment	15.9	16.5	16.6	16.6	16.5	16.4	16.2
Forest Land Remaining Forest Land	2.5	8.0	14.4	8.7	5.7	4.7	14.2
Rice Cultivation	7.1	6.8	6.2	7.2	7.3	8.6	6.6
Stationary Combustion	7.5	6.6	6.4	6.6	6.3	6.3	6.3
Abandoned Underground Coal Mines	6.0	5.5	5.3	5.3	5.1	5.0	4.8
Petrochemical Production	2.3	3.1	3.3	2.9	2.9	3.1	3.1
Mobile Combustion	4.6	2.4	2.1	1.9	1.8	1.8	1.7
Composting	0.3	1.6	1.7	1.7	1.6	1.5	1.5
Iron and Steel Production & Metallurgical Coke Production	1.0	0.7	0.7	0.6	0.4	0.5	0.6
Field Burning of Agricultural Residues	0.2	0.2	0.2	0.2	0.2	0.2	0.2
Ferroalloy Production	+	+	+	+	+	+	+
Silicon Carbide Production and Consumption	+	+	+	+	+	+	+
Incineration of Waste	+	+	+	+	+	+	+
International Bunker Fuels[c]	*0.1*	*0.1*	*0.1*	*0.1*	*0.1*	*0.1*	*0.1*
N_2O	**344.3**	**356.1**	**376.1**	**349.7**	**338.7**	**343.9**	**356.9**
Agricultural Soil Management	227.9	237.5	252.3	245.4	242.8	244.5	247.2
Stationary Combustion	12.3	20.6	21.2	21.1	20.7	22.6	22.0
Mobile Combustion	44.0	36.9	29.0	25.5	22.7	20.7	18.5
Manure Management	14.4	17.1	18.0	17.8	17.7	17.8	18.0
Nitric Acid Production	18.2	16.9	19.7	16.9	14.0	16.8	15.5
Forest Land Remaining Forest Land	2.1	6.9	12.1	7.4	5.0	4.2	11.9
Adipic Acid Production	15.8	7.4	10.7	2.6	2.8	4.4	10.6
Wastewater Treatment	3.5	4.7	4.8	4.9	5.0	5.1	5.2
N_2O from Product Uses	4.4	4.4	4.4	4.4	4.4	4.4	4.4
Composting	0.4	1.7	1.8	1.9	1.8	1.7	1.7
Settlements Remaining Settlements	1.0	1.5	1.6	1.5	1.4	1.5	1.5
Incineration of Waste	0.5	0.4	0.4	0.4	0.4	0.4	0.4
Field Burning of Agricultural Residues	0.1	0.1	0.1	0.1	0.1	0.1	0.1
Wetlands Remaining Wetlands	+	+	+	+	+	+	+
International Bunker Fuels[c]	*0.9*	*1.0*	*1.0*	*1.0*	*0.9*	*1.0*	*1.0*
HFCs	**36.9**	**115.0**	**120.0**	**117.5**	**112.0**	**121.3**	**129.0**
Substitution of Ozone Depleting Substances[d]	0.3	99.0	102.7	103.6	106.3	114.6	121.7
HCFC-22 Production	36.4	15.8	17.0	13.6	5.4	6.4	6.9
Semiconductor Manufacture	0.2	0.2	0.3	0.3	0.2	0.4	0.3
PFCs	**20.6**	**6.2**	**7.7**	**6.6**	**4.4**	**5.9**	**7.0**
Semiconductor Manufacture	2.2	3.2	3.8	3.9	2.9	4.4	4.1
Aluminum Production	18.4	3.0	3.8	2.7	1.6	1.6	2.9
SF_6	**32.6**	**15.0**	**12.3**	**11.4**	**9.8**	**10.1**	**9.4**
Electrical Transmission and Distribution	26.7	11.1	8.8	8.6	8.1	7.8	7.0
Magnesium Production and Processing	5.4	2.9	2.6	1.9	1.1	1.3	1.4
Semiconductor Manufacture	0.5	1.0	0.8	0.9	0.7	1.0	0.9
Total	**6,183.3**	**7,195.3**	**7,263.2**	**7,048.8**	**6,586.6**	**6,810.3**	**6,702.3**
Net Emissions (Sources and Sinks)	**5,388.7**	**6,197.4**	**6,334.0**	**6,146.2**	**5,704.0**	**5,921.5**	**5,797.3**

Source: *U.S. EPA, Inventory of U.S. Greenhouse Gas Emissions and Sinks: 1990–2011*

\+ Does not exceed 0.05 Tg CO_2 Eq.
[a] The net CO_2 flux total includes both emissions and sequestration, and constitutes a sink in the United States. Sinks are only included in net emissions total. Parentheses indicate negative values or sequestration.
[b] Emissions from Wood Biomass and Ethanol Consumption are not included specifically in summing energy sector totals. Net carbon fluxes from changes in biogenic carbon reservoirs are accounted for in the estimates for Land Use, Land-Use Change, and Forestry.
[c] Emissions from International Bunker Fuels are not included in totals.
[d] Small amounts of PFC emissions also result from this source.
Note: Totals may not sum due to independent rounding.

Table 2-2: Recent Trends in U.S. Greenhouse Gas Emissions and Sinks (Gg)

Gas/Source	1990	2005	2007	2008	2009	2010	2011
CO_2	**5,108,811**	**6,109,336**	**6,128,551**	**5,944,813**	**5,517,926**	**5,736,400**	**5,612,855**
Fossil Fuel Combustion	4,748,532	5,748,674	5,767,654	5,590,638	5,222,419	5,408,119	5,277,246
Electricity Generation	1,820,817	2,402,142	2,412,827	2,360,920	2,146,415	2,259,190	2,158,510
Transportation	1,493,968	1,891,744	1,904,652	1,815,999	1,749,166	1,763,870	1,745,001
Industrial	848,556	823,408	844,420	802,040	722,627	780,240	773,192
Residential	338,347	357,902	341,649	346,962	337,034	334,589	328,759
Commercial	218,963	223,510	218,874	223,759	223,358	220,616	222,098
U.S. Territories	27,882	49,968	45,232	40,959	43,818	49,615	49,685
Non-Energy Use of Fuels	117,414	142,701	134,887	139,484	123,977	132,839	130,554
Iron and Steel Production & Metallurgical Coke Production	99,781	66,666	71,277	66,822	43,029	55,746	64,259
Natural Gas Systems	37,665	29,923	30,851	32,622	32,187	32,313	32,344
Cement Production	33,278	45,197	44,538	40,531	29,018	30,924	31,632
Lime Production	11,488	14,322	14,579	14,345	11,164	13,145	13,795
Incineration of Waste	7,972	12,452	12,711	11,876	11,688	12,038	12,038
Other Process Uses of Carbonates	4,907	6,339	7,365	5,885	7,583	9,560	9,153
Ammonia Production	13,047	9,196	9,074	7,883	7,855	8,678	8,795
Cropland Remaining Cropland	7,084	7,854	8,222	8,638	7,236	8,351	8,117
Urea Consumption for Non-Agricultural Purposes	3,784	3,653	4,944	4,065	3,415	4,365	4,329
Petrochemical Production	3,429	4,330	4,070	3,572	2,833	3,455	3,505
Aluminum Production	6,831	4,142	4,251	4,477	3,009	2,722	3,292
Soda Ash Production and Consumption	2,822	2,960	2,937	2,960	2,569	2,697	2,712
Titanium Dioxide Production	1,195	1,755	1,930	1,809	1,648	1,769	1,903
Carbon Dioxide Consumption	1,416	1,321	1,867	1,780	1,784	2,203	1,811
Ferroalloy Production	2,152	1,392	1,552	1,599	1,469	1,663	1,663
Glass Production	1,535	1,928	1,536	1,523	1,045	1,481	1,299
Zinc Production	632	1,030	1,025	1,159	943	1,182	1,286
Phosphoric Acid Production	1,529	1,342	1,203	1,132	977	1,087	1,151
Wetlands Remaining Wetlands	1,033	1,079	1,012	992	1,089	1,010	918
Lead Production	516	553	562	547	525	542	538
Petroleum Systems	394	306	311	300	320	332	347
Silicon Carbide Production and	375	219	196	175	145	181	170
Land Use, Land-Use Change, and Forestry[a]	*(794,529)*	*(997,828)*	*(929,202)*	*(902,605)*	*(882,625)*	*(888,771)*	*(905,041)*
Wood Biomass and Ethanol Consumption[b]	*218,637*	*228,651*	*238,308*	*251,734*	*245,057*	*264,459*	*264,527*
International Bunker Fuels[c]	*103,463*	*113,139*	*115,345*	*114,342*	*106,410*	*116,992*	*111,316*
CH_4	**30,473**	**28,269**	**29,459**	**29,466**	**28,751**	**28,224**	**27,964**
Natural Gas Systems	7,678	7,572	8,018	7,782	7,178	6,838	6,893
Enteric Fermentation	6,321	6,522	6,751	6,731	6,693	6,632	6,542
Landfills	7,037	5,357	5,314	5,409	5,397	5,083	4,907
Coal Mining	4,003	2,710	2,756	3,196	3,348	3,447	3,011

Source: *U.S. EPA, Inventory of U.S. Greenhouse Gas Emissions and Sinks: 1990–2011*

Manure Management	1,499	2,265	2,493	2,452	2,403	2,466	2,478
Petroleum Systems	1,677	1,390	1,421	1,431	1,455	1,467	1,499
Wastewater Treatment	758	785	791	791	786	779	770
Forest Land Remaining Forest Land	118	383	684	413	271	222	675
Rice Cultivation	339	326	295	343	349	410	316
Stationary Combustion	355	315	305	313	298	301	300
Abandoned Underground Coal Mines	288	264	254	253	244	237	231
Petrochemical Production	108	150	155	137	138	146	148
Mobile Combustion	218	113	100	92	88	85	82
Composting	15	75	79	80	75	73	74
Iron and Steel Production & Metallurgical Coke Production	46	34	33	31	17	25	28
Field Burning of Agricultural Residues	10	8	11	11	11	11	10
Ferroalloy Production	1	+	+	+	+	+	+
Silicon Carbide Production and Consumption	1	+	+	+	+	+	+
Incineration of Waste	+	+	+	+	+	+	+
International Bunker Fuels[c]	*7*	*5*	*5*	*6*	*5*	*6*	*5*
N_2O	**1,111**	**1,149**	**1,213**	**1,128**	**1,093**	**1,109**	**1,151**
Agricultural Soil Management	735	766	814	792	783	789	797
Stationary Combustion	40	66	68	68	67	73	71
Mobile Combustion	142	119	94	82	73	67	60
Manure Management	46	55	58	57	57	57	58
Nitric Acid Production	59	55	64	54	45	54	50
Forest Land Remaining Forest Land	7	22	39	24	16	13	38
Adipic Acid Production	51	24	34	8	9	14	34
Wastewater Treatment	11	15	16	16	16	16	17
N_2O from Product Uses	14	14	14	14	14	14	14
Composting	1	6	6	6	6	5	6
Settlements Remaining Settlements	3	5	5	5	5	5	5
Incineration of Waste	2	1	1	1	1	1	1
Field Burning of Agricultural Residues	+	+	+	+	+	+	+
Wetlands Remaining Wetlands	+	+	+	+	+	+	+
International Bunker Fuels[c]	*3*	*3*	*3*	*3*	*3*	*3*	*3*
HFCs	**M**	**M**	**M**	**M**	**M**	**M**	**M**
Substitution of Ozone Depleting Substances[d]	M	M	M	M	M	M	M
HCFC-22 Production	3	1	1	1	+	1	1
Semiconductor Manufacture	+	+	+	+	+	+	+
PFCs	**M**	**M**	**M**	**M**	**M**	**M**	**M**
Semiconductor Manufacture	M	M	M	M	M	M	M
Aluminum Production	M	M	M	M	M	M	M
SF_6	**1**	**1**	**+**	**+**	**+**	**+**	**+**
Electrical Transmission and Distribution	1	+	+	+	+	+	+
Magnesium Production and Processing	+	+	+	+	+	+	+
Semiconductor Manufacture	+	+	+	+	+	+	+

+ Does not exceed 0.5 Gg.
M Mixture of multiple gases
[a] The net CO_2 flux total includes both emissions and sequestration, and constitutes a sink in the United States. Sinks are only included in net emissions total. Parentheses indicate negative values or sequestration.
[b] Emissions from Wood Biomass and Ethanol Consumption are not included specifically in summing energy sector totals. Net carbon fluxes from changes in biogenic carbon reservoirs are accounted for in the estimates for Land Use, Land-Use Change, and Forestry
[c] Emissions from International Bunker Fuels are not included in totals.

Source: *U.S. EPA, Inventory of U.S. Greenhouse Gas Emissions and Sinks: 1990–2011*

[d] Small amounts of PFC emissions also result from this source.
Note: Totals may not sum due to independent rounding.

Emissions of all gases can be summed from each source category into a set of six sectors defined by the Intergovernmental Panel on Climate Change (IPCC). Over the twenty-two-year period of 1990 to 2011, total emissions in the Energy, Industrial Processes, and Agriculture sectors grew by 478.4 Tg CO_2 Eq. (9.1 percent), 10.3 Tg CO_2 Eq. (3.3 percent), and 47.6 Tg CO_2 Eq. (11.5 percent), respectively. Emissions from the Waste and Solvent and Other Produce Use sectors decreased by 40.2 Tg CO_2 Eq. (23.9 percent) and less than 0.1 Tg CO_2 Eq. (0.4 percent), respectively. Over the same period, estimates of net C sequestration in the Land Use, Land-Use Change, and Forestry sector increased by 87.6 Tg CO_2 Eq. (11.2 percent).

Figure 2-4: U.S. Greenhouse Gas Emissions and Sinks by Chapter/IPCC Sector

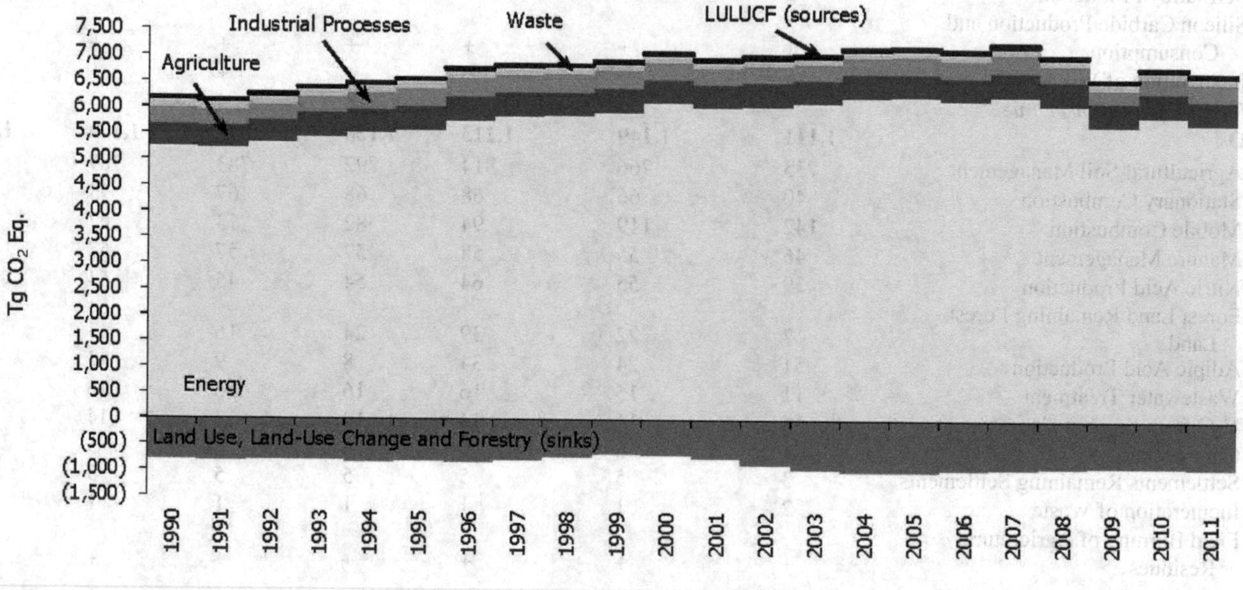

Table 2-3: Recent Trends in U.S. Greenhouse Gas Emissions and Sinks by Chapter/IPCC Sector (Tg CO_2 Eq.)

Chapter/IPCC Sector	1990	2005	2007	2008	2009	2010	2011
Energy	5,267.3	6,251.6	6,266.9	6,096.2	5,699.2	5,889.1	5,745.7
Industrial Processes	316.1	330.8	347.2	318.7	265.3	303.4	326.5
Solvent and Other Product Use	4.4	4.4	4.4	4.4	4.4	4.4	4.4
Agriculture	413.9	446.2	470.9	463.6	459.2	462.3	461.5
Land Use, Land-Use Change, and Forestry (Emissions)	13.7	25.4	37.3	27.2	20.4	19.7	36.6
Waste	167.8	136.9	136.5	138.6	138.1	131.4	127.7
Total Emissions	**6,183.3**	**7,195.3**	**7,263.2**	**7,048.8**	**6,586.6**	**6,810.3**	**6,702.3**
Net CO_2 Flux From Land Use, Land-Use Change and Forestry (Sinks)*	(794.5)	(997.8)	(929.2)	(902.6)	(882.6)	(888.8)	(905.0)
Net Emissions (Sources and Sinks)	**5,388.7**	**6,197.4**	**6,334.0**	**6,146.2**	**5,704.0**	**5,921.5**	**5,797.3**

* The net CO_2 flux total includes both emissions and sequestration, and constitutes a sink in the United States. Sinks are only included in net emissions total. Please refer to Table 2-9 for a breakout by source.
Note: Totals may not sum due to independent rounding.
Note: Parentheses indicate negative values or sequestration.

Source: *U.S. EPA, Inventory of U.S. Greenhouse Gas Emissions and Sinks: 1990–2011*

Energy

Energy-related activities, primarily fossil fuel combustion, accounted for the vast majority of U.S. CO_2 emissions for the period of 1990 through 2011. In 2011, approximately 87 percent of the energy consumed in the United States (on a Btu basis) was produced through the combustion of fossil fuels. The remaining 13 percent came from other energy sources such as hydropower, biomass, nuclear, wind, and solar energy (see Figure 2-5 and Figure 2-6). A discussion of specific trends related to CO_2 as well as other greenhouse gas emissions from energy consumption is presented in the Energy chapter. Energy-related activities are also responsible for CH_4 and N_2O emissions (43 percent and 11 percent of total U.S. emissions of each gas, respectively). Table 2-4 presents greenhouse gas emissions from the Energy chapter, by source and gas.

Figure 2-5: 2011Energy Chapter Greenhouse Gas Sources

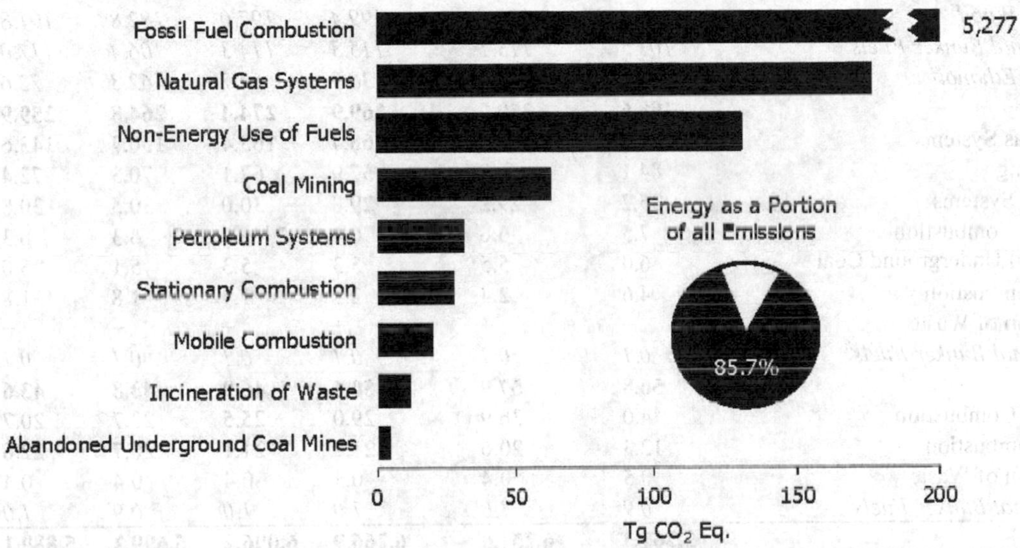

Figure 2-6: 2011 U.S. Fossil Carbon Flows (Tg CO_2 Eq.)

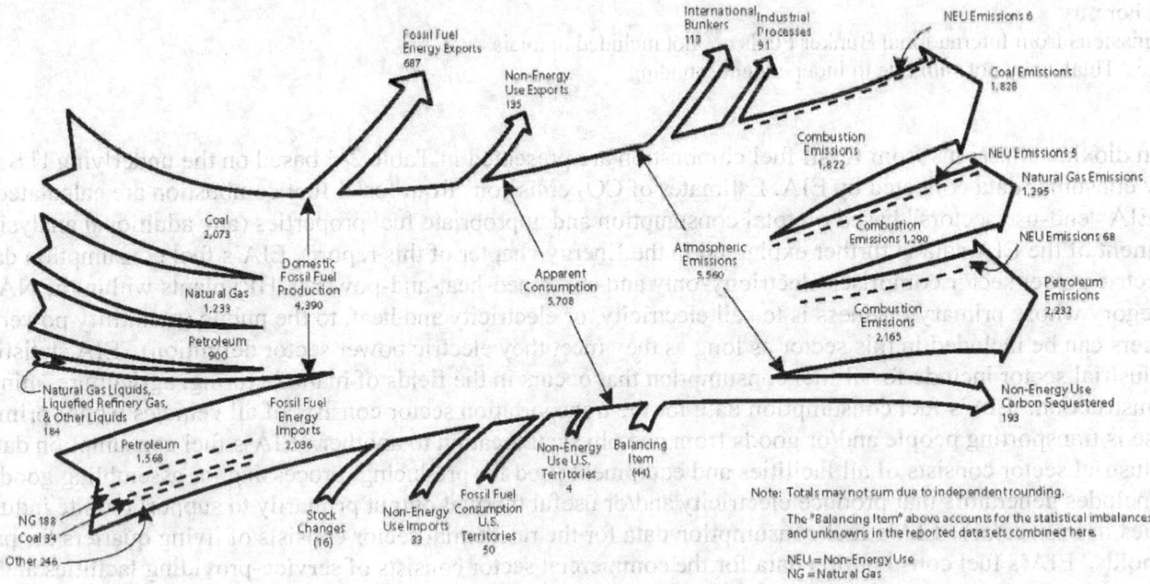

***Source:** U.S. EPA, Inventory of U.S. Greenhouse Gas Emissions and Sinks: 1990–2011*

Table 2-4: Emissions from Energy (Tg CO_2 Eq.)

Gas/Source	1990	2005	2007	2008	2009	2010	2011
CO_2	**4,912.0**	**5,934.1**	**5,946.4**	**5,774.9**	**5,390.6**	**5,585.6**	**5,452.5**
Fossil Fuel Combustion	4,748.5	5,748.7	5,767.7	5,590.6	5,222.4	5,408.1	5,277.2
Electricity Generation	1,820.8	2,402.1	2,412.8	2,360.9	2,146.4	2,259.2	2,158.5
Transportation	1,494.0	1,891.7	1,904.7	1,816.0	1,749.2	1,763.9	1,745.0
Industrial	848.6	823.4	844.4	802.0	722.6	780.2	773.2
Residential	338.3	357.9	341.6	347.0	337.0	334.6	328.8
Commercial	219.0	223.5	218.9	223.8	223.4	220.6	222.1
U.S. Territories	27.9	50.0	45.2	41.0	43.8	49.6	49.7
Non-Energy Use of Fuels	117.4	142.7	134.9	139.5	124.0	132.8	130.6
Natural Gas Systems	37.7	29.9	30.9	32.6	32.2	32.3	32.3
Incineration of Waste	8.0	12.5	12.7	11.9	11.7	12.0	12.0
Petroleum Systems	0.4	0.3	0.3	0.3	0.3	0.3	0.3
Biomass - Wood[a]	*214.4*	*205.7*	*199.4*	*197.0*	*182.8*	*191.8*	*191.8*
International Bunker Fuels[b]	*103.5*	*113.1*	*115.3*	*114.3*	*106.4*	*117.0*	*111.3*
Biomass - Ethanol[a]	*4.2*	*22.9*	*38.9*	*54.7*	*62.3*	*72.6*	*72.8*
CH_4	**298.6**	**259.7**	**269.9**	**274.4**	**264.8**	**259.9**	**252.3**
Natural Gas Systems	161.2	159.0	168.4	163.4	150.7	143.6	144.7
Coal Mining	84.1	56.9	57.9	67.1	70.3	72.4	63.2
Petroleum Systems	35.2	29.2	29.8	30.0	30.5	30.8	31.5
Stationary Combustion	7.5	6.6	6.4	6.6	6.3	6.3	6.3
Abandoned Underground Coal	6.0	5.5	5.3	5.3	5.1	5.0	4.8
Mobile Combustion	4.6	2.4	2.1	1.9	1.8	1.8	1.7
Incineration of Waste	+	+	+	+	+	+	+
International Bunker Fuels[b]	*0.1*	*0.1*	*0.1*	*0.1*	*0.1*	*0.1*	*0.1*
N_2O	**56.8**	**57.9**	**50.6**	**46.9**	**43.8**	**43.6**	**40.8**
Stationary Combustion	44.0	36.9	29.0	25.5	22.7	20.7	18.5
Mobile Combustion	12.3	20.6	21.2	21.1	20.7	22.6	22.0
Incineration of Waste	0.5	0.4	0.4	0.4	0.4	0.4	0.4
International Bunker Fuels[b]	*0.9*	*1.0*	*1.0*	*1.0*	*0.9*	*1.0*	*1.0*
Total	**5,267.3**	**6,251.6**	**6,266.9**	**6,096.2**	**5,699.2**	**5,889.1**	**5,745.7**

\+ Does not exceed 0.05 Tg CO_2 Eq.
[a] Emissions from Wood Biomass and Ethanol Consumption are not included specifically in summing energy sector totals. Net carbon fluxes from changes in biogenic carbon reservoirs are accounted for in the estimates for Land Use, Land-Use Change, and Forestry
[b] Emissions from International Bunker Fuels are not included in totals.
Note: Totals may not sum due to independent rounding.

Carbon dioxide emissions from fossil fuel combustion are presented in Table 2-5 based on the underlying U.S. energy consumer data collected by EIA. Estimates of CO_2 emissions from fossil fuel combustion are calculated from these EIA "end-use sectors" based on total consumption and appropriate fuel properties (any additional analysis and refinement of the EIA data is further explained in the Energy chapter of this report). EIA's fuel consumption data for the electric power sector comprises electricity-only and combined-heat-and-power (CHP) plants within the NAICS 22 category whose primary business is to sell electricity, or electricity and heat, to the public (nonutility power producers can be included in this sector as long as they meet they electric power sector definition). EIA statistics for the industrial sector include fossil fuel consumption that occurs in the fields of manufacturing, agriculture, mining, and construction. EIA's fuel consumption data for the transportation sector consists of all vehicles whose primary purpose is transporting people and/or goods from one physical location to another. EIA's fuel consumption data for the industrial sector consists of all facilities and equipment used for producing, processing, or assembling goods (EIA includes generators that produce electricity and/or useful thermal output primarily to support on-site industrial activities in this sector). EIA's fuel consumption data for the residential sector consists of living quarters for private households. EIA's fuel consumption data for the commercial sector consists of service-providing facilities and equipment from private and public organizations and businesses (EIA includes generators that produce electricity

Source: *U.S. EPA, Inventory of U.S. Greenhouse Gas Emissions and Sinks: 1990–2011*

and/or useful thermal output primarily to support the activities at commercial establishments in this sector). Table 2-5, Figure 2-7, and Figure 2-8 summarize CO_2 emissions from fossil fuel combustion by end-use sector.

Table 2-5: CO_2 Emissions from Fossil Fuel Combustion by End-Use Sector (Tg CO_2 Eq.)

End-Use Sector	1990	2005	2007	2008	2009	2010	2011
Transportation	**1,497.0**	**1,896.5**	**1,909.7**	**1,820.7**	**1,753.7**	**1,768.4**	**1,749.3**
Combustion	1,494.0	1,891.7	1,904.7	1,816.0	1,749.2	1,763.9	1,745.0
Electricity	3.0	4.7	5.1	4.7	4.5	4.5	4.3
Industrial	**1,535.3**	**1,560.4**	**1,559.9**	**1,499.3**	**1,324.6**	**1,421.3**	**1,392.1**
Combustion	848.6	823.4	844.4	802.0	722.6	780.2	773.2
Electricity	686.7	737.0	715.4	697.3	602.0	641.1	618.9
Residential	**931.4**	**1,214.7**	**1,205.2**	**1,189.9**	**1,123.5**	**1,175.0**	**1,125.6**
Combustion	338.3	357.9	341.6	347.0	337.0	334.6	328.8
Electricity	593.0	856.7	863.5	842.9	786.5	840.4	796.9
Commercial	**757.0**	**1,027.2**	**1,047.7**	**1,039.8**	**976.8**	**993.9**	**960.5**
Combustion	219.0	223.5	218.9	223.8	223.4	220.6	222.1
Electricity	538.0	803.7	828.8	816.0	753.5	773.3	738.4
U.S. Territories[a]	**27.9**	**50.0**	**45.2**	**41.0**	**43.8**	**49.6**	**49.7**
Total	**4,748.5**	**5,748.7**	**5,767.7**	**5,590.6**	**5,222.4**	**5,408.1**	**5,277.2**
Electricity Generation	**1,820.8**	**2,402.1**	**2,412.8**	**2,360.9**	**2,146.4**	**2,259.2**	**2,158.5**

Note: Totals may not sum due to independent rounding. Combustion-related emissions from electricity generation are allocated based on aggregate national electricity consumption by each end-use sector.

[a] Fuel consumption by U.S. Territories (i.e., American Samoa, Guam, Puerto Rico, U.S. Virgin Islands, Wake Island, and other U.S. Pacific Islands) is included in this report.

Figure 2-7: 2011 CO_2 Emissions from Fossil Fuel Combustion by Sector and Fuel Type

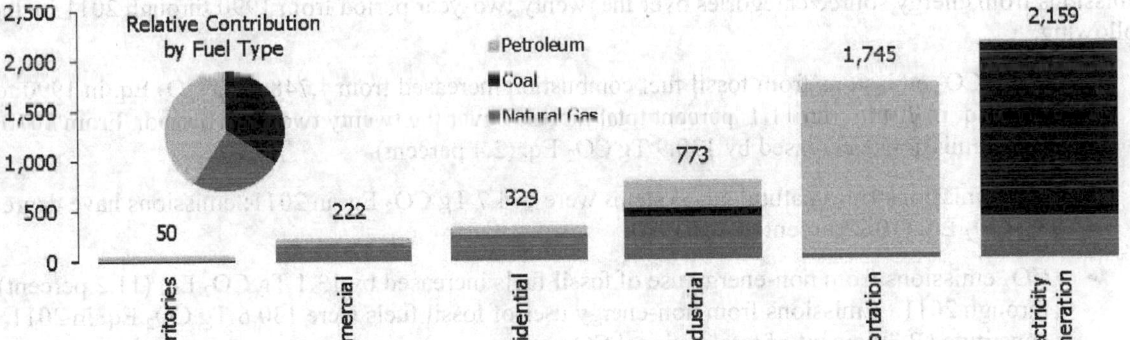

Source: U.S. EPA, Inventory of U.S. Greenhouse Gas Emissions and Sinks: 1990–2011

Figure 2-8: 2011 End-Use Sector Emissions from Fossil Fuel Combustion

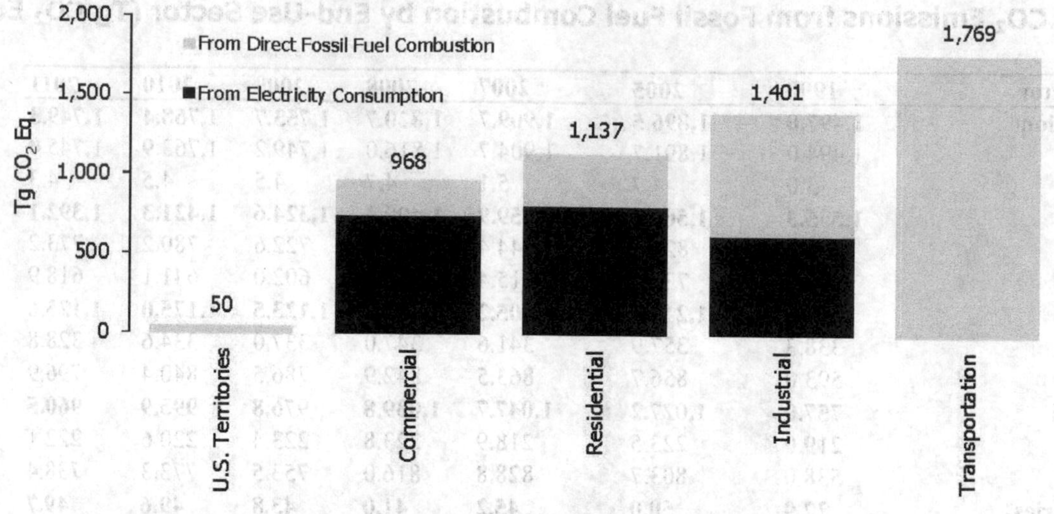

The main driver of emissions in the Energy sector is CO_2 from fossil fuel combustion. Electricity generation is the largest emitter of CO_2, and electricity generators consumed 36 percent of U.S. energy from fossil fuels and emitted 41 percent of the CO_2 from fossil fuel combustion in 2011. Electricity generation emissions can also be allocated to the end-use sectors that are consuming that electricity, as presented in Table 2-5. The transportation end-use sector accounted for 1,749.3 Tg CO_2 Eq. in 2011 or approximately 33 percent of total CO_2 emissions from fossil fuel combustion. The industrial end-use sector accounted for 26 percent of CO_2 emissions from fossil fuel combustion. The residential and commercial end-use sectors accounted for 21 and 18 percent, respectively, of CO_2 emissions from fossil fuel combustion. Both of these end-use sectors were heavily reliant on electricity for meeting energy needs, with electricity consumption for lighting, heating, air conditioning, and operating appliances contributing 71 and 77 percent of emissions from the residential and commercial end-use sectors, respectively. Significant trends in emissions from energy source categories over the twenty two-year period from 1990 through 2011 included the following:

- Total CO_2 emissions from fossil fuel combustion increased from 4,748.5 Tg CO_2 Eq. in 1990 to 5,277.2 Tg CO_2 Eq. in 2011 —an 11.1 percent total increase over the twenty two-year period. From 2010 to 2011, these emissions decreased by 130.9 Tg CO_2 Eq. (2.4 percent).
- CH_4 emissions from natural gas systems were 144.7 Tg CO_2 Eq. in 2011; emissions have decreased by 16.5 Tg CO_2 Eq. (10.2 percent) since 1990.
- CO_2 emissions from non-energy use of fossil fuels increased by 13.1 Tg CO_2 Eq. (11.2 percent) from 1990 through 2011. Emissions from non-energy uses of fossil fuels were 130.6 Tg CO_2 Eq. in 2011, which constituted 2.3 percent of total national CO_2 emissions.
- N_2O emissions from stationary combustion increased by 9.7 Tg CO_2 Eq. (79.3 percent) from 1990 through 2011. N_2O emissions from this source increased primarily as a result of an increase in the number of coal fluidized bed boilers in the electric power sector.
- CO_2 emissions from incineration of waste (12.0 Tg CO_2 Eq. in 2011) increased by 4.1 Tg CO_2 Eq. (51.0 percent) from 1990 through 2011, as the volume of plastics and other fossil carbon-containing materials in municipal solid waste grew.

The decrease in CO_2 emissions from fossil fuel combustion in 2011 was a result of multiple factors including: (1) a decrease in the carbon intensity of fuels consumed to generate electricity due to a decrease in coal consumption, with increased natural gas consumption and a significant increase in hydropower used; (2) a decrease in transportation-related energy consumption due to higher fuel costs, improvements in fuel efficiency, and a reduction in miles traveled; and (3) relatively mild winter conditions, especially in the South Atlantic Region of the United States where electricity is an important heating fuel, resulting in an overall decrease in electricity demand.

Source: *U.S. EPA, Inventory of U.S. Greenhouse Gas Emissions and Sinks: 1990–2011*

Industrial Processes

Greenhouse gas emissions are produced as the by-products of many non-energy-related industrial activities. For example, industrial processes can chemically transform raw materials, which often release waste gases such as CO_2, CH_4, and N_2O. These processes include iron and steel production and metallurgical coke production, cement production, ammonia production, urea consumption, lime production, other process uses of carbonates (e.g., flux stone, flue gas desulfurization, and glass manufacturing), soda ash production and consumption, titanium dioxide production, phosphoric acid production, ferroalloy production, CO_2 consumption, silicon carbide production and consumption, aluminum production, petrochemical production, nitric acid production, adipic acid production, lead production, and zinc production (see Figure 2-9). Industrial processes also release HFCs, PFCs and SF_6. In addition to their use as ODS substitutes, HFCs, PFCs, SF_6, and other fluorinated compounds are employed and emitted by a number of other industrial sources in the United States. These industries include aluminum production, HCFC-22 production, semiconductor manufacture, electric power transmission and distribution, and magnesium metal production and processing. Table 2-6 presents greenhouse gas emissions from industrial processes by source category.

Figure 2-9: 2011 Industrial Processes Chapter Greenhouse Gas Sources

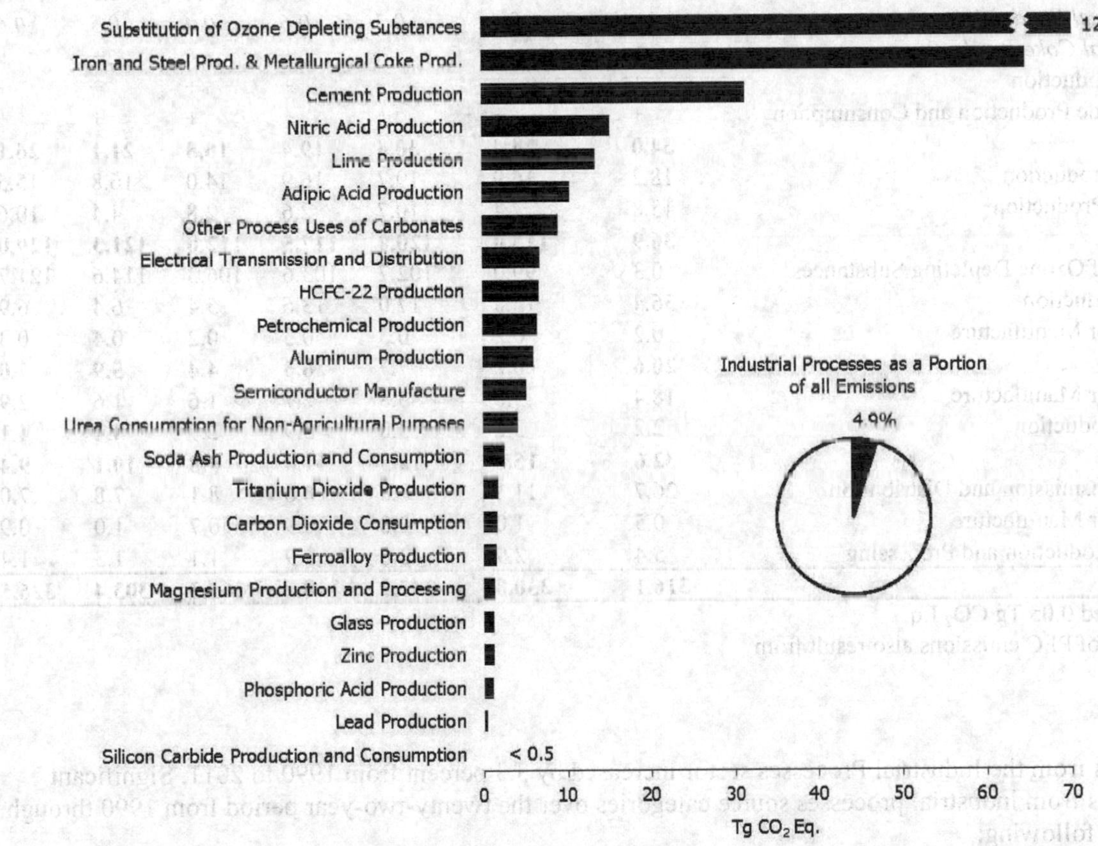

Table 2-6: Emissions from Industrial Processes (Tg CO_2 Eq.)

Gas/Source	1990	2005	2007	2008	2009	2010	2011
CO_2	**188.7**	**166.3**	**172.9**	**160.3**	**119.0**	**141.4**	**151.3**
Iron and Steel Production & Metallurgical Coke Production	99.8	66.7	71.3	66.8	43.0	55.7	64.3
Iron and Steel Production	*97.3*	*64.6*	*69.2*	*64.5*	*42.1*	*53.7*	*62.8*
Metallurgical Coke Production	*2.5*	*2.0*	*2.1*	*2.3*	*1.0*	*2.1*	*1.4*
Cement Production	33.3	45.2	44.5	40.5	29.0	30.9	31.6

Source: *U.S. EPA, Inventory of U.S. Greenhouse Gas Emissions and Sinks: 1990–2011*

Lime Production	11.5	14.3	14.6	14.3	11.2	13.1	13.8
Other Process Uses of Carbonates	4.9	6.3	7.4	5.9	7.6	9.6	9.2
Ammonia Production	13.0	9.2	9.1	7.9	7.9	8.7	8.8
Urea Consumption for Non-Agricultural Purposes	3.8	3.7	4.9	4.1	3.4	4.4	4.3
Petrochemical Production	3.4	4.3	4.1	3.6	2.8	3.5	3.5
Aluminum Production	6.8	4.1	4.3	4.5	3.0	2.7	3.3
Soda Ash Production and Consumption	2.8	3.0	2.9	3.0	2.6	2.7	2.7
Titanium Dioxide Production	1.2	1.8	1.9	1.8	1.6	1.8	1.9
Carbon Dioxide Consumption	1.4	1.3	1.9	1.8	1.8	2.2	1.8
Ferroalloy Production	2.2	1.4	1.6	1.6	1.5	1.7	1.7
Glass Production	1.5	1.9	1.5	1.5	1.0	1.5	1.3
Zinc Production	0.6	1.0	1.0	1.2	0.9	1.2	1.3
Phosphoric Acid Production	1.5	1.3	1.2	1.1	1.0	1.1	1.2
Lead Production	0.5	0.6	0.6	0.5	0.5	0.5	0.5
Silicon Carbide Production and Consumption	0.4	0.2	0.2	0.2	0.1	0.2	0.2
CH_4	**3.3**	**3.9**	**4.0**	**3.6**	**3.3**	**3.6**	**3.7**
Petrochemical Production	2.3	3.1	3.3	2.9	2.9	3.1	3.1
Iron and Steel Production & Metallurgical Coke	1.0	0.7	0.7	0.6	0.4	0.5	0.6
Iron and Steel Production	*1.0*	*0.7*	*0.7*	*0.6*	*0.4*	*0.5*	*0.6*
Metallurgical Coke Production	+	+	+	+	+	+	+
Ferroalloy Production	+	+	+	+	+	+	+
Silicon Carbide Production and Consumption	+	+	+	+	+	+	+
N_2O	**34.0**	**24.4**	**30.4**	**19.4**	**16.8**	**21.1**	**26.1**
Nitric Acid Production	18.2	16.9	19.7	16.9	14.0	16.8	15.5
Adipic Acid Production	15.8	7.4	10.7	2.6	2.8	4.4	10.6
HFCs	**36.9**	**115.0**	**120.0**	**117.5**	**112.0**	**121.3**	**129.0**
Substitution of Ozone Depleting Substances[a]	0.3	99.0	102.7	103.6	106.3	114.6	121.7
HCFC-22 Production	36.4	15.8	17.0	13.6	5.4	6.4	6.9
Semiconductor Manufacture	0.2	0.2	0.3	0.3	0.2	0.4	0.3
PFCs	**20.6**	**6.2**	**7.7**	**6.6**	**4.4**	**5.9**	**7.0**
Semiconductor Manufacture	18.4	3.0	3.8	2.7	1.6	1.6	2.9
Aluminum Production	2.2	3.2	3.8	3.9	2.9	4.4	4.1
SF_6	**32.6**	**15.0**	**12.3**	**11.4**	**9.8**	**10.1**	**9.4**
Electrical Transmission and Distribution	26.7	11.1	8.8	8.6	8.1	7.8	7.0
Semiconductor Manufacture	0.5	1.0	0.8	0.9	0.7	1.0	0.9
Magnesium Production and Processing	5.4	2.9	2.6	1.9	1.1	1.3	1.4
Total	**316.1**	**330.8**	**347.2**	**318.7**	**265.3**	**303.4**	**326.5**

+ Does not exceed 0.05 Tg CO_2 Eq.

[a] Small amounts of PFC emissions also result from this source.

Overall, emissions from the Industrial Processes sector increased by 3.3 percent from 1990 to 2011. Significant trends in emissions from industrial processes source categories over the twenty-two-year period from 1990 through 2011 included the following:

- Combined CO_2 and CH_4 emissions from iron and steel production and metallurgical coke production increased by 15.2 percent to 64.8 Tg CO_2 Eq. from 2010 to 2011, but have declined overall by 35.9 Tg CO_2 Eq. (35.6 percent) from 1990 through 2011, due to restructuring of the industry, technological improvements, and increased scrap steel utilization.

- CO_2 emissions from ammonia production (8.8 Tg CO_2 Eq. in 2011) decreased by 4.3 Tg CO_2 Eq. (32.6 percent) since 1990. This is due to a decrease in domestic ammonia production primarily attributed to market fluctuations. Urea consumption for non-agricultural purposes (4.3 Tg CO_2 Eq. in 2011) increased by 0.5 Tg CO_2 Eq. (14.4 percent) since 1990.

Source: *U.S. EPA, Inventory of U.S. Greenhouse Gas Emissions and Sinks: 1990–2011*

- N_2O emissions from adipic acid production were 10.6 Tg CO_2 Eq. in 2011, and have decreased significantly in recent years due to the widespread installation of pollution control measures. Emissions from adipic acid production have decreased by 32.9 percent since 1990 and by 39.6 percent since a peak in 1995.
- HFC emissions from ODS substitutes have been increasing from small amounts in 1990 to 121.7 Tg CO_2 Eq. in 2011. This increase results from efforts to phase out CFCs and other ODS' in the United States. In the short term, this trend is expected to continue, and will likely accelerate over the next decade as HCFCs—which are interim substitutes in many applications—are phased out under the provisions of the Copenhagen Amendments to the Montreal Protocol.
- PFC emissions from aluminum production decreased by about 84.0 percent (15.5 Tg CO_2 Eq.) from 1990 to 2011, due to both industry emission reduction efforts and lower domestic aluminum production.

Solvent and Other Product Use

Greenhouse gas emissions are produced as a by-product of various solvent and other product uses. In the United States, N_2O Emissions from Product Uses, the only source of greenhouse gas emissions from this sector, accounted for 4.4 Tg CO_2 Eq., or less than 0.1 percent of total U.S. greenhouse gas emissions in 2011 (see Table 2-7).

Table 2-7: N_2O Emissions from Solvent and Other Product Use (Tg CO_2 Eq.)

Gas/Source	1990	2005	2007	2008	2009	2010	2011
N_2O	4.4	4.4	4.4	4.4	4.4	4.4	4.4
N_2O from Product Uses	4.4	4.4	4.4	4.4	4.4	4.4	4.4
Total	4.4	4.4	4.4	4.4	4.4	4.4	4.4

In 2011, N_2O emissions from product uses constituted 1.2 percent of U.S. N_2O emissions. From 1990 to 2011, emissions from this source category decreased by 0.4 percent, though slight increases occurred in intermediate years.

Agriculture

Agricultural activities contribute directly to emissions of greenhouse gases through a variety of processes, including the following source categories: enteric fermentation in domestic livestock, livestock manure management, rice cultivation, agricultural soil management, and field burning of agricultural residues.

In 2011, agricultural activities were responsible for emissions of 461.5 Tg CO_2 Eq., or 6.9 percent of total U.S. greenhouse gas emissions. CH_4 and N_2O were the primary greenhouse gases emitted by agricultural activities. CH_4 emissions from enteric fermentation and manure management represented about 23.4 percent and 8.9 percent of total CH_4 emissions from anthropogenic activities, respectively, in 2011. Agricultural soil management activities, such as fertilizer application and other cropping practices, were the largest source of U.S. N_2O emissions in 2011, accounting for 69.3 percent.

Source: *U.S. EPA, Inventory of U.S. Greenhouse Gas Emissions and Sinks: 1990–2011*

Figure 2-10: 2011 Agriculture Chapter Greenhouse Gas Sources

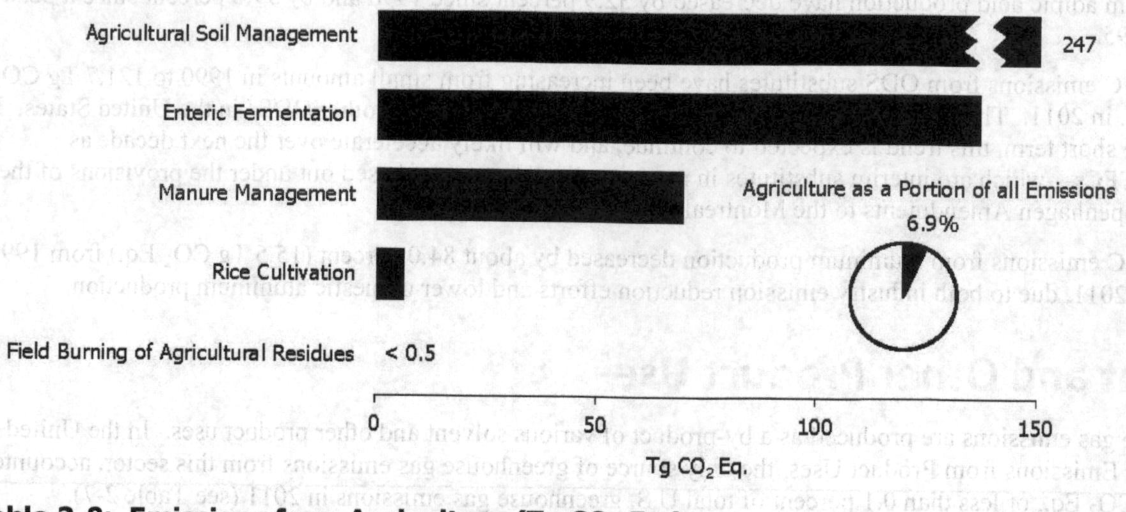

Table 2-8: Emissions from Agriculture (Tg CO_2 Eq.)

Gas/Source	1990	2005	2007	2008	2009	2010	2011
CH_4	**171.5**	**191.5**	**200.5**	**200.3**	**198.6**	**199.9**	**196.3**
Enteric Fermentation	132.7	137.0	141.8	141.4	140.6	139.3	137.4
Manure Management	31.5	47.6	52.4	51.5	50.5	51.8	52.0
Rice Cultivation	7.1	6.8	6.2	7.2	7.3	8.6	6.6
Field Burning of Agricultural Residues	0.2	0.2	0.2	0.2	0.2	0.2	0.2
N_2O	**242.3**	**254.7**	**270.4**	**263.3**	**260.6**	**262.4**	**265.2**
Agricultural Soil Management	227.9	237.5	252.3	245.4	242.8	244.5	247.2
Manure Management	14.4	17.1	18.0	17.8	17.7	17.8	18.0
Field Burning of Agricultural Residues	0.1	0.1	0.1	0.1	0.1	0.1	0.1
Total	**413.9**	**446.2**	**470.9**	**463.6**	**459.2**	**462.3**	**461.5**

Note: Totals may not sum due to independent rounding.

Some significant trends in U.S. emissions from Agriculture source categories include the following:

- Agricultural soils produced approximately 69.3 percent of N_2O emissions in the United States in 2011. Estimated emissions from this source in 2011 were 247.2 Tg CO_2 Eq. Annual N_2O emissions from agricultural soils fluctuated between 1990 and 2011, although overall emissions were 8.5 percent higher in 2011 than in 1990. Nitrous oxide emissions from this source have not shown any significant long-term trend, as their estimation is highly sensitive to the amount of N applied to soils, which has not changed significantly over the time-period, and to weather patterns and crop type.

- Enteric fermentation was the second largest source of CH_4 emissions in the United States in 2011, at 137.4 Tg CO_2 Eq. Generally, from 1990 to 1995 emissions increased and then decreased from 1996 to 2001. These trends were mainly due to fluctuations in beef cattle populations and increased digestibility of feed for feedlot cattle. Emissions generally increased from 2002 to 2007, though with a slight decrease in 2004., as both dairy and beef populations underwent increases and the literature for dairy cow diets indicated a trend toward a decrease in feed digestibility for those years. Emissions decreased again from 2008 to 2011 as beef cattle populations again decreased. Regarding trends in other animals, during the timeframe of this analysis, populations of sheep have decreased 52 percent while horse populations have almost doubled, with each annual increase ranging from about 2 to 6 percent. Goat and swine populations have increased 25 percent and 22 percent, respectively, during this timeframe, though with some slight annual decreases. The

Source: *U.S. EPA, Inventory of U.S. Greenhouse Gas Emissions and Sinks: 1990–2011*

populations of American bison and mules, burros, and donkeys have more than tripled and quadrupled, respectively.

- Overall, emissions from manure management increased 52.8 percent between 1990 and 2011. This encompassed an increase of 65.3 percent for CH_4, from 31.5 Tg CO_2 Eq. in 1990 to 52.0 Tg CO_2 Eq. in 2011; and an increase of 25.3 percent for N_2O, from 14.4 Tg CO_2 Eq. in 1990 to 18.0 Tg CO_2 Eq. in 2011. The majority of this increase was from swine and dairy cow manure, since the general trend in manure management is one of increasing use of liquid systems, which tends to produce greater CH_4 emissions.

Land Use, Land-Use Change, and Forestry

When humans alter the terrestrial biosphere through land use, changes in land use, and land management practices, they also alter the background carbon fluxes between biomass, soils, and the atmosphere. Forest management practices, tree planting in urban areas, the management of agricultural soils, and the landfilling of yard trimmings and food scraps have resulted in an uptake (sequestration) of carbon in the United States, which offset about 13.5 percent of total U.S. greenhouse gas emissions in 2011. Forests (including vegetation, soils, and harvested wood) accounted for approximately 92 percent of total 2011 net CO_2 flux, urban trees accounted for 8 percent, mineral and organic soil carbon stock changes accounted for 1 percent, and landfilled yard trimmings and food scraps accounted for 1 percent of the total net flux in 2011. The net forest sequestration is a result of net forest growth, increasing forest area, and a net accumulation of carbon stocks in harvested wood pools. The net sequestration in urban forests is a result of net tree growth and increased urban forest size. In agricultural soils, mineral and organic soils sequester approximately 5 times as much C as is emitted from these soils through liming and urea fertilization. The mineral soil C sequestration is largely due to the conversion of cropland to hay production fields, the limited use of bare-summer fallow areas in semi-arid areas, and an increase in the adoption of conservation tillage practices. The landfilled yard trimmings and food scraps net sequestration is due to the long-term accumulation of yard trimming and food scraps carbon in landfills.

Land use, land-use change, and forestry activities in 2011 resulted in a net C sequestration of 905.0 Tg CO_2 Eq. (246.8 Tg C) (Table 2-9). This represents an offset of approximately 16.1 percent of total U.S. CO_2 emissions, or 13.5 percent of total greenhouse gas emissions in 2011. Between 1990 and 2011, total land use, land-use change, and forestry net C flux resulted in a 13.9 percent increase in CO_2 sequestration, primarily due to an increase in the rate of net C accumulation in forest C stocks, particularly in aboveground and belowground tree biomass, and harvested wood pools.

Table 2-9: Net CO_2 Flux from Land Use, Land-Use Change, and Forestry (Tg CO_2 Eq.)

Sink Category	1990	2005	2007	2008	2009	2010	2011
Forest Land Remaining Forest Land	(696.8)	(905.0)	(859.3)	(833.3)	(811.3)	(817.6)	(833.5)
Cropland Remaining Cropland	(34.1)	(20.3)	(6.6)	(5.2)	(4.6)	(3.0)	(2.9)
Land Converted to Cropland	21.0	13.5	14.5	14.5	14.5	14.5	14.5
Grassland Remaining Grassland	(5.3)	(1.0)	7.1	7.2	7.3	7.3	7.4
Land Converted to Grassland	(7.7)	(10.2)	(9.0)	(9.0)	(8.9)	(8.8)	(8.8)
Settlements Remaining Settlements	(47.5)	(63.2)	(65.0)	(66.0)	(66.9)	(67.9)	(68.8)
Other (Landfilled Yard Trimmings and Food Scraps)	(24.2)	(11.6)	(10.9)	(10.9)	(12.7)	(13.3)	(13.0)
Total	**(794.5)**	**(997.8)**	**(929.2)**	**(902.6)**	**(882.6)**	**(888.8)**	**(905.0)**

Note: Totals may not sum due to independent rounding. Parentheses indicate net sequestration.

Land use, land-use change, and forestry source categories also resulted in emissions of CO_2, CH_4, and N_2O that are not included in the net CO_2 flux estimates presented in Table 2-9. The application of crushed limestone and dolomite to managed land (i.e., soil liming) and urea fertilization resulted in CO_2 emissions of 8.1 Tg CO_2 Eq. in 2011, an increase of about 14.6 percent relative to 1990. Lands undergoing peat extraction resulted in CO_2 emissions of 0.9 Tg CO_2 Eq. (918 Gg), and N_2O emissions of less than 0.05 Tg CO_2 Eq. N_2O emissions from the application of synthetic fertilizers to forest soils have increased from 0.1 Tg CO_2 Eq. in 1990 to 0.4 Tg CO_2 Eq. in 2011. Settlement soils in 2011 resulted in direct N_2O emissions of 1.5 Tg CO_2 Eq., a 51 percent increase relative to

Source: *U.S. EPA, Inventory of U.S. Greenhouse Gas Emissions and Sinks: 1990–2011*

1990. Emissions from forest fires in 2011 resulted in CH_4 emissions of 14.2 Tg CO_2 Eq., and in N_2O emissions of 11.6 Tg CO_2 Eq. (Table 2-10).

Table 2-10: Emissions from Land Use, Land-Use Change, and Forestry (Tg CO_2 Eq.)

Source Category	1990	2005	2007	2008	2009	2010	2011
CO_2	**8.1**	**8.9**	**9.2**	**9.6**	**8.3**	**9.4**	**9.0**
Cropland Remaining Cropland: Liming of Agricultural Soils	4.7	4.3	4.5	5.0	3.7	4.7	4.5
Cropland Remaining Cropland: Urea Fertilization	2.4	3.5	3.8	3.6	3.6	3.7	3.7
Wetlands Remaining Wetlands: Peatlands Remaining Peatlands	1.0	1.1	1.0	1.0	1.1	1.0	0.9
CH_4	**2.5**	**8.0**	**14.4**	**8.7**	**5.7**	**4.7**	**14.2**
Forest Land Remaining Forest Land: Forest Fires	2.5	8.0	14.4	8.7	5.7	4.7	14.2
N_2O	**3.1**	**8.4**	**13.7**	**8.9**	**6.4**	**5.6**	**13.4**
Forest Land Remaining Forest Land: Forest Fires	2.0	6.6	11.7	7.1	4.7	3.8	11.6
Forest Land Remaining Forest Land: Forest Soils	0.1	0.4	0.4	0.4	0.4	0.4	0.4
Settlements Remaining Settlements: Settlement Soils	1.0	1.5	1.6	1.5	1.4	1.5	1.5
Wetlands Remaining Wetlands: Peatlands Remaining Peatlands	+	+	+	+	+	+	+
Total	**13.7**	**25.4**	**37.3**	**27.2**	**20.4**	**19.7**	**36.6**

+ Less than 0.05 Tg CO_2 Eq.
Note: Totals may not sum due to independent rounding.

Other significant trends from 1990 to 2011 in emissions from land use, land-use change, and forestry source categories include:

- Net C sequestration by forest land (i.e., carbon stock accumulation in the five carbon pools) has increased by approximately 20 percent. This is primarily due to increased forest management and the effects of previous reforestation. The increase in intensive forest management resulted in higher growth rates and higher biomass density. The tree planting and conservation efforts of the 1970s and 1980s continue to have a significant impact on sequestration rates. Finally, the forested area in the United States increased over the past 20 years, although only at an average rate of 0.2 percent per year.
- Net sequestration of C by urban trees has increased by 44.9 percent over the period from 1990 to 2011. This is primarily due to an increase in urbanized land area in the United States.
- Annual C sequestration in landfilled yard trimmings and food scraps has decreased by 46.2 percent since 1990. This is due in part to a decrease in the amount of yard trimmings and food scraps generated. In addition, the proportion of yard trimmings and food scraps landfilled has decreased, as there has been a significant rise in the number of municipal composting facilities in the United States.

Waste

Waste management and treatment activities are sources of greenhouse gas emissions (see Figure 2-11). In 2011, landfills were the third largest source of U.S. anthropogenic CH_4 emissions, accounting for 17.5 percent of total U.S. CH_4 emissions.[45] Additionally, wastewater treatment accounts for 16.7 percent of Waste emissions, 2.8 percent of U.S. CH_4 emissions, and 1.5 percent of N_2O emissions. Emissions of CH_4 and N_2O from composting grew from 1990 to 2011, and resulted in emissions of 3.3 Tg CO_2 Eq. in 2011. A summary of greenhouse gas emissions from the Waste chapter is presented in Table 2-11.

---

[45] Landfills also store carbon, due to incomplete degradation of organic materials such as wood products and yard trimmings, as described in the Land Use, Land-Use Change, and Forestry chapter.

***Source:** U.S. EPA, Inventory of U.S. Greenhouse Gas Emissions and Sinks: 1990–2011*

Figure 2-11: 2011 Waste Chapter Greenhouse Gas Sources

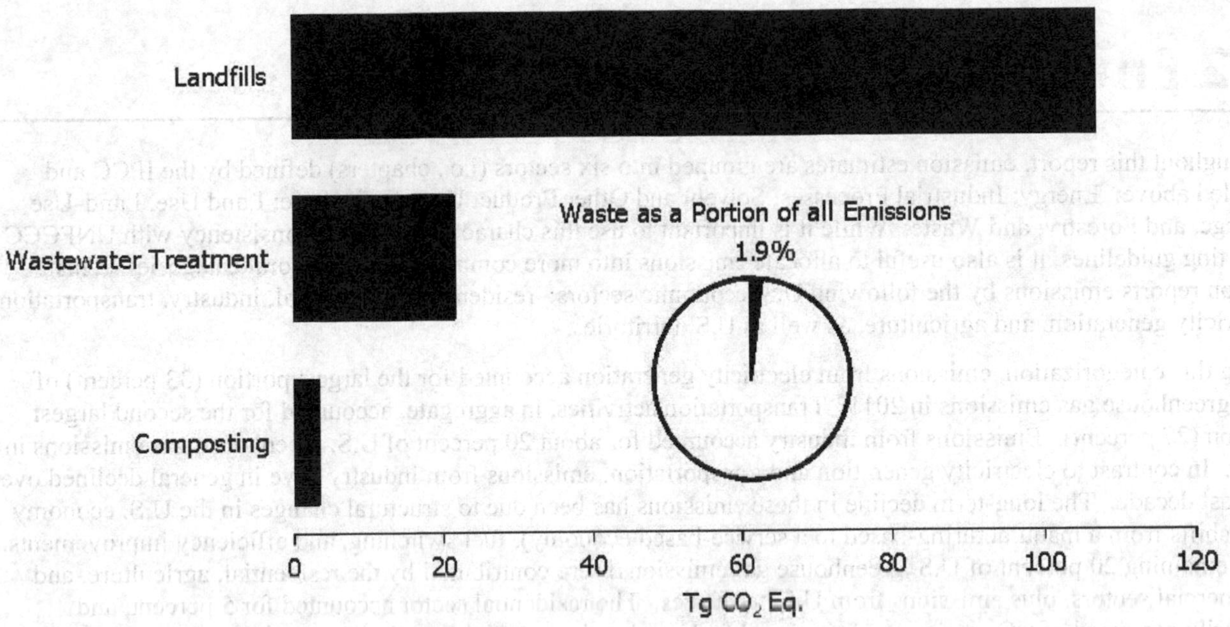

Overall, in 2011, waste activities generated emissions of 127.7 Tg CO_2 Eq., or 1.9 percent of total U.S. greenhouse gas emissions.

Table 2-11: Emissions from Waste (Tg CO_2 Eq.)

Gas/Source	1990	2005	2007	2008	2009	2010	2011
CH_4	**164.0**	**130.5**	**129.8**	**129.8**	**131.9**	**131.4**	**124.7**
Landfills	147.8	112.5	111.5	111.6	113.6	113.3	106.8
Wastewater Treatment	15.9	16.5	16.7	16.6	16.6	16.5	16.4
Composting	0.3	1.6	1.6	1.7	1.7	1.6	1.5
N_2O	**3.8**	**6.4**	**6.5**	**6.7**	**6.8**	**6.7**	**6.8**
Wastewater Treatment	3.5	4.7	4.8	4.8	4.9	5	5.1
Composting	0.4	1.7	1.8	1.8	1.9	1.8	1.7
Total	**167.8**	**136.9**	**136.5**	**138.6**	**138.1**	**131.4**	**127.7**

Note: Totals may not sum due to independent rounding.

Some significant trends in U.S. emissions from waste source categories include the following:

- From 1990 to 2011, net CH_4 emissions from landfills decreased by 44.7 Tg CO_2 Eq. (30.3 percent), with small increases occurring in interim years. This downward trend in overall emissions is the result of increases in the amount of landfill gas collected and combusted as well as reduction in the amount of decomposable materials (i.e., paper and paperboard, food scraps, and yard trimmings) discarded in MSW landfills over the time series,[46] which has more than offset the additional CH_4 emissions resulting from an increase in the amount of municipal solid waste landfilled.
- Combined CH_4 and N_2O emissions from composting have generally increased since 1990, from 0.7 Tg CO_2 Eq. to 3.3 Tg CO_2 Eq. in 2011, which represents slightly less than a five-fold increase over the time series.

[46] The CO_2 produced from combusted landfill CH_4 at landfills is not counted in national inventories as it is considered part of the natural C cycle of decomposition.

Source: U.S. EPA, Inventory of U.S. Greenhouse Gas Emissions and Sinks: 1990–2011

- From 1990 to 2011, CH_4 and N_2O emissions from wastewater treatment increased by 0.2 Tg CO_2 Eq. (1.6 percent) and 1.7 Tg CO_2 Eq. (49.7 percent), respectively.

2.2 Emissions by Economic Sector

Throughout this report, emission estimates are grouped into six sectors (i.e., chapters) defined by the IPCC and detailed above: Energy; Industrial Processes; Solvent and Other Product Use; Agriculture; Land Use, Land-Use Change, and Forestry; and Waste. While it is important to use this characterization for consistency with UNFCCC reporting guidelines, it is also useful to allocate emissions into more commonly used sectoral categories. This section reports emissions by the following U.S. economic sectors: residential, commercial, industry, transportation, electricity generation, and agriculture, as well as U.S. territories.

Using this categorization, emissions from electricity generation accounted for the largest portion (33 percent) of U.S. greenhouse gas emissions in 2011. Transportation activities, in aggregate, accounted for the second largest portion (27 percent). Emissions from industry accounted for about 20 percent of U.S. greenhouse gas emissions in 2011. In contrast to electricity generation and transportation, emissions from industry have in general declined over the past decade. The long-term decline in these emissions has been due to structural changes in the U.S. economy (i.e., shifts from a manufacturing-based to a service-based economy), fuel switching, and efficiency improvements. The remaining 20 percent of U.S. greenhouse gas emissions were contributed by the residential, agriculture, and commercial sectors, plus emissions from U.S. territories. The residential sector accounted for 5 percent, and primarily consisted of CO_2 emissions from fossil fuel combustion. Activities related to agriculture accounted for roughly 8 percent of U.S. emissions; unlike other economic sectors, agricultural sector emissions were dominated by N_2O emissions from agricultural soil management and CH_4 emissions from enteric fermentation, rather than CO_2 from fossil fuel combustion. The commercial sector accounted for roughly 6 percent of emissions, while U.S. territories accounted for less than 1 percent. Carbon dioxide was also emitted and sequestered (in the form of C) by a variety of activities related to forest management practices, tree planting in urban areas, the management of agricultural soils, and landfilling of yard trimmings.

Table 2-12 presents a detailed breakdown of emissions from each of these economic sectors by source category, as they are defined in this report. Figure 2-12 shows the trend in emissions by sector from 1990 to 2011.

Figure 2-12: Emissions Allocated to Economic Sectors

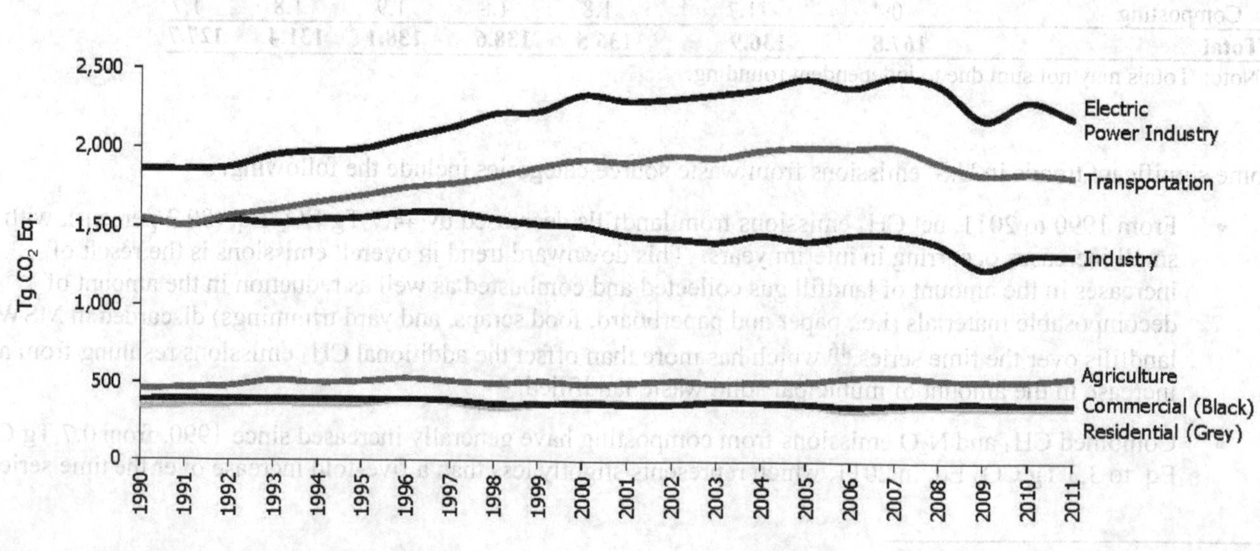

Table 2-12: U.S. Greenhouse Gas Emissions Allocated to Economic Sectors (Tg CO_2 Eq. and Percent of Total in 2011)

Source: *U.S. EPA, Inventory of U.S. Greenhouse Gas Emissions and Sinks: 1990–2011*

Sector/Source	1990	2005	2007	2008	2009	2010	2011	Percent[a]
Electric Power Industry	**1,866.1**	**2,445.7**	**2,455.6**	**2,402.0**	**2,187.6**	**2,303.0**	**2,200.9**	**32.8%**
CO_2 from Fossil Fuel Combustion	1,820.8	2,402.1	2,412.8	2,360.9	2,146.4	2,259.2	2,158.5	32.2%
Stationary Combustion	7.7	16.5	17.2	17.3	17.2	18.9	18.4	0.3%
Incineration of Waste	8.4	12.9	13.1	12.2	12.1	12.4	12.4	0.2%
Electrical Transmission and Distribution	26.7	11.1	8.8	8.6	8.1	7.8	7.0	0.1%
Other Process Uses of Carbonates	2.5	3.2	3.7	2.9	3.8	4.8	4.6	0.1%
Transportation	**1,553.2**	**2,012.3**	**2,013.1**	**1,916.0**	**1,840.6**	**1,852.3**	**1,829.4**	**27.3%**
CO_2 from Fossil Fuel Combustion	1,494.0	1,891.7	1,904.7	1,816.0	1,749.2	1,763.9	1,745.0	26.0%
Substitution of Ozone Depleting Substances	+	72.9	68.8	64.9	60.2	58.4	57.1	0.9%
Mobile Combustion	47.4	37.5	29.3	25.6	22.7	20.5	18.3	0.3%
Non-Energy Use of Fuels	11.8	10.2	10.2	9.5	8.5	9.5	9.0	0.1%
Industry	**1,538.8**	**1,416.2**	**1,456.1**	**1,398.8**	**1,244.2**	**1,331.8**	**1,332.0**	**19.9%**
CO_2 from Fossil Fuel Combustion	817.5	776.6	796.0	756.6	676.0	732.6	723.8	10.8%
Natural Gas Systems	198.9	188.9	199.2	196.0	182.9	175.9	177.1	2.6%
Non-Energy Use of Fuels	99.9	124.5	117.5	121.3	111.5	115.2	113.4	1.7%
Iron and Steel Production	100.7	67.4	72.0	67.5	43.4	56.3	64.8	1.0%
Coal Mining	84.1	56.9	57.9	67.1	70.3	72.4	63.2	0.9%
Petroleum Systems	35.6	29.5	30.1	30.3	30.9	31.1	31.8	0.5%
Cement Production	33.3	45.2	44.5	40.5	29.0	30.9	31.6	0.5%
Nitric Acid Production	18.2	16.9	19.7	16.9	14.0	16.8	15.5	0.2%
Substitution of Ozone Depleting Substances	+	6.4	7.8	8.5	10.9	13.5	15.0	0.2%
Lime Production	11.5	14.3	14.6	14.3	11.2	13.1	13.8	0.2%
Adipic Acid Production	15.8	7.4	10.7	2.6	2.8	4.4	10.6	0.2%
Ammonia Production	13.0	9.2	9.1	7.9	7.9	8.7	8.8	0.1%
HCFC-22 Production	36.4	15.8	17.0	13.6	5.4	6.4	6.9	0.1%
Petrochemical Production	5.7	7.5	7.3	6.5	5.7	6.5	6.6	0.1%
Aluminum Production	25.3	7.1	8.1	7.2	4.6	4.3	6.2	0.1%
Semiconductor Manufacture	2.9	4.4	4.9	5.1	3.8	5.7	5.3	0.1%
Abandoned Underground Coal Mines	6.0	5.5	5.3	5.3	5.1	5.0	4.8	0.1%
Other Process Uses of Carbonates	2.5	3.2	3.7	2.9	3.8	4.8	4.6	0.1%
N_2O from Product Uses	4.4	4.4	4.4	4.4	4.4	4.4	4.4	0.1%
Urea Consumption for Non-Agricultural Purposes	3.8	3.7	4.9	4.1	3.4	4.4	4.3	0.1%
Stationary Combustion	4.9	4.6	4.3	4.2	3.7	4.1	4.0	0.1%
Soda Ash Production and Consumption	2.8	3.0	2.9	3.0	2.6	2.7	2.7	+
Titanium Dioxide Production	1.2	1.8	1.9	1.8	1.6	1.8	1.9	+
Carbon Dioxide Consumption	1.4	1.3	1.9	1.8	1.8	2.2	1.8	+
Ferroalloy Production	2.2	1.4	1.6	1.6	1.5	1.7	1.7	+
Magnesium Production and Processing	5.4	2.9	2.6	1.9	1.1	1.3	1.4	+
Mobile Combustion	0.9	1.3	1.3	1.3	1.3	1.4	1.4	+
Glass Production	1.5	1.9	1.5	1.5	1.0	1.5	1.3	+
Zinc Production	0.6	1.0	1.0	1.2	0.9	1.2	1.3	+
Phosphoric Acid Production	1.5	1.3	1.2	1.1	1.0	1.1	1.2	+
Lead Production	0.5	0.6	0.6	0.5	0.5	0.5	0.5	+
Silicon Carbide Production and Consumption	0.4	0.2	0.2	0.2	0.2	0.2	0.2	+
Agriculture	**458.0**	**517.4**	**555.6**	**535.3**	**525.4**	**528.7**	**546.6**	**8.2%**
N_2O from Agricultural Soil Management	227.9	237.5	252.3	245.4	242.8	244.5	247.2	3.7%
Enteric Fermentation	132.7	137.0	141.8	141.4	140.6	139.3	137.4	2.0%
Manure Management	45.8	64.6	70.3	69.3	68.2	69.5	70.0	1.0%
CO_2 from Fossil Fuel Combustion	31.0	46.8	48.4	45.4	46.7	47.6	49.4	0.7%
CH_4 and N_2O from Forest Fires	4.5	14.6	26.1	15.7	10.4	8.5	25.7	0.4%
Rice Cultivation	7.1	6.8	6.2	7.2	7.3	8.6	6.6	0.1%
Liming of Agricultural Soils	4.7	4.3	4.5	5.0	3.7	4.7	4.5	0.1%
Urea Fertilization	2.4	3.5	3.8	3.6	3.6	3.7	3.7	0.1%
CO_2 and N_2O from Managed Peatlands	1.0	1.1	1.0	1.0	1.1	1.0	0.9	+
Mobile Combustion	0.3	0.5	0.5	0.5	0.5	0.5	0.5	+

Source: *U.S. EPA, Inventory of U.S. Greenhouse Gas Emissions and Sinks: 1990–2011*

Stationary Combustion	0.1	0.4	0.4	0.4	0.4	0.4	0.4	+
N_2O from Forest Soils	0.3	0.2	0.3	0.3	0.3	0.3	0.3	+
Field Burning of Agricultural Residues	+	+	+	+	+	+	+	+
Commercial	**388.1**	**374.1**	**372.0**	**380.9**	**382.9**	**376.9**	**378.0**	**5.6%**
CO_2 from Fossil Fuel Combustion	219.0	223.5	218.9	223.8	223.4	220.6	222.1	3.3%
Landfills	147.8	112.5	111.6	113.6	113.3	106.8	103.0	1.5%
Substitution of Ozone Depleting Substances	+	12.3	15.4	17.2	20.1	23.6	27.0	0.4%
Wastewater Treatment	15.9	16.5	16.6	16.6	16.5	16.4	16.2	0.2%
Human Sewage	3.5	4.7	4.8	4.9	5.0	5.1	5.2	0.1%
Composting	0.7	3.3	3.5	3.5	3.3	3.2	3.3	+
Stationary Combustion	1.3	1.3	1.3	1.3	1.3	1.3	1.3	+
Residential	**345.4**	**371.3**	**358.2**	**366.0**	**358.1**	**359.6**	**357.3**	**5.3%**
CO_2 from Fossil Fuel Combustion	338.3	357.9	341.6	347.0	337.0	334.6	328.8	4.9%
Substitution of Ozone Depleting Substances	0.3	7.3	10.7	12.9	15.1	19.1	22.6	0.3%
Stationary Combustion	5.7	4.6	4.4	4.7	4.5	4.4	4.4	0.1%
Settlement Soil Fertilization	1.0	1.5	1.6	1.5	1.4	1.5	1.5	+
U.S. Territories	**33.7**	**58.2**	**52.6**	**49.8**	**47.9**	**58.0**	**58.0**	**0.9%**
CO_2 from Fossil Fuel Combustion	27.9	50.0	45.2	41.0	43.8	49.6	49.7	0.7%
Non-Energy Use of Fuels	5.7	8.1	7.2	8.7	3.9	8.2	8.2	0.1%
Stationary Combustion	0.1	0.2	0.2	0.2	0.2	0.2	0.2	+
Total Emissions	**6,183.3**	**7,195.3**	**7,263.2**	**7,048.8**	**6,586.6**	**6,810.3**	**6,702.3**	**100.0%**
Sinks	**(794.5)**	**(997.8)**	**(929.2)**	**(902.6)**	**(882.6)**	**(888.8)**	**(905.0)**	**-13.5%**
CO_2 Flux from Forests	(696.8)	(905.0)	(859.3)	(833.3)	(811.3)	(817.6)	(833.5)	-12.4%
Urban Trees	(47.5)	(63.2)	(65.0)	(66.0)	(66.9)	(67.9)	(68.8)	-1.0%
Landfilled Yard Trimmings and Food Scraps	(24.2)	(11.6)	(10.9)	(10.9)	(12.7)	(13.3)	(13.0)	-0.2%
CO_2 Flux from Agricultural Soil Carbon Stocks	(26.0)	(18.0)	6.0	7.6	8.3	10.0	10.3	0.2%
Net Emissions	**5,388.7**	**6,197.4**	**6,334.0**	**6,146.2**	**5,704.0**	**5,921.5**	**5,797.3**	**86.5%**

Note: Includes all emissions of CO_2, CH_4, N_2O, HFCs, PFCs, and SF_6. Parentheses indicate negative values or sequestration. Totals may not sum due to independent rounding.

ODS (Ozone Depleting Substances)

+ Does not exceed 0.05 Tg CO_2 Eq. or 0.05 percent.

[a] Percent of total emissions for year 2011.

[b] Includes the effects of net additions to stocks of carbon stored in harvested wood products.

Emissions with Electricity Distributed to Economic Sectors

It can also be useful to view greenhouse gas emissions from economic sectors with emissions related to electricity generation distributed into end-use categories (i.e., emissions from electricity generation are allocated to the economic sectors in which the electricity is consumed). The generation, transmission, and distribution of electricity, which is the largest economic sector in the United States, accounted for 33 percent of total U.S. greenhouse gas emissions in 2011. Emissions increased by 18 percent since 1990, as electricity demand grew and fossil fuels remained the dominant energy source for generation. Electricity generation-related emissions decreased from 2010 to 2011 by 4.4 percent, primarily due to decreased CO_2 emissions from fossil fuel combustion. Electricity sales to the residential and commercial end-use sectors in 2011 decreased approximately 1.5 percent and 0.8 percent, respectively. The trend in the residential and commercial sectors can largely be attributed to milder, less energy-intensive winter conditions compared to 2010. Electricity sales to the industrial sector in 2011 increased approximately 0.5 percent. Overall, in 2011, the amount of electricity generated (in kWh) decreased by 0.8 percent from the previous year. As a result, CO_2 emissions from the electric power sector decreased by 4.4 percent as the consumption of coal and petroleum for electricity generation decreased by 5.7 percent and 19.9 percent, respectively, in 2011 and the consumption of natural gas for electricity generation, increased by 2.5 percent. Table 2-13 provides a detailed summary of emissions from electricity generation-related activities.

Source: *U.S. EPA, Inventory of U.S. Greenhouse Gas Emissions and Sinks: 1990–2011*

Table 2-13: Electricity Generation-Related Greenhouse Gas Emissions (Tg CO_2 Eq.)

Gas/Fuel Type or Source	1990	2005	2007	2008	2009	2010	2011
CO_2	**1,831.2**	**2,417.8**	**2,429.2**	**2,375.7**	**2,161.9**	**2,276.0**	**2,175.1**
Fossil Fuel Combustion	1,820.8	2,402.1	2,412.8	2,360.9	2,146.4	2,259.2	2,158.5
Coal	*1,547.6*	*1,983.8*	*1,987.3*	*1,959.4*	*1,740.9*	*1,827.6*	*1,722.7*
Natural Gas	*175.3*	*318.8*	*371.3*	*361.9*	*372.2*	*399.0*	*408.8*
Petroleum	*97.5*	*99.2*	*53.9*	*39.2*	*33.0*	*32.2*	*26.6*
Geothermal	*0.4*	*0.4*	*0.4*	*0.4*	*0.4*	*0.4*	*0.4*
Incineration of Waste	8.0	12.5	12.7	11.9	11.7	12.0	12.0
Other Process Uses of Carbonates	2.5	3.2	3.7	2.9	3.8	4.8	4.6
CH_4	**0.3**	**0.5**	**0.5**	**0.5**	**0.4**	**0.5**	**0.4**
Stationary Combustion*	0.3	0.5	0.5	0.5	0.4	0.5	0.4
Incineration of Waste	+	+	+	+	+	+	+
N_2O	**7.8**	**16.4**	**17.1**	**17.2**	**17.2**	**18.8**	**18.3**
Stationary Combustion*	7.4	16.0	16.7	16.8	16.8	18.5	17.9
Incineration of Waste	0.5	0.4	0.4	0.4	0.4	0.4	0.4
SF_6	**26.7**	**11.1**	**8.8**	**8.6**	**8.1**	**7.8**	**7.0**
Electrical Transmission and Distribution	26.7	11.1	8.8	8.6	8.1	7.8	7.0
Total	**1,866.1**	**2,445.7**	**2,455.6**	**2,402.0**	**2,187.6**	**2,303.0**	**2,200.9**

Note: Totals may not sum due to independent rounding.
* Includes only stationary combustion emissions related to the generation of electricity.
\+ Does not exceed 0.05 Tg CO_2 Eq.

To distribute electricity emissions among economic end-use sectors, emissions from the source categories assigned to the electricity generation sector were allocated to the residential, commercial, industry, transportation, and agriculture economic sectors according to each economic sector's share of retail sales of electricity consumption (EIA 2011 and Duffield 2006). These source categories include CO_2 from Fossil Fuel Combustion, CH_4 and N_2O from Stationary Combustion, Incineration of Waste, Other Process Uses of Carbonates, and SF_6 from Electrical Transmission and Distribution Systems. Note that only 50 percent of the Other Process Uses of Carbonates emissions were associated with electricity generation and distributed as described; the remainder of Other Process Uses of Carbonates emissions were attributed to the industrial processes economic end-use sector.[47]

When emissions from electricity are distributed among these sectors, industry activities account for the largest share of total U.S. greenhouse gas emissions (28.3 percent), followed closely by emissions from transportation (27.4 percent). Emissions from the residential and commercial sectors also increase substantially when emissions from electricity are included. In all sectors except agriculture, CO_2 accounts for more than 80 percent of greenhouse gas emissions, primarily from the combustion of fossil fuels.

Table 2-14 presents a detailed breakdown of emissions from each of these economic sectors, with emissions from electricity generation distributed to them. Figure 2-13 shows the trend in these emissions by sector from 1990 to 2011.

[47] Emissions were not distributed to U.S. territories, since the electricity generation sector only includes emissions related to the generation of electricity in the 50 states and the District of Columbia.

Source: U.S. EPA, Inventory of U.S. Greenhouse Gas Emissions and Sinks: 1990–2011

Figure 2-13: Emissions with Electricity Distributed to Economic Sectors

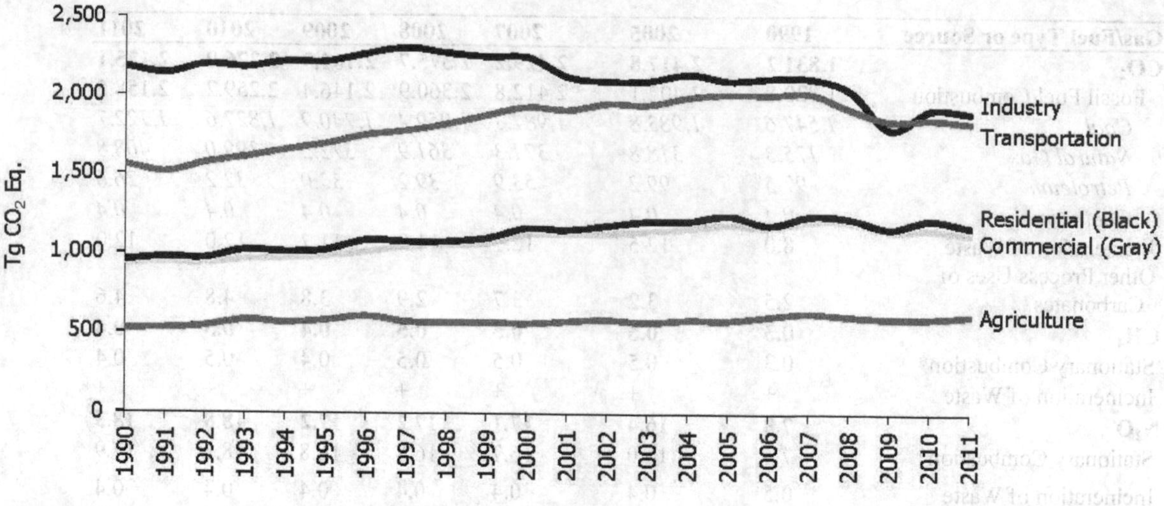

Table 2-14: U.S. Greenhouse Gas Emissions by Economic Sector and Gas with Electricity-Related Emissions Distributed (Tg CO_2 Eq.) and Percent of Total in 2011

Sector/Gas	1990	2005	2007	2008	2009	2010	2011	Percent[a]
Industry	**2,181.3**	**2,102.4**	**2,113.6**	**2,036.3**	**1,789.8**	**1,916.9**	**1,897.2**	**28.3%**
Direct Emissions	1,538.8	1,416.2	1,456.1	1,398.8	1,244.2	1,331.8	1,332.0	19.9%
CO_2	1,146.5	1,096.3	1,115.4	1,068.9	935.3	1,017.2	1,016.7	15.2%
CH_4	291.5	256.2	267.0	271.0	261.4	256.9	249.5	3.7%
N_2O	42.4	33.0	39.0	27.8	24.9	29.5	34.4	0.5%
HFCs, PFCs, and	58.4	30.6	34.6	31.1	22.6	28.3	31.5	0.5%
Electricity-Related	642.4	686.2	657.5	637.6	545.7	585.0	565.1	8.4%
CO_2	630.4	678.4	650.4	630.6	539.3	578.2	558.5	8.3%
CH_4	0.1	0.1	0.1	0.1	0.1	0.1	0.1	+
N_2O	2.7	4.6	4.6	4.6	4.3	4.8	4.7	0.1%
SF_6	9.2	3.1	2.4	2.3	2.0	2.0	1.8	+
Transportation	**1,556.3**	**2,017.2**	**2,018.2**	**1,920.8**	**1,845.2**	**1,856.9**	**1,833.7**	**27.4%**
Direct Emissions	1,553.2	2,012.3	2,013.1	1,916.0	1,840.6	1,852.3	1,829.4	27.3%
CO_2	1,505.8	1,901.9	1,914.9	1,825.5	1,757.7	1,773.4	1,754.0	26.2%
CH_4	4.4	2.1	1.8	1.6	1.5	1.5	1.4	+
N_2O	43.03	35.43	27.54	23.96	21.17	19.08	16.88	0.3%
HFCs[b]	+	72.9	68.8	64.9	60.2	58.4	57.1	0.9%
Electricity-Related	3.1	4.8	5.2	4.8	4.6	4.6	4.3	0.1%
CO_2	3.1	4.8	5.1	4.7	4.5	4.5	4.3	0.1%
CH_4	+	+	+	+	+	+	+	+
N_2O	+	+	+	+	+	+	+	+
SF_6	+	+	+	+	+	+	+	+
Commercial	**939.5**	**1,192.4**	**1,215.6**	**1,211.1**	**1,150.8**	**1,165.2**	**1,131.0**	**16.9%**
Direct Emissions	388.1	374.1	372.0	380.9	382.9	376.9	378.0	5.6%
CO_2	219.0	223.5	218.9	223.8	223.4	220.6	222.1	3.3%
CH_4	164.9	131.5	130.8	132.8	132.4	125.6	121.7	1.8%
N_2O	4.2	6.8	7.0	7.1	7.1	7.1	7.2	0.1%
HFCs	+	12.3	15.4	17.2	20.1	23.6	27.0	0.4%
Electricity-Related	551.4	818.3	843.5	830.2	767.9	788.3	752.9	11.2%
CO_2	541.1	808.9	834.5	821.2	758.9	779.0	744.1	11.1%
CH_4	0.1	0.2	0.2	0.2	0.2	0.2	0.2	+
N_2O	2.3	5.5	5.9	5.9	6.0	6.4	6.3	0.1%
SF_6	7.9	3.7	3.0	3.0	2.8	2.7	2.4	+
Residential	**953.1**	**1,243.6**	**1,237.1**	**1,223.6**	**1,159.6**	**1,216.3**	**1,169.8**	**17.5%**
Direct Emissions	345.4	371.3	358.2	366.0	358.1	359.6	357.3	5.3%

Source: *U.S. EPA, Inventory of U.S. Greenhouse Gas Emissions and Sinks: 1990–2011*

CO_2	338.3	357.9	341.6	347.0	337.0	334.6	328.8	4.9%
CH_4	4.6	3.6	3.5	3.7	3.6	3.5	3.5	0.1%
N_2O	2.1	2.4	2.5	2.4	2.3	2.4	2.4	+
HFCs	0.3	7.3	10.7	12.9	15.1	19.1	22.6	0.3%
Electricity-Related	607.8	872.3	878.8	857.6	801.6	856.7	812.5	12.1%
CO_2	596.4	862.3	869.4	848.2	792.2	846.7	803.0	12.0%
CH_4	0.1	0.2	0.2	0.2	0.2	0.2	0.2	+
N_2O	2.6	5.8	6.1	6.1	6.3	7.0	6.8	0.1%
SF_6	8.7	4.0	3.2	3.1	3.0	2.9	2.6	+
Agriculture	**519.4**	**581.6**	**626.2**	**607.1**	**593.3**	**597.1**	**612.6**	**9.1%**
Direct Emissions	458.0	517.4	555.6	535.3	525.4	528.7	546.6	8.2%
CO_2	39.2	55.7	57.7	55.1	55.0	57.0	58.5	0.9%
CH_4	174.1	199.7	215.1	209.1	204.4	204.7	210.6	3.1%
N_2O	244.7	262.0	282.8	271.1	266.0	266.9	277.6	4.1%
Electricity-Related	61.4	64.1	70.6	71.8	67.9	68.5	65.9	1.0%
CO_2	60.2	63.4	69.9	71.0	67.1	67.7	65.2	1.0%
CH_4	+	+	+	+	+	+	+	+
N_2O	0.3	0.4	0.5	0.5	0.5	0.6	0.5	+
SF_6	0.9	0.3	0.3	0.3	0.3	0.2	0.2	+
U.S. Territories	**33.7**	**58.2**	**52.6**	**49.8**	**47.9**	**58.0**	**58.0**	**0.9%**
Total	**6,183.3**	**7,195.3**	**7,263.2**	**7,048.8**	**6,586.6**	**6,810.3**	**6,702.3**	**100.0%**

Note: Emissions from electricity generation are allocated based on aggregate electricity consumption in each end-use sector.
Totals may not sum due to independent rounding.
+ Does not exceed 0.05 Tg CO_2 Eq. or 0.05 percent.
[a] Percent of total emissions for year 2011.
[b] Includes primarily HFC-134a.

Industry

The industrial end-use sector includes CO_2 emissions from fossil fuel combustion from all manufacturing facilities, in aggregate. This sector also includes emissions that are produced as a by-product of the non-energy-related industrial process activities. The variety of activities producing these non-energy-related emissions includes methane emissions from petroleum and natural gas systems, fugitive CH_4 emissions from coal mining, by-product CO_2 emissions from cement manufacture, and HFC, PFC, and SF_6 by-product emissions from semiconductor manufacture, to name a few. Since 1990, industrial sector emissions have declined. The decline has occurred both in direct emissions and indirect emissions associated with electricity use. However, the decline in direct emissions has been sharper. In theory, emissions from the industrial end-use sector should be highly correlated with economic growth and industrial output, but heating of industrial buildings and agricultural energy consumption are also affected by weather conditions. In addition, structural changes within the U.S. economy that lead to shifts in industrial output away from energy-intensive manufacturing products to less energy-intensive products (e.g., from steel to computer equipment) also have a significant effect on industrial emissions.

Transportation

When electricity-related emissions are distributed to economic end-use sectors, transportation activities accounted for 27 percent of U.S. greenhouse gas emissions in 2011. The largest sources of transportation greenhouse gases in 2011 were passenger cars (41.2 percent), light duty trucks, which include sport utility vehicles, pickup trucks, and minivans (17.4 percent), freight trucks (21.0 percent), rail (6.5 percent), and commercial aircraft (6.1 percent). These figures include direct emissions from fossil fuel combustion, as well as HFC emissions from mobile air conditioners and refrigerated transport allocated to these vehicle types.

Although average fuel economy over this period increased slightly due primarily to the retirement of older vehicles, average fuel economy among new vehicles sold annually gradually declined from 1990 to 2004. The decline in new vehicle fuel economy between 1990 and 2004 reflected the increasing market share of light duty trucks, which grew from about one-fifth of new vehicle sales in the 1970s to slightly over half of the market by 2004. Increasing fuel

Source: U.S. EPA, Inventory of U.S. Greenhouse Gas Emissions and Sinks: 1990–2011

prices have since decreased overall light duty truck sales, and average new vehicle fuel economy has improved since 2005 as the market share of passenger cars increased. Over the 1990s through early this decade, growth in vehicle travel substantially outweighed improvements in vehicle fuel economy; however, the rate of Vehicle Miles Traveled (VMT) growth slowed considerably starting in 2005 (and declined rapidly in 2008) while average vehicle fuel economy increased. In 2011, fuel VMT fell by 0.7 percent.[48] Additionally, consumption of diesel fuel has continued to decrease recently, due in part to a decrease in commercial activity and freight trucking as a result of the economic recession. Table 2-15 provides a detailed summary of greenhouse gas emissions from transportation-related activities with electricity-related emissions included in the totals.

In terms of the overall trend, from 1990 to 2011, transportation emissions rose by 19 percent due, in large part, to increased demand for travel and the stagnation of fuel efficiency across the U.S. vehicle fleet. The number of vehicle miles traveled by light-duty motor vehicles (passenger cars and light-duty trucks) increased 34 percent from 1990 to 2011, as a result of a confluence of factors including population growth, economic growth, urban sprawl, and low fuel prices over much of this period.

Then, from 2008 to 2009, CO_2 emissions from the transportation end-use sector declined 4 percent. The decrease in emissions can largely be attributed to decreased economic activity in 2009 and an associated decline in the demand for transportation. Modes such as medium- and heavy-duty trucks were significantly impacted by the decline in freight transport. From 2009 to 2011, CO_2 emissions from the transportation end-use sector stabilized even as economic activity rebounded slightly.

Almost all of the energy consumed for transportation was supplied by petroleum-based products, with more than half being related to gasoline consumption in automobiles and other highway vehicles. Other fuel uses, especially diesel fuel for freight trucks and jet fuel for aircraft, accounted for the remainder. The primary driver of transportation-related emissions was CO_2 from fossil fuel combustion, which increased by 17 percent from 1990 to 2011. This rise in CO_2 emissions, combined with an increase in HFCs from close to zero emissions in 1990 to 57.1 Tg CO_2 Eq. in 2011, led to an increase in overall emissions from transportation activities of 18 percent.

Table 2-15: Transportation-Related Greenhouse Gas Emissions (Tg CO2 Eq.)

Gas/Vehicle	1990	2005	2007	2008	2009	2010	2011
Passenger Cars	**657.4**	**709.5**	**847.4**	**807.0**	**798.7**	**794.1**	**787.4**
CO_2	629.3	662.3	804.4	769.3	766.0	763.8	759.0
CH_4	2.6	1.1	1.1	1.0	0.9	0.9	0.8
N_2O	25.4	17.8	17.3	14.7	12.4	10.9	9.4
HFCs	+	28.4	24.6	22.1	19.3	18.6	18.3
Light-Duty Trucks	**336.6**	**551.3**	**366.4**	**347.0**	**349.5**	**348.0**	**331.4**
CO_2	321.1	505.9	330.1	312.8	317.4	317.6	302.6
CH_4	1.4	0.7	0.3	0.3	0.3	0.3	0.3
N_2O	14.1	13.7	5.9	5.2	5.2	4.7	4.0
HFCs	+	31.0	30.1	28.6	26.6	25.4	24.5
Medium- and Heavy-Duty Trucks	**231.1**	**408.4**	**444.7**	**427.0**	**389.2**	**402.9**	**401.1**
CO_2	230.1	396.0	431.6	413.9	376.3	390.0	388.3
CH_4	0.2	0.1	0.1	0.1	0.2	0.1	0.1
N_2O	0.8	1.1	1.4	1.4	1.1	1.1	1.0
HFCs	+	11.1	11.5	11.6	11.6	11.6	11.7
Buses	**8.4**	**12.1**	**18.0**	**17.4**	**16.5**	**16.3**	**17.4**
CO_2	8.4	11.8	17.6	17.0	16.1	15.9	16.9

48 VMT and fuel use by vehicle class (VM-1 table) were not available from FHWA for 2011, but trends in overall diesel and gasoline consumption were released in FHWA's Table MF-21 and MF-27. Fuel use in vehicle classes that are predominantly gasoline was estimated to fall by the rate of decrease in gasoline consumption between 2010 and 2011. Fuel use in vehicle classes that were predominantly diesel was estimated to grow by the same rate of diesel fuel consumption increase in 2011. The 2010-2011 change in VMT from FHWA's Traffic Volume Trends was then distributed to vehicle classes based on these fuel consumption estimates, assuming no relative change in MPG between vehicle classes.

Source: *U.S. EPA, Inventory of U.S. Greenhouse Gas Emissions and Sinks: 1990–2011*

CH_4	+	+	+	+	+	+	+
N_2O	+	+	+	+	+	+	+
HFCs	+	0.2	0.3	0.4	0.4	0.4	0.4
Motorcycles	**1.8**	**1.7**	**4.3**	**4.5**	**4.3**	**3.8**	**3.7**
CO_2	1.7	1.6	4.3	4.4	4.2	3.8	3.6
CH_4	+	+	+	+	+	+	+
N_2O	+	+	+	+	+	+	+
Commercial Aircraft[a]	**110.9**	**134.0**	**141.0**	**128.5**	**120.7**	**114.4**	**115.7**
CO_2	109.9	132.7	139.7	127.3	119.5	113.3	114.6
CH_4	+	+	+	+	+	+	+
N_2O	1.1	1.3	1.3	1.2	1.1	1.1	1.1
Other Aircraft[b]	**78.3**	**59.7**	**42.4**	**48.2**	**36.8**	**40.5**	**34.2**
CO_2	77.5	59.1	42.0	47.8	36.4	40.1	33.8
CH_4	0.1	+	+	+	+	+	+
N_2O	0.7	0.6	0.4	0.4	0.3	0.4	0.3
Ships and Boats[c]	**45.1**	**45.2**	**55.2**	**45.4**	**40.8**	**44.1**	**48.2**
CO_2	44.5	44.5	54.4	44.7	40.2	43.4	47.4
CH_4	+	+	+	+	+	+	+
N_2O	0.6	0.6	0.8	0.6	0.6	0.6	0.7
HFCs	+	+	+	+	+	+	+
Rail	**39.0**	**53.0**	**54.4**	**50.7**	**43.4**	**46.3**	**48.0**
CO_2	38.5	50.3	51.6	47.9	40.7	43.5	45.3
CH_4	0.1	0.1	0.1	0.1	0.1	0.1	0.1
N_2O	0.3	0.4	0.4	0.4	0.3	0.3	0.4
HFCs	+	2.2	2.2	2.3	2.3	2.3	2.3
Other Emissions from Electricity Generation[d]	0.1	0.1	0.1	+	+	+	+
Pipelines[e]	**36**	**32.2**	**34.2**	**35.6**	**36.7**	**37.1**	**37.7**
CO_2	36	32.2	34.2	35.6	36.7	37.1	37.7
Lubricants	**11.8**	**10.2**	**10.2**	**9.5**	**8.5**	**9.5**	**9.0**
CO_2	11.8	10.2	10.2	9.5	8.5	9.5	9.0
Total Transportation	**1,556.30**	**2,017.2**	**2,018.2**	**1,920.8**	**1,845.2**	**1,856.9**	**1,833.7**
International Bunker Fuels[f]	104.5	*114.3*	*116.5*	*115.5*	*107.5*	*118.2*	*112.4*

Note: Totals may not sum due to independent rounding. Passenger cars and light-duty trucks include vehicles typically used for personal travel and less than 8500 lbs; medium- and heavy-duty trucks include vehicles larger than 8500 lbs. HFC emissions primarily reflect HFC-134a.

+ Does not exceed 0.05 Tg CO_2 Eq.

[a] Consists of emissions from jet fuel consumed by domestic operations of commercial aircraft (no bunkers).

[b] Consists of emissions from jet fuel and aviation gasoline consumption by general aviation and military aircraft.

[c] Fluctuations in emission estimates are associated with fluctuations in reported fuel consumption, and may reflect data collection problems.

[d] Other emissions from electricity generation are a result of waste incineration (as the majority of municipal solid waste is combusted in "trash-to-steam" electricity generation plants), electrical transmission and distribution, and a portion of Other Process Uses of Carbonates (from pollution control equipment installed in electricity generation plants).

[e] CO_2 estimates reflect natural gas used to power pipelines, but not electricity. While the operation of pipelines produces CH_4 and N_2O, these emissions are not directly attributed to pipelines in the US Inventory.

[f] Emissions from International Bunker Fuels include emissions from both civilian and military activities; these emissions are not included in the transportation totals.

Commercial

The commercial sector is heavily reliant on electricity for meeting energy needs, with electricity consumption for lighting, heating, air conditioning, and operating appliances. The remaining emissions were largely due to the direct consumption of natural gas and petroleum products, primarily for heating and cooking needs. Energy-related emissions from the residential and commercial sectors have generally been increasing since 1990, and are often correlated with short-term fluctuations in energy consumption caused by weather conditions, rather than prevailing

Source: *U.S. EPA, Inventory of U.S. Greenhouse Gas Emissions and Sinks: 1990–2011*

economic conditions. Landfills and wastewater treatment are included in this sector, with landfill emissions decreasing since 1990 and wastewater treatment emissions increasing slightly.

Residential

The residential sector is heavily reliant on electricity for meeting energy needs, with electricity consumption for lighting, heating, air conditioning, and operating appliances. The remaining emissions were largely due to the direct consumption of natural gas and petroleum products, primarily for heating and cooking needs. Emissions from the residential sectors have generally been increasing since 1990, and are often correlated with short-term fluctuations in energy consumption caused by weather conditions, rather than prevailing economic conditions. In the long-term, this sector is also affected by population growth, regional migration trends, and changes in housing and building attributes (e.g., size and insulation).

Agriculture

The agriculture sector includes a variety of processes, including enteric fermentation in domestic livestock, livestock manure management, and agricultural soil management. In 2011, agricultural soil management was the largest source of N_2O emissions, and enteric fermentation was the second largest source of CH_4 emissions in the United States. This sector also includes small amounts of CO_2 emissions from fossil fuel combustion by motorized farm equipment like tractors. The agriculture sector is less reliant on electricity than the other sectors.

Box 2-1: Methodology for Aggregating Emissions by Economic Sector

In presenting the Economic Sectors in the annual Inventory of U.S. Greenhouse Gas Emissions and Sinks, the Inventory expands upon the standard IPCC sectors common for UNFCCC reporting. Discussing greenhouse gas emissions relevant to U.S.-specific sectors improves communication of the report's findings.

In the Electricity Generation economic sector, CO_2 emissions from the combustion of fossil fuels included in the EIA electric utility fuel consuming sector are apportioned to this economic sector. Stationary combustion emissions of CH_4 and N_2O are also based on the EIA electric utility sector. Additional sources include CO_2, CH_4, and N_2O from waste incineration, as the majority of municipal solid waste is combusted in "trash-to-steam" electricity generation plants. The Electricity Generation economic sector also includes SF_6 from Electrical Transmission and Distribution, and a portion of CO_2 from Other Process Uses of Carbonates (from pollution control equipment installed in electricity generation plants).

In the Transportation economic sector, the CO_2 emissions from the combustion of fossil fuels included in the EIA transportation fuel consuming sector are apportioned to this economic sector (additional analyses and refinement of the EIA data is further explained in the Energy chapter of this report). Additional emissions are apportioned from the CH_4 and N_2O from Mobile Combustion, based on the EIA transportation sector. Substitutes of Ozone Depleting Substitutes are apportioned based on their specific end-uses within the source category, with emissions from transportation refrigeration/air-conditioning systems to this economic sector. Finally, CO_2 emissions from Non-Energy Uses of Fossil Fuels identified as lubricants for transportation vehicles are included in the Transportation economic sector.

For the Industry economic sector, the CO_2 emissions from the combustion of fossil fuels included in the EIA industrial fuel consuming sector, minus the agricultural use of fuel explained below, are apportioned to this economic sector. Stationary and mobile combustion emissions of CH_4 and N_2O are also based on the EIA industrial sector, minus emissions apportioned to the Agriculture economic sector described below. Substitutes of Ozone Depleting Substitutes are apportioned based on their specific end-uses within the source category, with most emissions falling within the Industry economic sector (minus emissions from the other economic sectors). Additionally, all process-related emissions from sources with methods considered within the IPCC Industrial Process guidance have been apportioned to this economic sector. This includes the process-related emissions (i.e., emissions from the actual process to make the material, not from fuels to power the plant) from such activities as Cement Production, Iron and Steel Production and Metallurgical Coke Production, and Ammonia Production.

Source: *U.S. EPA, Inventory of U.S. Greenhouse Gas Emissions and Sinks: 1990–2011*

Additionally, fugitive emissions from energy production sources, such as Natural Gas Systems, Coal Mining, and Petroleum Systems are included in the Industry economic sector. A portion of CO_2 from Other Process Uses of Carbonates (from pollution control equipment installed in large industrial facilities) are also included in the Industry economic sector. Finally, all remaining CO_2 emissions from Non-Energy Uses of Fossil Fuels are assumed to be industrial in nature (besides the lubricants for transportation vehicles specified above), and are attributed to the Industry economic sector.

As agriculture equipment is included in EIA's industrial fuel consuming sector surveys, additional data is used to extract the fuel used by agricultural equipment, to allow for accurate reporting in the Agriculture economic sector from all sources of emissions, such as motorized farming equipment. Energy consumption estimates are obtained from Department of Agriculture survey data, in combination with separate EIA fuel sales reports. This supplementary data is used to apportion CO_2 emissions from fossil fuel combustion, and CH_4 and N_2O emissions from stationary and mobile combustion (all data is removed from the Industrial economic sector, to avoid double-counting). The other emission sources included in this economic sector are intuitive for the agriculture sectors, such as N_2O emissions from Agricultural Soils, CH_4 from Enteric Fermentation (i.e., exhalation from the digestive tracts of domesticated animals), CH_4 and N_2O from Manure Management, CH_4 from Rice Cultivation, CO_2 emissions from Liming of Agricultural Soils and Urea Application, and CH_4 and N_2O from Forest Fires. N_2O emissions from the Application of Fertilizers to tree plantations (termed "forest land" by the IPCC) are also included in the Agriculture economic sector.

The Residential economic sector includes the CO_2 emissions from the combustion of fossil fuels reported for the EIA residential sector. Stationary combustion emissions of CH_4 and N_2O are also based on the EIA residential fuel consuming sector. Substitutes of Ozone Depleting Substitutes are apportioned based on their specific end-uses within the source category, with emissions from residential air-conditioning systems to this economic sector. N_2O emissions from the Application of Fertilizers to developed land (termed "settlements" by the IPCC) are also included in the Residential economic sector.

The Commercial economic sector includes the CO_2 emissions from the combustion of fossil fuels reported in the EIA commercial fuel consuming sector data. Stationary combustion emissions of CH_4 and N_2O are also based on the EIA commercial sector. Substitutes of Ozone Depleting Substitutes are apportioned based on their specific end-uses within the source category, with emissions from commercial refrigeration/air-conditioning systems to this economic sector. Public works sources including direct CH_4 from Landfills and CH_4 and N_2O from Wastewater Treatment and Composting are included in this economic sector.

Box 2-2: Recent Trends in Various U.S. Greenhouse Gas Emissions-Related Data

Total emissions can be compared to other economic and social indices to highlight changes over time. These comparisons include: (1) emissions per unit of aggregate energy consumption, because energy-related activities are the largest sources of emissions; (2) emissions per unit of fossil fuel consumption, because almost all energy-related emissions involve the combustion of fossil fuels; (3) emissions per unit of electricity consumption, because the electric power industry—utilities and non-utilities combined—was the largest source of U.S. greenhouse gas emissions in 2011; (4) emissions per unit of total gross domestic product as a measure of national economic activity; or (5) emissions per capita.

Table 2-16 provides data on various statistics related to U.S. greenhouse gas emissions normalized to 1990 as a baseline year. Greenhouse gas emissions in the United States have grown at an average annual rate of 0.4 percent since 1990. This rate is slightly faster than that for total energy consumption and slightly slower than growth in national population since 1990 and much slower than that for electricity consumption and overall gross domestic product, respectively. Total U.S. greenhouse gas emissions are growing at a rate similar to that of fossil fuel consumption since 1990 (see Table 2-16).

Table 2-16: Recent Trends in Various U.S. Data (Index 1990 = 100)

Chapter/IPCC Sector	1990		2005		2007	2008	2009	2010	2011	Growth[a]
Greenhouse Gas Emissions [e]	100		116		117	114	107	110	108	0.4%
Energy Consumption [c]	100		119		120	117	111	115	102	0.1%
Fossil Fuel Consumption [c]	100		119		119	116	109	112	101	0.1%

Source: *U.S. EPA, Inventory of U.S. Greenhouse Gas Emissions and Sinks: 1990–2011*

Electricity Consumption [c]	100	134	137	136	131	137	136	1.5%
GDP [b]	100	157	165	164	159	163	166	2.5%
Population [d]	100	118	121	122	123	124	125	1.1%

[a] Average annual growth rate
[b] Gross Domestic Product in chained 2005 dollars (BEA 2012)
[c] Energy-content-weighted values (EIA 2012)
[d] U.S. Census Bureau (2012)
[e] GWP-weighted values

Figure 2-14: U.S. Greenhouse Gas Emissions Per Capita and Per Dollar of Gross Domestic Product

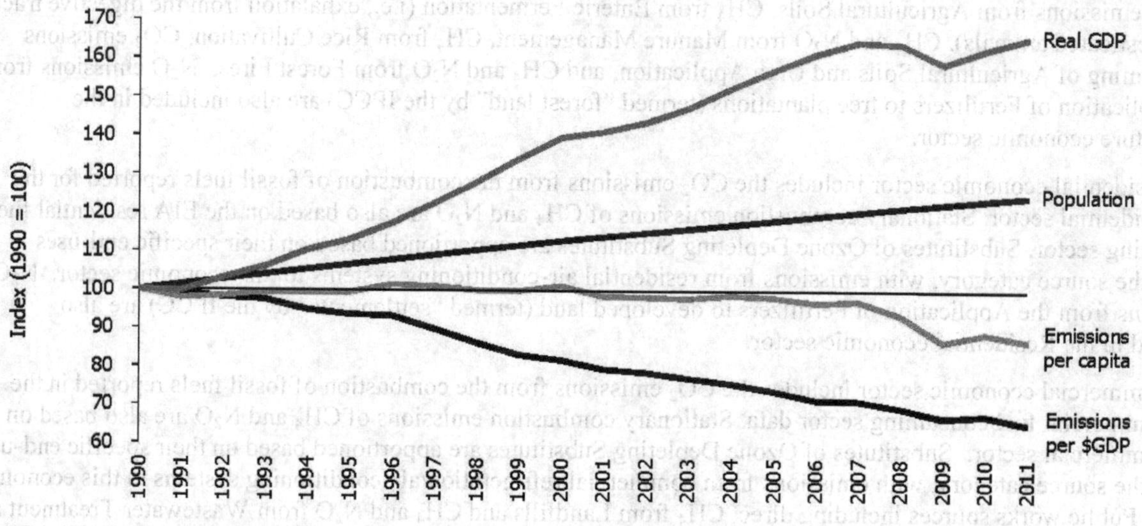

Source: BEA (2011), U.S. Census Bureau (2011), and emission estimates in this report.

2.3 Indirect Greenhouse Gas Emissions (CO, NO_x, NMVOCs, and SO_2)

The reporting requirements of the UNFCCC[49] request that information be provided on indirect greenhouse gases, which include CO, NO_x, NMVOCs, and SO_2. These gases do not have a direct global warming effect, but indirectly affect terrestrial radiation absorption by influencing the formation and destruction of tropospheric and stratospheric ozone, or, in the case of SO_2, by affecting the absorptive characteristics of the atmosphere. Additionally, some of these gases may react with other chemical compounds in the atmosphere to form compounds that are greenhouse gases. Carbon monoxide is produced when carbon-containing fuels are combusted incompletely. Nitrogen oxides (i.e., NO and NO_2) are created by lightning, fires, fossil fuel combustion, and in the stratosphere from N_2O. Non-CH_4 volatile organic compounds—which include hundreds of organic compounds that participate in atmospheric chemical reactions (i.e., propane, butane, xylene, toluene, ethane, and many others)—are emitted primarily from transportation, industrial processes, and non-industrial consumption of organic solvents. In the United States, SO_2 is primarily emitted from coal combustion for electric power generation and the metals industry. Sulfur-containing

[49] See <http://unfccc.int/resource/docs/2006/sbsta/eng/09.pdf>.

Source: U.S. EPA, Inventory of U.S. Greenhouse Gas Emissions and Sinks: 1990–2011

compounds emitted into the atmosphere tend to exert a negative radiative forcing (i.e., cooling) and therefore are discussed separately.

One important indirect climate change effect of NMVOCs and NO_x is their role as precursors for tropospheric ozone formation. They can also alter the atmospheric lifetimes of other greenhouse gases. Another example of indirect greenhouse gas formation into greenhouse gases is CO's interaction with the hydroxyl radical—the major atmospheric sink for CH_4 emissions—to form CO_2. Therefore, increased atmospheric concentrations of CO limit the number of hydroxyl molecules (OH) available to destroy CH_4.

Since 1970, the United States has published estimates of emissions of CO, NO_x, NMVOCs, and SO_2 (EPA 2010, EPA 2009),[50] which are regulated under the Clean Air Act[51]. Table 2-17 shows that fuel combustion accounts for the majority of emissions of these indirect greenhouse gases. Industrial processes—such as the manufacture of chemical and allied products, metals processing, and industrial uses of solvents—are also significant sources of CO, NO_x, and NMVOCs.

Table 2-17: Emissions of NO_x, CO, NMVOCs, and SO_2 (Gg)

Gas/Activity	1990	2005	2007	2008	2009	2010	2011
NO_x	**21,781**	**16,143**	**14,817**	**13,809**	**11,641**	**11,610**	**11,897**
Mobile Fossil Fuel Combustion	10,862	9,012	7,965	7,441	6,206	6,206	6,206
Stationary Fossil Fuel Combustion	10,023	5,858	5,432	5,148	4,159	4,159	4,159
Industrial Processes	591	569	537	520	568	568	568
Forest Land Remaining Forest Land	76	102	436	263	173	142	431
Oil and Gas Activities	139	321	318	318	393	393	393
Waste Combustion	82	129	114	106	128	128	128
Agricultural Burning	6	6	8	7	7	8	7
Solvent Use	1	3	4	4	3	3	3
Waste	+	2	2	2	2	2	2
CO	**132,671**	**79,500**	**79,180**	**69,387**	**57,611**	**56,494**	**66,773**
Mobile Fossil Fuel Combustion	119,360	62,692	55,253	51,533	43,355	43,355	43,355
Forest Land Remaining Forest Land	2,695	3,650	15,568	9,394	6,180	5,062	15,364
Stationary Fossil Fuel Combustion	5,000	4,649	4,744	4,792	4,543	4,543	4,543
Industrial Processes	4,125	1,555	1,640	1,682	1,549	1,549	1,549
Waste Combustion	978	1,403	1,421	1,430	1,403	1,403	1,403
Oil and Gas Activities	302	318	320	322	345	345	345
Agricultural Burning	205	166	225	224	226	227	205
Waste	1	7	7	7	7	7	7
Solvent Use	5	2	2	2	2	2	2
NMVOCs	**20,930**	**13,761**	**13,423**	**13,254**	**9,313**	**9,313**	**9,313**
Mobile Fossil Fuel Combustion	10,932	6,330	5,742	5,447	4,151	4,151	4,151
Solvent Use	5,216	3,851	3,839	3,834	2,583	2,583	2,583
Industrial Processes	2,422	1,997	1,869	1,804	1,322	1,322	1,322
Oil and Gas Activities	554	510	509	509	599	599	599
Stationary Fossil Fuel Combustion	912	716	1,120	1,321	424	424	424
Waste Combustion	222	241	234	230	159	159	159
Waste	673	114	111	109	76	76	76
Agricultural Burning	NA	NA	NA	NA	NA	NA	NA
SO_2	**20,935**	**13,466**	**11,799**	**10,368**	**8,599**	**8,599**	**8,599**
Stationary Fossil Fuel Combustion	18,407	11,541	10,172	8,891	7,167	7,167	7,167

50 NO_x and CO emission estimates from field burning of agricultural residues were estimated separately, and therefore not taken from EPA (2009) and EPA (2010).

51 Due to redevelopment of the information technology systems for the National Emission Inventory (NEI), publication of the most recent emissions for these pollutants was not available for this report. For an overview of the activities and the schedule for developing the 2011 National Emissions Inventory, with the goal of producing Version 1 in the summer of 2013, see < http://www.epa.gov/ttn/chief/eis/2011nei/2011plan.pdf>

Source: *U.S. EPA, Inventory of U.S. Greenhouse Gas Emissions and Sinks: 1990–2011*

Industrial Processes	1,307	831	807	795	798	798	798
Mobile Fossil Fuel Combustion	793	889	611	472	455	455	455
Oil and Gas Activities	390	181	184	187	154	154	154
Waste Combustion	38	24	24	23	24	24	24
Waste	+	1	1	1	1	1	1
Solvent Use	+	+	+	+	+	+	+
Agricultural Burning	NA	NA	NA	NA	NA	NA	NA

Source: (EPA 2010, EPA 2009) except for estimates from field burning of agricultural residues.

NA (Not Available)

Note: Totals may not sum due to independent rounding.

+ Does not exceed 0.5 Gg.

Box 2-3: Sources and Effects of Sulfur Dioxide

Sulfur dioxide (SO_2) emitted into the atmosphere through natural and anthropogenic processes affects the earth's radiative budget through its photochemical transformation into sulfate aerosols that can (1) scatter radiation from the sun back to space, thereby reducing the radiation reaching the earth's surface; (2) affect cloud formation; and (3) affect atmospheric chemical composition (e.g., by providing surfaces for heterogeneous chemical reactions). The indirect effect of sulfur-derived aerosols on radiative forcing can be considered in two parts. The first indirect effect is the aerosols' tendency to decrease water droplet size and increase water droplet concentration in the atmosphere. The second indirect effect is the tendency of the reduction in cloud droplet size to affect precipitation by increasing cloud lifetime and thickness. Although still highly uncertain, the radiative forcing estimates from both the first and the second indirect effect are believed to be negative, as is the combined radiative forcing of the two (IPCC 2001). However, because SO_2 is short-lived and unevenly distributed in the atmosphere, its radiative forcing impacts are highly uncertain.

Sulfur dioxide is also a major contributor to the formation of regional haze, which can cause significant increases in acute and chronic respiratory diseases. Once SO_2 is emitted, it is chemically transformed in the atmosphere and returns to the earth as the primary source of acid rain. Because of these harmful effects, the United States has regulated SO_2 emissions in the Clean Air Act.

Electricity generation is the largest anthropogenic source of SO_2 emissions in the United States, accounting for 60 percent in 2011. Coal combustion contributes nearly all of those emissions (approximately 92 percent). Sulfur dioxide emissions have decreased in recent years, primarily as a result of electric power generators switching from high-sulfur to low-sulfur coal and installing flue gas desulfurization equipment.

Source: *U.S. EPA, Inventory of U.S. Greenhouse Gas Emissions and Sinks: 1990–2011*

Green Metro Area Rankings by Category

Metro Area	State	Air Quality[1]	Toxic Releases[2]	Superfund Sites[3]	Energy Use[4]	Motor Vehicle Use[5]	Mass Transit Use[6]	Overall Score[7]	Overall Rank[8]
Akron	OH	12	23	39	61	52	61	248	47
Albany	NY	5	28	62	72	58	35	260	55
Albuquerque	NM	51	2	45	40	17	21	176	19
Allentown	PA	44	56	70	53	16	62	301	66
Atlanta	GA	62	37	1	24	63	14	201	23
Austin	TX	13	6	1	23	21	27	91	2
Bakersfield	CA	65	66	30	12	1	60	234	35
Baltimore	MD	39	31	41	45	42	12	210	28
Baton Rouge	LA	40	74	48	13	54	68	297	64
Birmingham	AL	46	72	21	25	73	69	306	67
Boston	MA	30	9	67	49	35	6	196	22
Buffalo	NY	29	38	47	66	31	29	240	39
Charleston	SC	24	69	53	14	20	65	245	45
Charlotte	NC	28	44	55	28	55	26	236	36
Chicago	IL	72	58	28	68	12	5	243	43
Cincinnati	OH	61	61	44	48	59	45	318	71
Cleveland	OH	63	63	8	60	34	23	251	49
Columbus	OH	33	46	13	52	40	55	239	37
Dallas-Ft. Worth	TX	48	19	11	32	48	31	189	20
Dayton	OH	16	26	74	56	57	53	282	62
Denver	CO	53	42	51	57	18	11	232	34
Detroit	MI	55	65	33	64	45	48	310	69
El Paso	TX	57	41	1	27	5	30	161	13
Fresno	CA	66	12	60	15	8	34	195	21
Grand Rapids	MI	6	18	72	73	56	43	268	56
Greensboro	NC	9	36	1	33	72	64	215	29
Greenville	SC	20	29	64	26	36	75	260	48
Hartford	CT	26	14	52	62	43	47	244	44
Honolulu	HI	1	35	42	22	3	4	107	3
Houston	TX	52	70	46	16	29	28	241	40
Indianapolis	IN	64	64	36	54	69	67	354	75
Jacksonville	FL	8	54	59	8	67	46	242	41
Kansas City	MO	67	52	40	58	65	59	341	73
Knoxville	TN	36	57	37	31	66	72	299	65
Las Vegas	NV	54	30	1	38	6	24	153	11
Little Rock	AR	47	27	16	34	71	63	258	53
Los Angeles	CA	73	20	18	2	33	9	155	12
Louisville	KY	59	67	27	44	60	52	309	68
Memphis	TN	34	53	49	35	51	56	278	60
Miami	FL	18	5	25	18	38	18	122	4
Milwaukee	WI	42	50	50	74	13	25	254	52
Minneapolis-St. Paul	MN	32	48	56	75	47	17	275	59
Nashville	TN	37	47	9	36	74	51	254	51
New Orleans	LA	50	73	32	11	4	37	207	25
New York-Northern NJ	NY	56	8	61	46	2	1	174	18
Oklahoma City	OK	43	11	29	41	75	73	272	58
Omaha	NE	58	59	24	70	9	70	290	63
Orlando	FL	3	16	35	9	61	40	164	15
Oxnard	CA	41	1	31	3	19	32	127	6
Philadelphia	PA	70	40	75	47	7	8	247	46
Phoenix	AZ	74	25	14	39	23	33	208	26
Pittsburgh	PA	68	71	19	55	11	19	243	42
Portland	OR	10	45	54	20	10	10	149	10
Providence	RI	17	22	71	51	24	42	227	33
Raleigh	NC	14	10	34	30	64	57	209	27

Metro Area	State	Air Quality[1]	Toxic Releases[2]	Superfund Sites[3]	Energy Use[4]	Motor Vehicle Use[5]	Mass Transit Use[6]	Overall Score[7]	Overall Rank[8]
Richmond	VA	11	60	43	37	62	58	271	57
Riverside	CA	75	13	22	6	39	50	205	24
Rochester	NY	4	43	38	67	30	41	223	32
Sacramento	CA	38	7	26	7	14	38	130	7
Saint Louis	MO	71	62	65	50	68	20	336	72
Salt Lake City	UT	35	75	69	59	25	16	279	61
San Antonio	TX	22	32	10	21	28	22	135	8
San Diego	CA	69	4	7	1	32	13	126	5
San Francisco	CA	27	21	15	4	15	2	84	1
San Jose	CA	23	3	73	5	26	15	145	9
Seattle	WA	25	24	57	17	41	7	171	16
Springfield	MA	21	17	17	71	37	54	217	30
Syracuse	NY	2	33	63	69	46	39	252	50
Tampa-St. Petersburg	FL	19	34	58	10	50	49	220	31
Toledo	OH	15	68	1	65	44	66	259	54
Tucson	AZ	31	49	12	19	27	36	174	17
Tulsa	OK	49	55	23	42	70	71	310	70
Virginia Beach	VA	7	39	68	29	53	44	240	38
Washington	DC	60	15	20	43	22	3	163	14
Youngstown	OH	45	51	66	63	49	74	348	74

Note: *The Green Metro Index compares 75 major metropolitan areas in the U.S. on measures of environmental quality and performance appropriate to metro areas as a whole. The index is based on federal and private data for six environmental measures including: air quality, toxic releases, superfund sites, energy use, mass transit use and motor vehicle use; The figures above rank how each metro area fared in each category. Lower numbers are better; (1) Based on the percent of days the Air Quality Index (AQI) was in the "Good" range in 2012; (2) Calculated by adding the total toxic releases for each metro area and dividing by the metro area population. Data is from the Environmental Protection Agency's Toxic Release Inventory for 2011; (3) Based on the per capita number of final and proposed Superfund Sites located within each metro area. Data is from the Environmental Protection Agency's Superfund National Priorities list (data extracted 8/30/2013); (4) Based on total heating and cooling degree days per year. Data is from Weather America, A Thirty-Year Summary of Statistical Weather Data and Rankings, 2011; (5) Based on the DVMT (daily vehicle-miles of travel) per capita for each urbanized area. Data is from the Department of Transportation's Urbanized Areas: 2011 Selected Characteristics report; (6) Calculated by dividing the total mass transit passenger miles by the population of the urbanized area. Data is from the Federal Transit Administration's 2011 National Transit Summaries and Trends report; (7) The overall score was calculated by combining the rankings of all six environmental indicators, giving equal weight to each indicator; (8) 1=best, 75=worst*

Sources: *U.S Environmental Protection Agency; U.S. Department of Transportation; Federal Transit Administration; Grey House Publishing, Weather America, A Thirty-Year Summary of Statistical Weather Data and Rankings, 2011*

Green Metro Area Overall Rankings

Metro Area	State	Overall Rank[1]	Overall Score[2]
San Francisco	CA	1	84
Austin	TX	2	91
Honolulu	HI	3	107
Miami	FL	4	122
San Diego	CA	5	126
Oxnard	CA	6	127
Sacramento	CA	7	130
San Antonio	TX	8	135
San Jose	CA	9	145
Portland	OR	10	149
Las Vegas	NV	11	153
Los Angeles	CA	12	155
El Paso	TX	13	161
Washington	DC	14	163
Orlando	FL	15	164
Seattle	WA	16	171
Tucson	AZ	17	174
New York-Northern NJ	NY	18	174
Albuquerque	NM	19	176
Dallas-Ft. Worth	TX	20	189
Fresno	CA	21	195
Boston	MA	22	196
Atlanta	GA	23	201
Riverside	CA	24	205
New Orleans	LA	25	207
Phoenix	AZ	26	208
Raleigh	NC	27	209
Baltimore	MD	28	210
Greensboro	NC	29	215
Springfield	MA	30	217
Tampa-St. Petersburg	FL	31	220
Rochester	NY	32	223
Providence	RI	33	227
Denver	CO	34	232
Bakersfield	CA	35	234
Charlotte	NC	36	236
Columbus	OH	37	239
Virginia Beach	VA	38	240
Buffalo	NY	39	240
Houston	TX	40	241
Jacksonville	FL	41	242
Pittsburgh	PA	42	243
Chicago	IL	43	243
Hartford	CT	44	244
Charleston	SC	45	245
Philadelphia	PA	46	247
Akron	OH	47	248
Greenville	SC	48	250
Cleveland	OH	49	251
Syracuse	NY	50	252
Nashville	TN	51	254
Milwaukee	WI	52	254
Little Rock	AR	53	258
Toledo	OH	54	259
Albany	NY	55	260

Metro Area	State	Overall Rank[1]	Overall Score[2]
Grand Rapids	MI	56	268
Richmond	VA	57	271
Oklahoma City	OK	58	272
Minneapolis-St. Paul	MN	59	275
Memphis	TN	60	278
Salt Lake City	UT	61	279
Dayton	OH	62	282
Omaha	NE	63	290
Baton Rouge	LA	64	297
Knoxville	TN	65	299
Allentown	PA	66	301
Birmingham	AL	67	306
Louisville	KY	68	309
Detroit	MI	69	310
Tulsa	OK	70	310
Cincinnati	OH	71	318
Saint Louis	MO	72	336
Kansas City	MO	73	341
Youngstown	OH	74	348
Indianapolis	IN	75	354

Note: *The Green Metro Index compares 75 major metropolitan areas in the U.S. on measures of environmental quality and performance appropriate to metro areas as a whole. The index is based on federal data for six environmental measures including: air quality, toxic releases, superfund sites, energy use, mass transit use and motor vehicle use; (1) A lower number indicates better environmental quality or performance; (2) The overall score was calculated by combining the rankings of all six environmental indicators, giving equal weight to each indicator.*
Sources: *U.S Environmental Protection Agency; U.S. Department of Transportation; Federal Transit Administration; Grey House Publishing, Weather America, A Thirty-Year Summary of Statistical Weather Data and Rankings, 2011*

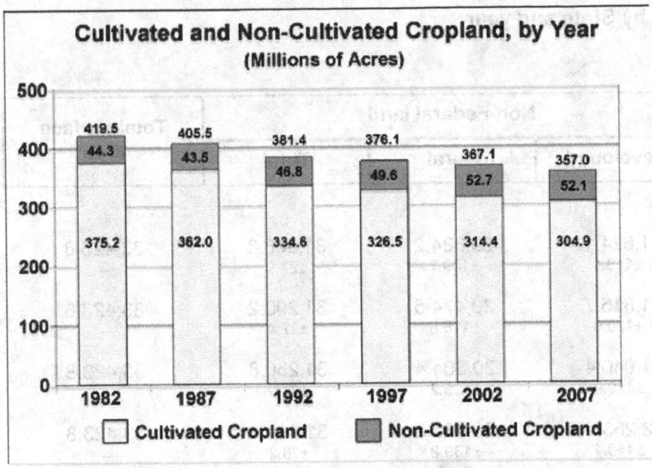

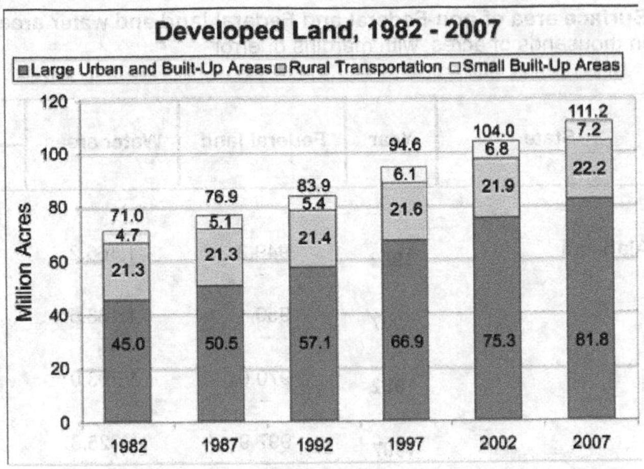

- Soil erosion on cropland decreased 43 percent between 1982 and 2007. Water (sheet and rill) erosion declined from 1.68 billion tons per year to 960 million tons per year, and erosion due to wind decreased from 1.38 billion to 765 million tons per year.

- About 24 percent (or 326 million acres) of the non-Federal rural land base is classified as prime farmland. This represents a 14-million-acre loss since 1982; most of this loss was due to development.

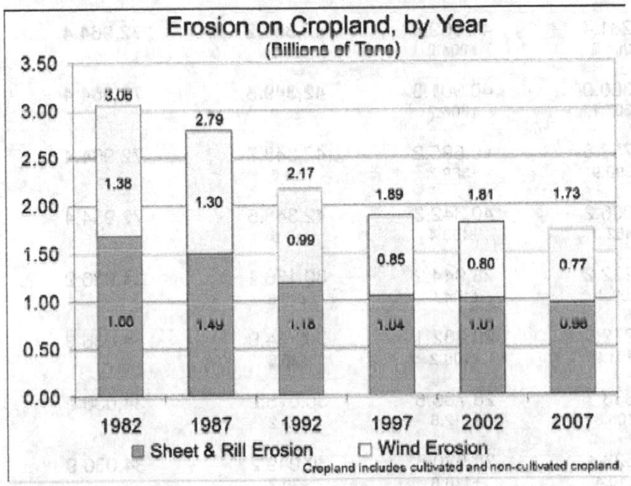

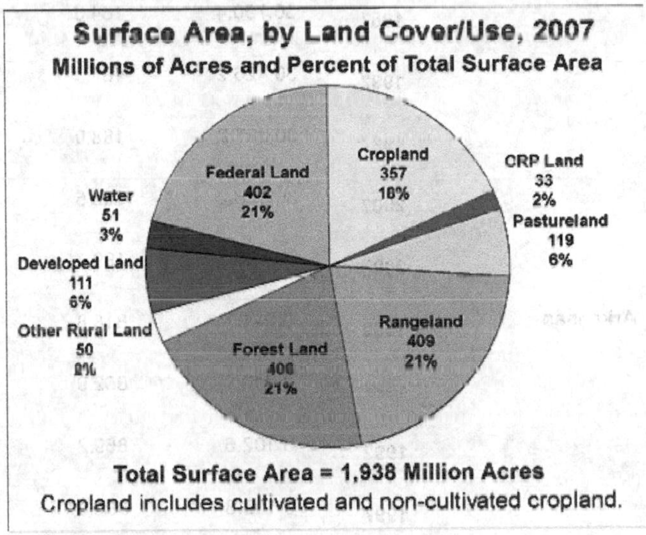

- About 40 million acres of land were newly developed between 1982 and 2007, bringing the total to about 111 million acres; that represents a 56 percent increase. This means that more than one-third of all land that has ever been developed in the lower 48 states was developed during the last quarter century.

- Cropland acreage declined from 420 million acres in 1982 to 357 million acres in 2007. About half of the reduction in cropland acreage is due to enrollments of environmentally sensitive cropland in the Conservation Reserve Program. The share of noncultivated cropland — permanent hayland and horticultural cropland — increased from 11 percent to 15 percent of all U.S. cropland over the period.

U.S. Department of Agriculture. 2009. *Summary Report: 2007 National Resources Inventory*, Natural Resources Conservation Service, Washington, DC, and Center for Survey Statistics and Methodology, Iowa State University, Ames, Iowa. 123 pages.

Surface area of non-Federal and Federal land and water areas, by State and year
In thousands of acres, with margins of error

State	Year	Federal land	Water areas	Non-Federal land			Total surface area
				Developed	Rural	Total	
Alabama	1982	949.3 --	1,166.2 --	1,624.1 ±113.1	29,684.2 ±109.7	31,308.3 ±27.8	33,423.8 --
	1987	950.1 --	1,183.5 --	1,815.7 ±120.0	29,474.5 ±115.8	31,290.2 ±27.4	33,423.8 --
	1992	970.0 --	1,203.0 --	1,946.4 ±129.9	29,304.4 ±125.2	31,250.8 ±27.9	33,423.8 --
	1997	997.9 --	1,225.8 --	2,263.6 ±140.4	28,936.5 ±139.2	31,200.1 ±28.2	33,423.8 --
	2002	997.9 --	1,278.1 --	2,673.5 ±207.9	28,474.3 ±213.9	31,147.8 ±35.8	33,423.8 --
	2007	997.9 --	1,290.1 --	2,942.9 ±203.7	28,192.9 ±214.9	31,135.8 ±146.4	33,423.8 --
Arizona	1982	31,005.4 --	182.9 --	1,018.1 ±271.0	40,758.0 ±270.9	41,776.1 ±7.5	72,964.4 --
	1987	30,790.4 --	184.6 --	1,184.8 ±287.3	40,804.6 ±286.7	41,989.4 ±7.6	72,964.4 --
	1992	30,426.2 --	187.0 --	1,281.4 ±294.8	41,069.8 ±294.2	42,351.2 ±8.7	72,964.4 --
	1997	30,426.2 --	188.9 --	1,388.0 ±307.1	40,961.3 ±306.7	42,349.3 ±8.9	72,964.4 --
	2002	30,426.2 --	189.5 --	1,753.5 ±390.9	40,595.2 ±389.7	42,348.7 ±8.6	72,964.4 --
	2007	30,426.2 --	189.7 --	2,006.2 ±462.3	40,342.3 ±460.4	42,348.5 ±8.5	72,964.4 --
Arkansas	1982	3,041.7 --	818.8 --	1,232.2 ±98.4	28,944.2 ±104.5	30,176.4 ±26.6	34,036.9 --
	1987	3,049.1 --	852.9 --	1,272.8 ±101.9	28,862.1 ±108.2	30,134.9 ±26.8	34,036.9 --
	1992	3,102.5 --	859.2 --	1,338.7 ±106.8	28,736.5 ±112.6	30,075.2 ±27.2	34,036.9 --
	1997	3,102.8 --	884.9 --	1,528.4 ±110.4	28,520.8 ±116.8	30,049.2 ±30.2	34,036.9 --
	2002	3,104.2 --	897.6 --	1,687.2 ±125.5	28,347.9 ±132.0	30,035.1 ±30.7	34,036.9 --
	2007	3,104.2 --	902.1 --	1,809.3 ±142.2	28,221.3 ±142.0	30,030.6 ±59.9	34,036.9 --
California	1982	46,007.5 --	1,856.2 --	4,082.8 ±342.6	49,563.7 ±341.5	53,646.5 ±28.3	101,510.2 --
	1987	46,029.0 --	1,866.5 --	4,344.6 ±359.3	49,270.1 ±357.0	53,614.7 ±28.4	101,510.2 --
	1992	46,633.4 --	1,869.1 --	4,836.9 ±371.7	48,170.8 ±368.0	53,007.7 ±28.2	101,510.2 --
	1997	46,633.4 --	1,860.2 --	5,381.9 ±370.7	47,634.7 ±368.1	53,016.6 ±28.2	101,510.2 --
	2002	46,639.0 --	1,867.6 --	5,807.2 ±391.3	47,196.4 ±387.3	53,003.6 ±27.9	101,510.2 --
	2007	46,639.0 --	1,874.9 --	6,173.8 ±403.8	46,822.5 ±401.9	52,996.3 ±29.2	101,510.2 --

State	Year	Federal land	Water areas	Non-Federal land: Developed	Non-Federal land: Rural	Non-Federal land: Total	Total surface area
Colorado	1982	23,606.8 –	327.3 –	1,187.4 ±109.5	41,503.0 ±108.9	42,690.4 ±21.7	66,624.5 –
	1987	23,741.2 –	328.9 –	1,329.4 ±140.8	41,225.0 ±138.3	42,554.4 ±21.5	66,624.5 –
	1992	23,802.9 –	328.4 –	1,472.1 ±148.9	41,021.1 ±147.1	42,493.2 ±21.9	66,624.5 –
	1997	23,793.8 –	329.4 –	1,577.6 ±165.2	40,923.7 ±163.9	42,501.3 ±22.2	66,624.5 –
	2002	23,796.9 –	330.9 –	1,778.7 ±203.8	40,718.0 ±203.4	42,496.7 ±21.9	66,624.5 –
	2007	23,796.9 –	332.1 –	1,934.3 ±222.5	40,561.2 ±223.1	42,495.5 ±22.1	66,624.5 –
Connecticut	1982	9.7 –	127.0 –	823.0 ±33.4	2,235.0 ±34.9	3,058.0 ±5.6	3,194.7 –
	1987	14.3 –	126.9 –	874.3 ±34.3	2,179.2 ±35.4	3,053.5 ±5.5	3,194.7 –
	1992	14.5 –	127.9 –	916.3 ±34.9	2,136.0 ±36.0	3,052.3 ±5.3	3,194.7 –
	1997	14.5 –	128.2 –	958.8 ±33.1	2,090.2 ±34.0	3,052.0 ±5.2	3,194.7 –
	2002	14.5 –	128.2 –	1,016.2 ±38.5	2,036.8 ±39.4	3,052.0 ±5.3	3,194.7 –
	2007	14.5 –	128.6 –	1,051.6 ±41.4	2,000.0 ±42.1	3,051.6 ±5.4	3,194.7 –
Delaware	1982	31.1 –	288.1 –	158.7 ±26.5	1,055.6 ±27.0	1,214.3 ±2.8	1,533.5 –
	1987	31.0 –	288.3 –	175.4 ±29.0	1,038.8 ±29.5	1,214.2 ±2.8	1,533.5 –
	1992	31.0 –	288.4 –	192.5 ±29.9	1,021.6 ±30.1	1,214.1 ±3.0	1,533.5 –
	1997	31.0 –	288.7 –	214.4 ±31.7	999.4 ±31.7	1,213.8 ±3.3	1,533.5 –
	2002	31.0 –	289.4 –	251.0 ±32.4	962.1 ±32.3	1,213.1 ±3.2	1,533.5 –
	2007	31.0 –	290.2 –	280.1 ±35.3	932.2 ±35.7	1,212.3 ±3.3	1,533.5 –
Florida	1982	3,630.9 –	3,041.4 –	2,771.8 ±239.6	28,089.6 ±241.1	30,861.4 ±26.2	37,533.7 –
	1987	3,656.2 –	3,048.8 –	3,081.9 ±246.1	27,746.8 ±247.3	30,828.7 ±24.8	37,533.7 –
	1992	3,784.2 –	3,076.0 –	3,677.3 ±272.1	26,996.2 ±273.5	30,673.5 ±26.7	37,533.7 –
	1997	3,784.2 –	3,071.4 –	4,368.2 ±295.9	26,309.9 ±304.3	30,678.1 ±31.7	37,533.7 –
	2002	3,784.2 –	3,096.2 –	4,945.7 ±331.0	25,707.6 ±342.9	30,653.3 ±34.5	37,533.7 –
	2007	3,784.2 –	3,133.6 –	5,515.2 ±405.5	25,100.7 ±422.2	30,615.9 ±37.1	37,533.7 –

State	Year	Federal land	Water areas	Non-Federal land			Total surface area
				Developed	Rural	Total	
Georgia	1982	2,099.9 –	949.8 –	2,227.1 ±116.0	32,463.7 ±114.1	34,690.8 ±24.5	37,740.5 –
	1987	2,107.0 –	956.4 –	2,469.1 ±128.4	32,208.0 ±125.9	34,677.1 ±24.8	37,740.5 –
	1992	2,125.6 –	990.6 –	2,910.5 ±139.2	31,713.8 ±138.8	34,624.3 ±24.4	37,740.5 –
	1997	2,124.0 –	1,012.6 –	3,702.2 ±158.6	30,901.7 ±159.7	34,603.9 ±25.7	37,740.5 –
	2002	2,124.0 –	1,046.3 –	4,233.0 ±205.6	30,337.2 ±206.9	34,570.2 ±28.1	37,740.5 –
	2007	2,124.0 –	1,059.3 –	4,639.9 ±220.6	29,917.3 ±227.4	34,557.2 ±35.0	37,740.5 –
Idaho	1982	33,601.8 –	545.3 –	562.2 ±48.3	18,778.2 ±50.6	19,340.4 ±10.9	53,487.5 –
	1987	33,395.5 –	548.1 –	624.9 ±52.5	18,919.0 ±54.9	19,543.9 ±10.8	53,487.5 –
	1992	33,480.9 –	550.8 –	680.0 ±59.8	18,775.8 ±61.5	19,455.8 ±10.4	53,487.5 –
	1997	33,563.3 –	552.9 –	777.2 ±66.8	18,594.1 ±67.8	19,371.3 ±10.0	53,487.5 –
	2002	33,563.3 –	554.0 –	830.4 ±67.2	18,539.8 ±67.6	19,370.2 ±9.9	53,487.5 –
	2007	33,563.3 –	557.6 –	907.3 ±75.3	18,459.3 ±75.7	19,366.6 ±11.2	53,487.5 –
Illinois	1982	476.4 –	723.6 –	2,622.5 ±115.2	32,236.2 ±120.6	34,858.7 ±24.0	36,058.7 –
	1987	477.1 –	719.2 –	2,759.7 ±123.7	32,102.7 ±129.6	34,862.4 ±21.9	36,058.7 –
	1992	492.1 –	715.7 –	2,855.2 ±125.3	31,995.7 ±128.3	34,850.9 ±20.5	36,058.7 –
	1997	490.3 –	711.0 –	3,092.9 ±125.5	31,764.5 ±126.2	34,857.4 ±20.6	36,058.7 –
	2002	491.1 –	725.4 –	3,226.3 ±136.3	31,615.9 ±136.6	34,842.2 ±19.2	36,058.7 –
	2007	491.1 –	732.5 –	3,383.3 ±166.3	31,451.8 ±166.1	34,835.1 ±19.4	36,058.7 –
Indiana	1982	473.3 –	348.6 –	1,778.3 ±92.1	20,558.2 ±94.5	22,336.5 ±18.1	23,158.4 –
	1987	472.3 –	357.9 –	1,892.7 ±92.0	20,435.5 ±95.3	22,328.2 ±17.8	23,158.4 –
	1992	473.5 –	361.6 –	1,997.0 ±99.2	20,326.3 ±102.0	22,323.3 ±17.4	23,158.4 –
	1997	472.4 –	358.5 –	2,186.7 ±110.8	20,140.8 ±113.8	22,327.5 ±17.3	23,158.4 –
	2002	472.4 –	366.5 –	2,328.1 ±112.5	19,991.4 ±115.7	22,319.5 ±17.2	23,158.4 –
	2007	472.4 –	373.1 –	2,446.0 ±123.8	19,866.9 ±125.1	22,312.9 ±18.5	23,158.4 –

State	Year	Federal land	Water areas	Non-Federal land			Total surface area
				Developed	Rural	Total	
Iowa	1982	151.1 --	447.9 --	1,634.1 ±95.3	33,783.4 ±92.8	35,417.5 ±17.4	36,016.5 --
	1987	152.2 --	451.5 --	1,661.4 ±102.3	33,751.4 ±100.9	35,412.8 ±17.5	36,016.5 --
	1992	150.7 --	463.6 --	1,689.8 ±103.4	33,712.4 ±102.1	35,402.2 ±17.6	36,016.5 --
	1997	172.0 --	470.5 --	1,765.6 ±106.0	33,608.4 ±103.8	35,374.0 ±18.4	36,016.5 --
	2002	172.4 --	479.7 --	1,838.7 ±103.5	33,525.7 ±103.5	35,364.4 ±17.7	36,016.5 --
	2007	172.4 --	485.9 --	1,892.3 ±111.5	33,465.9 ±112.0	35,358.2 ±19.6	36,016.5 --
Kansas	1982	494.1 --	518.8 --	1,732.4 ±69.3	49,915.5 ±73.3	51,647.9 ±17.8	52,660.8 --
	1987	494.8 --	519.3 --	1,759.6 ±68.9	49,887.1 ±73.8	51,646.7 ±17.7	52,660.8 --
	1992	504.0 --	519.3 --	1,860.0 ±70.9	49,777.5 ±75.0	51,637.5 ±18.7	52,660.8 --
	1997	504.0 --	530.3 --	1,959.2 ±70.8	40,667.3 ±77.0	51,626.5 ±20.0	52,660.8 --
	2002	504.0 --	538.6 --	2,033.5 ±78.9	49,584.7 ±82.2	51,618.2 ±19.2	52,660.8 --
	2007	504.0 --	554.4 --	2,095.7 ±94.0	49,506.7 ±96.8	51,602.4 ±22.9	52,660.8 --
Kentucky	1982	1,107.1 --	585.4 --	1,124.0 ±69.9	23,046.9 ±73.2	24,170.9 ±16.2	25,863.4 --
	1987	1,148.5 --	589.6 --	1,312.5 ±79.7	22,812.8 ±84.6	24,125.3 ±16.0	25,863.4 --
	1992	1,187.2	605.4 --	1,470.1 ±84.6	22,600.7 ±89.8	24,070.8 ±17.0	25,863.4 --
	1997	1,187.2 --	613.1 --	1,703.0 ±97.0	22,360.1 ±99.0	24,063.1 ±16.0	25,863.4 --
	2002	1,295.4 --	625.8 --	1,952.4 ±98.7	21,989.8 ±101.5	23,942.2 ±18.8	25,863.4 --
	2007	1,295.4 --	630.9 --	2,093.1 ±105.9	21,844.0 ±110.7	23,937.1 ±18.9	25,863.4 --
Louisiana	1982	1,180.7 --	3,684.1 --	1,232.1 ±57.2	25,279.9 ±70.7	26,512.0 ±36.0	31,376.8 --
	1987	1,239.7 --	3,730.5 --	1,381.3 ±58.9	25,025.3 ±68.5	26,406.6 ±34.0	31,376.8 --
	1992	1,308.1 --	3,769.3 --	1,454.6 ±61.9	24,844.8 ±70.7	26,299.4 ±35.0	31,376.8 --
	1997	1,308.1 --	3,779.7 --	1,594.7 ±65.8	24,694.3 ±75.1	26,289.0 ±39.8	31,376.8 --
	2002	1,310.0 --	3,822.4 --	1,738.7 ±68.8	24,505.7 ±84.6	26,244.4 ±45.0	31,376.8 --
	2007	1,310.0 --	3,924.2 --	1,862.8 ±80.0	24,279.8 ±92.0	26,142.6 ±49.1	31,376.8 --

State	Year	Federal land	Water areas	Non-Federal land: Developed	Non-Federal land: Rural	Non-Federal land: Total	Total surface area
Maine	1982	168.0 –	1,254.5 –	506.8 ±68.5	19,036.9 ±74.5	19,543.7 ±25.5	20,966.2 –
	1987	193.4 –	1,255.5 –	552.7 ±73.1	18,964.6 ±79.7	19,517.3 ±25.6	20,966.2 –
	1992	197.7 –	1,256.1 –	595.6 ±77.2	18,916.8 ±83.2	19,512.4 ±25.7	20,966.2 –
	1997	207.1 –	1,255.8 –	704.7 ±85.9	18,798.6 ±90.9	19,503.3 ±26.0	20,966.2 –
	2002	207.2 –	1,256.1 –	797.9 ±89.6	18,705.0 ±110.3	19,502.9 ±68.1	20,966.2 –
	2007	207.2 –	1,256.6 –	851.1 ±97.2	18,651.3 ±116.0	19,502.4 ±68.2	20,966.2 –
Maryland	1982	161.5 –	1,651.4 –	963.3 ±115.6	5,093.7 ±114.8	6,057.0 ±7.8	7,869.9 –
	1987	161.9 –	1,653.9 –	1,047.6 ±120.6	5,006.5 ±119.9	6,054.1 ±7.6	7,869.9 –
	1992	168.9 –	1,655.6 –	1,116.8 ±123.8	4,928.6 ±123.2	6,045.4 ±7.9	7,869.9 –
	1997	168.9 –	1,658.0 –	1,306.1 ±127.5	4,736.9 ±127.2	6,043.0 ±7.9	7,869.9 –
	2002	168.9 –	1,659.5 –	1,408.2 ±126.4	4,633.3 ±126.6	6,041.5 ±7.7	7,869.9 –
	2007	168.9 –	1,661.6 –	1,496.7 ±130.0	4,542.7 ±130.2	6,039.4 ±8.1	7,869.9 –
Massachusetts	1982	97.3 –	368.3 –	1,086.1 ±65.6	3,787.3 ±65.4	4,873.4 ±14.2	5,339.0 –
	1987	97.7 –	368.6 –	1,196.5 ±68.7	3,676.2 ±68.3	4,872.7 ±13.9	5,339.0 –
	1992	97.7 –	370.3 –	1,332.4 ±69.0	3,538.6 ±68.6	4,871.0 ±13.7	5,339.0 –
	1997	97.7 –	368.9 –	1,554.7 ±70.7	3,317.7 ±71.7	4,872.4 ±12.9	5,339.0 –
	2002	97.1 –	368.7 –	1,644.4 ±74.6	3,228.8 ±75.2	4,873.2 ±13.0	5,339.0 –
	2007	97.1 –	366.6 –	1,716.4 ±83.3	3,158.9 ±84.3	4,875.3 ±12.8	5,339.0 –
Michigan	1982	3,194.5 –	1,099.7 –	2,839.5 ±129.0	30,215.5 ±135.9	33,055.0 ±28.4	37,349.2 –
	1987	3,228.2 –	1,097.9 –	3,050.2 ±140.3	29,972.9 ±147.8	33,023.1 ±28.3	37,349.2 –
	1992	3,274.7 –	1,102.3 –	3,320.1 ±148.9	29,652.1 ±155.1	32,972.2 ±28.0	37,349.2 –
	1997	3,274.7 –	1,101.5 –	3,700.9 ±161.3	29,272.1 ±170.3	32,973.0 ±29.0	37,349.2 –
	2002	3,273.6 –	1,112.4 –	4,030.0 ±162.5	28,933.2 ±170.0	32,963.2 ±24.3	37,349.2 –
	2007	3,273.6 –	1,120.8 –	4,227.6 ±168.1	28,727.2 ±176.2	32,954.8 ±24.5	37,349.2 –

State	Year	Federal land	Water areas	Non-Federal land			Total surface area
				Developed	Rural	Total	
Minnesota	1982	3,326.3 --	3,125.8 --	1,715.6 ±77.0	45,842.2 ±87.0	47,557.8 ±29.0	54,009.9 --
	1987	3,342.3 --	3,133.6 --	1,839.0 ±82.1	45,695.0 ±91.1	47,534.0 ±28.6	54,009.9 --
	1992	3,336.3 --	3,136.8 --	1,949.9 ±88.7	45,586.9 ±97.0	47,536.8 ±28.8	54,009.9 --
	1997	3,336.3 --	3,135.0 --	2,181.3 ±98.7	45,357.3 ±106.9	47,538.6 ±30.9	54,009.9 --
	2002	3,336.3 --	3,142.6 --	2,305.6 ±107.4	45,225.4 ±115.8	47,531.0 ±32.1	54,009.9 --
	2007	3,336.1 --	3,144.9 --	2,395.2 ±116.7	45,133.7 ±124.2	47,528.9 ±33.7	54,009.9 --
Mississippi	1982	1,634.6 --	723.8 --	1,123.3 ±95.8	27,045.6 ±97.8	28,168.9 ±28.8	30,527.3 --
	1987	1,673.5 --	794.2 --	1,197.0 ±96.8	26,862.6 ±105.0	28,059.6 ±34.4	30,527.3 --
	1992	1,751.9 --	832.6 --	1,269.3 ±96.7	26,673.5 ±105.5	27,942.8 ±33.5	30,527.3 --
	1997	1,709.7 --	857.4 --	1,475.4 ±106.7	26,424.8 ±117.2	27,900.2 ±32.8	30,527.3 --
	2002	1,794.8 --	892.3 --	1,656.7 ±117.9	26,183.5 ±138.2	27,840.2 ±38.7	30,527.3 --
	2007	1,794.8 --	889.9 --	1,811.9 ±124.4	26,030.7 ±142.5	27,842.6 ±38.8	30,527.3 --
Missouri	1982	1,920.0 --	766.2 --	2,150.8 ±93.4	39,776.9 ±95.7	41,927.7 ±17.1	44,613.9 --
	1987	1,889.9 --	797.0 --	2,256.8 ±96.0	39,670.2 ±96.6	41,927.0 ±17.7	44,613.9 --
	1992	1,904.5 --	812.2 --	2,373.9 ±101.9	39,523.3 ±103.9	41,897.2 ±18.3	44,613.9 --
	1997	1,916.1 --	825.8 --	2,609.4 ±115.5	39,262.6 ±115.5	41,872.0 ±18.1	44,613.0 --
	2002	1,919.4 --	847.9 --	2,777.2 ±118.8	39,069.4 ±115.0	41,846.6 ±21.2	44,613.9 --
	2007	1,919.4 --	866.3 --	2,931.5 ±204.8	38,896.7 ±198.9	41,828.2 ±21.3	44,613.9 --
Montana	1982	27,273.5 --	1,053.0 --	820.2 ±91.7	64,963.3 ±98.1	65,783.5 ±38.5	94,110.0 --
	1987	27,183.6 --	1,047.6 --	828.7 ±91.9	65,050.1 ±99.0	65,878.8 ±38.6	94,110.0 --
	1992	27,089.7 --	1,038.5 --	877.7 ±96.5	65,104.1 ±106.9	65,981.8 ±35.4	94,110.0 --
	1997	27,089.7 --	1,027.6 --	935.9 ±101.2	65,056.8 ±111.4	65,992.7 ±32.6	94,110.0 --
	2002	27,092.0 --	1,028.5 --	972.6 ±104.1	65,016.9 ±117.2	65,989.5 ±35.0	94,110.0 --
	2007	27,092.0 --	1,039.4 --	1,047.0 ±119.5	64,931.6 ±132.5	65,978.6 ±35.8	94,110.0 --

State	Year	Federal land	Water areas	Non-Federal land: Developed	Non-Federal land: Rural	Non-Federal land: Total	Total surface area
Nebraska	1982	575.8 –	455.5 –	1,030.7 ±104.1	47,447.6 ±109.7	48,478.3 ±19.7	49,509.6 –
	1987	583.2 –	463.5 –	1,043.0 ±107.3	47,419.9 ±113.1	48,462.9 ±19.4	49,509.6 –
	1992	649.5 –	465.5 –	1,060.6 ±111.2	47,334.0 ±117.0	48,394.6 ±19.5	49,509.6 –
	1997	647.6 –	470.0 –	1,107.2 ±112.6	47,284.8 ±118.7	48,392.0 ±18.9	49,509.6 –
	2002	647.6 –	474.2 –	1,132.2 ±111.1	47,255.6 ±117.2	48,387.8 ±20.8	49,509.6 –
	2007	647.6 –	476.2 –	1,156.5 ±108.6	47,229.3 ±116.1	48,385.8 ±21.5	49,509.6 –
Nevada	1982	59,871.3 –	423.9 –	237.8 ±64.1	10,230.1 ±65.0	10,467.9 ±6.4	70,763.1 –
	1987	59,779.8 –	430.4 –	278.2 ±69.6	10,274.7 ±71.6	10,552.9 ±6.4	70,763.1 –
	1992	59,870.7 –	431.4 –	307.5 ±69.9	10,153.5 ±72.0	10,461.0 ±6.4	70,763.1 –
	1997	59,870.7 –	431.7 –	330.7 ±71.8	10,130.0 ±74.4	10,460.7 ±6.4	70,763.1 –
	2002	59,868.9 –	430.8 –	493.7 ±113.7	9,969.7 ±114.7	10,463.4 ±5.6	70,763.1 –
	2007	59,868.9 –	431.1 –	582.9 ±138.0	9,880.2 ±138.5	10,463.1 ±5.4	70,763.1 –
New Hampshire	1982	735.1 –	234.0 –	386.9 ±45.8	4,585.0 ±50.0	4,971.9 ±12.6	5,941.0 –
	1987	735.3 –	234.2 –	479.7 ±58.3	4,491.8 ±62.3	4,971.5 ±12.7	5,941.0 –
	1992	756.3 –	235.0 –	538.0 ±59.2	4,411.7 ±63.6	4,949.7 ±12.7	5,941.0 –
	1997	763.2 –	236.0 –	603.4 ±63.5	4,338.4 ±68.0	4,941.8 ±12.8	5,941.0 –
	2002	763.2 –	235.9 –	646.6 ±63.1	4,295.3 ±67.9	4,941.9 ±12.6	5,941.0 –
	2007	763.2 –	236.2 –	695.5 ±63.1	4,246.1 ±68.6	4,941.6 ±12.8	5,941.0 –
New Jersey	1982	135.6 –	514.5 –	1,178.5 ±65.8	3,387.0 ±68.3	4,565.5 ±9.6	5,215.6 –
	1987	138.4 –	516.3 –	1,384.7 ±70.3	3,176.2 ±74.1	4,560.9 ±9.4	5,215.6 –
	1992	148.3 –	519.5 –	1,453.8 ±70.5	3,094.0 ±74.2	4,547.8 ±9.3	5,215.6 –
	1997	148.3 –	523.5 –	1,653.0 ±75.7	2,890.8 ±78.3	4,543.8 ±8.7	5,215.6 –
	2002	148.3 –	525.4 –	1,782.4 ±79.2	2,759.5 ±83.1	4,541.9 ±9.4	5,215.6 –
	2007	148.3 –	526.0 –	1,849.3 ±83.6	2,692.0 ±87.3	4,541.3 ±10.0	5,215.6 –

State	Year	Federal land	Water areas	Non-Federal land			Total surface area
				Developed	Rural	Total	
New Mexico	1982	25,645.6 --	149.8 --	707.0 ±95.9	51,320.9 ±99.1	52,027.9 ±16.2	77,823.3 --
	1987	26,186.2 --	150.4 --	772.1 ±103.9	50,714.6 ±108.3	51,486.7 ±16.3	77,823.3 --
	1992	26,448.5 --	146.6 --	829.1 ±116.7	50,399.1 ±120.6	51,228.2 ±16.5	77,823.3 --
	1997	26,448.5 --	151.7 --	995.4 ±126.7	50,227.7 ±129.5	51,223.1 ±15.8	77,823.3 --
	2002	26,448.5 --	152.8 --	1,190.3 ±158.8	50,031.7 ±160.0	51,222.0 ±15.8	77,823.3 --
	2007	26,448.5 --	153.1 --	1,261.9 ±180.9	49,959.8 ±182.5	51,221.7 ±15.2	77,823.3 --
New York	1982	219.3 --	1,257.6 --	2,808.9 ±123.3	27,075.0 ±126.7	29,883.9 ±20.6	31,360.8 --
	1987	218.7 --	1,259.0 --	2,915.5 ±129.6	26,967.6 ±133.0	29,883.1 ±20.7	31,360.8 --
	1992	208.9 --	1,264.9 --	3,058.9 ±132.9	26,828.1 ±135.6	29,887.0 ±21.2	31,360.8 --
	1997	208.9 --	1,267.4 --	3,400.3 ±142.9	26,484.2 ±145.9	29,884.5 ±20.9	31,360.8 --
	2002	205.3 --	1,282.7 --	3,657.3 ±155.7	26,215.5 ±160.2	29,872.8 ±23.7	31,360.8 --
	2007	205.3 --	1,289.9 --	3,793.9 ±160.6	26,071.7 ±165.8	29,865.6 ±24.4	31,360.8 --
North Carolina	1982	2,181.2 --	2,724.4 --	2,317.5 ±107.6	26,486.2 ±101.2	28,803.7 ±16.8	33,709.3 --
	1987	2,335.9 --	2,741.0 --	2,731.1 ±116.8	25,901.3 ±110.1	28,632.4 ±17.3	33,709.3 --
	1992	2,506.6 --	2,748.8 --	3,191.3 ±144.3	25,262.6 ±139.3	28,453.9 ±18.1	33,709.3 --
	1997	2,507.5 --	2,757.4 --	3,673.0 ±165.6	24,771.4 ±164.7	28,444.4 ±20.7	33,709.3 --
	2002	2,507.5 --	2,772.2 --	4,404.7 ±209.6	24,024.9 ±206.1	28,429.6 ±20.9	33,709.3 --
	2007	2,507.5 --	2,783.3 --	4,796.7 ±245.7	23,621.8 ±243.1	28,418.5 ±22.7	33,709.3 --
North Dakota	1982	1,727.1 --	971.1 --	902.1 ±69.4	41,650.4 ±71.3	42,552.5 ±16.9	45,250.7 --
	1987	1,743.2 --	968.4 --	910.9 ±69.0	41,628.2 ±71.2	42,539.1 ±16.5	45,250.7 --
	1992	1,785.0 --	967.3 --	924.7 ±70.4	41,573.7 ±73.0	42,498.4 ±16.8	45,250.7 --
	1997	1,785.0 --	1,033.9 --	954.2 ±71.7	41,477.6 ±76.5	42,431.8 ±17.0	45,250.7 --
	2002	1,784.8 --	1,087.3 --	967.5 ±71.3	41,411.1 ±76.2	42,378.6 ±18.4	45,250.7 --
	2007	1,784.8 --	1,088.6 --	973.2 ±69.5	41,404.1 ±75.2	42,377.3 ±18.8	45,250.7 --

State	Year	Federal land	Water areas	Non-Federal land			Total surface area
				Developed	Rural	Total	
Ohio	1982	352.5 --	382.4 --	2,867.0 ±116.8	22,842.9 ±119.2	25,709.9 ±12.5	26,444.8 --
	1987	350.0 --	386.8 --	3,073.5 ±121.6	22,634.5 ±124.6	25,708.0 ±12.2	26,444.8 --
	1992	373.3 --	390.9 --	3,342.9 ±134.4	22,337.7 ±137.5	25,680.6 ±12.3	26,444.8 --
	1997	373.3 --	390.5 --	3,718.5 ±147.7	21,962.5 ±151.2	25,681.0 ±12.4	26,444.8 --
	2002	373.3 --	400.5 --	3,938.3 ±147.4	21,732.7 ±151.3	25,671.0 ±12.9	26,444.8 --
	2007	373.3 --	408.5 --	4,140.3 ±164.6	21,522.7 ±169.6	25,663.0 ±14.9	26,444.8 --
Oklahoma	1982	1,161.6 --	1,003.9 --	1,448.7 ±89.7	41,123.9 ±97.5	42,572.6 ±24.7	44,738.1 --
	1987	1,148.7 --	1,021.0 --	1,522.4 ±88.4	41,046.0 ±95.8	42,568.4 ±23.0	44,738.1 --
	1992	1,148.3 --	1,043.2 --	1,584.2 ±96.5	40,962.4 ±102.0	42,546.6 ±27.1	44,738.1 --
	1997	1,148.3 --	1,054.0 --	1,734.0 ±108.9	40,801.8 ±114.2	42,535.8 ±28.7	44,738.1 --
	2002	1,148.3 --	1,075.2 --	1,913.2 ±121.4	40,601.4 ±127.6	42,514.6 ±35.7	44,738.1 --
	2007	1,148.3 --	1,088.7 --	2,056.8 ±128.4	40,444.3 ±134.4	42,501.1 ±38.4	44,738.1 --
Oregon	1982	31,095.9	806.8 --	967.9 ±100.3	29,290.4 ±98.8	30,258.3 ±18.4	62,161.0 --
	1987	31,114.3 --	923.1 --	1,057.8 ±110.6	29,065.8 ±109.9	30,123.6 ±18.5	62,161.0 --
	1992	31,275.4 --	658.1 --	1,134.5 ±115.5	29,093.0 ±113.9	30,227.5 ±18.6	62,161.0 --
	1997	31,260.4 --	819.5 --	1,241.0 ±122.3	28,840.1 ±123.3	30,081.1 ±18.2	62,161.0 --
	2002	31,260.4 --	824.8 --	1,323.4 ±134.1	28,752.4 ±135.7	30,075.8 ±19.6	62,161.0 --
	2007	31,260.4 --	826.8 --	1,389.6 ±141.1	28,684.2 ±142.8	30,073.8 ±20.1	62,161.0 --
Pennsylvania	1982	719.9 --	466.8 --	2,763.8 ±103.4	25,044.7 ±109.8	27,808.5 ±19.1	28,995.2 --
	1987	721.2 --	468.6 --	2,944.5 ±111.6	24,860.9 ±119.5	27,805.4 ±19.4	28,995.2 --
	1992	723.9 --	471.5 --	3,375.3 ±130.0	24,424.5 ±136.1	27,799.8 ±19.1	28,995.2 --
	1997	723.9 --	472.9 --	3,911.8 ±145.3	23,886.6 ±150.1	27,798.4 ±18.2	28,995.2 --
	2002	724.3 --	477.1 --	4,173.6 ±160.0	23,620.2 ±163.8	27,793.8 ±18.3	28,995.2 --
	2007	724.3 --	480.8 --	4,360.7 ±173.3	23,429.4 ±177.4	27,790.1 ±19.1	28,995.2 --

State	Year	Federal land	Water areas	Non-Federal land			Total surface area
				Developed	Rural	Total	
Rhode Island	1982	6.0 –	151.3 –	171.6 ±12.4	484.4 ±12.5	656.0 ±2.3	813.3 –
	1987	6.2 –	151.1 –	181.4 ±13.7	474.6 ±14.0	656.0 ±2.2	813.3 –
	1992	6.8 –	151.4 –	198.5 ±13.8	456.6 ±14.0	655.1 ±2.2	813.3 –
	1997	3.5 –	151.3 –	205.1 ±14.2	453.4 ±14.4	658.5 ±2.3	813.3 –
	2002	3.5 –	151.3 –	221.7 ±15.4	436.8 ±15.6	658.5 ±2.3	813.3 –
	2007	3.5 –	151.3 –	232.2 ±17.0	426.3 ±17.4	658.5 ±2.3	813.3 –
South Carolina	1982	1,032.2 –	773.8 –	1,359.2 ±77.8	16,774.1 ±77.1	18,133.3 ±18.5	19,939.3 –
	1987	1,029.2 –	784.0 –	1,525.1 ±91.3	16,601.0 ±90.5	18,126.1 ±18.3	19,939.3 –
	1992	1,036.2 –	787.0 –	1,749.6 ±101.6	16,366.5 ±101.0	18,116.1 ±18.8	19,939.3 –
	1997	1,036.2 –	791.3 –	2,117.5 ±111.5	15,994.3 ±112.6	18,111.8 ±19.6	19,939.3 –
	2002	1,030.2 –	803.4 –	2,447.1 ±102.0	15,652.6 ±105.1	18,099.7 ±18.6	19,939.3 –
	2007	1,036.2 –	811.6 –	2,672.6 ±112.9	15,418.9 ±114.6	18,091.5 ±19.3	19,939.3 –
South Dakota	1982	3,029.5 –	865.5 –	811.6 ±63.2	44,651.4 ±64.1	45,463.0 ±13.7	49,358.0 –
	1987	3,065.0 –	872.7 –	817.6 ±64.3	44,602.7 ±65.5	45,420.3 ±13.6	49,358.0 –
	1992	3,107.9 –	875.0 –	870.6 ±89.7	44,504.5 ±90.7	45,375.1 ±14.0	49,358.0 –
	1997	3,107.9 –	879.6 –	921.6 ±99.0	44,448.9 ±100.7	45,370.5 ±14.0	49,358.0 –
	2002	3,112.5 –	879.0 –	939.2 ±103.6	44,427.3 ±104.7	45,366.5 ±14.2	49,358.0 –
	2007	3,112.2 –	879.4 –	962.8 ±110.4	44,403.6 ±112.4	45,366.4 ±14.6	49,358.0 –
Tennessee	1982	1,212.7 –	758.9 –	1,640.0 ±98.7	23,362.0 ±97.0	25,002.0 ±11.5	26,973.6 –
	1987	1,233.7 –	760.8 –	1,875.1 ±105.7	23,104.0 ±105.2	24,979.1 ±11.0	26,973.6 –
	1992	1,232.2 –	769.0 –	2,157.9 ±111.3	22,814.5 ±110.1	24,972.4 ±10.7	26,973.6 –
	1997	1,232.2 –	773.9 –	2,606.3 ±129.8	22,361.2 ±130.0	24,967.5 ±10.9	26,973.6 –
	2002	1,302.6 –	784.3 –	2,811.6 ±137.3	22,075.1 ±136.6	24,886.7 ±9.6	26,973.6 –
	2007	1,302.6 –	790.8 –	3,038.3 ±158.7	21,841.9 ±159.2	24,880.2 ±10.8	26,973.6 –

State	Year	Federal land	Water areas	Non-Federal land			Total surface area
				Developed	Rural	Total	
Texas	1982	2,769.2 –	3,691.4 –	5,073.1 ±180.7	159,518.2 ±185.5	164,591.3 ±43.3	171,051.9 –
	1987	2,813.9 –	3,836.4 –	5,572.4 ±196.9	158,829.2 ±200.5	164,401.6 ±46.9	171,051.9 –
	1992	2,909.9 –	3,960.9 –	6,102.0 ±234.2	158,079.1 ±237.5	164,181.1 ±48.4	171,051.9 –
	1997	2,909.9 –	4,041.9 –	6,770.0 ±257.1	157,330.1 ±264.6	164,100.1 ±46.2	171,051.9 –
	2002	2,909.9 –	4,080.7 –	7,710.9 ±291.0	156,350.4 ±294.0	164,061.3 ±47.5	171,051.9 –
	2007	2,909.9 –	4,126.1 –	8,515.7 ±345.2	155,500.2 ±352.1	164,015.9 ±56.7	171,051.9 –
Utah	1982	34,508.1 –	1,767.3 –	433.7 ±89.4	17,629.8 ±107.1	18,063.5 ±30.4	54,338.9 –
	1987	34,153.3 –	2,356.2 –	474.6 ±99.0	17,354.8 ±115.9	17,829.4 ±30.2	54,338.9 –
	1992	34,278.2 –	1,786.3 –	530.5 ±109.4	17,743.9 ±124.2	18,274.4 ±30.3	54,338.9 –
	1997	34,278.2 –	1,800.5 –	601.1 ±118.9	17,659.1 ±132.7	18,260.2 ±30.4	54,338.9 –
	2002	34,278.8 –	1,800.5 –	682.7 ±133.1	17,576.9 ±148.0	18,259.6 ±21.8	54,338.9 –
	2007	34,278.8 –	1,800.7 –	744.6 ±139.6	17,514.8 ±153.4	18,259.4 ±21.7	54,338.9 –
Vermont	1982	321.9 –	261.2 –	261.9 ±23.4	5,308.6 ±27.0	5,570.5 ±7.7	6,153.6 –
	1987	353.0 –	261.7 –	303.8 ±25.0	5,235.1 ±27.8	5,538.9 ±7.7	6,153.6 –
	1992	370.9 –	262.1 –	332.2 ±26.6	5,188.4 ±28.7	5,520.6 ±7.6	6,153.6 –
	1997	392.4 –	261.2 –	345.4 ±27.3	5,154.6 ±29.7	5,500.0 ±7.6	6,153.6 –
	2002	422.6 –	261.8 –	372.9 ±28.8	5,096.3 ±29.8	5,469.2 ±5.1	6,153.6 –
	2007	422.6 –	261.9 –	393.2 ±30.8	5,075.9 ±32.2	5,469.1 ±5.6	6,153.6 –
Virginia	1982	2,608.3 –	1,917.8 –	1,841.9 ±108.0	20,719.1 ±107.6	22,561.0 ±13.6	27,087.1 –
	1987	2,626.2 –	1,920.2 –	2,082.7 ±107.4	20,458.0 ±106.6	22,540.7 ±13.8	27,087.1 –
	1992	2,646.4 –	1,927.9 –	2,285.3 ±115.5	20,227.5 ±114.5	22,512.8 ±14.8	27,087.1 –
	1997	2,646.4 –	1,929.1 –	2,627.7 ±111.9	19,883.9 ±111.5	22,511.6 ±15.6	27,087.1 –
	2002	2,646.4 –	1,934.4 –	2,901.3 ±113.6	19,605.0 ±115.1	22,506.3 ±15.5	27,087.1 –
	2007	2,646.4 –	1,943.1 –	3,101.2 ±127.5	19,396.4 ±130.0	22,497.6 ±17.4	27,087.1 –

State	Year	Federal land	Water areas	Non-Federal land			Total surface area
				Developed	Rural	Total	
Washington	1982	11,897.9 --	1,536.9 --	1,594.7 ±147.8	29,005.8 ±154.7	30,600.5 ±21.4	44,035.3 --
	1987	11,917.9 --	1,537.7 --	1,675.3 ±148.3	28,904.4 ±155.2	30,579.7 ±21.2	44,035.3 --
	1992	11,921.9 --	1,537.2 --	1,897.2 ±162.6	28,679.0 ±168.7	30,576.2 ±21.5	44,035.3 --
	1997	11,923.4 --	1,536.5 --	2,150.5 ±176.4	28,424.9 ±181.7	30,575.4 ±20.0	44,035.3 --
	2002	11,923.5 --	1,541.7 --	2,357.7 ±186.6	28,212.4 ±190.9	30,570.1 ±22.8	44,035.3 --
	2007	11,923.5 --	1,544.0 --	2,464.5 ±192.7	28,103.3 ±197.8	30,567.8 ±23.0	44,035.3 --
West Virginia	1982	1,107.3 --	163.7 --	633.2 ±44.9	13,604.0 ±47.6	14,237.2 ±8.5	15,508.2 --
	1987	1,120.5 --	164.4 --	674.8 ±46.3	13,548.5 ±48.9	14,223.3 ±8.5	15,508.2 --
	1992	1,210.4 --	168.1 --	759.4 ±51.5	13,370.3 ±53.7	14,129.7 ±8.1	15,508.2 --
	1997	1,211.4 --	171.4 --	958.7 ±59.6	13,166.7 ±62.3	14,125.4 ±9.1	15,508.2 --
	2002	1,211.9 --	178.1 --	1,079.5 ±58.3	13,038.7 ±60.6	14,118.2 ±11.4	15,508.2 --
	2007	1,211.9 --	180.6 --	1,151.6 ±57.3	12,964.1 ±58.5	14,115.7 ±11.9	15,508.2 --
Wisconsin	1982	1,819.6 --	1,289.1 --	1,974.2 ±103.2	30,837.1 ±112.2	32,811.3 ±28.3	35,920.0 --
	1987	1,826.5 --	1,290.2 --	2,087.4 ±108.6	30,715.9 ±117.8	32,803.3 ±29.5	35,920.0 --
	1992	1,845.3 --	1,288.5 --	2,213.5 ±114.2	30,572.7 ±123.1	32,786.2 ±28.1	35,920.0 --
	1997	1,845.3 --	1,283.1 --	2,400.2 ±122.1	30,391.4 ±130.2	32,791.6 ±29.2	35,920.0 --
	2002	1,845.3 --	1,287.7 --	2,555.8 ±142.6	30,231.2 ±151.1	32,787.0 ±30.3	35,920.0 --
	2007	1,845.3 --	1,292.2 --	2,724.9 ±172.3	30,057.6 ±180.7	32,782.5 ±29.9	35,920.0 --
Wyoming	1982	28,700.7 --	436.2 --	535.8 ±67.8	32,930.1 ±66.7	33,465.9 ±14.7	62,602.8 --
	1987	28,700.3 --	438.1 --	578.8 ±68.7	32,885.6 ±70.2	33,464.4 ±15.6	62,602.8 --
	1992	28,748.0 --	438.3 --	590.3 ±71.2	32,826.2 ±73.3	33,416.5 ±16.0	62,602.8 --
	1997	28,748.0 --	438.4 --	621.5 ±73.7	32,794.9 ±76.8	33,416.4 ±16.0	62,602.8 --
	2002	28,748.0 --	440.2 --	640.5 ±78.5	32,774.1 ±82.1	33,414.6 ±16.0	62,602.8 --
	2007	28,748.0 --	441.1 --	681.1 ±92.7	32,732.6 ±98.0	33,413.7 ±16.3	62,602.8 --

State	Year	Federal land	Water areas	Non-Federal land			Total surface area
				Developed	Rural	Total	
Total	1982	399,076.8 --	48,657.9 --	70,964.1 ±768.3	1,418,965.4 ±805.0	1,489,929.5 ±163.0	1,937,664.2 --
	1987	399,419.5 --	49,837.4 --	76,871.0 ±837.6	1,411,536.3 ±871.0	1,488,407.3 ±161.8	1,937,664.2 --
	1992	401,517.0 --	49,414.1 --	83,902.3 ±960.8	1,402,830.8 ±976.9	1,486,733.1 ±154.6	1,937,664.2 --
	1997	401,685.7 --	49,902.8 --	94,578.9 ±993.5	1,391,496.8 ±1,022.8	1,486,075.7 ±159.0	1,937,664.2 --
	2002	401,937.4 --	50,426.2 --	104,030.8 ±1,274.8	1,381,269.8 ±1,300.0	1,485,300.6 ±174.5	1,937,664.2 --
	2007	401,936.9 --	50,817.3 --	111,251.2 ±1,499.4	1,373,658.8 ±1,500.2	1,484,910.0 ±252.4	1,937,664.2 --

Notes:

• Acreages for Federal land, water areas, and total surface area are established through geospatial processes and administrative records; therefore, statistical margins of error are not applicable and shown as a dashed line (--).

U.S. Department of Agriculture. 2009. *Summary Report: 2007 National Resources Inventory*, Natural Resources Conservation Service, Washington, DC, and Center for Survey Statistics and Methodology, Iowa State University, Ames, Iowa. 123 pages.

Land Cover/use of non-Federal rural land, by State and year
In thousands of acres, with margins of error

State	Year	Cropland	CRP land	Pastureland	Rangeland	Forest land	Other rural land	Total rural land
Alabama	**1982**	4,472.2 ±176.4	--	3,826.0 ±195.8	73.6 ±54.3	20,828.4 ±183.0	484.0 ±65.6	29,684.2 ±109.7
	1987	3,957.9 ±189.1	206.1 --	3,643.9 ±166.9	72.6 ±52.2	21,115.4 ±178.4	478.6 ±60.6	29,474.5 ±115.8
	1992	3,122.8 ±188.9	534.4 --	3,746.2 ±160.4	72.5 ±52.2	21,205.8 ±185.2	622.7 ±74.7	29,304.4 ±125.2
	1997	2,921.9 ±202.4	521.9 --	3,549.5 ±145.3	73.5 ±53.2	21,281.5 ±199.5	588.2 ±67.7	28,936.5 ±139.2
	2002	2,475.2 ±215.0	467.8 --	3,459.1 ±266.0	*73.3 ±147.7*	21,546.7 ±267.4	452.2 ±111.6	28,474.3 ±213.9
	2007	2,221.9 ±219.2	456.6 --	3,464.2 ±297.5	*73.3 ±73.3*	21,529.4 ±389.2	447.5 ±130.2	28,192.9 ±214.9
Arizona	**1982**	1,247.3 ±130.1	--	86.1 ±48.7	32,421.9 ±1,136.7	4,405.0 ±963.0	2,597.7 ±581.8	40,758.0 ±270.9
	1987	1,244.8 ±123.6	0.0 --	75.9 ±38.4	32,413.3 ±1,138.7	4,383.2 ±966.8	2,687.4 ±588.9	40,804.6 ±286.7
	1992	1,203.9 ±124.1	0.0 --	82.0 ±34.5	32,799.8 ±1,157.1	4,230.2 ±985.4	2,754.1 ±568.0	41,069.8 ±294.2
	1997	1,197.5 ±122.8	0.0 --	72.1 ±33.4	32,605.5 ±1,202.6	4,159.5 ±998.7	2,926.7 ±563.1	40,961.3 ±306.7
	2002	846.5 ±196.5	0.0 --	78.3 ±52.7	32,608.4 ±1,166.4	4,114.7 ±963.2	2,947.3 ±558.7	40,595.2 ±389.7
	2007	753.4 ±196.3	0.0 --	90.8 ±72.7	32,497.2 ±1,206.5	4,094.8 ±982.4	2,906.1 ±535.3	40,342.3 ±460.4
Arkansas	**1982**	8,063.2 ±442.5	--	5,634.5 ±326.0	*41.5 ±57.2*	14,887.0 ±454.7	318.0 ±44.7	28,944.2 ±104.5
	1987	7,969.5 ±431.3	99.4 --	5,569.8 ±321.8	*41.5 ±57.2*	14,851.6 ±458.3	330.3 ±42.3	28,862.1 ±108.2
	1992	7,724.5 ±436.3	233.9 --	5,505.7 ±324.1	*37.6 ±52.1*	14,892.1 ±457.6	342.7 ±43.7	28,736.5 ±112.0
	1997	7,608.7 ±429.8	230.2 --	5,301.0 ±295.4	*37.6 ±52.1*	14,977.3 ±464.3	366.0 ±52.4	28,520.8 ±116.8
	2002	7,520.9 ±468.8	148.1 --	5,278.1 ±332.3	*37.6 ±52.2*	14,985.1 ±462.0	378.1 ±59.6	28,347.9 ±132.0
	2007	7,379.5 ±489.2	156.3 --	5,167.5 ±420.2	*37.6 ±37.6*	15,095.9 ±426.1	384.5 ±85.1	28,221.3 ±142.0
California	**1982**	10,430.7 ±548.9	--	1,356.6 ±224.2	19,132.1 ±993.6	14,853.8 ±791.3	3,790.5 ±651.1	49,563.7 ±341.5
	1987	10,174.3 ±592.5	117.5 --	1,447.0 ±251.6	18,842.6 ±1,039.4	14,866.6 ±818.8	3,822.1 ±659.1	49,270.1 ±357.0
	1992	10,066.0 ±575.8	180.7 --	1,115.1 ±237.9	18,274.6 ±976.3	14,625.1 ±825.0	3,909.3 ±655.1	48,170.8 ±368.0
	1997	9,659.1 ±609.8	173.0 --	1,071.7 ±234.0	18,284.8 ±1,031.1	14,428.1 ±817.3	4,018.0 ±657.5	47,634.7 ±368.1
	2002	9,572.6 ±678.0	174.3 --	1,156.4 ±252.6	17,757.3 ±1,015.0	14,401.9 ±692.8	4,133.9 ±603.9	47,196.4 ±387.3
	2007	9,489.4 ±662.5	174.3 --	1,119.5 ±272.0	17,531.9 ±1,129.1	14,389.9 ±801.0	4,117.5 ±609.1	46,822.5 ±401.9

State	Year	Cropland	CRP land	Pastureland	Rangeland	Forest land	Other rural land	Total rural land
Colorado	1982	10,626.9 ±632.5	--	1,062.3 ±142.0	25,368.2 ±791.8	3,629.4 ±436.7	816.2 ±154.9	41,503.0 ±108.9
	1987	9,720.9 ±651.1	1,112.5 --	1,053.4 ±142.5	24,906.0 ±777.5	3,575.8 ±427.9	856.4 ±168.4	41,225.0 ±138.3
	1992	8,877.2 ±606.3	1,913.5 --	1,098.2 ±152.6	24,845.3 ±787.8	3,391.3 ±442.3	895.6 ±165.3	41,021.1 ±147.1
	1997	8,817.7 ±600.0	1,890.2 --	1,133.3 ±146.7	24,833.3 ±772.6	3,350.2 ±441.9	899.0 ±163.4	40,923.7 ±163.9
	2002	8,162.7 ±610.9	2,203.9 --	947.2 ±191.1	25,245.2 ±787.1	3,253.3 ±430.1	905.7 ±174.5	40,718.0 ±203.4
	2007	7,609.4 ±645.2	2,446.9 --	1,032.9 ±203.9	25,275.8 ±788.0	3,243.8 ±636.4	952.4 ±188.5	40,561.2 ±223.1
Connecticut	1982	235.3 ±39.4	--	117.4 ±23.6	0.0 --	1,776.2 ±57.3	106.1 ±22.2	2,235.0 ±34.9
	1987	222.7 ±34.9	0.0 --	116.1 ±26.3	0.0 --	1,735.1 ±55.0	105.3 ±22.1	2,179.2 ±35.4
	1992	216.4 ±34.5	0.0 --	110.7 ±21.6	0.0 --	1,707.4 ±54.0	101.5 ±20.0	2,136.0 ±36.0
	1997	198.5 ±32.7	0.0 --	107.9 ±21.2	0.0 --	1,689.8 ±52.6	97.0 ±18.8	2,093.2 ±34.0
	2002	177.3 ±32.4	0.0 --	109.5 ±23.6	0.0 --	1,650.9 ±54.4	98.1 ±18.4	2,035.8 ±39.4
	2007	172.0 ±33.5	0.0 --	105.2 ±24.9	0.0 --	1,620.4 ±55.5	102.4 ±18.6	2,000.0 ±42.1
Delaware	1982	525.6 ±38.3	--	34.5 ±10.5	0.0 --	372.3 ±43.6	123.2 ±25.3	1,055.6 ±27.0
	1987	515.3 ±37.8	0.0 --	32.3 ±10.0	0.0 --	368.7 ±45.2	122.5 ±25.1	1,038.8 ±29.5
	1992	506.8 ±38.1	0.9 --	27.2 ±8.4	0.0 --	362.3 ±43.8	124.4 ±24.6	1,021.6 ±30.1
	1997	489.9 ±35.6	0.9 --	24.2 ±8.1	0.0 --	356.1 ±41.2	128.3 ±24.6	999.4 ±31.7
	2002	463.8 ±35.6	0.0 --	29.7 ±8.4	0.0 --	345.6 ±40.6	123.0 ±26.7	962.1 ±32.3
	2007	420.5 ±41.4	0.0 --	37.4 ±16.4	0.0 --	339.4 ±40.3	134.9 ±29.4	932.2 ±35.7
Florida	1982	3,622.1 ±235.5	--	4,373.1 ±252.6	4,388.3 ±322.6	13,254.2 ±352.2	2,451.9 ±296.9	28,089.6 ±241.1
	1987	3,236.5 ±247.4	92.4 --	4,678.2 ±280.6	4,060.2 ±333.3	13,220.6 ±368.6	2,458.9 ±301.6	27,746.8 ±247.3
	1992	3,078.9 ±263.5	122.5 --	4,592.2 ±309.5	3,524.2 ±294.8	13,205.8 ±375.5	2,472.6 ±313.3	26,996.2 ±273.5
	1997	2,813.0 ±273.4	119.8 --	4,391.9 ±331.4	3,211.9 ±321.4	13,124.2 ±392.3	2,649.1 ±340.5	26,309.9 ±304.3
	2002	2,961.9 ±333.3	88.2 --	3,908.8 ±353.5	2,881.3 ±333.1	13,258.2 ±372.2	2,609.2 ±317.7	25,707.6 ±342.9
	2007	2,880.4 ±459.0	82.8 --	3,633.1 ±508.0	2,636.0 ±360.5	13,169.7 ±454.3	2,698.7 ±400.2	25,100.7 ±422.2

State	Year	Cropland	CRP land	Pastureland	Rangeland	Forest land	Other rural land	Total rural land
Georgia	1982	6,580.1 ±210.6	--	2,945.5 ±169.3	0.0 --	22,027.2 ±380.6	910.9 ±118.3	32,463.7 ±114.1
	1987	5,973.9 ±207.8	307.1 --	2,897.7 ±151.0	0.0 --	22,144.7 ±355.8	884.6 ±113.3	32,208.0 ±125.9
	1992	5,207.1 ±252.0	610.9 --	3,040.5 ±162.3	0.0 --	21,981.9 ±386.4	873.4 ±108.0	31,713.8 ±138.8
	1997	4,759.9 ±192.8	595.3 --	2,881.3 ±170.7	0.0 --	21,805.0 ±373.8	860.2 ±122.5	30,901.7 ±159.7
	2002	4,412.5 ±224.0	316.8 --	2,791.8 ±238.3	0.0 --	21,968.6 ±369.4	847.5 ±124.9	30,337.2 ±206.9
	2007	3,995.0 ±415.3	300.3 --	2,809.7 ±339.7	0.0 --	21,963.9 ±409.2	848.4 ±164.9	29,917.3 ±227.4
Idaho	1982	6,400.2 ±314.8	--	1,204.2 ±161.4	6,691.9 ±363.4	3,998.3 ±347.2	483.6 ±112.3	18,778.2 ±50.6
	1987	6,044.4 ±306.6	448.8 --	1,210.2 ±144.3	6,621.0 ±353.6	4,089.6 ±345.3	505.0 ±111.0	18,919.0 ±54.9
	1992	5,571.1 ±311.3	826.7 --	1,242.4 ±155.0	6,591.8 ±355.0	4,028.1 ±349.5	515.7 ±113.1	18,775.8 ±61.5
	1997	5,488.1 ±315.8	784.3 --	1,259.4 ±150.6	6,556.6 ±363.4	3,967.7 ±342.2	538.0 ±117.1	18,594.1 ±67.8
	2002	5,378.2 ±334.5	785.4 --	1,276.3 ±168.3	6,519.6 ±367.8	4,019.8 ±316.0	560.5 ±114.4	18,539.8 ±67.6
	2007	5,246.1 ±360.1	797.2 --	1,307.6 ±209.0	6,514.3 ±384.1	4,015.9 ±333.9	578.2 ±122.4	18,459.3 ±75.7
Illinois	1982	24,745.6 ±268.1	--	3,203.1 ±223.7	0.0 --	3,631.8 ±169.5	655.7 ±33.7	32,236.2 ±120.6
	1987	24,749.8 ±260.8	120.4 --	2,918.4 ±208.8	0.0 --	3,653.9 ±170.9	660.2 ±37.8	32,102.7 ±129.6
	1992	24,138.0 ±251.8	710.8 --	2,781.1 ±202.8	0.0 --	3,708.6 ±172.2	657.2 ±41.3	31,995.7 ±128.3
	1997	24,069.2 ±223.0	725.0 --	2,522.8 ±191.7	0.0 --	3,803.5 ±166.5	644.0 ±45.7	31,764.5 ±126.2
	2002	24,116.6 ±287.6	655.9 --	2,256.2 ±242.6	0.0 --	3,924.0 ±164.3	663.2 ±66.2	31,615.9 ±136.6
	2007	23,910.5 ±285.1	664.6 --	2,249.5 ±238.6	0.0 --	3,934.8 ±191.1	692.4 ±93.6	31,451.8 ±166.1
Indiana	1982	13,834.9 ±189.1	--	2,203.5 ±120.2	0.0 --	3,798.5 ±139.8	721.3 ±69.3	20,558.2 ±94.5
	1987	13,899.8 ±197.3	144.3 --	1,917.8 ±116.1	0.0 --	3,810.9 ±139.4	662.7 ±69.0	20,435.5 ±95.3
	1992	13,577.2 ±204.6	415.1 --	1,844.1 ±112.3	0.0 --	3,816.3 ±143.2	673.6 ±75.7	20,326.3 ±102.0
	1997	13,476.8 ±221.7	378.6 --	1,835.0 ±108.6	0.0 --	3,802.8 ±144.0	647.6 ±65.0	20,140.8 ±113.8
	2002	13,380.1 ±226.6	239.7 --	1,887.7 ±168.3	0.0 --	3,833.0 ±151.7	650.9 ±94.0	19,991.4 ±115.7
	2007	13,219.9 ±309.2	213.1 --	1,926.1 ±197.3	0.0 --	3,829.2 ±184.7	678.6 ±128.8	19,866.9 ±125.1

State	Year	Cropland	CRP land	Pastureland	Rangeland	Forest land	Other rural land	Total rural land
Iowa	1982	26,385.2 ±243.4	--	4,549.9 ±179.4	0.0 --	1,919.0 ±146.4	929.3 ±64.0	33,783.4 ±92.8
	1987	25,651.8 ±231.5	1,235.2 --	3,992.8 ±186.7	0.0 --	1,987.4 ±145.9	884.2 ±63.6	33,751.4 ±100.9
	1992	24,923.7 ±225.7	2,087.6 --	3,711.7 ±193.2	0.0 --	2,122.7 ±155.3	866.7 ±62.5	33,712.4 ±102.1
	1997	25,246.3 ±229.0	1,738.4 --	3,530.9 ±180.4	0.0 --	2,223.5 ±160.1	869.3 ±61.6	33,608.4 ±103.8
	2002	25,396.0 ±237.5	1,508.1 --	3,424.6 ±201.2	0.0 --	2,329.2 ±148.5	867.8 ±76.0	33,525.7 ±103.5
	2007	25,446.2 ±250.0	1,427.5 --	3,304.8 ±237.6	0.0 --	2,354.7 ±136.8	932.7 ±114.2	33,465.9 ±112.0
Kansas	1982	29,097.4 ±393.9	--	2,113.5 ±146.9	16,528.2 ±340.6	1,491.0 ±100.8	685.4 ±65.2	49,915.5 ±73.3
	1987	28,467.8 ±391.2	637.7 --	2,162.3 ±142.0	16,443.4 ±336.8	1,495.0 ±102.2	680.9 ±67.0	49,887.1 ±73.8
	1992	26,483.5 ±404.8	2,875.8 --	2,322.2 ±144.1	15,831.5 ±337.5	1,575.8 ±105.9	688.7 ±60.6	49,777.5 ±75.0
	1997	26,490.2 ±412.3	2,848.8 --	2,317.2 ±142.9	15,730.6 ±348.9	1,584.5 ±102.3	696.0 ±63.5	49,667.3 ±77.0
	2002	26,397.3 ±432.7	2,663.7 --	2,383.0 ±209.0	15,810.0 ±412.9	1,609.6 ±107.3	721.1 ±84.2	49,584.7 ±82.2
	2007	25,635.6 ±525.1	3,164.9 --	2,497.6 ±348.9	15,787.5 ±553.8	1,685.5 ±185.2	735.6 ±89.7	49,506.7 ±96.8
Kentucky	1982	5,907.9 ±157.2	--	5,954.4 ±160.8	0.0 --	10,508.9 ±187.5	675.7 ±62.1	23,046.9 ±73.2
	1987	5,428.3 ±184.8	205.2 --	5,920.3 ±163.9	0.0 --	10,558.1 ±203.4	700.9 ±66.8	22,812.8 ±84.6
	1992	5,094.9 ±165.0	421.0 --	5,894.7 ±140.2	0.0 --	10,626.1 ±208.5	564.0 ±55.9	22,600.7 ±89.8
	1997	5,186.0 ±151.9	332.2 --	5,679.3 ±124.3	0.0 --	10,701.1 ±211.0	461.5 ±40.8	22,360.1 ±99.8
	2002	5,307.5 ±327.3	273.5 --	5,214.4 ±293.1	0.0 --	10,657.2 ±208.3	537.2 ±73.2	21,989.8 ±101.5
	2007	5,173.0 ±394.9	285.0 --	5,242.1 ±303.1	0.0 --	10,590.9 ±246.5	553.0 ±144.9	21,844.0 ±110.7
Louisiana	1982	6,431.2 ±193.5	--	2,343.3 ±160.5	214.2 ±42.3	13,321.2 ±242.2	2,970.0 ±160.8	25,279.9 ±70.7
	1987	6,268.4 ±161.5	43.3 --	2,338.8 ±163.3	210.4 ±40.8	13,153.9 ±226.3	3,010.5 ±156.0	25,025.3 ±68.5
	1992	5,958.4 ±170.9	147.9 --	2,412.3 ±146.0	208.7 ±36.7	13,120.9 ±230.5	2,996.6 ±148.9	24,844.8 ±70.7
	1997	5,616.4 ±156.6	140.3 --	2,516.6 ±140.4	202.2 ±33.7	13,218.1 ±220.3	3,000.7 ±151.5	24,694.3 ±75.1
	2002	5,338.2 ±187.1	201.8 --	2,423.9 ±151.1	224.7 ±62.2	13,302.5 ±244.9	3,014.6 ±150.0	24,505.7 ±84.6
	2007	5,107.3 ±250.6	226.6 --	2,458.1 ±198.8	221.2 ±88.4	13,306.5 ±337.0	2,960.1 ±144.1	24,279.8 ±92.0

State	Year	Cropland	CRP land	Pastureland	Rangeland	Forest land	Other rural land	Total rural land
Maine	1982	518.5 ±102.2	--	283.1 ±47.7	0.0 --	17,669.6 ±185.5	565.7 ±136.9	19,036.9 ±74.5
	1987	507.1 ±97.4	0.0 --	230.3 ±46.9	0.0 --	17,670.9 ±183.1	556.3 ±135.0	18,964.6 ±79.7
	1992	447.4 ±85.6	35.6 --	168.4 ±53.6	0.0 --	17,683.2 ±186.7	582.2 ±119.0	18,916.8 ±83.2
	1997	425.0 ±81.4	29.7 --	139.1 ±38.8	0.0 --	17,706.0 ±204.1	498.8 ±118.3	18,798.6 ±90.9
	2002	391.9 ±87.5	29.7 --	144.8 ±32.1	0.0 --	17,655.3 ±217.3	483.3 ±142.9	18,705.0 ±110.3
	2007	372.8 ±92.8	29.7 --	141.6 ±45.8	0.0 --	17,632.1 ±211.7	475.1 ±150.9	18,651.3 ±116.0
Maryland	1982	1,771.8 ±88.3	--	540.7 ±43.6	0.0 --	2,441.4 ±108.6	339.8 ±28.7	5,093.7 ±114.8
	1987	1,717.2 ±83.2	1.2 --	559.9 ±36.3	0.0 --	2,411.4 ±106.2	316.8 ±31.2	5,006.5 ±119.9
	1992	1,657.5 ±83.8	17.8 --	554.5 ±36.2	0.0 --	2,384.2 ±106.1	314.6 ±30.7	4,928.6 ±123.2
	1997	1,590.2 ±82.4	18.9 --	477.7 ±36.5	0.0 --	2,338.4 ±102.5	311.7 ±31.6	4,736.9 ±127.2
	2002	1,486.0 ±98.1	13.9 --	454.7 ±59.2	0.0 --	2,340.2 ±109.9	338.5 ±29.8	4,633.3 ±126.6
	2007	1,413.0 ±108.4	10.7 --	463.4 ±71.4	0.0 --	2,317.4 ±124.9	338.2 ±32.7	4,542.7 ±130.2
Massachusetts	1982	285.5 ±50.5	--	187.0 ±38.4	0.0 --	3,062.0 ±103.8	252.8 ±36.4	3,787.3 ±65.4
	1987	277.0 ±51.7	0.0 --	161.7 ±33.7	0.0 --	2,978.7 ±102.8	258.8 ±38.2	3,676.2 ±68.3
	1992	258.1 ±52.5	0.0 --	162.4 ±33.7	0.0 --	2,866.4 ±101.7	251.7 ±37.1	3,538.6 ±68.6
	1997	263.0 ±50.8	0.0 --	129.7 ±27.0	0.0	2,692.0 ±100.5	233.0 ±35.9	3,317.7 ±71.7
	2002	239.8 ±51.3	0.0 --	136.7 ±33.5	0.0 --	2,040.0 ±106.3	200.5 ±39.4	3,228.8 ±75.2
	2007	237.7 ±63.8	0.0 --	135.4 ±31.8	0.0 --	2,589.0 ±110.4	196.8 ±50.0	3,158.9 ±84.3
Michigan	1982	9,382.1 ±282.3	--	2,938.4 ±182.1	0.0 --	15,847.7 ±283.3	2,047.3 ±132.0	30,215.5 ±135.9
	1987	9,246.5 ±253.6	56.6 --	2,614.6 ±185.2	0.0 --	16,036.7 ±267.8	2,018.5 ±134.3	29,972.9 ±147.8
	1992	8,935.1 ±247.7	261.4 --	2,402.3 ±169.2	0.0 --	16,051.1 ±260.8	2,002.2 ±132.7	29,652.1 ±155.1
	1997	8,478.8 ±262.6	321.0 --	2,054.9 ±137.3	0.0 --	16,326.5 ±258.6	2,090.9 ±137.2	29,272.1 ±170.3
	2002	8,118.5 ±256.1	258.9 --	2,099.1 ±142.2	0.0 --	16,570.3 ±267.0	1,886.4 ±165.6	28,933.2 ±170.0
	2007	7,844.1 ±344.5	192.0 --	2,213.9 ±239.9	0.0 --	16,568.3 ±284.5	1,908.9 ±175.8	28,727.2 ±176.2

State	Year	Cropland	CRP land	Pastureland	Rangeland	Forest land	Other rural land	Total rural land
Minnesota	1982	22,959.2 ±479.0	--	3,822.7 ±255.9	0.0 --	16,347.2 ±613.2	2,713.1 ±207.9	45,842.2 ±87.0
	1987	22,342.9 ±475.0	778.7 --	3,576.4 ±241.4	0.0 --	16,240.6 ±626.9	2,756.4 ±208.3	45,695.0 ±91.1
	1992	21,342.7 ±463.4	1,810.1 --	3,375.4 ±213.4	0.0 --	16,306.9 ±626.0	2,751.8 ±204.2	45,586.9 ±97.0
	1997	21,408.8 ±490.0	1,543.7 --	3,366.9 ±197.1	0.0 --	16,399.9 ±595.7	2,638.0 ±182.3	45,357.3 ±106.9
	2002	21,084.1 ±527.9	1,436.5 --	3,540.5 ±341.4	0.0 --	16,467.9 ±598.7	2,696.4 ±189.4	45,225.4 ±115.8
	2007	20,693.9 ±539.3	1,453.8 --	3,759.8 ±477.1	0.0 --	16,541.2 ±586.2	2,685.0 ±188.3	45,133.7 ±124.2
Mississippi	1982	7,379.3 ±264.1	--	3,980.6 ±218.1	0.0 --	15,351.4 ±309.7	334.3 ±38.1	27,045.6 ±97.8
	1987	6,638.7 ±252.4	292.4 --	3,864.5 ±213.6	0.0 --	15,736.9 ±317.8	330.1 ±37.6	26,862.6 ±105.0
	1992	5,686.2 ±241.6	778.1 --	3,937.5 ±212.5	0.0 --	15,944.0 ±321.3	327.7 ±37.0	26,673.5 ±105.5
	1997	5,346.7 ±232.9	797.6 --	3,680.2 ±176.2	0.0 --	16,227.7 ±301.7	372.6 ±47.1	26,424.8 ±117.2
	2002	4,925.7 ±266.3	805.3 --	3,360.1 ±243.4	0.0 --	16,675.3 ±300.6	417.1 ±82.0	26,183.5 ±138.2
	2007	4,703.9 ±261.2	780.0 --	3,249.3 ±305.6	0.0 --	16,826.8 ±343.7	470.7 ±113.4	26,030.7 ±142.5
Missouri	1982	14,885.0 ±281.2	--	12,538.4 ±356.4	129.0 ±46.3	11,557.1 ±298.9	667.4 ±49.0	39,776.9 ±95.7
	1987	14,321.1 ±281.3	567.9 --	12,121.8 ±353.4	92.2 ±39.5	11,916.8 ±303.8	650.4 ±45.6	39,670.2 ±96.6
	1992	13,212.7 ±307.0	1,599.9 --	11,842.5 ±310.3	87.5 ±39.8	12,143.9 ±305.2	636.8 ±47.9	39,523.3 ±103.9
	1997	13,564.4 ±278.3	1,605.9 --	10,919.8 ±292.1	77.8 ±38.8	12,462.9 ±307.7	631.8 ±49.1	39,262.6 ±115.5
	2002	13,533.6 ±285.7	1,486.9 --	10,762.0 ±407.2	77.7 ±39.3	12,548.5 ±368.5	660.7 ±80.1	39,069.4 ±115.0
	2007	13,285.7 ±339.7	1,463.3 --	10,950.4 ±474.3	83.1 ±39.7	12,430.1 ±496.2	684.1 ±102.5	38,896.7 ±198.9
Montana	1982	17,014.5 ±870.0	--	3,288.5 ±344.9	37,851.2 ±981.7	5,496.5 ±524.4	1,312.6 ±214.1	64,963.3 ±98.1
	1987	16,168.1 ±839.5	1,488.5 --	3,215.2 ±258.2	37,368.7 ±1,007.5	5,501.9 ±519.7	1,307.7 ±211.2	65,050.1 ±99.0
	1992	15,027.3 ±870.7	2,785.4 --	3,403.1 ±325.0	37,094.7 ±985.0	5,501.9 ±528.5	1,291.7 ±212.5	65,104.1 ±106.9
	1997	15,139.8 ±837.0	2,720.8 --	3,523.9 ±363.2	36,841.0 ±965.9	5,516.6 ±519.0	1,314.7 ±213.4	65,056.8 ±111.4
	2002	14,480.5 ±852.3	3,262.1 --	3,659.4 ±440.6	36,834.4 ±1,004.4	5,496.4 ±518.7	1,284.1 ±203.1	65,016.9 ±117.2
	2007	13,930.5 ±1,032.0	3,315.7 --	3,960.1 ±663.5	36,953.4 ±991.4	5,488.1 ±507.8	1,283.8 ±222.0	64,931.6 ±132.5

State	Year	Cropland	CRP land	Pastureland	Rangeland	Forest land	Other rural land	Total rural land
Nebraska	1982	20,232.0 ±446.2	--	1,970.8 ±127.2	23,691.1 ±489.9	807.1 ±97.4	746.6 ±52.0	47,447.6 ±109.7
	1987	19,966.3 ±401.6	587.4 --	1,881.7 ±141.4	23,407.7 ±463.9	823.8 ±97.9	753.0 ±56.2	47,419.9 ±113.1
	1992	19,296.3 ±395.6	1,365.2 --	1,871.7 ±139.3	23,213.2 ±463.4	826.6 ±99.2	761.0 ±58.0	47,334.0 ±117.0
	1997	19,499.5 ±405.0	1,244.4 --	1,785.5 ±122.3	23,158.8 ±457.1	839.7 ±100.0	756.9 ±62.7	47,284.8 ±118.7
	2002	19,529.6 ±428.9	1,101.6 --	1,810.9 ±140.0	23,174.6 ±455.9	824.7 ±97.6	814.2 ±71.4	47,255.6 ±117.2
	2007	19,526.2 ±573.0	1,198.3 --	1,773.5 ±140.4	23,107.0 ±557.3	823.7 ±100.2	800.6 ±88.8	47,229.3 ±116.1
Nevada	1982	815.7 ±165.2	--	293.6 ±87.2	8,360.9 ±205.8	364.6 ±135.6	395.3 ±89.8	10,230.1 ±65.0
	1987	786.7 ±167.1	0.0 --	301.9 ±89.5	8,404.8 ±209.3	373.0 ±135.6	408.3 ±96.0	10,274.7 ±71.6
	1992	746.8 ±162.8	1.4 --	288.5 ±88.4	8,358.6 ±198.8	372.9 ±136.0	385.3 ±97.8	10,153.5 ±72.0
	1997	686.6 +156.3	2.4 --	280.3 ±91.7	8,437.5 ±203.6	310.6 ±118.8	412.6 ±91.3	10,130.0 ±74.4
	2002	602.3 ±151.0	0.0 --	259.5 ±83.7	8,357.4 ±217.1	312.1 ±119.1	438.4 ±100.6	9,969.7 ±114.7
	2007	469.8 ±204.3	0.0 --	248.8 ±94.9	8,400.2 ±273.9	312.1 ±118.6	449.3 ±128.4	9,880.2 ±138.5
New Hampshire	1982	160.1 ±26.7	--	130.7 ±29.3	0.0 --	4,122.7 ±73.7	171.5 ±34.4	4,585.0 ±50.0
	1987	147.2 ±26.6	0.0 --	116.7 ±28.5	0.0 --	4,047.6 ±75.1	180.3 ±32.0	4,491.8 ±62.3
	1992	140.0 ±26.8	0.0 --	112.2 ±28.6	0.0 --	3,976.7 ±78.6	182.8 ±34.6	4,411.7 ±63.6
	1997	132.6 ±25.5	0.0 --	107.2 ±29.8	0.0 --	3,933.1 ±82.9	165.5 ±31.5	4,338.4 ±68.0
	2002	123.2 ±27.1	0.0 --	100.1 ±27.8	0.0 --	3,902.0 ±88.6	170.0 ±39.9	4,295.3 ±67.9
	2007	109.7 ±27.9	0.0 --	107.9 ±32.0	0.0 --	3,879.8 ±85.7	148.7 ±37.7	4,246.1 ±68.6
New Jersey	1982	818.1 ±59.6	--	225.3 ±36.8	0.0 --	1,951.5 ±62.1	392.1 ±44.0	3,387.0 ±68.3
	1987	704.5 ±54.8	0.0 --	174.8 ±25.3	0.0 --	1,907.6 ±68.6	389.3 ±41.7	3,176.2 ±74.1
	1992	665.2 ±52.5	0.6 --	159.8 ±25.0	0.0 --	1,883.0 ±72.7	385.4 ±43.2	3,094.0 ±74.2
	1997	601.6 ±52.7	0.6 --	129.8 ±20.9	0.0 --	1,777.8 ±70.7	381.0 ±44.0	2,890.8 ±78.3
	2002	540.0 ±60.4	0.0 --	120.6 ±26.0	0.0 --	1,713.4 ±77.5	385.5 ±45.5	2,759.5 ±83.1
	2007	487.8 ±67.6	0.0 --	141.0 ±35.2	0.0 --	1,677.7 ±87.6	385.5 ±47.6	2,692.0 ±87.3

State	Year	Cropland	CRP land	Pastureland	Rangeland	Forest land	Other rural land	Total rural land
New Mexico	1982	2,384.2 ±167.5	--	*157.8* *±176.8*	41,819.5 ±935.6	5,237.3 ±775.3	1,722.1 ±368.3	51,320.9 ±99.1
	1987	1,937.2 ±183.3	430.1 --	193.7 ±177.2	41,237.7 ±945.7	5,080.4 ±764.8	1,835.5 ±372.6	50,714.6 ±108.3
	1992	1,894.8 ±188.1	482.7 --	220.8 ±176.5	40,627.3 ±877.7	5,277.3 ±750.0	1,896.2 ±390.1	50,399.1 ±120.6
	1997	1,868.3 ±174.0	467.0 --	230.5 ±179.2	40,206.6 ±944.1	5,565.3 ±794.8	1,890.0 ±407.8	50,227.7 ±129.5
	2002	1,541.7 ±234.6	590.9 --	243.0 ±182.0	40,255.3 ±1,026.9	5,457.8 ±868.9	1,943.0 ±391.8	50,031.7 ±160.0
	2007	1,465.5 ±257.9	585.1 --	212.7 ±196.4	40,323.6 ±1,087.8	5,444.5 ±930.6	1,928.4 ±414.5	49,959.8 ±182.5
New York	1982	5,873.5 ±229.4	--	3,888.5 ±160.2	0.0 --	16,662.9 ±219.0	650.1 ±66.6	27,075.0 ±126.7
	1987	5,738.0 ±223.2	17.8 --	3,426.4 ±163.5	0.0 --	16,986.7 ±229.1	798.7 ±67.6	26,967.6 ±133.0
	1992	5,579.5 ±207.8	57.0 --	3,077.5 ±143.8	0.0 --	17,327.9 ±244.5	786.2 ±66.1	26,828.1 ±135.6
	1997	5,357.8 ±218.1	53.7 --	2,737.2 ±131.5	0.0 --	17,570.0 ±251.0	765.5 ±73.4	26,484.2 ±145.9
	2002	5,233.1 ±216.8	51.0 --	2,632.5 ±184.8	0.0 --	17,504.0 ±279.6	794.9 ±82.8	26,215.5 ±160.2
	2007	5,000.0 ±240.5	49.3 --	2,693.8 ±230.6	0.0 --	17,518.9 ±310.9	809.7 ±95.2	26,071.7 ±165.8
North Carolina	1982	6,680.5 ±258.4	--	1,935.8 ±120.5	0.0 --	17,104.7 ±290.3	765.2 ±98.7	26,486.2 ±101.2
	1987	6,405.2 ±275.5	30.2 --	1,927.1 ±132.6	0.0 --	16,760.1 ±267.3	778.7 ±98.9	25,901.3 ±110.1
	1992	5,984.3 ±257.7	138.2 --	1,976.5 ±118.3	0.0 --	16,375.4 ±274.9	788.2 ±99.8	25,262.6 ±139.3
	1997	5,664.4 ±252.9	131.4 --	2,041.0 ±127.2	0.0 --	16,119.9 ±271.3	814.7 ±95.5	24,771.4 ±164.7
	2002	5,457.1 ±258.6	85.5 --	1,897.3 ±196.3	0.0 --	15,728.2 ±294.1	856.8 ±104.8	24,024.9 ±206.1
	2007	5,240.0 ±287.9	85.9 --	1,869.7 ±187.8	0.0 --	15,546.7 ±316.8	879.5 ±137.2	23,621.8 ±243.1
North Dakota	1982	26,985.2 ±403.8	--	1,200.7 ±166.0	11,526.2 ±376.3	462.2 ±83.9	1,476.1 ±127.4	41,650.4 ±71.3
	1987	27,021.6 ±384.3	525.5 --	1,192.4 ±130.8	10,957.1 ±377.7	460.2 ±83.8	1,471.4 ±115.3	41,628.2 ±71.2
	1992	24,651.6 ±398.8	2,906.2 --	1,169.6 ±142.0	10,912.2 ±392.2	456.7 ±83.2	1,477.4 ±114.0	41,573.7 ±73.0
	1997	24,932.0 ±368.1	2,802.1 --	1,040.1 ±139.4	10,758.6 ±395.7	447.8 ±80.6	1,497.0 ±121.4	41,477.6 ±76.5
	2002	24,153.1 ±412.8	3,205.0 --	1,059.9 ±181.1	11,022.1 ±407.7	466.2 ±89.2	1,504.8 ±121.4	41,411.1 ±76.2
	2007	23,951.6 ±568.2	3,211.3 --	1,194.9 ±221.9	11,018.8 ±549.8	466.3 ±95.4	1,561.2 ±176.2	41,404.1 ±75.2

State	Year	Cropland	CRP land	Pastureland	Rangeland	Forest land	Other rural land	Total rural land
Ohio	1982	12,385.5 ±161.6	--	2,772.0 ±135.6	0.0 --	6,671.4 ±184.5	1,014.0 ±63.7	22,842.9 ±119.2
	1987	12,269.8 ±173.6	60.0 --	2,461.4 ±121.0	0.0 --	6,901.6 ±204.5	941.7 ±71.2	22,634.5 ±124.6
	1992	11,859.3 ±164.5	317.2 --	2,311.5 ±124.6	0.0 --	6,930.4 ±215.8	919.3 ±56.9	22,337.7 ±137.5
	1997	11,593.9 ±200.2	322.8 --	2,020.9 ±150.9	0.0 --	7,051.7 ±206.0	973.2 ±48.3	21,962.5 ±151.2
	2002	11,277.1 ±206.8	257.2 --	2,196.6 ±132.0	0.0 --	7,128.2 ±227.0	873.6 ±101.5	21,732.7 ±151.3
	2007	11,055.1 ±291.6	221.9 --	2,276.4 ±184.1	0.0 --	7,087.1 ±298.1	882.2 ±108.1	21,522.7 ±169.6
Oklahoma	1982	11,570.2 ±329.1	--	7,149.1 ±217.8	15,118.1 ±410.5	6,869.4 ±280.5	417.1 ±52.3	41,123.9 ±97.5
	1987	10,963.2 ±348.0	593.8 --	7,533.9 ±196.1	14,492.4 ±411.7	7,025.0 ±290.0	437.7 ±54.1	41,046.0 ±95.8
	1992	10,173.2 ±350.9	1,159.3 --	7,777.1 ±210.5	14,217.7 ±413.6	7,171.2 ±299.8	463.9 ±54.0	40,962.4 ±102.0
	1997	9,750.5 ±353.2	1,137.6 --	7,998.3 ±209.9	14,129.2 ±422.1	7,339.6 ±288.1	446.6 ±51.2	40,801.8 ±114.2
	2002	9,106.1 ±426.3	1,044.1 --	8,394.8 ±294.5	14,164.4 ±454.3	7,445.7 ±261.5	446.3 ±61.1	40,601.4 ±127.6
	2007	8,785.3 ±499.4	1,059.6 --	8,420.8 ±426.0	14,193.4 ±543.9	7,486.7 ±359.1	498.5 ±103.5	40,444.3 ±134.4
Oregon	1982	4,348.5 ±290.1	--	2,037.2 ±255.0	9,528.6 ±632.6	12,767.7 ±466.8	608.4 ±144.5	29,290.4 ±98.8
	1987	3,941.6 ±312.8	400.3 --	2,001.9 ±253.9	9,351.0 ±632.4	12,760.9 ±474.0	610.1 ±146.5	29,065.8 ±109.9
	1992	3,746.9 ±312.7	528.2 --	2,014.6 ±249.0	9,465.5 ±635.4	12,736.3 ±495.1	601.5 ±134.8	29,093.0 ±113.9
	1997	3,733.3 ±296.8	482.8 --	1,963.7 ±233.2	9,311.1 ±645.1	12,685.3 ±500.8	663.9 ±141.9	28,840.1 ±123.3
	2002	3,636.4 ±336.1	474.4 --	1,812.1 ±233.7	9,381.3 ±625.7	12,743.6 ±511.7	704.6 ±156.9	28,752.4 ±135.7
	2007	3,601.8 ±320.9	526.0 --	1,717.2 ±223.1	9,381.1 ±681.6	12,739.4 ±609.0	718.7 ±189.8	28,684.2 ±142.8
Pennsylvania	1982	5,878.1 ±251.6	--	2,652.5 ±150.4	0.0 --	15,583.4 ±282.7	930.7 ±91.9	25,044.7 ±109.8
	1987	5,747.3 ±251.2	15.7 --	2,491.1 ±168.6	0.0 --	15,656.7 ±291.8	950.1 ±93.3	24,860.9 ±119.5
	1992	5,585.0 ±252.3	92.4 --	2,305.9 ±152.7	0.0 --	15,512.9 ±290.6	928.3 ±88.9	24,424.5 ±136.1
	1997	5,467.7 ±259.1	90.2 --	1,872.7 ±147.4	0.0 --	15,559.3 ±301.1	896.7 ±92.8	23,886.6 ±150.1
	2002	5,101.2 ±291.5	55.1 --	2,037.4 ±178.9	0.0 --	15,639.6 ±316.3	786.9 ±98.7	23,620.2 ±163.8
	2007	4,935.9 ±325.0	51.4 --	2,050.1 ±175.3	0.0 --	15,590.1 ±341.5	801.9 ±121.1	23,429.4 ±177.4

State	Year	Cropland	CRP land	Pastureland	Rangeland	Forest land	Other rural land	Total rural land
Rhode Island	1982	26.8 ±6.6	--	35.0 ±11.6	0.0 --	399.3 ±19.4	23.3 ±8.6	484.4 ±12.5
	1987	23.6 ±6.9	0.0 --	35.1 ±10.7	0.0 --	395.4 ±20.8	20.5 ±8.5	474.6 ±14.0
	1992	22.9 ±7.0	0.0 --	25.6 ±8.5	0.0 --	386.3 ±20.3	21.8 ±8.4	456.6 ±14.0
	1997	19.3 ±6.8	0.0 --	26.6 ±7.5	0.0 --	385.3 ±19.9	22.2 ±8.6	453.4 ±14.4
	2002	18.0 ±7.8	0.0 --	26.5 ±8.1	0.0 --	375.6 ±20.1	16.7 ±8.6	436.8 ±15.6
	2007	17.6 ±6.3	0.0 --	22.1 ±7.6	0.0 --	366.7 ±23.2	19.9 ±10.7	426.3 ±17.4
South Carolina	1982	3,554.7 ±124.2	--	1,173.3 ±119.6	0.0 --	11,335.7 ±164.6	710.4 ±72.0	16,774.1 ±77.1
	1987	3,296.2 ±121.2	97.6 --	1,148.3 ±110.2	0.0 --	11,339.0 ±158.3	719.9 ±78.1	16,601.0 ±90.5
	1992	2,953.2 ±109.5	264.1 --	1,149.9 ±108.1	0.0 --	11,273.0 ±163.8	726.3 ±81.0	16,366.5 ±101.0
	1997	2,570.6 ±103.8	262.0 --	1,161.0 ±99.8	0.0 --	11,244.4 ±176.8	756.3 ±79.4	15,994.3 ±112.6
	2002	2,425.2 ±102.2	186.2 --	1,065.2 ±133.6	0.0 --	11,208.7 ±169.9	767.3 ±85.6	15,652.6 ±105.1
	2007	2,230.1 ±176.1	170.6 --	1,070.3 ±190.9	0.0 --	11,167.9 ±243.9	780.0 ±87.0	15,418.9 ±114.6
South Dakota	1982	17,009.8 ±308.2	--	2,645.7 ±237.4	22,974.5 ±429.5	529.5 ±108.4	1,491.9 ±142.5	44,651.4 ±64.1
	1987	17,567.2 ±372.7	358.1 --	2,244.4 ±207.6	22,412.7 ±443.5	529.5 ±106.1	1,490.8 ±140.2	44,602.7 ±65.5
	1992	16,428.3 ±366.9	1,756.3 --	2,164.2 ±195.2	22,140.7 ±444.1	524.7 ±104.7	1,490.3 ±138.9	44,504.5 ±90.7
	1997	16,747.6 ±367.2	1,685.2 --	2,042.5 ±173.0	21,944.3 ±456.1	512.5 ±105.3	1,516.8 ±144.0	44,448.9 ±100.7
	2002	17,025.9 ±389.0	1,297.0 --	2,017.8 ±306.7	22,029.7 ±483.9	530.7 ±112.1	1,526.2 ±153.7	44,427.3 ±104.7
	2007	16,764.4 ±528.3	1,342.3 --	2,089.5 ±313.2	22,189.7 ±572.9	524.2 ±121.3	1,493.5 ±154.9	44,403.6 ±112.4
Tennessee	1982	5,525.3 ±156.7	--	5,289.6 ±210.3	0.0 --	12,060.5 ±276.0	486.6 ±62.0	23,362.0 ±97.0
	1987	5,296.7 ±146.1	173.7 --	5,077.3 ±209.1	0.0 --	12,092.7 ±273.5	463.6 ±52.0	23,104.0 ±105.2
	1992	4,765.8 ±141.3	440.8 --	5,099.8 ±195.5	0.0 --	12,062.4 ±264.6	445.7 ±48.3	22,814.5 ±110.1
	1997	4,573.7 ±170.6	374.2 --	4,912.3 ±211.2	0.0 --	11,978.0 ±264.2	523.0 ±52.4	22,361.2 ±130.0
	2002	4,505.3 ±238.8	240.5 --	4,837.4 ±295.3	0.0 --	11,938.5 ±284.6	553.4 ±74.9	22,075.1 ±136.6
	2007	4,142.4 ±278.8	255.3 --	4,977.6 ±352.1	0.0 --	11,834.6 ±341.5	632.0 ±93.8	21,841.9 ±159.2

State	Year	Cropland	CRP land	Pastureland	Rangeland	Forest land	Other rural land	Total rural land
Texas	1982	33,542.9 ±705.2	--	17,000.6 ±455.8	97,318.3 ±911.7	9,785.7 ±242.3	1,870.7 ±170.9	159,518.2 ±185.5
	1987	31,389.3 ±725.5	1,587.5 –	16,764.9 ±486.0	96,817.7 ±975.4	10,268.6 ±296.6	2,001.2 ±171.6	158,829.2 ±200.5
	1992	28,525.8 ±713.2	3,973.1 –	16,682.2 ±513.1	96,369.1 ±1,006.7	10,483.1 ±302.6	2,045.8 ±175.6	158,079.1 ±237.5
	1997	27,227.9 ±697.5	3,905.1 –	16,016.6 ±464.4	97,041.2 ±954.1	10,960.0 ±347.6	2,179.3 ±181.8	157,330.1 ±264.6
	2002	25,830.9 ±748.6	4,044.4 –	16,207.3 ±533.1	97,247.5 ±949.8	10,778.5 ±375.7	2,241.8 ±153.3	156,350.4 ±294.0
	2007	24,003.6 ±942.8	4,020.7 –	16,329.8 ±746.2	98,070.3 ±1,288.3	10,650.6 ±470.8	2,425.2 ±230.2	155,500.2 ±352.1
Utah	1982	2,051.8 ±284.9	--	533.8 ±81.0	10,854.4 ±693.8	1,818.6 ±441.4	2,371.2 ±531.9	17,629.8 ±107.1
	1987	1,907.2 ±309.5	152.1 –	598.5 ±87.5	10,677.7 ±684.7	1,805.1 ±444.9	2,214.2 ±531.4	17,354.8 ±115.9
	1992	1,830.3 ±316.1	222.6 –	639.2 ±95.2	10,908.8 ±680.3	1,765.2 ±440.1	2,377.8 ±529.2	17,743.9 ±124.2
	1997	1,678.1 ±312.4	216.5 –	695.4 ±100.5	10,775.4 ±716.3	1,894.6 ±511.2	2,399.1 ±519.9	17,659.1 ±132.7
	2002	1,618.8 ±273.0	200.3 –	695.9 ±118.8	10,772.6 ±711.9	1,902.8 ±518.1	2,386.5 ±527.4	17,576.9 ±148.0
	2007	1,421.1 ±282.9	208.2 –	695.1 ±147.7	10,898.0 ±715.9	1,902.5 ±500.1	2,389.9 ±527.2	17,514.8 ±153.4
Vermont	1982	643.5 ±53.7	--	444.9 ±50.2	0.0 --	4,137.8 ±72.6	82.4 ±17.4	5,308.6 ±27.0
	1987	641.0 ±61.9	0.0 –	378.4 ±49.2	0.0 --	4,136.1 ±72.3	79.6 ±16.4	5,235.1 ±27.8
	1992	627.2 ±64.5	0.0 –	347.3 ±38.0	0.0 --	4,131.8 ±69.9	82.1 ±19.0	5,188.4 ±28.7
	1997	506.0 ±61.7	0.0 –	343.0 ±38.0	0.0 --	4,129.3 ±71.3	86.3 ±20.8	5,154.6 ±29.7
	2002	558.0 ±59.4	0.0 –	320.7 ±46.1	0.0 --	4,128.0 ±76.0	99.0 ±22.1	5,006.3 ±29.8
	2007	540.6 ±62.0	0.0 –	308.1 ±47.4	0.0 --	4,113.4 ±81.6	113.8 ±24.0	5,075.9 ±32.2
Virginia	1982	3,392.8 ±172.4	--	3,238.2 ±158.2	0.0 --	13,473.1 ±225.8	615.0 ±53.5	20,719.1 ±107.6
	1987	3,071.2 ±181.2	22.7 –	3,238.2 ±155.0	0.0 --	13,536.8 ±224.4	589.1 ±56.0	20,458.0 ±106.6
	1992	2,889.2 ±176.1	73.8 –	3,208.1 ±153.8	0.0 --	13,497.1 ±215.8	559.3 ±49.1	20,227.5 ±114.5
	1997	2,886.7 ±179.3	70.5 –	2,994.3 ±161.9	0.0 --	13,362.7 ±211.7	569.7 ±47.2	19,883.9 ±111.5
	2002	2,849.1 ±190.0	42.1 –	2,941.1 ±173.9	0.0 --	13,216.8 ±214.7	555.9 ±63.6	19,605.0 ±115.1
	2007	2,757.6 ±250.8	42.9 –	2,948.3 ±195.2	0.0 --	13,060.0 ±256.8	587.6 ±96.8	19,396.4 ±130.0

State	Year	Cropland	CRP land	Pastureland	Rangeland	Forest land	Other rural land	Total rural land
Washington	**1982**	7,759.3 ±410.2	--	1,287.1 ±168.7	6,090.1 ±366.7	13,075.0 ±398.4	794.3 ±120.7	29,005.8 ±154.7
	1987	7,243.7 ±415.4	459.9 --	1,357.0 ±203.3	6,073.4 ±358.0	12,995.3 ±393.3	775.1 ±116.6	28,904.4 ±155.2
	1992	6,765.8 ±403.5	1,027.4 --	1,339.9 ±217.5	5,874.7 ±350.2	12,882.7 ±385.2	788.5 ±111.3	28,679.0 ±168.7
	1997	6,654.0 ±405.3	1,017.0 --	1,237.6 ±176.5	5,903.7 ±368.9	12,756.0 ±380.2	856.6 ±117.8	28,424.9 ±181.7
	2002	6,592.9 ±483.7	1,214.2 --	971.1 ±150.0	5,921.1 ±373.9	12,654.4 ±396.9	858.7 ±126.1	28,212.4 ±190.9
	2007	6,465.1 ±398.9	1,360.8 --	897.7 ±199.1	5,927.0 ±372.1	12,587.0 ±411.9	865.7 ±141.9	28,103.3 ±197.8
West Virginia	**1982**	1,084.0 ±85.6	--	1,899.4 ±116.7	0.0 --	10,388.4 ±157.7	232.2 ±39.0	13,604.0 ±47.6
	1987	987.0 ±80.9	0.6 --	1,753.4 ±112.6	0.0 --	10,562.2 ±156.4	245.3 ±42.6	13,548.5 ±48.9
	1992	904.1 ±77.8	0.6 --	1,646.5 ±110.1	0.0 --	10,544.5 ±152.4	274.6 ±53.7	13,370.3 ±53.7
	1997	856.3 ±79.2	0.0 --	1,521.0 ±104.0	0.0 --	10,523.2 ±149.0	266.2 ±41.6	13,166.7 ±62.3
	2002	785.8 ±100.8	0.6 --	1,495.5 ±128.9	0.0 --	10,516.9 ±150.5	239.9 ±113.4	13,038.7 ±60.6
	2007	760.4 ±144.5	0.6 --	1,440.3 ±166.8	0.0 --	10,510.3 ±193.8	252.5 ±109.7	12,964.1 ±58.5
Wisconsin	**1982**	11,437.5 ±285.5	--	3,520.7 ±178.4	0.0 --	14,262.1 ±238.9	1,616.8 ±135.5	30,837.1 ±112.2
	1987	11,318.1 ±312.3	217.0 --	3,191.8 ±196.4	0.0 --	14,352.2 ±245.4	1,636.8 ±134.4	30,715.9 ±117.8
	1992	10,826.5 ±290.1	664.7 --	3,070.2 ±205.7	0.0 --	14,376.3 ±245.3	1,635.0 ±132.0	30,572.7 ±123.1
	1997	10,591.2 ±305.6	661.9 --	3,009.2 ±208.6	0.0 --	14,478.2 ±267.3	1,650.9 ±127.6	30,391.4 ±130.2
	2002	10,237.3 ±281.4	603.3 --	3,078.3 ±242.5	0.0 --	14,578.4 ±282.8	1,733.9 ±157.4	30,231.2 ±151.1
	2007	10,022.9 ±341.4	540.9 --	3,161.4 ±277.3	0.0 --	14,599.3 ±312.2	1,733.1 ±175.3	30,057.6 ±180.7
Wyoming	**1982**	2,585.2 ±306.4	--	826.7 ±360.5	27,777.7 ±437.5	1,033.9 ±269.2	706.6 ±237.3	32,930.1 ±66.7
	1987	2,430.9 ±331.0	129.8 --	912.4 ±363.6	27,670.2 ±461.8	1,034.1 ±265.7	708.2 ±235.3	32,885.6 ±70.2
	1992	2,261.2 ±329.5	251.7 --	987.8 ±378.1	27,460.6 ±471.8	1,038.4 ±265.5	826.5 ±253.5	32,826.2 ±73.3
	1997	2,192.6 ±338.8	246.6 --	1,127.7 ±415.1	27,421.2 ±478.2	1,029.5 ±252.7	777.3 ±214.6	32,794.9 ±76.8
	2002	2,184.1 ±320.8	276.4 --	777.2 ±562.6	27,813.7 ±511.1	963.6 ±248.3	759.1 ±217.5	32,774.1 ±82.1
	2007	2,127.3 ±331.6	277.8 --	*648.7 ±938.1*	27,999.0 ±606.9	963.2 ±250.7	716.6 ±433.1	32,732.6 ±98.0

State	Year	Cropland	CRP land	Pastureland	Rangeland	Forest land	Other rural land	Total rural land
Total	1982	419,546.9 ±1,988.1	--	130,896.3 ±1,357.3	417,899.5 ±3,366.1	403,379.6 ±2,664.4	47,243.1 ±1,379.4	1,418,965.4 ±805.0
	1987	405,545.4 ±1,936.5	13,815.0 --	126,722.0 ±1,327.5	412,574.3 ±3,359.3	405,335.0 ±2,833.7	47,544.6 ±1,448.8	1,411,536.3 ±871.0
	1992	381,440.6 ±1,942.1	34,093.5 --	125,018.8 ±1,274.6	408,916.4 ±3,247.2	405,294.8 ±2,845.0	48,066.7 ±1,346.6	1,402,830.8 ±976.9
	1997	376,138.1 ±2,010.1	32,690.5 --	119,780.7 ±1,278.1	407,542.4 ±3,386.4	406,596.7 ±2,893.8	48,748.4 ±1,279.7	1,391,496.8 ±1,022.8
	2002	367,099.6 ±2,269.2	31,990.3 --	117,783.0 ±1,629.8	408,209.2 ±3,494.5	407,256.4 ±2,689.3	48,931.3 ±1,225.7	1,381,269.8 ±1,300.0
	2007	357,023.5 ±2,688.7	32,850.2 --	118,615.7 ±2,347.0	409,119.4 ±3,992.9	406,410.4 ±3,065.4	49,639.6 ±1,359.1	1,373,658.8 ±1,500.2

Notes:
- Acreages for Conservation Reserve Program (CRP) land are established through geospatial processes and administrative records; therefore, statistical margins of error are not applicable and shown as a dashed line (--). CRP was not implemented until 1985.
- Cropland includes cultivated and noncultivated cropland.
- When the estimate is 0.0, margins of error are not applicable and shown as a dashed line (--).
- Instances where the margin of error is greater than or equal to the estimate are displayed in italics indicating that the confidence interval includes zero and that the estimate should not be used.

U.S. Department of Agriculture. 2009. *Summary Report: 2007 National Resources Inventory*, Natural Resources Conservation Service, Washington, DC, and Center for Survey Statistics and Methodology, Iowa State University, Ames, Iowa. 123 pages.

Changes in land cover/use between 2002 and 2007
In thousands of acres, with margins of error

Land cover/use in 2002	Land cover/use in 2007								
	Cropland	**CRP land**	**Pastureland**	**Rangeland**	**Forest land**	**Other rural land**	**Developed land**	**Water areas & Federal land**	**2002 total**
Cropland	352,866.1 ±2,667.8	1,729.3 --	7,974.4 ±850.0	1,279.6 ±528.3	673.7 ±352.1	828.0 ±211.9	1,657.3 ±138.3	91.2 --	367,099.6 ±2,242.8
CRP land	365.9 --	31,008.7 --	347.5 --	77.5 --	182.1 --	4.7 --	0.5 --	3.4 --	31,990.3 --
Pastureland	2,975.4 ±558.5	110.4 --	109,574.8 ±2,079.6	1,508.4 ±708.9	1,865.0 ±504.4	367.6 ±138.0	1,310.2 ±182.9	71.2 --	117,783.0 ±1,770.8
Rangeland	449.4 ±297.4	0.9 --	69.4 ±45.2	405,891.3 ±3,805.1	*307.2* *±374.6*	326.3 ±191.6	1,112.3 ±176.5	52.4 --	408,209.2 ±3,713.4
Forest land	*55.6* *±59.1*	0.9 --	348.7 ±185.3	*105.5* *±149.5*	402,874.8 ±3,002.2	453.0 ±210.3	3,236.1 ±131.0	181.8 --	407,256.4 ±3,020.5
Other rural land	227.0 ±61.6	0.0 --	231.9 ±121.2	220.4 ±158.7	346.2 ±255.3	47,649.6 ±1,342.4	174.9 ±28.3	81.3 --	48,931.3 ±1,332.4
Developed land	58.7 ±12.0	0.0 --	54.6 ±9.0	31.1 ±7.6	124.9 ±15.5	*8.1* *±11.8*	103,753.0 ±1,261.9	0.4 --	104,030.8 ±1,269.0
Water areas & Federal land	25.4 --	0.0 --	14.4 --	5.6 --	36.5 --	2.3 --	6.9 --	452,272.5 --	452,363.6 --
2007 total	357,023.5 ±2,688.7	32,850.2 --	118,615.7 ±2,347.0	409,119.4 ±3,992.9	406,410.4 ±3,065.4	49,639.6 ±1,359.1	111,251.2 ±1,499.4	452,754.2 --	1,937,664.2 ±163.8

Notes:
- Acreages for Conservation Reserve Program (CRP) Land and Water areas and Federal land are established through geospatial processes and administrative records; therefore, statistical margins of error are not applicable and shown as a dashed line (--). CRP was not implemented until 1985.
- Cropland includes cultivated and noncultivated cropland.
- When the estimate is 0.0, margins of error are not applicable and shown as a dashed line (--).
- Instances where the margin of error is greater than or equal to the estimate are displayed in italics indicating that the confidence interval includes zero and that the estimate should not be used.

2002 land cover/use totals are listed in the right hand vertical column, titled 2002 total. 2007 land cover/use totals are listed in the bottom horizontal row, titled 2007 total. The number at the intersection of rows and columns with the same land cover/use designation represents acres that did not change from 2002 to 2007. Reading to the right or left of this number are the acres that were lost to another cover/use by 2007. Reading up or down from this number are the acres that were gained from another cover/use by 2007.

U.S. Department of Agriculture. 2009. *Summary Report: 2007 National Resources Inventory*, Natural Resources Conservation Service, Washington, DC, and Center for Survey Statistics and Methodology, Iowa State University, Ames, Iowa. 123 pages.

Changes in land cover/use between 1982 and 2007
In thousands of acres, with margins of error

Land cover/use in 1982	Land cover/use in 2007: Cropland	CRP land	Pastureland	Rangeland	Forest land	Other rural land	Developed land	Water areas & Federal land	1982 total
Cropland	326,196.4 ±2,675.3	30,168.6 --	30,344.7 ±1,148.8	6,895.4 ±1,025.2	8,922.7 ±617.8	4,136.4 ±428.5	11,117.5 ±403.8	1,765.2 --	419,546.9 ±2,441.3
CRP land	--	--	--	--	--	--	--	--	--
Pastureland	18,526.6 ±1,055.1	1,351.6 --	78,372.2 ±2,050.0	5,085.3 ±943.5	17,760.5 ±1,039.9	2,036.1 ±384.5	6,845.0 ±338.0	919.0 --	130,896.3 ±1,493.8
Rangeland	7,430.8 ±1,292.5	1,124.5 --	3,369.1 ±719.4	391,615.0 ±3,681.9	3,379.4 ±802.1	2,272.5 ±565.5	5,201.0 ±544.1	3,507.2 --	417,899.5 ±3,741.7
Forest land	2,121.7 ±328.4	144.4 --	4,847.6 ±841.7	2,175.6 ±970.1	371,660.4 ±2,942.2	2,229.1 ±464.3	17,083.5 ±417.1	3,117.3 --	403,379.6 ±2,731.8
Other rural land	1,685.2 ±231.3	56.4 --	1,159.0 ±265.6	915.5 ±422.1	3,310.2 ±372.2	38,734.9 ±1,262.4	1,077.8 ±110.2	304.1 --	47,243.1 ±1,308.6
Developed land	264.1 ±22.3	0.0 --	163.7 ±19.1	176.6 ±22.9	442.6 ±27.7	18.4 ±6.9	69,896.9 ±783.7	1.8 --	70,964.1 ±779.7
Water areas & Federal land	798.7 --	4.7 --	359.4 --	2,256.0 --	934.6 --	212.2 --	29.5 --	443,139.6 --	447,734.7 --
2007 total	357,023.5 ±2,688.7	32,850.2 --	118,615.7 ±2,347.0	409,119.4 ±3,992.9	406,410.4 ±3,065.4	49,639.6 ±1,359.1	111,251.2 ±1,499.4	452,754.2 --	1,937,664.2 ±163.8

Notes:
- Acreages for Conservation Reserve Program (CRP) Land and Water areas and Federal land are established through geospatial processes and administrative records; therefore, statistical margins of error are not applicable and shown as a dashed line (--). CRP was not implemented until 1985.
- Cropland includes cultivated and noncultivated cropland.
- When the estimate is 0.0, margins of error are not applicable and shown as a dashed line (--)

1982 land cover/use totals are listed in the right hand vertical column, titled 1982 total. 2007 land cover/use totals are listed in the bottom horizontal row, titled 2007 total. The number at the intersection of rows and columns with the same land cover/use designation represents acres that did not change from 1982 to 2007. Reading to the right or left of this number are the acres that were lost to another cover/use by 2007. Reading up or down from this number are the acres that were gained from another cover/use by 2007.

U.S. Department of Agriculture. 2009. *Summary Report: 2007 National Resources Inventory*, Natural Resources Conservation Service, Washington, DC, and Center for Survey Statistics and Methodology, Iowa State University, Ames, Iowa. 123 pages.

Wetlands and deepwater habitats on water areas and non-Federal land in 2007, by State
In thousands of acres, with margins of error

State	Palustrine and Estuarine wetlands			Other aquatic habitats			Total
	Palustrine	Estuarine	Total	Lacustrine	Other (*)	Total	
Alabama	3,669.5 ±206.7	0.0 –	3,669.5 ±206.7	514.9 ±17.1	601.2 ±22.3	1,116.1 ±25.7	4,785.6 ±213.4
Arizona	*60.1* *±62.7*	0.0 –	*60.1* *±62.7*	139.9 ±2.2	204.2 ±154.0	344.1 ±153.7	404.2 ±154.5
Arkansas	3,084.0 ±283.2	0.0 –	3,084.0 ±283.2	579.5 ±24.5	263.1 ±34.6	842.6 ±39.5	3,926.6 ±292.8
California	1,205.6 ±259.9	96.7 ±59.6	1,302.3 ±244.8	1,151.8 ±128.4	773.1 ±90.3	1,924.9 ±103.9	3,227.2 ±283.9
Colorado	552.0 ±129.4	0.0 –	552.0 ±129.4	199.5 ±7.7	124.4 ±20.8	323.9 ±22.3	875.9 ±134.2
Connecticut	363.2 ±39.0	22.7 ±19.6	385.9 ±34.0	60.5 ±3.4	47.9 ±4.3	108.4 ±4.7	494.3 ±33.7
Delaware	161.5 ±28.9	100.8 ±26.2	262.3 ±42.6	24.4 ±0.0	261.2 ±2.5	285.6 ±2.5	547.9 ±43.3
Florida	7,885.4 ±326.4	478.7 ±190.2	8,364.1 ±318.4	1,111.6 ±17.5	1,852.3 ±26.9	2,963.9 ±28.1	11,328.0 ±312.1
Georgia	6,093.6 ±248.4	437.6 ±144.5	6,531.2 ±231.0	565.6 ±28.7	350.1 ±19.1	915.7 ±34.0	7,446.9 ±223.4
Idaho	665.3 ±162.7	0.0 –	665.3 ±162.7	434.2 ±3.3	108.1 ±31.2	542.3 ±32.2	1,207.6 ±176.1
Illinois	1,182.3 ±109.2	0.0 –	1,182.3 ±109.2	346.8 ±9.7	298.6 ±16.3	645.4 ±16.3	1,827.7 ±115.4
Indiana	733.5 ±108.8	0.0 –	733.5 ±108.8	173.2 ±6.7	143.9 ±15.1	317.1 ±16.0	1,050.6 ±114.4
Iowa	953.0 ±144.0	0.0 –	953.0 ±144.0	194.5 ±6.5	241.9 ±14.5	436.4 ±17.6	1,389.4 ±146.2
Kansas	841.9 ±88.4	0.0 –	841.9 ±88.4	220.1 ±9.1	207.3 ±28.6	427.4 ±28.5	1,269.3 ±103.7
Kentucky	446.3 ±45.3	0.0 –	446.3 ±45.3	285.1 ±7.2	265.4 ±12.6	550.5 ±13.7	996.8 ±48.4
Louisiana	7,743.9 ±255.4	2,464.1 ±237.9	10,208.0 ±251.6	1,145.2 ±34.4	2,598.4 ±20.4	3,743.6 ±40.8	13,951.6 ±256.2
Maine	5,613.1 ±465.5	*13.1* *±27.2*	5,626.2 ±470.3	893.3 ±8.3	352.2 ±19.7	1,245.5 ±23.9	6,871.7 ±472.4
Maryland	724.5 ±71.7	231.4 ±35.9	955.9 ±76.0	36.8 ±2.0	1,585.8 ±7.1	1,622.6 ±6.7	2,578.5 ±77.8
Massachusetts	528.3 ±56.6	36.5 ±25.7	564.8 ±63.9	136.3 ±8.7	221.6 ±6.4	357.9 ±11.2	922.7 ±66.3
Michigan	6,003.2 ±322.8	0.0 –	6,003.2 ±322.8	841.1 ±17.8	217.1 ±12.2	1,058.2 ±23.0	7,061.4 ±324.7
Minnesota	10,876.2 ±456.2	0.0 –	10,876.2 ±456.2	2,430.3 ±27.0	635.9 ±14.4	3,066.2 ±28.8	13,942.4 ±461.2

State	Palustrine and Estuarine wetlands			Other aquatic habitats			Total
	Palustrine	Estuarine	Total	Lacustrine	Other (*)	Total	
Mississippi	4,546.1 ±259.2	50.3 ±42.8	4,596.4 ±254.9	371.4 ±12.9	291.0 ±20.6	662.4 ±24.1	5,258.8 ±253.6
Missouri	948.6 ±194.7	0.0 --	948.6 ±194.7	427.8 ±9.4	229.0 ±11.7	656.8 ±15.5	1,605.4 ±194.3
Montana	1,168.2 ±261.1	0.0 --	1,168.2 ±261.1	699.0 ±23.4	323.2 ±63.9	1,022.2 ±75.5	2,190.4 ±273.1
Nebraska	1,183.2 ±276.1	0.0 --	1,183.2 ±276.1	221.8 ±10.2	205.6 ±24.3	427.4 ±27.9	1,610.6 ±278.7
Nevada	386.3 ±154.9	0.0 --	386.3 ±154.9	365.2 ±1.8	63.3 ±4.7	428.5 ±4.9	814.8 ±156.1
New Hampshire	485.2 ±54.4	*13.8* *±15.1*	499.0 ±52.0	168.1 ±6.9	48.6 ±8.5	216.7 ±13.1	715.7 ±54.6
New Jersey	514.7 ±62.4	222.7 ±58.1	737.4 ±75.7	75.1 ±8.1	444.6 ±15.9	519.7 ±18.1	1,257.1 ±73.3
New Mexico	43.9 ±16.6	0.0 --	43.9 ±16.6	83.4 ±4.8	75.9 ±23.1	159.3 ±22.6	203.2 ±30.1
New York	3,547.7 ±161.6	*2.6* *±6.6*	3,550.3 ±162.1	677.4 ±15.5	554.9 ±31.4	1,232.3 ±35.3	4,782.6 ±172.2
North Carolina	4,536.2 ±195.6	181.9 ±90.0	4,718.1 ±174.7	362.8 ±10.2	2,342.6 ±17.0	2,705.4 ±20.4	7,423.5 ±175.6
North Dakota	3,493.0 ±187.3	0.0 --	3,493.0 ±187.3	855.7 ±13.4	158.7 ±28.0	1,014.4 ±29.5	4,507.4 ±189.8
Ohio	898.7 ±77.3	0.0 --	898.7 ±77.3	196.1 ±7.5	168.5 ±10.6	364.6 ±11.6	1,263.3 ±79.5
Oklahoma	402.9 ±59.1	0.0 --	402.9 ±59.1	629.2 ±20.2	295.4 ±55.0	924.6 ±60.5	1,327.5 ±80.2
Oregon	1,391.6 ±251.3	*28.6* *±46.3*	1,420.2 ±241.9	531.8 ±9.3	380.7 ±73.7	912.5 ±72.9	2,332.7 ±273.0
Pennsylvania	918.2 ±92.7	0.0 --	918.2 ±92.7	223.3 ±8.8	228.1 ±14.5	451.4 ±18.5	1,369.6 ±93.1
Rhode Island	89.1 ±13.4	*6.2* *±6.3*	95.3 ±15.0	20.9 ±1.7	128.2 ±1.2	149.1 ±2.0	244.4 ±14.9
South Carolina	3,276.1 ±137.6	422.4 ±84.5	3,698.5 ±135.6	375.0 ±14.5	396.4 ±49.9	771.4 ±49.9	4,469.9 ±140.1
South Dakota	2,150.0 ±189.7	0.0 --	2,150.0 ±189.7	632.3 ±8.1	151.9 ±10.2	784.2 ±13.1	2,934.2 ±194.0
Tennessee	642.1 ±62.7	0.0 --	642.1 ±62.7	472.5 ±6.0	234.7 ±9.4	707.2 ±9.2	1,349.3 ±63.7
Texas	4,791.8 ±361.9	372.5 ±108.7	5,164.3 ±339.6	1,547.0 ±43.2	2,357.2 ±79.6	3,904.2 ±87.4	9,068.5 ±377.4
Utah	1,118.4 ±404.0	0.0 --	1,118.4 ±404.0	2,047.7 ±839.6	*61.0* *±615.8*	2,108.7 ±373.6	3,227.1 ±580.3
Vermont	560.5 ±53.0	0.0 --	560.5 ±53.0	226.5 ±3.3	28.8 ±3.9	255.3 ±4.8	815.8 ±53.3

State	Palustrine and Estuarine wetlands			Other aquatic habitats			Total
	Palustrine	Estuarine	Total	Lacustrine	Other (*)	Total	
Virginia	1,388.0 ±88.5	165.9 ±51.8	1,553.9 ±96.8	146.9 ±7.2	1,739.9 ±17.2	1,886.8 ±19.6	3,440.7 ±98.9
Washington	925.8 ±140.4	*44.6* *±90.5*	970.4 ±163.7	770.4 ±13.6	785.3 ±45.6	1,555.7 ±46.5	2,526.1 ±173.1
West Virginia	98.2 ±25.4	0.0 --	98.2 ±25.4	71.9 ±7.5	102.3 ±6.9	174.2 ±11.3	272.4 ±30.1
Wisconsin	5,581.1 ±298.0	0.0 --	5,581.1 ±298.0	919.5 ±19.6	293.2 ±22.6	1,212.7 ±30.8	6,793.8 ±306.6
Wyoming	806.4 ±223.7	0.0 --	806.4 ±223.7	357.6 ±15.8	67.5 ±21.0	425.1 ±19.5	1,231.5 ±223.9
Total	105,278.4 ±1,429.8	5,393.1 ±337.1	110,671.5 ±1,358.7	24,960.9 ±870.2	23,510.2 ±633.6	48,471.1 ±474.7	159,142.6 ±1,405.3

Notes:
- (*) includes Estuarine deepwater, and all Riverine and Marine systems.
- When the estimate is 0.0, margins of error are not applicable and shown as a dashed line (--).
- Instances where the margin of error is greater than or equal to the estimate are displayed in italics indicating that the confidence interval includes zero and that the estimate should not be used.

U.S. Department of Agriculture. 2009. *Summary Report: 2007 National Resources Inventory*, Natural Resources Conservation Service, Washington, DC, and Center for Survey Statistics and Methodology, Iowa State University, Ames, Iowa. 123 pages.

Superfund National Priorities List

St.	City/Area	County	Site Name	Status	Score[1]
AK	Adak	Aleutians West Census Are	Adak Naval Air Station	Final	51.37
AK	Anchorage	Anchorage	Standard Steel & Metal Salvage Yard (usdot)	Deleted	–
AK	Anchorage	Anchorage Borough	Elmendorf Air Force Base	Final	45.91
AK	Anchorage	Anchorage Borough	Fort Richardson (USARMY)	Final	50.00
AK	Fairbanks	Fairbanks North Star	Alaska Battery Enterprises	Deleted	–
AK	Fairbanks	Fairbanks North Star Boro	Arctic Surplus	Deleted	–
AK	Fairbanks	Fairbanks North Star	Eielson Air Force Base	Final	48.14
AK	Fort Wainwright	Fairbanks North Star Boro	Fort Wainwright	Final	42.40
AK	Thorne Bay	Outer Ketchikan	Salt Chuck Mine	Final	50.00
AL	Anniston	Calhoun	Anniston Army Depot (Southeast Industrial Area)	Final	51.91
AL	Axis	Mobile	Stauffer Chemical Co. (LeMoyne Plant)	Final	32.34
AL	Bucks	Mobile	Stauffer Chemical Co. (Cold Creek Plant)	Final	46.77
AL	Childersburg	Talladega	Alabama Army Ammunition Plant	Final	36.83
AL	Greenville	Butler	Mowbray Engineering Co.	Deleted	–
AL	Headland	Henry	American Brass	Final	55.61
AL	Huntsville	Madison	Redstone Arsenal (USARMY/NASA)	Final	50.00
AL	Leeds	Jefferson	Interstate Lead Co. (ILCO)	Final	42.86
AL	Limestone/morgan	Morgan, Limestone, Madison	Triana/Tennessee River	Final	61.42
AL	McIntosh	Washington	Ciba-Geigy Corp. (McIntosh Plant)	Final	53.42
AL	McIntosh	Washington	Olin Corp. (McIntosh Plant)	Final	39.71
AL	Montgomery	Montgomery	Capitol City Plume	Proposed	50.00
AL	Montgomery	Montgomery	T.H. Agriculture & Nutrition Co. (Montgomery Plant)	Final	44.46
AL	Perdido	Baldwin	Perdido Ground Water Contamination	Final	30.29
AL	Saraland	Mobile	Redwing Carriers, Inc. (Saraland)	Final	30.83
AL	Vincent	Shelby	Alabama Plating Company, Inc.	Final	30.20
AR	Edmondsen	Crittenden	Gurley Pit	Deleted	–
AR	El Dorado	Union	Popile, Inc.	Final	50.03
AR	Fort Smith	Sebastian	Industrial Waste Control	Deleted	–
AR	Jacksonville	Lonoke	Jacksonville Municipal Landfill	Deleted	–
AR	Jacksonville	Pulaski	Rogers Road Municipal Landfill	Deleted	–
AR	Jacksonville	Pulaski	Vertac, Inc.	Final	65.46
AR	Mena	Polk	Mid South Wood Products	Final	45.87
AR	Newport	Jackson	Cecil Lindsey	Deleted	–
AR	Ola/birta	Yell	Midland Products	Final	30.77
AR	Omaha	Boone	Arkwood, Inc.	Final	28.95
AR	Paragould	Greene	Monroe Auto Equipment Co. (Paragould Pit)	Final	46.01
AR	Plainview	Yell	Mountain Pine Pressure Treating	Final	41.93
AR	Reader	Ouachita	Ouachita Nevada Wood Treater	Final	50.00
AR	Walnut Ridge	Lawrence	Frit Industries	Deleted	–
AR	West Helena	Phillips	Cedar Chemical Corporation	Final	–
AR	West Memphis	Crittenden	South 8th Street Landfill	Deleted	–
AS	Pago Pago	[blank County]	Taputimu Farm	Deleted	–
AZ	Chandler	Maricopa	Williams Air Force Base	Final	37.93
AZ	Dewey-humboldt	Yavapai	Iron King Mine - Humboldt Smelter	Final	52.69
AZ	Glendale	Maricopa	Luke Air Force Base	Deleted	
AZ	Globe	Gila	Mountain View Mobile Home Estates	Deleted	–
AZ	Goodyear	Maricopa	Phoenix-Goodyear Airport Area	Final	45.91
AZ	Hassayampa	Maricopa	Hassayampa Landfill	Final	42.79
AZ	Phoenix	Maricopa	Motorola, Inc. (52nd Street Plant)	Final	40.83
AZ	Phoenix	Maricopa	Nineteenth Avenue Landfill	Deleted	–
AZ	Saint David	Cochise	Apache Powder Co.	Final	39.09
AZ	Scottsdale	Maricopa	Indian Bend Wash Area	Final	42.24
AZ	Tucson	Pima	Tucson International Airport Area	Final	57.80
AZ	Yuma	Yuma	Yuma Marine Corps Air Station	Final	32.24
CA	Alameda	Alameda	Alameda Naval Air Station	Final	50.00
CA	Alhambra	Los Angeles	San Gabriel Valley (Area 3)	Final	28.90

St.	City/Area	County	Site Name	Status	Score[1]
CA	Alviso	Santa Clara	South Bay Asbestos Area	Final	44.68
CA	Arvin	Kern	Brown & Bryant, Inc. (Arvin Plant)	Final	53.36
CA	Baldwin Park	Los Angeles	San Gabriel Valley (Area 2)	Final	42.24
CA	Barstow	San Bernardino	Barstow Marine Corps Logistics Base	Final	37.93
CA	Camp Pendleton	San Diego	Camp Pendleton Marine Corps Base	Final	33.79
CA	Casmalia	Santa Barbara	Casmalia Resources	Final	30.00
CA	Clearlake Oaks	Lake	Sulphur Bank Mercury Mine	Final	44.42
CA	Cloverdale	Sonoma	MGM Brakes	Final	34.70
CA	Coalinga	Fresno	Atlas Asbestos Mine	Final	45.55
CA	Coalinga	Fresno	Coalinga Asbestos Mine	Deleted	–
CA	Concord	Contra Costa	Concord Naval Weapons Station	Final	50.00
CA	Crescent City	Del Norte	Del Norte Pesticide Storage	Deleted	–
CA	Cupertino	Santa Clara	Intersil Inc./Siemens Components	Final	28.90
CA	Davis	Solano	Lab for Energy-Related Health Res./Old Campus Landfill (USDOE)	Final	50.00
CA	Davis	Yolo	Frontier Fertilizer	Final	35.04
CA	Edwards Afb	Kern	Edwards Air Force Base	Final	33.62
CA	El Monte	Los Angeles	San Gabriel Valley (Area 1)	Final	42.24
CA	El Toro	Orange	El Toro Marine Corps Air Station	Final	37.43
CA	Fillmore	Ventura	Pacific Coast Pipe Lines	Final	46.01
CA	Fresno	Fresno	Fresno Municipal Sanitary Landfill	Final	35.57
CA	Fresno	Fresno	Industrial Waste Processing	Final	51.13
CA	Fresno	Fresno	T.h. Agriculture & Nutrition Co.	Deleted	–
CA	Fullerton	Orange	McColl	Final	41.77
CA	Glendale	Los Angeles	San Fernando Valley (Area 2)	Final	42.24
CA	Glendale	Los Angeles	San Fernando Valley (area 3)	Deleted	–
CA	Hoopa	Humboldt	Celtor Chemical Works	Deleted	–
CA	Idria	San Benito	New Idria Mercury Mine	Final	31.66
CA	Imperial	Imperial	Stoker Company	Proposed	70.94
CA	La Puente	Los Angeles	San Gabriel Valley (Area 4)	Final	28.90
CA	Lathrop	San Joaquin	Sharpe Army Depot	Final	42.24
CA	Livermore	Alameda	Lawrence Livermore Laboratory (USDOE)	Final	42.24
CA	Los Angeles	Los Angeles	Del Amo	Final	47.12
CA	Los Angeles	Los Angeles	San Fernando Valley (Area 4)	Final	35.57
CA	Malaga	Fresno	Purity Oil Sales, Inc.	Final	43.27
CA	Marina	Monterey	Fort Ord	Final	42.24
CA	Markleeville	Alpine	Leviathan Mine	Final	50.00
CA	Mather	Sacramento	Mather Air Force Base (AC&W Disposal Site)	Final	28.90
CA	Maywood	Los Angeles	Pemaco Maywood	Final	45.23
CA	Mcclellan Afb	Sacramento	McClellan Air Force Base (Ground Water Contamination)	Final	57.93
CA	Merced	Merced	Castle Air Force Base (6 Areas)	Final	37.93
CA	Mira Loma	Riverside	Stringfellow	Final	–
CA	Modesto	Stanislaus	Modesto Ground Water Contamination	Final	28.90
CA	Moffett Field	Santa Clara	Moffett Naval Air Station	Final	29.49
CA	Monterey Park	Los Angeles	Operating Industries, Inc., Landfill	Final	57.22
CA	Mountain View	Santa Clara	CTS Printex, Inc.	Final	33.62
CA	Mountain View	Santa Clara	Fairchild Semiconductor Corp. (Mountain View Plant)	Final	31.94
CA	Mountain View	Santa Clara	Intel Corp. (Mountain View Plant)	Final	29.76
CA	Mountain View	Santa Clara	Jasco Chemical Corp.	Final	35.36
CA	Mountain View	Santa Clara	Raytheon Corp.	Final	29.76
CA	Mountain View	Santa Clara	Spectra-Physics, Inc.	Final	37.20
CA	Mountain View	Santa Clara	Teledyne Semiconductor	Final	35.35
CA	Nevada City	Nevada	Lava Cap Mine	Final	33.66
CA	North Hollywood	Los Angeles	San Fernando Valley (Area 1)	Final	42.24
CA	Oakland	Alameda	AMCO Chemical	Final	50.00
CA	Oroville	Butte	Koppers Co., Inc. (Oroville Plant)	Final	33.73
CA	Oroville	Butte	Louisiana-pacific Corp.	Deleted	–
CA	Oroville	Butte	Western Pacific Railroad Co.	Deleted	–
CA	Oxnard	Ventura	Halaco Engineering Company	Final	58.31
CA	Palo Alto	Santa Clara	Hewlett-Packard (620-640 Page Mill Road)	Final	29.76

St.	City/Area	County	Site Name	Status	Score[1]
CA	Pasadena	Los Angeles	Jet Propulsion Laboratory (NASA)	Final	50.00
CA	Paso Robles	San Luis Obispo	Klau/Buena Vista Mine	Final	50.00
CA	Petaluma	Sonoma	Sola Optical USA, Inc.	Final	33.39
CA	Porterville	Tulare	Beckman Instruments (Porterville Plant)	Final	34.21
CA	Rancho Cordova	Sacramento	Aerojet General Corp.	Final	54.63
CA	Redding	Shasta	Iron Mountain Mine	Final	56.16
CA	Rialto	San Bernardino	B.F. Goodrich	Final	50.00
CA	Richmond	Contra Costa	Liquid Gold Oil Corp.	Deleted	–
CA	Richmond	Contra Costa	United Heckathorn Co.	Final	38.49
CA	Riverbank	Stanislaus	Riverbank Army Ammunition Plant	Final	63.94
CA	Riverside	Riverside	Alark Hard Chrome	Final	50.50
CA	Riverside	Riverside	March Air Force Base	Final	31.94
CA	Rogue River-siskiyou Nf	Siskiyou	Blue Ledge Mine	Final	50.28
CA	Sacramento	Sacramento	Jibboom Junkyard	Deleted	–
CA	Sacramento	Sacramento	Sacramento Army Depot	Final	44.46
CA	Salinas	Monterey	Crazy Horse Sanitary Landfill	Final	37.93
CA	Salinas	Monterey	Firestone Tire & Rubber Co. (salinas Plant)	Deleted	–
CA	San Bernardino	San Bernardino	Newmark Ground Water Contamination	Final	35.57
CA	San Bernardino	San Bernardino	Norton Air Force Base	Final	39.65
CA	San Francisco	San Francisco	Treasure Island Naval Air Station - Hunters Point Annex	Final	48.77
CA	San Jose	Santa Clara	Fairchild Semiconductor Corp. (South San Jose Plant)	Final	44.46
CA	San Jose	Santa Clara	Lorentz Barrel & Drum Co.	Final	30.94
CA	Santa Clara	Santa Clara	Applied Materials	Final	31.94
CA	Santa Clara	Santa Clara	Intel Corp. (Santa Clara III)	Final	31.94
CA	Santa Clara	Santa Clara	Intel Magnetics	Final	31.94
CA	Santa Clara	Santa Clara	National Semiconductor Corp.	Final	35.57
CA	Santa Clara	Santa Clara	Synertek, Inc. (Building 1)	Final	31.94
CA	Santa Fe Springs	Los Angeles	Waste Disposal, Inc.	Final	34.60
CA	Scotts Valley	Santa Cruz	Watkins-Johnson Co. (Stewart Dvision Plant)	Final	28.90
CA	Selma	Fresno	Selma Treating Co.	Final	48.83
CA	South Gate	Los Angeles	Cooper Drum Company	Final	50.00
CA	South Gate	Los Angeles	Jervis B. Webb Co.	Final	45.76
CA	South Gate	Los Angeles	Southern Avenue Industrial Area	Final	50.00
CA	Stockton	San Joaquin	McCormick & Baxter Creosoting Co.	Final	74.00
CA	Sunnyvale	Santa Clara	Advanced Micro Devices, Inc.	Final	37.93
CA	Sunnyvale	Santa Clara	Advanced Micro Devices, Inc. (Building 915)	Final	31.94
CA	Sunnyvale	Santa Clara	Monolithic Memories	Final	35.57
CA	Sunnyvale	Santa Clara	TRW Microwave, Inc. (Building 825)	Final	31.94
CA	Sunnyvale	Santa Clara	Westinghouse Electric Corp. (Sunnyvale Plant)	Final	39.93
CA	Torrance	Los Angeles	Montrose Chemical Corp.	Final	32.10
CA	Tracy	San Joaquin	Lawrence Livermore National Laboratory (Site 300) (USDOE)	Final	31.58
CA	Tracy	San Joaquin	Tracy Defense Depot (USARMY)	Final	37.16
CA	Travis Afb	Solano	Travis Air Force Base	Final	29.49
CA	Turlock	Stanislaus	Valley Wood Preserving, Inc.	Final	32.01
CA	Ukiah	Mendocino	Coast Wood Preserving	Final	44.73
CA	Victorville	San Bernardino	George Air Force Base	Final	33.62
CA	Visalia	Tulare	Southern California Edison Co. (visalia Poleyard)	Deleted	–
CA	Weed	Siskiyou	J.H. Baxter & Co.	Final	34.78
CA	Westminster	Orange	Ralph Gray Trucking Co.	Deleted	–
CA	Whittier	Los Angeles	Omega Chemical Corporation	Final	30.94
CO	Adams County	Adams	Rocky Mountain Arsenal (USARMY)	Final	58.15
CO	Aspen	Pitkin	Smuggler Mountain	Deleted	–
CO	Aurora	Arapahoe	Lowry Landfill	Final	48.36
CO	Boulder	Boulder	Marshall Landfill	Final	–
CO	Canon City	Fremont	Lincoln Park	Final	31.31
CO	Commerce City	Adams	Sand Creek Industrial	Deleted	–
CO	Commerce City	Adams	Woodbury Chemical Co.	Deleted	–
CO	Creede	Mineral	Nelson Tunnel/Commodore Waste Rock	Final	48.03
CO	Denver	Adams	ASARCO, Inc. (Globe Plant)	Proposed	70.71
CO	Denver	Adams	Broderick Wood Products	Final	35.13

St.	City/Area	County	Site Name	Status	Score[1]
CO	Denver	Denver	Chemical Sales Co.	Final	37.93
CO	Denver	Denver	Denver Radium Site	Final	44.11
CO	Denver	Denver	Vasquez Boulevard and I-70	Final	50.00
CO	Golden	Jefferson	Rocky Flats Plant (USDOE)	Final	64.32
CO	Gunnison National Forest	Gunnison	Standard Mine	Final	50.00
CO	Idaho Springs	Clear Creek	Central City, Clear Creek	Final	51.39
CO	Leadville	Lake	California Gulch	Final	55.84
CO	Littleton	Jefferson	Air Force Plant PJKS	Final	42.93
CO	Minturn	Eagle	Eagle Mine	Final	47.19
CO	Rio Grande County	Rio Grande	Summitville Mine	Final	50.00
CO	Salida	Chaffee	Smeltertown Site	Proposed	58.56
CO	Uravan	Montrose	Uravan Uranium Project (Union Carbide Corp.)	Final	43.53
CO	Ward	Boulder	Captain Jack Mill	Final	50.56
CT	Barkhamsted	Litchfield	Barkhamsted-New Hartford Landfill	Final	38.05
CT	Beacon Falls	New Haven	Beacon Heights Landfill	Final	46.77
CT	Canterbury	Windham	Yaworski Waste Lagoon	Final	36.72
CT	Cheshire	New Haven	Cheshire Ground Water Contamination	Deleted	–
CT	Durham	Middlesex	Durham Meadows	Final	33.94
CT	East Windsor	Hartford	Broad Brook Mill	Proposed	54.35
CT	Naugatuck Borough	New Haven	Laurel Park, Inc.	Final	–
CT	New London	New London	New London Submarine Base	Final	36.53
CT	Norwalk	Fairfield	Kellogg-Deering Well Field	Final	39.92
CT	Plainfield	Windham	Gallup's Quarry	Final	46.29
CT	Southington	Hartford	Old Southington Landfill	Final	54.35
CT	Southington	Hartford	Solvents Recovery Service of New England	Final	44.93
CT	Sterling	Windham	Revere Textile Prints Corp.	Deleted	–
CT	Stratford	Fairfield	Raymark Industries, Inc.	Final	–
CT	Vernon	Tolland	Precision Plating Corp.	Final	49.10
CT	Waterbury	New Haven	Scovill Industrial Landfill	Final	50.00
CT	Wolcott	New Haven	Nutmeg Valley Road	Deleted	–
CT	Woodstock	Windham	Linemaster Switch Corp.	Final	33.71
DC	Washington	District Of Columbia	Washington Navy Yard	Final	48.57
DE	Cheswold	Kent	Coker's Sanitation Service Landfills	Deleted	–
DE	Dover	Kent	Chem-Solv, Inc.	Final	37.93
DE	Dover	Kent	Dover Air Force Base	Final	35.89
DE	Dover	Kent	Dover Gas Light Co.	Final	35.57
DE	Dover	Kent	Wildcat Landfill	Deleted	–
DE	Kirkwood	New Castle	Harvey & Knott Drum, Inc.	Final	30.77
DE	Laurel	Sussex	Sussex County Landfill No. 5	Deleted	–
DE	Middletown	New Castle	Sealand Limited	Deleted	–
DE	Millsboro	Sussex	Millsboro TCE	Proposed	50.00
DE	Millsboro	Sussex	NCR Corp. (Millsboro Plant)	Final	38.21
DE	New Castle	New Castle	Army Creek Landfill	Final	69.92
DE	New Castle	New Castle	Delaware City PVC Plant	Final	30.55
DE	New Castle	New Castle	Delaware Sand & Gravel Landfill	Final	46.60
DE	New Castle	New Castle	Halby Chemical Co.	Final	30.90
DE	New Castle	New Castle	New Castle Spill	Deleted	–
DE	New Castle	New Castle	New Castle Steel	Deleted	–
DE	New Castle	New Castle	Standard Chlorine of Delaware, Inc.	Final	35.42
DE	New Castle	New Castle	Tybouts Corner Landfill	Final	–
DE	Newport	New Castle	E.I. du Pont de Nemours & Co., Inc. (Newport Pigment Plant Landfill)	Final	51.91
DE	Newport	New Castle	Koppers Co., Inc. (Newport Plant)	Final	33.56
DE	Smyrna	Kent	Tyler Refrigeration Pit	Deleted	–
FL	Baldwin	Duval	Yellow Water Road	Deleted	–
FL	Brandon	Hillsborough	Sydney Mine Sludge Ponds	Final	38.93
FL	Cantonment	Escambia	Dubose Oil Products Co.	Deleted	–
FL	Clermont	Lake	Tower Chemical Co.	Final	44.03
FL	Cottondale	Jackson	Sapp Battery Salvage	Final	47.70
FL	Davie	Broward	Davie Landfill	Deleted	–

St.	City/Area	County	Site Name	Status	Score[1]
FL	Deland	Volusia	Sherwood Medical Industries	Final	39.83
FL	Duval County	Duval	Hipps Road Landfill	Deleted	–
FL	Fort Lauderdale	Broward	Florida Petroleum Reprocessors	Final	50.00
FL	Fort Lauderdale	Broward	Hollingsworth Solderless Terminal	Final	44.53
FL	Fort Lauderdale	Broward	Wingate Road Municipal Incinerator Dump	Final	31.72
FL	Gainesville	Alachua	Cabot/Koppers	Final	36.69
FL	Hialeah	Miami-dade	B&B Chemical Co., Inc.	Final	35.35
FL	Hialeah	Miami-dade	Northwest 58th Street Landfill	Deleted	–
FL	Hialeah	Miami-dade	Standard Auto Bumper Corp.	Deleted	–
FL	Homestead Air Force Base	Miami-dade	Homestead Air Force Base	Final	42.40
FL	Indiantown	Martin	Florida Steel Corp.	Final	45.92
FL	Jacksonville	Duval	Fairfax St. Wood Treaters	Final	50.00
FL	Jacksonville	Duval	Jacksonville Naval Air Station	Final	32.08
FL	Jacksonville	Duval	Kerr-McGee Chemical Corp - Jacksonville	Final	70.71
FL	Jacksonville	Duval	Pickettville Road Landfill	Final	42.94
FL	Jacksonville	Duval	Cecil Field Naval Air Station	Final	31.99
FL	Lake Alfred	Polk	Callaway & Son Drum Service	Deleted	–
FL	Lake Park	Palm Beach	Bmi-textron	Deleted	–
FL	Lake Park	Palm Beach	Trans Circuits, Inc.	Final	50.00
FL	Lakeland	Polk	Alpha Chemical Corp.	Deleted	–
FL	Lakeland	Polk	Landia Chemical Company	Final	50.00
FL	Live Oak	Suwannee	Brown Wood Preserving	Deleted	–
FL	Longwood	Seminole	General Dynamics Longwood	Final	50.00
FL	Madison	Madison	Madison County Sanitary Landfill	Final	37.93
FL	Marianna	Jackson	United Metals, Inc.	Final	33.73
FL	Medley	Miami-dade	Pepper Steel & Alloys, Inc.	Final	31.92
FL	Miami	Miami-dade	Airco Plating Co.	Final	42.47
FL	Miami	Miami-dade	Anaconda Aluminum Co./milgo Electronics Corp.	Deleted	–
FL	Miami	Miami-dade	Continental Cleaners	Final	50.00
FL	Miami	Miami-dade	Gold Coast Oil Corp.	Deleted	–
FL	Miami	Miami-dade	Miami Drum Services	Final	53.56
FL	Miami	Miami-dade	Varsol Spill	Deleted	–
FL	Milton	Santa Rosa	Whiting Field Naval Air Station	Final	50.00
FL	Mount Pleasant	Gadsden	Parramore Surplus	Deleted	–
FL	North Miami	Miami-dade	Munisport Landfill	Deleted	–
FL	North Miami Beach	Miami-dade	Anodyne, Inc.	Final	31.03
FL	Orlando	Orange	Chevron Chemical Co. (Ortho Division)	Final	50.00
FL	Orlando	Orange	City Industries, Inc.	Final	32.00
FL	Palm Bay	Brevard	Harris Corp. (Palm Bay Plant)	Final	35.57
FL	Panama City	Bay	Tyndall Air Force Base	Final	50.00
FL	Pembroke Park	Broward	Petroleum Products Corp.	Final	40.11
FL	Pensacola	Escambia	Agrico Chemical Co.	Final	44.98
FL	Pensacola	Escambia	American Creosote Works (Pensacola Plant)	Final	58.41
FL	Pensacola	Escambia	Beulah Landfill	Deleted	–
FL	Pensacola	Escambia	Escambia Wood - Pensacola	Final	50.00
FL	Pensacola	Escambia	Pensacola Naval Air Station	Final	42.40
FL	Plant City	Hillsborough	Schuylkill Metals Corp.	Deleted	–
FL	Pompano Beach	Broward	Chemform, Inc.	Deleted	–
FL	Pompano Beach	Broward	Flash Cleaners	Final	50.00
FL	Pompano Beach	Broward	Wilson Concepts Of Florida, Inc.	Deleted	–
FL	Port Salerno	Martin	Solitron Microwave	Final	50.00
FL	Princeton	Miami-dade	Woodbury Chemical Co. (princeton Plant)	Deleted	–
FL	Ruskin	Hillsborough	JJ Seifert Machine	Final	50.00
FL	Sanford	Seminole	Sanford Dry Cleaners	Final	50.00
FL	Seffner	Hillsborough	Taylor Road Landfill	Final	51.37
FL	Tampa	Hillsborough	Alaric Area Ground Water Plume	Final	41.91
FL	Tampa	Hillsborough	Helena Chemical Co. (Tampa Plant)	Final	30.19
FL	Tampa	Hillsborough	Kassauf-kimerling Battery Disposal	Deleted	–
FL	Tampa	Hillsborough	MRI Corp (Tampa)	Final	37.62

St.	City/Area	County	Site Name	Status	Score[1]
FL	Tampa	Hillsborough	Peak Oil Co./Bay Drum Co.	Final	58.15
FL	Tampa	Hillsborough	Raleigh Street Dump	Final	50.00
FL	Tampa	Hillsborough	Reeves Southeastern Galvanizing Corp.	Final	58.75
FL	Tampa	Hillsborough	Sixty-second Street Dump	Deleted	–
FL	Tampa	Hillsborough	Southern Solvents, Inc.	Final	50.00
FL	Tampa	Hillsborough	Stauffer Chemical Co (Tampa)	Final	59.81
FL	Tampa	Hillsborough	Tri-city Oil Conservationist, Inc	Deleted	–
FL	Tarpon Springs	Pinellas	Stauffer Chemical Co. (Tarpon Springs)	Final	50.00
FL	Temple Terrace	Hillsborough	Normandy Park Apartments	Proposed	49.98
FL	Thonotosassa	Hillsborough	Arkla Terra Property	Final	50.00
FL	Vero Beach	Indian River	Piper Aircraft Corp./Vero Beach Water & Sewer Department	Final	31.13
FL	Warrington	Escambia	Pioneer Sand Co.	Deleted	–
FL	Whitehouse	Duval	Coleman-Evans Wood Preserving Co.	Final	46.18
FL	Whitehouse	Duval	Whitehouse Oil Pits	Final	52.58
FL	Zellwood	Orange	Zellwood Ground Water Contamination	Final	51.91
FM	Palau	[blank County]	Pcb Wastes	Deleted	–
GA	Albany	Dougherty	Firestone Tire & Rubber Co. (Albany Plant)	Final	30.08
GA	Albany	Dougherty	Marine Corps Logistics Base	Final	44.65
GA	Albany	Dougherty	T.H. Agriculture & Nutrition Co. (Albany Plant)	Final	40.93
GA	Athens	Clarke	Luminous Processes, Inc.	Deleted	–
GA	Augusta	Richmond	Alternate Energy Resources	Final	50.00
GA	Augusta	Richmond	Monsanto Corp. (augusta Plant)	Deleted	–
GA	Augusta	Richmond	Peach Orchard Road PCE Ground Water Plume	Final	50.00
GA	Brunswick	Glynn	Brunswick Wood Preserving	Final	54.49
GA	Brunswick	Glynn	Hercules 009 Landfill	Final	52.58
GA	Brunswick	Glynn	LCP Chemicals Georgia	Final	–
GA	Brunswick	Glynn	Terry Creek Dredge Spoil Areas/Hercules Outfall	Proposed	50.18
GA	Camilla	Mitchell	Camilla Wood Preserving Company	Final	50.00
GA	Cedartown	Polk	Cedartown Industries, Inc.	Deleted	–
GA	Cedartown	Polk	Cedartown Municipal Landfill	Deleted	–
GA	Cedartown	Polk	Diamond Shamrock Corp. Landfill	Final	35.60
GA	Fort Valley	Peach	Woolfolk Chemical Works, Inc.	Final	42.24
GA	Houston County	Houston	Robins Air Force Base (Landfill #4/Sludge Lagoon)	Final	51.66
GA	Kensington	Walker	Mathis Brothers Landfill (South Marble Top Road)	Final	30.78
GA	Macon	Bibb	Armstrong World Industries	Final	50.00
GA	Macon	Bibb	Macon Naval Ordnance Plant	Final	48.97
GA	Peach County	Peach	Powersville Site	Deleted	–
GA	Tifton	Tift	Marzone Inc./Chevron Chemical Co.	Final	30.26
GU	Agana	Guam	Ordot Landfill	Final	–
GU	Yigo	Guam	Andersen Air Force Base	Final	50.00
HI	Kunia	Honolulu	Del Monte Corp. (Oahu Plantation)	Final	50.00
HI	Pearl Harbor	Honolulu	Pearl Harbor Naval Complex	Final	70.82
HI	Schofield	Honolulu	Schofield Barracks (usarmy)	Deleted	–
HI	Wahiawa	Honolulu	Naval Computer & Telecom Area Master Station Eastern Pacific	Final	50.00
IA	Camanche	Clinton	Lawrence Todtz Farm	Final	52.11
IA	Cedar Rapids	Linn	Electro-Coatings, Inc.	Final	42.24
IA	Charles City	Floyd	Labounty	Deleted	–
IA	Charles City	Floyd	Shaw Avenue Dump	Final	30.01
IA	Charles City	Floyd	White Farm Equipment Co. Dump	Deleted	–
IA	Des Moines	Polk	Des Moines TCE	Final	42.28
IA	Dubuque	Dubuque	Peoples Natural Gas Co.	Final	46.24
IA	Fairfield	Jefferson	Fairfield Coal Gasification Plant	Final	38.05
IA	Hospers	Sioux	Farmers' Mutual Cooperative	Deleted	–
IA	Kellogg	Jasper	Midwest Manufacturing/North Farm	Final	32.04
IA	Keokuk	Lee	Sheller-globe Corp. Disposal	Deleted	–
IA	Mason City	Cerro Gordo	Mason City Coal Gasification Plant	Final	69.33
IA	Mason City	Cerro Gordo	Northwestern States Portland Cement Co.	Deleted	–
IA	Maurice	Sioux	Vogel Paint & Wax Co.	Final	31.45
IA	Middletown	Des Moines	Iowa Army Ammunition Plant	Final	29.73

St.	City/Area	County	Site Name	Status	Score[1]
IA	Mineola	Mills	Aidex Corp.	Deleted	–
IA	Ottumwa	Wapello	John Deere (ottumwa Works Landfills)	Deleted	–
IA	Red Oak	Montgomery	Red Oak City Landfill	Deleted	–
IA	Sergeant Bluff	Woodbury	Mid-america Tanning Co.	Deleted	–
IA	Waterloo	Black Hawk	Waterloo Coal Gasification Plant	Proposed	50.00
IA	West Des Moines	Polk	Railroad Avenue Groundwater Contamination	Final	50.00
IA	West Point	Lee	E.i. Du Pont De Nemours & Co., Inc. (county Road X23)	Deleted	–
ID	Idaho Falls	Butte, Clark, Jefferson	Idaho National Engineering Laboratory (USDOE)	Final	51.91
ID	Lemhi County	Lemhi	Blackbird Mine	Proposed	50.00
ID	Mountain Home	Elmore	Mountain Home Air Force Base	Final	57.80
ID	Pocatello	Bannock	Pacific Hide & Fur Recycling Co.	Deleted	–
ID	Pocatello	Bannock	Union Pacific Railroad Co.	Deleted	–
ID	Pocatello	Power, Bannock	Eastern Michaud Flats Contamination	Final	57.80
ID	Rathdrum	Kootenai	Arrcom (drexler Enterprises)	Deleted	–
ID	Smelterville	Shoshone	Bunker Hill Mining & Metallurgical Complex	Final	54.76
ID	Soda Springs	Caribou	Kerr-McGee Chemical Corp. (Soda Springs Plant)	Final	51.91
ID	Soda Springs	Caribou	Monsanto Chemical Co. (Soda Springs Plant)	Final	54.77
ID	St. Maries	Benewah	St. Maries Creosote	Proposed	50.00
ID	Stibnite	Valley	Stibnite/Yellow Pine Mining Area	Proposed	50.00
IL	Antioch	Lake	H.O.D. Landfill	Final	34.68
IL	Beckemeyer	Clinton	Circle Smelting Corp	Proposed	70.71
IL	Belvidere	Boone	Belvidere Municipal Landfill	Final	28.62
IL	Belvidere	Boone	MIG/Dewane Landfill	Final	49.91
IL	Belvidere	Boone	Parsons Casket Hardware Co.	Final	55.58
IL	Byron	Ogle	Byron Salvage Yard	Final	33.93
IL	Carterville	Williamson	Sangamo Electric Dump/Crab Orchard Natl Wildlife Refuge (USDOI)	Final	40.70
IL	Chicago	Cook	Lake Calumet Cluster	Final	30.00
IL	Danville	Vermilion	Hegeler Zinc	Final	50.00
IL	Depue	Bureau	DePue/New Jersey Zinc/Mobil Chemical Corp.	Final	70.71
IL	Dupage County	Dupage	Kerr-McGee (Kress Creek/West Branch of DuPage River)	Final	39.05
IL	East Cape Girardeau	Alexander	Ilada Energy Co.	Deleted	–
IL	Galena	Jo Daviess	Bautsch-Gray Mine	Final	48.97
IL	Galesburg	Knox	Galesburg/Koppers Co.	Final	34.78
IL	Granite City	Madison	Jennison-Wright Corporation	Final	40.30
IL	Granite City	Madison	NL Industries/Taracorp Lead Smelter	Final	00.11
IL	Greenup	Cumberland	A & F Material Reclaiming, Inc.	Deleted	–
IL	Hartford	Madison	Chemetco	Final	30.00
IL	Hillsboro	Montgomery	Eagle Zinc Co Div T L Diamond	Final	50.00
IL	Joliet	Will	Amoco Chemicals (Joliet Landfill)	Final	39.44
IL	Joliet	Will	Joliet Army Ammunition Plant (Load-Assembly-Packing Area)	Final	35.23
IL	Joliet	Will	Joliet Army Ammunition Plant (Manufacturing Area)	Final	32.08
IL	La Salle	La Salle	LaSalle Electric Utilities	Final	42.06
IL	La Salle	La Salle	Matthiessen and Hegeler Zinc Company	Final	50.00
IL	Lawrenceville	Lawrence	Indian Refinery-Texaco Lawrenceville	Final	56.67
IL	Lemont	Dupage	Lenz Oil Service, Inc.	Final	42.33
IL	Libertyville	Lake	Petersen Sand & Gravel	Deleted	–
IL	Marshall	Clark	Velsicol Chemical Corp. (Marshall Plant)	Final	48.78
IL	Morristown	Winnebago	Acme Solvents Reclaiming, Inc. (Morristown Plant)	Final	31.98
IL	Ottawa	La Salle	Ottawa Radiation Areas	Final	50.00
IL	Pembroke Township	Kankakee	Cross Brothers Pail Recycling (Pembroke)	Final	42.04
IL	Quincy	Adams	Adams County Quincy Landfills 2&3	Final	34.21
IL	Rantoul	Champaign	Chanute Air Force Base	Proposed	48.30
IL	Rockford	Winnebago	Interstate Pollution Control, Inc.	Final	46.01
IL	Rockford	Winnebago	Pagel's Pit	Final	45.91
IL	Rockford	Winnebago	Southeast Rockford Ground Water Contamination	Final	42.24
IL	Rockton	Winnebago	Beloit Corp.	Final	52.08
IL	Sandoval	Marion	Sandoval Zinc Company	Final	30.00
IL	Sauget	St. Clair	Sauget Area 1	Proposed	50.00
IL	Sauget	St. Clair	Sauget Area 2	Proposed	50.00

St.	City/Area	County	Site Name	Status	Score[1]
IL	Savanna	Jo Daviess	Savanna Army Depot Activity	Final	42.20
IL	South Elgin	Kane	Tri-County Landfill Co./Waste Management of Illinois, Inc.	Final	42.76
IL	Taylor Springs	Montgomery	ASARCO Taylor Springs	Final	30.00
IL	Taylorville	Christian	Central Illinois Public Service Co.	Final	28.95
IL	Warrenville	Dupage	DuPage County Landfill/Blackwell Forest	Final	35.57
IL	Wauconda	Lake	Wauconda Sand & Gravel	Final	53.42
IL	Waukegan	Lake	Johns-Manville Corp.	Final	38.20
IL	Waukegan	Lake	Outboard Marine Corp.	Final	–
IL	Waukegan	Lake	Yeoman Creek Landfill	Final	33.23
IL	West Chicago	Dupage	Kerr-mcgee (reed-keppler Park)	Deleted	–
IL	West Chicago	Dupage	Kerr-McGee (Residential Areas)	Final	38.15
IL	West Chicago	Dupage	Kerr-mcgee (sewage Treatment Plant)	Deleted	–
IL	Woodstock	Mchenry	Woodstock Municipal Landfill	Final	50.10
IN	Bloomington	Monroe	Bennett Stone Quarry	Final	32.55
IN	Bloomington	Monroe	Lemon Lane Landfill	Final	29.31
IN	Bloomington	Monroe	Neal's Landfill (Bloomington)	Final	42.93
IN	Claypool	Kosciusko	Lakeland Disposal Service, Inc.	Final	34.10
IN	Columbia City	Whitley	Wayne Waste Oil	Final	42.33
IN	Columbus	Bartholomew	Columbus Old Municipal Landfill #1	Final	45.31
IN	Columbus	Bartholomew	Tri-state Plating	Deleted	–
IN	East Chicago	Lake	U.S. Smelter and Lead Refinery, Inc.	Final	58.31
IN	Elkhart	Elkhart	Conrail Rail Yard (Elkhart)	Final	42.24
IN	Elkhart	Elkhart	Himco Dump	Final	42.31
IN	Elkhart	Elkhart	Lane Street Ground Water Contamination	Final	40.53
IN	Elkhart	Elkhart	Lusher Street Ground Water Contamination	Final	50.00
IN	Elkhart	Elkhart	Main Street Well Field	Final	42.49
IN	Evansville	Vanderburgh	Jacobsville Neighborhood Soil Contamination	Final	35.52
IN	Fort Wayne	Allen	Fort Wayne Reduction Dump	Final	42.47
IN	Garden City	Bartholomew	Garden City Ground Water Plume	Proposed	50.00
IN	Gary	Lake	Gary Development Landfill	Final	30.00
IN	Gary	Lake	Lake Sandy Jo (M&M Landfill)	Final	38.21
IN	Gary	Lake	MIDCO I	Final	46.44
IN	Gary	Lake	MIDCO II	Final	30.16
IN	Gary	Lake	Ninth Avenue Dump	Final	40.32
IN	Griffith	Lake	American Chemical Service, Inc.	Final	34.98
IN	Hancock County	Hancock	Poer Farm	Deleted	–
IN	Indianapolis	Marion	Carter Lee Lumber Co.	Deleted	–
IN	Indianapolis	Marion	Keystone Corridor Ground Water Contamination	Proposed	50.00
IN	Indianapolis	Marion	Reilly Tar & Chemical Corp. (Indianapolis Plant)	Final	34.03
IN	Indianapolis	Marion	Southside Sanitary Landfill	Deleted	–
IN	Kokomo	Howard	Continental Steel Corp.	Final	31.85
IN	La Porte	La Porte	Fisher-Calo	Final	52.05
IN	Lafayette	Tippecanoe	Tippecanoe Sanitary Landfill, Inc	Final	42.24
IN	Lebanon	Boone	Wedzeb Enterprises, Inc.	Deleted	–
IN	Marion	Grant	Marion (Bragg) Dump	Final	35.25
IN	Martinsville	Morgan	Pike and Mulberry Streets PCE Plume	Final	50.00
IN	Michigan City	La Porte	Waste, Inc., Landfill	Deleted	–
IN	Mishawaka	St. Joseph	Douglass Road/Uniroyal, Inc., Landfill	Final	36.61
IN	Osceola	St. Joseph	Galen Myers Dump/Drum Salvage	Final	42.24
IN	Seymour	Jackson	Seymour Recycling Corp.	Final	–
IN	South Bend	St. Joseph	Beck's Lake	Proposed	50.00
IN	South Bend	St. Joseph	Whiteford Sales & Service Inc./nationalease	Deleted	–
IN	Spencer	Owen	Neal's Dump (spencer)	Deleted	–
IN	Terre Haute	Vigo	Elm Street Ground Water Contamination	Final	50.00
IN	Terre Haute	Vigo	International Minerals (e. Plant)	Deleted	–
IN	Vincennes	Knox	Prestolite Battery Division	Final	40.63
IN	Westville	La Porte	Cam-Or Inc.	Final	58.91
IN	Zionsville	Boone	Envirochem Corp.	Final	46.44
IN	Zionsville	Boone	Northside Sanitary Landfill, Inc.	Final	46.04

St.	City/Area	County	Site Name	Status	Score[1]
KS	Arkansas City	Cowley	Arkansas City Dump	Deleted	–
KS	Colby	Thomas	Ace Services	Final	50.00
KS	Delavan	Morris	Tri-County Public Airport	Proposed	50.00
KS	El Dorado	Butler	Pester Refinery Co.	Final	30.16
KS	Galena	Cherokee	Cherokee County	Final	58.15
KS	Great Bend	Barton	Plating, Inc.	Final	50.00
KS	Hutchinson	Reno	Obee Road	Final	33.62
KS	Iola	Allen	Former United Zinc & Associated Smelters	Final	50.00
KS	Junction City	Geary	Fort Riley	Final	33.79
KS	Olathe	Johnson	Chemical Commodities, Inc.	Final	50.00
KS	Shawnee Mission	Johnson	Doepke Disposal (Holliday)	Final	47.46
KS	Topeka	Shawnee	Hydro-flex Inc.	Deleted	–
KS	Wichita	Sedgwick	29th & Mead Ground Water Contamination	Deleted	–
KS	Wichita	Sedgwick	57th and North Broadway Streets Site	Final	50.00
KS	Wichita	Sedgwick	Big River Sand Co.	Deleted	–
KS	Wichita	Sedgwick	Johns' Sludge Pond	Deleted	–
KS	Winfield	Cowley	Strother Field Industrial Park	Final	33.62
KS	Wright	Ford	Wright Ground Water Contamination	Final	50.00
KY	Auburn	Logan	Caldwell Lace Leather Co., Inc.	Final	34.21
KY	Brooks	Bullitt	A.I. Taylor (valley Of Drums)	Deleted	–
KY	Brooks	Bullitt	Smith's Farm	Final	32.69
KY	Calvert City	Marshall	Airco	Final	33.29
KY	Calvert City	Marshall	B.F. Goodrich	Final	33.01
KY	Dayhoit	Harlan	National Electric Coil Co./Cooper Industries	Final	50.00
KY	Hawesville	Hancock	National Southwire Aluminum Co.	Final	50.00
KY	Hillsboro	Fleming	Maxey Flats Nuclear Disposal	Final	31.71
KY	Howe Valley	Hardin	Howe Valley Landfill	Deleted	–
KY	Island	Mclean	Brantley Landfill	Final	52.73
KY	Jefferson County	Jefferson	Distler Farm	Final	34.62
KY	Louisville	Jefferson	Lee's Lane Landfill	Deleted	–
KY	Maceo	Daviess	Green River Disposal, Inc.	Final	29.12
KY	Mayfield	Graves	General Tire & Rubber Co. (mayfield Landfill)	Deleted	–
KY	Newport	Campbell	Newport Dump	Deleted	–
KY	Olaton	Ohio	Fort Hartford Coal Co. Stone Quarry	Final	40.04
KY	Paducah	Mccracken	Paducah Gaseous Diffusion Plant (USDOE)	Final	56.95
KY	Peewee Valley	Oldham	Red Penn Sanitation Co. Landfill	Deleted	–
KY	Shepherdsville	Bullitt	Tri-City Disposal Co.	Final	33.82
KY	West Point	Hardin	Distler Brickyard	Final	44.77
LA	Abbeville	Vermilion	D.I. Mud, Inc.	Deleted	–
LA	Abbeville	Vermilion Parish	Gulf Coast Vacuum Services	Deleted	–
LA	Abbeville	Vermilion Parish	Pab Oil & Chemical Service, Inc.	Deleted	–
LA	Alexandria	Rapides Parish	Ruston Foundry	Deleted	–
LA	Ascension Parish	Ascension Parish	Dutchtown Treatment Plant	Deleted	–
LA	Bayou Sorrel	Iberville Parish	Bayou Sorrel	Deleted	–
LA	Bossier City	Bossier Parish	Highway 71/72 Refinery	Proposed	50.00
LA	Darrow	Ascension Parish	Old Inger Oil Refinery	Deleted	–
LA	Denham Springs	Livingston Parish	Combustion, Inc.	Final	33.79
LA	Doyline	Webster Parish	Louisiana Army Ammunition Plant	Final	30.26
LA	Grand Cheniere	Cameron Parish	Mallard Bay Landing Bulk Plant	Deleted	–
LA	Jennings	Acadia	EVR-Wood Treating/Evangeline Refining Company	Final	48.20
LA	Lake Charles	Calcasieu Parish	Gulf State Utilities-North Ryan Street	Proposed	50.43
LA	Madisonville	St. Tammany	Madisonville Creosote Works	Final	48.01
LA	Marion	Union Parish	Marion Pressure Treating	Final	50.00
LA	New Orleans	Orleans Parish	Agriculture Street Landfill	Final	50.00
LA	Ponchatoula	Tangipahoa Parish	Delatte Metals	Deleted	–
LA	Scotlandville	East Baton Rouge	Devil's Swamp Lake	Proposed	50.00
LA	Scotlandville	East Baton Rouge Parish	Petro-Processors of Louisiana, Inc.	Final	41.44
LA	Slaughter	East Feliciana Parish	Central Wood Preserving Co.	Deleted	–
LA	Slidell	St. Tammany	Bayou Bonfouca	Final	29.78
LA	Slidell	St. Tammany Parish	Southern Shipbuilding	Deleted	–

St.	City/Area	County	Site Name	Status	Score[1]
LA	Sorrento	Ascension Parish	Cleve Reber	Deleted	–
LA	Winnfield	Winn Parish	American Creosote Works, Inc. (Winnfield Plant)	Final	50.70
MA	Acton	Middlesex	W.R. Grace & Co., Inc. (Acton Plant)	Final	59.31
MA	Ashland	Middlesex	Nyanza Chemical Waste Dump	Final	69.22
MA	Attleboro	Bristol	Walton & Lonsbury Inc.	Final	58.30
MA	Bedford	Middlesex	Hanscom Field/Hanscom Air Force Base	Final	50.00
MA	Bedford	Middlesex	Naval Weapons Industrial Reserve Plant	Final	50.00
MA	Billerica	Middlesex	Iron Horse Park	Final	42.93
MA	Bridgewater	Plymouth	Cannon Engineering Corp. (CEC)	Final	39.89
MA	Concord	Middlesex	Nuclear Metals, Inc.	Final	58.31
MA	Danvers	Essex	Creese & Cook Tannery (Former)	Final	60.57
MA	Dartmouth	Bristol	Re-Solve, Inc.	Final	47.71
MA	Fairhaven	Bristol	Atlas Tack Corp.	Final	42.60
MA	Falmouth	Barnstable	Otis Air National Guard Base/Camp Edwards	Final	45.92
MA	Fort Devens	Worcester, Middlesex	Fort Devens	Final	42.24
MA	Groveland	Essex	Groveland Wells	Final	40.74
MA	Haverhill	Essex	Haverhill Municipal Landfill	Final	30.29
MA	Holbrook	Norfolk	Baird & McGuire	Final	66.35
MA	Lanesboro	Berkshire	Rose Disposal Pit	Final	33.03
MA	Lowell	Middlesex	Silresim Chemical Corp.	Final	42.72
MA	Mansfield	Bristol	Hatheway and Patterson Company	Final	56.60
MA	Natick	Middlesex	Natick Laboratory Army Research, Development & Engineering Ctr	Final	50.00
MA	New Bedford	Bristol	New Bedford Site	Final	–
MA	New Bedford	Bristol	Sullivan's Ledge	Final	32.77
MA	Norton/attleboro	Bristol	Shpack Landfill	Final	29.45
MA	Norwood	Norfolk	Norwood Pcbs	Deleted	–
MA	Palmer	Hampden	PSC Resources	Final	38.66
MA	Pittsfield	Berkshire	GE - Housatonic River	Proposed	70.71
MA	Plymouth	Plymouth	Plymouth Harbor/cannon Engineering Corp.	Deleted	–
MA	Salem	Essex	Salem Acres	Deleted	–
MA	Sudbury	Middlesex	Fort Devens-sudbury Training Annex	Deleted	–
MA	Tewksbury	Middlesex	Sutton Brook Disposal Area	Final	57.12
MA	Tyngsborough	Middlesex	Charles-George Reclamation Trust Landfill	Final	47.20
MA	Walpole	Norfolk	Blackburn and Union Privileges	Final	50.00
MA	Watertown	Middlesex	Materials Technology Laboratory (usarmy)	Deleted	–
MA	Westborough	Worcester	Hocomonco Pond	Final	44.80
MA	Weymouth	Norfolk	South Weymouth Naval Air Station	Final	50.00
MA	Wilmington	Middlesex	Olin Chemical	Final	50.00
MA	Woburn	Middlesex	Industri-Plex	Final	72.42
MA	Woburn	Middlesex	Wells G&H	Final	42.71
MD	Aberdeen	Harford	Aberdeen Proving Ground (Michaelsville Landfill)	Final	31.09
MD	Abingdon	Harford	Bush Valley Landfill	Final	40.30
MD	Andrews Air Force Base	Prince George's	Andrews Air Force Base	Final	50.00
MD	Annapolis	Anne Arundel	Middletown Road Dump	Deleted	–
MD	Baltimore	Anne Arundel	Curtis Bay Coast Guard Yard	Final	50.00
MD	Baltimore	Baltimore City	Chemical Metals Industries, Inc.	Deleted	–
MD	Baltimore	Baltimore City	Kane & Lombard Street Drums	Final	30.15
MD	Beltsville	Prince George's	Beltsville Agricultural Research Center (USDA)	Final	50.00
MD	Brandywine	Prince George's	Brandywine DRMO	Final	50.15
MD	Colora	Cecil	Woodlawn County Landfill	Final	48.13
MD	Cumberland	Allegany	Limestone Road	Final	30.54
MD	Dundalk	Baltimore	Sauer Dump	Final	50.00
MD	Edgewood	Harford	Aberdeen Proving Ground (Edgewood Area)	Final	53.57
MD	Elkton	Cecil	Dwyer Property Ground Water Plume	Final	50.00
MD	Elkton	Cecil	Sand, Gravel and Stone	Final	41.08
MD	Elkton	Cecil	Spectron, Inc.	Final	51.42
MD	Fort Detrick	Frederick	Fort Detrick Area B Ground Water	Final	49.52
MD	Hagerstown	Washington	Central Chemical (Hagerstown)	Final	50.00
MD	Harmans	Anne Arundel	Mid-atlantic Wood Preservers, Inc.	Deleted	–

St.	City/Area	County	Site Name	Status	Score[1]
MD	Hollywood	St. Mary's	Southern Maryland Wood Treating	Deleted	–
MD	Indian Head	Charles	Indian Head Naval Surface Warfare Center	Final	50.00
MD	North East	Cecil	Ordnance Products, Inc.	Final	32.15
MD	Odenton	Anne Arundel	Fort George G. Meade	Final	51.44
MD	Patuxent River	St. Mary's	Patuxent River Naval Air Station	Final	50.00
MD	Rosedale	Baltimore City	68th Street Dump	Proposed	50.00
ME	Augusta	Kennebec	O'Connor	Final	31.86
ME	Brooksville (cape Rosier)	Hancock	Callahan Mine	Final	50.00
ME	Brunswick	Cumberland	Brunswick Naval Air Station	Final	43.38
ME	Corinna	Penobscot	Eastland Woolen Mill	Final	70.71
ME	Gray	Cumberland	McKin Co.	Final	60.97
ME	Kittery	York	Portsmouth Naval Shipyard	Final	50.00
ME	Leeds	Androscoggin	Leeds Metal	Final	32.25
ME	Limestone	Aroostook	Loring Air Force Base	Final	34.49
ME	Meddybemps	Washington	Eastern Surplus	Final	50.00
ME	Plymouth	Penobscot	West Site/Hows Corners	Final	50.00
ME	Saco	York	Saco Municipal Landfill	Final	29.49
ME	Saco	York	Saco Tannery Waste Pits	Deleted	–
ME	South Hope	Knox	Union Chemical Co., Inc.	Final	32.11
ME	Washburn	Aroostook	Pinette's Salvage Yard	Deleted	–
ME	Winthrop	Kennebec	Winthrop Landfill	Final	35.62
MI	Adrian	Lenawee	Anderson Development Co.	Deleted	–
MI	Albion	Calhoun	Albion-Sheridan Township Landfill	Final	33.79
MI	Albion	Calhoun	McGraw Edison Corp.	Final	33.42
MI	Allegan	Allegan	Rockwell International Corp. (Allegan Plant)	Final	52.15
MI	Battle Creek	Calhoun	Verona Well Field	Final	40.00
MI	Bay City	Bay	Bay City Middlegrounds	Proposed	50.00
MI	Belding	Ionia	H & K Sales	Deleted	–
MI	Benton Harbor	Berrien	Aircraft Components (D & L Sales)	Final	–
MI	Brighton	Livingston	Rasmussen's Dump	Final	31.80
MI	Bronson	Branch	North Bronson Industrial Area	Final	33.93
MI	Buchanan	Berrien	Electrovoice	Final	35.36
MI	Cadillac	Wexford	Kysor Industrial Corp.	Final	33.04
MI	Cadillac	Wexford	Northernaire Plating	Final	57.93
MI	Charlevoix	Charlevoix	Charlevoix Municipal Well	Deleted	–
MI	Clare	Clare	Clare Water Supply	Final	38.43
MI	Dalton Township	Muskegon	Duell & Gardner Landfill	Final	34.68
MI	Dalton Township	Muskegon	Ott/Story/Cordova Chemical Co.	Final	53.41
MI	Davisburg	Oakland	Springfield Township Dump	Final	51.97
MI	Detroit	Wayne	Carter Industrials, Inc.	Deleted	–
MI	Filer City	Manistee	Packaging Corp. of America	Final	51.91
MI	Grand Ledge	Eaton	Parsons Chemical Works, Inc.	Final	31.32
MI	Grand Rapids	Kent	Butterworth #2 Landfill	Final	50.31
MI	Grand Rapids	Kent	Folkertsma Refuse	Deleted	–
MI	Grand Rapids	Kent	H. Brown Co., Inc.	Final	39.88
MI	Grand Rapids	Kent	State Disposal Landfill, Inc.	Final	42.24
MI	Grandville	Kent	Organic Chemicals, Inc.	Final	32.93
MI	Green Oak Township	Livingston	Spiegelberg Landfill	Deleted	–
MI	Greilickville	Leelanau	Grand Traverse Overall Supply Co.	Final	35.53
MI	Hartford	Van Buren	Burrows Sanitation	Final	30.59
MI	Highland	Oakland	Hi-Mill Manufacturing Co.	Final	49.54
MI	Holland	Ottawa	Waste Management Of Michigan (holland Lagoons)	Deleted	–
MI	Houghton County	Houghton	Torch Lake	Final	46.72
MI	Howard Township	Cass	U.S. Aviex	Final	33.66
MI	Howell	Livingston	Shiawassee River	Final	31.01
MI	Ionia	Ionia	American Anodco, Inc.	Final	57.99
MI	Ionia	Ionia	Ionia City Landfill	Final	31.31
MI	Kalamazoo	Kalamazoo	Allied Paper, Inc./Portage Creek/Kalamazoo River	Final	36.41
MI	Kalamazoo	Kalamazoo	Auto Ion Chemicals, Inc.	Final	32.07

St.	City/Area	County	Site Name	Status	Score[1]
MI	Kalamazoo	Kalamazoo	Michigan Disposal Service (Cork Street Landfill)	Final	37.93
MI	Kalamazoo	Kalamazoo	Roto-Finish Co., Inc.	Final	40.70
MI	Kent City	Kent	Kent City Mobile Home Park	Deleted	–
MI	Kentwood	Kent	Kentwood Landfill	Final	35.39
MI	Lake Ann	Benzie	Metal Working Shop	Deleted	–
MI	Lansing	Ingham	Adam's Plating	Final	29.64
MI	Lansing	Ingham	Barrels, Inc.	Final	42.24
MI	Lansing Township	Ingham	Motor Wheel, Inc.	Final	48.91
MI	Macomb Township	Macomb	South Macomb Disposal Authority (Landfills #9 and #9A)	Final	33.67
MI	Mancelona Township	Antrim	Tar Lake	Final	48.55
MI	Marquette	Marquette	Cliff/dow Dump	Deleted	–
MI	Metamora	Lapeer	Metamora Landfill	Final	35.51
MI	Muskegon	Muskegon	Bofors Nobel, Inc.	Final	53.42
MI	Muskegon	Muskegon	Kaydon Corp.	Final	34.21
MI	Muskegon	Muskegon	Peerless Plating Co.	Final	43.94
MI	Muskegon	Muskegon	Thermo-Chem, Inc.	Final	53.36
MI	Muskegon Heights	Muskegon	SCA Independent Landfill	Final	34.75
MI	Oscoda	Iosco	Hedblum Industries	Final	37.29
MI	Oscoda	Iosco	Wurtsmith Air Force Base	Proposed	50.00
MI	Oshtemo Township	Kalamazoo	K&L Avenue Landfill	Final	38.10
MI	Ossineke	Alpena	Ossineke Ground Water Contamination	Deleted	–
MI	Otisville	Genesee	Forest Waste Products	Final	38.64
MI	Park Township	Ottawa	Southwest Ottawa County Landfill	Final	39.66
MI	Pere Marquette Twp	Mason	Mason County Landfill	Deleted	–
MI	Petoskey	Emmet	Petoskey Municipal Well Field	Final	42.68
MI	Pleasant Plains Twp	Lake	Wash King Laundry	Final	40.03
MI	Rochester Hills	Oakland	J & L Landfill	Final	31.65
MI	Rose Center	Oakland	Cemetery Dump	Deleted	–
MI	Rose Township	Oakland	Rose Township Dump	Final	50.92
MI	Sault Ste Marie	Chippewa	Cannelton Industries, Inc.	Final	30.16
MI	Sparta Township	Kent	Sparta Landfill	Final	32.00
MI	St. Clair Shores	Macomb	Ten-Mile Drain	Final	48.88
MI	St. Joseph	Berrien	Bendix Corp./Allied Automotive	Final	37.27
MI	St. Louis	Gratiot	Gratiot County Golf Course	Deleted	–
MI	St. Louis	Gratiot	Gratiot County Landfill	Final	–
MI	St. Louis	Gratiot	Gratiot County Golf Course	Final	29.54
MI	St. Louis	Gratiot	Velsicol Chemical Corp.(Michigan)	Final	52.29
MI	Sturgis	St. Joseph	Sturgis Municipal Wells	Final	42.24
MI	Swartz Creek	Genesee	Berlin & Farro	Deleted	–
MI	Temperance	Monroe	Novaco Industries	Deleted	–
MI	Traverse City	Grand Traverse	Avenue E Ground Water Contamination	Deleted	–
MI	Utica	Macomb	G&H Landfill	Final	49.09
MI	Utica	Macomb	Liquid Disposal, Inc.	Final	63.28
MI	Whitehall	Muskegon	Muskegon Chemical Co.	Final	34.19
MI	Whitehall	Muskegon	Whitehall Municipal Wells	Deleted	–
MI	Wyandotte	Wayne	Lower Ecorse Creek Dump	Deleted	–
MI	Wyoming	Kent	Spartan Chemical Co.	Final	41.05
MI	Wyoming Township	Kent	Chem Central	Final	38.20
MN	Adrian	Nobles	Adrian Municipal Well Field	Deleted	–
MN	Andover	Anoka	South Andover Site	Final	35.41
MN	Andover	Anoka	Waste Disposal Engineering	Deleted	–
MN	Baytown Township	Washington	Baytown Township Ground Water Plume	Final	35.62
MN	Bemidji	Beltrami	Kummer Sanitary Landfill	Deleted	–
MN	Brainerd/baxter	Crow Wing	Burlington Northern (Brainerd/Baxter Plant)	Final	46.77
MN	Brooklyn Center	Hennepin	Joslyn Manufacturing & Supply Co.	Final	44.30
MN	Burnsville	Dakota	Freeway Sanitary Landfill	Final	45.91
MN	Cannon Falls	Dakota	Dakhue Sanitary Landfill	Deleted	–
MN	Cass Lake	Cass	St. Regis Paper Co.	Final	52.88
MN	Dakota County	Dakota	Pine Bend Sanitary Landfill	Deleted	–

St.	City/Area	County	Site Name	Status	Score[1]
MN	East Bethel Township	Anoka	East Bethel Demolition Landfill	Deleted	–
MN	Fairview Township	Cass	Agate Lake Scrapyard	Deleted	–
MN	Faribault	Rice	Nutting Truck & Caster Co.	Final	37.87
MN	Fridley	Anoka	Boise Cascade/onan Corp./medtronics, Inc.	Deleted	–
MN	Fridley	Anoka	FMC Corp. (Fridley Plant)	Final	65.50
MN	Fridley	Anoka	Fridley Commons Park Well Field	Final	50.00
MN	Fridley	Anoka	Kurt Manufacturing Co.	Final	31.41
MN	Fridley	Anoka	Naval Industrial Reserve Ordnance Plant	Final	30.83
MN	Hermantown	St. Louis	Arrowhead Refinery Co.	Final	43.75
MN	Lagrand Township	Douglas	Lagrand Sanitary Landfill	Deleted	–
MN	Lake Elmo	Washington	Washington County Landfill	Deleted	–
MN	Lehillier	Blue Earth	Lehillier/Mankato Site	Final	42.49
MN	Long Prairie	Todd	Long Prairie Ground Water Contamination	Final	31.94
MN	Minneapolis	Hennepin	General Mills/Henkel Corp.	Final	36.28
MN	Minneapolis	Hennepin	South Minneapolis Residential Soil Contamination	Final	44.58
MN	Minneapolis	Hennepin	Twin Cities Air Force Reserve Base (small Arms Range Landfill)	Deleted	–
MN	Minneapolis	Hennepin	Union Scrap Iron & Metal Co.	Deleted	–
MN	Minneapolis	Hennepin	Whittaker Corp.	Deleted	–
MN	Morris	Stevens	Morris Arsenic Dump	Deleted	–
MN	New Brighton	Ramsey	MacGillis & Gibbs/Bell Lumber & Pole Co.	Final	48.33
MN	New Brighton	Ramsey	New Brighton/Arden Hills/TCAAP (USARMY)	Final	59.16
MN	Oak Grove Township	Anoka	Oak Grove Sanitary Landfill	Deleted	–
MN	Oakdale	Washington	Oakdale Dump	Final	55.71
MN	Oronoco	Olmsted	Olmsted County Sanitary Landfill	Deleted	–
MN	Perham	Otter Tail	Perham Arsenic Site	Final	37.98
MN	Pine Bend	Dakota	Koch Refining Co./nrren Corp.	Deleted	–
MN	Rosemount	Dakota	University Of Minnesota (rosemount Research Center)	Deleted	–
MN	Sebeka	Wadena	Ritari Post & Pole	Final	29.81
MN	St. Augusta Township	Stearns	St. Augusta Sanitary Landfill/engen Dump	Deleted	–
MN	St. Louis County	St. Louis	St. Louis River Site	Final	32.08
MN	St. Louis Park	Hennepin	NI Industries/taracorp/golden Auto	Deleted	–
MN	St. Louis Park	Hennepin	Reilly Tar & Chemical Corp. (St. Louis Park Plant)	Final	–
MN	St. Paul	Ramsey	Koppers Coke	Final	55.05
MN	Waite Park	Stearns	Waite Park Wells	Final	31.94
MN	Windom	Cottonwood	Windom Dump	Deleted	–
MO	Amazonia	Andrew	Wheeling Disposal Service Co., Inc., Landfill	Deleted	–
MO	Annapolis	Iron	Annapolis Lead Mine	Final	56.67
MO	Bridgeton	St. Louis	Westlake Landfill	Final	29.85
MO	Caledonia	Washington	Washington County Lead District - Furnace Creek	Final	50.00
MO	Cape Girardeau	Cape Girardeau	Kem-pest Laboratories	Deleted	–
MO	Cape Girardeau	Cape Girardeau	Missouri Electric Works	Final	31.20
MO	Desloge	St. Francois	Big River Mine Tailings/St. Joe Minerals Corp.	Final	84.91
MO	Ellisville	St. Louis	Ellisville Site	Final	–
MO	Fredericktown	Madison	Madison County Mines	Final	58.41
MO	Granby	Newton	Newton County Mine Tailings	Final	50.00
MO	Imperial	Jefferson	Minker/Stout/Romaine Creek	Final	36.78
MO	Independence	Jackson	Lake City Army Ammunition Plant (Northwest Lagoon)	Final	33.62
MO	Jefferson County	Jefferson	Southwest Jefferson County Mining	Final	70.71
MO	Joplin	Jasper	Oronogo-Duenweg Mining Belt	Final	46.20
MO	Joplin	Newton	Newton County Wells	Final	50.00
MO	Kansas City	Jackson	Conservation Chemical Co.	Final	29.85
MO	Liberty	Clay	Lee Chemical	Final	46.81
MO	Malden	Dunklin	Bee Cee Manufacturing Co.	Final	28.59
MO	Moscow Mills	Lincoln	Shenandoah Stables	Deleted	–
MO	Neosho	Newton	Pools Prairie	Final	50.00
MO	New Haven	Franklin	Riverfront	Final	50.00
MO	North Kansas City	Clay	Armour Road	Final	50.00
MO	Old Mines	Washington	Washington County Lead District - Old Mines	Final	76.81
MO	Potosi	Washington	Washington County Lead District - Potosi	Final	50.00

St.	City/Area	County	Site Name	Status	Score[1]
MO	Republic	Greene	Solid State Circuits, Inc.	Final	37.93
MO	Richwoods	Washington	Washington County Lead District - Richwoods	Final	76.81
MO	Rogersville	Greene	Compass Plaza Well TCE	Final	50.00
MO	Sikeston	Scott	Quality Plating	Final	40.70
MO	Springfield	Greene	Fulbright Landfill	Final	40.60
MO	Springfield	Greene	North-u Drive Well Contamination	Deleted	–
MO	St. Charles	St. Charles	Weldon Spring Former Army Ordnance Works	Final	30.26
MO	St. Charles	St. Charles	Weldon Spring Quarry/Plant/Pits (USDOE/Army)	Final	58.60
MO	St. Louis	St. Louis	St. Louis Airport/Hazelwood Interim Storage/Futura Coatings Co.	Final	38.31
MO	Sullivan	Franklin	Oak Grove Village Well	Final	50.00
MO	Times Beach	St. Louis	Times Beach	Deleted	–
MO	Valley Park	St. Louis	Valley Park TCE	Final	35.57
MO	Verona	Lawrence	Syntex Facility	Final	43.78
MO	Vienna	Maries	Vienna Wells	Final	50.00
MP	Garapan	Saipan	Pcb Warehouse	Deleted	–
MS	Canton	Madison	Southeastern Wood Preserving	Final	48.03
MS	Clarksdale	Coahoma	Red Panther Chemical Company	Final	39.43
MS	Columbia	Marion	Newsom Brothers/old Reichhold Chemicals, Inc.	Deleted	–
MS	Columbus	Lowndes	Kerr-McGee Chemical Corp - Columbus	Final	52.47
MS	Flowood	Rankin	Flowood Site	Deleted	–
MS	Flowood	Rankin	Sonford Products	Final	31.66
MS	Greenville	Washington	Walcotte Chemical Co. Warehouses	Deleted	–
MS	Gulfport	Harrison	Chemfax, Inc.	Final	38.40
MS	Hattiesburg	Lamar	Davis Timber Company	Final	48.57
MS	Louisville	Winston	American Creosote Works, Inc.	Final	62.20
MS	Picayune	Pearl River	Picayune Wood Treating	Final	51.03
MS	Wesson	Copiah	Potter Co.	Proposed	50.00
MT	Anaconda	Deer Lodge	Anaconda Co. Smelter	Final	58.71
MT	Basin	Jefferson	Basin Mining Area	Final	61.15
MT	Billings	Yellowstone	Lockwood Solvent Ground Water Plume	Final	45.69
MT	Black Eagle	Cascade	ACM Smelter and Refinery	Final	54.26
MT	Bozeman	Gallatin	Idaho Pole Co.	Final	38.29
MT	Butte	Silver Bow	Montana Pole and Treating	Final	33.03
MT	Butte	Silver Bow, Deer Lodge	Silver Bow Creek/Butte Area	Final	63.76
MT	Columbus	Stillwater	Mouat Industries	Final	31.66
MT	East Helena	Lewis And Clark	East Helena Site	Final	61.65
MT	Helena	Lewis And Clark	Upper Tenmile Creek Mining Area	Final	50.00
MT	Libby	Lincoln	Libby Asbestos	Final	–
MT	Libby	Lincoln	Libby Ground Water Contamination	Final	37.67
MT	Livingston	Park	Burlington Northern Livingston Shop Complex	Proposed	50.00
MT	Milltown	Missoula	Milltown Reservoir Sediments	Final	43.78
MT	Missoula	Missoula	Smurfit-Stone Mill	Proposed	50.00
MT	Monarch	Cascade, Judith Basin	Barker Hughesville Mining District	Final	50.00
MT	Neihart	Cascade	Carpenter Snow Creek Mining District	Final	50.00
MT	Superior	Mineral	Flat Creek IMM	Final	51.33
NC	210 Miles Of Roads	Warren	Roadside Pcb Spill	Deleted	–
NC	Aberdeen	Moore	Aberdeen Contaminated Ground Water	Final	50.00
NC	Aberdeen	Moore	Aberdeen Pesticide Dumps	Final	52.70
NC	Aberdeen	Moore	Geigy Chemical Corp. (Aberdeen Plant)	Final	33.02
NC	Arden	Buncombe	Blue Ridge Plating Company	Final	38.67
NC	Ashe County	Ashe	Ore Knob Mine	Final	50.00
NC	Asheville	Buncombe	CTS of Asheville, Inc.	Final	38.40
NC	Belmont	Gaston	Jadco-Hughes Facility	Final	42.00
NC	Castle Hayne	New Hanover	Reasor Chemical Company	Final	32.14
NC	Charlotte	Mecklenburg	Martin-marietta, Sodyeco, Inc.	Deleted	–
NC	Charlotte	Mecklenburg	Ram Leather Care	Final	40.43
NC	Concord	Cabarrus	Bypass 601 Ground Water Contamination	Final	37.93
NC	Cordova	Richmond	Charles Macon Lagoon & Drum Storage	Final	47.10
NC	East Flat Rock	Henderson	General Electric Co/Shepherd Farm	Final	70.71

St.	City/Area	County	Site Name	Status	Score[1]
NC	Fayetteville	Cumberland	Cape Fear Wood Preserving	Final	34.09
NC	Fayetteville	Cumberland	Carolina Transformer Co.	Final	33.76
NC	Gastonia	Gaston	Davis Park Road TCE	Final	33.50
NC	Gastonia	Gaston	Hemphill Road TCE	Proposed	50.00
NC	Havelock	Craven	Cherry Point Marine Corps Air Station	Final	70.71
NC	Hazelwood	Haywood	Benfield Industries, Inc.	Final	31.67

Notes: *(1) Federal Register Hazard Rankings System (HRS) score. The HRS is a model that is used to evaluate the relative threats to human health and the environment posed by actual or potential releases of hazardous substances, pollutants, and contaminants. The HRS criteria take into account the population at risk, the hazard potential of the substances, as well as the potential for contamination of drinking water supplies, direct human contact, destruction of sensitive ecosystems, damage to natural resources affecting the human food chain, contamination of surface water used for recreation or potable water consumption, and contamination of ambient air. The higher the score, the higher the potential threat to human health or the environment.*
Source: *U.S. Environmental Protection Agency, CERCLIS Hazardous Waste Sites, August 29, 2013*

2011 ATSDR Substance Priority List

2011 Rank	Substance Name	Totals Points	2007 Rank	CAS Number[1]
1	Arsenic	1665.5	1	007440-38-2
2	Lead	1529.1	2	007439-92-1
3	Mercury	1460.9	3	007439-97-6
4	Vinyl Chloride	1361.1	4	000075-01-4
5	Polychlorinated Biphenyls	1344.1	5	001336-36-3
6	Benzene	1332.0	6	000071-43-2
7	Cadmium	1318.7	7	007440-43-9
8	Benzo(a)Pyrene	1305.7	9	000050-32-8
9	Polycyclic Aromatic Hydrocarbons	1282.3	8	130498-29-2
10	Benzo(b)Fluoranthene	1252.4	10	000205-99-2
11	Chloroform	1207.5	11	000067-66-3
12	Aroclor 1260	1190.0	14	011096-82-5
13	DDT, p,p'-	1183.0	12	000050-29-3
14	Aroclor 1254	1171.7	13	011097-69-1
15	Dibenzo(a,h)Anthracene	1155.2	15	000053-70-3
16	Trichloroethylene	1151.1	16	000079-01-6
17	Chromium, Hexavalent	1146.6	18	018540-29-9
18	Dieldrin	1143.1	17	000060-57-1
19	Phosphorus, White	1141.9	19	007723-14-0
20	Hexachlorobutadiene	1128.5	22	000087-68-3
21	DDE, p,p'-	1127.2	21	000072-55-9
22	Chlordane	1126.4	20	000057-74-9
23	Coal Tar Creosote	1124.8	23	008001-58-9
24	Aroclor 1242	1123.8	29	053469-21-9
25	Aldrin	1115.8	24	000309-00-2
26	DDD, p,p'-	1114.2	25	000072-54-8
27	Aroclor 1248	1103.9	27	012672-29-6
28	Heptachlor	1101.1	34	000076-44-8
29	Aroclor	1099.4	30	012767-79-2
30	Benzidine	1090.6	26	000092-87-5
31	Acrolein	1088.5	37	000107-02-8
32	Toxaphene	1087.7	31	008001-35-2
33	Tetrachloroethylene	1077.4	33	000127-18-4
34	Hexachlorocyclohexane, Gamma-	1074.7	32	000058-89-9
35	Cyanide	1071.9	28	000057-12-5
36	Hexachlorocyclohexane, Beta-	1053.5	36	000319-85-7
37	Benzo(a)Anthracene	1047.6	39	000056-55-3
38	Disulfoton	1047.2	38	000298-04-4
39	1,2-Dibromoethane	1041.9	35	000106-93-4
40	Endrin	1038.3	41	000072-20-8
41	Diazinon	1036.7	56	000333-41-5
42	Hexachlorocyclohexane, Delta-	1034.8	43	000319-86-8
43	Beryllium	1032.7	42	007440-41-7
44	Endosulfan	1028.0	54	000115-29-7
45	Aroclor 1221	1027.1	48	011104-28-2
46	1,2-Dibromo-3-Chloropropane	1025.8	44	000096-12-8
47	Heptachlor Epoxide	1021.4	46	001024-57-3
48	Endosulfan, Alpha	1018.4	57	000959-98-8
49	Cis-Chlordane	1016.1	59	005103-71-9
50	Carbon Tetrachloride	1015.5	47	000056-23-5
51	Aroclor 1016	1011.9	51	012674-11-2
52	Cobalt	1010.9	49	007440-48-4
53	Pentachlorophenol	1009.0	45	000087-86-5
54	DDT, o,p'-	1007.9	50	000789-02-6
55	Methoxychlor	1006.3	61	000072-43-5

2011 Rank	Substance Name	Totals Points	2007 Rank	CAS Number[1]
56	Endosulfan Sulfate	1003.9	55	001031-07-8
57	Nickel	998.7	53	007440-02-0
58	Di-N-Butyl Phthalate	997.3	52	000084-74-2
59	Endrin Ketone	992.0	63	053494-70-5
60	Dibromochloropropane	983.0	60	067708-83-2
61	Benzo(k)Fluoranthene	972.2	62	000207-08-9
62	Xylenes, Total	969.2	58	001330-20-7
63	Trans-Chlordane	968.3	64	005103-74-2
64	Endosulfan, Beta	967.6	67	033213-65-9
65	Chlorpyrifos	963.9	127	002921-88-2
66	Chromium(vi) Oxide	960.0	65	001333-82-0
67	Aroclor 1232	958.2	68	011141-16-5
68	Endrin Aldehyde	957.7	69	007421-93-4
69	Methane	953.4	66	000074-82-8
70	2-Hexanone	941.4	72	000591-78-6
71	2,3,7,8-Tetrachlorodibenzo-P-Dioxin	940.9	73	001746-01-6
72	3,3'-Dichlorobenzidine	940.6	40	000091-94-1
73	Benzofluoranthene	935.7	70	056832-73-6
74	Toluene	924.1	71	000108-88-3
75	Zinc	919.1	74	007440-66-6
76	Di(2-Ethylhexyl)Phthalate	908.0	76	000117-81-7
77	Pentachlorobenzene	906.8	155	000008-93-5
78	Chromium	897.5	77	007440-47-3
79	Aroclor 1240	888.3	81	071328-89-7
80	Naphthalene	881.4	78	000091-20-3
81	1,1-Dichloroethene	879.5	79	000075-35-4
82	2,4,6-Trinitrotoluene	877.5	82	000118-96-7
83	2,4,6-Trichlorophenol	866.4	86	000088-06-2
84	Bis(2-Chloroethyl) Ether	866.3	88	000111-44-4
85	Bromodichloroethane	866.2	83	000683-53-4
86	Methylene Chloride	865.6	80	000075-09-2
87	DDD, o,p'-	865.6	151	000053-19-0
88	Hydrazine	000.0	04	000302-01-2
89	2,4-Dinitrophenol	858.4	87	000051-28-5
90	4,4'-Methylenebis(2-Chloroaniline)	857.2	152	000101-14-4
91	1,2-Dichloroethane	853.6	85	000107-06-2
92	Thiocyanate	845.8	89	000302-04-5
93	Hexachlorobenzene	844.3	93	000118-74-1
94	Asbestos	841.4	90	001332-21-4
95	Radium-226	833.3	95	013982-63-3
96	Cyclotrimethylenetrinitramine (RDX)	831.8	92	000121-82-4
97	Uranium	831.8	98	007440-61-1
98	2,4-Dinitrotoluene	831.2	94	000121-14-2
99	Ethion	829.9	96	000563-12-2
100	Radium	827.7	100	007440-14-4
101	4,6-Dinitro-O-Cresol	827.3	102	000534-52-1
102	Thorium	823.4	101	007440-29-1
103	Dimethylarsinic Acid	821.2	75	000075-60-5
104	Chlorine	820.6	91	007782-50-5
105	Radon	818.6	105	010043-92-2
106	1,3,5-Trinitrobenzene	818.6	103	000099-35-4
107	Hexachlorocyclohexane, Alpha-	817.3	115	000319-84-6
108	Radium-228	815.3	106	015262-20-1
109	Thorium-230	813.7	107	014269-63-7
110	1,1,1-Trichloroethane	812.4	97	000071-55-6
111	Uranium-235	812.1	107	015117-96-1
112	Uranium-234	809.6	111	013966-29-5
113	Thorium-228	809.5	113	014274-82-9
114	Radon-222	809.3	114	014859-67-7

2011 Rank	Substance Name	Totals Points	2007 Rank	CAS Number[1]
115	Coal Tars	808.2	118	008007-45-2
116	Ethylbenzene	807.7	99	000100-41-4
117	Chlorobenzene	807.0	104	000108-90-7
118	N-Nitrosodi-N-Propylamine	806.9	112	000621-64-7
119	Chrysotile Asbestos	806.2	119	012001-29-5
120	Methylmercury	806.0	123	022967-92-6
120	Plutonium-239	806.0	121	015117-48-3
122	Polonium-210	805.6	122	013981-52-7
123	Plutonium-238	805.2	124	013981-16-3
124	Lead-210	805.1	125	014255-04-0
125	Copper	804.7	128	007440-50-8
126	Barium	804.7	109	007440-39-3
127	Amosite Asbestos	804.3	131	012172-73-5
127	Plutonium	804.3	126	007440-07-5
127	Strontium-90	804.3	119	010098-97-2
130	Radon-220	804.2	130	022481-48-7
131	Americium-241	803.8	129	086954-36-1
132	Tributyltin	802.9	134	000688-73-3
133	Fluoranthene	802.6	110	000206-44-0
134	Guthion	802.6	135	000086-50-0
135	Chlordecone	802.1	138	000143-50-0
136	Neptunium-237	801.9	136	013994-20-2
137	Hydrogen Cyanide	801.5	133	000074-90-8
138	Plutonium-240	801.4	138	014119-33-6
139	1,2,3-Trichlorobenzene	800.3	116	000087-61-6
140	Manganese	799.4	117	007439-96-5
141	S,S,S-Tributyl Phosphorotrithioate	797.6	141	000078-48-8
142	Chrysene	793.4	137	000218-01-9
143	2,4,5-Trichlorophenol	790.4	222	000095-95-4
144	Polybrominated Biphenyls	784.3	143	067774-32-7
145	Dicofol	783.8	144	000115-32-2
146	Selenium	778.3	147	007782-49-2
147	1,1,2,2-Tetrachloroethane	777.5	146	000079-34-5
148	Heptachlorodibenzo-P-Dioxin	773.8	154	037871-00-4
149	Parathion	773.5	145	000056-38-2
150	Hexachlorocyclohexane, Technical Grade	773.2	148	000608-73-1
151	Trichlorofluoroethane	772.4	149	027154-33-2
152	Bromine	770.1	142	007726-95-6
153	Heptachlorodibenzofuran	755.5	166	038998-75-3
154	Trifluralin	754.3	150	001582-09-8
155	1,3-Butadiene	750.4	156	000106-99-0
156	1,2,3,4,6,7,8,9-Octachlorodibenzofuran	742.9	162	039001-02-0
157	Ammonia	741.8	157	007664-41-7
158	2-Methylnaphthalene	728.9	158	000091-57-6
159	1,4-Dichlorobenzene	725.5	159	000106-46-7
160	1,1-Dichloroethane	725.0	160	000075-34-3
161	2,3,4,7,8-Pentachlorodibenzofuran	723.6	168	057117-31-4
162	Naled	720.6	235	000300-76-5
163	Hexachlorocyclopentadiene	718.1	165	000077-47-4
164	1,2-Diphenylhydrazine	717.9	167	000122-66-7
165	1,1,2-Trichloroethane	717.0	163	000079-00-5
166	Phorate	715.2	225	000298-02-2
167	Trichloroethane	713.8	164	025323-89-1
168	Acenaphthene	711.8	161	000083-32-9
169	Tetrachlorobiphenyl	709.2	169	026914-33-0
170	Oxychlordane	705.5	171	027304-13-8
171	Palladium	705.4	180	007440-05-3
172	Cresol, Para-	704.8	170	000106-44-5

2011 Rank	Substance Name	Totals Points	2007 Rank	CAS Number[1]
173	Indeno(1,2,3-Cd)Pyrene	702.6	174	000193-39-5
174	Gamma-Chlordene	701.9	175	056641-38-4
175	1,2-Dichlorobenzene	698.0	172	000095-50-1
176	Tetrachlorophenol	697.0	177	025167-83-3
177	1,2-Dichloroethene, Trans-	695.5	173	000156-60-5
178	Chloroethane	688.9	183	000075-00-3
179	Phenol	688.4	182	000108-95-2
180	P-Xylene	686.6	185	000106-42-3
181	Aluminum	684.7	187	007429-90-5
182	Carbon Disulfide	683.0	176	000075-15-0
183	Carbon Monoxide	682.2	189	000630-08-0
184	2,4-Dimethylphenol	680.5	188	000105-67-9
185	Dibenzofuran	677.3	186	000132-64-9
186	Acetone	676.5	184	000067-64-1
187	Hexachloroethane	669.4	197	000067-72-1
188	Bis(2-Methoxyethyl) Phthalate	667.4	194	034006-76-3
189	Chloromethane	666.3	193	000074-87-3
190	Hexachlorodibenzofuran	660.1	181	055684-94-1
191	Butyl Benzyl Phthalate	659.1	195	000085-68-7
192	Hydrogen Sulfide	656.3	191	007783-06-4
193	Dichlorvos	655.5	240	000062-73-7
194	Cresol, Ortho-	653.4	190	000095-48-7
195	Dibenzofurans, Chlorinated	653.0	236	042934-53-2
196	Hexachlorodibenzo-P-Dioxin	651.7	153	034465-46-8
197	Vanadium	649.9	198	007440-62-2
198	N-Nitrosodimethylamine	648.3	199	000062-75-9
199	1,2,4-Trichlorobenzene	647.4	200	000120-82-1
200	Ethoprop	643.7	236	013194-48-4
201	Tetrachlorodibenzo-P-Dioxin	641.5	202	041903-57-5
202	Bromoform	635.1	201	000075-25-2
203	Pentachlorodibenzofuran	631.7	192	030402-15-4
204	1,3-Dichlorobenzene	628.6	203	000541-73-1
205	Pentachlorodibenzo-P-Dioxin	625.9	204	036088-22-9
206	N-Nitrosodiphenylamine	625.8	205	000086-30-6
207	2,3,7,8-Tetrachlorodibenzofuran	618.9	207	051207-31-9
208	2,4-Dichlorophenol	618.5	209	000120-83-2
209	2,3-Dimethylnaphthalene	617.5	New	000581-40-8
210	1,4-Dioxane	613.5	210	000123-91-1
211	Fluorine	613.3	211	007782-41-4
212	2-Butanone	611.1	208	000078-93-3
213	1,2-Dichloroethylene	610.4	206	000540-59-0
214	Cesium-137	610.0	213	010045-97-3
214	Chromium Trioxide	610.0	215	007738-94-5
216	Nitrite	609.0	212	014797-65-0
217	Silver	608.1	214	007440-22-4
218	Potassium-40	607.6	217	013966-00-2
219	Dinitrotoluene	607.3	218	025321-14-6
220	Nitrate	606.0	216	014797-55-8
221	Coal Tar Pitch	605.2	220	065996-93-2
222	Thorium-227	605.0	221	015623-47-9
223	Arsenic Acid	604.3	223	007778-39-4
224	Arsenic Trioxide	603.8	224	001327-53-3
225	Benzopyrene	602.9	226	073467-76-2
226	Chlordane, Technical	602.5	228	012789-03-6
227	Strobane	602.5	230	008001-50-1
228	4-Aminobiphenyl	602.4	232	000092-67-1
228	Pyrethrum	602.4	232	008003-34-7
230	Arsine	602.4	234	007784-42-1

2011 Rank	Substance Name	Totals Points	2007 Rank	CAS Number[1]
230	Dimethoate	602.4	229	000060-51-5
232	Antimony	602.2	219	007440-36-0
233	Carbophenothion	601.9	238	000786-19-6
234	Alpha-Chlordene	601.4	238	056534-02-2
234	Iodine-131	601.4	132	010043-66-0
234	Mercuric Chloride	601.4	241	007487-94-7
234	Sodium Arsenite	601.4	241	007784-46-5
234	Uranium-233	601.4	178	013968-55-3
239	Dibromochloromethane	600.5	249	000124-48-1
240	Cresols	597.1	227	001319-77-3
241	Formaldehyde	596.0	244	000050-00-0
242	Dichlorobenzene	595.4	254	025321-22-6
243	2,4-D Acid	594.5	248	000094-75-7
244	2-Chlorophenol	591.1	245	000095-57-8
245	Butylate	589.9	251	002008-41-5
246	Phenanthrene	588.3	246	000085-01-8
247	Dimethyl Formamide	585.3	252	000068-12-2
248	4-Nitrophenol	580.0	257	000100-02-7
249	Diuron	578.7	250	000330-54-1
250	Tetrachloroethane	576.7	190	025322-20-7
251	Dichloroethane	567.8	256	001300-21-6
252	Ethyl Ether	565.2	255	000060-29-7
253	Pyrene	564.1	253	000129-00-0
254	Dimethylaniline	561.8	New	000121-69-7
255	1,3-Dichloropropene, Cis-	561.0	258	010061-01-5
256	1,2,3,4,6,7,8-Heptachlorodibenzo-P-Dioxin	558.9	263	035822-46-9
257	Phosphine	555.2	259	007803-51-2
258	Trichlorobenzene	555.1	260	012002-48-1
259	2,6-Dinitrotoluene	554.4	261	000606-20-2
260	Fluoride Ion	549.9	262	016984-48-8
261	1,2,3,4,6,7,8-Heptachlorodibenzofuran	548.8	273	067562-39-4
262	Pentaerythritol Tetranitrate	548.2	265	000078-11-5
263	1,3-Dichloropropene, Trans-	548.0	266	010061-02-6
264	Acrylonitrile	543.2	274	000107-13-1
265	Bis(2-Ethylhexyl)Adipate	542.4	267	000103-23-1
266	Carbazole	538.6	268	000086-74-8
267	Metolachlor	538.2	New	051218-45-2
268	2-Chloroaniline	537.9	New	000095-51-2
269	1,2,3-Trichloropropane	536.1	New	000096-18-4
270	Carbaryl	535.5	272	000063-25-2
271	1,2-Dichloroethene, Cis-	533.8	270	000156-59-2
272	Methyl Isobutyl Ketone	529.6	269	000108-10-1
273	Styrene	529.4	271	000100-42-5
274	Thallium	525.3	New	007440-28-0
275	1,2,3,7,8,9-Hexachlorodibenzofuran	524.3	New	072918-21-9

Notes: *Substances were assigned the same rank when two (or more) substances received equivalent total scores; (1) CAS Number = Chemical Abstracts Service registry number*

The Comprehensive Environmental Response, Compensation, and Liability Act (CERCLA) section 104 (i), as amended by the Superfund Amendments and Reauthorization Act (SARA), requires ATSDR and the EPA to prepare a list, in order of priority, of substances that are most commonly found at facilities on the National Priorities List (NPL) and which are determined to pose the most significant potential threat to human health due to their known or suspected toxicity and potential for human exposure at these NPL sites. This substance priority list is revised and published on a 2-year basis, with a yearly informal review and revision. (No list was published in 2009 while ATSDR transitioned to a new agency science database.) Each substance on the list is a candidate to become the subject of a toxicological profile prepared by ATSDR. The listing algorithm prioritizes substances based on frequency of occurrence at NPL sites, toxicity, and potential for human exposure to the substances found at NPL sites. It should be noted that this priority list is not a list of "most toxic" substances, but rather a prioritization of substances based on a combination of their frequency, toxicity, and potential for human exposure at NPL sites. Thus, it is possible for substances with low toxicity but high NPL frequency of occurrence and exposure to be on this priority list. The objective of this priority list is to rank substances across all NPL hazardous waste sites to provide guidance in selecting which substances will be the subject of toxicological profiles prepared by ATSDR.

Source: *Center for Disease Control, Agency for Toxic Substances & Disease Registry, 2011 ATDSR 2011 Substance Priority List*

TRI On-site and Off-site Reported Disposed of or Otherwise Released (in pounds), for Facilities in All Industries, for All Chemicals, by State, U.S., 2011

State	Total On-site Disposal or Other Releases[1]	Total Off-site Disposal or Other Releases[2]	Total On- and Off-site Disposal or Other Releases
Alabama	70,676,466	13,404,861	84,081,327
Alaska	1,048,115,535	634,749	1,048,750,284
Arizona	97,054,741	647,543	97,702,283
Arkansas	28,239,725	7,003,901	35,243,627
California	32,269,164	6,032,345	38,301,509
Colorado	21,669,208	4,662,108	26,331,316
Connecticut	1,193,691	882,895	2,076,587
Delaware	3,916,566	2,243,122	6,159,688
District of Columbia	29,112	1,171	30,283
Florida	70,467,699	3,256,011	73,723,710
Georgia	68,623,355	3,109,369	71,732,725
Hawaii	2,382,866	214,203	2,597,069
Idaho	53,643,313	809,931	54,453,244
Illinois	56,494,085	48,905,487	105,399,572
Indiana	98,084,145	51,152,498	149,236,643
Iowa	31,288,770	8,740,864	40,029,635
Kansas	20,609,351	2,585,598	23,194,949
Kentucky	73,037,156	10,566,530	83,603,686
Louisiana	122,169,927	8,583,201	130,753,129
Maine	8,500,795	2,307,766	10,808,561
Maryland	8,420,447	2,833,244	11,253,691
Massachusetts	1,905,939	1,296,493	3,202,432
Michigan	50,425,702	31,132,641	81,558,342
Minnesota	19,813,081	5,401,300	25,214,381
Mississippi	52,362,485	3,925,635	56,288,120
Missouri	71,036,700	2,373,982	73,410,681
Montana	32,411,363	1,362,847	33,774,210
Nebraska	24,072,282	2,935,611	27,007,893
Nevada	520,201,331	2,998,984	529,280,315
New Hampshire	1,975,741	135,116	2,110,057
New Jersey	11,186,235	2,963,135	14,149,370
New Mexico	14,308,466	97,079	14,405,545
New York	13,758,809	5,145,300	18,904,109
North Carolina	51,138,920	7,853,843	58,992,762
North Dakota	14,354,365	6,655,076	21,009,441
Ohio	114,219,113	36,246,430	150,465,543
Oklahoma	38,208,415	1,440,778	39,649,192
Oregon	22,495,524	787,744	23,283,268
Pennsylvania	54,483,641	46,394,756	100,878,396
Rhode Island	137,042	255,372	392,414
South Carolina	41,652,823	9,525,727	51,178,550
South Dakota	5,672,273	234,025	5,906,298
Tennessee	76,223,561	11,459,379	87,682,940
Texas	191,331,403	17,688,112	209,019,514
Utah	195,360,086	1,622,343	196,982,429
Vermont	176,984	189,831	366,815
Virginia	42,489,999	3,643,124	46,133,123
Washington	15,300,817	3,778,647	19,079,464
West Virginia	31,711,519	7,101,229	38,812,748
Wisconsin	19,686,261	16,383,875	36,070,136
Wyoming	17,748,749	1,346,505	19,095,254
American Samoa	5	0	5
Guam	276,453	0	276,453
Northern Mariana Isl	3,224	0	3,224
Puerto Rico	3,930,049	737,391	4,667,440

State	Total On-site Disposal or Other Releases[1]	Total Off-site Disposal or Other Releases[2]	Total On- and Off-site Disposal or Other Releases
Virgin Islands	1,777,745	36,295	1,814,040
Total	3,674,803,221	411,726,004	4,086,529,225

Notes: *TRI = Toxic Release Inventory; Reporting year (RY) 2011 is the most recent TRI data available. Facilities reporting to TRI were required to submit RY 2011 data to EPA by July 1, 2012. This dataset includes revisions processed by EPA as of October 10, 2012 for the years 1988 to 2011. Revisions submitted to EPA after this time are not included.*

(1) On-site Disposal or Other Releases include Underground Injection to Class I Wells (Section 5.4.1), RCRA Subtitle C Landfills (5.5.1A), Other Landfills (5.5.1B), Fugitive or Non-point Air Emissions (5.1), Stack or Point Air Emissions (5.2), Surface Water Discharges (5.3), Underground Injection to Class II-V Wells (5.4.2), Land Treatment/Application Farming (5.5.2), RCRA Subtitle C Surface Impoundments (5.5.3A), Other Surface Impoundments (5.5.3B), and Other Land Disposal (5.5.4). Off-site Disposal or Other Releases include from Section 6.2 Class I Underground Injection Wells (M81), Class II-V Underground Injection Wells (M82, M71), RCRA Subtitle C Landfills (M65), Other Landfills (M64, M72), Storage Only (M10), Solidification/Stabilization - Metals and Metal Category Compounds only (M41 or M40), Wastewater Treatment (excluding POTWs) - Metals and Metal Category Compounds only (M62 or M61), RCRA Subtitle C Surface Impoundments (M66), Other Surface Impoundments (M67, M63), Land Treatment (M73), Other Land Disposal (M79), Other Off-site Management (M90), Transfers to Waste Broker - Disposal (M94, M91), and Unknown (M99) and, from Section 6.1 Transfers to POTWs (metals and metal category compounds only).

(2) Off-site disposal or other releases show only net off-site disposal or other releases, that is, off-site disposal or other releases transferred to other TRI facilities reporting such transfers as on-site disposal or other releases are not included to avoid double counting.

This report may not include all states in the US. A state may not be included in this report for two reasons: 1) there are no facilities reporting to TRI in the particular state; or 2) the facilities reporting to TRI in the particular state did not report to TRI for the user-specified selection criteria.

Users of TRI information should be aware that TRI data reflect releases and other waste management activities of chemicals, not whether (or to what degree) the public has been exposed to those chemicals. Release estimates alone are not sufficient to determine exposure or to calculate potential adverse effects on human health and the environment. TRI data, in conjunction with other information, can be used as a starting point in evaluating exposures that may result from releases and other waste management activities which involve toxic chemicals. The determination of potential risk depends upon many factors, including the toxicity of the chemical, the fate of the chemical, and the amount and duration of human or other exposure to the chemical after it is released.

Source: U.S. Environmental Protection Agency, *TRI Explorer, August 29, 2013*

TRI On-site and Off-site Reported Disposed of or Otherwise Released (in grams), for Facilities in All Industries, Dioxin and Dioxin-like Compounds, by State, U.S., 2011

State	Total On-site Disposal or Other Releases[1]	Total Off-site Disposal or Other Releases[2]	Total On- and Off-site Disposal or Other Releases
Alabama	253.26	72.12	325.38
Alaska	0.78	0.00	0.78
Arizona	15.30	0.00	15.30
Arkansas	38.30	0.25	38.55
California	57.74	67.43	125.17
Colorado	15.75	0.34	16.09
Connecticut	0.47	0.00	0.47
Delaware	11.58	669.36	680.94
District of Columbia	0.15	0.00	0.15
Florida	57.69	1.16	58.86
Georgia	68.48	0.37	68.85
Hawaii	3.25	0.99	4.23
Idaho	1.50	9.48	10.97
Illinois	28.76	81.85	110.61
Indiana	200.54	87.41	287.95
Iowa	24.33	0.04	24.37
Kansas	12.45	0.00	12.45
Kentucky	188.12	2,592.68	2,780.80
Louisiana	354.66	514.40	869.06
Maine	6.61	2.02	8.62
Maryland	35.64	0.00	35.64
Massachusetts	2.65	0.00	2.65
Michigan	82.54	64.51	147.05
Minnesota	29.40	354.27	383.67
Mississippi	1,206.18	140.60	1,346.78
Missouri	53.71	0.01	53.72
Montana	7.64	1.60	9.24
Nebraska	3.58	0.00	3.58
Nevada	5.47	0.00	5.47
New Hampshire	0.17	0.00	0.17
New Jersey	1.23	16.02	17.24
New Mexico	4.01	0.00	4.01
New York	29.06	2.31	31.37
North Carolina	114.75	1.18	115.93
North Dakota	15.19	0.00	15.19
Ohio	2,360.80	108.63	2,469.43
Oklahoma	38.05	32.94	70.99
Oregon	956.73	142.12	1,098.85
Pennsylvania	54.94	6.72	61.66
South Carolina	45.68	2.31	47.98
South Dakota	10.22	0.00	10.22
Tennessee	1,197.48	60.42	1,257.89
Texas	9,042.48	24,382.55	33,425.03
Utah	7,270.29	21.21	7,291.50
Virginia	11.38	6.87	18.25
Washington	52.31	262.54	314.85
West Virginia	15.54	37.44	52.98
Wisconsin	33.67	781.02	814.69
Wyoming	17.80	0.00	17.80
Guam	0.16	0.00	0.16
Puerto Rico	13.22	0.01	13.22
Virgin Islands	2.26	0.00	2.26
Total	24,053.94	30,525.15	54,579.09

Notes: *TRI = Toxic Release Inventory; Reporting year (RY) 2011 is the most recent TRI data available. Facilities reporting to TRI were required to submit RY 2011 data to EPA by July 1, 2012. This dataset includes revisions processed by EPA as of October 10, 2012 for the years 1988 to 2011. Revisions submitted to EPA after this time are not included.*

(1) On-site Disposal or Other Releases include Underground Injection to Class I Wells (Section 5.4.1), RCRA Subtitle C Landfills (5.5.1A), Other Landfills (5.5.1B), Fugitive or Non-point Air Emissions (5.1), Stack or Point Air Emissions (5.2), Surface Water Discharges (5.3), Underground Injection to Class II-V Wells (5.4.2), Land Treatment/Application Farming (5.5.2), RCRA Subtitle C Surface Impoundments (5.5.3A), Other Surface Impoundments (5.5.3B), and Other Land Disposal (5.5.4). Off-site Disposal or Other Releases include from Section 6.2 Class I Underground Injection Wells (M81), Class II-V Underground Injection Wells (M82, M71), RCRA Subtitle C Landfills (M65), Other Landfills (M64, M72), Storage Only (M10), Solidification/Stabilization - Metals and Metal Category Compounds only (M41 or M40), Wastewater Treatment (excluding POTWs) - Metals and Metal Category Compounds only (M62 or M61), RCRA Subtitle C Surface Impoundments (M66), Other Surface Impoundments (M67, M63), Land Treatment (M73), Other Land Disposal (M79), Other Off-site Management (M90), Transfers to Waste Broker - Disposal (M94, M91), and Unknown (M99) and, from Section 6.1 Transfers to POTWs (metals and metal category compounds only).

(2) Off-site disposal or other releases show only net off-site disposal or other releases, that is, off-site disposal or other releases transferred to other TRI facilities reporting such transfers as on-site disposal or other releases are not included to avoid double counting.

This report may not include all states in the US. A state may not be included in this report for two reasons: 1) there are no facilities reporting to TRI in the particular state; or 2) the facilities reporting to TRI in the particular state did not report to TRI for the user-specified selection criteria.

Users of TRI information should be aware that TRI data reflect releases and other waste management activities of chemicals, not whether (or to what degree) the public has been exposed to those chemicals. Release estimates alone are not sufficient to determine exposure or to calculate potential adverse effects on human health and the environment. TRI data, in conjunction with other information, can be used as a starting point in evaluating exposures that may result from releases and other waste management activities which involve toxic chemicals. The determination of potential risk depends upon many factors, including the toxicity of the chemical, the fate of the chemical, and the amount and duration of human or other exposure to the chemical after it is released.

Source: *U.S. Environmental Protection Agency, TRI Explorer, August 29, 2013*

TRI On-site and Off-site Reported Disposed of or Otherwise Released (in pounds), for Facilities in All Industries, for All Chemicals, Top 75 Counties, 2011

Rank	County	State	Total On-site Disposal or Other Releases[1]	Total Off-site Disposal or Other Releases[2]	Total On- and Off-site Disposal or Other Releases
1	Northwest Arctic	Alaska	989,392,511	38	989,392,549
2	Salt Lake	Utah	169,370,831	676,108	170,046,939
3	Humboldt	Nevada	137,200,673	607	137,201,280
4	Eureka	Nevada	122,552,680	852	122,553,532
5	White Pine	Nevada	99,127,554	1,712	99,129,266
6	Lander	Nevada	86,082,079	1,437	86,083,517
7	Gila	Arizona	66,194,105	387,819	66,581,924
8	Juneau	Alaska	47,056,479	0	47,056,479
9	Brazoria	Texas	36,587,883	546,222	37,134,105
10	Escambia	Florida	35,165,159	175,153	35,340,312
11	Elko	Nevada	34,705,671	8,786	34,714,457
12	Wayne	Michigan	10,861,057	23,666,543	34,527,599
13	Pershing	Nevada	34,409,159	0	34,409,159
14	Harris	Texas	26,737,881	5,155,867	31,893,748
15	Lake	Indiana	15,923,999	15,446,263	31,370,261
16	Spencer	Indiana	24,736,431	962,828	25,699,259
17	Humphreys	Tennessee	21,020,033	4,412,091	25,432,124
18	Shoshone	Idaho	23,440,041	23,244	23,463,285
19	Calhoun	Texas	21,271,422	27,026	21,298,448
20	Harrison	Mississippi	20,933,694	6,624	20,940,318
21	St Charles	Louisiana	19,587,750	295,572	19,883,325
22	Reynolds	Missouri	19,870,960	0	19,870,960
23	Allegheny	Pennsylvania	5,264,530	14,347,887	19,612,418
24	Peoria	Illinois	1,956,378	17,586,613	19,542,991
25	Iron	Missouri	18,524,238	115,964	18,640,201
26	Ascension	Louisiana	17,035,340	1,000,330	18,035,670
27	Silver Bow	Montana	17,819,992	29,345	17,849,337
28	Jefferson	Louisiana	12,669,487	3,866,193	16,535,680
29	Beaver	Pennsylvania	2,120,755	13,839,571	15,960,326
30	Montgomery	Tennessee	15,294,494	143,702	15,438,196
31	Tooele	Utah	13,948,967	1,319,704	15,268,672
32	Calcasieu	Louisiana	14,073,312	483,169	14,556,481
33	Carroll	Kentucky	9,744,137	4,240,190	13,984,327
34	Richmond	Georgia	13,903,740	47,334	13,951,073
35	Allen	Ohio	13,158,875	490,898	13,649,773
36	Jefferson	Alabama	10,169,641	3,478,662	13,648,304
37	Gilliam	Oregon	13,370,492	62	13,370,554
38	Montgomery	Virginia	13,117,084	250,337	13,367,420
39	Cook	Illinois	4,120,414	9,091,631	13,212,046
40	Jefferson	Texas	9,004,600	3,276,915	12,281,515
41	Fairbanks North Star	Alaska	11,352,424	525,302	11,877,726
42	Ashtabula	Ohio	10,970,745	489,880	11,460,625
43	Marion	Indiana	2,148,684	9,243,376	11,392,060
44	Rosebud	Montana	10,970,923	408,255	11,379,178
45	Washington	Ohio	9,366,672	1,773,538	11,140,210
46	De Soto	Louisiana	11,112,379	0	11,112,379
47	Monroe	Michigan	10,725,654	323,953	11,049,606
48	Ouachita	Louisiana	10,787,308	53,155	10,840,463
49	San Juan	New Mexico	7,289,916	3,478,550	10,768,466
50	Cuyahoga	Ohio	3,928,609	6,825,469	10,754,078
51	Nye	Nevada	10,575,510	11,097	10,586,607
52	Monroe	Mississippi	10,556,280	27,934	10,584,214
53	Owyhee	Idaho	10,201,935	328	10,202,263
54	Kern	California	10,135,146	26,160	10,161,305
55	Jefferson	Kentucky	9,239,853	754,285	9,994,139

Rank	County	State	Total On-site Disposal or Other Releases[1]	Total Off-site Disposal or Other Releases[2]	Total On- and Off-site Disposal or Other Releases
56	Sandusky	Ohio	9,924,750	55,707	9,980,457
57	Major	Oklahoma	9,439,686	0	9,439,686
58	Will	Illinois	6,709,212	2,585,873	9,295,085
59	Jefferson	Missouri	9,102,139	91,353	9,193,492
60	East Baton Rouge	Louisiana	8,263,837	919,975	9,183,812
61	Muhlenberg	Kentucky	9,055,577	316	9,055,893
62	St Clair	Michigan	8,375,842	507,183	8,883,025
63	Madison	Illinois	5,956,638	2,858,362	8,815,000
64	Jefferson	Ohio	6,939,196	1,796,023	8,735,219
65	Indiana	Pennsylvania	8,654,469	10,200	8,664,670
66	Los Angeles	California	3,800,969	4,732,422	8,533,392
67	Garfield	Oklahoma	8,381,017	1	8,381,018
68	Coshocton	Ohio	7,070,325	1,256,740	8,327,065
69	Gallia	Ohio	7,973,474	5,996	7,979,470
70	Posey	Indiana	2,748,252	5,161,237	7,909,489
71	Harrison	Texas	7,574,660	150,944	7,725,604
72	Mercer	North Dakota	2,722,627	4,925,938	7,648,565
73	Sullivan	Tennessee	7,195,884	421,324	7,617,208
74	Lee	Iowa	6,321,266	1,242,505	7,563,772
75	Iberville	Louisiana	5,560,363	1,776,822	7,337,184

Notes: *TRI = Toxic Release Inventory; Reporting year (RY) 2011 is the most recent TRI data available. Facilities reporting to TRI were required to submit RY 2011 data to EPA by July 1, 2012. This dataset includes revisions processed by EPA as of October 10, 2012 for the years 1988 to 2011. Revisions submitted to EPA after this time are not included.*

(1) On-site Disposal or Other Releases include Underground Injection to Class I Wells (Section 5.4.1), RCRA Subtitle C Landfills (5.5.1A), Other Landfills (5.5.1B), Fugitive or Non-point Air Emissions (5.1), Stack or Point Air Emissions (5.2), Surface Water Discharges (5.3), Underground Injection to Class II-V Wells (5.4.2), Land Treatment/Application Farming (5.5.2), RCRA Subtitle C Surface Impoundments (5.5.3A), Other Surface Impoundments (5.5.3B), and Other Land Disposal (5.5.4). Off-site Disposal or Other Releases include from Section 6.2 Class I Underground Injection Wells (M81), Class II-V Underground Injection Wells (M82, M71), RCRA Subtitle C Landfills (M65), Other Landfills (M64, M72), Storage Only (M10), Solidification/Stabilization - Metals and Metal Category Compounds only (M41 or M40), Wastewater Treatment (excluding POTWs) - Metals and Metal Category Compounds only (M62 or M61), RCRA Subtitle C Surface Impoundments (M66), Other Surface Impoundments (M67, M63), Land Treatment (M73), Other Land Disposal (M79), Other Off-site Management (M90), Transfers to Waste Broker - Disposal (M94, M91), and Unknown (M99) and, from Section 6.1 Transfers to POTWs (metals and metal category compounds only).

(2) Off-site disposal or other releases show only net off-site disposal or other releases, that is, off-site disposal or other releases transferred to other TRI facilities reporting such transfers as on-site disposal or other releases are not included to avoid double counting.

This report may not include all states in the US. A state may not be included in this report for two reasons: 1) there are no facilities reporting to TRI in the particular state; or 2) the facilities reporting to TRI in the particular state did not report to TRI for the user-specified selection criteria.

Users of TRI information should be aware that TRI data reflect releases and other waste management activities of chemicals, not whether (or to what degree) the public has been exposed to those chemicals. Release estimates alone are not sufficient to determine exposure or to calculate potential adverse effects on human health and the environment. TRI data, in conjunction with other information, can be used as a starting point in evaluating exposures that may result from releases and other waste management activities which involve toxic chemicals. The determination of potential risk depends upon many factors, including the toxicity of the chemical, the fate of the chemical, and the amount and duration of human or other exposure to the chemical after it is released.

Source: *U.S. Environmental Protection Agency, TRI Explorer, August 29, 2013*

TRI On-site and Off-site Reported Disposed of or Otherwise Released (in grams), for Facilities in All Industries, Dioxin and Dioxin-like Compounds, Top 75 Counties, 2011

Rank	County	State	Total On-site Disposal or Other Releases[1]	Total Off-site Disposal or Other Releases[2]	Total On- and Off-site Disposal or Other Releases
1	Harris	Texas	19.23	23,897.01	23,916.23
2	Brazoria	Texas	8,925.23	0.00	8,925.23
3	Tooele	Utah	7,258.33	1.24	7,259.57
4	Marshall	Kentucky	18.16	2,478.79	2,496.95
5	Ashtabula	Ohio	2,271.38	1.41	2,272.79
6	Humphreys	Tennessee	1,165.65	0.02	1,165.67
7	Gilliam	Oregon	946.36	0.00	946.36
8	Harrison	Mississippi	840.86	0.01	840.87
9	Sheboygan	Wisconsin	9.12	742.73	751.85
10	New Castle	Delaware	11.45	669.36	680.81
11	Iberville	Louisiana	221.79	247.81	469.60
12	San Patricio	Texas	3.86	366.36	370.22
13	Dakota	Minnesota	11.09	354.04	365.13
14	Monroe	Mississippi	324.11	0.00	324.11
15	Pierce	Washington	1.77	226.37	228.14
16	Kemper	Mississippi	13.17	139.90	153.07
17	Lane	Oregon	2.07	140.30	142.37
18	Calcasieu	Louisiana	23.17	116.08	139.25
19	Sumter	Alabama	124.17	0.00	124.17
20	Calhoun	Texas	2.15	121.94	124.09
21	Wabash	Indiana	123.82	0.00	123.82
22	Butler	Kentucky	121.47	0.00	121.47
23	Barren	Kentucky	1.06	110.47	111.52
24	Ascension	Louisiana	8.97	100.26	109.23
25	Tuscarawas	Ohio	4.75	90.07	94.82
26	Porter	Indiana	13.15	63.60	76.75
27	Branch	Michigan	3.36	63.84	67.20
28	Peoria	Illinois	0.76	60.82	61.58
29	Lucas	Ohio	58.69	0.00	58.69
30	Los Angeles	California	2.64	55.73	58.37
31	St Clair	Alabama	3.03	53.78	56.81
32	Midland	Michigan	52.54	0.27	52.81
33	Etowah	Alabama	0.59	49.88	50.48
34	Mecklenburg	North Carolina	48.95	0.00	48.95
35	East Baton Rouge	Louisiana	30.81	12.80	43.61
36	Maury	Tennessee	3.21	35.00	38.21
37	St Charles	Louisiana	13.71	21.76	35.47
38	Tyler	West Virginia	1.76	33.50	35.26
39	Catawba	North Carolina	35.14	0.00	35.14
40	Creek	Oklahoma	1.74	32.94	34.68
41	Rapides	Louisiana	20.99	11.72	32.71
42	Allen	Indiana	32.35	0.00	32.35
43	Lake	Indiana	12.06	20.19	32.25
44	Mccurtain	Oklahoma	30.63	0.00	30.63
45	Kern	California	30.11	0.00	30.11
46	Spokane	Washington	24.35	5.54	29.89
47	Orange	Texas	29.64	0.00	29.64
48	Jefferson	Alabama	6.30	21.97	28.27
49	Bibb	Alabama	26.10	0.00	26.10
50	Eau Claire	Wisconsin	0.00	25.24	25.24
51	Pike	Missouri	24.85	0.00	24.85
52	Cook	Illinois	2.67	21.01	23.67
53	San Bernardino	California	11.27	11.08	22.35
54	York	South Carolina	20.89	0.00	20.89
55	Cass	Texas	20.77	0.00	20.77

Rank	County	State	Total On-site Disposal or Other Releases[1]	Total Off-site Disposal or Other Releases[2]	Total On- and Off-site Disposal or Other Releases
56	Weber	Utah	0.13	19.97	20.09
57	Baltimore	Maryland	20.05	0.00	20.05
58	Escambia	Alabama	20.00	0.00	20.00
59	Cowlitz	Washington	3.24	16.33	19.58
60	Washington	Louisiana	17.05	1.19	18.24
61	Lancaster	Pennsylvania	11.90	5.45	17.35
62	Walla Walla	Washington	14.29	0.00	14.29
63	Warren	New York	13.11	0.87	13.98
64	Schuylkill	Pennsylvania	13.61	0.00	13.61
65	Bergen	New Jersey	0.00	12.61	12.61
66	Henderson	Kentucky	12.49	0.00	12.49
67	Racine	Wisconsin	0.42	12.05	12.47
68	Columbiana	Ohio	0.05	12.40	12.45
69	Loudon	Tennessee	0.78	11.50	12.28
70	Snohomish	Washington	0.53	11.46	11.99
71	Putnam	Florida	11.71	0.00	11.71
72	Mercer	North Dakota	11.68	0.00	11.68
73	Platte	Wyoming	11.49	0.00	11.49
74	Wilcox	Alabama	11.13	0.00	11.13
75	San Joaquin	California	11.04	0.00	11.04

***Notes:** TRI = Toxic Release Inventory; Reporting year (RY) 2011 is the most recent TRI data available. Facilities reporting to TRI were required to submit RY 2011 data to EPA by July 1, 2012. This dataset includes revisions processed by EPA as of October 10, 2012 for the years 1988 to 2011. Revisions submitted to EPA after this time are not included.*

(1) On-site Disposal or Other Releases include Underground Injection to Class I Wells (Section 5.4.1), RCRA Subtitle C Landfills (5.5.1A), Other Landfills (5.5.1B), Fugitive or Non-point Air Emissions (5.1), Stack or Point Air Emissions (5.2), Surface Water Discharges (5.3), Underground Injection to Class II-V Wells (5.4.2), Land Treatment/Application Farming (5.5.2), RCRA Subtitle C Surface Impoundments (5.5.3A), Other Surface Impoundments (5.5.3B), and Other Land Disposal (5.5.4). Off-site Disposal or Other Releases include from Section 6.2 Class I Underground Injection Wells (M81), Class II-V Underground Injection Wells (M82, M71), RCRA Subtitle C Landfills (M65), Other Landfills (M64, M72), Storage Only (M10), Solidification/Stabilization - Metals and Metal Category Compounds only (M41 or M40), Wastewater Treatment (excluding POTWs) - Metals and Metal Category Compounds only (M62 or M61), RCRA Subtitle C Surface Impoundments (M66), Other Surface Impoundments (M67, M63), Land Treatment (M73), Other Land Disposal (M79), Other Off-site Management (M90), Transfers to Waste Broker - Disposal (M94, M91), and Unknown (M99) and, from Section 6.1 Transfers to POTWs (metals and metal category compounds only).

(2) Off-site disposal or other releases show only net off-site disposal or other releases, that is, off-site disposal or other releases transferred to other TRI facilities reporting such transfers as on-site disposal or other releases are not included to avoid double counting.

This report may not include all states in the US. A state may not be included in this report for two reasons: 1) there are no facilities reporting to TRI in the particular state; or 2) the facilities reporting to TRI in the particular state did not report to TRI for the user-specified selection criteria.

Users of TRI information should be aware that TRI data reflect releases and other waste management activities of chemicals, not whether (or to what degree) the public has been exposed to those chemicals. Release estimates alone are not sufficient to determine exposure or to calculate potential adverse effects on human health and the environment. TRI data, in conjunction with other information, can be used as a starting point in evaluating exposures that may result from releases and other waste management activities which involve toxic chemicals. The determination of potential risk depends upon many factors, including the toxicity of the chemical, the fate of the chemical, and the amount and duration of human or other exposure to the chemical after it is released.

***Source:** U.S. Environmental Protection Agency, TRI Explorer, August 29, 2013*

TRI On-site and Off-site Reported Disposed of or Otherwise Released (in pounds), for Facilities in All Industries, for All Chemicals, Top 75 Zipcodes, 2011

Rank	Zip	City	State	Total On-site Disposal or Other Releases[1]	Total Off-site Disposal or Other Releases[2]	Total On- and Off-site Disposal or Other Releases
1	99752	Kotzebue	Alaska	989,392,511	38	989,392,549
2	84006	Bingham Canyon	Utah	145,318,456	1,971	145,320,427
3	89414	Golconda	Nevada	135,531,353	6	135,531,359
4	89803	Elko	Nevada	115,863,448	1,717	115,865,164
5	89822	Carlin	Nevada	107,686,602	15	107,686,617
6	99801	Juneau	Alaska	47,056,479	0	47,056,479
7	89820	Battle Mountain	Nevada	46,922,642	44	46,922,686
8	85135	Hayden	Arizona	44,292,342	226	44,292,568
9	89821	Crescent Valley	Nevada	39,284,864	1,393	39,286,257
10	32533	Cantonment	Florida	33,916,225	174,587	34,090,812
11	89419	Lovelock	Nevada	33,718,627	0	33,718,627
12	77512	Alvin	Texas	29,827,049	100	29,827,149
13	65440	Boss	Missouri	27,350,129	113,018	27,463,147
14	47635	Rockport	Indiana	24,726,563	962,828	25,689,391
15	37134	New Johnsonville	Tennessee	19,799,840	4,335,192	24,135,032
16	84044	Magna	Utah	23,447,134	6,704	23,453,838
17	85532	Claypool	Arizona	21,869,859	385,485	22,255,345
18	77979	Port Lavaca	Texas	18,354,642	4,827	18,359,469
19	59701	Butte	Montana	17,819,992	29,345	17,849,337
20	70070	Luling	Louisiana	17,550,778	233	17,551,011
21	83846	Mullan	Idaho	17,059,136	22,621	17,081,757
22	39571	Pass Christian	Mississippi	15,795,516	9	15,795,525
23	37040	Clarksville	Tennessee	15,294,494	143,694	15,438,188
24	46312	East Chicago	Indiana	792,639	14,273,199	15,065,838
25	89316	Eureka	Nevada	14,740,651	0	14,740,651
26	46402	Gary	Indiana	13,738,837	929,989	14,668,826
27	41045	Ghent	Kentucky	9,673,250	4,100,133	13,773,384
28	97812	Arlington	Oregon	13,370,492	61	13,370,553
29	45804	Lima	Ohio	13,106,067	200,066	13,306,133
30	24141	Radford	Virginia	13,078,654	95,145	13,173,798
31	61615	Peoria	Illinois	13,474	12,755,842	12,769,316
32	70094	Westwego	Louisiana	12,604,404	41,453	12,645,857
33	89319	Ruth	Nevada	12,640,545	0	12,640,545
34	15104	Braddock	Pennsylvania	96,013	12,286,946	12,382,959
35	15061	Monaca	Pennsylvania	773,797	11,527,501	12,301,297
36	84029	Grantsville	Utah	11,449,949	407,117	11,857,065
37	59323	Colstrip	Montana	10,970,923	408,122	11,379,045
38	44004	Ashtabula	Ohio	10,853,308	330,284	11,183,593
39	71052	Mansfield	Louisiana	11,111,723	0	11,111,723
40	30901	Augusta	Georgia	11,061,163	44,546	11,105,709
41	39746	Hamilton	Mississippi	10,408,655	0	10,408,655
42	48161	Monroe	Michigan	10,061,055	321,393	10,382,448
43	83624	Grand View	Idaho	10,201,929	1	10,201,930
44	93206	Buttonwillow	California	9,854,172	7,856	9,862,028
45	73860	Waynoka	Oklahoma	9,439,686	0	9,439,686
46	48120	Dearborn	Michigan	86,364	9,336,578	9,422,943
47	43464	Vickery	Ohio	9,253,272	15,132	9,268,404
48	46231	Indianapolis	Indiana	5,263	9,173,890	9,179,153
49	70734	Geismar	Louisiana	8,716,201	330,933	9,047,134
50	71280	Sterlington	Louisiana	8,628,375	6,795	8,635,170
51	77536	Deer Park	Texas	8,167,570	416,396	8,583,966
52	99737	Delta Junction	Alaska	8,401,174	150	8,401,324
53	42337	Drakesboro	Kentucky	8,367,272	44	8,367,316
54	73701	Enid	Oklahoma	8,270,300	0	8,270,300
55	48229	Ecorse	Michigan	390,152	7,731,697	8,121,849

Rank	Zip	City	State	Total On-site Disposal or Other Releases[1]	Total Off-site Disposal or Other Releases[2]	Total On- and Off-site Disposal or Other Releases
56	70346	Donaldsonville	Louisiana	7,983,198	0	7,983,198
57	45620	Cheshire	Ohio	7,973,454	5,496	7,978,950
58	63048	Herculaneum	Missouri	7,923,074	24,513	7,947,587
59	47620	Mount Vernon	Indiana	2,748,252	5,161,236	7,909,488
60	70805	Baton Rouge	Louisiana	6,952,113	735,104	7,687,216
61	48054	East China	Michigan	7,213,208	0	7,213,209
62	55308	Becker	Minnesota	7,189,113	93	7,189,205
63	63633	Centerville	Missouri	6,997,897	0	6,997,897
64	70665	Sulphur	Louisiana	6,922,268	40,798	6,963,066
65	82001	Cheyenne	Wyoming	6,694,900	0	6,694,900
66	70669	Westlake	Louisiana	6,623,551	66,383	6,689,934
67	47665	Owensville	Indiana	6,637,030	5	6,637,035
68	41230	Louisa	Kentucky	6,498,609	1,140	6,499,749
69	43812	Coshocton	Ohio	5,163,669	1,254,055	6,417,724
70	77856	Franklin	Texas	6,239,267	0	6,239,267
71	77905	Victoria	Texas	5,991,906	227,573	6,219,479
72	45715	Beverly	Ohio	6,192,891	7,602	6,200,494
73	37662	Kingsport	Tennessee	6,000,256	134,675	6,134,930
74	60436	Joliet	Illinois	4,659,212	1,388,463	6,047,675
75	58530	Center	North Dakota	4,327,045	1,664,495	5,991,540

Notes: *TRI = Toxic Release Inventory; Reporting year (RY) 2011 is the most recent TRI data available. Facilities reporting to TRI were required to submit RY 2011 data to EPA by July 1, 2012. This dataset includes revisions processed by EPA as of October 10, 2012 for the years 1988 to 2011. Revisions submitted to EPA after this time are not included.*

(1) On-site Disposal or Other Releases include Underground Injection to Class I Wells (Section 5.4.1), RCRA Subtitle C Landfills (5.5.1A), Other Landfills (5.5.1B), Fugitive or Non-point Air Emissions (5.1), Stack or Point Air Emissions (5.2), Surface Water Discharges (5.3), Underground Injection to Class II-V Wells (5.4.2), Land Treatment/Application Farming (5.5.2), RCRA Subtitle C Surface Impoundments (5.5.3A), Other Surface Impoundments (5.5.3B), and Other Land Disposal (5.5.4). Off-site Disposal or Other Releases include from Section 6.2 Class I Underground Injection Wells (M81), Class II-V Underground Injection Wells (M82, M71), RCRA Subtitle C Landfills (M65), Other Landfills (M64, M72), Storage Only (M10), Solidification/Stabilization - Metals and Metal Category Compounds only (M41 or M40), Wastewater Treatment (excluding POTWs) - Metals and Metal Category Compounds only (M62 or M61), RCRA Subtitle C Surface Impoundments (M66), Other Surface Impoundments (M67, M63), Land Treatment (M73), Other Land Disposal (M79), Other Off-site Management (M90), Transfers to Waste Broker - Disposal (M94, M91), and Unknown (M99) and, from Section 6.1 Transfers to POTWs (metals and metal category compounds only).

(2) Off-site disposal or other releases show only net off-site disposal or other releases, that is, off-site disposal or other releases transferred to other TRI facilities reporting such transfers as on-site disposal or other releases are not included to avoid double counting.

This report may not include all states in the US. A state may not be included in this report for two reasons: 1) there are no facilities reporting to TRI in the particular state; or 2) the facilities reporting to TRI in the particular state did not report to TRI for the user-specified selection criteria.

Users of TRI information should be aware that TRI data reflect releases and other waste management activities of chemicals, not whether (or to what degree) the public has been exposed to those chemicals. Release estimates alone are not sufficient to determine exposure or to calculate potential adverse effects on human health and the environment. TRI data, in conjunction with other information, can be used as a starting point in evaluating exposures that may result from releases and other waste management activities which involve toxic chemicals. The determination of potential risk depends upon many factors, including the toxicity of the chemical, the fate of the chemical, and the amount and duration of human or other exposure to the chemical after it is released.

Source: *U.S. Environmental Protection Agency, TRI Explorer, August 29, 2013*

TRI On-site and Off-site Reported Disposed of or Otherwise Released (in grams), for Facilities in All Industries, Dioxin and Dioxin-like Compounds, Top 75 Zipcodes, 2011

Rank	Zip	City	State	Total On-site Disposal or Other Releases[1]	Total Off-site Disposal or Other Releases[2]	Total On- and Off-site Disposal or Other Releases
1	99752	Kotzebue	Alaska	989,392,511	38	989,392,549
2	84006	Bingham Canyon	Utah	145,318,456	1,971	145,320,427
3	89414	Golconda	Nevada	135,531,353	6	135,531,359
4	89803	Elko	Nevada	115,863,448	1,717	115,865,164
5	89822	Carlin	Nevada	107,686,602	15	107,686,617
6	99801	Juneau	Alaska	47,056,479	0	47,056,479
7	89820	Battle Mountain	Nevada	46,922,642	44	46,922,686
8	85135	Hayden	Arizona	44,292,342	226	44,292,568
9	89821	Crescent Valley	Nevada	39,284,864	1,393	39,286,257
10	32533	Cantonment	Florida	33,916,225	174,587	34,090,812
11	89419	Lovelock	Nevada	33,718,627	0	33,718,627
12	77512	Alvin	Texas	29,827,049	100	29,827,149
13	65440	Boss	Missouri	27,350,129	113,018	27,463,147
14	47635	Rockport	Indiana	24,726,563	962,828	25,689,391
15	37134	New Johnsonville	Tennessee	19,799,840	4,335,192	24,135,032
16	84044	Magna	Utah	23,447,134	6,704	23,453,838
17	85532	Claypool	Arizona	21,869,859	385,485	22,255,345
18	77979	Port Lavaca	Texas	18,354,642	4,827	18,359,469
19	59701	Butte	Montana	17,819,992	29,345	17,849,337
20	70070	Luling	Louisiana	17,550,778	233	17,551,011
21	83846	Mullan	Idaho	17,059,136	22,621	17,081,757
22	39571	Pass Christian	Mississippi	15,795,516	9	15,795,525
23	37040	Clarksville	Tennessee	15,294,494	143,694	15,438,188
24	46312	East Chicago	Indiana	792,639	14,273,199	15,065,838
25	89316	Eureka	Nevada	14,740,651		14,740,651
26	46402	Gary	Indiana	13,738,837	929,989	14,668,826
27	41045	Ghent	Kentucky	9,673,250	4,100,133	13,773,384
28	97812	Arlington	Oregon	13,370,492	61	13,370,553
29	45804	Lima	Ohio	13,106,067	200,066	13,306,133
30	24141	Radford	Virginia	13,078,654	95,145	13,173,798
31	61615	Peoria	Illinois	13,474	12,755,842	12,769,316
32	70094	Westwego	Louisiana	12,604,404	41,453	12,645,857
33	89319	Ruth	Nevada	12,640,545	0	12,640,545
34	15104	Braddock	Pennsylvania	96,013	12,286,946	12,382,959
35	15061	Monaca	Pennsylvania	773,797	11,527,501	12,301,297
36	84029	Grantsville	Utah	11,449,949	407,117	11,857,065
37	59323	Colstrip	Montana	10,970,923	408,122	11,379,045
38	44004	Ashtabula	Ohio	10,853,308	330,284	11,183,593
39	71052	Mansfield	Louisiana	11,111,723	0	11,111,723
40	30901	Augusta	Georgia	11,061,163	44,546	11,105,709
41	39746	Hamilton	Mississippi	10,408,655	0	10,408,655
42	48161	Monroe	Michigan	10,061,055	321,393	10,382,448
43	83624	Grand View	Idaho	10,201,929	1	10,201,930
44	93206	Buttonwillow	California	9,854,172	7,856	9,862,028
45	73860	Waynoka	Oklahoma	9,439,686	0	9,439,686
46	48120	Dearborn	Michigan	86,364	9,336,578	9,422,943
47	43464	Vickery	Ohio	9,253,272	15,132	9,268,404
48	46231	Indianapolis	Indiana	5,263	9,173,890	9,179,153
49	70734	Geismar	Louisiana	8,716,201	330,933	9,047,134
50	71280	Sterlington	Louisiana	8,628,375	6,795	8,635,170
51	77536	Deer Park	Texas	8,167,570	416,396	8,583,966
52	99737	Delta Junction	Alaska	8,401,174	150	8,401,324
53	42337	Drakesboro	Kentucky	8,367,272	44	8,367,316
54	73701	Enid	Oklahoma	8,270,300	0	8,270,300
55	48229	Ecorse	Michigan	390,152	7,731,697	8,121,849

Rank	Zip	City	State	Total On-site Disposal or Other Releases[1]	Total Off-site Disposal or Other Releases[2]	Total On- and Off-site Disposal or Other Releases
56	70346	Donaldsonville	Louisiana	7,983,198	0	7,983,198
57	45620	Cheshire	Ohio	7,973,454	5,496	7,978,950
58	63048	Herculaneum	Missouri	7,923,074	24,513	7,947,587
59	47620	Mount Vernon	Indiana	2,748,252	5,161,236	7,909,488
60	70805	Baton Rouge	Louisiana	6,952,113	735,104	7,687,216
61	48054	East China	Michigan	7,213,208	0	7,213,209
62	55308	Becker	Minnesota	7,189,113	93	7,189,205
63	63633	Centerville	Missouri	6,997,897	0	6,997,897
64	70665	Sulphur	Louisiana	6,922,268	40,798	6,963,066
65	82001	Cheyenne	Wyoming	6,694,900	0	6,694,900
66	70669	Westlake	Louisiana	6,623,551	66,383	6,689,934
67	47665	Owensville	Indiana	6,637,030	5	6,637,035
68	41230	Louisa	Kentucky	6,498,609	1,140	6,499,749
69	43812	Coshocton	Ohio	5,163,669	1,254,055	6,417,724
70	77856	Franklin	Texas	6,239,267	0	6,239,267
71	77905	Victoria	Texas	5,991,906	227,573	6,219,479
72	45715	Beverly	Ohio	6,192,891	7,602	6,200,494
73	37662	Kingsport	Tennessee	6,000,256	134,675	6,134,930
74	60436	Joliet	Illinois	4,659,212	1,388,463	6,047,675
75	58530	Center	North Dakota	4,327,045	1,664,495	5,991,540

Notes: *TRI = Toxic Release Inventory; Reporting year (RY) 2011 is the most recent TRI data available. Facilities reporting to TRI were required to submit RY 2011 data to EPA by July 1, 2012. This dataset includes revisions processed by EPA as of October 10, 2012 for the years 1988 to 2011. Revisions submitted to EPA after this time are not included.*

(1) On-site Disposal or Other Releases include Underground Injection to Class I Wells (Section 5.4.1), RCRA Subtitle C Landfills (5.5.1A), Other Landfills (5.5.1B), Fugitive or Non-point Air Emissions (5.1), Stack or Point Air Emissions (5.2), Surface Water Discharges (5.3), Underground Injection to Class II-V Wells (5.4.2), Land Treatment/Application Farming (5.5.2), RCRA Subtitle C Surface Impoundments (5.5.3A), Other Surface Impoundments (5.5.3B), and Other Land Disposal (5.5.4). Off-site Disposal or Other Releases include from Section 6.2 Class I Underground Injection Wells (M81), Class II-V Underground Injection Wells (M82, M71), RCRA Subtitle C Landfills (M65), Other Landfills (M64, M72), Storage Only (M10), Solidification/Stabilization - Metals and Metal Category Compounds only (M41 or M40), Wastewater Treatment (excluding POTWs) - Metals and Metal Category Compounds only (M62 or M61), RCRA Subtitle C Surface Impoundments (M66), Other Surface Impoundments (M67, M63), Land Treatment (M73), Other Land Disposal (M79), Other Off-site Management (M90), Transfers to Waste Broker - Disposal (M94, M91), and Unknown (M99) and, from Section 6.1 Transfers to POTWs (metals and metal category compounds only).

(2) Off-site disposal or other releases show only net off-site disposal or other releases, that is, off-site disposal or other releases transferred to other TRI facilities reporting such transfers as on-site disposal or other releases are not included to avoid double counting.

This report may not include all states in the US. A state may not be included in this report for two reasons: 1) there are no facilities reporting to TRI in the particular state; or 2) the facilities reporting to TRI in the particular state did not report to TRI for the user-specified selection criteria.

Users of TRI information should be aware that TRI data reflect releases and other waste management activities of chemicals, not whether (or to what degree) the public has been exposed to those chemicals. Release estimates alone are not sufficient to determine exposure or to calculate potential adverse effects on human health and the environment. TRI data, in conjunction with other information, can be used as a starting point in evaluating exposures that may result from releases and other waste management activities which involve toxic chemicals. The determination of potential risk depends upon many factors, including the toxicity of the chemical, the fate of the chemical, and the amount and duration of human or other exposure to the chemical after it is released.

Source: *U.S. Environmental Protection Agency, TRI Explorer, August 29, 2013*

MUNICIPAL SOLID WASTE IN THE UNITED STATES: 2011 FACTS AND FIGURES

EXECUTIVE SUMMARY

OVERVIEW

This report describes the national municipal solid waste (MSW) stream based on data collected for 1960 through 2011. The historical perspective is useful for establishing trends in types of MSW generated and in the ways it is managed. In this Executive Summary, we briefly describe the methodology used to characterize MSW in the United States and provide the latest facts and figures on MSW generation, recycling, and disposal.

In the United States, we generated 250 million tons of MSW in 2011—six million tons less than generated in 2007, which was a peak year for waste generation. Excluding composting, 66.2 million tons of MSW were recycled, an increase of 3 million tons from 2007. This is a 5 percent increase in recycling of MSW. The tons of food waste and yard trimmings recovered for composting were 20.7 million tons in 2011 compared to 21.7 million tons in 2007. This is a 5 percent decrease in food waste and yard trimmings recovered for composting. The recovery rate for recycling (including composting) was 34.7 percent in 2011, up from 33.1 percent in 2007. (See Table ES-1.)

MSW generation in 2011 declined to 4.40 pounds per person per day. This is a decrease of 6 percent from 2007 to 2011. The recycling rate in 2011 was 1.53 pounds per person per day compared to 1.54 pounds per person per day in 2007. Discards sent for combustion with energy recovery decreased about 12 percent from 0.58 pounds per person per day in 2007 to 0.51 pounds per person per day in 2011. Discards sent to landfills after recycling and combustion with energy recovery declined to 2.36 pounds per person per day in 2011. This is a decrease of 7 percent from 2007 to 2011.

Figure ES-1 shows a decrease in MSW generation in recent years. Figure ES-2 shows an increase in recycling over time. The state of the economy has a strong impact on consumption and waste generation. Waste generation increases during times of strong economic growth and decreases during times of economic decline.

Source: *U.S. EPA, Municipal Solid Waste in the United States, 2011 Facts and Figures*

Table ES-1. Generation, Materials Recovery, Composting, Combustion with Energy Recovery, and Discards of Municipal Solid Waste, 1960 – 2011

(In thousands of tons and percent of total generation)

	1960	1970	1980	1990	2000	2005	2007	2009	2010	2011
Thousands of Tons										
Generation	88,120	121,060	151,640	208,270	243,450	253,730	256,500	244,270	250,500	250,420
Recovery for recycling	5,610	8,020	14,520	29,040	53,010	59,240	63,100	61,640	64,960	66,200
Recovery for composting*	Neg.	Neg.	Neg.	4,200	16,450	20,550	21,710	20,750	20,170	20,700
Total Materials Recovery	5,610	8,020	14,520	33,240	69,460	79,790	84,810	82,390	85,130	86,900
Discards after recovery	82,510	113,040	137,120	175,030	173,990	173,940	171,690	161,880	165,370	163,520
Combustion with energy recovery**	0	400	2,700	29,700	33,730	31,620	31,970	29,010	29,260	29,260
Discards to landfill, other disposal†	82,510	112,640	134,420	145,330	140,260	142,320	139,720	132,870	136,110	134,260
Pounds per Person per Day										
Generation	2.68	3.25	3.66	4.57	4.74	4.69	4.66	4.36	4.44	4.40
Recovery for recycling	0.17	0.22	0.35	0.64	1.03	1.10	1.15	1.10	1.15	1.16
Recovery for composting*	Neg.	Neg.	Neg.	0.09	0.32	0.38	0.39	0.37	0.36	0.37
Total Materials Recovery	0.17	0.22	0.35	0.73	1.35	1.48	1.54	1.47	1.51	1.53
Discards after recovery	2.51	3.03	3.31	3.84	3.39	3.21	3.12	2.89	2.93	2.87
Combustion with energy recovery**	0.00	0.01	0.07	0.65	0.66	0.58	0.58	0.52	0.52	0.51
Discards to landfill, other disposal†	2.51	3.02	3.24	3.19	2.73	2.63	2.54	2.37	2.41	2.36
Population (thousands)	179,979	203,984	227,255	249,907	281,422	296,410	301,621	307,007	309,051	311,592
Percent of Total Generation										
Generation	100.0%	100.0%	100.0%	100.0%	100.0%	100.0%	100.0%	100.0%	100.0%	100.0%
Recovery for recycling	6.4%	6.6%	9.6%	14.0%	21.8%	23.3%	24.6%	25.2%	25.9%	26.4%
Recovery for composting*	Neg.	Neg.	Neg.	2.0%	6.7%	8.1%	8.5%	8.5%	8.1%	8.3%
Total Materials Recovery	6.4%	6.6%	9.6%	16.0%	28.5%	31.4%	33.1%	33.7%	34.0%	34.7%
Discards after recovery	93.6%	93.4%	90.4%	84.0%	71.5%	68.6%	66.9%	66.3%	66.0%	65.3%
Combustion with energy recovery**	0.0%	0.3%	1.8%	14.2%	13.9%	12.5%	12.5%	11.9%	11.7%	11.7%
Discards to landfill, other disposal†	93.6%	93.1%	88.6%	69.8%	57.6%	56.1%	54.4%	54.4%	54.3%	53.6%

* Composting of yard trimmings, food waste and other MSW organic material. Does not include backyard composting.

** Includes combustion of MSW in mass burn or refuse-derived fuel form, and combustion with energy recovery of source separated materials in MSW (e.g., wood pallets and tire-derived fuel). 2011 includes 25,930 MSW, 520 wood, and 2,810 tires (1,000 tons)

† Discards after recovery minus combustion with energy recovery. Discards include combustion without energy recovery.

Details may not add to totals due to rounding.

Source: *U.S. EPA, Municipal Solid Waste in the United States, 2011 Facts and Figures*

Figure ES-1. MSW Generation Rates, 1960 to 2011

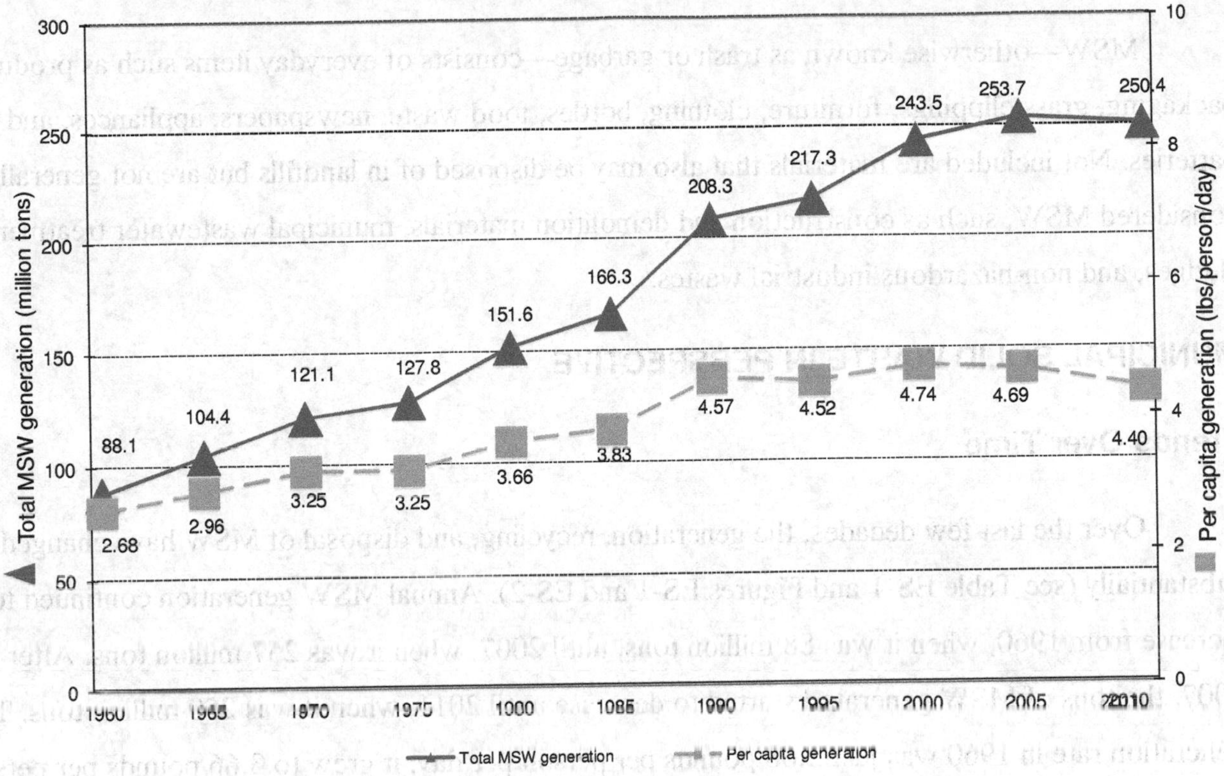

Figure ES-2. MSW Recycling Rates, 1960 to 2011

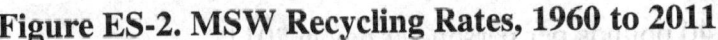

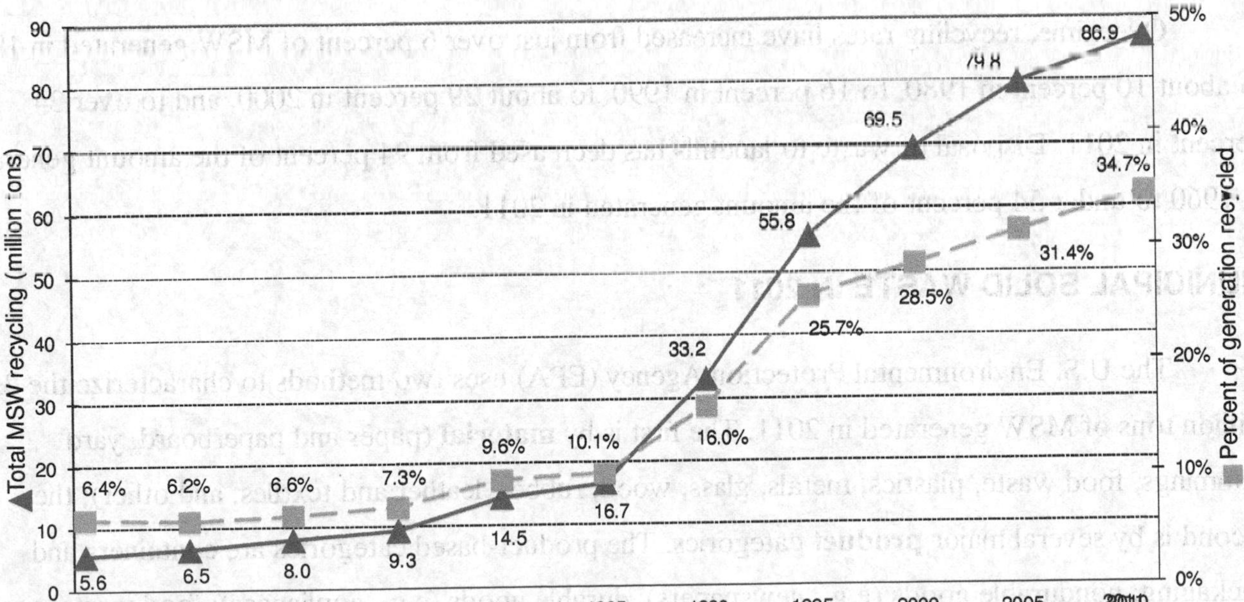

Source: *U.S. EPA, Municipal Solid Waste in the United States, 2011 Facts and Figures*

WHAT IS INCLUDED IN MUNICIPAL SOLID WASTE?

MSW—otherwise known as trash or garbage—consists of everyday items such as product packaging, grass clippings, furniture, clothing, bottles, food waste, newspapers, appliances, and batteries. Not included are materials that also may be disposed of in landfills but are not generally considered MSW, such as construction and demolition materials, municipal wastewater treatment sludges, and non-hazardous industrial wastes.

MUNICIPAL SOLID WASTE IN PERSPECTIVE

Trends Over Time

Over the last few decades, the generation, recycling, and disposal of MSW have changed substantially (see Table ES-1 and Figures ES-1 and ES-2). Annual MSW generation continued to increase from 1960, when it was 88 million tons, until 2007, when it was 257 million tons. After 2007, the tons of MSW generated started to decrease until 2011, when it was 250 million tons. The generation rate in 1960 was just 2.68 pounds per person per day; it grew to 3.66 pounds per person per day in 1980, reached 4.74 pounds per person per day in 2000, and decreased to 4.69 pounds per person per day in 2005. Since 2005, MSW generation per capita rate has continued to decrease. The generation rate was 4.40 pounds per person per day in 2011.

Over time, recycling rates have increased from just over 6 percent of MSW generated in 1960 to about 10 percent in 1980, to 16 percent in 1990, to about 29 percent in 2000, and to over 34 percent in 2011. Disposal of waste to landfills has decreased from 94 percent of the amount generated in 1960 to under 54 percent of the amount generated in 2011.

MUNICIPAL SOLID WASTE IN 2011

The U.S. Environmental Protection Agency (EPA) uses two methods to characterize the 250 million tons of MSW generated in 2011. The first is by **material** (paper and paperboard, yard trimmings, food waste, plastics, metals, glass, wood, rubber, leather and textiles, and other); the second is by several major **product** categories. The product-based categories are containers and packaging; nondurable goods (e.g., newspapers); durable goods (e.g., appliances); food waste; yard trimmings; and other materials. See Figure 1-B in Chapter 1 for product category definitions.

Source: *U.S. EPA, Municipal Solid Waste in the United States, 2011 Facts and Figures*

Materials in MSW

A breakdown, by weight, of the MSW **materials** generated in 2011 is provided in Figure ES-3. Paper and paperboard made up the largest component of MSW generated (28.0 percent), food waste was the second-largest component (14.5 percent) and yard trimmings were the third largest (13.5 percent). Metals, plastics, and wood each constituted between 6 and 13 percent of the total MSW generated. Rubber, leather, and textiles combined made up 8.2 percent of MSW, glass made up 4.6 percent, while other miscellaneous wastes made up 3.3 percent of the MSW generated in 2011.

Figure ES-3. Materials Generation in MSW, 2011
250 Million Tons (before recycling)

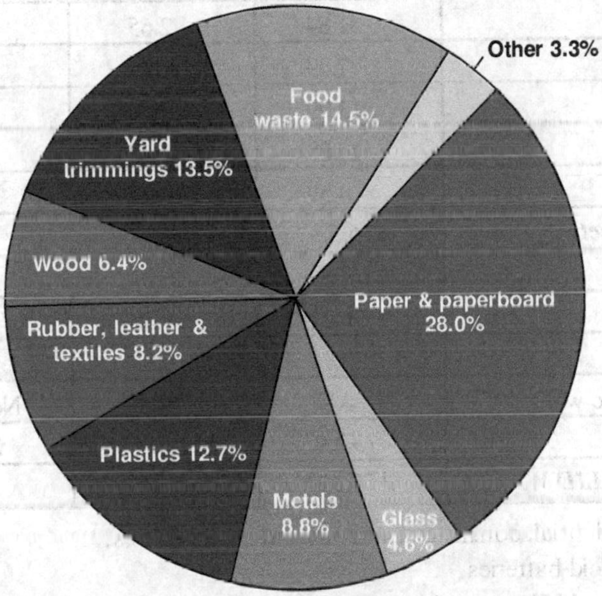

A portion of each material category in MSW was recycled or composted in 2011. The highest rates of recovery were achieved with paper and paperboard, yard trimmings, and metals. Over 65 percent (45.9 million tons) of paper and paperboard was recovered for recycling in 2011. About 57 percent (19.3 million tons) of yard trimmings was recovered for composting or mulching in 2011. This represents almost a five-fold increase since 1990. Recycling paper and paperboard and yard trimmings alone diverted about 26 percent of municipal solid waste generated from landfills and combustion facilities. In addition, about 7.5 million tons, or 34.2 percent, of metals were recovered for recycling. Recycling rates for all materials categories in 2011 are listed in Table ES-2.

Source: *U.S. EPA, Municipal Solid Waste in the United States, 2011 Facts and Figures*

Table ES-2. Generation, Recovery, and Discards of Materials in MSW, 2011

(In millions of tons and percent of generation of each material)

Material	Weight Generated	Weight Recovered	Recovery As a Percent of Generation	Weight Discarded
Paper and paperboard	70.02	45.90	65.6%	24.12
Glass	11.47	3.17	27.6%	8.30
Metals				
Steel	16.52	5.45	33.0%	11.07
Aluminum	3.47	0.72	20.7%	2.75
Other nonferrous metals*	1.96	1.34	68.4%	0.62
Total metals	*21.95*	*7.51*	*34.2%*	*14.44*
Plastics	31.84	2.65	8.3%	29.19
Rubber and leather	7.49	1.31	17.5%	6.18
Textiles	13.09	2.00	15.3%	11.09
Wood	16.08	2.38	14.8%	13.70
Other materials	4.59	1.28	27.9%	3.31
Total Materials in Products	*176.53*	*66.20*	*37.5%*	*110.33*
Other wastes				
Food, other**	36.31	1.40	3.9%	34.91
Yard trimmings	33.71	19.30	57.3%	14.41
Miscellaneous inorganic wastes	3.87	Negligible	Negligible	3.87
Total Other Wastes	*73.89*	*20.70*	*28.0%*	*53.19*
TOTAL MUNICIPAL SOLID WASTE	***250.42***	***86.90***	***34.7%***	***163.52***

Includes waste from residential, commercial, and institutional sources.
* Includes lead from lead-acid batteries.
** Includes recovery of other MSW organics for composting.
Details may not add to totals due to rounding.
Neg. = Less than 5,000 tons or 0.05 percent.

Figures ES-4 and ES-5 depict each material as a percent of total recovery and total discards, respectively. As a percent of total recovery, paper and paperboard make up over half of the materials recovered at 52.8 percent. Yard trimmings comprise the next largest portion of total materials recovery at 22.2 percent. All other materials account for less than 10 percent each of total recovery.

Food waste is the largest material in discards at 21.3 percent. Plastic is next largest at 17.8 percent followed by paper and paperboard at 14.8 percent and rubber, leather, and textiles at 10.6 percent. As a percent of total discards, the other materials account for less than 10 percent each.

Source: *U.S. EPA, Municipal Solid Waste in the United States, 2011 Facts and Figures*

Figure ES-4. Materials Recovery in MSW, 2011
87 Million Tons

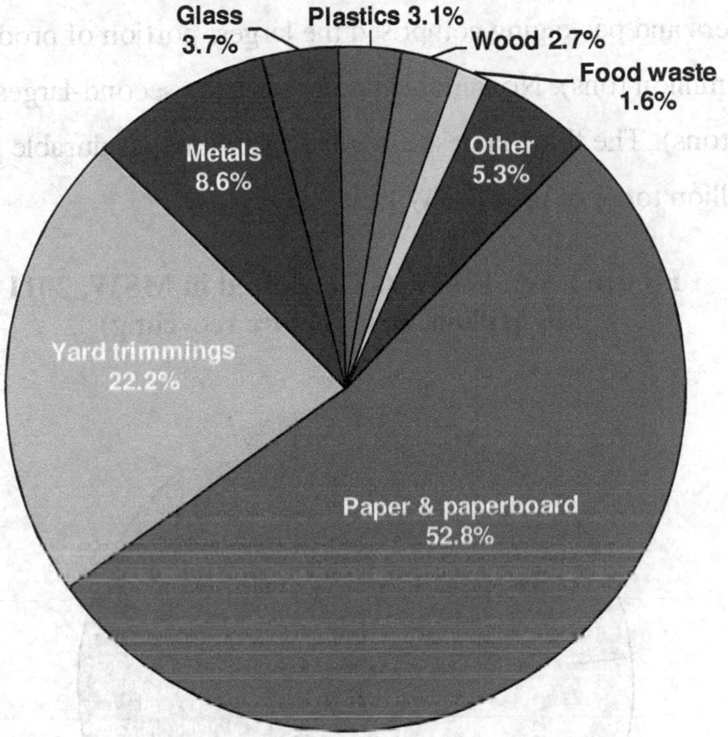

Figure ES-5. Material Discards in MSW, 2011
164 Million Tons (after recycling and composting)

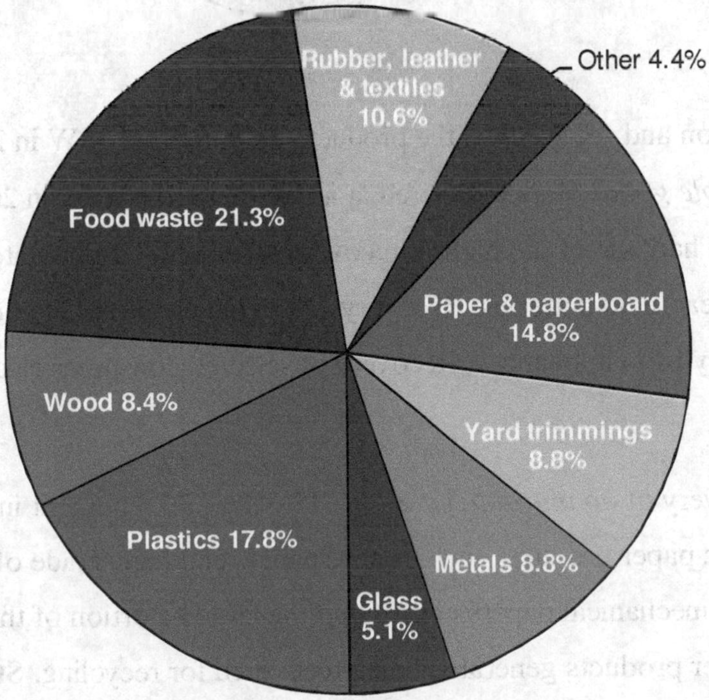

Source: *U.S. EPA, Municipal Solid Waste in the United States, 2011 Facts and Figures*

Products in MSW

The breakdown, by weight, of **product categories** generated in MSW in 2011 is shown in Figure ES-6. Containers and packaging comprised the largest portion of products generated in MSW, at 30.2 percent (75.6 million tons). Nondurable goods were the second-largest fraction, at 20.6 percent (51.6 million tons). The third-largest category of products is durable goods, which made up 19.7 percent (49.3 million tons) of total MSW generation.

Figure ES-6. Products Generated in MSW, 2011
250 Million Tons (before recycling)

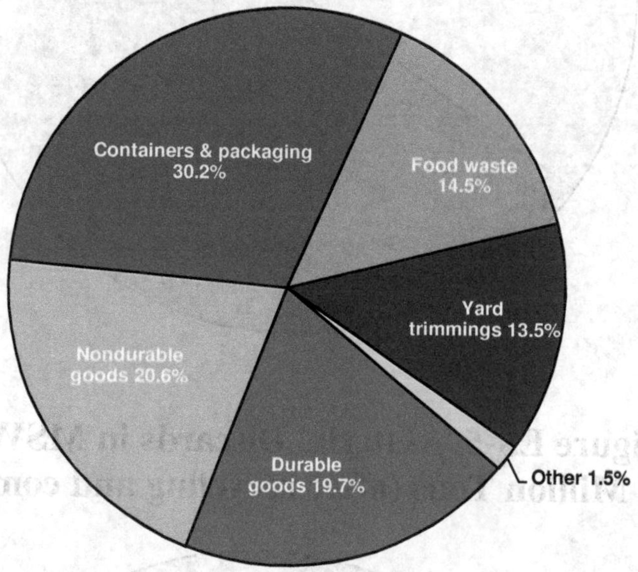

The generation and recovery of the product categories in MSW in 2011 are shown in Table ES-3. Overall, *durable goods* were recovered at a rate of 18.4 percent in 2011. Nonferrous metals other than aluminum had one of the highest recovery rates, at 68.4 percent, due to the high rate of lead recovery from lead-acid batteries. Recovery of steel in all durable goods was 27.1 percent, with high rates of recovery from appliances. Recovery of selected consumer electronic products was 24.9 percent.

Overall recovery of *nondurable goods* in MSW was 36.5 percent in 2011. Most of this recovery comes from paper products such as newspapers and high-grade office papers (e.g., white papers). Newspaper/mechanical papers constituted the largest portion of this recovery, with 72.5 percent of these paper products generated being recovered for recycling. Starting in 2010,

Source: *U.S. EPA, Municipal Solid Waste in the United States, 2011 Facts and Figures*

newspapers (including newsprint and groundwood inserts) were expanded to include directories and other mechanical papers previously counted as Other Commercial Printing. An estimated 46.6 percent of other nondurable paper products were recovered in 2011. Total nondurable paper and paperboard product recovery is at 53.9 percent. The nondurable goods category also includes clothing and other textile products—over 16 percent of these combined products were recovered for recycling or export in 2011.

Table ES-3 shows that recovery of containers and packaging was the highest of the three product categories—50.7 percent of containers and packaging generated in MSW in 2011 were recovered for recycling. Over 54 percent of all aluminum cans in MSW was recovered (38.9 percent of all aluminum packaging, including foil), while 72.0 percent of steel packaging (mostly cans) in MSW was recovered. Paper and paperboard containers and packaging were recovered at a rate of 75.4 percent; corrugated containers accounted for most of that amount.

Approximately 34 percent of glass containers in MSW were recovered, while about 24 percent of wood packaging (mostly wood pallets removed from service) was recovered for recycling. About 13 percent of plastic containers and packaging in MSW were recovered—mostly bottles and jars. Polyethylene terephthalate (PET) bottles and jars were recovered at about 29 percent. Recovery of high density polyethylene (HDPE) natural (white translucent) bottles was also estimated at about 29 percent.

The results of recovering containers and packaging are illustrated in Figures ES-7 and ES-8. Corrugated boxes account for 39 percent of total containers and packaging generation but, due to a high recovery rate, only account for seven percent of discards. Wood packaging makes up 13 percent of containers and packaging generation and 20 percent of discards. Plastic bags, sacks, and wraps are five percent of generation and nine percent of discards. Although steel and aluminum containers and packaging have high recovery rates (see Table ES-3), each account for two to three percent of generation and discards. This is due to the relatively small amounts of these products generated.

One of the products with a very high recovery rate was lead-acid batteries, recovered at a rate of about 96 percent in 2011. Other products with particularly high recovery rates were corrugated boxes (91 percent), newspapers/mechanical papers (72.5 percent), steel packaging (72.0 percent), major appliances (64.2 percent), aluminum cans (54.5 percent), yard trimmings (57.3), and mixed paper (46.6 percent). About 45 percent of rubber tires in MSW were recovered for recycling. (Other

Source: *U.S. EPA, Municipal Solid Waste in the United States, 2011 Facts and Figures*

tires were retreaded, and shredded rubber tires were made into tire-derived fuel.) See Chapter 2 of this report for additional detail on product recovery rates.

Table ES-3. Generation, Recovery, and Discards of Products in MSW by Material, 2011

(In millions of tons and percent of generation of each product)

Products	Weight Generated	Weight Recovered	Recovery as a Percent of Generation	Weight Discarded
Durable Goods				
Steel	14.34	3.88	27.1%	10.46
Aluminum	1.43	Negligible	Negligible	1.43
Other non-ferrous metals*	1.96	1.34	68.4%	0.62
Glass	2.19	Negligible	Negligible	2.19
Plastics	11.42	0.74	6.5%	10.68
Rubber and leather	6.44	1.31	20.3%	5.13
Wood	6.03	Negligible	Negligible	6.03
Textiles	3.84	0.52	13.5%	3.32
Other materials	1.69	1.28	75.7%	0.41
Total durable goods	*49.34*	*9.07*	*18.4%*	*40.27*
Nondurable Goods				
Paper and paperboard	31.99	17.24	53.9%	14.75
Plastics	6.52	0.11	1.7%	6.41
Rubber and leather	1.05	Negligible	Negligible	1.05
Textiles	8.95	1.48	16.5%	7.47
Other materials	3.10	Negligible	Negligible	3.10
Total nondurable goods	*51.61*	*18.83*	*36.5%*	*32.78*
Containers and Packaging				
Steel	2.18	1.57	72.0%	0.61
Aluminum	1.85	0.72	38.9%	1.13
Glass	9.28	3.17	34.2%	6.11
Paper and paperboard	38.02	28.66	75.4%	9.36
Plastics	13.90	1.80	12.9%	12.10
Wood	10.00	2.38	23.8%	7.62
Other materials	0.35	Negligible	Negligible	0.35
Total containers and packaging	*75.58*	*38.30*	*50.7%*	*37.28*
Other Wastes				
Food, other**	36.31	1.40	3.9%	34.91
Yard trimmings	33.71	19.30	57.3%	14.41
Miscellaneous inorganic wastes	3.87	Negligible	Negligible	3.87
Total other wastes	*73.89*	*20.70*	*28.0%*	*53.19*
TOTAL MUNICIPAL SOLID WASTE	***250.42***	***86.90***	***34.7%***	***163.52***

Includes waste from residential, commercial, and institutional sources.

* Includes lead from lead-acid batteries.

** Includes recovery of other MSW organics for composting.

Details may not add to totals due to rounding.

Neg. = Less than 5,000 tons or 0.05 percent.

***Source:** U.S. EPA, Municipal Solid Waste in the United States, 2011 Facts and Figures*

Figure ES-7. Containers and Packaging Generated in MSW, 2011
75.6 Million Tons (before recycling)

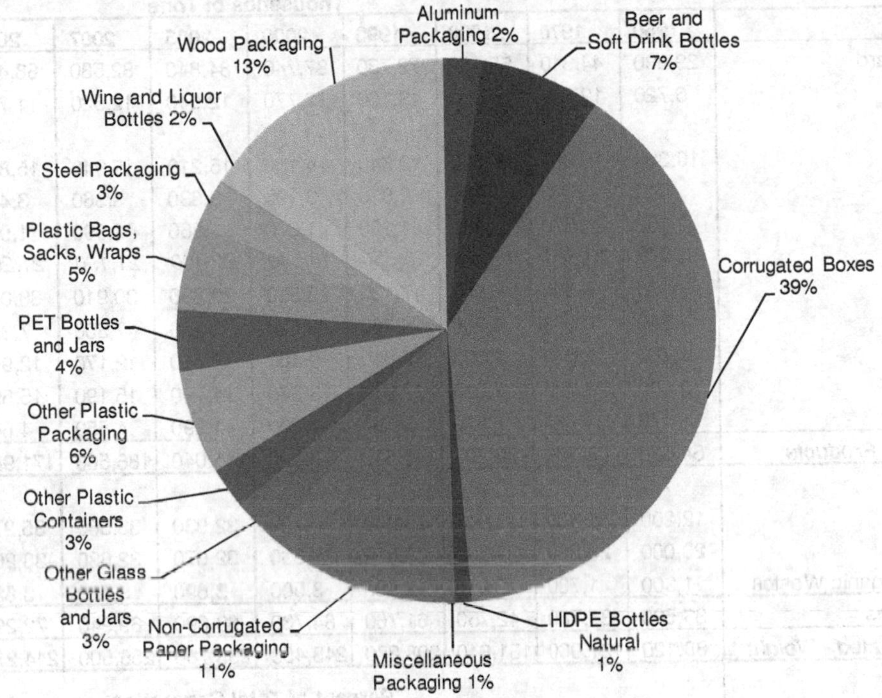

Figure ES-8. Containers and Packaging Discarded* in MSW, 2011
37.3 Million Tons (after recycling)

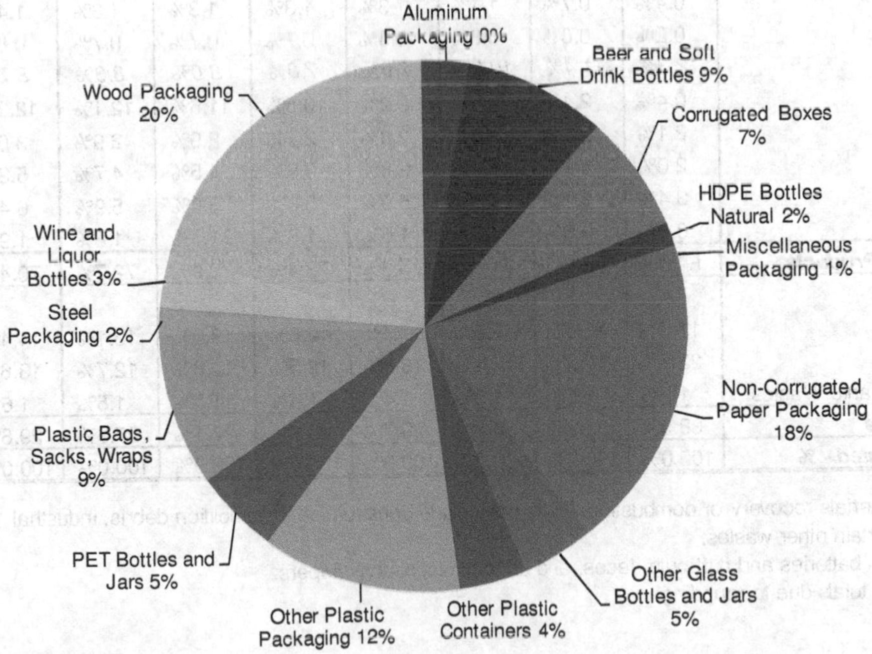

*Discards in this figure include combustion with energy recovery.

Source: *U.S. EPA, Municipal Solid Waste in the United States, 2011 Facts and Figures*

MATERIALS GENERATED* IN THE MUNICIPAL WASTE STREAM, 1960 TO 2011
(In thousands of tons and percent of total generation)

	Thousands of Tons									
Materials	**1960**	**1970**	**1980**	**1990**	**2000**	**2005**	**2007**	**2009**	**2010**	**2011**
Paper and Paperboard	29,990	44,310	55,160	72,730	87,740	84,840	82,530	68,430	71,310	70,020
Glass	6,720	12,740	15,130	13,100	12,770	12,540	12,520	11,780	11,530	11,470
Metals										
Ferrous	10,300	12,360	12,620	12,640	14,150	15,210	15,940	15,860	16,820	16,520
Aluminum	340	800	1,730	2,810	3,190	3,330	3,360	3,440	3,500	3,470
Other Nonferrous	180	670	1,160	1,100	1,600	1,860	1,890	1,900	2,000	1,960
Total Metals	*10,820*	*13,830*	*15,510*	*16,550*	*18,940*	*20,400*	*21,190*	*21,200*	*22,320*	*21,950*
Plastics	390	2,900	6,830	17,130	25,550	29,380	30,910	30,050	31,290	31,840
Rubber and Leather	1,840	2,970	4,200	5,790	6,670	7,290	7,500	7,350	7,400	7,490
Textiles	1,760	2,040	2,530	5,810	9,480	11,510	12,170	12,940	13,100	13,090
Wood	3,030	3,720	7,010	12,210	13,570	14,790	15,190	15,590	15,880	16,080
Other **	70	770	2,520	3,190	4,000	4,290	4,550	4,640	4,690	4,590
Total Materials in Products	54,620	83,280	108,890	146,510	178,720	185,040	186,560	171,980	177,520	176,530
Other Wastes										
Food Waste	12,200	12,800	13,000	23,860	30,700	32,930	33,560	35,270	35,740	36,310
Yard Trimmings	20,000	23,200	27,500	35,000	30,530	32,070	32,630	33,200	33,400	33,710
Miscellaneous Inorganic Wastes	1,300	1,780	2,250	2,900	3,500	3,690	3,750	3,820	3,840	3,870
Total Other Wastes	33,500	37,780	42,750	61,760	64,730	68,690	69,940	72,290	72,980	73,890
Total MSW Generated - Weight	88,120	121,060	151,640	208,270	243,450	253,730	256,500	244,270	250,500	250,420

	Percent of Total Generation									
Materials	**1960**	**1970**	**1980**	**1990**	**2000**	**2005**	**2007**	**2009**	**2010**	**2011**
Paper and Paperboard	34.0%	36.6%	36.4%	34.9%	36.0%	33.4%	32.2%	28.0%	28.5%	28.0%
Glass	7.6%	10.5%	10.0%	6.3%	5.2%	4.9%	4.9%	4.8%	4.6%	4.6%
Metals										
Ferrous	11.7%	10.2%	8.3%	6.1%	5.8%	6.0%	6.2%	6.5%	6.7%	6.6%
Aluminum	0.4%	0.7%	1.1%	1.3%	1.3%	1.3%	1.3%	1.4%	1.4%	1.4%
Other Nonferrous	0.2%	0.6%	0.8%	0.5%	0.7%	0.7%	0.7%	0.8%	0.8%	0.8%
Total Metals	*12.3%*	*11.4%*	*10.2%*	*7.9%*	*7.8%*	*8.0%*	*8.3%*	*8.7%*	*8.9%*	*8.8%*
Plastics	0.4%	2.4%	4.5%	8.2%	10.5%	11.6%	12.1%	12.3%	12.5%	12.7%
Rubber and Leather	2.1%	2.5%	2.8%	2.8%	2.7%	2.9%	2.9%	3.0%	3.0%	3.0%
Textiles	2.0%	1.7%	1.7%	2.8%	3.9%	4.5%	4.7%	5.3%	5.2%	5.2%
Wood	3.4%	3.1%	4.6%	5.9%	5.6%	5.8%	5.9%	6.4%	6.3%	6.4%
Other **	0.1%	0.6%	1.7%	1.5%	1.6%	1.7%	1.8%	1.9%	1.9%	1.8%
Total Materials in Products	62.0%	68.8%	71.8%	70.3%	73.4%	72.9%	72.7%	70.4%	70.9%	70.5%
Other Wastes										
Food Waste	13.8%	10.6%	8.6%	11.5%	12.6%	13.0%	13.1%	14.4%	14.3%	14.5%
Yard Trimmings	22.7%	19.2%	18.1%	16.8%	12.5%	12.6%	12.7%	13.6%	13.3%	13.5%
Miscellaneous Inorganic Wastes	1.5%	1.5%	1.5%	1.4%	1.4%	1.5%	1.5%	1.6%	1.5%	1.5%
Total Other Wastes	38.0%	31.2%	28.2%	29.7%	26.6%	27.1%	27.3%	29.6%	29.1%	29.5%
Total MSW Generated - %	100.0%	100.0%	100.0%	100.0%	100.0%	100.0%	100.0%	100.0%	100.0%	100.0%

* Generation before materials recovery or combustion. Does not include construction & demolition debris, industrial process wastes, or certain other wastes.

** Includes electrolytes in batteries and fluff pulp, feces, and urine in disposable diapers.
Details may not add to totals due to rounding.

Source: *U.S. EPA, Municipal Solid Waste in the United States, 2011 Facts and Figures*

RECOVERY* OF MUNICIPAL SOLID WASTE, 1960 TO 2011
(In thousands of tons and percent of generation of each material)

	Thousands of Tons									
Materials	**1960**	**1970**	**1980**	**1990**	**2000**	**2005**	**2007**	**2009**	**2010**	**2011**
Paper and Paperboard	5,080	6,770	11,740	20,230	37,560	41,960	44,480	42,500	44,570	45,900
Glass	100	160	750	2,630	2,880	2,590	2,880	3,000	3,130	3,170
Metals										
Ferrous	50	150	370	2,230	4,680	5,020	5,280	5,310	5,760	5,450
Aluminum	Neg.	10	310	1,010	860	690	730	690	680	720
Other Nonferrous	Neg.	320	540	730	1,060	1,280	1,300	1,300	1,390	1,340
Total Metals	*50*	*480*	*1,220*	*3,970*	*6,600*	*6,990*	*7,310*	*7,300*	*7,830*	*7,510*
Plastics	Neg.	Neg.	20	370	1,480	1,780	2,110	2,120	2,500	2,650
Rubber and Leather	330	250	130	370	820	1,050	1,140	1,310	1,300	1,310
Textiles	50	60	160	660	1,320	1,830	1,920	1,970	2,010	2,000
Wood	Neg.	Neg.	Neg.	130	1,370	1,830	2,020	2,200	2,300	2,380
Other **	Neg.	300	500	680	980	1,210	1,240	1,240	1,320	1,280
Total Materials in Products	5,610	8,020	14,520	29,040	53,010	59,240	63,100	61,640	64,960	66,200
Other Wastes										
Food Waste	Neg.	Neg.	Neg.	Neg.	680	690	810	850	970	1,400
Yard Trimmings	Neg.	Neg.	Neg.	4,200	15,770	19,860	20,900	19,900	19,200	19,300
Miscellaneous Inorganic Wastes	Neg.	Neg.	Neg.	Neg.	Neg.	Neg.	Neg.	Neg.	Neg.	Neg.
Total Other Wastes	Neg.	Neg.	Neg.	4,200	16,450	20,550	21,710	20,750	20,170	20,700
Total MSW Recovered - Weight	5,610	8,020	14,520	33,240	69,460	79,790	84,810	82,390	85,130	86,900

	Percent of Generation of Each Material									
Materials	**1960**	**1970**	**1980**	**1990**	**2000**	**2005**	**2007**	**2009**	**2010**	**2011**
Paper and Paperboard	16.9%	15.3%	21.3%	27.8%	42.8%	49.5%	53.9%	62.1%	62.5%	65.6%
Glass	1.5%	1.3%	5.0%	20.1%	22.6%	20.7%	23.0%	25.5%	27.1%	27.6%
Metals										
Ferrous	0.5%	1.2%	2.9%	17.6%	33.1%	33.0%	33.1%	33.5%	34.2%	33.0%
Aluminum	Neg.	1.3%	17.9%	35.9%	27.0%	20.7%	21.7%	20.1%	19.4%	20.7%
Other Nonferrous	Neg.	47.8%	46.6%	66.4%	66.3%	68.8%	68.8%	68.4%	69.5%	68.4%
Total Metals	*0.5%*	*3.5%*	*7.9%*	*24.0%*	*34.8%*	*31.3%*	*34.5%*	*34.4%*	*35.1%*	*34.2%*
Plastics	Neg.	Neg.	0.3%	2.2%	5.8%	6.1%	6.8%	7.1%	8.0%	8.3%
Rubber and Leather	17.9%	8.4%	3.1%	6.4%	12.3%	14.4%	15.2%	17.8%	17.6%	17.5%
Textiles	2.8%	2.9%	6.3%	11.4%	13.9%	15.9%	15.8%	15.2%	15.3%	15.3%
Wood	Neg.	Neg.	Neg.	1.1%	10.1%	12.4%	13.3%	14.1%	14.5%	14.8%
Other **	Neg.	39.0%	19.8%	21.3%	24.5%	28.2%	27.3%	26.7%	28.1%	27.9%
Total Materials in Products	10.3%	9.6%	13.3%	19.8%	29.7%	32.0%	33.8%	35.8%	36.6%	37.5%
Other Wastes										
Food, Other^	Neg.	Neg.	Neg.	Neg.	2.2%	2.1%	2.4%	2.4%	2.7%	3.9%
Yard Trimmings	Neg.	Neg.	Neg.	12.0%	51.7%	61.9%	64.1%	59.9%	57.5%	57.3%
Miscellaneous Inorganic Wastes	Neg.	Neg.	Neg.	Neg.	Neg.	Neg.	Neg.	Neg.	Neg.	Neg.
Total Other Wastes	Neg.	Neg.	Neg.	6.8%	25.4%	29.9%	31.0%	28.7%	27.6%	28.0%
Total MSW Recovered - %	6.4%	6.6%	9.6%	16.0%	28.5%	31.4%	33.1%	33.7%	34.0%	34.7%

* Recovery of postconsumer wastes; does not include converting/fabrication scrap.
** Recovery of electrolytes in batteries; probably not recycled.
Neg. = Less than 5,000 tons or 0.05 percent.
^ Includes recovery of paper and mixed MSW for composting.
Details may not add to totals due to rounding.

Source: *U.S. EPA, Municipal Solid Waste in the United States, 2011 Facts and Figures*

MATERIALS DISCARDED* IN THE MUNICIPAL WASTE STREAM, 1960 TO 2011
(In thousands of tons and percent of total discards)

	Thousands of Tons									
Materials	**1960**	**1970**	**1980**	**1990**	**2000**	**2005**	**2007**	**2009**	**2010**	**2011**
Paper and Paperboard	24,910	37,540	43,420	52,500	50,180	42,880	38,050	25,930	26,740	24,120
Glass	6,620	12,580	14,380	10,470	9,890	9,950	9,640	8,780	8,400	8,300
Metals										
Ferrous	10,250	12,210	12,250	10,410	9,470	10,190	10,660	10,550	11,060	11,070
Aluminum	340	790	1,420	1,800	2,330	2,640	2,630	2,750	2,820	2,750
Other Nonferrous	180	350	620	370	540	580	590	600	610	620
Total Metals	*10,770*	*13,350*	*14,290*	*12,580*	*12,340*	*13,410*	*13,880*	13,900	*14,490*	*14,440*
Plastics	390	2,900	6,810	16,760	24,070	27,600	28,800	27,930	28,790	29,190
Rubber and Leather	1,510	2,720	4,070	5,420	5,850	6,240	6,360	6,040	6,100	6,180
Textiles	1,710	1,980	2,370	5,150	8,160	9,680	10,250	10,970	11,090	11,090
Wood	3,030	3,720	7,010	12,080	12,200	12,960	13,170	13,390	13,580	13,700
Other **	70	470	2,020	2,510	3,020	3,080	3,310	3,400	3,370	3,310
Total Materials in Products	49,010	75,260	94,370	117,470	125,710	125,800	123,460	110,340	112,560	110,330
Other Wastes										
Food Waste	12,200	12,800	13,000	23,860	30,020	32,240	32,750	34,420	34,770	34,910
Yard Trimmings	20,000	23,200	27,500	30,800	14,760	12,210	11,730	13,300	14,200	14,410
Miscellaneous Inorganic Wastes	1,300	1,780	2,250	2,900	3,500	3,690	3,750	3,820	3,840	3,870
Total Other Wastes	33,500	37,780	42,750	57,560	48,280	48,140	48,230	51,540	52,810	53,190
Total MSW Discarded - Weight	82,510	113,040	137,120	175,030	173,990	173,940	171,690	161,880	165,370	163,520
	Percent of Total Discards									
Materials	**1960**	**1970**	**1980**	**1990**	**2000**	**2005**	**2007**	**2009**	**2010**	**2011**
Paper and Paperboard	30.2%	33.2%	31.7%	30.0%	28.8%	24.7%	22.2%	16.0%	16.2%	14.8%
Glass	8.0%	11.1%	10.5%	6.0%	5.7%	5.7%	5.6%	5.4%	5.1%	5.1%
Metals										
Ferrous	12.4%	10.8%	8.9%	5.9%	5.4%	5.9%	6.2%	6.5%	6.7%	6.8%
Aluminum	0.4%	0.7%	1.0%	1.0%	1.3%	1.5%	1.5%	1.7%	1.7%	1.7%
Other Nonferrous	0.2%	0.3%	0.5%	0.2%	0.3%	0.3%	0.3%	0.4%	0.4%	0.4%
Total Metals	*13.1%*	*11.8%*	*10.4%*	*7.2%*	*7.1%*	*7.7%*	*8.1%*	*8.6%*	*8.8%*	*8.8%*
Plastics	0.5%	2.6%	5.0%	9.6%	13.8%	15.9%	16.8%	17.3%	17.4%	17.9%
Rubber and Leather	1.8%	2.4%	3.0%	3.1%	3.4%	3.6%	3.7%	3.7%	3.7%	3.8%
Textiles	2.1%	1.8%	1.7%	2.9%	4.7%	5.6%	6.0%	6.8%	6.7%	6.8%
Wood	3.7%	3.3%	5.1%	6.9%	7.0%	7.5%	7.7%	8.3%	8.2%	8.4%
Other **	0.1%	0.4%	1.5%	1.4%	1.7%	1.8%	1.9%	2.1%	2.0%	2.0%
Total Materials in Products	59.4%	66.6%	68.8%	67.1%	72.3%	72.3%	71.9%	68.2%	68.1%	67.5%
Other Wastes										
Food Waste	14.8%	11.3%	9.5%	13.6%	17.3%	18.5%	19.1%	21.3%	21.0%	21.3%
Yard Trimmings	24.2%	20.5%	20.1%	17.6%	8.5%	7.0%	6.8%	8.2%	8.6%	8.8%
Miscellaneous Inorganic Wastes	1.6%	1.6%	1.6%	1.7%	2.0%	2.1%	2.2%	2.4%	2.3%	2.4%
Total Other Wastes	40.6%	33.4%	31.2%	32.9%	27.7%	27.7%	28.1%	31.8%	31.9%	32.5%
Total MSW Discarded - %	100.0%	100.0%	100.0%	100.0%	100.0%	100.0%	100.0%	100.0%	100.0%	100.0%

* Discards after materials and compost recovery. In this table, discards include combustion with energy recovery.
Does not include construction & demolition debris, industrial process wastes, or certain other wastes.

** Includes electrolytes in batteries and fluff pulp, feces, and urine in disposable diapers.
Details may not add to totals due to rounding.

Source: *U.S. EPA, Municipal Solid Waste in the United States, 2011 Facts and Figures*

PAPER AND PAPERBOARD PRODUCTS IN MSW, 2011
(In thousands of tons and percent of generation)

Product Category	Generation (Thousand tons)	Recovery (Thousand tons)	Recovery (Percent of generation)	Discards (Thousand tons)
Nondurable Goods				
Newspapers/Mechanical Papers†	9,150	6,630	72.5%	2,520
Books	930			
Magazines	1,510			
Office-type Papers*	5,100			
Standard Mail**	3,750			
Other Commercial Printing	2,710			
Tissue Paper and Towels	3,510			
Paper Plates and Cups	1,340			
Other Nonpackaging Paper***	3,940			
Subtotal Nondurable Goods excluding Newspaper/Mechanical Papers§	22,790	10,610	46.6%	12,180
Total Paper and Paperboard Nondurable Goods	31,940	17,240	54.0%	14,700
Containers and Packaging				
Corrugated Boxes	29,440	26,800	91.0%	2,640
Gable Top/Aseptic Cartons‡	540			
Folding Cartons	5,540			
Other Paperboard Packaging	80			
Bags and Sacks	750			
Other Paper Packaging	1,670			
Subtotal Containers and Packaging excluding Corrugated Boxes§	8,580	1,860	21.7%	6,720
Total Paper and Paperboard Containers and Packaging	38,020	28,660	75.4%	9,360
Total Paper and Paperboard^	69,960	45,900	65.6%	24,060

† Starting in 2010, newsprint and groundwood inserts expanded to include directories and other mechanical papers previously counted as Other Commercial Printing.
* High-grade papers such as copy paper and printer paper; both residential and commercial.
** Formerly called Third Class Mail by the U.S. Postal Service.
*** Includes paper in games and novelties, cards, etc.
§ Valid default values for separating out paper and paperboard sub-categories for recovery and discards were not available.
‡ Includes milk, juice, and other products packaged in gable top cartons and liquid food aseptic cartons.
^ Table 4 does not include 10,000 tons of paper used in durable goods and 50,000 tons tissue in disposable diapers (Table 1).
Neg. = Less than 5,000 tons or 0.05 percent.

***Source:** U.S. EPA, Municipal Solid Waste in the United States, 2011 Facts and Figures*

Figure 3. Paper and paperboard generation and recovery, 1960 to 2011

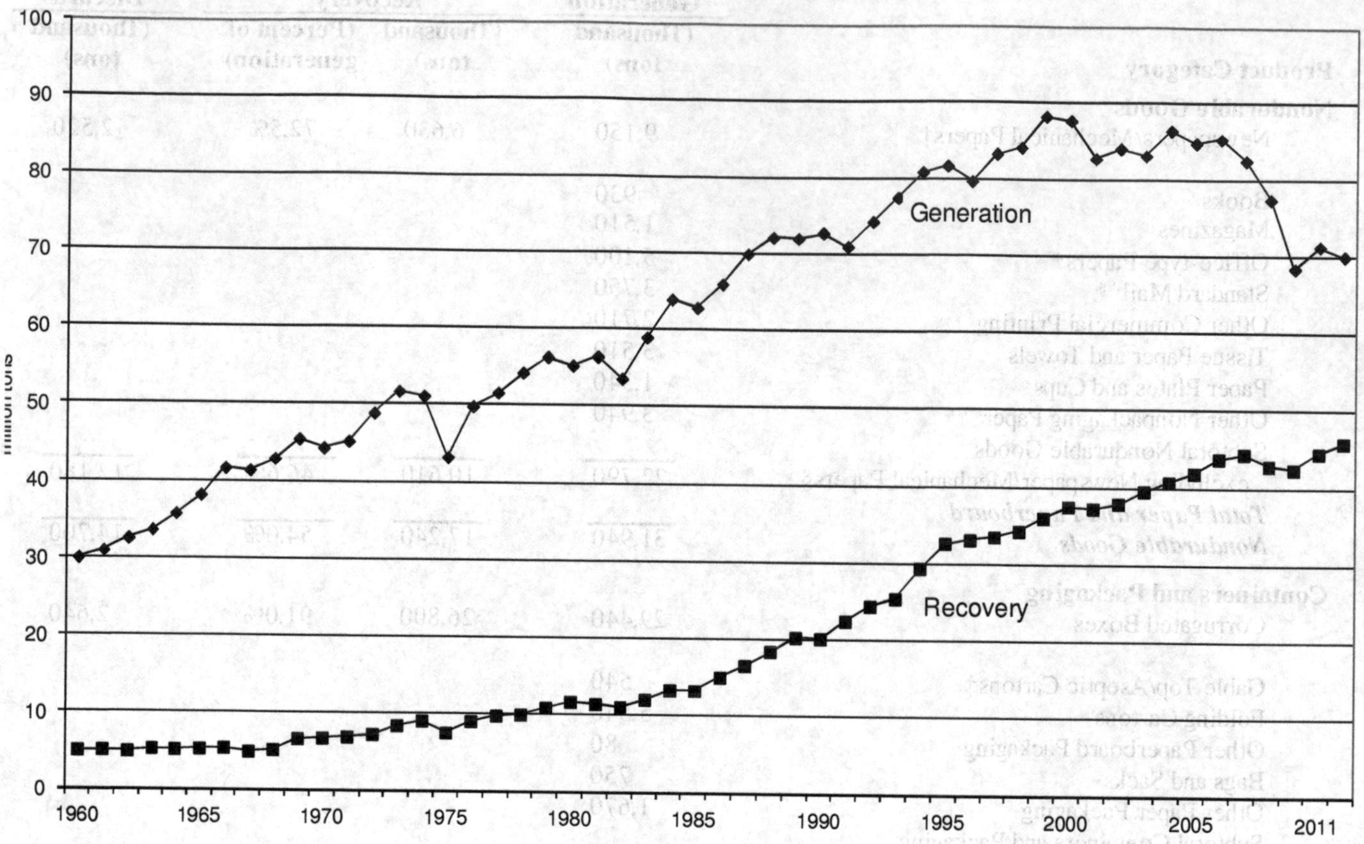

Source: *U.S. EPA, Municipal Solid Waste in the United States, 2011 Facts and Figures*

GLASS PRODUCTS IN MSW, 2011
(In thousands of tons and percent of generation)

Product Category	Generation (Thousand tons)	Recovery (Thousand tons)	Recovery (Percent of generation)	Discards (Thousand tons)
Durable Goods*	2,190	Neg.	Neg.	2,190
Containers and Packaging				
Beer and Soft Drink Bottles**	5,520	2,270	41.1%	3,250
Wine and Liquor Bottles	1,770	600	33.9%	1,170
Other Bottles and Jars	1,990	300	15.1%	1,690
Total Glass Containers	9,280	3,170	34.2%	6,110
Total Glass	11,470	3,170	27.6%	8,300

* Glass as a component of appliances, furniture, consumer electronics, etc.

** Includes carbonated drinks and non-carbonated water, teas, flavored drinks, and ready-to-drink alcoholic coolers and cocktails.

Neg. = Less than 5,000 tons or 0.05 percent.

Details may not add to totals due to rounding.

Source: *U.S. EPA, Municipal Solid Waste in the United States, 2011 Facts and Figures*

Figure 5. Glass generation and recovery, 1960 to 2011

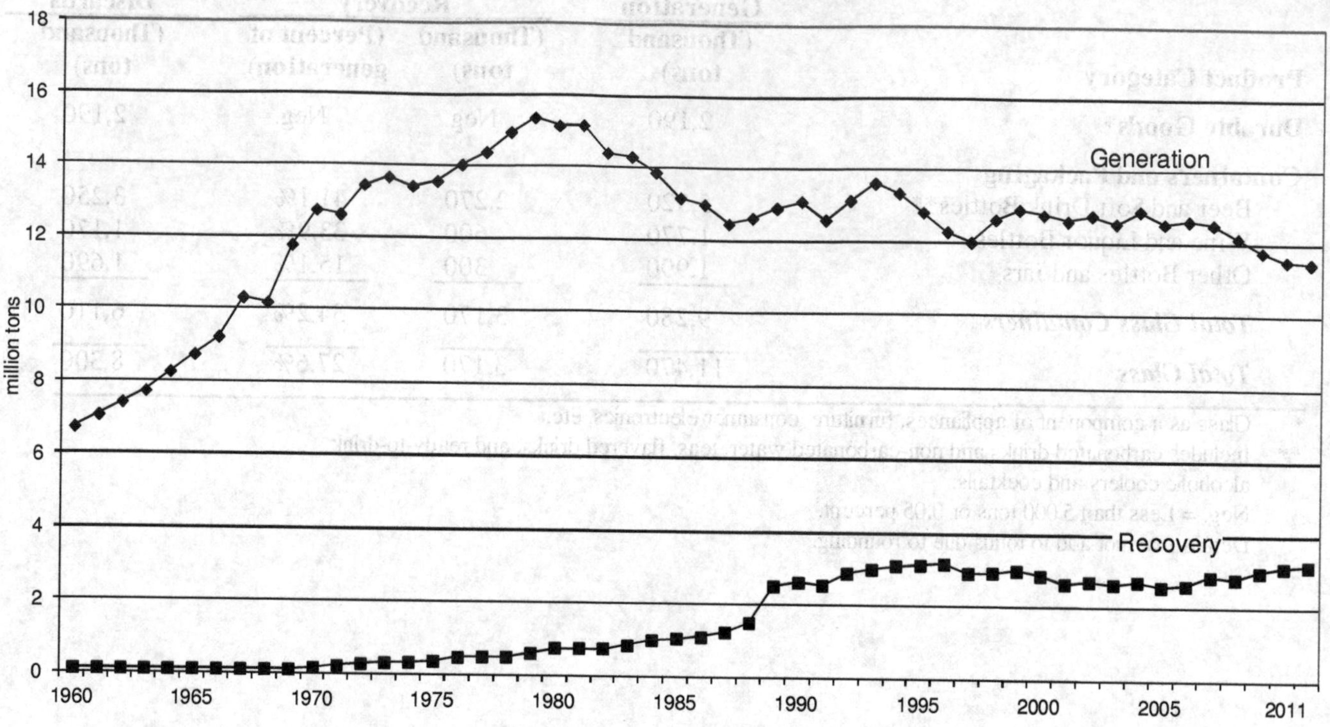

Source: *U.S. EPA, Municipal Solid Waste in the United States, 2011 Facts and Figures*

METAL PRODUCTS IN MSW, 2011
(In thousands of tons and percent of generation)

Product Category	Generation (Thousand tons)	Recovery (Thousand tons)	Recovery (Percent of generation)	Discards (Thousand tons)
Durable Goods				
Ferrous Metals*	14,340	3,880	27.1%	10,460
Aluminum**	1,430	NA		1,430
Lead†	1,390	1,340	96%	50
Other Nonferrous Metals‡	570	Neg.	Neg.	570
Total Metals in Durable Goods	17,730	5,220	29.4%	12,510
Nondurable Goods				
Aluminum	190	Neg.	Neg.	190
Containers and Packaging				
Steel				
Cans	1,800	1,270	70.6%	530
Other Steel Packaging	380	300	78.9%	80
Total Steel Packaging	2,180	1,570	72.0%	610
Aluminum				
Beer and Soft Drink Cans§	1,320	720	54.5%	600
Other Cans	70	NA		70
Foil and Closures	460	NA		460
Total Aluminum Packaging	1,850	720	38.9%	1,130
Total Metals in Containers and Packaging	4,030	2,290	56.8%	1,740
Total Metals	21,950	7,510	34.2%	14,440
Ferrous	16,520	5,450	33.0%	11,070
Aluminum	3,470	720	20.7%	2,750
Other nonferrous	1,960	1,340	68.4%	620

* Ferrous metals (iron and steel) in appliances, furniture, tires, and miscellaneous durables.
** Aluminum in appliances, furniture, and miscellaneous durables.
† Lead in lead-acid batteries.
‡ Other nonferrous metals in appliances and miscellaneous durables.
§ Aluminum can recovery does not include used beverage cans imported to produce new beverage cans.
Neg. = Less than 5,000 tons or 0.05 percent. NA = Not Available
Details may not add to totals due to rounding.

Source: *U.S. EPA, Municipal Solid Waste in the United States, 2011 Facts and Figures*

Figure 7. Metals generation and recovery, 1960 to 2011

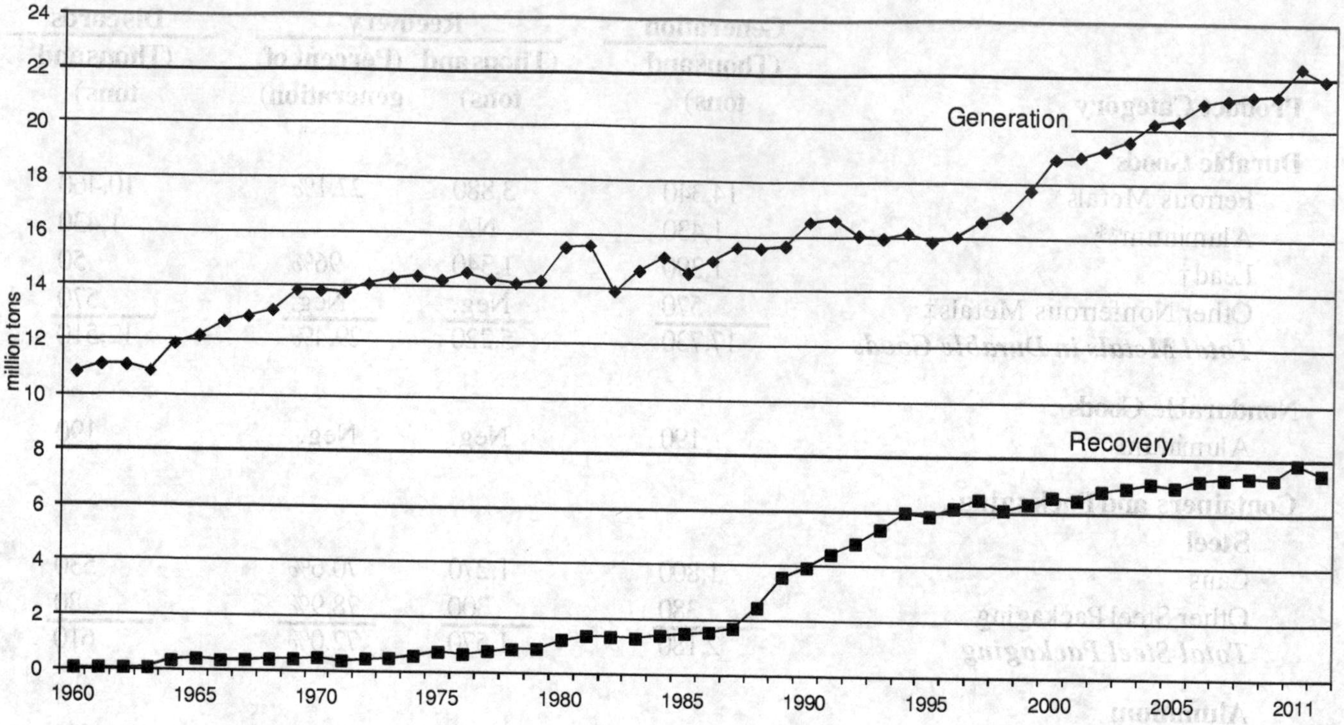

Source: *U.S. EPA, Municipal Solid Waste in the United States, 2011 Facts and Figures*

PLASTICS IN PRODUCTS IN MSW, 2011
(In thousands of tons, and percent of generation by resin)

Product Category	Generation (Thousand tons)	Recovery (Thousand tons)	Recovery (Percent of Gen.)	Discards (Thousand tons)
Durable Goods				
PET	270			
HDPE	1,270			
PVC	240			
LDPE/LLDPE	2,000			
PP	3,820			
PS	630			
Other resins	3,190			
Total Plastics in Durable Goods	**11,420**	**740**	**6.5%**	**10,680**
Nondurable Goods‡				
Plastic Plates and Cups§				
LDPE/LLDPE	20			20
PLA	10			10
PP	160			160
PS	840			840
Subtotal Plastic Plates and Cups	1,030	Neg.	Neg.	1,030
Trash Bags				
HDPE	220			220
LDPE/LLDPE	790			790
Subtotal Trash Bags	1,010			1,010
All other nondurables*				
PET	480			
HDPE	500			
PVC	260			
LDPE/LLDPE	1,190			
PLA	30			
PP	1,240			
PS	200			
Other resins	580			
Subtotal All Other Nondurables	4,480	110	2.5%	4,370
Total Plastics in Nondurable Goods, by resin				
PET	480			
HDPE	720			
PVC	260			
LDPE/LLDPE	2,000			
PLA	40			
PP	1,400			
PS	1,040			
Other resins	580			
Total Plastics in Nondurable Goods	**6,520**	**110**	**1.7%**	**6,410**
Plastic Containers & Packaging				
Bottles and Jars**				
PET	2,740	800	29.2%	1,940
Natural Bottles†				
HDPE	770	220	28.6%	550

‡ Nondurable goods other than containers and packaging.

§ Due to source data aggregation, PET cups are included in "Other Plastic Packaging".

* All other nondurables include plastics in disposable diapers, clothing, footwear, etc.

** Injection stretch blow molded PET containers as defined in the *2010 Report on Postconsumer PET Container Recycling Activity Final Report*. National Association for PET Container Resources.
Recovery includes caps, lids, and other material collected with PET bottles and jars.

† White translucent homopolymer bottles as defined in the *2007 United States National Postconsumer Plastics Bottles Recycling Report.* American Chemistry Council and the Association of Postconsumer Plastic Recyclers.
Neg. = negligible, less than 5,000 tons

Source: *U.S. EPA, Municipal Solid Waste in the United States, 2011 Facts and Figures*

PLASTICS IN PRODUCTS IN MSW, 2011
(In thousands of tons, and percent of generation by resin)

Product Category	Generation (Thousand tons)	Recovery (Thousand tons)	Recovery (Percent of Gen.)	Discards (Thousand tons)
Plastic Containers & Packaging, cont.				
Other plastic containers				
HDPE	1,480	270	18.2%	1,210
PVC	30	Neg.		30
LDPE/LLDPE	30	Neg.		30
PP	240	20	8.3%	220
PS	90	Neg.		90
Subtotal Other Containers	**1,870**	**290**	**15.5%**	**1,580**
Bags, sacks, & wraps				
HDPE	700	60	8.6%	640
PVC	50			50
LDPE/LLDPE	2,350	370	15.7%	1,980
PP	660			660
PS	120			120
Subtotal Bags, Sacks, & Wraps	**3,880**	**430**	**11.1%**	**3,450**
Other Plastics Packaging‡				
PET	790	30	3.8%	760
HDPE	650	Neg.		650
PVC	320	Neg.		320
LDPE/LLDPE	1,140	Neg.		1,140
PLA	10	Neg.		10
PP	1,060	10	0.9%	1,050
PS	290	20	6.9%	270
Other resins	380	Neg.		380
Subtotal Other Packaging	**4,640**	**60**	**1.3%**	**4,580**
Total Plastics in Containers & Packaging, by resin				
PET	3,530	830	23.5%	2,700
HDPE	3,600	550	15.3%	3,050
PVC	400	Neg.		400
LDPE/LLDPE	3,520	370	10.5%	3,150
PLA	10	Neg.		10
PP	1,960	30	1.5%	1,930
PS	500	20	4.0%	480
Other resins	380	Neg.		380
Total Plastics in Cont. & Packaging	**13,900**	**1,800**	**12.9%**	**12,100**
Total Plastics in MSW, by resin				
PET	4,280	830	19.4%	3,450
HDPE	5,590	550	9.8%	5,040
PVC	900			900
LDPE/LLDPE	7,520	370	4.9%	7,150
PLA	50			50
PP	7,180	30	0.4%	7,150
PS	2,170	20	0.9%	2,150
Other resins	4,150	850	20.5%	3,300
Total Plastics in MSW	**31,840**	**2,650**	**8.3%**	**29,190**

HDPE = High density polyethylene
LDPE = Low density polyethylene
LLDPE = Linear low density polyethylene
PET = Polyethylene terephthalate
PLA = Polylactide
PP = Polypropylene
PS = Polystyrene
PVC = Polyvinyl chloride

‡ Other plastic packaging includes coatings, closures, lids, PET cups, caps, clamshells, egg cartons, produce baskets, trays, shapes, loose fill, etc.
PP caps and lids recovered with PET bottles and jars are included in the recovery estimate for PET bottles and jars.
Other resins include commingled/undefined plastic packaging recovery.
Some detail of recovery by resin omitted due to lack of data.

Source: *U.S. EPA, Municipal Solid Waste in the United States, 2011 Facts and Figures*

Figure 9. Plastics generation and recovery, 1960 to 2011

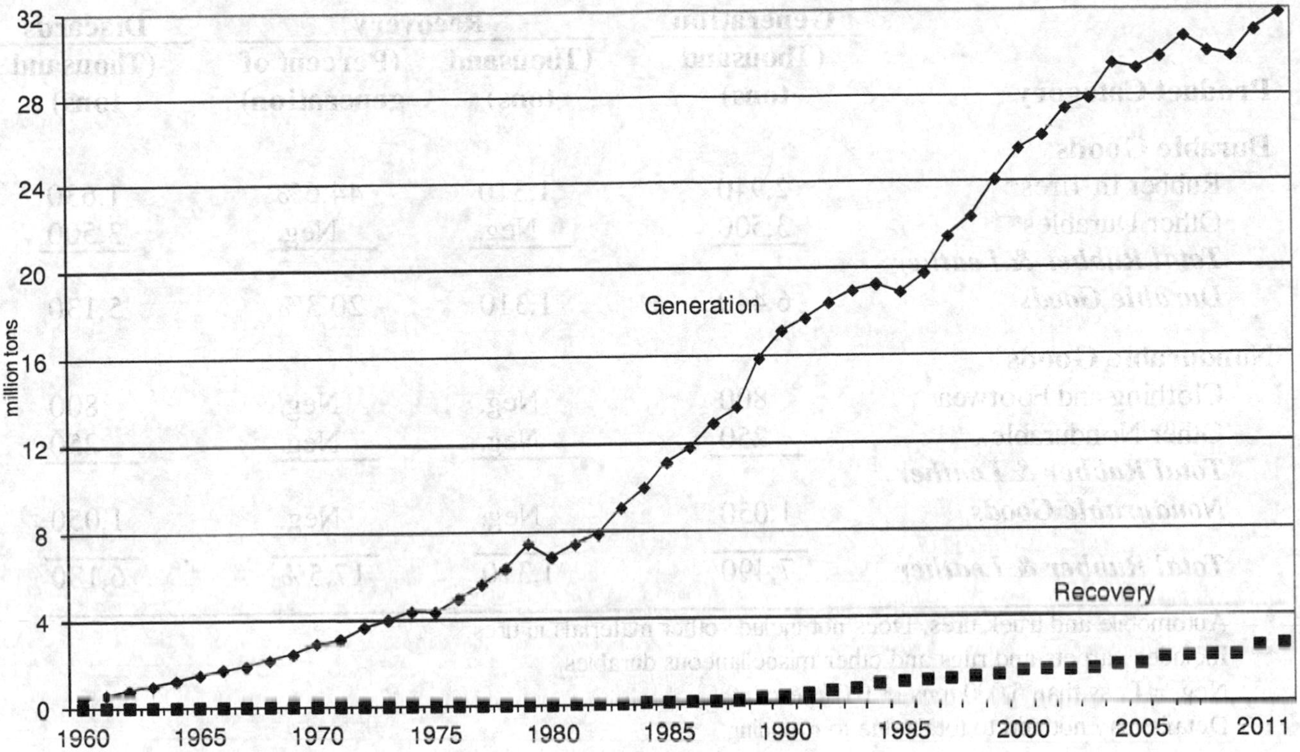

Source: *U.S. EPA, Municipal Solid Waste in the United States, 2011 Facts and Figures*

RUBBER AND LEATHER PRODUCTS IN MSW, 2011
(In thousands of tons and percent of generation)

Product Category	Generation (Thousand tons)	Recovery (Thousand tons)	Recovery (Percent of generation)	Discards (Thousand tons)
Durable Goods				
Rubber in Tires*	2,940	1,310	44.6%	1,630
Other Durables**	3,500	Neg.	Neg.	3,500
Total Rubber & Leather Durable Goods	6,440	1,310	20.3%	5,130
Nondurable Goods				
Clothing and Footwear	800	Neg.	Neg.	800
Other Nondurables	250	Neg.	Neg.	250
Total Rubber & Leather Nondurable Goods	1,050	Neg.	Neg.	1,050
Total Rubber & Leather	7,490	1,310	17.5%	6,180

* Automobile and truck tires. Does not include other materials in tires.
** Includes carpets and rugs and other miscellaneous durables.
Neg. = Less than 5,000 tons or 0.05 percent.
Details may not add to totals due to rounding.

Source: *U.S. EPA, Municipal Solid Waste in the United States, 2011 Facts and Figures*

Figure 10. Generation of materials in MSW, 1960 to 2011

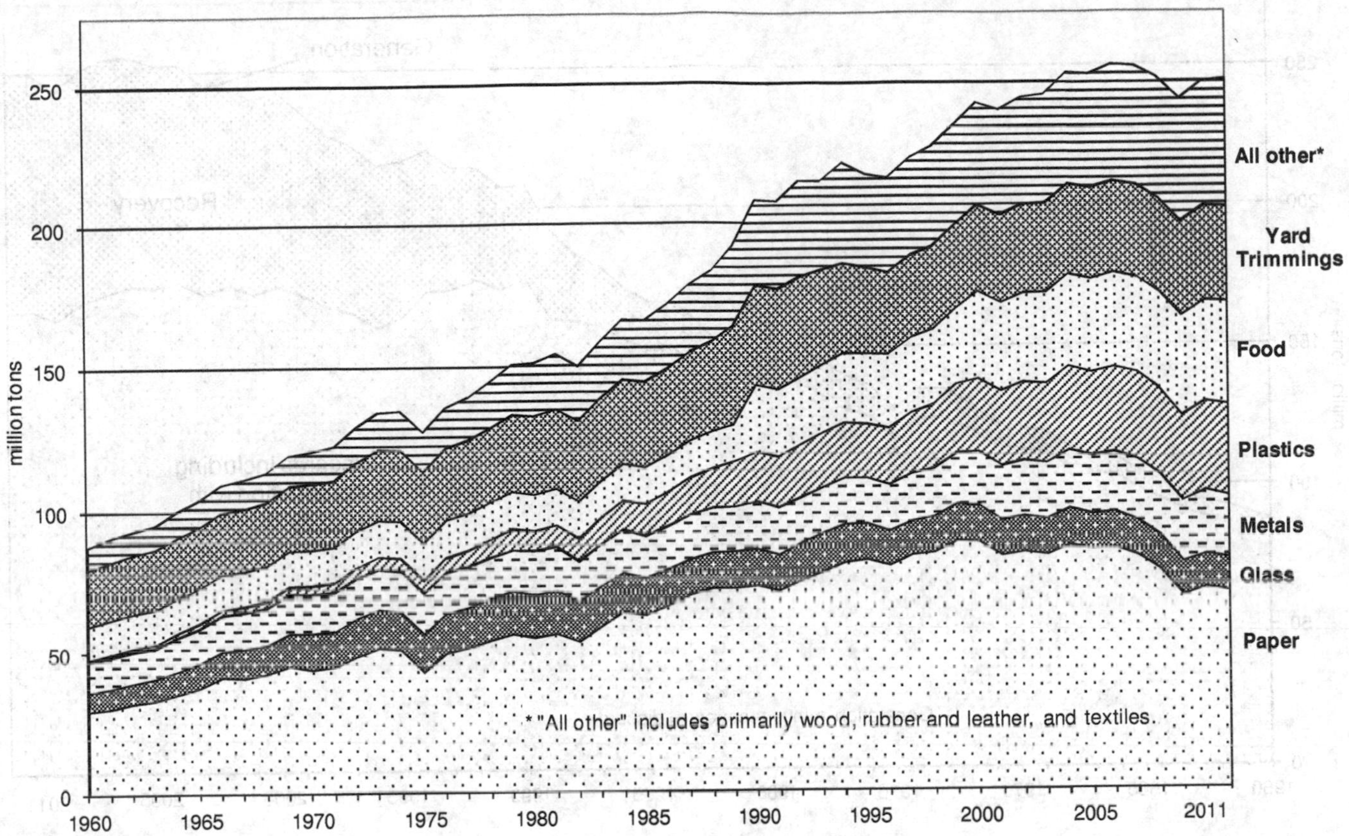

Source: *U.S. EPA, Municipal Solid Waste in the United States, 2011 Facts and Figures*

Figure 11. Recovery and discards of materials in MSW, 1960 to 2011

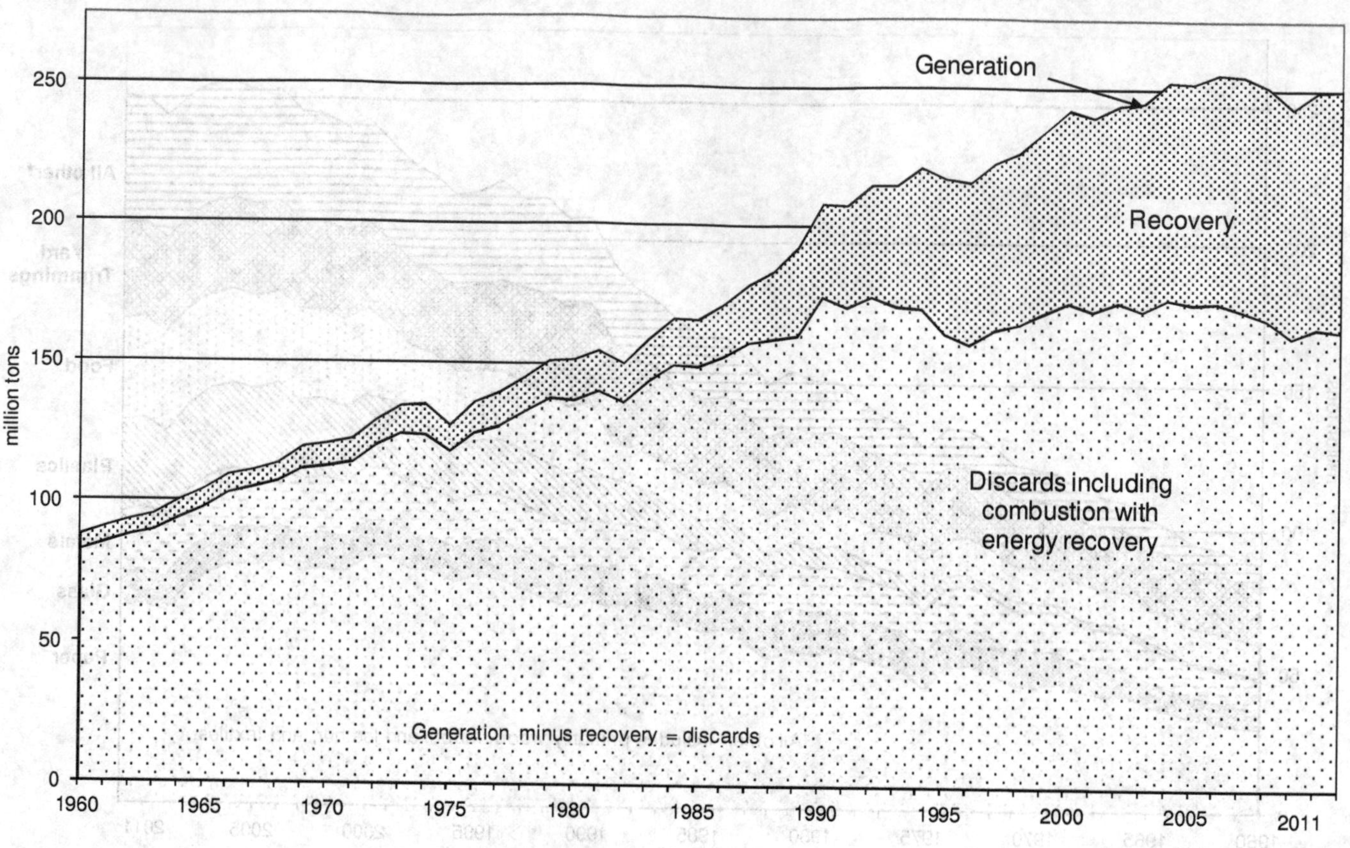

Source: *U.S. EPA, Municipal Solid Waste in the United States, 2011 Facts and Figures*

Figure 12. Materials recovery in MSW,* 2011
87 Million tons

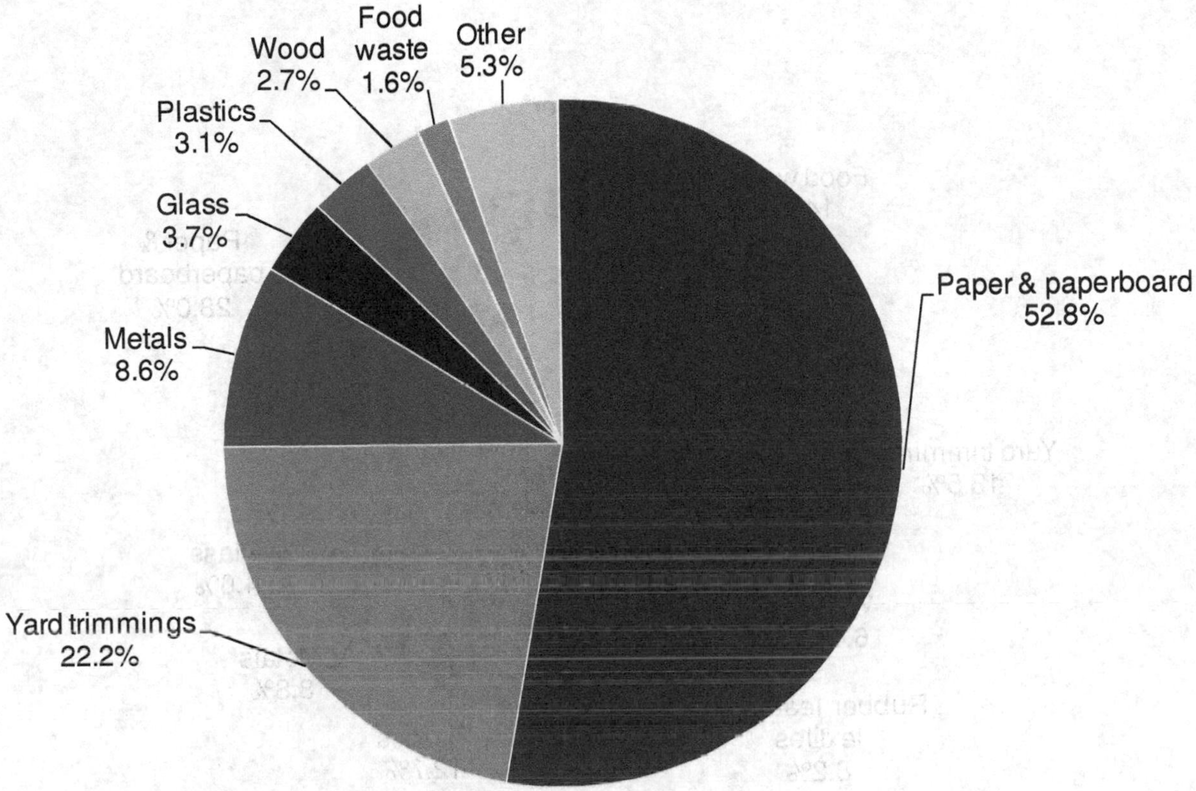

* In percent by weight of total recovery

Source: *U.S. EPA, Municipal Solid Waste in the United States, 2011 Facts and Figures*

Figure 13. Materials generated and discarded* in municipal solid waste, 2011 (In percent of total generation and discards)

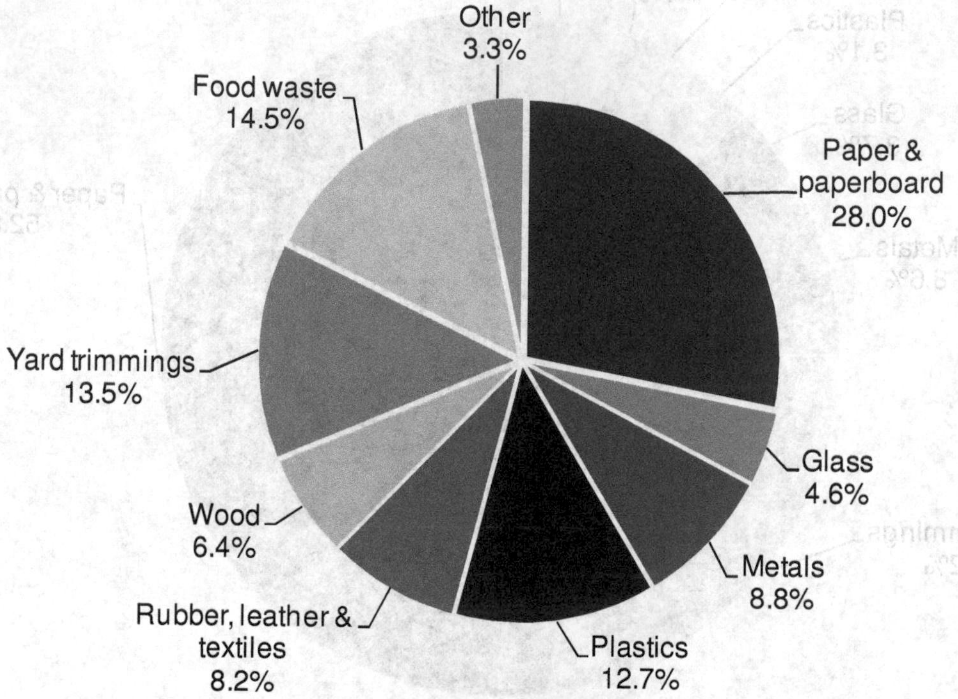

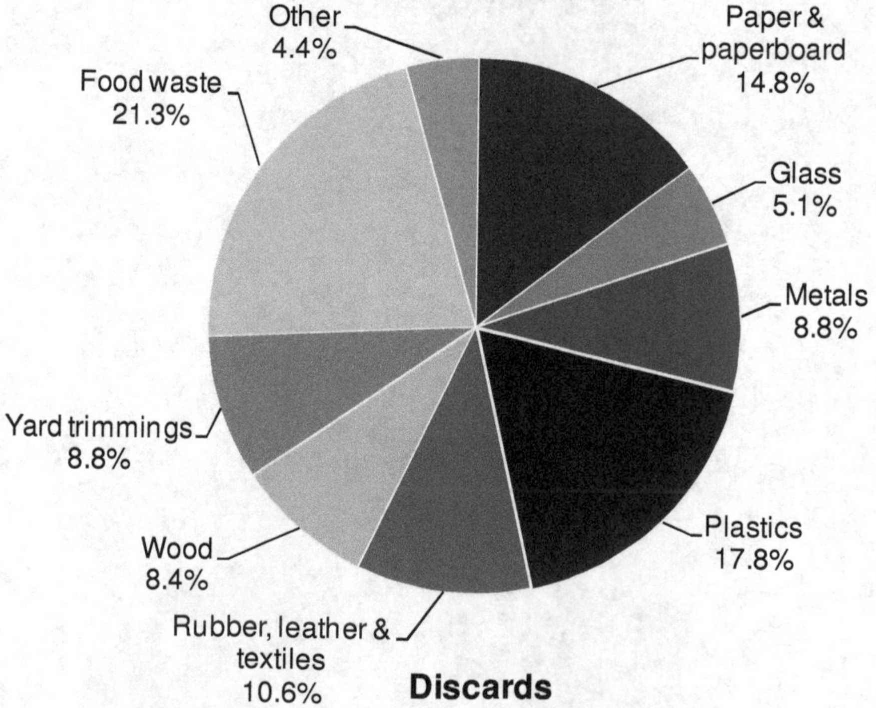

*Discards in this figure include combustion with energy recovery.

Source: *U.S. EPA, Municipal Solid Waste in the United States, 2011 Facts and Figures*

CATEGORIES OF PRODUCTS GENERATED* IN THE MUNICIPAL WASTE STREAM, 1960 TO 2011
(In thousands of tons and percent of total generation)

	Thousands of Tons									
Products	**1960**	**1970**	**1980**	**1990**	**2000**	**2005**	**2007**	**2009**	**2010**	**2011**
Durable Goods	9,920	14,660	21,800	29,810	38,870	45,060	46,430	47,220	48,680	49,340
(Detail in Table 12)										
Nondurable Goods	17,330	25,060	34,420	52,170	64,010	63,650	61,760	53,440	53,200	51,610
(Detail in Table 15)										
Containers and Packaging	27,370	43,560	52,670	64,530	75,840	76,330	78,370	71,320	75,640	75,580
(Detail in Table 18)										
Total Product** Wastes	54,620	83,280	108,890	146,510	178,720	185,040	186,560	171,980	177,520	176,530
Other Wastes										
Food Waste	12,200	12,800	13,000	23,860	30,700	32,930	33,560	35,270	35,740	36,310
Yard Trimmings	20,000	23,200	27,500	35,000	30,530	32,070	32,630	33,200	33,400	33,710
Miscellaneous Inorganic Wastes	1,300	1,780	2,250	2,900	3,500	3,690	3,750	3,820	3,840	3,870
Total Other Wastes	33,500	37,780	42,750	61,760	64,730	68,690	69,940	72,290	72,980	73,890
Total MSW Generated - Weight	88,120	121,060	151,640	208,270	243,450	253,730	256,500	244,270	250,500	250,420

	Percent of Total Generation									
Products	**1960**	**1970**	**1980**	**1990**	**2000**	**2005**	**2007**	**2009**	**2010**	**2011**
Durable Goods	11.3%	12.1%	14.4%	14.3%	16.0%	17.8%	18.1%	19.3%	19.4%	19.7%
(Detail in Table 12)										
Nondurable Goods	19.7%	20.7%	22.7%	25.0%	26.3%	25.1%	24.1%	21.9%	21.2%	20.6%
(Detail in Table 15)										
Containers and Packaging	31.1%	36.0%	34.7%	31.0%	31.2%	30.1%	30.6%	29.2%	30.2%	30.2%
(Detail in Table 19)										
Total Product** Wastes	62.0%	68.8%	71.8%	70.3%	73.4%	72.9%	72.7%	70.4%	70.9%	70.5%
Other Wastes										
Food Waste	13.8%	10.6%	8.6%	11.5%	12.6%	13.0%	13.1%	14.4%	14.3%	14.5%
Yard Trimmings	22.7%	19.2%	18.1%	16.8%	12.5%	12.6%	12.7%	13.6%	13.3%	13.5%
Miscellaneous Inorganic Wastes	1.5%	1.5%	1.5%	1.4%	1.4%	1.5%	1.5%	1.6%	1.5%	1.5%
Total Other Wastes	38.0%	31.2%	28.2%	29.7%	26.6%	27.1%	27.3%	29.6%	29.1%	29.5%
Total MSW Generated - %	100.0%	100.0%	100.0%	100.0%	100.0%	100.0%	100.0%	100.0%	100.0%	100.0%

* Generation before materials recovery or combustion. Does not include construction & demolition debris, industrial process wastes, or certain other wastes.

** Other than food products.

Details may not add to totals due to rounding.

Source: *U.S. EPA, Municipal Solid Waste in the United States, 2011 Facts and Figures*

RECOVERY* OF MUNICIPAL SOLID WASTE, 1960 TO 2011
(In thousands of tons and percent of generation of each category)

Products	Thousands of Tons									
	1960	1970	1980	1990	2000	2005	2007	2009	2010	2011
Durable Goods	350	940	1,360	3,460	6,580	7,970	8,230	8,540	9,070	9,070
(Detail in Table 13)										
Nondurable Goods	2,390	3,730	4,670	8,800	17,560	19,770	20,970	18,890	19,190	18,830
(Detail in Table 16)										
Containers and Packaging	2,870	3,350	8,490	16,780	28,870	31,500	33,900	34,210	36,700	38,300
(Detail in Table 20)										
Total Product** Wastes	5,610	8,020	14,520	29,040	53,010	59,240	63,100	61,640	64,960	66,200
Other Wastes										
Food, Other^	Neg.	Neg.	Neg.	Neg.	680	690	810	850	970	1,400
Yard Trimmings	Neg.	Neg.	Neg.	4,200	15,770	19,860	20,900	19,900	19,200	19,300
Miscellaneous Inorganic Wastes	Neg.	Neg.	Neg.	Neg.	Neg.	Neg.	Neg.	Neg.	Neg.	Neg.
Total Other Wastes	Neg.	Neg.	Neg.	4,200	16,450	20,550	21,710	20,750	20,170	20,700
Total MSW Recovered - Weight	5,610	8,020	14,520	33,240	69,460	79,790	84,810	82,390	85,130	86,900

Products	Percent of Generation of Each Category									
	1960	1970	1980	1990	2000	2005	2007	2009	2010	2011
Durable Goods	3.5%	6.4%	6.2%	11.6%	16.9%	17.7%	17.7%	18.1%	18.6%	18.4%
(Detail in Table 13)										
Nondurable Goods	13.8%	14.9%	13.6%	16.9%	27.4%	31.1%	34.0%	35.3%	36.1%	36.5%
(Detail in Table 16)										
Containers and Packaging	10.5%	7.7%	16.1%	26.0%	38.1%	41.3%	43.3%	48.0%	48.5%	50.7%
(Detail in Table 21)										
Total Product** Wastes	10.3%	9.6%	13.3%	19.8%	29.7%	32.0%	33.8%	35.8%	36.6%	37.5%
Other Wastes										
Food, Other^	Neg.	Neg.	Neg.	Neg.	2.2%	2.1%	2.4%	2.4%	2.7%	3.9%
Yard Trimmings	Neg.	Neg.	Neg.	12.0%	51.7%	61.9%	64.1%	59.9%	57.5%	57.3%
Miscellaneous Inorganic Wastes	Neg.	Neg.	Neg.	Neg.	Neg.	Neg.	Neg.	Neg.	Neg.	Neg.
Total Other Wastes	Neg.	Neg.	Neg.	6.8%	25.4%	29.9%	31.0%	28.7%	27.6%	28.0%
Total MSW Recovered - %	6.4%	6.6%	9.6%	16.0%	28.5%	31.4%	33.1%	33.7%	34.0%	34.7%

* Recovery of postconsumer wastes; does not include converting/fabrication scrap.
** Other than food products.
^ Includes recovery of paper and mixed MSW for composting.
Details may not add to totals due to rounding. Neg. = Less than 5,000 tons or 0.05 percent.

Source: *U.S. EPA, Municipal Solid Waste in the United States, 2011 Facts and Figures*

CATEGORIES OF PRODUCTS DISCARDED* IN THE MUNICIPAL WASTE STREAM, 1960 TO 2011
(In thousands of tons and percent of total discards)

	Thousands of Tons									
Products	**1960**	**1970**	**1980**	**1990**	**2000**	**2005**	**2007**	**2009**	**2010**	**2011**
Durable Goods	9,570	13,720	20,440	26,350	32,290	37,090	38,200	38,680	39,610	40,270
(Detail in Table 14)										
Nondurable Goods	14,940	21,330	29,750	43,370	46,450	43,880	40,790	34,550	34,010	32,780
(Detail in Table 17)										
Containers and Packaging	24,500	40,210	44,180	47,750	46,970	44,830	44,470	37,110	38,940	37,280
(Detail in Table 22)										
Total Product** Wastes	49,010	75,260	94,370	117,470	125,710	125,800	123,460	110,340	112,560	110,330
Other Wastes										
Food Waste	12,200	12,800	13,000	23,860	30,020	32,240	32,750	34,420	34,770	34,910
Yard Trimmings	20,000	23,200	27,500	30,800	14,760	12,210	11,730	13,300	14,200	14,410
Miscellaneous Inorganic Wastes	1,300	1,780	2,250	2,900	3,500	3,690	3,750	3,820	3,840	3,870
Total Other Wastes	33,500	37,780	42,750	57,560	48,280	48,140	48,230	51,540	52,810	53,190
Total MSW Discarded - Weight	82,510	113,040	137,120	175,030	173,990	173,940	171,690	161,880	165,370	163,520

	Percent of Total Discards									
Products	**1960**	**1970**	**1980**	**1990**	**2000**	**2005**	**2007**	**2009**	**2010**	**2011**
Durable Goods	11.6%	12.1%	14.9%	15.1%	18.6%	21.3%	22.2%	23.9%	24.0%	24.6%
(Detail in Table 14)										
Nondurable Goods	18.1%	18.9%	21.7%	24.8%	26.7%	25.2%	23.8%	21.3%	20.6%	20.0%
(Detail in Table 17)										
Containers and Packaging	29.7%	35.6%	32.2%	27.3%	27.0%	25.8%	25.9%	22.9%	23.5%	22.8%
(Detail in Table 23)										
Total Product** Wastes	59.4%	66.6%	68.8%	67.1%	72.3%	72.3%	71.9%	68.2%	68.1%	67.5%
Other Wastes										
Food Waste	14.8%	11.3%	9.5%	13.6%	17.3%	18.5%	19.1%	21.3%	21.0%	21.3%
Yard Trimmings	24.2%	20.5%	20.1%	17.6%	8.5%	7.0%	6.8%	8.2%	8.6%	8.8%
Miscellaneous Inorganic Wastes	1.6%	1.6%	1.6%	1.7%	2.0%	2.1%	2.2%	2.4%	2.3%	2.4%
Total Other Wastes	40.6%	33.4%	31.2%	32.9%	27.7%	27.7%	28.1%	31.8%	31.9%	32.5%
Total MSW Discarded - %	100.0%	100.0%	100.0%	100.0%	100.0%	100.0%	100.0%	100.0%	100.0%	100.0%

* Discards after materials and compost recovery. In this table, discards include combustion with energy recovery.
Does not include construction & demolition debris, industrial process wastes, or certain other wastes.
** Other than food products.
Details may not add to totals due to rounding.

Source: *U.S. EPA, Municipal Solid Waste in the United States, 2011 Facts and Figures*

PRODUCTS GENERATED* IN THE MUNICIPAL WASTE STREAM, 1960 TO 2011
(WITH DETAIL ON DURABLE GOODS)
(In thousands of tons and percent of total generation)

Products	1960	1970	1980	1990	2000	2005	2007	2009	2010	2011
	Thousands of Tons									
Durable Goods										
Major Appliances	1,630	2,170	2,950	3,310	3,640	3,610	3,620	3,760	4,020	4,080
Small Appliances**				460	1,040	1,180	1,390	1,630	1,720	1,770
Furniture and Furnishings	2,150	2,830	4,760	6,790	8,120	9,340	9,930	10,500	10,820	11,130
Carpets and Rugs**				1,660	2,460	2,960	3,170	3,550	3,720	3,830
Rubber Tires	1,120	1,890	2,720	3,610	4,930	4,910	5,020	4,570	4,600	4,600
Batteries, Lead-Acid	Neg.	820	1,490	1,510	2,280	2,750	2,820	2,810	2,990	2,890
Miscellaneous Durables										
Selected Consumer Electronics***					1,900	2,630	3,010	3,190	3,320	3,410
Other Miscellaneous Durables					14,500	17,680	17,470	17,210	17,490	17,630
Total Miscellaneous Durables	5,020	6,950	9,880	12,470	16,400	20,310	20,480	20,400	20,810	21,040
Total Durable Goods	9,920	14,660	21,800	29,810	38,870	45,060	46,430	47,220	48,680	49,340
Nondurable Goods	17,330	25,060	34,420	52,170	64,010	63,650	61,760	53,440	53,200	51,610
(Detail in Table 15)										
Containers and Packaging	27,370	43,560	52,670	64,530	75,840	76,330	78,370	71,320	75,640	75,580
(Detail in Table 18)										
Total Product Wastes†	54,620	83,280	108,890	146,510	178,720	185,040	186,560	171,980	177,520	176,530
Other Wastes										
Food Waste	12,200	12,800	13,000	23,860	30,700	32,930	33,560	35,270	35,740	36,310
Yard Trimmings	20,000	23,200	27,500	35,000	30,530	32,070	32,630	33,200	33,400	33,710
Miscellaneous Inorganic Wastes	1,300	1,780	2,250	2,900	3,500	3,690	3,750	3,820	3,840	3,870
Total Other Wastes	33,500	37,780	42,750	61,760	64,730	68,690	69,940	72,290	72,980	73,890
Total MSW Generated - Weight	88,120	121,060	151,640	208,270	243,450	253,730	256,500	244,270	250,500	250,420
	Percent of Total Generation									
Products	**1960**	**1970**	**1980**	**1990**	**2000**	**2005**	**2007**	**2009**	**2010**	**2011**
Durable Goods										
Major Appliances	1.8%	1.8%	1.9%	1.6%	1.5%	1.4%	1.4%	1.5%	1.6%	1.6%
Small Appliances**				0.2%	0.4%	0.5%	0.5%	0.7%	0.7%	0.7%
Furniture and Furnishings	2.4%	2.3%	3.1%	3.3%	3.3%	3.7%	3.9%	4.3%	4.3%	4.4%
Carpets and Rugs**				0.8%	1.0%	1.2%	1.2%	1.5%	1.5%	1.5%
Rubber Tires	1.3%	1.6%	1.8%	1.7%	2.0%	1.9%	2.0%	1.9%	1.8%	1.8%
Batteries, Lead-Acid	Neg.	0.7%	1.0%	0.7%	0.9%	1.1%	1.1%	1.2%	1.2%	1.2%
Miscellaneous Durables										
Selected Consumer Electronics***					0.8%	1.0%	1.2%	1.3%	1.3%	1.4%
Other Miscellaneous Durables					6.0%	7.0%	6.8%	7.0%	7.0%	7.0%
Total Miscellaneous Durables	5.7%	5.7%	6.5%	6.0%	6.7%	8.0%	8.0%	8.4%	8.3%	8.4%
Total Durable Goods	11.3%	12.1%	14.4%	14.3%	16.0%	17.8%	18.1%	19.3%	19.4%	19.7%
Nondurable Goods	19.7%	20.7%	22.7%	25.0%	26.3%	25.1%	24.1%	21.9%	21.2%	20.6%
(Detail in Table 15)										
Containers and Packaging	31.1%	36.0%	34.7%	31.0%	31.2%	30.1%	30.6%	29.2%	30.2%	30.2%
(Detail in Table 19)										
Total Product Wastes†	62.0%	68.8%	71.8%	70.3%	73.4%	72.9%	72.7%	70.4%	70.9%	70.5%
Other Wastes										
Food Waste	13.8%	10.6%	8.6%	11.5%	12.6%	13.0%	13.1%	14.4%	14.3%	14.5%
Yard Trimmings	22.7%	19.2%	18.1%	16.8%	12.5%	12.6%	12.7%	13.6%	13.3%	13.5%
Miscellaneous Inorganic Wastes	1.5%	1.5%	1.5%	1.4%	1.4%	1.5%	1.5%	1.6%	1.5%	1.5%
Total Other Wastes	38.0%	31.2%	28.2%	29.7%	26.6%	27.1%	27.3%	29.6%	29.1%	29.5%
Total MSW Generated - %	100.0%	100.0%	100.0%	100.0%	100.0%	100.0%	100.0%	100.0%	100.0%	100.0%

* Generation before materials recovery or combustion. Does not include construction & demolition debris, industrial process wastes, or certain other wastes.

** Not estimated separately prior to 1990.

† Other than food products.

Neg. = Less than 5,000 tons or 0.05 percent.

*** Not estimated separately prior to 1999. For more information on consumer electronics see the website http://www.epa.gov/waste/conserve/materials/ecycling/manage.htm which references the report Electronics Management in the U.S. Through 2009. This 2009 electronics report shows a lower generation tonnage for consumer electronics than does the table above, due to examining a smaller selection of types of electronics.

Source: *U.S. EPA, Municipal Solid Waste in the United States, 2011 Facts and Figures*

RECOVERY* OF PRODUCTS IN MUNICIPAL SOLID WASTE, 1960 TO 2011
(WITH DETAIL ON DURABLE GOODS)
(In thousands of tons and percent of generation of each product)

	Thousands of Tons									
Products	**1960**	**1970**	**1980**	**1990**	**2000**	**2005**	**2007**	**2009**	**2010**	**2011**
Durable Goods										
Major Appliances	10	50	130	1,070	2,000	2,420	2,430	2,510	2,610	2,620
Small Appliances**				10	20	20	20	110	120	120
Furniture and Furnishings	Neg.	Neg.	Neg.	Neg.	Neg.	Neg.	Neg.	10	10	10
Carpets and Rugs**				Neg.	190	250	280	260	270	270
Rubber Tires	330	250	150	440	1,290	1,640	1,770	2,040	2,050	2,050
Batteries, Lead-Acid	Neg.	620	1,040	1,470	2,130	2,640	2,700	2,700	2,880	2,780
Miscellaneous Durables										
Selected Consumer Electronics***					190	360	550	600	650	850
Other Miscellaneous Durables					760	640	480	310	480	370
Total Miscellaneous Durables	10	20	40	470	950	1,000	1,030	910	1,130	1,220
Total Durable Goods	350	940	1,360	3,460	6,580	7,970	8,230	8,540	9,070	9,070
Nondurable Goods	2,390	3,730	4,670	8,800	17,560	19,770	20,970	18,890	19,190	18,830
(Detail in Table 16)										
Containers and Packaging	2,870	3,350	8,490	16,780	28,870	31,500	33,900	34,210	36,700	38,300
(Detail in Table 20)										
Total Product Wastes†	5,610	8,020	14,520	29,040	53,010	59,240	63,100	61,640	64,960	66,200
Other Wastes										
Food Waste	Neg.	Neg.	Neg.	Neg.	680	690	810	850	970	1,400
Yard Trimmings	Neg.	Neg.	Neg.	4,200	15,770	19,860	20,900	19,900	19,200	19,300
Miscellaneous Inorganic Wastes	Neg.	Neg.	Neg.	Neg.	Neg.	Neg.	Neg.	Neg.	Neg.	Neg.
Total Other Wastes	Neg.	Neg.	Neg.	4,200	16,450	20,550	21,710	20,750	20,170	20,700
Total MSW Recovered - Weight	5,610	8,020	14,520	33,240	69,460	79,790	84,810	82,390	85,130	86,900
	Percent of Generation of Each Product									
Products	**1960**	**1970**	**1980**	**1990**	**2000**	**2005**	**2007**	**2009**	**2010**	**2011**
Durable Goods										
Major Appliances	0.6%	2.3%	4.4%	32.3%	54.9%	67.0%	67.1%	66.8%	64.9%	64.2%
Small Appliances**				2.2%	1.9%	1.7%	1.4%	6.7%	7.0%	6.8%
Furniture and Furnishings	Neg.	Neg.	Neg.	Neg.	Neg.	Neg.	Neg.	0.1%	0.1%	0.1%
Carpets and Rugs**				Neg.	7.7%	8.4%	8.8%	7.3%	7.3%	7.0%
Rubber Tires	29.5%	13.2%	5.5%	12.2%	26.2%	33.4%	35.3%	44.6%	44.6%	44.6%
Batteries, Lead-Acid	Neg.	75.6%	69.8%	97.4%	93.4%	96.0%	95.7%	96.1%	96.3%	96.2%
Miscellaneous Durables										
Selected Consumer Electronics***					10.0%	13.7%	18.3%	18.8%	19.6%	24.9%
Other Miscellaneous Durables					5.2%	3.6%	2.7%	1.8%	2.7%	2.1%
Total Miscellaneous Durables	0.2%	0.3%	0.4%	3.8%	5.8%	4.9%	5.0%	4.5%	5.4%	5.8%
Total Durable Goods	3.5%	6.4%	6.2%	11.6%	16.9%	17.7%	17.7%	18.1%	18.6%	18.4%
Nondurable Goods	13.8%	14.9%	13.6%	16.9%	27.4%	31.1%	34.0%	35.3%	36.1%	36.5%
(Detail in Table 16)										
Containers and Packaging	10.5%	7.7%	16.1%	26.0%	38.1%	41.3%	43.3%	48.0%	48.5%	50.7%
(Detail in Table 21)										
Total Product Wastes†	10.3%	9.6%	13.3%	19.8%	29.7%	32.0%	33.8%	35.8%	36.6%	37.5%
Other Wastes										
Food Waste	Neg.	Neg.	Neg.	Neg.	2.2%	2.1%	2.4%	2.4%	2.7%	3.9%
Yard Trimmings	Neg.	Neg.	Neg.	12.0%	51.7%	61.9%	64.1%	59.9%	57.5%	57.3%
Miscellaneous Inorganic Wastes	Neg.	Neg.	Neg.	Neg.	Neg.	Neg.	Neg.	Neg.	Neg.	Neg.
Total Other Wastes	Neg.	Neg.	Neg.	6.8%	25.4%	29.9%	31.0%	28.7%	27.6%	28.0%
Total MSW Recovered - %	6.4%	6.6%	9.6%	16.0%	28.5%	31.4%	33.1%	33.7%	34.0%	34.7%

* Recovery of postconsumer wastes; does not include converting/fabrication scrap.
** Not estimated separately prior to 1990.
† Other than food products.
Neg. = Less than 5,000 tons or 0.05 percent.

*** Not estimated separately prior to 1999. For more information on consumer electronics see the website http://www.epa.gov/waste/conserve/materials/ecycling/manage.htm which references the report Electronics Management in the U.S. Through 2009. The EPA website referenced above and the 2009 electronics report show a higher recovery rate for consumer electronics than does the table above, due to examining a smaller selection of types of electronics.

Source: *U.S. EPA, Municipal Solid Waste in the United States, 2011 Facts and Figures*

PRODUCTS DISCARDED* IN THE MUNICIPAL WASTE STREAM, 1960 TO 2011
(WITH DETAIL ON DURABLE GOODS)
(In thousands of tons and percent of total discards)

Products	Thousands of Tons									
	1960	1970	1980	1990	2000	2005	2007	2009	2010	2011
Durable Goods										
Major Appliances	1,620	2,120	2,820	2,240	1,640	1,190	1,190	1,250	1,410	1,460
Small Appliances**				450	1,020	1,160	1,370	1,520	1,600	1,650
Furniture and Furnishings	2,150	2,830	4,760	6,790	8,120	9,340	9,930	10,490	10,810	11,120
Carpets and Rugs**				1,660	2,270	2,710	2,890	3,290	3,450	3,560
Rubber Tires	790	1,640	2,570	3,170	3,640	3,270	3,250	2,530	2,550	2,550
Batteries, Lead-Acid	Neg.	200	450	40	150	110	120	110	110	110
Miscellaneous Durables										
Selected Consumer Electronics***					1,710	2,270	2,460	2,590	2,670	2,560
Other Miscellaneous Durables					13,740	17,040	16,990	16,900	17,010	17,260
Total Miscellaneous Durables	5,010	6,930	9,840	12,000	15,450	19,310	19,450	19,490	19,680	19,820
Total Durable Goods	9,570	13,720	20,440	26,350	32,290	37,090	38,200	38,680	39,610	40,270
Nondurable Goods *(Detail in Table 17)*	14,940	21,330	29,750	43,370	46,450	43,880	40,790	34,550	34,010	32,780
Containers and Packaging *(Detail in Table 22)*	24,500	40,210	44,180	47,750	46,970	44,830	44,470	37,110	38,940	37,280
Total Product Wastes†	49,010	75,260	94,370	117,470	125,710	125,800	123,460	110,340	112,560	110,330
Other Wastes										
Food Waste	12,200	12,800	13,000	23,860	30,020	32,240	32,750	34,420	34,770	34,910
Yard Trimmings	20,000	23,200	27,500	30,800	14,760	12,210	11,730	13,300	14,200	14,410
Miscellaneous Inorganic Wastes	1,300	1,780	2,250	2,900	3,500	3,690	3,750	3,820	3,840	3,870
Total Other Wastes	33,500	37,780	42,750	57,560	48,280	48,140	48,230	51;540	52,810	53,190
Total MSW Discarded - Weight	82,510	113,040	137,120	175,030	173,990	173,940	171,690	161,880	165,370	163,520

Products	Percent of Total Discards									
	1960	1970	1980	1990	2000	2005	2007	2009	2010	2011
Durable Goods										
Major Appliances	2.0%	1.9%	2.1%	1.3%	0.9%	0.7%	0.7%	0.8%	0.9%	0.9%
Small Appliances**				0.3%	0.6%	0.7%	0.8%	0.9%	1.0%	1.0%
Furniture and Furnishings	2.6%	2.5%	3.5%	3.9%	4.7%	5.4%	5.8%	6.5%	6.5%	6.8%
Carpets and Rugs**				0.9%	1.3%	1.6%	1.7%	2.0%	2.1%	2.2%
Rubber Tires	1.0%	1.5%	1.9%	1.8%	2.1%	1.9%	1.9%	1.6%	1.5%	1.6%
Batteries, Lead-Acid	Neg.	0.2%	0.3%	0.0%	0.1%	0.1%	0.1%	0.1%	0.1%	0.1%
Miscellaneous Durables										
Selected Consumer Electronics***					1.0%	1.3%	1.4%	1.6%	1.6%	1.6%
Other Miscellaneous Durables					7.9%	9.8%	9.9%	10.4%	10.3%	10.6%
Total Miscellaneous Durables	6.1%	6.1%	7.2%	6.9%	8.9%	11.1%	11.3%	12.0%	11.9%	12.1%
Total Durable Goods	11.6%	12.1%	14.9%	15.1%	18.6%	21.3%	22.2%	23.9%	24.0%	24.6%
Nondurable Goods *(Detail in Table 17)*	18.1%	18.9%	21.7%	24.8%	26.7%	25.2%	23.8%	21.3%	20.6%	20.0%
Containers and Packaging *(Detail in Table 23)*	29.7%	35.6%	32.2%	27.3%	27.0%	25.8%	25.9%	22.9%	23.5%	22.8%
Total Product Wastes†	59.4%	66.6%	68.8%	67.1%	72.3%	72.3%	71.9%	68.2%	68.1%	67.5%
Other Wastes										
Food Waste	14.8%	11.3%	9.5%	13.6%	17.3%	18.5%	19.1%	21.3%	21.0%	21.3%
Yard Trimmings	24.2%	20.5%	20.1%	17.6%	8.5%	7.0%	6.8%	8.2%	8.6%	8.8%
Miscellaneous Inorganic Wastes	1.6%	1.6%	1.6%	1.7%	2.0%	2.1%	2.2%	2.4%	2.3%	2.4%
Total Other Wastes	40.6%	33.4%	31.2%	32.9%	27.7%	27.7%	28.1%	31.8%	31.9%	32.5%
Total MSW Discarded - %	100.0%	100.0%	100.0%	100.0%	100.0%	100.0%	100.0%	100.0%	100.0%	100.0%

* Discards after materials and compost recovery. In this table, discards include combustion with energy recovery.
** Not estimated separately prior to 1990.
† Other than food products.
Neg. = Less than 5,000 tons or 0.05 percent.
*** Not estimated separately prior to 1999. For more information on consumer electronics see the website http://www.epa.gov/waste/conserve/materials/ecycling/manage.htm which references the report Electronics Management in the U.S. Through 2009. This 2009 electronics report shows a lower discards tonnage for consumer electronics than does the table above, due to examining a smaller selection of types of electronics.

Source: *U.S. EPA, Municipal Solid Waste in the United States, 2011 Facts and Figures*

PRODUCTS GENERATED* IN THE MUNICIPAL WASTE STREAM, 1960 TO 2011
(WITH DETAIL ON NONDURABLE GOODS)
(In thousands of tons and percent of total generation)

	Thousands of Tons									
Products	**1960**	**1970**	**1980**	**1990**	**2000**	**2005**	**2007**	**2009**	**2010**	**2011**
Durable Goods	9,920	14,660	21,800	29,810	38,870	45,060	46,430	47,220	48,680	49,340
(Detail in Table 12)										
Nondurable Goods										
Newspapers/Mechanical Papers†	7,110	9,510	11,050	13,430	14,790	12,790	10,780	7,760	9,880	9,150
Directories†**				610	680	660	760	650	-	-
Other Paper Nondurable Goods										
Books and Magazines	1,920	2,470	3,390							
Books**				970	1,240	1,100	1,270	960	990	930
Magazines**				2,830	2,230	2,580	2,550	1,450	1,590	1,510
Office-Type Papers***	1,520	2,650	4,000	6,410	7,420	6,620	6,060	5,380	5,260	5,100
Standard Mail§				3,820	5,570	5,830	5,910	4,650	4,340	3,750
Other Commercial Printing†	1,260	2,130	3,120	4,460	7,380	6,440	6,200	3,490	2,480	2,710
Tissue Paper and Towels	1,090	2,080	2,300	2,960	3,220	3,460	3,500	3,490	3,490	3,510
Paper Plates and Cups	270	420	630	650	960	1,160	1,230	1,170	1,350	1,340
Other Nonpackaging Paper	2,700	3,630	4,230	3,840	4,250	4,490	4,260	4,420	4,190	3,940
Total Other Paper Nondurable Goods									23,690	22,790
Disposable Diapers	Neg.	350	1,930	2,700	3,230	3,410	3,730	3,810	3,700	3,630
Plastic Plates and Cups§			190	650	870	930	860	900	890	1,030
Trash Bags**				780	850	1,060	1,070	1,000	980	1,010
Clothing and Footwear	1,360	1,620	2,170	4,010	6,470	7,890	8,320	9,080	9,050	9,020
Towels, Sheets and Pillowcases**				710	820	980	1,100	1,230	1,290	1,310
Other Miscellaneous Nondurables	100	200	1,410	3,340	4,030	4,250	4,160	4,000	3,720	3,670
Total Nondurable Goods	17,330	25,060	34,420	52,170	64,010	63,650	61,760	53,440	53,200	51,610
Containers and Packaging	27,370	43,560	52,670	64,530	75,840	76,330	78,370	71,320	75,640	75,680
(Detail in Table 18)										
Total Product Wastes‡	54,620	83,280	108,890	146,510	178,720	185,040	186,560	171,980	177,520	176,530
Other Wastes	33,500	37,780	42,750	61,760	64,730	68,690	69,940	72,290	72,980	73,890
Total MSW Generated - Weight	88,120	121,060	151,640	208,270	243,450	253,730	256,500	244,270	250,500	250,420
	Percent of Total Generation									
Products	**1960**	**1970**	**1980**	**1990**	**2000**	**2005**	**2007**	**2009**	**2010**	**2011**
Durable Goods	11.3%	12.1%	14.4%	14.3%	16.0%	17.8%	18.1%	19.3%	19.4%	19.7%
(Detail in Table 12)										
Nondurable Goods										
Newspapers/Mechanical Papers†	8.1%	7.9%	7.3%	6.4%	6.1%	5.0%	4.2%	3.2%	3.9%	3.7%
Directories†**				0.3%	0.3%	0.3%	0.3%	0.3%	-	-
Other Paper Nondurable Goods										
Books and Magazines	2.2%	2.0%	2.2%							
Books**				0.5%	0.5%	0.4%	0.5%	0.4%	0.4%	0.4%
Magazines**				1.4%	0.9%	1.0%	1.0%	0.6%	0.6%	0.6%
Office-Type Papers***	1.7%	2.2%	2.6%	3.1%	3.0%	2.6%	2.4%	2.2%	2.1%	2.0%
Standard Mail§				1.8%	2.3%	2.3%	2.3%	1.9%	1.7%	1.5%
Other Commercial Printing†	1.4%	1.8%	2.1%	2.1%	3.0%	2.5%	2.4%	1.4%	1.0%	1.1%
Tissue Paper and Towels	1.2%	1.7%	1.5%	1.4%	1.3%	1.4%	1.4%	1.4%	1.4%	1.4%
Paper Plates and Cups	0.3%	0.3%	0.4%	0.3%	0.4%	0.5%	0.5%	0.5%	0.5%	0.5%
Other Nonpackaging Paper	3.1%	3.0%	2.8%	1.8%	1.7%	1.8%	1.7%	1.8%	1.7%	1.6%
Total Other Paper Nondurable Goods									9.5%	9.1%
Disposable Diapers	Neg.	0.3%	1.3%	1.3%	1.3%	1.3%	1.5%	1.6%	1.5%	1.4%
Plastic Plates and Cups§			0.1%	0.3%	0.4%	0.4%	0.3%	0.4%	0.4%	0.4%
Trash Bags**				0.4%	0.3%	0.4%	0.4%	0.4%	0.4%	0.4%
Clothing and Footwear	1.5%	1.3%	1.4%	1.9%	2.7%	3.1%	3.2%	3.7%	3.6%	3.6%
Towels, Sheets and Pillowcases**				0.3%	0.3%	0.4%	0.4%	0.5%	0.5%	0.5%
Other Miscellaneous Nondurables	0.1%	0.2%	0.9%	1.6%	1.7%	1.7%	1.6%	1.6%	1.5%	1.5%
Total Nondurables	19.7%	20.7%	22.7%	25.0%	26.3%	25.1%	24.1%	21.9%	21.2%	20.6%
Containers and Packaging	31.1%	36.0%	34.7%	31.0%	31.2%	30.1%	30.6%	29.2%	30.2%	30.2%
(Detail in Table 19)										
Total Product Wastes‡	62.0%	68.8%	71.8%	70.3%	73.4%	72.9%	72.7%	70.4%	70.9%	70.5%
Other Wastes	38.0%	31.2%	28.2%	29.7%	26.6%	27.1%	27.3%	29.6%	29.1%	29.5%
Total MSW Generated - %	100.0%	100.0%	100.0%	100.0%	100.0%	100.0%	100.0%	100.0%	100.0%	100.0%

* Generation before materials recovery or combustion. Does not include construction & demolition debris, industrial process wastes, or certain other wastes. Details may not add to totals due to rounding.
† Starting in 2010, newsprint and groundwood inserts expanded to include directories and other mechanical papers previously counted as Other Commercial Printing.
** Not estimated separately prior to 1990.
*** High-grade paper such as printer paper; generated in both commercial and residential sources.
§ Standard Mail: Not estimated separately prior to 1990. Formerly called Third Class Mail and Standard (A) Mail by the U.S. Postal Service.
§ Plastic Plates and Cups: Not estimated separately prior to 1980.
‡ Other than food products.
\- Detailed data not available.
Neg. = Less than 5,000 tons or 0.05 percent.

Source: *U.S. EPA, Municipal Solid Waste in the United States, 2011 Facts and Figures*

RECOVERY* OF PRODUCTS IN MUNICIPAL SOLID WASTE, 1960 TO 2011
(WITH DETAIL ON NONDURABLE GOODS)
(In thousands of tons and percent of generation of each product)

Products	Thousands of Tons									
	1960	1970	1980	1990	2000	2005	2007	2009	2010	2011
Durable Goods *(Detail in Table 13)*	350	940	1,360	3,460	6,580	7,970	8,230	8,540	9,070	9,070
Nondurable Goods										
Newspapers/Mechanical Papers†	1,820	2,250	3,020	5,110	8,720	9,360	8,550	6,840	7,070	6,630
Directories†**				50	120	120	140	240	-	-
Other Paper Nondurable Goods										
Books and Magazines	100	260	280							
Books**				100	240	270	360	320	-	-
Magazines**				300	710	960	1,010	780	-	-
Office-Type Papers***	250	710	870	1,700	4,090	4,110	4,300	3,990	-	-
Standard Mail§				200	1,830	2,090	2,380	2,950	-	-
Other Commercial Printing†	130	340	350	700	810	1,440	2,790	2,310	-	-
Tissue Paper and Towels	Neg.	Neg.	Neg.	Neg.	Neg.	Neg.	Neg.	Neg.	-	-
Paper Plates and Cups	Neg.	Neg.	Neg.	Neg.	Neg.	Neg.	Neg.	Neg.	-	-
Other Nonpackaging Paper	40	110	Neg.	Neg.	Neg.	Neg.	Neg.	Neg.	-	-
Total Other Paper Nondurable Goods									10,650	10,610
Disposable Diapers				Neg.	Neg.	Neg.	Neg.	Neg.	Neg.	Neg.
Plastic Plates and Cups§			Neg.	Neg.	Neg.	Neg.	Neg.	Neg.	Neg.	Neg.
Trash Bags**				Neg.	Neg.	Neg.	Neg.	Neg.	Neg.	Neg.
Clothing and Footwear	50	60	150	520	900	1,250	1,250	1,250	1,250	1,250
Towels, Sheets and Pillowcases**				120	140	170	190	210	220	230
Other Miscellaneous Nondurables	Neg.	Neg.	Neg.	Neg.	Neg.	Neg.	Neg.	Neg.	Neg.	110
Total Nondurable Goods	2,390	3,730	4,670	8,800	17,560	19,770	20,970	18,890	19,190	18,830
Containers and Packaging *(Detail in Table 20)*	2,870	3,350	8,490	16,780	28,870	31,500	33,900	34,210	36,700	38,300
Total Product Wastes‡	5,610	8,020	14,520	29,040	53,010	59,240	63,100	61,640	64,960	66,200
Other Wastes	Neg.	Neg.	Neg.	4,200	16,450	20,550	21,710	20,750	20,170	20,700
Total MSW Recovered - Weight	5,610	8,020	14,520	33,240	69,460	79,790	84,810	82,390	85,130	86,900

Products	Percent of Generation of Each Product									
	1960	1970	1980	1990	2000	2005	2007	2009	2010	2011
Durable Goods *(Detail in Table 13)*	3.5%	6.4%	6.2%	11.6%	16.9%	17.7%	17.7%	18.1%	18.6%	18.4%
Nondurable Goods										
Newspapers/Mechanical Papers†	25.6%	23.7%	27.3%	38.0%	59.0%	73.2%	79.3%	88.1%	71.6%	72.5%
Directories†**				8.2%	17.6%	18.2%	18.4%	36.9%	-	-
Other Paper Nondurable Goods										
Books and Magazines	5.2%	10.5%	8.3%							
Books**				10.3%	19.4%	24.5%	28.3%	33.3%	-	-
Magazines**				10.6%	31.8%	37.2%	39.6%	53.8%	-	-
Office-Type Papers***	16.4%	26.8%	21.8%	26.5%	55.1%	62.1%	71.0%	74.2%	-	-
Standard Mail§				5.2%	32.9%	35.8%	40.3%	63.4%	-	-
Other Commercial Printing†	10.3%	16.0%	11.2%	15.7%	11.0%	22.4%	45.0%	66.2%	-	-
Tissue Paper and Towels	Neg.	Neg.	Neg.	Neg.	Neg.	Neg.	Neg.	Neg.	-	-
Paper Plates and Cups	Neg.	Neg.	Neg.	Neg.	Neg.	Neg.	Neg.	Neg.	-	-
Other Nonpackaging Paper	1.5%	3.0%	Neg.	Neg.	Neg.	Neg.	Neg.	Neg.	-	-
Total Other Paper Nondurable Goods									45.0%	46.6%
Disposable Diapers				Neg.	Neg.	Neg.	Neg.	Neg.	Neg.	Neg.
Plastic Plates and Cups§			Neg.	Neg.	Neg.	Neg.	Neg.	Neg.	Neg.	Neg.
Trash Bags**				Neg.	Neg.	Neg.	Neg.	Neg.	Neg.	Neg.
Clothing and Footwear	Neg.	Neg.	Neg.	13.0%	13.9%	15.8%	15.0%	13.8%	13.8%	13.9%
Towels, Sheets and Pillowcases**				16.9%	17.1%	17.3%	17.3%	17.1%	17.1%	17.6%
Other Miscellaneous Nondurables	Neg.	Neg.	Neg.	Neg.	Neg.	Neg.	Neg.	Neg.	Neg.	Neg.
Total Nondurables	13.8%	14.9%	13.6%	16.9%	27.4%	31.1%	34.0%	35.3%	36.1%	36.5%
Containers and Packaging *(Detail in Table 21)*	10.5%	7.7%	16.1%	26.0%	38.1%	41.3%	43.3%	48.0%	48.5%	50.7%
Total Product Wastes‡	10.3%	9.6%	13.3%	19.8%	29.7%	32.0%	33.8%	35.8%	36.6%	37.5%
Other Wastes	Neg.	Neg.	Neg.	6.8%	25.4%	29.9%	31.0%	28.7%	27.6%	28.0%
Total MSW Recovered - %	6.4%	6.6%	9.6%	16.0%	28.5%	31.4%	33.1%	33.7%	34.0%	34.7%

* Recovery of postconsumer wastes; does not include converting/fabrication scrap. Details may not add to totals due to rounding.
† Starting in 2010, newsprint and groundwood inserts expanded to include directories and other mechanical papers previously counted as Other Commercial Printing.
** Not estimated separately prior to 1990.
*** High-grade paper such as printer paper; generated in both commercial and residential sources.
§ Standard Mail: Not estimated separately prior to 1990. Formerly called Third Class Mail and Standard (A) Mail by the U.S. Postal Service.
§ Plastic Plates and Cups: Not estimated separately prior to 1980.
‡ Other than food products.
- Detailed data not available.

Neg. = Less than 5,000 tons or 0.05 percent.

Source: *U.S. EPA, Municipal Solid Waste in the United States, 2011 Facts and Figures*

PRODUCTS DISCARDED* IN THE MUNICIPAL WASTE STREAM, 1960 TO 2011
(WITH DETAIL ON NONDURABLE GOODS)
(In thousands of tons and percent of total discards)

	Thousands of Tons									
Products	**1960**	**1970**	**1980**	**1990**	**2000**	**2005**	**2007**	**2009**	**2010**	**2011**
Durable Goods	9,570	13,720	20,440	26,350	32,290	37,090	38,200	38,680	39,610	40,270
(Detail in Table 14)										
Nondurable Goods										
Newspapers/Mechanical Papers†	5,290	7,260	8,030	8,320	6,070	3,430	2,230	920	2,810	2,520
Directories†**				560	560	540	620	410	-	-
Other Paper Nondurable Goods										
Books and Magazines	1,820	2,210	3,110							
Books**				870	1,000	830	910	640	-	-
Magazines**				2,530	1,520	1,620	1,540	670	-	-
Office-Type Papers***	1,270	1,940	3,130	4,710	3,330	2,510	1,760	1,390	-	-
Standard Mail§				3,620	3,740	3,740	3,530	1,700	-	-
Other Commercial Printing†	1,130	1,790	2,770	3,760	6,570	5,000	3,410	1,180	-	-
Tissue Paper and Towels	1,090	2,080	2,300	2,960	3,220	3,460	3,500	3,490	-	-
Paper Plates and Cups	270	420	630	650	960	1,160	1,230	1,170	-	-
Other Nonpackaging Paper	2,660	3,520	4,230	3,840	4,250	4,490	4,260	4,420	-	-
Total Other Paper Nondurable Goods									13,040	12,180
Disposable Diapers	Neg.	350	1,930	2,700	3,230	3,410	3,730	3,810	3,700	3,630
Plastic Plates and Cups§			190	650	870	930	860	900	890	1,030
Trash Bags**				780	850	1,060	1,070	1,000	980	1,010
Clothing and Footwear	1,310	1,560	2,020	3,490	5,570	6,640	7,070	7,830	7,800	7,770
Towels, Sheets and Pillowcases**				590	680	810	910	1,020	1,070	1,080
Other Miscellaneous Nondurables	100	200	1,410	3,340	4,030	4,250	4,160	4,000	3,720	3,560
Total Nondurable Goods	14,940	21,330	29,750	43,370	46,450	43,880	40,790	34,550	34,010	32,780
Containers and Packaging	24,500	40,210	44,180	47,750	46,970	44,830	44,470	37,110	38,940	37,280
(Detail in Table 22)										
Total Product Wastes‡	49,010	75,200	94,370	117,470	125,710	125,800	123,460	110,340	112,560	110,330
Other Wastes	33,500	37,780	42,750	57,560	48,280	48,140	48,230	51,540	52,810	53,190
Total MSW Discarded - Weight	82,510	113,040	137,120	175,030	173,990	173,940	171,690	161,880	165,370	163,520

	Percent of Total Discards									
Products	**1960**	**1970**	**1980**	**1990**	**2000**	**2005**	**2007**	**2009**	**2010**	**2011**
Durable Goods	11.6%	12.1%	14.9%	15.1%	18.6%	21.3%	22.2%	23.9%	24.0%	24.6%
(Detail in Table 14)										
Nondurable Goods										
Newspapers/Mechanical Papers†	6.4%	6.4%	5.9%	4.8%	3.5%	2.0%	1.3%	0.6%	1.7%	1.5%
Directories†**				0.3%	0.3%	0.3%	0.4%	0.3%	-	-
Other Paper Nondurable Goods										
Books and Magazines	2.2%	2.0%	2.3%							
Books**				0.5%	0.6%	0.5%	0.5%	0.4%	-	-
Magazines**				1.4%	0.9%	0.9%	0.9%	0.4%		
Office-Type Papers***	1.5%	1.7%	2.3%	2.7%	1.9%	1.4%	1.0%	0.9%	-	-
Standard Mail§				2.1%	2.1%	2.2%	2.1%	1.1%	-	-
Other Commercial Printing†	1.4%	1.6%	2.0%	2.1%	3.8%	2.9%	2.0%	0.7%	-	-
Tissue Paper and Towels	1.3%	1.8%	1.7%	1.7%	1.9%	2.0%	2.0%	2.2%	-	-
Paper Plates and Cups	0.3%	0.4%	0.5%	0.4%	0.6%	0.7%	0.7%	0.7%	-	-
Other Nonpackaging Paper	3.2%	3.1%	3.1%	2.2%	2.4%	2.6%	2.5%	2.7%	-	-
Total Other Paper Nondurable Goods									7.9%	7.4%
Disposable Diapers	Neg.	0.3%	1.4%	1.5%	1.9%	2.0%	2.2%	2.4%	2.2%	2.2%
Plastic Plates and Cups§			0.1%	0.4%	0.5%	0.5%	0.5%	0.6%	0.5%	0.6%
Trash Bags**				0.4%	0.5%	0.6%	0.6%	0.6%	0.6%	0.6%
Clothing and Footwear	1.6%	1.4%	1.5%	2.0%	3.2%	3.8%	4.1%	4.8%	4.7%	4.8%
Towels, Sheets and Pillowcases**				0.3%	0.4%	0.5%	0.5%	0.6%	0.6%	0.7%
Other Miscellaneous Nondurables	0.1%	0.2%	1.7%	1.9%	2.3%	2.4%	2.4%	2.5%	2.2%	2.2%
Total Nondurables	18.1%	18.9%	21.7%	24.8%	26.7%	25.2%	23.8%	21.3%	20.6%	20.0%
Containers and Packaging	29.7%	35.6%	32.2%	27.3%	27.0%	25.8%	25.9%	22.9%	23.5%	22.8%
(Detail in Table 23)										
Total Product Wastes‡	59.4%	66.6%	68.8%	67.1%	72.3%	72.3%	71.9%	68.2%	68.1%	67.5%
Other Wastes	40.6%	33.4%	31.2%	32.9%	27.7%	27.7%	28.1%	31.8%	31.9%	32.5%
Total MSW Discarded - %	100.0%	100.0%	100.0%	100.0%	100.0%	100.0%	100.0%	100.0%	100.0%	100.0%

* Discards after materials and compost recovery. In this table, discards include combustion with energy recovery.
Does not include construction & demolition debris, industrial process wastes, or certain other wastes. Details may not add to totals due to rounding.
† Starting in 2010, newsprint and groundwood inserts expanded to include directories and other mechanical papers previously counted as Other Commercial Printing.
** Not estimated separately prior to 1990.
*** High-grade paper such as printer paper; generated in both commercial and residential sources.
§ Standard Mail: Not estimated separately prior to 1990. Formerly called Third Class Mail and Standard (A) Mail by the U.S. Postal Service.
§ Plastic Plates and Cups: Not estimated separately prior to 1980.
‡ Other than food products.
\- Detailed data not available.

Neg. = Less than 5,000 tons or 0.05 percent.

Source: *U.S. EPA, Municipal Solid Waste in the United States, 2011 Facts and Figures*

PRODUCTS GENERATED* IN THE MUNICIPAL WASTE STREAM, 1960 TO 2011
(WITH DETAIL ON CONTAINERS AND PACKAGING)
(In thousands of tons)

	Thousands of Tons									
Products	**1960**	**1970**	**1980**	**1990**	**2000**	**2005**	**2007**	**2009**	**2010**	**2011**
Durable Goods *(Detail in Table 12)*	9,920	14,660	21,800	29,810	38,870	45,060	46,430	47,220	48,680	49,340
Nondurable Goods *(Detail in Table 15)*	17,330	25,060	34,420	52,170	64,010	63,650	61,760	53,440	53,200	51,610
Containers and Packaging										
Glass Packaging										
Beer and Soft Drink Bottles**	1,400	5,580	6,740	5,640	5,710	6,540	6,760	6,000	5,670	5,520
Wine and Liquor Bottles	1,080	1,900	2,450	2,030	1,910	1,630	1,620	1,710	1,700	1,770
Other Bottles & Jars	3,710	4,440	4,780	4,160	3,420	2,290	2,030	1,950	1,990	1,990
Total Glass Packaging	6,190	11,920	13,970	11,830	11,040	10,460	10,410	9,660	9,360	9,280
Steel Packaging										
Beer and Soft Drink Cans	640	1,570	520	150	Neg.	Neg.	Neg.	Neg.	Neg.	Neg.
Cans	3,760	3,540	2,850	2,540	2,630	2,130	2,430	1,880	2,300	1,800
Other Steel Packaging	260	270	240	200	240	240	240	360	440	380
Total Steel Packaging	4,660	5,380	3,610	2,890	2,870	2,370	2,670	2,240	2,740	2,180
Aluminum Packaging										
Beer and Soft Drink Cans	Neg.	100	850	1,550	1,520	1,450	1,420	1,360	1,370	1,320
Other Cans	Neg.	60	40	20	50	80	30	60	70	70
Foil and Closures	170	410	380	330	380	400	430	460	460	460
Total Aluminum Packaging	170	570	1,270	1,900	1,950	1,930	1,880	1,880	1,900	1,850
Paper & Paperboard Pkg										
Corrugated Boxes	7,330	12,760	17,080	24,010	30,210	30,930	31,230	27,190	29,050	29,440
Other Paper & Paperboard Pkg										
Gable Top/Aseptic Cartons‡			790	510	550	500	500	460	540	540
Folding Cartons			3,820	4,300	5,820	5,530	5,530	4,980	5,470	5,540
Other Paperboard Packaging	3,840	4,830	230	290	200	160	150	90	90	80
Bags and Sacks			3,380	2,440	1,490	1,120	1,140	910	1,040	750
Wrapping Papers			200	110	Neg.	Neg.	Neg.	Neg.	Neg.	Neg.
Other Paper Packaging	2,940	3,810	850	1,020	1,670	1,400	1,390	1,310	1,490	1,670
Subtotal Other Paper & Paperboard Pkg									8,630	8,580
Total Paper & Board Pkg	14,110	21,400	26,350	32,680	39,940	39,640	39,940	34,940	37,680	38,020
Plastics Packaging										
PET Bottles and Jars			260	430	1,720	2,540	2,840	2,570	2,670	2,740
HDPE Natural Bottles			230	530	690	800	820	760	800	770
Other Containers	60	910	890	1,430	1,740	1,420	1,910	1,750	1,830	1,870
Bags and Sacks			390	940	1,650	1,640	1,010	660	770	
Wraps			840	1,530	2,550	2,810	3,180	3,190	3,160	
Subtotal Bags, Sacks, and Wraps			1,230	2,470	4,200	4,450	4,190	3,850	3,930	3,880
Other Plastics Packaging	60	1,180	790	2,040	2,840	3,210	3,870	3,600	4,450	4,640
Total Plastics Packaging	120	2,090	3,400	6,900	11,190	12,420	13,630	12,530	13,680	13,900
Wood Packaging	2,000	2,070	3,940	8,180	8,610	9,230	9,520	9,790	9,940	10,000
Other Misc. Packaging	120	130	130	150	240	280	320	280	340	350
Total Containers & Pkg	27,370	43,560	52,670	64,530	75,840	76,330	78,370	71,320	75,640	75,580
Total Product Wastes†	54,620	83,280	108,890	146,510	178,720	185,040	186,560	171,980	177,520	176,530
Other Wastes										
Food Waste	12,200	12,800	13,000	23,860	30,700	32,930	33,560	35,270	35,740	36,310
Yard Trimmings	20,000	23,200	27,500	35,000	30,530	32,070	32,630	33,200	33,400	33,710
Miscellaneous Inorganic Wastes	1,300	1,780	2,250	2,900	3,500	3,690	3,750	3,820	3,840	3,870
Total Other Wastes	33,500	37,780	42,750	61,760	64,730	68,690	69,940	72,290	72,980	73,890
Total MSW Generated - Weight	88,120	121,060	151,640	208,270	243,450	253,730	256,500	244,270	250,500	250,420

* Generation before materials recovery or combustion.
** Includes carbonated drinks and non-carbonated water, teas, flavored drinks, and ready-to-drink alcoholic coolers and cocktails.
† Other than food products.
‡ Includes milk, juice, and other products packaged in gable top cartons and liquid food aseptic cartons.
Details may not add to totals due to rounding.
Neg. = Less than 5,000 tons or 0.05 percent.
- Detailed data not available.

Source: *U.S. EPA, Municipal Solid Waste in the United States, 2011 Facts and Figures*

PRODUCTS GENERATED* IN THE MUNICIPAL WASTE STREAM, 1960 TO 2011
(WITH DETAIL ON CONTAINERS AND PACKAGING)
(In percent of total generation)

	Percent of Total Generation									
Products	**1960**	**1970**	**1980**	**1990**	**2000**	**2005**	**2007**	**2009**	**2010**	**2011**
Durable Goods	11.3%	12.1%	14.4%	14.3%	16.0%	17.8%	18.1%	19.3%	19.4%	19.7%
(Detail in Table 12)										
Nondurable Goods	19.7%	20.7%	22.7%	25.0%	26.3%	25.1%	24.1%	21.9%	21.2%	20.6%
(Detail in Table 15)										
Containers and Packaging										
Glass Packaging										
Beer and Soft Drink Bottles**	1.6%	4.6%	4.4%	2.7%	2.3%	2.6%	2.6%	2.5%	2.3%	2.2%
Wine and Liquor Bottles	1.2%	1.6%	1.6%	1.0%	0.8%	0.6%	0.6%	0.7%	0.7%	0.7%
Other Bottles & Jars	4.2%	3.7%	3.2%	2.0%	1.4%	0.9%	0.8%	0.8%	0.8%	0.8%
Total Glass Packaging	7.0%	9.8%	9.2%	5.7%	4.5%	4.1%	4.1%	4.0%	3.7%	3.7%
Steel Packaging										
Beer and Soft Drink Cans	0.7%	1.3%	0.3%	0.1%	Neg.	Neg.	Neg.	Neg.	Neg.	Neg.
Cans	4.3%	2.9%	1.9%	1.2%	1.1%	0.8%	0.9%	0.8%	0.9%	0.7%
Other Steel Packaging	0.3%	0.2%	0.2%	0.1%	0.1%	0.1%	0.1%	0.1%	0.2%	0.2%
Total Steel Packaging	5.3%	4.4%	2.4%	1.4%	1.2%	0.9%	1.0%	0.9%	1.1%	0.9%
Aluminum Packaging										
Beer and Soft Drink Cans	Neg.	0.1%	0.6%	0.7%	0.6%	0.6%	0.6%	0.6%	0.5%	0.5%
Other Cans	Neg.	Neg.	Neg.	Neg.	Neg.	Neg.	0.01%	0.02%	0.03%	0.03%
Foil and Closures	0.2%	0.3%	0.3%	0.2%	0.2%	0.2%	0.2%	0.2%	0.2%	0.2%
Total Aluminum Packaging	0.2%	0.5%	0.8%	0.9%	0.8%	0.8%	0.7%	0.8%	0.8%	0.7%
Paper & Paperboard Pkg										
Corrugated Boxes	8.3%	10.5%	11.3%	11.5%	12.4%	12.2%	12.2%	11.1%	11.6%	11.8%
Other Paper & Paperboard Pkg										
Gable Top/Aseptic Cartons‡			0.5%	0.2%	0.2%	0.2%	0.2%	0.2%	0.2%	0.2%
Folding Cartons			2.5%	2.1%	2.4%	2.2%	2.2%	2.0%	2.2%	2.2%
Other Paperboard Packaging	4.4%	4.0%	0.2%	0.1%	0.1%	0.1%	0.1%	0.0%	0.0%	0.0%
Bags and Sacks			2.2%	1.2%	0.6%	0.4%	0.4%	0.4%	0.4%	0.3%
Wrapping Papers			0.1%	0.1%	Neg.	Neg.	Neg.	Neg.	Neg.	Neg.
Other Paper Packaging	3.3%	3.1%	0.6%	0.5%	0.7%	0.6%	0.5%	0.5%	0.6%	0.7%
Subtotal Other Paper & Paperboard Pkg									3.4%	3.4%
Total Paper & Board Pkg	16.0%	17.7%	17.4%	15.7%	16.4%	15.6%	15.6%	14.3%	15.0%	15.2%
Plastics Packaging										
PET Bottles and Jars			0.2%	0.2%	0.7%	1.0%	1.1%	1.1%	1.1%	1.1%
HDPE Natural Bottles			0.2%	0.3%	0.3%	0.3%	0.3%	0.3%	0.3%	0.3%
Other Containers	0.1%	0.8%	0.6%	0.7%	0.7%	0.6%	0.7%	0.7%	0.7%	0.7%
Bags and Sacks			0.0%	0.5%	0.7%	0.6%	0.4%	0.3%	0.3%	0.0%
Wraps			0.6%	0.7%	1.0%	1.1%	1.2%	1.3%	1.3%	0.0%
Subtotal Bags, Sacks, and Wraps			0.8%	1.2%	1.7%	1.8%	1.6%	1.6%	1.6%	1.5%
Other Plastics Packaging	0.1%	1.0%	0.5%	1.0%	1.2%	1.3%	1.5%	1.5%	1.8%	1.9%
Total Plastics Packaging	0.1%	1.7%	2.2%	3.3%	4.6%	4.9%	5.3%	5.1%	5.5%	5.6%
Wood Packaging	2.3%	1.7%	2.6%	3.9%	3.5%	3.6%	3.7%	4.0%	4.0%	4.0%
Other Misc. Packaging	0.1%	0.1%	0.1%	0.1%	0.1%	0.1%	0.1%	0.1%	0.1%	0.1%
Total Containers & Pkg	31.1%	36.0%	34.7%	31.0%	31.2%	30.1%	30.6%	29.2%	30.2%	30.2%
Total Product Wastes†	62.0%	68.8%	71.8%	70.3%	73.4%	72.9%	72.7%	70.4%	70.9%	70.5%
Other Wastes										
Food Waste	13.8%	10.6%	8.6%	11.5%	12.6%	13.0%	13.1%	14.4%	14.3%	14.5%
Yard Trimmings	22.7%	19.2%	18.1%	16.8%	12.5%	12.6%	12.7%	13.6%	13.3%	13.5%
Miscellaneous Inorganic Wastes	1.5%	1.5%	1.5%	1.4%	1.4%	1.5%	1.5%	1.6%	1.5%	1.5%
Total Other Wastes	38.0%	31.2%	28.2%	29.7%	26.6%	27.1%	27.3%	29.6%	29.1%	29.5%
Total MSW Generated - %	100.0%	100.0%	100.0%	100.0%	100.0%	100.0%	100.0%	100.0%	100.0%	100.0%

* Generation before materials recovery or combustion.
** Includes carbonated drinks and non-carbonated water, teas, flavored drinks, and ready-to-drink alcoholic coolers and cocktails.
† Other than food products.
‡ Includes milk, juice, and other products packaged in gable top cartons and liquid food aseptic cartons.
Details may not add to totals due to rounding.
Neg. = Less than 5,000 tons or 0.05 percent.
- Detailed data not available.

Source: *U.S. EPA, Municipal Solid Waste in the United States, 2011 Facts and Figures*

RECOVERY* OF PRODUCTS IN MUNICIPAL SOLID WASTE, 1960 TO 2011
(WITH DETAIL ON CONTAINERS AND PACKAGING)
(In thousands of tons)

Products	Thousands of Tons									
	1960	1970	1980	1990	2000	2005	2007	2009	2010	2011
Durable Goods	350	940	1,360	3,460	6,580	7,970	8,230	8,540	9,070	9,070
(Detail in Table 13)										
Nondurable Goods	2,390	3,730	4,670	8,800	17,560	19,770	20,970	18,890	19,190	18,830
(Detail in Table 16)										
Containers and Packaging										
Glass Packaging										
Beer and Soft Drink Bottles**	90	140	730	1,890	1,530	2,000	2,340	2,340	2,350	2,270
Wine and Liquor Bottles	10	10	20	210	430	250	240	430	540	600
Other Bottles & Jars	Neg.	Neg.	Neg.	520	920	340	300	230	240	300
Total Glass Packaging	100	150	750	2,620	2,880	2,590	2,880	3,000	3,130	3,170
Steel Packaging										
Beer and Soft Drink Cans	10	20	50	40	Neg.	Neg.	Neg.	Neg.	Neg.	Neg.
Cans	20	60	150	590	1,530	1,340	1,570	1,240	1,540	1,270
Other Steel Packaging	Neg.	Neg.	Neg.	60	160	160	160	290	350	300
Total Steel Packaging	30	80	200	690	1,690	1,500	1,730	1,530	1,890	1,570
Aluminum Packaging										
Beer and Soft Drink Cans	Neg.	10	320	990	830	650	690	690	680	720
Other Cans	Neg.	Neg.	Neg.	Neg.	Neg.	Neg.	Neg.	NA	NA	NA
Foil and Closures	Neg.	Neg.	Neg.	20	30	40	40	NA	NA	NA
Total Aluminum Pkg	Neg.	10	320	1,010	860	690	730	690	680	720
Paper & Paperboard Pkg										
Corrugated Boxes	2,520	2,760	6,390	11,530	20,330	22,100	22,980	22,100	24,690	26,800
Other Paper & Paperboard Pkg										
Gable Top/Aseptic Cartons‡			Neg.	Neg.	Neg.	Neg.	Neg.	30		-
Folding Cartons			520	340	410	1,190	1,550	2,490	-	-
Other Paperboard Packaging			Neg.	Neg.	Neg.	Neg.	Neg.	Neg.	-	-
Bags and Sacks			Neg.	200	300	320	420	450	-	-
Wrapping Papers			Neg.	Neg.	Neg.	Neg.	Neg.	Neg.	-	-
Other Paper Packaging	220	350	300	Neg.	Neg.	Neg.	Neg.	Neg.	-	-
Subtotal Other Paper & Paperboard Pkg									2,160	1,860
Total Paper & Board Pkg	2,740	3,110	7,210	12,070	21,040	23,610	24,950	25,070	26,850	28,660
Plastics Packaging										
PET Bottles and Jars			10	140	380	590	700	720	780	800
HDPE Natural Bottles			Neg.	20	210	230	230	220	220	220
Other Containers	Neg.	Neg.	Neg.	20	170	140	190	290	300	290
Bags and Sacks										
Wraps										
Subtotal Bags, Sacks, and Wraps			Neg.	60	180	230	380	360	450	430
Other Plastics Packaging	Neg.	Neg.	Neg.	20	90	90	90	130	100	60
Total Plastics Packaging	Neg.	Neg.	10	260	1,030	1,280	1,590	1,720	1,850	1,800
Wood Packaging	Neg.	Neg.	Neg.	130	1,370	1,830	2,020	2,200	2,300	2,380
Other Misc. Packaging	Neg.	Neg.	Neg.	Neg.	Neg.	Neg.	Neg.	Neg.	Neg.	Neg.
Total Containers & Pkg	2,870	3,350	8,490	16,780	28,870	31,500	33,900	34,210	36,700	38,300
Total Product Wastes†	5,610	8,020	14,520	29,040	53,010	59,240	63,100	61,640	64,960	66,200
Other Wastes										
Food Waste	Neg.	Neg.	Neg.	Neg.	680	690	810	850	970	1,400
Yard Trimmings	Neg.	Neg.	Neg.	4,200	15,770	19,860	20,900	19,900	19,200	19,300
Miscellaneous Inorganic Wastes	Neg.	Neg.	Neg.	Neg.	Neg.	Neg.	Neg.	Neg.	Neg.	Neg.
Total Other Wastes	Neg.	Neg.	Neg.	4,200	16,450	20,550	21,710	20,750	20,170	20,700
Total MSW Recovered - Weight	5,610	8,020	14,520	33,240	69,460	79,790	84,810	82,390	85,130	86,900

* Recovery of postconsumer wastes; does not include converting/fabrication scrap. Details may not add to totals due to rounding.
** Includes carbonated drinks and non-carbonated water, teas, flavored drinks, and ready-to-drink alcoholic coolers and cocktails.
† Other than food products.
‡ Includes milk, juice, and other products packaged in gable top cartons and liquid food aseptic cartons.
Neg. = Less than 5,000 tons or 0.05 percent. NA = Not Available
\- Detailed data not available.

Source: *U.S. EPA, Municipal Solid Waste in the United States, 2011 Facts and Figures*

RECOVERY* OF PRODUCTS IN MUNICIPAL SOLID WASTE, 1960 TO 2011
(WITH DETAIL ON CONTAINERS AND PACKAGING)
(In percent of generation of each product)

	Percent of Generation of Each Product									
Products	**1960**	**1970**	**1980**	**1990**	**2000**	**2005**	**2007**	**2009**	**2010**	**2011**
Durable Goods	3.5%	6.4%	6.2%	11.6%	16.9%	17.7%	17.7%	18.1%	18.6%	18.4%
(Detail in Table 13)										
Nondurable Goods	13.8%	14.9%	13.6%	16.9%	27.4%	31.1%	34.0%	35.3%	36.1%	36.5%
(Detail in Table 16)										
Containers and Packaging										
Glass Packaging										
Beer and Soft Drink Bottles**	6.4%	2.5%	10.8%	33.5%	26.8%	30.6%	34.6%	39.0%	41.4%	41.1%
Wine and Liquor Bottles	Neg.	Neg.	Neg.	10.3%	22.5%	15.3%	14.8%	25.1%	31.8%	33.9%
Other Bottles & Jars	Neg.	Neg.	Neg.	12.5%	26.9%	14.8%	14.8%	11.8%	12.1%	15.1%
Total Glass Packaging	1.6%	1.3%	5.4%	22.1%	26.1%	24.8%	27.7%	31.1%	33.4%	34.2%
Steel Packaging										
Beer and Soft Drink Cans	1.6%	1.3%	9.6%	26.7%	Neg.	Neg.	Neg.	Neg.	Neg.	Neg.
Cans	Neg.	1.7%	5.3%	23.2%	58.2%	62.9%	64.6%	66.0%	67.0%	70.6%
Other Steel Packaging	Neg.	Neg.	Neg.	30.0%	66.7%	66.7%	66.7%	80.6%	79.5%	78.9%
Total Steel Packaging	Neg.	1.5%	5.5%	23.9%	58.9%	63.3%	64.8%	68.3%	69.0%	72.0%
Aluminum Packaging										
Beer and Soft Drink Cans	Neg.	10.0%	37.6%	63.9%	54.6%	44.8%	48.6%	50.7%	49.6%	54.5%
Other Cans	Neg.	Neg.	Neg.	Neg.	Neg.	Neg.	Neg.	NA	NA	NA
Foil and Closures	Neg.	Neg.	Neg.	6.1%	7.9%	10.0%	9.3%	NA	NA	NA
Total Aluminum Pkg	Neg.	1.8%	25.2%	53.2%	44.1%	35.8%	38.8%	36.7%	35.8%	38.9%
Paper & Paperboard Pkg										
Corrugated Boxes	34.4%	21.6%	37.4%	48.0%	67.3%	71.5%	73.6%	81.3%	85.0%	91.0%
Other Paper & Paperboard Pkg										
Gable Top/Aseptic Cartons‡			Neg.	Neg.	Neg.	Neg.	Neg.	6.5%	-	-
Folding Cartons			Neg.	Neg.	7.0%	21.5%	28.0%	50.0%	-	-
Other Paperboard Packaging			Neg.	Neg.	Neg.	Neg.	Neg.	Neg.	-	-
Bags and Sacks			Neg.	Neg.	20.1%	28.6%	36.8%	49.5%	-	-
Wrapping Papers			Neg.	Neg.	Neg.	Neg.	Neg.	Neg.	-	-
Other Paper Packaging	7.5%	9.2%	35.3%	Neg.	Neg.	Neg.	Neg.	Neg.	-	-
Subtotal Other Paper & Paperboard Pkg									25.0%	21.7%
Total Paper & Board Pkg	19.4%	14.5%	27.4%	36.9%	52.7%	59.6%	62.5%	71.8%	71.3%	75.4%
Plastics Packaging										
PET Bottles and Jars			3.8%	32.6%	22.1%	23.2%	24.6%	28.0%	29.2%	29.2%
HDPE Natural Bottles			Neg.	3.8%	30.4%	28.8%	28.0%	28.9%	27.5%	28.6%
Other Containers	Neg.	Neg.	Neg.	1.4%	9.8%	9.9%	9.9%	16.6%	16.4%	15.5%
Bags and Sacks										
Wraps										
Subtotal Bags, Sacks, and Wraps			Neg.	2.4%	4.3%	5.2%	9.1%	9.4%	11.5%	11.1%
Other Plastics Packaging	Neg.	Neg.	Neg.	1.0%	3.2%	2.8%	2.3%	3.6%	2.2%	1.3%
Total Plastics Packaging	Neg.	Neg.	Neg.	3.8%	9.2%	10.3%	11.7%	13.7%	13.5%	12.9%
Wood Packaging	Neg.	Neg.	Neg.	1.6%	15.9%	19.8%	21.2%	22.5%	23.1%	23.8%
Other Misc. Packaging	Neg.	Neg.	Neg.	Neg.	Neg.	Neg.	Neg.	Neg.	Neg.	Neg.
Total Containers & Pkg	10.5%	7.7%	16.1%	26.0%	38.1%	41.3%	43.3%	48.0%	48.5%	50.7%
Total Product Wastes†	10.3%	9.6%	13.3%	19.8%	29.7%	32.0%	33.8%	35.8%	36.6%	37.5%
Other Wastes										
Food Waste	Neg.	Neg.	Neg.	Neg.	2.2%	2.1%	2.4%	2.4%	2.7%	3.9%
Yard Trimmings	Neg.	Neg.	Neg.	12.0%	51.7%	61.9%	64.1%	59.9%	57.5%	57.3%
Miscellaneous Inorganic Wastes	Neg.	Neg.	Neg.	Neg.	Neg.	Neg.	Neg.	Neg.	Neg.	Neg.
Total Other Wastes	Neg.	Neg.	Neg.	6.8%	25.4%	29.9%	31.0%	28.7%	27.6%	28.0%
Total MSW Recovered - %	6.4%	6.6%	9.6%	16.0%	28.5%	31.4%	33.1%	33.7%	34.0%	34.7%

* Recovery of postconsumer wastes; does not include converting/fabrication scrap. Details may not add to totals due to rounding.
** Includes carbonated drinks and non-carbonated water, teas, flavored drinks, and ready-to-drink alcoholic coolers and cocktails.
† Other than food products.
‡ Includes milk, juice, and other products packaged in gable top cartons and liquid food aseptic cartons.
Neg. = Less than 5,000 tons or 0.05 percent. NA = Not Available
- Detailed data not available.

Source: *U.S. EPA, Municipal Solid Waste in the United States, 2011 Facts and Figures*

PRODUCTS DISCARDED* IN THE MUNICIPAL WASTE STREAM, 1960 TO 2011
(WITH DETAIL ON CONTAINERS AND PACKAGING)
(In thousands of tons)

	Thousands of Tons									
Products	**1960**	**1970**	**1980**	**1990**	**2000**	**2005**	**2007**	**2009**	**2010**	**2011**
Durable Goods	9,570	13,720	20,440	26,350	32,290	37,090	38,200	38,680	39,610	40,270
(Detail in Table 14)										
Nondurable Goods	14,940	21,330	29,750	43,370	46,450	43,880	40,790	34,550	34,010	32,780
(Detail in Table 17)										
Containers and Packaging										
Glass Packaging										
Beer and Soft Drink Bottles**	1,310	5,440	6,010	3,750	4,180	4,540	4,420	3,660	3,320	3,250
Wine and Liquor Bottles	1,070	1,890	2,430	1,820	1,480	1,380	1,380	1,280	1,160	1,170
Other Bottles & Jars	3,710	4,440	4,780	3,640	2,500	1,950	1,730	1,720	1,750	1,690
Total Glass Packaging	6,090	11,770	13,220	9,210	8,160	7,870	7,530	6,660	6,230	6,110
Steel Packaging										
Beer and Soft Drink Cans	630	1,550	470	110	Neg.	Neg.	Neg.	Neg.	Neg.	Neg.
Cans	3,740	3,480	2,700	1,950	1,100	790	860	640	760	530
Other Steel Packaging	260	270	240	140	80	80	80	70	90	80
Total Steel Packaging	4,630	5,300	3,410	2,200	1,180	870	940	710	850	610
Aluminum Packaging										
Beer and Soft Drink Cans	Neg.	90	530	560	690	800	730	670	690	600
Other Cans	Neg.	60	40	20	50	80	30	60	70	70
Foil and Closures	170	410	380	310	350	360	390	460	460	460
Total Aluminum Pkg	170	560	950	890	1,090	1,240	1,150	1,190	1,220	1,130
Paper & Paperboard Pkg										
Corrugated Boxes	4,810	10,000	10,690	12,480	9,880	8,830	8,250	5,090	4,360	2,640
Other Paper & Paperboard Pkg										
Gable Top/Aseptic Cartons‡			790	510	550	500	500	430	-	-
Folding Cartons			3,300	3,960	5,410	4,340	3,980	2,490	-	-
Other Paperboard Packaging	3,840	4,830	230	290	200	160	150	90	-	-
Bags and Sacks			3,380	2,240	1,190	800	720	460	-	-
Wrapping Papers			200	110	Neg.	Neg.	Neg.	Neg.	-	-
Other Paper Packaging	2,720	3,460	550	1,020	1,670	1,400	1,390	1,310	-	-
Subtotal Other Paper & Paperboard Pkg									6,470	6,720
Total Paper & Board Pkg	11,370	18,290	19,140	20,610	18,900	16,030	14,990	9,870	10,830	9,360
Plastics Packaging										
PET Bottles and Jars			250	290	1,340	1,950	2,140	1,850	1,890	1,940
HDPE Natural Bottles			230	510	480	570	590	540	580	550
Other Containers	60	910	890	1,410	1,570	1,280	1,720	1,460	1,530	1,580
Bags and Sacks										
Wraps										
Subtotal Bags, Sacks, and Wraps			1,230	2,410	4,020	4,220	3,810	3,490	3,480	3,450
Other Plastics Packaging	60	1,180	790	2,020	2,750	3,120	3,780	3,470	4,350	4,580
Total Plastics Packaging	120	2,090	3,390	6,640	10,160	11,140	12,040	10,810	11,830	12,100
Wood Packaging	2,000	2,070	3,940	8,050	7,240	7,400	7,500	7,590	7,640	7,620
Other Misc. Packaging	120	130	130	150	240	280	320	280	340	350
Total Containers & Pkg	24,500	40,210	44,180	47,750	46,970	44,830	44,470	37,110	38,940	37,280
Total Product Wastes†	49,010	75,260	94,370	117,470	125,710	125,800	123,460	110,340	112,560	110,330
Other Wastes										
Food Waste	12,200	12,800	13,000	23,860	30,020	32,240	32,750	34,420	34,770	34,910
Yard Trimmings	20,000	23,200	27,500	30,800	14,760	12,210	11,730	13,300	14,200	14,410
Miscellaneous Inorganic Wastes	1,300	1,780	2,250	2,900	3,500	3,690	3,750	3,820	3,840	3,870
Total Other Wastes	33,500	37,780	42,750	57,560	48,280	48,140	48,230	51,540	52,810	53,190
Total MSW Discarded - Weight	82,510	113,040	137,120	175,030	173,990	173,940	171,690	161,880	165,370	163,520

* Discards after materials and compost recovery. In this table, discards include combustion with energy recovery.
Does not include construction & demolition debris, industrial process wastes, or certain other wastes. Details may not add to totals due to rounding.
** Includes carbonated drinks and non-carbonated water, teas, flavored drinks, and ready-to-drink alcoholic coolers and cocktails.
† Other than food products.
‡ Includes milk, juice, and other products packaged in gable top cartons and liquid food aseptic cartons.
Neg. = Less than 5,000 tons or 0.05 percent.
\- Detailed data not available.

Source: *U.S. EPA, Municipal Solid Waste in the United States, 2011 Facts and Figures*

PRODUCTS DISCARDED* IN THE MUNICIPAL WASTE STREAM, 1960 TO 2011
(WITH DETAIL ON CONTAINERS AND PACKAGING)
(In percent of total discards)

	Percent of Total Discards									
Products	**1960**	**1970**	**1980**	**1990**	**2000**	**2005**	**2007**	**2009**	**2010**	**2011**
Durable Goods	11.6%	12.1%	14.9%	15.1%	18.6%	21.3%	22.2%	23.9%	24.0%	24.6%
(Detail in Table 14)										
Nondurable Goods	18.1%	18.9%	21.7%	24.8%	26.7%	25.2%	23.8%	21.3%	20.6%	20.0%
(Detail in Table 17)										
Containers and Packaging										
Glass Packaging										
Beer and Soft Drink Bottles**	1.6%	4.8%	4.4%	2.1%	2.4%	2.6%	2.6%	2.3%	2.0%	2.0%
Wine and Liquor Bottles	1.3%	1.7%	1.8%	1.0%	0.9%	0.8%	0.8%	0.8%	0.7%	0.7%
Other Bottles & Jars	4.5%	3.9%	3.5%	2.1%	1.4%	1.1%	1.0%	1.1%	1.1%	1.0%
Total Glass Packaging	7.4%	10.4%	9.6%	5.3%	4.7%	4.5%	4.4%	4.1%	3.8%	3.7%
Steel Packaging										
Beer and Soft Drink Cans	0.8%	1.4%	0.3%	0.1%	Neg.	Neg.	Neg.	Neg.	Neg.	Neg.
Cans	4.5%	3.1%	2.0%	1.1%	0.6%	0.5%	0.5%	0.4%	0.5%	0.3%
Other Steel Packaging	0.3%	0.2%	0.2%	0.1%	0.0%	0.0%	0.0%	0.0%	0.1%	0.0%
Total Steel Packaging	5.6%	4.7%	2.5%	1.3%	0.7%	0.5%	0.5%	0.4%	0.5%	0.4%
Aluminum Packaging										
Beer and Soft Drink Cans	Neg.	0.1%	0.4%	0.3%	0.4%	0.5%	0.4%	0.4%	0.4%	0.4%
Other Cans	Neg.	Neg.	Neg.	Neg.	Neg.	Neg.	Neg.	Neg.	Neg.	Neg.
Foil and Closures	0.2%	0.4%	0.3%	0.2%	0.2%	0.2%	0.2%	0.3%	0.3%	0.3%
Total Aluminum Pkg	0.2%	0.5%	0.7%	0.5%	0.6%	0.7%	0.7%	0.7%	0.7%	0.7%
Paper & Paperboard Pkg										
Corrugated Boxes	5.8%	8.8%	7.8%	7.1%	5.7%	5.1%	4.8%	3.1%	2.6%	1.6%
Other Paper & Paperboard Pkg										
Gable Top/Aseptic Cartons‡			0.6%	0.3%	0.3%	0.3%	0.3%	0.3%	-	-
Folding Cartons			2.4%	2.3%	3.1%	2.5%	2.3%	1.5%	-	-
Other Paperboard Packaging	4.7%	4.3%	0.2%	0.2%	0.1%	0.1%	0.1%	0.1%	-	-
Bags and Sacks			2.5%	1.3%	0.7%	0.5%	0.4%	0.3%	-	-
Wrapping Papers			0.1%	0.1%	Neg.	Neg.	Neg.	Neg.	-	-
Other Paper Packaging	3.3%	3.1%	0.4%	0.6%	1.0%	0.8%	0.8%	0.8%	-	-
Subtotal Other Paper & Paperboard Pkg									3.9%	4.1%
Total Paper & Board Pkg	13.8%	16.2%	14.0%	11.8%	10.9%	9.2%	8.7%	6.1%	6.5%	5.7%
Plastics Packaging										
PET Bottles and Jars			0.2%	0.2%	0.0%	1.1%	1.2%	1.1%	1.1%	1.2%
HDPE Natural Bottles			0.2%	0.3%	0.3%	0.3%	0.3%	0.3%	0.4%	0.3%
Other Containers	0.1%	0.8%	0.6%	0.8%	0.9%	0.7%	1.0%	0.9%	0.9%	1.0%
Bags and Sacks										
Wraps										
Subtotal Bags, Sacks, and Wraps			0.9%	1.4%	2.3%	2.4%	2.2%	2.2%	2.1%	2.1%
Other Plastics Packaging	0.1%	1.0%	0.6%	1.2%	1.6%	1.8%	2.2%	2.1%	2.6%	2.8%
Total Plastics Packaging	0.1%	1.8%	2.5%	3.8%	5.8%	6.4%	7.0%	6.7%	7.2%	7.4%
Wood Packaging	2.4%	1.8%	2.9%	4.6%	4.2%	4.3%	4.4%	4.7%	4.6%	4.7%
Other Misc. Packaging	0.1%	0.1%	0.1%	0.1%	0.1%	0.2%	0.2%	0.2%	0.2%	0.2%
Total Containers & Pkg	29.7%	35.6%	32.2%	27.3%	27.0%	25.8%	25.9%	22.9%	23.5%	22.8%
Total Product Wastes†	59.4%	66.6%	68.8%	67.1%	72.3%	72.3%	71.9%	68.2%	68.1%	67.5%
Other Wastes										
Food Waste	14.8%	11.3%	9.5%	13.6%	17.3%	18.5%	19.1%	21.3%	21.0%	21.3%
Yard Trimmings	24.2%	20.5%	20.1%	17.6%	8.5%	7.0%	6.8%	8.2%	8.6%	8.8%
Miscellaneous Inorganic Wastes	1.6%	1.6%	1.6%	1.7%	2.0%	2.1%	2.2%	2.4%	2.3%	2.4%
Total Other Wastes	40.6%	33.4%	31.2%	32.9%	27.7%	27.7%	28.1%	31.8%	31.9%	32.5%
Total MSW Discarded - %	100.0%	100.0%	100.0%	100.0%	100.0%	100.0%	100.0%	100.0%	100.0%	100.0%

* Discards after materials and compost recovery. In this table, discards include combustion with energy recovery. Does not include construction & demolition debris, industrial process wastes, or certain other wastes. Details may not add to totals due to rounding.
** Includes carbonated drinks and non-carbonated water, teas, flavored drinks, and ready-to-drink alcoholic coolers and cocktails.
† Other than food products.
‡ Includes milk, juice, and other products packaged in gable top cartons and liquid food aseptic cartons.
Neg. = Less than 5,000 tons or 0.05 percent. Details may not add to totals due to rounding.
\- Detailed data not available.

Source: *U.S. EPA, Municipal Solid Waste in the United States, 2011 Facts and Figures*

Figure 14. Generation of products in MSW, 1960 to 2011

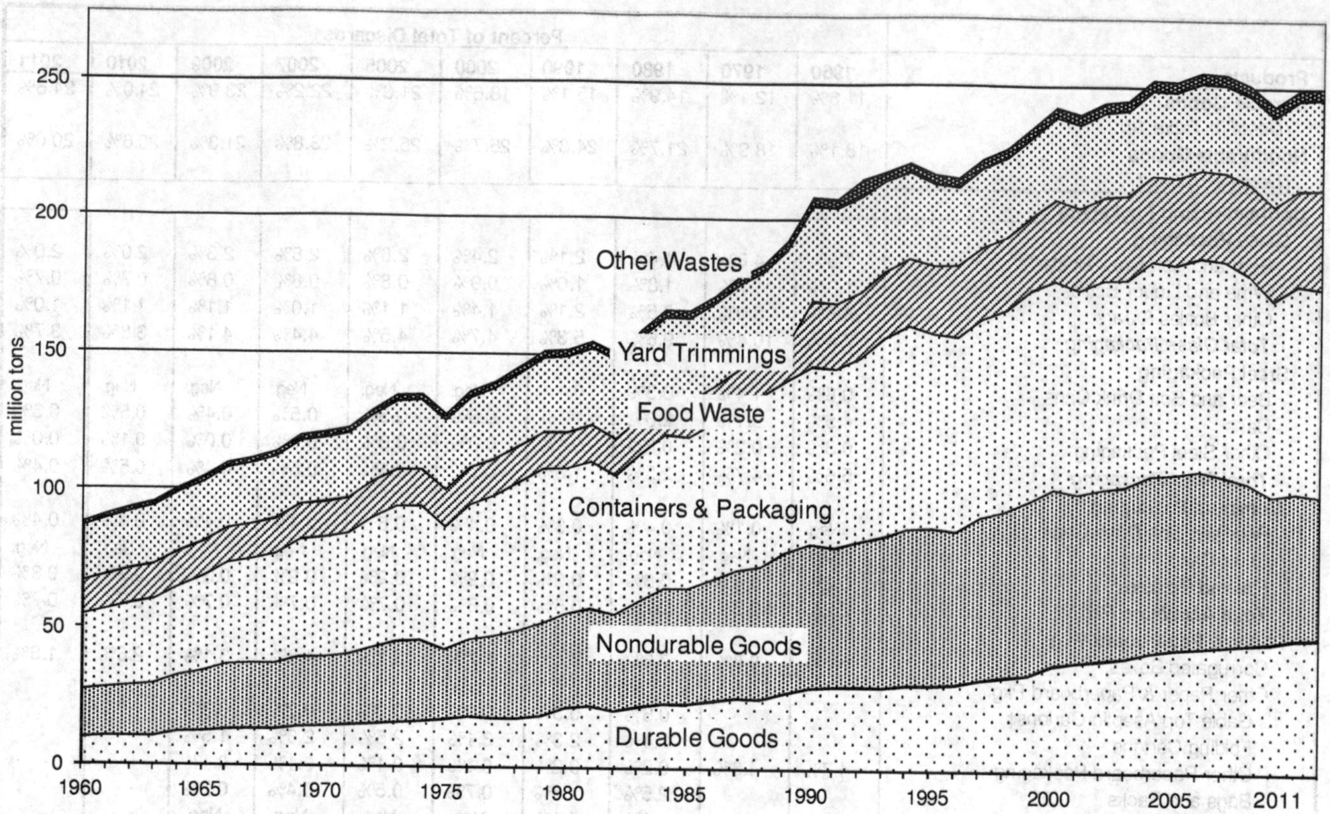

Source: *U.S. EPA, Municipal Solid Waste in the United States, 2011 Facts and Figures*

Figure 15. Nondurable goods generated and discarded* in municipal solid waste, 2011 (In percent of total generation and discards)

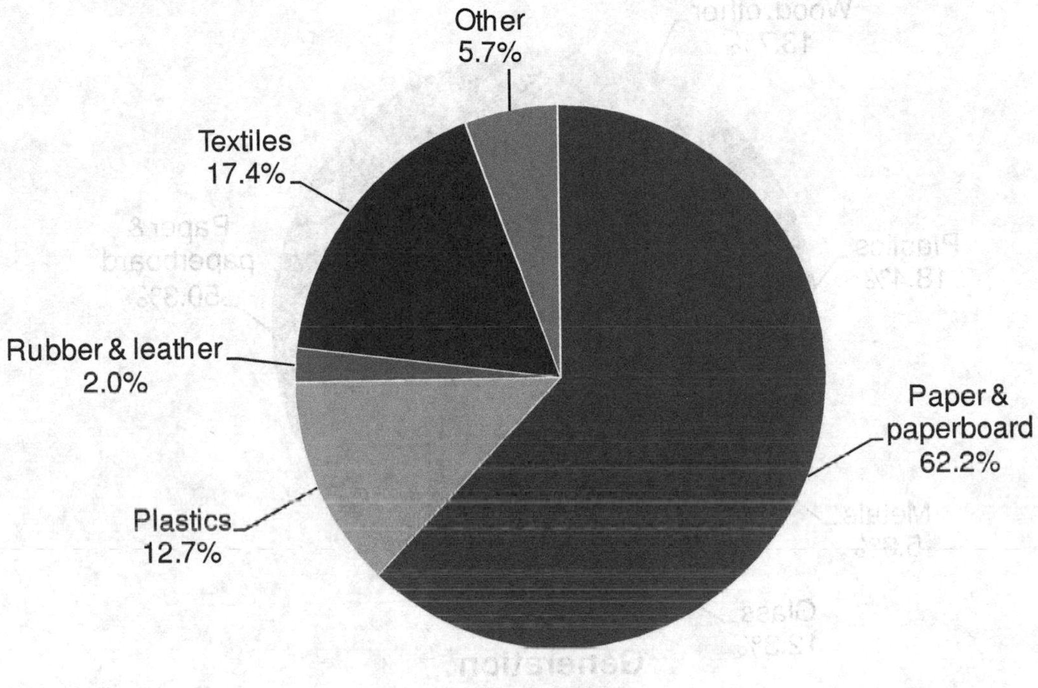

Generation

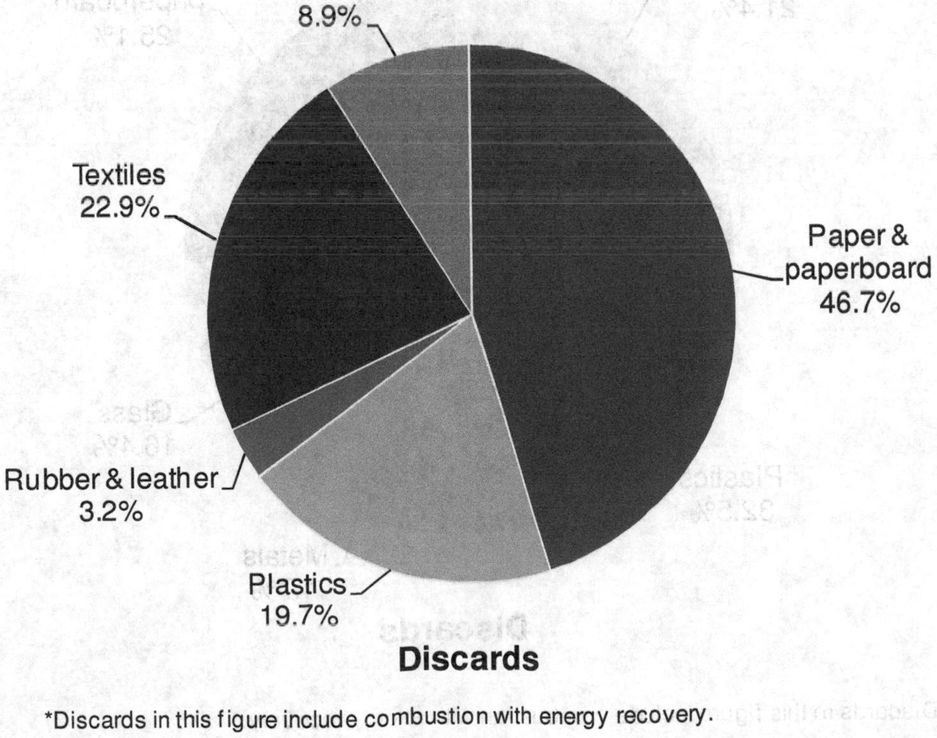

Discards

*Discards in this figure include combustion with energy recovery.

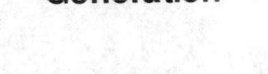

Source: *U.S. EPA, Municipal Solid Waste in the United States, 2011 Facts and Figures*

Figure 16. Containers and packaging materials generated and discarded* in municipal solid waste, 2011 (In percent of total generation and discards)

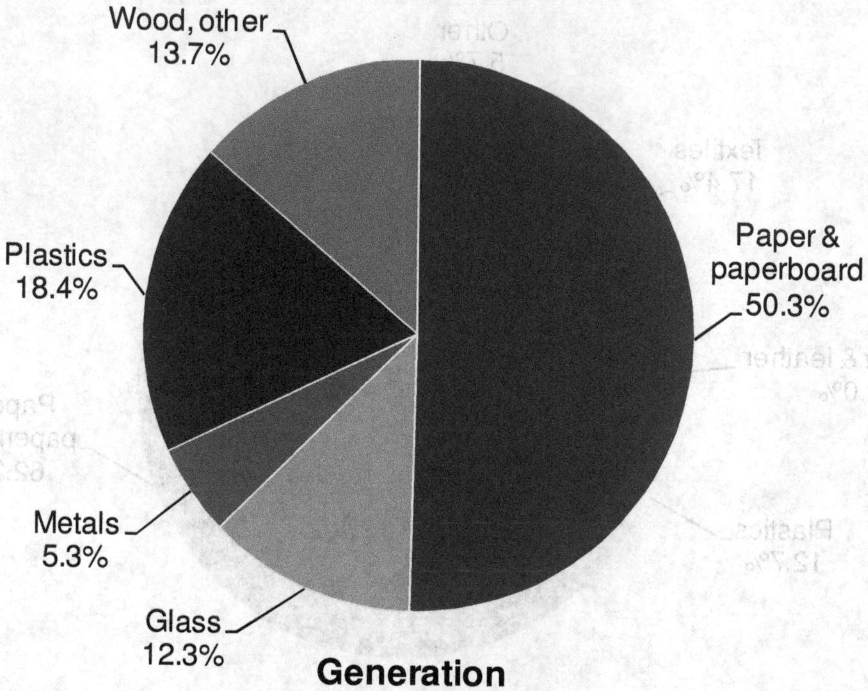

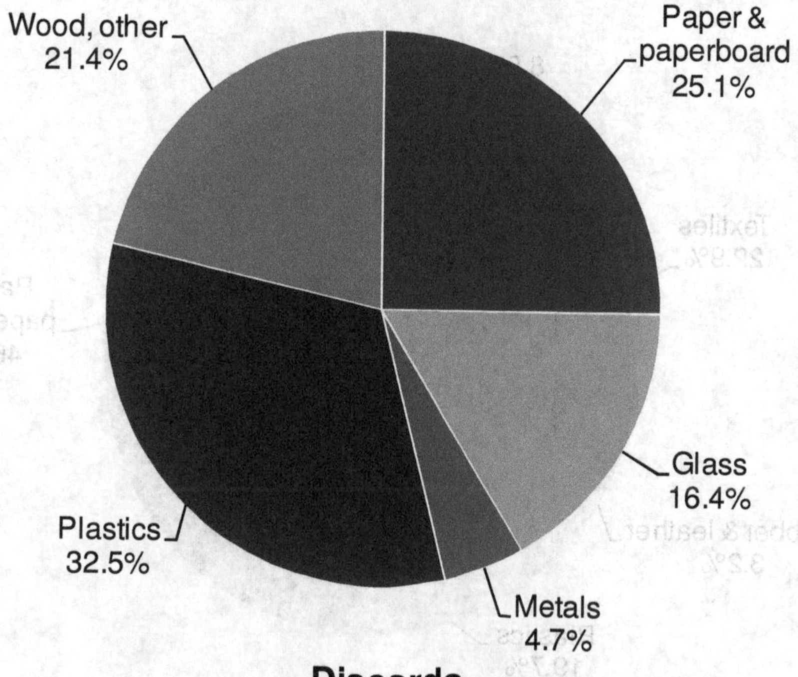

*Discards in this figure include combustion with energy recovery.

Source: *U.S. EPA, Municipal Solid Waste in the United States, 2011 Facts and Figures*

Figure 17. Containers and packaging generated and discarded* in municipal solid waste, 2011 (In percent of total generation and discards)

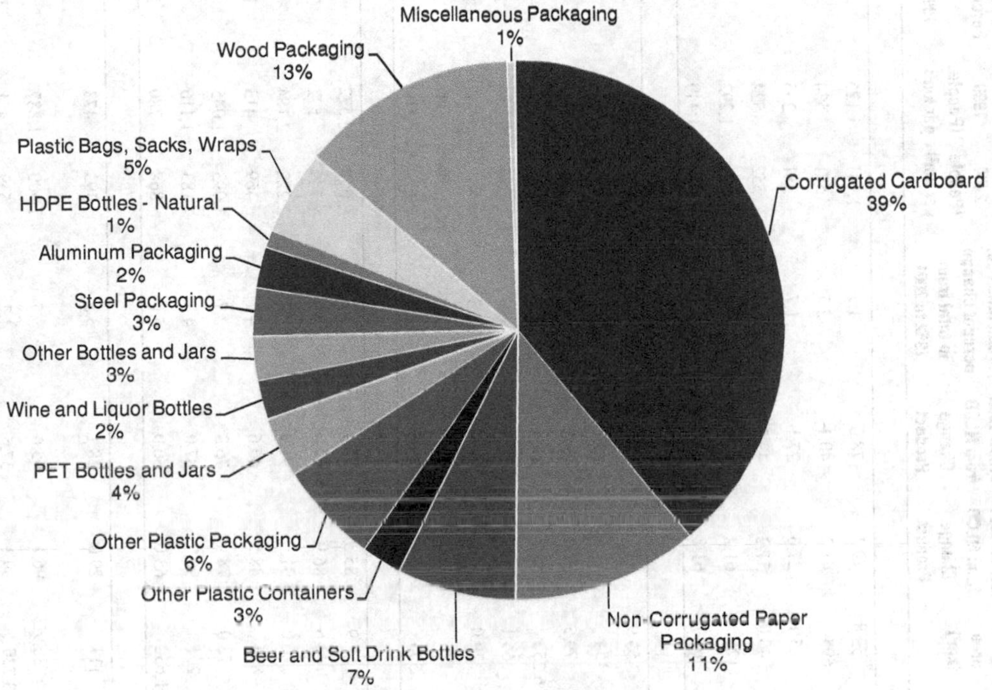

Generation

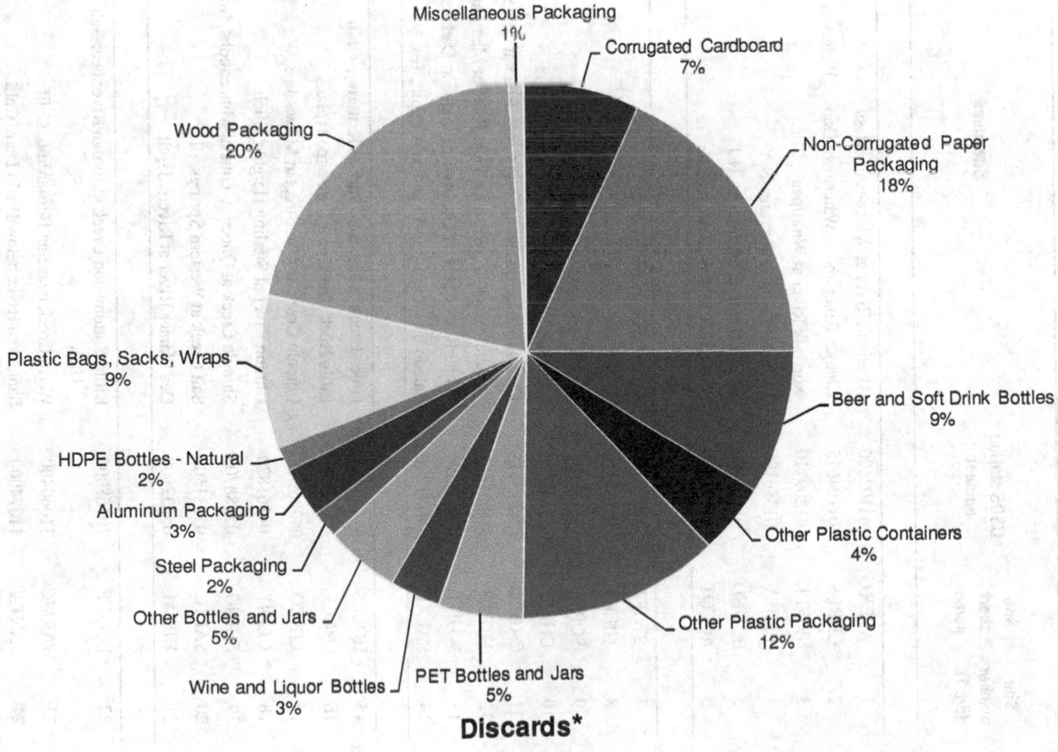

Discards*

Source: *U.S. EPA, Municipal Solid Waste in the United States, 2011 Facts and Figures*

Selected information for stream sites dominated by urban land use and selected for pesticide trend analysis, 1992–2008.

[USGS, U.S. Geological Survey; km², square kilometers; basins were delineated by a number of USGS hydrologists and geographers in National Water-Quality Assessment Program study units using a variety of methods using data sources at multiple scales and were current as of December 2009 (N. Nakagaki, U.S. Geological Survey, 2009, written commun.); NLCD, National Landcover Database, U.S. Geological Survey, 2007, and Fry and others, 2009; population data based on 1990 and 2000 population counts (U.S. Bureau of the Census, 1992, and Geolytics, Inc., 2001) and 1990 and 2000 census block group boundaries (U.S. Bureau of the Census, 2001a and 2001b)]

Site number (fig. 1)	Site short name	USGS station number	Site name	Drainage area (km²)	Percent land use			Population density		
					Urban 2001 from NLCD Change Product	Urban 1992 from NLCD Change Product	Urban land use, percent change in total from 1992 to 2001	2000 (People per km²)	1990 (People per km²)	Percent change from 1990 to 2000
			Northeast							
1	ABERJ	01102500	Aberjona River at Winchester, Mass.	59.8	79.3	78.0	1.7	1,141	1,126	1.3
2	CHRLS	01104615	Charles River above Watertown Dam at Watertown, Mass.	695	41.2	40.1	2.7	571	534	6.9
3	NRWLK	01209710	Norwalk River at Winnipauk, Conn.	85.1	27.6	27.1	1.7	281	255	10.2
4	LISHA	01356190	Lisha Kill near Niskayuna, N.Y.	40.0	51.2	49.3	3.9	552	524	5.3
5	BOUND	01403900	Bound Brook at Middlesex, N.J.	126	61.2	60.3	1.6	1,391	1,292	7.7
6	ACCOT	01654000	Accotink Creek near Annandale, Va.	60.7	61.8	59.0	4.8	1,610	1,440	11.8
			South							
7	SWIFT	02087580	Swift Creek near Apex, N.C.	53.9	73.9	64.4	14.8	726	489	48.5
8	GILLS	02169570	Gills Creek at Columbia, S.C.	154	51.8	50.7	2.2	481	445	8.1
9	SOPEC	02335870	Sope Creek near Marietta, Ga.	79.5	74.4	68.3	9.0	902	793	13.7
10	CHATT	02338000	Chattahoochee River near Whitesburg, Ga.	6,250	28.8	25.4	13.3	311	231	34.6
11	CAHAB	0242354750	Cahaba Valley Creek at Cross Creek Road at Pelham, Ala.	66.1	30.2	28.4	6.4	275	216	27.3
12	FLTCH	07031692	Fletcher Creek at Sycamore View Road at Memphis, Tenn.	79.0	85.0	70.7	20.3	847	442	91.6
13	WHITE	08057200	White Rock Creek at Greenville Avenue at Dallas, Tex.	173	91.2	77.1	18.2	1,510	987	53.0
14	SALAD	08178800	Salado Creek at Loop 13 at San Antonio, Tex.	506	53.7	46.1	16.6	624	508	22.8
			Midwest							
15	HOLES	393944084120700	Holes Creek at Huffman Park at Kettering, Ohio	51.9	85.5	82.4	3.8	650	572	13.6
16	LBUCK	03353637	Little Buck Creek near Indianapolis, Ind.	44.6	86.9	71.9	20.9	749	572	30.9
17	LINCO	040869415	Lincoln Creek at 47th Street at Milwaukee, Wis.	26.0	91.6	91.0	.7	2,222	2,184	1.7
18	CLINT	04161820	Clinton River at Sterling Heights, Mich.	803	48.5	46.6	4.1	469	413	13.6
19	SHING	05288705	Shingle Creek at Queen Avenue at Minneapolis, Minn.	73.0	78.4	76.3	2.7	1,093	1,045	4.6
20	SALTC	05531500	Salt Creek at Western Springs, Ill.	291	90.7	87.0	4.3	1,183	1,116	6.0
21	DPLAI	05532500	Des Plaines River at Riverside, Ill.	1,630	63.0	60.0	5.0	868	780	11.3
			West							
22	LCOTT	10168000	Little Cottonwood Creek at Jordan River near Salt Lake City, Utah	117	29.0	28.1	3.3	493	473	4.2
23	WARMC	11060400	Warm Creek near San Bernardino, Calif.	30.9	96.1	95.6	.5	1,900	1,887	.7
24	SANTA	11074000	Santa Ana River below Prado Dam, Calif.	3,730	39.1	37.5	4.2	539	451	19.5
25	ARCAD	11447360	Arcade Creek near Del Paso Heights, Calif.	81.5	100.0	97.9	2.1	2,034	1,986	2.4
26	THORN	12128000	Thornton Creek near Seattle, Wash.	29.2	95.8	95.7	.1	2,364	2,205	7.2
27	FANNO	14206950	Fanno Creek at Durham, Oreg.	80.7	87.0	85.2	2.1	1,502	1,202	25.0

Source: U.S. Geological Survey, Trends in Pesticide Concentrations in Urban Streams in the United States, 1992–2008

Number of uncensored concentrations for pesticides in urban-stream samples, 1992–2008.

[Shaded cells indicate site/pesticide samples with at least 10 uncensored concentrations during the trend assessment period; DCPA, dimethyl tetrachloroterephthalate; --, indicates that fipronil and its degradates were not considered for trend analysis in the first two periods because samples were not analyzed for fipronil and its degradates until 1999]

Trend assess-ment period	Site number (fig. 1)	Site short name	Number of uncensored concentrations								
			Simazine	Prometon	Atrazine	Deethylatrazine	Metolachlor	Trifluralin	Pendimethalin	Tebuthiuron	Dacthal (DCPA)
1992–2000	3	NRWLK	43	97	80	42	32	10	1	0	11
	6	ACCOT	76	78	64	48	74	11	29	6	21
	9	SOPEC	78	39	75	36	9	8	23	61	5
	16	LBUCK	113	118	118	112	118	29	21	46	47
1996–2004	1	ABERJ	21	51	40	17	28	16	7	9	0
	2	CHRLS	5	14	29	8	3	0	1	0	4
	3	NRWLK	28	112	88	58	42	13	0	1	1
	5	BOUND	45	66	67	58	52	16	13	28	20
	6	ACCOT	104	112	88	64	99	25	30	10	12
	8	GILLS	77	71	76	68	19	0	4	74	1
	9	SOPEC	92	57	88	64	5	11	23	90	7
	10	CHATT	88	67	87	43	13	1	4	60	2
	11	CAHAB	86	30	85	82	6	12	10	12	0
	12	FLTCH	56	43	54	51	54	13	20	19	2
	13	WHITE	120	114	120	120	117	11	66	37	16
	14	SALAD	43	70	70	65	15	0	3	69	2
	15	HOLES	74	99	104	94	73	27	23	0	0
	16	LBUCK	96	116	116	110	112	11	13	8	8
	18	CLINT	58	60	69	63	63	6	4	1	7
	19	SHING	6	82	73	51	56	8	4	32	19
	20	SALTC	44	59	66	63	54	11	5	2	5
	21	DPLAI	30	50	53	51	48	9	3	25	3
	22	LCOTT	11	68	54	45	0	7	17	39	26
	23	WARMC	12	36	2	2	2	0	0	18	25
	25	ARCAD	50	69	16	0	48	18	13	23	41
	26	THORN	30	68	17	0	0	6	0	1	1
2000–2008	2	CHRLS	4	13	38	15	7	0	1	0	0
	3	NRWLK	10	73	54	37	20	8	0	1	0
	4	LISHA	8	39	29	16	33	1	3	0	0
	5	BOUND	20	45	48	37	34	5	4	14	3
	6	ACCOT	85	93	70	51	78	17	21	7	4
	7	SWIFT	83	74	69	36	44	7	9	8	1
	8	GILLS	56	53	58	52	23	0	0	53	1
	9	SOPEC	109	82	106	85	4	9	24	105	5
	10	CHATT	106	82	105	69	23	2	5	76	5
	11	CAHAB	81	24	81	78	5	9	7	6	0
	13	WHITE	107	92	107	107	96	9	60	13	8
	14	SALAD	59	80	80	77	9	3	8	76	7
	17	LINCO	24	64	70	63	51	1	11	60	3
	18	CLINT	37	44	53	47	47	3	2	1	1
	19	SHING	2	67	59	44	45	1	3	26	6
	20	SALTC	37	62	75	72	63	11	6	2	2
	22	LCOTT	7	62	49	47	0	7	12	39	24
	24	SANTA	83	69	59	37	16	1	2	6	48
	25	ARCAD	53	76	12	2	60	20	26	17	44
	26	THORN	22	61	7	0	0	11	0	1	6
	27	FANNO	87	71	83	43	48	24	6	57	2

Number of uncensored concentrations for pesticides in urban-stream samples, 1992–2008.—Continued

[Shaded cells indicate site/pesticide samples with at least 10 uncensored concentrations during the trend assessment period; DCPA, dimethyl tetrachloro-terephthalate; --, indicates that fipronil and its degradates were not considered for trend analysis in the first two periods because samples were not analyzed for fipronil and its degradates until 1999]

Trend assessment period	Site number (fig. 1)	Site short name	Number of uncensored concentrations						
			Chlorpyrifos	Malathion	Diazinon	Fipronil	Fipronil sulfide	Desulfinyl-fipronil	Carbaryl
1992–2000	3	NRWLK	2	2	30	--	--	--	26
	6	ACCOT	41	11	75	--	--	--	49
	9	SOPEC	39	10	70	--	--	--	33
	16	LBUCK	64	26	109	--	--	--	36
1996–2004	1	ABERJ	3	0	55	--	--	--	38
	2	CHRLS	0	0	21	--	--	--	13
	3	NRWLK	3	1	36	--	--	--	28
	5	BOUND	24	7	59	--	--	--	37
	6	ACCOT	25	11	105	--	--	--	69
	8	GILLS	32	32	63	--	--	--	21
	9	SOPEC	20	5	76	--	--	--	30
	10	CHATT	9	3	81	--	--	--	44
	11	CAHAB	22	2	60	--	--	--	15
	12	FLTCH	30	25	47	--	--	--	37
	13	WHITE	54	22	120	--	--	--	55
	14	SALAD	12	9	52	--	--	--	24
	15	HOLES	18	8	90	--	--	--	36
	16	LBUCK	18	12	111	--	--	--	34
	18	CLINT	8	1	51	--	--	--	17
	19	SHING	1	4	54	--	--	--	19
	20	SALTC	2	6	54	--	--	--	26
	21	DPLAI	1	3	41	--	--	--	21
	22	LCOTT	1	11	64	--	--	--	29
	23	WARMC	5	3	40	--	--	--	5
	25	ARCAD	42	33	71	--	--	--	58
	26	THORN	3	6	55	--	--	--	15
2000–2008	2	CHRLS	0	0	12	11	19	16	19
	3	NRWLK	1	1	24	0	4	2	18
	4	LISHA	1	1	31	0	1	1	31
	5	BOUND	3	0	30	13	16	19	18
	6	ACCOT	6	8	69	36	21	27	52
	7	SWIFT	4	0	50	52	49	52	39
	8	GILLS	3	15	31	16	18	19	16
	9	SOPEC	15	4	58	43	42	40	35
	10	CHATT	5	2	62	49	40	41	55
	11	CAHAB	17	1	31	31	31	27	20
	13	WHITE	30	26	87	48	36	46	49
	14	SALAD	3	7	32	16	20	26	26
	17	LINCO	0	2	45	0	1	5	16
	18	CLINT	1	0	28	6	1	1	20
	19	SHING	0	2	36	4	8	17	19
	20	SALTC	9	5	33	33	24	29	29
	22	LCOTT	1	3	46	0	1	1	26
	24	SANTA	3	9	39	23	31	41	23
	25	ARCAD	39	35	77	58	50	56	60
	26	THORN	0	1	21	5	4	16	22
	27	FANNO	17	2	61	22	26	30	62

Source: U.S. Geological Survey, Trends in Pesticide Concentrations in Urban Streams in the United States, 1992–2008

Trends, in percent per year, for simazine, prometon, atrazine, and deethylatrazine for the 1996–2004 period.

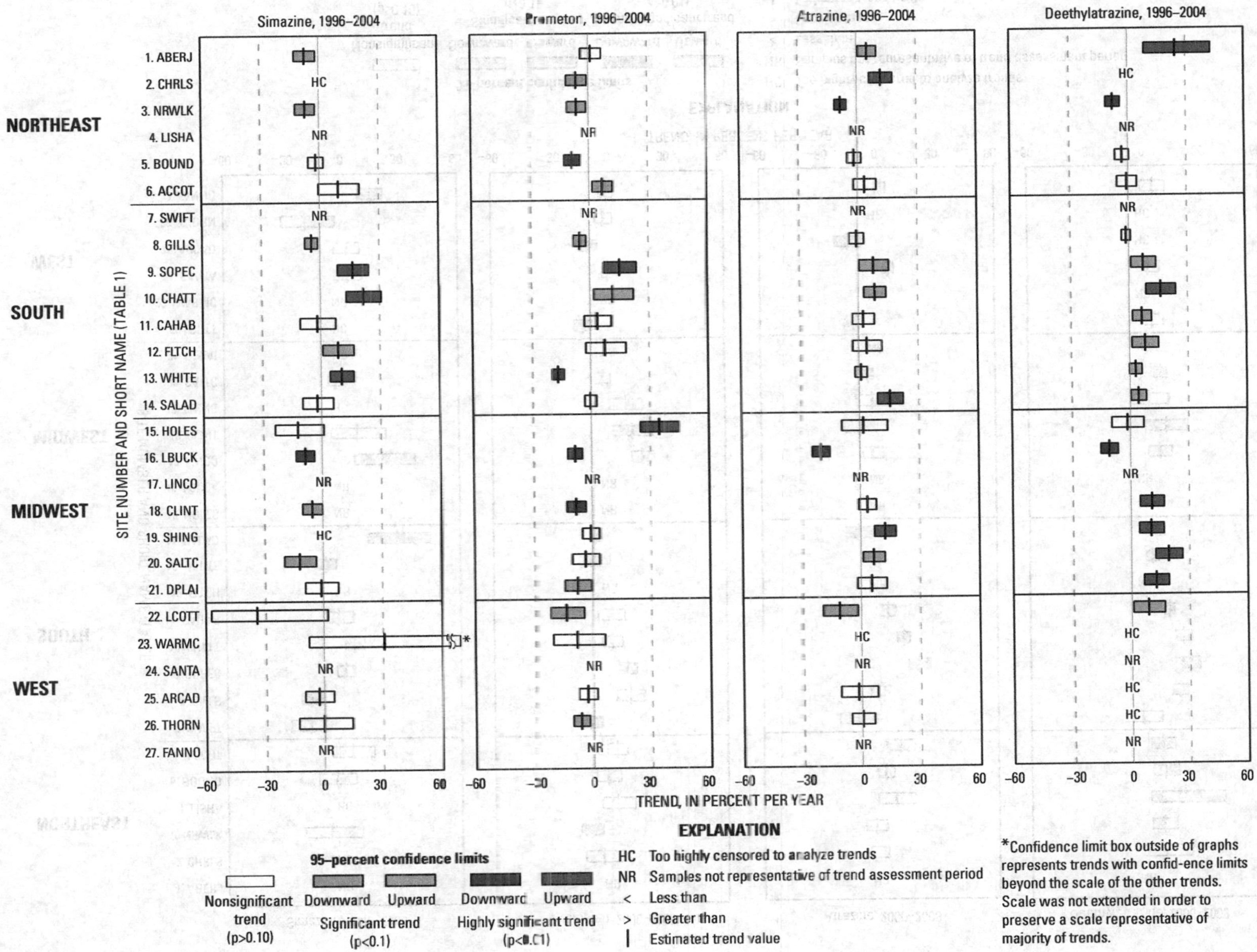

Source: U.S. Geological Survey, Trends in Pesticide Concentrations in Urban Streams in the United States, 1992–2008

Trends, in percent per year, for simazine, prometon, atrazine, and deethylatrazine for the 2000–2008 period.

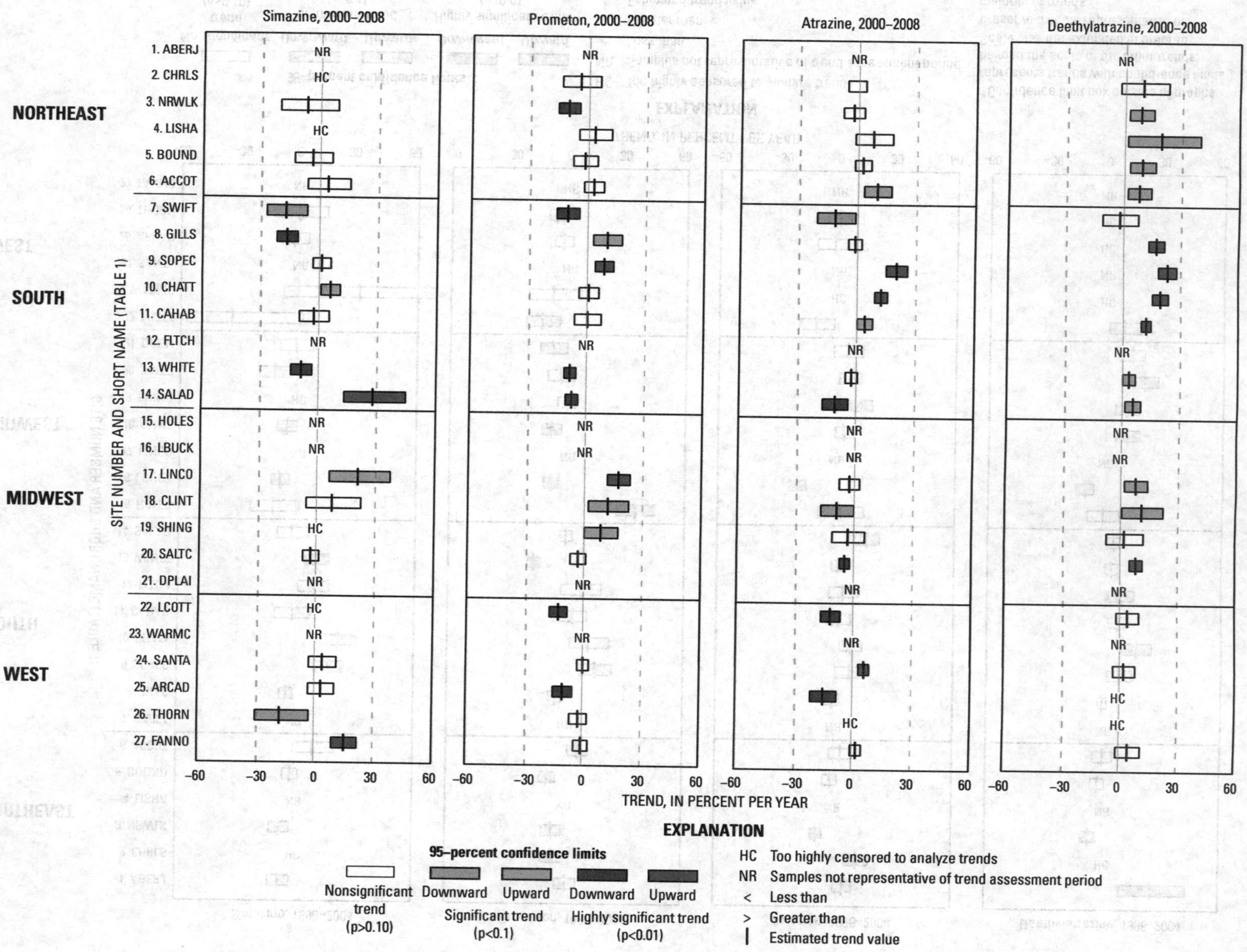

Source: U.S. Geological Survey, Trends in Pesticide Concentrations in Urban Streams in the United States, 1992–2008

Trends, in percent per year, for chlorpyrifos, diazinon, and carbaryl for the 1996–2004 period.

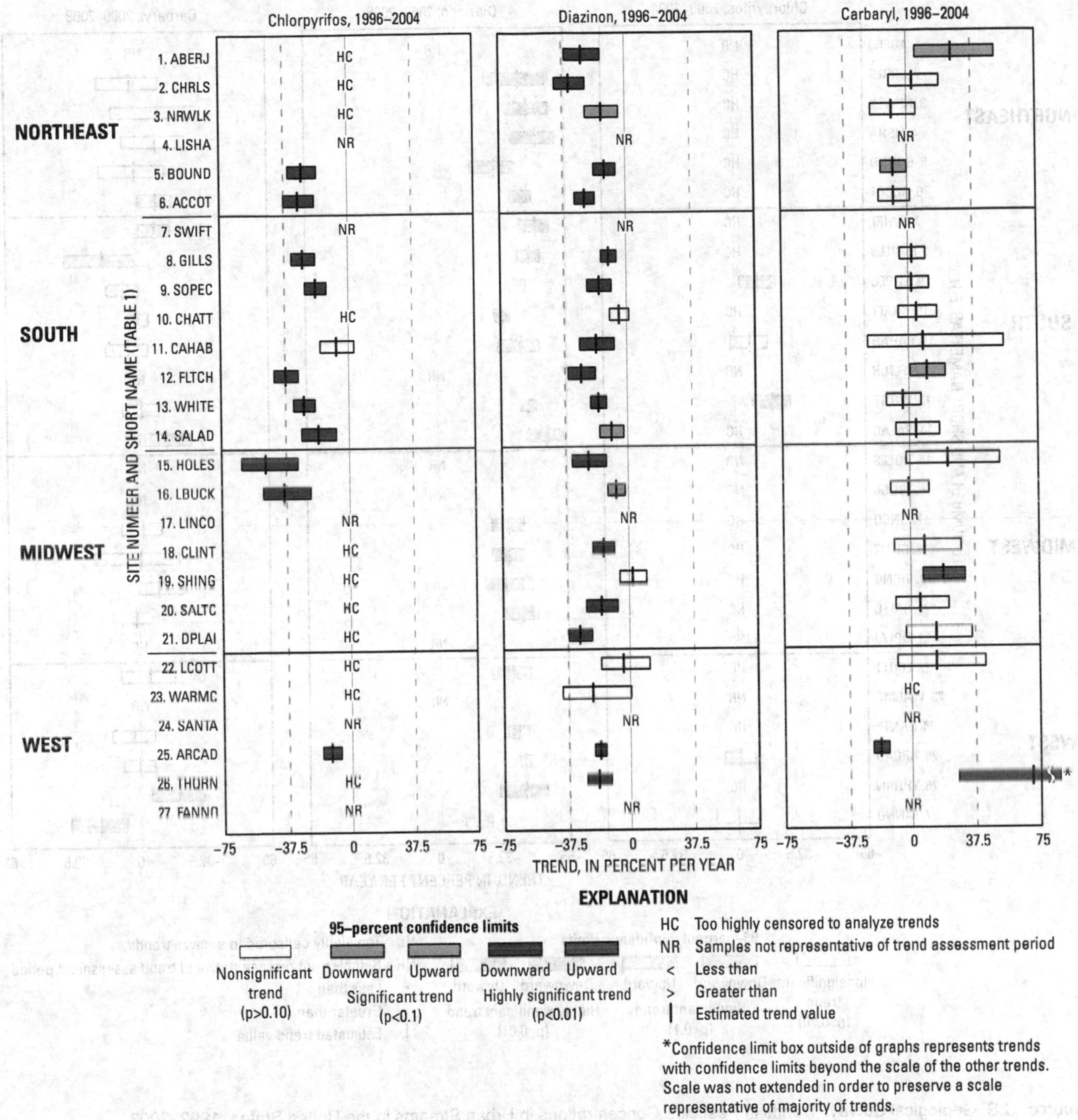

Source: U.S. Geological Survey, Trends in Pesticide Concentrations in Urban Streams in the United States, 1992–2008

Trends, in percent per year, for chlorpyrifos, diazinon, and carbaryl for the 2000–2008 period.

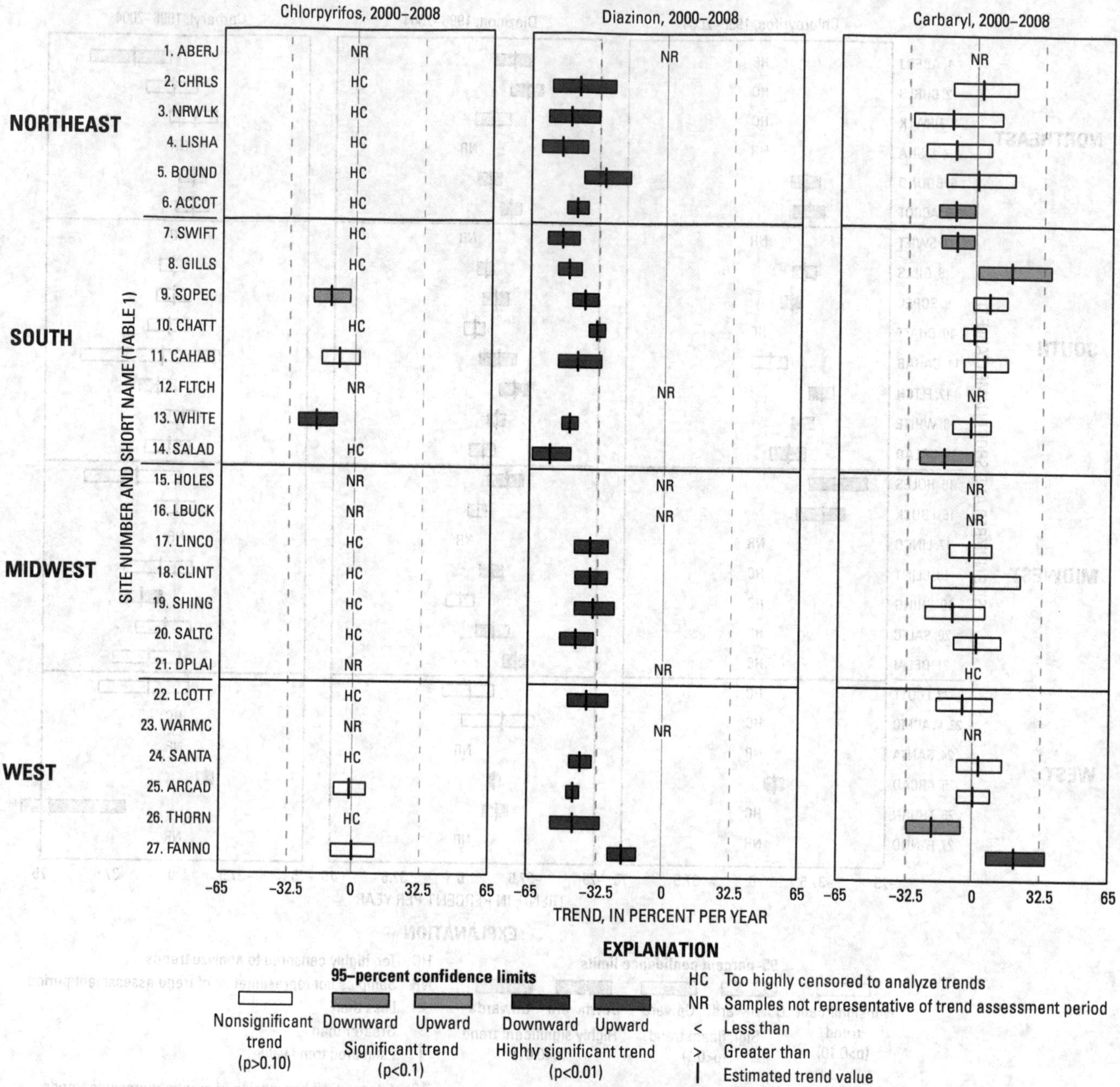

Source: U.S. Geological Survey, Trends in Pesticide Concentrations in Urban Streams in the United States, 1992–2008

Flow-adjusted trends, in percent per year, for fipronil, fipronil sulfide, and desulfinylfipronil for the 2000–2008 period.

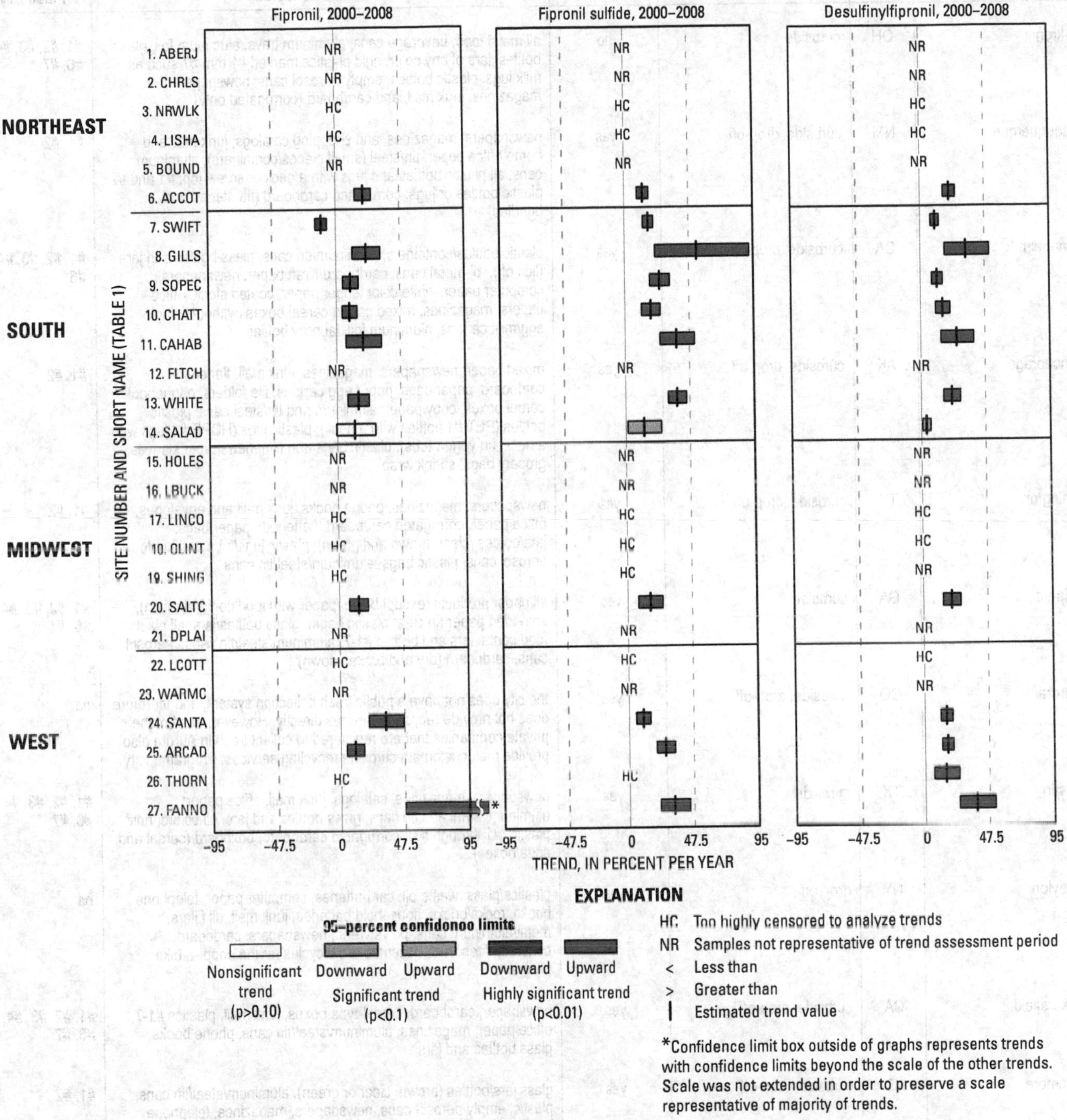

Source: U.S. Geological Survey, Trends in Pesticide Concentrations in Urban Streams in the United States, 1992–2008

Recycling Profiles of 100 Major U.S. Cities

City	State	System Type	Voluntary	Materials Collected	Plastic Types
Akron	OH	curbside	no	all metal food, beverage cans, aluminum trays, aluminum foil, glass bottles, jars of any color, rigid plastics marked #1 thru #7 such as milk jugs, plastic bottles, empty aerosol cans, newspapers, magazines, junk mail, and cardboard (corrugated only)	#1, #2, #3, #4, #5, #6, #7
Albuquerque	NM	curbside, drop-off	yes	newspapers, magazines, and shopping catalogs; junk mail and home office paper; tin/steel (small pieces/containers); aluminum cans; all plastic bottles and jugs with a neck or screw top; #1 and #2 plastic bottles or jugs; corrugated cardboard (fla ttened and bundled)	#1, #2
Anaheim	CA	curbside, drop-off	yes	plastic bottles/containers, aluminum/tin cans, glass bottles and jars (lids off), bi-metal cans, cardboard/Kraft paper, newspapers, computer paper, white/color ledger paper, coated stock, office papers, magazines, mixed paper, cereal boxes (without lining), egg/milk cartons, aluminum foil, laundry bottles	#1, #2, #3, #4, #5, #6
Anchorage	AK	curbside, drop-off	yes	mixed paper: newspapers, magazines, junk mail, flattened cardboard, paper bags, paper egg cartons, file folders, phonebooks, cereal boxes, copy paper; aluminum and tin/steel cans; plastic bottles (PET #1 bottles with a neck); plastic jugs (HDPE #2 jugs with a neck, no yogurt tubs); plastic bags and film: newspaper sleeves, grocery bags, shrink wrap	#1, #2
Arlington	TX	curbside, drop-off	yes	newspapers, magazines, phone books, junk mail and envelopes, office paper, corrugated cardboard (flattened), paper bags, jars/bottles (clear, brown and green), plastic jugs/tubs and bottles, aerosol cans, plastic bags, aluminum/steel/tin cans	#1, #2
Atlanta	GA	curbside	yes	all paper products (except boxes/paper with food contamination), shredded paper (in clear plastic bags), glass bottles/jars, all plastic food containers and bottles #1-7, aluminum/steel/tin cans, aerosol cans, cardboard (dry and broken down)	#1, #2, #3, #4, #5, #6, #7
Aurora	CO	curbside, drop-off	yes	the city does not have a public trash collection system, and therefore does not provide recycling services directly. However, most of the private companies that are registered to collect trash in Aurora also provide their customers curbside recycling services. Programs vary.	na
Austin	TX	curbside	yes	newspapers, magazines, catalogs, junk mail, office paper; aluminum, steel and tin cans; glass bottles and jars, all colors; rigid plastic (#1 through #7); corrugated cardboard; boxboard (cereal and soda boxes)	#1, #2, #3, #4, #5, #6, #7
Babylon	NY	drop-off	yes	plastics/glass, waste oil, car batteries, computer paper, telephone books, rocks/bricks, household batteries, junk mail, oil filters, metal/aluminum cans, polystyrene, newspapers, cardboard, concrete, tires. Also accepted are bicycles for the adopt-a-bike program.	na
Bakersfield	CA	curbside, drop-off	yes	newspaper, cardboard, cereal-type boxes, junk mail, plastics #1-7, office paper, magazines, aluminum/steel/tin cans, phone books, glass bottles and jars	#1, #2, #3, #4, #5, #6, #7
Baltimore	MD	curbside, drop-off	yes	glass jars/bottles (brown, clear or green), aluminum/steel/tin cans, plastic, empty aerosol cans, newspapers, magazines, telephone books, ad mail, cardboard/boxes, mixed paper, cartons (waxed), books	#1, #2
Baton Rouge	LA	curbside, drop-off	yes	newspaper, magazines, scrap paper, cardboard, glass, plastics with a 1 - 7 inside the triangular recycle symbol, milk cartons, juice boxes, detergent refill containers, aluminum/tin/metal alloy cans and metal lids	#1, #2, #3, #4, #5, #6, #7
Birmingham	AL	curbside, drop-off	yes	glass (all types); mixed paper (cereal boxes, box packaged foods, phone books, magazines, office paper, junk mail, etc.); newspaper; corrugated cardboard (broken down); aluminum, steel and tin cans; plastics #1 thru #7; At drop-off—cell phones; printer and ink toner cartridges; batteries (rechargeable and single-use). E-waste: computers, monitors (no TV's) printers, peripherals, other plug-in electronics	#1, #2

City	State	System Type	Voluntary	Materials Collected	Plastic Types
Boston	MA	curbside, drop-off	yes	newspaper (with inserts); magazines/catalogs; junk mail (remove free samples; plastic envelope window is ok); white and colored paper/brown bags; telephone books; flattened food boxes; paperback books; milk and juice cartons; juice/soy milk boxes; cardboard boxes; pizza boxes (empty); glass bottles/jars; tin and aluminum cans, foil, and pie plates; all plastic containers (no motor oil or chemical containers); cardboard/spiral cans; rigid plastics	#1, #2, #3, #4, #5, #6, #7
Brookhaven	NY	curbside, drop-off	no	glass bottles (clear and colored), aluminum/bimetallic/ tin cans, aerosol spray cans, plastic, aluminum foil/containers, newspapers, Kraft & PC paper, corrugated cardboard cartons, mixed low grade paper, phone books	#1, #2
Buffalo	NY	curbside	yes	paper (newspaper, office paper, cardboard, and other paper types); glass bottles and jars (clear, green, and amber); aluminum and steel cans; plastics (soda bottles, milk jugs, bags, detergent containers, etc.)	#1, #2, #3, #4, #5, #6, #7
Charlotte	NC	curbside, drop-off	yes	all glass containers, paper, shopping catalogs, milk and juice cartons, newspapers and inserts, cardboard, plastics #1-5 and #7, liquor bottles, spiral paper cans, aluminum/steel/tin cans, telephone books, office paper	#1, #2, #3, #4, #5, #7
Chesapeake	VA	curbside, drop-off	yes	aluminum and steel cans; pie plates and foil; glass jars and bottles; newspapers; #1 and #2 plastic bottles; gift wrapping paper; cardboard (flattened); cereal boxes, paper towel rolls, etc.	#1, #2
Chicago	IL	curbside, drop-off	yes	city-served blue cart program (clean paper, newspaper, magazines, junk mail, cardboard, clean food boxes, phone books, catalogs, brown paper bags, gift wrap, glass jars and bottles, empty aluminum/tin/steel cans, empty aerosol cans, rinsed aluminum foil and pie plates, milk, juice, plastic bottles and containers #1-5 and 7)	#1, #2, #3, #4, #5, #7
Cincinnati	OH	curbside, drop-off	yes	newspaper; office paper; junk mail and envelopes; cardboard (broken down 3' X 3'); paperboard (such as cereal boxes); brown paper bags; magazines; plastic bottles and jugs; aluminum and steel cans; empty aerosol cans (remove lids) ps); glass bottles and jars (remove lids)	#1, #2
Cleveland	OH	curbside (pilot program), drop-off	yes	glass bottles and jars (rinsed), metal cans (rinsed), plastic containers, newspapers, mixed paper, cardboard (flattened)	#1, #2, #3, #4, #5, #6, #7
Colorado Springs	CO	drop-off	yes	magazines, glass, plastic bags, aluminum, appliances, tires, electronics, metals, motor oil, automotive batteries, paint, hazardous chemicals	#1, #2, #3, #4, #5, #6, #7
Columbus	OH	curbside, drop-off	yes	newspaper, including all inserts; magazines, catalogs and telephone books; mail, scrap paper and envelopes (windows ok); brown paper bags; paperboard (such as cereal or snack boxes); cardboard boxes (flattened); bottles and jars; plastic bottles (any); glass bottles and jars; aluminum/tin/steel cans; aerosol cans	#1, #2, #3, #4, #5, #6, #7
Corpus Christi	TX	curbside, drop-off	yes	newspapers (with ads and inserts); junk mail and envelopes, magazines, catalogs and phone books, paperboard boxes (like cereal boxes), shoe boxes and other similar paper; corrugated cardboard (flattened to less than 2ft square); No Glass; aluminum, tin and steel; plastic bottles and containers, #1-7	#1, #2
Dallas	TX	curbside, drop-off	yes	newspapers and inserts, mixed paper, magazines, junk mail, home/office paper, chipboard, glass containers, plastic bottles, aluminum cans, steel/tin food cans, empty aerosol cans	#1, #2, #3, #4, #5, #6, #7
Denver	CO	curbside, drop-off	yes	newspapers and inserts, mixed paper, magazines, junk mail, home/office paper, glass containers, aluminum cans, steel/tin food cans, cardboard (flattened and no larger than 2ft x 2ft), phone books, plastic bottles/jars/containers #1-7, empty aerosol cans	#1, #2, #3, #4, #5, #6, #7
Des Moines	IA	curbside, drop-off	yes	glass bottles and jars, wire hangers, newspapers and inserts, brown paper bags, corrugated cardboard, junk mail, contained shredded paper, telephone books, magazines, catalogs, paperback books, folders and window envelopes, aluminum/tin cans, plastic containers (with twist off tops)	#1, #2

City	State	System Type	Voluntary	Materials Collected	Plastic Types
Detroit	MI	drop-off, pick-up (select communities/businesses)	yes	newspaper; mixed paper (items that CAN NOT be recycled are: tissue paper, receipts, napkins, wrapping paper, and paper towel); glossy paper; books; cardboard and clean chipboard; glass; all metals; plastic (#1 and #2 plastics together, and #4, #5, #6, and #7 plastics together); Styrofoam; aseptic containers; batteries; computers and electronics; # 1, #2, and #4 plastic bags	#1, #2, #4, #5, #6, #7
El Paso	TX	curbside, drop-off	no	corrugated cardboard, brown paper bags, newspapers and inserts, magazines, junk mail, white/colored bond paper, computer paper, plastic (lids removed), aluminum/steel/tin cans, aluminum foil and pie plates, copper, brass, iron, aluminum, (No Glass)	#1, #2, #3, #4, #5, #6, #7
Fort Wayne	IN	curbside	yes	newspapers, magazines, catalogs, cardboard, fiberboard, phonebooks, paperback books, plastic #1-7, glass (brown, clear, green), cans (aluminum, bi-metal, tin, steel), aluminum foil and pie pans	#1, #2, #3, #4, #5, #6, #7
Fort Worth	TX	curbside	yes	paper, cardboard, catalogs, envelopes, junk mail, magazines, newspapers (all sections), paper bags, telephone books, aluminum cans/baking tins, steel/tin food cans/lids, empty aerosol cans, steel paint cans (empty), glass bottles and jars, pots/pans, plastic bottles/cups/jars	#1, #2, #3, #4, #5, #6, #7
Fremont	CA	curbside, drop-off	yes	newspapers and inserts, most white/colored paper, magazines, junk mail, brown paper bags, catalogs, window envelopes, paper egg cartons, telephone books, flattened cereal/cracker/shoe boxes, glass bottles and jars, plastic containers, aluminum/steel/tin cans, yard waste, food scraps	#1, #2, #3, #4, #5, #6, #7
Fresno	CA	curbside, drop-off	no	aluminum/tin/aerosol cans, small appliances, cardboard, catalogs, chipboard, glass bottles and jars (all colors), junk mail (including envelopes), magazines, newspapers and inserts, plastic bottles (clear/green plastic soda and water bottles, plastic containers, phone books, yard waste	#1, #2, #3, #4, #5, #7
Garland	TX	curbside, drop-off	yes	newspapers and inserts, magazines, aluminum/steel/tin cans, empty aerosol cans, glass bottles and jars (lids removed), plastic, corrugated cardboard, junk mail, brown paper bags, telephone books, white office/computer paper, chipboard	#1, #2, #3, #4, #5, #7
Glendale	AZ	curbside, drop-off	yes	aluminum cans/foil/foil baking pans, empty aerosol cans, cardboard, cartons, chipboard (without inserts), magazines, junk mail, catalogs, brown paper bags, telephone directories, newspapers and inserts, plastic containers, steel/tin cans (all rinsed, clean and dry)	#1, #2, #3, #4, #5, #6, #7
Grand Rapids	MI	curbside, drop-off (at participating locations)	yes	aluminum/steel cans, glass bottles and jars (all colors), plastic bottles, newspapers and inserts, junk mail, corrugated cardboard, magazines, telephone books, white ledger paper, cereal boxes (with liners removed), colored/mixed paper	#1, #2, #3, #4, #5, #6, #7
Greensboro	NC	curbside, drop-off	yes	plastic bottles and jugs, newspapers, magazines, all aluminum beverage cans/pans/foil, office paper, mail, notebook paper, corrugated cardboard, chipboard, brown/gray egg cartons, all steel beverage and food cans, glass (all colors, shapes and sizes), aerosol cans (empty)	#1, #2, #3, #4, #5, #6, #7
Hempstead	NY	curbside, drop-off	yes	newspapers and inserts (tied or paper bagged), magazines, catalogs, box board, cans, all rigid plastic, bottles/glass, aluminum foil/pans/cans, corrugated cardboard (flattened and tied)	#1, #2
Hialeah	FL	curbside	yes	newspapers, aluminum/steel/tin cans, plastics, glass bottles and jars, plastic coated cardboard, six-pack rings, milk and juice containers	#1, #2, #3, #4, #5, #6, #7
Honolulu	HI	drop-off, curbside (pilot program)	man	newspaper (inserts and magazines removed), corrugated cardboard (flattened), office paper, glass bottles and jars, aluminum/steel cans, plastic containers, grass, tree and hedge trimmings, christmas trees	#1, #2
Houston	TX	curbside, drop-off	no	newspapers, magazines, telephone books, aluminum and tin cans, junk mail, corrugated cardboard, plastic soft drink/milk/water containers, used oil	#1, #2, #3, #4, #5, #7
Indianapolis	IN	curbside, drop-off	yes	glass; #1-#7 plastics; aluminum, tin, and steel beverage and food cans; newspapers; cardboard and magazines; phone books; empty aerosol cans	#1, #2, #3, #4, #5, #6, #7

City	State	System Type	Voluntary	Materials Collected	Plastic Types
Islip	NY	curbside	yes	newspapers, magazines, junk mail, tin/beverage cans, plastic, bottles/glass, corrugated cardboard	#1, #2
Jacksonville	FL	curbside	yes	plastic, glass bottles and jars, metal and aluminum cans, empty aerosol cans, newspapers and inserts, magazines, catalogs, phone books, paperboard cartons, brown paper bags, corrugated cardboard	#1, #2, #3, #4, #5, #6, #7
Jersey City	NJ	curbside, drop-off	no	mixed newspaper, magazines, junk mail, office paper, telephone books, cardboard boxes, corrugated and laundry detergent boxes, glass bottles, aluminum cans, metal cans, milk cartons, drink boxes, water containers, food containers, household cleaner containers, laundry detergent bottles, shampoo bottles, and other related plastic containers	na
Kansas City	MO	curbside, drop-off	yes	aluminum cans, household (dry cell) batteries, corrugated cardboard, clothing (dry), foil/pie pans, glass bottles (accepted at drop-off locations), magazines, newspapers, mixed office paper, paperboard, plastic bottles, tin cans, telephone books, scrap metal, yard waste	#1, #2, #3, #4, #5, #6, #7
Las Vegas	NV	curbside, drop-off	yes	newspaper, magazines, mixed paper, glass/plastic containers, aluminum/tin cans and scrap, copper, radiators, corrugated cardboard, phone books, dry/clean clothing and shoes	#1, #2, #3, #4, #5, #6, #7
Lexington-Fayette	KY	curbside	no	boxboard, brown paper bags, catalogs, corrugated cardboard, magazines, newspapers/inserts, office paper, telephone books, junk mail, empty aerosol cans, aluminum/steel cans, plastic bottles/jugs only, glass bottles and jars (blue, brown, clear, and green)	na
Lincoln	NE	drop-off, curbside (private collection)	yes	newspaper, glass containers, aluminum/steel/tin cans, paperboard and corrugated cardboard, mixed residential paper, plastic	#1, #2, #3, #4, #5
Long Beach	CA	curbside, drop-off	yes	glass, aluminum, steel, tin, plastic, clean polystyrene (Styrofoam(r)), empty aerosol and paint cans, mixed paper, bundled newspapers, corrugated cardboard, used motor oil (collected by request only)	#1, #2, #3, #4, #5, #6, #7
Los Angeles	CA	curbside, drop-off	yes	paper, all cardboard boxes and chipboard, all aluminum, tin, metal, and bi-metal cans, pie tins, clean aluminum foils; empty paint and aerosol cans with plastic caps removed, and wire hangers, all glass bottles and jars, plastics 1 through 7, polystyrene (Styrofoam(r))	#1, #2, #3, #4, #5, #6, #7
Louisville	KY	curbside, drop-off	yes	junk mail, brown paper bags, telephone books, magazines, catalogs, newspapers and inserts, flattened cardboard, glass bottles and jars (clear, brown, green and blue) aluminum/steel/tin cans, empty aerosol cans, aluminum foil/pie and cake pans, plastic, office paper and envelopes	#1, #2, #3, #4, #5, #6, #7
Lubbock	TX	drop-off	yes	glass (clear and colored), plastic, aluminum and beverage cans, tin food cans, corrugated cardboard, newspaper (no inserts), computer paper (green bar or shredded), white ledger paper, yard waste, used motor oil (under 5 gallons)	#1, #2
Madison	WI	curbside, drop-off	no	newspapers, corrugated cardboard, magazines, catalogs, brown paper bags, telephone books, glass bottles and jars only, aluminum/tin/steel cans, plastic containers, empty paint cans, #1 clam shells and blister packs, metal pots/pans	#1, #2, #3, #4, #5, #6, #7
Memphis	TN	curbside, drop-off	yes	aluminum/steel cans, empty aerosol cans, plastic bottles, glass bottles and jars (clear, brown and green), newspapers and inserts, magazines, telephone books, office paper, junk mail, white/colored paper, envelopes, manila folders, stationery, yard waste	#1, #2
Mesa	AZ	curbside, drop-off	yes	aluminum, cardboard, chipboard, glass food and beverage jars and bottles, metal cans, newspapers, magazines, mixed paper, plastic bottles/jugs/jars, telephone books	#1, #2, #3, #4, #5, #6, #7
Miami	FL	curbside	yes	glass/plastic bottles, aluminum/steel cans, magazines, office/mixed paper, corrugated cardboard, white goods, yard trash, tires	na
Milwaukee	WI	curbside	yes	plastic, glass jars and bottles (all colors), aluminum containers/foil/pans, bulky #2 plastics (like 5-gallon buckets), cartons, metal pots/pans, newspaper, magazines, catalogs, phone books, steel food cans, empty aerosol cans	#1, #2, #4, #5

City	State	System Type	Voluntary	Materials Collected	Plastic Types
Minneapolis	MN	curbside, drop-off	yes	dry boxboard, office paper, mail, cans, corrugated cardboard, glass, household batteries, magazines, newspapers, telephone books, plastic bottles, cartons	#1, #2, #3, #4, #5, #6, #7
Mobile	AL	drop-off	yes	plastic beverage containers, aluminum beverage cans, steel cans, corrugated cardboard, newspapers, magazines, junk mail, telephone books, computer paper, cereal boxes, glass jars (brown/amber, green/blue and clear), styrofoam packing peanuts, pine straw	#1, #2
Montgomery	AL	drop-off	yes	aluminum, paper, cardboard; additional programs for recycling: recharcheable batteries, tires, used motor oil, christmas trees, mobile phones, plastic bags, shredded paper	#1, #2
Nashville	TN	curbside, drop-off (glass must be dropped off)	yes	paper (newspaper, magazines, junk mail, phone books, paperback books, paperboard, cereal boxes, freezer food boxes); cardboard, aluminum and steel cans, plastic containers (plastic bottles, and dairy containers labeled #1 through #7); glass bottles should be taken to one of the drop-off or convenience centers or arrange for separate curbside collection	#1, #2, #3, #4, #5, #6, #7
New Orleans	LA	curbside, drop-off	yes	newspapers, magazines, telephone books, catalogs, brown paper bags, plastic, aluminum/steel/tin cans, glass, clean, unsoiled corrugated boxes	#1, #2, #3, #4, #5, #6, #7
New York	NY	curbside, drop-off	no	paper, mail and envelopes, wrapping paper, smooth cardboard, paper bags, cardboard egg cartons and trays, newspapers, magazines, catalogs, phone books, softcover books, corrugated cardboard, metal cans, aluminum foil, household metals, bulk metal (metal furniture, cabinets, large appliances, etc.), glass bottles and jars, plastic bottles and jugs, milk cartons and juice boxes, leaf program (fall)	na
Newark	NJ	curbside, drop-off	no	glass bottles and jars, cans, bottles, corrugated cardboard, newspapers, magazines, mixed high-grade white paper, aluminum and bimetal cans, used motor oil, leaves	na
Norfolk	VA	curbside, drop-off	yes	aluminum cans/pie plates/foil, glass bottles and jars, corrugated cardboard and chipboard (flattened), phone books, unwanted mail, household batteries, newspapers, plastic soda/water bottles, plastic milk/water/detergent jugs, steel cans, mixed office paper	na
North Hempstead	NY	curbside, drop-off	yes	newspapers/inserts, magazines, direct mail, catalogs, construction/wrapping paper, index/greeting cards, paperback books, plastic, food/beverage cans, aluminum foil/pie tins, glass (clear and colored)	#1, #2, #4, #5, #6
Oakland	CA	curbside, drop-off	yes	glass bottles and jars, plastic bottles and jugs, tin and aluminum cans/foil/pie plates, milk cartons, empty spray cans, empty and dry metal latex paint containers, newspapers, catalogs, magazines, paper egg cartons, holiday trees (seasonal)	na
Oklahoma City	OK	curbside, drop-off	yes	plastic milk jugs and beverage bottles, aluminum and steel food and beverage cans, glass food and beverage jars and bottles, newspapers and inserts, paper bags, magazines	#1, #2, #3, #4, #5, #6, #7
Omaha	NE	curbside, drop-off	yes	newspapers and inserts, magazines, catalogs, telephone books, junk mail, detergent boxes, wrapping paper, paperback books, office/school paper, plastic, glass bottles and jars (drop-off only), aluminum/steel/tin cans, corrugated cardboard	#1, #2, #3, #5
Oyster Bay	NY	curbside, drop-off	yes	newspapers and inserts (tied and separated), mixed paper and magazines (tied and separated); food and beverage cans, plastics (rigid only), bottles/glass	na
Philadelphia	PA	curbside, drop-off	no	mixed paper (newspapers including inserts, junk mail, envelopes, telephone books, magazines and catalogs, cereal type boxes - no liners, home office paper, stationery and other clean paper); metal cans, aluminum cans, empty aerosol cans (no caps), empty paint cans (air dried), paint can lids (separated from the paint cans), glass bottles and jars, plastic and cardboard, (clean foam #6 materials ok for drop-off)	#1, #2, #3, #4, #5, #6, #7

City	State	System Type	Voluntary	Materials Collected	Plastic Types
Phoenix	AZ	curbside, drop-off	yes	telephone books, plastic, food/glass bottles/jars, office paper, newspapers, magazines, cardboard, chipboard, milk/juice cartons, juice boxes, junk mail, aluminum cans/pie plates/foil, steel cans, metal hangers, scrap metal, aerosol cans, shredded paper (placed in clear bags)	#1, #2, #3, #4, #5, #6, #7
Pittsburgh	PA	curbside, drop-off	no	plastic/metal containers, newspapers and inserts, corrugated cardboard, magazines, catalogs, glossy paper, white office paper, glass (clear and colored), all metal cans, empty aerosol and paint cans, aluminum foil/containers, plastic bottles, jugs, and jars	#1, #2, #3, #4, #5
Plano	TX	curbside, drop-off	yes	newspapers, magazines, catalogs, junk mail, telephone books, brown paper bags, chipboard/ boxboard, corrugated cardboard boxes, aluminum/ steel/tin cans, plastic, aerosol cans, glass jars/ containers/dishes/drinking glasses/vases (any color), office paper	#1, #2, #3, #4, #5, #6, #7
Portland	OR	curbside, drop-off	no	newspapers, scrap paper, glass bottles and jars, magazines, corrugated cardboard, Kraft paper, plastic bottles (including milk jugs), steel/tin cans, used motor oil (in jugs)	na
Raleigh	NC	curbside, drop-off	yes	newspapers and inserts, magazines, catalogs, junk mail, food and beverage cans, plastic, glass food and beverage containers, aseptic boxes, aluminum foil/trays/ cans (clean), phone books	#1, #2, #3, #4, #5, #7
Richmond	VA	curbside, drop-off	yes	newspapers, mixed paper, aluminum cans/foil, steel cans, glass bottles and jars, milk cartons, juice boxes, plastic, cardboard	#1, #2
Riverside	CA	curbside, drop-off	yes	aluminum/tin cans, CRV and non-CRV glass, polystyrene, newspapers, white office paper, computer paper, cardboard, magazines, junk mail; C.U.R.E. program: gas run equipment, air conditioners, refrigerators, car batteries, appliances, electronics	#1, #2, #3, #4, #5, #6, #7
Rochester	NY	curbside	no	newspapers and inserts, magazines, glossy catalogs, corrugated cardboard, laundry baskets, glass, CD jewel cases, plastic food and beverage containers, milk/juice cartons, empty aerosol cans, aluminum/tin/bi-metal cans, durable kitchen cookware	#1, #2, #3, #4, #5, #6, #7
Sacramento	CA	curbside	yes	glass bottles and jars (all colors), newspapers, junk mail, envelopes, telephone books, magazines, catalogs, brown paper bags, paper egg cartons, shoe boxes, computer/colored paper, paper 6-pk containers and boxes, cardboard, aluminum/tin cans, plastic	#1, #2, #3, #4, #5, #6, #7
Saint Louis	MO	curbside, drop-off	yes	aluminum cans, glass bottles and jars (clear, green and brown), newspapers and inserts, magazines, thin catalogs, steel food cans, plastic bottles and jugs, paperboard, office paper, corrugated cardboard	#1, #2, #3, #4, #5, #7
Saint Paul	MN	curbside, drop-off	yes	newspapers/inserts, mail, envelopes, magazines, catalogs, office/school paper, boxboard, corrugated cardboard boxes, glass bottles and jars (clear/colors), metal cans/lids, jar lids, bottle caps, aluminum foil/trays, good clothes/linens	#1, #2
Saint Petersburg	FL	curbside, drop-off	yes	mixed paper; newspapers; glass and plastic bottles; metal/aluminum cans; food and beverage cartons; corrugated cardboard boxes (flattened); drop-off: appliances, mixed metal, yard waste	#1, #2, #3, #4, #5, #6, #7
San Antonio	TX	curbside, drop-off	yes	paper (ad circulars, catalogs, carbonless paper, dry goods packaging with liners removed, envelopes, file folders, cardboard, junk mail, magazines, newspapers, office paper, paperback books, paper bags, paper towel/toilet paper cores, phone books, non-metallic gift wrap); plastics (#1 through #7); glass (bottles and jars all colors); metal (aluminum, steel and tin beverage and food cans)	#1, #2, #3, #4, #5, #6, #7
San Diego	CA	curbside, drop-off	no	glass bottles and jars, empty aerosol cans, plastic bottles and jars, cardboard, aluminum cans, paper bags, aluminum foil, foil trays, bagged shredded paper, newspapers, metal cans, phone books, paper or frozen food boxes, mail and magazines, paper and catalogs	na
San Francisco	CA	curbside, drop-off	no	paper, envelopes (windows okay), corrugated cardboard, aluminum cans and foil, cereal boxes (without lining), glass bottles and jars, egg cartons (paper only), plastic bottles (#1 through #7), plastic tubs and lids (#2, #4 and #5), junk mail and brochures, spray cans (must be empty), magazines, steel (tin) cans, newspapers, phone books, wrapping paper	#1, #2, #3, #4, #5, #6, #7

City	State	System Type	Voluntary	Materials Collected	Plastic Types
San Jose	CA	curbside	yes	metal cans, milk and juice cartons, glass bottles and jars (brown, clear and green), plastic, carbonless paper, cardboard, catalogs, envelopes, junk mail, magazines, newspapers and inserts, paper bags, polystyrene, scrap metals, textiles	#1, #2, #3, #4, #5, #6, #7
Santa Ana	CA	curbside, drop-off	yes	newspaper, mixed/white paper, cardboard, junk mail, magazines, telephone books, cereal/tissue boxes, glass/plastic bottles and jars, aluminum/steel/tin cans, empty aerosol cans, pie tins, plastic milk containers	na
Scottsdale	AZ	curbside, drop-off	yes	aseptic boxes, corrugated cardboard/chipboard, glass (clear, green, amber), magazines, telephone books, aluminum/steel/tin cans, empty aerosol cans, newspapers/inserts, junk mail, brown paper bags, plastic jugs/bottles (regardless of recycling #)	#1, #2, #3, #4, #5, #6, #7
Seattle	WA	curbside, drop-off	yes	cardboard, magazines, junk mail, envelopes, aseptic packaging, telephone books, glass bottles and jars (all colors), steel/tin cans, plastic bottles/jugs/jars, milk and juice cartons, aluminum, used motor oil	na
Shreveport	LA	curbside, drop-off	yes	paper; plastic and glass bottles; metal cans; magazines; cardboard; corrugated boxes; newspaper; catalogs; detergent bottles	#1, #2, #3, #4, #5, #6, #7
Stockton	CA	curbside, drop-off	yes	aluminum beverage containers, steel/tin cans, glass bottles/jars, plastic, newspapers, telephone books	#1, #2
Tampa	FL	curbside	yes	glass bottles and jars (all colors), newspapers, aluminum/steel cans, milk and juice cartons made from paper, plastic containers, phone books, paperback books, cardboard	#1, #2, #3, #4, #5, #6, #7
Toledo	OH	curbside	yes	junk mail, paper, boxboard, corrugated cardboard, newspapers, magazines, milk/juice cartons, glass bottles, tin and aluminum cans	#1, #2, #3, #4, #5, #6, #7
Tucson	AZ	curbside, drop-off	yes	white/colored paper, envelopes, junk mail, magazines, catalogs, paperboard/chipboard, phone books, fiberboard, cartons, newspapers, brown paper bags, corrugated cardboard, plastic, steel/tin cans, aluminum cans/foil/baking pans, glass food/beverage containers	#1, #2, #3, #4, #5, #6, #7
Tulsa	OK	curbside, drop-off	yes	glass jars and bottles (green, brown and clear), plastic #1-7, aluminum/steel cans, newspapers and inserts, magazines, office paper, box board	#1, #2, #3, #4, #5, #6, #7
Virginia Beach	VA	curbside, drop-off	yes	newspapers, cardboard, chipboard, junk mail, catalogs, magazines, telephone books, glass bottles and jars (clear, green and brown), plastic bottles with a spout only, aluminum/steel/tin cans	na
Washington	DC	curbside	yes	glass jars and bottles; metals (aluminum pie plates, tin, aluminum and steel cans); aerosol cans; plastic bottles (all narrow-necked or screw-topped bottles marked with a #1 or #2); paper (white and colored papers, envelopes, forms, file folders, tablets, junk mail, cereal boxes, shoeboxes, wrapping paper, shredded paper/mail, catalogs, magazines, paperback books and phone books); newspaper (including inserts); corrugated cardboard; brown paper bags	#1, #2, #3, #4, #5, #6, #7
Wichita	KS	curbside (private-no public trash collection)	yes	aluminum cans; ammunition; appliances; batteries; books; carpet pad; catalogs; cellular phones; clothes hangers; clothing; compact fluorescent light bulbs; computers; curbside recycling; eyeglasses; fluorescent lights; furniture; glass; hazardous materials; hearing aids; magazines; medication; metal; motor oil; packaging material; paper items; phone directories; plastics; plastic bags; printer cartridges; televisions; tires; unsolicited mail; wood and yard waste	#1, #2, #3, #4, #5, #6, #7

***Source:** Independent research by the editors, August 2013*

Occupational and Environmental Exposures Capable of Causing Illness

Common Name/Synonym	Primary Name	AOEC Code[1]	Use[2]	Asthmagen[3]	Asthma Detail[3]
1,1,1-Trichloroethane	Methyl Chloroform	190.08	S		
1,1,2-Trichloroethane	1,1,2-Trichloroethane	190.12	S		
1,1-Azobisformamide	Azodicarbamide	260.18		Yes	Rs
1,2,3-Trihydroxybenzene	1,2,3-Trihydroxybenzene	180.06			
1,2,4-Benzenetricarboxylic Acid 1,2-Anhydride	Trimellitic Anhydride	151.03		Yes	Rs
1,2,4-Triazole-3-carboxamide	Ribaviran	321.32			
1,2,4-Trichlorobenzene	1,2,4-Trichlorobenzene	201.02			
1,2-benzenedicarboxaldehyde	Ortho-phthalaldehyde	120.10			R
1,2-Benzisothiazol-3(2H)one	Saccharin	320.38			R
1,2-Dibromoethane	Ethylene Dibromide	191.01	P		
1,2-Dichloroethane	Ethylene Dichloride	190.07	S		
1,2-Dichloroethylene	1,2-Dichloroethylene	190.06	S		
1,2-Dichloropropane	Propylene Dichloride	190.11	S		
1,2-Ethanediol	Ethylene Glycol	080.011			
1,3-Butylene Glycol	1,3-Butylene Glycol	080.04			
1,3-Dichloro-1,1,2,2,3-pentafluoropropane	1,3-Dichloro-1,1,2,2,3-pentafluoropropane	192.022			
1,3-Dichloro-2-Propanol	1,3-Dichloro-2-Propanol	190.17			
1,3-Dihydroxy-2-propanone	Dihydroxyacetone	130.08			
1,4 Benzenediamine	1,4-Benzenediamine	251.061			R
1,4-Dioxane	Dioxane	100.04	S		
1,5-Naphthylene Ester Isocyanic Acid	Naphthalene Diisocyanate	221.03		Yes	G
1,6 Diisocyanato Hexane	Hexamethylene Diisocyanate	221.04		Yes	G
1,6-Hexanediamine	Hexamethylenediamine	232.10			R
1-Allyl-3-Methoxy-4-Hydroxybenzene	Eugenol	100.07		Yes	Rs
1-beta-D-ribofuranosyl-	Ribaviran	321.32			
1-Bromo-3-chloro-5,5-dimethylhydantoin	1-Bromo-3-chloro-5,5-dimethylhydantoin	191.04			R
1-Butanol	N-Butyl Alcohol	070.04	S		
1-Chloro-2,3-Epoxypropane	Epichlorohydrin	110.01			
1-Hydroxy-2-methoxybenzene	Gualacol	100.09			
1 Methyl-2-Pyrrolidinone	1-Methyl-2-Pyrrolidinone	260.120			
1-Pentanol	Amyl Alcohol	070.02			
1-Propanol	Propyl Alcohol	070.08	S		
1-Propyl Chloride	Chloropropane	190.05	S		
2,3,7,8-TCDD	2,3,7,8-Tetrachlorodibenzodioxin	200.041	P		
2,3,7,8-Tetrachlorodibenzodioxin	2,3,7,8-Tetrachlorodibenzodioxin	200.041	P		
2,4,5-T	2,4,5-T	200.011	P		
2,4,6-Trinitrophenol	Picric Acid	250.09			
2,4-D	2,4-D	200.012	P		
2,6-Dichlorobenzonitrile	2,6-Dichlorobenzonitrile	200.10	P		
2-Aminoethanol	Monoethanolamine	231.01		Yes	Rs
2-Aminopropane	Isopropylamine	230.03			
2-Butanone	Methyl Ethyl Ketone	130.03	S		
2-Butoxyethanol	2-Butoxyethanol	091.03	S		R
2-Chloroacetophenone	Mace	320.27			
2-Chloroethanol	Beta-Chloroethyl Alcohol	070.03			
2-Chloroethylphosphonic Acid	Ethephon	291.12	P		
2-Ethoxyethanol	Ethylene Glycol Monoethyl Ether	091.02	S		
2-Ethoxyethyl Acetate	2-Ethoxyethyl Acetate	141.05			
2-Ethylhexyl Nitrate	2-Ethylhexyl Nitrate	260.31			
2-Furanmethanol	Furfuryl Alcohol	070.090			R
2-Hydroxyethanethiol	Mercaptoethanol	310.04			
2-Hydroxypropyl Acrylate	2-Hydroxypropyl Acrylate	142.09			
2-Methylpropane	Isobutane	060.04			
2-Naphthylamine	Beta-Naphthylamine	251.05			
2-Nitropropane	2-Nitropropane	260.141			

Common Name/Synonym	Primary Name	AOEC Code[1]	Use[2]	Asthmagen[3]	Asthma Detail[3]
2-Oxetanone	Beta-Propiolactone	320.04			
2-Propanol	Isopropyl Alcohol	070.06	S		
2-Propanone	Acetone	130.01	S		
2-Propen-1-ol	Allyl Alcohol	070.01			
2-Propenal	Acrolein	120.02			
2-Thiocarbamide	2-Thiocarbamide	310.071			
3,3'-Dichlorobenzidene & Salts	3,3'-Dichlorobenzidene & Salts	250.13			
3,3-Dichloro-1,1,1,2,2-pentafluoropropane	3,3-Dichloro-1,1,1,2,2-pentafluoropropane	192.021			
3-Amino-5-mercapto-1,2,4-triazole	3-Amino-5-mercapto-1,2,4-triazole	260.30		Yes	Rs
3-Dimethylamino Propylamine	3-Dimethylamino Propylamine	232.05			R
3-DMAPA	3-Dimethylamino Propylamine	232.05			R
3-mercaptopropionate	3-mercaptopropionate	310.13			
3-mercaptopropionic Acid	3-mercaptopropionic Acid	310.12			
3-thiopropionic Acid	3-mercaptopropionic Acid	310.12			
4,4'-Methylenebis(2-Chloroaniline)	4,4'-Methylenebis(2-Chloroaniline)	250.03			
4,4-Aminodiphenyl	Benzidine	251.03			
4,4-Diaminodiphenylmethane	Methylenedianiline	250.16			
4-Hydroxyaniline	Para-Aminophenol	251.01			
4-Methyl-2-Pentanone	Methyl Isobutyl Ketone	130.04	S		
4-PC	4-Phenylcyclohexene	060.11			
4-Phenylcyclohexene	4-Phenylcyclohexene	060.11			
5-chloro-2-(2,4-dichlorohydroxy) phenol	Triclosan	181.03			
5-Nonanone	Butyl Ketone	130.06	S		
7 ACA	7-aminocephalosporanic acid	321.064			R
7-Amino-3-thiomethyl-3-cephalosporanic acid	7-Amino-3-thiomethyl-3-cephalosporanic acid	321.065			R
7-aminocephalosporanic acid	7-aminocephalosporanic acid	321.064			R
7CTD	Tosyalate dihydrate	321.069			R
7TACA	7-Amino-3-thiomethyl-3-cephalosporanic acid	321.065			R
8-Hydroxyquinoline	8-Hydroxyquinoline	250.02			
8-Quinolinol	8-Hydroxyquinoline	250.02			
90% Uncured methacrylate ester monomers	Optigard	142.13			
Abiruana	Abiruana	373.08		Yes	
Abrasives, NOS	Abrasives, NOS	010.01			
ABS Copolymer	Acrylonitrile-Butadiene-Styrene Copolymer	270.29			R
Acacia	Gum Arabic	372.01		Yes	Rs
Acarian	Acarian	382.11		Yes	
Acephate	Acephate	291.11	P	Yes	
Acetaldehyde	Acetaldehyde	120.01			
Acetamide	Acetamide	260.01			
Acetates, NOS	Acetates, NOS	141.00			
Acetic Acid	Glacial Acetic Acid	050.34		Yes	Rrs
Acetic Acid Ethyl Ester	Ethyl Acetate	141.03	S		
Acetic Anhydride	Acetic Anhydride	151.09			
Acetic Ether	Ethyl Acetate	141.03	S		
Acetic Oxide	Acetic Anhydride	151.09			
Acetone	Acetone	130.01	S		
Acetonitrile	Acetonitrile	210.01			
Acetophenone	Mace	320.27			
Acetylene	Acetylene	060.01			
Acetylene Dichloride	1,2-Dichloroethylene	190.06	S		
Acetylene Trichloride	Trichloroethylene	190.13	S		
Acid & Base Mixture	Acid & Base Mixture	050.33			
Acid Solder	Acid Solder	050.26			
Acid Stripper	Acid Stripper	050.25			
Acids, Bases, Oxidizers, NOS	Acids, Bases, Oxidizers, NOS	050.00			
Acridine	Acridine	250.15			
Acrolein	Acrolein	120.02			
Acrylamide	Acrylamide	260.02			
Acrylate	Acrylic Monomer	142.01			

Common Name/Synonym	Primary Name	AOEC Code[1]	Use[2]	Asthmagen[3]	Asthma Detail[3]
Acrylates, NOS	Acrylates, NOS	142.00			
Acrylic Acid	Acrylic Acid	150.08		Yes	Rs
Acrylic Acid Butyl Ester	Butyl Acrylate	142.02			R
Acrylic Acid Polymer	Acrylics	270.01			
Acrylic Acid, 1,1,1-(Trihydroxymethyl) Propane Triester	Trimethylolpropane Triacrylate	142.08			
Acrylic Acid, 2(Diethylamino)ethyl Ester	Diethylaminoethyl Acrylate	142.06			
Acrylic Acid, 2-Hydroxypropylester	2-Hydroxypropyl Acrylate	142.09			
Acrylic Aldehyde	Acrolein	120.02			
Acrylic Amide	Acrylamide	260.02			
Acrylic Monomer	Acrylic Monomer	142.01			
Acrylic Resins	Acrylics	270.01			
Acrylics	Acrylics	270.01			
Acrylonitrile	Acrylonitrile	210.02			
Acrylonitrile-Butadiene-Styrene Copolymer	Acrylonitrile-Butadiene-Styrene Copolymer	270.29			R
Acrylonitrile-Butadiene-Styrene-Polyvinyl Chloride	Acrylonitrile-Butadiene-Styrene-Polyvinyl Chloride	270.30			
Actibon	Activated Carbon	010.041			
Activated Carbon	Activated Carbon	010.041			
Activol	Para-Aminophenol	251.01			
Adding Machine	Keyboard Use	360.02			
Adhesive, Epoxy	Adhesive, Epoxy	110.06		Yes	G
Adhesive, NOS	Glues, NOS	320.110			
Aerosolized Pentamidine	Pentamidine	321.23			
Aflotoxins	Aflotoxins	391.091			
African Maple	African Maple	373.09		Yes	
African Zebrawood	African Zebrawood	373.13		Yes	
Agent Orange	Agent Orange	200.010	P		
AIDS Exposure	HIV Exposure	390.08			
Air Bag Discharge Products	Air Bag Discharge Products	320.44			
Air Freshener	Air Freshener	320.42			
Air Pollutants, Indoor	Air Pollutants, Indoor	320.01			
Air Pollutants, Indoor, from Building Renovation	Indoor Air Pollutants from Building Renovation	320.33			
Air Pollutants, Outdoor	Air Pollutants, Outdoor	320.02			
Air Pressure, Changes	Air Pressure, Changes	350.07			
Albuterol Aerosol	Proventil	021.01			
Alcohol	Ethanol	070.05	S		
Alcohols, NOS	Alcohols, NOS	070.00	S		
Aldrin	Aldrin	280.01	P		
Alicyclic Hydrocarbons, NOS	Alicyclic Hydrocarbons, NOS	060.002			
Aliphatic Hydrocarbons, NOS	Aliphatic Hydrocarbons, NOS	060.001			
Alkyd Resins	Alkyd Resins	270.21			
Alkyl Dimethyl Benzyl Ammonium Chloride	Alkyl Dimethyl Benzyl Ammonium Chloride	322.326		Yes	Rs
alkylamine ethoxylate,alkyleneoxy diamine, ethylenediamine	Surfactant-Specific amines	320.191		Yes	Rs
Alkylcyanoacrylates, NOS	Cyanoacrylates, NOS	142.07		Yes	Rs
Allyl Alcohol	Allyl Alcohol	070.01			
Allylguaiacol	Eugenol	100.07		Yes	Rs
Alpha Amylase	Fungal Amylase	324.09		Yes	Rs
Alpha-Chlorotoluene	Benzyl Chloride	200.02			
Alpha-Naphthylamine	Alpha-Naphthylamine	251.04			
Alternaria	Alternaria	391.12		Yes	Rs
Alternaria Aleternata	Alternaria	391.12		Yes	Rs
Alternaria Alternata Toxin	Alternaria	391.12		Yes	Rs
Alternaria spp	Alternaria	391.12		Yes	Rs
Alumina	Aluminum Oxide	020.02		Yes	Rs
Aluminum	Aluminum	020.011		Yes	Rs
Aluminum Chloride	Aluminum Chloride	020.012		Yes	Rs
Aluminum Compounds	Aluminum Compounds	020.010		Yes	Rs
Aluminum Hydroxide	Aluminum Hydroxide	050.30			
Aluminum Oxide	Aluminum Oxide	020.02		Yes	Rs

Common Name/Synonym	Primary Name	AOEC Code[1]	Use[2]	Asth-magen[3]	Asthma Detail[3]
Aluminum Oxide, Corundum	Aluminum Oxide, Corundum	020.021		Yes	Rs
Aluminum Phosphide	Aluminum Phosphide	040.31	P		
Amaranth	Amaranth	252.01			
Amino Acids, NOS	Amino Acids, NOS	250.19			
Amino Resins	Amino Resins	270.22			
Aminobenzene	Aniline	250.01			
Aminoethyl Ethanolamine	Aminoethyl Ethanolamine	231.03		Yes	Rs
Aminophen	Aniline	250.01			
Ammonia	Ammonium Hydroxide, NOS	322.07		Yes	Rs
Ammonia Solution (10%)	Ammonia Solution (10%)	322.09		Yes	Rs
Ammonia Solution (29%)	Ammonia Solution (29%)	322.08		Yes	Rs
Ammonia Solution, NOS	Ammonium Hydroxide, NOS	322.07		Yes	Rs
Ammonia, Household	Ammonia Solution (10%)	322.09		Yes	Rs
Ammonium Bichromate	Ammonium Bichromate	022.02		Yes	Rs
Ammonium Chloride	Ammonium Chloride	052.031			
Ammonium chloroplatinate	Ammonium Hexachloroplatinate (IV)	024.01		Yes	Rs
Ammonium Hexachloroplatinate (IV)	Ammonium Hexachloroplatinate (IV)	024.01		Yes	Rs
Ammonium Hydroxide, NOS	Ammonium Hydroxide, NOS	322.07		Yes	Rs
Ammonium Persulfate	Ammonium Persulfate	052.04			
Ammonium Phosphate	Ammonium Phosphate	040.32	P		
Ammonium Salts	Ammonium Salts	052.030			
Ampicillin	Ampicillin	321.041		Yes	G
Amprolium	Amprolium	321.11		Yes	
AMT	3-Amino-5-mercapto-1,2,4-triazole	260.30		Yes	Rs
Amyl Acetate	Amyl Acetate	141.01			
Amyl Alcohol	Amyl Alcohol	070.02			
Amyl Nitrite	Amyl Nitrite	260.27			
Ananase	Bromelain	324.07		Yes	Rs
Anesthetic Ethers, NOS	Anesthetic Ethers, NOS	190.155			R
Anesthetic Gases, Halogenated	Anesthetic Gases, Halogenated	190.154			R
Anesthetic Gases, NOS	Anesthetic Gases, NOS	320.03			
Anhydride, NOS	Anhydride, NOS	151.00			
Anhydrous Ammonia	Anhydrous Ammonia	052.011		Yes	Rr
Aniline	Aniline	250.01			
Aniline Dyes, NOS	Aniline Dyes, NOS	251.00			
Animal Material, NOS	Animal Material, NOS	380.00			R
Animal Material, NOS (see specific animals)	Animal Material, NOS	380.00			R
Anisakis simplex	Anisakis simplex	382.26		Yes	Rs
Anthracene	Anthracene	161.01			
Antifreeze	Antifreeze	080.010			
Antigens, Animal	Antigens, Animal	380.01			
Antigens, Animal (see specific animals)	Antigens, Animal	380.01			
Antimony	Antimony	020.031			
Antimony Compounds	Antimony Compounds	020.030			
Antimony Hydride	Antimony Hydride	020.04			
Arabidopsis Thaliana	Arabidopsis Thaliana	370.52		Yes	Rs
Argon	Argon	040.01			
Arochlor	Polychlorinated Biphenyls	200.07			
Aromatic Hydrocarbons, NOS	Aromatic Hydrocarbons, NOS	160.00	S		
Aromatic Solvents, NOS	Aromatic Hydrocarbons, NOS	160.00	S		
Arsenic	Arsenic	020.051			
Arsenic Compounds	Arsenic Compounds	020.050			
Arsine	Arsine	020.06			
Arthropod, NOS	Insect, NOS	382.00			
Asbestos, Amosite	Asbestos, Amosite	010.021			
Asbestos, Chrysotile	Asbestos, Chrysotile	010.023			
Asbestos, Crocidolite	Asbestos, Crocidolite	010.024			
Asbestos, NOS	Asbestos, NOS	010.020			

Common Name/Synonym	Primary Name	AOEC Code[1]	Use[2]	Asthmagen[3]	Asthma Detail[3]
Asbestos, Tremolite	Asbestos, Tremolite	010.025			
Ash, NOS	Ash, NOS	010.16			
Ashwood	Ashwood	373.17		Yes	
Aspergillus	Aspergillus	391.020			
Aspergillus Flavus	Aspergillus Flavus	391.021			
Aspergillus Fumigatus	Aspergillus Fumigatus	391.022			
Aspergillus Glaucus	Aspergillus Glaucus	391.023			
Aspergillus Niger	Aspergillus Niger	391.024			
Aspergillus Versicolor	Aspergillus Versicolor	391.025			
Asphalt	Asphalt	061.07			
Asphyxiant Gases, NOS	Asphyxiant Gases, NOS	040.25			
Assault, Physical	Assault, Physical	353.12			
Astral Oil	Astral Oil	061.032	S		
Auramine	Auramine	251.02			
Auto Accident	Motor Vehicle Accident	353.05			
Avian Material, NOS	Avian Material, NOS	380.16			
Ayruvedic Medications	Ayruvedic Medications	321.35			
Azabenzene	Pyridine	250.14			
Azine	Pyridine	250.14			
Aziridine	Ethylenimine	260.101			
Azo Compounds, NOS	Azo Compounds, NOS	252.00			
Azo Dyes, NOS	Azo Compounds, NOS	252.00			
Azobisformamide	Azodicarbamide	260.18		Yes	Rs
Azodicarbamide	Azodicarbamide	260.18		Yes	Rs
B-Galactosidase	Lactase	324.14			
B-Mercaptoethanol	Mercaptoethanol	310.04			
Baby's Breath	Baby's Breath	370.17		Yes	
Bacillus Subtilis Enzymes	Bacillus Subtilis Enzymes	324.010		Yes	Rs
Bacillus Thurigiensis	Bacillus Thurigiensis	390.14	P		
Bacteria	Infectious Agents, NOS	390.070			
Balfourodendron Riedelianum	Pau Marfim	373.18		Yes	
Baquacil	Polyhexamethylene Biguanide	260.29	P		
Barium	Barium	020.071			
Barium Compounds	Barium Compounds	020.070			
Barn Dust	Manure	380.02			
Barn Mite	Barn Mite	382.15		Yes	
Barometric Pressure, Changes	Air Pressure, Changes	350.07			
Bat Guano	Bat Guano	380.12		Yes	
Baygon	Propoxur	292.04	P		
BCDMH	1-Bromo-3-chloro-5,5-dimethylhydantoin	191.04			R
BCME	Bis Chloromethyl Ether	100.01			
Bee Moth	Bee Moth	382.05		Yes	
Bee Sting	Venom	380.05			
Bending	Posture, Body - Dynamic	362.03			
Benlate Fungicide	Benomyl	260.03	P		
Benomyl	Benomyl	260.03	P		
Benzalkonium Chloride	Benzalkonium Chloride	322.321		Yes	Rs
Benzamide	N,N-diethyl-m-toluamide	260.26	P		
Benzene	Benzene	160.01	S		
Benzenediamine	Benzenediamine	251.060			R
Benzenediazonium Chloride	Diazonium Chloride	252.031		Yes	Rs
Benzidine	Benzidine	251.03			
Benzoic Acid	Benzoic Acid	150.02			
Benzol	Benzene	160.01	S		
Benzoyl Chloride	Benzoyl Chloride	200.09			
Benzoyl Peroxide	Benzoyl Peroxide	050.27			
Benzyl Chloride	Benzyl Chloride	200.02			
Benzyl-C10-16-alkyldimethyl, chlorides	Benzyl-C10-16-alkyldimethyl, chlorides	322.3210		Yes	Rs
Benzyl-C12-16-alkyldimethyl, chlorides	Benzyl-C12-16-alkyldimethyl, chlorides	322.328		Yes	Rs

Common Name/Synonym	Primary Name	AOEC Code[1]	Use[2]	Asthmagen[3]	Asthma Detail[3]
Benzyl-C12-18-alkyldimethyl, chlorides	Benzyl-C12-18-alkyldimethyl, chlorides	322.327		Yes	Rs
Benzyl-C16-18-alkyldimethyl, chlorides	Benzyl-C16-18-alkyldimethyl, chlorides	322.329		Yes	Rs
Benzyldimethylstearylammonium Chloride	Benzyldimethylstearylammonium Chloride	322.3214		Yes	Rs
Beryllium	Beryllium	020.081			
Beryllium Compounds	Beryllium Compounds	020.080			
Beta-Chloroethyl Alcohol	Beta-Chloroethyl Alcohol	070.03			
Beta-Galactosidase	Lactase	324.14			
Beta-Lactosidase	Lactase	324.14			
Beta-mercaptopropionic Acid	3-mercaptopropionic Acid	310.12			
Beta-Naphthylamine	Beta-Naphthylamine	251.05			
Beta-Propiolactone	Beta-Propiolactone	320.04			
Beta-thiopropionic Acid	3-mercaptopropionic Acid	310.12			
Bioaerosols	Microorganisms, NOS	390.00			
Bis 2-Chloroethyl Ether	Dichloroethyl Ether	100.03			
Bis Chloromethyl Ether	Bis Chloromethyl Ether	100.01			
Bis-2-Chloroethyl Sulfide	Mustard Gas	190.16			
Bismuth	Bismuth	020.091			
Bismuth Compounds	Bismuth Compounds	020.090			
Bitrex	Denatonium Benzoate	320.37			
Black GR	Rifazol Black GR	325.08		Yes	Rs
Bleach	Sodium Hypochlorite	322.10		Yes	Rs
Bleach plus Acid (mixture)	Bleach plus Acid (mixture)	322.11			R
Bleach plus Ammonia (Mixture)	Bleach plus Ammonia (Mixture)	322.12			R
Bleaching Powder	Calcium Hypochloride	322.13			
Blood Exposure (Unknown Infection Status)	Body Fluid Exposure (Unknown Infection Status)	390.16			
Bloodworm	Bloodworm	382.18			
Bodily Reaction	Bodily Reaction	360.07			
Body Fluid Exposure (Unknown Infection Status)	Body Fluid Exposure (Unknown Infection Status)	390.16			
Boric Acid	Boric Acid	020.101			
Boron	Boron	020.102			
Boron Compounds	Boron Compounds	020.100			
Boron Hydride	Diborane	020.11			
Borrelium Virus	Borrelium Virus	390.15			
Bovine Serum Albumin	Bovine Serum Albumin	380.13		Yes	Rs
BPL	Beta-Propiolactone	320.04			
Brass	Brass	020.43			
Brazil Ginseng	Brazil Ginseng	370.53		Yes	Rs
Brazilian Ginseng	Brazil Ginseng	370.53		Yes	Rs
Brazing, NOS	Brazing, NOS	023.002			
Brick Oil	Creosote	180.01			
Brilliant Orange 3R	Rifazol Brilliant Orange 3R	325.07		Yes	Rs
Brilliant Yellow 160	Remazol Brilliant Yellow 4GL	325.27			R
Bromelain	Bromelain	324.07		Yes	Rs
Bromelin	Bromelain	324.07		Yes	Rs
Brominated Fluorocarbon	Brominated Fluorocarbon	192.03			
Brominated Pesticides, NOS	Brominated Pesticides, NOS	191.00	P		
Bromine	Bromine	030.01			
Bromomethane	Methyl Bromide	191.03	P		
Bt	Bacillus Thurigiensis	390.14	P		
BTC 776	BTC 776	322.325		Yes	Rs
BTC 927	BTC 927	322.3211		Yes	Rs
Buckwheat	Buckwheat	371.01		Yes	G
Building Renovation	Indoor Air Pollutants from Building Renovation	320.33			
Burning Fume	Welding, NOS	023.001			
Burnt Lime	Calcium Oxide	050.05			
Butadiene & Styrene	Butadiene & Styrene	271.01			
Butyl Acetate	Butyl Acetate	141.02	S		
Butyl Acrylate	Butyl Acrylate	142.02			R

Common Name/Synonym	Primary Name	AOEC Code[1]	Use[2]	Asth-magen[3]	Asthma Detail[3]
Butyl Ketone	Butyl Ketone	130.06	S		
Butyl-Cellosolve	2-Butoxyethanol	091.03	S		R
C. Carnea	Chrysoperla Carnea	382.22		Yes	
C.I. Pigment Red 48:1	Red BBN	325.22		Yes	Rs
C.I. Reactive Black 5	Remazol Black B	325.11			R
C.I. Reactive Blue 203	Remazol Marine Blue GG	325.24			R
C.I. Reactive Yellow 145	Rifafix Yellow 3 RN	325.06		Yes	Rs
C.I. Reactive Yellow 39	Lanasol Yellow 4G	325.09		Yes	Rs
Cabreuva	Cabreuva	373.23		Yes	
Cacoon Seed	Cacoon Seed	370.32		Yes	
Caddis Flies	Caddis Flies	382.27		Yes	Rs
Cadmium	Cadmium	020.121			
Cadmium Compounds	Cadmium Compounds	020.120			
Cadmium Salts	Cadmium Salts	020.122			
Caesalpinia Echinata	Fernambouc	373.16		Yes	
Calcium Bisulfite	Calcium Bisulfite	050.03			
Calcium Carbide	Calcium Carbide	050.36			
Calcium Carbonate	Calcium Carbonate	050.35			
Calcium Chloride	Calcium Chloride	041.01			
Calcium Cyanamide	Calcium Cyanamide	260.04			
Calcium Hypochloride	Calcium Hypochloride	322.13			
Calcium Oxide	Calcium Oxide	050.05			
Calcium Salts, NOS	Calcium Salts, NOS	040.02			
Calculator	Keyboard Use	360.02			
California Redwood	California Redwood	373.02		Yes	
Camphor Oil	Camphor Oil	320.48			R
Capsicum	Capsicum	370.35			
Captan	Captan	260.05	P		
Car Accident	Motor Vehicle Accident	353.05			
Car Crash	Motor Vehicle Accident	353.05			
Carbamate Pesticides, NOS	Carbamate Pesticides, NOS	292.00	P		
Carbaryl	Carbaryl	292.02	P		
Carbazotic Acid	Picric Acid	250.09			
Carbinol	Methanol	070.07	C		
Carbolic Acid	Phenol	180.04			
Carbon Black	Carbon Black	010.042			
Carbon Dioxide	Carbon Dioxide	040.03			
Carbon Disulfide	Carbon Disulfide	310.01			
Carbon Monoxide	Carbon Monoxide	040.04			
Carbon Tetrachloride	Carbon Tetrachloride	190.01	S		
Carbonless Paper	Carbonless Paper	320.05			
Carbopol	Carbopol, NOS	270.36			
Carbopol, NOS	Carbopol, NOS	270.36			
Carborundum	Silicon Carbide	010.18			
Carene	Carene	060.21		Yes	Rs
Carmine	Carmine	320.24			
Carminic Acid	Carmine	320.24			
Carpet Dust	Carpet Dust	320.35			
Carpet Fibers	Carpet Dust	320.35			
Carrying	Lifting	361.02			
Casein	Casein	380.11		Yes	
Cash Register Use	Keyboard Use	360.02			
Castor Bean	Castor Bean	370.13		Yes	
Cat	Cat	380.22		Yes	Rs
Catalysts, NOS	Enzymes, NOS	324.00			
Caught In or Between Objects	Caught In or Between Objects	353.10			
Caustic Soda	Sodium Hydroxide	050.18			
Ceclor	Ceclor	321.26			

Common Name/Synonym	Primary Name	AOEC Code[1]	Use[2]	Asth-magen[3]	Asthma Detail[3]
Cedar of Lebanon	Cedar of Lebanon	373.03		Yes	
Cedrus Libani	Cedar of Lebanon	373.03		Yes	
Cefaclor	Ceclor	321.26			
Cefadroxil	Cefadroxil	321.061			R
Ceftazidine	Ceftazidine	321.062			R
Ceiba Pentandra Gaertner	Kapok	370.43		Yes	
Celery	Celery	370.011			
Cellosolve	Ethylene Glycol Monoethyl Ether	091.02	S		
Cement Dust	Cement Dust	010.03			R
Central American Walnut	Central American Walnut	373.11		Yes	
Cephalexin	Cephalexin	321.063			R
Cephalosporins	Cephalosporins	321.060			R
Cerium	Cerium	020.131			
Cerium Compounds	Cerium Compounds	020.130			
Cetalkonium Chloride	Cetalkonium Chloride	322.324		Yes	Rs
Cetane	Cetane	061.10			
CFC	Chlorofluorocarbon, NOS	192.020			
Chamomile	Chamomile	370.54		Yes	Rs
Chemical Dust, NOS	Chemicals, NOS	320.06			
Chemicals, NOS	Chemicals, NOS	320.06			
Chemicals, Unknown	Chemicals, NOS	320.06			
Chemotherapeutic Drugs	Chemotherapeutic Drugs	321.01			
Chicken	Chicken	380.07		Yes	
Chicory	Cichorium intybus	370.18		Yes	Rs
Chil-Perm CP-30	Chil-Perm CP-30	320.31	S		
Chloramide	Chloramine	030.09			R
Chloramine	Chloramine	030.09			R
Chloramine compounds, NOS	Chloramine compounds, NOS	030.090			
Chloramine T	Chloramine T	260.21		Yes	Rs
Chlorbenzol	Chlorobenzene	201.04	S		
Chlordane	Chlordane	280.02	P		
Chlorex	Dichloroethyl Ether	100.03			
Chlorhexidine	Chlorhexidine	200.08		Yes	Rs
Chlorimide	Dichloramine	030.1			R
Chlorinated Benzenes, NOS	Chlorinated Benzenes, NOS	201.00			
Chlorinated Dibenzodioxins	Chlorinated Dibenzodioxins	200.040			
Chlorinated Dibenzodioxins (except TCDD)	Chlorinated Dibenzodioxins	200.040	P		
Chlorinated Hydrocarbons, NOS	Chlorinated Hydrocarbons, NOS	190.00	S		
Chlorinated Naphthalene	Chlorinated Naphthalene	200.03			
Chlorinated Phenols, NOS	Chlorinated Phenols, NOS	181.00			
Chlorinated Solvents, NOS	Chlorinated Hydrocarbons, NOS	190.00	S		
Chlorine	Chlorine	030.02		Yes	Rrs
Chlorine Dioxide	Chlorine Dioxide	030.06			
Chlorine Trifluoride	Chlorine Trifluoride	030.05			
Chlorobenzene	Chlorobenzene	201.04	S		
Chlorobutadiene	Chloroprene	190.04			
Chlorodiphenyl	Polychlorinated Biphenyls	200.07			
Chloroethane	Chloroethane	190.02	S		
Chloroethene	Vinyl Chloride Monomer	190.14			
Chlorofluorocarbon, NOS	Chlorofluorocarbon, NOS	192.020			
Chloroform	Chloroform	190.03			
Chloromethyl Ether	Bis Chloromethyl Ether	100.01			
Chloromethyl Methyl Ether	Chloromethyl Methyl Ether	100.02			
Chlorophenoxy Herbicides, NOS	Chlorophenoxy Herbicides, NOS	200.11	P		
Chlorophora Excelsa	Iroko	373.05		Yes	
Chloropicrin	Chloropicrin	260.06	P		
Chloroprene	Chloroprene	190.04			
Chloropropane	Chloropropane	190.05	S		
Chlorothalonil	Chlorothalonil	210.03	P	Yes	Rs

Common Name/Synonym	Primary Name	AOEC Code[1]	Use[2]	Asthmagen[3]	Asthma Detail[3]
Chlorous Acid	Chlorous Acid	030.07			
Chlorpyrifos	Chlorpyrifos	291.05	P		R
Chorella Algae	Chorella Algae	370.36		Yes	
Chromic Acid	Chromic Acid	022.04		Yes	Rs
Chromium Compounds	Chromium Compounds	020.140		Yes	Rs
Chromium Metal	Chromium Metal	020.141		Yes	Rs
Chromium, Hexavalent, NOS	Chromium, Hexavalent, NOS	022.00		Yes	Rs
Chromium, Not Hexavalent	Chromium, Not Hexavalent	020.142		Yes	Rs
Chrysonilia sitophilia	Chrysonilia sitophilia	390.111		Yes	Rs
Chrysoperla Carnea	Chrysoperla Carnea	382.22		Yes	
Cibachrome Brilliant Scarlet 3R	Cibachrome Brilliant Scarlet 3R	325.03		Yes	Rs
Cichorium intybus	Cichorium intybus	370.18		Yes	Rs
Cidex OPA	Ortho-phthalaldehyde	120.10			R
Cigarette Smoke	Cigarette Smoke	330.01			R
Cimetidine	Cimetidine	321.17		Yes	
Cinnamene	Styrene	160.04	S	Yes	Rs
Cinnamic Aldehyde	Cinnamic Aldehyde	120.080			
Cinnamic Oil	Cinnamon Oil	120.089			
Cinnamomum Zeylanicum	Cinnamon	373.22		Yes	
Cinnamon	Cinnamon	373.22		Yes	
Citric Acid	Citric Acid	050.07			
Clam	Clam	381.10		Yes	
Clandestine Drug laboratory	Methamphetamine Laboratory	320.40			
Clay	Clay	010.051			
Clay 347	Clay	010.051			
Clay, NOS	Clay, NOS	010.050			
Cleaner, Citric	Cleaner, Citric	322.36			
Cleaners, Abrasive	Cleaners, Abrasive	322.14			
Cleaners, Acid	Cleaners, Acid	322.15			
Cleaners, Carpet	Cleaners, Carpet	322.16			
Cleaners, Caustic (excluding Lye)	Cleaners, Caustic (excluding Lye)	322.17			
Cleaners, Detergent, NOS	Cleaners, Detergent, NOS	022.10			
Cleaners, Disinfectant, NOS	Cleaners, Disinfectant, NOS	322.19			
Cleaners, Drain	Cleaners, Drain	322.20			
Cleaners, Floor Stripping	Cleaners, Floor Stripping	322.21			
Cleaners, Graffiti Removing	Cleaners, Graffiti Removing	322.22	S		
Cleaners, Household, General Purpose	Cleaners, Household, General Purpose	322.04			
Cleaners, Laundry Soap/Detergent	Cleaners, Laundry Soap/Detergent	322.23			
Cleaners, Lye	Cleaners, Lye	322.24			
Cleaners, Oven	Cleaners, Oven	322.25			
Cleaners, Pine Oil	Cleaners, Pine Oil	322.26			
Cleaners, Solvent-Based	Cleaners, Solvent-Based	322.06	S		
Cleaners, Tile	Cleaners, Tile	322.27			
Cleaners, Toilet Bowl	Cleaners, Toilet Bowl	322.28			
Cleaners, Wallpaper	Cleaners, Wallpaper	322.29			
Cleaning Fluids, Photocopier	Cleaning Fluids, Photocopier	322.03			
Cleaning Fluids/Spot Removers	Cleaning Fluids/Spot Removers	322.30	S		
Cleaning Materials, NOS	Cleaning Materials, NOS	322.00			
Cleaning Mixtures (excluding Bleach plus Acid or Ammonia)	Cleaning Mixtures (excluding Bleach plus Acid or Ammonia)	322.31			
Clove Oil	Oil of Clove	160.06			
CMME	Chloromethyl Methyl Ether	100.02			
CO	Carbon Monoxide	040.04			
Coal	Coal	010.06			
Coal Naphtha	Benzene	160.01	S		
Coal Tar	Polycyclic Aromatic Hydrocarbons, NOS	161.00			
Coal Tar Oil	Creosote	180.01			
Coating, Epoxy	Paint, Epoxy	110.05			
Cobalt	Cobalt	020.151		Yes	Rs

Common Name/Synonym	Primary Name	AOEC Code[1]	Use[2]	Asthmagen[3]	Asthma Detail[3]
Cobalt Compounds	Cobalt Compounds	020.150		Yes	G
Cocabolla	Cocabolla	373.04		Yes	
Cocoa	Cocoa Bean	370.47			
Cocoa Bean	Cocoa Bean	370.47			
Cocobolo	Cocabolla	373.04		Yes	
Coconut	Coconut	370.009			
Codeine	Codeine	321.182		Yes	Rs
Coffee Bean	Coffee Bean	370.12		Yes	
Coke Oven Emissions	Polycyclic Aromatic Hydrocarbons, NOS	161.00			
Cold	Cold	350.02			
Colistin	Colistin	321.34		Yes	Rs
Collodion	Collodion	270.39			
Collodium	Collodion	270.39			
Colophony	Colophony	023.05		Yes	G
Color Index No. 0-16	Rifazol Brilliant Orange 3R	325.07		Yes	Rs
Color Index No. 0-20	Rifacion Orange HE 2G	325.05		Yes	Rs
Color Index No. BK-5	Rifazol Black GR	325.08		Yes	Rs
Colorado Potato Beetle	Leptinotarsa Decemlineata	382.23		Yes	
Combustion Products, NOS	Smoke, NOS	330.03			
Computer Keyboard	Keyboard Use	360.02			
Computer Mouse Use	Keyboard Use	360.02			
Contact Pressure	Contact Pressure	360.01			
Coolants	Lubricants, NOS	320.14			
Copper	Copper	020.161			
Copper Compounds	Copper Compounds	020.160			
Copper Phthalocyanine	Copper Phthalocyanine	020.49			
Copper Sulfate	Copper Sulfate	020.51			
Copper Sulfate (Anhydrous)	Copper Sulfate	020.51			
Corn Dust	Corn Dust	370.51			
Corn Mint Oil	Corn Mint Oil	320.47			R
Corn Starch	Corn Starch	371.06			
Corrosive Preventative	Corrosive Preventative	060.23			
Cosmetics, NOS	Cosmetics, NOS	320.28			R
Cosmetology Chemicals, NOS	Cosmetics, NOS	320.28			R
Cotton Dust	Cotton Dust	370.02			
Coumarin	Coumarin	321.03			
Cow Dander	Cow Dander	380.041		Yes	
Crab	Crab	381.02		Yes	G
Creosote	Creosote	180.01			
Cresol	Cresol	180.02			
Cresylic Acid	Cresol	180.02			
Cricket	Cricket	382.04		Yes	
Crotonaldehyde	Crotonaldehyde	120.09			
CRT Radiation	Radiation, Electromagnetic	352.01			
Crude oil	Crude oil	170.04			
Cuprilinic Blue	Copper Phthalocyanine	020.49			
Cutting Oils	Cutting Oils	170.01		Yes	G
Cutting or Piercing Object, Except Blood-Contam. Sharps	Cutting or Piercing Object, Except Blood-Contam. Sharps	353.11			
Cuttlefish	Cuttlefish	381.06		Yes	
Cyanides, NOS	Cyanides, NOS	211.00			
Cyanoacrylates, NOS	Cyanoacrylates, NOS	142.07		Yes	Rs
Cyanurotramide	Melamine	260.28			
Cyclohexane	Cyclohexane	060.14	S		
Cyclohexanediamine_(1,2-diaminocyclohexane)	Cyclohexanediamine_(1,2-diaminocyclohexane)	060.25			R
Cyclohexanone	Cyclohexanone	130.07	S		
Cyclohexylamine	Cyclohexylamine	230.06			
Cyclopentadiene	Cyclopentadiene	060.13			
Cyclophosphamide	Cyclophosphamide	321.29			

Common Name/Synonym	Primary Name	AOEC Code[1]	Use[2]	Asthmagen[3]	Asthma Detail[3]
Cytoxan	Cyclophosphamide	321.29			
D-Limonene	D-Limonene	060.18	S		R
Dalbergia Retusa	Cocabolla	373.04		Yes	
Dander, Animal (NOS)	Dander, Animal (NOS)	380.040			
Daphnia	Daphnia	382.10		Yes	
DCB	Dichlorobenzene	201.010	P		
DDT	DDT	280.03	P		
DEA (Diethanolamine)	Diethanolamine	231.041		Yes	Rs
DEA (Diethylaniline)	Diethylaniline	250.18			
DEET	N,N-diethyl-m-toluamide	260.26	P		
Degreaser, NOS	Degreaser, NOS	171.04			
Denatonium Benzoate	Denatonium Benzoate	320.37			
Deodorizer, Aerosol	Air Freshener	320.42			
Dermasorb	Dimethyl Sulfoxide	310.14			
DHA	Dihydroxyacetone	130.08			
di-Halo	1-Bromo-3-chloro-5,5-dimethylhydantoin	191.04			R
Diacetyl	Diacetyl	130.09			
Diacetyl morphine	Diacetyl morphine	321.185		Yes	Rs
Dialkyl Methyl Benzyl Ammonium Chloride	Dialkyl Methyl Benzyl Ammonium Chloride	322.3212		Yes	Rs
Diamines, NOS	Diamines, NOS	233.00			
Diatomaceous Earth	Silica, Amorphous	010.12			
Diazinon	Diazinon	291.03	P	Yes	
Diazomethane	Diazomethane	260.23			
Diazonium Chloride	Diazonium Chloride	252.031		Yes	Rs
Diazonium Salt, NOS	Diazonium Salt, NOS	252.030			R
Diazonium Tetrafluoroborate	Diazonium Tetrafluoroborate	252.032		Yes	Rs
Diborane	Diborane	020.11			
Dichlobenil	2,6-Dichlorobenzonitrile	200.10	P		
Dichloramine	Dichloramine	030.1			R
Dichlorobenzene	Dichlorobenzene	201.010	P		
Dichlorodiphenyltrichloroethane	DDT	280.03	P		
Dichloroethyl Ether	Dichloroethyl Ether	100.03			
Dichloromethane	Methylene Chloride	190.09	O		
Dichloromethyl Ether	Bis Chloromethyl Ether	100.01			
Dichlorosilane	Dichlorosilane	040.270			
Dichlorvos	Dichlorvos	291.10	P		R
Dicumyl-peroxide	Dicumyl-peroxide	050.141		Yes	Rs
Didecyl Dimethyl Ammonium Chloride	Didecyl Dimethyl Ammonium Chloride	322.323		Yes	Rs
Dieldrin	Dieldrin	280.04	P		
Diesel Exhaust	Diesel Exhaust	331.01			R
Diesel Fuel	Diesel Fuel	061.060	S		
Diesel Oil	Diesel Oil	061.061	S		
Diethanolamine	Diethanolamine	231.041		Yes	Rs
Diethyl Ether	Ethyl Ether	100.05			
Diethyl Formamide	Diethyl Formamide	260.24	S		
Diethyl Silicate	Diethyl Silicate	140.02			
Diethyl Sulfate	Diethyl Sulfate	310.02			
Diethylamine	Diethylamine	230.02			
Diethylaminoethyl Acrylate	Diethylaminoethyl Acrylate	142.06			
Diethylaniline	Diethylaniline	250.18			
Diethylene Glycol	Diethylene Glycol	080.02			
Diethylenediamine	Piperazine	260.190		Yes	Rs
Diethylenetriamine	Diethylenetriamine	232.07			
Diethyltoluamide	N,N-diethyl-m-toluamide	260.26	P		
Difluoroethane	Difluoroethane	192.05			
Dihydroxyacetone	Dihydroxyacetone	130.08			
Diisocyanates, NOS	Diisocyanates, NOS	221.00		Yes	G
Dimethoate	Dimethoate	291.07	P	Yes	
Dimethyl Ethyl Benzyl Ammonium Chloride	Dimethyl Ethyl Benzyl Ammonium Chloride	322.3213		Yes	Rs

Common Name/Synonym	Primary Name	AOEC Code[1]	Use[2]	Asth-magen[3]	Asthma Detail[3]
Dimethyl Ketone	Acetone	130.01	S		
Dimethyl Methane	Propane	060.20			
Dimethyl Sulfate	Dimethyl Sulfate	310.03			
Dimethyl Sulfide	Dimethyl Sulfide	165.01			
Dimethyl Sulfoxide	Dimethyl Sulfoxide	310.14			
Dimethylacetamide	N,N-Dimethylacetamide	260.07			
Dimethylamine	Dimethylamine	230.04			
Dimethylaminoethanol	Dimethylethanolamine	231.042		Yes	Rs
Dimethylbenzene	Xylene	160.03	S		
Dimethylethanolamine	Dimethylethanolamine	231.042		Yes	Rs
Dimethylhydrazine	Dimethylhydrazine	260.09			
Dinitro-o-Cresol	Dinitro-o-Cresol	250.06			
Dinitrobenzene	Dinitrobenzene	250.05			
Dinitrobenzol	Dinitrobenzene	250.05			
Dinitrol	Dinitro-o-Cresol	250.06			
Dinitrophenol	Dinitrophenol	250.12			
Dinitrotoluene	Dinitrotoluene	250.07			
Dinitrotoluol	Dinitrotoluene	250.07			
Dioctylphthalate	Dioctylphthalate	140.03			
Dioscorea Batatas	Dioscorea Batatas	370.39		Yes	
Diospyros Crassiflora	Ebony	373.20		Yes	
Dioxane	Dioxane	100.04	S		
Dioxin	Chlorinated Dibenzodioxins	200.040			
Dipentene	Limonene	060.05	S		
Diphenylmethane Diisocyanate	Methylene Bisphenyl Diisocyanate	221.02		Yes	G
Dipropylene Glycol Methyl Ether	Dipropylene Glycol Methyl Ether	090.011	S		
Disinfectants, NOS	Disinfectants, NOS	050.28			
DMAC	N,N-Dimethylacetamide	260.07			
DMF	N,N-Dimethylformamide	260.08	S		
DMN	N-Nitrosodimethylamine	240.01			
DMNA	N-Nitrosodimethylamine	240.01			
DMS	Dimethyl sulfide	165.01			
DMSO	Dimethyl Sulfoxide	310.14			
DNOC	Dinitro-o-Cresol	250.06			
DNT	Dinitrotoluene	250.07			
Dodecanedioic Acid	Dodecanedioic Acid	270.40		Yes	Rs
Dodecyl-dimethyl-benzylammonium Chloride	Dodecyl-dimethyl-benzylammonium Chloride	322.322		Yes	Rs
Dodecylphenol	Dodecylphenol	180.08			
Drilling mud, mineral oil based	Drilling mud, mineral oil based	168.02			
Drilling Mud, NOS	Drilling Mud, NOS	168.00			
Drilling mud, oil based NOS	Drilling mud, oil based NOS	168.04			
Drilling mud, synthetic based	Drilling mud, synthetic based	168.05			
Drilling mud, vegetable oil based	Drilling mud, vegetable oil based	168.03			
Drilling mud, water based	Drilling mud, water based	168.01			
Drimaren Brilliant Blue K-BL	Drimaren Brilliant Blue K-BL	325.04		Yes	Rs
Drimaren Brilliant Yellow-K-3GL	Drimaren Brilliant Yellow K-3GL	325.02		Yes	Rs
Drimarene Brilliant Blue K-BL	Drimaren Brilliant Blue K-BL	325.04		Yes	Rs
Drimarene Brilliant Yellow K-3GL	Drimaren Brilliant Yellow K-3GL	325.02		Yes	Rs
Dry Air	Humidity, Low	350.04			
Dry Cleaning Fluid, NOS	Dry Cleaning Fluid, NOS	322.34	S		
Drywall Mud	Drywall Mud	010.23			
Dursban	Chlorpyrifos	291.05	P		R
Dust, NOS	Dust, NOS	010.00			
Dye Intermediates, NOS	Dyes, NOS	250.170			
Dyes, NOS	Dyes, NOS	250.170			
E. Kuehniella	Ephestia Kuehniella	382.25		Yes	
Eastern White Cedar	Eastern White Cedar	373.19		Yes	G
Ebony	Ebony	373.20		Yes	

Common Name/Synonym	Primary Name	AOEC Code[1]	Use[2]	Asth-magen[3]	Asthma Detail[3]
Echinodorus Larva	Fish Feed	381.09		Yes	
EDB	Ethylene Dibromide	191.01	P		
EDTA/Edetic Acid	Ethylenediamine Tetraacetic Acid	232.08			
EGBE	2-Butoxyethanol	091.03	S		R
EGEE	Ethylene Glycol Monoethyl Ether	091.02	S		
Egg Lysozyme	Egg Lysozyme	324.08		Yes	
Egg Protein	Egg Protein	380.06		Yes	G
EGME	Ethylene Glycol Monomethyl Ether	091.01	S		
Electrical Shock	Electrical Shock	353.01			
Electricity	Electrical Shock	353.01			
Electromagnetic Fields	Radiation, Electromagnetic	352.01			
Electroplating Chemicals, NOS	Electroplating Chemicals, NOS	320.07			
ELF	Radiation, Electromagnetic	352.01			
EMF	Radiation, Electromagnetic	352.01			
Enamel Thinner	Thinner	171.02	S		
Endotoxin	Endotoxin	391.13			
Endrin	Endrin	280.05	P		
Enflurane	Enflurane	190.151		Yes	Rs
Engine Exhaust	Engine Exhaust	331.02			
Environmental Tobacco Smoke	Cigarette Smoke	330.01			R
Enzymes, NOS	Enzymes, NOS	324.00			
Ephestia Kuehniella	Ephestia Kuehniella	382.25		Yes	
Epichlorohydrin	Epichlorohydrin	110.01			
Epigallocatechin gallate	Tea	370.14		Yes	Rs
EPO 60	EPO 60	232.06		Yes	Rs
Epoxies	Epoxy Resins	110.02		Yes	G
Epoxy Resin Hardeners	Epoxy Resins	110.02		Yes	G
Epoxy Resins	Epoxy Resins	110.02		Yes	G
Ergonomic Factors, NOS	Ergonomic Factors, NOS	360.00			
Esperase	Esperase	324.10		Yes	
Estrogens	Estrogens	321.02			
Ethane Trichloride	1,1,2-Trichloroethane	190.12	S		
Ethanedioic Acid	Oxalic Acid	150.03			
Ethanol	Ethanol	070.05	S		
Ethanol Ethylene Diamine	Aminoethyl Ethanolamine	231.03		Yes	Rs
Ethanolamines, NOS	Ethanolamines, NOS	231.00		Yes	Rs
Ethephon	Ethephon	291.12	P		
Ether	Ethyl Ether	100.05			
Ethidium Bromide	Ethidium Bromide	250.171			
Ethine	Acetylene	060.01			
Ethoxyethane	Ethyl Ether	100.05			
Ethyl 2-hydroxypropionate	Ethyl lactate	140.07			
Ethyl Acetate	Ethyl Acetate	141.03	S		
Ethyl Acrylate	Ethyl Acrylate	142.05			
Ethyl Alcohol	Ethanol	070.05	S		
Ethyl Benzene	Ethyl Benzene	160.07	S		
Ethyl Chloride	Chloroethane	190.02	S		
Ethyl Ether	Ethyl Ether	100.05			
Ethyl lactate	Ethyl lactate	140.07			
Ethyl Methacrylate	Ethyl Methacrylate	142.03			R
Ethyl Methyl Ether	Ethyl Methyl Ether	100.06			
Ethyl Oxide	Ethyl Ether	100.05			
Ethyl Sulfate	Diethyl Sulfate	310.02			
Ethylene Chlorohydrin	Beta-Chloroethyl Alcohol	070.03			
Ethylene Dibromide	Ethylene Dibromide	191.01	P		
Ethylene Dichloride	Ethylene Dichloride	190.07	S		
Ethylene Glycol	Ethylene Glycol	080.011			
Ethylene Glycol Ethers, NOS	Ethylene Glycol Ethers, NOS	091.00	S		

Common Name/Synonym	Primary Name	AOEC Code[1]	Use[2]	Asthmagen[3]	Asthma Detail[3]
Ethylene Glycol Monobutyl Ether	2-Butoxyethanol	091.03	S		R
Ethylene Glycol Monoethyl Ether	Ethylene Glycol Monoethyl Ether	091.02	S		
Ethylene Glycol Monomethyl Ether	Ethylene Glycol Monomethyl Ether	091.01	S		
Ethylene Oxide	Ethylene Oxide	110.03		Yes	Rr
Ethylenediamine	Ethylenediamine	232.01		Yes	Rs
Ethylenediamine Tetraacetic Acid	Ethylenediamine Tetraacetic Acid	232.08			
Ethylenimine	Ethylenimine	260.101			
Ethyne	Acetylene	060.01			
ETO	Ethylene Oxide	110.03		Yes	Rr
ETS	Cigarette Smoke	330.01			R
Eucalyptus Oil	Eucalyptus Oil	320.36			R
Eucalyptus Scent	Eucalyptus Oil	320.36			R
Eugenol	Eugenol	100.07		Yes	Rs
European Corn Borer	Ostrinia Nubilalis	382.24		Yes	
Exercise	Exercise	360.06			
Exhaust, NOS	Exhaust, NOS	331.00			
Explosion	Explosion	353.02			
Extranase	Bromelain	324.07		Yes	Rs
Extremely Low Frequency Elctromagnetic Radiation	Radiation, Electromagnetic	352.01			
Fall From Height	Fall, NOS	353.03			
Fall, NOS	Fall, NOS	353.03			
Fats	Oils, NOS	170.03			
FC 113	Trichlorotrifluoroethane	192.04			
FD&C Red No. 2	Amaranth	252.01			
Feldspar Dust	Feldspar Dust	010.131			
Fenthion	Fenthion	291.13	P	Yes	Rs
Fenugreek	Fenugreek	370.42		Yes	
Fernambouc	Fernambouc	373.16		Yes	
Ferric Chloride	Ferric Chloride	020.201			
Fertilizers, NOS	Fertilizers, NOS	320.09			
Fiberglass	Fiberglass	010.091			
Fibrous Glass	Fiberglass	010.091			
Ficam	Ficam	292.03	P		
Fingerprint Powder	Fingerprint Powder	320.34			
Fire Extinguisher Discharge	Fire Extinguisher Discharge	320.100			
Fire retardant	Halon	320.101			
Fish Feed	Fish Feed	381.09		Yes	
Fish Feed, Mosquito Larva	Fish Feed	381.09		Yes	
Fixer	Photo Developing Chemicals, NOS	320.17			
Flaviastase	Flaviastase	324.06		Yes	
Floor Finish	Floor Wax	322.35			
Floor Wax	Floor Wax	322.35			
Flour, NOS	Flour, NOS	371.00		Yes	G
Flumetsulam	N-(2,6-difluorophenyl)-5-methyl-(1,2,4) triazolo (1,5-a) pyrimidine-2-sulfonomide	320.131	P		
Fluorescent Lamp Phosphor	Fluorescent Lamp Phosphor	040.33			
Fluorine	Fluorine	030.03		Yes	
Fluorocarbons, NOS	Fluorocarbons, NOS	192.00			
Fluosilicic Acid	Hydrofluosilicic Acid	050.44			
Fluxes, NOS	Fluxes, NOS	040.05			
Fly Ash	Fly Ash	010.07			
Forceful Movements, NOS	Forceful Movements, NOS	361.01			
Formaldehyde	Formaldehyde	120.03		Yes	G
Formalin	Formaldehyde	120.03		Yes	G
Formates, NOS	Formates, NOS	140.01			
Formic Acid	Formic Acid	150.01			
Fowl Mite	Fowl Mite	382.14		Yes	
Fraxinus Americana	Ashwood	373.17		Yes	
Freesia	Freesia	370.30		Yes	

Common Name/Synonym	Primary Name	AOEC Code[1]	Use[2]	Asthmagen[3]	Asthma Detail[3]
Freon, Heated	Freon, Heated	192.06		Yes	Rs
Freon, NOS	Freon, NOS	192.01			
Freon, Unheated	Freon, Unheated	192.07			
Frog	Frog	380.09		Yes	
Fruit Fly	Fruit Fly	382.07		Yes	
Fruit Juices	Fruit Juices	370.05			
Fulvin P/G	Griseofulvin	321.27			
Fumes, NOS	Smoke, NOS	330.03			
Fungal Amylase	Fungal Amylase	324.09		Yes	Rs
Fungal Amyloglucosidase	Fungal Amyloglucosidase	324.11		Yes	
Fungal Hemicellulase	Fungal Hemicellulase	324.12		Yes	
Fungi, NOS	Mold, NOS	391.01			R
Fungicide, NOS	Fungicide, NOS	320.08	P		
Furfural	Furfural	120.04			
Furfuryl Alcohol	Furfuryl Alcohol	070.090			R
Furfuryl alcohol mixed with a catalyst	Furfuryl alcohol mixed with a catalyst	070.092		Yes	Rs
Garlic Dust	Garlic Dust	370.21		Yes	
Garlon 4	Garlon 4	260.25	P		
Gas Metal Arc Welding on Uncoated Mild Steel	Gas Metal Arc Welding on Uncoated Mild Steel	023.07		Yes	Rs
Gasoline	Gasoline	061.04	S		
Gasoline Exhaust	Engine Exhaust	331.02			
Germanium	Germanium	020.171			
Germanium Compounds	Germanium Compounds	020.170			
Glacial Acetic Acid	Glacial Acetic Acid	050.34		Yes	Rrs
Glues, NOS	Glues, NOS	320.110			
Glutaraldehyde	Glutaraldehyde	120.051		Yes	Rs
Gluten	Gluten	371.02		Yes	G
Glyceryl Trinitrate	Nitroglycerin	261.01			
Glycol Ethers, NOS	Glycol Ethers, NOS	090.00	S		
Glycol Monoethyl Ether Acetate	2-Ethoxyethyl Acetate	141.05			
Glyphosate	Glyphosate	320.132			
Gold	Gold	020.181			
Gold Compounds	Gold Compounds	020.180			
Gonystylus Bancanus	Ramin	373.14		Yes	
Grain Alcohol	Ethanol	070.05	S		
Grain Dust	Grain Dust	370.03		Yes	G
Grain Mite	Grain Mite	382.16		Yes	
Grain Parasite	Grain Mite	382.16		Yes	
Granite	Granite	011.01			
Granola, NOS	Granola, NOS	370.002			
Graphite	Graphite	010.08			
Grass Cuttings	Grass Cuttings	370.07			
Greases	Oils, NOS	170.03			
Green Beans	Green Beans	370.37		Yes	
Green Coffee Bean	Coffee Bean	370.12		Yes	G
Green Lacewing	Chrysoperla Carnea	382.22		Yes	
Grinding Dust	Abrasives, NOS	010.01			
Gripping, Forceful	Gripping, Forceful	361.03			
Gris-PEG	Griseofulvin	321.27			
Grisactin-Ultra	Griseofulvin	321.27			
Griseofulvin	Griseofulvin	321.27			
Guaiacol	Guaiacol	100.09			
Guar	Guar	372.04		Yes	
Guinea Pig Antigens	Guinea Pig Antigens	380.17		Yes	G
Gum Acacia	Gum Arabic	372.01		Yes	Rs
Gum Arabic	Gum Arabic	372.01		Yes	Rs
Gutta-percha	Gutta-percha	372.06		Yes	
Gypsophilia Paniculata	Baby's Breath	370.17		Yes	

Common Name/Synonym	Primary Name	AOEC Code[1]	Use[2]	Asth-magen[3]	Asthma Detail[3]
Gypsum	Gypsum	010.171			
Gypsum, NOS	Gypsum, NOS	010.170			
H2S	Hydrogen Sulfide	040.06			
Habanolide	Habanolide	320.43			
Hair Products	Hair Products	320.12			
Hair Solutions	Hair Products	320.12			
Hair Spray	Hair Products	320.12			
Halon	Halon	320.101			
Halothane	Halothane	190.153			R
Halowax	Chlorinated Naphthalene	200.03			
Hand-Arm Posture	Posture, Upper Extremity	362.01			
Hand-Arm Vibration	Vibration, Regional	354.01			
Handwriting	Gripping, Forceful	361.03			
Haptachlorine	Heptachlor	280.08	P		
Hard Metal	Tungsten Compounds	020.52			
Hardwood, Tropical, NOS	Hardwood, Tropical, NOS	373.24			
Hay	Hay	370.08			
HBR	Hydrobromic Acid	050.09			
HCFC-225ca	3,3-Dichloro-1,1,1,2,2-pentafluoropropane	192.021			
HCFC-225cb	1,3-Dichloro-1,1,2,2,3-pentafluoropropane	192.022			
HCL	Hydrochloric Acid	050.10		Yes	Rr
HCN	Hydrogen Cyanide	211.01			
HDI	Hexamethylene Diisocyanate	221.04		Yes	G
HDI Prepolymers	HDI Prepolymers	221.08		Yes	
Heat	Heat	350.03			
Heat Shrink Wrapping	Heat Shrink Wrapping	326.02			R
Heated Electrostatic Polyester Paint	Polyethylene Terephthalate/Polybutylene Terephthal	270.25		Yes	Rs
Heavy Lifting	Lifting	361.02			
Heavy Metals, NOS	Heavy Metals, NOS	020.46			
Henna	Henna	370.27		Yes	
Hepatitis B	Hepatitis B	390.09			
Hepatitis C	Hepatitis C	390.12			
Heptachlor	Heptachlor	280.08	P		
Heptane	Heptane	060.03	S		
Herbal Tea, NOS	Herbal Tea, NOS	370.001			R
Herbicides, NOS	Herbicides, NOS	320.13	P		
Heroin	Diacetyl morphine	321.185		Yes	Rs
Hexachlorobenzene	Hexachlorobenzene	201.03	P		
Hexachlorophene	Hexachlorophene	181.02		Yes	Rs
Hexahydrophthalic Anhydride	Hexahydrophthalic Anhydride	151.08		Yes	Rs
Hexamethylene Diisocyanate	Hexamethylene Diisocyanate	221.04		Yes	G
Hexamethylenediamine	Hexamethylenediamine	232.10			R
Hexamethylenetetramine	Hexamethylenetetramine	232.02			R
Hexane	Hexane	060.02	S		
Hexone	Methyl Isobutyl Ketone	130.04	S		
Hexylene Glycol	Hexylene Glycol	080.03			
HF	Hydrofluoric Acid	050.11			
High Force	Forceful Movements, NOS	361.01			
High Temperature	Heat	350.03			
Himic Anhydride	Himic Anhydride	151.07		Yes	Rs
Histoplasma Capsulatum	Histoplasma Capsulatum	390.03			
HIV Exposure	HIV Exposure	390.08			
Honeybee	Honeybee	382.08		Yes	
Hops	Hops	370.16		Yes	
Hot Liquid	Heat	350.03			
Hoya	Hoya	381.04			R
Humidity, High	Humidity, High	350.05			
Humidity, Low	Humidity, Low	350.04			
Hydralazine	Hydralazine	321.14		Yes	

Common Name/Synonym	Primary Name	AOEC Code[1]	Use[2]	Asth-magen[3]	Asthma Detail[3]
Hydraulics	Lubricants, NOS	320.14			
Hydrazine	Hydrazine	260.110			
Hydrazine Derivatives	Hydrazine Derivatives	260.119			
Hydrazoic Acid	Hydrazoic Acid	050.08			
Hydrobromic Acid	Hydrobromic Acid	050.09			
Hydrocarbons, NOS	Hydrocarbons, NOS	170.00			
Hydrochloric Acid	Hydrochloric Acid	050.10		Yes	Rr
Hydrocodone	Hydrocodone	321.187		Yes	Rs
Hydrofluoric Acid	Hydrofluoric Acid	050.11			
Hydrofluosilicic Acid	Hydrofluosilicic Acid	050.44			
Hydrogen Bromide	Hydrobromic Acid	050.09			
Hydrogen Chloride	Hydrochloric Acid	050.10		Yes	Rr
Hydrogen Cyanide	Hydrogen Cyanide	211.01			
Hydrogen Fluoride	Hydrofluoric Acid	050.11			
Hydrogen Peroxide	Hydrogen Peroxide	050.12			
Hydrogen Sulfate	Sulfuric Acid	050.24		Yes	Rr
Hydrogen Sulfide	Hydrogen Sulfide	040.06			
Hydroquinone	Hydroquinone	180.030			
Hydroxybenzene	Phenol	180.04			
Hypoxia	Hypoxia	353.04			
ILA Soap	Cleaners, Solvent-Based	322.06	S		
Imidacloprid	Imidacloprid	320.451	P		
Imipenem	Imipenem	321.20			
Incense Smoke	Incense Smoke	330.07			
Incinerator Fume, NOS	Incinerator Fume, NOS	330.04			
Indium	Indium	020.191			
Indium Compounds	Indium Compounds	020.190			
Indoor Air Pollutants from Building Renovation	Indoor Air Pollutants from Building Renovation	320.33			
Infectious Agents, NOS	Infectious Agents, NOS	390.070			
Inflamen	Bromelain	324.07		Yes	Rs
Infrared Light	Infrared Light	352.05			
INH	Isonicotinic Acid Hydrazide	321.13		Yes	Rs
Inks, NOS	Inks, NOS	170.02			
Inorganic Acids, NOS	Acids, Bases, Oxidizers, NOS	050.00			
Inorganic Compounds, NOS	Inorganic Compounds, NOS	040.00			
Inorganic Dust, NOS	Dust, NOS	010.00			
Insect Bite, NOS	Insect Bite, NOS	382.21			
Insect, NOS	Insect, NOS	382.00			
Insecticides, NOS	Insecticides, NOS	320.450	P		
Iodine	Iodine	030.04			
Iodophors	Iodophors	322.05			
IPDI	Isophorone Diisocyanate	221.05		Yes	Rs
Ipecac	Ipecacuanha	321.16		Yes	
Ipecacuanha	Ipecacuanha	321.16		Yes	
IR	Infrared Light	352.05			
IR Light	Infrared Light	352.05			
Irgasan	Triclosan	181.03			
Iroko	Iroko	373.05		Yes	
Iron	Iron	020.202			
Iron Compounds	Iron Compounds	020.200			
Irritant Gases, NOS	Irritant Gases, NOS	040.24			
Isoamyl Nitrite	Amyl Nitrite	260.27			
Isobutane	Isobutane	060.04			
Isocyanates, NOS	Isocyanates, NOS	220.00			
Isolyzer	Isolyzer	120.050		Yes	Rs
Isoniazid	Isonicotinic Acid Hydrazide	321.13		Yes	Rs
Isonicotinic Acid Hydrazide	Isonicotinic Acid Hydrazide	321.13		Yes	Rs
Isononanoyl Oxybenzene Sulfonate	Isononanoyl Oxybenzene Sulfonate	322.331			

Common Name/Synonym	Primary Name	AOEC Code[1]	Use[2]	Asthmagen[3]	Asthma Detail[3]
Isooctane	Isooctane	060.12			
Isophorone diamine	Isophorone diamine	232.09			R
Isophorone Diisocyanate	Isophorone Diisocyanate	221.05		Yes	Rs
Isophthalic Acid Chloride	Isophthaloyl Chloride	200.05			
Isophthaloyl Chloride	Isophthaloyl Chloride	200.05			
Isopropanol	Isopropyl Alcohol	070.06	S		
Isopropyl Alcohol	Isopropyl Alcohol	070.06	S		
Isopropylamine	Isopropylamine	230.03			
Jalapeno Pepper	Jalapeno Pepper	370.46			
Jet Exhaust	Jet Exhaust	331.03			
Jet Fuel	Jet Fuel	061.05	S		
Job Control	Stress	360.04			
Job Demand	Stress	360.04			
Joint replacement, elevated chromium	Joint replacement, elevated chromium	020.601			
Joint replacement, elevated cobalt	Joint replacement, elevated cobalt	020.602			
Joint replacement, toxicity NOS	Joint replacement, toxicity NOS	020.600			
Juglans Olanchana	Central American Walnut	373.11		Yes	
Kanechlor	Polychlorinated Biphenyls	200.07			
Kaolin	Clay	010.051			
Kapok	Kapok	370.43		Yes	
Karaya	Karaya	372.03		Yes	
Kejaat	Kejaat	373.12		Yes	
Kerosene	Kerosene	061.031	S		
Kerosine	Kerosene	061.031	S		
Ketones, NOS	Ketones, NOS	130.00	S		
Kevlar	Poly (P-Phenylenediamine)	270.35			
Key Punching	Keyboard Use	360.02			
Keyboard and Mouse Use	Keyboard Use	360.02			
Keyboard Use	Keyboard Use	360.02			
Kneeling	Posture, Body - Static	362.02			
KOH	Potassium Hydroxide	050.17			
Kotibe	Kotibe	373.21		Yes	
L. Caesar Larva	L. Caesar Larva	382.19		Yes	
L. Decemlineata	Leptinotarsa Decemlineata	382.23		Yes	
Laboratory Animals, NOS (see specific animals)	Animal Material, NOS	380.00			R
Lacquer	Lacquer	171.07			
Lacquer Thinner	Thinner	171.02	S		
Lactase	Lactase	324.14			
lactic acid, ethyl ester	Ethyl lactate	140.07			
Lactoserum	Lactoserum	380.10		Yes	
Lanasol Blue 3G	Lanasol Blue 3G	325.29			R
Lanasol Blue 3R	Lanasol Blue 3G	325.29			R
Lanasol Brown G	Lanasol Brown G	325.30			R
Lanasol Orange G	Lanasol Orange G	325.33			R
Lanasol Orange R	Lanasol Orange R	325.16			R
Lanasol Red 2G	Lanasol Red 2G	325.31			R
Lanasol Red 5B	Lanasol Red 5B	325.14			R
Lanasol Red B	Lanasol Red B	325.13			R
Lanasol Red G	Lanasol Red G	325.15			R
Lanasol Scarlet 2R	Lanasol Scarlet 2R	325.32			R
Lanasol Yellow 4G	Lanasol Yellow 4G	325.09		Yes	Rs
Laser cutting, stainless	Laser cutting, stainless	023.011			
Lasers	Lasers	352.02			
Latex Gloves, NOS	Latex, Natural Rubber	270.02		Yes	G
Latex, Natural Rubber	Latex, Natural Rubber	270.02		Yes	G
Latex, Synthetic	Latex, Synthetic	270.030			
Lathyrus Sativus	Lathyrus Sativus	370.29		Yes	
Lauryl Dimethyl Benzyl Ammonium Chloride	Dodecyl-dimethyl-benzylammonium Chloride	322.322		Yes	Rs

Common Name/Synonym	Primary Name	AOEC Code[1]	Use[2]	Asthmagen[3]	Asthma Detail[3]
Leachate	Leachate	323.02			
Lead, Inorganic Compounds	Lead, Inorganic Compounds	020.210			
Lead, Metal	Lead, Metal	020.211			
Lead, Organic	Lead, Organic	020.221			
Lead, Organic Compounds	Lead, Organic Compounds	020.220			
Lead-based Paint	Lead-based Paint	020.212			
Leather Dust	Leather Dust	380.03			
Leptinotarsa Decemlineata	Leptinotarsa Decemlineata	382.23		Yes	
Lesser Mealworm	Lesser Mealworm	382.09		Yes	
Levafix Black 5-GA	Levafix Black 5-GA	325.18			R
Levafix Black EB	Remazol Black B	325.11			R
Levafix Black EG	Levafix Black EG	325.17			R
Levafix Brilliant Blue K-BL	Drimaren Brilliant Blue K-BL	325.04		Yes	Rs
Levafix Brilliant Yellow E36	Levafix Brilliant Yellow E36	325.01		Yes	Rs
Levafix Golden Yellow E-3GA	Levafix Goldgelb E-3GA	325.20			R
Levafix Goldgelb E-3GA	Levafix Goldgelb E-3GA	325.20			R
Levafix Marinblau E-2BA	Levafix Marinblau E-2BA	325.19			R
Levafix Orange	Levafix Orange	325.12		Yes	Rs
Lifting	Lifting	361.02			
Lightning Powder	Fingerprint Powder	320.34			
Lime	Calcium Oxide	050.05			
Lime Chloride	Calcium Hypochlorite	322.13			
Limonene	Limonene	060.05	S		
Limonium Tataricum	Limonium Tataricum	370.38		Yes	
Lindane	Lindane	280.00	P		
Linseed Oil	Linseed Oil	060.15			
Linseed Oilcake	Linseed Oilcake	060.24		Yes	Rs
Local Vibration	Vibration, Regional	354.01			
Locust	Locust	382.02		Yes	
Low Temperature	Cold	350.02			
LPG	Propane	060.20			
Lubricants, NOS	Lubricants, NOS	320.14			
Lycopodium	Lycopodium	070.25		Yes	
Lye	Sodium Hydroxide	050.18			
m-Delphene	N,N-diethyl-m-toluamide	260.26	P		
Mace	Mace	320.27			
Magenta	Magenta	251.07			
Magnesium	Magnesium	020.231			
Magnesium Aluminum Silicate	Magnesium Aluminum Silicate	020.232			
Magnesium Compounds	Magnesium Compounds	020.230			
Mahogany	Mahogany	373.07		Yes	
Malathion	Malathion	291.01	P	Yes	
Maleic Anhydride	Maleic Anhydride	151.02		Yes	Rs
Malt	Malt	370.56		Yes	Rs
Man-Made Mineral Fibers	Man-Made Mineral Fibers	010.092			
Man-Made Mineral Fibers, NOS	Man-Made Mineral Fibers, NOS	010.090			
Manganese	Manganese	020.241			
Manganese Compounds	Manganese Compounds	020.240			
Manure	Manure	380.02			
MAP	Ammonium Phosphate	040.32	P		
Marijuana Smoke	Marijuana Smoke	330.05			
Marinblau E-2BA	Levafix Marinblau E-2BA	325.19			R
MBK	Methyl N-Butyl Ketone	130.05	S		
MDA	Methylenedianiline	250.16			
MDI	Methylene Bisphenyl Diisocyanate	221.02		Yes	G
ME-MDA	4,4'-Methylenebis(2-Chloroaniline)	250.03			
Mechanical Pressure	Contact Pressure	360.01			
MEK	Methyl Ethyl Ketone	130.03	S		
MEK Peroxide	MEK Peroxide	130.02			

Common Name/Synonym	Primary Name	AOEC Code[1]	Use[2]	Asthmagen[3]	Asthma Detail[3]
Melamine	Melamine	260.28			
Menta Arvensis Piperadcens	Corn Mint Oil	320.47			R
Mental Factors	Stress	360.04			
Menthol	Menthol	370.61			R
Mercaptans, NOS	Mercaptans, NOS	311.00			
Mercaptoethanol	Mercaptoethanol	310.04			
Mercaptopropionic Acid	3-mercaptopropionic Acid	310.12			
Mercuric Chloride	Mercuric Chloride	020.251			
Mercuric Salts	Mercuric Salts	020.252			
Mercury, Inorganic Compounds	Mercury, Inorganic Compounds	020.250			
Mercury, Organic	Mercury, Organic	020.261			
Mercury, Organic Compounds	Mercury, Organic Compounds	020.260			
Metal Carbonyls	Metal Carbonyls	020.44			
Metal Dust, NOS	Metal Dust, NOS	021.00			
Metal Fumes, NOS	Metal Fumes, NOS	020.00			
Metal Polish, Tarnish Remover, or Preventative	Metal Polish, Tarnish Remover, or Preventative	322.02			
Metal Working Fluids	Cutting Oils	170.01		Yes	G
Metallic Oxides, NOS	Metal Fumes, NOS	020.00			
Metals, NOS	Metals, NOS	020.47			
Metam Sodium	Sodium N-methyldithiocarbamate	292.01	P		
Methamphetamine Laboratory	Methamphetamine Laboratory	320.40			
Methane	Methane	060.06			
Methanol	Methanol	070.07	S		
Methaoxyethanol	Ethylene Glycol Monomethyl Ether	091.01	S		
Methoxychlor	Methoxychlor	280.07	P		
Methoxyflurane	Methoxyflurane	190.152			R
Methoxymethane	Ethyl Methyl Ether	100.06			
Methyl 2-Hydroxybenzoate Acrylate Acid	Methyl Salicylate	140.05			R
Methyl Alcohol	Methanol	070.07	S		
Methyl Blue	Methyl Blue	325.10		Yes	
Methyl Bromide	Methyl Bromide	191.03	P		
Methyl Carbinol	Ethanol	070.05	S		
Methyl Cellosolve	Ethylene Glycol Monomethyl Ether	091.01	S		
Methyl Chloroform	Methyl Chloroform	190.08	S		
Methyl Dichlorosilane	Methyl Dichlorosilane	040.271			
Methyl Ester Isocyanic Acid	Methyl Isocyanate	220.01			
Methyl Ethyl Ketone	Methyl Ethyl Ketone	130.03	S		
Methyl Ethyl Ketone Peroxide	MEK Peroxide	130.02			
Methyl Isobutyl Ketone	Methyl Isobutyl Ketone	130.04	S		
Methyl Isocyanate	Methyl Isocyanate	220.01			
Methyl Isothiocyanate	Methyl Isothiocyanate	220.02	P		
Methyl Mercury due to Fish Consumption	Methyl Mercury, Organic	020.262			
Methyl Mercury, Organic	Methyl Mercury, Organic	020.262			
Methyl Methacrylate	Methyl Methacrylate	142.04		Yes	Rs
Methyl N-Butyl Ketone	Methyl N-Butyl Ketone	130.05	S		
Methyl Pyrrolidone	Methyl Pyrrolidone	260.121			
Methyl Salicylate	Methyl Salicylate	140.05			R
Methyl Sulfoxide	Dimethyl Sulfoxide	310.14			
Methyl Tertiary Butyl Ether	Methyl Tertiary Butyl Ether	100.08			
Methyl Tetrahydrophthalic Anhydride	Methyl Tetrahydrophthalic Anhydride	151.05		Yes	Rs
Methyl-4-Isopropenyl Cyclohexene-1	Limonene	060.05	S		
Methylbenzene	Toluene	160.02	S		
Methylcatechol	Guaiacol	100.09			
Methyldopa	Methyldopa	321.09		Yes	
Methylene Bisphenyl Diisocyanate	Methylene Bisphenyl Diisocyanate	221.02		Yes	G
Methylene Chloride	Methylene Chloride	190.09	S		
Methylene Dichloride	Methylene Chloride	190.09	S		
Methylenedianiline	Methylenedianiline	250.16			

Common Name/Synonym	Primary Name	AOEC Code[1]	Use[2]	Asth-magen[3]	Asthma Detail[3]
Methylphenol	Cresol	180.02			
Methylstyrene	Vinyl Toluene	160.08	S		
Methylthiomethane	Dimethyl sulfide	165.01			
Methylvinylbenzene	Vinyl Toluene	160.08	S		
Mexican Bean Weevil	Mexican Bean Weevil	382.06		Yes	
MGK 264	N-Octyl Bicycloheptene Dicarboximide	320.30	P		
MIBK	Methyl Isobutyl Ketone	130.04	S		
MIC	Methyl Isocyanate	220.01			
Mice	Mice	380.14		Yes	G
Micotil	Micotil	321.30			
Microberlinia	African Zebrawood	373.13		Yes	
Microorganisms, NOS	Microorganisms, NOS	390.00			
Mineral Naphtha	Benzene	160.01	S		
Mineral Oil	Mineral Oil	060.07			
Mineral Oil Mist	Mineral Oil	060.07			
Mineral Spirits	Petroleum Spirits	061.011	S		
Mineral Thinner	Naptha	061.012	S		
Mineral Turpentine	Naptha	061.012	S		
Mineral Wool	Rockwool	010.093			
MINT X Rodent repellant trash bags	MINT X Rodent repellant trash bags	320.50			R
Mites, NOS	Mites, NOS	382.13		Yes	G
Mixed DCB	Mixed DCB	201.011	P		
MMMF	Man-Made Mineral Fibers	010.092			
MMMF, NOS	Man-made Mineral Fibers, NOS	010.090			
MOCA	4,4'-Methylenebis(2-Chloroaniline)	250.03			
Moisture	Humidity, High	350.05			
Mold, NOS	Mold, NOS	391.01			R
Molybdenum	Molybdenum	020.271			
Molybdenum Compounds	Molybdenum Compounds	020.270			
Monoammonium Phosphate	Ammonium Phosphate	040.32	P		
Monobromomethane	Methyl Bromide	191.03	P		
Monochloroethane	Chloroethane	190.02	S		
Monochloroethylene	Vinyl Chloride Monomer	190.14			
Monoethanolamine	Monoethanolamine	231.01		Yes	Rs
Morphine	Morphine	321.181		Yes	Rs
Mosquito Bite	Insect Bite, NOS	382.21			
Motor Oil, Synthetic	Motor Oil, Synthetic	170.05			
Motor Vehicle Accident	Motor Vehicle Accident	353.05			
MTBE	Methyl Tertiary Butyl Ether	100.08			
Multiple Chemicals	Chemicals, NOS	320.06			
Multiple Solvents	Solvents, NOS	171.00	S		
Muriatic Acid	Hydrochloric Acid	050.10		Yes	Rr
Mushrooms, NOS	Mushrooms, NOS	391.10			R
Mustard Gas	Mustard Gas	190.16			
Mustargen	Mustargen HCL	321.28			
Mustargen HCL	Mustargen HCL	321.28			
Mycotoxins	Mycotoxins	391.090			
Mylar	Polyethylene Terephthalate	270.26			
Myrocarpus Fastigiatus Fr. All.	Cabreuva	373.23		Yes	
N,N-diethyl-3-methyl-	N,N-diethyl-m-toluamide	260.26	P		
N,N-diethyl-m-toluamide	N,N-diethyl-m-toluamide	260.26	P		
N,N-Diethylethanamine	Triethylamine	230.05			
N,N-Dimethylacetamide	N,N-Dimethylacetamide	260.07			
N,N-Dimethylethanolamine	Dimethylethanolamine	231.042		Yes	Rs
N,N-Dimethylformamide	N,N-Dimethylformamide	260.08	S		
N,N-Dimethylnitrosamine	N-Nitrosodimethylamine	240.01			
N-(2,6-difluorophenyl)-5-methyl-(1,2,4) triazolo (1,5-a) pyrimidine-2-sulfonomide	N-(2,6-difluorophenyl)-5-methyl-(1,2,4) triazolo (1,5-a) pyrimidine-2-sulfonomide	320.131	P		

Common Name/Synonym	Primary Name	AOEC Code[1]	Use[2]	Asthmagen[3]	Asthma Detail[3]
N-Amyl Acetate	Amyl Acetate	141.01			
N-Amyl Alcohol	Amyl Alcohol	070.02			
N-Butyl Acetate	Butyl Acetate	141.02	S		
N-Butyl Acrylate	Butyl Acrylate	142.02			R
N-Butyl Alcohol	N-Butyl Alcohol	070.04	S		
N-Butyl Mercaptan	N-Butyl Mercaptan	311.01			
N-Butylamine	N-Butylamine	230.01			
N-Chloropropane	Chloropropane	190.05	S		
N-Heptane	Heptane	060.03	S		
N-Hexane	Hexane	060.02	S		
N-Hexyl Acrylate	N-Hexyl Acrylate	142.12			
N-Methylmorpholine	N-Methylmorpholine	260.20			R
N-Nitrosodimethylamine	N-Nitrosodimethylamine	240.01			
N-Octyl Bicycloheptene Dicarboximide	N-Octyl Bicycloheptene Dicarboximide	320.30	P		
N-Pentane	Pentane	060.19	S		
N-Pentyl Acetate	Amyl Acetate	141.01			
N2O	Nitrous Oxide	040.09			
NaClO	Sodium Hypochlorite	322.10		Yes	Rs
Nacre Dust	Nacre Dust	370.22		Yes	
Nail Care Products	Nail Care Products	320.41			
NaOH	Sodium Hydroxide	050.18			
Naphtha	Naphtha	061.02	S		
Naphthalene	Naphthalene	160.05			
Naphthalene Diisocyanate	Naphthalene Diisocyanate	221.03		Yes	G
Naphthalin	Naphthalene	160.05			
Naptha	Naptha	061.012	S		
Natural Gas	Natural Gas	060.080			
Navy Blue HER	Navy Blue HER	325.21			R
NCR Paper	Carbonless Paper	320.05			
NDI	Naphthalene Diisocyanate	221.03		Yes	G
Nemacur	Nemacur	291.06	P	Yes	
Neoprene	Neoprene	271.020			
Neosar	Cyclophosphamide	321.29			
Nerve Gas	Nerve Gas	291.04			
Nesorgordonia Papaverifera	Kotibe	373.21		Yes	
Neurospora	Neurospora	390.11		Yes	Rs
New Carpet Odor	4-Phenylcyclohexene	060.11			
New Mexico Range Moth Caterpillar	New Mexico Range Moth Caterpillar	382.20		Yes	
Nickel	Nickel	020.281		Yes	Rs
Nickel Compounds	Nickel Compounds	020.280		Yes	Rs
Nicotine Sulfate	Nicotine Sulfate	260.13	P		
Ninhydrin	Ninhydrin	320.25			
Nitramine	Tetryl	250.10			
Nitric Acid	Nitric Acid	050.13			
Nitric Oxide	Nitric Oxide	040.081			
Nitrobenzene	Nitrobenzene	250.04			
Nitrobenzol	Nitrobenzene	250.04			
Nitroethane	Nitroethane	260.142			
Nitrogen	Nitrogen	040.07			
Nitrogen chloride	Trichloramine	030.11		Yes	Rs
Nitrogen Dioxide	Nitrogen Dioxide	040.082			
Nitrogen Mustard Hydrochloride	Mustargen HCL	321.28			
Nitrogen Mustard, NOS	Nitrogen Mustard, NOS	050.061			
Nitrogen Oxide	Nitric Oxide	040.081			
Nitrogen Oxides, NOS	Nitrogen Oxides, NOS	040.080			
Nitroglycerin	Nitroglycerin	261.01			
Nitromethane	Nitromethane	260.143			
Nitroparaffins	Nitroparaffins	260.140			
Nitrophenol	Nitrophenol	250.11			

Common Name/Synonym	Primary Name	AOEC Code[1]	Use[2]	Asthmagen[3]	Asthma Detail[3]
Nitrous Oxide	Nitrous Oxide	040.09			
NO	Nitric Oxide	040.081			
No. 1 Fuel Oil	Kerosene	061.031	S		
No. 2 Fuel Oil	No. 2 Fuel Oil	061.062	S		
NO2	Nitrogen Dioxide	040.082			
Noise	Noise	350.01			
Nonoxynol	Nonoxynol	320.461			
Nuclear Reactor Release	Nuclear Reactor Release	351.02			
Nylon	Nylon	270.17			
Nylon Flock	Nylon Flock	010.22			R
o-methoxyphenol	Guaiacol	100.09			
O. Nubilalis	Ostrinia Nubilalis	382.24		Yes	
Oak	Oak	373.06		Yes	
Octacide 264	N-Octyl Bicycloheptene Dicarboximide	320.30	P		
Octopus	Octopus	381.12		Yes	Rs
Odors	Odors	320.15			
Oil Mist	Cutting Oils	170.01		Yes	G
Oil of Clove	Oil of Clove	160.06			
Oil of Mirbane	Nitrobenzene	250.04			
Oil of Wintergreen	Methyl Salicylate	140.05			R
Oil Orange SS	Oil Orange SS	252.02			
Oils, NOS	Oils, NOS	170.03			
Oils, Vegetable	Oils, Vegetable	370.34			
Omite	Propargite	310.060	P		
Omite Cr	Omite Cr	310.061	P		
OPA	Ortho-phthalaldehyde	120.10			R
Opiate Compounds	Opiate Compounds	321.180		Yes	Rs
Optigard	Optigard	142.13			
Orange 3R	Rifazol Brilliant Orange 3R	325.07		Yes	Rs
Orange HE 2G	Rifacion Orange HE 2G	325.05		Yes	Rs
Organic Chemicals, NOS	Hydrocarbons, NOS	170.00			
Organic Dusts, NOS	Organic Dusts, NOS	370.003			
Organic Phosphates, Nonpesticide	Organic Phosphates, Nonpesticide	300.00			
Organochlorine Insecticides, NOS	Organochlorine Pesticides, NOS	280.00	P		
Organochlorine Pesticides, NOS	Organochlorine Pesticides, NOS	280.00	P		
Organophosphate Pesticides, NOS	Organophosphate Pesticides, NOS	291.00	P		R
Orthene	Acephate	291.11	P	Yes	
Ortho-phthalaldehyde	Ortho-phthalaldehyde	120.10			R
Orthophenylphenol	Orthophenylphenol	180.07	P		R
Osmium	Osmium	020.291			
Osmium Compounds	Osmium Compounds	020.290			
Ostrinia Nubilalis	Ostrinia Nubilalis	382.24		Yes	
Oxacyclohexedecen-2-one	Habanolide	320.43			
Oxalic Acid	Oxalic Acid	150.03			
Oxycodone	Oxycodone	321.186		Yes	Rs
Oxygen Deficiency	Hypoxia	353.04			
Oxygen Propane Torch	Oxygen Propane Torch	023.012			
Oxygen, Liquid	Oxygen, Liquid	040.10			
Ozone	Ozone	040.11			
P-Dichlorobenzene	Dichlorobenzene	201.010	P		
P-Dihydroxybenzene	Hydroquinone	180.030			
P-Hydroxyphenol	Hydroquinone	180.030			
P-Mentha-1,8-Diene	Limonene	060.05	S		
PAH	Polycyclic Aromatic Hydrocarbons, NOS	161.00			
Paint Thinner	Thinner	171.02	S		
Paint, Acrylic	Acrylics	270.01			
Paint, Epoxy	Paint, Epoxy	110.05			
Paint, Latex	Paint, Latex	171.05			

Common Name/Synonym	Primary Name	AOEC Code[1]	Use[2]	Asthmagen[3]	Asthma Detail[3]
Paint, NOS	Paint, NOS	171.01	S		
Paint, Oil-Based	Paint, Oil-Based	171.06			
Pancreatin	Pancreatin	324.05		Yes	
PAP	Para-Aminophenol	251.01			
Papain	Papain	324.03		Yes	G
Papaverine	Papaverine	321.184		Yes	Rs
Paper Dust	Paper Dust	370.010			
Paprika	Paprika	370.31		Yes	
Para-Aminophenol	Para-Aminophenol	251.01			
Paraffin	Paraffin	060.09			
Paraffin Oil	Mineral Oil	060.07			
Paraffin Wax	Paraffin	060.09			
Paraformaldehyde	Paraformaldehyde	120.06		Yes	G
Paraldehyde	Paraldehyde	120.07			
Paraquat	Paraquat	260.15	P		
Parasites, NOS	Parasites, NOS	382.17			
Parathion	Parathion	291.02	P		R
Pau Marfim	Pau Marfim	373.18		Yes	
PCBs	Polychlorinated Biphenyls	200.07			
PCP	Pentachlorophenol	181.01			
PE, NOS	Polyethylene, NOS	270.06			
Pectin	Pectin	370.23		Yes	
Penicillamine	Penicillamine	321.05		Yes	
Penicillins	Penicillins	321.042		Yes	G
Penicillium	Penicillium	391.03		Yes	Rs
Pentachloronitrobenzene	Pentachloronitrobenzene	200.06	P		
Pentachlorophenol	Pentachlorophenol	181.01			
Pentaerythritol Tetrakis	3-mercaptopropionate	310.13			
Pentaerythritol Tetranitrate	Pentaerythritol Tetranitrate	261.02			
Pentamidine	Pentamidine	321.23			
Pentane	Pentane	060.19	S		
Pepper Spray	Capsicum	370.35			
Peppermint (mentha piperita)	Menthol	370.61			R
Pepsin	Pepsin	324.04		Yes	G
Perc	Perchlorethylene	190.10	S		
Perchlorethylene	Perchlorethylene	190.10	S		
Perchlorobenzene Fungicide	Hexachlorobenzene	201.03	P		
Perchloroethylene	Perchlorethylene	190.10	S		
Perfume, NOS	Perfume, NOS	320.23			
Perlite	Perlite	010.15			
Peroxidase Catalyst	Peroxidase Catalyst	324.13			
Peroxide 2-Butanone	MEK Peroxide	130.02			
Peroxides	Peroxides	050.140			
Peroxyacetic Acid	Peroxyacetic Acid	050.42		Yes	Rs
Persulfate Salts	Persulfate Salts	040.26		Yes	G
Pesticides, NOS	Pesticides, NOS	320.16	P		
PETN	Pentaerythritol Tetranitrate	261.02			
Petrochemicals, NOS	Hydrocarbons, NOS	170.00			
Petrol	Gasoline	061.04	S		
Petrolatum Liquid	Mineral Oil	060.07			
Petroleum Distillates, NOS	Petroleum Fractions, NOS	061.00	S		
Petroleum Fractions, NOS	Petroleum Fractions, NOS	061.00	S		
Petroleum Naphtha	Naphtha	061.02	S		
Petroleum Spirits	Petroleum Spirits	061.011	S		
PFA	Polyfunctional aziridine	260.102		Yes	Rs
Pharmaceuticals, NOS	Pharmaceuticals, NOS	321.00			
Phenol	Phenol	180.04			
Phenol Formaldehyde	Phenol Formaldehyde	120.11			

Common Name/Synonym	Primary Name	AOEC Code[1]	Use[2]	Asthmagen[3]	Asthma Detail[3]
Phenolic Resins	Phenolics	270.04			
Phenolics	Phenolics	270.04			
Phenols, NOS	Phenols, NOS	180.00			
Phenyl Chloride	Chlorobenzene	201.04	S		
Phenylamine	Aniline	250.01			
Phenylene Diamine	Benzenediamine	251.060			R
Phenylglycine Acid Chloride	Phenylglycine Acid Chloride	321.07		Yes	
Phenylmethane	Toluene	160.02	S		
Phosgene	Phosgene	040.12			
Phosphate Ester, NOS	Phosphate Ester, NOS	140.06			
Phosphine	Phosphine	040.13	P		
Phosphoric Acid	Phosphoric Acid	050.15			
Phosphorus Bromide	Phosphorus Bromide	050.32			
Phosphorus Pentasulfide	Phosphorus Pentasulfide	040.14			
Phosphorus Sulfide	Phosphorus Pentasulfide	040.14			
Phosphorus Tribromide	Phosphorus Bromide	050.32			
Phosphorus Trichloride	Phosphorus Trichloride	050.16			
Phostoxin	Aluminum Phosphide	040.31	P		
Photo Developer, Black & White	Photo Developer, Black & White	180.031			
Photo Developer, Color	Photo Developing Chemicals, NOS	320.17			
Photo Developing Chemicals, NOS	Photo Developing Chemicals, NOS	320.17			
Phthalate Ester	Phthalate Ester	140.04			
Phthalic Acid Anhydride	Phthalic Anhydride	151.01		Yes	Rs
Phthalic Aldehyde	Ortho-phthalaldehyde	120.10			R
Phthalic Anhydride	Phthalic Anhydride	151.01		Yes	Rs
Phthaloyl Chloride	Isophthaloyl Chloride	200.05			
Physical Factors, NOS	Physical Factors, NOS	350.00			
Pickle Processing (Unknown Causal Agent)	Pickle Processing (Unknown Causal Agent)	326.01			
Picric Acid	Picric Acid	250.09			
Pig	Pig	380.08		Yes	
Pigeon Droppings	Pigeon Droppings	380.21			
Pinching	Gripping, Forceful	361.03			
Pine Wood Dust	Pine Wood Dust	373.25			
Pinellia Ternata	Pinellia Ternata	370.40		Yes	
Piperazine	Piperazine	260.100		Yes	Rs
Piperazine Citrate	Piperazine Citrate	260.192		Yes	Rs
Piperazine Hydrochloride	Piperazine Hydrochloride	260.191		Yes	Rs
Piperonyl Butoxide	Piperonyl Butoxide	290.01	P		
Plant Material, NOS	Plant Material, NOS	370.004			
Plant Waste	Grass Cuttings	370.07			
Plasmopara	Plasmopara	391.05			
Plasmopara Viticola	Plasmopara	391.05			
Plaster	Plaster	010.10			
Plaster of Paris	Plaster of Paris	010.172			
Plastic Dust	Plastic Dust	010.143			
Plastic Smoke	Plastic Smoke	330.02			
Plasticizers	Plasticizers	270.13			
Plastics, NOS	Polymers, NOS	270.00			
Plastics, Pre-Polymer	Polymers, NOS	270.00			
Platinum	Platinum	020.301			
Platinum Compounds	Platinum Compounds	020.300			
Plexiglass Dust	Plexiglass Dust	270.18		Yes	
Plutonium	Plutonium	351.01			
PMMA	Polymethyl Methacrylate	142.11		Yes	Rs
PNA	Polycyclic Aromatic Hydrocarbons, NOS	161.00			
Poison Ivy	Poisonous Plants	370.06			
Poison Oak	Poisonous Plants	370.06			
Poison Sumac	Poisonous Plants	370.06			
Poisonous Plants	Poisonous Plants	370.06			

Common Name/Synonym	Primary Name	AOEC Code[1]	Use[2]	Asthmagen[3]	Asthma Detail[3]
Pollen	Pollen	370.10			
Pollution from Acts of Terrorism/War	World Trade Center Pollution	320.39			
Poly (P-Phenylenediamine)	Poly (P-Phenylenediamine)	270.35			
Polyamide Fibers	Nylon Flock	010.22			R
Polyamine EPO 60	EPO 60	232.06		Yes	Rs
Polyamines, NOS	Polyamines, NOS	232.00			
Polycarbamate	Polycarbamate	270.071			
Polychlorinated Biphenyls	Polychlorinated Biphenyls	200.07			
Polychlorobutadiene	Polychlorobutadiene	271.021			
Polychloroprene	Neoprene	271.020			
Polycyclic Aromatic Hydrocarbons, NOS	Polycyclic Aromatic Hydrocarbons, NOS	161.00			
Polydimethyl Siloxane	Polydimethyl Siloxane	270.031			
Polyester Resin	Polyester Resin	270.05			
Polyethylamine	Polyethylamine	230.07			
Polyethylene Glycol Stearates	Polyethylene Glycol Stearates	320.192			
Polyethylene Terephthalate	Polyethylene Terephthalate	270.26			
Polyethylene Terephthalate/Polybutylene Terephthal	Polyethylene Terephthalate/Polybutylene Terephthal	270.25		Yes	Rs
Polyethylene, Heated	Polyethylene, Heated	270.31			R
Polyethylene, NOS	Polyethylene, NOS	270.06			
Polyethylene, Unheated	Polyethylene, Unheated	270.32			
Polyfunctional aziridine	Polyfunctional aziridine	260.102		Yes	Rs
Polyhexamethylene Biguanide	Polyhexamethylene Biguanide	260.29	P		
Polyimides	Polyimides	270.19			
Polymer Fume	Plastic Smoke	330.02			
Polymers, NOS	Polymers, NOS	270.00			
Polymethyl Methacrylate	Polymethyl Methacrylate	142.11		Yes	Rs
Polymethylene Polyphenylisocyanate	Polymethylene Polyphenylisocyanate	221.06		Yes	
Polynuclear Aromatics	Polycyclic Aromatic Hydrocarbons, NOS	161.00			
Polypropylene, Heated	Polypropylene, Heated	270.33		Yes	Rs
Polypropylene, NOS	Polypropylene, NOS	270.24			
Polypropylene, Unheated	Polypropylene, Unheated	270.34			
Polystyrene	Polystyrene	270.20			
Polysulphide Polymer Adhesive	Polysulphide Polymer Adhesive	320.111			
Polytetrafluoroethylene	Polytetrafluoroethylene	270.12			
Polytetrafluoroethylene, Thermal Decomposition Products	Polytetrafluoroethylene, Thermal Decomposition Products	270.37			
Polyurethane	Polyurethane	270.079			
Polyurethane Coating	Polyurethane Coating	270.073			
Polyvinyl Alcohol	Polyvinyl Alcohol	270.08			
Polyvinyl Butyral Resins	Polyvinylbutyral	270.28			
Polyvinyl Chloride (heated)	Polyvinyl Chloride (heated)	270.091		Yes	Rs
Polyvinyl Chloride (Non-heated)	Polyvinyl Chloride (Non-heated)	270.092		Yes	Rs
Polyvinyl Chloride Dust	Polyvinyl Chloride Dust	010.141			
Polyvinyl Chloride, Thermal Decomposition Products	Polyvinyl Chloride, Thermal Decomposition Products	270.38		Yes	Rs
Polyvinyl Pyrrolidone	Polyvinyl Pyrrolidone	270.14			
Polyvinylbutyral	Polyvinylbutyral	270.28			
Poppers	Amyl Nitrite	260.27			
Porcelain	Porcelain	010.11			
Portland Cement	Cement Dust	010.03			R
Posture, Body - Dynamic	Posture, Body - Dynamic	362.03			
Posture, Body - Static	Posture, Body - Static	362.02			
Posture, NOS	Posture, NOS	362.00			
Posture, Upper Extremity	Posture, Upper Extremity	362.01			
Potassium Bicarbonate	Potassium Bicarbonate	050.19			
Potassium Carbonate	Potassium Carbonate	050.41			
Potassium Chlorate	Potassium Chlorate	040.16			
Potassium Cyanide	Potassium Cyanide	211.02			
Potassium Dichromate	Potassium Dichromate	022.01			
Potassium Hydroxide	Potassium Hydroxide	050.17			

Common Name/Synonym	Primary Name	AOEC Code[1]	Use[2]	Asthmagen[3]	Asthma Detail[3]
Potassium Nitrate	Potassium Nitrate	042.01			
Potassium Permanganate	Potassium Permanganate	050.39			
Potassium Salts, NOS	Potassium Salts, NOS	040.15			
Pouteria	Abiruana	373.08		Yes	
PPI	Polymethylene Polyphenylisocyanate	221.06		Yes	
Prawn	Prawn	381.03		Yes	G
Printing Chemicals, NOS	Printing Chemicals, NOS	320.29			
Producer Gas Residue	Polycyclic Aromatic Hydrocarbons, NOS	161.00			
Prolonged Position	Posture, Body - Static	362.02			
Propane	Propane	060.20			
Propane Exhaust	Propane Exhaust	331.04			
Propanol	Isopropyl Alcohol	070.06	S		
Propargite	Propargite	310.060			
Propenamide	Acrylamide	260.02			
Propenenitrile	Acrylonitrile	210.02			
Propetamphos	Safrotin	291.08	P	Yes	
Propionic Acid	Propionic Acid	310.15			
Propoxur	Propoxur	292.04	P		
Propyl Alcohol	Propyl Alcohol	070.08	S		
Propyl Hydride	Propane	060.20			
Propylene Dichloride	Propylene Dichloride	190.11	S		
Propylene Glycol Ethers	Propylene Glycol Ethers	000.012	S		
Propylene Oxide	Propylene Oxide	110.07			
Protease	Protease	324.011			
Proteolytic Enzymes, NOS	Enzymes, NOS	324.00			
Protozoa Giardia	Protozoa Giardia	390.13			
Proventil	Proventil	321.31			
Psychological Factors	Stress	360.04			
Psyllium	Psyllium	321.08		Yes	
Pteridine	Pteridine	250.20			
Pterocarpus Angolensis	Kejaat	373.12		Yes	
PTFE	Polytetrafluoroethylene	270.12			
Pulling	Forceful Movements, NOS	361.01			
Pulp Mill Effluent	Pulp Mill Effluent	070.006			
Pushing	Forceful Movements, NOS	361.01			
PVA	Polyvinyl Alcohol	270.08			
PVC (heated)	Polyvinyl Chloride (heated)	270.091		Yes	Rs
PVC (Non-heated)	Polyvinyl Chloride (Non-heated)	270.092		Yes	Rs
PVC Dust	Polyvinyl Chloride Dust	010.141			
Pyrethrins	Pyrethrins	320.181	P	Yes	Rs
Pyrethroids	Pyrethroids	320.182	P		R
Pyrfon	Pyrfon	291.09	P	Yes	
Pyridine	Pyridine	250.14			
Pyrogallic Acid	1,2,3-Trihydroxybenzene	180.06			
Pyrogallol	1,2,3-Trihydroxybenzene	180.06			
Pyromellitic Acid Dianhydride	Pyromellitic Dianhydride	151.04		Yes	Rs
Pyromellitic Dianhydride	Pyromellitic Dianhydride	151.04		Yes	Rs
Quartz Dust	Quartz Dust	010.132			
Quaternary Ammonium Compounds, NOS	Quaternary Ammonium Compounds, NOS	322.320		Yes	Rs
Quercus Rubra	Oak	373.06		Yes	
Quicklime	Calcium Oxide	050.05			
Quillaja Bark	Quillaja Bark	373.15		Yes	Rs
Quinone	Quinone	180.05			
Rabbit Antigens	Rabbit Antigens	380.15		Yes	
Radiation, Electromagnetic	Radiation, Electromagnetic	352.01			
Radiation, Ionizing, NOS	Radiation, Ionizing, NOS	351.00			
Radiation, Microwave	Radiation, Microwave	352.03			
Radiation, Nonionizing, NOS	Radiation, Nonionizing, NOS	352.00			

Common Name/Synonym	Primary Name	AOEC Code[1]	Use[2]	Asthmagen[3]	Asthma Detail[3]
Radiation, Ultraviolet	Radiation, Ultraviolet	352.04			
Radio Frequency Radiation	Radiation, Microwave	352.03			
Radiographic Fixative	Radiographic Fixative	320.32		Yes	
Radioisotopes	Therapeutic Radiation	351.04			
Radon	Radon	351.03			
Ramin	Ramin	373.14		Yes	
Raspberries	Fruit Juices	370.05			
Rat Antigens	Rat Antigens	380.18		Yes	G
Rat Feces	Rat Feces	380.20			
Reactice Red 78	Lanasol Scarlet 2R	325.32			R
Reactive Blue 114	Drimaren Brilliant Blue K-BL	325.04		Yes	Rs
Reactive Blue 171	Navy Blue HER	325.21			R
Reactive Blue 50	Lanasol Blue 3G	325.29			R
Reactive Brown 47	Lanasol Brown G	325.30			R
Reactive Dyes, NOS	Reactive Dyes, NOS	325.00			R
Reactive Orange 29	Lanasol Orange G	325.33			R
Reactive Orange 67	Levafix Goldgelb E-3GA	325.20			R
Reactive Orange 68	Lanasol Orange R	325.16			R
Reactive Orange 82	Remazol Brilliant Orange FR	325.26			R
Reactive Red 116	Lanasol Red 2G	325.31			R
Reactive Red 65	Lanasol Red B	325.13			R
Reactive Red 66	Lanasol Red 5B	325.14			R
Reactive Red 83	Lanasol Red G	325.15			R
Reactive Yellow 107	Remazol Gold Yellow RNL	325.25			R
Red BBN	Red BBN	325.22		Yes	Rs
Red HE 3B	Red HE 3B	325.23			R
Red Soft Coral	Red Soft Coral	381.05		Yes	
Refined Petroleum Solvent	Refined Petroleum Solvent	061.013	S		
Refractory Ceramic Fiber	Refractory Ceramic Fiber	010.094			
Remazol Black B	Remazol Black B	325.11			R
Remazol Black GF	Remazol Black B	325.11			R
Remazol Black GR	Rifazol Black GR	325.08		Yes	Rs
Remazol Brilliant Orange 3R	Rifazol Brilliant Orange 3R	325.07		Yes	Rs
Remazol Brilliant Orange FR	Remazol Brilliant Orange FR	325.26			R
Remazol Brilliant Yellow 4GL	Remazol Brilliant Yellow 4GL	325.27			R
Remazol Gold Yellow RNL	Remazol Gold Yellow RNL	325.25			R
Remazol Marine Blue GG	Remazol Marine Blue GG	325.24			R
Remazol Navy Blue GG	Remazol Marine Blue GG	325.24			R
Repetitive Lifting	Lifting	361.02			
Repetitive Motion	Repetitive Motion	360.03			
Repetitive Trauma	Repetitive Motion	360.03			
Resin containing furfuryl alcohol	Resin containing furfuryl alcohol	070.091		Yes	Rs
Resin Systems, NOS	Resin Systems, NOS	270.150			
Resins, NOS	Resins, NOS	270.151			
Rhodium	Rhodium	020.53		Yes	Rs
Ribaviran	Ribaviran	321.32			
Rice Dust	Rice Dust	370.48		Yes	Rs
Rice Flour	Rice Flour	371.07			
Rifacion Orange HE 2G	Rifacion Orange HE 2G	325.05		Yes	Rs
Rifafix Yellow 3 RN	Rifafix Yellow 3 RN	325.06		Yes	Rs
Rifazol Black GR	Rifazol Black GR	325.08		Yes	Rs
Rifazol Brilliant Orange 3R	Rifazol Brilliant Orange 3R	325.07		Yes	Rs
Road Pitch	Asphalt	061.07			
Road Tar	Asphalt	061.07			
Rock, NOS	Rock, NOS	011.00			
Rockwool	Rockwool	010.093			
Roofing Tar	Asphalt	061.07			
Rose Hips	Rose Hips	370.19		Yes	
Rotating Shifts	Stress	360.04			

Common Name/Synonym	Primary Name	AOEC Code[1]	Use[2]	Asth-magen[3]	Asthma Detail[3]
Round Up	Glyphosate	320.132			
Rubber Dust	Rubber Dust	010.142			
Rubber, NOS	Rubber, NOS	271.00			
Rust Inhibitor	Rust Inhibitor	060.22			
Rye Dust	Rye Dust	370.49			
Rye Flour	Rye Flour	371.03		Yes	G
Saccharin	Saccharin	320.38			R
Safrotin	Safrotin	291.08	P	Yes	
Salbutamol Intermediate	Salbutamol Intermediate	321.21		Yes	
Salicylate	Salicylic Acid	321.25			
Salicylic Acid	Salicylic Acid	321.25			
Salmo salar	Salmon	381.13		Yes	Rs
Salmon	Salmon	381.13		Yes	Rs
SBR	Butadiene & Styrene	271.01			
Scopthalmus maximus	Turbot	381.14		Yes	Rs
Screw Worm Fly	Screw Worm Fly	382.03		Yes	
Sec-Propyl Alcohol	Isopropyl Alcohol	070.06	S		
Selenium	Selenium	020.311			
Selenium Compounds	Selenium Compounds	020.310			
Senna	Senna	321.19			
Sequoia Sempervirens	California Redwood	373.02		Yes	
Sericin	Sericin	370.26		Yes	
Sesame Seed Dust	Sesame Seed Dust	370.45			
Sevin	Carbaryl	292.02	P		
Sewage	Sewer Water	323.03			
Sewer Gas	Sewer Gas	040.061			
Sewer Water	Sewer Water	323.03			
Shale	Shale	061.08			
Shark Cartilage	Shark Cartilage	381.11			R
Sharps	HIV Exposure	390.08			
Sheep Blowfly	Sheep Blowfly	382.12		Yes	
Shellfish	Shellfish	381.01			
Shrimp	Shrimp Meal	381.07		Yes	
Shrimp Meal	Shrimp Meal	381.07		Yes	
Sick Building	Air Pollutants, Indoor	320.01			
Silage Microorganisms, NOS	Silage Microorganisms, NOS	391.11			
Silica Flour	Quartz Dust	010.132			
Silica Sand	Silica, Cystalline	010.133			
Silica, Amorphous	Silica, Amorphous	010.12			
Silica, Crystalline	Silica, Crystalline	010.133			
Silica, Crystalline, NOS	Silica, Crystalline, NOS	010.130			
Silica, Vitreous	Silica, Vitreous	010.135			
Silicon Carbide	Silicon Carbide	010.18			
Silicon Dioxide	Silica, Crystalline	010.133			
Silicone	Silicone	270.10			
Silicone Fluid	Silicone	270.10			
Silicone Rubber	Silicone	270.10			
Silkworm	Silkworm	382.01		Yes	
Silkworm Larva	Silkworm	382.01		Yes	
Siloxanes	Silicone	270.10			
Silver	Silver	020.321			
Silver Compounds	Silver Compounds	020.320			
Silver Sulfate	Silver Sulfate	020.322			
Sitting	Posture, Body - Static	362.02			
Skin Contact	Contact Pressure	360.01			
Slime Mold	Slime Mold	391.06			
Slime Mold Dictyostelium Discoideum	Slime Mold	391.06			
Slip, Trip, or Fall on Same Level	Fall, NOS	353.03			

Common Name/Synonym	Primary Name	AOEC Code[1]	Use[2]	Asth-magen[3]	Asthma Detail[3]
Smoke Inhalation	Smoke, NOS	330.03			
Smoke, Lead-Containing	Smoke, Lead-Containing	330.06			
Smoke, NOS	Smoke, NOS	330.03			
Snake Bite	Venom	380.05			
Snappers	Amyl Nitrite	260.27			
SO2	Sulfur Dioxide	040.201			
Soap, excluding Laundry Soap/Detergent	Soap, excluding Laundry Soap/Detergent	322.01			
Soapbark	Quillaja Bark	373.15		Yes	Rs
Soda Ash	Soda Ash	050.211			
Sodium Azide	Sodium Azide	211.04			
Sodium Benzoate	Sodium Benzoate	050.31			
Sodium Bisulfate	Sodium Bisulfate	050.40			
Sodium Bisulfite	Sodium Bisulfite	040.18			
Sodium Borohydride	Sodium Borohydride	040.29			
Sodium Carbonate	Sodium Carbonate	050.210			
Sodium Carboxymethyl Cellulose	Sodium Carboxymethyl Cellulose	270.11			
Sodium Chloride	Sodium Chloride	041.02			
Sodium Chlorite	Sodium Chlorite	030.08			
Sodium Cyanide	Sodium Cyanide	211.03			
Sodium Dichromate	Sodium Dichromate	022.03			
Sodium Hydroxide	Sodium Hydroxide	050.18			
Sodium Hypochlorite	Sodium Hypochlorite	322.10		Yes	Rs
Sodium Metabisulfite	Sodium Metabisulfite	040.28		Yes	Rs
Sodium Metasilicate	Sodium Metasilicate	050.22			
Sodium N-methyldithiocarbamate	Sodium N-methyldithiocarbamate	292.01	P		
Sodium Nitrate	Sodium Nitrate	042.02			
Sodium Oxide	Sodium Oxide	050.45			
Sodium Salts, NOS	Sodium Salts, NOS	040.17			
Sodium Silicate	Sodium Silicate	050.23			
Sodium Sulfide	Sodium Sulfide	040.19			
Sodium Sulfite	Sodium Bisulfite	040.18			
Sodium Tripolyphosphate	Sodium Tripolyphosphate	050.38			
Soldering flux (heated) Alkyl Aryl Polyether Alcohol/Polypropylene Glycol Mixt.	Soldering flux (heated) Alkyl Aryl Polyether Alcohol/Polypropylene Glycol	070.10		Yes	Rs
Soldering Flux (heated) Zinc Chloride/Ammonium Chloride	Soldering Flux (heated) Zinc Chloride/Ammonium Chloride	023.08		Yes	Rs
Soldering Flux, NOS	Soldering Flux, NOS	023.04			
Soldering, NOS	Soldering, NOS	023.10			
Soluble Halogenated Platinum Compounds, NOS	Soluble Halogenated Platinum Compounds, NOS	024.00		Yes	G
Solvent Naphtha	Naptha	061.012	S		
Solvents, NOS	Solvents, NOS	171.00	S		
Sour gas	Sour gas	060.081			
Soya Flour	Soya Flour	371.05		Yes	G
Soybean Lecithin	Soybean Lecithin	370.41		Yes	
Soybean Lectin	Soybean Lecithin	370.41		Yes	
Spider Bite	Insect Bite, NOS	382.21			
Spiramycin	Spiramycin	321.10		Yes	
Spirits of Turpentine	Turpentine	060.10	S	Yes	Rs
Stachybotrys	Stachybotrys	391.07			
Standing	Posture, Body - Static	362.02			
Staph Aureus	Staph Aureus	390.071			
Steam	Heat	350.03			
Stearic Acid	Stearic Acid	150.05			
Stibine	Antimony Hydride	020.04			
Stick Welding	Stick Welding	023.09			
Stoddard Solvent	Stoddard Solvent	061.014	S		
Stooping	Posture, Body - Dynamic	362.03			
Stress	Stress	360.04			
Stripper	Stripper	171.03	S		
Strontium	Strontium	020.501			

Common Name/Synonym	Primary Name	AOEC Code[1]	Use[2]	Asth-magen[3]	Asthma Detail[3]
Strontium Compounds	Strontium Compounds	020.500			
Struck Against/Struck By Objects or Persons	Struck Against/Struck By Objects or Persons	353.09			
Struck by Falling Object	Struck by Falling Object	353.08			
Struck by Motor Vehicle (Road)	Struck by Motor Vehicle (Road)	353.06			
Struck by Vehicle or Equipment (Non-road)	Struck by Vehicle or Equipment (Non-road)	353.07			
Struck By/Against Object as Result of Fall	Fall, NOS	353.03			
Strychnine	Strychnine	260.16	P		
Styrene	Styrene	160.04	S	Yes	Rs
Styrene Monomer	Styrene	160.04	S	Yes	Rs
Styrene-Butadiene Copolymer	Butadiene & Styrene	271.01			
Styrene-Maleic Anhydride Polymer	Styrene-Maleic Anhydride Resin	270.23			
Styrene-Maleic Anhydride Resin	Styrene-Maleic Anhydride Resin	270.23			
Subtilisin	Bacillus Subtilis Enzymes	324.010		Yes	Rs
Suffocation	Hypoxia	353.04			
Sulfites, NOS	Sulfites, NOS	310.10			
Sulfonates, NOS	Sulfonates, NOS	322.330			
Sulfur Chloride	Sulfur Chloride	040.22			
Sulfur Dioxide	Sulfur Dioxide	040.201			
Sulfur Gas	Sulfur Gas	040.21			
Sulfur Hydrocarbons, NOS	Sulfur Hydrocarbons, NOS	165.00			
Sulfur Monochloride	Sulfur Chloride	040.22			
Sulfur Oxides, NOS	Sulfur Oxides, NOS	040.200			
Sulfur, Elemental	Sulfur, Elemental	010.21			
Sulfuric Acid	Sulfuric Acid	050.24		Yes	Rr
Sulfuric Acid Diethyl Ester	Diethyl Sulfate	310.02			
Sulfuric Acid Dimethyl Ester	Dimethyl Sulfate	310.03			
Sunflower	Sunflower	370.20		Yes	
Surfactant-Specific amines	Surfactant-Specific amines	320.191		Yes	Rs
Surfactants, NOS	Surfactants, NOS	320.190			
Talc	Talc	012.00			
Talc, Fibrous	Talc, Fibrous	012.01			
Talc, Nonasbestiform	Talc, Nonasbestiform	012.02			
Tall Oil, Crude	Tall Oil, Crude	110.041		Yes	Rs
Tall Oil, Fatty Acids	Tall Oil, Fatty Acids	110.043			R
Tall Oil, Rosin	Tall Oil, Rosin	110.042		Yes	Rs
Tanganyika Aningre	Tanganyika Aningre	373.10		Yes	
Tannic Acid	Tannic Acid	150.06			
Tar Camphor	Naphthalene	160.05			
Tartaric Acid	Tartaric Acid	150.07			
TDI	Toluene Diisocyanate	221.01		Yes	G
TDI Prepolymers	TDI Prepolymers	221.07		Yes	
Tea	Tea	370.14		Yes	Rs
Tear Gas	Mace	320.27			
Teflon	Polytetrafluoroethylene	270.12			
Teflon, Thermal Decomposition Products	Polytetrafluoroethylene, Thermal Decomposition Products	270.37			
Tellurium	Tellurium	020.331			
Tellurium Compounds	Tellurium Compounds	020.330			
Terpene	Terpene	060.17	S		R
Terra Cotta	Terra Cotta	010.052			
Tetrachloro-Isophthalonitrile	Chlorothalonil	210.03	P	Yes	Rs
Tetrachloroethylene	Perchlorethylene	190.10	S		
Tetrachloromethane	Carbon Tetrachloride	190.01	S		
Tetrachlorophthalic Anhydride	Tetrachlorophthalic Anhydride	151.06		Yes	Rs
Tetracycline	Tetracycline	321.12		Yes	
Tetraethyl Lead	Tetraethyl Lead	020.222			
Tetrahydrofuran	Tetrahydrofuran	060.16			
Tetramethrin	Tetramethrin	320.183	P	Yes	Rs
Tetrazene	Tetrazene	260.22		Yes	Rs

Common Name/Synonym	Primary Name	AOEC Code[1]	Use[2]	Asth-magen[3]	Asthma Detail[3]
Tetryl	Tetryl	250.10			
Textile Dust, NOS	Textile Dust, NOS	320.22			
Thallium Compounds	Thallium Salts	040.23	P		
Thallium Salts	Thallium Salts	040.23	P		
Thapsia Garganica L	Thapsigargin	370.33			
Thapsigargin	Thapsigargin	370.33			
Theatrical Fog, Glycol-Based	Theatrical Fog, Glycol-Based	320.21			
Theatrical Fog, NOS	Theatrical Fog, NOS	320.20			
Thebaine	Thebaine	321.183		Yes	Rs
Theophylline	Theophylline	321.24			
Therapeutic Radiation	Therapeutic Radiation	351.04			
Thermal cutting of stainless steel	Thermal cutting of stainless steel	023.011			
Thermal Energy	Heat	350.03			
Thermophilic Actinomyces	Thermophilic Actinomyces	390.05			
Thiamine	Thiamine	370.60		Yes	Rs
Thinner	Thinner	171.02	S		
Thioglycol	Mercaptoethanol	310.04			
Thiophosphoric Anhydride	Phosphorus Pentasulfide	040.14			
Thiourea	Thiourea	310.070			
Thiram	Thiuram	310.08			
Thiuram	Thiuram	310.08			
Thorium	Thorium	020.341			
Thorium Compounds	Thorium Compounds	020.340			
THU	Thiourea	310.070			
Thuja Occidentalis	Eastern White Cedar	373.19		Yes	G
Thuja Plicata	Western Red Cedar	373.01		Yes	G
Thyme	Thyme	370.007		Yes	Rs
Thymol	Thymol	370.005			R
Thymus Vulgaris	Thyme	370.007		Yes	Rs
Tilmicosin Phosphate	Micotil	321.30			
Tin, Inorganic	Tin, Inorganic	020.351			
Tin, Inorganic Compounds	Tin, Inorganic Compounds	020.350			
Tin, Organic	Tin, Organic	020.361			R
Tin, Organic Compounds	Tin, Organic Compounds	020.360			R
Titanium	Titanium	020.481			
Titanium Compounds	Titanium Compounds	020.480			
TMA	Trimellitic Anhydride	151.03		Yes	Rs
TMPTA	Trimethylolpropane Triacrylate	142.08			
TNT	Trinitrotoluene	250.08			
Tobacco Leaf	Tobacco Leaf	370.15		Yes	G
Toluene	Toluene	160.02	S		
Toluene Diisocyanate	Toluene Diisocyanate	221.01		Yes	G
Toluene-2,4-Diisocyanate	Toluene Diisocyanate	221.01		Yes	G
Toluol	Toluene	160.02	S		
Tomato	Tomato	370.55			R
Toner, Copier	Toner, Copier	010.040			
Tooth Enamel Dust	Tooth Enamel Dust	010.19			R
Tosyalate dihydrate	Tosyalate dihydrate	321.069			R
Tragacanth	Tragacanth	372.02		Yes	
Transmission Fluid	Lubricants, NOS	320.14			
Trauma, Acute, NOS	Trauma, Acute, NOS	353.00			
Traumanase	Bromelain	324.07		Yes	Rs
Trental	Trental	321.22			
Triazines, NOS	Triazines, NOS	260.17	P		
Tributyl Tin Oxide	Tributyl Tin Oxide	020.363	P	Yes	Rs
Trichloramine	Trichloramine	030.11		Yes	Rs
Trichloroacetic Acid	Trichloroacetic Acid	050.43			
Trichloroethylene	Trichloroethylene	190.13	S		

Common Name/Synonym	Primary Name	AOEC Code[1]	Use[2]	Asth-magen[3]	Asthma Detail[3]
Trichloromethane	Chloroform	190.03			
Trichloronitromethane	Chloropicrin	260.06	P		
Trichlorotrifluoroethane	Trichlorotrifluoroethane	192.04			
Trichoderma	Trichoderma	391.08			
Trichoderma Koningii	Trichoderma	391.08			
Triclosan	Triclosan	181.03			
Tricresyl phosphate	Tricresyl phosphate	291.14			
Triethanolamine	Triethanolamine	231.02		Yes	Rs
Triethylamine	Triethylamine	230.05			
Triethylenetetramine	Triethylenetetramine	232.03		Yes	Rs
Trifluoroacetic Acid	Trifluoroacetic Acid	050.37			
Trifluorotrichloroethane	Trichlorotrifluoroethane	192.04			
Triglycidyl Isocyanurate	Triglycidyl Isocyanurate	270.41		Yes	Rs
Trimellitic Anhydride	Trimellitic Anhydride	151.03		Yes	Rs
Trimethylhexane-1,6-diamine/Isophorondiamine Mixture	Trimethylhexane-1,6-diamine/Isophorondiamine Mixture	232.04		Yes	Rs
Trimethylhexanediamine/Isophorondiamine Mixture	Trimethylhexane-1,6-diamine/Isophorondiamine Mixture	232.04		Yes	Rs
Trimethylolpropane Triacrylate	Trimethylolpropane Triacrylate	142.08			
Trimethylolpropane Triacrylate/2-Hydroxypropyl Acrylate	Trimethylolpropane Triacrylate/2-Hydroxypropyl Acrylate	142.10		Yes	Rs
Trinitroglycerin	Nitroglycerin	261.01			
Trinitrotoluene	Trinitrotoluene	250.08			
Trinitrotoluol	Trinitrotoluene	250.08			
Triplochiton Scleroxylon	African Maple	373.09		Yes	
Tris	Tris	300.01			
Tris 2,3-Dibromopropyl Phosphate	Tris	300.01			
Trisodium Phosphate	Trisodium Phosphate	050.20			
Trout	Trout	381.08		Yes	Rs
Trypsin	Trypsin	324.02		Yes	
Tuberculosis	Tuberculosis	390.10			
Tungsten Carbide	Tungsten Carbide	020.37		Yes	Rs
Tungsten Carbide/Cobalt	Tungsten Carbide/Cobalt	020.451		Yes	Rs
Tungsten Compounds	Tungsten Compounds	020.52			
Turbot	Turbot	381.14		Yes	Rs
Turpentine	Turpentine	060.10	S	Yes	Rs
Twisting	Posture, Body - Dynamic	362.03			
Tylosin Tartrate	Tylosin Tartrate	321.15		Yes	
Typewriter	Keyboard Use	360.02			
Typing	Keyboard Use	360.02			
Ultrasound	Ultrasound	350.06			
Unspecified Solvents	Solvents, NOS	171.00	S		
Upper Extremity Awkward Positions	Posture, Upper Extremity	362.01			
Uranium	Uranium	351.05			
Urea Formaldehyde	Urea Formaldehyde	270.16		Yes	
Urea Formaldehyde Resin	Urea Formaldehyde	270.16		Yes	
Urethane	Urethane	270.070			
Urethane Enamel Paint	Urethane Enamel Paint	270.072			
UV Light	Radiation, Ultraviolet	352.04			
UV Radiation	Radiation, Ultraviolet	352.04			
Vanadium	Vanadium	020.381			
Vanadium Compounds	Vanadium Compounds	020.380			
Vanadium Hydroxide Oxide Phosphate	Vanadium Hydroxide Oxide Phosphate	040.30			
Vancomycin	Vancomycin	321.33		Yes	Rs
Vapam	Sodium N-methyldithiocarbamate	292.01	P		
Varethane Paint	Polyurethane Coating	270.073			
Varnish	Lacquer	171.07			
Varnish Makers' & Painters' Naphtha	Naptha	061.012	S		
Varsol	Naptha	061.012	S		
VDT Keyboard	Keyboard Use	360.02			
VDT Radiation	Radiation, Electromagnetic	352.01			
VDT Screen/Visual	VDT Screen/Visual	360.05			

Common Name/Synonym	Primary Name	AOEC Code[1]	Use[2]	Asth-magen[3]	Asthma Detail[3]
VDT Typing	Keyboard Use	360.02			
Vegetable Dust	Vegetable Dust	370.04			
Vegetable Juices	Fruit Juices	370.05			
Venom	Venom	380.05			
Ventilation, Inadequate	Air Pollutants, Indoor	320.01			
Vermiculite	Vermiculite	010.20			
Vetch	Vicia Sativa	370.11		Yes	
Vibration, NOS	Vibration, NOS	354.00			
Vibration, Regional	Vibration, Regional	354.01			
Vibration, Whole Body	Vibration, Whole Body	354.02			
Vicia Sativa	Vicia Sativa	370.11		Yes	
Vinegar	Vinegar	050.46			R
Vinyl Acetate	Vinyl Acetate	141.04			
Vinyl Carbinol	Allyl Alcohol	070.01			
Vinyl Chloride Monomer	Vinyl Chloride Monomer	190.14			
Vinyl Cyanide	Acrylonitrile	210.02			
Vinyl Dust	Polyvinyl Chloride Dust	010.141			
Vinyl Fumes	Plastic Smoke	330.02			
Vinyl Monomer	Vinyl Chloride Monomer	190.14			
Vinyl Plastic Wrap	Vinyl Plastic Wrap	270.27			
Vinyl Toluene	Vinyl Toluene	160.08	S		
Vinyl Trichloride	1,1,2-Trichloroethane	190.12	S		
Vinyl, NOS	Vinyl, NOS	010.140			
Vinylbenzene	Styrene	160.04	S	Yes	Rs
Violence, Other than Physical Assault	Violence, Other than Physical Assault	353.13			
Violence, Physical Assault	Assault, Physical	353.12			
Virazole	Ribaviran	321.32			
Viruses	Infectious Agents, NOS	390.070			
VM & P Naphtha	Naptha	061.012	S		
VOC, NOS	Hydrocarbons, NOS	170.00			
Walking	Walking	360.08			
Waste, Hazardous	Waste, Hazardous	323.01			
Waste, Hazardous Acid	Waste, Hazardous	323.01			
Waste, NOS	Waste, NOS	323.00			
Waste, Treated Human Sludge	Waste, Treated Human Sludge	323.04			
Water Chlorination Byproducts	Water Chlorination Byproducts	327.01			
Water Contamination, Inorganic	Water Contamination, Inorganic	327.02			
Water Contamination, NOS	Water Contamination, NOS	327.00			
Water Contamination, Organic	Water Contamination, Organic	327.03			
Waxes, NOS	Waxes, NOS	170.06			
Weeping Fig	Weeping Fig	370.24		Yes	
Welding Freon	Freon, Heated	192.06		Yes	Rs
Welding Fume, Copper/Nickel	Welding Fume, Copper/Nickel	023.03			
Welding Fume, Galvanized Metal	Welding Fume, Galvanized Metal	023.06			
Welding Fume, Iron or Steel	Welding Fume, Iron or Steel	023.02			
Welding Fume, NOS	Welding Fume, NOS	023.000			
Welding Fume, Stainless Steel	Welding Fume, Stainless Steel	023.010		Yes	G
Welding, NOS	Welding, NOS	023.001			
Western Red Cedar	Western Red Cedar	373.01		Yes	G
Wet Weather	Humidity, High	350.05			
Wheat Dust	Wheat Dust	370.50			
Wheat Flour	Wheat Flour	371.04		Yes	G
White Oil	Mineral Oil	060.07			
White Spirits	Petroleum Spirits	061.011	S		
White Tar	Naphthalene	160.05			
Wood Alcohol	Methanol	070.07	S		
Wood Ash	Ash, NOS	010.16			
Wood Bark, NOS	Wood Dust, NOS	373.00			

Common Name/Synonym	Primary Name	AOEC Code[1]	Use[2]	Asth-magen[3]	Asthma Detail[3]
Wood Dust, NOS	Wood Dust, NOS	373.00			
Wood Spirits	Methanol	070.07	S		
Wool Dust	Wool Dust	370.44			
Word Processing	Keyboard Use	360.02			
World Trade Center Dust	World Trade Center Pollution	320.39			
World Trade Center Pollution	World Trade Center Pollution	320.39			
X-Ray Developer	X-Ray Developer	180.032			
Xrays	Therapeutic Radiation	351.04			
Xylene	Xylene	160.03	S		
Xylol	Xylene	160.03	S		
Yeast	Yeast	370.28			
Yellow 3 RN	Rifafix Yellow 3 RN	325.06		Yes	Rs
Yellow 3R	Yellow 3R	325.28			R
Yellow 4GL	Remazol Brilliant Yellow 4GL	325.27			R
Yellow GR	Yellow 3R	325.28			R
Zeolite	Zeolite	324.15			
Zinc	Zinc	020.391			R
Zinc Chloride	Zinc Chloride	020.40			
Zinc Compounds	Zinc Compounds	020.390			R
Zinc Oxide	Zinc Oxide	020.393		Yes	Rs
Zirconium	Zirconium	020.411			
Zirconium Compounds	Zirconium Compounds	020.410			

Note: *(1) Association of Occupational & Environmental Clinics code; (2) S=Solvent, P=Pesticide; (3) A supplemental designation for asthmagens (indicated by an "A") is included on the list. Formal criteria for the asthmagen designation were first established for sensitizer-induced asthma in 2002, and for irritant-induced asthma (Reactive Airways Dysfunction Syndrome (RADS) in 2008. These criteria were developed in collaboration with experts in occupational and pulmonary medicine. An * in the asthmagen designation field means that specific substances within this generic category meet the AOEC criteria for an asthmagen. There are many other specific substances within this category that have not been studied as to whether or not they cause asthma. Clinicians evaluating patients with exposure to other substances in this category should have a high level of suspicion that specific substances within this category that have not been studied may also cause asthma. Exposures designated with an "A" for asthmagen are further classified by which criteria they meet. Exposures reviewed and meeting criteria for sensitizer-induced asthma are designated "Rs"; those reviewed and meeting criteria for RADS are designated "Rr"; those reviewed and not meeting either set of criteria are designated "R". Should any exposures be reviewed and determined to meet both criteria they will be designated "Rrs". Substances that are generally accepted as asthmagens are designated "G".*

The Association of Occupational and Environmental Clinics (AOEC) Exposure Code List was first developed in 1994, for use by AOEC members in order to help systematically identify both existing and emerging occupational and environmental health concerns. The AOEC Exposure Code List includes a wide range of exposures including not only chemicals but exposures to metals, dusts, plants, animals etc. as well as physical hazards e.g. falls, lifting, repetitive strains, etc. Neither the AOEC exposure code list nor the asthmagen designations are considered an official document of any governmental agency.

Source: *Association of Occupational & Environmental Clinics, August 30, 2013*

Serum Cotinine

Metabolite of nicotine (component of tobacco smoke)

Geometric mean and selected percentiles of serum concentrations (in ng/mL) for the ***non-smoking U.S. population from the National Health and Nutrition Examination Survey.

	Survey years	Geometric mean (95% conf. interval)	Selected percentiles (95% confidence interval) 50th	75th	90th	95th	Sample size
Total	99-00	*	.060 (<LOD-.080)	.240 (.190-.302)	1.02 (.770-1.28)	1.96 (1.60-2.62)	5999
	01-02**	.062 (.050-.077)	< LOD	.160 (.120-.220)	.930 (.740-1.17)	2.20 (1.83-2.44)	6819
	03-04	.071 (.057-.089)	.050 (.040-.070)	.210 (.140-.310)	.990 (.740-1.30)	2.17 (1.81-2.54)	6320
	05-06	.054 (.047-.061)	.040 (.030-.040)	.120 (.100-.150)	.630 (.460-.870)	1.47 (1.15-1.92)	6347
	07-08	.057 (.048-.068)	.040 (.030-.040)	.130 (.100-.180)	.760 (.550-1.09)	1.81 (1.45-2.43)	6197
	09-10	.041 (.037-.046)	.030 (.020-.030)	.070 (.070-.090)	.450 (.350-.580)	1.29 (1.04-1.61)	6678
Age group							
3-11 years	99-00	.164 (.115-.234)	.110 (.066-.188)	.500 (.260-1.16)	1.88 (.997-3.44)	3.44 (1.42-4.79)	1174
	01-02**	.110 (.076-.160)	.070 (<LOD-.130)	.570 (.310-1.00)	2.23 (1.63-2.78)	3.23 (2.53-4.01)	1415
	03-04	.137 (.088-.213)	.120 (.060-.220)	.620 (.310-1.20)	2.04 (1.38-2.94)	3.35 (2.12-4.68)	1252
	05-06	.078 (.062-.097)	.050 (.040-.070)	.220 (.160-.350)	1.22 (.880-1.82)	2.42 (1.63-3.46)	1296
	07-08	.095 (.067-.136)	.060 (.040-.100)	.380 (.170-.840)	1.67 (1.10-2.54)	2.81 (2.26-3.54)	1337
	09-10	.060 (.047-.075)	.040 (.030-.050)	.160 (.110-.250)	.920 (.560-1.58)	2.15 (1.35-3.00)	1355
12-19 years	99-00	.163 (.142-.187)	.110 (.080-.163)	.540 (.428-.660)	1.66 (1.50-1.95)	2.62 (2.09-3.39)	1773
	01-02**	.086 (.059-.126)	.050 (<LOD-.110)	.350 (.190-.580)	1.53 (1.09-2.12)	3.12 (2.47-3.99)	1902
	03-04	.110 (.087-.139)	.080 (.060-.120)	.510 (.350-.670)	1.55 (1.21-1.93)	2.68 (1.96-4.02)	1783
	05-06	.074 (.060-.092)	.050 (.040-.060)	.230 (.150-.350)	1.16 (.860-1.69)	2.26 (1.69-2.72)	1714
	07-08	.081 (.061-.106)	.050 (.030-.070)	.350 (.170-.550)	1.25 (.930-1.99)	2.54 (2.04-2.94)	934
	09-10	.056 (.044-.072)	.030 (.020-.040)	.130 (.080-.230)	.980 (.510-1.80)	2.49 (1.31-3.65)	1042
20 years and older	99-00	*	.050 (<LOD-.061)	.167 (.140-.193)	.630 (.533-.820)	1.50 (1.28-1.66)	3052
	01-02**	.052 (<LOD-.063)	< LOD	.110 (.090-.150)	.630 (.470-.790)	1.42 (1.14-1.89)	3502
	03-04	.058 (.047-.071)	.040 (.030-.050)	.140 (.100-.200)	.630 (.480-.840)	1.54 (1.26-1.92)	3285
	05-06	.047 (.042-.053)	.030 (.030-.040)	.100 (.080-.120)	.440 (.310-.620)	1.14 (.870-1.41)	3337
	07-08	.049 (.043-.057)	.030 (.030-.040)	.100 (.080-.120)	.490 (.390-.640)	1.37 (.970-1.70)	3926
	09-10	.037 (.034-.040)	.020 (.020-.030)	.070 (.060-.070)	.310 (.240-.390)	.990 (.700-1.24)	4281
Gender							
Males	99-00	.124 (.106-.145)	.080 (.060-.110)	.308 (.220-.410)	1.20 (.950-1.49)	2.39 (1.66-3.22)	2789
	01-02**	.075 (.059-.094)	.050 (<LOD-.070)	.230 (.160-.320)	1.17 (.960-1.49)	2.44 (2.23-2.99)	3152
	03-04	.087 (.070-.108)	.060 (.040-.080)	.280 (.190-.360)	1.23 (.910-1.68)	2.63 (2.09-3.19)	2937
	05-06	.064 (.055-.074)	.040 (.040-.050)	.150 (.120-.190)	.720 (.550-1.07)	1.85 (1.42-2.24)	2922
	07-08	.068 (.056-.081)	.040 (.040-.050)	.170 (.120-.240)	1.07 (.690-1.39)	2.52 (1.84-2.92)	2948
	09-10	.046 (.042-.051)	.030 (.030-.030)	.080 (.070-.100)	.550 (.410-.700)	1.60 (1.19-2.38)	3181
Females	99-00	*	< LOD	.180 (.148-.230)	.850 (.600-1.14)	1.85 (1.33-2.45)	3210
	01-02**	.053 (<LOD-.066)	< LOD	.120 (.090-.180)	.710 (.540-.990)	1.77 (1.32-2.20)	3667
	03-04	.060 (.047-.077)	.040 (.030-.060)	.160 (.110-.260)	.860 (.580-1.15)	1.76 (1.32-2.22)	3383
	05-06	.047 (.040-.054)	.030 (.030-.040)	.100 (.070-.130)	.510 (.300-.830)	1.23 (1.04-1.52)	3425
	07-08	.050 (.042-.059)	.030 (.030-.040)	.110 (.080-.150)	.630 (.400-.900)	1.40 (1.09-1.87)	3249
	09-10	.037 (.033-.042)	.020 (.020-.030)	.070 (.050-.080)	.380 (.270-.570)	1.03 (.720-1.61)	3497

Limit of detection (LOD, see Data Analysis section) for Survey years 99-00, 01-02, 03-04, 05-06, 07-08, and 09-10 are 0.05, 0.05, 0.015, 0.015, 0.015, and 0.015 respectively..

** In the 2001-2002 survey period, 83% of measurements had an LOD of 0.015 ng/mL, and 17% had an LOD of 0.05 ng/mL.

< LOD means less than the limit of detection, which may vary for some chemicals by year and by individual sample.

* Not calculated: proportion of results below limit of detection was too high to provide a valid result.

***Non-smoking is defined as a serum cotinine concentration of 10 ng/mL or less.

Biomonitoring Summary: http://www.cdc.gov/biomonitoring/Cotinine_BiomonitoringSummary.html

Factsheet: http://www.cdc.gov/biomonitoring/Cotinine_FactSheet.html

Source: *Centers for Disease Control & Prevention, Fourth National Report on Human Exposure to Environmental Chemicals, Updated Tables, March 2013*

Serum Cotinine

Metabolite of nicotine (component of tobacco smoke)

Geometric mean and selected percentiles of serum concentrations (in ng/mL) for the ***non-smoking U.S. population from the National Health and Nutrition Examination Survey.

	Survey years	Geometric mean (95% conf. interval)	Selected percentiles (95% confidence interval) 50th	75th	90th	95th	Sample size
Race/ethnicity							
Mexican Americans	99-00	*	< LOD	.140 (.110-.180)	.506 (.370-.726)	1.21 (.900-1.70)	2241
	01-02**	.060 (<LOD-.084)	< LOD	.160 (.080-.310)	.730 (.480-1.19)	2.12 (1.19-2.96)	1878
	03-04	.054 (.043-.068)	.030 (.020-.050)	.120 (.080-.180)	.690 (.430-1.00)	2.65 (1.87-3.57)	1707
	05-06	.047 (.038-.059)	.030 (.020-.040)	.100 (.070-.150)	.500 (.370-.730)	1.54 (.830-2.49)	1807
	07-08	.044 (.033-.057)	.030 (.020-.040)	.080 (.060-.120)	.480 (.290-.880)	1.59 (1.00-3.07)	1412
	09-10	.038 (.032-.045)	.020 (.020-.030)	.060 (.050-.080)	.360 (.230-.640)	1.35 (.710-2.25)	1615
Non-Hispanic blacks	99-00	.175 (.153-.201)	.131 (.111-.150)	.505 (.400-.625)	1.43 (1.21-1.75)	2.34 (1.84-3.50)	1333
	01-02**	.164 (.137-.197)	.130 (.110-.160)	.580 (.450-.770)	1.77 (1.55-2.05)	3.15 (2.50-4.30)	1602
	03-04	.144 (.104-.198)	.120 (.080-.180)	.520 (.350-.770)	1.54 (1.20-2.14)	2.77 (2.18-3.54)	1704
	05-06	.114 (.085-.153)	.080 (.060-.120)	.440 (.240-.690)	1.42 (.900-2.03)	2.45 (1.70-3.70)	1630
	07-08	.094 (.079-.112)	.060 (.050-.090)	.320 (.250-.390)	1.19 (.980-1.46)	2.37 (1.75-2.88)	1244
	09-10	.095 (.074-.122)	.070 (.050-.090)	.320 (.210-.540)	1.33 (.900-2.05)	2.85 (1.97-3.60)	1129
Non-Hispanic whites	99-00	*	.050 (<LOD-.073)	.216 (.154-.312)	.950 (.621-1.40)	1.92 (1.48-3.02)	1950
	01-02**	.052 (<LOD-.068)	< LOD	.120 (.090-.180)	.800 (.570-1.11)	1.88 (1.48-2.30)	2847
	03-04	.066 (.050-.087)	.040 (.030-.070)	.180 (.120-.300)	.920 (.630-1.33)	2.01 (1.70-2.49)	2500
	05-06	.049 (.042-.056)	.030 (.030-.040)	.100 (.080-.130)	.530 (.330-.800)	1.27 (.980-1.62)	2404
	07-08	.056 (.043-.073)	.040 (.030-.050)	.130 (.080-.240)	.750 (.440-1.27)	1.70 (1.24-2.54)	2485
	09-10	.037 (.033-.043)	.020 (.020-.030)	.070 (.050-.080)	.350 (.240-.560)	1.06 (.780-1.60)	2743

Limit of detection (LOD, see Data Analysis section) for Survey years 99-00, 01-02, 03-04, 05-06, 07-08, and 09-10 are 0.05, 0.05, 0.015, 0.015, 0.015, and 0.015 respectively.
** In the 2001-2002 survey period, 83% of measurements had an LOD of 0.015 ng/mL, and 17% had an LOD of 0.05 ng/mL.
< LOD means less than the limit of detection, which may vary for some chemicals by year and by individual sample.
* Not calculated: proportion of results below limit of detection was too high to provide a valid result.
*** Non-smoking is defined as a serum cotinine concentration of 10 ng/mL or less.

Biomonitoring Summary: http://www.cdc.gov/biomonitoring/Cotinine_BiomonitoringSummary.html
Factsheet: http://www.cdc.gov/biomonitoring/Cotinine_FactSheet.html

Source: *Centers for Disease Control & Prevention, Fourth National Report on Human Exposure to Environmental Chemicals, Updated Tables, March 2013*

Urinary NNAL (4-(methylnitrosamino)-1-(3-pyridyl)-1-butanol)

Metabolite of (4-(methylnitrosamino)-1-(3-pyridyl)-1-butanone) (NNK)

Geometric mean and selected percentiles of urine concentrations (in pg/mL) for the **non-smoking U.S. population from the National Health and Nutrition Examination Survey.

	Survey years	Geometric mean (95% conf. interval)	Selected percentiles (95% confidence interval) 50th	75th	90th	95th	Sample size
Total	07-08	*	< LOD	2.80 (2.20-3.70)	11.1 (8.80-14.4)	24.5 (18.0-30.4)	5212
	09-10	*	< LOD	1.90 (1.60-2.40)	7.30 (6.40-8.50)	16.7 (13.9-19.6)	6067
Age group							
6-11 years	07-08	*	1.30 (.600-2.60)	8.50 (4.70-13.8)	31.4 (17.5-49.8)	60.6 (37.1-75.7)	875
	09-10	*	.600 (<LOD-1.00)	3.10 (2.20-5.00)	15.5 (10.4-22.8)	29.3 (18.1-59.4)	937
12-19 years	07-08	*	1.20 (.600-2.10)	5.00 (3.80-9.20)	20.0 (11.9-27.5)	39.1 (20.6-60.9)	843
	09-10	*	.900 (<LOD-1.50)	3.70 (2.70-5.20)	12.5 (6.90-25.5)	29.1 (13.9-51.4)	1004
20 years and older	07-08	*	< LOD	2.10 (1.70-2.50)	8.20 (6.90-9.80)	16.6 (13.9-21.5)	3494
	09-10	*	< LOD	1.60 (1.30-1.90)	6.10 (5.10-6.90)	13.1 (10.7-15.8)	4126
Gender							
Males	07-08	*	< LOD	3.80 (3.00-4.50)	12.6 (10.6-15.0)	27.5 (18.9-38.1)	2463
	09-10	*	< LOD	2.40 (1.90-3.00)	8.30 (7.20-9.90)	19.3 (15.2-22.5)	2903
Females	07-08	*	< LOD	2.10 (1.50-2.90)	9.70 (7.10-13.6)	21.6 (16.6-28.0)	2749
	09-10	*	< LOD	1.60 (1.30-1.90)	6.50 (4.70-8.80)	14.0 (10.7-19.0)	3164
Race/ethnicity							
Mexican Americans	07-08	*	< LOD	2.00 (1.20-3.10)	6.90 (4.90-9.00)	13.9 (10.8-17.3)	1206
	09-10	*	< LOD	1.60 (1.20-2.20)	4.90 (3.70-7.00)	11.1 (5.70-18.4)	1476
Non-Hispanic blacks	07-08	*	.800 (<LOD-1.90)	4.90 (3.60-6.30)	14.0 (11.6-17.2)	26.1 (18.5-33.2)	1057
	09-10	1.81 (1.30-2.54)	1.40 (<LOD-2.40)	5.90 (3.80-8.10)	18.9 (11.7-26.1)	34.0 (18.9-61.9)	1004
Non-Hispanic whites	07-08	*	< LOD	2.80 (1.90-4.10)	11.9 (8.20-17.7)	27.5 (19.6-35.4)	2047
	09-10	*	< LOD	1.80 (1.40-2.40)	6.80 (5.40-8.40)	15.2 (11.9-19.3)	2514

Limit of detection (LOD, see Data Analysis section) for Survey years 07-08 and 09-10 are 0.6 and 0.6 respectively.
< LOD means less than the limit of detection, which may vary for some chemicals by year and by individual sample.
*Not calculated: proportion of results below limit of detection was too high to provide a valid result.
**Non-smoking is defined as a serum cotinine concentration of 10 ng/mL or less.

Biomonitoring Summary: http://www.cdc.gov/biomonitoring/NNAL_BiomonitoringSummary.html
Factsheet: http://www.cdc.gov/biomonitoring/NNAL_FactSheet.html

Source: Centers for Disease Control & Prevention, Fourth National Report on Human Exposure to Environmental Chemicals, Updated Tables, March 2013

NNAL (4-(methylnitrosamino)-1-(3-pyridyl)-1-butanol) (creatinine corrected)

Metabolite of (4-(methylnitrosamino)-1-(3-pyridyl)-1-butanone) (NNK)

Geometric mean and selected percentiles of urine concentrations (in pg/mg of creatinine) for the **non-smoking U.S. population from the National Health and Nutrition Examination Survey.

	Survey years	Geometric mean (95% conf. interval)	Selected percentiles (95% confidence interval) 50th	75th	90th	95th	Sample size
Total	07-08	*	< LOD	2.79 (2.31-3.50)	10.3 (7.36-14.0)	20.5 (16.4-27.5)	5210
	09-10	*	< LOD	2.05 (1.88-2.28)	6.40 (5.71-7.41)	14.6 (11.5-17.3)	6066
Age group							
6-11 years	07-08	*	2.15 (1.38-3.22)	10.7 (5.95-17.9)	38.3 (21.2-57.1)	60.9 (46.4-72.1)	875
	09-10	*	1.19 (<LOD-1.52)	4.25 (2.88-6.37)	19.2 (11.0-28.8)	37.2 (22.9-53.0)	936
12-19 years	07-08	*	1.14 (.710-1.75)	4.40 (2.59-7.36)	14.2 (10.5-23.1)	29.2 (15.6-41.9)	841
	09-10	*	1.05 (<LOD-1.26)	3.08 (1.96-4.37)	10.0 (6.02-15.2)	20.7 (12.3-30.2)	1004
20 years and older	07-08	*	< LOD	2.34 (2.00-2.73)	6.82 (5.49-8.65)	15.1 (11.8-17.7)	3494
	09-10	*	< LOD	1.84 (1.71-2.00)	5.21 (4.57-6.07)	11.4 (8.42-14.1)	4126
Gender							
Males	07-08	*	< LOD	2.98 (2.39-3.71)	10.5 (7.57-12.9)	20.9 (15.7-29.0)	2462
	09-10	*	< LOD	2.00 (1.86-2.25)	6.61 (6.00-7.83)	15.1 (11.7-19.8)	2902
Females	07-08	*	< LOD	2.67 (2.14-3.37)	9.07 (6.79-14.9)	20.0 (15.7-27.9)	2748
	09-10	*	< LOD	2.09 (1.82-2.36)	6.15 (4.88-8.21)	12.7 (9.26-17.3)	3164
Race/ethnicity							
Mexican Americans	07-08	*	< LOD	2.16 (1.55-3.00)	5.91 (4.32-8.30)	13.3 (8.36-17.9)	1205
	09-10	*	< LOD	1.73 (1.36-2.11)	5.00 (3.72-6.84)	10.0 (6.79-14.7)	1476
Non-Hispanic blacks	07-08	*	.960 (<LOD-1.42)	3.70 (2.50-5.31)	11.5 (9.18-14.2)	20.8 (14.5-28.8)	1056
	09-10	1.40 (.982-2.01)	1.21 (<LOD-2.06)	3.96 (2.78-5.99)	12.2 (7.29-20.3)	23.4 (14.3-35.4)	1003
Non-Hispanic whites	07-08	*	< LOD	2.93 (2.22-4.00)	11.4 (7.22-17.1)	23.9 (17.1-32.0)	2047
	09-10	*	< LOD	1.96 (1.82-2.15)	6.09 (5.00-7.83)	14.7 (10.0-18.2)	2514

< LOD means less than the limit of detection for the urine levels not corrected for creatinine.
*Not calculated: proportion of results below limit of detection was too high to provide a valid result.
**Non-smoking is defined as a serum cotinine concentration of 10 ng/mL or less.

Biomonitoring Summary: http://www.cdc.gov/biomonitoring/NNAL_BiomonitoringSummary.html
Factsheet: http://www.cdc.gov/biomonitoring/NNAL_FactSheet.html

Source: *Centers for Disease Control & Prevention, Fourth National Report on Human Exposure to Environmental Chemicals, Updated Tables, March 2013*

Urinary Bisphenol A (2,2-bis[4-Hydroxyphenyl] propane)

Geometric mean and selected percentiles of urine concentrations (in µg/L) for the U.S. population from the National Health and Nutrition Examination Survey.

	Survey years	Geometric mean (95% conf. interval)	Selected percentiles (95% confidence interval) 50th	75th	90th	95th	Sample size
Total	03-04	**2.64** (2.38-2.94)	**2.80** (2.50-3.10)	**5.50** (5.00-6.20)	**10.6** (9.40-12.0)	**16.0** (14.4-17.2)	2517
	05-06	**1.90** (1.79-2.02)	**2.00** (1.90-2.00)	**3.70** (3.50-3.90)	**7.00** (6.40-7.60)	**11.5** (10.0-13.6)	2548
	07-08	**2.08** (1.92-2.26)	**2.10** (1.90-2.30)	**4.10** (3.60-4.60)	**7.70** (6.80-8.70)	**13.0** (10.0-15.6)	2604
	09-10	**1.83** (1.72-1.94)	**1.90** (1.70-2.00)	**3.50** (3.30-3.80)	**6.60** (6.00-7.20)	**9.60** (8.50-11.3)	2749
Age group							
6-11 years	03-04	**3.55** (2.95-4.29)	**3.80** (2.70-5.00)	**6.90** (6.00-8.30)	**12.6** (9.50-15.1)	**16.0** (11.5-23.3)	314
	05-06	**2.86** (2.52-3.24)	**2.70** (2.30-2.90)	**5.00** (4.40-5.80)	**13.5** (9.30-16.8)	**22.8** (13.6-34.6)	356
	07-08	**2.48** (2.21-2.77)	**2.40** (1.90-3.00)	**4.50** (3.70-5.50)	**7.60** (6.30-9.50)	**13.4** (8.80-17.8)	389
	09-10	**1.81** (1.55-2.10)	**1.70** (1.50-2.00)	**3.40** (3.00-4.00)	**6.50** (4.30-9.70)	**9.20** (6.50-15.1)	415
12-19 years	03-04	**3.74** (3.31-4.22)	**4.30** (3.60-4.60)	**7.80** (6.50-9.00)	**13.5** (11.8-15.2)	**16.5** (15.2-20.9)	715
	05-06	**2.42** (2.18-2.68)	**2.40** (2.10-2.70)	**4.30** (3.90-5.20)	**8.40** (6.50-10.8)	**11.9** (10.7-14.8)	702
	07-08	**2.45** (2.14-2.80)	**2.40** (2.10-2.60)	**4.40** (3.60-5.50)	**9.70** (7.30-11.9)	**12.2** (9.70-19.0)	401
	09-10	**2.11** (1.86-2.40)	**2.20** (1.90-2.40)	**3.80** (3.20-4.50)	**6.90** (4.70-10.8)	**11.1** (6.90-21.0)	420
20 years and older	03-04	**2.41** (2.15-2.72)	**2.60** (2.30-2.80)	**5.10** (4.50-5.70)	**9.50** (8.10-11.3)	**15.2** (12.4-18.1)	1488
	05-06	**1.75** (1.62-1.89)	**1.80** (1.70-2.00)	**3.40** (3.10-3.70)	**6.40** (5.80-7.50)	**10.7** (8.80-12.1)	1490
	07-08	**1.99** (1.82-2.18)	**2.00** (1.80-2.30)	**3.90** (3.40-4.60)	**7.40** (6.60-8.50)	**13.2** (9.10-15.7)	1814
	09-10	**1.79** (1.67-1.93)	**1.80** (1.60-2.00)	**3.50** (3.30-3.70)	**6.50** (6.00-7.20)	**9.60** (8.30-11.3)	1914
Gender							
Males	03-04	**2.92** (2.63-3.24)	**3.20** (2.70-3.60)	**6.10** (5.40-6.60)	**10.4** (9.50-11.6)	**16.0** (12.7-17.6)	1229
	05-06	**2.09** (1.92-2.28)	**2.10** (2.00-2.30)	**3.70** (3.40-4.20)	**7.70** (6.80-9.30)	**12.8** (10.1-15.8)	1270
	07-08	**2.20** (2.01-2.41)	**2.10** (1.90-2.40)	**4.00** (3.60-4.70)	**8.10** (6.70-9.70)	**14.0** (8.70-20.8)	1294
	09-10	**1.94** (1.82-2.07)	**1.90** (1.70-2.00)	**3.70** (3.40-4.10)	**6.90** (5.90-7.90)	**10.9** (8.40-13.5)	1399
Females	03-04	**2.41** (2.11-2.75)	**2.50** (2.20-2.80)	**5.00** (4.20-6.20)	**10.6** (8.70-12.5)	**15.9** (13.5-20.1)	1288
	05-06	**1.74** (1.55-1.95)	**1.80** (1.60-2.00)	**3.70** (3.10-4.00)	**6.20** (5.80-7.60)	**10.4** (7.70-14.7)	1278
	07-08	**1.97** (1.80-2.16)	**2.00** (1.80-2.20)	**4.10** (3.60-4.60)	**7.40** (6.80-8.20)	**12.0** (9.60-14.1)	1310
	09-10	**1.73** (1.60-1.87)	**1.80** (1.60-2.00)	**3.40** (3.20-3.70)	**6.50** (5.60-7.10)	**9.20** (8.00-11.2)	1350
Race/ethnicity							
Mexican Americans	03-04	**2.58** (2.15-3.08)	**2.60** (2.10-3.20)	**5.20** (4.40-6.50)	**9.90** (7.30-13.9)	**15.4** (10.2-19.7)	613
	05-06	**2.05** (1.75-2.40)	**2.00** (1.70-2.40)	**3.60** (3.00-4.20)	**6.90** (5.40-10.1)	**12.2** (8.00-15.6)	637
	07-08	**2.09** (1.94-2.26)	**2.00** (1.80-2.30)	**3.80** (3.30-4.30)	**7.10** (6.10-8.60)	**11.7** (7.70-14.6)	531
	09-10	**1.92** (1.69-2.19)	**2.10** (1.80-2.30)	**3.50** (3.10-4.10)	**6.50** (5.20-7.50)	**9.00** (6.90-16.2)	566
Non-Hispanic blacks	03-04	**4.24** (3.73-4.82)	**4.30** (3.80-5.10)	**8.20** (7.10-9.80)	**14.2** (11.7-16.9)	**20.6** (14.9-25.2)	652
	05-06	**2.50** (2.25-2.77)	**2.70** (2.30-3.00)	**4.60** (4.00-5.00)	**8.00** (6.80-9.30)	**11.3** (8.90-14.2)	678
	07-08	**2.66** (2.38-2.97)	**2.80** (2.60-3.10)	**5.40** (4.40-6.40)	**9.10** (7.50-10.4)	**13.3** (10.0-15.1)	597
	09-10	**2.51** (2.22-2.83)	**2.60** (2.30-3.00)	**4.40** (3.80-5.00)	**7.30** (6.10-8.80)	**10.3** (7.90-13.6)	516
Non-Hispanic whites	03-04	**2.51** (2.26-2.79)	**2.70** (2.50-3.00)	**5.20** (4.70-5.80)	**9.60** (8.30-10.9)	**15.1** (12.6-16.7)	1092
	05-06	**1.76** (1.62-1.91)	**1.80** (1.60-2.00)	**3.50** (3.20-3.80)	**6.80** (5.90-7.60)	**11.0** (8.80-13.7)	1038
	07-08	**2.06** (1.87-2.27)	**2.00** (1.80-2.30)	**4.00** (3.40-4.70)	**7.80** (6.70-8.90)	**13.7** (9.80-16.1)	1077
	09-10	**1.73** (1.60-1.87)	**1.70** (1.60-1.90)	**3.40** (3.10-3.70)	**6.40** (5.40-7.60)	**9.20** (8.20-11.2)	1206

Limit of detection (LOD, see Data Analysis section) for Survey years 03-04, 05-06, 07-08 and 09-10 are 0.4, 0.4, 0.4, and 0.4 respectively.

Biomonitoring Summary: http://www.cdc.gov/biomonitoring/BisphenolA_BiomonitoringSummary.html
Factsheet: http://www.cdc.gov/biomonitoring/BisphenolA_FactSheet.html

Source: *Centers for Disease Control & Prevention, Fourth National Report on Human Exposure to Environmental Chemicals, Updated Tables, March 2013*

Urinary Bisphenol A (2,2-bis[4-Hydroxyphenyl] propane) (creatinine corrected)

Geometric mean and selected percentiles of urine concentrations (in µg/g of creatinine) for the U.S. population from the National Health and Nutrition Examination Survey.

	Survey years	Geometric mean (95% conf. interval)	Selected percentiles (95% confidence interval) 50th	75th	90th	95th	Sample size
Total	03-04	**2.58** (2.36-2.82)	**2.50** (2.31-2.80)	**4.29** (3.88-4.75)	**7.67** (6.62-8.66)	**11.2** (9.78-12.4)	2514
	05-06	**1.86** (1.79-1.92)	**1.71** (1.64-1.79)	**3.01** (2.86-3.20)	**5.73** (5.29-6.36)	**9.70** (8.31-10.9)	2548
	07-08	**2.10** (1.95-2.25)	**1.95** (1.84-2.03)	**3.45** (3.02-3.83)	**6.09** (5.10-7.45)	**10.0** (7.48-13.2)	2604
	09-10	**1.91** (1.79-2.04)	**1.76** (1.67-1.84)	**3.06** (2.80-3.33)	**5.33** (4.68-6.06)	**8.03** (6.94-10.0)	2749
Age group							
6-11 years	03-04	**4.32** (3.63-5.14)	**4.29** (3.63-5.23)	**7.14** (5.83-9.56)	**12.2** (9.84-14.8)	**15.7** (12.2-23.2)	314
	05-06	**3.14** (2.79-3.54)	**2.80** (2.55-3.06)	**5.04** (4.46-5.71)	**15.6** (8.15-22.4)	**24.6** (19.9-48.5)	356
	07-08	**3.05** (2.73-3.41)	**2.69** (2.38-3.12)	**5.06** (4.33-5.60)	**11.9** (6.30-17.4)	**20.8** (12.7-26.3)	389
	09-10	**2.36** (2.09-2.65)	**2.18** (2.00-2.53)	**3.70** (3.14-4.29)	**5.97** (4.57-9.15)	**9.57** (6.52-13.7)	415
12-19 years	03-04	**2.80** (2.52-3.11)	**2.74** (2.35-3.22)	**4.74** (4.21-5.09)	**7.79** (6.41-8.87)	**11.8** (8.05-14.2)	713
	05-06	**1.80** (1.67-1.95)	**1.65** (1.50-1.76)	**2.73** (2.41-2.98)	**5.71** (4.07-7.50)	**8.52** (6.94-12.2)	702
	07-08	**1.90** (1.72-2.10)	**1.69** (1.50-2.00)	**2.94** (2.38-3.60)	**5.10** (4.17-6.82)	**7.72** (5.32-13.9)	401
	09-10	**1.70** (1.47-1.95)	**1.60** (1.34-1.88)	**2.63** (2.11-3.58)	**4.47** (3.76-6.19)	**6.71** (4.40-17.8)	420
20 years and older	03-04	**2.39** (2.17-2.64)	**2.36** (2.15-2.59)	**3.93** (3.44-4.33)	**6.64** (5.97-7.74)	**10.0** (9.01-11.4)	1487
	05-06	**1.75** (1.67-1.84)	**1.64** (1.56-1.75)	**2.84** (2.67-3.08)	**5.38** (4.89-5.87)	**8.54** (7.58-9.77)	1490
	07-08	**2.04** (1.90-2.20)	**1.92** (1.79-2.03)	**3.36** (2.91-3.78)	**6.02** (4.88-7.48)	**9.32** (7.48-12.1)	1814
	09-10	**1.90** (1.76-2.05)	**1.76** (1.66-1.84)	**3.04** (2.76-3.24)	**5.33** (4.67-6.11)	**8.00** (6.97-10.0)	1914
Gender							
Males	03-04	**2.38** (2.15-2.63)	**2.31** (2.08-2.70)	**4.19** (3.81-4.64)	**7.10** (6.41-8.28)	**9.94** (9.06-11.7)	1228
	05-06	**1.68** (1.57-1.80)	**1.56** (1.45-1.64)	**2.73** (2.43-3.14)	**5.27** (4.64-6.04)	**8.40** (6.81-11.4)	1270
	07-08	**1.85** (1.71-2.01)	**1.77** (1.57-1.91)	**2.97** (2.59-3.33)	**5.41** (4.47-7.51)	**9.52** (6.29-13.4)	1294
	09-10	**1.74** (1.62-1.87)	**1.60** (1.48-1.72)	**2.76** (2.53-2.96)	**5.00** (4.16-5.86)	**7.50** (6.22-9.00)	1399
Females	03-04	**2.78** (2.50-3.08)	**2.68** (2.40-2.94)	**4.41** (3.81-5.15)	**7.93** (6.48-10.2)	**12.4** (9.29-18.2)	1286
	05-06	**2.04** (1.95-2.14)	**1.85** (1.76-2.02)	**3.21** (2.98-3.39)	**6.47** (5.51-7.50)	**9.86** (8.62-11.8)	1278
	07-08	**2.36** (2.17-2.57)	**2.14** (1.98-2.33)	**3.77** (3.43-4.31)	**6.67** (5.41-7.83)	**10.5** (7.45-15.2)	1310
	09-10	**2.09** (1.92-2.27)	**1.93** (1.80-2.15)	**3.33** (2.94-3.84)	**5.19** (4.87-6.74)	**8.80** (6.47-12.5)	1350
Race/ethnicity							
Mexican Americans	03-04	**2.34** (2.02-2.71)	**2.38** (2.00-2.65)	**3.85** (3.24-4.55)	**7.09** (5.00-9.04)	**10.9** (8.50-14.3)	612
	05-06	**1.84** (1.66-2.04)	**1.62** (1.45-1.84)	**2.99** (2.56-3.60)	**6.00** (4.51-8.00)	**10.3** (6.84-14.9)	637
	07-08	**2.04** (1.86-2.24)	**1.88** (1.72-2.11)	**3.33** (2.96-3.95)	**5.68** (5.05-6.59)	**8.90** (6.30-11.8)	531
	09-10	**1.91** (1.71-2.13)	**1.76** (1.67-1.87)	**3.13** (2.63-3.57)	**5.51** (4.72-6.97)	**8.71** (5.86-14.4)	566
Non-Hispanic blacks	03-04	**2.92** (2.58-3.32)	**2.95** (2.51-3.27)	**4.90** (4.07-6.13)	**8.64** (7.53-9.63)	**11.9** (10.2-13.3)	651
	05-06	**1.76** (1.62-1.90)	**1.68** (1.53-1.92)	**2.82** (2.67-3.04)	**4.56** (3.85-5.43)	**6.81** (5.00-9.27)	678
	07-08	**2.06** (1.91-2.23)	**2.03** (1.83-2.25)	**3.24** (2.86-3.78)	**5.71** (5.15-6.54)	**8.59** (6.54-10.9)	597
	09-10	**1.82** (1.65-2.01)	**1.70** (1.56-1.89)	**2.90** (2.39-3.17)	**4.94** (4.02-6.03)	**6.74** (5.95-8.09)	516
Non-Hispanic whites	03-04	**2.58** (2.37-2.81)	**2.55** (2.32-2.80)	**4.30** (3.93-4.67)	**7.58** (6.32-8.87)	**11.0** (9.34-12.4)	1091
	05-06	**1.85** (1.75-1.96)	**1.70** (1.60-1.82)	**3.08** (2.78-3.31)	**5.80** (5.13-6.72)	**9.77** (7.87-11.5)	1038
	07-08	**2.15** (1.97-2.35)	**1.97** (1.84-2.11)	**3.50** (3.04-3.95)	**6.44** (5.04-8.00)	**10.9** (7.47-14.5)	1077
	09-10	**1.94** (1.79-2.10)	**1.78** (1.67-1.92)	**3.16** (2.80-3.59)	**5.45** (4.67-6.94)	**8.55** (6.73-10.0)	1206

Biomonitoring Summary: http://www.cdc.gov/biomonitoring/BisphenolA_BiomonitoringSummary.html
Factsheet: http://www.cdc.gov/biomonitoring/BisphenolA_FactSheet.html

***Source:** Centers for Disease Control & Prevention, Fourth National Report on Human Exposure to Environmental Chemicals, Updated Tables, March 2013*

Urinary Triclosan (2,4,4'-Trichloro-2'-hydroxyphenyl ether)

Geometric mean and selected percentiles of urine concentrations (in µg/L) for the U.S. population from the National Health and Nutrition Examination Survey.

	Survey years	Geometric mean (95% conf. interval)	Selected percentiles (95% confidence interval) 50th	75th	90th	95th	Sample size
Total	03-04	**13.0** (11.6-14.6)	**9.20** (7.90-10.9)	**47.4** (38.2-58.4)	**249** (188-304)	**461** (383-522)	2517
	05-06	**18.5** (16.1-21.3)	**15.1** (11.8-18.5)	**76.2** (57.9-97.6)	**334** (279-402)	**655** (573-739)	2548
	07-08	**15.3** (13.5-17.4)	**12.1** (10.2-13.8)	**57.2** (46.1-65.9)	**225** (176-288)	**494** (371-615)	2604
	09-10	**14.5** (12.6-16.6)	**10.7** (8.80-12.6)	**51.2** (39.4-67.7)	**238** (200-284)	**483** (398-569)	2749
Age group							
6-11 years	03-04	**8.16** (6.20-10.8)	**6.00** (4.00-8.50)	**20.7** (14.3-31.6)	**123** (36.4-163)	**157** (113-380)	314
	05-06	**12.8** (9.89-16.7)	**10.3** (8.30-17.2)	**35.4** (23.9-65.8)	**97.6** (67.4-181)	**246** (99.5-462)	356
	07-08	**11.8** (7.57-18.2)	**9.80** (6.70-13.9)	**27.7** (14.8-52.2)	**98.5** (40.5-364)	**296** (67.4-826)	389
	09-10	**10.9** (9.35-12.8)	**9.90** (7.10-11.9)	**28.3** (22.1-35.5)	**95.5** (71.5-117)	**200** (114-474)	415
12-19 years	03-04	**14.5** (11.0-19.1)	**10.3** (8.20-13.1)	**39.0** (26.5-86.4)	**304** (134-566)	**655** (310-890)	715
	05-06	**18.8** (14.9-23.8)	**15.4** (11.0-21.0)	**67.5** (45.3-100)	**330** (174-461)	**566** (389-707)	702
	07-08	**18.2** (13.8-23.8)	**13.8** (9.40-20.1)	**63.2** (38.7-110)	**296** (144-395)	**401** (308-853)	401
	09-10	**11.7** (9.89-13.8)	**8.80** (7.30-10.9)	**30.2** (24.3-40.6)	**165** (56.7-289)	**301** (220-431)	420
20 years and older	03-04	**13.6** (12.0-15.3)	**9.60** (8.20-11.5)	**51.7** (39.6-65.7)	**261** (198-317)	**472** (406-522)	1488
	05-06	**19.3** (16.4-22.6)	**15.5** (11.8-19.4)	**84.3** (61.0-114)	**366** (289-462)	**738** (583-864)	1490
	07-08	**15.4** (13.7-17.3)	**12.3** (10.1-14.4)	**60.1** (48.5-69.0)	**225** (185-286)	**504** (378-573)	1814
	09-10	**15.5** (12.9-18.5)	**11.1** (8.60-14.2)	**61.8** (41.8-86.0)	**262** (214-327)	**544** (415-621)	1914
Gender							
Males	03-04	**16.2** (13.4-19.6)	**11.7** (9.30-14.8)	**84.9** (50.6-111)	**317** (231-433)	**574** (461-716)	1229
	05-06	**21.3** (17.6-25.7)	**17.6** (11.9-23.2)	**103** (69.9-143)	**446** (366-488)	**738** (601-873)	1270
	07-08	**15.2** (12.9-17.9)	**12.3** (9.50-15.3)	**60.6** (45.8-72.8)	**236** (159-338)	**467** (367-636)	1294
	09-10	**14.8** (12.7-17.4)	**10.9** (8.60-13.3)	**55.1** (40.4-77.5)	**243** (214-295)	**455** (327-600)	1399
Females	03-04	**10.6** (9.29-12.1)	**7.60** (6.10-9.10)	**33.2** (27.1-39.4)	**144** (96.5-250)	**380** (258-430)	1288
	05-06	**16.2** (13.9-18.8)	**12.6** (10.1-15.6)	**58.7** (41.5-81.9)	**226** (169-304)	**513** (310-773)	1278
	07-08	**15.5** (12.6-18.9)	**12.0** (9.90-14.1)	**52.1** (37.1-74.4)	**210** (133-367)	**504** (285-648)	1310
	09-10	**14.2** (12.0-16.8)	**10.5** (8.70-12.6)	**50.0** (34.4-63.8)	**235** (149-302)	**488** (332-661)	1350
Race/ethnicity							
Mexican Americans	03-04	**14.6** (10.6-20.1)	**8.80** (5.40-17.5)	**65.4** (32.8-127)	**357** (225-456)	**597** (372-992)	613
	05-06	**26.7** (21.2-33.7)	**18.7** (13.5-25.5)	**196** (99.4-269)	**668** (475-759)	**866** (750-1180)	637
	07-08	**17.1** (12.9-22.6)	**11.8** (8.40-17.8)	**67.4** (42.5-106)	**358** (208-474)	**556** (363-856)	531
	09-10	**14.9** (12.2-18.3)	**10.2** (8.20-12.8)	**54.7** (33.3-86.5)	**345** (260-494)	**691** (443-1180)	566
Non-Hispanic blacks	03-04	**14.4** (11.4-18.2)	**11.1** (8.70-16.1)	**37.6** (30.2-58.0)	**203** (87.5-341)	**450** (254-750)	652
	05-06	**17.3** (13.3-22.4)	**14.0** (10.4-19.0)	**59.2** (37.7-98.3)	**258** (138-460)	**541** (273-1190)	678
	07-08	**13.7** (11.7-16.1)	**11.3** (8.80-13.9)	**41.4** (28.9-49.6)	**150** (93.5-265)	**480** (190-757)	597
	09-10	**12.8** (10.8-15.0)	**9.30** (7.70-11.7)	**34.3** (24.0-44.6)	**168** (88.4-263)	**451** (202-959)	516
Non-Hispanic whites	03-04	**12.9** (11.2-14.9)	**9.20** (7.40-11.0)	**49.2** (37.8-63.4)	**245** (163-334)	**461** (383-527)	1092
	05-06	**17.5** (14.9-20.6)	**15.1** (10.9-19.0)	**74.3** (54.1-90.3)	**288** (231-366)	**569** (462-693)	1038
	07-08	**15.0** (12.6-17.7)	**12.3** (9.80-14.5)	**59.6** (41.9-73.4)	**197** (147-266)	**408** (296-537)	1077
	09-10	**14.0** (11.8-16.7)	**10.5** (8.30-12.9)	**51.7** (33.1-79.2)	**216** (174-266)	**431** (301-565)	1206

Limit of detection (LOD, see Data Analysis section) for Survey years 03-04, 05-06, 07-08 and 09-10 are 2.3, 2.3, 2.3, and 2.3 respectively.

Biomonitoring Summary: http://www.cdc.gov/biomonitoring/Triclosan_BiomonitoringSummary.html
Factsheet: http://www.cdc.gov/biomonitoring/Triclosan_FactSheet.html

Source: *Centers for Disease Control & Prevention, Fourth National Report on Human Exposure to Environmental Chemicals, Updated Tables, March 2013*

Urinary Triclosan (2,4,4'-Trichloro-2'-hydroxyphenyl ether) (creatinine corrected)

Geometric mean and selected percentiles of urine concentrations (in µg/g of creatinine) for the U.S. population from the National Health and Nutrition Examination Survey.

	Survey years	Geometric mean (95% conf. interval)	Selected percentiles (95% confidence interval) 50th	75th	90th	95th	Sample size
Total	03-04	**12.7** (11.5-14.1)	**9.48** (8.22-10.4)	**43.9** (33.8-60.6)	**212** (172-241)	**368** (294-463)	2514
	05-06	**18.0** (16.0-20.3)	**13.0** (11.5-16.1)	**73.2** (57.3-91.6)	**304** (240-364)	**532** (434-674)	2548
	07-08	**15.5** (13.7-17.5)	**12.4** (10.6-14.2)	**50.4** (40.2-59.8)	**233** (171-300)	**443** (330-559)	2604
	09-10	**15.1** (13.2-17.4)	**10.9** (9.41-12.4)	**49.4** (37.0-67.3)	**256** (191-322)	**454** (352-557)	2749
Age group							
6-11 years	03-04	**9.93** (7.43-13.3)	**7.55** (4.72-13.4)	**25.1** (15.3-35.6)	**116** (39.9-236)	**236** (115-336)	314
	05-06	**14.1** (10.8-18.5)	**13.5** (7.97-18.5)	**38.6** (26.0-54.1)	**108** (62.4-169)	**241** (108-598)	356
	07-08	**14.5** (9.47-22.1)	**13.0** (8.00-17.5)	**33.1** (17.5-72.4)	**132** (52.7-331)	**331** (131-599)	389
	09-10	**14.2** (12.4-16.4)	**12.0** (8.84-15.0)	**37.1** (27.0-47.3)	**129** (89.1-155)	**300** (148-469)	415
12-19 years	03-04	**10.9** (8.32-14.2)	**7.45** (5.48-10.7)	**31.8** (21.9-61.1)	**193** (90.7-318)	**356** (169-580)	713
	05-06	**14.0** (11.0-17.8)	**11.1** (8.68-13.6)	**51.0** (33.0-73.4)	**193** (125-306)	**385** (203-739)	702
	07-08	**14.1** (11.0-18.1)	**11.0** (7.87-14.4)	**50.2** (27.1-78.8)	**206** (95.3-293)	**378** (238-571)	401
	09-10	**9.38** (7.86-11.2)	**7.71** (5.71-9.21)	**23.2** (17.3-29.3)	**153** (63.0-201)	**247** (166-379)	420
20 years and older	03-04	**13.4** (12.0-15.1)	**10.0** (8.89-11.4)	**50.0** (36.0-73.8)	**224** (186-272)	**385** (308-506)	1487
	05-06	**19.3** (16.9-22.0)	**13.7** (11.6-17.0)	**86.1** (64.0-109)	**343** (262-411)	**581** (440-718)	1490
	07-08	**15.8** (14.0-17.8)	**12.6** (10.7-14.5)	**52.3** (43.8-64.6)	**244** (186-309)	**484** (336-568)	1814
	09-10	**16.4** (13.7-19.6)	**11.5** (9.63-14.8)	**57.1** (38.4-80.2)	**279** (202-364)	**504** (372-601)	1914
Gender							
Males	03-04	**13.2** (11.3-15.6)	**9.21** (6.86-12.1)	**73.1** (45.8-85.9)	**237** (175-294)	**384** (294-506)	1228
	05-06	**17.1** (14.1-20.7)	**12.4** (10.0-18.5)	**82.6** (58.2-109)	**308** (232-368)	**472** (355-721)	1270
	07-08	**12.8** (10.9-15.0)	**10.0** (8.12-13.0)	**45.7** (32.1-57.3)	**191** (132-241)	**330** (253-456)	1294
	09-10	**13.3** (11.3-15.7)	**9.21** (7.40-11.7)	**43.9** (33.5-67.4)	**230** (178-276)	**345** (276-429)	1399
Females	03-04	**12.2** (10.6-14.2)	**9.54** (8.45-10.4)	**32.3** (26.2-46.6)	**182** (138-217)	**336** (225-480)	1286
	05-06	**19.0** (16.1-22.6)	**13.8** (11.7-16.7)	**64.0** (47.6-89.8)	**301** (209-434)	**619** (418-898)	1278
	07-08	**18.5** (15.6-22.0)	**14.4** (12.4-16.8)	**55.3** (38.5-77.0)	**300** (182-435)	**571** (359-729)	1310
	09-10	**17.1** (14.6-20.1)	**12.3** (10.7-14.8)	**50.6** (37.0-71.3)	**300** (187-422)	**556** (422-668)	1350
Race/ethnicity							
Mexican Americans	03-04	**13.3** (9.38-18.8)	**9.18** (5.45-13.9)	**66.7** (28.8-112)	**292** (151-432)	**453** (263-1150)	612
	05-06	**24.1** (19.3-29.9)	**17.6** (13.3-22.8)	**154** (96.4-242)	**440** (379-601)	**736** (601-818)	637
	07-08	**16.6** (12.2-22.6)	**12.6** (8.51-16.5)	**60.1** (39.6-80.3)	**325** (182-475)	**637** (368-828)	531
	09-10	**14.8** (12.1-18.2)	**9.38** (7.63-12.4)	**45.4** (32.2-110)	**352** (244-458)	**578** (402-737)	566
Non-Hispanic blacks	03-04	**9.94** (7.92-12.5)	**7.74** (5.50-10.0)	**30.2** (25.6-37.3)	**132** (78.0-213)	**260** (127-513)	651
	05-06	**12.2** (9.47-15.6)	**9.50** (7.64-11.8)	**41.0** (23.3-77.4)	**179** (106-243)	**352** (203-674)	678
	07-08	**10.6** (8.91-12.7)	**8.34** (6.47-10.1)	**28.6** (22.3-36.7)	**120** (71.0-203)	**266** (151-407)	597
	09-10	**9.23** (7.62-11.2)	**6.62** (5.63-8.18)	**22.7** (16.9-29.1)	**136** (63.6-240)	**356** (180-689)	516
Non-Hispanic whites	03-04	**13.3** (11.6-15.1)	**9.82** (8.11-11.5)	**47.0** (34.3-67.7)	**213** (160-272)	**358** (276-480)	1091
	05-06	**18.4** (16.0-21.2)	**13.5** (11.6-17.0)	**73.4** (56.8-97.0)	**282** (231-343)	**472** (367-699)	1038
	07-08	**15.6** (13.1-18.7)	**13.0** (10.7-14.8)	**50.4** (35.9-65.9)	**222** (129-303)	**418** (262-586)	1077
	09-10	**15.8** (13.1-19.0)	**11.4** (9.41-14.8)	**52.0** (37.0-71.3)	**242** (159-323)	**410** (317-547)	1206

Biomonitoring Summary: http://www.cdc.gov/biomonitoring/Triclosan_BiomonitoringSummary.html
Factsheet: http://www.cdc.gov/biomonitoring/Triclosan_FactSheet.html

Source: *Centers for Disease Control & Prevention, Fourth National Report on Human Exposure to Environmental Chemicals, Updated Tables, March 2013*

Blood Lead

Geometric mean and selected percentiles of blood concentrations (in µg/dL) for the U.S. population from the National Health and Nutrition Examination Survey.

	Survey years	Geometric mean (95% conf. interval)	Selected percentiles (95% confidence interval) 50th	75th	90th	95th	Sample size
Total	99-00	**1.66** (1.60-1.72)	**1.60** (1.60-1.70)	**2.50** (2.40-2.60)	**3.80** (3.60-4.00)	**5.00** (4.70-5.50)	7970
	01-02	**1.45** (1.39-1.51)	**1.40** (1.40-1.50)	**2.20** (2.10-2.30)	**3.40** (3.20-3.60)	**4.50** (4.20-4.70)	8945
	03-04	**1.43** (1.36-1.50)	**1.40** (1.30-1.50)	**2.10** (2.10-2.20)	**3.20** (3.10-3.30)	**4.20** (3.90-4.40)	8373
	05-06	**1.29** (1.23-1.36)	**1.27** (1.20-1.34)	**2.01** (1.91-2.11)	**3.05** (2.86-3.22)	**3.91** (3.64-4.18)	8407
	07-08	**1.27** (1.21-1.34)	**1.22** (1.18-1.30)	**1.90** (1.80-2.00)	**2.80** (2.67-2.96)	**3.70** (3.50-3.90)	8266
	09-10	**1.12** (1.08-1.16)	**1.07** (1.03-1.12)	**1.70** (1.62-1.77)	**2.58** (2.45-2.71)	**3.34** (3.14-3.57)	8793
Age group							
1-5 years	99-00	**2.23** (1.96-2.53)	**2.20** (1.90-2.50)	**3.40** (2.80-3.90)	**4.90** (4.00-6.60)	**7.00** (6.10-8.30)	723
	01-02	**1.70** (1.55-1.87)	**1.60** (1.50-1.80)	**2.50** (2.20-2.90)	**4.20** (3.50-5.20)	**5.80** (4.70-6.90)	898
	03-04	**1.77** (1.60-1.95)	**1.70** (1.50-1.90)	**2.50** (2.30-2.80)	**3.90** (3.30-4.60)	**5.10** (4.10-6.60)	911
	05-06	**1.46** (1.36-1.57)	**1.43** (1.34-1.55)	**2.10** (1.97-2.20)	**2.98** (2.72-3.32)	**3.80** (3.49-4.54)	968
	07-08	**1.51** (1.37-1.66)	**1.43** (1.30-1.60)	**2.20** (1.98-2.31)	**3.20** (2.65-3.85)	**4.10** (3.40-5.19)	817
	09-10	**1.17** (1.08-1.26)	**1.15** (1.03-1.27)	**1.70** (1.50-1.87)	**2.39** (2.08-2.65)	**3.37** (2.63-4.11)	836
6-11 years	99-00	**1.51** (1.36-1.66)	**1.40** (1.30-1.60)	**2.10** (1.80-2.50)	**3.30** (2.80-3.80)	**4.50** (3.40-6.20)	905
	01-02	**1.25** (1.14-1.36)	**1.20** (1.00-1.30)	**1.70** (1.60-2.00)	**2.80** (2.50-3.10)	**3.70** (3.00-4.70)	1044
	03-04	**1.25** (1.12-1.39)	**1.20** (1.10-1.40)	**1.80** (1.50-2.10)	**2.60** (2.10-3.10)	**3.30** (2.50-4.60)	856
	05-06	**1.02** (.948-1.10)	**.970** (.890-1.01)	**1.40** (1.28-1.55)	**2.06** (1.80-2.72)	**3.00** (2.26-3.81)	934
	07-08	**.988** (.914-1.07)	**.960** (.880-1.07)	**1.31** (1.22-1.49)	**1.90** (1.70-2.11)	**2.50** (2.10-2.88)	1011
	09-10	**.838** (.792-.887)	**.810** (.740-.840)	**1.13** (1.06-1.21)	**1.64** (1.45-1.84)	**2.01** (1.88-2.25)	1009
12-19 years	99-00	**1.10** (1.04-1.17)	**1.10** (1.00-1.20)	**1.50** (1.40-1.70)	**2.30** (2.10-2.40)	**2.90** (2.70-3.00)	2135
	01-02	**.942** (.899-.986)	**.900** (.900-1.00)	**1.30** (1.20-1.40)	**2.00** (1.90-2.10)	**2.70** (2.40-2.90)	2231
	03-04	**.946** (.878-1.02)	**.900** (.800-1.00)	**1.30** (1.20-1.40)	**1.90** (1.70-2.10)	**2.60** (2.20-3.00)	2081
	05-06	**.797** (.746-.852)	**.740** (.690-.790)	**1.08** (.990-1.20)	**1.69** (1.50-1.85)	**2.23** (1.98-2.46)	1996
	07-08	**.800** (.744-.859)	**.760** (.720-.820)	**1.04** (.980-1.16)	**1.50** (1.35-1.70)	**1.90** (1.70-2.32)	1074
	09-10	**.680** (.636-.727)	**.660** (.590-.700)	**.910** (.840-.990)	**1.29** (1.19-1.43)	**1.72** (1.52-1.86)	1183
20 years and older	99-00	**1.75** (1.68-1.81)	**1.70** (1.60-1.80)	**2.60** (2.50-2.70)	**3.90** (3.70-4.10)	**5.20** (4.80-5.60)	4207
	01-02	**1.56** (1.49-1.62)	**1.60** (1.50-1.60)	**2.30** (2.30-2.40)	**3.60** (3.40-3.70)	**4.60** (4.30-5.00)	4772
	03-04	**1.52** (1.45-1.60)	**1.50** (1.40-1.60)	**2.30** (2.20-2.40)	**3.30** (3.20-3.50)	**4.30** (4.00-4.60)	4525
	05-06	**1.41** (1.34-1.48)	**1.41** (1.33-1.48)	**2.17** (2.04-2.31)	**3.22** (3.05-3.43)	**4.12** (3.82-4.38)	4509
	07-08	**1.38** (1.31-1.46)	**1.34** (1.26-1.42)	**2.06** (1.94-2.18)	**3.00** (2.80-3.14)	**3.90** (3.68-4.23)	5364
	09-10	**1.23** (1.19-1.28)	**1.20** (1.14-1.25)	**1.85** (1.78-1.93)	**2.77** (2.60-2.93)	**3.57** (3.29-3.84)	5765
Gender							
Males	99-00	**2.01** (1.93-2.09)	**1.90** (1.90-2.00)	**2.90** (2.80-3.00)	**4.50** (4.10-4.80)	**6.00** (5.50-6.50)	3913
	01-02	**1.78** (1.71-1.86)	**1.80** (1.70-1.80)	**2.70** (2.50-2.80)	**3.90** (3.80-4.10)	**5.40** (5.00-5.50)	4339
	03-04	**1.69** (1.62-1.75)	**1.60** (1.50-1.70)	**2.50** (2.40-2.60)	**3.70** (3.40-3.90)	**4.80** (4.50-5.20)	4132
	05-06	**1.52** (1.42-1.62)	**1.49** (1.41-1.58)	**2.30** (2.12-2.51)	**3.48** (3.20-3.75)	**4.36** (4.04-4.76)	4092
	07-08	**1.47** (1.39-1.56)	**1.40** (1.32-1.50)	**2.17** (2.00-2.30)	**3.21** (3.01-3.53)	**4.41** (4.10-4.88)	4147
	09-10	**1.31** (1.25-1.36)	**1.26** (1.20-1.32)	**1.96** (1.89-2.03)	**2.93** (2.72-3.15)	**3.84** (3.54-4.39)	4366
Females	99-00	**1.37** (1.32-1.43)	**1.30** (1.30-1.40)	**2.00** (1.90-2.10)	**3.10** (2.90-3.30)	**4.00** (3.80-4.20)	4057
	01-02	**1.19** (1.14-1.25)	**1.20** (1.10-1.20)	**1.80** (1.70-1.90)	**2.60** (2.50-2.80)	**3.60** (3.10-4.00)	4606
	03-04	**1.22** (1.14-1.31)	**1.20** (1.10-1.30)	**1.80** (1.70-2.00)	**2.70** (2.50-3.00)	**3.50** (3.10-3.80)	4241
	05-06	**1.11** (1.05-1.17)	**1.06** (.980-1.15)	**1.73** (1.61-1.84)	**2.59** (2.44-2.74)	**3.25** (3.12-3.44)	4315
	07-08	**1.11** (1.06-1.16)	**1.09** (1.00-1.14)	**1.64** (1.54-1.74)	**2.41** (2.35-2.50)	**3.00** (2.81-3.20)	4119
	09-10	**.966** (.929-1.01)	**.940** (.890-.970)	**1.43** (1.36-1.53)	**2.18** (2.08-2.30)	**2.81** (2.63-2.93)	4427

Limit of detection (LOD, see Data Analysis section) for Survey years 99-00, 01-02, 03-04, 05-06, 07-08, and 09-10 are 0.3, 0.3, 0.28, 0.25, 0.25, and 0.25 respectively.

Biomonitoring Summary: http://www.cdc.gov/biomonitoring/Lead_BiomonitoringSummary.html
Factsheet: http://www.cdc.gov/biomonitoring/Lead_FactSheet.html

Source: *Centers for Disease Control & Prevention, Fourth National Report on Human Exposure to Environmental Chemicals, Updated Tables, March 2013*

Blood Lead

Geometric mean and selected percentiles of blood concentrations (in µg/dL) for the U.S. population from the National Health and Nutrition Examination Survey.

	Survey years	Geometric mean (95% conf. interval)	Selected percentiles (95% confidence interval) 50th	75th	90th	95th	Sample size
Race/ethnicity							
Mexican Americans	99-00	**1.83** (1.75-1.91)	**1.80** (1.70-1.90)	**2.80** (2.60-2.90)	**4.20** (3.90-4.60)	**5.80** (5.10-6.60)	2742
	01-02	**1.46** (1.34-1.60)	**1.50** (1.30-1.60)	**2.30** (2.10-2.60)	**3.60** (3.40-4.20)	**5.40** (4.40-6.70)	2268
	03-04	**1.55** (1.43-1.69)	**1.50** (1.40-1.60)	**2.30** (2.10-2.50)	**3.50** (2.90-4.20)	**4.90** (3.90-6.40)	2085
	05-06	**1.29** (1.21-1.38)	**1.26** (1.15-1.36)	**2.00** (1.87-2.20)	**3.16** (2.79-3.58)	**4.22** (3.47-5.36)	2236
	07-08	**1.25** (1.15-1.36)	**1.20** (1.10-1.31)	**1.88** (1.70-2.06)	**2.81** (2.60-3.20)	**3.92** (3.20-5.00)	1712
	09-10	**1.14** (1.03-1.28)	**1.04** (.940-1.18)	**1.76** (1.52-1.99)	**2.93** (2.63-3.30)	**3.92** (3.60-4.69)	1966
Non-Hispanic blacks	99-00	**1.87** (1.75-2.00)	**1.80** (1.70-2.00)	**2.80** (2.60-3.00)	**4.30** (4.00-4.60)	**5.70** (5.20-6.10)	1842
	01-02	**1.65** (1.52-1.80)	**1.60** (1.40-1.70)	**2.60** (2.30-2.90)	**4.20** (3.80-4.70)	**5.80** (5.30-6.50)	2219
	03-04	**1.69** (1.52-1.89)	**1.60** (1.40-1.80)	**2.60** (2.20-3.00)	**4.10** (3.50-4.70)	**5.30** (4.60-6.60)	2293
	05-06	**1.39** (1.26-1.53)	**1.31** (1.19-1.45)	**2.16** (1.95-2.42)	**3.48** (3.19-3.80)	**4.65** (4.21-5.14)	2193
	07-08	**1.39** (1.30-1.48)	**1.30** (1.20-1.42)	**2.10** (2.00-2.20)	**3.22** (3.08-3.50)	**4.50** (4.00-4.80)	1746
	09-10	**1.24** (1.18-1.30)	**1.19** (1.12-1.25)	**1.87** (1.76-1.99)	**2.90** (2.68-3.18)	**3.86** (3.57-4.29)	1593
Non-Hispanic whites	99-00	**1.62** (1.55-1.69)	**1.60** (1.50-1.70)	**2.40** (2.30-2.50)	**3.60** (3.40-3.90)	**5.00** (4.40-5.70)	2716
	01-02	**1.43** (1.37-1.48)	**1.40** (1.30-1.50)	**2.20** (2.10-2.20)	**3.20** (3.10-3.40)	**4.20** (3.90-4.50)	3806
	03-04	**1.37** (1.32-1.43)	**1.30** (1.30-1.40)	**2.10** (2.00-2.10)	**3.00** (2.80-3.20)	**3.80** (3.60-4.30)	3478
	05-06	**1.28** (1.19-1.37)	**1.27** (1.17-1.38)	**1.97** (1.86-2.14)	**2.99** (2.73-3.25)	**3.82** (3.41-4.20)	3310
	07-08	**1.24** (1.16-1.33)	**1.20** (1.10-1.30)	**1.86** (1.72-2.00)	**2.70** (2.54-2.90)	**3.50** (3.20-3.89)	3461
	09-10	**1.10** (1.04-1.16)	**1.07** (1.00-1.15)	**1.67** (1.59-1.76)	**2.49** (2.35-2.63)	**3.14** (2.99-3.36)	3760

Limit of detection (LOD, see Data Analysis section) for Survey years 99-00, 01-02, 03-04, 05-06, 07-08, and 09-10 are 0.3, 0.3, 0.28, 0.25, 0.25, and 0.25 respectively.

Biomonitoring Summary: http://www.cdc.gov/biomonitoring/Lead_BiomonitoringSummary.html
Factsheet: http://www.cdc.gov/biomonitoring/Lead_FactSheet.html

Source: *Centers for Disease Control & Prevention, Fourth National Report on Human Exposure to Environmental Chemicals, Updated Tables, March 2013*

Urinary Lead

Geometric mean and selected percentiles of urine concentrations (in µg/L) for the U.S. population from the National Health and Nutrition Examination Survey.

	Survey years	Geometric mean (95% conf. interval)	Selected percentiles (95% confidence interval) 50th	75th	90th	95th	Sample size
Total	99-00	**.766** (.708-.828)	**.800** (.800-.900)	**1.40** (1.30-1.50)	**2.20** (2.00-2.30)	**2.90** (2.60-3.30)	2465
	01-02	**.677** (.637-.718)	**.700** (.700-.800)	**1.20** (1.20-1.30)	**2.00** (1.90-2.20)	**2.70** (2.50-2.80)	2690
	03-04	**.636** (.595-.680)	**.640** (.580-.690)	**1.04** (.960-1.12)	**1.73** (1.52-1.86)	**2.29** (2.03-2.62)	2558
	05-06	**.554** (.523-.587)	**.570** (.540-.600)	**.990** (.910-1.05)	**1.58** (1.44-1.73)	**2.14** (1.94-2.45)	2576
	07-08	**.493** (.467-.520)	**.500** (.470-.530)	**.850** (.790-.910)	**1.38** (1.23-1.58)	**1.97** (1.75-2.17)	2627
	09-10	**.458** (.441-.476)	**.470** (.450-.480)	**.790** (.750-.830)	**1.24** (1.11-1.38)	**1.65** (1.46-1.84)	2848
Age group							
6-11 years	99-00	**1.07** (.955-1.20)	**1.10** (.900-1.30)	**1.50** (1.40-1.70)	**2.40** (1.80-3.10)	**3.40** (2.40-5.00)	340
	01-02	**.753** (.661-.857)	**.800** (.600-.900)	**1.20** (1.10-1.40)	**2.10** (1.60-2.40)	**2.60** (2.10-3.70)	368
	03-04	**.795** (.671-.941)	**.790** (.640-.900)	**1.35** (.970-1.86)	**2.27** (1.62-4.09)	**3.33** (2.23-4.41)	290
	05-06	**.508** (.447-.579)	**.510** (.440-.560)	**.740** (.620-.980)	**1.33** (1.00-1.86)	**1.90** (1.33-2.60)	355
	07-08	**.494** (.411-.593)	**.520** (.410-.590)	**.790** (.660-.900)	**1.23** (.980-1.73)	**1.90** (1.51-2.18)	394
	09-10	**.443** (.399-.493)	**.460** (.430-.490)	**.710** (.630-.820)	**1.09** (.880-1.33)	**1.40** (1.06-1.82)	378
12-19 years	99-00	**.659** (.579-.749)	**.700** (.600-.800)	**1.10** (.900-1.30)	**1.80** (1.40-2.20)	**2.20** (1.90-2.80)	719
	01-02	**.564** (.526-.605)	**.600** (.500-.600)	**1.00** (.800-1.10)	**1.60** (1.40-1.70)	**2.00** (1.80-2.40)	762
	03-04	**.604** (.553-.660)	**.630** (.570-.680)	**.920** (.810-1.02)	**1.32** (1.14-1.80)	**1.86** (1.44-2.29)	725
	05-06	**.472** (.421-.530)	**.490** (.450-.540)	**.780** (.710-.830)	**1.19** (1.10-1.45)	**1.65** (1.34-1.80)	701
	07-08	**.386** (.346-.431)	**.380** (.350-.410)	**.640** (.560-.720)	**1.03** (.870-1.24)	**1.38** (1.09-1.91)	376
	09-10	**.320** (.283-.361)	**.320** (.270-.370)	**.530** (.460-.630)	**.830** (.710-1.10)	**1.16** (.860-1.37)	451
20 years and older	99-00	**.752** (.691-.818)	**.800** (.700-.900)	**1.40** (1.30-1.50)	**2.20** (2.00-2.40)	**2.90** (2.60-3.30)	1406
	01-02	**.688** (.641-.738)	**.700** (.700-.800)	**1.20** (1.20-1.30)	**2.00** (1.90-2.30)	**2.80** (2.50-2.90)	1560
	03-04	**.625** (.579-.674)	**.620** (.560-.700)	**1.04** (.960-1.11)	**1.70** (1.52-1.80)	**2.21** (2.04-2.49)	1543
	05-06	**.574** (.539-.612)	**.600** (.560-.640)	**1.02** (.970-1.13)	**1.65** (1.53-1.81)	**2.21** (1.99-2.57)	1520
	07-08	**.512** (.485-.540)	**.530** (.490-.560)	**.900** (.820-.950)	**1.49** (1.29-1.64)	**2.01** (1.78-2.33)	1857
	09-10	**.486** (.465-.507)	**.490** (.470-.520)	**.830** (.780-.880)	**1.32** (1.16-1.46)	**1.71** (1.52-2.03)	2019
Gender							
Males	99-00	**.923** (.822-1.04)	**.900** (.900-1.00)	**1.60** (1.40-1.80)	**2.50** (2.20-2.90)	**3.40** (2.90-3.80)	1227
	01-02	**.808** (.757-.862)	**.800** (.800-.900)	**1.40** (1.30-1.50)	**2.50** (2.20-2.70)	**3.20** (2.90-3.50)	1335
	03-04	**.731** (.680-.785)	**.730** (.680-.800)	**1.17** (1.07-1.27)	**2.03** (1.78-2.22)	**2.66** (2.33-2.91)	1281
	05-06	**.672** (.638-.707)	**.690** (.620-.760)	**1.16** (1.04-1.28)	**1.78** (1.60-2.00)	**2.45** (2.00-2.97)	1271
	07-08	**.560** (.518-.606)	**.570** (.530-.620)	**.930** (.840-1.02)	**1.63** (1.36-1.97)	**2.30** (1.97-3.07)	1327
	09-10	**.527** (.491-.566)	**.540** (.480-.580)	**.880** (.820-.960)	**1.41** (1.25-1.58)	**1.83** (1.62-2.21)	1398
Females	99-00	**.642** (.589-.701)	**.700** (.600-.800)	**1.20** (1.10-1.30)	**1.90** (1.60-2.20)	**2.40** (2.10-3.00)	1238
	01-02	**.573** (.535-.613)	**.600** (.600-.600)	**1.10** (1.00-1.10)	**1.60** (1.50-1.80)	**2.20** (1.90-2.40)	1355
	03-04	**.558** (.506-.616)	**.540** (.480-.620)	**.920** (.820-1.04)	**1.49** (1.24-1.75)	**1.82** (1.59-2.30)	1277
	05-06	**.461** (.425-.499)	**.460** (.430-.510)	**.810** (.730-.880)	**1.27** (1.17-1.46)	**1.86** (1.54-2.17)	1305
	07-08	**.436** (.412-.461)	**.430** (.400-.480)	**.760** (.690-.830)	**1.22** (1.05-1.34)	**1.67** (1.44-1.81)	1300
	09-10	**.400** (.378-.424)	**.420** (.390-.440)	**.690** (.660-.740)	**1.05** (.990-1.13)	**1.42** (1.26-1.59)	1450

Limit of detection (LOD, see Data Analysis section) for Survey years 99-00, 01-02, 03-04, 05-06, 07-08, and 09-10 are 0.1, 0.1, 0.33, 0.1, 0.1, and 0.1 respectively.

Biomonitoring Summary: http://www.cdc.gov/biomonitoring/Lead_BiomonitoringSummary.html
Factsheet: http://www.cdc.gov/biomonitoring/Lead_FactSheet.html

Source: *Centers for Disease Control & Prevention, Fourth National Report on Human Exposure to Environmental Chemicals, Updated Tables, March 2013*

Urinary Lead

Geometric mean and selected percentiles of urine concentrations (in µg/L) for the U.S. population from the National Health and Nutrition Examination Survey.

	Survey years	Geometric mean (95% conf. interval)	Selected percentiles (95% confidence interval) 50th	75th	90th	95th	Sample size
Race/ethnicity							
Mexican Americans	99-00	**1.02** (.915-1.13)	**1.10** (.900-1.20)	**1.80** (1.60-1.90)	**2.90** (2.50-3.40)	**4.30** (3.10-5.40)	884
	01-02	**.833** (.745-.931)	**.900** (.700-1.00)	**1.50** (1.20-1.70)	**2.50** (2.00-2.90)	**3.30** (2.70-3.80)	683
	03-04	**.815** (.710-.935)	**.840** (.700-.990)	**1.31** (1.18-1.59)	**2.19** (1.86-2.50)	**2.66** (2.13-3.97)	618
	05-06	**.729** (.653-.815)	**.770** (.680-.860)	**1.32** (1.15-1.59)	**2.22** (1.81-2.64)	**3.08** (2.50-4.03)	652
	07-08	**.607** (.528-.698)	**.610** (.530-.690)	**.990** (.890-1.21)	**1.76** (1.37-2.17)	**2.29** (1.82-2.80)	515
	09-10	**.546** (.483-.618)	**.520** (.460-.580)	**.930** (.800-1.09)	**1.66** (1.34-1.89)	**2.16** (1.80-2.87)	613
Non-Hispanic blacks	99-00	**1.11** (1.00-1.23)	**1.10** (1.00-1.20)	**1.90** (1.50-2.10)	**3.00** (2.40-3.50)	**4.20** (3.30-5.70)	568
	01-02	**.940** (.833-1.06)	**.900** (.800-1.00)	**1.60** (1.30-1.80)	**2.70** (2.10-3.40)	**3.70** (2.90-4.80)	667
	03-04	**.848** (.729-.986)	**.850** (.710-1.00)	**1.40** (1.10-1.72)	**2.14** (1.78-2.64)	**2.82** (2.31-3.89)	723
	05-06	**.666** (.604-.734)	**.660** (.590-.760)	**1.09** (.980-1.18)	**1.62** (1.42-1.85)	**2.24** (1.65-2.90)	692
	07-08	**.618** (.558-.685)	**.620** (.560-.690)	**1.01** (.920-1.13)	**1.56** (1.38-1.90)	**2.06** (1.88-2.60)	589
	09-10	**.560** (.522-.601)	**.550** (.490-.600)	**.910** (.830-1.01)	**1.53** (1.26-1.71)	**1.96** (1.68-2.80)	544
Non-Hispanic whites	99-00	**.695** (.625-.773)	**.700** (.700-.900)	**1.30** (1.10-1.40)	**2.00** (1.80-2.40)	**2.70** (2.30-3.10)	822
	01-02	**.610** (.572-.651)	**.700** (.600-.700)	**1.10** (1.10-1.20)	**1.90** (1.70-2.00)	**2.40** (2.30-2.60)	1132
	03-04	**.601** (.566-.628)	**.600** (.540-.660)	**.900** (.810-1.00)	**1.52** (1.40-1.75)	**2.14** (1.78-2.61)	1074
	05-06	**.520** (.477-.566)	**.540** (.490-.580)	**.950** (.820-1.05)	**1.53** (1.30-1.76)	**2.07** (1.78-2.45)	1041
	07-08	**.452** (.422-.485)	**.460** (.430-.490)	**.780** (.700-.880)	**1.23** (1.03-1.50)	**1.79** (1.58-1.97)	1095
	09-10	**.431** (.406-.458)	**.450** (.410-.480)	**.750** (.690-.820)	**1.11** (1.05-1.24)	**1.51** (1.39-1.67)	1225

Limit of detection (LOD, see Data Analysis section) for Survey years 99-00, 01-02, 03-04, 05-06, 07-08, and 09-10 are 0.1, 0.1, 0.33, 0.1, 0.1, and 0.1 respectively

Biomonitoring Summary: http://www.cdc.gov/biomonitoring/Lead_BiomonitoringSummary.html
Factsheet: http://www.cdc.gov/biomonitoring/Lead_FactSheet.html

Source: *Centers for Disease Control & Prevention, Fourth National Report on Human Exposure to Environmental Chemicals, Updated Tables, March 2013*

Urinary Lead (creatinine corrected)

Geometric mean and selected percentiles of urine concentrations (in µg/g of creatinine) for the U.S. population from the National Health and Nutrition Examination Survey.

	Survey years	Geometric mean (95% conf. interval)	Selected percentiles (95% confidence interval) 50th	75th	90th	95th	Sample size
Total	99-00	**.721** (.700-.742)	**.701** (.677-.725)	**1.11** (1.05-1.15)	**1.70** (1.62-1.85)	**2.38** (2.22-2.79)	2465
	01-02	**.639** (.603-.677)	**.635** (.588-.676)	**1.03** (.963-1.08)	**1.52** (1.43-1.61)	**2.03** (1.89-2.22)	2689
	03-04	**.632** (.603-.662)	**.622** (.594-.655)	**.979** (.920-1.03)	**1.49** (1.33-1.64)	**1.97** (1.73-2.26)	2558
	05-06	**.546** (.520-.573)	**.530** (.510-.560)	**.860** (.810-.900)	**1.27** (1.15-1.37)	**1.71** (1.50-1.89)	2576
	07-08	**.514** (.482-.548)	**.500** (.460-.530)	**.800** (.720-.880)	**1.30** (1.23-1.42)	**1.85** (1.73-1.96)	2627
	09-10	**.488** (.466-.512)	**.470** (.440-.500)	**.760** (.710-.810)	**1.16** (1.08-1.28)	**1.53** (1.41-1.62)	2848
Age group							
6-11 years	99-00	**1.17** (.975-1.41)	**1.06** (.918-1.22)	**1.55** (1.22-1.97)	**2.71** (1.67-4.66)	**4.66** (1.97-18.0)	340
	01-02	**.918** (.841-1.00)	**.870** (.800-.933)	**1.27** (1.12-1.43)	**2.33** (1.59-3.64)	**3.64** (1.89-5.56)	368
	03-04	**.926** (.812-1.06)	**.914** (.781-1.03)	**1.45** (1.17-1.72)	**2.14** (1.62-3.47)	**3.47** (2.19-5.31)	290
	05-06	**.628** (.563-.701)	**.590** (.530-.680)	**.870** (.770-.940)	**1.29** (1.03-1.82)	**1.96** (1.32-2.42)	355
	07-08	**.643** (.543-.763)	**.630** (.530-.730)	**1.02** (.770-1.24)	**1.50** (1.24-2.02)	**2.04** (1.70-2.58)	394
	09-10	**.604** (.551-.662)	**.580** (.520-.650)	**.870** (.780-1.00)	**1.32** (1.09-1.51)	**1.60** (1.38-1.75)	378
12-19 years	99-00	**.496** (.460-.535)	**.469** (.408-.508)	**.709** (.655-.828)	**1.11** (.981-1.28)	**1.65** (1.15-2.79)	719
	01-02	**.404** (.380-.428)	**.375** (.342-.400)	**.603** (.541-.702)	**.990** (.882-1.18)	**1.41** (1.07-1.63)	762
	03-04	**.432** (.404-.461)	**.404** (.383-.436)	**.623** (.551-.730)	**.938** (.828-1.06)	**1.23** (1.09-1.35)	725
	05-06	**.363** (.333-.395)	**.340** (.310-.360)	**.510** (.460-.600)	**.800** (.690-.930)	**1.07** (.940-1.23)	701
	07-08	**.302** (.270-.337)	**.290** (.250-.340)	**.430** (.400-.490)	**.670** (.550-.790)	**.900** (.700-1.09)	376
	09-10	**.299** (.273-.328)	**.290** (.260-.320)	**.420** (.370-.490)	**.620** (.550-.760)	**.880** (.740-1.01)	451
20 years and older	99-00	**.720** (.683-.758)	**.712** (.667-.739)	**1.10** (1.02-1.18)	**1.69** (1.53-1.87)	**2.31** (2.15-2.62)	1406
	01-02	**.658** (.617-.703)	**.652** (.608-.702)	**1.05** (.992-1.11)	**1.51** (1.40-1.61)	**2.00** (1.85-2.19)	1559
	03-04	**.641** (.606-.679)	**.633** (.605-.670)	**.988** (.917-1.04)	**1.47** (1.28-1.63)	**1.94** (1.72-2.12)	1543
	05-06	**.573** (.548-.600)	**.570** (.530-.600)	**.890** (.850-.960)	**1.32** (1.22-1.41)	**1.77** (1.53-1.94)	1520
	07-08	**.545** (.513-.579)	**.530** (.490-.570)	**.840** (.760-.910)	**1.36** (1.27-1.49)	**1.92** (1.78-2.08)	1857
	09-10	**.514** (.489-.539)	**.500** (.460-.530)	**.790** (.730-.840)	**1.22** (1.10-1.35)	**1.57** (1.46-1.71)	2019
Gender							
Males	99-00	**.720** (.679-.763)	**.693** (.645-.734)	**1.10** (.992-1.22)	**1.68** (1.50-2.09)	**2.43** (2.15-3.03)	1227
	01-02	**.639** (.607-.673)	**.638** (.586-.686)	**1.01** (.957-1.08)	**1.55** (1.41-1.61)	**2.06** (1.88-2.43)	1334
	03-04	**.615** (.588-.644)	**.593** (.561-.639)	**.914** (.862-.977)	**1.44** (1.25-1.53)	**2.00** (1.71-2.28)	1281
	05-06	**.551** (.522-.582)	**.530** (.510-.580)	**.830** (.770-.910)	**1.25** (1.13-1.39)	**1.77** (1.42-2.20)	1271
	07-08	**.501** (.471-.534)	**.490** (.450-.530)	**.750** (.700-.810)	**1.29** (1.15-1.49)	**1.88** (1.71-1.98)	1327
	09-10	**.481** (.458-.505)	**.450** (.430-.490)	**.740** (.690-.800)	**1.15** (1.04-1.29)	**1.56** (1.37-1.70)	1398
Females	99-00	**.722** (.681-.765)	**.707** (.667-.746)	**1.11** (1.05-1.18)	**1.74** (1.50-2.02)	**2.38** (2.03-2.88)	1238
	01-02	**.639** (.594-.688)	**.625** (.571-.682)	**1.03** (.946-1.11)	**1.50** (1.39-1.61)	**1.98** (1.85-2.15)	1355
	03-04	**.648** (.601-.698)	**.649** (.604-.718)	**1.03** (.938-1.10)	**1.56** (1.34-1.73)	**1.96** (1.72-2.20)	1277
	05-06	**.541** (.507-.577)	**.530** (.500-.580)	**.880** (.820-.940)	**1.28** (1.12-1.41)	**1.64** (1.38-1.91)	1305
	07-08	**.527** (.489-.568)	**.500** (.470-.550)	**.840** (.740-.960)	**1.34** (1.23-1.47)	**1.79** (1.56-2.08)	1300
	09-10	**.495** (.466-.526)	**.480** (.450-.520)	**.780** (.710-.830)	**1.20** (1.08-1.32)	**1.52** (1.39-1.62)	1450

Biomonitoring Summary: http://www.cdc.gov/biomonitoring/Lead_BiomonitoringSummary.html
Factsheet: http://www.cdc.gov/biomonitoring/Lead_FactSheet.html

Source: *Centers for Disease Control & Prevention, Fourth National Report on Human Exposure to Environmental Chemicals, Updated Tables, March 2013*

Urinary Lead (creatinine corrected)

Geometric mean and selected percentiles of urine concentrations (in µg/g of creatinine) for the U.S. population from the National Health and Nutrition Examination Survey.

	Survey years	Geometric mean (95% conf. interval)	Selected percentiles (95% confidence interval) 50th	75th	90th	95th	Sample size
Race/ethnicity							
Mexican Americans	99-00	**.940** (.876-1.01)	**.887** (.796-1.03)	**1.43** (1.37-1.58)	**2.38** (2.08-2.77)	**3.46** (2.78-4.18)	884
	01-02	**.810** (.731-.898)	**.774** (.702-.893)	**1.29** (1.09-1.44)	**2.05** (1.75-2.50)	**2.78** (2.56-3.33)	682
	03-04	**.755** (.681-.838)	**.708** (.612-.851)	**1.18** (1.09-1.31)	**1.86** (1.50-2.26)	**2.31** (1.98-2.92)	618
	05-06	**.686** (.638-.737)	**.680** (.620-.740)	**1.00** (.930-1.13)	**1.63** (1.39-1.88)	**2.20** (1.77-3.20)	652
	07-08	**.607** (.514-.717)	**.590** (.500-.690)	**.970** (.770-1.19)	**1.56** (1.25-2.07)	**2.20** (1.78-2.46)	515
	09-10	**.573** (.526-.623)	**.540** (.470-.610)	**.950** (.780-1.06)	**1.59** (1.41-1.82)	**2.02** (1.82-2.40)	613
Non-Hispanic blacks	99-00	**.722** (.659-.790)	**.671** (.583-.753)	**1.11** (.988-1.20)	**2.00** (1.56-2.51)	**2.83** (2.20-3.88)	568
	01-02	**.644** (.559-.742)	**.608** (.510-.710)	**.962** (.853-1.20)	**1.79** (1.36-2.33)	**2.75** (2.04-3.98)	667
	03-04	**.609** (.529-.701)	**.569** (.492-.698)	**.900** (.793-1.03)	**1.48** (1.11-1.97)	**2.24** (1.65-2.88)	723
	05-06	**.483** (.459-.508)	**.470** (.440-.490)	**.740** (.670-.820)	**1.18** (1.06-1.29)	**1.60** (1.37-1.85)	692
	07-08	**.452** (.414-.492)	**.440** (.400-.490)	**.710** (.610-.780)	**1.13** (.930-1.33)	**1.57** (1.21-1.88)	589
	09-10	**.444** (.417-.473)	**.420** (.390-.470)	**.680** (.600-.740)	**1.07** (.940-1.18)	**1.51** (1.18-1.65)	544
Non-Hispanic whites	99-00	**.696** (.668-.726)	**.677** (.645-.718)	**1.07** (.997-1.14)	**1.66** (1.50-1.83)	**2.31** (1.94-2.82)	822
	01-02	**.615** (.579-.654)	**.621** (.571-.667)	**1.00** (.933-1.07)	**1.46** (1.37-1.52)	**1.88** (1.62-2.03)	1132
	03-04	**.623** (.592-.655)	**.618** (.587-.657)	**.971** (.914-1.03)	**1.44** (1.25-1.61)	**1.85** (1.64-2.10)	1074
	05-06	**.541** (.500-.585)	**.530** (.490-.580)	**.850** (.790-.920)	**1.24** (1.12-1.37)	**1.62** (1.37-1.94)	1041
	07-08	**.506** (.466-.550)	**.490** (.460-.540)	**.790** (.700-.880)	**1.27** (1.15-1.42)	**1.81** (1.59-1.96)	1095
	09-10	**.482** (.448-.518)	**.460** (.430-.500)	**.740** (.690-.820)	**1.15** (1.01-1.30)	**1.46** (1.32-1.59)	1225

Biomonitoring Summary: http://www.cdc.gov/biomonitoring/Lead_BiomonitoringSummary.html
Factsheet: http://www.cdc.gov/biomonitoring/Lead_FactSheet.html

Source: *Centers for Disease Control & Prevention, Fourth National Report on Human Exposure to Environmental Chemicals, Updated Tables, March 2013*

Total Blood Mercury

Geometric mean and selected percentiles of blood concentrations (in µg/L) for the U.S. population from the National Health and Nutrition Examination Survey.

	Survey years	Geometric mean (95% conf. interval)	Selected percentiles (95% confidence interval) 50th	75th	90th	95th	Sample size
Total	03-04	**.797** (.703-.903)	**.800** (.700-.900)	**1.70** (1.50-1.90)	**3.30** (2.90-3.90)	**4.90** (4.30-5.50)	8373
	05-06	**.863** (.787-.946)	**.830** (.760-.920)	**1.66** (1.48-1.93)	**3.20** (2.87-3.54)	**4.64** (4.17-5.25)	8407
	07-08	**.769** (.689-.859)	**.740** (.660-.830)	**1.48** (1.29-1.69)	**2.95** (2.46-3.59)	**4.64** (3.74-5.79)	8266
	09-10	**.863** (.792-.941)	**.790** (.730-.880)	**1.68** (1.49-1.91)	**3.43** (3.07-3.84)	**5.13** (4.57-5.67)	8793
Age group							
1-5 years	03-04	**.326** (.285-.372)	**.300** (.300-.300)	**.500** (.500-.700)	**1.00** (.800-1.60)	**1.80** (1.30-2.50)	911
	05-06	*	**< LOD**	**.500** (.470-.550)	**.940** (.820-1.24)	**1.43** (1.25-1.59)	968
	07-08	*	**< LOD**	**.440** (.380-.540)	**.830** (.620-1.12)	**1.32** (.960-2.40)	817
	09-10	*	**< LOD**	**.490** (.430-.590)	**.890** (.740-1.08)	**1.30** (1.08-1.52)	836
6-11 years	03-04	**.419** (.363-.484)	**.400** (.400-.500)	**.700** (.700-.900)	**1.30** (1.00-1.60)	**1.90** (1.40-3.50)	856
	05-06	*	**.410** (.330-.460)	**.740** (.630-1.00)	**1.43** (1.21-1.87)	**2.34** (1.53-3.42)	934
	07-08	*	**.380** (.340-.440)	**.700** (.600-.790)	**1.21** (.970-1.36)	**1.56** (1.34-1.80)	1011
	09-10	*	**.360** (<LOD-.400)	**.670** (.590-.770)	**1.22** (1.05-1.45)	**1.88** (1.43-2.61)	1009
12-19 years	03-04	**.490** (.418-.574)	**.500** (.400-.600)	**1.00** (.800-1.20)	**1.80** (1.40-2.30)	**2.60** (2.10-3.30)	2081
	05-06	**.513** (.461-.570)	**.460** (.390-.530)	**.850** (.740-1.04)	**1.66** (1.31-1.98)	**2.41** (2.12-2.90)	1996
	07-08	**.469** (.426-.516)	**.440** (.390-.490)	**.800** (.670-.970)	**1.55** (1.30-1.72)	**2.05** (1.77-2.34)	1074
	09-10	**.534** (.473-.602)	**.450** (.370-.540)	**.910** (.770-1.11)	**2.04** (1.53-2.55)	**3.01** (2.53-3.63)	1183
20 years and older	03-04	**.979** (.860-1.12)	**1.00** (.800-1.10)	**2.00** (1.70-2.30)	**3.80** (3.20-4.40)	**5.40** (4.60-6.70)	4525
	05-06	**1.06** (.967-1.15)	**1.03** (.930-1.15)	**1.98** (1.73-2.22)	**3.64** (3.33-4.01)	**5.31** (4.82-5.67)	4509
	07-08	**.944** (.833-1.07)	**.890** (.780-1.03)	**1.73** (1.47-2.09)	**3.41** (2.82-4.17)	**5.32** (4.32-6.72)	5364
	09-10	**1.04** (.956-1.14)	**.970** (.870-1.08)	**2.00** (1.80-2.20)	**3.96** (3.55-4.27)	**5.75** (5.14-6.50)	5765
Gender							
Males	03-04	**.814** (.714-.927)	**.800** (.700-.900)	**1.80** (1.50-2.00)	**3.70** (3.20-4.30)	**5.40** (4.60-6.50)	4132
	05-06	**.864** (.783-.954)	**.810** (.720-.940)	**1.69** (1.48-2.01)	**3.30** (2.86-3.73)	**4.83** (4.08-5.45)	4092
	07-08	**.809** (.709-.923)	**.760** (.670-.850)	**1.56** (1.31-1.81)	**3.21** (2.72-4.06)	**5.16** (4.12-6.97)	4147
	09-10	**.883** (.810-.962)	**.790** (.730-.870)	**1.75** (1.54-2.02)	**3.84** (3.35-4.26)	**5.65** (5.13-6.34)	4366
Females	03-04	**.781** (.689-.886)	**.800** (.700-.900)	**1.60** (1.40-1.80)	**3.00** (2.50-3.50)	**4.40** (3.60-5.30)	4241
	05-06	**.864** (.791-.943)	**.850** (.770-.920)	**1.63** (1.44-1.89)	**3.09** (2.75-3.46)	**4.51** (4.01-5.28)	4315
	07-08	**.748** (.677-.827)	**.720** (.660-.810)	**1.42** (1.24-1.60)	**2.70** (2.27-3.27)	**3.93** (3.17-5.16)	4119
	09-10	**.845** (.772-.924)	**.800** (.720-.880)	**1.61** (1.43-1.81)	**3.13** (2.76-3.48)	**4.43** (4.04-5.11)	4427
Race/ethnicity							
Mexican Americans	03-04	**.563** (.472-.672)	**.600** (.500-.700)	**1.00** (.800-1.30)	**1.90** (1.60-2.40)	**3.00** (2.20-3.80)	2085
	05-06	**.597** (.524-.679)	**.580** (.490-.670)	**1.04** (.870-1.24)	**1.70** (1.40-2.12)	**2.58** (1.96-3.31)	2236
	07-08	**.594** (.536-.658)	**.580** (.520-.670)	**1.03** (.900-1.17)	**1.73** (1.49-2.04)	**2.48** (2.10-2.91)	1712
	09-10	**.613** (.571-.659)	**.580** (.540-.630)	**1.01** (.890-1.15)	**1.63** (1.47-1.90)	**2.45** (2.03-2.93)	1966
Non-Hispanic blacks	03-04	**.877** (.753-1.02)	**.900** (.800-1.00)	**1.60** (1.40-1.80)	**3.00** (2.30-4.00)	**4.40** (3.30-6.00)	2293
	05-06	**.823** (.697-.972)	**.800** (.670-.940)	**1.50** (1.21-1.92)	**2.72** (2.14-3.59)	**4.09** (3.22-5.16)	2193
	07-08	**.766** (.711-.825)	**.780** (.710-.830)	**1.32** (1.23-1.42)	**2.25** (1.99-2.58)	**3.42** (2.74-3.90)	1746
	09-10	**.928** (.805-1.07)	**.900** (.800-1.02)	**1.67** (1.38-1.96)	**2.93** (2.20-4.21)	**4.56** (3.34-6.69)	1593
Non-Hispanic whites	03-04	**.776** (.655-.919)	**.800** (.700-.900)	**1.70** (1.40-2.00)	**3.20** (2.60-3.90)	**4.70** (4.00-5.60)	3478
	05-06	**.891** (.801-.992)	**.870** (.770-1.00)	**1.74** (1.50-2.10)	**3.37** (2.88-3.76)	**4.76** (4.18-5.37)	3310
	07-08	**.743** (.651-.847)	**.720** (.620-.820)	**1.43** (1.18-1.70)	**2.79** (2.33-3.41)	**4.18** (3.57-4.83)	3461
	09-10	**.856** (.766-.957)	**.790** (.690-.920)	**1.70** (1.46-1.98)	**3.43** (2.94-3.94)	**4.92** (4.30-5.65)	3760

Limit of detection (LOD, see Data Analysis section) for Survey years 03-04, 05-06, 07-08 and 09-10 are 0.2, 0.33, 0.33, and 0.33 respectively.
< LOD means less than the limit of detection, which may vary for some chemicals by year and by individual sample.
* Not calculated: proportion of results below limit of detection was too high to provide a valid result.

Biomonitoring Summary: http://www.cdc.gov/biomonitoring/Mercury_BiomonitoringSummary.html
Factsheet: http://www.cdc.gov/biomonitoring/Mercury_FactSheet.html

Source: *Centers for Disease Control & Prevention, Fourth National Report on Human Exposure to Environmental Chemicals, Updated Tables, March 2013*

Inorganic Blood Mercury

Geometric mean and selected percentiles of blood concentrations (in µg/L) for the U.S. population from the National Health and Nutrition Examination Survey.

	Survey years	Geometric mean (95% conf. interval)	Selected percentiles (95% confidence interval) 50th	75th	90th	95th	Sample size
Total	03-04	*	< LOD	< LOD	.600 (.500-.600)	.700 (.700-.700)	8147
	05-06	*	< LOD	< LOD	.540 (.500-.580)	.660 (.620-.710)	8371
	07-08	*	< LOD	.350 (<LOD-.370)	.520 (.500-.540)	.650 (.620-.690)	8162
	09-10	*	< LOD	< LOD	.390 (.360-.430)	.510 (.480-.570)	8733
Age group							
1-5 years	03-04	*	< LOD	< LOD	< LOD	.500 (<LOD-.600)	792
	05-06	*	< LOD	< LOD	.430 (<LOD-.470)	.510 (.430-.670)	948
	07-08	*	< LOD	< LOD	.350 (<LOD-.450)	.500 (.410-.550)	726
	09-10	*	< LOD	< LOD	< LOD	.360 (<LOD-.460)	789
6-11 years	03-04	*	< LOD	< LOD	< LOD	.600 (.500-.600)	842
	05-06	*	< LOD	< LOD	.450 (<LOD-.520)	.560 (.470-.640)	932
	07-08	*	< LOD	< LOD	.380 (.350-.410)	.470 (.420-.520)	1010
	09-10	*	< LOD	< LOD	< LOD	.380 (.350-.440)	1006
12-19 years	03-04	*	< LOD	< LOD	.500 (<LOD-.500)	.600 (.500-.600)	2060
	05-06	*	< LOD	< LOD	.430 (.410-.460)	.540 (.480-.590)	1984
	07-08	*	< LOD	< LOD	.370 (<LOD-.400)	.480 (.410-.530)	1069
	09-10	*	< LOD	< LOD	< LOD	.420 (.350-.500)	1184
20 years and older	03-04	*	< LOD	< LOD	.600 (.500-.600)	.700 (.700-.800)	4453
	05-06	*	< LOD	< LOD	.570 (.530-.610)	.690 (.650-.750)	4507
	07-08	*	< LOD	.380 (.360-.390)	.550 (.530-.570)	.700 (.660-.730)	5357
	09-10	*	< LOD	< LOD	.420 (.390-.450)	.540 (.490-.600)	5754
Gender							
Males	03-04	*	< LOD	< LOD	.500 (.500-.600)	.600 (.600-.700)	4015
	05-06	*	< LOD	< LOD	.480 (.450-.520)	.600 (.550-.640)	4076
	07-08	*	< LOD	< LOD	.500 (.470-.520)	.600 (.570-.650)	4093
	09-10	*	< LOD	< LOD	.370 (<LOD-.420)	.500 (.440-.560)	4336
Females	03-04	*	< LOD	< LOD	.600 (.500-.600)	.700 (.700-.800)	4132
	05-06	*	< LOD	< LOD	.580 (.550-.640)	.700 (.670-.780)	4295
	07-08	*	< LOD	.380 (.360-.390)	.550 (.520-.570)	.700 (.670-.740)	4069
	09-10	*	< LOD	< LOD	.410 (.380-.440)	.530 (.490-.600)	4097
Race/ethnicity							
Mexican Americans	03-04	*	< LOD	< LOD	.500 (.500-.600)	.700 (.600-.800)	2007
	05-06	*	< LOD	< LOD	.530 (.470-.580)	.670 (.560-.830)	2224
	07-08	*	< LOD	< LOD	.430 (.400-.480)	.560 (.520-.610)	1685
	09-10	*	< LOD	< LOD	< LOD	.470 (.390-.530)	1947
Non-Hispanic blacks	03-04	*	< LOD	< LOD	.600 (.500-.600)	.700 (.600-.800)	2240
	05-06	*	< LOD	< LOD	.530 (.470-.600)	.670 (.600-.760)	2183
	07-08	*	< LOD	< LOD	.490 (.450-.530)	.610 (.560-.650)	1729
	09-10	*	< LOD	< LOD	.370 (.350-.390)	.480 (.410-.530)	1580
Non-Hispanic whites	03-04	*	< LOD	< LOD	.600 (.500-.600)	.700 (.600-.700)	3406
	05-06	*	< LOD	< LOD	.540 (.500-.580)	.650 (.610-.710)	3298
	07-08	*	< LOD	.360 (<LOD-.390)	.530 (.500-.550)	.660 (.620-.700)	3421
	09-10	*	< LOD	< LOD	.410 (.370-.450)	.520 (.480-.590)	3739

Limit of detection (LOD, see Data Analysis section) for Survey years 03-04, 05-06, 07-08 and 09-10 are 0.42, 0.4, 0.35, and 0.35 respectively.
< LOD means less than the limit of detection, which may vary for some chemicals by year and by individual sample.
* Not calculated: proportion of results below limit of detection was too high to provide a valid result.

Biomonitoring Summary: http://www.cdc.gov/biomonitoring/Mercury_BiomonitoringSummary.html
Factsheet: http://www.cdc.gov/biomonitoring/Mercury_FactSheet.html

Source: *Centers for Disease Control & Prevention, Fourth National Report on Human Exposure to Environmental Chemicals, Updated Tables, March 2013*

Urinary Mercury

Geometric mean and selected percentiles of urine concentrations (in µg/L) for the U.S. population from the National Health and Nutrition Examination Survey.

	Survey years	Geometric mean (95% conf. interval)	Selected percentiles (95% confidence interval) 50th	75th	90th	95th	Sample size
Total	03-04	**.447** (.406-.492)	**.420** (.360-.480)	**1.00** (.870-1.14)	**2.08** (1.78-2.42)	**3.19** (2.76-3.55)	2538
	05-06	**.468** (.426-.514)	**.460** (.410-.510)	**1.03** (.900-1.12)	**2.11** (1.88-2.36)	**2.94** (2.58-3.26)	2578
	07-08	**.443** (.408-.482)	**.440** (.400-.470)	**.880** (.760-1.00)	**1.74** (1.62-1.96)	**2.66** (2.29-3.08)	2634
	09-10	*	**.400** (.360-.450)	**.850** (.770-.910)	**1.53** (1.30-1.81)	**2.42** (2.07-2.72)	2865
Age group							
6-11 years	03-04	**.254** (.213-.304)	**.200** (.160-.250)	**.440** (.330-.580)	**1.16** (.610-1.61)	**1.96** (1.13-2.97)	287
	05-06	**.333** (.267-.416)	**.320** (.250-.390)	**.650** (.470-.840)	**1.32** (.930-1.88)	**2.18** (1.28-3.40)	355
	07-08	**.301** (.260-.347)	**.290** (.230-.340)	**.520** (.430-.620)	**1.03** (.770-1.23)	**1.87** (1.03-3.48)	398
	09-10	*	**.260** (.220-.320)	**.510** (.430-.620)	**1.03** (.730-1.31)	**1.58** (1.18-1.88)	379
12-19 years	03-04	**.358** (.313-.408)	**.330** (.290-.370)	**.700** (.530-.840)	**1.60** (1.14-2.52)	**2.93** (1.88-3.66)	722
	05-06	**.372** (.286-.486)	**.350** (.270-.470)	**.740** (.580-.920)	**1.61** (.970-2.81)	**2.59** (1.40-4.45)	703
	07-08	**.364** (.326-.406)	**.380** (.320-.450)	**.590** (.550-.650)	**1.24** (.830-1.71)	**1.82** (1.41-2.29)	375
	09-10	*	**.290** (.230-.360)	**.530** (.470-.630)	**1.09** (.890-1.31)	**1.73** (1.28-2.31)	455
20 years and older	03-04	**.495** (.442-.555)	**.480** (.410-.570)	**1.12** (.930-1.29)	**2.20** (1.85-2.65)	**3.33** (2.76-3.88)	1529
	05-06	**.505** (.468-.545)	**.510** (.460-.560)	**1.11** (1.04-1.16)	**2.23** (1.97-2.50)	**3.11** (2.64-3.37)	1520
	07-08	**.477** (.435-.523)	**.470** (.430-.520)	**.970** (.850-1.10)	**1.89** (1.69-2.20)	**2.82** (2.33-3.56)	1861
	09-10	*	**.450** (.390-.510)	**.890** (.810-1.00)	**1.66** (1.40-2.01)	**2.53** (2.21-2.84)	2031
Gender							
Males	03-04	**.433** (.405-.463)	**.400** (.350-.460)	**.940** (.840-1.05)	**1.88** (1.63-2.18)	**2.68** (2.34-3.05)	1266
	05-06	**.464** (.411-.523)	**.450** (.400-.520)	**.980** (.860-1.11)	**2.03** (1.57-2.48)	**3.00** (2.48-3.37)	1270
	07-08	**.457** (.417-.501)	**.460** (.400-.520)	**.880** (.780-1.01)	**1.68** (1.53-1.77)	**2.40** (2.11-2.76)	1326
	09-10	*	**.410** (.340-.480)	**.860** (.750-.950)	**1.46** (1.29-1.66)	**2.21** (1.93-2.53)	1404
Females	03-04	**.460** (.396-.534)	**.430** (.330-.530)	**1.07** (.870-1.28)	**2.26** (1.77-2.90)	**3.54** (2.76-4.31)	1272
	05-06	**.472** (.424-.525)	**.470** (.390-.550)	**1.07** (.900-1.19)	**2.14** (1.84-2.50)	**2.89** (2.60-3.38)	1308
	07-08	**.431** (.388-.478)	**.430** (.380-.460)	**.870** (.710-1.05)	**1.88** (1.55-2.38)	**2.92** (2.27-4.17)	1308
	09-10	*	**.390** (.360-.450)	**.840** (.730-.940)	**1.61** (1.29-2.03)	**2.61** (2.16-3.12)	1461
Race/ethnicity							
Mexican Americans	03-04	**.416** (.340-.509)	**.360** (.280-.430)	**.960** (.700-1.23)	**2.19** (1.39-3.24)	**3.16** (1.99-6.30)	619
	05-06	**.451** (.369-.551)	**.420** (.310-.560)	**1.01** (.780-1.25)	**2.22** (1.48-2.64)	**3.00** (2.27-4.01)	651
	07-08	**.409** (.349-.480)	**.370** (.330-.450)	**.780** (.700-.950)	**1.82** (1.26-1.97)	**2.55** (1.87-3.08)	514
	09-10	*	**.350** (.280-.430)	**.670** (.520-.890)	**1.53** (1.06-1.84)	**2.29** (1.81-2.76)	615
Non-Hispanic blacks	03-04	**.476** (.413-.549)	**.430** (.360-.530)	**.890** (.770-1.00)	**1.96** (1.60-2.31)	**3.09** (2.03-4.89)	713
	05-06	**.453** (.384-.533)	**.450** (.380-.550)	**.890** (.710-1.13)	**1.78** (1.34-2.29)	**2.57** (2.21-3.15)	691
	07-08	**.478** (.411-.556)	**.460** (.380-.540)	**.910** (.770-1.06)	**1.85** (1.42-2.41)	**2.76** (1.97-4.19)	589
	09-10	*	**.410** (.340-.490)	**.840** (.650-1.08)	**1.66** (1.34-1.95)	**2.64** (1.88-3.30)	546
Non-Hispanic whites	03-04	**.441** (.382-.509)	**.420** (.330-.520)	**1.01** (.840-1.23)	**2.08** (1.67-2.46)	**3.24** (2.67-3.60)	1066
	05-06	**.459** (.409-.513)	**.440** (.400-.510)	**1.00** (.860-1.12)	**2.07** (1.77-2.40)	**2.81** (2.47-3.37)	1044
	07-08	**.431** (.378-.493)	**.430** (.380-.480)	**.880** (.700-1.07)	**1.71** (1.50-2.18)	**2.70** (2.18-3.59)	1100
	09-10	*	**.390** (.330-.470)	**.850** (.750-.950)	**1.52** (1.26-2.01)	**2.42** (1.93-2.85)	1225

Limit of detection (LOD, see Data Analysis section) for Survey years 03-04, 05-06, 07-08 and 09-10 are 0.14, 0.11, 0.08, and 0.08 respectively.
* Not calculated: proportion of results below limit of detection was too high to provide a valid result.

Biomonitoring Summary: http://www.cdc.gov/biomonitoring/Mercury_BiomonitoringSummary.html
Factsheet: http://www.cdc.gov/biomonitoring/Mercury_FactSheet.html

Source: *Centers for Disease Control & Prevention, Fourth National Report on Human Exposure to Environmental Chemicals, Updated Tables, March 2013*

Urinary Mercury (creatinine corrected)

Geometric mean and selected percentiles of urine concentrations (in µg/g of creatinine) for the U.S. population from the National Health and Nutrition Examination Survey.

	Survey years	Geometric mean (95% conf. interval)	Selected percentiles (95% confidence interval) 50th	75th	90th	95th	Sample size
Total	03-04	**.443** (.404-.486)	**.447** (.392-.498)	**.909** (.785-1.00)	**1.65** (1.40-1.86)	**2.35** (1.88-2.85)	2537
	05-06	**.460** (.414-.511)	**.450** (.410-.510)	**.870** (.790-1.00)	**1.63** (1.44-1.75)	**2.26** (2.12-2.50)	2578
	07-08	**.462** (.425-.502)	**.450** (.400-.490)	**.820** (.750-.960)	**1.57** (1.38-1.73)	**2.32** (2.00-2.89)	2634
	09-10	*	**.409** (.367-.459)	**.793** (.691-.893)	**1.43** (1.24-1.67)	**2.09** (1.79-2.39)	2865
Age group							
6-11 years	03-04	**.297** (.246-.358)	**.276** (.208-.347)	**.485** (.391-.630)	**1.25** (.667-1.79)	**1.79** (1.11-2.61)	286
	05-06	**.411** (.323-.524)	**.390** (.290-.500)	**.710** (.510-.960)	**1.30** (.990-2.12)	**2.55** (1.38-3.50)	355
	07-08	**.393** (.351-.440)	**.350** (.300-.440)	**.630** (.540-.770)	**1.15** (.860-1.50)	**1.68** (1.18-2.99)	398
	09-10	*	**.357** (.306-.406)	**.632** (.500-.750)	**1.04** (.863-1.26)	**1.62** (1.19-1.98)	379
12-19 years	03-04	**.255** (.225-.289)	**.217** (.196-.275)	**.464** (.376-.535)	**1.06** (.714-1.39)	**1.67** (1.13-2.03)	722
	05-06	**.286** (.230-.356)	**.260** (.200-.320)	**.500** (.380-.660)	**1.09** (.660-1.70)	**1.76** (1.11-2.67)	703
	07-08	**.284** (.251-.320)	**.280** (.230-.300)	**.500** (.400-.550)	**.890** (.620-1.08)	**1.18** (.980-1.36)	375
	09-10	*	**.226** (.202-.287)	**.481** (.429-.553)	**.917** (.736-1.18)	**1.41** (1.12-1.62)	455
20 years and older	03-04	**.508** (.455-.566)	**.525** (.447-.616)	**1.00** (.875-1.09)	**1.76** (1.46-2.11)	**2.54** (2.04-3.00)	1529
	05-06	**.503** (.461-.549)	**.510** (.470-.550)	**.940** (.850-1.07)	**1.69** (1.50-1.86)	**2.31** (2.12-2.54)	1520
	07-08	**.507** (.463-.555)	**.500** (.450-.560)	**.940** (.810-1.02)	**1.69** (1.51-2.01)	**2.56** (2.09-3.17)	1861
	09-10	*	**.454** (.395-.517)	**.861** (.731-.988)	**1.51** (1.29-1.85)	**2.15** (1.88-2.57)	2031
Gender							
Males	03-04	**.365** (.333-.400)	**.362** (.309-.417)	**.696** (.620-.784)	**1.31** (1.18-1.44)	**1.87** (1.51-2.30)	1266
	05-06	**.380** (.336-.431)	**.390** (.330-.440)	**.740** (.600-.890)	**1.27** (1.09-1.47)	**1.73** (1.62-1.85)	1270
	07-08	**.408** (.374-.445)	**.390** (.350-.450)	**.730** (.650-.810)	**1.22** (1.11-1.36)	**1.69** (1.54-2.11)	1326
	09-10	*	**.337** (.298-.391)	**.675** (.585-.802)	**1.19** (1.06-1.29)	**1.50** (1.33-1.78)	1404
Females	03-04	**.532** (.472-.599)	**.545** (.455-.652)	**1.06** (.969-1.21)	**1.88** (1.64-2.30)	**2.77** (2.12-3.56)	1271
	05-06	**.552** (.494-.617)	**.540** (.490-.620)	**1.09** (.850-1.27)	**1.96** (1.72-2.14)	**2.78** (2.35-3.17)	1308
	07-08	**.520** (.469-.576)	**.490** (.460-.540)	**.960** (.820-1.11)	**1.92** (1.58-2.24)	**2.83** (2.24-3.50)	1308
	09-10	*	**.475** (.423-.552)	**.890** (.771-1.07)	**1.81** (1.43-2.09)	**2.57** (2.09-2.94)	1461
Race/ethnicity							
Mexican Americans	03-04	**.384** (.307-.480)	**.365** (.280-.455)	**.768** (.619-.990)	**1.62** (1.23-2.16)	**2.32** (1.78-4.01)	618
	05-06	**.425** (.337-.536)	**.400** (.310-.490)	**.840** (.560-1.29)	**1.82** (1.30-2.47)	**2.63** (2.22-3.20)	651
	07-08	**.409** (.350-.479)	**.380** (.310-.480)	**.790** (.690-.850)	**1.55** (1.08-1.98)	**2.03** (1.55-2.70)	514
	09-10	*	**.333** (.272-.400)	**.660** (.494-.861)	**1.29** (1.02-1.54)	**1.95** (1.52-2.89)	615
Non-Hispanic blacks	03-04	**.343** (.301-.391)	**.306** (.265-.368)	**.587** (.522-.687)	**1.28** (.964-1.63)	**2.13** (1.41-2.87)	713
	05-06	**.328** (.285-.378)	**.320** (.270-.370)	**.610** (.470-.780)	**1.15** (.930-1.40)	**1.64** (1.29-1.96)	691
	07-08	**.350** (.303-.404)	**.330** (.280-.380)	**.590** (.490-.690)	**1.10** (.840-1.46)	**1.85** (1.13-2.77)	589
	09-10	*	**.317** (.259-.393)	**.582** (.500-.659)	**1.05** (.900-1.30)	**1.55** (1.18-1.96)	546
Non-Hispanic whites	03-04	**.463** (.400-.537)	**.476** (.385-.588)	**.970** (.800-1.07)	**1.67** (1.32-2.11)	**2.40** (1.88-2.90)	1066
	05-06	**.475** (.426-.531)	**.490** (.440-.540)	**.890** (.820-1.02)	**1.61** (1.42-1.75)	**2.23** (1.98-2.50)	1044
	07-08	**.481** (.423-.546)	**.480** (.390-.540)	**.890** (.750-1.03)	**1.58** (1.34-2.02)	**2.49** (1.89-3.18)	1100
	09-10	*	**.434** (.370-.500)	**.833** (.689-1.04)	**1.50** (1.26-1.87)	**2.12** (1.80-2.64)	1225

* Not calculated: proportion of results below limit of detection was too high to provide a valid result.

Biomonitoring Summary: http://www.cdc.gov/biomonitoring/Mercury_BiomonitoringSummary.html

Factsheet: http://www.cdc.gov/biomonitoring/Mercury_FactSheet.html

Source: *Centers for Disease Control & Prevention, Fourth National Report on Human Exposure to Environmental Chemicals, Updated Tables, March 2013*

UV Index for 58 U.S. Cities

City	State	Clear Sky UV Index					UV Index Forecast				
		Extreme	Very High	High	Moderate	Low	Extreme	Very High	High	Moderate	Low
Albuquerque	NM	110	68	41	100	32	83	81	37	107	43
Anchorage	AK	0	0	3	127	221	0	0	0	101	250
Atlanta	GA	49	121	47	111	23	2	130	52	95	72
Atlantic City	NJ	1	122	52	74	102	0	62	74	87	128
Baltimore	MD	1	126	51	73	100	0	64	72	79	136
Billings	MT	0	90	59	65	137	0	68	50	85	148
Bismarck	ND	0	74	58	73	146	0	47	61	80	163
Boise	ID	18	97	48	63	125	1	97	43	62	148
Boston	MA	0	99	52	80	120	0	60	59	86	146
Buffalo	NY	0	93	57	78	123	0	44	71	80	156
Burlington	VT	0	86	56	69	140	0	42	57	74	178
Charleston	SC	36	133	60	115	7	2	136	60	99	54
Charleston	WV	3	133	51	69	95	0	86	61	65	139
Cheyenne	WY	47	93	34	72	105	17	99	46	76	113
Chicago	IL	0	102	65	59	125	0	64	59	81	147
Cleveland	OH	0	103	63	69	116	0	58	74	76	143
Concord	NH	0	95	52	80	124	0	52	51	86	162
Dallas	TX	56	117	48	111	19	4	121	35	117	74
Denver	CO	57	94	35	73	92	34	97	36	93	91
Des Moines	IA	0	115	57	57	122	0	61	65	71	154
Detroit	MI	0	96	63	66	126	0	53	64	85	149
Dover	DE	2	125	50	73	101	0	64	72	85	130
Hartford	CT	0	104	52	79	116	0	60	59	83	149
Honolulu	HI	150	96	102	3	0	124	112	94	21	0
Houston	TX	91	104	48	108	0	14	148	41	107	41
Indianapolis	IN	2	124	47	72	106	0	72	69	75	135
Jackson	MS	69	110	53	116	3	9	136	51	100	55
Jacksonville	FL	66	125	50	110	0	18	145	46	113	29
Las Vegas	NV	63	100	39	101	48	15	119	53	87	77
Little Rock	AR	36	129	43	100	43	1	120	40	106	84
Los Angeles	CA	100	71	45	113	22	54	108	40	96	53
Louisville	KY	4	132	50	72	93	0	90	53	80	128
Memphis	TN	35	123	47	96	50	1	115	58	90	87
Miami	FL	120	110	59	62	0	79	126	50	88	8
Milwaukee	WI	0	95	64	65	127	0	55	64	76	156
Minneapolis	MN	0	85	63	64	139	0	40	55	88	168
Mobile	AL	78	115	48	110	0	25	142	54	98	32
New Orleans	LA	90	108	45	108	0	37	141	37	107	29
New York	NY	0	114	50	79	108	0	63	65	78	145
Norfolk	VA	7	131	58	79	76	0	101	59	75	116
Oklahoma City	OK	32	128	37	98	56	1	114	32	111	93
Omaha	NE	1	116	53	60	121	0	70	64	71	146
Philadelphia	PA	0	121	51	74	105	0	56	71	89	135
Phoenix	AZ	100	75	43	115	18	46	117	39	112	37
Pittsburgh	PA	1	118	55	69	108	0	65	66	73	147
Portland	ME	0	88	55	79	129	0	44	56	82	169
Portland	OR	0	87	55	76	133	0	51	46	78	176
Providence	RI	0	103	54	78	116	0	58	62	80	151
Raleigh	NC	18	125	60	86	62	0	103	60	83	105
Saint Louis	MO	4	134	42	74	97	0	87	58	78	128
Salt Lake City	UT	58	86	41	72	94	35	83	51	70	112
San Francisco	CA	7	132	48	80	84	2	122	46	75	106
San Juan	PR	197	101	53	0	0	169	114	65	3	0
Seattle	WA	0	55	66	85	145	0	17	68	86	180
Sioux Falls	SD	0	97	65	60	129	0	49	64	78	160

City	State	Clear Sky UV Index					UV Index Forecast				
		Extreme	Very High	High	Moderate	Low	Extreme	Very High	High	Moderate	Low
Tampa	FL	96	114	47	94	0	56	129	50	106	10
Washington	DC	2	126	55	69	99	0	75	63	79	134
Wichita	KS	14	137	40	71	89	0	112	31	92	116

Notes: *Figures are the number of days in each exposure category; The days may not add up to 366 due to missing data.*

The UV Index is a next day forecast of the amount of skin damaging UV radiation expected to reach the earth's surface at the time when the sun is highest in the sky (solar noon). The amount of UV radiation reaching the surface is primarily related to the elevation of the sun in the sky, the amount of ozone in the stratosphere, and the amount of clouds present. The UV Index can range from 0 (when it is night time) to 15 or 16 (in the tropics at high elevations under clear skies). UV radiation is greatest when the sun is highest in the sky and rapidly decreases as the sun approaches the horizon. The higher the UV Index, the greater the dose rate of skin damaging (and eye damaging) UV radiation. Consequently, the higher the UV Index, the smaller the time it takes before skin damage occurs.

Source: *NOAA, Climate Prediction Center, UV Index: Annual Time Series, 2012*

Acronyms & Abbreviations

A

A&I: Alternative and Innovative (Wastewater Treatment System)

AA: Accountable Area; Adverse Action; Advices of Allowance; Assistant Administrator; Associate Administrator; Atomic Absorption

AAEE: American Academy of Environmental Engineers

AANWR: Alaskan Arctic National Wildlife Refuge

AAP: Asbestos Action Program

AAPCO: American Association of Pesticide Control Officials

AARC: Alliance for Acid Rain Control

ABEL: EPA's computer model for analyzing a violator's ability to pay a civil penalty.

ABES: Alliance for Balanced Environmental Solutions

AC: Actual Commitment. Advisory Circular

A&C: Abatement and Control

ACA: American Conservation Association

ACBM: Asbestos-Containing Building Material

ACE: Alliance for Clean Energy

ACE: Any Credible Evidence

ACEEE: American Council for an Energy Efficient Economy

ACFM: Actual Cubic Feet Per Minute

ACL: Alternate Concentration Limit. Analytical Chemistry Laboratory

ACM: Asbestos-Containing Material

ACP: Agriculture Control Program (Water Quality Management); ACP: Air Carcinogen Policy

ACQUIRE: Aquatic Information Retrieval

ACQR: Air Quality Control Region

ACS: American Chemical Society

ACT: Action

ACTS: Asbestos Contractor Tracking System

ACWA: American Clean Water Association

ACWM: Asbestos-Containing Waste Material

ADABA: Acceptable Data Base

ADB: Applications Data Base

ADI: Acceptable Daily Intake

ADP: AHERA Designated Person; Automated Data Processing

ADQ: Audits of Data Quality

ADR: Alternate Dispute Resolution

ADSS: Air Data Screening System

ADT: Average Daily Traffic

AEA: Atomic Energy Act

AEC: Associate Enforcement Counsels

AEE: Alliance for Environmental Education

AEERL: Air and Energy Engineering Research Laboratory

AEM: Acoustic Emission Monitoring

AERE: Association of Environmental and Resource Economists

AES: Auger Electron Spectrometry

AFA: American Forestry Association

AFCA: Area Fuel Consumption Allocation

AFCEE: Air Force Center for Environmental Excellence

AFS: AIRS Facility Subsystem

AFUG: AIRS Facility Users Group

AH: Allowance Holders

AHERA: Asbestos Hazard Emergency Response Act

AHU: Air Handling Unit

AI: Active Ingredient

AIC: Active to Inert Conversion

AICUZ: Air Installation Compatible Use Zones

AID: Agency for International Development

AIHC: American Industrial Health Council

AIP: Auto Ignition Point

AIRMON: Atmospheric Integrated Research Monitoring Network

AIRS: Aerometric Information Retrieval System

AL: Acceptable Level

ALA: Delta-Aminolevulinic Acid

ALA-O: Delta-Aminolevulinic Acid Dehydrates

ALAPO: Association of Local Air Pollution Control Officers

ALARA: As Low As Reasonably Achievable

ALC: Application Limiting Constituent

ALJ: Administrative Law Judge

ALMS: Atomic Line Molecular Spectroscopy

ALR: Action Leakage Rate

AMBIENS: Atmospheric Mass Balance of Industrially Emitted and Natural Sulfur

AMOS: Air Management Oversight System

AMPS: Automatic Mapping and Planning System

AMSA: Association of Metropolitan Sewer Agencies

ANC: Acid Neutralizing Capacity

ANPR: Advance Notice of Proposed Rulemaking

ANRHRD: Air, Noise, & Radiation Health Research Division/ORD

ANSS: American Nature Study Society

AOAC: Association of Official Analytical Chemists

AOC: Abnormal Operating Conditions

AOD: Argon-Oxygen Decarbonization

AOML: Atlantic Oceanographic and Meteorological Laboratory

AP: Accounting Point

APA: Administrative Procedures Act

APCA: Air Pollution Control Association

APCD: Air Pollution Control District

APDS: Automated Procurement Documentation System

APHA: American Public Health Association

APRAC: Urban Diffusion Model for Carbon Monoxide from Motor Vehicle Traffic

APTI: Air Pollution Training Institute

APWA: American Public Works Association

AQ-7: Non-reactive Pollutant Modelling

AQCCT: Air-Quality Criteria and Control Techniques

AQCP: Air Quality Control Program

AQCR: Air-Quality Control Region

AQD: Air-Quality Digest

AQDHS: Air-Quality Data Handling System

AQDM: Air-Quality Display Model

AQMA: Air-Quality Maintenance Area

AQMD: Air Quality Management District

AQMP: Air-Quality Maintenance Plan; Air-Quality Management Plan

AQSM: Air-Quality Simulation Model

AQTAD: Air-Quality Technical Assistance Demonstration

AR: Administrative Record

A&R: Air and Radiation

ARA: Assistant Regional Administrator; Associate Regional Administrator

ARAC: Acid Rain Advisory Committee

ARAR: Applicable or Relevant and Appropriate Standards, Limitations, Criteria, and Requirements

ARB: Air Resources Board

ARC: Agency Ranking Committee

ARCC: American Rivers Conservation Council

ARCS: Alternative Remedial Contract Strategy

ARG: American Resources Group

ARIP: Accidental Release Information Program

ARL: Air Resources Laboratory

ARM: Air Resources Management

ARNEWS: Acid Rain National Early Warning Systems

ARO: Alternate Regulatory Option

ARRP: Acid Rain Research Program

ARRPA: Air Resources Regional Pollution Assessment Model

ARS: Agricultural Research Service

ARZ: Auto Restricted Zone

AS: Area Source

ASC: Area Source Category

ASDWA: Association of State Drinking Water Administrators

ASHAA: Asbestos in Schools Hazard Abatement Act

ASHRAE: American Society of Heating, Refrigerating, and Air-Conditioning Engineers

ASIWCPA: Association of State and Interstate Water Pollution Control Administrators

ASMDHS: Airshed Model Data Handling System

ASRL: Atmospheric Sciences Research Laboratory

AST: Advanced Secondary (Wastewater) Treatment

ASTHO: Association of State and Territorial Health Officers

ASTM: American Society for Testing and Materials

ASTSWMO: Association of State and Territorial Solid Waste Management Officials

AT: Advanced Treatment. Alpha Track Detection

ATERIS: Air Toxics Exposure and Risk Information System

ATS: Action Tracking System; Allowance Tracking System

ATSDR: Agency for Toxic Substances and Disease Registry

ATTF: Air Toxics Task Force

AUSM: Advanced Utility Simulation Model

A/WPR: Air/Water Pollution Report

AWRA: American Water Resources Association

AWT: Advanced Wastewater Treatment

AWWA: American Water Works Association

AWWARF: American Water Works Association Research Foundation.

B

BAA: Board of Assistance Appeals

BAC: Bioremediation Action Committee; Biotechnology Advisory Committee

BACM: Best Available Control Measures

BACT: Best Available Control Technology

BADT: Best Available Demonstrated Technology

BAF: Bioaccumulation Factor

BaP: Benzo(a)Pyrene

BAP: Benefits Analysis Program

BART: Best Available Retrofit Technology

BASIS: Battelle's Automated Search Information System

BAT: Best Available Technology

BATEA: Best Available Treatment Economically Achievable

BCT: Best Control Technology

BCPCT: Best Conventional Pollutant Control Technology

BDAT: Best Demonstrated Achievable Technology

BDCT: Best Demonstrated Control Technology

BDT: Best Demonstrated Technology

BEJ: Best Engineering Judgement. Best Expert Judgment

BF: Bonafide Notice of Intent to Manufacture or Import (IMD/OTS)

BID: Background Information Document. Buoyancy Induced Dispersion

BIOPLUME: Model to Predict the Maximum Extent of Existing Plumes

BMP: Best Management Practice(s)

BMR: Baseline Monitoring Report

BO: Budget Obligations

BOA: Basic Ordering Agreement (Contracts)

BOD: Biochemical Oxygen Demand. Biological Oxygen Demand

BOF: Basic Oxygen Furnace

BOP: Basic Oxygen Process

BOPF: Basic Oxygen Process Furnace

BOYSNC: Beginning of Year Significant Non-Compliers

BP: Boiling Point

BPJ: Best Professional Judgment

BPT: Best Practicable Technology. Pest Practicable Treatment

BPWTT: Best Practical Wastewater Treatment Technology

BRI: Building-Related Illness

BRS: Bibliographic Retrieval Service

BSI: British Standards Institute

BSO: Benzene Soluble Organics

BTZ: Below the Treatment Zone

BUN: Blood Urea Nitrogen

C

CA: Citizen Act. Competition Advocate. Cooperative Agreements. Corrective Action

CAA: Clean Air Act; Compliance Assurance Agreement

CAAA: Clean Air Act Amendments

CAER: Community Awareness and Emergency Response

CAFE: Corporate Average Fuel Economy

CAFO: Concentrated Animal Feedlot; Consent Agreement/Final Order

CAG: Carcinogenic Assessment Group

CAIR: Clean Air Interstate Rule: Comprehensive Assessment of Information Rule

CALINE: California Line Source Model

CAM: Compliance Assurance Monitoring rule; Compliance Assurance Monitoring

CAMP: Continuous Air Monitoring Program

CAN: Common Account Number

CAO: Corrective Action Order

CAP: Corrective Action Plan. Cost Allocation Procedure. Criteria Air Pollutant

CAPMoN: Canadian Air and Precipitation Monitoring Network

CAR: Corrective Action Report

CAS: Center for Automotive Safety; Chemical Abstract Service

CASAC: Clean Air Scientific Advisory Committee

CASLP: Conference on Alternative State and Local Practices

CASTNet: Clean Air Status and Trends Network

CATS: Corrective Action Tracking System

CAU: Carbon Adsorption Unit; Command Arithmetic Unit

CB: Continuous Bubbler

CBA: Chesapeake Bay Agreement. Cost Benefit Analysis

CBD: Central Business District

CBEP: Community Based Environmental Project

CBI: Compliance Biomonitoring Inspection; Confidential Business Information

CBOD: Carbonaceous Biochemical Oxygen Demand

CBP: Chesapeake Bay Program; County Business Patterns

CCA: Competition in Contracting Act

CCAA: Canadian Clean Air Act

CCAP: Center for Clean Air Policy; Climate Change Action Plan

CCEA: Conventional Combustion Environmental Assessment

CCHW: Citizens Clearinghouse for Hazardous Wastes

CCID: Confidential Chemicals Identification System

CCMS/NATO: Committee on Challenges of a Modern Society/North Atlantic Treaty Organization

CCP: Composite Correction Plan

CC/RTS: Chemical Collection/ Request Tracking System

CCTP: Clean Coal Technology Program

CD: Climatological Data

CDB: Consolidated Data Base

CDBA: Central Data Base Administrator

CDBG: Community Development Block Grant

CDD: Chlorinated dibenzo-p-dioxin

CDF: Chlorinated dibenzofuran

CDHS: Comprehensive Data Handling System

CDI: Case Development Inspection

CDM: Climatological Dispersion Model; Comprehensive Data Management

CDMQC: Climatological Dispersion Model with Calibration and Source Contribution

CDNS: Climatological Data National Summary

CDP: Census Designated Places

CDS: Compliance Data System

CE: Categorical Exclusion. Conditionally Exempt Generator

CEA: Cooperative Enforcement Agreement; Cost and Economic Assessment

CEAT: Contractor Evidence Audit Team

CEARC: Canadian Environmental Assessment Research Council

CEB: Chemical Element Balance

CEC: Commission for Environmental Cooperation

CECATS: CSB Existing Chemicals Assessment Tracking System

CEE: Center for Environmental Education

CEEM: Center for Energy and Environmental Management

CEI: Compliance Evaluation Inspection

CELRF: Canadian Environmental Law Research Foundation

CEM: Continuous Emission Monitoring

CEMS: Continuous Emission Monitoring System

CEPA: Canadian Environmental Protection Act

CEPP: Chemical Emergency Preparedness Plan

CEQ: Council on Environmental Quality

CERCLA: Comprehensive Environmental Response, Compensation, and Liability Act (1980)

CERCLIS: Comprehensive Environmental Response, Compensation, and Liability Information System

CERT: Certificate of Eligibility

CESQG: Conditionally Exempt Small Quantity Generator

CEST: Community Environmental Service Teams

CF: Conservation Foundation

CFC: Chlorofluorocarbons

CFM: Chlorofluoromethanes

CFR: Code of Federal Regulations

CHABA: Committee on Hearing and Bio-Acoustics

CHAMP: Community Health Air Monitoring Program

CHEMNET: Chemical Industry Emergency Mutual Aid Network

CHESS: Community Health and Environmental Surveillance System

CHIP: Chemical Hazard Information Profiles

CI: Compression Ignition. Confidence Interval

CIAQ: Council on Indoor Air Quality

CIBL: Convective Internal Boundary Layer

CICA: Competition in Contracting Act

CICIS: Chemicals in Commerce Information System

CIDRS: Cascade Impactor Data Reduction System

CIMI: Committee on Integrity and Management Improvement

CIS: Chemical Information System. Contracts Information System

CKD: Cement Kiln Dust

CKRC: Cement Kiln Recycling Coalition

CLC: Capacity Limiting Constituents

CLEANS: Clinical Laboratory for Evaluation and Assessment of Toxic Substances

CLEVER: Clinical Laboratory for Evaluation and Validation of Epidemiologic Research

CLF: Conservation Law Foundation

CLI: Consumer Labelling Initiative

CLIPS: Chemical List Index and Processing System

CLP: Contract Laboratory Program

CM: Corrective Measure

CMA: Chemical Manufacturers Association

CMB: Chemical Mass Balance

CME: Comprehensive Monitoring Evaluation

CMEL: Comprehensive Monitoring Evaluation Log

CMEP: Critical Mass Energy Project

CNG: Compressedd Natural Gas

COCO: Contractor-Owned/ Contractor-Operated

COD: Chemical Oxygen Demand

COH: Coefficient Of Haze

CPDA: Chemical Producers and Distributor Association

CPF: Carcinogenic Potency Factor

CPO: Certified Project Officer

CQA: Construction Quality Assurance

CR: Continuous Radon Monitoring

CROP: Consolidated Rules of Practice

CRP: Child-Resistant Packaging; Conservation Reserve Program

CRR: Center for Renewable Resources

CRSTER: Single Source Dispersion Model

CSCT: Committee for Site Characterization

CSGWPP: Comprehensive State Ground Water Protection Program

CSI: Common Sense Initiative; Compliance Sampling Inspection

CSIN: Chemical Substances Information Network

CSMA: Chemical Specialties Manufacturers Association

CSO: Combined Sewer Overflow

CSPA: Council of State Planning Agencies

CSRL: Center for the Study of Responsive Law

CTARC: Chemical Testing and Assessment Research Commission

CTG: Control Techniques Guidelines

CTSA: Cleaner TechnologiesSubstitutess Assessment

CV: Chemical Vocabulary

CVS: Constant Volume Sampler

CW: Continuous working-level monitoring

CWA: Clean Water Act (aka FWPCA)

CWAP: Clean Water Action Project

CWTC: Chemical Waste Transportation Council

CZMA: Coastal Zone Management Act

CZARA: Coastal Zone Management Act Reauthorization Amendments

D

DAPSS: Document and Personnel Security System (IMD)

DBP: Disinfection By-Product

DCI: Data Call-In

DCO: Delayed Compliance Order

DCO: Document Control Officer

DDT: DichloroDiphenylTrichloroethane

DERs: Data Evaluation Records

DES: Diethylstilbesterol

DfE: Design for the Environment

DI: Diagnostic Inspection

DMR: Discharge Monitoring Report

DNA: Deoxyribonucleic acid

DNAPL: Dense Non-Aqueous Phase Liquid

DO: Dissolved Oxygen

DOW: Defenders Of Wildlife

DPA: Deepwater Ports Act

DPD: Method of Measuring Chlorine Residual in Water

DQO: Data Quality Objective

DRE: Destruction and Removal Efficiency

DRES: Dietary Risk Evaluation System

DRMS: Defense Reutilization and Marketing Service

DRR: Data Review Record

DS: Dichotomous Sampler

DSAP: Data Self Auditing Program

DSCF: Dry Standard Cubic Feet

DSCM: Dry Standard Cubic Meter

DSS: Decision Support System; Domestic Sewage Study

DT: Detectors (radon) damaged or lost; Detention Time

DU: Decision Unit. Ducks Unlimited; Dobson Unit

DUC: Decision Unit Coordinator

DWEL: Drinking Water Equivalent Level

DWS: Drinking Water Standard

DWSRF: Drinking Water State Revolving Fund

E

EA: Endangerment Assessment; Enforcement Agreement; Environmental Action; Environmental Assessment;. Environmental Audit

EAF: Electric Arc Furnaces

EAG: Exposure Assessment Group

EAO: Emergency Administrative Order

EAP: Environmental Action Plan

EAR: Environmental Auditing Roundtable

EASI: Environmental Alliance for Senior Involvement

EB: Emissions Balancing

EC: Emulsifiable Concentrate; Environment Canada; Effective Concentration

ECA: Economic Community for Africa

ECAP: Employee Counselling and Assistance Program

ECD: Electron Capture Detector

ECHH: Electro-Catalytic Hyper-Heaters

ECHO: Enforcement and Compliance History Online

ECL: Environmental Chemical Laboratory

ECOS: Environmental Council of the States

ECR: Enforcement Case Review

ECRA: Economic Cleanup Responsibility Act

ED: Effective Dose

EDA: Emergency Declaration Area

EDB: Ethylene Dibromide

EDC: Ethylene Dichloride

EDD: Enforcement Decision Document

EDF: Environmental Defense Fund

EDRS: Enforcement Document Retrieval System

EDS: Electronic Data System; Energy Data System

EDTA: Ethylene Diamine Triacetic Acid

EDX: Electronic Data Exchange

EDZ: Emission Density Zoning

EEA: Energy and Environmental Analysis

EECs: Estimated Environmental Concentrations

EER: Excess Emission Report

EERL: Eastern Environmental Radiation Laboratory

EERU: Environmental Emergency Response Unit

EESI: Environment and Energy Study Institute

EESL: Environmental Ecological and Support Laboratory

EETFC: Environmental Effects, Transport, and Fate Committee

EF: Emission Factor

EFO: Equivalent Field Office

EFTC: European Fluorocarbon Technical Committee

EGR: Exhaust Gas Recirculation

EH: Redox Potential

EHC: Environmental Health Committee

EHS: Extremely Hazardous Substance

EI: Emissions Inventory

EIA: Environmental Impact Assessment. Economic Impact Assessment

EIL: Environmental Impairment Liability

EIR: Endangerment Information Report; Environmental Impact Report

EIS: Environmental Impact Statement; Environmental Inventory System

EIS/AS: Emissions Inventory System/Area Source

EIS/PS: Emissions Inventory System/Point Source

EJ: Environmental Justice

EKMA: Empirical Kinetic Modeling Approach

EL: Exposure Level

ELI: Environmental Law Institute

ELR: Environmental Law Reporter

EM: Electromagnetic Conductivity

EMAP: Environmental Mapping and Assessment Program

EMAS: Enforcement Management and Accountability System

EMR: Environmental Management Report

EMS: Enforcement Management System

EMSL: Environmental Monitoring Support Systems Laboratory

EMTS: Environmental Monitoring Testing Site; Exposure Monitoring Test Site

EnPA: Environmental Performance Agreement

EO: Ethylene Oxide

EOC: Emergency Operating Center

EOF: Emergency Operations Facility (RTP)

EOP: End Of Pipe

EOT: Emergency Operations Team

EP: Earth Protectors; Environmental Profile; End-use Product; Experimental Product; Extraction Procedure

EPAA: Environmental Programs Assistance Act

EPAAR: EPA Acquisition Regulations

EPCA: Energy Policy and Conservation Act

EPACT: Environmental Policy Act

EPACASR: EPA Chemical Activities Status Report

EPCRA: Emergency Planning and Community Right to Know Act

EPD: Emergency Planning District

EPI: Environmental Policy Institute

EPIC: Environmental Photographic Interpretation Center

EPNL: Effective Perceived Noise Level

EPRI: Electric Power Research Institute

EPTC: Extraction Procedure Toxicity Characteristic

EQIP: Environmental Quality Incentives Program

ER: Ecosystem Restoration; Electrical Resistivity

ERA: Economic Regulatory Agency

ERAMS: Environmental Radiation Ambient Monitoring System

ERC: Emergency Response Commission. Emissions Reduction Credit, Environmental Research Center

ERCS: Emergency Response Cleanup Services

ERDA: Energy Research and Development Administration

ERD&DAA: Environmental Research, Development and Demonstration Authorization Act

ERL: Environmental Research Laboratory

ERNS: Emergency Response Notification System

ERP: Enforcement Response Policy

ERT: Emergency Response Team

ERTAQ: ERT Air Quality Model

ES: Enforcement Strategy

ESA: Endangered Species Act. Environmentally Sensitive Area

ESC: Endangered Species Committee

ESCA: Electron Spectroscopy for Chemical Analysis

ESCAP: Economic and Social Commission for Asia and the Pacific

ESECA: Energy Supply and Environmental Coordination Act

ESH: Environmental Safety and Health

ESP: Electrostatic Precipitators

ET: Emissions Trading

ETI: Environmental Technology Initiative

ETP: Emissions Trading Policy

ETS: Emissions Tracking System; Environmental Tobacco Smoke

ETV: Environmental Technology Verification Program

EUP: End-Use Product; Experimental Use Permit

EWCC: Environmental Workforce Coordinating Committee

EXAMS: Exposure Analysis Modeling System

ExEx: Expected Exceedance

F

FACA: Federal Advisory Committee Act

FAN: Fixed Account Number

FATES: FIFRA and TSCA Enforcement System

FBC: Fluidized Bed Combustion

FCC: Fluid Catalytic Converter

FCCC: Framework Convention on Climate Change

FCCU: Fluid Catalytic Cracking Unit

FCO: Federal Coordinating Officer (in disaster areas); Forms Control Officer

FDF: Fundamentally Different Factors

FDL: Final Determination Letter

FDO: Fee Determination Official

FE: Fugitive Emissions

FEDS: Federal Energy Data System

FEFx: Forced Expiratory Flow

FEIS: Fugitive Emissions Information System

FEL: Frank Effect Level

FEPCA: Federal Environmental Pesticide Control Act; enacted as amendments to FIFRA.

FERC: Federal Energy Regulatory Commission

FES: Factor Evaluation System

FEV: Forced Expiratory Volume

FEV1: Forced Expiratory Volume—one second; Front End Volatility Index

FF: Federal Facilities

FFAR: Fuel and Fuel Additive Registration

FFDCA: Federal Food, Drug, and Cosmetic Act

FFEO: Federal Facilities Enforcement Office

FFF: Firm Financial Facility

FFFSG: Fossil-Fuel-Fired Steam Generator

FFIS: Federal Facilities Information System

FFP: Firm Fixed Price

FGD: Flue-Gas Desulfurization

FID: Flame Ionization Detector

FIFRA: Federal Insecticide, Fungicide, and Rodenticide Act

FIM: Friable Insulation Material

FINDS: Facility Index System

FIP: Final Implementation Plan

FIPS: Federal Information Procedures System

FIT: Field Investigation Team

FLETC: Federal Law Enforcement Training Center

FLM: Federal Land Manager

FLP: Flash Point

FLPMA: Federal Land Policy and Management Act

FMAP: Financial Management Assistance Project

F/M: Food to Microorganism Ratio

FML: Flexible Membrane Liner

FMP: Facility Management Plan

FMP: Financial Management Plan

FMS: Financial Management System

FMVCP: Federal Motor Vehicle Control Program

FOE: Friends Of the Earth

FOIA: Freedom Of Information Act

FOISD: Fiber Optic Isolated Spherical Dipole Antenna

FONSI: Finding Of No Significant Impact

FORAST: Forest Response to Anthropogenic Stress

FP: Fine Particulate

FPA: Federal Pesticide Act

FPAS: Foreign Purchase Acknowledgement Statements

FPD: Flame Photometric Detector

FPEIS: Fine Particulate Emissions Information System

FPM: Federal Personnel Manual

FPPA: Federal Pollution Prevention Act

FPR: Federal Procurement Regulation

FPRS: Federal Program Resources Statement; Formal Planning and Supporting System

FQPA: Food Quality Protection Act

FR: Federal Register. Final Rulemaking

FRA: Federal Register Act

FREDS: Flexible Regional Emissions Data System

FRES: Forest Range Environmental Study

FRM: Federal Reference Methods

FRN: Federal Register Notice. Final Rulemaking Notice

FRS: Formal Reporting System

FS: Feasibility Study

FSA: Food Security Act

FSS: Facility Status Sheet; Federal Supply Schedule

FTP: Federal Test Procedure (for motor vehicles)

FTS: File Transfer Service

FTTS: FIFRA/TSCA Tracking System

FUA: Fuel Use Act

FURS: Federal Underground Injection Control Reporting System

FVMP: Federal Visibility Monitoring Program

FWCA: Fish and Wildlife Coordination Act

FWPCA: Federal Water Pollution and Control Act (aka CWA). Federal Water Pollution and Control Administration

FY: Fiscal Year

G

GAAP: Generally Accepted Accounting Principles

GAC: Granular Activated Carbon

GACT: Granular Activated Carbon Treatment

GAW: Global Atmospheric Watch

GCC: Global Climate Convention

GC/MS: Gas Chromatograph/ Mass Spectograph

GCVTC: Grand Canyon Visibility Transport Commission

GCWR: Gross Combination Weight Rating

GDE: Generic Data Exemption

GEI: Geographic Enforcement Initiative

GEMI: Global Environmental Management Initiative

GEMS: Global Environmental Monitoring System; Graphical Exposure Modeling System

GEP: Good Engineering Practice

GFF: Glass Fiber Filter

GFO: Grant Funding Order

GFP: Government-Furnished Property

GICS: Grant Information and Control System

GIS: Geographic Information Systems; Global Indexing System

GLC: Gas Liquid Chromatography

GLERL: Great Lakes Environmental Research Laboratory

GLNPO: Great Lakes National Program Office

GLP: Good Laboratory Practices

GLWQA: Great Lakes Water Quality Agreement

GMCC: Global Monitoring for Climatic Change

G/MI: Grams per mile

GOCO: Government-Owned/ Contractor-Operated

GOGO: Government-Owned/ Government-Operated

GOP: General Operating Procedures

GOPO: Government-Owned/ Privately-Operated

GPAD: Gallons-per-acre per-day

GPG: Grams-per-Gallon

GPR: Ground-Penetrating Radar

GPRA: Government Performance and Results Act

GPS: Groundwater Protection Strategy

GR: Grab Radon Sampling

GRAS: Generally Recognized as Safe

GRCDA: Government Refuse Collection and Disposal Association

GRGL: Groundwater Residue Guidance Level

GT: Gas Turbine

GTN: Global Trend Network

GTR: Government Transportation Request

GVP: Gasoline Vapor Pressure

GVW: Gross Vehicle Weight

GVWR: Gross Vehicle Weight Rating

GW: Grab Working-Level Sampling. Groundwater

GWDR: Ground Water Disinfection Rule

GWM: Groundwater Monitoring

GWP: Global Warming Potential

GWPC: Ground Water Protection Council

GWPS: Groundwater Protection Standard; Groundwater Protection Strategy

H

HA: Health Advisory

HAD: Health Assessment Document

HAP: Hazardous Air Pollutant

HAPEMS: Hazardous Air Pollutant Enforcement Management System

HAPPS: Hazardous Air Pollutant Prioritization System

HATREMS: Hazardous and Trace Emissions System

HAZMAT: Hazardous Materials

HAZOP: Hazard and Operability Study

HBFC: Hydrobromofluorocarbon

HC: Hazardous Constituents; Hydrocarbon

HCCPD: Hexachlorocyclo-pentadiene

HCFC: Hydrochlorofluorocarbon

HCP: Hypothermal Coal Process

HDD: Heavy-Duty Diesel

HDDT: Heavy-duty Diesel Truck

HDDV: Heavy-Duty Diesel Vehicle

HDE: Heavy-Duty Engine

HDG: Heavy-Duty Gasoline-Powered Vehicle

HDGT: Heavy-Duty Gasoline Truck

HDGV: Heavy-Duty Gasoline Vehicle

HDPE: High Density Polyethylene

HDT: Highest Dose Tested in a study. Heavy-Duty Truck

HDV: Heavy-Duty Vehicle

HEAL: Human Exposure Assessment Location

HECC: House Energy and Commerce Committee

HEI: Health Effects Institute

HEM: Human Exposure Modeling

HEPA: High-Efficiency Particulate Air

HEPA: Highly Efficient Particulate Air Filter

HERS: Hyperion Energy Recovery System

HFC: Hydrofluorocarbon

HHDDV: Heavy Heavy-Duty Diesel Vehicle

HHE: Human Health and the Environment

HHV: Higher Heating Value

HI: Hazard Index

HI-VOL: High-Volume Sampler

HIWAY: A Line Source Model for Gaseous Pollutants

HLRW: High Level Radioactive Waste

HMIS: Hazardous Materials Information System

HMS: Highway Mobile Source

HMTA: Hazardous Materials Transportation Act

HMTR: Hazardous Materials Transportation Regulations

HOC: Halogenated Organic Carbons

HON: Hazardous Organic NESHAP

HOV: High-Occupancy Vehicle

HP: Horse Power

HPLC: High-Performance Liquid Chromatography

HPMS: Highway Performance Monitoring System

HPV: High Priority Violator

HQCDO: Headquarters Case Development Officer

HRS: Hazardous Ranking System

HRUP: High-Risk Urban Problem

HSDB: Hazardous Substance Data Base

HSL: Hazardous Substance List

HSWA: Hazardous and Solid Waste Amendments

HT: Hypothermally Treated

HTP: High Temperature and Pressure

HVAC: Heating, Ventilation, and Air-Conditioning system

HVIO: High Volume Industrial Organics

HW: Hazardous Waste

HWDMS: Hazardous Waste Data Management System

HWGTF: Hazardous Waste Groundwater Task Force; Hazardous Waste Groundwater Test Facility

HWIR: Hazardous Waste Identification Rule

HWLT: Hazardous Waste Land Treatment

HWM: Hazardous Waste Management

HWRTF: Hazardous Waste Restrictions Task Force

HWTC: Hazardous Waste Treatment Council

I

I/A: Innovative/Alternative

IA: Interagency Agreement

IAAC: Interagency Assessment Advisory Committee

IADN: Integrated Atmospheric Deposition Network

IAG: Interagency Agreement

IAP: Incentive Awards Program. Indoor Air Pollution

IAQ: Indoor Air Quality

IARC: International Agency for Research on Cancer

IATDB: Interim Air Toxics Data Base

IBSIN: Innovations in Building Sustainable Industries

IBT: Industrial Biotest Laboratory

IC: Internal Combustion

ICAIR: Interdisciplinary Planning and Information Research

ICAP: Inductively Coupled Argon Plasma

ICB: Information Collection Budget

ICBN: International Commission on the Biological Effects of Noise

ICCP: International Climate Change Partnership

ICE: Industrial Combustion Emissions Model. Internal Combustion Engine

ICP: Inductively Coupled Plasma

ICR: Information Collection Request

ICRE: Ignitability, Corrosivity, Reactivity, Extraction

ICRP: International Commission on Radiological Protection

ICRU: International Commission of Radiological Units and Measurements

ICS: Incident Command System. Institute for Chemical Studies; Intermittent Control Strategies.; Intermittent Control System

ICWM: Institute for Chemical Waste Management

IDEA: Integrated Data for Enforcement Analysis

IDLH: Immediately Dangerous to Life and Health

IEB: International Environment Bureau

IEMP: Integrated Environmental Management Project

IES: Institute for Environmental Studies

IFB: Invitation for Bid

IFCAM: Industrial Fuel Choice Analysis Model

IFCS: International Forum on Chemical Safety

IFIS: Industry File Information System

IFMS: Integrated Financial Management System

IFPP: Industrial Fugitive Process Particulate

IGCC: Integrated Gasification Combined Cycle

IGCI: Industrial Gas Cleaning Institute

IIS: Inflationary Impact Statement

IINERT: In-Place Inactivation and Natural Restoration Technologies

IJC: International Joint Commission (on Great Lakes)

I/M: Inspection/Maintenance

IMM: Intersection Midblock Model

IMPACT: Integrated Model of Plumes and Atmosphere in Complex Terrain

IMPROVE: Interagency Monitoring of Protected Visual Environment

INPUFF: Gaussian Puff Dispersion Model

INT: Intermittent

IOB: Iron Ore Beneficiation

IOU: Input/Output Unit

IPCS: International Program on Chemical Safety

IP: Inhalable Particles

IPM: Inhalable Particulate Matter. Integrated Pest Management

IPP: Implementation Planning Program. Integrated Plotting Package; Inter-media Priority Pollutant (document); Independent Power Producer

IPCC: Intergovernmental Panel on Climate Change

IPM: Integrated Pest Management

IRG: Interagency Review Group

IRLG: Interagency Regulatory Liaison Group (Composed of EPA, CPSC, FDA, and OSHA)

IRIS: Instructional Resources Information System. Integrated Risk Information System

IRM: Intermediate Remedial Measures

IRMC: Inter-Regulatory Risk Management Council

IRP: Installation Restoration Program

IRPTC: International Register of Potentially Toxic Chemicals

IRR: Institute of Resource Recovery

IRS: International Referral Systems

IS: Interim Status

ISAM: Indexed Sequential File Access Method

ISC: Industrial Source Complex

ISCL: Interim Status Compliance Letter

ISCLT: Industrial Source Complex Long Term Model

ISCST: Industrial Source Complex Short Term Model

ISD: Interim Status Document

ISE: Ion-specific electrode

ISMAP: Indirect Source Model for Air Pollution

ISO: International Organization for Standardization

ISPF: (IBM) Interactive System Productivity Facility

ISS: Interim Status Standards

ITC: Innovative Technology Council

ITC: Interagency Testing Committee

ITRC: Interstate Technology Regulatory Coordination

ITRD: Innovative Treatment Remediation Demonstration

IUP: Intended Use Plan

IUR: Inventory Update Rule

IWC: In-Stream Waste Concentration

IWS: Ionizing Wet Scrubber

J

JAPCA: Journal of Air Pollution Control Association

JCL: Job Control Language

JEC: Joint Economic Committee

JECFA: Joint Expert Committee of Food Additives

JEIOG: Joint Emissions Inventory Oversight Group

JLC: Justification for Limited Competition

JMPR: Joint Meeting on Pesticide Residues

JNCP: Justification for Non-Competitive Procurement

JOFOC: Justification for Other Than Full and Open Competition

JPA: Joint Permitting Agreement

JSD: Jackson Structured Design

JSP: Jackson Structured Programming

JTU: Jackson Turbidity Unit

L

LAA: Lead Agency Attorney

LADD: Lifetime Average Daily Dose; Lowest Acceptable Daily Dose

LAER: Lowest Achievable Emission Rate

LAI: Laboratory Audit Inspection

LAMP: Lake Acidification Mitigation Project

LC: Lethal Concentration. Liquid Chromatography

LCA: Life Cycle Assessment

LCD: Local Climatological Data

LCL: Lower Control Limit

LCM: Life Cycle Management

LCRS: Leachate Collection and Removal System

LD: Land Disposal. Light Duty

LD L0: The lowest dosage of a toxic substance that kills test organisms.

LDAR: Leak Detection and Repair

LDC: London Dumping Convention

LDCRS: Leachate Detection, Collection, and Removal System

LDD: Light-Duty Diesel

LDDT: Light-Duty Diesel Truck

LDDV: Light-Duty Diesel Vehicle

LDGT: Light-Duty Gasoline Truck

LDIP: Laboratory Data Integrity Program

LDR: Land Disposal Restrictions

LDRTF: Land Disposal Restrictions Task Force

LDS: Leak Detection System

LDT: Lowest Dose Tested. Light-Duty Truck

LDV: Light-Duty Vehicle

LEL: Lowest Effect Level. Lower Explosive Limit

LEP: Laboratory Evaluation Program

LEPC: Local Emergency Planning Committee

LERC: Local Emergency Response Committee

LEV: Low Emissions Vehicle

LFG: Landfill Gas

LFL: Lower Flammability Limit

LGR: Local Governments Reimbursement Program

LHDDV: Light Heavy-Duty Diesel Vehicle

LI: Langelier Index

LIDAR: Light Detection and Ranging

LIMB: Limestone-Injection Multi-Stage Burner

LLRW: Low Level Radioactive Waste

LMFBR: Liquid Metal Fast Breeder Reactor

LMOP: Landfill Methane Outreach Program

LNAPL: Light Non-Aqueous Phase Liquid

LOAEL: Lowest-Observed-Adverse-Effect-Level

LOD: Limit of Detection

LQER: Lesser Quantity Emission Rates

LQG: Large Quantity Generator

LRTAP: Long Range Transboundary Air Pollution

LUIS: Label Use Information System

M

MAC: Mobile Air Conditioner

MACT: Maximum Achievable Control Technology

MAPSIM: Mesoscale Air Pollution Simulation Model

MATC: Maximum Acceptable Toxic Concentration

MBAS: Methylene-Blue-Active Substances

MCL: Maximum Contaminant Level

MCLG: Maximum Contaminant Level Goal

MCS: Multiple Chemical Sensitivity

MDL: Method Detection Limit

MEC: Model Energy Code

MEI: Maximally (or most) Exposed Individual

MEP: Multiple Extraction Procedure

MHDDV: Medium Heavy-Duty Diesel Vehicle

MOBILE5A: Mobile Source Emission Factor Model

MOE: Margin Of Exposure

MOS: Margin of Safety

MP: Manufacturing-use Product; Melting Point

MPCA: Microbial Pest Control Agent

MPI: Maximum Permitted Intake

MPN: Maximum Possible Number

MPWC: Multiprocess Wet Cleaning

MRBMA: Mercury-Containing and Rechargeable Battery Management Act

MRF: Materials Recovery Facility

MRID: Master Record Identification number

MRL: Maximum-Residue Limit (Pesticide Tolerance)

MSW: Municipal Solid Waste

MTBE: Methyl tertiary butyl ether

MTD: Maximum Tolerated Dose

MUP: Manufacturing-Use Product

MUTA: Mutagenicity

MWC: Machine Wet Cleaning

N

NAA: Nonattainment Area

NAAEC: North American Agreement on Environmental Cooperation

NAAQS: National Ambient Air Quality Standards

NACA: National Agricultural Chemicals Association

NACEPT: National Advisory Council for Environmental Policy and Technology

NADP/NTN: National Atmospheric Deposition Program/National Trends Network

NAMS: National Air Monitoring Stations

NAPAP: National Acid Precipitation Assessment Program

NAPL: Non-Aqueous Phase Liquid

NAPS: National Air Pollution Surveillance

NARA: National Agrichemical Retailers Association

NARSTO: North American Research Strategy for Tropospheric Ozone

NAS: National Academy of Sciences

NASA: National Aeronautics and Space Administration

NASDA: National Association of State Departments of Agriculture

NCAMP: National Coalition Against the Misuse of Pesticides

NCEPI: National Center for Environmental Publications and Information

NCWS: Non-Community Water System

NEDS: National Emissions Data System

NEIC: National Enforcement Investigations Center

NEPA: National Environmental Policy Act

NEPI: National Environmental Policy Institute

NEPPS: National Environmental Performance Partnership System

NESHAP: National Emission Standard for Hazardous Air Pollutants

NIEHS: National Institute for Environmental Health Sciences

NETA: National Environmental Training Association

NFRAP: No Further Remedial Action Planned

NICT: National Incident Coordination Team

NIOSH: National Institute of Occupational Safety and Health

NIPDWR: National Interim Primary Drinking Water Regulations

NISAC: National Industrial Security Advisory Committee

NMHC: Nonmethane Hydrocarbons

NMOC: Non-Methane Organic Component

NMVOC: Non-methane Volatile Organic Chemicals

NO: Nitric Oxide

NOý: Nitrogen Dioxide

NOA: Notice of Arrival

NOAA: National Oceanographic and Atmospheric Agency

NOAC: Nature of Action Code

NOAEL: No Observable Adverse Effect Level

NOEL: No Observable Effect Level

NOIC: Notice of Intent to Cancel

NOIS: Notice of Intent to Suspend

N_2O: Nitrous Oxide

NOV: Notice of Violation

NO_x: Nitrogen Oxides

NORM: Naturally Occurring Radioactive Material

NPCA: National Pest Control Association

NPDES: National Pollutant Discharge Elimination System

NPHAP: National Pesticide Hazard Assessment Program

NPIRS: National Pesticide Information Retrieval System

NPMS: National Performance Measures Strategy

NPTN: National Pesticide Telecommunications Network

NRD: Natural Resource Damage

NRDC: Natural Resources Defense Council

NSDWR: National Secondary Drinking Water Regulations

NSEC: National System for Emergency Coordination

NSEP: National System for Emergency Preparedness

NSPS: New Source Performance Standards

NSR: New Source Review

NSR/PSD: National Source Review/Prevention of Significant Deterioration

NTI: National Toxics Inventory

NTIS: National Technical Information Service

NTNCWS: Non-Transient Non-Community Water System

NTP: National Toxicology Program

NTU: Nephlometric Turbidity Unit

O

O_3: Ozone

OAQPS: Office of Air Quality Planning and Standards

OCD: Offshore and Coastal Dispersion

ODP: Ozone-Depleting Potential

ODS: Ozone-Depleting Substances

OECA: Office of Enforcement and Compliance Assurance

OECD: Organization for Economic Cooperation and Development

OF: Optional Form

OI: Order for Information

OLC: Office of Legal Counsel

OLTS: On Line Tracking System

O&M: Operations and Maintenance

ORE: Office of Regulatory Enforcement

ORM: Other Regulated Material

ORP: Oxidation-Reduction Potential

OTAG: Ozone Transport Assessment Group

OTC: Ozone Transport Commission

OTIS: Online Tracking Information System

OTR: Ozone Transport Region

P

P2: Pollution Prevention

PAG: Pesticide Assignment Guidelines

PAH: Polynuclear Aromatic Hydrocarbons

PAI: Performance Audit Inspection (CWA); Pure Active Ingredient compound

PAM: Pesticide Analytical Manual

PAMS: Photochemical Assessment Monitoring Stations

PAT: Permit Assistance Team (RCRA)

PATS: Pesticide Action Tracking System; Pesticides Analytical Transport Solution

Pb: Lead

PBA: Preliminary Benefit Analysis (BEAD)

PCA: Principle Component Analysis

PCB: Polychlorinated Biphenyl

PCE: Perchloroethylene

PCM: Phase Contrast Microscopy

PCN: Policy Criteria Notice

PCO: Pest Control Operator

PCSD: President's Council on Sustainable Development

PDCI: Product Data Call-In

PFC: Perfluorated Carbon

PFCRA: Program Fraud Civil Remedies Act

PHC: Principal Hazardous Constituent

PHI: Pre-Harvest Interval

PHSA: Public Health Service Act

PI: Preliminary Injunction. Program Information

PIC: Products of Incomplete Combustion

PIGS: Pesticides in Groundwater Strategy

PIMS: Pesticide Incident Monitoring System

PIN: Pesticide Information Network

PIN: Procurement Information Notice

PIP: Public Involvement Program

PIPQUIC: Program Integration Project Queries Used in Interactive Command

PIRG: Public Interest Research Group

PIRT: Pretreatment Implementation Review Task Force

PIT: Permit Improvement Team

PITS: Project Information Tracking System

PLIRRA: Pollution Liability Insurance and Risk Retention Act

PLM: Polarized Light Microscopy

PLUVUE: Plume Visibility Model

PM: Particulate Matter

PMAS: Photochemical Assessment Monitoring Stations

$PM_{2.5}$: Particulate Matter Smaller than 2.5 Micrometers in Diameter

PM_{10}: Particulate Matter (nominally 10m and less)

PM_{15}: Particulate Matter (nominally 15m and less)

PMEL: Pacific Marine Environmental Laboratory

PMN: Premanufacture Notification

PMNF: Premanufacture Notification Form

PMR: Pollutant Mass Rate

PMR: Proportionate Mortality Ratio

PMRS: Performance Management and Recognition System

PMS: Program Management System

PNA: Polynuclear Aromatic Hydrocarbons

PO: Project Officer

POC: Point Of Compliance

POE: Point Of Exposure

POGO: Privately-Owned/ Government-Operated

POHC: Principal Organic Hazardous Constituent

POI: Point Of Interception

POLREP: Pollution Report

POM: Particulate Organic Matter. Polycyclic Organic Matter

POP: Persistent Organic Pollutant

POR: Program of Requirements

POTW: Publicly Owned Treatment Works

POV: Privately Owned Vehicle

PP: Program Planning

PPA: Planned Program Accomplishment

PPB: Parts Per Billion

PPE: Personal Protective Equipment

PPG: Performance Partnership Grant

PPIC: Pesticide Programs Information Center

PPIS: Pesticide Product Information System; Pollution Prevention Incentives for States

PPMAP: Power Planning Modeling Application Procedure

PPM/PPB: Parts per million/ parts per billion

PPSP: Power Plant Siting Program

PPT: Parts Per Trillion

PPTH: Parts Per Thousand

PQUA: Preliminary Quantitative Usage Analysis

PR: Pesticide Regulation Notice; Preliminary Review

PRA: Paperwork Reduction Act; Planned Regulatory Action

PRATS: Pesticides Regulatory Action Tracking System

PRC: Planning Research Corporation

PRI: Periodic Reinvestigation

PRM: Prevention Reference Manuals

PRN: Pesticide Registration Notice

PRP: Potentially Responsible Party

PRZM: Pesticide Root Zone Model

PS: Point Source

PSAM: Point Source Ambient Monitoring

PSC: Program Site Coordinator

PSD: Prevention of Significant Deterioration

PSES: Pretreatment Standards for Existing Sources

PSI: Pollutant Standards Index; Pounds Per Square Inch; Pressure Per Square Inch

PSIG: Pressure Per Square Inch Gauge

PSM: Point Source Monitoring

PSNS: Pretreatment Standards for New Sources

PSU: Primary Sampling Unit

PTDIS: Single Stack Meteorological Model in EPA UNAMAP Series

PTE: Potential to Emit

PTFE: Polytetrafluoroethylene (Teflon)

PTMAX: Single Stack Meteorological Model in EPA UNAMAP series

PTPLU: Point Source Gaussian Diffusion Model

PUC: Public Utility Commission

PV: Project Verification

PVC: Polyvinyl Chloride

PWB: Printed Wiring Board

PWS: Public Water Supply/ System

PWSS: Public Water Supply System

Q

QAC: Quality Assurance Coordinator

QA/QC: Quality Assistance/ Quality Control

QAMIS: Quality Assurance Management and Information System

QAO: Quality Assurance Officer

QAPP: Quality Assurance Program (or Project) Plan

QAT: Quality Action Team

QBTU: Quadrillion British Thermal Units

QC: Quality Control

QCA: Quiet Communities Act

QCI: Quality Control Index

QCP: Quiet Community Program

QL: Quantification Limit

QNCR: Quarterly Noncompliance Report

QUA: Qualitative Use Assessment

QUIPE: Quarterly Update for Inspector in Pesticide Enforcement

R

RA: Reasonable Alternative; Regulatory Alternatives; Regulatory Analysis; Remedial Action; Resource Allocation; Risk Analysis; Risk Assessment

RAATS: RCRA Administrate Action Tracking System

RAC: Radiation Advisory Committee. Raw Agricultural Commodity; Regional Asbestos Coordinator. Response Action Coordinator

RACM: Reasonably Available Control Measures

RACT: Reasonably Available Control Technology

RAD: Radiation Adsorbed Dose (unit of measurement of radiation absorbed by humans)

RADM: Random Walk Advection and Dispersion Model; Regional Acid Deposition Model

RAM: Urban Air Quality Model for Point and Area Source in EPA UNAMAP Series

RAMP: Rural Abandoned Mine Program

RAMS: Regional Air Monitoring System

RAP: Radon Action Program; Registration Assessment Panel; Remedial Accomplishment Plan; Response Action Plan

RAPS: Regional Air Pollution Study

RARG: Regulatory Analysis Review Group

RAS: Routine Analytical Service

RAT: Relative Accuracy Test

RB: Request for Bid

RBAC: Re-use Business Assistance Center

RBC: Red Blood Cell

RC: Responsibility Center

RCC: Radiation Coordinating Council

RCDO: Regional Case Development Officer

RCO: Regional Compliance Officer

RCP: Research Centers Program

RCRA: Resource Conservation and Recovery Act

RCRIS: Resource Conservation and Recovery Information System

RD/RA: Remedial Design/ Remedial Action

R&D: Research and Development

RD&D: Research, Development and Demonstration

RDF: Refuse-Derived Fuel

RDNA: Recombinant DNA

RDU: Regional Decision Units

RDV: Reference Dose Values

RE: Reasonable Efforts; Reportable Event

REAP: Regional Enforcement Activities Plan

REE: Rare Earth Elements

REEP: Review of Environmental Effects of Pollutants

RECLAIM: Regional Clean Air Initiatives Marker

RED: Reregistration Eligibility Decision Document

REDA: Recycling Economic Development Advocate

ReFIT: Reinvention for Innovative Technologies

REI: Restricted Entry Interval

REM: (Roentgen Equivalent Man)

REM/FIT: Remedial/Field Investigation Team

REMS: RCRA Enforcement Management System

REP: Reasonable Efforts Program

REPS: Regional Emissions Projection System

RESOLVE: Center for Environmental Conflict Resolution

RF: Response Factor

RFA: Regulatory Flexibility Act

RFB: Request for Bid

RfC: Reference Concentration

RFD: Reference Dose Values

RFI: Remedial Field Investigation

RFP: Reasonable Further Programs. Request for Proposal

RHRS: Revised Hazard Ranking System

RI: Reconnaissance Inspection

RI: Remedial Investigation

RIA: Regulatory Impact Analysis; Regulatory Impact Assessment

RIC: Radon Information Center

RICC: Retirement Information and Counseling Center

RICO: Racketeer Influenced and Corrupt Organizations Act

RI/FS: Remedial Investigation/ Feasibility Study

RIM: Regulatory Interpretation Memorandum

RIN: Regulatory Identifier Number

RIP: RCRA Implementation Plan

RISC: Regulatory Information Service Center

RJE: Remote Job Entry

RLL: Rapid and Large Leakage (Rate)

RMCL: Recommended Maximum Contaminant Level (this phrase being discontinued in favor of MCLG)

RMDHS: Regional Model Data Handling System

RMIS: Resources Management Information System

RMP: Risk Management Plan

RNA: Ribonucleic Acid

ROADCHEM: Roadway Version that Includes Chemical Reactions of BI, NO_2, and O_3

ROADWAY: A Model to Predict Pollutant Concentrations Near a Roadway

ROC: Record Of Communication

RODS: Records Of Decision System

ROG: Reactive Organic Gases

ROLLBACK: A Proportional Reduction Model

ROM: Regional Oxidant Model

ROMCOE: Rocky Mountain Center on Environment

ROP: Rate of Progress; Regional Oversight Policy

ROPA: Record Of Procurement Action

ROSA: Regional Ozone Study Area

RP: Radon Progeny Integrated Sampling. Respirable Particulates. Responsible Party

RPAR: Rebuttable Presumption Against Registration

RPM: Reactive Plume Model. Remedial Project Manager

RQ: Reportable Quantities

RRC: Regional Response Center

RRT: Regional Response Team; Requisite Remedial Technology

RS: Registration Standard

RSCC: Regional Sample Control Center

RSD: Risk-Specific Dose

RSE: Removal Site Evaluation

RTCM: Reasonable Transportation Control Measure

RTDF: Remediation Technologies Development Forum

RTDM: Rough Terrain Diffusion Model

RTECS: Registry of Toxic Effects of Chemical Substances

RTM: Regional Transport Model

RTP: Research Triangle Park

RUP: Restricted Use Pesticide

RVP: Reid Vapor Pressure

RWC: Residential Wood Combustion

S

S&A: Sampling and Analysis. Surveillance and Analysis

SAB: Science Advisory Board

SAC: Suspended and Cancelled Pesticides

SAEWG: Standing Air Emissions Work Group

SAIC: Special-Agents-In-Charge

SAIP: Systems Acquisition and Implementation Program

SAMI: Southern Appalachian Mountains Initiative

SAMWG: Standing Air Monitoring Work Group

SANE: Sulfur and Nitrogen Emissions

SANSS: Structure and Nomenclature Search System

SAP: Scientific Advisory Panel

SAR: Start Action Request. Structural Activity Relationship (of a qualitative assessment)

SARA: Superfund Amendments and Reauthorization Act of 1986

SAROAD: Storage and Retrieval Of Aerometric Data

SAS: Special Analytical Service. Statistical Analysis System

SASS: Source Assessment Sampling System

SAV: Submerged Aquatic Vegetation

SBC: Single Breath Cannister

SC: Sierra Club

SCAP: Superfund Consolidated Accomplishments Plan

SCBA: Self-Contained Breathing Apparatus

SCC: Source Classification Code

SCD/SWDC: Soil or Soil and Water Conservation District

SCFM: Standard Cubic Feet Per Minute

SCLDF: Sierra Club Legal Defense Fund

SCR: Selective Catalytic Reduction

SCRAM: State Consolidated RCRA Authorization Manual

SCRC: Superfund Community Relations Coordinator

SCS: Supplementary Control Strategy/System

SCSA: Soil Conservation Society of America

SCSP: Storm and Combined Sewer Program

SCW: Supercritical Water Oxidation

SDC: Systems Decision Plan

SDWA: Safe Drinking Water Act

SDWIS: Safe Drinking Water Information System

SBS: Sick Building Syndrome

SEA: State Enforcement Agreement

SEA: State/EPA Agreement

SEAM: Surface, Environment, and Mining

SEAS: Strategic Environmental Assessment System

SEDS: State Energy Data System

SEGIP: State Environmental Goals and Improvement Project

SEIA: Socioeconomic Impact Analysis

SEM: Standard Error of the Means

SEP: Standard Evaluation Procedures

SEP: Supplementary Environmental Project

SEPWC: Senate Environment and Public Works Committee

SERC: State Emergency Planning Commission

SES: Secondary Emissions Standard

SETAC: Society for Environmental Toxicology and Chemistry

SETS: Site Enforcement Tracking System

SF: Standard Form. Superfund

SFA: Spectral Flame Analyzers

SFDS: Sanitary Facility Data System

SFFAS: Superfund Financial Assessment System

SFIP: Sector Facility Indexing Project

SFIREG: State FIFRA Issues Research and Evaluation Group

SFS: State Funding Study

SHORTZ: Short Term Terrain Model

SHWL: Seasonal High Water Level

SI: International System of Units. Site Inspection. Surveillance Index. Spark Ignition

SIC: Standard Industrial Classification

SICEA: Steel Industry Compliance Extension Act

SIMS: Secondary Ion-Mass Spectrometry

SIP: State Implementation Plan

SITE: Superfund Innovative Technology Evaluation

SLAMS: State/Local Air Monitoring Station

SLN: Special Local Need

SLSM: Simple Line Source Model

SMART: Simple Maintenance of ARTS

SMCL: Secondary Maximum Contaminant Level

SMCRA: Surface Mining Control and Reclamation Act

SME: Subject Matter Expert

SMO: Sample Management Office

SMOA: Superfund Memorandum of Agreement

SMP: State Management Plan

SMR: Standardized Mortality Ratio

SMSA: Standard Metropolitan Statistical Area

SNA: System Network Architecture

SNAAQS: Secondary National Ambient Air Quality Standards

SNAP: Significant New Alternatives Project; Significant Noncompliance Action Program

SNARL: Suggested No Adverse Response Level

SNC: Significant Noncompliers

SNUR: Significant New Use Rule

SO_2: Sulfur Dioxide

SOC: Synthetic Organic Chemicals

SOCMI: Synthetic Organic Chemicals Manufacturing Industry

SOFC: Solid Oxide Fuel Cell

SOTDAT: Source Test Data

SOW: Scope Of Work

SPAR: Status of Permit Application Report

SPCC: Spill Prevention, Containment, and Countermeasure

SPE: Secondary Particulate Emissions

SPF: Structured Programming Facility

SPI: Strategic Planning Initiative

SPLMD: Soil-pore Liquid Monitoring Device

SPMS: Strategic Planning and Management System; Special Purpose Monitoring Stations

SPOC: Single Point Of Contact

SPS: State Permit System

SPSS: Statistical Package for the Social Sciences

SPUR: Software Package for Unique Reports

SQBE: Small Quantity Burner Exemption

SQG: Small Quantity Generator

SR: Special Review

SRAP: Superfund Remedial Accomplishment Plan

SRC: Solvent-Refined Coal

SRF: State Revolving Fund

SRM: Standard Reference Method

SRP: Special Review Procedure

SRR: Second Round Review. Submission Review Record

SRTS: Service Request Tracking System

SS: Settleable Solids. Superfund Surcharge. Suspended Solids

SSA: Sole Source Aquifer

SSAC: Soil Site Assimilated Capacity

SSC: State Superfund Contracts

SSD: Standards Support Document

SSEIS: Standard Support and Environmental Impact Statement; Stationary Source Emissions and Inventory System.

SSI: Size Selective Inlet

SSMS: Spark Source Mass Spectrometry

SSO: Sanitary Sewer Overflow; Source Selection Official

SSRP: Source Reduction Review Project

SSTS: Section Seven Tracking System

SSURO: Stop Sale, Use and Removal Order

STALAPCO: State and Local Air-Pollution Control Officials

STAPPA: State and Territorial Air Pollution

STAR: Stability Wind Rose. State Acid Rain Projects

STARS: Strategic Targeted Activities for Results System

STEL: Short Term Exposure Limit

STEM: Scanning Transmission-Electron Microscope

STN: Scientific and Technical Information Network

STORET: Storage and Retrieval of Water-Related Data

STP: Sewage Treatment Plant. Standard Temperature and Pressure

STTF: Small Town Task Force (EPA)

SUP: Standard Unit of Processing

SURE: Sulfate Regional Experiment Program

SV: Sampling Visit; Significant Violater

SW: Slow Wave

SWAP: Source Water Assessment Program

SWARF: Waste from Metal Grinding Process

SWC: Settlement With Conditions

SWDA: Solid Waste Disposal Act

SWIE: Southern Waste Information Exchange

SWMU: Solid Waste Management Unit

SWPA: Source Water Protection Area

SWQPPP: Source Water Quality Protection Partnership Petitions

SWTR: Surface Water Treatment Rule

SYSOP: Systems Operator

T

TAD: Technical Assistance Document

TAG: Technical Assistance Grant

TALMS: Tunable Atomic Line Molecular Spectroscopy

TAMS: Toxic Air Monitoring System

TAMTAC: Toxic Air Monitoring System Advisory Committee

TAP: Technical Assistance Program

TAPDS: Toxic Air Pollutant Data System

TAS: Tolerance Assessment System

TBT: Tributyltin

TC: Target Concentration. Technical Center. Toxicity Characteristics. Toxic Concentration:

TCDD: Dioxin (Tetrachlorodibenzo-p-dioxin)

TCDF: Tetrachlorodi-benzofurans

TCE: Trichloroethylene

TCF: Total Chlorine Free

TCLP: Total Concentrate Leachate Procedure. Toxicity Characteristic Leachate Procedure

TCM: Transportation Control Measure

TCP: Transportation Control Plan; Trichloropropane;

TCRI: Toxic Chemical Release Inventory

TD: Toxic Dose

TDS: Total Dissolved Solids

TEAM: Total Exposure Assessment Model

TEC: Technical Evaluation Committee

TED: Turtle Excluder Devices

TEG: Tetraethylene Glycol

TEGD: Technical Enforcement Guidance Document

TEL: Tetraethyl Lead

TEM: Texas Episodic Model

TEP: Typical End-use Product. Technical Evaluation Panel

TERA: TSCA Environmental Release Application

TES: Technical Enforcement Support

TEXIN: Texas Intersection Air Quality Model

TGO: Total Gross Output

TGAI: Technical Grade of the Active Ingredient

TGP: Technical Grade Product

THC: Total Hydrocarbons

THM: Trihalomethane

TI: Temporary Intermittent

TI: Therapeutic Index

TIBL: Thermal Internal Boundary Layer

TIC: Technical Information Coordinator. Tentatively Identified Compounds

TIM: Technical Information Manager

TIP: Technical Information Package

TIP: Transportation Improvement Program

TIS: Tolerance Index System

TISE: Take It Somewhere Else

TITC: Toxic Substance Control Act Interagency Testing Committee

TLV: Threshold Limit Value

TLV-C: TLV-Ceiling

TLV-STEL: TLV-Short Term Exposure Limit

TLV-TWA: TLV-Time Weighted Average

TMDL: Total Maximum Daily Limit; Total Maximum Daily Load

TMRC: Theoretical Maximum Residue Contribution

TNCWS: Transient Non-Community Water System

TNT: Trinitrotoluene

TO: Task Order

TOA: Trace Organic Analysis

TOC: Total Organic Carbon/ Compound

TOX: Tetradichloroxylene

TP: Technical Product; Total Particulates

TPC: Testing Priorities Committee

TPI: Technical Proposal Instructions

TPQ: Threshold Planning Quantity

TPSIS: Transportation Planning Support Information System

TPTH: Triphenyltinhydroxide

TPY: Tons Per Year

TQM: Total Quality Management

T-R: Transformer-Rectifier

TRC: Technical Review Committee

TRD: Technical Review Document

TRI: Toxic Release Inventory

TRIP: Toxic Release Inventory Program

TRIS: Toxic Chemical Release Inventory System

TRLN: Triangle Research Library Network

TRO: Temporary Restraining Order

Acronyms & Abbreviations

TSA: Technical Systems Audit

TSCA: Toxic Substances Control Act

TSCATS: TSCA Test Submissions Database

TSCC: Toxic Substances Coordinating Committee

TSD: Technical Support Document

TSDF: Treatment, Storage, and Disposal Facility

TSDG: Toxic Substances Dialogue Group

TSI: Thermal System Insulation

TSM: Transportation System Management

TSO: Time Sharing Option

TSP: Total Suspended Particulates

TSS: Total Suspended (non-filterable) Solids

TTFA: Target Transformation Factor Analysis

TTHM: Total Trihalomethane

TTN: Technology Transfer Network

TTO: Total Toxic Organics

TTY: Teletypewriter

TVA: Tennessee Valley Authority

TVOC: Total Volatile Organic Compounds

TWA: Time Weighted Average

TWS: Transient Water System

TZ: Treatment Zone

U

UAC: User Advisory Committee

UAM: Urban Airshed Model

UAO: Unilateral Administrative Order

UAPSP: Utility Acid Precipitation Study Program

UAQI: Uniform Air Quality Index

UARG: Utility Air Regulatory Group

UCC: Ultra Clean Coal

UCCI: Urea-Formaldehyde Foam Insulation

UCL: Upper Control Limit

UDMH: Unsymmetrical Dimethyl Hydrazine

UEL: Upper Explosive Limit

UF: Uncertainty Factor

UFL: Upper Flammability Limit

ug/m^3: Micrograms Per Cubic Meter

UIC: Underground Injection Control

ULEV: Ultra Low Emission Vehicles

UMTRCA: Uranium Mill Tailings Radiation Control Act

UNAMAP: Users' Network for Applied Modeling of Air Pollution

UNECE: United Nations Economic Commission for Europe

UNEP: United Nations Environment Program

USC: Unified Soil Classification

USDA: United States Department of Agriculture

USDW: Underground Sources of Drinking Water

USFS: United States Forest Service

UST: Underground Storage Tank

UTM: Universal Transverse Mercator

UTP: Urban Transportation Planning

UV: Ultraviolet

UVA, UVB, UVC: Ultraviolet Radiation Bands

UZM: Unsaturated Zone Monitoring

V

VALLEY: Meteorological Model to Calculate Concentrations on Elevated Terrain

VCM: Vinyl Chloride Monomer

VCP: Voluntary Cleanup Program

VE: Visual Emissions

VEO: Visible Emission Observation

VHS: Vertical and Horizontal Spread Model

VHT: Vehicle-Hours of Travel

VISTTA: Visibility Impairment from Sulfur Transformation and Transport in the Atmosphere

VKT: Vehicle Kilometers Traveled

VMT: Vehicle Miles Traveled

VOC: Volatile Organic Compounds

VOS: Vehicle Operating Survey

VOST: Volatile Organic Sampling Train

VP: Vapor Pressure

VSD: Virtually Safe Dose

VSI: Visual Site Inspection

VSS: Volatile Suspended Solids

W

WA: Work Assignment

WADTF: Western Atmospheric Deposition Task Force

WAP: Waste Analysis Plan

WAVE: Water Alliances for Environmental Efficiency

WB: Wet Bulb

WCED: World Commission on Environment and Development

WDROP: Distribution Register of Organic Pollutants in Water

WENDB: Water Enforcement National Data Base

WERL: Water Engineering Research Laboratory

WET: Whole Effluent Toxicity test

WHO: World Health Organization

WHP: Wellhead Protection Program

WHPA: Wellhead Protection Area

WHWT: Water and Hazardous Waste Team

WICEM: World Industry Conference on Environmental Management

WL: Warning Letter; Working Level (radon measurement)

WLA/TMDL: Wasteload Allocation/Total Maximum Daily Load

WLM: Working Level Months

WMO: World Meteorological Organization

WP: Wettable Powder

WPCF: Water Pollution Control Federation

WQS: Water Quality Standard

WRC: Water Resources Council

WRDA: Water Resources Development Act

WRI: World Resources Institute

WS: Work Status

WSF: Water Soluble Fraction

WSRA: Wild and Scenic Rivers Act

WSTB: Water Sciences and Technology Board

WSTP: Wastewater Sewage Treatment Plant

WWEMA: Waste and Wastewater Equipment Manufacturers Association

WWF: World Wildlife Fund

WWTP: Wastewater Treatment Plant

WWTU: Wastewater Treatment Unit

Z

ZEV: Zero Emissions Vehicle

ZHE: Zero Headspace Extractor

ZOI: Zone Of Incorporation

ZRL: Zero Risk Level

***Note:** Some acronyms have more than one meaning. Multiple meanings are listed, separated by semi-colons.*

***Source:** U.S. Environmental Protection Agency, "Terms of Environment"*

Glossary of Environmental Terms

A

Abandoned Well: A well whose use has been permanently discontinued or which is in a state of such disrepair that it cannot be used for its intended purpose.

Abatement: Reducing the degree or intensity of, or eliminating, pollution.

Abatement Debris: Waste from remediation activities.

Absorbed Dose: In exposure assessment, the amount of a substance that penetrates an exposed organism's absorption barriers (e.g. skin, lung tissue, gastrointestinal tract) through physical or biological processes. The term is synonymous with internal dose.

Absorption: The uptake of water , other fluids, or dissolved chemicals by a cell or an organism (as tree roots absorb dissolved nutrients in soil.)

Absorption Barrier: Any of the exchange sites of the body that permit uptake of various substances at different rates (e.g. skin, lung tissue, and gastrointestinal-tract wall)

Accident Site: The location of an unexpected occurrence, failure or loss, either at a plant or along a transportation route, resulting in a release of hazardous materials.

Acclimatization: The physiological and behavioral adjustments of an organism to changes in its environment.

Acid: A corrosive solution with a pH less than 7.

Acid Aerosol: Acidic liquid or solid particles small enough to become airborne. High concentrations can irritate the lungs and have been associated with respiratory diseases like asthma.

Acid Deposition: A complex chemical and atmospheric phenomenon that occurs when emissions of sulfur and nitrogen compounds and other substances are transformed by chemical processes in the atmosphere, often far from the original sources, and then deposited on earth in either wet or dry form. The wet forms, popularly called "acid rain," can fall to earth as rain, snow, or fog. The dry forms are acidic gases or particulates.

Acid Mine Drainage: Drainage of water from areas that have been mined for coal or other mineral ores. The water has a low pH because of its contact with sulfur-bearing material and is harmful to aquatic organisms.

Acid Neutralizing Capacity: Measure of ability of a base (e.g. water or soil) to resist changes in pH.

Acid Rain: (See: acid deposition.)

Acidic: The condition of water or soil that contains a sufficient amount of acid substances to lower the pH below 7.0.

Action Levels: 1. Regulatory levels recommended by EPA for enforcement by FDA and USDA when pesticide residues occur in food or feed commodities for reasons other than the direct application of the pesticide. As opposed to "tolerances" which are established for residues occurring as a direct result of proper usage, action levels are set for inadvertent residues resulting from previous legal use or accidental contamination. 2. In the Superfund program, the existence of a contaminant concentration in the environment high enough to warrant action or trigger a response under SARA and the National Oil and Hazardous Substances Contingency Plan. The term is also used in other regulatory programs. (See: tolerances.)

Activated Carbon: A highly adsorbent form of carbon used to remove odors and toxic substances from liquid or gaseous emissions. In waste treatment, it is used to remove dissolved organic matter from waste drinking water. It is also used in motor vehicle evaporative control systems.

Activated Sludge: Product that results when primary effluent is mixed with bacteria-laden sludge and then agitated and aerated to promote biological treatment, speeding the breakdown of organic matter in raw sewage undergoing secondary waste treatment.

Activator: A chemical added to a pesticide to increase its activity.

Active Ingredient: In any pesticide product, the component that kills, or otherwise controls, target pests. Pesticides are regulated primarily on the basis of active ingredients.

Activity Plans: Written procedures in a school's asbestos-management plan that detail the steps a Local Education Agency (LEA) will follow in performing the initial and additional cleaning, operation and maintenance-program tasks; periodic surveillance; and reinspection required by the Asbestos Hazard Emergency Response Act (AHERA).

Acute Effect: An adverse effect on any living organism which results in severe symptoms that develop rapidly; symptoms often subside after the exposure stops.

Acute Exposure: A single exposure to a toxic substance which may result in severe biological harm or death. Acute exposures are usually characterized as lasting no longer than a day, as compared to longer, continuing exposure over a period of time.

Acute Toxicity: The ability of a substance to cause severe biological harm or death soon after a single exposure or dose. Also, any poisonous effect resulting from a single short-term exposure to a toxic substance. (See: chronic toxicity, toxicity.)

Adaptation: Changes in an organism's physiological structure or function or habits that allow it to survive in new surroundings.

Add-on Control Device: An air pollution control device such as carbon absorber or incinerator that reduces the pollution in an exhaust gas. The control device usually does not affect the process being controlled and thus is "add-on" technology, as opposed to a scheme to control pollution through altering the basic process itself.

Adequately Wet: Asbestos containing material that is sufficiently mixed or penetrated with liquid to prevent the release of particulates.

Administered Dose: In exposure assessment, the amount of a substance given to a test subject (human or animal) to determine dose-response relationships. Since exposure to chemicals is usually inadvertent, this quantity is often called potential dose.

Administrative Order: A legal document signed by EPA directing an individual, business, or other entity to take corrective action or refrain from an activity. It describes the violations and actions to be taken, and can be enforced in court. Such orders may be issued, for example, as a result of an administrative complaint whereby the respondent is ordered to pay a penalty for violations of a statute.

Administrative Order On Consent: A legal agreement signed by EPA and an individual, business, or other entity through which the violator agrees to pay for correction of violations, take the required corrective or cleanup actions, or refrain from an activity. It describes the actions to be taken, may be subject to a comment period, applies to civil actions, and can be enforced in court.

Administrative Procedures Act: A law that spells out procedures and requirements related to the promulgation of regulations.

Administrative Record: All documents which EPA considered or relied on in selecting the response action at a Superfund site, culminating in the record of decision for remedial action or, an action memorandum for removal actions.

Adsorption: Removal of a pollutant from air or water by collecting the pollutant on the surface of a solid material; e.g., an advanced method of treating waste in which activated carbon removes organic matter from waste-water.

Adulterants: Chemical impurities or substances that by law do not belong in a food, or pesticide.

Adulterated: 1. Any pesticide whose strength or purity falls below the quality stated on its label. 2. A food, feed, or product that contains illegal pesticide residues.

Advanced Treatment: A level of wastewater treatment more stringent than secondary treatment; requires an 85-percent reduction in conventional pollutant concentration or a significant reduction in non-conventional pollutants. Sometimes called tertiary treatment.

Advanced Wastewater Treatment: Any treatment of sewage that goes beyond the secondary or biological water treatment stage and includes the removal of nutrients such as phosphorus and nitrogen and a high percentage of suspended solids. (See primary, secondary treatment.)

Adverse Effects Data: FIFRA requires a pesticide registrant to submit data to EPA on any studies or other information regarding unreasonable adverse effects of a pesticide at any time after its registration.

Advisory: A non-regulatory document that communicates risk information to those who may have to make risk management decisions.

Aerated Lagoon: A holding and/or treatment pond that speeds up the natural process of biological decomposition of organic waste by stimulating the growth and activity of bacteria that degrade organic waste.

Aeration: A process which promotes biological degradation of organic matter in water. The process may be passive (as when waste is exposed to air), or active (as when a mixing or bubbling device introduces the air).

Aeration Tank: A chamber used to inject air into water.

Aerobic: Life or processes that require, or are not destroyed by, the presence of oxygen. (See: anaerobic.)

Aerobic Treatment: Process by which microbes decompose complex organic compounds in the presence of oxygen and use the liberated energy for reproduction and growth. (Such processes include extended aeration, trickling filtration, and rotating biological contactors.)

Aerosol: 1. Small droplets or particles suspended in the atmosphere, typically containing sulfur. They are usually emitted naturally (e.g. in volcanic eruptions) and as the result of anthropogenic (human) activities such as burning fossil fuels. 2. The pressurized gas used to propel substances out of a container.

Aerosol: A finely divided material suspended in air or other gaseous environment.

Affected Landfill: Under the Clean Air Act, landfills that meet criteria for capacity, age, and emissions rates set by the EPA. They are required to collect and combust their gas emissions.

Affected Public: 1.The people who live and/or work near a hazardous waste site. 2. The human population adversely impacted following exposure to a toxic pollutant in food, water, air, or soil.

Afterburner: In incinerator technology, a burner located so that the combustion gases are made to pass through its flame in order to remove smoke and odors. It may be attached to or be separated from the incinerator proper.

Age Tank: A tank used to store a chemical solution of known concentration for feed to a chemical feeder. Also called a day tank.

Agent: Any physical, chemical, or biological entity that can be harmful to an organism (synonymous with stressors.)

Agent Orange: A toxic herbicide and defoliant used in the Vietnam conflict, containing 2,4,5-trichlorophen-oxyacetic acid (2,4,5-T) and 2-4 dichlorophenoxyacetic acid (2,4-D) with trace amounts of dioxin.

Agricultural Pollution: Farming wastes, including runoff and leaching of pesticides and fertilizers; erosion and dust from plowing; improper disposal of animal manure and carcasses; crop residues, and debris.

Agricultural Waste: Poultry and livestock manure, and residual materials in liquid or solid form generated from the production and marketing of poultry, livestock or fur-bearing animals; also includes grain, vegetable, and fruit harvest residue.

Agroecosystem: Land used for crops, pasture, and livestock; the adjacent uncultivated land that supports other vegetation and wildlife; and the associated atmosphere, the underlying soils, groundwater, and drainage networks.

AHERA Designated Person (ADP): A person designated by a Local Education Agency to ensure that the AHERA requirements for asbestos management and abatement are properly implemented.

Air Binding: Situation where air enters the filter media and harms both the filtration and backwash processes.

Air Changes Per Hour (ACH): The movement of a volume of air in a given period of time; if a house has one air change per hour, it means that the air in the house will be replaced in a one-hour period.

Air Cleaning: Indoor-air quality-control strategy to remove various airborne particulates and/or gases from the air. Most common methods are particulate filtration, electrostatic precipitation, and gas sorption.

Air Contaminant: Any particulate matter, gas, or combination thereof, other than water vapor. (See: air pollutant.)

Air Curtain: A method of containing oil spills. Air bubbling through a perforated pipe causes an upward water flow that slows the spread of oil. It can also be used to stop fish from entering polluted water.

Air Exchange Rate: The rate at which outside air replaces indoor air in a given space.

Air Gap: Open vertical gap or empty space that separates drinking water supply to be protected from another water system in a treatment plant or other location. The open gap protects the drinking water from contamination by backflow or back siphonage.

Air Handling Unit: Equipment that includes a fan or blower, heating and/or cooling coils, regulator controls, condensate drain pans, and air filters.

Air Mass: A large volume of air with certain meteorological or polluted characteristics—e.g., a heat inversion or smogginess—while in one location. The characteristics can change as the air mass moves away.

Air Monitoring: (See: monitoring.)

Air/Oil Table: The surface between the vadose zone and ambient oil; the pressure of oil in the porous medium is equal to atmospheric pressure.

Air Padding: Pumping dry air into a container to assist with the withdrawal of liquid or to force a liquefied gas such as chlorine out of the container.

Air Permeability: Permeability of soil with respect to air. Important to the design of soil-gas surveys. Measured in darcys or centimeters-per-second.

Air Plenum: Any space used to convey air in a building, furnace, or structure. The space above a suspended ceiling is often used as an air plenum.

Air Pollutant: Any substance in air that could, in high enough concentration, harm man, other animals, vegetation, or material. Pollutants may include almost any natural or artificial composition of airborne matter capable of being airborne. They may be in the form of solid particles, liquid droplets, gases, or in combination thereof. Generally, they fall into two main groups: (1) those emitted directly from identifiable sources and (2) those produced in the air by interaction between two or more primary pollutants, or by reaction with normal atmospheric constituents, with or without photoactivation. Exclusive of pollen, fog, and dust, which are of natural origin, about 100 contaminants have been identified. Air pollutants are often grouped in categories for ease in classification; some of he categories are: solids, sulfur compounds, volatile organic chemicals, particulate matter, nitrogen compounds, oxygen compounds, halogen compounds, radioactive compound, and odors.

Air Pollution: The presence of contaminants or pollutant substances in the air that interfere with human health or welfare, or produce other harmful environmental effects.

Air Pollution Control Device: Mechanism or equipment that cleans emissions generated by a source (e.g. an incinerator, industrial smokestack, or an automobile exhaust system) by removing pollutants that would otherwise be released to the atmosphere.

Air Pollution Episode: A period of abnormally high concentration of air pollutants, often due to low winds and temperature inversion, that can cause illness and death. (See: episode, pollution.)

Air Quality Control Region:

Air Quality Criteria: The levels of pollution and lengths of exposure above which adverse health and welfare effects may occur.

Air Quality Standards: The level of pollutants prescribed by regulations that are not be exceeded during a given time in a defined area.

Air Sparging: Injecting air or oxygen into an aquifer to strip or flush volatile contaminants as air bubbles up through The ground water and is captured by a vapor extraction system.

Air Stripping: A treatment system that removes volatile organic compounds (VOCs) from contaminated ground water or surface water by forcing an airstream through the water and causing the compounds to evaporate.

Air Toxics: Any air pollutant for which a national ambient air quality standard (NAAQS) does not exist (i.e. excluding ozone, carbon monoxide, PM-10, sulfur dioxide, nitrogen oxide) that may reasonably be anticipated to cause cancer; respiratory, cardiovascular, or developmental effects; reproductive dysfunctions, neurological disorders, heritable gene mutations, or other serious or irreversible chronic or acute health effects in humans.

Airborne Particulates: Total suspended particulate matter found in the atmosphere as solid particles or liquid droplets. Chemical composition of particulates varies widely, depending on location and time of year. Sources of airborne particulates include: dust, emissions from industrial processes, combustion products from the burning of wood and coal, combustion products associated with motor vehicle or non-road engine exhausts, and reactions to gases in the atmosphere.

Airborne Release: Release of any pollutant into the air.

Alachlor: A herbicide, marketed under the trade name Lasso, used mainly to control weeds in corn and soybean fields.

Alar: Trade name for daminozide, a pesticide that makes apples redder, firmer, and less likely to drop off trees before growers are ready to pick them. It is also used to a lesser extent on peanuts, tart cherries, concord grapes, and other fruits.

Aldicarb: An insecticide sold under the trade name Temik. It is made from ethyl isocyanate.

Algae: Simple rootless plants that grow in sunlit waters in proportion to the amount of available nutrients. They can affect water quality adversely by lowering the dissolved oxygen in the water. They are food for fish and small aquatic animals.

Algal Blooms: Sudden spurts of algal growth, which can affect water quality adversely and indicate potentially hazardous changes in local water chemistry.

Algicide: Substance or chemical used specifically to kill or control algae.

Aliquot: A measured portion of a sample taken for analysis. One or more aliquots make up a sample. (See: duplicate.)

Alkaline: The condition of water or soil which contains a sufficient amount of alkali substance to raise the pH above 7.0.

Alkalinity: The capacity of bases to neutralize acids. An example is lime added to lakes to decrease acidity.

Allergen: A substance that causes an allergic reaction in individuals sensitive to it.

Alluvial: Relating to and/or sand deposited by flowing water.

Alternate Method: Any method of sampling and analyzing for an air or water pollutant that is not a reference or equivalent method but that has been demonstrated in specific cases-to EPA's satisfaction-to produce results adequate for compliance monitoring.

Alternative Compliance: A policy that allows facilities to choose among methods for achieving emission-reduction or risk-reduction instead of command-and control regulations that specify standards and how to meet them. Use of a theoretical emissions bubble over a facility to cap the amount of pollution emitted while allowing the company to choose where and how (within the facility) it complies.(See: bubble, emissions trading.)

Alternative Fuels: Substitutes for traditional liquid, oil-derived motor vehicle fuels like gasoline and diesel. Includes mixtures of alcohol-based fuels with gasoline, methanol, ethanol, compressed natural gas, and others.

Alternative Remedial Contract Strategy Contractors: Government contractors who provide project management and technical services to support remedial response activities at National Priorities List sites.

Ambient Air: Any unconfined portion of the atmosphere: open air, surrounding air.

Ambient Air Quality Standards: (See: Criteria Pollutants and National Ambient Air Quality Standards.)

Ambient Measurement: A measurement of the concentration of a substance or pollutant within the immediate environs of an organism; taken to relate it to the amount of possible exposure.

Ambient Medium: Material surrounding or contacting an organism (e.g. outdoor air, indoor air, water, or soil, through which chemicals or pollutants can reach the organism. (See: biological medium, environmental medium.)

Ambient Temperature: Temperature of the surrounding air or other medium.

Amprometric Titration: A way of measuring concentrations of certain substances in water using an electric current that flows during a chemical reaction.

Anaerobic: A life or process that occurs in, or is not destroyed by, the absence of oxygen.

Anaerobic Decomposition: Reduction of the net energy level and change in chemical composition of organic matter caused by microorganisms in an oxygen-free environment.

Animal Dander: Tiny scales of animal skin, a common indoor air pollutant.

Animal Studies: Investigations using animals as surrogates for humans with the expectation that the results are pertinent to humans.

Anisotropy: In hydrology, the conditions under which one or more hydraulic properties of an aquifer vary from a reference point.

Annular Space, Annulus: The space between two concentric tubes or casings, or between the casing and the borehole wall.

Antagonism: Interference or inhibition of the effect of one chemical by the action of another.

Antarctic "Ozone Hole": Refers to the seasonal depletion of ozone in the upper atmosphere above a large area of Antarctica. (See: Ozone Hole.)

Anti-Degradation Clause: Part of federal air quality and water quality requirements prohibiting deterioration where pollution levels are above the legal limit.

Anti-Microbial: An agent that kills microbes.

Applicable or Relevant and Appropriate Requirements (ARARs): Any state or federal statute that pertains to protection of human life and the environment in addressing specific conditions or use of a particular cleanup technology at a Superfund site,

Applied Dose: In exposure assessment, the amount of a substance in contact with the primary absorption boundaries of an organism (e.g. skin, lung tissue, gastrointestinal track) and available for absorption.

Aqueous: Something made up of water.

Aqueous Solubility: The maximum concentration of a chemical that will dissolve in pure water at a reference temperature.

Aquifer: An underground geological formation, or group of formations, containing water. Are sources of groundwater for wells and springs.

Aquifer Test: A test to determine hydraulic properties of an aquifer.

Aquitard: Geological formation that may contain groundwater but is not capable of transmitting significant quantities of it under normal hydraulic gradients. May function as confining bed.

Architectural Coatings: Coverings such as paint and roof tar that are used on exteriors of buildings.

Area of Review: In the UIC program, the area surrounding an injection well that is reviewed during the permitting process to determine if flow between aquifers will be induced by the injection operation.

Area Source: Any source of air pollution that is released over a relatively small area but which cannot be classified as a point source. Such sources may include vehicles and other small engines, small businesses and household activities, or biogenic sources such as a forest that releases hydrocarbons.

Aromatics: A type of hydrocarbon, such as benzene or toluene, with a specific type of ring structure. Aromatics are sometimes added to gasoline in order to increase octane. Some aromatics are toxic.

Arsenicals: Pesticides containing arsenic.

Artesian (Aquifer or Well): Water held under pressure in porous rock or soil confined by impermeable geological formations.

Asbestos: A mineral fiber that can pollute air or water and cause cancer or asbestosis when inhaled. EPA has banned or severely restricted its use in manufacturing and construction.

Asbestos Abatement: Procedures to control fiber release from asbestos-containing materials in a building or to remove them entirely, including removal, encapsulation, repair, enclosure, encasement, and operations and maintenance programs.

Asbestos Assessment: In the asbestos-in-schools program, the evaluation of the physical condition and potential for damage of all friable asbestos containing materials and thermal insulation systems.

Asbestos Program Manager: A building owner or designated representative who supervises all aspects of the facility asbestos management and control program.

Asbestos-Containing Waste Materials (ACWM): Mill tailings or any waste that contains commercial asbestos and is generated by a source covered by the Clean Air Act Asbestos NESHAPS.

Asbestosis: A disease associated with inhalation of asbestos fibers. The disease makes breathing progressively more difficult and can be fatal.

Ash: The mineral content of a product remaining after complete combustion.

Assay: A test for a specific chemical, microbe, or effect.

Assessment Endpoint: In ecological risk assessment, an explicit expression of the environmental value to be protected; includes both an ecological entity and specific attributed thereof. entity (e.g. salmon are a valued ecological entity; reproduction and population maintenance—the attribute—form an assessment endpoint.)

Assimilation: The ability of a body of water to purify itself of pollutants.

Assimilative Capacity: The capacity of a natural body of water to receive wastewaters or toxic materials without deleterious effects and without damage to aquatic life or humans who consume the water.

Association of Boards of Certification: An international organization representing boards which certify the operators of waterworks and wastewater facilities.

Attainment Area: An area considered to have air quality as good as or better than the national ambient air quality standards as defined in the Clean Air Act. An area may be an attainment area for one pollutant and a non-attainment area for others.

Attenuation: The process by which a compound is reduced in concentration over time, through absorption, adsorption, degradation, dilution, and/or transformation. an also be the decrease with distance of sight caused by attenuation of light by particulate pollution.

Attractant: A chemical or agent that lures insects or other pests by stimulating their sense of smell.

Attrition: Wearing or grinding down of a substance by friction. Dust from such processes contributes to air pollution.

Availability Session: Informal meeting at a public location where interested citizens can talk with EPA and state officials on a one-to-one basis.

Available Chlorine: A measure of the amount of chlorine available in chlorinated lime, hypochlorite compounds, and other materials used as a source of chlorine when compared with that of liquid or gaseous chlorines.

Avoided Cost: The cost a utility would incur to generate the next increment of electric capacity using its own resources; many landfill gas projects' buy back rates are based on avoided costs.

A-Scale Sound Level: A measurement of sound approximating the sensitivity of the human ear, used to note the intensity or annoyance level of sounds.

B

Back Pressure: A pressure that can cause water to backflow into the water supply when a user's waste water system is at a higher pressure than the public system.

Backflow/Back Siphonage: A reverse flow condition created by a difference in water pressures that causes water to flow back into the distribution pipes of a drinking water supply from any source other than the intended one.

Background Level: 1. The concentration of a substance in an environmental media (air, water, or soil) that occurs naturally or is not the result of human activities. 2. In exposure assessment the concentration of a substance in a defined control area, during a fixed period of time before, during, or after a data-gathering operation..

Backwashing: Reversing the flow of water back through the filter media to remove entrapped solids.

Backyard Composting: Diversion of organic food waste and yard trimmings from the municipal waste stream by composting hem in one's yard through controlled decomposition of organic matter by bacteria and fungi into a humus-like product. It is considered source reduction, not recycling, because the composted materials never enter the municipal waste stream.

Barrel Sampler: Open-ended steel tube used to collect soil samples.

BACT - Best Available Control Technology: An emission limitation based on the maximum degree of emission reduction (considering energy, environmental, and economic impacts) achievable through application of production processes and available methods, systems, and techniques. BACT does not permit emissions in excess of those allowed under any applicable Clean Air Act provisions. Use of the BACT concept is allowable on a case by case basis for major new or modified emissions sources in attainment areas and applies to each regulated pollutant.

Bacteria: (Singular: bacterium) Microscopic living organisms that can aid in pollution control by metabolizing organic matter in sewage, oil spills or other pollutants. However, bacteria in soil, water or air can also cause human, animal and plant health problems.

Bactericide: A pesticide used to control or destroy bacteria, typically in the home, schools, or hospitals.

Baffle: A flat board or plate, deflector, guide, or similar device constructed or placed in flowing water or slurry systems to cause more uniform flow velocities to absorb energy and to divert, guide, or agitate liquids.

Baffle Chamber: In incinerator design, a chamber designed to promote the settling of fly ash and coarse particulate matter by changing the direction and/or reducing the velocity of the gases produced by the combustion of the refuse or sludge.

Baghouse Filter: Large fabric bag, usually made of glass fibers, used to eliminate intermediate and large (greater than 20 PM in diameter) particles. This device operates like the bag of an electric vacuum cleaner, passing the air and smaller particles while entrapping the larger ones.

Bailer: A pipe with a valve at the lower end, used to remove slurry from the bottom or side of a well as it is being drilled, or to collect groundwater samples from wells or open boreholes. 2. A tube of varying length.

Baling: Compacting solid waste into blocks to reduce volume and simplify handling.

Ballistic Separator: A machine that sorts organic from inorganic matter for composting.

Band Application: The spreading of chemicals over, or next to, each row of plants in a field.

Banking: A system for recording qualified air emission reductions for later use in bubble, offset, or netting transactions. (See: emissions trading.)

Bar Screen: In wastewater treatment, a device used to remove large solids.

Barrier Coating(s): A layer of a material that obstructs or prevents passage of something through a surface that is to be protected; e.g., grout, caulk, or various sealing compounds; sometimes used with polyurethane membranes to prevent corrosion or oxidation of metal surfaces, chemical impacts on various materials, or, for example, to prevent radon infiltration through walls, cracks, or joints in a house.

Basal Application: In pesticides, the application of a chemical on plant stems or tree trunks just above the soil line.

Basalt: Consistent year-round energy use of a facility; also refers to the minimum amount of electricity supplied continually to a facility.

Bean Sheet: Common term for a pesticide data package record.

Bed Load: Sediment particles resting on or near the channel bottom that are pushed or rolled along by the flow of water.

BEN: EPA's computer model for analyzing a violator's economic gain from not complying with the law.

Bench-scale Tests: Laboratory testing of potential cleanup technologies (See: treatability studies.)

Benefit-Cost Analysis: An economic method for assessing the benefits and costs of achieving alternative health-based standards at given levels of health protection.

Benthic/Benthos: An organism that feeds on the sediment at the bottom of a water body such as an ocean, lake, or river.

Bentonite: A colloidal clay, expansible when moist, commonly used to provide a tight seal around a well casing.

Beryllium: An metal hazardous to human health when inhaled as an airborne pollutant. It is discharged by machine shops, ceramic and propellant plants, and foundries.

Best Available Control Measures (BACM): A term used to refer to the most effective measures (according to EPA guidance) for controlling small or dispersed particulates and other emissions from sources such as roadway dust, soot and ash from woodstoves and open burning of rush, timber, grasslands, or trash.

Best Available Control Technology (BACT): For any specific source, the currently available technology producing the greatest reduction of air pollutant emissions,taking into account energy, environmental, economic, and other costs.

Best Available Control Technology (BACT): The most stringent technology available for controlling emissions; major sources are required to use BACT, unless it can be demonstrated that it is not feasible for energy, environmental, or economic reasons.

Best Demonstrated Available Technology (BDAT): As identified by EPA, the most effective commercially available means of treating specific types of hazardous waste. The BDATs may change with advances in treatment technologies.

Best Management Practice (BMP): Methods that have been determined to be the most effective, practical means of preventing or reducing pollution from non-point sources.

Bimetal: Beverage containers with steel bodies and aluminum tops; handled differently from pure aluminum in recycling.

Bioaccumulants: Substances that increase in concentration in living organisms as they take in contaminated air, water, or food because the substances are very slowly metabolized or excreted. (See: biological magnification.)

Bioassay: A test to determine te relative strength of a substance by comparing its effect on a test organism with that of a standard preparation.

Bioavailability: Degree of ability to be absorbed and ready to interact in organism metabolism.

Biochemical Oxygen Demand (BOD): A measure of the amount of oxygen consumed in the biological processes that break down organic matter in water. The greater the BOD, the greater the degree of pollution.

Bioconcentration: The accumulation of a chemical in tissues of a fish or other organism to levels greater than in the surrounding medium.

Biodegradable: Capable of decomposing under natural conditions.

Biodiversity: Refers to the variety and variability among living organisms and the ecological complexes in which they occur. Diversity can be defined as the number of different items and their relative frequencies. For biological diversity, these items are organized at many levels, ranging from complete ecosystems to the biochemical structures that are the molecular basis of heredity. Thus, the term encompasses different ecosystems, species, and genes.

Biological Contaminants: Living organisms or derivates (e.g. viruses, bacteria, fungi, and mammal and bird antigens) that can cause harmful health effects when inhaled, swallowed, or otherwise taken into the body.

Biological Control: In pest control, the use of animals and organisms that eat or otherwise kill or out-compete pests.

Biological Integrity: The ability to support and maintain balanced, integrated, functionality in the natural habitat of a given region. Concept is applied primarily in drinking water management.

Biological Magnification: Refers to the process whereby certain substances such as pesticides or heavy metals move up the food chain, work their way into rivers or lakes, and are eaten by aquatic organisms such as fish, which in turn are eaten by large birds, animals or humans. The substances become concentrated in tissues or internal organs as they move up the chain. (See: bioaccumulants.)

Biological Measurement: A measurement taken in a biological medium. For exposure assessment, it is related to the measurement is taken to related it to the established internal dose of a compound.

Biological Medium: One of the major component of an organism; e.g. blood, fatty tissue, lymph nodes or breath, in which chemicals can be stored or transformed. (See: ambient medium, environmental medium.)

Biological Oxidation: Decomposition of complex organic materials by microorganisms. Occurs in self-purification of water bodies and in activated sludge wastewater treatment.

Biological Oxygen Demand (BOD): An indirect measure of the concentration of biologically degradable material present in organic wastes. It usually reflects the amount of oxygen consumed in five days by biological processes breaking down organic waste.

Biological pesticides: Certain microorganism, including bacteria, fungi, viruses, and protozoa that are effective in controlling pests. These agents usually do not have toxic effects on animals and people and do not leave toxic or persistent chemical residues in the environment.

Biological Stressors: Organisms accidentally or intentionally dropped into habitats in which they do not evolve naturally; e.g. gypsy moths, Dutch elm disease, certain types of algae, and bacteria.

Biological Treatment: A treatment technology that uses bacteria to consume organic waste.

Biologically Effective Dose: The amount of a deposited or absorbed compound reaching the cells or target sites where adverse effect occur, or where the chemical interacts with a membrane.

Biologicals: Vaccines, cultures and other preparations made from living organisms and their products, intended for use in diagnosing, immunizing, or treating humans or animals, or in related research.

Biomass: All of the living material in a given area; often refers to vegetation.

Biome: Entire community of living organisms in a single major ecological area. (See: biotic community.)

Biomonitoring: 1. The use of living organisms to test the suitability of effluents for discharge into receiving waters and to test the quality of such waters downstream from the discharge. 2. Analysis of blood, urine, tissues, etc. to measure chemical exposure in humans.

Bioremediation: Use of living organisms to clean up oil spills or remove other pollutants from soil, water, or wastewater; use of organisms such as non-harmful insects to remove agricultural pests or counteract diseases of trees, plants, and garden soil.

Biosensor: Analytical device comprising a biological recognition element (e.g. enzyme, receptor, DNA, antibody, or microorganism) in intimate contact with an electrochemical, optical, thermal, or acoustic signal transducer that together permit analyses of chemical properties or quantities. Shows potential development in some areas, including environmental monitoring.

Biosphere: The portion of Earth and its atmosphere that can support life.

Biostabilizer: A machine that converts solid waste into compost by grinding and aeration.

Biota: The animal and plant life of a given region.

Biotechnology: Techniques that use living organisms or parts of organisms to produce a variety of products (from medicines to industrial enzymes) to improve plants or animals or to develop microorganisms to remove toxics from bodies of water, or act as pesticides.

Biotic Community: A naturally occurring assemblage of plants and animals that live in the same environment and are mutually sustaining and interdependent. (See: biome.)

Biotransformation: Conversion of a substance into other compounds by organisms; includes biodegredation.

Blackwater: Water that contains animal, human, or food waste.

Blood Products: Any product derived from human blood, including but not limited to blood plasma, platelets, red or white corpuscles, and derived licensed products such as interferon.

Bloom: A proliferation of algae and/or higher aquatic plants in a body of water; often related to pollution, especially when pollutants accelerate growth.

BOD5: The amount of dissolved oxygen consumed in five days by biological processes breaking down organic matter.

Body Burden: The amount of a chemical stored in the body at a given time, especially a potential toxin in the body as the result of exposure.

Bog: A type of wetland that accumulates appreciable peat deposits. Bogs depend primarily on precipitation for their water source, and are usually acidic and rich in plant residue with a conspicuous mat of living green moss.

Boiler: A vessel designed to transfer heat produced by combustion or electric resistance to water. Boilers may provide hot water or steam.

Boom: 1. A floating device used to contain oil on a body of water. 2. A piece of equipment used to apply pesticides from a tractor or truck.

Borehole: Hole made with drilling equipment.

Botanical Pesticide: A pesticide whose active ingredient is a plant-produced chemical such as nicotine or strychnine. Also called a plant-derived pesticide.

Bottle Bill: Proposed or enacted legislation which requires a returnable deposit on beer or soda containers and provides for retail store or other redemption. Such legislation is designed to discourage use of throw-away containers.

Bottom Ash: The non-airborne combustion residue from burning pulverized coal in a boiler; the material which falls to the bottom of the boiler and is removed mechanically; a concentration of non-combustible materials, which may include toxics.

Bottom Land Hardwoods: Forested freshwater wetlands adjacent to rivers in the southeastern United States, especially valuable for wildlife breeding, nesting and habitat.

Bounding Estimate: An estimate of exposure, dose, or risk that is higher than that incurred by the person in the population with the currently highest exposure, dose, or risk. Bounding estimates are useful in developing statements that exposures, doses, or risks are not greater than an estimated value.

Brackish: Mixed fresh and salt water.

Breakpoint Chlorination: Addition of chlorine to water until the chlorine demand has been satisfied.

Breakthrough: A crack or break in a filter bed that allows the passage of floc or particulate matter through a filter; will cause an increase in filter effluent turbidity.

Breathing Zone: Area of air in which an organism inhales.

Brine Mud: Waste material, often associated with well-drilling or mining, composed of mineral salts or other inorganic compounds.

British Thermal Unit: Unit of heat energy equal to the amount of heat required to raise the temperature of one pound of water by one degree Fahrenheit at sea level.

Broadcast Application: The spreading of pesticides over an entire area.

Brownfields: Abandoned, idled, or under used industrial and commercial facilities/sites where expansion or redevelopment is complicated by real or perceived environmental contamination. They can be in urban, suburban, or rural areas. EPA's Brownfields initiative helps communities mitigate potential health risks and restore the economic viability of such areas or properties.

Bubble: A system under which existing emissions sources can propose alternate means to comply with a set of emissions limitations; under the bubble concept, sources can control more than required at one emission point where control costs are relatively low in return for a comparable relaxation of controls at a second emission point where costs are higher.

Bubble Policy: (See: emissions trading.)

Buffer: A solution or liquid whose chemical makeup is such that it minimizes changes in pH when acids or bases are added to it.

Buffer Strips: Strips of grass or other erosion-resisting vegetation between or below cultivated strips or fields.

Building Cooling Load: The hourly amount of heat that must be removed from a building to maintain indoor comfort (measured in British thermal units (Btus).

Building Envelope: The exterior surface of a building's construction—the walls, windows, floors, roof, and floor. Also called building shell.

Building Related Illness: Diagnosable illness whose cause and symptoms can be directly attributed to a specific pollutant source within a building (e.g. Legionnaire's disease, hypersensitivity, pneumonitis.) (See: sick building syndrome.)

Bulk Sample: A small portion (usually thumbnail size) of a suspect asbestos-containing building material collected by an asbestos inspector for laboratory analysis to determine asbestos content.

Bulky Waste: Large items of waste materials, such as appliances, furniture, large auto parts, trees, stumps.

Burial Ground (Graveyard): A disposal site for radioactive waste materials that uses earth or water as a shield.

Buy-Back Center: Facility where individuals or groups bring reyclables in return for payment.

By-product: Material, other than the principal product, generated as a consequence of an industrial process or as a breakdown product in a living system.

C

Cadmium (Cd): A heavy metal that accumulates in the environment.

Cancellation: Refers to Section 6 (b) of the Federal Insecticide, Fungicide and Rodenticide Act (FIFRA) which authorizes cancellation of a pesticide registration if unreasonable adverse effects to the environment and public health develop when a product is used according to widespread and commonly recognized practice, or if its labeling or other material required to be submitted does not comply with FIFRA provisions.

Cap: A layer of clay, or other impermeable material installed over the top of a closed landfill to prevent entry of rainwater and minimize leachate.

Capacity Assurance Plan: A statewide plan which supports a state's ability to manage the hazardous waste generated within its boundaries over a twenty year period.

Capillary Action: Movement of water through very small spaces due to molecular forces called capillary forces.

Capillary Fringe: The porous material just above the water table which may hold water by capillarity (a property of surface tension that draws water upwards) in the smaller void spaces.

Capillary Fringe: The zone above he water table within which the porous medium is saturated by water under less than atmospheric pressure.

Capture Efficiency: The fraction of organic vapors generated by a process that are directed to an abatement or recovery device.

Carbon Absorber: An add-on control device that uses activated carbon to absorb volatile organic compounds from a gas stream. (The VOCs are later recovered from the carbon.)

Carbon Adsorption: A treatment system that removes contaminants from ground water or surface water by forcing it through tanks containing activated carbon treated to attract the contaminants.

Carbon Monoxide (CO): A colorless, odorless, poisonous gas produced by incomplete fossil fuel combustion.

Carbon Tetrachloride (CC14): Compound consisting of one carbon atom ad four chlorine atoms, once widely used as a industrial raw material, as a solvent, and in the production of

CFCs. Use as a solvent ended when it was discovered to be carcinogenic.

Carboxyhemoglobin: Hemoglobin in which the iron is bound to carbon monoxide(CO) instead of oxygen.

Carcinogen: Any substance that can cause or aggravate cancer.

Carrier: 1.The inert liquid or solid material in a pesticide product that serves as a delivery vehicle for the active ingredient. Carriers do not have toxic properties of their own. 2. Any material or system that can facilitate the movement of a pollutant into the body or cells.

Carrying Capacity: 1. In recreation management, the amount of use a recreation area can sustain without loss of quality. 2. In wildlife management, the maximum number of animals an area can support during a given period.

CAS Registration Number: A number assigned by the Chemical Abstract Service to identify a chemical.

Case Study: A brief fact sheet providing risk, cost, and performance information on alternative methods and other pollution prevention ideas, compliance initiatives, voluntary efforts, etc.

Cask: A thick-walled container (usually lead) used to transport radioactive material. Also called a coffin.

Catalyst: A substance that changes the speed or yield of a chemical reaction without being consumed or chemically changed by the chemical reaction.

Catalytic Converter: An air pollution abatement device that removes pollutants from motor vehicle exhaust, either by oxidizing them into carbon dioxide and water or reducing them to nitrogen.

Catalytic Incinerator: A control device that oxidizes volatile organic compounds (VOCs) by using a catalyst to promote the combustion process. Catalytic incinerators require lower temperatures than conventional thermal incinerators, thus saving fuel and other costs.

Categorical Exclusion: A class of actions which either individually or cumulatively would not have a significant effect on the human environment and therefore would not require preparation of an environmental assessment or environmental impact statement under the National Environmental Policy Act (NEPA).

Categorical Pretreatment Standard: A technology-based effluent limitation for an industrial facility discharging into a municipal sewer system. Analogous in stringency to Best Availability Technology (BAT) for direct dischargers.

Cathodic Protection: A technique to prevent corrosion of a metal surface by making it the cathode of an electrochemical cell.

Cavitation: The formation and collapse of gas pockets or bubbles on the blade of an impeller or the gate of a valve; collapse of these pockets or bubbles drives water with such force that it can cause pitting of the gate or valve surface.

Cells: 1. In solid waste disposal, holes where waste is dumped, compacted, and covered with layers of dirt on a daily basis. 2. The smallest structural part of living matter capable of functioning as an independent unit.

Cementitious: Densely packed and nonfibrous friable materials.

Central Collection Point: Location were a generator of regulated medical waste consolidates wastes originally generated at various locations in his facility. The wastes are gathered together for treatment on-site or for transportation elsewhere for treatment and/or disposal. This term could also apply to community hazardous waste collections, industrial and other waste management systems.

Centrifugal Collector: A mechanical system using centrifugal force to remove aerosols from a gas stream or to remove water from sludge.

CERCLIS: The federal Comprehensive Environmental Response, Compensation, and Liability Information System is a database that includes all sites which have been nominated for investigation by the Superfund program.

Channelization: Straightening and deepening streams so water will move faster, a marsh-drainage tactic that can interfere with waste assimilation capacity, disturb fish and wildlife habitats, and aggravate flooding.

Characteristic: Any one of the four categories used in defining hazardous waste: ignitability, corrosivity, reactivity, and toxicity.

Characterization of Ecological Effects: Part of ecological risk assessment that evaluates ability of a stressor to cause adverse effects under given circumstances.

Characterization of Exposure: Portion of an ecological risk assessment that evaluates interaction of a stressor with one or more ecological entities.

Check-Valve Tubing Pump: Water sampling tool also referred to as a water Pump.

Chemical Case: For purposes of review and regulation, the grouping of chemically similar pesticide active ingredients (e.g. salts and esters of the same chemical) into chemical cases.

Chemical Compound: A distinct and pure substance formed by the union or two or more elements in definite proportion by weight.

Chemical Element: A fundamental substance comprising one kind of atom; the simplest form of matter.

Chemical Oxygen Demand (COD): A measure of the oxygen required to oxidize all compounds, both organic and inorganic, in water.

Chemical Stressors: Chemicals released to the environment through industrial waste, auto emissions, pesticides, and other human activity that can cause illnesses and even death in plants and animals.

Chemical Treatment: Any one of a variety of technologies that use chemicals or a variety of chemical processes to treat waste.

Chemnet: Mutual aid network of chemical shippers and contractors that assigns a contracted emergency response company to provide technical support if a representative of the firm whose chemicals are involved in an incident is not readily available.

Chemosterilant: A chemical that controls pests by preventing reproduction.

Chemtrec: The industry-sponsored Chemical Transportation Emergency Center; provides information and/or emergency assistance to emergency responders.

Child Resistant Packaging (CRP): Packaging that protects children or adults from injury or illness resulting from accidental contact with or ingestion of residential pesticides that meet or exceed specific toxicity levels. Required by FIFRA regulations. Term is also used for protective packaging of medicines.

Chiller: A device that generates a cold liquid that is circulated through an air-handling unit's cooling coil to cool the air supplied to the building.

Chilling Effect: The lowering of the Earth's temperature because of increased particles in the air blocking the sun's rays. (See: greenhouse effect.)

Chisel Plowing: Preparing croplands by using a special implement that avoids complete inversion of the soil as in conventional plowing. Chisel plowing can leave a protective cover or crops residues on the soil surface to help prevent erosion and improve filtration.

Chlorinated Hydrocarbons: 1. Chemicals containing only chlorine, carbon, and hydrogen. These include a class of persistent, broad-spectrum insecticides that linger in the environment and accumulate in the food chain. Among them are DDT, aldrin, dieldrin, heptachlor, chlordane, lindane, endrin, Mirex, hexachloride, and toxaphene. Other examples include TCE, used as an industrial solvent. 2. Any chlorinated organic compounds including chlorinated solvents such as dichloromethane, trichloromethylene, chloroform.

Chlorinated Solvent: An organic solvent containing chlorine atoms(e.g. methylene chloride and 1,1,1-trichloromethane). Uses of chlorinated solvents are include aerosol spray containers, in highway paint, and dry cleaning fluids.

Chlorination: The application of chlorine to drinking water, sewage, or industrial waste to disinfect or to oxidize undesirable compounds.

Chlorinator: A device that adds chlorine, in gas or liquid form, to water or sewage to kill infectious bacteria.

Chlorine-Contact Chamber: That part of a water treatment plant where effluent is disinfected by chlorine.

Chlorofluorocarbons (CFCs): A family of inert, nontoxic, and easily liquefied chemicals used in refrigeration, air conditioning, packaging, insulation, or as solvents and aerosol propellants. Because CFCs are not destroyed in the lower atmosphere they drift into the upper atmosphere where their chlorine components destroy ozone. (See: fluorocarbons.)

Chlorophenoxy: A class of herbicides that may be found in domestic water supplies and cause adverse health effects.

Chlorosis: Discoloration of normally green plant parts caused by disease, lack of nutrients, or various air pollutants.

Cholinesterase: An enzyme found in animals that regulates nerve impulses by the inhibition of acetylcholine. Cholinesterase inhibition is associated with a variety of acute symptoms such as nausea, vomiting, blurred vision, stomach cramps, and rapid heart rate.

Chromium: (See: heavy metals.)

Chronic Effect: An adverse effect on a human or animal in which symptoms recur frequently or develop slowly over a long period of time.

Chronic Exposure: Multiple exposures occurring over an extended period of time or over a significant fraction of an animal's or human's lifetime (Usually seven years to a lifetime.)

Chronic Toxicity: The capacity of a substance to cause long-term poisonous health effects in humans, animals, fish, and other organisms. (See: acute toxicity.)

Circle of Influence: The circular outer edge of a depression produced in the water table by the pumping of water from a well. (See: cone of depression.)

Cistern: Small tank or storage facility used to store water for a home or farm; often used to store rain water.

Clarification: Clearing action that occurs during wastewater treatment when solids settle out. This is often aided by centrifugal action and chemically induced coagulation in wastewater.

Clarifier: A tank in which solids settle to the bottom and are subsequently removed as sludge.

Class I Area: Under the Clean Air Act. a Class I area is one in which visibility is protected more stringently than under the national ambient air quality standards; includes national parks, wilderness areas, monuments, and other areas of special national and cultural significance.

Class I Substance: One of several groups of chemicals with an ozone depletion potential of 0.2 or higher, including CFCS, Halons, Carbon Tetrachloride, and Methyl Chloroform (listed in the Clean Air Act), and HBFCs and Ethyl Bromide (added by EPA regulations). (See: Global warming potential.)

Class II Substance: A substance with an ozone depletion potential of less than 0.2. All HCFCs are currently included in this classification. (See: Global warming potential.)

Clay Soil: Soil material containing more than 40 percent clay, less than 45 percent sand, and less than 40 percent silt.

Clean Coal Technology: Any technology not in widespread use prior to the Clean Air Act Amendments of 1990. This Act will achieve significant reductions in pollutants associated with the burning of coal.

Clean Fuels: Blends or substitutes for gasoline fuels, including compressed natural gas, methanol, ethanol, and liquified petroleum gas.

Cleaner Technologies Substitutes Assessment: A document that systematically evaluates the relative risk, performance, and cost trade-offs of technological alternatives; serves as a repository for all the technical data (including methodology and results) developed by a DfE or other pollution prevention or education project.

Cleanup: Actions taken to deal with a release or threat of release of a hazardous substance that could affect humans and/or the environment. The term "cleanup" is sometimes used interchangeably with the terms remedial action, removal action, response action, or corrective action.

Clear Cut: Harvesting all the trees in one area at one time, a practice that can encourage fast rainfall or snowmelt runoff, erosion, sedimentation of streams and lakes, and flooding, and destroys vital habitat.

Clear Well: A reservoir for storing filtered water of sufficient quantity to prevent the need to vary the filtration rate with variations in demand. Also used to provide chlorine contact time for disinfection.

Climate Change (also referred to as 'global climate change'): The term 'climate change' is sometimes used to refer to all forms of climatic inconsistency, but because the Earth's climate is never static, the term is more properly used to imply a significant change from one climatic condition to another. In some cases, 'climate change' has been used synonymously with the term, 'global warming'; scientists however, tend to use the term in the wider sense to also include natural changes in climate. (See: global warming.)

Cloning: In biotechnology, obtaining a group of genetically identical cells from a single cell; making identical copies of a gene.

Closed-Loop Recycling: Reclaiming or reusing wastewater for non-potable purposes in an enclosed process.

Closure: The procedure a landfill operator must follow when a landfill reaches its legal capacity for solid ceasing acceptance of solid waste and placing a cap on the landfill site.

Co-fire: Burning of two fuels in the same combustion unit; e.g., coal and natural gas, or oil and coal.

Coagulation: Clumping of particles in wastewater to settle out impurities, often induced by chemicals such as lime, alum, and iron salts.

Coal Cleaning Technology: A precombustion process by which coal is physically or chemically treated to remove some of its sulfur so as to reduce sulfur dioxide emissions.

Coal Gasification: Conversion of coal to a gaseous product by one of several available technologies.

Coastal Zone: Lands and waters adjacent to the coast that exert an influence on the uses of the sea and its ecology, or whose uses and ecology are affected by the sea.

Code of Federal Regulations (CFR): Document that codifies all rules of the executive departments and agencies of the federal government. It is divided into fifty volumes, known as titles. Title 40 of the CFR (referenced as 40 CFR) lists all environmental regulations.

Coefficient of Haze (COH): A measurement of visibility interference in the atmosphere.

Cogeneration: The consecutive generation of useful thermal and electric energy from the same fuel source.

Coke Oven: An industrial process which converts coal into coke, one of the basic materials used in blast furnaces for the conversion of iron ore into iron.

Cold Temperature CO: A standard for automobile emissions of carbon monoxide (CO) emissions to be met at a low temperature (i.e. 20 degrees Fahrenheit). Conventional automobile catalytic converters are not efficient in cold weather until they warm up.

Coliform Index: A rating of the purity of water based on a count of fecal bacteria.

Coliform Organism: Microorganisms found in the intestinal tract of humans and animals. Their presence in water indicates fecal pollution and potentially adverse contamination by pathogens.

Collector: Public or private hauler that collects nonhazardous waste and recyclable materials from residential, commercial, institutional and industrial sources. (See: hauler.)

Collector Sewers: Pipes used to collect and carry wastewater from individual sources to an interceptor sewer that will carry it to a treatment facility.

Colloids: Very small, finely divided solids (that do not dissolve) that remain dispersed in a liquid for a long time due to their small size and electrical charge.

Combined Sewer Overflows: Discharge of a mixture of storm water and domestic waste when the flow capacity of a sewer system is exceeded during rainstorms.

Combined Sewers: A sewer system that carries both sewage and storm-water runoff. Normally, its entire flow goes to a waste treatment plant, but during a heavy storm, the volume of water may be so great as to cause overflows of untreated mixtures of storm water and sewage into receiving waters. Storm-water runoff may also carry toxic chemicals from industrial areas or streets into the sewer system.

Combustion: 1. Burning, or rapid oxidation, accompanied by release of energy in the form of heat and light. 2. Refers to controlled burning of waste, in which heat chemically alters organic compounds, converting into stable inorganics such as carbon dioxide and water.

Combustion Chamber: The actual compartment where waste is burned in an incinerator.

Combustion Product: Substance produced during the burning or oxidation of a material.

Command Post: Facility located at a safe distance upwind from an accident site, where the on-scene coordinator, responders, and technical representatives make response decisions, deploy manpower and equipment, maintain liaison with news media, and handle communications.

Command-and-Control Regulations: Specific requirements prescribing how to comply with specific standards defining acceptable levels of pollution.

Comment Period: Time provided for the public to review and comment on a proposed EPA action or rulemaking after publication in the Federal Register.

Commercial Waste: All solid waste emanating from business establishments such as stores, markets, office buildings, restaurants, shopping centers, and theaters.

Commercial Waste Management Facility: A treatment, storage, disposal, or transfer facility which accepts waste from a variety of sources, as compared to a private facility which normally manages a limited waste stream generated by its own operations.

Commingled Recyclables: Mixed recyclables that are collected together.

Comminuter: A machine that shreds or pulverizes solids to make waste treatment easier.

Comminution: Mechanical shredding or pulverizing of waste. Used in both solid waste management and wastewater treatment.

Common Sense Initiative: Voluntary program to simplify environmental regulation to achieve cleaner, cheaper, smarter results, starting with six major industry sectors.

Community: In ecology, an assemblage of populations of different species within a specified location in space and time. Sometimes, a particular subgrouping may be specified, such as the fish community in a lake or the soil arthropod community in a forest.

Community Relations: The EPA effort to establish two-way communication with the public to create understanding of EPA programs and related actions, to ensure public input into decision-making processes related to affected communities, and to make certain that the Agency is aware of and responsive to public concerns. Specific community relations activities are required in relation to Superfund remedial actions.

Community Water System: A public water system which serves at least 15 service connections used by year-round residents or regularly serves at least 25 year-round residents.

Compact Fluorescent Lamp (CFL): Small fluorescent lamps used as more efficient alternatives to incandescent lighting. Also called PL, CFL, Twin-Tube, or BIAX lamps.

Compaction: Reduction of the bulk of solid waste by rolling and tamping.

Comparative Risk Assessment: Process that generally uses the judgement of experts to predict effects and set priorities among a wide range of environmental problems.

Complete Treatment: A method of treating water that consists of the addition of coagulant chemicals, flash mixing, coagulation-flocculation, sedimentation, and filtration. Also called conventional filtration.

Compliance Coal: Any coal that emits less than 1.2 pounds of sulfur dioxide per million Btu when burned. Also known as low sulfur coal.

Compliance Coating: A coating whose volatile organic compound content does not exceed that allowed by regulation.

Compliance Cycle: The 9-year calendar year cycle, beginning January 1, 1993, during which public water systems must monitor. Each cycle consists of three 3-year compliance periods.

Compliance Monitoring: Collection and evaluation of data, including self-monitoring reports, and verification to show whether pollutant concentrations and loads contained in permitted discharges are in compliance with the limits and conditions specified in the permit.

Compliance Schedule: A negotiated agreement between a pollution source and a government agency that specifies dates and procedures by which a source will reduce emissions and, thereby, comply with a regulation.

Composite Sample: A series of water samples taken over a given period of time and weighted by flow rate.

Compost: The relatively stable humus material that is produced from a composting process in which bacteria in soil mixed with garbage and degradable trash break down the mixture into organic fertilizer.

Composting: The controlled biological decomposition of organic material in the presence of air to form a humus-like material. Controlled methods of composting include mechanical mixing and aerating, ventilating the materials by dropping them through a vertical series of aerated chambers, or placing the compost in piles out in the open air and mixing it or turning it periodically.

Composting Facilities: 1. An offsite facility where the organic component of municipal solid waste is decomposed under controlled conditions; 2.an aerobic process in which organic materials are ground or shredded and then decomposed to humus in windrow piles or in mechanical digesters, drums, or similar enclosures.

Compressed Natural Gas (CNG): An alternative fuel for motor vehicles; considered one of the cleanest because of low hydrocarbon emissions and its vapors are relatively non-ozone producing. However, vehicles fueled with CNG do emit a significant quantity of nitrogen oxides.

Concentration: The relative amount of a substance mixed with another substance. An example is five ppm of carbon monoxide in air or 1 mg/l of iron in water.

Condensate: 1.Liquid formed when warm landfill gas cools as it travels through a collection system. 2. Water created by cooling steam or water vapor.

Condensate Return System: System that returns the heated water condensing within steam piping to the boiler and thus saves energy.

Conditional Registration: Under special circumstances, the Federal Insecticide, Fungicide, and Rodenticide Act (FIFRA) permits registration of pesticide products that is "conditional" upon the submission of additional data. These special circumstances include a finding by the EPA Administrator that a new product or use of an existing pesticide will not significantly increase the risk of unreasonable adverse effects. A product containing a new (previously unregistered) active ingredient may be conditionally registered only if the Administrator finds that such conditional registration is in the public interest, that a reasonable time for conducting the additional studies has not elapsed, and the use of the pesticide for the period of conditional registration will not present an unreasonable risk.

Conditionally Exempt Generators (CE): Persons or enterprises which produce less than 220 pounds of hazardous waste per month. Exempt from most regulation, they are required merely to determine whether their waste is hazardous, notify appropriate state or local agencies, and ship it by an authorized transporter to a permitted facility for proper disposal. (See : small quantity generator.)

Conductance: A rapid method of estimating the dissolved solids content of water supply by determining the capacity of a water sample to carry an electrical current. Conductivity is a measure of the ability of a solution to carry and electrical current.

Conductivity: A measure of the ability of a solution to carry an electrical current.

Cone of Depression: A depression in the water table that develops around a pumped well.

Cone of Influence: The depression, roughly conical in shape, produced in a water table by the pumping of water from a well.

Cone Penterometer Testing (CPT): A direct push system used to measure lithology based on soil penetration resistance. Sensors in the tip of the cone of the DP rod measure tip resistance and side-wall friction, transmitting electrical signals to digital processing equipment on the ground surface. (See: direct push.)

Confidential Business Information (CBI): Material that contains trade secrets or commercial or financial information that has been claimed as confidential by its source (e.g. a pesticide or new chemical formulation registrant). EPA has special procedures for handling such information.

Confidential Statement of Formula (CSF): A list of the ingredients in a new pesticide or chemical formulation. The list is submitted at the time for application for registration or change in formulation.

Confined Aquifer: An aquifer in which ground water is confined under pressure which is significantly greater than atmospheric pressure.

Confluent Growth: A continuous bacterial growth covering all or part of the filtration area of a membrane filter in which the bacteria colonies are not discrete.

Consent Decree: A legal document, approved by a judge, that formalizes an agreement reached between EPA and potentially responsible parties (PRPs) through which PRPs will conduct all or part of a cleanup action at a Superfund site; cease or correct actions or processes that are polluting the environment; or otherwise comply with EPA initiated regulatory enforcement actions to resolve the contamination at the Superfund site involved. The consent decree describes the actions PRPs will take and may be subject to a public comment period.

Conservation: Preserving and renewing, when possible, human and natural resources. The use, protection, and improvement of natural resources according to principles that will ensure their highest economic or social benefits.

Conservation Easement: Easement restricting a landowner to land uses that that are compatible with long-term conservation and environmental values.

Constituent(s) of Concern: Specific chemicals that are identified for evaluation in the site assessment process

Construction and Demolition Waste: Waste building materials, dredging materials, tree stumps, and rubble resulting from construction, remodeling, repair, and demolition of homes, commercial buildings and other structures and pavements. May contain lead, asbestos, or other hazardous substances.

Construction Ban: If, under the Clean Air Act, EPA disapproves an area's planning requirements for correcting nonattainment, EPA can ban the construction or modification of any major stationary source of the pollutant for which the area is in nonattainment.

Consumptive Water Use: Water removed from available supplies without return to a water resources system, e.g. water used in manufacturing, agriculture, and food preparation.

Contact Pesticide: A chemical that kills pests when it touches them, instead of by ingestion. Also, soil that contains the minute skeletons of certain algae that scratch and dehydrate waxy-coated insects.

Contaminant: Any physical, chemical, biological, or radiological substance or matter that has an adverse effect on air, water, or soil.

Contamination: Introduction into water, air, and soil of microorganisms, chemicals, toxic substances, wastes, or wastewater in a concentration that makes the medium unfit for its next intended use. Also applies to surfaces of objects, buildings, and various household and agricultural use products.

Contamination Source Inventory: An inventory of contaminant sources within delineated State Water-Protection Areas. Targets likely sources for further investigation.

Contingency Plan: A document setting out an organized, planned, and coordinated course of action to be followed in case of a fire, explosion, or other accident that releases toxic chemicals, hazardous waste, or radioactive materials that threaten human health or the environment. (See: National Oil and Hazardous Substances Contingency Plan.)

Continuous Discharge: A routine release to the environment that occurs without interruption, except for infrequent shutdowns for maintenance, process changes, etc.

Continuous Sample: A flow of water, waste or other material from a particular place in a plant to the location where samples are collected for testing. May be used to obtain grab or composite samples.

Contour Plowing: Soil tilling method that follows the shape of the land to discourage erosion.

Contour Strip Farming: A kind of contour farming in which row crops are planted in strips, between alternating strips of close-growing, erosion-resistant forage crops.

Contract Labs: Laboratories under contract to EPA, which analyze samples taken from waste, soil, air, and water or carry out research projects.

Control Technique Guidelines (CTG): EPA documents designed to assist state and local pollution authorities to achieve and maintain air quality standards for certain sources (e.g. organic emissions from solvent metal cleaning known as degreasing) through reasonably available control technologies (RACT).

Controlled Reaction: A chemical reaction under temperature and pressure conditions maintained within safe limits to produce a desired product or process.

Conventional Filtration: (See: complete treatment.)

Conventional Pollutants: Statutorily listed pollutants understood well by scientists. These may be in the form of organic waste, sediment, acid, bacteria, viruses, nutrients, oil and grease, or heat.

Conventional Site Assessment: Assessment in which most of the sample analysis and interpretation of data is completed off-site; process usually requires repeated mobilization of equipment and staff in order to fully determine the extent of contamination.

Conventional Systems: Systems that have been traditionally used to collect municipal wastewater in gravity sewers and convey it to a central primary or secondary treatment plant prior to discharge to surface waters.

Conventional Tilling: Tillage operations considered standard for a specific location and crop and that tend to bury the crop residues; usually considered as a base for determining the cost effectiveness of control practices.

Conveyance Loss: Water loss in pipes, channels, conduits, ditches by leakage or evaporation.

Cooling Electricity Use: Amount of electricity used to meet the building cooling load. (See: building cooling load.)

Cooling Tower: A structure that helps remove heat from water used as a coolant; e.g., in electric power generating plants.

Cooling Tower: Device which dissipates the heat from water-cooled systems by spraying the water through streams of rapidly moving air.

Cooperative Agreement: An assistance agreement whereby EPA transfers money, property, services or anything of value to a state, university, non-profit, or not-for-profit organization for the accomplishment of authorized activities or tasks.

Core: The uranium-containing heart of a nuclear reactor, where energy is released.

Core Program Cooperative Agreement: An assistance agreement whereby EPA supports states or tribal governments with funds to help defray the cost of non-item-specific administrative and training activities.

Corrective Action: EPA can require treatment, storage and disposal (TSDF) facilities handling hazardous waste to undertake corrective actions to clean up spills resulting from failure to follow hazardous waste management procedures or other mistakes. The process includes cleanup procedures designed to guide TSDFs toward in spills.

Corrosion: The dissolution and wearing away of metal caused by a chemical reaction such as between water and the pipes, chemicals touching a metal surface, or contact between two metals.

Corrosive: A chemical agent that reacts with the surface of a material causing it to deteriorate or wear away.

Cost/Benefit Analysis: A quantitative evaluation of the costs which would have incurred by implementing an environmental regulation versus the overall benefits to society of the proposed action.

Cost Recovery: A legal process by which potentially responsible parties who contributed to contamination at a Superfund site can be required to reimburse the Trust Fund for money spent during any cleanup actions by the federal government.

Cost Sharing: A publicly financed program through which society, as a beneficiary of environmental protection, shares part of the cost of pollution control with those who must actually install the controls. In Superfund, for example, the government may pay part of the cost of a cleanup action with those responsible for the pollution paying the major share.

Cost-Effective Alternative: An alternative control or corrective method identified after analysis as being the best available in terms of reliability, performance, and cost. Although costs are one important consideration, regulatory and compliance analysis does not require EPA to choose the least expensive alternative. For example, when selecting or approving a method for cleaning up a Superfund site, the Agency balances costs with the long-term effectiveness of the methods proposed and the potential danger posed by the site.

Cover Crop: A crop that provides temporary protection for delicate seedlings and/or provides a cover canopy for seasonal soil protection and improvement between normal crop production periods.

Cover Material: Soil used to cover compacted solid waste in a sanitary landfill.

Cradle-to-Grave or Manifest System: A procedure in which hazardous materials are identified and followed as they are produced, treated, transported, and disposed of by a series of permanent, linkable, descriptive documents (e.g. manifests). Commonly referred to as the cradle-to-grave system.

Criteria: Descriptive factors taken into account by EPA in setting standards for various pollutants. These factors are used to determine limits on allowable concentration levels, and to limit the number of violations per year. When issued by EPA, the criteria provide guidance to the states on how to establish their standards.

Criteria Pollutants: The 1970 amendments to the Clean Air Act required EPA to set National Ambient Air Quality Standards for certain pollutants known to be hazardous to human health. EPA has identified and set standards to protect human health and welfare for six pollutants: ozone, carbon monoxide, total suspended particulates, sulfur dioxide, lead, and nitrogen oxide. The term, "criteria pollutants" derives from the requirement that EPA must describe the characteristics and potential health and welfare effects of these pollutants. It is on the basis of these criteria that standards are set or revised.

Critical Effect: The first adverse effect, or its known precursor, that occurs as a dose rate increases. Designation is based on evaluation of overall database.

Crop Consumptive Use: The amount of water transpired during plant growth plus what evaporated from the soil surface and foliage in the crop area.

Crop Rotation: Planting a succession of different crops on the same land rea as opposed to planting the same crop time after time.

Cross Contamination: The movement of underground contaminants from one level or area to another due to invasive subsurface activities.

Cross-Connection: Any actual or potential connection between a drinking water system and an unapproved water supply or other source of contamination.

Crumb Rubber: Ground rubber fragments the size of sand or silt used in rubber or plastic products, or processed further into reclaimed rubber or asphalt products.

Cryptosporidium: A protozoan microbe associated with the disease cryptosporidiosis in man. The disease can be transmitted through ingestion of drinking water, person-to-person contact, or other pathways, and can cause acute diarrhea, abdominal pain, vomiting, fever, and can be fatal as it was in the Milwaukee episode.

Cubic Feet Per Minute (CFM): A measure of the volume of a substance flowing through air within a fixed period of time. With regard to indoor air, refers to the amount of air, in cubic feet, that is exchanged with outdoor air in a minute's time; i.e. the air exchange rate.

Cullet: Crushed glass.

Cultural Eutrophication: Increasing rate at which water bodies "die" by pollution from human activities.

Cultures and Stocks: Infectious agents and associated biologicals including cultures from medical and pathological laboratories; cultures and stocks of infectious agents from research and industrial laboratories; waste from the production of biologicals; discarded live and attenuated vaccines; and culture dishes and devices used to transfer, inoculate, and mix cultures. (See: regulated medical waste.)

Cumulative Ecological Risk Assessment: Consideration of the total ecological risk from multiple stressors to a given eco-zone.

Cumulative Exposure: The sum of exposures of an organism to a pollutant over a period of time.

Cumulative Working Level Months (CWLM): The sum of lifetime exposure to radon working levels expressed in total working level months.

Curb Stop: A water service shutoff valve located in a water service pipe near the curb and between the water main and the building.

Curbside Collection: Method of collecting recyclable materials at homes, community districts or businesses.

Cutie-Pie: An instrument used to measure radiation levels.

Cuttings: Spoils left by conventional drilling with hollow stem auger or rotary drilling equipment.

Cyclone Collector: A device that uses centrifugal force to remove large particles from polluted air.

D

Data Call-In: A part of the Office of Pesticide Programs (OPP) process of developing key required test data, especially on the long-term, chronic effects of existing pesticides, in advance of scheduled Registration Standard reviews. Data Call-In from manufacturers is an adjunct of the Registration Standards program intended to expedite re-registration.

Data Quality Objectives (DQOs): Qualitative and quantitative statements of the overall level of uncertainty that a decision-maker will accept in results or decisions based on environmental data. They provide the statistical framework for planning and managing environmental data operations consistent with user's needs.

Day Tank: Another name for deaerating tank. (See: age tank.)

DDT: The first chlorinated hydrocarbon insecticide chemical name: Dichloro-Diphenyl-Trichloroethane. It has a half-life of 15 years and can collect in fatty tissues of certain animals. EPA banned registration and interstate sale of DDT for virtually all but emergency uses in the United States in 1972 because of its persistence in the environment and accumulation in the food chain.

Dead End: The end of a water main which is not connected to other parts of the distribution system.

Deadmen: Anchors drilled or cemented into the ground to provide additional reactive mass for DP sampling rigs.

Glossary of Environmental Terms

Decant: To draw off the upper layer of liquid after the heaviest material (a solid or another liquid) has settled.

Decay Products: Degraded radioactive materials, often referred to as "daughters" or "progeny"; radon decay products of most concern from a public health standpoint are polonium-214 and polonium-218.

Dechlorination: Removal of chlorine from a substance.

Decomposition: The breakdown of matter by bacteria and fungi, changing the chemical makeup and physical appearance of materials.

Decontamination: Removal of harmful substances such as noxious chemicals, harmful bacteria or other organisms, or radioactive material from exposed individuals, rooms and furnishings in buildings, or the exterior environment.

Deep-Well Injection: Deposition of raw or treated, filtered hazardous waste by pumping it into deep wells, where it is contained in the pores of permeable subsurface rock.

Deflocculating Agent: A material added to a suspension to prevent settling.

Defluoridation: The removal of excess flouride in drinking water to prevent the staining of teeth.

Defoliant: An herbicide that removes leaves from trees and growing plants.

Degasification: A water treatment that removes dissolved gases from the water.

Degree-Day: A rough measure used to estimate the amount of heating required in a given area; is defined as the difference between the mean daily temperature and 65 degrees Fahrenheit. Degree-days are also calculated to estimate cooling requirements.

Delegated State: A state (or other governmental entity such as a tribal government) that has received authority to administer an environmental regulatory program in lieu of a federal counterpart. As used in connection with NPDES, UIC, and PWS programs, the term does not connote any transfer of federal authority to a state.

Delist: Use of the petition process to have a facility's toxic designation rescinded.

Demand-side Waste Management: Prices whereby consumers use purchasing decisions to communicate to product manufacturers that they prefer environmentally sound products packaged with the least amount of waste, made from recycled or recyclable materials, and containing no hazardous substances.

Demineralization: A treatment process that removes dissolved minerals from water.

Denitrification: The biological reduction of nitrate to nitrogen gas by denitrifying bacteria in soil.

Dense Non-Aqueous Phase Liquid (DNAPL): Non-aqueous phase liquids such as chlorinated hydrocarbon solvents or petroleum fractions with a specific gravity greater than 1.0 that sink through the water column until they reach a confining layer. Because they are at the bottom of aquifers instead of floating on the water table, typical monitoring wells do not indicate their presence.

Density: A measure of how heavy a specific volume of a solid, liquid, or gas is in comparison to water. depending on the chemical.

Depletion Curve: In hydraulics, a graphical representation of water depletion from storage-stream channels, surface soil, and groundwater. A depletion curve can be drawn for base flow, direct runoff, or total flow.

Depressurization: A condition that occurs when the air pressure inside a structure is lower that the air pressure outdoors. Depressurization can occur when household appliances such as fireplaces or furnaces, that consume or exhaust house air, are not supplied with enough makeup air. Radon may be drawn into a house more rapidly under depressurized conditions.

Dermal Absorption/Penetration: Process by which a chemical penetrates the skin and enters the body as an internal dose.

Dermal Exposure: Contact between a chemical and the skin.

Dermal Toxicity: The ability of a pesticide or toxic chemical to poison people or animals by contact with the skin. (See: contact pesticide.)

DES: A synthetic estrogen, diethylstilbestrol is used as a growth stimulant in food animals. Residues in meat are thought to be carcinogenic.

Desalination: [Desalinization] (1) Removing salts from ocean or brackish water by using various technologies. (2) Removal of salts from soil by artificial means, usually leaching.

Desiccant: A chemical agent that absorbs moisture; some desiccants are capable of drying out plants or insects, causing death.

Design Capacity: The average daily flow that a treatment plant or other facility is designed to accommodate.

Design Value: The monitored reading used by EPA to determine an area's air quality status; e.g., for ozone, the fourth highest reading measured over the most recent three years is the design value.

Designated Pollutant: An air pollutant which is neither a criteria nor hazardous pollutant, as described in the Clean Air Act, but for which new source performance standards exist. The Clean Air Act does require states to control these pollutants, which include acid mist, total reduced sulfur (TRS), and fluorides.

Designated Uses: Those water uses identified in state water quality standards that must be achieved and maintained as required under the Clean Water Act. Uses can include cold water fisheries, public water supply, and irrigation.

Designer Bugs: Popular term for microbes developed through biotechnology that can degrade specific toxic chemicals at their source in toxic waste dumps or in ground water.

Destination Facility: The facility to which regulated medical waste is shipped for treatment and destruction, incineration, and/or disposal.

Destratification: Vertical mixing within a lake or reservoir to totally or partially eliminate separate layers of temperature, plant, or animal life.

Destroyed Medical Waste: Regulated medical waste that has been ruined, torn apart, or mutilated through thermal treatment, melting, shredding, grinding, tearing, or breaking, so that it is no longer generally recognized as medical waste, but has not yet been treated (excludes compacted regulated medical waste).

Destruction and Removal Efficiency (DRE): A percentage that represents the number of molecules of a compound removed or destroyed in an incinerator relative to the number of molecules entering the system (e.g. a DRE of 99.99 percent means that 9,999 molecules are destroyed for every 10,000 that enter; 99.99 percent is known as "four nines." For some pollutants, the RCRA removal requirement may be as stringent as "six nines").

Destruction Facility: A facility that destroys regulated medical waste.

Desulfurization: Removal of sulfur from fossil fuels to reduce pollution.

Detectable Leak Rate: The smallest leak (from a storage tank), expressed in terms of gallons- or liters-per-hour, that a test can reliably discern with a certain probability of detection or false alarm.

Detection Criterion: A predetermined rule to ascertain whether a tank is leaking or not. Most volumetric tests use a threshold value as the detection criterion. (See: volumetric tank tests.)

Detection Limit: The lowest concentration of a chemical that can reliably be distinguished from a zero concentration.

Detention Time: 1. The theoretical calculated time required for a small amount of water to pass through a tank at a given rate of flow. 2. The actual time that a small amount of water is in a settling basin, flocculating basin, or rapid-mix chamber. 3. In storage reservoirs, the length of time water will be held before being used.

Detergent: Synthetic washing agent that helps to remove dirt and oil. Some contain compounds which kill useful bacteria and encourage algae growth when they are in wastewater that reaches receiving waters.

Development Effects: Adverse effects such as altered growth, structural abnormality, functional deficiency, or death observed in a developing organism.

Dewater: 1. Remove or separate a portion of the water in a sludge or slurry to dry the sludge so it can be handled and disposed of. 2. Remove or drain the water from a tank or trench.

Diatomaceous Earth (Diatomite): A chalk-like material (fossilized diatoms) used to filter out solid waste in wastewater treatment plants; also used as an active ingredient in some powdered pesticides.

Diazinon: An insecticide. In 1986, EPA banned its use on open areas such as sod farms and golf courses because it posed a danger to migratory birds. The ban did not apply to agricultural, home lawn or commercial establishment uses.

Dibenzofurans: A group of organic compounds, some of which are toxic.

Dicofol: A pesticide used on citrus fruits.

Diffused Air: A type of aeration that forces oxygen into sewage by pumping air through perforated pipes inside a holding tank.

Diffusion: The movement of suspended or dissolved particles (or molecules) from a more concentrated to a less concentrated area. The process tends to distribute the particles or molecules more uniformly.

Digester: In wastewater treatment, a closed tank; in solid-waste conversion, a unit in which bacterial action is induced and accelerated in order to break down organic matter and establish the proper carbon to nitrogen ratio.

Digestion: The biochemical decomposition of organic matter, resulting in partial gasification, liquefaction, and mineralization of pollutants.

Dike: A low wall that can act as a barrier to prevent a spill from spreading.

Diluent: Any liquid or solid material used to dilute or carry an active ingredient.

Dilution Ratio: The relationship between the volume of water in a stream and the volume of incoming water. It affects the ability of the stream to assimilate waste.

Dimictic: Lakes and reservoirs that freeze over and normally go through two stratifications and two mixing cycles a year.

Dinocap: A fungicide used primarily by apple growers to control summer diseases. EPA proposed restrictions on its use in 1986 when laboratory tests found it caused birth defects in rabbits.

Dinoseb: A herbicide that is also used as a fungicide and insecticide. It was banned by EPA in 1986 because it posed the risk of birth defects and sterility.

Dioxin: Any of a family of compounds known chemically as dibenzo-p-dioxins. Concern about them arises from their potential toxicity as contaminants in commercial products. Tests on laboratory animals indicate that it is one of the more toxic anthropogenic (man-made) compounds.

Direct Discharger: A municipal or industrial facility which introduces pollution through a defined conveyance or system such as outlet pipes; a point source.

Direct Filtration: A method of treating water which consists of the addition of coagulent chemicals, flash mixing, coagulation, minimal flocculation, and filtration. Sedimentation is not uses.

Direct Push: Technology used for performing subsurface investigations by driving, pushing, and/or vibrating small-diameter hollow steel rods into the ground/ Also known as direct drive, drive point, or push technology.

Direct Runoff: Water that flows over the ground surface or through the ground directly into streams, rivers, and lakes.

Discharge: Flow of surface water in a stream or canal or the outflow of ground water from a flowing artesian well, ditch, or spring. Can also apply tp discharge of liquid effluent from a facility or to chemical emissions into the air through designated venting mechanisms.

Disinfectant: A chemical or physical process that kills pathogenic organisms in water, air, or on surfaces. Chlorine is often used to disinfect sewage treatment effluent, water supplies, wells, and swimming pools.

Disinfectant By-Product: A compound formed by the reaction of a disinfenctant such as chlorine with organic material in the water supply; a chemical byproduct of the disinfection process..

Disinfectant Time: The time it takes water to move from the point of disinfectant application (or the previous point of residual disinfectant measurement) to a point before or at the point where the residual disinfectant is measured. In pipelines, the time is calculated by dividing the internal volume of the pipe by he maximum hourly flow rate; within mixing basins and storage reservoirs it is determined by tracer studies of an equivalent demonstration.

Dispersant: A chemical agent used to break up concentrations of organic material such as spilled oil.

Displacement Savings: Saving realized by displacing purchases of natural gas or electricity from a local utility by using landfill gas for power and heat.

Disposables: Consumer products, other items, and packaging used once or a few times and discarded.

Disposal: Final placement or destruction of toxic, radioactive, or other wastes; surplus or banned pesticides or other chemicals; polluted soils; and drums containing hazardous materials from removal actions or accidental releases. Disposal may be accomplished through use of approved secure landfills, surface impoundments, land farming, deep-well injection, ocean dumping, or incineration.

Disposal Facilities: Repositories for solid waste, including landfills and combustors intended for permanent containment or destruction of waste materials. Excludes transfer stations and composting facilities.

Dissolved Oxygen (DO): The oxygen freely available in water, vital to fish and other aquatic life and for the prevention of odors. DO levels are considered a most important indicator of a water body's ability to support desirable aquatic life. Secondary and advanced waste treatment are generally designed to ensure adequate DO in waste-receiving waters.

Dissolved Solids: Disintegrated organic and inorganic material in water. Excessive amounts make water unfit to drink or use in industrial processes.

Distillation: The act of purifying liquids through boiling, so that the steam or gaseous vapors condense to a pure liquid. Pollutants and contaminants may remain in a concentrated residue.

Disturbance: Any event or series of events that disrupt ecosystem, community, or population structure and alters the physical environment.

Diversion: 1. Use of part of a stream flow as water supply. 2. A channel with a supporting ridge on the lower side constructed across a slope to divert water at a non-erosive velocity to sites where it can be used and disposed of.

Diversion Rate: The percentage of waste materials diverted from traditional disposal such as landfilling or incineration to be recycled, composted, or re-used.

DNA Hybridization: Use of a segment of DNA, called a DNA probe, to identify its complementary DNA; used to detect specific genes.

Dobson Unit (DU): Units of ozone level measurement. measurement of ozone levels. If, for example, 100 DU of ozone were brought to the earth's surface they would form a layer one millimeter thick. Ozone levels vary geographically, even in the absence of ozone depletion.

Domestic Application: Pesticide application in and around houses, office buildings, motels, and other living or working areas.(See: residential use.)

Dosage/Dose: 1. The actual quantity of a chemical administered to an organism or to which it is exposed. 2. The amount of a substance that reaches a specific tissue (e.g. the liver). 3. The amount of a substance available for interaction with metabolic processes after crossing the outer boundary of an organism. (See: absorbed dose, administered dose, applied dose, potential dose.)

Dose Equivalent: The product of the absorbed dose from ionizing radiation and such factors as account for biological differences due to the type of radiation and its distribution in the body in the body.

Dose Rate: In exposure assessment, dose per time unit (e.g. mg/day), sometimes also called dosage.

Dose Response: Shifts in toxicological responses of an individual (such as alterations in severity) or populations (such as alterations in incidence) that are related to changes in the dose of any given substance.

Dose Response Curve: Graphical representation of the relationship between the dose of a stressor and the biological response thereto.

Dose-Response Assessment: 1. Estimating the potency of a chemical. 2. In exposure assessment, the process of determining the relationship between the dose of a stressor and a specific biological response. 3. Evaluating the quantitative relationship between dose and toxicological responses.

Dose-Response Relationship: The quantitative relationship between the amount of exposure to a substance and the extent of toxic injury or disease produced.

Dosimeter: An instrument to measure dosage; many so-called dosimeters actually measure exposure rather than dosage. Dosimetry is the process or technology of measuring and/or estimating dosage.

DOT Reportable Quantity: The quantity of a substance specified in a U.S. Department of Transportation regulation that triggers labeling, packaging and other requirements related to shipping such substances.

Downgradient: The direction that groundwater flows; similar to "downstream" for surface water.

Downstream Processors: Industries dependent on crop production (e.g. canneries and food processors).

DP Hole: Hole in the ground made with DP equipment. (See: direct push.)

Draft: 1. The act of drawing or removing water from a tank or reservoir. 2. The water which is drawn or removed.

Draft Permit: A preliminary permit drafted and published by EPA; subject to public review and comment before final action on the application.

Drainage: Improving the productivity of agricultural land by removing excess water from the soil by such means as ditches or subsurface drainage tiles.

Drainage Basin: The area of land that drains water, sediment, and dissolved materials to a common outlet at some point along a stream channel.

Drainage Well: A well drilled to carry excess water off agricultural fields. Because they act as a funnel from the surface to the groundwater below. Drainage wells can contribute to groundwater pollution.

Drawdown: 1. The drop in the water table or level of water in the ground when water is being pumped from a well. 2. The amount of water used from a tank or reservoir. 3. The drop in the water level of a tank or reservoir.

Dredging: Removal of mud from the bottom of water bodies. This can disturb the ecosystem and causes silting that kills aquatic life. Dredging of contaminated muds can expose biota to heavy metals and other toxics. Dredging activities may be subject to regulation under Section 404 of the Clean Water Act.

Drilling Fluid: Fluid used to lubricate the bit and convey drill cuttings to the surface with rotary drilling equipment. Usually composed of bentonite slurry or muddy water. Can become contaminated, leading to cross contamination, and may require special disposal. Not used with DP methods

Drinking Water Equivalent Level: Protective level of exposure related to potentially non-carcinogenic effects of chemicals that are also known to cause cancer.

Drinking Water State Revolving Fund: The Fund provides capitalization grants to states to develop drinking water revolving loan funds to help finance system infrastructure improvements, assure source-water protection, enhance operation and management of drinking-water systems, and otherwise promote local water-system compliance and protection of public health.

Drive Casing: Heavy duty steel casing driven along with the sampling tool in cased DP systems. Keeps the hole open between sampling runs and is not removed until last sample has been collected.

Drive Point Profiler: An exposed groundwater DP system used to collect multiple depth-discrete groundwater samples. Ports in the tip of the probe connect to an internal stainless steel or teflon tube that extends to the surface. Samples are collected via suction or airlift methods. Deionized water is pumped down through the ports to prevent plugging while driving the tool to the next sampling depth.

Drop-off: Recyclable materials collection method in which individuals bring them to a designated collection site.

Dual-Phase Extraction: Active withdrawal of both liquid and gas phases from a well usually involving the use of a vacuum pump.

Dump: A site used to dispose of solid waste without environmental controls.

Duplicate: A second aliquot or sample that is treated the same as the original sample in order to determine the precision of the analytical method. (See: aliquot.)

Dustfall Jar: An open container used to collect large particles from the air for measurement and analysis.

Dynamometer. A device used to place a load on an engine and measure its performance.

Dystrophic Lakes: Acidic, shallow bodies of water that contain much humus and/or other organic matter; contain many plants but few fish.

E

Ecological Entity: In ecological risk assessment, a general term referring to a species, a group of species, an ecosystem function or characteristic, or a specific habitat or biome.

Ecological/Environmental Sustainability: Maintenance of ecosystem components and functions for future generations.

Ecological Exposure: Exposure of a non-human organism to a stressor.

Ecological Impact: The effect that a man-caused or natural activity has on living organisms and their non-living (abiotic) environment.

Ecological Indicator: A characteristic of an ecosystem that is related to, or derived from, a measure of biotic or abiotic variable, that can provide quantitative information on ecological structure and function. An indicator can contribute to a measure of integrity and sustainability.

Ecological Integrity: A living system exhibits integrity if, when subjected to disturbance, it sustains and organizes self-correcting ability to recover toward a biomass end-state that is normal for that system. End-states other than the pristine or naturally whole may be accepted as normal and good.

Ecological Risk Assessment: The application of a formal framework, analytical process, or model to estimate the effects of human actions(s) on a natural resource and to interpret the significance of those effects in light of the uncertainties identified in each component of the assessment process. Such analysis includes initial hazard identification, exposure and dose-response assessments, and risk characterization.

Ecology: The relationship of living things to one another and their environment, or the study of such relationships.

Economic Poisons: Chemicals used to control pests and to defoliate cash crops such as cotton.

Ecosphere: The "bio-bubble" that contains life on earth, in surface waters, and in the air. (See: biosphere.)

Ecosystem: The interacting system of a biological community and its non-living environmental surroundings.

Ecosystem Structure: Attributes related to the instantaneous physical state of an ecosystem; examples include species population density, species richness or evenness, and standing crop biomass.

Ecotone: A habitat created by the juxtaposition of distinctly different habitats; an edge habitat; or an ecological zone or boundary where two or more ecosystems meet.

Effluent: Wastewater—treated or untreated—that flows out of a treatment plant, sewer, or industrial outfall. Generally refers to wastes discharged into surface waters.

Effluent Guidelines: Technical EPA documents which set effluent limitations for given industries and pollutants.

Effluent Limitation: Restrictions established by a state or EPA on quantities, rates, and concentrations in wastewater discharges.

Effluent Standard: (See: effluent limitation.)

Ejector: A device used to disperse a chemical solution into water being treated.

Electrodialysis: A process that uses electrical current applied to permeable membranes to remove minerals from water. Often used to desalinize salty or brackish water.

Electromagnetic Geophysical Methods: Ways to measure subsurface conductivity via low-frequency electromagnetic induction.

Electrostatic Precipitator (ESP): A device that removes particles from a gas stream (smoke) after combustion occurs. The ESP imparts an electrical charge to the particles, causing them to adhere to metal plates inside the precipitator. Rapping on the plates causes the particles to fall into a hopper for disposal.

Eligible Costs: The construction costs for wastewater treatment works upon which EPA grants are based.

EMAP Data: Environmental monitoring data collected under the auspices of the Environmental Monitoring and Assessment Program. All EMAP data share the common attribute of being of known quality, having been collected in the context of explicit data quality objectives (DQOs) and a consistent quality assurance program.

Emergency and Hazardous Chemical Inventory: An annual report by facilities having one or more extremely hazardous substances or hazardous chemicals above certain weight limits.

Emergency (Chemical): A situation created by an accidental release or spill of hazardous chemicals that poses a threat to the safety of workers, residents, the environment, or property.

Emergency Episode: (See: air pollution episode.)

Emergency Exemption: Provision in FIFRA under which EPA can grant temporary exemption to a state or another federal agency to allow the use of a pesticide product not registered for that particular use. Such actions involve unanticipated and/or severe pest problems where there is not time or interest by a manufacturer to register the product for that use. (Registrants cannot apply for such exemptions.)

Emergency Removal Action: 1. Steps take to remove contaminated materials that pose imminent threats to local residents (e.g. removal of leaking drums or the excavation of explosive waste.) 2. The state record of such removals.

Emergency Response Values: Concentrations of chemicals, published by various groups, defining acceptable levels for short-term exposures in emergencies.

Emergency Suspension: Suspension of a pesticide product registration due to an imminent hazard. The action immediately halts distribution, sale, and sometimes actual use of the pesticide involved.

Emission: Pollution discharged into the atmosphere from smokestacks, other vents, and surface areas of commercial or industrial facilities; from residential chimneys; and from motor vehicle, locomotive, or aircraft exhausts.

Emission Cap: A limit designed to prevent projected growth in emissions from existing and future stationary sources from eroding any mandated reductions. Generally, such provisions require that any emission growth from facilities under the restrictions be offset by equivalent reductions at other facilities under the same cap. (See: emissions trading.)

Emission Factor: The relationship between the amount of pollution produced and the amount of raw material processed. For example, an emission factor for a blast furnace making iron would be the number of pounds of particulates per ton of raw materials.

Emission Inventory: A listing, by source, of the amount of air pollutants discharged into the atmosphere of a community; used to establish emission standards.

Emission Standard: The maximum amount of air polluting discharge legally allowed from a single source, mobile or stationary.

Emissions Trading: The creation of surplus emission reductions at certain stacks, vents or similar emissions sources and the use of this surplus to meet or redefine pollution requirements applicable to other emissions sources. This allows one source to increase emissions when another source reduces them, maintaining an overall constant emission level. Facilities that reduce emissions substantially may "bank" their "credits" or sell them to other facilities or industries.

Emulsifier: A chemical that aids in suspending one liquid in another. Usually an organic chemical in an aqueous solution.

Encapsulation: The treatment of asbestos-containing material with a liquid that covers the surface with a protective coating or embeds fibers in an adhesive matrix to prevent their release into the air.

Enclosure: Putting an airtight, impermeable, permanent barrier around asbestos-containing materials to prevent the release of asbestos fibers into the air.

End User: Consumer of products for the purpose of recycling. Excludes products for re-use or combustion for energy recovery.

End-of-the-pipe: Technologies such as scrubbers on smokestacks and catalytic convertors on automobile tailpipes that reduce emissions of pollutants after they have formed.

End-use Product: A pesticide formulation for field or other end use. The label has instructions for use or application to control pests or regulate plant growth. The term excludes products used to formulate other pesticide products.

Endangered Species: Animals, birds, fish, plants, or other living organisms threatened with extinction by anthropogenic (man-caused) or other natural changes in their environment. Requirements for declaring a species endangered are contained in the Endangered Species Act.

Endangerment Assessment: A study to determine the nature and extent of contamination at a site on the National Priorities List and the risks posed to public health or the environment. EPA or the state conducts the study when a legal action is to be taken to direct potentially responsible parties to clean up a site or pay for it. An endangerment assessment supplements a remedial investigation.

Endrin: A pesticide toxic to freshwater and marine aquatic life that produces adverse health effects in domestic water supplies.

Energy Management System: A control system capable of monitoring environmental and system loads and adjusting HVAC operations accordingly in order to conserve energy while maintaining comfort.

Energy Recovery: Obtaining energy from waste through a variety of processes (e.g. combustion).

Enforceable Requirements: Conditions or limitations in permits issued under the Clean Water Act Section 402 or 404 that, if violated, could result in the issuance of a compliance order or initiation of a civil or criminal action under federal or applicable state laws. If a permit has not been issued, the term includes any requirement which, in the Regional Administrator's judgement, would be included in the permit when issued. Where no permit applies, the term includes any requirement which the RA determines is necessary for the best practical waste treatment technology to meet applicable criteria.

Enforcement: EPA, state, or local legal actions to obtain compliance with environmental laws, rules, regulations, or agreements and/or obtain penalties or criminal sanctions for violations. Enforcement procedures may vary, depending on the requirements of different environmental laws and related implementing regulations. Under CERCLA, for example, EPA will seek to require potentially responsible parties to clean up a Superfund site, or pay for the cleanup, whereas under the Clean Air Act the Agency may invoke sanctions against cities failing to meet ambient air quality standards that could prevent certain types of construction or federal funding. In other situations, if investigations by EPA and state agencies uncover willful violations, criminal trials and penalties are sought.

Enforcement Decision Document (EDD): A document that provides an explanation to the public of EPA's selection of the cleanup alternative at enforcement sites on the National Priorities List. Similar to a Record of Decision.

Engineered Controls: Method of managing environmental and health risks by placing a barrier between the contamination and the rest of the site, thus limiting exposure pathways.

Enhanced Inspection and Maintenance (I&M): An improved automobile inspection and maintenance program—aimed at reducing automobile emissions—that contains, at a minimum, more vehicle types and model years, tighter inspection, and better management practices. It may also include annual computerized or centralized inspections, under-the-hood inspection—for signs of tampering with pollution control equipment—and increased repair waiver cost.

Enrichment: The addition of nutrients (e.g. nitrogen, phosphorus, carbon compounds) from sewage effluent or agricultural runoff to surface water, greatly increases the growth potential for algae and other aquatic plants.

Entrain: To trap bubbles in water either mechanically through turbulence or chemically through a reaction.

Environment: The sum of all external conditions affecting the life, development and survival of an organism.

Environmental Assessment: An environmental analysis prepared pursuant to the National Environmental Policy Act to determine whether a federal action would significantly affect the environment and thus require a more detailed environmental impact statement.

Environmental Audit: An independent assessment of the current status of a party's compliance with applicable environmental requirements or of a party's environmental compliance policies, practices, and controls.

Environmental/Ecological Risk: The potential for adverse effects on living organisms associated with pollution of the environment by effluents, emissions, wastes, or accidental chemical releases; energy use; or the depletion of natural resources.

Environmental Equity/Justice: Equal protection from environmental hazards for individuals, groups, or communities regardless of race, ethnicity, or economic status. This applies to the development, implementation, and enforcement of environmental laws, regulations, and policies, and implies that no population of people should be forced to shoulder a disproportionate share of negative environmental impacts of pollution or environmental hazard due to a lack of political or economic strength levels.

Environmental Exposure: Human exposure to pollutants originating from facility emissions. Threshold levels are not necessarily surpassed, but low-level chronic pollutant exposure is one of the most common forms of environmental exposure (See: threshold level).

Environmental Fate: The destiny of a chemical or biological pollutant after release into the environment.

Environmental Fate Data: Data that characterize a pesticide's fate in the ecosystem, considering factors that foster its degradation (light, water, microbes), pathways and resultant products.

Environmental Impact Statement: A document required of federal agencies by the National Environmental Policy Act for major projects or legislative proposals significantly affecting the environment. A tool for decision making, it describes the positive and negative effects of the undertaking and cites alternative actions.

Environmental Indicator: A measurement, statistic or value that provides a proximate gauge or evidence of the effects of environmental management programs or of the state or condition of the environment.

Environmental Justice: The fair treatment of people of all races, cultures, incomes, and educational levels with respect to the development and enforcement of environmental laws, regulations, and policies.

Environmental Lien: A charge, security, or encumbrance on a property's title to secure payment of cost or debt arising from response actions, cleanup, or other remediation of hazardous substances or petroleum products.

Environmental Medium: A major environmental category that surrounds or contacts humans, animals, plants, and other organisms (e.g. surface water, ground water, soil or air) and through which chemicals or pollutants move. (See: ambient medium, biological medium.)

Environmental Monitoring for Public Access and Community Tracking: Joint EPA, NOAA, and USGS program to provide timely and effective communication of environmental data and information through improved and updated technology solutions that support timely environmental monitoring reporting, interpreting, and use of the information for the benefit of the public. (See: real-time monitoring.)

Environmental Response Team: EPA experts located in Edison, N.J., and Cincinnati, OH, who can provide around-the-clock technical assistance to EPA regional offices and states during all types of hazardous waste site emergencies and spills of hazardous substances.

Environmental Site Assessment: The process of determining whether contamination is present on a parcel of real property.

Environmental Sustainability: Long-term maintenance of ecosystem components and functions for future generations.

Environmental Tobacco Smoke: Mixture of smoke from the burning end of a cigarette, pipe, or cigar and smoke exhaled by the smoker. (See: passive smoking/secondhand smoke.)

Epidemiology: Study of the distribution of disease, or other health-related states and events in human populations, as related to age, sex, occupation, ethnicity, and economic status in order to identify and alleviate health problems and promote better health.

Epilimnion: Upper waters of a thermally stratified lake subject to wind action.

Episode (Pollution): An air pollution incident in a given area caused by a concentration of atmospheric pollutants under meteorological conditions that may result in a significant increase in illnesses or deaths. May also describe water pollution events or hazardous material spills.

Equilibrium: In relation to radiation, the state at which the radioactivity of consecutive elements within a radioactive series is neither increasing nor decreasing.

Equivalent Method: Any method of sampling and analyzing for air pollution which has been demonstrated to the EPA Administrator's satisfaction to be, under specific conditions, an acceptable alternative to normally used reference methods.

Erosion: The wearing away of land surface by wind or water, intensified by land-clearing practices related to farming, residential or industrial development, road building, or logging.

Established Treatment Technologies: Technologies for which cost and performance data are readily available. (See: Innovative treatment technologies.)

Estimated Environmental Concentration: The estimated pesticide concentration in an ecosystem.

Estuary: Region of interaction between rivers and near-shore ocean waters, where tidal action and river flow mix fresh and salt water. Such areas include bays, mouths of rivers, salt marshes, and lagoons. These brackish water ecosystems shelter and feed marine life, birds, and wildlife. (See: wetlands.)

Ethanol: An alternative automotive fuel derived from grain and corn; usually blended with gasoline to form gasohol.

Ethylene Dibromide (EDB): A chemical used as an agricultural fumigant and in certain industrial processes. Extremely toxic and found to be a carcinogen in laboratory animals, EDB has been banned for most agricultural uses in the United States.

Glossary of Environmental Terms

Eutrophic Lakes: Shallow, murky bodies of water with concentrations of plant nutrients causing excessive production of algae. (See: dystrophic lakes.)

Eutrophication: The slow aging process during which a lake, estuary, or bay evolves into a bog or marsh and eventually disappears. During the later stages of eutrophication the water body is choked by abundant plant life due to higher levels of nutritive compounds such as nitrogen and phosphorus. Human activities can accelerate the process.

Evaporation Ponds: Areas where sewage sludge is dumped and dried.

Evapotranspiration: The loss of water from the soil both by evaporation and by transpiration from the plants growing in the soil.

Exceedance: Violation of the pollutant levels permitted by environmental protection standards.

Exclusion: In the asbestos program, one of several situations that permit a Local Education Agency (LEA) to delete one or more of the items required by the Asbestos Hazard Emergency Response Act (AHERA); e.g. records of previous asbestos sample collection and analysis may be used by the accredited inspector in lieu of AHERA bulk sampling.

Exclusionary Ordinance: Zoning that excludes classes of persons or businesses from a particular neighborhood or area.

Exempt Solvent: Specific organic compounds not subject to requirements of regulation because they are deemed by EPA to be of negligible photochemical reactivity.

Exempted Aquifer: Underground bodies of water defined in the Underground Injection Control program as aquifers that are potential sources of drinking water though not being used as such, and thus exempted from regulations barring underground injection activities.

Exemption: A state (with primacy) may exempt a public water system from a requirement involving a Maximum Contaminant Level (MCL), treatment technique, or both, if the system cannot comply due to compelling economic or other factors, or because the system was in operation before the requirement or MCL was instituted; and the exemption will not create a public health risk. (See: variance.)

Exotic Species: A species that is not indigenous to a region.

Experimental Use Permit: Obtained by manufacturers for testing new pesticides or uses thereof whenever they conduct experimental field studies to support registration on 10 acres or more of land or one acre or more of water.

Experimental Use Permit: A permit granted by EPA that allows a producer to conduct tests of a new pesticide, product and/or use outside the laboratory. The testing is usually done on ten or more acres of land or water surface.

Explosive Limits: The amounts of vapor in the air that form explosive mixtures; limits are expressed as lower and upper limits and give the range of vapor concentrations in air that will explode if an ignition source is present.

Exports : In solid waste program, municipal solid waste and recyclables transported outside the state or locality where they originated.

Exposure: The amount of radiation or pollutant present in a given environment that represents a potential health threat to living organisms.

Exposure Assessment: Identifying the pathways by which toxicants may reach individuals, estimating how much of a chemical an individual is likely to be exposed to, and estimating the number likely to be exposed.

Exposure Concentration: The concentration of a chemical or other pollutant representing a health threat in a given environment.

Exposure Indicator: A characteristic of the environment measured to provide evidence of the occurrence or magnitude of a response indicator's exposure to a chemical or biological stress.

Exposure Level: The amount (concentration) of a chemical at the absorptive surfaces of an organism.

Exposure Pathway: The path from sources of pollutants via, soil, water, or food to man and other species or settings.

Exposure Route: The way a chemical or pollutant enters an organism after contact; i.e. by ingestion, inhalation, or dermal absorption.

Exposure-Response Relationship: The relationship between exposure level and the incidence of adverse effects.

Extraction Procedure (EP Toxic): Determining toxicity by a procedure which simulates leaching; if a certain concentration of a toxic substance can be leached from a waste, that waste is considered hazardous, i.e."EP Toxic."

Extraction Well: A discharge well used to remove groundwater or air.

Extremely Hazardous Substances: Any of 406 chemicals identified by EPA as toxic, and listed under SARA Title III. The list is subject to periodic revision.

F

Fabric Filter: A cloth device that catches dust particles from industrial emissions.

Facilities Plans: Plans and studies related to the construction of treatment works necessary to comply with the Clean Water Act or RCRA. A facilities plan investigates needs and provides information on the cost-effectiveness of alternatives, a recommended plan, an environmental assessment of the recommendations, and descriptions of the treatment works, costs, and a completion schedule.

Facility Emergency Coordinator: Representative of a facility covered by environmental law (e.g, a chemical plant) who participates in the emergency reporting process with the Local Emergency Planning Committee (LEPC).

Facultative Bacteria: Bacteria that can live under aerobic or anaerobic conditions.

Feasibility Study: 1. Analysis of the practicability of a proposal; e.g., a description and analysis of potential cleanup alternatives for a site such as one on the National Priorities List. The feasibility study usually recommends selection of a cost-effective alternative. It usually starts as soon as the remedial investigation is underway; together, they are commonly referred to as the "RI/FS". 2. A small-scale investigation of a problem to ascertain whether a proposed research approach is likely to provide useful data.

Fecal Coliform Bacteria: Bacteria found in the intestinal tracts of mammals. Their presence in water or sludge is an indicator of pollution and possible contamination by pathogens.

Federal Implementation Plan: Under current law, a federally implemented plan to achieve attainment of air quality standards, used when a state is unable to develop an adequate plan.

Federal Motor Vehicle Control Program: All federal actions aimed at controlling pollution from motor vehicles by such efforts as establishing and enforcing tailpipe and evaporative emission standards for new vehicles, testing methods development, and guidance to states operating inspection and maintenance programs. Federally designated area that is required to meet and maintain federal ambient air quality standards. May include nearby locations in the same state or nearby states that share common air pollution problems.

Feedlot: A confined area for the controlled feeding of animals. Tends to concentrate large amounts of animal waste that cannot be absorbed by the soil and, hence, may be carried to nearby streams or lakes by rainfall runoff.

Fen: A type of wetland that accumulates peat deposits. Fens are less acidic than bogs, deriving most of their water from groundwater rich in calcium and magnesium. (See: wetlands.)

Ferrous Metals: Magnetic metals derived from iron or steel; products made from ferrous metals include appliances, furniture, containers, and packaging like steel drums and barrels. Recycled products include processing tin/steel cans, strapping, and metals from appliances into new products.

FIFRA Pesticide Ingredient: An ingredient of a pesticide that must be registered with EPA under the Federal Insecticide, Fungicide, and Rodenticide Act. Products making pesticide claims must register under FIFRA and may be subject to labeling and use requirements.

Fill: Man-made deposits of natural soils or rock products and waste materials.

Filling: Depositing dirt, mud or other materials into aquatic areas to create more dry land, usually for agricultural or commercial development purposes, often with ruinous ecological consequences.

Filter Strip: Strip or area of vegetation used for removing sediment, organic matter, and other pollutants from runoff and wastewater.

Filtration: A treatment process, under the control of qualified operators, for removing solid (particulate) matter from water by means of porous media such as sand or a man-made filter; often used to remove particles that contain pathogens.

Financial Assurance for Closure: Documentation or proof that an owner or operator of a facility such as a landfill or other waste repository is capable of paying the projected costs of closing the facility and monitoring it afterwards as provided in RCRA regulations.

Finding of No Significant Impact: A document prepared by a federal agency showing why a proposed action would not have a significant impact on the environment and thus would not require preparation of an Environmental Impact Statement. An FNSI is based on the results of an environmental assessment.

Finished Water: Water is "finished" when it has passed through all the processes in a water treatment plant and is ready to be delivered to consumers.

First Draw: The water that comes out when a tap is first opened, likely to have the highest level of lead contamination from plumbing materials.

Fix a Sample: A sample is "fixed" in the field by adding chemicals that prevent water quality indicators of interest in the sample from changing before laboratory measurements are made.

Fixed-Location Monitoring: Sampling of an environmental or ambient medium for pollutant concentration at one location continuously or repeatedly.

Flammable: Any material that ignites easily and will burn rapidly.

Flare: A control device that burns hazardous materials to prevent their release into the environment; may operate continuously or intermittently, usually on top of a stack.

Flash Point: The lowest temperature at which evaporation of a substance produces sufficient vapor to form an ignitable mixture with air.

Floc: A clump of solids formed in sewage by biological or chemical action.

Flocculation: Process by which clumps of solids in water or sewage aggregate through biological or chemical action so they can be separated from water or sewage.

Floodplain: The flat or nearly flat land along a river or stream or in a tidal area that is covered by water during a flood.

Floor Sweep: Capture of heavier-than-air gases that collect at floor level.

Flow Rate: The rate, expressed in gallons -or liters-per-hour, at which a fluid escapes from a hole or fissure in a tank. Such measurements are also made of liquid waste, effluent, and surface water movement.

Flowable: Pesticide and other formulations in which the active ingredients are finely ground insoluble solids suspended in a liquid. They are mixed with water for application.

Flowmeter: A gauge indicating the velocity of wastewater moving through a treatment plant or of any liquid moving through various industrial processes.

Flue Gas: The air coming out of a chimney after combustion in the burner it is venting. It can include nitrogen oxides, carbon oxides, water vapor, sulfur oxides, particles and many chemical pollutants.

Flue Gas Desulfurization: A technology that employs a sorbent, usually lime or limestone, to remove sulfur dioxide from the gases produced by burning fossil fuels. Flue gas desulfurization is current state of the art technology for major SO_2 emitters, like power plants.

Fluidized: A mass of solid particles that is made to flow like a liquid by injection of water or gas is said to have been fluidized. In water treatment, a bed of filter media is fluidized by backwashing water through the filter.

Fluidized Bed Incinerator: An incinerator that uses a bed of hot sand or other granular material to transfer heat directly to waste. Used mainly for destroying municipal sludge.

Flume: A natural or man-made channel that diverts water.

Fluoridation: The addition of a chemical to increase the concentration of fluoride ions in drinking water to reduce the incidence of tooth decay.

Fluorides: Gaseous, solid, or dissolved compounds containing fluorine that result from industrial processes. Excessive amounts in food can lead to fluorosis.

Fluorocarbons (FCs): Any of a number of organic compounds analogous to hydrocarbons in which one or more hydrogen atoms are replaced by fluorine. Once used in the United States as a propellant for domestic aerosols, they are now found mainly in coolants and some industrial processes. FCs containing chlorine are called chlorofluorocarbons (CFCs). They are believed to be modifying the ozone layer in the stratosphere, thereby allowing more harmful solar radiation to reach the Earth's surface.

Flush: 1. To open a cold-water tap to clear out all the water which may have been sitting for a long time in the pipes. In new homes, to flush a system means to send large volumes of water gushing through the unused pipes to remove loose particles of solder and flux. 2. To force large amounts of water through a system to clean out piping or tubing, and storage or process tanks.

Flux: 1. A flowing or flow. 2. A substance used to help metals fuse together.

Fly Ash: Non-combustible residual particles expelled by flue gas.

Fogging: Applying a pesticide by rapidly heating the liquid chemical so that it forms very fine droplets that resemble smoke or fog. Used to destroy mosquitoes, black flies, and similar pests.

Food Chain: A sequence of organisms, each of which uses the next, lower member of the sequence as a food source.

Food Processing Waste: Food residues produced during agricultural and industrial operations.

Food Waste: Uneaten food and food preparation wastes from residences and commercial establishments such as grocery stores, restaurants, and produce stands, institutional cafeterias and kitchens, and industrial sources like employee lunchrooms.

Food Web: The feeding relationships by which energy and nutrients are transferred from one species to another.

Formaldehyde: A colorless, pungent, and irritating gas, CH20, used chiefly as a disinfectant and preservative and in synthesizing other compounds like resins.

Formulation: The substances comprising all active and inert ingredients in a pesticide.

Fossil Fuel: Fuel derived from ancient organic remains; e.g. peat, coal, crude oil, and natural gas.

Fracture: A break in a rock formation due to structural stresses; e.g. faults, shears, joints, and planes of fracture cleavage.

Free Product: A petroleum hydrocarbon in the liquid free or non aqueous phase. (See: non-aqueous phase liquid.)

Freeboard: 1. Vertical distance from the normal water surface to the top of a confining wall. 2. Vertical distance from the sand surface to the underside of a trough in a sand filter.

Fresh Water: Water that generally contains less than 1,000 milligrams-per-liter of dissolved solids.

Friable: Capable of being crumbled, pulverized, or reduced to powder by hand pressure.

Friable Asbestos: Any material containing more than one-percent asbestos, and that can be crumbled or reduced to powder by hand pressure. (May include previously non-friable material which becomes broken or damaged by mechanical force.)

Fuel Economy Standard: The Corporate Average Fuel Economy Standard (CAFE) effective in 1978. It enhanced the national fuel conservation effort imposing a miles-per-gallon floor for motor vehicles.

Fuel Efficiency: The proportion of energy released by fuel combustion that is converted into useful energy.

Fuel Switching: 1. A precombustion process whereby a low-sulfur coal is used in place of a higher sulfur coal in a power plant to reduce sulfur dioxide emissions. 2. Illegally using leaded gasoline in a motor vehicle designed to use only unleaded.

Fugitive Emissions: Emissions not caught by a capture system.

Fume: Tiny particles trapped in vapor in a gas stream.

Fumigant: A pesticide vaporized to kill pests. Used in buildings and greenhouses.

Functional Equivalent: Term used to describe EPA's decision-making process and its relationship to the environmental review conducted under the National Environmental Policy Act (NEPA). A review is considered functionally equivalent when it addresses the substantive components of a NEPA review.

Fungicide: Pesticides which are used to control, deter, or destroy fungi.

Fungistat: A chemical that keeps fungi from growing.

Fungus (Fungi): Molds, mildews, yeasts, mushrooms, and puffballs, a group of organisms lacking in chlorophyll (i.e. are not photosynthetic) and which are usually non-mobile, filamentous, and multicellular. Some grow in soil, others attach themselves to decaying trees and other plants whence they obtain nutrients. Some are pathogens, others stabilize sewage and digest composted waste.

Furrow Irrigation: Irrigation method in which water travels through the field by means of small channels between each groups of rows.

Future Liability: Refers to potentially responsible parties' obligations to pay for additional response activities beyond those specified in the Record of Decision or Consent Decree.

G

Game Fish: Species like trout, salmon, or bass, caught for sport. Many of them show more sensitivity to environmental change than "rough" fish.

Garbage: Animal and vegetable waste resulting from the handling, storage, sale, preparation, cooking, and serving of foods.

Gas Chromatograph/Mass Spectrometer: Instrument that identifies the molecular composition and concentrations of various chemicals in water and soil samples.

Gasahol: Mixture of gasoline and ethanol derived from fermented agricultural products containing at least nine percent ethanol. Gasohol emissions contain less carbon monoxide than those from gasoline.

Gasification: Conversion of solid material such as coal into a gas for use as a fuel.

Gasoline Volatility: The property of gasoline whereby it evaporates into a vapor. Gasoline vapor is a mixture of volatile organic compounds.

General Permit: A permit applicable to a class or category of dischargers.

General Reporting Facility: A facility having one or more hazardous chemicals above the 10,000 pound threshold for planning quantities. Such facilities must file MSDS and emergency inventory information with the SERC, LEPC, and local fire departments.

Generally Recognized as Safe (GRAS): Designation by the FDA that a chemical or substance (including certain pesticides) added to food is considered safe by experts, and so is exempted from the usual FFDCA food additive tolerance requirements.

Generator: 1. A facility or mobile source that emits pollutants into the air or releases hazardous waste into water or soil. 2. Any person, by site, whose act or process produces regulated medical waste or whose act first causes such waste to become subject to regulation. Where more than one person (e.g. doctors with separate medical practices) are located in the same building, each business entity is a separate generator.

Genetic Engineering: A process of inserting new genetic information into existing cells in order to modify a specific organism for the purpose of changing one of its characteristics.

Genotoxic: Damaging to DNA; pertaining to agents known to damage DNA.

Geographic Information System (GIS): A computer system designed for storing, manipulating, analyzing, and displaying data in a geographic context.

Geological Log: A detailed description of all underground features (depth, thickness, type of formation) discovered during the drilling of a well.

Geophysical Log: A record of the structure and composition of the earth encountered when drilling a well or similar type of test hold or boring.

Geothermal/Ground Source Heat Pump: These heat pumps are underground coils to transfer heat from the ground to the inside of a building. (See: heat pump; water source heat pump)

Germicide: Any compound that kills disease-causing microorganisms.

Giardia Lamblia: Protozoan in the feces of humans and animals that can cause severe gastrointestinal ailments. It is a common contaminant of surface waters.

Glass Containers: For recycling purposes, containers like bottles and jars for drinks, food, cosmetics and other products. When being recycled, container glass is generally separated into color categories for conversion into new containers, construction materials or fiberglass insulation.

Global Warming: An increase in the near surface temperature of the Earth. Global warming has occurred in the distant past as the result of natural influences, but the term is most often used to refer to the warming predicted to occur as a result of increased emissions of greenhouse gases. Scientists generally agree that the Earth's surface has warmed by about 1 degree Fahrenheit in the past 140 years. The Intergovernmental Panel on Climate Change (IPCC) recently concluded that increased concentrations of greenhouse gases are causing an increase in the Earth's surface temperature and that increased concentrations of sulfate aerosols have led to relative cooling in some regions, generally over and downwind of heavily industrialized areas. (See: climate change)

Global Warming Potential: The ratio of the warming caused by a substance to the warming caused by a similar mass of carbon dioxide. CFC-12, for example, has a GWP of 8,500, while water has a GWP of zero. (See: Class I Substance and Class II Substance.)

Glovebag: A polyethylene or polyvinyl chloride bag-like enclosure affixed around an asbestos-containing source (most often thermal system insulation) permitting the material to be removed while minimizing release of airborne fibers to the surrounding atmosphere.

Gooseneck: A portion of a water service connection between the distribution system water main and a meter. Sometimes called a pigtail.

Grab Sample: A single sample collected at a particular time and place that represents the composition of the water, air, or soil only at that time and place.

Grain Loading: The rate at which particles are emitted from a pollution source. Measurement is made by the number of grains per cubic foot of gas emitted.

Granular Activated Carbon Treatment: A filtering system often used in small water systems and individual homes to remove organics. Also used by municipal water treatment plantsd. GAC can be highly effective in lowering elevated levels of radon in water.

Grasscycling: Source reduction activities in which grass clippings are left on the lawn after mowing.

Grassed Waterway: Natural or constructed watercourse or outlet that is shaped or graded and established in suitable vegetation for the disposal of runoff water without erosion.

Gray Water: Domestic wastewater composed of wash water from kitchen, bathroom, and laundry sinks, tubs, and washers.

Greenhouse Effect: The warming of the Earth's atmosphere attributed to a buildup of carbon dioxide or other gases; some scientists think that this build-up allows the sun's rays to heat the Earth, while making the infra-red radiation atmosphere opaque to infra-red radiation, thereby preventing a counterbalancing loss of heat.

Greenhouse Gas: A gas, such as carbon dioxide or methane, which contributes to potential climate change.

Grinder Pump: A mechanical device that shreds solids and raises sewage to a higher elevation through pressure sewers.

Gross Alpha/Beta Particle Activity: The total radioactivity due to alpha or beta particle emissions as inferred from measurements on a dry sample.

Gross Power-Generation Potential: The installed power generation capacity that landfill gas can support.

Ground Cover: Plants grown to keep soil from eroding.

Ground Water: The supply of fresh water found beneath the Earth's surface, usually in aquifers, which supply wells and springs. Because ground water is a major source of drinking water, there is growing concern over contamination from leaching agricultural or industrial pollutants or leaking underground storage tanks.

Ground Water Under the Direct Influence (UDI) of Surface Water: Any water beneath the surface of the ground with: 1. significant occurence of insects or other microorganisms, algae, or large-diameter pathogens; 2. significant and relatively rapid shifts in water characteristics such as turbidity, temperature, conductivity, or pH which closely correlate to climatological or surface water conditions. Direct influence is determined for individual sources in accordance with criteria established by a state.

Ground-Penetrating Radar: A geophysical method that uses high frequency electromagnetic waves to obtain subsurface information.

Ground-Water Discharge: Ground water entering near coastal waters which has been contaminated by landfill leachate, deep well injection of hazardous wastes, septic tanks, etc.

Ground-Water Disinfection Rule: A 1996 amendment of the Safe Drinking Water Act requiring EPA to promulgate national primary drinking water regulations requiring disinfection as for all public water systems, including surface waters and ground water systems.

Gully Erosion: Severe erosion in which trenches are cut to a depth greater than 30 centimeters (a foot). Generally, ditches deep enough to cross with farm equipment are considered gullies.

H

Habitat: The place where a population (e.g. human, animal, plant, microorganism) lives and its surroundings, both living and non-living.

Habitat Indicator: A physical attribute of the environment measured to characterize conditions necessary to support an organism, population, or community in the absence of pollutants; e.g. salinity of estuarine waters or substrate type in streams or lakes.

Half-Life: 1. The time required for a pollutant to lose one-half of its original coconcentrationor example, the biochemical half-life of DDT in the environment is 15 years. 2. The time required for half of the atoms of a radioactive element to undergo self-transmutation or decay (half-life of radium is 1620 years). 3. The time required for the elimination of half a total dose from the body.

Halogen: A type of incandescent lamp with higher energy-efficiency that standard ones.

Halon: Bromine-containing compounds with long atmospheric lifetimes whose breakdown in the stratosphere causes depletion of ozone. Halons are used in firefighting.

Hammer Mill: A high-speed machine that uses hammers and cutters to crush, grind, chip, or shred solid waste.

Hard Water: Alkaline water containing dissolved salts that interfere with some industrial processes and prevent soap from sudsing.

Hauler: Garbage collection company that offers complete refuse removal service; many will also collect recyclables.

Hazard: 1. Potential for radiation, a chemical or other pollutant to cause human illness or injury. 2. In the pesticide program, the inherent toxicity of a compound. Hazard identification of a given substances is an informed judgment based on verifiable toxicity data from animal models or human studies.

Hazard Assessment: Evaluating the effects of a stressor or determining a margin of safety for an organism by comparing the concentration which causes toxic effects with an estimate of exposure to the organism.

Hazard Communication Standard: An OSHA regulation that requires chemical manufacturers, suppliers, and importers to assess the hazards of the chemicals that they make, supply, or import, and to inform employers, customers, and workers of these hazards through MSDS information.

Hazard Evaluation: A component of risk evaluation that involves gathering and evaluating data on the types of health injuries or diseases that may be produced by a chemical and on the conditions of exposure under which such health effects are produced.

Hazard Identification: Determining if a chemical or a microbe can cause adverse health effects in humans and what those effects might be.

Hazard Quotient: The ratio of estimated site-specific exposure to a single chemical from a site over a specified period to the estimated daily exposure level, at which no adverse health effects are likely to occur.

Hazard Ratio: A term used to compare an animal's daily dietary intake of a pesticide to its LD 50 value. A ratio greater than 1.0 indicates that the animal is likely to consume an a dose amount which would kill 50 percent of animals of the same species. (See: LD 50 /Lethal Dose.)

Hazardous Air Pollutants: Air pollutants which are not covered by ambient air quality standards but which, as defined in the Clean Air Act, may present a threat of adverse human health effects or adverse environmental effects.Such pollutants include asbestos, beryllium, mercury, benzene, coke oven emissions, radionuclides, and vinyl chloride.

Hazardous Chemical: An EPA designation for any hazardous material requiring an MSDS under OSHA's Hazard Communication Standard. Such substances are capable of producing fires and explosions or adverse health effects like cancer and dermatitis. Hazardous chemicals are distinct from hazardous waste.(See: Hazardous Waste.)

Hazardous Ranking System: The principal screening tool used by EPA to evaluate risks to public health and the environment associated with abandoned or uncontrolled hazardous waste sites. The HRS calculates a score based on the potential of hazardous substances spreading from the site through the air, surface water, or ground water, and on other factors such as density and proximity of human population. This score is the primary factor in deciding if the site should be on the National Priorities List and, if so, what ranking it should have compared to other sites on the list.

Hazardous Substance: 1. Any material that poses a threat to human health and/or the environment. Typical hazardous substances are toxic, corrosive, ignitable, explosive, or chemically reactive. 2. Any substance designated by EPA to be reported if a designated quantity of the substance is spilled in the waters of the United States or is otherwise released into the environment.

Hazardous Waste: By-products of society that can pose a substantial or potential hazard to human health or the environment when improperly managed. Possesses at least one of four characteristics (ignitability, corrosivity, reactivity, or toxicity), or appears on special EPA lists.

Hazardous Waste Landfill: An excavated or engineered site where hazardous waste is deposited and covered.

Hazardous Waste Minimization: Reducing the amount of toxicity or waste produced by a facility via source reduction or environmentally sound recycling.

Hazards Analysis: Procedures used to (1) identify potential sources of release of hazardous materials from fixed facilities or transportation accidents; (2) determine the vulnerability of a geographical area to a release of hazardous materials; and (3) compare hazards to determine which present greater or lesser risks to a community.

Hazards Identification: Providing information on which facilities have extremely hazardous substances, what those chemicals are, how much there is at each facility, how the chemicals are stored, and whether they are used at high temperatures.

Headspace: The vapor mixture trapped above a solid or liquid in a sealed vessel.

Health Advisory Level: A non-regulatory health-based reference level of chemical traces (usually in ppm) in drinking water at which there are no adverse health risks when ingested over various periods of time. Such levels are established for one day, 10 days, long-term and life-time exposure periods. They contain a wide margin of safety.

Health Assessment: An evaluation of available data on existing or potential risks to human health posed by a Superfund site. The Agency for Toxic Substances and Disease Registry (ATSDR) of the Department of Health and Human Services (DHHS) is required to perform such an assessment at every site on the National Priorities List.

Heat Island Effect: A "dome" of elevated temperatures over an urban area caused by structural and pavement heat fluxes, and pollutant emissions.

Heat Pump: An electric device with both heating and cooling capabilities. It extracts heat from one medium at a lower (the heat source) temperature and transfers it to another at a higher temperature (the heat sink), thereby cooling the first and warming the second. (See: geothermal, water source heat pump.)

Heavy Metals: Metallic elements with high atomic weights; (e.g. mercury, chromium, cadmium, arsenic, and lead); can damage living things at low concentrations and tend to accumulate in the food chain.

Heptachlor: An insecticide that was banned on some food products in 1975 and in all of them 1978. It was allowed for use in seed treatment until 1983. More recently it was found in milk and other dairy products in Arkansas and Missouri where dairy cattle were illegally fed treated seed.

Herbicide: A chemical pesticide designed to control or destroy plants, weeds, or grasses.

Herbivore: An animal that feeds on plants.

Heterotrophic Organisms: Species that are dependent on organic matter for food.

High End Exposure (dose) Estimate: An estimate of exposure, or dose level received anyone in a defined population that is greater than the 90th percentile of all individuals in that population, but less than the exposure at the highest percentile in that population. A high end risk descriptor is an estimate of the risk level for such individuals. Note that risk is based on a combination of exposure and susceptibility to the stressor.

High Intensity Discharge: A generic term for mercury vapor, metal halide, and high pressure sodium lamps and fixtures.

High-Density Polyethylene: A material used to make plastic bottles and other products that produces toxic fumes when burned.

High-Level Nuclear Waste Facility: Plant designed to handle disposal of used nuclear fuel, high level radioactive waste, and plutonium waste.

High-Level Radioactive Waste (HLRW): Waste generated in core fuel of a nuclear reactor, found at nuclear reactors or by nuclear fuel reprocessing; is a serious threat to anyone who comes near the waste without shielding. (See: low-level radioactive waste.)

High-Line Jumpers: Pipes or hoses connected to fire hydrants and laid on top of the ground to provide emergency water service for an isolated portion of a distribution system.

High-Risk Community: A community located within the vicinity of numerous sites of facilities or other potential sources of envienvironmental exposure/health hazards which may result in high levels of exposure to contaminants or pollutants.

High-to-Low-Dose Extrapolation: The process of prediction of low exposure risk to humans and animals from the measured high-exposure-high-risk data involving laboratory animals.

Highest Dose Tested: The highest dose of a chemical or substance tested in a study.

Holding Pond: A pond or reservoir, usually made of earth, built to store polluted runoff.

Holding Time: The maximum amount of time a sample may be stored before analysis.

Hollow Stem Auger Drilling: Conventional drilling method that uses augurs to penetrate the soil. As the augers are rotated, soil cuttings are conveyed to the ground surface via augur spirals. DP tools can be used inside the hollow augers.

Homeowner Water System: Any water system which supplies piped water to a single residence.

Homogeneous Area: In accordance with Asbestos Hazard and Emergency Response Act (AHERA) definitions, an area of surfacing materials, thermal surface insulation, or miscellaneous material that is uniform in color and texture.

Hood Capture Efficiency: Ratio of the emissions captured by a hood and directed into a control or disposal device, expressed as a percent of all emissions.

Host: 1. In genetics, the organism, typically a bacterium, into which a gene from another organism is transplanted. 2. In medicine, an animal infected or parasitized by another organism.

Household Hazardous Waste: Hazardous products used and disposed of by residential as opposed to industrial consumers. Includes paints, stains, varnishes, solvents, pesticides, and other materials or products containing volatile chemicals that can catch fire, react or explode, or that are corrosive or toxic.

Household Waste (Domestic Waste): Solid waste, composed of garbage and rubbish, which normally originates in a private home or apartment house. Domestic waste may contain a significant amount of toxic or hazardous waste.

Human Equivalent Dose: A dose which, when administered to humans, produces an effect equal to that produced by a dose in animals.

Human Exposure Evaluation: Describing the nature and size of the population exposed to a substance and the magnitude and duration of their exposure.

Human Health Risk: The likelihood that a given exposure or series of exposures may have damaged or will damage the health of individuals.

Hydraulic Conductivity: The rate at which water can move through a permeable medium. (i.e. the coefficient of permeability.)

Hydraulic Gradient: In general, the direction of groundwater flow due to changes in the depth of the water table.

Hydrocarbons (HC): Chemical compounds that consist entirely of carbon and hydrogen.

Hydrogen Sulfide (H2S): Gas emitted during organic decomposition. Also a by-product of oil refining and burning. Smells like rotten eggs and, in heavy concentration, can kill or cause illness.

Hydrogeological Cycle: The natural process recycling water from the atmosphere down to (and through) the earth and back to the atmosphere again.

Hydrogeology: The geology of ground water, with particular emphasis on the chemistry and movement of water.

Hydrologic Cycle: Movement or exchange of water between the atmosphere and earth.

Hydrology: The science dealing with the properties, distribution, and circulation of water.

Hydrolysis: The decomposition of organic compounds by interaction with water.

Hydronic: A ventilation system using heated or cooled water pumped through a building.

Hydrophilic: Having a strong affinity for water.

Glossary of Environmental Terms

Hydrophobic: Having a strong aversion for water.

Hydropneumatic: A water system, usually small, in which a water pump is automatically controlled by the pressure in a compressed air tank.

Hypersensitivity Diseases: Diseases characterized by allergic responses to pollutants; diseases most clearly associated with indoor air quality are asthma, rhinitis, and pneumonic hypersensitivity.

Hypolimnion: Bottom waters of a thermally stratified lake. The hypolimnion of a eutrophic lake is usually low or lacking in oxygen.

Hypoxia/Hypoxic Waters: Waters with dissolved oxygen concentrations of less than 2 ppm, the level generally accepted as the minimum required for most marine life to survive and reproduce.

I

Identification Code or EPA I.D. Number: The unique code assigned to each generator, transporter, and treatment, storage, or disposal facility by regulating agencies to facilitate identification and tracking of chemicals or hazardous waste.

Ignitable: Capable of burning or causing a fire.

IM240: A high-tech, transient dynamometer automobile emissions test that takes up to 240 seconds.

Imhoff Cone: A clear, cone-shaped container used to measure the volume of settleable solids in a specific volume of water.

Immediately Dangerous to Life and Health (IDLH): The maximum level to which a healthy individual can be exposed to a chemical for 30 minutes and escape without suffering irreversible health effects or impairing symptoms. Used as a "level of concern." (See: level of concern.)

Imminent Hazard: One that would likely result in unreasonable adverse effects on humans or the environment or risk unreasonable hazard to an endangered species during the time required for a pesticide registration cancellation proceeding.

Imminent Threat: A high probability that exposure is occurring.

Immiscibility: The inability of two or more substances or liquids to readily dissolve into one another, such as soil and water. Immiscibility The inability of two or more substances or liquids to readily dissolve into one another, such as soil and water.

Impermeable: Not easily penetrated. The property of a material or soil that does not allow, or allows only with great difficulty, the movement or passage of water.

Imports: Municipal solid waste and recyclables that have been transported to a state or locality for processing or final disposition (but that did not originate in that state or locality).

Impoundment: A body of water or sludge confined by a dam, dike, floodgate, or other barrier.

In Situ: In its original place; unmoved unexcavated; remaining at the site or in the subsurface.

In-Line Filtration: Pre-treattment method in which chemicals are mixed by the flowing water; commonly used in pressure filtration installations. Eliminates need for flocculation and sedimentation.

In-Situ Flushing: Introduction of large volumes of water, at times supplemented with cleaning compounds, into soil, waste, or ground water to flush hazardous contaminants from a site.

In-Situ Oxidation: Technology that oxidizes contaminants dissolved in ground water, converting them into insoluble compounds.

In-Situ Stripping: Treatment system that removes or "strips" volatile organic compounds from contaminated ground or surface water by forcing an airstream through the water and causing the compounds to evaporate.

In-Situ Vitrification: Technology that treats contaminated soil in place at extremely high temperatures, at or more than 3000 degrees Fahrenheit.

In Vitro: Testing or action outside an organism (e.g. inside a test tube or culture dish.)

In Vivo: Testing or action inside an organism.

Incident Command Post: A facility located at a safe distance from an emergency site, where the incident commander, key staff, and technical representatives can make decisions and deploy emergency manpower and equipment.

Incident Command System (ICS): The organizational arrangement wherein one person, normally the Fire Chief of the impacted district, is in charge of an integrated, comprehensive emergency response organization and the emergency incident site, backed by an Emergency Operations Center staff with resources, information, and advice.

Incineration: A treatment technology involving destruction of waste by controlled burning at high temperatures; e.g., burning sludge to remove the water and reduce the remaining residues to a safe, non-burnable ash that can be disposed of safely on land, in some waters, or in underground locations.

Incineration at Sea: Disposal of waste by burning at sea on specially-designed incinerator ships.

Incinerator: A furnace for burning waste under controlled conditions.

Incompatible Waste: A waste unsuitable for mixing with another waste or material because it may react to form a hazard.

Indemnification: In the pesticide program, legal requirement that EPA pay certain end-users, dealers, and distributors for the cost of stock on hand at the time a pesticide registration is suspended.

Indicator: In biology, any biological entity or processes, or community whose characteristics show the presence of specific environmental conditions. 2. In chemistry, a substance that shows a visible change, usually of color, at a desired point in a chemical reaction. 3.A device that indicates the result of a measurement; e.g. a pressure gauge or a moveable scale.

Indirect Discharge: Introduction of pollutants from a non-domestic source into a publicly owned waste-treatment system. Indirect dischargers can be commercial or industrial facilities whose wastes enter local sewers.

Indirect Source: Any facility or building, property, road or parking area that attracts motor vehicle traffic and, indirectly, causes pollution.

Indoor Air: The breathable air inside a habitable structure or conveyance.

Indoor Air Pollution: Chemical, physical, or biological contaminants in indoor air.

Indoor Climate: Temperature, humidity, lighting, air flow and noise levels in a habitable structure or conveyance. Indoor climate can affect indoor air pollution.

Industrial Pollution Prevention: Combination of industrial source reduction and toxic chemical use substitution.

Industrial Process Waste: Residues produced during manufacturing operations.

Industrial Sludge: Semi-liquid residue or slurry remaining from treatment of industrial water and wastewater.

Industrial Source Reduction: Practices that reduce the amount of any hazardous substance, pollutant, or contaminant entering any waste stream or otherwise released into the environment. Also reduces the threat to public health and the environment associated with such releases. Term includes equipment or technology modifications, substitution of raw materials, and improvements in housekeeping, maintenance, training or inventory control.

Industrial Waste: Unwanted materials from an industrial operation; may be liquid, sludge, solid, or hazardous waste.

Inert Ingredient: Pesticide components such as solvents, carriers, dispersants, and surfactants that are not active against target pests. Not all inert ingredients are innocuous.

Inertial Separator: A device that uses centrifugal force to separate waste particles.

Infectious Agent: Any organism, such as a pathogenic virus, parasite, or or bacterium, that is capable of invading body tissues, multiplying, and causing disease.

Infectious Waste: Hazardous waste capable of causing infections in humans, including: contaminated animal waste; human blood and blood products; isolation waste, pathological waste; and discarded sharps (needles, scalpels or broken medical instruments).

Infiltration: 1. The penetration of water through the ground surface into sub-surface soil or the penetration of water from the soil into sewer or other pipes through defective joints, connections, or manhole walls. 2. The technique of applying large volumes of waste water to land to penetrate the surface and percolate through the underlying soil. (See: percolation.)

Infiltration Gallery: A sub-surface groundwater collection system, typically shallow in depth, constructed with open-jointed or perforated pipes that discharge collected water into a watertight chamber from which the water is pumped to treatment facilities and into the distribution system. Usually located close to streams or ponds.

Infiltration Rate: The quantity of water that can enter the soil in a specified time interval.

Inflow: Entry of extraneous rain water into a sewer system from sources other than infiltration, such as basement drains, manholes, storm drains, and street washing.

Influent: Water, wastewater, or other liquid flowing into a reservoir, basin, or treatment plant.

Information Collection Request (ICR): A description of information to be gathered in connection with rules, proposed rules, surveys, and guidance documents that contain information-gathering requirements. The ICR describes what information is needed, why it is needed, how it will be collected, and how much collecting it will cost. The ICR is submitted by the EPA to the Office of Management and Budget (OMB) for approval.

Information File: In the Superfund program, a file that contains accurate, up-to-date documents on a Superfund site. The file is usually located in a public building (school, library, or city hall) convenient for local residents.

Inhalable Particles: All dust capable of entering the human respiratory tract.

Initial Compliance Period (Water): The first full three-year compliance period which begins at least 18 months after promulgation.

Injection Well: A well into which fluids are injected for purposes such as waste disposal, improving the recovery of crude oil, or solution mining.

Injection Zone: A geological formation receiving fluids through a well.

Innovative Technologies: New or inventive methods to treat effectively hazardous waste and reduce risks to human health and the environment.

Innovative Treatment Technologies: Technologies whose routine use is inhibited by lack of data on performance and cost. (See: Established treatment technologies.)

Inoculum: 1. Bacteria or fungi injected into compost to start biological action. 2. A medium containing organisms, usually bacteria or a virus, that is introduced into cultures or living organisms.

Inorganic Chemicals: Chemical substances of mineral origin, not of basically carbon structure.

Insecticide: A pesticide compound specifically used to kill or prevent the growth of insects.

Inspection and Maintenance (I/M): 1. Activities to ensure that vehicles' emission controls work properly. 2. Also applies to wastewater treatment plants and other anti-pollution facilities and processes.

Institutional Waste: Waste generated at institutions such as schools, libraries, hospitals, prisons, etc.

Instream Use: Water use taking place within a stream channel; e.g., hydro-electric power generation, navigation, water quality improvement, fish propagation, recreation.

Integrated Exposure Assessment: Cumulative summation (over time) of the magnitude of exposure to a toxic chemical in all media.

Integrated Pest Management (IPM): A mixture of chemical and other, non-pesticide, methods to control pests.

Integrated Waste Management: Using a variety of practices to handle municipal solid waste; can include source reduction, recycling, incineration, and landfilling.

Interceptor Sewers: Large sewer lines that, in a combined system, control the flow of sewage to the treatment plant. In a storm, they allow some of the sewage to flow directly into a receiving stream, thus keeping it from overflowing onto the streets. Also used in separate systems to collect the flows from main and trunk sewers and carry them to treatment points.

Interface: The common boundary between two substances such as a water and a solid, water and a gas, or two liquids such as water and oil.

Interfacial Tension: The strength of the film separating two immiscible fluids (e.g. oil and water) measured in dynes per, or millidynes per centimeter.

Interim (Permit) Status: Period during which treatment, storage and disposal facilities coming under RCRA in 1980 are temporarily permitted to operate while awaiting a permanent permit. Permits issued under these circumstances are usually called "Part A" or "Part B" permits.

Internal Dose: In exposure assessment, the amount of a substance penetrating the absorption barriers (e.g. skin, lung tissue, gastrointestinal tract) of an organism through either physical or biological processes. (See: absorbed dose)

Interstate Carrier Water Supply: A source of water for drinking and sanitary use on planes, buses, trains, and ships operating in more than one state. These sources are federally regulated.

Interstate Commerce Clause: A clause of the U.S. Constitution which reserves to the federal government the right to regulate the conduct of business across state lines. Under this clause, for example, the U.S. Supreme Court has ruled that states may not inequitably restrict the disposal of out-of-state wastes in their jurisdictions.

Interstate Waters: Waters that flow across or form part of state or international boundaries; e.g. the Great Lakes, the Mississippi River, or coastal waters.

Interstitial Monitoring: The continuous surveillance of the space between the walls of an underground storage tank.

Intrastate Product: Pesticide products once registered by states for sale and use only in the state. All intrastate products have been converted to full federal registration or canceled.

Inventory (TSCA): Inventory of chemicals produced pursuant to Section 8 (b) of the Toxic Substances Control Act.

Inversion: A layer of warm air that prevents the rise of cooling air and traps pollutants beneath it; can cause an air pollution episode.

Ion: An electrically charged atom or group of atoms.

Ion Exchange Treatment: A common water-softening method often found on a large scale at water purification plants that remove some organics and radium by adding calcium oxide or calcium hydroxide to increase the pH to a level where the metals will precipitate out.

Ionization Chamber: A device that measures the intensity of ionizing radiation.

Ionizing Radiation: Radiation that can strip electrons from atoms; e.g. alpha, beta, and gamma radiation.

IRIS: EPA's Integrated Risk Information System, an electronic data base containing the Agency's latest descriptive and quantitative regulatory information on chemical constituents.

Irradiated Food: Food subject to brief radioactivity, usually gamma rays, to kill insects, bacteria, and mold, and to permit storage without refrigeration.

Irradiation: Exposure to radiation of wavelengths shorter than those of visible light (gamma, x-ray, or ultra- violet), for medical purposes, to sterilize milk or other foodstuffs, or to induce polymerization of monomers or vulcanization of rubber.

Irreversible Effect: Effect characterized by the inability of the body to partially or fully repair injury caused by a toxic agent.

Irrigation: Applying water or wastewater to land areas to supply the water and nutrient needs of plants.

Irrigation Efficiency: The amount of water stored in the crop root zone compared to the amount of irrigation water applied.

Irrigation Return Flow: Surface and subsurface water which leaves the field following application of irrigation water.

Irritant: A substance that can cause irritation of the skin, eyes, or respiratory system. Effects may be acute from a single high level exposure, or chronic from repeated low-level exposures to such compounds as chlorine, nitrogen dioxide, and nitric acid.

Isoconcentration: More than one sample point exhibiting the same isolate concentration.

Isopleth: The line or area represented by an isoconcentration.

Isotope: A variation of an element that has the same atomic number of protons but a different weight because of the number of neutrons. Various isotopes of the same element may have different radioactive behaviors, some are highly unstable..

Isotropy: The condition in which the hydraulic or other properties of an aquifer are the same in all directions.

J

Jar Test: A laboratory procedure that simulates a water treatment plant's coagulation/flocculation units with differing chemical doses, mix speeds, and settling times to estimate the minimum or ideal coagulant dose required to achieve certain water quality goals.

Joint and Several Liability: Under CERCLA, this legal concept relates to the liability for Superfund site cleanup and other costs on the part of more than one potentially responsible party (i.e. if there were several owners or users of a site that became contaminated over the years, they could all be considered potentially liable for cleaning up the site.)

K

Karst: A geologic formation of irregular limestone deposits with sinks, underground streams, and caverns.

Kinetic Energy: Energy possessed by a moving object or water body.

Kinetic Rate Coefficient: A number that describes the rate at which a water constituent such as a biochemical oxygen demand or dissolved oxygen rises or falls, or at which an air pollutant reacts.

L

Laboratory Animal Studies: Investigations using animals as surrogates for humans.

Lagoon: 1. A shallow pond where sunlight, bacterial action, and oxygen work to purify wastewater; also used for storage of wastewater or spent nuclear fuel rods. 2. Shallow body of water, often separated from the sea by coral reefs or sandbars.

Land Application: Discharge of wastewater onto the ground for treatment or reuse. (See: irrigation.)

Land Ban: Phasing out of land disposal of most untreated hazardous wastes, as mandated by the 1984 RCRA amendments.

Land Disposal Restrictions: Rules that require hazardous wastes to be treated before disposal on land to destroy or immobilize hazardous constituents that might migrate into soil and ground water.

Land Farming (of Waste): A disposal process in which hazardous waste deposited on or in the soil is degraded naturally by microbes.

Landfills: 1. Sanitary landfills are disposal sites for non-hazardous solid wastes spread in layers, compacted to the smallest practical volume, and covered by material applied at the end of each operating day. 2. Secure chemical landfills are disposal sites for hazardous waste, selected and designed to minimize the chance of release of hazardous substances into the environment.

Glossary of Environmental Terms

Landscape: The traits, patterns, and structure of a specific geographic area, including its biological composition, its physical environment, and its anthropogenic or social patterns. An area where interacting ecosystems are grouped and repeated in similar form.

Landscape Characterization: Documentation of the traits and patterns of the essential elements of the landscape.

Landscape Ecology: The study of the distribution patterns of communities and ecosystems, the ecological processes that affect those patterns, and changes in pattern and process over time.

Landscape Indicator: A measurement of the landscape, calculated from mapped or remotely sensed data, used to describe spatial patterns of land use and land cover across a geographic area. Landscape indicators may be useful as measures of certain kinds of environmental degradation such as forest fragmentation.

Langelier Index (LI): An index reflecting the equilibrium pH of a water with respect to calcium and alkalinity; used in stabilizing water to control both corrosion and scale deposition.

Large Quantity Generator: Person or facility generating more than 2200 pounds of hazardous waste per month. Such generators produce about 90 percent of the nation's hazardous waste, and are subject to all RCRA requirements.

Large Water System: A water system that services more than 50,000 customers.

Laser Induced Fluorescence: A method for measuring the relative amount of soil and/or groundwater with an in-situ sensor.

Latency: Time from the first exposure of a chemical until the appearance of a toxic effect.

Lateral Sewers: Pipes that run under city streets and receive the sewage from homes and businesses, as opposed to domestic feeders and main trunk lines.

Laundering Weir: Sedimention basin overflow weir.

LC 50/Lethal Concentration: Median level concentration, a standard measure of toxicity. It tells how much of a substance is needed to kill half of a group of experimental organisms in a given time. (See: LD 50.)

LD 50/ Lethal Dose: The dose of a toxicant or microbe that will kill 50 percent of the test organisms within a designated period. The lower the LD 50, the more toxic the compound.

Ldlo: Lethal dose low; the lowest dose in an animal study at which lethality occurs.

Leachate: Water that collects contaminants as it trickles through wastes, pesticides or fertilizers. Leaching may occur in farming areas, feedlots, and landfills, and may result in hazardous substances entering surface water, ground water, or soil.

Leachate Collection System: A system that gathers leachate and pumps it to the surface for treatment.

Leaching: The process by which soluble constituents are dissolved and filtered through the soil by a percolating fluid. (See: leachate.)

Lead (Pb): A heavy metal that is hazardous to health if breathed or swallowed. Its use in gasoline, paints, and plumbing compounds has been sharply restricted or eliminated by federal laws and regulations. (See: heavy metals.)

Lead Service Line: A service line made of lead which connects the water to the building inlet and any lead fitting connected to it.

Legionella: A genus of bacteria, some species of which have caused a type of pneumonia called Legionaires Disease.

Lethal Concentration 50: Also referred to as LC50, a concentration of a pollutant or effluent at which 50 percent of the test organisms die; a common measure of acute toxicity.

Lethal Dose 50: Also referred to as LD50, the dose of a toxicant that will kill 50 percent of test organisms within a designated period of time; the lower the LD 50, the more toxic the compound.

Level of Concern (LOC): The concentration in air of an extremely hazardous substance above which there may be serious immediate health effects to anyone exposed to it for short periods

Life Cycle of a Product: All stages of a product's development, from extraction of fuel for power to production, marketing, use, and disposal.

Lifetime Average Daily Dose: Figure for estimating excess lifetime cancer risk.

Lifetime Exposure: Total amount of exposure to a substance that a human would receive in a lifetime (usually assumed to be 70 years).

Lift: In a sanitary landfill, a compacted layer of solid waste and the top layer of cover material.

Lifting Station: (See: pumping station.)

Light Non-Aqueous Phase Liquid (LNAPL): A non-aqueous phase liquid with a specific gravity less than 1.0. Because the specific gravity of water is 1.0, most LNAPLs float on top of the water table. Most common petroleum hydrocarbon fuels and lubricating oils are LNAPLs.

Light-Emitting Diode: A long-lasting illumination technology used for exit signs which requires very little power

Limestone Scrubbing: Use of a limestone and water solution to remove gaseous stack-pipe sulfur before it reaches the atmosphere.

Limit of Detection (LOD): The minimum concentration of a substance being analyzed test that has a 99 percent probability of being identified.

Limited Degradation: An environmental policy permitting some degradation of natural systems but terminating at a level well beneath an established health standard.

Limiting Factor: A condition whose absence or excessive concentration, is incompatible with the needs or tolerance of a species or population and which may have a negative influence on their ability to thrive.

Limnology: The study of the physical, chemical, hydrological, and biological aspects of fresh water bodies.

Lindane: A pesticide that causes adverse health effects in domestic water supplies and is toxic to freshwater fish and aquatic life.

Liner: 1. A relatively impermeable barrier designed to keep leachate inside a landfill. Liner materials include plastic and dense clay. 2. An insert or sleeve for sewer pipes to prevent leakage or infiltration.

Lipid Solubility: The maximum concentration of a chemical that will dissolve in fatty substances. Lipid soluble substances are insoluble in water. They will very selectively disperse through the environment via uptake in living tissue.

Liquefaction: Changing a solid into a liquid.

Liquid Injection Incinerator: Commonly used system that relies on high pressure to prepare liquid wastes for incineration by breaking them up into tiny droplets to allow easier combustion.

List: Shorthand term for EPA list of violating facilities or firms debarred from obtaining government contracts because they violated certain sections of the Clean Air or Clean Water Acts. The list is maintained by The Office of Enforcement and Compliance Monitoring.

Listed Waste: Wastes listed as hazardous under RCRA but which have not been subjected to the Toxic Characteristics Listing Process because the dangers they present are considered self-evident.

Lithology: Mineralogy, grain size, texture, and other physical properties of granular soil, sediment, or rock.

Litter: 1. The highly visible portion of solid waste carelessly discarded outside the regular garbage and trash collection and disposal system. 2. leaves and twigs fallen from forest trees.

Littoral Zone: 1. That portion of a body of fresh water extending from the shoreline lakeward to the limit of occupancy of rooted plants. 2. A strip of land along the shoreline between the high and low water levels.

Local Education Agency (LEA): In the asbestos program, an educational agency at the local level that exists primarily to operate schools or to contract for educational services, including primary and secondary public and private schools. A single, unaffiliated school can be considered an LEA for AHERA purposes.

Local Emergency Planning Committee (LEPC): A committee appointed by the state emergency response commission, as required by SARA Title III, to formulate a comprehensive emergency plan for its jurisdiction.

Low Density Polyethylene (LOPE): Plastic material used for both rigid containers and plastic film applications.

Low Emissivity (low-E) Windows: New window technology that lowers the amount of energy loss through windows by inhibiting the transmission of radiant heat while still allowing sufficient light to pass through.

Low NO_x Burners: One of several combustion technologies used to reduce emissions of Nitrogen Oxides (NO_x.)

Low-Level Radioactive Waste (LLRW): Wastes less hazardous than most of those associated with a nuclear reactor; generated by hospitals, research laboratories, and certain industries. The Department of Energy, Nuclear Regulatory Commission, and EPA share responsibilities for managing them. (See: high-level radioactive wastes.)

Lower Detection Limit: The smallest signal above background noise an instrument can reliably detect.

Lower Explosive Limit (LEL): The concentration of a compound in air below which the mixture will not catch on fire.

Lowest Acceptable Daily Dose: The largest quantity of a chemical that will not cause a toxic effect, as determined by animal studies.

Lowest Achievable Emission Rate: Under the Clean Air Act, the rate of emissions that reflects (1) the most stringent emission limitation in the implementation plan of any state for such source unless the owner or operator demonstrates such limitations are not achievable; or (2) the most stringent emissions limitation achieved in practice, whichever is more stringent. A proposed new or modified source may not emit pollutants in excess of existing new source standards.

Lowest Observed Adverse Effect Level (LOAEL): The lowest level of a stressor that causes statistically and biologically significant differences in test samples as compared to other samples subjected to no stressor.

M

Macropores: Secondary soil features such as root holes or desiccation cracks that can create significant conduits for movement of NAPL and dissolved contaminants, or vapor-phase contaminants.

Magnetic Separation: Use of magnets to separate ferrous materials from mixed municipal waste stream.

Major Modification: This term is used to define modifications of major stationary sources of emissions with respect to Prevention of Significant Deterioration and New Source Review under the Clean Air Act.

Major Stationary Sources: Term used to determine the applicability of Prevention of Significant Deterioration and new source regulations. In a nonattainment area, any stationary pollutant source with potential to emit more than 100 tons per year is considered a major stationary source. In PSD areas the cutoff level may be either 100 or 250 tons, depending upon the source.

Majors: Larger publicly owned treatment works (POTWs) with flows equal to at least one million gallons per day (mgd) or servicing a population equivalent to 10,000 persons; certain other POTWs having significant water quality impacts. (See: minors.)

Man-Made (Anthropogenic) Beta Particle and Photon Emitters: All radionuclides emitting beta particles and/or photons listed in Maximum Permissible Body Burdens and Maximum Permissible Concentrations of Radonuclides in Air and Water for Occupational Exposure.

Management Plan: Under the Asbestos Hazard Emergency Response Act (AHERA), a document that each Local Education Agency is required to prepare, describing all activities planned and undertaken by a school to comply with AHERA regulations, including building inspections to identify asbestos-containing materials, response actions, and operations and maintenance programs to minimize the risk of exposure.

Managerial Controls: Methods of nonpoint source pollution control based on decisions about managing agricultural wastes or application times or rates for agrochemicals.

Mandatory Recycling: Programs which by law require consumers to separate trash so that some or all recyclable materials are recovered for recycling rather than going to landfills.

Manifest: A one-page form used by haulers transporting waste that lists EPA identification numbers, type and quantity of waste, the generator it originated from, the transporter that shipped it, and the storage or disposal facility to which it is being shipped. It includes copies for all participants in the shipping process.

Manifest System: Tracking of hazardous waste from "cradle-to-grave" (generation through disposal) with accompanying documents known as manifests.(See: cradle to grave.)

Manual Separation: Hand sorting of recyclable or compostable materials in waste.

Manufacturer's Formulation: A list of substances or component parts as described by the maker of a coating, pesticide, or other product containing chemicals or other substances.

Manufacturing Use Product: Any product intended (labeled) for formulation or repackaging into other pesticide products.

Margin of Safety: Maximum amount of exposure producing no measurable effect in animals (or studied humans) divided by the actual amount of human exposure in a population.

Margin of Exposure (MOE): The ratio of the no-observed adverse-effect-level to the estimated exposure dose.

Marine Sanitation Device: Any equipment or process installed on board a vessel to receive, retain, treat, or discharge sewage.

Marsh: A type of wetland that does not accumulate appreciable peat deposits and is dominated by herbaceous vegetation. Marshes may be either fresh or saltwater, tidal or non-tidal. (See: wetlands.)

Material Category: In the asbestos program, broad classification of materials into thermal surfacing insulation, surfacing material, and miscellaneous material.

Material Safety Data Sheet (MSDS): A compilation of information required under the OSHA Communication Standard on the identity of hazardous chemicals, health, and physical hazards, exposure limits, and precautions. Section 311 of SARA requires facilities to submit MSDSs under certain circumstances.

Material Type: Classification of suspect material by its specific use or application; e.g., pipe insulation, fireproofing, and floor tile.

Materials Recovery Facility (MRF): A facility that processes residentially collected mixed recyclables into new products available for market.

Maximally (or Most) Exposed Individual: The person with the highest exposure in a given population.

Maximum Acceptable Toxic Concentration: For a given ecological effects test, the range (or geometric mean) between the No Observable Adverse Effect Level and the Lowest Observable Adverse Effects Level.

Maximum Available Control Technology (MACT): The emission standard for sources of air pollution requiring the maximum reduction of hazardous emissions, taking cost and feasibility into account. Under the Clean Air Act Amendments of 1990, the MACT must not be less than the average emission level achieved by controls on the best performing 12 percent of existing sources, by category of industrial and utility sources.

Maximum Contaminant Level: The maximum permissible level of a contaminant in water delivered to any user of a public system. MCLs are enforceable standards.

Maximum Contaminant Level Goal (MCLG): Under the Safe Drinking Water Act, a non-enforceable concentration of a drinking water contaminant, set at the level at which no known or anticipated adverse effects on human health occur and which allows an adequate safety margin. The MCLG is usually the starting point for determining the regulated Maximum Contaminant Level. (See: maximum contaminant level.)

Maximum Exposure Range: Estimate of exposure or dose level received by an individual in a defined population that is greater than the 98th percentile dose for all individuals in that population, but less than the exposure level received by the person receiving the highest exposure level.

Maximum Residue Level: Comparable to a U.S. tolerance level, the Maximum Residue Level the enforceable limit on food pesticide levels in some countries. Levels are set by the Codex Alimentarius Commission, a United Nations agency managed and funded jointly by the World Health Organization and the Food and Agriculture Organization.

Maximum Tolerated Dose: The maximum dose that an animal species can tolerate for a major portion of its lifetime without significant impairment or toxic effect other than carcinogenicity.

Measure of Effect/ Measurement Endpoint: A measurable characteristic of ecological entity that can be related to an assessment endpoint; e.g. a laboratory test for eight species meeting certain requirements may serve as a measure of effect for an assessment endpoint, such as survival of fish, aquatic, invertebrate or algal species under acute exposure.

Measure of Exposure: A measurable characteristic of a stressor (such as the specific amount of mercury in a body of water) used to help quantify the exposure of an ecological entity or individual organism.

Mechanical Aeration: Use of mechanical energy to inject air into water to cause a waste stream to absorb oxygen.

Mechanical Separation: Using mechanical means to separate waste into various components.

Mechanical Turbulence: Random irregularities of fluid motion in air caused by buildings or other nonthermal, processes.

Media: Specific environments—air, water, soil—which are the subject of regulatory concern and activities.

Medical Surveillance: A periodic comprehensive review of a worker's health status; acceptable elements of such surveillance program are listed in the Occupational Safety and Health Administration standards for asbestos.

Medical Waste: Any solid waste generated in the diagnosis, treatment, or immunization of human beings or animals, in research pertaining thereto, or in the production or testing of biologicals, excluding hazardous waste identified or listed under 40 CFR Part 261 or any household waste as defined in 40 CFR Sub-section 261.4 (b)(1).

Medium-size Water System: A water system that serves 3,300 to 50,000 customers.

Meniscus: The curved top of a column of liquid in a small tube.

Mercury (Hg): Heavy metal that can accumulate in the environment and is highly toxic if breathed or swallowed. (See:heavy metals.)

Mesotrophic: Reservoirs and lakes which contain moderate quantities of nutrients and are moderately productive in terms of aquatic animal and plant life.

Metabolites: Any substances produced by biological processes, such as those from pesticides.

Metalimnion: The middle layer of a thermally stratified lake or reservoir. In this layer there is a rapid decrease in temperature with depth. Also called thermocline.

Methane: A colorless, nonpoisonous, flammable gas created by anaerobic decomposition of organic compounds. A major component of natural gas used in the home.

Methanol: An alcohol that can be used as an alternative fuel or as a gasoline additive. It is less volatile than gasoline; when blended with gasoline it lowers the carbon monoxide emissions but increases hydrocarbon emissions. Used as pure fuel, its emissions are less ozone-forming than those from gasoline. Poisonous to humans and animals if ingested.

Method 18: An EPA test method which uses gas chromatographic techniques to measure the concentration of volatile organic compounds in a gas stream.

Method 24: An EPA reference method to determine density, water content and total volatile content (water and VOC) of coatings.

Method 25: An EPA reference method to determine the VOC concentration in a gas stream.

Method Detection Limit (MDL): See limit of detection.

Methoxychlor: Pesticide that causes adverse health effects in domestic water supplies and is toxic to freshwater and marine aquatic life.

Methyl Orange Alkalinity: A measure of the total alkalinity in a water sample in which the color of methyl orange reflects the change in level.

Microbial Growth: The amplification or multiplication of microorganisms such as bacteria, algae, diatoms, plankton, and fungi.

Microbial Pesticide: A microorganism that is used to kill a pest, but is of minimum toxicity to humans.

Microclimate: 1. Localized climate conditions within an urban area or neighborhood. 2. The climate around a tree or shrub or a stand of trees.

Microenvironmental Method: A method for sequentially assessing exposure for a series of microenvironments that can be approximated by constant concentrations of a stressor.

Microenvironments: Well-defined surroundings such as the home, office, or kitchen that can be treated as uniform in terms of stressor concentration.

Million-Gallons Per Day (MGD): A measure of water flow.

Minimization: A comprehensive program to minimize or eliminate wastes, usually applied to wastes at their point of origin. (See: waste minimization.)

Mining of an Aquifer: Withdrawal over a period of time of ground water that exceeds the rate of recharge of the aquifer.

Mining Waste: Residues resulting from the extraction of raw materials from the earth.

Minor Source: New emissions sources or modifications to existing emissions sources that do not exceed NAAQS emission levels.

Minors: Publicly owned treatment works with flows less than 1 million gallons per day. (See: majors.)

Miscellaneous ACM: Interior asbestos-containing building material or structural components, members or fixtures, such as floor and ceiling tiles; does not include surfacing materials or thermal system insulation.

Miscellaneous Materials: Interior building materials on structural components, such as floor or ceiling tiles.

Miscible Liquids: Two or more liquids that can be mixed and will remain mixed under normal conditions.

Missed Detection: The situation that occurs when a test indicates that a tank is "tight" when in fact it is leaking.

Mist: Liquid particles measuring 40 to 500 micrometers (pm), are formed by condensation of vapor. By comparison, fog particles are smaller than 40 micrometers (pm).

Mitigation: Measures taken to reduce adverse impacts on the environment.

Mixed Funding: Settlements in which potentially responsible parties and EPA share the cost of a response action.

Mixed Glass: Recovered container glass not sorted into categories (e.g. color, grade).

Mixed Liquor: A mixture of activated sludge and water containing organic matter undergoing activated sludge treatment in an aeration tank.

Mixed Metals: Recovered metals not sorted into categories such as aluminum, tin, or steel cans or ferrous or non-ferrous metals.

Mixed Municipal Waste: Solid waste that has not been sorted into specific categories (such as plastic, glass, yard trimmings, etc.)

Mixed Paper: Recovered paper not sorted into categories such as old magazines, old newspapers, old corrugated boxes, etc.

Mixed Plastic: Recovered plastic unsorted by category.

Mobile Incinerator Systems: Hazardous waste incinerators that can be transported from one site to another.

Mobile Source: Any non-stationary source of air pollution such as cars, trucks, motorcycles, buses, airplanes, and locomotives.

Model Plant: A hypothetical plant design used for developing economic, environmental, and energy impact analyses as support for regulations or regulatory guidelines; first step in exploring the economic impact of a potential NSPS.

Modified Bin Method: Way of calculating the required heating or cooling for a building based on determining how much energy the system would use if outdoor temperatures were within a certain temperature interval and then multiplying the energy use by the time the temperature interval typically occurs.

Modified Source: The enlargement of a major stationary pollutant sources is often referred to as modification, implying that more emissions will occur.

Moisture Content: 1.The amount of water lost from soil upon drying to a constant weight, expressed as the weight per unit of dry soil or as the volume of water per unit bulk volume of the soil. For a fully saturated medium, moisture content indicates the porosity. 2. Water equivalent of snow on the ground; an indicator of snowmelt flood potential.

Molecule: The smallest division of a compound that still retains or exhibits all the properties of the substance.

Molten Salt Reactor: A thermal treatment unit that rapidly heats waste in a heat-conducting fluid bath of carbonate salt.

Monitoring: Periodic or continuous surveillance or testing to determine the level of compliance with statutory requirements and/or pollutant levels in various media or in humans, plants, and animals.

Monitoring Well: 1. A well used to obtain water quality samples or measure groundwater levels. 2. A well drilled at a hazardous waste management facility or Superfund site to collect ground-water samples for the purpose of physical, chemical, or biological analysis to determine the amounts, types, and distribution of contaminants in the groundwater beneath the site.

Monoclonal Antibodies (Also called MABs and MCAs): 1. Man-made (anthropogenic) clones of a molecule, produced in quantity for medical or research purposes. 2. Molecules of living organisms that selectively find and attach to other molecules to which their structure conforms exactly. This could also apply to equivalent activity by chemical molecules.

Monomictic: Lakes and reservoirs which are relatively deep, do not freeze over during winter, and undergo a single stratification and mixing cycle during the year (usually in the fall).

Montreal Protocol: Treaty, signed in 1987, governs stratospheric ozone protection and research, and the production and use of ozone-depleting substances. It provides for the end of production of ozone-depleting substances such as CFCS. Under the Protocol, various research groups continue to assess the ozone layer. The Multilateral Fund provides resources to developing nations to promote the transition to ozone-safe technologies.

Moratorium: During the negotiation process, a period of 60 to 90 days during which EPA and potentially responsible parties may reach settlement but no site response activities can be conducted.

Morbidity: Rate of disease incidence.

Mortality: Death rate.

Most Probable Number: An estimate of microbial density per unit volume of water sample, based on probability theory.

Muck Soils: Earth made from decaying plant materials.

Mudballs: Round material that forms in filters and gradually increases in size when not removed by backwashing.

Mulch: A layer of material (wood chips, straw, leaves, etc.) placed around plants to hold moisture, prevent weed growth, and enrich or sterilize the soil.

Multi-Media Approach: Joint approach to several environmental media, such as air, water, and land.

Multiple Chemical Sensitivity: A diagnostic label for people who suffer multi-system illnesses as a result of contact with, or proximity to, a variety of airborne agents and other substances.

Multiple Use: Use of land for more than one purpose; e.g., grazing of livestock, watershed and wildlife protection, recreation, and timber production. Also applies to use of bodies of water for recreational purposes, fishing, and water supply.

Multistage Remote Sensing: A strategy for landscape characterization that involves gathering and analyzing information at several geographic scales, ranging from generalized levels of detail at the national level through high levels of detail at the local scale.

Municipal Discharge: Discharge of effluent from waste water treatment plants which receive waste water from households, commercial establishments, and industries in the coastal drainage basin. Combined sewer/separate storm overflows are included in this category.

Municipal Sewage: Wastes (mostly liquid) orginating from a community; may be composed of domestic wastewaters and/or industrial discharges.

Municipal Sludge: Semi-liquid residue remaining from the treatment of municipal water and wastewater.

Municipal Solid Waste: Common garbage or trash generated by industries, businesses, institutions, and homes.

Mutagen/Mutagenicity: An agent that causes a permanent genetic change in a cell other than that which occurs during normal growth. Mutagenicity is the capacity of a chemical or physical agent to cause such permanent changes.

N

National Ambient Air Quality Standards (NAAQS): Standards established by EPA that apply for outdoor air throughout the country. (See: criteria pollutants, state implementation plans, emissions trading.)

National Emissions Standards for Hazardous Air Pollutants (NESHAPS): Emissions standards set by EPA for an air pollutant not covered by NAAQS that may cause an increase in fatalities or in serious, irreversible, or incapacitating illness. Primary standards are designed to protect human health, secondary standards to protect public welfare (e.g. building facades, visibility, crops, and domestic animals).

National Environmental Performance Partnership Agreements: System that allows states to assume greater responsibility for environmental programs based on their relative ability to execute them.

National Estuary Program: A program established under the Clean Water Act Amendments of 1987 to develop and implement conservation and management plans for protecting estuaries and restoring and maintaining their chemical, physical, and biological integrity, as well as controlling point and nonpoint pollution sources.

National Municipal Plan: A policy created in 1984 by EPA and the states in 1984 to bring all publicly owned treatment works (POTWs) into compliance with Clean Water Act requirements.

National Oil and Hazardous Substances Contingency Plan (NOHSCP/NCP): The federal regulation that guides determination of the sites to be corrected under both the Superfund program and the program to prevent or control spills into surface waters or elsewhere.

National Pollutant Discharge Elimination System (NPDES): A provision of the Clean Water Act which prohibits discharge of pollutants into waters of the United States unless a special permit is issued by EPA, a state, or, where delegated, a tribal government on an Indian reservation.

National Priorities List (NPL): EPA's list of the most serious uncontrolled or abandoned hazardous waste sites identified for possible long-term remedial action under Superfund. The list is based primarily on the score a site receives from the Hazard Ranking System. EPA is required to update the NPL at least once a year. A site must be on the NPL to receive money from the Trust Fund for remedial action.

National Response Center: The federal operations center that receives notifications of all releases of oil and hazardous substances into the environment; open 24 hours a day, is operated by the U.S. Coast Guard, which evaluates all reports and notifies the appropriate agency.

National Response Team (NRT): Representatives of 13 federal agencies that, as a team, coordinate federal responses to nationally significant incidents of pollution—an oil spill, a major chemical release, or a - superfund response action—and provide advice and technical assistance to the responding agency(ies) before and during a response action.

National Secondary Drinking Water Regulations: Commonly referred to as NSDWRs.

Navigable Waters: Traditionally, waters sufficiently deep and wide for navigation by all, or specified vessels; such waters in the United States come under federal jurisdiction and are protected by certain provisions of the Clean Water Act.

Necrosis: Death of plant or animal cells or tissues. In plants, necrosis can discolor stems or leaves or kill a plant entirely.

Negotiations (Under Superfund): After potentially responsible parties are identified for a site, EPA coordinates with them to reach a settlement that will result in the PRP paying for or conducting the cleanup under EPA supervision. If negotiations fail, EPA can order the PRP to conduct the cleanup or EPA can pay for the cleanup using Superfund monies and then sue to recover the costs.

Nematocide: A chemical agent which is destructive to nematodes.

Nephelometric: Method of of measuring turbidity in a water sample by passing light through the sample and measuring the amount of the light that is deflected.

Netting: A concept in which all emissions sources in the same area that owned or controlled by a single company are treated as one large source, thereby allowing flexibility in controlling individual sources in order to meet a single emissions standard. (See: bubble.)

Neutralization: Decreasing the acidity or alkalinity of a substance by adding alkaline or acidic materials, respectively.

New Source: Any stationary source built or modified after publication of final or proposed regulations that prescribe a given standard of performance.

New Source Performance Standards (NSPS): Uniform national EPA air emission and water effluent standards which limit the amount of pollution allowed from new sources or from modified existing sources.

New Source Review (NSR): A Clean Air Act requirement that State Implementation Plans must include a permit review that applies to the construction and operation of new and modified stationary sources in nonattainment areas to ensure attainment of national ambient air quality standards.

Nitrate: A compound containing nitrogen that can exist in the atmosphere or as a dissolved gas in water and which can have harmful effects on humans and animals. Nitrates in water can cause severe illness in infants and domestic animals. A plant nutrient and inorganic fertilizer, nitrate is found in septic systems, animal feed lots, agricultural fertilizers, manure, industrial waste waters, sanitary landfills, and garbage dumps.

Nitric Oxide (NO): A gas formed by combustion under high temperature and high pressure in an internal combustion engine; it is converted by sunlight and photochemical processes in ambient air to nitrogen oxide. NO is a precursor of ground-level ozone pollution, or smog..

Nitrification: The process whereby ammonia in wastewater is oxidized to nitrite and then to nitrate by bacterial or chemical reactions.

Nitrilotriacetic Acid (NTA): A compound now replacing phosphates in detergents.

Nitrite: 1. An intermediate in the process of nitrification. 2. Nitrous oxide salts used in food preservation.

Nitrogen Dioxide (NO_2): The result of nitric oxide combining with oxygen in the atmosphere; major component of photochemical smog.

Nitrogen Oxide (NO_x): The result of photochemical reactions of nitric oxide in ambient air; major component of photochemical smog. Product of combustion from transportation and stationary sources and a major contributor to the formation of ozone in the troposphere and to acid deposition.

Nitrogenous Wastes: Animal or vegetable residues that contain significant amounts of nitrogen.

Nitrophenols: Synthetic organopesticides containing carbon, hydrogen, nitrogen, and oxygen.

No Further Remedial Action Planned: Determination made by EPA following a preliminary assessment that a site does not pose a significant risk and so requires no further activity under CERCLA.

No Observable Adverse Effect Level (NOAEL): An exposure level at which there are no statistically or biologically significant increases in the frequency or severity of adverse effects between the exposed population and its appropriate control; some effects may be produced at this level, but they are not considered as adverse, or as precurors to adverse effects. In an experiment with several NOAELs, the regulatory focus is primarily on the highest one, leading to the common usage of the term NOAEL as the highest exposure without adverse effects.

No Till: Planting crops without prior seedbed preparation, into an existing cover crop, sod, or crop residues, and eliminating subsequent tillage operations.

No-Observed-Effect-Level (NOEL): Exposure level at which there are no statistically or biological significant differences in the frequency or severity of any effect in the exposed or control populations.

Noble Metal: Chemically inactive metal such as gold; does not corrode easily.

Noise: Product-level or product-volume changes occurring during a test that are not related to a leak but may be mistaken for one.

Non-Aqueous Phase Liquid (NAPL): Contaminants that remain undiluted as the original bulk liquid in the subsurface, e.g. spilled oil. (See: fee product.)

Non-Attainment Area: Area that does not meet one or more of the National Ambient Air Quality Standards for the criteria pollutants designated in the Clean Air Act.

Non-Binding Allocations of Responsibility (NBAR): A process for EPA to propose a way for potentially responsible parties to allocate costs among themselves.

Non-Community Water System: A public water system that is not a community water system; e.g. the water supply at a camp site or national park.

Non-Compliance Coal: Any coal that emits greater than 3.0 pounds of sulfur dioxide per million BTU when burned. Also known as high-sulfur coal.

Non-Contact Cooling Water: Water used for cooling which does not come into direct contact with any raw material, product, byproduct, or waste.

Non-Conventional Pollutant: Any pollutant not statutorily listed or which is poorly understood by the scientific community.

Non-Degradation: An environmental policy which disallows any lowering of naturally occurring quality regardless of preestablished health standards.

Non-Ferrous Metals: Nonmagnetic metals such as aluminum, lead, and copper. Products made all or in part from such metals include containers, packaging, appliances, furniture, electronic equipment and aluminum foil.

Non-ionizing Electromagnetic Radiation: 1. Radiation that does not change the structure of atoms but does heat tissue and may cause harmful biological effects. 2. Microwaves, radio waves, and low-frequency electromagnetic fields from high-voltage transmission lines.

Non-Methane Hydrocarbon (NMHC): The sum of all hydrocarbon air pollutants except methane; significant precursors to ozone formation.

Non-Methane Organic Gases (NMOG): The sum of all organic air pollutants. Excluding methane; they account for aldehydes, ketones, alcohols, and other pollutants that are not hydrocarbons but are precursors of ozone.

Non-Point Sources: Diffuse pollution sources (i.e. without a single point of origin or not introduced into a receiving stream from a specific outlet). The pollutants are generally carried off the land by storm water. Common non-point sources are agriculture, forestry, urban, mining, construction, dams, channels, land disposal, saltwater intrusion, and city streets.

Non-potable: Water that is unsafe or unpalatable to drink because it contains pollutants, contaminants, minerals, or infective agents.

Non-Road Emissions: Pollutants emitted by combustion engines on farm and construction equipment, gasoline-powered lawn and garden equipment, and power boats and outboard motors.

Non-Transient Non-Community Water System: A public water system that regularly serves at least 25 of the same non-resident persons per day for more than six months per year.

Nondischarging Treatment Plant: A treatment plant that does not discharge treated wastewater into any stream or river. Most are pond systems that dispose of the total flow they receive by means of evaporation or percolation to groundwater, or facilities that dispose of their effluent by recycling or reuse (e.g. spray irrigation or groundwater discharge).

Nonfriable Asbestos-Containing Materials: Any material containing more than one percent asbestos (as determined by Polarized Light Microscopy) that, when dry, cannot be crumbled, pulverized, or reduced to powder by hand pressure.

Nonhazardous Industrial Waste: Industrial process waste in wastewater not considered municipal solid waste or hazardous waste under RARA.

Notice of Deficiency: An EPA request to a facility owner or operator requesting additional information before a preliminary decision on a permit application can be made.

Notice of Intent to Cancel: Notification sent to registrants when EPA decides to cancel registration of a product containing a pesticide.

Notice of Intent to Deny: Notification by EPA of its preliminary intent to deny a permit application.

Notice of Intent to Suspend: Notification sent to a pesticide registrant when EPA decides to suspend product sale and distribution because of failure to submit requested data in a timely and/or acceptable manner, or because of imminent hazard. (See: emergency suspension.)

Nuclear Reactors and Support Facilities: Uranium mills, commercial power reactors, fuel reprocessing plants, and uranium enrichment facilities.

Nuclear Winter: Prediction by some scientists that smoke and debris rising from massive fires of a nuclear war could block sunlight for weeks or months, cooling the earth's surface and producing climate changes that could, for example, negatively affect world agricultural and weather patterns.

Nuclide: An atom characterized by the number of protons, neturons, and energy in the nucleus.

Nutrient: Any substance assimilated by living things that promotes growth. The term is generally applied to nitrogen and phosphorus in wastewater, but is also applied to other essential and trace elements.

Nutrient Pollution: Contamination of water resources by excessive inputs of nutrients. In surface waters, excess algal production is a major concern.

O

Ocean Discharge Waiver: A variance from Clean Water Act requirements for discharges into marine waters.

Odor Threshold: The minimum odor of a water or air sample that can just be detected after successive dilutions with odorless water. Also called threshold odor.

OECD Guidelines: Testing guidelines prepared by the Organization of Economic and Cooperative Development of the United Nations. They assist in preparation of protocols for studies of toxicology, environmental fate, etc.

Off-Site Facility: A hazardous waste treatment, storage or disposal area that is located away from the generating site.

Office Paper: High grade papers such as copier paper, computer printout, and stationary almost entirely made of uncoated chemical pulp, although some ground wood is used. Such waste is also generated in homes, schools, and elsewhere.

Offsets: A concept whereby emissions from proposed new or modified stationary sources are balanced by reductions from existing sources to stabilize total emissions. (See: bubble, emissions trading, netting)

Offstream Use: Water withdrawn from surface or groundwater sources for use at another place.

Oil and Gas Waste: Gas and oil drilling muds, oil production brines, and other waste associated with exploration for, development and production of crude oil or natural gas.

Oil Desulfurization: Widely used precombustion method for reducing sulfur dioxide emissions from oil-burning power plants. The oil is treated with hydrogen, which removes some of the sulfur by forming hydrogen sulfide gas.

Oil Fingerprinting: A method that identifies sources of oil and allows spills to be traced to their source.

Oil Spill: An accidental or intentional discharge of oil which reaches bodies of water. Can be controlled by chemical dispersion, combustion, mechanical containment, and/or adsorption. Spills from tanks and pipelines can also occur away from water bodies, contaminating the soil, getting into sewer systems and threatening underground water sources.

Oligotrophic Lakes: Deep clear lakes with few nutrients, little organic matter and a high dissolved-oxygen level.

On-Scene Coordinator (OSC): The predesignated EPA, Coast Guard, or Department of Defense official who coordinates and directs Superfund removal actions or Clean Water Act oil- or hazardous-spill response actions.

On-Site Facility: A hazardous waste treatment, storage or disposal area that is located on the generating site.

Onboard Controls: Devices placed on vehicles to capture gasoline vapor during refueling and route it to the engines when the vehicle is starting so that it can be efficiently burned.

Onconogenicity: The capacity to induce cancer.

One-hit Model: A mathematical model based on the biological theory that a single "hit" of some minimum critical amount of a carcinogen at a cellular target such as DNA can start an irreversible series events leading to a tumor.

Opacity: The amount of light obscured by particulate pollution in the air; clear window glass has zero opacity, a brick wall is 100 percent opaque. Opacity is an indicator of changes in performance of particulate control systems.

Open Burning: Uncontrolled fires in an open dump.

Open Dump: An uncovered site used for disposal of waste without environmental controls. (See: dump.)

Operable Unit: Term for each of a number of separate activities undertaken as part of a Superfund site cleanup. A typical operable unit would be removal of drums and tanks from the surface of a site.

Operating Conditions: Conditions specified in a RCRA permit that dictate how an incinerator must operate as it burns different waste types. A trial burn is used to identify operating conditions needed to meet specified performance standards.

Operation and Maintenance: 1. Activities conducted after a Superfund site action is completed to ensure that the action is effective. 2. Actions taken after construction to ensure that facilities constructed to treat waste water will be properly operated and maintained to achieve normative efficiency levels and prescribed effluent limitations in an optimum manner. 3. On-going asbestos management plan in a school or other public building, including regular inspections, various methods of maintaining asbestos in place, and removal when necessary.

Operator Certification: Certification of operators of community and nontransient noncommunity water systems, asbestos specialists, pesticide applicators, hazardous waste transporter, and other such specialists as required by the EPA or a state agency implementing an EPA-approved environmental regulatory program.

Optimal Corrosion Control Treatment: An erosion control treatment that minimizes the lead and copper concentrations at users' taps while also ensuring that the treatment does not cause the water system to violate any national primary drinking water regulations.

Oral Toxicity: Ability of a pesticide to cause injury when ingested.

Organic: 1. Referring to or derived from living organisms. 2. In chemistry, any compound containing carbon.

Organic Chemicals/Compounds: Naturally occuring (animal or plant-produced or synthetic) substances containing mainly carbon, hydrogen, nitrogen, and oxygen.

Organic Matter: Carbonaceous waste contained in plant or animal matter and originating from domestic or industrial sources.

Organism: Any form of animal or plant life.

Organophosphates: Pesticides that contain phosphorus; short-lived, but some can be toxic when first applied.

Organophyllic: A substance that easily combines with organic compounds.

Organotins: Chemical compounds used in anti-foulant paints to protect the hulls of boats and ships, buoys, and pilings from marine organisms such as barnacles.

Original AHERA Inspection/Original Inspection/Inspection: Examination of school buildings arranged by Local Education Agencies to identify asbestos-containing-materials, evaluate their condition, and take samples of materials suspected to contain asbestos; performed by EPA-accredited inspectors.

Original Generation Point: Where regulated medical or other material first becomes waste.

Osmosis: The passage of a liquid from a weak solution to a more concentrated solution across a semipermeable membrane that allows passage of the solvent (water) but not the dissolved solids.

Other Ferrous Metals: Recyclable metals from strapping, furniture, and metal found in tires and consumer electronics but does not include metals found in construction materials or cars, locomotives, and ships. (See: ferrous metals.)

Other Glass: Recyclable glass from furniture, appliances, and consumer electronics. Does not include glass from transportation products (cars trucks or shipping containers) and construction or demolition debris. (See: glass.)

Other Nonferrous Metals: Recyclable nonferrous metals such as lead, copper, and zinc from appliances, consumer electronics, and nonpackaging aluminum products. Does not include nonferrous metals from industrial applications and construction and demolition debris. (See: nonferrous metals.)

Other Paper: For Recyclable paper from books, third-class mail, commercial printing, paper towels, plates and cups; and other nonpackaging paper such as posters, photographic papers, cards and games, milk cartons, folding boxes, bags, wrapping paper, and paperboard. Does not include wrapping paper or shipping cartons.

Other Plastics: Recyclable plastic from appliances, eating utensils, plates, containers, toys, and various kinds of equipment. Does not include heavy-duty plastics such as yielding materials.

Other Solid Waste: Recyclable nonhazardous solid wastes, other than municipal solid waste, covered under Subtitle D of RARA. (See: solid waste.)

Other Wood: Recyclable wood from furniture, consumer electronics cabinets, and other nonpackaging wood products. Does not include lumber and tree stumps recovered from construction and demolition activities, and industrial process waste such as shavings and sawdust.

Outdoor Air Supply: Air brought into a building from outside.

Outfall: The place where effluent is discharged into receiving waters.

Overburden: Rock and soil cleared away before mining.

Overdraft: The pumping of water from a groundwater basin or aquifer in excess of the supply flowing into the basin; results in a depletion or "mining" of the groundwater in the basin. (See: groundwater mining)

Overfire Air: Air forced into the top of an incinerator or boiler to fan the flames.

Overflow Rate: One of the guidelines for design of the settling tanks and clarifers in a treatment plant; used by plant operators to determine if tanks and clarifiers are over or under-used.

Overland Flow: A land application technique that cleanses waste water by allowing it to flow over a sloped surface. As the water flows over the surface, contaminants are absorbed and the water is collected at the bottom of the slope for reuse.

Oversized Regulated Medical Waste: Medical waste that is too large for plastic bags or standard containers.

Overturn: One complete cycle of top to bottom mixing of previously stratified water masses. This phenomenon may occur in spring or fall, or after storms, and results in uniformity of chemical and physical properties of water at all depths.

Oxidant: A collective term for some of the primary constituents of photochemical smog.

Oxidation Pond: A man-made (anthropogenic) body of water in which waste is consumed by bacteria, used most frequently with other waste-treatment processes; a sewage lagoon.

Oxidation: The chemical addition of oxygen to break down pollutants or organizac waste; e.g., destruction of chemicals such as cyanides, phenols, and organic sulfur compounds in sewage by bacterial and chemical means.

Oxidation-Reduction Potential: The electric potential required to transfer electrons from one compound or element (the oxidant) to another compound (the reductant); used as a qualitative measure of the state of oxidation in water treatment systems.

Oxygenated Fuels: Gasoline which has been blended with alcohols or ethers that contain oxygen in order to reduce carbon monoxide and other emissions.

Oxygenated Solvent: An organic solvent containing oxygen as part of the molecular structure. Alcohols and ketones are oxygenated compounds often used as paint solvents.

Ozonation/Ozonator: Application of ozone to water for disinfection or for taste and odor control. The ozonator is the device that does this.

Ozone (O_3): Found in two layers of the atmosphere, the stratosphere and the troposphere. In the stratosphere (the atmospheric layer 7 to 10 miles or more above the earth's surface) ozone is a natural form of oxygen that provides a protective layer shielding the earth from ultraviolet radiation.In the troposphere (the layer extending up 7 to 10 miles from the earth's surface), ozone is a chemical oxidant and major component of photochemical smog. It can seriously impair the respiratory system and is one of the most wide- spread of all the criteria pollutants for which the Clean Air Act required EPA to set standards. Ozone in the troposphere is produced through complex chemical reactions of nitrogen oxides, which are among the primary pollutants emitted by combustion sources; hydrocarbons, released into the atmosphere through the combustion, handling and processing of petroleum products; and sunlight.

Ozone Depletion: Destruction of the stratospheric ozone layer which shields the earth from ultraviolet radiation harmful to life. This destruction of ozone is caused by the breakdown of certain chlorine and/or bromine containing compounds (chlorofluorocarbons or halons), which break down when they reach the stratosphere and then catalytically destroy ozone molecules.

Ozone Hole: A thinning break in the stratospheric ozone layer. Designation of amount of such depletion as an "ozone hole" is made when the detected amount of depletion exceeds fifty percent. Seasonal ozone holes have been observed over both the Antarctic and Arctic regions, part of Canada, and the extreme northeastern United States.

Ozone Layer: The protective layer in the atmosphere, about 15 miles above the ground, that absorbs some of the sun's ultraviolet rays, thereby reducing the amount of potentially harmful radiation that reaches the earth's surface.

P

Packaging: The assembly of one or more containers and any other components necessary to ensure minimum compliance with a program's storage and shipment packaging requirements. Also, the containers, etc. involved.

Packed Bed Scrubber: An air pollution control device in which emissions pass through alkaline water to neutralize hydrogen chloride gas.

Packed Tower: A pollution control device that forces dirty air through a tower packed with crushed rock or wood chips while liquid is sprayed over the packing material. The pollutants in the air stream either dissolve or chemically react with the liquid.

Packer: An inflatable gland, or balloon, used to create a temporary seal in a borehole, probe hole, well, or drive casing. It is made of rubber or non-reactive materials.

Palatable Water: Water, at a desirable temperature, that is free from objectionable tastes, odors, colors, and turbidity.

Pandemic: A widespread epidemic throughout an area, nation or the world.

Paper: In the recycling business, refers to products and materials, including newspapers, magazines, office papers, corrugated containers, bags and some paperboard packaging that can be recycled into new paper products.

Paper Processor/Plastics Processor: Intermediate facility where recovered paper or plastic products and materials are sorted, decontaminated, and prepared for final recycling.

Parameter: A variable, measurable property whose value is a determinant of the characteristics of a system; e.g. temperature, pressure, and density are parameters of the atmosphere.

Paraquat: A standard herbicide used to kill various types of crops, including marijuana. Causes lung damage if smoke from the crop is inhaled..

Parshall Flume: Device used to measure the flow of water in an open channel.

Part A Permit, Part B Permit: (See: Interim Permit Status.)

Participation Rate: Portion of population participating in a recycling program.

Particle Count: Results of a microscopic examination of treated water with a special "particle counter" that classifies suspended particles by number and size.

Particulate Loading: The mass of particulates per unit volume of air or water.

Particulates: 1. Fine liquid or solid particles such as dust, smoke, mist, fumes, or smog, found in air or emissions. 2. Very small solids suspended in water; they can vary in size, shape, density and electrical charge and can be gathered together by coagulation and flocculation.

Partition Coefficient: Measure of the sorption phenomenon, whereby a pesticide is divided between the soil and water phase; also referred to as adsorption partition coefficient.

Parts Per Billion (ppb)/Parts Per Million (ppm): Units commonly used to express contamination ratios, as in establishing the maximum permissible amount of a contaminant in water, land, or air.

Passive Smoking/Secondhand Smoke: Inhalation of others' tobacco smoke.

Passive Treatment Walls: Technology in which a chemical reaction takes place when contaminated ground water comes in contact with a barrier such as limestone or a wall containing iron filings.

Pathogens: Microorganisms (e.g., bacteria, viruses, or parasites) that can cause disease in humans, animals and plants.

Pathway: The physical course a chemical or pollutant takes from its source to the exposed organism.

Pay-As-You-Throw/Unit-Based Pricing: Systems under which residents pay for municipal waste management and disposal services by weight or volume collected, not a fixed fee.

Peak Electricity Demand: The maximum electricity used to meet the cooling load of a building or buildings in a given area.

Peak Levels: Levels of airborne pollutant contaminants much higher than average or occurring for short periods of time in response to sudden releases.

Percent Saturatiuon: The amount of a substance that is dissolved in a solution compared to the amount that could be dissolved in it.

Perched Water: Zone of unpressurized water held above the water table by impermeable rock or sediment.

Percolating Water: Water that passes through rocks or soil under the force of gravity.

Percolation: 1. The movement of water downward and radially through subsurface soil layers, usually continuing downward to ground water. Can also involve upward movement of water. 2. Slow seepage of water through a filter.

Performance Bond: Cash or securities deposited before a landfill operating permit is issued, which are held to ensure that all requirements for operating ad subsequently closing the landfill are faithful performed. The money is returned to the owner after proper closure of the landfill is completed. If contamination or other problems appear at any time during operation, or upon closure, and are not addressed, the owner must forfeit all or part of the bond which is then used to cover clean-up costs.

Performance Data (For Incinerators): Information collected, during a trial burn, on concentrations of designated organic compounds and pollutants found in incinerator emissions. Data analysis must show that the incinerator meets performance standards under operating conditions specified in the RCRA permit. (See: trial burn; performance standards.)

Performance Standards: 1. Regulatory requirements limiting the concentrations of designated organic compounds, particulate matter, and hydrogen chloride in emissions from incinerators. 2. Operating standards established by EPA for various permitted pollution control systems, asbestos inspections, and various program operations and maintenance requirements.

Periphyton: Microscopic underwater plants and animals that are firmly attached to solid surfaces such as rocks, logs, and pilings.

Permeability: The rate at which liquids pass through soil or other materials in a specified direction.

Permissible Dose: The dose of a chemical that may be received by an individual without the expectation of a significantly harmful result.

Permissible Exposure Limit: Also referred to as PEL, federal limits for workplace exposure to contaminants as established by OSHA.

Permit: An authorization, license, or equivalent control document issued by EPA or an approved state agency to implement the requirements of an environmental regulation; e.g. a permit to operate a wastewater treatment plant or to operate a facility that may generate harmful emissions.

Persistence: Refers to the length of time a compound stays in the environment, once introduced. A compound may persist for less than a second or indefinitely.

Persistent Pesticides: Pesticides that do not break down chemically or break down very slowly and remain in the environment after a growing season.

Personal Air Samples: Air samples taken with a pump that is directly attached to the worker with the collecting filter and cassette placed in the worker's breathing zone (required under OSHA asbestos standards and EPA worker protection rule).

Personal Measurement: A measurement collected from an individual's immediate environment.

Personal Protective Equipment: Clothing and equipment worn by pesticide mixers, loaders and applicators and re-entry workers, hazmat emergency responders, workers cleaning up Superfund sites, et. al., which is worn to reduce their exposure to potentially hazardous chemicals and other pollutants.

Pest: An insect, rodent, nematode, fungus, weed or other form of terrestrial or aquatic plant or animal life that is injurious to health or the environment.

Pest Control Operator: Person or company that applies pesticides as a business (e.g. exterminator); usually describes household services, not agricultural applications.

Pesticide: Substances or mixture there of intended for preventing, destroying, repelling, or mitigating any pest. Also, any substance or mixture intended for use as a plant regulator, defoliant, or desiccant.

Pesticide Regulation Notice: Formal notice to pesticide registrants about important changes in regulatory policy, procedures, regulations.

Pesticide Tolerance: The amount of pesticide residue allowed by law to remain in or on a harvested crop. EPA sets these levels well below the point where the compounds might be harmful to consumers.

PETE (Polyethylene Terepthalate): Thermoplastic material used in plastic soft drink and rigid containers.

Petroleum: Crude oil or any fraction thereof that is liquid under normal conditions of temperature and pressure. The term includes petroleum-based substances comprising a complex blend of hydrocarbons derived from crude oil through the process of separation, conversion, upgrading, and finishing, such as motor fuel, jet oil, lubricants, petroleum solvents, and used oil.

Petroleum Derivatives: Chemicals formed when gasoline breaks down in contact with ground water.

pH: An expression of the intensity of the basic or acid condition of a liquid; may range from 0 to 14, where 0 is the most acid and 7 is neutral. Natural waters usually have a pH between 6.5 and 8.5.

Pharmacokinetics: The study of the way that drugs move through the body after they are swallowed or injected.

Phenolphthalein Alkalinity: The alkalinity in a water sample measured by the amount of standard acid needed to lower the pH to a level of 8.3 as indicated by the change of color of the phenolphthalein from pink to clear.

Phenols: Organic compounds that are byproducts of petroleum refining, tanning, and textile, dye, and resin manufacturing. Low concentrations cause taste and odor problems in water; higher concentrations can kill aquatic life and humans.

Phosphates: Certain chemical compounds containing phosphorus.

Phosphogypsum Piles (Stacks): Principal byproduct generated in production of phosphoric acid from phosphate rock. These piles may generate radioactive radon gas.

Phosphorus: An essential chemical food element that can contribute to the eutrophication of lakes and other water bodies. Increased phosphorus levels result from discharge of phosphorus-containing materials into surface waters.

Phosphorus Plants: Facilities using electric furnaces to produce elemental phosphorous for commercial use, such as high grade phosphoric acid, phosphate-based detergent, and organic chemicals use.

Photochemical Oxidants: Air pollutants formed by the action of sunlight on oxides of nitrogen and hydrocarbons.

Photochemical Smog: Air pollution caused by chemical reactions of various pollutants emitted from different sources. (See: photochemical oxidants.)

Photosynthesis: The manufacture by plants of carbohydrates and oxygen from carbon dioxide mediated by chlorophyll in the presence of sunlight.

Physical and Chemical Treatment: Processes generally used in large-scale wastewater treatment facilities. Physical processes may include air-stripping or filtration. Chemical treatment includes coagulation, chlorination, or ozonation. The term can also refer to treatment of toxic materials in surface and ground waters, oil spills, and some methods of dealing with hazardous materials on or in the ground.

Phytoplankton: That portion of the plankton community comprised of tiny plants; e.g. algae, diatoms.

Phytoremediation: Low-cost remediation option for sites with widely dispersed contamination at low concentrations.

Phytotoxic: Harmful to plants.

Phytotreatment: The cultivation of specialized plants that absorb specific contaminants from the soil through their roots or foliage. This reduces the concentration of contaminants in the soil, but incorporates them into biomasses that may be released back into the environment when the plant dies or is harvested.

Picocuries Per Liter pCi/L): A unit of measure for levels of radon gas; becquerels per cubic meter is metric equivalent.

Piezometer: A nonpumping well, generally of small diameter, for measuring the elevation of a water table.

Pilot Tests: Testing a cleanup technology under actual site conditions to identify potential problems prior to full-scale implementation.

Plankton: Tiny plants and animals that live in water.

Plasma Arc Reactors: devices that use an electric arc to thermally decompose organic and inorganic materials at ultra-high temperatures into gases and a vitrified slag residue. A plasma arc reactor can operate as any of the following:

- integral component of chemical, fuel, or electricty production systems, processing high or medium value organic compounds into a synthetic gas used as a fuel

- materials recovery device, processing scrap to recover metal from the slag
- destruction or incineration system, processing waste materials into slag and gases ignited inside of a secondary combustion chamber that follows the reactor

Plasmid: A circular piece of DNA that exists apart from the chromosome and replicates independently of it. Bacterial plasmids carry information that renders the bacteria resistant to antibiotics. Plasmids are often used in genetic engineering to carry desired genes into organisms.

Plastics: Non-metallic chemoreactive compounds molded into rigid or pliable construction materials, fabrics, etc.

Plate Tower Scrubber: An air pollution control device that neutralizes hydrogen chloride gas by bubbling alkaline water through holes in a series of metal plates.

Plug Flow: Type of flow the occurs in tanks, basins, or reactors when a slug of water moves through without ever dispersing or mixing with the rest of the water flowing through.

Plugging: Act or process of stopping the flow of water, oil, or gas into or out of a formation through a borehole or well penetrating that formation.

Plume: 1. A visible or measurable discharge of a contaminant from a given point of origin. Can be visible or thermal in water, or visible in the air as, for example, a plume of smoke. 2 The area of radiation leaking from a damaged reactor. 3. Area downwind within which a release could be dangerous for those exposed to leaking fumes.

Plutonium: A radioactive metallic element chemically similar to uranium.

PM-10/PM-2.5: PM 10 is measure of particles in the atmosphere with a diameter of less than ten or equal to a nominal 10 micrometers. PM-2.5 is a measure of smaller particles in the air. PM 10 has been the pollutant particulate level standard against which EPA has been measuring Clean Air Act compliance. On the basis of newer scientific findings, the Agency is considering regulations that will make PM-2.5 the new "standard".

Pneumoconiosis: Health conditions characterized by permanent deposition of substantial amounts of particulate matter in the lungs and by the tissue reaction to its presence; can range from relatively harmless forms of sclerosis to the destructive fibrotic effect of silicosis.

Point Source: A stationary location or fixed facility from which pollutants are discharged; any single identifiable source of pollution; e.g. a pipe, ditch, ship, ore pit, factory smokestack.

Point-of-Contact Measurement of Exposure: Estimating exposure by measuring concentrations over time (while the exposure is taking place) at or near the place where it is occurring.

Point-of-Disinfectant Application: The point where disinfectant is applied and water downstream of that point is not subject to recontamination by surface water runoff.

Point-of-Use Treatment Device: Treatment device applied to a single tap to reduce contaminants in the drinking water at the one faucet.

Pollen: The fertilizing element of flowering plants; background air pollutant.

Pollutant: Generally, any substance introduced into the environment that adversely affects the usefulness of a resource or the health of humans, animals, or ecosystems..

Pollutant Pathways: Avenues for distribution of pollutants. In most buildings, for example, HVAC systems are the primary pathways although all building components can interact to affect how air movement distributes pollutants.

Pollutant Standard Index (PSI): Indicator of one or more pollutants that may be used to inform the public about the potential for adverse health effects from air pollution in major cities.

Pollution: Generally, the presence of a substance in the environment that because of its chemical composition or quantity prevents the functioning of natural processes and produces undesirable environmental and health effects.Under the Clean Water Act, for example, the term has been defined as the man-made or man-induced alteration of the physical, biological, chemical, and radiological integrity of water and other media.

Pollution Prevention: 1. Identifying areas, processes, and activities which create excessive waste products or pollutants in order to reduce or prevent them through, alteration, or eliminating a process. Such activities, consistent with the Pollution Prevention Act of 1990, are conducted across all EPA programs and can involve cooperative efforts with such agencies as the Departments of Agriculture and Energy. 2. EPA has initiated a number of voluntary programs in which industrial, or commercial or "partners" join with EPA in promoting activities that conserve energy, conserve and protect water supply, reduce emissions or find ways of utilizing them as energy resources, and reduce the waste stream. Among these are: Agstar, to reduce methane emissions through manure management. Climate Wise, to lower industrial greenhouse-gas emissions and energy costs. Coalbed Methane Outreach, to boost methane recovery at coal mines. Design for the Environment, to foster including environmental considerations in product design and processes. Energy Star programs, to promote energy efficiency in commercial and residential buildings, office equipment, transformers, computers, office equipment, and home appliances. Environmental Accounting, to help businesses identify environmental costs and factor them into management decision making. Green Chemistry, to promote and recognize cost-effective breakthroughs in chemistry that prevent pollution. Green Lights, to spread the use of energy-efficient lighting technologies. Indoor Environments, to reduce risks from indoor-air pollution. Landfill Methane Outreach, to develop landfill gas-to-energy projects. Natural Gas Star, to reduce methane emissions from the natural gas industry. Ruminant Livestock Methane, to reduce methane emissions from ruminant livestock. Transportation Partners, to reduce carbon dioxide emissions from the transportation sector. Voluntary Aluminum Industrial Partnership, to reduce perfluorocarbon emissions from the primary aluminum industry. WAVE, to promote efficient water use in the lodging industry. Wastewi$e, to reduce business-generated solid waste through prevention, reuse, and recycling. (See: Common Sense Initiative and Project XL.)

Polychlorinated Biphenyls: A group of toxic, persistent chemicals used in electrical transformers and capacitors for insulating purposes, and in gas pipeline systems as lubricant. The sale and new use of these chemicals, also known as PCBs, were banned by law in 1979.

Portal-of-Entry Effect: A local effect produced in the tissue or organ of first contact between a toxicant and the biological system.

Polonium: A radioactive element that occurs in pitchblende and other uranium-containing ores.

Polyelectrolytes: Synthetic chemicals that help solids to clump during sewage treatment.

Polymer: A natural or synthetic chemical structure where two or more like molecules are joined to form a more complex molecular structure (e.g. polyethylene in plastic).

Polyvinyl Chloride (PVC): A tough, environmentally indestructible plastic that releases hydrochloric acid when burned.

Population: A group of interbreeding organisms occupying a particular space; the number of humans or other living creatures in a designated area.

Population at Risk: A population subgroup that is more likely to be exposed to a chemical, or is more sensitive to the chemical, than is the general population.

Porosity: Degree to which soil, gravel, sediment, or rock is permeated with pores or cavities through which water or air can move.

Post-Chlorination: Addition of chlorine to plant effluent for disinfectant purposes after the effluent has been treated.

Post-Closure: The time period following the shutdown of a waste management or manufacturing facility; for monitoring purposes, often considered to be 30 years.

Post-Consumer Materials/Waste: Recovered materials that are diverted from municipal solid waste for the purpose of collection, recycling, and disposition.

Post-Consumer Recycling: Use of materials generated from residential and consumer waste for new or similar purposes, e.g. converting wastepaper from offices into corrugated boxes or newsprint.

Potable Water: Water that is safe for drinking and cooking.

Potential Dose: The amount of a compound contained in material swallowed, breathed, or applied to the skin.

Potentially Responsible Party (PRP): Any individual or company—including owners, operators, transporters or generators—potentially responsible for, or contributing to a spill or other contamination at a Superfund site. Whenever possible, through administrative and legal actions, EPA requires PRPs to clean up hazardous sites they have contaminated.

Potentiation: The ability of one chemical to increase the effect of another chemical.

Potentiometric Surface: The surface to which water in an aquifer can rise by hydrostatic pressure.

Precautionary Principle: When information about potential risks is incomplete, basing decisions about the best ways to manage or reduce risks on a preference for avoiding unnecessary health risks instead of on unnecessary economic expenditures.

Pre-Consumer Materials/Waste: Materials generated in manufacturing and converting processes such as manufacturing scrap and trimmings and cuttings. Includes print overruns, overissue publications, and obsolete inventories.

Pre-Harvest Interval: The time between the last pesticide application and harvest of the treated crops.

Prechlorination: The addition of chlorine at the headworks of a treatment plant prior to other treatment processes. Done mainly for disinfection and control of tastes, odors, and aquatic growths, and to aid in coagulation and settling,

Precipitate: A substance separated from a solution or suspension by chemical or physical change.

Precipitation: Removal of hazardous solids from liquid waste to permit safe disposal; removal of particles from airborne emissions as in rain (e.g. acid precipitation).

Glossary of Environmental Terms

Precipitator: Pollution control device that collects particles from an air stream.

Precursor: In photochemistry, a compound antecedent to a pollutant. For example, volatile organic compounds (VOCs) and nitric oxides of nitrogen react in sunlight to form ozone or other photochemical oxidants. As such, VOCs and oxides of nitrogen are precursors.

Preliminary Assessment: The process of collecting and reviewing available information about a known or suspected waste site or release.

Prescriptive: Water rights which are acquired by diverting water and putting it to use in accordance with specified procedures; e.g. filing a request with a state agency to use unused water in a stream, river, or lake.

Pressed Wood Products: Materials used in building and furniture construction that are made from wood veneers, particles, or fibers bonded together with an adhesive under heat and pressure.

Pressure Sewers: A system of pipes in which water, wastewater, or other liquid is pumped to a higher elevation.

Pressure, Static: In flowing air, the total pressure minus velocity pressure, pushing equally in all directions.

Pressure, Total: In flowing air, the sum of the static and velocity pressures.

Pressure, Velocity: In flowing air, the pressure due to velocity and density of air.

Pretreatment: Processes used to reduce, eliminate, or alter the nature of wastewater pollutants from non-domestic sources before they are discharged into publicly owned treatment works (POTWs).

Prevalent Level Samples: Air samples taken under normal conditions (also known as ambient background samples).

Prevalent Levels: Levels of airborne contaminant occurring under normal conditions.

Prevention of Significant Deterioration (PSD): EPA program in which state and/or federal permits are required in order to restrict emissions from new or modified sources in places where air quality already meets or exceeds primary and secondary ambient air quality standards.

Primacy: Having the primary responsibility for administering and enforcing regulations.

Primary Drinking Water Regulation: Applies to public water systems and specifies a contaminant level, which, in the judgment of the EPA Administrator, will not adversely affect human health.

Primary Effect: An effect where the stressor acts directly on the ecological component of interest, not on other parts of the ecosystem. (See: secondary effect.)

Primary Standards: National ambient air quality standards designed to protect human health with an adequate margin for safety. (See: National Ambient Air Quality Standards, secondary standards.)

Primary Treatment: First stage of wastewater treatment in which solids are removed by screening and settling.

Primary Waste Treatment: First steps in wastewater treatment; screens and sedimentation tanks are used to remove most materials that float or will settle. Primary treatment removes about 30 percent of carbonaceous biochemical oxygen demand from domestic sewage.

Principal Organic Hazardous Constituents (POHCs): Hazardous compounds monitored during an incinerator's trial burn, selected for high concentration in the waste feed and difficulty of combustion.

Prions: Microscopic particles made of protein that can cause disease.

Prior Appropriation: A doctrine of water law that allocates the rights to use water on a first-come, first-served basis.

Probability of Detection : The likelihood, expressed as a percentage, that a test method will correctly identify a leaking tank.

Process Variable: A physical or chemical quantity which is usually measured and controlled in the operation of a water treatment plant or industrial plant.

Process Verification: Verifying that process raw materials, water usage, waste treatment processes, production rate and other facts relative to quantity and quality of pollutants contained in discharges are substantially described in the permit application and the issued permit.

Process Wastewater: Any water that comes into contact with any raw material, product, byproduct, or waste.

Process Weight: Total weight of all materials, including fuel, used in a manufacturing process; used to calculate the allowable particulate emission rate.

Producers: Plants that perform photosynthesis and provide food to consumers.

Product Level: The level of a product in a storage tank.

Product Water: Water that has passed through a water treatment plant and is ready to be delivered to consumers.

Products of Incomplete Combustion (PICs): Organic compounds formed by combustion. Usually generated in small amounts and sometimes toxic, PICs are heat-altered versions of the original material fed into the incinerator (e.g. charcoal is a P.I.C. from burning wood).

Project XL: An EPA initiative to give states and the regulated community the flexibility to develop comprehensive strategies as alternatives to multiple current regulatory requirements in order to exceed compliance and increase overall environmental benefits.

Propellant: Liquid in a self-pressurized pesticide product that expels the active ingredient from its container.

Proportionate Mortality Ratio (PMR): The number of deaths from a specific cause in a specific period of time per 100 deaths from all causes in the same time period.

Proposed Plan: A plan for a site cleanup that is available to the public for comment.

Proteins: Complex nitrogenous organic compounds of high molecular weight made of amino acids; essential for growth and repair of animal tissue. Many, but not all, proteins are enzymes.

Protocol: A series of formal steps for conducting a test.

Protoplast: A membrane-bound cell from which the outer wall has been partially or completely removed. The term often is applied to plant cells.

Protozoa: One-celled animals that are larger and more complex than bacteria. May cause disease.

Public Comment Period: The time allowed for the public to express its views and concerns regarding an action by EPA (e.g. a Federal Register Notice of proposed rule-making, a public notice of a draft permit, or a Notice of Intent to Deny).

Public Health Approach: Regulatory and voluntary focus on effective and feasible risk management actions at the national and community level to reduce human exposures and risks, with priority given to reducing exposures with the biggest impacts in terms of the number affected and severity of effect.

Public Health Context: The incidence, prevalence, and severity of diseases in communities or populations and the factors that account for them, including infections, exposure to pollutants, and other exposures or activities.

Public Hearing: A formal meeting wherein EPA officials hear the public's views and concerns about an EPA action or proposal. EPA is required to consider such comments when evaluating its actions. Public hearings must be held upon request during the public comment period.

Public Notice: 1. Notification by EPA informing the public of Agency actions such as the issuance of a draft permit or scheduling of a hearing. EPA is required to ensure proper public notice, including publication in newspapers and broadcast over radio and television stations. 2. In the safe drinking water program, water suppliers are required to publish and broadcast notices when pollution problems are discovered.

Public Water System: A system that provides piped water for human consumption to at least 15 service connections or regularly serves 25 individuals.

Publicly Owned Treatment Works (POTWs): A waste-treatment works owned by a state, unit of local government, or Indian tribe, usually designed to treat domestic wastewaters.

Pumping Station: Mechanical device installed in sewer or water system or other liquid-carrying pipelines to move the liquids to a higher level.

Pumping Test: A test conducted to determine aquifer or well characteristics.

Purging: Removing stagnant air or water from sampling zone or equipment prior to sample collection.

Putrefaction: Biological decomposition of organic matter; associated with anaerobic conditions.

Putrescible: Able to rot quickly enough to cause odors and attract flies.

Pyrolysis: Decomposition of a chemical by extreme heat.

Q

Qualitative Use Assessment: Report summarizing the major uses of a pesticide including percentage of crop treated, and amount of pesticide used on a site.

Quality Assurance/Quality Control: A system of procedures, checks, audits, and corrective actions to ensure that all EPA research design and performance, environmental monitoring and sampling, and other technical and reporting activities are of the highest achievable quality.

Quench Tank: A water-filled tank used to cool incinerator residues or hot materials during industrial processes.

R

Radiation: Transmission of energy though space or any medium. Also known as radiant energy.

Radiation Standards: Regulations that set maximum exposure limits for protection of the public from radioactive materials.

Radio Frequency Radiation: (See non-ionizing electromagnetic radiation.)

Radioactive Decay: Spontaneous change in an atom by emission of of charged particles and/or gamma rays; also known as radioactive disintegration and radioactivity.

Radioactive Substances: Substances that emit ionizing radiation.

Radioactive Waste: Any waste that emits energy as rays, waves, streams or energetic particles. Radioactive materials are often mixed with hazardous waste, from nuclear reactors, research institutions, or hospitals.

Radioisotopes: Chemical variants of radioactive elements with potentially oncogenic, teratogenic, and mutagenic effects on the human body.

Radionuclide: Radioactive particle, man-made (anthropogenic) or natural, with a distinct atomic weight number. Can have a long life as soil or water pollutant.

Radius of Vulnerability Zone: The maximum distance from the point of release of a hazardous substance in which the airborne concentration could reach the level of concern under specified weather conditions.

Radius of Influence: 1. The radial distance from the center of a wellbore to the point where there is no lowering of the water table or potentiometric surface (the edge of the cone of depression); 2. the radial distance from an extraction well that has adequate air flow for effective removal of contaminants when a vacuum is applied to the extraction well.

Radon: A colorless naturally occurring, radioactive, inert gas formed by radioactive decay of radium atoms in soil or rocks.

Radon Daughters/Radon Progeny: Short-lived radioactive decay products of radon that decay into longer-lived lead isotopes that can attach themselves to airborne dust and other particles and, if inhaled, damage the linings of the lungs.

Radon Decay Products: A term used to refer collectively to the immediate products of the radon decay chain. These include Po-218, Pb-214, Bi-214, and Po-214, which have an average combined half-life of about 30 minutes.

Rainbow Report: Comprehensive document giving the status of all pesticides now or ever in registration or special reviews. Known as the "rainbow report" because chapters are printed on different colors of paper.

Rasp: A machine that grinds waste into a manageable material and helps prevent odor.

Raw Agricultural Commodity: An unprocessed human food or animal feed crop (e.g., raw carrots, apples, corn, or eggs.)

Raw Sewage: Untreated wastewater and its contents.

Raw Water: Intake water prior to any treatment or use.

Re-entry: (In indoor air program) Refers to air exhausted from a building that is immediately brought back into the system through the air intake and other openings.

Reactivity: Refers to those hazardous wastes that are normally unstable and readily undergo violent chemical change but do not explode.

Reaeration: Introduction of air into the lower layers of a reservoir. As the air bubbles form and rise through the water, the oxygen dissolves into the water and replenishes the dissolved oxygen. The rising bubbles also cause the lower waters to rise to the surface where they take on oxygen from the atmosphere.

Real-Time Monitoring: Monitoring and measuring environmental developments with technology and communications systems that provide time-relevant information to the public in an easily understood format people can use in day-to-day decision-making about their health and the environment.

Reasonable Further Progress: Annual incremental reductions in air pollutant emissions as reflected in a State Implementation Plan that EPA deems sufficient to provide for the attainment of the applicable national ambient air quality standards by the statutory deadline.

Reasonable Maximum Exposure: The maximum exposure reasonably expected to occur in a population.

Reasonable Worst Case: An estimate of the individual dose, exposure, or risk level received by an individual in a defined population that is greater than the 90th percentile but less than that received by anyone in the 98th percentile in the same population.

Reasonably Available Control Measures (RACM): A broadly defined term referring to technological and other measures for pollution control.

Reasonably Available Control Technology (RACT): Control technology that is reasonably available, and both technologically and economically feasible. Usually applied to existing sources in nonattainment areas; in most cases is less stringent than new source performance standards.

Recarbonization: Process in which carbon dioxide is bubbled into water being treated to lower the pH.

Receiving Waters: A river, lake, ocean, stream or other watercourse into which wastewater or treated effluent is discharged.

Receptor: Ecological entity exposed to a stressor.

Recharge: The process by which water is added to a zone of saturation, usually by percolation from the soil surface; e.g., the recharge of an aquifer.

Recharge Area: A land area in which water reaches the zone of saturation from surface infiltration, e.g., where rainwater soaks through the earth to reach an aquifer.

Recharge Rate: The quantity of water per unit of time that replenishes or refills an aquifer.

Reclamation: (In recycling) Restoration of materials found in the waste stream to a beneficial use which may be for purposes other than the original use.

Recombinant Bacteria: A microorganism whose genetic makeup has been altered by deliberate introduction of new genetic elements. The offspring of these altered bacteria also contain these new genetic elements; i.e. they "breed true."

Recombinant DNA: The new DNA that is formed by combining pieces of DNA from different organisms or cells.

Recommended Maximum Contaminant Level (RMCL): The maximum level of a contaminant in drinking water at which no known or anticipated adverse effect on human health would occur, and that includes an adequate margin of safety. Recommended levels are nonenforceable health goals. (See: maximum contaminant level.)

Reconstructed Source: Facility in which components are replaced to such an extent that the fixed capital cost of the new components exceeds 50 percent of the capital cost of constructing a comparable brand-new facility. New-source performance standards may be applied to sources reconstructed after the proposal of the standard if it is technologically and economically feasible to meet the standards.

Reconstruction of Dose: Estimating exposure after it has occurred by using evidence within an organism such as chemical levels in tissue or fluids.

Record of Decision (ROD): A public document that explains which cleanup alternative(s) will be used at National Priorities List sites where, under CERCLA, Trust Funds pay for the cleanup.

Recovery Rate: Percentage of usable recycled materials that have been removed from the total amount of municipal solid waste generated in a specific area or by a specific business.

Recycle/Reuse: Minimizing waste generation by recovering and reprocessing usable products that might otherwise become waste (.i.e. recycling of aluminum cans, paper, and bottles, etc.).

Recycling and Reuse Business Assistance Centers: Located in state solid-waste or economic-development agencies, these centers provide recycling businesses with customized and targeted assistance.

Recycling Economic Development Advocates: Individuals hired by state or tribal economic development offices to focus financial, marketing, and permitting resources on creating recycling businesses.

Recycling Mill: Facility where recovered materials are remanufactured into new products.

Recycling Technical Assistance Partnership National Network: A national information-sharing resource designed to help businesses and manufacturers increase their use of recovered materials.

Red Bag Waste: (See: infectious waste.)

Red Border: An EPA document undergoing review before being submitted for final management decision-making.

Red Tide: A proliferation of a marine plankton toxic and often fatal to fish, perhaps stimulated by the addition of nutrients. A tide can be red, green, or brown, depending on the coloration of the plankton.

Redemption Program: Program in which consumers are monetarily compensated for the collection of recyclable materials, generally through prepaid deposits or taxes on beverage containers. In some states or localities legislation has enacted redemption programs to help prevent roadside litter. (See: bottle bill.)

Reduction: The addition of hydrogen, removal of oxygen, or addition of electrons to an element or compound.

Reentry Interval: The period of time immediately following the application of a pesticide during which unprotected workers should not enter a field.

Reference Dose (RfD): The RfD is a numerical estimate of a daily oral exposure to the human population, including sensitive subgroups such as children, that is not likely to cause harmful effects during a lifetime. RfDs are generally used for health effects that are thought to have a threshold or low dose limit for producing effects.

Reformulated Gasoline: Gasoline with a different composition from conventional gasoline (e.g., lower aromatics content) that cuts air pollutants.

Refueling Emissions: Emissions released during vehicle re-fueling.

Refuse: (See: solid waste.)

Refuse Reclamation: Conversion of solid waste into useful products; e.g., composting organic wastes to make soil conditioners or separating aluminum and other metals for recycling.

Regeneration: Manipulation of cells to cause them to develop into whole plants.

Regional Response Team (RRT): Representatives of federal, local, and state agencies who may assist in coordination of activities at the request of the On-Scene Coordinator before and during a significant pollution incident such as an oil spill, major chemical release, or Superfund response.

Registrant: Any manufacturer or formulator who obtains registration for a pesticide active ingredient or product.

Registration: Formal listing with EPA of a new pesticide before it can be sold or distributed. Under the Federal Insecticide, Fungicide, and Rodenticide Act, EPA is responsible for registration (pre-market licensing) of pesticides on the basis of data demonstrating no unreasonable adverse effects on human health or the environment when applied according to approved label directions.

Registration Standards: Published documents which include summary reviews of the data available on a pesticide's active ingredient, data gaps, and the Agency's existing regulatory position on the pesticide.

Regulated Asbestos-Containing Material (RACM): Friable asbestos material or nonfriable ACM that will be or has been subjected to sanding, grinding, cutting, or abrading or has crumbled, or been pulverized or reduced to powder in the course of demolition or renovation operations.

Regulated Medical Waste: Under the Medical Waste Tracking Act of 1988, any solid waste generated in the diagnosis, treatment, or immunization of human beings or animals, in research pertaining thereto, or in the production or testing of biologicals. Included are cultures and stocks of infectious agents; human blood and blood products; human pathological body wastes from surgery and autopsy; contaminated animal carcasses from medical research; waste from patients with communicable diseases; and all used sharp implements, such as needles and scalpels, and certain unused sharps. (See: treated medical waste; untreated medical waste; destroyed medical waste.)

Relative Ecological Sustainability: Ability of an ecosystem to maintain relative ecological integrity indefinitely.

Relative Permeability: The permeability of a rock to gas, NAIL, or water, when any two or more are present.

Relative Risk Assessment: Estimating the risks associated with different stressors or management actions.

Release: Any spilling, leaking, pumping, pouring, emitting, emptying, discharging, injecting, escaping, leaching, dumping, or disposing into the environment of a hazardous or toxic chemical or extremely hazardous substance.

Remedial Action (RA): The actual construction or implementation phase of a Superfund site cleanup that follows remedial design.

Remedial Design: A phase of remedial action that follows the remedial investigation/feasibility study and includes development of engineering drawings and specifications for a site cleanup.

Remedial Investigation: An in-depth study designed to gather data needed to determine the nature and extent of contamination at a Superfund site; establish site cleanup criteria; identify preliminary alternatives for remedial action; and support technical and cost analyses of alternatives. The remedial investigation is usually done with the feasibility study. Together they are usually referred to as the "RI/FS".

Remedial Project Manager (RPM): The EPA or state official responsible for overseeing on-site remedial action.

Remedial Response: Long-term action that stops or substantially reduces a release or threat of a release of hazardous substances that is serious but not an immediate threat to public health.

Remediation: 1. Cleanup or other methods used to remove or contain a toxic spill or hazardous materials from a Superfund site; 2. for the Asbestos Hazard Emergency Response program, abatement methods including evaluation, repair, enclosure, encapsulation, or removal of greater than 3 linear feet or square feet of asbestos-containing materials from a building.

Remote Sensing: The collection and interpretation of information about an object without physical contact with the object; e.g., satellite imaging, aerial photography, and open path measurements.

Removal Action: Short-term immediate actions taken to address releases of hazardous substances that require expedited response. (See: cleanup.)

Renewable Energy Production Incentive (REPI): Incentive established by the Energy Policy Act available to renewable energy power projects owned by a state or local government or nonprofit electric cooperative.

Repeat Compliance Period: Any subsequent compliance period after the initial one.

Reportable Quantity (RQ): Quantity of a hazardous substance that triggers reports under CERCLA. If a substance exceeds its RQ, the release must be reported to the National Response Center, the SERC, and community emergency coordinators for areas likely to be affected.

Repowering: Rebuilding and replacing major components of a power plant instead of building a new one.

Representative Sample: A portion of material or water that is as nearly identical in content and consistency as possible to that in the larger body of material or water being sampled.

Reregistration: The reevaluation and relicensing of existing pesticides originally registered prior to current scientific and regulatory standards. EPA reregisters pesticides through its Registration Standards Program.

Reserve Capacity: Extra treatment capacity built into solid waste and wastewater treatment plants and interceptor sewers to accommodate flow increases due to future population growth.

Reservoir: Any natural or artificial holding area used to store, regulate, or control water.

Residential Use: Pesticide application in and around houses, office buildings, apartment buildings, motels, and other living or working areas.

Residential Waste: Waste generated in single and multi-family homes, including newspapers, clothing, disposable tableware, food packaging, cans, bottles, food scraps, and yard trimmings other than those that are diverted to backyard composting. (See: Household hazardous waste.)

Residual: Amount of a pollutant remaining in the environment after a natural or technological process has taken place; e.g., the sludge remaining after initial wastewater treatment, or particulates remaining in air after it passes through a scrubbing or other process.

Residual Risk: The extent of health risk from air pollutants remaining after application of the Maximum Achievable Control Technology (MACT).

Residual Saturation: Saturation level below which fluid drainage will not occur.

Residue: The dry solids remaining after the evaporation of a sample of water or sludge.

Resistance: For plants and animals, the ability to withstand poor environmental conditions or attacks by chemicals or disease. May be inborn or acquired.

Resource Recovery: The process of obtaining matter or energy from materials formerly discarded.

Response Action: 1. Generic term for actions taken in response to actual or potential health-threatening environmental events such as spills, sudden releases, and asbestos abatement/management problems. 2. A CERCLA-authorized action involving either a short-term removal action or a long-term removal response. This may include but is not limited to: removing hazardous materials from a site to an EPA-approved hazardous waste facility for treatment, containment or treating the waste on-site, identifying and removing the sources of ground-water contamination and halting further migration of contaminants. 3. Any of the following actions taken in school buildings in response to AHERA to reduce the risk of exposure to asbestos: removal, encapsulation, enclosure, repair, and operations and maintenance. (See: cleanup.)

Responsiveness Summary: A summary of oral and/or written public comments received by EPA during a comment period on key EPA documents, and EPA's response to those comments.

Restoration: Measures taken to return a site to pre-violation conditions.

Restricted Entry Interval: The time after a pesticide application during which entry into the treated area is restricted.

Restricted Use: A pesticide may be classified (under FIFRA regulations) for restricted use if it requires special handling because of its toxicity, and, if so, it may be applied only by trained, certified applicators or those under their direct supervision.

Restriction Enzymes: Enzymes that recognize specific regions of a long DNA molecule and cut it at those points.

Retrofit: Addition of a pollution control device on an existing facility without making major changes to the generating plant. Also called backfit.

Reuse: Using a product or component of municipal solid waste in its original form more than once; e.g., refilling a glass bottle that has been returned or using a coffee can to hold nuts and bolts.

Reverse Osmosis: A treatment process used in water systems by adding pressure to force water through a semi-permeable membrane. Reverse osmosis removes most drinking water contaminants. Also used in wastewater treatment. Large-scale reverse osmosis plants are being developed.

Reversible Effect: An effect which is not permanent; especially adverse effects which diminish when exposure to a toxic chemical stops.

Ribonucleic Acid (RNA): A molecule that carries the genetic message from DNA to a cellular protein-producing mechanism.

Rill: A small channel eroded into the soil by surface runoff; can be easily smoothed out or obliterated by normal tillage.

Ringlemann Chart: A series of shaded illustrations used to measure the opacity of air pollution emissions, ranging from light grey through black; used to set and enforce emissions standards.

Riparian Habitat: Areas adjacent to rivers and streams with a differing density, diversity, and productivity of plant and animal species relative to nearby uplands.

Riparian Rights: Entitlement of a land owner to certain uses of water on or bordering the property, including the right to prevent diversion or misuse of upstream waters. Generally a matter of state law.

Risk: A measure of the probability that damage to life, health, property, and/or the environment will occur as a result of a given hazard.

Risk (Adverse) for Endangered Species: Risk to aquatic species if anticipated pesticide residue levels equal one-fifth of LD10 or one-tenth of LC50; risk to terrestrial species if anticipated pesticide residue levels equal one-fifth of LC10 or one-tenth of LC50.

Risk Assessment: Qualitative and quantitative evaluation of the risk posed to human health and/or the environment by the actual or potential presence and/or use of specific pollutants.

Risk Characterization: The last phase of the risk assessment process that estimates the potential for adverse health or ecological effects to occur from exposure to a stressor and evaluates the uncertainty involved.

Risk Communication: The exchange of information about health or environmental risks among risk assessors and managers, the general public, news media, interest groups, etc.

Risk Estimate: A description of the probability that organisms exposed to a specific dose of a chemical or other pollutant will develop an adverse response, e.g., cancer.

Risk Factor: Characteristics (e.g., race, sex, age, obesity) or variables (e.g., smoking, occupational exposure level) associated with increased probability of a toxic effect.

Risk for Non-Endangered Species: Risk to species if anticipated pesticide residue levels are equal to or greater than LC50.

Risk Management: The process of evaluating and selecting alternative regulatory and non-regulatory responses to risk. The selection process necessarily requires the consideration of legal, economic, and behavioral factors.

Risk-based Targeting: The direction of resources to those areas that have been identified as having the highest potential or actual adverse effect on human health and/or the environment.

Risk-Specific Dose: The dose associated with a specified risk level.

River Basin: The land area drained by a river and its tributaries.

Rodenticide: A chemical or agent used to destroy rats or other rodent pests, or to prevent them from damaging food, crops, etc.

Rotary Kiln Incinerator: An incinerator with a rotating combustion chamber that keeps waste moving, thereby allowing it to vaporize for easier burning.

Rough Fish: Fish not prized for sport or eating, such as gar and suckers. Most are more tolerant of changing environmental conditions than are game or food species.

Route of Exposure: The avenue by which a chemical comes into contact with an organism, e.g., inhalation, ingestion, dermal contact, injection.

Rubbish: Solid waste, excluding food waste and ashes, from homes, institutions, and workplaces.

Run-Off: That part of precipitation, snow melt, or irrigation water that runs off the land into streams or other surface-water. It can carry pollutants from the air and land into receiving waters.

Running Losses: Evaporation of motor vehicle fuel from the fuel tank while the vehicle is in use.

S

Sacrifical Anode: An easily corroded material deliberately installed in a pipe or intake to give it up (sacrifice it) to corrosion while the rest of the water supply facility remains relatively corrosion-free.

Safe: Condition of exposure under which there is a practical certainty that no harm will result to exposed individuals.

Safe Water: Water that does not contain harmful bacteria, toxic materials, or chemicals, and is considered safe for drinking even if it may have taste, odor, color, and certain mineral problems.

Safe Yield: The annual amount of water that can be taken from a source of supply over a period of years without depleting that source beyond its ability to be replenished naturally in "wet years."

Safener: A chemical added to a pesticide to keep it from injuring plants.

Salinity: The percentage of salt in water.

Salt Water Intrusion: The invasion of fresh surface or ground water by salt water. If it comes from the ocean it may be called sea water intrusion.

Salts: Minerals that water picks up as it passes through the air, over and under the ground, or from households and industry.

Salvage: The utilization of waste materials.

Sampling Frequency: The interval between the collection of successive samples.

Sanctions: Actions taken by the federal government for failure to provide or implement a State Implementation Plan (SIP). Such action may include withholding of highway funds and a ban on construction of new sources of potential pollution.

Sand Filters: Devices that remove some suspended solids from sewage. Air and bacteria decompose additional wastes filtering through the sand so that cleaner water drains from the bed.

Sanitary Landfill: (See: landfills.)

Sanitary Sewers: Underground pipes that carry off only domestic or industrial waste, not storm water.

Sanitary Survey: An on-site review of the water sources, facilities, equipment, operation and maintenance of a public water system to evaluate the adequacy of those elements for producing and distributing safe drinking water.

Sanitary Water (Also known as gray water): Water discharged from sinks, showers, kitchens, or other non-industrial operations, but not from commodes.

Sanitation: Control of physical factors in the human environment that could harm development, health, or survival.

Saprolite: A soft, clay-rich, thoroughly decomposed rock formed in place by chemical weathering of igneous or metamorphic rock. Forms in humid, tropical, or subtropical climates.

Saprophytes: Organisms living on dead or decaying organic matter that help natural decomposition of organic matter in water.

Saturated Zone: The area below the water table where all open spaces are filled with water under pressure equal to or greater than that of the atmosphere.

Saturation: The condition of a liquid when it has taken into solution the maximum possible quantity of a given substance at a given temperature and pressure.

Science Advisory Board (SAB): A group of external scientists who advise EPA on science and policy.

Scrap: Materials discarded from manufacturing operations that may be suitable for reprocessing.

Scrap Metal Processor: Intermediate operating facility where recovered metal is sorted, cleaned of contaminants, and prepared for recycling.

Screening: Use of screens to remove coarse floating and suspended solids from sewage.

Screening Risk Assessment: A risk assessment performed with few data and many assumptions to identify exposures that should be evaluated more carefully for potential risk.

Scrubber: An air pollution device that uses a spray of water or reactant or a dry process to trap pollutants in emissions.

Secondary Drinking Water Regulations: Non-enforceable regulations applying to public water systems and specifying the maximum contamination levels that, in the judgment of EPA, are required to protect the public welfare. These regulations apply to any contaminants that may adversely affect the odor or appearance of such water and consequently may cause people served by the system to discontinue its use.

Secondary Effect: Action of a stressor on supporting components of the ecosystem, which in turn impact the ecological component of concern. (See: primary effect.)

Secondary Materials: Materials that have been manufactured and used at least once and are to be used again.

Secondary Standards: National ambient air quality standards designed to protect welfare, including effects on soils, water, crops, vegetation, man-made (anthropogenic) materials, animals, wildlife, weather, visibility, and climate; damage to property; transportation hazards; economic values, and personal comfort and well-being.

Secondary Treatment: The second step in most publicly owned waste treatment systems in which bacteria consume the organic parts of the waste. It is accomplished by bringing together waste, bacteria, and oxygen in trickling filters or in the activated sludge process. This treatment removes floating and settleable solids and about 90 percent of the oxygen-demanding substances and suspended solids. Disinfection is the final stage of secondary treatment. (See: primary, tertiary treatment.)

Secure Chemical Landfill: (See:landfills.)

Secure Maximum Contaminant Level: Maximum permissible level of a contaminant in water delivered to the free flowing outlet of the ultimate user, or of contamination resulting from corrosion of piping and plumbing caused by water quality.

Glossary of Environmental Terms

Sediment: Topsoil, sand, and minerals washed from the land into water, usually after rain or snow melt.

Sediment Yield: The quantity of sediment arriving at a specific location.

Sedimentation: Letting solids settle out of wastewater by gravity during treatment.

Sedimentation Tanks: Wastewater tanks in which floating wastes are skimmed off and settled solids are removed for disposal.

Sediments: Soil, sand, and minerals washed from land into water, usually after rain. They pile up in reservoirs, rivers and harbors, destroying fish and wildlife habitat, and clouding the water so that sunlight cannot reach aquatic plants. Careless farming, mining, and building activities will expose sediment materials, allowing them to wash off the land after rainfall.

Seed Protectant: A chemical applied before planting to protect seeds and seedlings from disease or insects.

Seepage: Percolation of water through the soil from unlined canals, ditches, laterals, watercourses, or water storage facilities.

Selective Pesticide: A chemical designed to affect only certain types of pests, leaving other plants and animals unharmed.

Semi-Confined Aquifer: An aquifer partially confined by soil layers of low permeability through which recharge and discharge can still occur.

Semivolatile Organic Compounds: Organic compounds that volatilize slowly at standard temperature (20 degrees C and 1 atm pressure).

Senescence: The aging process. Sometimes used to describe lakes or other bodies of water in advanced stages of eutrophication. Also used to describe plants and animals.

Septic System: An on-site system designed to treat and dispose of domestic sewage. A typical septic system consists of tank that receives waste from a residence or business and a system of tile lines or a pit for disposal of the liquid effluent (sludge) that remains after decomposition of the solids by bacteria in the tank and must be pumped out periodically.

Septic Tank: An underground storage tank for wastes from homes not connected to a sewer line. Waste goes directly from the home to the tank. (See: septic system.)

Service Connector: The pipe that carries tap water from a public water main to a building.

Service Line Sample: A one-liter sample of water that has been standing for at least 6 hours in a service pipeline and is collected according to federal regulations.

Service Pipe: The pipeline extending from the water main to the building served or to the consumer's system.

Set-Back: Setting a thermometer to a lower temperature when the building is unoccupied to reduce consumption of heating energy. Also refers to setting the thermometer to a higher temperature during unoccupied periods in the cooling season.

Settleable Solids: Material heavy enough to sink to the bottom of a wastewater treatment tank.

Settling Chamber: A series of screens placed in the way of flue gases to slow the stream of air, thus helping gravity to pull particles into a collection device.

Settling Tank: A holding area for wastewater, where heavier particles sink to the bottom for removal and disposal.

7Q10: Seven-day, consecutive low flow with a ten year return frequency; the lowest stream flow for seven consecutive days that would be expected to occur once in ten years.

Sewage: The waste and wastewater produced by residential and commercial sources and discharged into sewers.

Sewage Lagoon: (See: lagoon.)

Sewage Sludge: Sludge produced at a Publicly Owned Treatment Works, the disposal of which is regulated under the Clean Water Act.

Sewer: A channel or conduit that carries wastewater and storm-water runoff from the source to a treatment plant or receiving stream. "Sanitary" sewers carry household, industrial, and commercial waste. "Storm" sewers carry runoff from rain or snow. "Combined" sewers handle both.

Sewerage: The entire system of sewage collection, treatment, and disposal.

Shading Coefficient: The amount of the sun's heat transmitted through a given window compared with that of a standard 1/8- inch-thick single pane of glass under the same conditions.

Sharps: Hypodermic needles, syringes (with or without the attached needle), Pasteur pipettes, scalpel blades, blood vials, needles with attached tubing, and culture dishes used in animal or human patient care or treatment, or in medical, research or industrial laboratories. Also included are other types of broken or unbroken glassware that were in contact with infectious agents, such as used slides and cover slips, and unused hypodermic and suture needles, syringes, and scalpel blades.

Shock Load: The arrival at a water treatment plant of raw water containing unusual amounts of algae, colloidal matter. color, suspended solids, turbidity, or other pollutants.

Short-Circuiting: When some of the water in tanks or basins flows faster than the rest; may result in shorter contact, reaction, or settling times than calculated or presumed.

Sick Building Syndrome: Building whose occupants experience acute health and/or comfort effects that appear to be linked to time spent therein, but where no specific illness or cause can be identified. Complaints may be localized in a particular room or zone, or may spread throughout the building. (See: building-related illness.)

Signal: The volume or product-level change produced by a leak in a tank.

Signal Words: The words used on a pesticide label—Danger, Warning, Caution—to indicate level of toxicity.

Significant Deterioration: Pollution resulting from a new source in previously "clean" areas. (See: prevention of significant deterioration.)

Significant Municipal Facilities: Those publicly owned sewage treatment plants that discharge a million gallons per day or more and are therefore considered by states to have the potential to substantially affect the quality of receiving waters.

Significant Non-Compliance: (See significant violations.)

Significant Potential Source of Contamination: A facility or activity that stores, uses, or produces compounds with potential for significant contaminating impact if released into the source water of a public water supply.

Significant Violations: Violations by point source dischargers of sufficient magnitude or duration to be a regulatory priority.

Silt: Sedimentary materials composed of fine or intermediate-sized mineral particles.

Silviculture: Management of forest land for timber.

Single-Breath Canister: Small one-liter canister designed to capture a single breath. Used in air pollutant ingestion research.

Sink: Place in the environment where a compound or material collects.

Sinking: Controlling oil spills by using an agent to trap the oil and sink it to the bottom of the body of water where the agent and the oil are biodegraded.

SIP Call: EPA action requiring a state to resubmit all or part of its State Implementation Plan to demonstrate attainment of the require national ambient air quality standards within the statutory deadline. A SIP Revision is a revision of a SIP altered at the request of EPA or on a state's initiative. (See: State Implementation Plan.)

Site: An area or place within the jurisdiction of the EPA and/or a state.

Site Assessment Program: A means of evaluating hazardous waste sites through preliminary assessments and site inspections to develop a Hazard Ranking System score.

Site Inspection: The collection of information from a Superfund site to determine the extent and severity of hazards posed by the site. It follows and is more extensive than a preliminary assessment. The purpose is to gather information necessary to score the site, using the Hazard Ranking System, and to determine if it presents an immediate threat requiring prompt removal.

Site Safety Plan: A crucial element in all removal actions, it includes information on equipment being used, precautions to be taken, and steps to take in the event of an on-site emergency.

Siting: The process of choosing a location for a facility.

Skimming: Using a machine to remove oil or scum from the surface of the water.

Slow Sand Filtration: Passage of raw water through a bed of sand at low velocity, resulting in substantial removal of chemical and biological contaminants.

Sludge: A semi-solid residue from any of a number of air or water treatment processes; can be a hazardous waste.

Sludge Digester: Tank in which complex organic substances like sewage sludges are biologically dredged. During these reactions, energy is released and much of the sewage is converted to methane, carbon dioxide, and water.

Slurry: A watery mixture of insoluble matter resulting from some pollution control techniques.

Small Quantity Generator (SQG-sometimes referred to as "Squeegee"): Persons or enterprises that produce 220-2200 pounds per month of hazardous waste; they are required to keep more records than conditionally exempt generators. The largest category of hazardous waste generators, SQGs, include automotive shops, dry cleaners, photographic developers, and many other small businesses. (See: conditionally exempt generators.)

Smelter: A facility that melts or fuses ore, often with an accompanying chemical change, to separate its metal content. Emissions cause pollution. "Smelting" is the process involved.

Smog: Air pollution typically associated with oxidants. (See: photochemical smog.)

Smoke: Particles suspended in air after incomplete combustion.

Soft Detergents: Cleaning agents that break down in nature.

Soft Water: Any water that does not contain a significant amount of dissolved minerals such as salts of calcium or magnesium.

Soil Adsorption Field: A sub-surface area containing a trench or bed with clean stones and a system of piping through which treated sewage may seep into the surrounding soil for further treatment and disposal.

Soil and Water Conservation Practices: Control measures consisting of managerial, vegetative, and structural practices to reduce the loss of soil and water.

Soil Conditioner: An organic material like humus or compost that helps soil absorb water, build a bacterial community, and take up mineral nutrients.

Soil Erodibility: An indicator of a soil's susceptibility to raindrop impact, runoff, and other erosive processes.

Soil Gas: Gaseous elements and compounds in the small spaces between particles of the earth and soil. Such gases can be moved or driven out under pressure.

Soil Moisture: The water contained in the pore space of the unsaturated zone.

Soil Sterilant: A chemical that temporarily or permanently prevents the growth of all plants and animals,

Solder: Metallic compound used to seal joints between pipes. Until recently, most solder contained 50 percent lead. Use of solder containing more than 0.2 percent lead in pipes carrying drinking water is now prohibited.

Sole-Source Aquifer: An aquifer that supplies 50-percent or more of the drinking water of an area.

Solid Waste: Non-liquid, non-soluble materials ranging from municipal garbage to industrial wastes that contain complex and sometimes hazardous substances. Solid wastes also include sewage sludge, agricultural refuse, demolition wastes, and mining residues. Technically, solid waste also refers to liquids and gases in containers.

Solid Waste Disposal: The final placement of refuse that is not salvaged or recycled.

Solid Waste Management: Supervised handling of waste materials from their source through recovery processes to disposal.

Solidification and Stabilization: Removal of wastewater from a waste or changing it chemically to make it less permeable and susceptible to transport by water.

Solubility: The amount of mass of a compound that will dissolve in a unit volume of solution. Aqueous Solubility is the maximum concentration of a chemical that will dissolve in pure water at a reference temperature.

Soot: Carbon dust formed by incomplete combustion.

Sorption: The action of soaking up or attracting substances; process used in many pollution control systems.

Source Area: The location of liquid hydrocarbons or the zone of highest soil or groundwater concentrations, or both, of the chemical of concern.

Source Characterization Measurements: Measurements made to estimate the rate of release of pollutants into the environment from a source such as an incinerator, landfill, etc.

Source Reduction: Reducing the amount of materials entering the waste stream from a specific source by redesigning products or patterns of production or consumption (e.g., using returnable beverage containers). Synonymous with waste reduction.

Source Separation: Segregating various wastes at the point of generation (e.g., separation of paper, metal and glass from other wastes to make recycling simpler and more efficient).

Source-Water Protection Area: The area delineated by a state for a Public Water Supply or including numerous such suppliers, whether the source is ground water or surface water or both.

Sparge or Sparging: Injection of air below the water table to strip dissolved volatile organic compounds and/or oxygenate ground water to facilitate aerobic biodegradation of organic compounds.

Special Local-Needs Registration: Registration of a pesticide product by a state agency for a specific use that is not federally registered. However, the active ingredient must be federally registered for other uses. The special use is specific to that state and is often minor, thus may not warrant the additional cost of a full federal registration process. SLN registration cannot be issued for new active ingredients, food-use active ingredients without tolerances, or for a canceled registration. The products cannot be shipped across state lines.

Special Review: Formerly known as Rebuttable Presumption Against Registration (RPAR), this is the regulatory process through which existing pesticides suspected of posing unreasonable risks to human health, non-target organisms, or the environment are referred for review by EPA. Such review requires an intensive risk/benefit analysis with opportunity for public comment. If risk is found to outweigh social and economic benefits, regulatory actions can be initiated, ranging from label revisions and use-restriction to cancellation or suspended registration.

Special Waste: Items such as household hazardous waste, bulky wastes (refrigerators, pieces of furniture, etc.) tires, and used oil.

Species: 1. A reproductively isolated aggregate of interbreeding organisms having common attributes and usually designated by a common name.2. An organism belonging to belonging to such a category.

Specific Conductance: Rapid method of estimating the dissolved solid content of a water supply by testing its capacity to carry an electrical current.

Specific Yield: The amount of water a unit volume of saturated permeable rock will yield when drained by gravity.

Spill Prevention, Containment, and Countermeasures Plan (SPCP): Plan covering the release of hazardous substances as defined in the Clean Water Act.

Spoil: Dirt or rock removed from its original location—destroying the composition of the soil in the process—as in strip-mining, dredging, or construction.

Sprawl: Unplanned development of open land.

Spray Tower Scrubber: A device that sprays alkaline water into a chamber where acid gases are present to aid in neutralizing the gas.

Spring: Ground water seeping out of the earth where the water table intersects the ground surface.

Spring Melt/Thaw: The process whereby warm temperatures melt winter snow and ice. Because various forms of acid deposition may have been stored in the frozen water, the melt can result in abnormally large amounts of acidity entering streams and rivers, sometimes causing fish kills.

Stabilization: Conversion of the active organic matter in sludge into inert, harmless material.

Stabilization Ponds: (See: lagoon.)

Stable Air: A motionless mass of air that holds, instead of dispersing, pollutants.

Stack: A chimney, smokestack, or vertical pipe that discharges used air.

Stack Effect: Air, as in a chimney, that moves upward because it is warmer than the ambient atmosphere.

Stack Effect: Flow of air resulting from warm air rising, creating a positive pressure area at the top of a building and negative pressure area at the bottom. This effect can overpower the mechanical system and disrupt building ventilation and air circulation.

Stack Gas: (See: flue gas.)

Stage II Controls: Systems placed on service station gasoline pumps to control and capture gasoline vapors during refuelling.

Stagnation: Lack of motion in a mass of air or water that holds pollutants in place.

Stakeholder: Any organization, governmental entity, or individual that has a stake in or may be impacted by a given approach to environmental regulation, pollution prevention, energy conservation, etc.

Standard Industrial Classification Code: Also known as SIC Codes, a method of grouping industries with similar products or services and assigning codes to these groups.

Standard Sample: The part of finished drinking water that is examined for the presence of coliform bacteria.

Standards: Norms that impose limits on the amount of pollutants or emissions produced. EPA establishes minimum standards, but states are allowed to be stricter.

Start of a Response Action: The point in time when there is a guarantee or set-aside of funding by EPA, other federal agencies, states or Principal Responsible Parties in order to begin response actions at a Superfund site.

State Emergency Response Commission (SERC): Commission appointed by each state governor according to the requirements of SARA Title III. The SERCs designate emergency planning districts, appoint local emergency planning committees, and supervise and coordinate their activities.

State Environmental Goals and Indication Project: Program to assist state environmental agencies by providing technical and financial assistance in the development of environmental goals and indicators.

State Implementation Plans (SIP): EPA approved state plans for the establishment, regulation, and enforcement of air pollution standards.

State Management Plan: Under FIFRA, a state management plan required by EPA to allow states, tribes, and U.S. territories the flexibility to design and implement ways to protect ground water from the use of certain pesticides.

Static Water Depth: The vertical distance from the centerline of the pump discharge down to the surface level of the free pool while no water is being drawn from the pool or water table.

Static Water Level: 1. Elevation or level of the water table in a well when the pump is not operating. 2. The level or elevation to which water would rise in a tube connected to an artesian aquifer or basin in a conduit under pressure.

Stationary Source: A fixed-site producer of pollution, mainly power plants and other facilities using industrial combustion processes. (See: point source.)

Sterilization: The removal or destruction of all microorganisms, including pathogenic and other bacteria, vegetative forms, and spores.

Sterilizer: One of three groups of anti-microbials registered by EPA for public health uses. EPA considers an antimicrobial to be a sterilizer when it destroys or eliminates all forms of bacteria, viruses, and fungi and their spores. Because spores are considered the most difficult form of microorganism to destroy, EPA considers the term sporicide to be synonymous with sterilizer.

Storage: Temporary holding of waste pending treatment or disposal, as in containers, tanks, waste piles, and surface impoundments.

Storm Sewer: A system of pipes (separate from sanitary sewers) that carries water runoff from buildings and land surfaces.

Stratification: Separating into layers.

Stratigraphy: Study of the formation, composition, and sequence of sediments, whether consolidated or not.

Stratosphere: The portion of the atmosphere 10-to-25 miles above the earth's surface.

Stressors: Physical, chemical, or biological entities that can induce adverse effects on ecosystems or human health.

Strip-Cropping: Growing crops in a systematic arrangement of strips or bands that serve as barriers to wind and water erosion.

Strip-Mining: A process that uses machines to scrape soil or rock away from mineral deposits just under the earth's surface.

Structural Deformation: Distortion in walls of a tank after liquid has been added or removed.

Subchronic: Of intermediate duration, usually used to describe studies or periods of exposure lasting between 5 and 90 days.

Subchronic Exposure: Multiple or continuous exposures lasting for approximately ten percent of an experimental species lifetime, usually over a three-month period.

Submerged Aquatic Vegetation: Vegetation that lives at or below the water surface; an important habitat for young fish and other aquatic organisms.

Subwatershed: Topographic perimeter of the catchment area of a stream tributary.

Sulfur Dioxide (SO_2): A pungent, colorless, gasformed primarily by the combustion of fossil fuels; becomes a pollutant when present in large amounts.

Sump: A pit or tank that catches liquid runoff for drainage or disposal.

Superchlorination: Chlorination with doses that are deliberately selected to produce water free of combined residuals so large as to require dechlorination.

Supercritical Water: A type of thermal treatment using moderate temperatures and high pressures to enhance the ability of water to break down large organic molecules into smaller, less toxic ones. Oxygen injected during this process combines with simple organic compounds to form carbon dioxide and water.

Superfund: The program operated under the legislative authority of CERCLA and SARA that funds and carries out EPA solid waste emergency and long-term removal and remedial activities. These activities include establishing the National Priorities List, investigating sites for inclusion on the list, determining their priority, and conducting and/or supervising cleanup and other remedial actions.

Superfund Innovative Technology Evaluation (SITE) Program: EPA program to promote development and use of innovative treatment and site characterization technologies in Superfund site cleanups.

Supplemental Registration: An arrangement whereby a registrant licenses another company to market its pesticide product under the second company's registration.

Supplier of Water: Any person who owns or operates a public water supply.

Surface Impoundment: Treatment, storage, or disposal of liquid hazardous wastes in ponds.

Surface Runoff: Precipitation, snow melt, or irrigation water in excess of what can infiltrate the soil surface and be stored in small surface depressions; a major transporter of non-point source pollutants in rivers, streams, and lakes..

Surface Uranium Mines: Strip mining operations for removal of uranium-bearing ore.

Surface Water: All water naturally open to the atmosphere (rivers, lakes, reservoirs, ponds, streams, impoundments, seas, estuaries, etc.)

Surface-Water Treatment Rule: Rule that specifies maximum contaminant level goals for Giardia lamblia, viruses, and Legionella and promulgates filtration and disinfection requirements for public water systems using surface-water or ground-water sources under the direct influence of surface water. The regulations also specify water quality, treatment, and watershed protection criteria under which filtration may be avoided.

Surfacing ACM: Asbestos-containing material that is sprayed or troweled on or otherwise applied to surfaces, such as acoustical plaster on ceilings and fireproofing materials on structural members.

Surfacing Material: Material sprayed or troweled onto structural members (beams, columns, or decking) for fire protection; or on ceilings or walls for fireproofing, acoustical or decorative purposes. Includes textured plaster, and other textured wall and ceiling surfaces.

Surfactant: A detergent compound that promotes lathering.

Surrogate Data: Data from studies of test organisms or a test substance that are used to estimate the characteristics or effects on another organism or substance.

Surveillance System: A series of monitoring devices designed to check on environmental conditions.

Susceptibility Analysis: An analysis to determine whether a Public Water Supply is subject to significant pollution from known potential sources.

Suspect Material: Building material suspected of containing asbestos; e.g., surfacing material, floor tile, ceiling tile, thermal system insulation.

Suspended Loads: Specific sediment particles maintained in the water column by turbulence and carried with the flow of water.

Suspended Solids: Small particles of solid pollutants that float on the surface of, or are suspended in, sewage or other liquids. They resist removal by conventional means.

Suspension: Suspending the use of a pesticide when EPA deems it necessary to prevent an imminent hazard resulting from its continued use. An emergency suspension takes effect immediately; under an ordinary suspension a registrant can request a hearing before the suspension goes into effect. Such a hearing process might take six months.

Suspension Culture: Cells growing in a liquid nutrient medium.

Swamp: A type of wetland dominated by woody vegetation but without appreciable peat deposits. Swamps may be fresh or salt water and tidal or non-tidal. (See: wetlands.)

Synergism: An interaction of two or more chemicals that results in an effect greater than the sum of their separate effects.

Synthetic Organic Chemicals (SOCs): Man-made (anthropogenic) organic chemicals. Some SOCs are volatile; others tend to stay dissolved in water instead of evaporating.

System With a Single Service Connection: A system that supplies drinking water to consumers via a single service line.

Systemic Pesticide: A chemical absorbed by an organism that interacts with the organism and makes the organism toxic to pests.

T

Tail Water: The runoff of irrigation water from the lower end of an irrigated field.

Tailings: Residue of raw material or waste separated out during the processing of crops or mineral ores.

Tailpipe Standards: Emissions limitations applicable to mobile source engine exhausts.

Tampering: Adjusting, negating, or removing pollution control equipment on a motor vehicle.

Technical Assistance Grant (TAG): As part of the Superfund program, Technical Assistance Grants of up to $50,000 are provided to citizens' groups to obtain assistance in interpreting information related to clean-ups at Superfund sites or those proposed for the National Priorities List. Grants are used by such groups to hire technical advisors to help them understand the site-related technical information for the duration of response activities.

Technical-Grade Active Ingredient (TGA): A pesticide chemical in pure form as it is manufactured prior to being formulated into an end-use product (e.g. wettable powders, granules, emulsifiable concentrates). Registered manufactured products composed of such chemicals are known as Technical Grade Products.

Technology-Based Limitations: Industry-specific effluent limitations based on best available preventive technology applied to a discharge when it will not cause a violation of water quality standards at low stream flows. Usually applied to discharges into large rivers.

Technology-Based Standards: Industry-specific effluent limitations applicable to direct and indirect sources which are developed on a category-by-category basis using statutory factors, not including water-quality effects.

Teratogen: A substance capable of causing birth defects.

Teratogenesis: The introduction of nonhereditary birth defects in a developing fetus by exogenous factors such as physical or chemical agents acting in the womb to interfere with normal embryonic development.

Terracing: Dikes built along the contour of sloping farm land that hold runoff and sediment to reduce erosion.

Tertiary Treatment: Advanced cleaning of wastewater that goes beyond the secondary or biological stage, removing nutrients such as phosphorus, nitrogen, and most BOD and suspended solids.

Theoretical Maximum Residue Contribution: The theoretical maximum amount of a pesticide in the daily diet of an average person. It assumes that the diet is composed of all food items for which there are tolerance-level residues of the pesticide. The TMRC is expressed as milligrams of pesticide/kilograms of body weight/day.

Therapeutic Index: The ratio of the dose required to produce toxic or lethal effects to the dose required to produce nonadverse or therapeutic response.

Thermal Pollution: Discharge of heated water from industrial processes that can kill or injure aquatic organisms.

Thermal Stratification: The formation of layers of different temperatures in a lake or reservoir.

Thermal System Insulation (TSI): Asbestos-containing material applied to pipes, fittings, boilers, breeching, tanks, ducts, or other interior structural components to prevent heat loss or gain or water condensation.

Thermal Treatment: Use of elevated temperatures to treat hazardous wastes. (See: incineration; pyrolysis.)

Thermocline: The middle layer of a thermally stratified lake or reservoir. In this layer, there is a rapid decrease in temperatures in a lake or reservoir.

Threshold: The lowest dose of a chemical at which a specified measurable effect is observed and below which it is not observed.

Threshold: The dose or exposure level below which a significant adverse effect is not expected.

Threshold Level: Time-weighted average pollutant concentration values, exposure beyond which is likely to adversely affect human health. (See: environmental exposure)

Threshold Limit Value (TLV): The concentration of an airborne substance to which an average person can be repeatedly exposed without adverse effects. TLVs may be expressed in three ways: (1) TLV-TWA—Time weighted average, based on an allowable exposure averaged over a normal 8-hour workday or 40-hour work- week; (2) TLV-STEL—Short-term exposure limit or maximum concentration for a brief specified period of time, depending on a specific chemical (TWA must still be met); and (3) TLV-C—Ceiling Exposure Limit or maximum exposure concentration not to be exceeded under any circumstances. (TWA must still be met.)

Threshold Odor: (See: Odor threshold)

Threshold Planning Quantity: A quantity designated for each chemical on the list of extremely hazardous substances that triggers notification by facilities to the State Emergency Response Commission that such facilities are subject to emergency planning requirements under SARA Title III.

Thropic Levels: A functional classification of species that is based on feeding relationships (e.g. generally aquatic and terrestrial green plants comprise the first thropic level, and herbivores comprise the second.)

Tidal Marsh: Low, flat marshlands traversed by channels and tidal hollows, subject to tidal inundation; normally, the only vegetation present is salt-tolerant bushes and grasses. (See: wetlands.)

Tillage: Plowing, seedbed preparation, and cultivation practices.

Time-weighted Average (TWA): In air sampling, the average air concentration of contaminants during a given period.

Tire Processor: Intermediate operating facility where recovered tires are processed in preparation for recycling.

Tires: As used in recycling, passenger car and truck tires (excludes airplane, bus, motorcycle and special service military, agricultural, off-the-road and-slow speed industrial tires). Car and truck tires are recycled into rubber products such as trash cans, storage containers, rubberized asphalt or used whole for playground and reef construction.

Tolerance Petition: A formal request to establish a new tolerance or modify an existing one.

Tolerances: Permissible residue levels for pesticides in raw agricultural produce and processed foods. Whenever a pesticide is registered for use on a food or a feed crop, a tolerance (or exemption from the tolerance requirement) must be established. EPA establishes the tolerance levels, which are enforced by the Food and Drug Administration and the Department of Agriculture.

Tonnage: The amount of waste that a landfill accepts, usually expressed in tons per month. The rate at which a landfill accepts waste is limited by the landfill's permit.

Topography: The physical features of a surface area including relative elevations and the position of natural and man-made (anthropogenic) features.

Total Dissolved Phosphorous: The total phosphorous content of all material that will pass through a filter, which is determined as orthophosphate without prior digestion or hydrolysis. Also called soluble P. or ortho P.

Total Dissolved Solids (TDS): All material that passes the standard glass river filter; now called total filtrable residue. Term is used to reflect salinity.

Total Petroleum Hydrocarbons (TPH): Measure of the concentration or mass of petroleum hydrocarbon constituents present in a given amount of soil or water. The word "total" is a misnomer—few, if any, of the procedures for quantifying hydrocarbons can measure all of them in a given sample. Volatile ones are usually lost in the process and not quantified and non-petroleum hydrocarbons sometimes appear in the analysis.

Total Recovered Petroleum Hydrocarbon: A method for measuring petroleum hydrocarbons in samples of soil or water.

Total Suspended Particles (TSP): A method of monitoring airborne particulate matter by total weight.

Total Suspended Solids (TSS): A measure of the suspended solids in wastewater, effluent, or water bodies, determined by tests for "total suspended non-filterable solids." (See: suspended solids.)

Toxaphene: Chemical that causes adverse health effects in domestic water supplies and is toxic to fresh water and marine aquatic life.

Toxic Chemical: Any chemical listed in EPA rules as "Toxic Chemicals Subject to Section 313 of the Emergency Planning and Community Right-to-Know Act of 1986."

Toxic Chemical Release Form: Information form required of facilities that manufacture, process, or use (in quantities above a specific amount) chemicals listed under SARA Title III.

Toxic Chemical Use Substitution: Replacing toxic chemicals with less harmful chemicals in industrial processes.

Toxic Cloud: Airborne plume of gases, vapors, fumes, or aerosols containing toxic materials.

Toxic Concentration: The concentration at which a substance produces a toxic effect.

Toxic Dose: The dose level at which a substance produces a toxic effect.

Toxic Pollutants: Materials that cause death, disease, or birth defects in organisms that ingest or absorb them. The quantities and exposures necessary to cause these effects can vary widely.

Toxic Release Inventory: Database of toxic releases in the United States compiled from SARA Title III Section 313 reports.

Toxic Substance: A chemical or mixture that may present an unreasonable risk of injury to health or the environment.

Toxic Waste: A waste that can produce injury if inhaled, swallowed, or absorbed through the skin.

Toxicant: A harmful substance or agent that may injure an exposed organism.

Toxicity: The degree to which a substance or mixture of substances can harm humans or animals. Acute toxicity involves harmful effects in an organism through a single or short-term exposure. Chronic toxicity is the ability of a substance or mixture of substances to cause harmful effects over an extended period, usually upon repeated or continuous exposure sometimes lasting for the entire life of the exposed organism. Subchronic toxicity is the ability of the substance to cause effects for more than one year but less than the lifetime of the exposed organism.

Toxicity Assessment: Characterization of the toxicological properties and effects of a chemical, with special emphasis on establishment of dose-response characteristics.

Toxicity Testing: Biological testing (usually with an invertebrate, fish, or small mammal) to determine the adverse effects of a compound or effluent.

Toxicological Profile: An examination, summary, and interpretation of a hazardous substance to determine levels of exposure and associated health effects.

Transboundary Pollutants: Air pollution that travels from one jurisdiction to another, often crossing state or international boundaries. Also applies to water pollution.

Transfer Station: Facility where solid waste is transferred from collection vehicles to larger trucks or rail cars for longer distance transport.

Transient Water System: A non-community water system that does not serve 25 of the same nonresidents per day for more than six months per year.

Transmission Lines: Pipelines that transport raw water from its source to a water treatment plant, then to the distribution grid system.

Transmissivity: The ability of an aquifer to transmit water.

Transpiration: The process by which water vapor is lost to the atmosphere from living plants. The term can also be applied to the quantity of water thus dissipated.

Transportation Control Measures (TCMs): Steps taken by a locality to reduce vehicular emission and improve air quality by reducing or changing the flow of traffic; e.g. bus and HOV lanes, carpooling and other forms of ride-shairing, public transit, bicycle lanes.

Transporter: Hauling firm that picks up properly packaged and labeled hazardous waste from generators and transports it to designated facilities for treatment, storage, or disposal. Transporters are subject to EPA and DOT hazardous waste regulations.

Trash: Material considered worthless or offensive that is thrown away. Generally defined as dry waste material, but in common usage it is a synonym for garbage, rubbish, or refuse.

Trash-to-Energy Plan: Burning trash to produce energy.

Treatability Studies: Tests of potential cleanup technologies conducted in a laboratory (See: bench-scale tests.)

Treated Regulated Medical Waste: Medical waste treated to substantially reduce or eliminate its pathogenicity, but that has not yet been destroyed.

Treated Wastewater: Wastewater that has been subjected to one or more physical, chemical, and biological processes to reduce its potential of being health hazard.

Treatment: (1) Any method, technique, or process designed to remove solids and/or pollutants from solid waste, waste-streams, effluents, and air emissions. (2) Methods used to change the biological character or composition of any regulated medical waste so as to substantially reduce or eliminate its potential for causing disease.

Treatment Plant: A structure built to treat wastewater before discharging it into the environment.

Treatment, Storage, and Disposal Facility: Site where a hazardous substance is treated, stored, or disposed of. TSD facilities are regulated by EPA and states under RCRA.

Tremie: Device used to place concrete or grout under water.

Trial Burn: An incinerator test in which emissions are monitored for the presence of specific organic compounds, particulates, and hydrogen chloride.

Trichloroethylene (TCE): A stable, low boiling-point colorless liquid, toxic if inhaled. Used as a solvent or metal degreasing agent, and in other industrial applications.

Trickle Irrigation: Method in which water drips to the soil from perforated tubes or emitters.

Trickling Filter: A coarse treatment system in which wastewater is trickled over a bed of stones or other material covered with bacteria that break down the organic waste and produce clean water.

Trihalomethane (THM): One of a family of organic compounds named as derivative of methane. THMs are generally by-products of chlorination of drinking water that contains organic material.

Troposhpere: The layer of the atmosphere closest to the earth's surface.

Trust Fund (CERCLA): A fund set up under the Comprehensive Environmental Response, Compensation and Liability Act (CERCLA) to help pay for cleanup of hazardous waste sites and for legal action to force those responsible for the sites to clean them up.

Tube Settler: Device using bundles of tubes to let solids in water settle to the bottom for removal by conventional sludge collection means; sometimes used in sedimentation basins and clarifiers to improve particle removal.

Tuberculation: Development or formation of small mounds of corrosion products on the inside of iron pipe. These tubercules roughen the inside of the pipe, increasing its resistance to water flow.

Tundra: A type of treeless ecosystem dominated by lichens, mosses, grasses, and woody plants. Tundra is found at high latitudes (arctic tundra) and high altitudes (alpine tundra). Arctic tundra is underlain by permafrost and is usually water saturated. (See: wetlands.)

Turbidimeter: A device that measures the cloudiness of suspended solids in a liquid; a measure of the quantity of suspended solids.

Turbidity: 1. Haziness in air caused by the presence of particles and pollutants. 2. A cloudy condition in water due to suspended silt or organic matter.

U

Ultra Clean Coal (UCC): Coal that is washed, ground into fine particles, then chemically treated to remove sulfur, ash, silicone, and other substances; usually briquetted and coated with a sealant made from coal.

Ultraviolet Rays: Radiation from the sun that can be useful or potentially harmful. UV rays from one part of the spectrum (UV-A) enhance plant life. UV rays from other parts of the spectrum (UV-B) can cause skin cancer or other tissue damage. The ozone layer in the atmosphere partly shields us from ultraviolet rays reaching the earth's surface.

Uncertainty Factor: One of several factors used in calculating the reference dose from experimental data. UFs are intended to account for (1) the variation in sensitivity among humans; (2) the uncertainty in extrapolating animal data to humans; (3) the uncertainty in extrapolating data obtained in a study that covers less than the full life of the exposed animal or human; and (4) the uncertainty in using LOAEL data rather than NOAEL data.

Unconfined Aquifer: An aquifer containing water that is not under pressure; the water level in a well is the same as the water table outside the well.

Underground Injection Control (UIC): The program under the Safe Drinking Water Act that regulates the use of wells to pump fluids into the ground.

Underground Injection Wells: Steel- and concrete-encased shafts into which hazardous waste is deposited by force and under pressure.

Underground Sources of Drinking Water: Aquifers currently being used as a source of drinking water or those capable of supplying a public water system. They have a total dissolved solids content of 10,000 milligrams per liter or less, and are not "exempted aquifers." (See: exempted aquifer.)

Underground Storage Tank (UST): A tank located at least partially underground and designed to hold gasoline or other petroleum products or chemicals.

Unreasonable Risk: Under the Federal Insecticide, Fungicide, and Rodenticide Act (FIFRA), "unreasonable adverse effects" means any unreasonable risk to man or the environment, taking into account the medical, economic, social, and environmental costs and benefits of any pesticide.

Unsaturated Zone: The area above the water table where soil pores are not fully saturated, although some water may be present.

Upper Detection Limit: The largest concentration that an instrument can reliably detect.

Uranium Mill Tailings Piles: Former uranium ore processing sites that contain leftover radioactive materials (wastes), including radium and unrecovered uranium.

Uranium Mill-Tailings Waste Piles: Licensed active mills with tailings piles and evaporation ponds created by acid or alkaline leaching processes.

Urban Runoff: Storm water from city streets and adjacent domestic or commercial properties that carries pollutants of various kinds into the sewer systems and receiving waters.

Urea-Formaldehyde Foam Insulation: A material once used to conserve energy by sealing crawl spaces, attics, etc.; no longer used because emissions were found to be a health hazard.

Use Cluster: A set of competing chemicals, processes, and/or technologies that can substitute for one another in performing a particular function.

Used Oil: Spent motor oil from passenger cars and trucks collected at specified locations for recycling (not included in the category of municipal solid waste).

User Fee: Fee collected from only those persons who use a particular service, as compared to one collected from the public in general.

Utility Load: The total electricity demand for a utility district.

V

Vadose Zone: The zone between land surface and the water table within which the moisture content is less than saturation (except in the capillary fringe) and pressure is less than atmospheric. Soil pore space also typically contains air or other gases. The capillary fringe is included in the vadose zone. (See: Unsaturated Zone.)

Valued Environmental Attributes/Components: Those aspects(components/processes/functions) of ecosystems, human health, and environmental welfare considered to be important and potentially at risk from human activity or natural hazards. Similar to the term "valued environmental components" used in environmental impact assessment.

Vapor: The gas given off by substances that are solids or liquids at ordinary atmospheric pressure and temperatures.

Vapor Capture System: Any combination of hoods and ventilation system that captures or contains organic vapors so they may be directed to an abatement or recovery device.

Vapor Dispersion: The movement of vapor clouds in air due to wind, thermal action, gravity spreading, and mixing.

Vapor Plumes: Flue gases visible because they contain water droplets.

Vapor Pressure: A measure of a substance's propensity to evaporate, vapor pressure is the force per unit area exerted by vapor in an equilibrium state with surroundings at a given pressure. It increases exponentially with an increase in temperature. A relative measure of chemical volatility, vapor pressure is used to calculate water partition coefficients and volatilization rate constants.

Vapor Recovery System: A system by which the volatile gases from gasoline are captured instead of being released into the atmosphere.

Variance: Government permission for a delay or exception in the application of a given law, ordinance, or regulation.

Vector: 1. An organism, often an insect or rodent, that carries disease. 2. Plasmids, viruses, or bacteria used to transport genes into a host cell. A gene is placed in the vector; the vector then "infects" the bacterium.

Vegetative Controls: Non-point source pollution control practices that involve vegetative cover to reduce erosion and minimize loss of pollutants.

Vehicle Miles Travelled (VMT): A measure of the extent of motor vehicle operation; the total number of vehicle miles travelled within a specific geographic area over a given period of time.

Ventilation Rate: The rate at which indoor air enters and leaves a building. Expressed as the number of changes of outdoor air per unit of time (air changes per hour (ACH), or the rate at which a volume of outdoor air enters in cubic feet per minute (CFM).

Ventilation/Suction: The act of admitting fresh air into a space in order to replace stale or contaminated air; achieved by blowing air into the space. Similarly, suction represents the admission of fresh air into an interior space by lowering the pressure outside of the space, thereby drawing the contaminated air outward.

Venturi Scrubbers: Air pollution control devices that use water to remove particulate matter from emissions.

Vinyl Chloride: A chemical compound, used in producing some plastics, that is believed to be oncogenic.

Virgin Materials: Resources extracted from nature in their raw form, such as timber or metal ore.

Viscosity: The molecular friction within a fluid that produces flow resistance.

Volatile: Any substance that evaporates readily.

Volatile Liquids: Liquids which easily vaporize or evaporate at room temperature.

Volatile Organic Compound (VOC): Any organic compound that participates in atmospheric photochemical reactions except those designated by EPA as having negligible photochemical reactivity.

Volatile Solids: Those solids in water or other liquids that are lost on ignition of the dry solids at 550ø centigrade.

Volatile Synthetic Organic Chemicals: Chemicals that tend to volatilize or evaporate.

Volume Reduction: Processing waste materials to decrease the amount of space they occupy, usually by compacting, shredding, incineration, or composting.

Volumetric Tank Test: One of several tests to determine the physical integrity of a storage tank; the volume of fluid in the tank is measured directly or calculated from product-level changes. A marked drop in volume indicates a leak.

Vulnerability Analysis: Assessment of elements in the community that are susceptible to damage if hazardous materials are released.

Vulnerable Zone: An area over which the airborne concentration of a chemical accidentally released could reach the level of concern.

W

Waste: 1. Unwanted materials left over from a manufacturing process. 2. Refuse from places of human or animal habitation.

Waste Characterization: Identification of chemical and microbiological constituents of a waste material.

Waste Exchange: Arrangement in which companies exchange their wastes for the benefit of both parties.

Waste Feed: The continuous or intermittent flow of wastes into an incinerator.

Waste Generation: The weight or volume of materials and products that enter the waste stream before recycling, composting, landfilling, or combustion takes place. Also can represent the amount of waste generated by a given source or category of sources.

Waste Load Allocation: 1. The maximum load of pollutants each discharger of waste is allowed to release into a particular waterway. Discharge limits are usually required for each specific water quality criterion being, or expected to be, violated. 2. The portion of a stream's total assimilative capacity assigned to an individual discharge.

Waste Minimization: Measures or techniques that reduce the amount of wastes generated during industrial production processes; term is also applied to recycling and other efforts to reduce the amount of waste going into the waste stream.

Waste Piles: Non-containerized, lined or unlined accumulations of solid, nonflowing waste.

Waste Reduction: Using source reduction, recycling, or composting to prevent or reduce waste generation.

Waste Stream: The total flow of solid waste from homes, businesses, institutions, and manufacturing plants that is recycled, burned, or disposed of in landfills, or segments thereof such as the "residential waste stream" or the "recyclable waste stream."

Waste Treatment Lagoon: Impoundment made by excavation or earth fill for biological treatment of wastewater.

Waste Treatment Plant: A facility containing a series of tanks, screens, filters and other processes by which pollutants are removed from water.

Waste Treatment Stream: The continuous movement of waste from generator to treater and disposer.

Waste-Heat Recovery: Recovering heat discharged as a byproduct of one process to provide heat needed by a second process.

Waste-to-Energy Facility/Municipal-Waste Combustor: Facility where recovered municipal solid waste is converted into a usable form of energy, usually via combustion.

Wastewater: The spent or used water from a home, community, farm, or industry that contains dissolved or suspended matter.Water Pollution: The presence in water of enough harmful or objectionable material to damage the water's quality.

Wastewater Infrastructure: The plan or network for the collection, treatment, and disposal of sewage in a community. The level of treatment will depend on the size of the community, the type of discharge, and/or the designated use of the receiving water.

Wastewater Operations and Maintenance: Actions taken after construction to ensure that facilities constructed to treat wastewater will be operated, maintained, and managed to reach prescribed effluent levels in an optimum manner.

Wastewater Treatment Plan: A facility containing a series of tanks, screens, filters, and other processes by which pollutants are removed from water. Most treatments include chlorination to attain safe drinking water standards.

Water Purveyor: A public utility, mutual water company, county water district, or municipality that delivers drinking water to customers.

Water Quality Criteria: Levels of water quality expected to render a body of water suitable for its designated use. Criteria are based on specific levels of pollutants that would make the water harmful if used for drinking, swimming, farming, fish production, or industrial processes.

Water Quality Standards: State-adopted and EPA-approved ambient standards for water bodies. The standards prescribe the use of the water body and establish the water quality criteria that must be met to protect designated uses.

Water Quality-Based Limitations: Effluent limitations applied to dischargers when mere technology-based limitations would cause violations of water quality standards. Usually applied to discharges into small streams.

Water Quality-Based Permit: A permit with an effluent limit more stringent than one based on technology performance. Such limits may be necessary to protect the designated use of receiving waters (e.g. recreation, irrigation, industry or water supply).

Water Solubility: The maximum possible concentration of a chemical compound dissolved in water. If a substance is water soluble it can very readily disperse through the environment.

Water Storage Pond: An impound for liquid wastes designed to accomplish some degree of biochemical treatment.

Water Supplier: One who owns or operates a public water system.

Water Supply System: The collection, treatment, storage, and distribution of potable water from source to consumer.

Water Table: The level of groundwater.

Water Treatment Lagoon: An impound for liquid wastes designed to accomplish some degree of biochemical treatment.

Water Well: An excavation where the intended use is for location, acquisition, development, or artificial recharge of ground water.

Water-Soluble Packaging: Packaging that dissolves in water; used to reduce exposure risks to pesticide mixers and loaders.

Water-Source Heat Pump: Heat pump that uses wells or heat exchangers to transfer heat from water to the inside of a building. Most such units use ground water. (See: groundsource heat pump; heat pump.)

Waterborne Disease Outbreak: The significant occurence of acute illness associated with drinking water from a public water system that is deficient in treatment, as determined by appropriate local or state agencies.

Watershed: The land area that drains into a stream; the watershed for a major river may encompass a number of smaller watersheds that ultimately combine at a common point.

Watershed Approach: A coordinated framework for environmental management that focuses public and private efforts on the highest priority problems within hydrologically-defined geographic areas taking into consideration both ground and surface water flow.

Watershed Area: A topographic area within a line drawn connecting the highest points uphill of a drinking waterintake into which overland flow drains.

Weight of Scientific Evidence: Considerations in assessing the interpretation of published information about toxicity—quality of testing methods, size and power of study design, consistency of results across studies, and biological plausibility of exposure-response relationships and statistical associations.

Weir: 1. A wall or plate placed in an open channel to measure the flow of water. 2. A wall or obstruction used to control flow from settling tanks and clarifiers to ensure a uniform flow rate and avoid short-circuiting. (See: short-circuiting.)

Well: A bored, drilled, or driven shaft, or a dug hole whose depth is greater than the largest surface dimension and whose purpose is to reach underground water supplies or oil, or to store or bury fluids below ground.

Well Field: Area containing one or more wells that produce usable amounts of water or oil.

Well Injection: The subsurface emplacement of fluids into a well.

Well Monitoring: Measurement by on-site instruments or laboratory methods of well water quality.

Well Plug: A watertight, gastight seal installed in a bore hole or well to prevent movement of fluids.

Well Point: A hollow vertical tube, rod, or pipe terminating in a perforated pointed shoe and fitted with a fine-mesh screen.

Wellhead Protection Area: A protected surface and subsurface zone surrounding a well or well field supplying a public water system to keep contaminants from reaching the well water.

Wetlands: An area that is saturated by surface or ground water with vegetation adapted for life under those soil conditions, as swamps, bogs, fens, marshes, and estuaries.

Wettability: The relative degree to which a fluid will spread into or coat a solid surface in the presence of other immiscible fluids.

Wettable Powder: Dry formulation that must be mixed with water or other liquid before it is applied.

Wheeling: The transmission of electricity owned by one entity through the facilities owned by another (usually a utility).

Whole-Effluent-Toxicity Tests: Tests to determine the toxicity levels of the total effluent from a single source as opposed to a series of tests for individual contaminants.

Wildlife Refuge: An area designated for the protection of wild animals, within which hunting and fishing are either prohibited or strictly controlled.

Wire-to-Wire Efficiency: The efficiency of a pump and motor together.

Wood Packaging: Wood products such as pallets, crates, and barrels.

Wood Treatment Facility: An industrial facility that treats lumber and other wood products for outdoor use. The process employs chromated copper arsenate, which is regulated as a hazardous material.

Wood-Burning-Stove Pollution: Air pollution caused by emissions of particulate matter, carbon monoxide, total suspended particulates, and polycyclic organic matter from wood-burning stoves.

Working Level (WL): A unit of measure for documenting exposure to radon decay products, the so-called "daughters." One working level is equal to approximately 200 picocuries per liter.

Working Level Month (WLM): A unit of measure used to determine cumulative exposure to radon.

X

Xenobiota: Any biotum displaced from its normal habitat; a chemical foreign to a biological system.

Y

Yard Waste: The part of solid waste composed of grass clippings, leaves, twigs, branches, and other garden refuse.

Yellow-Boy: Iron oxide flocculant (clumps of solids in waste or water); usually observed as orange-yellow deposits in surface streams with excess iron content. (See: floc, flocculation.)

Yield: The quantity of water (expressed as a rate of flow or total quantity per year) that can be collected for a given use from surface or groundwater sources.

Z

Zero Air: Atmospheric air purified to contain less than 0.1 ppm total hydrocarbons.

Zooplankton: Small (often microscopic) free-floating aquatic plants or animals.

Zone of Saturation: The layer beneath the surface of the land containing openings that may fill with water.

Source: *U.S. Environmental Protection Agency, "Terms of Environment"*

A

Entry Name Index

Entry Name Index

B

Entry Name Index

C

Entry Name Index

D

E

G

H

I

J

Entry Name Index

M

N

Entry Name Index

O

P

Q

R

S

U

V

W

X

Y

Z

Alabama

Alaska

Arizona

Arkansas

California

Colorado

Connecticut

Delaware

District of Columbia

Florida

Georgia

Hawaii

Idaho

Illinois

Indiana

Iowa

Kansas

Kentucky

Louisiana

Maine

Maryland

Massachusetts

Michigan

Minnesota

Mississippi

Missouri

Montana

Nebraska

Nevada

New Hampshire

New Jersey

New Mexico

New York

North Carolina

North Dakota

Ohio

Oklahoma

Oregon

Pennsylvania

Rhode Island

South Carolina

South Dakota

Tennessee

Texas

Utah

Vermont

Virginia

Washington

West Virginia

Wisconsin

Wyoming

Canada

Acid rain
(See also: Air pollution; Water pollution)

Agricultural Engineering

Agricultural conservation
(See also: Soil conservation)

Agricultural ecology
(See also: Agricultural conservation)

Agriculture
(See also: Sustainable agriculture & maps on pages 467-474)

Air pollution
(See also: Acid rain; Aerosols; Pollution, Environmental effects of)

Air quality
(See also: Air pollution and charts on pages 475-484)

Alternative fuels

Animal conservation

Animal ecology

Antarctica

Aquaculture

Aquatic ecology
(See also: Marine ecology)

Architecture and energy conservation

Arctic ecology

Arid regions

Asbestos

Atmospheric sciences

Biology-Ecology

Biomass energy

Biotechnology

Biotic communities (See also: Plant communities)

Botanical ecology

Brownfields (See also: charts on pages 485-490)

Buildings, Environmental engineering of

Chemical toxicology

Children's Environmental Health (See also: charts on pages 491-522)

Coastal engineering (See also: Coastal zone management)

Coastal zone management (See also: Coastal engineering)

Coasts (See also: Coastal engineering)

Conservation of natural resources

Coral reef ecology

Deforestation

Dolphins

Drinking water
(See also: charts on pages 523-546)

Ecological preserves

Ecology
(See also: Conservation of natural resources)

Ecology, Tropical

Endangered species, Animals
(See also: charts on pages 547-549)

Endangered species, Plants
(See also: charts on pages 547-549)

Energy conservation

Energy consumption
(See also: charts on pages 550-669)

Energy conversion

Energy economics

Energy management

Energy policy

Energy resources
(See also: Biomass energy)

Energy technology

Environmental chemistry (See also: Air pollution)

Environmental compliance

Environmental design

Environmental economics (See also: Energy economics)

Environmental education

Environmental engineering (See also: Environmental design)

Environmental Ethics

Environmental Finances
(See also: charts on pages 670-692)

Environmental Health
(See also: Air pollution)

Environmental impact analysis

Environmental monitoring

Environmental policy

Environmental protection

Environmental quality

Environmental sciences

Estuaries

Fertilizers

Fire ecology

Fish feeding and feeds

Fish habitat

Fish reproduction and growth

Fisheries

Fishery management

Fishery policy

Fishes

Food science and technology

Forest ecology

Forest management (See also: Fire ecology)

Forests and forestry (See also: National forests)

Fuels (See also: Biomass energy)

Geographic information systems

Geothermal resources

Glaciology

Global warming (See also: charts on pages 693-724)

Green metro areas (See also: charts on pages 725-728)

Groundwater

Habitat, Ecology (See also: charts on pages 729-760)

Harbors

Hazardous substances

Hazardous waste (See also: charts on pages 761-792)

Hazardous waste management

Human ecology (See also: Conservation of natural resources)

Hydrocarbons

Hydrogen as fuel

Hydrology

Industrial hygiene

Industrial safety

Inhalation toxicology

Lake renewal

Lakes

Land use (See also: Agricultural conservation)

Law, Environmental (See also: Acid rain; Air pollution)

Litter (Trash)

Livestock

Marine biology (See also: Marine ecology)

Marine ecology (See also: Coral reef ecology)

Marine engineering

Marine mammals (See also: Dolphins; Whales)

Marine resources

Marine sciences

Maritime law

Materials testing

Mines and mineral resources

Mountain ecology

Municipal waste (See also: charts on pages 793-839)

National forests (See also: Forests and forestry)

National parks and reserves (See also: Parks)

Ozone

Parks (See also: National parks and reserves)

Pest control, Integrated

Pesticides (See also: charts on pages 840-847)

Pesticides and the environment

Petroleum

Plant communities

Plant conservation

Plants, Protection of (See also: Plant conservation)

Plastics

Polar regions (See also: Arctic ecology)

Pollution (See also: Air pollution)

Pollution control

Pollution, Environmental effects of

Population

Prairie ecology

Public awareness/information programs

Pulp and paper technology

Radiation effects

Radioactive pollution (See also: Radioactive wastes)

Radioactive wastes (See also: Hazardous waste management)

Radon

Rain forest

Recreation areas

Recycling (See also: Energy conservation, and charts on pages 848-854)

Renewable energy sources (See also: Solar energy, Wind energy)

Renewable natural resources

Reservoirs (See also: Water resources)

Risk

Rivers (See also: Estuaries; Water pollution; Watersheds)

Salmon

Sand dune ecology

Sanitary engineering (See also: Pollution; Water resources)

Sewage sludge

Soil conservation

Soil pollution

Solar energy

Solid waste

Solid waste management

Speleology

Sustainable agriculture

Technology and the environment

Thermal energy

Tourism and recreation

Toxicology (See also: charts on pages 855-907)

Tropical ecology (See also: Ecology, Tropical)

Tropical forestry

UV index (See also: chart on page 908)

Urban ecology (Biology)

Urban wildlife

Waste disposal

Waste management

Waste products (See also: Recycling Waste, etc.)

Waste treatment

Wastewater treatment

Water conservation (See also: Water quality control)

Water pollution (See also: Acid rain)

Water quality (See also: Water pollution; Water quality control)

Water quality control (See also: Water reclamation)

Water reclamation (See also: Water use)

Water resources (See also: Groundwater; Reservoirs)

Water treatment (See also: Water reclamation)

Water use (See also: Water reclamation)

Waterfowl

Watersheds

Wetlands (See also: Estuaries)

Whales

Wilderness area

Wildlife (See also: Animal ecology; Wildlife management)

Wildlife management

Wind energy

Grey House Publishing

2013 Title List

Visit **www.greyhouse.com** for Product Information, Table of Contents and Sample Pages

Grey House Publishing

General Reference

America's College Museums
American Environmental Leaders: From Colonial Times to the Present
An African Biographical Dictionary
An Encyclopedia of Human Rights in the United States
Constitutional Amendments
Encyclopedia of African-American Writing
Encyclopedia of the Continental Congress
Encyclopedia of Gun Control & Gun Rights
Encyclopedia of Invasions & Conquests
Encyclopedia of Prisoners of War & Internment
Encyclopedia of Religion & Law in America
Encyclopedia of Rural America
Encyclopedia of the United States Cabinet, 1789-2010
Encyclopedia of War Journalism
Encyclopedia of Warrior Peoples & Fighting Groups
From Suffrage to the Senate: America's Political Women
Nations of the World
Political Corruption in America
Speakers of the House of Representatives, 1789-2009
The Environmental Debate: A Documentary History
The Evolution Wars: A Guide to the Debates
The Religious Right: A Reference Handbook
The Value of a Dollar: 1860-2009
The Value of a Dollar: Colonial Era
This is Who We Were: A Companion to the 1940 Census
This is Who We Were: The 1910s
This is Who We Were: The 1950s
US Land & Natural Resource Policy
Weather America
Working Americans 1770-1869 Vol. IX: Revol. War to the Civil War
Working Americans 1880-1999 Vol. I: The Working Class
Working Americans 1880-1999 Vol. II: The Middle Class
Working Americans 1880-1999 Vol. III: The Upper Class
Working Americans 1880-1999 Vol. IV: Their Children
Working Americans 1880-2003 Vol. V: At War
Working Americans 1880-2005 Vol. VI: Women at Work
Working Americans 1880-2006 Vol. VII: Social Movements
Working Americans 1880-2007 Vol. VIII: Immigrants
Working Americans 1880-2009 Vol. X: Sports & Recreation
Working Americans 1880-2010 Vol. XI: Inventors & Entrepreneurs
Working Americans 1880-2011 Vol. XII: Our History through Music
Working Americans 1880-2012 Vol. XIII: Education & Educators
World Cultural Leaders of the 20th & 21st Centuries

Business Information

Complete Television, Radio & Cable Industry Directory
Directory of Business Information Resources
Directory of Mail Order Catalogs
Directory of Venture Capital & Private Equity Firms
Environmental Resource Handbook
Food & Beverage Market Place
Grey House Homeland Security Directory
Grey House Performing Arts Directory
Hudson's Washington News Media Contacts Directory
New York State Directory
Sports Market Place Directory
The Rauch Guides – Industry Market Research Reports
Sweets Directory by McGraw Hill Construction

Health Information

Comparative Guide to American Hospitals
Complete Directory for Pediatric Disorders
Complete Directory for People with Chronic Illness
Complete Directory for People with Disabilities
Complete Mental Health Directory
Diabetes in America: A Geographic & Demographic Analysis
Directory of Health Care Group Purchasing Organizations
Directory of Hospital Personnel
HMO/PPO Directory
Medical Device Register
Obesity in America: A Geographic & Demographic Analysis
Older Americans Information Directory
Pharmaceutical Industry Directory

Statistics & Demographics

America's Top-Rated Cities
America's Top-Rated Small Towns & Cities
America's Top-Rated Smaller Cities
American Tally
Ancestry & Ethnicity in America
Comparative Guide to American Hospitals
Comparative Guide to American Suburbs
Profiles of America
Profiles of... Series – State Handbooks
The Hispanic Databook

Education Information

Charter School Movement
Comparative Guide to American Elementary & Secondary Schools
Complete Learning Disabilities Directory
Educators Resource Directory
Special Education

Financial Ratings Series

TheStreet.com Ratings Guide to Bond & Money Market Mutual Funds
TheStreet.com Ratings Guide to Common Stocks
TheStreet.com Ratings Guide to Exchange-Traded Funds
TheStreet.com Ratings Guide to Stock Mutual Funds
TheStreet.com Ratings Ultimate Guided Tour of Stock Investing
Weiss Ratings Consumer Box Set
Weiss Ratings Guide to Banks & Thrifts
Weiss Ratings Guide to Credit Unions
Weiss Ratings Guide to Health Insurers
Weiss Ratings Guide to Life & Annuity Insurers
Weiss Ratings Guide to Property & Casualty Insurers

Bowker's Books In Print® Titles

Books In Print®
Books In Print® Supplement
American Book Publishing Record® Annual
American Book Publishing Record® Monthly
Books Out Loud™
Bowker's Complete Video Directory™
Children's Books In Print®
Complete Directory of Large Print Books & Serials™
El-Hi Textbooks & Serials In Print®
Forthcoming Books®
Law Books & Serials In Print™
Medical & Health Care Books In Print™
Publishers, Distributors & Wholesalers of the US™
Subject Guide to Books In Print®
Subject Guide to Children's Books In Print®

Canadian General Reference

Associations Canada
Canadian Almanac & Directory
Canadian Environmental Resource Guide
Canadian Parliamentary Guide
Financial Services Canada
Governments Canada
Libraries Canada
The History of Canada

Grey House Publishing
4919 Route 22, PO Box 56, Amenia NY 12501-0056 | (800) 562-2139 | www.greyhouse.com | books@greyhouse.com